THEOLOGICAL DICTIONARY
OF THE
NEW TESTAMENT

THEOLOGICAL DICTIONARY
OF THE
NEW TESTAMENT

EDITED BY

GERHARD KITTEL

Translator and Editor

GEOFFREY W. BROMILEY, D. LITT., D. D.

Volume I

Α—Γ

WM. B. EERDMANS PUBLISHING COMPANY

GRAND RAPIDS, MICH. / LONDON

THEOLOGICAL DICTIONARY OF THE NEW TESTAMENT
Published by
Wm. B. Eerdmans Publishing Company
255 Jefferson, S.E.
Grand Rapids, Michigan, U.S.A.
United Kingdom Office:
16 Victoria Road, Surbiton, Surrey

COPYRIGHT © 1964 BY WM. B. EERDMANS PUBLISHING CO.
All rights reserved
Library of Congress Catalog Card Number: 64-15136

Translated from
THEOLOGISCHES WÖRTERBUCH ZUM NEUEN TESTAMENT
Erster Band: A–Γ, herausgegeben von Gerhard Kittel
Published by
W. KOHLHAMMER VERLAG
Stuttgart, Germany

PRINTED IN THE NETHERLANDS

To Adolf Schlatter

Preface

The *Theological Dictionary of the New Testament* stems from the great labours of Hermann Cremer and Julius Kögel. The goal before its contributors cannot be better formulated than in the introductory words of Cremer's preface to his *Biblico-Theological Dictionary of New Testament Greek Usage* (1883) in which he refers to the new force and impress and energy given to Greek words as "the horizons of those who spoke and wrote them changed with the point of departure and termination of all thinking." The true aim of the present book is to bring out in our discussions this new content of individual terms.

For all our inner agreement with Cremer's aims, and our astonishment at his achievement, we are forced to say, of course, that there have been great changes in the standpoints and methods of modern lexical research. Kögel could still devote many years of unassuming labour to re-editing the work of his teacher. After mature investigation it has seemed better to us to abandon the original idea of a fresh edition and to try to create a new work in every respect. It is in this way that I myself think we may best and most justly redeem the pledge once given to Kögel not to abandon the dictionary. When I recall the unimpeachable integrity of our departed friend, I am confident that we should have his full approval in doing this in a different way from that first intended. It has been a particular joy to me that Mrs. Kögel placed at our disposal the papers gathered by her husband and assured us that in our present work we are genuinely preserving the heritage bequeathed by these men.

In the *Theological Dictionary of the New Testament* we plan to treat every word of religious or theological significance. The number is much greater than that handled by Cremer and Kögel. We have included many proper names from the Old Testament borne by men of theological importance (e.g., Abel, Abraham, Adam etc.); and also some of the theologically more important prepositions (ἀντί, διά, ἐν, εἰς, σύν etc.) and numbers (εἷς, ἑπτά, δώδεκα etc.). Under A we have also included such words as ἀββᾶ, ἄδω, ἀήρ, αἰνέω-αἶνος, αἴνιγμα, αἰσχύνη, αἰχμάλωτος, ἅλας, ἁλληλούϊα, ἄμπελος, ἀνάγκη-ἀναγκάζω, ἀνήρ, ἀνταπό-δομα, ἄξιος-ἀξιόω, ἀπατάω-ἀπάτη, ἀποφθέγγομαι, ἀρκέω, ἀσέλγεια, ἀστήρ, ἀστραπή, ἀσφάλεια-ἀσφαλής, αὐτάρκεια-αὐτάρκης, αὐτόπτης.

External lexicographical matters are either taken for granted or treated very briefly. This may be done the more readily as students may now be assumed to have such excellent aids as the Preuschen-Bauer *Dictionary* and the Schmoller *Concordance*. Our own task begins in some sort where these break off, namely, with internal lexicography.

The order of words is generally by roots. But this principle has been interpreted with some elasticity, so that derived words with independent meanings are often treated at their own place in the alphabet. Since the limit is hard to define, it has seemed best in practice to include at least a reference to every word treated in due alphabetical order.

A distinctive feature of the work is the large number of contributors. It is inevitable that individual style should thus characterise the articles, and this the more so the more seriously the articles seek to penetrate to the inwardness of the New Testament words. Nevertheless we are confident that it is possible to create a work which is rounded and unitary for all the variety, not merely in the sense of a certain agreement in form, nor of a common application of historical and philological methods of scholarly work, but in a deeper sense. The unity arises as each contributor does not seek to write an individual monograph but to make a contribution to a total work which as a whole has its norm only in the New Testament.

The historical study of New Testament terms is at the moment a highly specialised one. The co-operation of many workers from other than the New Testament field has been sought to safeguard the standards of the work. According to a selection made by Rudolf Kittel shortly before his death, the more important Old Testament terms were independently treated by colleagues in this field. In addition, all the manuscripts have been sent to specialists who have weighed and added to them from their own particular standpoints : Gottfried Quell and Gerhard von Rad in that of the Old Testament ; Georg Bertram in that of the Septuagint ; Albert Debrunner and Hermann Kleinknecht in that of philology, secular usage and Hellenistic religion ; Hans Heinrich Schaeder in the field of Persian and Semitic studies ; Gerhard Kittel, Karl Georg Kuhn and Karl Heinrich Rengstorf in that of Rabbinics. The resultant annotations have been placed at the disposal of the main contributor prior to printing, though naturally he himself has carried full responsibility for the final form of his article. From the materials amassed by Kögel the contributors have had access to two further important manuscript aids. Adolf Schlatter added parallels from Rabbinic literature and Josephus by hand to extensive parts of an interleaved copy of Cremer-Kögel, and he has allowed us to make free use of these. In addition, Erik Peterson has found varying numbers of references for almost every word from his own collections of material.

It is essential that we should express our particular gratitude to these fellow-workers, since much of their work does not appear on the surface. This gives us all the more reason to mention here how great is the part played by these colleagues in the work.

In addition, we owe may literary references to Stephan Lösch of Tübingen in the sphere of Roman Catholic literature, to Otto Weinreich of Tübingen in that of philological literature, to F. W. Grosheide of Amsterdam and Arthur Nock of Cambridge (Mass.) in that of foreign literature. We express to them our grateful thanks for help already received and hope for further help in the future.

The list of abbreviations in the first edition was prepared by Gerhard Delling and Walter Grundmann, and in the final edition by Hermann Kleinknecht and Albrecht Stumpf.

Loyal service has been rendered in proof correction by W. Grundmann, C. Horovitz, H. Kleinknecht, O. Rühle, G. Schlichting, A. Stumpff and W. Vogel.

Finally, a special word of thanks is due to our publisher, Dr. Walter Kohlhammer. The work could hardly have been begun in these days, let alone executed in the present form, if it had not been that his material interest, his outstanding generosity scorning all pettiness, and his constant readiness to help, had seen us through every difficulty and smoothed the way for us at every turn. Sir Edwyn C. Hoskyns justly wrote in the English journal "Theology" (26, 87, 1933): "In conclusion, it is difficult not to be envious of a country possessed . . . of a publisher willing to print the book so magnificently at a time when its production can hardly be an economic adventure."

Our work has thus far met with a friendly response in scholarly and ecclesiastical criticism. If what has sometimes been said should prove true, namely, that it should not only advance research but also help the pastor in his study of Holy Scripture and pulpit ministry, this would be the finest reward that could be given us.

The dedicatory page, bearing the name of Cremer's friend, indicates the relationship with the older work referred to at the outset. It also reminds us that *Der Glaube im Neuen Testament* is a model for the investigation of biblical theological terms. And it perhaps expresses to this eighty year old scholar the thanks which the Church and theology and especially New Testament scholarship owe to his life's work.

Tübingen, New Year 1932, July 1933.   *Kittel*

Editor's Preface

From the publication of the first volume, and during the years of its long and arduous composition, the *Theologisches Wörterbuch zum Neuen Testament*, familiarly known as Kittel or abbreviated as *TWNT*, has secured for itself a solid place in biblical scholarship, not only as a reference work or a starting-point for further research, but also as a formative contribution to theology.

There has, of course, been some misunderstanding of its role. While it is not a simple lexicon, it obviously cannot replace either the full commentary or the biblical theology. Its task is to mediate between ordinary lexicography and the specific task of exposition, more particularly at the theological level. For this reason attention is concentrated on theologically significant terms, and on the theologically significant usage of these terms.

When this is understood, Kittel is safeguarded against the indiscriminate enthusiasm which would make it a sole and absolute authority in lexical and exegetical matters. It is also safeguarded against the resultant criticism that it involves an illegitimate task for which it uses improper means. Its more limited, yet valid and invaluable role, can be appreciated, and its learning and insights incorporated into the great task of New Testament interpretation.

Hitherto access to the great bulk of *TWNT* has been only in the original language. Some of the more important articles have been translated in the *Key Words* series, and by virtue of the significance of the words selected this series has performed a most useful service. Yet even the chosen articles have undergone some abridgment and editorial redaction, quite apart from the fact that the main part of Kittel has not been translated at all.

By contrast, the present rendering aims to present the whole of *TWNT* in a faithful reproduction of the original. At the cost of less felicity, for German scholarship is no guarantee of stylistic elegance, the rendering is more closely tied to the German. Quotations are fully given in the original Hebrew, Greek and Latin, and the references are left as they are apart from essential changes. For scholars who may wish to consult the original, even the pagination is retained except for a slight fluctuating variation of no more than two or three pages either way. The external size of the volumes has been much reduced, however, and costs have been trimmed so as to provide the student with maximum material at minimum price.

It need hardly be said that the translation and publication of Kittel is no necessary endorsement of everything contained in it. Written by many scholars over a long period, Kittel naturally contains articles of unequal value and varying outlook. Indeed, there are internal disagreements as regards basic presuppositions, historical assumptions and specific interpretations. The ultimate worth of the undertaking lies in its fundamental orientation and its objective findings; for these it is now presented in translation.

In the preparation of the volumes particular thanks are due to Professor F. F. Bruce of the University of Manchester for his many valuable suggestions and corrections in the course of laborious proof-reading. Also deserving of mention in this instance are the publishers for the courage and helpfulness which they have displayed in so monumental an enterprise, and the printers for the skill with which they have handled such difficult material. In spite of every effort, it would be presumptuous to suppose that all errors have been avoided, and the help of readers will be appreciated in detecting and eliminating those that remain.

Pasadena, California, 1963.

G. W. Bromiley

Contents

Contents

Contributors

Editor:

Gerhard Kittel, Tübingen.

Contributors:

Otto Bauernfeind, Tübingen.
Friedrich Baumgärtel, Greifswald.
Johannes Behm, Göttingen.
Georg Bertram, Giessen.
Hermann Wolfgang Beyer, Greifswald.
Friedrich Büchsel, Rostock.
Rudolf Bultmann, Marburg.
Albert Debrunner, Jena.
Kurt Deissner, Greifswald.
Gerhard Delling, Glachau (Saxony).
Werner Foerster, Münster.
Ernst Fuchs, Bonn.
Heinrich Greeven, Greifswald.
Walter Grundmann, Oberlichtenau (Saxony).
Friedrich Hauck, Erlangen.
Johannes Herrmann, Münster.
Joachim Jeremias, Greifswald.
Hermann Kleinknecht, Tübingen.
Karl Georg Kuhn, Tübingen.
Albrecht Oepke, Leipzig.
Erik Peterson, Munich.
Herbert Preisker, Breslau.
Otto Procksch, Erlangen.
Gottfried Quell, Rostock.
Gerhard von Rad, Leipzig.
Karl Heinrich Rengstorf, Tübingen.
Oskar Rühle, Stuttgart.
Hermann Sasse, Erlangen.
Hans Heinrich Schaeder, Berlin.
Heinrich Schlier, Marburg.
Karl Ludwig Schmidt, Bonn.
Johannes Schneider, Berlin.
Julius Schniewind, Königsberg.
Gottlob Schrenk, Zürich.
Hans Freiherr von Soden, Marburg.
Gustav Stählin, Leipzig, and Gurukul Theological Seminary, Madras, India.
Ethelbert Stauffer, Halle.
Artur Weiser, Tübingen.
Hans Windisch, Kiel.

Abbreviations

The editions mentioned in this list indicate where citations are to be found as quoted in the *Dictionary*. Wherever possible the latest are used, but the reader may consult more recent philological editions for himself. As a rule two editions are mentioned only when a fresh edition has begun to appear but is not yet completed.

AAB = *Abhandlungen der Kgl. Preussi-schen Akademie der Wissenschaften zu Berlin (Phil.-hist. Klasse)*, 1804 ff.

Ab. = *Pirqe Abot,*
Mishnah-, Tosefta-, Talmudtractate *Sayings of the Fathers* (Strack, *Einl.,* 54).

Ab RNat = Abot of Rabbi Nathan — an extracanonical Rabbinic tractate (Strack, *Einl.,* 72).

Ac. = Acts of the Apostles.

acc. = accusative.

Achill. Tat. = Achilles Tatius of Alexandria (4th. century A.D.), sophist and Christian, the last novelist of antiquity, ed. G. A. Hirschig, in *Erotici Scriptores,* 1856.

Act. = *Acta,* apocryphal Acts of the Apostles, consisting in part of writings which go back to the post-apostolic period and try to invest highly heretical traditions with apostolic sanction, ed. R. A. Lipsius and M. Bonnet, 1891 ff.

Act. Andr. = *Acts of Andrew.*
Andr. et Matth. = *Acts of Andrew and Matthias.*
Barn. = *Acts of Barnabas.*
Jn. = *Acts of John.*
Phil. = *Acts of Philip.*
Pl. = *Acts of Paul.*
Pl. and Thekl. = *Acts of Paul and Thekla.*
Pt. = *Acts of Peter.*
Pt. Verc. = *Acts of Peter of Vercellae.*
Thom. = *Acts of Thomas.*

adj. = adjective.

adv. = adverb.

Ael. = Claudius Aelianus (c. 175-235 A.D.), Roman author, writing in Greek, of the so-called Second Sophistic school, ed. R. Hercher, 1864 ff.
Ep. = *Epistulae.*
Nat. An. = *De Natura Animalium.*
Tact. = *Tactica.*
Var. Hist. = *Varia Historia.*

Ael. Arist. = Aelius Aristides, of Adrianutherai in Mysia (129-189 A.D.), celebrated rhetorician and credulous votary of Aesculapius, one of the best known representatives of later Hellenistic piety in literature (cf. his prose hymns to different deities), ed. W. Dindorf, 1829 ; ed. B. Keil, 1898.
Or. = *Orationes.*
Or. Sacr. = *Orationes Sacrae.*

Aen. Tact. = Aeneas Tacticus, contemporary of Xenophon, who wrote his technical military work (τακτικὸν ὑπόμνημα) c. 360 B.C., ed. H. Schöne, 1911.

Aesch. = Aeschylus, of Eleusis near Athens (525-456 B.C.), the first of the three great Attic dramatists, ed. U. v. Wilamowitz, 1915 ; Fragments, ed. A. Nauck in Tragicorum Graecorum Fragmenta, 1889.
Ag. = *Agamemnon.*
Choeph. = *Choephori.*
Eleg. = *Fragmenta Elegiaca.*
Eum. = *Eumenides.*
Pers. = *Persae.*
Prom. = *Prometheus Vinctus.*
Suppl. = *Supplices.*
Sept. c. Theb. = *Septem contra Thebas.*

Aeschin. = Aeschines, Athenian orator and politician (c. 390-314 B.C.), who gained fame by opposing Demosthenes. The letters ascribed to him are not authentic, ed. F. Blass, 1896.
Ep. = *Epistulae.*
Fals. Leg. = *De Falsa Legatione.*
Tim. = *Oratio in Timarchum.*

AGG = *Abhandlungen der Kgl. Gesellschaft der Wissenschaften zu Göttingen (phil.-hist. Klasse)*, 1838 ff., 1893 ff.

Agr. = Agraphon.

Alciphr. = Alciphron, Sophist of the 2nd century A.D., distinguished for his epistolary sketches of Attic life, ed. M. A. Schepers, 1905.
Ep. = *Epistulae.*

Alex. Aphr. = Alexander Aphrodisiensis, of Aphrodisias, peripatetic and author of commentaries on Aristotle, as also of some independent works (2nd and 3rd centuries A.D.), ed. J. Bruns in *Supplementum Aristotelicum,* 1887.

An. = *De Anima.*
Fat. = *De Fato.*
Am. = Amos.
Ambr. = Ambrosius of Treves (340-397), Bishop of Milan.
Amm. Marc. = Ammianus Marcellinus, of Antioch, born c. 332 A.D., officer under Julian, and the last great historian of imperial Rome (from Nerva to Valens), ed. L. Traube and W. Heraeus, 1910 ff.
Ammonius, *v.* Pseud.-Ammon.
Anacr. = Anacreon, of Teos, early Greek lyric poet, of the middle of the 6th century B.C., ed. E. Diehl, in *Anthologia Lyrica,* I, 1925.
Anal. Boll. = *Analecta Bollandiana,* continuing series of sources of ecclesiastical history prepared by the Jesuits, 1882 ff.
Anax. = Anaxagoras of Klazomenae (500-428 B.C.), mediator of Ionic philosophy to Athens, where he belongs to the circle of Pericles, ed. H. Diels, in *Die Fragmente der Vorsokratiker,* I⁴, 1922.
Anaxim. = Anaximenes, of Miletus, Ionic natural philosopher of the middle of the 6th century B.C., ed. H. Diels in *Die Fragmente der Vorsokratiker,* I⁴, 1922.
Anaximand. = Anaximander, of Miletus, Ionic natural philosopher of the 6th century B.C., ed. H. Diels, in *Die Fragmente der Vorsokratiker,* I⁴, 1922.
Andoc. = Andocides, one of the ten Attic orators of the end of the 5th century B.C. The most interesting of his four extant speeches is that *On the Mysteries* (399 B.C.), ed. F. Blass, 1906; W. J. Hickie, 1915.
Anecd. Graec. = *Anecdota Graeca,* ed. I. Bekker, 1814 ff.
Angelos = Angelos, Archiv für nt.liche Zeitgeschichte und Kulturkunde, 1925 ff.
Anth. Pal. = *Anthologia Palatina,* a collection of minor Hellenistic poetry based on ancient collections of epigrams, assembled by Konstantinos Kephales in Byzantium in the 10th century A.D., and so called because the only MS. is in Heidelberg Library, ed. H. Stadtmüller and F. Bucherer, 1906.
Antike = Die Antike, Zeitschrift für Kunst u. Kultur des klassischen Altertums, 1925 ff.
Antiph. = Antiphanes, of Athens, significant comic dramatist of the 4th century B.C., ed. T. Kock in *Comicorum atticorum Fragmenta,* II, 1884.
Lyc. = *Lycion.*
Antiphon = Antiphon, of Athens, at the end of the 5th century B.C., Sophist,

large sections of whose chief work *Truth* have recently been discovered on papyri at Oxyrhynchos, ed. H. Diels in *Die Fragmente der Vorsokratiker,* II⁴, 1922.
Anz Subsidia = H. Anz, *Subsidia ad cognoscendum Graecorum sermonem vulgarem e Pentateuchi versione Alexandrina repetita,* 1894.
AO = *Der alte Orient,* 1900 ff.
AOB = H. Gressmann, *Altorientalische Bilder zum AT²,* 1927.
aor. = aorist.
AOT = H. Gressmann, *Altorientalische Texte zum AT²,* 1926.
Ap. = Apostle.
ap. = apostolic.
Apc. Abr. = *Apocalypse of Abraham.*
Elias = *of Elias.*
Mos. = *of Moses.*
Pt. = *of Peter.*
Apcr. = Apocrypha.
APF = *Archiv für Papyrusforschung,* 1901 ff.
Apollon. Dyscol. = Apollonius Dyscolus, important Greek grammarian of the Hadrian-Antoninus period in Alexandria, ed. R. Schneider and G. Uhlig in Grammatici Graeci, II, 1878 ff.
Apoll. Rhod. = Apollonius Rhodius, of Naucratis or Alexandria (c. 295-215 B.C.), called after his main place of residence and a famous exponent of the Hellenistic epic, ed. M. Gillies, 1928.
App. = Appendix.
Appian. = Appianus, of Alexandria, imperial governor, who in 24 volumes wrote a Roman history up to his own times (c. 160 A.D.), much of which is lost, ed. L. Mendelssohn, 1879 ff.
Rom. Hist. = *Romanae Historiae.*
Apul. = Apuleius, of Madaura in Numidia, novelist, rhetorician and philosopher with strong religious interests (2nd century A.D.), ed. R. Helm, 1907.
Met. = *Metamorphoses.*
Ar. = *Arachim,* Mishnah-, Tosefta-, Talmud tractate *Appraisals (Estimates of the Basis of a Vow)* (Strack, *Einl.,* 57).
Arab. = Arabic.
Aram. = Aramaic.
Arat. = Aratus, of Soloi in Cilicia (c. 310-245 B.C.), Stoic, later at the Macedonian court, the author of a didactic epic in astronomy on heavenly phenomena, ed. E. Maass, 1893.
Phaen. = *Phaenomena.*
Archiloch. = Archilochus, of Pharos, early Greek lyric poet of the 7th century B.C.,

ed. E. Diehl in *Anthologia Lyrica*, I, 1925.

Ar. Did. = Arius Didymus, of Alexandria, Stoic of the age of Augustus, doxograph, ed. H. Diels in *Doxographi Graeci*, 1879.

Aret. = Aretaeus Medicus, of Cappadocia, physician in the Roman Empire, probably in the 2nd century, A.D., ed. C. Hude in *Corpus Medicorum Graecorum*, 1923.

Arg. = Argumentum.

Aristid. = Aristides, the first Christian Apologist, who addressed his defence of Christianity to Antoninus Pius c. 140 A.D., ed. E. Goodspeed, in *Die ältesten Apologeten*, 1914.
    Apol. = *Apologia*.

Aristoph. = Aristophanes, of Athens (c. 446-385 B.C.), the main representative of the older Attic comedy, who reached his height during the Peloponnesian War, ed. V. Coulon and H. van Daele, 1923 ff.
    Ach. = *Àcharnenses*.
    Av. = *Aves*.
    Eccl. = *Ecclesiazusae*.
    Eq. = *Equites*.
    Lys. = *Lysistrata*.
    Nu. = *Nubes*.
    Pax
    Pl. = *Plutus*.
    Ra. = *Ranae*.
    Thes. = *Thesmophoriazusae*.
    Vesp. = *Vespae*.

Aristot. = Aristotle, of Stageiros (c. 384-322 B.C.), with his teacher Plato the greatest of the Greek philosophers and the founder of the peripatetic school, quoted in each case from the comprehensive edition of the Academia Regia Borussica, 1831 ff.
    An. = *De Anima*.
    An. Post. = *Analytica Posteriora*.
    An. Pri. = *Analytica Priora*.
    Cael. = *De Caelo*.
    Cat. = *Categoriae*.
    Eth. Eud. = *Ethica Eudemia*.
    Eth. Nic. = *Ethica Nicomachea*.
    Gen. An. = *De Generatione Animalium*.
    Gen. Corr. = *De Generatione et Corruptione*.
    Hist. An. = *Historia Animalium*.
    Metaph. = *Metaphysica*.
    Meteor. = *Meteorologicum*.
    Mot. An. = *De Motu Animalium*.
    Oec. = *Oeconomica*.
    Part. An. = *De Partibus Animalium*.
    Phys. = *Physica*.
    Poet. = *Poetica*.
    Pol. = *Politica*.
    Probl. = *Problemata*.

Rhet. = *Rhetorica*.
Spir. = *De Spiritu*.

Pseud.-Arist. = Pseudo-Aristotle.

Mund. = *De Mundo*, a popular work of philosophy written by a later author under the influence of the Syrian Posidonius of Apamea (c. 135-51 B.C.), the main representative of Middle Stoicism.

Rhet. Al. = *Rhetorica ad Alexandrum*, written by the historian and rhetorician Anaximenes of Lampsacos at the time of Alexander the Great.

v. Arnim = J. v. Arnim, *Stoicorum veterum Fragmenta*, 1921 f.

ARPs = *Archiv für Religionspsychologie*, 1914 f.

Art. = Articles.

Artemid. = Artemidorus, of Ephesus, interpreter of dreams in the days of Hadrian, author of a book on dreams with examples of fulfilled dreams, ed. R. Hercher, 1864.
    Oneirocr. = *Oneirocriticum*.

ARW = *Archiv für Religionswissenschaft*, 1898 ff.

Asc. Is. = *Ascension of Isaiah*, Christian version of an originally Jewish legend (Schürer, III, 386 f.), ed. R. Charles, 1900.

ASG = *Abhandlungen d. Kgl. Sächsischen Gesellschaft d. Wissenschaften (phil.-hist. Klasse)*, 1850 ff.

Ass. Mos. = *Assumptio Mosis*, Jewish apocalypse of the time of the death of Herod the Great (Schürer, III, 294 ff.), ed. R. Charles, 1897.

Athen. = Athenaeus, of Naucratis, at the end of the 2nd century B.C., whose *Feast of Sophists* is a formless but valuable book of extracts of the type of variegated writing so common in later antiquity, ed. G. Kaibel, 1887 ff.

Athenag. = Athenagoras, of Athens, Christian Apologist, who came over from Platonism and wrote a defence of Christianity to the Emperor Marcus Aurelius in 177, ed. E. Goodspeed in *Die ältesten Apologeten*, 1914.
    Suppl. = *Supplicatio*.

Ath. Mitt. = *Mitteilungen des Kaiserlich Deutschen Archäologischen Instituts, Athenische Abteilung*, 1876 ff.

Audollent, Def. Tab. = A. Audollent, *Defixionum Tabellae*, 1914.

Aug. = Aurelius Augustinus, of Thagaste, Numidia (354-430 A.D.), ed. in MPL, 32-47, 1845; ed. by different editors in *Corpus Scriptorum Ecclesiasticorum La-*

tinorum, 1887 ff.
    Civ. D. = *De Civitate Dei.*
    Cresc. = *Contra Cresconium.*
    Ep. = *Epistulae.*
    Faust. = *Contra Faustum Manichae-um.*
    In Joh. Ev. Tract. = *In Johannis Evangelium Tractatus.*
    Sct. Virg. = *De Sancta Virginitate.*
    Serm. = *Sermones.*
AZ = *Aboda Zara,* Mishnah-, Tosefta-, Talmud tractate *Idolatry* (Strack, *Einl.,* 54).
b. = ben, when between the personal and family names of rabbis.
b. = Babylonian Talmud when before tractates from the Mishnah.
Bacchyl. = Bacchylides, of Ceos (505-450 B.C.), the most important writer of Greek odes after Pindar, ed. F. Blass, 1904.
Bar. = *Baraita* (in quotations from the Talmud), *Extra-Mishnaic Tradition of Tannaites* (Strack, *Einl.,* 2).
Bar. = Baruch, disciple of Jeremiah and supposed author of many works (Schürer, III, 305 ff.).
    Bar. = The Book of Baruch, apocryphal work in the LXX.
    Gr. Bar. = The Greek-Slavic Apocalypse of Baruch, a description of Baruch's journey to heaven (2nd century A.D.), ed. M. R. James in Greek, 1897 and St. Novakovitsch in Slavic, 1886.
    S. Bar. = Syrian Apocalypse of Baruch, originally Hebrew and strongly dependent on 4 Esdras (c. 100 A.D.), ed. R. Charles, 1896.
Barn. = *Epistle of Barnabas.*
Bas. = Basil of Caesarea (330-379 A.D.), one of the three Cappadocian fathers and an outstanding representative of early Christian culture, ed. in MPG, 29-32, 1886.
    Ep. = *Epistulae.*
    Spir. Sct. = *De Spiritu Sancto.*
Bau. J. = W. Bauer, *Kommentar z. Johannesev.*[2] 1925; [3] 1933.
BB = *Baba Batra,* Mishnah-, Tosefta-, Talmud tractate *Last Gate* (Legal Questions, Immovables) (Strack, *Einl.,* 51).
BCH = *Bulletin de Correspondance Hellénique,* 1877 ff.
BchmK = P. Bachmann, *Kommentar z. d. Korintherbriefen* I[2], 1910; II, 1909.
Bek. = *Bekorot,* Mishnah-, Tosefta-, Talmud tractate *Primogeniture* (Strack, *Einl.,* 32).

BFTh = *Beiträge zur Förderung christlicher Theologie,* 1897 ff.
BGU = *Ägyptische Urkunden aus den Kgl. Museen zu Berlin,* 1895 ff.
BHK[2], [3] = *Biblia Hebraica,* ed. R. Kittel[2], 1909; [3] 1929 ff.
Bibl. = Bibliography.
Bik. = *Bikkurim,* Mishnah-, Tosefta-, Talmud tractate *First-fruits* (Strack, *Einl.,* 36).
Bl.-Debr. = F. Blass, *Grammatik des neutestamentlichen Griechisch,* revised by A. Debrunner[5], 1921; [6] 1931.
BM = *Baba Mezia,* Mishnah-, Tosefta-, Talmud tractate *Middle Gate* (Legal Questions concerning Movables) (Strack, *Einl.,* 50).
BMI = Collection of Ancient Greek Inscriptions in the British Museum, 1874 ff.
Boisacq = E. Boisacq, *Dictionnaire étymologique de la langue Grecque*[2], 1923.
Bousset-Gressm. = W. Bousset, *Die Religion des Judentums im späthellenistischen Zeitalter,* ed. H. Gressmann[3], 1926.
BQ = *Baba Qamma,* Mishnah-, Tosefta-, Talmud tractate *First Gate,* (Legal Questions concerning Injuries) (Strack, *Einl.,* 49).
BrthR = K. Barth, *Kommentar z. Römerbrief*[5], 1926.
Bruder = C. H. Bruder, *Concordantiae Novi Testamenti*[5], 1900.
Bss. Apk. = W. Bousset, *Kommentar z. Apokalypse*[6], 1906.
BSt. = *Biblische Studien,* 1896 ff.
BüJ (1, 2, 3) = F. Büchsel, *Kommentar z. d. Johannesbriefen,* 1933.
Bultmann Trad. = R. Bultmann, *Die Geschichte der synoptischen Tradition*[2], 1931.
Buttmann = A. Buttmann, *Grammatik des nt.lichen Sprachgebrauchs,* 1859.
BW = H. Guthe, *Kurzes Bibelwörterbuch,* 1903.
BWANT = *Beiträge zur Wissenschaft vom Alten und Neuen Testament,* 1908 ff., 1926 ff.
BZ = *Biblische Zeitschrift,* 1903 ff.
C (1, 2) = Corinthians (1, 2).
c. = chapter.
c. = circa.
CAF = *Comicorum Atticorum Fragmenta,* ed. T. Kock, 1880 ff.
Callim. = Callimachus, of Cyrene (c. 310-240 B.C.), typical representative and acknowledged master of Hellenistic poetry, called by Ptolemy II to direct the

library in Alexandria. There is no single edition, but for individual pieces, cf. Liddell-Scott, XVIII.
  Hymn. = *Hymni.*
Cant. = Song of Solomon.
Cant. r. = *Canticum rabba, Midrash on Song of Solomon* (Strack, *Einl.*, 213).
Catal. Cod. Astr. Graec. = *Catalogus Codicum Astrologorum Graecorum,* 1898 ff.
Cath. Ep. = Catholic Epistles.
Ceb. = Cebes, the name adopted by the author of a book "πίναξ," a moralising and allegorical description of life in the Neo-Platonic spirit, probably 1st century A.D., ed. K. Prächter.
  Tab. = *Tabula.*
Cels. = A. Cornelius Celsus, wrote a comprehensive encyclopedia in the reign of Tiberius (14-37 A.D.), of which we still have 8 books on medicine, ed. F. Marx in *Corpus Medicorum Latinorum,* 1915.
  Med. = *Medicina.*
CGF = *Comicorum Graecorum Fragmenta,* ed. G. Kaibel, 1899 ff.
Ch. (1, 2) = Chronicles (1, 2).
Chag. = *Chagiga,* Mishnah-, Tosefta-, Talmud tractate *Feasts* (in relation to pilgrimages) (Strack, *Einl.,* 44).
Chant. de la Saussaye = P. D. Chantepie de la Saussaye, *Lehrbuch der Religionsgeschichte*[4], 1924 ff.
Chrys. = John Chrysostom, of Antioch (344-401 A.D.), bishop of Constantinople, whose sermons mark the climax of early Christian homiletics, ed. in MPG, 47-64, 1862 ff.
  Hom. in Hb., Col., Mt., Phil. = Homilies on Hebrews, Colossians, Matthew and Philippians.
  Liturg. = Liturgy of Chrysostom, in *Liturgies Eastern and Western,* ed. F. E. Brightman, I, 1896.
  Sacerdot. = *De Sacerdotio.*
Chul. = *Chullin,* Mishnah-, Tosefta-, Talmud tractate *Profane* (the killing of non-sacrificial animals) (Strack, *Einl.,* 56).
CIA = *Corpus Inscriptionum Atticarum* (→ IG, I-III), 1873 ff.
Cic. = M. Tullius Cicero, of Arpinum (106-43 B.C.), orator, politician and cultural philosopher of the last days of the Roman Republic, Teubner-Leipzig edition, 1925 ff.
  Att. = *Ad Atticum.*
  De Orat. = *De Oratore.*
  Divin. = *De Divinatione.*
  Fam. = *Ad Familiares.*
  Fin. = *De Finibus Bonorum et Malorum.*
  Lael. = *Laelius.*

Mil. = *Pro Milone.*
Nat. Deor. = *De Natura Deorum.*
Off. = *De Officiis.*
Or. = *Orationes.*
Orator = *Orator ad M. Brutum.*
Rep. = *De Re Publica.*
Som. Scip. = *Somnium Scipionis.*
Tusc. = *Tusculanae Disputationes.*
Verr. = *In Verrem.*
CIG = *Corpus Inscriptionum Graecarum,* 1828 ff.
CIL = *Corpus Inscriptionum Latinarum,* 1862 ff.
CI (1, 2) = *Epistle of Clement* (1, 2).
  Ps.-Clem. Hom. = *Pseudoclementine Homilies,* a narrative describing and defending the doctrine of the apostle Peter, ed. P. A. de Lagarde, 1865.
  Ps.-Clem. Recg. = *Pseudoclementine Recognitions,* the title of a novel which is partly made out of the Acts of Peter and which tells the story of a Roman family called Clemens, ed. P. A. de Lagarde, 1861.
Cl. Al. = T. Flavius Clemens Alexandrinus, of Athens, but doing his main work in Alexandria (150-215 A.D.), a leading representative of Christian culture, ed. O. Stählin, 1905 ff.
  Ecl. Proph. = *Eclogae Propheticae.*
  Exc. Theod. = *Excerpta ex Theodoto.*
  Paed. = *Paedagogus.*
  Prot. = ,*Protrepticus.*
  Quis Div. Salv. = *Quis Dives Salvetur.*
  Strom. = *Stromata.*
Class. Philol. = *Classical Philology,* Chicago, 1906 ff.
Class. Rev. = *Classical Review,* London, 1887 ff.
Clemen = C. Clemen, *Religionsgeschichtliche Erklärung des NT*[2], 1924.
Cod. = Codex.
Col. = Colossians.
col. = column.
comm. = commentary.
conj. = conjunction.
Const. Ap. = *Constitutiones Apostolorum,* a collection of early Christian writings (3rd-4th century A.D.), ed. F. X. Funk, 1905 ff.
Const. Porphyrog. = Constantinus Porphyrogenitus, Byzantine Emperor of the 10th century A.D. (912-959), who caused a collection of excerpts to be made from the classical Greek historians, ed. in MPG, 112-113, 1864.

constr. = construction.

Copt. = Coptic.

Corn. Nep. = Cornelius Nepos, of Upper Italy (c. 99-27 B.C.), friend of Cicero, antiquary and author of historical biographies with a strongly moralising and panegyrical flavour, ed. K. Halm, 1871.
>   Att. = *T. Pomponius Atticus.*
>   Vit. = *Vitae.*

Cornut. = L. Annaeus Cornutus, of Leptis in Africa, at the time of Nero, who in his *Hellenistic Theology* gives us a picture of later Stoic theology and allegory, ed. A. Nock, 1926.
>   Theol. Graec. = *Theologia Graeca.*

Corp. Gloss. Lat. = *Corpus Glossariorum Latinorum,* 1888 ff.

Corp. Herm. = *Corpus Hermeticum,* collection of Hermetic writings (Poimandres and others), late anonymous products of Hellenistic-Egyptian mysticism, the teachings of which may be found already in the 1st century A.D., ed. W. Scott, 1924.

Corp. Ref. = *Corpus Reformatorum,* 1834 ff.

Corp. Script. Christ. Or. = *Corpus Scriptorum Christianorum Orientalium,* 1903 ff.

CPR = *Corpus Papyrorum Raineri archiducis I,* ed. C. Wessely, 1895.

Cr.-Kö. = H. Cremer, *Biblisch-theologisches Wörterbuch des nt.lichen Griechisch,* revised by J. Kögel[11], 1923.

CSEL = *Corpus Scriptorum Ecclesiasticorum Latinorum,* 1866 ff.

Cyr. = Cyril of Jerusalem (c. 315-386 A.D.), ed. in MPG, 33 (1857).
>   Cat. Myst. = *Catechesis Mystagogica.*
>   Hom. = *Homiliae.*

d. = died.

Da. = Daniel.

DAC = *Dictionary of the Apostolic Church,* ed. J. Hastings, 1915 ff.

Dalman Gr. = G. Dalman, *Grammatik des jüdisch-palästinensischen Aramäisch*[2], 1924.

Dalman WJ = G. Dalman, *Worte Jesu,* I[2], 1930.

Dalman Wört. = G. Dalman, *Aramäisch-neuhebräisches Wörterbuch,* 1901.

Damasc. = *Damascus Document,* a Hebrew work discovered in 1910, partly admonitory and partly legal (Halacha) in content, possibly originating in Hasmonean or Roman times, ed. S. Schechter, 1910.

dat. = dative.

Dausch Synpt. = P. Dausch, *Kommentar z. d. älteren drei Evangelien*[2], 1930.

DCG = *Dictionary of Christ and the Gospels,* ed. J. Hastings[2], 1923 f.

Debr. Griech. Wortb. = A. Debrunner, *Griechische Wortbildungslehre,* 1917.

Def. = Definition.

Deissmann B. = A. Deissmann, *Bibelstudien,* 1895.

Deissmann LO = A. Deissmann, *Licht vom Osten*[4], 1923.

Deissmann NB = A. Deissmann, *Neue Bibelstudien,* 1897.

Demetr. Eloc. → Pseud.-Demetr.

Demetr. Phal. → Pseud.-Demetr.

Democr. = Democritus, of Abdera, in the second half of the 5th century B.C., the leading representative of atomism in ancient philosophy, ed. H. Diels in *Die Fragmente der Vorsokratiker,* II, 1922.

Demosth. = Demosthenes, of Athens (384-322 B.C.), ed. F. Blass, 1903 ff.
>   Or. = *Orationes.*
>   Ep. = *Epistulae.*

Dep. = Deponens.

Dessau Inscr. Lat. Select. = *Inscriptiones Latinae Selectae,* ed. H. Dessau, 1892.

Dg. = *Epistle to Diognetus.*

Dib. Gefbr. = M. Dibelius, *Kommentar z. d. Gefangenschaftsbriefen*[2], 1927.

Dib. Jk. = M. Dibelius, *Kommentar z. Jakobusbrief*[7], 1921.

Dib. Past. = M. Dibelius, *Kommentar z. d. Pastoralbriefen*[2], 1931.

Dib. Th. = M. Dibelius, *Kommentar z. d. Thessalonicherbriefen*[2], 1925.

Did. = *Didache.*

Didasc. = Syrian *Didascalia,* a comprehensive pre-Constantinian Church order contained in Const. Ap. (q.v.).

Didym. = Didymus, of Alexandria (c. 309-344/5 A.D.), one of the last instructors and principals of the Catechetical School, posthumously condemned (680) for his Origenistic tendencies, ed. in MPG, 39, 1863.
>   Trin. = *De Trinitate.*

Diehl = E. Diehl, *Anthologia Lyrica Graeca,* 1925.

Diels = H. Diels, *Die Fragmente der Vorsokratiker*[4], 1922.

Dio C. = Dio Cassius Cocceianus, of Nicea in Bithynia (c. 155-235 A.D.), a high Roman official, the author of a history of Rome in 80 books from Aeneas to his own time, ed. P. Boissevain, 1894 ff.

Dio Chrys. = Dion, of Prusa in Bithynia (c. 40-120 A.D.), later called Chrysostomus, the most important representative of the so-called Second Sophistic school in the Roman Empire, ed. H. v. Arnim, 1893 ff.

    Or. = *Orationes.*

Diod. S. = Diodorus Siculus, of Agyrion in Sicily, in the days of Augustus, author of a popular history of the world in 40 books in his *Historical Library,* ed. F. Vogel, 1888.

Diog. L. = Diogenes Laertius, author in the 3rd century A.D. of a not very critical history of Greek philosophy in 10 books, ed. H. G. Huebner, 1828.

Dion. Hal. = Dionysius of Halicarnassus, from 30 B.C. a teacher of rhetoric in Rome, Atticist and historian, author of an old Roman history, ed. C. Jacoby, 1885.

    Ant. Roma. = *Antiquitates Romanae.*

    Compos. Verb. = *De Compositione Verborum.*

    Pseud.-Dion. Hal. = *Pseudo-Dionysius Halicarnassensis.*

    Art. Rhet. = *De Arte Rhetorica.*

Dion. Thr. = Dionysius Thrax, Greek grammarian and rhetorician in Rhodes (170-90 B.C.), ed. G. Uhlig, 1883.

    Art. Gramm. = *De Arte Grammatica.*

Diosc. = Dioscurides, of Anazarbos in Cilicia, contemporary of the elder Pliny (1st century A.D.), author of a pharmacological work περὶ ὕλης ἰατρικῆς, ed. M. Wellmann, 1907 ff.

    Mat. Med. = *De Materia Medica.*

Diss. = Dissertation.

Diss. phil. Hall. = *Dissertationes philologicae Halenses,* 1873 ff.

Ditt. Or. = W. Dittenberger, *Orientis Graecae Inscriptiones,* 1902 ff.

Ditt. Syll. = W. Dittenberger, *Sylloge Inscriptionum Graecarum*², 1898 ff.;³, 1915 ff.

DLZ = *Deutsche Literaturzeitung,* 1880 ff.

Dob. Th. = E. Dobschütz, *Kommentar z. d. Thessalonicherbriefen*⁷, 1909.

Dt. = Deuteronomy.

Dt. Is. = Deutero-Isaiah.

Dt. r. = *Deuteronomium rabba* (= *Debarim rabba*), Homiletic Midrash on Deuteronomy (Strack, *Einl.,* 206).

Dtsch. Ev. Bl. = *Deutsch-evangelische Blätter,* 1876 ff.

E. = Elohist.

EB = *Encyclopaedia Biblica,* ed. T. K. Cheyne and S. J. Black, 1899 ff.

Ed. = *Edujot,* Mishnah-, Tosefta-, Talmud tractate *Witnesses* (later teachers on older authorities) (Strack, *Einl.,* 53).

EJ = *Encyclopaedia Judaica,* 1928 ff.

Eka r. = *Eka rabbati,* Midrash on Lamentations (Strack, *Einl.,* 212).

Emped. = Empedocles, of Acragas in Sicily (c. 495-435 B.C.), a philosopher who with his doctrine of the elements is to be placed among the physicists and mystics of the 5th century B.C., ed. H. Diels in *Die Fragmente der Vorsokratiker,* I, 1922.

En. = Enoch, patriarch, introduced into many later Jewish writings, the oldest of which date from the 2nd century B.C. (Schürer, III, 268 ff.).

    Eth. En. = Ethiopian Enoch, ed. A. Dillmann, 1851; R. Charles, 1906.

    Gr. En. = Greek Enoch. containing 32 chapters of the former in a MS discovered, 1886-7.

    Hb. En. = Hebrew Enoch, ed. H. Odeberg, 1928.

    Sl. En. = Slavic Enoch, ed. St. Novakovitsch, 1884.

ep. = *epistulae.*

Ep. Ar. = *Epistle of Aristeas,* apocryphal Jewish account of the origin of the LXX (2nd or 1st century B.C.), ed. P. Wendland, 1900.

Ep. Claud. ad Alex. = *Epistula Claudii ad Alexandrinos,* ed. H. Idris Bell, 1924.

Eph. = Ephesians.

Ephr. = Ephraim.

Epic. = Epicurus, of Samos (341-270 B.C.), established a philosophical school in Athens in 306, ed. H. Usener, 1887.

    (Ad) Men. = *Ad Menoeceum.*

Epict. = Epictetus, Phrygian slave of Hierapolis in the days of Nero (50-130 A.D.), freed at the imperial palace, Stoic of the younger school and preacher of ethics tinged with religion. From his lectures his pupil Arrian collected 8 books of diatribes which have been preserved, ed. H. Schenkl², 1916.

    Diss. = *Dissertationes.*

    Ench. = *Enchiridion.*

    Gnom. Stob. = *Gnomologium Stobaei.*

Ep. Jer. = *Epistle of Jeremiah,* Jewish apocryphal writing, in LXX attached to the Book of Baruch as the sixth chapter (3rd-2nd century B.C.), probably originating in the Babylonian *diaspora.*

Epigr. Graec. = *Epigrammata Graeca ex lapidibus conlecta,* ed. G. Kaibel, 1878.

epil. = *epilogium.*

Epiph. = Epiphanius, of Eleutheropolis in Palestine, bishop of Constantia in Cyprus (298-403 A.D.), opponent of 80 Christian, Jewish and Gnostic heresies in his rich and comprehensive work Πανάριον κατὰ πασῶν τῶν αἱρέσεων, ed. K. Holl, 1922.

    Haer. = *Haereses.*

Er(ub) = *Erubin,* Mishnah-, Tosefta-, Talmud tractate *Interminglings* (evasions of the Sabbath commandment) (Strack, *Einl.,* 38 f.).

ERE = *Encyclopaedia of Religion and Ethics,* ed. J. Hastings, 1908 ff.

esp. = especially.

4 Esr. = 4 Esdras (arranged as in the Vulgate), a most important Jewish apocalypse which originated at the end of the 1st century A.D. under the shattering impact of the destruction of Jerusalem, ed. B. Violet, 1910.

Est. = Esther.

ET or Exp. T. = *The Expository Times,* Edinburgh 1900 ff.

Etym. Gud. = *Etymologicum Gudianum,* etymological compilation of the Middle Ages (*c.* 1150 A.D.), named after Gude, the former owner of the Wolfenbüttler MS, ed. F. W. Sturz, 1818; E. A. de Stefani, 1909.

Etym. M. = *Etymologicum Magnum,* etymological compilation of the Middle Ages (*c.* 1100 A.D.), ed. T. Gaisford, 1848.

Eur. = Euripides, of Salamis nr. Athens (480-406 B.C.), tragic dramatist and philosopher of the stage, ed. G. Murray, 1901 ff.

   Alc. = *Alcestis.*
   Andr. = *Andromache.*
   Antiop. = *Antiope.*
   Archel. = *Archelaus.*
   Ba. = *Bacchae.*
   Cret. = *Cretes.*
   Cyc. = *Cyclops.*
   El. = *Electra.*
   Epigr. = *Epigrammata.*
   Hec. = *Hecuba.*
   Hel. = *Helena.*
   Herac. = *Heraclidae.*
   Herc. Fur. = *Hercules Furens.*
   Hipp. = *Hippolytus.*
   Hyps. = *Hypsipyle.*
   Ion
   Iph. Aul. = *Iphigenia Aulidensis.*
   Iph. Taur. = *Iphigenia Taurica.*
   Med. = *Medea.*
   Melan. Capt. = *Melanippe Captiva.*
   Melan. Sap. = *Melanippe Sapiens.*
   Oen. = *Oeneus.*
   Or. = *Orestes.*
   Phaët. = *Phaëthon.*
   Phoen. = *Phoenissae.*
   Pirith. = *Pirithous.*
   Rhes. = *Rhesus.*
   Sthen. = *Sthenoboea.*
   Suppl. = *Supplices.*
   Tro. = *Troades.*

Eus. = Eusebius of Caesarea (260-340 A.D.), ecclesiastical historian, ed. by different scholars in *Die Griech. christl. Schriftsteller der ersten 3 Jahrhunderte,* 1902 ff.

   Dem. Ev. = *Demonstratio Evangelica.*
   Hist. Eccl. = *Historia Ecclesiastica.*
   Marc. Fragm. = *Marcelli Fragmenta.*
   Praep. Ev. = *Praeparatio Evangelica.*
   Theoph. = *Theophania.*
   Vit. Const. = *Vita Constantini.*

Eustath. Thessal. = Eustathius Thessalonicensis (1175, archbishop of Thessalonica), the last allegorical commentator on the Iliad and the Odyssey, ed. G. Stallbaum, 1827 ff.

   Comm. in Il., Od. = *Commentarii in Homeri Iliadem, Odysseam.*

Euthymius Zig. = Euthymius Zigabenus, Byzantine theologian of the 12th century A.D. (died after 1118), author of exegetical and polemical dogmatic works, ed. in MPG, 128-131, 1864 ff.

   Commentary on the New Testament Epistles, ed. N. Calogeras, 1887.

Ev. Eb. = *Gospel of the Ebionites.*
   Hebr. = *Gospel of the Hebrews.*
   Naz. = *Gospel of the Nazarenes.*
   Pet. = *Gospel of Peter.*
   Remains of non-canonical and mostly heretical Gospels of the 2nd century A.D. existing only in fragments or quotations in the fathers, ed. E. Preuschen in *Antilegomena*[2], 1905.

Ew. Gefbr. = P. Ewald, *Kommentar z. d. Gefangenschaftsbriefen*[2], 1910.

Ex. = Exodus.

Exp. = *The Expositor,* London, 1882 ff.

Exp. T. *v.* ET.

Ex. r. = *Exodus rabba (Shemot rabba),* Midrash on Exodus (Strack, *Einl.,* 208).

Ez. = Ezekiel.

Ezr. = Ezra.

fem. = feminine.

Festschr. = *Festschrift.*

fig. etym. = figura etymologica.

Firm. Mat. = Julius Firmicus Maternus, of Syracuse, Latin author of the 4th century A.D., converted from Neo-Platonism to Christianity and a sharp opponent of the ancient cults and mysteries, ed. W. Kroll, F. S. Kutsch and K. Ziegler, 1897 ff.

   Err. Prof. Rel. = *De Errore Profanarum Religionum.*

Fr. (fr.) = Fragmenta (-um).

FRL = *Forschungen zur Religion und Literatur des AT und NT,* 1903 ff.

fut. = future.

Gal. = Claudius Galenus, of Pergamon (129-199 A.D.), the most renowned and from the literary standpoint the most productive of all the physicians of imperial Rome, ed. C. G. Kühn, 1821 ff.; H. Diels in *Corpus Medicorum Graecorum*, 1914 f.

GDI = Collection of Greek Dialect Inscriptions, ed. H. Collitz and F. Bechtel, 1884 ff.

Gelas. = Gelasius, of Cycicus, compiler (c. 475 A.D. in Bithynia) of an ecclesiastical history only partially extant, ed. G. Loeschcke and M. Heinemann, 1918.
    Hist. Eccl. = *Historia Ecclesiastica*.

gen. obj. = objective genitive.

gen. subj. = subjective genitive.

Geogr. Graec. Min. = *Geographi Graeci Minores*, ed. C. Müller, 1855 ff.

Ges.-Bergst. = W. Gesenius, *Hebräische Grammatik*, revised by G. Bergsträsser[29], 1918 ff.

Ges.-Buhl = W. Gesenius-F. Buhl, *Hebräisches und aramäisches Handwörterbuch zum AT*[16], 1915.

Ges.-K. = W. Gesenius, *Hebräische Grammatik*, revised by E. Kautzsch[28], 1909.

GGA = *Göttingische Gelehrte Anzeigen*, 1739 ff.

Git. = Gittin.

Gl. = Galatians.

Glotta = *Glotta, Zeitschrift für griechische und lateinische Sprache*, 1909 ff.

Gn. = Genesis.

Gnom. = J. A. Bengel, *Gnomon NT*[8] (1887).

Gn. r. = *Genesis rabba* (*Bereshit rabba*), Midrash on Genesis (Strack, *Einl.*, 209 ff.).

Gorg. = Gorgias, of Leontini in Sicily (c. 483-375 B.C.), one of the main representatives of classical sophistic and rhetoric in Athens (cf. Plato's dialogue *Gorgias*). From his rhetorical handbook two model speeches have come down to us, the deliverance of Helena and the defence of Palamedes, ed. H. Diels in *Die Fragmente der Vorsokratiker*, II[4], 1922.
    Hel. = *Helena*.
    Pal. = *Palamedes*.

Greg. Naz. = Gregory Nazianzus (c. 330-390 A.D.), one of the three great Cappadocian fathers and the most important Christian poet of his day, ed. in MPG, 35-38, 1857 f.
    Or. Theol. = *Orationes Theologicae*.

Greg. Nyss. = Gregory of Nyssa, brother of Basil of Caesarea (d.c. 394 A.D.), the most profound thinker of the three Cap-

padocians, ed. in MPG, 44-46, 1863.
    Apoll. = *Contra Apollonium*.
    Beat. Or. = *De Beatitudinibus Orationes*.
    (Ctr.) Eunom. = *Contra Eunomium*.
    Virg. = *De Virginitate*.

Gk. = Greek.

Hab. = Habakkuk.

Had. Apk. = W. Hadorn, *Kommentar z. Apokalypse*, 1928.

Hag. = Haggai.

Harnack Dg. = A. v. Harnack, *Lehrbuch d. Dogmengeschichte*[4], 1909 f.

Hastings DB = J. Hastings, *Dictionary of the Bible*, 1898 ff.

Hatch-Redp. = E. Hatch and H. Redpath, *A Concordance to the Septuagint*, 1897 ff.

Haupt Gefbr. = E. Haupt, *Kommentar z. d. Gefangenschaftsbriefen*[7], 1902.

Hb. = Hebrews.

Hbr. Un. Coll. = *Hebrew Union College Annual* (Cincinnati, 1924 ff.).

Hck. Jk. = F. Hauck, *Kommentar z. Jakobusbrief*, 1926.

Hck. Mk. = F. Hauck, *Kommentar z. Markusev.*, 1931.

Hdt. = Herodotus, of Halicarnassus (c. 484-425 B.C.), the first real Greek historian, described as early as Cicero as the father of history. His work deals with the conflicts between the Greeks and the barbarians from earliest times to the Persian Wars, ed. H. Kallenberg, 1926 ff.
    Pseud.-Hdt. = Pseudo-Herodotus.
    Vit. Hom. = *De Vita Homeri*.

Heb. = Hebrew.

Helbing = R. Helbing, *Grammatik der Septuaginta*, 1907.

Heliodor. = Heliodorus, of Emesa (3rd century B.C.), writer of stories, his Aethiopica consisting of Ethiopian tales of Theagenes and Charicleia, ed. I. Bekker, 1855.
    Aeth. = *Aethiopica*.

Hennecke = E. Hennecke, *Nt.liche Apokryphen*[2], 1923 f.

Heracl. = Heraclitus, of Ephesus (535-475 B.C.), pre-Socratic philosopher, ed. H. Diels in *Die Fragmente der Vorsokratiker*, I, 1922.

Heracl. = Heraclitus, Stoic philosopher, perhaps of the age of Augustus, author of Ὁμηρικαὶ Ἀλληγορίαι, ed. Soc. Phil. Bonn, 1910.
    Hom. All. = Homeri Allegoriae.

Herm. = *Hermes, Zeitschrift für klassische Philologie*, 1866 ff.

Herm. = *Pastor Hermae.*
   m. = *mandata.*
   s. = *similitudines.*
   v. = *visiones.*

Herm. Trismeg. = Hermes Trismegistus, the godhead of the corpus of 18 mystical and syncretistic writings known as the *Hermetica* (*v.* Corp. Herm.), ed. W. Scott, 1924 ff. *v.* Reitzenstein Poim.

Herodian = Herodianus, of Syria, official and historian under Septimius Severus, wrote 8 books from the death of Aurelius to 238 A.D., ed. K. Stavenhagen, 1922.
   Hist. = *Historiae.*

Herond. = Herondas, Greek poet, probably of Cos (*c.* 250 B.C.), who gives us realistic scenes from everyday life in his *Mimes,* of which eight have recently been discovered on papyri, ed. R. Herzog, 1926.
   Mim. = *Mimiambi.*

Hes. = Hesiodus, of Ascra in Boetia (*c.* 700 B.C.), the oldest Greek poet to emerge as a tangible figure. In his *Pastoral Calendar* ἔργα καὶ ἡμέραι he proclaims the pastoral ideal of life. His Theogony is a speculative work on the origin and descent of the gods, ed. A. Rzach, 1913.
   Op. = *Opera et Dies.*
   Theog. = *Theogonia.*

Hesych. = Hesychius, of Alexandria (5th century A.D.), lexicographer, ed. M. Schmidt, 1858 ff.

Hier. = Hieronymus (Jerome), of Dalmatia (*c.* 340-420 A.D.), who after study in Rome lived as a monk in the Near East and engaged in extensive scholarly work, particularly on the text of the Bible, ed. in MPL 22-30, 1865 ff.; *Epistulae,* ed. J. Hilberg, 1910 ff.
   (Comm.) in Is. = *Commentarii in Isaiam Prophetam.*
   (Ad) Gal. = *Ad Galatas.*
   (Ad.) Pelag. = *Adversus Pelagium.*

Hierocl. = Hierocles, of Alexandria, distinguished Neo-Platonist and contemporary of Proclus (410-485 A.D.), author of a long explanation of the *Golden Sayings* of Pythagoras, ed. F. W. A. Mullach, I, 1853.
   Carm. Aur. = *In Aureum Pythagorae Carmen Commentarius.*

Hipp. = Hippolytus (*c.* 160-235 A.D.), disciple of Irenaeus. His main work *A Refutation of all Heresies* in 10 books is directed against Greek philosophy as the mother of all heresies, ed. by different scholars in *Die griech. christl. Schriftsteller der ersten 3 Jahrhunderte,* 1897 ff.
   Philos. = *Philosophumena.*

   Ref. = *Refutatio Omnium Haeresium.*

Hippocr. = Hippocrates, of Cos (*c.* 460 B.C.), the founder of the scientific medicine of the Greeks. The authenticity of many of the works handed down under his name is disputed, ed. E. Littré, 1839 ff.; J. Ilberg and H. Kühlewein, 1899 ff.; J. L. Heiberg in *Corpus Medicorum Graecorum,* 1927.
   Acut. = *De Ratione Victus in Morbis Acutis.*
   Epid. = *Epidemiae.*
   Morb. = *De Morbis.*
   Mul. = *De Morbis Mulierum.*
   Progn. = *Prognosticum.*
   Vet. Med. = *De Vetere Medicina.*
   Vict. = *De Ratione Victus Salubris.*

Hist. Aug. *v.* Script. Hist. Aug.

Hom. = Homer, of Chios (?), the classical Greek epic poet, around whose name were grouped the older epics of the Ionians in the 9th and 8th centuries B.C., ed. G. Monro and T. W. Allen, 1908 ff.
   Il. = *Iliad.*
   Od. = *Odyssey.*

Hom. Hymn. = *Homerici Hymni,* deriving from the 7th century B.C., regarded by the ancients as Homeric, and used as an introduction to the recital of Homeric poems, ed. T. Allen, 1911.
   Hymn. Ap. = *Hymnus ad Apollinem.*
   Bacch. = *ad Bacchum.*
   Cer. = *ad Cererem.*
   Mart. = *ad Martem.*
   Merc. = *ad Mercurium.*
   Pan. = *ad Panem.*
   Ven. = *ad Venerem.*

Hor. = *Horajot,* Mishnah-, Tosefta-, Talmud tractate *Decisions* (erroneous) (Strack, *Einl.,* 54).

Horat. = Q. Horatius Flaccus, of Venusia (65-8 B.C.), with Vergil the best known and most important representative of the great Augustan era in Roman poetry.
   Sat. = *Satirae.*

Hos. = Hosea.

HT = Hebrew Text.

Iambl. = Iamblichus, of Chalcis in Syria, at the time of Constantine the Great, founder of the Syrian school of Neo-Platonism, and reputed author of a work on the Egyptian mysteries, ed. H. Pistelli, 1894; *De Mysteriis,* ed. G. Parthey, 1857.
   Comm. Math. Scient. = *De Communi Mathematica Scientia.*
   Myst. = *De Mysteriis.*
   Protr. = *Protrepticus.*
   Theol. Arithm. = *Theologia Arithmetica.*
   Vit. Pyth. = *Vita Pythagorae.*

IG = *Inscriptiones Graecae,* ed. *Preussische*

Akademie d. Wissenschaften zu Berlin, 1873 ff.

Ign. = Ignatius.
    Eph. = Epistula ad Ephesios.
    Mg. = ad Magnesios.
    Phld. = ad Philadelphenses.
    R. = ad Romanos.
    Sm. = ad Smyrnaeos.
    Tr. = ad Trallianos.
imp. = imperative.
impf. = imperfect.
ind. = indicative.
indecl. = indeclinable.
inf. = infinitive.

Inscr. Hierap. = Hierapolis Inscription, ed. W. Judeich, 1898.

Inscr. Magn. = Inscriptions of Magnesia on the Meander, ed. O. Kern, 1900.

Inscr. Perg. = Inscriptions of Pergamon, ed. M. Fränkel, 1900.

Insc(h)r. Priene = Priene Inscriptions, ed. F. Hiller v. Gärtringen, 1906.
int. = interdum.
intr. = intransitive.

IPE = Inscriptiones Orae Septentrionalis Ponti Euxini, ed. B. Latyschev, 1885.

Iren. = Irenaeus, of Asia Minor, bishop of Lyons, martyred 202 A.D. during the persecution under Severus, ed. in MPG, 7, 1882.
    Epid. = Epideixis.
Is. = Isaiah.

Isoc. = Isocrates, of Athens (436-338 B.C.), originally a barrister and writer of political pamphlets, later in connection with the Sophists an outstanding representative of general culture in the 4th century, ed. F. Blass, 1913 ff.
    Areop. = Areopagiticus.

J = Jahwist.

Jad. = Jadajim, Mishnah-, Tosefta-, Talmud tractate Hands (uncleanness and washing of the hands) (Strack, Einl., 64).

Jbch. f. Phil. = Neue Jahrbücher für Philologie und Pädagogik, 1831 ff.

Jbch. pr. Th. = Jahrbücher für protestantische Theologie, 1875 ff.

JBL = Journal of Biblical Literature, New Haven, 1881 ff.

Jd. = Epistle of Jude.

Jdt. = Judith.

Jeb. = Jebamot, Mishnah-, Tosefta-, Talmud tractate Marriage of those related by Marriage (Strack, Einl., 45).

Jer. = Jeremiah.

Jew. Enc. = Jewish Encyclopaedia, 1901 ff.

JHS = The Journal of Hellenic Studies,
London, 1880 ff.

Jl. = Joel.

Jm. = Epistle of James.

Jn. = John's Gospel.

Jn. (1, 2, 3) = Epistles of John (1, 2, 3).

Joh. = John.

Joh. = Johannine.

Joh. Lyd. = Johannes Laurentius Lydus, court official under the emperor Justinian, after 522 devoted to antiquarian studies of a chronological and astrological nature (e.g., De Mensibus), ed. I. Bekker in Corpus Scriptorum Historiae Byzantinae, 1837.

Joh. Mosch. = Johannes Moschus, Byzantine monk (6th century A.D.), whose work Λειμών (Pratum Spirituale) is a collection of anecdotes intended as a contribution to the ascetic life in the form of a description of the exemplary works of famous men, ed. in MPG, 87, 3, 1865.

Joh. W. 1 K. = Johannes Weiss, Kommentar z. 1. Korintherbrief[9] (1910).

Jon. = Jonah.

Jos. = Joshua.

Jos(eph). = Flavius Josephus, Jewish author (c. 37-97 A.D.) in Palestine and later Rome, author in Greek of the Jewish War and Jewish Archaeology, which treat of the period from creation to Nero, ed. B. Niese, 1887 ff.
    Ant. = Antiquitates.
    Ap. = Contra Apionem.
    Bell. = Bellum Judaicum.
    Vit. = Vita.

JPOS = Journal of the Palestine Oriental Society, Jerusalem, 1920 ff.

JQR = Jewish Quarterly Review, London-Philadelphia, 1905 ff.

JRS = Journal of Roman Studies, London, 1911 ff.

JThSt. = Journal of Theological Studies, London, 1899 ff.

Ju. = Judges.

Jud. = Judaism.

Jüd. Lex. = Jüdisches Lexikon, 1927 ff.

Jul. = Julian the Apostate (361-363 A.D.), who attempted by a fusion of polytheism and Neo-Platonism to restore decaying paganism, Orationes, ed. F. C. Hertlein, 1875 ff.; Epistulae, ed. J. Bidez-F. Cumont, 1922.
    Conv. = Convivium (= Caesares).
    Ep. = Epistulae.
    Gal. = Contra Galilaeos.
    Or. = Orationes.

Jülicher Gl. J. = A. Jülicher, *Die Gleichnis-reden Jesu²*, 1910.

Just. = Justin Martyr, executed c. 165 A.D., author of an apology against the attacks on Christians, and also of a discussion with Judaism in the *Dialogue with Trypho*, ed. E. Goodspeed in *Die ältesten Apologeten*, 1914; ed. G. Krüger, 1915.
    Apol. = *Apologia*.
    Dial. (c. Tryph.) = *Dialogus cum Tryphone Judaeo*.
    Epit. = *Epitome*.
Pseud-Just. = Pseudo-Justinus.
    Quaest. et Resp. ad Orth. = *Quaestiones et Responsiones ad Orthodoxos*.

Juv. = D. Junius Juvenalis, c. 58-138 A.D., the last great Roman satirist, ed. O. Jahn, F. Bücheler and F. Leo³, 1910.

K (1, 2) = Kings (1, 2).

Kassovsky = H. J. Kassovsky, *Concordantiae totius Mischnae*, 1927.

KAT = E. Schrader, *Die Keilschriften und das Alte Testament³*, ed. H. Zimmern and A. Winckler, 1903.

Kautzsch = *Die heilige Schrift des Alten Testaments*, tr. E. Kautzsch, ed. A. Bertholet, 1921 ff.

Kautzsch Apkr. u. Pseudepigr. = *Apokryphen und Pseudepigraphen des Alten Testamentes*, tr. E. Kautzsch, 1900.

Kern. Orph. *v.* Orph. Fr. Kern.

Ket. = *Ketubbot*, Mishnah-, Tosefta-, Talmud tractate *Rules for Marriage* (Strack, *Einl.*, 46).

Kg. Pt. = Kerygma Petri.

Khl. R. = E. Kühl, *Kommentar z. Römerbrief*, 1913.

Kid. *v.* Qid.

Kil. = *Kilajim*, Mishnah-, Tosefta, Talmud tractate *Two Things* (unlawful mixture of things of a different kind) (Strack, *Einl.*, 33).

Kittel Probleme = G. Kittel, *Die Probleme des palästinensischen Spätjudentums*, 1926.

Kl. Lk. = E. Klostermann, *Kommentar z. Lukasev.²* 1929.

Kl. Mk. = E. Klostermann, *Kommentar z. Markusev.²* 1926.

Kl. Mt. = E. Klostermann, *Kommentar z. Matthäusev.²* 1927.

Kl. T. = *Kleine Texte für Vorlesungen und Übungen*, ed. H. Lietzmann, 1902 ff.

Kn. Pt. = R. Knopf, *Kommentar z. d. Petrusbriefen⁷*, 1912.

Kühner-Blass-Gerth = *Ausführliche Grammatik der griechischen Sprache*, by R.

Kuhner³ I, 1890; II, 1892; rev. F. Blass, 1898; rev. B. Gerth.

Lact. = Lactantius, probably of Africa (3rd-4th century A.D.), later called by Diocletian to Nicomedia as a teacher of rhetoric and the most widely read Latin father, ed. S. Brandt, 1890 ff.
    Inst. = *Divinae Institutiones*.

Lat. = Latin.

Levy Chald. Wört. = J. Levy, *Chaldäisches Wörterbuch über die Targumim*, 1867 f.

Levy Wört. = J. Levy, *Neuhebräisches und chaldäisches Wörterbuch über die Talmudim und Midraschim*, 1876 f., new imp. 1924.

Lex. Th. K. = *Lexikon für Theologie und Kirche¹*, 1907 ff.; ² 1930 ff.

Lib. = Libanius, of Antioch (314-393 A.D.), teacher of Julian, one of the 4th century Sophists, of whom we have the autobiography, a comprehensive collection of letters and many addresses, ed. R. Förster, 1903 ff.
    Ep. = *Epistulae*.
    Or. = *Orationes*.

Liddell-Scott = H. Liddell and R. Scott, *Greek-English Lexicon*, New ed. by H. St. Jones, 1925 ff.

Lidz. Ginza = M. Lidzbarski, *Ginza*, 1925.

Lidz. Joh. = M. Lidzbarski, *Das Johannesbuch der Mandäer*, 1915.

Lidz. Liturg. = M. Lidzbarski, *Mandäische Liturgien*, 1920.

Lit. = Literature.

Liv. = Titus Livius, of Padua (59 B.C.-17 A.D.), the great historian of Augustan Rome, ed. G. Weissenborn and M. Müller, 1926 ff.

Lk. = Luke's Gospel.

Loh. Apk. = E. Lohmeyer, *Kommentar z. Apokalypse*, 1926.

Loh. Kol. = E. Lohmeyer, *Kommentar z. Kolosserbrief⁸*, 1930.

Loh. Phil. = E. Lohmeyer, *Kommentar z. Philipperbrief⁸*, 1928.

Loh. Phlm. = E. Lohmeyer, *Kommentar z. Philemonbrief⁸*, 1930.

Longus = Longus, of Lesbos (end of the 2nd century A.D.), Greek novelist, ed. R. Hercher in *Erotici Scriptores*, 1858.

Ltzm. Gl. = H. Lietzmann, *Kommentar z. Galaterbrief³*, 1932.

Ltzm. K. = H. Lietzmann, *Kommentar z. d. Korintherbriefen³*, 1931.

Ltzm. R. = H. Lietzmann, *Kommentar z. Römerbrief³*, 1928.

Luc. = Lucianus, of Samosata in Syria (120-180 A.D.), best-known, though re-

negade, representative of the Second Sophistic School, rhetorician and lively satirist of his epoch, ed. C. Jacobitz, 1836; W. Dindorf, 1858.
> Alex. = *Alexander sive Pseudomantis.*
> Demon. = *Demonax.*
> Dial. Mar. = *Dialogi Marini.*
> Eun. = *Eunuchus.*
> Hermot. = *Hermotimus.*
> Icaromenipp. = *Icaromenippus.*
> Indoct. = *Adversus Indoctum.*
> Jup. Conf. = *Juppiter Confutatus.*
> Jup. Trag. = *Juppiter Tragicus.*
> Nec. = *Necyomantia.*
> Pergr. Mort. = *De Peregrini Morte.*
> Pseudolol. = *Pseudologista.*
> Salt. = *De Saltatione.*
> Soloec. = *De Soloecismo.*
> Syr. D. *v.* Pseud. Luc.
> Tim. = *Timon.*
> Tyr. = *Cataplus sive Tyrannus.*
> Vit. Auct. = *Vitarum Auctio.*
> Zeux. = *Zeuxis sive Antiochus.*
> Pseud. Luc. = Pseudo-Lucianus.
> Asin. = *De Asino.*
> Ocyp. = *Ocypus.*
> Syr. Dea = *De Syria Dea.*

Lv. = Leviticus.

Lv. r. = *Leviticus rabba* (= *Wajjikra rabba*), Midrash on Leviticus (Strack, *Einl.*, 204).

Lyc. = Lycurgus, Attic orator and statesman (338-327 B.C.), ed. C. Scheibe and F. Blass, 1899.

Lys. = Lysias, of Athens (445-380 B.C.), belongs to the canon of the 10 Attic orators, ed. T. Thalhelm, 1901.

Maas. = *Maasrot,* Mishnah-, Tosefta-, Talmud tractate *The Tithe* (Strack, *Einl.*, 35).

Macc. (1, 2, 3, 4) = Maccabees (1, 2, 3, 4).

Macrob. = Macrobius Theodosius, an antiquary concerned in the movement of pagan restoration *c.* 400 A.D., ed. F. Eyssenhardt[2], 1893.
> Sat. = *Saturnalia.*

Mak. = *Makkot,* Mishnah-, Tosefta-, Talmud tractate *Scourging* (Strack, *Einl.*, 52).

Mak. = Makarios, Alexandrian, monk in the Nitric Hills (4th century A.D.). The homily ascribed to him was perhaps written by another monk, ed. in MPG, 34, 1848.

Maksh. = *Makshirin,* Mishnah-, Tosefta-, Talmud tractate *What Qualifies* (on becoming unclean) (Strack, *Einl.*, 63).

Mal. = Malachi.

Mandelkern = S. Mandelkern, *Veteris Testamenti Concordantiae Hebraicae atque Chaldaicae*[2], 1925.

M. Ant. = Marcus Aurelius Antoninus, emperor and philosopher (161-180 A.D.), influenced by Epictetus and one of the younger Stoics. His *Meditations* (τὰ εἰς ἑαυτόν) in 12 books are the last significant product of Stoicism, ed. H. Schenkl, 1913).

Marin. = Marinus, Neo-Platonist, successor of his teacher Proclus (410-485 A.D.), whose biography he wrote, and teacher of philosophy at Athens, ed. J. F. Boissonade, 1814.
> Vit. Procl. = *Vita Procli.*

Mark Liturg. = Liturgy of Mark, in *Liturgies Eastern and Western,* ed. F. E. Brightman, 1896.

Mart. = M. Valerius Martialis, of Spain, the most famous Latin epigrammatist in the 1st century of imperial Rome, ed. W. Heraeus, 1925.

Mart. = *Martyrium.*
> Is. = *Iesaiae* (*v.* Asc. Is.).
> Mt. = *Matthaei.*
> Pl. = *Pauli.*
> Pol. = *Polycarpi.*
> Pt. = *Petri.*

Mas. = Masora.

masc. = masculine.

Maxim. Conf. = Maximus Confessor, of Constantinople (580-662 A.D.), monk, theologian and mystic, who played a prominent part in the christological controversies of his day, being condemned and silenced for his Dyotheletism, ed. MPG, 90, 1865.
> Quaest. ad Thalass. = *Quaestiones ad Thalassium.*

Max. Tyr. = Maximus of Tyre, in Rome at the time of Commodus (180-192 A.D.), Sophist and wandering philosophical orator, an eclectic Platonist with Cynical and Stoic tendencies, author of philosophical essays in the style of diatribes (διαλέξεις), ed. H. Hobein, 1910.

Mayser = E. Mayser, *Grammatik d. Griech. Papyri aus der Ptolemäerzeit,* 1906.

Meg. = *Megilla,* Mishnah-, Tosefta-, Talmud tractate *Esther Scroll* (reading for the feast of Purim) (Strack, *Einl.*, 43).

Meinertz Gefbr. = M. Meinertz and F. Tillmann, *Die Gefangenschaftsbriefe des hl. Paulus*[4], 1931.

Meinertz Kath. Br. = M. Meinertz and W. Vrede, *Die Katholischen Briefe*[4], 1932.

Meinertz Past. = M. Meinertz, *Die Pastoralbriefe des hl. Paulus*[4], 1931.

Mek. R. Sim. = *Mekilta of Rabbi Simeon*

ben Jochai, reconstruction of an old Midrash on Exodus (Strack, *Einl.,* 200).

Men. = *Menachot,* Mishnah-, Tosefta-, Talmud tractate *Meat Offerings* (Strack, *Einl.,* 55 f.).

Menand. = Menander, of Athens (343-290 B.C.), recognised master of the new Attic comedy, ed. T. Kock in *Comicorum Atticorum Fragmenta* III, 1888; C. A. Jensen, 1929.

    Cith. = *Citharistes.*
    Col. = *Colax.*
    Con. = *Coneazomenae.*
    Epit. = *Epitrepontes.*
    Fab. Inc. = *Fabula Incerta.*
    Georg. = *Georgos.*
    Her. = *Heros.*
    Mis. = *Misumenae.*
    Mon. = *Monostichi.*
    Per. = *Perinthia.*
    Peric. = *Periciromena.*
    Phasm. = *Phasma.*
    Sam. = *Samia.*

Method. = Methodius, bishop of Olympus, martyred 311 A.D. Of his writings the only one that has come down to us complete in Greek is the *Symposion,* though others exist in translation, ed. MPG, 18, 1857.

    Resurrect. = *De Resurrectione.*
    Symp. = *Symposion.*

M. Ex. = *Mekilta Exodus,* Tannaitic Midrash on Exodus (Strack, *Einl.,* 201). ed. J. Rabin, 1929 ff.

Meyer Ursprung = E. Meyer, *Ursprung und Anfänge des Christentums,* 1921 ff.

MGWJ = *Monatsschrift für Geschichte und Wissenschaft des Judentums,* 1869 ff.

Mi. = Micah.

Mid. = *Middot,* Mishnah-, Tosefta-, Talmud tractate *Measures* (of the temple) (Strack., *Einl.,* 59).

mid. = middle.

Midr. = Midrash, Jewish expositions or homilies on books of the Old Testament (Strack, *Einl.,* 196 ff.).

Midr. HL = Midrash on the Song of Solomon (Strack, *Einl.,* 213).

Midr. Prv. = Midrash on Proverbs (Strack, *Einl.,* 216).

Midr. Ps. = Midrash on Psalms (Strack, *Einl.,* 215).

Midr. Qoh. = Midrash on Ecclesiastes (Strack, *Einl.,* 213).

Mimn. = Mimnermus, of Colophon, Ionic poet of the second half of the 7th century B.C., ed. E. Diehl in *Anthologia Lyrica,* I, 1925.

Miq. = *Miqvaot,* Mishnah-, Tosefta-, Talmud tractate *Plunge Baths* (Strack, *Einl.,* 62).

Mithr. Liturg. = A. Dieterich, *Eine Mithrasliturgie*[3], 1923.

Mitteis-Wilcken = L. Mitteis and U. Wilcken, *Grundzüge und Chrestomathie der Papyruskunde,* 1912.

Mk. = Mark's Gospel.

Moore = G. F. Moore, *Judaism,* 1927 ff.

Moult. Mill. = J. H. Moulton and G. Milligan, *The Vocabulary of the Greek Testament,* 1915 ff.

Moulton = J. H. Moulton, *Einleitung in die Sprache des NT,* 1911.

MPER = *Mitteilungen aus der Sammlung d. Papyrus Erzherzog Rainer,* 1887 ff.

MPG = *Patrologia, Series Graeca,* ed. J. P. Migne, 1844 ff.

MPL = *Patrologia, Series Latina,* ed. J. P. Migne, 1844 ff.

MQ = *Moed qatan,* Mishnah-, Tosefta-, Talmud tractate, *Intervening Festivals* (Strack, *Einl.,* 44).

MS = *Maaser Scheni,* Mishnah-, Tosefta-, Talmud tractate *The Second Tithe* (Strack, *Einl.,* 35).

Mt. = Matthew's Gospel.

Muson. = C. Musonius Rufus, of Volsinii in Etruria at the time of Nero, Stoic with cynical tendencies, ed. O. Hense, 1905.

Na. = Nahum.

Nägeli = T. Nägeli, *Der Wortschatz des Apostels Paulus,* 1905.

NAMZ = *Neue Allgemeine Missions-Zeitschrift,* 1924 ff.

Ned. = *Nedarim,* Mishnah-, Tosefta-, Talmud tractate *Vow* (Strack, *Einl.,* 46).

Neg. = *Negaim,* Mishnah-, Tosefta-, Talmud tractate *Leprosy* (Strack, *Einl.,* 61).

Neh. = Nehemiah.

Nestle = *Novum Testamentum Graece,* curavit E. Nestle, elaboravit Erwin Nestle[15], 1932.

Nestle Dobsch. = E. Nestle, *Einführung in das griechische NT,* ed. E. Dobschütz[4], 1923.

neutr. = neuter.

New Heb. = New Hebrew.

NGG = *Nachrichten von der Kgl. Gesellschaft der Wissenschaften zu Göttingen,* 1894 ff.

N. Jbch. Kl. Alt. = *Neue Jahrbücher des Klassischen Altertums,* 1898 ff.

N. Jbch. Wiss. u. Jugendbildung = *Neue Jahrbücher für Wissenschaft und Jugendbildung,* 1925 ff.

Nicand. = Nicander, of Colophon (3rd/2nd century B.C.), Hellenistic poet, grammarian and author of medical writings, ed. O. Schneider, 1856.
    Alexipharm. = *Alexipharmaca.*

Nk. Z. = *Neue kirchliche Zeitschrift,* 1890 ff.

No. (no.) = number.

Nonnus = Nonnus, of Panapolis in Egypt, a Christian, but author in the 4th century A.D. of a Dionysus epic in 48 books, ed. A. Ludwich, 1909 ff.
    Dionys. = Dionysiaca.

N. Ph. U. = *Neue philologische Untersuchungen,* 1926 ff.

N. pr. = proper name.

NT = New Testament.

NT Deutsch = *Das Neue Testament Deutsch,* ed. P. Althaus and J. Behm, 1932 ff.

Nu. = Numbers.

Nu. r. = *Numbers rabba* (= *Bemidbar rabba*), Midrash on Numbers (Strack, *Einl.,* 207).

Ob. = Obadiah.

obj. = object.

Oestr. Jhft. = *Jahreshefte d. Österreichischen Archäologischen Instituts,* 1898 ff.

OLZ = *Orientalistische Literatur-Zeitung,* 1898 ff.

opp. = oppositum.

Oppian Cyn. *v.* Pseud.-Oppian.

Or. = *Oratio* (*nes*).

Orig. = Origen, of Alexandria (185-254 A.D.), pupil of Clement of Alexandria, and most learned and fruitful representative of ancient Christian scholarship and culture, ed. by different scholars in *Die griech. christl. Schriftsteller der ersten 3 Jahrhunderte,* 1899 ff.
    Cels. = *Contra Celsum.*
    Comm. in Joh. = *In Johannem Commentarius.*
    Comm. in Ps. = *In Psalmos Commentarii.*
    Hom. in Ex. Jer. Jos. Lv. = *Homilies on Exodus, Jeremiah, Joshua and Leviticus.*
    Orat. = *De Oratione.*
    Philocal. = *Philocalia.*
    Princ. = *De Principiis.*

Orph. (Abel) = *Orphica,* Orphic hymns, of which 88 have survived, belonging to later antiquity but containing many older materials, and cultic in character, ed. E. Abel, 1885.

Orph. Fr. (Kern) = *Orphicorum Fragmenta,* ed. O. Kern, 1922.

O. Sol. = *Odes of Solomon,* Christian-Gnostic collection of songs of the 2nd century, extant in Syriac, ed. J. Rendel Harris, 1916 ff.

Ostraka = U. Wilcken, *Griechische Ostraka,* 1912.

OT = Old Testament.

Ovid. = P. Ovidius Naso, of Sulmo in Italy (43 B.C.-18 A.D.), the great elegiast of Augustan Rome, ed. C. Postgate, 1894.
    Fast. = *Fasti.*

Palaeph. = Palaephatus, author of a work on the rationalistic interpretation of myths somewhere between the 4th and 2nd century B.C., ed. M. Festa in *Mythographi Graeci,* 1902.

Pall. = Palladius Helenopolitanus, of Galatia (368-*c.* 431 A.D.), monk and bishop of Helenopolis, later of Aspruna (Galatia), close to Origen in outlook. He dedicated a collection of edifying biographies of monks to a chamberlain Lausos (*Historia Lausiaca*), and was possibly the author of a *Vita Chrysostomi.*
    Hist. Laus. = *Historia Lausiaca,* ed. D. C. Buttler, 1898 ff.

Pap. = Papyrus, shortened to P. when specific editions are quoted.
    P. Amh. = *The Amherst Papyri,* ed. B. Grenfell and A. Hunt, 1900 ff.
    P. Eleph. = *Elephantine Papyri,* ed. O. Rubensohn, 1907.
    P. Fay. = *Fayûm Towns and their Papyri,* ed. B. Grenfell, A. Hunt and D. Hogarth, 1900.
    P. Flor. = *Papyri Florentini,* I, ed. G. Vitelli, 1906; II, ed. D. Comparetti, 1908 ff.
    P. Gen. = *Les Papyrus de Genève,* ed. J. Nicole, 1896 ff.
    P. Giess. = *Griechische Papyri zu Giessen,* ed. O. Eger, E. Kornemann and P. M. Meyer, 1910 ff.
    P. Greci e Latini = *Papyri Greci e Latini,* Pubblicazioni della Società Italiana, 1911 ff.
    P. Hal. = *Papyrus-Sammlung d. Universität Halle,* ed. Graeca Halensis in Dikaiomata, 1913.
    P. Hamb. = *Griechische Papyrusurkunden der Hamburger Stadtbibliothek,* ed. P. M. Meyer, 1911 ff.
    P. Herm. = *Corpus Papyrorum Hermopolitanarum,* ed. C. Wessely, 1905.
    P. Hern. = *Papyruspublikationen,* ed. C. Wessely in *Jahresberichte d. K. K. Staatsgymnasiums in Hernals,* Vol. XIV, XVI.
    P. Hibeh = *The Hibeh Papyri,* ed. B. Grenfell and A. Hunt, 1906.

P. klein. Form. = *Griechische Papyrus-urkunden kleineren Formats,* ed. C. Wessely, 1904 ff.

P. Leid. = *Papyri Graeci Musei anti-quarii publici Lugduni-Batavi,* ed. C. Leemanns, 1843 ff.

P. Leipz. = *Die griechischen Papyri Sachsens,* ed. C. Wessely, 1885.

P. Lille = *Papyrus Grecs Lille,* ed. P. Jouguet, P. Collart and others, 1912.

P. Lips. = *Griechische Urkunden der Papyrussammlung zu Leipzig,* ed. L. Mitteis, 1906.

P. Lond. = *Greek Papyri in the British Museum,* ed. F. G. Kenyon and others, 1893 ff.

P. Magd. = *Papyrus de Magdola,* ed. J. Lesquier in P. Lille (*q.v.*).

P. Masp. = *Papyrus Grecs d'époque Byzantine,* ed. J. Maspéro, 1911 ff.

P. Oxy. = *The Oxyrhynchus Papyri,* ed. B. Grenfell and A. Hunt, 1898 ff.

P. Par. = *Les Papyrus Grecs du Musée du Louvre,* ed. W. Brunet de Presle and E. Egger, 1866.

P. Petr. = *The Flinders Petrie Papyri,* ed. J. P. Mahaffy and J. G. Smyly, 1891 ff.

P. Ryl. = *Catalogue of the Greek Pa-pyri in the John Rylands Library at Manchester,* ed. A. Hunt and others, 1911.

P. Tebt. = *The Tebtunis Papyri,* ed. B. Grenfell, A. Hunt and others, 1920 ff.

P. Tor. = *Papyri Graeci Regii Tauri-nensis Musei Aegyptii,* ed. A. Peyron, 1926 ff.

Pape = W. Pape, *Griechisch-Deutsches Handwörterbuch*[3], ed. M. Sengebusch, 1880.

par. = parallel.

Paral. Jerem. = *Paralipomena Jeremiae,* Jewish writing revised in a Christian sense (Schürer, III, 393 ff.).

Parm(en). = Parmenides, of Italian Elea (*c.* 500 B.C.), pre-Socratic head of the Eleatic school, ed. H. Diels in *Die Frag-mente der Vorsokratiker,* I, 1922.

part. = participle.

pass. = passive.

Pass. (-Cr.) = F. Passow, *Wörterbuch der griechischen Sprache*[5], 1841 ff., com-pletely revised by W. Crönert, 1913 ff.

Pass. Perp. et Fel. = *Passio Perpetuae et Felicitatis,* ed. J. A. Robinson, 1891.

Pass. Sct. Scilit. = *Passio Sanctorum Scili-tanorum,* ed. A. Robinson, 1891.

Past. = Pastoral Epistles.

Paul. = Pauline.

Paul. Diac. = Paulus Diaconus (*c.* 720-799 A.D.), the most important of the learned

Langobards at the court of Charlemagne, formerly a monk at Monte Cassino, and particularly significant for his historical works (*Geschichte der Langobarden*). His writings have never been collected into a complete edition (cf. RE[3], 15, p. 88).

(Pauli) Exc. (ex lib.) Pomp. Fest. = *Pauli Diaconi Excerpta ex Libro Pompei Festi,* ed. M. Lindsay, 1913.

Pauly-W. = A. Pauly, *Realencyclopädie der klassischen Altertumswissenschaften,* rev. ed., commenced by G. Wissowa, ed. W. Kroll and K. Mittelhaus, 1892 ff.

Paus. = Pausanias, the Periegete, probably of Magnesia by Mt. Sipylos, author un-der the emperor Commodus of his *Jour-ney through Greece* (Περιήγησις Ἑλ-λάδος) in 10 books, ed. J. Schubart, 1881; F. Spiro, 1903 ff.

PEFQ = *Palestine Exploration Fund Quar-terly Statements* (London), 1911 ff.

Pent. = Pentateuch.

perf. = perfect.

pers. = person.

Pes. = *Pesachim,* Mishnah-, Tosefta-, Tal-mud tractate *The Passover* (Strack, *Einl.,* 39).

Pesikt. = *Pesikta* (*de Rab. Kahana*), col-lection of homilies (Strack, *Einl.,* 202 f.).

Pesikt. r. = *Pesikta rabbati,* collection of homilies (Strack, *Einl.,* 205 f.).

Phil. = Philippians.

Philo = Philo, of Alexandria (*c.* 20 B.C.-50 A.D.), ed. L. Cohn and P. Wendland.
Abr. = *De Abrahamo.*
Aet. Mund. = *De Aeternitate Mundi.*
Agric. = *De Agricultura.*
Cher. = *De Cherubim.*
Conf. Ling. = *De Confusione Lin-guarum.*
Congr. = *De Congressu Eruditionis Gratia.*
Decal. = *De Decalogo.*
Det. Pot. Ins. = *Quod Deterius Po-tiori insidiari soleat.*
Deus Imm. = *Quod Deus sit Immu-tabilis.*
Ebr. = *De Ebrietate.*
Exsecr. = *De Exsecrationibus.*
Flacc. = *In Flaccum.*
Fug. = *De Fuga et Inventione.*
Gig. = *De Gigantibus.*
Jos. = *De Josepho.*
Leg. All. = *Legum Allegoriae.*
Leg. Gaj. = *Legatio ad Gajum.*
Migr. Abr. = *De Migratione Abra-hami.*
Mut. Nom. = *De Mutatione Nomi-num.*

Omn. Prob. Lib. = *Quod omnis Probus Liber sit.*
Op. Mund. = *De Opificio Mundi.*
Plant. = *De Plantatione.*
Poster. C. = *De Posteritate Caini.*
Praem. Poen. = *De Praemiis et Poenis.*
Quaest. in Ex. = *Quaestiones in Exodum.*
Rer. Div. Her. = *Quis Rerum Divinarum Heres sit.*
Sacr. AC. = *De Sacrificiis Abelis et Caini.*
Sobr. = *De Sobrietate.*
Som. = *De Somniis.*
Spec. Leg. = *De Specialibus Legibus.*
Virt. = *De Virtutibus.*
Vit. Cont. = *De Vita Contemplativa.*
Vit. Mos. = *De Vita Mosis.*
Philodem. Philos. = Philodemus Philosophus, of Gadara (*c.* 110-28 B.C.), popular philosopher of Epicurean tendencies. There is no complete edition. For individual writings, *v.* Liddell-Scott, XXX.
Philol. = *Philologus,* 1846 ff.
Philol. Wochenschr. = *Philologische Wochenschrift,* 1882 ff.
Philostr. = Flavius Philostratus, of Lemnos, representative of the Second Sophistic School, author as commissioned by the empress Julia Domna (d. 217), wife of Septimius Severus, of a life, containing many marvellous happenings, of the Neo-Platonic philosopher and thaumaturge, Apollonius of Tyana. His *Heroicus* is written in the same strain, ed. C. L. Kayser, 1870.
Heroic. = *Heroicus.*
Vit. Ap. = *Vita Apollonii.*
Vit. Soph. = *Vitae Sophistarum.*
Phlm. = Philemon.
Phot. = Photius, patriarch of Constantinople (858-886 A.D.), author of a lexicon (λέξεων συναγωγή) to aid readers of the classics and the Bible, ed. S. A. Naber, 1864 f.
Lex. = *Lexicon.*
Phryn. = Phrynichus, of Bithynia, lexicographer and Atticist, at the time of Commodus. Only small fragments of his great work in 37 volumes (σοφιστικὴ παρασκευή) have come down to us, ed. G. Rutherford, 1881.
Ecl. = *Eclogae Nominum et Verborum Atticorum.*
Ph. U. = *Philologische Untersuchungen,* 1880 ff.
PJB = *Palästina-Jahrbuch,* 1905 ff.
Pind. = Pindar, of Cynoscephalae, near Thebes (518-446 B.C.), the most impor-

tant author of Greek odes, and preacher of the ideal of nobility still held at the beginning of the 5th century. His most important surviving poems are the *Epinicia,* in praise of victors in the national games, ed. O. Schroeder, 1930.
Isthm. = *Isthmia.*
Nem. = *Nemea.*
Olymp. = *Olympia.*
Pyth. = *Pythia.*
Pist. Soph. = *Pistis Sophia,* original Gnostic work in Coptic (3rd. century A.D.), ed. C. Schmidt, 1925.
Pl. = Paul.
Plat. = Plato, of Athens (428/7-348/7 B.C.), ed. J. Burnet, 1905.
Alc. *v.* Pseud.-Plat.
Ap. = *Apologia.*
Ax. *v.* Pseud.-Plat.
Charm. = *Charmides.*
Clit. = *Clitopho.*
Crat. = *Cratylus.*
Critias.
Crito.
Def. *v.* Pseud.-Plat.
Ep. = *Epistulae.*
Epigr. = *Epigrammata.*
Eryx. *v.* Pseud.-Plat.
Euthyd. = *Euthydemus.*
Euthyphr. = *Euthyphro.*
Gorg. = *Gorgias.*
Hi. = *Hippias,* I *Maior,* II *Minor.*
Hipp. *v.* Pseud.-Plat.
Ion.
Just. *v.* Pseud.-Plat.
La. = *Laches.*
Leg. = *Leges.*
Lys. = *Lysis.*
Men. = *Meno.*
Menex. = *Menexenus.*
Min. *v.* Pseud.-Plat.
Parm. = *Parmenides.*
Phaed. = *Phaedo.*
Phaedr. = *Phaedrus.*
Phileb. = *Philebus.*
Polit. = *Politicus.*
Prot. = *Protagoras.*
Resp. = *Respublica.*
Sis. *v.* Pseudo.-Plat.
Soph. = *Sophista.*
Symp. = *Symposion.*
Theaet. = *Theaetetus.*
Theag. *v.* Pseud.-Plat.
Tim. = *Timaeus.*
Tim. Locr. = *Timaeus Locreus.*
Virt. *v.* Pseud.-Plat.
Pseud.-Plat. = Pseudo-Plato.
Alc. = *Alcibiades,* I *Maior,* II *Minor.*
Amat. = *Amatores.*
Ax. = *Axiochus.*
Def. = *Definitiones.*
Demod. = *Demodocus.*

Ep. = *Epistulae.*
Epin. = *Epinomis.*
Eryx. = *Eryxias.*
Hipp. = *Hipparchus.*
Just. = *Justus.*
Min. = *Minos.*
Sis. = *Sisyphus.*
Theag. = *Theages.*
Virt. = *De Virtute.*

Plaut. = T. Maccius Plautus, of Sarsina in Umbria (c. 251-184 B.C.), the most important Roman comic dramatist, ed. M. Lindsay, 1904 f.

Plin. (The Eld.) = C. Plinius Secundus, of Comum in Upper Italy (23/4-79 A.D.), historian, natural scientist and geographer, ed. S. Mayhoff, 1875 ff.
  Hist. Nat. = *Naturalis Historia.*

Plin. (The Y.) = C. Plinius Caecilius Secundus, of Comum (61/2-c. 113 A.D.), Roman official and author, his only surviving works being his letters and an address to Trajan.

Plot. = Plotinus, of Lycopolis in Egypt (204-270 A.D.), the last great thinker of antiquity who brought Neo-Platonism to systematic completion, ed. R. Volkmann, 1883 ff.
  Enn. = *Enneads.*

plur. = plural.

Plut. = Plutarchus, of Chaeronea (c. 50-120 A.D.), best known for his parallel biographies, but emerging in his ethical and religious writings as an eclectic with predominant Platonic and Neo-Pythagorean tendencies. The *Vitae* are indicated by I, ed. T. Doehner and F. Dübner, 1877 ff., and the *Moralia* by II, ed. D. Wyttenbach, 1796 ff.
  Adulat. = *De Adulatore et Amico.*
  Aem. = *De Aemilio.*
  Ages. = *De Agesilao.*
  Alex. = *De Alexandro.*
  Alex. Fort. Virt. = *De Alexandri Fortuna aut Virtute.*
  Amat. = *Amatorius Liber.*
  Amat. Narr. = *Amatoriae Narrationes.*
  Anton. = *De Antonio.*
  Apophth. = *Apophthegmata Regum et Imperatorum.*
  Apophth. Lac. = *Apophthegmata Laconica.*
  Aud. = *De Recta Ratione Audiendi.*
  Aud. Poet. = *De Audiendis Poetis.*
  Carn. Es. = *De Carnium Esu.*
  Cato Maior. = *De Catone Maiore.*
  Cato Minor. = *De Catone Minore.*
  C. Gracch. = *De Gajo Graccho.*
  Cim. = *De Cimone.*
  Col. = *Adversus Colotem.*

Comm. Not. = *De Communibus Notitiis.*
Cons. ad Apoll. = *Consolatio ad Apollonium.*
Crass. = *De Crasso.*
Def. Orac. = *De Defectu Oraculorum.*
De Isid. et Os. v. Is. et Os.
Demetr. = *De Demetrio.*
Ei (ap.) Delph. = *De Ei apud Delphos.*
Fab. Max. = *De Fabio Maximo.*
Fac. Lun. = *De Facie in Orbe Lunae.*
Galb. = *De Galba.*
Gen. Socr. = *De Genio Socratis.*
Is. et Os. = *De Iside et Osiride.*
Lat. Viv. = *An recte dictum sit latenter esse vivendum.*
Lib. Educ. = *De Liberis Educandis.*
Lucull. = *De Lucullo.*
Mar. = *De Mario.*
Non Posse Suav. Viv. Sec. Epic. v. Suav. Viv. Epic.
Pelop. = *De Pelopida.*
Pericl. = *De Pericle.*
Philop. = *De Philopoemene.*
Phoc. = *De Phocione.*
Pomp. = *De Pompeio.*
Praec. Coniug. = *Praecepta Coniugialia.*
Praec. Ger. Reip. = *Praecepta Gerendae Reipublicae.*
Pyth. Or. = *De Pythiae Oraculis.*
Quaest. Conv. = *Quaestiones Convivales.*
Quaest. Graec. = *Quaestiones Graecae.*
Quaest. Nat. = *Quaestiones Naturales.*
Quaest. Rom. = *Quaestiones Romanae.*
Sept. Sap. Conv. = *Septem Sapientium Convivium.*
Ser. Num. Pun. = *De iis qui sero a numine puniuntur.*
Stoic. Rep. = *De Stoicorum Repugnantiis.*
Suav. Viv. Epic. = *Non posse suaviter vivi secundum Epicurum.*
Superst. = *De Superstitione.*
Them. = *De Themistocle.*
Thes. = *De Theseo.*
Tib. Gracch. = *De Tiberio et Gaio Gracchis.*
Tit. = *De Tito.*
Tranq. An. = *De Tranquillitate Animi.*
Vit. Dec. Orat. = *Vitae Decem Oratorum.*
Pseud.-Plut. = Pseudo-Plutarchus.
  Vit. Poes. Hom. = *De Vita et Poesi Homeri.*

Pogn. Inscr. Sém. = H. Pognon, *Inscriptions Sémitiques*, 1907.

Pol. = *Epistle of Polycarp.*

Poll. = Julius Pollux (Polydeuces), of Naucratis in Egypt (178 A.D.), professor of rhetoric in Athens, Atticist lexicographer and grammarian, ed. I. Bekker, 1846; E. Bethe, I, 1900.
> Onom. = *Onomasticum.*

Polyaen. = Polyaenus, of Macedonia, author of a curious work on the arts of war dedicated in 162 A.D. to Marcus Aurelius, ed. E. Woelfflin, R. Schoell and F. Melber, 1887.
> Strat. = *Strategica.*

Polyb. = Polybius, of Megalopolis, in Arcadia (c. 210-120 B.C.), hostage of Rome in 167, general and statesman, and the greatest historian of Hellenism. In 40 books he depicts in essentials the rise of Roman world dominion in the period 221-168 B.C., ed. T. Büttner-Wobst, 1905.

Porphyr. = Porphyrius, of Tyre (232-304 A.D.), Neo-Platonic philosopher, the most important pupil of Plotinus, ed. A. Nauck[2], 1886.
> Abst. = *De Abstinentia.*
> Antr. Nymph. = *De Antro Nympharum.*
> Christ. = *Adversus Christianos.*
> (Ad) Marc. = *Ad Marcellam.*
> Vit. Plot. = *Vita Plotini.*
> Vit. Pyth. = *Vita Pythagorae.*

Pos. = Posidonius, of Apamea in Syria, (c. 135-51 B.C.), natural scientist, geographer, historian and philosopher of Middle Stoicism, ed. J. Bake and D. Wyttenbach, 1810.

praef. = *praefatio.*

Pr. Ag. = E. Preuschen, *Kommentar z. Apostelgeschichte*, 1912.

Pr. Bauer = E. Preuschen, *Griechisch-deutsches Wörterbuch zu den Schriften des NT und der übrigen urchristlichen Literatur*, rev. W. Bauer[2], 1928.

Preisigke Fachwörter = F. Preisigke, *Fachwörter des öffentlichen Verwaltungsdienstes Ägyptens in den griechischen Papyrusurkunden*, 1915.

Preisigke Namenbuch = F. Preisigke, *Namenbuch*, 1922.

Preisigke Sammelbuch = F. Preisigke, *Sammelbuch griechischer Urkunden aus Ägypten*, 1915 ff.

Preisigke Wört. = F. Preisigke, *Wörterbuch der griechischen Papyrusurkunden*, 1925 ff.

Preis. Zaub. = K. Preisendanz, *Papyri Graecae Magicae*, 1928 ff.

Prellwitz, Etym. Wört. = W. Prellwitz, *Etymologisches Wörterbuch der griechischen Sprache*[2], 1905.

prep. = preposition.

Pr (euss). Jahrb. = *Preussische Jahrbücher*, 1858 ff.

Pr. M. = *Protestantische Monatshefte*, 1897 ff.

Procl. = Proclus, of Constantinople (410-485 A.D.), the last great representative of Neo-Platonism in Athens, his main works being his *Elementary Theology* and *Commentary on Plato's Timaeus;* there is no complete ed. and for individual works cf. Liddell-Scott, XXXII.
> In Eucl. = *in Euclidem Commentarius.*
> in Rem Pub. = *in Platonis Rem Publicam Commentarius.*
> in Tim. = *in Platonis Timaeum Commentarius.*
> Inst. Theol. = *Institutio Theologica.*

Procop. Gaz. = Procopius of Gaza (495-557 A.D.), one of the three heads of the oratorical school of Gaza and a final representative of ancient Sophism, ed. MPG, 87, 1-3, 1860.

Proc. Soc. Bibl. Arch. = *Proceedings of the Society of Biblical Archaeology*, London, 1878 ff.

pron. = pronoun.

prooem = *prooemium.*

Prop. = Sextus Propertius, Roman poet of the Augustan era, ed. C. Hosius, 1932.

Prot. Ev. Jk. = *Protevangelium des Jakobus.*

Prud. = Aurelius Prudentius Clemens, Spanish by birth (c. 348-405 A.D.), official under Theodosius, then Latin poet of remarkable originality. Spanish and Roman martyrs are honoured in the collection *Peristephanon*, ed. A. Dressel, 1860.

Prv. = Proverbs.

Prv. r. v. Midr. Prv.

Ps. = Psalms.

psdepgr. = pseudepigraphical.

Ps. or Pseud. = Pseudo, often grouped under the names of the supposed authors, e.g., Ps.- or Pseud.-Plat. under Plato.

Pseud.-Ammon = Pseudo-Ammonius.
> Adfin. Vocab. Diff. = *De adfinium Vocabulorum Differentia*, dictionary of synonyms, c. 100 A.D., ed. R. Valckenaer, 1822.

Pseud.-Apollod. = Pseudo-Apollodor, ed. R. Wagner in *Mythographi Graeci*, 1926.
> Bibl. = *Bibliotheca.*

Pseud.-Aristid. = Pseudo-Aristides, ed. L. Spengel in *Rhetores Graeci*, I, 1856.

Pseud.-Callisth. = Pseudo-Callisthenes. In the name of Callisthenes of Olynthus, nephew of Aristotle, who accompanied Alexander the Great, we have a historical novel on Alexander which has a colourful and interesting history, ed. J. Kroll, 1926.

Pseud.-Demetr. = Pseudo-Demetrius. Demetrius of Phaleron, peripatetic, brought Greek learning from Athens to Alexandria 308/7 B.C. He is not the author of the work which has been handed down in his name (Περὶ ἑρμηνείας, On Oratorical Expression), but it probably dates from c. 100 A.D., ed. L. Radermacher, 1901.

Ps. Sol. = Psalms of Solomon, Pharisaic collection of the 1st century B.C., consisting of 18 songs, ed. O. Gebhardt, 1895.

Pt. (1, 2) = Epistle of Peter (1, 2).

Ptr. = Petrine.

Qid. = Qidduschin, Mishnah-, Tosefta-, Talmud tractate Betrothal (Strack, Einl., 49).

Qoh. = Ecclesiastes, or the Preacher.

Qoh. r. = Qohelet rabba, Midrash on Ecclesiastes (Strack, Einl., 213).

Quint. = M. Fabius Quintilianus, of Calagurris in Spain (c. 35-95 A.D.), rhetorician and author in Rome in the early days of the Empire, ed. L. Radermacher, 1907.

Inst. Orat. = Institutio Oratoria.

R. (before the names of rabbis) = Rabbi.

R. = Epistle to the Romans.

Rabb. = Rabbis.

Rabb. = Rabbinic.

Radermacher = L. Radermacher, Neutestamentliche Grammatik[1], 1911; [2] 1925.

RE[3] = Realencyclopaedie für protestantische Theologie und Kirche, ed. J. Herzog, rev. A. Hauck[3], 1896 ff.

Reinhold = H. Reinhold, De Graecitate Patrum Apostolicorum Librorumque Apocryphorum Novi Testamenti quaestiones Grammaticae, 1898.

REJ = Revue des Etudes Juives, 1880 ff.

Reitzenstein Hell. Myst. = R. Reitzenstein, Die Hellenistischen Mysterienreligionen[3], (1927).

Reitzenstein Ir. Erl. = R. Reitzenstein, Iranisches Erlösungsmysterium, 1921.

Reitzenstein Poim. = R. Reitzenstein, Poimandres, 1904.

Rev. = Book of Revelation.

Rev. Byz. = Revue Byzantine, 1915 ff.

RGG = Die Religion in Geschichte und Gegenwart[1], 1909 ff.; [2], 1927 ff.

Rgg. Hb. = R. Riggenbach, Kommentar z. Hebräerbrief, 1913.

RH = Rosch haschana.

Rhet. Graec. = Rhetores Graeci, ed. L. Spengel, 1853 ff.

RHR = Revue de l'Histoire des Religions, 1880 ff.

Röm. Mitt. = Mitteilungen des Kaiserlich Deutschen Archäologischen Instituts, Römische Abteilung, 1886 ff.

Rohr Hb., Rohr Off. = I. Rohr, Der Hebräerbrief und die Geheime Offenbarung des hl. Johannes[4], 1932.

Roscher = W. H. Roscher, Ausführliches Lexikon der griechischen und römischen Mythologie, 1884 ff.

Rt. = Ruth.

Rt. r. = Ruth rabba, Midrash on Ruth (Strack, Einl., 213).

RVV = Religionsgeschichtliche Versuche und Vorarbeiten, 1903 ff.

RW — Biblisches Realwörterbuch, by G. B. Winer[3], 1847 f.

S (1, 2) = Samuel (1, 2).

SAB = Sitzungsberichte der Preussischen Akademie der Wissenschaften zu Berlin (phil.-hist. Klasse), 1882 ff., 1922 ff.

SAH = Sitzungsberichte der Heidelberger Akademie der Wissenschaften (phil.-hist. Klasse), 1910 ff.

Sallust. = Sallustius, contemporary and friend of the emperor Julian (361-363 A.D.), who in his book Περὶ θεῶν καὶ κόσμου has left a catechism of the theology of the Neo-Platonists, ed. A. Nock.

Sanh. = Sanhedrin, Mishnah-, Tosefta-, Talmud tractate On the court of justice and its procedure (Strack, Einl., 51 f.).

SBE = Sacred Books of the East, ed. M. Müller, 1879 ff.

S(c)hab. = Shabbat, Mishnah-, Tosefta-, Talmud tractate Sabbath (Strack, Einl., 37).

S(c)hebi. = Shebiit, Mishnah-, Tosefta-, Talmud tractate Seventh Year (Strack, Einl., 34).

S(c)hebu. = Shebuot, Mishnah-, Tosefta-, Talmud tractate Oaths (Strack, Einl., 52).

S(c)heq. = Sheqalim, Mishnah-, Tosefta-, Talmud tractate Shekel Tax (Strack, Einl., 40).

Schleusner = J. F. Schleusner, Novus Thesaurus philologocriticus in LXX et reliquos interpretes Graecos ac scriptores apocryphos Veteris Testamenti, 1820 f.

Schl. Gesch. d. erst. Chr. = A. Schlatter, Die Geschichte der ersten Christenheit, 1926.

Schl. Gesch. d. Chr. = A. Schlatter, *Die Geschichte des Christus*[2], 1923.

Schl. Gesch. Isr. = A. Schlatter, *Die Geschichte Israels von Alexander bis Hadrian*[3], 1925.

Schl. J. = A. Schlatter, *Kommentar z. Johannesev.*, 1930.

Schl. Jk. = A. Schlatter, *Kommentar z. Jakobusbrief*, 1932.

Schl. Lk. = A. Schlatter, *Kommentar z. Lukasev.*, 1931.

Schl. Mt. = A. Schlatter, *Kommentar z. Matthäusev.*, 1929.

Schl. Theol. d. Ap. = A. Schlatter, *Die Theologie der Apostel*[2], 1922.

Schl. Theol. d. Judt. = A. Schlatter, *Die Theologie des Judentums nach d. Bericht d. Josefus*, 1932.

Schn. Euang. = J. Schniewind, *Euangelion*, 1927 ff.

Schol. = *Scholion* (-a).

Schriften d. NT = *Die Schriften des Neuen Testaments*, ed. J. Weiss and others[3], 1917 ff.

Schürer = E. Schürer, *Geschichte des jüdischen Volkes im Zeitalter Jesu Christi*[3, 4] 1901 ff.

Script. Hist. Aug. = *Scriptores Historiae Augustae*, collection of biographies in Latin of Roman emperors from Hadrian to Numerian (117-284 A.D.), a series of excerpts by different authors c. 330 A.D., later revised, ed. E. Hohl, 1927.

S. Dt. = *Sifre Deuteronomium*, Tannaitic Midrash on Deuteronomy (Strack, *Einl.*, 200 f.).

sec. Gk. = secular Greek.

Sen. = L. Annaeus Seneca, of Cordova in Spain (*c.* 4 B.C.-65 A.D.), politician, poet and moral philosopher of the later Stoa, ed. C. Hosius and E. Hermes, 1914 ff.
> Ben. = *De Beneficiis*.
> Marc. = *Dialogus ad Marcellam*.

Sen. Rhet. = Seneca Rhetor, father of the well-known philosopher, whose *Controversiae* give us an excellent picture of Roman rhetoric in early imperial Rome, ed. A. Kiessling, 1872.
> Contr. = *Controversiae*.

Sess. = *Sessio*.

Sext. Emp. = Sextus Empiricus, originally a physician probably practising in Alexandria (*c.* 200 A.D.), who summed up the whole development of ancient scepticism in his *Pyrrhonic Elements* and in 11 books against the mathematicians, directed against individual sciences and the dogmatic philosophical schools, ed.

I. Bekker, 1842; H. Mutschmann, 1912 ff.
> Gramm. = *Adversus Grammaticos*.
> Math. = *Adversus Mathematicos*.
> Pyrrh. Hyp. = *Pyrrhoneae Hypotyposes*.

Sib. = Sibyllines, the Sibylline Oracles in 14 books, collected in the 5th or 6th century A.D. for the propagation of Judaism or Christianity, composed at various periods, and predominantly Jewish but partly Christian in derivation.

Sickb. R., Sickb. K. = J. Sickenberger, *Die Briefe des hl. Paulus an die Römer und Korinther*[4], 1932.

sing. = singular.

Sir. = Jesus Sirach.

S. Lv. = *Sifra Leviticus*, Tannaitic Midrash on Leviticus (Strack, *Einl.*, 200).

S. Nu. = *Sifre Numeri*, Tannaitic Midrash on Numbers (Strack, *Einl.*, 201), ed. H. G. Horovitz, 1917.

Soph. = *Sopherim*, extra-canonical Talmud tractate *Scribes* (Strack, *Einl.*, 72).

Soph. = Sophocles, of Athens (496-406 B.C.), the real poet of the Athens of Pericles, ed. A. C. Pearson, 1924.
> Ai. = *Aiax*.
> Ant. = *Antigone*.
> El. = *Electra*.
> Oed. Col. = *Oedipus Coloneus*.
> Oed. Tyr. = *Oedipus Tyrannus*.
> Phil. = *Philoctetes*.
> Trach. = *Trachiniae*.

st. abs. = *status absolutus*.

st. c. = *status constructus*.

Stob. = Johannes Stobaeus, named after his home-town Stoboi in Macedonia (5th century A.D.), author of an anthology of extracts from Greek poets and prose writers, ed. C. Wachsmuth and O. Hense, 1884 ff., quoted by the volumes (I-IV) and pages.
> Ecl. = *Ecloge*.

Strack, Einl. = H. L. Strack, *Einleitung in Talmud und Midrasch*,[5] 1921.

Str.-B. = H. L. Strack and P. Billerbeck, *Kommentar zum NT aus Talmud und Midrasch*, 1922 ff.

Stud. Or. = *Studia Orientalia* ed. *Societas Orientalis Fennica*, 1925 ff.

subst. = substantive.

Suet. = C. Suetonius Tranquillus, high Roman official under Hadrian, historian and author of biographies of the emperors from Caesar to Domitian, ed. R. D. Robinson, 1925; J. R. Rietza, 1928.
> (Aug.) Caes. = *De Vita Caesarum*.

Suic. Thes. = J. C. Suiceri, *Thesaurus Ecclesiasticus e Patribus Graecis*, 1728.

Suid. = Suidas, author in the 10th century A.D. of the most comprehensive Greek lexicon, ed. G. Bernhardy, 1853; A. Adler, 1928 ff.

Suppl. Com. = *Supplementum Comicum,* ed. J. Demianczuk, 1912.

Sus. = Susanna.

s.v. = *sub voce.*

synon. = synonym.

Synpt. = Synoptist.

synpt. = synoptic.

Syr. = Syriac.

S. zutta Nu. = *Sifre zutta Numeri,* fragmentary Midrash on Numbers (Strack, *Einl.,* 200 f.).

T. = Tosefta (Strack, *Einl.,* 74 ff.), ed. G. Kittel-H. Rengstorf, 1933 ff.

Taan. = *Taanit,* Mishnah-, Tosefta-, Talmud tractate *Fasts* (Strack, *Einl.,* 43).

Tanch. = *Tanchuma,* collection of homilies named after R. Tanchuma (Strack, *Einl.,* 204 f.). The edition by S. Buber in 1885 has important textual variations from other editions.

Tat. = Tatian, of Syria, won to Christianity in Rome by Justin, author c. 152 of an address to the Greeks in which he sharply attacks Greek culture, ed. E. Goodspeed in *Die Ältesten Apologeten,* 1914. Or. Graec. = *Oratio ad Graecos.*

Teh. = *Tehorot,* Mishnah-, Tosefta-, Talmud tractate *Purities* (euphemistic for impurities) (Strack, *Einl.,* 61).

Tem. = *Temura,* Mishnah-, Tosefta-, Talmud tractate *Substitution* (of a sacrifice) (Strack, *Einl.,* 57).

Ter. = *Terumot,* Mishnah-, Tosefta-, Talmud tractate *Heave Offerings* (Strack, *Einl.,* 34).

Tertullian = Q. Septimius Tertullianus Florens, of Carthage (160-220 A.D.), ed. A. Reifferscheid and G. Wissowa, 1890 ff.

    Bapt. = *De Baptismo.*
    Marc. = *Adversus Marcionem.*
    Mart. = *Ad Martyras.*
    Nat. = *Ad Nationes.*
    Praescr. Haer. = *De Praescriptione Haereticorum.*
    Pud. = *De Pudicitia.*
    Scapul. = *Ad Scapulam.*
    Val. = *Contra Valentinianos.*
    Virg. Vel. = *De Virginibus Velandis.*

Test. XII = Testaments of the Twelve Patriarchs, Jewish work, slightly revised in a Christian sense, dating from the 2nd or 1st century A.D. and consisting of addresses of the twelve sons of Jacob to their descendants, ed. R. H. Charles, 1908.

    Test. A. = *Testament of Asher.*
    B. = of *Benjamin.*
    D. = of *Dan.*
    G. = of *Gad.*
    Jos. = of *Joseph.*
    Iss. = of *Issachar.*
    Jud. = of *Judah.*
    L. = of *Levi.*
    N. = of *Napthali.*
    R. = of *Reuben.*
    S. = of *Simeon.*
    Zeb. = of *Zebulon.*
    Test. Abr. = *Test. of Abraham.*
    Ad. = of *Adam.*
    Sol. = of *Solomon.*

Tg. = Targum, Aramaic translation or paraphrase of the OT.
    Tg. I Est. = Targum I on Esther.
    Tg. II Est. = Targum II on Esther (Targum sheni).
    Tg. J. I = Targum Pseudo-Jonathan.
    Tg. O. = Targum Onkelos.
    Tg. Pal. = Palestinian Targum of the Pentateuch.
    Tg. Pro. = Targum of the Prophets.

TGF = *Tragicorum Graecorum Fragmenta,* ed. A. Nauck, 1889.

Th. (1, 2) = Thessalonians (1, 2).

Thackeray = H. St. J. Thackeray, *A Grammar of the Old Testament in Greek according to the Septuagint,* 1909.

Thackeray Lex. Jos. = H. St. J. Thackeray, *Lexicon to Josephus,* 1930 ff.

ThBl = *Theologische Blätter,* 1922 ff.

Thdr. = Theodorus Lector, Church historian (6th century A.D.), who in his history in three parts deals with the period from Constantine to 518 A.D., ed. MPG, 86, 1865.

Thdrt. = Theodoretus, author in 448/9 A.D. of a Church history in 5 books and one of those who thus continued the work of Eusebius, ed. L. Parmentier, 1911.

Themist. = Themistius, the Paphlagonian (c. 317-388 A.D.), city prefect of Constantinople, a pagan Sophist with a strong interest in the philosophy of the ancients, ed. W. Dindorf, 1832.

Theocr. = Theocritus, of Syracuse (born c. 305 B.C.), celebrated Hellenistic poet and master of bucolic poetry (the idyll), later at court in Alexandria under Ptolemaeus II Philadelphus, ed. U. Wilamowitz in *Bucolici Graeci,* 1905.
    Idyll. = *Idyllia.*

Theod. Stud. = Theodorus Studita, of Byzantium (759-826 A.D.), monk and ecclesiastic, consistent advocate of the freedom of a Church separated from the state, ed. MPG, 99, 1860.

Enc. Theoph. = *Encomium in Theophanem.*

Theogn. = Theognis, of Megara (c. 500 B.C.), poet and preacher of a definitely aristocratic ideal. Many later works have been added to the collection of poems grouped under his name, ed. E. Diehl in *Anthologia Lyrica,* I, 1925.

Theol. Quart. = *Theologische Quartalschrift,* 1819 ff.

Theophan. = Theophanes Confessor, Byzantine monk (c. 757-817 A.D.), whose *Chronography* deals with the period 284-813, ed. C. de Boor, 1883 ff.

Chronogr. = *Chronographia.*
Hom. = *Homiliae.*

Theophil. = Theophilus, Christian Apologist (167-177 A.D.), of Antioch, author of a controversial work against Autolycus some time after 186, ed. J. Otto, 1861.

(Ad) Autol. = *Ad Autolycum.*

Theophr. = Theophrastus, of Eresos on Lesbos (c. 372-287 B.C.), pupil of Aristotle and important scholar, succeeding him as head of the peripatetic school in Athens, ed. F. Wimmer, 1854 ff.; *Charact.,* ed. O. Immisch, 1923 ; *De Igne,* ed. A. Gercke, 1896.

Char. = *Characteres.*
Ign. = *De Igne.*

Thes. Ling. Lat. = *Thesaurus Linguae Latinae,* 1604 ff.

Thes. Steph. = H. Stephanus, *Thesaurus Graecae Linguae,* 1831 ff.

ThLBl = *Theologisches Literaturblatt,* 1866 ff.

ThLZ = *Theologische Literatur-Zeitung,* 1876 ff.

Thom. Mag. = Thomas Magister, really Theodulus of Thessalonica (?), a teacher of rhetoric and monk in the 14th century A.D., ed. MPG, 145, 1904.

Thr. = *Threni* = Lamentations.

ThR = *Theologische Rundschau,* 1898 ff., New Series, 1929 ff.

ThSt = *Theologische Studiën,* Utrecht, 1883 ff.

ThStKr = *Theologische Studien und Kritiken,* 1828 ff.

ThT = *Theologisch Tijdschrift,* Leiden, 1867 ff.

Thuc. = Thucydides, of Athens (c. 460-396 B.C.), the classic historian of the Greeks, who as a contemporary wrote a history of the Peloponnesian War, ed. C. Hude, 1898 ff.

Tib. = Albius Tibullus, Roman poet of the Augustan era, ed. W. Levy, 1927.

Tillm. Gefbr. = M. Meinertz and F. Tillmann, *Die Gefangenschaftsbriefe des hl. Paulus*[4], 1931.

Tillm. J. = F. Tillmann, *Das Johannesevangelium*[4], 1931.

Tm. (1, 2) = Epistle to Timothy (1, 2).

Tob. = Tobit.

tr. = translation.

trans. = transitive.

Trench = R. C. Trench, *Synonyma des NT,* 1907.

Tr. Is. = Trito-Isaiah.

tt. (term. techn.) = *terminus technicus.*

Tt. = Epistle to Titus.

TU = *Texte und Untersuchungen zur Geschichte der altchristlichen Literatur,* 1883 f.

UNT = *Untersuchungen zum NT,* 1912 ff.

v. (V.) = verse.

v. = *vide.*

Vergil. = P. Vergilius Maro, of Andes near Mantua (70-19 B.C.), the greatest epic and national poet of Rome in the Augustan era.

Aen. = *Aeneis.*
Ecl. = *Ecloge.*
Buc. = *Bucolica.*

Vett. Val. = Vettius Valens, later Greek astrologist (2nd century A.D.), ed. W. Kroll, 1908.

Vis. Esr. = *Visio Esrae,* 5/6 book of Ezra ; two small apocalypses of the 2nd and 3rd centuries A.D.

Vis. Is. = *Visio Iesaiae* (v. Asc. Is.).

Vit. Ad. = *Vita Adae et Evae,* Latin work from the Jewish-Christian group of writings on Adam (Schürer, III, 396 ff.), ed. W. Meyer, 1878.

vl. (*vl.*) = *varia lectio.*

Vol. = Volume.

Vrede Kath. Br. = M. Meinertz and W. Vrede, *Die Katholischen Briefe*[4], 1932.

Wbg. Mk. = G. Wohlenberg, *Kommentar z. Markusev.,* 1910.

Wbg. Past. = G. Wohlenberg, *Kommentar z. d. Pastoralbriefen,* 1906.

Wbg. Pt. = G. Wohlenberg, *Kommentar z. d. Petrusbriefen*[3], 1923.

Wbg. Th. = G. Wohlenberg, *Kommentar z. d. Thessalonicherbriefen,* 1903.

Wdt. Ag. = H. H. Wendt, *Kommentar z. Apostelgeschichte*[9], 1913.

Weber = F. Weber, *Jüdische Theologie auf Grund des Talmud und verwandter Schriften*[2], 1897.

Wendland Hell. Kult. = P. Wendland, *Die hellenistisch-römische Kultur*[2, 3], 1912.

Wettstein = *Novum Testamentum Graecum ... opera et studio J. J. Wetstenii*, 1752 f.

Wilke-Grimm. = C. L. W. Grimm, *Lexicon Graeco-Latinum in Libros NT*[4], 1903 (*G. Wilcii Clavis NT Philologica.*).

Wilcken Ptol. = U. Wilcken, *Urkunden der Ptolemäerzeit*, 1922 ff.

Winer (Schmiedel) = G. B. Winer, *Grammatik des nt.lichen Sprachidioms*[7], 1867, rev. P. Schmiedel, 1894 ff.

Wis. = Book of Wisdom.

Wnd. Hb. = H. Windisch, *Kommentar z. Hebräerbrief*[2], 1931.

Wnd. J. (1, 2, 3) = H. Windisch, *Kommentar z. d. Johannesbriefen* (1, 2, 3)[2], 1930.

Wnd. Jk. = H. Windisch, *Kommentar z. Jakobusbrief*[2], 1930.

Wnd. 2 K. = H. Windisch, *Kommentar z. 2. Korintherbrief*[9], 1924.

Wnd. Kath. Br. = H. Windisch, *Kommentar z. d. katholischen Briefen*[2], 1930.

Wnd. Pt. = H. Windisch, *Kommentar z. d. Petrusbriefen*[2], 1930.

WZKM = *Wiener Zeitschrift für die Kunde des Morgenlandes*, 1887 ff.

Xenoph. = Xenophon, of Athens (c. 430-354 B.C.), pupil of Socrates, author of various historical, philosophical and scholarly works, ed. E. C. Marchant, 1900 ff.

    Ag. = *Agesilaus.*
    An. = *Anabasis.*
    Ap. = *Apologia Socratis.*
    Ath. *v.* Pseud.-Xenoph. Resp. Ath.
    Cyn. *v.* Pseud.-Xenoph.
    Cyrop. = *Cyropaedia.*
    Ep. *v.* Pseud.-Xenoph.
    Eq. = *De Equitandi Ratione.*
    Eq. Mag. = *De Equitum Magistro.*
    Hier. = *Hiero.*
    Hist. Graec. = *Historia Graeca.*
    Mem. = *Memorabilia Socratis.*
    Oec. = *Oeconomicus.*
    Resp. Lac. = *Republica Lacedaemoniorum.*
    Sym. = *Symposion.*
    Vect. = *De Vectigalibus.*
    Venat. = *De Venatione.*

Pseud.-Xenoph. = Pseudo-Xenophon.
    Cyn. = *Cynegeticus.*
    Ep. = *Epistulae.*
    Resp. Ath. = *Respublica Athenien-*

sium, the party political work of an Athenian oligarch (end of the 5th century B.C.).

Yr. = Yearbook.

Zahn Einl. = T. Zahn, *Einleitung in das NT*, 1906.

Zahn Forsch. = T. Zahn, *Forschungen zur Geschichte des nt.lichen Kanons*, 1881 ff.

Zahn Kan. = T. Zahn, *Geschichte des nt.-lichen Kanons*, 1888 ff.

ZAW = *Zeitschrift für die at.liche Wissenschaft*, 1881 ff.

ZDMG = *Zeitschrift der Deutschen Morgenländischen Gesellschaft*, 1847 ff.

ZDPV = *Zeitschrift des Deutschen Palästina-Vereins*, 1878 ff.

Z. d. Z. = *Zwischen den Zeiten*, 1923 ff.

Zeb. = *Zebachim*, Mishnah-, Tosefta-, Talmud tractate *Sacrifices* (Strack, *Einl.*, 55).

Zech. = Zechariah.

Zeph. = Zephaniah.

ZhTh = *Zeitschrift für die historische Theologie*, 1832 ff.

ZKG = *Zeitschrift für Kirchengeschichte*, 1877 ff.

ZMR = *Zeitschrift für Missionskunde und Religionswissenschaft*, 1886 ff.

Zn. Ag. = T. Zahn, *Kommentar z. Apostelgeschichte*, 1919 ff.

Zn. Apk. = T. Zahn, *Kommentar z. Apokalypse*, 1924 ff.

Zn. Gl. = T. Zahn, *Kommentar z. Galaterbrief*[2], 1907.

Zn. J. = T. Zahn, *Kommentar z. Johannesev.*[3, 4], 1912.

Zn. Lk. = T. Zahn, *Kommentar z. Lukasev.*, 1913.

Zn. Mt. = T. Zahn, *Kommentar z. Matthäusev.*[2], 1905.

Zn. R. = T. Zahn, *Kommentar z. Römerbrief*, 1910.

ZNW = *Zeitschrift für die nt.liche Wissenschaft und die Kunde des Urchristentums*, 1900 ff.

ZPK = *Zeitschrift für Protestantismus und Kirche*, 1838 ff.

ZSTh = *Zeitschrift für systematische Theologie*, 1923 ff.

ZThK = *Zeitschrift für Theologie und Kirche*, 1891 ff.

ZWL = *Zeitschrift für kirchliche Wissenschaft und kirchliches Leben*, 1880 ff.

ZwTh = *Zeitschrift für wissenschaftliche Theologie*, 1858 ff.

N.B. 1. Where verse references from the Septuagint differ from those of the Hebrew, they are usually preceded by an indication in Greek. Thus ψ 18:9 = Ps. 19:9; ᾽Ιερ.

25:15 = Jer. 49:35; 4 Βασ. 16:4 = 2 K. 16:4. In many cases the other reference is also given in brackets.

2. Most textual critical annotations are borrowed from BHK[3] and Nestle[15] and are not therefore noted in the list of abbreviations.

3. → always indicates reference to a passage or article within the *Theological Dictionary.*

4. Only the page numbers are given where the reference is to the same volume of the *Theological Dictionary.*

5. † before the heading of an article indicates that all the New Testament passages are mentioned in it.

6. Names of contributors in [] indicate reference to unpublished oral or written material.

† ΑΩ (→ πρῶτος, ἔσχατος).

The juxtaposition of the first and last letters of the Greek alphabet peculiar to Rev. It is used on the lips of God in 1:8 : ἐγώ εἰμι τὸ ἄλφα[1] καὶ τὸ ὦ,[2] λέγει κύριος ὁ θεός, ὁ ὢν καὶ ὁ ἦν καὶ ὁ ἐρχόμενος, ὁ παντοκράτωρ, and also in 21:6 : ἐγὼ τὸ ἄλφα καὶ τὸ ὦ, ἡ ἀρχὴ καὶ τὸ τέλος; and on the lips of Christ in 22:13 : ἐγὼ τὸ ἄλφα καὶ τὸ ὦ, ὁ πρῶτος καὶ ὁ ἔσχατος, ἡ ἀρχὴ καὶ τὸ τέλος.[3] It is also applied to Christ in 1:17 : ἐγώ εἰμι ὁ πρῶτος καὶ ὁ ἔσχατος καὶ ὁ ζῶν, and 2:8 : τάδε λέγει ὁ πρῶτος καὶ ὁ ἔσχατος.

The meaning of α/ω is fixed by its conjunction with ἀρχή/τέλος and πρῶτος/ ἔσχατος. It shows us that God or Christ is the One who begins and the One who ends, the Creator and the Consummator, the One from whom and to whom are all things. It is probable that the alphabetic designation may be traced back to Hellenistic speculations, the echoes of which came to the Apocalyptist either directly on the soil of Asia Minor or, as some think, indirectly through the mediation of Palestinian Judaism. Of the content of these speculations (the predicates of the Aeon-God) there is hardly anything present or at least discernible in his work. For him the α/ω is nothing more than a useful, pregnant and striking alternative to the OT πρῶτος/ἔσχατος. It corresponds to the basic view of the early Christian author that he can use of both God and Christ this predicate of divine majesty developed from the view of God found in the OT prophets. No less striking is the fact that the thought of the πρῶτος/ἔσχατος lying in the α/ω can be further expressed in the phrase ὁ ἦν καὶ ὁ ἐρχόμενος as an extension of the OT divine name ὁ ὤν. Here, too, an early Christian note is struck with the reference to the ἐρχόμενος. The reference to the *parousia* gives to the more general religious notion of Godhead eternally existing as beginning and end[4] a dynamic quality peculiar to the early Christian conception of God and Christ.

πρῶτος καὶ ἔσχατος is an OT expression, but not its indication by the use of the first and last letters. Is. 41:4 LXX : ἐγὼ θεὸς πρῶτος, καὶ εἰς τὰ ἐπερχόμενα ἐγώ εἰμι; 44:6 Mas. : "I am the first, and I am the last (אֲנִי רִאשׁוֹן וַאֲנִי אַחֲרוֹן); and beside me there is no God" ; LXX : ἐγὼ πρῶτος καὶ ἐγὼ μετὰ ταῦτα, πλὴν ἐμοῦ οὐκ

Α Ω. Commentaries on Rev.: Bss., 190, 458 ; Charles (1920), I, 20 ; II, 220 ; Zn., 178 ; Loh., 11, 165, 176 ; Str.-B., I, 156, 814 f. ; II, 362, 546, 693 ; III, 157, 789. F. Boll, *Sphaera* (1903) 469 ff.; F. Boll, *Aus. d. Off. Joh.* (1914), 26 f.; Reitzenstein, *Poim.,* 256 f.; *Iran. Erlös.,* 244 ; F. Dornseiff, *Das Alphabet in Mystik u. Magie*² (1925), 17 f., 122 ff., A. Schlatter, *Das AT i.d. joh. Apk.* (1912), 13 ; Kauffmann-Kohler, JE, I (1901), 438 f.

[1] It is written thus (ἄλφα as a word and ὦ as a sign) in all the early tradition : H. C. Hoskier, *Concerning the Text of the Apocalypse,* II (1929), 36 ; since the name ὦ μέγα only arose much later, at the time of the NT it could only be written as ω. Cf. E. Nestle, *Philologus,* 70 (1911), 155 f.

[2] rec + ἀρχὴ καὶ τέλος.

[3] Cf. 1:11 (on the lips of Christ) rec + ἐγώ εἰμι τὸ Α καὶ τὸ Ω, ὁ πρῶτος καὶ ὁ ἔσχατος.

[4] Cited as an ancient or Orphic saying in Plat. Leg., IV, 715d and the accompanying scholion (Charles, II, 220). A Palestinian form, though obviously borrowed and not native, is found in Jos. Ap., 2, 190 ; Ant., 8, 280. For Indian parallels to this widespread thought, cf. Weinreich, ARW, 19 (1916/19), 181.

ἔστιν θεός; 48:12 Mas.: "I am he;[5] I am the first, I also am the last"; LXX: ἐγώ εἰμι πρῶτος καὶ ἐγώ εἰμι εἰς τὸν αἰῶνα. The LXX certainly has πρῶτος, but does not venture to link ἔσχατος with God as given by the Hebrew אַחֲרוֹן. It uses a paraphrase instead. Thus the Apocalyptist returns to the original text with his ἔσχατος (Schlatter), as do most of the Rabbinic passages which quote Is. 44:6 in connexion with the symbolism of numbers (infra).

Reitzenstein points to the Mandaean parallels in Lidz. Lit., 130 f.: "Thou art the first, Thou art the last. Thou art the future One who is to come".[6] But the reference is superfluous in view of the plain OT link. For the rest, the literal form of the Mandaean saying ("who is to come") seems rather to suggest dependence on the NT.[7]

The symbolism of numbers is to be found in Hellenism as well as Rabbinic Judaism. Hellenism denoted the religious 12 or 24 hour day of the Egyptians by the letters of the Greek alphabet, and also established a link with the 12 signs of the Zodiac. Since the Greek alphabet has 24 letters, 2 have to be devoted to each sign. Two systems thus arise. In the first 1 and 13, 2 and 14 etc. are conjoined (ram = α/ν, steer = β/ξ etc.), and in the second 1 is linked with 24, 2 with 23 etc. (α/ω, β/ψ etc.), the latter combination being also applied by the Gnostic Marcus to the ἀλήθεια (head = α/ω, neck = β/ψ etc.). The whole system thus denotes the totality, the κόσμος, the Αἰών. The apocalyptic application of the letters to God and Christ may thus be regarded as an application of the predicates of the Aeon-God.[8]

Rabbinic thought used the first and last letters in four different ways. 1. We have the turn of speech: "To keep the Torah from א to ת", i.e., "to keep it fully". In bShab. 55a the introduction of תני רב יוסף shows that R. Joseph (d. 333) is quoting a Tannaitic tradition. Since the Apocalyptist does not equate Christ with the Torah, there is no possible connexion here. 2. Men. 8, 1 ff.; T. Men., 9, 5: Alpha (אַלְפָא), is a place, i.e., the best, with abundance of oil, flour, wine etc. Since the Greek name for the letter is used here even in a Hebrew setting, the turn of speech must either originate with the Greek alphabet or in discussion with Greeks.[9] Both expressions show that a symbolical use of the first and last letters was not strange to Judaism of the Tannaitic period. 3. In the 3rd century A.D. we have the letter systems of Albam and Athbash. The former equates 1 and 12 (ל/א), 2 and 13 (מ/ב), 11 and 22 (ת/כ); the latter 1 and 22 (ת/א), 2 and 21 (ש/ב), 11 and 12 (ל/כ), cf. Shab. 104a; Nu. r., 13 on 7:19; 18 on 16:35. Here the use of letters for numbers is simply for the purpose of secrecy or even perhaps of exercising the memory, and there is no astrological content; yet in form we notice an exact correspondence to the existing Hellenistic astrological systems. The two systems can hardly have arisen independently of these Hellenistic systems, especially as the tradition itself refers to their foreign origin.[10] 4. A speculation that אֱמֶת "truth" is the seal of God because it consists of א, the first, מ, the middle and ת, the last letters of the alphabet, all found in Is. 44:6, can be traced back only to the 3rd century A.D.,

---

[5] On the meaning of הוּא, cf. Ges.-K. § 135a, 1.

[6] "The first" alone quite often in Lidz. Ginza, 6, 16 f. ("He is the high King of light . . . from the beginning to all eternity, the first from all beginnings, the Creator") etc.

[7] Similarly there is obvious dependence on Rev. 22:13 in the Manichaean Fragment M, 10 cited by Andreas in Reitzenstein, Das Mandäische Buch (1919), 47.

[8] Boll, Sphaera, 469 ff.; Reitzenstein, Poim. 261.

[9] To this there corresponds the fact that, when the Greek letters and numbers זיטא אפסא איטא אוכטא were used as proof in a discussion on the seventh and eighth month of pregnancy, they were expressly introduced by the formula: "I will prove it from your own lips", thus indicating that the discussion was with those who spoke Greek (Gn. r., 14 on 2:7; 30 on 3:16; Nu. r., 4 on 3:40; jJeb., 5d n.).

[10] bShab., 104a: "The Rabbis said to R. Joshua b. Levi: 'Children have come into the house of instruction and said things which were not said even in the days of Joshua the son of Nun'." Cf. also Dornseiff, 17 f.

though this does not prove that it might not be of earlier origin (Gn. r., 81, on 35:1; Cant. r. on 1:9; jSanh., 18). The use of the letter m, which is the middle only of the 24 letter Greek alphabet and not of the 22 letter Hebrew, shows that elements have here been borrowed from Hellenistic speculation, including the interpretation, not offered by Is. 44:6 but present in Greek, of the "middle" interjected between the "first" and the "last". As against this, the connexion with Is. 44:6 is Jewish, as is also the reference of alphabetic speculation to the "truth", the similarity being only applicable to the Hebrew form of the word. The Gnostic Marcus, a contemporary of Irenaeus, who is responsible for the Hellenistic application to ἀλήθεια, is thus necessarily dependent either directly or indirectly on Jewish or Christian linguistic usage. We may conclude that Jewish אֱמֶת-speculation is older than Marcus, and therefore older than the fixing of the tradition as it has come to us.

The α/ω symbolism probably came to the early Christian Apocalyptist, not directly from Hellenistic sources, but through the mediation of Palestinian thought. In favour of this view it may be argued: 1. that as in Jewish speculation there is a connexion with the πρῶτος καὶ ἔσχατος of Is. 44:6; and 2. that the reference is to the Hebrew rather than the LXX text of this saying.

Kittel

Ἀαρών

1. Hb. 5:1-9: Christ is High-priest. This is indicated by the comparison with the high-priesthood of Aaron and his descendants. a. Aaron does not have this office of men, but by the call of God (5:4).[1] b. The Aaronic high-priest can μετριοπαθεῖν τοῖς ἀγνοοῦσιν καὶ πλανωμένοις, ἐπεὶ καὶ αὐτὸς περίκειται ἀσθένειαν (5:2).[2] Yet Christ's high-priesthood is much higher than the perishable (Hb. 7:23 ff.) and inadequate (7:27) Aaronic priesthood. Indeed, it is quite different in character, not being κατὰ τὴν τάξιν Ἀαρών,[3] but κατὰ τὴν τάξιν → Μελχισέδεκ (7:11, cf. ψ 109:4).

2. Hb. 9:4: The rod of Aaron, which miraculously budded (Nu. 17:16-26) lay beside the pot with manna and the tables of the Law in the ark of the covenant within the Holiest of all. Its position within rather than alongside the ark is based on Nu. 17:25 (לִפְנֵי הָעֵדוּת). Yet this expression simply tells us that the rod of Aaron was placed in the Holy of Holies before the ark.

This at least is how it was understood by Jewish tradition (T. Yoma, 3, 7; Str.-B., III, 739). In the exact description of the contents of the ark, i.e., the tables of the Law and the roll of the Torah, and in the list of these objects within it (bBB, 14 a/b), there is no mention of the rod or the pot with manna. It may thus be concluded with certainty

---

Ἀαρών. Article "Aaron" in EJ, I, 11 ff., esp. 13-21.
[1] Cf. Ex. 28:1, Nu. 18:1; also for the same thought Tanch. קרח 218a (Par: Midr., Ps. 2 § 3 (13a), Str.-B., III, 304, 688); also Jos. Ant. 3, 190: ὁ θεὸς Ἀαρῶνα τῆς τιμῆς ἄξιον ἔκρινε καὶ τοῦτον ᾕρηται ἱερέα.
[2] This thought is lacking in Judaism; it acquires significance for the author only because of the comparison with Christ (Heb. 5:8 f.).
[3] Ἀ. is indeclinable in LXX and NT (Bl.-Debr., § 53, 1; Helbing, 58).

that they were not in the ark according to Rabbinic opinion. [4] It is only with mediaeval Rabbis that discussion arises whether or not they were in the ark. [5]

3. Lk. 1:5: Elisabeth ἐκ τῶν θυγατέρων Ἀ. = of priestly descent. The expression is formed analogously to the OT turn of speech בְּנֵי אַהֲרֹן the priests (Lv. 1:5 and *passim*). It is found neither in the OT nor in Philo, Josephus or the Rabbis, and is not therefore in line with Jewish linguistic usage.

Rabbinic literature uses either בַּת כֹּהֵן (e.g., Ter., 7, 2; cf. Lv. 21:9) or כּוֹהֶנֶת (e.g., Sota, 3, 7). Similarly Philo in Spec. Leg., I, 111 has ἱερέων θυγατέρες alongside ἱέρεια (110). bEr. 53b אהרונית = "Aaronidin" cannot be adduced in this connexion, since there is here a play on words.

Kuhn

| † Ἀβαδδών |

In NT found only in Rev. 9:11. The name of an angel of the underworld, of the king of the scorpion centaurs who will plague men in the last days. The name is rendered → Ἀπολλύων "the Destroyer" in Greek. It is part of the cryptic style of the Apocalyptist to use the Hebrew name in the Greek text.

The name is taken from the OT. In Job 26:6; 28:22; Prv. 15:11 and Ps. 88:12 אֲבַדּוֹן (the "place of destruction", from אָבַד) is used to describe the world of the dead (→ ᾅδης); [1] LXX ἀπώλεια. The personification of אֲבַדּוֹן, found in Job 28:22, where אֲבַדּוֹן and מָוֶת are introduced as speakers, has given rise to the notion of an angel of hell who in Rev. 9:11 is identified with the prince of the underworld (Eth. En., 20, 2; Apc. Elias, Steindorff, 10, 7 ff.; [2] bSanh. 52a; bShab. 104a; bAr. 15b). [3]

The Greek rendering of the name as Ἀπολλύων is influenced 1. by the LXX ἀπώλεια and 2. by the thought of Apollyon in his quality as the God of plague and the destroying angel; already in Aesch. Ag., 1082 the name of the God is derived from ἀπόλλυμι.

Joachim Jeremias

---

[4] T. Sota, 13, 1 (Par. bYoma, 52b; bHor. 12a; Ab. of R.N. § 41) says nothing about its being kept either in or beside the ark; but see Rgg. Hb. 246, n. 85 and F. Delitzsch, *Comm. z. Briefe a.d. Hebr.* (1857), 361.

[5] The former view is championed, e.g., by Levi b. Gerson (13th century); cf. the commentary on 1 K. 8:9 in Rabbinic Bibles.

Ἀ β α δ δ ώ ν. Comm. on Rev.: Bss., 301; Loh., 77 f., Str.-B., III, 809 f., IV, 1088, 1091 f.

[1] In Rabbinic literature אֲבַדּוֹן as appellative signifies "destruction" and as proper noun the "place of destruction" = Gehinnom (Str.-B., III, 810, IV, 1078).

[2] TU, 17, 3a (1899).

[3] Str.-B., III, 809; IV, 1088, 1091f.

ἀ β β ᾶ. Zn. R., 395, n. 93; Schl. Mt., 383, 479, 670; Str.-B., I, 393 ff., 918 f.; II, 49 f.; A. Geiger, *Lehrbuch z. Sprache der Mischnah* (1845), 50; Dalman, WJ, I, 156 ff.

† ἀββᾶ   (→ πατήρ).

A. אַבָּא in Judaism.

An Aramaic determination אַבָּא from אַב "father", which in the more settled usage of the period of the Mishnah and the Targum takes two forms, first with the pronominal suffix of the 1st person singular ("my father"),[1] and second with that of the 1st person plural ("our father"). The word also serves as a title[2] and a proper name.[3] It is almost never used, however, in relation to God, the form אָבִי (→ πατήρ) being used in the formula: "My father, who is in heaven".

The secular use of אַבָּא is so strong that it is not merely found in the rendering of the Hebrew אָבִי by the Aramaic Targums (Tg. O. Gn. 20:12 etc.) but has even penetrated into the Hebrew of the Mishnah[4], e.g., in the mouth of the Rabbi Gamaliel etc.: בֵּית אַבָּא "house of my father" (Pea., 2, 4 etc.). It is particularly striking that in direct proximity to אַבָּא there may be found not merely the Hebrew הָאָב, without suffix, but also the forms אָבִיךָ, בְּנִי, אָחִי with the usual suffix. Ned., 11, 4: "That I do nothing for my father (אַבָּא) or thy father (אָבִיךָ), for my brother (אָחִי) or thy brother (אָחִיךָ),, Git., 7, 6: "There is a bill of divorce with the condition that thou servest my father (אַבָּא) and carest for my son (בְּנִי) ... If the son (הַבֵּן) dies, or if the father (הָאָב) dies..." The Mishnah also shows that אַבָּא can also be said in the name of several children and can thus have the meaning of "our father". BB, 9, 3: "They said, 'See what our father (אַבָּא) has left us'." Sheb., 7, 7: "We swear that our father (אַבָּא) did not direct us (in his will), nor did our father (אַבָּא) tell us earlier, nor have we found instructions in the papers of our father (אַבָּא), that this promissory note should be paid".

The use of אַבָּא in religious speech is attested only in few and later passages, and even so it is always accompanied by an addition which emphasises the distance of man, namely, "who is in heaven" (אבא דבשמיא, Tg. Job, 34, 36 ff.[5] or אבא שבשמים, Lv. r., 32 on 24:10).[6]

---

[1] Aram. אַבִי in Dan. 5:13.

[2] For a list of Rabbis who bore the title, cf. Str.-B., I, 918 ff.; cf. also the title "Sayings of the Fathers".

[3] Examples are given in Strack, Einl., 230. According to W. Bacher, REJ, 36 (1898), 103 ff., Abba as a proper name is a contraction of Abraham, which is not found among the Rabbis. But Moses is not found either. In reality both names are avoided out of reverence. In any case the proper name Acha (אַחָא ⸗ brother) is also found (cf. T. Jeb., 14, 4; b Ar., 22b etc., Strack, loc. cit.).

[4] Cf. Kassovsky, 5. In the same way אִמָא for "my mother", Ned., 2, 1.

[5] Cf. Levy, Chald. Wört., I, 1; Str.-B., II, 50.

[6] Characteristically only in a later addition to the original Midrash. As the parallel M. Ex., 20, 5 shows, the original tradition consists in the following sentence of Lv. r., which like M. Ex. has the customary אבי שבשמים.

B. ἀββᾶ in Early Christianity.

As concerns the usage of Jesus, the probability is that He employed the word אַבָּא not merely where it is expressly attested (Mk. 14:36) but in all cases, and particularly in address to God, where the Evangelists record Him as saying ὁ πατήρ,[7] πάτερ,[8] ὁ πατήρ μου,[9] πάτερ μου,[10] and even perhaps πάτερ ἡμῶν.[11] In so doing He applies to God a term which must have sounded familiar and disrespectful to His contemporaries because used in the everyday life of the family. In other words, He uses the simple "speech of the child to its father".[12]

When the Aramaic term is used in the Greek Epistles of Paul (R. 8:15; Gl. 4:6), there may well underlie it a liturgical reminiscence,[13] possibly the beginning of the Lord's Prayer.[14] In any case there can be no doubt that the use of the word in the community is linked with Jesus' term for God and thus denotes an appropriation of the relationship proclaimed and lived out by Him. Jewish usage shows how this Father-child relationship to God far surpasses any possibilities of intimacy assumed in Judaism, introducing indeed something which is wholly new.

Kittel

---

† Ἄβελ — Κάϊν

A. The Tradition of Judaism.

The account of Cain's murder of Abel in Gn. 4:3 ff. contains no hint of any difference in the piety or moral conduct of the two brothers. It simply says that God accepted Abel's sacrifice and not Cain's, and that Cain was so angry that he slew his brother. Nevertheless later Jewish exegesis always understood the story in terms of some such distinction, Abel being regarded as religious and Cain as ungodly. The story is thus brought into the dominant dualistic schema of later Judaism which divides men into the צַדִּיקִים and the רְשָׁעִים (δίκαιοι-πονηροί).[1] So Jos. Ant., 1, 53: Ἄβελος μὲν ... δικαιοσύνης ἐπεμελεῖτο ... Κάϊς δὲ τά τε ἄλλα πονηρότατος ἦν. Tanch. (Buber) בלק 16, p. 140 f.: "There were 7 righteous men who built 7 altars from Adam to Moses, and they were accepted: 1. Adam, 2. Abel ..." Similarly, T. Sota, 4, 19 includes Cain in a list of the ungodly. This distinction is also deduced from the dispute between the two which preceded the

---

[7] Mt. 11:26; Jn. 5:36. Cf. Mk. 14:36; R. 8:15; Gl. 4:6.
[8] Mt. 11:25; Lk. 11:2; 23:34; Jn. 11:41; 12:27 f.; 17:5.
[9] Mt. 11:27; 26:53.
[10] Mt. 26:39, 42.
[11] Mt. 6:9.
[12] Dalman, 157. According to Chrys., Thdr., Thdrt., who were Syrians, little children used to call their fathers "Abba" (Zahn).
[13] Ltzm. R. on 8:15.
[14] Since ἀ. can imply "our father" as well as "my father", it is no argument to the contrary that, as in other sayings of Jesus, Luke has here given us the beginning of the Lord's Prayer literally and Matthew more freely though correctly. Cf. Kittel, *Probleme*, 53 ff. Cf. also Ephr. and Jer. acc. to Zn. on Gl. 4:6.
Ἄβελ. V. Aptowitzer, *"Kain und Abel in der Agada, den Apokryphen, der hellenist., christl. und muhammed. Literatur"*, Publication of the Kohut Memorial Foundation, I, 1922. Article "Abel" in EJ, I, 207 ff., esp. 210 f.
[1] v. Bousset-Gressm., 183; Moore, I, 494.

murder according to J. I. Gn. 4:8 (and similarly J. II).[2] In Philo it is interwoven into the system of Stoic ethics (Abel is ἀρετή, Cain is κακία, Sacr. AC, 14 ; Det. Pot. Ins., *passim*). The question how acceptance and rejection were known is also left open in Gn. 4:4. Only in Theodotion and then in the fathers are we told that fire came down from heaven and consumed Abel's sacrifice but not Cain's (Θ Gn. 4:4 f. יִשַׁע = ἐνεπύρισεν). The Rabbinic writings, Philo and Josephus do not know this explanation, and it is not found until mediaeval Jewish exegetes.[3]

Why did God accept Abel's sacrifice and not Cain's? Jos. Ant., 1, 54 gives a rationalist answer : God has more pleasure τοῖς αὐτομάτοις καὶ κατὰ φύσιν γεγονόσι than τοῖς κατ᾽ ἐπίνοιαν ἀνθρώπου πλεονέκτου βίᾳ πεφυκόσιν. Gn. r. 22 on 4:3 has a different solution : "Cain brought of the fruits of the earth, which were of less value".[4] Phil. Sacr. AC, 88 takes a similar view : Abel brought a different sacrifice from Cain : ἀντὶ μὲν ἀψύχων ἔμψυχα, ἀντὶ δὲ νεωτέρων καὶ δευτερείων πρεσβύτερα καὶ πρῶτα, ἀντὶ δὲ ἠσθενηκότων ἐρρωμένα καὶ πιότερα. The quality of the sacrifice is thus regarded as determinative in relation to its acceptance or rejection, and this implicitly involves the quality of the one who offers it (cf. *supra*). That the religious and moral attitude of the one who offers it is decisive is stated explicitly only in J. I. Gn. 4:8, in which Abel says to Cain : "Because the fruits of my actions were better than thine, and preceded thine, my offering was accepted as well-pleasing".

B. Cain and Abel in the NT.

In accordance with the Jewish understanding, Mt. 23:35 and par., in which there is reference to the righteous Abel, conceive of the contrast in purely ethical terms, the brothers being δίκαιος or πονηρός in virtue of their works. The same is true of Jd. 11, which says of the errorists : τῇ ὁδῷ τοῦ Κάϊν ἐπορεύθησαν. As against this, there is a profounder metaphysical dualism in 1 Jn. 3:12 : Cain was ἐκ τοῦ πονηροῦ ; in the ἔργα πονηρά or δίκαια of the two there was expressed only their true nature. With a similar absolute contrast between faith and unbelief, Hb. 11:4 lists Abel among the witnesses of faith : "By faith Abel offered unto God a more excellent (πλείονα) sacrifice than Cain" ; in virtue of his faith (δι᾽ ἧς) God bore witness that he was righteous by accepting his offering. (How God did this, we are not told.)[5] The concluding words of the verse : ἀποθανὼν ἔτι λαλεῖ point back to Gn. 4:10 : φωνὴ αἵματος τοῦ ἀδελφοῦ σου βοᾷ πρός με ἐκ τῆς γῆς. The blood of the murdered Abel cries for vengeance until the murder is expiated by the death of the murderer.[6] This basic thought is explained by Hb. 11:4 to mean that Abel[7] still (ἔτι)[8] appeals to the righteousness of God until he shall have attained to full redress for his innocent death in the consummated kingdom of

---

[2] In many Rabbinic writings the distinction is dropped again. Abel and Cain are simply mentioned together without any judgment on them, possibly in apologetic answer to the magnifying of Abel in Christianity (Aptow., 23 f.).

[3] Aptow., 41 f.; Str.-B., III, 744.

[4] For similar Rabbinic references *v.* Aptow., 39, n. 162, 163.

[5] As Gn. 4:4 ; cf. *supra*.

[6] In Rabbinic Judaism we find the notion that the blood of an innocent victim of murder is in movement, welling up and not being absorbed in the ground, until the murderer is dead (jTaan, 69a, 56 and par. ; Dt. r., 2 on 4:41; *v.* Str.-B., I, 940 ff.

[7] i.e., his ψυχή, cf. Rev. 6:9, though also his blood (Gn. 4:10).

[8] βοᾷ (Gn. 4:10) is thus understood as a constant present.

God (cf. Rev. 6:9-11). [9] Similarly in Hb. 12:24 the blood of Abel can serve as an OT type for that of Jesus. The αἷμα ῥαντισμοῦ of Jesus, which makes atonement, speaks more strongly than that of Abel (παρὰ τὸν "A.), which demands expiation.

Kuhn

Ἀβραάμ

A. Abraham in Judaism.

אַבְרָהָם אָבִינוּ [1] in later Judaism is the celebrated national and religious hero of the people. His figure is surrounded by innumerable legends and miracle stories [2] in his honour, and his grave in Hebron is revered as a holy place. [3] Descent from Abraham is the pride of Israel. [4]

Abraham's religious significance is manifold. a. Within an idolatrous race he saw the enormity of idolatry and disseminated worship of the one true God. [5] He is thus the first proselyte and missionary. b. He is the illuminating example of perfect [6] obedience to the commands of God [7] rendered out of love [8]. He keeps the whole Torah, as yet unwritten, [9] and belongs to the righteous who have not sinned. [10] Hellenistic Judaism also likes to depict him as a fulfilment of the Greek ideal of virtue. [11] c. In particular he is a model of unshakeable believing trust in God maintained in ten temptations [12] and imputed to him by God as meritorious achievement. [13] d. In reward for his merits he is made, as God's friend, [14] the recipient of the promise and the covenant on which the prerogative of Israel stands. [15] His merit avails representatively for Israel in the present and helps Israel to eternal life, descent from Abraham being of decisive significance in this connexion. [16]

---

[9] A. Schlatter, *Der Glaube im NT*[3], 533, n. 1.

Ἀβραάμ. P. Billerbeck, *Abrahams Leben und Bedeutung für das Reich Gottes nach Auffassung der älteren Haggada, Nathanael* (1899), 43 ff., 118 ff., 137 ff., 161 ff., (1900), 33 ff., 65 ff.; O. Schmitz, "Abraham im Spätjudentum und im Urchristentum", in *Aus Schrift und Geschichte, Theol. Abhandlungen A. Schlatter dargebracht* (1922), 99 ff.; Dib. Jk., 157 ff.; Str.-B., Index under Abraham, esp. III, 34 ff., 186 ff., 212 ff.

[1] Thus already Jochanan b. Zakkai, bChag., 14b.

[2] Jub. 11:18-22; deliverance from the fiery furnace of the Chaldees, bPes., 118a and par.; victory over enemies by dust and chaff, bSanh., 108b and par., etc.

[3] Jos. Bell., 4, 531 f. Pilgrimage to the patriarch's grave in Hebron, bBB, 58a.

[4] Ps. Sol. 9:17, 3 Macc. 6:3 etc.

[5] Jub. 11:16 ff.; 12:1-21; 20:7-10; 21:3-5, 21-25; 22:6; Jos. Ant., 1, 155; Hebr. Test. N., 8-9; Apc. Abr., 1-8; Gn. r., 38 on 11:28.

[6] Jub. 23:10: "Abraham was perfect in all his dealings with God".

[7] Sir. 44:20; Jud. 8:26; 1 Macc. 2:52; Jub. 6:19; 18; 21:2 etc.; 4 Macc. 16:20; Syr. Bar., 57, 1 ff.

[8] Ab., 5, 3; S. Dt., 32 on 6:5.

[9] Jub. 16:28; Syr. Bar., 57, 2; Qid., 4, 14.

[10] Pray. Man. 8; bBB, 16b/17a; Str.-B., III, 187.

[11] Wis. 10:5-6; 4 Macc. 16:20; Jos. Ant., 1, 256; Philo Abr., 52-54; Sib., III, 218 ff.

[12] Jub. 19:8; Ab. 5, 3 etc.

[13] Str.-B., III, 186 ff., esp. 200 f.

[14] Is. 41:8; 2 Ch. 20:7; Jm. 2:23; 1 Cl., 10, 1; cf. LXX, Da, 3:35; Str.-B., III, 755.

B. Abraham in the NT.

In the NT Abraham is next to Moses the most frequently mentioned OT figure.
1. In the Gospels his significance in salvation history is conceded (Mt. 8:11 and
par.; Mk. 12:26 and par.; Lk. 16:22 ff.; 19:9 and all early Christianity). On the other
hand, the panegyric glorification of Abraham is contested. Jesus is superior to
him (Jn. 8:52-59), and Peter as the bearer of revelation takes his place [17] as a
cosmic rock (Mt. 16:18). [18] The Abrahamic descent of Israel is granted by Jesus
and the early Christians (Lk. 13:16; 16:24 ff.; 19:9 etc.), but it is argued that the
appeal of unrepentant Jews to it is self-deception (Jn. 8:33 ff. and Mt. 3:9). It is
also denied that Abraham can save his children from Hades (Lk. 16:26), and above
all table fellowship with him is also promised to the Gentiles (cf. Lk. 16:22 ff.).
2. Whereas in Jn. 8:39 f. and Jm. 2:21-24 Abraham is mentioned as an example
of obedience to the will of God, Paul in his conflict with judaising Christianity
finds in Abraham an example of the man who is justified by faith alone (R. 4:1 ff.;
Gl. 3:6 ff.), and can thus see in Christians both of Jewish and Gentile descent the
true children of Abraham and heirs of the Abrahamic promise (R. 4:1, 12; 9:7 f.;
Gl. 3:7, 9, 29; 4:22 ff.; and cf. Jm. 2:21; Hb. 2:16; 6:13 ff.). The decisive thing is no
longer physical but spiritual descent.

Joachim Jeremias

---

† ἄβυσσος (→ ᾅδης).

A description of the underworld as a. the "place of imprisonment for disobedient
spirits" (Lk. 8:31; Rev. 9:1, 2, 11; 11:7; 17:18; 20:1, 3) and b. the "realm of the
dead" (Rom. 10:7).

ἡ ἄβυσσος (originally adj. to a γῆ which is to be filled up but is never completely covered = "unfathomably deep") is used in later Greek to describe the
depths of original time (Preis. Zaub., III, 554; IV, 2835; Corp. Herm., III, 1, XVI,
5), the primitive ocean (Test. Sol., II, 8, B. C. MacCown, 15*), and the world of
the dead (Diog. L. 4, 5, 27). In LXX it is mostly used for תְּהוֹם, which in the OT
describes the original flood or floods of water, and is once used in the plural to
denote the realm of the dead (Ps. 71:20). In later Judaism תְּהוֹם signified 1. the
original flood; [1] 2. the depth of the earth, or interior of the earth, in which are
corpses causing defilement; [2] and 3., under the influence of Persian and Hellenistic
conceptions, [3] the place in which runagate spirits are confined (Jub. 5:6 ff.; Eth.
En., 10:4 ff.; 11 ff.; 18:11 ff. etc.; Jd. 6; 2 Pt. 2:4).

---

[15] Sir. 44:21; Jub. 1:7; 12:22-24; 13:3, 19-21; 14; 15 etc.; 4 Esd. 3:13-15; Syr. Bar.,
57, 1 ff.
[16] Str.-B., I, 116-121.
[17] For Abraham as a cosmic rock, Yalquṭ Shimoni, I, § 766 on Nu. 23:9.
[18] J. Jeremias, *Golgotha* (1926), 68 ff.
ἄβυσσος. Pr. B., 3; Str.-B., III, 281 f., 809; A. Schlatter, *Das AT i.d. joh. Apk.*
(1912), 85 f.
[1] For references, cf. Jeremias, *Golgotha* (1926), 54-58, 62-64, 74.
[2] Cf. Mishnah, e.g., Pes., 7, 7, and *passim*.
[3] Beer, in Kautzsch, *Pseudepigraphen* (1900), 242; Loh. Apk., 158.

In the NT 1. ἄβυσσος is thought of as a "prison for spirits" (Rev. 9:1; 20:1, 3
→ κλείς; cf. Pray. Man. 3). A well-like abyss[4] forms the entrance, from which
when it is opened there ascends the smoke of hell-fire (Rev. 9:1-2).[5] Its inmates
until their release in the tribulation before the end are Antichrist (Rev. 11:7; 17:8
→ θηρίον cf. Act. Thom., 32), the prince of the underworld (Rev. 9:11 → ᾽Αβαδ-
δών), demons (Lk. 8:31) and scorpion centaurs (Rev. 9:3 ff.).[6] After the *parousia*
Satan will be shut up in it during the millennial kingdom (20:1, 3). The fact that
God has power and control over the world of hostile spirits is clearly expressed in
this idea of a spirit prison.

2. R. 10:7 the term תְּהֹמֹת (LXX ἄβυσσοι, ψ 106:26) signifies the "realm of
the dead",[7] descent into which is contrasted with ascension into heaven; here, as
in bGit., 84a, Bar.,[8] τίς καταβήσεται εἰς τὴν ἄβυσσον is an expression for something which is impossible.

Joachim Jeremias

ἀγαθός, ἀγαθοεργέω, ἀγαθοποιέω, -ός, -ία,
ἀγαθωσύνη, φιλάγαθος, ἀφιλάγαθος

ἀγαθός

Καὶ μὴν τό γε ἀγαθόν, τοῦτο τῆς φύσεως πάσης τῷ ἀγαστῷ βούλεται τὸ
ὄνομα ἐπικεῖσθαι Plat. Crat., 412c. As an adjective or substantive ἀγαθός or τὸ
ἀγαθόν expresses the significance or excellence of a thing or person. This is made
plain by the punning etymology of Plato.

Accordingly, 1. as an adjective it means "excellent" or "fine" or "good". As a purely
formal concept, it is given its content by the substantive with which it is linked. Applied
to persons, it signifies the excellence of the person in his existing position ... ἀγαθοὺς
τέκτονας, χαλκέας ἀγαθούς, ζωγράφους ἀγαθούς, ἀνδριαντοποιούς, καὶ τὰ
ἄλλα τὰ τοιαῦτα ... Xenoph. Oec., 6, 13, or in the NT, e.g., δοῦλε ἀγαθέ (Mt.
25:21). Applied to things, it implies the quality of the thing referred to, e.g., ἀγαθὴ
γῆ, often used in the LXX of the land given to Israel, or δένδρον ἀγαθόν (Mt. 7:17),

---

[4] Cf. פִּי נֵיהִנֹּם bMen., 99b/100; Str.-B., IV, 1087 ff.; also S. Nu. 88 on 11:6-7.

[5] bMen., 99b: the smoke at the entrance to Gehinnom.

[6] Cf. the description of the plague of mice which overtook the Philistines (1 Sam. 6:4)
as given in S. Nu., 88 on 11:6-7. The destroying beasts come from the abyss (תְּהֹום) as in
Rev. 9:1 ff. Cf. also the Egyptian plague of frogs in Ex. r., 10 on 7:29.

[7] According to the Rabbinic view She'ol lies under Tehom: Tanch. (Buber), בשלח
15 p. 62; נֹח 8 p. 33.

[8] Str.-B., III, 281.

ἀ γ α θ ό ς. O. Dittrich, *Geschichte der Ethik* (1926), I, II, *v.* Index; K. Praechter, *Die
Philosophie des Altertums*[12] (1926), 387 ff.; C. Ritter, *Die Kerngedanken der platonischen
Philosophie* (1931), 18 ff., 55 ff.; J. Stenzel, *Platon der Erzieher* (1928), 249 ff.; Strack-
Billerbeck, *Zur Bergpredigt Jesu; Der gute und der böse Trieb; Die altjüdische Privat-
wohltätigkeit; Die altjüdische Liebeswerke*, IV, 1 ff., 466 ff., 563 ff., 559 ff.; A. Juncker,
Die Ethik d. Apostels Paulus (1904), I; W. G. Kümmel, *Römer 7 und die Bekehrung des
Paulus* (1929), 56 ff.; G. Kuhlmann, *Theologia naturalis bei Philo und Paulus* (1930), 84 ff.

or δόματα ἀγαθά (Mt. 7:11). The worthiness or excellence can be more closely defined by the added accusative of relation ... ἐγένοντο καὶ τέχνας καὶ λόγους καὶ πολέμους ἀγαθοί Xenoph. Venat., 1, 14. 2. Substantively, τὸ ἀγαθόν or τὰ ἀγαθά denotes "the good" or "goods", i.e., things which relate to man's well-being. The formal concept is in such cases filled out according to the understanding of existence. In Lk. 12:18 valuables from the standpoint of a materialistic understanding are described as τὰ ἀγαθά (cf. χώρα ... μεστὴ ... οἰῶν καὶ αἰγῶν καὶ βοῶν καὶ ἵππων καὶ σίτου καὶ πάντων ἀγαθῶν ... Xenoph. Cyrop., IV, 4, 4). The humanistic outlook of Greek philosophy declares τὸ γένος τῶν περὶ σῶμα ἀγαθῶν ὡς μὴ ἀγαθῶν, Sext. Adv. Math., XI, 46, and applies the terms to spiritual and moral magnitudes. The religious outlook of Hellenism and the biblical writings uses them with the significance of salvation. With these basic meanings the words ἀγαθός and τὸ ἀγαθόν may be found over the whole Greek-speaking world.

A. ἀγαθός in Greek philosophy.

In Greek philosophy with its humanistic attitude the concept of the ἀγαθόν is most important. The concern of the philosopher is to understand it as the magnitude which gives meaning to existence. Democritus makes the statement: ἀνθρώποις πᾶσι τωὐτὸν ἀγαθὸν καὶ ἀληθές· ἡδὺ δὲ ἄλλωι ἄλλο (Diels, II, 77, 1) — an insight which is adopted by Plato in his search for the good. In his struggle with the Sophists, who equate the good with the pleasant, Plato comes to formulate the idea of the good as the central idea: ... ἐν τῷ γνωστῷ τελευταία ἡ τοῦ ἀγαθοῦ ἰδέα καὶ μόγις ὁρᾶσθαι, ὀφθεῖσα δὲ συλλογιστέα εἶναι ὡς ἄρα πᾶσι πάντων αὕτη ὀρθῶν τε καὶ καλῶν αἰτία, ἔν τε ὁρατῷ φῶς καὶ τὸν τούτου κύριον τεκοῦσα, ἔν τε νοητῷ αὐτὴ κυρία ἀλήθειαν καὶ νοῦν παρασχομένη, καὶ ὅτι δεῖ ταύτην ἰδεῖν τὸν μέλλοντα ἐμφρόνως πράξειν ἢ ἰδίᾳ ἢ δημοσίᾳ, Resp., VII, 517bc, and: Οὐκοῦν εἰ μὴ μιᾷ δυνάμεθα ἰδέᾳ τὸ ἀγαθὸν θηρεῦσαι, σὺν τρισὶ λαβόντες, κάλλει καὶ ξυμμετρίᾳ καὶ ἀληθείᾳ, Phileb., 65a. Aristotle attacks the Platonic notion of the good. On the basis of his doctrine of categories, he raises the objection that the good as well as the existent is manifold rather than single. Thus in the category of essence it is divinity or reason, in that of quality virtue, in that of quantity measure, in that of relation the necessary, in that of time *kairos* etc. (Eth. Nic., I, 4, p. 1096a, 11 ff.). Thus the good is clearly recognised to be a formal concept. With the rejection of the good as a unitary idea, the humanistic view of life triumphed; the religious note still sounded in the Platonic doctrine of ideas is lost;[1] the supreme good is determined from within the human sphere ... τέλος τῶν ἀγαθῶν καὶ τελειότατον εἶναι, ἡ εὐδαιμονία, καὶ τοῦτο ταὐτό φαμεν εἶναι τῷ εὖ πράττειν καὶ εὖ ζῆν (Eth. M., I, 3, p. 1148b, 7 ff.). As εὐδαιμονία the good is the goal of life: Πᾶσα τέχνη καὶ πᾶσα μέθοδος, ὁμοίως δὲ πρᾶξίς τε καὶ προαίρεσις, ἀγαθοῦ τινος ἐφίεσθαι δοκεῖ· διὸ καλῶς ἀπεφήναντο τἀγαθὸν οὗ πάντ᾽ ἐφίεται (Eth. Nic., I, 1, p. 1094a, 1 ff., also Eth. M., I, 1, p. 1182a, 32 ff.).[2]

The same basic humanistic tendency is to be found in Stoicism. The Stoic definition of the ἀγαθόν is given by Sextus: ἦσαν δὲ οἱ φάσκοντες ἀγαθὸν ὑπάρχειν

---

[1] The humanistic attitude emerges in a statement such as this: ... λεκτέον ... ὑπὲρ ἀγαθοῦ οὐ τοῦ ἁπλῶς ἀλλὰ τοῦ ἡμῖν· οὐ γὰρ τοῦ θεῶν ἀγαθοῦ... (Eth. M., I, 1, p. 1182b, 3 ff.), a statement which separates the world of deity from that of man. It is also to be seen in the synonyms, τὸ καλόν, τὸ χρήσιμον, τὸ ἡδύ.

[2] Cf. esp. Rhet., I, 6, p. 1362a, 15 ff., where the different possible definitions of the ἀγαθόν and the resultant ἀγαθά are expressed.

τὸ δι' αὐτὸ αἱρετόν. οἱ δ' οὕτως "ἀγαθόν ἐστι τὸ συλλαμβανόμενον πρὸς εὐδαιμονίαν", τινὲς δὲ "τὸ συμπληρωτικὸν εὐδαιμονίας"· εὐδαιμονία δέ ἐστιν,
ὡς οἵ τε περὶ τὸν Ζήνωνα καὶ Κλεάνθην καὶ Χρύσιππον ἀπέδοσαν, εὔροια βίου
(Adv. Math., XI, 30); and also by Diogenes Laertius: ἀγαθὸν δὲ κοινῶς μὲν τὸ
τὶ ὄφελος, ἰδίως δὲ ἤτοι ταὐτὸν ἢ οὐχ ἕτερον ὠφελείας (VII, 94).[3] From the
concept of the good, whether conceived as idea or accepted as a formal principle,
there derives the doctrine of goods. In Stoicism the ἀγαθά corresponding to the
ἀγαθόν are divided into three classes: τὰ περὶ ψυχήν· ἀρεταὶ καὶ σπουδαῖαι
πράξεις (φρόνησις, σωφροσύνη, δικαιοσύνη, ἀνδρεία καὶ πᾶν ὅ ἐστιν ἀρετὴ ἢ
μετέχον ἀρετῆς (Stob. Ecl., II, 57, 19 W) τὰ ἐκτός· φίλος καὶ ὁ σπουδαῖος
ἄνθρωπος καὶ τὰ σπουδαῖα τέκνα καὶ γονεῖς καὶ τὰ ὅμοια, τὰ οὔτε περὶ ψυχὴν
οὔτε ἐκτός· αὐτὸς ὁ σπουδαῖος ἄνθρωπος ὡς πρὸς ἑαυτόν (Sext. Adv. Math.,
XI, 46).[4] The first class is thought to be necessary to εὐδαιμονία (καὶ τῶν ἀγαθῶν τὰ μὲν ἀναγκαῖα εἶναι πρὸς εὐδαιμονίαν, τὰ δὲ μή. καὶ ἀναγκαῖα μὲν
τάς τε ἀρετὰς πάσας καὶ τὰς ἐνεργείας τὰς χρηστικὰς αὐτῶν, Stob. Ecl., II,
77, 6). Whoever disposes of these goods is good. ἀγαθὸν ... οὗ παρόντος ἀγαθοί ἐσμεν ... Ἀλλὰ μὴν ἀγαθοί γε ἐσμὲν καὶ ἡμεῖς καὶ τἆλλα πάντα ὅσα
ἀγαθά ἐστιν, ἀρετῆς τινος παραγενομένης (Plat. Gorg., 506cd). The way thereto is by instruction, which has as its goal the mediation of φρόνησις from which
action springs quite naturally. It belongs to the humanistic understanding of existence that the one who has insight into ἀγαθόν becomes ἀγαθός. Of this man
alone can it be said that he is happy. τὸν μὲν γὰρ καλὸν κἀγαθὸν ἄνδρα καὶ
γυναῖκα εὐδαίμονα εἶναί φημι, τὸν δὲ ἄδικον καὶ πονηρὸν ἄθλιον (Plat. Gorg.,
470e). This humanistic attitude was threatened by the aristocratic tendency of
Greek life which Heraclitus expressed as follows: ... οὐκ εἰδότες ὅτι οἱ πολλοὶ
κακοί, ὀλίγοι δὲ ἀγαθοί (Diels, I, 98, 8 f.), and also by the thought of *heimar-
mene*, the influence of which on Stoicism is attested in the following sentence:
... οἱ δὲ φάσκοντες ἐξ ἀνάγκης ἡμᾶς εἶναί τε καὶ γίνεσθαι τοιούτους (sc.
ἀγαθοὺς ἢ κακούς) καὶ μὴ καταλιπόντες ἡμῖν τὴν ἐξουσίαν τοῦ ταῦτα πράττειν τε καὶ μή, δι' ὧν ἂν τοιοῦτοι γενοίμεθα (Alex. Aphr. Fat., 28, p. 199, 7 ff.,
ed. Bruns).

B. ἀγαθός in Hellenism.

With the general shattering of the ancient attitude, the concept acquires in
Hellenism a religious flavour in which ἀγαθόν signifies "salvation"[5] and ἀγαθός
"pleasing to God" as applied to man, or "kind" and "good" as applied to God.
Closer definition is provided by that in which salvation is sought or what is
pleasing to God perceived. For the Hermetic writings, which constitute one
significant literary deposit of Hellenism, salvation is divinisation. τοῦτο ἔστι
τὸ ἀγαθόν, <τοῦτο τὸ> τέλος τοῖς γνῶσιν ἐσχηκόσι, [θεωθῆναι] (Corp.

---

[3] In the statement of Chrysipp. handed down by Plutarch we have evidence of this
humanistic understanding of existence: ... ὥσπερ τῷ Διὶ προσήκει σεμνύνεσθαι ἐπ'
αὐτῷ τε καὶ τῷ βίῳ καὶ μέγα φρονεῖν, καί, εἰ δεῖ οὕτως εἰπεῖν, ὑψαυχεῖν καὶ
κομᾶν καὶ μεγαληγορεῖν, ἀξίως βιοῦντι μεγαληγορίας· οὕτως τοῖς ἀγαθοῖς πᾶσι
ταῦτα προσήκει, κατ' οὐθὲν προεχομένοις ὑπὸ τοῦ Διός (Stoic. Rep., 13).

[4] Cf. Plat. Leg., I, 631bc; Arist. Rhet., I, 6, p. 1362b, 3 ff.

[5] Where Greek thinking has a religious character, the terms ἀγαθόν and ἀγαθά are
also used with this meaning, e.g., ... ὅτι δοκεῖ τῇ βουλῆι, τὰ μὲν ἀγαθὰ δέχεσθαι
τὸν δῆμον ἃ ἀπαγγέλλουσι ὁ ἱερεὺς καὶ οἱ ἱεροποιοὶ γεγονέναι ἐν τοῖς ἱεροῖς οἷς
ἔθυον (Ditt. Syll.[3], 289, 11 ff.

Herm., I, 26). The *nous* helps towards this: ὁ γὰρ νοῦς ψυχῶν ἐστιν εὐεργέτης ἀνθρώπων· ἐργάζεται γὰρ αὐτ<α>ῖς [εἰς] τὸ ἀγαθόν ... νόσος δὲ μεγάλη ψυχῆς ἀθεότης· ἐπεί τα<ῖς τῶν ἀθέων> δόξα[ε]ις πάντα τὰ κακὰ ἐπακολουθεῖ, καὶ ἀγαθὸν οὐδέν. ἆρ᾽ οὖν ὁ νοῦς, ἀντιπράσσων αὐτῇ, τὸ ἀγαθὸν περιποιεῖται τῇ ψυχῇ (XII, 2 ff.).[6] The humanistic view is here overthrown to the extent that salvation is not proper to any earthly being, nor is the quality of being pleasing to God immanent in any such (II, 14 ff.; μόνον οὖν ... τὸ ὄνομα τοῦ ἀγαθοῦ ἐν ἀνθρώποις, τὸ δὲ ἔργον οὐδαμοῦ ... ὁ γὰρ κόσμος πλήρωμά ἐστι τῆς κακίας, ὁ δε θεὸς τοῦ ἀγαθοῦ, VI, 3 f.). The good strictly appertains only to the Godhead: ὁ οὖν θεὸς <τὸ> ἀγαθόν, καὶ τὸ ἀγαθὸν ὁ θεός (II, 16). It is the Godhead which creates salvation: ... οὐδὲ ὁ θεὸς δύναται μὴ ποιῶν τὸ ἀγαθόν (XI, 17c). He is ἀγαθός (I, 17) who mortifies the operations of matter. This overthrow of the humanistic attitude derives from a cosmological dualism.

In Hellenism there is a pantheon of gods and demons, personal beings to which man is delivered up. The deities from which he expects salvation are given the title of ἀγαθός; hence the expressions ἀγαθὸς θεός (Ditt. Syll.³, 526, 1; 685, 1; Act. Andr. et Matth., 6, in which Jesus is called ἀγαθός θεός), ἀγαθὸς δαίμων (Ditt. Syll.³, 985, 10; 1044, 35; Corp. Herm., XII, 1, 8 as a deity of revelation),[7] and ἀγαθὴ τύχη (Ditt. Or., 214, 30). Behind these formulae there stands the yearning of humanity threatened in its existence and seeking salvation.

Philo shares the Hellenistic attitude, but imparts Jewish elements. To him divinity is the supreme good. "I, the Lord", means: ἐγὼ τὸ τέλειον καὶ ἄφθαρτον καὶ πρὸς ἀλήθειαν ἀγαθόν (Gig., 45). Beside the neutral Greek form there stands the personal Jewish: ἀγαθὸς γὰρ ὢν ὁ θεός (Leg. All., I, 47; Som. I, 149). The activity corresponding to this understanding follows with the attainment of the goods corresponding to the supreme good: ἐγκράτεια, the supreme and most perfect good which man can achieve (Spec. Leg., I, 149);[8] εὐσέβεια, the cause of the highest of goods, since it brings us knowledge of the service of God (Spec. Leg., IV, 147); ἡ πρὸς θεὸν πίστις, the one infallible and certain good (Abr., 268); σοφία, the good by which the soul moves up from the world to its master and father (Rer. Div. Her., 98). The possibility of such activity is assumed by Philo with his trust in the help of God.

C. ἀγαθός in the OT and Judaism.

The OT and Judaism share with Hellenism a religious attitude to life. But in them its structure is completely different. Everything is now determined by knowledge of the personal God who reveals Himself to His people in its history and has elected it in this revelation. Accordingly, the use of the terms ἀγαθός and τὸ ἀγαθόν, which in the LXX are the normal equivalents of טוב, is quite different. The idea of the good in the Greek and Hellenistic sense is not present. The basic confession which constantly recurs and corresponds to the personal concept of

---

[6] Cf. also XIII, 9, where τὸ ἀγαθόν is linked with ἀλήθεια in accordance with the Greek tradition. The whole of the 13th tractate deals with the mystery of divinisation.

[7] *v.* Reitzenstein, Iran. Erl., 191, n. 2; 193, n. 1; Poim., Index; Roscher, I, 98 f. (Agathodaimon); Pauly-W., I, 746 f. (Agathodaimon), Suppl. III, 37 ff.; Ditt. Syll.³, p. 116, n. 11.

[8] In the high estimation of ἐγκράτεια there is revealed the Hellenistic foundation of the attitude, which is determined by cosmological dualism.

God is as follows: ...   הוֹדוּ לַיהוָה כִּי טוֹב   ἐξομολογεῖσθε τῷ κυρίῳ ὅτι ἀγαθόν... (1 Ch. 16:34 ; 2 Ch. 5:13 ; 2 Es. 3:11 f.; Ps. 118 [ψ 117:1 ff.] etc.). [9] The
Rabbis have the constant formula :   הַטּוֹב וְהַמֵּיטִיב   (e.g., Ber., 9, 2). This confession
expresses the perfectly good being of God which consists in His goodness. [10] By
revelation the understanding of existence is so determined that it has its roots in
the salvation experienced in history, that it has its goal in the final salvation which
is still awaited, and that it orientates its activity by this salvation under the direction of the Law as a manifestation of the will of God. The exodus from Egypt
and entry into the promised land, as well as the preservation experienced in history,
are sometimes expressed in the words טוב or טוֹבָה (Ex. 18:9 ; Nu. 10:29 ff.; Hos.
8:3 ; 14:3). The expression is particularly common in Jeremiah, for whom it signifies both national and personal salvation in relation to Yahweh (8:15 ; 14:11, 19 ;
17:6 etc.). It is Jeremiah, too, who gives the term an eschatological flavour. It is
said of the promised new covenant :   לְטוֹב לָהֶם וְלִבְנֵיהֶם   ("For the good of them,
and of their children after them", 32:39), and he is given the solemn assurance :
"I will bring upon them all the good" (32:42). The term is used in a similar way
in Is. 52:7, where there is reference to the   מְבַשֵּׂר טוֹב, the "good messenger". Both
passages have been understood Messianically: טוֹב == ἀγαθόν conceived as Messianic salvation.

Between these two given factors there takes place activity determined by the
Law enshrining God's will. In unequivocal terms the well-known saying of Micah
tells us what God requires of man and therefore what is good, namely, to do justly,
to love mercy and to walk humbly before the Lord (6:8). As a revelation of the
will of God the Law is that which brings salvation (Dt. 30:15). The Rabbis describe it quite simply as the good: ... "The upright shall have good things in
possession" (Prv. 28:10). "The good simply means the Torah" (Ab., 6, 3 etc.). [11]
The resultant ethic is simple. Those who do the will of God as contained in the
Law do good, and are therefore good, and will receive blessing and salvation from
the Lord (Ps. 34:14 f.; 37:27; 2 Ch. 19:11). The possibility of keeping the Law is
presupposed. There is division of opinion whether the help of Yahweh is necessary
for this purpose, the OT and the Pharisees thinking that it is but the Sadducees
rejecting such necessity (Jos. Bell., 2, 163-165). [12]

> The Wisdom literature, in which the terms ἀγαθός, τὸ ἀγαθόν and τὰ ἀγαθά are
> the most numerous from the purely lexicographical standpoint, introduces Hellenistic
> ideas which are linked with Jewish thoughts, and forms a bridge to Philo. It is thus in
> this literature especially that the question is raised what is good and evil, and what is
> good for man. In Qoh, which strips off every human illusion, the insight occurs that
> there is no other good for man than   [וְלַעֲשׂוֹת טוֹב] לִשְׂמוֹחַ, (to rejoice in what is given

---

[9] Except in ψ 117 the Hebrew adj. טוב is translated by the subst. ἀγαθόν in the LXX.
This translation has its origin in the Greek and Hellenistic spirit, for which Yahweh the
good (adj.) becomes Yahweh the good (subst.).
[10] v. n. 16.
[11] The connexion between the Law and the good, as also between the concept of Law
on the one side and those of wisdom and power on the other, may be traced back to Prv.
4:2 (cf. Str.-B., I, 809 ; III, 238). Cf. Neh. 9:13 : προστάγματα καὶ ἐντολὰς ἀγαθάς...;
Jos. Ant., 4, 295 : ... νόμοις οὓς ἀγαθοὺς δοκιμάσας ὁ θεὸς παραδίδωσι ...
[12] We often have the conjunction "good and evil" in different forms with the signification of everything as opposed to nothing ; cf. Gn. 3:5 ; 31:24, 29 ; Nu. 14:23 ; 32:11 (these
two are only in the LXX); Dt. 1:39 ; Zeph. 1:12.

[and to do good], 3:13; 5:17; 8:15), but also the insight, which brings the same shattering to Jewish existence as is found in Hellenistic, that "there is not a just man upon earth, that doeth good, and sinneth not" (7:20).

Rabbinic theology pursues further the ethical problems. It describes man as the theatre of conflict between good and evil impulse. His goal in life is to overcome the latter by the former. The control of the evil impulse by the good is the prerequisite for participation in the life of the future world. The good impulse is simply the conscience of the Israelite as this is bound to God. Its norm is the will of God consisting in the commands of the Torah. [13] In this theory there is disclosed the Judaistic view of life as particularly fashioned by the Torah. [14] In addition Rabbinic theology has a developed theory of good works set alongside the fulfilment of the command. [15] These Rabbinic good works are works of love done to the neighbour. They are valued very highly. Only those who perform them may be called good. [16] "Only the man who is good both to God and to creatures is a good righteous man; the man who is good to God but not to creatures is a righteous man, but not good ..." (bQid., 40a).

D. ἀγαθός in the NT.

a. The NT shares with Hellenism and Judaism a predominantly religious basic attitude. This is determined by God, to whom are referred by Jesus the most important words enshrining the OT declaration: εἷς ἐστιν ὁ ἀγαθός (Mt. 19:17, or: οὐδεὶς ἀγαθὸς εἰ μὴ εἷς ὁ θεός, Mk. and Lk.). The personal concept of God makes it impossible to use neutral expressions. ἀγαθός expresses the essential goodness of God which consists in His goodness or kindness.

It is from this God that there comes the salvation which is the central point of NT thinking, namely, the revelation of the salvation of God in Jesus Christ. ἀγαθόν is used in this sense in Hb. 9:11: Χριστὸς παραγενόμενος ἀρχιερεὺς τῶν μελλόντων ἀγαθῶν, [17] and 10:1: σκιὰν γὰρ ἔχων ὁ νόμος τῶν μελλόντων ἀγαθῶν. The μέλλοντα ἀγαθά or goods which belong to the future world, and which are related to those mediated through the Torah as the reality to types and shadows, are now given to the community in Christ. They consist in αἰωνία λύτρωσις and the possibility of λατρεύειν θεῷ ζῶντι, i.e., of being delivered from the dominion of sin and death and set in the fellowship and service of the living God. In R. 10:15 the Deutero-Isaianic prophecy of the מְבַשֵּׂר טוֹב is adopted and applied to the apostolic office. The content of apostolic proclamation is Messianic salvation.

The much debated question of the sinlessness of Jesus is linked with Mt. 19:17 and par. [18]. As against Mark and Luke, which run: "Why callest thou me good?", Mt. has the altered form: "Why askest thou me concerning the good?" It must be admitted that

---

[13] Cf. Str.-B., III, 92 f.

[14] Cf. the excursus in Str.-B., IV, 466 ff.

[15] Cf. the excursus in Str.-B., IV, 536 ff.; also in 559 ff.

[16] In this there is revealed the basic insight that kindness is part of goodness, and that true goodness is achieved in the I-Thou relationship. This insight is also to be found in a passage like the following: πρέπειν ἀνδράσιν ἀγαθοῖς μὴ μόνον συμβουλεύειν, ἀλλὰ ... βοηθεῖν, Jos. Vit., 288. We also find it in Greek literature: οἱ πλεῖστοι ὁρίζονται τοὺς εὐεργέτας ἑαυτῶν ἄνδρας ἀγαθοὺς εἶναι, Xenoph. Cyrop., VII, 3, 12. Cf. Lk. 23:50: ἀνὴρ ἀγαθός καὶ δίκαιος.

[17] This reading is to be preferred to the other. Cf. Rgg, Hb. ad loc.

[18] Wb. Mk., 162; Kl. Mk., 114; Hck. Mk., 122; Dalman, WJ, I, 277; W. Wagner, "In welchem Sinne hat Jesus das Prädikat ἀγαθός von sich abgewiesen?" ZNW (1907), 8, 143 ff.; F. Spitta, "Jesu Weigerung sich als 'gut' bezeichnen zu lassen", ZNW (1908), 9, 12 ff.; K. Bornhäuser, Das Wirken des Christus (1921), 147 ff.

Mt. alters the tradition maintained in the other two, since the opposite course is in-conceivable. Mt. is concerned in his version to avoid the misunderstanding that Jesus is repudiating His own sinlessness or goodness as compared with that of God. Even if he does amend the wording, he surely interprets correctly the intention of Jesus, who is not raising the question of His own sinlessness but rather of the honour of God. That is to say, His answer to the questioner is conditioned by the message of the lordship of God. The questioner is to be referred to God as the One who alone is good, bowing before Him and giving Him the glory.

b. The two statements, 1. that God alone and no other is ἀγαθός and 2. that the μέλλοντα ἀγαθά are the only real ἀγαθά because in them sin and death are done away, give us the insight that strictly speaking there is nothing in this world that deserves the predicate ἀγαθόν, and that there is no one who has the predi-cate ἀγαθός. This insight is completed by the statement of Paul which deals a mortal blow to every other humanistic or religious conception of life : οἶδα γὰρ ὅτι οὐκ οἰκεῖ ἐν ἐμοί, τοῦτ᾽ ἔστιν ἐν τῇ σαρκί μου, ἀγαθόν ... οὐ γὰρ ὃ θέλω ποιῶ ἀγαθόν, ἀλλὰ ὃ οὐ θέλω κακὸν τοῦτο πράσσω (R. 7:18 f.). The natural existence of man is excluded from the good, and cannot attain it in spite of every longing. What it does attain in its ποιεῖν and πράττειν is κακόν, i.e., θάνατος. In the Law an ἀγαθόν is certainly given to man : ἡ ἐντολὴ ... ἀγαθή — τὸ ἀγαθόν, says Paul in agreement with Judaism (R. 7:12 f.). But the ἁμαρτία which possesses and controls man, which is the reality of his existence, works θάνατος for him through the Law. The NT view of life sees man hopelessly delivered up to death and sin, and therefore to the sphere in which there is no possibility of goodness or salvation. This dualism, however, is not cosmologically grounded as in the case of Hellenism. It arises in face of the revelation of God in Christ, and is religious and ethical. It is no argument against this insight that moral distinctions remain in the NT. Jesus does, of course, perceive that there are good and bad on whom God causes His sun to rise (Mt. 5:45). He distinguishes between what is good and what is evil (Mt. 12:34 and par.). He acknowledges the keeping of the commandments to be an ἀγαθόν to the extent that in them there is revealed the will of God which is good. Paul invests the powers that be with the task of being θεοῦ διάκονος εἰς τὸ ἀγαθόν (R. 13:4). Yet beyond these moral distinctions of this cosmos the insight remains that they are relative and disappear before God.

c. With the revelation of salvation in Christ a radically new possibility of life is introduced : μεταμορφοῦσθε τῇ ἀνακαινώσει τοῦ νοός, εἰς τὸ δοκιμάζειν ὑμᾶς τί τὸ θέλημα τοῦ θεοῦ, τὸ ἀγαθὸν καὶ εὐάρεστον καὶ τέλειον (R. 12:2). The testing insight into the will of God which is the good carries with it the real-isation of this insight. It may be said of the Christian : κτισθέντες ἐν Χριστῷ Ἰησοῦ ἐπὶ ἔργοις ἀγαθοῖς, οἷς προητοίμασεν ὁ θεὸς ἵνα ἐν αὐτοῖς περιπατή-σωμεν (Eph. 2:10). ... περιπατῆσαι ... ἐν παντὶ ἔργῳ ἀγαθῷ καρποφοροῦντες (Col. 1:10 etc.). Paul demands the realisation of this possibility of existence : ... πάντοτε τὸ ἀγαθὸν διώκετε εἰς ἀλλήλους καὶ εἰς πάντας (1 Th. 5:15). This formulation shows us clearly in what the ἀγαθόν consists. It is the love which the Christian is enabled to exercise and which is the innermost purpose of the Law. The good is achieved in concrete I-Thou relationships. This new possibility of existence is the meaning of the life of the Christian. It is the purpose which it must realise. There thus obtains in all its fulness that which Paul formulates as the clear Law of God : δόξα ... καὶ τιμὴ καὶ εἰρήνη παντὶ τῷ ἐργαζομένῳ τὸ ἀγαθόν (R. 2:10).

In this self-fulfilling life the Christian who grasps this new possibility has the ἀγαθὴ συνείδησις. Paul can say of himself : ἐγὼ πάσῃ συνειδήσει ἀγαθῇ πεπολίτευμαι τῷ θεῷ (Ac. 23:1). There is reference to the ἀγαθὴ συνείδησις in 1 Tm. 1:5, 19 and 1 Pt. 3:16, 21. At the same time the Christian has the certainty that salvation is the goal and determinative magnitude of his life : οἴδαμεν δὲ ὅτι τοῖς ἀγαπῶσιν τὸν θεὸν πάντα συνεργεῖ [ὁ θεὸς] εἰς [τὸ] ἀγαθόν (R. 8:28). This certainty, which is proper to all Jewish piety [19] and derives from its consciousness of God, acquires here its fulness from the action of God. Hence we are given an expression which fully comprehends this whole understanding of life when Paul proclaims his confidence to the Philippians : ὁ ἐναρξάμενος ἐν ὑμῖν ἔργον ἀγαθὸν ἐπιτελέσει ἄχρι ἡμέρας Χριστοῦ ᾽Ιησοῦ (Phil. 1:6).

† ἀγαθοεργέω.

This is a rare word, which is not found in the LXX or Josephus. In the admonition to the rich in 1 Tm. 6:18, it signifies a demand for good action consisting in the demonstration of love to others. It refers to God in Ac. 14:17, in which He is described as the One who acts kindly. In this verse the contraction ἀγαθουργέω is used.

† ἀγαθοποιέω, ἀγαθοποιός, ἀγαθοποιῖα.

The verb and adjective are found as astrological terms. In a London papyrus (ed. Kenyon, P. Lond., p. 66, 48), it is said of an astrological constellation : μετὰ ἀγαθοποιων. Kenyon has the following comment : "An astrological term, used also by Artemidorus and Proclus, for stars of benign influence ; Proclus specifies Jupiter as being such." Cf. Plut. De Iside et Os., 42 : ῎Οσιρις ἀγαθοποιός· καὶ τοὔνομα πολλὰ φράζει, οὐχ ἥκιστα δὲ κράτος ἐνεργοῦν καὶ ἀγαθοποιὸν ὃ λέγουσι, a passage which indicates the connexion between astrology and contemplation of the gods. Hermes is called ἀγαθοποιός in a papyrus (Wessely, Neue gr. Zauber Pap., p. 55, 16). It is not unlikely that the use of the words in 1 Pt. is influenced by this application.

ἀγαθοποιέω corresponds rather to the Hebrew הֵיטִיב which expresses the realisation of the good by action (cf. הַטּוֹב וְהַמֵּטִיב Ber., 9, 2). It is often used in this sense in the LXX, where it is the consistent rendering of הֵיטִיב It is not found in Josephus or classical Greek. It passes from the LXX into the NT and the language of the Church, e.g., Lk. 6:9, 33.

ἀγαθοποιέω is particularly common in 1 Pt. (2:15, 20; 3:6, 17). John describes the ἀγαθοποιῶν as coming from God (3 Jn. 11). Sometimes it suggests the demonstration of love which will not suffer any restriction.

ἀγαθοποιός is the one who performs good actions. In the NT (1 Pt. 2:14) it is used with κακοποιός to indicate the two different categories of men distinguished by their ethical quality and not by their being in Christ. The view of the author is that Christians belong to the ἀγαθοποιοί.

---

[19] We find this insight in the OT. Joseph says to his brethren : "Fear not ; for I am under the Lord. But as for you, ye thought evil against me ; but God meant it unto good (לְטֹבָה)" (Gen. 50:19 f.). In Rabbinic literature, in which frequent use is made of the formula : "This or that happened unto me for good" (cf. Str.-B., III, 255), there occurs the statement : "A man should always be in the habit of saying, 'All that the All-merciful does, He does for good' " (bBer., 60b).

ἀγαθοποιΐα is good action (1 Pt. 4:19). In it alone consists the one possible preparation of Christians for final deliverance.

† ἀγαθωσύνη.

This word has come down from the LXX into the NT and the Greek of the Church. It indicates the quality which a man has who is ἀγαθός and therefore moral excellence as well as goodness. It is καρπὸς τοῦ πνεύματος (Gl. 5:22). It belongs with δικαιοσύνη and ἀλήθεια to the καρπὸς τοῦ φωτός (Eph. 5:9). Its possession constitutes the content of the life of the Christian : ... καὶ αὐτοὶ μεστοί ἐστε ἀγαθωσύνης (R. 15:14; cf. also 2 Th. 1:11). This use is controlled by what we described above as the Christian's radically new possibility of life.

† φιλάγαθος.

This is a quality demanded of the bishop in Tt. 1:8. According to the interpretation of the early Church it relates to the unwearying activity of love.

Aristotle calls φιλάγαθος the man who, in contrast to the φίλαυτος who is φαῦλος, places his ego under the good (Eth. M., II, 14, p. 1212b, 18 ff.). Philo demands φιλάγαθον of the law-giver together with the qualities of φιλάνθρωπον, φιλοδίκαιον and μισοπόνηρον (Vit. Mos., II, 9). The word plays a greater role in the Hellenistic period in the Greek societies [1] on the north coast of Asia Minor and the Bosphorus. It is "a title of honour to describe the disposition of the worthy brother in the society" (Ziebarth). It thus corresponds to the much more common φιλότιμος. But unlike the latter it is perhaps related to an official function (cf. καὶ ἰδίᾳ καὶ κοινεῖ φιλάγαθος ὢν ἐμ παντὶ καιρῷ, CIA, IV, 2, 623e). We have no information concerning the function of the one who bears the title φιλάγαθος. Hence the question of a possible relationship of this usage to Tt. 1:8 must be left open.

† ἀφιλάγαθος.

A hapaxlegomenon. In 2 Tm. 3:1 ff. the seriousness of the last time is depicted by express reference to the attitude of men towards it. To this attitude it belongs that they are ἀφιλάγαθοι. This word is distinguished from φίλαυτος (the opposite of φιλάγαθος), the term which introduces the description, in the sense that it says of the φίλαυτοι that as men who know only themselves they seem to have no knowledge of love or pity. It is part of the NT description of the last time that in it lovelessness celebrates its triumph.

Grundmann

φ ι λ ά γ α θ ο ς. [1] Cf. Ziebarth, *Das griechische Vereinswesen,* 1896, 155 ; Poland, *Geschichte des griechischen Vereinswesens,* 1904, 411 ff.

ἀγαλλιάομαι, ἀγαλλίασις

A. ἀγάλλω in Greek literature.

Ἀγαλλιάω, or the much more common mid., is a new construct from ἀγάλλω or ἀγάλλομαι,[1] and is found only in the language of the Bible and the early Church (with the single exception of P. Oxy., 1592, 4, 4th century A.D., possibly under Christian influence). The word ἀγάλλω, and esp. the mid., is of long standing in Greek poetry and prose (with ἄγαλμα and composites), and may be found also in P. Masp., 3, 8, 6th century A.D. In ancient Christian literature the term ἀγάλλομαι occurs as a variant in 1 Cl., 33, 2. Otherwise the word is replaced by ἀγαλλιάομαι under LXX influence, the sense of the latter term being determined by that of the Greek ἀγάλλεσθαι.

As ἀγάλλω means "to make resplendent" or "adorn," so the mid. means "to preen or plume oneself", "to be proud". Thus what the term denotes is not so much a mood of satisfied joy as a consciousness of joyful pride expressed in the whole attitude. The expression of this joy, to which there does not have to be any reference in the word, has the character of demonstration rather than impartation. Thus ἀγάλλεσθαι appears as the opposite of αἰσχύνεσθαι in Hdt., I, 143; Thuc., III, 82; Xenoph., Ag., 5, 5, or alongside μεγαλύνεσθαι in Xenoph. Oec., 21, 5. But as ἀγάλλω is specifically the celebration of a god (Eur. Herc. Fur., 379; Aristoph. Pax, 399; Thesm., 128; Plat. Leg., XI, 931 ad; Eleusin. Law in Porphyr. Abst., IV, 22), so ἀγάλλομαι is cultic and perhaps ecstatic festal joy (Eur. Ba., 157; Tro., 452).

B. ἀγαλλιάομαι in the LXX and Judaism.

Accordingly, in the LXX ἀγαλλιᾶσθαι or its derivative ἀγαλλίασις (and ἀγαλλίαμα) seems to be used as a rendering for גִּיל (possibly selected because of the similarity of sound) and רָנַן, rather less frequently of other verbs like הָלַל (Hitp.) and שׂוּשׂ or of the related substantives. But this use is almost entirely restricted to the Psalms and the poetic parts of the Prophets. The meaning of the word is the cultic joy which celebrates and extols the help and acts of God, whether shown to the people or community or to the individual (cf. ψ 50:14: ἀπόδος μοι τὴν ἀγαλλίασιν τοῦ σωτηρίου σου).[2] Even when it is no longer a question of cultic rejoicing in the narrower sense, the word still retains its "religious" meaning and indicates either joy in God or joy before Him. The praise

---

ἀ γ α λ λ ι ά ο μ α ι κτλ. [1] According to Debrunner ἀγαλλιᾶν is a variation of ἀγάλλειν after the pattern of "verbs of sickness" such as ὀφθαλμιᾶν, ἀγωνιᾶν, δειλιᾶν, ἰλλιγγιᾶν etc. (Debrunner, Gr. Wortb., 92). Hence the basic meaning is "to be self-satisfied in a pathological way," "to be gay to the point of madness." It is obviously a popular word used in jest.

[2] A good parallel is the use of *prangen* in the Austrian Alps to signify the arrangement of a procession.

of God and the pride of the community or the pious individual constitute a distinctive unity. As the μεγαλυνθῆναι of God attained by ἀγ. (ψ 34:27; 91:5 f.) is also a μεγαλυνθῆναι of the pious individual (ψ 19:6); as God's ὑψωθῆναι (ψ 96:8 f., Is. 12:6) corresponds to the ὑψωθῆναι of the community (ψ 88:17), so ἀγ. can be referred to God Himself (Is. 65:19; Tob. 13:13). Like ὑψωθῆναι and μεγαλυνθῆναι, εὐφραίνεσθαι, καυχᾶσθαι and related verbs are often conjoined with ἀγ. Especially striking is the linking up with it of ἐξομολογεῖσθαι (for הֹדָה) and ἐξ- (ἀν-) αγγέλλειν. The ἀγ. declares the acts of God. Antonyms are αἰσχυνθῆναι, ταπεινοῦσθαι, κλαυθμός, δάκρυα, etc. The demonstrative character of ἀγ. finds particular expression in the fact that in poetic language cosmic magnitudes like heaven and earth and mountains and islands are summoned to participate in ἀγ. (ψ 88:3; 95:11 f. etc.; also Test. L., 18, 5). Finally, ἀγ. is used as an eschatological term. It denotes the joy of the last time represented as cultic festivity (ψ 95:11 f.; 96:1, 8; 125:2, 5 f.; Is. 12:6; 25:9 etc.; also Test. L., 18, 14; Jud. 25, 5; B. 10, 6). Thus even on the Rabbinic view perfect joy and rejoicing characterise the future world. [3] If ἀγ. is lacking in Jos., who has ἀγάλλεσθαι = "to plume oneself" (Ant., 16, 64; 17, 112; 18, 66; 19, 191), and also in Aristeas, it is found in Sir. (in the profane sense) and Test. XII (v. supra).

C. ἀγαλλιάομαι in the NT.

In the NT ἀγαλλιᾶσθαι (and the act. in the same sense in Lk. 1:47 and Rev. 19:7 v.l.) and ἀγαλλίασις are used in the same way as in the LXX. The term signifies profane joy supremely in Jn. 5:35 : ἠθελήσατε ἀγαλλιαθῆναι πρὸς ὥραν ἐν τῷ φωτὶ αὐτοῦ. God's help is always the theme of the ἀγ. which is a jubilant and thankful exultation. As related terms we find χαίρειν (Mt. 5:12; Lk. 1:14; Jn. 8:56; 1 Pt. 1:8; 4:13; Rev. 19:7), διδόναι δόξαν (Rev. 19:7), and μεγαλύνειν (Lk. 1:46 f.). It is indeed the eschatological act of divine salvation which is supremely the theme of rejoicing, as is seen most clearly in the song of Revelation 19:7: χαίρωμεν καὶ ἀγαλλιῶμεν καὶ δώσομεν τὴν δόξαν αὐτῷ ὅτι ἦλθεν ὁ γάμος τοῦ ἀρνίου. When the δόξα of Christ is manifested, we shall rejoice : ἀγαλλιώμενοι (1 Pt. 4:13), and according to Jd. 24 we shall stand before the δόξα of God : ἄμωμοι ἐν ἀγαλλιάσει. But this ἀγ. is anticipated in faith. That there may be hesitation whether the ἀγαλλιᾶσθε of 1 Pt. 1:6, 8 is meant to be present or future is grounded in the character of faith ; both are possible. Mt. 5:12 is to be understood in the same way, and perhaps also Jn. 8:56 : ('Αβρ.) ἠγαλλιάσατο, ἵνα ἴδῃ τὴν ἡμέραν τὴν ἐμήν (infra). Even when ἀγ. is the individual joy of Zacharias and Elisabeth at the birth of John (Lk. 1:14), it is still eschatological joy; for John is the fore-runner, and therefore he rejoices (ἐσκίρτησεν ἐν ἀγ.) in his mother's womb when he meets the mother of the Messiah (Lk. 1:44), as does also Elisabeth that the divine work of salvation begins in her (Lk. 1:47). The word thus characterises the consciousness of the community that it is the community of the last time constituted by the saving act of God. If the word is not found in Paul, this is because καυχᾶσθαι (q.v.) is sometimes used instead The thing itself is perhaps to be found in 1 C. 11:26, where καταγγέλλειν perhaps corresponds to ἀγ.

---

[3] Str.-B., IV, 851 k, 852 m.

In connexion with the eschatological sense ἀγ. has a cultic. Nor does this mean only that the time of salvation has the aspect of a cultic festival. In the cultus the community actually celebrates and acknowledges the divine act of salvation. It celebrates its meals ἐν ἀγ. (Ac. 2:46; cf. 16:34; on 1 C. 11:26 supra). It is said in Ac. 2:26 (following ψ 15:9) and Hb. 1:9 (following ψ 44:8) that the person of Christ Himself is characterised by ἀγ. Worthy of note is Lk. 10:21: ἐν αὐτῇ τῇ ὥρᾳ ἠγαλλιάσατο τῷ πνεύματι τῷ ἁγίῳ καὶ εἶπεν, where ἀγ. seems to have the meaning of inspiration (cf. also Jn. 8:56?).

Analogies may perhaps be seen in Eur. Ba., 157, and Tro., 452, in which the feasts of Phoibos or Dionysus might be regarded as ecstatic. Above all we may refer to jSukka, 55 and other Rabbinic passages [4] in which ecstatic joy at the feast of the drawing of water within the Feast of Tabernacles is related to the outpouring of the Holy Spirit (following Is. 12:3).

D. ἀγαλλιάομαι in the early Church.

'Αγ. is often used by Ign. to characterise the eschatological community and its living expression, as in Phld., passim; Eph., 9, 2; Mg., 1, 1; but cf. also 1 Cl., 63, 2; Barn., 1, 6, and esp. Herm., where ἀγ., like ἱλαρότης, belongs to the very essence of the πνεῦμα of the pious man, m., V, 1, 2; 2, 3; s., IX, 24, 2. The cultic sense emerges in M.Pol., 18, 3, the eschatological in M. Pol., 19, 2. The word bears a more general sense in Cl. A. Paed., I, 8, 70, 1: οὗ γὰρ τὸ πρόσωπον κυρίου ἐπιβλέπει, εἰρήνη καὶ ἀγαλλίασις, οὗ δὲ ἀπέστραπται, παρείσδυσις γίνεται πονηρίας.

Bultmann

| ἀγαπάω, ἀγάπη, ἀγαπητός | → φιλέω |

A. Love in the OT.

1. Lexical analysis shows that the main word employed to express the concept of love in the OT is the root אהב [1] with its derivatives אֹהֵב, אֲהָבִים, אַהֲבָה. Like the English word, this is used with reference to persons as well as things and actions, and there is

---

[4] Str.-B., I, 643; II, 804 p, 805 ff.

ἀγαπάω κτλ. On A: J. Ziegler, *Die L. Gottes bei den Propheten* (1930); G. Winter, ZAW, 9 (1889), 211 ff. On B: W. Lütgert, *Die L. im NT.* (1905); B. B. Warfield, "Love in the NT," Princ. Th. Rev., 16 (1918), 153 ff.; P. Batiffol, *Études d'histoire et de théologie positive*, I (1926), 283 ff.; H. Preisker, *Die urchristliche Botschaft von d. Liebe Gottes* (1930); A. Nygren, *Eros und Agape* (1930); E. Stauffer, "Sittlichkeit des Urchristentums," RGG, V, 530 ff. Maximus Confessor, Κεφάλαια περὶ ἀγάπης, MSG, 90, 960 ff.; S. Kierkegaard, *Leben und Walten d. Liebe*, tr. Dorner-Schrempf (1924); M. Scheler, *Wesen und Formen der Sympathie* (1926); K. Koepp, *Panagape*, I/II (1927 ff.); H. Scholz, *Eros und Caritas* (1929); L. Grünhut, *Eros und Agape* (1931).

[1] The etymology is obscure; cf. the list of various attempts at elucidation in Ziegler, *op. cit.*, 13 f.

a most informative religious as well as a profane use. LXX mostly renders it ἀγαπᾶν, [2] and only seldom and in a secular context φιλεῖν (10 times; φιλία 5 times for אַהֲבָה), ἐρᾶσθαι (twice) or φιλιάζειν (once). The next term which calls for notice is the common Semitic root רחם which is used as a verb in the OT with one exception [3] in the piel. In most cases this restricts the concept of love to that of pity for the needy, [4] and it is often used, therefore, to denote the love of God. In almost every case God alone is called רָחוּם ("merciful"). [5] In translation of רחם the LXX uses ἀγαπᾶν only 5 times, in other cases using ἐλεεῖν as the most common rendering (26 times) or οἰκτείρειν (10 times). To this circle also belong the roots חפץ [6] (in the LXX mostly ἐθέλειν, otherwise βούλεσθαι, βουλεύεσθαι, εὐδοκεῖν and ἀγαπᾶν) and רצה [7] (LXX εὐδοκεῖν, προσδέχεσθαι, παραδέχεσθαι, εὐλογεῖν, and ἀγαπᾶν). These cause the person or thing by which the emotion is evoked to be followed by בְּ "to have pleasure in." Mention may also be made of חשק [8] "to adhere to someone in love" (LXX, προαιρεῖσθαι, ἐνθυμεῖσθαι, ἐλπίζειν), and חבב [9] which in the OT is found only in Dt. 33:3, but which is common in Aramaic. Limited to the secular sphere is עגב which denotes the sensually demanding [10] love of the female, being used of the male only in Jer. 4:30. So, too, are the nouns דּוֹדִים and יְדִידֹת.יָדִיד "beloved" is used only in the phrase יְדִיד יהוה "beloved of Yahweh." [11]

From this analysis we learn that love in the OT is basically a spontaneous feeling [12] which impels to self-giving [13] or, in relation to things, to the seizure of the object which awakens the feeling, or to the performance of the action in which

---

[2] This word, which is widely used in the LXX, is in the overwhelming majority of cases a rendering of אהב and derivatives, being used only seldom for רחם (5 times), for חפץ (twice), for רצה (once) or for other roots which sometimes stand in partial connexion (e.g., סות hi, פתה pi, שעע pilp), sometimes in no connexion at all (e.g., בוא 2 Βασ 7:18, 1 Ch. 17:16, where a theological interpretation is given, חטא and עשה) with the thought expressed by the translation. The noun ἀγάπη occurs some 20 times along with ἀγάπησις (some 10 times), and the two are often interchanged in MSS. Both are renderings of אַהֲבָה except in Hab. 3:4, where ἀγάπησις is a theological or erroneous equivalent for חֶבְיוֹן "cover." A Hebrew equivalent is lacking in Wis. 3:9; 6:18; Sir. 48:11.

[3] Ps. 18:2 qal of love for God.

[4] The relation of the verb to the noun רֶחֶם "mother-love" and the abstract plural רַחֲמִים "mercy" is obscure and debatable, cf. Ziegler, op. cit., 36 ff. It is certainly not possible to draw from this any conclusions as regards the interpretation of individual passages.

[5] Ps. 112:4 is an exception. Much favoured is the conjunction ר' וְחַנּוּן.

[6] In the erotic sense Gn. 34:19; Dt. 21:14; Est. 2:14; for friendship 1 S. 19:1 etc. For the religious use, v. n. 55. In 1 S. 18:22 there is interchange with אהב.

[7] In רצה there is strong emphasis on the element of recognition. רָצוּי is less "loved" than "liked" or "favoured" (Dt. 33:24; Job 20:10; Est. 10:3); cf. hitp. "to gain for oneself favour" (1 S. 29:4). Hence the aptness of the word for cultic usage, cf. n. 54.

[8] In the erotic sense Gn. 34:8; Dt. 21:11. With the subject God only in Dt. 7:7; 10:15, where it is near to בחר "to elect." Of the pious Ps. 91:14. Otherwise more weakly in the sense of "desire" in 1 K. 9:1, 19; 2 Ch. 8:6. For pi and pu constructions, v. Ex. 27:17; 38:17, 28.

[9] LXX ἐφείσατο. חֹב "bosom" becomes inf. in metonym. use, cf. E. König, Wörterbuch.

[10] LXX ἐπιτίθεσθαι, "to entice."

[11] V. n. 52 and 53.

[12] Cf. e.g., Jer. 31:20: הָמוּ מֵעַי. Also Ex. 33:19: רִחַמְתִּי אֶת־אֲשֶׁר אֲרַחֵם can be understood in this most untheological way.

[13] Cf. Lv. 19:18, 34: וְאָהַבְתָּ... כָּמוֹךָ.

pleasure is taken. Love is an inexplicable power of soul given in the inward person: מְאֹד (Dt. 6:5). One loves "with all one's heart and soul and strength" (Dt. 6:5; 13:4) if one does justice to the feeling of love. Love and hate are the poles of life (Qoh. 3:8; 9:6). To the natural basis residing in sexuality [14] it best corresponds that the power of love is directed to persons, so that the numerous statements about love for things or actions seem at once to belong to a weaker or more metaphorical usage. [15] Indeed, it may be concluded that only where there is reference to the love of persons for persons does the living basis emerge on which the concept rests. This is present, of course, in the religious use. For the authors of the OT the love of God is always a correlative of His personal nature, just as love for Him is quite strictly love for His person, and only for His Word or Law or temple etc. on this basis of love for His person. Nevertheless love is such a powerful expression of personal life that even the metaphorical use of the term in relation to things hardly ever loses its passionate note except perhaps in the case of lesser objects. [16]

In the OT the thought of love is both profane or immanent and religious or theological. The former usage relates primarily to the mutual relation of the sexes, then to parents and children, then to friends, to masters and servants and society generally. It is natural that we should use this group to interpret the numerically less frequent but for that very reason much more significant passages in which it is used religiously. For it is easier to grasp the content of the thought in the immanent sphere, and to judge the scope and bearing of the religious statements accordingly.

2. The Profane and Immanent Conception of love.

a. The most obvious passages calling for notice are those in which love unambiguously signifies the vital impulse of the sexes towards one another. For here we can see at a glance the impelling element behind it and its uniqueness, especially its complete difference from law. Sexuality is often strongly emphasised, and most strongly by Ezekiel, who uses אהב almost exclusively in the piel to denote sexual desire. [17] Hosea and Jeremiah, too, often speak of love in this sense, [18] and when the imperative אֱהַב occurs in Hos. 3:1 it is simply denoting the sexual act even if in an obviously euphemistic form. [19]

---

[14] For lack of any sure indication of its etymology, this may be concluded in the case of אהב from its more extended use in the erotic sense.

[15] Of the many instances, cf. Gn. 27:4: Isaac loves a savoury dish; Is. 56:10; Prov. 20:13: there is love of sleep; Prv. 21:17: of wine; 18:21: of the tongue; 15:12: of correction; 29:3: of wisdom; Ps. 109:17: of cursing; 11:5: of violence; Am. 4:5: of idolatry; Hos. 9:1: of the reward of whoring etc. Even the love of good or evil may be mentioned in this connexion (Am. 5:15; Ps. 52:3 etc.).

[16] This certainly applies in the case of חפץ and רצה for which numerous examples might be cited.

[17] Qal only Ez. 16:37, otherwise always pt piel: 16:33, 36, 37; 23:5, 9, 22. The use of עגב is also restricted to Ezekiel 23 (Ohola and Oholiba) except for Jer. 4:30.

[18] Hos. 2:7; 3:1; 4:18; 9:10 etc. Jer. 22:20, 22; 30:14; qal 2:25. Cf. בִּקֵּשׁ אַהֲבָה = "to follow the impulsion" (Jer. 2:33).

[19] Similarly in the same sentence אֲהֶבֶת רֵעַ.

But even where there is no emphasising of its unrestricted nature, the love of man and woman, [20] and particularly of husband and wife, [21] is generally recognised quite simply as a given natural reality, and the fact that in Israel, too, it contributed to the ennoblement of life may be seen from its elevation to the theme of poetic glorification. [22] The most forceful expression of the passion of love, almost hymnic in style, is to be found in the Song of Solomon 8:6 : עַזָּה כַמָּוֶת אַהֲבָה Love is the positive power which in the erotic sphere is confronted by negating hatred as a primitive force of equally unknown origin. The story of Amnon and Tamar presents the brutal nature of both impulses with undisguised clarity (2 S. 13:1-22), and in the hysterical words of the bride of Samson: רַק שְׂנֵאתַנִי וְלֹא אֲהַבְתָּנִי (Ju. 14:16; cf. 16:15; Gn. 29:31, 33), the same element finds haunting expression. Finally, even the Law has had cause to concern itself with the erotic symptoms of love and aversion (Dt. 21:15 ff.; 22:13 ff.; 24:1 ff.).

b. We seem to be dealing with something quite different when the same words אהב, רצה or חפץ are used to denote personal relationships which have no connexion with sexuality. Parenthood, blood relationship, friendship and legal partnership are the spheres in which the love which is free of the libido applies. Their connexion with sexual love is admitted to be very difficult to explain psychologically, and it may be that OT usage, like our own, relates under these modes of expression things which intrinsically have nothing to do with one another, so that in the analysis of such expressions we are rightly forced to speak metaphorically. That is to say, using the same words for sexual love and for non-sexual social relationships, we necessarily compare the latter with the love which bears an erotic emphasis. Yet this is perhaps going too far when we remember that in Hebrew, so far as we can see, there is absolutely no possibility of expressing, even though it may be felt (2 S. 1:26), the distinction between the two magnitudes of ἔρως and ἀγάπη. This means that the element common to both must have controlled the conceptions of the OT authors so strongly that they did not feel any need for verbal variation. Hence we should find particularly instructive for a perception of this normative element in the content of the word those passages which indicate the spontaneous and irrational nature of love as a feeling which wells up from personality. Jonathan loves David אַהֲבַת נַפְשׁוֹ, i.e., with the love which is proper to his own soul and which flows out from it (1 S. 20:17). Saul loves David מְאֹד, i.e., after the manner of a force which asserts itself in him (1 S. 16:21). Or Jonathan loves David כְּנַפְשׁוֹ ("as his own soul," 1 S. 18:1, 3), i.e., his relation to David was not merely close, but just as much impelled by and necessary to life as his relationship to his own soul. He was identical with David in the same way as a man is identical with his soul. If it would seem that there could be almost no way of emulating this simple comparison as an expression of spiritual communion, the poetic form of the same thought in David's lament for his friend is the more impressive : נִפְלְאַתָה אַהֲבָתְךָ לִי [23] ("thy love to me was wonderful"). For here the

---

[20] Cf. e.g., Gn. 29:18, 20, 30, 32; 34:3; Ju. 16:4 etc. The account of Solomon in 1 K. 11:1-3, if it is not meant to be a mild caricature, reveals in the enumeration a shallow and juristically coloured conception of love in the sense of legal sexual intercourse.

[21] E.g., 1 S. 1:5, 8.

[22] The famous praise of the virtuous woman in Prv. 31:10 ff. has, of course, a quiet undertone of irony, since the real answer to the question where a virtuous woman is to be found is that strictly no such woman is to be found anywhere.

[23] 2 S. 1:26.

irrational element in the experience is more strongly emphasised, though there is not strictly any religious connexion. [24]

c. We cannot always gather from the language the same intensity of feeling, nor perhaps is it always present, when the friend [25] or relative [26] is simply described as אֹהֵב.[27] But it constitutes the greatness of the OT ethos that it can always orientate itself by the thought of love. Love is regarded as the inalienable constituent of humanity, and for this reason it is declared to be the norm of social intercourse and set under the impress and protection of the theonomic law. Basically, it is of little consequence that such regulations apply only to compatriots and fellowcitizens. The legal character of the statements, their claim to validity within a definite circle of jurisdiction, makes it necessary that there should be specific reference to certain legally defined persons — a form which is necessarily felt to be an alien restriction when the living basis of the term אהב reminds us of the inner paradox of attempting to apply a non-legal word in a legal direction. [28] Hence a statement like Lv. 19:18: וְאָהַבְתָּ לְרֵעֲךָ כָּמוֹךָ, although couched in the legal style of the usual demand, and containing the legally very closely circumscribed term רֵעַ, is not really a legal statement, because the attitude denoted by the word אהב is one of natural feeling which cannot be legally directed. If the statement were really to have the force of law, then the word אהב would have to be taken purely phenomenologically as an injunction to act as one usually does in love. It is obvious, however, that even on this side it cannot be taken seriously as a legal ordinance, and in the analogous command to hate [29] the observation בִּלְבָבְךָ reveals that what is envisaged is a disposition. Hence all claim to legal competence must be renounced, and we are not to see in the legal form any more than an oxymoron designed to make the reader sharply aware that the ultimate concern of social legislation is to protect, foster and sometimes awaken the sense of brotherliness. This should be the basis of the legal relations, and to fulfil the command of love can only consist in not hindering the feeling of love, the rise of which is not connected with any act of will, but rather in accepting it in relation to the רֵעַ as though dealing with oneself: כָּמוֹךָ. [30] If the concern of the legislator is to order social life, he knows that all his ordinances in this direction can only be half measures if they are purely legal, and that the thought of power will always have a disruptive effect on society. Hence, whether or not he perceives its legal incongruity, he formulates the paradoxical command to love.

[24] The author of Qoh. 9:1 prepares the way for such a connexion when, having pointed to the hand of God which ordains the action of the righteous and the wise, he reverently maintains that man's most elemental feelings of love and hate remain mysterious to himself.

[25] E.g., אֹהֲבֵי עָשִׁיר in Prv. 14:20 means hypocrisy. But sayings like אַהֲבָה עַל־כָּל־פְּשָׁעִים תְּכַסֶּה in Prv. 10:12 or וְיֵשׁ אֹהֵב דָּבֵק מֵאָח in Prv. 18:24 show how the Wisdom literature maintains a high level in its handling of the concept.

[26] Cf. conjunctions like אֹהֲבַי וְרֵעַי in Ps. 38:11; 88:18.

[27] Especially the assertion of gradations of love occasions a serious weakening of the concept, cf. Gn. 37:4 (and its sexual counterpart in Gn. 29:30).

[28] The use of אֲנִי יהוה to give force to the theonomy hardly alters the fact, since it characterises the style of the so-called Holiness Code and does not usually influence the substance of the statements.

[29] Lv. 19:17; cf. also Zech. 8:17.

[30] This motive is found in Sir. 34:15 (31:18) even in a simple rule of conduct fixing good manners at table: νόει τὰ τοῦ πλησίον ἐκ σεαυτοῦ.

There is the obvious danger that in this way there might be established a much weakened and therefore legally competent concept of love in the sense of favouring etc. [31] But if we tried to interpret it along these lines, we should have great difficulty in proving it from analogous legal expressions. For Lv. 19:34, which gives us in the same form a command to love in relation to resident aliens (גֵּר), is burdened with the same difficulties. [32] It seems rather that the conception of Jesus, namely, that this is one of the two commands on which the whole Law depends (Mt. 22:40), does more justice to the meaning of what is said. Jesus isolates the command to love from the other legal materials, and protects it from all attempts at juristic interpretation, which in any case can only be forced. For a command to love arrayed in the garb of law reduces the law *ad absurdum,* since it indicates the limit at which all divine or human legislation must halt, and demands a moral direction of life transcending that of law.

This observation leads us to a definite judgment concerning particularism, which lies in a restriction to fellow-nationals rather than to fellow-residents. In his apparently exclusive concern with the wholly concrete relations of law, the legislator introduces into his definitions a thought which presses rather beyond the actual wording when he specifically envisages as neighbours not merely those who are such by law but simply men who are worthy of an act of love. The LXX translator is hardly guilty of a material error when he greatly weakens the legal sound of רֵעֶךָ with his rendering ὁ πλησίον σου. The real concern is in fact with men who live in the most immediate vicinity.

On this basis the interpretation can move confidently to the conclusion that the רֵעַ or גֵּר can from the human standpoint signify an enemy or hater and yet the attitude to him must be determined by love. The remarkable mutual interrelation of the two passages Dt. 22:1-4 and Ex. 23:4 f. seems at any rate to be concerned with and to give grounds for some such consideration. The passage in Dt. imposes an obligation of assistance in the case of a brother, i.e., a fellow-national, that in the book of the covenant in the case of an enemy. Whether we understand Ex. 23:4 f. as a development of Dt. 22:1-4, or the latter conversely as a weakening of the former, there can be no doubt that a comparison of the passages indicates the possibility of love of enemies as well being incorporated into the command to love in Lv. 19:18. The רֵעַ may be a friend or a foe, but he is to be the object of the feeling of love and not of legal definition. This implies a primacy of the man over the legal person. In this form the demands of Ex. 23:4 f., and perhaps to an even higher degree the basic statements in Prv. 25:21: אִם רָעֵב שֹׂנַאֲךָ הַאֲכִילֵהוּ לֶחֶם וְאִם־צָמֵא הַשְׁקֵהוּ מָיִם,[33] are designed to serve the practical inculcation of love for enemies, not being concerned directly with the disposition towards them, but making obligatory a specific line of conduct. The example of Joseph in the Joseph

---

[31] Mt. 5:43 refers to a "popular maxim" (Str.-B. *ad loc.*): "Thou shalt love thy neighbour and hate thine enemy." In this the unfortunate possibility is actually realised.

[32] Similarly Dt. 10:19. אהב in imp. only in Prv. 4:6.

[33] The following words in v. 22: גֶּחָלִים אַתָּה חֹתֶה עַל־רֹאשׁוֹ, deal ironically with the natural desire for revenge. Food and drink are the coals of fire which the wise and self-controlled man will heap on the head of him that hates him in order to destroy him. Prv. 24:17 may be cited in the same connexion: "Rejoice not when thine enemy falleth, and let not thine heart be glad when he stumbleth," although v. 18 shows that this is perhaps more a rule of prudence.

stories provides a practical illustration of the repayment of evil with good which also calls attention to Joseph's obedience to God (Gn. 50:19).

It is also true, of course, that the OT indicates the limits of love towards enemies, [34] most impressively in the anguished 109th Psalm. The petitioner remembers his love, [35] but this can only serve to nourish his late in dreadful illustration of the sentence in Sir. 37:2: הלא דין מגיע עד־מות ריע כנפש נהפך לצר. Even to the poor it often happened as described in the cutting saying in Proverbs (14:20), [36] and it seemed almost impossible to attain a personal and human relation to the foreigner in view of the tribal organisation and cultic exclusivism. [37] Yet the occasional visible clashes between theory and practice cannot destroy the greatness of the ethical demand, especially when it is recalled that it is proclaimed with divine authority and that there is also a place in the OT for the living value of love in religious experience as well.

3. The Religious Conception of Love.

a. From what we have seen already of the nearness to life of the concept of love it is surely obvious that it must have high theological value once it comes to be used in the language of religion. This is generally true even in the OT, although it is applied here only in statements concerning the mutual relation between God and man which are either very restrained or constricted by thelogical speculation and therefore easily underestimated. This restraint has its basis in the powerful predominance of the concept of the covenant, which asserts itself so strongly in the theological thinking of the biblical writers that they can seldom free themselves from the legal way of thinking which conditions this theory, and represent in its religious significance and with its unique force the thought of love as an expression of physical reality alien to the legal world. Nevertheless, there can be no doubt that the thought of the covenant (→ διαθήκη) is itself an expression in juridical terms of the experience of the love of God. Hence the concept of love is the ultimate foundation of the whole covenant theory. [38] It is a mark of Israelite religion that this connexion is for the most part only tacitly recognised, as though there were a fear of finding so typical a creaturely emotion and its resultant power in the nature of God, or of estimating too highly such an experience in dealings with God. No less striking are the attempts to approximate the thought of love to such concepts, imported into theology from law, as חֶסֶד, מִשְׁפָּט, צֶדֶק, אֱמֶת, etc., which are preferred to describe ethical and religious conduct. These do, in fact, bring about a levelling of the whole heritage of religious thought, and effectively hinder the fruitfulness of the concept of love in the OT. Yet they

---

[34] Cf. Joab's honest if rough remark to David in 2 S. 19:7.

[35] In Ps. 109:4 f. v. 4 b. is corrupt. "But I pray for them" is a rendering contrary to the sense. At most it could only be retained in the preterite.

[36] גַּם לְרֵעֵהוּ יִשָּׂנֵא רָשׁ.

[37] Elisha's advice concerning the captured Aramaeans in 2 K. 6:22 might be regarded as an upsurge of human feeling against the ban. That it is a Cushite, i.e., a ger of inferior rights and estimation, who out of impulsive sympathy rescues Jeremiah (Jer. 38:7-13) when the latter is abandoned by his own people is perhaps a kind of prior illustration of the parable of the Good Samaritan.

[38] The same is to be noted in respect of the related concept of election and also the religious use of the legal term חֶסֶד (→ χάρις), which affords the widest possible scope for the thought of love.

do not block it so completely that it cannot emerge in its full greatness in occasional statements.

These statements tell us on the one side that man loves God, and on the other that God loves man. Rather strikingly, no logical relationship is established between the two groups, and only the teacher of Deuteronomy attempts anything along these lines, sometimes demanding Israel's love for Yahweh on the ground of Yahweh's love for the fathers (Dt. 10:14-16), and sometimes promising Yahweh's love as a reward for covenant faithfulness (Dt. 7:14). It is not advisable, however, to investigate a thought in the light of its hortatory evaluation. Hence in what follows we shall take each group alone irrespective of any order of rank.

b. Love as a basic feeling of the pious in relation to the Godhead is accepted in the OT without any attempt to define the content of this feeling by way of instruction. If sometimes it is brought into connexion with fear, [39] this is obviously an improper use for the sake of plerophory of expression. For love in the OT is a contrary feeling to fear, [40] striving to overcome distance [41] and thus participating as a basic motive in prayer. [42] To love God is to have pleasure in Him and to strive impulsively after Him. [43] Those who love God are basically the pious whose life of faith bears the stamp of originality and genuineness and who seek God for His own sake. If, then, Abraham is called a אֹהֵב יהוה on account of his intimate intercourse with God, he is a model of piety. [44] As men of a distinctive inner life, members of the community of Yahweh in general can then be called אֹהֲבֵי יהוה [45] This designation embraces religion on its active side, although without slipping over into the cultic and ethical. Quite evidently it is not in any sense a mere theologoumenon, but its origin lies in simple experience. It attempts to describe a vital religious process [46] of an active kind which leads beyond or even apart from passive creaturely feeling to the distinctive joy of faith which the pious man needs and to which he gives expression in every hymnic motif. [47] Love finds salvation in the Godhead, and is the strongest basis of confidence. [48] The

---

[39] In Dt. 10:12 אַהֲבָה with לֶכֶת בְּכָל־דְּרָכָיו and עָבַד is one of the elements of יִרְאָה. The terms are already wellworn and tend to intercross. Classical expression is given to the conflict between love and fear in David's words in 1 S. 24:14.

[40] Cf. in the NT 1 Jn. 4:18; 2 Tm. 1:7.

[41] Cf. Dt. 11:22 etc.: לְדָבְקָה־בּוֹ.

[42] Typical is אֶרְחָמְךָ in Ps. 18:1, also the absolute אהבתי in Ps. 116:1, which it is better not to replace by our own poetry, however fine (cf. Gunkel, ad loc.), in spite of the difficulty of the text.

[43] Cf. Jer. 2:2 : אַהֲבַת כְּלוּלוֹתַיִךְ Ps. 91:14 חשׁק.

[44] Is. 41:8. The LXX takes this passively: ὃν ἠγάπησα. Cf. 2 Ch. 20:7: אֹהַבְךָ ἠγαπημένος (but Jm. 2:23 φίλος); Jdt. 8:22 Vlg.: amicus.

[45] אהב even in heathen religion, Jer. 8:2.

[46] Unfortunately there are objections against using for analysis the grandiose comparison in Ju. 5:31: אֹהֲבָיו כְּצֵאת הַשֶּׁמֶשׁ בִּגְבוּרָתוֹ, since it is an antithesis to the destruction of the foes of Yahweh. But the image of an irresistible process of nature is perhaps broken by the poet by the use of the slogan אֹהֲבָיו.

[47] We are concerned with one form of the experience of the so-called fascinosum, cf. R. Otto, Das Heilige, c. 6.

[48] Ps. 40:16; 70:4. Whether the frequent recollection in Psalms of complaint that the fathers had already experienced this salvation (Ps. 40:5) awakens this confidence or simply supports the emergent feeling cannot be decided, since in the life of prayer both possibilities alternate with the moods.

wealth of hymnic motifs which we find in the OT allows us to deduce the high significance and rich cultivation of this form of piety in the religion of Yahweh, which we might otherwise fail to appreciate in view of the fact that when the formal concept of love occurs, especially outside the prophetic books, it is almost always turned to exhortatory or confessional use and thus seems to be more of a rational product than is really the case. Thus we find such favourite combinations as to love Yahweh and keep His commandments,[49] or to love Him and serve Him (Dt. 10:12; 11:13; Is. 56:6), or to love Him and walk in His ways (Dt. 10:12; 11:22; 19:9; 30:16; Jos. 22:5; 23:11). These powerfully link love with cultic and ethical conduct and thus militate to some degree against a deeper understanding.[50] As against this, Dt. 30:6 impressively teaches us to understand love for God as a deeply inward and finally God-given experience. Yahweh circumcises the heart of Israel so that Israel loves Him with all its heart and soul. The prophetic picture (Jer. 4:4), which is in every respect a polemic against the secularisation of the concept of the covenant, serves, with a characteristic modification in sense of Jer. 31:33 (and also of Ez. 11:19), to indicate the irrational origin of the most powerful vital forces of the community.

But often the usage, as our examples have shown, is utterly alien to this thought. When the love of God is considered, the tendency in most authors is for the act, i.e., the ethical expression, to be ranked above the feeling, so that the impression is left that man himself decides whether or not to love. This impression is most strongly left by the command which Jesus calls the greatest in the Law : וְאָהַבְתָּ אֵת יְהוה אֱלֹהֶיךָ בְּכָל־לְבָבְךָ וּבְכָל־נַפְשְׁךָ וּבְכָל־מְאֹדֶךָ. (Dt. 6:5). The paradoxical element is the same as in the commands of Lv. 19:18, 34, and what we said in relation to these applies here too. There is ordered as a law[51] that which cannot be the subject of legal enactment. This cannot, of course, be understood by those who lack the spiritual power to which the command refers. The command presupposes and demands this in order to be raised. All the emphasis is placed on the threefold כֹּל (totality), and we may rightly paraphrase as follows : Thou shalt recognise the totality of the power indwelling thee, producing from the emotion of love a disposition which determines the total direction of thy life, and placing thy whole personality, לֵבָב and נֶפֶשׁ in the service of the relationship to Yahweh. It is true that this relationship already exists as a wholly personal (אֱלֹהֶיךָ) one. Man loves his God. But the concern of the law-giver is to make clear that there is contained therein a demand and a duty. As an instructor and leader he realises that whatever does not issue in action is worthless. He thus seeks by paradoxical formulation to make the most positive power in religion fruitful for covenant faithfulness. Yahweh Himself will test the seriousness of love (Dt. 13:3). In such thoughts the Deuteronomist is at one with Jeremiah, who bases the new fellowship between God and the people, the covenant of the coming age, on the law inscribed upon the heart and therefore on a law which is no true law any more (Jer. 31:33). He means nothing other than the free impulsion of love for God.

---

[49] E.g., Ex. 20:6; Dt. 5:10; 7:9; 11:1; 1 K. 3:3; Da. 9:4; Neh. 1:5.

[50] In such cases one is tempted to take the conjoining waw as an explicative : To love Him is to keep His commandments etc. May it be that this is the true meaning ?

[51] Dt. 30:16 emphasises אָנֹכִי מְצַוְּךָ. The thought is easier as poetically expressed in Ps. 31:23.

c. The message of the love of God takes on a national and an individual form in the OT. If chronological priority must be ascribed to the former, the nature of love finds purer and more instructive expression in the latter. It is striking how seldom the OT says that God loves a specific person. Only on two occasions do we meet with the expression יְדִיד יהוה, loved of Yahweh,[52] while turns of phrase with אהב are to be found only three times, and they are there used in relation to the rulers Solomon (2 S. 12:24; Neh. 13:26) and Cyrus (Is. 48:14?), so that they may well be linked with the theory of the divine sonship of kings which came to be accepted in Israel but which had an indisputable origin in pagan mythology in spite of the purification of its form.[53] For this reason these passages can hardly be explained from within the circle of ideas proper to the religion of Yahweh. Elsewhere אהב is completely avoided in statements concerning God's love. Instead, רצה is used, which as a sacrifical expression does not indicate anything like the same immediacy of feeling,[54] or חפץ, which does at least carry within it the element of recognition.[55] It may thus be concluded that basically the love of Yahweh is not usually related to individuals. For even those who pray prefer the thoughts of Yahweh's majesty, power or kindness to that of His love when they seek favour in respect of their personal affairs, or else in addresses like מַלְכִּי[56] they conceal as it were in the suffix "my" their desire for the loving remembrance of their God.

To this there corresponds the fact that for the most part only collective objects of the love of God are mentioned. On the borderline there stand the designations in the singular of certain types of persons such as fellow-citizens, the pure in heart, those who seek after righteousness etc.,[57] whom God loves or directs as does a father his son (Prv. 3:12). Behind such instructive statements there may perhaps stand certain experiences of faith such as emerge in the motifs of confidence in the Psalms, but their true religious content is hard to fix, since in them love approximates so closely to recognition or even to patronage in the case of the people of the land.[58] Again the pedagogic debasement of the father-son relationship in its more pedantic application[59] militates against a deeper conception

---

[52] Ps. 127:2 of a private individual, Dt. 33:12 as an attribute of the tribe of Benjamin (plur. Ps. 60:5).

[53] Cf. 2 S. 7:14; Ps. 89:27 f.; 2:7 (v. Gunkel, ad loc.). Perhaps even the name Solomon יְדִידְיָה (2 S. 12:25) is meant to stress his ordination to succeed to the throne.

[54] Cf., e.g., Lev. 7:18; Am. 5:22; Jer. 14:12; Ez. 43:27. Similarly the courtly formula יִרְצֶךָ יהוה in 2 S. 24:23 desires a successful offering. In Job 33:26 רצה is hearing of prayer. In Prv. 16:7 the pious life is a merit which Yahweh recognises.

[55] In Ps. 18:19 חָפֵץ בִּי, as we learn from the following verse in which the petitioner alleges his righteousness, is meant in the sense of דַּרְכִּי יֶחְפָּץ in Ps. 37:23. Cf. also Ps. 41:11 with v. 12. The courtly formula of the queen of Sheba: יְהִי יהוה בָּרוּךְ אֲשֶׁר חָפֵץ בְּךָ, in 1 K. 10:9 and 2 Ch. 9:8 is to be adjudged like the passages adduced above on p. 29. Cf. also 2 Ch. 2:10 (Hiram of Tyre to Solomon).

[56] Ps. 5:2; cf. Hos. 2:23.

[57] Dt. 10:18; Prv. 22:11 LXX; 15:9. Yet Wis. 7:28: οὐθὲν γὰρ ἀγαπᾷ ὁ θεὸς εἰ μὴ τὸν σοφίᾳ συνοικοῦντα, plainly indicates the trend towards exclusivism which characterises many such sayings.

[58] Ps. 68:6 may be quoted here. Yahweh is a Father to orphans and a Judge to widows, Ps. 103:13.

[59] Cf. the same teaching in the mouth of Eliphaz, Job 5:17.

of love in such a connexion. The thought of fatherhood does not penetrate to the private piety of ancient Israel. [60]

d. What the OT has to say about the love of God moves for the most part in national trains of thought, where it finds its natural soil. Love as a basic motif in Yahweh's dealings with His people seems first to have been experienced and depicted by Hosea, so far as we can see. To be sure, the thought of the Father-God is also found in Isaiah (1:4; 30:1, 9), but for him the emphasis falls rather on the element of authority than on the inner feeling of attraction, as may be seen in the bitter words of Yahweh concerning the ingratitude of His sons. [61] As against this, Hosea clearly perceives at the depths of the thought of the election and the covenant the spontaneous love of the acting God. Seeing that the forms and guarantees of law are inadequate to express the way in which Yahweh is bound to His people, he depicts this God as a man who against custom, legal sense and reason woos a worthless woman (Hos. 3:1). Hosea has to love the adulteress as Yahweh loves the children of Israel. This means that the whole of official religion has long since disintegrated, and that only an unfathomable power of divine love, apparently grotesque to sound common-sense, still sustains the existence of His people. Even the experience with Gomer, if we do not include chapter 3 in this, expresses something of the same. The prophet is to take a harlot to wife, for only a marriage which is nonsensical in the eyes of men and dishonouring to the husband can really give a faithful picture of the relationship of Yahweh to the land of Israel (Hos. 1:2). The threatening character of the names of the children, Not-beloved and Not-my-people, gives us an insight that the attitude of the husband is, of course, far from passive or supine, that the adulterous wife is lightly playing with fire, that she is unsuspectingly (2:8: "she did not know") moving towards the fate of one who is accused by her own children (2:2). She becomes an object of pity. The One who stands over the whole miserable situation knows her wretched plight better than she does herself, and takes her under His legal protection (2:19: ארש) for ever (בְּרַחֲמִים). Then she will "know" Him in the full sense (2:20). This is how Hosea seeks to understand the rule of God. He pulls down the structure of the covenant theory in order to lay bare its foundation in the love of God and then to build it again with צֶדֶק, מִשְׁפָּט, חֶסֶד and אֱמוּנָה. But the foundation stone is רַחֲמִים or mercy. [62]

With the same tenderness and depth Hosea introduces the thought of God's love in other motifs which cause us to think of fatherly love, although the actual terms father and son are perhaps deliberately avoided and we are simply given a picture of the fatherly instructor who is disappointed but who for this very reason

---

[60] If in Jer. 2:27 we have a caricature of the Canaanite form of address in prayer (אָבִי), it may be suspected that under prophetic influence private piety came to repudiate consciously the idea of God as Father on the ground that this necessarily implies naturalistic conceptions when related to the individual relationship of prayer. Cf. J. Begrich, ZAW, NF 5, (1928), 256.

[61] Of a different category are passages like Ex. 4:22: "Israel is my firstborn," or Dt. 14:1: "Ye are the children of the Lord your God," since these statements set aside the emotional content of the words and establish the claims of Yahweh on the basis of family rights.

[62] It must always be an open question how far a peculiar emotional sensibility may have predisposed Hosea for the task of symbolising ἀγάπη by ἔρως. Cf. A. Allwohn, *Die Ehe des Propheten Hosea in psychoanalytischer Beleuchtung* (1926), 54 ff.

loves the more passionately. [63] Israel has had a time of childhood and has thus won the love of Yahweh (11:1). Ephraim has learned to put its arm in His (11:3), and thus to be drawn by cords of love, [64] with no calling nor direction. Hence when he stands before a destruction brought upon himself, and it seems to be for Yahweh almost a duty to fulfil His righteous wrath, the love of God breaks through in terms of lament: "How shall I give thee up, Ephraim? how shall I deliver thee, Israel?... mine heart is turned within me, my repentings are kindled within me. I will not execute the fierceness of mine anger, I will not turn to destroy Ephraim: for I am God and not man; the Holy One in the midst of thee" (11:8-9). In this basic statement we may justly see the final fulfilment of the OT thought of love. A precedence of divine love over human is affirmed. It is to be found only in the fact that divine love does not let itself be affected by emotions or doubts which threaten it. It works irresistibly as an original force in the nature of God. When He acts in love, God demonstrates no less than His proper character as the holy God. Hence He suffers under the lovelessness of His people, whose covenant faithfulness is only like the morning dew which quickly dispels (6:4). In face of its sin He is overcome by a kind of helplessness: "O Ephraim, what shall I do unto thee? O Judah, what shall I do unto thee?"

This motif of the suffering love of God gives a peculiar note to all the threats in Hosea. It helps us to understand the degree of comfortlessness in such sayings as 9:15: לֹא אוֹסֵף אַהֲבָתָם "I will love them no more." [65] They have for him the significance of God's ceasing to be God, and therefore of absolute chaos. If the concluding chapter withdraws all these threats with the saying: אֹהֲבֵם נְדָבָה (14:4), there can be no doubt that this is spoken in the sense of the basic tendency of his message, whatever may be the relation of this chapter to the rest of the prophecy.

In a rather different and, as it seems to be, somewhat weakened form, the motif of the suffering love of God is also used in Jeremiah (12:7-9). Yahweh hates His heritage because it roars against Him like a lion. Nevertheless He calls it יְדִדוּת נַפְשִׁי and the whole poem is a lament. Yahweh Himself cannot say why Ephraim is to Him such a dear son that He is inwardly moved when He thinks of him and has to have mercy on him. [66] He loves His wife Israel with an eternal love, and this love is the basis of His faithfulness (31:3). In other places, too, Jeremiah adopts the motif of Hosea — whether consciously or unconsciously we need not decide. He thinks of a youth of Jerusalem-Judah celebrated with Yahweh in love like a honeymoon, and in this connexion he describes the Word of Yahweh as the fountain of living water (2:2 ff., 13). He shows how Yahweh waited in vain to hear from His beloved the tender word "my father" (3:19), and how He must feel it that she speaks to Him only hypocritically (3:4), and yet how He does not cease to call her to repentance (4:1).

---

[63] In fixing the meaning of the image less depends on the uncertain word בְּנִי (11:1) than on the expression תִּרְגַּלְתִּי (11:3): "to teach a little child to go." This does not fit in too well with נַעַר etc.

[64] 11:4. Textual corruption makes it difficult to interpret the picture with any certainty. Perhaps the mention of עֹל "yoke" suggests that it is based upon the "span." But this is not very satisfying.

[65] Cf. 1:6: לֹא רֻחָמָה and 13:14: נֹחַם יִסָּתֵר מֵעֵינָי.

[66] Jer. 31:20; cf. also 31:9.

Deutero-Isaiah, too, takes up the theme of the beloved of youth adopted again by God with eternal mercy (Is. 54:5-8), but he distinctively rejects the motif of the harlot. Instead, the wife of Yahweh has been left by her Husband for a עֲזוּבָה וַעֲצוּבַת רוּחַ, a moment. It is not she who has left Him; He has left her in wrath, as is now sadly interjected, though without specifying the reason for this wrath. The conception of Zion as the wife of Yahweh is perhaps also in the background when Deutero-Isaiah gives his emotionally most effective description of God's love in comparing it to, and even rating it above, motherly love. It may be, says Yahweh to Zion, that mothers sometimes forget their children, "yet will not I forget thee." [67] The theme of the father and son is also introduced as a variation when Yahweh addresses Israel in the masculine and declares to him his redemption: "I gave Egypt for thy ransom, Ethiopia and Seba for thee, since thou wast precious in my sight, and art worthy, and I love thee" (Is. 43:3 f.).

If in spite of varying estimates of their originality the prophetic passages all prove to be elemental expressions of piety untrammeled by theorising, [68] the sayings in Deuteronomy concerning the love of God display a different character. They attempt to make the lofty thought fruitful by pedagogic presentation, though this necessarily entails a certain weakening, since the fulness of experience out of which the prophets speak is obscured by the style of Torah. The experience is transformed into dogma. As we have seen already, the thought of love in Dt. serves predominantly to undergird the thought of election and the covenant. The irrational singularity of love is presented, therefore, in a way which is strictly formal and ineffective. Thus we are told that Yahweh has chosen Israel of all the nations on earth as His peculiar people. It was not because Israel was more numerous than others, on the contrary, it is the smallest of all peoples — but because He loved Israel that He bound Himself (חשׁק) to it (Dt. 7:6 ff.). In the same breath, however, we go on to read of the oath which Yahweh swore to the fathers, so that the impression is only too easily given that the legal guarantee given in the oath is the truly valuable and estimable feature, and the expression can thus become and be used as an exhortation to perceive from all this that Yahweh, the true God, is also the faithful God, who binds Himself by covenant to all those who for their part love Him and keep His commandments. Indeed, Dt. 7:13 links the love of God with blessing as a reward which Yahweh will give for covenant faithfulness. Hence the thought of love unintentionally acquires a note of *Do ut des* which it does not have in the prophets. It is integrated into the way of life of the pious man, and thus robbed of its best part, of its freedom. The integration is more happily made in Dt. 10:14 ff., because there the thought of the oath is dropped and it is simply stated that Yahweh had a delight in the fathers to love them, and that He elected their seed after them. [69] If the circumcision of the foreskin of the heart is demanded, this seems to be more in keeping with the message of the love of God, since it does not enter the sphere of law. The thought of the father best corresponds to the educative purpose of Dt. "Consider also in

---

[67] Is. 49:15. The same motif recurs in 66:13: "As one whom his mother comforteth, so will I comfort you." Dt. 32:18: "the God who hath borne thee," seems to belong to a different tradition.

[68] Zeph. 3:17 is highly corrupt and therefore not very clear. Ezekiel inclines to a cultic mediation of the good-pleasure of Yahweh, cf. 20:40 f.; 43:27. Cf. also Ps. 147:11; 149:4.

[69] Similarly the note in Dt. 23:5.

thine heart," we read in Dt. 8:5, "that, as a man brings up (יסר pi) his son, so Yahweh will bring up thee." But obviously even in this form the thought is rather different from what we find in Hosea. [70]

The clear development of the concept of love into a dogma in Dt. has some most important consequences. This fact is bound up specifically with the close interrelating to the dogma of election, so that it is involved in the process of hardening which the latter doctrine undergoes. We can see this by way of example in the use made of the thought in Malachi. At the beginning, we have a statement which startles us by its very simplicity : "I love you, saith Yahweh" (1:2). This message, however, is not understood with the depth and consequent breadth to be found in the word אהב, but it provides the occasion for a remarkable discussion of the question how this love works itself out and what is its basis. [71] This can hardly be meant as a question of truth, but only as a question of law. Enquiry is made into the circumstances which have the fact אֲהַבְתָּנוּ as consequence or presupposition. Thus the tenderness of the thought is violated and its force shattered. As the continuation shows, the good news is unfortunately estimated according to its legal implications. These are shown to consist in the privileged status of Jacob as compared with Esau. The misfortune of Esau-Edom discloses that he is hated by Yahweh, whereas Jacob should learn to regard the fact that he is spared the same fate as a proof of the "love" of Yahweh. If the use of the usual marital terms אֲהוּבָה and שְׂנוּאָה may have had some influence in producing this antithesis, [72] there is still every reason to deplore the distortion of the thought of love in the argumentation : Yahweh loves because He hates. Even the thought of the father is mutilated in this book. It is expounded as a legal claim against the priests : "If then I be a father," says Yahweh to them, "where is mine honour ?" (Mal. 1:6). Or it is almost completely reduced to a relationship of service such as obtains between a father and the son who works in his business (Mal. 3:17).

e. Yet the prophetic concept of the love of God is powerful enough of itself to be able to paralyse such distortions. To the same degree as the prophetic thought of God, it ultimately bears within itself the tendency to universality. Naturally, we do not find in the OT any direct expressions of a love of God which reaches beyond Israel. To interpret it in this way we should have to try to see it against Messianic contexts in which it may perhaps be presumed. [73] Yet this would mean wresting our exposition, since even where Messianic conceptions escape from particularism and lead to the idea of humanity they are too pale and general to find a place for such a vital motif.

The short statement in Dt. 33:3 : אַף חֹבֵב עַמִּים can in itself, according to Mas. and most versions, be interpreted in an absolutely universalist sense. But the context shows that it is not intended in this way, and that there is thus some corruption in it. In any case it is questionable whether עַמִּים can mean "nations." Again, the international question of Malachi 2:10 : "Have we not all one father ?", does not refer to the love of

---

[70] It is to be found also in Dt. 32:6, but only with the emphasis on God's creation.

[71] בַּמָּה אֲהַבְתָּנוּ can mean : "On what basis dost thou love us ?" or : "How dost thou show thy love to us ?" The following verses show that the second meaning is correct.

[72] Cf. Dt. 21:15 ff.

[73] Possibly Is. 42:6 is the least open to objection. בְּרִית־עָם means "covenant of humanity," as may be seen from the use of עַם humanity in v. 5. אֲבִי־עַד in Is. 9:5 is rather too obscure.

God but to His creative work, as is shown by the second question : "Hath not one God created us ?" The story of the tower of Babel in Gn. 11:1-9 indicates actual opposition to the idea of humanity.

Quell

B. The Words for Love in Pre-biblical Greek.

Basically, there are three expressions for love in pre-biblical Greek : ἐρᾶν, φιλεῖν, and ἀγαπᾶν. 1. ἐρᾶν is passionate love which desires the other for itself. In every age the Greeks sung glowing hymns to sensually joyous and daemonic ἔρως, the god who is compelled by none but compels all. This god played a great role in the cult, became in philosophy from the time of Plato the epitome of the uttermost fulfilment and elevation of life, and was completely sublimated and spiritualised in the mysticism of Plotinus to signify desire for union with the ἕν.

What the Greek seeks in *eros* is intoxication, and this is to him religion. To be sure, reflecton is the finest of the gifts which the heavenly powers have set in the heart of man (Soph. Ant., 683 ff.); it is the fulfilment of humanity in measure. More glorious, however, is the *eros* which puts an end to all reflection, which sets all the senses in a frenzy, which bursts the measure and form of all humanistic humanity and lifts man above himself. The great tragic dramatists estimate it with no less horror than enthusiasm : ἔρως ἀνίκατε μάχαν... ὁ δ' ἔχων μέμηνεν. Σὺ καὶ δικαίων ἀδίκους φρένας παρασπᾶς ἐπὶ λώβᾳ (*op. cit.*, 781 ff.). It is a god, and he is powerful even above the gods : τύραννος θεῶν τε κἀνθρώπων (Eur. Fr., 132, Nauck). All the forces of heaven and earth are forces of second rank compared with the one and only supreme power of *eros*. No choice is left, nor will, nor freedom, to the man who is seized by its tyrannical omnipotence, and he finds supreme bliss in being mastered by it.

Where the daemonism of sensual intoxication is celebrated with religious enthusiasm, there conversely religion itself seeks the supreme point of experience in this ecstasy. Creative *eros* stands at the heart of the fertility rites, and prostitution flourishes in the temples of the great goddesses, often under oriental influence. The sexual unions of gods and men narrated in mythology find current actualisation in the cultus. In the ἱερὸς γάμος (→ γάμος) the devotees experience physical union with the world of the gods. [74] Religion and ecstasy come together in religiously transmuted eroticism.

But the intoxication sought by the Greek in *eros* is not necessarily sensual. Already in the Greek mysteries, as so often in mysticism, erotic concepts are spiritualised in many ways as images and symbols for the encounter with the suprasensual. Plato works in this direction, devoting a whole dialogue to *eros*. For him, too, *eros* is an ecstasy which transports man beyond rationality (cf. Phaedr., 237 ff., 242 ff.), which has its source in an elemental need, and which finally issues in creative inspiration (Symp., 200, 206). But corporal beauty, which enkindles *eros*, is only a signpost to the αὐτὸ τὸ θεῖον καλόν which is intended and sought in all loving, to eternal being and the true good (Symp., 210 f.). Plato decisively lifts *eros* above everything sensual. Similarly, Aristotle frees it from the merely experiential and understands it as a cosmic function. It is the power

---

[74] O. Kern, *Religion der Griechen*, I (1926), 53 ff.; *Griech. Mysterien der klassischen Zeit* (1927), 71 ff.; A. Dieterich, *Mithrasliturgie*[3] (1923), 121 ff., 244.

of attraction in virtue of which the original principle maintains all being in order and movement: κινεῖ δὲ ὡς ἐρώμενον. This loving which inwardly holds the world together has nothing more to do with intoxication. It is an act which is strictly volitional in character. The πρῶτον κινοῦν is not ἐπιθυμητόν but βουλητὸν πρῶτον, just because τὸ ὂν καλόν (Metaph., XII, 7, p. 1072a, 27 f.).

In later Platonism, too, there is a tendency to purge eros of its original daemonic characteristics, and to subject it to the ideal of humanity. In typical fashion, the tractate τίς ἡ Σωκράτους ἐρωτική by Maximus of Tyre, who is more Platonic than Plato himself (Symp., 181 f., 208/9), contrasts the desire of the senses and the desire for beauty: ἐκεῖνος Ἑλληνικός, βαρβαρικὸς οὗτος. ὁ μὲν ἄκων νοσεῖ, ὁ δὲ ἑκὼν ἐρᾷ (Max. Tyr., XIX, 4, Hobein); and more fully: ἔρως... ἐστὶν χρῆμα... ἐλεύθερον (XX, 2). The mystical understanding of eros recurs in Plotinus (Enn., III, 5 π. ἔρωτος, Volkmann), in whom it finds its fullest expression. For him the true eros, the meaning of all love, is the impulsion of the soul beyond the world of sense and reason to the ὑπερβαλόν and ὑπερσχόν (cf. V, 5, 8), beyond all limitations to the point of coincidence: ἐράσμιον καὶ ἔρως ὁ αὐτὸς καὶ αὑτοῦ ἔρως (VI, 8, 15). The eros which celebrated its orgies in the social life of the time, which was on the look-out for piquant adventures in the myths of the gods, and which led to adventures in the temples, was developed humanistically by Maximus and sublimated mystically by Plotinus. Nevertheless it is the same eros, the natural impulse to the transcending of one's own life. Hence the original form of erotic religion is sensual intoxication and the supreme form ecstasy.

2. φιλεῖν/φιλία, on the contrary, signifies for the most part the inclination or solicitous love of gods for men, or friends for friends. It means the love which embraces everything that bears a human countenance; the love of Antigone's συμφιλεῖν ἔφυν. [75] Here we see most clearly the nobility of love. It is not an impulse or intoxication which overcomes man, but an order or task which he may evade (→ φιλεῖν).

3. In the word ἀγαπᾶν the Greek finds nothing of the power or magic of ἐρᾶν and little of the warmth of φιλεῖν. Its etymology is uncertain, and its meaning weak and variable. Often it means no more than "to be satisfied with something;" [76] often it means "to receive" or "to greet" or "to honour," i.e., in terms of external attitude. It relates more to the inward attitude in its meaning of "seeking after something," or "desiring someone or something." [77] The verb is often used to denote regard or friendship between equals, or sometimes sympathy. [78] Particularly characteristic are the instances in which ἀγαπᾶν takes on the meaning of "to prefer," "to set one good or aim above another," "to esteem one person more highly than another." Thus ἀγαπᾶν may be used of the preference of God for a particular man. [79] The ἠγαπημένος ὑπὸ τοῦ θεοῦ has a

---

[75] Soph. Ant., 523. Here φιλία is used, in 683 ff. eros, and both in the name of an ἀλήθεια which gains the victory over impulse and reason.

[76] Suid., s.v. ἀγαπᾶν: ἀρκεῖσθαί τινι καὶ μηδὲν πλέον ἐπιζητεῖν.

[77] Themistios, Περὶ φιλανθρωπίας, 9a (Dindorf), φίλοι γὰρ ἀλλήλων οἱ τὰ αὐτὰ ἀγαπῶντες.

[78] Hierocles, Carm. Aur., p. 56 (Mullach).

[79] Cf. also Dio Chrys. Or., 33:21: (Zeus) τῶν ὑπὸ τὸν ἥλιον πόλεων ἐκείνην ἔφη μάλιστα ἀγαπῆσαι.

position of preference before God. He is blessed by God with particular gifts and possessions. [80]

The specific nature of ἀγαπᾶν becomes apparent at this point. Ἔρως is a general love of the world seeking satisfaction wherever it can. Ἀγαπᾶν is a love which makes distinctions, choosing and keeping to its object. Ἔρως is determined by a more or less indefinite impulsion towards its object. Ἀγαπᾶν is a free and decisive act determined by its subject. Ἐρᾶν in its highest sense is used of the upward impulsion of man, of his love for the divine. [81] Ἀγαπᾶν relates for the most part to the love of God, to the love of the higher lifting up the lower, elevating the lower above others. [82] Eros seeks in others the fulfilment of its own life's hunger. Ἀγαπᾶν must often be translated "to show love"; it is a giving, active love on the other's behalf.

The use of ἀγαπητός, too, moves for the most part in the same sphere and enables us to trace the nuances of meaning of the verb. Ἀγαπητός can be applied to a thing which is right or a person who is dear. It is used above all of an only and precious child.

Yet the meaning of ἀγαπᾶν etc. is still imprecise, and its individuation still tentative, as may be seen when it is conjoined or interchanged with ἐρᾶν or φιλεῖν. For in these cases ἀγαπᾶν is often a mere synonym which is set alongside the other two for the sake of emphasis or stylistic variation. [83] To be sure, in Plotinus ἀγαπᾶν seems to be consciously used for condescending and ἐρᾶν for upsoaring love. [84] But whereas eros consistently engages the thinking of poets and philosophers from Homer to Plotinus, ἀγαπᾶν hardly ever emerges as a subject of radical deliberation. It is indeed striking that the substantive ἀγάπη is almost completely lacking in pre-biblical Greek.

The examples of ἀγάπη thus far adduced are few in number, and in many cases doubtful or hard to date. The reference in older indexes to Plut. Quaest. Conv. VII, 6, 2 (II, 709e): φιλίας καὶ ἀγάπης, cannot be sustained, Wyttenbach already having found the correct solution to ΑΓΑΠΗΣΩΝ: τοῦτο φιλίας ποιησόμενος ἀρχὴν καὶ ἀγαπήσων (instead of ἀγάπης ὤν) τὸ ῥαδίως... ἀφικέσθαι (finally adopted in Plut. ed. Dübner, p. 865). The scholion on Thucydides, II, 51, 5 (Hude, p. 142): ἀρετῆς: φιλανθρωπίας, ἀγάπης, is obviously late. Late and uncertain, too, is the appearance of ἀγάπη on a heathen inscription from Pisidia: πένψει δ' εἰς ἀγά[πη]ν σε φιλομμειδὴς Ἀφροδείτη. [85] Pre-Christian, but by no means certain, is Philodem. περὶ

---

[80] U. Wilcken, Chrestom, I, 109 (Ptolemaios, IV): αἰωνόβιος ἠγαπημένος ὑπὸ τῆς Ἴσιδος; Or. 90:4 (The Rosetta dedication, Ptol., V): ἠγαπημένος ὑπὸ τοῦ ΦΘᾶ together with αἰωνόβιος (cf. 90:8 f., 37:49). Constant. Porphyrog., De ceremoniis, I, 97 cd, Reiske, p. 443 (greeting of the president of the senate at the Byzantine court): καλῶς ἦλθες, ὁ πιστὸς δοῦλος καὶ φίλος τοῦ βασιλέως ἀναφανείς... ἠγαπημένε τῷ βασιλεῖ... ἠγαπημένε τῷ Καίσαρι.

[81] Dio Chrys. Or., 12:60: ἰσχυρὸς ἔρως... ἐγγύθεν τιμᾶν τὸ θεῖον. Cf. 12:61: ἄνθρωποι ἀγαπῶντες δικαίως.

[82] Plotin. Enn., V, 1:6: ποθεῖ δὲ πᾶν τὸ γεννῆσαν [τὸ γεγεννημένον] καὶ τοῦτο ἀγαπᾷ, καὶ μάλιστα ὅταν ὦσιν μόνοι τὸ γεννῆσαν καὶ τὸ γεγεννημένον.

[83] Xenoph. Mem., II, 7:12: ὡς κηδεμόνα ἐφίλουν, ὡς ὠφελίμους ἠγάπα. Corp. Herm., I, 19: ὁ ἀγαπήσας ἐκ πλάνης ἔρωτος σῶμα. Dio Chrys. Or., 13:32: θαυμάζειν καὶ ἀγαπᾶν τὸ δαιμόνιον.

[84] Cf. VI, 7:31 passim, but also VI, 5:10: ὁ Ἔρως ἀγαπῶν ἀεὶ οὕτως ὡς δύναται μετασχεῖν... τὸ γὰρ ὅλον ἦν τὸ ἐρώμενον.

[85] Papers of the Americ. School, 2, 57; W. H. Hatch in JBL, 27, 2 (1908), 134 ff. reads ἀγάπην; others read ἀγαθόν; v. Deissmann, LO. 17 n. 3.

παρρησίας, 13, 3 : δι' ἀ[γ]άπης. [86] Most important [87] is the recent discovery of a papyrus from the early 2nd century A.D. containing an ancient Isis litany. It lists the cultic names with which Isis is invoked at different points : 1. 27 f. : ε[ν Θώνι ἀγά-π[ην ...] ω, 1. 109 f. ἐν 'Ιταλίᾳ ἀ[γά]πην θεῶν (so P. Oxy., XI (1915), 1380. In the second passage, of course, revised collation gives us the reading ἀ[γα]θην, ἄθολον (Α[...]ΤΗΝ ΑΘ-ΟΛΟΝ), [88] cf. ἀγάθην, 1. 95. But there can be little doubt that ἀγάπην is used as a cultic name for Isis in 1. 28, cf. 1. 94, φιλίαν. [89] On the other hand, ἀγαπησμός and ἀγάπησις are more numerous, obviously older and at any rate more certain than ἀγάπη. These both mean love or the demonstration of love. [90]

C. Love in Judaism.

1. The picture changes completely when we turn to the OT (→ A.). אהב, the main word for love in the Hebrew text, applies to the passionate love between man and woman (Cant. 8:6 f.), to the selfless loyalty of friendship (1 S. 20), and to resolute adherence to righteousness (Ps. 45:8). The Hebrew word thus covers all the wealth of the three Greek terms. But there is lacking one feature, i.e., religious eroticism, and this lack distinguishes OT religion no less sharply from the fertility cults of surrounding nations than from the Greek world. The love of God for Israel (Dt. 7:13) is not impulse but will; the love for God and the neighbour demanded of the Israelite (Dt. 6:5; Lv. 19:18) is not intoxication but act.

The distinctive characteristic of Israelite אֲהֲבָה is, of course, its tendency to exclusivism. Greek eros is from the very outset a universal love, generous, unbound and non-selective. The love extolled in the OT is the jealous love which chooses one among thousands, holds him with all the force of passion and will, and will allow no breach of loyalty. It is in קִנְאָה that there is revealed the divine power of אֲהֲבָה. Not for nothing does Cant. 8:6 link in its parallelism the love which is as strong as death with the jealousy which is as hard as hell. Jacob has two wives, but his love belongs only to the one (Gn. 29); he has twelve sons, but he loves one above all the rest (Gn. 37:3). God has set many nations in the world, but His love is for the elect people. With this people He has made a covenant which He faithfully keeps and jealously guards like a bond of marriage (Hos. 1 ff.). Transgression of the provisions of the covenant is a breach of faith, and the worship of false gods is adultery provoking the passionate קִנְאָה of Yahweh. For He is a jealous God, punishing guilt, but showing grace (חֶסֶד) to those who love Him and keep His commandments (Ex. 20:2 ff.).

The same exclusive motif asserts itself in the principle of love for the neighbour. It is a love which makes distinctions, which chooses, which prefers and overlooks. It is not a cosmopolitan love embracing millions. The Israelite begins his social

---

[86] Philodem., c. 60 B.C., from the charred papyri of Herculaneum, ed. by Olivier (1914), 52.

[87] Cf. also *Berliner Klassikertexte*, 2 (1905), 55, P.Par., 49. For A.D. *v*. Reitzenstein, Poim., 297; NGG, (1919), 18, 138 f.; P. M. Meyer, Jurist. Pap. (1920), 30; Preisigke Wört., *s.v.*

[88] G. de Manteuffel, in *Revue de Philologie*, 54 (1928), 163, no. 10.

[89] R. Reitzenstein, NGG (1917), 130 f. compares with this IG, XII, 5, 217: ἐγὼ [Isis] γυναῖκα καὶ ἄνδρα συνήγαγα... ἐγὼ στέργεσθαι γυναῖκας ὑπ' ἀνδρῶν ἡνάγκασα.

[90] Suīd., *s.v.* ἀγαπησμός: ἀγαπησμὸν λέγουσιν καὶ ἀγάπησιν τὴν φιλοφροσύνην ... Cf. also Pass. (-Cr), *s.v.*

action at home. He loves his people with the same preferential love as is shown it by God. He extends his love to foreigners only is so far as they are incorporated into his house or nation (Ex. 20:10; 22:20 etc.). Even the enemy (שׂנא) is to have my assistance when in difficulty, and is expressly referred to my help (cf. Ex. 23:4 f.). It will be seen that the organic relationship and concrete situation are always normative for social responsibility. The general love of the Hellenistic cosmopolitan is eccentric. Neighbourly love for the native Israelite is concentric.

The LXX almost always renders the אהב of the Hebrew text by ἀγαπᾶν (→ p. 21). [91] To the substantive אהבה there corresponds the Greek ἀγάπη, which now comes into use. Ἔρως and φιλία and derivatives are strongly suppressed. The harmless ἀγαπᾶν carries the day, mainly because by reason of its prior history it is the best adapted to express the thoughts of selection, of willed address and of readiness for action. But the true victor in the competition is the ancient אהב, which impresses upon the colourless Greek word its own rich and strong meaning. It was once thought that ἀγάπη was a completely new word coined by the LXX. This no longer seems likely. Much more significant, however, is the fact that the whole group of words associated with ἀγαπᾶν is given a new meaning by the Greek translation of the OT.

2. Hellenistic Judaism.

a. In the wide circle of the Jewish world the predominant influence of the OT intermingles with modes of thought and expression partly from a Greek and partly an oriental background. [92] There is much reference to the love of God. God loves His creation more than any man can do so. Above all, however, He loves Israel: ἡ ἀγάπη σου ἐπὶ σπέρμα Ἀβραάμ. [93] His particular good-pleasure again rests on the pious (ἠγαπημένος, Da. 3:35 etc.). In Greek fashion, Josephus uses "the good" for "the pious," [94] but when his thought takes more biblical lines he says "the penitent" (Ant., 2, 23). In the Wisdom literature and related writings the fulfilment of the commandments and mercy are the way to earn God's love. He who treats orphans like a father will be loved by God like a son (Sir. 4:10 f.; cf. Test. N. 8:4, 10). Supremely, however, ἀγάπη is a relationship of faithfulness between God and man. Οἱ πιστοὶ ἐν ἀγάπῃ προσμενοῦσιν αὐτῷ. The martyr who decides unconditionally for God and accepts all kinds of torments for His sake will experience the more deeply in all his sufferings the faithfulness of God, and will receive eternal life in the future world. [95] πιστὸς κύριος τοῖς ἀγαπῶσιν αὐτὸν ἐν ἀληθείᾳ τοῖς ὑπομένουσιν... παιδείαν αὐτοῦ. [96] Hence the love of

---

[91] מְאַהֵב in Zech. 13:6 by ἀγαπητός.

[92] Cf. for what follows, Kauffmann-Kohler in JE, VIII (1904), 188 ff.

[93] Ps. Sol. 18:4. Cf. Jos. Ant., 8, 173: θεὸν ἀγαπήσαντα... τὴν χώραν. A. Schlatter in Wie sprach Josephus von Gott? (1910), p. 63 ff., compares with Josephus' use of ἀγαπᾶν the Rabbinic חבב.

[94] Ant., 8, 314: τὸ θεῖον... ἀγαπᾷ τοὺς ἀγαθοὺς μισεῖ δὲ τοὺς πονηρούς. How Greek is the spirit of this sentence may be seen from a comparison with Julian Ep., 89 b, p. 129, 4 (Bidez-Cumont).

[95] Wis. 3:9; Da. (LXX) 9:4; Bel 37 (38); 4 Macc. 16:19 ff.; 15:2: τὴν εὐσέβειαν μᾶλλον ἠγάπησε (more than the saving of life).

[96] Ps. Sol. 14:1, as a formula; cf. 4:29; 6:9. On love for God cf. also Tob. 14:7.

God includes love for God. The source, however, is to be found in God, as is emphasised in the epistle of Aristeas. ἀγάπη, which constitutes the power of piety, is the gift of God (Ep. Ar., 229). Similar references are made to the love of wisdom or truth as to love for God (Sir. 4:12). He who loves wisdom keeps the commandments (Wis. 6:18 f.). Love wisdom, and it will protect you (Test. R. 3:9). Josephus in particular loves descriptions which have a metaphysical ring, and speaks eloquently of the διάνοια ... τὸ θεῖον ἀγαπῶσα. [97] This echoes the Greek religion of culture. Philo speaks in mystical tones of ἀγάπη, the turning to true being, in which man overcomes all fear and attains to true life (Deus Imm., 69); ἀνάβηθι, ὦ ψυχή, πρὸς τὴν τοῦ ὄντος θέαν, ἀφόβως ... ἀγαπητικῶς (Migr. Abr., 169; cf. Cher., 73 : τὸν νοῦν ἠγαπηκέναι).

b. Love for one's neighbour is a favourite theme of Hellenistic Judaism. This is not merely the command of God ; like love for God, it is rooted in God Himself. Hatred derives from the devil, love from God. Only the man who loves God is secure against the assaults of Beliar (Test. G. 5:2; B. 3:4; cf. 8:2). Hatred leads to death, love by forbearance to deliverance (Test. G. 4:7). In many cases, the reference here is to family love, [98] but more frequently to neighbourly love in the more general sense, as when "Menander" introduces the Golden Rule. [99] Even love for enemies is expressly enjoined (Ep. Ar., 227). For the rest, the synthesis between the older Jewish concept of love and the Hellenistic ideal of humanity caused many difficulties to the Jews of the Dispersion. Philo in Virt., 51 ff. devotes to this problem a long chapter with the distinctive title : περὶ φιλανθρωπίας; and comparison with Josephus Ap., 2, 209 ff. makes it probable that we have before us here a solid τόπος of Jewish apologetic. All that deliberate exegesis can glean from the OT by way of philanthropic motifs is here picked out by Philo and fused into a systematic presentation. In the centre stand compatriots, including proselytes, [100] and fellow-residents, then in widening circles (109 ff.) enemies, slaves, animals and plants, until love embraces all creation. This must have been impressive even to the Greeks. Yet consciously or unconsciously there still emerges in this structure the singularity of Jewish neighbourly love, its fundamentally concentric character. For all the desire for adaptation in externals, even Hellenistic Judaism remains on the soil of the older Jewish understanding of love.

In any case there is a full differentiation from the ἔρως of the "unchaste Greeks" (Sib., 3, 171). [101] Eros is not a god, but a corrupter (Phokylides, 194). The most powerful enemy of all passion or eroticism is the purity of ἀγάπη (Test. B. 8:2).

---

[97] Ant., 7, 269 ; Ap., 296 : ἀλήθειαν ἀγαπᾶν. Rather differently Ant., 16, 158 : συνείθισται τὸ δίκαιον ἀντὶ τοῦ πρὸς δόξαν ἠγαπηκέναι (cf. μᾶλλον ἀγ. supra, n. 95). Typically Greek in Bell., 5, 438 : ἀγαπητόν, something which causes satisfaction. Occasionally Josephus like the secular Greek authors uses ἀγαπᾶν promiscue with ἐρᾶν, φιλεῖν, or one of their derivatives ; cf., e.g., Bell., 4, 319 : Ἄνανος ... ἠγαπηκὼς τὸ ἰσότιμον καὶ πρὸς τοὺς ταπεινοτάτους φιλελεύθερός τε καὶ δημοκρατίας ἐραστής.
[98] Test. S. 4:7. Cf. also ἀγαπητοῦ καὶ μόνου παιδός, Philo Som., I, 194 ; Abr., 168 ; Vit. Mos., I, 3.
[99] Men., 40 in the negative form. Also Tob. 4:15 and Philo in Euseb. Pr. Ev., VIII, 7, 6 ; for hints of the positive version, e.g., Ep. Ar., 207. Cf. Kittel, Probleme, 109 f.
[100] 103 : κελεύει δὴ τοῖς ἀπὸ τοῦ ἔθνους ἀγαπᾶν τοὺς ἐπηλύτας μὴ μόνον ὡς φίλους καὶ συγγενεῖς ἀλλὰ ὡς ἑαυτούς.
[101] Josephus loves piquant stories, but he recites them to his readers in a tone of moral edification, e.g., Ant., 18, 72 ff.

The substantive ἀγάπη is more common in Test. XII (G. 4:7; 5:2; B. 8:2; R. 6:8 f.),
but it occurs only once in Ps. Sol. (18:4), in Ep. Ar. (229) and in Philo (Deus. Imm., 69),
and not at all in Josephus, who also does not use ἀγάπησις. [102] Cf. also Wis. 3:9;
6:18 f.; Sib., 6, 25.

3. Rabbinic Judaism.

a. In the Hebrew-speaking world אָהֵב remains the basic term for love. Alongside
it there establishes itself in Rabbinic texts the Aramaic חִיֵּב [103] The energy of will
and religious strictness are maintained in both words, being much deepened indeed
by the suffering endured in times of persecution and the centuries long discipline
of will and action.

Love determines the relationship between God and man, but especially between
God and the people of God. "Man is loved (חֲבִיב) because he is made in the
image of God ... Israel is loved because they are called the children of God, and
loved especially because it is declared to them that they are called the children
of God." This is how Akiba puts it (Ab., 3, 14; cf. also bJoma, 52a). Other
depictions bring out even more clearly the inwardness and fidelity of this love.
God's steadfast and merciful love for Israel is like the love of a king who after
a short time seeks out again with grace his repudiated but favourite wife (Ex. r. 51
on 38:21). God is the Beloved of the Song of Solomon, always near, and always
ready to pardon (bShab., 88b). Hence Israel must love its God with all its heart
and soul and strength (Dt. 6:5). The Schᵉma' plays just as great a role in later
Jewish piety as in Rabbinic exegesis and theology. [104]

A striking proof of God's love for His people is given by the Torah: "Beloved
is Israel, because He gave them a gift by which the world was created; and
beloved especially because it is declared to them that He gave them this gift ...
Indeed, it is said: I gave you good doctrine; do not forsake my Law" (Akiba in
Ab., 3, 15). The Torah is the patent of Israel's nobility, but like all the gifts of
God's grace it carries with it obligations. God and the people of God (חֲבִיב in
bMen., 99b) meet in love for the Torah, and love for the Law of God, which
finds classical examples in men like Moses or Jethro, [105] is a powerful incentive
to self-sacrificing fulfilment of the commandments and unconditional faithfulness
to the Law (bShab., 130 etc.).

The point at which love between God and the people of God is particularly
revealed is that of suffering and especially martyrdom. "Dear are the chastisements." [106] For sufferings are the correction of the man who loves God, and must
be understood as loving chastisements (M. Ex. 20:23; bBer., 5b). Indeed, sufferings
are a means to earn the good-pleasure of God, atoning for sin and being a pledge
of participation in the coming world of God. [107] Above all, they are the decisive

---

[102] Cf. Thackeray, Lex. Jos.
[103] Cf. already the blessing of Moses in Dt. 33:3: אַף חֹבֵב עַמִּים. With אהב and חבב also
רחם, etc. Cf. Levy Wört.
[104] Cf. Tg. O, Dt. 6:5 (here רחם) S. Dt. 32 on 6:5 (Kittel, 54 ff.); Str.-B., IV, 189 ff.
[105] bSota, 13a etc.
[106] S. Dt. 6:5. חביב); as a formula in Ex. r. 27 on 18:1; Dt. r. 5; bJoma, 52a etc.
[107] Lv. r. 32 on 24:10: "These blows are the reason why I am loved (אהב) of my Father

fiery trial of our love for the Law of God and for God Himself. "Concerning those who are humiliated without humiliating others, who listen to insults without replying, who fulfil the commandments out of love and rejoice in chastisement, the Scripture says that those who love Him are as the sun rising in its glory." [108] It is obvious that this faithfulness to God cannot fail to have its influence on the future destiny of the martyrs. Yet the decisive thing is that God wills to be loved for His own sake. Tradition tells us that Akiba was controlled his whole life long by the thought that love with all one's soul as required by the Sch^ema' can find its final attestation and fulfilment only in martyrdom. He taught the Law untroubled by any fear of death. It was in the hour of the reading of the Sch^ema' that he was brought to the place of judgment, and he died under the iron wheel with the אֶחָד of the conclusion of the first sentence of the Sch^ema' on his lips (bBer., 61b). Nowhere do we have more glorious expression than in this story of the strength of will, the purity and the unreservedness of the love of suffering Israel for its God.

But the thinking of the Rabbis constantly returns to the love of God. This stands supreme. It is perhaps concealed in this age of stress, but it will the more gloriously manifest itself in its own time. It is strong as death. Only the victorious words of the Song of Solomon are adequate to convey the elementary force of this love. And in a broad exposition of the Song of Solomon there is expression again of all the needs and experiences and truths which stand before the trampled people of God when it speaks of the love of God. The love of God is strong as death for a generation undergoing religious persecution. His jealousy is as hard as hell in the hour of idolatrous worship. Many waters cannot quench love, nor can the nations pluck Israel away from the love of its God. If a man would give all the substance of his house for love, he would be scornfully rejected. The love with which Akiba and his fellows sacrificed themselves is more precious than all the treasures of the world. [109] Romantic love has always sought mystical sensations in the Song of Songs. Judaism has made of it a hymn to the defiant and faithful love between God and His maltreated people.

b. Another note is sounded by the Judaistic expressions for love when it refers to the relationship between man and man. [110] If love for God finds fulfilment in suffering, love for fellow-men does so in active and helpful work "To exercise love is to do beneficent works." [111]

Who is the neighbour who has a claim to the help of the Israelite ? First, it is the compatriot or the full proselyte in the sense of the concentric conception of the duty of love in ancient Israel. [112] Again in the sense of the OT, a readiness to help is demanded in the case of enemies who belong to the people, or even sometimes

in heaven." Also M. Ex. 20:6 (Wünsche, 213), and M. Ex. 20:23 : "Beloved are sufferings, for they procure the Torah, the land and the future world..." Also S. Dt. 6:5 (Kittel, 54 ff.) and bSanh., 101 a/b. Most striking is the answer to the question : "Are chastisements dear to thee ? Neither they nor their reimbursement !" (bBer., 5b, חביב). Cf. O. Wichmann, *Die Leidenstheologie* (1930).

[108] bSchab., 88b; cf. also M. Ex. 20:33 (Wünsche, 227 f.).
[109] Cant. r., 8:8 f. (Wünsche, 183 f.); cf. also Pesikta, 28 (Wünsche, 262).
[110] Sexual love, e.g., bKet., 56a (חיבה).
[111] bSukk., 49b; cf. גמילות חסדים in bBer., 5b etc.
[112] Numerous instances are given in Str.-B., I, 353 ff.; cf. also IV, 536 ff., 559 ff.

in the case of national enemies (M. Ex. 23:4). [113] Yet this last demand was contested by some. The neighbourly love of which Judaism speaks does not for the most part extend beyond the borders of the people of God. It is thus consistent that the love for God's creatures so finely expressed by Hillel should be an incentive to the spreading of the Law and therefore the extension of the people of God : "Love (אהב) peace. Seek after it. Love creatures — lead them to the Law" (Ab., 1, 12). The concentric reference is thus preserved again.

In its original sense Jewish neighbourly love is the attitude which the members of the people of God owe one another. But there is accorded to it as such the highest significance. "The world stands on three things, the Law, the service of God and works of love" (Simon the Righteous in Ab., 1, 2). Akiba declared neighbourly love to be the great and comprehensive general rule in the Torah (S. Lv. 19:18). [114] Hillel did the same when he summed up all the commandments in the Golden Rule : "Do not do to thy neighbour what is hateful to thee. This is the whole Law. All else is explanation." [115]

Yet the Rabbis are by no means content to estimate the significance of neighbourly love and to set up a formal canon for it. They also speak of the motives and reasons for the command to love. "Discharge the duties of love that men may discharge them to thee . . ." [116] More profound is the thought that love itself rather than prudent calculation should inspire our action. Love itself gives decisive meaning and content to the duty of love. "All that ye do should be done only out of love." [117] Clearly something is here demanded which cannot in fact be demanded. This love cannot be regulated or enforced by legislation. It must have a deeper basis. The Rabbis discovered this basis, and gave neighbourly love a foundation in which the understanding of love came to fruition in later Judaism.

c. The love of which the Rabbis speak is neither love between God and man exclusively, nor love between man and man exclusively, nor the two alongside, but both together and at the same time. It is the basic principle of the threefold relationship of God, man and man. "As the Holy One, blessed be He, clothes the naked, visits the sick, comforts the sorrowful and buries the dead, so do thou clothe the naked, visit the sick, comfort the sorrowful and bury the dead" (bSota, 14a). And again : "He who has mercy (רחם) on his fellow, heaven has mercy on him." [118] Hence mercy between men is no other than emulation of the mercy of God, [119] or entry into the form of the divine action. Again, God Himself acts towards man according to the principle followed by man himself in his dealings with his fellows. Love is the principle laid down by God for the relationship between God, I and Thou. It must determine all dealings within this threefold relationship, or the

---

[113] For this and other important passages, v. Kittel Probleme, 110 ff. Historical material may be found in H. Haas, Feindesliebe i.d. ausserchristl. Welt (1927).

[114] But. cf. the parity of all the commandments in 4 Macc. 5:20.

[115] bSchab., 31a; J. I. Lv. 19:18. Positive formulations in Ab. R. Nathan, 15, 1 f.; 16, 2, cf. Kittel Probleme, 110.

[116] Cf. G. Klein, D. älteste christl. Katechismus (1908), 86, n. 1; cf. for the thought of reward, Str.-B., IV, 562 ff.

[117] S. Dt. 41 on 11:13, Str.-B., III, 306.

[118] bShab., 151b; cf. bBer., 5b. Works of love (גמילות חסדים) serve to wash away sin. In this sense they are comparable to the sufferings of martyrs.

[119] Cf. also A. Marmorstein, "Die Nachahmung Gottes," in Jüd. Stud. f. J. Wohlgemuth (1928), 25 ff.; G. F. Moore, Judaism, II, 109 ff.

relationship is snapped. First and finally it is God who asserts the principle. But it can also be man's affair to assert this divine principle, the measure of goodness, before God. This is, perhaps, one of the boldest thoughts thus far conceived by Judaism. Yet it is no mere thought; it is a cry of need.

> Thus "Ezra" raises his voice at the climax of the powerful third dialogue with the angel of God : "Yet I know that the Most High is ... the Merciful God, for He has mercy on those who are not yet come into the world ... If He did not ordain in His goodness that sinners should be released from their sins, not even a ten thousandth part of humanity would attain to life" (4 Esr. 7:132, 138). It makes no difference that the angel repulses him : "Thou art still lacking in much to love creation more strongly than I" (8, 47). The fact remains that it is Ezra who must appeal to God's mercy, declaring that the greater part of humanity would inevitably perish if God were to weigh by the standard of justice and not of love. [120] In Rabbinic Judaism, too, we meet with the same insight or attitude. The pious man, who loves righteousness and hates iniquity, intercedes for God's creatures with confidence that the mercy of God will be greater than the sin of Israel, and with the clear recognition that God cannot order the world aright without love. [121]

This insight could not establish itself in its full scope without shaking the foundations of the Jewish view of God, the world and life. It did not do so. The lofty sayings about love remain isolated. The underlying basis of Judaistic theology and ethics is still righteousness — in spite of everything. [122] Jesus alone broke free from the old foundations and ventured a radically new structure.

D. Jesus.

1. The New Demand.

a. Jesus summed up in two sentences the meaning of the old and new righteousness : ἀγαπήσεις τὸν θεόν, ἀγαπήσεις τὸν πλησίον Mk. 12:28 ff.; Mt. 22:40. Both are well-known OT sayings, frequently and impressively emphasised by the Rabbis. And the new formula advanced by Jesus for the practice of neighbourly love is only distinguished by its positive conception from Hillel's famous rule. [123] Jesus stands plainly and consciously in the moral tradition of His people. But He demands love with an exclusiveness which means that all other commands lead up to it and all righteousness finds in it its norm. For Jesus, too, love is a matter

---

[120] Cf. the obvious echoes and developments in Apc. Sedrach, 8, Texts and Studies, II (1893), 2, 3, p. 133 ; Apc. Elias, 17, TU, 17 (1899), 3a, p. 63.

[121] Pesiq., 16 f. (Wünsche, 171 f., 178). For another turn of the thought of intercession for the wicked, cf. bSanh., 37a.

[122] Rather strikingly, the same is true of the Parsee religion. "The best good known to man is that of Zarathustra ... : that Ahura Mazda will invest him with splendours by Asa (righteous order) ... and so, too, those who exercise and observe the words and works of his good religion ..." "All those who in future will disregard the daevas and men who disregard him, to them will the helper's holy daena be a friend, brother or father." Gathas (Bartholomae), 17, 1; 10, 11; cf. 4, 14 ff. Yasna (Wolff, Avesta), 52, 3 f.; 70, 2 ff. Videvdat (ibid.), 3 ff. Minokherd, 37; 63 (SBE, Vol. 24, p. 73 ff.; 113).

[123] v. n. 115.

of will and action. But He demands decision and readiness for God and for God alone in an unconditional manner which startles His hearers.

The possibility of love for God stands under a radical Either/Or : οὐδεὶς δύναται δυσὶν κυρίοις [124] δουλεύειν· ἢ γὰρ τὸν ἕνα μισήσει καὶ τὸν ἕτερον ἀγαπήσει, ἢ ἑνὸς ἀνθέξεται καὶ τοῦ ἑτέρου καταφρονήσει (Mt. 6:24 ff.). To love God is to exist for Him as a slave for his lord (cf. Lk. 17:7 ff.). It is to listen faithfully and obediently to His orders, to place oneself under His lordship, to value above all else the realisation of this lordship (cf. Mt. 6:33). It also means, however, to base one's whole being on God, to cling to Him with unreserved confidence, to leave with Him all care or final responsibility, [125] to live by His hand. It is to hate and despise all that does not serve God nor come from Him, to break with all other ties, to cut away all that hinders (Mt. 5:29 f.), to snap all bonds except that which binds to God alone.

Two forces particularly are mentioned by Jesus as forces which man must renounce and fight against if he is to love God, namely, mammon and vainglory. He who would heap up riches is a heathen of little faith who is of no use in the kingdom of God (Mt. 6:24b, 30 ff.). And Jesus pronounces a woe on the Pharisees : ὅτι ἀγαπᾶτε τὴν πρωτοκαθεδρίαν ἐν ταῖς συναγωγαῖς καὶ τοὺς ἀσπασμοὺς ἐν ταῖς ἀγοραῖς. [126] The love of prestige is incompatible with the love of God. Yet there is also a third danger which threatens this love, i.e., the stress of persecution. Like the great Jewish martyr theologians, e.g., Akiba, Jesus sees that the assaults and afflictions, the insults and sufferings, which will necessarily break over the heads of His disciples, will be a decisive fiery test of their loyalty to God (cf. Mt. 10:17 ff.; 5:10 ff.). When the great and final agony of death comes on humanity : τότε σκανδαλισθήσονται [127] πολλοὶ καὶ... ψυγήσεται ἡ ἀγάπη τῶν πολλῶν. ὁ δὲ ὑπομείνας εἰς τέλος, οὗτος σωθήσεται. [128] In these words the character of love for God is clear and conclusive. It is a glowing passion for God, the passion of a little flock which perseveres faithfully and unshakeably, in spite of every puzzle, power or threat, until He is manifested whom it loves.

b. Love for God is the great and basic demand made by Jesus. δευτέρα ὁμοία αὐτῇ : ἀγαπήσεις τὸν πλησίον σου ὡς σεαυτόν (Mt. 22:39). Jesus, too, accepts the Jewish sobriety which is neither an extravagant universal love of humanity nor a high-flown love ὑπὲρ τὴν ψυχήν σου (so Barnabas, 19, 5), but which requires loving one's neighbour as oneself. Yet He frees neighbourly love once and for all from its restriction to compatriots. He concentrates it again on the helpless man whom we meet on our way. He makes the legal and contentious question a question of the heart with an urgency which there can be no escaping.

---

[124] N.B. ἀγ. κύριον in Mt. 22:37.
[125] On the problem of ἀγάπη and μέριμνα cf. W. Koepp's debate with Heidegger in *Seeberg-Festschrift* (1929), 99 ff.
[126] Lk. 11:43. In Mt. 23:6 φιλεῖν. In any case the underlying word is אהב cf. אהב in Ab. 1, 10 : "Love work and hate office."
[127] Cf. Mt. 5:29 f. and → σκάνδαλον.
[128] Mt. 24:10, 12 f. On the absolute use of ἀγάπη, cf. also Ep. Ar., 229 (*supra*, 41).

By itself, the Golden Rule (Mt. 7:12; Lk. 6:31) might be misunderstood in terms of general philanthropy, and it has in fact been wrongly evaluated along such lines throughout the whole course of humanistic ethics from Aristotle to Kant. But the story of the Good Samaritan makes such an understanding impossible (Lk. 10:29 ff.). The scribe asks : "Who is my neighbour ?" Jesus does not answer by giving a systematic list of the various classes of men from my fellow-national who is nearest to me to the foreigner who is farthest away (Philo, *supra,* 40). Nor does He reply by extolling the eccentric love of those who are most distant, to which all men are brothers. He answers the question of the νομικός by reversing the question : "Who is nearest to the one in need of help ?" This means that He shatters the older concentric grouping in which the I is at the centre, but maintains the organising concept of the neighbour, and by means of this concept sets up a new grouping in which the Thou is at the centre. This order, however, is not a system which applies schematically to all men and places. It consists only in absolute concreteness. It is built up from case to case around a man in need. Whoever stands closest to the man in need κατὰ συγκυρίαν, the same has a neighbourly duty towards him. Three men are equally near to the man who has fallen among thieves in his distress. Which of them fulfils his neighbourly duty ? The alien Samaritan. Why ? Ἰδὼν ἐσπλαγχνίσθη. The heart makes the final decision. He fulfils his neighbourly duty whose heart detects the distress of the other. At the decisive moment the two others hold back and thus violate their neighbourly duty. The introduction of this ἐσπλαγχνίσθη, however, does not imply emotional extravagance in neighbourly love. What is demanded is the most unsentimental imaginable readiness to help. The Samaritan does in all sobriety what the moment demands, taking care for the immediate future, no more and no less. He is an ἔλεος ποιήσας, who neither throws everything aside nor wastes words on the duties or guilt of others. He is one who does what has to be done, and what he can do. This is what gives to the story its inescapable urgency : πορεύου καὶ σὺ ποίει ὁμοίως.

c. In one demand Jesus consciously opposed Jewish tradition, namely, the demand to love one's enemies. Even in the brief words of Mt. 5:43 f. and Lk. 6:32 f. the threefold determination of the demand is clear. First, it is the new demand of a new age ("it was said by them of old time . . . But I say unto you," Mt. 5:21, 43). Second, it points to a χάρις (μισθός, περισσόν, Mt. 5:46 f.). Third, it applies to a host of ἀκούοντες (cf. Lk. 6:27) sharply distinguished from ἁμαρτωλοί (τελῶναι, ἐθνικοί, Mt. 5:46 f.). The love of enemies which Jesus demands is the attitude of the children of the new people of God, to whom the future belongs, in relation to the children of this world and age. They should show love without expecting it to be returned, lend where there is little hope of repayment, give without reserve or limit. They should accept the enmity of the world willingly, unresistingly and sacrificially (Lk. 6:28). Indeed, they should do good to those who hate them, giving blessing for cursing and praying for their persecutors (Lk. 6:27 ff.; Mt. 5:44). To some of these demands individually we can find isolated parallels in the Rabbinic world. But these are of no significance as compared with this full and resolute programme. Even the martyr spirit of the Jewish community, of the ancient people of God, is far surpassed by this unheard of will for martyrdom. A new intercession is here made the task of the martyr, namely, intercession for the hostile world, which hates God and destroys His faithful people.

There have always been Utopians. But here speaks the One who without illusion or sentimentality has introduced the ideal of neighbourly love into reality. He speaks of these impossible demands with the same tone of steady seriousness and sense of reality as of that which every man should and can do. There have always been enthusiasts for brotherly love and a better world. Jesus knows this world, and He thus calls for a life within it wholly grounded in love. He does so with sober realism and certainty. The fact that it is now so self-evident is what is so strange about His demand for love. This is where its secret surely lies.

2. The New Situation.

a. The fact that His demand for love is now so self-evident is an indication that He has more to proclaim than a new demand. He proclaims and creates a new world situation. He proclaims the mercy of God, not as a disposition which God always and in all possible ways expresses — *pardonner, c'est son métier* — but as an unheard of event which has the basis of its possibility in God alone, but which now places man in a completely different situation. Jesus brings forgiveness of sins, and in those who experience it a new and overflowing love is released. It is in this sense that Jesus says of the woman who sinned much: ἀφέωνται αἱ ἁμαρτίαι αὐτῆς αἱ πολλαί, ὅτι ἠγάπησεν πολύ. [129]

It is striking that in this passage ἀγαπᾶν is twice used without any precise indica-tion of object, the more so as this absolute use of the verb is otherwise confined to the First Epistle of John. It brings out the more clearly what is at issue in Lk. 7:47, namely, that a new life is awakened and the person now has love, is filled with it, and is guided by it in all his actions, rather than that he is to show it to such and such people. Love here is a spontaneous movement up to the One by whom it is released (cf. also the absolute use of ἀγάπη in Ep. Ar., 229 and Mt. 24:12, where the orientation on God is also dominant). But this is not the decisive element in the story, and it is certainly not the final goal of the divine act of forgiveness.

By His act of forgiveness God has instituted for humanity a new order which removes and supersedes the old worldly order of rank and thus creates as many new tasks as possibilities. The new relationship of God to man lays the founda-tion for a new relationship of man to man: Γίνεσθε οἰκτίρμονες, καθὼς ὁ πατὴρ ὑμῶν οἰκτίρμων ἐστίν (Lk. 6:36). Peacemakers are called the children of God. [130] But those who judge their fellows place themselves outside the new order and thus fall victim to the merciless judgment of God. ᾧ γὰρ μέτρῳ μετρεῖτε, ἀντιμετρηθήσεται ὑμῖν. [131] The constantly necessary request for the forgiveness of sins presupposes a constantly new readiness to forgive παντὶ ὀφείλοντι ἡμῖν. [132]

The synoptic Jesus hardly ever [133] uses of the love of God either the substantive ἀγάπη or the verb ἀγαπᾶν (or indeed φιλία or φιλεῖν). He proclaims and brings ἄφεσις and speaks of God's ἐλεεῖν, οἰκτίρμων εἶναι). Accordingly, in all passages where it is a matter of following God in the threefold relationship of God, man and man, primary emphasis is placed on the call for mercy and a spirit of reconciliation.

---

[129] Lk. 7:47. The following sentence provides the noetic basis; v. Kl. Lk., *ad loc.*
[130] Mt. 5:9; cf. υἱοί in Mt. 5:45.
[131] Lk. 6:38; cf. Mt. 5:22 ff.
[132] Lk. 11:4; cf. also Mt. 5:7; 18:21 ff.
[133] With Lk. 11:42: τὴν κρίσιν καὶ τὴν ἀγάπην τοῦ θεοῦ, we might perhaps compare Ps. Sol. 18:3: τὰ κρίματα ... καὶ ἡ ἀγάπη σου. But v. Mt. 23:23: τὴν κρίσιν καὶ τὸ ἔλεος.

b. The love of God which in this great historical moment is directed to the world of humanity is pardoning love. But Jesus also knows a different kind of divine love, namely, the preferential love which includes separation and special calling. This is God's love as directed exclusively to Jesus Himself. It is in this sense that in the parable of the wicked husbandmen Jesus speaks of the υἱὸς ἀγαπητός (Mk. 12:5; cf. Mt. 12:18). The calling of the only Son (→ υἱός) is a calling to tread to the end the way which the prophets took and on which they met their deaths. The ἀγαπητὸς υἱός is the one Martyr [134] at the turning point of the times whose death is an exercise of judgment on the whole world and lays the foundation of the new order of all things (12:8 ff.). Jesus Himself thereby becomes the Founder of the new people of God, so that it is by relationship to Him that membership of the coming world is decided. Hence the love which is ready to help even the least of brethren is equivalent to readiness to help the Son of Man, whereas lovelessness is the same as contempt for Him. Both will be judged by the Son of Man in His day (Mt. 10:40 ff.; 25:31 ff.). For this reason, Jesus can call blessed the disciples who must suffer persecutions for His sake (Lk. 6:22 f.). For the same reason He can demand unconditional attachment to Himself even to death with the same radicalism as He calls for readiness for God: ὁ φιλῶν πατέρα ἢ μητέρα ὑπὲρ ἐμὲ οὐκ ἔστιν μου ἄξιος· ... καὶ ὃς οὐ λαμβάνει τὸν σταυρὸν αὐτοῦ καὶ ἀκολουθεῖ ὀπίσω μου, οὐκ ἔστιν μου ἄξιος (Mt. 10:37 ff.; cf. Lk. 14:26 f.).

At this point everything that Jesus says concerning love is finally clarified and unified. God sends the ἀγαπητὸς υἱός into the world κηρύξαι ἐνιαυτὸν κυρίου δεκτόν. The Son brings the remission of sins to which man replies with grateful love and to which he should respond with an unconditional readiness to help and forgive his fellows. The Son calls for unreserved decision for God, and gathers around Him a band of "storm-troopers" (Mt. 11:12) who leave everything, follow Him and love God with passionate devotion. He creates a new people of God which renounces all hatred and force and with an unconquerable resolve to love treads the way of sacrifice in face of all opposition. And He Himself dies, as the ancient traditions tells us, with a request for the hostile world (Lk. 23:34).

The synoptic tradition uses ἀγαπητός wholly in the sense of Jesus when it places the saying about the ἀγαπητὸς υἱός at the beginning of His ministry and then again at the commencement of His passion (Mk. 1:11; 9:7). And Mark makes clear at a single stroke the relationship between love, election and heightened demand in the short phrase introduced in 10:21: ἐμβλέψας αὐτῷ ἠγάπησεν αὐτὸν καὶ εἶπεν ... Jesus loves the rich young ruler with the love of God which summons men to the very highest. But the one who is called starts back. For the rest, the Synoptists use ἀγαπᾶν only once [135] outside the sayings of Jesus, and ἀγάπη never. Acts is even more reserved, for in it we find only ἀγαπητός (15:25), [136] φίλος used in the same sense (27:3), and especially ἀδελφός (1:16). Neither ἀγάπη nor ἀγαπᾶν occurs at all, though we do find ἀφίημι (8:22 ff.), negatively expressed in the prayer of the first Christian martyr for his enemies in 7:60: κύριε, μὴ στήσῃς αὐτοῖς ταύτην τὴν ἁμαρτίαν.

---

[134] We seem to have here echoes of ancient ideas of the last martyr, cf. ZSTh, 8 (1930/31), 212, n. 4.
[135] Lk. 7:4 f.: ἄξιός ἐστιν ... ἀγαπᾷ γὰρ τὸ ἔθνος ἡμῶν (cf., however, Mt. 10:37).
[136] In the same section, the Golden Rule is later applied (15:29).

E. The Apostolic Period.

1. Paul.

a. Paul clearly sees and sketches the new situation created by the loving work of God. The great argument of Romans on the theme of the new epoch which has now dawned rightly culminates in a hymn which, beginning with the love of the elect for God, moves on to the love of Christ, and finally closes with the assurance τῆς ἀγάπης τοῦ θεοῦ τῆς ἐν Χριστῷ Ἰησοῦ τῷ κυρίῳ ἡμῶν (R. 8:28, 31 ff.). This assurance rests on three facts. The first is that God has sent His only Son [137] and that this act of love found fulfilment on the cross in the self-offering of the Son, τοῦ ἀγαπήσαντος ἡμᾶς. The second is that God has called the apostle and continually calls those whom He has chosen; His loving will is directed to them; they are ἠγαπημένοι, ἀγαπητοί. The third is that the ἀγάπη of God is shed abroad in our hearts and is thus the decisive reality in our existence.

As Jesus did not distinguish His activity from that of God, but did what only God can do, forgiving sins, so Paul regards the love of God as basically one with that of His Christ (R. 8:37; 2 Th. 2:16). The loving action of God is revealed and executed in that of Christ: συνίστησιν... τὴν ἑαυτοῦ ἀγάπην εἰς ἡμᾶς ὁ θεός, ὅτι Χριστὸς ὑπὲρ ἡμῶν ἀπέθανεν (R. 5:8). The eternal love of God becomes in the love of Christ a world-changing event of which Paul usually speaks in verbal forms and then always in the aorist. [138]

The love of God implies election. Paul quotes OT passages which refer to God's unconditional sovereignty in loving and hating, electing and rejecting (R. 9:13, 25), and he uses ἀγαπητοί and κλητοί, or even ἐκλεκτοὶ καὶ ἠγαπη-μένοι in formal parallelism (R. 1:7; Col. 3:12). It is natural that in the concept of electing love there should also be expressed the two basic thoughts of pre-temporal ordination [139] and temporal calling in the sign of the Christ event: ἀδελφοὶ ἠγαπημένοι ὑπὸ κυρίου, ὅτι εἵλατο ὑμᾶς ὁ θεὸς ἀπ' ἀρχῆς εἰς σωτηρίαν ἐν ἁγιασμῷ πνεύματος... εἰς ὃ καὶ ἐκάλεσεν ὑμᾶς διὰ τοῦ εὐαγ-γελίου ἡμῶν εἰς περιποίησιν (2 Th. 2:13; cf. also Eph. 1:4 f.).

The community of the elect which God in His χρηστότης and ἀποτομία has now separated from the mass of ἁμαρτωλοί stands in indissoluble fellowship with the God τῆς ἀγάπης καὶ εἰρήνης. In its midst He is at work in living power (R. 8:35; 2 C. 13:11 ff.). Love holds us captive (2 C. 5:14), or rather, ἡ ἀγάπη τοῦ θεοῦ ἐκκέχυται ἐν ταῖς καρδίαις ἡμῶν διὰ πνεύματος ἁγίου τοῦ δοθέντος ἡμῖν (R. 5:5). The reality of this new and vital power could hardly be more forcefully expressed than in these words of Paul.

The meaning of the Pauline concept of ἀγάπη θεοῦ is plain. It is the orientation of the sovereign will of God to the world of men and the deliverance of this world. The work of love is God's goal from the very first. From the days of Abraham God has foreseen a people free from the bondage of the Law. He has created this people by the sending of the Son and finally the Spirit. This Spirit, however,

---

[137] ἴδιος υἱός (R. 8:32); υἱὸς τῆς ἀγάπης (Col. 1:13); cf. Eph. 1:6: ὁ ἠγαπημένος. Paul never uses ἀγαπητός of Christ.

[138] Ἀγαπήσαντος (R. 8:37; 2 Th. 2:16; also Gl. 2:20). The outworking is seen in Eph. 5:2 etc. On Eph. 2:4: ἀγάπῃ ἣν ἠγάπησεν, cf. אַהֲבָה שֶׁאֲהֵבָם (T. Ber., 3, 7).

[139] Cf. ἐκλογή in 1 Th. 1:4 (ἠγαπημένοι); R. 11:28 (ἀγαπητοί); R. 9:11 ff.

is represented in the great closing section of Galatians (5:2-6:10) as the Spirit of love (5:22). Thus the thoughts of the Epistle leave the path of history.

b. The goal of the work of divine love is the new man. But this goal is not attained without man and his work of love. For all God's work, whether in creation or redemption, presupposes both the possibility and the necessity of human action. God's will does not exclude human volition. It includes it, finding its purest fulfilment in its fullest exercise. The imperious call of God is a call to freedom. This basic law, which is most clearly visible in the fact of Jesus and which according to Paul everywhere determines the relationship between divine and human work (cf. also Phil. 2:12 f.), is decisive for an understanding of what the apostle says concerning the relationship between divine and human love.

God has the first word. He establishes the relationship. This is laid down once and for all in R. 8. His resolve, election and calling are decisive. From Him proceeds everything that may be called ἀγάπη. The love of the ἀγαπῶντες τὸν θεόν is nothing but the direct flowing back of the heavenly love which has been poured out upon the κλητός. More accurately, it is an act of decision, like the basic act of love itself. In it there is fulfilled the covenant which God has concluded with His elect and which defies all the powers of heaven and earth : τοῖς ἀγαπῶσιν θεὸν πάντα συνεργεῖ εἰς ἀγαθόν — τοῖς κατὰ πρόθεσιν κλητοῖς οὖσιν (R. 8:28, cf. 37).

The same fundamental relationship brings Paul in 1 C. 8:3 to the pregnant formulation : εἰ δέ τις ἀγαπᾷ τὸν θεόν, οὗτος ἔγνωσται ὑπ᾽ αὐτοῦ. We are capable of active orientation on God only to the extent that we are passive before Him. The same schema of passive and active is used in the service of the same guiding thought in Gl. 4:9; 1 C. 13:12; Phil. 3:12.

God creates for us the life which first makes us in any true sense men of will and action. God awakens in man the faith in which he is wholly referred to God. But πίστις only comes into action and finds true actualisation δι᾽ ἀγάπης (Gl. 5:6). God pours forth the πνεῦμα into His elect (v. supra R. 5:5; 2 Th. 2:13). Again, man is passive. But the πνεῦμα liberates man for supreme activity in love. Freedom constrains and completes itself in love.

> That the πνεῦμα precedes ἀγάπη, which is thereby liberated, is classically expressed in Gl. 5:22 : καρπὸς τοῦ πνεύματος ἀγάπη ..., but also in combinations like ἀγάπη πνεύματος (R. 15:30) and ἀγάπη ἐν πνεύματι... (Col. 1:8), and more elegantly in 1 C. 4:21. For the relation of πνεῦμα and freedom, cf. R. 8:2; and for ἀγάπη as the measure and goal of freedom, cf. Gl. 5:13. It is decisive that in the liberation for love the Law is fulfilled, transcended and overcome, and a new order set up which cannot suffer any retrogression or violation.

However, it is not the goal of love that our love should respond to God, [140] nor that we should attain freedom for our own sake. Its goal is that the man who is called should place his life in love and freedom in the service of his neighbour : διὰ τῆς ἀγάπης δουλεύετε ἀλλήλοις. ὁ γὰρ πᾶς νόμος ἐν ἑνὶ λόγῳ πεπλήρωται· ἀγαπήσεις τὸν πλησίον σου ὡς σεαυτόν. [141] Paul takes up

---

[140] Paul speaks only rarely of love for God. Apart from R. 8:28 and 1 C. 8:3, cf. 2 Th. 3:5. In the verse 2 Th. 2:10, which is strongly influenced by tradition, we have ἀγάπη τῆς ἀληθείας (→ 40, 3 ff.). In Phlm. 5 the ἀγάπη is to be chiastically related to the ἅγιοι. Finally, cf. Eph. 6:24 (4:15).

[141] Gl. 5:13 f. For neighbourly love, v. also R. 13:8 ff. (cf. 1 Th. 3:12).

the command of Jesus that we should love our neighbours, and establishes it in the same way as the Lord. But his true interest is concentrated on brotherly love: ἐργαζώμεθα τὸ ἀγαθὸν πρὸς πάντας, μάλιστα δὲ πρὸς τοὺς οἰκείους τῆς πίστεως (Gl. 6:10). The organic principle which is given once and for all with the orientation of love to the neighbour is here worked out in terms of organisation. Neighbourly love, once a readiness to help compatriots in the covenant people of Israel, is now service rendered to fellow-citizens in the new people of God. It implies making the welfare of the brotherhood the guiding principle of conduct. [142] Ἀγαπητός and ἀδελφός become interchangeable terms (1. Th. 2:8; Phlm. 16).

Decisive definition is given to brotherly love, however, by the cosmic, historical καιρός (cf. Gl. 6:10; R. 13:11) which demands it. Brotherly love is the only relevant and forward-looking attitude in this time of decision between the cross and the τέλος. It stands under the sign of the cross. It is a readiness for service and sacrifice, for forgiveness and consideration, for help and sympathy, for lifting up the fallen and restoring the broken, [143] in a fellowship which owes its very existence to the mercy of God and the sacrificial death of Christ. [144] The highest possible goal for the apostle himself is imitation of Christ for the good of the Church. He is ready to suffer what is still lacking of the sufferings of Christ. [145] But this also means the requirement of even the most unassuming work of human love in the service of the great work of divine love according to the basic relationship between divine and human action which is fundamental for Paul. In love the work of God and the work of man unite. Love builds up (1 C. 8:1). It builds the work of the future. Ἀγάπη stands under the sign of the τέλος. This is the great truth of 1 C. 13. For this reason love is the heavenly gift surpassing all others, the καθ' ὑπερβολὴν ὁδός, which not only stands at the heart of the trinity of faith, love and hope but is also greater than the other two. Faith and hope bear the marks of this defective aeon. Ἡ ἀγάπη οὐδέποτε πίπτει. [146] With love the power of the future age already breaks into the present form of the world. As for Jesus, so for Paul ἀγάπη is the only vital force which has a future in this aeon of death.

The triad faith, love and hope seems to be a formula; cf. πίστις, ἀγάπη, ἐλπίς in 1 Th. 1:3; 5:8; Col. 1:4 f. [147] In all cases ἀγάπη is in the middle. Always where the interrelationship of the three is given with any precision, the emphasis falls wholly on ἀγάπη. Thus on the one side in Gl. 5:6: πίστις δι' ἀγάπης ἐνεργουμένη, and on the other in R. 5:5: ἡ ἐλπὶς οὐ καταισχύνεται, ὅτι ἡ ἀγάπη... ἐκκέχυται... πίστις and ἐλπίς are both unequivocally and naturally ascribed by Paul to this present era, as in 2 C. 5:7: διὰ πίστεως γὰρ περιπατοῦμεν, οὐ διὰ εἴδους, and R. 8:25: ὃ

---

[142] For brotherly love, v. 1 Th. 4:9; Col. 1:4; Phlm. 5, cf. Eph. 4:2; 6:23. Ἀγαπᾶν is used for marital love in the household tables, Col. 3:19 (Eph. 5:25). Cf. Delatte Anecdota, I (1927), 423, 11: ἀγάπην ἀνδρὸς πρὸς φιλίαν τῶν γυναικῶν.

[143] Gl. 5:25 ff.; R. 12:9 f.; 1 C. 13:4 ff.

[144] Phil. 2:1 ff.; 1 C. 8:11; Col. 3:14 f. (Eph. 5:2, and also marital love in this connexion, Eph. 5:25 → γάμος).

[145] 2 C. 1:3 ff. (8:7 f.); Col. 1:24 ff.

[146] Only for the mode of expression should we compare Ab., 5, 18: The love which does not have a sensual object "never ceases."

[147] On the triad, A. Harnack, Pr. Jahrb., 164 (1916), 1 ff.; R. Reitzenstein, in many places, esp. NGG, 1917, 130 ff.: P. Corssen, in Sokrates 7 (1919), 18 ff.; Ltzm. K. ad loc.; A. Brieger, Die urchristl. Trias G.L.H., Diss. Heidelberg (1925).

οὐ βλέπομεν ἐλπίζομεν. As against this, the triumphant love of God delivers us in every distress and our own love for God overcomes every assault (R. 8:28, 35 ff.). In 1 C. 13 it is brotherly love which gives value and content to all other action or gifts. With ἡ ἀγάπη οὐδέποτε πίπτει in v. 8 the train of thought fixes on the last time when all other gifts will be pointless. The transitory and ultimately perishable nature of *gnosis* is brought out in similar expressions, as is also the temporary character of πίστις and ἐλπίς. The conclusion begins with the typically eschatological concept of μένειν, which, e.g., in 1 C. 13:14 has the sense of outlasting. νυνὶ δὲ μένει — after all that has preceded, and all that Paul has said elsewhere, we should expect this to be followed by ἀγάπη, since this is the leading thought in the chapter which the whole hymn is designed to extol. Instead, there follows the favourite triad, which is stylistically most impressive but which is hardly justified materially nor prepared syntactically with its inclusion of three subjects in a singular predicate. To all appearances Paul has here sacrificed precision of thought to loftiness of expression. But he must then save his culminating thought by a subsidiary clause which forms a fine stylistic conclusion but which is overshadowed materially by the originally cosmic-historical opening: μείζων δὲ τούτων ἡ ἀγάπη. However, even if what was originally intended is temporarily obscured by the triad, it is adequately safeguarded, for love alone is seen to be no longer of this world but to stretch into the future aeon. [148]

2. James.

Faith acquires living force to the extent that it is active in love. This is perceived in essential necessity by Paul in Gl. 5:6. James translates this truth into practical commands which in sober yet unambiguous fashion prevent any pious or comfortable escape. Love implies primarily fulfilling immediate duties to our neighbours and not withholding rights from labourers (5:1 ff.). It means taking seriously the basic affirmation that all who love God are my brothers and are not to be put in the background even though they come shabbily dressed (2:14), since God has thought them good enough to be called into His βασιλεία (2:5). Love is indeed the Law of the new kingdom, the νόμος βασιλικός (2:8). This love is the work of faith, demanded by it, made possible by it, and counted for righteousness on account of it (2:14 ff.). The love for God which stands behind all brotherly love is also a work of faith. It holds fast to God, to His commands in the warfare against passions and to His promises in the long periods of tribulation and affliction. It is strong in ὑπομονή (1:2 ff.).

3. John.

For Paul ἀγάπη is the principle of the future; for John it is the principle of the world of Christ which is being built up in the cosmic crisis of the present. Οὕτως ἠγάπησεν ὁ θεὸς τὸν κόσμον, ὥστε τὸν υἱὸν τὸν μονογενῆ ἔδωκεν ἵνα (Jn. 3:16; 1 Jn. 4:9 f.). In this basic thought John and Paul (R. 8:32) are at one. But there is a difference in the way in which John constantly speaks of the love of the Father for the Son. [149] All love is concentrated on Him. He is wholly the Mediator of the love of God. In contrast, John hardly ever speaks of the love of the Son for the Father (Jn. 14:31). He emphasises the more strongly, however,

---

[148] On 1 C. 13 : 1 Cl., 49 f.; Apc. Sedrach, 1; Augustine, *Sermo 350 de caritate* (MPL, 39, 1533); Melanchthon's Comment. (C.R., XV, 1134 ff.); Calvin's Comment. (ed. A. Tholuck, V, 1834); A. Harnack, SAB, 1911, 132 ff.; E. Lehmann-A. Fridrichsen, Th. St. Kr., 94 (1922), 55 ff.
[149] Jn. 3:35; 10:17 (ἀγαπᾶν). Ἀγαπητός is never used in this connexion.

the love of the Son for those whom the Father has given Him, for His "friends." Through the Son the love of God reaches the world of men. [150] This love is at once crowned and released by His death. Through the death of the Son God reaches His goal of salvation for the world. [151]

Johannine ἀγάπη is quite explicitly condescending love (→ 37), or rather a heavenly reality which in some sense descends from stage to stage into this world. This heavenly reality, however, achieves revelation and victory in moral action. It is thus that John sees that which Paul clarifies in terms of the interrelation of divine work and human. The world of light and life is expressed in this world in the form of love. Hence John not only can but must emphasise the active character of ἀγάπη both in the life of Christ and in that of Christians.

It is quite of a piece that John, too, allows love for God or for Christ [152] to be overshadowed by love for the brethren which has its origin in God and its example in Christ. [153] In brotherly love the circle of the Father, the Son and the people of the Son constitutes a fellowship which is not of this world. The love of God is the final reality for the life of this fellowship, and abiding in His love is the law of its life. [154] Ὁ μὴ ἀγαπῶν μένει ἐν τῷ θανάτῳ. [155] Ἀγαπᾶν remains without any definition of object, and not merely in this verse. The absolute positing of ἀγαπᾶν, of which we have an isolated instance in Lk. 7:47, is in common use in the First Epistle of John (3:18; 4:7 f., 19). This love is a vital movement, a form of existence, an actualisation of God in this world.

To this there corresponds the fact that the law of love has drawn into itself all detailed requirements and is constantly repeated and set before the reader with magnificent monotony. Only occasionally is the demand for love more precisely defined by such expressions as to "love in deed and in truth." [156] More commonly in the Johannine Epistles exhortations are interrupted and emphasised by the urgent call ἀγαπητέ and ἀγαπητοί, which here has nothing to do with the thought of election but refers quite simply to the relation of brother to brother (3 Jn. 5; 1 Jn. 4:7).

In Revelation the demand for brotherly love (cf. 2:19) is completely overshadowed by the passionate call to cling fast to God in this hour of division and distress, even to death. Here the understanding of what love means is completely determined by the thinking of a theology of martyrdom which has come to new life in the needs of the day. At the beginning of the book there is a hymn to the faithful witness, τῷ ἀγαπῶντι ἡμᾶς (1:5), followed by an alternation of eschatological pictures of the beloved city (3:9; 20:9) and the glory of those who have maintained πίστις and ἀγάπη and loved not their lives to the death (12:11) with threats against the enemies of God and the complaint τὴν ἀγάπην σου τὴν πρώτην ἀφῆκας (2:4). The time has come when the love of many has grown cold (Mt. 24:12).

---

[150] Jn. 17:23 ff.; 14:21 ff.; 1 Jn. 4:19. For the affective, v. Jn. 11:5; 13:23; cf. φιλεῖν.
[151] On Jn. 13:1, A. Debrunner in *Gnomon,* 4 (1928), 444. On Jn. 15:13, Dibelius in *Festschrift f. Deissmann* (1927), 168 ff. Cf. also 1 Jn. 4:9 f., 3:16.
[152] Jn. 5:42; 8:42; 14:28.
[153] Jn. 13:34 f.; 14:15 ff.; 21:15 ff. (ἀγ.-φιλεῖν); 1 Jn. 4:20 (ἀγ.-μισεῖν).
[154] Jn. 15:9 f.; 1 Jn. 2:10; 3:10; 4:11 ff.; cf. R. Schütz. *Die Vorgeschichte d. Johanneischen Formel* θεὸς ἀγάπη ἐστίν, Diss. Kiel (1917).
[155] So 1 Jn. 3:14 with B ℵ A. Cf. also 2:15 ff.; 3:17; Jn. 3:19.
[156] 1 Jn. 3:18; cf. 2 Jn. 1; Test. G. 6:1.

F. The Post-Apostolic Period.

In the post-apostolic period the early Christian formulae are partly handed down in authoritative fashion and partly transcended by bold speculations. Under the old name of ἀγάπη ideals which are partly stricter and partly freer have found entry. The unity of breadth of theological outlook with stringency of demand, achieved in the Johannine writings, is now broken. But for all this there remained alive in the developing Church a respectful awareness, πῶς μέγα καὶ θαυμαστόν ἐστιν ἡ ἀγάπη, and an earnest practical sense of the significance of ἀγάπη for the community and the world. The hymn in 1 Clement (49 f.) is the finest testimony to this.

ἀγάπη and ἀγαπᾶν become basic terms for the attitude and action of God towards man, for the work of Christ. [157] ἠγαπημένος and ἀγαπητός are favourite terms for Jesus, sometimes linked with υἱός or παῖς, sometimes used as an independent title, the Only-Beloved. [158] The Church and Christians are also loved and elected by God, and His good-pleasure rests upon them. [159]

Again, ἀγάπη and ἀγαπᾶν are often used in this period to sum up Christian piety. [160] This is the response of love to the προαγαπήσας and the imitation of His φιλανθρωπία; ἀγαπῶμεν ἃ ἠγάπησεν, ἀπεχόμενοι... [161] Love for God demands scorn and hatred of the world. This tension can invite to martyrdom, which here, as in Judaism, is highly estimated as an extreme expression of piety and love of God. [162] In his most passionate epistle Ignatius seizes on the Greek term *Eros* to force it in abrupt antithesis to serve the thought of martyrdom: ζῶν... γράφω..., ἐρῶν τοῦ ἀποθανεῖν. ὁ ἐμὸς ἔρως ἐσταύρωται. [163] In another form the tension between God and the σχῆμα τοῦ κόσμου τούτου, between heavenly and earthly love, can lead to asceticism. ἀγαπᾶν becomes a term for the disciplined and sometimes even abstemious life, or indeed for ascetic exercises. ἀγάπη ἀγνή is more powerful than erotic love. [164]

The most common use of ἀγάπη and its derivatives, however, is in the sense of brotherly love. [165] The ancient sayings concerning faith, love and hope, concerning the meaning and fulfilment of the Law and concerning the love of enemies, are highly esteemed and applied. [166] οὐ μισήσεις πάντα ἄνθρωπον, ἀλλὰ οὓς μὲν ἐλέγξεις,

---

[157] Ign. R., 7, 3; Tr., 8, 1; Act. Thom., 132, p. 239, 26.

[158] 2 Pt. 1:17; Herm. s., 5, 2, 6; 9, 12, 5; 1 Cl., 59, 2 f.; M. Pol., 14, 1; Dg., 8, 11; Barn., 3, 6; 4, 3; Asc. Is., 1, 4; Act. Phil., 4 p. 3, 19.

[159] Jd. 1; 1 Cl., 8, 5 etc.

[160] Ign. Mg., 1, 1; 1 Pt. 1:8; C. Schmidt, "Gespr. Jesu," TU, 43 (1919), 121, 4. ἀγαπᾶν abs. in the Agraphon (?) in Didym. Trin., I, 16, MPG, 39, 333b, and in Ps. Clem. Hom., 3 p. 38, 6.

[161] Pol., 2, 2; Herm. m., 5, 2, 8; Dg., 8, 7; 9, 2; 10, 2 ff.

[162] 2 Tm. 4:8 ff.; Hb. 1:9; 1 Pt. 3:10; 2 Pt. 2:15; Jn. 3:16 (1 Jn. 4:9 f.).

[163] Ign. R., 7, 2 (cf. 2, 1; ad Pol., 4, 3). *Ad loc., v.* Origen, Comm. on Cant. Prol. (Baehrens, p. 71, 25); on the problem φιλία, ἀγάπη, ἔρως, *v.* also Justin Dial., 8, 1; Cl. Al. Strom., VI, 9, 73, 3; Orig. Comm. on Lam. 1:2, Fragm., XI (Klosterm.). Cf. also Harnack, SAB (1918), 81 ff.

[164] 1 Cl., 21, 8; Pol., 4, 2; Herm. s., 9, 11, 3 (cf. on this Hier., Ep. 22, 14, p. 161, 17, Hilberg: *agapetarum pistis*); Act. Joh., 29; 63 ff.; 68; 109; 114; Act. Pls., 6; 9 ff. But asceticism without ἀγάπη is valueless: Act. Gr. S. Melaniae iun. Anal. Boll (1903), p. 30 f. § 43.

[165] Cf. 1 Pt. 1:22; 2 Pt. 1:7; 1 Cl., 47, 5; 48, 1 (φιλαδελφία); 1 Pt. 2:17 (ἀδελφότης); Test. of the 40 Mart., 2, 4.

[166] Did., 1, 2 f. (Gold. Rule in negative form); Pol., 3, 2 f. (triad); Dg., 5, 11; 2 Cl., 13, 4 (love of enemies, cf. Cl. Al. Strom., IV, 13, 93, 3); 2 Cl., 16, 4 (alms, cf. J. Nicole, *Pap. d. Genève,* I [1896], 14, 7); 2 Cl., 4, 3 (ἀγ. ἑαυτούς, cf. Test. of the 40 Mart., 1, 6); Dio Chr. Or., 74, 5, II, p. 194, 8; 47, 20, II, p. 86, 12 ff.; Barn., 1, 4; 19, 5 (ὑπὲρ τὴν ψυχὴν); Herm. v., 3, 8, 5; 7; s., 9, 15, 2 ('Αγάπη); Did., 16, 3 (ἀγ. στραφήσεται...).

<οὓς δὲ ἐλεήσεις>, περὶ δὲ ὧν προσεύξῃ, οὓς δὲ ἀγαπήσεις ὑπὲρ τὴν ψυχήν σου (Did., 2, 7). In all cases to love the brethren means : μὴ μόνον ἑαυτὸν θέλειν σῴζεσθαι, ἀλλὰ καὶ πάντας τοὺς ἀδελφούς (M. Pol., 1, 2). The leaders of the community are unwearyingly concerned to strengthen the will for brotherly fellowship in service, in conciliatoriness and in the overcoming of evil with good. [167] Ἀγαπητός is a current form of address. [168] Ἀγάπη becomes a technical term for the fraternal love-feast which develops out of the beginnings of table fellowship and finds significant outworking even in a social sense. [169]

Ἀγαπᾶν in the Greek sense is respect and sympathy between equals. Christian ἀγάπη derives from a consciousness of equal unworthiness before God and His mercy. By this spirit of *caritas* the attitude and intercourse of the brethren are determined. These young brotherhoods thus grow up within a world which perishes through *Eros* and which vainly seeks to transcend itself by means of a sublimated *Eros*. In other words, there grows up a Church which knows of a love that does not desire but gives. The twilight of the sensual and suprasensual mystery cults yields before the clarity of the μυστήρια τῆς ἀγάπης. [170]

Stauffer

---

† Ἄγαρ

The name הָגָר of the maid of Sarah, the mother of Ishmael, introduced in Gn. 16, is used in Gl. 4:24 f. as an allegory of the Law-giving on Sinai and of the associated Jewish race (τῇ νῦν → Ἰερουσαλήμ). Over against her there stands Sarah, the free wife of Abraham, in whose person there is typified the mother of believers of the new covenant (ἡ ἄνω Ἰερουσαλήμ). In the Pauline allegory there is reflected the unparalleled conversion of the onetime Pharisee to the extent that for the pure Jew the relationship is the exact opposite. Sarah as the mother of Isaac is the ancestress of pure Judaism and Hagar as the mother of Ishmael (the wrong-doer) [1] the ancestress of the depraved descendants of Abraham. In the fact that Hagar allegorises the νῦν Ἰερουσαλήμ may be seen a thoroughgoing change in the understanding of true Judaism.

---

[167] 1 Pt. 4:7 ff.; 1 Cl., 49 ff.; Barn., 1, 6.
[168] Ἀγαπητοί esp. in 1 Cl. ἀξιαγάπητος (not vocative) in 1 Cl. 1; 21, 7. προφήτας ἀγαπῶμεν, Ign. Phld., 5, 2. Cf. esp. M. Pol., 17, 2 f. (against the suspicion of a cult of martyrs): τὸν Χριστὸν... προσκυνοῦμεν, τοὺς δὲ μάρτυρας ὡς μαθητὰς καὶ μιμητὰς τοῦ κυρίου ἀγαπῶμεν.
[169] Cf. the much discussed verses Jd. 12; 2 Pt. 2:13; Ign. Sm., 8, 2, and on this point Leclercq in *Dict. d'archéol. chrét.*, I (1907), 775 ff.; R. L. Cole, *Love Feasts, History of the Christ.* ἀγάπη (1916); R. Schütz, ZNW, 18 (1918), 224; Lietzmann on 1 C. 11:23; K. Völker, *Mysterium u. Agape* (1927).
[170] Reference to μυστήρια τ. ἀ. is found in Cl. Al. Quis Div. Salv., 37, 1. The Stromata are particularly rich in discussions of the spontaneous love for true being which finds fulfilment in the true Gnostic. Various motifs are at work here which are also found in Philo, Plotinus, the Hermetic writings, the Odes of Solomon and Mandaean Liturgies. There emerges a typical Alexandrian synthesis between mystical ἀγάπη and pneumatic ἔρως — a synthesis which recurs in all Romantic religion.
Ἄ γ α ρ. J. B. Lightfoot, Gal. (1910), 193-200; Zn. Gl., 230-235, 296-299 (Excursus II); Ltzm. Gl., 29; O Michel, *Pls. u. s. Bibel* (1929), 98.
[1] So, e.g., Gn. r., 62 on 25:12 ff.

In Judaism Hagar herself is esteemed to some extent for the revelation given to her (Gn. 16:13), e.g., by R. Samuel b. Nachman, Gn. r. 45 on 16:13 : "It is like the matron to whom the king said : Pass before me. So she passed before him, leaning on the maid and with covered face, so that only the maid and not she herself saw the king." [2] By contrast the judgment on the descendants of the two is unanimous, as, e.g., in R. Jizchaq, Gn. r. 47 on 17:20 f., who explains that the descendants of Isaac as descendants of the mistress Sarah are the twelve tribes, whereas those of Ishmael as descendants of the maid Hagar are twelve נְשִׂיאִם (Gn. 17:20), which according to Prv. 25:14 means twelve clouds full of wind but with no rain. To this there corresponds exactly the estimation of Philo according to his own particular outlook : σοφίαν μὲν 'Ισαάκ, σοφιστείαν δὲ 'Ισμαὴλ κεκλήρωται, Sobr., 9. [3]

So far as can be determined from the rather uncertain text, [4] the equating of Hagar with Sinai is suggested either by the location of Sinai in Arabia, the land of Ishmael and his progeny, [5] or by the linguistic similarity of an Arabian word ḥajar (rock or cliff), with which certain place names on the Sinaitic peninsula seem to be related. [6]

Kittel

| ἀγγελία, ἀγγέλλω, ἀν-, ἀπ-, δι-, ἐξ-, κατ-, προκαταγγέλλω, καταγγελεύς |

In view of the strong emphasis placed upon the concept of message as a sacral concept in NT days it is necessary to subject the individual words deriving from the root ἀγγελ- to a close historical examination. Only then can we appreciate the distinctive pregnancy of the NT words. To be sure, ἐπαγγελ-, εὐαγγελ- are in a different category. These central terms are most strongly individual. In the other ἀγγελ-words the important thing is that which is common to them for all the differences.

The words are to a large extent interchangeable, both in general and in detail. [1] Common to all is the main signification of "telling" or "declaring" or "proclaiming." [2] In the linguistic usage of Hellenistic religion there is a relationship

---

[2] The text of current editions is corrupt, though there can be no doubt as to the meaning. Cf. the tradition given in J. Theodor, Ber Rabba (1912 ff.), 458 n.

[3] For the Philo material, cf. Lightfoot, 198 ff.

[4] Cf. on the one side Ltzm., on the other Zn., *ad loc.* The most solid reason for the assumption that the second Ἄγαρ is secondary is Zahn's statement (233, n. 42): "The fact that in the Onomastika Hagar and Sinai are not brought into any personal relationship confirms the fact that this combination has penetrated into Gl. only from the time of Origen."

[5] Jos. Ant., 1, 220 f. says that the possessions of the Ishmaelites extend from the Euphrates to the Red Sea, the Sinaitic peninsula being thus obviously included.

[6] Baedecker, *Palästina*[6] (1904), 163, 179; cf. also Lightfoot, 193 ff. Rather curiously, Tg. O. Gn. 16:7, 14 (and J. I. Gn. 16:7) replaces the names שׁוּר and בֶּרֶד by חגרא.

ἀ γ γ ε λ ί α κ τ λ. J. Schniewind, *Euangelion,* I (1927); II (1931).

[1] ἐξαγγέλλω cf. ἀναγγέλλω; ἀπαγγέλλω, καταγγέλλω cf. διαγγέλλω, ἐπαγγέλλω. παραγγέλλω stands alone.

[2] Liddell-Scott translates all the words by "proclaim."

a. to sacred *agones* and sacrifice, b. to the cult of the ruler, often c. to aretalogy, and sometimes d. to the Hermes belief.

The words are all synonyms of εὐαγγελίζεσθαι, from secular usage to the supreme sacral use in the cult of the ruler. In Hellenism as in the NT εὐαγγελ- is the central concept and the others are satellites. Yet it is from the synonyms that we gain our understanding of εὐαγγέλιον. The Word of God is message, not *ratio*, ecstasy, dogma, nor speculation. The terminology is taken neither from the language of philosophy, [3] nor from that of high religion nor mysticism, but from the language of public life, the games and government. The rule of God and the rule of the Messiah is proclaimed. In the Word of God there breaks in the lordship of God. The apostolic word is the message of the risen Lord as *Kurios*.

The sacral evaluation of the messenger derives in Hellenism from the high estimation of government. [4] In the cult of the ruler we thus have a direct anti- thesis to the lordship of God and Χριστός. Even in the religious awareness of mission to be found in both Socrates and Epictetus (ἄγγελος καὶ κατάσκοπος καὶ κῆρυξ τοῦ θεοῦ), [5] and in the missionary word of the aretalogies, the parallel to NT speech is plain. Yet the miracle stories of aretalogy may be distinguished from the NT message in the same way as the Κύριοι therein proclaimed (→ ἀναγ- γέλλω, 62 f.). And the mission of the prophetic philosopher is quite different from that of the Messiah and His messengers.

Expectation of the coming divine messenger, of the one coming divine messenger, seems to be known to Hellenism. [6] This hope is presupposed in the NT (→ ἀγ- γελία, ἀν-, ἀπαγγέλλω). Nor is it any accident that it is nowhere directly related to Jesus, but only indirectly. Jesus as the Messiah cannot possibly be called ἄγγελος, since He is exalted above all ἄγγελοι (Hebr. 1:4 ff.; 2:5 ff. → ἄγγελος, 85). The ἄγγελος hope is presupposed esp. in the Johannine writings; the difference between expectation and fulfilment is to be seen at a glance in the Johannine picture of Christ (→ ἀπαγγέλλω, 66).

The picture of expectation becomes richer and the history of early Christianity clearer if we may also assume a pre-Christian Gnostic Jewish hope. The Mandaean writings speaks time and again of the high messenger of heaven or messenger of light etc., and the latest work on this question (Peterson, Lietzmann) does not preclude the possibility that early Christianity was antedated by this expecta- tion. [7]

---

[3] Socrates and Epictetus (→ n. 5) do not speak here as philosophers but as prophets.

[4] Schn. *Euang.,* II, 130 ff., 147 ff.

[5] Epict. Diss., III, 69 p. 306, 19 f. Sch.²; also III, 1, 37 p. 238, 2 and III, 22, 23; 38, p. 298, 7 and 301, 6. Epictetus appeals in these passages to Socrates: III, 1, 19; 42, p. 234, 8 and 238, 16; III, 22, 26, p. 298, 21. On Socrates' mission (Xen. Ap., 12 f.) → διαγγέλλω, ἐξαγ- γέλλω 66, 27; 68, 15.

[6] The material has been best assembled by G. P. Wetter, *Der Sohn Gottes* (1926), 26 ff. There should be added (→ also ἀπαγγέλλω, n. 11, 15) Or. c. Cels., II, 70 p. 192, 12 f., Koetschau (Bau J.², 206). Celsus says: τίς δὲ πώποτε πεμφθεὶς ἄγγελος, δέον ἀγγέλ- λειν τὰ κεκελευσμένα, κρύπτεται, as Jesus did. Also LXX Is. 9:6: μεγάλης βουλῆς ἄγγελος, as a title of the Messiah would be most important (Mas. יוֹעֵץ אֵל) if we could detect a definite view behind it; but perhaps the LXX is only "guessing" (Duhm, *ad loc.*). At any rate Volz (*Jüd. Eschat.*, 1903, 217) can refer to En. 46:1, where the face of the Messiah is "like that of a holy angel."

[7] Bultmann, ZNW, 24 (1925), 100 ff.; he defends his dating in ThLZ, (1931), 577 ff. against Lietzmann, SAB, (1930), 596 ff. (cf. Peterson, ZNW, 25 [1926], 236 ff.; 27 [1928], 55 ff.).

At any rate, there are points of contact between the OT and Palestinian Judaism on the one side and Hellenism on the other. Sending and mission stand behind the OT. There is a direct parallel between the piety of the Psalms and aretalogy (→ ἀναγγέλλω, 62). In virtue of their sending the prophets can be given the title מַלְאָךְ (ἄγγελος). [8] Moses is called *magnus nuntius* in the Assumption. [9] Deutero-Isaiah at least speaks as though in declaration of a message. [10] The expectation of a coming messenger, presupposed in the OT, [11] remains alive in Judaism in the form of hope for Elias, the coming prophet, the future me^ebasser. The thought of the "Word" is always associated with it. [12]

In this connexion it is wrong to ask whether the language of the NT derives from Judaism or Hellenism. Message and mission are known in both. The real question is who sends and who is sent, and what is signified by the sending and message. The NT gathers it all up in the ὄνομα Jesus. It may be asked, of course, whether the individual terms can be divided between the two spheres. We find the strongest LXX attestation for the words (ἀν-, ἀπ-, ἐξαγγέλλω) which are least prominent in the NT, but the Hellenistic attestation is no stronger, and there seems no evident reason why the main emphasis in the NT should fall on καταγγέλλω. What is finally clear is that in the NT as in earlier usage the verbal form of expression heavily outweighs the substantive. [13] This is in keeping with the dramatic nature of the whole idea, which grows directly out of living action, i.e., the action of proclaiming.

† ἀγγελία.

A. ἀγγελία in the NT.

1 Jn. 1:5: καὶ ἔστιν αὕτη ἡ ἀγγελία, ἣν ἀκηκόαμεν ἀπ᾽ αὐτοῦ καὶ ἀναγγέλλομεν ὑμῖν, ὅτι ὁ θεὸς φῶς ἐστιν κτλ.; 1 Jn. 3:11: αὕτη ἐστὶν ἡ ἀγγελία ἣν ἠκούσατε ἀπ᾽ ἀρχῆς, ἵνα ἀγαπῶμεν ἀλλήλους.

We bring these two passages together, although according to Bultmann's analysis they belong to different strata, the former to the original document and the latter to the author. For it is impossible to distinguish two theologies. The original and the author share in common the attestation of God, the antitheses ζωή/θάνατος and ἀλήθεια/ψεῦδος, the antithesis to antinomian Gnosis, the conjunction of self-judgment

---

[8] Hag. 1:13 (ἄγγελος Κυρίου); Mal. 3:1 (ἄγγελός μου, ἀγγ. διαθήκης). These passages are disputed, but the meaning given is possible in the light of n. 10. Similarly the priest in Mal. 2:7 is ἀγγ. Κυρίου. An incontestable passage is 2 Ch. 36:15 f., where ἄγγελοι = προφῆται (also Mas.). The LXX alone: (2 Ch. 36:15 f. =) 1 Ezr. 1:48 (ἄγγελος) and 1:49 (ἄγγελοι).

[9] Ass. Mos., 11, 17 (p. 14, 5 f., Clemen): *quomodo Monse erat magnus nuntius.*

[10] L. Köhler, Beih. ZAW (1923), 102 ff. M. Noth in a verbal communication traces this further through the prophets.

[11] Mal. 3:1, 23 f.; Is. 40:3. On Is. 40:9 etc. → εὐαγγ. Zech. 12:8 (the house of David ὡς οἶκος θεοῦ, ὡς ἄγγελος Κυρίου ἐνώπιον αὐτῶν) does not signify with any certainty a specific form of Messianic expectation (Is. 9:6 LXX), for cf. Mas. and 2 Sam. 14:17.

[12] 2 Ch. 36:16: μυκτηρίζοντες τοὺς ἀγγέλους αὐτοῦ καὶ ἐξουδενοῦντες τοὺς λόγους αὐτοῦ. Ass. Mos., 11, 16 (p. 13, 25; 14, 1, Clemen): *dominum uerbi fidelem in omnia.* Also Mal. 2:7 (χείλη γνῶσις, στόμα νόμος).

[13] On ἐπαγγελία, εὐαγγέλιον *s.v.*

and non-sinning, μένειν, ἀγάπη, etc. Thus any stylistic peculiarities in the passages adduced may be explained in terms of a basic form of the ἀγγελία entrusted to the readers which for some fresh reason is worked out either by the same author or in the same school (?).

The use of ἀγγελία is striking, since the *koine* prefers compounds to simple forms.[1] Above all, the majority of ἀγγελ- verbs and substantives, at any rate after classical times, are in their most pregnant use variants of → εὐαγγελίζεσθαι, εὐαγγέλιον. There has grouped around εὐαγγελ- a self-enclosed world with a particular outlook reflected in the usage of the remaining ἀγγελ- words.[2] Thus in 1:5 ἀγγελία = εὐαγγέλιον, the only point being that the Gospel and Epistles of John[3] apparently avoid εὐαγγελ-. It is hard to see any reason for this. Perhaps it is to be explained by the fact that the conflict against a Gnosis which hoped for a coming messenger (→ 57 f.) made it advisable not to use εὐαγγελ-.[4] The reading ἐπαγγελία (1:5: Cminn; 3:11 א Cminn) is a mistaken commentary. In 3:11 we should expect παραγγελία (command); but → παραγγ. can have much the same content as εὐαγγ., and in John ἐντολὰς τηρεῖν is a development of τὸν λόγον τηρεῖν. Hence it is no accident that in 3:11 the same sonorous word is used as in 1:5. Proclamation includes both news about God and command. In 1:5 it is the Word of Jesus that is meant, in 3:11 the preaching (μαρτυρία) which underlies the community (ἀρχή). The two coincide for the author. There is explicit statement in 1:5 (ἀκηκόαμεν ἀπ᾽ αὐτοῦ καὶ ἀναγγέλλομεν ὑμῖν), whereas in 3:11 there is no more than indication through the parallels in 2:7 f. and Jn. 13:34.

In view of what has been said, it might be asked whether we should not prefer the reading ἐπαγγελία in 3:11. The attestation is better than in 1:5, especially since the ᴅ- group C 1739 etc. is here strengthened by א (in 1:5 there is only C 33). Again, the explanation attempted above is more difficult than in 1:5, for ἐπαγγελία would have to have the sense of παραγγελία (→ *supra*), which is, however, linguistically rare (→ παραγγελία), and a mechanical adoption from 2:25 (Soden) is unlikely. It would be quite different, however, if ἐπαγγελία were the original reading. Then the command to love would be defined as promise, and this would correspond to the basic view of λόγος, which accomplishes what it commands (2:14; 5:3 f. etc.), and to the parallels in 2:7 f. (ἀληθὲς ἐν αὐτῷ) and Jn. 13:34 (καθὼς ἠγάπησα).

B. The Linguistic History of ἀγγελία.

The linguistic history confirms and extends what has been noted. According to Liddell-Scott N.E. *s.v.* it already signifies in classical usage "announcement" or "proclamation" no less than "command" or "order".[5] The word can signify the act of declaring[6] (and

---

ἀ γ γ ε λ ί α. R. Bultmann, "Analyse des ersten Johannesbriefes," *Jülicher-Festschr.* (1927), 138 ff.

[1] Moult.-Mill. *s.v.* ἀναγγέλλειν; this is even more true of the verbs.

[2] Schn. Euang., II, 249.

[3] We can see from Rev. 10:7; 14:6 that all the Johannine writings consciously avoid εὐαγγ.

[4] With → εὐαγγελίζεσθαι, εὐαγγέλιον there is primarily bound up expectation of the coming messenger with glad tidings.

[5] For the first meaning cf. Hom. Od., 5, 150; 7, 263 etc.; for the second, cf. Pind. Ol., 8, 81 f. (106 f.) p. 136 Schröder. Angelia is personified as the daughter of Hermes. The following examples are confined to the Hellenistic field.

[6] Jos. Ant., 7, 247; Bell., 4, 230 and 232 (ἔδει τάχους εἰς τὴν ἀγγελίαν).

specifically rhetorical art⁷) no less than what is declared, though the latter is more frequent (cf. 1 Jn. 1:5). ⁸

The same duality of meaning ⁹ is found in the case of → εὐαγγέλιον; The relationship to εὐαγγέλιον may be seen from the common addition ἀγγελία ἀγαθή, ¹⁰ as also from the content, ἀγγελία being used like εὐαγγέλιον of political news and favourable incidents. ¹¹ It is hard to prove any distinctive religious use. ¹²

In the LXX it is used for good news (ἀγγελία ἀγαθή, Prv. 12:25; 25:25), ¹³ but also for very bad news, 1 S. 4:19 (the loss of the ark); 2 S. 4:4 (death of Samuel and Saul); 2 K. 19:7 = Is. 37:7; Ez. 7:26; 21:7. Except in Prv. 12:25 (דָּבָר) it is always used for שְׁמוּעָה. It is significant in the verses from Proverbs that good news is always of value in itself, this corresponding again to the conception of Euangelion. ¹⁴ The other passages approximate to a religious use in the sense that disaster comes from Yahweh. In Is. 28:9 we finally have the same use as in 1 Jn. 1:5 ἀναγγέλλειν ἀγγελίαν (הוֹרָה דֵעָה) of the message of the prophets. Is there a direct influence ?

Schlatter ¹⁵ thinks it possible to affirm that ἀγγελία in 1 Jn. 1:5 is an equivalent for Aggada : "The theologians of M(ekilta) have for the doctrine of Scripture, which includes the sacred history, the fixed formula : 'God or Scripture proclaims מַגִּיד'." הִגִּיד however, is the equivalent of → ἀναγγέλλω, which in 1 Jn. 1:5 seems to be linked with ἀγγελία. "From this there developed the substantive" ; Schlatter translates it "proclamation" ¹⁶ and gives examples from the Tannaitic Midrashim : S. Dt., 49 on 11:22 ¹⁷ (syn. "to know God" cf. John); M. Ex., 15:26 : "proclamations heard by the ears of all" (cf. ὃ ἀκηκόαμεν, 1 Jn. 1:1, ἀγγελία ἣν ἀκηκόαμεν, 1:5). If this understanding of הַגָּדָה and the Johannine passages is right, ¹⁸ then the author has chosen a supreme expression of Judaism as his master concept for the Christian message. The word ἀγγελία resembled in sound the Hebrew equivalent, and was already stamped in advance (cf. Josephus). ¹⁹ Its relationship to εὐαγγέλιον thus commended it if the latter had to be avoided.

† ἀγγέλλω.

In Jn. 4:51 Nestle and Soden read with BL : οἱ δοῦλοι ὑπήντησαν αὐτῷ λέγοντες, ὅτι ὁ παῖς αὐτοῦ ζῇ. Against this א Dlat. : ὑπηντ. αὐτ. καὶ ἤγγειλαν ὅτι, ACℜ : καὶ ἀνήγγειλαν (λ 33 καὶ ἀπήγγειλαν) λέγοντες ὅτι. Tischendorf VIII (I, 782) pleads for אD : the rare ἤγγειλαν is replaced either by λέγοντες or by ἀνήγγ- or ἀπήγγ-, and thus both emendations are blended. But neither Tischendorf nor Soden knows any text which offers ἀναγγ. or ἀπαγγ. without the elucidating λέγοντες;

---

⁷ Περὶ ὕψους, 43, 3 p. 78, 1 Jahn-Vahlen : τῇ θαυμαστῇ... ἀγγελίᾳ, is an incredible combination. Toupius conjectured ἀπαγγελία, "expression," "style."
⁸ Jos. Vit., 380 : τῆς ἀγγελίας ἀκούσαντες.
⁹ Noted of ἀγγελία since Thes. Steph.
¹⁰ Schn. Euang., II, 250 n. 1 → n. 13.
¹¹ Jos. Ant. 18, 325 (ἀγγ. τῆς μάχης); Österr. Jahresh., 23 (1926), Beibl. Sp., 285, 11 f., Ephes. inscript., c. 44 A.D., ed. Keil : ἱλαρωτέρα ἀγγελία comes from Rome. Jos. Bell., 3, 144 (μέγιστον εὐτύχημα). Schn. Euang., II, 130 ff., 145 ff., 151 ff.
¹² One might adduce Ael. Arist. Or., 53 (55), 3 (II, p. 468, 16, Keil), where an ἀγγελία is owed to Zeus (Schn. Euang., II, 202 ff.). But no particular significance can be attached to the word ἀγγελία.
¹³ In early Christianity, only Herm. v., 3, 13, 2.
¹⁴ Schn. Euang., I, 31 ff.; II, 122 ff., 168 ff.
¹⁵ Sprache und Heimat des vierten Evangelisten (1902), 145.
¹⁶ Cf. also the definition of Haggadoth in Str.-B., I, 561.
¹⁷ Kittel, Sifre, 131 f., and n. 6, 7.
¹⁸ Yet there is room for doubt, cf. W. Bacher, Agada der Tannaiten, I² (1903), 451 ff.
¹⁹ → n. 6 ff.

hence the rise of deviations is more readily explained from the Nestle text. In any case, whether originally or by way of correction, the ἤγγειλαν indicates a solemn development. It is to be explained by what has been said about ἀναγγέλλειν and ἀπαγγέλλειν in accounts of miracles, and it thus denotes the proclamation of miracles.

The only sure attestation of ἀγγέλλω in the NT is in Jn. 20:18. It is never used in the apostolic fathers. Its rarity is to be explained by what we have noted concerning ἀγγελία. Indeed even in this one passage ἀναγγέλλειν and ἀπαγγέλλειν occur as variants.[1] Is the rare and intentional word felt to be sacral? It is in an Easter story that we read: ἔρχεται Μαριὰμ ἡ Μαγδαληνὴ ἀγγέλλουσα τοῖς μαθηταῖς ὅτι ἑώρακα τὸν κύριον καὶ ταῦτα εἶπεν αὐτῇ. Mary Magdalene proclaims "what she has seen and heard": cf. 1 Jn. 1:1, 3, where the reference is also to the risen Lord and the word → ἀπαγγέλλω, which often occurs in the resurrection narratives. Resurrection and proclamation belong closely together → εὐαγγέλιον (R. 1:3 f.; 10:9; 1 C. 15:1 ff. etc.) and μάρτυς, μαρτύριον.[2] The thought of Gospel also seems to be present in ἀγγέλλειν (as in the ἀγγελία of 1 Jn. 1:5).

This is confirmed by the history of the term. Schlatter gives instances of its secular use in Josephus, in whom "running" (Bell., 6, 254) and φύλακες (Bell., 6, 294) again remind us of the resurrection narratives, as also an ἀγγέλλοντες αὐτοῖς πάντα (Bell., 4, 196; cf. Lk. 24:9). "Running" is a constant feature in secular εὐαγγελ-, and the announcement of the birth of Moses (a hierogrammateus ἀγγέλλει) in Ant., 2, 205 corresponds to both secular and sacral Euangelion.[3] The LXX has the verb only 5 times, and only in individual MSS, always corrected by ἀναγγ., ἀπαγγ., διαγγ., and always used in a secular sense. In 2 Βασ. 18:11 it occurs in the context of the delivery of a message, in which εὐαγγ. is repeatedly used.[4]

The word has a religious tone in an ancient Eleusis document, in which the approach of a solemn procession is announced (220 A.D.; Ditt. Syll.,³ 885, 17). In a magic papyrus the name of the one cursed is "named."[5] Above all, in the Giess. Hadrian papyrus we find ἀγγέλλειν used poetically instead of the cultic εὐαγγελίζεσθαι for the "proclamation" of the rule of the new divine lord.[6] Jesus, however, is instituted Messiah-King and Lord in the resurrection, and the εὐαγγέλιον proclaims Him.

† ἀναγγέλλω.

A. ἀναγγέλλω outside the NT.

This is commonly used in the *koine* instead of the classical ἀγγέλλειν, though the equivalent ἀπαγγέλλειν is more common.[1] In the MSS tradition the two words seem to be interchangeable in many authors. In the NT the only passage which has come down without variants is Jn. 16:13-15.[2] In Attic ἀπαγγέλλειν is preferred; hence in

---

ἀ γ γ ε λ λ ω. [1] ἀναγγ. EG, 33 al, ἀπαγγ. אD pm, ἀγγ. BאA pc.
[2] Photius (MPG, 101, 989, 11 f.) can still call Mary Magdalene an εὐαγγελίστρια τῆς ἀναστάσεως.
[3] Schn. Euang., I, 98 f.; II, 141, 154 ff.
[4] *Op. cit.,* I, 30 f., 64 f.
[5] Audollent Def. Tab. No. 198, 15 f.: ὡς [σ]αφῶς ἀγγέ[λλω] with the textual note of the editor on p. 274.
[6] P. Giess, I, 3, 4 (p.19): ἄνακτα καινὸν Ἀδριανὸν ἀγγελῶ[ν]; Schn. Euang., I, 88 ff.
ἀ ν α γ γ έ λ λ ω. [1] Moult.-Mill. *s.v.*
[2] In Mk. 5:19 both alongside διαγγέλλειν, in Jn. 4:51 alongside ἀγγέλλειν.

non-Attic *koine* MSS, as also in the LXX and NT, we should always decide for ἀναγγέλλειν. [3]

The verb is frequently used in a secular sense. With the meaning of "proclamation" it is used of the proclamation [4] or declaration [5] of a king ; of the reports of envoys ; [6] of an unconcealed message of sorrow ; [7] of communications. [8] But in a weaker sense it is often used in letters [9] simply for "to tell," and it almost == εἰπεῖν. [10]

It can take on a sacral tone : a. ἀναγγέλλειν χρησμούς, Aesch. Prom., 661 f.; though this is not a technical term for the pronouncements of oracles [11] (unlike the word group εὐαγγελ- [12]). b. as used in connexion with Hellenistic divine festivals in Asia Minor : the κῆρυξ ἀναγγέλλει (proclaims) the rewards of εὐεργέται, rewards for the σωτηρία of the πόλις, [13] and esp. wreaths of honour. Synonyms can be used for both ἀναγγέλλειν and κῆρυξ. But the fact of sacral proclamation remains, and it is an important parallel to the NT development of the term in relation to the common root ἀγγελ- ; c. the same *anangelia* in the Diadochi period at the honouring of divine rulers [14] whose own message can have the force of divine ἀναγγελία ; [15] proclamation in honour of a Magna-Mater-priest (Samos, *c* 100 B.C., Ditt. Syll.³ 1047, 23; 27; 30), there being no reason to suspect a special usage in connexion with the Mysteries. [16]

It is very common in the LXX, being used predominantly for הגיד. [17] In religious use [18] it occurs most frequently, like many biblico-theological terms, in Ps. and Dt.

---

[3] Moult.-Mill.; H. Anz, *Subsidia ad cognosc. Graec. serm. e pentateuchi versione Alexandrine repetita* (Diss. Hal., 1894), 283 f.

[4] Liddell-Scott, N.E. *s.v.* : "proclaim." Jos. Ant., 17, 274 βασιλεὺς ἀναγγελθείς (of the rebel Simon).

[5] BCH, 20 (1896), p. 506, 13 f. (Delos, c. 300 B.C.): Damaratos ἀναγγέλλει... τὴν τοῦ βασιλέως Λυσιμάχου εὔνοιαν.

[6] E.g., IG, XII, 5, 532, 1 f.: ἐπειδὴ ἀναγγέλλουσιν οἱ πρέσβεις οἱ ἀποσταλέντες, GDI, 4254, 10 f.: ἐπειδὴ ἀνάγγελλον οἱ πρεσβέες οἱ ἐς 'Ρώμαν πορευθέντες. The circle of ideas (πρέσβεις, ἀποστάλεντες) corresponds to the missionary language of the early Church, *v.* Wnd., 2 K, 195 f.

[7] Test. N. 7: ἐκαιόμην ἐν σπλάγχνοις ἀναγγεῖλαι ("to publish," Schnapp): that Joseph is sold, Zn. Lk. 725, n. 68).

[8] αἱ προηγούμεναι φαντασίαι ἀναγγέλλουσιν, M. Anton, 8, 49, 1, p. 104, 9 f. (Schenkl).

[9] P. Petr., II, No. VIII (3), 1 etc. (*v.* Moult.-Mill.).

[10] Such is the usage, says H. Anz, in Gn. Ex., "*ut plerisque locis nihil intersit inter* ἀναγγέλλειν *et* εἰπεῖν".

[11] Schn. Euang., II, 254, 257 f. The only comparable passage is Hom. Hymn. Apoll., 394.

[12] Schn. Euang., I, 83 f., 98 ff.; II, 194 ff., 254 ff.

[13] There are many examples in inscriptions from the end of the 4th to the 1st century B.C., 37 alone being found in those of Magn. and Priene. Similarities to NT synonymous constructions with (εὐ)ἀγγελ- are found in IG, XII, 5, 714, 10 (4th cent. B.C.), cf. 6 εὐεργ., 8 ἀρετή; IG, XII, 5, 802, 6 f. (3rd. cent. B.C.), cf. 4 ἀπαγγεῖλαι, 8 f. ἐπαγγελία; Inscr. Magn. 53, 30, cf. 10 εὐεργ., 19, 58 ἐπιφάνεια, 20 παρακαλεῖν, 30 ἀποσταλέντες, 35 f. σωτηρία; Priene, 108, 330 f., 342 f. (after 129 B.C.), cf. 339 f. σωτηρία εὐεργεσία, 115 ἐπαγγελία.

[14] Ditt. Or., 6, 30 (Antigonus): ἀναγγεῖλαι στεφάνους; but there is a reminiscence here of the εὐαγγελ-concept of the imperial cult, εὐαγγέλια being offered (31 f.) for the word of peace (8, 16) of the divine ruler. For an understanding of the inscription, Ditt. n. 6; Schn. Euang., II, 132 ff. Similarly Ditt. Or., 332, 43 f. (Attalus III), where we find cultic honouring 6-13; he is Εὐεργέτης, 22; 24 f.; 30; 44 f.

[15] Cf. the inscription quoted in n. 5 : Lysimachos is divine ruler, and his εὔνοια (1 ff.) applies to a ἱερόν.

[16] Cl. Al. Protr., 8, 80, 1: τί σοι σοφίας ἀναγγέλλω μυστήρια καὶ ῥήσεις ἐκ παιδὸς 'Εβραίου σεσοφισμένου.

[17] In Hatch 4 columns altogether ; 184 times (including Da. Θ) for הגיד.

[18] The secular use is very common in the history books (cf. n. 10, Anz).

Is. [19] a. The Lord declares (ὁ λαλῶν δικαιοσύνην καὶ ἀναγγέλλων ἀλήθειαν) that which is to come (Is. 42:9; 46:10 etc.) as false gods cannot do (τὰ ἐπερχό-μενα... ἀναγγειλάτωσαν, 44:7 etc.). God's message through the prophets to Israel, e.g., Is. 53:1 f.: κύριε, τίς ἐπίστευσεν τῇ ἀκοῇ ἡμῶν ... ἀνηγγείλαμεν ὡς παιδίον ἐναντίον αὐτοῦ, Jer. 16:10 (ἄπαντα τὰ ῥήματα ταῦτα); [20] Is. 21:10; Mi. 6:8 (εἰ ἀνηγγέλη [20] σοι, ἄνθρωπε, τί καλόν); Is. 58:1 (ἁμαρτήματα), cf. Ez. 23:36; [20] also to the nations, Is. 2:3 (יֵרֶה hiph); 12:5; Ιερ 26:14; (synon. πα-ραγγ.); 27:2; Is. 52:15 (directly before Is. 53:1 f.), οἷς οὐκ ἀνηγγέλη περὶ αὐτοῦ ὄψονται, καὶ οἳ οὐκ ἀκηκόασιν συνήσουσιν; and to the prophets, 43:3. [20] Note especially Am. 4:13: ἀναγγέλλων εἰς ἀνθρώπους τὸν χριστὸν αὐτοῦ. [20] b. Cultic proclamation in the Ps.: There is declared God's δικαιοσύνη (ψ 21:31 f.; 70:15); [20] His ἀλήθεια (29:10); His ἔργα (63:10, cf. θαυμαστά 70:17); His ἔλεος (91:3, cf. 16); His ὄνομα (101:22); His αἴνεσις (50:17); to the nations (95:3, cf. Is. 42:12 : τὰς ἀρετὰς αὐτοῦ ἐν ταῖς νήσοις ἀναγγελοῦσιν).

This religious usage is distinguished from the Hellenistic by the reference to God's command and to His historical or eschatological act, as also by the fact that the latter is declared in the cultus in connexion with a list of synonyms all of which are alien to Hellenism (δικαιοσύνη, ἀλήθεια, θαυμαστά, ἔλεος, ὄνομα). [21] The Hellenistic parallel is aretalogy (→ ἀρετή), in which the mighty acts of a god are recounted. It has not been fully elucidated whether there is terminological affinity. [22] The similarity lies in the matter, which may derive from a common oriental source or perhaps develops spontaneously. But there is a great difference between the historical plan of Yahweh leading to the judgments of the last day and, e.g., the individual miracles of Aescul. Even the ἀναγγέλλειν of the Ps. is not merely the recounting of miracles, since the narration is retrospective re-collection of a long divine history. [23]

In later Judaism these thoughts seem to return. In Test. L. 10, 1: [24] ὅσα ἐγὼ ἤκουσα παρὰ τῶν πατέρων μου (Jn. 15:15) ἀνήγγειλα ὑμῖν reminds us of the concept of παράδοσις. With reference to the proclamation of eschatological occurrence, Gr. Bar., 1, p. 84, 20 (James): the angel is sent ὅπως ἀναγγείλω καὶ ὑποδείξω σοι πάντα <τὰ> τοῦ θεοῦ. Similarly the recurring adnuntiare of 4 Esdras [25] is direct proclamation rather than mere promise. [26]

---

[19] Ps. 23 times; Dt. Is. 27; Trit. Is. 2, Is. 1-39, 19; Jer. 23, but more than half of these are secular. → ἀπαγγέλλω, n. 21.

[20] Much textual variation as between ἀναγγ. and ἀπαγγ., and sometimes ἐξαγγ.

[21] The proclamation of the acts of Yahweh (Dt. Is.) and its echoes in the cultus (Ps.), are even more closely linked in בשׂר (→ εὐαγγελίζεσθαι).

[22] The word is not used technically for aretalogies. κηρύσσειν, ἀπαγγέλλειν, καταγ-γέλλειν seem to be preferred. For other verbs, cf. E. Peterson, Εἷς Θεός (1926), 191 ff., though he does not have ἀναγγέλλειν. The strongest affinity is in Is. 42:12 (supra). But there is reason to ask whether here and in Is. 43:21 ἀρεταί is not to be translated "laudes." Unique is Da. 3:99, LXX Θ: aretalogy through an opponent; ἀναγγ. used as elsewhere → διαγγ.

[23] Cf. the whole tenor of the historical Psalms.

[24] Wnd. on 1 Jn. 1:5.

[25] At any rate in 7:99 (3, 12, 13 V): ordo animarum, ut amodo ("ἀπ' ἄρτι" Rev. 14:13, Violet., II, ad loc.) adnuntiatur. Similarly 2, 10; 48 (from the Christian 5 Esdras), like ἀναγγ. in the prophets, while in 8, 36 like the Ps. (11:16 : → εὐαγγελίζεσθαι).

[26] So Gunkel on 7:99.

B. ἀναγγέλλω in the NT.

In the NT Mt. 28:11 inclines more to the secular use (א D pc read ἀναγγ.), whereas Jn. 5:15 [27] and Ac. 16:38 [28] incline strongly to the religious.

1. Mk. 5:14: οἱ βόσκοντες... ἀνήγγειλαν [29] belongs to the category of miracle stories, [30] and Mt. 28:11 and Jn. 5:15 might perhaps be regarded in the same way.

2. Not far removed is the usage in Ac. 14:27; 15:4, which reminds us both of aretalogy and the Psalms (63:10; 70:17). The apostles recount what God has done through them — a knowledge of the present act of God corresponding to that of the prophets. To the same group belongs 2 C. 7:7, in which Titus "tells" (cf. 1 Th. 3:6; → εὐαγγελίζομαι) the ἔργον of God. In 1 P. 1:12 it is used synon. with εὐαγγελίζεσθαι to record that Christ has appeared (in contrast with the mere expectation of the prophets and angels). A similar use may be seen in R. 15:21. Here Is. 52:15 is quoted (→ 58, 63) in the context of a great εὐαγγέλιον passage (15:14 ff., 18-20). In Ac. 20:20 f., 27 it is synon. with διδάξαι and διαμαρτύρεσθαι, having as its content συμφέροντα, μετάνοια and πίστις, the whole βουλή of God. Here we have the strongest analogy to its use in the prophets.

Under the same OT influence — 1 Cl. quotes Is. 53:2; Ps. 51:15 [31] — the post-apost. fathers almost use the word as a t.t. for divinely ordained proclamation. [32]

3. An isolated case is Ac. 19:18 (ἐξομολογούμενοι καὶ ἀναγγέλλοντες τὰς πράξεις αὐτῶν) where it is used of the confession of sins (cf. Is. 58:1; Ez. 23:36?).

4. In 1 Jn. 1:5 ἀναγγέλλειν (synon. with μαρτυρεῖν, ἀπαγγέλλειν, 2 f.) is the verb for ἀγγελία, which declares the λόγος τῆς ζωῆς as it has now become visible and audible (1:1, 3). Anaphorically repeated three times in Jn. 16:13-15, it is used of the speech of the Paraclete. The proclamation of the Paraclete is prophetically eschatological (cf. OT and apocalyptic): [33] τὰ ἐρχόμενα ἀναγγελεῖ (16:13, cf. Is. 44:7); He leads ἐν τῇ ἀληθείᾳ πάσῃ (so א D, cf. ψ 29:10?); He takes only of the things of Jesus (16:14 f.). In the coming ὥρα, says Jesus in 16:25, παρρησίᾳ περὶ τοῦ πατρὸς ἀναγγελῶ ὑμῖν. Do we not have in all these cases an indefinite use of the verb? The Samaritan woman says of the coming Messiah (Ta'eb) in 4:25: ἀναγγελεῖ ἡμῖν ἅπαντα. Is the coming messenger (→ 57 f.) meant? Or is there a direct reminiscence of Dt. 18:18?

† ἀπαγγέλλω.

A. ἀπαγγέλλω outside the NT.

Meaning the same as ἀναγγέλλω, and often replaced by it in the koine. A messenger brings news; the following of an order or a secret plan is recounted; [1] or it is used

---

27 εἶπεν אC al, ἀνήγγ. Bא al, ἀπήγγ. Dφ 33 al.

28 We read ἀναγγ. rather than ἀπαγγ. in spite of poor and meagre attestation.

29 With Soden the א reading ἀναγγ. is to be preferred to the "better" attested ἀπαγγ. It maintains the rougher non-Attic quality. Cf. also Jn. 16:25.

30 To be sure, Bultmann, Trad., 236 ff. and Peterson, op. cit., 193 ff. call this declaring rather than telling. But it has all the features of aretalogy indicated by Peterson.

31 1 Cl., 16, 3; 18, 15. Moreover ψ 18:3 = 1 Cl., 27, 7: νὺξ νυκτὶ ἀναγγέλλει γνῶσιν.

32 Herm. v., 2, 1, 3; 3, 3, 1; M. Pol., 15, 1; 1 Cl., 17, 7.

33 H. Windisch, Jülicher Festschrift (1927), 121, cf. the Comm.

ἀ π α γ γ έ λ λ ω. 1 Jos. Vit., 51: ἐκπέμπει μετ' ἐπιστολῶν... τὸν ἀπαγγελοῦντα

of reports, [2] of information given in letters etc., [3] often in official [4] or judicial [5] style (→ παραγγέλλω, ἐπαγγέλλω). On the whole the word is more official than ἀναγγέλλω, e.g., to signify the activity of envoys: πρέσβεις, [6] cf. the image in 2 C. 5:20; Eph. 6:20. Already in classical secular use εὐαγγελ- and ἀπαγγελ- occur as synonyms. [7] ἀπαγγέλλειν can have much the same meaning as "to speak," whether generally, [8] or more particularly to speak ἀληθῶς, λόγους ἀληθεῖς, τὴν ἀλήθειαν, πάντα ἐξ ἀληθείας. [9]

There is an approximation to religious speech when what is announced is liberation from a cultic κατοχή, [10] or magic, [11] or a favourable time to make war, [12] or a decree from the "God" Trajan. [13] Directly religious is its use a. to characterise Hermes (Phrygian inscript. from 1st cent. A.D.): Ἑρμῆν τε... ἀπαγγέλλοντα βροτοῖσιν Ὄσσα Ζεὺς φρονέ[ει]. [14] Similarly ἄγγελος ἀγγέλλειν and even Εὐάγγελος εὐαγγελίζεσθαι are used of Hermes. [15] b. In honours lists (esp. from Athens in 3rd to 2nd cent. B.C.) the success of a sacrifice dispensing σωτηρία is declared by solemn ἀπαγγέλλειν. [16] c. Occasionally in aretalogies, [17] esp. P. Oxy., XI, 1381, extolling Imouthes-Aesculapius (beginning of the 2nd cent. A.D.): ἀπαγγέλλειν δυνάμεις, synon. διηγεῖσθαι δυνάμεις, κηρύσσειν εὐεργεσίας, προφητεύειν ἐπίνοιαν. [18] d. In Epictetus' sense of mission: the ἄγγελος τοῦ Διός should ἀπαγγεῖλαι τἀληθῆ, synon. ἐξαγγέλλειν. [19]

In the LXX the word is almost as common as ἀναγγέλλειν, [20] usually as a rendering of הגיד. From this we may see that the terms are equivalent. Yet the

---

... τί τὸ συμβεβηκὸς εἴη τῷ ἀποσταλέντι (recalling the NT Epistles); Ant., 9, 49 (= 4 Βασ. 4:7); Ant., 15, 47: Sabbion ἀπαγγέλλει to Herod the plan of Alexandra.

[2] Herm. s., 5, 2, 11; also (ὑπὸ ... συγγραφέων ἀπηγγελμένα) Jos. Bell., 1, 13.

[3] P. Petr., II, No. II (3) 5 etc., as elsewhere ἀναγγέλλειν (→ n. 9). Men. Peric., 298, p. 61, Jensen.

[4] P. Oxy., I, 106, 4: ἀπήγγειλα ὑμεῖν (a declaration of Trajan).

[5] = "to appeal," P. Oxy., I, 33, V (2nd cent.), 2; 8; = "to intimate" (death), P. Magd., 8, 9 f.

[6] Explicitly, e.g., Ditt. Syll.[3], 206, 10 f.; 17 f.; 370, 43 f.: 46. Cf. Schn. Euang., II, 249, n. 4.

[7] Schn. Euang., II, 250, n. 1 (Demosthenes, Lycurg.).

[8] Alciphr. Ep., II, 17 (III, 20), 2 p. 38, 11, Schepers: τοιαῦτα καὶ εἰδέναι καὶ ἀπαγγέλλειν κακός; Philo Leg. All, II, 62: ψυχῆς τροπὴν ἔξω ἀπήγγειλε; and the whole discussion in Philo Leg. All., III, 118-121 (ἀπαγγεῖλαι, 120).

[9] Philo Leg. All., III, 120, p. 140, 1 CW; cf. p. 139, 26 and 139, 19 (Ex. 28:26); Men. Peric., 77 f., p. 50, Jensen; Polyb., I, 14, 1 (I, p. 17, 22, Büttner-Wobst); P. Lond., 46 (= Preis. Zaub., V), 302 f.

[10] P. Lond., 42, 26 (168 B.C.).

[11] P. Lond., 46 (→ n. 9; 4th cent. A.D.), 302 f., synon. ἐξαγγ., 294; cf. ἐγώ εἰμι ἄγγελος τοῦ Φαπρώ, 113 f.

[12] Alciphr. Ep., I, 14 (I, 11), p. 16 Schepers: μαστῆρες ("investigators") μέλλουσιν ἀπαγγέλλειν ὅτε δεῖ ἀπιέναι πολεμήσοντας: oracles? Even if the verse is a gloss (Hermann), the point remains.

[13] P. Oxy, I, 106, 4 (→ n. 4) "Θεός", line 11.

[14] Ramsay, Cities and Bishoprics of Phrygia, I (1895), 308, No. 120/1.

[15] Schn. Euang., I, 86; II, 197 ff., 218 ff. Hermes is the λόγος ἀγγελτικός, says Justin.

[16] Syll.[3], 289, 2 ff.; 299, 11 ff. etc. (cf. index): περὶ ὧν ἀπαγγέλλουσιν those honoured, ὑπὲρ τῶν θυσιῶν ὧν ἔθυον etc. Similarly Herodian, VIII, 3, 7, p. 209, 21. Stavenh. (Syria, 3rd cent. A.D.): ἱερὰ αἴσια ἀπαγγελλόντων. Cf. Axel Boethius, Die Pythaïs (Uppsala, 1918), 120. The ἀπαγγέλλοντες are there θεωροί (119 ff.) whose task is otherwise that of ἐπαγγέλλεσθαι (or καταγγέλλειν).

[17] → ἀναγγέλλω, 62.

[18] Lines 88-90, 215-222; cf. 42, 137, 145, 170.

[19] III, 22 (23), 25; on τἀληθῆ → n. 9; on the parallel III, 21, 16 → ἐξαγγέλλω.

[20] Hatch, 4 cols.

secular use easily predominates.[21] The religious use is wholly analogous to ἀναγγέλλειν.[22] It refers a. to God's message : Is. 44:8; ψ 147:8 : τὸν λόγον αὐτοῦ, cf. 7 (ἀποστελεῖ); to oracles : 1 S. 9:6, 8 ; to prophetic proclamation : 1 S. 9:19; 12:7; Mi. 3:8; Sir. 44:3; also Wis. 6:22; Sir. 16:25 (a Hellenistic awareness of inspiration ?); b. To cultic proclamation : God's δύναμις (ψ 144:4), arm (70:18, synon. ἀναγγ. θαυμάσια, 17), ἀλήθεια (88:2), ἔργα (104:1, twice for ידע hiph), διαλογισμοί (39:6), and αἰνέσεις (77:4, מַסֵּפ) are all declared. Synonyms are διηγεῖσθαι in 54:18 and also εὐαγγελίζεσθαι in Na. 1:15 (both times מַשְׁמִיעַ). Here again we have terminological echoes of aretalogy (διηγεῖσθαι, δυνάμεις).

B. ἀπαγγέλλω in the NT.

The word is found 25 times in Lucan writings, and about 14 times elsewhere (Mk. 16 twice). Literary style is an influence in Luke,[23] esp. in substitution for λέγειν, υ. what follows. Secular usage is found at : Mt. 2:8; 14:12; cf. Lk. 13:1; 14:21 ("to narrate or report"); Lk. 8:20 (= λέγειν, Mk. 3:32); 18:37; Ac. 5:22; 25 (infra); 16:36; 22:26; 23:16 f., 19; 28:21.

Religious use is found in the NT 1. in accounts of miracles, Mt. 8:33 = Lk. 8:34 (= Mk. 5:14, ἀναγγ.); cf. Lk. 8:36 (= διηγεῖσθαι, Mk. 5:16) and 8:47 (= εἰπεῖν... ἀλήθειαν, Mk. 5:33). Similarly, Ac. 11:13; 12:14, 17, in association with the thought of God's work (→ ἀναγγ.), as in Ac. 4:23. Hearers record the impression of the Word of God in 1 C. 14:25; 1 Th. 4:9. As with ἀναγγ., the usage remains much the same in the post-apostolic period, cf. 1 Cl., 65, 1. In Ign. Phld., 10, 1 a solemn account is given of the "peace" of the communities, with perhaps an echo of the thought of the Gospel, εὐαγγ. and εἰρήνη having been synon. since Is. 52:7.

The resurrection accounts are similar. In view of Lk. 9:36 (οὐδὲν ἀπήγγειλαν ἐν ἐκείναις ταῖς ἡμέραις), Mt. 28:8, 10 = Lk. 24:9 (Mk. 16:10, 13) might almost suggest the message of the resurrection in a specialised sense (→ ἀγγέλλω). To be sure, in the same (Mt. 28:11 ἀναγγ.) or similar contexts (Ac. 5:22, 25) the word seems to be secular, but it might well be asked, as with ἀναγγ., whether even the report of the neutral or the opponent is not thought to be sacral in a miracle story.

2. The message of God in the narrowest sense is also meant in Mt. 11:4 = Lk. 7:22 : ἀπαγγείλατε 'Ιωάννῃ,[24] cf. εὐαγγελίζεσθαι (Mt. v. 5 = Lk. v. 22), as it certainly is in Ac. 26:20 : τοῖς ἔθνεσιν ἀπήγγελλον μετανοεῖν καὶ ἐπιστρέφειν ἐπὶ τὸν θεόν (cf. 20:20 f. ἀναγγ. διδάξαι διαμαρτύρεσθαι; Mk. 1:4 κηρύσσειν). Similarly Ac. 17:30 tells us that God Himself ἀπαγγέλλει (παραγγέλλει in 𝔎 pm is a softening) τοῖς ἀνθρώποις... μετανοεῖν. In 1 Jn. 1:2, 3 we have a highly specialised use : ὃ ἑωράκαμεν καὶ ἀκηκόαμεν, ἀπαγγέλλομεν καὶ ὑμῖν (→ ἀναγγέλλω, ἀγγελία).

---

[21] Dt. Is. only twice (in Is. 48:20 read ἀναγγ.); in Ps. only 9 times.

[22] Since in principle we prefer ἀναγγ., some references given in Hatch are omitted. As the words are interchangeable, this makes no material difference.

[23] The certainty of this conclusion is restricted by the fact that ἀναγγ. and ἀπαγγ. appear very seldom in Philo. We owe the passages quoted to H. Leisegang ; they are not listed in the Index.

[24] In the same connexion Lk. 7:18 : ἀπήγγειλαν 'Ιωαν. οἱ μαθηταὶ αὐτ. (secondary in D); the passage would belong to 1. ("the work of God"), but all "dispositions" are fleeting.

3. Jesus Himself is the Messenger of God κατ' ἐξοχήν according to Mt. 12:18; Hb. 2:12 : two loose quotations from the LXX, first from Is. 42:1: κρίσιν τοῖς ἔθνεσιν ἀπαγγελεῖ (= יוֹצִיא, LXX ἐξοίσει), and then from Ps. 22:22 : ἀπαγγελῶ τὸ ὄνομά σου [25] τοῖς ἀδελφοῖς μου (= אֲסַפְּרָה, LXX διηγήσομαι). We probably have here the influence of Palestinian tradition, i.e., that the Messiah will be the prophet of Dt. 18:15, 18 [26] and the εὐαγγελιζόμενος of Is. 52:7; cf. Jn. 4:25 ἀναγγελεῖ, Hb. 3:1 ἀπόστολος. The Hellenistic (Jewish-Gnostic ?) expectation of the coming divine messenger (→ 57 f.) derives from the same root. The difference lies in the estimation of the "Word." Will the final Word of God, and therefore His last message, mean judgment and remission (OT, Palestine, NT), or will it mean an overflowing of the divine substance (Hellenism)? As distinct from both expectations Jesus signifies not merely fulfilment but also σκάνδαλον. Mt. 11:5 f. applies to the Jewish hope, and the whole of John's Gospel is in opposition to the Gnostic-Hellenistic hope, Jesus the Son being subordinate to the Father and not a θεῖος. [27]

† διαγγέλλω.

A. διαγγέλλω outside the NT.

Rare in Hellenism, but shares with ἐξαγγέλλειν, καταγγέλλειν and εὐαγγελίζεσθαι the solemn use [1] of the ἀγγελ-verbs. The word is used in Josephus for an important military announcement (Vit., 98, also Ant., 7, 201) and a solemn "proclamation" of the emperor (Bell., 6, 96). In Philo as in Josephus it is synon. with εὐαγγελίζεσθαι, [2] in both cases in purely Hellenistic contexts. It is linked with κήρυγμα [3] and λόγος. [4]

Religiously, the word is used a. of the herald ministry of Iris and Hermes, [5] Hermes occurring repeatedly with (εὐ)αγγελ-, κηρυγ-, λόγος. [6] It is also used b. of the Pythia: τὰ περὶ τοῦ θεοῦ διαγγέλλει; though Socrates under the power of the daemon can proclaim ἀληθέστερα, τοῖς φίλοις ἐξαγγείλας τὰ τῶν θεῶν συμβου-

---

[25] Cf. ψ 101, 22 ἀναγγ.
[26] The paucity of Rabbinic examples (Str.-B., II, 479 f., 626) is to be explained by the frequently recognisable tendency (Str.-B., IV, 452 ff. on Ps. 110; IV, 1223, Index s.v. Elias etc.) to expunge traditions welcome to Christianity. The attempt to explain the expectation of the one → προφήτης solely from Hellenism (Fascher, Prophetes, 1927) leaves open many questions. No strict derivation can be given, but the quotation from Dt. 18 and its appearance in non-Hellenistic contexts, e.g., the primitive community, call for explanation.
[27] Wetter, op. cit., 172-180; Lütgert, Die joh. Christologie² (1916).
δ ι α γ γ έ λ λ ω. [1] Used stylistically (instead of ἀναγγέλλειν etc.) in Philo Som., I, 27: ἄγγελοι διανοίας εἰσὶ (the senses) διαγγέλλουσαι χρώματα κτλ. Det. Pot. Ins., 13: υἱὸν... διαγγέλλοντα περὶ τῶν ἄλλων παίδων.
[2] Philo Leg. Gai., 99: ἀγαθὰ διαγγέλλειν synon. εὐαγγελίζεσθαι (Schn. Euang., I, 85 f.); Jos. Bell., 4, 618 : διήγγελλον αἱ φῆμαι τὸν ... αὐτοκράτορα, where ἑορτάζειν εὐαγγέλια follows at once, and where the whole outlook is determined by the εὐαγγέλιον of the imperial cult (ibid., I, 104 ff.).
[3] Herodian, II, 6, 6, p. 51, 11, Stavenhagen.
[4] Plat. Tim., 37b. ὅταν... ὁ τοῦ θατέρου κύκλος ὀρθὸς ἰὼν εἰς πᾶσαν αὐτοῦ τὴν ψυχὴν διαγγείλῃ. The whole treats of the λόγος ... περί τε θάτερον ὃν καὶ περὶ τὸ ταὐτόν. The text and meaning are doubtful (Taylor, A Comment. on Plato's Timaeus, Oxf. 1928, 180 f.). The → ἀλήθεια concept recurs repeatedly in the context.
[5] Etymologicum Gudianum, p. 71, 51 f., Sturzius; Cornut. Theol. Graec., 16, p. 21 (18) 19 f., Lang (Wetter, op. cit., 35). Similarly Philo Leg. Gai., 99 ff. (→ n. 2 ; the passage treats of Hermes). Also to be noted in this connexion is Philo's application of the verb to heavenly ἄγγελοι, Som., I, 141; Abr., 115.
[6] Schn. Euang., I, 85 ff., II, 197 ff., 218 ff.

λεύματα (Xenoph. Ap. 12 f.). Similarly we find in popular Greek religion [7] the psalm-catena: βροντή... ἡ μετὰ τὸ βάπτισμα τοῦ εὐαγγελίου διαγγελία. [8] Josephus is moving in the sphere of Hellenistic religion when in a διαγγελία (address against suicide) he seeks to declare the προστάγματα τοῦ θεοῦ before threatening death (Bell., 3, 361; 362-382), or when he uses the verb in the sense of εὐαγγελ- to proclaim the enthronement of the divine emperor (Bell., 4, 618).

In LXX it is always sacral (9 times). A miracle is reported to the Persian king (2 Macc. 1:33); the sabbatical year (עבר hi, Lv. 25:9) and the shouting at Jericho (אמר Jos. 6:10) are announced. [9] The dominion of the Kurios is proclaimed to the whole world. In Ex. 9:16 διετηρήθης (Pharaoh) that I may show my ἰσχύς καὶ ὅπως διαγγελῇ τὸ ὄνομά μου ἐν πάσῃ τῇ γῇ. Similarly of Heliodorus in 2 Macc. 3:34: σὺ δὲ ... μεμαστιγωμένος διάγγελλε πᾶσι τὸ μεγαλεῖον τοῦ θεοῦ κράτος; also ψ 58:13: διαγγελήσονται (14) συντέλειαι... καὶ γνώσονται ὅτι ὁ θεὸς τοῦ Ἰακὼβ δεσπόζει τῶν περάτων τῆς γῆς. Above all, Ps. 2:7: διαγγέλλων (διαγγελῶν, A) τὸ πρόσταγμα [10] Κυρίου. Κύριος εἶπεν πρός μέ Υἱός μου εἶ σύ κτλ. We are again reminded of the Hellenistic cult of the ruler; the same connexion, even of the Hebrew text, with this cult is found in the case of → εὐαγγελίζεσθαι. [11] The lordship of Yahweh and the coronation of the king are proclaimed. In Ps. 2:7 with its reference to the Messiah and its formula of adoption, the parallel is even stronger. [12]

B. διαγγέλλω in the NT.

In the NT it is used for "cultic announcement" in Ac. 21:26: διαγγέλλων (in the temple) τὴν ἐκπλήρωσιν τῶν ἡμερῶν τοῦ ἁγνισμοῦ (the Naziritic vow). In the other three instances it has much the same sense as in the LXX. Ex. 9:16 is quoted in R. 9:17. [13] In Mk. 5:19: διάγγειλον [14] αὐτοῖς, ὅσα ὁ Κύριός σοι πεποίηκεν, the miraculous act of the God of Israel is proclaimed in the heathen land. In Lk. 9:60: σὺ δὲ ... διάγγελλε τὴν βασιλείαν τοῦ θεοῦ, [15] corresponds to the Lucan εὐαγγελίζεσθαι τὴν βασιλείαν τοῦ θεοῦ, which has its roots in the Palestinian Jewish tradition. The meaning is not simply that the disciples announce the imminent βασιλεία τ.θ., but that the eschatological lordship of God is proclaimed, beginning in the word of proclamation. Thus it is said expressly of the word of the disciples in Lk. 10:9: ἤγγικεν ἐφ᾽ ὑμᾶς ἡ βασιλεία τοῦ θεοῦ. In the same sense we are to understand such sayings of the Lord as in Mt. 11:5 f. (πτωχοὶ εὐαγγελίζονται καὶ μακάριός ἐστιν ὃς ἐὰν μὴ σκανδαλισθῇ ἐν

---

[7] Alongside the Pythia are birds, thunderings, voices: φῆμαι (→ n. 2, Jos.), βρονταί, Xenoph. Apol., 12.

[8] Cf. the catena in Ps. I, 491, 19.

[9] Cf. the obscure Sir. 43:2: ἥλιος ἐν ὀπτασίᾳ διαγέλλων ἐν ἐξόδῳ. Smend: The sun when it arises radiates warmth (מביע חמה). How wonderful is the work of the Lord!

[10] Supra, Jos. Bell., 3, 361, either mere coincidence or imposed by the matter itself.

[11] Schn. Euang. I, 25 f., II, 180 ff.

[12] The content is the same in Mas. even though the text be emended (Gunkel, ad loc.). So, too, in Ex. 9:16. On the other hand, in ψ 58:13 f. the LXX goes its own way.

[13] LXX variations do not affect, διαγγελ.

[14] So. Dminn, against ἀπαγγελ. ۞ and ἀναγγελ. ℵ. Synon. κηρύσσειν in v. 20.

[15] "Simply a Greek variant for κηρύσσειν" (Dalman W. J., I, 86 = אַכְרֵיז or בַּשֵּׂר). In view of the parallel indicated in the text, this seems happier than Dalman's second suggestion, אוֹדִיעַ, "to make known."

ἐμοί); [16] Lk. 9:26 (ὃς ἂν ἐπαισχυνθῇ με [16] καὶ τοὺς ἐμοὺς λόγους); and Mk. 4:2-32. Indeed, this is the significance of the word in the sayings of the synoptic Jesus generally. Only along these lines can we perceive the parallel to the LXX as well as to the imperial cult, the whole of Jesus' preaching of the kingdom constituting an antithetical parallelism in the case of the latter. [17] All the ἀγγελ-words, however, signify proclamation.

Early Christian echoes of this synonymous usage are still to be found in the supplement to Dg. (11, 5): οὗτος ὁ ἀεί, ὁ "σήμερον υἱὸς" λογισθείς (Ps. 2:7) by whom the χάρις ἁπλουμένη ἐν ἁγίοις πληθύνεται... διαγγέλλουσα καιρούς (the fulfilment of the promises). [18] This is conjoined with such terms (1-8) as λόγος, μυστήρια, κηρύσσειν and εὐαγγέλια (the Gospels), all in characteristic reshaping of original Christian contents.

† ἐξαγγέλλω.

This is found only in 1 Pt. 2:9 in the sense of "publishing abroad" [1] or solemn ἀγγέλλειν: ὅπως τὰς ἀρετὰς ἐξαγγείλητε τοῦ... ὑμᾶς καλέσαντος. The style is that of aretalogy, [2] and there is allusion to Is. 43:21: λαόν μου ὃν περιεποιησάμην τὰς ἀρετάς μου διηγεῖσθαι. It is mere chance that it does not occur elsewhere in the NT or the apostolic fathers. In view of the uniformity of the whole ἀγγελ-stem, the history of this term is also given.

We see its secular use in tragedy, the ἐξάγγελος being a messenger who proclaims abroad... what is concealed from the gaze of the spectators. [3] The particular meaning [4] of imparting something unknown or declaring something concealed is illustrated by Schlatter from Jos.; [5] cf. also Pseud.-Call., Hist. Alex. Magn., I, p. 16, 18 (scroll from the jar of Nectanebos).

Religiously, a. the latter notion is seen in the ὅρκος inscriptions of early Hellenism, perjured transgressors of the nomos or unravelled conspiracies being published. [6] b. Both Socrates (Xenoph. Apol., 13) and Epictetus think of themselves as prophetic declarers of what is secret; Epictetus compares a bad philosopher to a poor κῆρυξ of mysteries: ἐξαγγέλλεις αὐτὰ παρὰ καιρόν (Diss., III, 21, 16, p. 293, 9, Sch.²). Philo uses the word of the λόγος προφορικός (Migr. Abr., 73 cf. 71), and a magic papyrus of the 4th century A.D. uses it of the proclamation of προγεγονότα. [7] c. It is also used in much the same sense as in aretalogy (Aelius Aristides), the epiphany, parousia and δυνάμεις of Aesculapius being extolled. [8] d. It is used of the sayings of

---

[16] Jesus is the αὐτοβασιλεία (Feine, Theol., [4] [5] 80). But in most recent studies it is recognised that the β.τ.θ. is present. This is the significance of the "Word."

[17] Many observations might be made such as those of Windisch, ZNW, 24 (1925), 240 ff.

[18] Bauer, s.v. διαγγελ.

ἐ ξ α γ γ έ λ λ ω. [1] Bauer, s.v.

[2] → ἀναγγ., n. 22.

[3] Pape, s.v.

[4] Examples can be found of its use in the sense of "betray" from the time of Homer.

[5] It is used of "betrayed" court intrigues (Bell., 1, 443: Ant., 17, 5; 44); of a strategic situation (Bell., 3, 317) or a threatening danger (Vit. 137) which is perceived.

[6] Ditt. Or., 226, 34 ff.; Syll.³, 145, 26; 360, 16 ff. (equivalent to εἰσαγγέλλειν, "to indicate," 35); 527, 73. All these are from the 4th to 3rd cent. B.C.

[7] P. Lond., 46 (Preis. Zaub., V), 294 = ἀπαγγείλω, 302 f.; cf. ἄγγελος τοῦ Φαπρώ, 113 f. (ἀπαγγέλλω, n. 11).

[8] Ael. Arist. Or. Sacr., II, 20, p. 399, 8, Keil: ἐξηγγέλθη τὰ τῆς ἐπιφανείας, ibid., 30, p. 401, 20 f. ἐξήγγελλεν ἱερὰν καὶ παρουσίαν καὶ δυνάμεις τινὰς τοῦ θεοῦ. Perhaps we should cite in the same connexion Jos. Ant., 10, 35: τούτων μὲν αὖθις ἐξαγγελοῦμεν ἕκαστον, i.e., the acts of the prophets.

rulers. Thus εὐαγγέλια are offered for the announcement of the victory (ἐξηγγελ-μένα) of Demetrius Poliorcetes, the message itself being clearly regarded as sacral. [9] Again, Antiochus of Commagene thinks of himself as the prophetic enunciator of a divine *nomos*. [10] In both these cases we have approximations to the use of εὐαγγέλιον in the cult of the ruler (→ ἀγγελία, ἀγγέλλω, ἀναγγέλλω, διαγγέλλω).

In the LXX we have only one case of the secular use of ἐξαγγέλειν (in Prv.). It is used 8 times for cultic declaration in the Psalms (= סֵפֶּר) and 3 times in Sir. The meaning is much the same as that of ἀναγγ. or ἀπαγγ.: αἰνέσ(ε)ις ψ 9:15; 72:28; Sir. 39:10 = 44:15 (ἔθνη, σοφία, ἐκκλησία); ἔργα ψ 106:22 (*par.* θυσία αἰνέσεως); Sir. 18:4; δικαιοσύνην (א ἀναγγ.) ψ 70:15 (*par.* σωτηρίαν); ὁδούς ψ 118:26; and in connexion with ἐπαγγελία, ῥῆμα and λόγος ψ 55:9, 11.

† κατ-, προκαταγγέλλω, καταγγελεύς.

A. καταγγέλλω outside the NT.

In the secular field the word can be used of official reports [1] or the process of cognition. [2] It can signify "maintaining" (Epict. Diss., IV, 8, 26, p. 429, 9, Sch.[2]) or "pronouncing" (Jos. Ant., 11, 222, cf. 229) something about oneself (on both → ἐπαγ-γέλλομαι). As with all the ἀγγελ-verbs, however, it has the constant sense of "pro-claiming."

This can be used religiously a. in the sense of the intimation of sacral *agones*. The usual term for this is ἐπαγγέλλεσθαι, but there are many examples of καταγγέλλειν in both earlier and later Hellenism, [3] especially in the proclamation of a sacred festival. It is very occasionally used of general promises to the deity [4] like the regular ἐπαγ-γέλλεσθαι. b. Philo thinks of his philosophical or religious proclamation (Omn. Prob. Lib., 71: ἔνδειαν σοφίας καταγγέλλοντες), as does also Cl. Al. in relation to the corybants (Protr., II, 19, 4: τελετὴν Καβειρικὴν καταγγέλλουσιν). Do we have here a distinctive usage of the mysteries? [5] c. It is used in honour of the emperors (37 A.D.): [6] ἡ κατ' εὐχὴν πᾶσιν ἀνθρώποις ἐλπισθεῖσα ... Καίσαρος ... ἡγεμονία κατήγγελ-ται. This is the proclamation of imperial rule more usually described in terms of

---

[9] Ditt. Syll.[3], 352 (Ephesus 302/1 B.C.), 2-6: συνησθ[ῆναι ἐπὶ τοῖς ἐξηγ]γελμένοις ἀγαθοῖς ... καὶ στεφανηφορεῖν ... ἐπὶ τοῖς εὐτυχήμασιν τοῖς ἐξηγγελμένοις· [θύειν δὲ καὶ εὐ]αγγέλια. In exposition, *v.* Schn. Euang., II, 134, 171, 168 ff. Sacral in the sense of the ἀναγγέλλειν-inscriptions is GDI, 3092 (Megaris, date unknown): the nomination of an εὐεργέτης (lines 7; 11 f.); the Psephisma, 15, ἐξαγγειλάντων the polemarchs.

[10] Ditt. Or., 383 (1st. cent. B.C.), 121 f.: νόμον δὲ τοῦτον φωνὴ μὲν ἐξήγγειλεν ἐμή, νοῦς δὲ θεῶν ἐκύρωσεν.

κ α τ α γ γ έ λ λ ω κτλ. [1] P. Oxy., X, 1274, 6: news of death; Jos. Ant., 20, 72: decla-ration of wars.

[2] Philo Op. Mund., 106: τὸν ἕβδομον ἀριθμὸν ... ἀμφοτέρας τὰς ἰσότητας καταγ-γέλλοντα.

[3] Boesch, ΘΕΩΡΟΣ (Ditt. Zür., 1908), 11, 2 for examples from the 2nd century B.C. To be noted are Ditt. Or., 319, 13: καταγγελία = ἐπηγγελμένα, 14. Similarly later, Epict. Diss., I, 29, 36, p. 105, 12 Sch.[2] (→ ἀγών metaphorically); Plut. Quaest. Conv., I, 4 (II, 622a): with κῆρυξ; this throughout. An ἀγών of the gods Ὁμήρῳ καταγγέλλεται on account of his despising of the gods, Pseud.-Heraclit. Quaest. Hom., I, 4 f. ed. Soc. Phil. Bon.

[4] P. Oxy., XI, 1381, 150: κατηγγελμένην ὑπόσχεσιν of an oath. In the same context ἀπαγγ. (*q.v.*, n. 18) and other words of sacral intimation.

[5] This is open to question, like the ἀναγγ. passage in Clement (*q.v.*, n. 16). Reference might be made to Heliodor. Aeth., III, 1, p. 78, 16 f., Bekker: αὐλοῦ ... τελεστικόν τε μέλος καὶ καταγγελτικὸν τῆς θυσίας; but what has been said under a. is enough to explain this, as also Philo.

[6] Ditt. Syll.[3], 797, 5 f. The inscription is also found in Wendland, *Hell. Kultur,* [2, 3] 410, No. 11.

εὐαγγελίζεσθαι, but also denoted by ἀγγέλλειν and διαγγέλλειν (→ 61, 62, 67 and 68).

The LXX makes no contribution. The only certain instances are in 2 Macc. 8:36 and 9:17, where Nicanor and Antiochus must declare the divine omnipotence. [7] Here we have a form of aretalogy usually conveyed by διαγγέλλειν, in which the opponent must be the messenger. Origen's Sexta has καταγγέλλειν for the important διαγέλλειν of LXX ψ 2:7. [8]

In Josephus καταγγέλλειν is used of God's promise to Abraham and through the prophets. [9] Here, too, the usage is synonym with ἐπαγγέλλεσθαι, but there is no case of a promise of God in Hellenism. This idea (→ ἐπαγγελία) is first found in Judaism.

B. καταγγέλλω in the NT.

In the NT the term is found 6 times in Paul and 11 in Acts. It is also used twice in Ignatius and once in Polycarp. It is always sacral.

The sense of promise is as infrequent as in Hellenism or Judaism. Only in Ac. 3:24 could it have this meaning: the prophets κατήγγειλαν τὰς ἡμέρας ταύτας (v. n. 12). In Ign. Phld., 5, 2; 9, 2, where we are to love the OT prophets διὰ τὸ καὶ αὐτοὺς εἰς τὸ εὐαγγέλιον κατηγγελκέναι, and where we are also told: προφῆται κατήγγειλαν εἰς αὐτόν, the word seems to mean "prophesy," as suggested by the context of 9, 2. [10] All the same, the intransitive use is striking; the thought of solemn proclamation is uppermost. [11] We should also construe Ac. 3:24 along similar lines; "promise" is → προκαταγγέλλω in v. 18. [12] The prophets are thought of as → καταγγελεῖς or heralds.

This seems to be the usual sense. The language of mission [13] loves such expressions as τὸν Χριστὸν καταγγέλλειν (Phil. 1:17; Col. 1:28), or Χριστὸς καταγγέλλεται (Phil. 1:18). These are equivalents of Χριστὸν κηρύσσειν (Phil. 1:15 etc.) and εὐαγγελίζεσθαι (Gl. 1:16 ff.). Similar phrases are τὸ εὐαγγέλιον καταγγέλλειν (1 Cor. 9:14), τὸν λόγον τοῦ θεοῦ (Ac. 13:5 and 17:13), τοῦ κυρίου (15:36), [14] in the sense of τὸ μαρτύριον [15] τοῦ θεοῦ (1 Cor. 2:1, synon. with λόγος, κήρυγμα, v. 4, cf. 1:18, 21). We should not distinguish a "weaker missionary meaning" in 1 C. 9:14 from the emphatic meaning in 1 C. 2:1 etc. [16] καταγγέλλειν shares with → εὐαγγέλιον and → λόγος "the emphatic meaning of a solemn religious message or teaching."

This sense is that of the proclamation or declaration of a completed happening rather than instruction marked off from others by distinctive formulations. The

---

[7] 8, 36: κατήγγελλεν ὑπέρμαχον ἔχειν τὸν θεὸν τοὺς Ἰουδ. (τὸν θεὸν V; om A, supported by the context) 9, 17: καταγγέλλοντα τὸ τοῦ θεοῦ κράτος.
[8] καταγγέλλων εἰς θεὸν διαθήκην. In ψ 39:6 Σ has καταγγέλλω instead of ἐλάλησα (LXX).
[9] Jos. Ant., 1, 183: παῖδα αὐτῷ γενήσεσθαι καταγγέλλει; 10, 61: οὐδὲν ἐψεύδετο τούτων ὧν αὐτὸς διὰ τῶν προφητῶν κατήγγειλε.
[10] οἱ γὰρ ἀγαπητοὶ προφῆται κατήγγειλαν εἰς αὐτόν· τὸ δὲ εὐαγγέλιον ἀπάρτισμά ἐστιν ἀφθαρσίας. The antithesis, however, is not καταγγέλλειν/εὐαγγέλιον, but εἰς αὐτόν/ἀπάρτισμα.
[11] Krüger in Hennecke² renders "prophesy" in both cases, W. Bauer in Hdbuch only in 9:2, but in WB in both cases "direct their proclamation to."
[12] C²pc Kosmas introduce it in v. 24 as well.
[13] Joh. W. 1 K. 45.
[14] ἐκηρύξαμεν C minn. cat.
[15] → μαρτύριον like → μυστήριον (vl) is a synon. for → εὐαγγέλιον.
[16] Joh. W., op. cit. He links with 1 C. 2:1 the verse 1 C. 11: 26 and 6 passages in Acts.

synonyms make this clear in Paul, and in Acts καταγγέλλειν reflects directly the language of mission. In 4:2 : καταγγέλλειν ἐν τῷ 'Ιησοῦ τὴν ἀνάστασιν τὴν ἐκ νεκρῶν : [17] the expectation of the ἀνάστασις νεκρῶν has become a reality "in Jesus" and is now declared. Similarly when Paul preaches to the Jews in 17:3 : ὅτι οὗτός ἐστιν ὁ Χριστός, ὁ 'Ιησοῦς, ὃν ἐγὼ καταγγέλλω ὑμῖν : the expected Messiah is now present. In both cases expectation is fulfilled in the name of Jesus. Synonymous is κηρύσσειν or εὐαγγελίζεσθαι τὸν 'Ιησοῦν, twice used in Acts. [18] In 13:38, too, ἄφεσις ἁμαρτιῶν means that the supreme expectation of the OT is fulfilled (cf. 10:43 etc.). [19] Similarly, when Paul preaches to the Gentiles in 17:23, that which is honoured in ἄγνοια, τοῦτο ἐγὼ καταγγέλλω ὑμῖν. It may thus be deduced that the formulae ὁδὸν σωτηρίας in 16:17 [20] and ἔθη καταγγέλλειν (Jewish) in 16:21 do not imply instruction on religious rules of life, but declaration or preaching. [21]

Christian liturgical language is seen in Ac. 26:23 (Is. 42:6, 9 ?): [22] ὁ Χρ... πρῶτος ἐξ ἀναστάσεως νεκρῶν φῶς μέλλει καταγγέλλειν τῷ τε λαῷ καὶ τοῖς ἔθνεσιν. With the eschatological raising of the dead commencing in Χριστός (R. 1:4), the intimation [23] goes out to all men that light has appeared, cf. 4:2. In 1 C. 11:26 : Τὸν θάνατον τοῦ Κυρίου καταγγέλλετε (indicative) does not refer to the Lord's Supper as an action. [24] This would be in keeping neither with the meaning of καταγγέλλειν nor with the Passover and mysteries. [25] We are rather to think of the words proclaimed in the Lord's Supper ; the death of the Lord is solemnly intimated. [26] A similar church usage is to be found in R. 1:8 : ἡ πίστις ὑμῶν καταγγέλλεται ἐν ὅλῳ τῷ κόσμῳ (cf. Pol. 1, 2); [27] καταγγ., like ἀναγγ., ἀπαγγ. and εὐαγγελ. in other places (→ 64; 65) means the declared work of God.

If καταγγέλλειν does not imply teaching of Christian content, nevertheless it does also include *paradosis* as in 1 C. 11:23 (→ n. 26), or νουθετεῖν and διδάσκειν as in Col. 1:28. [28] This corresponds to the basic OT view. Teaching and tradition are taken up into the word which proclaims the *Kurios Christos*. By its very nature, declaring the unique historical reality of Jesus, this word must also be instruction, admonition and tradition. But it is teaching which participates in the eschatological and dramatic character of the message.

---

[17] ἀναγγ. τὸν 'Ιησοῦν ἐν τῇ ἀναστάσει τῶν νεκρῶν in D is a twofold softening.
[18] κηρ. 9:20 (as Son of God); 19:13 : εὐαγγ. 5:42 (τὸν Χρ. 'Ι.); 8:35. Only once κηρ. τὸν Χρ., 8:5 and εὐαγγ. τὸν Κύριον 'Ιησοῦν, 11:20.
[19] καὶ μετάνοια D al., certainly a weakening (context !); derives from 5:31 etc.
[20] εὐαγγελίζοντες D*.
[21] → καταγγελεύς. Joh. W. also reckoned these passages emphatic.
[22] 6 leg. εἰς φῶς ἐθνῶν (despite B); 9 ἀναγγέλλω ἀναγγειλαι.
[23] The Comm. all relate καταγγέλλειν to the Gospel message But perhaps ὁ Χρ. Himself as the risen Lord is the message. Cf. Eph. 2:17: ἐλθὼν εὐηγγελίσατο κτλ. The Exalted, of course, speaks in the apostles (→ εὐαγγέλιον Χριστοῦ).
[24] This has mostly been accepted since Ltzm, Joh. W. 1 K.
[25] The Passover formulae (Str.-B., IV, 67 ff.), like the ancient liturgies (A. Dieterich, *Mithrasliturgie*[3] 1923, 213 ff.) prove that there is nowhere a δρώμενον without a significant word. Paul alludes to such a liturgy, traces of which may be seen again in the ἄχρι οὗ ἔλθῃ of v. 16.
[26] We then understand παρέλαβον, παρέδωκα (v. 23) of true *paradosis*, with Joh. W. *ad loc.*; Kittel Probleme, 63 f.; cf. H. Lietzmann, *Messe und Herrnmahl* (1926), 255.
[27] βεβαία τῆς πίστεως ὑμῶν ῥίζα, ἐξ ἀρχαίων καταγγελλομένη χρόνων.
[28] ὃν ἡμεῖς καταγγέλλομεν νουθετοῦντες πάντα ἄνθρωπον καὶ διδάσκοντες πάντα ἄνθρωπον.

C. προκαταγγέλλω, καταγγελεύς.

προκαταγγέλλω is found in the NT only[29] in Ac. 3:18: ὁ... θεὸς ἃ προκατήγγειλεν διὰ στόματος... τῶν προφητῶν, παθεῖν τὸν Χρ. αὐτοῦ, ἐπλήρωσεν and Ac. 7:52: ἀπέκτειναν τοὺς προκαταγγείλαντας περὶ τῆς ἐλεύσεως τοῦ δικαίου. In both cases the word of the prophets is a προκαταγγέλλειν.[30] In 3:18 it is God Himself who gives prior intimation. Cf. → ἐπαγγέλλεσθαι and → εὐαγγελίζεσθαι, though neither verb would be suitable here (παθεῖν τὸν Χρ.).[31]

Josephus, too, uses the phrase προκατηγγελμένα ὑπὸ τοῦ θεοῦ (of the birth of Moses).[32] It is also used of the ἄγγελος message to Hagar,[33] and of Joseph's prophecy to the cupbearer.[34]

καταγγελεύς is found in the NT only in Ac. 17:18: ξένων δαιμονίων καταγγελεὺς δοκεῖ εἶναι. These words repeat "what the Greek may often have said about the similar declaration of a new belief."[35] Yet καταγγελεύς is one who declares in the sense of a herald rather than a teacher.[36] Deissmann has shown this from a decree honouring Augustus, which calls those who declare the sacral *agones* καταγγελεῖς.[37] Similarly, on an inscription from the 1st century A.D., the κατα[γ]γε[λ]εύς of a sacred *agon* for the distribution of wreaths is call a "pious initiate."[38] Our conclusions concerning καταγγέλλειν are thus confirmed. In its Hellenistic sacral usage, it is preponderantly agonistic.[39] It rises to a higher status when it is adopted for the imperial cult[40] and the mysteries.[41] The messenger of Christ is also a herald. The word thus signifies the self-declaration of Christians (→ κῆρυξ), and is taken in this sense by contemporaries. Thus Ac. 17:18 confirms all that we have noted in the ἀγγελ-articles as a whole.

Schniewind

---

[29] In Ac. 3:24 and 2 C. 9:5 the attestation is poor and the true reading (→ καταγγέλλειν, n. 12, → προεπαγγέλλειν) is obvious. Though infrequently attested, the term seems to be a favourite one in ecclesiastical Greek, cf. examples in Thes. Steph and the dictionaries of Sophocles and Herwerden.

[30] Can we in 7:42 (Bengel, *ad loc.*) oppose the προ- to the νῦν (οὗ ὑμεῖς νῦν προδόται...)?

[31] Synon., however, προμαρτύρεσθαι in 1 Pt. 1:11.

[32] Ant., 2, 218. Here God Himself is the speaker (Traum, 212 ff.); previously (205 → ἀγγέλλειν) a ἱερογραμματεύς.

[33] Ant., 1, 219 (ἀγαθά, σωτηρία, προκατηγγελμένα).

[34] Ant., 2, 68 (προκαταγγείλαντός σοι τὰ ἀγαθά).

[35] Reitzenstein, *Nachr. Ges. Gött.* (1917), 134, 5.

[36] Deissmann, LO,[4] 77; cf. Liddell-Scott, *s.v.*; "one who proclaims," "herald."

[37] Ditt. Or., 456 (= IG, XII, 2, 58; Mytilene), 10: καταγγελεῖς τῶν πρώτων ἀ(χ)θησο[μένων ἀγώνων].

[38] IG, XII, 8, 190, 39 f.; cf. 37 f., 40-45.

[39] Cf. here too the relationship with ἐπαγγέλλεσθαι: καταγγελεύς = ἐπαγγελτήρ, *v.* Boesch, *op. cit.*

[40] In Ditt. Or., 456, 35-48: δόξα, τύχη, φύσις, θεοποιεῖν.

[41] ἀγὼν τῶν πυθ[ί]ων, IG, XII, 8, 190, 43-45.

ἄγγελος, ἀρχάγγελος,
ἰσάγγελος

---

† ἄγγελος.

A. ἄγγελος in the Greek and Hellenistic World.

1. The ἄγγελος is "one who brings a message," a "messenger." This meaning
is clear already in Homer (e.g., ὅτε τ᾽ ἤλυθε ... ἄγγελος ἐς Θήβας, Il., 5, 804,
cf. 18, 2). And in the time of Homer the role of the messenger is sacral. He stands
under the special protection of the gods (e.g., χαίρετε, κήρυκες, Διὸς ἄγγελοι
ἠδὲ καὶ ἀνδρῶν, Il., 1, 334, cf. 7, 274).[1] It is for this reason that Achilles does
not vent his wrath on the messengers of Agamemnon (Il., 1, 334 ff.). The task of
the messenger is to deliver messages. Since this is the only possibility of intercourse between men, he is accorded special divine protection.

Ἄγγελοι continue to play an important role in Greek life. Sophocles gives in
the Trachiniae a depiction of the work of the messenger. As the messenger of joy
he appears καταστεφής (178). He delivers his message and answers question
associated with it (180 ff.). He then asks for his reward (190 f.). On the messenger of joy, cf. also Xenoph. Hist. Graec., VI, 4, 19: ἔπεμψαν... ἄγγελον
ἐστεφανωμένον, καὶ ἅμα μὲν τῆς νίκης τὸ μέγεθος ἔφραζον, ἅμα δὲ βοηθεῖν
ἐκέλευον. ἄγγελος is also a technical term for an emissary, cf. Hdt., I, 36; Xenoph.
Hist. Graec., II, 1, 7 (ἀπεπέμφθησαν πρέσβεις, ξὺν αὐτοῖς καὶ παρὰ Κύρου
ταῦτα λέγοντες ἄγγελοι); I, 4, 2. The inscriptions give information on his
functions. He concludes treaties and delivers official messages (Ditt. Syll.[3], 273,
24 f.). He receives the tribute (ibid., 330, 26) and also the oath of the contracting
party (ibid., 229, 19 f., 25 : ὀρκῶσαι δὲ ἀγγέλους... ὀμόσαι δι᾽ ἀγγέλων βοη-
θήσειν, and 581, 93 : ὁ δὲ αἱρεθεὶς (sc. ἄγγελος) ... ὀρκιζάτω αὐτούς). The
last function brings out most clearly the sacral character of the ἄγγελος. In both
public and private dealings there is place for this office.

As messengers sent to men by the gods, birds play a great part, cf. Hom. Il.,
24, 292 : αἴτει δ᾽ οἰωνόν, ταχὺν ἄγγελον, Theogn., 549 f. : Ἄγγελος ἄφθογγος
πόλεμον πολύδακρυν ἐγείρει, Κύρν᾽, ἀπὸ τηλαυγέος φαινόμενος σκοπιῆς,

---

ἄ γ γ ε λ ο ς. On the whole article, O. Everling, Die paul. Angelologie u. Dämonologie
(1888); E. Cremer, RE,[3] V (1898), 364 ff.; M. Dibelius, Die Geisterwelt i. Glauben d. Pls.
(1909); Cr.-Kö., 19 ff.; F. Andres, Die Engellehre d. griech. Apologeten d. 2. Jhdts. u. ihr
Verhältnis z. griech.-röm. Dämonologie (1914); G. Kurze, Der Engels- und Teufelsglaube
d. Ap. Pls. (1915). On A, J. Schniewind, Euangelion, II (1931), 218 ff.; F. Andres, Pauly-
W., Suppl. III (1918), 101 ff.; T. Hopfner, Griech.-ägypt. Offenbarungszauber (1922/25),
v. Index ; F. Cumont, RHR, 72 (1915), 159 ff. On B, R. Smend., At.liche Religionsgesch.[2]
(1899), 122 ff., 449 ff.; G. Hölscher, Gesch. d. isr. u. jüd. Rel. (1922), 151 ff., 164, 183 f.;
W. H. Kosters, "De Mal'ach Jahwe", ThT, 9 (1875), 369 ff., 10 (1876), 34 ff., 113 ff.;
A. Jirku, Die Dämonen u. ihre Abwehr im AT (1912); H. Duhm, Die bösen Geister im AT
(1914). On C, A. Kohut, Über d. jüd. Angelologie u. Dämonologie in ihrer Abhängigkeit
v. Parsismus (1866); P. Volz, Jüd. Eschatologie (1903), v. Index, 384 ; B. Stade-A. Bertholet, Die jüd. Religion von d. Zeit Esras bis zur Zeit Christi (1911), 374 ff.; Meyer,
Ursprung, II, 106 ff.; Bousset-Gressm., 320 ff.; Moore, I, 401 ff., III, 123 f.; Str.-B., v.
Index, IV, 1223 f.; A. Marmorstein, "Anges et hommes dans l'Agada," REJ, 84 (1927),
37 ff., 138 ff.; EJ, VI (1930), 630 ff.
[1] On the synon. nature of → κῆρυξ and ἄγγελος cf. Hom. Od., 16, 468 f.; Xenoph. An.,
II, 3, 1-4.

Plut. Pyth. Or., 22 (II, 405d): θεῶν ἄγγελοι καὶ κήρυκες (sc. ἐρωδιοὶ καὶ τρόχιλοι καὶ κόρακες), and cf. also Xenoph. Symp., 4, 48 : (θεοὶ) πέμποντες ἀγγέλους φήμας, καὶ ἐνύπνια καὶ οἰωνούς. In Epictetus the philosopher himself appears finally as the ἄγγελος καὶ κατάσκοπος καὶ κῆρυξ τῶν θεῶν (Diss., III, 22, 69, p. 306, 19 f., Sch.).

2. "The earthly sacral ἄγγελος is the prototype of the heavenly ἄγγελοι." [2] The heavenly ἄγγελος in the strict sense is Hermes. Plato attempts to bring his name into relation with his function : ... ἔοικε περὶ λόγον τι εἶναι ὁ ᾽"Ἑρμῆς," καὶ τὸ ἑρμηνέα εἶναι καὶ τὸ ἄγγελον ... (Crat., 407e). In Homer he is addressed by Zeus as follows : σὺ γὰρ αὖτε τά τ᾽ ἄλλα περ ἄγγελός ἐσσι᾽, Od. 5, 29, [3] cf. Hom. Hymn. Cer., 407: ἐριούνιος ἄγγελος ὠκύς, Hymn. Merc. 3 : ἄγγελος ἀθανάτων ἐριούνιος cf. Kern Orph., 297a, 1: Ἑρμῆς δ᾽ ἑρμηνεὺς τῶν πάντων ἄγγελός ἐστι. Alongside Hermes other divine messengers are occasionally mentioned. [4]

There are chthonic as well as heavenly ἄγγελοι. Plato mentions the messenger from the underworld (ὁ ἐκεῖθεν ἄγγελος, Resp., X, 619b). As psychopomp Hermes is given the title ἄγγελος, cf. ᾽Άγγελε Φερσεφονῆς, Ἑρμῆ ... [5] Nemesis is called by Plato Δίκης ... ἄγγελος, Leg., IV, 717d. Similarly, Hecate herself, who is linked with Artemis, is described as ἄγγελος. [6] Together with these, there are the ἄγγελοι of the underworld. They are found on the Attic curse-tables, e.g., καταγράφω καὶ κατατίθω ἀνγέλοις καταχθονίοις Ἑρμῆ καταχθονίῳ καὶ Ἑκάτη καταχθονίᾳ Πλούτωνι καὶ Κόρη (another has δαίμοσι for ἀνγέλοις). [7] Frequent mention is also found on the gravestones of Thera, where ἄγγελος is everywhere present. [8] These final examples brings us into the time of post-Christian Hellenism, with its syncretistic character, and there is always the possibility here of Christian Jewish influence. Schniewind remarks on the whole evidence : "The basic view of divine messengers must be very old. It spread over the whole of the Greek world with no spatial restrictions." [9] Greek and Hellenistic religion thus felt itself to be in connexion with divinity through the divine messengers.

The magic papyri belong to the syncretistic field, which was strongly permeated by Christian Jewish influences. On magic incantations we find ὃν ἐκάλεσας ἄγγελον πεμφθέντα σοι, θεῶν δὲ βουλὰς συντόμως γνώσῃ, it being even said of the ἄγγελος : λέγε ταῦτα πρὸς τὸν ἄγγελον᾽ λαλήσει γάρ σοι συντόμως, πρὸς ὃ ἐὰν βούλῃ Preis. Zaub., I, 76 ff. Some ἄγγελος is conjured up: ὁρκίζω σε, τὸν ἐν τῷ τόπῳ τούτῳ μὲν ἄγγελον κραταιὸν καὶ ἰσχυρὸν τοῦ ζώου τούτου (III, 71 f.). This ἄγγελος, too, is to accomplish his task. In the Mithras liturgy there is reference to θεοὶ ἢ ἄγγελοι (IV, 570) and ἀρχάγγελος (IV, 483). Clear Jewish influence may be discerned in I, 206, III, 339 and especially IV, 2357.

3. Thus far we have been concerned with popular religion. We must now turn to that of the philosophers. It has a developed *logos* theology. The connexion

---

[2] Schn. Euang., 216.
[3] Elsewhere in Homer Iris is the ἄγγελος of the gods (Il., 2, 786; 3, 121).
[4] Cf. Schn. Euang., 222 ff.
[5] On a stone in Naples, *v.* Schn. Euang., 226 — the only example.
[6] Cf. Schn. Euang., 225, where there are other references.
[7] Cf. Dibelius, 212 for examples.
[8] IG, XII, 3, 933-974; cf. on this Schn. Euang., 233 f.
[9] Schn. Euang., 237.

→ λόγος/ἄγγελος [10] is present. This is brought about by the relating of the *logos* theology to Hermes. The link is fully made by Philo, to whom it is suggested by his allegorising of the Hebrew מַלְאָךְ which is, however, divested of its Jewish character : τὸν δὲ ἄγγελον, ὅς ἐστι λόγος, ὥσπερ ἰατρὸν κακῶν, Leg. All., III, 177; cf. Som., I, 239 : τὴν τοῦ θεοῦ εἰκόνα, τὸν ἄγγελον αὐτοῦ λόγον and Mut. Nom., 87: ἄγγελος ὑπηρέτης θεοῦ, λόγος... Thus, where a single angel is introduced in the Bible, he can be identified by Philo with the *logos*. Philo adopts Jewish angelology in general and links it with Greek and Hellenistic demonology. Angels and demons are depicted as powers and movements of the universe. Cf. Gig., 16 : ψυχὰς οὖν καὶ δαίμονας καὶ ἀγγέλους ὀνόματα μὲν διαφέροντα, ἓν δὲ καὶ ταὐτὸν ὑποκείμενον διανοηθείς (*v.* also Gig., 6); concerning their function, cf. Plant., N 14... ἃς (sc. ψυχαὶ καθαρώταται) οἱ μὲν παρ' Ἕλλησι φιλοσοφήσαντες ἥρωας καλοῦσι, Μωυσῆς δὲ ὀνόματι εὐθυβόλῳ χρώμενος ἀγγέλους προσαγορεύει, πρεσβευομένας καὶ διαγγελλούσας τά τε παρὰ τοῦ ἡγεμόνος τοῖς ὑπηκόοις ἀγαθὰ καὶ τῷ βασιλεῖ ὧν εἰσιν οἱ ὑπήκοοι χρεῖοι. Spec. Leg., I, 66 : ... ἱερέας δὲ τοὺς ὑποδιακόνους αὐτοῦ τῶν δυνάμεων ἀγγέλους... and Conf. Ling., 28 : κατὰ τῶν θείων καὶ ἱερῶν λόγων... οὓς καλεῖν ἔθος ἀγγέλους.

4. Josephus, the Greek speaking Palestinian, uses the term ἄγγελος in the twofold sense of "messenger" and "angel."

In the first sense it is used in, e.g., Ant. 7, 249 : ... τοῦ δ' ἄγγελον εἶναι φήσαντος ἀγαθῶν... ἀγαθῶν ἄγγελον τοῦτον ἔφησεν εἶναι. When questioned, the messenger delivers his message : καὶ πυθομένῳ περὶ τῆς μάχης νίκην εὐαγγελίζεται καὶ κράτος, 250. This is wholly in accord with Greek custom. Yet the agreement does not arise so much from dependence as from the necessities of intercourse.

But the word is also used in the sense of angel. Here Josephus adopts OT views, but he also contributes his own thoughts, as when he calls the angel (ἄγγελος θεῖος) which met Balaam θεῖον πνεῦμα (Ant., 4, 108), when he causes Agrippa solemnly to declare : μαρτύρομαι... τὰ ἅγια καὶ τοὺς ἱεροὺς ἀγγέλους τοῦ θεοῦ καὶ πατρίδα τὴν κοινήν (Bell., 2, 401), or when, following Palestinian tradition, he introduces angels at the giving of the Law : ... ἡμῶν τὰ κάλλιστα τῶν δογμάτων καὶ τὰ ὁσιώτατα τῶν ἐν τοῖς νόμοις δι' ἀγγέλων παρὰ τοῦ θεοῦ μαθόντων... (Ant., 15, 136). Some speculations concerning angels are alien to him (→ 80), though he attributes them expressly to the Essenes (Bell., 2, 142). "Josephus shows... how firmly in the case of the Jews the term ἄγγελος was bound up with the notion of angels... Hellenistic rationalism resists this notion... and in his evaluation of angels Josephus is dominated by the Hellenistic outlook." [11]

Grundmann

B. מַלְאָךְ in the OT.

מַלְאָךְ, which is found also in Phoenician, is a nominal construction from the root לאך of which there are no examples in Hebrew (Arab. *la'aka* "to send with a commission"). The basic element of meaning in the nominal is that of one who is sent, though originally the thought was perhaps abstract.

---

[10] Cf. καὶ τὴν ἀποστελλομένην Ἶριν ἄγγελον τοῦ Διὸς τὸν αἴροντα λόγον ὑφίσταται..., Pseud.-Heracl. Quaest. Hom., 28, p. 43, 8 (cf. Pauly-W., XIII, 1065).
[11] A. Schlatter, *Wie sprach Josephus von Gott?* (1910), 33 f.; on Josephus' conception of angels, *ibid.*, 32; cf. also Schl. Lk., 633 f.

Hence מַלְאָךְ. is a. the "messenger" sent by a man, or less frequently God. [12] Any man who has a special commission to fulfil is a מ'. Concerning the use of the term for a man there is no need for further discussion. The word also signifies b. a "heavenly being charged by God with some commission," i.e., "an angel." In this sense, too, the word retains its inherent meaning of being sent with a commission. [13]

1. The most important angelic form, most frequently mentioned, almost always attested in the OT in distinction from other angelic beings who occur only occasionally and collectively, [14] and supremely sent by God with a commission, is the מַלְאַךְ יְהֹוה the angel of Yahweh. The מ' י' is the one figure in the angelic world of the OT which is more personal, and sketched in more precise religious terms. To gain a clearer picture it is best to start with the more popular attestation rather than with passages which betray a theological tendency. In the faith of older Israel this angel is not a terrifying being, but a friendly and helpful messenger of God (2 S. 14:17, 20; 1 S. 29:9) in whom one may confide (2 S. 19:28). He smites the foes of Israel (2 K. 19:35), helps Elijah (1 K. 19:7), resists Balaam (Nu. 22:22), protects Israel at the Red Sea (Ex. 14:19), guides the people (Ex. 23:20), and fulfils many other commissions (Ju. 6:11 ff.; 13:3 ff.; 2 K. 1:3, 15). This older idea, which was certainly very popular, is retained in even the most complex theological passages. In Zechariah the מ' י' has basically no other task [15] than in the earliest periods. He helpfully represents the interests of Israel (1:12 and esp. 3:2).

The מ' י', however, is not a messenger, like other angelic beings in different circumstances. His significance is to be an express instrument of the particular relationship of grace which Yahweh has with Israel. He is the personification of Yahweh's assistance to Israel. Only in exceptional circumstances does he have to turn against Israel (2 S. 24:17), [16] the prospering of Israel being otherwise his exclusive office.

In some stories, especially in Genesis, there is such striking reference to the מ' י' that these passages deserve special mention. We refer to Gn. 16:7 ff.; 21:17 ff.; 22:11 ff.; 31:11 ff.; Ex. 3:2 ff.; Ju. 2:1 ff. What distinguishes these passages from the others is that it is impossible in them to differentiate between the מ' י' and Yahweh Himself. The One who speaks or acts, i.e., Yahweh or the מ' י', is obviously one and the same person. Yet in the apparently haphazard alternation between the two there is a certain system. When the reference is to God apart from man, Yahweh is used; when God enters the apperception of man, the מ' י' is introduced. Thus in Gn. 21:17 ff. God hears the cry of Hagar, the angel calls to her, and God opens her eyes. This obvious trend explains the peculiar facts.

---

[12] E.g., prophets, Hag. 1:13; Is. 44:26; 2 Ch. 36:15, or priests. Mal. 2:7, Ecc. 5:5.

[13] Babylonian religion, too, speaks of divine messengers, the son of the existing god usually being his messenger. However, the Accadian word does not correspond etymologically to the Hebrew מַלְאָךְ. There are serious linguistic and material objections to the attempt by Schröder (ZAW, 34, 172 f.) to understand מַלְאָךְ as an Amorite name for God.

[14] The attestation becomes rare only in post-canonical writings, though there is none at all in pre-exilic prophecy.

[15] However, there is here a certain broadening in the sense that in Zechariah the מַלְאַךְ יְהֹוה stands at the head of the entourage of Yahweh as well as having his particular office in relation to Israel.

[16] The parallel in Chronicles shows that at this later date he was thought to be of superhuman size (1 Chr. 21:16), standing between heaven and earth with his sword stretched out over Jerusalem. In distinction from 2 S. 24 he also blossoms out here as *angelus interpres*.

Originally the stories probably referred quite naively to purely sensual theophanies. The editors then softened this primitive tradition in the interests of strict transcendence by interposing the figure of the מ' י' as Yahweh's mode of manifestation. [17] This speculative reshaping of older traditions, which is so striking in the OT, is an important literary theologisation, but it does not express any widespread belief, and cannot therefore be claimed as the specific conception of the מ' י' current in Israel.

In yet another form theological reflection has taken control of this otherwise simple figure of popular belief. When Yahweh was angry at Horeb, He refused to guide Israel through the wilderness in case His holiness consumed the people. He thus sent His angel as guide (Ex. 33:2 f.). Here, too, the מ' י' is an executive of the covenant of grace; Yahweh conceals His glory from Israel and sends the mediator for the preservation of the people. [18]

2. In addition to the מ' י' the older Israelite view introduces other heavenly beings, though it is only rarely that these are called מַלְאָכִים. Nevertheless, it is justifiable not merely to refer to the passages which expressly speak of מַלְאָכִים but also to discuss those which mention heavenly beings which might be called מ', or which obviously are, even though the term itself is not used. The beings seen by Jacob in his dream ascending and descending the ladder, or the members of the heavenly court coming in and going out before Yahweh, [19] may be described at once as מַלְאָכִים even though they are called בְּנֵי הָאֱלֹהִים, which roughly means heavenly beings. [20] The notion that Yahweh is surrounded by a host of heavenly beings who assist in His world governance and praise Him etc. is quite current even in pre-exilic Israel, though it is only at rare moments of vision that they enter the perception of man. A distinctive feature of this heavenly entourage of Yahweh is its warlike character. [21] Perhaps the יְהוָה צְבָאוֹת refers to these beings.

The fact that especially stories which contain older ἱεροὶ λόγοι of shrines treat so readily of the entry of such heavenly beings leads us to suspect that there is at least an enrichment of the heavenly court from the Canaanite religion native to Palestine prior to the conquest. It is thus the more surprising that in no case do these angelic beings have autonomous functions or spheres of influence alongside Yahweh, and that they are never objects of worship. Belief in the overpowering uniqueness of Yahweh has reduced these beings, who must surely have played a much more significant role in the older stories, [22] to little more than supernumeraries, yet with no violation of the absolute transcendence of Yahweh.

3. A strange phenomenon, for which there is as yet no adequate explanation from the standpoint of the history of religion, is the development of the previously

---

[17] The Elohist goes a step further in this direction by causing the מ' י' to call down from heaven (Gn. 21:17; 22:11), whereas in the Jahwist men meet him on earth.

[18] It is impossible to decide whether Malachi's מ' הַבְּרִית (3:1) is meant to be the מ' י'. In view of the fact that he is called מַלְאָכִי i.e., מ' י', and that the conclusion of a covenant is ascribed to the מ' י' in Ju. 2:1 ff., this is quite likely. In any case, this figure, too, is an executive of Yahweh's particular relationship of grace.

[19] Job 1. The framework of the Book of Job, the popular tale, is almost certainly pre-exilic.

[20] בֵּן is never used in this connexion in the physical or genealogical sense, but in that of "belonging to." Cf. בְּנֵי הַנְּבִיאִים for disciples of the prophets rather than sons.

[21] Cf. Gn. 32:1 f.; Jos. 5:13; Ju. 5:20; 1 K. 22:19; 2 K. 6:17.

[22] E.g., in Gn. 18 f.; 28:12; 32:1 f.

restricted belief in angels after the exile, leading ultimately to a veritable angelology. We are faced by the fact that for a long period, under pressure from polytheism, Israel had had no angelology. In exilic and post-exilic times the belief in angels then became more prominent. More intensive contact with outside religions undoubtedly had some influence, yet hardly explains the matter. We have also to reckon with the fact that in a unique religious situation suppressed illegitimate gods or demons may sometimes have re-emerged in harmless forms. [23] In Israel itself the increasingly austere transcendentalising of Yahweh may have favoured the interest in concrete mediatorial beings. Yet when we investigate the attestation in exilic and early post-exilic Scripture, we are hardly justified in speaking of an angelology in the narrower sense. We must be careful not to construct a system where there is no need for it.

An insight into the new outlook is afforded by the Book of Job, which speaks of the angelic world with no dogmatic pretensions. The verdict as to their nature is expressed in their description as קְדֹשִׁים [24] Yet their holiness is limited; they are not pure compared with God (Job 4:18; 15:15). They were witnesses of creation, which they greeted with songs of joy (Job 38:7). They could be called upon in times of need (Job 5:1), some of them possibly being intercessors (Job 33:23). The angel of death came to the dying (Job 33:22; Prv. 16:14). Similar references may be found in the Psalter. [25]

The prophets, in whose proclamation so many fused mythologoumena have been retained, give full attestation of the change indicated, though one should not generalise from their detailed statements. Ezekiel is the first prophet in whose visions an interpreting mediatorial being (אִישׁ) is introduced (40:3 ff.). A distinctive world opens up in Zechariah, in whom the מַלְאַךְ יְהֹוָה blossoms out as an *angelus interpres* and who also introduces heavenly riders, smiths and winged creatures, all at the command of Yahweh. Nevertheless these visions bear a strongly individual imprint. Even some of the later Psalms know nothing of such sharply delineated heavenly figures, and the priestly code, in whose theology there is no place for angels, stands as a possible bulwark against the growing incorporation of heavenly beings into the faith of Israel.

Concerning the period immediately following the first post-exilic age we know very little in certain respects. For instance, we cannot say how long interest in the angelic world remained slight in theological circles. The apocalyptic trend already emerging in Ezekiel and Zechariah indicates a different outlook. Yet the angelic beings in whom the speakers in Job believe do not in any sense belong to the sphere of the religious problem discussed. In Daniel there is unfolded a picture which indicates the operation of opposing heavenly forces. To the partly increased interest in these forces there corresponds the fact that here for the first time the angels are named. [26] Directly under God stand the archangels (שַׂר). Michael is the guardian angel of Israel, and there are references also to the guardian angels of other countries (Da. 10:13, 20), to guardian angels generally (Da. 4:10, 14, 20), and to hundreds of thousands of angelic servants surrounding the throne (Da. 7:10). There thus opens a new phase in the history of the Jewish

---

[23] Esp. angelic beings which betray some connection with the stars may embody such a heritage, cf. Is. 24:21; Job 38:7; Da. 4:10.
[24] Job 5:1; 15:15; Ps. 89:6, 8; Zech. 14:5; Da. 8:13.
[25] Ps. 78:49; 89:6, 8; 9:11; 103:20; 148:2.
[26] Da. 10:13, 21; 12:1, Michael; 8:15 f.; 9:21, Gabriel.

belief in angels. Though there are still variations in detail, a constant doctrine of the heavenly hierarchy begins to take shape, and here at last, in the final book of the OT canon, we can speak of OT angelology.

> Externally, these heavenly messengers are depicted by the Hebrews in human form and without wings. [27] In OT literature there are also references to beings in the form of animals, the seraphim and cherubim, though these are not to be counted as מַלְאָכִים. [28] The cherubim, mixed creatures like birds which are known to the whole of the ancient Orient, indicate where they occur the proximity of the Godhead. [29] Even more clearly outside the sphere of the present discussion are the earthly demonic beings [30] sometimes mentioned in the OT. Quite apart from the fact that they are not to be thought of as heavenly beings, they do not have the slightest religious significance. At this point, in contrast with Babylonian and Egyptian religion, in which everyday life was a tormenting struggle with demons, we are confronted by a distinctive element in OT belief, namely, that Yahweh is the only creative causality in nature and history. In principle, therefore, the belief in demons is strangled. Israel attributes to Yahweh happenings which other religions attributed at once to demons. [31] This is ultimately a result of the OT concept of creation, which is never violated at any point; even the OT belief in angels bears strong witness to it in its specific form and more particularly in the circumspection with which it is developed.
>
> *von Rad*

C. The Doctrine of Angels in Judaism.

1. The development within Judaism is not uniform. To be sure, the tradition concerning the angel of Yahweh is present, and hardly anywhere is it completely set aside. But while the OT tradition on the one side was being broadened and refashioned into a full-scale angelology, under the influence of Greek rationalism influences were asserting themselves which so fully suppressed the idea of angels as almost completely to destroy it.

The OT apocryphal writings, with the exception of Tobit, remain for the most part within the limits of what was passed down from the OT. In them we still find the ἄγγελος τοῦ θεοῦ (κυρίου) [32] which elsewhere tends to be submerged under the individualising and naming of angels. In the free-thinking of the Sadducees speculations concerning angels certainly played no part, even though the charge in Ac. 23:8 may be a little exaggerated. [33] Josephus was no Sadducee, and basically he did not deny the existence of angels (→ 76), but in many of the OT stories he substituted visions (φάντασμα) for angelic appearances. [34] Thus in him, too,

---

[27] They need a leader (Gn. 28:12) and can be described quite easily as אִישׁ (Jos. 5:13; Ez. 40:3; Da. 10:5).

[28] The distinction is hard to make, of course, for in Is. 6 the seraphim have the same essential function as the בְּנֵי הָאֱלֹהִים.

[29] Only later Judaism incorporated these beings and other things (ophannim) into its angelology.

[30] שֵׁדִים, שְׂעִירִים etc.

[31] Any recollections of demonic beings and operations which still survived from pre-Israelite tradition were absorbed into the Israelite concept of Yahweh; cf. Gn. 32:25 ff.

[32] Sus. 55, 59; Bel. 34. In Ex. 3:2 the Tg. J. I. introduces the name Zagzag'el (to be read for זגנוגאל) Ex. r., 2 on 3:2 (R. Jochanan and R. Chanina) bring in the names Michael and Gabriel; Str.-B., II, 680.

[33] There is no direct evidence that the Sadducees completely denied the existence of angels.

[34] Bell., 5, 381; Ant., 1, 331; 5, 213 (Schl. Lk., 634).

we can see rationalistic influence. It is worth noting that he reports preoccupation with the names of angels to be an inner concern of the Essenes. [35]

It is in apocalyptic from the days of Daniel [36] that we find the starting-point and centre of more developed angelic speculation. Once the immediacy of early prophecy comes to an end, the angels serve to mediate the secrets of nature, the heavenly world and the last age. At the same time the example of the heroes of other religions may have strengthened the inclination to describe the intercourse of such figures as Enoch with members of the heavenly world. [37] Above all, the influence of dualism, which contributed so strongly to the nature and character of apocalyptic, helped to develop the fact of the divine מַלְכוּת in terms of the counter-notion of the other kingdom. In this as in other connection the Essenes participated in the dualistic movement. [35] There can be little doubt that this, and the associated development of the doctrine of angels, may be traced back to oriental and particularly Parsee influence. [38] Even Rabbinic tradition preserves a recollection that at this point there is an outworking amongst the Jews of the exile in Babylon. [39]

It appears that contemporaneously or very shortly afterwards the new angelic doctrine became part of popular piety as reflected, e.g., in the Book of Tobit. The syncretistic belief in spirits and demons may have helped to further this process. Nevertheless, the strength of the development can be explained only by the fact that the new aspects were not thought to be new or strange, but rather to fulfil the meaning of OT teaching. Only in this way at any rate can we understand the ease with which the Rabbis accepted angelology. It became a general possession of pious circles maintaining biblical belief. This sense was undoubtedly strengthened by the contrary tendency of the rationalism which they contested to dissolve the whole belief in angels. In this antithesis lay further legitimation for the Rabbis to affirm angelology even when the original interest in its acceptance had long since disappeared.

2. For the Rabbis the test of the acceptability of a doctrine is its relation to belief in God. Aversion to Gnosticism has its basis in the fact that this can lead to the theory of a second god. [40] The doctrine of angels is recognised to be a legitimate development of OT ideas because it never entails the independent divinisation of angels, nor even seems to show tendencies in this direction. Here, indeed, we see the basic difference from the good spirits met with in other religious circles. The angels of Judaistic angelology are always a naive representation of the omnipresent and omniscient Word and will of Yahweh. "Wherever Michael appears, is the Shekinah glory," Ex. r., 2 on 3:2. Even in the most developed angelology the angels only serve to execute and reveal the power and deity of Yahweh; [41] they are His court, and train, and ambassadors.

---

[35] These names were kept secret within the sect.

[36] Many examples from Enoch, Baruch and Test. XII are given in Bousset-Gressm.

[37] Cf. EJ, 631 for a reference to the Babylonian legends concerning the intercourse between gods and heroes.

[38] Cf. esp. Meyer, Hölscher, op. cit.; also Moore, I, 404.

[39] jRH, 56d E: "Even the names of angels are brought back with them from Babylon"; Str.-B., II, 90.

[40] Esp. plain in the story of the 4 Rabbis who entered Paradise (bChag., 14b/15a); Acher comes to exclaim that perhaps there are two deities.

[41] So esp. Moore, I, 404 f.

Hence in much of Rabbinic literature [42] the angels are simply introduced to give colour to the OT stories without any sense of modifying the sense or meaning. God consults them at the creation of man; [43] they express doubts at the offering of Isaac (Gn. r., 56 on 22:9); they appear at Sinai and take part in the giving of the Law. [44] They rule nature and the natural orders, [45] and guide the nations. [46] They accompany and protect man, [47] having a role in his death and final judgment. [46]

But Rabbinic teaching always sees to it that they do not detract from God and His rule. Even the angels of the foes of Israel must bow to His will. [48] The fact that they are thought to have taken part in creation does not alter the truth that they themselves were created in the course of creation, [49] and indeed that God daily creates or destroys angels to His own praise (Gn. r., 78 on 32:26; bChag., 14a). Everywhere, for all the strong differences of opinion, we see the attempt to keep angels subordinate in relation to God. Along with the view underlying Mt. 18:10, i.e., that angels see the face of God, [50] the contrary view is represented (S. Lv. 1:1) in Tannaitic discussion in the circle of Aqiba. Sometimes it is emphasised that they know what is concealed and future, [51] sometimes that they do not know it, [52] and in part that they learn it from the righteous, [53] so that the latter are above angels. The reason for such vacillation is obviously the constantly felt need to stress their subordination to God.

This concern expressed in all angelic speculation naturally works together with the common concept of God to affect the relation between angels and men. In large measure the guiding or guardian angels are representatives and executors of the divine care and direction, especially in the case of the pious. [47] They speak on behalf of God, [54] especially Michael. [55] They convey prayers from all the synagogues to God, and set them like crowns on His head. [56] But nowhere in true Judaism [57] is the awareness lost that in reality the prayer of the pious is ultimately a matter between God and man alone. "When necessity arises, a man should not call on Michael or Gabriel, but he should call on Me and I will answer him" (jBer., 13a).

---

[42] If angels do not appear in the Mishnah, this is because of its essentially halachic character. They are not avoided in the contemporary tannaitic Midrashim.

[43] bSanh., 38b, etc.; Str.-B., I, 203; III, 249, 681, 782.

[44] S.Nu., 102 on 12:5 (the reference to the giving of the Law derives from a quotation from Ps. 68:17, in which Sinai is mentioned). Cf. also M. Ex. 20:18; Pes. r., 21 (p. 104a) etc. → 83; n. 64. Further examples are given by Marmorstein EJ, 643.

[45] Str.-B., III, 819 f.

[46] Str.-B., IV, 1224 (Index).

[47] On the idea of the guardian angel, cf. Str.-B., I, 781 ff., III, 437 ff.; Schl. Mt., 551. Cf. also → 86.

[48] Gn. r., 56 on 22:9; God binds but also releases them.

[49] For the creation of the angels before Eden, Gn. r., 21 on 3:24; on the second day of creation, Ex. r., 15 on 12:12; Gn. r., 11 on 2:3.

[50] Schl. Mt., 551 compares the angel who is שַׂר הַפָּנִים = ἄρχων τοῦ προσώπου, Tanch. (Buber), ואתחנן, 6, p. 12.

[51] bSanh., 38b; jSanh., 18 (Str.-B., I, 961).

[52] 4 Esr. 4:52; bSanh., 99a.

[53] Tanch. בלק 14; Tanch. (Buber) בלק 23, p. 145; jShab., 8d M.

[54] Tg. Job 33:23; Test. XII: L, 5; D, 6; jQid., 61d M; bShab., 32a (Str.-B., 560 f.).

[55] W. Lueken, Michael (1898).

[56] Ex. r., 21 on 14:15. Cf. also good works, gBar., 11 ff.; misdeeds, En. 99:3.

[57] Cf. the conclusions on the cult of angels in popular religion in Bousset-Gressm., 330 f.

D. ἄγγελος in the NT.

1. The meaning of human messenger plays only a very small role in the NT. The scouts sent out by Joshua to Jericho in Jm. 2:25, the men sent by John to Jesus in Lk. 7:24 and by Jesus to the Samaritan village in Lk. 9:52, are the only cases in which men sent by other men are called ἄγγελοι in the NT.

Jesus in Mt. 11:10 par. (cf. Mk. 1:2), applying the OT promise,[58] interprets John the Baptist to be the messenger of the covenant preceding the day of the Lord. Originally the expectation may have been focused on either a human messenger or a heavenly angel,[59] but it is now linked with the concrete person of the Baptist as the messenger of God. The passage shows how the different meanings may merge into one another. The possibility has also to be considered that the application of the promise to the Baptist is conditioned by the various influences on the conception of message discussed in the earlier article on the root ἀγγελ-. This ἄγγελος is a predecessor to prepare the way, bearing the proclamation of Christ (→ 57 f.).

If there are no other instances in which the term is used of human messengers, this is not accidental. It simply derives from the fact that ἄγγελος is now mostly used for angels. In many cases messengers are now denoted by such simple alternatives as πεμφθείς in Lk. 7:10 or ἀπεσταλμένος in Lk. 19:32. Those sent are in many cases identical with men elsewhere described as ἀπόστολοι and μαθηταί (Mt. 10:5, 16; 11:2; Mk. 6:7 etc.).

2. a. The OT Jewish view of angels as representatives of the heavenly world and messengers of God is taken over quite naturally by the men of the NT. The angels represent the other world[60] (Hb. 12:22; 1 Tm. 5:21). To be like them is to reflect this world (Ac. 6:15). To be compared with them is to be compared with what is divine (Gl. 4:14). To be a spectacle to them is to offer such to all who dwell in heaven (1 C. 4:9).[61]

As in Judaism, there is reference to OT scenes involving angels, e.g., the visits of the angels to Abraham (Gn. 18) and Lot (Gn. 19)[62] in Hb. 13:2; or the appearance of the angel to Moses (Ex. 3:2)[63] in Ac. 7:30, 35; or the part of the angels in the giving of the Law in Ac. 7:53, Gl. 3:19 and Hb. 2:2.

The latter tradition is intimated already in LXX Dt. 33:2. Pes. r., 21 traces it back to an early tradition. The task of the angels is variously explained,[64] but always in such a way as to stress the importance of the process. The application of the idea in Gl. 3:19 and Hb. 2:2 to prove the inferiority of the Law which is given "only" by angels is not Jewish, but indicates the specific Christianising of the tradition (→ n. 44), strengthened perhaps by recollections of non-Christian and non-Jewish ἄγγελοι (→ 57). In contrast, Ac. 7:38 brings out the uniform estimation of the role of angel probably characteristic of pre-Pauline, Jewish Christianity. Jd. 9 makes use of another Jewish tradition[65] concerning the conflict between Michael (→ ἀρχάγγελος) and the

---

[58] It is obvious that the quotation from Mal. 3:1 stands under the influence of Ex. 23:20.

[59] → n. 18; cf. now O. Holtzmann, ARW, 29 (1931), 1 ff.

[60] The world in which there is no marriage, Mk. 12:25 and par.

[61] The thought present in Sl. En., 62, 12 intertwines with a favourite Stoic picture, Sen. Prv., 2, 9; Ltzm., ad loc.; A. Schweitzer, Die Mystik d. Ap. Pls. (1930), 149.

[62] Cf. Philo Abr., 107 ff.; Josephus Ant., 1, 196; For the discussion of the rabbis at the marriage of the son of R. Gamaliel II, bQid., 32b.

[63] Cf. Ex. r., 2 on 3:2.

[64] For various instances and interpretations of the tradition, v. Str.-B., III, 554 ff.

[65] For the connection with Ass. Mos., cf. Schürer, III, 294 ff.; Wnd. Jd., ad loc.; Lueken 120 ff.

devil over the body of Moses, but this reference is already suppressed in 2 Pt. 2:11, probably because it does not derive from the canonical OT. The true interest in Jude is to emphasise that even the archangel does not anticipate the judgment of God (ἐπι- τιμήσαι σοι κύριος). In the parable of Jesus, too, we find the idea of the angels as God's messengers bringing the dead to Abraham's bosom (Lk. 16:22).

b. Jesus is for early Christianity the presence of God and His lordship. This view finds expression in the fact that the early Christian narratives see an angelic accompaniment of the story of Jesus. Angels appear particularly in the birth and resurrection stories. Otherwise their ministry is mentioned only at special points such as the temptation (Mt. 4:11 and par.) and Gethsemane (Lk. 22:43), though it was always regarded as possible (Mt. 26:53). For the Evangelists it confirms and expresses the nature of Jesus. This is shown in Jn. 1:51 by the comparison with Jacob's ladder; [66] the Son of Man is surrounded by angels signifying His union with God. The restraint of the accounts is equally striking. Only in the later strata (Mt. 28:2 f.) do we find any tendency to speak of the independent activity of angels or to describe their figures. [67] There is no permeation of the Gospel narrative as a whole with angelic appearances of different kinds. In so far as they do not serve Jesus directly, the angels are occasional heralds of the divine action. The infancy stories, in which angelic appearances play the strongest role, are content to introduce only Gabriel (Lk. 1:26 ff.) or the angel of the Lord known to the OT (Mt. 1:20 ff.; 2:13; Lk. 1:11 ff.; 2:9), who in Lk. 2:13 is simply ac- companied by the πλῆθος στρατιᾶς οὐρανίου. In these accounts we find no trace of individual angels, nor is there any interest in angelology in abstraction from God.

The active participation of angels seems to be most strongly assumed in relation to events of the last time. Here Jesus Himself ascribes to them the role of ac- companying hosts who come with the Judge, who act with Him and for Him, [68] and who are present at the judgment (Lk. 12:8 f.). Paul presupposes the same view (2 Th. 1:7; cf. 1 Th. 4:16). The Revelation of John thus paints on a broad canvas that which is common to all early Christianity when in the description of events of the last days it introduces angels at many points and in many ways, describing in a most varied manner both their appearance and function.

In Rabbinic literature there is an almost complete absence of any thought of the co-operation of angels in the judgment. [69] It seems to be crowded out by the rather different thought of the participation of Israel. [70] In the Apocalypse, however, it is not merely emphasised that God will be accompanied by angels at the judgment, but that they will also assist in it. Yet in the Apocalypse there is no mention of the angels accompanying the Messiah [71] as emphatically presupposed elsewhere in the NT, where the angels can be called the angels of Christ the Son of Man as well as the angels of

---

[66] Cf. Joachim Jeremias, Angelos 3 (1928), 2 ff.; H. Odeberg, The Fourth Gospel (1929), 33 ff.; H. Windisch, ZNW, 30 (1931), 215 ff.

[67] The white robes of Mk. 16:5; Lk. 24:4; Jn. 20:12 and Ac. 1:10 are not so much de- scriptive as an expression of the transcendent character of their δόξα. Cf. Lk. 2:9; Mk. 9:3 and par.

[68] Angels as reapers, Mt. 13:39, 49; the Son of Man comes with His angels, Mt. 16:27; with the holy angels, Mk. 8:38 (cf. Lk. 9:23); Mt. 25:31; sends His angels (Mt. 13:41; 24:31; Mk. 13:27.

[69] So also Str.-B., I. 672 f.; only Tanch. שופטים 9 = Tanch (Buber) שופטים, 10, p. 32.

[70] Midr. Ps. 8 § 1; Pes. Kah., 187a (Str.-B., I, 672 n.).

[71] For examples, v. Str.-B., I, 973 f.

God (Mt. 16:27 etc. → n. 68; also 2 Th. 1:7: ἐν τῇ ἀποκαλύψει τοῦ κύριου Ἰησοῦ ἀπ᾽ οὐρανοῦ μετ᾽ ἀγγέλων τῆς δυνάμεως αὐτοῦ).

Thus to early Christianity the action of the angels is essentially action for Christ and in the service of His history. They are λειτουργικὰ πνεύματα εἰς διακονίαν ἀποστελλόμενοι διὰ τοὺς μέλλοντας κληρονομεῖν σωτηρίαν (Hb. 1:14), [72] σύνδουλοι τῶν ἀδελφῶν τῶν ἐχόντων τὴν μαρτυρίαν Ἰησοῦ (Rev. 19:10). They thus take a dynamic part in the processes of this salvation history, which is described not merely in the nativity anthem (Lk. 2:14) or the eschatological anthems (Rev. 5:11 ff.; 19:1 ff.) corresponding to Is. 6:2 ff., but also as χαρά at the development of the individual within this history (Lk. 15:10).

The participation of angels in the activities of the apostolic community assumed by the narrative in certain parts of Acts is based on the same presuppositions as their participation in the nativity and resurrection. Here, too, it is only the ἄγγελος τοῦ θεοῦ or τοῦ κυρίου who acts on behalf of the apostles (5:19; 12:7 ff.), or declares to them the will of God or of the *Kurios* (8:26; 10:3 ff.; 27:23), or punishes the enemy of the community (12:23). The extent to which the angel has ceased to play any autonomous part is shown, e.g., by a comparison of 18:9 and 27:23; the ἄγγελος simply takes the place of the κύριος whose message he has to bring.

c. It is thus self-evident that throughout the NT there can be no question of any equality of the angels with Christ. The Messiah is not an angelic being. As the Son He has a radically different origin and position (Mk. 13:32 and par.; Hb. 1:4 ff.). This fact, as shown by the spatial proximity in Hebrews, is not overthrown by the further fact of the βραχύ τι παρ᾽ ἀγγέλους ἐλαττοῦσθαι which is accomplished in the death of Jesus (Hb. 2:5 ff.). On the contrary, this declaration only serves to emphasise the absolute otherness and superiority of commission. It is indeed possible that the peculiarly strong emphasis in Hebrews on the essential distinction between Christ and the angels is given added point by the antithesis between the NT Gospel of Christ and the many ideas of messengers and messages current in the surrounding world of religion (→ 57).

To this there corresponds a tendency, particularly evident in Paul, to emphasise the comparative unimportance of angelology. The positive thought of the angel as the messenger of God, as found in the Gospels and also in Acts, is relatively little used in his Epistles. For him the whole stress falls on the complete overshadowing of angels by the fact of Christ. Thus he comes to attach a lesser significance to what was originally thought to be the significant participation of angels in the giving of the Law (Gl. 3:19; cf. also Hb. 2:2; → 83), the point being that he measures this now by the all-normative action of Christ. Along the same lines, there arises from his union with Christ a consciousness of his own superiority to angels as an apostle. His mission, for example, is superior to any possible mission of an ἄγγελος ἐξ οὐρανοῦ (Gl. 1:8), and his charismatic endowment fulfilled in ἀγάπη is superior to all γλῶσσαι τῶν ἀγγέλων (1 C. 13:1). As the Son is more and other than all categories of angels, so is the believer with and by Him. What is allotted to him, ἐπιθυμοῦσιν ἄγγελοι παρακῦψαι (1 Pt. 1:12); it is to human flesh and blood rather than to angels that the redemptive act of Christ has reference (Hb. 2:16).

---

[72] Cf. Cr.-Kö., 23

3. This depreciation of angels in comparison with the fact of Christ is strength-ened in Paul by his opposition to Gnostic teaching concerning them. We can hardly take Col. 2:18 to mean anything other than that a cult of angels had to be contested in the early Pauline communities. In the world of syncretism the belief in angels seems to have been partly divorced from the belief in God with which it has been indissolubly bound and to which it had been subordinate in its first beginnings. The ἄγγελοι can be reckoned with the θρόνοι, κυριότητες, ἀρχαί and ἐξουσίαι (Col. 1:16). They can thus be regarded as among the forces which threaten man (R. 8:38). What are in view are the elemental or natural angels which were widely accepted in Judaism [73] and which might in isolation become ungodly and demonic powers. Also in view are the earlier pagan gods, which in part came to be identified with the guardian angels under which God placed the nations. [74]. Paul is not concerned to contest their reality. His only concern is to assert the full and definitive overcoming of their influence in Christ. What is to be consummated eschatologically, ὅταν καταργήσῃ πᾶσαν ἀρχὴν καὶ πᾶσαν ἐξουσίαν καὶ δύναμιν (1 C. 15:24), is, like all eschatology, the present possession of the believer as ἀπαρχή in his πέπεισμαι (R. 8:38).

4. Fallen Angels → δαίμων.

5. The idea of the guardian, or better the directing and ministering angel, is taken over from Judaism, [75] which had long since forgotten the animistic roots of the notion. [76] Ac. 12:15 assumes a likeness in appearance and voice between the ἄγγελος and the man concerned. [77] In Mt. 18:10 recollection of the angels τῶν μικρῶν τούτων who constantly behold the face of God serves to describe the all-embracing love of God to which these μικροί are important, and thus to drive home our human responsibility to regard them as important too. [78] In the verse concerning the → ἐξουσία on the head of the woman demanded διὰ τοὺς ἀγγέ-λους (1 C. 11:10), we perhaps have a warning against the erotic desires of angels based on Gn. 6:1 ff. [79] More probably, however, it implies that regard should be had to the propriety required by accompanying angels. [80] Similar regard is had to accompanying angels in Judaism (bBer., 60b), which portrays the angels as guard-ians of good manners (bShab., 119b).

A particular exegetical question is posed by the ἄγγελοι τῶν ἑπτὰ ἐκκλησιῶν of Rev. 1:20 and Rev. 2 f. The only explanations which demand serious considera-tion are those which see a reference to bishops [81] or to real angels. [82] Since else-where in the Apocalypse ἄγγελοι are always angels, the latter seems more likely. This is supported by the fact that in NT days the ἐπίσκοπος was always regarded as a member of the community and never exalted above it, as would be de-manded by the conjunction of images, i.e., community-candlestick, ἄγγελος-star. On this ground, too, the reference would seem to be to angels representing the

---

[73] Str.-B., III, 819 ff.
[74] Ibid., 48 ff.
[75] Ibid., I, 781 ff.; III, 437 → n. 47.
[76] Bousset-Gressm., 324.
[77] For parallels, v. Str.-B., II, 707. Zn. Ag., 391, n. 49 contests any reference to guardian angels, but he gives no reasons.
[78] A. Schlatter, Erlaüterungen zum NT, ad loc.
[79] So already Tert. Virg. Vel., 7; Ltzm. ad loc.; Everling, 32 ff.
[80] Cf. G. Kittel, Rabbinica (1920), 17 ff.; Str.-B., III, 437 ff.
[81] Above all Zn. Apk., 209 ff.; Nk. Z., 37 (1926), 758; Had. Apk., 38 f.; Str.-B., III, 791.
[82] Comm. Bss., 200 f.; Loh., 18; Charles, I, 34 f.; A. Schlatter, Erlaüterungen zum NT, ad loc.; Gesch. d. ersten Christenheit (1927), 329; Cr.-Kö., 19 f. (hesitantly).

communities. These correspond to the angels of the nations already found in Judaism, [83] and to Michael as the angel of Israel, [84] but also to the description of angels, common to the whole Book of Revelation, as mediators of the divine action.

† ἀρχάγγελος.

The OT has an early reference to the ἀρχιστράτηγος δυνάμεως κυρίου in Jos. 5:14. In Da. 10:13 and 12:1 Michael is the εἷς τῶν ἀρχόντων or ὁ ἄγγελος (Θ: ἄρχων) ὁ μέγας. The first mention of seven special angels is found in Ez. 9:2 ff., [1] then in Tob. 12:15; Test. L. 8; Gr. En., 20; Tg. JI, Gn. 11:7; Rev. 8:2, 6 (cf. 1:4, 20; 3:1; 4:5; 5:6). Six are also mentioned in Eth. En., 20; Tg. JI, Dt. 34:6; and four in Eth. En., 9, 1 etc.; Sib., 2, 215; Pes. r., 46, Str.-B., III, 806. [2] The term is not found in the LXX, but occurs in Gr. En., 20, 8; 4 Esr. 4:36; Proseuche Joseph (bOr. Joh., II, 25), as also in Philo, who uses it to describe the *logos* (Conf. Ling., 146; Rer. Div. Her., 205). If both name and thing also play a role in the Gnostic magic literature [3] and Iamblichus the Neo-Platonist (Myst., 2, 3, p. 70, 10, Parthey), there can be no doubt that they derive from Jewish Christian sources. The Milesian theatre inscription CIG, 2895 has an invocation of the ἀρχάγγελοι as a late Christian protective charm. [4]

The development of the doctrine of archangels has its basis in the tendency to give prominence to certain leading and individualised angels. It is worth noting, however, that there is virtually no interest in this aspect in the NT. The paucity of occurrences is striking. The majority, though without the term ἀρχάγγελοι, occur in the Book of Revelation (→ 84): ἐνώπιον τοῦ θεοῦ, i.e., as part of the divine manifestation and in execution of the divine will. Paul mentions only once in 1 Th. 4:16 the φωνὴ ἀρχαγγέλου which will ring out at the *parousia*, and since this is brought into connection with the coming of the κύριος (the ἐν of accompaniment), it has no more significance than the σάλπιγξ θεοῦ which will be sounded at the same time. Even the archangel, then, is simply an accompanying manifestation of the eschatologically returning Christ. On Jd. 9 → 83.

† ἰσάγγελος.

This rare word corresponds to such analogous constructions as ἰσόθεος and ἰσοβασιλεύς. It is found in Iambl., Περὶ ψυχῆς; Stob. Ecl., I, p. 457, 9 W; Hierocles Carm. Aur., 49, p. 44, 9, Mullach; Christian epitaph, Kaibel, 542, 6 f. Materially equivalent are ἴσος ἀγγέλοις γεγονώς (Abraham after his death), Philo Sacr. AC, 5; ὥσπερ ἄγγελος θεοῦ, P. Greci et Latini, I, 26, 10, cf. 18 (5th century A.D.).

In the NT the only occurrence is in Lk. 20:36, which tells us that the resurrected will know neither mortality nor sexual intercourse, since they are like angels (Mt. 22:30; Mk. 12:25 : ὡς ἄγγελοι ἐν τ. οὐρ.). But cf. also Ac. 6:15 : ὡσεὶ πρόσωπον ἀγγέλου.

Kittel

---

[83] Str.-B., IV, 1224 (Index).
[84] Bousset-Gressm., 327; Str.-B., III, 813; Above all, Lueken, *ad loc.*
ἀρχάγγελος. Nägeli, 48, 72; Lueken, *ad loc.;* Everling, 79 ff.; Bousset-Gressm., 325 ff.; EJ, VI, 632 f.
[1] Six men and a seventh dressed as a scribe. H. Gunkel, ARW, 1 (1898), 294 ff., traces this back to the stellar deities of Babylon, in the midst of which was the scribal god Nabu.
[2] For the traditional names of the archangels, cf. Bousset-Gressm., 325 ff.; Str.-B., III, 805 ff.
[3] Preis Zaub., IV, 1203; VII, 257; XIII, 744, 929, 973.
[4] So Deissmann LO, 393 ff.

ἀγενεαλόγητος → γενεά.

ἅγιος — ἁγιάζω — ἁγιασμός
ἁγιότης — ἁγιωσύνη

The ΑΓ-family of Greek words is most extensive. In biblical Greek it is found not only in words like ἅγιος, ἁγιάζειν, ἁγιαστήριον, ἁγιότης and ἁγιωσύνη, but also in such words as ἁγνός, ἁγνίζειν, ἅγνισμα, ἁγνισμός, ἁγνεία and ἁγνότης. Here, indeed, it enjoys its most significant history. [1]

ἅγιος.

A. In Greek and Hellenistic Writings.

The old Greek word ἅγος signifies the object of awe (Williger, Pass.-Crö.), whether in the sense of reverence (Hom. Hymn. Cer., 479 : μέγα γάρ τι θεῶν ἅγος ἰσχάνει αὐδήν), or in that of aversion (Aesch. Choeph., 154 f.: ἀπότροπον ἅγος ἀπεύχετον, cf. Soph. Oed. Tyr., 1426). The adjective ἁγής (Diels,[4] I, 160, 12 f.; 244, 3) approximates to the sense of καθαρός, "clean." From the time of the Attic tragic dramatists this sense came to be less attached to the ἅγος stem than to the ἁγνός stem, which is linked with the verbal adjective. [2] The verb ἅζω, "to shrink from," usually found in the medial ἅζομαι (Soph. Oed. Col., 134 etc.), does not occur at all in the Bible.

The first certain attestation of the adjective ἅγιος is in Herodotus, who brings it into close relationship with the sanctuary (5, 119 : μέγα τε καὶ ἅγιον ἄλσος, and also 2, 41; 44). Plato distinguishes κακά ... διαφερόντως αὖ μεγάλα, ὅταν εἰς δημόσια καὶ ἅγια <sc. γίγνωνται> (Leg., X, 884a). It is used of sanctuaries (Demosth., 59, 77: ὑπὲρ τοίνυν ἁγίων καὶ σεμνῶν ἱερῶν), a distinction being made between βωμοί, οἱ μὲν κάλλιστοι καὶ ἁγιώτατοι ἐν αὐτῇ τῇ ψυχῇ τῇ ἑκάστου καὶ τῇ φύσει, οἱ δὲ καὶ κοινῇ τοῖς πᾶσι τιμᾶν ἱδρυμένοι (Demosth., 25, 35), so that the most beautiful and sacred things are not accessible to the public. Similarly Isocrates speaks of the ἁγιώτατα τῶν ἱερῶν, Areop. 29. [3] The Hellenistic inscriptions confirm this usage, particularly for oriental sanctuaries (IG, XII, 1, 694, 14 : ἐν τῷ ἱερῷ τῷ ἁγιωτάτῳ, Ditt. Syll.[3], 768, 16 : τῶν ἱερῶν τῶν ἁγιωτάτων).

ἅ γ ι ο ς. J. C. K. v. Hofmann, *Schriftbeweis*, I[2] (1857), 81 ff.; G. Menken, *Schriften* (1858), III, 305 ff., VI, 46 ff.; L. Diestel, "Die Heiligkeit Gottes," Jbch. pr. Th. (1859), 3 ff.; W. W. Graf Baudissin, *Studien z. semitischen Religionsgeschichte*, II (1876); G. Wobbermin, *Religionsgeschichtliche Studien* (1896); A. Fridrichsen, "Hagios-Qados," *Skrifter av Videnskaps Selskabet*, II, 3 (1916); E. Williger, "Hagios," RVV, 19 (1922); H. Leisegang, *Der Heilige Geist*, I (1919); *Pneuma Hagion* (1922); R. Asting, *Die Heiligkeit im Urchristentum* (1930); U. Bunzel, *Der Begriff der Heiligkeit im AT* (1914); E. Issel, *Der Begriff der Heiligkeit im NT* (1887); J. Hänel, *Die Religion der Heiligkeit* (1931); Cr.-Kö., 34 ff.; Pass.-Crö., *s.v.*

[1] In Indo-germanic, though this is disputed (cf. Boisacq, *s.v.* ἅγιος), a related term is found in the old Indian yaj = "to sacrifice" (cf. ἅζεται = Skt. yájati, "he sacrifices." ἅγιος = Skt. yájyah, "worthy of reverence." ἁγνός = yajñāḥ, "sacrifice," Debrunner). While the sacrificial meaning predominates in Indian, it is the sacramental which comes to the fore in Greek.

[2] Brugmann-Thumb, *Griechische Grammatik* ([4]1913), 223.

[3] Pausanias (Wobbermin, 62 ff.) says of the Kabira sanctuary at Thebes : οὕτω μὲν τὸ ἱερὸν τοῦτό ἐστιν ἐξ ἀρχῆς ἅγιον (IX, 25, 8); of the sanctuary at Tithorea : ἱερὸν Ἴσιδος ἁγιώτατον (X, 32, 13); as against Herodotus he makes much use of the superlative (Williger). His dependence on Herodotus (Kroll) is contested. Fridrichsen (44) gives other examples.

In the Hellenistic period ἅγιος is used as an epithet of the gods as well,[4] preferably in the case of Egyptian and Syrian, and therefore again oriental deities, such as Isis, Serapis and Baal (e.g., Ditt. Or., 620, 2 : Διὶ ἁγίῳ βεελβεσώρῳ [Gerasa], 590, 1 f.: Θεῷ ἁγίῳ Βὰλ καὶ θεᾷ Ἥρᾳ [Beirut], just as in the Roman cultus Syrian deities are given the predicate sanctus = ἅγιος.[5] From the oriental deities the phrase ἅγιος ἁγιώτατος seems only at a later date to have been transferred to the Greek gods.[6] On the other hand the word ἅγιος never seems to have been applied in pure Greek to men connected with the cultus, its place being taken by ἁγνός in this respect.

It may be added that it was used of customs connected with religion, especially the mysteries (e.g., Aristoph. Nu., 304: ἐν τελεταῖς ἁγίαις, Demosth., 25, 11: τὰς ἁγιωτάτας ἡμῖν τελετὰς καταδείξας etc.).

Only in the Hellenistic period does ἅγιος come into more common use. Probably this is due to the influence of the oriental concept of holiness, as best seen in the LXX. Here ἅγιος is used as the equivalent of the Hebrew in all applications of this Hebrew term, so that in the usage of the Bible we must everywhere recognise the Semitic background.

B. The Use of the Term Holiness in the OT.

The root קדשׁ is probably not originally Hebrew but Canaanite, being thus taken over from an alien religious circle, while the native Hebrew חרם acquires the significance of "what is banned" and thus becomes predominantly negative. The actual meaning of קדשׁ is hard to determine etymologically. We cannot accept the earlier theory of its kinship with חדשׁ, which contradicts the Semitic laws of sound. Fleischer, on the other hand, has rightly pointed to the basic קד, "to divide,"[7] which would cause us to think of what is marked off from the secular. The antithetical term is חל or "profane" (1 S. 21:5 f.; Ez. 22:26; 42:20; 44:23), i.e., that which is not under the ban of holiness. In contrast to קדשׁ this appertains to ordinary life, and thus self-evidently comes to mean "common" (κοινόν) as distinct from the cultic. Most closely related materially to קדשׁ or holiness is the term טהר ("purity"). The substantive (qōdeš : ṭōhar), adjective (qādōš : ṭāhōr) and verb (qādeš : ṭāher) all show the same basic forms. קדשׁ is related to טהר like ἅγιος to ἁγνός. Yet while קדשׁ is the basic cultic term, טהר is the ritual. There is always an energy in the holy which is lacking in the pure or clean. If both קדשׁ and טהר may be brought under the concept of the religious, both are distinct from the ethical, with which the religious is not to be equated. The ethical has its root in the human sphere rather than the divine. It is only with the increasing spiritualisation of thought that the two great vital streams come together.

From the very first קדשׁ is very closely linked with the cultic. Anything related to the cultus, whether God, man, things, space or time, can be brought under the term קדשׁ.

In analogy to the nominal construction טֹהַר אָדֹם, גֹּדֶל the substantive קֹדֶשׁ always denotes a state and not an action. In Genesis, where the cultus does not play any

---

[4] Williger, 81.

[5] Cumont, Die orientalischen Religionen (³1931), 266, n. 65. Fridrichsen, 30. Delehaye, Sanctus (1927), 22 ff.

[6] Williger, 82 f. It is only in mockery that ἅγιος is used of animals (Aristoph. Av., 522; Antiph. Lyk., 147, CAF, II, p. 80).

[7] Baudissin, I, 19 ff.

significant role, it is not found ; but it occurs only the more frequently in the story of Moses. Already at Sinai the J source has the expression (Ex. 3:5, אַדְמַת קֹדֶשׁ). The ground around the burning bush is holy ground, as is also Gilgal before Jericho (Jos. 5:15), and esp. Jerusalem (Is. 48:2; 52:1; Neh. 11:1, 18), the site of the temple (Is. 11:9; 56:7: הַר הַקֹּדֶשׁ), the temple itself (Is. 64:10; 1 Ch. 29:3 : בֵּית הַקֹּדֶשׁ cf. Ps. 5:7; 79:1; 138:2 : הֵיכַל הַקֹּדֶשׁ) and everything appertaining to it, the holiest of holies (Ps. 28:2 : דְּבִיר הַקֹּדֶשׁ), the chambers (Ez. 42:13; 46:19 לִשְׁכוֹת הַקֹּדֶשׁ) and the courts (Is. 62:9). In relation to the temple קדש comes to mean sanctuary rather than holiness, and within it a distinction is made between the sanctuary (Ex. 26:33; Lv. 4:6 : הַקֹּדֶשׁ) and the holiest of holies (Ex. 26:34; Nu. 18:10). The holy time as well as the holy place is called קֹדֶשׁ (Is. 58:13; Neh. 10:32 : יוֹם הַקֹּדֶשׁ, cf. Ex. 16:23; Neh. 9:14 : שַׁבַּת הַקֹּדֶשׁ). Reference is also made to holy offerings, and therefore to sacrifices (1 S. 21, 5-7; cf. Lv. 22:12; 3:11: לֶחֶם קֹדֶשׁ) and tithes (Dt. 26:13). The more deeply we penetrate into the priestly literature of the Pentateuch, the more common the word becomes, evidence being thus given of an increasing "catholicising" of the OT concept of holiness under priestly rule. The status merges more and more into the matter of the cultus, so that the Law no less than the cultus itself comes under the threat of a purely material conception of holiness.

The adjective קָדוֹשׁ is more fluid than the substantive קֹדֶשׁ. Whereas קֹדֶשׁ is a material concept with no personal element, קָדוֹשׁ can be used outside the place and time of the cultic (Lv. 6:9, 19 ff. etc.) of persons. Characteristically it is not applied to thinks like sacrifices, garments or vessels etc., [8] and in regard to cultic status God can be called קָדוֹשׁ as well as man. To be sure, the cultic nature of קָדוֹשׁ is somewhat evaporated when it is used of God, since the angels, who have no cultus, can sometimes be described as קְדֹשִׁים (Job 5:1; 15:15). As a predicate of God, קָדוֹשׁ comes to have the meaning of divine, and thus becomes an adjective for God (Is. 5:16; 6:3; Hos. 11:9 etc.; cf. קְדוֹשׁ יִשְׂרָאֵל Is. 1:4 etc.). But the personal character of God gives a spiritual turn to the whole concept, a development chiefly attributable to the prophets. Even as a human predicate קָדוֹשׁ acquires a new sense, for in man the holy comes into contact with the ethical, though there is no simple equation. The relationship of God and man thus gives to the adjective קָדוֹשׁ a historical element as distinct from the impersonal קֹדֶשׁ. [9]

Finally, the verb קָדֵשׁ is the most versatile form of the root. The relatively infrequent qal form denotes exclusively cultic holiness with no moral element. In contrast the niph'al form, of which God alone is the subject, denotes the self-representation of His holiness (Is. 5:16; Ez. 20:41; 28:22, 25; 36:23; 38:16; 39:27; Nu. 20:13) in Israel in face of the Gentile world. What is indicated is not so much entry into a state of holiness as the expression of the essence of divine holiness. In contrast again, the comparative stem is inchoative: "to set in a state of holiness." The subject here may be God, who sanctifies in the eyes of the nations His name defiled by Israel (Ez. 36:23), or who restores the holiness of Israel itself (Ez.

---

[8] In Nu. 5:17, according to the LXX ὕδωρ καθαρὸν ζῶν, we should read מַיִם טְהוֹרִים חַיִּים instead of מַיִם קְדוֹשִׁים.

[9] A distinction should be made between the Hebrew adjective קָדוֹשׁ and the Canaanite קָדֵשׁ. which became a proper name in place-names, and was also used of the hierodules, thus being brought into connection with pagan cults.

20:12; 37:28), or who declares the Sabbath to be holy (Gn. 2:3); but it may also be Moses, who sanctifies the people (Ex. 19:10, 14), or Joshua (Jos. 7:13), or Job (1:5), or Samuel (1 S. 16:5), as they sanctify either the nation or individuals. When the people as such enters a state of holiness, the middle hitpa'el is found (Jos. 3:5; 2 S. 11:4 : הִתְקַדֵּשׁ). In this case the concept never implies more than cultic qualification. Finally, the causative has the sense of "dedicate," not with the implication of cultic qualification, but rather of transfer to the possession of God, to whom the person or thing dedicated now exclusively belongs.

C. The History of the Term in the OT.

1. The Pre-prophetic Period.

The history of the term is linked with the substantive קֹדֶשׁ, though not so much in the sense of sanctuary with reference to the centre of the cultus, old though this use is (Ex. 3:5; Jos. 5:15), as in that of holiness with reference to the name of God. For God's name is an expression for His personal essence as present in the sanctuary and people. Taken up into the personal being of Yahweh, however, קֹדֶשׁ acquires a moral bearing alien to it by nature. Amos already causes Yahweh to swear by His holiness (4:2), and therefore by His innermost essence, which is different from everything creaturely, let alone unclean or sinful. Similarly he finds a mortal human sin in the defilement of the name of Yahweh's holiness even within the sphere of the cultus (2:7). The phrase שֵׁם קֹדֶשׁ יהוה is particularly common in the priestly literature, whether in the pre-exilic holiness code of P (Lv. 20:3; 22:2) or in the priestly prophet Ezekiel (Ez. 36:20 ff.). In the Psalter, too, where we again encounter the holiness of the name of Yahweh (Ps. 33:21; 103:1 etc., cf. also 1 Chr. 16:10, 35), it is used in connection with worship. Here the cultic element has certainly not disappeared, since the theological feeling of priestly circles is cultically emphasised. Again, the name itself is prescribed for invocation in the cultus; for the cultus is possible only where the name of God is acknowledged, the name in some sense taking the place of the cultic image in the OT. Nevertheless, with the emphasising of the name holiness becomes far more personal than cultic, as may be seen particularly clearly in Ezekiel and the Psalter.

In the process, however, the concept of holiness merges into that of divinity, so that Yahweh's holy name contrasts with everything creaturely. The phrases דְּבַר קָדְשׁוֹ (Ps. 105:42) and רוּחַ קָדְשׁוֹ (Is. 63:10 ff.; Ps. 51:11) follow the same pattern. The name, Word and Spirit of God are all forms of His revelation, but as קֹדֶשׁ they are set in antithesis to everything worldly or creaturely, so that even the cultic is almost consumed by the divine. God's holiness thus becomes an expression for His perfection of being which transcends everything creaturely. As we have seen, the revelation of His holiness is expressed by niph'al נִקְדַּשׁ; "to sanctify oneself," God alone being the subject (Lv. 10:3; Ex. 29:43; 22:32; Is. 5:16; Ez. 20:41). Even in the Lord's Prayer, the request ἁγιασθήτω τὸ ὄνομά σου corresponds to the Hebrew נִקְדַּשׁ, so that it is God Himself who demonstrates His name to be holy.

As the name of Yahweh is disclosed at Sinai, so it is at Sinai that Israel as His people has its origin in the divine covenant (Ex. 24:4-8). Thus the concept of holiness is linked with the relationship between God and His people, with the national religion. Because God dwells in the midst of the people, Israel, too, is to be a עַם קָדוֹשׁ (Dt. 7:6; 26:19; cf. Jer. 2:3). It must have no contact with the cults or rites of other nations. It must worship Yahweh as its only God (Dt. 6:4). In the concept of the עַם קָדוֹשׁ (cf. Ex. 19:6 : גּוֹי קָדוֹשׁ) the cultic and national elements are indissolubly merged. Probably developing out of a holy amphictyonic league, [9a] centred upon the ark, Israel is in Deuteronomy the people of God in an absolute sense, established on the basis of the divine covenant (Dt. 17:2) and election (7:1 ff.) in contrast to the heathenism of other nations. Indeed, within the one term קָדוֹשׁ Israelite and heathen conceptions of holiness are brought into mortal combat, since in the עַם קָדוֹשׁ there must be neither קָדֵשׁ nor קְדֵשָׁה (Dt. 23:18). These hierodules belong to the Canaanite cultus, the holiness of which cannot be better characterised than by the fact that it includes "holy" licence. The thought of the holy people emerges even more clearly in the Holiness Code (Lv. 17-26) than in Deuteronomy. Here everything derives from the basic statement in Lv. 19:2 : Ye shall be קְדֹשִׁים כִּי קָדוֹשׁ אֲנִי יְהוָה אֱלֹהֵיכֶם. Yahweh's holiness demands the holiness of His people as a condition of intercourse. If the cultic character of holiness is prominent in this code, c. 19 shows us that cultic qualification is inconceivable without purity. Cultic purity, however, demands personal purity. The ἅγιοι must be ἁγνοί. Hence the sphere of ethics is taken up into that of religion.

This form of the concept of holiness is thus determined by the cultus. At its heart stands the ark, which from Sinai on is linked with the sanctuary, like a mobile house in which God is thought to dwell. After a long detour by Shiloh it comes at length to Jerusalem, finding a permanent abode in the holiest of holies in Solomon's temple (1 K. 8:13), so that the sanctuary which shelters it is filled with its holiness, and the presence of God is thought to be enthroned above the ark, which is screened by the cherubim. It is worth noting that Yahweh appears for the first time as הָאֱלֹהִים הַקָּדוֹשׁ (1 S. 6:20) in connection with the ark. In stories like 1 S. 5 and 6, and 2 S. 6, the holiness is still impersonal and natural in character. The ark is as it were charged with sacred electricity which strikes what is profane like lightning. Only those in a state of קֹדֶשׁ may touch it.

On the older Hebrew view, such a state is the holy war in which the ark originally found its sphere of operation (Nu. 10:35 f.; Jos. 6). That God's war, which the ark symbolises, is holy, derives also from the fact that the warrior is in a state of קֹדֶשׁ, being allowed to eat the consecrated temple bread which otherwise only the priests as holy persons may eat (cf. Mt. 12:3 ff. and par.). It is along such lines that we are to understand the formula קַדֵּשׁ מִלְחָמָה ("to declare holy war," Mi. 3:5; Jer. 6:4). Similarly, the camp is holy (Dt. 23:15), since Yahweh dwells in it (v. 10 ff.). He Himself is described as a man of war by Moses (Ex. 15:3 : יהוה איש מלחמה). The holy war under the sign of the ark is the origin of the history of Israel.

Yet the ark is also the centre of national worship in time of peace, for Shiloh its first dwelling-place (Jos. 18:1; cf. Jer. 7:26), and Jerusalem to which David brought it permanently (2 S. 6), as the places where Yahweh causes His name to dwell (Dt. 12:5 etc.), are centres of the national cultus which Deuteronomy alone sanctions as compared with the tribal or family shrines, or the nature shrines on the "high places."

2. Prophetic Theology.

a. If in the national religion the holy still has a natural as well as a historical element, this disappears completely in prophetic theology. God as קָדוֹשׁ is now contrasted with the human and creaturely in all the fulness of His divine personality. It is noteworthy that it is in Hosea, who breaks completely with the cultic element in religion, that Yahweh as קָדוֹשׁ appears in moral antithesis to the nature of man : "I am God, and not man, holy (קָדוֹשׁ) in the midst of thee" (11:9). Israel has followed the cult of Baal, and in favour of Baal has become Kadesh

---

[9a] M. Noth, *System der zwölf Stämme Israels* (1930), 61 ff.

(קְדֵשָׁה, 4:14; 12:1). In this holy licence it commits mortal sin against Yahweh, who is קָדוֹשׁ in the opposite sense. But if the destruction of Israel must follow from this collision of קָדוֹשׁ with קְדֵשָׁה (cf. 14:1), this destruction will itself be destroyed by God as קָדוֹשׁ. In the holiness of God there is the deathdealing element which must destroy (cf. 5:3; 6:10; 9:4) uncleanness (טֻמְאָה; cf. 2 S. 11:4), but there is also the creative element which makes God a tree of life (14:8). Hosea finds the essence of God in suprahuman love (→ ἀγαπάω, 31 ff.).

The opposition of God's holiness to Israel thus works itself out in His love which is quite incomprehensible to human nature. In Hosea, therefore, the concept of holiness takes up into itself as the fulness of deity the thought of love — an insight never again attained in the OT. As Hosea himself in his shattered happiness learned to know love as the indestructible force which could save even his lost wife, so Yahweh's holiness as the sum of His being must contain the creative love which slays but also makes alive again (cf. 6:1 f.). In the older Hebrew concept the divine stands in mortal opposition to the human and especially the sinful. This opposition remains in Hosea's view of God, but it is absorbed into the opposition of holy love to unholy nature. What God in virtue of His holiness may do to love unholy nature, no man may do, and therefore the antithesis between God and man consists in the very love which overcomes it.

b. The concept of holiness is central to the whole theology of Isaiah. The Trisagion of his initial vision (Is. 6:3) remained normative for his picture of God. It shows that Yahweh Sabaoth is as it were thrice holy. Whereas Yahweh's כָּבוֹד His *gravitas,* is the φανερὸν τοῦ θεοῦ which appears in all the world as in a transparency, His holiness denotes His innermost and secret essence. The fearfulness of the holy God, the *numen tremendum,* is inimitably expressed in the holy awe of Isaiah. His trembling seems to shake the threshold on which he stands at the entrance to the sanctuary, and in the manifestation of the divine he feels the mortal contrast to his own nature, since he is טָמֵא, ἀκάθαρτος, unclean, and he thinks that he must perish. The continuation of the vision shows that this is a moral rather than a physical uncleanness, for there is reference to the taking away of guilt and the purging of sin (6:7). Atonement (כפר) is needed; the thought of it occurs here in the setting of the holy. To be sure, atonement is always implicitly demanded where there is question of the cultic encounter of man with the holy God. But here the atonement does not come from man's side by the offering of sacrifice. It comes from God's side, God Himself effecting it through the seraph by means of a coal from the altar used as a holy means. When in the state of reconciliation, Isaiah does not actually call himself קָדוֹשׁ, but we may thus describe him, since in his prophetic role he stands in direct contact with God (cf. 2 K. 4:9). At any rate, he himself calls the final state of the redeemed on Mount Sion קָדוֹשׁ (4:3), and it is characteristic that this is a state of life (כָּתוּב לַחַיִּים), whereas the contemplation of what is holy in a state of ἀκαθαρσία brings death (6:5).

From the concept of holiness Isaiah forged the expression קְדוֹשׁ יִשְׂרָאֵל for Yahweh. As is well known, it occurs only in Isaiah apart from a few dependent passages (e.g., 2 K. 19:22; Jer. 50:29 etc.). It is distributed more or less equally through the two parts, and is also highly esteemed by the editors (12:6; 17:7; 29:19). The expression is obviously paradoxical, for as קָדוֹשׁ Yahweh stands in antithesis to both natural and historical creation. If Yahweh as קְדוֹשׁ יִשְׂרָאֵל binds Himself to Israel, He sets up a relationship which must have as its goal a עַם קָדוֹשׁ obviously seen (4:3) only in a remnant of the people (שְׁאָר יָשׁוּב 10:21). To all the unholy, the light of Israel will be a fire and the Holy One a flame (10:16) by which it will be consumed and destroyed. In itself supreme grace, the establishment of the קְדוֹשׁ יִשְׂרָאֵל in His people will be judgment destroying the mass and purifying a remnant. Thus in face of the unholiness of the people it is supremely the divine Judge who is introduced in the קְדוֹשׁ יִשְׂרָאֵל. Once he is called הָאֵל הַקָּדוֹשׁ (5:16), in a corrupt passage in which, however, the thought of judgment is again present. As אֵל קָדוֹשׁ Yahweh shows Himself to be holy (נִקְדָּשׁ [10]).

c. Along the lines of Isaiah, the concept of the קְדוֹשׁ יִשְׂרָאֵל is further developed in Deutero-Isaiah. But whereas the name was formerly linked predominantly with judgment, the contrast between Yahweh and Israel being thus expressed, it is now brought into connection with the thought of redemption. For now the Holy One of Israel has executed His judgment, and behind it stands redemption as the final goal. Yahweh as קָדוֹשׁ is quite incomparable (Is. 40:25; cf. 57:15). As in Hosea, He is God and not man. In His holiness lies His divine mystery (45:15). This mystery is disclosed, however, in redemption (45:18 ff.). As קְדוֹשׁ יִשְׂרָאֵל Yahweh is the Creator (41:20; 45:11) and the Redeemer (41:14; 43:3, 14; 47:4) of Israel. As גֹּאֵל, He acknowledges Himself to be bound and committed to Israel, thus guaranteeing the freedom of Israel. Thus the thought of redemption is central to the theology of Deutero-Isaiah, and the Holy One of Israel is to be seen in the light of it. A connection is here established between salvation and holiness, though there is no linguistic relationship (as in German). The train of thought is similar to that of Hosea. For since Yahweh as קָדוֹשׁ is God and not man, since He stands in antithesis to the natural law of creation, since His thoughts and ways are different from those of men (55:8 f.), His holiness corresponds to a καινὴ κτίσις in which He is all in all, the רִאשׁנוֹת or τὰ ἀρχαῖα having passed away and all things become new.

3. The Post-exilic Period.

a. In post-exilic Judaism the concept of holiness gives evidence of two intermingling streams, the priestly and cultic on the one hand and the prophetic and ethical on the other. The former is predominant in the legal literature, the latter in the poetic. In the Jewish priest-state, the Israelite Law became more and more a ceremonial Law in which the popular elements were overshadowed by the cultic. In consequence the thought of holiness with its various derivatives plays a dominating role. At the head of Israel, which is to be a מַמְלֶכֶת כֹּהֲנִים וְגוֹי קָדוֹשׁ (Ex. 19:6), stands the high-priest as קְדוֹשׁ יהוה (Ps. 106:16), bearing on his breastplate the inscription : קֹדֶשׁ לַיהוה (Ex. 28:36). But in descending degrees not only he, but all the priests are holy (Lv. 21:6 f., cf. Nu. 16:5, 7), as are also the Levites who are offered as a wave-offering to Yahweh, and then the whole people (Lv. 11:44 f. etc.; Nu. 15:40). The power of holiness is imparted to men and things dwelling within the radius of the sanctuary, and there is a difference between קֹדֶשׁ and קֹדֶשׁ קָדָשִׁים. The danger of a materialisation of the concept is obvious, and Jesus had later to combat this (Mt. 23:17, 19).

---

[10] The addition בְּצְדָקָה certainly suggests a prophecy of salvation, for צְדָקָה "righteousness" always implies favour. But the train of thought (v. 15; v. 16) and the metre require the excision of בִּצְדָקָה.

On the basis of this cultic system, however, there is built in the Psalter a more spiritual world which has drawn from the riches of prophecy and especially Deutero-Isaiah, and in which the holy is conceived personally, whether in the person of the Holy One of Israel (Ps. 71:22; 78:41; 89:18) or of the saints of Israel (34:9; 89:5). Yet there is still frequent mention of the sanctuary of God (5:7; 138:2). And if the priesthood remains relatively in the background, it is easy to see that the collection of the Psalter belongs to the same period as the formation of the priest-state. The cultus was the envelope of faith, though without any sense of conflict between them. Indeed, we can see what power cultic festivals in the temple could exercise on pious minds, for in the sanctuary God could be seen (Ps. 27:4; 42:2; 63:2 etc.) and His presence enjoyed. The sacrifice in its many forms was the sign of reconciliation between God and the people. It did not express human invention, but divine institution, and as such it could be a source of comfort. The Holy Spirit (Ps. 51:11; cf. 143:10 [LXX] רוּחַ הַקֹּדֶשׁ) was present within Israel (Is. 63:10 f.) as the Spirit of reconciliation shed abroad by God in the heart (Ez. 36:26 f.) whose withdrawal was to be feared (Ps. 51:11).

b. The cultic basis of the ἅγιος-concept, however, is maintained not merely in the canonical literature but also in the apocryphal writings of Hellenism. The holiness of Jerusalem (1 Macc. 2:7; 2 Macc. 1:12; 3 Macc. 6:5; Tob. 13:9), of the temple (1 Esr. 1:53; 2 Macc. 1:29; 5:15 [ἁγιώτατον ἱερόν]; 3 Macc. 3:16), of the sanctuary (τὰ ἅγια, 1 Macc. 3:43, 51, 58 f. etc.; Jdt. 4:12 f.), of the altar (2 Macc. 14:3; Sir. 50:11), of the Sabbath (2 Macc. 5:25; Tob. 2:1), of holy objects such as garments (Sir. 45:10), candlesticks (26:17), oil (45:15), swords (2 Macc. 15:16), and books (1 Macc. 12:9), of the priesthood (1 Macc. 2:54), of the people (1 Macc. 10:39, 44; Wis. 18:9) and of the covenant (1 Macc. 1:15, 63) is firmly rooted in the OT. The same is true of the referring of ἅγιος to God (2 Macc. 14:36; 3 Macc. 2:2; Sir. 23:9; Tob. 12:12, 15), even if the address "Thou Holy One" is striking, as also to the divine names (Tob. 3:11; 8:5 f. etc.), to heaven (Wis. 9:10), to the angels (Tob. 11:14; 12:15), and to the Spirit (Wis. 1:5; Sir. 48:12), though the Wisdom of Solomon, plainly under the influence of Stoic philosophy, understands by πνεῦμα ἅγιον something rather different from what is meant by רוּחַ קָדְשׁ<י> (Is. 63:10 f., Ps. 51:11).

In general we may conclude that the apocryphal literature remains within the canonical conception of ἅγιος. This is supported by the almost invariable usage of the LXX translators, who rightly employed the relatively little used Greek ἅγιος as a rendering of the Hebrew קדשׁ. Nor did they allow the Hebrew קדש to be coloured by the Greek meaning of ἅγιος, but impressed ἅγιος wholly into the service of the Hebrew קדש. This is particularly obvious in the translating of the temple sanctuary by τὸ ἅγιον or τὰ ἅγια, whereas the normal Greek word ἱερόν does not occur at all in the LXX. Hence "we may see a conscious attempt to avoid the usual term for heathen sanctuaries," [11] though it is to be noted that already under Ptolemy III τὸ ἅγιον is used for a pagan sanctuary. [12] The plural ἅγια is found only in Hebrews outside the LXX, [13] except that Josephus uses it for the Jerusalem temple — an obvious Hebraism. It has been suggested that ἅγιος sometimes emphasises what is exalted or worthy of reverence, [14] and that

---

[11] M. Flashar in ZAW, 32 (1929), 245, n. 2.
[12] Ditt. Or., 56, 59; Flashar, op. cit.
[13] Flashar, op. cit.
[14] Asting, 37.

it is much used in this sense in the NT; but this rests on a misunderstanding. To the extent that what is exalted or worthy of reverence contains an element of the נוֹרָא or awful, it might sometimes be expressed by ἅγιος = קדשׁ but hardly in the sense of כָּבוֹד = *majestas*.

4. Philo and Josephus.

In post-biblical Judaism the authors to claim our attention are Philo and Josephus. Both these went beyond the frontiers of legal Judaism into the Hellenistic world, the one as a philosopher, the other as a historian. Both were much influenced thereby.

Philo starts with the Pentateuch as the basis of his theology, but he everywhere interprets it allegorically. His view of God is taken from Judaism. Hence God appears to him as ἅγιος (Sacr., 101; Som., I, 254; Praem. Poen., 123), and he also knows τὸ ἁγιώτατον καὶ θεῖον ὄνομα (Vit. Mos., II, 208) and describes the divine wisdom (σοφία) as ἁγία (Fug., 196). He realises that ἅγιος has its basis in the Hebrew קדשׁ. Hence the whole sphere of the cultus is brought under this term as in Hebrew, including the temple (Leg. Gai., 278: ὁ τοῦ ὑψίστου θεοῦ νεὼς ἅγιος; Leg. All., III, 125: τὸ ἅγιον), the holiest of holies (Mut. Nom., 192: τὰ ἅγια τῶν ἁγίων), the forecourt (Vit. Cont., 81: ἐν τῷ ἁγίῳ προνάῳ), the precincts (Rer. Div. Her., 75: τῶν ... τεμενῶν τὸ ἁγιώτερον), but also including the actions (Post. C., 96: ἅγιον πρᾶγμα ..., Som., I, 82: ... τελεταῖς ..., Som., II, 34: λειτουργίαι), which in the OT are not called קדשׁ. Similarly he knows the sacred number (Vit. Cont., 65) in relation to the Sabbath (Spec. Leg., II, 194) and other things (Vit. Mos., II, 80), and the Law (νόμος), like the cultus, is holy (Spec. Leg., III, 119), this being counted among the ἅγιαι γραφαί by Palestinian Jews also. Among Israelites Moses is ἱερώτατός τε καὶ ἅγιος (Spec. Leg., IV, 105). Yet Israel as such is ordained a holy people (Praem. Poen., 123), and the firstborn are to be counted as ἅγιοι (Sacr. A.C., 134), so that the whole people is to be reckoned holy as in Deuteronomy and the Holiness Code.

For Philo, of course, the Law is an allegory of the philosophical world, and the Hebrew root of his concept of God is indissolubly intertwined with a Greek derivation from Hellenistic philosophy. There thus ensues a transfer of the Hebrew predicate of holiness (ἅγιος) to philosophical concepts with which it has no basic connection. The cosmos is as τὸ πρεσβύτατον καὶ τελειότατον ἔργον ἅγιον (Rer. Div. Her., 199). It is a reflection of the Holy One (Plant., 50: ἁγίων ἀπαύγασμα). And as heaven is holy in the macrocosm, so is νοῦς in the microcosm (Som., I, 34). The ἅγιον has here lost its original sense and come to mean the lofty aspect (σεμνόν, Som., II, 251: σεμνότερον καὶ ἁγιώτερον ... οἶκον) borne by the creation of God. Hence Philo can arrive at his own distinctive view of the soul as the sanctuary of God (Som., I, 149: θεοῦ οἶκον γενέσθαι, ἱερὸν ἅγιον). There cannot be found for God any σεμνότερον καὶ ἁγιώτερον ... οἶκον than φιλοθεάμονα διάνοιαν (Som., II, 251). Like the διάνοια, the γνῶμαι (Leg. All., III, 125) and κινήσεις αἱ κατ᾽ ἀρετήν (Sacr. A.C., 109) can be called holy (ἅγιαι). Here the Philonic meaning of ἅγιος merges into that of ἁγνός or "pure" (Exsecr., 159: ψυχή ... ἁγνὴ παρθένος), but loses that of קדשׁ.

The usage of Josephus is quite different. In distinction from Philo, who does not avoid ἅγιος but gives it a different meaning from that of the OT, Josephus uses it sparingly, no doubt because ἅγιος "must have sounded strange in Greek ears." [15] This is revealed by a comparison of the third book of the Antiquities,

---

[15] Schl. Mt., 12.

which deals with the cultic arrangements under Moses, with the relevant sections of the source in Leviticus. In the latter the term ἅγιος = קָדוֹשׁ is extremely frequent, the so-called Holiness Code (Lv. 17-26) being named after it. But in Josephus it loses its prominence, and the same is true in all his writings. [16] He uses it most frequently of the Jerusalem temple, saying of the ναός that it ἅγιον ἐκαλεῖτο, τὸ δὲ ἄβατον ... τοῦ ἁγίου τὸ ἅγιον (Ant., 3, 125). He also uses it of the holiest of holies (Bell., 1, 152: ἀόρατον ἅγιον), and of the sanctuary with the forecourt and walls of the temple (Bell., 4, 171; 6, 95; Ant., 12, 413). The holy land is also called ἅγιον (Bell., 4, 163; 5, 400). Whereas πλῆθος is used of people of every kind, only the people of God is called πληθύς; [17] to it alone can the predicate ἅγιος be applied (Bell., 6, 425) as a precondition of its participation in the cultus. Josephus is much more liberal in his use of ἁγνός and its cognates (Ant., 15, 418; Bell., 6, 425 [ἅγιος]). The verb ἁγιάζειν, which is mostly restricted to biblical Greek, though it is found also in Philo, he replaces by ἁγνίζειν (Ant., 3, 262; 9, 272). As an intransitive we find ἁγνεύειν (Ant., 3, 152) in approximation to Greek usage. Here, too, Josephus shows that for the sake of his readers he has weakened the basic Jewish terms and ideas which sought expression in ἅγιος and ἁγιάζειν, as is most evident, of course, in his way of speaking of God. [18]

Procksch

D. The Concept of Holiness in Rabbinic Judaism.

a. In Rabbinic Judaism the application of the root קדשׁ is for the most part controlled by the OT. Thus, in accordance with OT custom, the following are called holy: the temple (מִקְדָּשׁ); the priests; the sacrifices (distinguished as קָדְשֵׁי קָדָשִׁים, most holy offerings, and קָדָשִׁים קַלִּים, offerings of a lesser degree of holiness); the feast-days; the Sabbath; the people Israel; Palestine etc. Yet in this usage the term קדשׁ is never given any precision of content. Often there is evidence of an attempt to systematise the OT statements. Thus Kel., 1, 6 ff. offers a series of ten items of increasing holiness, including the land, Jerusalem, [19] the temple hill, the courts of women, men and priests, and the temple itself. Meg., 3, 1 offers the following series: 1. the city square, where divine festivals might be held; 2. the synagogue; 3. the ark of the Torah within it; 4. the veils of Holy Scripture within this; 5. the scrolls of Nebiim and Ketubim; and 6. the scroll of the Torah. [20]

Occasionally the Rabbis venture new constructions within the framework of the OT concept of cultic holiness. Thus S. Nu., 25 on 6:5 speaks of the holiness of the hair to indicate that the Nazirite must cut off his hair because it is dedicated to God (Nu. 6:5, 18), and of the holiness of the body to indicate that there must be no defilement by corpses (Nu. 6:6 f.).

Mention should also be made of a secular use: קִדֵּשׁ c. acc. mul. et לְ viri = "to espouse a wife," [21] lit. "to select or separate to oneself a wife." For this is the

[16] Brüne, *Flavius Josephus* (1913).
[17] *Ibid.,* 118.
[18] A. Schlatter, *Wie sprach Josephus von Gott?* (1910).
[19] Jerusalem = "the holy city," *v.* Str.-B., I, 150.
[20] → 99.
[21] For references, *v.* Kidd, *pass.*

basic meaning of קדש,[22] which is here secularised and apparently restricted to the selection of a wife.

This more or less exhausts the main occurrences of the root קדש in Rabbinic literature. For apart from this traditional and secular use קדש is not very frequent in passages of any theological relevance.

b. God is called holy as the pitilessly stern Judge, as the lofty King, as *rex tremendae maiestatis*, whom one may approach only with fear and trembling. The Jew prays daily to Him, the "great, powerful and dreadful God."[23] "Holy art Thou, and fearful is Thy name."[24] Thus the Rabbis speak much of the fear of God,[25] and frequently call God מֶלֶךְ מַלְכֵי הַמְּלָכִים, in indication of His majesty transcending everything earthly. This emphasis on the majesty and transcendence of God does not mean, however, that God is distant, unapproachable or remote for Judaism.[26] He reveals Himself to be holy majesty specifically and indeed exclusively when one draws near to Him. It is constantly said that God is present among His people (שְׁכִינָה עִמָּהֶם). Later Judaism also knows well enough a direct relationship of trust in God. But where there is genuine piety and not unworthy calculation, this believing confidence is always sustained by fear and trembling before the holy God.[27] Hence the Holy One is one of the commonest designations for God in Judaism, as in Sir. and En.,[28] and later in Rabbinic texts from the 3rd century onwards (usually now with the eulogy : הַקָּדוֹשׁ בָּרוּךְ הוּא).[29] Rather strangely, it is almost completely lacking in the older strata of Rabbinic tradition (1st and 2nd centuries A.D.).[30] Alongside it there is still found הַקֹּדֶשׁ (abstr. pro concreto) in the formula מִפִּי הַקֹּדֶשׁ, e.g., S. Nu., 112 on 15:31: "The whole Torah was spoken by Moses from the mouth of Holiness," i.e., exactly as God spoke it to him.

The Spirit of God is also called holy. Indeed, רוּחַ הַקֹּדֶשׁ[31] has become almost a fixed formula, and we never have instead רוּחַ הַמָּקוֹם (which would correspond to the OT רוּחַ יהוה),

Above all, the name of God is holy. This explains why in later Judaism the proper name (שֵׁם הַמְיוּחָד)[32] of God was never pronounced except in temple worship.[33] After the destruction of the temple it was not even known how to pronounce it. It was replaced by אֲדוֹנִי in the reading of Scripture and by שָׁמַיִם in more general use. But even these substitutes eventually became taboo. The reading אֲדוֹנִי for יהוה was restricted to liturgical use. In private reading הַשֵּׁם or "the name" was used. Similarly שָׁמַיִם came to be replaced by the very general הַמָּקוֹם or "place" (i.e., heaven = God).[34]

---

[22] Baudissin, II, 20 ff.

[23] Schemone-Esre, 1. Benediction.

[24] *Ibid.,* 3. Benediction.

[25] E.g., Ab., 1, 3; bBer., 28b; 30b; Midr. Ps. 100 § 3 (213a).

[26] This view prevailed for many years, but it has been exploded by Moore, *Judaism* (1927), I, 423 ff.

[27] Cf. the prayer of Raba in bBer., 17a (bJoma., 87b); the words of Johanan b. Zaccai in bBer., 28b; and esp. the passages from a prayer on the great day of atonement cited by Moore, *op. cit.*, II, 214.

[28] For examples, *v.* Str.-B., III, 762.

[29] *Ibid.*, II, 310, under k.

[30] A. Marmorstein, *The Old Rabbinic Doctrine of God* (1927), I, 97.

[31] In the OT, only Is. 63:10, 11; Ps. 51:11.

[32] W. Bacher, *Die exegetische Terminologie* (1905), I, 159.

[33] Str.-B., II, 311 ff.

[34] *Ibid.*, II, 308-319.

The holiness of the name of God, i.e., of God Himself, is particularly characterised by the expression "to hallow the name (of God)." This is often found in
prayers with God as subject: "Hallow Thy name" (Tanna de-bē Elijjahu, 21, E),
or, the same in substance though not in expression: "Hallowed be Thy name,"
synonymous with "Glorified be Thy name." [35] The two latter terms are found
together at the beginning of the Kaddish prayer: יִתְגַּדַּל וְיִתְקַדַּשׁ שְׁמָךְ רַבָּא "Hallowed and
glorified be Thy great name." "God sanctifies His name by showing His holiness
to the world," [36] and by forcing men to acknowledge His name. Quite often,
however, it is said of men, though usually only of Israelites, that they hallow the
name of God. They do this by "so living that men must see and say that the God
of Israel is the true God," [37] and especially by obeying the will of God in keeping
the commands of the Torah and studying to achieve a blameless walk in the eyes
of the world. Thus the hallowing of the name (קִידּוּשׁ הַשֵׁם) is "the chief principle
and motive of ethical action in Judaism." [37] In a special sense it is martyrs who
by their constancy to God's commands sanctify the name of God at the cost of
their lives. [38]

c. Scripture is holy as the Word of God, the Torah being more holy than the
rest because it is more strictly God's Word. [39] Cf. the mounting succession of
holiness from Meg., 3, 1.

To be sure, the description of the Torah or the rest of the OT as כִּתְבֵי הַקֹּדֶשׁ
is relatively infrequent in Rabbinic literature. [40] It is usually called quite simply
הַתּוֹרָה or הַכָּתוּב. But the matter itself is plain enough. The holiness of the Torah is
seen supremely in the fact that the reading of it stands at the heart of synagogue
worship encircled by a series of prayers referring to it. [41] The reading of the Torah
is a sacred, cultic action. But concern with it apart from worship is also felt to be
in some sense a sacred action: "If two sit together and occupy themselves with
the Torah, God's presence is among them" (Ab., 3, 2). The same is true of
solitary study of the Torah (Ab., 3, 6 par.). [42] The same thought is reflected in
the miraculous accounts of certain rabbis being encircled with fire as they studied
the Torah. [43]

Because Scripture is holy, so, too, are the individual scrolls, especially of the
Torah. The writing of them is itself a sacred task. We see this from the saying
(bEr., 13a) of R. Jishma'el to R. Meir, himself a copyist of the Torah: "My son,
be careful in thy work, for it is a work of God." For the same reason, R. 'Akiba
(S. Nu., 5, 23, § 16, E) demands that scrolls copied by heretics should be burned
"because they are not written in holiness," i.e., by a strict Jew and with sufficient
care.

---

[35] = "Glorify thy name," cf. Jn. 12, 28.
[36] Str.-B., I, 411. The demonstration may also be given by a miracle, as in the case of
the three in the burning fiery furnace in Da. 3:24 (cf. S. Lv., 18, 6 in Str.-B., I, 413 etc.
Cf. also Moore, II, 102).
[37] Moore, II, 103.
[38] Ibid., 105 f. Cf. esp. Midrash on Ps. 16:2 (61a).
[39] Str.-B., IV, 435 ff.
[40] For examples, ibid., III, 14.
[41] Ibid., IV, 154 ff.
[42] Ibid., I, 794.
[43] Ibid., II, 603. Fire is the sacred element. Hence also Midr. Ps., 90 § 12 (196a): The
Torah as pre-existent with God was written with black fire on white fire (Str.-B., I, 975).

The particular expression for the holiness of the scrolls in the Rabbinic writings is that "they make the hands unclean" (Zab., 5, 12; bShab, 13b etc.), i.e., a cultic washing of the hands is necessary after touching them, [44] the hands having become holy through the holiness of Scripture and needing to be made unclean again after contact.

d. Men are often called holy in Rabbinic literature. The man who fulfils God's commandments and leads a pious life pleasing to God is holy: Tanch. שלח § 31 (37b); S. Lv., 20, 7 (91d) קְדוּשַׁת כָּל הַמִּצְוֹת: "The holiness which consists in keeping all the commandments." Study of the Torah also belongs essentially to a life pleasing to God. Hence students are called עַם קָדוֹשׁ (bMeg., 27b; bJeb., 105b; bSanh., 7b). Jose b. Meshullam and Shim'on b. Menasia are called עֵדָה קְדוֹשָׁה "a holy community," because they lead a life which is to some extent the ideal of Jewish piety, dividing the day into three parts, one third for the Torah, one third for prayer and one third for work. [45] The righteous of the OT are also called holy, as the early patriarchs in Tanch. במדבר, Isaac in Gn. r., 65 and Abraham in Gn. r., 45.

Particular emphasis always falls on the negative side of the concept of holiness. To be holy is to be separated, S. Lv., 11, 44 (57b) etc. In the first instance this means separation from the Gentiles and their idolatry (S. Lv., 20:7; M. Ex. 19:6). Often, however, to be holy means to refrain from sin, especially from licentiousness. Thus Lv. r. 24:6 (34d), Jehuda b. Pazzi: "He who refrains from licentiousness is called holy." Similarly, Nu. r. 9 (151b). [46] Similarly, Rabbi Jehuda I is called holy "because not once in his life did he look on the place of his circumcision" (jMeg., 72b, 50), and Nahum b. Simai is called most holy because he never looked on naked heathen statues, nor on any image on a coin. [47] For later Judaism holy and chaste come to be synonymous. Maimonides (12th century) calls קדושה the portion of his Mishnah Torah which contains definitions of sexual matters, and Nachmanides (13th century) entitles his missive on the same commandments אגרת קדושה.

Kuhn

E. ἅγιος in the NT.

1. The Holiness of God.

In the NT, which everywhere rests on an OT foundation, the material element largely yields before the personal. As already in the OT, e.g., in the prophets, the ἅγιος predicate is referred to the person of God. Indeed, it contains the innermost description of God's nature (Is. 6:3). Thus the Trisagion recurs in the song of praise of the four beasts in Rev. 4:8. The vision of Isaiah is here filled out with elements taken from the vision at the call of Ezekiel (Ez. 1), but with the song of the heavenly creatures, who are to be thought of as holy like the ἄγγελοι ἅγιοι (cf. Rev. 14:10), it retains its basic character. The scene is set in heaven, and

---

[44] The reason given for this definition in bShab., 14a, and followed in Str.-B., IV, 433 f., is a late construction of no historical value.
[45] Str.-B., II, 692, under d.
[46] Str.-B., III, 632.
[47] *Ibid.*, II, 692, under e. For further examples, *v.* Fridrichsen, 60, n. 3.

therefore in the supra-creaturely realm of the worship of God, who Himself belongs to the holy sphere. Yahweh Sabaoth is rightly regarded as παντοκράτωρ, so that omnipotence is the external aspect of the holiness of God, to which eternity also belongs (ὁ ἦν καὶ ὁ ὢν καὶ ὁ ἐρχόμενος, cf. 9 f.). Holiness and glory thus combine to express the essence of the Godhead, and a holy awe permeates the whole scene. If God is invoked by martyrs as the avenger of innocent blood (Rev. 6:10), in His attributes as ὁ ἅγιος καὶ ἀληθινός there is found a guarantee of the detection of religious crimes which constitute sacrilege.

As in the Apocalypse, so in John's Gospel the holiness of God emerges in the πάτερ ἅγιε of Jesus (Jn. 17:11), which Jesus uses to descibe the innermost nature of God. [48] Elsewhere ἅγιος is applied to God in 1 Pt. 1:15 f.: κατὰ τὸν καλέσαντα ὑμᾶς ἅγιον, in which reference is made to Lv. 19:2 to deduce from the holiness of God a demand for holy conversation in His children to the extent that they are taken out of the world and await the ἀποκάλυψις Ἰησοῦ (v. 13). Finally, in the Lord's Prayer petition is made that God's name should be hallowed (Mt. 6:9; Lk. 11:12: ἁγιασθήτω τὸ ὄνομά σου). Here τὸ ὄνομα means the person in which God reveals Himself (cf. Mt. 28:19), but in which He is also distinct from the creaturely world. In the name of God the holy shows itself to be something personal which thus requires of the one who prays a personal attitude to the divine world. Thus the holiness of God the Father is everywhere presumed in the NT, though seldom stated. It is filled out in Jesus Christ as the ἅγιος τοῦ θεοῦ, and in the πνεῦμα ἅγιον.

2. Jesus Christ as ἅγιος.

The description of Jesus Christ as ἅγιος is rare (Mk. 1:24; Lk. 1:35; 4·34; Jn. 6:69; 1 Jn. 2:20; Rev. 3:7; Ac. 3:14; 4:27, 30). On the other hand, it is ancient and full of content. In Luke it is grounded upon His miraculous birth when the πνεῦμα ἅγιον came on Mary and the δύναμις ὑψίστου overshadowed her (διὸ καὶ τὸ γεννώμενον ἅγιον κληθήσεται υἱὸς θεοῦ, 1:35). With τὸ γεννώμενον, ἅγιον here belongs to the subject, for the predicate is υἱὸς θεοῦ; but the expression τὸ γεννώμενον ἅγιον is to be explained by the supranatural origin of the new life, which is called υἱὸς θεοῦ because of its origin, so that υἱὸς θεοῦ is here a predicate which is not grounded in the Messianic office of Christ but in His origin. Immediately alongside, Luke sets the establishment of the divine sonship of Christ by the reception of the Spirit (καταβῆναι τὸ πνεῦμα τὸ ἅγιον) at baptism. [49] In Luke, Jesus can in any case be called ἅγιος as a bearer of the Spirit. This is also the thought in the old Synoptic scene (Lk. 4:34; Mk. 1:24) where the ἄνθρωπος ἐν πνεύματι ἀκαθάρτῳ (Mk. ἔχων πνεῦμα δαιμόνιον ἀκάθαρτον) says to Jesus: οἶδά [οἴδαμέν] σε τίς εἶ, ὁ ἅγιος τοῦ θεοῦ. Jesus plainly confronts the unclean spirit as a bearer of the πνεῦμα ἅγιον; there is a mortal antithesis

---

[48] The name which the πατὴρ ἅγιος has given the Son (v. 11 f.) can only be the divine name itself (Mt. 28:19), in which the Father and the Son are one, this being the basis of the unity of Christian faith: ἵνα ὦσιν ἓν καθὼς ἡμεῖς.

[49] υἱός μου εἶ σύ, ἐγὼ σήμερον γεγέννηκά σε (Lk. 3:22, D latt.). This text, which as against the Marco-Matthean (Mt. 3:17; Mk. 1:11) that has mostly penetrated into Luke, we must regard as the older Synoptic (cf. Zahn), does not refer to the natural but to the Messianic birth of Christ (cf. Ps. 2:7), which is followed by the reception of the πνεῦμα ἅγιον at baptism (σήμερον).

between πνεῦμα ἅγιον and πνεῦμα ἀκάθαρτον which the demons recognise. [50] The predicate ὁ ἅγιος τοῦ θεοῦ, however, implies more than that Jesus is the popular Messiah, for there is no reference here to His national position, but to His pneumatic nature. As ἅγιος τοῦ θεοῦ He is the Firstborn and Inaugurator of the pneumatic age which will destroy the kingdom of demons.

In John, too, Jesus is called ὁ ἅγιος τοῦ θεοῦ (6:69), this time in the confession of Peter and therefore in an extraordinary place. The recognition of Jesus as ὁ ἅγιος τοῦ θεοῦ is here called a confession of faith (ἡμεῖς πεπιστεύκαμεν καὶ ἐγνώκαμεν), so that again more is at issue than the recognition of the popular Messiah. [51] As ὁ ἅγιος τοῦ θεοῦ Jesus is set by John at the side of God whom He addresses as πατὴρ ἅγιος (Jn. 17:11). The One whom the Father has sanctified (ἡγίασεν) and sent into the world, is rightly called υἱὸς τοῦ θεοῦ (Jn. 10:36). As the Holy One Christ is also in John the Dispenser of χρῖσμα, namely, of the anointing of the Spirit (1 Jn. 2:20). [52] Similarly in Revelation Christ as ὁ ἅγιος καὶ ὁ ἀληθινός (3:7) bears the same predicates as God Himself (6:10). Thus in all the passages adduced ἅγιος is used to describe the deity of Christ.

The case is rather different in the early Christian application of the predicate ὁ ἅγιος παῖς (Ac. 3:14; 4:27, 30) to Jesus. It is evident that in the expression ὁ παῖς, which elsewhere is used of Jesus only in Mt. 12:16 ff., we have a play on the עֶבֶד יְהוָה of Deutero-Isaiah, whose counterpart Jesus clearly showed Himself to be in Lk. 4:16 ff. and Lk. 22:37. If Jesus bears the ancient predicate of ὁ ἅγιος παῖς [θεοῦ] in the primitive community, this is less a reference to His divine origin, for which παῖς is hardly appropriate, than to His cultic mission; for the Servant of the Lord of Deutero-Isaiah is obviously a Messianic figure, since he is anointed with the Spirit of God (Is. 42:1; 61:1), to which there is reference in Ac. 4:27: ὃν ἔχρισας, and yet His Messianic sending is accomplished in vicarious sacrifice for others (Is. 53:10) and thus acquires a cultic content. The same meaning is indicated in the primitive community by emphasis on the suffering of the ἅγιος καὶ δίκαιος παῖς (3:14; 4:27). As the Servant of God Jesus is the holy sacrifice which, itself innocent, is offered vicariously for the guilt of the people of God (cf. 1 Pt. 1:18 f.) to open up access to the sanctuary.

This train of thought comes out most clearly in Hebrews (c. 9), except that the one Jesus is now both priest and victim. As the high-priest, who is here the figura Christi, went once a year into the holiest of holies (9:3: ἅγια ἁγίων), not without blood, to make atonement for himself and the people, so Christ has done

---

[50] It is arguable whether ὁ ἅγιος τοῦ θεοῦ is vocative or predicate in relation to τίς εἶ. It seems to be that the second is the case, for the former would leave it open who the ἅγιος τοῦ θεοῦ is, whereas the whole point is that the demons feel themselves to be mortally assailed (ἦλθες ἀπολέσαι ἡμᾶς) in the ἅγιος τοῦ θεοῦ.

[51] If we compare the Synoptic confession of Peter: σὺ εἶ ὁ Χριστός (Lk. + τοῦ θεοῦ), in Mk. 8:29 and par., and the Matthean addition ὁ υἱὸς τοῦ θεοῦ τοῦ ζῶντος (16:16), to which there corresponds in Matthew the ὁ πατὴρ ὁ ἐν τοῖς οὐρανοῖς of v. 17, so that Mt. 16:16b, 17-19 at least derive from a special source, the Johannine ὁ ἅγιος τοῦ θεοῦ is undoubtedly better explained by the Matthean ὁ υἱὸς τοῦ θεοῦ ζῶντος than by ὁ Χριστός, as ὁ υἱὸς τοῦ θεοῦ ζῶντος also corresponds better to the Matthean question who ὁ υἱὸς τοῦ ἀνθρώπου is (16:13). The υἱὸς τοῦ ἀνθρώπου as ὁ υἱὸς τοῦ θεοῦ is ὁ ἅγιος τοῦ θεοῦ (cf. Mk. 1:24; Lk. 4:34) not merely in the cultic (Ps. 106:16: ἅγιος κυρίου) but in the supraterrestrial sense (cf. Da. 7:27: קַדִּישֵׁי עֶלְיוֹנִין; Da. 7:13).

[52] The play on Χριστός in χρῖσμα is so obvious that the question, which is often left undecided, whether ὁ ἅγιος refers to God or to Christ, is surely to be answered in the latter sense.

by His own blood as both priest and victim (9:25 ff.). The holiest of holies is an antitype of heaven as the dwelling-place of God which Jesus has entered by His death and where He now represents Christians as a Priest, so that the new testament (v. 15, διαθήκη καινή) is now valid for the Christian world. In this connection it is to be noted that instead of ἁγνίζειν = קִדֵּשׁ, which signifies the self-sanctifying of the layman with a view to his cultic status (Jn. 11:55; Ac. 21:24, 26; 24:18 etc.), the verb ἁγιάζειν (Hb. 2:11; 9:13; 13:12 f.; cf. 10:10, 14, 29) is here used, which expresses expiatory sanctification by the sacrifice here offered in Christ. Only he who himself is ἅγιος, whether it be God, priest or victim, can exercise ἁγιάζειν. Hence Christ as ἁγιάζων (Hb. 2:11) must Himself be ἅγιος.

3. The Holy Spirit.

a. The holiness of the Spirit (→ πνεῦμα) is inseparable from that of Christ. The OT root is obviously רוּחַ הַקֹּדֶשׁ (Is. 63:10 f.; Ps. 51:11).

Though the expression is infrequent in the OT, its substance is common. In David רוּחַ has Messianic as well as prophetic content (2 S. 23:2); in Isaiah the Messiah is a bearer of the Spirit (Is. 11:2), and in Deutero-Isaiah the עֶבֶד יהוה is anointed with the Spirit (42:1; 61:1). As the Spirit is here a possession of the Messiah, so elsewhere of the prophets. Elijah bears the Spirit (2 K. 2:9), and Elisha asks of his master a double measure of the firstborn's portion of the Spirit (cf. Dt. 21:17). If Elisha is depicted as a holy man of God (2 K. 4:9), his holy character presumably rests on his possession of the Spirit. Hosea, too, is called אִישׁ הָרוּחַ (Hos. 9:7), and both Isaiah (30:1) and Micah (3:8) are conscious of being filled with the Spirit. In Ezekiel the Spirit of God becomes a possession of the community in the Messianic future (36:26 f.), and in Joel He is poured out on all flesh as a prelude to the last time (3:1), this passage being adopted by Peter in his preaching at Pentecost (Ac. 2:17 ff.). Yet the post-exilic people of God is already aware that it is indwelt by the Spirit of Yahweh (Hag. 2:5; Zech. 4:6; 7:12), as was also the Israel of the time of Moses (Is. 63:10 f.). The Psalmist is unmistakeably thinking of this common possession of the Spirit when in relation to Ezekiel's promise of a new heart and spirit (Ez. 36:26 f.) he prays for a clean heart and right spirit, and asks that he should not be expelled from the fellowship of the Holy Spirit (Ps. 51:10 f.).

b. In the NT there is the textual difficulty that in the Synoptics and Acts πνεῦμα ἅγιον is often an emendation of πνεῦμα alone (i.e., without ἅγιον). [53] In both Matthew and Luke τὸ πνεῦμα ἅγιον is the principle of the derivation of Christ even on the natural side (Mt. 1:18, 20; cf. Lk. 1:35) as distinct from πνεῦμα as an immanent potency. Above all, however, πνεῦμα ἅγιον plays an important role in the baptism story (Mt. 3:11 and par.); for according to the old Synoptic conception the Messiah is to baptise ἐν πνεύματι ἁγίῳ (cf. Ac. 1:5), with a clear forward reference to the fulfilment at Pentecost. [54] With the baptism of Christ the age of the Spirit begins in the full sense (Mt. 3:13 ff. and par.). As the dove of Noah after the flood indicates the dawn of a new epoch (Gn. 8:8 ff.), so the

---

[53] Luke especially loves the formula τὸ πνεῦμα τὸ ἅγιον in both his books, though this weakens to some extent the original sense of ἅγιον. Yet Mark, too, shows the same tendency (cf. 3:29 : Mt. 12:31; 12:36 : Mt. 22:43; 13:11: Mt. 10:20), so that Matthew seems to have here the earliest Synoptic text.

[54] John uses the expression πνεῦμα ἅγιον only in relation to the event of Pentecost, which he attributes directly to the risen Lord (20:22); for in Jn. 14:26 τὸ ἅγιον is an addition lacking in Syr. sin. The Hebrew concept of the holy comes out in this saying to the extent that there is binding and loosing of sin in the power of the πνεῦμα ἅγιον. The πνεῦμα ἅγιον excludes the hardened sinner but pardons the penitent.

dove-like form of the Spirit indicates the dawn of a new creation rising with Christ from the baptismal waters (cf. 1 Pt. 3:19 ff.). In the first instance the Spirit of God is linked exclusively with Christ; He is freed to be the Spirit of Christianity only by the resurrection of Christ (Jn. 20:22; Ac. 2:1 ff.; 4:27 ff.), being then imparted to the disciples as the Spirit of Pentecost. The promise of the πνεῦμα ἅγιον undoubtedly goes back to Jesus and is referred back by Him to John the Baptist (Mk. 1:8 and par.).

Even the obscure saying concerning the sin against the Holy Ghost (Mt. 12:32 f. par.) has a Pentecostal content.[55] In the υἱός τοῦ ἀνθρώπου God is present in hidden form. Hence sin against the Son of Man is committed in ignorance and may be pardoned. In the πνεῦμα ἅγιον of the Pentecostal age, however, God manifests Himself through Christ. Hence he who is apprehended by the πνεῦμα ἅγιον, but resists His power and thus blasphemes Him (βλασφημεῖ), commits unforgivable sin. The possibility of this sin thus arises only with the Pentecostal era when the Holy Spirit has been poured out by Jesus on the disciples and has become their indwelling possession.[56] Even the Trinitarian baptismal command, in which we have the divine name as πατήρ, υἱός and ἅγιον πνεῦμα, is linked with the Pentecostal age.

It thus follows that in the primitive Gospel πνεῦμα ἅγιον = רוּחַ [הַ]קֹּדֶשׁ is used only of the Pentecostal period, though Jesus Himself often enough spoke of πνεῦμα alone. The absolute *Pneuma* was fully adequate to express the matter, especially on Hebrew soil. Yet the ἅγιος τοῦ θεοῦ added the attribute ἅγιον in order to differentiate the Spirit from all ἀκαθαρσία.

c. Among the Evangelists Luke is most fond of the expression πνεῦμα ἅγιον, whether he uses the definite article and thus selects the formula τὸ πνεῦμα τὸ ἅγιον, or whether he has the indefinite πνεῦμα ἅγιον.[57] In general it may be said that the definite form reveals the Pentecostal Spirit manifested at the baptism of Jesus (Lk. 3:22), who at a supreme point broke forth from the lips of Jesus in rejoicing (Lk. 10:21), but only became the possession of the Christian community in the event of Pentecost (Ac. 4:31) in which He now works with sovereign creativity. On the other hand, the indefinite πνεῦμα ἅγιον works less as conscious will than as unconscious power of a creative (Lk. 1:35; 4:1) or prophetic nature (1:15, 41, 67 etc.), although this cannot be pressed too hard. In both cases Luke lays special emphasis on the attribute ἅγιον, though the liberal use perhaps weakens the material force of the expression. As the Holy Spirit, He is everywhere thought to be grounded in God, so that ἅγιον takes on almost the meaning of divine. The antithesis to demonic or natural spirit is thus underlined.

As a Greek nurtured on the mission field rather than in the homeland of the Gospel, Luke had particular reason to distinguish the Spirit of God from other spirits active in the pagan world. There can be no doubt that his conception of the Spirit corresponds to popular ideas in early missionary Christianity rather than Jewish Christianity, in which the cultic element is never completely lost, as shown by Matthew and Hebrews. His conception of the Spirit is shaped by the char-

---

[55] H. v. Baer, *Der Heilige Geist in den Lukasschriften* (1926), 75 f.

[56] The form of the saying in Mark and Matthew (Mk. 3:28 f.: Mt. 12:31) suppresses the contrast between ὁ υἱός τοῦ ἀνθρώπου and τὸ πνεῦμα τὸ ἅγιον.

[57] τὸ πνεῦμα [τὸ] ἅγιον Lk. 2:26; 3:22; 10:21; 12:10, 12; Ac. 1:8; 2:33; 4:31; 5:3; 7:51; 9:31; 10:44; 13:4; 15:8, 28; 16:6; 19:6; 20:23, 28; 28:25; πνεῦμα ἅγιον Lk. 1:15 (17), 35, 41, 67; 2:25; 3:16; 4:1; 11:13; Ac. 1:2; 4:25; 6:5; 7:55; 8:15, 17, 19; 10:38; 11:24; 19:2.

ismatic processes in the early Christian communities which found expression in the gift of tongues and the prophetic stimulation so dynamically depicted by Paul, especially in the Corinthian Epistles. The Holy Spirit in Luke often bears the character of eschatological unrest as described by Joel (Jl. 3:1 ff.) and as undoubtedly most frequently found in early Christianity in view of the expected end. His descriptions are thus more rewarding for investigators of the Pentecost movement in the broad strata of the apostolic age than for those who seek more clear-cut theological concepts.

d. Far more personal and noble is the conception of the Spirit in Paul, which has many points of contact with the Johannine view except that Paul makes far more use of the attribute ἅγιον, to which he gives a specific sense. Thinking in terms of the temple (1 C. 3:16; 6:19; Eph. 2:20), the sacrifice (Eph. 5:2) and the liturgy (R. 15:16), Paul maintains but spiritualises the cultic character of the holy.

In Christ there is established a holy temple (Eph. 2:21) in which Christians are built up as living stones, God Himself dwelling therein ἐν πνεύματι. The foundation of this building consists of the apostles and prophets (Eph. 2:20) to whom the mystery of Christ is revealed ἐν πνεύματι (Eph. 3:5). The integration of this living organism, in which the body of Christ is built up, is explicitly described (4:11 ff.). In I Corinthians this thought is individualised (6:19 : τὸ σῶμα ὑμῶν ναὸς τοῦ ἐν ὑμῖν ἁγίου πνεύματός ἐστιν, cf. 3:16). To the temple there corresponds the sacrifice which is brought in Christ and which has the character of holiness (1 C. 5:7). In Romans Paul compares himself as λειτουργὸς Ἰησοῦ Χριστοῦ with the priest who handles the Gospel (ἱερουργοῦντα τὸ εὐαγγέλιον τοῦ θεοῦ) in order that the Gentile world may be accepted as a sacrifice (προσφορά) by God, ἡγιασμένη ἐν πνεύματι ἁγίῳ (R. 15:16). Everywhere it is a matter of building the holy temple and setting up the holy cultus whose holiness consists in the πνεῦμα ἅγιον, in which the fellowship of Christianity is also grounded (2 C. 13:13; R. 5:5). As once in the Israel of the time of Moses (Is. 63:10 f.; cf. 1 C. 10:1 ff.), so now τὸ πνεῦμα τὸ ἅγιον dwells in Christianity (1 Th. 4:8; 2 Tm. 1:14) to the extent that it consists in a state of ἁγιασμός (2 Th. 2:13).

The signs of the new cultic community, of Christianity, created in the death of Christ, are baptism (1 C. 12:13 : ἐν ἑνὶ πνεύματι ἡμεῖς εἰς ἓν σῶμα ἐβαπτίσθημεν), in which the Holy Spirit effects the παλιγγενεσία and ἀνακαίνωσις of creation (Tt. 3:5), and the Lord's Supper (1 C. 12:13 : πάντες ἓν πνεῦμα ἐποτίσθημεν). Baptism as a fellowship with Christ in death signifies the death of the old life and the raising up of the new (R. 6:3; Col. 2:12). Similarly the communion of the Lord's Supper expresses fellowship with Christ in death (1 C. 11:26) from which there springs the new creation (2 C. 5:17: εἴ τις ἐν Χριστῷ, καινὴ κτίσις). Hence in the death of Christ there is advanced the thought of a cultic fellowship of Christianity. The cultic element in its spiritual form is contained in the concept of reconciliation (καταλλαγή), which is effected by the sacrificial death of Christ (R. 5:9 ff.; 2 C. 5:18 f.).

4. The Holiness of the ἐκκλησία.

The connection of the holy with the cultic may be clearly perceived in the NT, as we have already seen, not merely in the name of God but also in fellowship in divine service.

Here, too, the OT origin is obvious. Jerusalem is ἡ ἁγία πόλις (Mt. 4:5; 27:53; Rev. 11:2) where the great King dwells (Mt. 5:35). Like Sinai (Ac. 7:33) and the Mount of Transfiguration (2 Pt. 1:18), the Jerusalem temple is a τόπος ἅγιος (Mt. 24:15; Ac. 6:13); even Paul, if in a higher sense, calls the temple holy (1 C. 3:17; Eph. 2:21). As ἅγιος, it lends holiness even to the gold (Mt. 23:17), just as the altar does to the offering (Mt. 23:19 : ἁγιάζον, cf. 7:6 : ἅγιον). Along with the cultus, Scripture as the constitutional foundation of the people of God is reckoned holy (R. 1:2 : ἐν γραφαῖς ἁγίαις); the Law of Moses is the basic Scripture as developed in the commandments (ἐντολή) on the basis of the divine testament (Lk. 1:72; R. 7:12 : ὁ μὲν νόμος ἅγιος καὶ ἡ ἐντολὴ ἁγία καὶ δικαία). At this point the doctrine of the priests and scribes is taken over in the NT.

In the καινὴ κτίσις, however, the OT cult which is the starting-point is only ὑπόδειγμα καὶ σκιὰ τῶν ἐπουρανίων (Hb. 8:5), so that the Ἅγιον in the NT takes on a pneumatic sense. Christ as ὁ ἅγιος παῖς (→ 102) becomes the centre of a new sanctuary in which He Himself is the Priest, Sacrifice and Temple of God. His priestly character is especially emphasised in Hebrews (→ 102 f.).

The NT view as a whole corresponds to the brilliant sketch of Hebrews. Already the early Jerusalem community is constituted by the ἅγιος παῖς (Ac. 4:27, 30) a temple of the Holy Spirit (4:31: ἐπλήσθησαν ἅπαντες τοῦ ἁγίου πνεύματος). [58] There thus arises a new people of God within the old (cf. Hb. 13:12 ff.), which with reference to Ex. 19:6 is described as βασίλειον ἱεράτευμα, ἔθνος ἅγιον (1 Pt. 2:9), and to which the old saying applies : Ἅγιοι ἔσεσθε, ὅτι ἐγὼ ἅγιος (1 Pt. 1:16). [59] In the powerful historical sweep of Paul the concept of the people of God has burst its national limits and come to be equated with the Church of Christ. On the holy stump of the OT people of God the new branches from the Gentile world have been engrafted (R. 11:17), and they are sanctified by the stump. The stump is obviously Christ as ἡ ῥίζα τοῦ Ἰεσσαί (R. 15:12) ordained to rule over the Gentiles. He has given Himself for the ἐκκλησία, ἵνα αὐτὴν ἁγιάσῃ ... ἵνα ᾖ ἁγία καὶ ἄμωμος (Eph. 5:26). By Him it is sanctified not merely in the Jewish Christian trunk but also in the Gentile Christian grafts ; these are ἡγιασμένοι ἐν Χριστῷ Ἰησοῦ (1 C. 1:2; cf. 6:11), a προσφορά ... ἡγιασμένη ἐν πνεύματι ἁγίῳ (R. 15:16). The πολιτεία τοῦ Ἰσραήλ together with the διαθῆκαι τῆς ἐπαγγελίας (Eph. 2:12) is extended by Christ to the whole Christian world, so that now Gentile Christians are no longer ξένοι καὶ πάροικοι (= גֵּרִים וְתוֹשָׁבִים) but συμπολῖται τῶν ἁγίων καὶ οἰκεῖοι τοῦ θεοῦ (2:19), built on the corner-stone Christ over the foundation of the apostles and prophets. Here the ἅγιοι are to be sought in the πολιτεία τοῦ Ἰσραήλ, except that we are now dealing with an Ἰσραὴλ κατὰ πνεῦμα. Originally contained in Jewish Christianity, with which the ἅγιοι are often equated even in Acts (9:13, 32, 41; 26:10), the holy people of God now extends to the Gentile world.

We may thus understand quite simply Paul's frequent application of the term both to the mother community in Jerusalem (R. 15:25 f.; 1 C. 16:1, 15; 2 C. 8:4 etc.) and also to Gentile Christianity (R. 1:7; 1 C. 1:2). As members of the ἐκκλησία

---

[58] Here we perhaps have the oldest form of the Pentecost story which later came to be accompanied by the familiar one ; cf. A. Harnack, Die Apostelgeschichte (1908), 142 ff.
[59] K. Holl, "Der Osten" (Ges. Auf. z. Kirchengeschichte, II, 1928), 60, takes ἅγιοι to be a synon. of πτωχοί, both becoming standard names for the Christians at Jerusalem. He also equates ἅγιοι with ἐκλεκτοὶ τοῦ θεοῦ. But this is to empty ἅγιος of any specific content and to ignore the distinctive cultic element (cf. Asting. 154, n. 2). It is not in virtue of election but rather in virtue of the atonement that the Jerusalem Christians are called ἅγιοι. They are related as ἅγιοι to the ἅγιος τοῦ θεοῦ in the same sense as they are related as Χριστιανοί to Χριστός (Ac. 11:26).

ἁγία καὶ ἄμωμος (Eph. 5:27), individual ἐκκλησίαι are holy together with their members. Basically there is no distinction in Paul between the ἅγιοι of the mother community and those of the missionary Church, for in each case the holiness derives from Christ even though the πρῶτον ᾿Ιουδαῖοι καὶ ῞Ελληνες remains as a historical relationship. The same order obtains for all ἐκκλησίαι τῶν ἁγίων (1 C. 14:33), since they are all partial organisms in the organism of the ἐκκλησία. A distinctive phrase is κλητοὶ ἅγιοι in the address to the communities (R. 1:7; 1 C. 1:2), an apposition to ἐκκλησία in which we may seek the individualisation of κλητὴ ἁγία = מִקְרָא קֹדֶשׁ. [60] Yet while in the OT expression the stress falls on קֹדֶשׁ, in Paul it falls on κλητοί (R. 1:6: καὶ ἡμεῖς κλητοί; 1 C. 1:24: αὐτοῖς δὲ τοῖς κλητοῖς, ᾿Ιουδαίοις τε καὶ ῞Ελλησι; cf. Jd. 1). For it is not by nature but by divine calling that Christians are ἅγιοι; they owe their membership of the holy cultic community to the call of divine grace in Christ (Phil. 1:1: τοῖς ἁγίοις ἐν Χριστῷ).

As ἅγιοι they are members of a cultic circle grounded in the sacrifice of Christ ; as ἐκλεκτοὶ τοῦ θεοῦ ἅγιοι καὶ ἠγαπημένοι (Col. 3:12), a phrase in which the parallel terms ἅγιοι and ἠγαπημένοι belong to the ἐκλεκτοί as attributes, they are selected by God for this circle. If Acts 20:32 speaks of the κληρονομία ἐν τοῖς ἡγιασμένοις πᾶσιν, it refers to the inheritance of God (κληρονομία = נַחֲלָה, Dt. 9:26; 12:9; 19:14; 32:9) which is distributed among the saints so that each receives his portion. [61] Similarly Eph. 1:18 speaks of the κληρονομία αὐτοῦ ἐν τοῖς ἁγίοις whose glorious riches are to be known by Christians. Inseparably related is the verse in Colossians in which the Father enables Christians εἰς τὴν μερίδα τοῦ κλήρου τῶν ἁγίων ἐν τῷ φωτί (Col. 1:12); for κλῆρος like κληρονομία is the usual rendering of נַחֲלָה, and חֵלֶק "share" is the Hebrew equivalent of μερίς. The defining ἐν τῷ φωτί is set in opposition to ἐξουσία τοῦ σκότους and thus refers to the light of grace (cf. Eph. 5:7) rather than to that of heavenly glory; [62] for the translation into the βασιλεία τοῦ υἱοῦ τῆς ἀγάπης αὐτοῦ, the heavenly inheritance, is already achieved (μετέστησεν). Everywhere in the relation of the ἅγιοι to the κληρονομία we are concerned with the birthright of the people of God on the Deuteronomic pattern. [63]

5. The Holy Life of Christians.

As the Church is a ναὸς ἅγιος (1 C. 3:17; Eph. 2:21), so the life of Christians should be a θυσία ζῶσα ἁγία τῷ θεῷ (R. 12:1; 15:16). Paul describes himself as a drink-offering poured out at the sacrifice and service of the faith of his com-

---

[60] In the OT מִקְרָא קֹדֶשׁ is the cultic assembly, usually translated in the LXX, with concretum pro abstracto, by κλητὴ ἁγία (Ex. 12:16; Lv. 23:2 ff.). Paul has the concept κλῆσις ἁγία even with God as the Subject of calling (2 Tm. 1:9).

[61] The reference of ἡγιασμένοι (Ac. 20:32) cannot be to angels but only to men and therefore to members of the Church of Christ. Eph. 1:18, then, can hardly be interpreted in any other way, so that we have to think of the saints in heaven. Thus according to the ἡγιασμένοι of Ac. 20:32 the ἅγιοι are to be understood as Christians in whom the glory of the allotted inheritance will be manifested.

[62] As against Asting, 104 f., 138.

[63] In Dt. Israel is ordained to be עַם קָדוֹשׁ = λαὸς ἅγιος (7:6; 14:2 etc.) — a highly characteristic expression reflected in Ex. 19:6 : גּוֹי קָדוֹשׁ = ἔθνος ἅγιον, along with מַמְלֶכֶת כֹּהֲנִים = βασίλειον ἱεράτευμα (cf. 1 Pt. 2:9). Similarly the term נַחֲלָה = κληρονομία = κλῆρος (for examples, v. the text) emerges strongly in Dt., and the verb נָחַל = κληρονομεῖν is also a distinctive Deuteronomic word.

munity (Phil. 2:17: σπένδομαι ἐπὶ τῇ θυσίᾳ καὶ λειτουργίᾳ τῆς πίστεως ὑμῶν), the reference being to his death as a martyr. Yet not merely the death but the life of the Christian in the body counts as a θυσία. Here again the cultic element emerges in the thought of ἅγιος as applied to the individual Christian (Phil. 4:21) as well as to the whole community. In Christianity the material offering, distinct from the giver, is replaced by the personal offering of the body, of the earthly life, inseparable from the existence of the one who offers. It is at this point that the holy impinges on the ethical, with which it may so easily be equated. Yet on the basis of the thought of sacrifice the ethical is here to be thought of, not as צֶדֶק = δικαιοσύνη, but as טָהֳרָה = purity (Lv. 13:7; 14:23; Ez. 44:23), so that the cultic element is not lost. [64] In the personal offering of the Christian life, the ἁγιασμός logically precedes the καθαρισμός; Pindar's law is valid : γένοι' οἷός ἐσσι. [65] Already in the Sermon on the Mount Jesus fills out the concept of purity with ethical content (Mt. 5:8 : οἱ καθαροὶ τῇ καρδίᾳ), and this became normative for primitive Christianity (1 Tm. 1:5; 2 Tm. 2:22; Tt. 1:15; Jm. 1:27; cf. Mt. 23:26 etc.). Purity is innocence (Ac. 18:6; 20:26), i.e., static morality as opposed to the active, which appears as δικαιοσύνη. Christian morality does not arise on the basis of new action but on that of a new state which is best expressed as ἁγιασμός. [66]

As ἅγιοι Christians are ordained for a θυσία ζῶσα ἁγία τῷ θεῷ which is fulfilled in the bodily life of each, yet also for the mutual service of love. The loyalty owed to Christ is also normative between Christians as ἅγιοι (Eph. 1:15 א*AB; Phlm. 5); it is the πίστις δι' ἀγάπης ἐνεργουμένη (Gl. 5:6) with which they should serve one another (5:13; cf. Col. 1:4). The Church of Christ is built up πρὸς τὸν καταρτισμὸν τῶν ἁγίων εἰς ἔργον διακονίας κτλ. ... (Eph. 4:12): Paul constantly emphasises the διακονία τοῖς ἁγίοις (R. 15:25; 1 C. 16:15; 2 C. 8:4; 9:1; cf. Hb. 6:10). We are to receive the ἅγιοι suitably (R. 16:2) and to become participant in their needs (12:13 : ταῖς χρείαις τῶν ἁγίων κοινωνοῦντες, cf. 2 C. 9:12). The communion of saints is that of the reconciled in Christ mutually serving one another (2 C. 5:17), and the holy kiss (φίλημα ἅγιον) is the seal of this fellowship (1 C. 16:20; 2 C. 13:12; 1 Th. 5:26). The man who is ἡγιασμένος in Christ (1 C. 1:2) becomes the holy centre of his own immediate circle, so that the husband is sanctified in the wife and the wife in the husband, and the children of Christian parents are not ἀκάθαρτα but ἅγια. Here, too, ἅγιος implies a moral state in the sense of καθαρός. The same is true of the virgin, ἵνα ᾖ ἁγία καὶ τῷ σώματι καὶ τῷ πνεύματι (1 C. 7:34; cf. 1 Pt. 3:5). To the same effect is the expression καρδίαι ἄμεμπτοι ἐν ἁγιωσύνῃ (1 Th. 3:13), as also the parallel-ism ἅγιος καὶ ἄμωμος (Eph. 1:4; 5:27; Col. 1:22), since ἄμωμος is used of the sacrifice which is without cultic blemish (1 Pt. 1:19; Hb. 9:14) and thus denotes cultic qualification.

The opposite of this moral state is ἀκαθαρσία (Mt. 23:27; R. 1:24; 6:19 etc.),

---

[64] Purity (Hb. 9:13 : καθαρότης, cf. Mk. 1:44; Lk. 5:14; Jn. 2:6 : καθαρισμός) is strictly cultic qualification, the clean beasts (Gn. 7:2 ff.) being those which may be sacrificed, and which become קֹדֶשׁ by sacrifice.

[65] Cf. Asting, 217.

[66] Certainly one and the same person may be δίκαιος καὶ ἅγιος, as is said not only of God (Jn. 17:25, v. 11) but also of Christ (Ac. 3:14) and of his prophet John (Mk. 6:20); yet the two concepts belong to different orders of life which are to be basically distinguished (1 C. 6:11: ἀλλὰ ἡγιάσθητε, ἀλλὰ ἐδικαιώθητε), so that there can be no question of the Hellenistic δίκαιος καὶ ἅγιος (cf. Williger). They are related like justification and atonement.

which is revealed particularly in the sexual sins of the Gentile world, among whom the ἀκάθαρτον is at home (Ac. 10:14, 28; 11:8; Eph. 5:5), the OT already speaking of אֶרֶץ טְמֵאָה (Am. 7:17; Hos. 9:3). [67] These passages show us again that, whether under Hellenistic influence or not, the reference of holiness is always to the static morality of innocence rather than to ethical action. But this static morality is closely linked with cultic qualification. For this reason we should never translate ἁγιότης or ἅγιος as morality or moral, since this is to lose the element of the *religiosum*.

Finally in the last judgment the principle of holiness is normative; for οἱ ἅγιοι τὸν κόσμον κρινοῦσιν (1 C. 6:2). Since the reference is to men and not angels, we are to think of the ἐκκλησία τοῦ θεοῦ as the judge to whom are committed the keys of the kingdom of heaven (Mt. 16:17 ff.; 18:18; Jn. 20:23) with power to bind and to loose. Hence faith can be described as ἁγιωτάτη (Jd. 20). The believer stands outside the nexus of the world and will not be judged (cf. Jn. 12:47).

6. The Ecclesia triumphans.

a. Like the *Ecclesia militans*, the *Ecclesia triumphans* stands under the concept of holiness. To it belongs the world of angels, already called holy in the OT. ἄγγελοι ἅγιοι is an apocalyptic term found on the lips of Jesus (Mk. 8:38; Lk. 9:26; cf. Rev. 14:10; Jd. 14 : ἐν ἁγίαις μυριάσιν αὐτοῦ); the reference is to the return of the Son of Man with the holy angels, with suggestions of the picture of the last judgment in Da. 7:9 ff.

The angels are also intended in 1 Th. 3:13; cf. 2 Th. 1:7: ἐν τῇ παρουσίᾳ τοῦ κυρίου ἡμῶν Ἰησοῦ Χριστοῦ μετὰ πάντων ἁγίων αὐτοῦ; for the saints often mean angels in apocalyptic literature. [68] It is not impossible that the departed souls of the pious are included among the ἅγιοι as well as angels (4 Esr. 6:26; cf. Mt. 27:52 : σώματα τῶν κεκοιμημένων ἁγίων). [69] More difficult to decide is whether 2 Th. 1:10 : ἐνδοξασθῆναι ἐν τοῖς ἁγίοις αὐτοῦ refers to angels or to Christians. Since the genitive, οἱ ἅγιοι αὐτοῦ, seems to contain a differentiation from πάντες οἱ πιστεύσαντες, already found in the verbs ἐνδοξασθῆναι and θαυμασθῆναι, the term ἅγιοι (cf. 1 Th. 3:13) more likely denotes the angels who will accompany Christ at His final appearing to be adored by all the faithful. In the passage quoted from the Psalms (ψ 88:8): ἐνδοξαζόμενος ἐν βουλῇ ἁγίων, angels are obviously meant. Finally, it is clear from the Book of Revelation that heavenly creatures are numbered among the ἅγιοι. For in the invocation in Rev. 18:20 : εὐφραίνου ἐπ' αὐτῇ, οὐρανὲ καὶ οἱ ἅγιοι καὶ οἱ ἀπόστολοι καὶ οἱ προφῆται we have a natural sequence if the ἅγιοι who come after heaven and before the apostles and prophets, the pillars of the earthly theocracy (Eph. 2:20; 3:5), are regarded as the קַדִּישֵׁי עֶלְיוֹנִין (Da. 7:18, 21 ff.) and therefore as heavenly beings. [70] God vindicates against the world power of Babylon His own hierarchy represented by the saints in heaven and the apostles and prophets on earth.

---

[67] Naturally the holy state is to issue in a holy walk (ἀναστροφή) even outside the sexual sphere (1 Pt. 1:15, 22; 2 Pt. 3:11; 2 C. 1:12). Nevertheless, it is to be emphasised here that in 1 Pt. 1:15 the holy state is stressed as opposed to ἐπιθυμίαι which affect the sensual sphere, just as the parallel terms ἀναστροφὴ καὶ εὐσέβεια in 2 Pt. 3:11 and ἁγιότης(?) καὶ εἰλικρινία in 2 C. 1:12 suggest the meaning of the Hellenistic ἁγνός, since εὐσέβεια (Is. 11:2, 33:6; Prv. 1:7 = יִרְאַת יהוה) and εἰλικρινία (Wis. 7:25) in the LXX hardly have any Hebrew equivalents, unless in 2 C. 1:12 we ought to read ἁπλότης for ἁγιότης.
[68] Bousset-Gressm., 321.
[69] It is not said of departed saints that they go up to heaven some day to return with Jesus, so that we do better to restrict the heavenly ἅγιοι to angels.
[70] As against Asting, 292.

b. To the *Ecclesia triumphans* of the Apocalypse there also belong men as ἅγιοι. We are certainly to think of such in regard to the προσευχαὶ τῶν ἁγίων offered by the 24 elders (Rev. 5:6 ff.) and later by an angel (8:3, 4). In 11:18 they come between the prophets and the φοβούμενοι τὸ ὄνομα, and therefore are obviously men. Since the reference is to the judgment of the dead (ὁ καιρὸς τῶν νεκρῶν), we best equate the προφῆται with the OT prophets, after whom the ἅγιοι signify the narrower circle of primitive Christianity and the φοβούμενοι (═══ יִרְאֵי יהוה) the wider circle of Gentile proselytes. Again, the saints are obviously Christians in the reference in 14:12 (cf. 13:10) to the ὑπομονὴ τῶν ἁγίων, οἱ τηροῦντες τὰς ἐντολὰς τοῦ θεοῦ καὶ τὴν πίστιν Ἰησοῦ. The ὑπομονή indicates afflictions to which the ἅγιοι are exposed, as previously there is mention of their subjection to the beast (13:7). The bloody drink of Babylon-Rome refers to the martyrs of Jesus who have entered the *Ecclesia triumphans* by death: μεθύουσαν ἐκ τοῦ αἵματος τῶν ἁγίων καὶ ἐκ τοῦ αἵματος τῶν μαρτύρων Ἰησοῦ (17:6). In accordance with the division of the martyrs we are to distinguish two circles, the previously mentioned ἅγιοι being apostolic martyrs like Peter and Paul, and the μάρτυρες those who suffered under Nero's persecution; the city depicted is thus simply Rome.

Less precise is the combination without the article in 18:24: αἷμα προφητῶν καὶ ἁγίων καὶ πάντων τῶν ἐσφαγμένων ἐπὶ τῆς γῆς, as also in 16:6, where there is no spatial link with Rome. The varying position held by προφῆται and ἅγιοι does not support any order of rank (cf. 18:20) or time; we may think of either the older or the newer prophets, beside whom the ἅγιοι are named as Christian martyrs and the ἐσφαγμένοι as martyrs of every kind. [71] In the interval after the first resurrection comes the attack of Gog and Magog on τὴν παρεμβολὴν τῶν ἁγίων καὶ τὴν πόλιν τὴν ἠγαπημένην (20:9). According to the pattern set by Ezekiel (38 f.) the camp of the ἅγιοι can only be in Jerusalem (═══ ἐκύκλευσαν), so that we are reminded of early Christianity. Finally, in the separation of the good and the bad we have the statement (22:11): καὶ ὁ δίκαιος δικαιοσύνην ποιησάτω ἔτι· καὶ ὁ ἅγιος ἁγιασθήτω ἔτι. [72] According to the usage of ἁγιάζειν sanctification by God is meant rather than self-sanctification. In the δίκαιος and ἅγιος there is contained the essence of the Christian as he moves towards the last time.

We thus see that neither in the OT nor the NT is the cultic basis of the ἅγιος concept ever denied. In both a cultic element is retained in the people of God. This is spiritualised, but can never disappear. For it is present in the worship of the supramundane God, in reconciliation by Jesus Christ and in the new creation as the temple of the Holy Spirit. The nature of Christianity is thus centrally determined by the concept of the holy.

---

[71] Also witnesses of Christ are the ἅγιοι whose δικαιώματα is the robe of the bride (19:8); yet it may be that we here have a gloss in τὸ γὰρ βύσσινον τὰ δικαιώματα τῶν ἁγίων (Loh. Apk., *ad loc.*). To the interval after the first resurrection in the millennial kingdom belongs the beatitude of 20:6: μακάριος καὶ ἅγιος ἔχων μέρος ἐν τῇ ἀναστάσει τῇ πρώτῃ. But the predicate ἅγιος is lacking in the other six beatitudes of Revelation (1:3; 14:13; 16:15; 19:9; 22:7, 14). Indeed, ἅγιος never elsewhere occurs as a predicate in Revelation, but only as subject, so that καὶ ἅγιος may be an addition following Jub. 2:23 f. (cf. Loh. Apk., *ad loc.*).

[72] Characteristically we again see here the difference between δίκαιος and ἅγιος; the former is active (δικαιοσύνην ποιησάτω) and the latter passive (ἁγιασθήτω ἔτι).

ἁγιάζω.

The verb ἁγιάζω belongs almost exclusively to biblical Greek or Greek influenced by the Bible (Phil. Leg. All., I, 18; Spec. Leg., I, 167),[1] the form -άζειν occurring after ι instead of -ίζειν. We probably have here a denominative of קָדֵשׁ, קָדוֹשׁ = ἅγιος.[2]

In the LXX ἁγιάζειν is the usual rendering of the root קדשׁ, so that we are everywhere concerned with a cultic state, not only in the qal (Ex. 29:21; 30:29 etc.), and niph'al (Ex. 29:43; Lv. 10:3 etc.), but also in the causative (Ex. 28:34; Lv. 22:2 f. etc.) and comparative (Gn. 2:3; Ex. 13:2 etc.) of all three classes.[3] Yet according to the Hebrew stem forms there is also a shift of meaning, so that in the causative we have mostly to translate "consecrate" and in the comparative "sanctify," by which the LXX sometimes understands the ritual of expiation (Ex. 29:33, 36). Sanctifying can be achieved by cultic practices (Ex. 19:10, 14; Jos. 7:13 etc.), but also by celebration (Ex. 20:8; Dt. 5:12; cf. Is. 30:29); with a divine subject and object it can also be thought of declaratively (Gn. 2:3; Ex. 19:23; Nu. 20:12 f.), though we are always to think of effective operation.

In the derived stems of the verb the subject is always personal, whether God, judge or people; only in the qal can there also be a material subject of the taboo (Nu. 17:2, 3; Dt. 22:9). As object God is rare (Nu. 20:12; 27:14; Is. 29:23; cf. 8:13), and it can only be a question of acknowledging what God is in Himself. Mostly the objects are priests, people, and holy places and vessels. By sanctification they are separated from what is profane and set in a consecrated state. Sacrilege, or the violation of what is holy, does not come under human jurisdiction but under the judgment of God which normally means death.

In the NT we think supremely of the saying in the Lord's Prayer (Mt. 6:9; Lk. 11:2): ἁγιασθήτω τὸ ὄνομά σου.[4] The logical subject of sanctifying is God alone and not man. This may be seen by comparison with the petitions which follow. God's name is as little hallowed by men as His kingdom comes or His will is done. His name is His person, which is holy in itself and is to be revealed in its holiness (cf. Ez. 20:41; 38:16 : וְנִקְדַּשְׁתִּי לְעֵינֵיהֶם etc.). The revelation takes place eschatologically in the last judgment and historically in, though not by, believers. When God's deity is revealed to man in the mystery of worship (cf. Is. 6:3), then God is sanctified to him. The cultic element is here absorbed in the adoration in which God's deity is felt in contrast to all creatureliness.[5]

When Jesus sanctifies Himself (Jn. 17:19 : ὑπὲρ αὐτῶν ἁγιάζω ἐμαυτόν) or sanctifies the Church (Eph. 5:26 : ἵνα αὐτὴν ἁγιάσῃ καθαρίσας), this is a proof of His deity, and the same is true of the Holy Spirit (R. 15:16 : ἡγιασμένη ἐν πνεύματι ἁγίῳ). The sanctification of Christ by the Father (ὃν ὁ πατὴρ ἡγίασεν

ἁ γ ι ά ζ ω. [1] But v. the Mithras liturgy, ἁγίοις ἁγιασθεὶς ἁγιάσμασι ἅγιος (Preis. Zaub., IV, 523).

[2] Bl.-Debr., § 108.

[3] The occasional equivalents ברר (Da. 12:10), כפר (Ex. 29:33, 36), נזר (Lv. 25:11 etc.) do not affect this.

[4] For Rabbinic usage, → 99.

[5] Elsewhere in the NT, too, sanctification is exclusively of God; for even when the temple (Mt. 23:17), the altar (Mt. 23:19), or the sacrifice (Hb. 9:13) ἁγιάζει, the sanctifying power rests exclusively on the holiness of God.

καὶ ἀπέστειλεν, Jn. 10:36), as shown by the context, is achieved prior to the incarnation, as Jeremiah is also sanctified prior to his birth (Jer. 1:5). To it there corresponds the self-sanctification (Jn. 17:19) of the Holy God (cf. 6:69) with a view to the sanctification of the disciples (17:19 : ἵνα ὦσιν ἡγιασμένοι), which is sanctification in truth (ἐν ἀληθείᾳ), and which is accomplished in the atonement.

Christ's atoning sacrifice is very clearly depicted as a means of sanctification in Hebrews. Hb. 2:11: ὁ ἁγιάζων ... καὶ οἱ ἁγιαζόμενοι ἐξ ἑνὸς πάντες, tells us that Christ and Christians derive from one as children of common flesh and blood (v. 14). As the emphasis on physical relationship shows, this one is not God but Adam. Christ, however, is also ἅγιος, and He is thus ἁγιάζων to the ἁγιαζόμενοι. He achieves sanctification for the sanctified by His offering (10:10, 14). His blood is the means of reconciliation (10:29; 13:12) for them : ἵνα ἁγιάσῃ διὰ τοῦ ἰδίου αἵματος τὸν λαόν (13:12). There is here a clear connection between the concept of atonement and that of sanctification. [6]

In Paul the thought of justification overshadows sanctification (ἁγιάζειν) as a function of God. He applies the concept passively rather than actively, speaking of the sanctified. In him, too, the ἡγιασμένοι have their root ἐν Χριστῷ (1 C. 1:2); the Gentile Christians are a προσφορά, ἡγιασμένη ἐν πνεύματι ἁγίῳ (R. 15:16), so that again the concept of sanctification is linked with that of reconciliation. Sanctification is not moral action on the part of man, but a divinely effected state (1 C. 6:11: ἀλλὰ ἀπελούσασθε, ἀλλὰ ἡγιάσθητε, ἀλλὰ ἐδικαιώθητε), the baptismal washing showing that in the baptismal fellowship of Christ (R. 6:4 ; Col. 2:12) lies the basis of sanctification and justification (cf. 1 Cor. 1:30). That sanctification is a state emerges with particular clarity in the fact that a Christian partner effects a character of holiness in the pagan partner and also the children (1 C. 7:14), who are not themselves Christians. In the later Pauline literature, e.g., Ephesians (5:26 : ἁγιάσῃ καθαρίσας) and the Pastorals (1 Tm. 4:5; 2 Tm. 2:21) the concept of holiness approximates to that of purity in wholly Jewish style (cf. Eph. 1:14; Col. 1:22).

In Acts the expression ἡγιασμένοι is twice set on the lips of Paul (Ac. 20:32 : κληρονομίαν ἐν τοῖς ἡγιασμένοις πᾶσιν; 26:18 : κλῆρον ἐν τοῖς ἡγιασμένοις), and both times in allusion to Dt. 33:3 : πάντες οἱ ἡγιασμένοι ὑπὸ τὰς χεῖράς σου. This corresponds to the Pauline thought of the share of the Christian in the κλῆρος τῶν ἁγίων ἐν τῷ φωτί (Col. 1:12; cf. s.v. ἅγιος), except that the passive ἡγιασμένοι causes a heavier stress to fall on the setting up of the state of holiness. Finally, in 1 Pt. 3:15 Christians are summoned to the sanctification of Christ : Χριστὸν ἁγιάσατε ἐν ταῖς καρδίαις. The presupposition here is that they are ἅγιοι (1:16), so that Christ dwells in them as His temple, and will not suffer any impurity. Again, therefore, purity of heart is a condition of sanctification.

---

[6] Christians as ἅγιοι should continue to let the process of sanctification proceed in them (Rev. 22:11: ὁ ἅγιος ἁγιασθήτω ἔτι) even when they have been set in a state of holiness by Christ.

ἁγιασμός.

While ἁγιάζω is developed from the noun ἅγιος, the noun ἁγιασμός derives from the verb ἁγιάζειν as a *nomen actionis*. [1] Hence it signifies "sanctifying" rather than "sanctification," as we learn from the corresponding constructions βαπτισμός, ἐνταφιασμός, ὀνειδισμός, παροργισμός, etc. It is, of course, conceivable that a *nomen actionis* like βασανισμός or πλεονασμός might acquire a passive meaning, but philological investigation must begin with the active.

In the LXX ἁγιασμός is rare and has no clear-cut Hebrew equivalent (Ju. 17:3 : ἁγιασμῷ ἡγίασα : הַקְדֵּשׁ הִקְדַּשְׁתִּי ; Am. 2:11: εἰς ἁγιασμόν : לִנְזִרִים ; Jer. 6:16; Ez. 22:8; 45:4; Sir. 7:31; 17:10; 2 Macc. 2:17; 14:36; 3 Macc. 2:18). So far as sound comparisons suggest, the LXX knows ἁγιασμός both as "sanctifying" (Ju. 17:3) and also as "sanctification" (Sir. 7:31; 3 Macc. 2:18), and there is a strong connection with the cultus.

In the NT ἁγιασμός occurs only in the Epistles, preponderantly in the field of Gentile Christianity. The term "sanctifying" fits it better than "sanctification," in accordance with its construction. It must be remembered, however, that the operation of ἁγιασμός can be accomplished only by a holy person (cf. the verb ἁγιάζειν), so that in the case of self-sanctifying it is always assumed that it is accomplished on the basis of the state of sanctification attained in the atonement according to the standard of the statement in Revelation 22:11: ὁ ἅγιος ἁγιασθήτω ἔτι. In ἁγιασμός we thus have a process which has as its presupposition the religious process of atonement. ἁγιασμός is the will of God (1 Th. 4:3), and it consists again in purity of physical life, so that marital fellowship is fulfilled ἐν ἁγιασμῷ καὶ τιμῇ (4:4). The opposite of ἁγιασμός is ἀκαθαρσία (4:7), except that ἀκαθαρσία is a moral state which cannot possibly be linked with calling, (οὐ ... ἐπὶ ἀκαθαρσίᾳ), whereas ἁγιασμός is the moral form in which it is worked out. The body is to be serviceable to δικαιοσύνη εἰς ἁγιασμόν (R. 6:19), so that ἁγιασμός is again the moral goal of purity (cf. R. 6:22 : ἔχετε τὸν καρπὸν ὑμῶν εἰς ἁγιασμόν). In Christ is made possible δικαιοσύνη τε καὶ ἁγιασμός καὶ ἀπολύτρωσις (1 C. 1:30), and it is by Him or by the Spirit (2 Th. 2:13; 1 Pt. 1:2 : ἐν ἁγιασμῷ πνεύματος) that it comes into effect in Christians, so that the ἁγιασμός or sanctifying effected by the Spirit is the living form of the Christian state. In the phrase ἐν ἁγιασμῷ πνεύματος the emphasis does not fall on the character of the Spirit described as πνεῦμα ἅγιον, but on His operation, which consists in sanctification. Similarly, in the sequence ἐν πίστει καὶ ἀγάπῃ καὶ ἁγιασμῷ (1 Tm. 2:15) what is expressed is not the state but the conduct of children, and in Hebrews again (12:14 : διώκετε ... τὸν ἁγιασμόν) ὁ ἁγιασμός is a moral goal. If atonement is the basis of the Christian life, ἁγιασμός is the moral form which develops out of it and without which there can be no vision of Christ. The term ἁγιασμός is always distinguished from ἅγιος and ἁγιάζειν by the emphasis on the moral element.

ἁγιασμός. [1] Bl.-Debr., § 109.

† ἁγιότης.

This rare word (2 Macc. 15:2; 2 C. 1:12; Hb. 12:10; cf. Cl. Al., Strom., VII, 5, 29, 4; VI, 7, 57, 4) is in line with a favourite later construction [1] of adjectives and substantives of the second declension, [2] in this case of ἅγιος. The meaning is sanctification [3] as distinct from sanctifying (ἁγιασμός).

In the NT the holiness of God is thought of as His essential attribute in which the Christian must share and for which the heavenly Father prepares him by His instruction (Hb. 12:10 : εἰς τὸ μεταλαβεῖν τῆς ἁγιότητος αὐτοῦ). The goal is the same as in 1 Pt. 1:15 : ἅγιοι ἔσεσθε, ὅτι ἐγὼ ἅγιος.

A difficult verse is 2 C. 1:12 : ἐν ἁγιότητι καὶ εἰλικρινίᾳ τοῦ θεοῦ ... ἀνεστράφημεν ἐν τῷ κόσμῳ. If the text is correct, ἁγιότης and εἰλικρινία must be attributes of God by which Paul also orders his own conversation. Yet since ἁγιότης denotes a state, but εἰλικρινία (as sincerity) a disposition (1 C. 5:8; 2 C. 2:17) never elsewhere ascribed to God (cf. Phil. 1:10; 2 Pt. 3:1), the well-attested reading is questionable. The text is clearer if we read ἐν ἁπλότητι καὶ εἰλικρινίᾳ for ἐν ἁγιότητι καὶ εἰλικρινίᾳ (D min sy, cf. Chr. Thdt.). Then Paul speaks of walking in the simplicity and sincerity of God, i.e., as they correspond to God. If this is the case, the term ἁγιότης occurs in the NT only in Hebrews.

† ἁγιωσύνη.

This rare word, formed from the adjective ἅγιος by extension of the ο to ω after a short syllable as an abstract term of quality, [1] in the same way as δικαιοσύνη is formed from δίκαιος, is not found in pre-biblical Greek. It means "sanctification" or "holiness" rather than sanctifying, but as a quality rather than a state. In the LXX it is found only in ψ 29:5; 95:6; 96:12; 144:5; 2 Macc. 3:12. In these verses the element of glory (הוד — עז) is introduced together with that of holiness (קדש), though the two are not interchangeable.

In the NT only Paul uses the word (R. 1:4; 2 C. 7:1; 1 Th. 3:13). The best known verse is R. 1:4 : τοῦ ὁρισθέντος υἱοῦ θεοῦ ἐν δυνάμει κατὰ πνεῦμα ἁγιωσύνης ἐξ ἀναστάσεως νεκρῶν. Here κατὰ πνεῦμα ἁγιωσύνης is obviously set in antithesis to κατὰ σάρκα. According to the natural order (κατὰ σάρκα), Jesus Christ is a descendant of David; according to that of the πνεῦμα ἁγιωσύνης indwelling Him, He is declared to be the Son of God on the basis of the resurrection. The πνεῦμα ἁγιωσύνης is not a stronger form of πνεῦμα ἅγιον, [2] but an exact rendering [3] of the Hebrew רוּחַ הַקֹּדֶשׁ (Is. 63:10 f.; Ps. 51:11), which signifies

---

ἁ γ ι ό τ η ς. [1] C. A. Lobeck, Phrynichus (1820), 350.
[2] Bl.-Debr., § 110.
[3] In 2 Macc. 15:2 : ἡ προτετιμημένη ... μεθ' ἁγιότητος ἡμέρα, the Sabbath is described as the day characterised by holiness.

ἁ γ ι ω σ ύ ν η. [1] Bl.-Debr., § 110.
[2] As against Pr.-B., s.v.
[3] Thus Cr.-Kö.

the creative principle of life within the people of God in virtue of which this people does not belong to the natural order but to the καινὴ κτίσις. The deity of Christ is disclosed by the resurrection in which the new creation finds expression according to the principle of the πνεῦμα ἁγιωσύνης. Hence ἁγιωσύνη is here identical with deity.

In 2 C. 7:1: ἐπιτελοῦντες ἁγιωσύνην ἐν φόβῳ θεοῦ, ἁγιωσύνη is a human quality. Its basis is to be found in the atonement, in the power of which the ἔθνος ἅγιον exists. Yet this divinely created condition demands completion (ἐπιτελεῖν) in the moral dedication which is only possible on the basis of the fear of God (ἐν φόβῳ θεοῦ), fear being the normal attitude in the environs of the holy. The ἁγιωσύνη awakened in this way bears the form of κάθαρσις, which as pneumato-physical purity (σαρκὸς καὶ πνεύματος) stands opposed to all ἀκαθαρσία, especially in sexual matters. Hence ἁγιωσύνη like ἁγιασμός has an ethical character. The same is true in 1 Th. 3:13: εἰς τὸ στηρίξαι ὑμῶν τὰς καρδίας ἀμέμπτους ἐν ἁγιωσύνῃ. The aim of God is the strengthening of the heart in holiness. Here, too, holiness shows itself in purity of heart; it is the ἁγιωσύνη which is completed in ethical dedication and the origin of which is found in the atonement, wherein lies its cultic character.

Procksch

ἀγνοέω, ἀγνόημα, ἄγνοια, ἀγνωσία, ἄγνωστος

ἀγνοέω, ἀγνόημα.

ἀγνοεῖν (= "not to know") can be used with all the nuances of the Greek concept of knowledge (→ γινώσκω). Especially it can denote "being mistaken" or "in error" as the character of action. [1]

Polyb. XXXVIII, 9, 5: ποιήσασθαί τινα διόρθωσιν τῶν ἠγνοημένων (cf. I, 67, 11). So also in the LXX 2 Macc. 11:31: οὐδεὶς αὐτῶν κατ’ οὐδένα τρόπον παρενοχληθήσεται περὶ τῶν ἠγνοημένων. Da. 9:15: ἡμάρτομεν, ἠγνοήκαμεν (cf. Test. Jud. 19:4: ἐτύφλωσε γάρ με ὁ ἄρχων τῆς πλάνης καὶ ἠγνόησα ὡς ἄνθρωπος [καὶ ὡς σάρξ ?] ἐν ἁμαρτίαις φθαρείς; Jos. Ant., 4, 263). Similarly ἀγν. can be used for שׁגג (Lv. 5:18; Ez. 45:20) and שׁגה (Lv. 4:13, ἀκουσίως being added in 1 S. 26:21), while in Nu. 15:22-24 ἁμαρτάνειν is used for שׁגג. Ἀγνοῶν or ἠγνοηκώς can in fact mean "innocent" (Gn. 20:4; 3 Macc. 3:9).

Ἀγνόημα especially is used in this way. It signifies not merely "error" (in the LXX being used only in Gn. 43:12 for משׁגה) but "unconscious mistake." [1] As in P. Par., 63, XIII, 3 (2nd century B.C.) and P. Tebt., 5, 3 (118 B.C.) ἀγνοήματα is linked with ἁμαρτήματα, so in Sir. 23:2, 1 Macc. 13:39 and Tob. 3:3 it is linked with ἁμαρτίαι (cf. Jdt. 5:20; Sir. 51:19). In this sense we have ἀγνοήματα in Hb. 9:7; Herm. s., 5, 7, 3 f. (*par.* ἄγνοια). [2]

ἀγνοέω κτλ. [1] Cf. L. Wenger, APF II (1902), 483-485; P. M. Meyer, Jurist. Pap. (1920), 236 f. (No. 69); K. Latte, ARW, 20 (1920/21), 287, 1.
[2] Cf. Trench, 159 f.

A firm linguistic usage is established especially in Stoic writings (→ ἄγνοια), and there are no problems in the NT. It is used with reference to personal acquaintance (as in Wis. 14:18; 19:14) in Gl. 1:22; 2 C. 6:9 (ὡς ἀγνοούμενοι, meaning "obscure" rather than "unknown"); Dg., 5, 12. It signifies "not to understand" in Mk. 9:32 par.; Lk. 9:45; 1 C. 14:38 (εἴ τις ἀγνοεῖ, infra) and perhaps 2 Pt. 2:12, and "not to know" (as Wis. 7:12) in R. 2:4; 2 C. 2:11; Ac. 17:23 and perhaps 2 Pt. 2:12. The form found in 2 C. 2:11 is also common elsewhere (Wis. 12:10; 18:19, also Pap.), and is also to be found, corresponding to the ἢ οὐκ οἴδατε, in the epistolary formulae οὐ θέλω (δὲ) ὑμᾶς ἀγνοεῖν (R. 1:13; 11:25 etc.) and (ἢ) ἀγνοεῖτε (R. 6:3; 7:1). [3]

"Erroneous ignorance" characterising action is meant by ἀγνοῶν ἐποίησα (v. infra) in 1 Tm. 1:13; and in Hb. 5:2 ἀγνοεῖν has the sense of "ignorance of self." In 1 C. 14:38 (εἴ τις ἀγνοεῖ, i.e., "does not understand"; ἀγνοεῖται, namely, of God), we are to take the word in the OT sense in which knowledge means election and ignorance rejection, unless the true reading is ἀγνοείτω, which would signify that he should remain without understanding.

In accordance with the Jewish and Christian use of γινώσκω and γνῶσις (→ γινώσκω), ἀγνοεῖν can also relate to the "knowledge of God" (→ ἄγνοια), as in Wis. 15:11; Philo Spec. Leg., I, 332; Jos. Ant., 2, 172; 10, 142, and also R. 10:3: ἀγνοοῦντες γὰρ τὴν τοῦ θεοῦ δικαιοσύνην. It can also be used of knowledge of Christ in Ign. Sm., 5, 1; Just. Ap., 31, 7; 49, 1 and 5; 53, 6; Dial., 136, 3; and again of specifically Christian knowledge in Ac. 13:27; Ign. Eph., 17, 2; M. Pol., 11, 2; 2 Cl., 10, 4; Just. Ap., 13, 4; 52, 2. This meaning is also suggested in 1 Tm. 1:13 (→ ἄγνοια). As in γινώσκειν (→ γινώσκω) the practical element in this knowledge can be more or less strongly emphasised, R. 10:3 making it plain that ignorance is also disobedience. In the OT sense such ἀγνοεῖν is not merely "lack of information," which is excusable, but a "misunderstanding" which stands under the ὀργή of God and needs forgiveness, as expressed in 1 Tm. 1:13 f.: ἀλλὰ ἠλεήθην ... ὑπερεπλεόνασεν δὲ ἡ χάρις. Accordingly the knowledge by which ἀγν. is removed does not derive from human reflection or enquiry, but from the proclamation which demands faith (→ ἄγνοια).

ἄγνοια, ἀγνωσία.

1. The Philosophical and Legal Usage.

ἄγνοια, meaning "ignorance" in all the difference nuances of the Greek concept of knowledge (→ γινώσκω), is used in the first instance of ignorance of something specific. Yet the term was obviously used in Greek earlier than γνῶσις in an absolute sense to denote ignorance generally in the sense of not knowing essentials and therefore of being "uncivilised." In this sense it was either linked or parallel with ἀμαθία and ἀπαιδευσία, [1] and found its opposite not merely in γνῶσις (Plat. Theaet., 176c; Resp., V, 478c) but especially in σοφία (Plat. Prot., 360b ff.) and ἐπιστήμη (Plat. Resp., V, 477a). [2] This usage, and occasionally that of the

---

[3] Cf. R. Bultmann, Der Stil der paul. Predigt (1910), 13, 65; cf. 4 Macc. 10:2; Jos. Ant., 7, 266; 13, 354; Philo Op. Mund., 87; Rer. Div. Her., 301; Fug., 168; Abr., 26 and 53; Spec. Leg., I, 302; 2 Cl., 14, 2; P. Tebt., 314, 3 (2nd cent. A.D.): πιστεύω σε μὴ ἀγνοεῖν.

ἄγνοια κτλ. [1] Plat. Prot., 360b; Theaet., 176c; Epict. Diss., I, 11, 14; II, 1, 16.

[2] Occasionally φρόνησις as antonym (v. Arnim, III, 166, 27 ff.; M. Ant., V, 18, p. 57, 14, Stich), or γνώμη (M. Ant., IX, 22, p. 119, 16).

verb, is especially found in the Stoa, ἄγνοια being remote from the σοφός who has ἐπιστήμη. [3] It is not infrequently emphasised that ἑαυτὸν ἀγνοεῖν is part of this ἄγνοια. [4] If according to Diog. L., VII, 93 the Stoics teach: εἶναι δὲ ἀγνοίας τὰς κακίας, ὧν αἱ ἀρεταὶ ἐπιστῆμαι, this means that ignorance is the basis of wickedness ; v. Arnim, III, 23, 32 ff.; Epict. Diss., I, 26, 6 f.: τί οὖν ἐστι τὸ αἴτιον τοῦ ἁμαρτάνειν με; ἡ ἄγνοια etc. But ἄγνοια itself, since ἐπιστήμη belongs to the ἐφ' ἡμῖν, can also be described as the true κακία (v. Arnim, III, 60, 28 ff. etc.). That the knowledge of God also belongs to the essential knowledge concealed by ἄγνοια may be seen under ἄγνωστος.

We should also mention the legal usage, which rests on the antithesis of ἄγνοια and προαίρεσις. [5] In this ἄγνοια (anal. to ἀγνόημα → 116) signifies ignorance of law, as in the formula κατ' ἄγνοιαν = per ignorantiam. [6]

The LXX adopts this legal usage when it translates בִּשְׁגָגָה by κατ' ἄγνοιαν (Lv. 22:14), [7] but it extends it when it uses ἀγν. (like ἀγνόημα) for "unintentional sin" in Lv. 5:18, Qoh. 5:5; cf. also 2 Ch. 28:13 and 1 Esr. 8:72, where it is linked with ἁμαρτία. This usage is also found in Test. Jud. 19:3 (ἐν ἀγνοίᾳ, vl ἐν ἀγνωσίᾳ); L. 3:5; S. 1:5; G. 5:7; and also in Jos. Ant., 6, 92; 11, 130 (in both cases κατ' ἄγνοιαν) and Ap., 2, 174 (ὑπ' ἀγνοίας). Philo uses ἄγνοια in this sense in conjunction with διαμαρτίαι in Plant., 108, and in such expressions as κατὰ ἄγνοιαν (Leg. All., I, 35), ὑπ' ἀγνοίας (Vit. Mos., I, 273) and ἀγνοίᾳ (Leg. All., III, 91; Flacc., 7). If occasionally (Deus Imm., 134 f.) ἀμαθία appears alongside ἄγνοια and as the opposite of ἐπιστήμη (Flacc., 7), this is an indication of Stoic influence. The antithesis ἄγνοια-ἐπιστήμη is frequent in Philo. [8] Above all Ebr., 154-161 (cf. already 6) treats of ἀγν. and ἐπιστήμη in the sense of the Aristotelian-Stoic enlightenment, and in 162-205 in that of scepticism. [9] In 160 ἀγν. has the force of πάντων ἁμαρτημάτων αἰτία, as in the corresponding Stoic Leg. Gaj., 69 : φασὶ δὲ τὴν μὲν ἐπιστήμην εὐδαιμονίας, τὴν δὲ ἄγνοιαν κακοδαιμονίας αἰτίαν εἶναι. God is specially thought of as the object of ἄγνοια, as in Decal., 8; Spec. Leg., I, 15; cf. Fug., 8. But the Stoic usage has also penetrated the LXX in the modified sense that absolute ἄγνοια is used of the state of heathenism, God obviously being the object of ἀγν. (cf. Wis. 14:22; 2 Macc. 4:40; 4 Macc. 1:5; 2:24; and cf. also Jos. Ant., 10:142 : τὴν τῶν ἀνθρώπων ἄγνοιαν καὶ ἀπιστίαν). Judaism could adopt this usage, for among the Rabbis we find the

---

[3] v. Arnim, I, 20, 10 f.; II, 41, 12; III, 60, 28 ff.; 150, 15; 164, 31 ff. etc.
[4] Ibid., III, 150, 15; 166, 27 ff.; Epict. Diss., II, 14, 20; 24, 19 etc.
[5] Cf. Aristot. Eth. Nic., III, 2, p. 1110b, 17 ff.; V, 10, p. 1135a, 16 ff.
[6] Polyb., XII, 12, 4 and 5 → συγγνώμη ; Pap., cf. Preisigke Wört; P. M. Meyer, Jurist. Pap. (1920), 201 f., 331, 334 f.; F. Steinleitner, Die Beicht im Zusammenhange mit der sakralen Rechtspflege in der Antike (1913), 43.
[7] The LXX also uses ἄγνοια for אָשַׁם in Gn. 26:10; Ez. 40, 39; 42:13 (in the latter two in conjunction with ἁμαρτία) etc., while, e.g., in Ιερ. 28:5 it has ἀδικία, and in Nu. 5:7 and ψ 67:22 πλημμελία, for the same word. In ψ 24:7 ἄγνοια is used for פֶּשַׁע (together with ἁμαρτία), whereas the rendering in Gn. 31:36 and Ex. 22:8 is ἀδίκημα, in 1 S. 24:12 and Ps. 5:10 ἀσέβεια, and in ψ 88:33 and Prv. 10:19 ἁμαρτία. In Da. 9:16 we have ἄγνοια for עָוֹן (together with ἁμαρτία and ἀδικία), Gn. 15:16 and Is. 65:7 translating the same term by ἁμαρτία, Gn. 44:16 and Ez. 21:30 by ἀδικία, and ψ 35:3 and 50:7 by ἀνομία. On עָשָׂה בִּשְׁגָגָה in Rabbinic literature, cf. Str.-B., II, 264 on Lk. 23:34.
[8] Agric., 161 f.; Plant., 98; Fug., 36; Vit. Mos., I, 222; Spec. Leg., I, 15; IV, 70; Virt., 172, 180 etc.; cf. also ἀγν.-ἀμαθία, Poster C., 52; Gig., 30.
[9] Cf. W. Bousset, Jüdisch.-christl. Schulbetrieb in Alexandria u. Rom (1915), 94 f.

view worked out that education and knowledge, i.e., knowledge of the Torah and tradition, are the presupposition of piety. [10]

In early Christian literature the legal usage is found in Herm. s., 5, 7, 3, though in the NT we only have the formula κατὰ ἄγνοιαν in Ac. 3:17. More common is the Stoic and Jewish usage (→ γινώσκω; ἀγνοέω, 117), e.g., in Ac. 17:30 : τοὺς μὲν οὖν χρόνους τῆς ἀγνοίας ὑπεριδὼν ὁ θεός ...; Eph. 4:17 f.; 1 Pt. 1:14; Kg. Pt. Fr., 4; Ign. Eph., 19, 3; Just. Ap., 61, 10 (as also ἀγνωσία in the Christian addition to Test. L. 18:9, and cf. 1 Tm. 1:13). [11] What we said concerning ἀγνοέω on p. 116 applies to the guilty aspect of ἄγνοια. Wholly Stoic is e.g., Cl. Al. Strom., VII, 16, 101, 6 : δύο εἰσὶν ἀρχαὶ πάσης ἁμαρτίας, ἄγνοια καὶ ἀσθένεια, or the definition of ἄγνοια in Strom., I, 6, 35, 3 as ἀπαιδευσία and ἀμαθία.

> Often ἀγνωσία is given the same force as ἄγνοια. This word also means "ignorance" in its various nuances (cf. Pap., and Preisigke Wört.). It seems to have the same meaning in e.g., Plat. Resp., V, 477a (cf. 478c). It was not developed terminologically, and seems to be completely lacking in the Stoa and Philo. But it is found in the LXX, though with no distinctive features, at Job 35:16 and 3 Macc. 5:27, and cf. in the NT 1 Pt. 2:15. In Wis. 13:1 it is used, like ἄγνοια elsewhere, to describe the state of the Gentile world : ἀγνωσία θεοῦ.

2. The Dualistic Gnostic Usage of Hellenism.

Both ἀγνωσία and ἄγνοια (also ἀγνοεῖν) are used quite characteristically in the dualistic Gnostic language of Hellenism, which offers a parallel to the Stoic usage and is obviously influenced by it. [12] The term ἀγνωσία now signifies lack of the knowledge essential to the salvation of the soul, i.e., the knowledge of God, of the fate of the soul and of true direction for life (→ γινώσκω). Men are entangled in such ἀγνωσία before they receive revelation, i.e., before they believe, and so long as the λήθη and intoxication of the senses holds them captive. Hence ἀγνωσία is again κακία (τῆς ψυχῆς), except that now this is not equated with lack of culture, and we thus have a parallel to the Jewish modification of Stoic usage.

> So Corp. Herm., I, 27: ὦ λαοί, ἄνδρες γηγενεῖς, οἱ μέθῃ καὶ ὕπνῳ ἑαυτοὺς ἐκδεδωκότες [καὶ ?] τῇ ἀγνωσίᾳ τοῦ θεοῦ, νήψατε, παύσασθε δὲ κραιπαλῶντες <καὶ ?> θελγόμενοι ὕπνῳ ἀλόγῳ. Thus those drunk with ἀγνωσία (VII, 1) are summoned to sobriety when ἡ τῆς ἀγνωσίας κακία is described. Again, ἀγνωσία is described as κακία ψυχῆς (X, 8), and the ἀγνοήσασα ἑαυτήν (ψυχή) warned; cf. XI, 21: ἡ γὰρ τελεία κακία τὸ ἀγνοεῖν τὸ<ν> θε[ι]όν. Cf. O. Sol., 11, 8 : "But my intoxication was not that of supreme ignorance." The Κόρη κόσμου thus describes the state prior to the revelation of the supreme God : ἀγνωσία κατεῖχε τὰ ξύμπαντα (Corp. Herm., 4, p. 458, 11, Scott; cf. 53, p. 486, 10). This ignorance is described in Plot. Enn., V, 1, 1 as ἄγνοια τοῦ γένους (of the origin of the soul), as a forgetting of God and our heavenly derivation (cf. Hieroclis Carm. Aur., p. 26, 21 ff., Mullach, and the mythological side-piece in Iren., I, 21, 5; 30, 5 and 8 f. etc.). According to the Marcosites ὑστέρημα and πάθος derive from ἄγνοια (Iren., I, 21, 4). As Mart. Pauli,

---

[10] → γινώσκω and Str.-B., I, 191 f.

[11] Cf. Dib. Past. on 1 Tm. 1:13 f.

[12] Cf. R. Reitzenstein, *Hellenist. Mysterienreligionen*[3] (1927), 65, 2; 292 f.; E. Norden, *Agnostos Theos* (1913), 64, 67 f., 96; J. Kroll, *Die Lehren des Hermes Trismegistos* (1914), 353, 376 f., 412.

4, p. 114, 4 f. warns : ἄνδρες οἱ ὄντες ἐν τῇ ἀγνωσίᾳ καὶ τῇ πλάνῃ ταύτῃ, μετα-
βάλησθε καὶ σωθῆτε, so Cl. Al. Paed., II, 9, 80, 1 explains the μεθύσκεσθαι of 1 Th.
5:7: τουτέστι, ἐν τῷ τῆς ἀγνοίας σκότῳ (cf. on ἀγν. as σκότος Strom., VII, 7, 43, 6
and cf. Protr., XI, 114, 1: ἀφελώμεν τὴν λήθην τῆς ἀληθείας τὴν ἄγνοιαν καὶ τὸ
σκότος). Similiarly Or. c. Cels., VI, 66, p. 136, 24, Koetschau, links ἄγνοια and ἀσέβεια, and Porphyr. Marc., 13, p. 283, 4 ff. teaches : ἐφ' ὅσον τις τὸ σῶμα ποθεῖ καὶ
τὰ τοῦ σώματος σύμφυλα, ἐπὶ τοσοῦτον ἀγνοεῖ τὸν θεὸν καὶ τῆς ἐκείνου ἐνορά-
σεως ἑαυτὸν ἀπεσκότισε ... Yet in him the dualistic Gnostic view is conjoined with
the Stoic (ibid., p. 283, 1: κακία δὲ πᾶσα ὑπ' ἀγνοίας διέψευσται and Abst., II, 53,
p. 178, 21: τῶν θείων ἀμαθία). Stoic also is Cl. Al. Strom., V, 14, 140, 5 : (Empedocles)
γνῶσιν καὶ ἀγνωσίαν ὅρους εὐδαιμονίας καὶ κακοδαιμονίας τε θείως ἐδήλωσεν,
and again Corp. Herm., XIV, 8 : ὦ τῆς πολλῆς ἀνοίας καὶ ἀγνωσίας τῆς περὶ τὸν
θεόν, and notably the combination λήθη and ἄγνοια in 4 Macc. 1:5; 2:24.

In the NT Stoic influence has been seen in the passages already quoted from
Ac. 17:30, 1 Pt. 1:14 and especially Eph. 4:17 f. It is also plain in 1 C. 15:34 :
ἐκνήψατε δικαίως καὶ μὴ ἁμαρτάνετε· ἀγνωσίαν γὰρ θεοῦ τινες ἔχουσιν.
Early Christianity could accept this usage to the extent that it expresses the destiny
of the world's alienation from God, its fallen estate, and its dependence upon
revelation, and therefore to the extent that it rests on a view of man in which the
idealistic Greek understanding of man is broken. But the Christian usage is
naturally not the same as the Gnostic, since the ideas of sin and grace are very
different, as emerges in the conception of the positive correlative of γνῶσις
(→ γινώσκω). For this reason it is characteristic that early Christianity, like
Hellenistic Judaism, could appropriate the language of the Stoa, in which man's
responsibility for his knowledge is asserted.

† ἄγνωστος.

ἄγνωστος is found in the NT only in Ac. 17:23, and simply means "unknown" in
terms of the Jewish and Christian assumption that the heathen do not know God
(→ ἄγνοια). The term ἄγνωστος as such raises no problems. It can mean unknowable or unrecognised in all the nuances of ἀγνοεῖν or γινώσκειν (q.v.). In the sense
of "unknown" it is found in the LXX (Wis. 11:18; 18:3; 2 Macc. 1:19), and often in Philo
and Josephus.

The phrase ἄγνωστος θεός (Ac. 17:23) is alien to the OT, the LXX and Philo.
The idea of God being unknown is certainly possible in the OT so far as concerns
the heathen who know not God (Ps. 79:6), but it is not explicitly formulated, and
to the extent that it is present it is accompanied by the thought of the acknowledgment of God (→ γινώσκω C.). Israel knows God from its history; it does not

---

ἄ γ ν ω σ τ ο ς. F. Pfister, "Der Reliquienkult im Altert.," RVV, V, 1/2, 465, n. 83; P.
Wendland, Die Hellenist.-Röm. Kultur,[2] (1912), 128; E. Norden, Agnostos Theos (1913);
A. Harnack, TU, 39, 1 (1913); R. Reitzenstein, Neue Jahrb. f. d. klass. Altert., 31 (1913),
146 ff., 393 ff.; W. Jaeger, GGA, (1913), 569 ff.; O. Weinreich, DLZ (1913), 2949 ff.; De
dis ignotis (1914); ARW, 18 (1915), 1 ff.; Neue Jahrb. f. d. klass. Altert., 45 (1920), 185 f.;
P. Corssen, ZNW, 14 (1913), 309 ff.; T. Plüss, Wochenschrift f. klass. Phil., 30 (1913),
557; Festgabe f. H. Blümmer (1914), 36 ff.; T. Birt, RM, 69 (1914), 342 ff.; H. Lietzmann,
RM, 71 (1916), 280 f.; W. Schmid, Wochenschr. f. klass. Phil., 35 (1918), 256 ff.; L. Deubner, ARW, 20 (1921), 422, 1; A. Wickenhauser, "Die Ag. u. ihr Geschichtswert," Nt.liche
Abh., VIII, 3-5 (1921), 369 ff.; Meyer, Ursprung, III, 96, 2. E. Fascher, "Deus invisibilis,"
Marburger theol. Studien, I (1930); R. Bultmann, ZNW, 29 (1930), 169-192.

know other gods (Hos. 13:4; Dt. 11:28; 13:3). The Rabbis, too, do not develop any theory of the knowledge of God, since it is obvious to them that Adam and the early human race, especially Noah and his descendants, received 6 or 7 commandments from God, so that knowledge of God either is or might be present among the heathen. On the other hand, they are familiar with the idea of the ways or rule of God being unknown ; [1] the OT also speaks of His will as unsearchable (→ γινώσκω). The case is otherwise in Hellenistic Judaism and primitive Christianity, in which missionary preaching of monotheism contains an element of theoretical instruction (→ γινώσκω, ἀγνοέω, ἄγνοια).

As against this, the thought of the unknowability of God is necessarily alien to the OT, as indicated by the lack of the verbal adjective (as, e.g., for ἀόρατος). It is also more or less completely absent in Hellenistic Judaism and primitive Christianity. Except in Philo, we find it only in Jos. Ap., 2, 167: Moses αὐτὸν (sc. τ. θεόν) ἀπέφηνε καὶ ἀγέννητον καὶ πρὸς τὸν ἀίδιον χρόνον ἀναλλοίωτον, πάσης ἰδέας θνητῆς κάλλει διαφέροντα καὶ δυνάμει μὲν ἡμῖν γνώριμον, ὁποῖος δὲ κατ' οὐσίαν ἄγνωστον. In Philo the phrase θεὸς ἄγνωστος does not occur, but the thought is often expressed by him, [2] Gnostic influence being obviously at work. For the idea is alien to the Greek world as well. Later Greek philosophy after Plato certainly calls the deity ἀόρατος, ἀκατάληπτος etc. It means, however, that it is not accessible to the senses, not that it is radically unkowable. For if it is hard to know God (Plat. Tim., 28c), he may still be known by the νοῦς or λόγος (Tim., 28a; Ps. Arist. Mund., 6, p. 399a, 31). Otherwise he would not be existent, for only the non-existent is unknowable (Diels, I, 152, 12 f.; Plat. Resp., V, 477a). This is contested by scepticism (sophistry), but this doubts the possibility of any objective knowledge at all; thus Gorgias says of the ὄν that if it exists at all it is ἀκατάληπτον ἀνθρώπῳ or ἄγνωστόν τε καὶ ἀνεπινόητον (Diels, II, 243, 5 f.; 244, 30).

For the rest, a γινώσκειν can also have deity as its object in different senses. When Achilles pursues Apollos without recognising him, the latter says : οὐδέ νύ πώ με ἔγνως, ὡς θεός εἰμι (Hom. Il., 22, 9 f.); and Heraclitus (Diels, I, 78, 11 f.) says with reference to the nature of the gods : οὔτε γινώσκων θεοὺς οὐδ' ἥρωας οἵτινές εἰσι (cf. Diels, I, 95, 1 f.). Similarly Pausanias can often speak of βωμοὶ ἀγνώστων θεῶν; they are obviously altars of which it is no longer known to which gods they were once dedicated. Perhaps in some cases they bore the inscription : ἀγνώστοις θεοῖς, [3] but if so the meaning can only be the same as that of inscriptions like θεῷ or προσήκοντι θεῷ, i.e., that it is not certain to which special god the altar should apply. [4] Yet such expressions are rare, and the phrase γνῶσις θεοῦ is completely lacking in the earlier period. Only when the existence

---

[1] Cf. Str.-B., III, 33-36 and 294 f.

[2] Cf. R. Bultmann, ZNW, 29 (1930), 189-192, esp. 191, n. 1.

[3] Cf. the works already mentioned, and also A. Deissmann, *Paulus*[2] (1925), 226-229. The inscription here mentioned : θεοῖς ἀγ[νώστοις], might also be : θεοῖς ἀγ[ιωτάτοις], and is thus no proof. E. Norden is hardly justified in arguing from the expression in a speech of Apollonios (Philostr. Vit. Ap., VI, 3, 5): καὶ ταῦτα Ἀθήνησιν, οὗ καὶ ἀγνώστων δαιμόνων βωμοὶ ἵδρυνται, that Apollonios was referring to such inscriptions, and that the author of the Areopagite address in Ac. 17 depends on him, except that he changes the plur. into a sing.

[4] Cf. the exposition of Ac. 17:23 in Dionys. bar Salibi Corp. Script. Christ. Or., II, 101, Versio (1910), 75.

and nature of God became a problem in philosophical disputation against the sceptics and Epicureans did phrases of this kind become more common.

Already in the followers of Socrates we find the theory of the natural knowledge of God (Xenoph. Mem., IV, 3, 13 f.) which became so important in Stoicism. [5] In his dialogue on philosophy Aristotle adduced a teleological proof of God translated by Cicero in Nat. Deor., II, 95. The first point is to prove the existence of God, but then also, where this is resisted as in Epicurus, Ep. ad Men., p. 60, 4 f. Us.: θεοὶ μὲν γάρ εἰσιν· ἐναργὴς γὰρ αὐτῶν ἐστιν ἡ γνῶσις, to demonstrate his nature as the governor of the world in order to prove a πρόνοια. Cf. Zeno in Diog. L., VII, 147; Epict. Diss., II, 14, 11: λέγουσιν οἱ φιλόσοφοι, ὅτι μαθεῖν δεῖ πρῶτον τοῦτο, ὅτι ἔστι θεὸς καὶ προνοεῖ τῶν ὅλων (combined with OT ideas by Philo in Op. Mund., 170-172). Since the nature of God is essentially πρόνοια for Stoicism, the proofs of his existence and nature sometimes coincide. It is self-evident for Stoicism that a right knowledge of God is essential for man and that knowledge of God and piety belong together. Cf. Musonius, p. 134, 5 f., Hence: ἔκκοψον τὸ τεθηηκὸς τῆς ψυχῆς καὶ γνώσῃ τὸν θεόν. Epict. Ench. 31, 1: τῆς περὶ θεοὺς εὐσεβείας ἴσθι ὅτι τὸ κυριώτατον ἐκεῖνό ἐστιν, ὀρθὰς ὑπολήψεις περὶ αὐτῶν ἔχειν ὡς ὄντων καὶ διοικούντων τὰ ὅλα καλῶς καὶ δικαίως. Cic. Nat. Deor., II, 153 : cognitio deorum, e qua oritur pietas... Sen. Ep., 95, 47: deum colit qui novit ; 50 : primus est deorum cultus : deos credere, deinde reddere illis maiestatem suam, reddere bonitatem, sine qua nulla maiestas est. scire illos esse, qui praesident mundo. Also in Plut. Praec. Coniug., 19 (II, 140d) we see how closely conjoined are the σέβεσθαι and γινώσκειν θεούς. Cic. and Sen. often say agnoscere or nosse deum, and the former also notitia and cognitia dei or deorum (to which ἔννοια as well as γνῶσις may correspond). [6]

Nowhere, however, is the Gnostic idea of the ἄγνωστος θεός, i.e., the idea of the irrationality of God, and the corresponding idea of His supranatural revelation, either the presupposition or the cause of discussion, so that we cannot follow E. Norden in trying to trace back these thoughts or words to oriental influence mediated by Poseidonios. It is only in Plotinus, the Christian Alexandrians and the Corp. Herm., where such influences are undoubtedly present as in Philo, that God is irrational in the strict sense. [7]

Bultmann

---

[5] Cf. Ltzm. R. on R. 1:20 (with further literature); E. Norden, *Agnostos Theos*, 24-28; J. Kroll, *Die Lehren des Hermes Trismegistos* (1914), 37-43; K. Gronau, *Das Theodizeeproblem in der altchristl. Auffassung* (1922); G. Kuhlmann, "Theologia naturalis bei Philon und bei Paulus," *Nt.liche Forschungen*, I, 7 (1930), 65 ff.; → γινώσκω.

[6] Cf. also Max. Tyr., III, 6a, p. 36, 14, Hobein : ἡ τοῦ θείου γνῶσις; Iambl. Protr. III, p. 11, 14 ff.: ἡ γνῶσις τῶν θεῶν. Similarly Myst., 10, 5.

[7] On the ἄγνωστος θεός in Gnosticism, cf. W. Bousset, *Hauptprobl. d. Gnosis* (1907), 83-91; Pauly-W., VII, 1507 ff. For Plotinus God is ἐπέκεινα οὐσίας (so also in Plat. Resp., VI, 509b) καὶ νοήσεως (Enn., V, 3, 11-13). For Cl. Al., cf., e.g., Strom., V, 1, 1, 5 : ἡμεῖς ἄρα ἐσμὲν οἱ ἐν τῷ ἀπιστουμένῳ πιστοὶ καὶ οἱ ἐν τῷ ἀγνώστῳ γνωστικοί, τουτέστιν ἐν τῷ πᾶσιν ἀγνοουμένῳ καὶ ἀπιστουμένῳ, ὀλίγοις δὲ πιστευομένῳ τε καὶ γινωσκομένῳ γνωστικοί. γνωστικοὶ δὲ οὐ λόγῳ, ἔργα ἀπογραφόμενοι, ἀλλ' αὐτῇ τῇ θεωρίᾳ. For the Corp. Herm., cf. J. Kroll, *op. cit.,* 18-21 and 406. On Philo, v. n. 2.

┌─────────────────────────────┐
│ ἀγνός, ἀγνίζω, ἀγνεία   │
│ ἀγνότης, ἀγνισμός   │
└─────────────────────────────┘

† ἀγνός.

ἀγνός, like ἅγιος, is a verbal adjective of ἅζομαι. It originally signifies "that which awakens religious awe." Etymologically it is linked with the old Indian yaj ═ "to reverence" or "sacrifice," and not with the Latin *sacer*.

It is the proper term for "taboo." Thus the sanctuary is ἀγνός : λείψεις τόδ' ἀγνὸν τέμενος ἐναλίας θεοῦ, Eur. Andr., 253. It is an epithet for the gods, especially avenging gods (cf. Hom. Od., 12, 386 : Persephone). But the original meaning is soon softened. It comes to be used simply for things connected with deity. It then comes to signify "ritually clean" and in contrast to the positive synon. δίκαιος it refers negatively to the lack of defects arising, e.g., from bloodguiltiness (cf. Ἁγνὰς μέν, ὦ παῖ, χεῖρας αἵματος φέρεις, Eur. Hipp., 316 ; φόνου δὲ ἀγνὸν καὶ πάντων τῶν περὶ τὰ τοιαῦτα εἰς τὰ θεῖα ἁμαρτανομένων ... Plat. Leg., VI, 759c), contact with corpses, or — according to primitive ideas — sexual intercourse (cf. ἀγνεύειν· καθαρεύειν ἀπό τε ἀφροδισίων καὶ ἀπὸ νεκροῦ, Hesych ; Jos. Ap., 2, 198). This gives rise to the meaning "chaste." The originally purely externally religious concept now acquires a more ethical and inward significance. ἀγνός means "morally blameless" (ἀγνὸς γάρ εἰμι χεῖρας, ἀλλ' οὐ τὰς φρένας, Eur. Or., 1604 ; ἀνδρὸς θείου ἡ ἔσω καὶ ἡ ἐκτὸς ἀγνεία, Porphyr. Abst., II, 44). In this sense it is much used in Hellenism. In civic life ἀγνός is a term of honour denoting the blameless discharge of office (cf. ἀγορανομήσαντα τετράμηνον ἀγνῶς, OGIS, 524, 5).

The proper term for cultic purity in the LXX is → καθαρός. In contrast, ἀγνός ("clean") is used only 11 times (in translation of זך and טָהוֹר): of cultic things (πῦρ, σποδός, 2 Macc. 13:8); of divine words (ψ 11:7; Prv. 15:26); of inward disposition (καρδία, Prv. 20:9); and of chastity (4 Macc. 18:7 f.).

In the NT, too, it is not very important. We do not find it at all in the Synoptics, Hb. and Rev., and with its cognates it is more frequent only in the more linguistically Hellenistic Pastoral and Catholic Epistles. In the NT it never signifies cultic cleaness (though → ἀγνίζειν), but has the following meanings.

1. It signifies "moral purity and sincerity," as in relation to Christ in 1 Jn. 3:3. It is demanded especially of those who bear office in the community (1 Tm. 5:22 : σεαυτὸν ἀγνὸν τήρει; Tt. 2:5); of the conversation of Christian wives (1 Pt. 3:2); of the pious wisdom which avoids all self-seeking (Jm. 3:17). As a moral ideal ἀγνός is linked with δίκαιος in Phil. 4:8. In Phil. 1:17 it seems to be used of the blameless discharge of office, as in the Greek inscriptions.

2. It has the meaning of "innocence" in regard to a matter (2 C. 7:11).

3. It implies "chastity" in the narrower sense (2 C. 11:2): παρθένον ἁγνὴν παραστῆσαι τῷ Χριστῷ, chastity here being an expression of wholehearted inward dedication to Christ (11:3 : ἁπλότης εἰς Χριστόν).

ἀ γ ν ό ς κτλ. E. Fehrle, "Die kultische Keuschheit im Altertum," RVV, VI (1910), 42 ff., 235 ff.; E. Williger, "Hagios," RVV, XIX, 1 (1922), 37 ff.; E. Giertz, *De verborum* ἅζεσθαι, ἀγνός, ἅγιος *usu pagano* (unpublished Diss. Münster, 1920); G. Gerlach, *Griechische Ehreninschriften* (1908), 58 ff.

† ἁγνίζω.

In the LXX frequent only in Ch; 17 times, for טהר pi hithp in 2 Ch. 29:18; 30:18; קדש hi hithp in 1 Ch. 15:12, 14; 2 Ch. 29:5, 15, 34 etc. Otherwise rare, 14 times, esp. for חטא hithp in Nu. 8:21; 19:12 etc.; קדש pi in Ex. 9:10; hithp in Nu. 11:18; Jos. 3:5; Is. 66:17; Jer. 12:3 etc. The word means "to set in a state of cultic qualification," and thus applies to the various measures serving this end (e.g., washing garments in Ex. 19:10). [1]

In the NT ἁγνίζω is used in Jn. 11:55 of the cultic purification of the Jews prior to the passover. It is then used of cultic purification within the Jewish Christian community in Jerusalem which kept to the OT Law and laid on Paul a demand of this kind in Ac. 21:24, 26; 24:18. The ongoing participation of the primitive community in the temple cultus made observance of the traditional external cultic regulations unavoidable. In particular, visiting the temple after returning from the Gentile world demanded additional cultic purification. [2] NT religion did not fashion any such rules of its own. Hence this aspect drops away as NT religion attains fuller understanding of itself. However, the term occasionally finds a new use to denote full moral purity as the decisive presupposition for the reception of salvation (Jm. 4:8; 1 Pt. 1:22; 1 Jn. 3:3).

† ἁγνεία.

In secular Greek ἁγνεία denotes partly the "state of purity" according to the different meanings of the word → ἁγνός, and partly the "action of purifying" (expiatio, lustratio : ἁγνείας ἐπὶ ταῖς θυσίαις διείρηκεν ὁ νόμος ἀπὸ κήδους, ἀπὸ λέχους, ἀπὸ κοινωνίας τῆς πρὸς γυναῖκα καὶ πολλῶν ἄλλων, Jos. Ap., 2, 198 ; ἁγνεία δ' ἐστὶ φρονεῖν ὅσια Porphyr. Abstr., II, 19 ; ἀνδρὸς ἄρα θείου ἡ ἔσω καὶ ἡ ἐκτὸς ἁγνεία, ἀποσίτου μὲν παθῶν ψυχῆς σπουδάζοντος εἶναι, ἀποσίτου δὲ καὶ βρώσεων αἳ τὰ πάθη κινοῦσιν 2, 45; and again Jos. Ap.,1,199; Cl. Al. Strom., IV, 22, 141, 4; 142, 1-4; VII, 4, 27, 4. [1]

In the few OT and apocryphal passages the reference is to "cultic purity," e.g., in Nu. 6:2, 21 (נֶזֶר) the vow and dedicated state of the Nazirite, in 2 Ch. 30:19 (טָהֳרָה) the purity required for the sanctuary, and in 1 Macc. 14:36 the cultic purity of the sanctuary.

In the two NT references (1 Tm. 4:12; 5:2) the cultic element has disappeared and what seems to be meant is "moral purity and blamelessness" (→ ἁγνός).

ἁγνίζω. [1] For examples of the non-biblical use, v. Williger 48 f.; ἁγνός is, e.g., a technical term for the expiation of murder along with καθαίρειν (Eur. El., 794; Herc. Fur., 940).
[2] Str.-B., II, 757 f.
ἁγνεία. [1] For the difference from καθαρμός, v. T. Wächter, Reinheitsvorschriften im griechischen Kult (1910), 1 ff.; Fehrle, 42 ff.

† ἀγνότης.

This term, used neither in classical Greek[1] nor the LXX, denotes the quality of → ἀγνός in the general sense of "moral purity and blamelessness" (2 C. 6:6).

† ἀγνισμός.

This is a cultic word for "purification" or "consecration." In the OT it has a negative reference to the purification of that which is cultically disturbing (Nu. 8:7 for מֵי חַטָּאת), but also a positive for the dedication thereby achieved (Nu. 6:5). In the NT it occurs only in Ac. 21:26 (Nu. 6:5): ἡμερῶν τοῦ ἁγνισμοῦ, in the OT sense of cultic purification linked with the acceptance of a vow.[1]

Hauck

ἀγοράζω, ἐξαγοράζω

A. The Sacral Manumission of Slaves.

In sacral manumission, as particularly attested by the Delphic inscriptions, the god buys the slave to freedom from his owner. For the legal establishment of the liberation a purchase by the god is pretended. The owner actually receives the purchase price from a man, even if only mediately. The god does the slave no real favour, but simply mediates the freedom which he has mostly won for himself. Sacral manumission is for the most part only a legal form of self-manumission. A typical document is as follows: "Item, on behalf of the Pythian Apollo, NN purchased a male slave called XY, at a price of so many mina, to freedom (or, on the condition that he should be free)." There then follow special stipulations and the names of witnesses.[1] Particularly instructive is the Delphic inscription of 200/199 B.C.[2] in which Apollo is called the buyer but in which it is expressly said

---

ἀ γ ν ό τ η ς. [1] For non-biblical use, *v*. IG, IV, 588.
[2] In 2 C. 11:3 it is an old addition to the text (Cl. Or. vg sy in the narrower sense of chastity, cf. 11:2).
ἀ γ ν ι σ μ ό ς. [1] Str.-B., II, 757 ff. For non-biblical use, *v*. Ditt. Syll.³, 1219, 19.
ἀ γ ο ρ ά ζ ω κτλ. On the manumission of slaves, cf. Pauly-W., VII, 95 ff. *s.v.* "Freigelassene"; XIV, 1366 *s.v. "manumissio."* On sacral redemption, cf. Ditt. Syll.², 844 ff. (the inscriptions are not given in the 3rd ed.). Cf. also K. Latte, *Heiliges Recht* (1920), 109 ff.; Deissmann LO, 271 ff.
[1] Deissmann, 274 f.
[2] Ditt. Syll.², 845.

of the redeemed slave at the end: τὰν δὲ ὠνὰν ἐπίστευσε Νικαία τῷ ᾿Απόλλωνι ἐπ᾿ ἐλευθερίᾳ. Here it is evident that the purchase by Apollo was a mere fiction. In reality, the slave bought her own freedom, depositing the price with the priests who secured her freedom thereby. Apollo simply lent his name for the freeing of Nikaia, thus protecting her from any future demands that she should return to slavery. The importance of this sacral redemption, however, should not be over-estimated. Alongside it there was also secular manumission, probably much more practised. Hence we are not to think always of sacral manumission when we read of the purchase of a man to freedom.

The Jewish world too, though there is no evidence of sacral manumission in the temple,[3] is familiar with the religious application of the thought of redemption.[4] We may refer to S. Nu., 115 on 15:41: "When (the king) redeemed him (his friend's son), he did not buy him as a free man but as a slave, so that if he should order something and the other be unwilling to undertake it, he should be able to say, Thou art my slave... Similarly, when the Holy One, blessed be He, redeemed the seed of Abraham His friend, He did not buy them as children but as slaves, so that if He should order something and they be unwilling to undertake it, He should be able to say, Ye are my slaves" (→ δοῦλος).[5]

B. ἀγοράζω.

From ἀγορά, "market," this means "to buy," and is often used in the NT in relation to commercial life.

1. The almost verbal repetition of 1 C. 6:20: ἠγοράσθητε γὰρ τιμῆς, in 7:23: τιμῆς ἠγοράσθητε, and the rather abrupt way in which the phrase is introduced in both cases, shows that it is a kind of slogan of Paul's. In both verses the main point is that Christians are not free (6:19) but are the possession of Christ (7:23). Intentionally it is not said who has bought them, or from whom they are bought, or at what cost. The reference is simply to the fact of their redemption. The reverse side of Paul's consciousness of freedom, which does not permit of bondage to any man (7:23), is his consciousness of being bound to God and to Christ, and this is sharply expressed. Behind this slogan, though not expounded in it, is Paul's doctrine of salvation (→ ἐξαγοράζω). Since in these verses Christians are not thought of as free men but as slaves, so that no purchase ἐπ᾿ ἐλευθερίᾳ has taken place, it suffices by way of exposition to compare it with the usual manumission of slaves.[1] The details of sacral manumission need hardly be applied, though a comparison may be seen with the passage already quoted from S. Nu., 115 on 15:41.

In Rev. 5:9 (cf. 14:3, 4) the word celebrates the greatness of the achievement of the Lamb. It is thus indicated how, from what and for whom the Lamb has

---

[3] On manumission in the synagogue (ἐπὶ τῆς προσευχῆς), i.e., before the assembled community as witnesses, cf. Schürer, III, 93 f.

[4] Cf. also R. H. Rengstorf, Jebamot (1929), 89 ff.

[5] On the continuation of sacral redemption in the Church, cf. E. Dobschütz in RE, 18 (1906), 430.

ἀγοράζω. Comm. on 1 C. ad loc.: Joh. W.; Bchm; Ltzm.

[1] ἀπελεύθερος κυρίου in 1 C. 7:22 does not mean every Christian, but only the

purchased men (→ λύτρον). But no doctrine of salvation is to be sought in the hymn.

2. In Rev. 3:18 the community should ἀγοράσαι gold etc. from Christ. The thought here is not so much that of accepting what is given as in Is. 55:1 ("buy... without price"), but rather of the presence of sham possessions instead of real ones (3:17).

C. † ἐξαγοράζω.

1. The LXX does not use ἐξαγοράζω for "redeem," but it is found in secular speech, e.g., Diod .S., 362, Dindorf, V, 213 : ἐξηγόρασεν (a Roman knight) αὐτήν (a slave). No examples have been found in non-Christian cultic speech. Nor is it found in Josephus. On the Jewish estimation of the suffering of the pious as an expiation, → ἱλαστήριον and λύτρον. Among the Jews the particular image of manumission is lacking in this connection.

In the NT the word is used of the redeeming and liberating act of Christ (Gl. 3:13; 4:5). The idea is the same as in the case of ἀγοράζειν, except that now the purchase does not transfer to the possession of God or Christ, but to freedom. Standing under the Law and its curse is thought of as slavery (4:1, 3, 7). To this extent, the idea corresponds to the contemporary practice of sacral manumission.

In Paul, of course, the divine Purchaser does not pay only in appearance as in sacral redemption, but in the most bitter reality, so that the parallel breaks down at the decisive point and there is thus a great difference. In respect of the seriousness of the purchase, Christ is to be compared to the one who actually pays and not to the Delphic god who merely makes a fictional payment. And everything depends on this. In this liberation from the curse of the Law, the essential point is that it confers both an actual and also a legally established freedom ensuring against any renewal of slavery. The claim of the Law is satisfied. It can be dissolved because the Law is neither the first nor the last Word of God to man, and has thus only conditional validity (4:2; 3:17). The relationship of man to God which God willed earlier, and therefore properly, is justification by faith (3:6-14) and therefore sonship (3:24 f.; 4, 1-5).

Nevertheless, the transition from status under the Law to divine sonship and justification by faith is not accomplished merely by a declaration of God, but by redemption (3:13; 4:5). For the curse of the Law is an ordinance of God which truly corresponds to His holy will towards the sinner (→ κατάρα, ἐπικατάρα-

---

Christian slave, whereas the Christian freeman is δοῦλος Χριστοῦ. These concepts are correlative. Hence ἀπελεύθερος has no bearing on the meaning of ἀγοράζειν, as against Joh. W. on 1 C. 6:20.

ἐ ξ α γ ο ρ ά ζ ω. Comm. on Gl.: Zn., 155 f.; Ltzm. ad loc.; Sieffert (1899), 184, 244 (with good material on earlier exegesis). J. C. K. v. Hofmann, Die hl. Schrift d. NT, II, 1² (1872), 71. Also NT theologies by A. Schlatter, II (1910), 277 ff.; P. Feine⁵ (1931), 194 f.; J. Kaftan (1927), 119.

τος), as is shown by the fact that it remains eternally valid and effective in relation to the lost (R. 2:5-10 etc.). The fact that the holy will of God expressed in
the Law and its curse finds true and full recognition in the transition to divine
sonship and justification by faith, so that no man can find forgiveness in Christ
unless the judgment on his sinfulness is also revealed in the experience of Jesus
as the Crucified, [1] is what Paul expresses in his metaphorical use of redemption.
There can be no doubt that the use is metaphorical, since no mention is made of
any recipient of the purchase price.

If we take the ἐξηγόρασεν quite objectively, loosing it from any connection
with the "we" who by this act are brought into fellowship with God in penitence
and faith, then we make of it a commercial transaction between Christ and God
which affects us only in so far as we are the object of it. This raises, however,
the question of the necessity and possibility of any such transaction. Paul, however, does not answer this kind of question. His statements and thought are not
moving along the lines of objectivisation. He sees the process as something which
took place towards us and in our favour, [2] not as something which took place
towards God and in His favour. If for him the cross of Christ is also the service
of God by the Crucified, His obedience towards God (Phil. 2:8), the revelation
of God's righteousness and love (R. 3:25; 5:8), nevertheless for Paul God is not
the One who receives but the One who acts in the cross of Jesus (→ καταλλάσσω). [3] Thus, even though the significance and force of the ἐξηγόρασεν are
not to be found in human piety as a conscious attitude or historical process, even
though it has also validity before God and for Him, the service of Jesus being
rendered both to God and man, yet in the strict sense it is the execution of a
divine action towards man. Hence it is not service to God and man in the same
sense. We should not make of the ἐξηγόρασεν a myth, a word concerning a
process of some transcendent reality which only subsequently has significance for
us; it speaks of an action of God towards us in the history of salvation. Paul has
it in common with myths that he evidently speaks of divine fellowship. But he
does not speak of the transcendent God of religious fantasy; he speaks of "our"
God, i.e., of the God who acts towards us. [4]

The predominance of an objectivising understanding of ἐξηγόρασεν has led most of
the exegetical and biblico-theological work on the passage astray. If we are to objectivise, however, the orthodox form found in Lietzmann, in which the redeemed are
all men, is better than the Hofmann form present in Sieffert, Zahn and Kaftan, in which
the redeemed are the Jews. For the orthodox form does at least give us a living relation
to the first and all subsequent readers, whereas the Hofmann view excludes this and
thus impoverishes the passage.

---

[1] Cf. Schlatter, op. cit.
[2] Gl. 3:13: ἡμᾶς ἐξηγόρασεν. Formally, 4:5 speaks objectively (ἵνα τοὺς ὑπὸ νόμον
ἐξαγοράσῃ), but materially subjectively. For those under the law are "we"; cf. v. 3:
οὕτως καὶ ἡμεῖς and v. 5: ἵνα τὴν υἱοθεσίαν ἀπολάβωμεν. For Paul, all men stand
under the curse of the Law, since this is God's curse (cf. R. 1: 18 ff.).
[3] Obviously action and the experiencing or receiving of effects cannot be absolutely
separated, since Paul thinks of God as in a relationship of fellowship with man. But it makes
a great difference whether we think of God's acting as the primary and essential aspect,
or His receiving.
[4] → κατάρα and the bibliography there given.

2. ἐξαγοράζω also means, in accordance with the sense of the ἐκ in many composites, [5] an "intensive buying," i.e., a buying which exhausts the possibilities available. [6] It is used in this sense in Col. 4:5 and Eph. 5:16 : τὸν καιρὸν ἐξαγοραζόμενοι. καιρός here stands for the opportunities offered by time. These are to be tirelessly snapped up and used at the expense of effort.

There is no thought of making time empty. [7] Da. 2:8 : עִדָּנָא אַנְתּוּן זָבְנִין, is translated in the LXX and Θ by καιρὸν ὑμεῖς ἐξαγοράζετε : "that ye would buy the time," i.e., seek to win it. Possibly we have here the hint of a proverbial saying. But no matter how the Greek translators understood the Aramaic, their use of ἐξαγοράζω is different from that of Paul.

Büchsel

ἀγρυπνέω → ἐγείρω, γρηγορέω.

┌─────────────────────────────────┐
│ ἀγωγή, παράγω, προάγω   │
│   προσάγω, προσαγωγή   │
└─────────────────────────────────┘

† ἀγωγή.

In the NT this occurs only in 2 Tm. 3:10 : παρηκολούθησάς μου τῇ διδασκαλίᾳ, τῇ ἀγωγῇ, τῇ προθέσει, τῇ πίστει κτλ. The context shows that ἀγωγή, which literally means "guidance" or "direction," refers to the orientation of the writer, which is to be appropriated no less than διδασκαλία etc. by his readers. "Manner of life" thus seems to be the best translation. [1] The word can be both transitive and intransitive. In the sense of manner of life or conduct the word ἀγωγή is found in Attic prose, [2] in inscriptions, papyri, the LXX, and especially the later philosophy of antiquity and Jewish and Christian literature. A particular extension of the term ἀγωγή is to those who are to be guided or educated, i.e., children. [3] Cf. the title of the writing of Plut. : περὶ παίδων ἀγωγῆς. The instructor is thus called ὁ παιδαγωγός, and instruction ἡ παιδαγωγία, from which is derived παιδαγωγέω and other similar constructions. The Greek lexicographers have more closely defined ἀγωγή in this connection. [4] Suid. quotes from Polyb. (I, 32, 1): Λακεδαιμόνιον ἄνδρα τῆς Λακωνικῆς ἀγωγῆς μετεσχηκότα. Hesychius interprets ἀ. by τρόπος, ἀναστροφή. Julius Pollux relates : τὰ δὲ πράγματα, διδασκαλία, παίδευσις, ἐξήγησις, ὑφήγησις, ἡγεμονία, ἀγωγή, σοφιστική.

───────────────

[5] Cf. ἐξοπλίζειν = "to arm fully;" ἐκθερίζειν = "to finish harvesting," etc.
[6] E.g., Plut. Crass., 2, 5 (II, 543e): ἐξηγόραζε τὰ καιόμενα, καὶ γειτνιῶντα τοῖς καιομένοις.
[7] Loh. Kol., 4:5.
ἀ γ ω γ ή. [1] So Dib. Past. etc.
[2] Pass.: "The word occurs in Attic prose in every shade of meaning."
[3] The verb ἄγω often has the pregnant sense of "educate." There is reference to the good or bad training of animals (Xenoph. Mem., IV, 1, 3: τὰς καλῶς ἀχθείσας κύνας), but especially to the upbringing of men (Plat. Leg., VI, 782d): ἀνθρώποις ... ἀγομένοις ὀρθῶς).
[4] Cf. the detailed instances in Thes. Steph.

As these examples show, the reference to education may be decisive for an understanding of ἀ. even in the sense that it refers to the results of education rather than to education itself, [5] i.e., to the way in which the man who is guided conducts himself in life, to his breeding, behaviour, mode or manner of life. Hence there is frequent reference to βίου ἀγωγή. And even without the addition ἀ. can have this significance. Cf. Xenoph. Eq., 3, 4; Polyb., VI, 2, 13 : ἡ ἐκ παίδων ἀγωγή. There is particularly frequent reference (cf. the passage from Suid. already quoted) to the Spartan ἀ.; cf. ἤχθη τὴν λεγομένην ἀγωγὴν ἐν Λακεδαίμονι, Plut. Ages., 1, 2 (I, 596c), and more generally Ἑλληνικὴ ἀγωγή (e.g., Strabo). The philosophical schools are palpably distinguished by their ἀ.: Σκεπτικὴ ἀγωγή, Κυρηναϊκὴ ἀγωγή, Πρωταγόρειος ἀγωγή, Diog. L., I, 19 mentions together αἱρέσεις καὶ ἀγωγάς.

In the world around the NT we find the same usage though not with the preciseness finally mentioned : φαίνεσθε γὰρ καθόλου ἀγωγῇ ταύτῃ χρῆσθαι, Ditt. Or., 223, 15; 479, 9; 485, 3; P. Tebt., I, 24, 57; P. Par., 61, 12; 63, col. 9, 38. Ps.-Heracl. Ep., I, 16 (Bernays), where ἀ. is set alongside δίαιτα (it is also used in medical terminology in the sense of δίαιτα). Jos.: τὴν πάτριον ἀγωγὴν τῶν ἐθῶν ἀποσῴζειν, Ant., 12, 10 ; ζήτησις περὶ τῆς Ἰουδαίων ἀγωγῆς, 14, 195[6].

The LXX uses it in the same way : καὶ Ἐσθὴρ οὐ μετήλλαξεν τὴν ἀγωγὴν αὐτῆς, Est. 2:20; διηγεῖτο τὴν ἀγωγὴν παντὶ τῷ ἔθνει αὐτοῦ, 10:3; ἐξῆλουν τὰς ἀγωγάς, 2 Macc. 4:16; τὴν αὐτὴν ἀγωγὴν κατὰ τῶν Ἰουδαίων ἄγειν, 6:8; τὴν ἑαυτῶν ἀγωγὴν αἱρετίζοντας, 11:24; ἀγωγὴν ἐπιβούλων ... λαμβάνειν, 3 Macc. 4:10.

The Jewish writers finally mentioned (Jos., Ps.-Heracl. and LXX) thus apply a common Greek expression.

Since the Pastorals use other popular philosophical terms, the use of ἀγωγή in 2 Tm. 3:10 may well testify to this background. In a similar reference to Timothy, who is addressed in 2 Tm. 3:10, Paul says in 1 C. 4:17: τὰς ὁδούς μου τὰς ἐν Χριστῷ. As here the ὁδοί (= διδασκαλία) are Christianised both in form and content by the addition of ἐν Χριστῷ, so 1 Cl., 47, 6 refers to τῆς ἐν Χριστῷ ἀγωγῆς and 48, 1 to τὴν σεμνὴν τῆς φιλαδελφίας ἡμῶν ἁγνὴν ἀγωγήν.

† παράγω.

This transitive and intransitive word is found in the NT only in the latter sense; Mt. 9:9; 9:27; 20, 30; Mk. 1:16; 2:14; 15:21; Jn. 8:59; [1] 9:1; 1 C. 7:31. The passive or middle is found in 1 Jn. 2:8, 17. Apart from Mk. 15:21, it is always emphasised in the passages in the Gospels that Jesus "passes by." The similar καὶ παράγων in Mk. 1:16; 2:14; Jn. 9:1 might be regarded as the introductory phrase to a pericope.

1 C. 7:31: παράγει ... τὸ σχῆμα τοῦ κόσμου τούτου, reminds us of 1 Jn. 2:17: ὁ κόσμος παράγεται καὶ ἡ ἐπιθυμία αὐτοῦ. Perhaps the Johannine phrase echoes

---

[5] In modern Greek ἀ. means "education" or "discipline" : δὲν ἔχει ἀγωγήν = "he has no education."
[6] Further examples from ancient Greek and the contemporary NT world may be found in Pass.-Cr., s.v.
π α ρ ά γ ω. [1] Not in all MSS.

the Pauline. But perhaps the recurrence of the rare and almost technical παράγει (παράγεται) suggests reference to an apocalyptic commonplace. Both passages (cf. 1 Jn. 2:8) have the nuance of "passing away" or "disappearing." With the same eschatological significance there perhaps corresponds the *pertransire* of 4 Esr. 4:26. A similar sense is found in Mt. 5:18; 24:34 f.; 2 Pt. 3:10, παρέρχεσθαι.

The relevant Hebrew עָבַר is translated παράγειν in ψ 143:4: αἱ ἡμέραι αὐτοῦ ὡσεὶ σκιὰ παράγουσι = יָמָיו כְּצֵל עוֹבֵר. Cf. Is. 24:11, where עָבְרָה כָּל־שִׂמְחָה is rendered πέπαυται πᾶσα εὐφροσύνη. If in 1 C. 7:31 we give σχῆμα the theatrical sense of "part" or "role," then παράγειν might mean "introducing to the stage." We might then take Paul's meaning to be that the role of this world is played out and another σχῆμα has appeared on the scene. The present is to be noted; it tells us that the great eschatological change is already taking place.[2]

προάγω.

As elsewhere, προάγω is used in the NT both transitively and intransitively. It is often said of Jesus that He "precedes" His followers. This is perhaps a Christological expression. To the Christological event there corresponds on the part of men an ἀκολουθεῖν which means following in the deeper sense of discipleship. Cf. especially in the sense of following Christ's passion: ἦν προάγων αὐτοὺς ὁ Ἰησοῦς, καὶ ἐθαμβοῦντο, οἱ δὲ ἀκολουθοῦντες ἐφοβοῦντο, Mk. 10:32; προάξω ὑμᾶς εἰς τὴν Γαλιλαίαν, Mk. 14:28 (= Mt. 26:32); and cf. Mk. 16:7 (= Mt. 28:7). What applies in this way to the following of the death and resurrection applies also to the apostolic words of prophecy which go before (1 Tm. 1:18) and to the commandment which goes before (Hb. 7:18). Yet it may be we are reading too much into the two latter passages, and the πρό simply denotes temporal precedence. The same problem whether the πρό in προάγω is to be understood spatially with reference to those who follow or in a more general temporal sense[1] arises in relation to the contested explanation of 1 Tm. 5:24: αἱ ἁμαρτίαι ... προάγουσαι εἰς κρίσιν. In the former case we are reminded of parallels like Is. 58:8: προπορεύσεται ἔμπροσθέν σου ἡ δικαιοσύνη σου or Barn., 4, 12: ἐὰν ᾖ ἀγαθός, ἡ δικαιοσύνη αὐτοῦ προηγήσεται αὐτοῦ. A separate question is raised by 2 Jn. 9: πᾶς ὁ προάγων καὶ μὴ μένων ἐν τῇ διδαχῇ τοῦ Χριστοῦ θεὸν οὐκ ἔχει.

The reading παραβαίνων for προάγων makes quite good sense. In favour of this view, προάγειν trans. means "to seduce or mislead"; to this there corresponds an intrans. προάγειν as a synon. of παραβαίνειν in the sense of "going astray" in contrast to περιπατεῖν ἐν τῇ ἐντολῇ in v. 6 and as a predicate of πλάνοι in v. 7.[2] On the other hand, it is more likely that the reading παραβαίνων is simply an alternative for a genuine προάγων which it was found impossible to understand apart from the situation actually envisaged in the epistle. In this case, it may be that the reference is to a slogan of docetic or libertine opponents who like to think of themselves as advanced

---

[2] Cf. Joh. W. 1 K. *ad loc.*
π ρ ο ά γ ω. [1] The general temporal significance is, of course, intrinsically possible, as illustrated by, e.g.: ὅπερ ἐν ταῖς προαγούσαις γραφαῖς παρέδομεν, Jos. Ant., 19, 298; προάγειν ἀρχαιότητι, Jos. Ap., 2, 154.
[2] So Cr.-Kö.

or progressive in their teaching.[3] Polemically the expression is thus used *in malam partem*.

† προσάγω.

Three times used transitively in the NT (Lk. 9:41; Ac. 16:20 and 1 Pt. 3:18), and once intransitively (Ac. 27:27).[1]

It is only in 1 Pt. 3:18 that elucidation is needed and particular interest arises. In a kerygmatic statement, the meaning of the death of Christ, who died the Just for the unjust, is described as follows: ἵνα ὑμᾶς (or ἡμᾶς) προσαγάγῃ τῷ θεῷ. Both the expression and the context suggest that we have here a cultic term.

a. The word is used of gifts that are brought: δῶρά τινι. We may thus understand its sacrifical usage in the sense of "offer" = *offerre*. This is common to the whole range of Greek. Cf. θυσίας οἱ προσάγοντες, Hdt., III, 24; ἑκατὸν προσῆγε συμμιγῆ βοσκήματα, Soph. Trach., 762; ἑκατόμβας προσάγομεν, Luc. Jup. Conf., 5; ἑκατόμβην προσάγειν, Pollux, 1, 26; ἱερεῖα προσάγειν τοῖς βωμοῖς, *ibid.*, 1, 27; κἀγώ σοι τὸν βοῦν τὸν μέγαν προσαγάγω εἰς εὐχήν, Theophanes Confessor, 283, 19 f. Similarly two passages from the post-apostolic fathers: Ἰσαὰκ ... προσήγετο θυσία, 1 Cl., 31, 3; τὴν θρησκείαν προσάγουσιν αὐτῷ (sc. τῷ θεῷ), Dg., 3, 2. In most of these instances the idea of offering is quite plain. Occasionally, esp. when the gift is an animal or even a man, we may wonder whether the original precise meaning of "bring" is not adequate or even more suitable.[2]

The LXX usage is exactly the same as elsewhere. The term occurs esp. in Ex., Lv., and Nu. in a cultic sense, usually for the hiphil of קרב,[3] more rarely for בוא. From the many examples we may select the following: προσάξεις τὸν μόσχον ἐπὶ τὰς θύρας τῆς σκηνῆς τοῦ μαρτυρίου, Ex. 29:10; ἄρσεν ἄμωμον προσάξει, Lv. 1:3; προσάξουσιν ἀπὸ τῆς θυσίας τοῦ σωτηρίου κάρπωμα Κυρίῳ, τὸ στέαρ ... καὶ τοὺς νεφρούς, Lv. 3:3; προσάξει ἡ συναγωγὴ μόσχον ἐκ βοῶν ἄμωμον περὶ τῆς ἁμαρτίας, Lv. 4:14; προσαγάγῃ τὴν θυσίαν αὐτοῦ, Lv. 7:6 (cf. 2 Ch. 29:31 [here for וגש]; 1 Esr. 1:18; Sir. 31:20; 2 Macc. 3:22; 12:43 etc.); προσάξετε ὁλοκαυτώματα τῷ Κυρίῳ, Lv. 23:8; προσφορὰς Κυρίῳ ἀξίως πρόσαγε, Sir. 14:11; προσήγαγον τὸ μνημόσυνον τῆς προσευχῆς ὑμῶν ἐνώπιον τοῦ ἁγίου, Tob. 12:12. It is indicative of the great range of application of προσάγειν that it corresponds to a dozen Hebrew word stems. That the metaphorical sense of "offer" or "sacrifice" is present is plainly shown by the passages last mentioned, in which there can be no question of an animal which is to be brought.

---

[3] An analogous situation is perhaps depicted in 1 C. 4:6.

π ρ ο σ ά γ ω. [1] Here instead of προσάγειν we also have προσαχεῖν, *resonare*, προσανέχειν, προσεγγίζειν.

[2] Thes. Steph. says of the Lk. passage: *Sunt tamen qui interpretantur Adducunt.* And D. Tabachovitz, *Sprachliche und textkritische Studien zur Chronik des Theophanes Confessor* (Phil. Diss. Upsala, 1926), 39 f. contests the view of K. Krumbacher, *Geschichte der byzantinischen Literatur*[2] (1897), 792 f. that we ought to read: "Then will I offer Thee the great ox" (in satirical reference to a Byzantine emperor), suggesting as the true rendering: "Then will I bring the great ox to prayer." In this connection Tabachovitz postulates a special use of προσάγειν for the leading of the emperor in a procession, the usual words in such cases being διασῴζειν, "to conduct," or διριγεύειν, "to escort." If this not particularly obvious assumption is correct, it might help to explain 1 Pt. 3:18, or at least to give a distinctive shade of meaning to it.

[3] There are examples of the sacrificial use of קרב even outside the OT, as in the Elephantine-Pap. and epigraphically on consecrated gifts (Aramaic and Nabataean).

Yet the conjunction of προσάγειν with a personal object points in a specific direction which alone suffices to explain 1 Pt. 3:18. Ἀαρὼν καὶ τοὺς υἱοὺς προσάξεις ἐπὶ τὰς θύρας τῆς σκηνῆς τοῦ μαρτυρίου (in relation to the consecration of priests, Ex. 29:4 and cf. 29:8); cf. 40:12 (in relation to cleansing from sin); προσήγαγεν Μωυσῆς τοὺς υἱοὺς Ἀαρών (Lv. 8:24); προσάξεις τοὺς Λευίτας (Nu. 8:9, 10). In this 8th chapter of Numbers as in other chapters the object is sometimes the priest to be consecrated and sometimes the animal to be offered. At any rate a Christian reading 1 Pt. 3:18, and at home in the sacrificial terminology of the OT, is reminded by the parallel mode of expression of the approach of the cleansed priest to God, for Christians themselves are called to be a holy priesthood according to 1 Peter. [4]

b. We do not leave this circle if we affirm that προσάγειν also seems to be a legal term: προσάξει αὐτὸν ὁ κύριος (sc. of the slave) πρὸς τὸ κριτήριον τοῦ θεοῦ (Ex. 21:6); προσήγαγεν τὸν ἀδελφὸν αὐτοῦ πρὸς τὴν Μιδιανεῖτιν ἐναντίον Μωυσῆ καὶ ἔναντι πάσης συναγωγῆς υἱῶν Ἰσραήλ (Nu. 25:6); προσήγαγεν Μωυσῆς τὴν κρίσιν αὐτῶν ἔναντι κυρίου (Nu. 27:5). [5] In this connection we are also to think of Ac. 16:20, which we should not in the first instance connect with 1 Pt. 3:18. If in Ac. 16:20 we are concerned with a normal human judgment, so in 1 Pt. 3:18, as in the old covenant with its covenant people, in which the judgment of God is constantly worked out, we are concerned with the judgment of God to which Christ leads men, though at this point there is no cleavage between judgment and grace, since by His death Christ has reconciled God with men.

Christ is thus a προσαγωγεύς in a special sense. There are only a few instances of this word, and it is used both generally and specially and in malam as well as in bonam partem. On the one side the agents, messengers and spies of the Sicilian tyrant are προσαγωγεῖς as reported by Plut. But the title is also given to those who make friends of others, and therefore to mediators or reconcilers (cf. Demosth., 24, 161). Hence Christ could be given as a mark of honour the title of προσαγωγεύς, as also of παράκλητος, a word which derives from a related circle of ideas. In fact Greg. Naz. applies the term προσαγωγεύς to Christ in his polemic against Julian.

Our final discussions suggest, however, that we are now using the word προσάγειν more in the sense of courtly ceremonial than of law. Xenoph. Cyrop., I, 3, 8 (with which we should connect VII, 5, 45, where we find προσαγωγή, → 133) uses προσάγειν for the admission of ambassadors to audience with the great king. [6]

---

[4] This deduction is drawn by B. Weiss in his *Handausgabe des NT*, and in spite of the refutation by Cr.-Kö. there is much to be said for it.

[5] In the papyri the word προσάγειν is sometimes used of bringing someone before a judge either as defendant or witness; cf. Preisigke Wört. The legal term is also extended to things (cf. the German *beitreiben*). A. Steinwenter, *Studien zum römischen Versäumnisverfahren* (1914), 189 f.: "The προσάγειν of BGU, 2, 388, II, 14 and Lips., 38, II, 1 I take to mean bringing to judgment; cf. *citato et inducto Capitone* in P. Lips., 38, I, 12. Other instances of προσαγωγεύς and προσαγωγή in this sense may be given: Xenoph. Cyrop., 7, 5, 45; Paul to the Ephesians 2:18; Philostr. Vit. Soph., 2, 32 ..." This is the meaning of προσάγειν in modern Greek.

[6] It is hard to see why this reference is "as superfluous as it is inappropriate" in explanation of 1 Pt. 3:18 (Cr.-Kö.). If Christ is here thought of as the One who brings men to the King of all kings, this in no way affects the decisive sense of the passage with its reminder of the reconciling death of Christ.

c. Finally, προσάγειν in 1 Pt. 3:18 may be given another shade of meaning by the fact that we have ultimately to think always of the act of God. And the point here is that God reconciles man to Himself. This is expressed by means of προσάγεσθαι. This sense of bringing to one's side, whether in a good way or in a bad, is found in Greek generally, and it is specially, i.e., positively emphasised in the LXX: προσηγαγόμην ὑμᾶς πρὸς ἐμαυτόν, Ex. 19:4; οὓς ἐλέξατο ἑαυτῷ προσηγάγετο πρὸς ἑαυτόν, Nu. 16:5 (cf. 16:9, 10).

d. Materially the statement that God leads and reconciles men to Himself is identical with the statement in 1 Pt. 3:18 that Christ leads and reconciles men to God. That the word προσάγειν can still gather shades of meaning from sacrificial, legal and courtly usage without any disruptive intersecting of the various images is due not so much to the vagueness of the expression, or the overloading of a simple term by exegetes who do not observe the limits of the lexicographer, as to the event itself in its simplicity from above and its multiplicity from below, i.e., in the complexity which demands different images set alongside or superimposed on one another if it is to be properly grasped. What is true of the person of Christ, who is both subject and object, is also true of His work, which as the work of Χριστός (προσαγωγεύς) has the aim ἵνα ἡμᾶς προσαγάγῃ τῷ θεῷ, and which is thus the work of the θεὸς προσαγόμενος ἡμᾶς πρὸς ἑαυτόν.

† προσαγωγή.

The significance of this word, which occurs 3 times in the NT (R. 5:2; Eph. 2:18; 3:12), is for the most part expounded in our discussion of προσάγω, and all that is essential to explain the relevant passages has been said already. Is it not necessary, however, that we should consider the much ventilated question [1] whether it is used transitively or intransitively? Does not this question have some bearing on exegesis?

Like the basic ἄγειν and its various derivatives, the verb προσάγειν is sometimes used transitively and sometimes intransitively, and the same is true of the verbal substantives. Cf. what was said above concerning ἀγωγή. Thus, transitively the sense is that of "introduction" and intransitively of "access."

The lexical battle which of these is predominant and which is older is hampered by the inconclusiveness of statistical analysis and the difficulty of deciding which is the true meaning in many passages. This is particularly true in the oldest example in Hdt., II, 58: πανηγύρεις δὲ ἄρα καὶ πομπὰς καὶ προσαγωγὰς πρῶτοι Αἰγύπτιοί εἰσι οἱ ποιησάμενοι καὶ παρὰ τούτων Ἕλληνες μεμαθήκασι. Here an intransitive use yields the sense of "approaching," and particularly of the sacred approach to a sacrifice or other festival, i.e., a "procession" (Attic = πρόσοδος). A transitive use yields the sense of "bringing up," particularly in the case of a sacrifice (→ προσάγω, 131), and therefore again of a religious "procession." The word is used in another connection in the passage from Xenoph. Cyrop., already quoted (VII, 5, 45): ἐγὼ δὲ ἠξίουν τοὺς τοιούτους, εἴ τίς τι ἐμοῦ δέοιτο, θεραπεύειν ὑμᾶς τοὺς ἐμοὺς φίλους δεομένους προσαγωγῆς. Here the transitive sense seems most likely. The reference is to an

προσαγωγή. [1] Cf. in relation to R. 5:2, H. A. W. Meyer[3] (1859), and H. A. W. Meyer-B. Weiss[6] (1881), also Zn. R.

"audience." A good example of the intransitive is found in Plut. Aem., 13, 3 (I, 261e): ἱδρυμένος ἐπὶ χωρίων οὐδαμόθεν προσαγωγὴν ἐχόντων; as also in Polyb., X, 1, 6 : ἐκεῖνοι γὰρ θερινοὺς ἔχοντες ὅρμους καὶ βραχεῖάν τινα παντελῶς προσαγωγήν. Thus a "landfall" or "haven."

In the NT we have an absolute use of the term in Eph. 3:12, whereas R. 5:2 emphasises the relation to something εἴς τι, and Eph. 2:18 the relation to a person πρός τινα. The lexical question whether it is used transitively or intransitively has no importance from the standpoint of exegesis and biblical theology. For materially it makes no difference, nor could it possibly do so, whether the Christian moves towards grace, towards God the Father, or whether he is led. For the Christian does not in any case go of himself. He is led by Christ, so that his own movement is accomplished in Christ. We may prefer the possibly better attested and widespread translation "access." But we must always keep in view the fact just emphasised that, quite apart from any question of transitive or intransitive use, we are dealing concretely with what takes place in Christ. If it is access, then it is an access which is simply Christ Himself, who in Jn. 10 is called the door.

> Thes. Steph. : *Gregor. Christum Servatorem nostrum* προσαγωγέα *Dei patris, Emissarium, Conciliatorem et interpretem, vocavit, alludens ad verbum* προσαγωγῆς, *quo Paulus utitur, ap. quem quidam, ut mox dicam,* προσαγωγὴν *Admissionem verterunt ; in qua interpretatione, Admissio passive dicetur, qua admittimur : at* προσαγωγεύς *est Ille qui admittit, et aditum praebet.* W. Sanday and A. C. Headlam [2] : ". . . the idea is that of introduction to the presence-chamber of a monarch. The rendering 'access' is inadequate, as it leaves out of sight that we do not come in our own strength but need an 'introducer' — Christ." On the other hand, A. Pallis [3] lays all the emphasis on an intransitive rendering. He has a useful comment : "It has been a commonplace both in ancient and modern times to liken salvation to a haven" — a view which is not incompatible with the exegesis stressed above.

Karl Ludwig Schmidt

> ### ἀγών, ἀγωνίζομαι, † ἀντ-, † ἐπ-, † καταγωνίζομαι, ἀγωνία

(→ ἀθλέω).

This is a group of words much used in relation to the Greek stadium. They are rare in the LXX and NT, and are almost always used in writings tinged with Hellenism.

---

[2] The International Critical Commentary (1895) on R. 5:2.
[3] To the Romans (1920), *ad loc.*
ἀ γ ώ ν κ τ λ. J. Jüthner, *s.v.* "Gymnastik," Pauly-W., XIV, 2030 ff.; E. Norden, *Fleckeisens Jahrb. f. klass. Philol. Suppl.,* 18 (1892), 298 ff.; L. Schmid, *Der* ἀγών *bei Paulus* (unpublished Diss. Tübingen, 1921); F. J. Fölger, "Gladiatorenblut u. Märtyrerblut, Eine Szene der Passio Perpetuae in kultur- und religionsgeschichtlicher Beleuchtung," *Vortr. d. Bibl. Warburg,* III (1924).

ἀγών, ἀγωνίζομαι and Compounds.

A. Hellenistic Usage.

a. ἀγών originally means a "place of assembly," then a "place of contest" or "stadium," then the "contest" itself (including litigation and debate), and finally any kind of "conflict," Lat. *certamen*. [1] The word is often used metaphorically. The diatribe compares exercise in virtue and the moral struggle of life with the exertions and self-denials of the ἀγών. [2] The prize before the victor is ultimately beyond this life. Thus Plut. Gen. Socr. 24 (II, 593e): οἱ πεπαυμένοι τῶν περὶ τὸν βίον ἀγώνων δι' ἀρετὴν ψυχῆς γενόμενοι δαίμονες. In similar vein Philo speaks of the ἀγών τοῦ βίου, [3] and 4 Esr. refers to the conflict with the *sensus malus* in which man is to conquer. [4] Life is a deadly struggle the outcome of which will decide our future destiny: *Hoc est cogitamentum certaminis, quod certabit, qui super terram natus est homo, ut si victus fuerit, patiatur ..., si autem vicerit, recipiet, quod dico.* [5] The image of the ἀρετή, its conflict and reward is particularly worked out in Wis. 4:2, where it is said of the ἀτεκνία μετὰ ἀρετῆς: ἐν τῷ αἰῶνι στεφανοφοροῦσα πομπεύει τὸν τῶν ἀμιάντων ἄθλων ἀγῶνα νικήσασα. In this passage we can see quite clearly the Hellenistic origin of this whole outlook.

ἀγωνίζομαι means "to carry on a conflict, contest, debate or legal suit." Plut. Non Posse Suav. Viv. Sec. Epic., 28 (II, 1105c): ἀθληταί ... ἀγωνισάμενοι; 2 Macc. 13:14: γενναίως ἀγωνίσασθαι μέχρι θανάτου περὶ νόμων ... [6] Even when linked with ἀντί, σύν, etc., [7] the verb has the same shades of meaning as the noun, and is sometimes used literally, sometimes figuratively: ἕως θανάτου ἀγώνισαι περὶ τῆς ἀληθείας, καὶ κύριος ὁ θεὸς πολεμήσει ὑπὲρ σοῦ, Sir. 4:28.

b. Alongside these occasional metaphorical uses of the idea of the contest, in the literature of Hellenistic Judaism there are many examples of the use of this whole imagery and terminology of the arena in relation to the heroic struggle which the pious has to go through in this world. Philo likes to think of the ascetic achievements of the heroes of virtue, as in Agric., 112, 119: Τὸν ἐπιθυμίας καὶ ... ἀδικίας προτεθέντα ἀγῶνα, ὧ θεαταὶ καὶ ἀθλοθέται ... νενίκηκε ... οὑτοσί ... Ὁ τοίνυν Ὀλυμπιακὸς ἀγὼν μόνος ἂν λέγοιτο ἐνδίκως ἱερός, οὐχ ὅν τιθέασιν οἱ τὴν Ἦλιν οἰκοῦντες, ἀλλ' ὁ περὶ κτήσεως τῶν θείων καὶ ὀλυμπίων

---

[1] Herodot., IX, 60: ἀγῶνος προκειμένου. 2 Macc. 4:18: ἀγομένου δὲ πενταετηρικοῦ ἀγῶνος (game or tourney) ἐν Τύρῳ; 15:9: ἀγῶνας (battles) οὓς ἦσαν ἐκτετελεκότες. Jos. Bell., 1, 426: ἡ δόξα τῶν Ὀλυμπίασιν ἀγώνων.

[2] R. Heinze Philologus, 50 (1891), 458 ff.

[3] Som., II, 145. Cf. Jos. Ant., 17, 150: εὐσεβείας ἀγωνίσματα. 4 Macc. 12:15: ἀρετῆς ἀγωνισταί.

[4] 4 Esr. 7:92. Cf. also 4 Macc. 3:5: ὁ λογισμὸς τῶν παθῶν ἀνταγωνιστής; 15:29: ὦ μῆτερ ἔθνους ... τοῦ διὰ σπλάγχνων ἀγῶνος ἀθλοφόρε!

[5] 4 Esr. 7:127 f. We also have a psychologising use in 4 Macc. 13:15: μέγας γὰρ ψυχῆς ἀγὼν καὶ κίνδυνος ἐν αἰωνίῳ βασάνῳ κείμενος τοῖς παραβᾶσιν τὴν ἐντολὴν τοῦ θεοῦ.

[6] Cf. Test. J. 2:2; Jos. Ant., 7:14 etc.

[7] Ἀνταγωνίζομαι = "to meet in contest," Jos. Ap., 1, 56. καταγωνίζομαι, "to defeat," Jos. Ant., 16, 8. ἐπαγωνίζομαι, "to take up the fight again," "to fight for or against," Plut. Cim., 13 (I, 486e), Comm. Not., 31 (II, 1075d). συναγωνίζομαι, "to fight with," "to help with all one's power," Test. A. 6:2.

ὡς ἀληθῶς ἀρετῶν. Εἰς τοῦτον τὸν ἀγῶνα οἱ ἀσθενέστατοι τὰ σώματα, ἐρρωμενέστατοι δὲ τὰς ψυχὰς ἐγγράφονται πάντες. Praem. Poen., 5 f. : οἱ μὲν ἀθληταὶ ... ἀρετῆς ... βραβείων καὶ κηρυγμάτων καὶ τῶν ἄλλων ὅσα νικῶσιν δίδοται μετελάμβανον. οἱ δὲ οὐκ ἀστεφάνωτοι μόνον ἀπῆεσαν ἀλλὰ καὶ ἧτταν ἐπονείδιστον ἐνδεξάμενοι τῶν ἐν τοῖς γυμνικοῖς ἀγῶσιν ἀργαλεωτέραν· ἐκεῖ μὲν γὰρ ἀθλητῶν σώματα κλίνεται ... ἐνταῦθα δὲ ὅλοι βίοι πίπτουσιν ...

A counterpart to these graphic pictures of the struggle for virtue is offered by 4 Macc. with its comparing of the passion of martyrs to the contests of athletes. The comparison is the more relevant as the torturing and execution of martyrs often took place in the same arena and before the same spectators as the γυμνικοὶ ἀγῶνες. [8] Hence the picture and the reality frequently merge : ὦ ἱεροπρεποῦς ἀγῶνος, calls the sufferer, ἐφ᾽ ὃν διὰ τὴν εὐσέβειαν εἰς γυμνασίαν πόνων ... κληθέντες οὐκ ἐνικήθημεν. [9] And in 17:10 ff. the author paints the picture in all its fulness : ἐξεδίκησαν τὸ γένος εἰς θεὸν ἀφορῶντες καὶ μέχρι θανάτου τὰς βασάνους ὑπομείναντες. ἀληθῶς γὰρ ἦν ἀγὼν θεῖος ὁ δι᾽ αὐτῶν γεγενημένος· ἠθλοθέτει γὰρ τότε ἀρετὴ δι᾽ ὑπομονῆς δοκιμάζουσα. τὸ νῖκος ἀφθαρσία ἐν ζωῇ πολυχρονίῳ. Ἐλεάζαρ δὲ προηγωνίζετο, ἡ δὲ μήτηρ ... ἐνήθλει, οἱ δὲ ἀδελφοὶ ἠγωνίζοντο· ὁ τύραννος ἀντηγωνίζετο· ὁ δὲ κόσμος ... ἐθεώρει. θεοσέβεια δὲ ἐνίκα, [10] τοὺς ἑαυτῆς ἀθλητὰς στεφανοῦσα. τίνες οὐκ ἐθαύμασαν ... αὐτῶν ... τὴν ὑπομονήν, δι᾽ ἣν καὶ τῷ θείῳ νῦν παρεστήκασιν θρόνῳ. [11]

The Hellenistic type of the struggling hero of virtue and the Jewish type of the martyr fighting unto death seem to come together in the picture of the divine warrior Job as sketched in the Testamentum Iobi. [12] In the war of ὑπομονή and μακροθυμία Job stands manfully against all the θλίψεις which break upon him, like a boxer : ὡς ἀθλητὴς πυκτεύων καὶ καρτερῶν πόνους καὶ ἐκδεχόμενος τὸν στέφανον (Test. Iob. 4). But now the opponent who would knock him out is not merely the *sensus malus,* nor ἐπιθυμία, nor even a godless τύραννος, but no less than the devil himself. Yet Satan must finally give up the struggle against the unconquerable divine hero, and confess : ἐγένου γὰρ ὃν τρόπον ἀθλητὴς μετὰ ἀθλητοῦ καὶ εἰς τὸν ἕνα κατέρραξαν ... καὶ σύ, Ἰώβ, ὑποκάτω ἧς καὶ ἐν πληγῇ. ἀλλ᾽ ἐνίκησας τὰ πλευτρικά (sic, vl. παλαιστρικά) μου ἃ ἐπήγαγόν σοι (Test. Iob. 27). Literature of this kind obviously helped in large measure to fix the sense and application of ἀγών and its derivatives in early Christianity.

B. ἀγών, ἀγωνίζομαι in the NT.

Under the sign of the cross, the thought of the fight to which those who are faithful to God are called acquires a new seriousness. It is thus hardly

---

[8] Thus we are told concerning the martyrs of 3 Maccabees that they awaited their fate ἐν τῷ πρὸ τῆς πόλεως ἱπποδρόμῳ, which seemed to be particularly adapted πρὸς παραδειγματισμόν (4:11). We are also told concerning a gymnasium in Jerusalem in 1 Macc. 1:14; cf. 2 Macc. 4:12 ff.; 4 Macc. 4:20 etc. → n. 18.

[9] 11:20, cf. 16:16.

[10] καθάπερ γενναῖος ἀθλητὴς τυπτόμενος ἐνίκα τοὺς βασανίζοντας ὁ γέρων, 6:10.

[11] διὰ τῆσδε τῆς κακοπαθείας καὶ ὑπομονῆς τὰ τῆς ἀρετῆς ἆθλα οἴσομεν, καὶ ἐσόμεθα παρὰ θεῷ, δι᾽ ὃν καὶ πάσχομεν, 9:8; σὺν τῇ ἀθλοφόρῳ μητρὶ εἰς πατέρων χορὸν συναγελάζονται, 18:23. On the idea of the martyrs around God's throne, *v.* also bPes., 50a; Qoh. r., 3 on 9:10.

[12] M. R. James, "*Apocrypha anecdota,*" II, *Texts and Studies,* V, 1 (1899), 106; 120.

accidental that Paul particularly likes and brings into use the various ἀγών terms. [13] Five motifs of thought seems to be expressed by primitive Christianity in these concepts.

a. First is the thought of the goal which can be reached only with the full expenditure of all our energies. Thus already in the saying of the Lord in Lk. 13:24 ἀγωνίζεσθε εἰσελθεῖν is opposed to impotent ζητεῖν; the struggle for the kingdom of heaven allows of no indolence, indecision or relaxation. Only those who press into it can attain entrance (cf. Lk. 16:16). In full accordance with this, Paul likes to add an → εἰς and occasionally a → ἵνα to ἀγωνίζεσθαι and related verbs. His work for the Gospel is more than the faithful daily fulfilment of duty; it is an ἀγών (1 Th. 2:2), a tense exertion, [14] a passionate struggle, a constantly renewed concentration of forces on the attainment of the goal, as in Col. 1:29: ... ἵνα παραστήσωμεν πάντα ἄνθρωπων τέλειον ἐν Χριστῷ· εἰς ὃ καὶ κοπιῶ ἀγωνιζόμενος κατὰ τὴν ἐνέργειαν αὐτοῦ τὴν ἐνεργουμένην ἐν ἐμοὶ ἐν δυνάμει. The whole life of the apostle stands under this sign, and acquires value and meaning only from the final victory. It is thus that the master speaks according to the Pastorals: τὸν καλὸν ἀγῶνα ἠγώνισμαι, τὸν δρόμον τετέλεκα ... [15] ... λοιπὸν ἀπόκειταί μοι ὁ τῆς δικαιοσύνης στέφανος (2 Tm. 4:7 f.). And the follower is to take up the same conflict, to run the same race to the same goal: ἀγωνίζου τὸν καλὸν ἀγῶνα τῆς πίστεως, ἐπιλαβοῦ τῆς αἰωνίου ζωῆς, εἰς ἣν ἐκλήθης καὶ ὡμολόγησας τὴν καλὴν ὁμολογίαν ἐνώπιον [16] πολλῶν μαρτύρων (1 Tm. 6:12). Here already we can see the development of Hellenistic Jewish influence in later Pauline literature.

b. The struggle for the reward does not demand only full exertion but also rigid denial: πᾶς ... ὁ ἀγωνιζόμενος πάντα ἐγκρατεύεται, ἐκεῖνοι μὲν οὖν ἵνα φθαρτὸν στέφανον λάβωσιν, ἡμεῖς δὲ ἄφθαρτον (1 C. 9:25). The final assault is so exacting that all forces must be reserved, assembled and deployed in it. The final goal is so high and glorious that all provisional ends must fade before it. If the → βραβεῖον does not mean everything, nothing will be attained. If a man is not ready to set aside his egotistic needs and desires and claims and reservations, he is not fit for the arena: ὑπωπιάζω μου τὸ σῶμα καὶ δουλαγωγῶ, μή πως ... ἀδόκιμος γένωμαι (1 C. 9:27). This is not the asceticism of the monk suppressing the body; it is the manly discipline of the fighter controlling the body. The admonitions: νῆφε ἐν πᾶσιν (2 Tm. 4:5), and: γύμναζε ... σεαυτὸν πρὸς εὐσέβειαν· ἡ γὰρ σωματικὴ γυμνασία πρὸς ὀλίγον ἐστὶν ὠφέλιμος, are both determined by regard for the supreme goal: εἰς τοῦτο γὰρ κοπιῶμεν καὶ ἀγωνιζόμεθα, ὅτι ἠλπίκαμεν ἐπὶ θεῷ ζῶντι (1 Tm. 4:7 ff.). This is not contempt for the world. It is insight into the law of life that the better is the enemy of the best, so that even what is right and good may have to be renounced.

c. The thought of the antagonists, which is important in 4 Macc. and occasionally in the Test. of Job, is seldom expressed in the NT. Phil. 1:28 speaks of ἀντικείμενοι, Hb. 12:3 f. of ἀντιλογία and ἀνταγωνίζεσθαι. Hb. 11:33, in the style

---

[13] Apart from Lk. 13:24 and Jn. 18:36 the use of this group of words is restricted to the Pauline corpus.
[14] πόνος *v.* 1 Cl. 5:4; Mak. Homil., XV, 224b. κόπος and κοπιῶ are more common. *v.* J. B. Lightfoot, *The Ap. Fathers,* II, 2 (1889), 351 on Ign. Pol., 6.
[15] Cf. Marcus Diaconus, Vita Porphyrii p. 82:12: τὸν καλὸν ἀγῶνα τετελεκώς.
[16] Cf. 4 Macc. 12:16; 17:14.

of the books of Maccabees, refers to heroes of faith : κατηγωνίσαντο βασιλείας, though here the place of conflict seems to be the battleground rather than the arena (→ 135, n. 1). Nevertheless there seems to belong to the whole concept of ἀγωνίζεσθαι the thought of obstacles, dangers and catastrophes through which the Christian must fight his way. The missionary work which Paul calls an ἀγών in 1 Th. 2:2 is beset by a hundred perils, and full of outer and inner storms : ἔξωθεν μάχαι, ἔσωθεν φόβοι (2 C. 7:5). And when the field is won, the watchword must be : ἐπαγωνίζεσθαι τῇ ἅπαξ παραδοθείσῃ τοῖς ἁγίοις πίστει (Jd. 3).

d. The sharpest form of ἀγών which the man who is faithful to God must undergo on earth is the battle of suffering fulfilled in martyrdom. These are familiar Jewish conceptions which make a powerful impact on early Christianity in the age of the Pastorals and Hebrews. Ἐγὼ γὰρ ἤδη σπένδομαι, is the saying of Paul in the Pastorals, speaking of the warfare and victory of his own life (2 Tm. 4:6; cf. Phil. 2:17); and he summons Timothy : κακοπάθησον, [17] δίωκε ὑπομονήν, πραϋπαθίαν. ἀγωνίζου ... (1 Tm. 6:11). Hb. 10 ff. is shot through with the thought of martyrdom. In 10:32 f. we have a backward glance at the ἡμέραι, ἐν αἷς φωτισθέντες πολλὴν ἄθλησιν ὑπεμείνατε παθημάτων ... ὀνειδισμοῖς τε καὶ θλίψεσιν θεατριζόμενοι, [18] in 11 a consideration of the great victors of the past, [19] and in 12:1 ff. an exhortation to supreme resistance with the gaze fixed on Christ. Here, as in 4 Macc. 17, the motifs of conflict are found in profusion : ἔχοντες ... νέφος μαρτύρων ... τρέχωμεν τὸν προκείμενον ἡμῖν ἀγῶνα ἀφορῶντες ... And here the thought of the ἀντιλογία of the ἁμαρτωλοί is alive and powerful : οὔπω μέχρις αἵματος ἀντικατέστητε πρὸς τὴν ἁμαρτίαν ἀνταγωνιζόμενοι. [20]

e. The supreme goal for which we fight and work and suffer is not our own salvation alone; it is the salvation of many. The late epistles, which otherwise speak a great deal about the heavenly reward, are silent on this point. Yet it is intimated already in 4 Macc., and it finds clear enunciation in Paul. Paul cannot attain the goal of his own life without throwing in everything and sacrificing himself for the salvation of the people of God (Col. 1:29). Hence he does not link with the term ἀγωνίζεσθαι only a ἵνα, but also quite frequently a → ὑπέρ. His struggle is for his communities : ἡλίκον ἀγῶνα ἔχω ὑπὲρ ὑμῶν, ἵνα (Col. 2:1 f.). The one stands for the many, πάντοτε ἀγωνιζόμενος in both work and prayer (Col. 4:12 f.). Hence all must stand for the one, mustering around him in a loyal fellowship of battle. The ἀγωνίζεσθαι is extended by a → σύν: παρακαλῶ δὲ ὑμᾶς ... συναγωνίσασθαί μοι ἐν ταῖς προσευχαῖς ὑπὲρ ἐμοῦ ... ἵνα ῥυσθῶ

---

[17] 2 Tm. 4:5; cf. 2:3 ff.: συγκακοπαθεῖν with ἀθλεῖν and κακοπαθεῖν; cf. also 4 Macc. 9:8 : διὰ .... κακοπαθείας καὶ ὑπομονῆς.

[18] Cf. 1 C. 4:9 : θεὸς ἡμᾶς ... ἀπέδειξεν ὡς ἐπιθανατίους, ὅτι θέατρον ἐγενήθημεν τῷ κόσμῳ καὶ ἀγγέλοις καὶ ἀνθρώποις, and on this passage Lietzmann. 4 Macc. 17:14 : ὁ δὲ κόσμος καὶ ὁ τῶν ἀνθρώπων βίος ἐθεώρει, and the Gerasa inscription in H. J. Cadbury, ZNW, 29 (1930), 61: ἀγωνιζόμενοι ... καὶ ... θεατρίζοντες, ἐν ἀγῶνι ... θεωρίᾳ. Theatrum and spectaculum in Aug. Civ. D., 14, 9. Cf. also παραδειγματίζω in Hb. 6:6, and παραδειγματισμός in 3 Macc. 4:11; 7:14 → n. 8.

[19] Cf. 1 Macc. 2:49 ff.; 2 Macc. 15:9; 4 Macc. 16:16 ff. etc.

[20] On 12:2 : ἀντὶ τῆς προκειμένης αὐτῷ χαρᾶς ὑπέμεινεν σταυρόν, cf. 11:26, 35 and 4 Macc. 15:2 f.: δυεῖν προκειμένων, εὐσεβείας καὶ ... σωτηρίας προσκαίρου ... τὴν εὐσέβειαν μᾶλλον ἠγάπησε; also Aug., op. cit., 13, 4. On ἐν δεξιᾷ ... τοῦ θρόνου τοῦ θεοῦ, cf. 4 Macc. 17:17 f.; → n. 11.

ἀπὸ τῶν ἀπειθούντων (R. 15:30).²¹ Again the form of battle is prayer. In prayer there is achieved unity between the will of God and that of man, between human struggling and action and effective divine operation. In prayer, too, there is fulfilled the fellowship of conflict and destiny between man and man. In prayer one man becomes the representative of the other, so that there is here opened up the possibility of one standing in the breach for all and all for one.

As Paul speaks in Col. 4 and R. 15 of the alliance of those who pray, so in Phil. 1:27 ff. he speaks of unity in the Spirit : στήκετε ἐν ἑνὶ πνεύματι. And here all the motifs come together which are elsewhere treated in isolation in the image of ἀγών. There is need to stand together, μιᾷ ψυχῇ συναθλοῦντες τῇ πίστει τοῦ εὐαγγελίου. Where the Gospel is, there will be conflict and division (v. Lk. 2:34). There is thus need to resist the adversary, μὴ πτυρόμενοι ἐν μηδενὶ ὑπὸ τῶν ἀντικειμένων. Already those who are unafraid can see the approaching final victory, and they thus concentrate all their forces for the last effort, ἥτις ἐστὶν αὐτοῖς (i.e., your adversaries) ἔνδειξις ἀπωλείας, ὑμῶν δὲ σωτηρίας. The form of the conflict, however, is supremely suffering, and the meaning of suffering is sacrifice : ὅτι ὑμῖν ἐχαρίσθη τὸ ὑπὲρ Χριστοῦ ... πάσχειν, τὸν αὐτὸν ἀγῶνα ἔχοντες οἷον εἴδετε ἐν ἐμοί. Paul here uses the image of ἀγών along the lines of the martyr theology of later Judaism. But he no longer thinks of the battle waged by the martyrs in the stadium to God's glory. He thinks of the conflicts and sufferings of the Christian life itself as a life which in its totality stands under the sign of the cross and in this sign carries the cause of Christ to victory.

C. ἀγών, ἀγωνίζομαι in the Early Church.

The early Church took up with particular enthusiasm the theme of the warfare and triumph of the Christian, and applied it in new ways. Pauline modes of thought and expression are most faithfully reproduced in 1 Cl. : the thought of the goal in 35, 4 : ἀγωνισώμεθα ... ὅπως μεταλάβωμεν;²² that of discipline in 7, 1 f.: ἐν γὰρ τῷ αὐτῷ ἐσμὲν σκάμματι (!), καὶ ὁ αὐτὸς ἡμῖν ἀγὼν ἐπίκειται. διὸ ἀπολίπωμεν; that of intercession and representation in 2, 4 : ἀγὼν ἦν ὑμῖν ἡμέρας τε καὶ νυκτὸς ὑπὲρ πάσης τῆς ἀδελφότητος εἰς τὸ σῴζεσθαι. Barnabas brings his apocalyptic message of the ἄνομος καιρός and the final onslaught of darkness to a climax in the summons to conflict : ἀγωνιζώμεθα! (4. 11). 2 Cl., 7 offers a clear picture of ἀγών in the στάδιον, of ἀγωνίζεσθαι for righteousness, primarily in the style of the Hellenistic diatribe, but finally culminating in an eschatological admonition. According to the later conception, the warfare of the Christian deserves particular renown and reward where it takes ascetic forms.²³ But the truly decisive battle is seen in martyrdom, since the victor in this conflict does not merely attain his own blessedness like the self-sufficient ascetic, but reveals and accomplishes the triumph of the Church over all forces inimical to God. The young martyr Church quickly developed to their logical end the suggestions made by the martyr literature of Hellenistic Judaism and especially by the Epistle to the Hebrews. The picture of the victorious contestant became in all its individual features

---

²¹ For actual warfare we also have ἠγωνίζοντο ἵνα μὴ παραδοθῶ in Jn. 18:36 f., cf. Mt. 26:52 f.

²² Cf. in 37, 1 the analogous στρατευσώμεθα ... μετὰ πάσης ἐκτενείας. Similarly in 2 Tm. 2:3 ἀθλεῖν with στρατεύεσθαι.

²³ ἀσκητικοὺς ἀγῶνας, Theod. Stud. Enc. Theoph., Anal. Boll., 31 (1912), 22, 9 (→ ἀθλεῖν).

the glowing symbol of the heroic Christian martyr. Christ Himself came to be celebrated as the great ἀθλητής and Martyr who endured the contest of suffering on our behalf : ὁ εἰς πολλοὺς ἀγῶνας ὑπὲρ ἡμῶν ἀγωνιζόμενος. [24] It is for us to continue His conflict. Those who gain the victory here overthrow Satan himself : διὰ τῆς ὑπομονῆς καταγωνισάμενος τὸν ἄδικον ἄρχοντα καὶ οὕτως τὸν τῆς ἀφθαρσίας στέφανον ἀπολαβών. [25] The full terminology of the stadium is used to depict the martyr and his contest and triumph. And the full range of these specialised Greek terms is taken up into the vocabulary of the Latin literature of martyrdom. Thus it is a Latin writer who is our most valuable witness for the spread and significance of this group of words, Tert. Ad Mart., 3 : *Bonum agonem subituri estis, in quo agonothetes deus vivus est ... brabium angelicae substantiae ... Itaque epistates vester Christus Jesus, qui vos spiritu unxit et ad hoc scamma produxit, voluit vos ante diem agonis ad duriorem tractationem a liberiore conditione seponere. Nempe enim et athletae segregantur ad strictiorem disciplinam, ut robori aedificando vacent ; continentur a luxuria ...; coguntur, cruciantur, fatigantur : quanto plus in exercitationibus laboraverint, tanto plus de victoria sperant ... Carcerem nobis pro palaestra interpretemur, ut ad stadium tribunalis bene exercitati incommodis omnibus producamur.*

ἀγωνία.

If this word can sometimes denote "conflict," originally it means "inner tension" or "anxiety," and most strictly it indicates the "supreme concentration of powers" in face of imminent decisions or disasters. [1] φόβος πτώσεως ἢ ἥττης ἐπὶ τοῦ εἰς ἀγῶνα μέλλοντος ἀπιέναι. [2] To this there corresponds the usage in 2 Macc. 15:19 : ἦν ... ἀγωνία ταρασσομένοις τῆς ἐν ὑπαίθρῳ προσβολῆς, and the impressive image in 3:14 ff. : ἦν δὲ οὐ μικρὰ καθ’ ὅλην τὴν πόλιν ἀγωνία ... ἡ γὰρ ὄψις ἐνέφαινε τὴν κατὰ ψυχὴν ἀγωνίαν ... (δέος, ἄλγος) ... ἐλεεῖν δ’ ἦν τὴν τοῦ πλήθους παμμιγῆ πρόπτωσιν τήν τε τοῦ μεγάλως διαγωνιῶντος [3] ἀρχιερέως προσδοκίαν. [4]

It is in this sense that ἀγωνία must be understood in Lk. 22:44 : γενόμενος ἐν ἀγωνίᾳ ἐκτενέστερον προσηύχετο. This is not fear of death, but concern for victory in face of the approaching decisive battle on which the fate of the world depends. Hence it is not to be compared with the εὐλάβεια of Hb. 5:7, but with the saying of the Lord in Lk. 12:49 f. : πῦρ ἦλθον βαλεῖν ἐπὶ τὴν γῆν, καὶ τί θέλω εἰ ἤδη ἀνήφθη. βάπτισμα δὲ ἔχω βαπτισθῆναι, καὶ πῶς συνέχομαι ἕως ὅτου τελεσθῇ.

Stauffer

---

[24] Act. Thom., 39, cf. also Act. Ptr. et Pl., 5, 84, p. 218, 11.
[25] M. Pol., 19, 2, cf. Pass. S. Scilit., p. 117, 18; Pass. Perp. et Fel., 18, 2; Act. Thom., 39; Test. of the 40 Mart., 1, 1; 1, 5; Aug. De Agone Christiano, MPL, XL, 289 ff.
ἀγωνία. [1] Hence the prevalent significance of mortal conflict or anguish.
[2] Lex. Rhet. Pros., p. 663. Closely related are the definitions in Aristot. Probl., II 31, p. 869b, 6 f. (φόβος τις πρὸς ἀρχὴν ἔργου) and Diog. L., VII, 1, 13 (φόβος ἀδήλου πράγματος). Cf. also Aristot. Rhet., I, 9, p. 1367a, 15; Suid., s.v. φόβος; Etym. M., p. 15, 46.
[3] A reads ἀγωνιῶντος. ἀγωνιάω, "to be concerned for," v. Pass.-Cr., s.v.
[4] Cf. also Jos. Ant., 11, 241 and 326. Philo Leg. Gai., 243.

Ἀδάμ	(→ υἱὸς τοῦ ἀνθρώπου).

A. Early Christian Usage.

1. Adam as the First Man.

Adam (אָדָם) as the first man is mentioned in 1 Tm. 2:13-14 in connection with the order of the community set out in 1 Tm. 2:1-3:16. In the section which deals with the right conduct of the woman in the service of God (2:9-15) the demand that she should be subordinate to man (2:12) is given a basis in early biblical history. This establishes the supremacy of man at creation by the fact a. that he was created first (2:13), [1] and b. that Eve was first deceived (2:14), [2] in which there is perhaps a hint of the legend that Eve was sensually seduced by the serpent. [3] The order of God at creation is still His will for the community (cf. Mk. 10:6).

2. The NT Typology Adam/Christ.

Adam is an antitype of Christ in Mk. 1:13; R. 5:12-21; 1 C. 15:22, 45-49. The account of the temptation in Mark (1:13) shows how Jesus as the new man (→ υἱὸς τοῦ ἀνθρώπου) overcame the temptation which overthrew the first man. Jesus, like Adam, is tempted by Satan. Again, as Adam was once honoured by the beasts in Paradise according to the Midrash, [4] so Christ is with the wild beasts after overcoming temptation. He thus ushers in the paradisial state of the last days when there will be peace between man and beast (Is. 11:6-8; 65:25). [5] As Adam in Paradise enjoyed angels' food according to the Midrash, [6] so the angels give heavenly food to the new man. Jesus reopens the Paradise closed to the first man. This typology Adam/Christ perhaps underlies the tracing of the genealogy of Jesus back to Adam in Lk. 3:38 (as against Mt. 1:1-17). The fact that the temptation story follows immediately in Lk. 4:1 ff. seems to support this; it may well be that as a follower of Paul Luke knew the Pauline typology Adam/Christ.

Paul uses this typology a. to show the universality of grace in R. 5:12-21; Adam, through whom sin and death came on the race, is the τύπος τοῦ μέλλοντος (5:14), of the εἷς ἄνθρωπος Ἰησοῦς Χριστός (5:15), who brought life and grace to humanity; b. to establish the certainty of the resurrection (1 C. 15:22: ὥσπερ γὰρ ἐν τῷ Ἀδάμ [7] πάντες ἀποθνήσκουσιν, οὕτως καὶ ἐν τῷ Χριστῷ πάντες

Ἀδάμ. B. Murmelstein "Adam, ein Beitrag zur Messiaslehre," WZKM, XXXV (1928), 242-275; XXXVI (1929), 51-86; Ltzm. 1 K., Exc. on 1 C. 15:45-49; Str.-B., Index under Adam.

[1] Cf. S. Dt., 37 on 11:10: "All that is worthy precedes all else."
[2] Cf. Sl. En., Bonwetsch, 31, 6: "He (the devil) seduced Eve, but did not approach Adam."
[3] Gn. r., 18 on 3:1 etc. Cf. 4 Macc. 18:7-8; Philo Leg. All., III, 59 ff.; B. Murmelstein, op. cit., 284, n. 4.
[4] Apc. Mos., 16.
[5] Str.-B., III, 254; IV, 892, 964 f.
[6] bSanh., 59b par.; Vit. Ad., 4.
[7] ἐν τῷ Ἀδάμ is perhaps simply an analogous construction to ἐν τῷ Χριστῷ.

ζωοποιηθήσονται; c. to demonstrate the certainty of the spiritual resurrection body (1 C. 15:44b-49 : καθὼς ἐφορέσαμεν τὴν εἰκόνα τοῦ χοϊκοῦ, φορέσωμεν καὶ τὴν εἰκόνα τοῦ ἐπουρανίου, v. 49).

The latter of these two certainties, namely, that at the resurrection of Christians the image of Adam (the physical body) will be transformed into that of Christ (the spiritual body), is based by Paul on the Bible. He finds his Scripture proof in LXX Gn. 2:7: ἐγένετο ὁ ἄνθρωπος εἰς ψυχὴν ζῶσαν. In a paraphrase after the manner of the Targum he adds to this verse the two words πρῶτος and Ἀδάμ : ἐγένετο ὁ πρῶτος ἄνθρωπος Ἀδάμ εἰς ψυχὴν ζῶσαν. From the text as thus amplified, in conjunction with his common Messianic interpretation of the creation story (Col. 1:15 : LXX Gn. 1:26 f.; 1 C. 6:17 and Eph. 5:31 f.: LXX Gn. 2:24), and with the help of a קַל וְחֹמֶר conclusion [8] e contrario, [9] he achieves the statement : ὁ ἔσχατος Ἀδάμ εἰς πνεῦμα ζωοποιοῦν. Paul thus gives us the antitheses (1 C. 15:45, 47 f.):

v. 45 :	ὁ πρῶτος Ἀδάμ	ὁ ἔσχατος Ἀδάμ
	ψυχὴ ζῶσα	πνεῦμα ζωοποιοῦν
v. 47 :	ὁ πρῶτος ἄνθρωπος	ὁ δεύτερος ἄνθρωπος
v. 47 f.:	ἐκ γῆς, χοϊκός	ἐξ οὐρανοῦ, ἐπουράνιος.

According to their earthly bodies, Christians are like the first Adam ; according to their resurrection bodies they are like the last Adam (1 C. 15:48). Hence the historical sequence of the creation of the first man and the resurrection of the second [10] has a typical significance ; it is a type of the destiny of believers who, when they have first borne the image of the earthy, will then be transformed into the image of the heavenly (1 C. 15:49 ; cf. 44b, 46, 48).

B. The Origin of the Typology Adam/Christ.

As regards the origin of the idea, assumed to be familiar in this argumentation, that Adam is the prototype and antitype of Christ, we may first maintain that, although the designation of Adam as אָדָם הָרִאשׁוֹן or אָדָם הַקַּדְמוֹנִי א׳ (in distinction from the appellative אָדָם = man) is current in later Rabbinic literature, we never find the Redeemer described as the last Adam. [11] Yet though the term does not occur, there are certain material similarities between the Pauline conception of the last Adam and Jewish ideas. In both Palestinian and Hellenistic Judaism we find traces of an Eastern redeemer myth which finds in the first man partly the redeemer himself and partly a type of the reedemer (→ υἱὸς τοῦ ἀνθρώπου). Points which call for particular notice are a. the very widespread notion in Judaism in the NT period that the first man was an ideal man, together with the doctrine of the

---

[8] On this conclusion from the easier to the harder (a minori ad maius), very common in Rabbinic exposition, cf. Str.-B., III, 223 ff., IV, 1255 (Index).

[9] A similar conclusion is found in 1 C. 6:16 f. on LXX Gn. 2:24.

[10] And not, of course, the creation of the last Adam (→ 143), since the last Adam comes first (Col. 1:15).

[11] Str.-B., III, 477 f.

restitution by the Messiah of the glory which he lost at the fall; [12] and b. the doctrine of the pre-existent Messiah בַּר נָשָׁא, which resulted from a fusion of Messianic expectation with the doctrine of the first man as redeemer (→ υἱὸς τοῦ ἀνθρώπου).

Both theologoumena were known to Paul, and related by him to Christ. As regards the former idea of the first man as ideal, Philo used this also to explain the two Genesis accounts of the creation of man (Gn. 1:27; 2:7). As he sees it, in Gn. 1:27 we are told of the creation of ideal man in God's image (= the Logos), and in 2:7 of the creation of Adam. [13] In similar fashion Paul finds in Christ the divine image (Col. 1:15, cf. Gn. 1:27), while he refers 2:7, like Philo, to the creation of Adam. He also agrees with Philo as to the priority of the heavenly man (Col. 1:15: πρωτότοκος πάσης κτίσεως); the statement in 1 C. 15:46: ἀλλ᾽ οὐ πρῶτον τὸ πνευματικὸν ἀλλὰ τὸ ψυχικόν, ἔπειτα τὸ πνευματικόν, does not mean that Adam was created prior to Christ, but — with σῶμα as the subject, cf. 1 C. 15:44b — is really dealing with the bodily nature of the Christian, who first bears the physical body and will then receive the spiritual at the *parousia*.

The main difference between Paul and Philo arises in relation to the eschatological role of the firstborn heavenly man which also underlies the Pauline phrase ἔσχατος ᾽Αδάμ. This eschatological interpretation of the heavenly man in Paul is explained by the fact that in the light of Jesus' own description of Himself as → υἱὸς τοῦ ἀνθρώπου Paul finds in Jesus the pre-existent Messiah bar nāshā. Now it is true that in preaching to Gentiles and Gentile Christians Paul avoids this misleading expression, preferring to render the substance of bar nāshā by ὁ ἄνθρωπος (R. 5:15; 1 C. 15:21; Eph. 5:31 f.; cf. 1 Tm. 2:5). Nevertheless, there can be no doubt that he knew the self-description of Jesus, as appears plainly in his Messianic interpretation of Psalm 8 in 1 C. 15:27.

With his Adam/Christ antithesis Paul expresses the same thought as underlies Jesus' self-description as bar nāshā, namely, that Jesus is the firstborn of the new creation of God. As Adam stands at the head of the αἰὼν οὗτος as the first man, so the risen Christ stands at the head of the αἰὼν μέλλων as the Initiator of the perfect redeemed creation of God [14] (→ αἰών).

J. Jeremias

---

[12] Vit. Ad.; Sl. En., Bonwetsch 30, 12 f. etc.; B. Murmelstein, *op. cit.*, 225-258; 271-275; Bousset-Gressm., 352 ff.; Str.-B., I, 19, 801 f.; II, 173 f.; III, 247, 325, 478, 851; IV, 181, 405, 667 f., 887 f., 940 f., 943, 946 f., 1126 (Adam as ideal man); III, 10 (Adam as the first to be awakened by the Messiah).

[13] Philo Op. Mund., 134: διαφορὰ παμμεγέθης ἐστὶ τοῦ τε νῦν (Gn. 2:7) πλασθέντος ἀνθρώπου καὶ τοῦ κατὰ τὴν εἰκόνα θεοῦ γεγονότος πρότερον (Gn. 1:27). Leg. All., I, 31 ff. Conf. Ling., 146: ἀρχὴ καὶ ὄνομα θεοῦ καὶ ὁ κατ᾽ εἰκόνα ἄνθρωπος ... προσαγορεύεται (ὁ πρωτόγονος αὐτοῦ λόγος).

[14] J. Jeremias, *Jesus als Weltvollender* (1930), 53-57.

ἀδελφός, ἀδελφή, ἀδελφότης, φιλάδελφος,
φιλαδελφία, ψευδάδελφος

In the NT ἀδελφός and ἀδελφή denote either "physical brotherhood" in the strict sense or more generally the "spiritual brotherhood" of Israelites or Christians; the derivatives and compounds ἀδελφότης, φιλάδελφος, φιλαδελφία, ψευδάδελφος bring out the figurative significance of the basic term.

1. Physical Brotherhood.

References are found to the physical brothers of the patriarch Judah in Mt. 1:2, of Joseph in Ac. 7:13, of Jechoniah in Mt. 1:11, and of Herod in Lk. 3:1 and Mk. 6:17 and par. Among the disciples Simon and Andrew are also blood relations in this sense (Mk. 1:16 and par. = Jn. 1:41 f.; Mt. 10:2), as are also the sons of Zebedee James and John (Mk. 1:19 and par.; 3:17 and par.; 5:37; 10:35 and par.; Mt. 17:1; Ac. 12:2). The sisters Mary and Martha (Lk. 10:39 f.; Jn. 11:1 f.) have a brother Lazarus (Jn. 11:2 ff.). There is also mention, though no name is given, of a son of Paul's sister (Ac. 23:16), and Nereus and his sister appear in the list of those greeted in R. 16:15.

ἀδελφοί of Jesus are mentioned in Mk. 3:31 ff. and par.; Jn. 2:12; 7:3, 5, 10; Ac. 1:14; 1 C. 9:5;[1] Gl. 1:19, names being given in Mk. 6:3 and par.[2] ἀδελφαί are also referred to in Mk. 3:32;[3] 6:3 and par.; ἡ ἀδελφὴ τῆς μητρὸς αὐτοῦ, Jn. 19:25.[4] On account of the perpetual virginity the older Catholic Church would not allow that these were

---

ἀ δ ε λ φ ό ς κτλ. Ltzm. R. on 1:13; Reitzenstein Poim., 154; A. Dieterich, *Mithras-liturgie*[3] (1923), 149 f.; G. Wissowa, *Religion und Kultus der Römer*[2] (1912), 561; W. Liebenam, *Zur Gesch. u. Organisation des röm. Vereinswesens* (1890), 185; F. Poland, *Geschichte des griech. Vereinswesens* (1909), 54 f.; Deissmann B., 82 f., 140; Nägeli, 38; W. Otto, *Priester und Tempel*, I (1905), 142, n. 3; A. D. Nock, "The Historical Importance of Cult-Associations," *Class. Rev.*, 38 (1924), 105; H. Sedlaczek, "φιλαδελφία nach den Schriften des hl. Apostels Paulus," *Theol. Quart.*, 76 (1897), 272-295.

[1] Μὴ οὐκ ἔχομεν ἐξουσίαν ἀδελφὴν γυναῖκα περιάγειν, ὡς καὶ οἱ λοιποὶ ἀπόστολοι καὶ οἱ ἀδελφοὶ τοῦ κυρίου καὶ Κηφᾶς; to interpret ἀδελφοὶ τοῦ κυρίου in the more general sense of "brothers in the Lord" is excluded both by the linguistic form and the material context, though this view has been championed by those who would deny the historicity of Christ, e.g., A. Drews, *Christusmythe*, II (1911), 125 ff. In any case, brothers in the Lord or in Christ is not really a NT formula: in Phil. 1:14 the ἐν κυρίῳ belongs to πεποιθότας (cf. Gl. 5:10; Phil. 2:24; 2 Th. 3:4), and in Col. 1:2 ἐν Χριστῷ is to be linked with ἁγίοις καὶ πιστοῖς (cf. 1 C. 1:2; 4:17; Eph. 1:1).

[2] The names are Ἰάκωβος, Ἰωσῆς, Σίμων, Ἰούδας; the first two are the sons of another Mary (cf. the Comm.), James being distinguished as "the Less." We meet the first two names again in Mk. 15:40 (47) and par. In Mt. 13:55 Ἰωσήφ is better attested as a variant of Ἰωσῆς, and it has penetrated into the secondary texts of Mk. 6:3; 15:40, 47; Mt. 27:56. יוֹסִי is simply a short form of יוֹסֵף. Both forms are common in Rabbinical writings and seem to be used without distinction of one and the same person. In Mt. 13:55 alone Ἰωάννης also appears as a variant of Ἰωσῆς, an unhappy conjecture possibly based on Jn. 19:26. Jude calls himself ἀδελφός Ἰακώβου in Jd. 1, and James is called ἀδελφός τοῦ λεγομένου Χριστοῦ in Josephus Ant., 20, 200. On historical and extracanonical tradition, → n. 5.

[3] In Mk. 3:32 καὶ αἱ ἀδελφαί σου is not found in the Alex. and Caes. texts, nor in Mt. 12:47, which is no part of the original text; Lk. 8:20; Mk. 3:31 and par. The words are an addition on the basis of ἀδελφή in Mk. 3:35; Mt. 12:50 (as against Lk. 8:21).

[4] On the problem of the identification of the different designations of the women under the cross, cf. the Comm.; Bibl. → n. 5.

brothers and sisters in the full sense, arguing that they were either children of Joseph by a previous marriage or cousins. [5]

Further references to physical brothers may be seen in the question of the Sadducees as to marriage in the resurrection (Mk. 12:19 f. and par.), the parable of the Prodigal Son (Lk. 15:27, 32), the parable of Dives and Lazarus (Lk. 16:28), the story of the disputed inheritance (Lk. 12:13), the saying about hating brothers and sisters for Jesus' sake (Mk. 10:29 f. and par.; Lk. 14:26), and the sayings about the betrayal of brother by brother (Mk. 13:12 f.) and the inviting of guests (Lk. 14:12).

2. Spiritual Brotherhood.

In a more general sense ἀδελφός in the NT denotes "fellow-Christians" or "Christian brothers." Many instances may be given from all parts of the NT; there are some 30 in Acts and 130 in Paul. The usage plainly derives from Jewish religious custom. The old Israelite lament הוֹי אָחִי (Jer. 22:18) seems to contain a regular spontaneous address to fellow-Israelites. In Judaism, too, ἀδελφός means a co-religionist, who historically is identical with a compatriot. Yet the latter as such is also called רֵעַ = πλησίον, and in Rabbinic writings this is sometimes explicitly distinguished from אָח = ἀδελφός. [6] There can be no doubt, however, that ἀδελφός is one of the religious titles of the people of Israel taken over by the Christian community.

The Jewish usage is itself attested in the NT, not merely in OT quotations (Ac. 3:22; 7:37; Hb. 2:12; 7:5), but also directly (Mt. 5:22 f., 47; 7:3 ff. and par.; 18:15 ff. and par.; Ac. 7:23 ff.; R. 9:3; Hb. 7:5). [7] In accordance with this the apostles, like the synagogue preachers, address Jews as ἀδελφοί in Acts (2:29; 3:17; 7:2; 13:15, 26, 38; 22:1; 23:1 ff.; 28:17; cf. R. 9:3), and are themselves addressed in the same way (2:37); the usual form ἄνδρες ἀδελφοί is a rendering of the Jewish אַחֵינוּ. [8] In Mk. 3:33 ff. and par.; Mt. 25:40; 28:10; Jn. 20:17 Jesus calls His hearers or disciples His brethren, and He also uses the same term to describe the relations of the disciples to one another (Mt. 23:8; Lk. 22:32). As an address ἀδελφός does not, of course, occur on the lips of Jesus, and it may be asked whether there is some significance in this. Christians are certainly to see themselves as His brethren or people (R. 8:29; Hb. 2:11 ff.). [9] The specific relationship of brothers is that of love (1 Jn. 2 f.). ἀγαπητός or ἠγαπημένος is thus the most common name for them, though occasionally we have πιστός (Col. 4:9; 1 Tm. 6:2;

---

[5] Cf. T. Zahn, "Brüder und Vettern Jesu," Forschungen, VI (1900), 225 ff.; W. Bauer, Das Leben Jesu im Zeitalter der nt.lichen Apokryphen (1909), 7 f.; A. Meyer, in E. Hennecke, Nt.liche Apokryphen,² (1924), 103 ff. On official Roman Catholic doctrine, which maintains the virginity of Joseph too, and therefore regards the brethren as cousins of Jesus, cf. J. Pohle, Lehrbuch der Dogmatik, II⁶ (1915), 287 ff.; A. Schäfer, Die Gottesmutter in der Heiligen Schrift² (1900), 79 ff.

[6] S. Dt., 15, 2 § 112, 97b; Dt. r., 6, 203c; cf. Str.-B., I, 276.

[7] The Heb. equivalent for ἀδελφός in each sense is always אָח. In Gn. 43:33 and Jer. 31 (38):34 the LXX has ἀδελφός for רֵעַ. The meaning is physical brethren (i.e., the sons of Jacob). In Jer. 31 (38):34 רֵעֵהוּ is equated with the אָחִיו which follows immediately, but there are variants in this passage (πολίτης, πλησίον, v. Swete). In 2 Ch. 35:14, where we have ἀδελφός for כֹּהֵן we may have a variant, an error, or perhaps even a free translation according to the sense.

[8] Cf. the instances given in Str.-B., II, 766.

[9] On the other hand, the later usage "brothers in the Lord" rests on an understanding of Phil. 1:14 which is to be rejected; → n. 1.

1 Pt. 5:12), ἅγιος (only in Hb. 3:1), or the two together (Col. 1:2). Paul refers sharply to an ὀνομαζόμενος ἀδελφός in 1 C. 5:11. [10]

According to instances found in Josephus Bell., 2, 122, the more general sense of ἀδελφός is also found among the Essenes; indeed, it was common outside the Jewish and Christian world. Plato uses it for compatriots: ἡμεῖς δὲ καὶ οἱ ἡμέτεροι, μιᾶς μητρὸς πάντες ἀδελφοὶ φύντες (Menex., 239a); Xenophon for friends: ὑπισχνούμενος ... σε φίλῳ ... χρήσεσθαι καὶ ἀδελφῷ (An., VII, 2, 25); ἀδελφούς γε ποιήσομαι ... κοινωνοὺς ἁπάντων (38); Plotinus calls all the things in the world ἀδελφοί (Enn., II, 9, 18, p. 211, 7 ff., Volckmann). It is often used for members of a religious society, both in the papyri and inscriptions and also in literature; e.g., Vett. Val., IV, 11, p. 172, 31: ὁρκίζω σε, ἀδελφέ μου τιμιώτατε, καὶ τοὺς μυσταγωγουμένους ... ἐν ἀποκρύφοις ταῦτα συντηρῆσαι καὶ μὴ μεταδοῦναι τοῖς ἀπαιδεύτοις.

The general meaning underlies the compounds φιλάδελφος (in the NT only in 1 Pt. 3:8), [11] and φιλαδελφία (R. 12:10; 1 Th. 4:9; Hb. 13:1; 1 Pt. 1:22; 2 Pt. 1:7), [12] as also ψευδάδελφος (2 C. 11:26; Gl. 2:4). From this there also derives the designation ἀδελφότης for the Christian brotherhood in the concrete sense of denoting the ἀδελφοί (1 Pt. 2:17; 5:9). The same term appears in the LXX in the primary sense of physical relationship (so 4 Macc. 9:23; 10:3, 15; 13:19, 27), but also in that of the brotherhood established by covenant fellowship (1 Macc. 12:10, 17). ἀδελφότης in the sense of brotherly disposition also occurs in the lists of virtues. [13] There are no examples of this more general use of φιλαδελφία and φιλάδελφος outside Christian writings.

In a weakened form the biblical usage is taken over by the Church; cf. among many examples Luc. Mort. Peregr., 13: ὁ νομοθέτης ὁ πρῶτος ἔπεισεν αὐτοὺς (sc. τοὺς Χριστιανοὺς), ὡς ἀδελφοὶ πάντες εἶεν ἀλλήλων. It is worth noting that it sometimes acquires an ascetic significance: in Cl. Al. Strom., VI, 12, 100, 3 the γυνή is, for the γνωστικός, ἀδελφή μετὰ τὴν παιδοποιίαν ... τότε μόνον τοῦ ἀνδρὸς ἀναμιμνησκομένη, ὁπηνίκα ἂν τοῖς τέκνοις προσβλέπῃ; then in Greg. Nyss. Virg., 23 we read: γυναιξὶ ... συνοικοῦντες καὶ ἀδελφότητα τὴν τοιαύτην συμβίωσιν ὀνομάζοντες. In Palladius Hist. Laus., 43, 2, p. 130, 10, Butler, etc. all the monastic brethren are called ἀδελφότης.

von Soden

---

† ἅδης   (→ ἄβυσσος).

A. ἅδης in Later Judaism.

In the LXX ἅδης is almost always a rendering of שְׁאוֹל. In the OT this signifies the dark (Job 10:21 f.) "realm of the dead" which is set beneath the ocean (26:5) and which consigns all men indiscriminately (Ps. 89:49) behind its portals to an

---

[10] In a few cases the attestation is uncertain. In R. 15:15; 1 C. 15:31; Eph. 6:10 more or less reliable authorities leave out the address ἀδελφοί; in 1 C. 7:14 ἀνδρί for ἀδελφῷ is doubtless a secondary correction (in accordance with 14a).

[11] Cf. also the LXX 2 Macc. 15:14; 4 Macc. 13:21; 15:10; and again Sophocles, Xenophon, Plutarch. Cf. too the epithet φιλάδελφος ascribed to Ptolemy II.

[12] Thus also 4 Macc. 13:23, 26; 14:1.

[13] Hermes m., 8, 10; Vett. Val., I, 1, p. 2, 28; 4, 5.

ἅ δ η ς. Str.-B., IV, 1016-1029; G. Dalman, in RE³, VII, 295 ff.; G. Beer, "Der biblische Hades," in *Theol. Abhandlungen für H. J. Holtzmann* (1902), 3-29; Schürer, II, 639-643;

eternal (Job 7:9 f.; 16:22; Qoh. 12:5) shadowy existence (Is. 14:9), cf. 38:10; Job 38:17. This OT שאול idea is in essential agreement with the conception of the future world found in popular Babylonian belief. [1]

After the Exile this notion went through a sequence of incisive changes. [2] a. Belief in the resurrection (→ ἀνάστασις) resulted in a temporal limitation of the sojourn in the underworld for the souls of those to be resurrected, [3] the earliest instance of this being seen in Is. 26:19. b. Then under the influence of Persian and Hellenistic ideas concerning retribution after death the belief arose that the righteous and the godless would have very different fates, and we thus have the development of the idea of spatial separation in the underworld, the first instance being found in Eth. Enoch, 22. According to Jos. Ant., 18, 14 the Pharisees held this view. c. The penetration into Palestine, through the mediation of the *Diaspora*, of the belief in immortality [4] led to the idea that the souls of the righteous proceed at once to heavenly felicity after death, there to await their resurrection (→ παρά-δεισος). In consequence the term ᾅδης/שאול came to be used only of the "place of punishment" for ungodly souls in the underworld.

This third development was still taking place in the time of Jesus, as may be seen from the fact that Jesus Himself knows the second conception according to which the souls of the righteous are in the underworld as well as those of the ungodly (Lk. 16:23, 26), [5] and yet is also familiar with the third conception now in process of penetration, namely, that the souls of the righteous are in Paradise (Lk. 16:9; 23:43). A similar conjunction is to be found in Josephus, who tells us that the Pharisees locate the souls of both the righteous and the ungodly in Hades (Ant., 18, 14; Bell., 2, 163), and yet who also, himself a Pharisee, espouses the modern view that the souls of the righteous live in the heavenly world until the resurrection, and only the souls of the ungodly are to be found in Hades (Bell., 3, 375). To this co-existence of two conceptions of Hades in the time of the NT there corresponds a twofold use of the word ᾅδης/שאול. On the one side, in accordance with the older view, it denotes the whole sphere of the dead; [6] on the other, it denotes only the temporary sojourn of the souls of the ungodly. [7]

In respect of the duration of this sojourn, there can be no doubt that it was originally thought to be everlasting (→ n. 2). Independently of the changes in the conception of Hades mentioned, this view lived on where only a partial doctrine of the resurrection was taught. [8] On the other hand, where a general resurrection

---

Stade-Bertholet, *Biblische Theologie des AT,* II (1911), 397 f.; A. v. Harnack, "Der Spruch über Petrus als den Felsen der Kirche," in SAB, 32 (1918), 638-641; W. Bousset, *Kyrios Christos*[2] (1921), 26-33; H. Meusel, "Zur paulinischen Eschatologie" in NKZ, 34 (1923), 689-701; A. v. Gall, Βασιλεια του θεου (1926), 348-351; Bousset-Gressm., 293 ff.; Joach. Jeremias, *Golgotha* (1926), 70-77; Wnd. Pt., 71 f. Cf. also under n. 17.

[1] A. Jeremias, *Das AT im Lichte des Alten Orients*[4] (1930), 67.
[2] Str.-B., IV, 1016 f.
[3] On the two views of the resurrection of the righteous and the resurrection of all the dead → ἀνάστασις.
[4] Str.-B., IV, 1017, 1020-1022.
[5] *Ibid.,* 1019 f.
[6] Eth. En. 22:1-14; 51:1; 102:5; 103:7; 2 Macc. 6:23; the Pharisees acc. to Jos. Ant., 18, 14; Bell., 2, 163; 4 Esr. 4:41; 7:32; Syr. Bar., 11, 6; 21, 23.
[7] Eth. En. 63:10; Ps. Sol. 14:6; 15:11; Wis. 2:1; 17:14 (21); Philo Som., I, 151; Sl. En. 10; 40:12-42:2; Jos. Bell., 3, 375; Gr. Bar., 4.
[8] E.g., the whole of the apocal. and pseudepigr. literature except in the passages mentioned in n. 9; the Pharisees according to Jos. Ant., 18, 14; Bell., 2, 163; and in part the older Tannaites, cf. Str.-B., IV, 1166, 1182 ff.; W. Bacher, *Die Agada der Tannaiten*[2] (1903), 133 ff.

was expected, [9] the stay in Hades was thought to be limited in time, as everywhere in the NT.

The fact that there were these different views as to which souls are in Hades, and for how long, meant that there were great variations on this question in the Judaism of NT days.

B. ᾅδης in the NT.

1. The Link with Judaism.

The NT conception of Hades is closely linked with that of later Judaism. This comes out most clearly in Lk. 16:19-31, for here a conception of the time underlies the whole parable, [10] and even in detail, as a comparison with Eth. En., 22 reveals, the depiction of Hades corresponds to the average popular view. [11] This link with Judaism means that certain ideas of Hades are common to the whole of the NT.

a. The notion of a soul-sleep is just as foreign to the NT as to Judaism; the image of the sleep is introduced (Mk. 5:39 and par.; 1 Th. 5:10; Jn. 11:11-12 etc. → κοιμάω) simply as an euphemistic description of death. The soul is certainly separated from the body in death, but it experiences temporary retribution in the time between death and the resurrection. When the NT refers to Hades, the reference is to the abode of souls loosed from their bodies (cf. Ac. 2:26 f., 31).

b. The NT is also in agreement that Hades lies at the heart of the earth. In contrast to heaven as the highest height it signifies the deepest depth (Mt. 11:23; Lk. 10:15); it is the heart of the earth (Mt. 12:40); one goes down into it (Mt. 11:23; Lk. 10:15; cf. R. 10:7); it is called φυλακή as the underground (cf. Rev. 20:7 and 20:2 f.) prison of the souls of the ungodly (1 Pt. 3:19). The image of the πύλαι ᾅδου (Mt. 16:18; cf. Is. 38:10; Ps. Sol. 16:2; Wis. 16:13; 3 Macc. 5:51; [12] and cf. also the "keys of Hades" in Rev. 1:18 → κλείς) is to be understood in terms of the ancient oriental and biblical cosmology according to which the underworld, located in the hollow earth, is enclosed by sacred cliffs. [13] c. Finally, the NT agrees that the stay in Hades is limited, as may be seen from the sharp distinction between ᾅδης and γέεννα. Throughout the NT Hades serves only an interim purpose. It receives souls after death, [14] and delivers them up again at the resurrection (Rev. 20:13). The resurrection constitutes its end (20:14), and it is replaced by γέεννα (19:20; 20:10, 14 f.: λίμνη τοῦ πυρός) as the final place of punishment.

On the other hand, in another respect we seem to have a double view in the NT. In Ac. 2:27, 31 ᾅδης seems to be thought of as a place of assembly for all souls, and in Lk. 16:23 (cf. 26) all the dead are pictured as in the underworld, though Hades itself is used only of the place of punishment of the wicked. Yet there are other passages according to which only the souls of the ungodly are in the underworld (1 Pt. 3:19), whereas the righteous are in "everlasting habitations"

---

[9] E.g., the images used in Eth. En. 51:1 f.; Test. Benj. 10; Sib., IV, 178-190; 4 Esr. 5:45; 7:32 ff.; Syr. Bar. 50:2-51:3; Apc. Mos. 13, 41; and in part the older Tannaites, cf. Str.-B., IV, 1172 ff.; Bacher, op. cit., 133 ff.

[10] H. Gressmann, "Vom reichen Mann und armen Lazarus," SBA, 32 (1918).

[11] Str.-B., IV, 1019 f.

[12] For Rabbinic parallels, v. Str.-B., III, 790; IV, 1087, 1089 f.

[13] Joachim Jeremias, Golgotha, 68-77, 87 f.

[14] Lk. 16:23; hence Rev. 1:18; 6:8; 1 C. 15:55, together with θάνατος in a variant reading.

(Lk. 16:9), in Paradise (23:43), with the Lord (2 C. 5:8), united with Christ (Phil. 1:23), in the heavenly Jerusalem (Hb. 12:22), under the heavenly altar (Rev. 6:9, with reference to the souls of martyrs), and before the throne of God (Rev. 7:9 referring to martyrs and 14:3 to the unspotted). To this twofold conception, analogous to that found in Judaism of the NT period (→ 147), there corresponds the twofold use of ᾅδης in the NT. In some cases the term denotes the place of all the souls of the dead until the resurrection (Ac. 2:27, 31), whereas in others it denotes the place only of the souls of the ungodly (Lk. 16:23) or non-Christians (Rev. 20:13 f.). [15]

2. The Early Christian Reconstruction.

If the detailed conception of Hades in the NT is closely linked with contemporary views, these are basically altered by faith in Jesus and His resurrection. Two points are to be underlined.

In virtue of the promise of Jesus His community knows that it is secure from the powers of Hades (Mt. 16:18) because by faith in Him it has access to the kingdom of God (16:19 → κλείς). [16] In particular it knows that its dead are not in Hades, but in the presence of Jesus. This certainty, first declared in the saying to the dying thief on the cross (Lk. 23:43: μετ᾽ ἐμοῦ), is most sharply expressed by Paul in the phrase σὺν Χριστῷ εἶναι (Phil. 1:23).

The Christian community also knows, however, that Jesus is the Lord of Hades. This certainty, which has its roots in the preaching of Jesus (Mt. 16:18) and in faith in His resurrection (Ac. 2:31), is expressed in the doctrine of the descent to Hades [17] in the time between the death of Christ and His resurrection. This theologoumenon has points of contact with one aspect of ancient redeemer-mythology. Analogies may be found in Babylon (the descent of Ishtar), in Greece (descents in the mysteries), and among the Mandaeans (the descent of Hibil-Ziwa). [18] But there are two distinctive points in the NT, first, that Christ preached the Gospel to the souls in Hades (1 Pt. 3:19 ff.; 4:6), and second, that He has the keys of death and Hades (Rev. 1:18), in which there is reference to the preceding overthrow of the powers of death in conflict.

Joachim Jeremias

ἀδιάκριτος → κρίνω.

ἄδικος, ἀδικία,
ἀδικέω, ἀδίκημα

ἄδικος.

A. The Development of the Concept ἄδικος.

1. The ἄδικος is the "violator of law" in the widest sense. This is shown by the definition of Aristot. Eth. Nic., V, 2, p. 1129a, 32 ff.: δοκεῖ δὲ ὅ τε παράνομος ἄδικος

---

[15] The dead who belong to Christ are resurrected already at the beginning of the millennial kingdom (Rev. 20:4-5).

[16] J. Jeremias, *Jesus als Weltvollender* (1930), 63.

[17] W. Bousset, *Kyrios Christos*[2] (1921), 26-31; Wnd. Pt., 71 f. (For bibliography of the descent to Hades, v. Pr.-Bauer, 1081 f.; Wnd. Pt., *ad loc.*)

[18] Wnd. Pt., *ad loc.*

ἄδικος. E. Riggenbach, "Zur Exegese und Textkritik zweier Gleichnisse Jesu" in

εἶναι καὶ ὁ πλεονέκτης καὶ ἄνισος, ὥστε δῆλον ὅτι καὶ ὁ δίκαιος ἔσται ὅ τε νόμιμος καὶ ὁ ἴσος. The definition of Xenoph. Mem., IV, 4, 13 is along the same lines: ὁ μὲν ἄρα νόμιμος δίκαιός ἐστιν, ὁ δὲ ἄνομος ἄδικος. Cf. also Hdt., VI, 137: εἴτε δικαίως εἴτε ἀδίκως = iure an iniuria, and also Phil. Vit. Mos., I, 45 and the prayer for vengeance of Rheneia. [1] Similarly Plut. Apophth. Lac. Ag. Ult. (II, 216d) sets παρανόμως alongside ἀδίκως. What is in view, as in the case of → δίκαιος, is the relationship to law and rule and custom. Τὸ ἄδικον is not merely that which is unjust in the general sense (Jos. Bell., I, 215), nor that which is inimical (Jos. Ant., 5, 55), but more exactly that which is against law (Epict. Diss., I, 29, 17; II, 2, 9) and rule (Epict. Diss., II, 10, 26), i.e., that which comes up against the ἔθος. The opposition to custom is expressly stated in Epict. Diss., I, 6, 32: ἄδικοί τινες ἄνθρωποι καὶ θηριώδεις, where ἄδικος also means that which is uncivilised.

A distinction is also made between what is against custom and what is impious, e.g., in Xenoph. Cyr., VIII, 8, 5: τὸ ἀσεβὲς καὶ τὸ ἄδικον; Hist. Graec., II, 3, 53: περὶ ἀνθρώπους ἀδικώτατοι, ἀλλὰ καὶ περὶ θεοὺς ἀσεβέστατοι; Ap., 22: περὶ θεοὺς ἀσεβῆσαι — περὶ ἀνθρώπους ἄδικος φανῆναι. The differentiations in these passages show that ἄδικος can imply the violation of what is socially right as distinct from what is religious. Cf. also the distinction in Xenoph. Mem., I, 4, 19: ἀπέχεσθαι τῶν ἀνοσίων καὶ ἀδίκων καὶ αἰσχρῶν. This distinction discloses the view of the morally religious — this formula is in substance good Greek — in Hellenic spiritual life. The relationship to God is not sovereignly determinative in the field of ethics.

As in the case of δίκαιος, the rootage of the concept of ἄδικος in the legal world links the general usage with the biblical. In the LXX, too, ἄδικος is used as a synonym for ἄνομος, as in Job 5:22: ἀδίκων καὶ ἀνόμων καταγελάσῃ, and Ιεζ. 21:3 (Mas. 21:8): ἄδικον καὶ ἄνομον. [2] This grouping is later adopted especially by the apostolic fathers. [3] Even in Wis. 14:31 it is παράβασις which characterises the ἄδικοι. Similarly in Philo Conf. Ling., 83: ἐν τῇ τῶν ἀδίκων πράξεων κοινωνίᾳ, the ἄδικοι πράξεις are unlawful actions, except that in Philo and others we have the concept of natural law, as in Spec. Leg., IV, 204, where the ἄδικος perversely violates the νόμος φύσεως. In accordance with the doctrine of virtue in the case of δίκαιος, the doctrine of vices comes to be linked with ἄδικος. Together with ἄφρων, ἀκρατής, ἀκόλαστος and ἀνεπιστήμων, ἄδικος is included in the list of offences in Abr., 103, Sobr., 42, Gig., 2 etc., and appears as the opposite of → δίκαιος.

2. In spite of what has been said, ἄδικος does sometimes have a religious connotation. We see this already in Plat. Leg., IV, 716d: ὁ δὲ μὴ σώφρων ἀνόμοιός (opp. θεῷ φίλος) τε καὶ διάφορος καὶ ἄδικος. What ἄδικος implies here is dissimilarity from God or conflict with Him. Cf. also the religious application of ἄδικος (synon. ἀσεβής) in inscriptions as early as the 2nd century B.C. [4]

But these traces cannot in any sense be compared with the basic religious significance of the term acquired in the Jewish and Christian sphere under the influence of the OT. The essential difference from the Greek sphere is that now the main impulse derives from the strict application of the relationship to God in the assessment of human conduct. Even where there is an intermingling of Judaism and Hellenism, this OT influence is palpable. Thus we read in LXX Job 16:12: παρέδωκεν γάρ με ὁ κύριος εἰς χεῖρας ἀδίκου (a free rendering of עֲוִיל, ἐπὶ δὲ ἀσεβέσιν ἔρριψέν με, ἄδικος being synon. with ἀσεβής. Again, in Sir.

Aus Schrift und Geschichte, Thlg. Abh. f. A. Schlatter (1922), 17 ff.; R. Bultmann, ZNW, 27 (1928), 130 f.; BCH (1927), 380, 32 and 36 f.

[1] Deissmann LO, 354, 356.

[2] The Hebrew text (צַדִּיק וְרָשָׁע) gives no grounds for this.

[3] Pr.-Bauer, 27.

[4] Deissmann LO, 92.

10:7 the ἄδικον is related both to God and man. The Hellenistic Jews, in spite of their attachment to Greek ethics, were plainly influenced by this view. In Jos. Ant., 8, 251 ἄδικος and ἀσεβής are synonyms. Again, in Ant., 10, 83 : (Jehoiakim) τὴν φύσιν ἄδικος καὶ κακοῦργος καὶ μήτε πρὸς θεὸν ὅσιος μήτε πρὸς ἀνθρώπους ἐπιεικής, ἄδικος in conjunction with κακοῦργος is a title for ὅσιος (against God) and ἐπιεικής (against men). We do, of course, have a similar equation of ὅσιον, ἀνόσιον with ἄδικον, δίκαιον, e.g., in Epict. Diss., I, 29, 54. Philo relates ἄδικος and ἀσεβής in Spec. Leg., III, 209, and the two in the superlative in Rer. Div. Her., 90. The strongest religious significance is found in Conf. Ling., 129 : nothing is ἀδικώτερον than μετακλιθῆναι διάνοιαν ἀπὸ τῆς τοῦ θεοῦ τιμῆς. The same basic outlook is found in Vit. Mos., II, 107: the θυσίαι of the ἄδικος are ineffective. Even in Wisdom we find the same wholly religious use. The ἄδικοι are not subject to the Creator like the κτίσις ὑπηρετοῦσα (16:24); they are ἐν ἀφροσύνη ζωῆς (12:23) and their race will come to a bad end (3:19).

B. The Special Use of ἄδικος, especially in the NT.

The more forceful the influence of the OT, the more clearly the ἄδικος is the violator of divine law. That this fundamental view is adopted by the NT may be seen quite clearly from the fact (1) that the NT use is determined in the first instance by the OT antithesis of righteous and ungodly.

To be sure, we can see from Epict. Diss., II, 11, 5; III, 1, 8, that this is to some extent a common Greek view, though not with the religious concentration referred to under n. 2. In the LXX ἄδικος often stands for רָשָׁע the ungodly or transgressor, as in Ex. 23:1; Is. 57:20; Sir. 40:13. Josephus, too, has the antithesis δίκαιος/ἄδικος in Bell., 2, 139; 5, 407; and also Philo in Abr., 33 etc.

In the NT the antithesis δίκαιοι (צַדִּיקִים) and ἄδικοι (רְשָׁעִים) is to be found in Mt. 5:45 : βρέχει ἐπὶ δικαίους καὶ ἀδίκους, cf. LXX and → passages listed under δίκαιος. We might also refer to Ac. 24:15 : ἀνάστασιν δικαίων τε καὶ ἀδίκων, cf. again δίκαιος, where the relationship to Lk. 14:14 is discussed. In the oxymoron in 1 C. 6:1: κρίνεσθαι ἐπὶ τῶν ἀδίκων καὶ οὐχὶ ἐπὶ τῶν ἁγίων, the Gentiles are described in this way because as despisers of the divine law they cannot be expected to do justice. [5] In 1 C. 6:9 : ἄδικοι θεοῦ βασιλείαν οὐ κληρονομήσουσιν, the word means servants of iniquity or ungodly. The reference back to ἀδικεῖτε in 6:8, and the contrast to the θεοῦ which follows, give it its distinctive flavour in this verse. It is hardly a satisfactory explanation to say that the doctrine of justification is here left out of account in a return to the Synoptic preaching of repentance ; [6] we are rather brought up against the whole problem raised by the presence both of justification and of thoughts of judgment (→ δικαιοσύνη). In 1 Pt. 3:18 we read of Christ : ἀπέθανεν δίκαιος ὑπὲρ ἀδίκων. Here the thought of the substitution of Christ controls the schema δίκαιος/ἄδικος. We may also refer to 2 Pt. 2:9 : οἶδεν κύριος εὐσεβεῖς ἐκ πειρασμοῦ ῥύεσθαι, ἀδίκους δὲ εἰς ἡμέραν κρίσεως κολαζομένους τηρεῖν. Here the ἄδικοι, in contrast to the εὐσεβεῖς, denote the world which persists in wickedness and is ripe for the day of judgment (→ also n. 2).

It is also plain (2) that ἄδικος means "unjust" in the specific sense, especially with reference to rulers and judges, and in the negative to God. In Ps. Sol. 17:24

---

[5] Joh. W. 1 K., 146; Ltzm. *ad loc.*
[6] Joh. W. 1 K., 153.

it is said of the Messiah: θραῦσαι ἄρχοντας ἀδίκους. In R. 3:5 we read: μὴ ἄδικος ὁ θεὸς ὁ ἐπιφέρων τὴν ὀργήν; the suggestion that God falls short of the norm of righteousness is repudiated. Similarly Hb. 6:10: οὐ γὰρ ἄδικος ὁ θεὸς ἐπιλαθέσθαι τοῦ ἔργου ὑμῶν, emphasises that God will not be found wanting in His judicial righteousness, which recognises the labour of love.

Some other specific meanings may be mentioned. Thus it denotes "deceivers" in Sir. 19:25: ἔστιν πανουργία ἀκριβὴς καὶ αὕτη ἄδικος, cf. Epict. Diss., II, 21, 3; III, 17, 2; IV, 1, 2; "calumniators" in Sir. 51:6: βασιλεῖ διαβολὴ γλώσσης ἀδίκου; "unusable" (e.g., servants or horses etc.) in Xenoph. Cyrop., II, 2, 26; the opp. of δίκαιος in Mem., IV, 4, 5.

In Lk. 16:10: ὁ ἐν ἐλαχίστῳ ἄδικος καὶ ἐν πολλῷ ἄδικός ἐστιν, the ἄδικος is the "dishonest man" who is unfaithful to the trust laid on him, and is thus contrasted with the πιστός as the one who is reliable or faithful. In the prayer of the Pharisee in Lk. 18:11 the ἄδικοι are "hypocrites" in a more specialised sense.

3. As an attribute of concrete or abstract things, we find ἄδικος in the LXX, e.g. in ψ 118, 128: ὁδὸς ἄδικος; 118, 104: ὁδὸς ἀδικίας (for אֹרַח שָׁקֶר). It is linked with εἱμαρμένη in Jos. Bell., 1, 628; with ζῆλος in 1 Cl., 5, 4; with κρίσις in Pol., 6, 1; with ἐπιθυμία frequently in Jos. Ant., e.g., 1, 164; 6, 279; 7, 168. ἄρχειν χειρῶν ἀδίκων ("to mount an attack") is found in Lys., 4, 11; Xenoph. Cyrop., I, 5, 13; Philo Vit. Mos., I, 142 and 311. We find reference to unlawful possession in Eur. Fr., 56, Nauck: ἄδικον ὁ πλοῦτος. Cf. also Sir., 5:8: χρήμασιν ἀδίκοις (וְנִכְסֵי שָׁקֶר); Sir. 31:21: θυσιάζων ἐξ ἀδίκου; Eth. En. 63:10: "our soul is satiated with unlawful goods." In Jos. Ant., 2, 128 we have κέρδος ἄδικον (unlawful gain), as also πλοῦτος ἄδικος in Isocr., I, 38. Along the same lines, cf. also Philo Spec. Leg., I, 104: τὸ νόμισμα καθ' αὐτὸ οὐκ ἔνοχον. A rather different use is found in Jos. Ap., 2, 216: πρᾶσις ἄδικος, signifying dishonesty in business. νομὴ ἄδικος in P. Tebt., 2, 286, 7 (121-38 A.D.) means unlawfully acquired possession. Many other uses are found in the papyri, e.g., unjustifiable, incompetent, incorrect, false etc. [7]

Lk. 16:19 Dᵃ has ἐκ τοῦ ἀδίκου μαμωνᾶ instead of ἐκ τοῦ μαμωνᾶ τῆς ἀδικίας, rather along the lines of Sir. 5:8. In Lk. 16:11 we have the phrase: εἰ ἐν τῷ ἀδίκῳ μαμωνᾷ πιστοὶ οὐκ ἐγένεσθε, adj. f. ἀδίκιας, gen. qual. An exact parallel for the change (cf. supra) may be found in ὁδὸς ἄδικος or ἀδικίας in ψ 118:128, cf. also v. 104. The probable contrast here is between solid and illusory goods, for with the ἄδικος μαμωνᾶς there is contrasted τὸ ἀληθινόν as the true and essential good. [8]

4. On ἀδίκως cf. Jos. Ant., 2, 50: παθεῖν ἀδίκως (Joseph by Potiphar's wife); 1 Pt. 2:19: πάσχων ἀδίκως, opp. δικαίως πάσχειν in Test. Sym. 4:3 (→ δίκαιος).

5. The neut. τὸ ἄδικον, τὰ ἄδικα, is the opp. of δίκαιον. It is frequent in Philo: Jos., 143; Ebr., 187; Poster. C., 32. It is also found in Epict. Diss., IV, 1, 133 and 163. The contrast to ἀλήθεια is worth noting. [9] In Sir. 27:8-10, it is the opposite of δίκαιον, which corresponds to ἀλήθεια. The use of these two words as antonyms is particularly common in 1 Esr. 3:1-4, 63. The latter terms contains a reference to the revelation disclosed in the Jewish religion. The same antithesis is found in Jos. Ant., 11:55 with its reference to the superior power of truth — καὶ μηδὲν πρὸς αὐτὴν τὸ ἄδικον δυνάμενον. In Ant., 11:56 we read: ἡ ἀλήθεια διακρίνουσα ἀπ' αὐτῶν (namely, τὰ δίκαια καὶ τὰ νόμιμα) τὰ ἄδικα καὶ ἀπελέγχουσα.

---

[7] Preisigke Wört., 23 f.
[8] E. Riggenbach, Zur Exegese, 21, 23.
[9] R. Bultmann, ZNW, 27 (1928), 130 f.

ἀδικία.

A. ἀδικία outside the NT.

1. ἀδικία signifies (a) *in abstracto* "unrighteous action" or "unrighteousness" in general. In Plato Resp., X, 609c ἀδικία = πονηρία ψυχῆς; Polyb., XV, 21, 3 : διὰ τὴν τῶν πέλας ἀδικίαν; Sir., 7:3 : μὴ σπεῖρε ἐπ' αὔλακας ἀδικίας. It also signifies (b) concretely an "unjust act" or "transgression." The concrete meaning derives from the plural. [1] We may refer to Plat. Phaed., 82a : τοὺς δέ γε ἀδικίας τε καὶ τυραννίδας καὶ ἁρπαγὰς προτετιμηκότας. The definition of Aristotle in Rhet. Al., 5, p. 1427a, 31 f.: τὸ μὲν ἐκ προνοίας κακόν τι ποιεῖν ἀδικίαν τίθει, relates to the concrete sense and hardly sums up the current usage to the extent that the ἐκ προνοίας is not always in view. Aristotle is followed by Cl. Al. Strom., II, 15, 64, 5 : ἀτυχία δέ ἐστιν ἄλλου εἰς ἐμὲ πρᾶξις ἀκούσιος, ἡ δὲ ἀδικία μόνη εὑρίσκεται ἑκούσιος εἴτε ἐμὴ εἴτε ἄλλου; 64, 3 : ἀτύχημα μὲν οὖν παράλογός ἐστιν ἁμαρτία, ἡ δὲ ἁμαρτία ἀκούσιος ἀδικία, ἀδικία δὲ ἑκούσιος κακία. Thus in Sir. 14:9 covetousness is ἀδικία, or theft in Jos. Ant., 16, 1, or deception in Jos. Ant., 1, 301, or the wrong treatment of parents in Ap., 2, 217 or incest in Ant., 3, 274. The plural is very common in this respect, with the meaning of "unjust acts" or "transgressions," as in LXX, Jer., 38:34 : ἵλεως ἔσομαι ταῖς ἀδικίαις αὐτῶν ((לַעֲוֹנָם) quoted in Hb. 8:12), Ιωηλ 3:19 (חָמָס); ψ 139:3 : οἵτινες ἐλογίσαντο ἀδικίας ἐν καρδίᾳ (רָעוֹת). Sir. 17:20 : οὐκ ἐκρύβησαν αἱ ἀδικίαι αὐτῶν ἀπ' αὐτοῦ, and also in Philo Conf. Ling., 21: ἀφροσύναι καὶ δειλίαι ἀκολασίαι τε καὶ ἀδικίαι, Migr. Abr., 60 : ἀφροσύναι καὶ ἀδικίαι, etc. The term also signifies (c) "injury" or "harm," as in Test. Sol., 13:4 : ὀφθαλμῶν ἀδικία (var. -ίας), injury to the eyes; esp. pap. : ἐπ' ἀδικίᾳ, to the hurt : P. Oxy., 9, 1203, 24 (1st century A.D.), or BGU, 4, 1123, 11 (1st century B.C.). [2]

2. The content of the word is further defined (a) by the stressing of the element of "lawlessness" or "transgression." Thus ἀδικία and ἀνομία are often synonyms, e.g., in Epict. Diss., II, 16, 44 : Hercules περιῄει καθαίρων ἀδικίαν καὶ ἀνομίαν (cf. III, 26, 32), and also Is. 33:15 : μισῶν ἀνομίαν καὶ ἀδικίαν (מֹאֵס בְּבֶצַע מַעֲשַׁקּוֹת). In Sir. 41:18, too, περὶ ἀνομίας is linked with περὶ ἀδικίας. We may also refer to Philo Conf. Ling., 108. The relationship of concepts gives rise to variant readings. Thus in ψ 44:8 we find ἠγάπησας δικαιοσύνην καὶ ἐμίσησας ἀδικίαν (for ἀνομίαν) in A, and cf. also Hb. 1:9 in א A. Again, in ψ 88:33 S 1098 LA have ἀδικίας for ἐν ῥάβδῳ ἀνομίας (עֲוֹנָם): Cf., too, ψ 6:9 : οἱ ἐργαζόμενοι τὴν ἀνομίαν (אָוֶן), with which we should compare ψ 13:4 : οἱ ἐργαζόμενοι τὴν ἀδικίαν (1 Macc. 9:23). In Lk. 13:27, where ψ 6:9 is quoted, D Just. Or. have ἐργάται ἀνομίας. In 2 Macc. 10:12 we have ἀδικία as a violation of τὸ δίκαιον. Similarly Jos. Ant., 8, 314 links ἀδικία with παρανομία, and cf. Philo Abr., 242. [3]

Further definition is also given (b) by the opposing of ἀδικία to δικαιοσύνη. Cf. Isocr., 8:35 : θεοφιλέστερος ἡ δικαιοσύνη τῆς ἀδικίας; Corp. Herm., XIII, 9 : ἐδικαιώθημεν ἀδικίας ἀπούσης; LXX Dt. 32:4 : οὐκ ἔστιν ἀδικία (עָוֶל), and δίκαιος καὶ ὅσιος κύριος; ψ 51:5 : ἀδικίαν (שֶׁקֶר) ὑπὲρ τὸ λαλῆσαι δικαιοσύνην (צֶדֶק), Prv. 11:5 : δικαιοσύνη — ἀδικία (רִשְׁעָה). Prv. 16:8 (LXX 15:29): μετὰ δικαιοσύνης (בִּצְדָקָה), μετὰ ἀδικίας (בְּלֹא מִשְׁפָּט). Test. D. 6:10 : ἀπόστητε ἀπὸ πάσης

ἀδικία. E. Riggenbach, *Zur Exegese usw.* (→ under ἄδικος), 21 ff.; Andronicus Rhodius (1st century B.C.), *De Passione,* ed. K. Schuchardt (1883), p. 20, 13 f.; Defin. p. 30, 6 ff., 14 ff.

[1] Cf. Kühner-Gerth, II, 1 (1898), 17.
[2] Moult.-Mill., 10.
[3] For the ap. fathers, cf. Pr.-Bauer, 26.

ἀδικίας καὶ κολλήθητε τῇ δικαιοσύνῃ τοῦ θεοῦ; and cf. 4 Esd. 12:31-33, where the Messiah in judgment will speak with them *de iniustitiis*. In Philo, where the doctrine of virtue is determinative, ἀδικία as κακία is set over against δικαιοσύνη as ἀρετή, e.g., in Rer. Div. Her., 162 and 209; Gig., 5; Op. Mund., 73. We find the same antithesis in Jos. Ap., 2, 291: ἀδικίας ἐχθροί, δικαιοσύνης ἐπιμελεῖς. In him, too, ἀρετή is the opposite, as in Bell., 5, 414. ἀδικία is also a link in the chain of offences, being linked with ἀφροσύνη, ἀκολασία, δειλία, and the κακιῶν γένος in Philo Conf. Ling., 90. Cf. also Rer. Div. Her., 245; Op. Mund., 79 etc. The list often closes with the phrase καὶ τὰς ἄλλας κακίας. For Philo in Spec. Leg., II, 204 ἀνισότης is called ἡ δὲ ἀδικίας ἀρχή τε καὶ πηγή, or in Rer. Div. Her., 161 ἀδικία is called ἡ ἀνισότητος τῆς ἐχθίστης δημιουργός.

Important also (c) is the opposing of ἀδικία to ἀλήθεια. In this case ἀλήθεια is usually the antithesis of τὸ ἄδικον (τὰ ἄδικα), as in 1 Esr. 4:39 (→ 152). It is significant that in the LXX שֶׁקֶר in the sense of lying or untruthfulness in speech is often translated ἀδικία, as in ψ 51:5; 118:69 and 163; 143:8 and 11; and even more often ἄδικος or ἀδίκως (→ 152). In Lk. 13:27 ἀδικία is translated falsehood in sy^s.c.

3. We now turn to the express religious use, and here we must first consider (a) ἀδικία and ἀσέβεια. Outside the Bible (→ δίκαιος and ἄδικος, 150) we again find the separation and distinction between "what is against ethics" and "what is against religion," ἀδικία signifying "unlawful conduct towards men" and ἀσέβεια the "despising of God." This is seen in Xenoph. Cyrop., VIII, 8, 7: περὶ μὲν θεοὺς ἀσέβειαν, περὶ δὲ ἀνθρώπους ἀδικίαν. The mutual absorption of the two finds expression in Prv. 11:5: ἀσέβεια περιπίπτει ἀδικίᾳ. As against this we find in Jos. Bell., 7, 260: αἱ πρὸς θεὸν ἀσέβειαι καὶ αἱ εἰς τοὺς πλησίον ἀδικίαι, a mere conjunction as in Xenophon. Cf. Jos. Ap., 1, 316, in which Lysimachos gives laws περὶ θεῶν καὶ τῆς πρὸς ἀνθρώπους ἀδικίας. The two words often occur together in Philo, as in Spec. Leg., I, 215; Deus Imm., 112; Praem. Poen., 105. The Rabbis compare עֲבֵירוֹת שֶׁבֵּין אָדָם לַמָּקוֹם (sins between man and God) and עֲבֵירוֹת שֶׁבֵּין אָדָם לַחֲבֵירוֹ (sins between man and his neighbour), as in Yoma, 8, 9 (Str.-B., III, 31). Yet the Rabbis have only this one word for ἀσέβεια and ἀδικία. For them the ethical and religious elements are indissolubly linked.

We have also to notice (b) the influence of the OT conception of God on ἀδικία. It is a basic note in the OT that ἀδικία is sin against God. Thus in Is. 43:24 f. ἀδικίαι (עָוֹן) are equated with ἁμαρτίαι (חַטָּאָה). The same is true in Jer. 31:33 (LXX 38:34); 33:8 (LXX 40:8); Lam. 4:13; Ez. 28:18. It casts nets which sinfully entangle, as in Is. 58:6: λῦε πάντα σύνδεσμον ἀδικίας (פְּתֵּחַ חַרְצֻבּוֹת רֶשַׁע) cf. Hos. 13:12: συστροφὴν ἀδικίας (צָרוּר עָוֹן). The fact that ἀδικία is the usual translation of עָוֹן or "guilt" shows impressively how the term is affected by the conception of God. Cf. Jer. 2:22; 3:13; 11:10; 13:22 (in all cases עָוֹן). This is not contradicted by statements in which ἀδικία = עָוֶל ("dishonesty" or "injustice"), as in Ez. 18:18, 24; 28:18; 33:13), nor by those in which it is the equivalent of שֶׁקֶר ("disloyalty" or "unreliability"), as in ψ 118:29, 104. In Ez. it can also stand for מַעַל ("apostasy" or "breach of faith, as in 17:20 A; 39:26. And elsewhere it stands for רֶשַׁע: (Is. 58:6) or רָע: (Prv. 8:13). The same basic shade of meaning is found in Sir. 17:26: Cleave to the Highest and ἀπόστρεφε ἀπὸ ἀδικίας; in 32:5: ἀποστῆναι ἀπὸ ἀδικίας as a sin-offering; in Bar. 3:8, where ἀδικίαι means "apostasy from God." In Josephus, too, this religious sense is strongly to the forefront in addition to that already mentioned, as in Ant., 1, 45, where Adam hides from God συνειδὼς αὐτῷ τὴν ἀδικίαν; Ant., 2, 293, where Egypt and Pharaoh kindle God's wrath by ἀδικία; in Ant., 5, 168, where it is iniquity punished by God ; and in Ant., 11, 103, where the hindering of the building of the temple is ἀδικία.

4. Particular note should be taken of the apocalyptic use of the term. The whole period preceding the final Messianic revelation is viewed as a time of unrighteousness, as in 4 Esr. 4:51 ff.; En. 48:7, which speaks of this "world of unrighteousness"; 91:5 ff.; Mk. 16:14 W: ὁ αἰὼν οὗτος τῆς ἀνομίας. Relevant also are Corp. Herm., VI, 4 : ὁ γὰρ κόσμος πλήρωμά ἐστι τῆς κακίας; and 1 Jn. 5:19 : ὁ κόσμος ὅλος ἐν τῷ πονηρῷ κεῖται; Dg., 9, 1 f.: τῷ τῆς ἀδικίας καιρῷ. [4] The Messiah will then destroy the roots of iniquity, En. 91:8; Ps. Sol. 17:29 : καὶ οὐκ ἀφήσει ἀδικίαν ἐν μέσῳ αὐτῶν; 17:36 : καὶ οὐκ ἔστιν ἀδικία ἐν ταῖς ἡμέραις αὐτοῦ ἐν μέσῳ αὐτῶν. The phrase μισθὸς τῆς ἀδικίας (→ 156) is also eschatological.

5. We may refer finally to the Hebraic gen. of definition (Lk. 16:8; 18:6). [5] The gen. qual. takes the place of the adjective, cf. 2 S. 3:34; 7:10 : υἱοὶ (-ὸς) ἀδικίας (בְּנֵי־עַוְלָה). Rabbinic parallels to ὁ κριτὴς τῆς ἀδικίας (Lk. 18:6) may be found in Str.-B., II, 239. On μαμωνᾶς τῆς ἀδικίας (Lk. 16:9), → 157 and the parallels there adduced.

B. ἀδικία in the NT.

In the NT the word ἀδικία is first related to basic NT conceptions in Paul, then in John. The use of the term without the force of inner accentuation in 2 C. 12:13 : χαρίσασθε δέ μοι τὴν ἀδικίαν ταύτην, is exceptional. Here there is ironic reference to the concrete wrong or unjust action (→ 153), or the unjust nature of the action, that Paul has not burdened the Corinthians with his personal needs. Otherwise almost all the instances add something to the content of ἀδικία (→ A. 2).

1. a. It is an antonym to δικαιοσύνη (→ A. 2b). In R. 1:29 ἀδικία is put first in the list of offences as "violation of the divine law and its norm" (πεπληρωμένους πάσῃ ἀδικίᾳ, πονηρίᾳ, πλεονεξίᾳ, κακίᾳ). [6] The list itself is a new one. In similar lists in Philo we hardly ever miss ἀφροσύνη, nor is ἀδικία so much emphasised as in the Romans group, where it always comes first in spite of many textual variants. [7] In R. 9:14 : μὴ ἀδικία παρὰ τῷ θεῷ, [8] it is to be thought of as "legal injustice" or "partiality in judgment," and therefore as the opposite of the δικαιοσύνη demanded in a judge. In R. 3:5 : εἰ δὲ ἡ ἀδικία ἡμῶν θεοῦ δικαιοσύνην συνίστησιν, it is again opposed to δικαιοσύνη, but this time (cf. 3:3) with special emphasis on the element of unfaithfulness in contrast to the righteousness of God as His abiding faithfulness in the fulfilment of promise. It is in R. 6:13 however — ὅπλα ἀδικίας/ὅπλα δικαιοσύνης — that we reach the height of contrast to the solemn basic concept of the δικαιοσύνη θεοῦ. We do not have

---

[4] Cf. Str.-B., IV, 978 ff., where Rabbinic parallels are given : bSanh., 97a; Midr. Cant., 2, 13 (101a); Midr. Ps. 92 § 10 etc.
[5] Kühner-Gerth, II, 1 (1898), 264; Moulton, 113; Bl.-Debr., § 165.
[6] On the old Hebrew and Stoic lists, cf. Ltzm. ad loc.
[7] Ltzm. ad loc.
[8] But cf. Khl. R., 324 f.: "deviation from the norm."

here a gen. qual. [9] but a gen. auctoris : ἀδικία and δικαιοσύνη as two objective powers controlling man present their instruments or weapons.

b. It is also the opposite of ἀλήθεια (→ A. 2c). According to Jn. 7:18 : ὁ δὲ ζητῶν τὴν δόξαν τοῦ πέμψαντος αὐτόν, οὗτος ἀληθής ἐστιν καὶ ἀδικία ἐν αὐτῷ οὐκ ἔστιν, ἀδικία is present when we do not seek God's glory but our own reputation. Truth on the other hand consists in desiring the glory of the One who sends. Paul, too, makes great use of this contrast. In 2 Th. 2:10 the ἀπάτη ἀδικίας to which the ἀπολλύμενοι are subject is contrasted with salvation by receiving love of the truth. In 2 Th. 2:12 the contrast is between believing the truth, i.e., the Gospel and delighting in ἀδικία as wrongdoing. In both cases reception of the Gospel (ἀλήθεια) means a break with ἀδικία. In 1 C. 13:6 : οὐ χαίρει ἐπὶ τῇ ἀδικίᾳ, συγχαίρει δὲ τῇ ἀληθείᾳ, the antithesis is conceived in such a way that we see the relation between ἀλήθεια and δικαιοσύνη; for obedience to the truth is ἀγάπη, which is the direct opposite of ἀδικία. Again, in R. 2:8 : ἀπειθοῦσι τῇ ἀληθείᾳ πειθομένοις δὲ τῇ ἀδικίᾳ, ἀδικία as transgression of the divine law is set in emphatic contrast with the truth. Like the truth (cf. 6:13), it is a power which is obeyed. Hence in unrighteousness the truth is suppressed (1:18). Again, in 2 Tm. 2:19 : ἀποστήτω ἀπὸ ἀδικίας (a partial quotation from Is. 26:13), we have the same antithesis (cf. with περὶ τὴν ἀλήθειαν ἠστόχησαν in v. 18), the reference here being to denial of correct doctrine.

2. a. We find again the relationship to ἀσέβεια (→ A. 3a). In the thesis of Paul in R. 1:18 : ἀποκαλύπτεται γὰρ ὀργὴ θεοῦ ἐπὶ πᾶσαν ἀσέβειαν καὶ ἀδικίαν ἀνθρώπων, which stands at the head of the two sections vv. 19-23 (a perverted cultus = ἀσέβεια) and vv. 24-32 (sexual and social perversion = ἀδικία), a distinction is made between them. Yet the context as a whole makes it evident that ἀδικία arises out of the perversion of worship, and already in τῶν τὴν ἀλήθειαν ἐν ἀδικίᾳ κατεχόντων it is clearly stated that the nature which is against the norm and opposed to the will of God is fundamentally linked with the suppression of the truth. Thus the statement transcends the distinction between moral and religious to which we referred earlier (→ 150).

b. ἀδικία is also defined as "sin against God" (→ A. 3b). In Ac. 8:23 : σύνδεσμον ἀδικίας (→ 154), where the gen. is either poss. or auct., it obviously casts nets after the manner of sinful enticement. In 1 Jn. 1:9 ἀδικία is expressly linked with ἁμαρτία as unrighteousness against God. A definition along these lines is given in 1 Jn. 5:17: πᾶσα ἀδικία ἁμαρτία ἐστίν. Thus in 3:7 ff. ποιεῖν τὴν ἁμαρτίαν is the opposite of ποιεῖν τὴν δικαιοσύνην.

3. The term is also used apocalyptically (→ A. 4). In 2 Th. 2:10 mention is made of the ἀπάτη ἀδικίας in depiction of the operation of Antichrist. [10] Here we again have the Hebraic gen. instead of the adj. (on the relation to ἀλήθεια → B. 1b). In Jm. 3:6, though the text is corrupt, the tongue is linked with the eschatologically conceived κόσμος τῆς ἀδικίας. [11] Another eschatological concept is found in Ac. 1:18 : μισθὸς τῆς ἀδικίας ("reward of iniquity"). In 2 Pt. 2:13 ἀδικούμενοι μισθὸν ἀδικίας [12] means being harmed by the reward "paid for

---

[9] So Khl. R., 210.

[10] On the reading τῆς ἀδικίας, assimilated to Lk. 16:8 f.; 18:6, cf. Dob. Th., 288.

[11] A. Meyer, Rätsel d. Jk. (1930), 144, takes κόσμος here to be simply a place of assembly (Prv. 17:6), but the expression is rather too distinctive, cf. Wnd., ad loc., Hck. Jk., 160.

[12] B ℵ* P arm against κομιούμενοι ℵ.

unrighteousness" (cf. Rev. 2:11: ἀδικηθῇ ἐκ).[13] The phrase in 2 Pt. 2:15 : ὃς μισθὸν ἀδικίας ἠγάπησεν (with reference to Balaam) is to be understood in the same way.[14]

4. We find the Hebraic gen. of definition (→ A. 5.) in Lk. 16:8, where οἰκονόμος ἀδικίας (for ἄδικος) means a steward who is "guilty of official unfaithfulness"; or again in 18:6 : κριτὴς τῆς ἀδικίας = a judge who "perverts justice." Lk. 16:9 : μαμωνᾶς τῆς ἀδικίας,[15] raises serious problems. The idea that possessions as such are necessarily linked with a moral defect[16] is rather a crude conception which is open to the objection that in dealing with questions of meats and purification Jesus established the rule that nothing is unclean of itself. The parable certainly describes riches as an ἐλάχιστον (v. 10), as the opposite of ἀληθινόν (v. 11), as an ἀλλότριον (v. 12), and as not in the true sense ἡμέτερον. Yet it does not actually characterise possession as ἄδικον, even though the particular attitude of Lk. to earthly goods may have fostered a certain carelessness of expression. The Targums should be especially noted in this respect. In Tg. Hab. 2:9 we have מָמוֹן דִּרְשַׁע "mammon of iniquity" (Str.-B., II, 220). Again, in Tg. 1 S. 12:3 and Tg. Hos. 5:11 we have מָמוֹן דִּשְׁקַר (usually a rendering of the Heb. בֶּצַע "dishonest gain"). Hence we might see in the phrase μαμωνᾶς τῆς ἀδικίας a reference to the tax-gatherers of the time who had amassed their fortunes by lying and trickery.[17] Such a reference hardly fits the context of Lk. 16, but possibly a saying originally addressed to the publicans is here given a wider application. On the other hand, the many different renderings of שֶׁקֶר in the LXX[18] — as ἀδικία it might be either lying or deception in speech or unfaithfulness or unreliability (→ 154) — suggest at least the possibility of various meanings in the original Semitic. Thus the original sense might well be that of possessions which deceive their owner, or which are illusory and transitory, as in Mk. 4:19 : ἀπάτη τοῦ πλούτου.[19]

ἀδικέω.

A. ἀδικέω outside the NT.

1. ἀδικέω means to be ἄδικος, "to do wrong in the sense of transgression." It is found in Arist. Rhet., I, 10, p. 1368b, 6 f.: ἔστω τὸ ἀδικεῖν τὸ βλάπτειν ἑκόντα παρὰ τὸν νόμον; Rhet. Al., 5, p. 1427a, 36 f.: τὸ μὲν ἀδικεῖν εἶναι τῶν πονηρῶν ἀνθρώπων ἴδιον (→ ἀδίκημα, 161). It is also common in Herodot. and the Attic. In the sense of "wrongdoing" it is found in Epict. Diss., II, 10, 28 : ἀδικήσας, and IV, 1, 167: τοὺς ἀδικοῦντας; in Jos. Ant., 2, 26 : ὡς ἀδελφὸν οὐδὲ ἀδικήσαντα κτείνειν ὅσιον, Ant., 2, 146 : οἱ ἠδικηκότες, and Ant., 4, 297, of unjust aggression ; and in Philo Vit. Mos., I, 54, Gig., 46, and Agric., 92 etc. The pres. εἰ ἀδικῶ means "if I am in the wrong." Cf. LXX Ex. 2:13 : λέγει τῷ ἀδικοῦντι. In Plat. Charm., 156a εἰ μὴ ἀδικῶ means "if I am not mistaken."

---

[13] Thus correctly Wnd. Pt., 95. Kn. Pt., 298 offers the improbable "spoiled for the reward."

[14] Grammatically this might also be a gen. auct. (Kn. Pt., 301; Wnd. Pt., 97), or a gen. qual.: an unrighteous reward.

[15] Riggenbach, Zur Exegese etc. (→ 149, n.), 21 ff.

[16] Zn. Lk., 578. Cf. S. Nu., 119 on 18:20 : "Gold and silver take men out of this world and out of the future world." But cf. also Philo Spec. Leg., I, 104, and → 152.

[17] Lightfoot, Horae Hebr., I (ed. Carpzov Lips., 1864), p. 843 ff.; A. Merx, Die vier kan. Evgl., II, 2 (1905), 327 ff.

[18] Riggenbach, 25. מָמוֹן דִּשְׁקַר is obviously the Aramaic equivalent of the Hebrew נִכְסֵי שֶׁקֶר in Sir. 5:8 (χρήμασιν ἀδίκοις).

[19] Thus already Drusius, Michaelis, Wieseler, and more recently Riggenbach and others.

2. Relationship to God is also envisaged, as in Eur. Phoen., 958 : ἀδικεῖ τὰ τῶν θεῶν; Xenoph. Mem., I, 1, 1: ἀδικεῖ Σωκράτης, οὓς μὲν ἡ πόλις νομίζει θεοὺς οὐ νομίζων — naturally violating the honour of the gods is also a transgression of national duty.

In the LXX ἀδικεῖν is unconditionally used for the OT words which denote "sinning against God." Sometimes it is the rendering of חָטָא. Thus David in 2 S. 24:17 says : ἰδοὺ ἐγώ εἰμι, ἠδίκησα (חָטָאתִי). The meaning is religious rather than legal or social. [1] Or it sometimes stands for מָעַל: as in 2 Ch. 26:16 : ἠδίκησεν (וַיִּמְעַל) with reference to the offering of Uzziah as a sin against God. Or it may signify the breach of an oath, as in ψ 43:17 (Mas. 44:17): καὶ οὐκ ἠδικήσαμεν ἐν διαθήκῃ σου שִׁקַּרְנוּ Pi). It is often used to translate עָוָה, as in Jer. 3:21: The children of Israel ἠδίκησαν ἐν ταῖς ὁδοῖς αὐτῶν (הֶעֱווּ). The continuation : "They have forgotten the Lord their God," shows the Godward reference. We might also refer to Ιερ. 9:5 : Israel is unwearying in wrongdoing (ἠδίκησαν, הֶעֱוֵה). or 3 Βασ. 8:47 (= 2 Ch. 6:37), where it is synon. with ἁμαρτάνειν and ἀνομεῖν: ἡμάρτομεν, ἠδικήσαμεν, ἠνομήσαμεν (חָטָאנוּ וְהֶעֱוִינוּ רָשָׁעְנוּ). A changes the order to 1/3/2, and this suggests that all three Hebrew words might well be rendered ἀδικεῖν. In this connection note should also be taken of ψ 105:6 (Mas. 106:6), where we find the same verbs in the sequence 1/3/2, and הִרְשַׁעְנוּ is translated ἠδικήσαμεν. Da. 9:5, however, uses the Hellenistically apprehended ἠσεβήσαμεν together with ἡμάρτομεν and ἠδικήσαμεν (וְעָוִינוּ) as does also Bar. 2:12.

Josephus follows the usage of the LXX when he employs ἀδικεῖν to denote violation of the Law and disobedience to God. When Zambrias marries a foreign wife in Ant. 4, 150, this is called an ἀδικεῖν because it is contrary to the Law ; cf. in the same connection 4, 155 : ἀδικεῖν τῷ θεῷ δοκοῦντες, and also 4, 211. Saul's disobedience to God (Ant., 6, 151) leads to his admission : ἀδικεῖν ὡμολόγει καὶ τὴν ἁμαρτίαν οὐκ ἠρνεῖτο. Both views are found in Ant., 20, 44 : τὰ μέγιστα τοὺς νόμους καὶ δι᾽ αὐτῶν τὸν θεὸν ἀδικῶν. Philo, too, links ἠδίκουν and ἡμάρτανον in Leg. All., II, 68. In Gig., 47 ἀδικεῖν means sinning against the God who is close to hand and fills all things, and it results in the departure of the divine Spirit of wisdom. Philo devotes particular attention to συναδικεῖν as the common transgression of man, as in Decal., 123; Conf. Ling., 9 f.; Ebr., 25. For him the opposite of ἀδικεῖν is δικαιοπραγεῖν (Ebr. 26; Agric., 123). Within his teaching on offences (Det. Pot. Ins., 73) ἀδικεῖν is linked with ἄφρων and ἀφροσύνη (Deus Imm., 181; Conf. Ling., 119; Sobr., 69). The Sodomites are guilty of ἀδικεῖν, Conf. Ling., 27: ἐστειρωμένους σοφίαν καὶ τυφλοὺς διάνοιαν. It is a distinctive feature of Philo's ethics that the root of ἀδικεῖν is found in a lack of the sense of decorum and moderation.

3. Also envisaged is relationship to the social sense. In the LXX there is no cleavage between the social and the religious meaning, though there is a distinction. In Gn. 42:22 : μὴ ἀδικήσατε τὸ παιδάριον (אַל־תֶּחֶטְאוּ), Ex. 5:16 (the γραμματεῖς to Pharaoh): ἀδικήσεις τὸν λαόν σου (וְחָטָאת), Ιερ. 44:18 (Mas. 37:18, Jeremiah to the king): τί ἠδίκησά σε καὶ τοὺς παῖδάς σου, ἀδικεῖν takes place towards men, but is a rendering of חטא. Elsewhere in Greek there is not the same interfusion of the two standpoints; the constant reference to the divine command is specifically Hebrew. Thus ὁ ἀδικῶν (Jos. Ant., 1, 318; plur. Epict. Diss., II, 20, 23) is for the

---

ἀδικέω. [1] Thus Cr.-Kö., 339.

most part simply the wrongdoer, the one who is set in the wrong; and ἀδικεῖν is wrongdoing : Soph. Ant., 1059; Philo Poster. C., 82; Conf. Ling., 25 and 69; Spec. Leg., II, 11. Sometimes in legal terminology ἀδικεῖν means to have an unjust cause in the eyes of the law : Plat. Ap., 19b; Xenoph. Mem., I, 1, 1; Epict. Diss., II, 5, 29 : κρίνω σε ἀδικεῖν. In Ditt. Syll.³, 635, 22 we read : ἀποτεισάτω ὁ ἀδικῶν δισχιλίους στατῆρας. There is a reference to warlike hostilities in Jos. Ant., 1, 327: εἰ θέλοιεν ἀδικεῖν.

4. Other points may best be arranged in order of syntax. a. With acc. of object : [2] BGU, IV, 1138, 13 : ὃ ἠδίκησεν ἐμαρτύρησ(εν) (1st century B.C.); Jos. Ant., 6, 238 (Jonathan asking Saul concerning David): τί δ᾽ ἀδικοῦντα κολάσαι θέλεις; with περί, Philo Jos., 156 (concerning the chief baker): περὶ τὸ μέγιστον ἀδικήσαντα. μηδὲν ἀδικεῖν (Epict. Diss., II, 15, 11: ἀπολλύων ἄνθρωπον μηδὲν ἠδικηκότα); frequently in Jos. in protestation of innocence, as Jacob to Laban in Ant., 1, 319; the witch of Endor to Saul in Ant., 6, 331; or Antipater in Bell., 1, 639 : θεός ἐστίν μοι τοῦ μηδὲν ἀδικεῖν μάρτυς etc. b. Transitively with acc. of person[3] == "to do wrong to someone," "to treat someone unjustly" or "to do him an injury." In the LXX we may refer to Jdt. 11:4 : οὐ γὰρ ἔστιν ὃς ἀδικήσει σε, ἀλλ᾽ εὖ σε ποιήσει; Tobit 6:15 : ὅτι δαιμόνιον φιλεῖ αὐτὴν ὃ οὐκ ἀδικεῖ οὐδένα πλὴν τῶν προσαγόντων αὐτῇ; Test. Sol. 18:3, where the 36 στοιχεῖα say to Solomon : οὐ δύνασαι ἡμᾶς ἀδικῆσαι; ibid., MS, D, III, 8 (MacCown, 92): ἀδικῆσαι τοὺς ἀνθρώπους; Corp. Herm., X, 19a : μηδένα ἀνθρώπων ἀδικῆσαι; Epict. Diss., III, 24, 79 : μηδείς σε ἀδικῇ, cf. II, 17, 20 ; IV, 1, 95 ; Ditt. Syll., ³ 635, 8 f.; ἀδικεῖν μηδένα; amulet in Reitzenstein : [4] τοῦ μὴ ἀδικῆσαι ἢ βλάψαι ἢ προσεγγίσαι τὸν δοῦλον τοῦ θεοῦ; Jos. Ant., 4, 50 : τοῦ τὸν σὸν ἀδικῆσαι θελήσαντος λαόν; 11, 281: ἀδικήσαντας αὐτούς; 17, 109 : ἀδικεῖν τοὺς εὐεργέτας; though see 2, 245 and 15, 144 where it means "hurt" without accusative of either person or object. It is used in the sense of hostile operations in Ant., 13, 275 and of insult in Ap., 1, 98, where Rameses forbade τὴν βασιλίδα μητέρα ἀδικεῖν and Philo Leg. All., I, 51: ἑαυτὸν ἀδικεῖ. In Rabbinic usage the one who injures is מַזִּיק, and the injured party נִזָּק.[5] c. Transitively with accus. of object in the sense of "damaging something." [6] In this form it is mostly active, as in Thuc., II, 71: ἀ. γῆν; Xenoph. Eq., 6, 3 : ἵππον; Test. Sol. 18:7 f.: ὀφθαλμοὺς ἀδικῶ; Ditt. Syll., ³ 635, 8 ff.: τὴν δὲ λοιπὴν χώραν τὴν ἱερὰν τοῦ Ἀπόλλωνος τοῦ Πτῴου μὴ ἀδικεῖν μηδένα; BCH (1902), p. 217: ἐάν τις τὴν στήλην ἀδικήσει. d. With a double accusative in the sense of "hurting someone in some matter": Demosth. 21, 129 : ἃ πολλοὺς ὑμῶν ἠδίκησεν; in the LXX Lv. 6:2 : ἠδίκησέν τι τὸν πλησίον; Prv. 24:44 : ἅ με ἠδίκησεν; in Jos. Ant., 2, 138, of Joseph : οὐδὲν γὰρ αὐτὸν ἀδικεῖν; Ant., 3, 271, where the suspected adulteress must swear : μηδὲν ἠδικηκέναι τὸν ἄνδρα. Cf. Ant., 6, 297; 10, 2; Epict. Diss., III, 24, 81: τί σε ἠδίκησε Χρύσιππος.

e. Passively, in the sense of "suffering wrong or injury or damage," of "being wronged." Cf. Plat. Gorg., 509c, where ἀδικεῖν is the greater and ἀδικεῖσθαι the lesser evil ; [7] Polyb. XI, 28, 8 : ὑπὸ γονέως ἰδίου φάσκων εἰς ἀργυρίου λόγον ἀδικεῖσθαι; Corp. Herm., X, 21: slander, murder, maltreatment — δι᾽ ὧν ἄνθρωποι ἀδικοῦνται. Very frequently for עָשַׁק in the LXX in the sense of "oppress" or "defraud," as in Dt. 28:29, 33 : ἀδικούμενος (עָשׁוּק); ψ 102:6 (Mas. 103:6): ποιῶν ὁ κύριος κρίμα

---

[2] Many examples from the classical period are found in Liddell-Scott, 23; Pass.-Cr., 94 f.
[3] For classical examples, Liddell-Scott and Pass.-Cr., op. cit.
[4] Poim., 294, 6 f. Cf. further JRS, XIV (1924), p. 47, No. 37, 7 ff.; Audollent, Def. Tab., No. 2b, 4 f. Cumont-Anderson, Studia Pontica, III (1903 ff.), p. 20, No. 10g, 15.
[5] Schl. Mt., 590, where there is reference to jRH, 58a, BQ, 1, 2.
[6] Cf. H. B. Swete, Rev. (1907) on Rev. 2:11.
[7] Quoted from Philo Jos., 20.

πᾶσι τοῖς ἀδικουμένοις (לְכָל־עֲשׁוּקִים), ψ 145:7 (Mas. 146:7); Is. 1:17: ῥύσασθε ἀδικούμενον for אַשְּׁרוּ חָמוֹץ. Is. 25:3 : πόλεις ἀνθρώπων ἀδικουμένων (גּוֹיִם עָרִיצִים). The ἀδικούμενος as "the one who suffers wrong" is often found in Sir. 4:9 ; 13:3; 32:16 (Heb. 35:16). In Jos. Ant., 2, 22 we have συναδικεῖται, the father and mother being hurt by the death of Joseph ; Ant., 2, 260 : ἀδικουμένας of the girls badly treated by the shepherds at the well ; Philo Vit. Mos., I, 56. For ἀδικεῖσθαι, cf. Ant., 5, 258; 6, 144; 8, 27; Bell., 1, 124; 2, 351 f.; 5, 377. In Philo Abr., 96 God is the ὑπέρμαχος τῶν ἀδικουμένων. In Vit. Mos., I, 40 ἀδικούμενοι is used of oppression by forced labour ; and in I, 67 the burning bush is a σύμβολον τῶν ἀδικουμένων. In the pap. we often find ὁ ἠδικημένος, ἀδικούμενος used for "wronged or injured parties" in petitions, as in P. Tebt., I, 42, 5 (c. 114 B.C.); P. Eleph., 27a, 25 (3rd cent. B.C.). [8] But the transitive use with acc. of object, "to hurt something," also carries with it the corresponding passive, as in Wis. 14:29 : ἀψύχοις γὰρ πεποιθότες εἰδώλοις κακῶς ὀμόσαντες ἀδικηθῆναι οὐ προσδέχονται; or Jos. Ant., 4:76, where in respect of transit through Edom Moses gives the guarantee : ὑπὲρ τοῦ μηδὲν ἀδικηθήσεσθαι δώσειν ὁμολογῶν. A peculiar use is found in Corp. Herm., VI, 1b, where the impassibility of God is depicted as follows : οὔτε κρεῖττον αὐτοῦ ἐστιν οὐδέν, ὑφ' οὗ ἀδικηθεὶς πολεμήσει.

B. ἀδικέω in the NT.

It is a striking fact that apart from Col. 3:25 and Rev. 22:11, which are early exhortations shaped by the LXX, the NT usage does not reach this LXX level (→ A.2), and is little affected by any spirit of fresh evaluation. This is obviously due to the victory over ἀδικεῖν of its LXX rival ἁμαρτάνειν. ἀδικεῖν is thus as it were relegated to mundane speech to express what is usually signified by it in everyday affairs. In this respect the NT usage conforms to that of Greek in general.

a. The absolute use in the active (→ A. 1) is found in 2 C. 7:12 : οὐχ ἕνεκεν τοῦ ἀδικήσαντος, "he who has done wrong." [9] We may also refer to Ac. 25:11: εἰ μὲν οὖν ἀδικῶ, "I am in the wrong." Finally we may quote the words of exhortation in Col. 3:25, which are obviously applied in a religious sense as already mentioned : ὁ γὰρ (DᶜEKL : ὁ δὲ) ἀδικῶν κομίσεται ὃ ἠδίκησεν. Of the last verse, as of Rev. 22:11: ὁ ἀδικῶν ἀδικησάτω ἔτι, it has been rightly said [10] that the form of expression seems to derive from an early hortatory tradition. In Col. 3:25 we have a final warning in the address to slaves that all ἀδικεῖν should be set aside in view of the final judgment. [11] This saying is also an example of the use of the verb with acc. of object.

b. The use with acc. of person (→ A. 4b) occurs in Mt. 20:13 : ἑταῖρε, οὐκ ἀδικῶ σε — a milder, negative form of the thought that the conduct of the οἰκο-

---

[8] Cf. Moult.-Mill., 10; Preisigke Wört., 23.

[9] The arguments of Zahn (*Einl.*, I, 248) against the common rendering as the one who has offered insult are supported by the use in the pap. — cf. Preisigke Wört., II, 37 and 631 — where λοιδορέω and ὑβρίζω are used for "insult" and "libel."

[10] Loh. Apk., on the ground that elsewhere in Rev. ἀδικεῖν means to injure rather than to sin. Rev. 22:11 reminds us of the ἀνομήσωσιν ἄνομοι in Θ Dan. 12:10 (LXX : ἁμάρτωσιν οἱ ἁμαρτωλοί), cf. Bss. Apk., 457.

[11] The particular application to slaves is shown by the context. But the translation "wrong" in the sense of wronging the master cannot be justified (cf. Ew. Gefbr., 432) by the fact that Paul does not elsewhere use ἀδικεῖν in a religious sense. The extraordinary usage is explained by the adoption of the pulpit style of exhortation. But A. Debrunner comes down on the opposite side : "As in judicial life the rule obtains : ὁ ἀδικῶν κομίσεται ὃ ἠδίκησεν, without προσωπολημψία, so it is before God."

δεσπότης is wholly according to law and custom. [12] It is also found in Lk. 10:19 : καὶ οὐδὲν ὑμᾶς οὐ μὴ ἀδικήσει in which οὐδὲν is the subject and ὑμᾶς the acc. of person.[13]. Ac. 7:26 : ἱνατί ἀδικεῖτε; ὁ δὲ ἀδικῶν τὸν πλησίον, conforms to the LXX with its allusion to Ex. 2:13 : λέγει τῷ ἀδικοῦντι. In 1 C. 6:8 : ὑμεῖς ἀδικεῖτε καὶ τοῦτο ἀδελφούς and 2 C. 7:2 : οὐδένα ἠδικήσαμεν it is a question of wronging by hurting or making sick. The demonic locusts of Rev. 9:10 are given power ἀδικῆσαι τοὺς ἀνθρώπους μῆνας πέντε, a similar construction being found in Rev. 11:5 : εἴ τις θελήσῃ αὐτοὺς ἀδικῆσαι.

c. With acc. of object in the sense of "hurting" (→ A. 4c) ἀδικεῖν is a favourite term in Revelation as applied to acts of judgment on the cosmos. We may refer to 6:6 : τὸ ἔλαιον καὶ τὸν οἶνον μὴ ἀ.; 7:2 f.: ἀ. τὴν γῆν καὶ τὴν θάλασσαν; 9:4 : ἵνα μὴ ἀ. τὸν χόρτον τῆς γῆς; 9:19 : ἐν αὐταῖς i.e., their tails, ἀδικοῦσιν i.e., the horses.

d. The double acc. (→ A. 4d) is perhaps found in Lk. 10:19 (cf. supra), but it is certainly present in Ac. 25:10 : Ἰουδαίους οὐδὲν ἠδίκησα; Gl. 4:12 : οὐδέν με ἠδικήσατε; Phlm. 18 : εἰ δέ τι ἠδίκησέν σε, "if he has wronged thee in anything." [14]

e. For the passive (→ A. 4e) we turn to Ac. 7:24 : ἰδών τινα ἀδικούμενον, "the one who suffered wrong or violence"; 1 C. 6:7 : διὰ τί οὐχὶ μᾶλλον ἀδικεῖσθε; vg.: quare non magis iniuriam accipitis? 2 C. 7:12 : ἕνεκεν τοῦ ἀδικηθέντος, "the one who has suffered injustice." [15] For ἀδικεῖσθαι ἐκ, "to be injured by," cf. Rev. 2:11 : οὐ μὴ ἀδικηθῇ ἐκ τοῦ θανάτου τοῦ δευτέρου. For ἀδικεῖσθαι with acc. of object, cf. 2 Pt. 2:13 : ἀδικούμενοι (Bℵ* P arm) [16] μισθὸν ἀδικίας, "to be wronged or deceived by" — a very rare construction. [17]

ἀδίκημα.

A. ἀδίκημα outside the NT.

ἀδίκημα in secular Greek is the concrete term corresponding to ἀδικεῖν. It denotes the "completed act of wrong." This is expressed as follows in the definition of Aristot. Eth. Nic., V, 10, p. 1135a, 10 ff.: ἀδικον μὲν γάρ ἐστιν τῇ φύσει ἢ τάξει, αὐτὸ δὲ τοῦτο, ὅταν πραχθῇ, ἀδίκημά ἐστι, πρὶν δὲ πραχθῆναι, οὔπω ἀλλ' ἄδικον. Unlike ἀδικία, it cannot also denote wrong in the abstract. In this respect Xenoph. Mem., II, 2, 3 is instructive : αἱ πόλεις ἐπὶ τοῖς μεγίστοις ἀδικήμασι ζημίαν θάνατον πεποιήκασιν ὡς οὐκ ἂν μείζονος κακοῦ φόβῳ τὴν ἀδικίαν παύσαντες. And as distinct from ἀμάρτημα ("failing" or "defect") and ἀτύχημα ("unintentional fault") it implies predominantly a "deliberate act of wrongdoing." Cf. Aristot. Eth. Nic., V, 10, p. 1135b, 20 ff.; Rhet., I, 13, p. 1374b, 8 and cf. Eth. Nic., V, 10, p. 1135a, 21 ff.: ὅταν γὰρ ἑκούσιον ᾖ, ψέγεται, ἅμα δὲ καὶ ἀδίκημα τότε ἐστίν· ὥστ' ἔσται τι ἄδικον μὲν ἀδίκημα δ' οὔπω, ἐὰν μὴ τὸ ἑκούσιον προσῇ [1]. Thus ἀδίκημα is often used

12 Cf. Kl. Mt., 161.
13 Zn. Lk., 422. However, the double acc. (Kl. Lk., ad loc.) is also possible ("in nothing"). On the negations of the saying, cf. Bl.-Debr., § 431, 3.
14 Loh. Phlm., 190, whether by theft, neglect of duty, or poor work.
15 Cf. Zn., n. 9; Ltzm. K., 133.
16 ACℜ 33 vg syh have the weaker κομιούμενοι.
17 → ἀδικία, n. 13.
ἀ δ ί κ η μ α. Trench, 155. In defin., Themist. Or., 1 (15c).
1 This is the basis of Philo Leg. All., I, 35 : εἴ γε τὰ ἀκούσια καὶ κατὰ ἄγνοιαν

for misdeeds such as those of indisciplined troops (Polyb., I, 66, 6 and 8), the oppressions of foes (Philo Rer. Div. Her., 289), acts of violence (Vit. Mos., I, 149), the ill-treatment of a wife (in the pap. BGU, IV, 1098, 22 [1st cent. B.C.]: εἰς αὐτὴν ἀδίκημα), fraud and embezzlement (in the pap. P. Amh., II, 33, 13 c. 157 B.C.). ² This usage in the pap. shows us that the normal reference is to concrete violations of law. ³

The word is comparatively rare in the LXX, and it mostly implies "breach of the Law" or "misdeeds against God." It is often a rendering of עָוֹן "misdeed" — with a predominant reference to God — as in Is. 59:12 : καὶ τὰ ἀδικήματα (וַעֲוֹנֹתֵינוּ) ἡμῶν ἔγνωμεν; Jer. 16:17: οὐκ ἐκρύβη τὰ ἀδικήματα (עֲוֹנָם) αὐτῶν ἀπέναντι τῶν ὀφθαλμῶν μου; Ez., 14:10 : κατὰ τὸ ἀδίκημα (כַּעֲוֹן) τοῦ ἐπερωτῶντος. It is also used for מִשְׁפָּט : in Zeph. 3:15 : περιεῖλεν Κύριος τὰ ἀδικήματά σου; ⁴ for פֶּשַׁע "offence" or "fault" in Prv. 17:9 : ὃς κρύπτει ἀδικήματα, ζητεῖ φιλίαν. It is found in the special sense of the rustling of cattle in Εξ 22:9 (Mas. 22:8); in parallelism with ἁμάρτημα or ἁμαρτίαι in Gn. 31:36; Lv. 16:16; for עָוֹן in 1 S. 20:1: τί τὸ ἀδίκημά μου καὶ τί ἡμάρτηκα ἐνώπιον τοῦ πατρός σου; explicitly for offences against one's neighbour in Sir. 10:6 : ἐπὶ παντὶ ἀδικήματι μὴ μηνιάσῃς τῷ πλησίον; 28:2 : ἄφες ἀδίκημα τῷ πλησίον σου; and more generally in ep. Jer., 53 : οὐδὲ μὴ ῥύσωνται ἀδίκημα. ⁵

The word ἀδίκημα is plentiful in Josephus and Philo. It denotes for Josephus "action contrary to the law." But we could not say that this is meant only in the social sense. Thus, for the Pharisees it is an ἀδίκημα or violation of the Law for the priests at a time of famine to eat meal during the feast of unleavened bread (Ant., 3, 321). Again, in Bell., 1, 35 there is reference to ταῖς ὑπερβολαῖς τῶν ἀδικημάτων of Bacchides because he executes the unlawful orders of Antiochus. We may also refer to the acts of violence of Felix against the Jews (Ant., 20, 182); to the real wrong done to Joseph by his brothers (Ant., 2, 145); to the supposed wrong done to Saul by David (Ant., 6, 209); and then to such concrete matters as the theft of the cup (Ant., 2, 140; cf. also Philo Jos., 216); theft, plunder and robbery (Bell., 2, 581); perjury (Ant., 8, 20); unjust violations of agreements (Ant., 13, 265). All these correspond to the basic meaning indicated.

In contrast, we might refer to the passages in Jos. and Philo in which, as in Bell., 4, 150, τὰ εἰς ἀνθρώπους ἀδικήματα is opposed to ὕβρις ἐπὶ τὸ θεῖον; but here the reference is to violation of the cultus. Similarly, in Philo Decal., 2 there is distinction between τὰ πρὸς τὸ θεῖον ἀνοσιουργήματα and τὰ πρὸς ἀλλήλους ἀδικήματα, as also in Conf. Ling., 114 between τὰ ἀνθρωπεῖα ἀδικήματα and then successively ἀσέβεια and ἀθεότης; yet here again this amounts to little more than the difference between the two tables of the Law. If adultery is called τὸ μέγιστον τῶν ἀδικημάτων in Jos., 44, the same is said of the ὀλιγωρία of God in Spec. Leg., II, 38. For Philo

---

οὐδὲ ἀδικημάτων ἔχειν λόγον φασί τινες. But occasionally he can refer without difficulty to ἀκούσια ἀδικήματα, as in Poster. C., 48; Deus Imm., 128; Agric., 180. Indicative of the conscious differentiation between ἀδίκημα and ἀτύχημα is the textual alteration in Polyb., III, 20, 6, where Cod. C has ἀδικήματος for ἀτυχήματος.

² Cf. Moulton-Milligan, 10; Preisigke Wört., 23.

³ Concerning the prepositions (πρός τινα, εἴς τι, περί τι) linked with ἀδίκημα in classical usage, and other material not very relevant to the NT, cf. Liddell-Scott, s.v. under I; Pass.-Cr., s.v.

⁴ Mas. מִשְׁפָּטַיִךְ is vocalised by J. Wellhausen, Kl. Proph. (1898)³: מִשְׁפְּטַיִךְ. On this, cf. the comment of H. H. Schaeder : "That he is right in this may be seen with certainty from the corresponding אֹיְבֵךְ = אִיְבֵךְ. The translation of משפטיך by τὰ ἀδικήματά σου in the LXX is an attempt at exact rendering on the basis of an obvious misinterpretation of the relevant consonants expressed in the Mas. pointing."

⁵ Within the OT no distinction can be made between the religious and the social sense (Cr.-Kö., 339).

μοιχεία is self-evidently a despising of God. In Conf. Ling., 15, he can also describe sins εἰς τὸ θεῖον as ἀδικήματα. In Deus Imm., 138 it is parallel with ἁμαρτήματα. Ἀδίκημα is, in fact, used quite generally for sinful action. Thus in Decal., 173 ἐπιθυμία is ἡ τῶν ἀδικημάτων πηγή; in Spec. Leg., I, 229 the high-priest intercedes for the ἀμνηστία ἀδικημάτων; in I, 243 the Law comforts those who do not walk τὴν τῶν ἀδικημάτων ὁδόν. Indeed, Philo's pronouncements concerning universal sinfulness seem to make particular use of this expression. Thus in Ebr., 73, the life of man is filled with an overflowing mass of ἀδικήματα; and in Det. Pot. Ins., 170 the soul needs κάθαρσις τῶν ἀμυθήτων ἀδικημάτων. In Leg. All., II, 107 they occur οὐκ ἄνευ πανουργίας τῆς ἐσχάτης. The viewpoint (Decal., 91) that ἀθεότης is the πηγὴ πάντων ἀδικημάτων might also be described as dominant in Philo. God is wroth (Abr., 40 f.) concerning it; it is subject (Jos., 170) to the judgment τῆς ἐφόρου δίκης τῶν ἀνθρωπείων πραγμάτων; the Judge of all things (Abr., 133) condemns the Sodomites because of it. Ἀδικήματα (Conf. Ling., 30) stand in contrast to the ἑστὼς ἀεὶ θεός. But God redeems from them too (Rer. Div. Her., 186). Gratitude and reverence (Deus Imm., 7) are not affected by them. Finally, an important part is played by the psychological consideration that συνείδησις convicts concerning them (Det. Pot. Ins., 146; Spec. Leg., II, 49). Their beginning is ἡ σωμάτων ἡδονή (Op. Mund., 152). They produce (Sobr., 5) an intoxication which leads to possession. They overwhelm the soul and throw the νοῦς overboard (Agric., 89).

B. ἀδίκημα in the NT.

The word ἀδίκημα occurs only three times in the NT. It has the same meaning as that stated under → ἀδικεῖν (B). In Rev. 18:5 it is said of Babylon: ἐκολλήθησαν αὐτῆς αἱ ἁμαρτίαι ἄρχι τοῦ οὐρανοῦ καὶ ἐμνημόνευσεν ὁ θεὸς τὰ ἀδικήματα αὐτῆς. In this case, as in the LXX (→ 162), it is synon. with ἁμαρτίαι. Yet the LXX text of Ιερ. 28:6 (Mas. 51:6), of which there is a reminiscence in the image and in which we read ἐν τῇ ἀδικίᾳ αὐτῆς, undergoes an alteration by the use of the plur. ἀδικήματα, which serves to emphasise much more strongly than the abstract ἀδικία the blatant concreteness of countless open and unlawful misdeeds. [6]

In Ac. 24:20 (Paul before Felix) we read: οὗτοι εἰπάτωσαν τί εὗρον ἀδίκημα. Here what is meant is violation of the Jewish law. Again, in Ac. 18:14 (Gallio to the Jews) we have: εἰ μὲν ἦν ἀδίκημά τι ἢ ῥᾳδιούργημα πονηρόν. The meaning here is conscious and criminal violation from the standpoint of Roman law, whereas ῥᾳδιούργημα signifies frivolous action. [7]

Schrenk

ἀδόκιμος → δόκιμος.   ἀδύνατος, ἀδυνατέω → δύναμαι.

ἄδω, ᾠδή

---

† ἄδω.

"To sing." [1] a. Intr. LXX ψ 56:8 etc.; Herm. s., 9, 11, 5; Tat. 1, 1; 22, 2. b. Trans. LXX Ex. 15:1; Nu. 21:1 etc. "To sing of" (τινι): Ex. 15:21; ψ 67:5; Philo Agric., 79. "To celebrate something or someone in song": Tat., 33, 2; Ign. Eph., 4, 1; Mg., 1, 2;

---

[6] Zn. Apk., 572.
[7] Cf. ibid., 658.
ἄδω κτλ. J. Kroll, *Die christliche Hymnodik bis z. Cl. Al.* (1921); "Die Hymnendichtung des frühen Christentums," *Antike*, 2 (1926), 258-281.
[1] Pass.-Cr.; Liddell-Scott, s.v.

Dg., 11, 6. In this sense ᾄδειν is the opposite of λέγειν, as in Philo Som., I, 256 (cf. Xenoph. Cyr., III, 3, 55), though occasionally it can be used for λέγειν (Max Tyr., XXXV, 3), just as *carmen* can mean a formula as well as a song, and conversely, *dicere* can also mean "to sing." [2] Between the spoken word and song the distinction is fluid. As "to sing," ᾄδειν approximates to ὑμνῆσαι, ψάλλειν and αἰνεῖν. Indeed, it can be used interchangeably with these terms : Themist. Or., 1 (4a); Epict. Diss., I, 16, 15 f.; Ael. Arist. Or., 50 (26), 38 ff. (II, 435, 11 ff., Keil); LXX 1 Ch. 16:7-10; ψ 20:13; and later Or. c. Cels., 8, 67.

In the NT we have the phrases : ᾄδειν (τὴν) ᾠδήν (Rev. 5:9; 14:3; 15:3), and also : ᾄδειν ... τῷ θεῷ (τῷ κυρίῳ) (Col. 3:16; Eph. 5:19). The same idea is also conveyed in Revelation by λέγειν, as in Rev. 5:13 : λέγειν φωνῇ μεγάλῃ (cf. also λαλεῖν in Eph. 5:19). There is no distinction from ψάλλειν in Eph. 5:19 (Just. Dial., 74, 3).

† ᾠδή (→ ψαλμός, ὕμνος).

a. "Song" as such, or b. "a song" of any kind, accompanied by κιθάρα and αὐλός. [1] In the LXX what is meant is almost always, though not fundamentally, a "religious song" (or the ᾠδὴ πάτριος in 3 Macc. 6:32). Hence the very free alternation between ᾠδή, ψαλμός and ὕμνος. ψ 47 tit B ψαλμὸς ᾠδῆς, S ᾠδὴ ψαλμοῦ. In Philo Agric., 81 there is first mention of παράλιος ᾠδή, then ὕμνος, in relation to Ex. 15:1 ff. Cf. Epict. Diss., I, 16, 15 ff.; Philo Flacc., 22; Const. Ap., III, 7, 7; Mart. Mt., 25.

In the NT there is still no precise differentiation between ᾠδή, ψαλμός, and ὕμνος, e.g., in Col. 3:16 or Eph. 5:19, in contrast to a later time, when ᾠδή (*canticum*) came to be used only for biblical songs (apart from the Psalms) used in the liturgy. From the NT passages we may gather the following elements in the concept of the Christian ᾠδή as also illustrated and confirmed from other sources.

a. ᾠδαί are the cultic songs of the community. They are not sung by the individual, but by the community gathered for worship. In this respect they differ from the personal songs of the Gnostics most clearly illustrated in the Odes of Solomon. Of a piece with this is the anonymity of the early authors, as also the attachment to OT tradition. Only in the 2nd century are the authors sometimes mentioned. In the Didascalia, 2, p. 5, 29 f. we can still read : "If thou desirest hymns, thou hast the Psalms of David."

b. The ᾠδή is inspired. [2] This is shown by the epithet πνευματικός, though this does also indicate more generally its religious character. Hymns are to be numbered with heavenly things (Act. Thom., 76; Just. Dial., 118b). With the inspiration of hymns is linked their improvisation, e.g., in 1 C. 14:26 (cf. Ac. 4:24); Tert. adv. Marc., 5, 8; Apolog., 39, 18.

c. In virtue of its inspiration, the ᾠδή is not regarded as the "attempt at a fairly adequate expression of the lofty religious mood, ... at a representation of the new disposition of soul," [3] but as λόγος τοῦ Χριστοῦ (Col. 3:16). It is also a

---

[2] F. J. Dölger, *Sol Salutis*[2] (1925), 124. Cf. Act. Thom., 6.
ᾠ δ ή. [1] Pass.
[2] The character of inspiration is also indicated in the τῇ καρδίᾳ ὑμῶν of Eph. 5:19, or ἐν τῇ χάριτι ᾄδοντες ἐν ταῖς καρδίαις ὑμῶν of Col. 3:16. N. v. Arseniew, "Das innere Lied der Seele," ARW, 22 (1924), 266-283; on inspired singing, cf. E. Norden, *Geburt des Kindes* (1924), 104; H. Schlier, *Rel.gesch. Unters. zu d. Ignbriefen* (1929), 144 f.
[3] J. Kroll, in *Antike*, 2 (1926), 258.

mode of the Word in which Christ makes Himself heard. Cf. the fine expression in Ign. Eph., 4, 1: Ἰησοῦς Χριστὸς ᾄδεται. This does not exclude a participation of the members of the community. On the contrary, Christ finds utterance in the hearts of members of the community (ᾄδοντες ἐν ταῖς καρδίαις ὑμῶν τῷ θεῷ) who then express with their lips what is said by Him in the heart. The λόγος τοῦ Χριστοῦ means that ᾠδαὶ πνευματικαί are mostly songs about Christ, or about the saving acts of God enacted in Him. An example may be seen in 1 Tm. 3:16.

d. The distinction between this λόγος τοῦ Χριστοῦ and the λόγος τοῦ κυρίου which the apostle imparts in his *kerygma* and then in his διδαχή consists in the fact that in ᾠδαί the community mutually instructs and admonishes itself (διδά-σκοντες καὶ νουθετοῦντες ἑαυτοὺς ψαλμοῖς κτλ. Col. 3:16; or according to Eph. 5:19 it shares in λαλοῦντες ἑαυτοῖς ψαλμοῖς καὶ ὕμνοις καὶ ᾠδαῖς πνευ-ματικαῖς ᾄδοντες καὶ ψάλλοντες). The spiritual song of the Church is the Word of Christ uttered in the cultus in the form of alternating and reciprocal address. In this sense it fills the community with the Spirit. [4]

e. It is conceived as an eschatological process in the Apocalypse, e.g., 5:9; 14:3; 15:3, where there is also reference to an ᾠδὴ καινή. If it was true in Judaism: "Israel will sing a new song only in the days of the Messiah in praise of the wonders of His redemption," [5] these days have now come for the Christian community, and there sounds out on earth as in heaven thanksgiving and praise for the fulfilled wonders of God.

Schlier

ἄζυμος → ζύμη.

ἀήρ

According to the ancient conception of the earth, the sphere of the air reaches to the moon, where the ethereal region of the stars commences. The Greek made a distinction between the impure element of air and the purer ether, thus finding in the former a place of abode for imperfect spirits. [1] Like all animism, popular Greek belief peopled the air with all kinds of spirits, who had to be taken into account. Later Judaism sharply distinguished between angels and demons, and found in the air the abode of the latter. [2] In line with early Christian thinking, Paul links with this the idea of an organised kingdom under the single ruler Satan: ἀμαρ-τίαις ... ἐν αἷς ποτε περιεπατήσατε ... κατὰ τὸν ἄρχοντα τῆς ἐξουσίας τοῦ ἀέρος (Eph. 2:2). [3]

---

[4] The singing of the community is set on a level with prophecy in Conf. Cypriani, 17 (*v*. Dölger², *op. cit.*, 132 f.).

[5] Str.-B., III, 801.

ἀ ή ρ. [1] Yet there are many Greek conceptions. On this as on what follows → δαίμων. So far as concerns popular belief, it is worth noting that even to-day evil spirits are still called ἀερικά in Greece, F. Pfister, *Philologus*, 69 (1910), 427.

[2] Str.-B., IV, 515 ff.

[3] There is no kingdom of evil demons in the air according to Judaism. Test. B. 3:4: τοῦ ἀερίου πνεύματος τοῦ βελίαρ, is textually uncertain, and we cannot adduce Asc. Jes., → διάβολος. *v*. the Comm. *ad loc.*, and O. Everling, *D. pl. Angelologie u. Dämonologie* (1888), 105 ff., 111 f.; M. Dibelius, *Geisterwelt im Glauben d. Pls.* (1909), 156 f.; G. Kurze, *Engels- u. Teufelsglaube d. Ap. Pls.* (1915), 86/91.

Because of its middle position, the air in 1 Th. 4:17: εἰς ἀπάντησιν τοῦ κυρίου εἰς ἀέρα, is the sphere where believers will meet Christ on his coming to set up on earth the millennial kingdom. [4] We find a proverbial use of the term in 1 C. 14:9: ἔσεσθε γὰρ εἰς ἀέρα λαλοῦντες = "to speak into the air" (of those who speak with tongues). [5] In the declaration of Paul in 1 C. 9:26: οὕτως πυκτεύω ὡς οὐκ ἀέρα δέρων, the metaphor seems to imply that Paul is not engaged in sham conflict but in a true fight, [6] or that he is not striking aimlessly but hitting the target. [7] Both are linguistically possible. [8]

Foerster

ἀθανασία → θάνατος.

† ἀθέμιτος

Extra- and post-Attic = ἀθέμιστος. Opp. to θεμι(σ)τός, whence "contrary to statute," "illegal," or "criminal," always with the idea of a higher will. a. Cultic. νεκρὰ σώματα are ἀθέμιτα before Hera and Demeter, P. Turin, I, 2, 22 (2nd century B.C.). To the Jews unlawful sacrifices (2 Macc. 6:5), eating swine's flesh (2 Macc. 7:1), and leaving the doors of the temple open at night (Jos. Ap., 2, 119) are ἀθέμιτον. b. Moral and Religious. In this sphere we may refer to ξενοκτονίαι ἀθέμιστοι, Dion. Hal. Ant. Rom., 1, 41; to the smell of a roasted child, Jos. Bell., 6, 209; to prayer without the fulfilment of duty, Xenoph. Cyrop., I, 6, 6 (synon. παρὰ τοὺς τῶν θεῶν θεσμούς and παράνομος); to εὐχαὶ ἀθέμιτοι, Plut. Aem., 19 (I, 265c); to ungodly speech, 2 Macc. 10, 34; to shameless sexual intercourse, Vett. Val., 43, 27 Kroll; to anger, 1 Cl., 63, 2; to the works of Antichrist, Did., 16, 4. There is no sharp distinction between a. and b. Of persons: Orph. Frg., 232, Kern: λύσις προγόνων ἀθεμίστων. [1] ἀθέμιτόν ἐστιν with infin.: Plut. Sept. Sap. Conv., 5 (II, 150 f.); Jos. Bell., 1, 650; Ap., 2, 119.

In 1 Pt. 4:3 we find ἀθέμιτοι εἰδωλολατρίαι numbered with ἀσέλγειαι, ἐπιθυμίαι etc. as truly pagan evils. [2] In Ac. 10:25, with a reference back to the Pharisaic standpoint overcome in Christianity, we read: ἀθέμιτόν ἐστιν ἀνδρὶ Ἰουδαίῳ ... προσέρχεσθαι ἀλλοφύλῳ.

Oepke

---

[4] → ἀπάντησις. Cf. E. Peterson in ZSTh, 8 (1930), 682 ff. It follows from the context that the reference is to the coming of the millennial reign.
[5] For examples, v. Pr.-Bauer, s.v. ἀήρ.
[6] So Bchm. K., ad loc.
[7] So Joh. W., 1 K., ad loc.
[8] On the one side Theophil. Ad. Autol., III, 2 (MPG, VI, 1121b): τρόπῳ γάρ τινι οἱ τὰ ἄδηλα συγγράφοντες ἀέρα δέρουσι, and on the other Greg. Naz. Hom., XXI, 389 (MPG, XXXV, 1088b): τῶν ἀθλητῶν τοῖς ἀπείροις, οἳ τὸν ἀέρα πλείω παίοντες ἢ τὰ σώματα ...
ἀθέμιτος. Glotta, 4 (1913), 23, n. 2, 27; R. Hirzel, *Themis, Dike und Verwandtes* (1907), 1-56 (contestable).
[1] Tannery, *Revue de Philol.*, 23 (1899), 126 ff.: expiation of the wrong done in previous births.
[2] Cf. Jos. Bell., 1, 650: offence against the prohibition of images.

ἄθεος → θεός.

---

† ἄθεσμος

"Apart from or contrary to statute," "illegal," "impious" (rarely = *exlex,* Hesych.): in a general sense in Plut. Caes., 10 (I, 712b); more specifically of neglected offerings, Sext. Emp. Pyr. Hyp., III, 220, 223; unlawfull sexual intercourse: ἄθεσμοι γάμοι, Iambl. Vit. Pyth., 17, 78; μίξεις ἄθεσμοι, Philo Spec. Leg., II, 50; unsuccessful attacks on the Jews as ἄθεσμος πρόθεσις, 3 Macc. 5:12; ἄθεσμοι αἰκίαι, 3 Macc. 6:26; or the foods not allowed to Levites, Jos. Bell., 7, 264: τράπεζα ἄθεσμος. The word is not really popular but a term in philosophical ethics. Instances in the pap. (P. Oxy., 129, 8; P. Lond., 1678, 5) are late (6th cent. A.D.) and probably stand under Christian influence. Of persons: Sib., 5, 309: ἄνδρες ἄδικοι καὶ ἄθεσμοι. Subst.: "the malefactor," Philo Praem. Poen., 126.

In the NT it occurs only as a subst. and is peculiar to 2 Pt., being used in 2:7 of the Sodomites and in 3:17 of heretical leaders.

Oepke

ἀθετέω → τίθημι.

ἀθλέω, συναθλέω, ἄθλησις
(→ ἀγών).

ἀθλέω, "to engage in competition or conflict," whence later ἄθλησις, συναθλέω, often used metaphorically in diatribes. [1] In the LXX it is found only in later writings such as 4 Macc., where it denotes the conflict of martyrs. In the NT it is found only in the Pauline writings.

ἀθλέω occurs in 2 Tm. 2:5: ἐὰν δὲ καὶ ἀθλῇ τις, οὐ στεφανοῦται ἐὰν μὴ νομίμως ἀθλήσῃ. The fight in which the leader of the community is engaged demands not only extreme exertion and readiness for sacrifice, but also discipline and ordered conduct (νομίμως). [2]

συναθλέω is found twice in Phil., both times in connection with the Gospel, which is the source of the community and of opposition to it. In 1:27 those who fight together are companions in suffering, in 4:3 they are labourers together. The Gospel triumphs in the passion and action of the συναθλοῦντες.

ἄθλησις is used in Hb. 10:32 f.: πολλὴν ἄθλησιν ὑπεμείνατε παθημάτων. The final θεατριζόμενοι evokes the image of the crowd of spectators in the arena watching the spectacle of abuse and persecution. The image and reality merge into one another, as in 4 Macc. 17:14 ff.

ἀθλητής is the term used by Ignatius in his epistle to Polycarp to describe the leader of the community who is tested by battle and equal to every demand or conflict. The burden of the many rests on his strong shoulders (1, 3). For him, as for Timothy,

---

ἀ θ λ έ ω κτλ. [1] Themist. Or., 17 (213d). Wis. 4:2; Philo Congr., 165; Spec. Leg., II, 183; Jos., 82. For important examples, → ἀγών, 135.
[2] The overcoming of the world in 2 Cl., 20, 2 (ἀθλοῦμεν καὶ γυμναζόμεθα); flight from it in Cl. Al. Strom., VII, 11, 67, 4.

sobriety is a special duty (2, 3). He must defy all blows like an anvil : μεγάλου ἐστὶν ἀθλητοῦ τὸ δέρεσθαι καὶ νικᾶν (3, 1). In 1 Cl., 5, 1, in a passage which in the style of Hb. 11 speaks of the persecution of the δίκαιοι by the ζῆλος, [3] the apostles are called ἀθληταί who ἕως θανάτου ἤθλησαν. [4] The obvious decisive step is made in the Acts of Thomas (39), in which Christ Himself, our ἀθλητής, is the model of the perfect athlete.

Stauffer

---

† ἀΐδιος

"Everlasting," "eternal." Ps.-Plat. Def., 411a: ἀΐδιον τὸ κατὰ πάντα χρόνον καὶ πρότερον ὂν καὶ νῦν μὴ ἐφθαρμένον. Frequent in Arist., e.g., Cael., II, 1, p. 283b, 26 ff. of the οὐρανός : ἀΐδιος, ἀρχὴν ... καὶ τελευτὴν οὐκ ἔχων; Eth. Nic., VI, 3, p. 1139b, 23 f.: τὰ γὰρ ἐξ ἀνάγκης ὄντα ἁπλῶς πάντα ἀΐδια, τὰ δ᾽ ἀΐδια ἀγένητα καὶ ἄφθαρτα. It is of the essence of the ἀϊδιότης (subst. in Aristot. and Philo) to be without beginning or end. The term ἀΐδιος is very important in Philo. God is ἀΐδιος because He is ἀγένητος καὶ ἄφθαρτος (Jos., 265) and ὢν ὄντως (Spec. Leg., I, 28): Spec. Leg., IV, 73; Virt., 204; ἀΐδιος can be used for God without θεός : Spec. Leg., I, 20, II, 166; Decal., 41, 60 and 64 etc. [1] The Logos, too, is ἀΐδιος (Plant., 8, 18), as also everything which is ἀόρατον καὶ νοητόν. Sometimes → αἰώνιος is used with ἀΐδιος as a synon.: λόγος δὲ ὁ ἀΐδιος θεοῦ τοῦ αἰωνίου (Plant., 8). ἀΐδιος is also used with ζωή (Fug., 97). On inscriptions we find : τὸν ἀΐδιον χρόνον, Ditt. Syll., [3] 46; ἀΐδία ἀναγραφά, ibid., 622 B, 10; δωρεὰ ἀΐδιος, ibid., 672, 10 f. etc. We find it used of God in Corp. Herm., passim; Stob. Ecl., I, 34, 6 W; Julian Ep., 89b, p. 128, 14 Bidez-Cumont ; Sib., V, 66, VIII, 429. In the LXX it is a philosophical rather than popular term found only in Wis. 7:26 : ἀπαύγασμα γάρ ἐστι φωτὸς ἀΐδίου (of wisdom ; on φῶς ἀΐδιον cf. Clem. Al. Paed., I, 6, 32) and 4 Macc. 10:15 S : τὸν ἀΐδιον (AR ἀοίδιμον) τῶν εὐσεβῶν βίον.

In the NT ἀΐδιος in the sense of "eternal" occurs only in two passages. The first is R. 1:20 in a context which reminds us of Stoic ways of thought and also of Philo : τὰ γὰρ ἀόρατα αὐτοῦ ... τοῖς ποιήμασιν νοούμενα καθορᾶται, ἥ τε ἀΐδιος αὐτοῦ δύναμις καὶ θειότης (His eternal power). The second is Jd. 6: εἰς κρίσιν μεγάλης ἡμέρας δεσμοῖς ἀΐδίοις ὑπὸ ζόφον τετήρηκεν (in everlasting chains). Cf. for this expression Jos. Bell., 6, 434 : δεσμοῖς αἰωνίοις (of the lifelong imprisonment of John) and Philo Aet. Mund., 75 : αἰώνιος δεσμός (of the eternal bond which holds the cosmos together).

In the apostolic fathers we find ἀΐδιος only in Ign. Eph., 19, 3 : εἰς καινότητα ἀΐδίου ζωῆς.

Sasse

---

[3] → ἀγών, n. 19.
[4] Cf. also Test. of the 40 Mart., 1, 1 (ἆθλον); Eus. Hist. Eccl., VII, 12 : ἀγῶνα διηθλη-κέναι; the Index to Eus. (ed. Schwartz, II, 3, p. 159), s.v. ἀθλητής.
ἀ ΐ δ ι ο ς. Cr.-Kö., 80.
[1] Cf. Index of H. Leisegang in Cohn-Wendland, VII,[1] s.v.

---

† αἰδώς (→ αἰσχύνη).

A. The Greek Terms for Shame and Disgrace (αἰδώς, αἰσχύνη).

a. αἰδώς was originally a basic concept in the Greek understanding of existence. It became rare in the time of Hellenism, [1] but was brought back into use by the late Stoics. αἰδεῖσθαι was always in current use. αἰδώς comes on man because his existence stands in more than individual connections which surround and bind it with divine authority. It is regard for these connections, the bashful fear of breaking them. It is his attitude in face of the δεινόν, the awful, wherever and however manifested. It is dread of λίαν, of the violation of the μέτρον. Its opposite is ὕβρις. It is thus "reverence" before God, the priest, or an oath, so that αἰδώς can mean the same as εὐσέβεια and αἰδεῖσθαι as σέβεσθαι. It is respect for the one who is visited by the → χάρις of God and who is thus αἰδοῖος and δεινός. It is reverence for the king, for singers and orators, for parents and elders, for ξένοι and ἱκέται, the meaning here being much the same as that of → ἔλεος. It is respect for the law of hospitality and for the sanctity of the home and marriage. Above all, it expresses respect for the → δίκη which binds society together, for the → πόλις and its → νόμος. Hesiod complains (Op., 197 ff.) that Αἰδώς and Νέμεσις have left men, and the myth of Protagoras (Plat. Prot., 322b ff.) tells us that Zeus through Hermes sends Αἰδώς and Δίκη to men ἵν' εἶεν πόλεων κόσμοι τε καὶ δεσμοὶ φιλίας συναγωγοί. In what is said about education, instruction in αἰδώς plays a most important part, the Stoics setting the → κόσμος, → φύσις, or the → λόγος either in place of or alongside the πόλις. αἰδεῖσθαι can thus be synon. with τιμᾶν, and to the extent that in all αἰδώς there is an element of fear it is used as a parallel of δεδιέναι or φοβεῖσθαι (→ φόβος), by which it is later delimited (Plat. Euthyphr., 12a ff.; Arist. Eth. Nic., IV, 15, p. 1128 f., 10 ff. etc.), just as in definitions of the Platonic and Stoic school αἰδώς is defined as a specific form of φόβος or εὐλάβεια (e.g., ἀδοξίας or ὀρθοῦ ψόγου, cf. Ps.-Plat. Def., 412c; v. Arnim, III, 101, 29 ff., 105, 15 ff., 107, 20 ff.). Yet these definitions are artificial and do not correspond to the older usage of which living examples may still be found in Musonius, Epictetus and Philo.

The true development of the use of αἰδώς corresponds to that of Greek ethics, namely, that terms which first denoted the position of the individual in society or in specific situations came increasingly to describe the ἕξις of the individual and therefore his attitude towards himself, his disposition of soul. One can thus have αἰδώς without being confronted by an αἰδοῖον. Or rather it is in such confrontation that αἰδώς comes to expression. This is a very early conception, for already from the time of Homer αἰδώς is used for *pudor* or the "feeling of shame." [2] Yet there is a widening of usage, and αἰδώς also comes to signify a

---

α ἰ δ ώ ς. Trench, 42-47; R. Schultz, ΑΙΔΩΣ (Diss. Rostock, 1910); U. v. Wilamowitz-Moellendorff, Euripides Herakles, II (1895), 129 f.

[1] In prose we do not find αἰδώς between 300 B.C. and the time of the Empire (Nägeli, 16); αἰδεῖσθαι belongs to more carefully chosen speech (*ibid.*, 57). In the pap. αἰδώς is rare, αἰδεῖσθαι being more frequent, cf. Preisigke Wört.

[2] Especially as applied to women; cf. Hdt., I, 8 : ἅμα δὲ κιθῶνι ἐκδυομένῳ συνεκδύεται καὶ τὴν αἰδῶ γυνή. This has its basis in the fact that αἰδοῖα in the sexual sense are bearers of a δεινόν, but also in the fact that the fate which has overtaken one is a δεινόν which one is reluctant to display publicly. καλύπτεσθαι is frequently the symptom of αἰδώς.

feeling of honour and becomes synon. with → σωφροσύνη. An attempt at differentiation is made in Arist. Eth. Nic., II, 7, p. 1108a, 30 ff.; IV, 15, p. 1128b, 10 ff., but the later Stoa again uses the terms *promiscue*. [3] αἰδώς is thus the "attitude of the worthy man," and it is characteristic of the Greek conception of existence that αἰδώς is closely linked with → ἐλευθερία and therefore with παρρησία (Philo Jos.,107 and 222). Its opposite is ἀναίδεια, the shamelessness of the robber of temples, the lack of shame of the avaricious, or even sometimes θάρσος (→ θαρρέω) in the sense of insolence.

b. At an early stage αἰδώς came to be linked with αἰσχύνη, from which it was originally distinct [4] both in signification and also etymologically. [5] The Stoic distinction between αἰδώς as φόβος ἐπὶ προσδοκίᾳ ψόγου and αἰσχύνη as φόβος ἐπ' αἰσχρῷ πεπραγμένῳ (v. Arnim, III, 101, 34 ff.), repeated by John of Damascus in *De Fide Orthodoxa*, 2, 15, does not really correspond to the proper usage, in which αἰδώς, too, can signify shame after an action, and αἰσχύνη can mean shame at doing something as well as having done it, and indeed need not be related to an action at all, but may be motivated by a specific αἶσχος, e.g., a lowly origin or a humiliating destiny. For αἰσχύνη in the subjective sense is fear of the αἶσχος or αἰσχρόν, or shame because of it. The αἶσχος is that which is repugnant, primarily in the external sense; the αἰσχρόν is that which in δόξα must be regarded as disgraceful in words and deeds or in appearances and afflictions. Thus αἰσχύνη is fear of the αἰσχρόν and therefore of one's δόξα. [6] If αἰδώς might be described as originally a religious term, αἰσχύνη might be regarded as a sociological. Yet we can understand how the two came to be equated. For the δεινόν to which αἰδώς refers is primarily found in society. Again, the Sophists reduced religious concepts to the level of sociology by interpreting religious bonds as social. Hence the verbs especially soon came to be used interchangeably. [7] Yet the original distinction may still be seen in the fact that αἰσχύνη can have the objective meaning of "disgrace" as well as the subjective of "shame," so that it may well be identical with the αἶσχος or ὄνειδος which brings shame to the αἰσχυνόμενος. [8] Similarly, αἰσχύνω, which originally means "to disfigure" or "to make repugnant," can also mean "to bring into disgrace." Since the shame which clings to a man may be caused by his own shameful action, it seems as though

---

[3] In Epict. and M. Ant. we often find αἰδήμων with σώφρων, εὐσχήμων, κόσμιος, πιστός, γενναῖος etc. to denote a worthy moral attitude.

[4] Cf. Boisacq, *s.v.*

[5] This is seen already in the fact 1. that there can be no derivatives from αἶσχος corresponding to αἰδοῖος or αἰδέσιμος from αἰδώς; 2. that there is no analogy in the αἰδώς root to the act. αἰσχύνειν. Attention may also be drawn to the fact that Αἰδώς as a goddess has a cult, whereas Αἰσχύνη is never honoured cultically, though sometimes described as θεός. The difference was plainly detected by Demetrius in Περὶ ἑρμηνείας, 114 (p. 27, Raderm).

[6] There is frequent reference to λώβη or ὄνειδος as the object of αἰσχύνη. In contrast Democrit. (Diels, II, 78, 14 f.) admonishes ἑαυτὸν αἰσχύνεσθαι, but for him αἰσχύνεσθαι and αἰδεῖσθαι coincide in the opposite way (Diels, II, 114, 1 ff.). Cf. also Hierocl. Carm. Aur., p. 59, 1 ff., Mullach.

[7] It is also impossible to make any *a priori* distinction between ἀναιδής and ἀναίσχυντος. On ἀναισχυντία cf. Theophr. Char., 9.

[8] Here we have αἶσχος where previously αἶσχος was used. The subst. αἰσχύνη comes into use only in the 5th century (cf. U. v. Wilamowitz-Moellendorff, *op. cit.*, 281). It is formed from αἰσχύνεσθαι, and originally has the meaning of τὸ αἰσχύνεσθαι.

αἰσχύνη can sometimes mean "ignominy" or an "ignominious act," though this rendering does not correspond precisely to the Greek conception.

B. The Hellenistic Jewish Use of αἰδώς.

In the literature of Hellenistic Judaism we find αἰδώς (or αἰδεῖσθαι) particularly in Philo in the Greek and esp. the later Stoic sense. In the LXX αἰδώς, for which there is no Hebrew equivalent — יראת־יהוה perhaps corresponds to the original sense in passages like Gn. 20:11; Is. 11, 2; Prv. 1:7 — is rather strangely found only in 3 Macc. 1:19 (= *pudor*) and 4:5 ("respect" for age). In Sir. 29:14 we have αἰσχύνη instead (no Heb.). In Jos. Ant., 9, 226, again, αἰσχύνη (τοῦ συμβεβηκότος δεινοῦ) is used for αἰδώς (opp. παρρησία). αἰδεῖσθαι is more frequent. Prv. 24:38 uses it as a fairly suitable rendering of הַכֵּר־פָּנִים, the obj. being πρόσωπον. In 28:21, however, αἰσχύνεσθαι is used instead, and it is in fact mostly replaced either by αἰσχύνεσθαι (Job 32:21; 34:19) or φοβεῖσθαι. Elsewhere with no Heb. source it is used for fear of God (4 Macc. 12:11, 13); reverence for the king (4 Macc. 3:12, καταιδ.); respect for age (4 Macc. 5:6); respect for what is δίκαιον or fear of its violation (2 Macc. 4:34, cf. Jdt. 9:3); fear of one's enemies, φοβεῖσθαι being a parallel (1 Macc. 4:8, and cf. δειλοῦσθαι). In other words, it bears the Greek sense. Typical Stoic uses of αἰδήμων may be seen in 2 Macc. 15:12 and 4 Macc. 8:3 (with γενναῖος). A common word in the LXX is ἀναιδής = insolent, often with πρόσωπον, ὀφθαλμός or ψυχή.

C. The Early Christian Use of αἰδώς.

In the NT αἰδώς occurs for certain only in 1 Tm. 2:9 in the admonition to wives ἐν καταστολῇ κοσμίῳ, μετὰ αἰδοῦς καὶ σωφροσύνης κοσμεῖν ἑαυτάς. It thus denotes the "modest demeanour" of the wife, as in Greek, and the linking with σωφροσύνη and κοσμεῖν is wholly in line with Greek usage. [9] The older sense of αἰδώς may also be seen in the K reading of Hb. 12:28 : λατρεύειν μετὰ αἰδοῦς καὶ εὐλαβείας. [10] αἰδεῖσθαι is not found at all, → ἐντρέπεσθαι being used instead in Mk. 12:6 and par.; Lk. 18:2, 4; Hb. 12:9. Ign., Eph., 11, 1 and R., 9, 2 prefers αἰσχύνεσθαι. The word αἰδώς is not found at all in the apostolic fathers, αἰσχύνη being used instead in Did., 4, 11 and Barn., 19, 7. We find αἰδεσθῆναι in the Greek sense in 1 Cl., 21, 6 (τοὺς προηγουμένους) alongside ἐντραπῆναι (τὸν κύριον 'I. Χρ.) and τιμᾶν (τοὺς πρεσβυτέρους); and again in M. Pol., 9, 2 (τὴν ἡλικίαν = old age). The apologists use αἰδεῖσθαι more frequently, but αἰδώς occurs only in Athenagoras, 30, 2.

The most notable point, therefore, is that αἰδώς (like σωφροσύνη) does not really play any part in early Christianity. The reason for this is not merely that it had become a highbrow term, but especially that in Greek it had come to be used primarily of a ἕξις. The essence of the believer, however, is not a relationship to himself, a ἕξις or ἀρετή, but a being before God and towards his neighbour. To the extent that αἰδώς does, of course, include an attitude of respect and reserve towards others, this is very different from the Christian being towards the other. For the latter does not rest on a conception of the πόλις or κόσμος, but on the claim of the other as a neighbour. Hence the term αἰδώς is robbed of its fundamental significance ; αἰδήμων is replaced by πιστεύων and ἀγαπῶν.

Bultmann

---

[9] *v.* Dibelius, *ad loc.,* and Kaibel, Epigr. Gr., 648, 12.
[10] For μετὰ εὐλαβείας καὶ δέους in the H recension.

αἷμα, αἱματεκχυσία

αἷμα.

1. The basic physiological meaning is "blood," i.e., the blood of man. In this sense there is reference to the blood [1] of Jesus [2] in Jn. 19:34 : ἐξῆλθεν εὐθὺς αἷμα καὶ ὕδωρ. In the light of this fundamental sense the NT agrees with Jewish literature in describing man, according to the constituents of his body, as σάρξ καὶ αἷμα (→ σάρξ). Man is flesh and blood as a frail creature of earth in contrast to the majestic God : σὰρξ καὶ αἷμα οὐκ ἀπεκάλυψέν σοι ἀλλ᾽ ὁ πατήρ μου ὁ ἐν τοῖς οὐρανοῖς, Mt. 16:17. He is flesh and blood in his inability to oppose his own authority to the revelation of God : οὐ προσανεθέμην σαρκὶ καὶ αἵματι, Gl. 1:16. He is flesh and blood in his impotence and impermanence : σὰρξ καὶ αἷμα βασιλείαν θεοῦ κληρονομῆσαι οὐ δύναται, 1 C. 15:50; in his littleness in face of the spirit world : οὐκ ἔστιν ἡμῖν ἡ πάλη πρὸς αἷμα καὶ σάρκα, ἀλλὰ πρὸς τὰς ἀρχάς, Eph. 6:12; in his material and mortal nature : τὰ παιδία κεκοινώνηκεν αἵματος καὶ σαρκός, Hb. 2:14. Only in the last passage does the phrase seem designed to emphasise even more sharply the material aspect of man's earthly and corporeal nature. [3]

σάρξ καὶ αἷμα = בָּשָׂר וָדָם: an established Jewish (though not OT) term for man, whether as individual or species, in his creatureliness and distinction from God, Sir. 14:18 : ὡς φύλλον θάλλον ... οὕτως γενεὰ σαρκὸς καὶ αἵματος [דורות בשׂר ודם] ἡ μὲν τελευτᾷ, ἑτέρα δὲ γεννᾶται, Gr. En. 15:4; T. Ber., 7, 18 : מֶלֶךְ בָּשָׂר וָדָם a human as distinct from a divine king (cf. Mt. 18:23); S. Nu., 78 on 10:29; 84 on 10:35, 36 etc. [4] Greek authors who bring the words together think more of the actual constituents of the human body : Polyaen. Strat., III, 11, 1: ἀνθρώποις αἷμα καὶ σάρκας ἔχουσι; Porphyr. Abst., II, 46 : τῇ ἀκαθαρσίᾳ τῇ ἐκ σαρκῶν καὶ αἱμάτων; also Philo Rer. Div. Her., 57: αἵματι καὶ σαρκὸς ἡδονῇ ζώντων; Justin Dial., 135, 6 : τὸν μὲν ἐξ αἵματος καὶ σαρκός, τὸν δὲ ἐκ πίστεως, καὶ πνεύματος γεγεννημένον; Athenagoras, 27, 1: μόνον αἷμα καὶ σάρξ, οὐκέτι πνεῦμα καθαρόν; Herm. in Stob. Ecl., I, 68, p. 461, 12 W: πάσχουσιν (souls) σαρκὶ καὶ αἵματι βεβαπτισμέναι.

The notion that blood is the material of conception, "the bearer of the ongoing life of the species," [5] underlies the expression in Jn. 1:13 : ἐξ αἱμάτων ἐγεννήθησαν, "born of blood," the distinctive plur. αἵματα [6] indicating the union of the

---

αἷμα. Cr.-Kö., 82 ff.; W. Oesterley, DCG, I, 214 ff.; C. A. Beckwith, DAC, I, 153 f.; J. Hempel, RGG, I, 1154 ff.; H. L. Strack, Das Blut im Glauben u. Aberglauben der Menschheit,⁵/⁷ (1900); E. Bischoff, Das Blut im jüd. Schrifttum u. Brauch (1929); F. Rüsche, "Blut, Leben u. Seele" (Studien z. Geschichte u. Kultur des Altertums, Suppl. V, 1930), esp. 358 ff.
[1] On the early Christian ideas concerning the baptism of blood (martyrdom) which clustered around this verse, together with Lk. 12:50 and 1 Jn. 5:6, cf. F. J. Dölger, Antike u. Christentum, II (1930), 117 ff.
[2] In answer to Docetic ideas, Zn. Jn., 633.
[3] Rgg. Hb., 55, n. 35.
[4] For further Rabbinic examples, v. Str.-B., I, 731; Zn. Mt., 537, n. 58; Schl. Mt., 505.
[5] Zn. Jn., 76, n. 68.
[6] Eur. Ion, 693 : ἄλλων ἐξ αἱμάτων; plur. elsewhere of mass bloodshed (→ αἷμα, 3): Soph. Ant., 121; Aesch. Suppl., 265; Polyb., XV, 33, 1; 4 Βασ. 9:26; Jer. 19:4; Ez. 24:6 (for דָּמִים); 2 Macc. 14:18; Ep. Ar., 88 and 90; 1 Cl., 18, 14; Aristides Ap., 4, 3.

lifebearing blood of both parents in the child. [7] The same thought is found in Ac. 17:26 ℵ D : ἐποίησεν ἐξ ἑνὸς αἵματος [8] πᾶν ἔθνος ἀνθρώπων κατοικεῖν ἐπὶ ... τῆς γῆς, the blood of the progenitor of the race being the bond which unites humanity.

αἷμα denotes "descent" or "family" from the time of Homer : IG, XIV, 1003, 1: Διὸς 'Αλκμήνης τε αἷμα; Jos. Ant., 4, 310 : τὶς τῶν ἐξ αἵματος; 20, 226 : τὸν ἐξ αἵματος τοῦ 'Ααρῶνος; 2, 102 : ἐσμὲν ἀδελφοὶ καὶ κοινὸν ἡμῖν αἷμα; P. Leipz., 28, 16 : υἱὸν γνήσιον καὶ πρωτότοκον ὡς ἐξ ἰδίου αἵματος γεννηθέντα σοι; P. Masp., 67097, II, 59 of a disinherited daughter : ξένην διακεχωρισμένην ἀπὸ τοῦ ἐμοῦ αἵματος καὶ γένους. With reference to the act of conception, Gr. En. 15:4 : ἐν τῷ αἵματι τῶν γυναικῶν ἐμιάνθητε καὶ ἐν τῷ αἵματι σαρκὸς ἐγεννήσατε καὶ ἐν αἵματι ἀνθρώπων ἐπεθυμήσατε.

2. The OT belief in the sanctity of blood is the basis of the prohibition of eating the blood of animals in the Eastern text of the apostolic decree in Ac. 15:29 : ἀπέχεσθαι αἵματος (cf. 15:20; 21:25). [9] When an animal is sacrificed, its blood as the bearer of life is a means of expiation before God, Lv. 17:11. Hence the general prohibition of eating blood, Lv. 17:10, 14; 7:26 f.; 3:17; Dt. 12:23; Gn. 9:4. The validity of this prohibition is attested by such passages as 1 S. 14:32 ff.; Jub. 6:7, 12 ff.; 7:28 ff.; Damasc., 4, 6; Eth. En., 98:11; 7:5; Jos. Ant., 3, 260. [10]

3. To shed blood is to destroy the bearer of life and therefore life itself. Hence αἷμα signifies "outpoured blood," "violently destroyed life," "death" or "murder." In this sense it is used of the slaying of Jesus in Mt. 27:4, 24; Ac. 5:28, and of the prophets, saints and witnesses of Jesus in Mt. 23:30, 35; Lk. 11:50 f.; Rev. 16:6; 17:6; 18:24; 19:2. Along the same lines the OT, Jewish and Greek expression αἷμα ἐκχέειν or ἐκχύννειν is also used for "to kill," though with no specific reference to the actual shedding of blood, Lk. 11:50; Ac. 22:20; R. 3:15; Rev. 16:6. God avenges the blood shed in murder, Rev. 6:10 : ἐκδικεῖς τὸ αἷμα ἡμῶν; 19:2; Lk. 11:50 f.: ἐκζητηθῇ τὸ αἷμα ... ἀπὸ τῆς γενεᾶς ταύτης; Mt. 27:25 : τὸ αἷμα αὐτοῦ ἐφ' ἡμᾶς καὶ ἐπὶ τὰ τέκνα ἡμῶν; 23:35; Ac. 5:28; 18:6. According to the Western version of the apostolic decree the prohibition of murder : ἀπέχεσθαι αἵματος (Ac. 15:29), is one of the basic principles of Christian conduct. [11] The saying in Hb. 12:4 : οὔπω μέχρις αἵματος ἀντικατέστητε ("ye have not yet resisted unto blood") can hardly refer to the forfeiting of life in martyrdom, but denotes extreme resistance to sin in the military image of a conflict with its wounds. [12] In Ac. 20:26 : καθαρός εἰμι ἀπὸ τοῦ αἵματος πάντων (18:6), αἷμα is used in the sense of θάνατος or eternal death as judgment on the sinner (→ θάνατος).

For αἷμα ἐκχέειν, "to kill," cf. Aesch. Eum., 653 : τὸ μητρὸς αἷμ' ὅμαιμον ἐκχέας πέδοι. It is often found in the LXX as a rendering of דָּם שָׁפַךְ e.g., Gn. 9:6; 37:22;

---

[7] Aug. in Joh. Ev. Tract., II, 14 : ex sanguinibus homines nascuntur maris et feminae. Zn., op. cit. refers to Sanh., 4, 5, where the plur. דְּמֵי אָחִיךָ in Gn. 4:10 is taken to signify "his own blood and that of his descendants."

[8] ϑ-αἵματος. For the authenticity of αἵματος, Zn. Ag., I, 613, 69.

[9] K. Six, Das Aposteldekret (1912), 44 ff.; Zn. Ag., II, 528 ff.; Str.-B., II, 734 ff.

[10] Rabb. material : Str.-B., II, 734 ff. Mand. par. : Lidz. Ginza, 20, 4 : "Eat not the blood of animals."

[11] G. Resch. Das Aposteldekret (1905); A. v. Harnack, Ag. (1908), 188 ff.; Zn. Ag., II, 546 ff.

[12] Rgg. Hb., 394, referring to 2 Macc. 13:14 : ἀγωνίσασθαι μέχρι θανάτου, and Heliodor. Aeth., VII, 8 : τῆς ... μέχρις αἵματος στάσεως.

Dt. 19:10; 1 Βασ. 25:31; Is. 59:7 (= ψ 13:3). Cf. also Ditt. Syll.³, 1181, 5 f.: ἐχχέαντας αὐτῆς τὸ ἀναίτιον αἷμα (a Jewish prayer for vengeance from the 3rd cent. B.C.); [13] דָּמִים שֶׁנִּשְׁפָּךְ Sanh., 6:5 : "If God is so concerned at the blood of the ungodly shed (in execution), how much more at the blood of the righteous!" [14] For the deity as the avenger of murder, cf. Plat. Leg., VIII, 872e : ἡ τῶν ξυγγενῶν αἱμάτων τιμωρὸς δίκη; Dt. 32:43 : τὸ αἷμα τῶν υἱῶν αὐτοῦ ἐκδικᾶται; 4 Βασ. 9:7; ψ 78:10; Ditt. Syll.³, 1181, 12 : ἵνα ἐκδικήσῃς τὸ αἷμα τὸ ἀναίτιον. For בַּקֵּשׁ דָּם מִיַּד the LXX often has ἐκζητεῖν αἷμα ἐκ χειρός. For the curse of bloodguiltiness, cf. 2 Βασ. 1:16 : τὸ αἷμά σου ἐπὶ τὴν κεφαλήν σου; Ιερ. 28:35; Ez. 18:13; Test. L. 16:3 : τὸ ἀθῷον αἷμα ἐπὶ τῆς κεφαλῆς ὑμῶν ἀναδεχόμενοι; T. Sanh., 9, 5 : דָּמוֹ תָּלוּי בְּצַוַּאר עֵדָיו cf. also jSanh., 23b. [15] For the Rabbinic phrase דָּמוֹ בְּרֹאשׁוֹ (cf. 1 S. 1:16; 1 K. 2:33), v. jBer., 11 c E; bPes., 112a.

In Hebrews αἷμα often denotes the blood of animals shed in the sacrificial cultus and rites of the OT to ward off the destroying angel (11:28), to institute the divine order of the OT (9:18), to consecrate the tabernacle and the cultic vessels (9:21), and to effect atonement and purification (9:7, 12 f., 22, 25; 10:4; 13:11). [16]

4. In the NT αἷμα achieves its greatest theological significance in relation to the death of Christ : [17] αἷμα τοῦ Χριστοῦ, 1 C. 10:16; Eph. 2:13; Hb. 9:14 : Ἰησοῦ, Hb. 10:19; 1 Jn. 1:7; Ἰησοῦ Χριστοῦ, 1 Pt. 1:2; τοῦ κυρίου, 1 C. 11:27; τοῦ ἀρνίου, Rev. 7:14; 12:11. The interest of the NT is not in the material blood of Christ, but in His shed blood as the life violently taken from Him. Like the cross (→ σταυρός), the "blood of Christ" is simply another and even more graphic phrase for the death of Christ in its soteriological significance. According to the eucharistic words of institution the blood of Christ is a guarantee of the actualisation of the new divine order (→ διαθήκη): 1 C. 11:25 : τοῦτο τὸ ποτήριον ἡ καινὴ διαθήκη ἐστὶν ἐν τῷ ἐμῷ αἵματι, [18] "This cup is the new divine order in virtue of my blood"; Mk. 14:24 : τοῦτό ἐστιν τὸ αἷμά μου τῆς διαθήκης τὸ ἐκχυννόμενον ὑπὲρ πολλῶν (cf. Mt. 26:28), i.e., the violent death of Christ establishes and assures the validity of the new divine order promised in Jer. 31:31 ff., according to which God writes His will on the hearts of men and forgives their sins. As the old divine order of Sinai was sealed and inaugurated by blood (Hb. 9:18 ff., Ex. 24:8 : דַּם הַבְּרִית), so the new with its gifts is established and set in force by the blood of Jesus.

The same thought of the death of Christ as the guarantee of remission, one of the gifts of the διαθήκη, underlies the statements of Paul, 1 Peter, 1 John and Revelation concerning the blood of Christ : ὃν → προέθετο ὁ θεὸς → ἱλαστήριον ἐν τῷ αὐτοῦ αἵματι, R. 3:25; → δικαιωθέντες ἐν τῷ αἵματι αὐτοῦ, 5:9; → εἰρηνοποιήσας διὰ τοῦ αἵματος τοῦ σταυροῦ αὐτοῦ, Col. 1:20; τὴν → ἀπολύτρωσιν διὰ τοῦ αἵματος αὐτοῦ, Eph. 1:7; ἐγενήθητε → ἐγγὺς ἐν τῷ αἵματι τοῦ

---

[13] Deissmann LO, 351 ff.

[14] Always plur. דָּמִים, whereas in the OT sing. Gn. 9:6; Ez. 18:10. Plur. 1 Ch. 22:8 : דָּמִים רַבִּים "the blood of many men."

[15] Trans. Str.-B., I, 1033.

[16] O. Schmitz, Die Opferanschauung des späteren Judentums und die Opferaussagen des NT (1910); Wnd. Hb., 82 ff., 90 ff.; Str.-B., III, 176 ff.

[17] J. Behm, RGG,² I, 1156 f. In addition to the bibliography there given, cf. Wnd. Hb., 83 ff., 90 ff.; Rgg. Hb., 260, n. 19; C. A. Anderson Scott, Christianity according to St. Paul (1927), 85 ff.; J. Schneider, Die Passionsmystik des Pls. (1929), 28 ff., 120 ff.

Χριστοῦ, 2:13; [19] → ῥαντισμὸν αἵματος Ἰησοῦ Χριστοῦ, 1 Pt. 1:2; → ἐλυτρώ-θητε τιμίῳ αἵματι ὡς → ἀμνοῦ → ἀμώμου καὶ → ἀσπίλου Χριστοῦ, 1:19; τὸ αἷμα Ἰησοῦ ... → καθαρίζει ἡμᾶς ἀπὸ πάσης → ἁμαρτίας, 1 Jn. 1:7; ὁ ἐλθὼν δι' → ὕδατος (baptism) καὶ αἵματος (death), 5:6; cf. 5:8; τῷ ... → λύσαντι (𝔎 P → λούσαντι) ἡμᾶς ἐκ τῶν ἁμαρτιῶν ἡμῶν ἐν τῷ αἵματι αὐτοῦ, Rev. 1:5; ἐλεύκαναν αὐτὰς (τὰς στολὰς αὐτῶν) ἐν τῷ αἵματι τοῦ → ἀρνίου, 7:14; περι-βεβλημένος ἱμάτιον βεβαμμένον αἵματι, 19:13; → ἠγόρασας τῷ θεῷ ἐν τῷ αἵματί σου ἐκ πάσης φυλῆς, 5:9; → ἐνίκησαν αὐτὸν διὰ τὸ αἷμα τοῦ ἀρνίου, 12:11. These varied expressions include simple references to the fact of Christ's death, images taken from the sphere of law (acquittal, ransom and the conclusion of peace), and concepts which belong to the language of sacrifice (expiation, sprinkling, purification, lamb without spot or blemish). The presence of the latter does not mean, however, that cultic notions of sacrifice are bound up with the blood of Christ. Already in later Judaism the idea of sacrifice is weakened and spiritualised, so that it appears to be little more than a symbol of personal and ethical processes. Similarly, the early Christian representation of the blood of Christ as sacrificial blood is simply the metaphorical garment clothing the thought of the self-offering, the obedience to God, which Christ demonstrated in the crucifixion (Phil. 2:8; R. 5:19; Hb. 5:8). The history of belief in the atoning and purifying power of blood, esp. among the Israelites and Greeks, does not help us to understand the ideas which the NT links with the blood of Christ, since the latter is simply a pregnant verbal symbol for the saving work of Christ. Even in Hb., which compares the attributes of the old and new διαθήκη as type and antitype, and in which the blood of the heavenly High-priest Christ is thus the counterpart of the blood of animals (→ 174), the language is metaphorical: οὐδὲ δι' αἵματος τράγων καὶ μόσχων, διὰ δὲ τοῦ ἰδίου αἵματος εἰσῆλθεν ἐφάπαξ εἰς τὰ ἅγια, αἰωνίαν λύτρωσιν εὑράμενος, 9:12; τὸ αἷμα τράγων καὶ ταύρων ... ἁγιάζει πρὸς τὴν τῆς σαρκὸς καθαρότητα, ... τὸ αἷμα τοῦ Χριστοῦ, ὃς διὰ πνεύματος αἰωνίου ἑαυτὸν προσήνεγκεν ἄμωμον τῷ θεῷ, καθαριεῖ τὴν συνείδησιν ἡμῶν ἀπὸ νεκρῶν ἔργων εἰς τὸ λατρεύειν θεῷ ζῶντι, 9:13 f. (cf. v. 25 f.); ἔχοντες παρρησίαν εἰς τὴν εἴσοδον τῶν ἁγίων ἐν τῷ αἵματι Ἰησοῦ, 10:19; αἵματι ῥαντισμοῦ, 12:24; ἐν αἵματι διαθήκης αἰωνίου, [20] 13:20 (cf. v. 12). The real point is the religous and ethical significance of the blood of Christ cleansing the conscience from dead works (9:14, cf. 10:22). Again, when Paul in 1 C. 10:16 describes communion with the exalted Lord in the Lord's Supper as → κοινωνία τοῦ αἵματος and τοῦ → σώματος τοῦ Χριστοῦ, and when John in Jn. 6:54, 56 (53) speaks of the eating of the flesh and drinking of the blood of Christ: ὁ ... → πίνων μου τὸ αἷμα; v. 55: τὸ αἷμά μου ἀληθής ἐστιν → πόσις, the blood is only a graphic term for death; the Lord's Supper unites Christians with the Christ who gave up His life to death. There can be no question in either Paul or John of the kind of blood mysticism we find in the mysteries. The enhanced realism of sacramental thinking in John is to be explained in the light of the anti-docetic trend common to both the Gospel of John and the First Epistle (→ 172 on Jn. 19:34, and also τρώγω, σάρξ).

For the atoning power of blood in the OT, v. Lv. 17:4; the cleansing power, Lv. 14:1 ff., 10 ff. (leprosy); the sanctifying, Ex. 29:20 f. (dedication of priests); apotropaic,

---

[18] Cf. Lk. 22:20 𝔎.
[19] Cf. Ac. 20:28: τὴν ἐκκλησίαν τοῦ θεοῦ ... → περιεποιήσατο διὰ τοῦ αἵματος τοῦ ἰδίου.
[20] On αἷμα διαθήκης, cf. Zech. 9:11; Test. B. 3:8.

Ex. 12:22 f.; [21] in Greek religion, Eustath. in Od., 22, 494 and 797: δι' αἵματος ἦν κάθαρσις ... καὶ ἡ τῶν φονέων, οἳ αἵματι νιπτόμενοι καθάρσιον εἶχον αὐτό; Heracl. Frg., 5 (Diels, I, 78, 6 ff.): καθαίρονται ... αἵματι μιαινόμενοι. [22]

For a mystico-material view of Christ's blood, v. Cl. Al. Paed., II, 2, 19, 4 : διττὸν τὸ αἷμα τοῦ κυρίου ... σαρκικόν, ᾧ τῆς φθορᾶς λελυτρώμεθα, ... πνευματικόν, ... ᾧ κεχρίσμεθα· καὶ τοῦτ' ἔστι πιεῖν τὸ αἷμα τοῦ Ἰησοῦ, τῆς κυριακῆς μεταλαβεῖν ἀφθαρσίας. Hellenistic blood mysticism is to be seen in the Dionysus-Zagreus-cult, in which union with the god is achieved by eating the divine animal torn and consumed in a wild frenzy (Scholion on Cl. Al. Protr., 318, 5 : ὠμὰ ἤσθιον κρέα οἱ μυούμενοι Διονύσῳ), and esp. in the taurobolium and criobolium of the Attic mysteries, with their regeneration and divinisation of the devotee through the blood of the sacred animal sprinkled over him (Prudent. Perist., 10, 1011 ff.; Firm. Mat. Err. Prof. Rel., 27, 8). [23]

5. In the language of apocalyptic αἷμα signifies the red colour [24] similar to blood which indicates eschatological terrors in earth and heaven, such as war (Ac. 2:19), hail and fire, μεμιγμένα ἐν αἵματι (Rev. 8:7), the changing of water (Rev. 8:8; 11:6; 16:3 f.), the colouring of the moon (Rev. 6:12; Ac. 2:20), the judgment of the nations (Rev. 14:20 : ἐξῆλθεν αἷμα ἐκ τῆς ληνοῦ ἄχρι τῶν χαλινῶν τῶν ἵππων).

Ex. 7:17 ff. underlies the use of αἷμα (red colour) as a sign of disaster in the OT. This apocalyptic use is found in Jl. 3:3 f. (LXX 2:30 f.); Sib., 5, 378 : πῦρ καὶ αἷμα; Ass. Mos., 10, 5 : (luna) tota convertit se in sanguine; 4 Esr. 5:5 : de ligno sanguis stillabit; Barn., 12, 1; Herm. v., 4, 3, 3. Wine = αἷμα σταφυλῆς in Gn. 49:11; Dt. 32:14; Sir. 39:26; 50:15; 1 Macc. 6:34; αἷμα βοτρύων: Achill. Tat., 2, 2; αἷμα ἀμπέλου: Cl. Al. Paed, II, 19, 3; 29, 1; Strom., V, 8, 48, 8. [25] The wine harvest is also an eschatological picture in Is. 63:3; Jl. 4:13. On Rev. 14:20, cf. En. 100:3 : "The horse will wade up to the breast in the blood of sinners"; jTaan, 69a, 7: [26] "Until a horse sank in blood up to its nostrils;" Lidz. Ginza, 417, 16 f.: "His horse strides ... up to its saddle in blood, and the swirl of blood reaches up to the sides of its nose."

† αἷματεκχυσία.

This is found only in Hb. 9:22 : χωρὶς αἷματεκχυσίας οὐ γίνεται ἄφεσις, "without the shedding of blood there is no remission." As abs. αἷμα ἐκχέειν (→ αἷμα, 3) denotes "to put to death (by blood shedding)" in the LXX and NT (corresponding to ἔκχυσις αἵματος in 3 Βασ. 18:28; Sir. 27:15), so the word αἷματεκχυσία, found here for the first time, refers to the shedding of blood in slaying, and esp. in the offering of sacrifices under the OT cultus (v. 18 ff.). There is no specific reference to the pouring of blood at the altar (Lv. 4:7, 18, 25, 30, 34; 8:15; 9:9; Ex. 29:12), nor to the sprinkling on the altar (Ex. 24:6; Lv. 1:5, 11; 9:12), for which the LXX always has αἷμα ἐκ- or προσχέειν with prep., since

---

[21] Stade-Bertholet, Bibl. Theol. des AT, II (1911), 32 ff.; G. Hölscher, Geschichte der israel. u. jüd. Religion (1922), 16, n. 8; 28 ff.; 76 ff.

[22] E. Rohde, Psyche⁹/¹⁰ (1925), I, 271 ff., II, 77 f.; O. Gruppe, Gr. Mythologie u. Religionsgeschichte (1906), 891, 1552 f.; P. Stengel, Kultusaltertümer³ (1920), 127 ff.; K. Latte, ARW, 20 (1921/22), 254 ff.

[23] Rohde, op. cit., II, 14 ff.; H. Hepding, Attis (1903), 196 ff.; O. Gruppe, op. cit., 1552 ff.; F. Cumont, Mysterien des Mithra³ (1923), 169 ff.; Bau. Jn. ad loc.; R. Reitzenstein, Die hellen. Mysterienreligionen³ (1927), 45 f.; H. Gressmann, Die oriental. Religionen im hellen. röm. Zeitalter (1930), 105 ff.

[24] E. Wunderlich, "Die Bedeutung der roten Farbe im Kultus der Griechen und Römer," RVV, XX, 1 (1925), 4 ff.; 10 ff.

[25] K. Kircher, RVV, IX, 2 (1910), 32 ff.

[26] Trans. Str.-B., III, 817.

αἷματεκχυσία. Cr.-Kö., 84; Wnd. Hb., 82 f.; Rgg. Hb., 280 f.

such reference to particular rites, which would include the πρόσχυσις τοῦ αἵματος of Hb. 11:28 (Ex. 12:7, 13, 22 f.), would not fit the more general content of v. 22 as the conclusion of the train of thought from v. 18 ff. The main point is that the giving of life is the necessary presupposition of the remission of sins (→ ἄφεσις). This was prefigured in the animal sacrifices of the OT, but what could not be actualised in the OT (Hb. 10:4) has now been established as an eternal truth by the death of Christ (αἷμα, 4 → 174 f.).

Apart from Hb. 9:22, αἱματεκχυσία is found only in the fathers. It signifies the "shedding of blood" or "murder" in Tat., 23, 2; Epiph. Panar., 39, 9, 2, where αἱματεκχυσία is numbered among the major sins; Georg. Al. Vit. Chrys. (Chrys. Opp., VIII, 1612, 184, 26: φοβηθεὶς μήπως καὶ αἱματεκχυσίαι γένωνται εἰς τὸν λαόν etc., and cf. Thes. Steph., s.v.). It is found in the same sense in Joh. Mosch., 3005c; Theophan. Chronogr. (Bonn, 1839), 510, 16. Relevant also in אֵין כַּפָּרָה אֶלָּא בַדָּם in bYoma, 5a; bMen. 93b; bZeb., 6a.

Behm

αἰνέω, αἶνος

† αἰνέω.

There are two main meanings in secular use: [1] a. "to praise or extol" (Arist. Fr., 673; Hdt., V, 102; Corp. Hermet., XIII, 21); b. "to tell or commend" (Soph. Phil., 1380). Only the former, however, is relevant to our purpose. It occurs frequently in the LXX in a religious sense with reference to God: with acc. in ψ 148:1 ff. τὸν κύριον, or dat. =לְ with הוֹדָה and הִלֵּל in Jer. 20:13; 1 Ch. 16:36; 23:5; 2 Ch. 20:19; 2 Εσδρ. 3:10 f.; Ps. Sol. 5:1. It is often used with δοξάζειν, LXX Da. 4:34; ψ 21:22 f. and ὑμνεῖν (ὕμνος), Neh. 12:24; Ju. 16:24 (BS ὕμνησαν instead of ἤνεσαν) and also with ἐξομολογεῖσθαι in 1 Ch. 16:4.

There are eight occurrences in the NT, six in Luke and Acts, one in R. 15:11 = ψ 116:1, and one in Rev. 19:5 dat. It denotes the joyful praise of God expressed in doxology, hymn or prayer, whether by individuals (Lk. 2:20; Ac. 3:8 f.), the group of disciples (Lk. 19:37), the community (Ac. 2:47; Rev. 19:5) or the angels (Lk. 2:13).

Related or similar terms are found in M. Pol., 14, 3: ... σὲ αἰνῶ, σὲ εὐλογῶ, σὲ δοξάζω ...; Act. Joh., 77: δοξάζομέν σε καὶ αἰνοῦμεν καὶ εὐλογοῦμεν καὶ εὐχαριστοῦμεν; Act. Ptr., 39: αἰνοῦμέν σε, εὐχαριστοῦμέν σοι καὶ ἀνθομολογούμεθα, δοξάζοντές σε ... Cf. Lk. 2:20; 24:53 ℵ pl lat.; Just. Dial., 106, 1; Ap., 13, 1; Cl. Al. Strom., VII, 7, 35, 2.

† αἶνος.

a. "Story" or "fable," Aesch. Suppl., 534; Hes. Op., 202; b. "resolve," IG, IV, 926; c. "praise," Aesch. Ag., 1547; Hdt., VII, 107. In the LXX transl. of עֹז and הלל pi, ψ 8:2; 94 tit.; 2 Ch. 23:13: ὑμνοῦντες αἶνον; 3 Macc. 7:16: ἐν αἴνοις καὶ παμμελέσιν ὕμνοις.

It occurs twice in the NT (Mt. 21:16 = ψ 8:2 and Lk. 18:43) signifying "praise" in the religious sense.

α ἰ ν έ ω. [1] Thes. Steph.; Liddell-Scott, s.v.

In 2 Cl., 1, 5; 9, 10 we find αἶνον διδόναι = αἶνον ἀναπέμπειν in Just. Ap., I, 65, 3; Orig. De Orat., 13, 3. αἶνος is also found with εὐχαριστία, ὕμνος and δόξα in Just. Ap., I, 13, 1; 65, 3; Cl. Al. Strom., VII, 7, 49; Const. Ap., VII, 48, 3. Cf. Act. Joh., 109 : τίνα αἶνον ἢ ποίαν προσφορὰν ἢ τίνα εὐχαριστίαν … ἐπονομάσωμεν … αἶνος is the only praise which is worthy of God and the only sacrifice appropriate to Him in Just. Ap., I, 13, 1; Dial., 118, 2. Origen comments on Ps. 148:1 [2]: αἶνός ἐστιν ὕμνος εἰς θεὸν ἐπὶ θεωρίᾳ τῶν γεγονότων.

Schlier

---

† αἴνιγμα (ἔσοπτρον)

In the NT this occurs only in 1 C. 13:12, which contrasts our present (ἄρτι) imperfect seeing with perfect eschatological (τότε) seeing : βλέπομεν γὰρ ἄρτι δι᾽ ἐσόπτρου ἐν αἰνίγματι, τότε δὲ πρόσωπον πρὸς πρόσωπον. To understand this, we need to analyse the two terms αἴνιγμα and ἔσοπτρον.

αἴνιγμα first means "riddle." Since the mysterious elements in religious utterances can also be interpreted and understood as riddles, there is a material link between the concept and oracular or prophetic pronouncement. [1] This is true in the case of the Sphinx : Soph. Oed. Tyr., 1525; Eur. Phoen., 1688; the Pythia : Plut. Pyth. Or., 25 (II, 407b), 30 (II, 409c); the Sibylls : Sib., 3, 811. We may also refer to S. Nu., 103 on 12:8, which tells us that according to Ez. 17:2 the prophets speak to men, and according to Nu. 12:8 God speaks to the prophets, in riddles (בְּחִידֹת, LXX δι᾽ αἰνιγμάτων), the only exception being Moses. Among both Greeks and Jews the essence of prophetic utterance is thus speaking in riddles in the sense of saying things which require elucidation.

ἔσοπτρον. "To see in a glass" also means "to see prophetically." The Rabbis, when they compare Moses' knowledge of God with that of other prophets, explain that the latter saw God with the help of nine mirrors (Ez. 43:3) whereas Moses needed only one (Nu. 12:8), [2] and that the latter saw Him in clouded mirrors, but Moses in a clear one (Lv. r. 1 on 1:1). [3] Or it is maintained that God revealed Himself to the prophets according to Nu. 12:6, and again in distinction from His impartations to Moses according to 12:8, not in a clear glass but (only) by dreams and visions (Tanch. צו 143a). It is thus clear that seeing in a

---

[2] MPG, 12, 1677d.

αἴνιγμα. On 1 C. 13:12 : H. A. W. Meyer, Komm.[5] (1870), 370 f.; G. Heinrici, Sendschreiben (1880), 424 f.; Joh. W. 1 K., 319 f.; Bchm. 1 K., 402 ff.; Harnack, SAB (1911), 150, 157 f.; R. Seeberg, Ewiges Leben (1915), 103 ff.; S. Basset, JBL, 47 (1928), 232 ff.; J. Behm, Reinhold-Seeberg-Festschrift, I (1929), 314-342. On ἔσοπτρον : R. Reitzenstein, Historia Monachorum (1916), 243-254, 262; Festschr. f. F. C. Andreas (1916), 48 ff.; NGG (1916), 411; H. Achelis, Festschr. f. Bonwetsch (1918), 56-63; K. Bornhäuser, Bethel, XVIII (1926), 45 f.; Str.-B., III, 452 ff.; W. Theiler, "D. Vorbereitung des Neuplatonismus," in Problemata, I (1930), 148.

[1] On the material links, v. A. Jolles, Einfache Formen (1930), 139 (ref. of Peterson).

[2] The starting-point is found in the noun מראה, which in the vocalisation מַרְאָה in the OT (Ex. 38:8) and also in Rabbinic writings (cf. Str.-B., III, 452 for examples) signifies mirror. The idea of the one and nine mirrors is deduced from the fact that in Nu. 12:8 מַרְאָה occurs only once, whereas in Ez. 43:3 this and other forms of ראה are found nine times.

[3] For a similar statement, cf. bJeb., 49b; Mek. Sim. b. J. on Ex. 20:21, p. 114, Hoffmann. A rather different view is found in bSanh., 97b, bSuk., 45b. Most of the relevant passages may be found in Str.-B., op. cit. They usually rest on the mistranslation referred to in n. 5.

glass can denote participation in the divine revelation in a very lofty sense, as shown by the example of Moses.

The Rabbinic word אִסְפַּקְלַרְיָא = σπεκλάριον means "glass" (esp. Muscovy glass) as well as "mirror." There can be no disputing the fact that both meanings occur, [4] nor that this alien term alone is used to denote the wonderful mirror which points into the future or the beyond. This is the basis of the erroneous view, remarkably prevalent among Christians, that in the Rabbinic passages mentioned אספקלריא is to be rendered "glass" or "pane" or "window." [5] As against this, there can be no question that at least in Lv. r., 1 there is a plain link with the מראה of Nu. 12:8 which is always taken to be a "mirror." Again, it is hard to see any point in the comparing of the divine revelation to seeing through a window, and esp. through nine windows. On the other hand, we can see at once how the image of looking in a mirror arises from Hellenistic magical practices, particularly in view of the use of the alien word. If the number nine is more than an exegetical play on Ez. 43:3 (→ n. 2), it may well be linked with the fact that consulting mirrors was often unsuccessful at the first attempt, and had to be repeated until a clear picture was seen.

Light is shown on the origin of the image by the fact that in all the relevant Rabbinic passages the only word used out of all the possible terms for mirror is the alien אִסְפַּקְלַרְיָא. While this is applied only figuratively to the divine revelation, there can be no doubt that it is basically linked with the mirror gazing found in Hellenism. [6] There are many passages to show that this was known to Judaism, e.g., [7] Gn. r., 91 on 42:1 E : (Jacob) saw in a mirror that his hope (i.e., Joseph) was in Egypt.

In this image of looking into and seeing in mirrors there is no stress on the fact that the mirror gives only an indirect and clouded picture. The latter notion occurs only where less clear mirrors are distinguished from clear. [8] It is thus incorrect to maintain that one of the characteristics of the mirrors of antiquity was to give indistinct pictures. [9] Similarly, in the Rabbis as in Philo, we do not find the idea "that the mirror does not show us the thing itself, but only a reflection." [10] Moses is indeed extolled as the one who received the supreme and most direct revelation of God when he saw Him in a clear mirror.

From the examples adduced, it may be seen that both terms, i.e., the mirror and the riddle, are given their distinctive point as applied to prophetic revelation. The

---

[4] Cf. Str.-B., III, 452 f.

[5] Thus already Lambert Bos, Schöttgen etc. (cf. Meyer, Bchm.); more recently Bornhäuser, Str.-B. As above, S. Krauss, *Talmudische Archäologie* (1910), 68, 399; Bacher, Tann., II, 214.

[6] For bibl. on the mirror magic of antiquity : Pauly-W., XI, 27; F. Pfister, *Die Rel. d. Griech. u. Röm.* (1930), 317; ERE, IV, 351 ff.; examples in Achelis, *op. cit.* The most comprehensive discussion of the figurative usage of "mirror" in Hellenism and Gnosticism is found in Behm, 326-335.

[7] Cf. Str.-B.; esp. M. Ex. 18:21, where we do not have astrological practice (Str.-B., Behm, 325) but genuine consultation of mirrors. It might be that the word "mirror" is used for a rough piece of glass or polished stone. All that is needed for the magical practice is a bright surface, so that a dish of water or coloured vessel might serve. In the later usage the nature of the mirror was of no importance.

[8] → 178 and n. 3.

[9] Thus, e.g., BW, 634 : "whose image was never wholly clear" ; cf. Meyer, Heinrici, etc. But J. Weiss, 319, n. 1 and Achelis, 62, n. 1 show the archaeological unsoundness of this view. Cf. further Pauly-W., *op. cit.* Bornhäuser rightly points out that even Jm. 1:23 f. says nothing about any lack of clarity in the picture reflected ; nor does 2 C. 3:18.

[10] Thus J. Weiss argues that this is "always" the case in Philo, but in most of the instances adduced, as in the passages listed in Leisegang's Index, 299, 447, we find no trace of this idea. Cf. e.g., Abr., 153; Spec. Leg., 219. Behm might have been even sharper in his criticism on p. 332.

expressions thus signify that to see (→ βλέπειν) in the Spirit is to see prophetically. Yet, though their basic meaning is the same, the two words have different nuances, as appears very clearly in the Rabbinic discussion concerning Moses. ἐν αἰνίγματι βλέπειν is always used of the obscure seeing, hearing and speaking of the prophets, among whom Moses is not included. As against this, δι' ἐσόπτρου does not imply any depreciation of the revelation, and may be used of Moses as of all other prophets, the only difference being that his mirror is better than those of others. To this extent the two terms are not tautological, [11] but ἐν αἰνίγματι is a more precise form of the general δι' ἐσόπτρου to indicate what is less clear. Our pneumatic seeing is "only" ἐν αἰνίγματι (not "only" δι' ἐσόπτρου).

> The quotations also show that in relation to Nu. 12:8 Rabbinic exegesis spoke of the prophets speaking in riddles as well as seeing in a glass. To this there corresponds the clear connection of the Pauline statement with Nu. 12:8, [12] the relationship not being with the LXX but with the Mas. and Rabbinic exegesis. [13] Even the much discussed ἐν in conjunction with αἴνιγμα is not to be explained in terms of a Greek prepositional construction, [14] but in terms of the בְּ of the Heb. text which Paul followed.
>
> *Kittel*

αἱρέομαι, αἵρεσις, αἱρετικός, αἱρετίζω, διαιρέω, διαίρεσις

---

† αἱρέομαι.

αἱρέω act., means "to take," "win," "seize," and also "comprehend"; mid. "to take for or to oneself," "to select." [1] The mid. meaning of "choose" or "elect," which is the only use in the NT, is common both in the LXX and secular usage. Hebrew equivalents are בָּחַר, חָפֵץ, חָשַׁק, סוּר hi and אָמַר hi. [2] Synonyms are ἐκλέγεσθαι, εὐδοκεῖν, βούλεσθαι, θέλειν.

1. In Phil. 1:22 and Hb. 11:25 (μᾶλλον αἱρεῖσθαι ... ἤ) it indicates selective preference as between two possibilities.

2. In 2 Th. 2:13 αἱρεῖσθαι indicates the election of the community by God. Cf. Dt. 26:18: καὶ κύριος εἵλατό σε σήμερον γενέσθαι σε αὐτῷ λαὸν περιούσιον ... (cf. Herm. s., 5, 6, 6). There is no instance of this kind of religious election outside the biblical circle.

† αἵρεσις.

A. αἵρεσις in classical Usage and Hellenism.

αἵρεσις, from αἱρεῖν, is used in classical Greek to indicate: a. "seizure," e.g., of a city (Hdt., IV, 1); b. "choice" (αἱρέομαι mid.), in the general sense of choice of a

---

[11] For this reason there is no ground for eliminating the ἐν αἰν., as suggested by E. Preuschen, ZNW, I (1900), 180 f. and favoured by J. Weiss. Cf. on this point already Maxim. Conf. Quaest. ad Thalass., 46 (MPG, 90, 420b): τίς ἡ διαφορὰ τοῦ ἐσόπτρου πρὸς τὸ αἴνιγμα.

[12] Cf. already Tert. Adv. Prax., 14.

[13] Thus esp. Harnack, 158; as against Reitzenstein, 253.

[14] Achelis, 62.

α ἱ ρ έ ο μ α ι. [1] Pass.; Liddell-Scott, *s.v.*

[2] The introduction of 1 Ch. 21:10 under αἱρέω in Hatch-Redpath is an oversight. It should really come under αἴρω.

possibility or even to an office; "inclination" (opp. φυγή); and c. "resolve" or "enterprise," "effort directed to a goal," almost προαίρεσις (Plat. Phaedr., 256c). The last meaning persists in Hellenism and occasionally in Christian literature (Ditt. Syll.³, 675, 28; Herm. s., 9, 23, 5).

From this there develops in Hellenism the predominant objective use of the term to denote a. "doctrine" and especially b. "school." The αἵρεσις of the philosopher, which in antiquity always includes the choice of a distinctive Bios, is related to δόγματα to which others give their πρόσκλισις. It thus comes to be the αἵρεσις (teaching) of a particular αἵρεσις (school).[1] Cf. the title of a work by Antipater of Tarsus (2nd century B.C.) κατὰ τῶν αἱρέσεων, and the writing of Chrysipp. αἵρεσις πρὸς Γοργιππίδην (Diog. L., VII, 191); also the description of the philosophical schools as αἱρέσεις in Polyb., V, 93, 8 (Peripatetic), Dion. Hal. Compos. Verb., 19, p. 134, 3 f. (ἥ γ' Ἰσοκράτους καὶ τῶν ἐκείνῳ γνωρίμων αἵρεσις); Sext. Emp. Pyrrh. Hyp., 1, 16; Diog. L., I, 19 (τοῦ δὲ ἠθικοῦ [sc. μέρους τῆς φιλοσοφίας] γεγόνασιν αἱρέσεις δέκα: Ἀκαδημαική, Κυρηναική κτλ.). For the concept of such a fellowship — as well as αἱρέσεις κατὰ φιλοσοφίαν (Sext. Emp. Pyrrh. Hyp., I, 185) we also have κατὰ ἰατρικὴν αἱρέσεις (ibid., I, 237) — the following aspects are important: the gathering of the αἵρεσις from a comprehensive society and therefore its delimitation from other schools; the self-chosen authority of a teacher; the relatively authoritarian and relatively disputable doctrine; and the private character of all these features.

B. αἵρεσις and מִין in the LXX and Judaism.

In the LXX αἵρεσις is found occasionally in the general sense of "choice": ἐξ αἱρέσεως or κατὰ αἵρεσιν, of or by free choice, or voluntarily: Gn. 49:5; Lv. 22:18, 21; 1 Macc. 8:30.[2] The Hebrew equivalent is נְדָבָה. More important is the signification in Hellenistic and Rabbinic Judaism. We need not be surprised if in Philo it is used on the one side to denote a Greek philosophical school, as, e.g., in Plant., 151, and if on the other it is employed to depict what Philo calls the august philosophical society of the Therapeutics, as, e.g., in Vit. Cont., 29. In Josephus, too, αἵρεσις is used of the religious community of the Essenes (Bell., 2, 118). Indeed, Josephus sees all the Jewish religious schools in terms of the Greek philosophical schools, the Essenes, Sadducees and Pharisees being the τρεῖς παρ' ἡμῶν αἱρέσεις. After his investigation[3] of all three, Josephus resolved πολιτεύεσθαι τῇ τῶν Φαρισαίων αἱρέσει κατακολουθῶν, ἣ παραπλήσιός ἐστι τῇ παρ' Ἕλλησιν Στωϊκῇ λεγομένῃ (Vit., 12). Cf. for the linguistic usage Vit., 191 and 197; Ant., 13, 171 and 293. If the choice of the term is partly due to Josephus' bias towards assimilation, it was justified by the material relationship between the Palestinian Jewish and Greek schools in basic structure. The μόριόν τι Ἰουδαϊκόν (Ant., 17, 41) or σύνταγμά τι Ἰουδαίων (Bell., 1, 110) found a suitable designation in αἵρεσις.

The corresponding term in Rabbinic Judaism is מִין,[4] which can mean both

---

αἵρεσις. [1] αἵρ. = organised school or class in Ditt. Or., 176: οἱ ... ἐφηβευκότες τῆς Ἀμμωνίου αἱρέσεως.
[2] Neh. 12:40: αἱ δύο τῆς αἱρέσεως, perhaps ... αἰνέσεως as in v. 31, 38, otherwise = division. Cf. Ps.-Plat. Ax., 367a, commission; IG, IV, 937, embassy.
[3] Contested by G. Hölscher, Pauly-W., IX, 1936.
[4] On the etymology, cf. W. Bacher, REJ, 38, 45 f. What follows is substantially in accordance with the findings of K. G. Kuhn. Cf. his Excursus I ("Giljonim and Sifre minim") in Sifre Numeri.

αἵρεσις and αἱρετικός. [5] Like αἵρεσις in Josephus, מין denoted in the first instance the trends and parties within Judaism. But soon, when certain minim separated themselves from the orthodox Rabbinic tradition, it came to be used only of trends within Judaism opposed by the Rabbis, [6] and therefore *sensu malo*. The term thus stigmatised certain groups as "heretical." This sense is found in Rabbinic writings belonging to the end of the 1st and the early part of the 2nd century A.D., e.g., in the *birkat ha-minim* which was probably incorporated in the Prayer of Eighteen Petitions towards the end of the 1st century (bBer., 28b). [7] At the end of the 2nd century the term acquired a new meaning, being applied not so much to the members of a sect within Judaism as to the adherents of other faiths, and esp. Christians and Gnostics. [8] Rabbin. מֵחֲלוֹקֶת can also be compared (TSota, 14, 1 ff.; T. Sanh., 7, 1). [9] But this corresponds rather to the Greek σχίσμα with its main suggestion of personally motivated disputes, whereas מין is the exact equivalent of αἵρεσις.

C. αἵρεσις in the NT.

The NT statements concerning αἵρεσις are to be understood against the Hellenistic and Jewish background.

1. The usage in Acts corresponds exactly to that of Josephus and the earlier Rabbis. Cf. αἵρεσις τῶν Σαδδουκαίων in Ac. 5:17; αἵρεσις τῶν Φαρισαίων in 15:5; ὅτι κατὰ τὴν ἀκριβεστάτην αἵρεσιν τῆς ἡμετέρας θρησκείας ἔζησα Φαρισαῖος in 26:5. Christianity, too, is called a αἵρεσις by its opponents in 24:5 : πρωτοστάτης τῆς τῶν Ναζωραίων αἱρέσεως. Cf. 24:14; 28:22; also Just. Dial., 17:1; 108, 2; Act. Phil., 15. In these passages the term has the neutral flavour of "school."

2. Against this background, it is impossible to solve the problem of the derivation of the special Christian sense of heresy. For the development of the Christian concept is not wholly analogous to that of the Rabbinic מין, as though, in the process of the separation of non-orthodox groups, the heterodox parties came to be designated heresy. On the contrary, the word seems to have been suspect in Christianity from the very first, and when it is used as a Christian technical term in conscious or unconscious connection either with the Greek philosophical schools or the Jewish sects it denotes at once societies outside Christianity and the Christian Church. [10] Hence it does not owe its meaning to the development of an orthodoxy. The basis of the Christian concept of αἵρεσις is to be found

---

[5] מין does not usually mean "sect," but "member of a sect"; hence αἱρετικός and not αἵρεσις. Cf. Ign. Tr., 6, 1.

[6] Including Jewish Christians, but not exclusively Jewish Christians (as against Bacher). Cf. Str.-B., IV, 330.

[7] The noṣrim are mentioned as well as the minim. Since the former are Christians, it is obvious that the latter are not necessarily so.

[8] Cf. A. Büchler, "Über die Minim von Sephoris und Tiberias im 2. u. 3. Jhdt.", *Cohen-Festschrift Judaica* (1912), esp. 293 f. The conclusions of B. are not in complete agreement. The many parallels which he shows between the subjects discussed between the Rabbis and the minim and those debated in the Dial. of Justin indicate that the minim are for the most part Christians, and indeed Gentile Christians.

[9] Cf. Str.-B., III, 321 f., 443.

[10] When we read in the Edict of Milan (Eus. Hist. Eccl., X, 5, 2): κεκελεύκαμεν τοῖς ... Χριστιανοῖς τῆς αἱρέσεως καὶ τῆς θρησκείας τῆς ἑαυτῶν τὴν πίστιν φυλάττειν ..., αἵρεσις has just as much the sense of choice as of society, as the context shows.

in the new situation created by the introduction of the Christian ἐκκλησία. ἐκκλησία and αἵρεσις are material opposites. The latter cannot accept the former ; the former excludes the latter. This may be clearly seen in Gl. 5:20, where αἵρεσις is reckoned among the ἔργα τῆς σαρκός along with ἔρις, ἔχθραι, ζῆλος, θυμοί, ἐριθεῖαι and διχοστασίαι. Yet neither here nor elsewhere in the NT does αἵρεσις have a technical sense. In 1 C. 11:18 f. we see even more clearly the impossibility of αἵρεσις within Christianity. Mention of the cultic assembly in which the community gathers as ἐκκλησία brings Paul back to the σχίσματα of 1 C. 1:10 ff. σχίσματα are splits in the community caused by personally motivated disputes. Paul believes in part the accounts which have come to him of such divisions in the community. He does so because there must be (καὶ) αἱρέσεις ἐν ὑμῖν in order that the tested might be made manifest. It makes no difference whether Paul is here using an apocryphal saying of the Lord (cf. Just. Dial., 35, 3; Didasc., 118, 35). The statement is for him an eschatologico-dogmatic statement[11] in which αἵρεσις is understood as an eschatological magnitude. In this respect it is distinguished from σχίσμα,[12] and obviously indicates something more serious. The greater seriousness consists in the fact that αἱρέσεις affect the foundation of the Church in doctrine (2 Pt. 2:1), and that they do so in such a fundamental way as to give rise to a new society alongside the ἐκκλησία. This the Church cannot accept, since as the lawful public assembly of the whole people of God the Church embraces this people exclusively and comprehensively. By its very nature, however, αἵρεσις is a private magnitude with a limited validity. It is, in fact, a school or party. If the Church accedes to αἱρέσεις, it will itself become a αἵρεσις and thus destroy its comprehensive "political" claim ; the concept of party — to mention a close analogy — necessarily excludes that of the people or state.

D. αἵρεσις in the Early Church.

In the age which followed αἵρεσις was still understood as an eschatologically threatening magnitude essentially opposed to the ἐκκλησία. This may be seen clearly in Ign. Eph., 6, 2; Trall., 6, 1; Just. Dial., 51, 2. Here the term has already become technical. It is worth noting however — and this confirms what we have said about the material difference between ἐκκλησία and αἵρεσις — that within Christianity αἵρεσις always denotes hostile societies, and there is always consciousness of an inner relationship between heretics and the secular philosophical schools or Jewish sects (Justin Ap., I, 26, 8; Dial., 80, 4), which they also describe by the term αἵρεσις.[13] What the Church usually has in view is Gnosticism. As seen by the Church, the Gnostics form schools.[14] It is worth noting that when Celsus raises the charge of multiplicity against Christianity, the only defence that Origen can make (c. Cels., III, 12) is to point to the fact that οὐδενὸς πράγματος, οὗ μὴ σπουδαία ἐστὶν ἡ ἀρχὴ καὶ τῷ βίῳ χρήσιμος, γεγόνασιν αἱρέσεις

---

[11] Cf. Mk. 13:5 f. and par.; Ac. 20:29 f.; 2 Pt. 2:1; 1 Jn. 2:19.
[12] The distinction is here implicit which is made explicit in Iren., IV, 26, 2 and 33, 7, namely, between *haeretici et malae sententiae* and those *qui scindunt et separant unitatem ecclesiae.*
[13] Cf. Just. Dial., 62, 3; Theoph. Ad. Autol., II, 4 (MPG, 6, 1052a); Cl. Al. Strom, I, 15, 69, 6; VI, 15, 123, 3 etc.; Hipp. El., I, 2, 1 etc.; Orig. c. Cels., III, 80, in Joh. II, 3, 30.
[14] Cf. M. Pol. epil., 1 f.; Test. Sol., 6, 4 P; 8, 5; Iren., II, 19, 8 (*de schola eorum, qui sunt a Valentino et a reliquis haereticorum*); Theoph. Ad. Autol., II, 14 (MPG, 6, 1076c); Hipp. El. praef., 11; IV, 2, 3; X, 23, 1 etc.; Cl. Al. Strom., I, 19, 95, 6 (αὗται [sc. αἱρέσεις] δέ εἰσιν αἱ τὴν ἐξ ἀρχῆς ἀπολείπουσαι ἐκκλησίαν).

διάφοροι; as it is in medicine, Greek philosophy, and Jewish exegesis, so also in Christianity. Origen, therefore, has lost sight of the material distinction between the ἐκκλησία and a αἵρεσις.

† αἱρετικός.

In view of what we have said, this word need not detain us. It is found already in Greek usage in the sense of "one who can choose aright" (Ps.-Plat. Def., 412a).[1] It does not occur, however, in Josephus. In Christianity it seems to have been used technically from the very first, and denotes the "adherent of a heresy."[2] In the NT it is found in Tt. 3:9 f.: μωρὰς δὲ ζητήσεις καὶ γενεαλογίας καὶ ἔριν καὶ μάχας νομικὰς περιίστασο· εἰσὶν γὰρ ἀνωφελεῖς καὶ μάταιοι. αἱρετικὸν ἄνθρωπον μετὰ μίαν καὶ δευτέραν νουθεσίαν παραιτοῦ, εἰδὼς ὅτι ἐξέστραπται ὁ τοιοῦτος καὶ ἁμαρτάνει ὢν αὐτοκατάκριτος. For the early Church, cf. Didasc., 33, 31; 118, 33; Iren., III, 3, 4 (Polycarp πολλοὺς ἀπὸ τῶν προειρημένων αἱρετικῶν ἐπέστρεψεν εἰς τὴν ἐκκλησίαν τοῦ θεοῦ, μίαν καὶ μόνην ταύτην ἀλήθειαν κηρύξας ὑπὸ τῶν ἀποστόλων παρειληφέναι, τὴν ὑπὸ τῆς ἐκκλησίας παραδεδομένην); Cl. Al. Strom., I, 19, 95, 4 etc.; Hipp. El., IV, 47, 5 etc.

† αἱρετίζω.

Predominantly Hellenistic, act. and mid., meaning the same as αἱρεῖσθαι, but stronger. Common in the LXX for בָּחַר but also for חָפֵץ, סוּר, זָבַל, נָשָׂא, אָנָה pi, חָמַל. Cf. also 2 Cl. 14, 1: ὥστε οὖν αἱρετισώμεθα ἀπὸ τῆς ἐκκλησίας τῆς ζωῆς, ἵνα σωθῶμεν.

In the NT it occurs only in Mt. 12:18 in a quotation from Is. 42:1 (Mas. תָּמַךְ, LXX ἀντιλαμβάνεσθαι). Possibly in Mt. 12:18 it reflects the specific meaning of αἱρετίζω in 1 Ch. 28:6 (not v. 10); 1 Ch. 29:1; Hag. 2:23; Mal. 3:17 = "to adopt." This is also found in secular Greek. Cf. JPE, 2, 299 : αἱρετίσας πατήρ; of God, IG, III, 74.

† διαιρέω, † διαίρεσις.

διαιρέω has at least five meanings in secular usage : "to dissolve or break"; "to distinguish" both generally and logically ; "to decide"; "to distribute"; "to apportion." The last two are most common in the LXX. Cf. Gn. 4:7; 15:10; 32:7; Lv. 1:12 and Jos. 18:4 f.; Jdt. 16:24; 1 Macc. 1:6; 6:35 etc.

In the NT it obviously means "to apportion and distribute," as in Lk. 15:12 : τὸν βίον; 1 C. 12:11: τὸ ἓν καὶ τὸ αὐτὸ πνεῦμα, διαιροῦν ἰδίᾳ ἑκάστῳ καθὼς βούλεται. The πνεῦμα allots the gifts of the Spirit to the various members of the community according to His will.

διαίρεσις has three important meanings in secular Greek : "separation or dissolution"; "division" either generally or logically; and "distribution," as the apportionment of property or an estate in the pap.[1] In the LXX it means "distribution" in Jdt. 9:4; Sir. 14:5; or "what is distributed": a. a part in ψ 135:13 (parts of the sea), or Jos. 19:51

αἱρετικός. [1] Cf. Pr.-Bauer.
[2] The leader of a secular αἵρεσις, e.g., a medical school, is called a αἱρεσιάρχης, IG, XIV, 1759; Galen, 6, 372. The title then passed to the leader of a Christian heresy : Hipp. El., VI, 27, 1 etc. The member of a sect is also called αἱρετιστής in Jos. Bell., 2, 119 ; Iambl. Protr. 21 κα' (in secular usage also the founder of a philosophical school, Diog. L, IX, 6) or αἱρεσιώτης, Just. Dial., 80, 3 ; Porphyr. Abst., IV, 11.
διαιρέω κτλ. [1] Preisigke Wört.

= 19:8 f. (an inheritance); or b. a "division," as in Ju. 5:16 : εἰς διαιρέσεις Ῥουβήν = 5:15 : εἰς τὰς μερίδας Ῥουβήν = clan; 1 Ch. 24:1; 2 Ch. 8:14; 35:5, 10, 12; 2 Esr. 6:18: courses of priests; 1 Ch. 26:19: διαιρέσεις τῶν πυλωρῶν, 1 Ch. 27:1-15: divisions of the army.

So far as concerns 1 C. 12:4 ff., this can be decided only from the context. The plur. διαιρέσεις, the opposition to τὸ δὲ αὐτὸ πνεῦμα, and the parallelism with the basic concept of ἡ φανέρωσις τοῦ πνεύματος (v. 7) all favour "distribution" rather than "distinction." The one Spirit is manifested in apportionments of gifts of the Spirit, so that in the community the one χάρις of God is experienced by charismatics in these distributions (of χαρίσματα). The one concept διαίρεσις here includes both distribution and what is distributed.

In early patristic writing we find the peculiar use of διαίρεσις to denote the distinction in the intertrinitarian relationship. Cf. Athen. Suppl., 10:3 : τὴν ἐν τῇ ἑνώσει δύναμιν καὶ τὴν ἐν τῇ τάξει διαίρεσιν of the Father, Son and Holy Spirit. Cf. 12, 2; Tatian, 5, 1 f.; Orig. in Joh., II, 10, 74.

Schlier

αἴρω, ἐπαίρω

αἴρω.

a. "to lift from the ground": Test. Sol., 23, 3, McCown, 69; b. "to lift with a view to carrying": LXX, Gn. 40:16; 45:23 etc.; c. "to carry off or put away": LXX, Gn. 35:2; 44:1 etc.; P. Tebt., II, 417 etc. Figur. in LXX 1 Βασ. 15:25 : αἴρειν ἁμάρτημα, and 25:28 : αἴρειν ἀνόμημα, to signify remission.

1. The basic meaning of "to lift up" is used in the religious language of the NT to signify the raising of the hand in an oath : ἦρεν τὴν → χεῖρα αὐτοῦ τὴν δεξιάν (Rev. 10:5, cf. Dt. 32:40; Da. 12:7), the raising of the face to heaven in prayer : ἦρεν τοὺς → ὀφθαλμοὺς ἄνω (Jn. 11:41),[1] and the raising of the voice in prayer : ἦραν → φωνὴν πρὸς τὸν θεόν (Ac. 4:24, cf. Ju. 21:2).

2. The sense of "to take up and carry" is found in Mt. 11:29 : Ἄρατε τὸν → ζυγόν μου, in which it is contrasted with taking up the yoke of the Torah, the commandments etc. (Ac. 15:10; Gl. 5:1)[2] and signifies obedience to the will of God declared by Jesus. Ἀράτω τὸν → σταυρὸν αὐτοῦ in Mk. 8:34 and par. is a picture signifying readiness for self-denial and martyrdom in following Jesus : ἐπὶ χειρῶν ἀροῦσίν σε (Mt. 4:6 and par. → ψ 90:12) implies protection by the guardian angel.

3. The idea of "to carry off" occurs in many connections in the religious language of the NT, being used of death: αἴρεται ἀπὸ τῆς γῆς ἡ ζωὴ αὐτοῦ (Ac. 8:33 = Is. 53:8, cf. Jn. 10:18); again of death[3] rather than[4] snatching away

---

αἴρω, ἐπαίρω. Pr.-Bauer, 35 ff., 437 f.; Str.-B., II, 363-370.
[1] Cf. Mk. 6:41 and par.; 7:34; Jn. 11:41; 17:1. Also Lk. 18:13; Ps. 123:1; 1 Esr. 4:58; Jos. Ant., 11, 162; Gn. r., 33 on 8:1; bJeb., 105b.
[2] Str.-B., I, 608-610; Buechler, *Studies in Sin and Atonement* (1928), 52-118.
[3] So A. Schlatter, *Sprache u. Heimat d. vierten Evangelisten* (1902), 134.
[4] Rabbinic usage is against this, cf. Schl. J., 323.

or rapture : [5] οὐκ ἐρωτῶ ἵνα ἄρῃς αὐτοὺς ἐκ τοῦ κόσμου (Jn. 17:15); of the depriving of salvation : ἀρθήσεται ἀφ' ὑμῶν ἡ βασιλεία τοῦ θεοῦ (Mt. 21:43); of the depriving of knowledge : ἤρατε τὴν κλεῖδα τῆς γνώσεως (Lk. 11:52); of the taking away of judgment : ἡ κρίσις αὐτοῦ ἤρθη (Ac. 8:33 = Is. 53:8); of the removal of guilt by the cross : τὸ καθ' ἡμῶν → χειρόγραφον ἦρκεν ἐκ τοῦ μέσου (Col. 2:14); of the expiation of sin : ἵνα τὰς ἁμαρτίας ἄρῃ (1 Jn. 3:5).

It has long been disputed whether the second or the third is the true meaning in the phrase : ὁ αἴρων τὴν ἁμαρτίαν τοῦ κόσμου (Jn. 1:29). [6] In both cases it is a matter of setting aside the guilt of others. In the former, however, the means of doing this is by a substitutionary bearing of penalty; [7] in the latter sin is removed by a means of expiation. [8] If the reference in Jn. 1:29 is primarily to the Servant of the Lord (טַלְיָא דַאֲלָהָא), then what is meant (→ ἀμνός) [9] is the representative bearing of the punishment of sin (cf. Is. 53:12 LXX : καὶ αὐτὸς ἁμαρτίας πολλῶν ἀνήνεγκεν, he took to himself the sins of many; cf. also Is. 53:4, 6, 11). But the Evangelist, who renders טַלְיָא דא by ἀμνὸς τοῦ θεοῦ, is thinking of the setting aside of sin by the expiatory power of the death of Jesus, so that we should translate the statement as follows : "Behold the Lamb of God, which taketh away the sin of the world" (i.e., by the atoning power of His blood, cf. 1 Jn. 1:7).

ἐπαίρω.

In the LXX mostly used for נָשָׂא a. "to set or lift up"; and by extension pass. b. "to lift up oneself against someone" (κατά τινος): LXX, 2 Esr. 4:19 with ἐπί, or "to exalt oneself" (abs.): LXX ψ 36:35; 3 Βασ. 1:5.

1. In the sense of "to lift up" ἐπαίρειν is used religiously to denote the gesture of prayer : ἐπαίρειν ὁσίους χεῖρας (1 Tm. 2:8), [1] ἐπαίρειν τοὺς → ὀφθαλμοὺς εἰς τὸν οὐρανόν (Lk. 18:13; Jn. 17:1 → 185); the gesture of blessing at departure : ἐπαίρειν τὰς χεῖρας Lk. 24:50, and elsewhere of the priest who blesses); [2] and in a figurative sense the gesture of hope : ἐπαίρειν τὰς κεφαλάς (Lk. 21:28; cf. נְשׂוּ ראֹשׁ in Zech. 2:4 etc.; LXX, αἴρειν κεφαλήν).

2. In the figurative pass. sense of "to raise up oneself" or "to oppose" : πᾶν ὕψωμα ἐπαιρόμενον κατὰ τῆς γνώσεως τοῦ θεοῦ (2 C. 10:5), or "to exalt oneself" : ἀνέχεσθε ... εἴ τις ἐπαίρεται (2 C. 11:20). In both cases we have to do with human pride arrogantly asserting itself against God (2 C. 10:5) or man (11:20).

Joachim Jeremias

---

[5] So Pr.-Bauer, 36.

[6] Cf. Str.-B., II, 363-370.

[7] LXX, Is. 53:12 : ἁμαρτίας πολλῶν ἀνήνεγκεν.

[8] LXX, Lv. 10:17 of the eating of the flesh of the sin-offering : ἵνα ἀφέλητε τὴν ἁμαρτίαν. The eating of the priest counts as an expiatory, cultic act. S. Lv. 10:17; cf. Str.-B., II, 366.

[9] Burney, *The Aramaic Origin of the Fourth Gospel* (1922), 107 f. For greater detail, cf. → ἀμνός.

ἐπαίρω. [1] LXX, 2 Esr. 18(8):6 vl.; ψ 133:2; Str.-B., II, 261; Dib. 1 Tm. *ad loc.*; → ἐκτείνω.

[2] Lv. 9:22; Sir. 50:20 (22); Str.-B., IV, 238-249; II, 76; III, 456, 458, 645.

† αἰσθάνομαι, αἴσθησις,
αἰσθητήριον

A. The Linguistic Usage outside the NT.

If we are to understand the word, we must see how wide is the range of possible meanings of αἰσθάνομαι. It is used to denote a. "sensual perception"; b. "perception" generally, esp. "spiritual discernment"; and c. "intellectual understanding." Under a. there is an original sharp distinction from → συνίημι (cf. c.). Man alone understands (ξυνίησι), whereas other creatures perceive by the senses (αἰσθάνεται) but do not understand (Diels, I, 135, 8). On b. cf. Jos. Ant., 18, 148 (247) etc. But c. is also found in Plat. Gorg., 479c : ἆρ' αἰσθάνει τὰ συμβαίνοντα ἐκ τοῦ λόγου. The person questioned is summoned to a decision which is first logical but which approximates closely to being ethical, and not finally in consequence of the totality of the Socratic dialectic. Cf. Thuc., I, 71: οἱ αἰσθανόμενοι = those who have insight; Jos. Ant., 19, 168 : οἱ ἀρετῆς αἰσθανόμενοι = those who direct their inner attention to virtue.

αἴσθησις. a. In original distinction from → λόγος, αἴσθησις is ἄπιστον (Heracl. in Diels, I, 74, 38) as "sensual perception." Thus also in the Hermetic literature αἴσθησις is an organ of the σῶμα whereas gnosis is an organ of the νοῦς: ὁ δὲ νοῦς τῷ σώματι ἐναντίος, Corp. Herm., X, 10a. In its most general meaning αἴσθησις denotes "sense." Along these lines αἴσθησις can be understood rather less precisely as an "organ of sense" (as already in Plat.). b. Though the Stoics do not equate → νοῦς and αἴσθησις, they regard them as two different ways of considering the same capacity of soul (v. Arnim, II, 230 [849]). With this there is bound up on the one side the assertion of the trustworthiness of αἰσθήσεις (v. Arnim, II, 27 [78]), and on the other the clear division between αἰσθήσεις and moral acts (III, 16 [63]). Jos. in the first instance understands by αἴσθησις a capacity of soul. In Ap., 2, 178 = Bell., 7, 343 it is the "power of recollection" (hence Ant., 19, 119 where it is almost "news" or "information"). In Bell., 1, 650 it is the power to enjoy the good things of the last time. c. In Epictetus "judgment" concerning the moral valuelessness of an ἐπιθυμία can be called αἴσθησις (Diss., II, 18, 8).[1]

There is variety in Philo's use of the term, but in general it is regarded in later Platonic fashion as the cause of passions (Leg. All., II, 50). It deceives and pollutes (Cher., 52), and is thus resisted by those who love wisdom (Cher., 41, although Philo concedes the possibility of training αἴσθησις in Vit. Mos., II, 81 f. etc.). In Philo it is predominantly "sensual perception," but along the lines of b. it can also be "consciousness" with even a hint of moral consciousness (Som., II, 292). It is often opposed to νοῦς, and above all to the processes of religious awareness (Migr. Abr., 5). At best, it can only mediate to man a sense of his own littleness (Spec. Leg., I, 293). But these are not consistent deductions from the later Platonic

---

αἴσθησις. Isolated observations on the history of the term may be found in O. Immisch, "Agatharchidea," SHA, Phil.-hist. Kl. (1919), 98-100; Meyer[8] on Phil. 1:9. — αἰσθητήριον. P. Linde, De Epicuri vocabulis ... (1906), 32; Rgg. Hb. 5:14.

[1] Dib. Phil., 1, 9.

idea, fairly widely developed in individual works of Philo, that αἴσθησις is to be rejected along with matter because of its connection with it. When in Leg. Gaj., 21 the decision of νοῦς in action is made dependent on correct αἴσθησις, Philo is following the usage of the day, or possibly Palestinian usage, which in general does not see any distinction between spirit and experience. He is not speaking in the stricter terms of philosophical theology.

αἰσθητήριον. a. "instrument of sense," [2] as always in Philo. On the other hand, Plut. can call νοῦς an αἰσθητήριον or "organ" of the ψυχή in Non Posse Suav. Viv. Sec. Epic., 14 (II, 1096e). This shift of meaning goes rather beyond anything found in the NT or 4 Macc.

In the LXX αἰσθάνομαι occasionally means purely a. "sensual perception" (Ep. Jer. 19, 41; cf. Job 40:18). Mostly, however, it indicates not merely b. "reception into a state of knowledge" (Job 23:5) but also c. a "judgment," whether moral (Prv. 17:10), religious (Is. 49:26) or general (4 Macc. 8:4). It thus means a conscious affirmation (Wis. 11:13), an actual understanding (Is. 33:11), which finally presses towards or even includes a decision. We can thus understand how it is that in the LXX αἴσθησις (always used for נעת except in Ex. 28:3; Prv. 14:7) signifies conscious apperception and is mostly equivalent to wisdom (Prv.), with an emphasis on the element of moral discrimination. Particularly striking is Prv. 1:7: εὐσέβεια δὲ εἰς θεὸν ἀρχὴ αἰσθήσεως, in which αἴσθησις is compared with σοφία and παιδεία. αἰσθητήριον thus denotes the "organs of the soul" which mediate between νοῦς and (θυμοί) πάθη and ἤθη, and which constitute the psychological point at which moral decision becomes actual (4 Macc. 2:22).

B. The Word Group in the NT.

In Lk. 9:45 αἰσθάνομαι obviously has the meaning c. The disciples have no inner understanding of the prophecy of the passion.

In Phil. 1:9 αἴσθησις also has the meaning c. It indicates the power of moral discrimination and ethical judgment as distinct from religious, and as further developed in v. 10.

In Hb. 5:14 αἰσθητήριον has much the same sense as c. and 4 Macc. 2:22, except that the point of view is different. The αἰσθητήρια are the organs which are capable of, or at least susceptible to, discrimination between good and evil, the τέλειος having so trained them by exercise that they have become a corresponding *habitus*. Here the *pneuma* has replaced the νοῦς of 4 Macc. 2, and αἰσθητήρια indicates a plurality of capacities for moral decision which through ἕξις have already developed into specific qualities.

> It is only to Christians of this developed moral character that the doctrine of justification by faith can be preached (v. 13), since νήπιοι so easily misunderstand it after the manner of the Judaising opponents of Paul. The λόγος δικαιοσύνης seems almost to be an esoteric doctrine (5:13). But it cannot lead the τέλειοι into moral danger, for they cannot attain to a second repentance (6:4 ff.). If the picture were further developed in 5:14b, and if doctrines were meant by καλοῦ τε καὶ κακοῦ, the view of the author would be quite distorted. [3]

Delling

---

[2] Examples may be found in Linde.
[3] As against Rgg. and Meyer-Weiss, *ad loc.*

| αἰσχύνω, ἐπαισχύνω, καταισχύνω, αἰσχύνη, αἰσχρός, αἰσχρότης | (→ αἰδώς). |

A. The Linguistic Usage in the LXX.

In contrast to → αἰδώς and αἰδεῖσθαι, αἰσχύνη and αἰσχύνω (or αἰσχύνομαι) remained in common use even in the lower strata of Greek, and must often have replaced the less usual terms. As in all the literature of Hellenistic Judaism, they are thus common in the LXX (mostly in translation of בּוֹשׁ and בֹּשֶׁת). Nor are they used in a special sense, except that there is a one-sided application which gives them a certain nuance.

The verb αἰσχύνω, fully interchangeable with ἐπ- and esp. καταισχύνω, is often found act. in the sense of "to shame" or "to bring to shame" (mostly for בּוֹשׁ). Most frequently God is the subject, and the shame to which He brings is His judgment (ψ 43:9, v.l. ἐξουδενόω; 118:31, 116). The mid. is relatively uncommon, and has the common Greek sense of "being ashamed" (i.e., of doing something, 2 Esr. 8:22 etc., or of having done something, 2 Ch. 12:6). Mostly αἰσχύνεσθαι denotes experience of the judgment of God; and it is usually difficult to decide whether the form is mid. or pass., i.e., "to be shamed or confounded," or "to be ashamed" in the sense of "having to be ashamed." What is in view is not so much the state of soul of the αἰσχυνθείς but the situation into which he is brought and in which he is exposed to shame and has thus to be ashamed. That the thought is primarily of one's own despair rather than the δόξα of others is shown by the fact that → ἀγαλλιᾶσθαι and εὐφραίνεσθαι are the most common opposites (ψ 34:26 f.; 69:3-5 etc.); indeed, when δοξάζεσθαι (→ δόξα) and → καυχᾶσθαι are the opposites (Is. 45:24 f.; ψ 96:7 etc.), they do not have their Greek sense, but indicate pride rather than good repute. Characteristic are the combinations and parallelisms of αἰσχυνθῆναι with ἐντραπῆναι, ταραχθῆναι, ἀτιμωθῆναι, ὀνειδισθῆναι, καταγελασθῆναι, ἐπιστραφῆναι, ἀποστραφῆναι εἰς τὰ ὀπίσω, ἐκλείπειν, ἡττᾶσθαι, ματαιωθῆναι, ἀπολέσθαι, συντριβῆναι etc., which illustrate the breadth of meaning. Since the reference is mostly to the αἰσχυνθῆναι of those who are full of proud confidence and expectancy, or to the fact that those who trust in Yahweh will not be confounded, αἰσχυνθῆναι often has almost the meaning of "being disillusioned" (e.g., Jer. 2:36).

Accordingly, the subst. αἰσχύνη is very seldom used for the "feeling of shame." [1] It mostly denotes "disgrace," though sometimes with an emphasis on the fact that this also means being ashamed. Its primary reference is to the shame brought by the divine judgment. Here, too, the range of meaning is shown by the combinations with ἐντροπή, ὀνειδισμός, ἀτιμία, etc. It is also characteristic that αἰσχύνη is used for בַּעַל or for the equivalent בֹּשֶׁת.

B. The NT Usage.

This is primarily determined by that of the LXX or Judaism. The verb, again used interchangeably with ἐπ- and καταισχύνω, is found in the act. in the older sense of "to shame" (1 C. 11:4 f.: τὴν κεφαλήν; cf. v. 14: ἀτιμία αὐτῷ ἐστιν).

αἰσχύνη. Bibliography as for αἰδώς, where the Greek use of αἰσχύνη is also treated.

[1] αἰσχύνη is used in the sexual sense for עֶרְוָה in Is. 20:4 etc.

Mostly, however, it means "to bring to shame." If the Greek sense of "to shame" is found in 1 C. 11:22 (τοὺς μὴ ἔχοντας, cf. Jm. 2:6 : ἀτιμάζειν), we are wholly on OT ground in 1 C. 1:27: ἵνα καταισχύνῃ (sc. God) τοὺς σοφούς ... τὰ ἰσχυρά, as is plainly shown by the parallel expression in v. 28 : ἵνα καταργήσῃ. The same is true of R. 5:5 : ἡ δὲ ἐλπὶς οὐ καταισχύνει.

The mid. is found in the older sense of "being ashamed" of doing something in Lk. 16:3 (ἐπαιτεῖν); Hb. 2:11; 11:16; cf. Herm. s., 9, 11, 3; or of something bad in R. 6:21 (ἐφ' οἷς νῦν ἐπαισχύνεσθε), or of a dubious person or cause in Mk. 8:38 and par. (με καὶ τοὺς ἐμοὺς λόγους); R. 1:16 (τὸ εὐαγγέλιον); 2 Tm. 1:8, 16. It is found in the absol. in 2 Tm. 1:12; 1 Pt. 4:16 and 1 Jn. 2:28 : ἵνα ... σχῶμεν παρρησίαν καὶ μὴ αἰσχυνθῶμεν ἀπ' αὐτοῦ. If the word were not used as the opposite of παρρησία in 1 Jn. 2:28, we might well put it in the following group, in which αἰσχύνεσθαι bears the partly mid. and partly pass. sense of being ashamed as found in the OT. This sense is found not merely in the quotation from Is. 28:16 in R. 9:33 (cf. 10:11) and in 1 Pt. 2:6, but also in 2 C. 10:8 : ἐάν τε γὰρ περισσότερόν τι καυχήσωμαι ... οὐκ αἰσχυνθήσομαι (→ 189); and again in 2 C. 7:14 : εἴ τι ... κεκαύχημαι, οὐ κατῃσχύνθην (cf. the continuation : ἡ καύχησις ... ἀλήθεια ἐγενήθη). There can be no doubt that αἰσχυνθῆναι includes an enforced sense of shame in these passages, and cf. Phil. 1:20, where we find the sense of being disillusioned : κατὰ τὴν ἀποκαραδοκίαν καὶ ἐλπίδα μου, ὅτι ἐν οὐδενὶ αἰσχυνθήσομαι, ἀλλ' ἐν πάσῃ παρρησίᾳ ... μεγαλυνθήσεται Χριστός. Similarly in 2 C. 9:4 : μή πως ... καταισχυνθῶμεν ἡμεῖς ... ἐν τῇ ὑποστάσει ταύτῃ, where in view of the typical correspondence of expectation and being ashamed the contested → ὑπόστασις must surely be understood as confidence. Finally, in 1 Pt. 3:16 and Lk. 13:17 καταισχυνθῆναι has the sense of being put in a situation in which one has to be ashamed.

The subst. αἰσχύνη, which in Did., 4, 11 and Barn., 19, 7 is used for αἰδώς with φόβος, is found in the NT only in the sense of "disgrace," or at the most "shame" in Lk. 14:9 : ἄρξῃ μετ' αἰσχύνης τὸν ἔσχατον τόπον κατέχειν. If in Hb. 12:2 : ὑπέμεινεν σταυρὸν αἰσχύνης καταφρονήσας, αἰσχύνη is the disgrace brought on one by others, in Jd. 13 : ἐπαφρίζοντα τὰς ἑαυτῶν αἰσχύνας, it is the disgrace one brings on oneself by one's own action. This is perhaps the meaning in 2 C. 4:2 also : ἀπειπάμεθα τὰ κρυπτὰ τῆς αἰσχύνης, i.e., either hidden things which bring shame (gen. qual., αἰσχύνη thus corresponding to the ἀτιμία of R. 1:26), or hidden shameful things (gen. subj.). Otherwise, it might have the sense of things which shame hides (gen. subj.). Reference may also be made to Phil. 3:19 : ὧν ... ἡ δόξα ἐν τῇ αἰσχύνῃ αὐτῶν, and Rev. 3:18 : ἵνα περιβάλῃ καὶ μὴ φανερωθῇ ἡ αἰσχύνη τῆς γυμνότητός σου, where we find the meaning of disgrace, but in such a way that there is a play on the sexual sense of αἰσχύνη.

From the root αἰσχ- we also find αἰσχρός in the NT in the sense of "that which is disgraceful" in the judgment of men (1 C. 11:6; 14:35), especially as expressed in words (Eph. 5:12, cf. Herm. v., 1, 1, 7) or in relation to filthy lucre (Tt. 1:11). This corresponds to Greek usage, as does the use of the compounds αἰσχρολογία (Col. 3:8; Did., 5, 1), αἰσχρολόγος (Did., 3, 3) and αἰσχροκερδής (1 Tm. 3:3 [א] 8; Tt. 1:7; Adv. 1 Pt. 5:2) — words which are typical in the lists of vices, c. 30 of the Characters of Theophr. being devoted to αἰσχροκερδής. Perhaps αἰσχρολογία and αἰσχροκέρδεια may be described as more choice.[2] The

---

[2] Cf. Nägeli, 18.

rarer αἰσχρότης, [3] which is attested only in Attic literature, is found once in Eph. 5:4, where it occurs with μωρολογία and εὐτραπελία in the sense of αἰσχρολογία.

Bultmann

αἰτέω, αἴτημα, ἀπαιτέω,
ἐξαιτέω, παραιτέομαι

(→ εὔχομαι).

αἰτέω (αἰτέομαι).

Constructions [1] (act. and mid.): τι (Lk. 1:63), τινα (Mt. 5:42), τί τινα [2] (Mt. 7:9), τι ἀπό τινος (only act., Mt. 20:20), [3] τι παρά τινος (Ac. 3:2), with inf. (Eph. 3:13), acc. c. inf. (Lk. 23:23), with ἵνα (only mid., Col. 1:9). The Heb. equivalent in the OT is mostly שׁאל, the Aram. בעא (Θ Da. 2:49; 6:7, 12 f.), [4] both with the same twofold sense of "to demand" and "to request."

1. αἰτέω (αἰτέομαι) as "to demand."

Jos. Ant., 1, 224. LXX (mostly mid.): Dt. 10:12; Ju. 8:24, 26 (B: act.). NT: Lk. 1:63: αἰτήσας πινακίδιον ἔγραψεν; Ac. 16:29: αἰτήσας δὲ φῶτα εἰσεπήδησεν.

In the NT concrete demands are often given a religious application. Thus payment is demanded in financial transactions (P. Oxy. 54, 15); [5] in Lk. 12:48 [6] this is transferred to the sphere of ethical obligations: ᾧ παρέθεντο πολύ, περισσότερον αἰτήσουσιν [7] αὐτόν. Again, in public life accreditation is required (Jos. Ant., 19, 85); similarly in 1 C. 1:22 the Jews demand σημεῖα in proof of the Messiahship of Jesus. [8] Again, as λόγον αἰτεῖν τινα means to exact an account of someone (P. Hamb., 6, 8 f.), so it is in 1 Pt. 3:15: ἕτοιμοι ἀεὶ πρὸς ἀπολογίαν παντὶ τῷ αἰτοῦντι [9] ὑμᾶς λόγον περὶ τῆς ἐν ὑμῖν ἐλπίδος.

In Judaism, too, it was required that a man should be able to give an account of his religion; [10] cf. S. Dt., 34 on 6:7: "If a man ask thee ought (from the Torah), thou shalt not give a stammering or uncertain answer." [11]

2. αἰτέω (αἰτέομαι) as "to request."

a. For the transition from the former meaning to the latter, cf. Xenoph. An., II, 1, 10: θαυμάζω, πότερα ὡς κρατῶν βασιλεὺς αἰτεῖ τὰ ὅπλα ἢ ὡς διὰ φιλίαν δῶρα. In the NT there is vacillation between the two meanings in the par. passages Mt. 5:42 and Lk. 6:30: [12] τῷ αἰτοῦντί σε δός. In the sense of "to request" the act. is found as early as Homer, and the mid. from Herodotus.

---

[3] Cf. Nägeli, 14 and 85.

α ἰ τ έ ω. Bengel, 383 f.; Trench[12] (1894), 143 ff., and cf. E. Abbott, in *North American Review*, 114 (1872), 171-189, esp. 182 ff.; Cr.-Kö., 91 f.; EB, 3824; Bl. Debr. § 316, 2; Moulton, 251 f.; Mayor, Jk. (1892), 128 f.; also Exp., VIII, 3 (1912), 522-527; Dalman, WJ, I, 99 f.; on the Lat. par. *rogo*: Abbott, *op. cit.*, 196 f.; on *oro*: F. Heerdegen, *Unters. z. lat. Semasiologie*, III (1881). On the forms and contents of early Christian prayer → εὔχομαι.

[1] Buttmann § 131, 6; Bl. Debr. § 155, 2; 392, 1c.

[2] Also in the mid.: Jn. 11:22 (overlooked by Bl.-Debr. § 155, 2).

[3] א rec: παρ', so A rec in 1 Jn. 5:15.

[4] Cf. Dalman, WJ, I, 99 f.

[5] F. Preisigke, *Girowesen i. griech. Ägypten* (1910), 136 f.

[6] Zn. Lk., 511; Jülicher, *Gleichnisreden*, II² (1910), 156 f.

[7] D: ἀπαιτήσουσιν (→ ἀπαιτέω, 194).

[8] Zn. Mt., 467 f.; Schl. Mt., 413 ff.; Str.-B., I, 640 f.

[9] A: ἀπαιτοῦντι (→ ἀπαιτέω, 193).

[10] Str.-B., III, 765 f.

[11] Cf. S. Nu., 119 on 18:20; Ab., 2, 14; esp. bSan., 38b.

[12] A. Tholuck, *D. Bergrede Christi*⁵ (1872), 249: an unjustifiable request amounting almost to confiscation.

The NT knows this usage both in the secular and the religious sense. There is no striking distinction between the act. and the mid. The many distinctions sought by older grammarians [13] and more recent exegetes [14] are not for the most part supported by the sources. On the other hand, the mid. seems to be preferred in commercial [15] or official relationships.

As regards the former, the LXX uses the term in connection with things which are requested as a dowry (Jos. 15:18, though cf. Ju. 1:14 act.), as an inheritance (Jos. 19:50 = 21:40 [LXX, 42b]), as a condition of alliance (2 S. 3:13), or as the gift of a host (which is a transaction in the orient, cf. 1 K. 10:13). In the NT cf. Mk. 6:24 f. with v. 22 f.; the transaction began with the promise of Herod: αἴτησόν με ὃ ἐὰν θέλῃς, καὶ δώσω σοι. [16] As regards official relationships, cf. in the LXX 3 Βασ. 2:16, 20, 22 of Adonijah and Solomon; 1 Εσδρ. 4:42, 46 (8:51 A: act.); 2 Εσδρ. 8:22 of Ezra and the emperor. In the NT cf. Mk. 15:6 (rec), 8 and par. (Ac. 3:14); Lk. 23:23 (Ac. 13:28) of the people and Pilate; Mk. 15:43 and par. of Joseph of Arimathea and Pilate (Jn. 19:38, ἐρωτάω); Ac. 9:2 of Paul and the high-priest; 12:20 of the representatives of the cities and Herod. Cf. also Mt. 20:22 and par. with v. 20 and par. where Jesus speaks to the mother of the sons of Zebedee as the future King.

b. In religious usage it is almost impossible to distinguish between the mid. and act. [17] Such a distinction is often attempted on the basis of Jm. 4:2 f., the act. signifying prayer with the lips and the mid. prayer with the heart: [18] οὐκ ἔχετε διὰ τὸ μὴ αἰτεῖσθαι ὑμᾶς· αἰτεῖτε καὶ οὐ λαμβάνετε, διότι κακῶς αἰτεῖσθε. The variation is certainly striking, but the distinction is not borne out by the rest of the NT (cf. esp. 1 Jn. 5:15; Jn. 16:24, 26; also Mt. 21:22/Jn. 11:22). Hence we have no option but to explain it in terms of the formal structure of the sentence, i.e., the linking of its components into a kind of chain. [19]

The use of αἰτέομαι for petitionary prayer is naturally the most important theologically in the NT. But sometimes requests to men and to God are brought into juxtaposition, as in Mt. 7:9 ff.; Lk. 11:10 ff. The request of the human child brings out the unconditional nature (πᾶς) both of what we may ask and of its certain fulfilment by God.

Jesus uses αἰτέω only of the prayer of others, not of His own (cf. Jn. 16:26), which is always for Him an ἐρωτᾶν (Jn. 14:16 etc.) or δεῖσθαι (Lk. 22:32), [20] though Martha thinks nothing of applying the term αἰτεῖν to Him too (Jn. 11:22). Perhaps in explanation we might suggest that the basic meaning of αἰτέω is to want something, in the first instance for oneself. When Jesus prays, however, there is no question of His wanting things for Himself, but only for others. Again,

---

[13] Mid. "to request as a loan" (act. as a gift); so Suidas, s.v. αἰτούμενος; cf. also Valckenaer, *Animadv. ad Ammon. Grammat.*[2] (1822), §§ 12 ff. Mid. "to ask beseechingly"; so Favorianus, s.v. αἰτοῦμαι; cf. also Mayor and Hauck on Jm. 4:2 f. Artemidor, 4, 2: act. requests to man; mid. requests to God.

[14] Mid. (usually) "to ask for oneself"; so Cr.-Kö., 92, Radermacher,[2] 146, 2 (on Mk. 10:38). Act.: (usually) with the acc. of pers.; mid.: with the acc. of things; so Hort, Jm. (1909), 90 f.; cf. Mayor Exp., VIII, 3 (1912), 523 ff.

[15] Bl.-Debr. § 316, 2; Moulton, 251 f. and also Grammar, I[3] (1908), 160 f.

[16] Bl.-Debr., *op. cit.*

[17] For other usage, cf. Ps.-Plat. Eryx., 398e: προσευχόμενος αἰτεῖς παρὰ τῶν θεῶν δοῦναί σοι ἀγαθά; Xenoph. Cyrop., I, 6, 5: αἰτεῖσθαι τἀγαθὰ παρὰ τῶν θεῶν. Cf. also Jos. Ant., 9, 70; Herm. v., 3, 10, 7; m., 9, 4; Cl. Al. Strom., VI, 8, 63, 1 f.

[18] Mayor, Exp., 525; Jm., 128 f.: mid.: "a certain special diligence and earnestness"; act.: "without the spirit of prayer" (cf. Moulton, 251 f.). Similiarly Hauck Jk., 192.

[19] Cf. Dib. Jk., 201; also Bl.-Debr. § 316, 2; Powell Class. Rev., 28 (1914), 192 f.; Ropes Jk., 259; Wnd. Jk., 25.

[20] Bengel, 383 f.; Trench, 145.

αἰτέω might easily suggest a far from humble demanding, whereas Jesus never demands (Schlatter). Again, αἰτέω seems to presuppose a lesser degree of intimacy than ἐρωτάω; hence αἰτέω is used of the requests of the disciples to God, but ἐρωτάω of the requests of the disciples to Jesus, and of those of Jesus to God. [21]

In Mk. 10:35 αἰτέω is also used of a request of the disciples to Jesus, but codd D 1 rightly have ἐρωτάω here too; cf. also Jn. 14:13 f., where we have real prayer to Jesus in analogy to prayer to God.

† αἴτημα.

Verbal substant. of αἰτέω with -μα [1] in the passive sense [2] of "what is demanded or requested." 1. "Demand" : Plat. Resp., VIII, 566b : αἴτημα τυραννικόν, "demand of a tyrant"; cf. Plut. Demetr., 3 (I, 890b); Lk. 23:24 : Πιλᾶτος ἐπέκρινεν γενέσθαι τὸ αἴτημα αὐτῶν, i.e., the popular demand for the crucifixion, and therefore spec. a verbal substant. for official αἰτέομαι (before the procurator, → αἰτέω 192).

2. "Request," "petition" or "desire." Outside the NT it is found in this sense in Aristot. Rhet. Al., 20 p, 1433 b, 17 ff.; P. Flor., 296, 16 (a written petition); LXX, 3 Βασ. 12:24 d; Est. 7:2 f.: αἴτημα καὶ ἀξίωμα. The transition from requests to men to requests to God is illustrated in ΘDa. 6:7, 12. For requests to God, cf. LXX ψ 36:4; 105:15; ΘDa. 6:13; Ps. Sol. 6:8; Jos. Ant., 8, 24; Herm. m., 9, 2, 4 and 5; s., 4, 6.

In the NT it is esp. used of the individual petitions which constitute a prayer (προσευχή). [3] In distinction from δέησις, αἴτημα points to the content of the request. [4] So Phil. 4:6 : ἐν παντὶ τῇ προσευχῇ καὶ τῇ δεήσει μετὰ εὐχαριστίας τὰ αἰτήματα ὑμῶν γνωριζέσθω πρὸς τὸν θεόν; [5] 1 Jn. 5:15 : οἴδαμεν ὅτι ἔχομεν τὰ αἰτήματα ἃ ᾐτήκαμεν ἀπ᾽ [6] αὐτοῦ.

The fig. etym. αἰτέω (Θ NT) or αἰτέομαι (LXX) [7] αἴτημα has Semitic roots. [8] Cf. Ju. 8:24; 1 S. 1:17, 27: שׁאל שְׁאֵלָה; M. Ex. 17:14 : בקשׁ בקשׁות; S. Nu., 105 on 12:13 : בקשׁ שׁאלות. In the LXX : "to place a demand" in Ju. 8:24 B; or "to direct a request" (to men) in 3 Βασ. 12:24d; (to men and God). ΘDa. 6:7, 12; (to God) 1 S. 1:17, 27; 1 K. 3:5; Jos. Ant., 11, 58; Herm. m., 9, 7 and 8.

† ἀπαιτέω.

1. "To demand." Plut. Def. Orac., 14 (II, 417c); Jos. Ant., 6, 203; 7, 64 : ἀπαιτέω λόγον = αἰτέω λόγον (→ αἰτέω, 191). "To demand an account" : Plat.

---

[21] On the distinctions between αἰτέω, δέομαι, ἐρωτάω and προσεύχομαι, as also on the presuppositions and objects of petitionary prayer, → εὐχή, εὔχομαι.

α ἴ τ η μ α. Trench, 115 ff. (Eng.[12], 1894, 188 ff.); Cr.-Kö., 92.
[1] Bl. Debr. § 109, 3.
[2] Of course, αἴτησις is often used in the same sense, as in Ju. 8:24 A; Job 6:8; Ign. Tr., 13, 3.
[3] In the Lord's Prayer it is possible to distinguish 7 αἰτήματα or 3 εὐχαί and 4 αἰτήματα, cf. Trench, 191 (118).
[4] A. Klöpper, Phil. (1893) 236, 1; Loh. Phil., 169 f.
[5] For αἴτημα with προσευχή, though with no distinction, cf. also Ps. Sol. 6:8.
[6] A rec : παρ᾽ (as Mt. 20, 20).
[7] Cf. here in the same sense αἰτέομαι αἴτησιν (Ju. 8:24 A; 1 K. 2:16, 20).
[8] A. Schlatter, Sprache und Heimat des vierten Evangelisten (1902), 151.
ἀ π α ι τ έ ω. Schleusner, NT-Lex., s.v.; Cr.-Kö., 92. On the difference between ἀπαιτέω and αἰτέω, cf. Andoc. 2, 22 : ἃ γάρ μοι αὐτοὶ ... ἔδοτε, ὕστερον δὲ ... ἀφείλεσθε, ταῦθ᾽ ὑμᾶς εἰ μὲν βούλεσθε αἰτῶ, εἰ δὲ μὴ βούλεσθε ἀπαιτῶ. Cf. also Arist. Rhet., II, 6, p. 1383b, 29 f.; Favorinus, s.v. ἀπαιτίζω.

Resp., X, 599b; NT: 1 Pt. 3:15 A etc.: ἕτοιμοι ἀεὶ πρὸς ἀπολογίαν παντὶ τῷ ἀπαιτοῦντι ὑμᾶς λόγον περὶ τῆς ἐν ὑμῖν ἐλπίδος.

2. "To demand back," e.g., what has been stolen: Menand. Epit., 87, 97 and 100; Jos. Ant., 8, 29; Lk. 6:30 (→ αἰτέω, 191): ἀπὸ τοῦ αἴροντος τὰ σὰ μὴ ἀπαίτει. b. "To call in debts":[1] Dt. 15:2 f.; BGU, 183, 8. Hence in the parable it is used for the demand of God on man, Lk. 12:48 D (→ αἰτέω, 191): ᾧ παρέθεντο πολύ, πλέον ἀπαιτήσουσιν[2] αὐτόν. Again, according to the ancient view life is a loan of nature[3] or of God which has to be paid back at death.[4] Cf. Lk. 12:20: ἄφρων, ταύτῃ τῇ νυκτὶ τὴν ψυχήν σου ἀπαιτοῦσιν[5] (B: αἰτοῦσιν ἀπὸ σοῦ).

† ἐξαιτέω.

"To demand of." a. "to require": (act.) BGU, 944, 8; b. "To demand the freedom of": (mid.) Plut. Pericl., 32 (I, 169e); c. "To demand the surrender of": (act.) Jos. Ant., 5, 152 (= αἰτέω πρὸς τιμωρίαν, 5, 153); (mid.) Jos. Ant., 16, 272.

Lk. 22:31: ὁ σατανᾶς ἐξῃτήσατο ὑμᾶς τοῦ σινιάσαι ὡς τὸν σῖτον. A case may be made out here for a.[1] or b.[2]; but c. is more likely in the sense that the devil demands the test,[3] as in Job 1 f. to which Jesus clearly alludes. The devil is the anti-Messiah who winnows (cf. Mt. 3:12) or sifts the wheat.[4] He has the right to bring to light the evil in men[5] and to recall their guilt before God. He plays the role of the κατήγορος (q.v.),[6] just as in Zech 3:1 ff. he is portrayed as a heavenly official, and as an instrument of ethical detection[7] in Job 1 f.[8] In later Judaism, too, the devil is the accuser קטיגור = κατήγωρ.[9],[10] Jesus opposes His request (ἐδεήθην, v. 32) to the devilish demand (Bengel). The latter is conceded, but Jesus sees to it that Peter survives the test.[11]

Cf. Test. B 3:3: ἐὰν τὰ πνεύματα τοῦ βελίαρ εἰς πᾶσαν πονηρίαν τοῦ θλίβειν[12] ἐξαιτήσωνται ὑμᾶς ...; Plut. Def. Orac., 14 (II, 417d): ἰσχυροὶ καὶ βίαιοι δαίμονες ἐξαιτούμενοι ψυχὴν ἀνθρωπίνην.

---

[1] Cf. L. Wenger, Die Stellvertretung im Rechte d. Papyri (1906), 189 ff.
[2] D obviously has in view the parable of the talents (in the Mt. form). Because of the parallelism it is probably to be preferred to the usual αἰτήσουσιν.
[3] Cic. Resp., 1, 4 (5).
[4] Cf. Wis. 15:8: τὸ τῆς ψυχῆς ἀπαιτηθεὶς χρέος (also Epict. Diss., IV, 1, 172).
[5] Pers. plur. = "one" (God being intended); cf. on this use Str.-B., II, 221, and in the NT also Mt. 7:2; Lk. 6:38; 16:9.
ἐ ξ α ι τ έ ω. Zn. Lk., 683, n. 62; Cr.-Kö., 92.
[1] So Hofmann, 8, 529; Kl. Lk. ad loc. (trans.); Pr.-Bauer, s.v.
[2] So ad loc. Zn. ("to ask for"); Bengel; Holtzmann Hand-Comm.; J. Weiss, Schriften d. NT. Also Cr.-Kö., op. cit.
[3] Wünsche, RE,³ 19, 565.
[4] Metaphor of the hostile neighbour? cf. Mt. 13:25, 39.
[5] Hofmann, Schriftbeweis, I, 434.
[6] Cf. Schlatter, Nt.liche Theol., I (1910), 583; P. Fiebig, ZNW, 9 (1908), 311.
[7] Clemen, 112; Wünsche, op. cit.
[8] Cf. also the designation מַזְכִּיר עָוֹן for Egypt and Babylon in Ez. 21:28 f.; 29:16; and also the aversion from the man of God as the one who reminds of guilt in 1 K. 17:18.
[9] Cf. Str.-B., I, 136, 141 ff.
[10] Cf. also Βεε(λ)ζεβούλ.
[11] Godet, Lk. (Germ., 1872), 437.
[12] cj Charles, codd: θλίψεως.

† παραιτέομαι.

1. In all Greek the word can be used in the sense of "begging" (LXX, Est. 4:8) or "begging off" (Plut. Demetr., 9 [I, 893a]; Mk. 15:6 ‭א‬* B* etc.).[1] It can thus signify begging to be excused, e.g., an invitation : LXX, 1 S. 20:6, 28; Jos. Ant., 7, 175; and in the NT in the parable of the guests excusing themselves from the supper : Lk. 14:18a (mid.); 18b, 19 (pass.).

2. More important in the NT, however, is another group of meanings in which the prefix παρ- gives a nuance of aversion or repudiation. a. "To seek to turn aside by asking" (with inf. and pleon. μή)[2]: Plat. Resp., III, 387b; Jos. Ant., 10, 203. In the NT Hb. 12:19 : οἱ ἀκούσαντες παρητήσαντο μὴ προστεθῆναι αὐτοῖς λόγον. The request (Dt. 5:25; 18:16) originally dictated by humble fear of God and recognised by God to be justifiable (Dt. 18:17) is here understood to be a sinful repudiation of the divine revelation.[3] Similarly in Ac. 25:11 Paul will not try to avert punishment by entreaty.[4]

b. "To reject or repudiate" : P. Oxy, 1252 B, 28 (something); Jos. Ant., 7, 167 (someone). In the NT the word is used in this sense in relation to different actions in the the supervision of doctrine and the exercise of congregational discipline. It is noteworthy that it occurs only in the Pastorals. In 1 Tm. 4:7 it signifies the rebuttal of βέβηλοι καὶ γραώδεις μῦθοι, in 2 Tm. 2:23 the rejection of → ζητήσεις, and in 1 Tm. 5:11 the refusal to accept widows under 60 years of age on the list of ὄντως χῆραι.[5] From this rather forceful application there arises the meaning of expulsion in the sense of putting out disruptive elements and possibly of excommunication, as in Tt. 3:10 : αἱρετικὸν ἄνθρωπον μετὰ μίαν καὶ δευτέραν νουθεσίαν παραιτοῦ.[6] This is clearly linked, however, with the meaning already found elsewhere.

c. "To disdain," "to spurn" : Plut. Them., 3, 4 (I, 113b); Dg., 4, 2. In the NT this is used of turning from God[7] in Hb. 12:25 (cf. v.19): βλέπετε μὴ παραιτήσεσθε τὸν λαλοῦντα.

Stählin

> † αἰχμάλωτος, † αἰχμαλωτίζω,
> † αἰχμαλωτεύω, † αἰχμαλωσία,
> † συναιχμάλωτος

1. Proper Use.

In both OT and NT the "prisoner of war" is a miserable person who stands in special need of God's help (Ps. 79:11 etc.), having been swallowed up by a terrible enemy (Lk. 21:24; Rev. 13:10 ; par. to ἐν μαχαίρῃ ἀποκτανθῆναι). The national

---

π α ρ α ι τ έ ο μ α ι. Cr.-Kö., 93; Koelling, 1 Tm., II (1887), 274, 320; Wbg. Past., 159, n. 1.

[1] CDGW rec : αἰτέομαι; → 192, as also Bl. Debr. § 367.
[2] Bl.-Debr. § 429.
[3] Wnd. Hb., 113.
[4] Cf. 4 Macc. 11:2. Deissmann (in Kautzsch) translates "to give way to constraint," referring to 1 C. 6:7 and Blass, *Grammatik* (1896), 181. But comparison with Ac. 25:11 suggests "to try to evade."
[5] Koelling, 298 ff.; Dib. Past. on 1 Tm. 5:3-16; B. Weiss,[5] 203 takes a different view.
[6] Cf. Diog. L., VI, 82.
[7] Synon. the even stronger → ἀποστρέφεσθαι; cf. Rgg. Hb., 423, 51.

disaster of the exile made the αἰχμαλωσία Σιών a destiny which was particularly understood in religious terms (Ps. 126:1 etc.). Hence the κηρῦξαι αἰχμαλώτοις ἄφεσιν (Mas. לִקְרֹא לִשְׁבוּיִם דְּרוֹר)[1] is one of the tasks of the messenger in Is. 61:1, and is accepted by Jesus in Lk. 4:18 as a Messianic function. In the same way, visiting prisoners (ἐν φυλακῇ ὤν) is one of the duties of discipleship in the exercise of love according to Mt. 25:36 ff. (Hb. 10:34; 13:3 : μιμνῄσκεσθε τῶν δεσμίων ὡς συνδεδεμένοι).

In the OT the thought of imprisonment is always self-evidently linked with prayer for liberation. The same principle is illustrated by the Rabbinic anecdote about a great sinner who gained merit by helping a prisoner to freedom (jTaan., 64b). Josephus journeys to Rome (Vit., 13 ff.) to secure the liberation of imprisoned priests. In the NT, too, the freeing of prisoners is sought so earnestly that sometimes it is attributed to divine miracle (Ac. 5:19; 12:7; 16:26)[2] and is made an object of prayer (Phlm. 22). At any rate, Paul can raise the question whether ἀναλῦσαι καὶ σὺν Χριστῷ εἶναι is not to be preferred (Phil. 1:23). On the other hand, a new outlook arises when the idea of merit comes to be associated with martyrdom. Thus Ignatius passionately declines liberation (R., 2, 2; 4, 1).

2. Figurative Use.

The thought of imprisonment in war is carried over into the inner moral and religious struggle of man and for man. This use is not found in the OT.[3] In the NT it occurs only in Paul, who shows a partiality for military images (→ στρατεύομαι etc.). Paul applies it in different ways, e.g., to those who lead astray : αἰχμαλωτίζοντες γυναικάρια σεσωρευμένα ἁμαρτίαις (2 Tm. 3:6); to express subjection to sin : (ἕτερον νόμον) αἰχμαλωτίζοντά με ἐν τῷ νόμῳ τῆς ἁμαρτίας (R. 7:23); but also, along the lines of the δουλεύειν ἐν καινότητι πνεύματος of R. 7:6, to illustrate the subjection of our thoughts to Christ : αἰχμαλωτίζοντες πᾶν νόημα εἰς τὴν ὑπακοὴν τοῦ Χριστοῦ (2 C. 10:5); and also to express the subjection of spirits[4] to Christ : ᾐχμαλώτευσεν αἰχμαλωσίαν (Eph. 4:8, quoting Ps. 68:18).[5]

The same figurative use is found in the LXX at Jdt. 16:9. It occurs occasionally in the post-apostolic writings, Ign. Eph., 17, 1 referring to imprisonment by the ἄρχων τοῦ αἰῶνος τούτου, Phld., 2, 2 to imprisonment by wolves, Ir., I, praef. 1 by false teachers, Pall. Hist. Laus., 69 (p. 165, Butler) by temptation, O. Sol. 10:3 f. to the fact that Christ takes souls and the world captive, and Lidz. Ginza, 49, 33 to the fact that the tempter makes prisoners in the world and leads men astray by introducing to them his own wisdom.

In connection with this metaphorical use of αἰχμαλωτίζω we should also note the description of Paul's individual helpers as συναιχμάλωτος in R. 16:7, Col.

αἰχμάλωτος. [1] In the original the thought of liberation from captivity is even more strongly emphasised by the final part of the verse : וְלַאֲסוּרִים פְּקַח־קוֹחַ ("and liberation to them that are bound"); but this is paraphrased in LXX and Lk. by καὶ τυφλοῖς ἀνάβλεψιν. Similarly the Tg. paraphrases : "And the revelation of light to those who are blind." This allegorisation is traditional in the Synagogue, probably on the basis of Is. 42:7.

[2] Cf. O. Weinreich, Gebet und Wunder (1929), 281 ff.

[3] The image in Jer. 16:16 (followed in Mk. 1:17 and par.) has nothing to do with military service and is therefore quite different (as against Wnd. 2 K., 298).

[4] The interpretation in v. 9 ff. does not elucidate the ᾐχμαλώτευσεν αἰχμαλωσίαν, but in the context it is only possible to think of spirits, cf. Dib. Gfbr., 61.

[5] For the Rabbinic interpretation of the quotation, cf. Str.-B., III, 596.

4:10 and Phlm. 23. If he really meant literal imprisonment with him, σύνδεσμιος or συνδεσμώτης would be more likely, since Paul in his imprisonment never describes himself as αἰχμάλωτος, but always as → δέσμιος. Once again we most likely have the military image. This is suggested by Paul's recollections of battles and persecutions, and it is no accident that it is during his prison days that he uses it. Warfare and captivity carry with them a hint of the higher warfare and captivity along the lines of 2 C. 10:5 and Eph. 4:8. The one who has a particular part in the external conflict can be called → συστρατιώτης from the one standpoint and → συναιχμάλωτος from the other. The latter, however, is wholly equivalent in content to the → σύνδουλος (ἐν κυρίῳ) of Col. 1:7 and 4:7. The three συν- constructions are not applied to all fellow-workers, but have a special emphasis which singles out individuals. [6]

Kittel

αἰών, αἰώνιος

αἰών.

A. The Non-Biblical Use.

a. "Vital force," or "life" in Hom. Il., 9, 415; Od., 5, 152 etc.; cf. ψυχή τε καὶ αἰών, Il., 16, 453; Od., 9, 523; Pind. Fr. 111, 5 (Schroeder). b. "Lifetime": αἰών βίοιο, Hesiod. Fr., 161, 1 (Rzach); αἰών μόρσιμος, Pind. Olymp., II, 11; Hdt., I, 32; Thuc., I, 70, 8; Xenoph. Cyrop., VIII, 7, 1. c. "Age" or "generation" in Aesch. Sept. c. Theb., 742 and 771; Soph. Fr., 1021, 1 (Nauck); plur. Emped. Fr., 129, 6 (Diels, I, 272, 20). d. "Space of time" or "time," with ref. to the past in Demosth. Ep., 2, 7: ἐν ἅπαντι τῷ αἰῶνι; Or., 18, 203: πάντα τὸν αἰῶνα; to the future in 18, 199: δόξα ἢ προγόνων ἢ τοῦ μέλλοντος αἰῶνος; to the present in Psephisma of Assos Ditt. Syll.[3], 797, 9: αἰών ἐνεστώς; plur. μακροὺς αἰῶνας, Theocr., XVI, 43. e. "Eternity," since Plat. (*infra*); hyperbol. ἐξ ... αἰῶνος, "from eternity," Lycurg., 110, Diod. S., I, 63, 5; δι' αἰῶνος, Ps.-Demosth. Or., 60, 6; Diod. S., III, 8, 5; κατὰ ... αἰῶνος, Lycurg., 7; εἰς αἰῶνα, Lycurg., 106; εἰς ἅπαντα τὸν αἰῶνα "in eternity," *loc. cit.*

From the days of Heraclitus (αἰών παῖς ἐστι παίζων, Fr. 52, Diels, I, 88, 1) and Empedocles the philosophers made use of the term in discussions of the problem of time. The high-water mark of such discussions is found in Plato's Timaeus. Whereas Greek in general distinguishes between χρόνος and αἰών, using the former for time in itself and the latter for the relative time allotted to

---

[6] But cf. Hb. 13:3: ὡς συνδεδεμένοι (→ 196).

α ἰ ώ ν. C. Lackeit, *Aion. Zeit u. Ewigkeit in Sprache u. Religion d. Griechen,* I (1916); C. Clemen, "Aion," RGG², I, (1927), 171; Reitzenstein, Poim. *v.* Ind.; Iran Erl. *v.* Ind.; R. Wünsch, ARW, XII (1909), 32 ff.; K. Holl, "Ursprung d. Epiph.-Festes," SAB (1917), 402 ff.; O. Weinreich, "Aion in Eleusis," ARW, XIX (1916/19), 174 ff.; H. Junker, "Über iranische Quellen d. hellenist. Aionvorstellung," *Vorträge d. Bibliothek Warburg,* 1921/2 (1923), 125 ff.; H. Sasse, *Aion erchomenos* (unpub. Diss., Berlin, 1923); L. Troje, "Die Geburt des Aion," ARW, XXII (1923/4), 87 ff.; E. Norden, *Die Geburt des Kindes* (1924); R. Kittel, *D. hellenist. Mysterienrel. u. das AT* (1924); R. Reitzenstein and H. H. Schaeder, "Studien z. antiken Synkretismus. Aus Iran u. Griechenland." *Studien d. Bibliothek Warburg,* VII (1926); E. Meyer, *Ursprung u. Anfänge des Christentums,* II (1921), 83 ff.; F. Cumont, *Textes et Monuments relatifs aux mystères de Mithra* (1894-1900), I, 76 ff.; *Die Mysterien des Mithra* (Germ. transl. Gehrich)³ (1923), 96 ff.; A. Christensen, *Études sur le Zoroastrisme de la Perse antique* (1928), 45 ff.; H. Schaedel, *Die nt.liche Äonenlehre* (1930).

a being, Plato distinguishes between αἰών as timeless, ideal eternity, in which there are no days or months or years, and χρόνος as the time which is created with the world as a moving image of eternity (εἰκὼ κινητόν τινα αἰῶνος, Tim., 37d). From this view, which is rather singular in the Greek world, and which reminds us of the later Persian distinction between *zrvan akarana* ("endless time" or "eternity") and *zrvan dareghō-chvadhāta* (a "long period of time" with its own fixed span, i.e., the duration of the world), Aristotle returns to the conception of αἰών as the relative period of time allotted to each specific thing. In accordance with his doctrine of the eternity of the world, the αἰών of the world coincides with χρόνος ἄπειρος : ὅτι μὲν οὖν οὔτε γέγονεν ὁ πᾶς οὐρανὸς οὔτ' ἐνδέχεται φθαρῆναι ... ἀλλ' ἔστιν εἷς καὶ ἀΐδιος, ἀρχὴν μὲν καὶ τελευτὴν οὐκ ἔχων τοῦ παντὸς αἰῶνος, ἔχων δὲ καὶ περιέχων ἐν αὐτῷ τὸν ἄπειρον χρόνον, Cael., II, 1, p. 283b, 26 ff. To this there corresponds the definition in Cael., I, 9, p. 279a, 23 ff. : τὸ γὰρ τέλος τὸ περιέχον τὸν τῆς ἑκάστου ζωῆς χρόνον ... αἰὼν ἑκάστου κέκληται. Κατὰ τὸν αὐτὸν δὲ λόγον καὶ τὸ τοῦ παντὸς οὐρανοῦ τέλος καὶ τὸ τὸν πάντα χρόνον καὶ τὴν ἀπειρίαν περιέχον τέλος, αἰών ἐστιν, ἀπὸ τοῦ ἀεὶ εἶναι εἰληφὼς τὴν ἐπωνυμίαν, [1] ἀθάνατος καὶ θεῖος.

Under Plato's influence, Philo gives the following definition of αἰών : τὸ χρόνου παράδειγμα καὶ ἀρχέτυπον, Mut. Nom., 267; Deus Imm., 32; cf. Rer. Div. Her., 165. χρόνος is the βίος of the κόσμος αἰσθητός, αἰών the βίος of God and the κόσμος νοητός. It is of the nature of αἰών to be the eternal to-day, Fug., 57. It is ἀπέρατος (Fug., 57), ἄπειρος (Leg. Gaj., 85). In the sense of eternity or unending time both Plutarch (Cons. ad. Apoll., 17 [II, 111c]; Ei ap. Delph., 20 [II, 393a]) and the younger Stoics[2] are familiar with the term αἰών. [3]

In the Hellenistic age the word acquires religious significance in virtue of the fact that Αἰών becomes the name of a god of eternity whose mysteries are known to have been celebrated in Alexandria from c. 200 B.C. [4] (Ps.-Callisth., 30, 6, p. 27; Epiph. Haer., 51, 22). The αἰών speculations of Alexandria, where Judaism also picked up the Greek word αἰών, had a profound influence on syncretistic Gnosticism. Behind the Greek Αἰών stands the Persian *Zrvan akarana* or unlimited time, which Eudemos of Rhodes already recognised to be the supreme principle of Persian theology above even Ahuramazda and Ahriman (Damascius, I, 322, 8 ff., Ruelle) and which, personified in Persian fashion, occupied an important place among the later Parsee deities, esp. in the cult of Mithras.

B. αἰών in the Sense of Prolonged Time or Eternity.

1. The Formulae "from eternity" and "to eternity."

a. The concepts of time and eternity merge in the formulae in which αἰών is linked with a preposition to indicate an indefinite past or future, e.g., ἀπ' αἰῶνος (Lk. 1:70; Ac. 3:21; 15:18) and ἐκ τοῦ αἰῶνος (Jn. 9:32) in the sense of "from the ancient past" or "from eternity," or εἰς αἰῶνα (Jd. 13) and εἰς τὸν αἰῶνα (27 times, esp. common in Jn. e.g., 4:14) in the sense of "for ever" or "to all eternity." Only in the light of the context can it be said whether αἰών means "eternity" in the strict sense or simply "remote" or "extended" or "uninterrupted

---

[1] This etymology is naturally false. αἰών and ἀεί go back to the same root *aivo, āju* (cf. Lat. *aevum*, Sansk. *āyu*), which means "life," or "life force" or "lifetime"; v. Lackeit, *op. cit.*, 7 ff.

[2] Epict. Diss., II, 5, 13; Marc. Ant., 2, 12; 4, 43 and 50 etc.

[3] On αἰών in the Neo-Platonists (esp. Plotin. and Proclos), v. Lackeit, 69 ff.

[4] Thence spreading to Eleusis, cf. Ditt. Syll.[3], 1125, 8 (inscr. 73/74 B.C.) → n. 20.

time." Thus in Lk. 1:70 and Ac. 3:21 οἱ ἅγιοι ἀπ' αἰῶνος προφῆται means "the holy prophets of old time." The meaning is particularly weak when we have an αἰών formula in a negative statement. Thus Jn. 9:32 : ἐκ τοῦ αἰῶνος οὐκ ἠκούσθη, simply means that "it has never been heard," and οὐ (μὴ) ... εἰς τὸν αἰῶνα merely signifies "never" (cf. Jn. 13:8; 1 C. 8:13). The full significance of "eternity" is perhaps to be found in passages like Lk. 1:55; Jn. 6:51; 12:34; 14:16; 2 C. 9:9 (ψ 111, 9); Hb. 5:6; 7:17, 21 etc.; 1 Pt. 1:25; 1 Jn. 2:17; Jd. 13, if the question can ever be answered with any certainty.

In order to bring out more fully the stricter concept of eternity, religious usage generally prefers the plur. Esp. in doxologies we find : εἰς τοὺς αἰῶνας (Mt. 6:13 [Rd]; Lk. 1:33; R. 1:25; 9:5; 11:36; 2 C. 11:31; Hb. 13:8; and also εἰς πάντας τοὺς αἰῶνας with πρὸ παντὸς τοῦ αἰῶνος, Jd. 25). This plur. use is simply designed to emphasise the idea of eternity which is contained but often blurred in the sing. αἰών. Thus in Hebrews the εἰς τὸν αἰῶνα used under the influence of the LXX (e.g,. 5:6; 7:24) is materially identical with εἰς τοὺς αἰῶνας in 13:8. The plur. is also to be found in formulae which refer to the past. In 1 C. 2:7 it is said of the θεοῦ σοφία : ἣν προώρισεν ὁ θεὸς πρὸ τῶν αἰώνων ("from all eternity"); similarly in Col. 1:26 : ἀπὸ τῶν αἰώνων καὶ ἀπὸ τῶν γενεῶν, and Eph. 3:9 : ἀπὸ τῶν αἰώνων, cf. Eph. 3:11: κατὰ πρόθεσιν τῶν αἰώνων ἣν ἐποίησεν (= κατὰ πρόθεσιν ἣν ἐποίησεν πρὸ τῶν αἰώνων). In these cases the sing. ἀπὸ or πρὸ τοῦ αἰῶνος might well be used instead of the plur. But the plur. presupposes knowledge of a plurality of αἰῶνες, of ages and periods of time whose infinite series constitutes eternity. Thus the idea of prolonged but not unending time is also present in the αἰών formulae. Noteworthy in this respect is the parallel αἰῶνες/γενεαί in Col. 1:26. The concepts of limited and unlimited time merge in the word αἰών. The implied inner contradiction is brought to light in the expression χρόνοι αἰώνιοι which is used as an equivalent of the plur. in R. 16:25; 2 Tm. 1:9; Tt. 1:2; for eternal times is strictly a contradiction in terms.

Also designed to emphasise the concept of eternity is the twofold use of the term in the formula εἰς τὸν αἰῶνα τοῦ αἰῶνος (Hb. 1:8, ψ 44:6). In 21 passages this twofold use is linked with the plur., thus giving rise to the distinctive formula of the Pauline Epistles and Revelation (cf. also Hb. 13:21; 1 Pt. 4:11; 5:11): εἰς τοὺς αἰῶνας τῶν αἰώνων. Finally, there are cases in which the αἰών formulae are united with similar expressions. Thus in the phrase : εἰς πάσας τὰς γενεὰς τοῦ αἰῶνος τῶν αἰώνων Eph. 3:21 (cf. Col. 1:26), we can pick out the components εἰς πάσας τὰς γενεὰς and εἰς τὸν αἰῶνα τῶν αἰώνων; and εἰς ἡμέραν αἰῶνος (2 Pt. 3:18) can be dissected into the two constituents εἰς ἡμέραν (sc. κυρίου) and εἰς τὸν αἰῶνα.

b. These formulae contain nothing peculiar to the NT. From the time of the LXX they form part of the common usage of Hellenistic Judaism. The LXX uses αἰών to translate different Hebrew terms, among which the most important are עוֹלָם and עַד. While αἰών always contains the idea of a prolongation of time, in the first instance עוֹלָם means only hidden or distant time belonging to the remote and inscrutable past or future from the standpoint of the present. [5] The chronological distance is relative. Thus Amos in 9:11 can refer to the time of David as יְמֵי עוֹלָם "days of old" (LXX : ἡμέραι τοῦ αἰῶνος). If the thought of distance is to be expressed by עוֹלָם, expressions like מֵעוֹלָם, לְעוֹלָם etc. are often used. Only at a later time (demonstrably after Deutero-

---

[5] "A concept which takes over where our comprehension ceases," C. v. Orelli, *D. hebr. Synonyma d. Zeit u. Ewigkeit* (1871), 70.

Isaiah) does עוֹלָם begin to have the sense of endless time or eternity in the true sense. At the same period we begin to find the plur. עוֹלָמִים (Is. 45:17), which was unknown in earlier writings, and which signifies eternity, but on the assumption that the sing. means a long period of time. The idea of a stretch of time belongs from the very first to the word עַד,[6] which is a poetic term and, except in Job 20:4, denotes unlimited future. In translation of such Hebrew expressions as מֵעוֹלָם, לְעוֹלָם and לָעַד (or occasionally לָנֶצַח etc.), the LXX offers an incalculable wealth of examples of eternity formulae with the simple sing. αἰών, e.g., ἀπὸ (τοῦ) αἰῶνος, πρὸ (τοῦ) αἰῶνος, εἰς (τὸν) αἰῶνα etc.

The LXX can also afford examples of the twofold use of αἰών in these formulae. In a passage like ψ 44:6 (cf. Hb. 1:8) εἰς (τὸν) αἰῶνα (τοῦ) αἰῶνος is given as the translation of עוֹלָם וָעֶד. It is harder to explain why the simple לָעַד should be predominantly, though not exclusively, rendered εἰς αἰῶνα αἰῶνος, and לְעוֹלָם וָעֶד εἰς τὸν αἰῶνα καὶ εἰς τὸν αἰῶνα τοῦ αἰῶνος. We need hardly follow R. Kittel[7] in detecting here the influence of the *aion* theology of Alexandria. The most likely explanation is that עַד, as the strongest Hebrew term for an infinite future, demanded a special translation, and recourse was therefore had to the expression αἰὼν αἰῶνος.[8] This is to be understood in terms of linguistic psychology, possibly being suggested by the Hebrew עֲדֵי־עַד, which is often rendered εἰς (τὸν) αἰῶνα (τοῦ) αἰῶνος (ψ 82:18; 91:8; 131:14). The name Αἰὼν Αἰῶνος, which occurs in the Hermetic writings for the god of eternity Αἰών,[9] certainly developed out of these formulae as found in the LXX. Whether the translators coined the expression or found it cannot be decided. The plur. use of αἰών in such formulae does occur in the LXX, though infrequently.[10] The basis of this construction seems to be the Hebrew plur. עוֹלָמִים, though this is not usually rendered αἰῶνες, and never in Is. The combination of the plur. and a twofold use is extremely rare in the LXX, but there are a few examples, such as εἰς τοὺς αἰῶνας τῶν αἰώνων for עוֹד in ψ 83:5, and cf. Tob. 14:15 S; 4 Macc. 18:24. Similarly there are one or two instances of the interfusion of αἰών and γενεά formulae.

Hence it may be seen that the usage of the NT is distinguished from that of the LXX only by an intensification of the tendency already displayed in the LXX to replace the simple formulae by more complicated.[11]

2. The Eternity of God.

a. αἰών has the full significance of eternity when it is linked with the concept of God. Apart from the doxologies, this is the case in the description of God as the eternal God. In R. 16:26 we find this in the form ὁ αἰώνιος θεός (→ αἰώνιος). The phrase occurs already in the LXX: Gn. 21:33; Is. 26:4; 40:28; Bar. 4:8, 10 etc.;

---

[6] "If עוֹלָם is the dark abyss which swallows up time, עַד is the direct way to it," *ibid.*, 88.

[7] *D. hellenist. Mysterienreligion u. d. AT*, 73.

[8] Cf. the LXX formulae εἰς γενεὰν καὶ γενεάν and εἰς γενεὰς γενεῶν, and the multiplication of עוֹלָם in the doxologies of later Judaism, e.g., Kaddish, 4: לְעָלַם לְעָלְמֵי עָלְמַיָּא.

[9] Reitzenstein Poim., 23, 270; E. Peterson, ΕΙΣ ΘΕΟΣ (1926), 320.

[10] πρὸ τῶν αἰώνων for קֶדֶם in ψ 54:20; εἰς τοὺς αἰῶνας for עוֹלָמִים in 2 Ch. 6:2; ψ 60:5; for לְעוֹלָמִים in ψ 76:8; for לְעָלְמִין in Da. 3:9; cf. also Sir. 45:24; Wis. 3:8; Tob. 3:11; 8:5, 15 B; 11:14 AB; 13:1, and esp. the apocryphal addition to Daniel 3; εἰς πάντας τοὺς αἰῶνας in Tob. 13:4; 8:5 S; 8:15 AS; 11:14 S; 13:16 S; 13:18 A.

[11] On the non-biblical use of eternity formulae, *v.* Lackeit, *op. cit.*, 32; Peterson, *op. cit.*, 168 ff. Examples from the inscriptions are εἰς αἰῶνα, Ditt. Or., 515, 56; εἰς τὸν αἰῶνα, *ibid.*, 566, 21 f.; εἰς τὸν ἅπαντα αἰῶνα, 332, 33. The plur. is infrequent and late, cf. Peterson, *op. cit.*, 169.

Sus. 42; 2 Macc. 1:25; 3 Macc. 6:12; cf. Philo Plant., 8 and 74 and 89 (→ ἀΐδιος). We also find ὁ βασιλεὺς τῶν αἰώνων in 1 Tm. 1:17.

However we understand this expression, it originally means the eternal king ; cf. the common Jewish description of God as מֶלֶךְ עוֹלָם (first found in Jer. 10:10, lacking in the LXX), and similar expressions (e.g., רִבּוֹן כָּל־הָעוֹלָמִים bBer., 60b). As in many similar cases, the gen. is modelled on the Heb. stat. constr. Other examples of this use of αἰών are θεὸς τοῦ αἰῶνος in Eth. En. 1:4; θεὸς τῶν αἰώνων in Sir. 36:22; 1 Cl., 55, 6 (cf. αἰώνων θεός, P. Paris, 174, 629, Wessely); βασιλεὺς τοῦ αἰῶνος in Eth. En. 25:3, 5, 7, cf. "the eternal king" in Slav. En. 64:3 AB); βασιλεὺς τῶν αἰώνων in Eth. En. 22:14. Cf. also "the eternal Lord" in Slav. En. 1:8; dominus saeculorum in Jub. 31:13; δέσποτα παντὸς αἰῶνος in Jos. Ant., 1, 272 (cf. αἰώνων βασιλεῦ καὶ κύριε, Preis. Zaub., XII [P. Leid.] Col. VII, 36). Originally these Judaeo-Christian formulae were simply designed to express the eternity of God, but later all the other meanings of αἰών were read into them. Thus βασιλεὺς τῶν αἰώνων is also taken to mean "the King of the aeons," i.e., the One who rules over the αἰῶνες understood as periods of time or spheres of the cosmos (→ 204 on Hb. 1:2; 11:3), or perhaps even as personal beings. This is shown by expressions like πατὴρ τῶν αἰώνων in Just. Apol., 41, 2 (quoting 1 Ch. 16:28 in a text which deviates from both Mas. and LXX), or ὁ δημιουργὸς καὶ πατὴρ τῶν αἰώνων in 1 Cl., 35, 3, in which it would be impossible to substitute αἰώνιος for τῶν αἰώνων.

b. But how are we to understand the eternity ascribed to God in the term αἰών ?

In the older writings of the OT there is a very simple concept of eternity. The being of God reaches back into times past computation. God has always been. Hence He is the God of old, as we are really to construe the אֵל עוֹלָם of Gn. 21:33 (θεὸς αἰώνιος, LXX). [12] Again, He always will be. In contrast to men, who are subject to death (Gn. 6:3), He is the living God (e.g., Dt. 5:23; 32:40).

This primitive idea of eternity changes at a later date. In Deutero-Isaiah אֱלֹהֵי עוֹלָם really means θεὸς αἰώνιος (Is. 40:28), עוֹלָם no longer signifying merely the remote past, but unending time or eternity. In addition to the important description of God as אֱלֹהֵי עוֹלָם, which in similar forms is also used outside Judaism for Baalšamin as the god of the world and heaven, [13] Deutero-Isaiah also introduces a formula which is of great significance in religious history, namely, "I am the First and the Last." This, too, serves to describe the eternity of God (→ ΑΩ). As the Creator and Consummator God is the eternal One. His eternal being stretches beyond the time of the world. He is from eternity to eternity (ἀπὸ τοῦ αἰῶνος ἕως τοῦ αἰῶνος, ψ 89, 2). Before the world was created, He was (ψ 89:2); and when heaven and earth have vanished, He will be (ψ 101:26 ff., quoted with reference to Christ in Hb. 1:10). Thus the unending eternity of God and the time of the world, which is limited by its creation and conclusion, are contrasted with one another. Eternity is thought of as unending time — for how else can human

[12] Cf. אֱלֹהֵי קֶדֶם Dt. 33:27 etc.; "the Ancient of days," Da. 7:9.

[13] מרא עלמא: inscription in Palmyra, De Vogüé, Inscriptions Sémitiques (1868-77), No. 73, 1 (cf. M. Lidzbarski, Ephemeris, I, 257; Cooke, North Semitic Inscriptions, 295); another inscription from the vicinity of Palmyra bearing the same designation of God is given by Lidzbarski, loc. cit. למרא עלמא: inscription from the Diocl. camp of Palmyra, ibid., II, 298. With מרא עלמא there is also found מרא כל ibid., II, 296. עלמא can mean either "eternity" or "world." The former is attested by the frequent occurrence of לעלמא ibid., II, 296; cf. De Vogüé, op. cit., No. 74-88.

thought picture it ? — and the eternal being of God is represented as pre-existence and post-existence. Yet in later Judaism there are also attempts to make eternity the complete antithesis of time. Thus Slav. En. 65 describes the creation of time along with that of the world. "But when all creation comes to an end ... the times will be destroyed, and there will be no more months nor days nor hours ; [14] they will be dissolved and will be reckoned no more ; for the one aion will begin." Here eternity is thought of as timelessness, as in Plato. [15]

The NT took over the OT and Jewish view of divine eternity along with the ancient formulae. There was new development, however, to the extent that the statements concerning God's eternity were extended to Christ (cf. Hb. 1:10 ff.; 13:8; Rev. 1:17 f.; 2:8; 22:13). In the NT, too, eternity is thought of as the opposite of this cosmic time which is limited by creation and conclusion. Statements concerning the eternal being and action of God are thus expressed in terms of pre- and post- (cf. πρό and ἀπὸ τῶν αἰώνων, 1 C. 2:7; Col. 1:26; Eph. 3:9; πρὸ καταβολῆς κόσμου, Jn. 17:24; Eph. 1:4; 1 Pt. 1:20). To this context there also belongs the doctrine of the pre-existence of Christ.

C. αἰών in the Sense of the Time of the World.

1. αἰών as the Time of the World ; the End of the αἰών.

In the plur. αἰών formulae the meaning of αἰών merges into that of a long but limited stretch of time. In particular, αἰών in this sense signifies the time or duration of the world, i.e., time as limited by creation and conclusion. At this point we are confronted by the remarkable fact that in the Bible the same word αἰών is used to indicate two things which are really profoundly antithetical, namely, the eternity of God and the duration of the world. This twofold sense, which αἰών shares with the Heb. עוֹלָם, points back to a concept of eternity in which eternity is identified with the duration of the world.

Parseeism, too, uses the same word zrvan to denote both concepts. It may be assumed that both the zrvan concept and the new use of עוֹלָם which we suddenly find in Deutero-Isaiah have a common origin in an oriental and probably Babylonian concept of time and eternity. [16] In both cases, however, belief in creation brings about a separation between the concepts of eternity and duration. In distinction from the biblical usage, Parseeism also introduced a terminological differentiation. The distinction between zrvan akarana as eternity and zrvan dareghō-chvadhāta as the duration of the world (→ 197 f.) is first found on the epitaph of Antiochus of Commagene (34 B.C.; Ditt. Or., 383, 44), where we may recognise the former in εἰς τὸν ἄπειρον αἰῶνα, whereas χρόνος ἄπειρος is an incorrect rendering of the latter. It is not possible to trace back zrvan speculation beyond the 4th century B.C. Yet there can be little doubt that, even before the terms came to be fixed, the thought of creation as an absolute beginning had in-

---

[14] It is to be noted that the week is not mentioned as a measure of time; cf. also Plat. Tim., 37e : ἡμέρας γὰρ καὶ νύκτας καὶ μῆνας καὶ ἐνιαυτούς, οὐκ ὄντας πρὶν οὐρανὸν γενέσθαι; and Philo Op. Mund., 26 : χρόνος γὰρ οὐκ ἦν πρὸ κόσμου, ἀλλ᾽ ἢ σὺν αὐτῷ γέγονεν ἢ μετ᾽ αὐτόν, which is explained by the fact that time is διάστημα τῆς τοῦ κόσμου κινήσεως.

[15] Cf. also Ps. 90:4 and 2 Pt. 3:8, as also the destruction of the concept of time in the saying in Syr. Bar. 74 (E. Kautzsch, Pseudepigraphen [1900], 440) concerning the future aeon: "Because this time is the end of what is destructible and the beginning of what is indestructible ... it is far from the wicked and near to those who do not die."

[16] Cf. on this problem, H. H. Schaeder, "Parsismus und Judentum," RGG², IV, 1085 ff.

troduced a distinction between eternity and the duration of the world in Parseeism no less than Judaism. Only in Slav. En. 65 (→ 202) do we detect any direct influence of *zrvan* speculation on Jewish thought.

In the NT αἰών is used in the sense of the time of the world in the expression συντέλεια τοῦ αἰῶνος ("the end of the aeon") which Mt.[17] uses for the end of the world. The expression is to be explained by the penetration of the term into eschatological formulae (→ ἔσχατος, συντέλεια) in place of other temporal concepts like ἡμέραι, χρόνοι, καιροί, ἔτη.[18]

For other examples of συντέλεια τοῦ αἰῶνος, cf. Sir. 43:7 S (a misunderstanding of the original); Ass. Mos. 12:4 (*exitus saeculi*); 4 Esr. 6:25 (*finis saeculi*); S. Bar. 54:21; 69:4; 83:7; cf. ἕως πληρωθῶσιν καιροὶ αἰῶνος, Tob. 14:5 BA; μέχρι τέρματος αἰῶνος, Sib., 3, 756 f. For the use of αἰών in the sense of "the time of the world," cf. 4 Esr. 14:11: *saeculum perdidit iuventutem suam et tempora appropinquant senescere. Duodecim enim partibus divisum est saeculum* ...; Wis. 13:9: στοιχάσασθαι τὸν αἰῶνα ("to search out the course of the world"); 14:6: ἀπέλιπεν τῷ αἰῶνι σπέρμα ("left seed to the later time of the world"); 18:4: τῷ αἰῶνι ("to the course of the world"). There is an odd use of ὁ αἰὼν ὁ μέγας ("the great aeon") for the duration of the world in Eth. En. 16:1. But cf. the concept of the μέγας ἐνιαυτός, the Platonic and Stoic cosmic year: Cic. Nat. Deor., 2, 20 and 52; Arat. Phaenom., 458 etc.

This clear conception of αἰών as the time or duration of the world is obscured by the irruption of the plur. into such expressions. It hardly need be demonstrated that ἐπὶ συντελείᾳ τῶν αἰώνων in Hb. 9:26 (cf. συντέλεια τῶν αἰώνων, Test. L. 10) is identical with the sing. συντέλεια τοῦ αἰῶνος. The plur. has been formed here in analogy with the eternity formulae and other eschatological expressions. The same is true of τὰ τέλη τῶν αἰώνων in 1 C. 10:11.[19] These phrases naturally suggest that the course of the world, the great αἰών (*supra*), is made up of a series of smaller αἰῶνες. Thus we read in 4 Esr. 11:44: *respexit Altissimus super sua tempora et ecce finita sunt et saecula eius completa sunt* (cf. 14:11). On the other hand, αἰών has not yet become a fixed term for a specific portion of the course of the world.

2. αἰών as World.

The sense of "time or course of the world" can easily pass over into that of the "world" itself, so that αἰών approximates closely to κόσμος. In Mk. 4:19 and the par. Mt. 13:22 the phrase αἱ μέριμναι τοῦ αἰῶνος means "the cares of the world" (cf. ὁ γαμήσας μεριμνᾷ τὰ τοῦ κόσμου, 1C. 7:33). Paul uses as equivalent expressions σοφία τοῦ κόσμου, σοφία τοῦ αἰῶνος τούτου and σοφία τοῦ κόσμου τούτου (1 C. 1:20; 2:6; 3:19). To the description of the end of the world as συντέλεια τοῦ αἰῶνος there corresponds the description of its beginning as καταβολὴ κόσμου (→ κόσμος).

The equation of αἰών and κόσμος, also found in the Hellenistic mysteries,[20]

---

[17] Mt. 13:39, 40, 49; 24:3; 28:20. In the latter case the expression is used instead of an eternity formula.

[18] Cf. ἐπ᾽ ἐσχάτοις αἰῶσιν ("in the last times"), Eth. En. 27:3.

[19] The eschatological significance of τέλος counts against the view of Joh. W. 1 K., 254 and Pr.-Bauer that τὰ τέλη signifies the end of the present and the beginning of the future αἰών.

[20] Ditt. Syll.³, 1125, 8: Αἰὼν ὁ αὐτὸς ἐν τοῖς αὐτοῖς αἰεὶ φύσει θείαι μένων κόσμος τε εἰς κατὰ τὰ αὐτά, ὁποῖος ἔστι καὶ ἦν καὶ ἔσται, ἀρχὴν μεσότητα τέλος οὐκ ἔχων (Eleusis). This identification goes back to the *zrvan* conception if it is implied by Eudemos of Rhodes that the original being (*Zrvan*) is called either space (τόπος) or time (χρόνος). Cf. also the conjunction of αἰών and κόσμος in Philo Spec. Leg., I, 170.

is to be explained in the NT by Jewish linguistic usage. Only at a later stage did Hebrew develop the concept of the universe, and for it, in addition to the paraphrase "heaven and earth," it fashioned the terms הַכֹּל (the "universe") and עוֹלָם (Aram. עָלְמָא). Both occur in Qoh. 3:11, but in such a way that עֹלָם probably still has temporal significance.[21] Later the sense of "world" accrues to עוֹלָם as well. In 4 Esr. the spatial significance is just as definite as the temporal, as in expressions like *habitantes saeculum* (3:9 etc.) or *qui in saeculo seminati sunt* (8:41) etc. Both meanings are also found in the Greek version of S. Bar. In the Rabbinic writings there is only sparse attestation for עוֹלָם or עָלְמָא in the sense of the spatial world prior to the 1st century A.D., but there are several examples later. Indeed, in the later Rabbis the "world" in the spatial sense becomes the main meaning of עָלְמָא[22] — a process for which there are parallels in Syriac and Arabic. Even the eternity formulae are interpreted by the Rabbis in this sense.[23]

The plural αἰῶνες shares the change of meaning. Hence the αἰῶνες of Hb. 1:2 (δι' οὗ καὶ ἐποίησεν τοὺς αἰῶνας) and 11:3 (κατηρτίσθαι τοὺς αἰῶνας ῥήματι θεοῦ) are to be understood spatially as "worlds" or "spheres."

> In the case of Hb. 1:2 we should compare the reading ὃς ὕψωσε πάντας τοὺς αἰῶνας (Tob. 13:18 B) for εἰς ... αἰῶνας A (cf. also 3:2 S σὺ κρίνεις [AB εἰς] τὸν αἰῶνα). For Rabbinic examples of עוֹלָמִים in the same sense, v. Str.-B., III, 671 f.). It is often said that God has created the עוֹלָם (עָלְמָא) cf. Hb. 11:3; Tg. Dt. 33:28: בְּמֵימְרֵיהּ אִתְעֲבֵיד עָלְמָא ("by his word is the world made"). There is even reference to the creation of more worlds (עָלְמוֹת).[24] Thus it is said in Gn. r., 3 on 1:5 that the Holy One, before He created the present world, created others (בְּרָא עָלְמוֹת), but then destroyed them again because He took no pleasure in them.[25]

3. The Present and Future αἰών.

a. If αἰών means the time or duration of the world, and the plur. is firmly established, there is an obvious suggestion that the αἰών is not unique, but that there is a series of αἰῶνες in which all things flow in eternal recurrence. On this view, creation and conclusion are not to be taken in the sense of absolute beginning and end, but rather in the sense of transition from one aeon to the other.[26] Eternity would then be coincident with the infinite series of such αἰῶνες, just as in Aristotle it is identical with the time of the world. This is the doctrine of eternity found in oriental astrology with its thought of eternal recurrence. It can hardly be doubted that this view had some influence on that of the Bible, especially on its eschatological ideas.[27] In Ecclesiastes, in which the clear-cut statement לְכֹל זְמָן (3:1) gives classical formulation to the oriental view of the determination of all occurrence by time, the thought of recurrence is also expressed, namely,

---

[21] In favour of the correctness of this disputed text, and the sense of "the time of the world," we may refer to the mention of beginning and end in the same verse.
[22] Cf. Dalman, WJ, 120-27 and 132-46.
[23] Thus the fathers of the remote past become the fathers of the world (jChag., 77d, Dalman, 141) and the eternal King (God) becomes the King (God) of the world (Tg. O., Gn. 21:33, Dalman, 142).
[24] On the plur. v. Levy Wört., III, 656.
[25] Bereshit Rabba, ed. J. Theodor (1912), I, 23.
[26] This view is found in Ps.-Arist. Mund., 5, p. 397a, 9 ff.: ἡλίου τε καὶ σελήνης, κινουμένων ἐν ἀκριβεστάτοις μέτροις ἐξ αἰῶνος εἰς ἕτερον αἰῶνα. Cf. also Sir. 39:20.
[27] Cf. the eschatological principle τὰ ἔσχατα ὡς τὰ πρῶτα, Barn., 6, 13 (→ ἔσχατος), the concept of παλιγγενεσία etc.

that there is nothing new under the sun, and that what seems to be new has already taken place in the epochs (מֵעֹלָמִים, LXX ἐν τοῖς αἰῶσιν) before us (1:9 f.). The αἰῶνες here are the periods of the world[28] in their infinite succession. It was under the influence of such ideas, probably Babylonian, that the Heb. plural came to be used, and there can be no doubt that the same ideas influenced the understanding of αἰών and αἰῶνες.

Nevertheless, even though the αἰῶνες were often understood in this way in the eternity formulae and other expressions, this understanding is contrary to the biblical doctrine of time and eternity. The idea of eternal recurrence cannot be united with the understanding of the creation and end of the world as absolute beginning and absolute conclusion. The biblical view of the uniqueness of the course of the world, which is also the view of Persian religion, stands in antithesis to the pantheistic and astrological doctrine of recurrence with its confusion of God and the world, of eternity and time.

b. A combination of the dualistic doctrine of time and eternity with the terminology of the doctrine of recurrence is to be found in the inwardly self-contradictory view of the two aeons, the present and the future. The present αἰών is identical with the time of the world whose συντέλεια has come. The future αἰών, the future time of the world, is the new which follows. It is something inconceivable, to be represented only symbolically, e.g., as "the kingdom of God" in a historical image,[29] or as "the new heaven and the new earth" in a spatial,[30] or as "the new time of the world" in a temporal. The inward contradiction consists in trying to picture in the category of time that which stands in antithesis to it. For the present αἰών is related to the future as time to eternity.

In the NT the present and future aeons are mentioned in the Synoptic Gospels, in the Pauline writings, and in Hebrews. In Mk. 10:30 (Lk. 18:30) we read: ἐὰν μὴ λάβῃ ... νῦν ἐν τῷ καιρῷ τούτῳ οἰκίας ... καὶ ἐν τῷ αἰῶνι τῷ ἐρχομένῳ ζωὴν αἰώνιον, "... now in this time ... and in the coming aeon." In Lk. 16:8 the sons of this aeon (οἱ υἱοὶ τοῦ αἰῶνος τούτου) are contrasted with the sons of light, and in Lk. 20:34 f. with those who are counted worthy to take part in that aeon (τοῦ αἰῶνος ἐκείνου τυχεῖν) and in the resurrection. The saying in Mk. 3:29, according to which those who blaspheme against the Holy Ghost can never be forgiven, is reproduced in Mt. 12:32 in a form in which εἰς τὸν αἰῶνα is replaced by οὔτε ἐν τούτῳ τῷ αἰῶνι οὔτε ἐν τῷ μέλλοντι, "neither in this aeon nor in that which is to come." In Paul the phrase ὁ αἰὼν οὗτος occurs seven times (R. 12:2; 1 C. 1:20; 2:6 twice; 2:8; 3:18; 2 C. 4:4), and ὁ αἰὼν ὁ ἐνεστὼς πονηρός once (Gl. 1:4). This πονηρός is characteristic of the way in which Paul speaks of the present aeon as that of sin.[31] In the Synoptics (apart from Lk. 16:8) and Eph. 1:21 this additional sense is lacking, though it is found again in the references to ὁ νῦν αἰών in 1 Tm. 6:17; 2 Tm. 4:10; and Tt. 2:12. For ὁ αἰὼν οὗτος there can be substituted ὁ καιρὸς οὗτος (Mk. 10:30; Lk. 18:30); ὁ νῦν καιρός (R. 3:26; 8:18; 11:5; 2 C. 8:14); or ὁ κόσμος οὗτος (1 C. 3:19; 5:10; 7:31; Eph. 2:2). In the Johannine writings this expression is normally used instead of ὁ αἰὼν οὗτος, which does not occur (Jn. 8:23; 9:39; 11:9; 12:25, 31; 13:1; 16:11; 18:36; 1 Jn. 4:17). In the

---

[28] With this may be linked the view that the earth is everlasting (Qoh. 1:4). It is the theatre of world occurrence, as is also assumed in 4 Esr.

[29] Cf. the train of thought in Da. 7.

[30] I.e., as the new cosmos → γῆ, κόσμος.

[31] Cf. ὁ θεὸς τοῦ αἰῶνος τούτου (2 C. 4:4) and οἱ ἄρχοντες τοῦ αἰῶνος τούτου (1 C. 2:6).

Pauline writings the future aeon is found only in Eph. in the expression (1:21): οὐ μόνον ἐν τῷ αἰῶνι τούτῳ ἀλλὰ καὶ ἐν τῷ μέλλοντι (cf. Mt. 12:32), and in the remarkable phrase: ἐν τοῖς αἰῶσιν τοῖς ἐπερχομένοις, in which the plur. is to be understood in the light of the plur. eternity formulae. In Hb. 6:5 there is reference to the δυνάμεις μέλλοντος αἰῶνος, i.e., the pneumatic powers of the future world which believers have already experienced.

c. The NT borrowed the doctrine of the two aeons [32] from Jewish apocalyptic, [33] in which we find the same expressions from the 1st century B.C. onwards: Eth. En. 48:7 (prior to 64 B.C.): "this world of unrighteousness"; 71:15 (pre-Christian): "in the name of the future world." For "world" we are here to assume αἰών in the Gr. text. In Slav. En. (prior to 70 A.D.), originally written in Greek, κόσμος and αἰών seem to be used alongside one another. Along with the spatial dualism of this world and that (cf. 42:3) there are the two temporal αἰῶνες: "this aeon of woes" (66:6); "this aeon" (e.g., 66:7); "that aeon" (e.g., 43:3); "the one aeon" (65:8); "the great aeon" (e.g., 61:2); [34] "the endless aeon" (50:2; 66:6 A, ὁ ἄπειρος αἰών = zrvan akarana; cf. εἰς τὸν ἄπειρον αἰῶνα in the sense of "until the dawn of the zrvan akarana on the day of the resurrection," Ditt. Or., 383, 44, → 202). [35] The two αἰῶνες here are the time between the creation and conclusion of the world and the endless eternity which follows (65:3 ff.), though this temporal dualism is interfused with the spatial dualism between the visible world and the invisible, between this world and the world to come. The doctrine of the two aeons is found in its complete form in S. Bar. and esp. 4 Esr (at the end of the 1st century A.D.). In 4 Esr. the two aeons confront one another as hoc saeculum (e.g., 4:2), hoc tempus (7:113), hic mundus (9:19), praesens saeculum (7:112) and futurum saeculum (8:1), saeculum venturum (7:47), saeculum sequens (6:9); saeculum maius (= αἰών μέγας, 7:13). The alternation between saeculum, mundus and tempus corresponds exactly to the alternation between αἰών, κόσμος and καιρός in the NT. Here, too, there is an intermingling of temporal and spatial ideas, though in 4 Esr. the temporal conception of the two aeons, separated by a seven day silence (7:30 f.) and the ensuing day of resurrection and judgment (7:32 f., 113), is predominant. Syr. Bar. agrees with this view of the aeons, except that the spatial dualism is made more prominent by making heaven (instead of the earth as in 4 Esr.) the theatre of life in the coming aeon.

Among the Rabbis the two aeons are עוֹלָם הַזֶּה "this aeon" and עוֹלָם הַבָּא "the coming aeon." Prior to 70 A.D. the attestation is limited and uncertain: jBM, 8c (Shimeon b. Shetach, 90-70 B.C.): אֲגַר כָּל הָדֵין עָלְמָא "the winning of this whole aeon" (cf. Mk. 8:31 and par.); Ab., 2:7 (Hillel, 20 B.C.): חַיֵּי הָעוֹלָם הַבָּא "the life of the coming aeon"; Gn. r., 14 on 2:7 (school of Shammai) on the training of man, i.e., of his body: בָּעוֹלָם הַזֶּה "in this aeon", and לָעוֹלָם הַבָּא "in the future aeon"; T. Pea., 4, 18, on the heaping up of riches: בָּעוֹלָם הַזֶּה "in this aeon," and לָעוֹלָם הַבָּא "in the coming aeon" (according to a saying of King Monobazus, a proselyte, c. 50 A.D.). That לָעוֹלָם הַבָּא is said instead of בְּעוֹלָם shows the influence of the Heb. eternity formulae in these expressions. The Rabbis themselves brought the idea of the two עוֹלָמִים into connection with these formulae, as is shown by the story that originally עַד הָעוֹלָם was said in benedictions, but then, in opposi-

---

[32] Cf. for what follows the excursus "Diese Welt, die Tage des Messias und d. zukünftige Welt," Str.-B., IV, 799 ff. On the Semitic position of οὗτος, cf. Bl.-Debr.[6], 306 (suppl. to § 292).

[33] The LXX does not have these formulae except in Is. 9:5, where A and S have πατὴρ τοῦ μέλλοντος αἰῶνος for אֲבִי־עַד

[34] Cf. 4 Esr. 7:13; Sib., 3, 92; Eth. En. 16:1, where the great αἰών is the duration of the world (if the text is sound).

[35] H. Gressmann, "D. hellenist. Gestirnreligion," Beihefte z. AO, 5 (1925), 23; H. Junker, op. cit., 152.

tion to those who denied the resurrection and thus accepted only one עוֹלָם, the form was introduced : מִן הָעוֹלָם וְעַד הָעוֹלָם "from eternity to eternity" (T. Ber., 7, 21). [36] With υἱοὶ τοῦ αἰῶνος τούτου we may compare the common Rabbinic phrase "son of the future world" (e.g., S. Dt. § 333 on 32:43). [37] That the Rabbis understood the two aeons in the temporal sense is shown by the many attempts to integrate the old concept of the last time, "the days of the Messiah," into the framework of the doctrine of two aeons. In accordance with the change in meaning of the Aram. עָלְמָא, however, the spatial aspect becomes more and more prominent, the dualism of present and future merging into that of the visible and invisible worlds, of the present world and the world to come, as also happened in the history of Christian eschatology.

The origin of this Jewish mode of speaking of the present and future עוֹלָם is quite obscure. It is true that the Persian distinction between *zrvan daregho-chvadhata* and *zrvan akarana* lies behind the Jewish view of the aeons, but there are no parallels in Parseeism for speaking in terms of present and future aeons.

In connection with the oriental expectation of a redeemer and the doctrine of a rebirth of the world, we find the expression *saeculum venturum* in Vergil Ecl., IV, 52 : *adspice, venturo laetentur ut omnia saeclo* (cf. 4 f.: *ultima Cumaei venit iam carminis aetas ; magnus ab integro saeclorum nascitur ordo*). Again, in the language of emperor worship from the time of Augustus we find similar expressions, e.g., Ditt. Syll.[3], 797, 8 f. (Psephisma of Assos, 37 A.D.): τοῦ ἡδίστου ἀνθρώποις αἰῶνος νῦν ἐνεστῶτος (cf. Gl. 1:4); Dessau Inscr. Lat. Select., II, 1, 6043 : *felicitati saeculi instantis ;* Tacit. Agric., 44 : *beatissimi saeculi*. Here oriental forms intermingle with the Roman or Etruscan view of the *saeculum* as the highest conceivable age that man can attain to in his life-time, i.e., about 110 years. [38]

In its view of the two aeons the NT is in essential agreement with 1st century apocalyptic. The framework of eschatological notions is broken only by the fact that the αἰὼν μέλλων is no longer merely in the future. Believers are already redeemed from this present evil αἰών (Gl. 1:4) and have tasted the powers of the future αἰών (Hb. 6:5). If according to the teaching of Jewish and early Christian eschatology the resurrection of the dead implies the transition from the one aeon to the other and the beginning of the new and eternal creation, the new aeon has begun already, though as yet concealed from the eyes of men, in and with the resurrection of Christ, inasmuch as this is the beginning of the general resurrection (1 C. 15:20, 23).

There is an echo of the original Christian view of the two aeons, or a bit of secularised eschatology, in the western view that world history is split into two periods by the coming of Jesus Christ.

D. The Personification of Αἰών.

The idea of a personal Αἰών or personified αἰῶνες (→ 198), so important in Hellenistic syncretism, is alien to the NT. It may perhaps be found only in Eph. 2:2 : κατὰ τὸν αἰῶνα τοῦ κόσμου τούτου (cf. the continuation : κατὰ τὸν ἄρχοντα τῆς ἐξουσίας τοῦ ἀέρος), but certainly not in passages like Col. 1:26 or Eph. 2:7 or 3:9, as suggested by Reitzenstein. [39] On the other hand, we seem to have reference to personal αἰῶνες in Ign. Eph., 19, 2: πῶς ἐφανερώθη τοῖς αἰῶσιν (cf. 19, 1). Here, as in Eph. 2:2, we may perhaps see a penetration into Christian

---

[36] Dalman, WJ, 122 f.; cf. Str.-B., IV, 816.
[37] Str.-B., II, 219; IV, 837.
[38] Censorinus, De Die Natali, 17.
[39] Iran. Erl., 86, n. 3; 255 f.; and after him Pr.-Bauer, 42.

thinking of a mythological conception of syncretism which came to play a most important part in Gnosticism. In Judaism there is a personification of the two αἰῶνες in Slav. En., 25 f.

αἰώνιος.

Adj. with 2 and 3 endings: "eternal." Orphic. Hymn., 87, 5 (Abel); Plat. Leg., X, 904a; Resp. II, 363d; Tim., 37d and 38b: θεὸν τὸν αἰώνιον, Tim. Locr., 96c. In later poetry and prose αἰώνιος is also used in the sense of "lifelong" or "enduring," in accordance with the basic meaning of → αἰών: Callim. Hymn., 3, 6; 4, 130; Philodem. De Deis, III, 8, 22, Diels (AAB, 1916, 4); Dion. Hal. Ant. Rom., X, 36; Diod. S., I, 1, 5; IV, 63, 4; Max. Tyr., XLIII, 43, Dübner. [1] Cf. the distinction between νοῦσος χρονίη and αἰωνίη in Aretaios of Cappadocia (181, 7 Ermerins). Inscriptions: ἡ αἰώνιος καὶ ἀθάνατος τοῦ παντὸς φύσις, Inscr. Brit. Mus. (inscription in honour of Augustus from Halicarnass.); εἰς χρόνον αἰώνιον, Ditt. Or., 383, 11; πρὸς δόξαν καὶ μνήμην αἰώνιον, ibid., 438, 13 [2] and many similar formulations. [3] In the later empire αἰώνιος (aeternus) is applied to the emperors like many similar divine predicates, e.g., τῶν αἰωνίων Αὐγούστων, ibid., 580, 3; 619, 2; 722, 6. [4]

In the LXX עוֹלָם is often rendered adjectivally by αἰώνιος, the sense being thus affected, e.g., in ψ 23:7: πύλαι αἰώνιοι ("everlasting doors") instead of "ancient doors"; ψ 76:5: ἔτη αἰώνια ("eternal years") instead of "years long past"; Gn. 21:33: θεὸς αἰώνιος ("eternal God") instead of "God of old."

In the NT αἰώνιος (with the rare → ἀΐδιος) is used in the sense of eternal in three ways.

1. It is used of God: τοῦ αἰωνίου θεοῦ (R. 16:26, → αἰών, 200). As a predicate of God αἰώνιος contains not merely the concept of unlimited time without beginning or end, but also of the eternity which transcends time.

2. In the latter sense it is used also of divine possessions and gifts. In 2 C. 4:18 the things which are seen (τὰ βλεπόμενα) are compared to the things which are not seen as things temporal (πρόσκαιρα) to things eternal. [5] The same view is developed in Hb., e.g., in 9:14: the πνεῦμα is the πνεῦμα αἰώνιον ("eternal Spirit") because divine. In the same connection we should mention αἰώνιος δόξα, 2 Tm. 2:10; 1 Pt. 5:10; αἰώνιον βάρος δόξης, 2 C. 4:17; cf. Wis. 10:14; τιμὴ καὶ κράτος αἰώνιον (doxologically), 1 Tm. 6:16; εὐαγγέλιον αἰώνιον, Rev. 14:6; παράκλησις αἰωνία. 2 Th. 2:16; διαθήκη αἰώνιος, Hb. 13:20 (very common in the LXX, as in Gn. 9:16; 17:7; Ex. 31:16; Lv. 24:8; 2 Βασ. 23:5); σωτηρία αἰώνιος, Hb. 5:9; Mk. 16 (short ending); cf. Is. 45:17; αἰωνία λύτρωσις, Hb. 9:12; αἰώνιος κληρονομία, Hb. 9:15.

αἰώνιος. Cr.-Kö., 99; C. Lackeit, Aion, Zeit u. Ewigkeit in Sprache u. Religion d. Griechen, I (1916), 35 f., 106 ff.; B. Laum, Stiftungen in d. griech. u. röm. Antike, (1914), I, 46 ff.; Pauly-W., I, 694 ff. s.v. Aeternitas, Aeternus; F. Oertel, Liturgie (1917), 323; H. Major, JThSt, 18 (1917), 7 ff.; F. Tennant, ET, 29 (1917/18), 265-267; H. Linssen, Jahrb. f. Liturgiewiss., 8 (1928), 73 ff.

[1] For further examples, v. Ind. in Lackeit, 106 ff.
[2] Cf. εἰς μνημόσυνον αἰώνιον, ψ 111, 6.
[3] v. Index of passages in inscr. and pap., Lackeit, 106, 107.
[4] Cf. βασιλεὺς Πτολεμαῖος αἰωνόβιος, Ditt. Or., 90, 10 and the oriental royal greeting: ζήτω ὁ βασιλεὺς εἰς τὸν αἰῶνα, 3 Βασ. 1:31; Da. 2:4 etc.
[5] Cf. Philo's equation of ἀόρατος and → ἀΐδιος, and the contrasting of the visible and invisible, the temporal and eternal, in Slav. En. 24 etc.

3. The expression αἰώνιος βασιλεία (2 Pt. 1:11) [6] forms a transition to the use of αἰώνιος as a term for the object of eschatological expectation : ζωὴ αἰώνιος, [7] αἰώνιος κληρονομία, Hb. 9:15; αἰώνιοι σκηναί of the place of blessedness, Lk. 16:9; οἰκία αἰώνιος ἐν τοῖς οὐρανοῖς of the heavenly body, 2 C. 5:1. [8] If in such expressions αἰώνιος has the full sense of divine eternity, in τὸ πῦρ τὸ αἰώνιον, Mt. 18:8; 25:41; Jd. 7 (cf. 4 Macc. 12:12), κόλασις αἰώνιος, Mt. 25:46; ὄλεθρος αἰώνιος, 2 Th. 1:9; αἰώνιον ἁμάρτημα, Mk. 3:29 (eternally unforgivable sin) it has in the first instance only the sense of "unceasing" or "endless." But an expression like κρίμα αἰώνιον, Hb. 6:2 (cf. αἰωνίου κρίσεως, Mk. 3:29, ΑΚΜΠ) shows that here, too, it extends beyond the purely temporal meaning.

4. The concept of eternity is weakened in χρόνοι αἰώνιοι, R. 16:25; 2 Tm. 1:9; Tt. 1:2. This expression is simply a variant of αἰῶνες in the eternity formulae. The phrase in Phlm. 15 : ἵνα αἰώνιον αὐτὸν ἀπέχῃς ("that thou shouldest receive him for ever") reminds us of the non-biblical usage (→ 208) and of οἰκέτης εἰς τὸν αἰῶνα (עֶבֶד עוֹלָם) "slave for life" in Dt. 15:17.

Sasse

ἀκαθαρσία,

ἀκάθαρτος → καθαρός	ἀκαίρως → καιρός
ἄκακος → κακός	ἄκαρπος → καρπός
ἀκατάγνωστος → γινώσκω	ἀκατάκριτος → κρίνω
ἀκατάλυτος → λύω	ἀκαταστασία, ἀκατάστατος → καθίστημι

┌─────────────┐
│ † ἀκέραιος │
└─────────────┘

a. "Unravaged" or "unharmed" (cf. κεραΐζω ⊢ "to ravage" or "destroy"), [1] used of a country, city or walls : Demosth., 1, 28; Ditt. Syll.[3], 210, 13 ; Jos. Ant., 5, 47; Bell., 3, 257. b. Thence in a figurative sense "that which is still in its original state of intactness, totality or moral innocence." Thus "undivided attention" in Jos. Bell., 1, 621; the "incorruptibility of a judge" in Dion. Hal. Ant. Rom., 7, 4; "innocent harmlessness" as opposed to deceit and cunning : LXX St. on Est. 6:6; Jos. Ant., 1, 61. [2] c. In the Hellenist. period there arises the combination with οἶνος, χρυσός, etc., and therefore the sense of "pure" : Athen. II, 45e etc. [3]

In the NT it is always used in the figurative sense. In Phil. 2:15 it is set alongside → ἄμεμπτος and → ἄμωμος [4] in definition of the τέκνα θεοῦ μέσον γενεᾶς

---

[6] Cf. Da. 3:33; 7:27; 1 Macc. 2:57; Philo Som., II, 285 in another sense.

[7] → ζωή; cf. Da. 12:2; 2 Macc. 7:9, 36; Ps. Sol. 3:12; Eth. En. 37:4; 40:9; in Philo ζωή is found in conjunction with αἰώνιος only in Fug., 78 : οὐ ζωὴ μέν ἐστιν αἰώνιος.

[8] Cf. Qoh. 12:5 : εἰς οἶκον αἰῶνος αὐτοῦ (בֵּית עֹלָמוֹ) and Semitic epitaphs with בית עלם, as also the description of the temple as בֵּית הָעוֹלָמִים, jSota, 24b; S. Nu., 10 on 5:17.

ἀ κ έ ρ α ι ο ς. Boisacq; Pass.-Cr.; Moult.-Mill. *s.v.*; Zn. on Mt. 10:16; Schl. Mt., 338. [1] Also κηραίνω "to harm," ἀκήρατος, "unharmed." Cf. Boisacq, 35 as against the older dictionaries, many of which derive it from κεράννυμι. This derivation is formally impossible; "unadmixed" is ἄκρατος (Debrunner). Pass.-Cr. rightly compares γεραιός / ἀγήρατος.

[2] Not in Philo.

[3] Debrunner thinks it possible that there may sometimes have been a secondary influence of the like-sounding κεράννυμι; but cf. n. 1.

[4] Par. with εἰλικρινής, 1 Cl., 2, 5.

σκολιᾶς κτλ. In R. 16:19 Christians are to be ἀκέραιοι εἰς τὸ κακόν, possessors of an integrity [5] which they have kept in face of evil, the symbol of which is the sacrificial [6] dove (Mt. 10:16).

Kittel

ἀκολουθέω, ἐξ-, ἐπ-, παρ-, συνακολουθέω

ἀκολουθέω.

A. ἀκολουθεῖν and ἕπεσθαι in Greek Usage.

Already in secular Greek the ordinary sense of "following" or "going behind" someone has given rise to that of following in an intellectual, moral or religious sense. Thus one follows an orator in thought (γνώμῃ), Thuc., III, 38, 6; or the wise man, Aristot. Eth. M., II, 6, p. 1203b, 19 f.; or a friend, BGU, 1079, 10 and 26. Similarly the servant (ἀκόλουθος) or slave follows, Ps.-Aristid. in Rhet. Graec., II, 519, 11, Spengel; or the lover, Plat. Phaedr., 232a.

In religious and philosophical use we find ἀκολουθεῖν φύσει, Epict. Diss., I, 6, 15, or θεῷ, M. Ant., 7, 31; Epict. Diss., I, 30, 4. More commonly for the following of God, however, we find ἕπεσθαι, which does not occur in the NT. [1] This tells us that we become like God by acting as He does. [2] Plat. [3] Phaedr., 248a : ἡ μὲν ἄριστα (ψυχή) θεῷ ἑπομένη καὶ εἰκασμένη, cf. Symp. 197e; Leg., I, 636d. Xenoph. Cyrop., VII, 1, 3 : ἑψόμεθά σοι, ὦ Ζεῦ. It can be maintained by Epict.: τέλος ἐστὶ τὸ ἕπεσθαι θεοῖς, Diss., I, 20, 15; 12, 8. This religious goal of ἕπεσθαι is expressed particularly finely in the Stoic [4] verses which Epict. has preserved at the end of his Encheiridion (53, 1):

ἄγου δέ μ', ὦ Ζεῦ, καὶ σύ γ' ἡ Πεπρωμένη,
ὅποι ποθ' ὑμῖν εἰμι διατεταγμένος·
ὡς ἕψομαί γ' ἄοκνος· ἢν δέ γε μὴ θέλω,
κακὸς γενόμενος, οὐδὲν ἧττον ἕψομαι.

---

[5] Not "unadmixed with evil," (Zn. R., ad loc., as an alternative). Cf. Plat. Resp., III, 409a : ἀκέραιοι κακῶν ἠθῶν. At the same time the usual translation "simple in respect of evil," to counterbalance the preceding σοφοί, is a misunderstanding with no foundation in the true signification of the word.

[6] Cf. Cant. r. 2:14, Str.-B., I, 574 f.: תְּמִימִים כְּיוֹנִים sy[s] Mt. 10:16, תמימין.

ἀ κ ο λ ο υ θ έ ω. E. G. Gulin, "Die Nachf. Gottes," Stud. Or., I (Helsingfors, 1925), 34-50; A. Marmorstein, "Die Nachahmung Gottes in der Agada," Jüdische Studien, Festschr. f. J. Wohlgemuth (1928), 144-159; M. Buber, "Nachahmung Gottes," Morgen, I (1926), 638-647; W. Beyschlag, Leben Jesu, II² (1887), 184 ff.; J. Weiss, D. Nachfolge Christi u. d. Predigt d. Gegenwart (1895), Part A : F. Bosse, Prolegomena z. einer Geschichte d. Begriffs d. Nachf. Christi (1895), 83-104; A. Fischer, "Über Nachahmung u. Nachf.," ARPs I ; A. Runestam, Liebe, Glaube, Nachf. (1931), 147-183; Cr.-Kö., 101 f.; Schl. Mt., 119; Str.-B., I, 188, 528 f.

[1] Only συνέπομαι, Ac. 20:4; in the LXX only 3 Macc. 2:26; 5:48.
[2] Cf. Gulin, 45 f.
[3] ἀκολουθεῖν, ἐξακολουθεῖν of following God is not found in Plato. In Epict. it occurs only in the passage quoted, Diss., I, 30, 4.
[4] According to Simplicius the verses derive from the Stoic Cleanthes, the pupil of Zeno and teacher of Chrysippus.

B. Discipleship in the OT and Judaism.

The Hebrew term corresponding to ἀκολουθεῖν and ἕπεσθαι is הָלַךְ אַחֲרֵי. The LXX usually gives a literal translation: πορεύεσθαι ὀπίσω. From the Hebr. expression, however, there arises in the few cases where ἀκολουθεῖν is used the construction with ὀπίσω:[5] 3 Βασ. 19:20; Hos. 2:5 (7);[6] Is. 45:14: ὀπίσω σου ἀκολουθήσουσιν. This is found neither in secular Greek nor in Josephus,[7] who, e.g., out of וְאֵלְכָה אַחֲרֵיךְ = LXX ἀκολουθήσω (Elisha) ὀπίσω σου (3 Βασ. 19:20), makes the usual Gk. dative: ἠκολούθησεν Ἠλίᾳ, Ant., 8, 353.[8] On the other hand, in Mt. 10:38 we have ἀκολούθει ὀπίσω μου, which is a parallel and equivalent to ἔρχεσθε ὀπίσω μου in Mt. 16:24 and par.

1. The Following of God by the Righteous.

In the OT[9] the expression הָלַךְ אַחֲרֵי acquires its distinctive meaning from the fact that, esp. in Hosea, Jeremiah and the Deuteronomic writings, it is used as a technical term for apostasy into heathenism. Going after other gods is the basic sin of the people and the cause of all visitations, Ju. 2:12; Dt. 4:3; 6:14; 1 K. 21:26; Jer. 11:10 etc. In Hosea[10] the expression is bound up with the picture of adultery which dominates his preaching. Israel follows the paramour and forgets the husband, Hos. 1:2; 2:7, 13.[11]

The idea of following Yahweh is much less prominent. It occurs occasionally in a Deuteronomic context, Dt. 1:36; 13:5; 1 K. 14:8; 2 K. 23:3; 2 Ch. 34:31. The main Deuteronomic call, however, is not that Israel should go after Yahweh but that it should walk in His ways (Dt. 5:30 etc.). Only in 1 K. 18:21 is there any emphasis on the former picture. Here the relating of לְכוּ אַחֲרָיו to Yahweh arises out of the simultaneous reference to Baal and the demand of Elijah that a choice should be made between them. It is remarkable that no part is played by the suggestive thought of Ex. 13:21 f. that the Israelites followed Yahweh as He preceded them through the wilderness. The only occasion when there is reference to this following in the wilderness is in Jer. 2:2, and here the emphasis does not fall on the preceding of Yahweh but on the idea of the bridal relationship, so that the statement is reminiscent of Hosea, yet with a positive application: "I remember ... the love of thine espousals, when thou wentest after me in the wilderness." It almost appears that there are reservations against using the otherwise obvious picture of following in relation to Yahweh because of its particular sense of walking after other gods.[12] Possibly there were still lively recollections that the expression took its origin from the processions of the devotees of pagan cults behind the preceding images of the gods.[13] This perhaps explains why there is never any reference in a strongly religious sense[14] to following the ark, though

---

[5] On the other hand, ἐξακολουθεῖν is always construed with the dat., even as a transl. of הָלַךְ אַחַר, Jer. 2:2; Am. 2:4.

[6] B: πορεύσομαι ὀπίσω τῶν ...

[7] Here, as often, Jos. more strongly hellenises the Palestinian usage than the Evangelists.

[8] Cf. M. Johannessohn, D. Gebrauch d. Kasus. u. d. Präpos. in LXX (1910), 215 f.

[9] Cf. Gulin, op. cit., 39 ff.

[10] But cf. also passages like Dt. 8:19; Jer. 2:2, 23, 25, which approximate to the thought of Hosea.

[11] הָלַךְ אַחֲרֵי as applied to the erotic passion of the lover, Prv. 7:22.

[12] Gulin, 42.

[13] So P. Volz, Jeremia² (1928), 17. With qualifications, Gulin, 35.

[14] Jos. 3:3; 6:9, 13 have no cultic importance, as rightly observed by Gulin, 43, n. 3.

the ark certainly went on before in the wilderness journey (Nu. 10:33 ff.) and formed the focal point in the cultic processions in Jerusalem (1 S. 6:12 ff.). [15]

Our findings in relation to the Rabbis correspond to those in the OT field. The realism of this type of thinking cannot grasp concretely the thought of following God, which is strongly felt to be opposed to the idea of transcendence. If the image is suggested by exegesis, e.g., of Dt. 13:5, it is immediately explained and diverted along the rather different lines of imitation. "Is it then possible for a man to go behind the Shekinah? We read: 'For the Lord thy God is a consuming fire' (Dt. 4:24)," bSot., 14a. "Is it then possible for flesh and blood to go behind the Holy One, blessed be He? It is written of Him: 'Thy way is in the sea...' (Ps. 77:19) ... And is it then possible for flesh and blood to mount up to heaven and to cling to the Shekinah? Of this it is written: 'For the Lord thy God is a consuming fire' (Dt. 4:24)," Lv. r. 25 on 19:23. The true answer to the question is that we should "follow the qualities of God," bSot., 14a. This is expounded either in historical terms, e.g., that Israel should plant the land as God planted the Garden of Eden (Lv. r., 25), or in ethical terms, that the righteous should clothe the naked as God clothed Adam, visit the sick as God visited Abraham, comfort the sorrowful as God comforted Isaac, and bury the dead as God buried Moses, bSot., 14a. Thus the following of God is a mere *imitatio* for which other expressions (e.g., דמה "to resemble") [16] are normally used. The resultant problem for Rabbinic theology is the very different one whether man can really be like God already in this world, or whether this expression should be reserved for the world to come. [17]

> Philo, on the other hand, is in full agreement with Gk. usage in his application of ἀκολουθεῖν and ἕπεσθαι. For him, as for Epictet., the thought of following is dominated by the reference to God and to φύσις. συμβήσεσθαι τοῖς ἑπομένοις θεῷ, Praem. Poen., 98; τίς ἐμοὶ (sc. θεῷ) καὶ τοῖς ἐμοῖς βουλήμασιν ἕποιτο, Abr., 204; ἑπόμενος ἀκολουθίᾳ φύσεως, Spec. Leg., III, 180; φύσει γὰρ ἕπεσθαι καλόν, ἀκολουθίᾳ φύσεως δ' ἀντίπαλον ὄχλου φορά, IV, 46. [18] Migr. Abr., 128: ἀκολούθως τῇ φύσει ζῆν, identical with ἕπεσθαι θεῷ. In Josephus, however, no very significant role is played by the special use of ἀκολουθεῖν. The only mention of discipleship [19] is in the case of Elisha on the basis of the OT narrative, Ant., 8, 354. [20] The most common feature in Jos. is the linking of ἀκολουθία and ἀκόλουθος with the νόμος in the sense of "obedience to the divine Law," Ap., 2, 220; Ant., 9, 187; 11, 124 etc. [21]

2. The Following of the Disciple.

In the OT a following which in the first instance has no religious significance is following of a respected person. Thus the warrior follows a leader as the people followed Abimelech in Ju. 9:4, 49. Again, the wife follows her husband or the bride

---

[15] S. Mowinckel, *Psalmenstudien,* II (1922), 112 ff.; Gulin, 43.
[16] Cf. e.g., the saying of Abba Shaul, M. Ex. 15:2: "Be like Him. As He is merciful and gracious, so be thou merciful and gracious." The starting-point for the use of דמה is always provided, of course, by recollection of the דְּמוּת of Gn. 5:1.
[17] Cf. Marmorstein, *op. cit.,* 155 ff.
[18] For further examples, cf. Leisegang, Index, 74, 265.
[19] At most the saying in Ant., 20, 188, that the ἀκολουθήσαντες of a false prophet ἕπονται μέχρι τῆς ἐρημίας, only approximates to a more specialised use.
[20] There is perhaps a certain deeper significance in the ἀκολουθεῖν of the wife behind her husband, e.g., Ant., 1, 318, *v. infra.*
[21] For further examples, cf. Thackeray, Lex. Jos., 18.

her bridegroom in Jer. 2:2 (→ 211). The prophetic disciple Elisha follows his master Elijah in 1 K. 19:20 f.: וַיֵּלֶךְ אַחֲרֵי אֵלִיָּהוּ = LXX καὶ ἐπορεύθη ὀπίσω [22] 'Ηλείου. Even this following expresses little more [23] than a relationship of respect. This is fully confirmed by the phrase which follows : "and ministered unto him." The disciple follows his master as a servant in the strict sense.

This last type of following passed over into Rabbinic custom to the extent that this received its impress from the master-pupil relationship. In many stories handed down by tradition we always perceive the same order, the rabbi or rabbis going ahead, perhaps riding on an ass, and their pupils following on behind at an appropriate distance (והיו תלמידיו מהלכין אחריו S. Dt., 305 on 31:14). The form is fixed right through from the earlier [24] to the later texts, whether the master is one of the great figures of the first century like Gamaliel [25] or Jochanan ben Zakkai, [24] or whether it is one of the third century teachers like Eleazar ha-Qappar [26] or Rab Uqba. [27] Even when it is the son who follows the father as a pupil, it makes no difference : "R. Ismael, R. Eleazar ben Azarja and R. Aqiba went on the way, and Levi the director and R. Israel the son of R. Eleazar ben Azarja went on the way after them" (M. Ex. 31:12). At no point do we detect any impulse towards giving this notion any fuller significance or making it a theological concept.

C. ἀκολουθεῖν in the NT.

In the NT the idea of following is never applied to God (though → μιμεῖσθαι, μιμητής). This was not suggested by Palestinian usage, and early Christianity had all the less reason to coin the expression in view of the fact that from the root of the pupil relationship there arose within it the wholly new and distinctive concept of following after Christ. Even when Christianity entered the sphere of Hellenism, which was familiar with the religious and philosophical notion of following God, the verb ἀκολουθεῖν and the whole idea of following were so fully influenced by the thought of following Christ, and indeed of following the historical Jesus, that it was no longer possible to turn the words to any other religious use.

The distinctive statistical evidence shows that the special use of ἀκολουθεῖν is strictly limited to discipleship of Christ; [28] apart from a single reference in Revelation it is found exclusively in the four Gospels. To some extent it connotes an external following, as when the multitudes accompany Jesus in Mk. 3:7 and par., Mt. 8:10 and par., or the disciples in a narrower sense in Mt. 8:19 : ἀκολουθήσω σοι ὅπου ἐὰν ἀπέρχῃ. The disciple leaves everything to go after Jesus (Mk. 10:28; cf. 1:18; Lk. 5:11). This implies, however, that ἀκολουθεῖν signifies self-commitment in a sense which breaks all other ties (Mt. 8:22; Lk. 9:61 f.). The disciple does what the pupil of the rabbi does, externally in the same forms as the

---

[22] Jos. Ant., 8, 353 ἠκολούθησεν 'Ηλίᾳ (→ 211).

[23] As against Gulin, p. 42 f.: "Following makes the pupil like the teacher, the godliness of the teacher passing quasi-physically to the pupil."

[24] S. Dt., 305 on 31:14 : "It happened that R. Jochanan ben Zakkai rode on an ass, and his pupils went after him," cf. bKet., 66b.

[25] Gamaliel rides on an ass from Akko to Kesib. His slave Tabi goes before him and his pupil R. Elai behind. T. Pes., 1, 27; Lev. r., 37 on 27:2.

[26] bAZ, 43a.

[27] bKet., 72b.

[28] All other occurrences of ἀκ. in the NT speak of a following which has no religious significance.

latter, but internally in attachment to Jesus. Hence the word still has the sense of discipleship, but in relation to Jesus it acquires a new content and impress. The exclusiveness of the NT use arises from the fact that for primitive Christianity there is only one discipleship and therefore only one following, namely, the relationship to Jesus. The demand ἀκολούθει μοι in Mk. 2:14 and par. is a Messianic demand (→ συνακολουθέω).

Because it signifies following the Messiah, this discipleship is essentially a religious gift. ἀκολουθεῖν means participation in the salvation offered in Jesus. In Lk. 9:61 f. only he who εὔθετός ἐστιν τῇ βασιλείᾳ τοῦ θεοῦ can achieve ἀκολουθεῖν. In Mk. 10:17, 21 and par. ἀκολούθει μοι is an answer to the question concerning ζωὴ αἰώνιος. Similarly in Jn. 8:12: ὁ ἀκολουθῶν ἐμοὶ οὐ μὴ περιπατήσῃ ἐν τῇ σκοτίᾳ, ἀλλ᾽ ἕξει τὸ φῶς τῆς ζωῆς. The same thought is found in Rev. 14:4: οἱ ἀκολουθοῦντες τῷ ἀρνίῳ ... ἠγοράσθησαν τῷ θεῷ καὶ τῷ ἀρνίῳ.

Yet ἀκολουθεῖν also implies participation in the fate of Jesus. In Mt. 8:19 f. the answer to the ἀκολουθήσω σοι is ὁ υἱὸς τοῦ ἀνθρώπου οὐκ ἔχει ποῦ τὴν κεφαλὴν κλίνῃ. In Mk. 8:34 and par.: εἴ τις θέλει ὀπίσω μου ἐλθεῖν, ἀπαρνησάσθω ἑαυτὸν καὶ ἀράτω τὸν σταυρὸν αὐτοῦ, καὶ ἀκολουθείτω μοι. We see the same connection in Jn. 12:25, 26. These statements show clearly that this is not in any sense an imitation of the example of Jesus, as later ecclesiastical interpretation assumed,[29] but exclusively a fellowship of life and suffering with the Messiah which arises only in the fellowship of His salvation.[30]

How strong the figurative use of the term can be is revealed by the following consideration. On the one side the tradition quite naively retains sayings like Mt. 10:38: ὃς οὐ ... ἀκολουθεῖ ὀπίσω μου, οὐκ ἔστιν μου ἄξιος; Lk. 14:27: ὅστις οὐ ... ἔρχεται ὀπίσω μου, οὐ δύναται εἶναί μου μαθητής. On the other it equally naively presents the fact that there are disciples who do not exercise ἀκολουθεῖν in the sense of going around with Jesus. All the more remarkable is the third distinctive feature of the tradition, that the connection of the word with the concrete processes of the history of Jesus is so strongly felt and retained that no noun ever came into use corresponding to the concept of discipleship.[31] The NT simply has the active term, because what it is seeking to express is an action and not a concept. On this basis it is no accident that the word ἀκολουθεῖν is used only in the Gospels, that there is agreement as to its use in all four Gospels, and that they restrict the relationship signified by it to the historical Jesus. In the Epistles other expressions are used (→ σύν, ἐν) in which the emphasis falls on relationship to the exalted κύριος and His πνεῦμα. The only exception outside the Gospels (Rev. 14:4) is obviously an application of Mt. 10:38 to a specific class of believers.[32]

---

[29] Aug. Sct. Virg., 27: *quid est enim sequi nisi imitari?* Theophylact J., 21, p. 845: οἱ μιμούμενοι αὐτοῦ τὴν ἐν πᾶσιν ἀκρίβειαν, οὗτοι ἀκολουθοῦσιν αὐτῷ; Theophanes Hom., 41, p. 293: τὸ ἀκολουθῆσαι αὐτῷ τὸ τὴν ἐκείνου πολιτείαν, ὡς δυνατὸν ἀνθρώπῳ μιμήσασθαι, ὃς ἐπολιτεύσατο ἐπὶ τῆς γῆς γενόμενος ἄνθρωπος.

[30] A. Klostermann, Mk. (1867), 179: Discipleship as participation "in the inheritance of Christ" is "not the activity of going as such, but achievement with Him of the goal to which He goes."

[31] ἀκολούθησις might have been used for this purpose (Ps.-Plat. Def., 412b). Cf. also the use of παρακολούθησις in Stoic writings (Epict. Diss., I, 6, 13 etc.).

[32] Hence it is no surprise that this formed the starting-point for the concept of *imitatio Agni,* which was so important in the early Church and beyond; cf. Loh. Apk., 120.

Equally distinctive of the new content here given to the concept is the fact that in the apostolic period the picture of following never seems to have been applied to any but the disciples of Jesus. At any rate, Acts [33] as well as other sources avoids this kind of expression, though it is not unfamiliar with the master-pupil relationship, e.g., in the case of Barnabas and Mark, or of Paul and his circle.

† ἐξακολουθέω.

Like the simple form, this is used in both the literal and the figurative sense. In the NT it is found only in 2 Pt. in the latter sense: σεσοφισμένοις μύθοις, 1:16; ἀσελγείαις, 2:2; τῇ ὁδῷ τοῦ Βαλαάμ, 2:15.

Cf. ταῖς ὁδοῖς αὐτῶν, Is. 56:11; μύθοις, Jos. Ant., 1, 22; δαίμοσι πλάνης, Test. Jud. 23:1; πονηροῖς διαβουλίοις, Test. Iss. 6:2.

† ἐπακολουθέω.

This is partly used a. in the true sense of following, sometimes metaphorically: Mk. 16:20: διὰ τῶν ἐπακολουθούντων (ensuing as a result) [1] σημείων; 1 Pt. 2:21: τοῖς ἴχνεσιν αὐτοῦ (i.e., Christ's, expressing the fact that He is an example); 1 Tm. 5:24: the sin which follows after, i.e., which only manifests itself in the future, [2] in contrast to that which declares itself from the very first; and partly b. in the figurative sense of pursuing a matter, or concerning oneself with it: 1 Tm. 5:10: παντὶ ἔργῳ ἀγαθῷ.

As regards a. cf. LXX Jos. 6:8: ἡ κιβωτὸς τῆς διαθήκης κυρίου; Polyb., 30, 9, 10: μέμψις; BGU, 2, 14: ζημία; Philo Virt., 64: ἴχνεσιν. As regards b. cf. LXX Jos. 14:9: ὀπίσω κυρίου τοῦ θεοῦ ἡμῶν; 14:14: τῷ προστάγματι κυρίου; Jos. Ap., 1:6: ματαίαις δόξαις.

† παρακολουθέω.

a. The strict meaning is "to go along with (παρ-)" or "to accompany." Thus in Mk. 16:17 the miracles which accompany believers are σημεῖα τοῖς πιστεύσασιν ταῦτα παρακολουθήσει. b. A first figurative meaning is that of "pursuing or investigating a matter," as in Lk. 1:3: παρηκολουθηκότι ἄνωθεν πᾶσιν ἀκριβῶς. c. A second figurative meaning is that of "not letting a matter slip," of "concentrating" (either abs. or on something), of "following a teaching which has been grasped," as in 1 Tm. 4:6; 2 Tm. 3:10: διδασκαλίᾳ, ἀγωγῇ, προθέσει, πίστει. In both figurative meanings a strong emphasis is laid on the exactness or constancy of agreement indicated by the prefix.

With regard to a. τύχη, Demosth., 42, 21; ἔχθρα, 59, 98; δίκη, 2 Macc. 8:11; ᾿Αντί-πατρος ἡ τοῦ ὑπόθεσις, Jos. Bell., 1, 455; Papias in Eus. Hist. Eccl., III, 39, 4 and 15

---

[33] Ac. 13:43 hardly has any significance beyond that of accompanying in order to make themselves known.

ἐ π α κ ο λ ο υ θ έ ω. [1] As against Pr.-Bauer, 438; cf. Preisigke Wört., 526.

[2] Bengel: *interim patienter exspectandum, dum res se aperiat.*

π α ρ α κ ο λ ο υ θ έ ω. Zahn, *Einl.,* II, 388; A. Bonhöffer, "Epiktet u. das NT," RVV, X (1910), 210; Moult.-Mill., 485 f.; H. J. Cadbury in Jackson-Lake, *The Beginnings of Christianity,* I, 2 (1922), 501 f.; Ropes, JThSt, 25 (1923), 70 f.

for accompanying Jesus. With regard to b. πράξεσιν, Polyb., III, 32, 2; γεγονόσι, Jos. Ap., 1, 53; ἡμετέροις γράμμασιν, 1, 218; Vit. 357. With regard to c. this is "one of the most important technical terms in Epictetus" (Bonhöffer). Cf. esp. ἡμῖν δ' οἷς καὶ τὴν παρακολουθητικὴν δύναμιν ἔδωκεν, Diss., I, 6, 12 ff.; μὴ παρακ. λόγῳ μηδ' ἀποδείξει μηδὲ σοφίσματι, Diss. I, 7, 33; also τῇ περὶ τὸ θεῖον τῆς πόλεως θεραπείᾳ, Ditt. Syll.³, 885, 32.

† συνακολουθέω.

In the NT this refers only to those who accompany Jesus, though in two passages (Mk. 5:37; 14:51), and perhaps the third (Lk. 23:49), it signifies only "external accompanying." The pregnant sense of following as discipleship is reserved for the simple form → ἀκολουθέω. This is perhaps surprising in view of the fact that in secular Greek the compound συνακολουθέω can acquire the figurative meanings of "understanding" and "obeying" (Plat. Leg., I, 629 etc.). It is a further sign that in the use of the simple form there begins to develop a special term with particular religious significance.

Kittel

> ### ἀκούω, ἀκοή, εἰς-, ἐπ-, παρακούω,
> ### παρακοή, ὑπακούω, ὑπακοή,
> ### ὑπήκοος

ἀκούω (→ βλέπω, ὁράω).

The class. rule of the gen. (or prep. παρά, πρός, ἐκ) for the persons whom we hear, and the acc. for the persons or things about whom or which we hear, is applied even more systematically in the NT, where the acc. tends to replace the more common class. gen. even in the case of hearing a sound, though the latter still occurs. The position is similar in the LXX. Cf. 1 K. 10:8, 24 : Mas. הַשֹּׁמְעִים אֶת־חָכְמָתֶךָ/לִשְׁמֹעַ אֶת־חָכְמָתוֹ = LXX ἀκούοντες ... τὴν φρόνησιν / ἀκοῦσαι τῆς φρονήσεως. Ac. 9:4, 7; Rev. 14:2, 13 : ἀκ. φωνήν / ἀκ. φωνῆς.¹

A. The Hearing of Man.

The use of ἀκούω and its derivatives in the NT reflects something of the significance of the Word as it is spoken and as it is to be heard in the reciprocal NT relationship between God and man. The hearing of man represents correspondence to the revelation of the Word, and in biblical religion it is thus the essential form in which this divine revelation is appropriated.

ἀ κ ο ύ ω κτλ. W. W. Graf Baudissin, " 'Gott schauen' in d. at.lichen Rel.," ARW, 18 (1915), 173 ff.; J. Hänel, *Das Erkennen Gottes bei d. Schriftpropheten* (1923), esp. 19 ff.; 193 ff.; J. Hempel, *Gott u. Mensch im AT* (1926); F. Häussermann, *Wortempfang u. Symbol in d. at.lichen Prophetie* (1932). E. v. Dobschütz, "Die fünf Sinne im NT," JBL, 48 (1929), 378 ff.; R. Bultmann, θεὸν οὐδεὶς ἑώρακεν πώποτε, ZNW (1930), 169 ff.; E. Fascher, "Deus invisibilis," *Marburger Theol. Stud.*, I (1931), 41 ff.; G. Kittel, *Religionsgesch. u. Urchristentum* (1932), 95 ff.

¹ On the syntax, cf. Bl.-Debr., 103 f., 236; Zn. J., 357 f., n. 2; R. Helbing, *Die Kasussyntax der Verba bei den LXX* (1928), 150 ff.

1. The Hearing of Revelation outside the NT.

a. In the Greek mysteries and oriental Gnosticism[2] great stress is laid on the fact that man apprehends God by seeing. It is not as though there were no religious hearing ;[3] but the phenomena of sight are the more essential. For Philo the inter-relation of hearing and seeing is strikingly determined by the fact that the former can lead astray and deceive as distinct from the latter. Fug., 208 : ἀκοὴ δ' ὁρά-σεως τὰ δευτεραῖα φέρεται ... ἀκούειν μὲν γὰρ καὶ ψευδῶν ὡς ἀληθῶν ἔνεστιν, ὅτι ἀπατηλὸν ἀκοή, ἀψευδὲς δ' ὅρασις, ᾗ τὰ ὄντα ὄντως κατανοεῖται. In Apuleius many revelations of God are imparted which must be received by hearing.[4] At the point, however, where the true mystery is achieved, the reference is to vision, access and worship, with no reference to the fact that the devotee has heard a verbal revelation : *accessi confinium mortis et calcato Proserpinae limine per omnia vectus elementa remeavi, nocte media vidi solem candido coruscantem lumine, deos inferos et deos superos accessi coram et adoravi de proxumo*, Met., XI, 23. The content of revelation consists in seeing rather than hearing. Similarly in the so-called Mithras Liturgy all the emphasis is placed on the fact that ulti-mately God appears. Contemplation makes the devotee a παλινγενόμενος.[5] Al-ready in the Eleusinian mystery the climax was the moment when the bright light shone into the dark telesterion from above and a divine spectacle was witnessed.[6]

The monuments which have come down to us with pictures of religious acts also make it clear that the sacred moment of the mystery or cult is one of vision. If on the well-known terracottae and the picture in the Villa Item[7] the mysterious contents of the winnow are in the first instance covered with a cloth which is withdrawn at the solemn climax, this implies that the significance of the action depends upon the devotee seeing the symbolism of these contents.[8]

b. The emphasis is quite different in OT religion and in Judaism, which stems from it. These are religions of the Word which is either heard or to be heard. To be sure, the OT, too, speaks of seeing God and His face, especially in relation to the temple and its worship, but also in relation to the experience of God's help in daily emergencies. This form of speech, however, although it arose outside Israel in cults which had images, became so much a part of the religion of Israel, which had no images, that it no longer contained any serious emphasis on seeing in the strict sense. Hence it hardly enters into the present problem.[9] The true vision of God increasingly becomes for OT religion something exceptional and dangerous (Gn. 19:26; 32:31; Ex. 3:6; Ju. 6:23). When it takes place, its unusual nature is always underlined (Nu. 12:6 ff. → αἴνιγμα). Even in the case of Moses

---

[2] Cf. esp. for what follows v. Dobschütz, 396 ff. Concerning healings by "direction in dreams" amongst the Greeks and Romans, cf. O. Weinreich, "Antike Heilungswunder," RVV (1909), 110 ff.

[3] Cf. e.g., the very dramatic representation by ἀκοή demonstrated by Zingerle (→ 222).

[4] Met., XI, 5, 22 and 29.

[5] Preis. Zaub., IV (Paris), 695-723. That the continuation of the pap. causes God to prophesy merely shows us that we have here the voice of the revising magus, cf. A. Diete-rich-O. Weinreich, *Mithrasliturgie*³ (1923), 82.

[6] Cf. F. Noack, *Eleusis*, I (1927); Ill., 111.

[7] Cf. the ill. in J. Leipoldt, *Die Religionen in der Umwelt des Urchrts.* (1926), 170-172.

[8] On the Hanoverian terracotta it appears that the devotee is covered by the contents of the winnow (cf. Leipoldt, 171). Here too, however, the hanging cloth indicates the earlier disclosure of contents not previously seen, and the veiled eyes of those still to be initiated indicate that these may see only from the moment of dedication.

[9] → ὁράω; cf. G. Kittel, *op. cit.*, 100.

this is felt so strongly that the tradition that he saw the face of God and talked with him "face to face" (Ex. 33:11; Nu. 12:8) is toned down to suggest that he could only see His back (Ex. 33:20). Earthly and therefore unclean human eyes cannot see the holy God without perishing (Is. 6:5). Seeing God is an eschatological event which takes place when Yahweh comes to Zion and men are no longer of unclean lips (Is. 60:1 ff.; Job 19:26 f.; → ὁράω). [10]

The more seeing fades into the background, [11] the more hearing is emphasised. It is significant that the theophany of Moses is rather in the nature of speaking face to face (Ex. 33:11). Where there are accounts of seeing God, they simply provide the setting for the revelation of the Word (Is. 6:1 ff.; Ez. 1 f.; Am. 9:1 ff.; cf. also Ex. 3:1 ff.). When God appears, it is not for the sake of the theophany, but in order to send the prophet that he may pass on His Word, and consequently in order to cause Himself to be heard either indirectly or directly. The decisive religious statement is: "Hear the Word of the Lord" (Is. 1:10; Jer. 2:4; Am. 7:16); "Hear, O heavens, and give ear, O earth: for the Lord speaketh" (Is. 1:2). The decisive accusation is that of failure or unwillingness to hear (Jer. 7:13; Hos. 9:17).

This prevalence of hearing points to an essential feature of biblical religion. It is a religion of the Word, because it is a religion of action, of obedience to the Word. The prophet is the bearer of the Word of Yahweh which demands obedience and fulfilment. Man is not righteous as he seeks to apprehend or perceive God by way of thought and vision, but as he hears the command of God and studies to observe it. It is thus that he "seeks the Lord" (Jer. 29:13). "It hath been declared to thee, O man, what is good, and what doth the Lord require of thee, but to do justly, and to exercise love ..." (Mic. 6:8).

c. There are two lines in Judaism. In Apocalyptic the eschatological contemplation of symbols naturally comes to the forefront, though these are often bound up with words which are to be heard and which help to bring out the meaning (Da. 7:17 ff.; 8:16 ff.; 4 Esr. 4:26; 5:32; 9:38; 10:38). In the Rabbinic literature hearing is related in the first instance to the Word of God given in the sacred book. Since the text is not read quietly but recited and elucidated aloud, even externally its study involves hearing, for which the terminology of exegesis has several expressions: [12] שׁוֹמֵעַ אֲנִי "I hear (a text and its exposition)"; [13] שָׁמוּעַ (→ ἀκοή), "what is heard," i.e., the meaning of a passage; מִשְׁמָע "hearing," i.e., the meaning of a passage recognised in hearing; [14] שְׁמוּעָה (→ ἀκοή), "what is received," i.e., the Halachic tradition.

The strength of the underlying awareness that all hearing is referred to God and His will emerges most clearly in the use of the sch*e*ma, the "Hear, O Israel," [15] as a daily confession. [16] The three portions to be heard (Dt. 6:4-9; 11:13-21;

---

[10] Cf. R. Kittel, Psalmen[4] (1921), 59 (on Ps. 17:15; Job 19:26 etc.).

[11] A seeing of a very different kind is that whereby God is perceived in nature, which leads on at once to history as the action of God; cf. Is. 40:26 ff.; Job 38 ff.; Mt. 6:26 ff. → βλέπω, ὁράω.

[12] W. Bacher, Die exeget. Terminologie d. jüd. Traditionslit., I (1899), 189 f. On the Amorean use of שמע cf. II (1905), 219 ff.

[13] In this expression it is alway presupposed that the exposition appended is false; its untenability is always shown from another passage. Cf. Bacher, 198; K. G. Kuhn, Sifre Numeri, 69, n. 4.

[14] Bacher, 191.

[15] For material on the sch*e*ma, v. Str.-B., IV, 189; Schürer, II, 528 f.; 537 f.

[16] Even the fringes of Nu. 15:39 are merely to remind of the commandments.

Nu. 15:37-41) treat of the way in which God's commandments are to be observed. The seeing of God is reserved for the hour of death and the life beyond. [17] It is an impossible thought that any man, apart from Moses (Nu. 12:8), should presume to see Him on earth. [18] In this life, God's coming is simply by the study of the Torah and the fulfilment of the Law. The man who is righteous in the Law is "as (!) he who greets the face of the Shekina" (M. Ex. 18:12). [19] That seeing is here used for comparison shows more plainly than anything else how little it can be the theme of direct statement. Hence even when the "Palestinian soul" [20] does have immediate and physically perceptible apprehension of deity, there is no question of seeing but of hearing the voice from heaven, the Bath Qol. [21] This is what replaces the now extinct prophetic endowment. In it men experience decisions, warnings and consolations through hearing the echo of the voice of God (hence "daughter of the voice").

2. The Hearing of Revelation in the NT.

a. It is against this background that the use of ἀκούειν and ἀκοή in the NT acquires its force. The NT revelation, too, is a Word to be heard. It is message, proclamation. We must remember, of course, that events themselves are now a Word in a very different sense from that of Judaism with its exclusive emphasis on teaching. This is true of the Synoptic no less than the Johannine presentation, Mt. 11:4 ff., 20 ff. (→ δύναμις, λόγος, ὁράω, σημεῖον). On the other hand, there can be no doubt both that the OT word was heard by early Christianity in exactly the same physical sense as already described (Mt. 5:21 ff.: ἠκούσατε ὅτι ἐρρέθη; also Gl. 4:21: τὸν νόμον οὐκ ἀκούετε), and also that the mission of Jesus and the disciples was first regarded and treated as something to be received by way of hearing. Throughout the NT hearing is strongly emphasised, to some degree almost more so than seeing (Mk. 4:24; Mt. 11:4; 13:16; Lk. 2:20; Ac. 2:33; 1 Jn. 1:1). In the ἀκούσαντες of Hb. 2:3 we simply have another expression for the αὐτόπται of Lk. 1:2. There is no record concerning the appearance of Jesus, in which the first Christians showed no interest. The accounts tell of what He said and did, i.e., of what was heard. Even when there is reference to seeing, it is to the seeing of His acts, in which the nature of His mission in revealed. The parables of sowing, in which the actualisation of the βασιλεία τῶν οὐρανῶν is described (Mt. 13:1 ff.; Mk. 4:26), are parables of hearing. The NT often tells of things seen, but these usually acquire their true significance in what is heard, as in the case of the message of the nativity, the voice at the baptism, the voice at the transfiguration (Mk. 9:7: ἀκούετε αὐτοῦ), the visions of Paul (2 C. 12:3: ἤκουσεν ἄρρητα ῥήματα, Ac. 18:9 etc.) and the visions of the Apocalypse.

As in prophetic usage, ἀκούειν in the absolute can express the appropriation in which external hearing becomes true hearing, or which may be lacking in spite of external hearing: ὃς ἔχει ὦτα ἀκούειν ἀκουέτω, Mk. 4:9 etc.; ἀκούοντες

---

[17] Cf. Str.-B., I, 207 ff. Seeing in the hour of death naturally anticipates the vision of God both as the destruction of the guilty and the bliss of those called to salvation, esp. martyrs (→ ὁράω).

[18] In the apocalyptic story of the four rabbis who penetrated to Paradise (bChag, 14b), their analogous experience is expressed in the word יצה. "he saw." This is Gnosis, and thus the experience of the rabbis is characteristically regarded as suspect and dangerous.

[19] For further examples, cf. Str.-B., I, 207.

[20] So Schl. Mt., 92 in connection with the Bath Qol at the baptism of Jesus.

[21] For material, cf. Str.-B., I, 125 ff.

ἀκούωσιν καὶ μὴ συνιῶσιν, Mk. 4:12 and par.; ὦτα ἔχοντες οὐκ ἀκούετε, Mk. 8:18 (cf. Jer. 5:21; Ez. 12:2). In the apostolic era, however, ἀκοή becomes a technical term for the preaching without which there can be no faith, for the κήρυγμα of Christ (→ ἀκοή).

As is only natural, the content of hearing is determined by the content of the message. In the New Testament this is always the offering of salvation and ethical demand in one. Hearing, then, is always the reception both of grace and of the call to repentance. This means that the only marks to distinguish true hearing from purely physical hearing are faith (Mt. 8:10; 9:2; 17:20 etc.) and action (Mt. 7:16, 24, 26; R. 2:13 etc.). This is not the place to treat of the interrelationship of the two. It is surely evident, however, that NT hearing as reception of the declared will of God always implies affirmation of this will as the willing of salvation and repentance by the man who believes and acts. There thus arises, as the crowning concept of the obedience which consists in faith and the faith which consists in obedience, ὑπακοὴ πίστεως, R. 1:5; 16:26 (→ ὑπακοή).

b. It is in keeping with the OT model that throughout the NT eschatology is described in terms of seeing rather than hearing (Mt. 5:8; Mk. 14:62; 1 C. 13:12; Hb. 12:14 ff.; 1 Jn. 3:2; Rev. 22:4). The same holds good, however, of the accounts of the risen Lord; He is "seen" (1 C. 9:1; 15:5 ff.; cf. Mk. 16:7 and par.). In this respect, as in the general view of the NT, the Easter event proves to be eschatologically evaluated. [22] This explains why John can set alongside his strong emphasis on hearing (8:43; 18:37; 1 Jn. 2:7) an equally strong emphasis on seeing (Jn. 1:14; 1 Jn. 1:1). At this point, too, the Johannine picture of Christ arises as the earthly Jesus is seen and described in the light of the Easter experience.

This aspect is emphasised particularly strongly and thematically in John. Yet it is materially present in the other Evangelists as well. The message of Jesus to the Baptist runs as follows: ἀπαγγείλατε ἃ ἀκούετε καὶ βλέπετε (Mt. 11:4). The blessing of Jesus extends to ὀφθαλμοὶ ὅτι βλέπουσιν as well as ὦτα ὅτι ἀκούουσιν (Mt. 13:16). The condemnation is ἵνα βλέποντες βλέπωσιν καὶ μὴ ἴδωσιν as well as ἀκούοντες ἀκούωσιν καὶ μὴ συνιῶσιν (Mk. 4:12). Hearing is always to the fore, no less emphasised than in one of the prophets. But seeing also comes into account, and in the intermingling of hearing and seeing in relation to the person of Jesus there is expressed the fundamental distinction of the situation depicted by the Evangelists both from pedagogic Judaism and also from prophecy with its reception and proclamation of the revelation of the Word. When Jesus describes unrepentant cities, this is not merely in terms of their failure to hear His preaching but also of their failure to see the essential elements in His acts (Mt. 11:20 ff.). Already in His earthly presence with its Word and work there has come the dawn of eschatology in which seeing has a place alongside hearing. Thus in the use of the verbs denoting the sense-process described there is reflected the early Christian understanding of the revelation given in Jesus. The influence which here asserts itself as a new factor does not derive primarily from the motifs of Gnostic or Hellenistic theophany, but from the eschatological understanding of the fact of Christ. [23]

---

[22] Cf. v. Dobschütz, 402.
[23] What falls to be said concerning seeing is developed and established more fully under the relevant words, q.v., esp. ὁράω.

B. The Hearing of God.

ἀκούειν (→ εἰσακούω, ἐπακούω) also means God's hearing of the prayers which man undertakes to address to Him. It is not used very often in this sense in the NT. Possibly the purely passive use of εἰσακούω in this sense is the result of some scruple against ascribing "hearing" to God Himself. It is remarkable that there is almost no use of ἐπακούω, and none at all of ἐπήκοος, the word most commonly used in Hellenism for the hearing deity. [24] The attribute of the heathen θεοὶ ἐπήκοοι is avoided (→ 222).

Yet the underlying thought is completely in accord with the NT concept of God, and it is thus used quite freely in relation to Jesus (Jn. 11:41 f.; → εἰσακούω, Hb. 5:7), in quotation from the OT (Ac. 7:34 = Ex. 3:7; → ἐπακούω in 2 C. 6:2 = Is. 49:8), and even in relation to the God who hears man (Jn. 9:31; 1 Jn. 5:14 f.: οἴδαμεν ὅτι ἀκούει ἡμῶν).

ἀκοή.

This is a common word in every period of secular Greek, and also in the LXX (= עֵמַע, שֵׁמַע, שְׁמוּעָה, שֵׁמַע).

It has 1. the active signification of the "sense or organ of hearing" (Mk. 7:35 etc.).

It has also 2. the passive sense of a "rumour" or "report" which is heard (Mk. 1:28 etc.). In this sense ἀκοή approximates closely to → ἀγγελία (LXX = שְׁמוּעָה) and κήρυγμα, [1] and can be a technical term for "proclamation" or "preaching" (cf. also λόγος ἀκοῆς, 1 Th. 2:13; Hb. 4:2). The emphasis always falls, of course, on the one who hears the proclamation (R. 10:16 ff.: ἡ πίστις ἐξ ἀκοῆς ... ἀλλὰ λέγω, μὴ οὐκ ἤκουσαν; Hb. 4:2: ἀκοῆς ... ἀκούσασιν). With this signification there is a return to the prophetic usage (R. 10:16; Jn. 12:38 = Is. 53:1: τίς ἐπίστευσε τῇ ἀκοῇ ἡμῶν). Again, there is no doubt as to the meaning of Gl. 3:2: ἐξ ἔργων νόμου τὸ πνεῦμα ἐλάβετε ἢ ἐξ ἀκοῆς πίστεως (cf. v. 5). The true reading is not πίστις ἀκοῆς [2] but ἀκοὴ πίστεως, and in correspondence with ἔργα νόμου this does not mean "believing hearing" [3] but the "preaching of faith," i.e., proclamation which has faith as its content and goal.

3. In many cases ἀκοαί seem to be the ears which are fixed on the walls of sanctuaries or on altars and which symbolise "hearing" deity. [4] This custom started in Egypt and thence spread over the whole of the ancient world, for which it proved an eloquent representation of the θεὸς ἐπήκοος. Hence in the temple of Isis in Pompeii two stucco ears were modelled on the wall behind the statue of Dionysus Osiris. [5] We also find similar ears on altars from Delos (Atargatis), [6] Arles (Bona Dea), [7] etc., as also on numerous votive tablets, on which they may very occasionally be offerings for restored ears. [8] This also seems to be the reference of an inscription from Apollonia on the

---

[24] O. Weinreich, Θεοὶ ἐπήκοοι, Ath. Mitt., 37 (1912), 1-68.
ἀ κ ο ή. [1] Zn. Gl., 140, 83 : "Since one comes to hear only that which is said by others."
[2] Hofmann, Gl.[2] (1872), 49 : "Belief in a report."
[3] Zn., op. cit. Bengel : ex auditu fidei.
[4] Esp. O. Weinreich, Ath. Mitt., 37 (1912), 46 ff.; 57 ff.; Herm., 51 (1916), 624 ff. In relation to the examples cited, cf. also P. Wolters, Herm., 49 (1914), 151.
[5] Weinreich, Ath. Mitt., 49; A. Mau, Pompeji[2] (1908), 181.
[6] BCH, 6 (1882), 311, 487, 499.
[7] W. Altmann, Röm. Grabaltäre d. Kaiserzeit (1905), 185, Fig. 151; Weinreich, Ath. Mitt., 37, Ill. 4.
[8] Weinreich, Ath. Mitt., 52.

Rhyndacus : [9] ἀγαθῇ τύχῃ· ταῖς ἀκοαῖς τῆς θεοῦ ‘Ε<ρ>μιανὸς ... ἀπέδωκ<εν> εὐχαριστήριον τὰ ὦτα καὶ τὸν βωμόν; and also of an inscription from Aquileia : [10] auribus [11] b<onae> d<eae> d<edit> Petrusia Proba magistra. Again, the term ἀκοή sometimes denoted places in the temple where mysterious voices might be heard as described by Psellos Εἰς τὸ ἐν Νικομηδείᾳ ἠχεῖον (p. 58, Boiss). [12] In this sense there is a relative approximation to the biblical concept of the proclamation which derives from God. Cf. Ditt. Syll.[3], 1170, 15 : ἐξιέναι κατὰ τὰς ἀκοὰς ἐκ τοῦ ἀβάτου (cf. 10); and esp. Orph. fr., 249, Kern : οὔατά μοι καθαρὰς ἀκοάς τε πετάσσας κέκλυθι τάξιν ἅπασαν, ὅσην τεκμήρατο Δαίμων.

† εἰσακούω.

(LXX = שׁמע; ענה etc.), "to hear something or someone," [1] "to consent to" or "to gratify." a. "to obey" (secular Gk. and LXX): 1 C. 14:21 (cf. Is. 28:12); b. "to hear or answer" (LXX), always used passively in the NT (→ 221): Lk. 1:13: εἰσηκούσθη ἡ δέησίς σου; Mt. 6:7; Ac. 10:31; Hb. 5:7: (Christ) εἰσακουσθείς.

† ἐπακούω.

This word occurs in secular Gk. from the time of Homer. In a religious context it is the established technical term in the ancient language of prayer for the hearing deity. Aesch. Choeph., 725; Wilcken Ptol., 78, 23 f.: ἐλθέ μοι θεὰ θεῶν ... ἐπάκουσόν μου, ἐλέησον; Philo Det. Pot. Ins., 93. In the LXX it is used for שׁמע, ענה etc.

The word ἐπήκοος was a common epithet for oriental and Egyptian, Greek and Roman deities. First used in laudation, [1] under oriental influence it came to be applied specifically to gods who answer prayer. There are not many literary examples, [2] but all the more on inscriptions. [3]

In the NT the only instance is 2 C. 6:2 (cf. LXX, Is. 49:8): ἐπήκουσά σου, "I have heard thee." In view of the evidence in secular Gk., it is surprising that neither the adj. nor the verb occurs in the NT except in this one verse which is obviously influenced by the OT. There can be no material reason for avoiding the popular term, since early Christian piety unconditionally accepts the fact that God answers prayer (→ 221). The only explanation is an awareness of the need to differentiate from the θεοὶ ἐπήκοοι of popular syncretism.

---

[9] BCH, 25 (1901), 326, No. 4.
[10] CIL, V, 759. Cf. the similar inscription in CIL, III, 986.
[11] In Thes. Ling. Lat., II, 1505 the first word is incorrectly and misleadingly given as aures. Cf. Weinreich, Ath. Mitt., 53, n. 3.
[12] Wolters, Herm., 149 ff.; J. Zingerle, ARW, 27 (1929), 53 ff. Cf. also Marinos Vit. Procl., 32.
εἰσακούω. [1] Often like the simple form : LXX, Ex. 16:7: εἰσήκουσεν τὸν γογγυσμόν; Eur. El., 416 : ζῶντ’ εἰσακούσας, "hearing, that he live."
ἐπακούω. C. Ausfeld, "De Graecorum precationibus quaestiones," Jbch. f. klass. Phil. Suppl., 28 (1903), 503-547; O. Weinreich, Θεοὶ ἐπήκοοι, Ath. Mitt., 37 (1912), 1-68.
[1] F. Poland, Griech. Vereinswesen (1909), 238.
[2] On the grotesque description in Lucian, Ikaromenippos, 23 ff. of the ἐπηκοώτατον τοῦ οὐρανοῦ = the place in heaven where Zeus as θεὸς ἐπήκοος listens to prayers at a specific time of the day, and of the way in which he conducts himself in this place, cf. O. Weinreich, Gebet und Wunder (1929), 200 ff.
[3] Weinreich, Ath. Mitt., 5-25 gives 138 examples.

† **παρακούω**, † **παρακοή** (→ ἀπειθέω).

The verb means "to hear aside," either in the sense a. of "to overhear," i.e., "to hear something not intended for one" : Plat. Euthyd., 300d; Aristoph. Ra., 750 ; or b. "to hear incorrectly" (par. παριδεῖν): Plut. Philop., 16 (I, 365c); LXX, Est. 4:14; Σ Ps. 39:13 (חרשׁ); Act. Jn., 17; or, in the Hellenistic period, "not to be willing to hear," i.e., "to be disobedient" : Polyb., III, 15, 2; P. Hib., 170; Preis. Zaub., IV (Paris), 3037: διὰ τὸ παρακούειν αὐτόν; LXX, Est. 3:3 (עבר) ; 3:8 (אֵין שׁוֶֹה); Is. 65:12 (לֹא שׁמַעתֶּם); Tob. 3:4. The noun is rare in secular Gk., and has the sense of b., though it acquires also the sense of c. in post-Christian usage. [1] The noun is not found at all in the LXX, but the content of the NT term is fully given by the verb παρακούειν and by μὴ ὑπα-κούειν.

παρακούω occurs in Mk. 5:35 f., when in the Jairus incident there comes to the latter the message : ἡ θυγάτηρ σου ἀπέθανεν (v. 35). ὁ δὲ ᾿Ιησοῦς παρακού-σας [2] τὸν λόγον λαλούμενον λέγει τῷ ἀρχισυναγώγῳ· μὴ φοβοῦ, μόνον πίστευε (v. 36). Since Jesus did not ignore the message, but referred to it in His μὴ φοβοῦ, there can be no question either of His not hearing it properly in the sense of b., or of His disregarding it in the sense of c., [3] and therefore it must mean that He overheard it as under a. The word also occurs in Mt. 18:17: ἐὰν δὲ παρακούσῃ αὐτῶν ... ἐὰν δὲ καὶ τῆς ἐκκλησίας παρακούσῃ, but here it ob-viously has the sense of unwillingness to hear as under c.

παρακοή in the NT alway means "bad hearing" in consequence of unwillingness to hear (c.), and therefore in the guilty sense of disobedience which does not and will not proceed to the action by which hearing becomes genuine hearing (→ 219). A dramatic example of παρακοή is given in Ac. 7:57: συνέσχον τὰ ὦτα αὐτῶν. In this sense the word is par. to παράβασις : Hb. 2:2 (παρακοή to the λαληθεὶς λόγος, i.e., the Law), and is the opp. of ὑπακοή : R. 5:19 (the παρακοή of Adam); 2 C. 10:6 (παρακοή in the congregation).

† **ὑπακούω** (→ πειθαρχέω).

In secular Gk. with the gen. or dat. of person or thing ; in the LXX more often with the gen., more rarely with the dat., and very occasionally the acc. (Dt. 21:18); in the NT only the dat.

1. "To hearken at the door," i.e., "to open," t.t. of the θυρωρός, Ac. 12:13 (cf. [1] Plat. Phaed., 59e ; Xenoph. Symp., I, 11).

2. "To obey." This obedience first relates to persons such as children, slaves or wives who stand in a divinely willed relation of subordination (Eph. 6:1, 5; Col. 3:20, 22; 1 Pt. 3:6). It can thus also describe the relation of demons (Mk. 1:27) or nature (Mk. 4:41 and par.) to the omnipotence of Jesus and the authoritative faith of the disciples (Lk. 17:6). In the same sense, however, the term expresses the

---

π α ρ α κ ο ύ ω, κ τ λ. Trench, 155 f.
[1] Preisigke Wört., *s.v.* : 2 Byzant. pap. of the 8th century A.D.
[2] The early correction in ACD rec, which substituted the simple ἀκούσας, is an attempt to avoid the dilemma that Jesus might either have heard something not intended for Him or have missed something ; cf. Cr.-Kö., 108.
[3] Wbg., Mk. 165 f. (*neglexit*); Moult.-Mill., *s.v.*
ὑ π α κ ο ύ ω. Loh. Phil., 101; Helbing, *op. cit.,* 155 f.
[1] Pr.-Bauer, 1339.

position of man in relation to dominant moral or religious powers, whether in the good sense or the bad: R. 6:16 (δοῦλοί ἐστε ᾧ ὑπακούετε): ἐπιθυμίαις, v. 12; to the τύπος διδαχῆς, v. 17; πίστει, Ac. 6:7; εὐαγγελίῳ, R. 10:16; 2 Th. 1:8; λόγῳ; 2 Th. 3:14; αὐτῷ (τῷ Χριστῷ) in Hb. 5:9 (cf. 11:8: πίστει καλούμενος Ἀβραὰμ ὑπήκουσεν ἐξελθεῖν). Similarly at Phil. 2:12, in connection [2] with the obedience of Jesus in v. 8 (*infra*), recollection of the ὑπακούειν of the community can describe its positive religious state: καθὼς πάντοτε ὑπηκούσατε, just as believers in Ac. 5:32 can be called: οἱ πειθαρχοῦντες (θεῷ).

The frequent use of ὑπακούειν for שׁמע in the LXX shows how strongly the idea of hearing is still present for the translator in the Gk. ὑπακούειν. Hence ὑπακούειν and ὑπακοή as terms for religious activity are always to be thought of within the sphere of a religion which receives the divine Word by hearing and then translates it into action (→ ἀκούω, 1): ὑπήκουσας τῆς ἐμῆς φωνῆς, Gn. 22:18; Lv. 26:14; τοὺς μὴ βουλομένους ὑπακούειν τῶν λόγων μου, Jer. 13:10; ὑπακούσεται (לְהַקְשִׁיב) σοφίας τὸ οὖς σου, Prv. 2:2. Cf. also Test. Jud. 13:1: ὑπακούειν ἐντολὰς θεοῦ; 18:6: θεῷ ὑπακοῦσαι οὐ δύναται.

† ὑπακοή, † ὑπήκοος.

In the LXX the noun is found only in 2 Βασ. 22:36 (עֲנֹתְךָ). It is rare and late in secular Gk. [1] The adj. is common in secular Gk. and occurs several times in the LXX.

Except in Phlm. 21: ὑπακοή to the injunction of the apostle, ὑπακοή is always used in connection with religious decision, as in R. 6:16: ᾧ παριστάνετε ἑαυτοὺς δούλους εἰς ὑπακοήν. In general, however, this is measured by the attitude of obedience to God; it is the opp. of ἁμαρτία (R. 6:16), and of παρακοή (R. 5:19; 2 C. 10:6), and it is filled out positively as the ὑπακοή τῆς ἀληθείας (1 Pt. 1:22) and the ὑπακοή τοῦ Χριστοῦ (2 C. 10:5). [2] The act of Christ Himself is ὑπακοή (R. 5:19); ὑπακοή τοῦ ἑνός (Hb. 5:8). When used alone, however, the word also signifies the believing state of Christians as this consists in obedience: R. 15:18; 16:19 (ἡ γὰρ ὑμῶν ὑπακοὴ εἰς πάντας ἀφίκετο); 2 C. 7:15; 10:6; 1 Pt. 1:2. [3] In the first instance ὑπακοή does not denote an ethical attitude but the religious act from which this self-evidently springs (1 Pt. 1:14). It is in this sense, and therefore as gen. epexeg., that ὑπακοὴ πίστεως is to be understood in R. 1:5; 16:26, i.e., the message of πίστις which consists or works itself out in ὑπακοή. [4] Christians are τέκνα ὑπακοῆς in the sense that the essence of their sonship is to be found in ὑπακοή (1 Pt. 1:14). [5]

ὑπήκοος means "obedient," whether to God (Ac. 7:39) or the apostle (2 C. 2:9). In Phil. 2:8 it is used of the act of Christ (→ ὑπακοή, R. 5:19), though here the

---

[2] Although cf. Ew. Gefbr., 118.
ὑ π α κ ο ή κτλ. J. C. K. Hofmann, 1 Pt. (1875), 8 f.; Kn. Pt., 33 f., 63 f.
[1] Preisigke Wört., II, 639 for examples from the 6th cent. A.D.
[2] Gen. obj.; on εἰς cf. Lk. 21:24.
[3] There is no need to make the rather difficult (cf. Knopf *ad loc.*) connection of ὑπακοή with Ἰησοῦ Χριστοῦ, since in any case we have an abs. use in v. 14.
[4] Gen. epexeg.; Bengel: *obedientiam in ipsa fide consistentem*.
[5] Gen. qual.; as Eph. 2:2: υἱοῖς τῆς ἀπειθείας; also Eth. En. 91:3; 93:2: "children of righteousness."

μέχρι θανάτου of v. 8 and the μορφὴν δούλου λαβών of v. 7 set it in the context of the thought of fulfilment orientated to Is. 53. [6]

Kittel

| † ἀκροβυστία | (→ περιτομή).

1. The Etymology of the Word.

ἀκροβυστία (signifying "foreskin" or *praeputium*), [1] ἀκρόβυστος and ἀκροβυστέω are formed from the adj. ἄκρος (which denotes "running up to a point," or "that which stands on the outer edge"; "extreme" or "supreme") and the relatively infrequent verb βύω (meaning "to stop up" or "close"), with the related forms βύζω and βυνέω (the latter being specifically Attic).

Although this etymology seems to be clear and meaningful, it is rendered uncertain by the fact that elsewhere in Gk. the same thing is denoted by a much more pregnant term of similar sound. In Hippocrates, Aristotle and Pollux the foreskin is ἀκροποσθία (or ἀκροπόσθιον) derived from ἄκρος (as above) and πόσθη (or ποσθία, πόσθιον), which is used by the doctors of antiquity like Hippocrates and Galen, as also by Aristotle, to denote the "foreskin" or "male organ." Hence ἀκροποσθία comes to signify the "extreme foreskin" or the "foreskin" itself. The possibility has thus to be taken into account that ἀκροβυστία really derived from ἀκροποσθία, [2] the link with βύω [3] playing a primary, or more likely a secondary, role. Perhaps the Greek Jews, who first used ἀκροβυστία for ἀκροποσθία, had special reasons for so doing.

Cr.-Kö., 109 f.: "It has thus to be recognised with Winer [4] that ἀκροβυστία arises as an intentional reconstruction of ἀκροποσθία with a view to expressing the matter in a decorously indirect and veiled manner. The term is obviously fashioned by the Jews in opposition to περιτομή and perhaps in reminiscence of the Gk. ἀκροποσθία, as also with the Heb. בְּשָׂר in mind. It is used only by them (cf. Eph. 2:11: ὑμεῖς τὰ ἔθνη ἐν σαρκὶ οἱ λεγόμενοι ἀκροβυστία ὑπὸ τῆς λεγομένης περιτομῆς ἐν σαρκί)." In the attempt to establish a *vox mere biblica,* Cr.-Kö. seems at this point to read rather too much out of Eph. 2:11. Winer, to whom appeal is made, says of this passage among others: "Like all euphemistic expressions, it remains general; [5] those who used it knew what was meant."

E. Weidner: [6] "It may be that the word *baltu* = *bultu* = *buštu* contributed to the NT ἀκροβυστία ('foreskin'). This term might signify the *membrum virile.*" Weidner [7] also lists ἀκροβυστία as one of the Semitic words which came into Gk., seeing behind

---

[6] E. Lohmeyer, "Kyrios Jesus," SHA (1928), 41 f.
ἀ κ ρ ο β υ σ τ ί α. [1] So in *Corpus Glossariorum Latinorum,* II, 157 etc.
[2] The thesis of K. F. A. Fritzsche on R. 2:26, which is disputed by Cr.-Kö., namely, "*pronuntiarunt Alexandrini* τὴν βύστην *quam Graeci dixerunt* τὴν πόσθην," is far from certain. Pass.-Cr. thinks that ἀκροβυστία is perhaps a dialect form of ἀκροποσθία.
[3] So Bl.-Debr. § 120, 4 and Pr.-Bauer, *s.v.*
[4] G. B. Winer, *Gramm. d. nt.lichen Sprachidioms*⁷ (1867), 16, n. 4.
[5] By this means Winer overcomes the difficulty of the not very specific significance of βύω.
[6] OLZ, 34 (1931), 209.
[7] Glotta, 4 (1913), 303.

it the Babylonian *buštu* ("shame"). The Heb. בֹּשֶׁת corresponds to the Babylonian *buštu*. My own suspicion is that the similarity of sound played some part for Greek speaking Jews as in other cases like קָהָל = ἐκκλησία. [8]

2. The Occurrence of the Word.

The word is found only in biblical and ecclesiastical Greek.

Comparison of the different Gk. versions of the OT shows that ἀκροβυστία and ἀκρόβυστος are used both in a literal (physical) and a metaphorical (spiritual and ethical) sense, and that they are the opposites of περιτομή and περιτετμημένος.

In the LXX it is used 13 times for עׇרְלָה in Gn. 17:11, 14, 23, 24, 25; 34:14; Ex. 4:25; Lv. 12:3; Jos. 5:3; 1 Βασ. 18:25, 27; 2 Βασ. 3:14; Jer. 9:25 (24, also ᾽A). It also occurs in Gn. 34:24; Jdt. 14:10; 1 Macc. 1:15. In ᾽ΑΣΘ it is found in Lv. 19:23 (LXX: ἀκαθαρσία) in conjunction with the verb ἀκροβυστίζω, which is not found elsewhere. In ᾽A it occurs at Dt. 10:16 (LXX: σκληροκαρδία); Ex. 6:12: ἀκρόβυστος χείλεσιν (LXX: ἄλογος); Is. 52:1: ἀκρόβυστος (LXX: ἀπερίτμητος [καὶ ἀκάθαρτος]); Ez. 32:26 (ἀπερίτμητος), 27, 29 (also ΣΘ).

In the NT it occurs 20 times. Except for Ac. 11:3, it is found only in Paul, R. 2:25, 26 (twice), 27; 3:30; 4:9, 10 (twice), 11 (twice), 12; 1 C. 7:18, 19; Gl. 2:7; 5:6; 6:15; Eph. 2:11; Col. 2:13; 3:11. In early Christian literature it occurs in Barn., 9,5 and 13,7, in both cases in quotation of the OT, and more frequently in Justin; ἀκρόβυστος is found in Ign. Phld., 6, 1; Just. Dial., 19, 3.

The true range and biblico-theological sense of ἀκροβυστία in the linguistic usage of the LXX and NT can be worked out only in connection with its opposite περιτομή, and demands rather more than the lexicographical discussion given in this article.

K. L. Schmidt

ἀκρογωνιαῖος → γωνία   ἀκυρόω → κυρόω   ἄκων → ἑκών

---

† ἀλαζών, ἀλαζονεία

The ἀλαζών is the one who "makes more of himself" than the reality justifies, "ascribing to himself either more and better things than he has, or even what he does not possess at all"; [1] who "promises what he cannot perform"; [2] οὐκ ἐν τῇ δυνάμει ... ὁ ἀλαζών, ἀλλ᾽ ἐν τῇ προαιρέσει, Aristot. Eth. Nic., IV, 13, p. 1127b (cf. 1 C.

---

[8] Cf. K. L. Schmidt, "Die Kirche des Urchristentums," in *Festgabe für Adolf Deissmann* (1927), 263 f.; and also the comments of G. Stählin, *Skandalon* (1930), 44: "... a consideration ... which takes into account the similarities in sound rather than the semasiological relationship of the Hebrew and Greek equivalents. It has long been recognised that the translators of the LXX allowed themselves to be guided in their choice of words by formal similarities as well as by meaning."

ἀ λ α ζ ώ ν. O. Ribbeck, *Alazon* (1882).
[1] *Ibid.*, 4; Aristot. Eth. Nic., IV, 13, p. 1127a, 21 f.
[2] Ribbeck, 4; Xenoph. Cyrop., II, 2, 12.

4:20). Very often the orator, philosopher, poet, [3] magician, doctor, cook or officer is called ἀλαζών, and especially the last of these (cf. the *Miles gloriosus* of Plautus). Theophrastus defines ἀλαζονεία as "arousing of the expectation of certain ἀγαθά which are not in fact there" (Char., 23, 1). A religious connotation is suggested by the link with ὕβρις, which is always punished by the gods.

This line of thought is sometimes pursued in the LXX. Thus in Wis. 5:8 ἀλαζονεία is something which separates from God; in Hab. 2:5 (acc. to א etc.) the ἀλαζών is the man who does not put his confidence in God. In 4 Macc. 8:19 ἀλαζονεία is made a parallel of κενοδοξία, and in Prv. 21:24 the ἀλαζών is connected with the αὐθάδης.

In R. 1:30 and 2 Tm. 3:2 the ἀλαζόνες appear in lists of 12 or 18 [4] ethological terms which show traces of arrangement at least in R. (cf. 4 Macc. 1:26; 2:15). In both cases the term ἀλαζών is set directly alongside ὑπερήφανος, which seems to be a kind of equivalent (e.g., Wis. 5:8). In 2 Tm. another corresponding word is τετυφωμένοι, the cognates of which are elucidated by lexicographers together with those of ἀλ. Yet ἀλ. has its own special sense as declared above, and perhaps with the particular application made in the LXX.

This is certainly true of ἀλαζονεία. In 1 Jn. 2:16 this denotes the attitude of the cosmic man who does not ask concerning the will of the Father but tries to make out that he himself may sovereignly decide concerning the shape of his life, whereas in actuality the decision lies with God, as is seen in the passing away of the world (v. 17). This is worked out with an example in Jm. 4:16, where ἀλαζονεῖαι are expressions of the ἀλαζονεία which acts as if it could dispose of the future, whereas this is really under the control of the will of God (v. 15).

Delling

---

† ἀλαλάζω

The word group ἀλαλάζω, ἐλελίζω, ὀλολύζω etc. probably belongs to the cultural world preceding the Greek. [1] As terms of a past and foreign world they serve in the Gk. period to denote alien and extraordinary expressions of joy, applause, [2] or sorrow in which man transcends himself. In an attack in war we have the same phenomenon, so that the ἀλαλαί cry is the battle-cry (cf. ἀλαλάζειν in this sense in Jos Ant., 6, 191; 8, 283; 12, 372 and 427). [3] Such self-transcendence may also take place at a sacrifice, [4] and it may be linked with a hymn or lament. [5]

1. The word refers to "lamentation" in Mk. 5:38. We are not told whether the ἀλαλάζοντες are men or women. In Heliodor. Aeth., III, 5 a distinction is made

---

[3] Both of whom "pretend a knowledge which they do not possess," Ribbeck, 13.

[4] In 2 Tm. 5 of these are the same as in Philo Sacr. AC, 32. Such lists are very popular; there are about 150 of them in Philo.

ἀλαλάζω. [1] C. Theander, *Eranos*, 15 (1915), 99 ff., 20 (1921/22), 1 ff.

[2] Cf. esp. Herond. Mim., VIII, 46 f., ed. Headlam; Plut. Aud., 15 (II, 46c).

[3] On ἀλαλάζειν as φωνὴ ἐπινίκιος, cf. Orig. in Ps. 88(89):16 in Pitra, *Analecta Sacra*, III, 163, and also in Jos. Hom., VII, 2, p. 328, 13 ff., Bährens.

[4] *v.* Eitrem, *Beitr. z. Gr. Religionsgesch.*, III (Videnskapsselskapets Skrifter, II, 1919, Kristiania), 44 ff.; F. Schwenn, *Gebet und Opfer* (1927), 38 ff.

[5] ἀλαλάζειν for lament: *v.* Orig. In Jer. Hom., V, p. 47, 13 ff.

on the occasion of a cultic ὀλολυγή : ὠλόλυξαν μὲν αἱ γυναῖκες, ἠλάλαξαν δὲ οἱ ἄνδρες. But we cannot be sure that such a distinction is of general application. [6]

2. 1 C. 13:1 refers to a κύμβαλον ἀλαλάζον. Here the "ecstatic noise" in orgiastic cults is linked with the κύμβαλον used in these cults (esp. that of Cybele). [7] We may compare the use of the term ἀλαλάζειν for the noise of the Dionysiac winepress in Nonnos Dionys., XII, 354. [8]

ἀλαλάζειν has persisted in the Orient right up to the present time, cf. Konstantinides, [9] s.v. : Καὶ νῦν ἔτι ἐν Παλαιστίνη καὶ Αἰγύπτῳ αἱ γυναῖκες καὶ ἐν χαρᾷ καὶ ἐν πένθει ὀλολύζουσι, ἐκπέμπουσι διὰ τοῦ λάρυγγος ὀξεῖς ὀλολυγμούς.

Peterson

---

† ἅλας

In the ancient world salt has religious significance. Because of its purifying and seasoning (Job 6:6) and preserving qualities it is a symbol of endurance [1] and value. [2] It is linked with God, [3] as putrefaction and corruption are linked with demons. For this reason it was much used in worship, as in the OT. It was sprinkled on or mixed into the sacrifices (Ex. 30:35; Lv. 2:13; Ez. 43:21). Newborn children were rubbed with it (Ez. 16:4). It was used by Orientals to drive away evil spirits. [4] Lasting covenants were made by eating bread and salt, or salt alone (Nu. 18:19; 2 Ch. 13:5 : the covenant of salt). [5]

In the NT its cultic significance is lost. [6] The sacrificial ritual is simply a means to convey the truths of the religious and moral world. This seems to be the point

---

[6] For the ὀλολύζειν of a woman, cf. Ps.-Clem. Hom., XII, 22; Act. Pl. Thcl., 35.

[7] On the κύμβαλον in such cults, v. F. J. Dölger, *Antike u. Christentum*, I (1929), 184 ff. I might also refer to Mart. Ariad. (*Studi e testi*, VI, p. 124): The heathen festival was ἐν αὐλοῖς καὶ κυμβάλοις καὶ ᾠδαῖς ἀτάκτοις καὶ ἤχοις ἀλαλαγμῶν.

[8] ὀλολύζειν (B : ἀλαλάζειν) used of the sound of the σάλπιγξ, v. Ps.-Callisth., Hist. Alex. Magn., I, p. 20, 2, Kroll.

[9] A. Konstantinides : Μέγα λεξικὸν τῆς Ἑλλ. γλώσσης (1901/4).

ἅ λ α ς. M. J. Schleiden, *Das Salz* (1875); V. Hehn, *Das Salz*[2] (1901); S. Krauss, *Talmudische Archäol.*, I (1910), 119 f.; Str.-B., I, 232 ff.; W. Bousset, *Hauptprobleme d. Gnosis* (1907), Index, s.v.; Jülicher, Gl. J., II, 67-79; RW, II, 366.

[1] Philo Spec. Leg., I, 289 : ὡς γὰρ αἰτία τοῦ μὴ διαφθείρεσθαι τὰ σώματα ψυχή, καὶ οἱ ἅλες ἐπὶ πλεῖστον αὐτὰ συνέχοντες καὶ τρόπον τινὰ ἀθανατίζοντες.

[2] "The Torah is like salt ... the world cannot endure without salt," Soph., 15, 8, Str.-B., I, 235; as a symbol for what is witty or clever, Corn. Nep. Att., 13, 2.

[3] Plat. Tim., 60e : ἁλῶν ... θεοφιλὲς σῶμα. Plut. Quaest. Conv., V, 10, 1 and 3 (II, 684 f., 685d): θεοφιλὲς καὶ θεῖον ... τὴν αὐτὴν ἔχον τῷ θείῳ δύναμιν πυρὶ θεῖον ὑπέλαβον οἱ παλαιοί.

[4] T. Canaan, *Dämonenglaube im Land d. Bibel* (1929), 42.

[5] Cf. Aristot. Eth. Nic., VIII, 4, p. 1156b, 27 ff.; Cic. Lael., 19, 67.

[6] Also in Rabbinic Judaism; cf. the reinterpretation in S. Nu. § 118 on 18:19 : " 'This is an eternal contract with the Lord concluded with salt.' Scripture thus concludes a contract with Aaron by means of something which is powerful, and which even more can make other things (e.g., the contract) powerful."

of the obscure saying in Mk. 9:49. [7] The disciple must be seasoned with salt like the sacrifice. This will take place through trials (cf. the fire of 1 C. 3:13), and everything contrary to God will be purged away. Salt also typifies the religious and moral quality which must characterise the speech of the Christian (Col. 4:6), and esp. the quality which is an inner mark of the disciple and the loss of which will make him worthless (Lk. 14:34 f.; Mt. 5:13; Mk. 9:50).

Lk. gives us the original wording, linking the saying with serious demands made on the disciple. Mt. gives us, secondarily, a direct application to the disciples themselves. The saying seems to have in view conditions in Palestine. Salt from the Dead Sea, which is mixed with gypsum etc., acquires easily a stale and alkaline taste (cf. Plin., 31, 34: tabescit). There seems to be a scoffing reference to this saying of Jesus in bBek., 8b: "(R. Joshua b. Chananja (c. 90) was once asked to tell a story). He said: There was once a mule which had a foal. On this was hung a chain with the inscription that it should raise 100,000 Zuz from its father's family. He was asked: Can then a mule bear offspring? He said: These are fables. He was then asked: When salt loses its savour (סריא), wherewith shall it be salted? He answered: With the young of a mule. He was then asked: Does then the unfruitful mule have young? He answered: Can salt lose its savour?" [8]

Hauck

---

† ἀλείφω   (→ χρίω).

In the LXX ἀλείφειν (ἀλείφεσθαι) is used for three Heb. words: a. סוך "to anoint," Rt. 3:3: σὺ δὲ λούσῃ καὶ ἀλείψῃ καὶ περιθήσεις τὸν ἱματισμόν σου ἐπὶ σέ; cf. 2 Βασ. 12:20; 14:2; 4 Βασ. 4:2; 2 Ch. 28:15; Mi. 6:15; Jdt. 16:7: ἠλείψατο τὸ πρόσωπον αὐτῆς ἐν μυρισμῷ; b. טוח "to rub" or "to wash over": Ez. 13:10 ff.; c. משח Gn. 31:13: στήλην ἀλ. = "to pour an offering of oil over"; Nu. 3:3: οἱ ἱερεῖς οἱ ἠλειμμένοι; Ex. 40:13 (15): καὶ ἀλείψεις αὐτοὺς (the sons of Aaron) ... καὶ ἱερατεύσουσί μοι. In this as in other contexts, however, משח is usually rendered χρίω, with which the religious and theological significance of the concept of anointing came to be generally linked.

This is confirmed at once in the NT, where ἀλείφειν is used only of external, physical anointing and χρίειν in the figurative sense of anointing by God. [1] Yet the external action has its own inner meaning.

1. In Mt. 6:17 anointing is linked with bodily comfort, and according to Jewish custom expresses a mood of joy and festivity. Cf. LXX, Jdt. 16:7; 2 Βασ. 14:2. For Judaism anointing could not go hand in hand with fasting, but Jesus demands

---

[7] The text acc. to אBW sys; OLZ, 7 (1904), 111; ZNW, 19 (1919), 96.

[8] Cf. Str.-B., I, 236; Schl. Mt., 147.

ἀλείφω. Dib., Wnd. on Jm. 5:14; Str.-B., I, 426-9; II, 11 f.; III, 759; F. Kattenbusch, RE,³ 14, 304 ff., s.v. Ölung; W. Heitmüller, RGG,¹ IV, 874 f., s.v. Ölsalbung; L. Fendt, RGG,² IV, 641 f., s.v. Ölung; J. Hempel-E. Wissmann, ibid., V, 80 ff., s.v. Salbung; W. Bousset, Hauptprobleme d. Gnosis (1907), 297-305; F. J. Dölger, Der Exorzismus im altchr. Taufritual (1909), 137-159; F. Fenner, D. Krankheit i. NT (1930), 92.

[1] Pr.-Bauer, s.v.

that the sacrifice in fasting should be made so secretly that it should be an occasion of joy and festivity for others, and even for the one who fasts.

2. In Mt. 26:7; Lk. 7:38, 46; Jn. 11:2; 12:3 anointing is a mark of honour shown to a guest, as in Judaism. [2] In the first of the instances quoted it is also a prophetic action in the Gospels. By anointing the head (v. 7) of Jesus the woman has honoured Him in a deeper sense, anointing His body (v. 12) for burying. This anointing is a proleptic anointing of the Crucified in death. Reference is made to the anointing of the body in Mk. 16:1.

3. The Anointing of the Sick.

To understand Mk. 6:13 and Jm. 5:14 we must recall the practice and meaning of anointing with a view to healing in Hellenism and Judaism. Oil is applied a. medicinally to alleviate and cure various sicknesses : Jos. Bell., 1, 657 = Ant., 17, 172; Philo Som., II, 58; Is. 1:6; and Rabbinic examples of the use of oil for sciatic pains, skin afflictions, headaches, wounds etc.; [3] b. magico-medicinally, and especially as a means of exorcism. It is hard to draw the line between a. and b. Since sickness is ascribed very largely to demonic influence, it is easy to see why medicinal anointing should come to have the character of a victorious action in expulsion of demons. This is especially so in the case of afflictions with psychic manifestations or causes. Anointing against possession is mentioned by Celsus Med., III, 23, 3. In Test. Sol. 18:34 we read : ἐάν τις βαλεῖ ἅλας εἰς ἔλαιον καὶ ἐπαλείψει τὸν ἀσθενῆ λέγων· χερουβίμ, σεραφίμ, βοηθεῖτε, εὐθὺς ἀναχωρῶ (sc. the demon). Anointings at conjurations are found in jMS, 53b, 48 [4] and for the healing and release of one who is bewitched in Midr. Qoh., 1, 8, (9a). [5] c. A further step is taken when there is ascribed to oil a heavenly power to change or to dispense life. On this point, cf. esp. Vit. Ad., 36 and 40-42, and also Slav. En. 22:8 ff. (8, 5): "And the Lord said to Michael, Come forth, and divest Enoch of his earthly garments, rub him with a goodly salve and clothe him in the garments of my glory. And he did so ; and the appearance of that salve was more than a great light, its creaminess as the dew, its perfume as myrrh, and its shining as the rays of the sun. And I beheld myself, and I was as one of His glorious ones ..." This is the salve which in Iren., I, 21, 3 is called a τύπος τῆς ὑπὲρ τὰ ὅλα εὐωδίας. Cf. also Euseb. Hist. Eccl., V, 1, 35.

In the Christian sphere, too, we find the use of oil both as a medicine (Lk. 10:34) and for the combined purpose of medicine and exorcism, oil being consecrated for these uses. Cf. Act. Thom., 67, where Jesus is asked to come and anoint those who are troubled by demons : καὶ ἀλείψας αὐτὴν ἐλαίῳ ἁγίῳ θεράπευσον ἀπὸ τῶν ἑλκῶν καὶ διατήρησον αὐτὴν ἀπὸ τῶν λύκων τῶν διαρπαζόντων. The restoration of the Emperor Antoninus by a Christian by means of consecrated oil is described in Tertullian Ad Scapul., 4. Cf. Chrys. Hom. in Mt. 32 (33), 6 (MPG, 57, 384). One who is possessed is healed by means of anointing in Palladius, Hist. Laus., 18, p. 55, Butler. Naturally there is the same use in magic, as we learn from the great Paris magic papyrus (Preis. Zaub., IV), 3007 f. Alongside this magico-medicinal use there also developed a sacramental, a. in the form of a

---

[2] Cf. Str.-B., I, 427 and 986.
[3] v. Str.-B., I, 428 f.; II, 11 f.
[4] Str.-B., I, 429.
[5] Ibid., III, 759.

baptism in oil which is found among the Gnostics [6] either in place of [7] water baptism or alongside it; [8] b. as an exorcism prior to the act of baptism in the Church; and c. in the form of a sacrament of death, though this is found only among the Marcosites in Iren., I, 21, 5 and with Heracleon in Epiph. Haer., 36, 2, 4 ff., and it is uncertain whether "what is meant is really a sacrament for the dying or a consecration of the dead." [9] Outside Christianity the Mandaeans have a final anointing of the dying as well as a consecration with oil, cf. Lidz. Lit., 114 ff., Ginza, 326 f., 591, 12 f. and 28 f.

What conceptions of anointing and its effect here predominate may be seen from the different prayers over the oil. Cf., e.g., the prayer for healing oil in the euchologion of the Serapion of Thmuis: [10] ... "a means to drive away this sickness and weakness, to act as an antidote to the demon, to expel the unclean spirit, to exclude every evil spirit, to drive away the heat and cold of fever and all weakness, to mediate grace and remission of sins, to be a means of life and redemption, to be the health and portion of body, soul and spirit, to bring full strengthening ..." Or, in relation to baptism in oil (Act. Thom., 49): "Apostle of the Highest, give me the seal, that no foe may again turn against me ... O most Merciful, thou that glowest through the force of words, power of the wood, clothed with which men may overcome all their adversaries. Thou that crownest the victor, sign and joy of the sick (καμνόντων) ... Jesus, may thy victorious power descend and rest on this oil as thy power rested on the related wood ... may the gift with which Thou blewest on its enemies, and made them yield and fall, come to dwell in this oil over which we repeat Thy holy name." Or, in relation to the oil used before baptism (cf. Cyr. Cat. Myst., II, 3): "... so may this exorcised oil, by the invocation of God and prayer, not merely burn away and destroy the traces of sin, but repel all the invisible powers of evil." Or, in relation to extreme unction (cf. Iren., I, 21, 5): "That they may not be grasped nor seen by principalities or powers, and that their inner man may soar above the invisible ..." The conquering of supraterrestrial forces and the possession of heavenly goods are also guaranteed by extreme unction for the Mandaeans, as we see from Lidz. Ginza, 326 f. Cf. also Lidz. Lit., 35 ff. for the oil of baptismal consecration.

In the NT anointing with oil is used on the sick for purposes of both medicine and exorcism. In Mk. 6:13 the apostles heal in connection with their preaching of repentance and their expulsion of demons, and in this regard they are messengers and bearers of the inbreaking kingdom of God. In Jm. 5:14 the same kind of anointing is carried out by Church officials, and in the situation of the Church it brings healing of body and soul, i.e., the remission of sins, as in Mk. 6:13 health was mediated to make fit for the kingdom of God. The whole action is envisaged in Jm. 5:14 f. Anointing takes place in invocation of the name of God and is en-

---

[6] Tert. Adv. Marc., 1, 14, Marcionites; Iren., I, 21, 4, Marcosites; Or. c. Cels., VI, 27, Ophites; Act. Thom., 26 (?), 49.

[7] Hipp. Elench., V, 7, 1; 9, 22, Naassenes; *Kopt. Schriften*, II, Ieu 43; Act. Thom., 121, 132 and 157 in the present arrangement.

[8] It is doubtful whether we have a true prayer for the consecration of healing oil in the prayer over the oil of anointing in the Copt. fragment appended to the Didache, Ch. 10 ff. (cf. JThSt., 25 [1924] 225 ff.; ZNW, 24 [1925] 81 ff.). It might also be a prayer over the oil of baptism, esp. in the version of C (cf. K. Bihlmeyer, *Ap. Väter* [1924] XVIII f.). We should then have evidence in the Didache of the confluence of water baptism with baptism in oil, as in Act. Thom.

[9] K. Holl, *Epiphanius*, II (1922), 45.

[10] G. Wobbermin, "Altchristl. Stücke aus d. Kirche Ägyptens," TU, XVII, 3b (1898), 13 f., No. 17.

closed by prayer, which as the εὐχή τῆς πίστεως brings healing and forgiveness. Here the oil has the character of the matter of a sacrament.

From the anointing of the sick for purposes of medicine and exorcism there developed in the Eastern Church the anointing called εὐχέλαιον and in Roman Catholicism extreme unction. The customary emphasis on the thought of the remission of sins [11] and the reference to the dying, in conjunction with a sacramentalisation of the process, [12] produced *extrema unctio* or the *sacramentum exeuntium*. The title itself was used in the 12th century. Attempts at theological definition may be found in Hugh of St. Victor and Peter Lombard. At the Council of Florence in 1439 the sacrament was sanctioned by Eugenius IV. According to Trent Sess., XIV, 1 the sacrament, which removes the relics of sin and strengthens the soul, and which may sometimes be followed by recovery, is "insinuated" in Mk. 6:13 and "promulgated" in Jm. 5:14.

4. In Ignatius Eph., 17, 1 ἀλείφεσθαι is given a figurative sense in a pneumatic exegesis of Mk. 14:3 ff. The μύρον is the true gnosis with which we must be anointed in order that we may be led by its perfume to immortality. In similar passages [13] in Cl. Al. Paed., II, 8, 61 μυρίζειν or χρίειν is used for ἀλείφεσθαι. A variable use of ἀλ. is to be found also in Act. Thom., in which it is used 27 times for sacramental sealing in the literal sense; 67 ἔλαιον ἀλείφειν, a means of healing for sickness, i.e., possession; and 25 "bring them into thy flock," καθαρίσας αὐτοὺς τῷ σῷ λουτρῷ (baptism) καὶ ἀλείψας αὐτοὺς τῷ σῷ ἐλαίῳ (marking with oil) ἀπὸ τῆς περιεχούσης αὐτοὺς πλάνης (cf. 157).

Schlier

ἀλήθεια, ἀληθής,
ἀληθινός, ἀληθεύω

ἀλήθεια.

A. The OT Term אֱמֶת

1. The word אֱמֶת

The word אֱמֶת, occurs about 126 times. It is used absolutely to denote a reality which is to be regarded as אָמֵן "firm," and therefore "solid," "valid," or "binding." [1]

---

[11] Already in Orig. In Lev. Hom., II, 4 (MPG, 12, 419a) *infirmitas* is given a moral significance, as also in Chrys. Sacerd., III, 6 (MPG, 48, 644).

[12] Innocent I, Ep. 25, 11 (416 A.D.) calls the anointing of the sick a *genus sacramenti*.

[13] Reitzenstein Hell. Myst., 39, 6 f.; H. Schlier, *Relgesch. Untersuch. zu Ign.* (1929), 84. ἀλήθεια κτλ. On A: cf. V. Ryssel, *Die Synonyma des Wahren und Guten in den semit. Sprachen* (Diss. Leipzig, 1872); J. Pedersen, *Israel, Its Life and Culture* (1926), 338 ff. On B: cf. Moore, II, 188 ff.; Str.-B., II, 361 f., 522, 572; III, 76. On C and D: cf. R. Herbertz, *Das Wahrheitsproblem i. d. griech. Philosophie* (1913); G. Storz, *Gebrauch u. Bedeutungsentwicklung von* ἀλήθεια *u. begriffsverwandten Wörtern in d. griech. Literatur vor Plato* (unpub. Diss. Tüb., 1922); H. H. Wendt, ThStKr, 56 (1883), 511-547; *Die Johannesbriefe u. das johann. Christentum* (1925), 15 f., n. 2; F. Büchsel, *Der Begriff d. Wahrheit in dem Ev. u. d. Briefen des Joh.* (1911); H. v. Soden, *Was ist Wahrheit?* (1927); R. Bultmann, ZNW, 27 (1928), 113-163; E. Hoskyns-N. Davey, *The Riddle of the NT* (1931), 35 ff.

[1] The Hebrew says אָמֵן ("firm" or "sure") to denote that he accepts as authentic what is laid before him (1 K. 1:36; Neh. 5:13). It is then predominantly used in cultic situations

It thus signifies what is "true." When used of persons, it sometimes expresses that which predominantly characterises their speech, action or thought. The אִישׁ אֱמֶת is one whose conduct falls under the norm of truth and therefore a man of integrity, [2] a נֶאֱמָן (→ πίστις).

The noun is usually in the feminine (on Dt. 13:15; 17:4, → n. 6). Deriving from the root אמן ('amin), "to be firm or sure," it is constructed in the manner of fem. segolata, נ being assimilated to a fem. ת afformative. The process may still be seen in suffix constructions like אֲמִתּוֹ. The Hexapla transcription ημεθ (Ps. 31:6) seems to indicate a quantity on the first syllable lost in the Mas. It is probable that the vocalisation of the final syllable with segol is meant to differentiate it from אֲמַת, st. c. of אָמָה "maid," so that when the term is used in religious speech there should be no confusion with a purely secular word. [3] In the LXX ἀλήθεια is mostly used for אֱמֶת (87 times), ἀληθινός being also used (12 times), and occasionally ἀληθής, ἀληθῶς, and ἀληθεύειν. The equivalent in Gn. 24:49; Jos. 24:14; Is. 38:19; 39:8; Da. 8:12 and 9:13 is δικαιοσύνη, δίκαιος also occurring 4 times, and πίστις only in Jer. 35(28):9; 39(32):41; 40(33):6, while in Prv. 3:3; 14:22; 16:6 the plur. πίστεις is used for the combination חֶסֶד וֶאֱמֶת. On πιστός → n. 2. In Is. 38:18, 19 there is alternation between ἐλεημοσύνη and δικαιοσύνη; it is possible that this derives from an original deviation from the Mas. [4]

A related term is אֱמוּנָה (→ πίστις). [5] Both are close to the terms for wholeness, שָׁלוֹם (→ εἰρήνη) and תָּמִים (→ ἁπλοῦς) and the legal terms חֶסֶד (→ χάρις) and צֶדֶק, צְדָקָה (→ δίκη), and they are often used to elucidate these in the OT. They all indicate a "normal state," and אֱמֶת especially serves to express its "certainty and force." In detail the usage is rich in nuances, but the material does not allow us to fix exactly the historical development of the term.

2. אֱמֶת as a Legal Term.

a. אֱמֶת basically describes the "actual truth of a process or cause," most clearly in legal terminology. Thus we read in Dt. 22:20: וְאִם־אֱמֶת הָיָה הַדָּבָר "if the matter rests on authentic facts," on truth, and not on calumny, as in the previous case. In the same sense there is reference to אֱמֶת נָכוֹן, to something which is confirmed by enquiry, in Dt. 13:14 and 17:4. [6] An אוֹת אֱמֶת (Jos. 2:12) is a pledge for the validity of a promise, and דִּבְרֵי שָׁלוֹם וֶאֱמֶת "words of peace and truth," is used

---

whether of the community (Dt. 27:14 ff., cf. Jer. 11:5; Neh. 8:6; 1 Ch. 16:36; Ps. 41:13 etc.) or of the individual (Nu. 5:22), or with a distinctly religious accent (Jer. 28:6). The expression אֱלֹהֵי אָמֵן (Is. 65:16), "God of the Amen," derives from this liturgical use, if it is correctly pointed.

[2] The translation "faithfulness" nowhere commends itself, → n. 12. The LXX sometimes has δίκαιος (Ex. 18:21), sometimes ἀληθής (Neh. 7:2), but πιστός only in Prv. 14:25. It uses πιστός rather more frequently for נֶאֱמָן.

[3] Bauer-Leander, Hist. Gramm. der hebr. Sprache des AT, I (1922), § 77 j A.

[4] Cf. B. Duhm, Das Buch Jesaja[3] (1914), ad loc.

[5] In the full poetic expression in Is. 25:1 אֹמֶן is used side by side with it as a synonym.

[6] The masc. behind the fem. is to be understood as permutative apposition (Ges.-Kautzsch § 131 k). E. König (Komm., 123) interprets אֱמֶת as an accusative of manner or mode, though this is hardly to do justice to the usage in expressions like אֱמֶת הַדָּבָר and אֱמֶת הָיָה הַדָּבָר, on which both passages recline.

(Est. 9:30) for a valid report. Again, the legal term appears in the paraphrase: אֱמֶת הַדָּבָר, "it is really as I have heard" (1 K. 10:6; 2 Ch. 9:5, LXX: ἀληθινὸς ὁ λόγος). The same words are used to affirm that a revelation has really happened and is incontestable (Da. 10:1, cf. 8:26). In cases where אֱמֶת is applied to things, we are probably to see a metaphorical use of the legal term. In Gn. 24:48 the right way is the דֶּרֶךְ אֱמֶת, i.e., the one which proves to be successful among the many which offer. In Jer. 2:21 we have the same picture of judicial decision; the זֶרַע אֱמֶת is a genuine plant as distinct from נָכְרִיָּה, the degenerate growth.

But the use of the term is not restricted to such simple cases. An example like Gn. 42:16 (E): "Your words shall be proved" הַאֱמֶת אִתְּכֶם, indicates a tendency to abstract the concept from the concrete processes which it is supposed to elucidate, for it is open to question whether we should translate: "Whether the truth is as you say," or: "Whether there is any truth in you," i.e., veracity. Yet it is only rarely that there is any such explicit ambiguity, since אֱמֶת usually refers to a matter which is either described or indicated by the context and which is to be denoted as factual, impressive and beyond cavil, or else it occurs absolutely with a very different emphasis. In the former sense the Word of the Lord in the mouth of a prophet is called אֱמֶת, i.e., truly and indisputably present and therefore operative. Thus in 1 K. 17:24 the mother of the child who is delivered by Elijah sees from this event that the Word of Yahweh is in the mouth of Elijah. In Jer. 23:28 the prophet "which hath my word, speaketh my word as אֱמֶת" i.e., as a fact which shows itself to be such in operation, and not as a dream. [7] A עֵד אֱמֶת is a witness to the true facts which are to be disclosed by judicial trial, and as such he is a deliverer of souls (Prv. 14:25); or a נֶאֱמָן, one who has proved to be reliable: Jer. 42:5 (spoken of Yahweh). If in Is. 43:9 the nations speak אֱמֶת the context makes it plain that here again the thought is that of a judicial process of enquiry to establish the former things, so that אֱמֶת is here also the convincing "state of affairs." [8] We are to take in the same way the cases in which Zechariah insists that regard for אֱמֶת is an indispensable principle in the process of judgment. Thus in Zech. 7:9 we have: מִשְׁפַּט אֱמֶת שְׁפֹטוּ "pronounce judgment according to the true facts"; or in Zech. 8:16: "Speak ye every man the truth in process with his neighbour; judge truth, and salutary judgment in your gates." The latter passage brings out particularly well the connection between judicial findings and the judicial norm in the concept of אֱמֶת [9].

b. Not always, however, are the particular facts which count as אֱמֶת, and which are indicated by the term אֱמֶת, either supplied or specifically made known by the context. In such cases the word indicates a general and indefinite validity extending rather beyond the sphere of law. It has reference to facts which always demand recognition by all men as reality, to the normal state which corresponds to divine

---

[7] LXX: ἐπ' ἀληθείας, understands אֱמֶת here adverbially as an indication of the attitude of the prophet — a softening which can hardly be right. Cf. also Da. 8:26.

[8] In 1 K. 22:16 (2 Ch. 18:15) also we have an official hearing, and the king demands that Michaiah should say in the name of Yahweh only that which is actually so (רַק אֱמֶת),

[9] At least in the mind of the author of the gloss, who possibly inserted the second אֱמֶת. if such a vague assumption is really necessary.

and human order, and which is thus to be respected, [10] as it is similarly reflected in related terms such as צֶדֶק, צְדָקָה, שָׁלוֹם etc. In accordance with the sense it may then be rendered quite generally by "truth," or even by "veracity" as a normative concept.

3. אֱמֶת as a religious term.

a. Like other expressions important in the legal sphere, the concept of truth is particularly at home in the religious terminology of the OT. Yet it is more difficult to decide whether אֱמֶת is adopted as a rational legal concept than is usually the case with words which bear a strong legal impress. The religious use of אֱמֶת does not always have to be understood metaphorically, but may also have arisen out of religious perception. At any rate, there are many cases in which it unambiguously denotes a religious reality without any need to explain it in terms of its forensic use. The pious man, who is often juridically described as the righteous (→ δίκη), grounds his attitude to God on the incontestable fact of truth, and exercises truth, just as truth is the foundation in God's own acts and words. The truthfulness of God requires the truthfulness of man : Ps. 51:6 : אֱמֶת חָפַצְתָּ. The man who may dwell on the holy hill of Yahweh, i.e., who is cultically qualified, is the one who speaks אֱמֶת in his heart (Ps. 15:2), and who thus has a mind which is set on truth in the sense of the order of life pleasing to God. This mind is practically expressed in social life in Ez. 18:8 : "He hath executed true judgment between man and man" ; yet, as indicated in Ez. 18:9, he does this in commitment to the will of God : "He hath maintained my standards, as he hath executed truth." When Hosea (4:1) complains that there is no אֱמֶת in the land, by linking the concept with the knowledge of God (דַּעַת אֱלֹהִים) he maintains the line of thought along which he understands אֱמֶת (and חֶסֶד), namely, that in every sphere of life truthfulness grows out of unerring knowledge of God's will, and that such knowledge is for its part an actualisation of truthfulness.

Although poetic plerophory employs in its description of the pious such expressions as פֹּעַל צֶדֶק and הֹלֵךְ תָּמִים synonymously with דֹּבֵר אֱמֶת (Ps. 15:2), and although legal norms give precision to אֱמֶת (Ez. 18:9), yet in the last resort the rational element in the concept of אֱמֶת is not the essential feature, and there are many passages in which it should not be emphasised. In such cases אֱמֶת serves rather to express the reality immediately accessible to religious feeling, something which all unsought for impresses itself upon a man, the attitude corresponding to it, and then the result of apperceptive reflection, towards which the word has an unmistakeable bias. For with other words taken from the same forensic field it shares the partly advantageous and partly disadvantageous quality of stimulating and schooling religious thinking by its conceptual precision. This rational and pedagogic tendency of the word, which is linked with its legal nature, is plainly at work when it is said by way of instruction that the Word and Law of Yahweh are for man both the truth and the source of knowledge of the truth. In Ps. 119:160

---

[10] Pedersen, op. cit., 339 : "Truth is that which can be maintained by the soul, that which has the strength to exist and act in the entirety of the soul." The root of the concept is here rightly seen to be in the conception of the soul. Yet so far as the relation of אֱמֶת to this conception is concerned, the latter is rather too weak to serve as an interpretative key to all the evidence.

the sum or quintessence of the words of God is אֱמֶת; in Ps. 19:9 His judgments are אֱמֶת. It seems that the reference here is to Holy Scripture, and this conjecture is supported when an apocalyptic book may be simply described as כְּתָב אֱמֶת, the "record of truth" (Da. 10:21). Even expressions like walking in Thy truth (Ps. 25:5; 26:3; 86:11) may be reduced to solid rules of life which are called truth and which are the theme of divine instruction (cf. Ps. 86:11: "Teach me thy way, O Lord"). Along the same lines, there are times, especially in the Wisdom literature, when the rational element leads to an emphasising of the concept of truth by setting it in antithesis to שֶׁקֶר "deceit," or עַוְלָה "that which is corrupt," etc. (cf. Mal. 2:6; Prv. 11:18; 12:19; Jer. 9:4), while the contrast with רשׁע (Neh. 9:33) inclines more definitely in a religious direction. A poet may speak of אֱמֶת symbolically (Ps. 85:11: "אֱמֶת shall spring out of the earth, and צֶדֶק shall look down from heaven"), or personify it (Is. 59:14: "אֱמֶת is fallen in the street"), or appraise it as merchandise (Prv. 23:23). Symbolically we read in Da. 8:12 that truth is dashed to the ground, this passage being also noteworthy for the fact that אֱמֶת in its most pregnant sense seems to be used here as a kind of catchword for the true, i.e., the Jewish religion.[11] With the same rational emphasis the Chronicler speaks of Yahweh as אֱלֹהֵי אֱמֶת (2 Ch. 15:3) in the sense of the true, i.e., the absolute and exclusive God.

b. It indicates the multiple use of the term אֱמֶת, and its adaptability to the context in which it is set, that an almost identical expression in Ps. 31:5 (אֵל אֱמֶת) is used in an essentially different sense to denote trust or confidence. This passage is one of several in the OT which bring out the supreme signification of אֱמֶת by linking the legal with the ethical meaning or by going beyond both to make it a mark and goal of the divine action. Appeal is made to God as רַב חֶסֶד וֶאֱמֶת "rich in faithfulness and truth" (Ex. 34:6), as הָאֵל הַנֶּאֱמָן (Dt. 7:9), as אֵל אֱמֶת (Ps. 31:5), as the Guarantor of moral and legal standards. As such, God is worthy of the absolute confidence both of the righteous and of man generally. The thoughtful man sees his own littleness before the truthfulness of God which is declared in His promises (Gn. 32:11). God as צַדִּיק has always done אֱמֶת (Neh. 9:33). On Sinai He gave תּוֹרוֹת אֱמֶת, laws which establish the truth and are themselves truth (Neh. 9:13). The works of His hands are truth and right, and all His commands are unconditionally valid (Ps. 111:7). He swears אֱמֶת, i.e., irrevocably (Ps. 132:11), and keeps the norm of truthfulness for ever (Ps. 146:6).[12] Those who go down into the pit cannot hope any more for God's אֱמֶת (Is. 38:18;[13] cf. Ps. 30:9), for there is for them no divine promise to which they can appeal. If many of these

---

[11] Cf. Marti, ad loc. Da. 9:13 can be understood in the same way.
[12] The much favoured translation "faithfulness" is materially justifiable, since it is in fact a matter of proving the covenant faithfulness of God (cf. A. Dillmann, Handbuch der at.lichen Theologie [1895] 270). Yet in order that there should be differentiation from חֶסֶד which is the proper legal term for faithfulness to a compact (→ χάρις), I do not think it really suitable. This view is further supported by the frequent use of the expression חֶסֶד וֶאֱמֶת. For although this seems to make the terms almost synonymous, they are not synonymous. God confirms חֶסֶד by acting according to the norm of אֱמֶת. Truthfulness is thus the presupposition of faithfulness. Hence to use the latter term for אֱמֶת always implies a measure of refining and retouching, and ought to be avoided.
[13] Yet the LXX gives us grounds to contest the Mas., → 233.

statements include a more or less clear and conscious appeal to the thought of national election (→ διαθήκη), they all give evidence of the strong moral feeling which characterises the Israelite's faith in God and which finds its simplest expression in an older verse : אַתָּה־הוּא הָאֱלֹהִים וּדְבָרֶיךָ יִהְיוּ אֱמֶת (2 S. 7:28): "Thou art the God, namely, thy words be truth."

Quell

B. אֱמֶת in Rabbinic Judaism.

The Rabbinic use of אֱמֶת (or קוּשְׁטָא) follows essentially the same lines as that of the OT. In the first instance, the word denotes a human attitude, and on this basis it serves to express a divine mode of being.

In a popular legend traced back to Raba (4th century), קוּשְׁטָא is defined as follows: that a man should make no alteration in his word (bSanh., 97a), otherwise he is as an idolater (bSanh., 92a). Where אֱמֶת is maintained in this sense, there is peace (jTaan., 68a). A well-known statement of R. Simeon runs as follows: "The world rests on three things, on righteousness, on אֱמֶת and on peace" (Ab., 1, 18). As in the OT, אֱמֶת is the basis of all legal judgment; nor should we ignore the fact that this involves a religious statement, since the execution of law is a religious function. "The man who on the basis of אֱמֶת reaches a verdict which is אֱמֶת attains to the life of the world to come" (Tanch. שופטים 7, p. 31, Buber), and "causes the Shekinah to dwell in Israel"; whereas a judge who judges without אֱמֶת "causes the Shekinah to depart" (bSanh., 7a).

It is self-evident that the judgment of the divine Judge rests on the same foundation. "The judgment (of God) is a judgment of אֱמֶת" says Akiba Ab., 3, 16; or again: "He judges all thing according to אֱמֶת " M. Ex. 14:28; or again: "All should recognise and bear witness that His judgment is a judgment of אֱמֶת," Ex. r. on 6:2. Beyond this, however, the very essence of God is אֱמֶת, so that it may be said conversely that אֱמֶת has its essence in God. The "God of אֱמֶת" is the "Judge of אֱמֶת" (bBer., 46b). "As Thou art אֱמֶת so is Thy Word אֱמֶת, for it is said: 'For ever, O Lord, thy word is settled in heaven' (Ps. 119:89)" (Ex. r. on 29:1). Hence the Torah as the expression of the divine Word and essence is אֱמֶת (Midr. Ps. 25 § 11). This thought of the divine אֱמֶת finds powerful symbolical expression in the image of God's seal. "God's seal is אֱמֶת. What does אֱמֶת mean? That He, God, lives, and is an everlasting King" (jSanh., 18a).[14] אֱמֶת is formed from the initial letters of אֱלֹהִים and מֶלֶךְ תָּמִיד. From this process, and from its prior history (→ ΑΩ, 2), it is obvious that what we have here is not an infusion of content from the concept of God, but formal exegetical play which gives occasion to link with what is said about God a concept which is felt to be suitable for the purpose. There is an obvious difference at this point from Greek ἀλήθεια and the infusion of content essential to it.

When the term is used of God, an exegetical question arises concerning the relationship between חֶסֶד and אֱמֶת, i.e., concerning the God who is kind but who also judges. The real antithesis is between the words חֶסֶד and דִּין, but אֱמֶת can also

---

[14] For further examples, cf. Str.-B., II, 262, 431; cf. also ΑΩ, 2, where there is also a review of the rise of the notarikon.

be involved, and it thus comes to be synonymous with צֶדֶק. There are different ways in which the divine attributes may then be related. The two may sometimes be set alongside (bBer., 46b), [15] but sometimes it may be emphasised that אֱמֶת comes first and then, and therefore definitively, חֶסֶד (bRH, 17b). Yet it is always the concern of the Rabbi who interprets the Old Testament to show that both elements are essential in his view of God.

Kittel

C. The Greek and Hellenistic Use of ἀλήθεια.

The NT use of ἀλήθεια is partly determined by the Semitic use of אֱמֶת and partly by the Greek and Hellenistic use of ἀλήθεια. That the basic meanings of אֱמֶת and ἀλήθεια are not coincident is shown already by the fact that the LXX has to use πίστις, [16] δικαιοσύνη, etc. as well as ἀλήθεια to translate אֱמֶת. If ἀλήθεια is often selected, this is to be understood in the light of the Greek usage, which came to enjoy a high degree of flexibility in the course of its development.

1. The Original Greek Usage and its Differentiations.

Etymologically ἀλήθεια has the meaning of non-concealment. [17] It thus indicates a matter or state to the extent that it is seen, indicated or expressed, and that in such seeing, indication or expression it is disclosed, or discloses itself, as it really is, [18] with the implication, of course, that it might be concealed, falsified, truncated, or suppressed. ἀλήθεια, therefore, denotes the "full or real state of affairs." From the time of Homer the subst. and neut. of the adj. have been normally used as the acc. obj. of a *verbum dicendi*, and the adv. ἀληθῶς usually means "really" or "truly." As in judicial language the ἀλήθεια is the actual state of affairs to be maintained against different statements, so historians use it to denote real events as distinct from myths, and philosophers to indicate real being in the absolute sense.

> The adj. ἀληθής declares that a thing really is as it is seen or represented, and can take on, like ἀληθινός especially, the force of "proper" or "genuine." [19] If on the one side τὸ σαφές as that which is truly seen, and on the other τὸ ὄν, or in philosophy also ἡ φύσις, as that which truly is, are equivalents of ἡ ἀλήθεια or τὸ ἀληθές, the most common antonyms are → ψεῦδος ("deception") and → δόξα ("appearance" or "mere opinion"), which conceal or replace the truth. In opposition to these the ἀλήθεια must be sought and investigated, [20] and in philosophy the question arises whether the ἀλήθεια is ληπτή or ἄληπτος (Emped., Fr. 2 [Diels, I, 223, 16 ff.]), and how far the senses or the understanding suffice to grasp it.

---

[15] In the house of the sorrowing there is an appeal both to the Merciful and to the Judge of אֱמֶת.

[16] On this point, cf. A. Schlatter, *Der Glaube im NT*⁴ (1917), 551-561.

[17] Note the negative construction as in the related words ἀτρεκής, ἀψευδής, νημερτής.

[18] Cf. Xenoph. An., IV, 4, 15: ἀληθεῦσαι ... τὰ ὄντα τε ὡς ὄντα, καὶ τὰ μὴ ὄντα ὡς οὐκ ὄντα.

[19] There is no comprehensive investigation of ἀληθινός and ἀληθεύειν outside the OT and NT.

[20] E.g., κρίνειν τἀληθές, Anaxag., Fr. 21 (Diels, I, 409, 14); ἡ ζήτησις τῆς ἀληθείας, Thuc., I, 20.

Since in the practice of history, and in historical and philosophical enquiry, it is essentially the task of the λόγος to reveal and indicate, ἀλήθεια can also denote an aspect of the λόγος which is proper to this as ἀπόφανσις to the extent that it causes that which is to be seen; either it is ἀληθεύων or ἀληθής ("true"), or it is the opposite. Hence ἀληθής and → ὀρθός can be synonyms (e.g., Soph. Oed. Tyr., 1220), and in as much as we may be convinced by the ἀλήθεια itself as by true words, and may thus rely on it, there results a connection between ἀλήθεια and → πίστις; ἀλήθεια underlies πίστις ἀληθής (Parm., Fr. 1, 30; 8, 28 [Diels, I, 150, 9; 156, 14]). If πίστις ("conviction" and "demonstration") is never synonymous with ἀλήθεια, πιστὰ λέγειν can mean the same as ἀληθῆ λέγειν (Hdt., I, 182; II, 73), and, like πιστός, ἀληθής as a personal attribute can denote "trustworthiness." Thus ἀλήθεια acquires the meaning of "truthfulness" (Mimn., Fr. 8 [Anth. Lyr., I, p. 42, Diehl]: ἀληθείη δὲ παρέστω σοὶ καὶ ἐμοί, πάντων χρῆμα δικαιότατον), and the adj., synon. with εὐθύς, can characterise a man or the νοῦς (Homer Il., 12, 433; Pind. Ol., 2, 101).

It is thus understandable that ἀλήθεια can serve as a rendering of אֱמֶת in the sense of "veracity" or "reliability," even though אֱמֶת is not like ἀλήθεια understood as ἀρετή, as a personal quality. Further differentiations of the concept of ἀλήθεια make this even more possible, though in the first instance they bring out an ever greater distinction. For if there are intrinsically as many "truths" as there are facts, in the Greek world the question of *the* truth was raised (Plat. Phaedr., 248b: ἡ πολλὴ σπουδὴ τὸ ἀληθείας ἰδεῖν πεδίον οὗ ἐστιν). This is the question of true being in the absolute sense, which man must know if he is to find his way in his puzzling existence; cf. Plat. Gorg., 526d: χαίρειν οὖν ἐάσας τὰς τιμὰς τὰς τῶν πολλῶν ἀνθρώπων, τὴν ἀλήθειαν σκοπῶν πειράσομαι τῷ ὄντι ὡς ἂν δύνωμαι βέλτιστος ὢν καὶ ζῆν καὶ ἐπειδὰν ἀποθνήσκω ἀποθνήσκειν. This question of the truth is alien to the OT. Nevertheless, by means of it ἀλήθεια does acquire a significance related to that of אֱמֶת, since in the question: What is truth?, it is used to denote a norm, and according to the Greek understanding of existence it is self-evident that action should follow true knowledge or self-understanding. [21] For this reason ἀλήθεια can also have the sense of "correct doctrine," for this shows what the truth is. [22] Hence ἀλήθεια can be synon. with ἐπιστήμη, [23] and can be used to denote the teaching of a religious proclamation.

2. The Usage of Dualism.

If in philosophy ἀλήθεια is understood as true being in distinction from the worldly phenomena which in the first instance appear as being, and if in Plato especially this true being is understood as the world of ideas which is immune from becoming and perishing, which is concealed from the senses and which may be comprehended in thinking, ἀλήθεια takes on more and more the sense of "true and genuine reality," and its opposite becomes εἴδωλον ("reflection" or "appearance"). The only thing which is truly ἀληθές is that which always is, the

[21] Plat. Prot., 345d, e; 361b; Soph., 228c, d; Resp., III, 413a; Epict. Diss., I, 17, 14; 28, 4; II, 26, 1-5.
[22] Epict. Diss., I, 4, 31; III, 24, 40.
[23] Plut. De Isid. et Os., 1 (II, 351c, e); cf. Hierocl. Carm. Aur., p. 21-23, Mullach.

divine, the αὐτὸ καθ' αὐτὸ μεθ' αὐτοῦ μονοειδὲς ἀεὶ ὄν.[24] If Plato still uses ἀλήθεια formally to denote genuineness, or that which truly is, in Hellenism it comes to imply the "eternal" or "divine" in the sense of a cosmological dualism. It still retains the sense of genuineness, since the divine being is that in which man must come to share in order to be saved (→ σωτηρία) and thus to attain to his own genuine or proper being. Yet to different degrees in different strata the presupposition is abandoned that the ἀλήθεια is accessible to thought, since the true being of man is no longer seen in thinking. The ἀλήθεια is closed to man as such, and he comes to share in it only when the limits of humanity are transcended, whether in ecstasy or by revelation from the divine sphere. In this sense ἀλήθεια becomes an "eschatological" concept, and this dualistically eschatological understanding of ἀλήθεια is developed by Gnosticism, Philo and Plotinus.

In certain Herm. fragments handed down by Stob. (Scott, *Hermetica,* I, 380-392) an attempt is made to combine the Gnostic concept of ἀλήθεια with the Platonic. The Gnostic view is found in a pure form in individual parts of the Corp. Herm. and in the literature of Christian Gnosticism. There has obviously been some Persian influence ; the Gnostic ἀλήθεια corresponds to a large extent to כושטא in the Mandaean writings.[25]

Since Godhead is here represented as an eternal diaphanous substance, and at the same time as the miraculous power which effects → ἀφθαρσία, ἀλήθεια becomes synon. with οὐσία (= divine substance) and δύναμις, as with θεότης generally. And since ἀλήθεια has also the sense of revealed doctrine, doctrine itself is understood as the mighty efficacy and power of God. Since again γνῶσις corresponds to divine revelation, the γνῶσις effected by divine revelation also appears as divine power, so that there is a resultant equation of ἀλήθεια and γνῶσις. The usage is made even more complicated by the fact that the divine revelation both is and effects → ζωή and → φῶς. To the extent that ἀλήθεια means the divine essence, it is the equivalent of ζωή, and to the extent that this ζωή as φῶς is the divine power of revelation ἀλήθεια and ζωή are also coterminous. Indeed, since the divine sphere can also be described as → πνεῦμα, ἀληθινός comes to mean the same as πνευματικός, and since → νοῦς is often understood according to the analogy of πνεῦμα, it can also mean the same as νοητός and νοερός. Finally, ἀληθινός or ἀληθής is synon. with οὐσιώδης (= essential or divine), ἀόρατος, ἀσώματος, ἀγέννητος, ἄφθαρτος, and therefore with all the attributes which are intended to describe the divine side of cosmic duality.

As regards the richly variegated usage,[26] the following is the essential material. The character of ἀλήθεια as divine δύναμις is shown esp. by Corp. Herm., XIII, which treats of rebirth (→ παλιγγενεσία). The ἀληθές, the being opposed to the θνητόν, grows out of rebirth, which is described as γένεσις τῆς θεότητος. This takes place in such a way that the divine δυνάμεις draw together in man, the first being γνῶσις and the last ἀλήθεια, which completes regeneration: τῇ δὲ ἀληθείᾳ καὶ τὸ ἀγαθὸν

---

[24] Plat. Symp., 211b; 212a; Resp., X, 596d-605c; cf. 508d.
[25] Cf. Lidz. Joh., II, p. XVII f.; R. Reitzenstein-H. H. Schaeder, *Studien zum antiken Synkretismus* (1926), 327.
[26] Cf. the examples in R. Bultmann, ZNW, 27 (1928), 151-163.

ἐπεγένετο ἅμα ζωῇ καὶ φωτί. [27] According to Corp. Herm., VII revelation leads to the gates of γνῶσις, and from φθορά and θάνατος to the vision of ἀλήθεια. God's "word" brings "light" and "truth" to "those who know," and assures them of victory over darkness, falsehood and death, according to Od. Sol. 18. Similarly for Philo the ἀληθινή ζωή is divine and incorruptible life (Leg. All., I, 32 and 35; III, 52); Ignatius uses much the same terminology (Eph., 7, 2; Sm., 4, 1 etc.). Heaven is the place of ἀλήθεια, which is declared only by δήλωσις. The revelation of God causes its φέγγος to stream forth, and the αὐγή τῆς ἀληθείας shines forth φέγγει νοητῷ καὶ ἀσωμάτῳ (Spec. Leg., I, 89; Migr. Abr., I, 76; Vit. Mos., II, 271). To the one who is filled with striving for the ἀξιέραστος ἀλήθεια, the ὅρασις θεοῦ is granted as γέρας ἐξαίρετον (Praem. Poen., 36; cf. 46: ἀλήθειαν δὲ μετίασιν οἱ θεὸν θεῷ φαντασιωθέντες, φωτὶ φῶς, cf. Leg. All., III, 45 ff.). Led by ἀλήθεια, the soul is enticed by heavenly ἔρως and strides to ὄντως ὄν (Rer. Div. Her., 70). The human νοῦς could not tread this way εἰ μὴ καὶ θεῖον ἦν πνεῦμα τὸ ποδηγετοῦν πρὸς αὐτὴν τὴν ἀλήθειαν (Vit. Mos., II, 265). And in the same sense Plot. (Enn. VI, 9, 4, p. 513, 12, Volkmann) speaks of the φῶς ἀληθινόν by which the man is filled who soars up to the vision of Godhead (cf. I, 6, 9, p. 95, 28). He thus extols the ἀληθινή ζωή in which genuine ἔρως participates (VI, 9, 9, p. 522, 7). And the older Gk. concept of truth is completely set aside when according to V, 3, 5 (p. 184, 6 f.) the one who views has that which he views in such sort that he is one with it, and he thus has the truth in such a way that he actually is the truth: τὴν ἄρα ἀλήθειαν οὐχ ἑτέρου δεῖ εἶναι, ἀλλ', ὃ λέγει, τοῦτο καὶ εἶναι. In this sense we read in Porphyr. Ad Marcell., 13, p. 282, 24 ff., Nauck: κάλλος γὰρ ἐκείνου (of God) τὸ ἀκήρατον (καὶ?) φῶς τὸ ζωτικὸν ἀληθείᾳ διαλάμπον (cf. Abst., II, 52). In Vit. Pyth., 41, p. 38, 16 ff. he advances the speculation: ἐπεὶ καὶ τοῦ θεοῦ ... ὃν Ὡρομάζην καλοῦσιν ἐκεῖνοι (sc. οἱ μάγοι) ἐοικέναι τὸ μὲν σῶμα φωτί, τὴν δὲ ψυχὴν ἀληθείᾳ. For the Neo-Platonist Hierocles Carm. Aur., p. 21-23, Mullach, the ἀλήθεια is on one side the τῶν θείων γνῶσις which leads to ὁμοίωσις πρὸς θεόν, and on the other it is the divine essence itself; for γνῶσις leads here to τὸ τῆς ἀληθείας ἐνοπτρίσασθαι κάλλος. Alkinoos (Albinos) Isag., 10, p. 164, Hermann, defines the πρῶτος θεός as θειότης, οὐσιότης, ἀλήθεια, συμμετρία, ἀγαθόν. Corp. Herm., XIII, 6 defines the ἀληθές as τὸ μὴ θολούμενον, τὸ μὴ διοριζόμενον, τὸ ἀχρώματον, τὸ ἀσχημάτιστον, τὸ ἄτρεπτον, τὸ γυμνόν, τὸ φαῖνον (?), τὸ αὐτῷ καταληπτόν, τὸ ἀναλλοίωτον (ἀγαθόν), τὸ ἀσώματον. And in the language of magic θεσπίσματ' ἀληθῆ are words of magical potency (Preis. Zaub., II [Berlin] 7); the ἀλήθεια is here the divine essentiality (Preis. Zaub., III [Paris], 156; IV [Paris], 1014); yet the use of ἀλήθεια in magic is also under Semitic influence (Preis. Zaub., III [Paris], 156; V [London], 148 f.: ἐγώ εἰμι ἡ ἀλήθεια, ὁ μισῶν ἀδικήματα γίνεσθαι ἐν τῷ κόσμῳ), as also under Egyptian (Preis. Zaub., XII [Leiden] Col. VIII, 10, in which there is the invocation of the Most High God: ὁ ἔχων τὴν ἄψευστον ἀλήθειαν).

D. The Early Christian Use of ἀλήθεια.

Having considered the possibilities of use in the NT, we can now group the actual usage systematically. The meanings of the subst. ἀλήθεια may be arranged as follows, although sometimes the exact classification is open to question.

---

[27] Cf. Reitzenstein, Hell. Myst., 383-393. Cf. also Cl. Al. Strom., I, 7, 38, 4: ἄλλως τις περὶ ἀληθείας λέγει, ἄλλως ἡ ἀλήθεια ἑαυτὴν ἑρμηνεύει. ἕτερον στοχασμὸς ἀληθείας, ἕτερον ἡ ἀλήθεια, ἄλλο ὁμοίωσις, ἄλλο αὐτὸ τὸ ὄν, καὶ ἡ μὲν μαθήσει καὶ ἀσκήσει περιγίνεται, ἡ δὲ δυνάμει καὶ πίστει. We have here a clear formulation of the distinction between ἀλήθεια as the divine reality and ἀλήθεια as a given state of things in the world which is amenable to investigation. In this case the relationship between the two is, of course, interpreted Neo-Platonically through the term ὁμοίωσις.

1. ἀλήθεια as that which "has certainty and force" (in the sense of אֶמֶת).
a. ἀλήθεια seems to be used in the OT sense in Eph. 4:21: καθώς ἐστιν ἀλήθεια
ἐν τῷ Ἰησοῦ = as this is so in Jesus. We are to understand in the same way
Gl. 2:5 : ἵνα ἡ ἀλήθεια τοῦ εὐαγγελίου διαμείνῃ πρὸς ὑμᾶς, and Gl. 2:14: ὅτι
οὐκ ὀρθοποδοῦσιν πρὸς τὴν ἀλήθειαν τοῦ εὐαγγελίου. The truth is the "valid
norm," with perhaps a hint of the Gk. idea of what is "genuine" or "proper";
cf. Gl. 1:6 : εἰς ἕτερον εὐαγγέλιον, ὃ οὐκ ἔστιν ἄλλο. The demand of God is
the ἀλήθεια in R. 2:8 : τοῖς ... ἀπειθοῦσι τῇ ἀληθείᾳ (!), and R. 2:20 : ... ἔχοντα
τὴν μόρφωσιν τῆς γνώσεως καὶ τῆς ἀληθείας ἐν τῷ νόμῳ, γνῶσις here being
undoubtedly the equivalent of דַּעַת־יהוה (on 2 C. 13:8 → 244).

This is in line with the Rabbinic conception of God's אֶמֶת as the demand incorporated
in the Torah (→ 237); cf. the meaning of אֱמֶת, as the "seal" of God as a notarikon
which means "God the everlasting King" → 237. Cf. also Philo Vit. Mos., II, 273. In
Herm. m., 10, 1, 4-6 ἀλήθεια is combined with θεότης to denote the irrefragably valid
demand of God. The older meaning of "sureness" or "certainty" is also seen clearly
in Herm. v., 3, 4, 3 : ταῦτα πάντα ἐστὶν ἀληθῆ καὶ οὐθὲν ἔξωθέν ἐστιν τῆς ἀληθείας, ἀλλὰ πάντα ἰσχυρὰ καὶ βέβαια καὶ τεθεμελιωμένα ἐστίν. The characterisation of God as the θεὸς τῆς ἀληθείας (ψ 30:5) recurs in 2 Cl., 19, 1, and in 2 Cl., 3, 1;
20, 5 we have the corresponding πατὴρ τῆς ἀληθείας. On the other hand, (σέβεται)
τὸν κατ' ἀλήθειαν θεόν in Ep. Ar., 140 belongs under 3.

b. Like אֶמֶת, ἀλήθεια can also have the meaning of δικαιοσύνη as "judicial
righteousness"; cf. Da. 3:28 : God's judgments are κρίματα ἀληθείας, for He acts
ἀληθείᾳ καὶ κρίσει (cf. Tob. 3:2). [28] In the NT this sense is found only in the
case of → ἀληθινός; yet in Did., 16, 6 the σημεῖα τῆς ἀληθείας are the signs of
eschatological judgment. On R. 2:2 → 243.

c. Quite often ἀλήθεια, like אֶמֶת, takes on the weaker sense "uprightness," as
in the expression ποιεῖν ἀλήθειαν (Tob. 4:6; 13:6; Jn. 3:21; 1 Jn. 1:6; 1 Cl., 31, 2),
which corresponds to the Rabbinic עֲבַד קוּשְׁטָא (Tg. Hos. 4:1). Similarly, we have
πορεύεσθαι ἐν ἀληθείᾳ (3 Βασ. 2:4; Tob. 3:5) or περιπατεῖν ἐν ἀληθείᾳ (4 Βασ.
20:3; 2 Jn. 4; 3 Jn. 3 f.) in the sense of acting honestly. Along the same lines,
ἀλήθεια is the opposite of → ἀδικία in the NT (1 C. 13:6; R. 1:18, though → 243;
R. 2:8, though supra), and it is also combined with δικαιοσύνη (Eph. 4:24; 5:9;
6:14; cf. Tob. 14:7; Philo Vit. Mos., 237), and is perhaps sometimes to be understood in terms of it (Jm. 3:14; 5:19). Cf. also perhaps 1 Cl., 35, 5 (ὁδὸς τῆς
ἀληθείας); 60, 2; Herm. v., 3, 7, 3 (ἡ ἁγνότης τῆς ἀληθείας); s., 9, 19, 2 (καρπὸς
ἀληθείας par. καρπὸς δικαιοσύνης).

For the Jewish usage, cf. again Tob. 8:7 (opp. πορνεία); Wis. 5:6 (par. δικαιοσύνη); Sir. 27:8 f. (opp. v. 10 ἁμαρτία); Test. G. 3:1. In the song of praise to ἀλήθεια
in 1 Εσδρ. 4:36-40 this meaning is asserted within the total range of significance of
אֱמֶת, as also in the version of the story in Jos. Ant., 11, 56.

2. ἀλήθεια is also that "on which one can rely" (in the sense of אֱמֶת). a. It
signifies "reliability" or "trustworthiness." How closely this meaning is linked

---

[28] Cf. A. Schlatter, Die Sprache und Heimat des vierten Evangelisten (1902), 94; Schl. J.,
206; → 237.

with the former may be seen in R. 3:3-7, in which God's ἀλήθεια, opposed to man's ψεῦσμα (→ ψεῦδος) in v. 7 (cf. v. 4), is nothing other than His πίστις = faithfulness (v. 3), and between the πίστις and ἀλήθεια of God there again stands His δικαιοσύνη (v. 5) in opposition to human ἀδικία, the ὅπως ἂν δικαιωθῇς corresponding to the γινέσθω δὲ ὁ θεὸς ἀληθής (v. 4). This can be understood only in the light of the אֱמֶת concept. In the same connection we might also refer to R. 15:8 : ὑπὲρ τῆς ἀληθείας θεοῦ εἰς τὸ βεβαιῶσαι τὰς ἐπαγγελίας τῶν πατέρων.

On the Jewish use, cf. Sir. 7:20; 1 Macc. 7:18 and the Rabbinic use of קוּשְׁטָא.

b. It also signifies "sincerity" or "honesty" in 2 C. 7:14 (πάντα ἐν ἀληθείᾳ ἐλαλήσαμεν ὑμῖν); 11:10 (in the oath ἔστιν ἀλήθεια Χριστοῦ ἐν ἐμοὶ ὅτι). It is thus linked with εἰλικρινία in 1 C. 5:8, and opposed to πρόφασις in Phil. 1:18. Cf. Herm. m., 8, 9; s., 9, 15, 2. This is also how we are to take the formula ἐν ἀληθείᾳ (1 Βασ. 12:24; ψ 144:18), though ἀλήθεια has a broad sense in this case, being sometimes linked with a related term to form a hendiadys as in 1 Tm. 2:7 (ἐν πίστει καὶ ἀληθείᾳ, cf. also 1 Cl., 60, 4); and cf. ἐν φόβῳ καὶ ἀληθείᾳ in 1 Cl., 19, 1; στέργειν ἐν πάσῃ ἀληθείᾳ in Pol., 4, 2; πορεύεσθαι ἐν ἀληθείᾳ in Herm. m., 3, 4 (in a different sense from → supra). There is a play on this use in 2 Jn. 1 and 3 Jn. 1: ἀγαπᾶν ἐν ἀληθείᾳ, with which we should compare the epistolary formula φιλεῖν πρὸς ἀλήθειαν (P. Fay., 118, 26; 119, 26 f.).

3. ἀλήθεια implies the "real state of affairs" as disclosed (in the Gk. sense). The obvious usage in Wis. 6:22 (θήσω εἰς τὸ ἐμφανὲς τὴν γνῶσιν αὐτῆς [sc. τῆς σοφίας] καὶ οὐ μὴ παροδεύσω τὴν ἀλήθειαν) [29] gives us the sense in R. 1:18 : ... ἐπὶ πᾶσαν ἀσέβειαν καὶ ἀδικίαν ἀνθρώπων τῶν τὴν ἀλήθειαν ἐν ἀδικίᾳ κατεχόντων. To be sure, in this case we might understand ἀλήθεια either as the divine claim (→ 242) or as uprightness (δικαιοσύνη, → 242), but we can see from v. 19 : διότι τὸ γνωστὸν τοῦ θεοῦ φανερόν ἐστιν ἐν αὐτοῖς, that what is really meant is the "revealed reality" of God. R. 1:25 : μετήλλαξαν τὴν ἀλήθειαν τοῦ θεοῦ ἐν τῷ ψεύδει, is to be understood in the same way, unless ἀλήθεια τοῦ θεοῦ simply means the true or real God as opposed to the ψεῦδος, i.e., an idol. Similarly ἐν ἀληθείᾳ signifies "real" in Ju. 9:15, Ιερ. 33:15, Ign. Eph., 6, 2 and even Col. 1:6, as does also ἐπ' ἀληθείας in Ac. 4:27 and 10:34, and κατ' ἀλήθειαν in Ep. Ar., 140, while κατὰ τὴν ἀλήθειαν in R. 2:2 means "in accordance with reality" (as opposed to προσωπολημψία in v. 11). The contrast in 1 Jn. 3:18 : (μὴ ἀγαπῶμεν) λόγῳ μηδὲ τῇ γλώσσῃ ἀλλὰ ἔργῳ καὶ ἀληθείᾳ is a common one in Greek, cf. Thuc., II, 41; Isoc., 3, 33; and also Jos. Ant., 14, 68. Again, the old Greek expression "to tell" or "to show the truth" etc. is found, not only in the LXX (2 Ch. 18:15; Prv. 8:7; Tob. 7:10 etc.) and Jos. (Ant., 10, 124), but also in the NT (Mk. 5:33; R. 9:1; 2 C. 12:6 etc.). In Jn., too, we find λέγειν τὴν ἀλήθειαν at 8:40, 45 f.; 16:7, and the corresponding μαρτυρεῖν τῇ ἀληθείᾳ at 5:33; there is an intentional ambiguity at 8:40, 45 and 5:33, the discerning reader being meant to interpret the ἀλήθεια also as the divine revelation (→ 245).

---

[29] Cf. Jos. Ant., 1, 4; Herm. v., 3, 3, 5.

4. ἀλήθεια as "truth of statement" is found in the expression ῥήματα ἀληθείας in Ac. 26:25 (cf. Jdt. 10:13) and in the expositions in Herm. m., 3, 1 ff. The Gk. formula ἐπ' ἀληθείας, which commonly means "in accordance with the truth" in the pap., [30] has this sense in connection with λέγειν (Lk. 4:25), εἰπεῖν (Mk. 12:32), διδάσκειν (Mk. 12:14); in this sense it can also correspond to אֱמֶת (Lk. 22:59, where Mk. 14:70 and Mt. 26:73 have ἀληθῶς; and 1 Cl., 23, 5; 47, 3).

5. ἀλήθεια can also be used for "true teaching or faith." As in Da. 8:12 אֱמֶת means the true faith or the Jewish religion, so the proselyte is described in Philo Spec. Leg., IV, 178 as μεταναστὰς εἰς ἀλήθειαν καὶ τὴν τοῦ ἑνὸς τιμίου τιμὴν ἀπὸ μυθικῶν πλασμάτων καὶ πολυαρχίας. It is in this sense that the righteous are called the children of truth in Eth. En. 105:2, and there is a similar use in 1 Εσδρ. 4:36-40 (→ 242). We are to understand 2 C. 13:8 along the same lines: οὐ γὰρ δυνάμεθά τι κατὰ τῆς ἀληθείας ἀλλὰ ὑπὲρ τῆς ἀληθείας; ἀλήθεια here means true doctrine as opposed to a ἕτερον εὐαγγέλιον (cf. 11:4), as in Philo Poster. C., 101 etc. [31] unless we take it in the sense of 1 a. For this reason, Paul can call the Gospel in general the ἀλήθεια which he makes manifest by his activity (2 C. 4:2: τῇ φανερώσει τῆς ἀληθείας). ἀλήθεια in this case subsumes the concept λόγος τοῦ θεοῦ in terms of what precedes; cf. the objects of φανεροῦν: in 2 C. 2:14: τὴν ὀσμὴν τῆς γνώσεως αὐτοῦ; in Col. 4:3 f.: τὸ μυστήριον τοῦ θεοῦ; Tt. 1:3: τὸν λόγον. In the formal parallel in Jos. Bell., 1, 627: δόλοις τὴν ἀλήθειαν ἐπικαλύψειν, ἀλήθεια has only the formal sense of truth. Just as Paul can say ὑπακούειν τῷ εὐαγγελίῳ (R. 10:16), he can also say τῇ ἀληθείᾳ (μὴ) πείθεσθαι (Gl. 5:7), and the Christian faith can be called ὑπακοὴ τῆς ἀληθείας (1 Pt. 1:22). Again, the preaching of the Gospel can be called λόγος ἀληθείας (2 C. 6:7; Col. 1:5; Eph. 1:13 etc.), and to become a Christian is εἰς ἐπίγνωσιν ἀληθείας ἐλθεῖν (1 Tm. 2:4; 2 Tm. 3:7; cf. 1 Tm. 4:3; Hb. 10:26; 2 Jn. 1). In 2 Th. 2:10-12 the ἀλήθεια is the Christian revelation as opposed to the revelation of Antichrist, which is called ψεῦδος and ἀδικία. [32] In 1 Tm. 3:15 the ἐκκλησία is described as the στῦλος καὶ ἑδραίωμα τῆς ἀληθείας; and in 2 Pt. 1:12 the ἀλήθεια is simply Christianity. Harder to determine is ἀλήθεια ἐν παρρησίᾳ, which in 1 Cl., 35, 2 is enumerated with πίστις ἐν πεποιθήσει as one of the δῶρα τοῦ θεοῦ; but the implication seems to be the true faith which we possess with confidence, as also, perhaps, in the list of divine gifts in Act. Joh., 109, p. 208, 3. It is especially against error that ἀλήθεια is "true teaching" (1 Tm. 6:5; 2 Tm. 2:18; 3:8; 4:4; Tt. 1:14; and also Ign. Eph., 6, 2; Pol., 7, 3). Yet this usage is still determined by the אֱמֶת concept (cf. Gl. 5:7; 1 Pt. 1:22). As the concept of → πίστις is determined by the thought of obedience, so ἀλήθεια is "authoritative teaching." The way is thus prepared for the historical development which fashions the concept of dogma, in which truth and law are conjoined. [33]

---

[30] Preisigke Wört.

[31] Cf. Wnd., ad loc.

[32] To 2 Th. 2:10: τὴν ἀγάπην τῆς ἀληθείας, there are formal parallels in Jos. Ap., 2, 296; Bell., 1, 30: ἀγαπᾶν τὴν ἀλήθειαν, yet in these ἀλήθεια has the formal sense of truth (the "real state of affairs"), and the contrasting of ἀλήθεια with ἡδονή is common in older Gk. On the other hand, in the similar expression in Bell., 2, 141 ἀλήθεια means "probity."

[33] Cf. v. Soden, 23-26.

6. ἀλήθεια can also mean "genuineness," "divine reality," "revelation." Developing out of Hellenistic dualism (→ B), this usage determines the use of ἀληθινός in Hb. (→ 250) and the highly individual terminology of John. In John ἀλήθεια denotes "divine reality" with reference to the fact 1. that this is different from the reality in which man first finds himself, and by which he is controlled, and 2. that it discloses itself and is thus revelation. If there is here a good deal of agreement with Hellenistic dualism, John is distinguished from this by the fact that for him the antithesis between ἀλήθεια as divine power and ψεῦδος as anti-divine is not cosmological, in spite of the mythological form in which it is sometimes clothed (Jn. 8:44). ἀλήθεια and ψεῦδος are understood as genuine possibilities of human existence rather than substances. It is in keeping that revelation is determined by the thought of the Word and of hearing the Word, so that we again have a genuine possibility of existence. ἀλήθεια is thus the reality of God which is, of course, opposed and inaccessible to human existence as it has constituted itself through the fall from God, i.e., through sin, and revelation is a miraculous occurrence beyond the reach of the being which is alien to God. Yet in revelation there is disclosed to man the true possibility of his own being when, in face of the Word of revelation which encounters him, he decides to surrender himself. Thus the reception of ἀλήθεια is conditioned neither by rational or esoteric instruction on the one side nor psychical preparation and exercise on the other; it takes place in obedient faith. [34]

A distinctive feature is that almost all the elements infused into the ἀλήθεια concept by tradition can sometimes be combined, and yet in such a way that one of them is particularly emphasised. The antithesis between divine and anti-divine reality emerges at 8:44 in a formulation which derives from Gnostic mythology: ἐκεῖνος (the devil) ἀνθρωποκτόνος ἦν ἀπ' ἀρχῆς, καὶ ἐν τῇ ἀληθείᾳ οὐκ ἔστηκεν, ὅτι οὐκ ἔστιν ἀλήθεια ἐν αὐτῷ. But indirectly this asserts that the ἀλήθεια gives life, and that what is not determined by it leads to death. It is also asserted that when the ἀλήθεια is present it shows itself to be a determinative power in concrete conduct. Again, in what follows: ὅταν λαλῇ τὸ ψεῦδος, ἐκ τῶν ἰδίων λαλεῖ, ψεῦδος has the first and provisional meaning of a "lie" or "untruth," but the context shows clearly 1. that both divine and demonic reality is expressed in words, and 2. that these realities are actual as active modes of being, or conversely that every active mode of being is determined either by divine or demonic reality. The determination of being by the revealed reality of God is thus indicated in 1 Jn. 1:8 and 2:4 by the expression: "The ἀλήθεια is (or is not) in ..." This also means that such a determination must show itself in concrete action.

For this reason there can arise for John a distinctive ambiguity. When Jesus speaks the ἀλήθεια, this has first the formal meaning of "speaking the truth," but it also means "bringing the revelation in words" (8:40, 45; cf. v. 46, where in place

---

[34] Perhaps the usage is also determined by the fact that John thinks of the ἀλήθεια as the revelation given by Jesus in contrast to the Torah. To the best of my knowledge, the latter is not described absolutely as the קוּשְׁטָא; the most that can be said is that in the exegesis of the OT God's אֱמֶת is referred to the Torah (Str.-B., II, 361 on Jn. 1:14; → 237). Yet things are said of it analogous to what Jn. says of the ἀλήθεια: it gives life (Str.-B., III, 129 ff. on R. 3:1 f.); it is to be compared with light (Str.-B., II, 357 on Jn. 1:4); it makes free (Str.-B., II, 522 f. on Jn. 8:32).

of the antithetical concept ψεῦδος the more general ἁμαρτία is used, and esp. v. 47, where the term ἀλήθεια is replaced by τὰ ῥήματα τοῦ θεοῦ). The same twofold sense is present when it is said of the Baptist: μεμαρτύρηκεν τῇ ἀληθείᾳ (5:33). [35] It is also found in 18:37: ἐγὼ ... εἰς τοῦτο ἐλήλυθα εἰς τὸν κόσμον, ἵνα μαρτυρήσω τῇ ἀληθείᾳ, where Pilate's question gives emphasis to the word, and the continuation shows again that ἀλήθεια is the self-revealing divine reality, and that its comprehension is not a free act of existence, but is grounded in the determination of existence by divine reality: πᾶς ὁ ὢν ἐκ τῆς ἀληθείας ἀκούει μου τῆς φωνῆς. [36]

As revelation ἀλήθεια is the object of γινώσκειν (Jn. 8:32; 2 Jn. 1) or εἰδέναι (1 Jn. 2:21). What is primarily expressed is the character of the determinative power of revelation as a word which can be understood (Jn. 8:32: γνώσεσθε τὴν ἀλήθειαν, καὶ ἡ ἀλήθεια ἐλευθερώσει ὑμᾶς). For ἀλήθεια naturally does not mean the formal truth of the facts in question (as in Jos. Ant., 13, 291: γνῶναι τὴν ἀλήθειαν; cf. Ant., 2, 60). It would be a gross misunderstanding to take it here in the general and formal sense. What is meant is not knowledge generally, but the knowledge of revelation, just as ἐλευθερία does not mean the freedom of the human mind but freedom from sin (cf. 8:34). The same is true of Jn. 17:17, 19: ἁγίασον αὐτοὺς ἐν τῇ ἀληθείᾳ· ὁ λόγος ὁ σὸς (i.e., the proclamation of Jesus entrusted to Him by the Father) ἀλήθειά (i.e., revelation) ἐστιν ... ἵνα ὦσιν καὶ αὐτοὶ ἡγιασμένοι ἐν ἀληθείᾳ (i.e., taken from the "world" through revelation). The fact that the Word of revelation is not a complex of statements or ideas, that it is not cosmological or soteriological speculation, but an address fulfilled in concrete encounter, is shown by the fact that it cannot be separated from the person of Jesus and the events fulfilled in His history (17:17-19). He brings the ἀλήθεια, not simply as an impartation mediated by His Word, but as He sanctifies Himself for them, so that it can be said: ἐγώ εἰμι ἡ ὁδὸς καὶ ἡ ἀλήθεια καὶ ἡ ζωή (14:6). Hence revelation is not the means to an end; it is itself both the way and the goal (ζωή). In other words, it is taken seriously as a divine occurrence. That God is disclosed in revelation is stated in 1:14, 17, where the δόξα of the μονογενής is described as πλήρης χάριτος καὶ ἀληθείας, i.e., God's reality is given in it. [37]

We are to understand the demand for προσκυνεῖν ἐν πνεύματι καὶ ἀληθείᾳ (4:23 f.) along the same lines. For Jn. πνεῦμα as well as ἀλήθεια denotes the sphere of divine essence and occurrence as distinct from human (3:6-8). Hence the meaning is not that true worship takes place in spirituality and pure knowledge on the basis of a concept of God purged of anthropomorphic conceptions, but that it takes place as determined by God's own essence, i.e., by the πνεῦμα. If ἀλήθεια is added, this is an indication that such worship can take place only as determined by the revelation accomplished in Jesus (v. 25 f.), and consequently as deter-

---

[35] There is a characteristic difference from Jos. Vit., 367: τὴν ἀλήθειαν ἐμαρτύρει, in which ἀλήθεια simply has the unequivocal formal sense of truth; cf. Ant., 4, 219: τἀληθῆ μαρτυρῆσαι.

[36] Instructive again is the difference from Jos. Ant., 8, 33, where Solomon ἐπιγνοὺς τὰς ἑκατέρων φωνὰς (3 Βασ. 3:26) ἀπὸ τῆς ἀληθείας γεγενημένας, i.e., that the statements were based on the actual facts.

[37] I think it possible that in 1:14 there is a play on the חֶסֶד וֶאֱמֶת of Ex. 34:6, but this is not very likely, for we must remember 1. that the LXX rendering is πολυέλεος καὶ ἀληθινός, and 2. that Jn. does not bring out the idea of faithfulness which אמת has in this verse.

mined by the Revealer who is the only way of access to God (1:18; 14:6). The Paraclete promised by the departing Jesus is interpreted in 14:17; 15:26; 16:13, as the πνεῦμα τῆς ἀληθείας, [38] and there can be no doubt that this is how Jn. intends to understand the traditional concept of the πνεῦμα ἅγιον granted to the community (cf. esp. Mk. 13:11; Ac. 1:8). He himself selects the term Paraclete in 14:16. The πνεῦμα τῆς ἀληθείας does not simply mean the Spirit of God, for the sphere of God is denoted no less by ἅγιος than by ἀλήθεια (cf. 17:17-19; → 246). But when it is said of this πνεῦμα: ὁδηγήσει ὑμᾶς εἰς τὴν ἀλήθειαν πᾶσαν (16:13), this shows us that for John the divine truth is always that which works in revelation, so that the function of the παράκλητος who works as the πνεῦμα τῆς ἀληθείας is described as the revelation which continues to work in the community, and in 1 Jn. 5:6 the witnessing πνεῦμα is simply equated with the ἀλήθεια. In the same sense there is reference in 1 Jn. 4:6 to the πνεῦμα τῆς ἀληθείας in contrast to the πνεῦμα τῆς πλάνης, and the criterion for knowing whether something is of God or of anti-godly power is actual conduct, i.e., the hearing or non-hearing of the Word proclaimed in the community. Thus ἀλήθεια, in so far as it is proclaimed, can be right doctrine, and ψεῦδος error (1 Jn. 2:21), while ποιεῖν τὴν ἀλήθειαν in 1 Jn. 1:6, as the opposite of ψεύδεσθαι, characterises a way of life (→ 242), just as ἀλήθεια in 3 Jn. 3 denotes the way of life determined by revelation. Indeed, in 3 Jn. 12 the witness which one has ὑπὸ πάντων can be called the witness ὑπὸ αὐτῆς τῆς ἀληθείας, since revelation is the power which determines the community. [39] Along the same lines we might refer to 3 Jn. 8, where the community motivates its concrete Christian action by the admonition, ἵνα συνεργοὶ γινώμεθα τῇ ἀληθείᾳ. This determination unites individual believers, so that the author of 2 Jn., using an epistolary expression (→ 243), speaks of his readers thus: οὓς ἐγὼ ἀγαπῶ ἐν ἀληθείᾳ, καὶ οὐκ ἐγὼ μόνος ἀλλὰ καὶ πάντες οἱ ἐγνωκότες τὴν ἀλήθειαν, διὰ τὴν ἀλήθειαν τὴν μένουσαν ἐν ἡμῖν, καὶ μεθ' ἡμῶν ἔσται εἰς τὸν αἰῶνα, and he also greets them ἐν ἀληθείᾳ καὶ ἀγάπῃ (2 Jn. 1-3).

ἀληθής.

1. a. ἀληθής means "constant" or "valid," as in 1 Pt. 5:12: ταύτην εἶναι ἀληθῆ χάριν τοῦ θεοῦ, εἰς ἣν στῆτε (cf. Is. 43:9). As an attribute of God, ἀληθινός is more commonly used (→ 249), but ἀληθής is sometimes found (Jos. Ant., 8, 337 and 343; 10, 263: μόνον αὐτὸν εἶναι ... ἀληθῆ καὶ τὸ πάντων κράτος ἔχοντα; Sib., V, 499; Fr. 1, 10). Yet we cannot be sure that in such cases it does not have the sense discussed under 6.

---

[38] The πνεῦμα τῆς ἀληθείας of Herm. m., 3, 4 is no true parallel. The mode of conception in this phrase is animistic; ἀλήθεια signifies "truthfulness."

[39] Thus Papias seeks guidance (in Eus. Hist. Eccl., III, 39, 4) from those who hand down τὰς παρὰ τοῦ κυρίου τῇ πίστει δεδομένας καὶ ἀπ' αὐτῆς παραγινομένας τῆς ἀληθείας (ἐντολάς). On the other hand, in the formal parallel to 3 Jn. 12 which Windisch (Handbuch z. NT) finds in Demosth. z. NT, 59, 15, ἀλήθεια has only the formal sense of the actual state of affairs. Similarly in Jos. Ant., 16, 246: τὸν μὲν ὑπ' αὐτῆς τῆς ἀληθείας ἀναίτιον (proved innocent by the actual facts), and Ap., 2, 287: τοὺς ... πρὸς αὐτὴν ἀναιδῶς τὴν ἀλήθειαν πεφιλονεικηκότας, we have only formal parallels.

b. To describe the "judicial righteousness" of God, ἀληθινός is used in the NT (→ 249).

c. In the sense of "upright," ἀληθής occurs in Phil. 4:8 : ὅσα ἐστὶν ἀληθῆ, ὅσα σεμνά, ὅσα δίκαια ...

2. a. ἀληθής means "trustworthy" or "reliable" in R. 3:4 (→ 243). According to 1 Cl., 45, 2 the γραφαί are ἀληθεῖς. Cf. Neh. 7:2; Prv. 22:21.

b. In the sense of "sincere" or "honest" it is found in Mk. 12:14 : οἴδαμεν ὅτι ἀληθὴς εἶ καὶ οὐ μέλει σοι περὶ οὐδενός; 2 C. 6:8 : ὡς πλάνοι καὶ ἀληθεῖς; Jn. 3:33 : ἐσφράγισεν ὅτι ὁ θεὸς ἀληθής ἐστιν (→ infra); cf. 7:18; 8:26. See also Did., 15, 1; Pol. 1, 1 (ἀληθὴς ἀγάπη), as also Jos. Ant., 13, 191 (ὑπὸ ... γνώμης ἀληθοῦς).

3. ἀληθής means "real" in Ac. 12:9 : οὐκ ᾔδει ὅτι ἀληθές ἐστιν τὸ γενόμενον; Jn. 10:41; 1 Jn. 2:27 (as distinct from ψεῦδος); cf. Jos. Bell., 1, 254 (opp. πρόφασις). In this sense we have λέγειν ἀληθές in Jn. 4:18; 19:35; 1 Jn. 2:27; cf. Jos. Ant., 8, 404 etc. The adv. ἀληθῶς ("really") is found in Mk. 14:70; Mt. 26:73 etc. In 1 Jn. 2:8 we have πάλιν ἐντολὴν καινὴν γράφω ὑμῖν, ὅ ἐστιν ἀληθὲς ἐν αὐτῷ καὶ ἐν ὑμῖν, i.e., "which is really new," or, as the continuation shows, "which is reality, or has become real."

4. ἀληθής in indication that a statement is "true" is found in Tt. 1:13; Jn. 5:31 etc.; 3 Jn. 12 (of μαρτυρία, cf. Jos. Ant., 4, 219); 2 Pt. 2:22 (παροιμία). Cf. Da. 10:1; Herm. m., 3, 3; 11, 3 (ῥήματα); also pap. [40]

5. ἀληθής in indication of "correct doctrine" is never found in the NT.

6. ἀληθής in the sense of "genuine" or "proper" (of the divine reality) occurs in Jn. 6:55 : ἡ σάρξ μου ἀληθής (or ἀληθῶς) ἐστιν βρῶσις, where we can hardly think of it in terms of 3. This also seems to be the more obvious sense in Jn. 3:33 (→ supra under 2. b.), i.e., that the believer, by affirming the truthfulness of God, confirms that He gives revelation. Cf. also Jn. 7:18 : ὁ δὲ ζητῶν τὴν δόξαν τοῦ πέμψαντος αὐτὸν ἀληθής ἐστιν, where the point is, not merely that as One who is truthful He declares what is real, but that He Himself is genuine, that He is determined by the ἀλήθεια, and that He is therefore the Revealer. This is confirmed by what follows : καὶ ἀδικία ἐν αὐτῷ οὐκ ἔστιν, i.e., He belongs to the sphere of God. Again, Jn. 8:26 : ὁ πέμψας με ἀληθής ἐστιν, does not mean only that He is truthful, but also that He (alone) is the One who is real and who brings revelation, as is shown by the par. in 7:28 : ἀλλ᾽ ἔστιν ἀληθινὸς ὁ πέμψας με (→ 249; 250). If in 8:13 ἀληθής (with μαρτυρία) has the customary sense (→ supra under 4.), in v. 14 it immediately assumes on the lips of Jesus the further sense that My witness is revelation. This is plainly shown by the otherwise inexplicable argument.

That we have here a distinctive Johannine modification of Hellenistic usage may be seen from parallels such as Philo Leg. All., II, 93 : ἵνα ... ζήσῃ τὸν ἀληθῆ βίον; Leg. Gaj., 347: εἰς τὸν ὄντως ὄντα ἀληθῆ θεόν. [41] Cf. also Mart. Ptr., 8, p. 92, 10 ff.:

[40] Cf. Preisigke Wört. s.v.
[41] On Jos. Ant., 8, 337; Sib., V, 499; Fr., 1, 10 → 247.

παντὸς αἰσθητηρίου χωρίσατε τὰς ἑαυτῶν ψυχάς, παντὸς φαινομένου μὴ ὄντος ἀληθοῦς; Corp. Herm., XIII, 6: the ἀληθές is the ἀσώματον; Stob. Ecl., I, 275, 18: οὐδὲν ἐν σώματι ἀληθές, ἐν ἀσωμάτῳ τὸ πᾶν ἀψευδές.

ἀληθινός.

1. ἀληθινός is often used in the same sense as ἀληθής, sometimes with the meaning of "sincere," as in Hb. 10:22: μετὰ ἀληθινῆς καρδίας, or "upright," as in Herm. v., 3, 7, 1: τὴν ὁδὸν αὐτῶν τὴν ἀληθινήν. In respect of words ἀληθινός first means "true" or "correct," as in Jn. 4:37 (λόγος), [42] 19:35 (μαρτυρία); cf. Da. 10:1 (λόγος). This is how we are first to take it in Jn. 8:16: ἡ κρίσις (the verdict) ἡ ἐμὴ ἀληθινή (or ἀληθής) ἐστιν; in v. 17 ἀληθής is used instead, as in Soph. Oed. Tyr., 501: κρίσις οὐκ ἔστιν ἀληθής "this is not a correct verdict." On the other hand, when the λόγοι of revelation are called πιστοὶ καὶ ἀληθινοί in Rev. 21:5; 22:6, we have a hendiadys: "sure and certain." Rev. 19:9 might perhaps be taken in the same way: οὗτοι οἱ λόγοι ἀληθινοί [τοῦ θεοῦ?] εἰσιν, but it is better to translate: "These words are the real words of God." In Rev. 15:3; 16:7; 19:2, where God's ὁδοί (His rule) and κρίσεις are called ἀληθιναί and δίκαιαι, ἀληθινός is wholly controlled by אֱמֶת in the sense of God's valid demand or righteousness; cf. ψ 18:9; Tob. 3:2, 5; Da. 3:27 (Θ), where ἀληθινός occurs as an attribute of κρίσεις or κρίματα (for Rabbinic par., → ἀλήθεια, 237).

2. As an attribute of God, ἀληθινός is again controlled by אֱמֶת in the Judaeo-Christian sphere, Ex. 34:6; 2 Ch. 15:3; ψ 85:15; M. Pol., 14, 2: ὁ ἀψευδὴς καὶ ἀληθινὸς θεός (Herm. m., 3, 1 as an attribute of κύριος), where the meaning hovers between "trustworthy," "truthful" and "righteous"; cf. alongside one another, 1 Εσδρ. 8:86: κύριε ... ἀληθινὸς εἶ, and 2 Εσρ. 9:15: κύριε ... δίκαιος σύ; cf. Jos. Ant., 11, 55: God as ἀληθινός and δίκαιος. As against this, ἀληθινός is also used of God in the sense of "real" or "true" in contrast to the vanity of idols. This usage, too, is determined by אֱמֶת; thus Is. 65:16 (for בֵּאלֹהֵי אמן); 3 Macc. 6:18; Philo Spec. Leg., I, 332 (ἀγνοοῦντες τὸν ἕνα καὶ ἀληθινὸν θεὸν πολλοὺς ψευδωνύμους ἀναπλάττοντες); Leg. Gaj., 366 (the same antithesis); Sib. Fr., 1, 20; 3, 46; and cf. also 1 Th. 1:9: πῶς ἐπεστρέψατε πρὸς τὸν θεὸν ἀπὸ τῶν εἰδώλων δουλεύειν θεῷ ζῶντι καὶ ἀληθινῷ; 1 Cl., 43, 6: εἰς τὸ δοξασθῆναι τὸ ὄνομα τοῦ ἀληθινοῦ καὶ μόνου θεοῦ. In Rev. the word ἀληθινός is sometimes used of God (6:10), sometimes of Christ (3:7, 14; 19:11). The same usage is found in Jn. 7:28; 17:3; 1 Jn. 5:20, as also in Christian pap. [43] But the Gk. sense of genuine might give rise to the same usage, as when the Athenians greet Demetrius Poliorketes: ὡς εἴη μόνος θεὸς ἀληθινός, οἱ δ' ἄλλοι καθεύδουσιν ἢ ἀποδημοῦσιν ἢ οὐκ εἰσίν (Athen., VI, 62, cf. 63, p. 253c, e). At this point the Semitic usage approximates very closely to the Gk. use of ἀληθινός. The use of אֱמֶת obviously underlies Lk. 16:11: εἰ οὖν ἐν τῷ ἀδίκῳ μαμωνᾷ (═ הַשֶּׁקֶר בְּמָמוֹן) πιστοὶ οὐκ ἐγένεσθε, τὸ ἀληθινὸν (אֵת הָאֲמִתִּי) [44] τίς ὑμῖν πιστεύσει (cf. Philo Fug., 17; Praem.

---

[42] The classical par. to Jn. 4:37 have ἀληθής: Soph. Ai., 664: ἀλλ' ἔστ' ἀληθὴς ἡ βροτῶν παροιμία; Plat. Leg., VI, 757a: παλαιὸς γὰρ λόγος ἀληθὴς ὤν.

[43] Cf. Preisigke Wört. s.v.

[44] So F. Delitzsch, Hbr. NT, ad loc.

Poen., 104). In the case of the προφήτης and διδάσκαλος in Did., 11, 11 we see the same influence, though we are almost tempted to give the rendering "genuine." Orig. correctly finds the Gk. sense of ἀληθινός in Joh. II, 6, 48 : πρὸς ἀντιδιαστολὴν σκιᾶς καὶ τύπου καὶ εἰκόνος; cf. P. Oxy., 465, 108 : ἄγαλμα κυάνου ἀληθινοῦ ("an image of real lapis lazuli"). In this sense the LXX has ἀληθινὴ ἄμπελος in Jer. 2:21.

3. Yet in Hellenism ἀληθινός no longer means genuine in the general sense. In relation to divine things it has the sense of that which truly is, or of that which is eternal, and in relation to human conduct or being it signifies their more than earthly character as mediated by revelation or contact with the divine.

> Cf. Philo Leg. All., I, 32 f.: ὁ δὲ νοῦς οὗτος γεώδης ἐστὶ τῷ ὄντι καὶ φθαρτός, εἰ μὴ ὁ θεὸς ἐμπνεύσειεν αὐτῷ δύναμιν ἀληθινῆς ζωῆς· τότε γὰρ γίνεται ... εἰς νοερὰν καὶ ζῶσαν ὄντως (ψυχήν); for God has honoured the νοῦς of the θεῖον πνεῦμα. Vit. Mos., I, 289 : φησὶν ὁ ἄνθρωπος ὁ ἀληθινῶς ὁρῶν, ὅστις καθ᾽ ὕπνον ἐναργῆ φαντασίαν εἶδε θεοῦ τοῖς τῆς ψυχῆς ἀκοιμήτοις ὄμμασιν. In the same sense Plotin. Enn., VI, 9, 9 (II, 522, 7, Volkm.) speaks of the ἀληθινὴ ζωή, and Corp. Herm., I, 30 of the ἀληθινὴ ὅρασις. Similarly, in Corp. Herm., XIII, 2 regeneration is described as ἀληθινὸν ἀγαθόν. So, too, in magic ἀληθινός means genuine in the sense of magically potent : Preis. Zaub., VII (London), Col. XIX, 634 ff.: πέμψον μοι τὸν ἀληθινὸν Ἀσκλήπιον δίχα τινὸς ἀντιθέου πλανοδαίμονος, VIII (London), 20 and 46 : οἶδά σου καὶ τὰ βαρβαρικὰ ὀνόματα ... τὸ δὲ ἀληθινὸν ὄνομά σου.

This usage is found in Hb. 8:2, where the tabernacle in heaven is described as ἀληθινὴ σκηνή in contrast to the earthly, and also in Hb. 9:24, where the earthly cultic ordinances are called ἀντίτυπα τῶν ἀληθινῶν. [45] In Act. Thom., 88, p. 203, 15 the heavenly marriage is called the ἀληθινὴ κοινωνία. [46] In a characteristic development of this usage, the Johannine use of ἀληθινός again introduces a distinctive ambiguity. If the formal sense of genuine is to be seen in Jn. 4:23 (οἱ ἀληθινοὶ προσκυνηταί), it is with reference to the fact that such true worshippers are determined by revelation. In the images in which Jesus is described as the φῶς ἀληθινόν (1:9) and the ἄμπελος ἀληθινή (15:1), ἀληθινός has in the first instance the sense of "true" or "genuine," but genuine here means "divine" in contrast to human and earthly reality, and it also implies "containing" ἀλήθεια and therefore "dispensing revelation." The φῶς ἀληθινόν of Jn. 1:9; 1 Jn. 2:8, is the same as the φῶς τῆς ζωῆς of Jn. 8:12; and the ἄμπελος ἀληθινή is materially the same as the ἄρτος τῆς ζωῆς of Jn. 6:35, 48, with which we should also compare Jn. 6:32 : τὸν ἄρτον ἐκ τοῦ οὐρανοῦ τὸν ἀληθινόν. If in Jn. 7:28; 17:3, God is called ἀληθινός, in addition to the usual sense (→ 248, under 6.) this implies that He is the One who effects revelation. And when the κρίσις of Jesus is called ἀληθινή (Jn. 8:16), this does not mean only "true" or "trustworthy," but "proper" and "definitive." That is, the judgment of the event of revelation itself is fulfilled in it.

---

[45] The description of the earthly as σκία in distinction from ἀληθινόν (Hb. 8:5; 10:1) is also found in Philo (Dibelius on Col. 2:17; Windisch on Hb. 8:5; 10:1 in his Handbuch z. NT), and in Plotinus (Enn., I, 6, 8 [I, 94, 24 ff., Volkm.]).
[46] Cf. 12, p. 118, 7 f.: τὸν γάμον τὸν ἄφθαρτον καὶ ἀληθινόν.

† **ἀληθεύω.**

In Gl. 4:16 : ὥστε ἐχθρὸς ὑμῶν γέγονα ἀληθεύων ὑμῖν, this has perhaps the original Gk. sense of "speaking the truth," which is frequently found in Jos. (e.g., Vit., 132 and 338), cf. also Gn. 42:16; Cl. Al. Strom., VII, 9, 53, 1 (opp. ψεύδεσθαι). Yet it is more likely that it means "to preach the truth," i.e., the Gospel (→ 244). On the other hand, ἀληθεύειν ἐν ἀγάπῃ in Eph. 4:15 means "to be sincere in love," unless it means "to live by true faith in love." [47]

Bultmann

> **ἀλλάσσω, ἀντάλλαγμα, ἀπ-, δι-,**
> **καταλλάσσω, καταλλαγή,**
> **ἀποκατ-, μεταλλάσσω**

---

† **ἀλλάσσω.**

The basic meaning is "to make otherwise" (from → ἄλλος). Outside the NT we find both act. and med. in the trans. signif. of "to alter," "to give in exchange," or "to take in exchange," as also in the intrans. signif. of "to change." [1] In the NT we find only the trans. act. and pass., not med.

1. In the sense of "to alter or change" [2] it occurs at Ac. 6:14 : (Jesus) ἀλλάξει τὰ ἔθη ἃ παρέδωκεν ἡμῖν Μωϋσῆς; and also at Gl. 4:20, where Paul wishes that he could ἀλλάξαι τὴν φωνήν μου; his passionate complaint is about the manner, not the substance, of his speech. It also means "to change" at 1 C. 15:51 f., and we might refer to the eschatological ἀλλαγησόμεθα of Hb. 1:12.

2. In the sense of "to exchange" [3] we find it at R. 1:23 : ἤλλαξαν τὴν δόξαν τοῦ ἀφθάρτου θεοῦ ἐν ὁμοιώματι εἰκόνος φθαρτοῦ ἀνθρώπου, where there is allusion to ψ 105:20 : ἠλλάξαντο τὴν δόξαν αὐτῶν ἐν ὁμοιώματι μόσχου, and

---

[47] Dib., *ad loc.*: *Die Wahrheit treiben in Liebe.*
ἀ λ λ ά σ σ ω. Pass.-Cr., *s.v.*; Zn. R. (1910), 94 f.; Str.-B., III, 47 f.
[1] Cf. Pass.-Cr., 286 f.
[2] Also in Jos. Bell., 2, 113 etc. : τὴν χώραν ἀλλάσσειν, in ploughing.
[3] P. Oxy., 729, 43 : ἀλλάσσειν κτήνη ἢ πωλεῖν.

Jer. 2:11: ὁ δὲ λαός μου ἠλλάξατο τὴν δόξαν αὐτοῦ. [4] The construction with ἐν [5] in both the LXX and the NT derives from the Hebrew : הֵמִיר בְּ.

† ἀντάλλαγμα.

Like the simple ἄλλαγμα (from → ἀλλάσσειν in the sense of "to exchange"), this means "purchase-money," or abstr. "equivalent" or "substitute." Eur. Or., 1157: ἀλόγιστον δέ τι τὸ πλῆθος ἀντάλλαγμα γενναίου φίλου. Jos. Bell., 1, 355 = Ant., 14, 484 : καὶ ὡς ἐπὶ τοσούτων πολιτῶν φόνῳ βραχὺ καὶ τὴν τῆς οἰκουμένης ἡγεμονίαν ἀντάλλαγμα κρίνοι. The LXX generally uses it to translate מְחִיר ("purchase-price"), as in 3 Βασ. 20:2; Job 28:15; Jer. 15:13; cf. also Sir. 6:15 : φίλου πιστοῦ οὐκ ἔστιν ἀντάλλαγμα; 26:14 : οὐκ ἔστιν ἀντάλλαγμα πεπαιδευμένης ψυχῆς. It is also used for כֹּפֶר ("bribe") in Am. 5:12; for חֲלִיפוֹת (meaning uncertain) in ψ 54:19; for תַּחֲלִיף ("substitute") in Heb. Sir. 44:17; and for תְּמוּרָה ("exchange") in Ju. 4:7.

In the NT ἀντάλλαγμα is found only in Mk. 8:37 = Mt. 16:26 : τί γὰρ δοῖ ἄνθρωπος ἀντάλλαγμα τῆς ψυχῆς αὐτοῦ. The saying is drawn from Ps. 49:7, and expresses the infinite seriousness of the divine judgment which takes from man his life and therefore absolutely everything, so that any exchange is impossible. It does not treat of the infinite worth of the human soul as such, and certainly not of the soul in distinction from the body. [1] But it makes ridiculous the avaricious desire of man for possession and enjoyment. [2]

† ἀπαλλάσσω.

The basic meaning (→ ἀλλάσσω) is "to alter by removal," "to do away." Outside the OT and NT there is a varied and developed usage : in the act. a. trans. "to dismiss" or "liberate," b. intrans. "to absent oneself" or "retire"; in the med. "to withdraw," "to retire." [1] In the LXX ἀπαλλάσσω is used for הֵסִיר, "to remove" (Job 9:34; 27:5; 34:5; Ιερ. 39:31; for הִסְתִּיר "to conceal" (Job 3:10); for חָתַף, "to carry or sweep away" (Job 9:12); and also in a looser or mistaken rendering for various other words in Ex. 19:22; 1 Βασ. 14:29; Is. 10:7; Job 7:15; 10:19.

In the NT it occurs 1. in the trans. act. in the sense of "to liberate" in Hb. 2:15, according to common usage. [2]

---

[4] On the Rabbinic exposition and amendment of the text of both passages, cf. Str.-B., III, 47-48.

[5] Outside the LXX and NT we find only the dat., gen. or πρός, cf. Pass.-Cr., 286 f. ἀ ν τ ά λ λ α γ μ α. Zn. Mt.², 557, n. 87; Str.-B., I, 750 f.

[1] The Lucan par. has ἑαυτόν for ψυχήν.

[2] Cf. on this whole subject S. Dt., 329 on 32:39 (perhaps drawing on Ps. 49:7, like Mt. 16:26): "The soul is of great value, for if a man sins against it there is no payment for it" (אֵין לָהּ תַּשְׁלוּמִים).

ἀ π α λ λ ά σ σ ω. Pape, Pass., Preisigke Wört., s.v.; Rgg. Hb., 56, n. 44.

[1] Numerous examples are given by Pape and Pass.

[2] Cf. Wis. 12:2 : ἀπαλλαγέντες τῆς κακίας (the divine chastisement), cf. v. 20; Jos. Ant., 3, 83 : ἀπαλλάσσει (Moses) τοῦ δέους αὐτούς (the Israelites); 11, 270 : ἀπαλλάξαι τοῦ περὶ τῆς ζωῆς φόβου τὸ τῶν Ἰουδαίων ἔθνος; 13, 363 : τῆς ὑπὸ τοῖς ἐχθροῖς αὐτὰ δουλείας οὕτως ἀπαλλάττειν ἠναγκασμένοι; Isoc., 14, 18 : δουλείας ἀπηλλάγησαν; Phil. Spec. Leg., I, 77: δουλείας ἀπαλλαγήν.

It is also found 2. in the med. in the sense of "to withdraw" in Ac. 19:12 : ἀπαλλάσσεσθαι τὰς νόσους ἀπ᾽ αὐτῶν,[3] or "to escape" in Lk. 12:58 : δὸς ἐργασίαν ἀπηλλάχθαι ἀπ᾽ αὐτοῦ.

ἀπηλλάχθαι here is not perf. pass. but med., and therefore means "to break free" rather than "to be freed." Cf. P. Oxy., 889, 26, 31 (3rd century B.C.): ἀξιοῖ ἀπηλλάχθαι, "he proposed to break away, to be free." The perf. used here, as in Lk. 12:58, is stronger than the aor. or pres. Jos. Ant., 6, 198 also has the med. in the sense of "to escape" or "to become free": ἀπαλλαγήσομαι (Saul) (ἀπ᾽) αὐτοῦ (David) δι᾽ ἄλλων αὐτόν, ἀλλ᾽ οὐχὶ δι᾽ ἐμαυτοῦ κτείνας. In relation to marriage the med. is used as a technical term for the withdrawal of the wife from her husband on the occasion of divorce.[4] In this case ἀπαλλάσσομαι signifies the breach of a two-sided relationship. This may be one-sided but it has consequences for both parties (→ καταλλάσσω, 254).

† διαλλάσσω.

The usage varies so much that we cannot trace it back to a single basic meaning. a. It signifes "to alter or exchange" (like ἀλλάττω) in the act. and med. b. It means "to distinguish oneself" or "surpass," sometimes with the acc. of person.[1] c. It means "to reconcile" in the trans. act. and pass. and the intrans. med. Cf. Xenoph. Oec., XI, 23 : ... διαλλάττω τινὰς τῶν ἐπιτηδείων, πειρώμενος διδάσκειν, ὡς συμφέρει αὐτοῖς φίλους εἶναι μᾶλλον ἢ πολεμίους; Hist. Graec., I, 6, 7: διαλλάξειν Ἀθηναίους καὶ Λακεδαιμονίους; Jos. Bell., 1, 320 : τὸν βασιλέα πολλὰ δεηθεὶς ἑαυτῷ διαλλάττει etc.; Eur. Hel., 1235 : διαλλάχθητί μοι; Thuc., VIII, 70, 2 : ἐπεκηρυκεύοντο λέγοντες διαλλαγῆναι βούλεσθαι. P. Giess., 17, 13 (2nd century A.D.): διαλλάγηθι ὑμῖν; Jos. Ant., 16, 125 : Ἡρώδην δὲ παρεκάλει (the emperor) πᾶσαν ὑπόνοιαν ἐκβαλόντα διαλλάττεσθαι τοῖς παισίν; Ant., 7, 295 etc. On the reconciliation of God with man, cf. Ant., 7, 153 : ᾤκτειρεν ὁ θεὸς καὶ διαλλάττεται. Jos. refers in Bell., 5, 415 to τὸ θεῖον εὐδιάλλακτον ἐξομολογουμένοις καὶ μετανοοῦσιν. A distinction between διαλλάττειν and καταλλάττειν cannot be demonstrated. At the time of early Christianity καταλλάττειν had become the more common word.

In the LXX διαλλάσσω is used at Job 12:20, 24 for הֵסִיר "to remove"; at Job 5:12 for הֵפֵר, "to destroy"; at Ju. 19:3 (A): διαλλάξαι αὐτὴν ἑαυτῷ, for הֵשִׁיב, "to lead back"; at 1 Βασ. 29:4 we have διαλλαγήσεται for יִתְרַצֶּה, "to make oneself pleasing"; at 1 Εσδ. 4:31: ὅπως διαλλαγῇ αὐτῷ.

In the NT it occurs only at Mt. 5:24 : διαλλάγηθι τῷ ἀδελφῷ σου. Here διαλλαγῆναι means "to reconcile" in the sense of seeing to it that the angry brother, who neither seeks nor envisages reconciliation (v. 23), renounces his enmity. On the other hand, in BGU, 846, 10,[2] the letter of an errant son to his angry mother, the διαλλάγητί μοι denotes the action of the mother renouncing

---

[3] Cf. Ps.-Plat. Eryx., 401c : εἰ αἱ νόσοι ἀπηλλαγείησαν ἐκ τῶν σωμάτων. Jos., too, has the med. in the sense of "withdrawing" (Vit., 131: ἀπαλλαγέντων ... αὐτῶν) and ἀπαλλαγή in the sense of "going away" (Vit., 206 : περὶ τῆς ἀπαλλαγῆς; Ap., 1, 104 : τὴν ἐκεῖθεν ἀπαλλαγήν), and even of "dying" (Ant., 2, 150 : ἡ ἐκ τοῦ ζῆν ἀπαλλαγή).

[4] Mitteis-Wilcken, II, 2, 284, 12; P. Tebt., 104, 31; P. Oxy., 104, 26 f. In the latter it is the opp. of καταλλαγῆναι. Cf. Preisigke Wört. under ἀπαλλάσσω, 11.
δ ι α λ λ ά σ σ ω. Zn. on Mt. 5:24.
[1] There are many examples in Pape and Pass.
[2] Cf. Deissmann LO, 154 f., esp. 155, n. 13.

her anger against the son who seeks reconciliation. διαλλαγῆναι is thus a two-sided process in which the hostility is overcome on both sides.

† καταλλάσσω (→ δι-, ἀποκαταλλάσσω, καταλλαγή).

It is no more possible to find a basic meaning than in the case of διαλλάσσω. Yet the thought of change predominates. It means a. "to change" as reflex. act. : Ιερ. 31:39 : πῶς κατήλλαξεν; πῶς ἔστρεψεν νῶτον Μωάβ; b. "to exchange" as trans. act. and mid.: Plat. Phaed., 69a : φόβον πρὸς φόβον καταλλάττεσθαι; Herod., II, 13, 12 : ἐπ' ἀργυρίῳ κατηλλάξασθε; c. "to reconcile" as trans. act.; Aristot. Oec., II, 15, p. 1348b, 9 : κατήλλαξεν αὐτοὺς πρὸς ἀλλήλους; "to reconcile oneself" as intrans. mid. (with pass. aor. κατηλλάγην); Xenoph. An., I, 6, 2 : καταλλαγεὶς τῷ Κύρῳ; Jos. Ant., 7, 184 : τῷ σεαυτοῦ παιδὶ πρῶτον καταλλάγηθι, 11, 195 : καταλλαγῆναι αὐτῇ ... οὐκ ἐδύνατο, also with πρός, 5, 137: καταλλάττεται πρὸς αὐτήν. In the LXX καταλλάσσω is rare, occurring only in Ιερ. 31:39 (supra) and 2 Macc. 1:5; 7:33; 8:29 (infra).

A. The Religious Use of καταλλάσσω outside the NT.

καταλλάττειν and καταλλάττεσθαι play no essential part in even the expiatory rites (→ ἱλάσκομαι) of Greek and Hellenistic pagan religion, though they are used in a religious sense in e.g., Soph. Ai., 744 : θεοῖσιν ὡς καταλλαχθῇ χολῶν. The relation between divinity and humanity does not have this personal nearness. [1]

In Greek speaking Judaism καταλλάσσεσθαι occurs, but infrequently. If, as a result of the prayers or confession or conversion of men, God renounces His wrath and is gracious again, this is called a καταλλαγῆναι of God. Thus in 2 Macc. 1:5 : He might hear your requests and be reconciled to you (καταλλαγείη ὑμῖν); or in 7:33 : if He has been wroth for a time, He will again be reconciled to His servants (καταλλαγήσεται), cf. 8:28. In Jos. καταλλάττεσθαι is similarly used of God in Ant., 6, 143 : (Samuel) παρακαλεῖν ἤρξατο τὸν θεὸν καταλλάττεσθαι τῷ Σαούλῳ καὶ μὴ χαλεπαίνειν. ὁ δὲ τὴν συγγνώμην οὐκ ἐπένευσεν. Elsewhere Jos. uses διαλλάττεσθαι of God.

In the language of the Rabbis καταλλάσσειν corresponds to רָצָה and פֵּיֵּס. רָצָה, Aram. רְצִי, means "to make benevolent or well-disposed," "to placate"; הִתְרַצָּה : "to reconcile oneself," "to be reconciled or appeased"; אֲרְצִי Aram. "to be kindly disposed or reconciled." פֵּיֵּס, Aram. פַּיֵּיס, means "to appease" or "reconcile"; הִתְפַּיֵּיס, Aram., אִתְפַּיֵּיס "to let oneself be, or to be, reconciled." [2] These words refer to the relations between men, and between God and men. God is subject to the reconciling action of men in prayer, sacrifice, etc. (supra).

κ α τ α λ λ ά σ σ ω. A. Ritschl, *Rechtfertigung u. Versöhnung*, II⁴ (1900), 231 ff. NT theologies of P. Feine⁵ (1931), 234 ff., A. Schlatter, II (1910), 283 ff., H. Weinel⁴ (1928), 238 ff., J. Kaftan (1927), 122 f., Cr.-Kö., 129-133. Comm. on 2 C : Bchm., 252-274; Ltzm., 124 ff., Wnd., 191-199; on Romans : Zn., 257 ff., Ltzm., 57, Sickbg., 213; Str.-B., III, 519 f. On the concept of atonement in the OT → ἵλεως, κτλ.

[1] Not once do we find either δι-, or καταλλάττειν in the inscriptions collected by F. Steinleitner in *Die Beicht im Zshg. mit der sakralen Rechtspflege in der Antike* (1913), though there is reference to the chastisement of God and His becoming gracious again.

[2] Str.-B., III, 519, cf. II, 365.

B. καταλλάσσω in the NT.

1. Husband and Wife.

As in Gk. marriage records ἀπαλλάσσεσθαι is a technical term for the separation of married couples, so καταλλάσσεσθαι is used for their "reconciliation" in P. Oxy., 104, 27: ἐὰν ἀπαλλαγῇ τοῦ ἀνδρὸς ... καταλλαγῇ. As in 1 C. 7:11 καταλλαγῆναι is here an action on the part of the wife separated from her husband, and not merely something which happens to her, just as in Mt. 5:24 and BGU, 846, 10 διαλλαγῆναι (253) is something which is done by, and not merely something which happens to, those who are estranged. There is no reason to suppose that in 1 C. 7:11 the wife has left her husband more or less in a spirit of ill-will.

2. God and Man.

a. In the NT it is only Paul who uses the word of the relation between God and man, and καταλλάσσειν is used only of God, καταλλαγῆναι only of man. God reconciles us or the world to Himself in 2 C. 5:18 f. He is not reconciled. Nor does He reconcile Himself to us or to the world. On the other hand, we are reconciled to God in R. 5:10, or reconcile ourselves to Him in 2 C. 5:20. Thus God and man are not on equal terms in relation to reconciliation. Reconciliation is not reciprocal in the sense that both equally become friends where they were enemies. The supremacy of God over man is maintained in every respect.

καταλλάσσειν denotes a transformation or renewal of the state between God and man, and therewith of man's own state. In 2 C. 5:18 it is introduced as the basis of the most comprehensive renewal possible for man, namely, that he has become a new creature, that old things have passed away and that all things have become new. In R. 5:10, too, it denotes an incisive change. We are no longer ἐχθροί, ἀσεβεῖς, ἀσθενεῖς (v. 6), ἁμαρτωλοί (v. 8), but the love of God is shed abroad in our hearts (v. 5). There is a change, not merely in the disposition of man or his legal relationship to God, but in the total state of his life. On the other hand, it cannot be maintained that there has been any change of mind on the part of God, since His gracious will had been revealed long before in the OT.

b. We are reconciled by the death of Jesus (R. 5:10). As He was made sin for us, we were made the righteousness of God in Him (2 C. 5:21). To this extent reconciliation is parallel to justification (cf. also R. 5:10 in relation to 5:9). This is why λογίζεσθαι, which is vital to Paul's view of justification (R. 4:3, 4, 5, 6, 8, 9, 10, 11, 23, 24) occurs again in 2 C. 5:19: μὴ λογιζόμενος αὐτοῖς τὰ παραπτώματα αὐτῶν. Yet there can be no question that in reconciliation more takes place than a mere removal of the relationship of guilt. God has sent to men His messengers through whom He addresses men and who beseech them for Christ's sake: "Be ye reconciled to God" (2 C. 5:20). Through the revelation of the superabounding love of God which did not find the sacrifice of the Son too great, and which does not regard it as too humiliating to plead with men, we are renewed in the total state of our life. The love of Christ controls us, according to 2 C. 5:14. We no longer live for ourselves, but for the One who died for us and was raised again (v. 15). We judge that we have died like all others and are new creatures. By reconciliation our sinful self-seeking is overcome and the fellowship with God is created in which it is replaced by living for Christ. These are for Paul present realities which are revealed to the conscience and which can be adduced in answer to opponents (2 C. 5:11-15). They cannot be asserted in respect of a psychology abstracted from the conscience. But the fact that Paul speaks of the conscience, and makes this the basis of his self-vindication (v. 11, 12), shows that perception of these realities is more than a mere projection of faith on an object which in reality is not led to love by the love of God. If the new reality is both basically and continuously brought about by God's action towards man, and if man himself never ceases to be a sinner and carnal, nevertheless man is no mere point of transition of the divine activity. He is a person who is visited by the love of God and who is thus awakened to love.

This is particularly clear in R. 5:5. In us (the reconciled), the love of God has become a present and active reality, whereas previously we lived apart from it, and simply of ourselves. This has taken place through the Holy Spirit, who is given to us men who still live in the flesh. Thus both the old and the new are to be found in man, both his own heart and the Holy Spirit; yet considered in totality he has become new through the Spirit, and he is enabled to walk in the Spirit (R. 8:4).

It is often asked whether men are active or passive in reconciliation. The true answer is that they are made active. By the διακονία τῆς καταλλαγῆς, which conveys to them the loving act of God, God Himself makes them active, giving them both the right and the power to reconcile themselves to God. It is true that κατηλλάγημεν and καταλλαγέντες are undoubtedly to be taken in the pass., and not the mid., in R. 5:10. This is demanded by the parallel to the pass. δικαιω-θέντες in v. 9, as also by the context, which speaks of the work of the Spirit towards us, and not of our action. We have received reconciliation, yet not as blows are received, but in such a way that God has besought us (2 Cor. 5:20). The activity of a man cannot be conceived of in any higher way than in terms of causing him to ask for the acceptance of a gift. The fact that Paul speaks of the word of reconciliation as a request excludes any possibility of regarding man as merely passive in reconciliation. In reconciliation, too, man is a person. It is only because he is a person, and consequently an active being, that there can be any reconciliation for him at all. The analogy between the καταλλάγητε of 2 C. 5:20 and the καταλλαγήτω of 1 Cor. 7:11 also excludes any mere passivity of man in reconciliation. καταλλαγῆναι could not be enjoined on the wife if she were purely passive in relation to it. Even if she is not to attempt reconciliation, she must at least agree to the attempt of the husband. If she were purely passive, there could be no new fellowship, and therefore no reconciliation between herself and the husband.

c. Paul always speak of reconciliation in the form of a personal confession, namely, that "we" are reconciled (R. 5:9, 10; 2 C. 5:18). He refers to the reconciliation of the world only in 2 C. 5:19-20, and even here the world is not opposed to the "we," but represents precisely the same thing in its widest possible range. We and the world are the same in kind, because, apart from reconciliation, we, too, are simply weak and sinful and ungodly, and reconciliation is ordained for all without restriction. So long as reconciliation is thought to be engaged in an ongoing progress, it is the reconciliation of the world. This is how Paul conceives of it in 2 C. 5:19-20. For he could hardly think of his own work as διακονία τῆς καταλλαγῆς, nor of the content of his message as: "Be ye reconciled," if he believed that reconciliation was concluded in the death and resurrection of Jesus in such a way that what followed no longer formed any part of it. Since the διακονία τῆς καταλλαγῆς has not yet come to an end, and the world has not yet heard the λόγος τῆς καταλλαγῆς in all its members, reconciliation itself must not be thought of as concluded. Obviously there can be no question of any continuation or repetition of that which underlies reconciliation, i.e., the death and resurrection of Jesus. But the ministry of the divine messengers through whose work there is accomplished the renewal of the individuals who constitute the world, is the ongoing execution of reconciliation. "Our" reconciliation is concluded, and Paul can speak of it in the aorist (R. 5:9, 10 [11]; 2 C. 5:18). But this is not so with the reconciliation of the world. The phrase ἦν καταλλάσσων in 2 C. 5:19 does not denote a concluded work : "He was present to reconcile the world to Himself"; when and where this work will be concluded is not brought under consideration in 2 C. 5:19-20. For this reason we should not draw from the fact that Paul thinks of the world as the object of reconciliation the deduction that reconciliation for him consists exclusively in the removal of the relationship of guilt between man and God, since the world as a whole is not a new creation etc. This would amount to saying that what Paul explicitly calls the ministry of reconciliation and the self-reconciliation of man forms no part of reconciliation. Paul does not say that the world is reconciled (καταλλαγείς). The reconciliation of the world is as little finished as the ἀποβολή of the Jews. Both have been begun in the cross of Christ, and both are in course of fulfilment (→ 258). We can call the world reconciled in the Pauline sense only as we anticipate the execution of that which is present in the purpose of God and in the foundation. [3]

d. The state of hostility which precedes reconciliation is not mentioned at all in 2 C. 5, and it is only alluded to in R. 5. But there is no reason to understand the ἐχθροί of v. 10 unilaterally, to limit it to man's enmity against God. For in R. 1:18-32 Paul speaks quite plainly of the wrath of God as a present and manifest reality, though His patience is also manifest and operative (2:2, 5; 3:26). Indeed, in R. 11:28 the δι' ὑμᾶς and the parallel ἀγαπητοί show us that ἐχθροί is to be taken passively, i.e., "standing under the wrath of God." Paul never ascribes to man any lack of harmony or trust in relation to God. If something of the sort may perhaps be deduced from the analogy of 2 C. 5:10 to 1 C. 7:11, this is only secondary. In R. 8:7 the essential expression of hostility to God is disobedience, which in 2 C. 5:15 is called living to oneself. The essential features of man's state prior to reconciliation are his entanglement in a self-seeking which cannot fulfil the divine command of love (R. 8:7c) and his consequent standing under the divine displeasure (R. 8:8), wrath and judgment.

Reconciliation comes about through the death of Jesus (R. 5:10), which is obviously not merely something which takes place to our advantage, nor simply the revelation of the love of God (R. 5:8), but representative substitution for us (2 C. 5:20, 14 f.; → ὑπέρ, ἐξαγοράζω, ἱλαστήριον). The God who reconciles us to Himself is always at the same time the God who judges us. For this reason reconciliation includes justification both in 2 C. 5:21: ἵνα ἡμεῖς γενώμεθα δικαιο-

---

[3] θέμενος in 2 C. 5:19 is not to be subordinated to ἦν ... καταλλάσσων, along with μὴ λογιζόμενος τὰ παραπτώματα αὐτῶν. The change in tense is in itself an argument against this. Grammatically, it is a continuation of the finite verb by a part.; cf. Bl.-Debr. § 468, 1. Materially, the θέμενος ἐν ἡμῖν τὸν λόγον τῆς καταλλαγῆς denotes another part of reconciliation, since the word is called ὁ λόγος τῆς καταλλαγῆς.

σύνη θεοῦ ἐν αὐτῷ, and in v. 19: μὴ λογιζόμενος αὐτοῖς τὰ παραπτώματα αὐτῶν. Yet as the kindling of love it embraces more than the removal of guilt in forgiveness. If δικαιωθέντες and καταλλαγέντες are parallel in R. 5:9, 10 (cf. the repeated πολλῷ μᾶλλον ... σωθησόμεθα), this does not constitute any reason to reduce καταλλαγῆναι to δικαιωθῆναι. For to καταλλαγῆναι there belongs the kindling of love which does not lie in δικαιωθῆναι. It is in keeping with this that, although Paul brings faith into the closest connection with justification, he does not mention it in relation to reconciliation in either R. 5 or 2 C. 5, just as he does not derive love from justification.

† καταλλαγή.

The meaning of καταλλαγή corresponds to that of → καταλλάσσειν, i.e., "exchange," and then "reconciliation." [1] In the canonical books the LXX uses it only in Is. 9:5 (4), where there is deviation from the Mas. and the sense is obscure: ὅτι πᾶσαν στολὴν ἐπισυνηγμένην δόλῳ καὶ ἱμάτιον μετὰ καταλλαγῆς ἀποτείσουσιν. [2] The meaning "reconciliation" can be illustrated from non-biblical Gk.: Demosth. Or., 1, 4: πρὸς δὴ τὰς καταλλαγάς, ἃς ἂν ἐκεῖνος ποιήσαιτο ἄσμενος πρὸς 'Ολυνθίους; Jos. Ant., 7, 196: μετὰ τὴν τοῦ πατρὸς αὐτῷ καταλλαγήν etc. Yet the usual term for reconciliation elsewhere is διαλλαγή or συναλλαγή. In 2 Macc. 5:20 καταλλαγή is the opp. of the wrath of God, namely, the attitude of God turning to man again in His grace: ὁ καταλειφθεὶς ἐν τῇ τοῦ παντοκράτορος ὀργῇ πάλιν ἐν τῇ τοῦ μεγάλου δεσπότου καταλλαγῇ μετὰ δόξης ἐπανορθώθη.

In Paul, who alone uses the term in the NT, it always denotes a disposition or economy of God. Paul denotes the significance of his own word and work by calling it the word and ministry of reconciliation (2 C. 5:18, 19). It brings before men the action by which God takes them up again into fellowship with Himself (cf. v. 20: ὡς τοῦ θεοῦ παρακαλοῦντος δι' ἡμῶν). Those who have allowed this action to reach its goal in them, opening themselves to it, have received reconciliation (R. 5:11). In R. 11:15 the καταλλαγὴ κόσμου, like the ἀποβολὴ αὐτῶν (of the Jews), is an action of God on the world which does not belong only to the past but still continues (→ 257).

ἀποκαταλλάσσω.

ἀποκαταλλάσσω is found in the NT only in Col. and Eph., where → καταλλάσσω does not occur. Since it is never found prior to Paul, it is perhaps coined by him. Its meaning and use are essentially the same as those of καταλλάσσω. A difference is that in addition to God or the πλήρωμα (Col. 1:20) Christ is also the Subject of ἀποκαταλλάσσω (Col. 1:22; Eph. 2:16), whereas God alone is the Subject of καταλλάσσω. Yet in the case of ἀποκαταλλάσσω as well as καταλ-

---

κ α τ α λ λ α γ ή. For bibl. → καταλλάσσω.
[1] Cf. Pape and Pass., who give examples.
[2] Perhaps "to pay back a deposit" (cf. Preisigke Wört., s.v.).
ἀ π ο κ α τ α λ λ ά σ σ ω. For bibl. → καταλλάσσω. Cf. also Haupt, Ew., Dib., Loh., Gefbr., ad loc.

λάσσω God is never the acc. obj., but only men, or they and spirits. In Col. 1:22 also reconciliation is unmistakeably of God, since He is the Subject of ἀποκαταλλάσσειν in v. 20. In men ἀποκαταλλάσσειν is preceded by alienation and enmity (Col. 1:22). This enmity does not consist in discord or mistrust. It is "in the mind by wicked works." If ἀποκαταλλάσσειν applies to the one addressed, it is a completed fact. [1] Its purpose is that he might stand in the last judgment (Col. 1:22). Col. 1:20 speaks of the gracious purpose which God had demonstrated (εὐδόκησεν, v. 19) to reconcile the whole world to Himself; it does not speak of a reconciliation of the world already concluded. ἀποκαταλλάξαι cannot refer merely to the removal of a relationship of guilt by God, since it is plainly expounded as a conclusion of peace in Col. 1:20 and Eph. 2:15, and as a new creation in Eph. 2:15. Hence it is not something one-sided. It embraces the total life situation of man. It does not refer merely to his guilt before God. In Eph. 2:16 reconciliation to God also brings reconciliation between Jews and Gentiles, and in Col. 1:20 the reconciliation of men to God also carries with it that of supraterrestrial beings.

In Col. 1:20 ἀποκαταλλάξαι has often been given a wider significance. Ewald takes it to imply a restoration of orderly, right and original relationships; the object is creaturely being rather than conscious creatures. Dibelius finds in it the subjection of all things to Christ. All such attempts are shattered by the elucidation of ἀποκαταλλάξαι by εἰρηνοποιήσας. In 1:20 ἀποκαταλλάξαι means exactly the same as in 1:22 and Eph. 2:16. The εἰς αὐτόν is most simply related to God, as in 2 C. 5:19: κόσμον καταλλάσσω ἑαυτῷ. If this means that in the same sentence αὐτός is referred in one case to God and the other to Christ, this is in exact correspondence with v. 22, where the first αὐτοῦ can refer only to Christ and the second only to God. If we refer the εἰς αὐτόν in 1:20 to Christ, this yields the thought that the beings created in Christ (1:16) have found in Him their Head (2:10), so that the reconciliation of all things leads to their subjection to Christ, even though it does not consist in it.

† μεταλλάσσω.

"To alter," "to change," "to exchange," also intrans. [1] In R. 1:25 μετήλλαξαν ("they changed") is the equivalent of ἤλλαξαν in v. 23, as is shown by the same construction: "for" τὶ ἔν τινι, which goes back to the Hebrew (→ ἀλλάσσω, 252). ἡ ἀλήθεια τοῦ θεοῦ is here the self-revelation of God (v. 18-21), and therefore the truth about God which derives from God, whereas τὸ ψεῦδος is the idolatry which sets other beings in the place of God (v. 23). μετήλλαξαν in v. 26 takes up again the μετήλλαξαν in v. 25. The construction with εἰς corresponds to the usual πρός construction with ἀλλάσσω. The terrible perversion of the natural in the sexual field is a just punishment for the sinful perversion of facts in the religious.

Büchsel

---

[1] Cf. the aor. in Col. 1:22; Eph. 2:16.
μ ε τ α λ λ ά σ σ ω. [1] Cf. Pape, Pass., *s.v.*

† ἀλληγορέω

A. The Use of the Term.

The verb is first found in Philo and Jos., the Gk. subst. ἀλληγορία in Cicero Orat. 94. Plutarch tells us in Aud. Poet., 4 (II, 19e), cf. De Isid. et Os., 32 (II, 363d), that ὑπόνοια used to be the term for what is now called ἀλληγορία. ἀλληγορία and ἀλληγορεῖν thus derive from the Hellenistic period and probably from Cynic-Stoic philosophy. ἀλληγορεῖν means a. "to speak allegorically," and b. "to explain or denote allegorically." Philo Cher., 25 : τὰ μὲν δὴ Χερουβὶμ καθ' ἕνα τρόπον οὕτως ἀλληγορεῖται.[1] Plut. De Isid. et Os. ib. : οἱ Ἕλληνες Κρόνον ἀλληγοροῦσι τὸν χρόνον, Ἥραν δὲ τὸν ἀέρα. The former meaning fits Gl. 4:24 : ἅτινά ἐστιν ἀλληγορούμενα· αὗται γάρ εἰσιν δύο διαθῆκαι. That is, the OT story of Sarah and Hagar is allegorical.

B. The Application of Allegorical Exposition.

1. The allegorical exposition of ancient tradition is found among the Indians, Mohammedans, Greeks, Jews and Christians. It occurs with a certain regularity where an authoritative tradition is outstripped by development but is neither discarded nor interpreted historically. Among the Greeks[2] the myths came to be explained allegorically because many of them, esp. the Homeric tales of the gods, caused offence (Xenophanes, Pythagoras, Plato). Allegorical interpretation was supposed to constitute an antidote[3] or a "healing" of myth,[4] and was practised by Antisthenes, the Stoics and the Pergamenes. In method, e.g., in the handling of names, which plays a great role in Philo,[5] the Jewish and Christian interpretation of the OT is dependent on this allegorical exposition of Homer.

2. The first representative of Gk. Judaism whom we can certainly demonstrate to have undertaken the allegorical interpretation of the OT to any large extent is the Alexandrian Aristobulus about the middle of the 2nd century B.C.[6] It can hardly be doubted that he took over the allegorical method from the Greeks, for he is saturated with Greek culture and uses the same method to interpret Greek

---

ἀ λ λ η γ ο ρ έ ω. On A, cf. Pass.-Cr., 288. On B, K. Müller in Pauly-W. Suppl., IV, 16 ff. (where a fuller bibl. is given); C. Siegfried, Philo (1875); Schürer, Index, s.v., "Allegorie" ; Bousset-Gressm., 160-161; E. Stein, "D. allegor. Schriftauslegung d. Philo v. Al," ZAW, 51 (1929); H. Heinemann, Philons griech. u. jüd. Bildung (1932), 138 ff., 454 ff.; A. Schlatter, D. Theol. des Jdts. nach d. Bericht des Josephus (1932), 235 f.; Steinm. on Gl. 4:24; Str.-B., III, 385-399.

[1] Cf. Mut. Nom., 67; Som., II, 207.
[2] Pauly-W., op. cit. Relics of the resultant literature are to be seen in Heracl. Hom. All., Ps.-Plut. Vit. Poes. Hom., Cornutus De Natura Deorum.
[3] Heracl. Quaest. Hom., 22, p. 32, 18 f. (ed. Soc. Phil. Bonn).
[4] τοῦ μύθου θεράπευμα, Eustath. Thessal. Comm. in Hom. Il., p. 1504, 54.
[5] Cf. Stein, 53-61.
[6] Schürer, III, 384-392; A. Schlatter, Gesch. Isr.³ (1925), 82-90; Stein, 7-11.

poetry. [7] Self-evidently the method would not have been adopted by the Jews if they had not been long accustomed to understand Scripture in all its parts as the fount of mysterious divine wisdom concerning this world and the next, the tasks of the present and the events of the future, in short, as a supratemporal divine Word. Against a Greek derivation the argument has little weight that there are genuine allegories in the OT [8] which must have taught the scribes the art of interpretation. The ingenious skill with which cosmological or moral lessons are extracted from texts which do not seem to offer them is far too refined to be explained simply as a development of the exposition demanded by OT allegories. Judaism owes it to its contact with the Greeks. The allegorical interpretation of Scripture established itself in the time between Aristobulus and Philo. In the Epistle of Aristeas (148-171) it makes possible the extraction of profound ethical wisdom from the ritual definitions of the OT. [9] On the other hand, Philo himself tells us that before him there were expositors who accepted only the literal sense and rejected all allegorising. [10] Yet he also tells us that there were others who accepted only the allegorical sense and rejected the literal observance of the Law, so that Judaism was dissolved altogether into philosophical ethics and cosmology. [11] Against this background Philo personally emerges in his allegorising as a theologian of the centre who avoids extremes and can combine diverse elements. His significance is to be found in the main in his fruitfulness, though many of his actual interpretations may well be older. The breadth and depth with which he worked over the Greek cultural heritage made possible and natural this fruitfulness in the allegorical interpretation of the OT. [12] Rightly to evaluate his allegorising, we must not forget that, for all his arbitrariness in interpretation, Philo never surrenders the literal validity of the text. The Law is to be observed literally, and he accepts the factuality of what is narrated in the OT. For all his Greek culture and mystical piety, Philo is a convinced Jew ready to sacrifice himself for his faith. To maintain that the literal sense [13] of the OT commands and narratives is not essential in Philo, but that he is concerned only with the allegorical meaning, is to make deductions which he himself rejected.

Naturally, Philo was influenced by rationalising criticism of the OT. He rejected its anthropomorphisms and even criticised individual historical accounts. [14] Nevertheless, he maintained expressly and in all seriousness that those who could not bear the full truth declared by allegorical exposition should keep to the literal sense (Som., I, 231 ff.). Thus, those who could not love God as pure being should fear Him as the One who threatens and punishes (Deus Imm., 69). The literal

---

[7] Schlatter, *Gesch.*, 86 f.

[8] Cf. Gunkel, RGG², I, *s.v.* "*Allegorie.*"

[9] The dating of Aristeas is much contested. Schürer, III, 48 argues for *c.* 200 B.C.; E. Bickermann, ZNW, 29 (1930), 280 ff. for 145-100; Wendland in Kautzsch, *Apokryphen*, II, 3 for 96-63 (as also P. Riessler, *Altjüd. Schrifttum* [1928], 1277); Bousset-Gressm., 27 for 40 B.C.-30 A.D. The most commonly accepted date is *c.* 96 B.C. (cf. RGG², I, *s.v.* "Aristeas").

[10] Som., I, 92 ff.

[11] Migr. Abr., 89 ff.; Cf. Heinemann, 454.

[12] Cf. the material assembled on the basic principles of Philo's allegorising and their application in Siegfried, 166-199.

[13] Naturally, it is quite another question that in all probability Philo knew only the Gk. and not the Heb. text of the OT, cf. Schlatter, *Gesch.*, 31, n. 43; Heinemann, 524 ff.

[14] For examples, cf. Siegfried, 165-168.

sense has only a subordinate significance. Yet it is still essential, since those for whom it is present are always the majority. [15]

In this matter we should bear in mind the highly complicated nature of Philo's theology. It maintains an artificial balance between a legal and literalistic Judaism on the one side and an intellectual and spiritualistic mysticism on the other, never inclining too much to either the one or the other, but keeping the two in equilibrium.

3. The early vindication and practice of allegorical exposition even in scribal circles in Palestine is shown by the canonicity of the Song of Solomon. Only by means of allegorising could this collection of love songs be understood as a representation of the love which binds Israel to God. [16] The only question is whether there is a difference of degree or of principle between the Alexandrian and Palestinian theologians. The difference of degree is unmistakeable. Among the Palestinians allegorical interpretations [17] are both rarer and less arbitrary; the distance between the literal meaning and the allegorical is much less. In general, the Palestinians are not so well instructed as Aristobulus and Philo in cosmology, psychology and similar achievements of Greek learning. [18] Their concern is with questions more closely linked with the natural sense. For this reason they are less capable of allegorising, and have less need of it. Nevertheless, they applied it as needed, even in relation to the OT commands. [19]

The older contention [20] that allegorical interpretation is found in Palestine only in exceptional cases is now outdated. Similarly, attempts [21] to distinguish between the allegorical interpretation of the Alexandrians and the typological of the Palestinians in terms of an acceptance of historicity on the part of the latter and indifference to it on the part of the former, miss the decisive point. On the whole, Philo himself intends to maintain the historicity of what is narrated. [22] The decisive point is the attitude to the Greek Enlightenment and its biblical criticism. Philo was open to this, though not without reservations; the Palestinians were closed to it, though not completely. There is thus the same broken attitude on both sides; consequently a distinction only of degree and not of principle is to be discerned. [23]

---

[15] This is not sufficiently taken into account in Str.-B., III, 397 f.

[16] Schlatter, *Gesch.*, 356.

[17] On רֶמֶז, cf. Schürer, II³, 348 f. and F. Weber, *Jüd. Theol. auf Grund d. Talmud*² (1897), 118 ff.

[18] Cf. e.g., Schlatter, 356. The criticism of OT anthropomorphisms was not without its effect on the Palestinian Rabbis, as may be seen from the restriction of anthropomorphisms in the Targums, in which traces of other Gk. influence may also be detected, Schlatter, *Gesch.*, 306-308. On the other hand, they consciously and powerfully resisted such influences.

[19] Str.-B., III, 391 ff. shows that the application of allegorical methods to the pronouncements of the Law was often undertaken as a kind of "harmless, homiletical pastime," yet sometimes with serious intent. Schlatter, *Theol. d. Jdts.*, 235 also recognises that allegory seemed to be indispensable to the Jerusalem teachers in their interpretation of prophecy, and that they also applied it to the historical part of the Pentateuch.

[20] Bousset, 185 f.; E. Bréhier, *Les Idées philos. et relig. de Philon*² (1925), 45 f.

[21] Cf. EJ, II, 338; O. Michel, *Pls. und seine Bibel* (1929), 110.

[22] Cf. again Siegfried, 163.

[23] Michel correctly observes (111) that it is "obvious that there are many links between Philo and Palestinian exegesis."

The conception of Scripture is in essentials the same. For the Palestinians, too, it is in keeping with the dignity of Scripture that it has many meanings. "As the hammer causes many sparks to fly, so the word of Scripture has a manifold sense." [24] In view of all this, it seems overwhelmingly probable that the allegorical exposition of Scripture came to the Palestinians from the Alexandrians, so that in the last analysis it derives from Greek influence even in its Palestinian form. [25] There might well have been first steps in this direction in local Palestinian scholarship, [26] but further development came only under Greek influences by way of Alexandria.

Most instructive is the position of Josephus, who was writing for the Greek world, but was originally a Palestinian. As a historian he has little occasion to allegorise, Ant., 1, 25 ; and he can sometimes (Ap., 2, 255) speak sharply against τὰς ψυχρὰς προφάσεις τῶν ἀλληγοριῶν among the Greeks. Yet he unhesitatingly accepts the legitimacy of allegorical interpretation. Moses spoke allegorically μετὰ σεμνότητος (Ant., 1, 24). Accordingly, he himself interprets allegorically the tabernacle and its furnishings (Ant., 3, 179-187). His allegorising is wholly along Alexandrian lines. Because Moses gave τοσοῦτον φυσιολογίας in his giving of the Law and narration of history (Ant., 1, 18), the tabernacle and its furnishings must be evaluated as a representation τῶν ὅλων (Ant., 3, 180). He did not, of course, allegorise the *halachot* of the OT. [27] What we see in Josephus does not indicate, therefore, that there was any essential difference between Palestinian and Alexandrian allegorising.

4. There is no allegorical handling of Scripture either in the Synoptic sayings of Jesus or in John, but we find it in Paul in 1 C. 5:6-8; 1 C. 9:8-10; 1 C. 10:1-11; Gl. 4:21-31. Paul's allegorising is closer to the Palestinian than the Alexandrian, since he does not use it to extract cosmological, psychological or similar lessons from the text. Yet formally the distinction from Philo is only one of degree. He allegorises in the true sense. [28] If there is a distinctive feature as compared with Jewish allegorising, both Palestinian and Alexandrian, it is that he expounds Scripture as one who lives in the time of its fulfilment (1 C. 10:11), as one for whom the veil is thus removed which had previously lain over its reading (2 C. 3:14), so that the true sense of the OT may now be seen. Allegorising is thus a means to carry though his understanding of Scripture in terms of the centrality of Christ or the cross. In this regard Hebrews continues the work of Paul (7:1 ff.). Hence, for all the formal dependence of Christianity on Judaism and Hellenism, we really have a new beginning in this field which demonstrates the independence of Christianity.

Büchsel

---

[24] bSanh., 34a; bShab., 88b; M. Ex. 15:12. Cf. Kittel Probleme, 94 f. The much quoted statement : "The meaning of Scripture does not go beyond the sphere of the literal" (jShab., 63a), cannot be used in opposition, since the 7 rules of Hillel and the 13 of Ishmael (cf. Strack, Einl., 96 ff.) show what can be gleaned from the literal wording.

[25] Cf. Kittel, *op. cit.*, 85, who thinks it likely that Gk. philosophy had some effect on Palestinian Judaism.

[26] Schürer, III³, 548, n. 22.

[27] If Josephus interprets dreams allegorically (e.g., Ant., 17, 345) as ἀμφιβόλως ὑπὸ τοῦ θείου λεγόμενα (Bell., 3 352), this is simply along the lines of the OT itself. Cf. Schlatter, *Theol. d. Jdts.*, 235 f.

[28] As against Michel, *op. cit.*, 110.

† ἀλληλουϊά

Heb. הַלְלוּ־יָהּ, "praise Yahweh," found in the LXX in ψ 104-106, 110-112, 113-118, 134-135, 145-150. [1] It is doubtful whether it is a heading or a conclusion. [2] In favour of the latter view we might refer to a. Midr. Ps. 104 § 27 (224b), which attaches Hallelujah to v. 35 of Ps. 104 (Heb.); [3] b. the Odes of Solomon, which always conclude with Hallelujah ; c. the liturgical use in Jewish (Hellenistic) worship, which has it sung by the congregation and makes it an independent acclamation (Tob. 13:8; 3 Macc. 7:13). Christian worship adopted the same practice : Mart. Mt., 25 : ψάλλειν τὸ ἀλληλουϊά, and after a Psalm : πάντες ἐπέκραξαν· Ἀλληλουϊά. Ἀλληλουϊά is also a song of the angels (ib., 26).

In the NT it occurs only at Rev. 19:1, 3, 4, 6, where it introduces or merges into a hymn of victory and forms with ἀμήν (19:4) an independent response.

Schlier

ἄλλος, ἀλλότριος, ἀπαλλοτριόω, ἀλλογενής, ἀλλόφυλος

ἄλλος.

If even in ancient Greek it is very difficult to make a clear distinction between ὁ ἕτερος (the other where there are two) and ἄλλος (another where there are many), since the latter shades into the former and the former into the latter, [1] in the κοινή and the NT this kind of distinction becomes quite impossible. "Both words deny identity." [2] Neither Heb. nor Aram. has more than one word for "other" : אַחֵר, אָחֳרָן. ἕτερος is never found in the genuine Mk., the Epistles of Peter, or Rev., and only once in John (19:37). ἄλλος is often used where only two are in question, as in Mt. 5:39 (Lk. 6:29); 12:13; 27:61; 28:1; Jn. 18:16; 20:3, 4, 8; 19:32. ἄλλος and ἕτερος are also used interchangeably with no recognisable difference, as in Mt. 16:14; [3] 1 C. 12:8-10; 2 C. 11:4; Hb. 11:35-36. In Gl. 1:6, 7: εἰς ἕτερον εὐαγγέλιον, ὃ οὐκ ἔστιν ἄλλο, we again find the two in the same sense : "Unto

---

ἀ λ η λ ο υ ϊ ά. [1] η instead of ε : cf. Dalman Gr., 191, 2.

[2] It is probable that no general decision can be made. Cf. also H. B. Swete, *An Introduction to the Old Testament in Greek* (1900), 250 f.

[3] Str.-B., III, 497.

ἄ λ λ ο ς. Bl.-Debr. § 306; Zahn on Gl. 1:6, 7.

[1] Cf. Pass.-Cr., *s.v.* ἄλλος; and other dictionaries on ἄλλος and ἕτερος.

[2] Zn., *op. cit.*

[3] Schl. Mt., 503 compares : οἱ μὲν ... ἤγγελλον, οἱ δὲ ... ἕτεροι δὲ ἔλεγον, Jos. Bell., 6, 398.

another gospel which is not another," i.e., which is really no gospel at all, but [4] a human teaching.

† ἀλλότριος.

"What belongs to an ἄλλος," and therefore "strange," also "alien," "unsuitable," and even finally "hostile." [1] The LXX normally uses it to render נָכְרִי, and sometimes זָר.

In the NT it is mainly used to denote "what belongs to another": οἰκέτης (R. 14:4), κόποι (2 C. 10:15), κανών (2 C. 10:16), ἁμαρτίαι (1 Tm. 5:22), αἷμα (Hb. 9:25), γῆ (Ac. 7:6; Hb. 11:9). Substantively, τὸ ἀλλότριον is used as the opp. of τὸ ὑμέτερον in Lk. 16:12. [2] It can also denote that which does not form part of the subject in question, [3] and it is thus used in opp. to υἱοί in Mt. 17:25 and ποιμήν in Jn. 10:5. Finally, it has the sense of "hostile" in Hb. 11:34. In the NT, however, it is never used in the sense of alien to God.

† ἀπαλλοτριόω.

"To estrange or alienate." [1] ἀπαλλοτριοῦσθαι and ἀπαλλοτριωθῆναι usually have a pass. rather than a reflex. significance. Polyb., I, 79, 6: ἡ Σαρδὼ ... ἀπηλλοτριώθη Καρχηδόνος, is not reflex. but pass., as shown by the context, cf. I, 82, 7. As against this it must be conceded that in Ps. 58:3; Hos. 9:10; Is. 1:4 (Qᵐᵍ) ἀπηλλοτριώθησαν has the meaning that "they have estranged or alienated themselves." In the LXX the word renders נֵכַר, נוּד, נָזַר, זוּר. It is also found in Jos. (Ant., 4, 3; 11, 148).

In the NT we find only the part. perf. pass. and the word occurs only in the Prison Epistles at Col. 1:21 and Eph. 2:12; 4:18. It denotes the state prior to reconciliation. The parallel expressions make it plain that in all three passages it applies only to this state. Col. 1:12: ὄντας ἀπηλλοτριωμένους καὶ ἐχθροὺς τῇ διανοίᾳ ἐν τοῖς ἔργοις τοῖς πονηροῖς; Eph. 2:12: ἀπηλλοτριωμένοι τῆς πολιτείας τοῦ Ἰσραὴλ καὶ ξένοι τῶν διαθηκῶν τῆς ἐπαγγελίας κτλ.; Eph. 4:18: ἐσκοτωμένοι τῇ διανοίᾳ ὄντες ἀπηλλοτριωμένοι τῆς ζωῆς τοῦ θεοῦ. [2] There

---

[4] Examples of this meaning of εἰ μή may be found in Ditt. Or., 201, n. 33.

ἀ λ λ ό τ ρ ι ο ς. Pass.-Cr., Pr.-Bauer, Cr.-Kö., s.v.

[1] The fullest examples are given in Pass.-Cr. Under no. 4 there are examples of the sense of "alien," and under no. 5 of "hostile."

[2] Although there is good attestation for ἡμέτερον BL Orig. or ἐμόν 157e i1 Mcion, we must keep to the usual reading ὑμέτερον. To describe the eternal good as divine by means of ἡμέτερον (ἐμόν) is only to weaken the profound thought that the true possession of man is the eternal good ascribed to him by God; cf. Zn., ad loc.

[3] Correspondingly we find in Jos. Bell., 2, 409 that no sacrifice of ἀλλότριοι should be accepted; and in 7, 266 ἀλλότριοι is the opp. of οἰκειότατοι.

ἀ π α λ λ ο τ ρ ι ό ω. Cr.-Kö., s.v.

[1] Examples may be found in Pape and Pass.

[2] Cf. ψ 68:9: ἀπηλλοτριωμένος ἐγενήθην τοῖς ἀδελφοῖς μου καὶ ξένος τοῖς υἱοῖς τῆς μητρός μου; Ez. 14:5: κατὰ τὰς καρδίας αὐτῶν τὰς ἀπηλλοτριωμένας ἀπ' ἐμοῦ ἐν τοῖς ἐνθυμήμασιν αὐτῶν; Ps. Sol. 17:15: ἐν ἀλλοτριότητι ὁ ἐχθρὸς ἐποίησεν, ἐν ὑπερηφανίᾳ· καὶ ἡ καρδία αὐτοῦ ἀλλοτρία ἀπὸ τοῦ θεοῦ ἡμῶν. The meaning "excluded" or "expelled" is possible (Jos. Ant., 11, 148: ὡς τῶν ... οὐκ ἀπαντησάντων

is reference to a process or act which has brought about this state, whether we think of the judgment of God or the guilt of man, only to the extent that this state is culpable and worthy of condemnation; the presuppositions of the state are no longer expressly in view. As the parallels ἐχθρός and ξένος show, ἀπηλλοτριωμένος means almost the same as ἀλλότριος. Aristot. Pol., II, 8, p. 1268a, 40 : ἀλλότριον τῆς πολιτείας is a striking parallel to Eph. 2:12. Light is also shed on Eph. 4:18 by Pol., II, 8, since οὐδενὸς μετέχον in the latter is parallel to ἀλλότριον, and ἀπηλλοτριωμένος in the former means "without a share in (the life of God)."

† ἀλλογενής.

"Alien" or "foreign," the opp. of ἐγγενής and συγγενής, also εὐγενής, and par. to ἀλλόφυλος, ἀλλοεθνής, ἑτεροεθνής, also ἀλλοδαπός, ἀλλότριος. The word is found only in Jewish and Christian Gk.; there are no pagan examples. The LXX uses it for זָר Ex. 29:33; Nu. 16:40 (17:5); Lv. 22:10 (not of priestly descent); Jl. 3(4):17; Jer. 51(28):51; Ob. 11 (not of Israelite descent); or for בֶּן־(הַ)נֵּכָר ("son of an alien land"): Ex. 12:43; Lv. 22:25; Is. 56:3. 6; 60:10; Ez. 44:7, 9; also for מַמְזֵר ("bastard"): 1 Zech. 9:6. Philo has it in Som., I, 161; Spec. Leg., I, 124; IV, 16; Virt., 147, but it is not found in Josephus.

In the NT it is used only of the Samaritan who gives thanks in Lk. 17:18. Elsewhere it is found only on the inscription on the barrier in the temple at Jerusalem : [2] μηθένα ἀλλογενῆ εἰσπορεύεσθαι ἐντὸς τοῦ τρυφάκτου καὶ περιβόλου, ὃς δ᾽ ἂν ληφθῇ, ἑαυτῷ αἴτιος ἔσται διὰ τὸ ἐξακολουθεῖν θάνατον. With the help of the hypothesis that this inscription comes from the Roman government, [3] attempts have been made to show that ἀλλογενής also occurs in secular Gk. But since this hypothesis is palpably mistaken, we must accept the fact that, even if ἀλλογενής was not coined by the Jews, it was given its meaning by them. This is in full accord with the fact that genealogy, not in the sense of nationality but of descent from Abraham, had a significance for the Jews hardly paralleled among any other people. [4]

The inscription has come down intact ; cf. the illustration in Deissmann and quotations in Jos. Bell., 5, 194; 6, 124 f.; Ant., 15, 417. Its commencement is thus μηθένα ἀλλογενῆ, i.e., ἀλλογενής is used in the absolute. Consequently the inscription speaks from a Jewish rather than a Roman standpoint, and is thus Jewish in derivation. If it were Roman, the use of the absolute ἀλλογενής for non-Jews would be quite inexplicable. It would have run somewhat as follows : Access for Jews only, no alien may ... In addition, the Jews themselves, i.e., the priests and their officers, had control of the temple. [5] According to Jos., Titus says expressly that, as the Jews built the barrier, so

ἀπαλλοτριωθησομένων τοῦ πλήθους), but seems less likely in view of the parallels.
ἀ λ λ ο γ ε ν ή ς. Cr.-Kö., 237; Deissmann, LO, 61; Dausch Synopt., 528.
[1] In the sense of mixed descent, cf. Ges.-Buhl, s.v.
[2] Ditt. Or., 598; Schürer, II, 272 f.; Deissmann, LO, 61.
[3] T. Mommsen, Röm. Gesch.[4] (1894), 513, also Dittenberger and Deissmann.
[4] Cf. the emphasis placed by the Jews on genealogical records, 1 Chr. 1-9; Mt. 1 etc.; on this point cf. G. Kittel in ZNW, 20 (1921), 49 ff. Even the full proselyte could never describe the patriarchs as אֲבוֹתֵינוּ.
[5] Schürer, II, 271 ff. Mommsen and Dittenberger seem not to have considered this point.

they set up the Gk. and Lat. inscriptions (Bell., 6, 124 f.); the right to execute those who violated the prohibition was guaranteed by the Romans (126). The οὐχ ὑμεῖς in 124 and 125 (the Jews) and the οὐχ ἡμεῖς in 126 (the Romans) correspond too plainly to leave any doubt that the Romans invested the Jews with the right referred to but did not themselves put up the inscriptions. The use of Lat. shows regard for the Roman government but does not prove that the Romans were responsible for the inscriptions.

It is striking that Jos. does not use ἀλλογενής in any of his three versions of the inscription. He has no equivalent in Bell., 6, 125, ἀλλόφυλος in 5, 194 and ἀλλοεθνής in Ant., 15, 417. His reason for avoiding ἀλλογενής is that he is writing for non-Jews. Perhaps he or his revisers feared that the word might offend non-Jews by seeming to deny them εὐγένεια. It is improbable that it was avoided on literary grounds, since Philo, who writes a cultured and not a popular Gk., does not avoid it in writing for Jews.

† ἀλλόφυλος.

"Of alien descent," "foreign." It is found from the time of Aeschylus and Thucydides.[1] In the LXX it is used for בְּנֵי נֵכָר in Is. 61:5; for נָכְרִי in Is. 2:6; for פְּלִשְׁתִּים in 1 S. 13:3; Ps. 108:10 (cf. 1 Macc. 4:22). Jos. uses it in Ant., 9, 102 and 291; 11, 150; Bell., 5, 194.

In the NT it is found only at Ac. 10:28 to denote the Gentiles from the standpoint of the Jews. According to Dg., 5, 17 the Jews treat Christians as ἀλλόφυλοι.

Büchsel

ἀλλοτριεπίσκοπος → ἐπίσκοπος   ἄλογος → λέγω

ἁμαρτάνω, ἁμάρτημα, ἁμαρτία

A. Sin in the OT.

1. The Words used in the OT.

a. The concept of sin is linguistically expressed in many ways in the OT. Indeed, justice is hardly done to this variety either in the LXX with its summary

---

ἀ λ λ ό φ υ λ ο ς. Pr.-Bauer, Pape, s.v.; Cr.-Kö. under ἀλλογενής.
[1] Examples are given by Pape and Pass.-Cr.
ἁ μ α ρ τ ά ν ω, κτλ. It is to be noted that the authorship of these articles on the word group ἁμαρτ- is particularly complex. Examples from the OT and LXX were provided by G. Quell and G. Bertram. The basis of the MS. was provided by G. Stählin, but in his absence on a journey to India this was worked over by W. Grundmann and K. H. Rengstorf. Section D. was left virtually unaltered; sections C. and E. were much revised and extended by Grundmann, with contributions from H. Kleinknecht and K. G. Kuhn; and section F was completely recast by Grundmann. The articles on ἁμαρτωλός and ἀναμάρτητος, which were not originally planned as separate articles, were contributed by K. H. Rengstorf.
On A: K. Umbreit, *Die Sünde, ein Beitrag z. Theologie des AT* (1853); J. C. Matthes, ThT, 24 (1890), 225 ff.; J. Köberle, *Sünde u. Gnade im relig. Leben d. Volkes Israel* (1905);

use of ἁμαρτία, ἁμάρτημα, ἁμαρτωλός, ἁμαρτάνω, or ἀδικία, ἄδικος, ἀδικέω, or ἀνομία, ἀσέβεια, κακία and their derivatives, nor by our modern translations, which neither express the richness of the original nor even catch the decisive point in some cases. In English, for example, some Heb. expressions like אָשָׁם and עָוֹן, and sometimes others, are usually rendered "guilt" as indicating a distinctive aspect of sin, but in the Gk. Bible the same words (e.g., עָוֹן) [1] are usually translated by the terms adduced or sometimes (e.g., אָשָׁם) [2] by other equivalents which are even less appropriate. The following examination will indicate both the most important LXX usage and also the rich variety of the Heb. mode of expression.

ἁμαρτία is mostly used for חַטָּאת (238 times) and עָוֹן (70 times). Of the other derivatives of חטא, חֵטְא is translated by it 28 times, חֲטָאָה 8 times, and חַטָּאָה, חֲטָיָא, and the inf. חֲטֹא once each. In the case of other Heb. equivalents, it is used for פֶּשַׁע 19 times, for the verb פשׁע twice, for אָשָׁם, אַשְׁמָה and אָשֵׁם 4 times, twice and once. In addition, it is used twice for רֶשַׁע and תּוֹעֵבָה, and in what often seems to be a "theologisation" it is used once each for חֳלִי (Is. 53:4), מַחֲשָׁבָה (Is. 65:2), מְשׁוּבָה (Jer. 14:7), עֲלִילָה (Ez. 36:19), Aram. עִלָּה (Da. 6:5), רָעָה f (Prv. 26:26), טֻמְאָה (Lv. 14:19), דֶּרֶךְ (1 K. 22:53); Aram. חֲבוּלָה (Da. 6:23) and רשׁע in hi (Da. 11:32). ἁμάρτημα is mostly used for חַטָּאת, עָוֹן and פֶּשַׁע (8 and 4 times). It is also used once each for חֵטְא, רֶשַׁע, דֶּרֶךְ (Hos. 10:13) and קֶצֶף (Nu. 1:53 incorrectly). ἁμαρτωλός is used 72 times for רָשָׁע and twice for רֶשַׁע, also for חֵטְא (11 times), חַטָּאָה and חֹטֵא (once each), and for the verb חטא (twice); also once each for חָנֵף, רַע and חָרֵשׁ (ψ 128[129]:3 in a "theologisation"). ἁμαρτάνω occurs 162 times for חטא qal and twice for hi. It also represents the verbs פשׁע (Lam. 3:42), אָשֵׁם (3 times), מָעַל, שָׁחַת pi (once), עָשָׂה (in expressions like Nu. 5:7: הַחַטָּאתָם אֲשֶׁר עָשׂוּ) and רשׁע hi (each 3 times). It is only mistakenly or in intentionally free translations that nouns are rendered ἁμαρτάνω, e.g., חַטָּאת (in Gn. 4:7 ἥμαρτες incorrectly for חֵי רֹבֵץ; 1 S. 20:1 τί ἡμάρτηκα for מֶה חַטָּאתִי etc.), חֵטְא, חֹטֵא and פֶּשַׁע (each 3 times); also אָשָׁם, אַשְׁמָה, and רָשָׁע (each twice) and עָוֹן (once). ἀδικία has 36 equivalents, of which עָוֹן (50 times) is the most common, whereas פֶּשַׁע is found only 7 times and חַטָּאת (Da. 9:24) and אָשָׁם (Ιερ. 28[Jer. 51]:5) only once each. We also find עַוְלָה (14 times), עָוֶל (9), אָוֶן and חָמָס (8), שֶׁקֶר (7, confined to Psalms), רָעָה f and עֹשֶׁק (4). The only

W. Staerk, *Sünde u. Gnade nach d. Vorstellung d. älteren Judentums, bes. d. Dichter der sog. Busspsalmen* (1905); F. Bennewitz, *Die Sünde im alten Israel* (1907); H. Seeger, *Die Triebkräfte d. relig. Lebens in Israel u. Babylon* (1923), 87 ff.; J. Pedersen, *Israel, Its Life and Culture* (1926), 411 ff.; S. Mowinckel, *Psalmenstudien*, I (1921), 39 ff.; J. Hempel, "Sünde u. Offenbarung nach at. u. nt.licher Anschauung," *Z. syst. Th.*, 10 (1932), 163-199. On C: F. Weber, *Jüdische Theologie*[2] (1897); Moore, I, 445-552; Bousset-Gressm., 399-409; F. C. Porter, *The Yeçer Hara, A Study of the Jewish Doctrine of Sin, Bibl. and Sem. Studies of Yale Univ.* (1902), 93-156; A. Büchler, *Studies in Sin and Atonement in the Rabbin. Literature of the First Century* (1928). On E: K. Latte, "Schuld u. Sünde in der griechischen Religion," ARW, 20 (1920/21), 254-298; O. Hey, Ἁμαρτία, *Philologus*, 83 (1927), 1-17, 137-163; J. Stenzel, "Metaphysik des Altertums," *Hdbch. d. Philosophie* (1929/ 31), 17 ff.; H. Weinstock, *Sophokles* (1931); F. X. Steinleitner, *Die Beicht im Zshg. mit der sakralen Rechtspflege in d. Antike* (Diss. München, 1913). On D to F: Cr.-Kö., 136 ff.; Trench, 152 ff.; Ltzm. R., 75 ff.; E. de Witt-Burton, *Crit. and Exeg. Comm. on the Ep. to the Gal.* (1921), 436 ff.; M. Dibelius, *Die Geisterwelt im Glauben des Pls* (1909), 119 ff.; R. Otto, *Sünde und Urschuld* (1932). Cf. also the NT theologies.

[1] Only Gn. 4:13 is rendered by the most appropriate αἰτία (→ 280).

[2] πλημμέλεια, -λεῖν ("mistake in singing") is most commonly used (22 times); other equivalents are ἄγνοια (5), βάσανος (4), even ἱλασμός (Am. 8:14 fem.) and καθαρισμός (Prv. 14:9). ἁμαρτία is used only in Lv. 5:7; Nu. 18:9 (pl.); 2 K. 12:17; Is. 53:10; and ἀδικία in Jer. 28(51):5.

other equivalents of material interest, and occurring only once or twice each, are רֶשַׁע,
עָוֶה, (Ez. 21:32), עָוֶל, Aram. עֲוָיָא (Da. 4:24), רַע, מְטֶה, מִרְמָה and מַעֲשֶׂה, together
with the name of the well in Gn. 26:20 (עֵשֶׂק) and the abbreviation for בֵּית הַמְּרִי (Ez.
12:2). ἀδίκημα, too, is mostly used for עָוֹן (5 times) and פֶּשַׁע (4) and also עֹשֶׁק (twice)
and חָמָס, עַוְלָה, רַע, רָעָה and מִשְׁפָּט (once each). ἄδικος occurs 33 times for שֶׁקֶר (as
nomen rectum), 10 times for חָמָס, and 8 for עַוְלָה. It is also used for עָוֶל, רָשָׁע (4 each),
עַוָּל (3), מִרְמָה, אָוֶן, רַע, עֹשֶׁק (2 each), תַּהְפּוּכָה, נְבָלָה, רְמִיָּה and תֹּהוּ (1 each). ἀδικέω is
used for חטא (3 times), פֶּשַׁע, רֵעַ and רָשַׁע hi (1 each). On the other hand, it is used
14 times for עָשַׁק, 3 for מָעַל, (Da. 9:5 Θ [A] for מרד). Of relevant nouns, we may cite
חָמָס (twice) and מְשׁוּבָה (once). ἀνομία is used for 24 Heb. equivalents: 63 times for
עָוֹן, 26 for אָוֶן and תּוֹעֵבָה (only in Ez. apart from Jer. 16:18), 20 for פֶּשַׁע (Is. 53:12 verb),
8 or 5 for רִשְׁעָה and רֶשַׁע; 7 each for זִמָּה, חָמָס, עַוְלָה and חַטָּאת. More rarely it is used for
עֶצֶב, עָוֶל, סָרָה (Ps. 139:24 per- (Is. 5:7), מִשְׁפָּח, נְבָלָה, עֲלִילָה, מַעַל, הַוָּה, דֶּרֶךְ, בֶּצַע, בְּלִיַּעַל
haps for דְּבַר־עֶצֶב "injurious word," Gunkel), עָתָק, קָלוֹן and שֶׁקֶר, also once for the verb
שִׁחֵת hi. ἄνομος is used 31 times for רָשָׁע, but only once for חטא (Is. 33:14). It is also
used for אָוֶן (5 times), for הָלַל, חָנֵף, עַוָּל, and twice for עָוֹן. The infrequent ἀνόμημα
occurs sometimes for עָוֹן, פֶּשַׁע (3 times each), חַטָּאת, זִמָּה (twice each) and נְבָלָה, תּוֹעֵבָה
and תִּפְלָה (once). ἀνομεῖν translates רָשַׁע (qal and hi 8 times), פֶּשַׁע and שִׁחֵת (pi and hi)
three each. It is also used for עוה, מָעַל, חטא (ΘDa. 9:5?) and some nouns. ἀσέβεια,
which with ἁμαρτία has the strongest religious accentuation of all the equivalents, is
most commonly used for פֶּשַׁע, (27 times), then for רֶשַׁע and רִשְׁעָה (4 times), more rarely
for הַוָּה, זָדוֹן, זִמָּה, חָמָס, מִרְמָה, סָרָה, עֲלִילָה, רָעָה, תּוֹעֵבָה etc. It occurs only twice each for
חַטָּאת and עָוֹן, and even in these cases there is some textual doubt. ἀσεβής is mostly
the equivalent for רָשָׁע (14 times), other terms being of little significance. The case is
much the same with ἀσεβεῖν, except that now פֶּשַׁע is strongly represented (10 times)
and חטא does not occur at all. Worth noting is מרה in Lam. 3:42. κακία corresponds
for the most part to the derivates of רעע, but also, though the MSS differ, to עָוֹן,
in 1 Ch. 21:8; Jer. 16:18; 13:22 (A), to אָוֶן in Is. 29:20 and to חַטָּאת in Jer. 15:13 (A).
The same is true of κακός, for which, with רַע etc., the following equivalents deserve
mention: אָוֶן (3 times), זִמָּה (Prv. 10:23), עָמָל (Job 16:2), רֶשַׁע (Prv. 16:12), עַוְלָה (Job
22:23). κακοῦν is used in Is. 50:9 for רָשַׁע hi, κακοποιεῖν in 2 S. 24:17 (A) for עוה
hi. As equivalents for מרד or מרה in the religious sense we often find ἀθετεῖν, ἀφιστά-
ναι (both also for פֶּשַׁע), ἀμελεῖν (Jer. 4:17), ἐρίζειν (1 K. 12:14 f.), παραβαίνειν,
παροξύνειν (for מרה אֶת־פִּי יהוה Nu. 20:24), μὴ εἰσακούειν (Is. 1:20), and esp. παρα-
πικραίνειν (Ez. 2:3 for מרד and 18 times for מרה; in Ez. οἶκος παραπικραίνων
9 times for בֵּית מְרִי).

The reasons for these defects in translation are not to be sought only in the
methods of the translators but also in the peculiar difficulty of the Heb. usage. It
is obvious that among the many words to be considered none was exclusively
devoted to religious and theological use and therefore none constitutes an exact
equivalent to the English "sin." All the Heb. words in question had a secular as
well as a religious sense, and, disparate though the relation often is, the very fact
of this twofold usage constitutes a warning not to overestimate the purely religious
content of the term. On closer inspection all seem to be more or clearly the results
of rational reflection which is religious in content. They are theologoumena rather
than original terms of spontaneous experience, and the meaning falls into different
groups. This explains why the subjectivity of the translator plays a more important
role than is helpful. Sometimes a religious emphasis is imported where none was

meant,[3] and sometimes a secular word is used which weakens the religious content.[4] At any rate, the relatively rich linguistic differentiation in the Hebrew may be very largely discerned of itself by reason of the fact that only with the strongest reservations, if at all, can we count on a uniform and self-contained concept of sin in the authors of the OT; the problem of sin is complicated by a series of detailed questions of linguistic history.

b. The language of the OT gives us four different roots to which the concept of sin is usually attached and which we have usually to render as "to sin" or "sin" without being able to bring out the etymologically derived nuances of the Hebrew. These roots are as follows.

חטא. This verb is used 177 times in the qal including the infin. and part. forms, 32 times in the hiphil and 9 in the hithpael. We also find 15 forms of the piel, which always have denominative significance in the privat. sense "to put away sin."[5] Even some of the hithpael forms are reflexive in relation to the privat. piel: "to free oneself from sin." On the whole there are thus 233 examples of the verb, predominantly in a religious sense.[6] Of the nouns formed from חטא the most common is חַטָּאת (fem., only Gn. 4:7 masc. → n. 28), which occurs 289 times and seems to be strongly preferred to nouns from other roots. In large part,[7] of course, חַטָּאת follows the intensive constructions of the verb and has thus the privative significance of means to avert sin or its consequences. It thus denotes in many cases a specific form of sacrifice the occasion and ritual of which are described in Lv. 4:1-5; 13.[8] Elsewhere it simply means "sin" unless in certain cases we prefer a legal term like "misdemeanour" or "negligence." The various plural and suffix constructions of חַטָּאת can all be traced back to the sing. חַטָּאה, which in the absol. form occurs only twice (Ex. 34:7; Is. 5:18). We find חֵטְא 8 times[9] and the masc. חֵטְא 35 times.[10] The *nomen agentis* חַטָּא ("sinner") is found in the sing. only as a fem. (Amos 9:8); but the plur. either with or without suffix occurs 18 times.

פשע ("to rebel") is found as a verb 41 times, including 10 instance of the part. qal; as the noun פֶּשַׁע it is found 92 times (sing. and plur.).

עוה as a verb occurs in 17 forms, of which 6 (niph and pi forms) have either directly

---

[3] Cf. e.g., Prv. 1:31: ἀσέβεια for מוֹעֵצָה etc.

[4] Cf. e.g., Job 9:22 : δυνάστης for רָשָׁע etc.

[5] Cf. Bauer-Leander, *Hist. Grammatik d. heb. Spr.*, I (1922), 291; G. Bergsträsser, *Hebr. Gramm.*, II (1929), 94.

[6] For exceptions → 2a.

[7] B. Baentsch (Komm. zu Ex. 29:14) counts 101 instances.

[8] This meaning, and the corresponding meaning of אָשָׁם, are perhaps to be explained from the fact that חַטָּאת and אָשָׁם were catch-words in the priestly theology of the cultus and were thus adapted to serve as principles of classification in drawing up rubrics for the sacrifices. The oldest examples seem to occur in Ez. (cf. 40:39 and R. Smend, Komm. ad loc.). Baentsch (Lv., 321) sees a connection with the penal and penitential offerings already found prior to the Exile (כֶּסֶף חַטָּאוֹת 2 K. 12:17; perhaps this was the term for what was done by those who were expiated in Am. 2:8); yet these instances give us only analogies of the transference of meaning and do not provide stepping-stones in the development of technical cultic terms.

[9] Ps. 40:6, where חַטָּאה, seems to mean sin-offering, as elsewhere חַטָּאת and חַטָּאה, must have been pointed by someone who had in view a combination like אָוֶן וַעֲצָרָה (Is. 1:13).

[10] It often seems to merge into the concept of guilt, cf. נָשָׂא חֵטְא Lv. 19:17; 20:20; 22:9; 24:15; Nu. 9:13; 18:22; Is. 53:12; Ez. 23:49. → 279 ff.

or metaphorically the secular meaning of "to bend" (→ 279). The use of the noun עָוֹן[11] is much greater ; this is found in the sing. and the plur.(עֲוֹנוֹת)227 times and it has a stronger religious emphasis, the thought of guilt being forcefully asserted[12] (→ 3. and δικαιοσύνη). עֲוֹנוֹת are faults which establish guilt.

שׁגה ("to err") occurs 19 times as a verb, with the par. construction שׁגג (4 times), and also 19 instances of the noun שְׁגָגָה. Together these bring out a further characteristic of sin as creaturely conditioned error.[13]

Apart from מרד and מרה, which are particularly close in meaning to פשע, many of the roots mentioned under a., and esp. רשע, עול or אשם (→ ἱλάσκεσθαι and 279 f.) might be added to these four. And the four themselves, for all that they are used in what is essentially the same or a similar theological and religious way, give evidence of such strong qualitative differences among themselves that they alone are enough to prove the rich and varied nature of the thinking about sin either consciously or unconsciously expressed in their use. Hence a comparison of the content enclosed in these four main strands of usage will help us to a more or less accurate understanding of what the Hebrews meant by sin.

2. The Legal and Theological Content of the OT Concept of Sin.

a. As we have learned from the above statistics, the root חטא with its derivatives is the main word for sin. This seems to be in harmony with the fact that this root can give an obviously formal definition which suits well the conceptual significance. That is to say, the widespread religious and theological use of the root does not touch the motive and inner quality of sinful action but simply its formal peculiarity. The root is basically metaphorical, and all who used and heard it must have been aware of this. For in a limited way the OT uses the same word חטא in a secular sense as a verb of movement to indicate "missing the right point." Now it is impossible to think that this usage derives from the religious, legal, or ethical ; on the contrary, it is basic to the latter. Thus it can be said of the wayfarer in Prv. 19:2 : אָץ בְּרַגְלַיִם חוֹטֵא ("he that hasteth with his feet goeth astray"). Again, in Prv. 8:36 חטא, "to miss," is the opp. of מצא, "to find." We also read in Job 5:24 : לֹא תֶחֱטָא ("thou shalt not miss," i.e., fail to find what thou art seeking). The same meaning is to be found outside the Wisdom literature. Thus Ju. 20:16 says of the Benjamite slingers that they could sling stones at an hair breadth : וְלֹא יַחֲטִא ("and not miss").[14] There is an instructive example of confusion of meaning in Ps. 25:8. The Mas. reading חַטָּאִים understands those who are to be guided by Yahweh as "sinners," whereas there can be little doubt that the poet simply had in view those who had lost their way (חֹטְאִים בַּדֶּרֶךְ, cf. LXX : ἁμαρτάνοντας ἐν ὁδῷ), i.e., those who even with the best intentions were in difficulties. The one who supplied the pointing purposely introduced a theological significance in order

---

[11] Constructed with the afformative -ān on the concluding vowel, cf. J. Barth, *Die Nominalbildung in den semit. Sprachen* (1889), 326.

[12] Other derivatives like עִי, עָוֶים and מְעִי have little connection with religious speech, unless we appeal to Is. 19:14 : רוּחַ עִוְעִים (LXX : πνεῦμα πλανήσεως).

[13] Also שְׁגִיאָה in Ps. 19:12, מִשְׁגֶּה in Gn. 43:12 and מְשׁוּגָה in Job 19:4 may be cited in this connection.

[14] LXX : οὐκ ἐξαμαρτάνοντες.

to make it clear to the reader that even circles which follow closely the guidance of Yahweh still have a sense of sin. This subtlety could be easily introduced into the text, however, only because the verb of movement used by the author was already associated metaphorically with the "way." Although there are only a few instances of this secular usage, [15] they give us good grounds for concluding that חטא never quite lost in Hebrew its sense of erroneous action, and therefore that the most common Heb. term for sin did not have the predominantly religious emphasis proper to the English "sin."

This conjecture is strengthened by a comparative survey of the numerous passages in the OT in which חטא is used as a legal term either in judicial terminology or more popularly. If it is correct that basically the verb חטא is a verb of movement denoting erring or straying, it was well adapted to be used of all kinds of misdemeanours. We can see its adoption for this purpose in all cases where חטא denotes a missing of the legal norm which ought to obtain in the mutual dealings of men. The law about witnesses before the judgment in Dt. 19:15-21 uses the term חַטָּאת as well as עָוֹן in the comprehensive sense of offence against established practice. Thus we read that only many witnesses can be accepted לְכָל־עָוֹן וּלְכָל־חַטָּאת ("in respect of any iniquity or misdemeanour"). The addition בְּכָל־חֵטְא אֲשֶׁר יֶחֱטָא ("in respect of any offence of which he may be guilty," v. 15) expressly widens the reference to embrace all legal categories. There is certainly no thought of a purely religious or cultic transgression, since the authorities concerned are secular. [16] Similarly Dt. 21:22 includes חֵטְא without restriction under the concept of מִשְׁפָּט ("case of law"). [17] A specific reference to legal processes is also to be found in the threatening saying in Is. 29:21 concerning persons who force others to make false statements: מַחֲטִיאֵי אָדָם בְּדָבָר. Again, legal terminology is plainly recognisable when Hezekiah confesses to the king of Assyria his breach of the treaty in the word חָטָאתִי (2 K. 18:14). [18] The law of custom in the dealings of nations is certainly meant when Jephthah says to the Moabite king who attacks him: וְאָנֹכִי לֹא חָטָאתִי לָךְ (Ju. 11:27). Individual legal relationships are in view when it is said of the Egyptians whom Joseph met in prison: חָטְאוּ לַאֲדֹנֵיהֶם (Gn. 40:1, E ? J ?), i.e., they had failed in their duty; there had been חֲטָאִים or "failings" (Gn. 41:9). [19] In the same sense it is said of David, who had done nothing amiss as the vassal of Saul: לֹא חָטָא (1 S. 19:4). David himself, when he might have spared Saul but did him no harm, cried to him: לֹא חָטָאתִי לָךְ (1 S. 24:12). On the other hand, Saul admits his disloyalty to David: חָטָאתִי (1 S. 26:21). There are other cases where the forensic reference is strong even though it is to faults which are against an ethical rather than a strictly legal norm. Reuben warns his brothers

---

[15] Various interpretations are possible in the case of הַחוֹטֶא in Is. 65:20. What is meant is the one who has "missed" the full measure of his life, cf. the old man who has not yet filled his days. He is a sinner only to the extent that premature death is dogmatically thought to be a proof of sin.

[16] v. 17 has been unskilfully edited to give a spiritual character to the legal court, cf. the Comm. *ad loc.*

[17] Cf. also Dt. 22:26. On the other hand, in Dt. 15:9; 23:22; 24:15, the reference to the making of complaint to Yahweh gives the term חֵטְא a religious emphasis. Yahweh is the Guardian of the legal relationship and is thus affected by a breach of the norm which protects it.

[18] The obviously incorrectly pointed words in Ex. 5:16 (read: וְחַטָאת עַמֶּךָ [Σ]) also express a complaint at unlawful conduct on the part of officials.

[19] It is self-evident that the Heb. author is not alluding here to the supposed divine dignity of Pharaoh.

against doing violence to Joseph : אַל־תֶּחֶטְאוּ בַיֶּלֶד (Gn. 42:22 E), [20] and similarly Jonathan warns Saul against murdering David : לָמָּה תֶחֱטָא בְּדָם נָקִי (1 S. 19:5). If odd or ungracious treatment is suffered at the hands of someone, the dispute with him is opened with a question like that of Jacob to Laban : מַה־פִּשְׁעִי מַה חַטָּאתִי (Gn. 31:36) or Abimelech to Abram : מֶה־חָטָאתִי לְךָ (Gn. 20:9). Here חַטָּאת (or פֶּשַׁע) is simply that which a reasonable person does not do, for "actions which are not done" is on the lips of Abimelech a more stringent formulation of what he had already described as חטא and of what he could not affirm in respect of his own conduct. In this sense חטא can even denote a lasting state of guilt or moral boycott, as when Judah pledges the safety of Benjamin with the words : "If I bring him not unto thee," וְחָטָאתִי לְךָ כָּל־הַיָּמִים (Gn. 43:9 J; cf. 44:32), i.e. I will always count as disloyal before thee. It is self-evident that the speaker has in mind here certain unfavourable consequences for himself in the case envisaged.

b. This limited aspect of the usage of חטא [21] is fundamental to an understanding of the religious meaning of the term, and in essence of the whole thought of sin in the OT. For in the case of the other roots mentioned a theological and more generally religious usage has also developed from the content of secular usage in regard to interrelationships and law, though it is impossible to fix with any historical precision either the beginning or the progress of this development in the literature of the OT. The transference of the secular content to the processes of religious life is particularly instructive in this instance because the assumption must have been that this life was seen as one which was either ordered, or to be ordered, by legal norms, or at least by certain generally binding rules. If the religious life is accepted as one which is predominantly ordered, i.e., if the basic principle is accepted that the dealings of man with God must follow a prescribed pattern and no other, this is a specifically theological consideration. From it one can if one wishes deduce the process of a transference of meaning without any possibility of conflict with the declarations of the OT. There will remain, however, a certain basic suspicion against making theological reflection responsible for giving such a distinctive meaning to terms which were used so realistically by the authors, especially when roots like פשע ("to rebel") are not merely formal like חטא and עוה but express human volition.

Certainly פשע is the most active and the least formal of all the terms used for sin and sinning. It has been excellently equated by E. König [22] with "rebellion." In its secular and not necessarily forensic use it denotes the wilful breach of a relationship of peace or alliance, e.g., Israel's renouncing of the dynasty of David (1 K. 12:19), or the revolt of vassal peoples against the "hand" of their overlords (cf. esp. 2 K. 8:20 : פָּשַׁע אֱדוֹם מִתַּחַת יַד־יְהוּדָה). If, then, in Is. 1:2 the image of sons rebelling against parental authority is applied to the opposition of Israel to Yahweh, or if in Jer. 2:29 the revolt against God is compared with a legal process initiated against Him, this shows clearly that the origin of such conduct, i.e., of sin, is to

---

[20] Cf. the self-accusation of the brothers in v. 21: אֲנַחְנוּ אֲשֵׁמִים.

[21] A similar picture is presented by the use of רָשָׁע, which has an even stronger legal character. In legal terminology (e.g., Ex. 23:1 etc.) רָשָׁע denotes one who is in the wrong. This is the starting-point for all further shades of meaning. Cf. G. Marschall, *Die "Gottlosen" des ersten Psalmenbuches* (1929), 49 ff.

[22] E. König, Wört., s.v.

be found in a decision of the human will. [23] Along the same lines Amos (4:4) need only say פִּשְׁעוּ ("transgress") without any further explanation to denote this challenging and almost impetuous attitude towards God. There is unmistakeably reflected in this attitude towards God, and hence also in the corresponding expression, a basic "numinous" element in sin. Rebellion is a conscious and intentional "violation, not of purely arbitrary will, but of an actual object of numinous value, no matter what this may be." [24] Sin is thus a spontaneous human reaction to the holy and the divine.

The same thought, though with emphasis on an almost tragic element in human conduct, is to be found in the concept of man's going astray in his dealings with God. In a way which is often overlooked, this touches on the genuinely theological problem of sin and should not be omitted in the present context. Unfortunately, in the OT it mostly occurs with some degree of distortion in ritual terminology, or, conversely, we are to assume that it achieved its full development only as a few religious thinkers lifted it out of its relatively innocuous ritual setting. For, so far as the actual wording goes, שׁגה ("to err") with its derivatives seems to be the mildest expression for the reality of sin. This appearance is easily given because the root is predominantly used in the cultic and ritual sphere. In this sphere it denotes a misguided but not unconditionally negligent or culpable offence on the part of a "simple" person (פֶּתִי, Ez. 45:20) against ritual regulations which are concealed, i.e., which are not present to his consciousness (Lv. 4:13; cf. חטא בִּשְׁגָגָה "to sin through ignorance," Lv. 4:2 etc.). To this there corresponds in law an unpremeditated offence on provocation (בִּבְלִי דַעַת, Jos. 20:3; cf. Nu. 35:11). When the word is used in this way, however, full justice can hardly be done to the thought concealed in it. שׁגה is not really a mild expression. Its content is in fact much more serious than that of the formal "to be at fault" or the emotional "to rebel." For we can speak of error only on the assumption of the good will of the one who acts. If there is error, this is because of the circumstances, or, in religious terms, of God. Thus, the moment error is referred to as a religious concept outside the sphere of the cultic, there emerges an element of daemonic dread, which cannot indeed be entirely overlooked even when it is weakened by the possibility of cultic adjustment. When Job coins the statement (12:16) that the deceived as well as the deceiver is God's, he does not have in view an apparently innocuous thought, but the terrifying and tormenting one that man cannot attain to God by his own striving because God withholds from him the ability to do so. This bitter poet, pitilessly analysing his soul's life, ascribes decisively to God responsibility for the restricted destiny of man. Job thinks that he is quite right to complain against God on the point. The same thoughts seem to have been present in Isaiah too, though in him there is no such titanic outbreak of unrest. Is. warns against those who speak professionally of error and yet go astray themselves in frivolous in-

---

[23] Further examples may be found, e.g., in Hos. 7:13; 8:1 (rebellion against the Torah of Yahweh); Jer. 2:29; 3:13; Ez. 18:31; 20:38; Is. 43:27 (par. with חטא). The relationship of פשע to מרה, and the distinctive emphasis on will in both terms, emerges particularly clearly in Ps. 5:10. The plans of the adversaries which have led to their downfall correspond to their rebellions, and both are summed up in the concluding expression: מָרוּ בָךְ "they bade thee defiance."

[24] Cf. R. Otto, op. cit., 4.

toxication. With uncanny realism he draws out (Is. 28:7 f.) the twofold sense of
שגה as drunken wandering and as going astray on the way to God. He shows that
the irresistible wandering of the drunken seer in exercise of his calling to serve
the declaration of the will of God is partly culpable and partly brought about by
God. For him שגה implies a clouded mind which is incapable of comprehension and
therefore of dealings with God. God will speak to those who are in error "with
stammering lips and another tongue" which they cannot understand. They will
experience the same plight as Job, who, in spite of every human consolation, can
find no way out of his error, but must suffer the pain of the divine riddle (Job
19:4; 6:24). To be sure, many have not seen or wished to see the threatening
depths of the thought present in שגה. A quiet and simple man of prayer like the
author of Ps. 119 safely skirts such abysses, like the friends of Job. He realises
that he was once in error, but he is confident that the study of the Torah has instructed him and brought him out of his affliction (v. 67).

If, then, there is not lacking an irrational element in the thought of sin, as
indicated by פשע, מרה and שגה, yet we should not underestimate the importance of
the observation that in Hebrew usage apart from פשע this element, while it is incontestable, is not predominant. It is in the concept of "unclean" that the thought
of sin in the OT seems to have been most fully divested of this element. Basically,
the latter concept is not quite so "primitive," for it is at root theological, and it
is linked with a conception of God which has already attained to a certain stability.
To be sure, except in texts which are distinctively theological, like the Penta-
teuchal Law, we cannot say how far, if at all, rational theological ways of thinking
are consciously present in the authors. The logical structure of the concept usually
retreats in the measure that the term expresses lively personal feeling. Yet even
then we can recognise its content to be failure or opposition in respect of an imposed norm, and the corresponding theory can be easily reconstructed. The exegetical difficulty which lies in the danger of exaggeration, to use a typical phrase
of Gunkel, has thus to be taken seriously into account in all the OT passages
which speak of sinning or sin. Yet in the OT itself the addition בְּיָד רָמָה, "with a
high hand" (Nu. 15:30), sometimes betrays a need to give more body to the term
חטא and to rescue it from a more definitely formal sphere. The sin which, e.g., the
people of Sodom and Gomorrah committed (Gn. 18:20) was not sin in their own
eyes. It was first recognised to be such by the Israelite narrator on the basis of
a theological judgment. There are also many other statements about sin which
are more easily explained by the rational and theoretically ordered considerations
of the author than by basic feelings of a numinous kind. This must be taken into
account even in our interpretation of prayers in which sin is confessed. Thus in
Ps. 32, for example, we are taught that the one who prays was led to see and to
confess his sin by suffering. The thought suggests itself that such considerations
identify as sin much that was not really directed against God. It is presupposed
that God scrutinises sharply the *opus operatum* and the technical cultic ritual.

c. Scepticism in relation to the specifically religious character of the prevalent
OT concept of sin is further increased by the fact that Israelite wisdom usually
has a decidedly intellectual understanding of sin. If this is predominantly for
pedagogic reasons, we are still left with the impression that this teaching fell on
particularly fruitful soil, and that this way of thinking about the living questions
of religion was already scoffed at by the צַו לָצָו and קַו לָקַו of Isaiah (28:10). A

נָבָל [25] or fool is one who does not know what is fitting in relation to God, or who has this knowledge but does not see its applicability to his life (Ps. 14:1 f.). The sense of superiority enjoyed by the righteous then works itself out in a way which itself arouses suspicion even though such trains of thought are occasionally found in Jeremiah (4:22; 5:21), and even though there are warnings against this kind of folly in the song of Moses (Dt. 32:6). In spite of pastoral sympathy for a "foolish" people, the impulse and the distinctive character of sinful conduct hardly attain here to full and correct expression.

A profounder insight is to be seen in the phrase used in the augmented Decalogue (Ex. 20:5; Dt. 5:9) which describes those who resisted the directions of Yahweh in terms of hatred. For here it is brought out most forcefully that in sin we have a process which in the last resort cannot be explained, since the impelling forces of hatred are beyond human understanding. רְשָׁעִים [26] and לֵצִים both seem to be filled with hatred against God like many other kinds of ungodly whose designations are for the most part both etymologically and materially obscure. [27] It can hardly be denied that terms like תּוֹעֵבָה ("abomination"), זִמָּה ("device"), אָוֶן (mostly very colourlessly equated with "evil"), חָמָס ("act of violence"), מִרְמָה, רְמִיָּה ("deception"), בְּלִיַּעַל, [28] הוֹלְלִים etc. go back to conceptions of sin which have nothing to do with the typical concepts of the schools.

At any rate, they lack the distinctive pregnancy which is proper to the latter and which helped to make terms like חָטָא, פֶּשַׁע, and עָוֹן the common property of pious speech as simple metaphors unburdened by theological speculation. If this presentation seems to lead us to the conclusion that the developed and unmistakeable concept "sin" is a late growth on Israelite soil, this is not necessarily an argument against the correctness of the construction. [29] On the contrary, it testifies to a high maturity of the religious form of expression, which was grounded in firm and unshakeable categories whose validity no one in ancient Israel could contest with the instruments of current thought. The simple man could not be told more simply or clearly what was the significance of the unrest of his heart in the presence of the holy than by such terms as transgression, deviation from a required norm, repudiation of every norm, or error which is to be corrected thereby. Criticism of human conduct, the assertion of guilty action and above all the inescapable knowledge of a demanding will of deity all meet in these pregnant concepts and give them the force of powerful formulae which exhaustively interpret the significance of all the situations of human destiny controlled by creaturely feeling. If the religion of Israel recognised the will of God to be the supreme law

---

[25] Cf. also כְּסִיל in Prv. 3:35 etc.; he is dumb like the brutes (בַּעַר, Ps. 92:6; 49:11); נָבוּב (Job 11:12). It is striking that the "simple" (פֶּתִי) can also be religiously well-disposed when under the influence of the Law (Ps. 19:7; 119:130). If on the other hand the same group is often described as "cunning" etc., this is either in a purely tactical sense or it perhaps reflects more "primitive" views.

[26] The book of the covenant (Ex. 23:7) already emphasises Yahweh's aversion to the רָשָׁע, which must correspond to the aversion of the latter to Him (cf. also Ex. 9:27).

[27] Cf. on this point Mowinckel and Pedersen, op. cit., and Marschall, op. cit., esp. 125.

[28] Cf. esp. Ps. 18:3, where the reference is to a demon in Sheol. Similarly חַטָּאת in Gn. 4:7 indicates a demonic being, cf. H. Duhm, Die bösen Geister im AT (1904), 8 f. and the Comm. ad loc.

[29] That the term "sin" is lacking in the oldest accessible parts of the OT literature may be accidental, and cannot be used as a historical proof.

which determines every creature, then it had to try to express the apostasy of man from God, and his ungodly actions, in concepts which establish their claim to binding validity by indicating the lines along which human life ought to move. In a way which is inescapable for the Hebrew sense of language, such indication is given in the verb of movement חטא, or in עוה, in the thought of error, or in the legal conception which underlies פשע. Undoubtedly, the theological thinking of a whole series of generations was needed at least theoretically to establish this validity, and there can be no question that this development was narrowly linked with the thought of the covenant (→ διαθήκη) which is the basic pillar of Israelite religion. [30] In both cases the feeling of terror retreats before the awareness of responsibility, which grows with the greatness of God and extends to every area of life with the confession לְךָ לְבַדְּךָ חָטָאתִי ("against thee, thee only, have I sinned," Ps. 51:4).

At this point it emerges plainly what sin is as distinct from all other defective action. If sin is to be asserted, then we must exclude both our own and all other human opinion as to the significance of what has been done. Whether the transgression is slight or serious by human judgment, for the author its character as transgression is set beyond all possible doubt simply by the thought of God and of the order which is subject to His will. It is to Him and to no other authority that he must render an account. This is his "hidden wisdom" (v. 6). That he has violated the norm of God is the substance of his knowledge of sin. He has done that which is done in all sinning and which constitutes sinful action as such. In order to bring this out more sharply, he augments his confession with a final saying which is almost blasphemously bold : "I have sinned ... that thou mightest be justified ... and pure." The result of his action in terms of the knowledge of God is here described as the purpose of the sinner. His knowledge culminates in the insight that the objective fact of his sinning seems to serve a purpose by leading him to a recognition of the unconditional validity of the divine norm. If he now makes of this thought a rather unhappily negative and flattering motive : "I have sinned to the glory of God" (the positive motive is given in the following verse), this may seem repellent, and yet it has high theological value as a ruthless attempt to set human failure within the divine order and consequently to interpret it religiously as sin.

The view expressed by H. Gunkel [31] in his exposition of the Ps. can hardly be correct: "David, who has seduced a married woman and shamefully betrayed her husband to death, cannot truly say that he has sinned against God alone." To be sure, David did Uriah a great wrong. Nevertheless, it was only as an act against God that this Sultanlike action was sin. We cannot read with any certainty from v. 4 what the poet has either done or not done. For this reason we cannot use the statement as an argument against the correctness of what the heading describes as the occasion of the Psalm. If the heading does not prove suspect on other grounds, it might well be correct in relation to v. 4, since in this verse all significance is denied to what has actually been done, and only the religious situation created by the act is recognised to be essential. To weaken [32] the self-exculpation boldly expressed in the final clause by referring it to v. 3 rather than v. 4a ("I acknowledge or confess ... in order" etc.) is a vague

---

[30] Cf. the expression מַרְשִׁיעֵי בְרִית ("such as do wickedly against the covenant," Da. 11:32), and cf. Pedersen, op. cit., 415 : "The breach of the covenant is the kernel of sin."
[31] H. Gunkel, Psalmen (1926), 226, following B. Duhm, Psalmen² (1922), 211.
[32] Cf. Duhm, 211; Gunkel, 222 f.

exegetical device which convinces no one, since it does not take the author seriously
and throws doubt on a perfectly good text. Those who "take pleasure in the profundity" [33] of the author ought to ask themselves whether his statement is really quite
so confused as this hypothesis supposes. The theory of an "elliptical manner of speaking" [34] avoids having to recognise the blasphemous element in the flattering motive
and proclaims an understanding which many an Israelite or Jewish reader must have
introduced into the passage. Yet it is unquestionably an emendation, and if the author
had really had this in view he would surely have expressed himself more clearly. The
simplest and therefore the correct interpretation is given by W. Staerk. [35] How Paul
views this final statement is to be seen in R. 3:5a.

d. Taking the OT as a whole, we may thus maintain that for the authors of
the OT sin is a legal and theological term for what is contrary to the norm. If
in the main the theological use is very prominent, yet great significance must be
attached to the fact that it is not the only use of the expressions available. Similarly, attention should be paid to the circumstance that in its rational form the
concept belongs far less to religion itself, to the living dealings between God and
man, and far more to theology, to the theoretical clarification of religious processes. It is this which makes its impress on a term like sin, and which attempts
therewith to denote symbolically a distinct religious situation or psychical event,
explaining it as best it can in this way. For this reason it is in the very nature of
the case that the OT has a long series of different linguistic modes of expression
for sin. We best understand these as different theological formulae mediating
different basic theological insights. They are attempts to represent a religious
phenomenon whose roots escape human understanding.

The concept of sin itself, which emerges from all these formulae and gives both
cause and justification for bringing them together, acquires many shades of meaning
from this varied usage, yet there is not lacking a certain unity. This is emphasised
indeed by plerophoric expressions in the OT itself, which partly seem to stress the
synonymous nature of the words (cf. the poetically fashioned Ps. 32:5 : "I acknowledged my חַטָּאת unto thee, and my עָוֹן have I not hid. I said, I will confess my פְּשָׁעִים"),
partly seek to impress by conscious cumulation (cf. esp. Ex. 34:7: Yahweh remits
עָוֹן וָפֶשַׁע וְחַטָּאָה), [36] and partly serve either intentionally or unintentionally to bring
out certain nuances (as, e.g., in the development indicated in Job 34:37: "He addeth
פֶּשַׁע unto his חַטָּאת", or Lv. 16:21, also v. 16 etc., where the explanatory addition
לְכָל־חַטֹּאתָם draws attention to a particular aspect of the preceding terms עָוֹן and
פֶּשַׁע). [37] It is obvious that fundamentally all the variations indicate one and the
same thing, namely, the deviation from a required norm which is the sense of the
predominant root חטא. By the use of various roots, however, account is taken of
the many possibilities of viewing and assessing this basic content. Sometimes the
emphasis is put on the process of the soul itself, sometimes on the act described

---

[33] Gunkel, 225.
[34] R. Kittel, *Psalmen*[3, 4] (1922), 190.
[35] W. Staerk, "Lyrik" (*Schriften des AT*, III, 1)[2] (1920), 231.
[36] Cf. also Ez. 21:29 : יַעַן הַזְכַּרְכֶם עֲוֹנְכֶם בְּהִגָּלוֹת פִּשְׁעֵיכֶם לְהֵרָאוֹת חַטֹּאותֵיכֶם בְּכֹל עֲלִילוֹתֵיכֶם
and Da. 9:24 ; cf. on all these passages L. Köhler, ZAW, NF 5 (1928), 214.
[37] Less clear is Hos. 12:9 : עָוֹן, אֲשֶׁר חֵטְא where the pointing does not seem to be right,
cf. the Comm. *ad loc.*

as sinful, sometimes on the state which results from sinning. But as a rule it is not so much from the root selected as from the context in which it is used that we can fix the intellectual or emotional content of the individual statements, or place the religious accent which is not immediately obvious in itself.

In analysing these statements, therefore, we have to differentiate a whole series of possibilities ranging from sober intellectual assertion to the unmistakeable experience of being divinely seized. But even where the theology seems to be almost entirely eliminated from a religious expression, the term always retains a certain theoretical flavour. For it is always a concept, and as such it leads easily to a purely rational and legal conception of the matter. This is no doubt of pedagogic value, but it is always in danger of reducing to a common denominator the manifold phenomena of religious life which are so finely indicated by the alternation of forms of expression. A metaphorical nature which can hardly do justice to the religious process denoted is particularly characteristic of roots like חטא, עוה, also שגה, תעה, etc., which indicate deviation from a norm. They point to this process only as they factually denote the disorder incurred. On the other hand, a root like פשע ("to rebel") brings us closer to the heart of the true problem of sin, i.e., the question of the origin and significance of the religious process, since it unmistakeably describes the motive which determines the sinner. Yet even in this case, as in all others in which one of the usual terms occurs and there is thus express reference to sin, a certain intellectual order is imposed on an experience which was wholly irrational, so that retroactively a stronger or weaker irrational impulse is conveyed to intrinsically clear metaphorical concepts. Thus in prayers especially the irrational problem behind the concept emerges the more clearly, the further removed the language is from that of the schools and the more fully it takes the form of confession or complaint. In this connexion it is particularly instructive that in the story of the fall in Genesis, i.e., in the one great passage in the OT which deals thematically with the religious problem of sin, we do not find at all the customary terminology for sin, unless we are to count the very general term for evil. What sin is, is indicated in other ways in this passage.

3. Sin and Guilt.

Before we analyse this story and assess its contribution to the conception of sin in detail, we must first return to a point already mentioned, namely, that many of the Hebrew words for sin allude to it in such a way that the translation "guilt" seems to be justifiable or even necessary (→ δικαιοσύνη). This is always the case when the terms occur in passages in which it is plain that in his use of חטא, עָוֹן, רשע etc. the author is not thinking of an action but is speaking of the consequences of a sinful, i.e., a negative, erroneous and disruptive action, of the state which is brought about and determined by sinning, or of the inner attitude which stems from the sinful action. The promiscuity of usage in this respect teaches us that the Hebrews never attained to any sharp terminological distinction between sin and guilt, since there was not the slightest doubt as to the causal connection between abnormal action and the abnormal state.

In a plain and unequivocal way, the only religious terms to denote the state of guilt, or the guilt which burdens man, are the nouns אָשָׁם and אַשְׁמָה, to which there correspond the verb אשם ("to incur guilt" or "to be guilty") and the verbal adjective אָשֵׁם ("guilty"). This root is mostly used in the language of sacral law

(→ ἱλάσκεσθαι), and there are few examples of secular use. [38] The use which the priestly legislation makes of the concept underlying the root אשם makes clear the material and objective character of sacral guilt. It is identical with uncleanness. To incur guilt one does not have to be a sinner in the sense of a man who rebels against the divine order on the basis of a decision of the will. Guilt is incurred unintentionally through a mistake. The only point is that the ritual concept of error is essentially weakened in the sphere of casuistry, as already indicated (→ 274). Nevertheless, the consequences of such error are taken no less seriously than in the case of other sins. A transgression committed בִּשְׁגָגָה ("through ignorance"), i.e., unintentionally, whether out of negligence (Lv. 4:13, 22) or some other misapprehension (Lv. 4:2; 5:15, 18; Nu. 15:22 etc.), incurs no less guilt than a misdeed committed בְּיָד רָמָה i.e., with a high hand, or intentionally (Nu. 15:30, cf. בְּזֶה and הֵפֵר, v. 31). Even if the nature of the matter is concealed from the one who does it, he becomes unclean and guilty : וְנֶעְלַם מִמֶּנּוּ וְהוּא טָמֵא וְאָשֵׁם (Lv. 5:2). To set aside his guilt, the same ritual is used as that which restores cleanness (→ ἱλάσκεσθαι). [39]

The expressions which refer to guilt without using the technical term אשם are further removed from this dynamic circle of conception. In such cases the thought of guilt is usually linked with עָוֹן, and quite unequivocally when there is reference to bearing or taking away, both denoted by נשא. [40] The expressions brought together in Ps. 32:1 are particularly instructive : אַשְׁרֵי נְשׂוּי־פֶּשַׁע כְּסוּי חֲטָאָה אַשְׁרֵי־אָדָם לֹא יַחְשֹׁב יְהֹוָה לוֹ עָוֹן. We again encounter the three words פֶּשַׁע, חטא and עָוֹן (→ 278), the emphasis now falling unmistakeably on the element of guilt. Guilt is a "heavy burden" which man cannot bear (Ps. 38:4). It is the sum of debts incurred by individual acts of sin. In substance it is identical with the sufferings which may plague a man, and it is manifested in these afflictions. When Cain says (Gn. 4:13): גָּדוֹל עֲוֹנִי מִנְּשֹׂא, the thought underlying עָוֹן, as in many Psalms of complaint, is that the misfortune which is suspended as a punishment is linked with the state which opposes the divine norm. Sorrow at the guilt of sin is evoked by, or is identical with, the sorrow of suffering. In the construction of theories of expiation and retribution which have this view as a basis, the rational theological character of the OT concept of both guilt and sin comes out very strongly, since such construction is mostly undertaken from standpoints which are dominated by legal thinking. When legal thinking was applied to the relationship between God and the sinner, so far as concerned the idea of the righteousness of God and that of man the religious concept of guilt derived from a numinous root. For this reason, its full effect on the thinking of the OT authors is purposely developed in connection with these complexes.

---

[38] The reference in Gn. 26:10 is to marital rights. Guilt is brought (בוא hi) upon a man when he is led to violate another's marriage, cf. also Ju. 21:22. In the law of property expressions are used which are quite alien to the religious concept of guilt, e.g., מַשָּׂה, מַשָּׁא, חוֹב, נְשִׁי.

[39] Cf. A. Bertholet, Das Dynamistische im AT (1926), 36 f.

[40] Rather strangely, this seems to be almost completely ignored in the LXX (→ n. 3), where ἀδικία (80 times), ἀμαρτία (69) and ἀνομία (64) are excessively used as equivalents.

4. The Story of the Fall (Gn. 3).

The treatment which J has accorded to the problem of sin within the framework of the Paradise story in Gn. 3 stands aloof from all theories which are basically orientated to legal thinking, and is without influence on them. Perhaps making use of ancient mythological materials, [41] with no fear of their strangeness, subjecting them by the force of his own thinking, the author tells us with a simplicity which even children can understand, and therefore with absolutely convincing power, of the way in which sin originated, what it is and how it works itself out. As already noted, it is striking that in this story of the so-called Fall no use whatever is made of the usual technical terms apart from the particularly difficult רַע (→ κακός). Only from the matter itself do we know that the reference is to sin. [42] Because the author seeks to mediate a view and to describe processes of a typical kind, he must set aside these terms. Their pedagogic nature would be out of place in an attempt to observe and portray life rather than to give a theological presentation of the results. The latter is left to the theologically inclined reader ; only a few cautious indications are given of the lines along which his thinking should proceed if it is to be fruitful. The primary interest lies elsewhere. The attention of the hearer or reader is directed to the peculiar event itself which the pedagogic terms are designed in their own way to comprehend and explain. The point of the portrayal is to make it clear that our whole destiny as men is supremely shaped by this event. What is commonly called sin is thus integrated into a series of tense processes which bring out more clearly than any conceptual reflection the living and sinister reality of the matter with which theology, the cultus and piety are for the most part unsuspectingly concerned as they make use of the concept of sin.

If we dismiss all conjectures or possible conclusions concerning the history of the material, the basic ideas of the narrative may be presented as follows. A prohibition, sharpened by the reference to serious consequences, unequivocally expresses the will of Yahweh for man. In the first instance this remains inviolate, since the authority of deity would seem to be beyond human assault. Only the clever serpent perceives the disproportion between the seriousness of the consequences, i.e., death, and the triviality of the forbidden action. In order to initiate discussion of the point, it puts to the woman a leading question as to the scope of the prohibition. The loyal answer betrays as yet no trace of scepticism, but it does reveals a readiness for it, and the serpent goes on to entice her, creating the desired opportunity resolutely to renounce her literal conception of the prohibition. The thesis of the serpent is that the warning of Yahweh is not to be taken seriously. It is simply a purposeful threat. The prohibition and warning are not in man's interests but in those of Yahweh. God aims to restrain man by fear from

---

[41] For an analysis of the motifs, cf. the Comm., and esp. H. Gressmann in *Festgabe für Harnack* (1921), 24 ff.; R. Kittel, *Gesch. d. Volkes Israel,* I 5, 6 (1923), 220 f.; J. Feldmann, *Paradies und Sündenfall* (1913).

[42] It can hardly be correct that this was first seen by Deuteronomists and later scholars, as assumed by H. Schmidt, *Die Erzählung von Paradies und Sündenfall* (1931), 49 f. The narrator and all his readers were surely aware that sin lay at the very heart of the story. Cf. K. Budde, *Die biblische Urgeschichte* (1883), 72 : "If the author were to ask his readers what spiritual magnitude was brought before them, I for my part believe that there can be only one possible answer, namely, sin." On the whole complex of questions, cf. also K. Budde, *Die biblische Paradiesesgeschichte* (1932).

something which he might easily and safely take by transgression of the command. In so doing, man would become as God, knowing good and evil. The woman is already attracted by the external appearance of the forbidden fruit. Therefore like a fool she listens to this partially understood saying about becoming wise, and she violates the prohibition. The man silently participates in her act of wrongdoing. He, too, has heard about knowledge and becoming wise, for he is present with his wife. The first consequence of the forbidden action is that they become aware of their nakedness and try to cover it. The second is that they hide at the approach of Yahweh. The third is that, when examined, the man resorts to subterfuges in explanation of his action. The fourth is that all concerned fall under the penalty of Yahweh.

It is evident that in this fatal chain of events the emphasis falls on inner processes mysteriously indicated by the formulae "being as God" and "knowledge of good and evil." Men are as God when they set aside His prohibition. They do this the moment when they begin to doubt, first, that God's overruling is in their interests, and second, that God's will is unconditionally binding. In this context we need not pursue the fact that in the story these considerations seem to apply to varying degrees in respect of the man and the woman. The essential point is that they both perceive that they have only to decide and they can infringe the divine mandate. This is possible, however, only by a convincing material consideration from the authoritative standpoint of their own persons, to which the serpent helps them by an illuminating utterance which characterises the obedient attitude of faith as hopeless stupidity. If, therefore, sin is transgression of the divine order, the force which impels thereto is here perceived and described. The root of sinful action is the understanding and the need to exercise it, i.e., practical reason exalting man to be lord and God in his own personal life. This understanding is capable of despising all correctives, even those of religion, and of performing actions which do not ask concerning the judgment of God, though they are in fact subject to it.

For alongside this picture of the man who boldly asserts himself, and who is called to maturity of will, there is set the further picture which shows how that which is brought about by this self-assertion against God tries to avoid being called to account by God. The self-will of man is not strong enough to resist the summons to give account. It collapses miserably, and the man who would be as God finally stands there like a schoolboy who has been found out, defiant and full of evasions, yet also convicted.

The delicate sarcasm of the presentation is directed against these same men to the extent that they are יֹדְעֵי טוֹב וָרָע. This appositional expression, with its intentionally selected syntactical imprecision, seems essentially to be chosen to convey the same thing as "being as God," and there can be no doubt that, like the latter phrase, it is meant sarcastically to veil rather than instructively to reveal. For this reason we cannot say finally what its meaning is. The conjecture that there is a play on sexual maturity seems to rest mainly on the fact that the discovery of nakedness was the first consequence of the violation rather than on any connection of ידע with the terminology of sex. [43] It is quite impossible to bring *tob* and *ra'* into the sexual sphere. Nor is it readily conceivable that the Hebrews would immediately see a sexual meaning in the words; neither Prv. 31:12, Dt. 1:39, nor even 2 S. 19:36 offers any real proof in this regard. Hence the view

---

[43] Gressm., 46. Cf. E. König, *Genesis, ad loc.*

that the story is a depiction of the "rise of sensual love" [44] does not really help to explain it. The corresponding translation "full of desire and suffering" is much too strongly sentimental. It hardly does justice to a writer of the stature of J and smacks rather of the Klärchen of Goethe's *Egmont*. All things considered Wellhausens's robust explanation of *tob* and *ra'* in terms of what we usually call culture [45] still seems to be nearest the mark, and it has not yet been superseded by a better one.

The impression can hardly be avoided that the evident Prometheus motif is finally reduced *ad absurdum* by being linked with the sorry spectacle which follows. Yet it is part of the imperishable greatness of the story that, in spite of its clear recognition of the grotesquely misguided nature of the desire to be as God, it does not regard this as outrageous or disgraceful, but acknowledges it with the painful gentleness of an *expertus*. The formulations וִהְיִיתֶם כֵּאלֹהִים and נֶחְמָד לְהַשְׂכִּיל serve to bring out the tragic situation of man, attempting in his own power to transcend the narrowness of his existence, with a clarity which awakens motifs of longing in the simplest as well as the most mature, and which thus gives rise with shattering compulsion to an kind of apology of sin for itself. Nevertheless, as this effect is attained, with needle-like certainty there is a probing of the religious kernel of the problem of sin which is concealed from all conceptual thinking. This is found in the incontestable immanent right of the ungodly attitude of man in his hostility to God. There can be conviction of the reality of sin only as it is psychologically justified. None of the biblical authors has done this in so masterly or pregnant a way as the Jahwist. The human desire for culture, the work of creative thought obeying immanent laws, bold and compelling sensual desire seeking theoretical support — all these are positively apprehended by the narrator and set in the pitiless light of the concept of God. Two worlds meet, and the reader is left in no doubt that in every act which deviates from obedience to God there will take place the same encounter with the unfathomable distress to which it gives rise. The way of man as it is opened up by the possibilities of his being will always entail his venturing on to the heights with bold or clumsy audacity, and his final attempt at concealment from the glance of God. His divine likeness is a cause of anxiety when God calls him.

b. Thus we need do no violence to the story to see that it opens up a perspective on the totality of human existence. There are uneven passages, and it is subject to the cultural limitations of the period, for it is strongly shot through with mythologoumena. But for the kind of theological interpretation which we are attempting the unmistakeable unity of the whole complex must be normative. The story as we now have it is aetiologically fashioned and yet this orientation does not obtrude, nor does it weaken the convicting force of the content. We perceive it in the curses on the serpent (v. 14 f.), the woman (v. 16) and the man (v. 17b-19), and in the distinctive significance attached to nakedness. The curses relate to conditions which may be seen from simple observation and everyday experience. They thus explain the presence of inescapable difficulties as a consequence of the curse which the first pair brought down by their conduct. It is thus shown why

---

[44] H. Schmidt, *op. cit.*, 22.
[45] Prolegomena, 305 ff. (*Gesch. Isr.*, I [1878], 344 ff.).

the serpent is such a remarkable and detested animal, why the woman suffers in childbirth and lives in dependence, and why the man must toil for his bread and finally be reduced to dust. The sinning of the first couple against God is the explanation. [46] But if they come under something which is of general validity, and if they adopt a common custom like the use of clothing, the explanation given can carry conviction only if the underlying basis is not a contingent event outside normal experience, but if all men in the same circumstances can be trusted to act in exactly the same way as the two in Paradise. If, then, the two are types of humanity generally to the extent that they must take upon themselves what is borne by all, and learn the shame which is known by all, this typology becomes the more compellingly clear to the reader the more he begins to understand that the manner in which they act towards God *mutatis mutandis* is exactly the same as that in which all men become guilty in thought and action towards God. The aetiology of the story thus extends beyond the explanation of sorrow and labour and death as punishments inflicted by God, or of shame as the result of transgression, to the most important theme of the explanation of sin itself as the *primum movens* of all the unrest and unhappiness of man. [47]

The doubts expressed by Weiser [48] (following Gressmann) as to this aetiological conception hardly do justice to the relevance of the story. In it the field is cursed for man's sake, and therefore it is man himself who is indirectly cursed. Nor should we be so affected as to question the townsman's poetic fancy that the serpent eats dust. The concealing of nakedness is also to be understood aetiologically. The helpless perplexity of man when he has become unsure of himself is to be recognised as a feeling which is just as typically a consequence of sin as shame is the normal, impulsive reaction in a state of nakedness. The words: "They knew that they were naked," are in the style of the story a way of saying that the wrongdoers were suddenly conscious of a feeling of insecurity. This feeling the narrator thinks he can best interpret by the feeling of shame. At the same time he incidentally answers the question of the origin of this remarkable feeling by showing that it is a consequence of sin and very close to, although not identical with it. Without sin the man and woman would have had nothing to hide from one another. Because they transgressed, they lost this state even in the physical sphere. This train of thought makes it clear that the writer is operating with a specific, culturally conditioned view of nakedness, namely, the Israelite and Jewish, which is marked by a "wholly ritual fear of purely physical divestiture." [49] Yet this cannot weaken the impression that here, too, the purpose of the narrator is to say and explain something of general validity, and that in the last resort he is thus dealing with a living problem which naturally arises in all cultured society, namely, the sexual question in its widest sense.

c. The aetiological interpretation justifies us to some extent in building on the story of the fall a theory of original sin in the sense of the general sinfulness of man. [50] At any rate, a theological deduction of this kind does not run counter to

[46] The view of A. Menes (ZAW, NF 2 [1925], 39) that the creation of the woman is perhaps an act of divine wrath in "consequence of a sin" has no more value than can ever be ascribed to products of an unbridled delight in hypotheses. When J. Hempel (ZSTh., 9 [1931] 223) speaks of "tolerable certainty" in relation to this view, this seems to me to be a rash and distorted judgment.
[47] Though cf. M. Weber, *Ges. Aufsätze zur Religionssoziologie*, III (1921), 242.
[48] A. Weiser, *Religion u. Sittlichkeit in der Genesis* (1928), 36 f.
[49] Weber, *op. cit.*, 205, cf. 234, 245.
[50] The same author actually expresses this at the beginning and end of the flood story in Gn. 6:5; 8:21.

the meaning of the story. When the narrator motivates the fall of the first man by a general human impulse capable of a thousand variations, namely, the demand for knowledge and the desire to be clever, he is vitally impelled by the recognition that in virtue of this urge all normal men to-day will not merely be tempted along similar lines but will in fact be guilty of the same act. He sees that the uncontrolled intellect is in conflict with religion and that the freedom of the will and of thought prepare the ground for sin. If all share in the intellect and its destructive possibilities, all are participants in the act which brings guilt, and all are thus afflicted by the misery of existence.

By making the dramatic figure of the clever serpent the representative of the unrestricted and penetrating intellect, the narrator consciously emphasises the demonic nature of the thought which derives from doubt, which strives fanatically for knowledge and which for the sake of it tears down everything that would hamper it. He uses this genre of fable to stress the unfathomable duality which marks all sinful conduct. He gives us to understand that a kind of alien power comes over the man who sins, which he must obey against his better judgment because it convinces him by its assured manner and its correspondence with his own feeling. At any rate, no deeper purpose is served by the mythologoumenon of the serpent within the context of Gn. 3. The dualism concealed in it serves here only as a practical stylistic device to portray analytically the development of a very delicate process of the soul. For the fable motif is abandoned at once when it has fulfilled its purpose of expounding and explaining the origin of the novel action of the woman. The reader can now appreciate how the cold power of doubt, which proceeds from the understanding as thus personified, reinforces the existing sensual and intellectual feeling, and he is not at all surprised when an impulsive movement finally overthrows uncritical obedience.

The impossibility of making against this movement any thoroughgoing opposition grounded in experience, the overwhelming impression that the deviation of the human will and the corresponding action from the divinely established norm is a kind of necessity of the structure of man, compels every theological consideration to recognise the general validity of the phenomenon presented in the story. Because man seeks to be wise irrespective of God's authority, because he seeks to penetrate behind the thoughts of God and to anticipate them, because he not only wills to do this but is also able to do so within certain limits, a sphere of mistrust is opened up in which it is both possible and tempting for man to renounce the attitude appropriate to him as a creature, to regard the Creator with criticism and to think and act as himself God, unhampered, and in responsibility only to himself. Because reason and the ability to form his own judgments on man and the world are native to him, the motive for sinning is present and active with the same necessity and to the same degree as life generally.

The more strongly, however, this interpretation is theologically emphasised, the more clearly it must be stated that the aim of the author is not to give a correct theological account, but rather, if we may use the phrase, to popularise a basic theological concept. He attempts this without displaying any tendentiousness beyond that of the simple aetiology indicated. What is expressed in his spontaneous and uncomplicated representation is not so much theology as true and profound piety. An unsparing desire for truth gives it its unforgettable impress. Hardly anywhere else in the OT do we encounter discussion of a religious question which is so penetrating and yet sustained by such piety. From the manner in which J introduces the statement that humanity necessarily entails sinfulness one may easily detect that he is not spinning a theory. With a sense of vocation he is speaking out of the compelling experience of inner tension. Through this simple story he is trying to lead his readers to a knowledge of the fateful power of this serious situation which is inseparable from human existence, and consequently to self-knowledge. To the question which finally suggests itself because it is so much in line with the penetrating scrutiny of this observer, namely, why God so arranged it that the decision of activity either for or against God is laid upon man, he returns no answer. His religion is to be found in this silence.

Quell

B. Theological Nuances of ἁμαρτία in the LXX.

In sections A and D (→ 267 ff.; 293 ff.), and in section B of the art. on ἁμαρτωλός (→ 320 f.), there are reviews of the general usage of the LXX which it is the purpose of the present section to supplement by reference to theologically important nuances. These were partly due to misunderstandings and difficulties of the Heb. text, partly to the intentions of the translators.

In ψ 128:3 חֹרְשִׁים is altered into הָרְשָׁעִים in the light of the following verse. Similarly in the second half-verse the metaphorical language of the Mas. is changed by using ἀνομία [51] for מַעֲנוֹת, as often occurs in the LXX. There is a parallel to this in Dt. 29:18 (19), where the Mas. speaks of "the watered and the dry being rooted out." A similar image is used by Gk. translators outside the LXX. The latter replaces the image by the matter represented: ἵνα μὴ συναπολέσῃ ὁ ἁμαρτωλὸς τὸν ἀναμάρτητον. We may also refer to ψ 140:5, where the Mas. reads: "My head shall not refuse head ointment," [52] but the LXX changes רֹאשׁ into רָשָׁע: ἔλαιον δὲ ἁμαρτωλοῦ μὴ λιπανάτω τὴν κεφαλήν μου; it thus issues a warning against fellowship with sinners.

Greater prominence is given to presumption as a characteristic of sinners in the LXX. Thus in Sir. 11:9 זֵד ("arrogant"), and in 15:7 זָדוֹן ("arrogance") are rendered ἁμαρτωλός. In 11:9 the LXX expresses religious wisdom (cf. Ps. 1:1), whereas the Heb. is quite secular. If in Sir. 3:27 we ought to read מתהלל for מתחלל (Smend), [53] then here, too, arrogance is regarded as the sin *par excellence*. The sinful attitude thereby presupposed is depicted in Sir. 5:4, 5 (cf. also 10:12 f.). Again, in 35(32):12(16) the LXX merges the concepts of sin and presumption without any sure basis in the Heb. The latter reads: "And there speak what cometh into thy mind in the fear of God and not in ignorance." [54] But the Gk. writes: ἐκεῖ παῖζε καὶ ποίει τὰ ἐνθυμήματά σου, καὶ μὴ ἁμάρτῃς (א: ἁμαρτία καὶ) λόγῳ ὑπερηφάνῳ. A unitary view of sin is also asserted when Sir. 47:23 has ὁδὸς ἁμαρτίας for מכשול, and when ἁμαρτωλός is used for אנשי חמס in 15:12, for עול in 16:13 and for בליעל in 11:32. That the rich and powerful man is a sinner is a view occasionally found in the OT and NT (cf. Qoh. 2:26; Prv. 23:17), but in Hab. 3:14 this is forced into a translation of unknown origin when ראשׁ פְּרָזוֹ is rendered τοὺς ἀρχηγοὺς τῶν ἁμαρτωλῶν. Sin is also sickness; and this genuine OT insight causes חֳלִי to be rendered ἁμαρτία in Is. 53:4, so that the thought of v. 12 is anticipated. It is worth noting that Σ has a formulation which seems

---

[51] Deriv. from ענה pi, "to oppress" ?
[52] So A. Bertholet in Kautzsch, II⁴ (1923), 269; H. Gunkel, *Psalmen* (1926), *ad loc.* corrects the Mas. in accord. with the LXX.
[53] So R. Smend, *Die Weisheit d. Jesus Sirach erkl.* (1906), 32.
[54] Smend, 290 f.

to be determined by the NT concept of the sufferings of the Messiah as developed on the basis of the LXX : ὄντως τὰς ἁμαρτίας ἡμῶν αὐτὸς ἀνέλαβε, καὶ τοὺς πόνους ὑπέμεινεν, ἡμεῖς δὲ ἐλογισάμεθα αὐτὸν ἐν ἁφῇ ὄντα, πεπληγότα ὑπὸ θεοῦ καὶ τεταπεινωμένον. According to Procopius of Gaza, 'Α and Θ had the same text. The idea of the healing of sin, which corresponds to the equation of sin and sickness, is introduced by the LXX in Dt. 30:3. The Mas. reads : וְשָׁב יְהֹוָה אֱלֹהֶיךָ אֶת־שְׁבוּתְךָ ("Then the Lord thy God will turn thy destiny"). 'Α attempts a literal translation : καὶ ἐπιστρέψει κύριος, ὁ θεός σου, τὴν ἐπιστροφήν σου. Σ introduces a reference to salvation history : καὶ ἐπιστρέψει σοι κύριος, ὁ θεός σου, τὴν αἰχμαλωσίαν σου. [55] The LXX on the other hand independently emphasises the thought of the forgiveness of sins from the standpoint of a hamartologically determined piety : καὶ ἰάσεται κύριος τὰς ἁμαρτίας σου. 'Α and LXX here derive שְׁבוּת from the verb שׁוּב (so also Σ at Jer. 33:26), whereas Σ and Θ, and usually the LXX, have שָׁבָה in view. The negative understanding of שְׁבוּת by the LXX is important for the development of the concept of sin. This is also found in Ez. 16:53, where שְׁבוּת is translated ἀποστροφή ("apostasy"). In Jer. ἀποστροφή occurs 4 times for מְשׁוּבָה (5:6; 8:5; and 6:19 and 18:12, where it is wrongly read for מַחְשְׁבוֹת). The word מְשׁוּבָה for its part underlies ἁμαρτία in Jer. 14:7, where it is in keeping with the context. Similarly the LXX usually takes both שְׁבוּת and מְשׁוּבָה in the negative sense of apostasy. According to Dt. 30:3 and Jer. 14:7 apostasy is the basic sin from which deliverance and healing are expected and besought.

The LXX often seemed to avoid translating the formula שׁוּב שְׁבוּת. We may refer to Job 42:10, where one of the reasons is perhaps that the LXX is less interested in the restoration of the former wealth of Job than in the offence which the friends of Job have committed by their false accusations against (v. 8 : κατά) Job (→ 288 on ψ 108:5). Thus in Job 42 the LXX stresses the thought of forgiveness, which is only indicated in the Mas. In 42:7 the Mas. has : "My wrath is kindled against thee," but the LXX substitutes : ἥμαρτες σύ. In this way, it also avoids the anthropopathic view of God of the Mas. There is a similar change in v. 9, where the Mas. : "The Lord had regard unto Job," is paraphrased : καὶ ἔλυσεν τὴν ἁμαρτίαν αὐτοῖς διὰ 'Ιώβ. Again, in v. 10 the LXX introduces the thought : εὐξαμένου δὲ αὐτοῦ καὶ περὶ τῶν φίλων ἀφῆκεν αὐτοῖς τὴν ἁμαρτίαν. The translation of נשׂא by ἔλυσεν τὴν ἁμαρτίαν in v. 9 is perhaps due to the fact that נשׂא is a technical term for the remission of sins. This would also explain the change in Is. 1:14 : οὐκέτι ἀνήσω τὰς ἁμαρτίας ὑμῶν. Σ understands the technical term thus : ἐκοπώθην ἱλασκόμενος. [56] As in Job 42:7, so in Nu. 1:53 "sin" (ἁμάρτημα) is substituted for "wrath" (קֶצֶף). Instead of speaking theologically (Ju. 1:18), if also anthropopathically, of the wrath of God which the congregation might provoke, the LXX speaks psychologically of the transgression which it should avoid. According to Sh Σ (ὀργή) and Θ (θυμός) translated literally. The same alteration occurs in Is. 57:17 (קָצַפְתִּי = ἐλύπησα αὐτόν). God sends as a punishment for sin λύπη εἰς μετάνοιαν (2 K. 7:9 f.). A comparison with 1 Εσδρ. 6:14 is interesting, for here רגז (hafel), "to provoke to anger," is rendered παραπικράναντες ἁμαρτάνειν, although in 2 Εσδρ. 5:12 the same word is translated lit. παροργίζω. Even here, however, care is taken not to ascribe the emotion of wrath to God. παραπικραίνω without object is intrans. In 2 Ch. 12:2 the verb מָעַל ("to be unfaithful") is translated ἁμαρτάνειν. In 2 Ch. 30:7 ἀφίστημι is used for the same verb, so that here

---

[55] So also Θ, except that the σοι is lacking; 'Α, Σ, Θ have been trans. back by Field acc. to Masius.
[56] 'Α, followed by Jerome in the Vulgate, had a lit. trans. Cf. also the addition to the LXX : τὰς ἁμαρτίας ὑμῶν, in Is. 55:7. The Mas. simply has סלה.

again sin seems to be thought of as apostasy in accordance with the Chronicler's view of history (cf. Ju. 10:10). The same is true of 1 Εσδρ. 8:89. Here, too, ἁμαρτάνειν is used for מַעַל, whereas the corresponding passage 2 Εσδρ. 10:2 has ἀσυνθετεῖν, which is used 6 times for מַעַל and which indicates faithless conduct towards God (cf. v. 3 in contrast). The LXX rendering of Na. 3:6 is meant in the same sense. The Mas. reads: וְהִשְׁלַכְתִּי עָלַיִךְ שִׁקֻּצִים וְנִבַּלְתִּיךְ (pi of נבל "to revile"). "I (Yahweh) will cast filth upon thee and revile thee." [57] The LXX derives the form וְנִבַּלְתִּיךְ from the subst. נְבָלוּת and translates: καὶ ἐπιρίψω ἐπὶ σὲ βδελυγμὸν κατὰ τὰς ἁμαρτίας (א* ἀκαθαρσίας Β) σου. The fact that B has ἀκαθαρσίας (as also the LXX in Hos. 2:12, the only place where נְבָלוּת occurs in the Mas.) points to the sin of idolatry for which ἀκαθαρσία is the tech. term in the LXX. In Prv. it is found in a more psychological and ethical sense as a rendering of תּוֹעֵבָה, which is for the most part used cultically and often with reference to idols. A, which here has the original, uses ἁμαρτία for תּוֹעֵבָה in Ez. 8:6 and 16:51, whereas B has ἀνομία according to the usual translation. In both cases the reference is to the sin of idolatry or of a-whoring from Yahweh (Ez. 16:41 ff.). The Heb. stem טמא, mostly rendered ἀκαθαρσία or μιαίνειν, indicates cultic uncleanness. In Lv. 14:19, which refers to the uncleanness of a leper, the LXX intentionally replaces the cultic term by the moral and religious concept of sin. [58]

That folly is sin and wisdom piety is a familiar thought in OT wisdom. It is perhaps in this light that we are to understand the combination of ἁμαρτία and κακία in Prv. 26:11 as a twofold rendering of אִוֶּלֶת. אִוֶּלָא often has the additional sense of a defective knowledge of God which is guilty, and therefore of ungodliness. In the sphere of the OT doctrine of wisdom and the Law ignorance can imply sin generally (→ 274), as, for example, in Prv. 24:9 'ΑΘ: ἔννοια ἀφροσύνης ἁμαρτία. As previously in v. 8, the LXX here reads זִמָּה as מוּת and thus translates the Mas.: זִמַּת אִוֶּלֶת חַטָּאת as follows: ἀποθνήσκει δὲ ἄφρων ἐν ἁμαρτίαις.

In 3 Βασ. 5:18 B and 1 Βασ. 22:17 AB ἁμάρτημα or ἁμαρτάνειν has been intentionally or mistakenly introduced into the LXX as a rendering of פגע in place of ἀπάντημα or ἀπαντᾶν. In 3 Βασ. 5:18 ἁμάρτημα is thought of in terms of 1 Ch. 22:8 as an obstacle to the sacred work of building the temple. In Is. 66:4, again, the LXX introduces the thought of sin into the text. The Mas. reads: מְגוּרֹתָם אָבִיא לָהֶם ("I will bring that which they fear upon them"). Thus in the Mas. the reference is to punishment. But the LXX speaks of the cause of punishment: καὶ τὰς ἁμαρτίας ἀνταποδώσω αὐτοῖς. Here, too, idolatry or apostasy is the sin in question. Similarly in Is. 24:6 the Mas. reads: "Therefore a curse devours the earth, and they that dwell therein suffer (אָשֵׁם)." The LXX, however, runs as follows: διὰ τοῦτο ἀρὰ ἔδεται τὴν γῆν, ὅτι ἡμάρτοσαν οἱ κατοικοῦντες αὐτήν. A deepening of the consciousness of sin may be seen in ψ 139:8: אַל־תִּתֵּן יְהוָה מַאֲוַיֵּי רָשָׁע ("Grant not, O Lord, the desires of the ungodly," cf. Σ). Out of consciousness of one's own sinful desires, the LXX formulates the request: μὴ παραδῷς με, κύριε, ἀπὸ τῆς ἐπιθυμίας μου ἁμαρτωλῷ. Cf. ψ 108:5, where ἁμαρτωλός and διάβολος are used metaphysically by the LXX but not by the Mas. (2 Th. 2:3). A spiritualisation may be found in Ez. 23:49, where for the Heb. חֲטָאֵי גִלּוּלֵיכֶן ("the guilt incurred by your idols") the LXX has τὰς ἁμαρτίας τῶν ἐνθυμημάτων. According to Jer. 50(Ιερ. 27):7 the foes of Judah do not incur any guilt by attacking and destroying the Jews because the people sinned. According to the LXX they fulfil the will of God: μὴ ἀνῶμεν αὐτούς, ἀνθ' ὧν ἥμαρτον. In independence of the Mas. the LXX formulates Job 15:11: ὀλίγα, ὧν ἡμάρτηκας,

---

[57] H. Guthe in Kautzsch, II⁴, 70.

[58] Cf. the relationship between sickness and sin in the NT (Mk. 2:5; Jn. 5:14; 8:11).

μεμαστίγωσαι. What is here read into the text is the thought of the school of suffering so dear to Hellenistic Judaism. The piety of suffering expressed here presupposes a very strong consciousness of sin. This gives rise to the need to confess sins as, e.g., in Sir. 4:26, where in independence of the Heb.: אל תבוש לשוב מעון ("Be not ashamed to turn from sin"), the LXX coins the expression : μὴ αἰσχυνθῇς ὁμολογῆσαι ἐφ' ἁμαρτίαις σου. To the consciousness of sin there also corresponds the hope of divine grace. In Is. 27:9, where the Mas. refers to the destruction of pagan altars as the full fruit of purification, the LXX finds an entry for the religion of grace : καὶ τοῦτό ἐστιν ἡ εὐλογία αὐτοῦ, ὅταν ἀφέλωμαι τὴν ἁμαρτίαν αὐτοῦ.

Thus the LXX creates a unitary concept of sin. And the unity of word inclines to a unity of matter. Against the division of the sinfulness of man into individual sins, which is still characteristic of later Judaism, there are attempts to press forward to the basic sin which separates man from God as a power (Sir. 21:2; 27:10) which controls man so long as he does not allow God to save him.

Bertram

C. The Concept of Sin in Judaism. [59]

1. The concept of sin in Judaism is determined by the law (→ νόμος). The transgression of each individual command of the Torah is sin. For the Torah is the revelation of the will of God. Therefore all its definitions, including the civil and judicial which we might regard as secular, are *ius divinum*. On this basis all transgressions have a religious character. They are all rebellion against God. They are all sin.

To the sphere of sin as transgression in the religious sense there thus belong not only the sins more properly directed against God, but also cultic violations and errors, and criminal offences. [60] All these have a religious character and are offences against God. Judaism thus takes up the OT idea of sin as an outraging of God and makes it a constitutive element. In the religiously conceived Jewish concept of sin two opposing trends are at work, the one to level down and the other to differentiate. The first is inspired by the casuistry of the scribes, for whom even the slightest infringements, and certain religiously indifferent customs, are offences against the Law and therefore sins. [61] The second derives from the OT distinction between sins with a high hand and sins of ignorance. On the basis of Lv. 16:21 S. Lv. 16:6 distinguishes three kinds of sin : עֲוֹנֹת which are flagrant misdeeds ; פִּשְׁעֵיהֶם, which are acts of rebellion ; and חַטֹּאתָם which are unwitting offences (cf. also T. Joma, 2, 1; bJoma 36b). [62] According to the differentiating trend, the severity of a sin depends upon knowledge of the Law. In bBM the first part of Is. 58:1b : "Shew my people their transgression," is related to those who are instructed in

---

[59] Cf. Moore, I, 461. T. Shebu, 3, 6.

[60] The concept of crime or violation in the legal sense is not yet distinguished from that of sin in the religious sense. At most we have only the germ of this distinction in later Judaism. The reason for this is that the OT is the unconditional Word of God in both its functions, i.e., as a book which contains religious demands and as a valid code of civil law and penalties.

[61] For an example of such Rabbinic statutes, cf. Shab. 12, 3 ff.: "He who writes two letters (on the Sabbath) ... is guilty. He who writes on his body is guilty. He who writes with other fluids (which do not serve as ink), or on something on which the writing does not remain, is innocent." Cf. Schürer, II, 471 ff., Shebu, 1, 2-2, 5.

[62] Cf. Moore, I, 464.

the Law, so that "their unwitting faults are equal to serious sins," and the second part: "And the house of Jacob their sins," to those who do not know it, so that "their serious sins are equal to unwitting faults." [63] From this differentiation there derives even in the OT an isolation of mortal sins such as idolatry, licentiousness and bloodshed. These sins must not be committed in any circumstances. [64] The worst of all is idolatry (עבודה זרה). "It is of the very essence of rebellion, violating not only the first commandment of the Decalogue, 'Thou shalt have no other gods before me,' but the fundamental principle of the divine unity, the profession of faith solemnly pronounced by the Jew every time he repeated the Shema." [65] To commit this sin is to commit every sin (S. Nu., 111 on 15:22). While there is the possibility of expiating [66] other sins by rites of purification, good works, [67] and sufferings, [68] these serious sins can be atoned only by death (bSanh., 74a). [69]

2. Closely related to the concept of sin as orientated to the Law is the dominant tendency in Judaism to eliminate the idea of collective responsibility for sin and to link it firmly with the individual. This tendency begins with Ezekiel, who rejects the connection between the sins of the fathers and their children expressed in the saying: "The fathers have eaten sour grapes, and the children's teeth are set on edge," and who establishes the basic principle: "The soul that sinneth, it shall die" (Ez. 18:2-4). Sin is thus the current offence of the individual against the command of the Torah, with consequences for the man concerned both in this world and the next. The Law, the theory of merit and the concept of sin form an indissoluble whole. The resultant dismissal of the connection between the sins of the fathers and the fate of the children is expressed in the following passages from the Targum. Ex. 20:5 (Mas.) reads: "I am a jealous God, visiting the iniquity of the fathers upon the children unto the third and fourth generation." The Tg., however, has the alternative: "... requiting the guilt of sinful fathers on their refractory children." Dt. 5:9 is even clearer. The Mas. is the same as Ex. 20:5, but the Tg. reads: "... when the children proceed to sin according to their fathers." [70] Yet the idea of general responsibility is not completely dead. This may be seen from the comparison of the sinner with a man who bores a hole in a boat on the sea. When asked what he is doing, he says to his companions: "What is that to you? Am I not boring under myself?" And he receives the answer: "This is our affair, for

---

[63] Cf. also bTaan., 11a.

[64] Cf. the discussion at the conference of Rabbis at Lydda during the persecution under Hadrian, which decided that there could be no redeeming of life on the committal of one of these three sins (jSanh., 21b; bSanh., 74; cf. Moore, I, 467). Cf. also the apostolic decree in Ac. 15:29 and the preceding discussion.

[65] Moore, I, 466.

[66] → ἱλάσκεσθαι; cf. Moore, I, 497 ff.

[67] Cf. A. Schlatter, Jochanan ben Zakkai (1899), 39 f., esp. 41: "... with the confidence that the gift earns forgiveness as a reward."

[68] Cf. W. Wichmann, Die Leidenstheologie (1930).

[69] For expiation by death, as for other expiations, there applies the conclusion corresponding to the factor discussed in n. 60: When a man who commits an offence which comes under the death penalty according to Jewish law, i.e., the Torah (e.g., idolatry, bloodshed or licentiousness), is sentenced to death by a Jewish court, this is not merely a punishment for his offence, but the fulfilment of the penalty is also an expiation for his sin.

[70] L. Baeck, RGG², V, 883.

the water will come in and the boat will go down with us" (Lv. r., 4 on 4:1). [71]

As a whole Judaism accepts the view that sinning is general. [72] All men are sinful, cf. 4 Esr. 7:68 f.: "For all who are born are marred by ungodliness, full of sin and laden with guilt. And it would be better for us if after death we did not have to go to the judgment"; 9:36 : "We who receive the Law must perish because of our sins, along with our hearts in which they are committed." Ex. r., 31 on 22:24; Lv. r., 14 on 12:2 (on Ps. 51:5): "Even if a man were the most pious of the pious, he would still have one page of sin"; Philo Vit. Mos., II, 147: παντὶ γενητῷ ... συμφυὲς τὸ ἁμαρτάνειν ἐστίν; also Fug., 158. The Gentiles, too, come under this sinfulness as religious responsibility and guilt before God. According to Jewish theory they have the Adamic and Noachic commands in respect of theft, licentiousness, idolatry, blasphemy and the shedding of blood, S. Lv., 18, 4. Indeed, the Torah has been offered them, but they have refused it. R. Jochanan has stated : "This teaches (i.e., Dt. 33:2; Hab. 3:3) that God has published the Torah to every nation and language, but it was not accepted until He came to Israel and Israel accepted it" (bAZ, 2b). [73] For this reason they are not without guilt in their sin. On the other hand, this basic principle is not so sharply applied as might have been expected. 4 Esr. 7:48 says that almost all are sinners. Especially distinguished saints like Abraham, Moses and Elijah are accepted as without sin (cf. Test. Zeb., 1; Jos. Ant., 7, 153; Pesikt., 76a, ed. Buber). [74] This postulate of sinlessness is possible because of the individual freedom of the will and the gift of the Law. The observance of the Law makes possible a pure life. "Thus God ... has said to the Israelites, My children, I have created you with an evil impulse, but I have given you the Law as a means of salvation. So long as you occupy yourselves with it, that impulse will not rule over you" (S. Dt., 45 on 11:18). The testimony of Paul may be cited in this regard : κατὰ δικαιοσύνην τὴν ἐν νόμῳ γενόμενος ἄμεμπτος (Phil. 3:6). [75] If the sinlessness of isolated saints is maintained, and the possibility of a sinless life is provided by observance of the Law, it can almost be taken for granted that the sinlessness of the Messiah will be assumed. We read already of the Servant of the Lord in Dt.-Is. : "... he had done no violence, neither was any deceit in his mouth" (53:9). In Ps. Sol. 17:41 it is said of the Messiah : καὶ αὐτὸς καθαρὸς ἀπὸ ἁμαρτίας; and in Test. Jud. 2:4 (A): καὶ πᾶσα ἁμαρτία οὐχ εὑρεθήσεται ἐν αὐτῷ; cf. also Test. L. 18:9. Linked with this is the expectation of Jewish eschatology that sin will be set aside and the sinlessness of man established in the Messianic kingdom (cf. En. 5:8 f.; Ps. Sol. 17:32; Test. L. 18).

3. The rise and the consequences of sin are considered in post-biblical Judaism. A historical answer is given to the former question. Sin derives from Adam [76] or from Eve, and has spread from them and established its dominion over the whole race. Cor ... malignum baiulans, primus Adam transgressus et victus est, sed et omnes, qui de eo nati sunt. Et facta est permanens infirmitas et lex cum corde

---

[71] Cf. Moore, I, 471.

[72] Cf. Weber, 233 f.; Str.-B., III, 155 ff.

[73] Cf. Str.-B., III, 38-43. Cf. esp. 4 Esr. 7:20-24 : ... vias eius non cognoverunt et legem eius spreverunt, et sponsiones eius abnegaverunt, et in legitimis eius fidem non habuerunt, et opera eius non perfecerunt.

[74] Weber, 53 ff.; 224.

[75] → ἁμαρτωλός. Cf. also Ab. R. Nat., 59, where it is said of Jochanan's son : "He departed this world without sin" (cf. A. Schlatter, Jochanan ben Zakkai [1899], 20 f.).

populi, cum malignitate radicis; et discessit quod bonum est, et mansit malignum (4 Esr. 3:21 f.). Cf. also Sir. 25:34; 4 Esr. 3:26; 7:48 ff., esp. 118 : "Alas, Adam, what hast thou done ? When thou didst sin, thy fall came not upon thee alone, but upon us thy descendants." Cf. also S. Bar. 48:42, where sin is derived from Eve ; and esp. Bar. 54:15 : "If Adam first sinned and brought premature death on all, each of his descendants has incurred future pain." In these apocalyptic passages there is a view of sin, largely shared by the NT, as a power which profoundly shapes the world. A variation from the view which attributes sin to Adam is to be found in En. 10:4 ff.; 64:1 ff. and Mart. Is., 5, 3, in which its origin is found in the fallen angels of Gn. 6:1 ff. Alongside this historical explanation we should set the more basic view that the root of man's sin, the *fomes peccati,* lies in the evil impulse implanted in him by God. Cf. Sir. 15:14; 37:3; 4 Esr. 3:20; 4:4; 7:48 (*cor malignum*); [77] Pesikt., 38b-39a, ed. Buber; Vit. Ad., 19 (ἐπιθυμία ... ἐστὶ κεφαλὴ πάσης ἁμαρτίας).

It is this evil impulse which entices man to sin. Its overthrow by the observance of the Torah is the task of man. He who does not overcome it must bear the consequences of sin which consist in all kinds of suffering. The thought developed by Paul in R. 1:18 ff., namely, that God punishes sin with sinning, is known to Judaism in the form that sin begets sin : ὁ ἁμαρτωλὸς προσθήσει ἁμαρτίαν ἐφ᾽ ἁμαρτίαις (Ps. Sol. 3:12). It belongs to the consequences of sin that one sin gives rise to another, so that once a man begins sinning he will finally commit mortal sin : "To-day the evil impulse says to someone : Do this, and to-morrow : Do that, until it finally says : Pray to other gods, and he goes and does it" (bShab, 105b; cf. Ab., 4, 2; S. Nu., 112 on 15:30). To the consequences of sin there belongs separation from God. The worship of the golden calf made it impossible for the Israelites to see the glory of God. [78] Sin makes impossible any direct dealings with God face to face [79] (→ ἀκούω, 218). Sin constantly disrupts the gracious purpose of God for man. "When I desire to do you good, the heavenly power weakens in you... (examples are given from the history of the people in the wilderness)," S. Dt., 319; cf. Pesikt., 166a-b (ed. Buber). To the consequences of sin there belongs the punishment of sin. Between this and sin there is a close connection (cf. Ps. Sol. 2:17: ὅτι ἀπέδωκας τοῖς ἁμαρτωλοῖς, κατὰ τὰ ἔργα αὐτῶν καὶ κατὰ τὰς ἁμαρτίας αὐτῶν τὰς πονηρὰς σφόδρα; Philo Leg. All., I, 35 : κολαζόμενος ἐφ᾽ οἷς ἡμάρτανεν; Philo Vit. Mos., I, 96; Sacr. AC, 131). Sickness is a punishment for sin ; there is a formula that the sick man does not recover until all his sins are forgiven (by God), bNed., 41a. Death is another penalty ("no death without sin, and no chastisement without guilt," bShab, 55a; cf. Sir. 25:24; Wis. 1:13; 2:23 f.; Bar. 23:4; 4 Esr. 3:7; S. Dt., 305 on 31:14; Gn. r. 16:6, where death is brought into close connection with the fall). A further penalty is eternal damnation (ἡ ἀπώλεια τοῦ ἁμαρτωλοῦ εἰς τὸν αἰῶνα, Ps. Sol. 3:13). But in respect of all

---

[76] Cf. Tanch. Bereshith § 29, Hukkat § 39, ed. Buber. These passages express obvious annoyance at Adam for the trouble occasioned by his sin.

[77] Moore, I, 479 ff.; Weber, 221 f., 225 ff.; Porter, *op. cit.;* Büchler, *op. cit.;* K. Stier, "Pls über d. Sünde u. d. Judentum seiner Zeit," *Prot. Monatsh.,* II (1907), 104; Bousset-Gressm., 402 ff.; cf. also → πονηρός.

[78] Cf. the exposition of Ex. 24:17 and 34:30 by Simeon b. Jochai in S. Nu., 1 on 5:3.

[79] Gn. 3:8; Ex. 34:30; 2 S. 17:2; Cant. 3:7 f.; 1 S. 28:5; cf. Pesikt., 44b-45a (ed. Buber); also, with a rather different application, R. 3:3 : πάντες γὰρ ἥμαρτον καὶ ὑστεροῦνται τῆς δόξης τοῦ θεοῦ.

these penalties man has the opportunity to repent and to return to God. This is expressed with particular clarity in Tg. Qoh. 7:20, where in addition to the categorical statement : "There is none righteous on earth to do good and not sin," we have the further statement : "But God shows to the man who is guilty before him the way of conversion before he dies." [80]

Stählin/Grundmann

D. The Linguistic Usage and History of ἁμαρτάνω, ἁμάρτημα and ἁμαρτία before and in the NT.

1. ἁμαρτάνω ("not to hit" or "to miss") is synon. with ἀποτυγχάνειν (Suid.) and the opp. of τυγχάνειν (cf. Hom. Il., 5, 287: ἤμβροτες οὐδ' ἔτυχες, Hdt., I, 43). The word is found in the concrete sense from the time of Homer (Suid.: ἄσκοπα τοξεύειν), but it is also used metaphorically, esp. in the sense of "intellectual shortcoming" (Thuc., I, 33, 3; Philo Omn. Prob. Lib., 133 : γνώμης), and thence in the abs. sense of "error" (Dio Chrys. Or., 53, 3). The σοφός is the opp. of the ἁμαρτάνων (cf. Gorg. Pal., 26, Blass); the ἁμαρτίνοος is "the one who is in error" (e.g., Hes. Theog., 511). But already in Homer it denotes "erroneous action" (Od., 22, 154; Xenoph. Cyrop., V, 4, 19: τὸ γὰρ ἁμαρτάνειν ἀνθρώπους ὄντας οὐδὲν θαυμαστόν; cf. *errare humanum est*). There is also the beginning of moral evaluation in the sense of "doing wrong" (Il., 9, 501: ὅτε κέν τις ὑπερβήῃ καὶ ἁμάρτῃ; cf. Od., 13, 214).

The LXX (→ 268 ff.) occasionally uses ἁμαρτάνειν for פשׁע, אשׁם, רשׁע hiph., but mostly for חטא in accordance with the sense. Beyond its basic meaning of "missing" and its metaphorical sense of "going astray" or "not finding," חטא had come to have the predominant religious sense of "aberration" or "sinning." Only by its use for חטא in the LXX did ἁμαρτία itself become a distinctively religious term.

2. As a verbal subst. with -μα, ἁμάρτημα denotes the result of ἁμαρτάνειν, i.e., "fault" or "mistake," at first more in the sense of folly or blindness than wrongdoing, as in Soph. Ant., 1261 (→ συνείδησις with its analogous history). Aristotle (Eth. Nic., V, 10, p. 1135b, 18; Rhet., I, 13, p. 1374b, 5) defines ἁμάρτημα as a middle case between ἀδίκημα and ἀτύχημα, since it does not take place unexpectedly (μὴ παραλόγως), yet ἄνευ κακίας. In general usage and esp. in legal terminology, [81] however, it comes more and more to mean an offence which is committed with evil intent and which therefore occasions guilt (P. Tebt., 5, 3; Antiph., 1, 27: ἑκούσια καὶ ἐκ προνοίας ἀδικήματα καὶ ἁμαρτήματα).

In the LXX ἁμάρτημα is used esp. for חטאת though also for עון, פשׁע and רשׁע. It is particularly common in Wis. (2:12; 4:20 etc.), and always as an ethical and religious concept for the "sinful act," or "sin." It is set alongside ἀδίκημα in Gn. 31:36; ἀδικία in Dt. 19:15; Jer. 14:20; ἀσέβημα in Dt. 9:27; ἀνόμημα in Jos.

---

[80] → n. 70. With the thought of a change of heart there arises, alongside the dominant tendency to identify crime and sin, punishment and expiation, another tendency to concentrate on the purely religious concept, i.e., that sin is something which cannot be removed by judicial punishment but only in the relationship of the individual to God, i.e., by repentance, good works, suffering, death, or as God punishes it in the future life.
[81] Cf. R. Taubenschlag, *D. Strafrecht im Rechte d. Papyri* (1916), 8; L. Wenger, APF, II (1902), 483; Hey, Ἁμαρτία (→ Bibl.).

24:19; ἀνομία in Is. 58:1. It can also mean the "punishment of sin" (Is. 40:2). While it is more common in the secular sense than ἁμαρτία, it is far less frequent, significant or comprehensive in the Bible than the latter.

In the NT ἁμάρτημα ("the sinful act") is rare; it is found only in Mk. 3:28 f.; 4:12 Rec.; R. 3:25; 5:16 DG It Pesch (אB: ἁμαρτήσαντος); 1 C. 6:18; 2 Pt. 1:9.

3. ἁμαρτία, like ἁμάρτημα, is used from the very first (since Aeschylus) in a metaphorical sense, but in contrast it is often taken to denote the "nature of an act" (cf. Cl. Al. Strom., II, 15, 64, 3). [82] The term was at first used to describe the fact of ἁμαρτάνειν, but since the fact can be known only from the defective act it is natural that this distinction should be effaced even in the known beginnings of its use. Already in Aeschylus (Ag., 1197: παλαιᾶς τῶνδ' ἁμαρτίας δομῶν, sc. of the house of Atrides) ἁμαρτία is an "offence." As in the case of ἁμάρτημα, however, the question of guilt is not posed in the modern sense (→ 293). Even acts done out of good motives, if they are punishable and need to be atoned, are called ἁμαρτία, e.g., the robbing of Philoctetus in Soph. Phil., 1225 or the white lie in Trach., 483. It is of a piece with this that in the language of law and philosophy ἁμαρτία is a comprehensive and collective term, as in Pseud.-Plat. Def., 416a: πρᾶξις παρὰ τὸν ὀρθὸν λογισμόν, in which ὀρθός may be taken ethically but also in the more formal legal or even intellectual sense. As the counterpart of ὀρθότης (Plat. Leg., I, 627d: ὀρθότητός τε καὶ ἁμαρτίας περὶ νόμων, also II, 668c), ἁμαρτία means the nature of an unrighteous action (→ supra), but it is more often used for the action itself over the whole range from a simple error to a crime (Plat. Gorg., 525c; Aristot. Pol., IV, 16, p. 1336a, 1: ἀτιμίᾳ ζημιούσθω πρεπούσῃ πρὸς τὴν ἁμαρτίαν, "licentiousness").

Aristotle also defines ἁμαρτία (→ ἁμάρτημα) as a "missing of virtue, the desired goal, whether out of weakness, accident or defective knowledge" (→ ἄγνοια), Eth. Nic., II, 5, p. 1106b, 25 ff. This means "wrong without κακία" (III, 13, p. 1118b, 16 ff. etc.). It is thus intellectual deficiency working itself out morally according to the intellectual character of Greek ethics (III, 1, p. 1110b, 18 ff.). On the other hand, at a later period the thought of guilt, which is excluded by Aristotle, [83] is sometimes linked with ἁμαρτία, as in P. Lips., 1119, 3; Ditt. Syll.[3], 1042, 15: ὀφείλω ἁμαρτίαν.

In the LXX ἁμαρτία is for the most part a synon. of ἁμάρτημα, and it is normally used for חַטָּאת and חֲטָאָה, often for עָוֺן and occasionally for פֶּשַׁע, אָשָׁם, רֶשַׁע. In contrast to the indefinite, general and "tragic" use of Aristotle, ἁμαρτία, like ἁμαρτάνω, becomes a moral and religious concept of guilt in the LXX; there is seen in it an evil will and intention, i.e., a conscious apostasy from and opposition to God (synon. ἀδικία). Because this most general and least sharp secular word for wrong was selected as the main bearer of the pitiless biblical thought of sin, and partly by reason of its concrete relationship of meaning with חַטָּאת, ἁμαρτία became the most pregnant term among all its numerous synonyms, [84] being cal-

---

[82] Cr.-Kö., 139; Trench, 154 f.

[83] O. Hey, op. cit., shows how ἁμαρτία became a catch-word in the Aristot. theory of drama, but no true starting-point for the theory of "tragic guilt." When we compare the Aristot. exclusion of the thought of moral guilt in the modern sense with the biblical inclusion, we can see that "the word ἁμαρτία as variously conceived reflects the profound difference between two worlds of culture" (Hey, 163).

[84] Cf. Trench, 152.

culated to express the divine reference of sin much more purely than, e.g., such primarily ethical concepts as → ἀδικία and κακία. [85]

The NT follows the LXX in the meaning of the various ἁμαρτ- constructions. [86] It is almost always a matter of "offence in relation to God with emphasis on guilt," i.e., of "sin." Three main forms of ἁμαρτία are to be distinguished in the NT, a. sin as an individual act (= ἁμάρτημα), b. as a determination of the nature of man, and c. as a personal power. All three have earlier stages outside the NT, but the NT understanding of esp. b. and c. characterises the NT concept of sin. In the NT, in contrast to all earlier forms, sin is a magnitude which determines man and humanity in the sense of distance from God and opposition to Him.

a. ἁμαρτία is understood as an individual act (for earlier forms of this aspect → 294) consistently in the Synoptics, in Acts (2:38; 3:19; 7:60; 5:31; 10:43; 13:38; 22:16; 26:18), in the Past. (1 Tm. 5:22, 24; 2 Tm. 3:6), in Revelation (1:5; 18:4 f.), mostly in Hb. (1:3; 2:17; 5:1 etc.) and in the Cath. Ep. (Jm. 2:9; 4:17; 5:15, 20; 1 Pt. 2:22, 24; 3:18; 4:8; 2 Pt. 1:9; 2:14; 1 Jn. 1:9; 2:2, 12; 3:4 f., 8; 4:10; 5:16 f.). In the Synoptics it is almost always used (Mk. 1:5 and par. Mt. 1:21 being exceptions), and in Acts exclusively, in relation to the remission of sins (Mk. 2:5 and par.; Lk. 11:4 etc.; sing. only in Mt. 12:31; Ac. 7:60). Paul uses ἁμαρτία of individual sins for the most part only in quotations (R. 4:7 f. = ψ 31:1 f.; 11:27 = Is. 27:9) and borrowed formulae (1 C. 15:3 : Χριστὸς ἀπέθανεν ὑπὲρ τῶν ἁμαρτιῶν ἡμῶν κατὰ τὰς γραφάς; Gl. 1:4 : ... τοῦ δόντος ἑαυτὸν ὑπὲρ τῶν ἁμαρτιῶν ἡμῶν; Col. 1:14 : ἄφεσις τῶν ἁμαρτιῶν). R. 7:5; 2 C. 11:7; Eph. 2:1 are exceptions. The plur. is used in all these passages except R. 4:8 (a quotation) and 2 C. 11:7. In the Gospel John uses ἁμαρτία in this sense only in 8:24 (twice), 34a; 9:34 (an allusion to Ps. 51:5), but it is more common in the First Epistle, which in this respect also is nearer than the Gospel to the common world of Christian ideas and concepts. [87]

b. ἁμαρτία is used already to denote the defective nature of man in Plato (Leg., I, 627d, II, 668c), who speaks of the ὀρθότης and ἁμαρτία (→ 294) of laws or of works of musical or poetic art. A complete transformation takes place when the NT uses ἁμαρτία to denote the determination of human nature in hostility to God, esp. in Jn. in the synon. formulae ἔχειν ἁμαρτίαν (9:41; [88] 15:22, 24; 19:11; 1 Jn. 1:8) and ἁμαρτία ἔν τινί ἐστιν (1 Jn. 3:5; cf. Jn. 7:18), and similarly, though with a reversal of the spatial relationship, ἀποθανεῖν ἐν τῇ ἁμαρτίᾳ (8:21). [89] We also read in Jn. 8:24 : ἀποθανεῖν ἐν ταῖς ἁμαρτίαις (also Ez. 18:24); in 9:34 : γεννᾶσθαι ἐν ἁμαρτίαις; and again in 1 C. 15:17: ἔτι ἐστὲ ἐν ταῖς ἁμαρτίαις ὑμῶν. Man lives outside Christ and dies in sins. In these expressions the plur. is a comprehensive term similar to the sing. elsewhere in Jn. (also 9:41;

---

[85] Cf. Cr.-Kö., 137 f.

[86] Steinleitner (→ 268 n.), 85 : "Nowhere do we see more clearly the difference between paganism and Christianity than in the conception of sin."

[87] Here, too, the fig. etym. ἁμαρτάνω ἁμαρτίαν which derives from the LXX : Ex. 32:30 f.; Lv. 4:23; 5:6, 10, 13; Ez. 18:24; and Philo Mut. Nom., 233, Herm. v., 2, 2, 4. Secular Gk. usage prefers the more exact ἁ. ἁμάρτημα : Soph. Phil., 1249; Plat. Phaed., 113e; Dio Chrys. Or., 32, 3. Cf. M. Johannessohn, *Der Gebrauch der Kasus u. der Präpositionen i. d. LXX* (Diss. Berlin, 1910), 56 f.; Winer § 32, 2.

[88] Cf. Pesikt., 5, p. 55b (Buber) in Schl. J., 232.

[89] Cf. Ιερ. 38:30; bShab., 55b in Schl. J., 208.

1 Jn. 1:7) and also frequently in the Pauline literature (R. 3:20 : ἐπίγνωσις ἁμαρτίας; 5:13, 20; 6:1: ἐπιμένειν τῇ ἁμαρτίᾳ; 6:6a : τὸ σῶμα τῆς ἁμαρτίας; 7:7; 8:3 : σάρξ ἁμαρτίας; Hb. 4:15; 9:28, 26 : εἰς ἀθέτησιν τῆς ἁμαρτίας; 11:25; 1 Pt. 4:1: πεπαῦσθαι ἁμαρτίας; esp. 2 C. 5:21 shows ἁμαρτία to be a pregnant expression for the whole sinful nature of man.

c. Personifications of sin are found in the Paris Gk. magic papyrus and also in Judaism, the one referring to Ἁμαρτίαι χθόνιαι (Preis. Zaub., IV, 1448), a species of demons of the underworld, and the other to the woman of sin as in Zech. 5:5 ff. [90] and also to ἁμαρτίαι lurking like lions (Sir. 27:10), both within the framework of the currently developing view of a cosmic power of sin. [91] A similar idea is originally presupposed by the personal conception of ἁμαρτία (mostly with the art.) [92] which is often found in the NT, esp. in R. 5-7. [93] The initial reference is simply to the personal appearance of sin ; it came into the world (R. 5:12). Originally it was νεκρά (7:8), but ἡ ἁμαρτία ἀνέζησεν through the ἐντολή or the νόμος (v. 9). It receives from this the impulse (v. 7, 11) to deceive man (v. 11; also Hb. 3:13) and to "beset" him (Hb. 12:1, εὐπερίστατος); it dwells in him (R. 7:17, 20); it brings forth παθήματα (v. 5) and ἐπιθυμία (v. 8); and it thus becomes a demonic power ruling over him. Man is ὑφ᾽ ἁμαρτίαν (R. 3:9; Gl. 3:22; cf. R. 11:32); he is sold to it as a slave (R. 6:16, 20; 7:14; also Jn. 8:34; cf. Gl. 2:17); he serves according to its law (6:6; 7:23, 25; 8:3); he loans it his members as ὅπλα ἀδικίας (6:13). Its sphere of power is the σάρξ, where it exercises its dominion (κυριεύει, 6:14; βασιλεύει, 5:21; 6:12), which culminates in its giving man the wages (6:23) of death (5:21; 7:11; cf. Jm. 1:15). But through and with Christ man dies to sin (R. 6:2, 10), and is thus νεκρός for it (v. 11) and liberated from it (v. 7, 18, 22). Sin itself is condemned (8:3). Nevertheless, the battle against it must not cease (Hb. 12:4).

It is hard to say how far what we have here is the concrete notion of a demon "sin" (Dibelius) standing in place of Satan, who is not mentioned at all in R. 6 f., and how far it is simply poetic imagery (Feine). How fluid are the boundaries between these NT forms of the ἁμαρτία concept may be seen from John (cf. esp. Jn. 8:34; 1 Jn. 3:5; and e.g., Jn. 8:21 with v. 24).

Stählin

E. Sin and Guilt in Classical Greek and Hellenism.

1. The Christian view of sin is not found in classical Gk. In this we have no sin in the sense of man's enmity against God consisting in his refusal to understand and will the right. [94] In this section, therefore, it is as well not to use the term sin,

---

[90] Cf. R. Smend, *Lehrbuch d. at.l. Rel.-Gesch.*[2] (1899), 402.

[91] Cf. Köberle, 473 f.

[92] On the whole, the use of the art. with ἁμαρτία, which e.g., Cr.-Kö. selects as a principle for co-ordinating the meaning, is not very common ; cf. R. 6:6 with 8:3; 6:16 with v. 17 etc.

[93] Cf. Ltzm. R.[2], 65; M. Dibelius, *Die Geisterwelt i. Glben. d. Pls.* (1909), 119 ff.; P. Feine, *Theol. d. NT*[5] (1931), 200 f.

[94] S. Kierkegaard, *Die Krankheit z. Tode* (H. Gottsched and C. Schrempf[2], 1924), 89, where in the chapter "The Socratic Definition of Sin" we are given an analysis of the Gk. and Christian conceptions of sin.

but to introduce the Gk. conception of defect and guilt, since the stem ἁμαρτ-
(→ 293) means "missing a definite goal," whether mistakenly or guiltily, or by a
mistake which is itself guilt.

The terminology has a wide reference. It covers everything from crime to harmless faults. [95] It includes moral actions but also intellectual and artistic failings. The
same writers use it in many senses. [96] "ἁμαρτάνειν came to be a purely negative
term for doing something which is no → ὀρθόν, the word ὀρθόν being used in
the sense of morality, of formal law, or indeed of that which is intellectually or
technically correct." [97]

For a full grasp of the thought of guilt interwoven and expressed in the Gk.
ἁμαρτ-concept, other terms had to be introduced. Thus in early Gk. we have ἄτη,
a word which combines the thought of destiny and one's own act. [98] In the post-
Homeric period we also find the → ἀδικ- group. "Developing from the personal
experience of the poet (sc. Hesiod), the belief that all unrighteousness is sin constitutes the critical point of the 'works' of Hesiod." [99] On the basis of the life of
the state and society, which cannot exist without law, ἀδικία came to be understood as a violation of the norm of existence. Note should also be taken of the
cultically orientated ἄγος and μίασμα, of ὕβρις, and finally, in relation particularly to the philosophical literature, of κακός, κακία.

2. The concept of guilt in the earliest period is determined by an attitude to
life which has no distinctive awareness of self or freedom but gives itself joyfully
to what is given in the form of destiny and divine ordination (cf. Hom. Il., 19,
83 f.). [100] An incurred guilt is known from resultant misfortune (→ συνείδησις).
Guilt or misdemeanour is one's own action. In the Homeric period it consists in
cultic neglect, perjury and violation of the law of hospitality in opposition to divine
and human τιμή; in Hesiod the circle is widened to include the wounding or dishonouring of parents, divorce, oppression of orphans and social injustice generally
(Hes. Op., 327 ff.). Such things evoke the wrath of the gods who are the guardians
and guarantors of law and order. Cf. Hom. Od., 13, 214: Ζεὺς ... ἀνθρώπους
ἐφορᾷ καὶ τείνυται ὅστις ἁμάρτῃ. In relation to this early period of the Gk.
spirit the statement of Rohde is in every sense true: "They were hardly susceptible
to the infectious sickness of consciousness of sin in their greatest centuries." [101]

3. Into this Homeric world there flows in the 6th and 7th centuries B.C. a
broad wave of oriental religiosity and other feeling. The Greek becomes open to
the recognition of the sinful and mortal state of the world. [102] "Behind that which
is close to hand and of the day, man experiences night and the unfathomableness
of existence." [103] The questionable nature of human life, the inscrutability of fate

---

[95] Hey, Ἁμαρτία, 14.
[96] Cf. the many examples given in Hey, 7 ff., esp. from Thucydides and legal terminology
(14 f.) and from Aristotle (141 ff.).
[97] Hey, 15 f.
[98] Cf. W. Jaeger, "Solons Eunomie," SAB (1926).
[99] Latte, op. cit., 266.
[100] Cf. on this point Stenzel, op. cit., 17 ff.
[101] E. Rohde, Psyche⁹ [10] (1925), I, 319.
[102] Cf. Weinstock, op. cit., 275 ff., esp. 279 f.
[103] Ibid., 280.

and the inevitability of guilt enter the Greek field of vision. The mysteries, esp.
the Orphic, are linked with this experience. They rise everywhere, and men who
see their very existence threatened take refuge in them. In such circles life is felt
to be a consequence of guilt. "It is in expiation of a fault that the soul is exiled in
the body ; the payment for sin is earthly life, which is the death of the soul." [104]
Original guilt prior to life, and the sentence of death after it, [105] take a central
place and exert a wide influence in art and philosophy. Threatened in this way,
the Greek spirit wrestles with itself and is deepened and enriched. "The visible
and lasting result, with which the Greek spirit bears witness to the removal of the
threat in blessing, is tragedy." [106] The concept of guilt, which previously found it
in pure acts, is now understood in such a way as to denote by guilt an inward
factor in man (→ 299).

Human guilt is the confusion of the existing order, the disruption of an objectively given state, which man must make good by his suffering and the misfortune which strikes him, and sometimes by his destruction. This is not the guilt
of a man who has freedom to choose between good and evil. It is the guilt of a
blindness which in the last resort is posited with his existence. [107] Guilt is inevitable. It is at this point that the term → ἄγνοια, which is so essential to the
Gk. understanding of existence, attains its final depth of meaning. All guilt derives
from ἄγνοια, but this ἄγνοια is the limitation of human existence, which would
cease to be human existence if it possessed omniscience. The deep meaning of the
Oedipus tragedy, for example, consists in "the tragic limitation of human knowledge, which as such must remain fragmentary" and "with which there is posited
the tragedy of human action," "which is action in the full sense of the word only
when it is consciously directed to a goal and fashioned in clear knowledge." [108]
Human guilt follows from the limitation of human knowledge, not as personal
moral guilt, but as guilt given with existence itself. Since man "in his ignorance
is set to act, and by his action to have a part spatially and temporally in the unlimited nexus of cause and effect, with unforeseeable consequences for which he
is thus not responsible, all action is guilt." [109] In face of this situation, all that man
can do is to accept his guilt, [110] as Oedipus does, who takes from the gods his guilt
in his own existence and fate [111] and confesses himself guilty in his suffering. In
this suffering, however, there is disclosed to man the final meaning of his existence
generally. For like everything else, man's becoming guilty is set aside in the will

---

[104] Rohde, II, 126.
[105] Cf. Latte, 281 ff., where examples are given.
[106] Weinstock, 280.
[107] Cf. the scene in Soph. Ant., in which Creon comes out of the house with Haemon's
corpse. The chorus : μνῆμ' ἐπίσημον διὰ χειρὸς ἔχων ... οὐκ ἀλλοτρίας ἄτης, ἀλλ'
αὐτὸς ἁμαρτών. Creon : ἰὼ φρενῶν δυσφρόνων ἁμαρτήματα στερεὰ θανατόεντ' ...
ἐν δ' ἐμῷ κάρᾳ θεὸς τότ' ἄρα τότε μέγα βάρος μ' ἔχων ἔπαισεν, ἐν δ' ἔσεισεν
ἀγρίαις ὁδοῖς ... (1258 ff.). Not long before we have the words of Teiresias : ἀνθρώ-
ποισι γὰρ τοῖς πᾶσι κοινόν ἐστι τοὐξαμαρτάνειν (1023 f.).
[108] Weinstock, 149 ff., esp. 172 ff., and again 230 ff. The quotations are from 151.
[109] Ibid., 175.
[110] Cf. also the analysis of Sophocles' Ajax in W. Schadewaldt, "Sophokles, Aias und
Antigone," in Neue Wege zur Antike, 8 (1929), 70 ff., and esp. the concluding section with
what is said about greatness and guilt on p. 100 ff.
[111] Cf. Soph. Oed. Col., 974 : εἰ δ' αὖ φανεὶς δύστηνος, ὡς ἐγὼ φάνην ...

and counsel of the gods. For the Greeks, therefore, to become guilty and to suffer in consequence is simply to come to a deeper understanding of the world. (Aesch. Ag., 176 f.). This is Greek religion.

From the necessity of guilty action given with this understanding of existence, there arises the possibility of voluntary guilt confessed by Prometheus in Aeschylus' work of this name, when to the question of the leader of the chorus : οὐχ ὁρᾶς ὅτι ἥμαρτες; ὡς δ᾽ ἥμαρτες οὔτ᾽ ἐμοὶ λέγειν καθ᾽ ἡδονὴν σοί τ᾽ ἄλγος· (259 ff.), he answers : ἑκὼν ἑκὼν ἥμαρτον, οὐκ ἀρνήσομαι· θνητοῖς ἀρήγων αὐτὸς ηὑρόμην πόνους (266 f.). We here find a concept of guilt in accordance with which human existence is determined by existential guilt, and with it is set in a nexus of suffering.

In tragedy the thought of existential guilt is brought into connection with another line of thought which begins in the later Homeric period and which is clearly expressed in the acknowledged later part of the Odyssey, in which the following statement is put on the lips of Zeus : ὢ πόποι οἷον δή νυ θεοὺς βροτοὶ αἰτιόωνται· ἐξ ἡμέων γάρ φασι κάκ᾽ ἔμμεναι. οἱ δὲ καὶ αὐτοὶ σφῇσιν ἀτασθαλίῃσιν ὑπὲρ μόρον ἄλγε᾽ ἔχουσιν· (Hom. Od., 1, 32 ff.). Within the suffering which arises from fatal guilt and which is poised with fatal necessity, there is also misfortune incurred through personal guilt and self-created, even though warning is given by the gods and there is advance knowledge of the destruction which threatens for wrong-doing ; Hom. Od., 1, 37 f.: εἰδὼς αἰπὺν ὄλεθρον, ἐπεὶ πρό οἱ εἴπομεν ἡμεῖς. Here man gains an insight into the working of an immanent process of visible law — a thought which is first formulated by Solon : "According to immanent laws of developing reality, according to the law of time, the bad withers and the good flourishes and establishes itself." [112] The concept of ἄγνοια evoked by guilt is here a failure to know the good which leads to blessedness according to this immanent process of law. These thoughts were developed by philosophy. Democritus could already say: ἁμαρτίης αἰτίη ἡ ἀμαθίη τοῦ κρέσσονος (Fr., 83, Diels, II, 78, 13). Socrates based his work of instruction on the principle that ignorance is at the root of guilt and evil. It is thus self-evident for Greek philosophy that right understanding will lead to right action. Knowledge is an existential insight and not just an intellectual magnitude. The man who really understands and knows [113] acts rightly. Behind this assumption stands belief in the goodness (→ ἀρετή) of man. [114] This idea that insight fashions action underlies

---

[112] Stenzel, 27 acc. to Fr. 3, 30 ff. (Diehl, I, 24); 24, 3 (I, 35); 10 (I, 28 f.).

[113] On the inner dialectic of this Socratic ἄγνοια concept, cf. Kierkegaard : "If a man does not do right, he has not understood it ; his understanding is illusory; his certainty that he has understood it simply proves that he misunderstands what he thinks he has understood ... But then the definition is correct. If a man does right, he does not sin ; and if he does not do right, he has not understood it ; if he had truly understood it, it would have moved him to do it and made him a representative of its truth ; ergo sin is ignorance" (87).

[114] Kierkegaard shows that the Socratic definition of sin is no definition : "If, therefore, the Socratic definition of sin is correct, there is no sin" (84). And Kierkegaard goes on to ask very pertinently, disclosing the underlying belief in the natural goodness of man : "What is lacking in Socrates' definition of sin ? The will, the defiance. Greek intellectualism was too happy, too naive, too aesthetic, too ironic, too witty, too sinful, to be able to grasp that all of us consciously refrain from doing good and consciously, i.e., with knowledge of the good, do evil. The Greek world lays down an intellectual categorical imperative" (84 f.).

tragedy. Its strength lies "in belief that there is a unitary and intelligible world order in which it may be expected that evil and arrogance will co-operate but in which it is still possible to regulate one's action according to the definite, recognisable relationship between guilt and punishment, and therefore to achieve insight through the paradigms of great suffering in the mythical past or through one's own experience of its operations." [115] It is thus orientated to "the idea of polity and the thought of the state embodied in it." [116] This line of thought is, of course, intersected by that of existential guilt (→ 298) which can disturb all understanding, since there is a necessity about this guilt and ἄγνοια is blindness (ἄτη). But the two lines come together in the deepening of the idea that tragedy has a purpose of instruction by mediating the thought of ignorance and reverence before omniscient deity. [117] Plato's thinking concerning guilt is developed in terms of → ἀδικία, which is more or less equivalent to ἁμαρτία (cf. e.g., Gorg., 525c; Phaid., 113e; Leg. X, 906c), and of → κακόν. For him the thought of guilt in connection with that of destiny is turned in the very different direction already indicated in Hom. Od., 1, 32 f., namely, that men choose their own destinies. The guilt in misfortune concerns only those who choose, while deity is innocent (... αἰτία ἑλομένου· θεὸς ἀναίτιος, Resp., X, 617e). A new and sharp definition of what ἁμαρτία is in relation to ἀδικία is presented by Aristotle. [118] ἔστι ἀτυχήματα μὲν ὅσα παράλογα καὶ μὴ ἀπὸ μοχθηρίας, ἁμαρτήματα δὲ ὅσα μὴ παράλογα καὶ μὴ ἀπὸ πονηρίας, ἀδικήματα δέ, ὅσα μήτε παράλογα ἀπὸ πονηρίας τε ἐστίν (Rhet., I, 13, p. 1374b, 7 ff.). What are ἁμαρτήματα in this context ? The word group ἁμαρτ- is used with a wider reference but unambiguous meaning to denote artistic and intellectual defects, [119] technical and hygienic failings, [120] errors on the part of a legislator or judge, [121] and political blunders. [122] Finally it has an ethical significance. In the ethical field a ἁμαρτία is not an ἀδικία but a mistake made in an ethical action performed in good faith that it is right. It is the result of non-culpable ἄγνοια. Virtue for Aristotle is the mean between two extremes, while ἁμαρτία is deviation on the right hand or the left. [123] τὸ μὲν ἁμαρτάνειν πολλαχῶς ἐστι ... τὸ δὲ κατορθοῦν μοναχῶς ... ῥᾴδιον μὲν γὰρ τὸ ἀποτυχεῖν τοῦ σκοποῦ, χαλεπὸν δὲ τὸ ἐπιτυχεῖν (Eth. Nic., II, 5, p. 1106b, 28 ff.). No matter what the field in which it is committed, such ἁμαρτάνειν always rests on ἄγνοια (for the ethical field, cf. Eth. Eud., VIII, 1, p. 1246a, 32 ff.; Pol., III, 11, p. 1231b, 28). The word group is totally divested by Aristotle of its association with moral guilt. "The word or word group does not belong ...

---

[115] For this and the following quotation, v. Stenzel, 87.

[116] Cf. on this point the analysis of Aesch. Eum. in Stenzel, 84-87, where it is shown that the order of the state is a divine order : "The decisive development to the immanence of the suprasensual in the sensual, which was achieved by philosophy only after a long and severe struggle, was anticipated in poetry."

[117] Cf. the conclusion to Soph. Oed. Tyr. : ὥστε θνητὸν ὄντα κείνην τὴν τελευταίαν ἰδεῖν ἡμέραν ἐπισκοποῦντα μηδὲν ὀλβίζειν, πρὶν ἂν τέρμα τοῦ βίου περάσῃ μηδὲν ἀλγεινὸν παθών, 1528 ff. Cf. also how in the oracle — on this point v. Weinstock's interpretation (184 ff.) — the thought of the immanent system of law manifested in it recurs.

[118] Cf. esp. Hey, 137 ff.

[119] Hey, 141.

[120] Hey, 141 f.

[121] Hey, 143.

[122] Hey, 145.

[123] Hey, 147 ff., with many examples.

at all to the moral sphere, but to the intellectual." [124] But this is of a piece with the general rationalising of Greek thought present in Aristotle and developed in post-Aristotelian philosophy.

4. Thus the two lines in the Greek concept of guilt which were previously held together by the ἄγνοια concept and the thought of immanence, namely, existential guilt which is fate and the thought of error which takes place out of ἄγνοια and brings suffering, now fall apart. Rationalism becomes predominant in philosophy. All guilt derives from ἄγνοια, which can be removed by education. By φρόνησις man who is regarded as good can attain to the actualisation of good. τὸ δὲ ἁμαρ-τάνειν ἐκ τοῦ ἀγνοεῖν κρίνειν ὅ τι χρὴ ποιεῖν συνίσταται (Cl. Al. Strom., II, 15, 62, 3; cf. Epict. Diss., I, 26, 6). The rationalistic concept of knowledge of later philosophy destroys the serious concept of guilt of the classical period. [125]

Yet the concept of fate remained. It no longer attained the height of the classical period with its idea of the identity of fate and guilt. It now became an experience which disrupts the thought of guilt and delivers up human existence to caprice. The mystery religions, which in the Hellenistic period crowded into the Greek world in great numbers, are all designed to break through the barrier of fate and mortality. To the same context belongs Hellenistic mysticism, which finds ex-pression in the Corp. Herm. and which regards the world as the theatre of → κακία interpreted as a cosmic power, and man as one who has fallen victim to vices from which he can be rescued only by the gracious gift of γνῶσις. ἄγνοια and γνῶσις have here become metaphysical opposites. The result of this dominant thought of guilt is the retreat of guilt as personal responsibility; cf. e.g.: τύχη ... νοῦν ἔχοντα ἄνθρωπον ἁμαρτάνειν ἠνάγκασεν (Lib. Ep., 1025). Here the deci-sive factor in existence is no longer a man's knowledge or ignorance; it is his foreordained destiny, which is also the cause of his guilt. In consequence there is also a change in the ἁμαρτ- concepts. "How far the intellectual colouring of the word ἁμαρτάνειν is lost is shown by the 'amnesty' of Euergetes II, which supple-ments ἀγνοήματα by ἁμαρτήματα in its attempt to give a comprehensive de-scription of all offenders." [126] Under the pressure of fate ἁμαρτάνειν is simply human destiny in general. [127]

5. An exception to Greek and Hellenistic thought in general is to be found in the inscriptions from Asia Minor gathered by Steinleitner from the field of Phrygian and Lydian religion. [128] In these primitive religions we find a belief in God as the absolute lord of his devotees who wills their good and himself punishes every violation. ἁμαρτία or ἁμαρτάνειν, which can be conscious and inten-

---

[124] Hey, 160; cf. 161: "There is no adequate equivalent in our language for the concept of ἁμαρτία with its many nuances. In Aristotelian terms, it is for us an ἀνώνυμον. We can render it blunder, failure (but not fault), miscalculation, misunderstanding, oversight (but not transgression), misjudgment, aberration, absurdity or folly according to the character and severity of the 'Hamartia'."

[125] There can be no serious question of a rise of the idea of sin. "The word (sin) is not in keeping with the Stoic system" (Bonhöffer).

[126] P. Tebt., I, 5, 3 (cf. Latte, 287).

[127] Cf. οὐκ ἔστιν ἄνθρωπος, ὃς ζήσεται καὶ οὐχ ἁμαρτίσει, Preisigke Sammelbuch, 4949, 17 ff.; 5716, 17.

[128] F. S. Steinleitner, *Die Beicht im Zusammenhange mit der sakralen Rechtspflege in der Antike* (Diss. München, 1913). → also ἁμαρτωλός, 318.

tional or the reverse ([ἐξ] εἰδότων καὶ μὴ εἰδότων, No. 11 in Steinleitner ; κατ᾽ ἄγνοιαν No. 14), is a violation of deity. It is called καταφρονεῖν τοῦ θεοῦ (No. 22). The religious significance of this sin is thus clearly brought out.[129] Sin consists[130] in gratitude withheld from deity (No. 7), in insulting speech (No. 12), in transgression of regulations for cleanness (No. 13), in violation of the sanctuary (No. 14), in non-observance of required cultic chastity (No. 22, 23), in cultic misdemeanour (No. 25, 33), and in perjury (No. 3, 6, 8). A whole series of sins is ethical in character. The godhead reacts to each offence with some punishment. Sickness especially is regarded as a punishment for sin. Sin is a kind of "substance which brings sickness."[131] So far as the character of these sins is concerned, it is excellently described by Steinleitner in the words : "Since the concern in this conception of sin and guilt is only with cultic and ritual offences, not with laws of basic ethics, the objective fact of the sinful act alone constitutes the essence of sin. No regard is had to the moral guilt or innocence of the doer."[132] The aim and goal of the related act of expiation is "to make the sinner physically and cultically normal again." "It is not directed to the inward disposition of the man, but only to his outward habitus."[133] The καταφρονεῖν τοῦ θεοῦ is not an existential determination of man, but one of the acts described above.[134] Here too, then, there can be no question of any true consciousness of sin.

With this we should perhaps link what is said by Plutarch[135] on one occasion : ἔα με ... ἄνθρωπε, διδόναι δίκην, τὸν ἀσεβῆ, τὸν ἐπάρατον, τὸν θεοῖς καὶ δαίμοσι μεμισημένον, Superst., 7 (II, 168c).

Stählin/Grundmann

F. Sin in the NT.

1. The Synoptic Gospels and Acts.

a. In the Synoptic Gospels it is striking how slight is the role of terms for sin as compared with their application in other parts of the NT. If we investigate the terms and their place in these Gospels, we find certain significant features

---

[129] The religious connection is naturally present in the classical Greek world as well (Plat. Phaedr. 242c; Leg., X, 891e; Aesch. Prom., 945; Xenoph. Hist. Graec., I, 7, 19; later Muson, p. 78, 9 and 13). Greek humanism is religious. The deities are equated with the immanent system of law. They are forms of reality. But this is rather different.

[130] Cf. on this point Steinleitner, 83 ff.

[131] *Ibid.*, 99.

[132] Steinleitner, 92.

[133] *Ibid.*, 121.

[134] This concept of sin is also found in the examples quoted from the mysteries of Samothrace in J. Leipoldt, *Das Gotteserlebnis Jesu* (1927), 35 and "Der Sieg des Christentums über die antiken Religionen," *Festschr. f. L. Ihmels* (1928), 81 f. Cf. Plut. Apophth. Lac. Antalcidas, I (II, 217c d), Lysandros 10 (II, 229d), where confession for sin is demanded. Leipoldt comments : "Thus sinners, and sinners specifically, were welcomed at Samothrace, and undoubtedly their sins were remitted. We can hardly say, however, how far we are to think of cultic sin or of sin ethically understood. Those who know Gk. religion will see the difficulty. The attitude of Christianity is unambiguous. Jesus and Paul are indifferent to cultic matters..." ("Sieg des Christentums," 81 f.). Cf. also Steinleitner, 118 f.

[135] Latte, 294.

which may be reduced to the twofold statement, first, that Jesus did not speak of sin and its nature and consequences, but was conscious of its reality (e.g., in the Sermon on the Mount) and acted accordingly, and second, that in His acts and sayings He was conscious of being the Victor over sin. These features may be illustrated from the Gospels.

b. The mission of Jesus is the proclamation of the divine lordship fulfilled in His Word and action. The event achieved by this lordship is the overcoming of sin. As Jesus proclaims the Father in His proclamation, and declares His goodness in His works, there arises a recognition of the distance of God and the impurity of man, and a desire for God. This event achieved by the coming of Jesus is described in the parable of the Prodigal Son, who goes to his father and confesses: πάτερ, ἥμαρτον εἰς τὸν οὐρανὸν καὶ ἐνώπιόν σου (Lk. 15:18, 21). The parable shows us what Jesus understands by sin. It is going out from the father's house, i.e., godlessness and remoteness from God working itself out in a life in the world with all its desires and its filth. The event achieved through the coming of Jesus is recognition of this sin and conversion to God. Thus Jesus shows what penitence is as well as sin, namely, the way to God as the Father who receives the sinner with love. λέγω ὑμῖν ὅτι οὕτως χαρὰ ἐν τῷ οὐρανῷ ἔσται ἐπὶ ἑνὶ ἁμαρτωλῷ μετανοοῦντι ἢ ἐπὶ ἐνενήκοντα ἐννέα δικαίοις, οἵτινες οὐ χρείαν ἔχουσιν μετανοίας (Lk. 15:7, cf. v. 10). On the basis of this twofold knowledge Jesus does not speak of sin but proclaims God as the Father in His lordship, conscious that this proclamation goes right home to the sin which consists both in godlessness and in guilt towards one's neighbour, [136] and thus brings about the event of penitence. This sin is guilt towards God. Hence its bitter seriousness. [137]

The basic insight is confirmed in the attitude of Jesus. He describes His task to the Pharisees in the words: οὐ γὰρ ἦλθον καλέσαι δικαίους ἀλλὰ ἁμαρτωλούς (Mt. 9:13). [138] He knows that He is sent to those who live in guilt far from God in order to call them to God. From this task springs His attitude as described by the Evangelists: καὶ ἐγένετο αὐτοῦ ἀνακειμένου ἐν τῇ οἰκίᾳ, καὶ ἰδοὺ πολλοὶ τελῶναι καὶ ἁμαρτωλοὶ ἐλθόντες συνανέκειντο τῷ Ἰησοῦ καὶ τοῖς μαθηταῖς αὐτοῦ (Mt. 9:10; cf. v. 11 par.; Lk. 15, 1, 2; 19:7). From this attitude derives the judgment τελωνῶν φίλος καὶ ἁμαρτωλῶν (Mt. 11:19 and Lk. 7:34). [139] This attitude consists in acceptance of the closest fellowship known to the oriental world, i.e., table fellowship. In this attitude He is the Victor over sin, not merely by overcoming the gulf between the righteous and sinners, but by forgiving sin and thus overcoming the gulf between God and sinners and establishing a new fellowship with God by drawing sinners into fellowship with Himself. [140] This is the effect of the word of forgiveness which He speaks and which shows Him

---

[136] Cf. Mt. 18:23 ff.; 5:21 ff.; 6:14 f.; also → πονηρός.

[137] → ὀφείλημα, ὀφειλέτης, Mt. 6:12; 18:24.

[138] It is true that Jesus finds both δίκαιοι and ἁμαρτωλοί in His people. It is true that He thus sets alongside the prodigal son another who remains in his father's house and grumbles at the welcome given to his brother — a trait obviously based on experience. Yet it is also true that Jesus sees the universality of sinfulness. This emerges in His attitude to the δίκαιος. From this insight derive such verdicts as that of Mk. 8:38 (→ πονηρός); Lk. 6:32 ff.; 13:1-4. Cf. RGG², V, 885, 3.

[139] On the formula τελῶναι καὶ ἁμαρτωλοί, cf. Joachim Jeremias, ZNW, 30 (1931), 293 ff.

[140] Cf. esp. Schl. Mt., 304.

to be the Christ sitting on the right hand of God and endowed with omnipotence (→ ἄφεσις, ἐξουσία, cf. Mt. 9:2; Lk. 7:47 ff.). How the event described in the parable of the Prodigal Son is brought about by the attitude of Jesus, we see clearly from many narratives, such as that of the draught of fishes (Lk. 5:8), or of the woman who sinned much (Lk. 7:37 ff.), or of Zacchaeus (Lk. 19:1 f.). That God meets with fellowship this conversion to Himself is shown by Jesus in His verdict on the publican in the temple who confesses : ἱλάσθητί μοι τῷ ἁμαρτωλῷ (Lk. 18:13 ff.).

Neither Jesus' word of forgiveness nor His attitude can be taken for granted. They are in fact quite extraordinary. They constitute the overcoming of sin and therefore the irruption of the divine lordship. They are eschatological. This emerges particularly clearly in the Lord's Supper. The Lord's Supper is the declaration of the new covenant promised for the last time (Jer. 31:31-34). This new covenant is concluded with the coming of Jesus and set in force with His death. His blood is the blood of the covenant (τὸ αἷμα τῆς διαθήκης), of which it is said : τὸ περὶ πολλῶν ἐκχυννόμενον εἰς ἄφεσιν ἁμαρτιῶν (Mt. 26:28). [141] With it is fulfilled : ἵλεως ἔσομαι ταῖς ἀδικίαις αὐτῶν καὶ τῶν ἁμαρτιῶν αὐτῶν οὐ μὴ μνησθῶ ἔτι (Ιερ. 38:34 = 31:34 Mas.). But with it there is also fulfilled what Dt.-Is. writes concerning the Servant of the Lord : καὶ αὐτὸς ἁμαρτίας πολλῶν ἀνήνεγκε (Is. 53:12). [142] Jesus is the Servant of the Lord who by His death and passion bears away the sin of humanity. This is how He understood His mission. It means that by His coming, death and resurrection, sin is overcome and the foundation laid for the new world of God.

In this light we can understand the saying about the unforgivable sin (→ 104), irrespective of whether we regard it as a saying of Jesus, a product of the theology of the community, or a genuine saying refashioned by the community. The saying is as follows : πᾶσα ἁμαρτία καὶ βλασφημία ἀφεθήσεται τοῖς ἀνθρώποις, ἡ δὲ τοῦ πνεύματος βλασφημία οὐκ ἀφεθήσεται ... οὔτε ἐν τούτῳ τῷ αἰῶνι οὔτε ἐν τῷ μέλλοντι, Mt. 12:31 f. par. (Mk.: ... ἔνοχός ἐστιν αἰωνίου ἁμαρτήματος, 3:29). This sin is committed when a man recognises the mission of Jesus by the Holy Spirit but defies and resists and curses it. The saying shows the seriousness of the situation. It is the last time, in which the lordship of God breaks in.

c. Jesus as the Victor over sin — this is the Synoptic *kerygma* derived from the story of Jesus. This *kerygma* comes out with particular clarity in the saying of the angel to Joseph in the introductory story in Matthew — a saying which interprets the name of Jesus : αὐτὸς γὰρ σώσει τὸν λαὸν αὐτοῦ ἀπὸ τῶν ἁμαρτιῶν αὐτῶν (Mt. 1:21).

The history of Jesus was prepared by the emergence of the Baptist, which on any view must be seen as preparation. In the Baptist the thought of sin is central. We can see this from his preaching, which had the effect : ... ἐξομολογούμενοι τὰς ἁμαρτίας αὐτῶν (Mt. 3:6). We can see it also from his baptism, which Mk. and Lk. both call βάπτισμα μετανοίας εἰς ἄφεσιν ἁμαρτιῶν (Mk. 1:4; Lk. 3:3). In the song of praise of Zacharias his mission is described in the words : τοῦ

---

141 The addition εἰς ἄφεσιν ἁμαρτιῶν is found only in Mt., yet it is a meaningful interpretation of what is at issue.
142 Cf. also Is. 53:5, 6. The πολλοί of the words of institution in Mt. and Mk. unmistakeably reflects Is. 53:12.

δοῦναι γνῶσιν σωτηρίας τῷ λαῷ αὐτοῦ ἐν ἀφέσει ἁμαρτιῶν αὐτῶν (Lk. 1:77). Thus in the Baptist, under the impress of the coming kingdom of God, sin, repentance and remission are central. If things are otherwise with Jesus, we have seen that this is because, in distinction from the Baptist, He is the Fulfiller, i.e., the One who overcomes sin, who in every word and deed acts as the Forgiver of sins, and with whom the kingdom of God breaks in.

The history of Jesus is continued in the work of the apostles. Their proclamation is the proclamation of Christ as the gift of God's salvation to men. In clear agreement with the action of Jesus and its operation, they demand: μετανοήσατε, καὶ βαπτισθήτω ἕκαστος ὑμῶν ἐπὶ τῷ ὀνόματι 'Ιησοῦ Χριστοῦ εἰς ἄφεσιν τῶν ἁμαρτιῶν ὑμῶν (Ac. 2:38).¹⁴³ The distinction from Jesus is that there is now a summons to receive the remission of sins, whereas Jesus gave it directly in His action by drawing into dealings and fellowship with Himself. In this way we may distinguish the ἀπόστολοι and the κύριος. The distinction from the Baptist is that the latter summoned to such reception in the light of a future event, whereas the disciples speak on the basis of an event which has already occurred: ἐπὶ τῷ ὀνόματι 'Ιησοῦ Χριστοῦ. In Him sin is overcome and forgiveness is present; cf. esp. Ac. 5:31: τοῦτον ὁ θεὸς ἀρχηγὸν καὶ σωτῆρα ὕψωσεν τῇ δεξιᾷ αὐτοῦ τοῦ δοῦναι μετάνοιαν τῷ 'Ισραὴλ καὶ ἄφεσιν ἁμαρτιῶν. The Baptist and the apostles differ in respect of the situation in which they stand (cf. Ac. 10:43; → ἄφεσις).

It has already been pointed out (295) that in the Synoptic Gospels and Acts ἁμαρτία is always understood as an individual act. For this reason we have the plur. ἁμαρτίαι rather than the sing. ἁμαρτία. This lexicographical finding confirms our conclusions (302). Neither Jesus nor the primitive community asked concerning the nature of sin; they saw men in the reality of sins which were very definitely individual sins. The work of Christ is based on this reality. As shown again by the lexicographical findings, it was the theologian Paul who raised the theological question of sin as a power which determines the nature of man and the world, and who saw its actuality as such (295 and cf. also 308). John is nearer to the first group than to Paul.

2. John.

In the Christ *kerygma* of John¹⁴⁴ we again see the fact of the overcoming of sin by Christ as it is first displayed in the picture of the historical Jesus presented by the Synoptists. The significance of this fact is further developed by John. The mission of Jesus consists in the overcoming of sin: καὶ οἴδατε ὅτι ἐκεῖνος ἐφανερώθη ἵνα τὰς ἁμαρτίας ἄρῃ, καὶ ἁμαρτία ἐν αὐτῷ οὐκ ἔστιν (1 Jn. 3:5). Christ is the One who takes sin to Himself and bears it away. The reference here is primarily to His death, and the overcoming of sin is seen in terms of the picture of atonement deriving from the Jewish sacrificial system. This is brought out by the → αἴρειν which both occurs in the verse quoted and is also found in the picture of the Lamb of God¹⁴⁵ with its reference to sacrifice and its great thematic

---

¹⁴³ *v.* also Lk. 24:47; Ac. 3:19; 13:38; 22:16; 26:18.

¹⁴⁴ Cf. R. Seeberg, "Die Sünden und die Sündenvergebung nach dem ersten Brief des Johannes," *Festschr. f. L. Ihmels* (1928), 19 ff.

¹⁴⁵ Cf., however, Burney's explanation of ἀμνός as a mistranslation of "Servant of the Lord"; → 186, and ἀμνός.

significance : ἴδε ὁ ἀμνὸς τοῦ θεοῦ ὁ αἴρων τὴν ἁμαρτίαν τοῦ κόσμου (Jn. 1:29).
It is also brought out vividly by the expressions : καὶ αὐτὸς ἱλασμός ἐστιν περὶ
τῶν ἁμαρτιῶν ἡμῶν (1 Jn. 2:2; cf. 4:10), and : τὸ αἷμα Ἰησοῦ Χριστοῦ τοῦ
υἱοῦ αὐτοῦ καθαρίζει ἡμᾶς ἀπὸ πάσης ἁμαρτίας (1 Jn. 1:7). The overcoming
of the sin of the world by Christ consists in the fact that He makes atonement,
and is the One who atones. This mission of His bursts all human limits, whether
of nation, race or sex: ἱλασμός ἐστιν περὶ τῶν ἁμαρτιῶν ἡμῶν, οὐ περὶ τῶν
ἡμετέρων δὲ μόνον ἀλλὰ καὶ περὶ ὅλου τοῦ κόσμου (1 Jn. 2:2). This mission of
Jesus to the whole of humanity has its presupposition in His being : ἁμαρτία ἐν
αὐτῷ οὐκ ἔστιν (1 Jn. 3:5). As it makes and is atonement, His mission rests in
His sinlessness in which He is the man after the will of God, who is one with the
Father and who is therefore the Son. He can thus put to the Jews the question :
τίς ἐξ ὑμῶν ἐλέγχει με περὶ ἁμαρτίας (Jn. 8:46). In face of the signs which
reveal His Messianic glory the Jews must confess : πῶς δύναται ἄνθρωπος ἁμαρτωλὸς τοιαῦτα σημεῖα ποιεῖν (Jn. 9:16). [146]

The two sides of Christ's mission, the overcoming of sin by atonement and the
general human significance of this event, correspond to the Johannine concept of
sin. In two passages he gives a precise definition of what he means by sin : πᾶς
ὁ ποιῶν τὴν ἁμαρτίαν καὶ τὴν ἀνομίαν ποιεῖ, καὶ ἡ ἁμαρτία ἐστὶν ἡ ἀνομία
(1 Jn. 3:4); πᾶσα ἀδικία ἁμαρτία ἐστίν (5:17). Sin is action opposed to the
divine ordinance, which corresponds to the right. It is thus ἀνομία and ἀδικία.
As ἀδικία it is contradiction of what is right, and therefore of God's will, so that
it is also ἀνομία. It has its origin, therefore, in opposition to God, derives from
human godlessness, and finds expression in sins against one's neighbour. Thus the
basic character of the universality of sin is established. It is not merely a human
state. It involves guilt and brings about separation from God. The statement :
οἴδαμεν ὅτι ὁ θεὸς ἁμαρτωλῶν οὐκ ἀκούει, ἀλλ' ἐάν τις θεοσεβὴς ᾖ καὶ τὸ
θέλημα αὐτοῦ ποιῇ, τούτου ἀκούει (Jn. 9:31), necessarily implies that sin separates from God. This separation is absolute: ὁ ποιῶν τὴν ἁμαρτίαν ἐκ τοῦ
διαβόλου ἐστίν, ὅτι ἀπ' ἀρχῆς ὁ διάβολος ἁμαρτάνει (1 Jn. 3:8). In the opposition to God there is manifested the demonic character of man's sin as it binds him
to the διάβολος. We can thus understand quite well the familiar saying: ἀμὴν
ἀμὴν λέγω ὑμῖν ὅτι πᾶς ὁ ποιῶν τὴν ἁμαρτίαν δοῦλός ἐστιν τῆς ἁμαρτίας
(Jn. 8:34). This is not a general sentence, as we see from the twofold → ἀμήν,
but a perception of human existence in the light of Christ, namely, that human
sin is servitude to demonic power [147] and therefore complete separation from God.

The mission of Christ brings with it an entirely new situation best denoted by
the word κρίσις = division and decision. εἰ μὴ ἦλθον καὶ ἐλάλησα αὐτοῖς,
ἁμαρτίαν οὐκ εἴχοσαν· νῦν δὲ πρόφασιν οὐκ ἔχουσιν περὶ τῆς ἁμαρτίας αὐ-

---

[146] We can see both unity with and distinction from the Synoptists. The unity consists
in the *kerygma*. As Christ, Jesus is the Victor over sin. But while the Syn. bring this out
in His attitude and acts among the Jewish people, and thus give a living picture of His
coming, John forms the kerygmatic thesis of the propitiation of the sin of the world by the
death of Christ, and he thus stresses the final basis of the attitude of Jesus as this emerges
in the Lord's Supper.

[147] To understand these sayings we must note that Jesus shatters the Jewish prerogative
of being the σπέρμα Ἀβραάμ and shows to the Jews their demonic bondage.

τῶν. ὁ ἐμὲ μισῶν καὶ τὸν πατέρα μου μισεῖ. εἰ τὰ ἔργα μὴ ἐποίησα ἐν αὐτοῖς ἃ οὐδεὶς ἄλλος ἐποίησεν, ἁμαρτίαν οὐκ εἴχοσαν (Jn. 15:22-24). The coming of Jesus Christ means the revelation of sin as hatred of God. Before Him there is taken the decision concerning men and there is accomplished the division between them : εἰ τυφλοὶ ἦτε, οὐκ ἂν εἴχετε ἁμαρτίαν· νῦν δὲ λέγετε ὅτι βλέπομεν· ἡ ἁμαρτία ὑμῶν μένει (Jn. 9:41); cf. also 8:24 : εἶπον οὖν ὑμῖν ὅτι ἀποθανεῖσθε ἐν ταῖς ἁμαρτίαις ὑμῶν· ἐὰν γὰρ μὴ πιστεύσητε ὅτι ἐγώ εἰμι, ἀποθανεῖσθε ἐν ταῖς ἁμαρτίαις ὑμῶν. The man who refuses to bow to Christ or to believe in His ἐγώ εἰμι remains and dies in his sin and is excluded from the mission of Christ. All the sin of man is blindness as compared with this sin ; it is thus described as ἀδικία ... καὶ ἔστιν ἁμαρτία οὐ πρὸς θάνατον (1 Jn. 5:17). But the sin which arises in the presence of Christ is ἁμαρτία πρὸς θάνατον (1 Jn. 5:16).[148] This is the κρίσις which has come into the world with Christ. The situation of the last hour which means decision either for life or death could not be more plainly declared. The one possibility is seen in the Jews who reject Jesus with hatred, the other in those who believe in Him : ἐὰν ὁμολογῶμεν τὰς ἁμαρτίας ἡμῶν, πιστός ἐστιν καὶ δίκαιος, ἵνα ἀφῇ ἡμῖν τὰς ἁμαρτίας καὶ καθαρίσῃ ἡμᾶς ἀπὸ πάσης ἀδικίας (1 Jn. 1:9). The man who confesses his guilt before God receives the word of forgiveness. The man who does not cannot receive it because there is no truth in him and he makes God a liar. The diabolical character of sin is herein expressed (1 Jn. 1:8, 10; cf. Jn. 8:44).[149] This situation has not come to an end but still continues. For in the Paraclete Christ is present to His community. The work of the Paraclete continues the work of Christ : καὶ ἐλθὼν ἐκεῖνος ἐλέγξει τὸν κόσμον περὶ ἁμαρτίας καὶ περὶ δικαιοσύνης καὶ περὶ κρίσεως· περὶ ἁμαρτίας μέν, ὅτι οὐ πιστεύουσιν εἰς ἐμέ (Jn. 16:8 f.).

The mission of Christ to αἴρειν τὰς ἁμαρτίας attains its goal in the community which is delivered from sin. This deliverance from sin is basically maintained and is established by birth of God. The man who belongs to the community is born again of and by God in the fact that God has given him faith, and in faith the knowledge of God and His Christ. The new birth takes place with reference to Christ. For this reason the basic statements are true : πᾶς ὁ ἐν αὐτῷ μένων οὐχ ἁμαρτάνει· πᾶς ὁ ἁμαρτάνων οὐχ ἑώρακεν αὐτὸν οὐδὲ ἔγνωκεν αὐτόν ... πᾶς ὁ γεγεννημένος ἐκ τοῦ θεοῦ ἁμαρτίαν οὐ ποιεῖ, ὅτι σπέρμα αὐτοῦ ἐν αὐτῷ μένει· καὶ οὐ δύναται ἁμαρτάνειν, ὅτι ἐκ τοῦ θεοῦ γεγέννηται (1 Jn. 3:6, 9).[150] The new situation becomes effective in love, which is the total opposite of ἁμαρτία (→ ἀγάπη). These basic statements are guaranteed and made serious by the attitude of Jesus, cf. Jn. 5:14 : μηκέτι ἁμάρτανε, ἵνα μὴ χεῖρόν σοί τι γένηται.[151] But they contain a contradiction to the reality of the Christian community, which in practice is not without sin. Here is a serious problem. There is opposition to the new energy of love striving against sin. John, however, does not reflect on this problem, but, emphasising the fundamental sinlessness of the community, he present two points for consideration. First : ταῦτα γράφω ὑμῖν ἵνα

---

[148] As against Seeberg, op. cit., 23 ff.

[149] Cf. Hempel, op. cit., 183 in relation to Jn. 8:44 : "The effect of revelation, however, is to bring the facts to light and thus to commence with the destruction of the kingdom of Satan."

[150] Cf. W. Grundmann, Begriff der Kraft in d. nt.lichen Gedankenwelt (1932), 113, n. 8.

[151] The χεῖρον which can come on the one who is healed is θάνατος from the sin πρὸς

μὴ ἁμάρτητε· καὶ ἐάν τις ἁμάρτῃ, παράκλητον ἔχομεν πρὸς τὸν πατέρα, Ἰησοῦν Χριστὸν δίκαιον, καὶ αὐτὸς ἱλασμός ἐστιν περὶ τῶν ἁμαρτιῶν ἡμῶν... (1 Jn. 2:1 f.). Christ's atonement relates to the sin of the community. The community has a παράκλητος to make possible its situation in problematic tension. Again, there is a brotherly ministry of love: ἐάν τις ἴδῃ τὸν ἀδελφὸν αὐτοῦ ἁμαρτάνοντα ἁμαρτίαν μὴ πρὸς θάνατον, αἰτήσει, καὶ δώσει αὐτῷ ζωήν, τοῖς ἁμαρτάνουσιν μὴ πρὸς θάνατον (1 Jn. 5:16). The community can engage in intercessory prayer which will be heard. This is its second prop in that dubious position of tension. We can see from this how seriously John takes sin and how plain is its decisive significance for man in the light of Christ.

In the Book of Revelation, which bears John's name, the work of Christ is described as a work of love which has as its content His delivering of us from the sinful world order: ... τῷ λύσαντι ἡμᾶς ἐκ τῶν ἁμαρτιῶν ἡμῶν ἐν τῷ αἵματι αὐτοῦ (1:5). The blood of Christ has atoning power. The task of the people of God in the last time is to keep themselves from the increasing power of sin: ... ἵνα μὴ συγκοινωνήσατε ταῖς ἁμαρτίαις αὐτῆς (sc. Babylon), for the divine punishment destroying both sin and sinners is passed on all the sin of the world: ... ἐκολλήθησαν αὐτῆς αἱ ἁμαρτίαι ἄχρι τοῦ οὐρανοῦ, καὶ ἐμνημόνευσεν ὁ θεὸς τὰ ἀδικήματα αὐτῆς (18:4, 5). By a final and definitive act of God the universal dominion of sin, from which Christians are liberated, will be destroyed. This is the view of the author of Revelation.

3. Paul.

a. What Paul has to say about sin is orientated to the revelation of God in Christ. Hence it is not an empirical doctrine of sin based on pessimism. It is the judgment of God on man without God as this is ascertained from the revelation of Christ and revealed in full seriousness in the cross of Christ. This presupposition is essential for an understanding of what Paul says about sin. His view may thus be summarised in two propositions. 1. The Christ event comes upon man in a specific reality, i.e., his reality as a sinner. 2. It comes upon him as an event which rescues him from this reality and reconstitutes him. What was for Jesus Himself simply an event is here described and developed.[152] This is the difference between Jesus and Paul in the matter of sin.

b. The Pauline concept and understanding of sin are determined by Paul's own experience under the impress of the act of divine revelation accomplished in Christ. Paul said of himself: κατὰ δικαιοσύνην τὴν ἐν νόμῳ γενόμενος ἄμεμπτος (Phil. 3:6; cf. Gl. 1:14; → 291 and also → ἁμαρτωλός, 330). This was his Jewish self-awareness. Under the impress of the revelation of Christ on the Damascus road there arose the confession: ἐγὼ γάρ εἰμι ὁ ἐλάχιστος τῶν ἀποστόλων, ὃς οὐκ εἰμὶ ἱκανὸς καλεῖσθαι ἀπόστολος, διότι ἐδίωξα τὴν ἐκκλησίαν τοῦ θεοῦ (1 Cor. 15:9; cf. 1 Tm. 1:15). His sin is the persecution of the Christian

---

θάνατον (cf. Schl. J., 145). Thus the connection between sin, suffering and death is maintained. But the dominant schema which finds a guilty source for individual suffering is shattered (Jn. 9:2, 3), since it blinds us to the work of God as the One who blesses and endows.

152 Cf. G. Kittel, *Die Religionsgeschichte und das Urchristentum* (1932), 154 ff., n. 350. Here the general view is worked out of which we have given the particular application.

community (1 C. 15:9; Gl. 1:23; Phil. 3:6). But this persecution was simply the final result of his attempted self-justification through the works of the Law, of his zeal for it. This zeal was also judged in the judgment on the persecution of the community of God. With this judgment, he came to realise that his whole activity in Judaism was opposition to God's will and consequently active hostility to God. Both the persecution and the underlying zeal for the Law sprang from the tendency of man to assert himself against God and to try to will in independence of Him. This desire of man to dispose concerning himself [153] is opposition to the will of God. Once this became clear, he was insistent that sin is not merely a violation of the divine majesty, as he had already learned as a Jew, but active hostility to God and resistance to His will on the part of the man who wills to be independent and to rule his own life. This thought of hostility is the constitutive element in Paul's doctrine of sin.

How does Paul see the reality of sin in detail?

This question leads us to a presentation of the thoughts contained in R. 5-8, where from the purely lexical view we have the most frequent occurrence of the terms for sin in the NT. The Christ event is first depicted in the words: συνίστησιν δὲ τὴν ἑαυτοῦ ἀγάπην εἰς ἡμᾶς ὁ θεὸς ὅτι ἔτι ἁμαρτωλῶν ὄντων ἡμῶν Χριστὸς ὑπὲρ ἡμῶν ἀπέθανεν (R. 5:8). What this means we are told in 5:12 ff. in connection with what precedes: [154] ... ὥσπερ δι' ἑνὸς ἀνθρώπου ἡ ἁμαρτία εἰς τὸν κόσμον εἰσῆλθεν, καὶ διὰ τῆς ἁμαρτίας ὁ θάνατος, καὶ οὕτως εἰς πάντας ἀνθρώπους ὁ θάνατος διῆλθεν ἐφ' ᾧ πάντες ἥμαρτον. To the question of the origin of sin Paul gives the answer of Judaism that sin entered the world through Adam. The act of Adam in opposition to God is the beginning of sin. Sin thus derived from the freedom of man. With sin death also came into the world, as we read in the short statement: τὰ γὰρ ὀψώνια τῆς ἁμαρτίας θάνατος (6:23). Sin as the master gives its paid underlings the wages of death. Thus the dominant power of death in the world is attributed to sin (cf. 1 C. 15:56). The world in its being is not determined only by its creatureliness (R. 1:20) but also by sin. Paul differs from the Greek and Hellenistic world in the fact that, though he, too, can talk of the power of fate, for him the power of fate is closely linked with that of death, [155] and human sin is the basis of death's rule. Sin is the author of all evil: ... ἐβασίλευσεν ἡ ἁμαρτία ἐν τῷ θανάτῳ. Here we have a Christian rather than a Greek understanding. But from the sway of death there may also be discerned the universality of sin as hostile striving against God (3:9, 23; 5:9, 10; 8:7; Gl. 3:22). At this point Paul differs from Judaism. For Paul sin does not consist only in the individual act. Sin is for him a state which embraces all humanity. The individual is always in this all-embracing state of sin, and thus he

---

[153] R. Bultmann, "Römer 7 u. d. Anthropologie des Paulus" in Imago Dei, *Festschrift f. G. Krüger* (1932), 53 ff.; esp. 60 f.: "Sin is ... the desire of man to dispose concerning himself, his raising of his own claim, his will to be as God."

[154] The context of the chapter consists in the thought of endurance in affliction. This is demanded by the a minori ad maius conclusions (πολλῷ μᾶλλον) from the community's situation of salvation (5:7-11) and the new situation of the world (5:12-21).

[155] At any rate we should not overlook the fact that in Gk. and Hellenistic dualism — to use the phrase of E. Rohde (→ 297 f., esp. n. 104) — life is the wages of sin, so that a very different view of life is present from that of Christianity with its consciousness of sin and the statement that death is the wages of sin.

does not have the Jewish freedom of choice which constitutes the Jewish conception of sin (... διὰ τῆς παρακοῆς τοῦ ἑνὸς ἀνθρώπου ἁμαρτωλοὶ κατεστάθησαν οἱ πολλοί ... 5:19). There is an indissoluble connection between the act of Adam, the fate of death and the general state of sin. This does not mean that a doctrine of inherited sin is presented. It means that a judgment is pronounced on men in their being as such — a judgment which is certainly shaped by human reality but which is possible only in the light of Christ.

In what does this state consist? Paul continues: ἄχρι γὰρ νόμου ἁμαρτία ἦν ἐν κόσμῳ, ἁμαρτία δὲ οὐκ ἐλλογεῖται μὴ ὄντος νόμου (R. 5:13). This statement, with its relating of sin and Law, corresponds to Jewish thinking. The state of sin already present (ἁμαρτία ἦν ἐν κόσμῳ, cf. also χωρὶς γὰρ νόμου ἁμαρτία νεκρά in R. 7:8) is actualised through the command of the Law in transgression (cf. Gl. 3:19: τί οὖν ὁ νόμος; τῶν παραβάσεων χάριν προσετέθη → παράβασις). Thus the nature of sin becomes clear. Sin is the rejection of God by self-assertive man (cf. R. 1:21: ... γνόντες τὸν θεὸν οὐχ ὡς θεὸν ἐδόξασαν ἢ ηὐχαρίστησαν — this is the original sin). In this respect the sin of man in general corresponds to the sin of Adam. This sin, however, arises only in relation to the command as a declaration of the will of God. For this reason, between Adam and Moses sin is a μὴ ἁμαρτάνειν ἐπὶ τῷ ὁμοιώματι τῆς παραβάσεως Ἀδάμ (5:14). For this reason it may be said: οὐκ ἐλλογεῖται μὴ ὄντος νόμου. The function of the Law, therefore, is to actualise the sinful state in transgression and thus to reveal the character of sin, to show it to be ἔχθρα εἰς θεόν (R. 8:7), or, metaphorically, to transform the potential energy of the sinful state into the kinetic energy of the individual action, and thereby to bring into play the sentence of death passed on sin and to represent sin as responsible guilt before God. The reason why sin is for Paul the determinative reality of man is that it is guilt before God. At this point the element of truth in the Jewish concept of sin is adopted, but it is essentially deepened and brought into a new perspective. In agreement with this concept it is maintained that sin is action in the interrelation of sin and Law. But the Law now has the very opposite function from that ascribed to it in Judaism.

Paul speaks expressly of the interrelation of sin and Law in R. 7. The experience of Paul is stated generally in the sentence: ὅτε γὰρ ἦμεν ἐν τῇ σαρκί, τὰ παθήματα τῶν ἁμαρτιῶν τὰ διὰ τοῦ νόμου ἐνηργεῖτο ἐν τοῖς μέλεσιν ἡμῶν εἰς τὸ καρποφορῆσαι τῷ θανάτῳ (7:5). The carnal reality of man is his sinful reality, yet not for Paul in such a way that sin and the flesh are identical and sinfulness is constituted with corporeality (→ σάρξ, σῶμα), but rather in such a way that man is determined by sin in his carnal being, and has firmly linked himself to it. This union is disclosed by the Law: ... τὴν ἁμαρτίαν οὐκ ἔγνων εἰ μὴ διὰ νόμου· τήν τε γὰρ ἐπιθυμίαν οὐκ ᾔδειν εἰ μὴ ὁ νόμος ἔλεγεν· οὐκ ἐπιθυμήσεις· ἀφορμὴν δὲ λαβοῦσα ἡ ἁμαρτία διὰ τῆς ἐντολῆς κατηργάσατο ἐν ἐμοὶ πᾶσαν ἐπιθυμίαν· χωρὶς γὰρ νόμου ἁμαρτία νεκρά· ἐγὼ δὲ ἔζων χωρὶς νόμου ποτέ· ἐλθούσης δὲ τῆς ἐντολῆς ἡ ἁμαρτία ἀνέζησεν, ἐγὼ δὲ ἀπέθανον, καὶ εὑρέθη μοι ἡ ἐντολὴ ἡ εἰς ζωήν, αὕτη εἰς θάνατον (7:7-10). Different expressions are used to bring out the one fact that actual sin is by way of the Law. The Law awakens slumbering desire. At this point → ἐπιθυμία is not to be taken as merely a specifically carnal, i.e., sexual desire, but in a more comprehensive sense (πᾶσα ἐπιθυμία) as the yearning of man, kindled by the Law but opposed to it, for self-assertion against the claim of God. This is the nerve of every individual sin from the failure to acknowledge God, which is for Paul the original sin (R. 1:21), to that in which he sees the punishment of sin on the part of the God who punishes sin with sinning, i.e., to sexual perversity and expressions of the hatred which destroys fellowship (R. 1:24-31; 1 Th. 2:16). From this standpoint every individual sin committed by and against men acquires its significance before God and has before Him the character of guilt. [156]

It has already been noted that sin is here personified as a demon (→ 296). Sin has a demonic character. This demonic character emerges quite clearly in the fact that it uses the holy will of God to increase its power: ἡ ἁμαρτία, ἵνα φανῇ ἁμαρτία, διὰ τοῦ ἀγαθοῦ μοι κατεργαζομένη θάνατον, ἵνα γένηται καθ' ὑπερβολὴν ἁμαρτωλὸς ἡ ἁμαρτία διὰ τῆς ἐντολῆς (7:13). That is to say, the function which we assert the Law to have in the divine plan for the world is finally achieved when sin is unmasked in its demonic character as utter enmity against God. The state of the world and each individual since Adam has a demonic character as directed against God. Hence the situation of man is quite adequately described when Paul says of him: ἐγὼ δὲ σάρκινός εἰμι, πεπραμένος ὑπὸ τὴν ἁμαρτίαν (7:14). Man is a slave sold under sin, and therefore even before his physical death he is delivered up to the power of death (καὶ ὑμᾶς ὄντας νεκροὺς ... ταῖς ἁμαρτίαις ὑμῶν, Eph. 2:1). This situation of man emerges clearly in the inner conflict of man in his action — a conflict which is to be explained by the fact that he is possessed by demonic power: ... ὃ μισῶ τοῦτο ποιῶ· εἰ δὲ ὃ οὐ θέλω τοῦτο ποιῶ, σύμφημι τῷ νόμῳ ὅτι καλός ... εἰ δὲ ὃ οὐ θέλω ἐγὼ τοῦτο ποιῶ, οὐκέτι ἐγὼ κατεργάζομαι αὐτὸ ἀλλὰ ἡ οἰκοῦσα ἐν ἐμοὶ ἁμαρτία (7:15, 16, 20; cf. also v. 17). Man is under the Law as God's claim. But he cannot fulfil the Law. He is possessed by the demonic power of sin. Sin controls him and finally gives him the reward of death. [157] This train of thought introduces an essential feature in Paul. As we have seen above that the dominion of death is based on the reality of sin, so we now recognise that the demonology and satanology of Paul is not dualistic speculation, but a way of expressing the fact of sin. The demonological and satanological statements are all determined by the view of sin.

c. It is in this reality that the Christ event strikes man. [158] This event is the overcoming of sin ... ὁ θεὸς τὸν ἑαυτοῦ υἱὸν πέμψας ἐν ὁμοιώματι σαρκὸς

---

[156] The drawing out of desire and the disclosure of its inner being are the function of the Law, as we are told in 7:7: τὴν ἁμαρτίαν οὐκ ἔγνων εἰ μὴ διὰ νόμου, and 3:20: διὰ ... νόμου ἐπίγνωσις ἁμαρτίας. Yet we do not have here the functions ascribed to it in the dogmatic construction of a fourfold purpose of the Law, but a cosmic and historical function.

[157] On the question of R. 7 we share the thesis formulated by R. Bultmann in RGG², IV, 1022: "Rather Paul describes the situation of the Jew under the Law in its material sense as seen by the believer." We only ask whether it is the situation of the Jew alone. Bultmann has repeated this view more recently in his Römer 7 und d. Anthropologie d. Pls., 53: "The situation of man under the Law is here generally characterised as it has come to be seen by those whom Christ has freed from the Law." The same thesis has been adopted by W. G. Kümmel, Römer 7 u. d. Bekehrung des Paulus (1929). Arguments and bibliography may be found in these places and also in the commentaries ad loc.

[158] Cf. Hempel, op. cit., 181: "By this knowledge of sin in its awful form there is created a way to thankful acceptance (χάρις ... R. 7:25) and a distinctive background for the work of Jesus Himself."

ἁμαρτίας καὶ περὶ ἁμαρτίας κατέκρινεν τὴν ἁμαρτίαν ἐν τῇ σαρκί ... (R. 8:3). The aim of Christ's sending by God is to judge and destroy sin. This is the meaning of the incarnation. Paul states this graphically in the words: τὸν μὴ γνόντα ἁμαρτίαν ὑπὲρ ἡμῶν ἁμαρτίαν ἐποίησεν ... (2 C. 5:21). The sinlessness of Jesus is the presupposition of His mission. According to Paul's description of the mystery of the Christ event, this sinless Jesus became sin. All the sin of man rests on Him, whether past or present: ὃν προέθετο ὁ θεὸς ἱλαστήριον ... εἰς ἔνδειξιν τῆς δικαιοσύνης αὐτοῦ διὰ τὴν πάρεσιν τῶν προγεγονότων ἁμαρτημάτων ἐν τῇ ἀνοχῇ τοῦ θεοῦ (R. 3:25). For the sake of Christ and His victory over sin there has been and is the day of God's grace and the postponement of judgment. Christ's victory over sin is described as expiatory or propitiatory atonement. For this reason His death is essential. It was on the cross that there took place, in a way which is valid for all ages, the conquest of sin: ὃ γὰρ ἀπέθανεν, τῇ ἁμαρτίᾳ ἀπέθανεν ἐφάπαξ (R. 6:10; cf. 1 C. 15:3; Gl. 1:4). For this reason the cross is the sign of triumph over sin, over the dominion of death and demonic power. Hence the preaching of the cross is the δύναμις θεοῦ and the σοφία τοῦ θεοῦ (1 C. 1:18 f.). The cross cannot be separated from the resurrection. The mission of Christ would have been in vain without the resurrection: εἰ δὲ Χριστὸς οὐκ ἐγήγερται, ... ἔτι ἐστὲ ἐν ταῖς ἁμαρτίαις ὑμῶν (1 C. 15:17). This total event is representative or substitutionary (ὑπὲρ ἡμῶν, 2 C. 5:21; 1 C. 15:3; Gl.1:4). Because in virtue of the deed of Adam there is a fatal nexus of sin and death within humanity; because for Paul men are not individuals who can be considered in isolation but a society with a common destiny, this representation or substitution on the part of Christ is possible. The Christ event means for humanity the overcoming of sin and the beginning of the dominion of life. This is the cosmic alteration brought about by Christ: ... ὥσπερ ἐβασίλευσεν ἡ ἁμαρτία ἐν τῷ θανάτῳ, οὕτως καὶ ἡ χάρις βασιλεύσῃ διὰ δικαιοσύνης εἰς ζωὴν αἰώνιον διὰ Ἰησοῦ Χριστοῦ τοῦ κυρίου ἡμῶν (R. 5:21).

This Christ event comes to man as an event which releases him from the reality of sin and constitutes him anew. The content of the Gospel is that man is justified by faith and baptism, that he is made a new creature risen with Christ, that he is redeemed and reconciled, in short, that he has attained the remission of sins [159] (cf. Eph. 1:7). Through fellowship with Christ in His destiny (→ σύν), which is fulfilled in baptism and of which there is awareness in faith, it may be said of the Christian: ἀπεθάνομεν τῇ ἁμαρτίᾳ (R. 6:2). This is the theme of Romans 6, which deals with the question of Christ and sin. There is first laid down the basic insight that the Christian is freed from sin. This is brought out in different ways throughout the chapter. Christians are dead with Christ and have thus died to sin. In this the Christ event achieves its purpose: ἵνα καταργηθῇ τὸ σῶμα τῆς ἁμαρτίας (6:6). There is fulfilled in Christians the old and familiar thesis: ὁ γὰρ ἀποθανὼν δεδικαίωται ἀπὸ τῆς ἁμαρτίας (6:7). [160] Moreover: ἁμαρτία γὰρ

---

[159] The thought of ἄφεσις is found only in this passage (and perhaps also in the quotation in R. 4:7). On the question of redemption → βαπτίζω, δικαιόω, καταλλάσσω, ἀπολύτρωσις, σύν etc. In the present context only certain aspects can be expressed.

[160] K. G. Kuhn, ZNW, 30 (1931), 105 ff.: "Once we see that Paul is using a Rabbinic theologoumenon in R. 6:7, the train of thought in this passage becomes simple and clear. Our old man is crucified with Christ, and thereby the body of sin is destroyed, so that, in accordance with the principle that those who die are freed from sin in virtue of their death, we do not need to serve sin any longer."

ὑμῶν οὐ κυριεύσει· οὐ γάρ ἐστε ὑπὸ νόμον ἀλλὰ ὑπὸ χάριν (6:14). Redemption is simultaneously liberation from the Law and from its function as that which evokes sin. Finally, Christians are ἐλευθερωθέντες ... ἀπὸ τῆς ἁμαρτίας (6:18, 22), i.e., they are freed by Christ from the bondage to sin in which they found themselves — ... δοῦλοι ἦτε τῆς ἁμαρτίας (6:20). The Christian has to realise this fact: λογίζεσθε ἑαυτοὺς εἶναι νεκροὺς μὲν τῇ ἁμαρτίᾳ ... (6:11). He must draw the deductions from it according to the insight: δοῦλοί ἐστε ᾧ ὑπακούετε, ἤτοι ἁμαρτίας εἰς θάνατον ἢ ὑπακοῆς εἰς δικαιοσύνην (6:16). There is no more possibility of remaining in sin and sinning as if nothing had happened (6:1, 15). The only possible conclusion is to this effect: μὴ οὖν βασιλευέτω ἡ ἁμαρτία ἐν τῷ θνητῷ ὑμῶν σώματι εἰς τὸ ὑπακούειν ταῖς ἐπιθυμίαις αὐτοῦ (6:12). By liberation from sin, man is given the possibility of resisting the claim of sin, of not living to it and thus asserting himself against God, but rather: λογίζεσθε ἑαυτοὺς ... ζῶντας ... τῷ θεῷ ἐν Χριστῷ ᾿Ιησοῦ (6:11). To live to God is to be dead to sin and liberated from it. Paul describes this new possibility in various ways: μηδὲ παριστάνετε τὰ μέλη ὑμῶν ὅπλα ἀδικίας τῇ ἁμαρτίᾳ, ἀλλὰ παραστήσατε ἑαυτοὺς τῷ θεῷ ὡσεὶ ἐκ νεκρῶν ζῶντας καὶ τὰ μέλη ὑμῶν ὅπλα δικαιοσύνης τῷ θεῷ (6:13; cf. v. 18: ἐδουλώθητε τῇ δικαιοσύνῃ; 19: παραστήσατε τὰ μέλη ὑμῶν δοῦλα τῇ δικαιοσύνῃ εἰς ἁγιασμόν etc.). → ἁγιασμός, the life dedicated to God, is the goal of the Christ event (cf. the ἵνα in R. 8:3 f. and 2 C. 5:21). This ἁγιασμός is the life of faith. Freedom from sin is fulfilled in the obedience of faith (R. 14:23: πᾶν δὲ ὃ οὐκ ἐκ πίστεως ἁμαρτία ἐστίν). The life for God as a life of faith is manifested in love for the brethren which is the fulfilling of the Law, for: ἁμαρτάνοντες εἰς τοὺς ἀδελφοὺς ... εἰς Χριστὸν ἁμαρτάνετε (1 C. 8:12).

The Christian stands in the tension of a double reality. Basically freed from sin, redeemed, reconciled and sinless, he is actually at war with sin, threatened, attacked and placed in jeopardy by it. He must be called to ἁγιασμός. [161] The tension of this double reality is finally manifested in his life as follows: εἰ δὲ Χριστὸς ἐν ὑμῖν, τὸ μὲν σῶμα νεκρὸν διὰ τὴν ἁμαρτίαν, τὸ δὲ πνεῦμα ζωὴ διὰ δικαιοσύνην (8:10). In his somatic life the Christian is given up to death. This is the final outworking of sin. But the Christian has also a new pneumatic life deriving from the pneuma of Christ and received by death and resurrection with Him. He now lives his life in a new and pneumatic possession (διὰ τοῦ ἐνοικοῦντος αὐτοῦ πνεύματος ἐν ὑμῖν, 8:11; cf. in contrast 7:18, 20). This pneumatic life has overcome death and derives from the dominion of life which has commenced with Christ and which will be consummated with His coming again, when sin in its final outworking in death will be completely abolished (R. 8:11; 1 C. 15:26). The tense double reality is thus a state of expectation πρὸς τὴν μέλλουσαν δόξαν ἀποκαλυφθῆναι εἰς ἡμᾶς (8:18).

4. The Other NT Writings.

a. In Hebrews the question of sin is treated from the twofold standpoint of the high-priestly ministry and sacrifice, and consequently of the institution set up under the old covenant to make atonement for sin: πᾶς ... ἀρχιερεὺς ... ὑπὲρ

---

[161] On this situation, cf. Grundmann, op. cit., 79 f., 108 ff.

ἀνθρώπων καθίσταται τὰ πρὸς τὸν θεόν, ἵνα προσφέρῃ δῶρά τε καὶ θυσίας ὑπὲρ ἁμαρτιῶν (5:1). The proclamation of Hb. is that Christ is the eternal High-priest who has offered Himself as a sacrifice and thus made atonement and taken away sin. As such a High-priest He is distinguished from human high-priests (ἐξ ἀνθρώπων λαμβανόμενος, 5:1) by His sinlessness. Whereas the human high-priest needs πρότερον ὑπὲρ τῶν ἰδιῶν ἁμαρτιῶν θυσίας ἀναφέρειν (7:27; cf. 5:3), Christ is κεχωρισμένος ἀπὸ τῶν ἁμαρτωλῶν (7:26); πεπειρασμένος κατὰ πάντα ... χωρὶς ἁμαρτίας (4:15). And His offering is different from all cultic offerings. Whereas it must be said of the cultic offering : ἀδύνατον γὰρ αἷμα ταύρων καὶ τράγων ἀφαιρεῖν ἁμαρτίας (10:4; cf. 10:2, 3, 11), it may be said of His self-offering : νυνὶ δὲ ἅπαξ ἐπὶ συντελείᾳ τῶν αἰώνων εἰς ἀθέτησιν τῆς ἁμαρτίας διὰ τῆς θυσίας αὐτοῦ πεφανέρωται (9:26). With this offering the cultus has been abolished, for through the Christ event salvation consists in ἄφεσις : ὅπου δὲ ἄφεσις τούτων (sc. ἁμαρτιῶν καὶ ἀνομιῶν), οὐκέτι προσφορὰ περὶ ἁμαρτίας (10:18). With the sacrifice of Christ the beginning of the Messianic age has come (ἐπὶ συντελείᾳ τῶν αἰώνων) and this now moves to its consummation : ... ὁ Χριστός, ἅπαξ προσενεχθεὶς εἰς τὸ πολλῶν ἀνενεγκεῖν ἁμαρτίας, ἐκ δευτέρου χωρὶς ἁμαρτίας ὀφθήσεται τοῖς αὐτὸν ἀπεκδεχομένοις εἰς σωτηρίαν (9:28). With His victory over sin, depicted in priestly and cultic terms (cf. again 10:12 : μίαν ὑπὲρ ἁμαρτιῶν ... θυσίαν εἰς τὸ διηνεκὲς ... 1:3; 2:17), the Messianic age has come as promised by the prophets (8:12; 10:17). To the community which now passes through the affliction of persecution there is directed the admonition to set aside τὴν εὐπερίστατον ἁμαρτίαν and to fight πρὸς τὴν ἁμαρτίαν with a resistance even unto blood (12:1, 4), i.e., not to yield in different temptations and not to be afraid even of martyrdom (cf. 3:13 : ἵνα μὴ σκληρυνθῇ τις ἐξ ὑμῶν ἀπάτῃ τῆς ἁμαρτίας). The warning is underlined by a reference to the unforgivable sin which involves all the difficulties and disputes concerning penitence in the early Church : ἑκουσίως γὰρ ἁμαρτανόντων ἡμῶν μετὰ τὸ λαβεῖν τὴν ἐπίγνωσιν τῆς ἀληθείας, οὐκέτι περὶ ἁμαρτιῶν ἀπολείπεται θυσία (10:26). The unforgivable sin is here equated with wilful apostasy from the faith — a rather different conception from the sin against the Holy Ghost in the Synoptists, or the understanding in terms of κρίσις which we find in John. In this passage there thus emerges the readiness for martyrdom which characterised primitive Christianity.

b. The Epistle of James follows the lines of Judaism. The element which incites to sin in man is ἐπιθυμία, which corresponds to evil impulse. The rise of sin is described in terms of conception and birth. By ἐπιθυμία man is enticed to sin. The consent of the will to temptation signifies conception : εἶτα ἡ ἐπιθυμία συλλαβοῦσα τίκτει ἁμαρτίαν. But the process does not end here, for ἡ δὲ ἁμαρτία ἀποτελεσθεῖσα ἀποκύει θάνατον (1:15). There is a connection between desire, sin and death, and this is represented as a natural process. Sin is an isolated act. This emerges in other passages. Thus, when the wealthy man is preferred to the poor, ἁμαρτίαν ἐργάζεσθε, ἐλεγχόμενοι ὑπὸ τοῦ νόμου ὡς παραβάται (2:9) — this is a thoroughly Jewish concept of sin — εἰδότι οὖν καλὸν ποιεῖν καὶ μὴ ποιοῦντι, ἁμαρτία αὐτῷ ἐστιν (4:17). Failure to do what is good is also sin. At the end of the Epistle James gives some instructions on the practice of penance. Prayer brings forgiveness by God, confession before the brother is recommended, in the case of the sick this is seen to be a prerequisite of healing, and the keeping or rescuing of the brethren from sin is the task of the Christian and has atoning power (Jm. 5:15, 16, 19, 20). Here, too, we have evidence of the practical bent of the author.

c. In the First Epistle of Peter the sinless Christ is understood and proclaimed as the Victor over sin according to the Isaianic picture of the Servant of the Lord (2:22, 24; 3:18). It is also stated that separation from sin is manifested in the voluntary suffering of Christ, since here the desire which strives against God is subjected to the will of God.

Surveying the way which we have taken, we recognise that the most significant feature in the NT *kerygma* is that Christ is the Victor over sin, the final cause of eternal ruin. Thus a new situation has arisen. The decisive feature in the NT message is to be found in its eschatological consciousness of history, i.e., its realisation that Christ is the Victor over sin and that a new world has thus dawned. [162] It is not accidental, however, that the decisive statement is to the effect that Christ is the Victor over *sin*. R. Reitzenstein and K. Latte have shown us from the standpoint of religious history, and K. Holl and G. Kittel from that of theology, that what distinguishes Christianity is its attitude to sin.

> Reitzenstein, Poim., 180, n. 1: "That this redemption is not a mere curbing of evil passions and vices, nor a mere liberation from death and assurance of eternal life with God, but primarily a remission of sins, seems to me to be the new element. So far as I can see, the great seriousness of preaching about guilt and atonement is quite lacking in Hellenism ... It was only as the first community linked the death of Jesus with this profound feeling of guilt and faith in the remission of even the heaviest fault, that the Christian σωτήρ doctrine acquired its distinctive and world-conquering force, so that its Hellenistic rivals could only prepare the way for it through a world which had again come to have a consciousness of sin."

> K. Latte, *op. cit.*, 298 : "... as in Paul especially an exclusively ethical conception of sin comes to be clearly distinguished from all other evil, and the divine act of grace which covers human guilt and weakness is set in the forefront, redemption from evil becomes in the first instance the remission of sins ... In spite of all impulses in this direction, paganism had never clearly attained to this view. The new religion owed to it an essential part of its power of persuasion." By way of criticism we might point out esp. that the expression "exclusively ethical conception of sin" hardly does justice to the NT. The NT conception of sin is theological; it is ethical only to the extent that conduct towards one's neighbour stands under the claim of God. On this ground we might go on to criticise the rest of the terminology, even though it encloses a correct insight.

> K. Holl, "Urchristentum und Religionsgeschichte," ZSTh, 2 (1924), 399 ff.; cf. esp. 425: „A μυστήριον serving εἰς ἄφεσιν τῶν ἁμαρτιῶν would have been a monstrosity to the Hellenistic world."

---

[162] This point of view receives prominence in the debate between K. Holl and R. Bultmann, and has helped to clarify the relationship between early Christianity and the history of religion (R. Bultmann, "Urchristentum u. Religionsgeschichte," Th. R., NF, 4 [1932], 1 ff.). Cf. also Kittel, Probleme, 130 f.; *Relgesch. u. Urchr.*, 151 f., n. 315, where the thought more generally applied by Bultmann is claimed for Jesus and the Synoptists. This thought is in fact decisive, yet perhaps it does not need to entail such a radical rejection of Holl's concern as we find in Bultmann. For the eschatological consciousness of history found in the NT was expressed in a view of God, the world and man, which was wholly distinctive and which made full allowance for the consciousness of history on the basis of truth.

G. Kittel, *Die Lebenskräfte der ersten christlichen Gemeinden* (1926), 19 ff.: "In Christianity the leading problem is one which is absolutely and *a limine* different. Christianity is the religion of the sinner. The sinner stands before God, and God wants the sinner . . ."; cf. also Kittel's *Spätjudentum, Hellenismus* (1926), 27; ThLB, 50 (1929), 373 f. in answer to the objections raised by J. Leipoldt, *Das Gotteserlebnis Jesu* (1927), 35. Leipoldt himself, however, confirms this insight, → n. 134. His work is orientated to the history of ideas and lacking in eschatological perspective (→ n. 162); it thus leads to relativisations. More recently Kittel has worked out the point afresh in his work *Die Religionsgeschichte und das Urchristentum* (1932), 118 ff. "Though this religion does not cease for a moment to be ethical, it emphasises non-fulfilment (sc. of the demand of the divine commandment). It is the religion at whose heart stands the consciousness of not having done what one ought to have done, i.e., the consciousness of sin" (120). "The primary thing is . . . the overcoming of guilt or sin, and of death as the wages of sin" (122). "The message of forgiveness is always for early Christianity the message of Christ. In Christ we have both the holiness of God's judgment on sin and the love of God's saving of the sinner" (124).

Our deliberations have confirmed this view in three respects. We have seen (1) that sin is the reality which, with creatureliness, determines the nature of the world ; (2) that essentially sin is the rejection of the claim of God by self-assertive man, not merely in certain Promethean figures, but by its very nature and in a way which is generally determinative for all men ; and (3) that redemption is summed up in the remission of sins. This is what distinguishes the NT in relation to Hellenism and Judaism. This is the form in which the Christ event is known.

Grundmann

ἁμαρτωλός, ἀναμάρτητος

ἁμαρτωλός → τελώνης, ἀσεβής, ἄδικος.

The matter itself suggests that we should devote a special article to the "sinner" along with sin. For this term can be used in the sense of a general value judgment from the human standpoint as well as in the sense of a conclusive description of the natural relationship of man to God on the basis of the fact and experience of sin as a power hostile to God. The NT evidence inclines us in the same direction, for in addition to the way in which Paul speaks of "us" absolutely as sinners from the standpoint of the concept of ἁμαρτία, there is also a "naive" use of this pregnant word in the Synoptic Gospels to describe not so much those who resist the proclamation and claim of Jesus as a narrow segment of the people with whom He has constant dealings (τελῶναι καὶ ἁμαρτωλοί; e.g., Mt. 9:10; Mk. 2:16; Lk. 7:34). How is this divergence possible? What is its basis? Or is it only an apparent divergence? At any rate, it needs to be noted and clarified both in the interests of the word ἁμαρτωλός and also of the NT view of sin generally.

A. ἁμαρτωλός in the Greek and Hellenistic World.

1. In the adj. ἁμαρτωλός, -όν, which, like ἁμαρτία, is formed from ἁμαρτάνειν (ἁμαρτεῖν) and is not a further construction of ἁμαρτία[1], there is contained, as in the verb,[2] the thought of "not hitting" or "missing." ἁμαρτωλός is thus "the man who misses something." That is to say, he is ἁμαρτωλός "when he misses something." This gives us a twofold meaning of the term, which is usually restricted to the sphere of mental or spiritual life. It denotes a. intellectual inferiority and failure, e.g., by reason of deficient education (cf. Plut. Aud. Poet., 7 [II, 25c]: πάντως μὲν ἐν πᾶσιν ἁμαρτωλὸν εἶναι τὸν ἀμαθῆ, περὶ πάντα δ' αὖ κατορθοῦν[3] τὸν ἀστεῖον); and b. moral failings (cf. Aristoph. Thes., 1111 f.: ἁμαρτωλὴ γέρων καὶ κλέπτο καὶ πανοῦργο).[4] The word is extremely rare; there are only three known instances in Gk. literature[5] apart from those cited, namely, Aristot. Eth. Nic., II, 9, p. 1109a, 33,

---

ἁ μ α ρ τ ω λ ό ς. Cr.-Kö., 140; Pr.-Bauer, 68; Trench, 155; Deissmann, LO 91 f.; A. Bon-höffer, *Die Ethik des Stoikers Epictet* (1894), 133 ff.; I. Abrahams, "Publicans and Sinners" in *Studies in Pharisaism and the Gospels*, I (1917), 54 ff.; Moore, I, 445 ff.; Joach. Jeremias, "Zöllner und Sünder," ZNW, 30 (1931), 293 ff.; and cf. → ἁμαρτάνω, 267 n.

[1] A. Debrunner, *Griechische Wortbildungslehre* (1917), 164.
[2] → 293.
[3] On κατορθοῦν as the opp. of ἁμαρτάνειν in Stoicism — the two words first occur together in Aristot. Eth. Nic., II, 6, p. 1107a, 14 f. — cf. Bonhöffer, 193 ff. *passim;* H. Win-disch, *Taufe u. Sünde im ältesten Christentum bis auf Origenes* (1908), 51 f. Cf. also Philo Leg. All., I, 93 and Josephus Ant., 2, 51 and 10, 50 (where διορθοῦν is used).
[4] This is intentionally "barbaric" Gk.
[5] Liddell-Scott, 77.

where its meaning is general (τῶν γὰρ ἄκρων[6] τὸ μέν ἐστιν ἁμαρτωλότερον, τὸ δ' ἧττον); Philodem. Philos. De Ira (p. 73, Wilke), where it has the second meaning (δοῦλοι ἁμαρτωλοί, i.e., slaves of bad character); and Eupolis, 24, Demianczuk Suppl. Com., where the adv. is used in a condemnatory sense, since Photius interprets it by ἐπιρρηματικῶς, [7] though without giving the basis of the judgment.

2. In none of these passages can ἁμαρτωλός be given a deeper sense. On the other hand, the question of a religious tinge becomes vital when it is used in curses on the violators of graves, as on many Lycaonian inscriptions from imperial Rome : [8] ἁμαρτωλὸς ἔστω θεοῖς καταχθονίοις (CIG, III, 4307); ἁμαρτωλὸς ἔστω θεῶν πάντων καὶ Λητοῦς καὶ τῶν τέκνων αὐτῆς (CIG, 4259); ἁμαρτωλὸς ἔστω εἰς τὴν Λητὼ καὶ εἰς τοὺς λοιποὺς θεοὺς πάντας (CIG, 4303). [9] A similar usage is found in a decree from Telmessus in Lycaonia dating from the time of Ptolemy III Euergetes (247-221 B.C.): ἐὰν [δὲ] μὴ συντελῆι ὁ ἄρχων καὶ οἱ πολῖται τὴν [θυσί]αν κατ' ἐνιαυτόν, ἁμαρτωλοὶ ἔστωσαν [θεῶ]ν πάντων. [10] Steinleitner thinks that in this whole group ἁμαρτωλός is used to denote "the sinner in the religious sense," [11] and his judgment is typical. [12] But the context in which the term is used seems to be against this. With the curse there is usually put on the inscriptions a statement of the debt of the owner of the grave in the form of a specific sum which the community may exact. Often this reckoning is found alone, [13] and it occurs also on the Telmessus decree, where in place of the ordained yearly sacrifice for Zeus Soter, prevented perhaps by war, the ἄρχων has to make a payment of 1000 drachmas. This makes it doubtful whether in all these cases ἁμαρτωλός has a definitely religious sense. It is tempting to see first in the formulae the general thought of an offence against the dead, which is a violation of the underworld to which he now belongs and which is not prepared to allow such intrusions. At any rate, there is no reason to take ἁμαρτωλός substantively as "sinner" in the sense of a qualitative declaration ; nor should it be overlooked that on the inscriptions it is a matter of threats. Yet it is a striking fact that we have this frequent occurrence of the term in a narrow field and a sacral or equivalent context. It is impossible to explain this fact, however, and therefore we should not attach too great importance to these inscriptions in relation to the prior history of the NT ἁμαρτωλός. [14] In any case, the word as used in these formulae bears no relation to ἁμαρτία in the sense of sinfulness. It is also striking, and an added reason for caution, that ἁμαρτωλός has not yet been found where it might be expected as distinct from these burial inscriptions, namely, on the penitential inscriptions

---

[6] The reference is to the extremes which threaten the ἀρετὴ ἠθική, and of which the one stands closer than the other to the desired μεσότης.

[7] This might mean "in the manner of the ἐπίρρημα." The ἐπίρρημα is the part called parabasis in ancient Attic comedy (i.e., "the main work of the chorus interrupting the action and in part becoming a dialogue of the author with the spectators," Pauly-W., 11, 1242), which originally "consisted exclusively in the accusation of an individual" — a form which Eupolis seems to have maintained faithfully as distinct from Aristophanes (ibid., 1246). At any rate, in ἁμαρτωλὴ γέρων the word ἁμαρτωλός seems to be used as a term of opprobrium. (Acc. to Debrunner ἐπιρρηματικῶς is here to be taken as usual, i.e., as an adv.; but if so we could make no deductions from this passage.)

[8] Cf. F. S. Steinleitner, Die Beicht im Zusammenhange mit der sakralen Rechtspflege in d. Antike (Diss. München, 1913); Deissmann, op. cit.

[9] Many other instances are given by Steinleitner, 84.

[10] Ditt. Or., 55, 30 ff.

[11] Op. cit., 84.

[12] Cf. Cr.-Kö., 140; Pr.-Bauer, 68; Deissmann, op. cit.

[13] For instances, E. Petersen-F. v. Luschan, Reisen im südwestlichen Kleinasien, II (1889), 41, No. 77; 51, No. 91; 58, No. 113 etc.

[14] As against Deissmann, op. cit.

of Lycaonia, [15] although there is no doubt that in Asia Minor, and esp. Lycaonia, there was a vital if primitive, cultically orientated and magically tinged concept of sin. [16]

2. The Stoics do not use the term in their derogatory estimates of a man. Epictetus uses φαῦλος when he wishes to describe one who is not clear as to the importance or bearing of his action in contrast to the percipient because educated (ἀστεῖος, σπου-δαῖος) man. [17] In so doing he follows the usual Stoic pattern. [18] For the Stoics the φαῦλος is one who stumbles from one failing (ἁμαρτάνειν) to another, proving himself to be φαῦλος by his failings, even though he may occasionally give signs of rising above the level of utter worthlessness. [19] If there had been for Epictetus any connection between ἁμαρτωλός and the idea of specifically religious and moral inferiority, he could hardly have failed to make considerable use of it in his Diatribes. Yet the term is not found either in Epictetus or other Stoics. Nor does it occur in Philo; this is the more remarkable in view of his linking of the Stoic idea of the wise man with OT conceptions of sin and penitence, [20] his acquaintance with ἁμαρτωλός in the Gk. OT [21] and his regular use of ἁμαρτάνειν and the derived substantives ἁμαρτία, ἁμάρτημα, etc. The word is also lacking in Josephus, although he uses the formulae οἱ ἁμαρτάνοντες [22] and οἱ ἡμαρτηκότες [23] in a wholly religious sense.

4. We thus have the anomalous situation that the matter is there, and also the word which seems designed to express it, but the word is everywhere ignored, and it is ambiguous even when used (Lycaonia). [24] Is this to be explained by the content of the word or its history?

Concerning the content, the only point to be noted is that whenever we find ἁμαρτωλός the element of failure is the basis of the meaning. [25] This does not seem to help us. But further light is perhaps shed by a discussion of the wider context in which the term is used in the few available instances.

The first conclusion to be drawn from the material regarding the history of the word is that from the 5th century B.C. (Eupolis) [26] at least the word was known to the Greeks, though not extensively used in literary speech. The reason for this can be found only in the character of the term. Whenever it occurs in literature, a light is cast on it by the context. [27] Except perhaps in Aristotle, it always has an ironical and rather disreputable flavour. This emerges most clearly in Plutarch, who in the sentence quoted mounts a polemical and ironical attack on the Stoic

---

[15] Cf. Steinleitner, 84.

[16] → 301. This is perhaps influenced by oriental religions with their strong sense of sin; v. F. Cumont, *Die orientalischen Religionen im römischen Heidentum*³ (1931), 36 ff.

[17] Diss., IV, 1, 1 ff.; cf. Plutarch → 317.

[18] Cf. Bonhöffer, 216 ff.

[19] *Ibid.*, 222 ff.

[20] Cf. Windisch, 54 ff.

[21] → 320.

[22] Ant., 7, 266 (rising ag. David); 16, 376 (opp. to the good); Bell., 7, 12 (opp. to ἀρετή) etc.

[23] Ant., 5, 50 (rebellion of Korah); Bell., 2, 303 (part in a rising).

[24] The word has not so far been found on pre-Christian papyri, and it is rare in any case. For a possible occurrence in the Byzantine period, v. Preisigke Wört., I, 65; for a definite example from the 4th century, *ibid.*, 64.

[25] → 317.

[26] → 318.

[27] → 317.

doctrine of the wise and the simple. He is obviously selecting a strong expression to make his opponents ridiculous, though the context does not suggest that he used the word with any thought of guilt. The manner in which it appears in Aristophanes indicates a plebeian origin, for it occurs alongside other vulgar terms. It thus appears to be a non-literary word used for the instinctive characterisation of a man who either in fact or hypothetically is the very opposite of everything that is right and proper, in disposition as well as in other respects. So far as concerns the meaning of the word, this implies that materially as well as linguistically [28] we can find no connection with ἁμαρτία in the Greek world.

This thesis is confirmed not only by the Stoics but also by Philo and Josephus; for when it is a matter of positive ethical deliberations, or of judgments which have the aim of moral demand, there is naturally no place for this kind of term. [29] Along these lines we can also explain the Lycaonian inscriptions with their avoidance of the word in propitiatory and penitential inscriptions and its frequent occurrence in curses against possible violators of tombs; for no one would describe himself as a ἁμαρτωλός, whereas it is natural enough for the defenceless dead to use the word in delivering up the disturber of his rest and the violator of his property to the sentence and punishment of the gods, who like all right thinking men will want no dealings with him. When we see it in this light the character of the curses is safeguarded and yet the forced introduction of even a primitive awareness of the sinfulness of man is rendered superfluous. It is really only in Asia Minor that the "barbaric" force of the word is confirmed.

In the Greek world, therefore, ἁμαρτωλός as an adj. is always used with a strongly derogatory meaning, if not as an actual term of abuse. To give a summary translation is hardly possible. On the other hand, it is firmly established by the examples that the content of the word is determined by the idea of the negation of right and order and custom to an inordinate degree. Nor should it be overlooked that in right and order and custom divine intentions are ultimately expressed.

B. ἁμαρτωλός in the LXX and Its Hebrew Equivalents.

1. In the LXX (→ 268) ἁμαρτωλός is common both as an adj. and a subst., and it is predominantly used for the Heb. רָשָׁע. This is true of no less than 72 of the 94 occurrences, and since in 2 others it is used for רֶשַׁע (ψ 83:11; 124:3), [30] this means that in more than ³/₄ of the whole it relates to the stem רשׁע. In addition, it is often used for the subst. חַטָּא, (11 times), and once in the expression βασιλεία τῶν ἁμαρτωλῶν for מַמְלָכָה הַחַטָּאָה (Am. 9:8), 3 times for the part. חוֹטֵא (Is. 1:4; 65:20; Prv. 11:31, the text here is uncertain), and then once each for חָנֵף (Prv. 11:9 א, c. a), חָרָשׁ (ψ 128:3) [31] and רַע (Prv. 12:13). The total picture becomes even more uniform when we remember that ἁμαρτωλός occurs 68 times in the Psalter alone, and that in only 5

---

[28] → supra and also 317 and 321.

[29] Apart from some basis in exaggerated polemics against Stoicism such as those of Plutarch.

[30] In neither case, of course, is the Heb. text intact; cf. BHK², ad loc.

[31] The rendering partly blurs the picture in the original. Cf. also Δευτ. 29:19; ψ 140:5; Is. 1:31, where again there is no equivalent for ἁμαρτωλός and we are thus dependent on the exegesis of the translator.

of these occurrences is it not used for רָשָׁע (or רֶשַׁע); in 3 cases it is used for חֵטְא (1:1,5; ψ 103:35), and on one occasion it has no equivalent in the original (ψ 140:5). [32] It should be noted that ἁμαρτωλός is not the only LXX term for רָשָׁע; ἀσεβής is also very common, being used for רָשָׁע in 120 of its 180 occurrences. We may also mention ἄνομος, used in 32 of its 73 cases, and ἄδικος, used in only 5 of its 95 cases. It is interesting that in the Psalter ἀσεβής is used 16 times for רָשָׁע, ἄνομος only once (ψ 103:35) and ἄδικος not at all — an indication that there were perhaps special reasons for finding in ἁμαρτωλός the most suitable rendering of רְשָׁעִים in the Psalms. [33] Finally, it is not unimportant that חֵטְא is often rendered literally as (οἱ) ἁμαρτάνοντες (cf. the plur. 1 Βασ. 15:18; ψ 24:8; [34] and Prv. 13:21). This shows us that חֵטְא and ἁμαρτωλός are not full equivalents, and that here, too, there is some difference between ἁμαρτωλός and ἁμαρτάνειν.

2. The statistics show us that the רְשָׁעִים of the Psalms for the most part underlies the ἁμαρτωλός of the LXX. But the רְשָׁעִים are a definite religious type. Throughout the Psalter [35] they are the opposite of the pious, righteous and godly, in short, of those who with the author of Ps. 1 have made it the goal and content of their lives to serve God in His Law day and night with all their heart and soul and mind. It is evident that to a large extent they are Jews no less than the righteous. [36] Thus the רָשָׁע boasts of his portion in the Law of God and in God's covenant with Israel, but he does not regard or follow the Law as an absolutely binding expression of the will of God (Ps. 50:16 f.). He persistently breaks the commandments (10:7), shows no signs of repentance and boasts of his wickedness and ungodly folly (49:13), trusting in his own wealth and power instead of in God (49:6), and perhaps even going so far as to ignore God completely in his life (10:4; 36:1 etc.). Social oppression is particularly emphasised.

In this connection we need not ask who the רְשָׁעִים are in detail. But we may make two points. The first is that the statements of the Psalmist concerning them are undoubtedly polemical, and even very severely and unfairly so in their generalisation. There were obviously others besides rascals and saints in Israel. The basis of the distinction, however, is not to be found in the immoral or ungodly mode of life, but much deeper. This brings us to the second point. The basis of the distinction is the fundamentally different religious attitude. In the case of the pious this is regulated by the Law, whereas the רְשָׁעִים, though they do not repudiate the Law, adopt towards it a liberal attitude verging on laxity. From the time of the Exile, however, the Law had become the shibboleth of Israel and Judaism,

---

[32] The figures are all based on Hatch-Redpath, s.v. and do not take into account other Gk. renderings of the OT.

[33] It is also to be noted that ἀσεβής occurs for רָשָׁע only in Ps. 1-57 and occurs in 17 Psalms; that while ἄδικος is used only once for רָשָׁע in the Ps. it is the usual rendering in Ez., where there is only one firm attestation of ἁμαρτωλός, and where ἀσεβής is also unimportant. On the other hand, ἁμαρτωλός is used for רָשָׁע in 37 Psalms scattered over the whole book.

[34] Ps. 25:8 is textually uncertain; cf. BHK², ad loc. Perhaps ἁμαρτάνειν ἐν ὁδῷ means "to miss the way," or to be in danger of so doing (→ 271).

[35] Cf. W. Staerk, "Die Gottlosen in den Psalmen," ThStKr, 70 (1897), 449 ff.; J. Köberle, Sünde und Gnade im rel. Leben des Volkes Israel bis auf Christum (1905), 338 ff.; G. Marschall, Die "Gottlosen" des ersten Psalmenbuches (1929).

[36] Cf. Staerk, 468 ff.

and therefore the people were necessarily divided into two religious groups. So far as the meaning of רָשָׁע is concerned, this implies that from the very first it is negatively determined, i.e., by negation of the Torah as the only practical standard of Israel's life and thought. The חוֹטֵא, then, is one who does not have the right attitude to the Torah. But the man who has a wrong attitude to the Torah has a wrong attitude to God. For the Torah is the revelation of God's will. Even the one who tries to keep the Law in all things may sometimes be a רָשָׁע. and as such he, too, needs divine forgiveness, which he seeks through repentance (→ μετά-νοια), the bringing of sin offerings and the fulfilment of the rites of penance and purification. But on this account he is not by a long way a רָשָׁע. He becomes this only when he basically alters his positive attitude to the Law. For רָשָׁע denotes a man for whose life the Torah has no existential significance, so that his sin is not simply his *actus peccandi* but embraces his life as such. For the rest we gather from the Psalms, Proverbs etc. the impression that for the pious רָשָׁע approximates closely to a word of reproach, just as the opposite צַדִּיק is an honourable self-description which plainly expresses the positive attitude to the Torah conceived as → νόμος.

The usage here depicted continued into later Judaism. חָטָא is found only once in the Mishnah, namely, in the explanation of Gn. 13:13 (Sanhedrin, 10, 3), so that it has virtually disappeared. [37] It is replaced by חוֹטֵא, which often seems to mean ἁμαρτάνων or even more often ἡμαρτηκώς (cf., e.g., Challa, 2, 7; Shebi, 9, 9; Men., 1, 1 and 2; Sheq., 1, 4 etc.). [38] In contrast רָשָׁע is now exclusively a description of man's attitude before God. There is a good example in Ed., 5, 6. Here it is reported that the representatives of the Halacha wanted to make Akabia b. Mahalalel (in the time of Paul) judicial president of Israel [39] on the one condition that he revoked four statements of his which were in opposition to accepted teaching. [40] His answer was: "I would rather be called a fool [41] for the rest of my life than become for a single moment [42] a רָשָׁע before God, [43] [44] on the ground of revoking for the sake of position." Here we have the typical attitude of the righteous man of the Psalms (73:25).

---

[37] In its other occurrences חָטָא generally means guilty as opposed to innocent (זַכַּי; cf. Pesikt., 16 (128b, 2 ff. Buber).

[38] Sheq., 5, 3 is no exception in its usage. To be sure, it refers to the חוֹטֵא absolutely, but the context shows that behind the חוֹטֵא there lurks the leper who is characterised as חוֹטֵא i.e., as ἡμαρτηκώς by his leprosy. Leprosy is particularly a penalty for sins of the tongue (b. Ar., 16a: "There are seven reasons for leprosy, namely, evil gossip, bloodshed, perjury, incest..."). Cf. also the play on words in b. Ar., 15b: מוציא (שם) רע = מצורע, and also relevant is Jn. 9:2.

[39] אב בית דין לישראל, i.e., acc. to Chag., 2, 2 vice-president of the Sanhedrin.

[40] These are appended.

[41] שׁוֹטֶה; → μωρός. Cf. the antithesis between כסיל and רשע in T. Jeb., 1, 13, where along the same lines the student is called רשע if he uses the differences between the schools to alleviate the demands of the Law.

[42] שעה אחת; → ὥρα.

[43] הַמָּקוֹם → θεός.

[44] Implying that he would thus deny his teachers and act against his conscience, cf. Ab., 2, 13. Acc. to Ab., 4, 7 he who takes halachic decisions lightly is regarded as רָשָׁע

In the definition of the רָשָׁע regard for the Torah was even more important for the Rabbis that in earlier periods. This is natural enough as Judaism became a pure religion of Law. The best illustration of the trend is to be found in Ab., 5, 10-19. Here the חָסִיד is the correct seeker of the house of instruction and the no less correct representative of its ideal of life, in contrast to the רָשָׁע, who is the despiser of the Torah (v. esp. 5:14). [45] In the first part of the הַגָּדָה שֶׁל פֶּסַח, the liturgy for the evening of the Passover, which in its present form dates from the time of the completion of the Talmud (c. 500 A.D.), the רָשָׁע among the "questioners" is the opposite of the חָכָם, who is the representative of young people dedicated to the Torah; [46] this is wholly in accordance with the usage of the Rabbis for whom חֲכָמִים (→ σοφός) is a general term for scribal authorities. Only constant study of the Torah keeps from sin (Kid., 1, 10). For this reason the man who will not give himself to this is the seat of evil. This is also true of the 'am ha-ares: ὁ ὄχλος οὗτος ὁ μὴ γινώσκων τὸν νόμον ἐπάρατοί εἰσιν (Jn. 7:49: spoken by the Pharisees). [47] Such a man is bound to sin whether he wants to or not, and therefore it is best that he should die young in order to be kept from further sin which would increase his guilt (Sanh., 8, 5). It corresponds to his relationship to God — which for the Rabbis is the same as that to the Torah [48] — that after death he will inevitably go to hell and thus be far from God (Ed., 2, 10; cf. Gr. En., 22, 10 f.; cf. S. Dt., 357 on 34:5 etc.).

For the rest it naturally results that for the Rabbis the word רָשָׁע has lost nothing of the contemptuous accent that it has in the OT. Indeed, we are forced to say that, under the influence of a developing religious self-consciousness, this accent has become even more marked.

3. When we consider this history of the term on Jewish soil, it is obvious that no Gk. term was so well adapted to render רָשָׁע as ἁμαρτωλός. Both words denote an attitude which by its very nature is a basic negation of the order and custom either attained, or recognised and sought as a goal. It belongs to the nature of the case that in the Jewish world this attitude is conceived more in relation to its volitional and therefore guilty aspects. This is connected with the fact that Judaism had in the Torah a historical revelation of the divine will which forces each individual to decision, [49] whereas even at best the Greeks had as a corresponding factor only the purely humanistic ideal of καλοκἀγαθία. It is also connected with the fact that only as it was adopted by Hellenistic Judaism and came under the influence of רָשָׁע could the word become a religious term, but that in this sphere it was bound to do so, since, once it was linked with the Torah, [50] it was brought into relationship with the idea of God in Judaism and integrated into the

---

[45] Cf. the old classification רשעים—צדיקים (Sanh., 6, 5; 8, 5; 10, 5).
[46] This section dealing with the four questioning sons is old, however, and belongs to the time of the Tannaites (before 200 A.D.); cf. M. Ex. בא 18 on 13:14 (p. 73, 8 ff., Horovitz-Rabin) and D. Hoffmann, "Die Barajtha über die vier Söhne," in Magazin für die Wissenschaft des Judentums, 13 (1886), 191 ff.
[47] Every non-Pharisee is regarded as such by the Pharisee; cf. Str.-B., II, 494 ff.
[48] The word "thoralogy," coined by K. Bornhäuser, characterises this outlook very well; cf. Das Joh. Ev. eine Missionsschrift für Israel (1928), 6 ff.
[49] For the view that we have here the basic presupposition of the antithesis between the righteous and the ungodly in older Judaism (Psalms etc.), v. Köberle, 345 ff.
[50] On this point, cf. the correspondence between ἁμαρτωλός and ἀνομία already found in ψ 124:3; 128:3 etc.

religious and moral linguistic heritage of Greek speaking Jews. This inter-relating with the idea of God, however, is the starting-point for its further development. By means of this the term acquires for the first time the character of a positive declaration by coming to denote the man who is in opposition to God and in league with, or even helpless in the hands of, ungodly forces (→ ἁμαρτία).

The text shows that ἁμαρτωλός is always used as a religious term in the LXX. It has no secular use. The same is true of the Gk. pseudepigrapha (e.g., Gk. En. 22: 10 ff., p. 54, Fl.-Raderm.; [51] Ps. Sol. 2:17; 4:9, 27 etc.). In the Ps. Sol. the polemic associated with the word is directed against the Sadducees, but here too, quite outwith the sphere of the Jewish people and its religious divisions, a foreign ruler or general may be called a ἁμαρτωλός because he attacks Jerusalem and thus sets himself in open opposition to God (2:1). [52] How fixed the term has now become is shown by the use of ἁμαρτωλοὶ ἀσεβεῖς (Gk. En. 1:9, p. 20 Fl.-Raderm.), as though ἁμαρτωλοί alone were not strong enough.

C. The Development of the Concept of the Sinner in Later Judaism. [53]

1. a. What we have already said about the Rabbinic period (→ 322) by no means exhausts its significance for the history of the word ἁμαρτωλός. A second and most influential factor has also to be taken into account. This, too, is connected with the Torah as the religious centre of later Judaism.

For the Rabbis the Torah is not merely a code of behaviour for individuals or a collection of liturgical directions and ritual prescriptions which apply to the individual only in cases of need. It is also a manifestation of God to the whole people and, once completed to Israel, to the whole of humanity (→ νόμος). Israel has received the Torah according to the will of God, who in this way made it His people with the aim of sanctification (Ex. 19:5 f. etc.). He Himself is the Holy One, and therefore those who belong to Him are to be holy (Lv. 19:2). For the Rabbis, therefore, the thought of sanctification bound up with the Torah acquires a strong sociological element. Only the Jew who has the possibility of sanctification through the Law can be holy (→ ἅγιος). The Jew not only can be holy, but is already holy. Even though he neither is nor can be holy as an individual, he is holy as a member of the people to whom God has given the Law as an expression of the will of the holy God, and whom He has thus sanctified by this historical act of election. This thought is carried so far linguistically that the entry of a non-Jew into Judaism can be described as an entry into קְדֻשָּׁה, into the state of holiness (→ ἁγιωσύνη; Jeb., 11, 2; T. Jeb., 12, 2). [54] Hence it is quite impossible to be holy outside Judaism. Those who are without are by their very nature non-holy, since they are not in fellowship with the holy God as mediated by the Law. In the consciousness of קְדֻשָּׁה Israel's consciousness of election and its conviction of being

---

[51] Here we have again the old antithesis ἁμαρτωλοί—δίκαιοι → n. 45.

[52] The reference is probably to Pompey and to the destruction of the temple by him in 63 B.C.

[53] Cf. on the view of sin in later Judaism and the Rabbis Moore, I, 445 ff. and → 289 ff.

[54] Cf. on this point K. H. Rengstorf, *Jebamot* (1929), 137 ff., where further material is adduced, the full range of the view is sketched, and its significance for early Christian thinking is indicated.

essentially different from the Gentiles (→ ἔθνος) reached its climax in the Rabbis. If the Jews are by nature holy, the Gentiles are by nature sinners. [55]

b. The legal element behind these sociological ideas is amplified by the religious and moral. It is the firm conviction of Rabbinic teaching, and the basis of its perfectionism as an ethical postulate, that those who have and keep the Torah are kept from sin in the sense of transgression of the ordinances (עֲבֵרָה; → παράβασις) willed by God and fully revealed in the Law (→ δικαιοσύνη).

This is not merely true of the righteous of an earlier period (the patriarchs, Elijah etc.); [56] the Rabbis do not think it to be excluded in their own case. Thus the sick R. Eliezer (c. 90 A.D.) is not conscious of any sin to which to attribute his sickness (bSanh., 101a), and T.B.Q., 8, 13 tells of R. Jehuda b. Baba (d. c. 135) that on his deathbed he remembered only one sin, namely, that contrary to Rabbinic statute he had small cattle in the land of Israel, though in his favour this prohibition was still in dispute as late as 100 A.D. [57] The only sin of David was thought to be his adultery with Bathsheba, [58] and it was regarded as possible to purify him from this. [59] At any rate, Rabbinic Judaism was firmly of the view that it was possible to remain without sin with the help of the Torah. [60]

Those who did not belong to Israel had no such possibility. This was primarily their own fault, for the Torah did not come to Israel so self-evidently as might be supposed; it became the distinguishing mark of Israel only when the Gentiles had refused to accept it. [61] Nevertheless, the Jewish sense of difference from the Gentiles did not lay any particular stress on this point of guilt. More important to the rational piety of Judaism was the result of the rejection of the Torah by the non-Jewish world. By this rejection it forfeited the possibility of a life according to the will of God. This is shown in its idolatry. It is also shown in the inability of the Gentiles to fulfil the Jewish rites of purification which rest on the Law of God as such, and their consequent disqualification from table-fellowship with the Jews. [62] It is shown again in their supposed lack of any sexual ethics and their classification with slaves in this regard. [63] It is shown in their complete absence of any good qualities. [64] For the Jews, therefore, the Gentiles were to be equated quite simply with "sinners," i.e., with those whose basic attitude in no way corresponded with what God expects, and must expect, of man. To speak of Gentiles was to imply at once both the thought of uncleanness in external things and also that of a final personal impurity before God. Thus it came about that the word ἁμαρτωλός, destined in the Jewish sphere to describe a radical or practical aliena-

---

[55] For the distinction and separation of Israel from all other peoples, v. the passages in Str.-B., III, 126 ff.

[56] Cf. Str.-B., I, 815.

[57] Cf. T. Jeb., 3, 4 and my comm. ad loc.

[58] b. Shab., 30a, 56a; Jos. Ant., 7, 391. It is obviously felt to be serious, cf. b. Pes., 113a.

[59] b. Ket., 9b = b. Shab., 56a Bar.; a second attempt, b. Kid., 43a.

[60] For further material, cf. Str.-B., I, 814 ff. Rather strangely, this does not decide the question of assurance of salvation, as the dying Jochanan b. Zakkai shows (b. Ber., 28b); → σωτηρία. Cf. also A. Marmorstein, "Paulus und die Rabbinen," ZNW, 30 (1931), 271 ff.

[61] Cf. Str.-B., III, 36 ff.

[62] Ibid., IV, 374 ff.

[63] Cf. T. Jeb., 2, 6; 12, 2 and my comm. ad loc.

[64] Cf. Str.-B., III, 43 ff.

tion from the Jewish Law as a declaration of the will of the one holy God, [65] inevitably became a technical term for the Gentile. The Gentile was a ἁμαρτωλός in virtue of his not being a Jew and his failure to regulate his conduct according to the Torah. [66]

ἁμαρτωλός is occasionally used in the LXX in the sense of Gentile, yet not as a translation of גּוֹיִם, but of רְשָׁעִים (Is. 14:5). In other places, too, we can see how the literal application of רָשָׁע to the heathen forms a transition to the equation of ἁμαρτω-λοί and Gentiles (e.g., Ps. 9:15 ff., esp. v. 17); cf. also 1 Macc. 1:34 : καὶ ἔθηκαν ἐκεῖ ἔθνος ἁμαρτωλόν, ἄνδρας παρανόμους [!]. In 1 Macc. 2:48, 62 (cf. 1:10) ἁμαρτωλός denotes the Gentile king Antiochus as a personification of the heathen world in its hostility to God and to Israel (cf. ἄνθρωπος τῆς ἀνομίας, 2 Th. 2:3 f.). As against this, it is uncertain in 1 Macc. 2:44 whether the phrase ἁμαρτωλοὺς ... καὶ ἄνδρας ἀνόμους is used of Gentiles or apostate Israelites.

2. A question which demands brief consideration is whether our presentation thus far is not one-sided and exaggerated in so much that it makes possession of the Torah a hindrance to the development in the righteous of a personal conscious-ness of sin in the sense of being absolutely sinners. A review of all the available material, however, suggests that, in spite of apparent evidence to the contrary, the idea of being absolutely sinful before God is fundamentally alien both to earlier and probably also to later Judaism. This is proved both by extra-canonical Jewish writings and by the NT in certain Jewish testimonies therein preserved. In any case, even the sin of the Gentiles, which is plain enough from what we have al-ready seen, is not regarded as a kind of fate to which they are abandoned, but as guilt historically grounded and working itself out right up to the present. This is also the view of Paul (Rom. 1:18 ff.).

The pseudepigrapha do in fact refer to a general sinfulness which none escapes or can escape. [67] In so doing, they use the term sinner not so much of individuals as of certain national or religious groups, and perhaps even of man as such. Yet the con-sciousness of election [68] dominates even the author of 4 Esdras (5:23 ff.; 6:55 ff. etc.) to such a degree that he obviously differentiates himself and those like-minded with him — who in the last analysis represent Israel because they keep the Law and are righteous — from the impii (7:17, 102 etc.).

In the Rabbis, too, we can find the view that there are no men without sin, i.e., transgression of the divine commandments. [69] But this is found alongside the opinion already cited concerning the actual sinlessness of certain righteous and the possibility of this state for all. If no compromise was made between the two trends, [70] this was perhaps due to the fact that the events of 70 A.D. gave added vigour to the collective

---

[65] Cf. what is said about the LXX !

[66] Later Judaism has no word corresponding to ἁμαρτωλός in this sense unless this is the meaning of חַטְיָתָא as applied to the heathen queen Vashti in Est. r., 4, 10 on 1:20. In character, however, גּוֹי corresponds exactly to the Gk. term even to the extent of an under-tone of contempt. No need of a new word was thus felt.

[67] Cf. the passages from 4 Esr. and Slav. En. in Str.-B., III, 156.

[68] On the relationship of this to the view of the sinner → 324.

[69] Cf. Str.-B., III, 156 f.

[70] Cf. b. Shab, 55a and Str.-B., III, 157.

sense of the sin and guilt of Judaism, [71] but that leading religious circles could not be shaken by this judgment on the people from their conviction that the Torah has absolute saving significance, since they adopted the prophetic scheme of a causal connection between national decline and unsatisfactory service of God or even apostasy, except that they now thought more consistently in terms of the relationship of Israel to the Torah rather than to God.

As a typically Jewish figure in the NT, standing beyond personal sinfulness, no less a man than Paul must be set alongside the Pharisee praying in the temple (Lk. 18:11 f.). The terse depiction of his self-consciousness prior to conversion in Phil. 3:6 (κατὰ δικαιοσύνην τὴν ἐν νόμῳ γενόμενος ἄμεμπτος) agrees to the letter with what we have just said concerning the practical relationship of Rabbinic teaching to sin. It is thus both materially and methodologically unsound to try to adduce R. 7:14 ff. in favour of the opposite opinion. [72]

D. The New Testament.

1. The Lexical Evidence.

The different meanings of ἁμαρτωλός in the NT are easily explained by the history of the word. As in the LXX, the term is used both as adj. and subst., and always in expression of a derogatory judgment. The subst. means the "sinner" as a man who forfeits a correct relationship to God by his culpable attitude to the Jewish Law.

a. This may be in the sense of the ungodly of the OT, i.e., a man who lives in conscious or witting opposition to the divine will (Torah) as distinct from the righteous who makes submission to this will the content of his life. [73]

It is in this sense that we have the formula τελῶναι καὶ ἁμαρτωλοί (Mt. 9:10 etc.), in which ἁμαρτωλοί partly means those who live a flagrantly immoral life (murderers, robbers, deceivers etc.), and partly those who follow a dishonourable vocation or one which inclines them strongly to dishonesty. [74] The woman who anointed the feet of Jesus in the house of Simon is called a ἁμαρτωλός (Lk. 7:37, 39) [75] because she was a harlot (→ πόρνη), [76] though not an adulteress. [77] From sinners of this kind we are to differentiate not merely the Pharisees but ordinary people who maintain personal respectability (Mt. 11:19; Lk. 7:34, 39; 19:7). [78] We find the same usage in 1 Tm. 1:9, where it seems to be adopted without deliberation. It is also given a distinctively Christian form in James, for whom a man is a ἁμαρτωλός if he does not uncompromisingly (→ δίψυχος) subject himself to God and accept no other motives for conduct (4:8; 5:20). → μοιχαλίς, → κόσμος.

---

[71] The Rabbinic statements all come after 70 A.D., and the apocalypses are quite unthinkable in their present form apart from the destruction of Jerusalem and the temple.

[72] → ἁμαρτάνω, 308, also n. 153 and 157.

[73] Cf. at any rate the recurrence of the old antithesis δίκαιοι/ἁμαρτωλοί (→ 322, with n. 45 and 51).

[74] For fuller proof, cf. Jeremias, 295 ff.

[75] In any case, the word is to be taken here as a subst.

[76] In view of Rabbinic terminology, this is more likely than the view that her conduct did not conform to Pharisaic claims (→ n. 47); cf. Str.-B., II, 162.

[77] It is true that in Lk. 18:11 adulterers are mentioned as sinners (→ μοιχός), but the Pharisees would stone an adulteress (Jn. 8:7); cf. on the point Schl. Lk., 258 f.

[78] Jeremias (294) draws attention to this.

b. For the Pharisee, however, a ἁμαρτωλός is one who does not subject himself to the Pharisaic ordinances, i.e., the so-called 'am ha-ares. [79] He is not a sinner because he violates the Law, but because he does not endorse the Pharisaic interpretation. [80]

Since more or less the whole people is to be numbered among the 'am ha-ares, and since Jesus addresses the whole people rather than individuals, He necessarily has daily contact with ἁμαρτωλοί (Mt. 9:13 par.; Lk. 15:2 etc.). But according to the judgment of the Pharisees, Jesus and His disciples are also ἁμαρτωλοί, since they refuse to follow the Pharisaic [81] washing of hands before meals, which is not prescribed in the accepted Torah (Mt. 15:2; Mk. 7:5; Lk. 11:37 f.), and do not accept Pharisaic casuistry in relation to the Sabbath (Mt. 12:1 ff. par.; Jn. 9:16, 24 f., 31). [82]

c. According to the Jewish view derived from the νόμος (→ 325), οἱ ἁμαρτωλοί can also mean Gentiles in Mt. 26:45 (cf. Mk. 14:41): ὁ υἱὸς τοῦ ἀνθρώπου παραδίδοται εἰς χεῖρας ἁμαρτωλῶν, [83] where the reference can hardly be to Jewish sinners, but is obviously to the Roman soldiers who carry out the crucifixion for the Jews (Ac. 2:23). [84] The same usage is found in Paul, e.g., in Gl. 2:15, where the antithesis to φύσει Ἰουδαῖοι shows that ἐξ ἐθνῶν ἁμαρτωλοί is a single concept. Lk. 6:32 ff. has ἁμαρτωλοί where the par. in Mt. 5:47 has ἐθνικοί; if Jesus was speaking of גּוֹיִם, as is very possible, [85] then in both Evangelists we have a similar situation to that of Mt. 5:3; Lk. 6:20. Acts avoids the word and always uses → ἔθνη when speaking of the Gentiles.

d. We find some development beyond the pre-Christian history when the term is used to describe men from the standpoint that, apart from action on God's part, all without exception are separated from Him by sin, so that the reference is to guilty humanity which is without Christ and therefore unreconciled. Though we cannot trace a historical connection [86] with → ἁμαρτία at this point, it is obvious from the matter itself. R. 5:8: ἔτι ἁμαρτωλῶν ὄντων ἡμῶν Χριστὸς ὑπὲρ ἡμῶν ἀπέθανεν (cf. ὑπὲρ ἀσεβῶν, v. 6; ἐχθροί, v. 10; δικαιωθέντες, v. 1, 9; κατηλλάγημεν, v. 10); 5:19: ἁμαρτωλοὶ κατεστάθησαν οἱ → πολλοί; [87] and most clearly Gl. 2:16 ff., esp. 17: εἰ δὲ ζητοῦντες δικαιωθῆναι ἐν Χριστῷ, εὑρέθημεν καὶ αὐτοὶ ἁμαρτωλοί, ἄρα Χριστὸς ἁμαρτίας διάκονος; cf. also 1 Tm. 1:15, where ἁμαρτωλοί might be defined in terms of Jn. 3:16 as those who do not believe. [88] Also of material relevance are R. 3:23: πάντες γὰρ ἥμαρτον, and R. 5:12: ἐφ᾽ ᾧ πάντες ἥμαρτον.

---

[79] → 323.
[80] Note the γινώσκων of Jn. 7:49.
[81] Ed., 5, 6; cf. Jeremias, 294, n. 1; → παράδοσις.
[82] Cf. Str.-B., I, 615 ff.
[83] There are OT models for this expression, cf. ψ 70:4; 81:4; 96:10.
[84] Cf. Kl. Mk. on 14:31 and 15:15.
[85] Cf. Schl. Mt., 196. On ἁμαρτωλός and ἐθνικός as equivalents, v. also A. Meyer, Jesu Muttersprache (1896), 135 f.
[86] → 317.
[87] Here the old antithesis ἁμαρτωλοί/δίκαιοι is formally adopted, but filled with new meaning by the belief in justification.
[88] We should probably include in this group the ἁμαρτωλοὶ ἀσεβεῖς of Jd. 15, the OT derivation of which is plainly to be detected. The same pleonasm may be seen in Gr. En. 1:9; → 324.

e. A special group is formed by instances in which ἁμαρτωλός signifies one who has fallen into concrete guilt, so that the word is not such a technical term as in a.-d. but is already stereotyped and seems to mean much the same as ἡμαρτηκώς. [89]

This usage seems to be independent of d. and secondary. It is found esp. in Lk.; cf. 13:2: ἁμαρτωλοὶ παρὰ πάντας alongside the par. ὀφειλέται ... παρὰ πάντας in 13:4; again 15:7, 10; 18:13; Hb. 7:26. Yet in all these cases the religious character of the term is preserved by the context and it does not become a mere formula.

f. As an adj. ἁμαρτωλός means "guilty" or "sinful," always with a nuance corresponding to the various meanings of the subst. already listed: Mk. 8:38 (cf. 9:19; Mt. 12:39, 45; 16:4; 17:17 etc.): ἐν τῇ γενεᾷ ταύτῃ τῇ μοιχαλίδι καὶ ἁμαρτωλῷ (= d.); Lk. 5:8: ἀνὴρ ἁμαρτωλός εἰμι (Peter = b. [90] or e.). The word is sometimes used synon. with πονηρός (cf. Mt. 12:39, 45; 16, 4 etc.). It is striking that it is never self-applied in Matthew, Mark or John, but twice in Luke (5:8; 18:13; → 330).

Some difficulty is posed by R. 7:13: ἵνα γένηται καθ' ὑπερβολὴν ἁμαρτωλὸς ἡ ἁμαρτία διὰ τῆς ἐντολῆς. This is solved when we understand the peculiar mode of expression. Personified ἁμαρτία (→ 296; 311) only becomes aware of itself and its power through the → ἐντολή; but in the same way there is given the possibility of recognising it as such and of seeking liberation from it. [91]

2. The Attitude of Jesus.

a. It has been pointed out already (→ 303) that there are no pronouncements of Jesus on sin as such. He gave His disciples no doctrine of sin, nor did He engage in profound speculations concerning it. He never once told us what He meant by it. On the other hand, He reckoned with its reality, and undoubtedly referred all His work and teaching to it. Yet this reality was not the result of penetrating investigation. It was always present in the reality of the man who had fallen short. The attitude of Jesus to sin is closely linked with His attitude to the sinner.

This attitude is first characterised by the fact that He took over the contemporary formulae and used them to describe His goal. [92] He never contested nor avoided the distinction of the people into sinners and righteous which He met at every turn and in which He Himself was implicated according to the view of His opponents. [93] He did not even treat it ironically. [94] "We cannot understand what Jesus did if we devaluate the concept 'righteous' and thus divest it of its full

---

[89] Materially we might compare the question of the disciples to Jesus in Jn. 9:2.
[90] Cf. Schl. Lk., 232.
[91] Cf. A. Schlatter, Erläuterungen zum NT, ad loc.
[92] Cf. A. Schlatter, Die Geschichte des Christus (1921), 190; O. Schmitz, "Sünde und Schuld im NT" in RGG², V, 885 f.
[93] Cf. Mt. 15:2; Mk. 7:5 or Mt. 12:1 ff. par.; Jn. 9:16, 24 f., 31; → 328.
[94] So H. Weinel, Biblische Theologie des NT⁴ (1928), 149, and with some reservations Kl. Mk. on 2:17 etc.

seriousness as moral fitness. If it is made ironical, then the condemnation of the sinners whom Jesus opposes to the righteous is also robbed of its sting. The sick of whom He spoke were in His view seriously sick, and the healthy seriously healthy. Jesus admitted that the righteous genuinely obeyed God and did what He commanded ... If we weaken this judgment, we are involved on the other side of the antithesis in an idealisation of sin which is very far from the intention of Jesus." [95]

Jesus thus accepted as such those who were regarded as sinners by the community. It was just because they were sinners that He drew them to Himself. How little they understood such conduct is shown by Peter when, after the miraculous draft of fishes, he confesses to Jesus that as an ἀνὴρ ἁμαρτωλός he is not worthy to have dealings with Him (Lk. 5:8), [96] and Zacchaeus makes the same confession when he joyfully (χαίρων) welcomes Jesus (Lk. 19:6). Jesus Himself, however, acted on the assumption that men needed Him at this very point, and that the way to Him was open, since man's self-awareness does not bar the way to God, before whom alone man comes to an awareness of his guilt. It is rather the "righteous" who are hindered (→ δίκαιος), for they do not let themselves be placed before God, but measure themselves by a standard which finally derives from their own intuition, in face of which they have nothing to fear or renounce, and against the correctness of which they cannot entertain any doubts. [97]

b. It was the aim of Jesus to set men before the total reality of God and to mediate to them total fellowship with Him. [98] For this reason, however, He took them in their totality as He found them, and not just in accordance with certain appealing or repellent aspects. It is of a piece with this attitude that the Evangelists all agree in linking a confession of sins [99] with the baptism of John (→ βαπτίζω), but that nowhere in the dealings of Jesus with sinners do we read of any confession of specific sins. [100] Even where He Himself depicts sinners in contrast to the righteous (Lk. 18:9 ff.), He does not put any special confession in their mouth, but simply causes them to express their neediness before God (Lk. 18:13). [101] In this trait, which more clearly perhaps than any other brings out the unity of the complete devotion of Jesus to God on the one side and His complete devotion to sinners on the other, we detect the same attitude which underlies His rejection of Pharisaic casuistry in relation to the Sabbath (Mt. 12:1 ff. par.), which causes Him

---

[95] A. Schlatter, *Die Geschichte des Christus*, 190; cf. more expressly Schl. Mt. on 9:13; also Zn. Mt. on 9:13; H. J. Holtzmann, *Lehrbuch der nt.lichen Theologie*[2] (1911), I, 218 f. etc.

[96] As shown by the miracle, Jesus encounters him as "the prophet" (→ προφήτης) who reveals God ; for this reason it is inconceivable to Peter that He should seek his fellowship and not that of the righteous. We find the same attitude in the centurion (Mt. 8:8; Lk. 7:6).

[97] Cf. the judgment of Jesus on the Rabbis (Mt. 23:12; Lk. 14:11; 18:14). The procedure on the death of Rabbi Jochanan b. Zakkai (bBer., 28b) provides striking confirmation.

[98] Cf. Mt. 22:10 ff.; Lk. 15:11 ff., where table-fellowship (→ δεῖπνον) is a picture of total fellowship. The Fourth Gospel is very relevant in this connection.

[99] Mt. 3:6; Mk. 1:5; Lk. 3:3; cf. Jn. 1:29; 3:25.

[100] Zacchaeus never says what he has done, but what he is doing, or will do, to make restitution ; but this is not confession.

[101] I. Abrahams, 57 completely misses the point of Lk. 18:9 ff. when he argues that the prayer and gestures of the publican are typically Pharisaic, and on this interpretation finds in the parable a curiously grounded attack on ritualism.

to reject any concession to Pharisaic custom (Mt. 15:2; Mk. 7:5; cf. Mt. 23 *passim*) and which enables Him to accept the verdict of being Himself a "sinner" (Jn. 9:16, 24, 31 f.; → 328) without any violation of His direct relationship to God. By the very fact that He accepts no compromise, and does not even consider the possibility of exculpation, He shows Himself to be the One who helps His people out of its sins (Mt. 1:21). Those who are truly set before God are no longer able to speak of themselves as though they could lay the foundation of the new relationship to God with their own judgment on themselves. This foundation is laid when in the presence of God the impress of His kindness as well as His holiness and majesty causes them to renounce their own will and awakens them to readiness for absolute obedience (Lk. 15:17 ff.; 18:13), and Jesus is their Saviour to the extent that in His person, word and work God and His manner and goal are made clear to those who need such a new relationship to Him.

> This conception is predominantly based on the Synoptists, but it is in full agreement with what John causes Jesus to say about His task of witnessing to the Father (cf. in this connection esp. 8:21 ff.) and also with what Jesus here says about the presupposition of a pure relationship to God (9:41).
>
> For the rest, John does not use the term in relation to men or groups, but only in relation to Jesus (→ 328) on the lips of the Pharisees. John's acquaintance with Pharisaic terminology is thus illustrated. ἁμαρτωλός is used in self-description only in Luke, though even here it is rare (5:8; 18:13) and is hardly to be given any special emphasis (cf. 15:18, 21). This fact is important in our estimate of the situation, since it shows us how false it would be to see in the sayings of Jesus about sinners, and especially in the parables peculiar to Luke, the demand for a strongly accentuated awareness of sin in the sense of the most profound self-contempt and self-condemnation. This is obviously not the Christian ideal. To think and act in this way is to make oneself the centre of thought and action, and therefore to remain in the very position from which Jesus seeks to bring liberation when He sets the sinner in the presence of God and under the overpowering impress of His being.

c. Among those who need the new relationship to God Jesus also and especially numbers the righteous.[102] In so doing He does not dispute their righteousness (→ 330) or call it sin. But He judges it in respect of its nature.[103] In this regard He shares the outlook of the Baptist, who in hard words warns the pious of the impending judgment of God.[104] The reason for this is to be found in the egotistic nature of this righteousness, which is satisfied with the fulfilment of the divine commands and which thus becomes inwardly self-confident,[105] and outwardly proud[106] and pitiless.[107] Such emphasis on oneself and one's achievements inevitably leads to an attitude in which one does not bow before God but treats with Him,[108] leaving it to human perception to determine what is legitimate and

---

[102] Cf. for what follows, esp. A. Schlatter, *Die Geschichte des Christus*² (1923), 186 ff.
[103] Cf. Mt. 5:20 (→ δικαιοσύνη).
[104] Mt. 3:7 ff.; cf. Mt. 21:32; Lk. 7:29 ff.
[105] Lk. 18:11 ff.
[106] Mt. 6:1 ff.; 23:5 ff.; Lk. 14:7 ff.; 20:46; Mk. 12:38 f.
[107] Mt. 23:14, 23; 25:41 ff.
[108] Lk. 15:28 ff.

what is sinful before Him. [109] This profanation of the service of God Jesus casti-
gates severely, and His struggle with the Rabbis was designed to expose and
overcome it. [110] His ultimate accusation was that there is not here the serious
opposition to sin which is meet and proper for the sake of God, [111] so that a true
righteousness is achieved, but it is a righteousness which measures up only to
human standards and does not satisfy the divine judgment. [112] This insight leads
Jesus sharply to call the pious and righteous as well to repentance, [113] not for
their sin, but for their righteousness, which prevents them from seeing clearly
either the greatness of God or their own situation. [114]

Thus we can see already how Jesus transcended the view that only certain
individuals or groups are sinners, replacing it by the conception which regards the
emphasising of human autonomy, even under the guise of service of God and
devotion to Him, as that which makes man a sinner who needs divine forgiveness
and grace. But we also find in Him already the universal offer of forgiveness, and
therewith the establishment of a new relationship to God, in submission to His
will and judgment without regard to human assumptions, [115] to the degree that
there is a readiness for this attitude which is alone appropriate to the situation
(→ μετάνοια). [116] Since Jesus is the One who is sent by God to the guilty, the
removal of sin knows no limit apart from unwillingness that it should be removed. [117]

3. The Attitude of the New Testament Writers.

This can be summed up in a few sentences, since there are no basic differences
between the authors of the NT and Jesus as regards sinners. Only the standpoint
is different, since none of them can look away from himself and speak of the
sinner as a third person. From such apostasy they are kept by the cross of Jesus,
which is set up for them as well as for others. [118] It is perhaps connected with this
that outside the Synoptists the term ἁμαρτωλός is infrequent and does not occur
at all in Acts. On Jewish soil the history of the word had given it too strong an
overtone of superiority over sinners to allow of its general use in preaching to
non-Jews. Thus it is to be noted that in John it appears only on the lips of the
Pharisees as one of their theological terms, [119] and that it is rejected at once as
unjustifiable. Paul, too, uses it only as a particularly strong expression and always
in relation to himself. [120] The underlying matter is there, though not in the Jewish

---

[109] Mt. 15:3 ff.; 23:16 ff.
[110] Cf. esp. Mt. 23 par. → ὑποκριτής.
[111] Mt. 23:23; cf. Mt. 21:29.
[112] Lk. 18:14; cf. Mt. 23:13.
[113] In spite of 9:13, Mt. 23 is really an address calling for the repentance of the righteous; cf. also Mt. 21:32.
[114] Mt. 25:44; cf. Mt. 9:11 f. par.; Lk. 10:40 ff.; 15:25 ff.
[115] Mt. 22:9 ff.; Lk. 15:11 ff.
[116] Mt. 19:21; cf. 18:3 ff.
[117] Mt. 21:32.
[118] R. 4:25; 1 C. 15:3; 2 C. 5:21; Gl. 1:4; Col. 1:14; 1 Pt. 3:18; 1 Jn. 2:2; Hb. 2:17; Rev.
1:5 etc.
[119] Jn. 9:16, 24, 25, 31; → 328.
[120] R. 3:7; 5:8, 19; Gl. 2:15, 17.

formulae (→ ἁμαρτία). The basic description of the sinner has not changed. The sinner is the man who does not allow God supreme authority over his life and who withholds from Him total dedication and obedience. [121] If new words are found to state this, [122] no change in respect of the fundamental judgment is implied.

The new feature, however, is not simply that outside Jesus there is no longer any frontier between the sinners and the righteous. It really emerges in full force when the reference is to man prior to or without Jesus on the one side and the man who is united with Him on the other. Paul, although he is a man and in temptation and under sentence of death, is no longer conscious of sin in his state of union with Christ, [123] and he presupposes the same of all those who belong to Him and have a share in His work. [124] The same is true of John, who can already attest deliverance from involvement in the world of sin. [125] It need hardly be said that this implies a new gulf of unfathomable depth right across humanity. This is the gulf which separates those who are ἐν Χριστῷ, and who are thus rescued from the power of ἁμαρτία [126] and brought into His possession [127] and the service of God, [128] from those who are still "under sin" [129] or "in their sins," [130] neither knowing God [131] nor serving Him. [132] This gulf is deeper than that which existed between the righteous and sinners prior to the coming of Jesus, for it is not created or maintained by men, but has arisen and continually arises from the act of God in Christ. [133] From the same act of God, however, there also results the fact that in the NT the righteous or the justified have no consciousness of themselves as such, [134] but simply magnify the grace which has genuinely made sinners righteous, [135] and are full of zeal to point all men to this way of grace. [136]

† ἀναμάρτητος.

This word is found in Gk. from the time of Herodotus (V, 39, 2), and in contrast to ἁμαρτωλός (→ 317) it is quite common. [1] The etymon is again ἁμαρτάνειν or ἁμαρτεῖν, so that we are not to regard the word as a negation of ἁμαρτωλός. [2] The basic

---

[121] Cf. with R. 12:1 f.; 1 C. 1:19 f. etc. in Paul, Jm. 1:27.

[122] Cf. in Jn. expressions like → ἀγαπάω, → κόσμος, τηρεῖν τὸν λόγον (μου) etc.

[123] Cf. 1 C. 4:4, and the discussion of T. Schlatter, "Für Gott lebendig in Christi Kraft," in *Jahrbuch der Theolog. Schule Bethel* (1930: 116-144), 121 ff. Cf. 1 Jn. 3:6.

[124] Cf. esp. R. 6:1 ff.; also 5:1.

[125] Jn. 5:24; 1 Jn. 3:14 etc.; → ζωή (αἰώνιος).

[126] R. 6:10 f.; Hb. 9:26 ff.; → ἐξαγοράζω.

[127] R. 14:7 ff.; 2 C. 5:14 f. etc.

[128] R. 6:13, 22 etc.; → δουλεύω.

[129] R. 3:9; Gl. 3:22; cf. R. 6:17; Jn. 8:34.

[130] 1 C. 15:17.

[131] 1 Th. 4:5; 2 Th. 1:8; Gl. 4:8.

[132] Gl. 4:8. These statements really need to be discussed in a separate chapter.

[133] → σκάνδαλον, μωρία.

[134] It is striking that the self-declaration → ἀναμάρτητος is never found in the NT, though the presuppositions are present; cf. T. Schlatter, 141 ff.

[135] R. 5:1; 6:17 f.; 7:25; 8:1 etc.; → χάρις, πνεῦμα.

[136] 1 C. 9:16 ff.

ἀναμάρτητος. Pr.-Bauer; Liddell-Scott, 112; Thes. Steph. *s.v.*; Bau. Jn., 113 f.

[1] Many examples are given in the dictionaries.

[2] Ling. ἁμάρτημα is closest; → n. 9.

meaning is "without fault," primarily in a very general sense, as of the constitution of a city (Aristot. Pol., III, 1, p. 1275a, 38 ff.: τὰς δὲ πολιτείας ὁρῶμεν εἴδει διαφερούσας ἀλλήλων, καὶ τὰς μὲν ὑστέρας τὰς δὲ προτέρας οὔσας· τὰς γὰρ ἡμαρτημένας καὶ παρεκβεβηκυίας ἀναγκαῖον ὑστέρας εἶναι τῶν ἀναμαρτήτων, or of a project (προαίρεσις; Aristot. Eth. Eud., II, 11, p. 1227b, 12 f.: ... λέγωμεν πότερον ἡ ἀρετὴ ἀναμάρτητον ποιεῖ τὴν προαίρεσιν). In a figur. sense it means one who is without fault, though with no necessary restriction to the moral sphere in the narrower sense (Plut. Adulat., 33 [II, 72b]: ὡς αὐτὸς ἀπαθὴς ὢν ὑπ' ὀργῆς καὶ ἀναμάρτητος), [3] or one who has not failed (Xenoph. Hist. Graec., VI, 3, 10 : ὁρῶ γὰρ τῶν ἀνθρώπων οὐδένα ἀναμάρτητον διατελοῦντα), or finally one who does not need to fail (Plat. Resp., I, 339c: πότερον δὲ ἀναμάρτητοί εἰσιν οἱ ἄρχοντες ἐν ταῖς πόλεσιν ἑκάσταις ἢ οἷοί τι καὶ ἁμαρτεῖν). [4] Independent Christian development, more esp. on the basis of Paul, is again found in Cl. Al. (Strom., VI, 12, 101, 3; VII, 12, 80, 2), who equates ἀναμάρτητος with γνωστικός in the sense of one who cannot fail (or sin). [5] Such a religious use, coloured by the conception of God, is foreign to the word in secular usage so far as the evidence goes. This is true even in the case of Epictetus, for whom ἀναμάρτητον is a definition of the philosopher's humanistic and purely ethical ideal of personality (Diss., IV, 8, 6; 12, 19). [6]

In the LXX there are three occurrences. In 2 Macc. 12:42 the reference is definitely religious in the sense of remaining free from guilt before God. 2 Macc. 8:4 (τῶν ἀναμαρτήτων [7] νηπίων παρανομία ἀπώλεια) is doubtful. In Δευτ. 29:19 (→ 320, n. 31) it is the opposite of ἁμαρτωλός within a theological interpretation of the verse by the translator. In Symmachus it also occurs in ψ 58:4 as a self-declaration on the part of the righteous Psalmist (LXX : ἄνευ ἀνομίας). [8]

Philo uses the word with ἀνυπαίτιος in Mut. Nom., 51 in exposition of Gn. 17:1 (γίνου → ἄμεμπτος), and with ὀρθῶς, ἀμέμπτως, ἀνεπιλήπτως, ἀνυπευθύνως, ἀζημίως (adverbially) in Omn. Prob. Lib., 59. In neither case is there any special reference to God. [9] There is such reference, however, in the only case in Jos. noted by Thackeray [10] (Bell., 7, 329 : ἀναμάρτητοι πρὸς τὸν θεὸν γενόμενοι).

In the NT the only occurrence is in the challenge of Jesus in the story of the woman taken in adultery : ὁ ἀναμάρτητος ὑμῶν πρῶτος ἐπ' αὐτὴν βαλέτω λίθον (Jn. 8:7). What is meant is very generally the one who is not burdened by any guilt (→ ἁμαρτωλός); reference to God is the self-evident presupposition. The history of the word gives us no grounds for taking it to mean those who are not guilty of sexual sin, i.e., adultery, [11] after the pattern of a specific interpretation of ἁμαρτωλός in Lk. 7:37 and ἐπὶ ἁμαρτίᾳ in Jn. 8:3 D (instead of ἐν μοιχείᾳ).

---

[3] In Plut. ἀναμάρτητος takes on a distinctive flavour due to its frequent association with ἀπαθής in the sense of freedom from emotion; e.g., Aud. Poet., 7 (II, 25d); Pyth. Orac., 21 (II, 404c); Def. Orac., 16 (II, 419a) etc. Cf. also Jer. Adv. Pelag., Prolog., 1 (MPL, 23, 517a).

[4] This usage is still found in Jerome, though in a distinctively Christian sense (Adv. Pelag., II, 4, MPL, 23, 562b; II, 23, 587b). For him ἀναμάρτητος expresses in Gk. what Pelagius was saying in Latin with his posse hominem, si velit, esse sine peccato.

[5] As pointed out by G. Stählin.

[6] Materially, v. already Aristot. Eth. Nic., IX, 1, p. 1155a, 13 ff.

[7] At least in the sense of those who have not yet failed.

[8] On this point → 323, n. 50; 324.

[9] Materially, cf. also γυμνὸς ἁμαρτημάτων in Fug., 158.

[10] Lex. Jos., 39.

[11] Bau. J., 114; H. J. Holtzmann in his Hand-Commentar z. NT, ad loc.; and many older commentators.

Indeed, the context forbids this, for Jesus is dealing with the scribes and Pharisees, against whom the charge of adultery could hardly be levelled, [12] and no other sexual sin seems to be in question. [13] The best explanation of ἀναμάρτητος in this passage is thus the general but concrete ἄνευ ἀνομίας of ψ 58:4 (→ supra).

It is striking that the word is not used elsewhere in the NT, especially in relation to the asserted sinlessness of Jesus. [14] If it was not applied to Him, this was probably to avoid any suggestion of non posse peccare, and thus to safeguard the whole greatness of his ministry and sacrifice, though without throwing any doubt on the uniqueness of His relationship to God as free from any sin or guilt. [15]

Rengstorf

ἄμεμπτος → μέμφομαι   ἀμετανόητος → μετανοέω

ἀμήν

A. אָמֵן in the OT and Judaism.

In the OT [1] the word is used both by the individual and the community (1) to confirm the acceptance of a task allotted by men in the performance of which there is need of the will of God (1 K. 1:36), (2) to confirm the personal application of a divine threat or curse (Nu. 5:22; Dt. 27:15 ff.; Jer. 11:5; Neh. 5:13), and (3) to attest the praise of God in response to a doxology (1 Ch. 16:36; Neh. 8:6), as at the end of the doxologies of the first four books of the Psalms (Ps. 41:13; 72:19; 89:52 : אָמֵן וְאָמֵן; 106:48 : אָמֵן הַלְלוּ־יָהּ). In all these cases אָמֵן is the acknowledgment of a word which is valid, and the validity of which is binding for me

---

[12] Cf. Str.-B., I, 297 f.

[13] The reference in Lk. 7:37 is to a prostitute (→ 327), but here to one who is affianced ; on Rabbinic terminology, cf. Str.-B., I, 297.

[14] v. esp. Jn. 8:46; 2 C. 5:21; 1 Pt. 2:22.

[15] The fellowship of Jesus with sinners, and yet His radical difference from them, are expressed in a single phrase in R. 8:3 : ἐν ὁμοιώματι (→ ὁμοίωμα) σαρκὸς ἁμαρτίας; cf. also 2 C. 5:21; Phil. 2:5 ff. (→ μορφή, σχῆμα); Hb. 4:15; 9:28.

ἀμήν. Dalman WJ, I, 185 ff.; Dalman, Jesus-Jeschua (1922), 27 f.; Str.-B., I, 242 ff.; III, 456 ff.; E. Peterson, Εἷς Θεός (1926), Index; Dausch, Synpt., 128.

[1] On the Heb. root אמן ("to be firm or sure") → 232 f.

and then generally in this acknowledgment. Thus אָמֵן means that which is sure and valid.

In Judaism the use of Amen is widespread and firmly established. An extra-ordinary value is attached to its utterance.[2] In synagogue though not in temple worship it occurs as the response of the community "to the detailed praises which the leader utters with the prayers or on other occasions," and "to each of the three sections into which the priests divided the Aaronic blessing of Nu. 6:24-26."[3] It was the confession of the praise of God which was laid on the community and which the community was to affirm by its answer. And it was the confession of the blessing of God which was pronounced to the community and which the com-munity was to make operative by its Amen. Apart from divine service it was to be used in response to any prayer or praise uttered by another. The concluding Amen signified concurrence. Amen to a vow meant engagement to fulfil it. Amen to a curse implied either the cursing of what the other cursed or placing oneself under the curse. The same is true of Amen to a blessing (jSota, 18b).[4] If in these cases Amen retains its character as the response to a word spoken by another, and as a confirmation of it, there is a shift in meaning in the few instances in which it is a concluding wish at the end of one's own prayers (Tob. 8:7 f.; Taan., 4, 8 etc.).[5] In such cases it is not so much a confirmation of what is, but rather hope for what is desired.

This tendency is strengthened when the LXX mostly translates אָמֵן by γένοιτο (once in Ιερ. 35:6 with ἀληθῶς). In this way the inner dialectic of the concept is concealed to the degree that the γένοιτο still signifies what endures, or is true, of the spoken Word of God in the sense of its standing fast, but no longer brings out the fact that this "truth" constitutes a claim which binds me in my Amen. There are no material grounds why the Amen should be retained in 1 Ch. 16:36; 1 Esr. 9:47; Neh. 5:13; 8:6; Tob. 8:8; 14:15; 3 Macc. 7:23; 4 Macc. 18:24 (as often in Σ). Note should be taken of the rendering of אָמֵן as πεπιστωμένως in 'Α (Ιερ. 35:6: πιστωθήτω). This shows that אָמֵן for him approximates closely to "sure" or "reliable."

B. ἀμήν in the NT and Early Christianity.

In the NT and the surrounding Christian world the Heb. is usually taken over as it stands. It is used in three ways.

1. It is a liturgical acclamation in Christian worship (1 C. 14:16). As in the heavenly worship of Rev. 5:14 the four beasts respond to the praise of all creation with their Amen, so the congregation acclaims the εὐχαί and εὐχαριστία of the president with theirs (Just. Ap., 65, 3).[6] The Amen thus retains its character of response, since it is to another that the people (the ἰδιῶται of 1 C. 14:16) reply with their ἀμήν (Did., 10, 6; Act. Thom., 29 to the apostle; Act. Phil., 146 to the

---

[2] Str.-B., III, 457, 460 (under n.).
[3] Str.-B., III, 456.
[4] Str.-B., I, 242.
[5] *Ibid.*, I, 243.
[6] Cf. Prot. Ev. Jk., 6, 2.

heavenly voice; Act. Joh., 94 to the Christ-Logos). To say Amen is the right of the baptised λαός (Act. Phil., 147). And the Amen first makes the προσφορά perfect (Act. Phil., 143). Sometimes the president himself joins in this Amen (M. Pol., 15, 1; Act. Phil., 117 f.).

2. Christian prayers[7] and doxologies themselves mostly end with Amen. Cf. for prayers M. Pol., 14, 3; 1 Cl., 45, 8; 61, 3; 64; Mart. Ptr., 10; Act. Joh., 77; for doxologies R. 1:25; 9:5; 11:36; 16:27; Gl. 1:5; Eph. 3:21; Phil. 4:20; 1 Tm. 1:17; 6:16; 2 Tm. 4:18; Hb. 13:21; 1 Pt. 4:11; 5:11; Jd. 25; 1 Cl., 20, 12 etc.; 2 Cl., 20, 5; M. Pol., 21, 1; 22; 3; Dg., 12, 9 etc. This does not mean, however, the self-confirmation of the one who prays. It expresses the fact that in divine service prayer and doxology have their place before the people whose response they evoke or anticipate. We are to understand the ἀμήν in the same way when it comes at the end of a prophetic word (Rev. 1:7) or an epistle or book (R. 15:33; Gl. 6:18; Rev. 22:20). The last instances shows how a liturgical use can be turned to literary account. From the use of ἀμήν at the end of a doxology, in which it becomes part of the doxology or prayer, we can understand how it can come to have a place at the beginning as well, especially when it forms the link between a preceding doxology and that which follows (Rev. 7:12; Mart. Mt., 29). The combination with ἀλληλουϊά (Rev. 19:4; Mart. Mt., 26) may be explained by the acclamatory character of both terms and the tendency of acclamations to become more extensive. [8]

That this Christian Amen has retained its original inward meaning may be seen from three passages in the NT. In Rev. 1:7 it occurs in close proximity to ναί = Yes. But Rev. 22:20 shows that it is the answer of the ἐκκλησία to the divine Yes. The Yes does not here introduce the eschatological petition but acknowledges the divine promise which is the basis on which the petition can be made. The Amen of the community makes the divine Yes valid for it. The Amen of 2 C. 1:20 is to be seen in the same light. Because the ναί of God, the fulfilment of His promises, is declared in Christ, by Him (= by the ἐκκλησία) there is uttered the Amen or response of the community to the divine Yes, so that the divine Yes forms a sure foundation for them (βεβαιῶν, v. 21). In the same way, in reminiscence of Is. 65:16, Christ Himself can be called ὁ Ἀμήν in Rev. 3:14, and the meaning of this ὁ Ἀμήν is brought out by the addition: ὁ μάρτυς ὁ πιστὸς καὶ ἀληθινός, ἡ ἀρχὴ τῆς κτίσεως τοῦ θεοῦ. He Himself is the response to the divine Yes in Him. And to the extent that in Himself He acknowledges and obediently responds to the divine Yes which is Himself, He is the reliable and true Witness of God.

3. If, however, this meaning of Amen is retained in the Christian community, it is best preserved in the ἀμήν which Jesus places before His sayings in the Synoptic Gospels[9] (30 times in Mt., 13 in Mk. and 6 in Lk., though the latter also uses ἀληθῶς at 9:27; 12:44; 21:3 and ἐπ' ἀληθείας at 4:25), and also in John's Gospel (25 times, liturgically doubled). That Jesus' command not to swear played any part in its use[10] is nowhere indicated. For בְּקֻשְׁטָא or מִן קֻשְׁטָא might also have

---

[7] As also Jewish prayers, cf. Dalman WJ, I, 185, 3.
[8] On the apotrop. use of ἀμήν, cf. Peterson, op. cit.
[9] Schl. Mt., 155.
[10] Dalman WJ, I, 186 f.

been adopted. The point of the Amen before Jesus' own sayings is rather to show that as such they are reliable and true, and that they are so as and because Jesus Himself in His Amen acknowledges them to be His own sayings and thus makes them valid. These sayings are of varied individual content, but they all have to do with the history of the kingdom of God bound up with His person. Thus in the ἀμήν preceding the λέγω ὑμῖν of Jesus we have the whole of Christology *in nuce*. The one who accepts His word as true and certain is also the one who acknowledges and affirms it in his own life and thus causes it, as fulfilled by him, to become a demand to others.

Schlier

ἀμίαντος → μιαίνω

ἀμνός, ἀρήν, ἀρνίον

† ἀμνός.

Attested from classical times, it is mostly used in the LXX for the Heb. כֶּבֶשׂ, though occasionally for אַיִל, אִמֵּר, כֶּשֶׂב, עַתּוּד, צֹאן, קְשִׂיטָה, רָחֵל, שֶׂה.

In the NT it occurs 4 times (Jn. 1:29, 36; Ac. 8:32; 1 Pt. 1:19) and it is always applied to Jesus, who is compared with a lamb as the One who suffers and dies innocently and representatively.

The description of the Redeemer as a lamb is unknown to later Judaism; the only possible occurrence (Test. Jos. 19) falls under the suspicion of being a Christian interpolation. [1] The question of the derivation of the description of Jesus

---

ἀμνός. F. Spitta, *Streitfragen zur Geschichte Jesu* (1907), 172-224; O. Procksch, *Petrus und Johannes bei Mk. und Mt.* (1920), 125; C. F. Burney, *The Aramaic Origin of the Fourth Gospel* (1922), 107 f.; A. Schlatter, *Geschichte des Christus* (1923), 108 ff.; Str.-B., II, 367-370; Schl. J., 46-49; H. Wenschkewitz, "Die Spiritualisierung der Kultusbegriffe Tempel, Priester und Opfer im NT," *Angelos*, 4 (1932), 70-230.

[1] Test. Jos. 19:8 according to the Armenian version is as follows: "I saw in the middle of the horns (of the fourth beast) a virgin wearing a brightly coloured vestment, and from her went forth a lamb. On her right hand was the likeness of a lion. And all the wild beasts and serpents raged; the lamb conquered and destroyed them." F. Spitta, *op. cit.*, 187-194 and Loh. Apk., 51 f. regard the designation of the Messiah in this passage as a pre-Christian Jewish tradition.

as ἀμνός or → ἀρνίον thus arises. Two influences have perhaps been at work. The first is that both Jesus Himself and the primitive community of the very earliest period saw in Jesus the Servant of the Lord of Is. 53. The early nature of the designation of Jesus as → παῖς θεοῦ in the primitive community (Ac. 3:13; 4:27, 30) is guaranteed by the fact that offence was quickly taken at this title and it thus came to be avoided. [2] In Is. 53:7, however, the Servant who suffers patiently is compared to a lamb, and this comparison is expressly related to Jesus in Ac. 8:32 (→ Is. 53:7): ὡς ἀμνὸς ἐναντίον τοῦ κείραντος αὐτὸν ἄφωνος. Thus Is. 53:7 might well be the origin of the description of Jesus as ἀμνός. Yet a second influence is also to be seen. The crucifixion of Jesus took place at the Passover. First Paul and then John (19:36) thus compared Jesus to the Paschal lamb: τὸ πάσχα ἡμῶν ἐτύθη Χριστός (1 C. 5:7). To be sure, kids as well as lambs might be offered at the Passover; [3] yet it was more usual to sacrifice lambs. Thus the comparison of Jesus with the Passover sacrifice might well have resulted in His description as ἀμνός. More likely the two lines of influence interacted.

Yet it might well be that the adoption or even the derivation of the description of Jesus as the Lamb of God should be seen against a wider background. For the expression ὁ ἀμνὸς τοῦ θεοῦ (Jn. 1:29, 36) gives us a highly singular genitive combination which can be explained only in the light of the Aramaic. In Aramaic the word טַלְיָא has the twofold significance of a. lamb and b. boy or servant. Probably an Aramaic טַלְיָא דֵּאלָהָא in the sense of עֶבֶד יְהוָה underlies the Greek ὁ ἀμνὸς τοῦ θεοῦ, [4] the original reference thus being to Jesus as the servant of God. The translation of טַלְיָא as ἀμνός (instead of παῖς) thus gives us the strange construction ὁ ἀμνὸς τοῦ θεοῦ. If so, the double meaning of טַלְיָא has some part in the adoption, or even the origin, of the designation of Jesus as ἀμνός or ἀρνίον. The designation could thus arise only on bilingual or Greek speaking territory; this is supported by the fact that it is found exclusively [5] in the Johannine literature.

In the designation of Jesus as ἀμνός we thus have a creation of the community. This consideration has a bearing on our estimate of the historicity of the saying of the Baptist in Jn. 1:29, 36: ἴδε ὁ ἀμνὸς τοῦ θεοῦ, including in v. 29: ὁ αἴρων τὴν ἁμαρτίαν τοῦ κόσμου. If in the basic Aramaic the reference was to the servant of God, the most serious objections to its historicity are dispelled. In terms [6] of Is. 53 the Baptist was calling Jesus the Servant of the Lord [7] who takes away the sin of the world, and thus thinking (→ αἴρω) of the substitutionary suffering of the penalty of sin by the Servant of God. [8]

---

[2] A. v. Harnack, "Die Bezeichnung Jesu als 'Knecht Gottes' und ihre Geschichte in der alten Kirche," SAB (1926), 212-238.
[3] Ex. 12:3, 5; Pes., 8, 2; T. Pes., 4, 2 → πάσχα.
[4] Burney, op. cit., 107 f.; cf. Loh. Apk., 52.
[5] Ac. 8:32 and 1 Pt. 1:19 merely give us the comparison of Jesus with a lamb, but not His title as Lamb. The latter is found only in the Johannine writings; ἀμνός occurs twice (Jn. 1:29, 36) and ἀρνίον 28 times (in Rev.).
[6] Cf. Is. 53:12: וְהוּא חֵטְא־רַבִּים נָשָׂא.
[7] Cf. the reference to Is. 42:1 in the voice from heaven at the baptism (Mk. 1:11 par.).
[8] On the Messianic significance of Is. 53 in pre-Christian times cf. J. Jeremias, "Erlöser und Erlösung im Spätjudentum und Urchristentum," in Deutsche Theologie, II, Der Erlösungsgedanke (1929), 106-119. Cf. also → παῖς.

In the community the saying of the Baptist acquired a new significance when the Evangelist John, or the underlying tradition, rendered טַלְיָא דֵאלָהָא by ὁ ἀμνὸς τοῦ θεοῦ and thus described Jesus as the true Paschal lamb (cf. Jn. 19:36). At the same time αἴρειν (Jn. 1:29) took on the new meaning of blotting out by a means of expiation which removes guilt (→ αἴρω). The saying of the Baptist was thus taken to mean that Jesus as the Lamb of God blots out the sin of the world by the expiatory efficacy of His blood. The community expresses three things in describing Jesus as ἀμνός: 1. the patience of His suffering (Ac. 8:32); 2. His sinlessness (1 Pt. 1:19); and 3. the efficacy of His sacrificial death (Jn. 1:29, 36; 1 Pt. 1:19). With the patience of a sacrificial lamb, the Saviour dying on the cross went as a Substitute to death, and by the atoning power of His innocent dying He has cancelled the guilt — for this is the meaning of ἁμαρτία in Jn. 1:29 [9] — of the whole of humanity. Thus His dying means the dawn of the time of salvation (1 Pt. 1:20). As once the blood of the Passover lambs played a part in the redemption from Egypt, so by the atoning power of His blood He has accomplished redemption (ἐλυτρώθητε, 1 Pt. 1:18) from the bondage of sin (ἐκ τῆς ματαίας ὑμῶν ἀναστροφῆς πατροπαραδότου, 1 Pt. 1:18). But the atoning efficacy of His death is not limited to Israel like that of the Paschal lamb. As agnus Dei He makes atonement for the whole world, which, without distinction of race or religion, has come hopelessly under the judgment of God (Jn. 1:29 → κόσμος).

† ἀρήν.

LXX for גְּדִי, טָלֶה, טְלִי, כֶּבֶשׂ, כַּר, מְרִיא, עַתּוּד.

In the NT ἀρήν occurs only in Lk. 10:3: ἀποστέλλω ὑμᾶς ὡς ἄρνας (par. Mt. 10:16: πρόβατα) ἐν μέσῳ λύκων. The antithesis lambs/wolves expresses 1. the dangerous position of the defenceless disciples; cf. Ps. Sol. 8:28: καὶ οἱ ὅσιοι τοῦ θεοῦ ὡς → ἀρνία ἐν ἀκακίᾳ ἐν μέσῳ αὐτῶν (the nations of the earth); 2. the certainty of divine protection; cf. Tanch. תולדות 32b: "Hadrian said to R. Jehoshua (c. 90 A.D.): There is something great about the sheep (Israel) that can persist among 70 wolves (the nations). He replied: Great is the Shepherd who delivers it and watches over it and destroys them (the wolves) before them (Israel)."

ἀρνίον.

ἀρνίον is originally a dimin. of ἀρήν with the significance of a little lamb (Philippides, Fr. 29 [CAF, III, 310] ἀρνίου μαλακώτερος); but it no longer has this force in NT times. [1]

---

[9] Schl. J., 48.

ἀ ρ ή ν. Schl. Mt., 336 f.; Str.-B., I, 574; Dausch Synpt., 486.

ἀ ρ ν ί ο ν. A. Jeremias, Babylonisches im NT (1905), 8-18; F. Spitta, Streitfragen zur Geschichte Jesu (1907), 172-224; Clemen, 382-384; Loh. Apk., 51-53; Had. Apk., 76-78; H. Wenschkewitz, "Die Spiritualisierung der Kultusbegriffe Tempel, Priester und Opfer im NT," Angelos, 4 (1932), 213 ff.

[1] Cf. F. Boll, Aus der Off. Joh. (1914), 45, n. 6; Moult.-Mill., 78a.

Apart from Jn. 21:15 ἀρνίον is found only in Rev., where it occurs 29 times. The Jewish Greek usage is important for the NT. In the LXX it occurs 4 times, and always denotes "lamb": Jer. 11:19 for כֶּבֶשׂ; Ιερ. 27(50):45: τὰ ἀρνία τῶν προβάτων for צְעִירֵי הַצֹּאן; ψ 113:4, 6: ἀρνία προβάτων for בְּנֵי צֹאן. The same holds good in Aquila (Is. 40:11 for טְלָאִים), Ps. Sol. (8:28 → supra) and Josephus. [2]

There can be no doubt about the meaning "lamb" in Jn. 21:15: βόσκε τὰ ἀρνία μου, in view of the parallel word προβάτια[3] in v. 16 f. and the Syriac understanding. [4] What is meant by my lambs is the community as an object of the loving care of Jesus.

In Revelation, in which the exalted Christ is 28 times called the Lamb, and once (13:11) Antichrist as His anti-type, [5] the meaning of ἀρνίον is disputed. On the one side[6] it is argued that "ram" is the correct translation, since what is depicted is the wrath (6:16 f.) warfare and triumph (17:14) of the ἀρνίον. Along the same lines reference is made to the 7 horns (5:6; cf. 13:11), and there is a common inclination[7] to identify the ἀρνίον of Rev. with the zodiac and to explain its individual features astrologically. But reminiscence of Da. 8:3 (cf. Eth. En. 90:9, 37 and the number 7 in Zech. 4:10) might easily give us the 7 horns, and in any case the philological justification of the translation "ram" is highly doubtful. In Jewish Greek usage (→ supra) the only significance is "lamb," as also in Jn. 21:15 and 2 Cl., 5, 2-4. In addition the fact that the ἀρνίον is also described as "slain" (5:6; cf. 5:9, 12; 13:8) shows that we cannot separate the statements of Revelation from what the NT says about Jesus as the sacrificial Lamb (→ ἀμνός).

The statements of Revelation concerning Christ as ἀρνίον depict Him as Redeemer and Ruler, and in so doing bring out all the most important elements in His title as Deliverer. [8] a. The Lamb bears (on His neck) the mark of His slaughtering (5:6, 9, 12; 13:8); His blood flowed in atonement for sin (5:9; 7:14; 12:11). b. But the Lamb overcame death (5:5-6) and is omnipotent (→ κέρας) and omniscient (5:6). c. He takes over the government of the world by opening the book of destiny in the heavenly council (4:2 ff.; 5:7 ff.), receiving divine adoration (5:8 ff. etc.), establishing the rule of peace (7:9) on the heavenly mountain (14:1), overcoming demonic powers (17:14), exercising judgment (6:16 f.; 14:10) and making distinction on the basis of the book of life (13:8; 21:27). d. As Victor He is the Lord of lords and King of kings (17:14; 19:16), celebrating His marriage festival with the community (19:9) and ruling His own as partner of the throne of God (22:1, 3).

J. Jeremias

---

[2] Jos. in Ant., 3, 221, 251 renders the OT כֶּבֶשׂ (Nu. 7:15; 23:12) by ἀρνίον and distinguishes the ram as κριός.

[3] אD rec πρόβατα.

[4] Syr. sin pesch philox arm Ta: v. 15: lambs (= children), v. 16-17: sheep and rams (= women and men in the community); cf. A. Merx, Das Evg. des J. (1911), 466-468.

[5] B. Murmelstein, WZKM, 36 (1929), 83.

[6] Spitta, op. cit., 174; Cr.-Kö., 167; K. Bornhäuser, Wirken des Christus (1921), 244 ff.

[7] Boll, op. cit., 44 ff.

[8] Cf. A. Jeremias, op. cit., 8-18.

| ἄμπελος |

"Vine," applied metaphorically by Jesus to Himself in the NT (Jn. 15:1: ἐγώ εἰμι ἡ ἄμπελος ἡ ἀληθινή; v. 5: ἐγώ εἰμι ἡ ἄμπελος, ὑμεῖς τὰ κλήματα). The allegory of the vine tended by the gardener, from which the sap flows into the branches, denotes in the first instance the inner fellowship of the disciples with Jesus, which rests on their utter dependence and in which they must abide and bring forth fruit (v. 4 ff.). It then denotes the intensive nurture of the community of disciples by God (v. 1 ff.). If Jesus is the true vine which alone is worthy of the name (→ ἀληθινός), this is hardly in distinction from literal vines, but rather from others to whom the image had already been applied. It cannot be decided with any certainty whether or not the metaphor of Jn. 15:1 ff. should be linked with the saying at the Last Supper concerning the γένημα τῆς ἀμπέλου (Mk. 14:25 par.; cf. the ἁγία ἄμπελος Δαβίδ in Did., 9, 2).

The metaphor of the vine is common in Israelite and Judaic literature. It is used for the people of Israel in Hos. 10:1; Jer. 2:21 (ἄμπελον ἀληθινήν); Ez. 15:1 ff.; 19:10 ff.; Ps. 80:9 ff.; bChul., 92a; Lv. r., 36 on 26:42 (Str.-B., II, 495, 563); for the Messiah in S. Bar., 36 ff. (39:7: "the dominion of my Messiah, which is like a vine"); for wisdom in Sir. 24:17; for the wife in Ps. 128:3. In view of this usage the conception and execution of the image in Jn. can be regarded only as "new building on old foundation." [1] Indeed, in later texts the image is a common one throughout the Orient, as in the Dionysus cult (Εὐστάφυλος) [2] and esp. in the Mandaean religion, where not merely the heavenly messenger but a whole series of beings from the light world are spoken of in terms of the vine, and we find what is almost a metaphysics of the vine.

> Lidz. Ginza, 181, 27: "Mandā dHaijē revealed himself in Judea, a vine appeared in Jerusalem"; Lidz. Lit., 68, 7 (to Mandā dHaijē): "Thou art the vine"; Lidz. Ginza, 301, 11 ff.: "I (Hibil) am a soft vine ... and the great (life) was for me the planter"; Lidz. Lit., 218, 9 ff.: "On the bank of the great Jordan of the first life there stands the wondrous vine before which my daily prayers and praises ascend"; cf. 180:11 ff. [3]

ἄ μ π ε λ ο ς.   Zn. J., 576 ff.; Bau. J., 183 ff.; Tillm. J., 273; Clemen, 282 f.; F. Büchsel, *Joh. u. der hellenist. Synkretismus* (1928), 52 f.

[1] Büchsel, *op. cit.*, 53.

[2] R. Knopf on Did., 9, 2; W. Bousset, *Kyrios Christos*² (1921), 274; J. Grill, *Untersuchungen über die Entstehung des 4 Ev.*, II (1923), 106; H. Weinel, *Bibl. Theol. d. NT*⁴ (1928), 427; J. Leipoldt, *Dionysos* (1931), 51 f. etc. On the golden vine which plays a role earlier in the Phrygian Zeus myth, cf. A. B. Cook, *Zeus*, II (1925), 281, n. 4 and 1394 *s.v.* "Vine, golden."

[3] Lidz. Joh., Lit., Ginza, Index *s.v.* "Weinstock." Cf. W. Brandt, *Jbch. pr. Th.*, 18 (1892), 433 ff.; M. Lidzbarski, *Oriental. Studien Nöldeke gew.* (1906), 538. Gnostic Act. Thom., 36: ποτὸς τῆς ἀμπέλου τῆς ἀληθινῆς. Also *Actus Petri cum Simone*, 20 (p. 68 Lipsius)?

In some cases Jn. may well have provided the details of the conception, e.g., Lidz. Joh., 204, 34 ff.: "The vine which bears fruits arises, and that which does not is cut down ... whosoever will not be enlightened and instructed by me will be cut off"; Lidz. Lit., 253, 1: "Thy pure shoots ... shall be united with thee and shall not be cut off"; Lidz. Ginza, 24, 14 f.: "Root up the bad vine and bring a good and plant it instead." All these seem to be either paraphrases or applications of Jn. 15:2, 4 ff.

There are contacts between the Johannine use of the image and oriental analogies. The Johannine Jesus claims for Himself alone the symbolical predicate of other divine figures of that syncretistic period: "I am the true vine," and He develops the thought with creative depth.

Behm

ἄμωμος, ἀμώμητος → μῶμος   ἀναβαίνω → βαίνω
ἀναγγέλλω → 61 ff.   ἀναγεννάω → γεννάω

ἀναγινώσκω, ἀνάγνωσις

ἀναγινώσκω in Gk. means "to know exactly" or "to recognise," and for the most part it is used with the sense of reading or public reading (cf. both older usage and the pap.). In this sense it is by no means uncommon in the LXX, mostly for קרא.

In the NT ἀναγινώσκειν is used of the reading of a letter (Ac. 15:31; 23:34; 2 C. 1:13; 3:2; Eph. 3:4) and esp. of public reading in the congregation (1 Th. 5:27; Col. 4:16). In Jn. 19:20 it is used of reading the τίτλος on the cross. It is mainly used of the reading of the OT: Mk. 2:25 par.; 12:10 par.; Mt. 12:5; Ac. 8:28; Gl. 4:21 (vl) etc.; cf. esp. Mk. 13:14: ὁ ἀναγινώσκων νοείτω (whosoever reads the apocalypse in question — Daniel?). We find the same use in Jos. Ant., 4, 209; 10, 267; 20, 44 f. and later Christian literature. There is particular reference to the cultic reading of the OT in Lk. 4:16; Ac. 13:27; 15:21; 2 C. 3:15. In Rev. 1:3 the reference is to reading of the prophecy presented, and since the Epistles were already being publicly read in the early communities it is evident that the apostolic

---

ἀναγινώσκω κτλ. Pr.-Bauer, *s.v.*; Str.-B., IV, 154 ff. (Exc. 8); R. Knopf, ZNW, 3 (1902), 266 ff.; also on 2 Cl. 19, 1 in *Hdb. z. NT, Ergänzungsband* (1923); P. Glaue, *Die Vorlesung heil. Schriften im Gottesdienst*, I (1907). Also A. Harnack, "Über den privaten Brauch der heil. Schriften in der alten Kirche" in *Beitr. z. Einl. in d. NT*, V (1912).

literature was also an object of ἀναγινώσκειν as well as the OT (cf. 2 Cl., 19, 1; Just. Ap., 67, 3 f.).[1]

ἀνάγνωσις means "knowledge" or "recognition" and it is particularly used for reading or public reading (as in the pap.), esp. in law courts and other assemblies. In Judaism it was used for the public reading of the OT, cf. Philo Rer. Div. Haer., 253 and the synagogue inscription in Jerusalem: συναγωγὴν εἰς ἀνάγνωσιν νόμου.[2] We find the same usage in early Christianity: Ac. 13:15; 2 C. 3:14; 1 Tm. 4:13; and cf. also Cl. Al. Paed., II, 10, 96, 2; Strom., I, 21, 146, 1; VI, 14, 113, 3.

Bultmann

| ἀναγκάζω, ἀναγκαῖος, |
| ἀνάγκη |

A. ἀναγκ- outside the NT.

The question bound up with the root ἀναγκ-[1] is pursued by Aristotle in his Metaphysics when he explains what is meant by τὸ ἀναγκαῖον. It is ... οὗ ἄνευ οὐκ ἐνδέχεται ζῆν ... and therefore "all that which is part of the *conditio sine qua non* of being and life"; it is ἐναντίον ... τῇ κατὰ τὴν προαίρεσιν κινήσει καὶ κατὰ τὸν λογισμόν, and therefore all that which is apart from the true fashioning of life and which constricts and opposes it.[2] Both these meanings are rooted in a

---

[1] If in the LXX ἀναγινώσκειν is sometimes used for קרא when this can only mean "to call" or "proclaim" (Jer. 3:12; 11:6; 19:2), this perhaps rests on the fact that ἀναγινώσκειν already has the sense of cultic reading.

[2] Deissmann LO, 379.

ἀ ν α γ κ ά ζ ω κ τ λ. R. Hirzel, *Themis, Dike und Verwandtes* (1907), 426-428; R. Wünsch, *Sethianische Verfluchungstafeln* (1898), 94-96; Pauly-W., *s.v.* Ananke, I, 2057 f.; Str.-B., *Die Vorzeichen und Berechnung der Tage des Messias* (Excurs.), IV, 977 ff.; K. Benz, "Die ἐνεστῶσα ἀνάγκη in 1 K. 7:26," *Theol. u. Glaube*, 10 (1918), 388 ff.; P. Tischleder, "Nochmals die ἐνεστῶσα ἀνάγκη in 1 C. 7, 26," *ibid.*, 12 (1920), 225 ff.; Rohr, Hb. 33 ff. Def. ... τὸ δὲ ἀναγκαῖον καὶ ἀντίτυπον (*sc.* to the ἑκούσιον), παρὰ τὴν βούλησιν ὄν, τὸ περὶ τὴν ἁμαρτίαν ἂν εἴη καὶ ἀμαθίαν, ἀπείκασται δὲ τῇ κατὰ τὰ ἄγκη πορείᾳ, ὅτι δύσπορα καὶ τραχέα καὶ λάσια ὄντα ἴσχει τοῦ ἰέναι. ἐντεῦθεν οὖν ἴσως ἐκλήθη ἀναγκαῖον, τῇ διὰ τοῦ ἄγκους ἀπεικασθὲν πορείᾳ (Plat. Crat., 420d, e).

[1] No sure light is cast on the meaning by etymology. The Platonic definition quoted is of little worth. More probable is the connection with a Celtic word for "need" or "necessity"; cf. Walde-Pokorny, *Etym. Wört. d. indogerm. Sprachen*, I (1930), 60.

[2] The Platonic definition embraces only this part of the concept.

third and general meaning: τὸ μὴ ἐνδεχόμενον ἄλλως ἔχειν ἀναγκαῖόν φαμεν οὕτως ἔχειν, Metaph., IV, 5, p. 1015a, 20 ff.

Thus the different meanings of the terms are given. ἀνάγκη is compulsion or necessity and therefore the means of compulsion or oppression; ἀναγκαῖος is that which compels or makes necessary; ἀναγκάζω is to cause or compel someone in all the varying degrees from friendly pressure to forceful compulsion. [3]

In relation to the Greek and Hellenistic understanding of ἀνάγκη we have thus to take into account two different views. 1. As a *conditio sine qua non* it is recognised to be a cosmic principle. It has a divine character and is even a personification of the most forceful divinity of being. With the increasing rationalisation of Greek thinking it loses this character and becomes the rational concept of an immanent necessity. In Hellenism, *ananke* is identified with other deities and reemerges as a hypostasis or personified concept. κρατερὴ Ἀνάγκη controls being (Parmen. Fr., 8, 30, Diels, I, 157, 2). It is supreme power (κρεῖσσον οὐδὲν Ἀνάγκας ηὗρον, Eur. Alk., 965). In his myth of the hereafter in the Politeia Plato thinks of it as seated at the heart of the world (Resp., X, 616 ff.). It plays a great part in magic, e.g., ἐξορκίζω σε ... κατὰ τῆς Ἀνάγκης τῶν Ἀναγκαίων (Preis. Zaub., III, 120 f.). Its role is comparatively subordinate in the Hermetic literature: ... μέρη ἐστὶ <τοῦ> θεοῦ ... εἷμα<ρμένη> καὶ ἀνάγκη καὶ πρόνοια καὶ φύσις (Corp. Herm., XII, 21). What Philo says of the Chaldeans is true of the Greek world generally: εἱμαρμένην τε καὶ ἀνάγκην θεοπλαστήσαντες (Migr. Abr., 179). *Ananke* is thus a force which defies all knowledge, which controls all things and which conditions reality. 2. In the cosmological dualism of spirit and matter it is felt to be a constraint which is opposed to and resists the spirit. The rise of the world is conceivable only ἐξ ἀνάγκης τε καὶ νοῦ συστάσεως (Plat. Tim., 48a). [4] From ἀνάγκη derive the many different ἀνάγκαι: ἐρωτικαὶ ἀνάγκαι (Plat. Resp., V, 458d); αἱ τῆς φύσεως ἀνάγκαι (Aristoph. Nu., 1075; Philo Jos., 264; Leg. All., III, 151). These are hindrances to the soul. The main point in ethical and religious life is to control them and to bring them under the dominion of reason. The final basis of ἀνάγκη is the destiny of death (ὁ ἀναγκαῖος τρόπος, Eur. Herc. Fur., 282 f.). Of the immortal soul after physical death it may be said: ... ψυχῇ μηκέτι ταῖς σώματος ἀνάγκαις ἐνδεδεμένῃ (Philo Jos., 264).

The situation of man as thus understood may be described in terms of ἀνάγκη. The so-called Mithras Liturgy from the great Paris magic papyrus speaks of ἐνεστῶσα καὶ κατεπείγουσά με πικρὰ ἀνάγκη (Preis. Zaub., IV, 526 f.), and the reference is obviously to the natural situation of man.

Both in the OT and Josephus ἀνάγκη has the meaning of constraint. In the OT it is usually a rendering of צַר, צָרָה, a word which expresses narrowness and constraint. In contrast to the Greek and Hellenistic understanding, however, the situation of constraint does not lie in the natural condition produced by the dualism of spirit and matter, but in the afflictions and oppressions, divinely caused and interpreted as divine visitations, either of the people or of individuals in the form of

---

[3] On the individual meanings, cf. the lexicons.
[4] Cf. the very similar view of Philo with regard to the individual: ... ἄνωθεν ἀπ' οὐρανοῦ καταβὰς ὁ νοῦς ἐνδεθῇ ταῖς σώματος ἀνάγκαις (Rer. Div. Her., 274).

persecution, enmity, subjugation or sickness. It is in this sense that ἀνάγκη is used both in the OT and in Jos. (Bell., 5, 571; cf. also Test. Jos. 2:4). The meaning of ἀνάγκαι for the individual Israelite is made clear by the following verse : καὶ ἔκραξαν πρὸς κύριον ἐν τῷ θλίβεσθαι αὐτούς, καὶ ἐκ τῶν ἀναγκῶν αὐτῶν ἔσωσεν αὐτούς. καὶ ἐξήγαγεν αὐτοὺς ἐκ σκότους καὶ ἐκ σκιᾶς θανάτου καὶ τοὺς δεσμοὺς αὐτῶν διέρρηξεν (ψ 106:13 f.). When Zephaniah speaks of a ἡμέρα θλίψεως καὶ ἀνάγκης, his reference is to the day of Yahweh as a day of judgment (1:15).

Apocalyptic and Rabbinic theology speaks expressly of a Messianic tribulation known as the "sorrows of the Messiah." This tribulation consists in "commotion and war, pestilence and hunger, scarcity and famine, apostasy from God and His Torah, the inversion of all moral orders, the failure of even the laws of nature."[5] Cf. also the enumeration of ἀνάγκαι (צָרָה), given by R. Akiba in S. Nu., 76 on 10:9 :[6] "And when you go to war against the enemy who oppresses you (הַצַּר הַצֹּרֵר), and blow the alarm with the trumpet, you shall be remembered (i.e., helped) before God." He expounds as follows : "I have (there) only war, drought, failure of crops, and whence is difficulty in childbirth or helplessness in a storm at sea ? We find instruction in the phrase עַל הַצַּר הַצֹּרֵר (understood pleonastically): In face of every emergency (צָרה = ἀνάγκη) we should blow the trumpets and thus invoke God's aid that it should not afflict the community."

B. ἀναγκ- in the NT.

In the NT, as in the OT, there is no deification of ἀνάγκη. Recognition of God as Creator and Preserver of the world leaves no room for this. Except in so far as the general meanings already noted are conveyed, ἀνάγκη is used in the NT as in the OT.

1. It expresses a situation of need : a. the Messianic tribulation, Lk. 21:23 : ἔσται γὰρ ἀνάγκη μεγάλη ἐπὶ τῆς γῆς ... ; b. such afflictions as those experienced by the apostle Paul, or afflictions which derive from the tension between the new creation in Christ and the old cosmos (2 C. 12:10; 6:4; 1 Th. 3:7), or the afflictions of the community (1 C. 7:26)[7] which consist in the same tension as characterises the Christian situation.

2. At one point Paul uses ἀνάγκη to describe his apostolic office : ἀνάγκη γάρ μοι ἐπίκειται (1 C. 9:16). In this office Paul has the same experience as the prophets ; he is under a divine constraint[8] which he cannot escape. The content

---

[5] Cf. Str.-B., IV, 977 ff.

[6] Cf. K. G. Kuhn, Sifre Nu., 195.

[7] ἐνεστῶσα is "present" distress ; cf., e.g., the parallel expressions βοηθεῖν τῇ ἐνεστώσῃ ἀνάγκῃ, 3 Macc. 1:16; Preis. Zaub., IV, 526 f.; and finally κατὰ ... τὸ ἐνεστὸς κλωθώ, Ps.-Aristot. Mund., 7, p. 401b, 21.

[8] Contemporary Judaism knows the same divine constraint in its religious life : ... οὐδεμίαν ἀνάγκην βιαιοτέραν εἶναι νομίζομεν τῆς πρὸς τὸν νόμον ἡμῶν εὐπειθείας (4 Macc. 5:16); ... τὴν κατὰ τούτους (sc. νόμους) παραδεδομένην εὐσέβειαν ἔργον ἀναγκαιότατον παντὸς τοῦ βίου πεποιημένοι (Jos. Ap., 1, 60).

of this compulsion is that a part of the divine plan of salvation is committed to him, and its seriousness consists in the fact that he cannot evade it if he is not to bring on himself the woe of eternal perdition.

3. ἀνάγκη is used to denote the divine order of the world and its subjection to law (R. 13:5; Mt. 18:7) in the sense : It is necessary, or it must be.

Grundmann

ἀνάγνωσις → 343	ἀναδείκνυμι → δείκνυμι
ἀναζάω → ζωή	ἀνάθεμα,
ἀνακαινίζω,	ἀναθεματίζω, ἀνάθημα → ἀνατίθημι
ἀνακαινόω, ἀνακαίνωσις → καινός	ἀνακαλύπτω → καλύπτω
ἀνάκειμαι → κεῖμαι	ἀνακεφαλαιόω → κεφαλή
ἀνακράζω → κράζω	ἀναλαμβάνω, ἀνάλημψις → λαμβάνω
ἀνακρίνω, ἀνάκρισις → κρίνω	

---

† ἀναλογία

ἀνάλογος : corresponding to λόγος, or concurring with a given factor. Hence ἀναλογία, the "correspondence of a right relationship," or "proportion." κατὰ τὴν ἀναλογίαν (Plat. Polit., 257b; P. Flor., I, 50, 91 = κατὰ (τὸ) ἀνάλογον : P. Amh., II, 85, 17 f.; Philo Virt., 95 : legal fees κατὰ τὸ ἀνάλογον τῆς κτήσεως. Field, Hexapla on Lv. 27:18 Alius : [1] κατὰ ἀναλογίαν τῶν ἐτῶν τῶν ὑπολειφθέντων (LXX : ἐπὶ τὰ ἔτη τὰ ἐπίλοιπα).

In the NT statement in R. 12:6 it is clear at least that in its representative the χάρισμα τῆς προφητείας should stand in right "correspondence" to πίστις : κατὰ ἀναλογίαν τῆς πίστεως. The → πίστις which underlies this correspondence, however, is not the *regula fidei* of the objective content of Christian faith or the doctrine of faith (*quae creditur*). [2] This is proved beyond dispute by the parallelism both of ἑκάστῳ ὁ θεὸς ἐμέρισεν μέτρον [3] πίστεως (v. 3) and of κατὰ τὴν χάριν

ἀ ν α λ ο γ ί α. [1] Field, I, 217.
[2] For champions of this old and widespread view, cf. Meyer and B. Weiss, R. *ad loc.*
[3] syP uses the same word for ἀναλογία (v. 6) and μέτρον (v. 3). Cf. also Plat. Tim., 69b : ἀνάλογα καὶ ξύμμετρα.

τὴν δοθεῖσαν ἡμῖν (v. 6). Only the believer can exercise the χάρισμα; the power of the χάρισμα stands in ἀναλογία to the power of the faith appropriate to each. This is true of all χαρίσματα. But in others, e.g., the healing of the sick, the correspondence is externally visible, since the power of the χάρισμα disappears with the cessation of faith. In the case of προφητεία, however, which needs other special tests of its genuineness (1 C. 12:10; 14:29), there is the inherent temptation to exercise it without πίστις. [4] The reminder is thus needed that it is truly possible only κατὰ ἀναλογίαν πίστεως.

Kittel

ἀνάλυσις, ἀναλύω → λύω   ἀναμάρτητος → 333 ff.

---

† ἀνάμνησις, † ὑπόμνησις

ἀνάμνησις means "remembrance" or "recollection." Synon. ὑπόμνησις; cf. Philo Plant., 108. ἀνάμνησις is philosophically distinguished from μνήμη ("memory") as the "reliving of vanished impressions by a definite act of will" [1]: cf. Plat. Phileb., 34b; Leg., V, 732b: ἀνάμνησις δ' ἐστὶν ἐπιρροὴ φρονήσεως ἀπολειπούσης; Aristot. Hist. An., I, 1, p. 488b, 88; Philo Leg. All., III, 91-93; Congr., 39 f.; Virt., 176; *Berliner Klassikertexte*, 2 (1905), Index, *s.v.* ἀνάμνησις. The active element in ἀνάμνησις (ποιεῖν ... ἀνάμνησιν, e.g., burial inscription in Nicomedia from the imperial period) [2] leads on from the signification of a. "recollection in the consciousness" (Philo Vit. Mos., I, 21; Congr., 111; 1 Cl., 53. 1; Just. Ap., 44, 11) to that of b. "recollection by word" or "commemoration" (*commemoratio*), Lys. Or. 2, 39: θυσιῶν ἀναμνήσεις, and c. "recollection by act," i.e., "an action whereby the object is re-presented in memory" [3] (cf. Nu. 10:10, where זִכָּרוֹן before God is accomplished by the blowing of trumpets; and Wis. 16:6).

Hb. 10:3: ἐν αὐταῖς (ταῖς θυσίαις) ἀνάμνησις ἁμαρτιῶν κατ' ἐνιαυτόν, "by them there is a remembrance again made of sins every year." The annual sin offerings made on the day of atonement are inadequate to remove sins (v. 1 f.), but serve rather to remind of them by the very fact that they are offered. To the members of the community they make sins present *in actu* as a hindrance to

---

[4] Cf. Zn. R. *ad loc.*
ἀνάμνησις κτλ. [1] Trench, 38, n. 1.
[2] B. Laum, *Stiftungen in der griechischen u. römischen Antike*, II (1914), 141, No. 203.
[3] Bchm. 1 C., 369.

fellowship with God. This estimate of the sacrifice of the day of atonement is wholly opposed to the Jewish view in spite of Nu. 5:15: θυσία μνημοσύνου ἀναμιμνήσκουσα ἁμαρτίαν (cf. Jub. 34:19; Philo Vit. Mos., II, 107: [of the sacrifices of the unrighteous] οὐ λύσιν ἁμαρτημάτων, ἀλλ᾽ ὑπόμνησιν ἐργάζονται, Plant., 108). [4]

1 C. 11:24 (Lk. 22:19 𝔥𝔎): τοῦτο ποιεῖτε εἰς τὴν ἐμὴν ἀνάμνησιν, v. 25: τοῦτο ποιεῖτε, ὁσάκις ἐὰν πίνητε, εἰς τὴν ἐμὴν ἀνάμνησιν. Christians are to enact (→ ποιέω) the whole action of the Lord's Supper — this is the reference of the twofold τοῦτο — in recollection of Jesus, and this not merely in such sort that they simply remember, but rather, in accordance with the active sense of ἀνάμνησις and the explanation in v. 26, in such a way that they actively fulfil the ἀνάμνησις. The making present by the later community of the Lord who instituted the Supper, and who put the new → διαθήκη into effect by His death, is the goal and content of their action in which they repeat what was done by Jesus and His disciples on the eve of His crucifixion. [5]

Linguistically εἰς ἀνάμνησιν = לְהַזְכִּיר; ψ 37 tit.; ψ 69 tit.; Wis. 16:6; Just. Dial., 27:4; Lv. 24:7 for לְאַזְכָּרָה, whereas in Ex. 12:14, where the Passover is appointed a day of remembrance of deliverance from Egypt, לְזִכָּרוֹן is rendered μνημόσυνον. Materially, we may refer to the endowment of a feast of the dead εἰς τὴν ἡμῶν τε καὶ Μητροδώρου μνήμην in the testament of Epicurus in Diog. L, X, 18. [6] On anamnesis as an act of recollection of the death of Christ in the celebration of the eucharist in the early Church, [7] cf. already Just. Dial., 41, 1: εἰς ἀνάμνησιν τοῦ πάθους; 70, 4: περὶ τοῦ ἄρτου ὃν παρέδωκεν ... ὁ ... Χριστὸς ποιεῖν εἰς ἀνάμνησιν τοῦ τε σωματοποιήσασθαι αὐτὸν διὰ τοὺς πιστεύοντας εἰς αὐτόν, δι᾽ οὓς καὶ παθητὸς γέγονε, καὶ περὶ τοῦ ποτηρίου, ὃ εἰς ἀνάμνησιν τοῦ αἵματος αὐτοῦ παρέδωκεν εὐχαριστοῦντας ποιεῖν; 117, 3: ἐπ᾽ ἀναμνήσει τῆς τροφῆς αὐτῶν ..., ἐν ᾗ καὶ τοῦ πάθους ... μέμνηνται.

ὑπόμνησις in 2 Tm. 1:5; 2 Pt. 1:13; 3:1 [8] is substantially identical with ἀνάμνησις in the active sense.

Behm

---

[4] Rgg., Wnd. on Hb. 10:3.
[5] Bchm. 1 C. 368 f.; Ltzm. 1 C. ad loc.; D. Stone, DCG, II, 74a; cf. Sickbg., 1 C., 54.
[6] Older examples of such endowments are given by Ltzm. 1 C., 93 f.
[7] G. P. Wetter, Altchristl. Liturgien : Das christliche Mysterium (1921), 66 ff., 143 ff.; F. J. Dölger, ΙΧΘΥΣ, II (1922), 549 ff.; H. Lietzmann, Messe u. Herrenmahl (1926), 50 ff.; O. Casel, Jahrbuch für Liturgiewissenschaft, 6 (1926), 113 ff.
[8] Wbg., Past., 274, n. 1 is only true up to a point.

ἀνανεόω → νέος   ἀνάξιος → ἄξιος

ἀναπαύω, ἀνάπαυσις,
ἐπαναπαύω

(→ καταπαύω, κατάπαυσις).

† ἀναπαύω.

a. "to cause to cease," Hom. Il., 17, 550; Gr. Sir. 18:16; mid. "to cease with something," Xenoph. An., IV, 2, 4. b. "to give someone rest" or "to refresh someone," Xenoph. Cyrop., VII, 1, 4; LXX 2 Βασ. 7:11; 1 Ch. 22:18; Prv. 29:17; Gr. Sir., 3:6; Mark Lit., 129, 11 (Brightman); mid. "to rest from something," Plat. Critias, 106a; LXX Est. 9:16 (ἀπὸ τῶν πολεμίων). c. mid. "to rest," LXX Ex. 32, 12; of the dead, Gr. Sir. 22:11; IG, XIV, 1717; Act. Andr., 15 (83, 7); Anth. Pal., 12, 50; d. mid. "to remain at rest," LXX Da. 12:13. e. mid. "to rest on" (→ ἐπαναπαύομαι), LXX Is. 11:2 (the permanent resting of the Spirit of God in distinction from temporally limited filling with the Spirit); Cl. Al. Ecl. Proph., 56, 6 f.; Iambl. Comm. Math. Scient., 8, p. 33 (of the shadow).

In the NT ἀναπαύειν sometimes means corporal rest (c) in the usual sense, as in Mk. 6:31: ἀναπαύσασθε ὀλίγον; Mk. 14:41: καθεύδετε τὸ λοιπὸν καὶ ἀναπαύεσθε; Lk. 12:19: ἀναπαύου φάγε πίε (reproachfully in the last two cases). More commonly it denotes the refreshment (b) of the inner man, [1] as in 1 C. 16:18: ἀνέπαυσαν γὰρ τὸ ἐμὸν πνεῦμα; Phlm. 20: ἀνάπαυσόν μου τὰ σπλάγχνα pass.; 2 C. 7:13: ἀναπέπαυται τὸ πνεῦμα αὐτοῦ; Phlm. 7: τὰ σπλάγχνα τῶν ἁγίων ἀναπέπαυται. In Rev. it us used in relation to the hereafter, as in 14:13: ἀναπαήσονται [2] ἐκ τῶν κόπων αὐτῶν, to rest (b) from their labours; 6:11: ἵνα ἀναπαύσωνται ἔτι χρόνον μικρόν, to tarry at rest (d), to await. In 1 Pt. 4:14 the Spirit of God is the subject: τὸ πνεῦμα θεοῦ ἐφ᾽ ὑμᾶς ἀναπαύεται (e). Finally, in Mt. 11:28 the word comprehends the whole saving work of Jesus [3] (b; → ἀνάπαυσις b.).

† ἀνάπαυσις.

a. "Cessation" or "interruption," Plut. Lib. Educ., 13 (II, 9c); b. "rest," common in the LXX, Gr. Sir. 6:28, cf. 51:27, promised to the disciple of wisdom; Gr. Sir. 30:17 variant; 38:23, rest of the dead. c. "place of rest" (like ἀνάπαυμα), LXX Gn. 8:9; Nu. 10:33; Gr. Sir. 24:7, sought by wisdom; Ru. 3:1; [1] d. "day of rest" (Sabbath), Jos. Ap., 2, 174.

In place of the rest promised to the Jewish disciple of wisdom, Mt. 11:28 f., while it retains the older form of promise, emphatically sets the genuine rest (d)

ἀ ν α π α ύ ω. Schl. Mt., 385 f.
[1] Str.-B., III, 486; Plot. Enn., VI, 9:9 . ἀναπαύεται ψυχή.
[2] On the form, cf. Winer (Schmiedel) § 13, 9; Bl.-Debr. § 78.
[3] How slight is the connection here with the Rabbinic conception of the Messiah is shown by Str.-B., I, 607.
ἀ ν ά π α υ σ ι ς. Schl. Mt., 388; Dausch, Synopt. on Mt. 11:28 f.
[1] Cf. E. L. Hicks, JHSt., 12 (1891), 230.

which Jesus brings with the Gospel. To this rest are invited whose who in truth have found in Judaism only a burden (→ φορτίον, ζυγός) and no rest, Mt. 11:29 : εὑρήσετε ἀνάπαυσιν ταῖς ψυχαῖς ὑμῶν (11:28 → ἀναπαύομαι). In Rev. 4:8, cf. 14:11: ἀνάπαυσιν οὐκ ἔχουσιν ἡμέρας καὶ νυκτός means without cessation (a). Mt. 12:43 : ζητοῦν ἀνάπαυσιν means seeking a place of rest (c).

Cf. Ev. Naz. (Jer. on Is. 11:2), where the words of the Holy Ghost at the baptism of Jesus are as follows : Fili mi, in omnibus prophetis exspectabam te, ut venires et requiescerem in te. Tu enim es requies mea ...

† ἐπαναπαύω.

A late and rare word. Act. Ju. 16:26 A : ἐπανάπαυσόν με, synon. with ἄφες; elsewhere only in Ael. Nat. An., V, 56 and Procop. Gaz. (v. Ps.-Choricius, [1] ed. Boissonade, p. 170) in the sense of mid. a. Mid. a. "to rest on" (→ ἀναπαύω e.), Jos. Ant., 8, 84; LXX Is. 11:2 א Nu. 11:25 f. : ἐπανεπαύσατο τὸ πνεῦμα ἐπ᾽ αὐτούς. b. "to lean on," LXX 1 Macc. 8:12 : μετὰ δὲ τῶν φίλων αὐτῶν καὶ τῶν ἐπαναπαυομένων αὐτοῖς; Mi. 3:11: ἐπὶ τὸν κύριον ἐπανεπαύοντο. Cf. Epict. Diss., I, 9, 9 : τὸν δὲ φιλόσοφον ἡμῖν δεήσει ἄλλοις θαρροῦντα καὶ ἐπαναπαυόμενον ἀποδημεῖν.

Lk. 10:6 : ἐπαναπαήσεται ἐπ᾽ αὐτὸν ἡ εἰρήνη ὑμῶν, "to rest" (a); Ev. Hebr. (Cl. Al. Strom., II, 9, 45, 5; V, 14, 96, 3): ὁ βασιλεύσας ἐπαναπαήσεται, "to give oneself to rest" (a); R. 2:17: εἰ δὲ ἐπαναπαύῃ νόμῳ, "if thou restest in thy possession of the Law" (b).

Bauernfeind

ἀναπληρόω → πληρόω

ἀνασταυρόω → σταυρός

ἀνάστασις → ἀνίστημι

ἀναστρέφω, ἀναστροφή → στρέφω

ἀνατέλλω, ἀνατολή

---

† ἀνατέλλω.

Trans. "to cause to come forth or arise"; intrans. "to come forth or arise." This general meaning varies according to the relevant subject. There is no difference in this respect between Christian and secular usage. Aesch. Fr., 300 (Nauck, cf. Gn. 3:18) στάχυς; Pind. Isthm., 6, 75 ὕδωρ; 1 Cl., 20, 4 τροφή; Dg., 12, 1 ξύλον; LXX 2 Ch. 26:19 ἡ λέπρα; Lv. 13:37 θρίξ; Lk. 12:54 νεφέλη (rise); also abstr. ψ 71:7 δικαιοσύνη;

ἐπαναπαύω. [1] Cf. C. Kirsten, Quaestiones Choricianae, Bresl. phil. Abh., 7 (1895), 46 ff.

ἀνατέλλω κτλ. Str.-B., II, 113; A. Jacoby, Ἀνατολὴ ἐξ ὕψους, ZNW, 20 (1921), 205-214; F. J. Dölger, Sol salutis² (1925), 149 ff.

Philo Conf. Ling., 14 etc.; persons: ἀνέτειλε σωτήρ Epigr. Gr., 978; but mostly light: Mt. 4:16 = ψ 96:11; the stars LXX Job 3:9; Is. 14:12; Aristid., 4, 2; 6, 3; the sun Hdt., I, 204; IV, 40; LXX Gn. 32:31; Gr. Sir. 26:16; Mt. 5:45; 13:6; Mk. 16:2; Jm. 1:11. Preis. Zaub., IV (Paris), 2989 ff.

The Christian term ἀνατέλλειν is a translation of the subst. of צָמַח "to sprout" (צֶמַח "sprout"), and of זָרַח "to arise," and in connection with Jer. 23:5, Zech. 3:8 and 6:12 in the former case, and Nu. 24:17 (דָּרַךְ) [1] in the latter, it is used of the Messiah. In the process the two meanings merge, so that it is difficult to fix the precise sense. In Hb. 7:14: ἐξ 'Ιούδα ἀνατέταλκεν ὁ κύριος ἡμῶν, we must translate "sprout" or "spring forth" as in Test. G. 8 and Test. D. 5 (though in Test. Jud. 24 we have "arise"). Elsewhere, however, it is more in keeping with Christian usage to render "arise" or "shine forth" in relation to Christ: 2 Pt. 1:19; Ign. Mg., 9, 1: ἐν ᾗ (sc. ἡμέρᾳ) καὶ ἡ ζωὴ ἡμῶν (Christ = our life) ἀνέτειλεν δι' αὐτοῦ καὶ τοῦ θανάτου αὐτοῦ. Like Christ and the sun, the martyr, too, rises up to God (Ign. R., 2, 2).

Similarly in O. Sol. 7:15: "It shone forth in the son." On the other hand in O. Sol. 15:10 it is said of the Lord (i.e., the singer himself) as the sun (v. 1): "Immortal life grew in the land of the Lord." Cf. Lidz. Lit., 192: "The man of proven righteousness sprang forth and shone in the world."

† ἀνατολή.

1. The "rising of the stars": Eur. Phoen., 504; Plat. Polit., 269a; Mt. 2:2, 9; P. Tebt., 276, 38.

2. The "sunrise as a quarter of heaven," the "morning," or the "east." Sing. Rev. 7:2; 16:12; Act. Thom., 18 with ἡλίου; Rev. 21:13; 1 Cl., 10, 4; Mithr. Lit. (Dieterich), 4, 16 = Preis. Zaub., IV (Paris), 514; Act. Thom., 105. Anton. δύσις, 1 Cl., 5, 6: ἔν τε τῇ ἀνατολῇ καὶ ἐν τῇ δύσει. Plur. more common, Hdt., IV, 8; Polyb., II, 14, 4; Nu. 23:7 etc.; Mt. 2:1; 8:11; 24:27; Lk. 13:29 = "from the whole world." ἀνατολή = "the orient": Act. Thom., 108 ff.; Jos. Bell., 3, 3.

Often the east is the predominant quarter of the heavens in mostly a good but sometimes a bad sense. On the one side it is the location of Paradise acc. to Gn. 2:8; Eth. En. 32:2; of the Messiah, Sib., 3, 652; of the κυρία, Herm. v., 1, 4, 1 and 3; of the son of the king, the redeemed redeemer, Act. Thom., 108 ff. On the other side it is the point from which Antichrist comes (Act. Thom., 32) and the location of the headless demon (Test. Sol. 9:7 P). [1] In Rev. 7:2 ἀνατολή is the good locality from which there comes the angel with the seal, but in Rev. 16:12 it is the bad from which the kings proceed.

3. The term ἀνατολή is difficult to render in Lk. 1:78. In itself and according to the variously construed context, ἀνατολή ἐξ ὕψους might be equated with צֶמַח יהוה and rendered "Messiah of God." For in LXX Jer. 23:5 and Zech. 3:8 and 6:12 ἀνατολή is used for צֶמַח and on the basis of these passages this became

---

[1] Cf. BHK,² ad loc.

ἀνατολή. [1] On the antique conception, cf. Cl. Al. Protr., p. 80, 25 f. (= 11, 114, 4); Stählin in F. Boll, Aus der Offenbarung Joh. (1914), 20.

a name for the Messiah in the Synagogue. Yet it might also mean a "star shining from heaven." This usage is found in Philo Conf. Ling., 14, and in connection with Zech. 6:12 Philo understands the λόγος as ἀνατολή.[2] In favour of this view we might refer to v. 79, where ἀνατολή must be light (and not merely a bright shoot as צֶמַח might be). We might also refer to the exposition of Zech. 6:12 in Justin and Melito. Justin always understands the ἀνατολή of Zech. 6:12 (Dial., 100, 4; 106, 4; 121, 2; 126, 1) in terms of the ἀνατέλλειν of LXX Nu. 24:17, so that for him the advent of Christ is the rising of a star. And Melito construes Lk. 1:78 as follows: καὶ μόνος ἥλιος οὗτος ἀνέτειλεν ἀπ᾽ οὐρανοῦ. The visitation of the mercy of God has come with the dawn of heavenly light in the Messiah Christ as the sun of the world.

Schlier

> ἀνατίθημι, προσανατίθημι,
> ἀνάθεμα, ἀνάθημα,
> κατάθεμα, ἀναθεματίζω,
> καταθεματίζω

† ἀνατίθημι († προσανατίθημι).

ἀνατίθημι is found in the NT only in the mid. with dat. of person and acc. of object; "to set forth, impart or communicate one's cause" (Ac. 25:14: τῷ βασιλεῖ ἀνέθετο τὰ κατὰ τὸν Π.); "to expound with the request for counsel, approval or decision" (Gl. 2:2: ἀνεθέμην αὐτοῖς τὸ εὐαγγέλιον).

This meaning and construction are alien to class. Gr. but common in the *koine*, e.g., Mi. 7:5; Plut. Amat. Narr., 2, 1 (II, 722d): τὴν πρᾶξιν ἀνέθετο τῶν ἑταίρων τισίν; Alciphr. Ep., 3, 23, 2: πρὸς σὲ ὡς φίλον ἀναθέσθαι τὸ καινὸν τοῦτο ... φάσμα; P. Par., 69 D, 23: ἀναθέμενοι τὸ πρᾶγμα ἀκέραιον; Act. Barn., 4 (293, 10, Bonnet): ἀνεθέμην τὰ μυστήρια.

Anal. is προσανατίθημι mid. (originally "to present one's cause, i.e., something of oneself, to another"). Gl. 1:16: οὐ προσανεθέμην σαρκὶ καὶ αἵματι, "I did not expound it to men (→ αἷμα, 172 f.) for their approval or submit it to their judgment." Also Gl. 2:6: ἐμοὶ οἱ δοκοῦντες οὐδὲν προσανέθεντο, "Those who seemed to be somewhat did not impart anything to me,[1] i.e., submit anything to my consideration or judgment." Only Paul gave an account and asked for decision (2:2); there was no question of the leaders of the first community giving any account to him or making him their (partial?) judge.[2]

---

[2] Cf. the inscription on a gem: εἷς Ζεὺς Σάραπις, ἅγιον ὄνομα, σαβαώ, φῶς, ἀνατολή, χθών in E. Peterson, Εἷς Θεός (1926), 238 and 238, n. 2, where ἀνατολή is the rising sun.

ἀνατίθημι κτλ. Cr.-Kö., 1059; Pr.-Bauer, 97; Nägeli, 45; Zn. Gl.³, 65, n. 78; 99 f.; J. Weiss, *Urchristentum* (1917), 202; E. de Witt Burton on Gl. 1:16 and 2:2, 6.

[1] Euthymius Zig. (Calogeras, I, 511): οὐδὲν προσεδίδαξάν με.

[2] Cf. Zn. (who appeals to Thdrt.) and J. Weiss, *ad loc.*

The usual rendering that they added nothing to him [3] is linguistically insecure and hardly fits the context, where there is no question of mere impartation (as distinct from Ac. 15:28). The meaning "to expound or recount with the desire for counsel or decision" is supported by Chrysipp. De Divinat. (II, 344, 31 ff., v. Arnim): ὄναρ ... προσανα-θέσθαι ὀνειροκρίτῃ; Diod. S., XVII, 116, 4 : τοῖς μάντεσι προσαναθέμενος (περὶ τοῦ σημείου); Luc. Jup. Trag., 1, 3 : ἐμοὶ προσανάθου, λαβέ με σύμβουλον πόνων. The meaning "to impose an additional burden" is not supported by Xenoph. Mem., II, 1, 8 : προσαναθέσθαι τὸ καὶ τοῖς ἄλλοις πολίταις ὧν δέονται πορίζειν, since here we really have the mid. "to take on an additional burden."

† ἀνάθεμα, † ἀνάθημα, † κατάθεμα.

ἀνάθεμα is a new Hell. constr. for the Att. ἀνάθημα with no change of meaning. [1] It denotes "something dedicated or consecrated to the deity." It is used a. of the consecrated offerings laid up in the temple : CIG, 2693d, 12; Plut. Pelop., 25, 7 (I, 291b); 2 Macc. 2:13; Jdt. 16:19 A; elsewhere in the LXX we have ἀνάθημα, cf. also Philo Migr. Abr., 98; Rer. Div. Her., 200. It is also used b. of "something delivered up to divine wrath, dedicated to destruction and brought under a curse." In the latter sense ἀνάθεμα (more rarely ἀνάθημα) is found only in IG, III, 3, App., XIVb, 17 (a table of curses from Megara dating from the 1st or 2nd century A.D.) [2] outside the LXX etc., where it is used for the Heb. חֵרֶם (Lv. 27:28 f.; Dt. 7:26; 13:17; Jos. 6:17 f.; 7:11 ff.; Zech. 14:11 etc.). What comes under the "ban" [3] is taken out of ordinary human circulation and given up to destruction. Hence in the LXX we find such variants for חֵרֶם as ἀπώλεια (Is. 34:5), ἐξολέθρευμα (1 Βασ. 15:21), ἐκθλιβή (Mi. 7:2) and ἀφόρισμα (Ez. 44:29).

1. In the NT it is used in the sense of offering only in Lk. 21:5, where the Jerusalem temple ἀναθήμασιν (אD ἀναθέμασιν) κεκόσμηται.

2. The Pauline use of ἀνάθεμα is along the lines of the LXX. For Paul the word denotes the object of a curse. 1 C. 12:3 : οὐδεὶς ἐν πνεύματι θεοῦ λαλῶν λέγει· ἀνάθεμα Ἰησοῦς, "Accursed be Jesus!" It would be a self-contradiction for the Christian pneumatic to curse Jesus, i.e., to deliver Him up to destruction by God. The curse formula is also used in 1 C. 16:22 : εἴ τις οὐ φιλεῖ τὸν κύριον, ἤτω ἀνάθεμα, cf. Gl. 1:8 : ἀνάθεμα ἔστω; R. 9:3 : ηὐχόμην ἀνάθεμα εἶναι αὐτὸς ἐγὼ ἀπὸ τοῦ Χριστοῦ, "I could wish myself accursed from Christ and expelled from fellowship with Him." The controlling thought here is that of the delivering up to the judicial wrath of God of one who ought to be ἀνάθεμα because of his sin. We can hardly think of an act of Church discipline, [4] since the apostle uses

---

[3] Still found in Ltzm. Gl.[3], 12.

ἀνάθεμα κτλ. L. Brun, Segen u. Fluch im Urchristentum (1931); Schenkel, I, 351 ff.; Heinrici, RE[3], I, 493 ff.; XXIII, 40 f.; Cr.-Kö., 1059 ff.; Pr.-Bauer, 84 f.; Zn. R.[3], 430 f.; Gl.[3], 50 f.; Sickbg., R. 248; 1 C., 87 f.

[1] Moeris, Lex, 188, 30, Bekker (1833); Moulton, 68; Bl.-Debr. § 109, 3; Ditt. Syll.[3], IV, 208 s.v. Artificial attempts at separation are of a later date (cf. Thdrt. on R. 9:3).

[2] On this point, cf. A. Deissmann, ZNW, 2 (1901), 342; LO, 74; Nägeli, 49; Moult.-Mill., 33. For indications of earlier non-Jewish use, cf. C. T. Newton, Essays on Art and Archaeology (1880), 193 f. On ἀνάθεμα in modern Gk. = a cursing cairn, v. Philol. Wochenschr., 46 (1926), 133.

[3] Cf. H. Gressmann, RGG,[2] I, 754 f.

[4] Cf. the use of excommunication in the Synagogue (→ ἀποσυνάγωγος) and the anathema of the later Church against heretics, which may be traced back to Gl. 1:8 f. and 1 C. 16:22.

the phrase ἀπὸ τοῦ Χριστοῦ (R. 9:3) and also considers that an angel from heaven (Gl. 1:8) or even Jesus Himself (1 C. 12:3) might be accursed. That he would willingly see himself separated from Christ and given up to divine judgment ὑπὲρ τῶν ἀδελφῶν μου τῶν συγγενῶν μου κατὰ σάρκα (R. 9:3) is a supreme expression of the readiness of Paul for redemptive self-sacrifice for the people which excludes itself from the divine revelation of salvation (Ex. 32:32).

ἀνάθεμα corresponds to the Rabb. אֲרוּר.[5] For the thought of R. 9:3, cf. Neg., 2, 1: "The children of Israel — I will be an expiation for them אֲנִי כַּפָּרָתָן,"and other passages [6] where we do not have the חֵרֶם of the Synagogue ban. [7] Cf. also Jos. Bell., 5, 9: λάβετε μισθὸν τῆς ἑαυτῶν σωτηρίας τοὐμὸν αἷμα· κἀγὼ θνῄσκειν ἕτοιμος, εἰ μετ' ἐμὲ σωφρονεῖν μέλλετε.

Equivalent to ἀνάθεμα is the κατάθεμα of Rev. 22:3 (= Zech. 14:11, though this has ἀνάθεμα): καὶ πᾶν κατάθεμα οὐκ ἔσται ἔτι, there will no longer be "anything accursed" in the New Jerusalem, the Paradise of the last time (as there was in the shattered first Paradise according to Gn. 3:17 ff.). Cf. Did., 16, 5: σωθήσονται ὑπ' αὐτοῦ τοῦ καταθέματος, i.e., from Christ Himself, the Accursed (Gl. 3:13), believers will receive the blessing of salvation in the last days.

The rare κατάθεμα, which is probably another and sharper form of ἀνάθεμα (the κατα-frequently indicating a hostile influence), or which may be a contraction of κατανάθεμα, is not found outside early Christian texts (Act. Phil., 28, 15, 12, Bonnet) except on a Cyprian magic tablet of the 3rd century A.D.: θάψατε τὸν προγεγραμμένον ἐπὶ τοῦδε τοῦ φιμωτικοῦ καταθέματος = curse (Audollent Def. Tab., 22, 23; cf. IG, III, 3, p. XVII). There is an artificial distinction between ἀνάθεμα and κατάθεμα in Ps.-Just., Quaest. et Resp. ad Orth., 121 (III, 2³ [1881] 198, Otto). [8]

3. In Ac. 23:14: ἀναθέματι ἀνεθεματίσαμεν ἑαυτούς, ἀνάθεμα has the significance of a curse in the sense of a vow or solemn obligation the breach of which will bring under the ban (cf. infra).

† ἀναθεματίζω, † καταθεματίζω.

"To bring under the ἀνάθεμα," "to curse." Of the oath taken by the Jews against the life of Paul in Ac. 23:12, 21: ἀνεθεμάτισαν ἑαυτούς, we read in v. 14: ἀναθέματι ἀνεθεματίσαμεν ἑαυτούς (→ supra), "they accursed themselves," or "wished for themselves the curse of God," or "declared their lives forfeit," if they did not bend every effort to fulfil their voluntarily accepted obligation to kill Paul. Again, it is said of Peter in Mk. 14:71: ἤρξατο ἀναθεματίζειν καὶ ὀμνύναι; ἀναθεματίζειν is here intentionally left without object to denote both that he curses himself if he lies and also the people if they make out that he is a disciple. [1] In the parallel passage in Mt. 26:74 we have καταθεματίζειν in the same sense. [2]

---

[5] Str.-B., III, 446.
[6] Ibid., 261.
[7] Ibid., IV, 327 ff.; Schürer, II, 507 f.
[8] Cf. Bryennios in A. v. Harnack, Die Lehre der 12 Apostel (1884), 63 (n. on 16, 5).
ἀναθεματίζω κτλ. Cr.-Kö., 1061.
[1] Wbg. Mk., 365, n. 31; cf. Schl. Mt., 764.
[2] On κατάθεμα → supra. καταθεματίζω is not found in the LXX, but only in Christian

ἀναθεματίζειν, strengthened by ἀναθέματι in Dt. 13:15 and 20:17, is often used in the LXX for the Heb. הֶחֱרִים (perhaps also on the curse tablet of Megara, IG, III, 3, App. XIII f.: a5 and 8 and b8), but never of conditional self-cursing. There is a par. to Ac. 23:14 in Tanch. בלק § 30, p. 149, Buber, where Pinchas the zealot resolves to catch the wrongdoer Zimri red-handed and destroy him : "Then he stood forth from the assembly, i.e., the Sanhedrin, which was discussing the possibility of condemning Simri to death, and made the vow (ונתנדב)."

Behm

ἀναφέρω → φέρω   ἀνάψυξις → ψυχή
ἀνδρίζομαι → ἀνήρ

---

† ἀνέγκλητος

This term denotes a person or thing against which there can be no ἔγκλημα and which is thus "free from reproach," "without stain," "guiltless" ; cf.: ... ἀνεγκλήτους γὰρ δεῖ τὰς οὐσίας πρὸς ἀλλήλους κατασκευάζεσθαι, Plat. Leg., V, 737a. Plutarch relates of Epicurus that he pledged himself μὴ καταλιπεῖν ἀνέγκλητον τὴν κακίαν, while ἡ μὲν γὰρ κακία πάντως ἀνέγκλητός ἐστι κατὰ τὸν τοῦ Χρυσίππου λόγον, Stoic. Rep., 34 f. (II, 1049 f.). The word is common in everyday speech and thus comes to be more formal, e.g. : ἀνέγκλητον ἐχέτω τὴν ἑτερογνωμοσύνην, Jos. Ant., 10, 281. It is found in assertions of guilt or innocence, as in the sparing of Samaria by Varus διὰ τὸ ἀνέγκλητον ἐν τοῖς νεωτερισμοῖς εἶναι, Jos. Ant., 17, 289, and also in the same sense in 3 Macc. 5:31: ἀντὶ τῶν ἀνεγκλήτων ... Ἰουδαίων. The papyri esp. prove its common use, e.g. : θεραπεύειν ἀνεγκλήτως ("without blame"), P. Magd., 15, 3 (3rd century A.D.); ἵνα ἀνέγκλητος ὢν ("irreproachable") τὸν βίον ἔχω, P. Soc., 541, 6 (3rd century B.C.); ... ὄντος μου αὐτῶι ἀνεγκλήτου ("blameless"), BGU, 1347, 8 (2nd century B.C.). [1]

1. In the NT there are three examples of ordinary usage in the Pastorals. In Tt. 1:6 it is demanded that Titus should see to it in presbyters : εἴ τίς ἐστιν ἀνέγκλητος ... δεῖ γὰρ τὸν ἐπίσκοπον ἀνέγκλητον εἶναι ὡς θεοῦ οἰκονόμον (v. 7). The predicates which follow show us that in relation to these offices we have a demand for the blamelessness (in the sense of civic ethics) which they must have for their work as that of a θεοῦ οἰκονόμος. In 1 Tm. the same demand is made in relation to deacons : καὶ οὗτοι δὲ δοκιμαζέσθωσαν πρῶτον, εἶτα διακονείτωσαν ἀνέγκλητοι ὄντες (3:10).

2. The word has a religious character in two other instances in Paul : ... καὶ βεβαιώσει ὑμᾶς ἕως τέλους ἀνεγκλήτους ἐν τῇ ἡμέρᾳ τοῦ κυρίου ἡμῶν Ἰησοῦ [Χριστοῦ] (1 C. 1:8); νυνὶ δὲ ἀποκατήλλαξεν ... παραστῆσαι ὑμᾶς ἁγίους καὶ ἀμώμους καὶ ἀνεγκλήτους κατενώπιον αὐτοῦ (Col. 1:22). The situation of the

---

writers (Iren., I, 13, 4; 16, 3; Act. Phil., 17 (9, 23, Bonnet) ═ καταναθεματίζω (Just. Dial., 47). Dubious reflections on the difference between ἀναθεματίζειν in Mk. 14:71 and καταθεματίζειν in Mt. 26:74 may be found in Ps.-Just. Quaest. et Resp. ad Orth., 121 (III, 2³ [1881], 196, Otto).

ἀ ν έ γ κ λ η τ ο ς. [1] For further examples, *v.* Preisigke Wört., *s.v.*

last judgment is in view.[2] In it Christians will stand as such, and they will be ἀνέγκλητοι even before God. They are this in Jesus Christ. Yet this is not the whole story. 1 C. 1:8 includes a movement which finds its τέλος at the last judgment (βεβαιώσει ὑμᾶς ἕως τέλους), and Col. 1:22 stands under a νυνί. "This Now reaches to the day of Christ. As the work of reconciliation will only then come to fulfilment, so also the work of this representation. It is thus a Now as seen from the standpoint of God, before whom even the time which still runs on to the parousia is eternally present."[3] On the basis of the justification effected by the death and resurrection of Christ, Christians are spotless and irreproachable before God. No accusation can be brought against them. This will be disclosed at the last judgment. In this declaration we have a clear expression of the power of grace creating a wholly new situation. How the ἀνέγκλητος is to be understood is made perfectly plain by the question of R. 8:33 f. : τίς ἐγκαλέσει κατὰ ἐκλεκτῶν θεοῦ; θεὸς ὁ δικαιῶν; τίς ὁ κατακρινῶν; Χριστὸς Ἰησοῦς ὁ ἀποθανών, μᾶλλον δὲ ἐγερθείς, ὅς ἐστιν ἐν δεξιᾷ τοῦ θεοῦ, ὃς καὶ ἐντυγχάνει ὑπὲρ ἡμῶν. No reproach can be made against Christians. The presupposition according to 1 C. 1:8 is the help of God : ὃς βεβαιώσει ὑμᾶς, or according to Col. 1:22 : εἴ γε ἐπιμένετε τῇ πίστει τεθεμελιωμένοι καὶ ἑδραῖοι καὶ μὴ μετακινούμενοι ἀπὸ τῆς ἐλπίδος τοῦ εὐαγγελίου, i.e., a life of faith willed and effected by God.

Grundmann

ἀνεκτός → ἀνέχω   ἀνελεήμων, ἀνέλεος → ἔλεος

---

† ἀνεξερεύνητος

ἀνεξερεύνητος (or ἀνεξεραύνητος in post-classical Gk.)[1] means "inscrutable" (Heracl. Fr., 18 [Diels, I, 81, 17], of the way to the mystery), from ἐρευνάω "to track" (also of an animal) or "to search out." It is not found in the LXX.

It is used in R. 11:33 of the unsearchable mystery of God's way of judgment with Israel as this leads to grace. The exact connotation of the term implies the abandonment of all attempts to solve theoretically the question of the meaning of the judgment on Israel, so that Paul describes even his own answer as an attempt for which he cannot claim absolute validity.

Delling

---

[2] This is true in both passages, though Haupt Gefbr., 49 f. strongly maintains that the reference in Col. 1:22 is to the present. He fails to consider 1 C. 1:8, which is perfectly plain.
[3] Loh. Kol., 71.
ἀνεξερεύνητος. [1] On the change from ευ to αυ, cf. Bl.-Debr. § 30, 4 and Br. Olsson, *Papyrusbr.* (Diss. Uppsala, 1925), 65.

ἀνεξίκακος → κακός

---

† ἀνεξιχνίαστος

"Indetectable." Thus far this word has been found only in biblical and biblically dependent usage. [1] Suid. s.v. ἀνεξεύρητον οὖ μηδὲ ἴχνος ἐστὶν εὑρεῖν (p. 205, no. 2280, Adler), rightly emphasises the rhetorically mounting character of the construction. In the LXX we find the term in Job 5:9; 9:10; 34:24. It is also found in the apocr. Prayer of Manasses (Const. Apost., II, 22, 12 etc.). [2]

In the NT the word is used by Paul at R. 11:33 and Eph. 3:8. In the first passage the parallelism : ὡς ἀνεξερεύνητα τὰ κρίματα αὐτοῦ καὶ ἀνεξιχνίαστοι αἱ ὁδοὶ αὐτοῦ, suggests a poetic source. The terminology of the verse, however, indicates that this source was perhaps coloured by Gnostic terminology. [3] Eph. 3:8 : τὸ ἀνεξιχνίαστον πλοῦτος, points in the same direction, in conjunction with the verses which follow. In any context the term must be related to the divine οἰκονομία. [4]

The word was used by the Valentinians of the Πατήρ (Iren., I, 2, 2 : τὸ ἀνεξιχνίαστον τοῦ Πατρός), and it was also known to the Marcosites (Iren., I, 15, 5). In Iren., IV, 20, 5 : ὡς γὰρ τὸ μέγεθος αὐτοῦ ἀνεξιχνίαστον, οὕτως καὶ ἡ ἀγαθότης ἀνεξήγητος, the anti-Gnostic bias of the source of Iren. at this point [5] brings out even more clearly the connection with Gnosticism. Even the quotation from R. 11:33 in Iren., I, 10, 3 is linked with anti-Gnostic polemics. At an earlier period we find the term in 1 Cl., 20, 5 and Dg., 9, 5; cf. also Bas. Ep., 265, 1 (MPG, 32, p. 984b); Greg. Naz. Or. Theol., 2, 12 (MPG, 36, p. 40c). Its liturgical appearances are worth noting, e.g., in Sacrament. Serap., XIII, 2 (F. X. Funk, Didasc. et Constit. Apost., II [1905], p. 172, 6), Mark Lit., 137, 14 f. (Brightman), and the dependent Catal. Cod. Astr. Graec., VIII, 2 (1911), 156, 16. It plays a further role in the Eunomian controversy ; cf. Greg. Nyss. Eunom. MPG, 45, 604a and Beat. Or., 6, MPG, 44, 1268b and c, where it is said in reference to R. 11:33 : ἀνεξιχνιάστους τὰς ὁδοὺς αὐτοῦ ὁ μέγας ὀνομάζει ἀπόστο-

---

ἀνεξιχνίαστος. [1] It is to be noted that ἀνεξιχνίαστος, ἐξιχνιάζειν (for ἐξιχνεύειν) and ἐξιχνιασμός (for ἐξίχνευσις) are found only in the LXX. This indicates a common point of origin.

[2] Ps.-Callisth., II, 28, MS.C. (ed. C. Müller) causes Alexander the Gt. to revere μόνον ἕνα θεόν ἀθεώρητον, ἀνεξιχνίαστον. F. Pfister, "Eine jüdische Gründungsgeschichte Alexandrias" (SAH, phil.-hist. Kl., V, 1914, p. 4) has tried to trace back this chapter to a 1st century Jewish tradition. I do not think that he has proved his case. The textual evidence is against him, and when in II, 28 MS. C makes God out to be τρισαγίῳ φωνῇ δοξαζόμενον we can see the influence of the Byzantine liturgy (cf. Chrys. Lit., 369, 24, Brightman). Hence we cannot cite Ps.-Callisth., II, 28 as a Jewish example of the use of the word ἀνεξιχνίαστος. On the other hand it is very likely that in Const. Apost., VII, 35, 9, in the collection of Jewish prayers discovered by Bousset, we have an original use of the word and not a Christian interpolation as Bousset supposed (NGG, 1916, 440).

[3] E. Norden, Agnostos Theos (1913), 243, n. 3.

[4] We have reference to a βουλὴ ἀνεξιχνίαστος of God in the Gnostically coloured and related prayer given by C. Schmidt-W. Schubart, Altchr. Texte (1910), 113, 63 f.

[5] v. F. Loofs, "Theophilus von Antiochen Adversus Marcionem und die anderen theol. Quellen bei Iren.," TU, 46 (1930), 20.

λος, σημαίνων διὰ τοῦ λόγου τὸ ἀνεπίβατον εἶναι λογισμοῖς τὴν ὁδὸν ἐκείνην, ἢ πρὸς τὴν γνῶσιν τῆς θείας οὐσίας ἄγει.

Peterson

ἀνεπίλημπτος → λαμβάνω.
ἄνεσις → ἀνίημι.

---

† ἀνέχω, ἀνεκτός, ἀνοχή

In secular Gk. ἀνέχω is found with various shades of meaning in both act. and mid., trans. and intrans.[1] In the NT and related literature it occurs only in the mid., and in conjunction with ἀνεκτός and ἀνοχή it has two main senses.[2]

1. "To receive, take up, bear and endure." With a material object the reference is especially to receiving, e.g. the hearing of a word (Hb. 13:22; 2 Tm. 4:3; 2 C. 11:4), or more generally the receiving of τὰ σάββατα from God (Barn., 2, 5; 15, 8 = LXX Is. 1:13), of smell from men (2 Macc. 9:12), of punishment (Dg., 2, 9), of πάθη (4 Macc. 1:35 SR), of θλίψεις (2 Th. 1:4), of πάντα (1 Cl., 49, 5). More important are the cases when there is a personal object. Here the meaning ranges from accepting someone (2 C. 11:1, 19; Herm. m., 4, 4, 1) to the true bearing and taking to oneself of one's neighbour in the sense of tolerating his life. ἀνέχεσθαι is used of Jesus in this sense at Mk. 9:19 and par. in relation to the γενεὰ ἄπιστος. His being with men involves His putting up with them. In Eph. 4:2 and Col. 3:13 ἀνέχεσθαι ἀλλήλων ἐν ἀγάπῃ is an admonition to the community to apply to one another the love or the election which is theirs in Christ. Without object ἀνέχεσθαι has the absolute sense of "endure," as in LXX Job 6:11 and 1 C. 4:12. This endurance (in persecution) does not have the negative significance of a heroism which retreats into itself but implies a constant acceptance of the claims of others, as shown by the parallel εὐλογεῖν and παρακαλεῖν in the latter reference. In the absolute sense we also have the verbal adj. ἀνεκτός in Lk. 10:12 and par. and 10:14 and par. — a construction not found in the LXX. On the day of judgment it will be more tolerable for Tyre and Sidon and Sodom and Gomorrah than for the cities of Israel which do not believe in Jesus.

2. "To restrain oneself." God restrains Himself either to man's destruction (LXX Is. 64:12) or out of mercy (LXX Is. 42:14; Dg., 9, 1 f., par. ἐμακροθύμησεν). That this sense easily merges into the former may be seen from LXX Is. 63:15, where it is said that God forbears with us. The substantive ἀνοχή in R. 2:4 and 3:26 may be mentioned in this connection. ἀνοχή, which is put between the χρηστότης and the μακροθυμία of God in R. 2:4, is God's restraint in the

---

ἀ ν έ χ ω κ τ λ. [1] Pass.; Liddell-Scott, s.v.
[2] In Ac. 18:14 ἀνέχεσθαι is a technical legal term for accepting a complaint or accusation for further treatment.

outworking of His wrath, which with Christ has ceased to be an essential determination of the world.

Schlier

---

† ἀνήκει

(καθῆκον) imp. from the pers. ἀνήκω "to refer to" (Ditt. Or., 763, 36; Ign. Phld., 1, 1; Sm., 8, 1; 1 Cl., 62, 1 etc.) in the sense of "to be fitting or seemly," τὸ ἀνῆκον being that which is suitable or proper. In the LXX it is almost always (1 Βασ. 27:8) found in the legal or political sense (1 Macc. 10:42 : διὰ τὸ ἀνήκειν αὐτὰ τοῖς ἱερεῦσι τοῖς λειτουργοῦσι, 11:35; 2 Macc. 14:8. Cf. P. Tebt., 6, 42 : τῶν ἀνηκόντων τοῖς ἱεροῖς ...

In Phlm. 8 in the NT τὸ ἀνῆκον (with ἐπιτάσσειν) denotes not merely that which is fitting but that which is almost legally obligatory, although in a private matter. In Eph. 5:4 the ἃ οὐκ ἀνῆκεν[1] (DGKL min : τὰ οὐκ ἀνήκοντα) is that which does not belong, which is opposed to καθὼς πρέπει ἁγίοις. The unsuitable nature of an action is shown by the fact that those who perform it are ἅγιοι acting ἐν κυρίῳ. This unsuitability may concur with the judgment of the world (Col. 3:18) or it may contradict it (Eph. 5:4 : εὐτραπελία, for example, is accepted by the world, cf. Aristot. Eth. Nic., II, 7, p. 1108a, 23 ff.).

Schlier

ἀνήρ, † ἀνδρίζομαι

A. ἀνήρ outside the NT.

1. The word is common as the general designation of a man with adjectives and substantives denoting the function, e.g., ἀνὴρ μάντις, but also ἄνδρες λησταί.

2. The word is also used for the human species. This may be a. in distinction from fabled monsters like centaurs (Od., 21, 303) or gods. Ζεὺς πατὴρ ἀνδρῶν τε θεῶν τε (Il., 1, 544 etc.); the heralds are Διὸς ἄγγελοι ἠδὲ καὶ ἀνδρῶν (Il., 1, 334). We see a distinctive Hellenic self-awareness in the formula : ἄνδρες ἡμίθεοι (Il., 12, 23). But the phrase also occurs : θνητοὶ ἄνδρες (Od., 10, 306). Man should not strive against God (Eur. Ba., 635). b. The general equation of

---

ἀ ν ή κ ε ι. Liddell-Scott, Moult.-Mill., *s.v.* Cf. also Meinertz Eph., 93, Kol., 42.
[1] On the impf., Bl.-Debr., 358, 2; though cf. Loh. Kol., *ad loc.*
ἀ ν ή ρ. Fick-Bezzenberger-Stokes, *Vergl. Wörterbuch der indogermanischen Sprachen*[4], I (1890), 98; W. Prellwitz, *Etym. Wört.*[2] (1905), 40; J. Wackernagel, *Über einige antike Anredeformen* (Universit. Progr. Gött., 1912); P. Kretschmer, *Glotta*, 6 (1914/15), 296 f.; *Philol. Wochenschr.*, 46 (1926), 131; Bl.-Debr., § 242, → γυνή.

male and man is Homeric and poetic, but not Attic; nor is there any instance in the pap. [1] The original is discerned, however, when ἄνδρες is used for inhabitants or people. P. Oxy., IV, 719, 24 (2nd century A.D.): οἰκία καθαρὰ ἀπὸ ἀπογραφῆς ἀνδρῶν "a house that shelters no unreported dwellers"; BGU, 902, 2 (2nd century A.D.): etc.: ἄνδρας ἐκ τοῦ πλείστου ἐκλελοιπέναι "for the most part the inhabitants are no longer there." It is found with the gen. of place in Ju. 9:18; of Gentiles: Φοίνικες ἄνδρες etc. It is also frequently found (→ 1.) with adj. in general statements (ἀνὴρ συνετός, Prv. 12:23), or in such phrases as κατ' ἄνδρα, viritim, or in such expressions as we meet in Job 41:8. In the OT and NT such phrases betray Hebrew influence but cannot be regarded as simple Hebraisms.

3. The word signifies man as opposed to woman. Philo Abr., 137: τὰς μὲν κατὰ φύσιν ἀνδρῶν καὶ γυναικῶν συνόδους; ibid., 135: ἄνδρες ὄντες ἄρρεσιν ἐπιβαίνοντες. Male posterity is preferred: τῶν ἀνδρῶν ἄπαις (Plat. Leg., IX, 877e). Philo too emphasises the distinction of sexes. Cf. esp. Ebr., 59 ff.: ἡμεῖς δὲ ἔτι ὑπὸ τῆς ἀνάνδρου καὶ γυναικώδους συνηθείας τῆς περὶ τὰς αἰσθήσεις καὶ τὰ πάθη καὶ τὰ αἰσθητὰ νικώμενοι τῶν φανέντων οὐδενὸς κατεξαναστῆσαι δυνάμεθα (63). Woman's clothing is forbidden to man in order that he should not be tainted with anything feminine. The state for man, the house for woman! (Virt., 18-20). → γυνή.

4. The word also denotes the husband (LXX for בַּעַל, Ex. 21:22 etc.). πόσις refers to the legal, ἀνήρ to the actual position (Soph. Trach., 550 f.: μὴ πόσις μὲν Ἡρακλῆς ἐμὸς καλῆται, τῆς νεωτέρας δ' ἀνήρ). In antiquity marriage was less personal (→ γυνή). If the passage adduced reflects unhappiness in marriage, happiness is also seen. Od., 6, 182 ff.: οὐ μὲν γὰρ τοῦ γε κρεῖσσον καὶ ἄρειον / ἢ ὅθ' ὁμοφρονέοντε νοήμασιν οἶκον ἔχητον / ἀνὴρ ἠδὲ γυνή. To the burial inscription of Otacilia Polla in Pergamon (2nd century A.D.)[2] we have a counterpart on the Roman gravestone of Claudia Piste: [3] coniugi optimae sanctae et piae benemeritae. In Judaism the wife is strongly subordinated to the husband: "The power of the husband is on her" (T. Qid., 1, 11); [4] he is her "lord" (cf. 1 Pt. 3:6). On the other hand, the husband should "love his wife as himself, and honour her more than himself" (bJeb., 62b). [5]

5. The word can also denote an adult man as distinct from a boy (LXX for גֶּבֶר, Ex. 10:11), ἀνὴρ τέλειος (Xenoph. Cyrop., VIII, 7, 6; Philo Cher., 114 of the age of life; Sobr., 9 in terms of worth).

6. The word can also be used of full manhood (LXX for אָדוֹן, אִישׁ, נָשִׂיא, זָקֵן, גִּבּוֹר). In contrast to the eunuch ἀνήρ τε κοὐκ ἀνήρ ... τὸ δὲ εὐνοῦχος (Athen., X, p. 452c; cf. Cl. Al. Protr., 1, 3, 1). We can see from Priapus [6] and Hermes [7] how antiquity absolutised the natural force of manhood. On the ideal of manhood, cf.

---

[1] For the distinction of the male → infra.
[2] Deissmann LO, 267 f.
[3] Vatican Museum of Antiquities, No. 295.
[4] Str.-B., III, 436c.
[5] For further passages, ibid., 610a.
[6] H. Herter, "De Priapo," RVV, 23 (1932).
[7] For examples, v. A. Rumpf, "Die Religion der Griechen" (Haas' Bilderatlas zur Rel. Gesch., 13/14, 1928), 29, 30, 32, 67. On ancient pederasty, v. F. Lübker-J. Geffcken-E. Ziebarth, Reallexikon[8] (1914), 751; E. Bethe, Rhein. Mus., 62 (1907), 438 ff.; W. Kroll, Freundschaft und Knabenliebe (1924).

the satirical sayings in Aristoph.Ach., 77 ff.: οἱ βάρβαροι ἄνδρας ἡγοῦνται μόνους τοὺς πλεῖστα δυναμένους καταφαγεῖν ... ἡμεῖς δὲ λαικαστάς τε καὶ καταπύγονας, the Homeric ἀνέρες ἐστέ, φίλοι (Il., 5, 529 etc.), the Attic ὦ ἄνδρες Ἀθηναῖοι. Philostr. Vit. Apoll., I, 16 (p. 17, 2, Kaiser): Apollonius avoids frequented places, saying: οὐκ ἀνθρώπων ἑαυτῷ δεῖν, ἀλλ' ἀνδρῶν. In later usage ἀνήρ approximates to our "lord." BGU, 1022, 7 (2nd century A.D.): ἄνδρες κράτιστοι (βουλευταί); P. Oxy., I, 133, 6 (6th century A.D.): ὁ πανεύφημος ἀνήρ.

B. ἀνήρ in the NT.

In the NT ἀνήρ is most common in the Hellenistic Luke. Even elsewhere, however, it occurs in most of the senses mentioned. For 1. cf. Ac. 18:24: ἀνὴρ λόγιος; Mk. 6:20; Lk. 24:19: ἀνὴρ προφήτης; Ac. 3:14: ἄνδρα φονέα.

2. is more influential than sometimes supposed. Under a. Lk. 5:8: ἀνὴρ ἁμαρτωλός and Jm. 1:20 ὀργὴ ἀνδρός, are comparable, though there are obvious differences. For the most part the only contrast is to pure spirits (or animals) → ἄνθρωπος (Ac. 14:15; R. 1:23) or corresponding to בָּשָׂר[-כָּל] or the Rabb. בָּשָׂר וָדָם [πᾶσα] → σάρξ or σάρξ καὶ αἷμα (Mk. 13:20 and par.; Jn. 17:2; R. 3:20; 1 C. 1:29; Gl. 2:16; 1 C. 15:50; Gl. 1:16; Eph. 6:12). The pride in manhood is lacking and the sense of distance is stronger. [8] Statistics show that there is a more common use simply for men as under b. (Mt. 14:21; 15:38; Ac. 4:4; not Mk. 8:9, but cf. 6:44). [οἱ] ἄνδρες frequently denotes more or less the totality of population (with gen. τοῦ τόπου ἐκείνου, Mt. 14:35, of Gentiles, Mt. 12:41 and par.; Ac. 10:28; cf. 11:20, though cf. also 8:3, 12; 9:2). ἀνήρ with adj. in general statements occurs frequently in the Epistle of James (1:8, 12, 23; 3:2), cf. Mt. 7:24, 26. Paul gives the order (1 C. 11:3 ff.) God, Christ, man, woman, each preceding link being the → κεφαλή of that which follows, and each that follows the → δόξα of the preceding. [9]

Emphatic sexual differentiation (3.) is mostly expressed in biblical Gk. by ἄρσεν and θῆλυ (זָכָר וּנְקֵבָה, Gn. 1:27; Mk. 10:6 and par.; cf. R. 1:26 ff.), though ἄνδρα [οὐ] γινώσκειν is also used in correspondence with אִישׁ יָדַע (Ju. 11:39; Lk. 1:34). A new feature of Christianity is the equality of the sexes before God (Gl. 3:28; 1 Pt. 3:7). Yet this does not mean that they are put on the same level (→ supra).

Examples of 4. are found in Mk. 10:2, 12 and par.; R. 7:2, 3; 1 C. 7; [10] 14:35; in the house-tables in Eph. 5:22 ff.; Col. 3:18 f.; 1 Pt. 3:1 ff.; in the passages dealing with office-bearers in the Pastorals (1 Tm. 3:2, 12; 5:9; Tt. 1:6). [11] In marriage

---

[8] J. Hempel, Gott und Mensch im AT (1926), passim and esp. 1-27, 174.

[9] Since man and woman are here considered in relation to creation, we do not have meaning 4. So Bruder, s.v.; Bchm. 1 C. In favour of this view we might quote v. 10 (→ ἐξουσία), though v. 8 f. seem to be clearly against it. Joh. W 1 C. tries to excise v. 3. But this is indispensable. Vv. 5b-6 and 13-15 seem to be of Stoic derivation, but a double interpolation is surely unlikely. The difficulty remains.

[10] ἄνερ is for the most part used only as the wife's address to her husband (unlike → γύναι). 1 C. 7:16 is an easily understood exception. See further Wackernagel, op. cit., 24-26.

[11] μιᾶς γυναικὸς ἀνήρ, ἑνὸς ἀνδρὸς γυνή. This is a prohibition of immoral conduct, and especially an exclusion from office of those who have remarried after divorce. It does

Christianity demands the subordination of the wife (ὑποτάσσεσθαι τοῖς ἰδίοις ἀνδράσιν, Eph. 5:22, 24; Col. 3:18; 1 Pt. 3:1, 5 [v. 6 : κύριος]) but also unselfish love from the husband such as that shown by Christ for the Church (Eph. 5:25, 28; Col. 3:19; 1 Pt. 3:7). In accordance with Jewish marriage law,[12] the fiancé is already referred to as ἀνήρ (Mt. 1:19; Rev. 21:2; cf. 2 C. 11:2; Dt. 22:23 f.).

Meaning 5. underlies 1 C. 13:11: ὡς νήπιος ... ὅτε γέγονα ἀνήρ.[13] The NT uses ἀνὴρ τέλειος only metaphorically (e.g., Eph. 4:13 : μέχρι καταντήσωμεν ... εἰς ἄνδρα τέλειον, in spite of Mk. 10:13 ff. and par.; Mt. 18:3; 1 Pt. 2:2, → νήπιος). We find it in Jm. 3:2 without regard for age (→ 2b.) ═ מַשְׂכִּיל Prv. 10:19.

Meaning 6. does not occur in the NT in the sexual sense (Ac. 8:27 uses ἀνήρ primarily with Αἰθίοψ, → 2.), but in a higher sense. Lk. often refers to ἄνδρες Γαλιλαῖοι, Ἰουδαῖοι, Ἀθηναῖοι, ἀδελφοί (Ac. 1:11; 2:5; 17:22; 1:16; 7:2 etc.). He emphasises the dignity of the honourable and mature man (Lk. 23:50; Ac. 6:3, 5). The word ἀνδρεία is not found in the NT. 1 Cl., 6, 1 is the first emphatic reference to the apostles as men. But in face of the powers of darkness Paul admonishes ἀνδρίζεσθε, κραταιοῦσθε (1 C. 16:13). In this respect, as in so many others, he is echoing the LXX (ψ 30[31]:25;[14] 2 Βασ. 10:12; 1 Ch. 22:13 etc.). He might have used the same expression in Eph. 6:10 ff. and 1 Th. 5:8.

ἀνδρεία occurs in the LXX only in books strongly influenced by Hellenism, like Prv. (21:30); Qoh. (2:21; 4:4; 5:10); Wis. (8:7); Macc. (1, 9:10; 4, 1:4 etc.; 5:23; 17:23). The equivalents תְּבוּנָה and כִּשְׁרוֹן are perhaps themselves translations of terms for the Gk. cardinal virtues.

Oepke

---

not forbid second marriage for clergy. This is correctly stated in Dib. Past. on 1 Tm. 3:2, where there is a review of the whole discussion. The opposite arguments are not convincing as stated by J. B. Frey, "La signification des termes ΜΟΝΑΝΔΡΟΣ et *univira*," *Recherches de science religieuse*, 20 (1930), 48 ff. — a work which contains much relevant material from the inscriptions — and G. Delling, *Paulus' Stellung zu Frau und Ehe* (1931), 136 ff.

[12] Str.-B., II, 393 ff.
[13] Cf. Sickbg., 1 C., 66.
[14] ἀνδρίζεσθε καὶ κραταιούσθω ἡ καρδία ὑμῶν ═ חִזְקוּ וְיַאֲמֵץ לְבַבְכֶם (established terminology); cf. Dt. 31:6 etc.; Jos. 1:6 etc. (ἀνδρίζεσθαι ═ אָמֵץ).

ἀνθομολογέω → ὁμολογέω.   ἀνθρωπάρεσκος → ἀρέσκω.

| ἄνθρωπος, ἀνθρώπινος |

ἄνθρωπος.

1. "Man" as species a. as distinct from animals (Mt. 12:12), angels (1 C. 4:9), Jesus Christ (Gl. 1:12) and God (Mk. 11:30 and par.); b. with special emphasis on the transitoriness and sinfulness of human nature [1] as subject to physical weakness (Jm. 5:17) and death (Hb. 9:27), as sinful (R. 3:4; 5:12), full of evil (Mt. 10:17; Lk. 6:22), loving flattery (Lk. 6:26) and subject to human error Gl. 1:1, 11 f.; Col. 2:8, 22). Thus κατὰ ἄνθρωπον does not merely introduce the general analogy of human relations [2] and considerations of human logic (Gl. 3:15 in introduction of the figure of the human testament, or 1 C. 15:32 : εἰ κατὰ ἄνθρωπον ἐθηριομάχησα ἐν Ἐφέσῳ, where the κατὰ ἄνθρωπον might be amplified by a λέγω). In the NT it almost always expresses as well the limited nature of human thinking and conduct in contrast to God and His revelation. Thus Paul in R. 3:5 introduces κατὰ ἄνθρωπον λέγω as an epidiorthosis, in 1 C. 9:8 κατὰ ἄνθρωπον λαλῶ is set over against ὁ νόμος λέγει, and in Gl. 1:11 τὸ εὐαγγέλιον ... οὐκ ἔστιν κατὰ ἄνθρωπον is set over against δι' ἀποκαλύψεως Ἰησοῦ Χριστοῦ in 1:12. There is a particular emphasis on the sinful disposition of man in the κατὰ ἄνθρωπον of 1 C. 3:3 : κατὰ ἄνθρωπον περιπατεῖτε (par. σαρκικοί ἐστε), as also in the plural form in 1 Pt. 4:6 : ἵνα κριθῶσι μὲν κατὰ ἀνθρώπους (as they have deserved as men) σαρκί, ζῶσι δὲ κατὰ θεὸν πνεύματι, being delivered from the judgment of the intervening state.

2. The word is also used with the gen. in Semitic fashion to express relationship to something abstract or a relationship of possession. Thus ἄνθρωποι εὐδοκίας [3] in Lk. 2:14 signifies men of the divine good-pleasure and is used to denote the elect Messianic community of salvation. [4] Again, ὁ ἄνθρωπος τῆς ἀνομίας, [5] the lawless one, denotes Antichrist in 2 Th. 2:3. Again, ὁ ἄνθρωπος τοῦ θεοῦ, the man of God, is used of the Christian standing in the service of God (1 Tm. 6:11; 2 Tm. 3:17). [6]

ἄνθρωπος τοῦ θεοῦ is found a. in the LXX for אִישׁ־הָאֱלֹהִים, originally a prophet of God (3 Βασ. 12:22; 13:1; 17:18, 24 etc.), used also of Moses (Dt. 33:1), but more generally applied later to signify the elect of God (e.g., David in 2 Ch. 8:14). [7] It also

---

ἄ ν θ ρ ω π ο ς. Pr.-Bauer, 106-108.
[1] Common in the OT, e.g., Ps. 8:4; 2 S. 24:14. Cf. ἄνθρωπος ὢν ἥμαρτον (Menander Fr., 499, CAF, III, 143), also Herond. Mim., 5, 27; Eur. Hipp., 615; Philo Spec. Leg., I, 252.
[2] Cf. Diod. S., XVI, 11, 2 : μειζόνως ἢ κατ' ἄνθρωπον, Plut. Stoic. Rep., 17 (II, 1042a).
[3] In syrsin pesh bo 𝔖 we find the nomin. εὐδοκία (tristich arrangement of the Gloria in excelsis in Lk. 2:14).
[4] Joachim Jeremias, "Ἄνθρωποι εὐδοκίας, ZNW, 28 (1929), 13-20.
[5] ADGK ἁμαρτίας.
[6] The rec. of 2 Pt. 1:21 (א A 𝔖 vg. syph) calls the prophets ἅγιοι θεοῦ ἄνθρωποι.
[7] P. Joüon, Biblica, III (1922), 53-55.

occurs b. in Hellenistic Judaism, e.g., in Ep. Ar., 140 to designate a worshipper of the true God. Philo uses it of Abraham (on the basis of Gn. 17:1), as also of the ἱερεῖς καὶ προφῆται as types of the citizens of the νοητὸς κόσμος (Gig., 60-63), of Moses as a type of the τέλειος on the basis of Dt. 33:1 (Mut. Nom., 24 ff.; 125 ff.), of Elijah and the prophets as types of the Logos on the basis of 3 Βασ. 17:18 (Deus Imm., 138 f.), and of the Logos as the ideal man created after the divine image [8] (Conf. Ling., 41-43, cf. 146). It is obvious that where ἄνθρωπος τοῦ θεοῦ is found in Hellen. Judaism, it is not an independent construction, but has developed out of LXX usage. c. There are no exact parallels outside Hellen. Judaism. An echo is heard in the cry of the regenerate mystic in Corp. Herm., XIII, 20 : σὺ εἶ ὁ θεός· ὁ σὸς ἄνθρωπος ταῦτα βοᾷ. On the other hand, Preis. Zaub., IV, 1178/9 is not an instance, for with Preisendanz we should put a comma after ἄνθρωπος : ὅτι ἐγώ εἰμι ἄνθρωπος, θεοῦ τοῦ ἐν οὐρανῷ πλάσμα κάλλιστον. Hence the usage of the NT is not to be explained from mysticism, but from OT Judaism.

3. In the anthropological terminology of the Pauline literature ἄνθρωπος is used in the following expressions with antithetical adjectival or adverbial attributes.

a. ὁ ἔξω ἄνθρωπος and ὁ ἔσω ἄνθρωπος : ὁ ἔξω ἄνθρωπος according to his physical and mortal side ; ὁ ἔσω ἄνθρωπος (or ὁ κρυπτὸς τῆς καρδίας ἄνθρωπος, 1 Pt. 3:4) = man — including the non-Christian (R. 7:22) [9] as well as the Christian (2 C. 4:16; Eph. 3:16; cf. 1 Pt. 3:4) — according to his Godward, immortal side.

Already in Plat. Resp., IX, 589a we find the expression τοῦ ἀνθρώπου ὁ ἐντὸς ἄνθρωπος = Resp., IV, 439d : τὸ λογιστικὸν τῆς ψυχῆς = the capacity of thought identical with moral disposition ; cf. Plot. Enn., V, 1, 10 (II, p. 173, 24 f., Volkm.): οἷον λέγει Πλάτων τὸν εἴσω ἄνθρωπον. Later Plato calls the νοῦς : ὁ ἐν ἡμῖν πρὸς ἀλήθειαν ἄνθρωπος (Plant., 42) or : ὁ ἄνθρωπος ἐν ἀνθρώπῳ (Congr., 97); in Det. Pot. Ins., 22 f. he defines the λογικὴ διάνοια as ὁ πρὸς ἀλήθειαν ἄνθρωπος and ὁ ἄνθρωπος ἐν ἑκάστου τῇ ψυχῇ. In the Hermetic literature there is distinguished from Adam, the earthly body of the first man, ὁ ἔσω αὐτοῦ ἄνθρωπος ὁ πνευματικός called φῶς ; the ἔξω ἄνθρωπος (Adam) is its prison (Zosimos, in Reitzenstein Poim., 104 f.). [10] Thus each man bears in himself a divine being : ὁ οὐσιώδης ἄνθρωπος (Corp. Herm., I, 15) or ὁ ἔννους ἄνθρωπος (I, 18 and 21) or ὁ ἐνδιάθετος ἄνθρωπος (XIII, 7) which languishes in the body as in a prison. Finally, we should compare the anthropology of the Marcosites, who believe that the *interior homo* of the redeemed, the *filius a Patre*, ascends at death to the higher world, while the body remains in the world and the soul (*anima*) falls to the demiurge (Iren., I, 21, 5). Paul thus follows an idea widespread in the Hellenistic Gnosis and mysticism of his day, [11] though also known in Hellenistic Judaism.

b. Rather different is the antithesis of ὁ → παλαιὸς ἄνθρωπος and ὁ → καινὸς or ὁ → νέος ἄνθρωπος: ὁ παλαιὸς ἄνθρωπος (R. 6:6; Col. 3:9; Eph. 4:22) denotes the sinful being of the unconverted man, ὁ καινὸς (Eph. 2:15; 4:24) or ὁ νέος (Col. 3:10) ἄνθρωπος the renewed being of the convert to Christ. The picture of the

---

[8] H. Leisegang, *Der Heilige Geist*, I, 1 (1919), 80.

[9] Cf. Sickbg. R., 231.

[10] Similarly we read in the preaching of the Naassenes (Hipp. Ref., V, 7, 35 f.) that the ἔσω ἄνθρωπος (= Adamas-Hermes) is as it were imprisoned in the πλάσμα τῆς λήθης, i.e., the body, fashioned from earth and clay (cf. Gn. 2:7).

[11] Cf. Reitzenstein Ir. Erl., 54; Hell. Myst., 354 ff.; H. Schlier, *Christus und die Kirche im Eph.* (1930), 35, n. 2.

old and new man is first used in interpretation of baptism; the old man is crucified in baptism (R. 6:6). The picture is then transferred from the sacramental sphere to the ethical; the Christian has to put off the παλαιὸς ἄνθρωπος, i.e., the offences and lusts of his heathen past (Col. 3:5-9; Eph. 4:22), and to put on the καινὸς ἄνθρωπος created after the image of God (Col. 3:10; Eph. 4:24; cf. Dg., 2, 1: γενόμενος ὥσπερ ἐξ ἀρχῆς καινὸς ἄνθρωπος). The picture is finally used of the Church; Christ unites Jews and Gentiles εἰς ἕνα καινὸν ἄνθρωπον (Eph. 2:15; cf. 4:13 : εἰς ἄνδρα τέλειον). In this case the identifying of the Redeemer with the totality of the redeemed corresponds to the language of oriental and Hellenistic teaching concerning the redeemer God-man. [12] In all these different uses of the image it is assumed that Christ is *the* absolute καινὸς ἄνθρωπος (→ υἱὸς τοῦ ἀνθρώπου; cf. Ign. Eph., 20, 1), the Initiator of the consummated creation of God. [13]

c. ψυχικὸς ἄνθρωπος/πνευματικὸς ἄνθρωπος (1 C. 2:14 f.) → ψυχικός, πνευματικός.

4. ὁ ἄνθρωπος as a Messianic designation of Jesus (R. 5:15; 1 C. 15:21, 47; Eph. 5:32; 1 Tm. 2:5; Hb. 2:6; perhaps also Mt. 4:4 and par.) → υἱὸς τοῦ ἀνθρώπου.

ὁ πρῶτος/δεύτερος ἄνθρωπος (1 C. 15:45, 47) → Ἀδάμ and υἱὸς τοῦ ἀνθρώπου.

† ἀνθρώπινος.

1. This is used generally of man as part of the created world, as in Jm. 3:7 : ἡ φύσις ἡ ἀνθρωπίνη, where it signifies human as distinct from animal nature (cf. Da. 7:4, 8). In this connection we might also mention 1 Pt. 2:13. Since there is no instance of κτίσις in the sense of order or authority, ὑποτάγητε πάσῃ ἀνθρωπίνῃ κτίσει must be understood with the Syr. and one part of the Lat. attestation as a comprehensive admonition to be subject to "every human creature." [1]

2. It is used to mark off man from God (ὑπὸ χειρῶν ἀνθρωπίνων, Ac. 17:25), [2] with a strong emphasis in Paul on the corporal limits of human nature. [3] Thus R. 6:19 : ἀνθρώπινον λέγω διὰ τὴν ἀσθένειαν τῆς σαρκὸς ὑμῶν = κατὰ ἄνθρωπον → 364; 1 C. 2:13 : ἀνθρωπίνη σοφία (antith. πνεῦμα in 2:13 or θεοῦ σοφία in 2:7); 4:3 : ἀνθρωπίνη ἡμέρα (antith., the judgment day of the Messiah); and 10:13, where ἀνθρώπινος does not refer to the origin of temptation (i.e., its

---

[12] Reitzenstein Ir. Erl. and Hell. Myst., *loc. cit.*; H. Schlier, *Religionsgeschichtliche Untersuchungen zu den Ignatiusbriefen* (1929), 88 f., 173; also *Christus und die Kirche im Eph.* (1930). On the other hand, the extra-Christian provenance (Reitzenstein Ir. Erl., 153, n. 2; Schlier, *Religionsgesch. Untersuchungen zu den Ign.-Briefen,* 88, n. 2) of the image of the old and new man has never been proved. To be sure, we meet the image in Manichean literature (Aug. contra Faustum, 24, 1, p. 717-721, Zycha), but Mani borrowed it from Paul (K. Holl, *Urchristentum u. Religionsgeschichte*[2] [1927], 12 f.; H. H. Schaeder, "Urform und Fortbildung des mandäischen Systems," *Vortr. Bibl. Warburg* (1924/5 [1927]), 93, n. 1.

[13] J. Jeremias, *Jesus als Weltvollender* (1930), 53-57.

ἀ ν θ ρ ώ π ι ν ο ς. [1] O. Holtzmann, *Das NT* (1926), 847.

[2] Cf. Jos. Bell., 5, 400 : καταφρονεῖν χειρὸς ἀνθρωπίνης = ἐπιτρέπειν πάντα τῷ θεῷ δικάζειν; Bell., 5, 387 of Sennacherib : ἆρα χερσὶν ἀνθρωπίναις ἔπεσεν.

[3] Cf. Jos. Ant., 5, 215 : τὴν ἀνθρωπίνην φύσιν φίλαυτον οὖσαν.

derivation from man, which would be contrary to v. 13b), but to its puny strength, i.e., that it may be borne by the weakness of human nature. [4]

J. Jeremias

---

† ἀνίημι, † ἄνεσις

The basic meaning of the word ἀνίημι is the relaxation of tension, e.g., χορδῶν (Plat. Resp., I, 349e; opp. ἐπίτασις); the usage has many nuances in both the literal and figurative senses. Both the verb and the noun are rare in the NT, as also in the LXX, where ἀνίημι is more common and varied.

ἀνίημι occurs in the true sense of "to release" or "loose" (Ac. 16:26: τὰ δεσμά; 27:40 τὰς ζευκτηρίας); in the fairly common LXX sense of "to forsake" or "give up" (Hb. 13:5: οὐ μή σε ἀνῶ οὐδ' οὐ μή σε ἐγκαταλίπω; cf. Dt. 31:6); in the metaphorical sense of Eph. 6:9 (τὴν ἀπειλήν — a choice expression, [1] though often found in Gk., e.g., τὴν ἔχθραν, Thuc., 3, 10). The legal sense of "to remit," which occurs in Gk. [2] and the LXX, is not found in the NT.

ἄνεσις in the strict sense occurs in Ac. 24:23 as "mitigation," i.e., of imprisonment (τηρεῖσθαι αὐτὸν ἔχειν τε ἄνεσιν, cf. Jos. Ant., 18, 235: φυλακὴ μὲν γὰρ καὶ τήρησις ἦν, μετὰ μέντοι ἀνέσεως). Elsewhere it is found only in the metaphorical sense of "refreshment" or "rest," which is also common in Gk. (e.g., Plat. Leg., IV, 724a: opp. σπουδή; M. Ant., I, 16, 6: opp. ἔντασις). Cf. 2 C. 2:13: οὐκ ἔσχηκα ἄνεσιν τῷ πνεύματί μου; 7:5: οὐδεμίαν ἔσχηκεν ἄνεσις ἡ σὰρξ ἡμῶν, ἀλλ' ἐν παντὶ θλιβόμενοι; 8:13: οὐ γὰρ ἵνα ἄλλοις ἄνεσις, ὑμῖν θλῖψις; 2 Th. 1:7: ἀνταποδοῦναι τοῖς θλίβουσιν ὑμᾶς θλῖψιν, καὶ ὑμῖν τοῖς θλιβομένοις ἄνεσιν μεθ' ἡμῶν. In the last passage we might speak of an eschatological significance, comparing ἄνεσις with ἀνάψυξις (Ac. 3:20), with the eschatological ἀνάπαυσις (2 Cl., 5, 5; 6, 7 — found in Gnosticism but not in the NT) and with → ἀπολύτρωσις (cf. Schol. on Thuc., 1, 76, where the ἀνιέναι of the text is explained in terms of ἀπολύειν).

It is worth noting that ἄνεσις is not used for forgiveness (→ ἄφεσις, πάρεσις), as might have been expected from the use of ἀνιέναι in the LXX (e.g., Jos. 24:19; Is. 1:14). The fairly common Gk. sense of "self-abandonment" or "license" is found in early Christian literature only in Barn., 4, 2.

Bultmann

---

[4] Pollux, III, 131: ὃ οὐκ ἄν τις ὑπομένοιεν, ὃ οὐκ ἄν τις ἐνέγκοι — τὸ δὲ ἐναντίον κοῦφον, εὔφορον ... ἀνθρώπινον.
ἀ ν ί η μ ι. [1] Nägeli, 85.
[2] Pap., cf. Preisigke Wört.

ἄνιπτος → νίπτω.

| ἀνίστημι, † ἐξανίστημι, ἀνάστασις, † ἐξανάστασις |

→ ἐγείρω, ζωή.

ἀνίστημι, † ἐξανίστημι.

A. Meanings of ἀνιστάναι and ἐξανιστάναι.

In respect of the trans. and intrans. use the words follow the simple form, and the meaning in the Bible is in accord with general usage. a. trans. of persons (since Homer); "to raise up," e.g., one who is lying down or crouching (Ac. 9:41); "to awaken" one who is asleep; "to institute or instal" someone in a function, to "institute" a high-priest (Hb. 7:11, 15); "to deport" a people; of objects (post-Homeric): "to set up" pillars or altars; "to repair" walls. b. Intrans. "to rise up" or "to waken" from sleep (Ac. 12:7), from bed (Lk. 11:7); esp. of the sick (Lk. 4:39) and the lame (Mk. 9:27; Ac. 14:10); "to recover" ἐκ τῆς νόσου; "to rise up to speak" (Lk. 10:25; Ac. 5:34; 13:16; ἐξανίστασθαι, 15:5) in judgment as a judge or witness (Mk. 14:60 and par. 57); "to rise up in enmity" (Mk. 3:26; Ac. 5:17).

The following meanings are unique, or at least bear a unique emphasis, in biblical usage: a. the use of the intrans. in Hebrew fashion to mark the beginning of an action: Gn. 21:32: וַיֵּשְׁבוּ אֲ "וַיָּקָם ἀνέστη δὲ ᾿Α ... καὶ ἐπέστρεψαν; Ju. 13:11; 3 Βασ. 19:21. The part. is particularly common for this purpose: καὶ ἀναστὰς ἠκολούθησεν αὐτῷ (Mk. 2:14 and par.; 7:24; Ac. 8:27). We also find imperatives with the sense of "Up!" (→ ἐγερθείς and ἔγειρε). Gn. 13:17: הִתְהַלֵּךְ קוּם ἀναστὰς διόδευσον; 19:15; Nu. 22:20; 1 K. 17:9: לֵךְ קוּם ἀνάστηθι καὶ πορεύου; Jon. 3:2; Ez. 3:22; Lk. 17:19: ἀναστὰς πορεύου; Ac. 8:26: ἀνάστηθι καὶ πορεύου; 9:6. b. (ἐξ)ανιστάναι σπέρμα is a Semitism for זֶרַע הֵקִים. LXX Gn. 38:8, cf. Ju. 4:5, 10 (also וְרַע חַיָּה LXX Gn. 19:32, 34), i.e., to raise up seed to a dead brother by Levirate marriage,[1] as in Mt. 22:24 and par.

ἀνίστημι κτλ. On the general usage, cf. Liddell-Scott s.v. On the resurrection of the dead, RGG², I, 623-634 and RE³, II, 219-224. Apart from the works there mentioned, EJ, III, 665-667; Jüdisches Lexikon, I, 566-568; Schürer, II, 458 ff., 638 ff.; Bousset-Gressm., Index, esp. 269-274; F. Weber, Jüd. Theol. auf Grd. d. Talmud² (1897), 390 ff.; Str.-B. passim on the NT passages adduced, also IV, 1166-1198 (Excursus: Allgemeine oder teilweise Auferstehung der Toten?); G. Quell, Die Auffassung des Todes in Israel (1925); P. Volz, Jüdische Eschatologie von Daniel bis Akiba (1903); R. H. Charles, A Critical History of the Doctrine of a Future Life (1899); G. F. Moore, II, 279-395. On questions of religious history: E. Böklen, Die Verwandtschaft der jüdisch-christlichen und der parsischen Eschatologie (1902); A. Bertholet, "Zur Frage des Verhältnisses von persischem und jüdischem Auferstehungsglauben," Festschr. für F. K. Andreas (1916), 51 ff.; E. Sellin, "Die alttestamentliche Hoffnung auf Auferstehung und ewiges Leben," NkZ, 30 (1919), 232 ff.; E. Albert, Die israelitisch-jüdische Auferstehungshoffnung in ihren Beziehungen zum Parsismus (1910); Meyer, Ursprung, II, 58 ff.; Bousset-Gressm., 478 ff.; 506 ff.; E. Ebeling, "Tod und Leben nach den Vorstellungen der Babylonier," I, Texte (1931); E. Rohde, Psyche⁹⁻¹⁰ (1925); E. Benz, Das Todesproblem in der stoischen Philosophie (1929); F. Cumont, Die orient. Rel. im röm. Heidentum³ (1931) passim (the presentation of Cumont shows particularly impressively how close to the centre of Hellenistic religion is the thought of the future life → ζωή).

[1] Cf. on this point K. H. Rengstorf, Jebamot (1929), 28 ff.; 38 f.; also Str.-B., I, 886 f.

(a free quotation from Dt. 25:5 ff., which also borrows from Gn. 38:8). On the meaning of the term cf. Jos. Ant., 5, 46 : ἐπὶ τὴν μάχην ἐξανίστησιν. c. ἀνιστάναι τινά to introduce a personage (in history). LXX for קים with acc., Dt. 18:15, 18 : προφήτην ἀνιστάναι, cf. 1 Βασ. 2:35; 3 Βασ. 14:14; Jer. 23:4; 37(30):9; Ez. 34:23. In quotations Ac. 3:22; 7:37; Ac. 3:26 of the sending of Jesus. ² Comparable is Plut. Marc., 27 (I, 314a): ἀνιστάναι τινὰ ἐπὶ τὴν κατηγορίαν, to raise up someone as an accuser. Theologically the most important meaning is d. "to raise from the dead," or intrans. "to rise from the dead."

B. Resurrection in the Greek World.

Apart from transmigration of souls, for which ἀναβιώσκεσθαι is used in Plat. Phaed., 72d, the Gk. speaks of resurrection in a twofold sense. a. Resurrection is impossible. Hom. Il., 24, 551 (Achilles to Priam of Hector): οὐδέ μιν ἀνστήσεις; cf. *ibid.*, 756; 21, 56. Hdt., III, 62 : εἰ οἱ τεθνεῶτες ἀνεστᾶσι, προσδέκεό τοι καὶ 'Αστυάγεα τὸν Μῆδον ἐπαναστήσεσθαι. Aesch. Ag., 1360 f. : κἀγὼ τοιοῦτός εἰμ', ἐπεὶ δυσμηχανῶ λόγοισι τὸν θανόντ' ἀνιστάναι πάλιν. Soph. El., 137 ff. : ἀλλ' οὖτοι τὸν γ' ἐξ 'Αΐδα παγκοίνου λίμνας πατέρ' ἀνστάσεις οὔτε γόοις οὔτε λιταῖσιν. Aesch. Eum., 648 : ἅπαξ θανόντος οὔτις ἔστ' ἀνάστασις. With a transition to b. Eur. Herc. Fur., 719 : οὔκ, εἴ γε μή τις θεῶν ἀναστήσειέ νιν. b. Resurrection may take place as an isolated miracle. Plat. Symp., 179c : ἔδοσαν τοῦτο γέρας οἱ θεοί, ἐξ 'Αιδου ἀνεῖναι πάλιν τὴν ψυχήν. Luc. Salt., 45 : καὶ τὴν Τυνδάρεω ἀνάστασιν, καὶ τὴν Διὸς ἐπὶ τούτῳ κατ' 'Ασκληπιοῦ ὀργήν. Aesculapius the physician is also one who raises the dead. So in Ps.-Xenophon's work on dyeing (Cyn., 1, 6): 'Ασκληπιὸς δὲ <καὶ> μειζόνων ἔτυχεν, ἀνιστάναι μὲν τεθνεῶτας, νοσοῦντας δὲ ἰᾶσθαι. According to Paus., II, 26, 5 the shepherd who recognises the foundling Aesculapius in the lightning proclaims : ὅτι ἀνίστησι τεθνεῶτας (cf. II, 27, 4). The raising of an apparently dead girl in Rome by Apollonius of Tyana is recounted in Philostr. Vit. Ap., IV, 45, 150,000 denarii being contributed as additional endowment. The raisings reported in such apocryphal Acts as Act. Petr. Verc., 25-28 ³ are also essentially Hellenistic.

The idea of a general resurrection at the end of the age is alien to the Greeks. Indeed, it is perhaps attacked on a Phrygian inscription : [ο]ἴ δὴ δ[εἴλ]αιοι πάντ[ες] εἰς ἀνάστασιν (βλέποντες ?). ⁴ In Ac. 17:18 ἀνάστασις seems to be misunderstood by the hearers as a proper name (cf. 17:31 f.).

C. Resurrection in the OT and Judaism.

The OT recounts individual resurrections in 1 K. 17:17 ff.; 2 K. 4:18 ff.; 13:20 f. ⁵ There was inward preparation for the hope of general resurrection in its eschatological form (Ez. 37:1-14; Is. 53:10; Job 19:25 ff.; Ps. 73), but this did not come to formulation apart from Persian influence. ⁶ It first becomes palpable in Is. 26:19 : ἀναστήσονται οἱ νεκροί (LXX for יְחְיוּ מֵתֶיךָ, synon. ἐγερθήσονται

---

² Wdt. Ag., *ad loc.*

³ E. Hennecke, *Neutestamentl. Apokryphen*² (1924), 244.

⁴ W. M. Ramsay, *The Cities and Bishoprics of Phrygia*, No. 232 (Eumeneia). There is not sufficient evidence to prove that the author was an Epicurean Jew.

⁵ For Jewish accounts of resurrections, cf. P. Fiebig, *Jüdische Wundergeschichten* (1911), 16; Str.-B., I, 560, II, 545.

⁶ → Bibl. and → ζωή/θάνατος.

for יְקוּמוּ) and Da. 12:2 : πολλοὶ τῶν καθευδόντων ἐγερθήσονται (יָקִיצוּ). and is then more comprehensively developed in Apocalyptic. [7] Where the doctrine of an intermediate state obtains, the more immediately interesting resurrection of the righteous comes at the beginning and that of the wicked at the end.

The Sadducees and Samaritans rejected this hope (Mk. 12:18 and par.; Ac. 23:8; Jos. Bell., 2, 165; Ant., 18, 16). [8] The rejection constantly recurs : Ber., 9, 5 : "The Minim say that there is only one world" ; jChag., 77b, 4 : Elisa ben Abuja said : "There is no resurrection of the dead." Sanh., 10, 1 is directed against it : "Whosoever says that the resurrection of the dead cannot be deduced from the Torah has no part in the future world." The whole of later Judaism includes the hope of the resurrection as a firm and necessary part of its faith : Sch^emone Esre, 2. [9] In T. Ber., 7, 5 the doxology to be pronounced in a graveyard is as follows : "He will cause you to arise. Blessed be He who keeps His Word and raises the dead !" In Hellenistic Judaism the hope of the resurrection is spiritualised. Neither Josephus nor Philo uses ἀνάστασις in the sense of resurrection. Josephus interprets his hope of immortality in terms of Pharisaic dogma (Bell., 2, 163). Philo does not understand immortality as continuation of life but mystically as liberation from particularity, as the new birth (Quaest. in Ex. 2:46, Harris, p. 60 f.). [10] He describes the ascent of the soul in Sacr. AC, 5. Hell is separation from God already effective here and now (Cher., 2).

D. Resurrection in the NT.

1. The NT tells of individual resurrections from the dead. As one customarily calls someone who is asleep or sick, and takes him by the hand and raises him, so the miracle-worker does with the dead, and they arise (Mk. 5:42; cf. with 9:27; Ac. 9:40 f. with 9:34). As the NT itself teaches, such procedures are not strange to the thinking of the world around (Mk. 6:14; Hb. 11:35). Nevertheless, Ac. 20:10 ff. reveals a capacity to distinguish. The records from the life of Jesus in particular (Mk. 5:21-43 and par.; Lk. 7:11-17; Jn. 11:1-44) are marked by seriousness, sobriety and solemnity. The awakenings are signs of the Messianic age and are not therefore isolated miracles (Mt. 11:5; Jn. 11:25, 26, cf. 5:20 f.; 6:39, 40, 44, 54). Mt. 27:53 must be cited in the same connection.

2. The resurrection of Jesus (often, thought not always, with the addition ἐκ νεκρῶν) is announced by Jesus Himself [11] (Mk. 8:31 and par.; 9:9 and par.; 9:31 and par.; 10:34) and is described in the earliest proclamation as the work of the Father whereby the Crucified is exalted to Messianic δόξα [12] (Ac. 1:22; 2:24,

---

[7] Cf. esp. Str.-B., IV, 1166-1198.

[8] On the Samaritans, cf. Str.-B., I, 551 f.

[9] Schürer, II, 539; Str.-B., IV, 211.

[10] E. Bréhier, Les idées philosophiques et religieuses de Philon d'Alexandrie (1908), 240 ff.; R. Reitzenstein, Die Vorgeschichte der christlichen Taufe (1929), 111; H. H. Schaeder, Gnomon, 5 (1929), 353 ff.; Reitzenstein, ARW, 27 (1929), 241 ff.

[11] According to W. Michaelis, Taüfer, Jesus, Urgemeinde (1928), 100 f., the saying of Jesus about His resurrection cannot be clearly distinguished from that concerning His parousia. On the tendency for the resurrection, the sending of the Paraclete and the parousia to merge in John's Gospel, cf. the comm. and NT theologies.

[12] Acc. to G. Bertram, "Die Himmelfahrt Jesu vom Kreuze," Festgabe für Deissmann (1926), 187 ff.; E. Lohmeyer, Kyrios Jesus (1928), 48 f., the accent fell variously on the resurrection and the exaltation in Paul and the rest of the NT. Acc. to E. Fascher, ZNW,

31 f.; 4:33; 10:41; 13:33 f.; 17:3, 31; R. 1:4; 1 C. 15:1 ff.). On such questions as the significance of the resurrection for the *kerygma*, the dying and rising again of gods in Hellenism etc., → ἐγείρω, συζάω.

3. The general resurrection has that of Jesus as its first-fruits (Ac. 26:23: πρῶτος ἐξ ἀναστάσεως νεκρῶν; 1 C. 15:20: ἀπαρχὴ τῶν κεκοιμημένων; v. 21: δι' ἀνθρώπου ἀνάστασις νεκρῶν; Col. 1:18: ἀρχή, πρωτότοκος ἐκ τῶν νεκρῶν. In the NT, too, the inner logic of faith is towards the resurrection to life (1 C. 15:22; R. 8:11; Jn. 6:39, 40, 44, 54: ἀναστήσω αὐτὸν ἐν τῇ ἐσχάτῃ ἡμέρᾳ). Nevertheless, the predominant view is that of a double resurrection (Jn. 5:29: ἀνάστασις ζωῆς, κρίσεως; cf. R. 14:9; 2 C. 5:10). Possibly in Lk. 14:14: ἡ ἀνάστασις τῶν δικαίων, and certainly in Rev. 20:5, 6: ἡ ἀνάστασις ἡ πρώτη, Jewish tradition is followed and the resurrection to life is seen as a prior act in time at the beginning of the millennium. We are to take 1 C. 15:23 f. in the same way if τὸ τέλος does not signify the end of the world but the "rest" of the dead. [13] Similarly in 1 Th. 4:16 f. the union of resurrected believers and of those who are still alive with their Lord seems to take place without judgment. A different view seems to prevail in R. 2:16; 2 Th. 1:9, 10; 1 C. 4:5; 2 C. 5:10. The conceptions are fluid, as in Judaism.

Though it is already for believers a present possession, [14] the resurrection to life is still the goal of their hope and striving (Phil. 3:11: ἐξανάστασις, found only here in the NT). On the Gnostic error combatted in 2 Tm. 2:18: ἀνάστασιν ἤδη γεγονέναι, cf. Menander in Iren., I, 23, 5: *resurrectionem enim per id, quod est in eum baptisma, accipere eius discipulos, et ultra non posse mori, sed perseverare non senescentes et immortales.* [15] There is a strongly figurative use in Eph. 5:14: ἄναστα ἐκ τῶν νεκρῶν, καὶ ἐπιφαύσει σοι ὁ Χριστός.

Those who denied the resurrection in Corinth (1 C. 15:12) were probably repelled by the materialism of Jewish expectation [16] (→ ἐγείρω, σῶμα).

ἀνάστασις, † ἐξανάστασις.

The two words are equivalent. 1. Trans. a. the "erection" of statues, dams etc.: ep. Claud. ad Alex.; [1] Jos. Ant., 17, 151; 14, 473; 11, 19; cf. Bell., 5, 205; BGU, 362, VII, 3 (215 A.D.); b. "expulsion" from one's dwelling: Hdt., IX, 106; Polyb., II, 21, 9: τὴν τῶν δύο φυλῶν ἀνάστασιν; Jos. Ant., 10, 185; 2, 248; 16, 278; Bell., 6, 339. 2. Intrans. a. "arising": Aristot. Spir., 8, p. 485a, 18 f.; from sleep: Soph. Phil., 276; from bed in the morning: Porph. Vit. Pyth., 40; mid. "to go to stool": Hippocr. Epid., VI, 7, 1;

---

26 (1927), 1 ff. the only essential thing was the ἀπὸ θεοῦ, all the rest being merely "ideogram."

[13] This interpretation has gradually gained acceptance, cf. Joh. W., Bchm., Ltzm. 1 C. The older view that we should render: "Then cometh the end of the world," is to be found in Heinrici 1 C., *ad loc.* and K. Deissner, *Auferstehungshoffnung und Pneumagedanke bei Paulus* (1912), 23 ff.

[14] In R. 6:5, 8 we do not have a *futurum resurrectionis* (Barth R.², 175 f., 182 *ad loc.*) but *logicum*, Col. 2:12 f.; 3:1; cf. Khl. R., 204; Sickbg. R., 219.

[15] An essentially fuller version is found in Demas and Hermogenes, Act. Pl. et Thecl., 14 (E. Hennecke, *Ntl. Apokr.²*, 200), namely, that the resurrection has taken place in children.

[16] A. Schweitzer, *Die Mystik des Apostels Paulus* (1930), 93 f., has in view the representatives of an ultra-conservative eschatology who could offer hope of glorification at the *parousia* only to the living.

ἀνάστασις κτλ. [1] H. Idris Bell, *Jews and Christians in Egypt* (1924), 23 ff., line 31, 45.

Progn., 11. [2] There is no instance of its use for "recovery." b. "rising up" : Thuc., II, 14, or "departure" : Strabo, II, 3, 6. c. "rising" or "insurrection" : Demosth. Or., 1, 5.

Of these meanings, we find only 2a in Lk. 2:34 : οὗτος κεῖται εἰς πτῶσιν καὶ ἀνάστασιν [3] (for the fall and rising, i.e., the judgment and salvation). For the image, cf. Ps. 118:22, 23; Is. 8:14, 15; 28:16; R. 9:33; 1 Pt. 2:6; Mk. 12:10 and par.; Lk. 20:17 f.; for the fact, cf. 1 C. 1:18 ff.

Otherwise the term is used exclusively of the resurrection of Christ from the dead (Mk. 12:18 and par.; Jn. 5:29; Ac. 1:22; R. 1:4; Hb. 6:2; Rev. 20:5 f. etc. ἐξανάστασις — with the latter meaning — is found only in Phil. 3:11. On all material points → ἀνίστημι, ἐγείρω.

Oepke

ἄνοια → νοῦς. ἀνομία, ἄνομος → νόμος.
ἀνόσιος → ὅσιος. ἀνοχή → 359 f.
ἀνταγωνίζομαι → 134 ff. ἀντάλλαγμα → 252
ἀνταναπληρόω → πληρόω. ἀνταποδίδωμι, ἀνταπόδομα, ἀνταπόδοσις → δίδωμι.
ἀνταποκρίνομαι → κρίνω. ἀντέχω → ἔχω.

ἀντί

ἀντί is one of the prepositions whose use goes back to the Hellenistic period. In its basic meaning of "over against" it does not occur in the NT, but is mostly used in the sense of a. "in place of," often in figures like κακὸν ἀντὶ κακοῦ (R. 12:17; 1 Th. 5:15; 1 Pt. 3:9); χάριν ἀντὶ χάριτος (Jn. 1:16). [1] In this respect it makes little difference whether the word denotes an actual replacement, an intended replacement, or a mere equivalent in estimation (Hb. 12:16 : ἀντὶ βρώσεως μιᾶς ἀπέδετο τὰ πρωτοτόκια), or similarity (1 C. 11:15 : κόμη ἀντὶ περιβολαίου). From the meaning a. there develops b. "on behalf of" = ὑπέρ : Mt. 17:27: δοῦναι ἀντ' ἐμοῦ καὶ σοῦ, "for" = "to the account of" ; and also c. "for the sake of" in ἀντὶ τούτου = "for this cause," Eph. 5:31; ἀνθ' ὧν = "for the reason that" or "because," 2 Th. 2:10, and frequently in Lk. (Lk. 12:3 in the main clause, thus signifying "therefore").

---

[2] Do we have here the explanation of the strange use of ἐξανάστασις to denote a piece of furniture in BGU, 717, 11? It follows σκαφίον (chamber-pot ?). Cf. *Berichtigungen und Nachträge zu BGU*, III, 4.
[3] The suggestion of J. Weiss and Gressmann (Kl. Lk., *ad loc.*) that the words καὶ ἀνάστασιν should be deleted as an addition has little to support it.
ἀ ν τ ί. Bl.-Bebr. § 208; Radermacher, 138; Ditt. Syll.³, IV, 218, *s.v.* ἀντί; W. Kuhring, *De praepos. Graec. in chart. Aegypt. usu* (Diss. Bonn, 1906); K. Rossberg, *De praep. Graec. in chart. Aegypt. Ptolm. aet. usu* (Diss. Jena, 1909).
[1] Cf. Philo Poster C, 145 : διὸ τὰς πρώτας χάριτας ... ἑτέρας ἀντ' ἐκείνων καὶ τρίτας ἀντὶ τῶν δευτέρων καὶ ἀεὶ νέας ἀντὶ παλαιοτέρων ... ἐπιδίδωσι.

In Mk. 10:45 and par.: δοῦναι τὴν ψυχὴν αὐτοῦ λύτρον ἀντὶ πολλῶν, the position of ἀντὶ πολλῶν shows that it is dependent on λύτρον and not δοῦναι. It thus has the meaning of a. and not of b. in the sense of Mt. 17:27. The sacrificed life of Jesus is a sufficient price to redeem many. Even if we relate the ἀντὶ πολλῶν to δοῦναι and understand it in the sense of b., the saying still contains in substance the thought of representation or substitution. For the πολλοί have not merely forfeited a favourite possession but their very lives, themselves; and what Jesus gives them is His very life, Himself. What He does on their behalf is simply to take their place.

In Jos. Ant., 14, 107: τὴν δοκὸν αὐτῷ τὴν χρυσῆν λύτρον ἀντὶ πάντων ἔδωκεν, it is incontestable that ἀντί means "in place of." For the priest is not merely intending to give something for the good of the treasury. He is seeking to satisfy Crassus that the latter may take this ingot of gold instead of the treasury.

Büchsel

---

† ἀντίδικος

A. ἀντίδικος outside the NT.

1. ἀντίδικος is the "opponent at law" (plaintiff or defendant). Aeschin. Fals. Legat., 165. Plat. Phaedr., 261c.: ἐν δικαστηρίοις οἱ ἀντίδικοι τί δρῶσιν; 273c: ἔλεγχόν πη παραδοίη τῷ ἀντιδίκῳ; Leg., XI, 937b: τῶν ἀντιδίκων ἑκάτερος, both parties in a suit. Cf. also Epict. Diss., II, 2, 10: σκέπτου καὶ τὴν φύσιν τοῦ δικαστοῦ καὶ τὸν ἀντίδικον; III, 9, 5: ἆρ' οὖν πάντες ἔχομεν ὑγιῆ δόγματα καὶ σὺ καὶ ὁ ἀντίδικός σου; though ἀντίδικος can also mean the defendant: Antiphon Or., 1, 5; P. Oxy., 37, I, 8 (1st century A.D.) or the plaintiff: Lys., 7, 13. The opponents or parties in a legal dispute may be either individuals or groups (esp. common in the pap.). For opponents in a private suit, cf. P. Lips., 33, II, 4 (368 A.D.), where at the head of a record of proceedings we find ἀντιδί[κο]ις χαίρει[ν] after the names of the litigants. In Ditt. Syll.³, 656, 24, it is used of the party in a civic action, the citizens of Abdera in their appeal to Rome calling the Thracian king Kotys, who was trying to annex their city, ἀντίδικος. [1]

We find this direct sense in the LXX at Prv. 18:17: δίκαιος ἑαυτοῦ κατήγορος ἐν πρωτολογίᾳ· ὡς δ' ἂν ἐπιβάλῃ ὁ ἀντίδικος (רֵעֵהוּ) ἐλέγχεται. Cf. also Jos. Ant., 8, 30: τὸ δὲ τῆς ἀντιδίκου τεθνηκέναι, the women contesting for the παιδίον before Solomon. In Philo Aet. Mund., 142 the judge does not pronounce his verdict πρὶν [παρὰ] τῶν ἀντιδίκων ἀκοῦσαι. Similarly in Leg. Gaj., 350: ἑκατέρωθεν στῆναι τοὺς ἀντιδίκους μετὰ τῶν συναγορευσόντων (advocates); 361: γέλως ἐκ τῶν ἀντιδίκων κατερράγη. Cf. 362. The Rabbis simply borrowed the foreign word and described opponents at law as אַנְטִידִיקוֹס; Pesikt., 122b.; Dt. r., 5 on 16:18 of the contesting parties. [2] But in Heb. the contestant is also בַּעַל דִּין (Aram. בַּעַל דְּבָבָא): bScheb., 31a; bBer., 16b; Ab., 1, 8. [3]

ἀντίδικος. [1] For further examples, Moult.-Mill., 47; Preisigke Wört., 133.
[2] Str.-B., I, 288.
[3] *Ibid.*, II, 238.

2. This image of the court action is then applied in such a way that, originally with a conscious retention of the image, it is used metaphorically of any contesting parties. LXX : 1 Βασ. 2:10 (the song of Hannah): Κύριος ἀσθενῆ ποιήσει ἀντίδικον αὐτοῦ (מְרִיבוֹ) ; [4] Is. 41:11: ἀπολοῦνται πάντες οἱ ἀντίδικοί σου (אַנְשֵׁי רִיבֶךָ) — the enemies of Israel as opponents in a dispute. Ιερ. 27:34: κρίσιν κρινεῖ πρὸς τοὺς ἀντιδίκους αὐτοῦ (רִיבָם) — Yahweh conducts Israel's case against its opponents at law. The same use of the image is found at Jer. 50:34, except that the Mas. has Israel's opponent in view, the LXX (27:34) Yahweh's. The image is also found in the Rabbis : [5] Ab., 4, 22 : God is both litigant and judge ; Gn.r., 82 on 35:17: God is advocate in the judgment of the nations.

3. Very generally, the image having slipped into the background, ἀντίδικος simply means opponent, esp. in poetic usage. Aesch. Ag., 41: Πριάμου μέγας ἀντίδικος Μενέλαος ἄναξ. LXX : Est. 8:11: χρῆσθαι τοῖς ἀντιδίκοις αὐτῶν of the adversaries of the Jews. Sir. 33:9 (Heb. 36:7): ἔξαρον ἀντίδικον in a liturgical passage. Jos. Ant., 13, 413 : εἰ ἀρκεσθεῖεν τοῖς ἀνηρημένοις οἱ ἀντίδικοι. Philo Leg. All., I, 87: δικαιοσύνη οὐδενὸς οὖσα ἀντίδικος. Virt., 174 : God as ἀντίδικος. In the Rabbinic field : [5] Gn.r., 100 on 50:21. [6]

B. ἀντίδικος in the NT.

In the NT we never have ἀντίδικος in the direct and concrete sense of a litigant (1). On the other hand, we have the use of the image (2) in Mt. 5:25 : ἴσθι εὐνοῶν τῷ ἀντιδίκῳ σου — μήποτέ σε παραδῷ ὁ ἀντίδικος τῷ κριτῇ. This is not a prudent maxim of middle-class morality ; the ἀντίδικος is the brother with whom one must not squabble on the way to the judge — the background is eschatological. [7] The same eschatological content is to be found in the parable in Lk. 12:58 : ὡς γὰρ ὑπάγεις μετὰ τοῦ ἀντιδίκου σου ἐπ᾽ ἄρχοντα. The only point is that in Mt. the relationship to the neighbour is predominant, whereas in Lk. it is the relationship to God. [8] It seems that the comparison was contained in Q, but could be interpreted differently. [9]

The usage in 1 Pt. 5:8 : ὁ ἀντίδικος ὑμῶν διάβολος, hovers between 2. and 3. As the περιπατεῖ shows, the image of a court action is abandoned. Yet in the background there stands שָׂטָן, Aram. שָׂטָנָא, סִיטְנָא, סְטַן, which also means opponent, esp. at law (→ διάβολος, σατανᾶς). It is as such that Satan in Job 1:6 ff. and 2:1 ff. is prosecutor before the judgment seat of God, just as לְשִׂטְנוֹ = τοῦ ἀντικεῖσθαι αὐτῷ at Zech. 3:1 signifies the action of the accuser. The role of Satan is the same in Rev. 12:10 as in Job: ὁ κατηγορῶν αὐτοὺς ἐνώπιον τοῦ θεοῦ ἡμῶν ἡμέρας καὶ νυκτός. The διάβολος is the calumniator. Thus in 1 Pt. 5:8

---

[4] The later use of ποιεῖν κρίμα and κρινεῖ shows that the image is retained.

[5] Str.-B., I, 288 f.

[6] The verb : LXX Ju. 6:31 A : ὃς ἀντεδίκησεν; 12:2 A : ἀντιδικῶν. Pap. Preisigke Sammelbuch, 2055, 2 (4th-5th centuries A.D.). Concerning the point of the action, Ιερ. 28:36 (Mas. 51:36) has : ἐγὼ κρινῶ τὴν ἀντίδικόν σου (רָב אֶת־רִיבֵךְ.) In Philo Leg. All., II, 92 neutr. : τὸ ἀντίδικον τῆς ἡδονῆς.

[7] Schl. Mt., 174 f.

[8] God is here ἀντίδικος, κριτής and πράκτωρ all in one, as Godet rightly observes. The ἀντίδικος can hardly be Satan (Kl. Lk., ad loc.) as the Carpocratians believed according to Iren., I, 25, 4.

[9] Cf. Jülicher, Gl. J., 240 ff.

we no longer have the picture of the opponent at law; yet this picture originally gave colour to the expression.

The word is used very generally in the sense of opponent (3) in Lk. 18:3: ἐκδίκησόν με ἀπὸ τοῦ ἀντιδίκου μου, for in this case there is no opponent in court, but the widow is pleading with the judge alone.

Schrenk

ἀντίκειμαι → κεῖμαι.

┌───┐
│ † ἀντιλαμβάνομαι, ἀντίλημψις,   │
│   συναντιλαμβάνομαι   │
└───┘

ἀντιλαμβάνομαι in Att. prose means "to grasp," "to take up a matter," "to master": Xenoph. Cyrop., II, 3, 6: ἐρρωμένως ἀντιλήψονται τῶν πραγμάτων; "to take up helpfully" (Eur. Tro., 464). In the pap. it is often used for "to help" (cf. further Diod. S., XI, 13, though we do not find this meaning in Philo), as also in the more basic senses. ἀντίλημψις originally means "grasping" or "appropriation" (App. Rom. Hist. even uses it in the sense of "import," VIII, 89); and it is thus used in Plato and still in Philo. It takes the sense of "help" in Iambl. Myst., 7, 3 and frequently in the pap. (as early as the 2nd century B.C.). Deissmann's explanation [1] that the LXX application to religious relationships is based on its reference to rulers, who are honoured as divine, is materially unnecessary; in any case the cultus in Egypt has the invocation: ἀντιλαβοῦ, κύριε ... (CIG, 4712b = Ditt. Or., 697). συναντιλαμβάνομαι has the sense of "to take up with," cf. Diod. S., XIV, 8, 2, where Liddell-Scott again sees the thought of help. This sense seems to be at least possible, and even more probable, in the inscriptions and pap. quoted by Deissmann. [2]

In the LXX we often find the proper sense of "to grasp"; and the metaphorical sense of "to keep to" (Is. 26:3), or "to enter into alliance with" (Mi. 6:6), is also found. In 2 Macc. 11:26 ἀντίλημψις means "taking up something." Yet the idea of help is predominant. In relation to one's neighbour, ἀντιλαμβάνομαι is used about 14 times; of God ἀντιλαμβάνομαι is used 20 times, mostly in the Psalms, as also ἀντίλημψις (plur. "assistances"). συναντιλαμβάνομαι a. "to share a task with someone" (Ex. 18:22; Nu. 11:17); "to help someone in his work" (ψ 88:22 = R. 8:26).

In the NT ἀντιλαμβάνομαι is used 1. more in the original sense (*v.* Xenoph. Cyrop., II, 3, 6, → *supra*) of serious concern for a right relationship to the brother, esp. one's own Christian slave (1 Tm. 6:2), or of regard for the weak (Ac. 20:35).

2. It is also used in the LXX sense (Is. 41:9) for "divine help" (Lk. 1:54).

In 1 C. 12:28 ἀντίλημψις is not to be understood as the assumption of office (as in P. Oxy., 900, 13), since we have here a list of specific offices; what it means is "help," the gift or capacity being differentiated from those that precede

---

[1] Deissmann B, 87.
[2] Deissmann LO, 68.

by the fact that it does not have a miraculous character, and thus leads on to those that follow. The reference is obviously to the activity of love in the dealings of the community (cf. Ac. 6:1 ff.).

συναντιλαμβάνομαι means "to take up with." It is used in a secular sense in Lk. 10:40 and of the pneumatic prayer of the Christian assisting or replacing the noetic in R. 8:26. Here the pneuma is not thought of as *tertia persona* but as having become one with man. It has entered into union with the human καρδία and there fashions prayers which cannot be grasped by the human understanding and are not immediately adequate before God, but must first be searched out by Him. This pneumatic prayer is a charismatic dealing with God like speaking with tongues, whether with or without the corresponding forms (v. 26, στεναγμοῖς ἀλαλήτοις).

Delling

ἀντίλυτρον → λύω.

ἀντίτυπος → τύπος.

ἀνυπόκριτος → ὑποκρίνω.

ἀντιμισθία → μισθός.

ἀντίχριστος → χριστός.

ἀνυπότακτος → τάσσω.

| ἄνω, ἀνώτερον | (→ ἄνωθεν).

1. Adv. of place with the twofold meaning of "above" and "upward," and of time with the meaning of "earlier" (anton. κάτω); ἄνω denotes land (as opposed to sea), mountains, the atmosphere, heaven and its gods, and even the earth as opposed to the underworld.[1] In the NT it is normally used of heaven in its material (Jn. 11:41; Ac. 2:19) or religious sense (Jn. 8:23; Gl. 4:26; Phil. 3:14; Col. 3:1, 2).[2] For early Christianity, as for Judaism and Hellenism, it is natural to think of the Deity in heaven and thus to equate divine and heavenly. Thus expressions like the substant. τὰ ἄνω (Jn. 8:23; Phil. 3:14; Col. 3:1, 2) or the attribut. ἄνω (Gl. 4:26; Phil. 3:14) may be regarded as traditional. Similar expressions may be found both in Hellenistic[3] and Palestinian Judaism. The distinction between above and below (לְמַטָּה / לְמַעְלָה) plays an important role among the

---

ἄ ν ω. Lohmeyer on Col. 3:1; Str.-B., II, 116, 430.

[1] Cf. Pape, Liddell-Scott, *s.v.*

[2] The two cannot be separated. In prayer God is sought with an upward glance (Jn. 11:41; 17:1).

[3] Jos. Bell., 5, 400: τὸν ἄνω δικαστήν; Gr. Bar. 4: ἐν αὐτῷ μέλλουσιν τὴν ἄνω κλῆσιν προσλαβεῖν; Philo Rer. Div. Her., 70: (τῆς ψυχῆς) ἄνω πρὸς αὐτὸ (τὸ ὄντως ὄν) εἱλκυσμένης etc. (cf. the index to Leisegang).

Rabbis. A large measure of parallelism is maintained between what is and takes place above and what is and takes place below. [4]

2. In Philo the religious antithesis between God and the world is linked with a speculation which distinguishes an upper and a lower world. God is put in the upper and the lower is sub-divided so as to produce a varied but integrated whole with God at the head and matter at the foot. [5] Similar cosmological constructions are common in Hellenism, especially in Gnosticism. [6] To the degree that the thought of God remains weak, such metaphysical speculation may understand τὰ ἄνω as a higher world, until God is finally thought of as emanating from this world in a theogonic process.

There is no similar doctrine of the two worlds behind either Judaism or the NT. In both cases it is excluded by the concept of God in which the position of God as Creator and Lord of the world is unconditionally maintained. In the NT the antithesis between above and below is essentially religious. Above is God and His perfect revelation, below the world which is His creature but which stands in personal antithesis to Him. Thus the ἄνω κλῆσις in Phil. 3:14 is the call of God in Jesus Christ; the τὰ ἄνω of Col. 3:1, 2 can be more precisely defined: Where Christ is at the right hand of God; the opposite of this world denoted by the τὰ ἄνω of Jn. 8:23 is not that world [7] but the Father (13:1). The nature of the Jerusalem which is above (G. 4:26) is not described in cosmological but in religious terms, [8] and rather strangely its opposite is that which now is rather than a lower Jerusalem (v. 25). Naturally the NT has no doctrine of creation and consummation which establishes the relationship of the ἄνω to the present world. There are materials for a doctrine of two worlds. Indeed, we are given plastic descriptions of heaven, the new Jerusalem. [9] The air is the place of spirits where those who are perfected will meet Christ (→ ἀπάντησις, 380). [10] Yet in spite of these points of contact with the doctrine of two worlds, or with its mythical basis, the total view of the NT is determined by the religious antithesis between God as the holy and eternal and the world as the sinful and therefore transitory (→ κόσμος). There is no NT cosmology in the Philonic or Gnostic sense.

---

[4] E.g., Chag., 2, 1: Whosoever considers what is above and what is below, cf. Str.-B., II, 116, 430. יְרוּשָׁלֵם שֶׁל מַעְלָה, bTaan., 5a. S. Nu., 84 on 10:36: As the Shekinah above is always surrounded by thousands and tens of thousands (Ps. 68:17), so it is below (Nu. 10:36). S. Nu., 84 on 10:35: As the Israelites had to make bricks in Egypt, so they will also be made above.

[5] It is worth noting that Philo uses ἀνωτέρω and ἀνωτάτω together with ἄνω (Leisegang, Index). Neither word, however, is used in this sense in the NT (ἀνώτερον is used in Lk. 14:10 of the better place at table, and in Hb. 10:8 of the first part of a passage of Scripture). The air has special significance for Philo, since as a light material it moves upwards (Gig., 22), as do also souls (Som., I, 139).

[6] Plotinus often speaks of τὸ ἄνω in this sense: Enn., I, 6, 7: ἀναβαίνουσι πρὸς τὸ ἄνω; V, 9, 1: ἀδυνατήσαντες δὲ ἰδεῖν τὸ ἄνω.

[7] ὁ → κόσμος ἐκεῖνος and similar expressions are not found in the NT, where we simply have ὁ κόσμος οὗτος and, of course, ὁ μέλλων → αἰών etc.

[8] Even in the Pauline antithesis of flesh and spirit the decisive contrast is not cosmological but religious and ethical.

[9] Cf. Rev., also Lk. 16:19-31, but also 1 C. 15:35-49.

[10] Eph. 2:2; 1 Th. 4:17.

† ἄνωθεν.

Both in and outside the NT a. an adv. of place "from above" Mt. 27:51: ἀπ᾽ ἄνωθεν ἕως κάτω (the veil of the temple). b. adv. of time "from an earlier period" (Ac. 26:5; cf. Ditt. Syll.³, 685, 81: νόμοις γὰρ ἱεροῖς καὶ ἐπιτιμίαις ἄνωθεν διεκεκώλυτο ἵνα μηδείς ...; Jos. Ap., 1, 28: ἐκ μακροτάτων ἄνωθεν χρόνων etc.). c. "From the first" (Lk. 1:3; cf. Epict. Diss., II, 17, 27: ἄνωθεν ἄρξασθαι). d. "anew" (Gl. 4:9; cf. Artemid. Oneirocrit., 1, 13: ἄνωθεν ¹ αὐτὸς δόξειε γεννᾶσθαι; Jos. Ant., 1, 263: φιλίαν ἄνωθεν ποιεῖται πρὸς αὐτόν, of the renewal of an original friendship).

As regards Jn. 3:3, 7 the original usage does not help us to decide, but inclines in favour of a. "born from above." For it is only with a. that we can link Job 3:4: μὴ ἀναζητήσαι αὐτὴν ὁ κύριος ἄνωθεν (Jm. 1:17; 3:15, 17), and in Philo² a strong religious sense "of God." ³ It is decisive that elsewhere Jn. always uses ἄνωθεν in the sense of a. (3:31; 19:11, 23), and he always describes birth in terms of its origin, i.e., of God (1:13; 1 Jn. 2:29; 3:9; 4:7; 5:18), of the Spirit or flesh (3:6), of water and the Spirit (3:5). To presuppose an originally purely formal description of birth in the sense of d., and thus to make the misunderstanding of Nicodemus more pardonable, may correspond to modern sensibility but not to the dealings of Jesus with Nicodemus according to John. Recourse to an underlying Hebrew would suggest a., since מִלְמַעְלָה has this meaning.⁴ Declension from d. to c.⁵ gives a dreadful pleonasm. For at birth a life always begins at the beginning and not at some point in its course. The suggestion that both a. and d. are meant is both superfluous and unprovable. Distinguished representatives of ecclesiastical tradition testify that ἄνωθεν here means "from above." Orig. Fr., 35 (p. 510, Preuschen) and Chrys. Hom. in Joh. 24, 2 (MPG, 59, p. 145 f.) mention both a. and d. in relation to Jn. 3:5, and come down more or less decidedly in favour of the former. Cyr. does not consider any other meaning. The Syr. versions are overwhelmingly for a.: syrᶜ syrᵖᵃˡ syrᵖ ; though the Lat. and Copt. favour d., as also Tert. and Thdr. Just. has the form: ἂν μὴ ἀναγεννηθῆτε οὐ μὴ εἰσέλθητε εἰς τὴν βασιλείαν τῶν οὐρανῶν (Apol., I, 61), similarly Ps.-Clem. Hom., XI, 26, Recg., VI, 9 and Iren. Fr., 35, Stieren.

Büchsel

ἄ ν ω θ ε ν. ¹ So the MSS adduced by R. Hercher in the apparatus of his edition (1864). Hercher substitutes a mere ἄν.

² Rer. Div. Her., 64: ὁ καταπνευσθεὶς ἄνωθεν, οὐρανίου τε καὶ θείας μοίρας ἐπιλαχών etc., e.g., Fug., 138; Mut. Nom., 260.

³ Cf. also bYoma, 39a: The man who sanctifies himself below will be sanctified above מלמעלה (= God), and S. Nu., 45 on 7:5: Their purpose agreed with the higher purpose לדעת העליונה.

⁴ Gn.r., 51 on 19:24: אין דבר רע יורד מלמעלה and Tanch. מצורע 9:43: אני הוא שמטהר אתכם מלמעלה (I purify you from above, i.e., I, God, purify you, so that there is no possibility of relapse into uncleanness). The Aram. מִלְעֵילָא is also unambiguous.

⁵ Zn. J., ad loc.

ἄξιος, ἀνάξιος,
ἀξιόω, καταξιόω

† ἄξιος, ἀνάξιος.

Properly, "bringing up the other beam of the scales," "bringing into equilibrium," and therefore "equivalent": Philo Leg. All., III, 10: ἀξίως γὰρ οὐδεὶς τὸν θεὸν τιμᾷ, ἀλλὰ δικαίως μόνον· ὁπότε γὰρ οὐδὲ τοῖς γονεῦσιν ἴσας ἀποδοῦναι χάριτας ἐνδέχεται — ἀντιγεννῆσαι γὰρ οὐχ οἶόν τε τούτους —, πῶς οὐκ ἀδύνατον τὸν θεὸν ἀμείψασθαι ... κατὰ τὴν ἀξίαν τὸν τὰ ὅλα συστησάμενον; so R. 8:18: οὐκ ἄξια τὰ παθήματα τοῦ νῦν καιροῦ πρὸς τὴν μέλλουσαν δόξαν ἀποκαλυφθῆναι "they are not of equal weight." ἄξιόν ἐστιν "it is appropriate or reasonable" (1 Cor. 16:4; 2 Th. 1:3). The use of ἄξιος or ἀνάξιος shows that two distinct magnitudes are equal or equivalent; an act "deserves" praise or punishment: Jos. Bell., 5, 408: εἰ καὶ τὴν ἡμετέραν γενεὰν ἐλευθερίας ἢ Ῥωμαίους κολάσεως ἀξίους ἔκρινε; so in the NT: μισθοῦ, τιμῆς, τροφῆς, πληγῶν, δεσμῶν, θανάτου ἄξιος, Mt. 10:10, Lk. 10:7; 12:48; 23:15, 41; Ac. 23:29; 25:11, 25; 26:31; R. 1:32; 1 Tm. 5:18; 6:1; Rev. 16:6. As Inschr. Priene, 59, 3: ἐπιστροφῆς ἄξιος, "worthy of consideration," so 1 Tm. 1:15; 4:9: πάσης ἀποδοχῆς ἄξιος, "worthy in any wise to be received." Supremely, God is worthy to be praised: Rev. 4:11; 5:12, [1] or the Lamb to open the seal: Rev. 5:2, 4, 9. Yet the context suggests that in the latter passages ἄξιος almost has the sense of "in a position to" (cf. 1 C. 6:2). Figuratively we have καρποὶ ἄξιοι τῆς μετανοίας "corresponding to repentance" (Mt. 3:8 and par.; Ac. 26:20).

The thought of merit in later Judaism found expression in זַכַּי (זָכָה) which corresponds to ἄξιος. Thus Gn.r., 8 on 1:26: אם זכה אדם אומרים לו אתה קדמת למלאכי השרת. [2] In contrast the self-judgment in such passages as Lk. 15:19, 21; Jn. 1:27 and Ac. 13:25 is in terms of unworthiness. [3] A man is worthy of the Gospel of Christ as and because he receives it; all thought of merit is excluded by the nature of the Gospel (Mt. 10:11, 13; 22:8; 10:37 f.; Ac. 13:46; Hb. 11:38; Rev. 3:4).

In a series of expressions the gen. or infin. is linked with ἄξιος to indicate the sphere in which there is correspondence. We see this esp. in many pagan expressions like πομπεύσας δὲ ἀξίως μὲν τῶν πατρω[ίων θεῶν] ... ἀξίως δὲ καὶ τῶν πολιτῶν (Inschr. Priene, 109, 195), [4] cf. R. 16:2: προσδέξησθε ... ἀξίως τῶν ἁγίων. To the extent that this sphere has binding force for the man who acts, the expression "to act accordingly" can express a living self-determination. In pagan inscriptions [5] the judgment ἀξίως is passed on action, and sometimes

---

ἄ ξ ι ο ς. Dob. Th. on 1, 2:12; Joh. W. 1 K. on 11:27; Loh. Phil. on 1:27.

[1] The form shows affinity with the so-called acclamations, v. E. Peterson, Εἷς θεός (1926), 176/180, Loh. Apk. on 4:11. It is worth noting that ᾽A translates אֵל שַׁדַּי by ἄξιος καὶ ἱκανός (Str.-B., III, 491g).

[2] For further passages, v. Str.-B., I, 129, 8; II, 254; Dalman WJ, I, 97 f.; Schl. Mt. on 10:13; 24:35; also F. Weber, Jüd. Theol.[2] (1897), 277, 279. On the exact sense of זכה, cf. K. G. Kuhn, Sifre Nu. § 119, n. 68.

[3] Positively, only Lk. 7:4 (the Jews of the centurion at Capernaum).

[4] For further examples, v. index of Inschr. Priene (ed. F. Hiller v. Gaertringen [1906], s.v. ἀξίως.

[5] The expressions with ἀξίως are here fairly formal.

in Epictet. ἔση ἄξιος τῶν θεῶν συμπότης (Ench., 15) can be asserted as the motive of action. Paul uses the expression only by way of admonition περιπατεῖν, πολιτεύεσθαι ἀξίως τοῦ εὐαγγελίου, τῆς κλήσεως, τοῦ κυρίου (1 Th. 2:12; Phil. 1:27; Col. 1:10; Eph. 4:1; cf. also 3 Jn. 6), and therein links the motive and goal of all Christian action. Its motivating power lies only in the preceding action of God, which alone determines its content and thus distinguishes it from all legalism. Hence the warning not to receive the Lord's Supper τοῦ κυρίου ἀναξίως (1 C. 11:27) does not denote a moral quality but an attitude determined by the Gospel.

† ἀξιόω, † καταξιόω.

1. "To make worthy." This meaning must be accepted in the case of 2 Th. 1:11: ἵνα ὑμᾶς ἀξιώσῃ τῆς κλήσεως ὁ θεός, in view of the significance of κλῆσις. [1]

2. "To regard as worthy" and to act accordingly = "to value or appreciate" (even a punishment, Θ Da. 3:97; 2 Macc. 9:15; Lk. 7:7; 1 Tm. 5:17; Hb. 3:3; 10:29). Epictetus describes the calling, position and destiny of man as "being regarded as worthy of a post by Zeus", [2] whereas the NT with the exclusive use of the compound καταξιόω expresses unworthiness of the divine gift of grace: Lk. 20:35: οἱ δὲ καταξιωθέντες τοῦ αἰῶνος ἐκείνου τυχεῖν; and similarly Ac. 5:41; 2 Th. 1:5. [3]

3. "To regard as right" (Ac. 15:38); "to ask" (Ac. 28:22).

Foerster

ἀόρατος → ὁράω   ἀπαγγέλλω → 64
ἀπαίδευτος → παιδεύω   ἀπαιτέω → 193 f.
ἀπαλλάσσω → 252 f.   ἀπαλλοτριόω → 265 f.

ἀπάντησις

According to 1 Th. 4:17, at the second coming of the Lord, there will be a rapture εἰς ἀπάντησιν τοῦ κυρίου εἰς ἀέρα. The word ἀπάντησις (also ὑπάντησις, DG) is to be understood as a tech. term for a civic custom of antiquity whereby a public welcome was accorded by a city to important visitors. Similarly,

---

ἀ ξ ι ό ω. Dob. Th. on 2, 1:11.
[1] Cf. the same meaning in Dg., 9, 1.
[2] Diss., IV, 8, 30 : τοιοῦτος γάρ τίς ἐστιν ὁ Κυνικὸς τοῦ σκήπτρου ... ἠξιωμένος παρὰ τοῦ Διός; II, 1, 39 : τῷ ἄξιον τῆς χώρας ταύτης κεκρικότι. Similarly I, 29, 47 and 49; III, 22, 57.
[3] Vett. Val., IX, 1, p. 329, 20 ff., Kroll : ἤδη ποτὲ πελαγοδρομήσας καὶ πολλὴν ἔρημον διοδεύσας ἠξιώθην ἀπὸ θεῶν λιμένος ἀκινδύνου τυχεῖν.
ἀ π ά ν τ η σ ι ς. E. Peterson, "Die Einholung des Kyrios," ZSTh, 7 (1929/30), 682 ff., where the evidence from antiquity is given.

when Christians leave the gates of the world, they will welcome Christ in the ἀήρ, acclaiming Him as κύριος.

> P. Berol, II, 362, p. 7; Ditt. Or., 332; Polyb., V, 26, 8 etc.; Jos. Bell., 7, 100. The Gk. word was also adopted by the Rabbis as a loan word, e.g., Tanch. אמור 178a: "The great of the city moved out to meet the king" יוצאין לאפנטי של מלך.[1]

Peterson

ἅπαξ, ἐφάπαξ

† ἅπαξ.

1. ἅπαξ "once" a. as a strictly numerical concept.

ἅπαξ ἐλιθάσθην (2 C. 11:25); with a temporal definition: ἅπαξ τοῦ ἐνιαυτοῦ[1] (Hdt., II, 59; cf. IV, 105; LXX, Ex. 30:10; cf. 3 Macc. 1:11; Jos. Bell., 5, 236; Philo Ebr., 136; NT, Hb. 9:7). The expression ἅπαξ καὶ δίς = "repeatedly" (LXX, Dt. 9:13, cf. 1 Cl., 53, 3; 1 Macc. 3:30; cf. Dion. Hal. Ant. Rom., VIII, 56, 1: οὐχ ἅπαξ, ἀλλὰ [καὶ] δίς; in the NT, Phil. 4:16; 1 Th. 2:18; cf. Tt. 3:10: μετὰ μίαν καὶ δευτέραν νουθεσίαν "after more than one admonition").

The basic meaning of ἅπαξ in the NT is acquired when it refers to the uniqueness of Christ's work as something which cannot be repeated. Hb. 9:26: νυνὶ δὲ ἅπαξ ... ἐπὶ συντελείᾳ τῶν αἰώνων εἰς ἀθέτησιν τῆς ἁμαρτίας ... πεφανέρωται. As the uniqueness of Christ's appearing in the world is emphasised here, so is the unique birth of Νοῦς in Plotinus (Enn., VI, 8, 21 [II, 506, 16 f., Volkm.]). Cf. also the divine name Ἅπαξ ἐπέκεινα with the (ambiguous?) Δὶς ἐπέκεινα in one of the triads of Procl. (in Tim., 94c.; in Crat., 64, 3; 56, 8).[2] The once-for-all offering of Christ is contrasted with the annual visit of the Jewish high-priest to the Holiest of Holies (v. 25). The ἅπαξ is even more strongly emphasised 1. by the reference to the last time, when only that which is definitive will take place, 2. by the twofold repetition of ἅπαξ in v. 27 f., and 3. by the application of the thought of v. 26 in v. 28: ἅπαξ προσενεχθεὶς εἰς τὸ πολλῶν ἀνενεγκεῖν ἁμαρτίας.[3] Christ is not merely the unique High-priest but also the unique sacrifice (cf. Hb. 10:12, 14, → εἷς). Both in v. 26 and v. 28 the aim of the ἅπαξ of Christ in relation to sin is underlined. By His one coming and death sin is finally set aside (→ ἀθετέω, ἀναφέρω). The parallel to this passage is an argument in favour of Χριστὸς ἅπαξ περὶ ἁμαρτιῶν ἀπέθανεν at 1 Pt. 3:18 (instead of ἔπαθεν); for according to Hb. it was meaningful for Christians to emphasise the once-for-allness of Christ's death[4] (→ 383 on R. 6:10). Indeed, in the light of it they could point expressly to the general human analogy of the

---

[1] Cf. Levy Wört., I, 145.

ἅ π α ξ. Rgg. Hb., 155, 8; Kn. Pt., 144; Zn. Einl., 86, 3; Preisigke Wört. s.v. ἅπαξ.

[1] Cf. Rgg. Hb., 248, n. 91.

[2] Cf. W. Kroll, De oraculis Chaldaicis, Bresl. Philol. Abh., 7 (1894), 16 f.

[3] Bengel, ad loc.: suave antitheton: semel multorum, qui tot saeculis vixerunt.

[4] As opposed to Kn. Pt., 143.

one experience of death (Hb. 9:27: καθ' ὅσον ἀπόκειται τοῖς ἀνθρώποις ἅπαξ ἀποθανεῖν). [5]

As in relation to Christ's first coming, so in relation to His second ἅπαξ acquires a radical meaning in the NT ; for eschatological events are unique in the strict sense and cannot be repeated. In Hb. 12:26 the words of Hag. 2:6 are referred to the final catastrophe : ἔτι ἅπαξ ἐγὼ σείσω οὐ μόνον τὴν γῆν ἀλλὰ καὶ τὸν οὐρανόν. The phrase "yet once more," i.e., "for the last time," [6] denotes a final transformation of the world (v. 27) which will leave only that which cannot be transformed (→ supra on Hb. 9:26).

b. ἅπαξ as an indefinite concept of time : ("when," "after" etc.) "once," and therefore esp. after ἐάν, ἐπεί, ὅτε, etc., or in conjunction with the part. praet. : Aesch. Eum., 648; Ag., 1018; Amphis, 8 (CAF, II, 238): ἂν ἅπαξ τις ἀποθάνῃ, P. Oxy., 1102, 8; 471, 77; Jos. Ant., 4, 140; Herm. v., 3, 3, 4; Julian Or., 2, p. 91d. In the NT this form is found only in d cod. 69 at 1 Pt. 3:20 (?): ὅτε ἅπαξ ἐδέχετο ἡ τοῦ θεοῦ μακροθυμία, and perhaps in the part. constructions in Hb. 6:4; 10:2 (→ infra).

2. ἅπαξ "once-for-all" [7] (→ ἐφάπαξ, 2).

Mostly (and exclusively in the NT) before part praet. (in contrast v. ἐφάπαξ). P. Form., 1281: ἅπαξ δοθέντα "final reckoning," P. Leipz., 35, 19 : τὰ ἅπαξ τυπωθέντα ἐφ' ὑπομνημάτων, "that which is laid down once and for all by protocol"; Philo Ebr., 198; APF, 2 (1903), 433 (21, 14); possibly LXX ψ 88:36.

In the NT it signifies the definitiveness of the Christian state and the once-for-allness of the one baptism : [8] ἀδύνατον γὰρ τοὺς ἅπαξ φωτισθέντας γευσαμένους τε τῆς δωρεᾶς τῆς ἐπουρανίου ... καὶ παραπεσόντας πάλιν ἀνακαινίζειν εἰς μετάνοιαν (Hb. 6:4). The enlightenment and reception of the Holy Spirit [9] in baptism (→ φωτίζω) are so essentially unique that if they are lost there can be no repetition or restoration. The expression ἅπαξ γευσάμενος undoubtedly [10] derives from a proverbial saying similar to that about those who have once tasted blood ; hence the thought is also present that it is quite unnatural for anyone to let go again the heavenly gift.

In the ἅπαξ κεκαθαρισμένοι of Hb. 10:2 what is actually true of Christians is hypothetically stated of the Jews. In Judaism there was no once-for-all purification because no once-for-all sacrifice ; but Christianity has both [11] (→ ἐφάπαξ, 384).

---

[5] The truth that man dies only once had often been stated from the time of Homer : Od., 12, 22 : ἅπαξ θνήσκουσ' ἄνθρωποι; Soph. Fr., 64 (TGF, 114, Nauck): θανεῖν γὰρ οὐκ ἔξεστι τοῖς αὐτοῖσι δίς. Cf. Wis. 25.

[6] Ἔτι ἅπαξ, "for the last time," is found already in Aesch. Ag., 1322; LXX, Ju. 6:39; cf. also ἔτι τὸ ἅπαξ τοῦτο, "yet one more time," Ju. 16:18, 28. On this subst. ἅπαξ, cf. P. Jernstedt, "Sur la forme substantive ἅπαξ" (Russian), Rev. Byz., 2 (1916), 97-105 (numerous examples being given); APF, 6 (1920), 379 f. (on P. Ry., 435); Ditt. Or., 201, 2, 4 with n. 7 and 10, and on this Radermacher,[2] 13, 2; Deissmann LO, 185, 8 (on P. Lond., 417, 8 and 12).

[7] Semel is used in the same way, e.g. Horace Sat., II, 8, 24.

[8] Cf. Wnd. Hb.[2], 52 ff.

[9] Ibid., ad loc.

[10] As in Jos. Ant., 4, 140; Bell., 2, 158, though here the once-for-allness is not stressed.

[11] In the reading ℵ c Or Tert the washing only of the feet in Jn. 13:10 symbolises the once-for-all purification by Christ.

The Epistle of Jude [12] formulates the thought of Christian once-for-allness in a more rigid and intellectual manner. Christianity is now ἅπαξ παραδοθεῖσα τοῖς ἁγίοις πίστις (Jd. 3). The ἅπαξ underlines the concept of *fides, quae creditur*. Thus Christians are εἰδότες ἅπαξ πάντα, i.e., men who know everything necessary for salvation and who therefore, according to the author, possess it. Here there is no danger of loss. The thought is thus quite different from that of Hb., and we recall that Paul knows nothing of a πίστις given once and for all in this sense.

It is interesting that Philo on one occasion (Ebr., 198) censures πιστεύειν τοῖς ἅπαξ παραδοθεῖσι (i.e., believing as if laws were given once and for all).

If in Jd. 5 the reading of א 1739 Cl. Al. Pesh etc. is right, [13] the unique redemption of Israel out of Egypt is here advanced as a prototype of the one definitive redemption by Christ.

† ἐφάπαξ. [1]

1. ἐφάπαξ "at once" (= "together"). P. Lond., 1708, 242 : οὐκ ὑφ᾽ ἕν ἐφάπαξ, "not individually but together" ; 483, 88 : ἐφάπαξ ὁμολογεῖν, "to agree in the lump" ; P. Flor., II, 158, 10. [2] In the NT 1 C. 15:6.

2. ἐφάπαξ "once and for all." [3] In the NT this is a technical term for the definitiveness and therefore the uniqueness or singularity of the death of Christ and the redemption thereby accomplished : R. 6:10 : τῇ ἁμαρτίᾳ ἀπέθανεν ἐφάπαξ, where ἐφάπαξ, prepared and emphasised in v. 9 by οὐκέτι ἀποθνήσκει, θάνατος οὐκέτι κυριεύει, sharply expresses the basic significance of the death of Christ, namely, that sin and Christ are quits, and Christians with Christ, since His one death is of paradigmatic and dynamic effect for us. To the ἀποθανεῖν τῇ ἁμαρτίᾳ ἐφάπαξ in the case of Christ there corresponds νεκροὺς εἶναι (dead once and for all) τῇ ἁμαρτίᾳ. There here rules a divine causality mediated through baptism (→ βαπτίζω on R. 6:3). Like Christ, man can die this death only once (as he can rise again only once, → 383 on Hb. 6:4); there is a turning from sin to God which cannot subsequently be reversed. [4] The man who has died this death lives once and for all according to Paul, i.e., in eternity like Christ.

The same thought is expressed under the image of the sacrifice in Hb. 7:27: τοῦτο γὰρ ἐποίησεν ἐφάπαξ ἑαυτὸν ἀνενέγκας. The ἐφάπαξ acquires its force here from comparison with the (daily?) [5] sacrifice of the high-priest, for, quite apart from the fact that He is both Priest and offering, Christ is distinguished from the high-priest by the once and once-for-allness of His sacrifice ; the ἐφάπαξ excludes both the necessity and the possibility of repetition. Hb. 9:12 uses the same imagery : εἰσῆλθεν ἐφάπαξ εἰς τὰ ἅγια, αἰωνίαν λύτρωσιν εὑράμενος.

---

[12] Cf. Zn. Einl., *ad loc.*
[13] Cf. Wnd. Jd. *ad loc.* ; a contrary view is found in Kn. Jd., 220.
ἐ φ ά π α ξ. Winer, 393 f.; Zn. R., 306, 6; Preisigke Wört., *s.v.*; G. Schrenk, "D. Geschichtsanschauung d. Pls.," *Jbch. d. Theol. Schule Bethel,* 3 (1932), 61, n. 8.
[1] Bl.-Debr., 12, 3 : ἐφ᾽ ἅπαξ.
[2] In the MS itself we find ἀφάπαξ, which according to Vitelli (in Preisigke, *Berichtungsliste d. griech. Papyrusurkunden aus Ägypten,* I [1913/22], *ad loc.*) is a mistake for ἐφ᾽ ἅπαξ.
[3] Similarly καθάπαξ, εἰς ἅπαξ, P. Oxy., 1294, 14; πρὸς ἅπαξ, P. Oxy., 1138, 13.
[4] Brth. R², 188 f.
[5] Cf. Rgg. Hb., 212 on this error (?).

Here ἐφάπαξ corresponds to αἰώνιος. The priestly entry into the sanctuary accomplishes a transitory λύτρωσις, but the definitive entry of Christ a definitive. Thus the ἐφάπαξ not only of Christ's death but of its efficacy is emphasised in Hb. 10:10 : ἡγιασμένοι ἐσμὲν διὰ τῆς προσφορᾶς τοῦ σώματος Ἰησοῦ Χριστοῦ ἐφάπαξ (ἐφάπαξ relating to ἡγιασμένοι rather than προσφορά). There is here a more direct linking of the once-for-allness of the death of Christ with the once-for-allness of the sanctification of Christians than in R. 6. The sacrifice of Christ accomplishes our sanctification directly and gives it the same definitiveness as it has itself.

Stählin

ἀπαράβατος → παραβαίνω   ἀπαρνέομαι → ἀρνέομαι
ἀπαρχή → ἄρχω

ἀπατάω, ἐξαπατάω, ἀπάτη

† ἀπατάω, † ἐξαπατάω.

ἀπατάω, common since Homer; in the pap. found only in P. Greci e Latini, 152, 24 (2nd century A.D.) in connection with ψεῦδος, then not until P. Lond., 1345, 13 (8th century A.D.); not attested in the inscr., but found in Epicur., p. 298, 29, Usener : ἐὰν μή τις ταῖς κεναῖς δόξαις ἑαυτὸν ἀπατᾷ; in Plut. and Epictet. Diss., IV, 5, 32 : ἠπατημένοι περὶ τῶν μεγίστων. ἐξαπατάω was more common : Hippocr. Vet. Med., 2 : ἐξηπάτηται καὶ ἐξαπατᾶται; P. Oxy., 471, 42 (2nd century A.D. : ἐξαπατη-[θῆναι] ἢ καὶ δωρεὰ[ς λαβεῖν] φήσεις (deceived or corrupted ?); Ditt. Syll.³, 364, 37 (3rd century B.C.): ἐξαπατήσαντες τοὺς ὑστέρους δανειστάς; ibid., 884, 46 (3rd century A.D.): εἰ δέ τις ἐξαπατήσα[ς τῶν] ὀφειλόν[των ξένῳ ὑποθείη τι τῶν χωρίων τῶ]ν δημοσίων ...

Common in the LXX "to deceive" or "entice"; of the wives of Samson, Ju. 14:15; 16:5; of the instigation of God, 3 Βασ. 22:20 f.; cf. Jdt. 13:16; of God Himself as Deceiver, Jer. 4:10; 20:7: ἠπάτησάς με, κύριε, καὶ ἠπατήθην (profound temptation); but also in hostility to God, Gn. 3:13 : ὁ ὄφις ἠπάτησέν με; of the temptation to idolatry, Job 31:27 : εἰ ἠπατήθη λάθρα ἡ καρδία μου; of the deceitfulness of sensual desire, Sus. 56 : τὸ κάλλος σε ἠπάτησεν (Θ ἐξηπάτησεν), ἡ μικρὰ ἐπιθυμία.

The NT mostly uses the word in the last sense : 2 C. 11:3 : ὁ ὄφις ἐξηπάτησεν Εὔαν; 1 Tm. 2:14 : Ἀδὰμ οὐκ ἠπατήθη, ἡ δὲ γυνὴ ἐξαπατηθεῖσα. R. 7:11 [1] speaks of the deception of sin repeated in the life of each of us; Eph. 5:6 warns

---

ἀπατάω κτλ. [1] According to W. G. Kümmel, *Römer 7 und die Bekehrung des Paulus* (1929), 74, this passage is not to be interpreted either biographically or with reference to the Jewish people or the fall, but purely rhetorically (→ ἁμαρτία, 311, n. 157).

against being deceived : μηδεὶς ὑμᾶς ἀπατάτω, cf. R. 16:18; 2 Th. 2:3; 1 C. 3:18 speaks of sinful self-deception : μηδεὶς ἑαυτὸν ἐξαπατάτω; cf. Jm. 1:26 : ἀπατῶν καρδίαν ἑαυτοῦ.

† ἀπάτη.

a. "Deception" or "enticement." Pind. Fr., 213, Schroeder: σκολιαὶ ἀπάται; P. Oxy., 1020, 8 (2nd century A.D.): ἀγὼν τῆς ἀπάτης, an action because of deceitful conduct ; Luc. Tim., 27; Ceb. Tab., 5, 2 : ἀπάτη, ἡ πάντας τοὺς ἀνθρώπους πλανῶσα; 6, 2 : 'Απάτη personified ; 14, 3; Corp. Herm., XIII, 1: ἀπαλλοτριοῦν τὸ φρόνημα ἀπὸ τῆς τοῦ κόσμου ἀπάτης (cf. 7). b. "(Pleasant) illusion," e.g., (in the theatre etc.). Gorg. Fr., 23 (Diels, II, 265, 32 ff.): (Tragedy) παρασχοῦσα τοῖς μύθοις καὶ τοῖς πάθεσιν ἀπάτην, hence more generally "pleasure" : Moeris, p. 65, Pierson: ἀπάτη ἡ πλάνη παρ' 'Αττικοῖς ... ἡ τέρψις παρ' "Ελλησιν; Inschr. Priene, 113, 63 f. (84 B.C.): [2] κα[τατιθ]εὶς δὲ μὴ μόνον τὰ πρὸς ἡδον[ήν, ἀλλὰ καὶ βουλόμενος] ἐκ[τ]ὸς ἀπάτην χορηγῆσαι [τοῖς θεαταῖς, αὐλητήν?], "He did not provide only what ministers satisfaction, but, aiming also to delight his audience, he caused a fluteplayer to come (?)"; Polyb., II, 56, 12; IV, 20, 5. Even the woman's name 'Απάτη might well mean "delight." The evil connotation is not found in Hellenism, though cf. → supra Cebes, Corp. Herm., etc.

In the NT we have the meaning a. in Col. 2:8 : "Beware lest any man spoil you διὰ τῆς φιλοσοφίας καὶ κενῆς ἀπάτης; Hb. 3:13; 2 Th. 2:10. The meaning b. [3] is most likely in Mk. 4:19; Mt. 13:22 : ἡ μέριμνα τοῦ αἰῶνος καὶ ἡ ἀπάτη τοῦ πλούτου (Lk. 8:14 : ἡδονῶν) and 2 Pt. 2:13 : ἐντρυφῶντες ἐν ταῖς ἀπάταις (altern. reading ἀγάπαις) αὐτῶν, as also Eph. 4:22 : ("Put off the old man") φθειρόμενον κατὰ τὰς ἐπιθυμίας τῆς ἀπάτης. In distinction from Hellenism the NT lays great stress on the evil aspects of b. It is thus more strongly affected by a.

Oepke

ἀπάτωρ → πατήρ   ἀπαύγασμα → αὐγάζω
ἀπείθεια, ἀπειθέω, ἀπειθής → πείθω   ἀπείραστος → πειράζω
ἀπεκδέχομαι → δέχομαι   ἀπέκδυσις, ἀπεκδύω → δύω
ἀπελεύθερος → ἐλεύθερος   ἀπελπίζω → ἐλπίζω
ἀπερίτμητος → περιτομή   ἀπέχω → ἔχω
ἀπιστέω, ἀπιστία, ἄπιστος → πιστεύω

---

[2] Cf. on this J. Rouffiac, *Recherches* (1911), 38 f. The Latins translate ἀπάτη *delectationes, voluptas, delectamentum.*

[3] A. Deissmann, *Neue Jbch. f. d. klass. Altertum,* 6 (1903), 165, 5.

ἁπλοῦς, ἁπλότης

† ἁπλοῦς.

In addition to the original meaning a. "simple" : LXX, Wis. 16:27; Philo Congr., 36, there is a whole series of derived meanings : b. "open," "without ulterior motive" : hence the adv. ἁπλῶς, "unambiguously," "wholeheartedly" : M. Ant., V, 7, 2 : εὔχεσθαι ... ἁπλῶς καὶ ἐλευθέρως; cf. III, 6, 6; X, 8, 5; XI, 5, 6; then in addition to these more positive senses, the more intellectual c. "simple" in the negative sense : Isoc., 2, 46 : ἁπλοῦς ἡγοῦνται τοὺς νοῦν οὐκ ἔχοντας. The verb ἁπλόω, common only after the imperial period, thus means to "make simple," i.e., "to expound" (Lucillius, Ant. Pal., XI, 107), but then comes to signify amongst other things "to disseminate" (Dg., 11, 5 : δι᾽ οὗ πλουτίζεται ἡ ἐκκλησία καὶ χάρις ἁπλουμένη ἐν ἁγίοις πληθύνεται.

In Gk. translations of the OT ἁπλοῦς or → ἁπλότης (or ἁπλοσύνη) are equivalents [1] of ἀληθινός, ἄμωμος, ὅσιος, εἰρηνικός, καθαρὰ καρδία etc. in transl. of תֹּם, תָּם, יֹשֶׁר, יָשָׁר and כֵּן. Here as in Greek-speaking Judaism generally the word-group is most used to express such positive values as "free from inner discord," "innocent," "upright," "pure." The adj. ἁπλοῦς is found in the LXX only at Prv. 11:25 : ψυχὴ εὐλογημένη πᾶσα ἁπλῆ = נֶפֶשׁ בְּרָכָה תְדֻשָּׁן, where it is synon. with εὐσχήμων.

The intellectual depreciation of the "simple" was no less foreign to early Christianity than to Judaism. Hence in the NT the word-group is either neutral or expresses positive values as in Jewish literature. Mt. 6:22 : ἐὰν οὖν ᾖ ὁ ὀφθαλμός σου ἁπλοῦς, ὅλον τὸ σῶμά σου φωτεινὸν ἔσται· ἐὰν δὲ ὁ ὀφθαλμός σου πονηρὸς ᾖ, ὅλον τὸ σῶμά σου σκοτεινὸν ἔσται. If the words ἁπλοῦς and → πονηρός here describe physical states, [2] as seems most likely, then ἁπλοῦς must have the meaning of "healthy" as in Prv. 11:25. [3] If, however, the terms have ethical significance, [4] then we must translate ἁπλοῦς "pure" in the sense of a purity which is ready for sacrifice. In favour of this is the sense d. of ἁπλότης (perhaps the meaning of ἁπλόω mentioned above), as also the possibility of taking ὀφθαλμὸς ἁπλοῦς to be a specific antithesis to ὀφθαλμὸς πονηρός (= evil eye). [5] In Jm. 1:5 : αἰτείτω παρὰ τοῦ διδόντος θεοῦ πᾶσιν ἁπλῶς καὶ μὴ ὀνειδίζοντος, the meaning might well be "kind" or "generous." Yet the sense of "wholehearted" is perhaps nearer the mark, cf. Herm. m., 2, 4 : πᾶσιν ὑστερουμένοις δίδου ἁπλῶς, μὴ διστάζων τίνι δῷς ἢ τίνι μὴ δῷς. ἁπλούστατοι in Mt. 10:16 D (sense b.) is not original.

ἁπλότης.

Here, too, the basic meaning is a. "simplicity" : 2 Βασ. 15:11; 3 Macc. 3:21; Jos. Bell., 2, 151. And again this leads to such value concepts as b. "noble simplicity," "character-

---

ἁπλοῦς κτλ. W. Brandt, "Der Spruch vom lumen internum," ZNW, 14 (1913), esp. 189 ff.; Dib. Jk., 76 f.; Sickbg. R., 124; Bousset-Gressm., 418 ff.; K. Brugmann, Indogerm. Forsch., 38 (1917/20), 128-135.

[1] Brandt, op. cit., 189.

[2] Cf. esp. Jülicher Gl. J., II, 98 ff.

[3] Heb. תָּם or תָּמִים, as used in bBQ, 12b; M.S., 1, 2; bTem., 107b for unblemished sacrificial animals.

[4] Cf. Jos. Ap., 2, 190 : the commandments are ἁπλαῖ τε καὶ γνώριμοι.

[5] עַיִן טוֹבָה and עַיִן רָעָה, cf. Ab., 2, 9 and 11; 5, 13 and 19; Ter., 4, 3 etc. (Str.-B., I, 833 ff.); also earlier Prv. 22:9; 23:6.

istic of the psyche of heroes," [1] c. "purity" or "singleness of heart" : Jos. Bell., 5, 319 and often in M. Ant., related to ἀλήθεια, [2] and d. "sufficiency" which has something to spare for others, i.e., "generosity" : Jos. Ant., 7, 332; Test. Iss. 3:8 : πάντα γὰρ πένησι καὶ θλιβομένοις παρεῖχον ... ἐν ἁπλότητι καρδίας μου.

In the NT the usual meaning is c.: Eph. 6:5; Col. 3:22 : ὑπακούετε ... ἐν ἁπλότητι καρδίας, [3] "with pure hearts" ; 2 C. 11:3 : ... ἀπὸ τῆς ἁπλότητος τῆς εἰς Χριστόν, "sincere dedication to Christ." In R. 12:8, 2 C. 8:2 and 9:11, 13, however, we have sense d. — sacrificial "liberality."

In Cl. Al. Prot., 106, 3 (from the Apoc. Petr. ?): τάχα που ὁ κύριος ἁπλότητος ὑμῖν δωρήσεται πτερόν, ἁπλότης leads to heaven. It is mentioned particularly by Herm.

Bauernfeind

ἀπογίγνομαι → γίγνομαι ἀπόδεκτος, ἀποδέχομαι → δέχομαι
ἀποδίδωμι → δίδωμι ἀποδοκιμάζω → δόκιμος
ἀποδοχή → δέχομαι ἀποθνήσκω → θάνατος

ἀποκαθίστημι, ἀποκατάστασις

---

† ἀποκαθίστημι.

The basic meaning is "to restore to an earlier condition." From this derive the following main senses : 1. "to restore" or "return": a leasehold estate, P. Oxy., II, 278, 17 (17 A.D.); something borrowed, Xenoph. Resp. Lac., 6, 3 : ἱερὸν ἀποκατασταθῆναι αὐτοῖς; 2 Macc. 11:25; with a personal obj., P. Oxy., I, 38, 12 (49/50 A.D.): ὑφ᾽ οὗ καὶ ἀποκατεστάθη μοι ὁ υἱός; so also Hb. 13:19 : ἵνα τάχιον ἀποκατασταθῶ ὑμῖν, "that I may be restored to you the sooner."

2. "To restore" a. buildings etc., Inschr. Priene, 12, 8 : στήλη νῦν ἀποκαθισταμένη ; a canal, Ditt. Or., 672, *ibid.*, 90, 18 : ἀπεκατέστησεν εἰς τὴν καθήκουσαν τάξιν; b. mid. "to heal," Diosc. Mat. Med., I, 64, 4; esp. in the Bible, e.g., of lepers : Ex. 4:7; Lv. 13:16; Job 5:18; Mk. 3:5 and par. : ἀπεκατεστάθη ἡ χείρ, Mk. 8:25; cf. also the Mithras Liturgy in Preis. Zaub., IV (Paris), 629 f. : ὅταν ἀποκατασταθῇ σου ἡ ψυχή ; c. cosmologically "to renew the world," Herm. Trismeg., in Lact. Inst., VII, 18 (the demiurge of the first and only God after general expiation and purification) ἤγαγεν ἐπὶ τὸ ἀρχαῖον καὶ ἀποκατέστησεν τὸν ἑαυτοῦ κόσμον; d. politically

---

ἁ π λ ό τ η ς. [1] W. Schmid, *Philolog. Wochenschr.*, 46 (1926), 131, 144 (with examples). [2] R. Hirzel, *Themis, Dike und Verwandtes* (1907), 113, 3. [3] ἁπλότης καρδίας, also in 1 Ch. 29:17; Wis. 1:1; Test. XII : R. 4:1; S. 4:5; L. 13:1; Iss. 7:7.

ἀ π ο κ α θ ί σ τ η μ ι. On Elijah as the Restorer Schürer, II, 592, 610 ff.; Bousset-Gressm., 232 f.; the best collection of material is in Str. -B., IV, 764-798; B. Murmelstein, "Adam, ein Beitrag zur Messiaslehre," WZKM, 35 (1928), 242 ff.; 36 (1929), 51 ff., esp. 65 ff.; V. Aptowitzer, *Parteipolitik* (1927), 96-104, 244 f. A. Merx, *Der Messias oder Taëb der Samaritaner* (1909); for the older literature on this, cf. Schürer, II, 608 f. On Taxo, cf. Clement in Kautzsch, *Pseudepigr.*, 326. O. Procksch, "Wiederkehr und Wiedergeburt," *Ihmels-Festschr.* (1928), 1-18; J. Jeremias, *Jesus als Weltvollender* (1930). → ἀποκατάστασις.

"to reconstitute a state": Antiochus Epiphanes, 1 Macc. 15, 3 : ὅπως ἀποκαταστήσω αὐτήν (the kingdom of the fathers). Cf. Jos. Ant., 13, 261 and 408; Vit., 183.

From 2. d., and probably with some influence of 2. c., there developed the specific Messianic and ethical biblical usage. The term becomes a technical one for the restoration of Israel to its own land by Yahweh : Jer. 16:15 : ἀποκαταστήσω αὐτοὺς εἰς τὴν γῆν αὐτῶν; 23:8; 24:6 (Jos. Ant., 11, 2); Hos. 11:11, cf. Jer. 15:19; Ez. 16:55; with dat. and acc. ψ 15:5; Δα. 4:33. This was increasingly understood in a Messianic and eschatological sense. On the other hand, under prophetic influence it was more fully perceived that inner restitution is the condition and crown of the outer. The people must work for this (Am. 5:15). Yet from the time of Mal. 3:24 (4:5) the returning Elijah seems to have been expected as its true representative : ἀποκαταστήσει (הֵשִׁיב) καρδίαν πατρὸς πρὸς υἱόν κτλ. [1] There is a notable parallelism between the Heb. and the Gk. terminology. Both go back to an ancient oriental doctrine of the dissolving aeons and the saving restoration of all things to their original condition as created. Offshoots of this mythical conception of the world may be traced right up to the Fourth Eclogue of Vergil and the Metamorphoses of Ovid. The OT expression שׁוּב שְׁבוּת, not understood in the LXX, means technically "to execute a turn" or "to bring about a change of times" (Dt. 30:3; Jer. 31:23; Ps. 14:7 etc.). It no doubt comes from the hiphil of שׁוּב. Usually the LXX renders it ἀποκαθιστάναι, which would suggest → ἀποκατάστασις to the Gk. ear.

From the corresponding Aram. תוב the Samaritan Messiah derived his name Taheb. Although we have only later attestation of it, this expectation of the Taheb seems to be very old. It is possibly a relic of the Messianology which was not systematically connected with the house of David and which found an echo in Jewish expectation of Messiah ben Joseph. For the antiquity of this expectation of the Taheb we may refer not only to Jn. 4:25 but also to the legend of the concealment of the sacred vessels of the tabernacle in Gerizim as found in Samaritan texts and mentioned in Jos. Ant., 18, 85. Later Samaritan texts [2] attribute the name Taheb to the fact that the one who is expected will convert men, or even himself, as the "one who leads back" or the "penitent." Since, however, there is no instance of a causative significance for part. qal תָּהֵב,[3] and since the figurative use of תוב is highly uncertain, the basic meaning is simply he who returns ; the reference is to one of the princes of the past, usually Joshua. [4] Kingly and prophetic functions are ascribed to the Taheb, but he is subordinate to the priesthood. He will subdue eleven peoples and powerfully protect the true cult of Yahweh, also teaching and building a synagogue. After 110 years he will die and be buried, leaving his throne to his descendants. Only later did the doctrine of the resurrection, still denied by

---

[1] We need not decide at this point whether the second Elijah of later Jewish expectation fused with the Messiah and the returning original man to produce the World-redeemer, Prophet, Priest and King. Murmelstein has shown that there are many things pointing in this direction (op. cit.).

[2] Merx (op. cit.), 42, 72, 80, 82.

[3] שׁוּב שְׁבוּת is acc. of inner object. Thus שׁוּב is not caus. but intr. The rendering of Taheb as Restorer on the basis of the erroneous causative interpretation was never fully accepted (Bousset-Gressm.) and has been exploded by the researches of Merx.

[4] Here, then, we perhaps have the much sought for pre-Christian Saviour Joshua-Jesus. To contest the historicity of Jesus on this ground would be ridiculous in view of the fact that the name Jesus was so common in the NT period.

the Samaritans, and a cosmic eschatology come to be linked with this belief in the Messiah. In the interpretation of the name in terms of conversion we see a more inward turn of thought which reminds us us of the twofold meaning of ἀποκαθιστάναι in the Bible.

The name Taxo in the Ass. Mos., 9, 1 may be traced back to τάξων and signifies the "one who puts in order." Since he is of the tribe of Levi he is not the Messiah but His direct predecessor in the sense of Mal. 3:24, though without any reference to the prophet Elijah. [5]

The original politically Messianic sense of ἀποκαθιστάναι may be clearly seen in the question of the disciples to the risen Jesus in Ac. 1:6: εἰ καὶ ἀποκαθιστάνεις τὴν βασιλείαν τῷ 'Ισραήλ. The answer is worth noting, for, though it forbids inquisitive investigation of the times and seasons, it does not repudiate the expectation as such, but simply deprives it of political significance and refers it to the pneumatic sphere. We should also note that in all the other passages in the NT in which it occurs (though cf. → ἀποκατάστασις in Ac. 3:21), the concept of ἀποκαθιστάναι is not applied to the Messiah coming in power but to his forerunner, to John the preacher of repentance, in whom Jesus recognises the promised Elijah (Mk. 9:12 and par., cf. 6:15 and par.; 8:28 and par.; 1:2; Mt. 11:10, 14; Jn. 1:21). The πάντα in Mk. 9:12, which in itself is to be taken as comprehensively as possible in connection with the expectation depicted, is in fact restricted to the religious and ethical field. [6]

† ἀποκατάστασις.

The only passage in which this word appears in the NT is Ac. 3:20 f. : ὅπως ἄν ἔλθωσιν καιροὶ ἀναψύξεως ἀπὸ προσώπου τοῦ κυρίου καὶ ἀποστείλῃ τὸν προκεχειρισμένον ὑμῖν Χριστὸν 'Ιησοῦν, ὃν δεῖ οὐρανὸν μὲν δέξασθαι ἄχρι χρόνων ἀποκαταστάσεως πάντων ὧν ἐλάλησεν ὁ θεὸς διὰ στόματος τῶν ἁγίων ἀπ' αἰῶνος αὐτοῦ προφητῶν. On rather dubious grounds this statement has been the basis of the theological use of the word from the time of Origen.

A. ἀποκατάστασις in Secular Usage.

The basic meaning is "restitution to an earlier state" or "restoration" (e.g., of a temple, Ditt. Syll.[3], 695, 13 and 23 ; of a way, Ditt. Or., 483, 8 → 387). From this

---

[5] For other theories and the objections to them, v. Kautzsch, Pseudepigr., 326, ad loc.

[6] Though cf. 4 Esr. 13:26 of the Messiah : ipse est ..., qui per semetipsum liberabit creaturam suam, et ipse disponet qui derelicti sunt. On the misunderstanding of the Latin writer in the second half of the sentence, cf. H. Gunkel in Kautzsch, op. cit., 396.

ἀποκατάστασις. RGG[2], V, 1908 ff.; RE[3], I, 616 ff.; XIV, 467 ff., esp. 488; Wdt., Zn., Pr. on Ac. 3:20 f.; Zn., Khl., Ltzm. on R. 5:18; 11:32; Joh. W., Bchm., Ltzm. on 1 C. 15:22 f. NT theologies of Holtzmann[2] (1911), II, 190, 227 f.; Feine[5] (1931), 136, 302, 433; Weinel[4] (1928), 235, 255; Schlatter[2], II (1922), 365; Bousset-Gressm., 278, 502 ff.; A. Jeremias, Handb. d. altorientalischen Geisteskultur[2] (1929), 25 ff., 165 ff., 239 ff., 313 ff.; H. Brandes, Abhdlgen z. Gesch. d. Orients (1874), 123 ff.; J. Lepsius, "The Symbolic Language of the Revelation," Exp. Ser., 8, III (1912), 158 ff.; A. Harnack, Dogmengesch.[4] (1909), Index, esp. I, 681 ff., 693; F. Loofs, Dogmengesch.[4] (1906), 201 f.; R. Seeberg, Dogmengesch., II[2] (1910), 451 f.; L. Atzberger, Gesch. d. christl. Eschatologie (1896), 409 ff.; 451 ff.; E. R. Redepenning, Origenes, II (1846), 335 f.; 399 f.; 447 ff.; C. Bigg, The Christian Platonists of Alexandria (1886), 227 ff.; 292 ff.; E. de Faye, Origène, sa Vie, son Oeuvre, sa Pensée, III (1928), 249 ff., esp. 261 f.; O. Riemann, Die Lehre von der Apokatastasis (1889); P. Althaus, Die letzten Dinge[3] (1926), 203 ff. → ἀποκαθίστημι, → αἰών.

derive specialised uses: 1. in medicine, Aret., I, 10, 4, p. 13, 13; VII, 5, 16, p. 159, 14, Hude: τῆς φύσιος ἐς τὸ ἀρχαῖον ἀποκατάστασιν (→ 387); 2. in law (the returning of hostages to their own cities, Polyb., III, 99, 6; or tech. in pap. the restoration of property, P. Leid. B., 3a, 15; P. Oxy., I, 67, 9 [338 A.D.]; P. Flor., I, 43, 12 [370 A.D.], etc. → 387); 3. in politics, the reconstitution of the political order, Polyb., IV, 23, 1; Preisigke Sammelbuch, 4224, 3 (1st century B.C., → 387); also more generally of personal betterment, P. Par., 63, VIII, 40 f.: μετὰ τὴν ἀπὸ τῶν πραγμάτων νυνεὶ ἀποκατάστασειν (sic).

4. Also significant is the astronomical usage to describe the return of the constellations to their original position (→ ἀποκαθίστημι, 387). Vett. Val., II, 2, p. 57, 5, Kroll; Ps.-Plat. Ax., 370 b: The shining again of the sun or moon after obscuration. Esp. ἀποκατάστασις is a technical term for the restitution of the cosmic cycle, whether by the conjunction of Sirius and the sun after every 1461 years as in Egyptian chronology, [1] or by the reattainment of the original relation between the points of the equinox and the zodiac in consequence of the so-called procession of the sun, which the Babylonian astronomer Kidinnu had already worked out fairly accurately in 314 B.C. to involve the period of 25,800 years fixed by modern astronomy, [2] or finally in connection with the variously calculated periods of the Phoenix. [3] In Corp. Herm., VIII, 4 the maintenance of the order of the οὐράνια σώματα is attributed to ἀποκατάστασις. In Corp. Herm., XI, 2 ἀποκατάστασις and ἀνταποκατάστασις are called the ἐνέργεια τοῦ κόσμου. A period of time of this kind was called the great year (Arius Did. Fr., 37 [II, 184, 35, v. Arnim]: τὸν μέγιστον ἐνιαυτόν, Plin. Hist. Nat., X, 2: cum huius alitis [sc. Phoenicis] vita magni conversionem anni fieri prodit Manilius). The characteristic feature of this view of time, often advanced with political and Messianic expectations, is the fact that it entails belief in endless recurrence. This is the Stoic doctrine: γίνεσθαι τὴν ἀποκατάστασιν τοῦ παντὸς οὐχ ἅπαξ, ἀλλὰ πολλάκις· μᾶλλον δὲ εἰς ἄπειρον καὶ ἀτελεύτητον τὰ αὐτὰ ἀποκαθίστασθαι. Everything is restored exactly as it was before (II, 190, 19 f., v. Arnim). [4] Parsee belief seems to be the only exception with its hope that after the destruction of Ahriman there will be a new creation of all things (frashōkereti, frashegerd, "transfiguration"). This stimulated Judaism to the development of its teleological eschatology (→ ἀνίστημι, 368 f.).

5. ἀποκατάστασις is finally used of the individual soul, though rarely in the soteriological sense. Among the Neo-Platonists it seems to denote the new entry of not yet redeemed soul into the cycle of generations. To be sure, Joh. Lyd., IV, 149 says of Iamblichus: ἐν τῷ πρώτῳ τῆς περὶ καθόδου ψυχῆς πραγματείας καὶ τῆς ἀποκαταστάσεως αὐτῶν μέμνηται. Here ἀποκατάστασις is reached by way of καθαρμός. Yet the reference is not too precise. Iamblichus says (Myst., I, 10): τί δεῖται αὕτη (ἡ ψυχή) τῆς ἐν τῇ ἡδονῇ γενέσεως (conception) ἢ τῆς ἐν αὐτῇ εἰς φύσιν ἀποκαταστάσεως (return to earthly life) ὑπερφυὴς οὖσα καὶ τὴν ἀγέννητον ζωὴν διαζῶσα. To the same effect is Procl. Inst. Theol., 199:

---

[1] For examples and notes, v. H. Brandes, Abhdlgen zur Gesch. d. Orients (1874), 123 ff.

[2] Bousset-Gressm., 502 ff.

[3] RGG², IV, 1236 f.

[4] The expression "great year" occurs also in Poseidonius-Cicero. For a more detailed account of the Stoic doctrine of ekpyrosis, cf. P. Schubert, Die Eschatologie des Posidonius (1927), esp. 47 f.

πᾶσα ψυχὴ ἐγκόσμιος περιόδοις χρῆται τῆς οἰκείας ζωῆς καὶ ἀποκαταστά-σεσιν, if here too we are to think of reincarnations. Redemption in the Neo-Platonic sense is not so much the restoration of the soul as its release from matter. Yet the διάλυσις of the material body is called in Corp. Herm., VIII, 4 the ἀπο-κατάστασις of earthly beings and set in parallelism with the ἀποκατάστασις of the heavenly bodies. Clement of Alexandria knows this soteriological sense (Strom., VI, 9, 75, 2): γνωστικὴ ἀγάπη, δι' ἣν καὶ ἡ κληρονομία καὶ ἡ παντε-λὴς ἕπεται ἀποκατάστασις.

B. ἀποκατάστασις in Judaism.

The LXX does not use the word. It is rare in Judaism generally, and its technical meaning is weakly developed. In Ep. Ar., 123 the most that can be said is that certain religious yearnings intermingle with the reference to the return of Jewish emissaries to Jerusalem. When Josephus speaks of the ἀποκατάστασις τῶν 'Ιουδαίων he means the return from exile (Ant., 11, 63). Philo first thinks of the redemption from Egypt, but links with it a mystical reference to the ἀποκατάστασις ψυχῆς (Rer. Div. Her., 293). These meagre results may to some extent be accidental. The technical meaning of the verb is much more strongly attested (→ ἀποκαθίστημι, 387); and in any case the concept of Messianic restitution is current in Judaism. It is debatable whether the cosmological speculations of the world around exercised an influence on the expecta-tion and the linguistic usage. [5] Mention should be made of the fact that the beginning of a new "great year" was imminent at the time of the Barcochba revolt. [6] There is no record, however, that this helped to heighten the Messianic expectations of the Jews. [7]

C. ἀποκατάστασις in the NT.

Ac. 3:20 f. should be translated as follows: "That times of refreshing may come from the Lord, and that he may send the Messiah Jesus ordained for you, whom heaven must receive until the time of the restitution of all that of which (or, the establishment of all that which) God has previously spoken through his holy prophets."

Grammatically ὧν cannot be related to χρόνων but only to πάντων. This means further that πάντων can only be neut. and not masc. This also means that ἀπο-κατάστασις cannot denote the conversion of persons but only the reconstitution or establishment of things. For the concept of restoration, which is so strong in the term, does not strictly refer to the content of the prophetic promise, but to the relations of which it speaks. These are restored, i.e., brought back to the integrity of creation, while the promise itself is established or fulfilled. The difficulty arises from, but is also solved in, the fact that the two thoughts set out in the translation are linked in pregnant brevity. καιροὶ ἀναψύξεως and χρόνων ἀποκαταστάσεως stand in correspondence and mutually explain one another, but are not tautological. καιροί marks the beginning of the transformation, whereas χρόνων conveys the thought of the lasting nature of the renewed world. ἀναψύξεως denotes the subjective, ἀποκαταστάσεως the ob-jective side of the matter. The technical meaning of ἀποκατάστασις πάντων is limited by the dependent clause, yet also speaks through it. [8]

---

[5] Maintained by J. Lepsius, op. cit., 158 ff., and with reservations by Bousset-Gressm., 502 ff.

[6] Traditionally dated 139 A.D. Brandes (op. cit., 130) favours a year rather nearer the revolt, namely, 136 A.D.

[7] On the causes of the Jewish revolt under Hadrian (132-135), cf. Schürer, I, 671 ff.

[8] Cf. the comm. listed, and esp. Wdt. Ag.

Fundamentally we thus have the concept of the new Messianic creation which was current in Judaism. On the very different question whether the NT teaches a final restoration of all fallen sinners, and even of Satan, to the harmony of all created things in God, no light is shed by this particular text. In general such an idea is just as remote from the NT world of thought as the Jewish. Indeed, the latter thinks that the blessedness of the just is heightened by seeing the torture of the rejected (Ass. Mos., 10, 10; 4 Esr. 7:93, though cf. S. Bar. 52:6). Punishment is often declared to be unalterable (S. Bar. 85:12 ff.; also αἰώνιος Da. 12:2; Mt. 18:8; 25:41, 46; 2 Th. 1:9 and cf. Is. 66:24). The thought of destruction or the second death does not point in the opposite but in a similar direction (Eth. En., 97; Ps. Sol. 3:11; Rev. 20:14 → ἀπόλλυμι, ἀπώλεια). Paul sometimes emphasises so strongly the comprehensive saving work of the second Adam as to give rise to the appearance of a final restoration of all (R. 5:18: εἰς πάντας ἀνθρώπους εἰς δικαίωσιν ζωῆς, 11:32; 1 C. 15:22: ἐν τῷ Χριστῷ πάντες ζωοποιηθήσονται, cf. Eph. 1:10; Col. 1:20). Yet in truth the reference is only to a final hope, or perhaps only to a final tendency of the divine work of salvation. It is Paul who also emphasises most strongly the election of grace (R. 8:29; 9:11, 17; Eph. 1:4, 11 etc.). He knows that judgment will have a twofold outcome (R. 2:7 ff.; 2 C. 5:10), and expects the actualisation of the ὁ θεὸς πάντα ἐν πᾶσιν by means of the powerful overthrow of all opposition (1 C. 15:25 ff.). Thus there remains a strong tension throughout the NT, and, even if there is an underlying universalism, for reasons of admonition the main emphasis falls on the fact that few will be saved (Mt. 22:14; 7:13 f.; Lk. 13:23 ff.; 1 C. 9:24 ff.). [9]

This thought is stated rather more speculatively in 4 Esr. (8:3: "Many are created but few saved"; 8:41). In Parseeism the original dualism seems to have been partially replaced by an optimistic doctrine of *apocatastasis* which can find a place for the salvation of the evil serpent Azi Dahâka. [10]

D. Apocatastasis in the History of the Church.

From the time of Origen the term has been understood theologically to refer to the restoration of all created beings. In spite of several premises pointing in this direction, Marcion and Irenaeus do not draw such a conclusion, and at most Clement of Alexandria only hints at it. But it became a favourite teaching of the great successor of Clement. His ontological idealism equated the beginning and the end, and he could not, therefore, accept any end which does not lie wholly in God. An end of the world process is conceivable only if it means that all hostile *voluntas* is taken from that which is against God, even death and Satan, and that the substance which derives from God returns to Him. There are infinite possibilities of development both good and bad. Like aberration from God, theopanism is finally a fluid state. The author was not unaware that the *philosophi* shared this view, but he believed that their knowledge finally derived from the divine Scriptures (Princ., III, 6, 1). Exegetically he relied mainly on 1 C. 15:25 ff. (ὁ θεὸς πάντα ἐν πᾶσιν, Princ., III, 6, 1; 6, 2; 6, 6; 6, 8; in Joh., I, 16, 91); and also on Jn. 17:11 (ἵνα ὦσιν ἓν καθὼς ἡμεῖς, Princ., II, 3, 5). He

[9] Cf. apart from the works mentioned, A. Oepke, *Allg. ev.-luth. Kirch.-Zeitg.*, 60 (1927), 485, 499.
[10] Bousset-Gressm., 512.

took the term from Ac. 3:21, being influenced mainly by the current medical and political senses rather than the astronomical (Hom. in Jer., XIV, cf. also Princ., II, 3, 5 : ... *in* restitutione omnium, *cum ad perfectum finem universa pervenient ... omnium consummatio* ...). There is a good summary in the not very literal citation of Leontius of Byzantium from Princ., II, 10, 8, p. 182, 16 ff., Koetschau : γίνεται νεκρῶν ἀνάστασις, καὶ γίνεται κόλασις, ἀλλ᾽ οὐκ ἀπέραντος. κολαζομένου γὰρ τοῦ σώματος κατὰ μικρὸν καθαίρεται ἡ ψυχή, καὶ οὕτως ἀποκαθίσταται εἰς τὴν ἀρχαίαν τάξιν ... πάντων ἀσεβῶν ἀνθρώπων καὶ πρός γε δαιμόνων ἡ κόλασις πέρας ἔχει. καὶ ἀποκατασταθήσονται ἀσεβεῖς τε καὶ δαίμονες εἰς τὴν προτέραν αὐτῶν τάξιν. Longer expositions — in spite of the rule that it is dangerous to write such things, since most people do not need them and can be kept from evil only by fear of hell (c. Cels., VI, 26) — may be found in Princ., I, 6, 1-4; III, 6, 1-9; c. Cels., VIII, 72; cf. also Princ., II, 3, 1-5). Though rejected by official theology, esp. Western and particularly in respect of this doctrine, Origen has found disciples in many great Eastern theologians and even in such Westerners as Scotus Erigena, Hans Denck, J. A. Bengel, F. C. Oetinger, J. M. and P. M. Hahn, F. D. Schleiermacher and more recent Universalists, though not J. Böhme.

Oepke

ἀποκαλύπτω, ἀποκάλυψις → καλύπτω

† ἀποκαραδοκία

This word is made up of κάρα "head" and δέκομαι (Ion.) = δέχομαι (Att.) "to take" (perhaps origin. "to stretch," cf. δοκεύω/δοξάζω "to spy on," "to give heed to," and thus καραδόκος (not attested) "stretching the head forward," whence -κέω, -κία (Debrunner). There are no instances of the term except in Christian literature. The rare verb ἀποκαραδοκέω, hardly ever found prior to 200 B.C., means "to await" (either calmly or tensely). The simp. is class. It is not found in the LXX but cf. ψ 36:7 ᾽Α : "to wait humbly."

Linked with ἐλπίς in Phil. 1:20, the word [1] expresses confident expectation ; the ἐλπίς denotes well-founded hope and the ἀποκαραδοκία unreserved waiting. The same is true in R. 8, where the former word is used of Christians in v. 24 f. and the latter of the rest of creation in v. 19. It may be that Paul is here conscious of the anxious waiting of creation under the stress of the inner and reciprocal conflict of creatures and elements. Or it may be that he is simply drawing a theological conclusion from the dominion of anti-godly power over this aeon in consequence of the fall. [2]

Delling

ἀ π ο κ α ρ α δ ο κ ί α. [1] The simp. is poorly attested, cf. Comm. *ad loc.*
[2] Cf. Zn. R. on 8:20.

ἀποκαταλλάσσω → 258 f.   ἀποκατάστασις → 389 ff.
ἀπόκειμαι → κεῖμαι   ἀποκόπτω → κόπτω
ἀπόκριμα, ἀποκρίνω, ἀπόκρισις → κρίνω   ἀποκρύπτω, ἀπόκρυψος → κρύπτω

> ἀπόλλυμι, ἀπώλεια,
>   Ἀπολλύων

ἀπόλλυμι.

In exact correspondence with the Lat. *perdere* the word has two trans. meanings. There is also an intrans. mid., and note must be taken of the figurative NT use and its roots in the literal.

A. The Literal Use.

a. "To destroy or kill": in battle, Hom. Il., 5, 758 : ἀπώλεσε λαὸν Ἀχαιῶν; in prison, P. Petr., III, 36a (verso) 28 : μή με ἀπολέσηι τῶι λιμῶι; by torture, 4 Macc. 8:9 : διὰ τῶν βασάνων ἀπολέσαι; Mt. 2:13; 27:20; Mk. 3:6 and par.; 11:18 and par.; 9:22; Lk. 6:9; infrequ. with impersonal obj.: ἀπολῶ τὴν σοφίαν τῶν σοφῶν, Is. 29:14 = 1 C. 1:19. b. "To lose or suffer loss from": P. Oxy., IV, 743, 23 (2nd cent. B.C.): ἐγὼ ὅλως διαπονοῦμαι εἰ Ἕλενος χαλκοῦς ἀπόλεσεν (agitation about a lost penny); Lk. 15:4, 8; Mk. 9:41 and par.: οὐ μὴ ἀπολέσῃ τὸν μισθόν (freely quoted in P. Gen., 51, 11 [4th cent. A.D.]). c. Mid. with strong aor. mid. and strong perf. act. serves as intr. of a. and b. and hence "to perish": P. Petr., II, 4 (1), 4 (3rd cent. A.D.): νυνὶ δὲ ἀπολλύμεθα (stonebreakers complaining about their heavy work); inscript. on a Thracian sarcophagus : [1] ἄν τις δὲ ταύτην | ἀνύξῃ, ὅλη πανώ|λη ἀπόλοιτω; Mk. 4:38 and par.; Lk. 11:51; 13:3, 5, 33; 15:17; Mt. 26:52; 1 C. 10:9 f. etc.; of things, Jn. 6:12, 27. d. "To be lost," P. Masp., 166, 18 (6th cent. A.D.): διὰ τὸ ἀπολωλέναι τὸ πινάκιον (because the record is lost). Lk. 15:4, 6, 24, 32 of the lost sheep and the lost son (opp. εὑρεθῆναι). Passages like Mt. 5:29 f.; Mk. 2:22 and par.; Lk. 21:18; Ac. 27:34 show that these two meanings cannot be sharply distinguished but merge into one another.

B. The Figurative Use.

It is impossible to trace back the figurative use to any one of the meanings listed. In general we may say that b. and d. underlie statements relating to this world as in the Synoptists, whereas a. and c. underlie those relating to the next world, as in Paul and John. Yet there are exceptions, the more so as modifications are demanded by the Heb. background.

1. In the first case the soul of man is an object of value in which both man himself and God and His commissioned representative are interested. Underlying the saying of the Lord in Mk. 8:35 and par.; Mt. 10:39, is the familiar Jewish expression אִבֵּד נַפְשׁוֹ, which has the sense of "to trifle away one's life."

In אִבֵּד there is always an active element which may be lacking in "to lose" and which is not always present in the Gk. ἀπολλύναι, namely, the thought that the loss is

---

[1] *Jahreshefte des Oesterr. Arch. Inst. in Wien,* 23 (1926), *Beiblatt,* 136.

attributable to the will or fault of the one who suffers it. Cf. S. Nu. § 131, which refers to the execution of a disloyal centurion and a priest's daughter who became a harlot. Both spoiled their lives through their own acts (וֹפְשַׁ, cf. Mt. 16:26: ψυχήν), bringing themselves (וֹמְצַעַ, cf. Lk. 9:25: ἑαυτόν) to destruction.

This is what gives the Lord's saying its pregnant significance. He who seeks to save his life, i.e., to secure his existence (θέλῃ σῶσαι, Mk. 8:35 = ζητήσῃ περιποιήσασθαι, Lk. 17:33 = εὑρών, Mt. 10:39 = φιλῶν, Jn. 12:25), like the rich fool in Lk. 12:16 ff. or the denier in the storm of persecution, brings about his own destruction thereby (ἀπολέσει = אַבֵּד), whereas he who gives his life (אַבֵּד), not seeking any such security (in the sense of Mt. 8:19 ff. and Mt. 16:24), will thereby safeguard it in a deeper sense (σώσει, Mk. 8:35; Lk. 9:24 = ζωογονήσει, Lk. 17:33 = εὑρήσει, Mt. 10:39; 16:25 = φυλάξει, Jn. 12:25).[2] The profundity in comparison with ordinary speech lies in the ambivalent concept "life," with whose help the irreplaceability which is felt to be elemental for earthly existence is referred to eternal existence (Mk. 8:36 and par.; ζημιωθῆναι is not fully synon. with ἀπολέσει but emphasises its fateful consequences). The exposition of the saying in terms of a humanistic cult of personality contains an element of truth but is an undoubted softening.

The three parables in Lk. 15 are told from God's standpoint. The image of the sheep which is lost, far from the pasture and without a shepherd, is found already in the OT: ψ 118:176: ἐπλανήθην ὡσεὶ πρόβατον ἀπολωλός (אַבֵּד הֶשׂ), ζήτησον τὸν δοῦλόν σου; Ez. 34:4 (against the shepherds): τὸ ἀπολωλὸς οὐκ ἐζητήσατε. The basic word (אבד, "to wander around," "to perish") and the synon. (τὸ ἠσθενηκός, κακῶς ἔχον, συντετριμμένον, πλανώμενον) show how close is the thought of destruction here too. This is important for the NT passages. Mt. 10:6; 15:24: τὰ πρόβατα τὰ ἀπολωλότα οἴκου Ἰσραήλ, forms the transition to the simple τὸ ἀπολωλός of Lk. 19:10 (Mt. 18:11?), cf. Ez. 34:16: τὸ ἀπολωλὸς ζητήσω. As Jesus must seek what is lost, on the other hand He may not lose any of those whom the Father has given Him (Jn. 6:39, a Hebraism: πᾶν ὃ δέδωκέν μοι μὴ ἀπολέσω ἐξ αὐτοῦ; 18:9).

2. In addition there is a specifically NT usage which cannot be explained in the light of what has been said but which derives from sense a. or c. 1 C. 8:11: ἀπόλλυται ὁ ἀσθενῶν ἐν τῇ σῇ γνώσει; R. 2:12: ἀνόμως ἀπολοῦνται (synon. κριθήσονται); 1 C. 1:18; 2 C. 2:15; 4:3; 2 Th. 2:10: οἱ ἀπολλύμενοι (anton. οἱ σῳζόμενοι); 1 C. 15:18: οἱ κοιμηθέντες ἐν Χριστῷ ἀπώλοντο; Jn. 3:16: ἵνα πᾶς ὁ πιστεύων εἰς αὐτὸν μὴ ἀπόληται ἀλλ᾿ ἔχῃ ζωὴν αἰώνιον; Jn. 10:28: δίδωμι αὐτοῖς ζωὴν αἰώνιον, καὶ οὐ μὴ ἀπόλωνται εἰς τὸν αἰῶνα; cf. 17:12; 2 Pt. 3:9: μὴ βουλόμενός τινας ἀπολέσθαι ἀλλὰ πάντας εἰς μετάνοιαν χωρῆσαι. Luther here used the familiar and meaningful "be lost,"[3] but the synon. and anton. make it probable that what is really meant is "perish."[4] This is suggested further by the active use in sense a. as this is found in other NT writings. The subject may be a human or demonic destroyer of souls (R. 14:15, or the allegory in Jn. 10:10:

---

[2] Cf. → supra acc. to K. G. Kuhn, Sifre Numeri, § 131, n. 18. Cf. also Str.-B., I, 587 f.; A. Schlatter, Sprache und Heimat des vierten Evangelisten (1902), 118 f.; Schl. Mt., 351.

[3] Cf. also Weizsäcker, ad loc.

[4] The active element in אַבֵּד mentioned above (→ 394) should be noted in this connection; the transl. in some cases might well be "to bring oneself to eternal destruction."

ἵνα θύσῃ καὶ ἀπολέσῃ), or someone commissioned by God (Mk. 1:24: ἦλθες ἀπολέσαι ἡμᾶς, and the textually uncertain Lk. 9:56, anton. σῶσαι), or finally God Himself, who in such a case does not play the passive role of One who loses something, but exercises the supremely active function of Judge (= אָבֵּד), 1 C. 1:19: ἀπολῶ τὴν σοφίαν τῶν σοφῶν; Jd. 5: τοὺς μὴ πιστεύσαντας ἀπώλεσεν, anton. σῴζω; and more specifically of eternal destruction, Mt. 10:28: ἀπολέσαι ἐν γεέννῃ; Jm. 4:12: ὁ δυνάμενος σῶσαι καὶ ἀπολέσαι; and in the parables in Mt. 22:7 and Mk. 12:9 and par.). This usage has some links with the OT, the act. (e.g., Ἰερ. 29[47]:4, ψ 32:10 etc. being also relevant), but also the intrans. (Ps. 9:6, 7; ψ 36:20: οἱ ἁμαρτωλοὶ ἀπολοῦνται; 67:3; 72:27 etc.; Is. 41:11; 60:12). Yet in the OT the concept is in the first instance an immanent one to the degree that an earthly destruction is in view. It becomes increasingly transcendent as the concepts → ᾅδης, → θάνατος (→ also מָוֶת), → ἀπώλεια and → Ἀβαδδών take concrete form. The antithesis between life and death becomes a hostile one, and in this form it has a central place in NT religion, esp. in Paul and John. In contrast to σῴζεσθαι or to ζωὴ αἰώνιος, ἀπόλλυσθαι is definitive destruction, not merely in the sense of the extinction of physical existence, but rather of an eternal plunge into Hades and a hopeless destiny of death in the depiction of which such terms as ὀργή, θυμός, θλῖψις and στενοχωρία are used (R. 2:8 f.). This is pre-dated in Jd. 11.

The word is not found in this sense in the apocr. and pseudepigr. Nor are there real equivalents in the Rabbis.[5] Yet the idea is present.[6] Even in Epict. we find the antithesis ἀπολλύναι (ἀπόλλυσθαι)/σῴζειν, as also the combination ἀπόλωλεν ἡ ψυχή, though in a purely immanent sense.[7] Cf. also Ceb. Tab., 6, 2.

† ἀπώλεια.

Rare in secular Gk., a. from the act. (→ ἀπόλλυμι, sense a.) "destruction," "ruin," BGU, 1058, 35 "wearing out," also by misuse (= "squandering"), Polyb., VI, 11a: οἱ μὲν κτησάμενοι πρὸς τὴν τήρησιν, οἱ δ᾽ ἕτοιμα παραλαβόντες πρὸς τὴν ἀπώλειαν εὐφυεῖς εἰσιν; Mk. 14:4 and par.: εἰς τί ἡ ἀπώλεια αὕτη (τοῦ μύρου γέγονεν); b. from the intr. (→ ἀπόλλυμι, sense c.) "perishing," "destruction," Aristot. Eth. Nic., IV, 1, p. 1120a, 2 f.: δοκεῖ δ᾽ ἀπώλειά τις αὐτοῦ εἶναι καὶ ἡ τῆς οὐσίας φθορά, ὡς τοῦ ζῆν διὰ τούτων ὄντος; c. (from ἀπόλλυμι, sense b./d.), "loss," Ditt. Or., 229, 4 (246-226 B.C.); P. Lond., 1404, 5 (8th century A.D.): ἀπόλεια τῆς ψυχῆς καὶ ὑποστάσεως; also in Plutarch and Epict.

Common in the LXX in sense b. The concepts θάνατος, ᾅδης, ἀπώλεια etc. are all used together for it, being often personified as man's worst enemy. Job 26:6: ᾅδης (שְׁאוֹל) and ἀπώλεια (אֲבַדּוֹן); 28:22: ἡ ἀπώλεια καὶ ὁ θάνατος (אֲבַדּוֹן וּמָוֶת); cf. 31:12; ψ 87:12: τάφος (קֶבֶר) and ἀπώλεια (אֲבַדּוֹן); cf. ψ 15:10; Prv. 15:11: ᾅδης καὶ ἀπώλεια; 1 C. 15:55; Rev. 20:14 → Ἀβαδδών; bShab., 89a: אֲבַדּוֹן וּמָוֶת; Qoh.r. 5:9: the soul of Titus escaped לַאֲבַדּוֹן לִדְרָאוֹן עוֹלָם. Similarly Lidz. Liturg., 67, 10. Preis. Zaub., IV, 1247 f.: παραδίδωμί σε (the demon) εἰς τὸ μέλαν χάος ἐν ταῖς ἀπωλείαις, betrays Jewish Christian influence.

---

[5] It is striking that there are so few parallels in Str.-B. to the NT passages quoted.
[6] Schl. J., 98 on Jn. 3:16.
[7] A. Bonhöffer, "Epiktet und das Neue Testament," RVV, 10 (1911), 173 f.
ἀπώλεια. Nägeli, 35.

The strictly NT use links up with that of the OT. Thus εἶναι εἰς ἀπώλειαν in the curse of Ac. 8:20 has almost an OT ring. The term is used for eternal destruction in the Synoptics : Mt. 7:13 : ἡ ὁδὸς ... εἰς ἀπώλειαν (anton. ζωή), and esp. in Paul and John : R. 9:22 : σκεύη ... εἰς ἀπώλειαν (anton. δόξα); Phil. 1:28 : ἔνδειξις ἀπωλείας; 3:19 : ὧν τὸ τέλος ἀπώλεια; 1 Tm. 6:9 : εἰς ὄλεθρον καὶ ἀπώλειαν; Hb. 10:39; one who has fallen victim to destruction is called in Semitic fashion ὁ υἱὸς τῆς ἀπωλείας, as Judas in Jn. 17:12, Antichrist in 2 Th. 2:3. ἀπώλεια is a favourite word in 2 Peter (2:1, 3 : αἱρέσεις ἀπωλείας, ταχινὴν ἀπώλειαν, ἡ ἀπώλεια ... οὐ νυστάζει; 3:7: ἡμέρα κρίσεως καὶ ἀπωλείας; 3:16). Rev. 17:8, 11: εἰς ἀπώλειαν ὑπάγειν. What is meant here is not a simple extinction of existence (→ ἀπόλλυμι, 396), but an everlasting state of torment and death.

† ᾿Απολλύων (→ ᾿Αβαδδών).

Rev. 9:11: (the demonic locust-scorpions from the abyss) ἔχουσιν ἐπ᾽ αὐτῶν βασιλέα τὸν ἄγγελον τῆς ἀβύσσου, ὄνομα αὐτῷ ῾Εβραϊστὶ ᾿Αβαδδών, καὶ ἐν τῇ ῾Ελληνικῇ ὄνομα ἔχει ᾿Απολλύων. ᾿Απολλύων is a transl. and personification of אֲבַדּוֹן (→ ᾿Αβαδδών, 4:11) "destruction," for which the LXX uses → ἀπώλεια. It means the Exterminator or Destroyer, and from the time of Grotius has usually been taken as a play on Apollo, which is the actual reading in sy[ph]. [1]

The name of the god of pestilence is often linked with ἀπόλλυμι or ἀπολλύω : Aesch. Ag., 1081: ᾿Απόλλων ... ἀπόλλων ἐμός, ἀπώλεσας γὰρ οὐ μόλις τὸ δεύτερον; Archiloch Fr., 30 (Diehl, I, 219); Eur. Phaëth. in v. Arnim's Suppl. Eur. (Kl. T., 112), p. 75, 12; Menand. Peric., 440, Jensen. That this was usual is shown by Plat. Crat., 404e, 405e, though there are other derivations. Cf. also Firm. Mat. Err. Prof. Rel., 17, 3 : *Solem etiam quidam Apollinem dicunt, quia cottidie in occasu constitutus splendorem luminis perdat : perdere autem Graeci apollin dicunt.* From the time of the victory of Octavian at Actium under the temple of Apollo which was later enlarged by him, Apollo was especially regarded as the god of the empire. [2] The locust is his creature. [3] If the Apoc. is directed against the empire, there is thus a whole range of connections.

Oepke

ἀπολούω → λούω   ἀπολύτρωσις → λύω

ἀποσκίασμα → σκιά   ἀποστασία → ἀφίστημι

᾿Α π ο λ λ ύ ω ν. Comm. on Rev.: Bss., 301; Charles, I, 245 ff.; Zn., 400; Loh., 77 ff.; Had., 107; Rohr, 102; Str.-B., III, 810. W. Schmid, *Philol. Wochenschr.*, 47 (1927), Sp. 230; F. Boll, *Aus d. Off. Joh.* (1914), 68 ff., 71 f.: "The second half of the zodiac from Libra, i.e., the shears of the scorpion, is the Hades half of heaven according to a doctrine which Macrobius (Saturn., I, 21, 1) ascribes to the Assyrians and Phoenicians."

[1] According to Charles and Lohmeyer there are linguistic and metrical grounds for regarding the second half of the verse as a gloss.

[2] Hence the swan on the *Ara pacis* of Augustus (Rome, Thermes museum), cf. J. Durm, *Baukunst der Römer* (1905), 738; E. Petersen, *Ara pacis Augustae* (1902), 28; H. Luckenbach, *Kunst und Geschichte, grosse Ausgabe*, I (1913), 110 f.

[3] L. Preller, *Griech. Mythol.*[4], I (1894), 292 : "Feldmaus, Heuschrecke, Zikade" (no examples given). O. Gruppe, *Griech. Mythol. u. Rel. Geschichte* (1906), II, 1229, n. 3 tells us that Apollo protects the crops against locusts. This can also imply that he is one of those who sends them. Perhaps connected with Apollo is the locust on the coin of Sinope, F. Imhoof-Blumer, *Kleinasiat. Münzen* (1901), 7. Against the totemistic interpretation of the locust and mouse god by A. Lang, *Myth, Ritual and Rel.*, II (1887), 201, cf. Class. Rev., 6 (1892), 413.

ἀποστέλλω (πέμπω),
ἐξαποστέλλω, ἀπόστολος,
ψευδαπόστολος, ἀποστολή

ἀποστέλλω (πέμπω).

A. ἀποστέλλω and πέμπω in Secular Greek.

1. ἀποστέλλειν in its basic meaning "to send forth," together with the simp. στέλλειν and along with πέμπειν, is well attested both in the literature and the common speech of the classical period as well as Hellenism, and it is often used of the sending of persons as well as things. [1] As a compound of στέλλειν, it has an additional emphasis as compared with it. This emerges esp. when it is used figuratively [2] or almost technically. [3] Thus it is more sharply accentuated in relation to the consciousness of a goal or to effort towards its attainment. There is also a significant difference from πέμπειν. In the latter the point is the sending as such, i.e., the fact of sending, as in the transmission of an object or commission or the sending of a man. ἀποστέλλειν, however, expresses the fact that the sending takes place from a specific and unique standpoint which does not merely link the sender and recipient but also, in virtue of the situation, unites with the sender either the person or the object sent. To this extent it is only logical that ἀποστέλλειν should also carry with it the significance that the sending implies a commission bound up with the person of the one sent. This emerges more clearly in Hellenistic Gk. The expression: οἱ ἀπεσταλμένοι ὑπὸ τοῦ βασιλέως (3rd. century B.C.), in Dikaiomata ed. Graec. Hal., 1, 124; cf. 147 and 154, gives us already an interesting example of this development, the more so as the construction is purely verbal. [4] To be sure, the rulers of provinces sent from Rome are sometimes referred to as οἱ πεμπόμενοι (Ael. Arist. Or., 24 [14], 37 [II, p. 102, 12, Keil]); but the context is sufficient to show that what is in view is less the goal of their coming, i.e., the assumption of the office for which they are commissioned, than the fact of their coming from Rome as an impressive concretion of the empire. In relation to the distinction between πέμπω and ἀποστέλλω the different meanings of πομπή are also instructive, as is the fact that this word is never used in the NT and only once in the LXX in a very doubtful passage (ψ 43:14) which is attested only by Chrysostom (Field, Hexapla, ad loc.) and has no MS support. In general the word πομπή is only externally related to the basic term πέμπω, and in content it is closer to → θέατρον, 1 C. 4:9. Compounds in the LXX are ἀποπομπή, Lv. 16:10; παραπομπή, 1 Macc. 9:37; προπομπή, 1 Εσδρ. 8:51.

ἀ π ο σ τ έ λ λ ω. Cr.-Kö., 1018 f.; G. Heine, Synonymik des Nt.lichen Griechisch (1898), 180.

[1] Numerous examples may be found in Pass. s.v.

[2] Cf., e.g., Thuc., III, 89, 5: αἴτιον δ' ἔγωγε νομίζω τοῦ τοιούτου, ᾗ ἰσχυρότατος ὁ σεισμὸς ἐγένετο, κατὰ τοῦτο ἀποστέλλειν τε τὴν θάλασσαν καὶ ἐξαπίνης ... τὴν ἐπίκλυσιν ποιεῖν.

[3] Cf. e.g., Wilcken Ptol., 15, 24 (2nd cent. B.C.), where the meaning is "seconded." For other instances of this sense, cf. Dikaiomata ed. Graec. Hal., p. 86.

[4] The formula persisted, and thus shows itself to be different in content from → ἄγγελος. Thus in Jos. Bell., 4, 32 Titus is an ἀπεσταλμένος of his father, i.e., according to the context, "one who is on the way with a commission"; and in 1 Cl., 65, 1 the messengers from Rome to the Corinthian church are called οἱ ἀπεσταλμένοι ἀφ' ἡμῶν (→ ἀπόστολος, 443 f.). But v. also Lk. 19:32.

2. Already the formula ἀπεσταλμένοι ὑπὸ τοῦ βασιλέως links with the thought of sending the further thought of the associated authorisation of the one sent. The men thus described are representatives of their monarch and his authority. [5] Yet the use of ἀποστέλλειν in this sense is not in any way restricted to the legal sphere. On the contrary, it takes on its full sense when used, if we may put it thus, to express the impartation of full religious and ethical power. This takes place in the diatribe of the Cynics and Stoics, [6] though in this respect it is simply following a common usage of philosophical religion. [7] The Cynic knows himself to be an ἄγγελος καὶ κατάσκοπος καὶ κῆρυξ τῶν θεῶν (Epict. Diss., III, 22, 69), not because he is ordained such by himself or his pupils, but because he is certain that he is one who is divinely sent, an ἀποσταλείς, like Diogenes (I, 24, 6). Epictetus can lay it down as a rule (III, 22, 23 : τὸν ταῖς ἀληθείαις Κυνικὸν ... εἰδέναι δεῖ, ὅτι ἄγγελος ἀπὸ τοῦ Διὸς ἀπέσταλται ...) that the ultimate presupposition for genuine Cynicism is awareness of being divinely sent. In all these cases [8] ἀποστέλλειν is a technical term for divine authorisation, whereas πέμπειν is used when it is a matter of the charging of the Cynic with a specific task on human initiative [9] (I, 24, 3 : καὶ νῦν ἡμεῖς γε εἰς τὴν Ῥώμην κατάσκοπον πέμπομεν. οὐδεὶς δὲ δειλὸν κατάσκοπον πέμπει ...; ibid., I, 24, 5). [10] Even linguistically, however, it is another matter, and goes beyond the awareness of mission expressed by ἀποστέλλεσθαι, when Epictetus alleges as the only authority, even in face of the emperor and his representative, the καταπεπομφὼς αὐτὸν καὶ ᾧ λατρεύει, ὁ Ζεύς (III, 22, 56, cf. 59). This brings us close to a view which represents the divinity of the true philosopher and which is first emphatically proclaimed by the Cynics (θεῖος ἄνθρωπος) in adoption of a thought of Antisthenes. [11] We need not pursue this in the present context, but we must mention it because, in spite of the use of καταπέμπειν, it is better explained and understood in terms of ἀποστέλλειν than πέμπειν. The use of ἀποστέλλειν for entrusting with a religious commission is not confined, of course, to Epictetus. Thus Irenaeus summed up as follows the claim of Menander, the disciple of Simon Magus : ἑαυτὸν μὲν ὡς ἄρα εἴη ὁ σωτὴρ ἐπὶ τῇ τῶν ἀνθρώπων ἄνωθέν ποθεν ἐξ ἀοράτων αἰώνων ἀπεσταλμένος σωτηρίᾳ (I, 23, 5; cf. Eus. Hist. Eccl., III, 26, 1), and he can hardly have used the term unless it was suggested by the matter itself. Again, Philo knows and uses it in the same sense, as in Migr. Abr., 22. Here it is said of Joseph : τὸ φάναι μὴ πρὸς ἀνθρώπων ἀπεστάλθαι, ὑπὸ δὲ τοῦ θεοῦ κεχειροτονῆσθαι πρὸς τὴν τοῦ σώματος καὶ τῶν ἐκτὸς ἔννομον ἐπιστασίαν.

We thus have a religious use of the word in three men in widely varying circles of life and even in very different locations. We can hardly overestimate the

---

[5] Cf. Preisigke Fachwörter, 29.

[6] For material on this point, cf. E. Norden, "Beiträge z. Gesch. der griech. Philosophie," Jbch. f. Phil. Suppl., 19 (1893), 377 ff.; K. Holl, "Die schriftstellerische Form des griech. Heiligenlebens," N. Jbch. Kl. Alt., 29 (1912), 418 f.; K. Deissner, "Das Sendungsbewusstsein der Urchristenheit," ZSTh, 7 (1929/30), 783.

[7] → 76, n. 10.

[8] v., e.g., III, 23, 46; IV, 8, 31 (ἰδοὺ ἐγὼ ὑμῖν παράδειγμα ὑπὸ τοῦ θεοῦ ἀπέσταλμαι, words of the Cynic to his hearers).

[9] It is to be noted that on an inscr. discovered in Kefr Hauar (Syria) a slave praying for the protection of the Syrian goddess described himself as πεμφθείς by his mistress (BCH, 21 [1897], 60). Can we conclude that this is only a matter of commercial authorisation and not also of religious ?

[10] Note that in I, 24, 6 ἀποσταλείς is stated quite absolutely of Diogenes.

[11] Norden, 380.

significance of this fact for the linguistic expression of the early Christian awareness of mission (→ ἀπόστολος). Naturally, the original meaning of ἀποστέλλειν
did not come to be restricted to the exclusive significance of the divine sending
and authorisation of a man. Nevertheless, this constitutes the climax of the history
of the term, even though alongside it the original secular use continued well into
Christian times, as attested amongst other things by many non-literary sources. [12]

B. ἀποστέλλω and πέμπω in the LXX (OT) and Judaism.

1. In the LXX ἀποστέλλειν occurs more than 700 times, in many cases with the
variant ἐξαποστέλλειν. With few exceptions it is a rendering of the root שׁלח, usually
in its verbal forms. Similarly שׁלח is predominantly [13] translated ἀποστέλλειν or → ἐξαποστέλλειν. In contrast, the simp. στέλλειν and πέμπειν are almost completely
absent. Indeed, στέλλειν does not occur at all, but only → στέλλεσθαι, which we shall
ignore in this context. πέμπειν is found about 26 times, [14] but only in 6 cases does it
render a Heb. original ; [15] the other instances are in texts which exist only in Gk. The
compounds of πέμπειν are so infrequent [16] that they do not affect the picture. In the
LXX ἀποστέλλειν is the Gk. term for the OT שׁלח. There is no need to expound the
meaning of שׁלח, since our present concern is with the Gk. equivalent. In brief, however,
we may say that ἀποστέλλειν in the LXX corresponds to the original to the extent
that it is predominantly used where it is a matter of commissioning with a message or
task. מַלְאָךְ and שָׁלַח are conjoined in numerous instances, irrespective of whether the
task committed to the messenger is human [17] or divine. [18]

Moreover ἀποστέλλειν/שׁלח alone is a technical term for the sending of a
messenger with a special task ; the messenger himself does not have to be named. [19]
In other words, the emphasis rests on the fact of sending in conjunction with the
one who sends, not on the one who is sent. This aspect reaches its climax in the
description of the call of Isaiah. Here (6:8) God can ask : אֶת־מִי אֶשְׁלַח וּמִי יֵלֶךְ־לָנוּ,
meaning that He needs someone whom he may send as His plenipotentiary, even
though this does not have to be stated and is not actually expressed in Isaiah's
brief declaration of readiness (הִנְנִי שְׁלָחֵנִי). At this point we can see most clearly
what is the characteristic feature of שׁלח in all its meanings, namely, the volitional
and conscious element in a planned action of any kind. Thus שׁלח is less a statement

---

[12] So Preisigke Wört., I, 194.

[13] Exceptions are those cases in which the equation of שׁלח and ἀποστέλλειν would be
contrary to the sense, e.g., in the formula שָׁלַח יַד "to stretch forth the hand," where שׁלח
is usually rendered ἐκτείνειν (Gn. 3:22 etc.) or ἐπιβάλλειν (Gn. 22:12 etc.) according to
the detailed sense. → n. 16.

[14] As counted by Hatch-Redp., and once in Symmachus at Jer. 16:16.

[15] Gn. 27:42; 1 Βασ. 20:20; Ezr. 4:14; 5:17; Neh. 2:5 for שׁלח ; Est. 8:5 for כתב, since here
the reference is to a written communication.

[16] Of compounds ἀποπέμπειν occurs once, διαπέμπειν 6 times (= שׁלח),
εἰσπέμπειν once, ἐκπέμπειν 9 times (= שׁלח in Gn. 24:54, 56, 59; 1 Βασ. 20:20 [as a var.
of πέμπειν]; 24:20; 2 Βασ. 19:31; Prv. 17:11), ἐπιπέμπειν 3 times (Prv. 6:19 = שׁלח),
παραπέμπειν twice, προπέμπειν 5 times, mostly in cases where there is no original Heb.
In all these instances — on Prv. 17:11 → n. 34 — it would distort the sense to replace by
στέλλειν or one of its compounds.

[17] Gn. 32:4; Nu. 20:14; Jos. 7:22; Ju. 6:35; 7:24; 9:31 etc.

[18] 2 Ch. 36:15; Mal. 3:1.

[19] Gn. 31:4; 41:8, 14 etc.

concerning the mission than a statement concerning its initiator and his concern ; [20] the one who is sent is of interest only to the degree that in some measure he embodies in his existence as such the one who sends him. In principle, it does not matter who it is that sends, whether God or man, or who it is that is sent, whether a heavenly or an earthly messenger. Even in the consciousness of the bearer of the commission, the emphasis lies on its author, as we can see from such cases as Abraham (Gn. 12:1 ff.), Eliezer (Gn. 24:1 ff.), Moses and above all the prophets (→ ἀπόστολος, 414).

2. The usage of the LXX is marked by the consistency with which it pursues this thought. This emerges in the fact that there is no mechanical rendering of שלח by ἀποστέλλειν, [21] and yet that contrary to the literal sense ἀποστέλλειν is sometimes used for שלח in order to emphasise the purposive and authoritative element in the action concerned and the position of the one who acts.

Thus שלח as well as שלח יד can denote stretching forth the hand. According to the sense the LXX ought to choose one of the renderings listed under n. 13 when it encounters this short formula. But it does not always do so. Thus Ps. 18:16 says of God : יִשְׁלַח מִמָּרוֹם יִקָּחֵנִי, and Ps. 144:7 makes it indisputably clear that He is stretching out His hand to deliver the Psalmist. In ψ 17:17 the LXX has : ἐξαπέστειλεν (→ ἐξαποστέλλω) ἐξ ὕψους [22] καὶ ἔλαβέν με, although, as ψ 143:7 shows, ἐξαπέστειλεν τὴν χεῖρα αὐτοῦ would have met the data. In contrast, it is quite according to the sense that in 2 Βασ. 6:6 a simple וַיִּשְׁלַח is rendered : καὶ ἐξέτεινεν ... τὴν χεῖρα, while in Ob. 13 συνεπιτίθεσθαι is used for שלח, quite in accordance with the context and the shade of meaning. Apart from ψ 56:4; 143:7, [ἐξ]αποστέλλειν τὴν χεῖρα is used elsewhere for שלח יד only at Ex. 9:15; Job 2:5 and Cant. 5:4. Only in the last instance is it used of a man, and in this case it has the special sense of putting one's hand through the hole in the door. Conversely, ἐκτείνειν τὴν χεῖρα is used only in relation to man. [23] Behind this distinction there stands more than a spiritualised view of God. The limitation of ἀποστέλλειν to God expresses an essential feature of God, namely, the absoluteness of His will. It also brings out the fact that ἀποστέλλειν is not merely linked externally with שלח but has taken on its characteristic element of the awareness and the raising of a claim. In contrast ἐκτείνειν simply affirms the fact without any further interest in its subject. We thus have a similar situation to that of the purely Gk. relationship between ἀποστέλλειν and πέμπειν. [24]

Self-evidently the ἀποστέλλειν of the LXX cannot deny its linguistic origin. That which characterises the term in secular usage is not lost in biblical Greek but passes into it and links up with what is contributed by the OT equivalent. We may thus say that in the LXX the word is as little given a specifically religious flavour as שלח in the Heb. OT. Even in the accounts of the sending of

---

[20] It is to be noted that the basic meaning of the stem is to "let go" (cf. the dictionaries s.v.). Only in the intensified figurative sense does it come to mean "to send." This meaning gradually becomes predominant, yet the word can never wholly refute its origin, and even in the sense of "to send" this gives it its emphasis ; the acting subject stands in the forefront rather than the object.

[21] → n. 13.

[22] Cf. also ψ 56:4.

[23] There are no exceptions acc. to Hatch-Redp.; where ἐκτείνειν τὴν χεῖρα is used of God in the LXX, the original is נטה (Ex. 7:5; Zeph. 2:13), or נשא (Ex. 6:8), not שלח.

[24] → 398.

the prophets [25] we do not have a purely religious use. In such contexts the word simply denotes sending; it acquires a religious connotation only to the extent that the situation is religiously conditioned and the obedience of the one to be sent is seen as a self-evident attitude before God as the One who sends — an obedience not to be distinguished in its practical results from that which might be rendered, e.g., to a king. It is of a piece with this, and ought to be noted, that in the OT sphere there neither is nor can be any use of שלח or ἀποστέλλειν to describe a consciousness of mission such as that which is the climax of the self-consciousness of the Cynic; [26] for alongside the unconditional subordination to the will of Him who sends, which שׁלַח and ἀποστέλλειν here presuppose in the messenger, there is no place for this kind of exalted emotion. This may also help to explain why there is no need to restrict the significance and use of ἀποστέλλειν to the purely religious field, though the term has an assured place in most important religious contexts and there is a tendency to use the word only for divine sending. [27]

3. Rabbinic Judaism keeps within the sphere delineated in its use of שלח. Nowhere does it go beyond the secular use. A special position is occupied only by the derived subst. שליח or שׁלִיחַ (→ ἀπόστολος, 414). Josephus uses the word about 75 times. [28] On the one side he employs it more or less synon. with πέμπειν; [29] on the other it is used to denote an official mission as such. [30] In many cases πέμπειν is for Josephus a rather colourless omnibus word like the German lassen. [31] This never happens, however, in the case of ἀποστέλλειν. Even where this word is used interchangeably with πέμπειν, it still carries with it a reference to awareness of the action denoted. It is thus understandable that Josephus, too, uses ἀποστέλλειν when the reference is to sending by God, anal. to the usage of the LXX. [32] The same seems to be the case in 4 Esr., where the missus est (4:1; 5:31; 7:1; cf. misit, 6:33; misi, 14:4 etc.) with reference to the angel presupposes an ἀπεστάλη etc. in the Gk. We have already said [33] that in Philo, as in the Cynic-Stoic diatribe, we find an absol. use of ἀποστέλλειν or ἀποστέλλεσθαι; [34] in his case, as has now been shown, there is isolation from both

---

[25] Is. 6:8; Jer. 1:7; Ez. 2:3; cf. Hag. 1:12; Zech. 2:15 (11); 4:9; Mal. 2:23 (4:4); Ex. 3:10; Ju. 6:8, 14.

[26] → 399.

[27] Cf. also n. 34.

[28] Thackeray, Lex. Jos., 76. In many cases in Ant. Josephus simply takes over ἀποστέλλειν from the LXX, which he uses as a source.

[29] Cf. e.g., Ant. 7, 191; 11, 190 f.; 12, 181-183. Stylistic reasons explain the interchangeability of ἐκπέμπειν and ἀποστέλλειν in Ant., 20, 37; Vit., 51 etc.

[30] Cf. also Bell., 4, 32: Titus as an ἀπεσταλμένος of Vespasian; 7, 17 f. and 230: the sending of troops from specific standpoints; Ant., 12, 193: ἀποσταλησόμενοι = possible messengers.

[31] Cf., e.g., Ant., 13, 23.

[32] Bell., 7, 387: τούτων τὴν ἀνάγκην θεὸς ἀπέσταλκε ...; Ant., 7, 334: ὁ γὰρ θεὸς τὸν προφήτην ἀποστείλας πρὸς αὐτὸν (David) ... (God's promise that Solomon would build the temple planned by David in his place).

[33] → 399.

[34] Cf., e.g., Poster C., 44: δύο δ' ἐκ ταύτης παρίσταται τῆς φωνῆς, ἓν μὲν καθ' ὅ τινι ἐπιπέμπεται θάνατος, ἕτερον δὲ καθ' ὃ ἀπό τινος ἀποστέλλεται ... Here, too, the religious element lies in the use of the pass. In this connection it is to be noted that throughout the OT שלח in the nif'al occurs only at Est. 3:13, and even here in such a way that God is not hidden behind the pass. In the pu'al שלח occurs in the OT 10 times (Gn. 44:3 is missing in Mandelkern), but in the LXX it is translated in the pass. only twice, at Gn. 44:3 in a secular context (Joseph's brothers ἀπεστάλησαν, i.e., were sent away), and at Da. 10:11 as a statement of the angel to Daniel (ἀπεστάλην), where God may be

the Rabbis and Josephus, and in his use of ἀποστέλλειν he has not been influenced by שׁלח, since it is characterised by the fact that there is in it no religious note.

C. ἀποστέλλω and πέμπω in the NT.

1. In the NT ἀποστέλλειν occurs some 135 times. The distribution is such that outside the Gospels and Acts it is found only 12 times, 3 times in 1 Jn., 3 in Rev., 3 in Paul (R. 10:15; 1 C. 1:17; 2 C. 12:17), or 4 if we include 2 Tm. 4:12, once in Hb. 1:14 and once in 1 Pt. 1:12. In the Gospels and Acts the occurrence is more or less even in relation to the scope of the individual writings, and the word is obviously an acknowledged part of the vocabulary. Of the compounds, apart from → ἐξαποστέλλειν we find only συναποστέλλειν in 2 C. 12:18.

Alongside ἀποστέλλειν, πέμπειν occurs some 80 times. Of these 33 are in the Fourth Gospel and 5 in Rev. There are 10 occurrences in Lk. and 12 in Ac., while only 4 in Mt. and 1 in Mk. (5:12), the form in Mt. being always πέμψας with the following fin. verb. In contrast with ἀποστέλλειν the distribution is thus most uneven in the historical books.

When we review the material we first note that there is a special occurrence of πέμπειν in the Fourth Gospel which demands separate treatment (→ 2.). Otherwise the Lucan writings predominate. This is even clearer when we take into account the compounds of πέμπειν and their distribution in the NT. Thus we find ἀναπέμπειν 5 (4) times, 3 of which are in Lk. and 1 (?) in Ac.; ἐκπέμπειν twice (Ac.); μεταπέμπεσθαι 9 times (Ac.); προπέμπειν 9 times, 3 of which are in Ac. and none in the Gospels; συμπέμπειν twice (Paul). Thus of 27 instances no less than 18 are in Lk. and Ac., none in Mt. and Mk. and only one in the whole Johannine material (3 Jn. 6: προπέμπειν). The full bearing of these statistics only emerges, however, when we investigate the detailed material. Even for Lk., unlike Josephus, πέμπειν cannot be described as "the normal word throughout" for "to send"; [35] for even statistically ἀποστέλλειν is more common. Yet Lk. may be compared with Josephus to the extent that in addition to a specific usage of ἀποστέλλειν and πέμπειν he also seems to use the words as synonyms (→ 402). [36] Like Josephus, he thus seems to stand between a Semitic use of ἀποστέλλειν under the influence of the OT שׁלח (as in the LXX), and therefore its sharp distinction from πέμπειν, on the one side, and the less sharp and ultimately nonessential distinction from it in Hellenism on the other; yet always in such a way that he is nearer to the common NT usage than to Josephus.

We may also see kinship between Lk. and Josephus in the fact that for stylistic reasons both seem to use πέμπειν τινὰ λέγοντα or πέμπειν ... λέγων promiscue

---

seen behind the pass. as the One who sends. In Da. 5:24 the pass. part. שְׁלִיַח (שְׁלַח) is also kept in the pass. ἀπέσταλη : the hand which the king saw writing is given by this expression the significance of an angel. Of the other passages שׁלח is not translated ἀποστέλλειν in Job 18:8; Is. 16:2; 27:10; Prv. 29:15. In Prv. 17:11 יְשַׁלַּח seems to be clearer than ὁ κύριος ἐκπέμψει in the Gk. The reason for the selection of ἐκπέμπειν here is probably to be found in the fact that the reference is to the sending of an ἄγγελος ἀνελεήμων, and the translator did not wish to bind this so closely to God, either in the matter itself or its results, as he would have done by using ἀποστέλλειν, and as is done in the basic text. In Ju. 5:15 (where the text is uncertain), Ob. 1 and Is. 50:1 we have secular contexts for which the LXX has chosen the act. form.

[35] Thackeray, Lex. Jos., 76.
[36] Cf., e.g., οἱ πεμφθέντες (those sent by the Capernaum centurion) in Lk. 7:10 after ἀπέστειλεν in 7:3 with Jos. Vit., 180 f.

with ἀποστέλλειν. If this is so, then this formula denotes in them the giving of a commission (λέγειν) in spite of πέμπειν, though according to the sense more so in the first form than the second. This would support the view that neither Lk. nor Josephus has any true feeling for the special nature of ἀποστέλλειν. Cf. Lk. 7:6 with 7:3 (ἀπέστειλεν); 7:19 with 7:20 (ἀπέσταλκεν ἡμᾶς πρός σε λέγων); Ac. 15:22 (πέμψαι ... ἄνδρας ... γράψαντες διὰ χειρὸς αὐτῶν, cf. 25) with 15:27 (ἀπεστάλκαμεν οὖν ...) and 15:33 (ἀπελύθησαν ... πρὸς τοὺς ἀποστείλαντας αὐτούς); Jos. Ant., 18, 325 (καὶ πέμπει τὸν πιστευότατον ... λέγοντα) with 326 (βασιλεὺς ... ἀπέστειλέν με).

For the rest, the varying frequency and unequal distribution of the two terms in the NT may be explained by the religious character of this literature and therefore of its material, and by the difference in orientation resulting from their linguistic development (→ 398). Sometimes this may be seen even where there seems to be no difference in the use of ἀποστέλλειν and πέμπειν. [37] At any rate we can say in general that when πέμπειν is used in the NT the emphasis is on the sending as such, whereas when ἀποστέλλειν is used it rests on the commission linked with it, no matter whether the one who sends or the one who is sent claims prior interest. To the development of the usage as already noted in the LXX and Josephus there also corresponds the fact that the Synoptists never use πέμπειν but only ἀποστέλλειν of God, [38] and that Paul seems to follow the same pattern, unless we prefer to suspend judgment in his case in view of the infrequency of occurrence. [39]

2. A special position is obviously occupied by John's Gospel. Here ἀποστέλλειν seems to be used quite *promiscue* with πέμπειν. Thus, to denote His full authority both to the Jews [40] and the disciples [41] Jesus uses ἀποστέλλειν, since He thereby shows that behind His words and person there stands God and not merely His own pretension. Again, in prayer He uses the same term to describe His relationship to God. [42] Yet in close proximity to it He uses πέμπειν as well in such a way that there is no self-evident distinction. Closer investigation, however, shows us that when the Johannine Jesus uses πέμπειν in speaking of His sending by God He does so in such a way as to speak of God as the πέμψας με. This usage is wholly restricted to God, being sometimes amplified to ὁ πέμψας με πατήρ; [43] when speaking of Himself He uses other forms of πέμπειν. Except on the lips of Jesus the formula occurs only once, namely, in 1:33 on the lips of the Baptist (ὁ πέμψας με βαπτίζειν ἐν ὕδατι ...). Of the 33 πέμπειν passages in Jn., apart from the last mentioned no less than 26 fall into this category. [44] As against this, in Jn. God is never called ὁ ἀποστείλας με, but whenever ἀποστέλλειν is used of the sending of Jesus by God it occurs in a statement.

---

[37] Perhaps the distinction is not impossible even in a passage like Mt. 21:36 ff./Mk. 12:4 ff. as against Lk. 20:11 ff.

[38] Mt. 10:40; Mk. 9:37/Lk. 9:48; Mt. 15:24 (pass. self-declaration of Jesus); cf. Jn. 1:6.

[39] Of the two not wholly unambiguous passages, R. 8:3 certainly stresses the coming rather than the sending of Jesus as the act of God, so that there is here good reason for πέμπειν. On the other hand, a case might be made out for ἀποστέλλειν at 2 Th. 2:11.

[40] 5:36, 38; 6:29, 57; 7:29; 8:42; 10:36.

[41] 3:17; 20:21.

[42] 11:42; 17:3, 8, 18, 21, 23, 25.

[43] 5:37; 6:44; 8:18; 12:49; 14:24. The formula is so complex that in the course of textual history the simple ὁ πέμψας με has in many cases probably had πατήρ added; cf., e.g., 5:30; 6:29; 8:16.

At first sight this usage is extremely odd. It is to be explained as follows. In John's Gospel ἀποστέλλειν is used by Jesus when His concern is to ground His authority in that of God as the One who is responsible for His words and works and who guarantees their right and truth. On the other hand, He uses the formula ὁ πέμψας με (πατήρ) to affirm the participation of God in His work in the *actio* of His sending. This explanation is in full accord with the Johannine view of Jesus as the One whose "work originates in God's work" and by whom "God's work ... reaches its goal." [45]

Purely linguistically we have in this usage a fairly striking parallel to that of Epictetus in his statements concerning the sending of the Cynic by Zeus. As on the one side ἀποστέλλειν is used to characterise the sending as a mission, so on the other Zeus is for the Cynic the καταπεπομφὼς αὐτόν (Diss., III, 22, 56; → 399). But we should not overemphasise the parallel. For one thing, the formula occurs only once in Epictetus and is not to be given a false significance. Again, though there may be an external kinship, the drift is quite different from that of the ὁ πέμψας με (πατήρ) of the Johannine Jesus. For the Cynic it gives him a claim to exemption from all human authority ; as the messenger of God he must give account to Him alone. This is a thought which necessarily lies outwith the mode of thinking of the Fourth Gospel. It is excluded by the fact that between Jesus and the "Father" (→ πατήρ) is a unity in will [46] and action (10:30; 14:9) which leaves no room for "responsibility." And it is wholly and utterly excluded by the fact that alongside the formula ὁ πατήρ με ἀπέσταλκεν (5:36) Jesus with equal justification can use the formula ἦλθον (10:10; 12:47) or ἐλήλυθα (εἰς τὸν κόσμον) (12:46; 16:28; 18:37), which finds the basis of this unity in the time preceding His earthly life. We have here ideas which cannot possibly apply in the case of the Cynic.

As there is reflected in these findings the history of the terms outside the NT, so there is also disclosed the specifically Johannine Christology which emphasises as strongly as possibly the essential unity of Jesus with God by describing Him absolutely as the Son (→ υἱός). It is in the light of this that in some passages ἀποστέλλειν and πέμπειν acquire their distinctive meanings in the Fourth Gospel. We are not to say, however, that the terms themselves have helped to shape Johannine Christology. For, quite apart from what we have already stated, even in John the words are not fundamentally or essentially theological terms. They are rather taken out of their ordinary meaning by the specific context in which they are used — very forcibly so in this Gospel — and filled with religious significance.

Thus the view falls to the ground of itself that in Jn. ἀποστέλλειν is designed specifically to reveal "the divine sonship of Christ prior to His coming into the world." [47] It is not this which is confirmed in the sending of Jesus. On the contrary, it is from the

[44] With these we should also reckon 7:18 and 13:16, even though ὁ πέμψας αὐτόν refers very generally to a human sender ; for both statements grow out of the situation of Jesus characterised by the ὁ πέμψας με πατήρ, the first as an illustration, the second as a consequence for the inner and outer attitude of the "apostle."

[45] Schl. J., 130 on 4:34 (→ τελειόω). This distinction between ἀποστέλλειν and πέμπειν is confirmed in such passages as 5:36 ff. and 7:28 f. It is to be noted, esp. also from the standpoint of Christology, that πέμπειν and not ἀποστέλλειν is always used of the sending of the Spirit by Jesus (15:26; 16:7; cf. 14:26).

[46] In this connection we should note the version of the Gethsemane story in Jn. (18:1 f.) and esp. 18:11 in comparison with Mt. 26:38 f. and par.

[47] Cf., e.g., Cr.-Kö., 1018.

fact that Jesus is for John the υἱός that in this Gospel His mission acquires its ultimate meaning and pathos in its demand for the decision and division of men.

3. In relation to the general use of ἀποστέλλειν in the NT we must say finally that the word does begin to become a theological term [48] meaning "to send forth to service in the kingdom of God with full authority (grounded in God)." Yet this does not imply any real departure from its proper sense. [49] What we see here is rather the influence of the NT use of ἀπόστολος. In the NT field the history of ἀποστέλλειν thus merges into that of → ἀπόστολος.

† ἐξαποστέλλω.

First found in the "Epistle of Philip" in Demosthenes Or., 18, 77, this word became common in Gk. from the time of Polybius [1] with essentially the same meaning as ἀποστέλλειν. [2] In the LXX it is fully interchangeable with, though not so common as, the latter, as the many variants show. In Philo, too, there is no distinction between them, as may be seen from his explanation of Μαθουσάλα = מְתוּשָׁלַח (Gn. 5:21 ff.) partly as ἀποστολὴ θανάτου [3] and partly as ἐξαποστολὴ θανάτου. [4] The word also occurs in Josephus (Vit. 57, 147) [5] without having any special significance.

In the NT ἐξαποστέλλειν occurs 13 times, 11 in Luke (Lk. 1:53; 20:10, 11; 24:49; Ac. 7:12; 9:30; 11:22; 12:11; 13:26; 17:14; 22:21) and 2 in Paul (Gl. 4:4, 6). The verses in Luke's Gospel, apart from 24:49, give us the formula ἐξαποστέλλειν τινὰ κενόν, which is common in the LXX (Gn. 31:42; Dt. 15:13 etc.) but which does not give any special significance to ἐξαποστέλλειν. [6] In all the other passages what we have said concerning the simple ἀποστέλλειν applies to ἐξαποστέλλειν.

Linguistically there is no support for the thesis of Zn. [7] that in Gl. 4:4 [8] the ἐξ- in ἐξαποστέλλειν indicates that "prior to his sending the one sent was in the presence of the one who sent him," i.e., in this case "that prior to His sending, or prior to His birth, as the γενόμενον ἐκ γυναικός tells us, Jesus was παρὰ τῷ θεῷ (Jn. 17:5) or πρὸς τὸν θεόν (Jn. 1:1)." The truth is that in this passage in Paul, which reminds us of John, the verb for sending (→ ἀποστέλλειν, C. 2) does not in itself make any christological statement, but rather derives its christological flavour from the christological context in which it is used. We might also make the very pertinent observation that in Gl. 4:4, 6 Paul is not so much speaking of Christ as of God and of the event of salvation willed and in due time accomplished by Him.

---

[48] Mt. 10:5, 16; Lk. 22:35; R. 10:15; 1 C. 1:17.

[49] This is shown by the fact that in all the Gospels and throughout the NT the original usage persists alongside the beginning of restriction in the manner indicated. It is hardly necessary to give examples.

ἐ ξ α π ο σ τ έ λ λ ω. Anz Subsidia, 356 f.

[1] Anz, 356.

[2] Cf. also the examples in Preisigke Wört., I, 509.

[3] Poster C., 73: Μαθουσάλα, ὃς ἑρμηνευθεὶς ἦν ἀποστολὴ θανάτου.

[4] Poster C., 41: ἑρμηνεύεται ... Μαθουσάλα δ' ἐξαποστολὴ θανάτου; 44: Μαθουσάλα, ὃς ἦν ἐξαποστολὴ θανάτου.

[5] Schl. Lk., 121.

[6] In the parallel pass. to Lk. 20:10, Mk. (12:3) has ἀποστέλλειν κενόν.

[7] Zn. Gl., 199 ad loc., as also many other older and more recent commentators.

[8] Mutatis mutandis the thesis would also apply to 4:6: ἐξαπέστειλεν ... τὸ πνεῦμα τοῦ υἱοῦ αὐτοῦ.

ἀπόστολος (→ δώδεκα, μαθητής).

A. The Word and Concept ἀπόστολος in Classical Greek and Hellenism.

1. The Greek Usage.

Only occasionally in the Gk. field does ἀπόστολος have a meaning related or apparently related to that which it bears in the NT. For the most part the similarity is only external. The background of usage is basically different in the two cases. In the older period ἀπόστολος is one of the special terms bound up with sea-faring, and more particularly with military expeditions; it is almost a technical political term in this sense. Originally it was an adj., as shown by Plat. Ep., VII, 346a (ἐν τοῖς ἀποστόλοις πλοίοις πλεῖν). It was often combined with πλοῖον to mean a freighter or transport ship, though sometimes it could be used as a noun, i.e., without πλοῖον, for the same purpose (τὸ ἀπόστολον, Ps. Hdt. Vita Hom., 19). As the formula τὸ ἀπόστολον (πλοῖον) shows, the word obviously cannot be separated from → ἀποστέλλειν. The close material connection emerges in the common expression ὁ ἀπόστολος. In the first instances this simply denotes the despatch of a fleet (or army) on a military expedition, being simply a stronger form of the simp. στόλος (Lys. Or., 19, 21; Demosth. Or., 18, 107). [1] It then comes to be applied to the fleet itself and it thus acquires the meaning of a naval expedition (Demosth. Or., 18, 80; cf. 3, 5). [2] In this way it comes to be applied on the one side to a group of men sent out for a particular purpose, e.g., not merely to an army but to a band of colonists and their settlement (Dion. Hal. Ant. Rom., IX, 59), [3] and on the other to the commander of an expedition, e.g., the admiral (Hesychius, s.v.; Anecdota Graeca, ed. Bekker, 217, 26). [4]

A common feature of all these meanings is their predominantly passive character. In none of them do we find any suggestion either of initiative on the part of the ἀπόστο-

---

ἀ π ό σ τ ο λ ο ς. On the whole field, and C. and D.: W. Seufert, *Der Ursprung und die Bedeutung des Apostolates in der christlichen Kirche der ersten zwei Jhdte.* (1887); J. B. Lightfoot, *St. Paul's Epistle to the Galatians,*[10] (1890), 92 ff.; P. Batiffol, "L'Apostolat," Rev. Bibl., NS, 3 (1906), 520 ff.; J. Wellhausen, *Einleitung in die drei ersten Evv.*[2] (1911), 138 ff.; G. P. Wetter, "Der Sohn Gottes," FRL, 26 (1916); R. Schütz, *Apostel und Jünger* (1921); Meyer, *Ursprung,* I, 264 ff.; III, 255 ff.; K. Holl, "Der Kirchenbegriff des Pls. in seinem Verhältnis zu dem der Urgemeinde," SAB, 1921, 920 ff. = *Gesammelte Aufsätze zur Kirchengeschichte,* II: "Der Osten" (1928), 44 ff.; E. de Witt Burton, *Crit. and Exeget. Comm. on the Ep. to the Gal.* (1921), 363 ff.; F. Kattenbusch, "Die Vorzugsstellung des Petr. u. d. Charakter der Urgemeinde zu Jerusalem," in *Festgabe, Karl Müller ... zum 70. Geburtstag dargebracht* (1922), 322 ff.; F. Haase, "Apostel u. Evangelist. in d. orientalischen Überlieferungen" = *Nt.liche Abhandlungen,* IX, 1-3 (1922); A. v. Harnack, *Die Mission und Ausbreitung des Christentums in d. ersten 3 Jhdten,* I[4] (1923), esp. 332 ff.; J. Wagenmann, *Die Stellung d. Apostels Pls. neben den Zwölf in d. ersten zwei Jhdten* (1926); Ltzm. on R. 1:1; W. Mundle, "Das Apostelbild der Apostelgesch.," ZNW, 27 (1928), 36 ff.; K. Deissner, "Das Sendungsbewusstsein der Urchristenheit," ZSTh, 7 (1929/30), 772 ff. On A.: E. Norden, "Beiträge z. Geschichte d. gr. Philosophie," *Jbch. f. Phil. Suppl.,* 19 (1893), 365 ff.; K. Holl, "Die schriftstellerische Form d. gr. Heiligenlebens," N. Jbch. Kl. Alt., 29 (1912) 406 ff. = *Ges. Aufsätze z. KG,* II (1928), 249 ff.; C. Clemen, "Die Missionstätigkeit der nichtchristl. Religionen," ZMR, 44 (1929), 225 ff. On B.: S. Krauss, "Die jüdischen Apostel," JQR (1905), 370 ff.; H. Vogelstein, "Die Entstehung und Entwicklung des Apostolats im Judentum," MGWJ, 49 (1905), 427 ff. and "The Development of the Apostolate in Judaism and Its Transformation in Christianity," *Hbr. Un. Coll. Ann.,* 2 (1925), 99 ff.; S. Krauss, EJ, III (1929), 1 ff.; Str.-B., III, 2 ff.

[1] Cf. also the definition of Suid.: ἀπόστολοι δὲ αἱ τῶν νεῶν ἐκπομπαί.

[2] In Demosth. Or., 3, 5 the expression ἀφιέναι τὸν ἀπόστολον can be taken to signify either failure to send the triremes prepared or postponement of the expedition.

[3] It thus becomes almost a synon. of ἀποικία, which is the technical term for a colonising expedition; cf. Aeschin. Fals. Leg., 175, where there is reference to the ἀποστέλλειν of the ἀποικία.

[4] Pr.-Bauer, 156.

λος or of authorisation linked with the mission. The most that can be said it that the
word denotes the quality of being sent, unless we are to regard it as no more than
a stereotyped term. In this basic passive element the adj. derivation remains dominant
long after its application as a noun. Apart from the impersonality of its fundamental
meaning, it could not become the usual term for an emissary in the Gk. world, since
the Greeks had many others words which they could use for this purpose (→ ἄγγελος,
→ κῆρυξ, πρεσβευτής etc.). Thus its later Christian usage was an innovation to Gk.
ears or to those familiar with Gk.; this is shown by the fact that the Latins did not
translate it but took it over as a loan word into ecclesiastical Latin (apostolus).[5] Even
in the two isolated passages in which ἀπόστολος occurs, or seems to occur, on Ionic
soil in the sense of one who is sent (Hdt., I, 21; V, 38), the basic element is obviously
the quality of being sent; the idea of authorisation is not the point at issue and is quite
secondary.[6] Hence we are not to see any approach to NT usage in these passages.
Against such a thesis the LXX, Josephus and Philo all bear strong witness, since they
do not play in this respect the important role of links between secular and NT usage
which they frequently do elsewhere (→ 413). Instances of ἀπόστολος in the sense of
messenger belong to a much later period and obviously presuppose the Christian usage.[7]

How far normal usage differed from that of the NT in the first Christian period and
the time of the Early Church is shown by the papyri.[8] Here we find it in the technical
sense of an accompanying bill or invoice, e.g., for shipments of corn (P. Oxy., IX,
1197, 13 etc.),[9] as also in the sense of a passport (BGU, V, 64; cf. VI, 1303, 26). These
senses go rather beyond those mentioned above, yet do not refute kinship with them.
They rather develop more consistently the abstraction from the personal already noted,
so that we might almost speak of a complete mechanisation of the term. It is not
irrelevant that even in this final stage of its history we can still see evidence of the
background in maritime commerce from which the word derives or by which it is
originally characterised.

2. Religious Messengers in Hellenism.

a. If the connection between the ordinary Gk. and the early Christian ἀπόστολος is limited to the mere word, the material points of contact between the
apostolate and the Greek world are also very slight.

The earlier period has no parallel to the NT apostle. The Greek προφῆται are
proclaimers of a truth, and in so far as they belong to a sanctuary they are thus
mouthpieces for the deity which they serve.[10] This is true of the Pythian, who
is simply an intermediary between the deity and the believer who is anxious for
knowledge.[11] The very fact that she is anonymous and timeless shows that no
independent significance is attached to her. The whole problem of the authorisation of the intermediary remains in the background. This is self-explanatory, however, in view of her role, even when the mediation is accomplished through one

---

[5] → also 414.
[6] I, 21 of the κῆρυξ whom Alyattes sends to Miletus: ὁ μὲν δὴ ἀπόστολος ἐς τὴν
Μίλητον ἦν ...; ἀ. is here a pred. and approximates in meaning to the part. ἀπεσταλμένος (cf. K. W. Krüger in his ed. of Herodotus, Berlin, 1855 f., ad loc.). The case is much
the same in V, 38.
[7] Preisigke Wört., I, 195 furnishes only one example, which dates only from the 8th
century A.D. (P. Lond., IV). I do not know of any others.
[8] Cf. Preisigke Wört., I, 195; Fachwörter, 30.
[9] ἐξ ἀποστόλου or ἐξ ἀποστόλων corresponds to our "as per bill of lading"; examples
may be found in Preisigke Wört., I, 195.
[10] On this whole complex, v. E. Fascher, Προφήτης (1927), passim.
[11] Ibid., 14 and 68.

of the messenger-gods, as is usually the case in post-Christian Hellenism (→ 75). The words → ἄγγελος and → κῆρυξ, which usually occur along with πρέσβυς, πρεσβευτής etc. in this connection (cf. 1 Tm. 2:7; 2 Tm. 1:11), are a purely external expression of the fact that what is at issue is not a commission which must always be linked with a person, but the message which mediates fellowship as such, and in relation to which the bearer has only the significance of a supernumerary. This fact has its ultimate basis in the close relationship which Greek religion, so far as it is concerned with human intermediaries, sees between the divine office of the messenger and inspiration. [12] This also explains why it is that in the religious messenger of Hellenism there is no development of an awareness of mission or of a claim to full personal authority but there necessarily results a surrender of one's own consciousness and personality to the deity.

b. An exception is to be found to some degree in the representatives of Cynic-Stoic philosophy in so far as Epictetus [13] describes for us the reality and not merely the ideal of the true Cynic. For here we have a strong consciousness of mission and a related self-consciousness. The Cynic realises that he is "sent by Zeus," and Epictetus can even say that it is only this awareness of divine sending that makes the ταῖς ἀληθείαις Κυνικόν (Diss., III, 22, 23). [14] To be sure, → ἄγγελος and → κῆρυξ are here, too, the words used to describe this mission as regards its content (→ 399); but in addition, quite apart from the important part played by → ἀποστέλλειν as a technical term for commissioning and authorising by the deity, [15] there emerges as a third function that of the κατάσκοπος τῶν θεῶν. [16] As such he has to investigate (κατασκέπτεσθαι) quite exactly (ἀκριβῶς, III, 22, 25), and therefore as a true κατάσκοπος (I, 24, 3), how matters stand with men, and then ἀπαγγεῖλαι τἀληθῆ to them (III, 22, 25), as none has done but Diogenes, the first κατάσκοπος and the great example of the Cynic (I, 24, 6; III, 22, 24). [17] The Cynic thus observes men and seeks to fix on the points in their lives at which he can help as a "doctor of the soul, moral support and deliverer." [18] In so far as he does this, he becomes the ἐπισκοπῶν, [19] so that Epictetus can call true Cynics the ἐπισκοποῦντες πάντας κατὰ δύναμιν ἀνθρώπους, τί ποιοῦσιν, πῶς διάγουσιν, τίνος ἐπιμελοῦνται, τίνος ἀμελοῦσι παρὰ

---

[12] Cf. for the Pythian, Dio. Chrys. Or., 72, 12.

[13] Diss., III, 22 : περὶ κυνισμοῦ. Cf. on this pt., Wendland, Hell. Kult., 75 ff.

[14] → on this pt. and what follows 399 (s.v. ἀποστέλλω).

[15] → 398.

[16] The Cynic is ἄγγελος καὶ κατάσκοπος καὶ κῆρυξ τῶν θεῶν (III, 22, 69); as κατάσκοπος he is sent out into the world by his brethren in the order, e.g., to Rome (I, 24, 3 ff.). For further materials, cf. Deissner, 783 and esp. Norden, 377 f. (where we also have passages from Diog. L. and Plutarch).

[17] This self-designation is already found in Antisthenes, who links with it popular ideas of intermediaries between the gods and men (Norden, 373 ff., esp. 381).

[18] Holl, Ges. Aufsätze, II, 261; ibid. n. 1 for many examples, as also Pauly-W., XII, 14.

[19] Cf. on this point Norden, 378. For all their kinship κατάσκοπος and ἐπισκοπῶν should be distinguished, as emphatically shown by Norden, 378, n. 1. This emerges in the fact that the verb ἐπισκοπεῖν is always used and never the subst. → ἐπίσκοπος. ἐπισκοπεῖν is thus to some extent a function of the κατάσκοπος, while κατάσκοπος is essentially more than the designation of a function (supra). To be sure, in Diog. L., VI, 102 the Cynic Menedemos (c. 300 B.C.) is sometimes called an ἐπίσκοπος ... τῶν ἁμαρτανομένων who has come from Hades; but this instance is late (3rd century A.D.), and the term derives from ideas which differ at essential points from those of the older representatives of Cynicism (cf. Norden, 379).

τὸ προσῆκον (III, 22, 77).[20] The Cynic brings help as the κῆρυξ τῶν θεῶν;[21] in his κηρύσσειν, however, he shows himself to be ἐπισκοπῶν, which can only have meaning if he is truly a κατάσκοπος.

Hence the Cynic as ἄγγελος is the messenger of Zeus who sends him and stands behind him.[22] This is the purely passive side of his being as such. In addition, however, we see in the designation κατάσκοπος the initiative of the messenger which derives from his commissioning by Zeus (→ ἀποστέλλω, 399) and which expresses itself in the relevant *kerygma* in which the Cynic κῆρυξ to some extent proves himself to be the representative of the deity to men in the sense of their instructor in the divine standard (ἐπισκοπεῖν). Hence we can no longer speak of a purely passive attitude as in the case of the Greek prophets. This is clear from the relationship of the Cynic both to the one who commissions him and to those to whom he is sent. There is no doubt that he does not reckon himself among men. He sees them before him as a *massa perditionis*. He knows that he is exalted above them by his task and by his related freedom from worldly goods. It is not for nothing that he calls himself βασιλεὺς καὶ δεσπότης (Epict. Diss., III, 22, 49). He is controlled by a clear awareness of his remoteness from other men. Yet his distinguishing feature is not isolation; it is a strong sense of commitment to the *kerygma*, a strong sense of responsibility for humanity.[23] It seems almost an accident that the formal ὀφειλέτης by which Paul describes his relation to the non-Christian world (R. 1:14) is missing in Epictetus; the idea itself is there.[24] The strong sense of responsibility for humanity, however, is linked with a strong sense of responsibility towards Zeus. As the Cynic is absolutely free in relation to men, he is bound and committed to Zeus (399). He is his → ὑπηρέτης (III, 22, 82 and 95) who must hearken to him.[25] He is his → διάκονος (III, 22, 69). The sense of commitment by God and to men is the basis of the → παρρησία of the Cynic, of his candour (III, 22, 96), of his right always and everywhere to occupy himself with the affairs of others as with his own (III, 22, 97 ff.; cf. Horat. Sat., II, 3, 19), and of the certainty that he need not fear even the emperor when it is a matter of the cause represented by him (III, 22, 56). The word in which his commission and responsibility merge is κατάσκοπος. Here the initiative of the Cynic is both demanded and limited. If we want a term in which there is a material parallel to the NT use of ἀπόστολος, it is offered only by this word. The parallelism is emphasised by the fact that the terminology linked with the two words is very much the same,[26] even though in essentials the

---

[20] ἐπισκοπεῖν again in III, 22, 72 and 97.

[21] The Cynic as κῆρυξ τῶν θεῶν, Epict. Diss., III, 22, 69 (→ n. 16), κηρύσσειν, III, 13, 12; IV, 5, 24 (Deissner, 783); and cf. also III, 21, 13. For examples of similar usage outside Stoicism, cf. Pr.-Bauer, 674 f. and → κῆρυξ.

[22] Diogenes seems to have emphasised his divine mission even in connection with his name (Norden, 380, n. 1).

[23] Cf. on this pt. Deissner, 786 f. Important in this connection are the metaphors and self-designation taken from the medical world, esp. III, 23, 30 ff., Diog. L., VI, 6; cf. also Wendland, Hell. Kult., 82, n. 2; also v. Harnack, 129 ff. and → σῴζω, σωτήρ.

[24] Deissner, 786.

[25] Cf. the passages in Deissner, 784, esp. Diss., IV, 3, 9: ἐλεύθερος γάρ εἰμι καὶ φίλος τοῦ θεοῦ, ἵν᾽ ἑκὼν πείθωμαι αὐτῷ.

[26] The hints given above should be enough in this context. Cf. further the individual terms as discussed in this dictionary.

identity is again limited to form.[27] We can at least say that the Cynic-Stoic sage in his role as κατάσκοπος is the figure of the period which we can set in closest proximity to the apostle.

The Cynic's consciousness of mission has its prototype in Socrates as depicted by Plato in the Apology.[27] Socrates traces back his whole βίος and πρᾶγμα to the god of Delphi (τοῦ θεοῦ λατρεία, Plat. Ap., 23c) who has given him his life's task and to whom he owes obedience (Ap., 29d: πείσομαι δὲ μᾶλλον τῷ θεῷ ἢ ὑμῖν). For this reason his enemies and judges incur heavy responsibility, especially before God, when they seek to do away with him: μή τι ἐξαμάρτητε περὶ τὴν τοῦ θεοῦ δόσιν ὑμῖν ... ἐὰν γὰρ ἐμὲ ἀποκτείνητε, οὐ ῥᾳδίως ἄλλον τοιοῦτον εὑρήσετε ἀτεχνῶς, εἰ καὶ γελοιότερον εἰπεῖν, προσκείμενον τῇ πόλει ὑπὸ τοῦ θεοῦ, ὥσπερ ἵππῳ μεγάλῳ μὲν καὶ γενναίῳ, ὑπὸ μεγέθους δὲ νωθεστέρῳ καὶ δεομένῳ ἐγείρεσθαι ὑπὸ μύωπός τινος· οἷον δή μοι δοκεῖ ὁ θεὸς ἐμὲ τῇ πόλει προστεθεικέναι, τοιοῦτόν τινα, ὃς ὑμᾶς ἐγείρων καὶ πείθων καὶ ὀνειδίζων ἕνα ἕκαστον οὐδὲν παύομαι τὴν ἡμέραν ὅλην πανταχοῦ προσκαθίζων ... εἶτα τὸν λοιπὸν βίον καθεύδοντες διατελοῖτε ἄν, εἰ μή τινα ἄλλον ὁ θεὸς ὑμῖν ἐπιπέμψειεν κηδόμενος ὑμῶν (Plat. Ap., 30e-31a). Here, too, is the basis of the Stoic terminology, though ἀποστέλλειν is not found. Yet perhaps there is a certain distinction between Socrates and the Stoics in the fact that for him the source of the mission is far less important than its goal, whereas, e.g., Epictetus claims the authority of the God who sends him (→ 399).

The same is true of the external aspect of the Cynic, for like the apostle he goes through the world and tries to commend his doctrine, relying on the generosity of his hearers and well-wishers for support. The visit of Paul to Athens (Ac. 17:16 ff.) is fully after the manner of Cynic and Epicurean philosophers in their appeal to the public, as also of other wandering preachers trying to commend their convictions.[28] Because of this external similarity Paul himself after his departure from Thessalonica seems to have been suspected by ill-disposed elements of being a preacher of this type, and indeed of being one of the less reputable who for the sake of gold and fame were more interested in attaching followers to themselves than to their cause.[29] On Greek soil the apostles were not a new type but simply the champions of one religion alongside the innumerable missionaries of other cults and philosophies in this classical age of religious propaganda.[30] Nevertheless, there is no true parallel, for although these others used ἀποστέλλεσθαι to denote their authorisation,[31] they never gave linguistic formulation to the sense of mission and the related claim. This happened only in the case of the Cynics with their term κατάσκοπος.

This term, however, is most apt to denote the nature of the awareness thus described. To the extent that in it the Cynic himself is the acting subject, and not God[32] as in the case of ἄγγελος, this awareness is shown to be a consciousness of self rather than God. Externally this finds expression in the arrogant bearing

---

[27] For what follows, cf. the account given by H. Kleinknecht. Cf. also P. Friedländer, *Platon,* II (1930), 165 f.; E. Wolff, *Platos Apologie = Neue philologische Untersuchungen,* 6 (1929), 25 ff., 39 ff.

[28] Cf. Wendland, Hell. Kult., 92 ff.

[29] The so-called apology in 1 Th. 2:1-13 is perhaps occasioned by this.

[30] For a brief sketch cf. Dob. Th., 2 ff.; cf. H. Gressmann, "Heidnische Mission in der Werdezeit des Christentums," ZMR, 39 (1924), 14 ff.

[31] → 399.

[32] We can say this in view of the way in which Epictetus speaks of ὁ θεός.

of the Cynic, which often caused offence ; [33] internally in the need for religious assurance of his own authority beyond the mere fact of being sent. This was done by the adoption of the formula θεῖος ἄνθρωπος as a self-designation (→ 399), especially by the Stoics. [34] This rests on the old Cynic tradition [35] but with mystical echoes which it has as a constituent part of the language of the Mystery religions. [36] In the language of the philosophers this cannot be separated from their consciousness of mission (→ 399). Yet we can see from its presence that the latter had no ultimate metaphysical foundation, since it brought into rational philosophical piety an irrational element in which there is even a certain approximation, within the limits of the rational, to the enthusiasm of the Greek prophets. Yet since this element, too, gives clear evidence of its origin in Pantheism, which finally entails the absorption of the divine in the ego, we can see that it is not along these lines that the self-consciousness of the Cynic-Stoic philosopher passes over into a consciousness of mission which manifests its theonomic character in the uniting of an unlimited claim in the name of the sending God with a renunciation of any significance of the man who is highly favoured with this mission. The tension which necessarily results between the sense of mission and the person of the missionary could never be overcome by the Cynic-Stoic diatribe, since in the last resort this was always a human programme even when its representatives advanced a religious claim. That it was itself aware of this may be seen in the description of the messengers as κατάσκοποι. This is an admission that at the decisive point, namely, at the moment when the ἄγγελος θεῶν becomes the κῆρυξ θεῶν, the accent is still laid on human initiative and human judgment. For, although the ἀπεσταλμένος belongs to the deity as ὑπηρέτης, he is never absolutely dependent on it as its δοῦλος; [37] he rather stands alongside it as βασιλεὺς καὶ δεσπότης (→ 410), and he is thus almost equal to it in rank and dignity (θεῖος ἄνθρωπος). [38] Hence the relationship of the messenger to the deity never has the character of an unconditional appointment to which he is subject ; it is more like an agreement between two partners. [39] This is only possible, however, because in these circles there is no clear concept of God nor certainty of a definitive revelation of the will of God. But this is also the explanation why, for all its consciousness of mission and self-consciousness, the philosophical religion of the period never attains the claim to absoluteness which is the mark of all genuine religion and its messengers. [40]

Especially in view of the last point, we can finally add quite briefly that it is quite consistent that in the Gk. world no essential role, and perhaps no role of any kind, is

---

[33] For greater detail, cf. Pauly-W., XII, 14 f.

[34] A typical example is Dio. Chrys.; cf. Holl, 262.

[35] → 400 and n. 19.

[36] Holl, 262.

[37] δοῦλος τοῦ θεοῦ etc. is never used by the Cynics or Stoics as a self-designation and would be quite impossible from their standpoint. v. on this pt. Deissner, 787.

[38] Thus, like Zeus, he is some sense the father of all men (Epict. Diss., III, 22, 81).

[39] It is symptomatic that when the Cynic is scorned and insulted he always regards it as an attack on himself and not on the one whom he ostensibly represents (cf., e.g., Epict. Diss., III, 22, 53 ff.); the formula ἡ πρὸς θεοὺς ὁμιλία (III, 22, 22) is also relevant in this regard.

[40] This shows how appropriate is the choice of the term κατάσκοπος as the typical self-designation of the Cynic. It should be noted that κατάσκοπος (from κατασκέπτεσθαι) and ἀπόστολος (from ἀποστέλλεσθαι) are basically analogous constructions.

played by legal elements in the dealings of the gods with humanity through human intermediaries. This is quite obvious in the case of the Cynic (→ n. 39), but it applies
no less to others. Again, this results logically from the lack of a clear conception of
God and of a historical revelation as determinative factors. Mythical notions of God
and mystical divine union leave no place for concrete categories like the legal, nor for
the content of proclamation, whether in respect of those who execute it or of those
who are won by it. Further discussion of this point is thus unnecessary.

B. ἀπόστολος/ שָׁלִיחַ (שָׁלוּחַ) in Judaism.

1. ἀπόστολος among the Greek Jews.

In Gk. Judaism the term ἀπόστολος was not widely used. This is perhaps because
the sphere in which it arose (→ 407) was largely closed to Judaism. The Palestinians
had no direct access to the sea and were thus under no necessity of equipping or even
planning maritime expeditions. But even the Egyptian Jews never seem to have undertaken sea voyages to any great extent. At any rate we do not find the word in Philo.

The term occurs twice in Josephus, though the attestation is poor in one case.
First (Ant., 17, 300) it has the sense of the sending of emissaries,[41] and it thus stands
midway between the original sense (→ 407) and the NT meaning, but is quite different
from the usage of the papyri (→ 408). We can thus speak of an adaptation to the
particular background of Josephus, though it should not be overlooked that the reference
is to a Jewish embassy to Rome which would necessitate a sea-journey. Two elements
in the usage of Josephus call for notice : first, the strengthened influence of ἀποστέλλειν
on the word, as seen in its special application to the sending of men ; and secondly,
that he retains the traditional collective use. We cannot know how far Josephus was
here in line with the usage of the time. In the second passage (Ant., 1, 146) ἀπόστολος
is synon. with → ἀποστολή,[42] though it may not be the true reading.[43] In any case,
this sheds no light on the usage of Josephus.

The LXX[44] has the word only at 1 Βασ. 14:6 in the passage 14:1-20 which is missing
in the Vaticanus[45] and which is thus usually given according to the Alexandrinus :
ἐγώ εἰμι ἀπόστολος πρός σε σκληρός. These are the words of the prophet Ahijah
to the wife of king Jeroboam when she comes to ask concerning the fate of her sick son.
The Hebr. original is : אָנֹכִי שָׁלוּחַ אֵלַיִךְ קָשָׁה. It should be noted first that ἀπόστολος
is the rendering of שָׁלוּחַ, which is obviously taken as a noun, though it is really a pass.
part.,[46] for only on this assumption is the translation ἀπόστολος ... σκληρός possible.
ἀπόστολος thus attains an individual character in this passage. It makes no difference
that in the ἀπόστολος πρός σε we still have an echo of the verbal form of the original.
More important is the fact that ἀπόστολος is here the messenger of God in the technical
sense, since the word expresses the fact that Ahijah is commissioned to deliver a divine
message to the wife of the king.[47] Here we see the influence of שָׁלִיחַ, which describes
the authorisation of the prophet by God (→ שׁלח, 400). The secular meaning of שָׁלַח/
ἀποστέλλειν has thus given place to the theological, and it is this which gives its
meaning to ἀπόστολος. It should also be particularly noted that the word is used of a
נָבִיא (προφήτης), and furthermore that it is used in a concrete situation in his prophetic

---

[41] It has here almost the sense of "embassy."
[42] This is also attested as a variant.
[43] Perhaps we should read ἀποδασμός.
[44] Based on the findings of Hatch-Redp.
[45] This shows that the text is of more recent date.
[46] On the construction of the Heb. sentence, cf. Gesenius-Kautzsch, *Hebr. Gramm.*[27]
(1902), 393, n. 3.
[47] It should be noted that she comes to the prophet and not *vice versa*.

life. The addition of σκληρός shows that the term has not become static but is materially the same as ἀπεσταλμένος, which would be the usual rendering of שָׁלִיחַ. When this is taken into account, the usage is seen to go far beyond what we find in the two instances of the use of ἀπόστολος for "messenger" in Herod. (→ 408). For the rest, Aquila also has ἀπόστολος [48] at 1 Βασ. 14:6, thus underlining the equation of שָׁלוּחַ and ἀπόστολος. Finally, Symmachus gives us a further instance in Is. 18:2 by rendering הַשֹּׁלֵחַ בַּיָּם צִירִים ἀποστέλλων ἀποστόλους ἐν θαλάσσῃ. This is an isolated case, however, for the equation of ἀπόστολος and צִיר is not attested elsewhere. [49]

2. The Later Jewish Institution of the שָׁלִיחַ.

We are led a decisive step forward by Rabbinic Judaism. Here the term שָׁלִיחַ [50] has an assured place as a noun, and in such a way that we have in it the closest parallel to the NT ἀπόστολος. The material kinship was recognised by the fathers. Jerome [51] tells us that Slias is a title borne by Jews who may be compared to the ἀπόστολοι, and this is simply a Latinised form of שְׁלִיחָא. [52] The terminological agreement is proved by the fact that in the Syr. Church an apostle is called שְׁלִיחָא, while on a Jewish inscription at Venosa dating from the 5th or 6th century A.D. there is reference to *duo apostuli* with *duo rebbites*. [53] The relationship between ἀπόστολος and שָׁלִיחַ is thus recognised by the non-Christian world as well; otherwise the use of the Latinised *apostulus* would be impossible. [54] The Rabbis, however, did not adopt the Gk. word themselves [55] — a sign that the Semitic term was firmly rooted among them. Another possible reason was that from the middle of the 1st century the Gk. word has become a constituent part of the distinctively Christian vocabulary, and could not therefore be considered for Jewish use.

a. The legal institution of the שְׁלוּחִים is old. It may be proved from the time after the Exile (2 Ch. 17:7-9), but is probably older still. [56] Yet it is only around the 1st century that it takes distinctive shape. What characterises the שְׁלוּחִים of all periods is their commissioning with distinctive tasks which take them greater or

---

[48] Acc. to Wellhausen, 143, n. 2 Aquila is here the source of the LXX.

[49] For an assessment of this exegesis of Is. 18:1 f. in the early Church, cf. Lightfoot, 93, n. 2.

[50] This is the usual form. In the plur. and with suffixes שָׁלוּחַ is used (Str.-B., III, 2); שְׁלִיחָא is the corresponding Aram.

[51] Ad Gal. 1:1; there is here a full equation.

[52] Slias from שליחא as Messias from משיחא, Krauss, JQR, 17 (1905), 370, n. 4.

[53] CIL, IX, 648; cf. REJ, 6 (1882), 205 f.

[54] S. Krauss (JQR, 17 [1905], 370 ff.) was the first to develop the connection between ἀπόστολος and שליח in detail, following Lightfoot and in opposition to A. v. Harnack. Yet neither he nor H. Vogelstein (MGWJ, 49 [1905] 427 ff.) went beyond a comparison with individual forms of the institution. P. Billerbeck (esp. III, 2 ff.) first made a comparison with its essential nature and thus made possible a theological investigation in the light of Judaism. Holl's scepticism (Ges. Aufs., II, 51, n. 1) about the introduction of the Jewish parallel was refuted by B.

[55] M. Jastrow, *A Dictionary of the Targumim etc.*, I (1903), 101 has argued that in Taan., 4, 6 (. . . שֶׁבְּנֶה עָשָׂר אֶת הַתּוֹרָה) שָׂרַף אפסטמוס בְּתַמּוּז . . . (בְּשִׁבְעָה עָשָׂר) an ἀπόστολος is denoted by the אַפְּסְטֹמוֹס (?) who burns the Torah, and he finds in the passage a reminiscence of the event recorded in 2 Macc. 6:1 f. Yet in spite of obscurities in detail other explanations seem to be nearer the mark. Cf. S. Krauss, *Proc. Soc. Bibl. Arch.*, 25 (1903), 222 ff.; Jew. Enc., II, 21 f.

[56] Krauss, JQR, 382: post-Exilic. Vogelstein (Hbr. Un. Coll. Ann., 2 [1925], 100) traces it back to 419 B.C. (Elephantine Pap.).

lesser distances away from the residence of the one who gives them. Thus the point of the designation שְׁלוּחִים is neither description of the fact of sending nor indication of the task involved but simply assertion of the form of sending, i.e., of authorisation. This is the decisive thing. The task as such is of no significance for the quality as שָׁלִיחַ. Fundamentally, therefore, it matters little whether the task is to proclaim religious truths (2 Ch. 17:7 ff.) or to conduct financial business (T. Kid., 4, 2). The term is legal rather than religious, and if the שָׁלִיחַ has religious significance this is not because he is a שָׁלִיחַ but because as such he is entrusted with a religious task. In other words, we simply have a consistent application of the sense (→ 400) of שָׁלִיחַ (ἀποστέλλειν) irrespective of certain theological contexts in which it is given a particular flavour by the situation. The Rabbis traced back the institution to the Torah (bNed., 72b; → infra).

The legal element in שָׁלִיחַ thus lies in the very nature of the matter. None can be sent but one who is under orders or who places himself under orders. Thus with the commission there goes the necessary responsibility for the one who receives it. The man commissioned is always the representative of the man who gives the commission. He represents in his own person the person and rights of the other. The Rabbis summed up this basis of the שָׁלִיחַ in the frequently quoted statement: שְׁלוּחוֹ שֶׁל אָדָם כְּמוֹתוֹ, "the one sent by a man is as the man himself" (Ber., 5, 5), [57] i.e., the שָׁלִיחַ is as good as the שׁוֹלֵחַ in all that he says and does in execution of his commission.

> Thus one may become betrothed through a שָׁלִיחַ (Kid., 2, 1; T. Kid., 4, 2; T. Yeb., 4, 4). In such a case the one commissioned validly performs all the ceremonies in place of the bridegroom concerned. [58] Similarly there may be a valid execution of the ceremonial of divorce through a commissioned representative; the powers of the latter are so extensive that the divorce accomplished or initiated by him cannot be reversed by the husband (Git., 4, 1). *Mutatis mutandis* the same is true of any legal transaction (e.g., a purchase, T. Yeb., 4, 4, or the killing of the Passover lamb by a slave, Pes., 8, 2 etc.).

That the one sent should act in accordance with his commission is naturally an unconditional presupposition. At this point there might be sabotage of the commission by abuse of the plenary power entrusted, and this could not be prevented or its effects arrested (Kid., 3, 1). In other words, the transaction could not be properly conducted without a resolute subordination of the will of the representative to that of the one who commissioned him. In the Rabbinic institution of שָׁלִיחַ, therefore, we do not finally have the mechanistic fulfilment of an order but a conscious, active decision for the plan and commission of another. [59] It makes no difference that this takes place wholly in the legal sphere. This does not secularise the institution. On the contrary, it implies its religious confirmation and purification. On Jewish soil law and religion constitute an indissoluble unity. This is shown by the fact that it can sometimes be said that God is well-pleased with a שָׁלִיחַ who sacrifices his life for the cause in hand. [60] But it also emerges clearly in the further use of שָׁלִיחַ.

---

[57] For further instances, cf. Str.-B., III, 2.

[58] Incisive reasons are given in bKid., 41a-b.

[59] This rather exaggerated formulation is indispensable for a clear understanding of the facts.

[60] Nu.r., 16 on 13:2 (a reference given by H. Bornhäuser).

In its legal basis the whole circle of ideas bound up with the שָׁלִיחַ goes back to the Semitic law of the messenger as presupposed in the OT. Here the messenger fully represents in his person the one who sends him, usually the king ; and this is the original meaning of the sending of a plenipotentiary. The honour which belongs and is to be paid to his lord is paid to him. We see this in the case of Abigail, who, when the servants of David come to take her to him as his wife (דָּוִד שְׁלָחָנוּ אֵלַיִךְ לְקַחְתֵּךְ לֹו לְאִשָּׁה), washes their feet and thus shows that she is ready to perform this wifely service to him (1 S. 25:40 f.). On the other hand, shameful treatment of a messenger is not so much directed against him as against his lord, and cannot be ignored. Thus in 2 S. 10:1 f. the shaming of the messengers of David by the Ammonites is the cause of a war of extirpation against them. In these and similar cases we have practical applications of the theory of the שָׁלִיחַ as later formulated by the Rabbis (→ 415). Cf. on this point bBQ, 113b : "The emissary of a king is as the king himself" (Str.-B., I, 590); also S. Nu., 103 on 12:9 : "With what is the matter to be compared ? With a king of flesh and blood, who has an *epitropos* in the land. And the inhabitants of the land spoke against him. Then the king said : You have not spoken about my servant, but about me."

b. Thus far the reference of the institution has been to the relation between two men, i.e., to a purely private transaction. But the institution has a wider scope. On the same foundation the שָׁלִיחַ may represent in the same sense a number of individuals. Here the connection between law and religion in the person of the emissary emerges far more clearly than was hitherto possible, for in addition to a definite group he may represent the community as such or local congregations if empowered to do so. In some cases, therefore, it is a question of the interpretation or religious confirmation of existing offices with the help of the institution of the שָׁלִיחַ.

It is not unusual for a court to charge an individual with the conveyance or even the execution of its decisions. What is important is that the one who bears this commission is called שָׁלִיחַ (Git., 3, 6; cf. BQ, 9, 5 and Yoma, 1, 5). [61] Again, it is as plenipotentiaries of the great Sanhedrin that certain rabbis go to the *diaspora* with the task of regulating the calendar, i.e., of executing the intercalation made in Palestine by official decree (Yeb., 16, 7: Akiba ; T. Meg., 2, 5 : Meir). [62] Similarly, the beginning of the new month is made known by שְׁלוּחִים (RH, 1, 3 and 4 ; 2, 2) to the Syrian *diaspora,* who pass on the news to Babylon by fire signals (RH, 2, 4). Again, it is as an authorised representative of the local community (שָׁלִיחַ צִבּוּר) that the leader prays for the assembled congregation in the individual synagogue, and any lapse is a bad sign for those whom he has to represent before God (Ber., 5, 5). [63] Again, the high-priest acts as a fully accredited representative of the priesthood, which for its part is charged by the Sanhedrin to see that he correctly carries out the prescribed actions, and then on the Day of Atonement he represents the national community as a whole (Yoma, 1, 5). It is in this light that we are to understand the care which the Pharisees and their adherents among the priests displayed in following the ritual according to Pharisaic tradition (Yoma, 1, 1 ff.; cf. bYoma, 19b).

---

[61] שליח בית דין thus comes to mean an "agent of justice" (Mak. 2:2). In cases in which knowledge of the Halacha was necessary for the execution of the commission as well as trustworthiness, these agents were themselves scribes and they might alone constitute a court capable of pronouncing sentence (e.g., Men., 10, 3).

[62] The word שָׁלִיחַ is not used, but the thing itself is present ; for Akiba does not journey on his own authority. That only an acknowledged scribe could make the intercalation is easily explained by the importance of a common calendar for Judaism.

[63] The same is true *mutatis mutandis* of the intercessor in relation to the sick for whom he intercedes ; cf. the anecdotes about Chanina b. Dosa, bBer., 34b; jBer., 9d, 21 ff.

As representatives of the scribes, and in their name again of all Israel, we have to mention supremely the rabbis who were sent out to the whole *diaspora* by the central authorities ; for them the designation שְׁלוּחִים became an official title in the true sense (→ 414). Their commission was many-sided enough, but it was always made possible by the authority which stood behind them in the person of those who sent them. After 70 A.D. they made a voluntary collection for the Palestinian scribes, who could not have carried on without this help, so that the continued exposition of the Halacha, and therefore the achievement by the people of a life well-pleasing to God, would have been threatened with destruction. To this extent the gathering of money is a distinctly religious office.[64] Otherwise Akiba and other great rabbis would not have been willing to undertake it (jHor., 48a, 39 ff.). Their main task, however, was the visitation of the *diaspora*. According to jChag., 76c, 31 ff. and other passages[65] the patriarch Jehuda II (c. 250 A.D.) sent three leading rabbis to the districts of Palestine to appoint teachers of the Bible and the Mishna. Similar attempts to maintain through envoys the connection between the motherland and the *diaspora*, between the spiritual authorities and the congregations outside Palestine, seem to date from an earlier period. It is as one such שָׁלִיחַ of the central authorities that Paul, for example, goes to Damascus in Ac. 9:1 ff. His carrying of letters from those who commissioned him is fully in line with the custom of giving שְׁלוּחִים letters of accreditation.

We have one such document in jChag., 76d, 3 f. (cf. jNed., 42b, 22 f.).[66] It refers to R. Chijja bar Abba (c. 280) and commends him to the patriarch Jehuda II : "Lo, we send (שְׁלַחֲנוּ) you a great man (אָדָם גָּדוֹל) as our envoy (שְׁלוּחֵנוּ), equal to ourselves until he come to us." Naturally, more details were given of the person and tasks of the שָׁלִיחַ. Their nature was not unimportant even from the standpoint of the → ψευδαπόστολοι who competed with Paul (2 C. 11:13); this phenomenon could hardly be unknown in Judaism if accrediting letters were thought to be necessary.

Moreover the שְׁלוּחִים, who were usually ordained rabbis, were specially set apart for their task by the laying on of hands in the name of the community which sent them. Their mission thus acquired a religious as well as an official character (→ χειροτονέω).[67] Perhaps this final element is also specifically expressed in the fact that שְׁלוּחִים were not sent out alone but usually two or more together.[68]

Just. Dial., 108 refers to "selected men on whom hands have been laid" (χειροτονήσαντες), meaning Jewish שְׁלוּחִים (cf. also 17).[69] The laying on of hands (סְמִיכָה), with

---

[64] In time there developed a regular tax of the *diaspora*, the so-called patriarchal tax, which linked up with the earlier temple tax and replaced free will offerings (cf. Vogelstein, MGWJ, 438 ff.). Yet the collection still remained in the hands of scribal שְׁלוּחִים with the support of local authorities (*ibid.*, 441 f.), which had previously imposed and gathered the temple tax (cf. also Str.-B., III, 316 ff.).

[65] Cf. Krauss, JQR, 375 ff.; EJ, III, 5; Vogelstein, MGWJ, 437.

[66] Krauss, EJ, III, 3; Vogelstein, 435, n. 2.

[67] We also find χειροτονέω with ἀποστέλλω in quite a different connection in Philo Migr. Abr., 22 (→ 399).

[68] Cf. the Venosa inscription (→ n. 53): *duo apostuli et duo rebbites,* but esp. the passages in Schl. Mt., 325 f., and in the NT Mt. 11:2: two sent by the Baptist ; Mk. 6:7: the sending out (ἀποστέλλειν) of the disciples δύο δύο; and Lk. 10:1: the sending out of the 70 (ἀπέστειλεν) ἀνὰ δύο.

[69] Cf. v. Harnack, 65, n. 2, where we also have patristic references to Jewish ἀπόστολοι. But cf. what follows.

which, e.g., the representative high-priest on the Day of Atonement was designated for his supreme office (Yoma., 1, 1), but which was above all customary in ordination (T. Sanh., 1, 1), seems to have been later abandoned by the Jews in view of its adoption by Christians (Str.-B., II, 653 f.). Its earlier link with the institution of שְׁלוּחִים emphasises the importance of the latter.

On the other hand, it must be emphasised most strongly that Jewish missionaries, of whom there were quite a number in the time of Jesus, [70] are never called שְׁלוּחִים, and that in relation to them the words שָׁלֵחַ and ἀποστέλλειν play no part. Their work took place without authorisation by the community in the narrower sense, and it thus had a private character, though without detriment to its scope and significance. [71]

Even in Justin (→ 417) we still do not find ἀπόστολος used of Jewish missionaries (Dial., 108), though it would have been natural to use the term as ἀποστέλλειν came to be increasingly used of their authoritative sending by the spiritual authorities in Jerusalem (17). [72] We may thus conclude that ἀπόστολος was not regarded as the obvious Gk. equivalent of שָׁלִיחַ, and particularly that the Jews did not make this equation. [73] Against such a view we may mention, not only the failure of the Jews to use ἀπόστολος in the sense of "apostle" prior to NT usage, but also the fact that Jews as well as Christians came to use ἀπόστολος as a loan word in Latin (inscription of Venosa), [74] which would not have been necessary in the case of שָׁלִיחַ. [75]

Thus we cannot really speak of Jewish "apostles" at the time of Jesus; the only suitable term is "authorised representatives." If "apostles" is used, it is due to a mechanical transfer of Christian usage to Judaism in spite of the lack of any grounds on which to justify it; for, although older Judaism knew many different kinds of שְׁלוּחִים, it never linked the word with the missionary activity of its members. This was because the office of שָׁלִיחַ grew out of everyday needs within the community, and did not extend beyond its frontiers. By its whole nature and origin the institution was secular and not religious, so that even where it takes a religious form (→ c.) this is only by way of application. In relation to the provenance of the Christian apostolate the result is that we must be careful not to link it with Jewish missionary work. We are certainly guilty of error if we think of Paul as a missionary prior to his conversion, especially in the sense of one who was regularly called to preach the religion of his fathers. [76]

The fact that there were no authorised missionaries in Judaism prior to 70 A.D. may be explained by the Jewish consciousness of election as this found expression in the subordination of the concept of God to religious self-awareness and therefore in the very trait in Judaism which Jesus attacked, especially in the Sermon on the Mount. From this assured position the Jewish world had no interest in fostering the spread of its faith; it could let others seek it, but not propose it to them. Where missions were conducted,

---

[70] Cf. Mt. 23:15; on the question of origins, v. Str.-B., I, 926.

[71] A striking example is the conversion of the royal house of Adiabene through the Jewish merchant (a Pharisee; Str.-B., I, 926), Eleazar (Jos. Ant., 20, 17 ff.).

[72] On Justin's usage, → 424.

[73] As held by Harnack, 340, n. 1, mainly on the basis of an erroneous interpretation of Jos. Ant., 17, 300 (→ 413).

[74] → 414, with n. 53.

[75] *Legatus* would have been a suitable rendering.

[76] Cf. E. Barnikol, *Die vorchristliche und frühchristliche Zeit des Paulus* (1929), 18 ff.

they were backed by Pharisaic groups whose action in this respect, too, was grounded in the concept of merit rather than in a universalism of salvation. [77] The people or community no more thought of missions as a concern of Israel than the spiritual leaders and priests. [78] Even after 70 A.D. this was still essentially true. [79]

c. Further light is shed on the last statements by the fact that the Rabbis often used the term שָׁלִיחַ of one who was commissioned and authorised by God. Two groups might be mentioned in this connection, first, the impersonal one of the priesthood in the priest as such, and second, a small number of outstanding personalities, especially Moses, Elijah, Elisha and Ezekiel. [80]

In offering sacrifices the priest was the commissioned minister of God and not of the Jewish community (Rab. Huna b. Jehoshua, c. 350 A.D.; bKid., 23b). Behind this statement stands the whole שָׁלִיחַ idea that the one authoritatively commissioned is as the one who commissions him (→ 415). If the priest were the שָׁלִיחַ of the community, the latter might also offer sacrifice. But if so, the priest would be superfluous. Hence the priest can be only the שָׁלִיחַ of God. He is thus called שָׁלִיחַ דְּרַחֲמָנָא "accredited representative of the Merciful" (cf. bKid., 23b; Yoma, 19, a-b). There is here no contradiction of Lv. 16 (cf. 4:5 ff.) in as much as his action on behalf of the people is not hereby prejudiced; on the contrary, it is shown to be possible.

Moses, Elijah, Elisha and Ezekiel are called שְׁלוּחִים of God because there took place through them things normally reserved for God. [81] Moses causes water to flow out of the rock (bBM, 86b); Elijah brings rain and raises a dead man; Elisha "opens the mother's womb" and also raises a dead man; and Ezekiel receives the "key to the tombs at the reawakening of the dead" according to Ez. 37:1 ff. (Midr. Ps. 78 § 5; cf. bTaan. 2a; bSanh., 113a). [82]

These four were distinguished by the miracles which God empowered them to perform and which He normally reserved for Himself. Thus here too (→ supra) there is a deduction from cause and effect, with no very profound reflection on שָׁלִיחַ. In the background there may even be a tendency to clear the four of any violation of the divine prerogatives by showing them to be instruments.

In Ex. r., 5, 14 on 5:1 Moses and Aaron, when asked by Pharaoh who they are, style themselves שְׁלוּחָיו שֶׁל הַקָּדוֹשׁ בָּרוּךְ הוּא. At a first glance the formula seems to be far-reaching and to demand some such rendering as "accredited agents of God." But the context shows that it is simply a passive form of "God has sent us" as demanded by the question of Pharaoh (Gr. ἀπεσταλμένοι ὑπὸ θεοῦ). The situation is similar in the case of the angel of death (→ n. 82).

---

[77] Midr. HL, 1 on 1:3: "If anyone bring a creature (i.e., a man) under the wings of the Shekinah (i.e., makes him a proselyte), it is reckoned unto him (i.e., by God) as if he had created and formed and fashioned it."

[78] Under the Maccabees and their successors (cf. A. Schlatter, Geschichte Israels³ [1925], 132 ff.) special motives were operative.

[79] Cf. Str.-B., I, 926, where the reasons for the failure of missionary enterprise after 70 A.D. are found in the external situation of the Jews.

[80] Cf. the instances given in Str.-B., III, 5 f.

[81] Cf. on this pt. the Prayer of Eighteen Petitions, where God is especially extolled as the Raiser of the dead and the Giver of dew and rain. It is to be noted that in 1 Cl., 17, 1 only the first three of these are mentioned specifically along with the prophets generally.

[82] Naturally the angels are שְׁלוּחִים, as the angel of death in Dt. r., 9, 1 on 34:5 (שָׁלוּחוֹ שֶׁל מָקוֹם); but this is another question.

As missionaries do not count as שְׁלוּחִים of the community (→ 418), so the prophets are not reckoned as שְׁלוּחִים of God. Nowhere do the Rabbis describe a prophet as the שָׁלִיחַ of God, [83] though this might have been a good way of denoting his special commissioning by God and his representation of God, which was the only content of his life and result of his calling. Perhaps the reason is to be sought in the tendency of the Rabbis to lay increasing emphasis on the divine transcendence; yet this is hardly adequate, for in respect of the call of the prophets שָׁלַח was a technical term for authorisation by God (→ 400), and therefore שָׁלִיחַ was the obvious term to use. We can hardly avoid the conclusion that for later Judaism the sending of a man (שָׁלַח) by God did not have to imply that he is a שָׁלִיחַ. In other words, for the Rabbis שָׁלִיחַ was obviously not the proper word to express the ultimate meaning of the prophetic office. If we take missionaries and prophets together, we are thus forced to the view that the term was avoided in these cases because, although they speak about God and in the name of God, they are not His representatives in so far as they perform no action. The essence of the שָׁלִיחַ is that he should actively represent another.

The thesis that the prophet cannot be a שָׁלִיחַ because he merely speaks is in some sense confirmed by the fact that later Judaism interposed the Holy Spirit between the prophet and God; the Holy Spirit is, of course, a mere hypostasis of God and serves to emphasise His transcendence. But if the prophets are made a possession of the רוּחַ הַקּוֹדֶשׁ, [84] they become mere instruments and forfeit their own initiative, [85] which is essential to the nature of the שָׁלִיחַ even though he unites his own will with that of him who sends him. We need hardly say that with this mechanisation of prophecy in the interests of speculation the Rabbis grossly misunderstood it, and they did so in such a way that it finally became impossible to understand that the essence of this mission consists in the commissioning of a man to represent the divine Word and will in his whole person. Here we reach the rationalistically determined limit of the Jewish conception of the שָׁלִיחַ, and it is here that, for all the formal kinship, the NT ἀπόστολος both opposes and transcends this view.

C. The Use of ἀπόστολος in the NT.

1. Statistical Findings.

There are 79 fully attested occurrences, and some others, esp. in Lk. (→ 422; 428), where it is a secondary reading (Lk. 9:1; [86] Ac. 5:34 [87]). It is found only once each in Mt., Mk. and Jn., but 29 times in Paul (if we include 4 times in Eph. and once in Col., but exclude 5 times in the Past.), and 34 in Lk. (28 in Ac. and 6 in Lk.); the remaining occurrences are once each in Hb., 1 Pt. and Jd., twice in 2 Pt. and 3 times in Rev. It

---

[83] Ezekiel is not reckoned a שָׁלִיחַ because he is a prophet, but because he possesses miraculous power (→ 419).

[84] Cf. esp. T. Sota, 13, 2: When Haggai, Zechariah and Malachi, the last prophets, died, the Holy Spirit disappeared from Israel.

[85] Cf. the common Rabbinic formula: "This is what the Holy Spirit has said through ..." (Str.-B., I, 74 f.).

[86] Here it is fairly certainly an Alexandrian gloss (J. Weiss, Das Ev. des Lk.[9] [1901], ad loc.).

[87] V. Soden accepts ἀποστόλους, but v. Wdt. Ag., 53 and F. Blass, Acta apostolorum (1895), 88 ad loc.

will be seen that four-fifths of the occurrences are to be found in Paul and his pupil and companion Luke. Thus they are of particular importance in fixing the meaning. Another important feature is the use of the term at the head of epistles, 6 times in Paul and 3 times in Past., 1 Pt. and 2 Pt. In this regard we have to reckon with the possibility that the non-Pauline greetings were influenced by the Pauline both in the use of the formula χάρις καὶ εἰρήνη and also in that of the title of "apostle." [88]

2. The Meaning.

From the total material the following meanings emerge, partly in connection with the history of the word and concept, partly in anticipation of the results of our later deliberations, which in this case are indispensable even for those whose interest is purely lexical. [89]

a. There is now no trace of the common use of ἀπόστολος outside the Bible and in Josephus (→ A. 1 and B. 1). In the NT ἀπόστολος never means the act of sending, or figuratively the object of sending. It always denotes a man who is sent, and sent with full authority. Thus the Gk. gives us only the form of the NT concept; the שָׁלִיחַ of later Judaism provides the content.

We can say this quite exclusively because throughout the NT the word is used only of men, although according to the course of things (→ 430) women might also have been called apostles. Yet this would have been a self-contradiction, since שָׁלִיחַ is a legal term and women have very restricted legal competence in Judaism. Above all, they cannot act as witnesses (cf. S. Dt., 190 on 19:17). They are also inferior to slaves in the sense that the latter are the possession of their masters and may legally represent their will (e.g., in the representative slaying of the Paschal lamb, → 415). It is typical of the situation that with → μαθητής we also find → μαθήτρια for the woman Christian, although Judaism did not recognise women μαθηταί. In this case, however, the presuppositions were very different.

b. There is full identity between ἀπόστολος and שָׁלִיחַ at Jn. 13:16: οὐκ ἔστιν δοῦλος μείζων τοῦ κυρίου αὐτοῦ, οὐδὲ ἀπόστολος μείζων τοῦ πέμψαντος αὐτόν. Here ἀπόστολος is simply a rendering of the legal term in its purely legal sense of one who is lawfully charged to represent the person and cause of another (→ B 2a.).

This meaning is confirmed by the juxtaposition of the two pairs δοῦλος/κύριος and ἀπόστολος/πέμψας. The δοῦλος stands fully under the jurisdiction of his master and derives from him all that he is. But this is also a mark of the שָׁלִיחַ. Cf. Gn. r., 78 on 32:23: R. Shim'on (c. 150) has said: "From the fact that it is written 'Let me go' (שלחני, Gn. 32:27), deduce that the one who sends is greater than the one sent." [90]

---

[88] On the problem of the Pauline superscription and its development, cf. O. Roller, "Das Formular der paulinischen Briefe," BWANT, 4. Folge 9/10 (1933). On Paul's self-designation as an apostle in the salutation → 441 f.

[89] The situation is such that the meaning can be stated precisely only at the end and as the result of the enquiry which follows. But this would involve a very extended exposition. It is thus anticipated, and the later discussion of the origin of NT usage must serve as detailed corroboration.

[90] Str.-B., II, 558. It makes no difference that we here have משתלח (part. hithpael), with no mention of שליח. It is also worth noting that the Rabb. statement goes beyond the saying of Jesus in a way which throws typical light on the self-awareness of Jesus (→ ταπεινός).

c. Like שָׁלִיחַ (→ 416), ἀπόστολος denotes the "commissioned representative of a congregation."

Here we may refer to the phrase ἀπόστολοι ἐκκλησιῶν in 2 C. 8:23. This is used by Paul of the men who at his request were to accompany him to Jerusalem with the collection which he had organised among the Greek congregations for the poor "saints" (→ λογεία).[91] Along the same lines Epaphroditus is an ἀπόστολος of the Philippians to Paul (Phil. 2:25). In these instances the nature of the task, i.e., the conveyance of proofs of love, gives to the ἀπόστολος a religious rather than legal significance.

d. Finally, ἀπόστολοι is a comprehensive term for "bearers of the NT message." The name is first borne by the circle of the twelve, i.e., the original apostles (including Matthias brought in as a replacement in Ac. 1:26; cf. οἱ → δώδεκα, 1 C. 15:5). Their sending by Jesus is presupposed.

This use dominates the presentation of Lk. in the Gospel and esp. Acts. The twelve are here almost a closed college alongside that of the → πρεσβύτεροι (Ac. 15:2, 4, 6, 22 f.; 16:4). Among them the figure of Peter is pre-eminent (2:37; 5:29). Jerusalem is expressly stated to be their centre (Ac. 8:1). In Mt. 10:2 and Mk. 6:30 also the ἀπόστολοι are the first twelve disciples of Jesus. In all these cases the term is absolute and self-explanatory; and it is always in the plur. (→ on this pt. 435).

Yet the name is also applied to the first Christian missionaries or their most prominent representatives, including some who did not belong even to the wider groups of disciples.

Even in Acts we find this usage at least in 14:4, 14, where Paul and Barnabas are called ἀπόστολοι without any sense of impropriety on the part of the author.[92] Thus, although the twelve are ἀπόστολοι for Luke, they are not the only ἀπόστολοι. Paul esp. is an ἀπόστολος in this sense, and he constantly uses the word of himself, esp. in the salutations to his epistles. James, the Lord's brother, may also be mentioned (Gl. 1:19),[93] and like Paul he joined the community only after the death of Jesus. In R. 16:7 the word is used of Junias and Andronicus, two otherwise unknown fellow-workers of Paul of Jewish origin. A wider circle (including James, the Lord's brother) is mentioned in 1 C. 15:7.

In this connection we have side by side both sending by a congregation (e.g., Paul and Barnabas by Antioch in Ac. 13:2 ff.) and the more precise description of the ἀπόστολος as an ἀπόστολος Ἰησοῦ Χριστοῦ in the Pauline salutations. In both cases a link may be seen with the Jewish שָׁלִיחַ. Yet at this point the difference from the first group is also clear. If it is not expressed in the term, or in different estimations of the wider and the narrower circle, the reason must be sought in a basis of apostolate which is common to both and which cannot be anything other than encounter with the risen Lord and reception of the commission from Him personally ("sending"; → 430).

---

[91] Cf. Holl, Ges. Aufsätze, II, 60.

[92] Later readers found the term awkward, as the textual tradition of vv. 4, 14 shows. Yet there are no good reason for omitting ἀπόστολοι (Wagenmann, 76, n. 1; cf. Mundle, 38, n. 1), as we shall see on material grounds from what follows.

[93] That is, if we may link the εἰ μή with ἀποστόλων, and if a completely new statement does not follow in 19b. On Junias and Andronicus cf. Zn. R. on 16:7. On 1 C. 15:7 cf. A. Schlatter, Erläuterungen zum NT, ad loc., where special emphasis is laid on the commission of the risen Lord; → 423.

It is to be noted that although Barnabas of the original community (cf. 1 C. 9:5 f.), [94] James the Lord's brother and Paul's compatriots Junias and Andronicus (R. 16:7) are called ἀπόστολοι as well as Paul, this is not true of Apollos, although it would have been natural for Paul to give him this title in 1 C. 3:5 ff. Again, Timothy is not an ἀπόστολος, although he is actively and successfully engaged in missionary work (e.g., in Thessalonica). Instead he is called an ἀδελφός (2 C. 1:1; Col. 1:1; Phlm. 1), a δοῦλος Χριστοῦ ʼΙησοῦ (Phil. 1:1), and even a συνεργὸς τοῦ θεοῦ (1 Th. 3:2). [95] But these are no substitutes for the title of apostle. Again, the common enjoyment of a direct commission prevented a breach between Paul and the Jerusalem group represented by James, in spite of the serious differences between them (Ac. 15:1 ff.; cf. Gl. 2:9). That basis of the apostolate is commissioning by the risen Lord is expressly stated in 1 Cl., 42, 1 ff. For Paul, too, the sense of apostolate is linked with recollection of his encounter with the living Christ (1 C. 9:1 and esp. 15:8 ff.). [96]

According to Paul the ἀπόστολοι (1 C. 12:28 f.) are not officials of the congregation, let alone the chief of such officials; [97] they are officers of Christ by whom the Church is built. In this respect they may be compared with the prophets of the OT (Eph. 2:20; 3:5), whose office, on the basis of their commission, was to prepare the way for the One who was to come (→ ἀποστέλλω, 400; προφήτης). Here, then, a climax of apostolic awareness is reached which was only possible on the soil of early Christian eschatology, as we can see esp. in Paul (→ D. 3).

The context makes it quite plain that in the phrase ἐν τῇ ἐκκλησίᾳ (1 C. 12:28) Paul means the Church and not the Corinthian congregation. [98] For just before he refers to the → σῶμα Χριστοῦ. He never does this, however, in respect of the individual congregation, but always of the total organism whose Head (→ κεφαλή) is Christ (Eph. 1:22; cf. 2:11 f.; Col. 1:18 etc.; cf. R. 12:5). In any case, to interpret ἐκκλησία as the individual congregation would stamp Paul as the teacher of an interim ethics, which he never was, just as he never wrote of man or the community apart from Christ, but always considered their state and significance in relation to Him (→ ἐκκλησία). Cf. also Eph. 4:11.

e. In Hb. 3:1 Jesus Himself is called ὁ ἀπόστολος καὶ ἀρχιερεὺς τῆς ὁμολογίας ἡμῶν. Here the only possible meaning of ἀπόστολος is that in Jesus there has taken place the definitive revelation of God by God Himself (1:2).

Omission of an art. before → ἀρχιερεύς [99] shows that the phrase constitutes a unity. It gathers up what has been said about Jesus from the standpoint of the decision of the readers (→ ὁμολογία), namely, that He is the Son (→ υἱός) in whom God has finally spoken (1:1 ff.), and that He is the High-priest who has finally expiated the sins of His people (2:5 ff.). In this case ἀπόστολος goes far beyond → προφήτης, which is not used of Jesus; and in terms of the absolute ὁ υἱός (1:2) it is best explained by the later Jewish שָׁלִיחַ, i.e., that in the Son there speaks and acts God Himself (the term Father is avoided in Hb.; → πατήρ). We have seen already (→ 419) that the idea of the שָׁלִיחַ was applied to ordinary priests. We are here in the presence of analogous thoughts (3:5 ff.) which justify our adoption of the same conception. If this line of

---

[94] So Ltzm. K., ad loc. and esp. J. Wellhausen, NGG, 1907, 5, n. 1, as against Bchm. K., ad loc. and esp. Holl, Ges. Aufsätze, II, 51, n. 1.
[95] There are strong internal reasons for this reading, which is attested by D* 33 Ambst (cf. 1 C. 3:9 and → 442); it is much too bold to be a later intrusion.
[96] 1 C. 15:8 ff. is stronger than 9:1; this was overlooked by v. Harnack, 335, n. 5.
[97] So Pr.-Bauer, 156.
[98] Which many have taken to be self-evident.

reasoning is sound, the same thought, differently applied, lies behind the two parts of the one expression. This is the thought of absolute authority (ὁμολογία) on the basis of absolute authorisation for word (ἀπόστολος) and work (ἀρχιερεύς). The usage is unique, and yet it develops organically out of the customary usage of NT times.

If a different view is taken, then the only possibility is that in ἀπόστολος Jesus, "as the One uniquely sent by God, is contrasted with Moses, the greatest bearer of revelation in the OT," and in ἀρχιερεύς "with Aaron, the leading representative of the priesthood under the Law." [99] This would give us, however, a usage never found elsewhere in the NT and found only in Justin throughout the whole range of early Christian literature. Justin does sometimes call Jesus ἀπόστολος as well as ἄγγελος and διδάσκαλος (Apol., I, 12, 9 etc.), [100] adopting terms from the Gnostic myth according to which the final Redeemer is simply the One who is sent. It is worth noting, however, that the word is not used in John's Gospel, where we have echoes, or apparent echoes, of such ideas, [101] whereas it does occur in Hb., which gives no evidence of connection with this speculation. Above all, this view entails inevitable disruption in the description of Jesus (→ supra), since it involves the isolation of ἀπόστολος from ἀρχιερεύς, whereas the author is concerned to bring out their indivisibility and thus to show that the revelation accomplished in Jesus is characterised neither by Word alone on the one side nor by priestly office alone on the other, but by both in conjunction.

D. The Rise and Nature of the Apostolate in the NT.

1. Jesus and the First Circle of Disciples.

a. Quite apart from the fact that the group of disciples was the germ cell of the future community, and was viewed by Jesus Himself as such, [102] the question of the rise of the apostolate must begin here. It is to be noted first that from the purely external standpoint there was nothing to distinguish this group from similar groups gathered around other teachers. This is expressed even in the name → μαθηταί, which was used for the followers of Jesus as well as for the pupils of other rabbis. The difference consists in the way in which the circle came into being (→ καλέω, ἀκολουθέω) and in what developed out of it; it was created and formed neither by a special spiritual endowment nor by a special decision of the members, but solely on the initiative of Jesus. It is characteristic of Jesus that in the first instance He did not transfer this initiative to His adherents, but that they first became μαθηταί, and thus had to listen, even though the situation itself was crying out for action. [103] If the disciples nevertheless renounced all initiative, this was because "they sincerely and resolutely accepted His call to repentance."[104] They thus learned what obedience is, learning it from the fact that Jesus showed them God both as the Holy One and as the Father. [105] We can hardly understand the inner nature of the NT apostolate if we do not see this above all else. Here are the final reasons why it could not harden into an office even when Jesus died and the time came to establish a community with clear-cut ordinances. [106] This

---

[99] Rgg. Hb., 67 ad loc.

[100] Wetter, 28.

[101] Bau. J., 55 on 3:17; R. Bultmann, ZNW, 24 (1925), 105 ff. → E.

[102] Cf. A. Schlatter, Die Geschichte des Christus² (1923), 406 f.

[103] This is constantly shown by the behaviour of the disciples right up to the incident of Peter's sword (Jn. 18:10 and par.).

[104] Schlatter, op. cit., 312 and esp. 313, n. 1.

[105] Cf. the whole of the Sermon on the Mount and the great parables, esp. in Lk.

[106] The account of the transactions in Jerusalem in Ac. 15 gives clear evidence of a properly constituted community (→ πρεσβύτερος), though cf. also Ac. 6:1.

was not possible because it arose among a circle of believers who knew that they were under God's orders and who realised that the rule of love had become the only rule for dealings with their neighbours. [107] The result is that only those who belonged to the μαθηταί of Jesus in the full sense of the word could have this authoritative part in His work.

Materially, this is the essential point in the relation between οἱ μαθηταί, οἱ ἀπόστολοι and οἱ δώδεκα. The → μαθηταί are the larger fellowship because they are the more general group [108] without which there can be neither ἀπόστολοι nor δώδεκα. Presupposing the legitimate use of the term, an ἀπόστολος must always be a μαθητής, whereas not every μαθητής need be an ἀπόστολος. There are thus no material reasons for surprise at the use of the phrase οἱ δώδεκα ἀπόστολοι (Mt. 10:2). On the other hand, it does not force us to identify οἱ δώδεκα and οἱ ἀπόστολοι. Indeed, any such identification is ruled out by the conjoining of the two expressions, the more so as we have no grounds for suspecting a pleonasm in Mt. 10:2.

b. The activity of the disciples begins when Jesus determines to make them His fellow-workers. [109] The Synoptists agree in giving no reasons for this decision. Indeed, we cannot even speak of a specific decision in the strict sense, but only of the fact that Jesus called "the twelve" to Himself and "sent them out." Only Mk. uses → ἀποστέλλειν to describe this act, while Mt. and Lk., and Mk. in a later saying, emphasise the fact that endowment by Jesus with → ἐξουσία is the characteristic feature of the act. This shows us that we have here an authoritative sending in the sense of full delegation. From the way in which their mission is described, the men thus sent out are to be described as שְׁלוּחִים in the legal sense of the term. It is in full agreement that they later return and give an account (→ ἀπαγγέλλω, Mk. 6, 30; διηγέομαι, Lk. 9:10) of what they have done.

At this point we cannot discuss in detail whether the sending out of the twelve is a historical act of Jesus, or whether it is to be regarded as the invention of a later age designed to prove that the college of the δώδεκα ἀπόστολοι in the original community was authorised by Jesus Himself in His own life-time. [110] But in this form the question is perhaps wrongly put, since it presupposes the possibility, and perhaps even the necessity, of identifying οἱ δώδεκα and οἱ ἀπόστολοι, and apart from the formulae adduced, which can be explained differently, there are no reasons for this. We may only say that the historical relationships are made even more obscure if we do not accept a sending out of the twelve by Jesus, not least because there is no motive for the sending apart from the will of Jesus.

The derivation of the apostolate from Jesus Himself, however, is not linked only with the contested issue of the genuineness of the sending of the twelve. For apart from the account of the sending in the strict sense, there are two additional testimonies to an apostolate after the manner of the Jewish institution of the שָׁלִיהַ; and while these do not render the account superfluous, they form a welcome addition to the material on which to base a judgment.

---

[107] Cf. Mt. 22:37-40.
[108] Bultmann Trad., 390 f. refers esp. to the usage of Lk.
[109] Mt. 10:1; Mk. 6:7; Lk. 9:1.
[110] So again in recent times, following many earlier scholars, Schütz, 72 ff.; a brief sketch of the history of the problem is given on 71 f.

The first testimony is to be found in Mk. 9:38 ff.; Lk. 9:49 f. Here John complains to Jesus about an exorcist who is casting out demons in the name (→ ὄνομα) of Jesus without being one of His μαθηταί, and who will not allow the disciples to stop him. John could hardly speak as he did if it were only a matter of prestige or competence affecting Jesus Himself. He is obviously incensed that an outsider should arrogate to himself what is not his. The formula ἐν τῷ ὀνόματί σου (Mk.) or ἐπὶ τῷ ὀνόματί σου [111] shows us that in his miracles the stranger was using the power available to Jesus as if it were his own, but without authorisation. Only the disciples were authorised to use it. This is at least the view of John, and it is only possible if the authorisation of the disciples to work miracles [112] was not merely wishful thinking but a reality hitherto restricted to them and deriving from authorisation by Jesus Himself.

The second testimony is the saying of Jesus concerning the significance of the treatment of the disciples by men (Mt. 10:40 ff.; Mk. 9:41; Lk. 10:16). This presupposes the validity of the statement that the שָׁלִיחַ of a man is as the man himself, and what is done to the שָׁלִיחַ is done as to him (→ 415). Hence the saying is only possible if there has already been an authorisation of those addressed. It makes little difference that in this context, as distinct from Mk. 9:38 ff., there is no reference to miracles or to other special acts which might show that those addressed are authorised by Jesus. Lk. speaks only of preaching, Mk. of belonging to Christ or discipleship (cf. Mt. 10:42). There is no mention of ἀπόστολος in any of the three passages, or in Mk. 9:38 ff. par. Indeed, even ἀποστέλλειν is used only of the relationship of Jesus to God and not of the disciples. Nevertheless, the matter is wholly as we have learned to see it in the legal discussions of the Rabbis concerning the שָׁלִיחַ.

The two passages support an authorisation of the disciples which is linked with the person of Jesus, the more so as they take it for granted and do not seek to establish it. [113] They acquire added significance from the fact that, particularly in the first passage, Jesus has to correct the ideas of the disciples. Although the legal foundations of the apostolate are unmistakeably present, Jesus does not advance the claim that might be based on them. If the disciples are given full power "in the name of Jesus," i.e., to speak and act as He does, this does not give them a new right but implies the duty of serving the One who confers the power. The choice of examples in the second passage shows further that commissioning to represent Jesus and His cause means humiliation rather than exaltation. Thus in the sayings of Jesus we do not see only the apostolate as such. We also see its conjunction with service and humility and consequently the purification from any legal claim which is so characteristic of the view of the apostolic office found in Paul. We are thus prevented by the sayings of Jesus Himself from trying to deduce from His authorisation for word and action an official congregational office fulfilled in terms of law. To be precise, we should not use the word office

---

[111] On the usage cf. par. from Josephus in Schl. Lk., 109.

[112] In accordance with the mode of expression of the two Evangelists it is better to take this as generally as possible. The exorcist is not a rival of specific disciples such as the twelve, but of all of them as such; cf. Lk.: ὅτι οὐκ ἀκολουθεῖ μεθ' ἡμῶν.

[113] In the light of these passages the person of Jesus, and His relationship to His disciples during His ministry, are grossly misunderstood if we assume that "Jesus gathered around Him disciples who should go out to preach the kingdom of God and work miracles," without even considering the concept of the personal authority of Jesus, let alone making this authority, or the concept of God represented by it, the only standard of the conduct of the disciples as such (as against Schütz, 72). At very best, this could produce only a group of philosophical adherents but not a religious fellowship. Cf. on this pt. Wagenmann, 5 f., who refers to Judas as one of the twelve.

at all in this context; we should speak of commission in the sense of the authorisation which is limited in time and space, and which is conditioned materially rather than personally, as in the Jewish concept of שָׁלִיחַ.

How little we are concerned with office is shown by the fact that the authorisation was not restricted to the twelve, nor was any such restriction even suggested in the interests of the first apostles; otherwise the account of the sending of the 70 (μαθηταί, Lk. 10:1) could hardly have been tolerated in the tradition. On the other hand, even this story [114] makes it self-evident that the task of proclaiming the coming kingdom (→ κηρύσσω) was first committed to the immediate circle of the twelve who were closest to Jesus, though He obviously did not grant them any special position or personal privilege (→ 426). The fact that there is no office is also brought out by the obvious conclusion of the task with the return to Jesus. In Lk. 9:49 f. and par. the band of disciples is not at work, because it is with Jesus. We never hear of any activity of the disciples in His immediate presence. They are always "sent out" (ἀποστέλλειν) by Him. [115] When they are with Him, it is as hearers and ministers, [116] after the manner of the pupils of the rabbis. This is of decisive importance in relation to the early Christian view of the apostle, and it is obviously linked with שָׁלִיחַ. On this point, see what follows. [117]

It should be obvious that the apostolate as such has no religious character, but is simply a form. These apostles receive their religious impress from the One who gives them their commission, and always in such a way that the commission itself is the main thing and the apostles are only its bearers, according to the Rabbinic principle : שְׁלוּחוֹ שֶׁל אָדָם כְּמוֹתוֹ (→ 415; 421).

c. A more difficult question than that of the presence of authorisation is that of the presence of the name of "apostle" in the first group of disciples. The word ἀπόστολος is occasionally used in the Gospels of the men sent out by Jesus (→ 422) with the task of proclamation. In Mt. 10:2 the δώδεκα μαθηταί of 10:1 are called the δώδεκα ἀπόστολοι. Between the two different terms for the same men [118] lies the commissioning or the endowment with → ἐξουσία. This shows us why ἀπόστολος is used. The μαθηταί have become ἀπόστολοι by the decision of Jesus. The case is much the same in Mk. 6:30. This tells of the return of the ἀπόστολοι to Jesus; the terms ἀποστέλλειν and διδόναι ἐξουσίαν have been used to describe their sending (6:7). But then both Matthew [119] and Mark revert to the word μαθηταί for the rest of their Gospels. [120] This excludes the possibility that they saw in ἀπόστολος a description of office in the sense of a *character indelebilis*. [121] Yet this is not to say that Jesus did not use the word or refer to what it denotes, [122] as though the term implied the importation of a later status and title into His dealings with His disciples.

---

[114] Cf. on this Schl. Lk., 274 ff.

[115] Cf. also Lk. 10:17.

[116] Cf. Mt. 19:13 par.; 21:1 ff. par.; 26:17 ff. par.; but also Jn. 12:20 f. It is only in this light that we can see the full significance of the foot-washing (Jn. 13:1 ff.).

[117] On the sending of the apostles two by two, for which there are Jewish precedents, → 417 and n. 68.

[118] On their material relationship, → 425.

[119] Matthew does not describe the return.

[120] The account given by Wellhausen, 140 can only be described as a caricature.

[121] From this standpoint critical objections to the appearance of the word in the two passages would be quite justified.

[122] → 428.

There is perhaps something of this in Luke. In the Gospel the word is found 6 times. At 24:10 it is a fixed term for the first group of disciples, as also at 22:14, where it is used of the identical circle which gathered for the Last Supper. [123] In neither of these cases is there any reference to a mission. We thus have a fixed usage, and this is corroborated by the absence of the limiting [124] δώδεκα. In the other passages, however, those called ἀπόστολοι are truly sent out.

In 11:49 the word appears with προφῆται in a quotation, and has no reference either to the μαθηταί of Jesus or the twelve. In 9:10 is refers to the return of the twelve as in Mk. 6:30 (supra). In 17:5 it cannot be separated from the story of possession in Mt. 17:14 ff.; Mk. 9:14 ff., and it thus presupposes a general authorisation to heal [125] which is rendered nugatory by their → ὀλιγοπιστία. [126] Finally, the election and designation of the twelve as apostles in Lk. 6:12 f. is obviously with a view to their mission (9:1: οἱ δώδεκα), [127] from which they return as οἱ ἀπόστολοι in 9:10 (supra).

In Lk. we thus have on the whole a usage in which the inner connection between ἀπόστολος and ἀποστέλλειν is maintained. This usage is only conceivable in a situation in which ἀποστέλλεσθαι and not ἀπεστάλθαι or ἀποσταλῆναι is appropriate ; this is shown by the later fixing of the term. Yet from this standpoint, too, there can be little doubt that the word ἀπόστολος goes back to Jesus, obviously not in the Greek form, but in the Aramaic original שְׁלִיחָא. The latter point is not unimportant, for the Aramaic word does not have the suggestion of office which later came to attach to ἀπόστολος in consequence of the position of the twelve in the primitive community. Lk. 6:13 says expressly : καὶ ἐκλεξάμενος ἀπ' αὐτῶν δώδεκα, οὓς καὶ ἀποστόλους ὠνόμασεν. The relative clause is usually taken to be anachronistic. Some see assimilation to a similar phenomenon in the Synagogue, though others dismiss it altogether as an intrusion. [128] Yet neither view is necessary if we see in ἀπόστολος no more than a purely objective term to denote a fully accredited representative with a specific commission. Our preceding deliberations (→ 427 f.) have made this interpretation not merely possible but necessary, since otherwise we are involved in a serious misrepresentation of the relationship of the disciple to Jesus which inevitably leads, and has actually led, to glaring contradictions in the accounts. In any case, however, this interpretation has the support of the Gospel tradition itself.

When we compare Lk. 6:12 f. and Mk. 3:13 ff., we find that the words οὓς καὶ ἀποστόλους ὠνόμασεν in Lk. correspond to ἵνα ἀποστέλλῃ αὐτοὺς κηρύσσειν καὶ

---

[123] The reading οἱ δώδεκα ἀπόστολοι (22:14), attested by AC and the imper. text, is definitely secondary.
[124] → 425.
[125] So also Schl. Lk., 384 f.; cf. H. J. Holtzmann, Die Synoptiker³ (1901), 391 ad loc. Amongst other objections to the attempt to anchor the saying at any price in the context given by Lk. (Zn. Lk., ad loc.) we may mention that it is customary for Lk. to give his own introductions to sayings of Jesus (Bultmann Trad., 384 ff.). In this case, v. Schl. Lk., 385.
[126] The event takes place in the absence of Jesus (Mt. 17:1 ff.; Schl. Lk., 385), with which the → ὀλιγοπιστία is possibly connected, since it is preceded by the first intimations of the passion (Mt. 16:21 ff.).
[127] In the light of 6:12 f. this is the only possible comprehensive designation, for they are selected from the μαθηταί but cannot yet be called ἀπόστολοι since they have not actually been sent out. In general the usage is thus very similar to that of Mt. 10:1 f. (supra).
[128] As, for instance, in Kl. Lk., ad loc.

ἔχειν ἐξουσίαν … in Mk., just as ἐκλεξάμενος ἀπ' αὐτῶν in Lk. correspond to καὶ ἐποίησεν δώδεκα, ἵνα ὦσιν μετ' αὐτοῦ in Mk. In both Evangelists what follows shows that the true appointment as ἀπόστολοι comes later, at 6:7 in Mk. and 9:1 in Lk. Thus the creation of the inner circle of the twelve and their appointment as ἀπόστολοι are not coincident in time. Mt. is in full agreement on this point (Mt. 10:1; → 427). The selection made by Jesus is with a view to their future participation in His work. This is brought out expressly by Mk. in a final clause which points to the future. But the relative clause in Lk. can have only the same meaning unless the word ἀπόστολος — which here has no article — is completely divorced from the situation of the disciples as this is indicated by a comparison of 6:13 and 9:1 ff. It is even possible that the sources used by Lk. suggested that when Jesus selected the twelve He spoke to them about His plan, and that this is what is meant by the ὀνομάζειν αὐτοὺς ἀποστόλους; but this is pure conjecture.

Moreover, the relative clause in Lk. has a full par. in the textual tradition of Mk. 3:14 in as much as it is excellently attested (אBC*WΘφ sah min Tatian) for this passage after μετ' αὐτοῦ, though on account of Lk. 6:13 it has never been accepted as canonical in textual criticism. Possibly the difficulties created by the term ἀπόστολοι have also had something to do with its rejection. If it were interpreted as here proposed, the reading would perhaps command more confidence than it has thus far received.

It may thus be accepted not merely that the apostolate itself derives from Jesus but also that the name apostle is used by Him. If He did not use the Greek term, or speak in terms of an office, at least He applied the שָׁלִיחַ institution to the relationship between Him and His disciples at the time when, assigning them His fully authority, He brought them into full participation in His work.

d. A further point from the Gospels which is significant for the later period is the linking of שָׁלִיחַ/ἀπόστολος with the proclamation of the Word as the act of Jesus. Mk. tells us that the supreme task of the ἀπόστολοι according to the will of Jesus is → κηρύσσειν (3:14), and on their return they tell Him πάντα ὅσα ἐποίησαν καὶ ἐδίδαξαν. According to Lk. Jesus sends them out κηρύσσειν τὴν βασιλείαν τοῦ θεοῦ καὶ ἰᾶσθαι (9:2), and they are given the same task in Mt. in a rather fuller form and with closer reference to the work of Jesus (10:7 f.). The implication of this feature is that a supremely objective element is made the content of the apostolate. The ἀπόστολος has no personal influence on the inner form of his commission. When the saying ἤγγικεν ἡ βασιλεία τῶν οὐρανῶν is given to the disciples as the theme of their proclamation they are placed at the side of Jesus. They are thus brought under the will of God which destroys their autonomy [129] and leaves them no option but full and obedient dedication to their task. [130]

Indissolubly bound up with the commission to preach the Word is Jesus' empowering of His messengers to act (supra). Action, too, is essential, for in it the messenger has and gives proof that he is really the commissioned representative of Jesus. It is a characteristic of the disciples who take part in the first mission, and of their inward sobriety grounded in the Word and example of Jesus, that the miracles which they perform are never a subject of boasting, let alone of

---

[129] Cf. Mt. 10:9 ff. par. In this regard we might point to many things spoken to the μαθηταί as such and not as ἀπόστολοι, esp. Mt. 18:1 ff.
[130] Mt. 25:14 ff.; Lk. 19:12 ff. It is to be noted that the reference is to the departure of the man and to a commission given to his servants during his absence.

assessment according to the standard of individual performance. [131] Of the seventy, too, Lk. tells us that on their return they reported μετὰ χαρᾶς : καὶ τὰ δαιμόνια ὑποτάσσεται ἡμῖν ἐν τῷ ὀνόματί σου (10:17). Here is a complete ignoring of the person of the one commissioned and a complete absorption in the task. Here is the χαρά which obtains when man leaves the field to God and finds the meaning of life in serving Him (→ χαρά). Obviously Lk. was not here giving his own ideal of the apostle, but simply following his source. It is the more significant that here already the returning messengers joyfully extol their success as the success of Jesus, and that, like all other returning messengers in the Gospels, they say nothing at all of the difficulties which they have had to face when working in the name of Jesus, and of which Jesus has quite clearly warned them (cf., e.g., Mk. 6:11). This is important because it means that a decisive element in the attitude of Paul is already found among the first disciples of Jesus in relation to this appointment to responsible service.

2. The Early Christian Apostolate as a Gift of the Risen Lord.

a. The usage of the term and the situation of the disciples during their contact with Jesus show us that their task of preaching the imminent kingdom of God was limited to a set period (→ 427). Since we do not read of the twelve being sent out again, or of any continuing commission to represent Jesus, the departure of Jesus found them at a loss rather than ready for service. All that they had was the promise that death would not hold Him [132] and that His fellowship with them would continue. [133] Even this promise, however, did not keep them from flight, [134] denial, [135] fear, [136] and hopeless grief. [137] The Gospels and Acts make it quite clear that it was exclusively the act of the risen Lord that this scattered group became a community full of hope and ready for action. [138] The act of the risen Lord, however, was the renewal of the commission of the disciples in their definitive institution as ἀπόστολοι. [139]

Keeping to essentials, we may ignore the historical details, and also the geographical problem of Galilee or Jerusalem. [140] What matters is that the apostolate was not carried over into the developing community from the pre-Easter period. It was after His resurrection that Jesus, in the apostolate, made the community possible as a preaching community. [141] The apostles are witnesses of the resurrection, though not all witnesses of the resurrection are apostles. [142] The circle of

---

[131] It is a moot point whether such thoughts perhaps occasioned the conversation in Mt. 18:1 ff. par.; we hardly need assume this to understand the passage, since the question treated was always a live issue in the Synagogue (Schl. Mt., 543 f.).

[132] Mt. 16:21 par.; 17:23 par.; 20:19.

[133] Mt. 18:20; 26:29 par.

[134] Mt. 26:56; Mk. 14:50.

[125] Mt. 26:69 ff. par.

[136] None of the disciples takes part in His burial (Mt. 27:57 ff.). A few of the women close to Him come to see where He is laid (Mk. 15:47; cf. Lk. 23:55 f.; Mt. 27:61). The situation in Jn. 20:19 is typical.

[137] Lk. 24:4 (ἀπορεῖσθαι), 13 ff.

[138] Cf. esp. Lk. 24:36 ff.

[139] Mt. 28:16 ff.; Lk. 24:48 f.; Ac. 1:8.

[140] Cf. J. Weiss, Das Urchristentum (1917), 10 ff., and for bibl. on the problem of "Galilee on the Mt. of Olives" Pr.-Bauer, 236.

[141] v. A. Schlatter, Die Geschichte der ersten Christenheit (1926), 10; P. Feine, Der Apostel Paulus (1927), 222.

[142] Cf. Lk. 24:49 with 46 and esp. 1 C. 15:8 ff., but also Holl, Ges. Aufs., II, 51.

apostles does not seem to have been particularly large. It still did not include any women, though women were the first to see the risen Lord [143] and there were also women prophets. [144]

Thus it is very doubtful whether the "more than 500" of 1 C. 15:6 became apostles as a result of Jesus' appearance to them, though in 1 C. 15:8 f. the apostolate is linked with personal encounter with the risen Lord and the thought of the founding of the apostolate is prominent in the whole passage. [145] On the other hand, James the Lord's brother, who was never a → μαθητής but was a witness of the resurrection according to 1 C. 15:7, was one of the leaders of the Jerusalem church (Gl. 1:19; 2:9, 12) and was obviously regarded by Paul as one of the ἀπόστολοι, [146] though not actually given the title. [147]

With personal encounter with the risen Lord, personal commissioning by Him seems to have been the only basis of the apostolate. That this commission was given primarily to the twelve is connected with their participation in the history of the earthly Jesus, who specifically prepared them to take up and continue His preaching, yet now as the proclamation of Jesus as the One who had come in fulfilment of OT prophecy. [148] Materially, therefore, two elements are linked with the apostolate in the first community. By the commission of Jesus a number of men, especially those who were closest to Him during His life, became His representatives in the sense that they took His place and thus assumed an authoritative position in the little company of Christians. Yet the altered situation meant that they also became misssionaries, and this form of their work was what really characterised their office.

We do not know how large was the circle of the first ἀπόστολοι. It cannot have been too small. Paul and Acts show us indirectly that the missionary task dominated its life right into the inner circle of the twelve. At the time of Gl. 1:18 ff. there were no ἀπόστολοι in Jerusalem except Peter and James, who was not one of the twelve, although by now the scattering of the community in connection with the martyrdom of Stephen was long since past (Ac. 8:1 ff.). [149] At Ac. 15:1 ff. we have only οἱ ἀπόστολοι, not the twelve, and it must be remembered that James, the son of Zebedee, had been executed prior to the so-called Apostolic Council (Ac. 12:1 f.). Paul speaks especially of the misionary activity of Peter in 1 C. 9:5, if we are to take it that the περιάγειν refers to apostolic journeys; [150] the same verse speaks not only of the λοιποὶ ἀπόστολοι but also of the ἀδελφοὶ τοῦ κυρίου, who cannot be simply equated with the ἀπόστολοι. Perhaps Peter as a missionary was particularly connected with the Babylonian Jews. [151] It is striking that we know very little about most of the

---

[143] Mt. 28:1 ff. par.; Jn. 20:11 ff.
[144] Ac. 21:8 f. The Ac. Pl. et Thecl. give Thecla the title of apostle (ἡ τοῦ θεοῦ πρωτόμαρτυς καὶ ἀπόστολος καὶ παρθένος Θέκλα, p. 272, 20 f., Lipsius), but this is simply an approximation to the picture of Paul.
[145] "In Paul the Easter event is viewed exclusively from the standpoint that through it Jesus created His messengers" (A. Schlatter, Die Geschichte des Christus² [1923], 532).
[146] Cf. the emphatic τοῖς ἀποστόλοις πᾶσιν in 1 C. 15:7b.
[147] Gl. 1:19 is not decisive, since linguistically it is hard to tell whether the εἰ μή refers to the whole preceding clause or only to ἀποστόλων (v. Lightfoot ad loc.).
[148] Cf. the addresses in Ac. but also the κατὰ τὰς γραφάς of 1 C. 15:3 f.; also R. 1:2; 3:21.
[149] Ac. 8:1 states expressly that the ἀπόστολοι remained in Jerusalem at this period.
[150] Joh. W. 1 C., ad loc.
[151] Cf. 1 Pt. 5:13 and A. Schlatter, Erläuterungen zum NT, ad loc.; Einleitung in die Bibel⁴ (1923), 448 f.; but → Βαβυλών.

apostles after Pentecost. From Mt. 28:19 f. we can see clearly that they must have engaged in missionary enterprise, for the developing Church would hardly have kept this saying in the Gospel if it had not corresponded to the facts. [152]

This missionary element is something which radically distinguishes the NT apostolate from the Jewish שָׁלִיחַ institution. The same is true even of the form which it had assumed in the intercourse of Jesus with His disciples and in their participation in preparation for the coming → βασιλεία of God (→ 427). Here the basis was the same, but in the post-Easter situation it led to very different consequences from those prior to Easter. With the post-Easter situation, which cannot be separated from the experience of the absoluteness of Jesus in the circle of the disciples, there is linked the lasting character of the commission which they are now given. The risen Lord does not now appoint His representatives merely for a limited span but for the whole period, of unknown duration, [153] between Easter and His return. Yet He makes only the one appointment, and therefore it is only logical that the apostolate should be limited to the first generation and should not become an ecclesiastical office. For the rest, we have a repetition of what took place at the first commissioning of His messengers, namely, the endowment with → ἐξουσία[154] and also the imposition of a duty to render an account when the commission is given back into the hands of the One who gives it. [155] In both these points we can see that what counts is not the initiative of the apostle but his obedient observance of the line followed by Jesus Himself. This is classically fulfilled by Paul (→ 437).

Did., 11, 1 ff. [156] is no argument against the limitation of the apostolate to the generation of Paul in the technical sense of NT usage. For in the phrase ἀπόστολοι καὶ προφῆται the concern of the passage is only with the latter; [157] no warning is issued against false ἀπόστολοι. The term ἀπόστολος seems to be used merely to indicate that the true prophet does not come in his own name but in the name of Jesus [158] and in His Spirit, [159] i.e., as a member of His Church and its order. [160]

Because of the thought of God which works itself out in obedience, the Spirit is indispensable for the renewed apostolate. In the Spirit the community and especially the apostles receive assurance of the presence of Jesus and therewith the power of Jesus. [161] It is of the very essence of the early Christian apostolate

---

[152] But cf. also Paul at R. 1:5 ff.; 1 C. 9:16 (→ ἀνάγκη, 346).

[153] Ac. 1:6 f.

[154] Cf. the miracles in Ac., but also the formula σημεῖα τοῦ ἀποστόλου in 2 C. 12:12 and the material par. in 1 Th. 1:5.

[155] Mt. 25:14 ff. par.; 1 C. 4:4 (→ οἰκονόμος).

[156] Seufert, 119 sees in the ἀπόστολοι of the Didache "independent missionaries restlessly wandering from congregation to congregation to spread the γνῶσις κυρίου;" cf. also v. Harnack, 347 ff. This view, however, is impossible, since ἀπόστολος and independence are mutually exclusive (→ 415).

[157] Seufert failed to see this (119); → προφήτης.

[158] Did., 12, 1.

[159] A prophet is a true prophet ἐὰν ἔχῃ τοὺς τρόπους κυρίου (11, 8); it is thus, and not merely by his words, that one may perceive whether he has the Spirit.

[160] Cf. 11, 11. It is to be noted in this connection that the envoys from the Church of Rome to the Church of Corinth in 1 Cl., 65, 1 are not called ἀπόστολοι but ἀπεσταλμένοι.

[161] Cf. on this pt. W. Grundmann, Der Begriff der Kraft in der nt.lichen Gedankenwelt (1932), 92 ff. Power cannot be considered in itself, as Grundmann tends to handle it in his chapter on the disciples and apostles (92 ff.); is always linked with a person.

that the missionary activity of the disciples should begin with Pentecost. [162] In the Spirit, however, the apostle is also given a standard of what he himself is and does, and of what is done through him by God or Christ, [163] who has called him to be His instrument, though in full and conscious surrender of his own will and not in ecstatic abandonment to divine power. [164] For this reason, in the preaching of the apostles and evangelists [165] in Acts no less than in Jesus Himself, the central point is the faith of the hearers in Jesus and not the achievement of the preacher or worker of miracles. [166]

We completely misunderstand the significance of the possession of the Spirit, and especially the nature of the apostolate in primitive Christianity, if we explain the miracles of Acts [167] solely as later legends of the community told *in maiorem gloriam* of individual apostles, e.g., of Paul as compared with the acts of Peter in the first part of the book. At all points there is firm belief that Jesus Himself stands behind the miracles, that in them He displays His power through His messengers and that He thus endorses His messengers as such. If the messenger of a man is as the man himself, and if the NT apostolate is based on this principle, the absence of miracles would signify no less than the invalidity of the apostolic claim. It would show that the proclamation of the risen Christ is simply a human theorising and not a message concerning the divine act which transcends all human thought. To this extent the σημεῖα τοῦ ἀποστό-λου (2 C. 12:12) are indispensable for the sake of the cause itself, for Jesus' sake, rather than for the sake of His messengers. Those who think they may dispense with them must also interpret the miracles of Jesus as legends, or at least try to reduce them to natural processes which took on legendary form in the tradition. But this would also be to disclaim the apostolate as a religious, indeed, as the basic religious institution in the primitive community. It would leave only an institution which is a legal office, even though founded by Jesus. This true apostolate most definitely was not [168] either in its history or in important aspects of its outworking. [169] Naturally these considerations do not render superfluous an exact critical investigation of the miracles in Acts ; on the contrary, they make it genuinely necessary. [170]

The whole complex of ideas bound up with the idea of the σημεῖον of the ἀπόστο-λος has its final model in the Semitic office of messenger (→ 416). Moses is the typical divine messenger endorsed by signs ; in Ex. 3:12 we find שָׁלַח /ἐξαποστέλλειν accompanied by אוֹת /σημεῖον in the sense of legitimation by God. It is in keeping that → Jannes and → Jambres, the Egyptian magicians who opposed Moses, should also display σημεῖα (Ev. Nicodemi, 5, p. 235, ed. Tischendorf, 2nd. ed.; cf. Ex. 7:11, 22). But cf. also Is. 7:11 (Isaiah as envoy to Ahaz), or Ju. 6:17, where Gideon asks of the מַלְאַךְ יְהֹוָה (→ ἄγγελος, 76) an אוֹת /σημεῖον in confirmation of his authority to appoint

[162] Ac. 2:14 ff.
[163] Ac. 10:26; 14:15; 19:11, but also as early as 3:11 ff.
[164] Ac. 4:19 f. → παρρησία.
[165] Ac. 8:5 ff., 37 f.
[166] Ac. 3:16; 5:14 f.; 14:9 f. etc.
[167] The only miracles we read of are those of ἀπόστολοι, including Paul and perhaps also Stephen, who seems to have belonged to the community from the very first (Ac. 6:3, 8). We are also told of σημεῖα καὶ δυνάμεις μεγάλαι (8:13) in connection with Philip, though we do not know whether he bore the name of an apostle.
[168] At this pt. Holl is guilty of a grave error in his essay on the concept of the Church in the first community ; he does not fully recognise the pneumatic character of the apostolate.
[169] In this connection we may refer above all to the transmission of the Spirit (Ac. 8:14 ff.; 10:44 ff.; 19:1 ff.).
[170] Cf. Grundmann, *op. cit.*, 98, n. 7.

him a judge. [171] Appeal might be made even to Jesus Himself in this connection (Mt. 16:1 ff. par.; Jn. 6:29 ff.).

In any case, we must be on our guard at this point against schematically limiting to specific circles the powers at work in primitive Christianity. In this connection, too, it is indispensable to recognise that the community rather than individuals is the sphere where Jesus works as the risen Lord, and that His ἀπόστολοι can be His fully accredited representatives only as members of it. Yet we must also appreciate their close connection with Him and their significance as leaders of the movement linked with His name. As Jesus is exalted above all, and His goal is the all-embracing community, so their office is also universal. [172] It is in the universality of their commission, and the universal claim of those thus sent, that we may see finally how the new and definitive commissioning of the disciples by the risen Lord transcends their pre-Easter apostolate. He Himself stands behind all that they say and do. But because He has ascended to God, miracles cannot be separated from His messengers; yet in the last resort not they, but He who has sent them, must be the subject of the preaching of the Gospel to the world. [173]

b. Our findings thus far concerning the renewal of the apostolate by the risen Lord, its final and conclusive institution, and its linking with the possession of the Spirit, have been based especially upon the Synoptic Gospels and Acts. They are confirmed, however, in John's Gospel. This is the more significant because the word ἀπόστολος does not occur in this Gospel except for one passage in which it is used in the proper sense and with no restriction to the messengers of Jesus (→ 421). "In John the main part of the Easter narrative serves directly his central purpose; he shows how the risen Lord united the disciples to Himself by faith, and gave them full authority for their work." [174] This is true of Thomas (20:24 ff.), but especially of Peter, who also receives with the apostolate forgiveness for his denial (21:1 ff.).

Here, too, the point at issue is not independent achievement. It is authority to represent Jesus, and it is thus obedience and service. The community is not committed to Peter as such but as τὰ ἀρνία μου (21:15) and τὰ προβάτιά μου (21:16 f.), and his work is not described as that of ruling and deciding but βόσκειν and ποιμαίνειν. Yet here, too, the one commissioned does not become a mere instrument; he is burdened with a full load of responsibility which he can carry only where there is absolute commitment to Jesus (21:15, 16, 17: φιλεῖν). The parallel with the first three Evangelists, however, goes even further. In John, too, possession of the Spirit is the indispensable prerequisite for the discharge of apostolic functions. He thus causes reception of the Spirit and commissioning to take place simultaneously (20:21 ff.), formulating his statements in such a way as to leave no doubt that those commissioned go out with full authority as representatives (20:21).

Special attention should be paid to the form of 20:21. Jesus says: καθὼς ἀπέσταλκέν με ὁ πατήρ, κἀγὼ πέμπω ὑμᾶς. In relation to this we should remember what was said earlier (→ 403) about the relationship between ἀποστέλ-

---

[171] → σημεῖον.
[172] Cf. Schlatter, *Geschichte des Christus*, 534 f.
[173] Mt. 10:18 ff.; Lk. 12:11 f.
[174] Schlatter, *Geschichte des Christus*, 532. On the next sentence cf. also E. Hirsch, *Jesus Christus der Herr* (1926), 39 f.

λειν and πέμπειν in the Fourth Gospel. On the lips of Jesus ἀποστέλλειν is used
to describe His mission when He wishes to ground His authority in that of the
Father, whereas πέμπειν is used when He wants to establish the participation of
God in His work. This usage is followed exactly in 20:21, except that it is here
applied to the relationship of Jesus to His messengers. The work which they have
to do is finally His work, for He sends them.[175]

Thus in John the thought of the authorisation of the messengers is subsidiary
to that of the part of Jesus in their work, or rather to the consideration that it is
He who sustains both them and their apostolic office. This is why the figure of
the → παράκλητος comes to have fundamental significance in the commissioning
of the disciples. It is in Him that the presence and participation of Jesus in their
work are effected. He, too, is sent to take His place with them (πέμπειν, 14:26;
15:26).[176] Nor does Jesus represent His coming merely as an act of the Father
(14:16, 26). In the light of His own exaltation to be with the Father (παρὰ τοῦ
πατρός), He can say that He Himself will send the Spirit to His own (πέμψω,
15:26). In Him as the → πνεῦμα τῆς ἀληθείας (14:17) He Himself, who is the
→ ἀλήθεια in person, is still with them, though physically removed from them
(14:5 f.; 16:7). Thus in the Johannine picture of an apostle, the Evangelist combines
his basic christological belief that the Son stands alongside God and works beside
Him (→ υἱός), with the Jewish view of the fully accredited messenger. In so doing
he subordinates the latter, but only in so far as he may do so without making the
office of the messenger a mere matter of enthusiasm. John has no desire to do
this. On the contrary, his interest is to see the Son, and to cause his readers to
see Him, as the One who works from the beginning of all things to the end of
all things (→ λόγος). Perhaps on this account the word ἀπόστολος did not seem
to be suitable to him, since he saw in it at least the danger that by his own
assumption of power the → μαθητής might become a → κύριος instead of a
→ δοῦλος, and that the ἀπόστολος might forget that behind him there stood
a πέμψας who was also before him (13:16).

c. It is impossible to say definitely when the Greek term ἀπόστολος came
into use for שָׁלִיחַ. All that we can say with certainty is that it was not the Jews
who selected the term, since otherwise it would be better attested among them.
It is particularly strange that a term originally used for an act or a group with
no religious connotation should have come to be used for an individual with
expressly religious functions. Perhaps the word first began to be used in this way
in Antioch, being originally applied to the missionary expedition as such, then to
its individual members,[177] and finally, as a masculine noun, to the accredited
representative, as a recognised translation of שָׁלִיחַ. It is even possible that Paul had
some hand in this process of transition, which might have been much quicker
than suggested. Certainly he is the first in whom we find the term clearly used
of an individual messenger of Jesus in the singular; the Synoptists always use it in
the plural. In no case, however, is ἀπόστολος as a rendering of שָׁלִיחַ to be sepa-

---

[175] In Mt. (10:16) and Lk. (10:3) it is appropriately said of the sending of the disciples
by Jesus: ἀποστέλλω ὑμᾶς; for here they are to represent the earthly Jesus, not the
exalted Jesus.

[176] Cf. on this pt. H. Windisch, "Die fünf joh. Parakletsprüche" in Festgabe für
A. Jülicher (1927), 132 ff., esp. 134.

[177] Possibly linked with this is its exclusive use in the plur. except in Paul.

rated from ἀποστέλλειν/חֹלֵשׁ; it was possible at all only on the basis of the long-standing relationship between these two words. This relationship was to a large extent determined by the concept of God. If this was true from the very first in the early Christian use of ἀπόστολος, it is a direct fruit of the existing relationship.

A certain difficulty of terminology arises from the fact that our sources do not enable us to distinguish between ἀπόστολοι in the absolute and the ἀπόστολοι of the churches (cf. Ac. 13:1 ff.) who also preached the Gospel with full authority. Yet such a distinction is not unconditionally necessary, inasmuch as the Spirit, i.e., Jesus Himself as the Giver of the apostolic commission, is for primitive Christianity the normative principle of its action. It is significant that in Antioch the two set apart for the mission are not any two of the group called προφῆται καὶ διδάσκαλοι in Ac. 13:1, but Paul and Barnabas, of whom the first had certainly seen the risen Lord and most probably the second also (→ 422). Again, → ἀφορίζειν rather than ἀποστέλλειν is used to describe the act of the community, and the initiative is found in the prior decision of the → πνεῦμα τὸ ἅγιον, [178] so that the community has simply to give outward authorisation (13:2 f.). It is also conceivable that the two had apostolic ἐξουσία for a long time without exercising it. Moreover, we also see here the universal character of the NT apostolate, coupled with the universal claim of the community. The form of commissioning or ordination, i.e., with fasting, prayer and the laying on of hands, is Jewish (→ 417). Paul, however, quite distinctly did not regard himself as an apostle of the Christians of Antioch, but solely as an apostle of Jesus Christ (→ 437).

d. Our deliberations have now led us to the assured result that the basis of the NT apostolate as a whole is the will and commission of the risen Lord. Yet it should not be overlooked that from the very first this was not the one exclusive basis of the office in the primitive community. The account of the election of Matthias to the inner circle of the twelve in place of Judas shows us that together with the direction and will of the Spirit, who represented Jesus, another element played a decisive part, namely, the qualification of the one selected as an eye-witness. Luke tells us expressly that the substitute for Judas had to fulfil the condition of having been with the apostles "all the time that the Lord Jesus went in and out among us, beginning from the baptism of John, unto that same day that he was taken up from us" (Ac. 1:21 f.). Closest contact with Jesus during His life is thus the most important prerequisite for assuming the apostolate. In practice this means that the primitive community did not see in commissioning by the risen Lord anything radically new. Though lack of materials prevents us from fixing the relationship with any precision, we are perhaps nearest the heart of the matter if we say that for the early Church the new commissioning was simply a repetition or continuation of the first in the life-time of Jesus. We may thus conclude that the primitive community did not fully perceive the radical change in the world situation which consists in the fact that the risen Lord appointed men His representatives. Yet we may also see that from the very outset the history of Jesus was most important as history both for the content and the specific form of early proclamation. [179] The apostle of Jesus is always the witness to historical facts rather than to myths, and consciously and necessarily so in view of the fact that what he proclaims contradicts all human experience.

---

[178] Cf. also v. Harnack, 348, n. 1.
[179] Cf. on this pt. G. Kittel, "Der 'historische Jesus'" in *Mysterium Christi* (1931), 49 ff.

This connection of the apostle with personal participation in the history of Jesus affects Paul in two ways. First, the objection to his claim to be an equal of the twelve (→ 441 f.) seems to have here at least some relative justification. Paul was in fact inferior to the twelve in the sense that he had not had the contacts with the historical Jesus which they had been privileged to have. On the other hand, this led him to establish his apostolate in a way which saved him from a verdict of inferiority and at the same time proved to be of basic importance for the whole conception and claim of the early Christian apostolate (→ infra). Secondly, Paul attached himself to the primitive community in this respect by resolutely entering the stream of early Christian tradition concerning Jesus (1 C. 11:23 ff.; 15:1 ff. etc.). This bears witness to his inner commitment to the history of Jesus as the only foundation and content of his proclamation too, and the historical form of this proclamation shows us what constitutes the unity between Paul and the original apostles for all the differences between them (Ac. 15:12; cf. Gl. 2:9 and especially 1 C. 15:11).

3. The Classical Form of the Apostolate in the Person of Paul.

Paul is the classical representative of the apostolate in the NT. He is the only apostle who is to some extent known to us in his apostolic position; the others leave us no direct information concerning the manner of their apostolate. The reason is to be found partly in his special position in relation to the other ἀπόστολοι and partly in the extraordinary range of his activity. He belonged neither to the original circle of disciples nor to the first company of Christians who had intercourse with the risen Lord between Easter and the ascension. Yet he could say that he had laboured more than all others in the service of Jesus (1 C. 15:10). He was sustained in these labours by a strong sense of office which did not grow of itself but which was based on his experience of calling and which developed in conflict with those who disputed his right to be called an apostle of Jesus or to advance a claim to apostolic authority. Hence, when we undertake to depict the apostolic consciousness of Paul, we have to take two factors into account, namely, the peculiarity of his mode of life prior to his entry into apostolic work, and the peculiarity of his position as an apostle among the other accredited messengers of Jesus.

a. The first distinguishing mark of the Pauline apostolate is the break in the life of the apostle which accompanied his entry upon it. He himself could compare the process of his calling with the shining of the first ray of light at creation (2 C. 4:6); he indicated thereby that it transcended all human possibilities and could not be viewed from an autonomous standpoint. Paul as a Christian saw behind him the will of God from all eternity awaiting only the hour of its fulfilment (Gl. 1:15). The fact that his calling meant a complete upheaval in his life constitutes a basic difference between Paul and the other disciples of Jesus, who were certainly called away from their homes and families, but who hardly came to see the sharpest conceivable antithesis between their past and their ministry as Paul always did when he had occasion to speak of the beginnings of his apostolate (1 C. 15:9; Gl. 1:13, 23; Phil. 3:7 f.). In Paul's case, this is the more significant because in such contexts he is never a "sinner" who sharply condemns himself and his pre-Christian past; rather he speaks highly of his Jewish past (→ ἁμαρτωλός, 327), as he may well do, seeing that he was then just as obedient to God as at the moment of his conversion and afterwards as a Christian and apostle.

It thus follows that the apostolic consciousness of Paul is essentially determined by his encounter with Jesus on the Damascus road. In this, and in his immediate response to it, [180] lies the uniqueness of his apostolate as compared with the other apostles, who came to full dedication to Jesus only after much vacillation and a long course of instruction by Him. In the case of Paul we find no evidence of either vacillation or instruction. On the contrary, there is a sudden and yet no less resolute committal to the Messiah Jesus whom hitherto he had passionately persecuted. The reason for this is that the concept of God had from the very first determined the thinking and action of Paul, [181] and yet only outside Damascus did it attain to an absolutely dominating position. Only in this light can we understand the distinctive nature of his self-awareness and assurance of apostolic mission.

In this connection it does not matter exactly what took place on the Damascus road; [182] the important thing is how Paul regarded it in retrospect. It was for him quite unconditionally an act of God, an objective event, [183] not a visionary experience. [184] The subject of the process, however, was God rather than Christ, [185] though it was certainly Christ who encountered and addressed him. We can agree with Alfred Jeremias [186] that Paul became the apostle instead of the persecutor of Jesus at the moment when in the בַּת קוֹל (the divine voice of revelation since the extinction of prophecy with Haggai, Zechariah and Malachi) [187] he recognised the voice of Jesus, and was thus persuaded and cured of his error in relation to Him. Paul himself classically expresses this by describing himself as the ἀπόστολος Ἰησοῦ Χριστοῦ but with the addition that he is this (as κλητός) διὰ θελήματος θεοῦ (1 C. 1:1; 2 C. 1:1; Eph. 1:1; cf. 1:5; Col. 1:1). [188] It is to be noted that, so far as the sources go, Paul seems to be the first to trace back the apostolate to God Himself; 1 Pt. 1:2 (→ πρόγνωσις) is dependent on Pauline trains of thought.

The dominant role of the concept of God in Paul's sense of apostolic mission is particularly emphasised by the fact that he recognises himself to be ἀφωρισμένος εἰς εὐαγγέλιον θεοῦ (R. 1:1) and that he calls God the ἀφορίσας με ἐκ κοιλίας μητρός μου (Gl. 1:15). In these formulae he integrates himself into the world plan of God as a significant and indispensable member; his indispensability

---

[180] Gl. 1:16: εὐθέως οὐ προσανεθέμην σαρκὶ καὶ αἵματι ...

[181] On his attachment to the νόμος in Pharisaic Judaism (cf. Gl. 1:14; Phil. 3:6), → 324 s.v. ἁμαρτωλός. It should not be overlooked that to the best of our knowledge Paul as distinct from the twelve was the only apostle who came from learned circles and not from the ʿam ha-ares (→ ἁμαρτωλός, 322; 327).

[182] Similarly it makes no difference which of the three accounts in Acts is the most reliable (9:1 ff.; 22:5 ff.; 26:12 ff.). On this pt. cf. E. Hirsch, "Die drei Berichte der Ag. über die Bekehrung des Pls.," ZNW, 28 (1929), 305 ff.

[183] Gl. 1:15; R. 1:1.

[184] 1 C. 9:1; 15:8 are assertions of objective fact rather than impartations of ecstatic vision: → ὁράω.

[185] Gl. 1:15 f.: ὅτε δὲ εὐδόκησεν ὁ ἀφορίσας με ... ἀποκαλύψαι τὸν υἱὸν αὐτοῦ ἐν ἐμοί ... Cf. the way in which Pl. uses ὤφθη for the appearances of the risen Lord (1 C. 15:5 ff.), and how his disciple Luke follows him in this (Lk. 24:34; Ac. 13:31).

[186] In an address at the Fourth Conference on the Jewish Question at Nuremberg, Feb. 27 to March 1, 1929.

[187] T. Sota, 13, 2. Materially, → φωνή (ἐκ τῶν οὐρανῶν).

[188] In the Past. the apostolate is constituted by → ἐπιταγὴ θεοῦ (1 Tm. 1:1; Tt. 1:3); 2 Tm. 1:3 has the more familiar Pauline formula.

derives, not from himself, but from God (1 C. 3:5). [189] For this reason he has no option but to see in his apostolate (→ ἀποστολή) a proof of divine grace (→ χάρις) which is not linked to any presuppositions but which leads man to obedient subjection to God (1 C. 15:10). [190] It is at this point that Paul's sense of mission links up with that of the prophets, especially of Jeremiah and Deutero-Isaiah. This takes place in a way which can be understood only in terms of the particular mode of life of Paul. It can be regarded only as his own act, and in it the self-awareness not merely of the apostle but of early Christianity generally reaches its supreme point.

The parallels between Paul and Jeremiah have long been noted, [191] but predominantly from external angles [192] rather than from that of apostolic self-consciousness. Yet it is in this respect that Jeremiah was Paul's great predecessor.

The significance of Jeremiah in the history of OT prophecy consists in his radical rejection of any significance of man and his utter devotion to the given message, in clear recognition of the hopeless situation of the prophet. It is thus to be found in the absolute predominance of the concept of God. [193] This is expressed in the complete disappearance of the ecstatic element which had characterised the earlier prophets, [194] and even Isaiah, [195] and which reappeared in the successors of Jeremiah, [196] though less in revival of the older Israelite Nabiism than under the influence of incipient oriental and Hellenistic syncretism and its enthusiastic tendencies. Even when Jeremiah has visions (1:11 ff.; 4:19 ff.) it would be more correct to speak of visions of faith rather than of ecstatic rapture, just as it is characteristic of him to speak and act in symbols and parables which presuppose rational deliberation and a clear insight into the situation. "At first prophecy is quite passive in relation to its object." For this reason the persons of the prophets "are lost in the object; where they reflect upon it, they do so purely objectively and in such a way as only to impart the results of what they have seen." [197] In Jeremiah the prophetic ego awakens for the first time to a degree which makes him a religious thinker. This takes place so strongly that conflict cannot always be avoided between God and his own individuality. At any rate, we find incipient movements in this direction in the case of Jeremiah (20:7 ff.), e.g., when he resists the divine calling and commission; though it is only in Deutero-Isaiah that the ego really comes between God and the prophet to such a degree that in the ensuing period "a new person must be introduced to mediate between them in the form of the angelus interpres of Zechariah." [198]

From this standpoint Jeremiah marks a high point even in comparison with Deutero-Isaiah. This is fully apparent when we consider his consciousness of calling and study the manner of its execution. Just because there is in him no ecstatic element, the whole emphasis falls on his union with God and subjection to His will (20:7 ff.; cf. 15:19 ff.).

---

[189] The same thought underlies the formula κλητὸς ἀπόστολος (R. 1:1; 1 C. 1:1) and also Gl. 1:15 (καλέσας).

[190] Cf. also the εὐθέως at Gl. 1:16.

[191] Cf. most recently E. Lohmeyer, Grundlagen paulinischer Theologie (1929), 201.

[192] As suggested by the allusion to Jer. 1:5 in Gl. 1:15.

[193] Cf. for what follows R. Kittel, Geschichte des Volkes Israel, II[5, 6] (1925), 336 f.

[194] Elijah might be mentioned as well as Amos and Hosea.

[195] Isaiah still offers king Ahaz a miracle (אות/σημεῖον, Is. 7:11) in attestation of his mission; God is naturally the one who will perform it in vindication of His messenger as such (cf. Elijah in 1 K. 18:21 ff.).

[196] On Ezekiel, cf. R. Kittel, Geschichte des Volkes Israel, III (1927), 151 ff.

[197] Ibid., II, 336. Cf. also J. Hempel, Altes Testament und Geschichte (1930), 65 f.

[198] R. Kittel, op. cit., II, 337 and n. 1.

Hence his whole work is to proclaim the divine will, which does not have to be revealed to him from case to case but is continually present in his union with God. [199] There are two consequences. The first is that the prophetic calling embraces the whole life of Jeremiah and, since the people resists God and the prophet is faithful to Him, his whole life is consequently marked by suffering (e.g., 11:18 ff.; 15:10, 15 ff.; 20:14 ff., and also the actual sufferings in 20:1 ff.; 26:1 ff.; 37:1 ff.; 38:1 ff.). The other is that the Word alone determines the activity of the prophet and gives him power and authority (15:16 etc.). This restriction to the Word constitutes the true greatness of the prophecy of Jeremiah. In it his office coincides with his life and there is displayed the overriding power of the concept of God. God is everything, and man is what he is through God and to bear witness to God as such (1:9; 15:19 etc.).

It is difficult and perhaps even impossible to say whether Paul consciously or unconsciously followed Jeremiah in his sense of mission. Yet there is no doubt that he did so even in his evaluation of suffering as a divinely willed element in the life of the apostle, [200] his exclusive concentration on the preaching of the Word, [201] and his renunciation of any ecstatic basis for the apostolate.

We see this renunciation in 2 C. 12:1 ff., [202] where Paul distinguishes himself from opponents who preen themselves on their ecstatic experiences and seek to supplant and outbid him on this ground. The problem was acute only in the Greek congregations where enthusiasm played a great role (cf. esp. 1 C. 14:1 ff., but also 12:1 ff.). Here there was a danger that the divine authorisation of the apostle would be replaced by ecstatic experience with its exaltation of the individual, and consequently that the cult of man in terms of his piety, which Jesus had discarded (→ 329), would be revived in a new form, namely, in the veneration of the pneumatic or the pretended pneumatic. [203] It is essential that Paul should in fact be able to boast of ecstatic experiences of an extraordinary nature, [204] but that he should regard them as a purely personal concern and take strong steps to prevent them from being organically linked with his apostolate, [205] lest God and His act in Christ should again be set under the shadow of man and → χάρις obscured as the only principle which has unconditional validity. [206]

To the same context belongs the depreciation of the σημεῖα τοῦ ἀποστόλου (2 C. 12:12) in Paul. He speaks of them only when forced to do so or for pastoral reasons (R. 15:19; 1 Th. 1:5), never for their own sake or to give prominence to himself. Even in 2 C. 12:12 they serve only to demonstrate the justice of his cause and not the significance of his person.

The connection between the apostle's sense of mission and the prophetic sense of calling is no less significant for the cause represented by him. In it the revelatory character of his proclamation is very strongly emphasised and safeguarded against all human corruption. For this reason, whenever he has reason to speak authoritatively to his churches, Paul stresses in his salutations his apostolic authorisation

---

[199] Cf. the attack on visionaries in 23:25 ff.

[200] Cf. 2 C. 11:16 ff.; 12:10; Phil. 3:10 ff.; Gl. 6:17; but also 2 C. 4:6 ff.; 1 Th. 3:3 f. and Dob. Th., 135, ad loc.

[201] 1 C. 1:14 ff.; 2:1 ff. etc.

[202] Cf. A. Schlatter, Die Theologie der Apostel² (1922), 261 f.

[203] Cf. the spiritual gift of διακρίσεις πνευμάτων (1 C. 12:10) and the conflict of Paul with ὑπερλίαν ἀπόστολοι (2 C. 11:5; 12:11; → ψευδαπόστολος).

[204] 2 C. 12:1-4; 1 C. 14:18.

[205] 2 C. 12:5.

[206] 2 C. 12:9.

by Christ. What is at issue is not his own person but the cause for which he stands. Like the prophet, Paul as an apostle serves only his message, i.e., the preaching of the → λόγος τοῦ σταυροῦ (1 C. 1:18) which as such is the → λόγος τῆς καταλλαγῆς (2 C. 5:19). This explains his passionate attack on partisanship in Corinth, not in spite of, but just because of the involvement of his own name against his own will and against the meaning of the Gospel (1 C. 1-4, esp. 3:5 ff.). It also explains the lack of any tendency towards an *imitatio Christi* in his own life or in the life of Christians who imitate him (1 Th. 1:6), [207] though this quickly made its appearance in the early Church. [208] If Jesus in His earthly life and calling was in some sense an example for Paul in respect of his office as an apostle, [209] this was because he was His ἀπόστολος. He was thus pledged to Him in everything he did. His apostolate had not to be mere empty talk (→ 415). Nevertheless, the point at issue was the obedience which the → δοῦλος owes his lord, not a meritorious action. [210]

The parallel between the apostles and the prophets which we see in Paul rests on the fact that both are exclusively bearers of revelation, the prophets of revelation still in progress and the apostles of completed revelation. Perhaps the different temporal relationship to the same thing [211] explains why the NT preaching office could not use the ancient title for God's messengers (→ προφήτης) to describe the messengers of Jesus. It needed a new term corresponding to the new and altered situation and yet still referring to the commission which Jesus gave to His disciples. Yet here, too, we probably have the explanation of the linking of the two from the standpoint of their historical significance for the origin of the community as presented in Eph. 2:20. In the circumstance as we have outlined them, this mode of expression is possible not only on the lips of the first generation of Christians but also of Paul himself. [212]

It should be obvious that the NT προφῆται (1 C. 12:28 etc.) do not correspond at all to those of the OT. It should also be clear why they do not play a very prominent part, though they are highly respected in the time of the great Pauline Epistles.

b. The special nature of Paul's position among the other apostles of Jesus cannot be separated from his recovery of the prophetic sense of calling in the predominant position of the concept of God. It is not originally determined by this, but by his calling to be a messenger in the sense of the Jewish שָׁלִיחַ institution, as in the case of the other ἀπόστολοι. If this aspect and basis of his office came to be more strongly accentuated by Paul, one of the main contributory factors was the fact that opponents challenged his equality of status and dignity with the other apostles.

As we can see from the opening of Galatians, this had happened in Galatia; his authorisation was traced back either to the church (Antioch) from which he had come

---

[207] → ἀκολουθέω; → μιμέομαι.

[208] → 214, n. 29.

[209] Cf. on this pt. P. Feine, *Der Apostel Paulus* (1927), 407 ff.

[210] 1 C. 4:1 f.

[211] In R. 10:15, quoting Is. 52:7 (מְבַשֵּׂר טוֹב), Messianic deliverance is expressly made the subject of apostolic proclamation. Cf. also R. 1:15; 1 C. 1:17; 9:16; 15:1 f.; 2 C. 11:7 etc.

[212] For this reason the phrase is no decisive argument against the genuine Pauline nature of Eph.; all that it tells us is that the Epistle belongs to a period when a close relation was seen between the NT apostles and the OT prophets, and this is the time of the Pauline Epistles (→ 439).

(Ac. 13:1 ff.) or to Barnabas, who according to the tradition (Ac. 9:27) had introduced him into the original community. This is why Paul in Gl. 1:1 calls himself an ἀπόστο-λος οὐκ ἀπ' ἀνθρώπων οὐδὲ δι' ἀνθρώπου, ἀλλὰ διὰ 'Ιησοῦ Χριστοῦ, and then demonstrates in v. 10 f. the independence of his apostolate of men, and in 2:1 ff. his equality with the other apostles as recognised in Jerusalem.

Another important factor was the strong conception of his apostolic office in relation to the experience of Jesus as Messiah and to recognition of the significance of the Spirit (→ πνεῦμα) as the Spirit of Jesus [213] whom all Christians that are found in Him (→ ἐν Χριστῷ) possess without exception (1 C. 3:16; 6:19 etc.).

This leads Paul to the bold statement that in virtue of his apostolic office he can call men to reconciliation with God ὑπὲρ Χριστοῦ in the full sense of representing Christ (2 C. 5:20), or that this may be more precisely described as συνεργεῖν with Christ (2 C. 6:1).

Once again it is the concept of God which leads him to this climax. Paul traces the hand of God in his whole life. But the life and passion and death of Jesus, and the proclamation of Jesus, are also grounded in the will of God. [214] This is why Paul can call himself a συνεργὸς θεοῦ (1 C. 3:9) [215] and thereby affirm his own participation in the divine goal, not in the sense of an achievement, but as one who stands in the service of God and thus has a share in His work (1 C. 3:8, 11 ff.). Any breach at this point would be a breach with Christ and would imply contempt for the divine work of salvation in Him (Gl. 1:6 ff.; 5:1 ff.). Yet the basis does not lie in his own person. Only in virtue of his commission, and of the → κύριος who stands behind it, is Paul "anything"; [216] yet through Him he is everything that a man can be by the grace of God. [217] If he is not proud of this, it is because he considers himself His → δοῦλος for the sake of the cross, and recognises the apostolic responsibility laid on him with the grace given (1 C. 3:11 ff.), yet all in such a way that, because God is the Ruler of all history and Jesus is the Lord, there shines over all that the apostolic office involves as the apostolate of the Crucified, [218] the triumphant joy which is a mark of the apostle of the risen Lord. [219]

The idea that suffering and poverty are essential marks of the divine messenger is found in the Socrates of Plato's Apology (23b-c). Genuine in this case, it becomes almost a pose among the Cynics. Paul takes up the same thought, but it is now occasioned and determined by the particular basis of his apostolate (→ supra). It is thus

---

[213] R. 8:9 etc.

[214] Cf. simply the κατὰ τὰς γραφάς of 1 C. 15:3 f., and also the fact that, except in 1 Th. 1:14: ὅτι 'Ιησοῦς ἀπέθανεν καὶ ἀνέστη, Paul always says that Jesus was raised again by God (Gl. 1:1 etc.).

[215] Cf. also 1 Th. 3:2 and → 423, n. 95.

[216] Note the τί of 1 C. 3:5; the κύριος is naturally Jesus as the One who sends and authorises. Cf. also 1 C. 1:13.

[217] Instructive is the relationship between → ἀποστολή and → χάρις, which Paul uses almost synon. (→ 446).

[218] For the apostolate as the link between Paul's sufferings and those of Jesus, cf. Phil. 3:10.

[219] Cf. συνεργοί ἐσμεν τῆς χαρᾶς ὑμῶν in 2 C. 1:24 and also 2 C. 6:9 f.; 7:4. These verses occur in a strong letter in which Paul must struggle for recognition of his apostleship.

a bitter reality which is only tolerable because it, too, attests the close bond between the apostle and the κύριος who gives him his commission. This enables us to understand the paradox of 2 C. 12:10. The attitude of the early Church to suffering and poverty shows how very quickly the attitude of Paul is developed into a system of human merit. There thus takes place the same degeneration as from Socrates to Cynicism, except that the misconception is now more serious and inevitably has more serious consequences.

E. Jesus as One who was sent.

1. Only once is Jesus called ἀπόστολος in the NT, namely, in Hb. 3:1, which we have already considered (→ 423). Yet the question arises whether the reality is not present even though the actual term is not used. This is especially so in the case of John's Gospel. For here the statements of Jesus concerning His relation to God are very largely governed by the verb ἀποστέλλειν.[220] This gives rise to the question whether we may here detect the influence of oriental myths concerning the redeemer sent down from heaven, who is also the original man. The opening up of Mandaean sources[221] has made this a burning question,[222] and it may be briefly discussed from the linguistic standpoint.

In the Book of John, 66 there is a conversation at the moment of the sending of Mandā d'Hayyē to earth. Here we read: "My son, come and be my messenger (אשגאנדא), come and be my bearer (i.e., of commissions) ..." This envoy is then more precisely called "the ambassador of light" (Lidz. Ginza, 58, 17 and 23 etc.) or the "true ambassador" (ibid., 59, 1) or the "ambassador of life" (ibid., 59, 15). He himself says that he is "sent into the world" in the Manichaean Zarathustra fragment.[223] In the Mandaean source the messenger is always called אשגאנדא in these passages, and שאדאר is always used for his sending. This root is a common word in the Aramaic of the Babylonian Talmud and corresponds to πέμπειν rather than ἀποστέλλειν in the Gk.[224] Yet in the Gk. texts relating to the ambassador ἀποστέλλειν is used to denote his sending, as in Gk. Christian texts like the Acta Thomae.[225] Thus in the Gospel of Peter ἀποστέλλειν is used of the sending of Jesus, and it is logically followed by His return to the place of sending; the young man at the grave on Easter morning here gives to the women the reply: τίνα ζητεῖτε; ... ἀνέστη γὰρ καὶ ἀπῆλθεν ἐκεῖ ὅθεν ἀπεστάλη (56).[226] In this case the question even arises whether the thought of authorisation is predominant, as in LXX usage, or whether the reference is simply to spatial movement. Jesus is expressly called ἀπόστολος by Justin;[227] he is thus given a title which by this time has acquired solid content, as may be seen from 1 Cl., 65, 1, where the messengers of the Roman church are not called ἀπόστολοι, as in early

---

[220] For examples → 403 and also Wetter, 49.
[221] Lidz. Joh.; Lidz. Lit.; Lidz. Ginza.
[222] R. Bultmann, "Die Bedeutung der neuerschlossenen mandäischen und manichäischen Quellen für das Verständnis des Joh. Ev.," ZNW, 24 (1925), 100-146; Bau. J., 55 on 3:17; H. H. Schaeder in R. Reitzenstein und H. H. Schaeder, Studien zum antiken Synkretismus — Aus Iran und Griechenland (1926), 203 ff., esp. 306 ff.; H. Odeberg, The Fourth Gospel (1929), 117 ff.; G. P. Wetter (→ Bibl.).
[223] Cf. Reitzenstein Ir. Erl., 3; Bultmann, 106 and n. 7.
[224] Cf. the examples in Levy Wört., IV, 513b.
[225] Cf. the examples in Bultmann, 106.
[226] v. also Const. Ap., VIII, 1, 10: ἀνελήφθη πρὸς τὸν ἀποστείλαντα αὐτόν.
[227] → 424.

Christian usage (→ 398, n. 4; 432, n. 160), but ἀπεσταλμένοι. It is just conceivable, therefore, that Justin is here borrowing the idea of the ambassador from oriental myths and applying it to Jesus. Its popularity is attested not merely by the fact that Mani was the absolute ambassador for his followers [228] but that in Gk. Arab. papyri Mohammed is also sometimes called ἀπόστολος. [229] Indeed, a later age, following the example of Apollonius of Tyana, linked the person of Alexander the Great with the myth of the ambassador and accorded him special reverence. [230]

In all these cases the one who is given the name of divine messenger is also the preacher of truth. [231] Above all, he is the one who unites the divine and human worlds by speaking and leading men out of error. This is what Jesus does in the passages in which Justin calls him ἀπόστολος. As the ἄγγελος of God He has the task of imparting true knowledge to His hearers. His whole life and work serve this end. [232] The goal is perhaps different from that of the Mandaean or Manichean ambassador, and so, too, is the person, but there is still a material parallel. Thus neither in Justin nor in the Mandaean records nor Manichean fragments is the thought of authorisation predominant. When the ambassador appears, it is not that he speaks and acts as one who is commissioned by, or as a representative of, the one who sends him. What matters is that he comes from another sphere. This is the most important presupposition of his redemptive work. And it is finally his own mystery of which he gives only hints even to his followers. [233] It may be added that the selection of ἀποστέλλειν (ἀπόστολος) in Justin and other Christian writings plainly rests on a linguistic dependence on the Gospel of John.

2. The Gospel of John, however, is plainly opposed to this whole view, materially if not formally. Certainly Jesus is sent by the Father (→ 405). Nevertheless, this sending is designed simply to bring out the significance of His person and of the history enacted in Him, namely, that God Himself speaks by Him and acts in Him.

This is shown in three ways. a. In the → σημεῖον of the Johannine Jesus God manifests Jesus as the promised One and also manifests Himself as the One who works in and through Him (→ ἔργον). [234] b. The destiny of those who encounter Jesus is decided by the person of Jesus and their attitude to Him rather than to the doctrine taught by Him. [235] This is possible only if God is present in Him and He literally represents the Father in person. [236] c. Like all the other ἔργα effected by God, the death of Jesus cannot be separated from His Word. Indeed, in John His death and glorification (δοξάζω), i.e., His exaltation to the side of the Father to participate in

---

[228] Wetter, 15 ff. There are, of course, other ambassadors as well (cf. Bau. J., 55).

[229] Preisigke Sammelbuch, No. 7240, 5.

[230] Cf. on this pt. W. Bacher, *Nizâmî's Leben und Werke und der zweite Teil des Nizâmîschen Alexanderbuches* (Diss. Leipzig, 1871), 90.

[231] This is true even of Alexander, who is depicted as the representative of true religion (Bacher, *op. cit.*, 90 and 94 ff. *passim*).

[232] Ap., I, 63, 5 (p. 54, 4 ff., Krüger): God's Son καὶ ἄγγελος δὲ καλεῖται καὶ ἀπόστολος· αὐτὸς γὰρ ἀπαγγέλλει ὅσα δεῖ γνωσθῆναι, καὶ ἀποστέλλεται, μηνύσων ὅσα ἀγγέλλεται ... Justin also uses ἄγγελος for Jesus (Wetter, 28 f.).

[233] Cf. on this pt. more generally, and not with special reference to Jn., G. P. Wetter, " 'Ich bin es,' " ThStKr, 88 (1915), 224 ff. esp. 235.

[234] Cf. Jn. 4:34; 5:36; 9:3 f.; 10:37 etc.

[235] 3:18; cf. 3:17; 12:47, and in general the strength of the thought of judgment in Jn.

[236] 8:16, 29; cf. 5:36 f.; 8:18; 10:25; 12:49; 14:10 etc.

His → δόξα, and consequently His full manifestation as the Son (→ υἱός), constitute an indissoluble unity. [237]

What is said about Jesus in this Gospel is left hanging in the air if He is here analogous to the ambassadors of oriental Gnosticism. Jesus is essentially more than these, even though ἀποστέλλειν is one of the most important words which He uses to describe His office. This word is not identical in significance with the term used by the Mandaeans when they speak of the sending of Mandā d'Hayyē (→ 443). In any case, it should be noted in respect of the Jesus of the Fourth Gospel that πέμπειν as well as ἀποστέλλειν is used to express His consciousness of mission, and in such a way as to leave no doubt as to the relationship between the two terms (ἀποστέλλω, 404). Hence it must be stated that, in so far as the idea of the ambassador plays any role in John, it does not influence the Christology but is rather coloured by it. In this respect the whole complex is linked in John with the sending of the prophets, and derives its distinctive character from the fact that this ambassador is not a man, not even a pre-existent or primal man, but the Son in whom the Father attests His presence and Himself offers salvation or judgment.

† ψευδαπόστολος.

This word is one of the compounds with ψευδ(ο) of which → ψευδάδελφος, → ψευδοδιδάσκαλος, → ψευδόμαρτυς etc. are also found in the NT.[1] It does not occur elsewhere.

In the NT it occurs only at 2 C. 11:13, where Paul himself adds the explanation : μετασχηματιζόμενοι εἰς ἀποστόλους Χριστοῦ. By ψευδαπόστολοι he understands those who pretend to be apostles of Christ without being authorised by Him. The lack of authorisation is seen in the fact that they are not wholly and exclusively committed to Christ or God; they seek their own ends instead of offering unselfish service (cf. ἐργάται δόλιοι, 11:13). Not knowing that it is of the essence of the apostolate of Jesus that the one commissioned by Him should be lowly and suffer, they acquire the air of ὑπερλίαν ἀπόστολοι (11:5, 11), an expression which even linguistically brings out the impossible nature of such apostles, since an ἀπόστολος/שָׁלִיחַ (→ 427) of Jesus already has a position which is quite incomparable. In both expressions Paul had in view his Judaistic opponents who either disputed his apostleship (cf. Gl. 1:1 and → 441 f.) or set about to drive him from his churches by their own claims, though they had no any inner right to pass sentence on him.

---

[237] 12:23 ff. from this standpoint 18:1 ff. should be compared with Mt. 26:36 ff. par. and → ὑψόω.

ψ ε υ δ α π ό σ τ ο λ ο ς. On such compounds cf. the bibl. given by Pr.-Bauer, 1420, s.v. ψευδόμαρτυς, and on their history cf. Debr. Griech. Wortb., 37. More particularly on ψευδαπόστολος cf. K. Holl, ψευδόμαρτυς in *Gesammelte Aufsätze zur KG*, II : *Der Osten* (1928, 110-114), 114; Sick. K., 145.

[1] For their basic understanding, cf. esp. Holl, 110 ff.

The fact that the word is attested only in this passage is an argument not merely for the view that it is a Christian and even a Pauline construction but also for the conclusion that ἀπόστολος itself is coined in the Christian or Pauline vocabulary to meet the need for a new term for the new institution of messengers authorised by Jesus Himself (→ 435). Though Revelation does not have the word, it has its substance in 2:2 : καὶ ἐπείρασας τοὺς λέγοντας ἑαυτοὺς ἀποστόλους καὶ οὐκ εἰσίν.

† ἀποστολή (→ χάρις).

This word is relatively common in secular usage. It has many different senses corresponding to ἀποστέλλειν. Thus it is used a. for the "despatch of ships" (Thuc., VIII, 9 : ἀποστολὴ νεῶν); b. for any "sending," including the discharge of a missile (βέλους ἀποστολή : Philo Mechanicus Belopoica, p. 68, 33, Diels-Schramm [AAB, 1918, No. 13, 46]), but also active "separation from a man" (Aristot. Rhet., II, 23, p. 1400b, 11 f. : ἥμαρτε γὰρ ἡ Μήδεια περὶ τὴν ἀποστολὴν τῶν παίδων) or the "entombment of a mummy" (P. Oxy., 736, 13 : ἀποστολὴ ταφῆς). On the basis of ἀποστέλλεσθαι the word can also signify "expedition" (Thuc., VIII, 8 ; → ἀπόστολος, 407 and n. 3). In all these cases it is a noun of action.

In the Jewish sphere we find the usual meanings (cf. Ep. Ar., 15, where πρὸς τὴν ἀποστολήν = πρὸς τὸ ἀποστέλλειν). But the strongly developing influence of שׁלח/ἀποστέλλειν in the techn. sense (→ 417) can also give it the meaning of "tribute" in connection with the Jewish office of ἀπόστολοι (cf. Jul. Ep., 204, p. 281, 4, Bidez-Cumont).[1] It is found 12 times in the LXX,[2] always in connection with the root שׁלח when there is an original except at Ιερ. 39:36 (→ Jer. 32:36). In this case בַּחֶרֶב וּבְרָעָב וּבַדֶּבֶר is rendered ἐν μαχαίρᾳ καὶ ἐν λιμῷ καὶ ἐν ἀποστολῇ. The translator, on the basis of his historical knowledge, has here amended to read דֶּבֶר (pestilence) as דָּבָר (the divine address). In 1 K. 9:16 ἀποστολή almost signifies "gift" or "present," but elsewhere it is simply "sending" (ψ 77:49),[3] including more specifically the despatch of gifts. Josephus uses it in Ant., 20, 50 for a "ceremonial escort" (cf. Vit., 268).[4]

In the NT the term occurs 4 times. In Ac. 1:25 it is used with → διακονία, in R. 1:5 with → χάρις, in 1 C. 9:2 and Gl. 2:8 without addition. In all cases it clearly refers to the office of the ἀπόστολος of Jesus, technically conceived and discharged. In the NT, then, it is fully controlled by ἀπόστολος. It thus occupies a distinctive position in the history of the word and shows that the new term ἀπόστολος has a powerful tendency to make use of related concepts.

The way was perhaps prepared to some degree for this development. Thus the Armenian version of Test. N. 2 : "My father Jacob ordained me for this mission and message," presupposes a Gk. ἀποστολὴν καὶ ἀγγελίαν; there may be in ἀποστολήν an allusion to the שִׁלְחָה of Gn. 49:21;[5] yet the Gk. as edited by R. H. Charles simply

---

ἀ π ο σ τ ο λ ή. Cr. Kö., 1020; Preisigke Wört., I, 195; Liddell-Scott, 220.

[1] Cf. S. Krauss, JQR, 17 (1905), 375.

[2] Of these 3 are only partially attested (1 K. 4:34; 9:16; Cant. 4:13); cf. also 3 Macc. 4:4 : ἐξαποστολή.

[3] The fig. ἀποστολὴ χειρός is found in Aquila Is. 11:14, where Symmachus and Theodotion read ἔκτασις and the LXX has neither (τὰς χεῖρας ἐπιβαλοῦσιν).

[4] For these instances, cf. Thackeray Lex. Jos., 76.

[5] As suggested by F. Schnapp in Kautzsch Apkr. u. Pseudepigr. ad loc.

has εἰς πᾶσαν ἀγγελίαν. [6] In any case, ἀποστολή and ἀγγελία are here related. In Rabbinic sources the word שְׁלִיחוּת is occasionally found with reference to the despatch of messengers (angels : מַלְאָכִים). [7] This corresponds materially to ἀποστολή, but we cannot be sure that it is not derived from it.

Rengstorf

ἀποστρέφω → στρέφω   ἀποσυνάγωγος → συναγωγή
ἀποτάσσω → τάσσω

---

† ἀποφθέγγομαι

"To speak out loudly and clearly," "to speak with emphasis." ψ 58:8; Luc. Zeux., 1; Iambl. Vit. Pyth., 11, 55. Cf the philosopher, Philo Vit. Mos., II, 33; Diog. L., I, 63, 73, 79; Luc. Alex., 25 : χρησμὸν ἀπεφθέγξατο. Of the ecstatic, whether the giver of oracles, Diod. S., XVI, 27, 1; Plut. Pyth. Or., 23 (II, 405e), the diviner, Mi. 5:12; Zech. 10, 2; Vett. Val., II, 16, p. 73, 24 f.; II, 36, p. 112, 15; 113, 1, Kroll, the inspired singer, 1 Ch. 25:1 or the prophet, Ez. 13:9, 19; Catal. Cod. Astr. Graec., VIII, 4, 147, 15 etc. (often *sensu malo*).

In the NT it is found only in Ac. *sensu bono* of Christians who, filled with the Spirit, are ecstatically transported (2:4 : ἤρξαντο λαλεῖν ἑτέραις γλώσσαις, καθὼς τὸ πνεῦμα ἐδίδου ἀποφθέγγεσθαι αὐτοῖς) or inspired to speak prophetically (2:14; 26:25 : ἀληθείας καὶ σωφροσύνης ῥήματα ἀποφθέγγομαι). Its opposite is μαίνομαι (cf. 2 C. 5:13 : ἐξέστημεν ... σωφρονοῦμεν).

Behm

---

[6] *The Greek Versions of the Testaments of the Twelve Patriarchs* (1908), 145.
[7] Gn.r., 50, 1 on 19:1. For further information *v.* S. Rappaport, *Agada und Exegese bei Flavius Josephus* (1930), 105 and Levy Wört., IV, *s.v.*

ἀποψύχω → ψυχή   ἀπρόσκοπος → κόπτω
ἀπροσωπολήμπτως → προσωποληψία

┌─────────────────┐
│ † ἀπωθέω   │
└─────────────────┘

Used in Gk. poetry and prose from the time of Homer to the pap. with both the literal and figur. meaning of "to repel" or "reject." It occurs 6 times in the NT at Ac. 7:27, 39; 13:46; R. 11:1, 2; 1 Tm. 1:19, always in the mid. aor. 1: ἀπωσάμην.

The only passage of significance for biblical theology is R. 11:1, 2 : μὴ ἀπώσατο ὁ θεὸς τὸν λαὸν αὐτοῦ; The form of this question necessarily carries with it a negative answer. The decisive feature is the combination of ὁ θεός and τὸν λαὸν αὐτοῦ. Israel is God's people and therefore He cannot finally repudiate them. The reading of Codex G, which has τὴν κληρονομίαν (LXX) for τὸν λαόν, is a correct interpretation (→ λαός). [1] Three times in the LXX (1 Βασ. 12:22; ψ 93:14; 94:4) we have the promise : οὐκ ἀπώσεται Κύριος τὸν λαὸν αὐτοῦ. Paul reminds us of this promise when in R. 11:2 he expressly gives us the negative answer : οὐκ ἀπώσατο ὁ θεὸς τὸν λαὸν αὐτοῦ.

Karl Ludwig Schmidt

ἀπώλεια → 396

┌──────────────────────────────┐
│ ἀρά, καταράομαι, κατάρα,   │
│ ἐπικατάρατος, ἐπάρατος   │
└──────────────────────────────┘

† ἀρά.

Originally "wish" or "petition," though used in the sense of "curse" from the time of Homer. In the NT found only at R. 3:14 in free quotation of ψ 9:28.

† καταράομαι.

Since the simple form does not occur in the NT, and other compounds occur only as verbal adj., καταράομαι is with ἀναθεματίζω the usual word for "to curse." In the NT it is found only with the acc. of person (Lk. 6:28 and par. vl.; Jm. 3:9), and

---

ἀ π ω θ έ ω. [1] Cf. Bengel, *ad loc.* : *Ipsa populi eius appellatio rationem negandi continet.*
κ α τ α ρ ά ο μ α ι. [1] Cf. Pr.-Bauer, *s.v.*; Bl. Debr. § 152, 1.

therefore also in the pass. (Mt. 25:41: οἱ κατηραμένοι; and absol. καταρᾶσθε in R. 12:14). In non-biblical Gk. the dat. of person is more common than the acc. [1] With one exception the LXX always has the acc., but Jos. has the dat. (Bell., 3, 297; Ant., 1, 142; Ap., 1, 204), though also the pass. (Bell., 5, 401). Philo has the dat. (classically) and the acc. when following the LXX.

† κατάρα (→ ἐξαγοράζω, 126).

κατάρα, from καταρᾶσθαι "to enchant" or "bewitch," [1] means "curse." In the LXX it is a common rendering of קְלָלָה.

1. Curse (and Blessing).

Cursing and blessing are customs which can be traced through almost all religious history. [2] A curse is a directly expressed or indicated utterance which in virtue of a supernatural nexus of operation brings harm by its very expression to the one against whom it is directed. [3] For true cursing there is thus needed the special endowment possessed by priests, wizards, chiefs etc., a special situation like that of the dying man or someone unjustly persecuted, the use of special formulae such as the naming of names, or the observance of particular customs like the recording of the curse on leaden plates or in a holy place etc. The curse can overlap with prayer if its fulfilment is thought to be so dependent on a deity that it must be committed to this deity, and it may even become a prayer if it is requested from the deity. It can also find blatant expression, perhaps poetically, in a passionate surge of ill-will. For true cursing, however, faith is essential; fulfilment is implied in the act of cursing. This fulfilment may be thought to come in virtue of a mysterious nexus of operation independent of God, as amongst primitive peoples, or of a compulsion which he who curses exercises upon spirits, gods, etc., as amongst wizards of a higher type, or of an authority allegedly given him by God, as in the anathematising of the Synagogue or Roman Catholicism (→ ἀνάθεμα, ἀναθεματίζω). In the judicial procedures of ancient peoples curses play a significant role, e.g., in the execution of punishment, the enforcement of law etc.; the oath is originally a pledge or declaration on the condition of self-cursing. Jesus forbade His disciples to curse as an act of revenge (Lk. 6:28 and par. and cf. Jm. 3:9-12). Nor did He give them any authority to curse, but only to withhold remission (Jn. 20:23; Mt. 16:19; 18:18). The cursing of God, or of those whom He has authorised, of the prophets and Scripture, is designed to reveal the divine judgment in such a way that it is already initiated. The curse is thus a judicial action of God, or a consequence of human sin, as in Gl. 3:10, 13; Hb. 6:8; 2 Pt. 2:14. The emphasis here is not so much on the fact that the curse is pronounced as on the ineluctability of this consequence of sin, which is determined once and for all by the divine judgment.

κ α τ ά ρ α. L. Brun, *Segen und Fluch im Urchristentum* (1932). For bibl. on cursing as a phenomenon in religious history → n. 2; for bibl. on Gl. 3:10, 13 → ἐξαγοράζω, 126 n.

[1] Debr. Griech. Wortb., 21.

[2] Cf. A. Bertholet-E. Lehmann, *Lehrbuch d. Rel. Gesch.* (1925), Index, *s.v.* "Fluch"; also J. Hempel, "Die israel. Anschauungen v. Segen u. Fluch im Lichte altorient. Parallelen," ZDMG, 79 (1925), 20-110; R. Wünsch, *Antike Fluchtafeln, Kl. T.* 20 (1907); Pauly-W., VI (1909), 271 and Suppl., IV (1924), 454; K. Latte, *Heiliges Recht* (1920), 61-96.

[3] The common definition (e.g., H. Gunkel, RGG[1], II, 921) that a curse is the wishing of harm is incorrect; the wish must be expressed etc.

2. Gl. 3:13.

In Gl. 3:13 the curse is the curse of the Law, since the Law expresses it (Dt. 27:26; 21:23). Yet it is also the curse of God, for the Law is the revelation of God. This is in no sense affected by Gl. 3:19, 20. For Paul humanity stands under the wrath of God (R. 1:19-32) or the judgment of God (R. 5:18). For this reason we take away the foundation and destroy the very nerve of the passage if we restrict the "we" of Gl. 3:10, 13 to the Jews or to Jewish Christians. [4] Paul speaks personally or subjectively. If we make this personal confession objective, we rob it of its essence. According to Gl. 3:10, 13 no man is exempt from standing under the curse, for all men are sinners (R. 3:23). [5] To be a sinner is to stand already under the wrath and condemnation of God, not just to move forward to it. This is expressed in the saying about the curse of the Law.

In the curse of the Law ὀργή and κατάκριμα already press on man ; hence there is forgiveness only through strict release from the curse. Jesus accomplished this by becoming a curse on our behalf (→ ὑπέρ), i.e., by dying the death of the accursed on the cross. The distinctive mode of expression used by Paul in Gl. 3:13, i.e., *abstractum pro concreto,* is also found in the OT and in the literature of Jewish tradition. [6] Thus the key to the concept of substitution in Gl. 3:13 is not to be sought in the recurrence of the same formulation at 2 C. 5:21: ὑπὲρ ἡμῶν ἁμαρτίαν ἐποίησεν. This phrase expresses neither the inward nature of the union between the one who bears and what is borne, nor does it relativise the substitution to the divine ordination that He "should suffer what men did to Him in fulfilment of the curse which He had not brought down and which did not apply to Him." [7] The key is to be sought in the ὑπὲρ ἡμῶν which occurs in both passages, and especially in the insight (→ ἐξαγοράζω, 127) that Paul does not objectivise the thought of substitution. It is thus beside the point to differentiate between the curse which Jesus became and that which God in the Law decreed on transgressors of the Law. [8] For whatever may be the correct interpretation of the קִלְלַת אֱלֹהִים of Dt. 21:23, [9] both the LXX and Paul have here, not the abstract κατάρα, but the concrete, passive ἐπικατάρατος or κεκαταραμένος. The one who is hanged is thus regarded as accursed in the sense that, as "a publicly exposed example of the pitiless severity of the Law," [10] he stands under the very curse which the Law brings on those who transgress it. [11] Obviously, then, Paul is stating a view

---

[4] Hofmann, Sieffert, Zn., Kaftan etc.; → ἐξαγοράζω, 126, n.

[5] On the question whether and in what way all men, including the Gentiles, stand under the Law, cf. R. 2:12-16.

[6] Jer. 24:9; 42:18; Zech. 8:13; Ex.r., 38 on 29:1: "As Thou, God, art truth ..." ; S. Nu., 161 on 35:34 : "I am your atonement כַּפָּרַתְכֶם. Str.-B., III, 261 gives many examples of the expression : "I am an atonement for someone," e.g., Neg., 2, 1: "The children of Israel, I am their atonement ..." This singular but recurrent assurance of love shows how deeply rooted in Judaism is the thought that by voluntarily accepted sufferings one may free others from sufferings which are divinely imposed.

[7] Sieffert, *ad loc.* according to Hofmann.

[8] Zn. acc. to Hofmann, and even more clearly Sieffert.

[9] Cf. Zn. Gl., 156, n. 9.

[10] *Ibid.,* 157.

[11] Zn. himself shows that to distinguish between the curse which Jesus became and that which rests on transgressors of the Law obscures rather than elucidates the passage. But he also finds in the passage no statement concerning the way in which Jesus redeemed us from the curse by becoming a curse.

of substitution. Yet it is not the orthodox view which views the cross in the light of a purely objective legal transaction between God and Christ that does not concern man nor embrace him personally. Nor is any help to be found in the restrictions of a mediating theology which derives the curse only from the Law and not from God, or which applies it only to the Jews and not to "us." For Paul substitution is part of God's dynamic action towards us. It is the establishment of the new fellowship between God and us. It does not merely make this possible legally and objectively. It is also the effective creation of this fellowship subjectively in us. These statements of Paul can be understood only in the light of the new divine fellowship which is twosided, which is both objective and subjective, and which thus manifests itself in the workings of faith and conscience that are produced in us by the cross. It is not for nothing that Paul speaks of our redemption (Gl. 3:13), of our justification (R. 3:21 ff.), of our reconciliation (2 C. 5:17 ff.), in short of our new fellowship with God, before he speaks of Jesus as the One who became a curse, as the ἱλαστήριον, as the One who was made sin. This recurrent formal structure of his statements can hardly be accidental. If not, however, it shows us that He does not think in the purely objective manner of orthodoxy. That Jesus was made a curse for us implies, then, that He is set by God in our alienation from God in order that He might bring us out of it to fellowship with God (→ ὑπέρ).

The question whether and for what reason this penal substitution was necessary is neither raised nor answered in the Pauline Epistles. Paul accepts the fact that Jesus has died the death of the accursed and that He is thus the Initiator of new fellowship with God. He states this fact, but does not speculate on its necessity. Nevertheless, the punishment of sinners, as he sees it, is not merely threatened by the curse of the Law; it is already initiated, if not completed. Thus there can be no new divine fellowship for those who are accursed, i.e., for those who stand under punishment, except by way of penal substitution.

† ἐπικατάρατος, † ἐπάρατος (→ κατάρα).

ἐπικατάρατος is common in the LXX but in the NT it occurs only at Gl. 3:10, 13. Older non-biblical Gk. uses ἀρατός, ἐπάρατος,[1] κατάρατος.[2] Outside the Bible ἐπικατάρατος is found only from the 2nd century A.D.: Ditt. Syll.³, 1240, 2 f.: ἐπικατάρατος ὅστις μὴ φείδοιτο κατὰ τόνδε τὸν χῶρον τοῦδε τοῦ ἔργου, CIG, 2664. It is possible that it came into secular use by way of the LXX and NT.[3] Yet it can hardly be accidental that this double rather than single compound is first found in the LXX, from which the NT takes it. For the older period was not so fond of double compounds as the later.[4] On Gl. 3:13 → κατάρα, 450. The judgment on the people in Jn. 7:49 (ἐπάρατος) is in keeping with the inordinate scorn of the scribes for the unlearned; it is based on Dt. 27:26.[5]

Büchsel

ἐ π ι κ α τ ά ρ α τ ο ς. [1] Jos. Ant., 1, 58; 7, 208; Philo *passim.* Jos. does not have ἐπικατάρατος, though it is found in Philo Leg. All., 3, 111 and 113.
[2] Jos. Ant., 4, 126.
[3] Nägeli, 60.
[4] Deissmann LO, 74.
[5] Materially cf. Str.-B., II, 494-519, esp. 514-516; Deissmann LO, 74.

ἀργός, ἀργέω, καταργέω

† ἀργός, † ἀργέω.

ἀργός (= ἀ-εργός, Hom. Il., 9, 320) means "inactive" or "inoperative." It is used a. in the sense of "indolent" (Sir. 37:11), "unemployed," "useless," "unserviceable" (νῆες, Thuc., VII, 67), or pass. "unused" (Wis. 14:5) or "unworked," i.e., "raw" or "crude" (3 Βασ. 6:7; Sir. 38:28). It is also used b. in the sense of "incapable of action or of live operation." Thus in Emped. (Diels, I, 208, 7) it is used of the matter of the cosmos to signify its lack of potential energies; cf. Philo Spec. Leg., I, 21 with reference to the material of idols (cf. also on this pt. Wis. 15:15). It is used of the souls of lower animals, which have few functions (Op. Mund., 65; cf. Leg. All., I, 32). Corp. Herm., XI, 5 states that it is not proper to God, i.e., God is always active. It can also be used of a philosophical theorem (the ἀργὸς λόγος, v. Arnim, II, 277 f.; the context actually treats of this ἀργὸς λόγος) which blunts the (moral) power of action. It is also used of the ἐπιθυμίαι which are not capable of good = "bad" (Plat. Resp., IX, 572e).

ἀργέω is intr.; it can be used in the LXX for "to rest" (on the Sabbath, 2 Macc. 5:25), but also for "to be idle," or "to pause" (1 Esr. 2:25; 2 Esr. 4:24; Qoh. 12:3).

ἀργός in the NT is used in the secular sense of "unemployed" (Mt. 20:3), "inactive" (Mt. 20:6; 1 Tm. 5:13), or "idle" (Tt. 1:12). It is also used in the moral sense of "not accomplishing good," i.e., "bad" (→ supra, Plat. Resp., IX, 572e), of human words which come under judgment (Mt. 12:36, where it is obviously identical with → πονηρόν in v. 34, though cf. Stob. Ecl., III, p. 684, 8 f.). It is also found in the religious sense at 2 Pt. 1:8 (par. to ἄκαρπος) of those who will stand before Christ in the judgment with nothing to attest their Christian standing either in their individual life or the life of the community. What the author has in view is the expression of πίστις by ἀρετή. In a Jewish rather than a Greek phrase, this is most explicitly demanded in Jm. 2:20. According to this verse a faith which consists merely in convictions is unserviceable or worthless to the believer; only when it achieves in works the dynamic of συνεργεῖ (v. 22) does its attain the necessary fulness. Faith which is understood only intellectually is in some sense a mere cloak, and as such it is worthless, ἀργή. [1]

ἀργέω is used at 2 Pt. 2:3, οὐκ ἀργεῖ intrans. to signify the latent activity of judgment.

† καταργέω.

Trans. in the sense of "to render inactive," "to condemn to inactivity" (χέρα, Eur. Phoen., 753), "to put out of use" (Corp. Herm., XIII, 7: κατάργησον τοῦ σώματος τὰς → αἰσθήσεις). In the LXX it occurs only at 2 Εσδρ. (4 times) with the meaning "to destroy."

In the NT it is used with the secular meanings a. "to condemn to inactivity" (Lk. 13:7); b. "to destroy" (1 C. 13:11); and c. "to remove from the sphere of activity" (R. 7:2). [1]

ἀ ρ γ ό ς κ τ λ. [1] Better attested than the variant νεκρά, which misses the subtle play on words.
κ α τ α ρ γ έ ω. [1] Cf. Sickb. R.⁴, 225.

In the religious sense, which is almost exclusive to Paul, it means 1. "to make completely inoperative" or "to put out of use." As applied to God and Christ (a.), it signifies a religious benefit or liberation ; as applied to men (b.) it denotes offence against a religious order or ordinance.

a. Since the world view of Paul recognises several real destructive elements, it is radically refashioned by the new religion, so that the concept of καταργεῖν in the objective sense plays no inconsiderable role in the totality of the cosmic and extra-cosmic development theologically interpreted by him.

The remarkable observation of Paul in relation to the Corinthian church, i.e., that it is not composed of those who are noteworthy in the eyes of the world, leads him to the judgment that God's purpose is obviously to "render insignificant," "to set aside," "that which is," i.e., the values which count for the psychic (1 C. 1:28), in order that those who think that they count for something and make themselves out to be important should be deprived of their significance in His judgment. Thus the way of the Greeks to God, their "wisdom," is made totally inoperative by God, as is also the νόμος τῶν ἐντολῶν (Eph. 2:15). And it is stated expressly that a new valuation has been set up by the work of Christ. Christ Himself by His physical death has set aside the Jewish and OT Law with its detailed provisions and the expository pronouncements of the Rabbis. The way to God has thus been opened up for the Gentiles. To be sure, Paul does not wish to invalidate the Law as an ethical demand (cf. R. 2:14, or as given to the Jew) with his preaching of faith (R. 3:31). The point is that it cannot advance any claim which would make of none effect the promise of the righteousness of faith given to Abraham (Gl. 3:17). Behind all this there stand for Paul very real powers which control this aeon, the → ἀρχαί, → ἐξουσίαι, → δυνάμεις. Yet these, too, are robbed of their power for the Christian ; they have no more power over him (1 C. 2:6). Using καταργεῖν, Paul say this expressly even of death, which is a curse resting on the physical and intellectual and moral life of the natural, i.e., the carnal or psychic man (2 Tm. 1:10). The Epistle to the Hebrews fills out this declaration by stating that through the death of Christ even the one who has power over death, the διάβολος (2:14), is condemned to inactivity or ineffectiveness in relation to the Christian.

In individual terms, these Pauline statements concerning the new estimation of the existing world order apply with even greater precision to the carnal man. The crucifixion of this man with Christ implies that he is released from his bondage to sin, or more exactly — and here we see clearly the strong tension which can also be for Paul the tension between σῶμα and πνεῦμα — that the body of sin, the form of man's appearance in subjection to sin, is robbed of its power to affect the religious and moral attitude and development of man (R. 6:6). For the moment this liberation according to the will of God is not definitive ; the religious life of the Christian still assumes forms which will be ended, such as the prophetic utterances of the pneuma and indeed the gnosis which is highly estimated by Paul (only ἀγάπη will remain, 1 C. 13:8). For by these it is inevitable that only portions of the divine reality may be apprehended. With the fulfilment, this partial work loses its point (v. 10).

b. Subjectively, i.e., for himself and his sphere of activity — for Paul expressly denies the possibility of any objective operation of such disobedient καταργεῖν — man can render these divine acts of liberation ineffective by his disobedience to the resultant demands of faith, e.g., by maintaining that the fulfilment of the Law according to a Judaistic understanding is necessary for heirs of the βασιλεία

(R. 4:14), for instance, in such matters as circumcision (Gl. 5:11). The scandal of the cross is thus robbed of its effect, i.e., the offence which the Jew takes at justification, not by works, but by the cross of Christ.

2. The provisional disarming of demonic powers and the carnal man will obviously end with their complete destruction at the *parousia* (1 C. 15:24, 26; 2 Th. 2:8; 1 C. 6:13).

3. The deliberative use of the term, "to take from the sphere of operation," is found with the two references treated under 1a. : ἀπὸ τοῦ νόμου (R. 7:6) and ἀπὸ Χριστοῦ (Gl. 5:4).

4. The use in 2 C. 3 causes difficulties. In v. 7 and v. 13 we seem to have un-equivocal examples of 2. The external glow on the face of Moses, caused by the mediation of the Law, was transitory (pres. part. pass. as adj., formally as in v. 11). Again v. 14 may belong to 2. if we are to fill out the subj. of καταργεῖται to τὸ κάλυμμα (which conceals the passing nature of the δόξα of the service of the Law). Thus the deceptive appearance that the δόξα of the service of the Law still remains is destroyed in Christ. On the other hand, we get a clearer sense if we take παλαιὰ διαθήκη as the subject here. This is invalidated or devalued in Christ, i.e., by the given fact of Christ. In this case the καταργούμενον of v. 11 refers to the service of the Law as well. This was subjected to later devalua-tion ; it was deprived of its original value (→ *supra* 1.). It thus has only a borrow-ed δόξα and not one of its own, not even as the gift of faith. We see, therefore, that καταργεῖν often means "to put out of action" or "to deprive of power" in cases where there has been relative value and validity in the pre-Christian period. It is from the vacillation between the meanings 2. (v. 7, 13) and 1a. (v. 11, 14) that the train of thought in 2 C. 3:7-14 derives its cogency.

Delling

ἀρέσκω, ἀνθρωπάρεσκος, ἀρεσκεία,
ἀρεστός, εὐάρεστος, εὐαρεστέω

ἀρέσκω implies the establishment of a positive relationship between two factors and therefore "to make peace" or "to reconcile." From the original legal sphere the term passed into the aesthetic in the sense of "to please" someone. The various constructions from the present stem, e.g., ἄρεσκος, ἀρεσκεύω and ἀρεσκεία, express the action of trying to please, and easily come to have, though not exclusively, an unfavourable sense. Constructions from the general verbal stem, e.g., ἀρεστός, εὐάρεστος and εὐαρεστέω, denote something which positively evokes pleasure.

† ἀρέσκω.

a. Originally with the acc. "to make peace with" or "to reconcile" someone,[1] mid. "to be well disposed" to someone, as in Xenoph. Mem., IV, 3, 16 : ἱεροῖς θεοὺς ἀρέσκεσθαι, and similarly Jos. Ant., 6, 67; Bell., 1, 321; 5, 503. Hence pass. "to be satisfied by" or "to take pleasure in," M. Ant., III, 4, 9 etc. Then with the dat. b. "to take a pleasant attitude" to someone, Xenoph. Mem., II, 2, 12 : οὐκοῦν ... καὶ τῷ γείτονι βούλει σὺ ἀρέσκειν, ἵνα σοι καὶ πῦρ ἐναύῃ, ὅταν τούτου δέῃ; similarly Eur. Fr., 93 and often on inscriptions, as CIG, 4479, 5 : ἀρέσαντας τῇ πατρίδι καὶ τοῖς πατρίοις θεοῖς, also Epict. c. "to please" someone, as often in secular usage.

In the LXX ἀρέσκω always means "to please," and the compound εὐαρεστέω is used to translate הִתְהַלֵּךְ where this denotes the walk before God : Gn. 5:22, 24; 6:9; 17:1 (εὐαρέστει ἐναντίον ἐμοῦ καὶ γίνου ἄμεμπτος); 24:40; 48:15; Ps. 26:3; 35:14; 56:13; 116:9; Sir. 44:16.[2] In Gn. 39:4 it is used for שֵׁרֵת. This shows that the LXX uses εὐαρεστέω for an attitude.[3]

In the NT we have the meaning "to please" at Mk. 6:22 and par. and Ac. 6:5,[4] as also perhaps at 1 C. 7:32 ff. and 2 Tm. 2:4. In Paul, however, it mostly signifies to "please oneself," as in R. 15:1-3, where the opp. is not "to detest oneself"[5] but "to deny oneself." Similarly in 1 C. 10:33 the part. clause : καθὼς κἀγὼ πάντα πᾶσιν ἀρέσκω μὴ ζητῶν τὸ ἐμαυτοῦ σύμφορον, suggests that the reference is to an attitude. The same holds good in 1 Th. 2:4 and Gl. 1:10 : ἢ ζητῶ ἀνθρώποις ἀρέσκειν; εἰ ἔτι ἀνθρώποις ἤρεσκον, Χριστοῦ δοῦλος οὐκ ἂν ἤμην, where serving men and being the slave of Christ are brought into contrast. 1 Th. 2:15 and 4:1 are to be taken in the same way, and the context shows that the reference is to an attitude in R. 8:8.

ἀ ρ έ σ κ ω. Nägeli, 40; Joh. W. 1 K. on 10:33; Dob. Th. on 1 Th. 2:4; A. Robertson-A. Plummer, 1 Cor. (1911), on 10:33.

[1] Cf. the words ἀρεστήρ (savour of an expiatory offering) and ἀρεστήρια ἱερά (expiatory offering).

[2] Exceptions are 4 Βασ. 20:3 (περιπατεῖν) and Is. 38:3 (πορεύεσθαι).

[3] Rgg. Hb. on 11:5.

[4] On the construction with ἐνώπιον cf. 3 Βασ. 12:24; Jdt. 7:16, often whith ἐναντίον. Εὐαρεστέω occurs with ἐνώπιον in ψ 55:14. The MSS sometimes vacillate between ἐνώπιον and ἐναντίον.

[5] This is how the expression is used in Epict. Diss., II, 18, 19.

† ἀνθρωπάρεσκος.

Only in ψ 52:6 and Ps. Sol. 4:8, 10, 21, according to the context in the sense of one who reckons only with men and their power and who therefore seeks to please men and does not take God into account [1] (ψ 52:6 : ἐκεῖ φοβηθήσονται φόβον, οὗ οὐκ ἦν φόβος). Outside the Bible we have only ἄρεσκος. Def. in Aristot. Eth. Nic., II, 7, p. 1108a, 28; IV, 12, p. 1126b, 12 ff. : οἱ μὲν ἄρεσκοι δοκοῦσιν εἶναι οἱ πάντα πρὸς ἡδονὴν ἐπαινοῦντες καὶ οὐθὲν ἀντιτείνοντες, ἀλλ' οἰόμενοι δεῖν ἄλυποι τοῖς ἐντυγχάνουσιν εἶναι; cf. also Theophr. Char., 5. The word describes an attitude rather than a relation. It is to be distinguished from κόλαξ, which denotes one who seeks his own advantage by his attitude. In itself, however, ἄρεσκος too is *vox media*.

ἀνθρωπάρεσκος is the opposite of an incipient θεάρεσκος and denotes in Col. 3:22 and Eph. 6:6 one whose final norm, born of fear and quite natural in slaves, is striving to please those who are in superior authority. For Paul the service of men and the service of God are quite distinct, though the service of God points us back to calling.

† ἀρεσκεία.

This denotes the attitude of an ἄρεσκος, and like the latter it is often used *sensu malo*. Yet there are examples of a favourable sense in secular Gk. and Philo. [1] In the LXX it occurs only in Παροιμ. 29:48 parallel with κάλλος γυναικός.

Col. 1:10 : περιπατῆσαι ἀξίως τοῦ κυρίου εἰς πᾶσαν ἀρεσκείαν "to every kind of pleasing attitude" ; towards whom is not clearly specified.

† ἀρεστός.

"Acceptable" (used of the quality of goods [1] in the pap.), "pleasing," "agreeable," is found as early as Pythagoras in secular Gk. [2] In the LXX it denotes what God (or a man) accepts as pleasing, and it can thus be an expression of full freedom, Tob. 3:6 : κατὰ τὸ ἀρεστόν σου ποίησον μετ' ἐμοῦ.

In the NT it means "pleasing" as in Jn. 8:29; Ac. 6:2 (to God); 12:3 (to the Jews); 1 Jn. 3:22, where we have the par. τὰς ἐντολὰς αὐτοῦ τηρεῖν and τὰ ἀρεστὰ ἐνώπιον αὐτοῦ ποιεῖν. Elsewhere in the NT the compound is used.

† εὐάρεστος, † εὐαρεστέω.

εὐάρεστος, "well-pleasing," a term of the *koine*, common on inscr., Inschr. Priene, 114, 15 : γενηθεὶς δὲ εὐάρεσ[τος] ἐν τοῖς τῆς γυμνασιαρχίας ἀναλώμασιν. In Epict. it also means "content." As a note of quality it means "acceptable." In the LXX it occurs only in Wis. 4:10; 9:10.

ἀ ν θ ρ ω π ά ρ ε σ κ ο ς. Nägeli, 61.
[1] Theophil. Ad. Autol., III, 14 : τοὺς δὲ ποιοῦντας τὸ ἀγαθὸν διδάσκει (sc. Jesus) μὴ καυχᾶσθαι, ἵνα μὴ ἀνθρωπάρεσκοι ὦσιν, has rather a different slant.
ἀ ρ ε σ κ ε ί α. Deissmann NB, 51.
[1] P. Oxy., 729, 24 : ποιήσονται τοὺς ποτισμοὺς ... πρὸς ἀρεσκί[αν] τοῦ Σαραπίωνος. Philo Fug., 88 : ἕνεκα ἀρεσκείας Θεοῦ; cf. Op. Mund., 144; Spec. Leg., I, 176 and 317.
ἀ ρ ε σ τ ό ς. [1] P. Amh., II, 48, 8 (106 B.C.) of vessels.
[2] Stob. Ecl., IV, p. 277, 13 f.: οὐ γὰρ ἄλλα μὲν ἀρετὰ ποιεῖ τὰ ἀρεστὰ τῷ θεῷ.
ε ὐ α ρ ε σ τ έ ω. Rgg. Hb. on 11:5; Sickb. R.[4], 273.

In the NT it is used only once of acceptance by men, i.e., at Tt. 2:9 : δούλους ἰδίοις δεσπόταις ... εὐαρέστους εἶναι. Otherwise it is always used of God's attitude towards human conduct. It is characteristic of the NT, however, that only once is the judgment εὐάρεστος used retrospectively, i.e., at Phil. 4:18 : δεξάμενος ... θυσίαν δεκτήν, εὐάρεστον τῷ θεῷ. For Paul εὐάρεστος τῷ θεῷ (ἐνώπιον αὐτοῦ [Hb.], ἐν κυρίῳ) is a goal of the Christian walk, as in R. 12:1 f. : παραστῆσαι τὰ σώματα ὑμῶν θυσίαν ... τῷ θεῷ εὐάρεστον; R. 14:18 : ὁ ... ἐν τούτῳ δουλεύων τῷ Χριστῷ εὐάρεστος τῷ θεῷ; Col. 3:20 : ὑπακούετε τοῖς γονεῦσιν ... τοῦτο γὰρ εὐάρεστόν ἐστιν ἐν κυρίῳ; cf. Hb. 13:21: ποιῶν ἐν ἡμῖν τὸ εὐάρεστον ἐνώπιον αὐτοῦ. What is well-pleasing is affirmed in no casuistical sense to be what is ἄξιον τοῦ κυρίου. In both expressions Paul comprises both the goal and the motive of the Christian life, and he admonishes us in vital and continually new seeking to "test" what is εὐάρεστον, Eph. 5:10 : ὡς τέκνα φωτὸς περιπατεῖτε ... δοκιμάζοντες τί ἐστιν εὐάρεστον τῷ κυρίῳ, cf. 2 C. 5:9 : φιλοτιμούμεθα ... εὐάρεστοι αὐτῷ εἶναι; cf. also Hb. 12:28.

εὐαρεστέω (koine) in a sense often par. to ἀρέσκω. a. "to be well-pleasing" (secular Gk., Philo). b. "to take pleasure in something (τινί)," also "to be satisfied," as ἀρέσκεσθαί τινι, Diod. S., III, 55, 9 : τὴν μητέρα τῶν θεῶν εὐαρεστηθεῖσαν τῇ νήσῳ. c. "To walk well-pleasing" (in the LXX sometimes for הִתְהַלֵּךְ → ἀρέσκω).

Hb. 13:16 : τοιαύταις ... θυσίαις εὐαρεστεῖται ὁ θεός, as b. "to take pleasure in." Hb. 11:5 f. : μεμαρτύρηται (Enoch) εὐαρεστηκέναι τῷ θεῷ = c. "to walk well-pleasing," as shown by the continuation : χωρὶς δὲ πίστεως ἀδύνατον εὐαρεστῆσαι· πιστεῦσαι γὰρ δεῖ τὸν προσερχόμενον θεῷ, ὅτι ἔστιν καὶ τοῖς ἐκζητοῦσιν αὐτὸν μισθαποδότης γίνεται.

Foerster

† ἀρετή

A. ἀρετή outside the NT.

At the time of the NT the word ἀρετή had so many meanings that it gave rise to misunderstandings. When, e.g., we read Hesiod Op., 313 : πλούτῳ δ' ἀρετὴ

ἀ ρ ε τ ή. Deissmann LO, 270; B, 90 ff., 278; Clemen, 365 f.; U. v. Wilamowitz-Moellendorff, NGG (1898), 214 ff. and on this J. Ludwig, *Quae fuerit vocis* ἀρετή *vis ac natura ante Demosthenis exitum* (Diss. Leipzig, 1906); J. Stenzel, *Studien zur platonischen Dialektik, ... Arete und Diairesis* (1917). Art. "Sokrates," Pauly-W., 2 *Reihe*, III, 830; A. Kiefer, *Aretalogische Studien* (Diss. Freiburg, 1929), esp. 18 ff.; Nägeli, 69; A. Bonhöffer, *Epictet und das NT* (1911), 108 f.; L. Schmidt, *Die Ethik der alten Griechen*, I (1882), 295 ff.; E. Schwartz, *Das Geschichtswerk des Thucydides* (1919), esp. 351 ff.; also *Gnomon*, 2 (1926), 75 ff.; S. Reiter, "'Αρετή und der Titel von Philos 'Legatio'" in *Epitymbion, Heinrich Swoboda dargebracht* (1928), 228-237; Comm. on Phil. by Dib.[2] (1925) and Loh.[8] (1928). Def. : Aristot. Eth. Nic., II, 4 f.; cf. esp. p. 1106a, 14 ff. : ἡ τοῦ ἀνθρώπου ἀρετὴ εἴη ἂν ἕξις ἀφ' ἧς ἀγαθὸς ἄνθρωπος γίνεται καὶ ἀφ' ἧς εὖ τὸ ἑαυτοῦ ἔργον ἀποδώσει. Chrysipp. in Alex. Aphr. Fat., 26 (A. Gercke, *Jbch. f. klass. Phil. Suppl.*, 14 [1885], 740]; Plut. Aud. Poet., 6 (II, 24d). On the history of the meaning, M. Hoffmann, *Ethische Terminologie bei Homer, Hesiod, Jambikern und Tragikern* (Diss. Tübingen, 1914).

καὶ κῦδος ὀπηδεῖ, we might take it to mean that wealth and virtue are inseparably connected. Plutarch [1] at least credits such ideas of the young patrons of letters in his day. That later generations, for whom Greek was no longer their everyday speech, should be exposed to errors is obvious, and to this very day it is still difficult to decide in individual cases. [2]

Yet in spite of the ambiguity of the term we can pick out a single basic meaning. It might be rendered a. "eminence," [3] *quaelibet rei praestantia.* [4] It can refer to excellence of achievement, to mastery in a specific field, on the one side, or to endowment with higher power on the other, or often to both together. Thus a happy destiny is the result of fine achievement (Plut. → n. 1), and conversely achievement is a precondition of the good which is sought by all, of good fortune. [5]

The subject of achievement may be lands, animals, objects, parts of the body, but mostly it is man. Just as the ways in which the Greek world reflects on human achievement, on specifically human achievement, and indeed on man, are manifold and distinctive, so are the different contents of the word ἀρετή. Already in the time of Homer it is used to denote one particular human achievement, namely, b. "manliness" [6] or martial valour. In relation to the goal which it serves, this often comes to denote c. "merit," as in ἀρετῆς ἕνεκα with reference to rolls of honour. [7]

At the time of the Sophists the intellectual aspect of the term on the one side, and the ethical, dating from Socrates and Plato, on the other, achieve a prominence unknown in ancient Greece. It is now that the word acquires the particular meaning which becomes predominant and which primarily influences our own impression of it. ἀρετή becomes a leading tool in the language of Greek moral philosophy in the sense of d. "virtue." This is not the place for an evaluation either of this extraordinarily significant development or of the Greek concept of virtue. [8] It should be pointed out, however, that the concept could not be a matter of indifference to Hellenistic Judaism. It formed an important medium in the dealings of Judaism with the Hellenistic world, in its struggle for it and proselytising within it.

Philo made frequent and emphatic use of it. [9] In his case the concept remained

---

[1] In section 6 of the work Aud. Poet. (II, 24d), which is most instructive for the word ἀρετή.

[2] Cf. the excellent art. by Pass. and Pape in their more recent dictionaries.

[3] So also Cr.[1-3]. The word ἀρε-τή is etymologically connected with ἀρέ-σκω, ἤρε-σα, ἄρ-ιστος, cf. A. Walde, *Vergleichendes Wörterbuch der indogermanischen Sprachen,* I (1930), 69.

[4] F. W. Sturz, *Lex Xenophonteum* (1801 ff.) *s.v.*

[5] Hes. Op., 313 and in general 274-326, as also in the well-known statement: τῆς δ' ἀρετῆς ἱδρῶτα θεοὶ προπάροιθεν ἔθηκαν (289), cf. esp. Wilamowitz, *op. cit.* Cf. also ἀρετᾶν, Hom. Od., 8, 329; 19, 108.

[6] Common also in Jos. (Bell., 3, 380; 4, 325 etc.).

[7] IG, II², 107 etc.; cf. Xenoph. An., I, 4, 8 : τῆς πρόσθεν ἕνεκα περὶ ἐμὲ ἀρετῆς.

[8] Reference should be made particularly to the hymn of Aristotle : Ἀρετά, πολύμοχθε γένει βροτέωι ... Diehl, Anth. Lyr., I, 101, 16; here we have a grand and comprehensive review of the nature of Greek ἀρετή generally, both heroic and philosophical ; cf. U. v. Wilamowitz, *Aristoteles und Athen,* II (1893), 405 ff.; W. Jaeger, *Aristoteles* (1923), 119. On the whole theme, *v.* R. Eisler, *Wörterbuch der philosophischen Begriffe,* III, 4th ed. K. Koretz (1930), 274 ff.; L. Schmidt, E. Schwartz, *op. cit.*

[9] *v.* Index in Cohn-Wendland, VII. Cf. also Jos. on the content of the Baptist's preaching: ... τοὺς Ἰουδαίους κελεύοντα ἀρετὴν ἐπασκοῦντας βαπτισμῷ συνιέναι, Ant., 18, 117,

wholly within the limits set by Greek use. Yet this is hardly characteristic of Hellenistic Judaism generally. In other circles there are movements towards a more strongly religious use with more distinctive Jewish colouring. ἀρετή approximates to → δικαιοσύνη, which elsewhere is logically subordinate to it as one of the four cardinal virtues. Indeed, the two words become almost equivalents. [10] Moreover recollection of the great age of the Maccabees made ἀρετή a useful term to describe the fidelity of the heroes of faith in life and death.

In 2 Macc. 10:28 ἀρετή, together with ἐπὶ τὸν κύριον καταφυγή, is esp. a guarantee of victory as sheer θυμός (unless we are to take it as under f.); in 4 Macc. 7:22 we have the par. διὰ τὴν ἀρετὴν πάντα πόνον ὑπομένειν and ... περικρατήσειεν τῶν παθῶν διὰ τὴν εὐσέβειαν. 4 Macc. 9:8 : ... διὰ τῆσδε τῆς κακοπαθείας καὶ ὑπομονῆς τὰ τῆς ἀρετῆς ἆθλα οἴσομεν; cf. 1:8; 12:15; 9:18 : διὰ πασῶν γὰρ ὑμᾶς πείσω τῶν βασάνων, ὅτι μόνοι οἱ παῖδες Ἑβραίων ὑπὲρ ἀρετῆς εἰσιν ἀνίκητοι; 10:10 : ἡμεῖς ... διὰ παιδείαν καὶ ἀρετὴν θεοῦ ταῦτα πάσχομεν. [11] For ἀρετή without this special flavour, cf. 2 Macc. 15:12 : Ὀνίαν ... ἄνδρα καλὸν καὶ ἀγαθὸν ... ἐκ παιδὸς ἐκμεμελετηκότα τὰ τῆς ἀρετῆς οἰκεῖα; 4 Macc. 1:2 : τῆς μεγίστης ἀρετῆς, λέγω δὲ φρονήσεως; cf. Heracl. Fr., 112 (I, 99, 10, Diels): τὸ φρονεῖν ἀρετὴ μεγίστη. For divine ἀρετή in contrast to the impurity of pagan gods, cf. Jos. Ant., I, 23 : ἀκραιφνῆ τὴν ἀρετὴν ἔχοντα τὸν θεόν.

In the last resort the fidelity of the martyr is just as much a divine gift as a moral achievement. Though the concept is not uniform, and is perhaps more easily appreciated than stated, we undoubtedly have here a distinctive use which must have had quite a considerable influence, the more so as Wisdom and Maccabees, the books in which we find it, became biblical writings.

If meaning d. became the main meaning, others could still maintain themselves and develop alongside it. Religiously it is important that from a very early stage reference could be made to the ἀρετή of the gods. [12] Later the ἀρετή of a god often came to signify in particular e. his "self-declaration" as such. [13] ἀρετή thus came to be linked with → δύναμις, as a more comprehensive synonym, [14] in relation to powerful divine operation. This meaning was in view [15] when ἀρεταλογία was used in the religious sense.

---

and on this passage R. Eisler : Ἰησοῦς βασιλεὺς οὐ βασιλεύσας, II (1930), 59; Ap. 2, 151.

[10] Esp. Wis. 8:7: ... εἰ δικαιοσύνην ἀγαπᾷ τις, οἱ πόνοι ταύτης (scil. σοφίας) εἰσὶν ἀρεταί, and there then follow σωφροσύνη, φρόνησις, δικαιοσύνη (here as one of the cardinal virtues alongside others) and ἀνδρεία; 4 Macc. 13:24 : νόμῳ γὰρ τῷ αὐτῷ παιδευθέντες, καὶ τὰς αὐτὰς ἐξασκήσαντες ἀρετάς, καὶ τῷ δικαίῳ συντραφέντες βίῳ ... In Wis. 5:13 ἀρετή is the opp. of κακία; cf. also ἀρετὴ δικαιοσύνης, Herm. m., 1, 2 etc. (v. Pr.-Bauer).

[11] Cf. Cr.-Kö., 163.

[12] Hom. Il., 9, 498. ἀρετή is proper to supernatural beings ; the continuation of the verse quoted on p. 457 f. is as follows : δαίμονι δ' οἷος ἔησθα.

[13] Ditt. Syll.³, 1151, 2 : Ἀθηνάαι Μένεια ἀνέθηκεν ὄψιν ἰδοῦσα ἀρετὴν τῆς θεοῦ — acc. to Kiefer, op. cit., 21 at the latest from the middle of the 4th cent. B.C.; 1172, 10 (Note 8); 1173, 5 : ζῶσαι ἀρεταί; CIG, 2715 : ἀγάλματα ... παρέχοντα τῆς θείας δυνάμεως ἀρετάς from the earliest imperial period, cf. Deissmann B, 277 ff.; P. Oxy., XI, 1382; Philo Som., I, 256; Jos. Ant., 18, 266 : θεοῦ πεισθέντες ἀρετῇ; 17, 130; Preis. Zaub., V, 418 ff.: ὄφρα τε μαντοσύνας ταῖς σαῖς ἀρεταῖσι λάβοιμι.

[14] Philo Spec. Leg., I, 209 : τῶν θείων δυνάμεων καὶ ἀρετῶν; Vit. Cont., 26 : τῶν θείων ἀρετῶν καὶ δυνάμεων.

[15] Probably without corresponding in this respect to the true sense of the word ἀρεταλογία, v. Kiefer, op. cit., 37.

ἀρετή also means fortune, success (Hom. Od., 13, 45), a good worth seeking, especially in the sense of special prominence among men, i.e., f. "fame." [16] It thus comes to be synon. with → δόξα. [17] The Greek translation of the OT uses it only in this sense. It is the equivalent of הוֹד [18] and תְּהִלָּה. [19] From the simultaneous existence of meanings d. and f. we can see the extraordinary range of the term. The man of true virtue is above what others say; virtue and praise are radically different and even conflicting; [20] yet the one word can signify both.

B. ἀρετή in the NT.

To understand the few passages where ἀρετή is used in the NT it is important that the LXX applies the Greek concept of virtue in a distinctive way. Even more significant, however, is the negative fact that the LXX use is purely tentative and that there is no real place for ἀρετή = virtue in the translation of the OT. For a world in which man constantly saw himself morally responsible before a holy God the Greek concept of virtue could not finally fulfil its apparent promise. Though not irreligious, [21] it was far too anthropocentric and this-worldly in orientation. What both the OT and NT attest is not human achievements or merits but the acts of God. Thus in the whole of Pauline literature with its wealth of exhortation the word occurs only once and quite incidentally in Phil. 4:8: ... εἴ τις ἀρετὴ καὶ εἴ τις ἔπαινος, ταῦτα λογίζεσθε. Here the proximity of ἀρετή and ἔπαινος is perhaps Greek, [22] but hardly their co-ordination. And if the preceding concepts, ἀληθῆ σεμνά etc., are co-ordinated with ἀρετή rather than subordinated to it, there is a clear distinction between what Paul has in view and Greek ἀρετή (→ sense f.). The precise understanding depends upon whether we think the series has a more secular or a more religious ring. [23] If the latter, then we have an echo of the usage noted in the LXX. ἀρετή is the attitude which the righteous must maintain in life and death. The same is true in relation to the only other passage in which there is reference to human ἀρετή, i.e., 2 Pt. 1:5: ... ἐπιχορηγήσατε ἐν τῇ πίστει ὑμῶν τὴν ἀρετήν, ἐν δὲ τῇ ἀρετῇ τὴν γνῶσιν. Here a notable formal analogy points us to the secular world, [24] to the sphere of "virtue." Yet it is almost certain that in this passage πίστις is more than the secular parallel ("fidelity") and consequently a similar distinction is likely in the case of ἀρετή.

---

[16] → the passages mentioned on 457 f., and n. 1; Soph. Phil., 1420: ἀθάνατος ἀρετή.
[17] v. Wettstein on 1 Pt. 1:3.
[18] Hab. 3:3; Zech. 6:13.
[19] ἀρεταί = תְּהִלָּה, Is. 42:8, 12; 43:21: λαόν μου ὃν περιεποιησάμην τὰς ἀρετάς μου διηγεῖσθαι (cf. Εσθ. C. 21). ἀρεταί = תְּהִלֹּת, Is. 63:7: τὸν ἔλεον κυρίου ἐμνήσθην, τὰς ἀρετὰς Κυρίου ἐν πᾶσιν οἷς ὁ κύριος ἡμῖν ἀνταποδίδωσιν. In the two last passages the translator may also have had sense e. in view. In Sir. 36:19 the word ἀρεταλογία is used for הוֹד synon. with δόξα (→ n. 15) and here, too, we probably have a suggestion of both e. and f.
[20] Although naturally, in different words, they often occur together, e.g., Aristot. Eth. Nic., I, 13, p. 1103a, 4 ff.; Eth. M., I, 5, p. 1185b, 5 f.; Eth. Eud., II, 1, p. 1220a, 5 f. Cf. Loh. Phil., 175.
[21] L. Schmidt, op. cit.
[22] → n. 20. Cf. also the series in Cic. Tusc., V, 23, 67: bonum autem mentis est virtus ... hinc omnia, quae pulchra, honesta, praeclara sunt ... plena gaudiorum sunt.
[23] Cf. the comm. of Dib. and Loh.
[24] Ditt. Or., 438: ἄνδρα ἀγαθὸν γενόμενον καὶ διενένκαντα πίστει καὶ ἀρετῇ καὶ δικαιοσύνῃ καὶ εὐσεβείᾳ καὶ ... τὴν πλείστην εἰσενηνεγμένον σπουδήν.

In the same chapter we read just before with reference to God (v. 3): τοῦ καλέσαντος ἡμᾶς ἰδίᾳ δόξῃ καὶ ἀρετῇ. Here again there is a parallel[25] which points to close contact with the non-Christian world; in both cases the term is to be rendered according to sense e. In 1 Pt. 2:9: ὅπως τὰς ἀρετὰς ἐξαγγείλητε τοῦ ἐκ σκότους ὑμᾶς καλέσαντος, this is again the most likely meaning, though f. must also be considered in view of the clear echo of Is. 43:21 LXX (→ n. 19).

In the period after the NT Hermas especially used the term in sense d. (→ n. 10).

Bauernfeind

ἀρήν → 340

ἀριθμέω, ἀριθμός

In the NT these words are often used in the literal sense of "to count" or "to reckon," and "sum" or "number" (Mt. 10:30; Ac. 11:21; R. 9:27; Rev. 5:11).

1. Only in one passage in the NT (Rev. 13:17, 18) does ἀριθμός have special theological significance. These verses, which are variously interpreted, raise the difficult problem of sacred numbers.[1] This cannot be discussed in detail in the present context; some brief remarks must suffice. In spite of all the efforts of many investigators, no satisfactory solution has been found. There can be no doubt, however, that originally numbers are purely secular in character. They are a means of mastering many everyday matters. Counting is not originally an act of thought, but a process in concrete reality. Primitive man can count only when he uses his fingers and toes or such material aids as stones, sticks, knots, or notches. Before an abstract system of numbering was invented, man simply took as many pebbles as he had objects in view. The Lat. *calculus,* from which our word "to calculate" derives, points us back to this primitive sphere. It simply means pebble, or figuratively a stone for counting. In some way, however, man came to sense either a power or a regularity behind numbers, perhaps because some of them recur in definite sequences. Because he could not properly grasp this regularity, that which he could not comprehend in numbers was for him a mystery. He read a potency into them, as in the case of the letters of the alphabet.[2] Thus

---

[25] CIG, 2715 (1st cent. B.C.); cf. Deissmann LO, 270. There too, before the passage quoted in n. 13, as also in Ditt. Or., 438 (→ n. 24), and cf. 2 Pt. 1:5, we have the expression: σπουδὴν πᾶσαν εἰσφέρεσθαι.

ἀριθμέω κτλ. [1] The vast literature is briefly reviewed in O. Rühle, RGG², V (1931), 2068. Some of the most important books may be mentioned: E. Fettweis, *Das Rechnen der Naturvölker* (1927); W. Wundt, *Völkerpsychologie,* I, 2 (1900), 25 ff.; II, 3 (1909), 530 ff.; also *Elemente der Völkerpsychologie* (1912), 304 ff.; E. Cassirer, *Philosophie der symbolischen Formen,* III (1929), 396 ff.; ERE, IX, 406 ff.; RE³, XXI, 598 ff.

[2] F. Dornseiff, *Das Alphabet in Mystik und Magie²* (1925), where further bibl. data may be found.

we have the sacred numbers which meet us at every turn in magic and religion even though it cannot be said why individual numbers like 3, 7, 9 etc. should be given such preference.

The individual numbers which occur in the NT are treated in special articles (→ εἷς; → τρεῖς; → ἑπτά; → δέκα; → δώδεκα; → ἑβδομήκοντα). In general there are three characteristic features of the use of numbers in the NT. First, a new content has been given to them by NT events (1[Lord] and 3 [days]). Secondly, in accordance with the total situation of early Christianity as a fulfilment and yet also an offshoot of the religion of the OT, the inherited symbolism is refashioned (12). Thirdly, the symbolism has become predominantly formal, so that the numbers are either "round" numbers or purely stylistic (7 and 3½; 10 and 5).[3] In the present article our concern is with the meaning of Rev. 13:17, 18. In Revelation there is a strong and distinctive symbolism and mysticism of numbers.[4] The number 7 is particularly dominant (→ ἑπτά),[5] but 10 (→ δέκα), and also 12 and its multiple 144 (→ δώδεκα) may also be mentioned.

2. The special problem of Rev. 13:18 is the solving of the "gematric" puzzle behind the number 666. Gematria[6] is a procedure in which the letters of a word are given numerical values which together give the ἀριθμός of the word concerned. Conversely the word can be replaced by a numerical value and the gematric art consists in calculating it. This is a difficult task since every number presents us with a variety of possibilities. For this reason it was a favourite procedure in the ancient world to present numerically a name that one wished to keep secret. T. Zahn gives us an excellent and instructive example. In excavations at Pompeii a wall inscription was found with the declaration of love φιλῶ ἧς ἀριθμός φμε. "The name of the lover is concealed; the beloved will know it when she recognises her name in the sum of the numerical value of the 3 letters φμε, i.e., 545 (φ = 500 + μ = 40 + ε = 5). But the passing stranger does not know in the very least who the beloved is, nor does the 19th century investigator know which of the many Greek feminine names she bore. For he does not know how many letters there are in the name which gives us the total of 545 when added numerically."[7] It may also be recalled that in Sib., I, 326-330 the number 888 appears as a symbol for Jesus (ι = 10 + η = 8 + σ = 200 + ο = 70 + υ = 400 + σ = 200). In gematria a good deal depends on correct guessing. Hence it is well adapted for riddles, as shown by countless examples from classical and Hellenistic[8] and indeed Rabbinic literature.[9] The most important riddle of this kind is posed by Rev. 13:18 with the number 666.

---

[3] Cf. G. Kittel in *Rabbinica* (1920), 31-47. Instances from Roman literature may be found in T. Birt, *Rhein Museum für Philologie,* NF, 70 (1915), 253 ff.

[4] Apart from the comm., cf. esp. F. Boll, "Aus der Offenbarung Johannis," *Stoicheia,* 1 (1914).

[5] It is going too far to make 7 the formal principle of Rev., as Lohmeyer does.

[6] Cf. esp. Dornseiff, *op. cit.,* 91 ff. (§ 7).

[7] Zn. Apk., 461. Zn. gives many other pertinent examples from classical literature. Cf. esp. Dornseiff, *op. cit.,* 96 ff.

[8] Dornseiff, *op. cit.,* 108 ff.

[9] Weber, 121; Zn. Apk., 459 f.; A. Wuensche, "Pesikta des Rab. Kahana," in *Bibliotheca Rabbinica,* 30-32 (1885), 299 f.; EJ, VII (1931), 172 f.; JE, V, 589 ff. Some observations on numbers in older Judaism may be found in L. Blau, *Das altjüdische Zauberwesen* (1898), 44 ff., 73 f., 137 ff.

Interpretation is made more difficult by textual variation. C and some minusc. have 616 instead of 666. Yet the latter is better attested and is thus to be preferred.[10] Indeed, apart from textual evidence ἑξακόσιοι ἑξήκοντα ἕξ is more in keeping with the style of Rev. On the other hand, 616 is not a scribal error, as Iren. suggests (V, 30, 1). It is a deliberate correction with a view to linking the number with a particular emperor. Gaius Caesar, usually known as Caligula, is identified therein as antichrist. The numerical value of his name in Greek (Γαιος Καισαρ) gives us 616 (γ = 3 + α = 1 + ι = 10 + ο = 70 + σ = 200 + κ = 20 + α = 1 + ι = 10 + σ = 200 + α = 1 + ρ = 100, total 616).[11] Caligula reigned from 37 to 41 A.D. and was an archetype of cruelty, an arrogant blasphemer and irreligious tyrant, so that the champions of the reading 616 had material grounds for finding antichrist in him.[12] On the other hand, this interpretation would give us an impossibly early date for Revelation, and we must accept the reading 666.

Theologians have given free rein to their imagination in relation to this number. There can be no certainty whether it is based on the Gk. or the Heb. alphabet, and an infinite number of names can be deduced from it. Most of the more or less phantastic suggestions may be ignored;[13] we can only refer briefly to some of the most important. Irenaeus[14] vacillates between Εὐάνθας (no longer identifiable), Λατεῖνος (the Roman empire) and Τεῖταν (Titus). His vacillation shows that there was no fixed tradition at the end of the 2nd cent. Τεῖταν is orthographically impossible for Titus, and a collective like the Roman empire is quite out of the question, since the text tells us plainly that this is an ἀριθμὸς ἀνθρώπου. The latter consideration enables us to dismiss the conjectures of Gunkel,[15] who suggests the chaos of primeval time, and Deissmann,[16] who sees in the θηρίον the institution of Roman imperialism. It is true that θηρίον in Heb. gives us exactly the numerical value of 666 (ת = 400 + ר = 200 + י = 10 + ו = 6 + ן = 50),[17] but this in itself is not enough, since the text plainly indicates a human figure. Hugo Grotius[18] suggested the emperor Trajan, whose family name Ulpius, written in Gk., gives us the requisite 666.[19] There is greater intrinsic probability in the reference to Nero, which goes back to Hitzig and Reuss and is still supported by many scholars, including Hadorn.[20] If we use the Heb. alphabet, נרון קסר gives us the following addition: נ = 50 + ר = 200 + ו = 6 + ן = 50 + ק = 100 + ס = 60 + ר = 200, total 666. It is incontestable that by his character and evil actions Nero makes a realistic antichrist. Yet there are objections to this view. Even to write קסר for καισαρ is open to criticism on the ground that the omission of י is arbitrary. Above all T. Zahn[21] points out that it was only in the 2nd cent. A.D. that the legend of Nero *redivivus* arose.

---

[10] As against F. Spitta, *Off. Joh.* (1889), 392, who argues that 616 is original.

[11] Cf. Zn. Apk., 474.

[12] *Ibid.,* 475 ff.

[13] Lists may be found in Zn. Apk. and Bss. Apk., 370 ff. Where mere guessing may take us is satirically shown by G. Salmon (*Historical Introduction to the Books of the NT* [1885], 298 [quoted in Zn. Apk., 472, n. 93]) when he points out that the name of the Irish patriot Parnell gives us the number 666 if only we double the 'r' and write the name in Gk. Παρρνελλος.

[14] Iren., V, 30, 3.

[15] H. Gunkel, *Schöpfung und Chaos* (1895), 375 ff.

[16] Deissmann LO, 238.

[17] Had. Apk., 146.

[18] H. Grotius, *Annotationes ad NT* (1641). Cf. Zn. Apk., 502, n. 52.

[19] Hadorn originally took this view independently of Grotius (ZNW, 19 [1919/20], 11 ff.), but abandoned it in his comm. on Rev. on the decisive ground that the book could not have been written as late as the reign of Trajan (98-117).

[20] Had. Apk., 147.

[21] Zn. Apk., 490 ff.

A very different solution has been proposed by G. A. van den Bergh van Eysinga [22] on the basis of the so-called triangular number. This is the number which results as the sum of consecutive numbers from 1. Thus 10 is the triangular number of 4, since the sum of 1-4 is 10. On this reckoning 666 is the triangular number of 36 and 36 of 8. Now it belongs to the nature and symbolism of the triangular number that it has the same meaning as the last of the consecutive numbers which constitute it. Thus we have the equation 666 ⊨ 36 ⊨ 8. And there can be no doubt as to the meaning of 8 in the Apocalypse; it is the number of the beast from the abyss. Thus 666 is simply a symbolical way of referring to antichrist. [23] This explanation is not unattractive in view of the fact that the symbolism and magic of triangular numbers were common enough in the Hellenistic period. [24] It breaks down, however, on the simple requirement of the text: ἀριθμὸς ἀνθρώπου.

In conclusion, it may be said that all the solutions proposed are unsatisfactory. Indeed, it may be asked whether it is worth proceding along these lines, since all such attempts must be hypothetical. Ought we not to accept the fact that the divine was writing for his own age and that we are thus confronted with a puzzle which could be solved only by a few initiates from his own circle who were acquainted with his lines of thought? Or may it be that the whole passage is to be taken purely eschatologically in the sense that σοφία, the divine wisdom which we need for understanding in addition to νοῦς, will be given to believers only at the supposedly imminent end of the days, when they will see the mystery directly?

Rühle

| ἀρκέω, ἀρκετός, |
| αὐτάρκεια, αὐτάρκης |

ἀρκέω, ἀρκετός.

In the first instance this is an external [1] expression of "satisfaction" or "contentment". In philosophical and religious reflection, however, it has within itself the tendency to become a radical demand or admonition. This can take place in various ways.

1. The demand is that man should be content with the goods allotted to him by fate or by God; that he should exercise ἀρκεῖσθαι τοῖς παροῦσι; that he should ask no more than he is given. Such statements may be either Christian or non-Christian maxims. The difference lies in the general view which gives rise to them. Thus we may have merely the prudent suppression of passion and desire, as when Josephus, to avoid bloodshed, warns the rebels: ἀρκουμένους τοῖς

---

[22] ZNW, 13 (1912), 293 ff.
[23] More recently approved by Lohmeyer, cf. Loh. Apk. (1925), 114 f.
[24] Examples from Philo etc. may be found in Loh. Apk., 202 (App. 9).

ἀ ρ κ έ ω κτλ. Wnd. 2 K., 390 f.; Schl. Mt., 342, J., 294; G. A. Gerhard, Phoinix v. Kolophon (1909), 56 f.
[1] E.g., Mt. 25:9: (τὸ ἔλαιον) οὐ μὴ ἀρκέσῃ; Aesch. Pers., 278: οὐδὲν γὰρ ἦρκει τόξα.

ἑαυτῶν ἐφοδίοις, Vit., 244. Or we may have the freedom from want of the philosopher to whom external goods are incidental. A favourite expression is as follows: ἀρκεῖσθαι τοῖς παροῦσι (e.g., Teles, p. 11, 5; 38, 10; 41, 12, Hense; M. Ant., VI, 30, 9: ὡς ὀλίγοις ἀρκούμενος, οἷον οἰκήσει, στρωμνῇ, ἐσθῆτι, τροφῇ, ὑπηρεσίᾳ. Stob. Ecl., III, 273, 2: (Epaminondas) ὁ τούτοις ἀρκούμενος.

For the NT this freedom from want is grounded in God; His provision is sufficient. Hb. 13:5: ἀρκούμενοι τοῖς παροῦσιν (→ supra), "for he hath said, I will never leave thee, nor forsake thee"; 1 Tm. 6:8; cf. also Mt. 6:34: ἀρκετὸν τῇ ἡμέρᾳ ἡ κακία αὐτῆς (on the basis of v. 32: οἶδεν γὰρ ὁ πατὴρ ὑμῶν ...). The thought of content is underlined by reference to imminent retribution, as in the preaching of the Baptist in Lk. 3:14.

Between the philosopher and the eschatological believer of the NT stands the teacher of the Torah who from Sabbath to Sabbath is satisfied with a carob-bean, bTaan, 24b.: R. Jehuda in the name of Rab: "Every day a voice (בַּת־קוֹל)[2] rings out and says: the whole world is nourished for the sake of my son Chanina, and my son Chanina is satisfied (דַּי לוֹ)[3] with a carob-bean from the evening before the Sabbath to the next evening before the Sabbath."

2. The admonition to be content can easily change into a warning against becoming secure and complacent in the illusion of sufficiency. Epict. Diss., I, 6, 14: ἐκείνοις μὲν ἀρκεῖ τὸ ἐσθίειν καὶ πίνειν ... ἡμῖν δ' ... οὐκέτι ταῦτ' ἀπαρκεῖ. Biblical statements are numerous but for the most part they do not use the stem ἀρκ-. Cf. Hos. 12:8 f.; 13:6; Sir. 5:1 (→ αὐτάρκης); Lk. 6:25; 12:19; Rev. 3:17 (→ ἐμπεπλησμένος, πλούσιος etc.).

3. The religious connection is brought out when contentment is linked with a supreme philosophical or religious good. For here the statement concerning what suffices expresses particularly clearly the profoundest character of the underlying view of life. For the philosopher supreme content is to fashion his life in accordance with his φύσις or δαίμων. M. Ant., II, 13, 1: ὅτι ἀρκεῖ πρὸς μόνῳ τῷ ἔνδον ἑαυτοῦ δαίμονι εἶναι καὶ τοῦτον γνησίως θεραπεύειν. VIII, 1, 3: ἀρκέσθητι δέ, εἰ κἂν τὸ λοιπὸν τοῦ βίου ..., ὡς ἡ φύσις σου θέλει, βιώσῃ, IX, 26: ἀρκεῖσθαι τῷ σῷ ἡγεμονικῷ. To the degree that the force working in the philosopher is regarded as a gift of deity, the ἀρκεῖ μοι is related to it and the statement of content becomes a concentrated expression of religious union with God and the spirituality implanted in man by Him. Epict. Diss., I, 1, 12 f. (Zeus speaking to the philosopher): ἐδώκαμέν σοι μέρος τι ἡμέτερον, τὴν δύναμιν ταύτην τὴν ὁρμητικήν τε καὶ ἀφορμητικήν ... ἀρκῇ οὖν αὐτοῖς, IV, 10, 14 ff.: ἃς ἔλαβον ἀφορμὰς παρά σου ... ἐφ' ὅσον ἐχρησάμην τοῖς σοῖς, ἀρκεῖ μοι ... σὰ γὰρ ἦν πάντα, σύ μοι αὐτὰ δέδωκας. οὐκ ἀρκεῖ οὕτως ἔχοντα ἐξελθεῖν. Iambl. Vit. Pyth., 1: ἐξαρκεῖ ἡμῖν ἡ τῶν θεῶν βούλησις.

At certain levels OT piety knows similar moods, cf. Solomon's prayer in 1 K. 3:6 ff. with its description of the wisdom of moderation, or Ps. 131 with its

---

[2] Content is often enjoined by a divine voice, either through the direct Word of the κύριος (as in Dt. 3:26 and related Rabbinic exegesis; cf. also 2 C. 12:9), or by the voice from heaven, (as supra and cf. bMeg. 3a on R. Jonatan ben Uzziel).

[3] The use of the Heb. and Talmudic דַּי with suffix is close to the impers. ἀρκεῖ and fully equivalent in content (cf. Schlatter, op. cit.). Prv. 25:16: Mas דְּבַשׁ מָצָאתָ אֱכֹל דַּיֶּךָ= LXX μέλι εὑρὼν φάγε τὸ ἱκανόν.

depiction of the quiet content of the righteous. More powerful however, in accordance with the character of this religion, is recollection of the guidance of God and the resultant readiness to do His will (Ps. 73:23 ff.). For Jewish exegesis an excellent example of the demand for religious satisfaction in God is to be found in God's answer to Moses' request that he may enter the land. In the original Dt. 3:26 : רַב־לָךְ, LXX : ἱκανούσθω σοι, is simply a prohibition of any further asking. [4] In Rabbinic exegesis, however, it is partly related to previous divine guidance and partly to divine grace and the future eschatological gift with which Moses should be content. M. Ex., 17, 14 : "rab lak — be content (דַּיֶּיךָ) [3] for thyself thus far ; R. Joshua said : rab lak — be content with the coming world." Similarly S. Dt., 29 on 3:26; Midr. Tann., Dt. 3:26, p. 18, Hoffmann : "rab lak — be content that the evil impulse has no power over thee, yea rather that I will not deliver thee into the hand of the angel of death, but will Myself be with thee." The same basic structure may be seen in the fine paraphrase of Gn. 17:1 preserved in Gn. r., 46 : "Then spake the Holy One, blessed be He : Abraham, be content (דַּיֶּיךָ) that I am thy God, be content that I am thy Protector. And not thou only, but the whole world should be content (דַּיּוֹ) that I am its God ; the whole world should be content that I am its Protector." [5]

Similarly the corresponding NT passages are a faithful reflection of the view of God and the understanding of life mirrored in them. At Jn. 14:8 to be shown whose being is described by the name of πατήρ is the final ἀρκεῖν which embraces or renders superfluous all other gifts. At 2 C. 12:9 all the sufficiency of the apostle is found in participation in the χάρις given to the ἀσθενής — and here, too, we have a reflection of Paul's thinking on the nature of God and the nature of man, just as the opinion of the Stoics is similarly declared in analogous statements. [6]

† αὐτάρκεια, † αὐτάρκης.

1. The word is both a central concept in ethical discussion from the time of Socrates and yet also a well-worn term in ordinary usage. In Cynic and Stoic philosophy it denotes one who exercises → ἀρκεῖσθαι in relation to his own inner possibility and who thus becomes an independent man sufficient to himself and in need of none else. Aristot. Pol., VII, 5, p. 1326b, 29 f. : τὸ γὰρ πάντα ὑπάρχειν καὶ δεῖσθαι μηδενὸς αὐτάρκες. The word is par. to σωφροσύνη and εὐταξία : Epict. Gnom. Stob. Fr., 33, Elter (p. 481, Schenkl); to other virtues, M. Ant., III, 11, 3; to ἐλεύθερος and ἀπαθής, ibid., VI, 16, 8. It is the opp. of τρυφή, Epict., op. cit.; of φιλαργυρία, Gnom. Byz., 209, p. 200, Wachsm.; of ἐνδεής, Plat. Resp., II, 369b.

In everyday speech this pregnant sense is weakened to that of "satisfactory competence" or more generally "sufficient quantity." Jos. Ant., 2, 259 (sufficient water), Sir. 34:28 (wine), 40:18 (work), Παρ. 24:31 (livelihood). Ps. Sol. 5:18 : μνημονεύει ὁ

---

[4] It is already rather more in the LXX ; cf. Wnd. 2 K., 391.

[5] On the meanings of אֵל שַׁדַּי which to some degree point to αὐτάρκης, → αὐτάρκης, 467.

[6] Closest to Paul is the above-mentioned version of the Midr. Tannaim on Dt. 3:26. The philosophical statements may be said to "have a wholly Pauline ring" (Wnd., 390) only if we completely ignore their content.

α ὐ τ ά ρ κ ε ι α, α ὐ τ ά ρ κ η ς. Wnd. 2 K., 278; Loh. Phil., 180; Nägeli, 41 f.; Moult.-Mill., 93; H. J. Wicks, Exp. T., 29 (1917/18), 424.

θεὸς ἐν συμμετρίᾳ αὐταρκίας (sufficient). Sir. 5:1 warns those who rely on riches and says: αὐτάρκη μοί ἐστιν. Numerous examples are found in the pap. [1]

2. As distinct from the rich philosophical usage, the NT term seems first to have only the sense of a capacity for external contentment and privation. Yet this almost banal virtue of αὐτάρκεια is set in a new light by becoming a constituent part of εὐσέβεια (1 Tm. 6:6). What this means is made plain in Phil. 4:11-13. Πάντα ἰσχύω (v. 13) seems to be fully identical with the philosophical αὐτάρκης ἐν παντί, M. Ant., I, 16, 11. Yet the root is ἐν τῷ ἐνδυναμοῦντί με. From a concept of God and redemption which wholly affirms creation there arises a perspective on which even what is philosophically superfluous [2] is the gift and purpose of Christ. Not merely the πεινᾶν but also the χορτάζεσθαι, not merely the ταπεινοῦσθαι but also the περισσεύειν (v. 12), is the object of this new religious αὐτάρκεια. [3] How it works out is described in 2 C. 9:8. Enough means not only a sufficiency for oneself but what can also be given to one's brothers. The Christian αὐτός cannot be considered in isolation. His αὐτ-άρκεια arises only when the ἄλλος has a share in it.

3. The inner motifs of Judaism emerge clearly in the exegetical attempts at a clear interpretation of the divine name אֵל שַׁדָּי. The starting-point is the disjunction of the word into שֶׁ and דַּי (→ ἀρκέω), on the basis of which 'Α, Σ, Θ, and sometimes the LXX (Ju. 1:20 f.) translate ὁ ἱκανός. Here the philosophical ideal of the αὐτάρκης is transferred to God as the One who is independent in His omnipotence and self-sufficient. But such sufficiency can also be attributed by R. Levi to Abraham, in whom there is nothing blameworthy except his uncircumcision; [4] and this follows expressly [5] from the translation ἱκανός in 'Α. At the same time the interpretation of שדי = ἱκανός takes other directions: God, for whose Godhead the world and its fulness do not suffice (R. Eliezer b. Jacob); God who said to the world and heaven and earth: Enough! (R. Jishaq); God who said to human suffering: Enough! (R. Hoshaja). [6] In this exegesis, therefore, we not only have the motif of self-sufficiency either with reference to God or the righteous, but also the motifs of the Infinite, of the almighty Creator, and of the One who is merciful to man.

Kittel

---

[1] For examples, *v.* Preisigke Wört., 239 and Moult.-Mill., 93.
[2] For a different view, *v.* Windisch *ad loc.*: "Paul actualises the Stoic ideal."
[3] Loh., *ad loc.*: "Not impassibility but supreme passibility, not the unimportance but the importance of these things, is the motif in these statements."
[4] R. Levi explains this sufficiency by comparing it with the beauty of a woman whose only defect was that the nail of her little finger was too long: "Cut it off, and the defect is remedied." Hence the circumcision of Abraham.
[5] So Gn.r., 46 on 17:1: (ἱκανός) ואנקס (ἄξιος) תרגום אקילוס אכסיוס אקילוס אכסיוס.
[6] *Loc. cit.*; also Gn.r., 92 on 43:14.

---

† Ἀρ Μαγεδών [1]

Mt. Magedon (only at Rev. 16:16) is a Heb. name for the place where the kings of the whole earth (16:14) will assemble under the direction of demonic spirits (16:13) for the final battle. It is thus the mountain of the world which as the place of assembly of hostile forces is the counterpart of the mountain of God in Hb. 12:22 ff. It is also the place of the decisive battle (Rev. 16:14; 19:19) and consequently of world judgment (19:21).[2] The retention of the Heb. and failure to give an interpretation are part of the style of apocalyptic.

Thus far there has been no satisfactory explanation of the name. (a) Ἀρ Μαγεδών seems to comprise the name of the city Megiddo (מְגִדּוֹ; Zech. 12:11 with the final n: מְגִדּוֹן; LXX Μεγεδδώ, Ju. 5:19; Μαγεδδώ, Jos. 17:11; Μαγεδών, 2 Ch. 35:22). But we never hear of Mt. Megiddo, nor is Megiddo given eschatological significance in contemporary literature, nor does the earliest exegesis of Rev. 16:16 connect it with Megiddo. Loh.[3] tries to overcome the difficulty by translating "the Megiddo range" and referring it to Mt. Carmel, where according to Lidz. Ginza, 121, 13 ff. (125, 4; 132, 4; 197, 20) Ruha and the planets gather to concoct the mysteries of love. But this gives rise to the new problem of supposing that Carmel took on a new name, never attested elsewhere, from a ruined city which was situated about 7 miles away from its southern end, which had been ruined since 350 B.C. and which had now sunk into oblivion.[4] (b) F. Hommel[5] conjectures that Ἀρ Μαγεδών is originally a Gk. rendering of הַר־מוֹעֵד (mount of assembly), used in Is. 14:13 for the mountain on which the gods assemble and which the presumptuous king of Babylon seeks to climb in blasphemous pride. Ἀρ Μαγεδών is thus the demonic counterpart to the mount of assembly of the gods; the ending -ων is a later assimilation to Μαγεδών. This explanation fits the context well, but it does not show how we are to explain the rendering of y in מוֹעֵד by γ since no r underlies this y. Unless we are to ignore this difficulty, we must conclude that the riddle of Ἀρ Μαγεδών still awaits solution.

Joachim Jeremias

Ἀρ Μαγεδών. Bss. Apk., 399; Loh. Apk., 133 f.; Rohr Apk., 119; J. Jeremias, *Der Gottesberg* (1919); Clemen, 402 f.; Joachim Jeremias, "Har Magedon (Apc. 16:16)," ZNW, 31 (1932), 73-77; also "Ἀρ Μαγεδών und Megiddo," JPOS, 12 (1932), 49 f.; J. Sickenberger, Lex. Th. K., I, 657.

[1] In two words and with rough breathing (Westcott-Hort) on the basis of the Heb., cf. Ἑβραϊστί, Rev. 16:16.
[2] Joh. Jeremias, *Der Gottesberg* (1919), 93. Cf. Ez. 38:8, 21; 39:2, 4, 17.
[3] Rev., 134.
[4] Tell el-Mutesellim. C. S. Fisher, "The Excavation of Armageddon," *Or. Inst. of the Univ. of Chicago, Commun.* No. 4 (1929), 16; P. L. O. Guy, "New Light from Armageddon," *ibid.* No. 9 (1931), 5.
[5] Nk. Z., 1 (1890), 407 f.

† ἀρνέομαι

The basic meaning is "to say no," "to deny," in description of a negative attitude towards a question or a demand. a. "To say no" in relation to a question, either with or without object : Thuc., VI, 60; LXX Gn. 18:15; Jos. Ant., 6, 151. The anton. is ὁμολογεῖν "to agree." A clause dependent on ἀρνέομαι mostly in infin. (sometimes part.) either with or without μή : Jos. Ant., 7, 226 : ἰδεῖν οὐκ ἠρνήσατο. b. "To refuse" in relation to a demand or claim, in the absol. sense : Plut. Tib. Gr., 1 (I, 827d); Wis. 12:27 "not to be willing"; with obj. of thing or person raising a claim, "to resist" or "to reject," Demosth., 18, 282; 4 Macc. 8, 7; opp. "to accede," "to grant," for oneself or others : Hdt., III, 1, 2 : οὐκ εἶχε οὔτε δοῦναι οὔτε ἀρνήσασθαι. The negation in this twofold sense does not imply against better knowledge or right. Conceptually ἀρνέομαι does not include ψεύδεσθαι, although the context may impart this nuance. In the Rabbis it is the equiv. of כָּפַר "to negate" or "to reject," bBB, 154b : "to reject an opinion"; S. Lv., 26, 14 : to deny or resist the commandments (i.e., their fulfilment), bShab., 116a, bSanh., 102b : to deny or resist God. [1]

In the NT 1. we find senses a. and b. Thus a. ἀρνεῖσθαι "to deny" is found at Lk. 8:45; Ac. 4:16; Jn. 1:20 : John the Baptist καὶ ὡμολόγησεν καὶ οὐκ ἠρνήσατο, "he affirmed and denied not"; [2] Mk. 14:68, 70 and par.; Jn. 18:25, 27 (the denial of Peter); 1 Jn. 2:22 : "Who is a liar but he that denieth that Jesus is the Christ." Also Tt. 1:16; Ign. Mg., 9, 1; Herm. v., 2, 4, 2; Just. Apol., I, 11, 2; Dial., 49, 8; 78, 10. b. ἀρνεῖσθαι "to refuse" or "to reject" Hb. 11:24 : Moses refused to be called the son of Pharaoh's daughter; Tt. 2:12: deny ungodliness and worldly lusts; also Ac. 3:13 : παρεδώκατε καὶ ἠρνήσασθε, the rejection of Jesus by the Jews, like their rejection of Moses, the type of Jesus (Ac. 7:35).

2. In addition to these two meanings there is in the NT a third which became the main sense and gathered up the other two into it, i.e., "to deny." This concept receives its emphasis from the fact that the object whose claim is resisted and denied is in the NT supremely a person. Thus in the three passages already mentioned which refer to Jesus (Ac. 3:13; Jn. 1:20 and Mk. 14:68, 70) we already have the sense of denial. When the Jews reject Jesus before Pilate, it is their way of denying Him. The admission of the Baptist that he is not himself the Messiah is, as the Evangelist sees it, an indirect confession of Jesus; it is his way of not denying him. Peter's refusal to acknowledge Him is the moment of denial, and behind the ὁ δὲ ἠρνήσατο λέγων there stands the τρίς με ἀπαρνήσῃ of v. 30. Terminologically, however, ἀρνεῖσθαι first means "to deny" in the saying in Mt. 10:33 and par., just as it is in this saying that ὁμολογεῖσθαι acquires the pregnant sense of "to confess."

The following constitutive elements may be discerned in the concept of denial. a. It relates primarily to a person, so that properly one can speak only of denying someone and not something. Its tendency is to be linked with a person. Cf. Jn. 13:38 Ἰησοῦν; 2 Pt. 2:1: τὸν ἀγοράσαντα αὐτοὺς δεσπότην; 1 Jn. 2:22 f. τὸν υἱόν; Jd. 4 : τὸν μόνον δεσπότην καὶ κύριον ἡμῶν Ἰησοῦν Χριστόν. Cf. also

ἀρνέομαι. [1] v. Str.-B., I, 585; II, 518.
[2] Cf. Dt.r., 2 on 3:24; v. Str.-B., II, 363; Schl. J., 38.

2 Cl., 3, 1; 17, 7; Just. Apol., I, 31, 6; I, 50, 12 (Christ); Herm. v., 2, 2, 8; s., 9, 26, 6; 28, 8 etc. (τὸν κύριον); Herm. v., 2, 2, 7 (τὴν ζωήν); s., 8, 3, 7 (τὸν νόμον = Son of God) etc. But also, though not in the NT, it may refer to τὸν θεόν (Just. Apol., I, 26, 5; I, 58, 1; Dg., 10, 7). The λόγος or ὄνομα may also represent the person of Christ (Rev. 3:8), or His πίστις (faith, Rev. 2:13). He is present in these. On the other hand it must be asked whether the better rendering in 1 Tm. 5:8 is not : "He denies the faith," and in 2 Tm. 3:5 : "They deny that which gives power to godliness." ἀρνεῖσθαι can also be used absolutely in relation to this personal element; the implication is denial of Christ (2 Tm. 2:12; M. Pol., 9, 2; Herm. v., 2, 3, 4; s., 8, 8, 4 etc.).

b. ἀρνεῖσθαι implies a previous relationship of obedience and fidelity. It can take place only where there has first been acknowledgment and commitment. Hence in 2 Tm. 2:12 ἀρνεῖσθαι = ἀπιστεῖν, "to be unfaithful" ; and in Rev. 2:13; 3:8 κρατεῖν, τηρεῖν is the opp. of ἀρνεῖσθαι. In the strict sense, therefore, we cannot use the word of the Jews or of the Baptist, as we can of Peter.

c. ἀρνεῖσθαι, which is unfaithfulness to the person of Jesus Christ, takes three forms. The first is a failure to meet concretely the claim of Jesus Christ for a confession of discipleship (Mt. 10:33 and par.). The recorded instance is that of Peter's denial. Yet the same possibility often arose in the case of martyrs (Rev. 2:13; 3:8; Dg., 7, 7). In Mk. 8:38 we have ἐπαισχυνθῆναί με καὶ τοὺς ἐμοὺς λόγους, which gives the motive for such denial. This is anxiety born of doubt as to the truth of the Lord, lest the judgment of the world in which we live will be one of contempt. Being ashamed of the Lord in this way, and seeking honour from the world rather than from Him, we bring the Lord Himself into contempt, so that in this connection M. Pol., 9, 2 f. can speak of a λοιδορεῖν τὸν Χριστόν and a βλασφημεῖν τὸν βασιλέα (cf. Just. Apol., I, 31, 6).

The second form of denial consists in a failure to do justice to the claims of one's neighbours. This is clear from 2 Tm. 2:11 ff., where in a quotation (?) [3] we find συναποθνήσκειν and ὑπομένειν as opp. of ἀρνεῖσθαι. To deny Christ is not to be at His disposal to meet the needs and acknowledge the claims of one's neighbours. It thus follows that any unethical conduct may be described as a denial of Christ. There is an analysis of this connection in 2 Cl., 3 and 4. Cf. Tt. 1:16; 1 Tm. 5:8; 2 Tm. 3:5; Jd. 4. It is to be noted, however, that there is no question of the denial of Christ in the first three passages, and that in the last three the issue is not the personal immorality of the false teachers but a wrong theory and practice of the relationship between γνῶσις and πρᾶξις.

This leads us to the third form of denial, namely, the failure to acknowledge Jesus Christ in sound doctrine. Particularly when a statement about Christ has consequences for the practical decisions of life, it must be made correctly and cautiously. Nor is it merely the inner connection between teaching and practice which makes of heresy a denial of Christ (cf. 2 Pt. 2:1 ff.). In itself a false statement concerning Christ is a denial of Christ. For the claim of Christ extends to thinking, and where there is a false statement it implies that this claim is heard but not acknowledged. This gives us the clue to 1 Jn. 2:22. ἀρνεῖσθαι ὅτι ᾽Ιησοῦς οὐκ ἔστιν ὁ Χριστός is ἀρνεῖσθαι υἱόν.

---

[3] Cf. Dib., ad loc.

d. All these three forms of denial, however, contain the source which gives rise to it. This means, and is shown in the fact, that each individual denial is a failure of the whole man in respect of his total truth before God. In relation to discipleship we learn this from Mt. 10:33: ἀρνήσομαι κἀγὼ αὐτὸν ἔμπροσθεν τοῦ πατρός μου τοῦ ἐν τοῖς οὐρανοῖς; in relation to ethical practice from 2 Tm. 2:12: κἀκεῖνος ἀρνήσεται ἡμᾶς; in relation to doctrine from 1 Jn. 2:23: οὐδὲ τὸν πατέρα ἔχει. [4]

3. The one basic attitude which comprises ἀρνεῖσθαι may also be seen when it is no longer a matter of denying Christ but in a different sense of denying one's own person. a. 2 Tm. 2:13: "If we are unfaithful to him, he remains faithful, ἀρνήσασθαι γὰρ ἑαυτὸν οὐ δύναται." Here ἀρνεῖσθαι ἑαυτόν is to cease to be oneself. b. Mk. 8:34 and par.: "Whosoever will come after me, (ἀπ-)αρνησάσθω ἑαυτὸν καὶ ἀράτω τὸν σταυρὸν αὐτοῦ." I must not confess myself and my own being, nor cling to myself, but abandon myself in a radical renunciation of myself, and not merely of my sins. I must no longer seek to establish my life of myself but resolutely accept death and allow myself to be established by Christ in discipleship. Chrys. Hom. in Mt., 55, 1 (MPG, 58, 542): ἀπαρνησάσθω ἑαυτόν, τουτέστι, μηδὲν ἐχέτω κοινὸν πρὸς ἑαυτόν. This is already weakened in, e.g., Pall. Hist. Laus., 64 (MPG, 34, 1170a): σεαυτὸν τῷ κόσμῳ ἀπαρνεῖσθαι = τοῖς ἑαυτοῦ ἀποτάσσεσθαι.

ἀπαρνέομαι.

In the NT the compound in no sense differs from ἀρνεῖσθαι, whether by suggesting treachery[1] or by giving greater intensity. That the original intensification has been lost in the NT (as already in the classical age),[2] is proved a. by the interchangeability in par. passages: Lk. 9:23 = Mk. 8:34; Mt. 16:24; Mk. 14:30, 31, 72 and par. = Jn. 13:38; Mt. 10:33ab; Lk. 12:9a = Lk. 12:9b; b. by alternate use within the same sentence or short section: Lk. 12:9; Herm. s., 8, 8, 2 ff.; and c. by textual variants: Lk. 9:23 𝔖; Jn. 13:38 𝔖.

Schlier

---

[4] Cf. also Herm.v., 2, 2, 7 f.; Ign. Sm., 5, 1.

ἀπαρνέομαι. [1] So Cr.-Kö., s.v.

[2] There is no difference in secular Gk. It occurs often in Plato, e.g., Theaet., 165a; Resp., V, 468c. In the LXX it is found in Is. 31:7 (מַאְסֻן) in the same sense as in 4 Macc. 8:7.

ἀρνίον → 340

| ἁρπάζω, ἁρπαγμός |

† ἁρπάζω.

"To take something forcefully" (firmly, quickly or rapaciously). Thus a. "to steal" (Jos. Ant., 20, 214 of robbers). b. "To capture in war." [1] In the NT the word is used in parables which speak of the conflict between the kingdom of God and that of Satan : ὁ λύκος ἁρπάζει (steals) τὰ πρόβατα, Jn. 10:12; οὐχ ἁρπάσει (forcefully snatch) τις αὐτὰ ἐκ τῆς χειρός μου, Jn. 10:28, 29; Mt. 12:29 (the battle between the strong man and the stronger): τὰ σκεύη αὐτοῦ ἁρπάσαι. c. With the thought of speed : Jos. Ant., 6, 238 : ἁρπάσας τὸ δόρυ ἀνεπήδησεν (Saul); also Jd. 23 : to "snatch" out of the fire. d. "To take rapaciously" : Epict. Diss., IV, 7, 22 : ἰσχαδοκάρυά τις διαρριπτεῖ· τὰ παιδία ἁρπάζει. e. "To take a man by force" : Chrys. Beat. Philog., VI, 2 (MPG, 48, 751): ἐκ μέσης τῆς ἀγορᾶς ἁρπασθείς, Jn. 6:15; Ac. 23:10. Similarly in Mt. 13:19: "to take away." f. To denote the rapture of visions. In this sense it does not occur in the LXX, [2] which instead uses αἴρειν at 3 Βασ. 18:12; Ez. 3:14 and ἀναλαμβάνειν at Ez. 3:12. It is found, however, in the pseudepigr. : Apc. Mos. 37; Apc. Esr. 5:7; Gr. Bar. passim. [3] In the NT it occurs at 2 C. 12:2, 4 (vision); 1 Th. 4:17; Rev. 12:5 ("to catch up or away"); Ac. 8:39 — always expressing the mighty operation of God.

Since ἁρπάζω does not here mean either to bring in by force or to plunder, [4] only three alternatives are open in the difficult saying at Mt. 11:12 : [5] ἀπὸ τῶν ἡμερῶν ᾿Ιωάννου τοῦ βαπτιστοῦ ἕως ἄρτι ἡ βασιλεία τῶν οὐρανῶν βιάζεται, καὶ βιασταὶ ἁρπάζουσιν αὐτήν. a. It may mean that the kingdom of God is stolen, i.e., taken away from men and closed to them ; [6] b. it may mean that violent men culpably try to snatch it to themselves ; or c. it may mean that men forcefully take it in the good sense. Linguistically all three are possible (→ supra, a.-d.). The first and third are to be taken most seriously. The former is suggested by the emphatic use of βιάζομαι, by the correspondence between βιάζεται and βιασταί and perhaps by the Matthean context. The latter is supported by the fact that the decisively new thing since the appearance of John the Baptist [7] is the powerful

---

ἁ ρ π ά ζ ω. [1] Of the river which carries away, Test. Abr. (A), 19, p. 102, 1, James.
[2] Though here we have ἡρπάγη with ref. to death (Wis. 4:11).
[3] In others the Gk. text is missing.
[4] The accus. is always used of the thing stolen.
[5] Bibliography apart from comm. and theologies : Dalman, WJ, I, 115 f.; J. Weiss, *Jesu Predigt vom Reiche Gottes*², (1900), 192-197; A. Harnack, "Zwei Worte Jesu" (SAB, 1907), 942 ff.; D. Völter, *Johannes en Jesus in het licht van Mt. 11:12-15* (1909); W. Brandt, ZNW, 11 (1910), 247; H. Scholander, ZNW, 13 (1912), 172 ff.; M. Dibelius, *Die urchr. Überlieferung v. Joh. d. Täufer* (1911), 23 ff. Exegesis depends on the evaluation of the context in Mt. and the par. in Lk.
[6] Schl. Mt. *ad loc.*
[7] This is what is meant by ἀπὸ τῶν ἡμερῶν ᾿Ιωάννου.

irruption of the kingdom of God. This is the presupposition for its being taken. It demands resolute earnestness on the part of men if they are to enter it. Furthermore, the idea of men themselves taking away the kingdom of God is strange and is hardly supported by such parallels as Mt. 13:19, where the evil one snatches away the seed and not the kingdom, or Mt. 23:13, where closing the kingdom to men is not quite the same as taking it away. On this whole passage → βιάζομαι.

† ἁρπαγμός.

In the NT this is found only at Phil. 2:6 : οὐχ ἁρπαγμὸν ἡγήσατο τὸ εἶναι ἴσα θεῷ.

In common with other subst. formed with -μός, ἁρπαγμός first means a. the activity of ἁρπάζειν. [1] In non-Christian writings it is found only in this sense.

Plut. Lib. Educ., 15 (II, 11 f.); in the form ἁρπασμός, Plut. Quaest. Conv., II, 10, 2 (II, 644a). As a variant, Paus., I, 20, 3; Phryn. Ecl., 302, p. 407, Rutherford ; Vett. Val., II, 38, p. 122, 1, Kroll accord. to V. Stegemann in the same sense.

The word then took on the sense of the more common ἅρπαγμα and came to mean b. "what is seized," esp. plunder or booty. [2] Like ἅρπαγμα, it then came to be used in such related expressions as εὕρημα, ἕρμαιον, εὐτύχημα, ἅρπαγμα, ἁρπαγμόν τι ἡγεῖσθαι, ποιεῖσθαι, τίθεσθαι. These mean c. "to take up an attitude to something as one does to what presents itself as a prey to be grasped, a chance discovery, or a gift of fate, i.e., appropriating and using it, treating it as something desired and won." What is regarded as gain may be something which is already present and is utilised, or a possibility which is about to eventuate and is not to be let slip. Materially, therefore, the sense is no less "to utilise" than "to take." [3] The connection with what "everyone" does, which is present in the above expressions, may thus easily be set in antithesis to what is done by one who acts according to higher principles. [4] The figurative element in the expression still remains, and a οἷον or ὥσπερ is often put before it. [5] Although ἅρπαγμα = prey or valuable prey stands in the background, the meaning of the verb also asserts itself ("to grasp eagerly"), so that sometimes we are forced back on the sense of res rapienda : Eus. Hist. Eccl., VIII, 12, 2 : Those who

---

ἁ ρ π α γ μ ό ς. J. B. Lightfoot, St. Paul's Epistle to the Phil.[8] (1885), 111, 133 ff.; Haupt Gefbr.[7], 69 ff.; Tillm. Gefbr.[4], 144; A. Schlatter, Theologie d. Ap.[2] (1922), 341 f. Also T. Zahn, ZWL, 6 (1885), 243 ff.; J. Kögel, Christus der Herr, Erläuterungen zu Phil. 2:5-11 (1908); M. Dibelius, Die Geisterwelt im Glauben des Paulus (1909), 105 ff.; L. Saint-Paul, Rev. Bibl., NS, 8 (1911), 550 ff.; W. Lütgert, Die Vollkommenen im Phil. (1909), 591 ff.; W. Warren, JThSt, 12 (1911), 461 ff.; G. Kittel, ThStK, 85 (1912), 377 ff.; Meyer, Ursprung, III, 380, n. 2; W. Jaeger, Hermes, 50 (1915), 537 ff., and on this A. Jülicher, ZNW, 17 (1916), 1 ff.; P. W. Schmidt, Prot. Monatshefte, 20 (1916), 171 ff.; K. F. Proost, Th.T., 50 (1916), 373 ff.; H. Schumacher, Christus in s. Präexistenz u. Kenose, I (1914); F. Loofs, ThStK, 100 (1927/28), 1 ff.; E. Lohmeyer, "Kyrios Jesus," SHA, 18 (1927/8); A. Nock in Essays on the Trinity and the Incarnation, ed. A. E. J. Rawlinson (1928), 99. S. Reinach, Cultes, Mythes et Rel., V (1923), 304 ff. proposes οὐκ ἄπραγμον ἡγήσατο, but does not regard it as certain. So now F. Kattenbusch, ThStKr 104 (1932), 373-420.

[1] Kühner-Blass-Gerth, I, 2, 272.

[2] In this sense, in obvious dependence on Phil., it is used in Chrys. Hom. in Phil., 7, 1 (MPG, 62, 229): ὁ δὲ βασιλεὺς μετὰ πολλῆς ... ποιεῖ τῆς ἀσφαλείας (sc. temporarily to lay aside his dignity). Διὰ τί; ὅτι οὐχ ἁρπαγμὸν ἔχει τὴν ἀρχήν (as a prey).

[3] May we also appeal to the expression τὸν καιρὸν ἁρπάζειν = to grasp the hour or the opportunity ? Cf. Dio C., XLI, 44, 2; Plut. Philop., 15 (I, 364e) and Dio, 26 (I, 969c).

[4] So Plut. Alex. Fort. Virt., I, 8 (II, 330d). v. W. Jaeger, Hermes, 50 (1915), 550 f.

[5] Eus. Vit. Const., II, 31, 2; Herond. Mim., VI, 30; Plut. Alex. Fort. Virt., I, 8 (II, 330d).

evading the pains of martyrdom killed themselves, τὸν θάνατον ἅρπαγμα θέμενοι τῆς τῶν δυσσεβῶν μοχθηρίας = believing death to be preferable to torments.[6]

In Phil. 2:6 sense a. would imply that "He did not see equality with God in a snatching to Himself of the honour and glory bound up with it."[7] But the lack of an object makes this impossible; instead of ἁρπαγμός one would expect a verb which does not require an object, such as κυριεύειν. Sense b. is unintelligible unless we paraphrase as Chrysostom does in Phil., 7, 1 (MPG, 62, 229). It may thus be dismissed.[8] This leaves only c.,[9] which gives us the rendering: "He did not regard equality with God as a gain, either in the sense of something not to be let slip, or in the sense of something not to be left unutilised." The former nuance, championed among others by Schlatter and Loofs, refers the passage to the historical Jesus, especially in respect of the temptation. The ensuing ἐκένωσεν it takes to mean: "He denied himself." Yet the expression ἐν ὁμοιώματι ἀνθρώπων γενόμενος (cf. Rom. 8:3: ἐν ὁμοιώματι σαρκός) refers to a pre-temporal act, and what Schlatter, in the context of the Epistle, seeks in the whole passage from v. 6 onwards, the voluntary self-abnegation which runs through the whole life of Jesus, is amply expressed in v. 7b and 8. Hence we may translate: "He did not regard it as a gain to be equal with God." The negative formulation is readily understandable, for it is a great gain to be equal with God and "everyone" would utilise it. In justification of the negative formulation, therefore, we do not need think of the fall of Adam ("Ye shall be as God") or the fall of the devil. Nor is there any suggestion of a pre-temporal temptation of Christ, since the reference is not so much to temptation as to a free act, and in this connection we are not to link ἁρπαγμός with any thought of robbery or seizure by force. Against all expectation, Jesus did not regard equality with God as a gain to be utilised.

The expositions of the fathers, with dwindling exceptions, are all to be understood in terms of c.[10] Particularly those which consciously or less consciously give an independent paraphrase, i.e., one which is not dependent on the word group ἁρπάζειν etc., point in this direction. This must not be overlooked in relation to the passage.

Foerster

---

[6] We find the same comparative significance in Orig. Joh., I, 231: Christ showed His kindness more divinely when He humbled Himself, ἢ εἰ ἁρπαγμὸν ἡγήσατο τὸ εἶναι ἴσα θεῷ καὶ μὴ βουληθεὶς ἐπὶ τῇ τοῦ κόσμου σωτηρίᾳ γενέσθαι δοῦλος, than if He had thought it better to be equal with God and not freely to become a servant.

[7] Ew. Gefbr., ad loc., also P. W. Schmidt, op. cit. and G. Kittel, op. cit.

[8] The meaning which Schumacher, op. cit., tries to prove from the fathers, namely, that He did not need to regard equality with God as wrong, cannot be maintained linguistically and does not seem to be found in the fathers.

[9] So already Bengel, ad loc.

[10] Cf. W. Foerster, ZNW, 29 (1930), 115 ff.

---

† ἀρραβών[1]

A loan word from the Semitic, Heb. עֵרָבוֹן.[2] Gn. 38:17 ff. (LXX, ἀρραβών), Lat. *arrha* or *arrhabo* (ꝗ Gn. 38:17 ff.). The word is a commercial term (Isaeus 8:23; Aristot. Pol., I, 11, p. 1259a, 12; esp. pap.). It signifies a "pledge" which is later returned (only Gn. 38:17-20); a "deposit" which pays part of the total debt and gives a legal claim (BGU, 947, 6; Ostraka, II, 1168); "earnest-money" ratifying a compact (P. Oxy., 299, 2 f.; BGU, 446, 5). It always implies an act which engages to something bigger.[3] It occurs figur. in Antiph. Fr., 123, 6 (CAF, II, 60): ἔχοντες ἀρραβῶνα τὴν τέχνην τοῦ ζῆν; Menand. Fr., 697 (*ibid.*, III, 200): τοῦ δυστυχεῖν ... ἀρραβῶν' ἔχειν.

Paul uses it figuratively at 2 C. 1:22: ὁ ... δοὺς τὸν ἀρραβῶνα τοῦ πνεύματος ἐν ταῖς καρδίαις ἡμῶν; 5:5: ὁ δοὺς ἡμῖν τὸν ἀρραβῶνα τοῦ πνεύματος (→ πνεῦμα). In the latter τοῦ πνεύματος is gen. appos.: "the earnest, i.e., the Spirit" (like → ἀπαρχὴ τοῦ πνεύματος in R. 8:23). The Spirit whom God has given them is for Christians the guarantee of their full future possession of salvation. Similarly in Eph. 1:14: τῷ πνεύματι ..., ὅς[4] ἐστιν ἀρραβὼν τῆς → κληρονομίας ἡμῶν.

In 2nd century Christian literature it is found only in Pol., 8, 1: τῷ ἀρραβῶνι τῆς δικαιοσύνης ἡμῶν ὅς ἐστι Χριστὸς 'Ιησοῦς, Christ by His death is a pledge that Christians will attain to righteousness at the last judgment.

Behm

ἄρρητος → ἐρῶ
ἀρτιγέννητος → γεννάω

---

† ἄρτιος, † ἐξαρτίζω, † καταρτίζω,
† καταρτισμός, † κατάρτισις

In the LXX ἄρτιος is found only as an adv. of time meaning "until now" (2 Βασ. 15:34). Elsewhere it means a. "suitable" or "adapted" for something; b. "right," "faultless," "normal," "meeting demands" posed to the *subst. regens*: τοῖς σώμασιν, Diod. S., III, 33, 6; of movements of thought, Theogn., 946; in the ethical sense, Theogn., 154; more religiously, Philo Det. Pot. Ins., 7 (τὸ ἄρτιον ... ἀγαθόν); c. "evenness" in

---

ἀ ρ ρ α β ώ ν. Cr.-Kö., 171 f.; Pr.-Bauer, 171 f.; Deissmann B., 104 f.; Moult.-Mill., 79; Bchm. 2 K.⁴, 80; Wnd. 2 K., 73; Sickb. K.⁴, 97 f.; Meinertz Gefbr.⁴, 66 f.
[1] A secondary form is ἀραβών; cf. Winer (Schmiedel) § 5, 26c; Deissmann NB, 11; Bl.-Debr. § 40; Mayser, 40.
[2] Cf. Ges.-Buhl, *s.v.*
[3] Bchm., 80; Pr.-Bauer, 171.
[4] ὅς א B D is gramm. correct (Bl.-Debr. § 132, 1) as against ὅ אG.

mathematics; ἄρτιον and περιττόν are for the Pythagoreans partly στοιχεῖα of the basic principle of numbers, and partly one of the ten basic principles (Diels, I, 347, B5).

The deriv. are late; they are not found, e.g., in Philo, Jos., etc. ἐξαρτίζω, "to equip," found in the LXX only at Ex. 28:7: "to bind or unite." καταρτίζω (Ion.): a. "to regulate" (politically), "to order" (Preis. Zaub., IV, 1147: ὁ θεὸς ... ὁ τὸν κόσμον καταρτισάμενος). In the LXX "to establish," "to create" (ψ 39:6, quoted in Hb. 10:5); mid. "to prepare for oneself" (Ps. 8:2, quoted in Mt. 21:16), used also of God's direction of the steps of men (ψ 16:5; 17:33); b. "to equip." It is used absol. in Hdt., IX, 66 of the ability of a general, variant κατηρτημένως. To this there corresponds the use of καταρτισμός and κατάρτισις. Plut. Alex., 7 (I, 667 f.), of education; Plut. Them., 2 (I, 112e), with παιδεία (in both cases κατάρτισις). Neither word is found in the LXX.

At 2 Tm. 3:17 ἄρτιος is used in sense b. to denote what is right or proper, and more particularly what is becoming to a Christian, obviously with a moral accent, as shown by what follows.

At 2 Tm. 3:17 ἐξαρτίζω means to bring to a suitable state for Christian moral action. It is used in Ac. 21:5 in the secular sense of "to end as prescribed."

καταρτίζω [1] at Hb. 11:3 means a. "to order," of the aeons (→ supra, Preis. Zaub., IV, 1147); at R. 9:22 "to foreordain" (for destruction), [2] obviously along the lines of ψ 16:5 etc.). At 1 Th. 3:10, with reference to the πίστις of the Thessalonians, it means b. "to establish," "to confirm," especially in terms of Christian character worked out in the sense of unity of the members of the community (1 C. 1:10), or the restoration of the fallen brother (Gl. 6:1), but also ἐν παντὶ ἀγαθῷ (Hb. 13:21). The κατηρτισμένος (like the ἄρτιος) can thus denote the ideal of the Christian generally (Lk. 6:40). Members of the community are summoned to instruct and help one another with a view to confirmation (2 C. 13:11), though success is finally the work of God (1 Pt. 5:10). [3] (On Mt. 21:16; Hb. 10:5 → supra).

Along the same lines καταρτισμός is used at Eph. 4:12, in the context of the edifying of the body of Christ, to denote the equipment of the saints for the work of the ministry. The establishment of the community in work for the kingdom of God in the widest sense thus constitutes for Paul a material precondition of the upbuilding and consequently the actualisation of the community.

Similarly κατάρτισις denotes inner strength, whether of the community (οἰκοδομή) in its organic relationship, or of the character of its members, i.e., their maturity as Christians (2 C. 13:9).

Delling

ἄρτιος κτλ. [1] Secular use at Mt. 4:21 and par.; cf. Pr.-Bauer, s.v.

[2] B. Weiss (Meyer⁸), *ad loc.* suggests "ready or ripe for destruction," but with no philological justification.

[3] προκαταρτίζειν is used in the secular sense of "prepare" (the collection) at 2 C. 9:5, the only occurrence in the NT.

ἄρτος

This word is much used in the NT. It is of theological interest at the following points.

1. In the expressions λαμβάνειν, (κατα-)κλᾶν, (δια-, ἐπι-)διδόναι τὸν ἄρτον (Lk. 24:30; Jn. 21:13; Ac. 27:35; Mk. 6:41 par.; 8:19 par.; Jn. 6:11), it has the strict meaning "bread." The reference here is to the head of the house who at the beginning of a meal takes bread, gives thanks, breaks it and gives to those at table with him. [1] In this way it is used of the bread of the Last Supper in Mk. 14:22 and par.; 1 C. 11:23 f., 26 ff.; 10:16 f.; Ac. 2:42, 46; 20:7, 11 (→ λαμβάνω, → εὐ-χαριστέω, → εὐλογέω, → κλάω, → κλάσις, → δίδωμι). It is also used of the shew-bread of the OT sanctuary (οἱ ἄρτοι τῆς προθέσεως) at Mk. 2:26 and par. (Hb. 9:2 : ἡ πρόθεσις τῶν ἄρτων). [2]

In the koine ἄρτος is the main word for bread. Hippocr. Acut., 37 still distinguished ἄρτος (white bread) from μᾶζα (barley-bread). Philo Spec. Leg., I, 173 : ἄρτος ἐραστῇ σοφίας διαρκῆς τροφή. [3]

2. Bread can also signify nourishment generally (like the OT לֶחֶם). [4] ἄρτος ἐπιούσιος, Mt. 6:11 and par. (→ ἐπιούσιος). τὸν ἑαυτοῦ ἄρτον ἐσθίειν, 2 Th. 3:12 : "to keep oneself," in contrast to v. 8 : δωρεὰν ἄρτον φαγεῖν παρά τινος, "to be supported by someone for nothing." The fasting ascetic is called μὴ ἐσθίων ἄρτον μήτε πίνων οἶνον in Lk. 7:33, the guest at table ὁ τρώγων μου [5] τὸν ἄρτον in Jn. 13:18. [6]

3. The thought of participation in bliss (= feasting) underlies the φαγεῖν ἄρτον ἐν τῇ βασιλείᾳ τοῦ θεοῦ of Lk. 14:15 (→ ἐσθίω, → βασιλεία), and also the picture of Christ as the true ἄρτος ἐκ τοῦ οὐρανοῦ (surpassing the OT manna) in Jn. 6:31 ff., as the ἄρτος τῆς ζωῆς in v. 35, 48 (the bread which gives life) or ὁ ἄρτος ὁ ζῶν in v. 51 (→ οὐρανός, → ζωή), received by the believer in the Lord's Supper.

In the LXX the manna is called ἄρτος ἐκ τοῦ οὐρανοῦ at Neh. 9:15 (= 2 Εσδ. 19:15); Wis. 16:20 (ἀπ' οὐρανοῦ); Ex. 16:4 (ἄρτοι) ἄρτος οὐρανοῦ; ψ 77:24; 104:40. The idea of heavenly bread is seen already in the Babyl. Adapa-myth. [7] Judaism expected a second and eschatological miracle of manna: S. Bar. 29:8: "At that time stores of manna will again fall from above"; Sib. Fr., 3, 49, Geffck. γλυκὺν ἄρτον ἀπ' οὐρανοῦ; Rev. 2:17; Qoh. r., 1 on 1:9 : "As the first redeemer caused manna to come down, so will the last." In Philo manna is a type of the logos : Leg. All., III, 169 and 175 ; Det. Pot. Ins., 118; Rer. Div. Her., 79; Fug., 137; ἡ οὐράνιος τροφή, the nourishment of the soul, Sacr. AC, 86 etc. According to bJoma, 75b (Akiba) manna was "bread which ministering

---

ἄ ρ τ ο ς. [1] Cf. on this point Str.-B., IV, 620 ff.

[2] P. Volz, Die bibl. Altertümer² (1925), 118 f.; G. Hölscher, Geschichte der israel. u. jüd. Religion (1922), 77; Str.-B., III, 719 ff. An analogon may be seen in Ditt. Or., 56, 73.

[3] On this pt. L. Cohn, Die Werke Philos v. Alex. in deutscher Übersetzung, II (1910), 59, n. 1 and 2.

[4] Semit. Cf. A. Debrunner, Th.Bl., 8 (1929), 212.

[5] μετ' ἐμοῦ ℵ 𝔄 D.

[6] ψ 40:9 : ὁ ἐσθίων ἄρτους μου.

[7] A. Jeremias, Das AT im Lichte des alten Orients⁴ (1930), 47.

angels eat." The bread of life and living bread are peculiar to Jn. with no parallels in Judaism[8] or in ancient religions which speak of heavenly food that dispenses life; [9] though cf. the Adapa-myth, B 60 f.: "the food of life" (and 29 : "the food of death"). [10]

Behm

ἀρχάγγελος → 87   ἀρχιερεύς → ἱερεύς
ἀρχιποιμήν → ποιμήν   ἀρχισυνάγωγος → συναγωγή

ἄρχω, ἀρχή, ἀπαρχή,
ἀρχαῖος, ἀρχηγός, ἄρχων

ἄρχω.

Act. a. "to rule"; b. "to begin" (where others continue, though this is rare later, being found only 3 times in Jos. [Schlatter]); mid. "to begin" (and oneself continue). In non-biblical lit., except where it is a part., it is almost always used with the pres. infin.; so, too, in the NT and Jos.[1] In the LXX the act. always has the sense of "to rule" or "to be superior" (even in Sir. 47:21), except in the few cases where the reference is to singers (2 Ch. 35:25; Job 36:24). The mid. is predominant (perf. also in the pass. sense at 1 Macc. 5:31; 2 Ch. 31:10); it sometimes occurs in expressions which are to us superfluous.[2] It is worth noting that the inf. aor. is restricted to the canonical books. Hesseling[3] advances "the hypothesis that they (the translators) rediscovered the timeless character of the Hebrew infinitive in the Greek aorist infinitive."

1. In the NT the act. occurs only at Mk. 10:42; R. 15:12, "to rule." Jesus relativises the concept in relation to earthly rulers; He finds true power only in God and not in them.

2. In almost half the cases the mid. occurs in Lk. (41 times, of which only 3 are common with Mk. and 2 with Mt.).[4] It is usually a kind of auxiliary verb (Hunkin), as in half of the 10 cases in Ac., even in the polished chapter 24 (v. 2). Nevertheless, this use is more than a Semitism. The word is more pregnant at Jn. 13:5; 8:9. Pleonastically it usually serves to draw attention to a particular element in the story. The best course is simply to render by some such word as

---

[8] Str.-B., II, 482 ff.
[9] Bau. J.³, 100 f. and E. Waldschmidt-W. Lentz, "Die Stellung Jesu im Manichäismus" (AAB, 1926, 4), 65 draw attention to a Manichean text in which the soul calls the redeemer bread.
[10] AOT, 145.

ἄ ρ χ ω. D. C. Hesseling, "Zur Syntax von ἄρχομαι u. Verw.," *Byz. Ztschr.*, 20 (1911), 147-164; J. W. Hunkin, " 'Pleonastic' ἄρχομαι in the NT," JThSt, 25 (1923/24), 390-402.
[1] Hesseling, 148-150.
[2] A typical example is Ju. 19:6, where we have ἀρξάμενος in A and ἄγε δή in B.
[3] *Op. cit.,* 161 f.
[4] Mt. has 6 of 13 common with Mk. In the NT it is never used with part., cf. Bl.-Debr. § 414.

"moreover" or "indeed," or by even freer expressions suggested by the context, such as "were so bold" or "were forced to." The auxiliary character of the word appears most plainly where ἄρχομαι is used in connection with the evangelistic activity of Jesus (especially in Mt. and Lk.). Yet there are still some cases in which it has a more pregnant sense (always, of course, with ἀπό ...), more particularly in Lk. and in the Epistles (where it is found only at 2 C. 3:1 and 1 Pt. 4:17).

† ἀρχή (→ χρονός).

A. The General and Philosophical Use of ἀρχή.

ἀρχή always signifies "primacy," whether in time : "beginning," *principium,* or in rank : "power," "dominion," "office."

1. In its temporal significance, it denotes beginning in the exact sense, i.e., "the place in a temporal sequence at which something new, which is also finite, commences" : Melissus, I, 184, 29 ff., Diels ; Democrit., II, 23, 10 ff., Diels ; Gorg. Fr., 3, II, 243, 23 ff., Diels ; ἀρχή = γένεσις Chrysipp., III, 80, 34 ff., v. Arnim ; τοῦ δὲ ἀπείρου οὐκ ἔστιν ἀρχή, Aristot. Phys., III, 4, p. 203b, 7 concerning Anaximander. This precise use of the term is found again and again. How common it became is shown by the fact that even Philo consistently uses it to denote noneternity (Op. Mund., 54; Aet. Mund. [53;], 118; cf. Decal., 58).[1] From the parallel ἀρχή/γένεσις it may be seen that to the Greek the thought of τέλος/φθορά is also present ; both are part of the concept of οὐκ ἄπειρον.[2] Thus in discussions of ἄπειρον the beginning and the end form a circle. Everything proceeds from ἄπειρον and everything leads back to it (Anaximander, I, 17, 17 ff., Diels). Hence Hippocrates, imitating Heraclitus, can say : ἀρχὴ δὲ πάντων μία καὶ τελευτὴ πάντων μία καὶ ἡ αὐτὴ τελευτὴ καὶ ἀρχή (Diels, I, 111, 26): all occurrence which can be measured in time is simply a falling from the ἄπειρον.

The thought of the relativity of the time sequence also underlies the religious statement that God is ἀρχὴ καὶ τέλος (Preis.Zaub., IV, 2836 f.), a statement adopted by Greek Judaism (Philo Plant., 93; Jos. Ant., 8, 280).[3] There is an obvious connection with discussion of ἄπειρον when it is said of a god that he comprises ἀρχή and τέλος (συλλαβών : Skythinos [imitation of Heraclitus], I, 112, 20 f., Diels ; cf. Ael. Arist. Or., 8, 22 : ἀρχὰς καὶ πέρατα ἔχει).[4]

---

[5] 1:1: ὧν ἤρξατο = ἅ ... ἐποίησεν ἀπ' ἀρχῆς.

ἀ ρ χ ή. M. Dibelius, *Die Geisterwelt im Glauben des Pls.* (1909), esp. 99 ff.; G. Kurze, *Der Engels- und Teufelsglaube des Ap. Pls.* (1915), *passim* ; A. Schweitzer, *Mystik d. Ap. Pls.* (1930), 58 f., 305 f. For further lit., *v.* Pr.-Bauer, *s.v.,* though G. Teichmüller, *Studien z. Geschichte d. Begriffe* (1874), 48 ff., 560 ff. (Anaximander) is open to question ; cf. O. Dittrich, *Geschichte d. Ethik,* I and II (1926), Index *s.v.* "Prinzip." Def. Aristot. Metaph., IV, 1, p. 1012 f.

[1] Cf. the quotation from Phaedr., 245 d; → 480.

[2] Cf. Phaedr., 245d : what is ἀγένητον must necessarily be ἀδιάφθορον. → *supra.*

[3] On the other hand OT Judaism does not say that God *is* the beginning but that He *acts* in the beginning. Thus the concept of God is taken out of the category of beginning (→ A/Ω).

[4] The thought changes when it is said of God that He is the centre (Diels, II, 169, 5 f., 16; cf. Plat. Leg., IV, 715e; Jos. Ap., 2, 190), for He is then seen to be wholly immersed in historical occurrence.

As used in philosophy, the term ἀρχή is of greatest significance in cosmic physics. [5] Here it denotes the original material from which everything has evolved. [6] In this sense, however, it is gradually replaced by → στοιχεῖον. It is still reserved, however, for the fundamental laws which control the evolution of the world both in great things and small. [7] Amongst other things referred to as ἀρχή in this sense [8] are χρόνος in the later Orphics (Diels, II, 171, 26 f.); ἀριθμός in the Pythagoreans (ibid., I, 347, 12 f.); the νοῦς from which movement proceeds in Anaxagoras (I, 388, 39 f.); τὸ θεῖον as an unmoved and infinite ἀρχή in Melissos (I, 185, 1 f.); κενόν (and the atoms) in Democritus (II, 13, 18 ff.); ὕλη, εἶδος (λόγος), στέρησις in Aristotle (Metaph., XI, 2, p. 1069b, 32 ff.). The sense of temporal beginning often recurs in material definition, as when Anaximander defines ἄπειρον as ἀρχή because "everything proceeds from it and everything at destruction returns to it" (Diels, I, 17, 17 ff.). In the Platonic concept of ἀρχή, too, the temporal sense is prominent : ἀρχὴ δὲ ἀγένητον. ἐξ ἀρχῆς γὰρ ἀνάγκη πᾶν τὸ γιγνόμενον γίγνεσθαι, αὐτὴν δὲ μηδ᾿ ἐξ ἑνός· εἰ γὰρ ἔκ του ἀρχὴ γίγνοιτο, οὐκ ἂν ἔτι ἀρχὴ γίγνοιτο (Phaedr., 245d). [9]

Stoicism could make nothing of an idealistic conception of ἀρχή; [10] it viewed θεός and ὕλη (= ποιοῦν and πάσχον) as ἀρχαί. [11] The distinction into θεός and ὕλη is not to be taken antithetically. God penetrates matter (II, 156, 16 f., v. Arnim); He is identical with ἀρχή as with the λόγος, νοῦς, and κοινὸς νόμος of the Stoics, or perhaps more precisely with ἀρχὴ καὶ τέλος, the basic meaning and goal, the logos which penetrates and rules all being (M. Ant., V, 32). To know ἀρχὴ καὶ τέλος is thus the sum of the perfect understanding of the totality and goal of the Stoic (loc. cit.), so that even Judaism must make God say : ἀρχὴν καὶ τέλος οἶδα (Sib., 8, 375).

> The linguistic usage and conceptual content of Philo are not too clear. He calls the 4 elements of which the cosmos consists (Rer. Div. Her., 281) ὑλικαὶ ἀρχαί (Det. Pot. Ins., 153 f.); the atoms τῶν ὅλων ἀρχαί (Fug., 148); ἀρχή is the equivalent of original matter. He has in view the leading thought or principle when he describes the number one (Poster C., 65) or four (Op. Mund., 52) as ἀρχὴ τῶν ὅλων, obviously in dependence on the Pythagoreans (cf. Rer. Div. Her., 62 : ἀμήτωρ ἀρχή). Stoic influence may be seen in his description of the logos as ἀρχή (Conf. Ling., 146). With comparatively the greatest frequency God is called ἀρχή (Rer. Div. Her., 172; Decal., 52; Plant., 93; cf. 77; Leg. All., I, 5). This confusion naturally corresponds to the obscurity in general philosophical usage.
>
> 2. a. "Dominion" (often with the undertone of legality and material necessity, e.g., Diels, I, 368, 24 f. : ἀεί τινα ἐπιστατείαν ὑπάρχειν δεῖν καὶ ἀρχὴν νόμιμόν τε καὶ εὐσχήμονα, ἧς ὑπήκοος ἔσται ἕκαστος τῶν πολιτῶν; cf. v. Arnim, III, 81, 20 ff.; b. "realm" (e.g., in Hdt.); c. "authorities."

---

[5] Cf. the naturally uncritical and imperfect summary in Stob. Ecl., I, 118-130.

[6] So, e.g., Thales, ibid., I, 128, 16 ff.

[7] This usage is first found in Anaximander, Diels I, 15, 24.

[8] Together with a list of theogonic concepts encountered in many mythological systems, esp. the Orphic.

[9] The only new feature is the application of the term to the immortality of the soul.

[10] Thus sometimes in their polemics we even find the 4 elements described as ἀρχαί (II, 134, 39 ff., v. Arnim).

[11] According to their teaching from the time of Zeno (II, 111, v. Arnim); the 4 elements are expressly distinguished (Stob. Ecl., I, 126, 17 f.).

B. ἀρχή in the LXX.

In the LXX ἀρχή 1. usually denotes temporal beginning (also in the pre-positional expressions found in the NT). Occasionally it is a stock phrase for primeval time. Only rarely is it used spatially ("head" in Jer. 22:6; "tree-top" in Ez. 31:3, 10, 14; "ends" in Gn. 2:10 and other contexts). Many peculiarities and obscurities are caused by the often fairly automatic use of ἀρχή for ראשׁ.

2. Comparatively frequently ἀρχή is used for "dominion," "power," "position of power" (also "host" or "division of a host"; or "sphere of power"), whence "official posts" (Gn. 40:13, 20 f.), "leading position" (1 Ch. 26:10; 4 Macc. 4:17, of the office of the high-priest), and finally the "person who exercises influence" (leader in Neh. 9:17; captain in ᾽Ωσ. 1:11). In Dan. Θ 7 ἀρχή means "power," whether of the enemies of Israel (v. 12, 26) or of the One who stands at the side of God (v. 14). It is taken away from the former and given to the One like a man. In the blessed time of the end πᾶσαι αἱ ἀρχαί will render menial service to the people of the saints of the Most High (v. 27). Even though v. 27 shows that the translator is still thinking of the kingdoms of the earth, c. 10 shows that these are connected with those who wield power in the supraterrestrial sphere. Hence it was natural enough to understand by ἀρχή the dominion exercised by them and by their fellows in this realm.

C. ἀρχή in the NT.

1. ἀρχή = Beginning.

In the NT ἀρχή is most frequently used for "beginning" [12] a. in the formulas ἀπ᾽ and ἐξ ἀρχῆς [13] (κατ᾽ ἀρχάς in Hb. 1:10, quoting from the LXX ψ 101:26), often with no more precise indication, so that it simply denotes the first point of time according to the context, whether of creation (Hb. 1:10; Mt. 19:4, 8; 24:21 [Mk. 10:6; 13:19]; 2 Pt. 3:4), or of the first appearing of Jesus (Lk. 1:2; Jn. 15:27; 16:4), or of the beginning of being a Christian (1 Jn. 2:24; 3:11; 2:7; 2 Jn. 5, 6) etc. (Jn. 6:64; Ac. 26:4). In 6 cases it is not clear what point of beginning is in view. In 2 Th. 2:13 [14] the reference is to the election of those who are addressed, either from their birth or from all ages, presumably the latter. [15] The other passages are in the Johannine writings. In Jn. 8:44; [16] 1 Jn. 3:8 the devil is the subject, and therefore the meaning is obviously "from all ages." This does not imply that the devil is eternal, but that the beginning of his existence precedes earthly time, within which alone we can speak of time.

In 1 Jn. 1:1 the reference of ὃ ἦν ἀπ᾽ ἀρχῆς is to the Logos. The established Greek term *logos* is avoided; it is replaced by a neutral "it." This cannot be embraced in any concept; in it God gives Himself to men. It has become sensually perceptible to the disciples and it lives also in their proclamation. In 1 Jn. 2:13 f.

---

[12] Spatially it is used only in Ac. 10:11; 11:5.

[13] This occurs in Jn. 6:64; 16:4. In 16:4 the point of time is indicated; cf. on this S. Dt., 29 on 3:28: לא כך אמרתי למשה רבך מתחלה.

[14] The variant reading ἀπαρχήν championed in Dib. Th. gives a poorer sense and makes the εἵλατο difficult to understand. If it was not a mistake (as often in secular codices), it belongs to a recension which is a little too studied.

[15] Naturally not predestination in the later ecclesiastical sense.

[16] Bau. J., *ad loc.* suggests the fall (→ 245).

we have the masculine, but again without a noun, namely, He who is from before time. With reference to Christ, this includes the assertion of eternity, for that which or He who was from all ages can only be that which or He who is included in the being of God. This gives us pre-existence in the strict sense. [17]

b. This is even more plain in the parallel saying in Jn. 1:1 f. [18] Here, however, the term *logos* is used. In a Gospel it is almost impossible not to objectivise the It or He. The loaded term *logos* is an attempt to express formally what is said more exactly in 1 Jn. 1:1; 2:13 f. Here, then, that which is ἐν ἀρχῇ is that which is "before" all time, or, more correctly, that concerning which no temporal statement can be made (cf. the secular use, esp. Plat. Phaedr., 245d, and → *supra,* esp. n. 2). This strict concept of pre-existence does not seem to be present in Jewish thinking. At any rate, it is restricted to statements about God. [19] Even though the Torah was before the world, its age could be assigned. For the older Synagogue there was no thought of any "real pre-existence of the Messiah," restricted to Him alone. [20]

The two other ἐν ἀρχῇ phrases are meant relatively. Thus Phil. 4:15 refers to the first period of Paul's evangelistic activity and Ac. 11:15 to the early days of the Jerusalem church; ἀρχή has here acquired something of a romantic aura; → ἀρχαῖος, 486. [21]

c. τὴν ἀρχήν is used adverbially for "all the time" in Jn. 8:25. [22]

d. Ἀρχή in other constructions may indicate, as in 4 passages in the Gospels, the first occurrence in a series of similar or corresponding events (Mt. 24:8 = Mk. 13:8; Jn. 2:11). In Mk. 1:1 the preaching and baptism of John are the temporal starting-point of the evangelical preaching of Jesus (in spite of Hos. 1:2). Again, in 5 passages in Hb. the reference is to the beginning of Christian instruction and proclamation for those addressed (5:12; 6:1), or to the beginning of the confidence of faith (3:14). In 2:3 ἀρχή is related to the proclamation of salvation by Jesus Himself (cf. Mk. 1:1). In 7:3 expression is given to the fact that Christ is beyond time by saying that He has no ἀρχή or τέλος, as the Greeks elsewhere say of eternity (→ 479); cf. esp. Philo, of whom we also have an echo in the ἀμήτωρ (→ 479).

2. ἀρχή = Power.

a. In the sense of "dominion" or "force" ἀρχή is always (except at Jd. 6) coupled with ἐξουσία in the NT. At Lk. 12:11 and Tt. 3:1 it denotes the secular or spiritual authorities and at Lk. 20:20 it denotes the official power of the Roman procurator. At Tt. 3:1 (cf. R. 13) there is no suggestion that the ἀρχή of the

---

[17] Cf. Jn. 17:5; Zn. on Jn. 1:1.

[18] Cf. on this pt. Prv. 8:22 f.: πρὸ τοῦ αἰῶνος ἐθεμελίωσέν με ἐν ἀρχῇ; "But while it is said of wisdom that it was created, the Logos was" (Bau. on Jn. 1:1).

[19] Cf. the examples given in Str.-B., II, 353 f.

[20] Though there is, of course, the thought of an ideal pre-existence; Str.-B., II on Jn. 1:1, esp. 333 f.

[21] ἐν ἀρχῇ is not a Semit., in spite of the intentional par. to Gn. 1:1 in Jn. 1:1 (→ λόγος); cf. Ditt. Or., 56, 57; P. Petr., II, 37, 2b. Nor is it just attested in the *koine,* but classically; *v.* Thuc., I, 35, 5: ὥσπερ ἐν ἀρχῇ ὑπείπομεν; Eur. Med., 60; Plat. Tim., 28b.

[22] In the question in Ps.-Plat. Demod., 381d: ἀρχὴν δὲ τί δεῖ πάντως ἄλλους ξυμβουλεύειν ὑμῖν etc.; often in negated propositions in Plat., Xenoph., Jos. etc.; cf. also Pr.-Bauer, *s.v.;* Zn. Jn., *ad loc.*

state might represent a force inimical to God (→ 481). The Christian owes it obedience. [23]

b. In Da. 7 the reference of ἀρχαί is perhaps to supraterrestrial and demonic powers which are subdued by the Messiah (according to NT exegesis) and which cannot therefore hurt the people of God any more. It is, of course, a long way from these national angels [24] to the ἀρχή concept of Paul. This had been worked out by the *diaspora* prior to Paul. For Paul, however, there is no need to identify ἀρχαί with national angels, since the people of God is no longer the Jewish nation. The dominion of the ἀρχαί is thus widened, though we cannot say what functions they have — in distinction from the → ἐξουσίαι and → δυνάμεις ? — or whether they are wholly hostile to God, though this is probable in view of Eph. 1:21 and Col. 1:16. We may gather from Eph. 6:12 that different spheres of influence are allotted to them, probably by their over-lord (Eph. 2:2), according to the different spheres of life, e.g., the religious (1 C. 8:5; 10:20 f.), the sexual (1 C. 6:15 ff.; 7:14), the purely vital (1 C. 15:26), and the different social relationships in terms of the general context of Eph. 6. Strictly, however, the reference is not to dominion over other spirits — for in such cases we should expect ἄρχοντες — but to power over the rest of the cosmos, especially the earthly.

They are spiritual beings [25] (Eph. 6:12), related to angels according to R. 8:38. [26] For Paul this does not exclude the possession of another form (v. 12a) of corporeality (cf. 1 C. 15:35 ff.). In the plan of creation they were originally meant to be good spirits and were created as such (Col. 1:16). [27] Perhaps they were originally assigned to a higher heavenly sphere. Their abode is now the ἐπουράνια (Eph. 3:10), which is obviously the lowest of the different heavenly spheres (cf. 2 C. 12:2) from which σκότος comes into this world (Eph. 6:12). The powers of the air, i.e., of the lowest heavenly sphere, have, somewhat schematically, separated God and man until the coming of Christ. They believed that with the rejection of the human race by God (R. 1:24) they would become unconditional κοσμοκράτορες, until God's original plan of salvation was disclosed in and with the resurrection of Christ (Eph. 3:10). [28] By the crucifixion of Christ they have been deprived of their power (Col. 2:15; → ἄρχων, 489). The wall of partition, which their power over the world implied, has been broken down. Christ has subjected them to Himself (Col. 2:15; Eph. 1:21). He has now been revealed as their Lord (Col. 2:10), [29] as He has been from the very first as their Creator, archetype and ground of existence (Col. 1:16). This does not mean, of course, that their power is destroyed. Man is still engaged in continuing conflict with them (Eph. 6:12). They are not merely behind those who threaten Christians for their faith; [30] they are also behind all moral temptations. Yet they cannot decisively affect the relationship between the Christian and God (R. 8:38), and in the final

---

[23] On the corresponding secular use → 480.

[24] Dibelius, *op. cit.*, 10.

[25] Not special aeons or stellar powers (Reitzenstein Ir. Erl., 235 f. for Eph. or 1 C. 15). On the other hand, men can hardly be meant in Eph. 6:12 (Kurze, 82).

[26] On the basic attitude of Paul to angels, → ἄγγελος, 85 f.

[27] The doctrine of the fall of angels is tacitly assumed (cf. Jd. 6).

[28] The reference to "pure spirits of heaven" (Kurze, 92 f.) is meaningless.

[29] It can hardly be said that Paul is "primarily thinking of the elements" (Dibelius, *op. cit.*, 138).

[30] Dibelius, 164.

consummation they will be definitively stripped of all their influence (1 C. 15:24). [31]

3. In Col. 1:18 Christ is called the ἀρχή in parallelism with the statements that He is the εἰκὼν θεοῦ [32] and πρωτότοκος πάσης κρίσεως [33] who existed πρὸ πάντων. In this sense He is first the ἀρχή from which all creation has received its norm and in which it will result with the fulfilment of the plan of creation. This corresponds to the Stoic doctrine of the ἀρχή as the κοινὸς νόμος, the dominating world principle, which gives to each in the cosmos the place which is meaningful for the whole. In v. 16b we have another formulation of the ἀρχή καὶ τέλος principle. This significance of Christ is also demonstrated in the fact (ἵνα γένηται ἐν πᾶσιν αὐτὸς πρωτεύων) that He is the first to be raised from the dead.

It cannot be said with certainty whether ἀρχή is used in the same sense in Rev. 3:14. [34] This is not unlikely in view of 21:6; 22:13. The ἀρχή/τέλος statement in relation to God and Christ (→ A/Ω) is wholly along the lines of philosophical usage. In strongly eschatological thinking a certain kinship of outlook arose in virtue of the relativising of all historical occurrence (→ 479). Thus in Rev. the One who sits on the throne, or Christ, is the One who is pre-temporal and post-temporal, to whom the categories of time do not apply. [35]

† ἀπαρχή.

A. ἀπαρχή outside the NT.

In the oldest literary example (Hdt., I, 92) ἀπαρχή means not only a. the true "first-fruits" of natural products [1] but also b. the "proportionate gift" from the earnings or possessions of the pious giver, then "thankoffering" for any success, [2] and finally c. any "offering" to the deity or to the servants or sanctuary of the deity, whether as a special or a regular offering. Hence it is used even of the Jewish tax [3] (Jos. Ant., 16, 172), or first-fruits to the state, or an inheritance tax. For details, cf. the similar usage in the LXX. Figuratively it is used in Eur. Ion, 401 f.: προσφθεγμάτων ἀπαρχαί, for the first greeting or address (to Apollo). ἀπαρχή then comes to have, like ἀρχή, the sense of "beginning" (hence the textual variations between ἀπαρχή(ν) and ἀπ' ἀρχῆς), and finally the sense of certification of birth.

Religiously the offering of men as ἀπαρχή is of interest. To be sure, the expression is rare in this sense. [4] When used, it is often not subject to historical control, since it

---

[31] There is no express reference here to human ἀρχαί (Ltzm. C., ad loc.; → 482 on Tt. 3:1.

[32] In correspondence with Alexandrian exegesis of LXX Gn. 1:27, and perhaps in connection with the (Philonic) logos doctrine.

[33] Here we have an even plainer hint of the ideal man of Philo by whom all things were created, v. 16.

[34] "The principle and origin of creation" (Had. Apk., ad loc.). Otherwise the usage reflects Rabbinic influence and the Messiah is before the world, yet Himself created (→ 481 on Jn. 1:1).

[35] Reitzenstein Poim., 287 understands by ἀρχή καὶ τέλος the totality or πλήρωμα (of creation ?).

ἀ π α ρ χ ή. H. Beer, Ἀπαρχή (Diss. Würzbg., 1914); P. Stengel in Pauly-W., I (1894), 2666 f.

[1] Pauly-W., I, 2667.

[2] Beer, 11 f.

[3] v. Preisigke Wört., s.v.

[4] Plut. Thes., 16 (I, 6 f.); Pyth. Or., 16 (II, 402a); Quaest. Graec., 35 (II, 298 f.); K. F.

refers to the offerings of whole portions of the population of a city (usually to the Delphic Apoll.) with a view to colonisation. [5] Yet the clear impression remains that these are regarded as religious acts and are undertaken as such. [6] In addition we read that individuals are offered as → ἀνάθημα to a deity (Eur. Ion., 310, cf. Phoen. Schol. on 214); ἀπαρχή might easily be substituted; and men who dedicated themselves to the service of the sanctuary, or who were made over to the temple by their parents or masters (ἱερόδουλοι etc.; → δοῦλος), [7] were in fact called ἀπαρχή (cf. Diod. S., IV, 66, 6).

In the LXX ἀπαρχή is first used in the original sense a. of the "first-fruits" of the field or flocks which is offered to God (Dt. 18:4; 26:2, 10; Nu. 18:8-12; Neh. 10:37 ff.; cf. Ez. 45:13-16) and thus separated to Him and sanctified (Nu. 5:9). The fiction is maintained that the ἀπαρχαί of men and cattle also belong to God (Nu. 18:15). The meaning of first-fruits can even be carried so far that τῶν πρωτογενημάτων can be added to ἀπαρχή (Ex. 23:19; Sir. 45:20). The term also comes to signify, however, b. the "regular offering" to the temple or the priests [8] (2 Ch. 31:5 ff.). Finally, it means c. "special gifts" or "endowments" etc., also by pagans (more particularly for the sanctuary, Εξ. 39:1; Ex. 25:2 f.; 35:5; 36:6; 2 Esr. 8:25), or to idols (Ez. 20:31). Only rarely is the word used in a non-cultic sense. In 1 Βασ. 10:4; Dt. 33:21 it signifies "share" or "portion" and in ψ 77:51; 104:36 "firstborn." In Sir. 24:9 [9] it is used to indicate the extra-temporality or eternity of the hypostasis wisdom (thus ἀπαρχή is purely temporal): πρὸ τοῦ αἰῶνος ἀπαρχὴν ἔκτισέ με.

B. ἀπαρχή in the NT.

1. The OT ordinance to give a heave-offering of dough as first-fruits (Nu. 15:20 f.) forms the starting-point for the exhortation of Paul in R. 11:16. Dough is allowed to the Israelites if a portion is taken from the secular sphere and dedicated to Yahweh. Paul goes further and brings the whole into this state of desecularisation. Par. with the ῥίζα/κλάδοι image, he uses the ἀπαρχή/φύραμα image to try to make it clear that the election of the Jewish people continues even though a portion has fallen from it. By their membership of the race the first-fruits of faith (e.g., Abraham) [10] guarantee the maintenance by the whole (τὸ φύραμα) of its pre-eminent place in the divine plan of salvation.

2. Similarly the house of Stephanas baptised by Paul (1 C. 1:16) is called the first-fruits of Achaia (1 C. 16:15). The thought is the same as in R. 16:5, unless Paul means that, as formerly men were described as ἀνάθημα πόλεως (→ 484 f.), so now Asia has brought its first-fruits to Christ as an offering. This would include a special service rendered to the Gospel by this first-fruits. [11] To some extent we have a similar use in Jm. 1:18. The constancy of God is shown in the fact that He maintains His resolve in relation to Christianity by giving new birth to the writer and readers; thereby, in a paradoxical formulation, they are a first-

---

Hermann, Lehrb. d. gottesdienstl. Altertümer (1846), 86 ff., esp. 91; cf. P. Stengel, Die griech. Kultusaltert.[3] (1920), Index, s.v.

[5] Cf. Pauly-W., I, 2667.

[6] Plut. Quaest. Graec., 35 (II, 298 f., 299a): colonisation follows the failure of the Delphic offering.

[7] Cf. A. L. Hirt, Die Hierodulen (1818), 52 f., 64.

[8] This is later distinguished from the offering to the Levites, who receive the tithe (Neh. 12:44; 13:5; 2 Ch. 31:10, 12, 14).

[9] Variant for ἀπ᾿ ἀρχῆς.

[10] R. 4, esp. v. 16 — hardly the first Jewish Christians.

[11] As a special offering for Paul during his Ephes. imprisonment?

fruits of humanity to God, "free in relation to all men and subject only to God." [12]

The image of the redemption of the slave (→ ἀγοράζω, 125 ff.) merges into that of dedication to God in Rev. 14:4. [13] In both ways one could become the possession of God (cf. Eur. Ion, 310 : ἀνάθημα πόλεως ἤ τινος πραθεὶς ὕπο). The virgin 12 x 12,000 — even the continence of the ἱερόδουλοι παρθένοι [14] is thus maintained — form the cultic personnel of the Jerusalem which is above. They will always be in the presence of God. They alone can offer the mysterious music of the heavenly sanctuary (v. 2 f.). As ἱερόδουλοι they are τῶν ἄλλων δεσποτῶν καὶ ἀρχόντων ἐλεύθεροι καὶ ἄφετοι (Plut. Amat. Narr., 21 [II, 768a]); this particular position is their reward for offering themselves to God as ἀπαρχή. [15]

3. In R. 8:23 the relationship of giver and recipient [16] is reversed and ἀπαρχή is the first-fruits of God to man (cf. 2 C. 5:5). The gift of the *pneuma* is only provisional. [17] It is only the beginning which will ultimately be followed by υἱοθεσία, by the gift of the σῶμα πνευματικόν. It thus represents the final spiritualisation of man. If ἀπαρχή has temporal significance in R. 8:23, this is emphasised in 1 C. 15:20, 23 (in v. 23 almost statically in antithesis to τέλος). Christ is the first to be raised.

† ἀρχαῖος.

Mostly "from the very beginning" (τὰ ἀρχαῖα, "the earliest time," Plato Tim., 22a), then "belonging to a distant time," "past," "old," though also used of past events in the life of an individual. The word refers to that which is older than παλαιός and confers a romantic aura of dignity : Demetr. Phal. in Rhet. Graec., III, p. 300, 22 ff., Spengel : οἷον τὸ ἀρχαῖοι ἀντὶ τοῦ παλαιοὶ ἐντιμότερον· οἱ γὰρ ἀρχαῖοι ἄνδρες ἐντιμότεροι; (cf. Plat. Tim., 22b). It denotes nearness to nature, to origins (Arist. Rhet., II, 9, p. 1387a, 16 ff.). οἱ ἀρχαῖοι is a fixed formula which takes its sense from the context. Thus in Plat. it signifies "the ancient poets" (παρειλήφαμεν παρὰ ... τῶν ἀρχαίων, Theaet., 180c); in Aristotle "the forefathers" (Pol., III, 15, p. 1286b, 37; ἐπὶ τῶν ἀρχαίων, "in the time of our forefathers," Pol., V, 5, p. 1305a, 7); "the speculative philosophers" (Arist. Meteor., II, 1, p. 353a, 34 ff.); "the pre-Socratics." For Philo, Plato is τὶς τῶν ἀρχαίων (Rer. Div. Her., 181). [1]

In the LXX it is normally the rendering of קֶדֶם and cognates. It is often used for primeval days (thus also ἡμέραι ἀρχαῖαι in ψ 43:1), but also relatively for phases in individual life. Sometimes ἀρχαῖος (→ ἀρχή) can also mean things which happened pre-temporally in the strict sense, when the divine plans were formed (Is. 37:26; cf. 25:1); in such cases the ἀρχαῖα are set in antith. to the ἔσχατα or μέλλοντα (ψ 138:4 f.; Wis. 8:8).

---

[12] Hirt, 53 f. → *infra* on Rev. 14:4.
[13] It is most unlikely that the Jewish Christians are called ἀπαρχή.
[14] Hirt, 62; Eur. Phoen. Schol. on 224.
[15] Loh. Apk., as martyrs ; Had., temporally as the first-fruits.
[16] W. Schubart, *Raccolta di Scritti in Onore di Giacomo Lumbroso* (1925), is reminded of the Egyptian ἀπαρχή, i.e., the certification of noble birth ; he thus suggests the patent or certification of the Spirit. But this robs the phrase of its pregnancy, and it is unlikely that Paul, even if he knew it, would have given the word this specialised sense without explanation. Materially → ἀρραβών, πνεῦμα.
[17] πνεύματος, gen. part.

ἀρχαῖος. [1] Cf. Pesikt. Kah., 32 (198b): ראשונים (without subst.) = Noah, Moses, Abraham, Isaac, Jacob.

In the NT the ἀρχαῖος κόσμος is earthly creation prior to the flood (2 Pt. 2:5). In Mt. 5:21, (27), 33 οἱ ἀρχαῖοι are our (your) forefathers.[1] In Lk. 9:8, 19 the reference is to "one of the ancient prophets,"[2] who evoke implicit trust in contrast to contemporaries who come with a prophetic claim. Ac. 15:21 has in view the past of the people of Israel. On the other hand, in 15:7 the comparatively distant days of the first community in and around Jerusalem are intended, i.e., the time of the conversion of Cornelius, which is shown to be particularly venerable by the use of ἀρχαῖαι. ἀρχαῖος is again a predicate of honour in 21:16.[3]

In Paul (2 C. 5:17) τὰ ἀρχαῖα are all the religious relationships which obtained prior to the resurrection of Christ. Though these have all the honour which the Greeks give to what is old, they are abolished by the fact of Easter. Paul is first thinking of the attitude of contemporaries to the earthly Jesus, then of his own Pharisaic piety.

In Rev. 12:9; 20:2 ὁ ὄφις ὁ ἀρχαῖος is a name for Satan. It is taken over from the Rabbinic usage based on Gn. 3 (S. Dt., 323, on 32:32; Gn. r., 22 on 4:15; Tanch. מצורע 7 [47]).[4]

† ἀρχηγός.[1]

a. The "hero" of a city, who founded it, often gave it his name and became its guardian, as, e.g., Athene for Athens Ditt. Syll.³, 400, 16 (ἀρχηγέτις). This gives us already b. the "originator" or "author" (Zeus ἀρχηγὸς φύσεως, Cleanthes Fr., 537, 2 [I, 121, 35, v. Arnim]). It is then found in application to philosophy (Arist. Metaph., I, 3, p. 983b, 20 f.) and the cultus in the widest sense (Apollo ἀρχηγὸς τῆς εὐσεβείας, Ditt. Syll.³, 711, L 13)[2] and in even looser usage. On the other hand, the hero-ἀρχηγός concept also has the subsidiary sense of c. "captain." All three variations come together again in the NT. In Philo the term ἀρχηγέτης is mostly used for the patriarchs or Adam or Noah (a.). With special pride he calls Abraham the ἀρχηγέτης of the Jews (Abr., 9, 276; Vit. Mos., I, 7). On one occasion, however, he uses the word in a bold metaphor for God as the Creator and Father of all things (Ebr., 42).

In the LXX the ἀρχηγός is usually the political or military "leader" of the whole people, or of a part of it. It is usually the equivalent of רֹאשׁ, שַׂר, or נָשִׂיא; or of the קָצִין elected in time of emergency. In the Chronicler it is also used for רֹאשׁ as the "head" of the clan. It is used more figuratively only in 5 places: Mi. 1:13 (corr. to 1 Macc. 9:61): ἀρχηγὸς τῆς ἁμαρτίας (ἀρχηγοὶ τῆς κακίας): the ἀρχηγός is the leader and example in an action, who stirs others to follow. The superiority of the ἀρχηγός emerges in 1 Macc. 10:47, where only by his εἰρηνεύειν is it made possible for weaker parties to act at all. Cf. also Jer. 3:4; Lam. 2:10.

In the NT Christ is the ἀρχηγός. The term does not seem to be used as in Mi. 1:13. Yet it is thus that Christians, whose πολίτευμα is not of this world, answer the question of their eponymous hero (Plat. Tim., 21e). Because they bear His name, they may be certain not merely that He regards their affairs as

---

[2] Jos. Ant., 12, 413: ἀρχαῖοι προφῆται; M. Ex. 17:14: זקנים הראשונים; Tanch. B בלק § 21 (72a): אבות הראשונים; cf. also Sota, 9, 12; Tanch. B אחרי § 4 (30a). This use of ἀρχαῖος (and "ר") corresponds to the current tendency to ascribe the greater value to religious traditions the higher their claim to primitive revelation.

[3] Cf. ἀρχαῖος μύστης, Insc. Magn., 215b.

[4] Cf. Str.-B. on Rev. 12:9 and Mt. 4:1 (I, 138).

ἀρχηγός. [1] To the ἀρχηγός there corresponds ἀρχηγέτης (fem. ἀρχηγέτις).
[2] Par. to παραίτιος, e.g., Ditt. Syll.³, 704, 10 ff.

His but also that He gives them a share in His power and glory. It is in this sense that Christ is the ἀρχηγὸς καὶ σωτήρ (Ac. 5:31). In the par. saying which is part of the evangelistic preaching of Peter in 3:15 He is particularly the ἀρχηγὸς τῆς ζωῆς. By His resurrection Christians have the pledge that they will share the destiny of their Hero and Saviour.

The concept is more deeply rooted in the circle of specific Christian thinking at Hb. 2:10. Christ is the ἀρχηγὸς τῆς σωτηρίας. He leads many brethren to the honour or glory[3] which is the end of σωτηρία. By His suffering He accomplishes His work as the "Author" of salvation. In 12:2 He is similarly called the "Author" and "Founder" of Christian faith (ἀρχηγὸς τῆς πίστεως), and more particularly, according to the context, of the resultant moral consequences. Yet Jesus is also ἀρχηγὸς τῆς πίστεως in the sense that as the first man He gave an example of faith in God, that by His death He "fulfilled" this faith in God's unconditional love and its overcoming of the barrier of sin, and that He thereby gave this love concrete and once-for-all actualisation in the history of salvation.[4]

ἄρχων.

The ἄρχων has a prominent position in which he exercises authority; he is thus in the first instance a "high official." Most civic constitutions distinguish ἄρχοντες, βουλή and δῆμος (Jos. Ant., 16, 172 of Ephesus; 14, 190 of Sidon).[1] It is also used for consul and praefectus.

In religious usage the word is comparatively rare; Diels, I, 318, 7: ἔστι γὰρ ... ἄρχων ἁπάντων θεός (cf. Corp. Herm., XI, 7: πάσης τάξεως ἄρχοντος). More important is the fact that in a myth of Plato (Leg., X, 903b) we meet archontes who exercise a divinely willed oversight over individual parts of creation. These are cosmic rulers with specific spheres of authority: τούτοις δ' εἰσὶν ἄρχοντες προστεταγμένοι ἑκάστοις ... τέλος ἀπειργασμένοι; they are thus given a positive value. Cf. also Iamblichus Myst., II, 3.

In the LXX, too, the ἄρχων is one who exercises authoritative influence; the term is used for the national, local or tribal leader from Gn. to 2 Ch. In the historical books it is used for a general, though sometimes we also read of the ἄρχοντες τῶν ἱερέων (Neh. 12:7). In the later books it more often denotes officials of the overlord of Palestine (ἄρχων τοῦ βασιλέως, Da. 2:15).

In Da. Θ 10:13, 20 f. cf. 12:1 (also Da. LXX: 10:13) it denotes the celestial beings which guard and represent earthly states (popularly identified with the corresponding peoples), and on the rank and power (→ ἀρχή) of which in the spirit world the position of these states depends. The ἄρχων of Israel has the name of Michael. His victory (or that of the One like a man) over the ἄρχοντες of the Persians and Greeks leads to the dominion of the Jews over these peoples.[2] To a large extent the ἄρχοντες

---

[3] ἀγαγών = who has begun to lead (aor. ingress.) by His activity up to the cross (or part. aor. of identity, Bl.-Debr. § 339, 1).

[4] Otherwise ἀρχηγός means exactly the same as τελειωτής and is to be referred to the crucifixion as the causative presupposition of πίστις.

ἄ ρ χ ω ν. On the planetary deities as ἄρχοντες, cf. Reitzenstein Poim., 270 f. ἄρχων = "high official": Pauly-W., s.v. for an earlier period (esp. Athens); F. Preisigke, Städt. Beamtenwesen (Diss. Halle, 1903), 7-15 f. for a later period; cf. also APF, IV (1908), 119; H. Swoboda, Die griech. Volksbeschlüsse (1890), Index, s.v., esp. 205 f.; G. Busolt-H. Swoboda, Griech. Staatskunde (1920/26), esp. 1081 ff. For the civic organisation of Roman Jews, v. N. Müller, Jüd. Katak. am Monteverde (1919), Index, s.v.

[1] Jos. tries to apply this to Jerusalem in Bell., 2, 405, and so he does not call the high-priests ἄρχοντες (Cr.-Kö.). For the archontate, cf. esp. Athens.

[2] The One like a man seems to be the real leader in the conflict.

are opponents of the people of God who are resisted by the One like a man (later the Messiah) and His allies, and who will be defeated in the last days. In its conflict with earthly enemies the people of God is really engaged with these celestial powers. The same concept is found in Pesikt. Kah., 23 (150b-151a): שרי אמות העולם ἄρχοντες ἐθνῶν τοῦ κόσμου, of Babylon, Greece etc. Cf. also M. Ex., 15, 1 (36b, 6 f., Friedm.): In the future world God will call the princes (שריהם) of the kingdoms to account before He calls the kingdoms themselves.

In the NT ἄρχων 1. denotes Roman and Jewish officials of all kinds, often without specifying the particular office. In Jn. and Lk. the ἄρχοντες are groups in the Jewish people, distinguished by Lk. from the πρεσβύτεροι, γραμματεῖς, ἀρχιερεῖς, and by Jn. from the Pharisees (and sometimes even opposed to them, 12:42), though they may be fellow-members of religious ἀρχαί. Occasionally ἄρχων may simply mean "respected." There is a transition to a more religious sense in relation to Moses in Ac. 7:35.

2. It is used doxologically of the exalted Christ in Rev. 1:5: ἄρχων τῶν βασιλέων τῆς γῆς (the only application to Christ).

3. It denotes those who have at their command supernatural and ungodly powers. In the Synoptists the Pharisees try to counteract the impression of Jesus' healings of demoniacs by arguing that they are accomplished in the name of the ἄρχων of demons (→ Βεελζεβούλ in Mt. 12:24 and Lk. 11:15); the suggestion in Mk. 3:22 is that Beelzebub himself is active in Jesus. [3] Here we see already that for the NT the work of Jesus is a conflict with supernatural powers. In Jn. the tension is carried to the point of almost a transitory dualism. The whole κόσμος is ruled by this ἄρχων. [4] But the Father is with Jesus in the struggle, and his power is already broken (12:31). [5] Judgment is already accomplished on him (16:11). For he tries to put forth his power on the sinless One (14:30) and to engulf Him like a sinner in the destiny of death, his sphere of dominion. [6] Paul speaks of several ἄρχοντες [7] in 1 C. 2:6, 8. They have been rendered inoperative by treating the Lord of δόξα as their prey in ignorance of the divine plan of salvation. [8, 9] The πνεῦμα of the ἄρχων (Eph. 2:2) works irresistibly in non-Christians; only Christians, through the life given them by God (Eph. 2:5), have the power to withstand it. The chief of these personified powers is the ἄρχων of the power(s) of the air [10] (Eph. 2:2; → καταργέω, ἀρχή).

Delling

---

[3] Cf. on ἄρχων τῶν δαιμόνων, jPea., 21b, 27: רבהון דרוחיא; Lev. r., 5, 1 on 4:3: שריהון דרוחתא.

[4] שר העולם, Ex. r., 17, 4 on 12:23.

[5] ἐκβληθήσεται: in the present moment? from the lowest heaven to hell (cf. Rev. 20)? Zn. J. relates the saying to the judgment which is executed in the death of Jesus.

[6] This sphere can never be related to activity as the διάβολος or accuser in the way suggested in Zn. J. on 12:31 and 16:11.

[7] τοῦ αἰῶνος τούτου, gen. obj. not temp.; not, then, referring to earthly rulers. The arguments of Kurze (→ ἀρχή), 77 f. to the contrary are not convincing. Cf. Ltzm. Exc. on 1 C. 2:6; Joh. W., ad loc.; Sickb., ad loc.

[8] And perhaps also of the deity of Christ? Dibelius, op. cit., 90 ff.

[9] W. Bousset, ZNW, 19 (1919/20), 64, thinks that "the myth of the descent to Hades of a redeemer hero, and his conflict with demonic powers, is here applied to Christ's coming down to earth, His mortal conflict on the cross and the victory won by Him." Cf. Dibelius, op. cit., 92 ff.; 234 ff.

[10] Dib. Gefbr., 156: of the kingdom of the air; cf. Meinertz Gefbr.⁴, ad loc.

ἀσέβεια, ἀσεβής, ἀσεβέω → σέβομαι.

---

† ἀσέλγεια

"License," [1] mostly in the physical sphere : Polyb., XXXVI, 15, 4 : περὶ τὰς σωματι-κὰς ἐπιθυμίας; cf. LXX Wis. 14:26; 3 Macc. 2:26; but figuratively also of the soul : Demosth., 21, 1 (with ὕβρις); Philodem. Lib., 42, 12 (anton. κολακεία).

In the NT only the older and sensual sense of "voluptuousness" or "debauchery" is relevant (Mt. 7:22). Man necessarily falls victim to this when cut off from God. It characterises Sodom and Gomorrah (2 Pt. 2:7) and the pagan world generally (Eph. 4:19), also heresy and apostasy (Jd. 4; 2 Pt. 2:2, 18). The special sense of sexual excess is probable in Gl. 5:19 and certain in R. 13:13; 2 C. 12:21; 2 Pt. 2:2, 18; as also in Herm. m., 12, 4, 6; s., 9, 15, 3; v., 2, 2, 2; 3, 7, 2.

Bauernfeind

ἀσθενής, ἀσθένεια, ἀσθενέω, † ἀσθένημα

A. Linguistic Data.

The word group ἀσθενής, ἀσθένεια, ἀσθενέω, formed with ἀ *privativum* from σθένος and used from the time af Pindar, Herodotus and Euripides, signifies "weakness" or "impotence" of different kinds.

In the LXX [1] and esp. Theodotion [2] ἀσθενέω is often used for כשל (e.g., Θ Da. 11:41) and ἀσθένεια for מכשול, the latter esp. in the prophetic books (e.g., Jer. 6:21; 18:23 ?). The explanation of this striking rendering is to be found in the Aram. background of the translators. For the Aram. root תקל, normally used for כשל in the Targumim, means a. "to stumble," "to be weak" ; just as כשל sometimes approximates to this sense (e.g., Ps. 109:24; 31:11). From the fact that ἀσθενέω thus approximates for its part to the sense of "to stumble" (→ n. 9), it is easier to explain Paul's coupling of it with προσκόπτω and σκανδαλίζομαι in R. 14:21 BDG ﬡ. [2]

The part. οἱ ἀσθενοῦντες is often used in the NT for οἱ ἀσθενεῖς (e.g., Jn. 5:3) or interchangeably with it (cf. 1 C. 8:10 with v. 11 and Mt. 10:8 with Lk. 10:9). Similarly

---

ἀσέλγεια. [1] Etymology obscure ; for tentative suggestions : W. Havers, *Indogerm. Forsch.*, 28 (1911), 190 ff. (ἀ = ἐν + dial. σελγ = θελγ- "strike," cf. also A. Walde, *Vergl. Wört. d. indogerm. Sprache*, I [1930], 866); W. Prellwitz, *Zeitschr. f. vergl. Sprachforsch.*, 47 (1916), 295 f. (ἀ intens. + root *tvelg*-"strut"). In the first case the orig. meaning would perhaps be "demonic stroke" (cf. Philostr. Vit. Ap., IV, 20, the expulsion of the demon from the μειράκιον ἀσελγές).

ἀσθενής κτλ. M. Rauer, "Die 'Swachen' in Korinth und Rom nach den Paulusbriefen," BSt., XXI, 2/3 (1923). Bengel on R. 6:17; Nägeli, 31; 41 n. 1; 77.
[1] Cf. Helbing, 127; G. Stählin, *Skandalon* (1930), 111 ff.
[2] Stählin, 85, n. 1; 91, n. 1.

τὸ ἀσθενές is sometimes used for ἡ ἀσθένεια : Thuc., II, 61, 2 : τὸ ἀσθενὲς τῆς γνώμης; P. Oxy., 71, II, 4 : τὸ τῆς φύσεως ἀσθενές; Cl. Al. Strom., I, 1, 14, 2 : τὸ ἀσθενὲς τῆς μνήμης; and in the NT 1 C. 1:25 : τὸ ἀσθενὲς τοῦ θεοῦ; Hb. 7:18 : τὸ αὐτῆς (sc. ἐντολῆς) ἀσθενὲς καὶ ἀνωφελές.

ἀσθένημα is first attested in Arist. (Hist. An., X, 7, p. 638a, 37, Gen. An., I, 18, p. 726a, 15). It is a favourite expression in Hellenism, [3] cf. BGU, 903, 15. It is found once in the NT (R. 15:1) for the individual expression of religious ἀσθένεια (→ 492).

B. Material Data.

1. The first main meaning is "weak," or "weakness," or "to be weak," originally in the physical sense (cf. Cl. Al. Strom., II, 15, 62, 3 : ἀσθένεια σώματος). In the NT the words are hardly ever used of purely physical weakness, [4] but frequently a. in the comprehensive sense of the whole man, e.g., the "weaker sex" in 1 Pt. 3:7: συνοικοῦντες κατὰ γνῶσιν ὡς ἀσθενεστέρῳ σκεύει τῷ γυναικείῳ; cf. P. Lond., 971, 4 : ἀδύνατος γάρ ἐστιν ἡ γυνὴ διὰ ἀσθενίαν τῆς φύσεως; Cl. Al. Paed., II, 10, 107, 2 : πλεονεκτεῖ τὸ θῆλυ διὰ τὴν ἀσθένειαν; or the "unimpressive appearance" of Paul in 1 C. 2:3; 2 C. 10:10 : ἡ ... παρουσία τοῦ σώματος ἀσθενής.

It is often stated or suggested that man as a whole is an ἀσθενὲς ζῷον, as in Cl.Al. Exc. Theod., 73, 3; cf. Max. Tyr., II, 2, p. 20, 5, Hobein : ἀσθενὲς ὂν κομιδῇ τὸ ἀνθρώπειον; Cl. Al. Strom., II, 16, 72, 4 : ἀσθένεια τῶν ἀνθρώπων; Paed., III, 12, 86, 2. In the NT (→ σάρξ) we have the saying of Jesus in Mt. 26:41 that the flesh is ἀσθενής in contrast to the spirit which is πρόθυμον. [5] Paul has particularly in view the religious and moral weakness of the σάρξ, e.g., in R. 6:19 : ἀνθρώπινον λέγω διὰ τὴν ἀσθένειαν τῆς σαρκὸς ὑμῶν. [6] Here ἄνθρωπος, σάρξ and ἀσθένεια are correlative terms. Having the character of σάρξ, all creation shares in its weakness; cf. Philo Deus Imm., 80 : τῶν γεγονότων ... φυσικὴ ἀσθένεια; Spec. Leg., I, 293 f.; also Cl. Al. Strom., VII, 3, 16, 2 : ἀσθένεια ὕλης. In the NT cf. 1 C. 15:43 : σπείρεται ἐν ἀσθενείᾳ, ἐγείρεται ἐν δυνάμει.

b. The opp. of the ἀσθένεια of the σάρξ is the δύναμις of the πνεῦμα which συναντιλαμβάνεται τῇ ἀσθενείᾳ ἡμῶν (R. 8:26). Yet ἀσθένεια is not merely the opposite pole but in the Christian sphere can also be the place where the divine δύναμις is revealed on earth, as in 2 C. 12:9 : ἡ ... δύναμις ἐν ἀσθενείᾳ τελεῖται, "the power is fully expressed in weakness." The acts of God's election relate to the weak (1 C. 1:27: τὰ ἀσθενῆ τοῦ κόσμου ἐξελέξατο ὁ θεὸς ἵνα καταισχύνῃ τὰ ἰσχυρά). Thus Christ, to whom 2 C. 13:3 : οὐκ ἀσθενεῖ ἀλλὰ δυνατεῖ, properly refers, became weak as a man (Hb. 5:2 : καὶ αὐτὸς περίκειται ἀσθένειαν; 2 C. 13:4 : καὶ γὰρ ἐσταυρώθη ἐξ ἀσθενείας). Those who are in Christ share the same weakness (→ συμπάσχω): καὶ γὰρ ἡμεῖς ἀσθενοῦμεν ἐν αὐτῷ. This is the ἀσθενὲς τοῦ θεοῦ of which Paul says in 1 C. 1:25 that it is ἰσχυρότερον τῶν ἀνθρώπων. Thus, along the basic line of the NT paradox, weakness as a form of manifestation of the divine on earth is a mark of honour for the Christian. For he can say : ὅταν γὰρ ἀσθενῶ, τότε δυνατός εἰμι (2 C. 12:10). His weakness is a reason for boasting (2 C. 11:30; 12:5, 9 : ἥδιστα οὖν

---

[3] Nägeli, 41, 1.
[4] But → 493, ἀσθεν- "sickness."
[5] Cf. Cl. Al. Paed., I, 8, 62, 2 : ἀσθένεια τῆς σαρκός etc.
[6] Cf. Ltzm., ad loc.; the sense is very different in the same expression in Gl. 4:13 : ἀσθένεια τῆς σαρκός (→ 493).

μᾶλλον καυχήσομαι ἐν ταῖς ἀσθενείαις) and for joy (2 C. 12:10; 13:9 : χαίρομεν γὰρ ὅταν ἡμεῖς ἀσθενῶμεν). [7]

c. Alongside this weakness, which is accepted by God (1 C. 1:27), there is also a "weakness which must be overcome" (→ σκάνδαλον). This is a weakness of religious and moral condition. In this sense ἀσθενής etc. are not found prior to the NT ; [8] though cf. Epict. Diss., I, 8, 8 : τοῖς ἀπαιδεύτοις καὶ ἀσθενέσι; also Ps. Sol. 17:42 of the Messiah : οὐκ ἀσθενήσει ἐν ταῖς ἡμέραις αὐτοῦ ἐπὶ θεῷ αὐτοῦ, "He shall not be weak, nor waver in his trust in God" [9] (opp. in v. 38 : δυνατὸς ἐλπίδι θεοῦ). Thus used, the terms οἱ ἀσθενεῖς (ἀσθενοῦντες) etc. [10] (→ ἀδύνατος) are favourite expressions of Paul, [11] although with the exception of 1 Th. 5:14 they are limited to his chief epistles. [12] In them he was perhaps adopting slogans current in his churches, especially in Corinth and Rome and on the lips of the opposite group, the "strong," against whom he uses them as a weapon (R. 15:1). [13] More precisely these are the weak in faith, as in R.14:1 (cf. also 4:19): τὸν δὲ ἀσθενοῦντα τῇ πίστει προσλαμβάνεσθε, [14] though it is not usually necessary to say this, cf. 1 C. 8:9 ff.; 9:22; 2 C. 11:29, 30. It is common to the weak in both Corinth and Rome that they lack the γνῶσις of the full Christian (1 C. 8:7), and that they have not completely loosed themselves from their pre-Christian past. In Corinth [15] they are still bound by the συνήθεια τοῦ εἰδώλου, in Rome [16] by the διάκρισις of meats. To some extent the *locus minoris resistentiae* in them is the conscience, cf. 1 C. 8:7, 12 : συνείδησις ἀσθενής (ἀσθενοῦσα).

d. In a further development religious ἀσθένεια has almost the sense of "sin." Hb. 4:15 : ἀρχιερέα ... δυνάμενον συμπαθῆσαι ταῖς ἀσθενείαις ἡμῶν, "with our many infirmities" (→ 490), cf. also 7:28, where ἔχων ἀσθένειαν is the opp. of τετελειωμένος and has thus the sense of moral imperfection. Sinful seems to be the meaning of ἀσθενής in R. 5:6, for ὄντων ἡμῶν ἀσθενῶν is almost synon. with v. 8 : ἔτι ἁμαρτωλῶν ὄντων ἡμῶν.

2. As a special form of bodily weakness "sickness" etc. can also be the meaning of ἀσθένεια etc. [17] Indeed, these terms are the most common NT expressions for sickness. In secular usage νόσον is sometimes added to ἀσθενέω as an explanatory inner object. [18] For the most part, however, it is used absolutely, e.g., BGU,

---

[7] Philosophy demands at least an awareness of one's own weakness : Epict. Diss., II, 11, 1: ἀρχὴ φιλοσοφίας συναίσθησις τῆς αὐτοῦ ἀσθενείας. Cf. W. Grundmann, *Der Begriff der Kraft in der nt.lichen Gedankenwelt* (1932), 75, 87 f., 103 ff., 118. → δύναμις.
[8] Nägeli, 46.
[9] Cf. P. Volz, *Jüd. Eschat. v. Daniel bis Akiba* (1903), 232; R. Kittel in Kautzsch : *straucheln* ("to stumble").
[10] Cf. Rauer, *op. cit.,* 18 ff.; F. Godet, *Komm. zu R.*[2] (1892), II, 277 ff.; E. Hirsch, ZNW, 29 (1930), 75; Stählin, 238 f., 258; F. C. Baur, *Paulus* I (1845), 361 ff., thought the "weak" were Ebionites. A. Ritschl, *Entstehung der altkath. Kirche*[2] (1857), 184 ff., found a reference to the Essenes.
[11] Nägeli, 77.
[12] *Ibid.,* 80.
[13] Cf. Khl. R., 445.
[14] Cf. Sickb., *ad loc.*
[15] Cf. Rauer, *op. cit.,* 27 ff.
[16] *Ibid.,* 76 ff.
[17] Cf. F. S. Steinleitner, *Die Beicht* (→ 268, n.), 97 f.; Reitzenstein Poim., 19 n.
[18] Cf. Kühner-Blass, I, 305b.

594, 6 : μετὰ τὸν θερισμὸν ἐργολαβήσομαι, ἄρτι γὰρ ἀσθενῶ. This is what we often find in the NT, e.g., in Mk. 6:56 : ἐν ταῖς ἀγοραῖς ἐτίθεσαν τοὺς ἀσθενοῦντας. In the NT τῆς σαρκός is sometimes added to ἀσθένεια by way of explanation (Gl. 4:13), but normally it is absolute in both the sing. and the plur., [19] e.g., at Jn. 5:5 : ἔχων ἐν τῇ ἀσθενείᾳ; cf. Ac. 28:9 : οἱ ... ἔχοντες ἀσθενείας. For ἀσθενής (Lk. 10:9 : θεραπεύετε τοὺς ἐν αὐτῇ — sc. τῇ πόλει — ἀσθενεῖς) we often have ὁ ἀσθενῶν, as in the par. at Mt. 10:8 : ἀσθενοῦντας θεραπεύετε.

Regarding the cause of sickness there are two parallel views in the NT. a. It is the work of spirits, e.g., Mt. 17:18 and esp. Lk. 13:11: πνεῦμα ... ἀσθενείας. b. It is the penalty of sin, esp. 1 C. 11:30; Mk. 2:5 ff.; also Jm. 5:16. Both attempts at explanation are widespread [20] and are often found together. For the second, cf. esp. the penitential psalms of the OT (e.g., Ps. 31:10), [21] as also Ps. 107:17 f. and expiatory inscriptions from Asia Minor (e.g., ἁμαρτήσας καταπίπτω εἰς ἀσθένειαν). [22] There is an ἀσθένεια πρός θάνατον (Jn. 11:4) as there is also a ἁμαρτία πρὸς θάνατον (1 Jn. 5:16). But there are different ways of healing (θεραπεύειν ἀπὸ ἀσθενειῶν, Lk. 5:15; 8:2). Primarily in the NT we have the miracles of Jesus, τὰ σημεῖα ἃ ἐποίει ἐπὶ τῶν ἀσθενούντων (Jn. 6:2), on account of which Mt. (8:17) can sum up the work of Jesus in a literal translation and understanding of the saying in Is. 53:4 : αὐτὸς τὰς ἀσθενείας ἡμῶν ἔλαβεν καὶ τὰς νόσους ἐβάστασεν. In place of the healing methods of Jesus (cf. Lk. 13:12 f.) and the apostles (Mt. 10:8; Ac. 28:9), there arise in the Church others for which parallels may be found in religious history, such as anointing with oil (and prayer) in Jm. 5:14 (16), [23] the laying on of handkerchiefs and passing under the shadow of the apostles (Ac. 19:12; 5:15). [24]

3. Figuratively, ἀσθένεια can also mean "impotence" in the sense of "inner poverty" or "incapacity." Thus we read of the beggarly elemental spirits in Gl. 4:9 : τὰ ἀσθενῆ καὶ πτωχὰ στοιχεῖα; of the inability of the Law in respect of the salvation of men in R. 8:3 : τὸ ... ἀδύνατον τοῦ νόμου, ἐν ᾧ ἠσθένει διὰ τῆς σαρκός; Hb. 7:18 : ἀθέτησις ... γίνεται προαγούσης ἐντολῆς διὰ τὸ αὐτῆς ἀσθενὲς καὶ ἀνωφελές; of the insignificance of certain members of the body in 1 C. 12:22 : ἀλλὰ πολλῷ μᾶλλον τὰ δοκοῦντα μέλη τοῦ σώματος ἀσθενέστερα ὑπάρχειν ἀναγκαῖά ἐστιν. [25]

4. Finally ἀσθένεια can also mean "economic weakness" or literal "poverty," as in Ac. 20:35 : δεῖ ἀντιλαμβάνεσθαι τῶν ἀσθενούντων, cf. Aristoph. Pax, 636 ; Dg., 10, 5 (ἀσθενής).

Stählin

---

[19] In the plur., cf. the occasional distinction of 72 ἀσθένειαι. Cf. *Anecdota Graeco-Byzantina*, ed. Vassiliev (1893), 323 ff.

[20] Cf. O. Rühle, "Krankheit," RGG², III, 1277 ff.; Steinleitner, *op. cit.*, 99; F. J. Dölger, *D. heilige Fisch*, II (1922), 162 ff. On the whole question cf. also Jn. 9:2 and the new answer of Jesus in v. 3.

[21] Cf. H. Gunkel, *Ausgewählte Psalmen*⁴ (1917), *passim* ; H. Hehn, *Sünde und Erlösung nach bibl. u. babyl. Anschauung* (1903), 12 ff.

[22] Steinleitner, No. 20, p. 46.

[23] Cf. Dibelius, *ad loc.*; → ἀλείφω and δύναμις.

[24] Cf. Chant. de la Saussaye, I, 33, 56; among the Celts etc. healing power is attributed to contact with holy men and things.

[25] Cf. Cl. Al. Strom., VI, 18, 67, 5 : ἀσθενὴς δωρεά, "a poor gift."

---

† ἀσκέω

In the NT this is found only at Ac. 24:16 : ἐν τούτῳ καὶ αὐτὸς ἀσκῶ ἀπρόσκοπον συνείδησιν ἔχειν πρὸς τὸν θεὸν καὶ τοὺς ἀνθρώπους διὰ παντός in the sense of "I exercise or exert myself." In taking pains to have a conscience void of offence towards God and man, Paul is careful to listen constantly to the admonishing and warning voice of conscience in order not to offend God or man and not to neglect any obligations towards them.

This sense of ἀσκεῖν is already current in classical and Hellenistic Greek, and also in Jewish Hellenism.

Homer uses the term only in the sense of technical adornment and artistic effort. [1] From the time of Herodotus and Pindar, however, it acquires the more spiritual sense of exercising a virtue, e.g., Hdt., I, 96; VII, 209 : τὴν ἀληθείην ἀσκέειν; Plat. Euthyd., 283a : σοφίαν καὶ ἀρετὴν ἀσκεῖν; Gorg., 527e : δικαιοσύνην καὶ ... ἀρετήν; though naturally also in the opp. sense, as in Aesch. Prom., 1065 : κακότητ᾽ ἀσκεῖν. With the acc., ἀσκεῖν in this sense (e.g., in Ac. 24:16) has also an infin., e.g., Xenoph. Cyrop., V, 5, 12 : ἀσκῶν ... τοὺς φίλους ὡς πλεῖστα ἀγαθὰ ποιεῖν; Epict. Diss., III, 12, 10 : ἄσκησον, εἰ γοργὸς εἶ, λοιδορούμενος ἀνέχεσθαι, ἀτιμασθεὶς μὴ ἀχθεσθῆναι. An important special meaning develops in relation to σῶμα ἀσκεῖν, i.e., the training of the body in the sense of gymnastic and athletic exercises ; hence ἀσκητής = ἀθλητής (→ ἀθλέω), as may be seen clearly in Xenoph. Mem., I, 2, 19 : ὁρῶ γάρ, ὥσπερ τὰ τοῦ σώματος ἔργα τοὺς μὴ τὰ σώματα ἀσκοῦντας οὐ δυναμένους ποιεῖν, οὕτω καὶ τὰ τῆς ψυχῆς ἔργα τοὺς μὴ τὴν ψυχὴν ἀσκοῦντας οὐ δυναμένους. Thus ἀσκεῖν becomes synon. with → γυμνάζεσθαι (cf. Epict. Diss., III, 10, 7 : ἕνεκα τούτου ἐγυμναζόμην, ἐπὶ τοῦτο ἤσκουν), or with → μελετᾶν (cf. Epict. Diss., I, 25, 31; 1 Tm. 4:7). [2]

The Greek world was already familiar with spiritual asceticism in the sense of exercise in the taming of the passions and the doing of righteous acts, or of conscious and almost technical exercise in the control of thoughts and impulses. [3] We can see this in the older Sophists, who singled out ἄσκησις as a third factor (alongside φύσις and μάθησις) in the process of education. [4] Further examples are to be found especially in Epict. Diss., III, 3, 16 : καὶ τοῦτο εἰ ἐποιοῦμεν καὶ πρὸς τοῦτο ἠσκούμεθα καθ᾽ ἡμέραν ἐξ ὄρθρου μέχρι νυκτός, ἐγίνετο ἄν τι, νὴ τοὺς θεούς, and again in IV, 1, 81; III, 2, 1, where there is mention of the three τόποι in which the man who would be καλὸς καὶ ἀγαθός must exercise himself. Cf. also III, 12, 8. In Epictetus, however, we can already see indications of the later concept of asceticism, i.e., the voluntary adoption of renunciations, privations and self-chastenings, cf. Ench., 47.

Philo introduced both the term and the reality into theological ethics. He allots the three functions in the Sophist doctrine of education, i.e., μάθησις, φύσις and ἄσκησις, to the three patriarchs Abraham, Isaac and Jacob. [5] Jacob is for him the

---

ἀ σ κ έ ω . [1] So already in Athenagoras Suppl., 16, 1; 22, 8.

[2] Cf. also the connection with μανθάνειν in Plat. Leg., VIII, 831c; Gorg., 509a.

[3] K. Deissner, *Das Idealbild des stoischen Weisen* (1930), 5 f.; "Die Seelentechnik in der antiken Religion u. Sittlichkeit im Lichte d. Christentums," in *Von der Antike zum Christentum, Festschr. f. V. Schultze* (1931), 11 ff.

[4] For bibl. and examples, v. P. G. Gunning, *De Sophistis Graeciae praeceptoribus* (Diss. Amsterdam, 1915).

[5] K. Siegfried, *Philo v. Alex.* (1875), 258 ff.

model ἀσκητής = ἀθλητής, the spiritual wrestler (on the basis of Gn. 32:24 ff.); [6] cf. Leg. All., III, 190 ... πτερνισθήσεται πρὸς τοῦ πάλην ἠσκηκότος Ἰακώβ — πάλην δ’ οὐ τὴν σώματος, ἀλλ’ ἣν παλαίει ψυχή, πρὸς τοὺς ἀνταγωνιστὰς τρόπους αὐτῆς πάθεσι καὶ κακίαις μαχομένη. Here we have the foundation of the later ecclesiastical concept of asceticism to the degree that in this bodily and spiritual training the emphasis lies on the taming of desires and abstention from all enjoyment. [7] Philo already makes the link ὀλιγοδεῖαν καὶ ἐγκράτειαν ἀσκεῖν in Praem. Poen., 100, as also καθαρὰν εὐσέβειαν ἀσκεῖν in Abr., 129.

It is from him particularly that the fathers from the time of Clement of Alexandria and Origen adopt both the usage and the corresponding scriptural types (Jacob etc.). Cf. Cl. Al. Paed., I, 7, 57; Strom., I, 5, 31 (Jacob the ἀθλητής and ἀσκητής); Orig. Cels., VII, 48 (of Christians): ἀσκοῦσι τὴν παντελῆ παρθενίαν; and the ancient burial inscription : [8] τὸν μοναδικὸν ἀσκήσας βίον. [9] Yet already in Tat. Or. Graec., 19 there is reference to the θανάτου καταφρονεῖν καὶ τὴν αὐτάρκειαν ἀσκεῖν of the philosophers, which they preach but do not practise. ἄσκησις is here training and perseverance in renunciation and contempt for death. The asceticism of Christian monasticism has one of its roots in that of the NT. But it does not take from it either the despising of the body or the prescription of definite exercises.

Apart from Ac. 24:16, Paul never uses the word. Yet in substance we already find in Paul this training in bodily and spiritual self-discipline and renunciation, e.g., in 1 C. 9:25-27, where the words → ἐγκρατεύεσθαι and → ὑπωπιάζω μου τὸ σῶμα καὶ δουλαγωγῶ obviously depict the ἀσκεῖν of the spiritual athlete. This meaning is not so dramatically expressed in Ac. 24:16. It is obvious, however, that the concern of the apostle to have a conscience void of offence is a definite task which fully occupies him from morning to night in all the situations in which he has dealings with God and men.

In the LXX ἀσκεῖν and its derivatives are almost completely absent. Only in 2 Macc. 15:4 do we find ἀσκεῖν τὴν ἑβδομάδα, "to keep the Sabbath" (= → τηρεῖν in Rev. 1:3 and → παρατηρεῖν in Gl. 4:10); in 4 Macc. 13:22 ἄσκησις occurs in the sense of discipline and training in the keeping of the Law : καὶ αὔξονται σφοδρότερον διὰ συντροφίας καὶ τῆς καθ’ ἡμέραν συνηθείας καὶ τῆς ἄλλης παιδίας καὶ τῆς ἡμετέρας ἐν νόμῳ θεοῦ ἀσκήσεως. The word is strangely absent from the Test. XII, though in Ep. Ar., 168 we have a statement which almost reads like a commentary on Ac. 24:16 in its use of ἀσκεῖν: οὐδὲν εἰκῇ κατατέτακται διὰ τῆς γραφῆς οὐδὲ μυθωδῶς, ἀλλ’ ἵνα δι’ ὅλου τοῦ ζῆν καὶ ἐν ταῖς πράξεσιν ἀσκῶμεν δικαιοσύνην πρὸς πάντας ἀνθρώπους, μεμνημένοι τοῦ δυναστεύοντος θεοῦ. [10] Paul gives us an example of genuine Jewish Hellenism in Ac. 24:16 and the whole passage 24:14-18. Cf. also what the Jew Trypho is made to say in Just. Dial., 8, 3 : ἄμεινον δὲ ἦν φιλοσοφεῖν ἔτι σε τὴν Πλάτωνος ἢ ἄλλου του φιλοσοφίαν ἀσκοῦντα καρτερίαν καὶ σωφροσύνην ἢ λόγοις ἐξαπατηθῆναι ψευδέσι κτλ. This is undoubtedly the asceticism of Gk. philosophy, which is also included in Ac. 24:16. [11]

---

[6] Cf. H. Leisegang, Indices, 124 f., 61; Siegfried, 266 ff.
[7] E. Bréhier, Les Idées philosophiques et religieuses de Philon d'Alexandrie (1908), 265 ff.
[8] Preisigke Wört., 225.
[9] For ecclesiastical usage, cf. Canon. Apost., 53; Canones Gangra, 12 f., 21 (F. Lauchert, Die Kanones d. altkirchlichen Concilien [1896], 8, 82 f.). Cf. also Suic. Thes., s.v.
[10] Cf. again Ep. Ar., 225 : εὔνοιαν ἀσκεῖν; 255 : τὴν εὐσέβειαν ἀσκεῖν; 285.
[11] The Gk. δικαιοσύνην ἀσκεῖν is first found in Christian literature in Herm. m., 8, 10, cf. θεοσέβειαν ἀσκεῖν in 2 Cl., 20, 4. Both phrases express what is meant in Ac. 24:16. The synon. εὐσέβειαν ἀσκεῖν, according to Moult.-Mill., s.v., is found in a Paris Pap. (63, VIII, 24), 2nd cent. B.C.

It is perhaps surprising that when ἀσκεῖν is so common in Jewish Hellenism and Christian literature from the time of the post-apostolic fathers, it should occur only once in the NT, and its derivatives not at all. For Paul (cf. 1 C. 9:25 ff.), the author of Acts and above all the author of the Pastorals this is possibly a mere accident. Cf. especially 1 Tm. 4:7 f., where γύμναζε σεαυτόν seems to be the equivalent of ἄσκει and σωματικὴ γυμνασία of ἄσκησις, just as τὸ δὲ ἀσκεῖν εὐσέβειαν might well have been written for the antithetical ἡ δὲ εὐσέβεια.

Windisch

| ἀσπάζομαι, † ἀπασπάζομαι, ἀσπασμός |

A. ἀσπάζεσθαι and ἀσπασμός outside the NT.

ἀσπάζεσθαι (etymology uncertain) means to effect ἀσπασμός, i.e. mostly "to proffer the greeting" which is customary on entering a house or meeting someone on the street or parting. ἀσπασμός consists in such gestures as "embracing,"[1] "kissing,"[2] "offering the hand,"[3] and even sometimes *proskynesis*[4] (→ προσκυνεῖν). It also consists in words, especially a set form of greeting. There is a good example in Herm. v., 4, 2, 2: ἀσπάζεταί με λέγουσα· Χαῖρε σύ, ἄνθρωπε, καὶ ἐγὼ αὐτὴν ἀντησπασάμην· Κυρία, χαῖρε (cf. 1, 1, 4; 1, 2, 2 and Lk. 1:27, 29). A special, official form of ἀσπασμός is the "homage" paid to an overlord or superior. This can be accomplished a. by a visit: Jos. Ant., 1, 290; 6, 207. ἀσπάζεσθαι can thus mean "to pay someone a ceremonious call," "to pay an official visit to a high dignitary,"[5]; ἀσπασμός itself has here the force of an "official call," e.g., P. Flor., 296, 57: ἡ ἐποφειλομένη ὑμῖν προσκύνησις καὶ ἀσπασμός μου (cf. Ac. 25:13: ἀσπασάμενοι τὸν Φῆστον). Homage can also be paid b. by acclamation, cf. Plut. Pomp., 12 (I, 624e): αὐτοκράτορα τὸν Πομπήιον ἠσπάσαντο, 13 (I, 625c): μεγάλη φωνῇ Μάγνον ἠσπάσατο (cf. Mk. 15:18 in the NT). ἀσπασμός in a letter is a greeting from a distance, which is a substitute for greeting and embracing in personal encounter. It expresses sincere attachment in separation and thus serves to strengthen personal fellowship.[6] The custom of epistolary greeting was only gradually adopted in the sphere of Greek and Roman culture. In letters of the pre-Christian period greetings are not too common and there are no long series of greetings.[7]

ἀ σ π ά ζ ο μ α ι κ τ λ. [1] Plut. Tit., 11 (I, 375b): ἀσπαζόμενοι καὶ περιπλεκόμενοι.
[2] Plut. Ages., 11 (I, 602b): προσιόντος ὡς ἀσπασομένου καὶ φιλήσοντος, cf. 1 C. 16:20 etc. (→ 501); Just. Apol., I, 65, 2; Ps.-Luc. Asin., 17: φιλήμασιν ἠσπάζοντο ἀλλήλους.
[3] Plut. Phoc., 27 (I, 753e), Cato, 13 f. (I, 765a).
[4] Jos. Ant., 11, 331: (Alex. the Gt.) προσελθὼν μόνος προσεκύνησεν τὸ ὄνομα καὶ τὸν ἀρχιερέα πρῶτος ἠσπάσατο.
[5] Instances from the pap. in Preisigke Wört., s.v. "Jüdisches"; for Josephus v. Schl. Mt., 669 f.
[6] Ditt. Or., 219, 42 ff.; Ditt. Syll.³, 700, 40 ff.; 798, 20 ff.
[7] Cf. F. Ziemann, *De epistularum Graecarum formulis solemnibus* (Diss. Halle, 1911), 325 ff.; F. H. Exler, *The Form of the Ancient Greek Letter* (Diss. Washington, 1923), 111 f., 115, 136; O. Roller, *Das Formular der paulinischen Briefe* (1933), 67 ff.

Ziemann gives as the oldest instances Cic. Fam., XVI, 4, 5 (50 B.C.): *Lepta tibi salutem dicit et omnes,* and P. Oxy., IV, 745 : ἀσπάζου πάντας τοὺς παρ' ἡμῶν (25 B.C.). Roller, [8] however, has found rather more examples both from the last four centuries B.C. and the first century A.D. (to 70 A.D.). Thus he mentions other greetings in Cicero, e.g., Att., II, 9 : *Terentia tibi salutem,* καὶ Κικέρων ὁ μικρὸς ἀσπάζεται Τίτον 'Αθηναῖον. But only if the letters of Plato are genuine, esp. Ep. 13, do we really have examples of the custom in the 4th century B.C., and the letter in Witkowski Epist. priv. Graec. (1911), No. 37 (162 B.C.) is hardly relevant in relation to this custom.

Epistolary greetings are rather better attested in the oriental correspondence which has come down to us. Thus the religious wishing of salvation is already an established custom in the East at the time of the Amarna letters ; [9] cf. in the letter of Ribadda (Knudtzon, No. 68): "Ribadda spoke to his lord : The lady of Gubla give power to the king my lord ..." ; or in a letter found in Taanak : [10] "... May the lord of the gods protect thy life." Rather weaker is the phrase "many greetings" (שְׁלָם בְּלָא) in Ezr. 5:7, though this is also to be understood as a religious wish (LXX : Δαρείῳ τῷ βασιλεῖ εἰρήνη πᾶσα). More exactly this greeting corresponds to the salutations of the apostolic letters (χάρις καὶ εἰρήνη κτλ.). Greetings are also found in the Aramaic pap. letters from Elephantine (5th cent. B.C.). A special instance is the letter of Hošeh to a woman Slwh, [11] which consist almost entirely of greetings : "The gods ask concerning thy salvation שלמכי ישׁאלו ... and concerning the salvation (שׁלם) of my lord Menachem ..." This shows that the religious wishing of salvation in letters, of which the Gk. ἀσπάζομαι, ἀσπάζου, etc. is a secularised form, was customary in pre-Ptolemaic Judaism.

The basic meaning of the term seems to be "to embrace." It denotes the embrace of greeting as well as the erotic embrace of love, Plat. Symp., 209b : τά ... σώματα τὰ καλά ... ἀσπάζεται. That this meaning is echoed in epistolary greeting is shown in Ps.-Plato, Ep., 13 (363d): καὶ τοὺς συσφαιριστὰς ἀσπάζου ὑπὲρ ἐμοῦ, "embrace our fellow-players in my place." [12] From this original concrete meaning the more general sense follows, a. with a personal object, "to be fond of someone," "to like someone," "to agree to something," "to pay one's respects to someone" (Plat. Ap., 29d. : ὅτι ἐγὼ ὑμᾶς, ὦ ἄνδρες 'Αθηναῖοι, ἀσπάζομαι μὲν καὶ φιλῶ); b. with a material object, "to give oneself gladly to something," e.g., Ps.-Xenoph., Ep., 1, 2 : σοφίαν ἀσπάζεσθαι; Just. Apol., I, 39, 5; 45, 5; Test. G. 3:3 : καταλαλιὰν ἀσπάζεται, "to accept with pleasure a situation or event," Eur. Ion., 587 : ἐγὼ δὲ τὴν μὲν συμφορὰν ἀσπάζομαι; Jos. Ant., 6, 82 : Σαοῦλος δὲ τούτων μὲν ἠσπάζετο τὴν εὔνοιαν καὶ τὴν περὶ αὐτὸν προθυμίαν; 7, 187: τοὺς λόγους ἀσπασάμενος; "to welcome a given factor or a prospect." Hb. 11:13 : μὴ κομισάμενοι τὰς ἐπαγγελίας, ἀλλὰ πόρρωθεν αὐτὰς ἰδόντες καὶ ἀσπασάμενοι (sc. the promised city of 11:10), is mostly interpreted along these lines, but there seems to be rather closer analogy to greeting from a distance, cf. Plat. Charm., 153b : καί με ὡς εἶδον εἰσιόντα ἐξ ἀπροσδοκήτου εὐθὺς πόρρωθεν ἠσπάζοντο ἄλλος ἄλλοθεν. ἀσπασμός has the corresponding meaning of

---

[8] *Op. cit.,* 472 ff., n. 312.
[9] A suggestion of v. Rad.
[10] AOT, 371.
[11] P. 13, 462 in E. Sachau, *Aramäische Papyri und Ostraka aus ... Elephantine* (1911), 58 f.; W. Staerk, *Alte und neue aramäische Papyri, Kl. T.,* 94 (1912), 68 f.; A. Cowley, *Aramaic Papyri of the Fifth Century B.C.* (1923), No. 39.
[12] The rendering given by O. Apelt in his *Platons Briefe* (1918), 109 : "Give my sincere greetings ...," can hardly be right.

"embrace," "love," e.g., Plat. Leg., XI, 919e : τῷ ἐκείνων μίσει τε καὶ ἀσπασμῷ; b. "greeting," "visit," P. Oxy., 471, 67; P. Flor., 296, 57. [13]

In the LXX proper ἀσπάζεσθαι occurs only once at Ex. 18:7 in transl. of שָׁאַל לְשָׁלוֹם, "to ask concerning the welfare." The whole passage introduces fairly fully the customary greetings on a visit : [14] ἐξῆλθεν δὲ Μωυσῆς εἰς συνάντησιν τῷ γαμβρῷ, καὶ προσεκύνησεν αὐτῷ καὶ ἐφίλησεν αὐτόν, καὶ ἠσπάσαντο ἀλλήλους. [15] ἀσπασμός is not found at all in the LXX. ἀσπάζεσθαι in this sense is more common in the Apocrypha : Tob. 5:10; 9:6 א; 10:12 א of the parting greeting ἀπασπασάμενος, with the parting word βάδιζε εἰς εἰρήνην; 1 Macc. 7:29, 33; 11:6; 12:17; 3 Macc. 1:8 of solemn meeting and accompaniment, as in Jos. Vit., 325. In Ep. Ar. ἀσπάζεσθαι is used of the greeting of the king by ambassadors after their return (173), of the greeting of an embassy by the king (179), and of a friendly gesture of the king to his guests at table when they have given good answers to his questions (235). ἀσπασμός is the greeting at the beginning of an audience or session (246) and the attendance owed to the king at the commencement of the working day (304). In Philo ἀσπάζεσθαι occurs only once [16] in Rer. Div. Her., 44 : ἀγάπησον οὖν ἀρετὰς καὶ ἄσπασαι ψυχῇ τῇ σεαυτοῦ καὶ φίλησον ὄντως καὶ ἥκιστα βουλήσῃ τὸ φιλίας παράκομμα (caricature) ποιεῖν, καταφιλεῖν, cf. 40-43; the meaning is consciously spiritualised to signify spiritual embrace or reception, being connected with the winning of non-erotic love. ἀσπασμός is not found at all in Philo.

B. In the NT.

1. Jesus' Rules of Greeting.

For the Jews greeting is an important ceremony. This may be seen from Jesus' accusation that the scribes love τοὺς ἀσπασμοὺς ἐν ταῖς ἀγοραῖς (Mk. 12:38; Mt. 23:6 f.; Lk. 20:46; 11:43). Like the seat of honour in the synagogue or at a feast, greeting in the market-place is one of the distinctions to which rabbis raise claim by reason of the dignity of their office. A greeting is given on the street when שָׁלוֹם עָלֶיךָ is first addressed to the one who is to be honoured. In their desire for a greeting, the rabbis want to be greeted first and therefore publicly recognised as superiors (cf. Alexander and the high-priest in Jos. Ant., 11, 331, → 496, n. 4). Censuring the claim of the rabbis to ἀσπασμός, Jesus does not wish his disciples to be honoured by greetings but rather to greet others. It is known that this basic principle was taught and practised by many rabbis, especially Jochanan ben Zakkai. [17]

To offer rabbis the ἀσπασμός coveted by them was the impulse of all pious Jews. Only once (Mk. 9:15) do we read that the multitude respectfully greeted Jesus : ἰδόντες αὐτὸν ἐξεθαμβήθησαν, καὶ προστρέχοντες ἠσπάζοντο αὐτόν. But there is frequent mention of → προσκυνεῖν before Jesus, and this is a particularly respectful form of ἀσπασμός. The caricature of such greeting is the mocking of Jesus as the King of the Jews in Mk. 15:18 f. : καὶ ἤρξαντο ἀσπάζεσθαι αὐτόν· χαῖρε, βασιλεῦ τῶν Ἰουδαίων· ... καὶ τιθέντες τὰ γόνατα προσεκύνουν αὐτῷ (ἀσπάζεσθαι here means to "acclaim," → 496.

---

[13] → 496; Preisigke Wört., s.v.; very rare in the pap.

[14] On the Heb. ceremonies of greeting, cf. G. B. Winer, *Bibl. Realwörterbuch,* s.v. "Höflichkeit"; RE³, VII, 217 f.; BW, s.v. "Gruss."

[15] Ges.-Buhl, s.v. שׁאל. There is a literal transl. in Ju. 18:15 B : καὶ ἠρώτησαν αὐτὸν εἰς εἰρήνην (א :ἠσπάσαντο αὐτόν).

[16] H. Leisegang told me this personally ; the word does not occur in his Index to Philo.

[17] Str.-B., I, 382.

According to Mt. 5:47 the ἀσπάζεσθαι of brothers is also customary among the heathen ; it is a natural sign of the fellowship created by kinship and friendship. Jesus desires that we should greet on the street those who are not our brothers, and even our enemies, and thus draw them into the circle of our fellowship, not recognising the enmity. In just the same way R. Jochanan ben Zakkai tried to be the first to extend greetings even to a *Goy* (bBer., 17a).

How seriously Jesus took this matter of ἀσπάζεσθαι may be seen finally from the rule which He gave His envoys in Mt. 10:12 f.; Lk. 10:5 (for the ἀσπάσασθε αὐτήν of Mt. Lk. has the more concrete πρῶτον λέγετε· εἰρήνη τῷ οἴκῳ τούτῳ). The point at issue is that of greeting on entry into a strange house.[18] The customary → εἰρήνη σοι is the word of greeting.[19] This peace is presented quite realistically as a *dynamis*. If the family is worthy of it, i.e., if the messenger is received accordingly (Mt.), then the power of the greeting comes on it as the Spirit comes on man,[20] or blood[21] or a curse to his destruction.[22] Otherwise the εἰρήνη of the disciples will return to them. This part of their power of εἰρήνη will not, then, remain in the house, but will come back to the disciples for other use.[23] The εἰρήνη is thus a power with which the disciples can spread blessing but the withdrawal of which has the force of a curse. The power is linked with the word and corresponding gesture.[24] The greeting of apostles who are endued with ἐξουσία (Mt. 10:1) = δύναμις is thus a sacramental action.[25]

In a certain contrast to this high estimation of the greeting is the prohibition in Lk. 10:4 : μηδένα κατὰ τὴν ὁδὸν ἀσπάσησθε (without par.), i.e., Do not allow yourselves to be held up on the way by time-wasting ceremonies, do not enter into conversations on the streets, but hasten to the place where you are to stay and work (anal. 2 K. 4:29). The disciples are thus forbidden to make contacts by greeting in the course of their actual journeys.[26]

2. The ἀσπασμός in Religious Narrative.

According to Lk. 1:29 Mary wonders concerning the greeting of the angel : ποταπὸς εἴη ὁ ἀσπασμὸς οὗτος (ἀσπασμός is here a word of greeting). Each greeting has in fact its own ring. The Greek χαῖρε (→ 496), punningly deepened by κεχαριτωμένη, is related to the biblical ὁ κύριος μετὰ σοῦ of Ju. 6:12; Rt. 2:4. In the ἀσπασμός there is proclaimed already something of the wonderful message of grace which the future mother of Christ is at once to receive.

---

[18] Cf. Lk. 1:28 f., the ἀσπασμός of the angel in the house of Mary ; Lk. 1:40 f., the ἀσπασμός of Mary in the house of Elisabeth ; Herm. v., 1, 2, 2, the ἀσπασμός of the *ecclesia ; ibid.,* 4, 2, 2; 5, 1, that of the Shepherd at the bed of Hermas.

[19] Str.-B., I, 388 f., Schl. Mt., 333.

[20] Mt. 3:16; Ac. 19:6; Lk. 11:2 Marcion.

[21] Mt. 23:35; 27:25.

[22] L. Brun, *Segen und Fluch im Urchristentum* (1932), 33. Cf. Gn. 27:13; Ju. 9:57; ψ 108:17; Da. 9:11.

[23] Lk. (10:6) writes : If there is there a υἱὸς εἰρήνης, i.e., a man to whom the εἰρήνη can cleave ; and then in the next sentence : ἐπαναπαήσεται ἐπ' αὐτὸν ἡ εἰρήνη ὑμῶν. He is really thinking of the πνεῦμα, cf. Nu. 11:25 f.; Is. 11:2; 1 Pt. 4:14.

[24] Cf. the anal. ceremony of shaking off the dust in Mt. 10:14 and par. and Ac. 18:6, where the gesture seems to be linked with a curse. The house is thus given up to judgment.

[25] C. Clemen, *Die Reste der primitiven Religion im ältesten Christentum* (1916), 20 f.; L. Brun, *Segen und Fluch,* 33; A. Merx, *Ev. Mt.* (1902), 116.

[26] Hence J. Wellhausen, *Das Ev. Lucae* (1904), 40 : Do not make yourselves known before the time. The forbidding of χαίρειν λέγειν in 2 Jn. 10 is for other reasons.

A second greeting of profoundest importance and remarkable power is that with which Mary greets Elisabeth in Lk. 1:40-44. We are not told how it runs, but the φωνὴ τοῦ ἀσπασμοῦ of Mary stirs the child John in his mother's womb; it reveals to him the nearness of the mother of Christ. Through the greeting Elisabeth herself is filled with the "Holy Ghost." Thus here again there operates in the greeting a *dynamis* of divine character.

3. The Greeting of the Apostle.

In Ac. it is often emphasised that the apostle greets a congregation either on arrival (18:22; 21:7, 19) or at parting (20:1; 21:6). At Ac. 18:22 ἀναβὰς καὶ ἀσπασάμενος τὴν ἐκκλησίαν simply means that he visited the church. [27] On the other hand, κατηντήσαμεν εἰς Πτολεμαΐδα καὶ ἀσπασάμενοι τοὺς ἀδελφοὺς ἐμείναμεν ἡμέραν μίαν παρ' αὐτοῖς at 21:7 lays a certain emphasis on the scene of the greeting, i.e., in the assembly, while at 21:19 the report is preceded by a solemn greeting of the elders assembled in the house of James. Similarly, the greeting is significant at parting. According to Ac. 20:1 the ἀσπάσασθαι or parting greeting forms the conclusion of an exhortation to the assembled disciples. At 21:6, they knelt for prayer on the shore, and then parting from one another (ἀπησπασάμεθα[28] ἀλλήλους) took place prior to going aboard the ship. This moving ceremony would consist of embracing, kissing and the wishing of peace.

> The initial greeting of the apostle would again consist in a χαίρετε (Lk. 1:28; 2 Jn. 10 (→ χαίρειν) or an εἰρήνη ὑμῖν (→ εἰρήνη), as at the beginning of an address of greeting; though it may be that some of the greetings found at the beginning of the epistles (χάρις ὑμῖν καὶ εἰρήνη κτλ.) were also used. The concluding greeting would be εἰρήνη ὑμῖν or ὑπάγετε εἰς εἰρήνην, as at the end of epistles (Gl. 6:16; Eph. 6:23; 1 Pt. 5:14; 3 Jn. 15).

4. The ἀσπασμός in Epistles.

In the NT the most common use of ἀσπάζεσθαι is as an epistolary formula (47 times against 13 others). It occurs in almost all the epistles; the only exceptions are Gl., where relations were temporarily very strained, Eph., 1 Tm. and the Catholic Epistles Jm., 2 Pt., Jd. and 1 Jn. If our conclusion is correct that the custom of greeting in letters was rare prior to 70 A.D., Paul seems to have been the first to see great significance in it. [29] He welcomed it as an expression of the particular affection which he bore churches as a Christian and an apostle. It may be, however, that in the environment in which he grew up, and particularly his Jewish surroundings, the habit of epistolary greeting had been more fully adopted than we are now in a position to show (→ 497).

> We distinguish an imperative and an indicative form. In the imperative a. ἀσπά-σασθε is the most common term. The writer asks his readers, whether individuals or groups loved and esteemed by him, to present his greetings from a distance, as in the long series in R. 16:3 ff.; Col. 4:15: καὶ Νύμφαν καὶ τὴν κατ' οἶκον αὐτῆς ἐκ-κλησίαν; Hb. 13:24: πάντας τοὺς ἡγουμένους (only here is prominence given to

---

[27] Either Caesarea or Jerusalem.

[28] ἀπασπάσασθαι, a rare word, cf. Tob. 10:12 א; it is not found in Preisigke Wört.; cf. Pr.-Bauer, 128.

[29] Roller, *op. cit.*

the leaders as compared with the whole community, cf. Ign. Sm., 12, 2 : ἀσπάζομαι τὸν ... ἐπίσκοπον καὶ ... πρεσβυτέριον καὶ τοὺς ... διακόνους); b. ἀσπάσασθε as a greeting to all the members of the community, Phil. 4:21: πάντα ἅγιον ἐν Χριστῷ Ἰησοῦ; Col. 4:15 : τοὺς ἐν Λαοδικίᾳ ἀδελφούς; 1 Th. 5:26 : τοὺς ἀδελφοὺς πάντας; Hb. 13:24 : καὶ πάντας τοὺς ἁγίους. This formula does not occur in Ign. The greeting is naturally restricted to words. That purely human relations and evaluations are not expressed in it is plain from the characterisation of those who receive it. Either achievements are emphasised, as in R. 16, or they are described as saints and brothers, as in Phil. 4:21; Col. 4:15; 1 Th. 5:26. The greeting expresses and strengthens the bond of fellowship with those who are engaged in the same task and who serve the same Lord, i.e., with saints and brothers (cf. 1 Jn. 1:3). A variant of b. is c. the demand to the whole congregation ἀσπάσασθε ἀλλήλους ἐν ἁγίῳ φιλήματι, 1 C. 16:20; 2 C. 13:12; R. 16:16; 1 Pt. 5:14; cf. also 1 Th. 5:26 : ἀσπάσασθε τοὺς ἀδελφοὺς πάντας ἐν φιλήματι ἁγίῳ. Here there is added to the greeting the gesture of → φίλημα, [30] which is naturally linked with embracing, so that we may translate : "Embrace one another with the holy kiss" (→ 496, n. 2). It is to be assumed that the holy kiss was customary in the churches (Just. Apol., I, 65, 2). Hence the distinctive feature is that on the reading of the letter it should take place at the request of the absent apostle. The fellowship with one another and with him which is strengthened by obedient reading (cf. 1 Jn. 1:3) will then be sealed by the reciprocal ceremony. This ἀσπάζεσθαι, too, has within itself a holy *dynamis* and borders on a sacramental action. Finally, in letters to individuals d. we have the sing. ἄσπασαι, e.g., at 2 Tm. 4:19, which is just a friendly greeting ; at Tt. 3:15 : ἄσπασαι τοὺς φιλοῦντας ἡμᾶς ἐν πίστει, where the greeting is restricted to believing friends ; [31] and at 3 Jn. 15 : ἄσπασαι τοὺς φίλους κατ' ὄνομα, which is a purely secular formula. [32]

Indicative greetings are introduced either by ἀσπάζομαι, which is found only in Ign. [33] and corresponds to Paul's ἀσπάσασθε, or by ἀσπάζεται and ἀσπάζονται. They occur a. when individual fellow-Christians, absent at the time of writing, deliver their greetings. These are either mentioned by name (1 C. 16:19; R. 16:21-23, where we have the rare instance of a greeting in the first person : ἀσπάζομαι ὑμᾶς ἐγώ, from the actual scribe ; [34] Col. 4:10, 12, 14; Phlm. 23 f.; 2 Tm. 4:21), or referred to generally (Phil. 4:21: οἱ σὺν ἐμοὶ ἀδελφοί; Tt. 3:15: οἱ μετ' ἐμοῦ πάντες; 1 C. 16:20: οἱ ἀδελφοὶ πάντες). Such greetings help to give the readers a concrete picture of the situation in which the epistle is written and to include the friends and assistants of the apostle in the fellowship which he enjoys with them. b. Individual groups in the congregation may send their greetings where there is some particular relationship (Phil. 4:22: μάλιστα δὲ οἱ ἐκ Καίσαρος οἰκίας; Hb. 13:24: οἱ ἀπὸ τῆς Ἰταλίας; 2 Jn. 13 : τὰ τέκνα τῆς ἀδελφῆς σου (if these are nieces); 3 Jn. 15 : οἱ φίλοι; Ign. Mg., 15 : Ἐφέσιοι ἀπὸ Σμύρνης. Again c. the whole church where the apostle is staying when he writes may send greetings to the church to which he writes : οἱ ἅγιοι πάντες, 2 C. 13:12; Phil. 4:22; 1 Pt. 5:13 : ἡ ἐν Βαβυλῶνι συνεκλεκτή (if this is the church in Babylon); 2 Jn. 13 (if the sister is the church). It is here assumed that the church knows of the despatch of the epistle and has asked the apostle to send greetings. Furthermore d. there are ecumenical greetings, as in 1 C. 16:19 : ἀσπάζονται ὑμᾶς αἱ ἐκκλησίαι τῆς Ἀσίας, and even more comprehensively in R. 16:16 : ... αἱ ἐκκλησίαι

---

[30] Wnd. 2 C., 427; R. Asting, *Die Heiligkeit im Urchrtt.* (1930), 148; F. J. Dölger, in *Antike u. Christentum,* 1 (1930), 195 f.; 3 (1932), 79 f.

[31] Cf. P. Fay, 118.

[32] Examples are given in Ziemann, 329 f.; Pr.-Bauer, 185.

[33] This ἀσπάζομαι is directed either to the church (as in the introd. to Mg., Tr., Phld., Tr., 12, Pol., 8, 2), or to groups (as in Sm., 13, 1; Pol., 8, 2), or to individuals (as in Sm., 12, 1; 13, 2; Pol., 8, 2 f.).

[34] Cf. P. Oxy., 1067, 25 : κἀγὼ Ἀλέξανδρος ... ἀσπάζομαι ὑμᾶς πολλά.

πᾶσαι τοῦ Χριστοῦ. In the first case Paul speaks for the churches of the "province" of Asia, in the latter for all churches everywhere. He has no particular charge to do this, but is simply expressing the sure and certain fact that the churches are aware of their fellowship of faith with the church to which he writes. R. 16:16 is so strongly ecumenical or catholic that it may almost be asked whether it was not added in the later "catholic" redaction. [35] Ign. Mg., 15 may be quoted in the same connection : καὶ αἱ λοιπαὶ δὲ ἐκκλησίαι ἐν τιμῇ 'Ιησοῦ Χριστοῦ ἀσπάζονται ὑμᾶς.

Finally, we have a distinctive greeting e. in the formula : ὁ ἀσπασμὸς τῇ ἐμῇ χειρί (Παύλου) in 2 Th. 3:17; 1 C. 16:21; Col. 4:18. According to 2 Th. 3:17 this is a σημεῖον of authenticity in every letter. [36] It is a greeting in the apostle's own hand which is part of the normal style of a letter and yet which is also a requirement of the apostle, being materially identical with an ἀσπάσασθε (sc. from me) or an ἀσπάζομαι. The phrase gives to his greeting a certain solemnity. He performs the ceremony with a full sense of its inner significance. A striking feature is that this ἀσπασμός, i.e., the formula introduced, does not in fact occur in every letter. [37] Yet there can have been no rigidity about this, and we must also remember that many earlier and later letters of Paul which have perished probably contained it. Above all, he may well have added his own greeting or conclusion even in letters which do not have the formula ; this would be recognisable only in the original MS (cf. Gl. 6:11 ff.; R. 16:17-20). [38]

Windisch

---

† ἄσπιλος

1. "Without spot," "blameless," hence cultically "free from blemish," like the selected white horses of Elagabal in Herodian V, 6, 16; or stones : ὑγιεῖς λευκοὺς ἀσπίλους, IG, II, 5, 1054c, 4 (Eleusis c. 300 B.C.); μῆλον Anth. Pal., VI, 252, 3 (Antiphil.); Preis. Zaub., XIII (Leiden), [1] 369 f.: θῦε λ(ε)υκὸν ἀλέκτορα ἄσπιλον.

In 1 Pt. 1:19 we have the phrase : "Redeemed by the precious blood ὡς ἀμνοῦ ἀμώμου καὶ ἀσπίλου Χριστοῦ." The metaphor does not exclude but includes the thought of the sinlessness of Jesus. The holy God accepts only what is morally blameless. Hence this usage links with that which follows.

2. "Morally pure." This is found only in biblical literature and that influenced by it. [2] In the OT only Symmachus uses the word at Job 15:15 (deviating from the original בִּקְדֹשָׁיו לֹא יַאֲמִין). It is found in Jm. 1:27: ἄσπιλον ἑαυτὸν τηρεῖν ἀπὸ τοῦ κόσμου; 2 Pt. 3:14 : ἄσπιλοι καὶ ἀμώμητοι εὑρεθῆναι; 1 Tm. 6:14: τὴν ἐντολὴν ἄσπιλον τηρῆσαι. The term illustrates the way in which the NT gives new religious and moral content to originally cultic concepts.

Oepke

---

[35] Though cf. the no less comprehensive ecumenical statements in 1 Th. 1:6-8; R. 1:8.
[36] Cf. Dob. Th. and Dib. Th., *ad loc.*
[37] Cf., however, Roller, 70 ff., 78, 505 f. (n. 351 f.); also C. G. Bruns, "Die Unterschriften in den röm. Rechtsurkunden" (AAB, 1876).
[38] Cf. Roller, 72 f., 500 f. (n. 340 f.).
ἄ σ π ι λ ο ς. [1] Cf. A. Dieterich, *Abraxas* (1891), 170, 14 f.
[2] P. Grenf., II, 113 of the Virgin.

† ἀστατέω

"To be unsteady or restless." a. act. of a flickering glance : Hippiatrica, III, 3; morally "unreliable," "vacillating," Vett. Val., II, 37, p. 116, 30 : πολύκοιτοι καὶ ἀστατοῦντες περὶ τοὺς γάμους; esp. for the fickleness of fortune we have the adj. ἄστατος : Epicur. Ad Men., 3, 133; Ps.-Plut. Cons. ad Apoll., 5 (II, 103 f.); Jos. Ant., 20, 57: τὸ τῆς τύχης ἄστατον. b. pass. "to be set in commotion," Plut. Crass., 17 (I, 553b): ἀστατούσης χειμῶνι τῆς θαλάσσης, also spiritually ἄστατος καὶ ἐπίφοβος, Vett. Val., II, 2, p. 57, 6. c. "to wander around unsteadily," either act. or pass.; this is rare in secular usage, though cf. ᾽Α Is. 58:7: ἀστατοῦντας = LXX ἀστέγους = Mas. מְרוּדִים, "the homeless" (for which we should perhaps read מְרֹדִים, "the wandering").

Among various bodily and spiritual sufferings listed by Paul in 1 C. 4:11 we read : καὶ ἀστατοῦμεν. The meaning here is c. "we have no fixed abode." [1] Yet we should not emphasise too strongly the element of "wandering," [2] for, although this fits the sarcastic style of the whole section, it imparts rather too activist a character. The opp. ἐνδημῆσαι πρὸς τὸν κύριον in 2 C. 5:8 is in keeping with this sense. [3]

Oepke

ἀστήρ, ἄστρον

ἀστήρ almost always denotes a single "star," whereas ἄστρον can also be used for a "constellation." [1]

For the ancients, stars were "beings." In virtue of their spiritual constitution the Greeks regarded them as deities. Typical is the statement of Philo, who reproduced the view of Greek philosophy, Op. Mund., 73 : οὗτοι (οἱ ἀστέρες) γὰρ ζῷά τε εἶναι λέγονται καὶ ζῷα νοερά, μᾶλλον δὲ νοῦς αὐτὸς ἕκαστος, ὅλος δι᾽ ὅλων σπουδαῖος καὶ παντὸς ἀνεπίδεκτος κακοῦ. [2] Plat. Ap., 26d : οὐδὲ ἥλιον οὐδὲ σελήνην ἄρα νομίζω θεοὺς εἶναι, ὥσπερ οἱ ἄλλοι ἄνθρωποι. [3] On the other hand, for the OT and later Rabbinic Judaism the stars receive and execute the divine commands and declare the divine glory, Is. 40:26; 45:12; Ps. 19:1, 5 f.; 148:3; Gk. Sir. 43:9 f.; Apcr. Bar. 3:34 f.; Ep. Jer. 59; Eth. En. 18:13 ff.; 21:1 ff.; 41:5; 86:1 ff.; 4 Esr. 6:3; Gn. r., 6 on 1:44. [4] What obeys the command of God is

---

ἀ σ τ α τ έ ω. [1] Theophyl. : ἐλαυνόμεθα, φεύγομεν.
[2] Field, cf. Moult.-Mill.
[3] Cf. ἐβασιλεύσατε in v. 8, and on this pt. Joh. W. 1 K. and Sickb. K., 22.

ἀ σ τ ή ρ. [1] Examples in F. Boll, *Aus d. Offenb. Joh.* (1914), 99, n. 1; ZNW, 18 (1917/18), 41 ff.; O. Gerhardt, *Der Stern d. Messias* (1922), 79 f. If I have rightly understood the context, in Catal. Cod. Astr. Graec., III, 30 : δεῖ γινώσκει(ν) ὅτι τῶν καθ᾽ ἕν(α) καιρῶν ἕν πρὸς ἕν ζῴδιον βασιλεύει ... οὐχ ὁρμαθικῶς δὲ καὶ κυκλικῶς ἡ βασιλεία κυκλοῖ τῶν αὐτῶν, ἀλλὰ κατὰ διαστολήν τινα βαθμῶν ἄλλος ἀστὴρ ἄλλοτε βασιλεύει, ἀστήρ here refers to a zodiac.
[2] *v.* E. Pfeiffer, *Studien zum antiken Sternglauben* (1916).
[3] The continuation, in which Socrates alludes to Anaxagoras, provides the necessary qualification of the general view mentioned above.
[4] The moon has transgressed the command of God and penetrated the sphere of the sun; it is thus reduced in size.

not dead, even though it be the world of atoms. [5] This is expressed in pseud-epigraphical literature by the idea of angels set above the stars : Eth. En. 72:3; 75:3; 80:1, 6; Sl. En. 19:5; Test. Ad. 4:10. In 1 C. 15:40 f. we are led by the use of the term σῶμα, a parallel to living earthly σώματα, and also by the context (ποίῳ δὲ σώματι ἔρχονται οἱ νεκροί), to the conclusion that for Paul, too, the stars are ζῷα. Up to v. 41 he is giving images of the resurrection of human bodies. Hence we are not to think that for him the stellar form of existence is psychically or spiritually nearer to God. He stands rather in the OT tradition.

In apocalyptic contexts there is reference to the fall of stars from heaven (Mk. 13:25 and par. and Rev. 6:13, cf. Is. 34:4). Rev. 8:12 also speaks of the obscuring of some of the stars, for which there are many biblical and later Jewish parallels. [6] In Rev. 12:4 there is a reminiscence of Da. 8:10. In Rev. 8:10 the greatness and origin of their harmful working are symbolically depicted, while in the related image in Rev. 9:1 the star seems to represent a living being, perhaps a fallen (?) angel. [7] The seven stars of Rev. 1:16, 20; 2:1; 3:1 are either to be identified with the 7 planets which astrological belief supposed to be the shapers of destiny, [8] or with the Great or Little Bear as the ruler of the world. [9] Yet it is to be considered that the 7 candlesticks mentioned in Philo, [10] Josephus [11] and the Rabbis [12] are perhaps identical with 7 stars, so that Rev. is keeping to the image of the candlestick, and a parallelism may be discerned between the images for the ἄγγελοι (→ 86) and the ἐκκλησίαι. The image of the 12 stars is based on the zodiac, though related to the 12 tribes. [13]

What is meant by the reference to the morning star in Rev. 2:28 : καὶ δώσω αὐτῷ τὸν ἀστέρα τὸν πρωϊνόν, and 22:16 : ἐγώ εἰμι ... ὁ ἀστὴρ ὁ λαμπρὸς ὁ πρωϊνός, it is hard to say. Lohmeyer [14] attempts the equation of this star with the Holy Spirit. Boll [15] takes the first passage to mean that "He will have the strongest of the stellar angels as His servant." Schlatter [16] sees a current image for the dawn of the time of salvation. That the morning star occupies a prominent position may be seen from Preis. Zaub., IV, 3045/7: ὁρκίζω σε θεὸν φωσφόρον, ἀδάμαστον, τὰ ἐν καρδίᾳ πάσης ζωῆς ἐπιστάμενον. But there is also an old tradition that it was created before all other creatures. At ψ 109:3 LXX rendered the obscure text : πρὸ ἑωσφόρου ἐξεγέννησά σε = ℭ ante luciferum. Aug. Serm., 119, 14 (p. 260, Mai) took this to mean ante omnem creaturam. [17] At Rev. 22:16 it would then be the equivalent of ἀρχὴ

---

[5] The natural laws in which the commands of God clothe themselves to human vision both conceal and reveal this.
[6] Is. 13:10; Ez. 32:7; Jl. 2:10; 4:15; Ass. Mos. 10:5; Str.-B., IV, 977 ff.
[7] Cf. Eth. En. 86:1.
[8] Sen. Dial., VI, 18, 3 in Pauly-W., II, 1813.
[9] Suet. Aug., 80; Pauly-W., II, 1821; the work of Bolos of Mendes mentioned in Pauly-W., II, 1815; H. Cohen, Descr. hist. des monnaies frappées sous l'empire Romain² (1880 ff.): Hadrian, 507; Commodus, 245, 714; Loh. Apk. on 1:16.
[10] Rer. Div. Her., 221.
[11] Bell., 5, 217; Ant., 3, 146.
[12] Str.-B., III, 717.
[13] So also Bass Apk., ad loc. and Boll, Aus d. Offenbarung Joh., 99 ff.
[14] Apk., ad loc.
[15] Op. cit., 47 f.
[16] D. AT in d. joh. Apk. (1910), 51 f.; also Charles I, 77; cf. Rohr, ad loc.
[17] Cf. also 174, 1 (p. 391) and Prosp. in Ps. 109:3 (cf. F. Blatt, "Die lat. Bearbeitungen d. Act. And. et Mtth. apud anthropophagos," Beih. z. ZNW, 12 [1930], 121).

πάσης κτίσεως. Only a systematic investigation of the nature of the whole imagery of Rev. could give us any certainty in the matter.

As regards the star which appeared to the wise men, we have many instances of special heavenly manifestations which herald the birth of great rulers according to ancient belief.[18] Furthermore, on the basis of Nu. 24:17, later Judaism symbolised its Messianic expectations in a star.[19] Yet we still cannot be sure what the wise men saw or are reported to have seen, or how they interpreted it astrologically. O. Gerhardt[20] attempts such an interpretation; he suggests that they saw the Jews' star Saturn in a particular conjunction.

Foerster

† ἀστραπή

"Lightning," also "beam of light" (Lk. 11:36).[1] The word is often employed as a comparison in the NT. Thus it is used of the Easter angel in Mt. 28:3.[2] In Lk. 10:18: ἐθεώρουν τὸν σατανᾶν ὡς ἀστραπὴν ἐκ τοῦ οὐρανοῦ πεσόντα, the point of comparison is the suddenness of the divine working.[3] In Mt. 24:27 and par.: ὥσπερ γὰρ ἡ ἀστραπὴ ἐξέρχεται ἀπὸ ἀνατολῶν καὶ φαίνεται ἕως δυσμῶν, οὕτως ἔσται ἡ παρουσία τοῦ υἱοῦ τοῦ ἀνθρώπου, it is the inescapable visibility[4] and divine suddenness (?) of the coming of the Son of Man.

In the symbolical language of the Apocalypse (4:5; 8:5; 11:19; 16:18) the mention of lightning is a link with OT theophanies.[5] There are also echoes of the plagues of Egypt in the last three passages. The phenomena here mentioned (lightning, thunder, voices, hail and earthquakes) form a climax at the end of the three series of seven plagues and are meant to show that the Lord of nature stands behind the plagues, in which He reveals to created humanity on earth His supremacy and severity. Hence the same phenomena are encountered in 4:5, whereas they do not occur at the final judgment seat of God (20:11 ff.; cf. 19:11 ff.).

Foerster

---

[18] Herodian Hist., I, 14, 1; Plin. Hist. Nat., II, 28. For the birth star of Mithridates, Justinus Epit., XXXVII, 2, 1 f.; for Augustus, Suet. Aug., 94, 5; Dio C., XLV, 1, 3; for Alexander Severus, Lampridius, Alex. Sever., 13, 1 f. (in Script. Hist. Aug.). Cf. Schol. in Verg. Buc., IX, 47: *astrum, id est imperare coepit.*

[19] For the Messianic understanding of the star in Nu. 24:17, *v.* the Rabbinic passages in Str.-B., I, 13c, 76 f. Simon's coins after the revolt of 132 carry a star. For the later period, cf. H. W. Beyer and H. Lietzmann, *Die jüd. Katakombe der Villa Torlonia* (1930), 24; also Damasc., 7, 18 f.; also K. H. Rengstorf, ZNW, 31 (1932), 37 ff., 42.

[20] *D. Stern d. Messias* (1922).

ἀ σ τ ρ α π ή. [1] Aesch. Fr., 386.

[2] Cf. Da. 10:6.

[3] F. Spitta, ZNW, 9 (1908), 160 ff. sees here the reference to a descent of Satan to do battle against the kingdom of God, while the parallel passage in Rev. 12:9 refers to the future. But this is unlikely.

[4] Ps. 77:18; 97:4; Lv. r., 31 on 24:1 (Str.-B., I, 954, n. 2); Tanch בהעלותך, 7, 48 (Schl. Mt., *ad loc.*); the lightning illumines the earth.

[5] Esp. Ex. 19:16 ff.; cf. Ju. 5:4 f.; 2 S. 22:8 ff.; Ez. 1:13; Hab. 3:3 ff.; Ps. 18:7 ff.; 77:16 ff.; 97:2 ff.

ἄστρον → ἀστήρ   ἀσύνετος → συνίημι

| ἀσφάλεια, ἀσφαλής, |
| ἀσφαλῶς, ἀσφαλίζω |

All four words[1] are current in earlier and later Gk. in the sense of "firmness," "certainty," "firm," "certain," "to make firm" or "certain." They are used with the same meaning in the LXX and NT.

Lk. 1:4: λόγων τὴν ἀσφάλειαν = "the reliability of the words or teachings," reminds us of Xenoph. Mem., 6, 15: ἀσφάλεια λόγου.[2] To this there corresponds Ac. 25:26: ἀσφαλές τι γράψαι, and again Ac. 21:34; 22:30: γνῶναι τὸ ἀσφαλές = "to know the truth." The reference in Ac. 2:36: ἀσφαλῶς γινωσκέτω πᾶς οἶκος Ἰσραήλ, is to "certain, solid, or reliable knowledge." 1 Th. 5:3 has ἀσφάλεια with εἰρήνη in the sense of the security to which men should not yield in view of current eschatological events.[3]

Karl Ludwig Schmidt

| † ἄσωτος, † ἀσωτία |

Used in essentially the same sense from class. to Byzant. times. Aristot. Eth. Nic., IV, 1, p. 1119b, 31 ff.: τοὺς γὰρ ἀκρατεῖς καὶ εἰς ἀκολασίαν δαπανηροὺς ἀσώτους καλοῦμεν. διὸ καὶ φαυλότατοι δοκοῦσιν εἶναι· πολλὰς γὰρ ἅμα κακίας ἔχουσιν. οὐ δὴ οἰκείως προσαγορεύονται· βούλεται γὰρ ἄσωτος εἶναι ὁ ἔν τι κακὸν ἔχων, τὸ φθείρειν τὴν οὐσίαν· ἄσωτος γὰρ ὁ δι' αὐτὸν ἀπολλύμενος, δοκεῖ δ' ἀπώλειά τις αὐτοῦ εἶναι καὶ ἡ τῆς οὐσίας φθορά, ὡς τοῦ ζῆν διὰ τούτων ὄντος. The original meaning is a. "incurable": ἀσώτως ἔχειν, to be hopelessly sick, Aristot. Probl., 33, 9, p. 962b, 5; Plut. Quaest. Nat., 26 (II, 918d).[1] ἄσωτος then denotes b. "one who by his manner of life, esp. by dissipation, destroys himself"; ἀσωτία thus has the sense of "dissipation." This is the most common sense and therefore the only one found in definitions and comparisons, Plat. Resp., VIII, 560e, Aristot. Eth. Nic., II, 7, p. 1107b, 8 ff.: περὶ δὲ δόσιν χρημάτων καὶ λῆψιν μεσότης μὲν ἐλευθεριότης, ὑπερβολὴ δὲ καὶ ἔλλειψις ἀσωτία καὶ ἀνελευθερία. Plut. Adulat., 19 (II, 60d); Inim. Util., 5 (II, 88 f.), in both cases comparing ἄσωτος and ἀνελεύθερος; Plut. Pelop., 3, 2 (I, 279b); Galb., 16, 3 (I, 1060b), comparing ἀσωτία with μικρολογία; also in the collection of stories of ἄσωτοι, Athen., IV, 59 ff.

Yet the words also come to have derived and special meanings, perhaps, as Arist. maintains (*supra*), because hopeless dissipation is linked with other vices, or perhaps because of the influence of the original sense of incurable.[2] At any rate, the term

---

ἀσφάλεια κτλ. [1] Root σφαλ- with ἀ privativum.
[2] ἀσφάλεια is also used as a tech. legal term for "certainty" in Epict. Diss., II, 13, 7 and pap.
[3] Meyer's rendering of ἀσφάλεια as "full certainty of faith" in *Ursprung,* I, 10 (Lk. 1:4) is perhaps a little exaggerated, but gives the right impression.

ἄσωτος, ἀσωτία. Kl. Lk. and Zn. Lk. on 15:13.
[1] Cf. also Cyr. Hom., XIV (MPG, 77, 1073): ἀσωτοποσίας οἴνου, the unhealthy and immoderate drinking of wine.
[2] This derivation is already forgotten in Cl. Al. Paed., II, 1, 7, 5, where there is a concealed allusion to ἄσωτος.

suggests something unusual and unhealthy. Thus ἄσωτος is c. the "glutton" and ἀσωτία "gluttony." Dio C., LXXV, 15, 7: ἀσωτότατός τε ἀνθρώπων γενόμενος, ὥστε καὶ εὐωχεῖσθαι ἅμα καὶ ἐμεῖν; also Plut. Apophthegm (Cato maior, 1 [II, 198d]); Dio C., LXV, 20, 3. Again, it means d. a "voluptuary," and ἀσωτία "voluptuousness," Plut. Eumen., 13, 5 (I, 591c): τοὺς δὲ Μακεδόνας κολακεύοντες ἐκκεχυμένως καὶ καταχορηγοῦντες εἰς δεῖπνα καὶ θυσίας ὀλίγου χρόνου τὸ στρατόπεδον ἀσωτίας πανηγυριζούσης καταγώγιον ἐποίησαν; also Phil. Spec. Leg., IV, 91. Finally, ἄσωτος means e. "one who lives a wild and undisciplined life," ἀσωτία a "wild and undisciplined life." Going about in women's clothing and engaging in lighthearted vagabondage are described in Plut. Vit. Dec. Orat., 8, 59 (II, 847e) as ἀσώτως βιῶναι, and Polyb. speaks of the Ἰακὴ (read ἰακχικὴ) καὶ τεχνιτικὴ ἀσωτία, XXXII, 11, 10. Plut. Adul., 11 (II, 55c) has ἄσωτος with ἄτακτος, Dio C., LXVII, 6, 3 with ἀσελγής, Polyb., XL, 12, 7 ἀσωτία with ῥᾳθυμία, Athen., IV, 60 (p. 374, 14 f., Kaibel) with κιναιδία. [3]

In the OT ἄσωτος occurs only at Prv. 7:11 and ἀσωτία at Prv. 28:7 and 2 Macc. 6:4.

In terms of the general Gk. usage, ζῶν ἀσώτως at Lk. 15:7 speaks of the dissipated life of the Prodigal without specifying the nature of this life, cf. v. 30. It is simply depicted as carefree and spendthrift in contrast to the approaching dearth. Ἀσωτία occurs three times in the NT: at Eph. 5:18: μὴ μεθύσκεσθε οἴνῳ, ἐν ᾧ ἐστιν ἀσωτία; Tt. 1:6: (of the bishop) τέκνα ἔχων πιστά, μὴ ἐν κατηγορίᾳ ἀσωτίας ἢ ἀνυπότακτα; 1 Pt. 4:4: ξενίζονται μὴ συντρεχόντων ὑμῶν εἰς τὴν αὐτὴν τῆς ἀσωτίας ἀνάχυσιν. In all these passages the word signifies wild and disorderly rather than extravagant or voluptuous living. The manner of life which these passages have in view would probably not have been identified as ἀσωτία by the Greeks, since for them ἀσωτία is only what is particularly wasteful or luxurious or wild as compared with the average. We can see this in the much quoted P. Flor., 99, 6 ff. (1/2 cent. A.D.), where ἀσωτεύεσθαι means dissipating all one's resources. [4]

Foerster

ἀτακτέω, ἄτακτος → τάσσω

αὐγάζω, ἀπαύγασμα

† αὐγάζω.

[αὐγή means "radiance," and is used fig. in Philo Praem. Poen., 25: οἷς ἂν ὁ θεὸς αὐγὴν ἐπιλάμψῃ τῆς ἀληθείας. In the NT it is used only at Ac. 20:11 for "dawn."] αὐγάζω signifies a. "to shine forth." It is found in the LXX at Lv. 13:24 ff., 38 f.; 14:56 (αὐγάζοντα of the white spots in leprosy). Cf. also Preis. Zaub., III (Mimaut), 143; IV (Gr. Paris), 2558; also διαυγάζω at 2 Pt. 1:19. It also means b. "to illuminate": Philo Fug., 136; Jos., 68; and c. "to see": act. Soph. Phil., 217 f. and other poets; Philo Vit. Mos., II, 139; mid., Philo Migr. Abr., 189 etc.

---

[3] It must be stressed that ἄσωτος does not mean immoral in the narrower sense. In Test. A. 5:1 there is only one MS for ἐν τῷ γάμῳ ἡ ἀσωτία; the others have either ἀκρασία or ἀτεκνία.

[4] Ἐπεὶ ὁ υἱὸς ἡμῶν Κάστωρ μεθ᾽ ἑτέρων (the conjecture ἑταιρῶν in Zn. Lk. on 15:13 seems to be superfluous) ἀσωτευόμενος ἐσπάνισε τὰ αὐτοῦ πάντα.

α ὐ γ ά ζ ω. Wnd. 2 C. 136, n. 4; Cr.-Kö., 181; Nägeli, 25 f.

At 2 C. 4:4 : ὁ θεὸς τοῦ αἰῶνος τούτου ἐτύφλωσεν τὰ νοήματα τῶν ἀπίστων εἰς τὸ μὴ αὐγάσαι [1] τὸν φωτισμὸν τοῦ εὐαγγελίου τῆς δόξης, meaning b. does not come into consideration, but it is hard to decide between a. and c. Whereas the older transl. and the variants seem to assume a. ("that it should not shine"), parallelism to 3:13 : πρὸς τὸ μὴ ἀτενίσαι, is a strong argument in favour of c. ("that they should not see").

† ἀπαύγασμα.

a. "Effulgence" : LXX Wis. 7:26 (synon. ἀπόρροια); Philo Spec. Leg., IV, 123; Op. Mund., 146; Tatian, 15, 10. b. "reflection" : Plut. Fac. Lun., 21 (II, 934d) (ἀπαυγασμός); "image" ; Philo Plant., 50 (synon. εἰκών); cf. also Act. Thom., 6, 35.

The word is a later one. In the LXX it is used of the relation of wisdom to the eternal light (a), in Philo of its relation to the world (b), of that of man to God (a), and of the human spirit to the divine logos (a). We read of Christ in Hb. 1:3 : ὃς ὢν ἀπαύγασμα τῆς δόξης καὶ χαρακτὴρ τῆς ὑποστάσεως αὐτοῦ. Both meanings would be possible according to usage and context, yet patristic consensus favours the interpretation that Christ is the effulgence of the divine doxa, as sunshine is of the sun or light of light.

Greg. Nyss. Apoll., II, 47 ff. : ὥσπερ πρὸς τὸν ἥλιον ἀκτὶς καὶ πρὸς τὸν λύχνον τὸ ἀπαυγαζόμενον φῶς Chrys. Hom. in Hb. 2:2 (MPG, 63, 22): φῶς ἐκ φωτός.

Kittel

αὐθάδης

a. "Self-satisfied," Aristot. Eth. M., I, 28, p. 1192b, 30 ff.; Jos. Bell., 2, 356; 4, 96. Cf. the related noun αὐθάδεια (αὐθαδία) in Is. 24:8. There the Mas. runs : חָדַל שְׁאוֹן עַלִּיזִים; the LXX : πέπαυται αὐθαδία καὶ πλοῦτος ἀσεβῶν, giving two renderings of שָׁאוֹן. At Hab. 3:14 one reading in the Hexapla, without Mas. basis, has the formulation : τοὺς πεποιθότας ἐπὶ τῇ αὐθαδείᾳ αὐτῶν. [1] b. "Arbitrary," unconsidered" : Preisigke Sammelbuch, 4284; Jos. Ant., 1, 189; 4, 236; 16, 399; Philo Rer. Div. Her., 21: θρασύτης μὲν γὰρ αὐθάδους, φίλου δὲ θαρραλεότης οἰκεῖον. In Aesch. Prom., 1034 αὐθάδεια is the opp. of εὐβουλία; in Ael. Arist. Or., 45 (II, 80, 15, Dindorf) of φρόνησις. In Σ Qoh. 9:3 αὐθάδεια = הוֹלֵלוֹת, "madness." c. "Morose," "gruff": Theophr. Char., 15: the αὐθάδης soon ceases to pray δεινὸς δὲ καὶ τοῖς θεοῖς μὴ ἐπεύχεσθαι; Plat. Resp., IX, 590a : αὐθάδεια. d. "Blatant," "shameless": Aesch. Prom., 64; Ditt. Syll.[3], 1243, 25. In LXX Gn. 49:3, 7 עַז is translated αὐθάδης; in 49:3 the sense is thus turned into the opp. and σκληρός is made a parallel of αὐθάδης (as also in Θ). In LXX Prv. 21:24 αὐθάδης = יְהִיר. "The critical judgment (implied in αὐθάδης and related substantives) of the egocentric attitude, which as such necessarily leads to arrogance, is peculiar to the LXX and influences later translations" (Bertram).

---

[1] CD : καταυγάσαι, A Marcion : διαυγάσαι, Or vg sy rec : + αὐτοῖς.
ἀπαύγασμα. F. J. Dölger, "Sonne u. Sonnenstrahl als Gleichnis in der Logos-theologie des Altertums," *Antike u. Chrtt.*, 1 (1929), 269 ff.
αὐθάδης. A. Giesecke in *Theophrasts Charaktere,* ed. by the Phil. Ges. Leipzig (1897), 116-119.
[1] Field, ad loc.

In the two passages in which αὐθάδης occurs in the NT the reference is to human impulse violating obedience to the divine command. In both cases it is religious leaders who are exposed to this danger or succumb to it. At Tt. 1:7: δεῖ γὰρ τὸν ἐπίσκοπον ἀνέγκλητον εἶναι ... μὴ αὐθάδη, μὴ ὄργιλον, μὴ πάροινον. The related adjectives suggest meaning b. At 2 Pt. 2:10 heretics who are afraid of nothing are called αὐθάδεις, i.e., bold and shameless fellows (d.).

Cf. the blasphemies of the αὐθάδης in Did., 3, 6. In the similitudes of Hermas the αὐθάδης does not accept the hiddenness of divine mysteries (s., 5, 4, 2; 5, 5, 1; 9, 22, 1).

Bauernfeind

αὐτάρκεια, αὐτάρκης → 466   αὐτόπτης → ὁράω
αὐτοκατάκριτος → κρίνω   ἀφθαρσία, ἄφθαρτος → φθείρω

ἀφίημι, ἄφεσις, παρίημι, πάρεσις

A. The Greek Usage.

ἀφιέναι, "to send off," is richly attested in Gk. from an early period, and is used in every nuance, both lit. and figur., from "to hurl" (e.g., missiles) to "to release," "to let go," or "to let be." It may have either a material or a personal object, so that its meaning verges both on ἀνίημι (→ ἄνεσις) and παρίημι. To be emphasised is the legal use much attested in the pap. [1] ἀφιέναι τινά, "to release someone from a legal relation," whether office, marriage, obligation, or debt, though never in a religious sense. In the sense of "to pardon" it is construed with the accus. of person and gen. of object. Plat. Leg., IX,2869a : τὸν δράσαντα φόνου; Plut. Alex., 13 (I, 671b): πάσης αἰτίας; P. Tebt., 5, 2 (2nd cent. B.C.): πάντας ἀγνοημάτων ἁμαρτημάτων etc. In the sense of "to remit" it takes the acc. of object and dat. of person (Hdt., VI, 30 : αὐτῷ τὴν αἰτίην; Hdt., VIII, 140 : ὑμῖν τὰς ἁμαρτάδας, cf. Demosth., 59, 30; Polyb., XXI, 24, 8).

Corresponding is the use of the rarer subst. ἄφεσις, which often has the legal sense of "release" from office, marriage, obligation etc., as also from debt or punishment, though never religiously (Plat. Leg., IX, 869d : φόνου; Demosth., 24, 45 f. : ὀφλήματος or τῶν ὀφλημάτων); we find it in these senses in inscriptions and pap., e.g., as "pardon" in P. Greci e Lat., 392, 6 (3rd cent. B.C.): τοῦ βασιλέως ἐπιγράψαντος τὴν ἄφεσιν. [2]

παρίημι means "to send by" or "to cause to go past" both lit. and figur. and with many different nuances. As "to leave behind" or "to leave off" it has the same sense as ἀνίημι; cf. esp. παρειμένος, "debilitated," "tired." This sense is often found in the LXX, where παρεθῆναι and (ἐκ)λυθῆναι are not infrequently par. (cf. Polyb., I, 58, 9 : τήν τε δύναμιν παρελέλυντο καὶ παρεῖντο) and the subj. is often χεῖρες e.g., 2 Βασ. 4:1; Jer. 4:31; Sir. 2:12 f.; 25:23; as also Hb. 12:12 quoting Is. 35:3 (LXX ἀνειμ-); cf. 1 Cl., 34, 1 and 4. Similarly Jos. Ant., 13, 343. As "to leave" or "to let be" [3] it has much the same sense as ἀφιέναι (Ex. 14:12 πάρες as elsewhere ἄφες); simil. as "to abandon," "to give up" (4 Macc. 5:29 : ὅρκους; anal. ἀφιέναι in Mk. 7:8; Jos. Ant., 4, 130. The παριέναι of Lk. 11:42 corresponds to ἀφιέναι in Mt. 23:23). The legal sense of "to remit" is not so prominent, but it does occur. Cf. already Aristoph. Ra., 699; then Xenoph. Eq. Mag., 7, 10; Dion. Hal. Ant. Rom., II, 35, p. 310, 14; Ditt.

ἄφεσις. C. Vitringa, *Observationes sacrae* (1723), IV, 3-4.
[1] Cf. Preisigke Wört., *s.v.*
[2] *Ibid.*, Pr.-Bauer, Nägeli, 56.
[3] In the pap. "to resign," "to concede," cf. Preisigke Wört.

Syll.³, 742, 33 and 39; Or., 669, 50; Jos. Ant., 15, 48 : τὴν ἁμαρτίαν; in LXX Sir. 23:2 : τὰ ἁμαρτήματα; in 1 Macc. 11:35 *vl.,* taxes).

B. The Use of ἀφίημι, ἄφεσις, [4] in the LXX.

In the LXX ἀφιέναι is used for a whole series of Hebrew words, a. for those which denote either "release," "surrender" etc. or "leave," "leave in peace" etc. (esp. common for הִגִּיחַ הִנִּיחַ or הִנִּיחַ, e.g., Ju. 2:23; 3:1; 16:26; 2 Βασ. 16:11; 20:3; ψ 104:14; or for עָזַב, Ex. 9:21; 2 Βασ. 15:16 etc.; and נָתַן, e.g., Gn. 20:6; Ex. 12:23; Nu. 22:13 etc.); b. for verbs of "remission" and indeed for נָשָׂא, e.g., Gn. 4:13; Ex. 32:32; ψ 24:18; 31:5; for סָלַח, e.g., Lv. 4:20; 5:10, 13; Nu. 14:19; 15:25 f.; Is. 55:7; and כִּפֶּר, Is. 22:14. The object of remission is sin or guilt, mostly ἁμαρτία(ι), but also ἀνομία, ἀσεβεια, and in Gn. 4:13 αἰτία. The one who forgives is God; this is never so in Gk. usage, though it is naturally found in Josephus, e.g., Ant., 6, 92 (but more frequently in the secular sense). While the Gk. rendering corresponds in the first case, ἀφιέναι significantly modifies the verbs of remission or forgiveness, since the original sense of the Heb. verbs is that of the cultic removal and expiation of sin, while ἀφιέναι has a legal sense. The relationship of man to God is thus conceived of in legal terms, and this is quite alien to Greek thought.

The noun ἄφεσις is used in the LXX to translate יוֹבֵל in Lv. 25 and 27 and שְׁמִטָּה (or שְׁמַט) in Ex. 23:11; Dt. 15:1 ff.; 31:10. It is also used for "release" (דְּרוֹר etc.) in Lv. 25:10; Ἰερ. 41:8, 15, 17 etc.; esp. Is. 58:6; 61:1, where it denotes eschatological liberation. In Est. 2:18 it means "amnesty" or "exemption from taxation." It means "forgiveness" only in the translation of אֶת־הַשָּׂעִיר לַעֲזָאזֵל as τὸν χίμαρον τὸν διεσταλμένον εἰς ἄφεσιν at Lv. 16:26. Except in this legal sense ἄφεσις is correctly used for אָפִיק and פֶּלֶג.[5] Josephus uses ἄφεσις for human forgiveness in Bell., 1, 481, but mostly for release, as in Ant., 2, 67; 12, 40; 17, 185.

C. The NT Usage.

1. NT usage exhibits most of the possibilities. ἀφιέναι means "to let go" or "to leave" : Mk. 1:20 and par. (τὸν πατέρα); 10:28 f. and par. (πάντα etc.); 12:12 and par. (αὐτόν); Jn. 4:3 (τὴν Ἰουδαίαν); 16:28 (τὸν κόσμον) etc. ἀφῆκεν αὐτὴν ὁ πυρετός (Mk. 1:31; cf. Jn. 4:52) is also good Gk., as is ἀφιέναι φωνήν (Mk. 15:37) and τὸ πνεῦμα (Mt. 27:50).[6] So, too, is ἀφιέναι γυναῖκα or ἄνδρα in 1 C. 7:11-13 (cf. Hdt., V, 39). It also means "to leave or to set aside" : Mk. 7:8 (τὴν ἐντολήν); Mt. 23:23 (τὰ βαρύτερα τοῦ νόμου), cf. Jos. Ant., 4, 130 : ἀφέντας τοὺς πατρίους νόμους καὶ τὸν τούτους αὐτοῖς θέμενον τιμᾶν θεόν; 4 Macc. 5:29 (→ 509); again, Mt. 5:40 (τὸ ἱμάτιον); Mt. 23:38 (ὁ οἶκος ὑμῶν); 24:40 f. (εἷς παραλαμβάνεται καὶ εἷς ἀφίεται κτλ.); R. 1:27 (τὴν φυσικὴν χρῆσιν); Rev. 2:4 (τὴν ἀγάπην σου τὴν πρώτην). It is used for "to leave behind" in Mk. 1:18 and par. (τὰ δίκτυα); 12:19-22 (τέκνα or σπέρμα); Mt. 5:24 (τὸ δῶρόν σου ἔμπροσθεν τοῦ θυσιαστηρίου); 18:12 (τοὺς ἐνενήκοντα ἐννέα sc. πρόβατα); Jn. 4:28 (τὴν ὑδρίαν); 14:18 (ὑμᾶς ὀρφανούς); 27 (εἰρήνην); Hb. 6:1 (τὸν τῆς ἀρχῆς λόγον) etc. It can also mean "to leave in peace," "to let alone" : [7] Mk. 11:6; 14:6; Mt. 3:15; 19:14; Lk. 13:8; Jn. 11:48; Rev. 2:20

---

[4] παρίημι → 509.

[5] On ἄφεσις in the LXX, Deissmann B., 94-97.

[6] τὴν ψυχήν would, of course, be better Gk., cf. Jos. Ant., 1, 218; Bell., 2, 153 etc.

[7] This is good Gk.; occasionally it is used for שבק or נתן, cf. Schl. Mt., 88, 91, 289, 484, 650.

etc.; cf. Mk. 13:2 : οὐ μὴ ἀφεθῇ λίθος ἐπὶ λίθον; cf. Lk. 19:44. Similarly Ac. 14:17: οὐκ ἀμάρτυρον αὐτὸν ἀφῆκεν, and Hb. 2:8 : οὐδὲν ἀφῆκεν αὐτῷ ἀνυπότακτον. Finally, it can also mean "to allow" or "to permit" : Mk. 1:34 (οὐκ ἤφιε λαλεῖν τὰ δαιμόνια); 5:19, 37 and par. etc. Occasionally we also have the Hellenistic request formula ἄφες (or ἄφετε), e.g., in Mk. 7:27; 15:36 and par.; Mt. 3:15; 7:4 and par. [8]

2. There are also the instances in which ἀφιέναι means "to remit" or "to forgive," whether in the profane sense in Mt. 18:27 (τὸ δάνειον) and 32 (τὴν ὀφειλήν), or more often in the religious. The objects are τὰς ἁμαρτίας (Mk. 2:5 ff.; Lk. 7:47 ff.; Jn. 20:23 etc.); τὰ ἁμαρτήματα (Mk. 3:28); τὰ παραπτώματα (Mt. 6:14 f.); αἱ ἀνομίαι (R. 4:7 quoting ψ 31:1); ἡ ἐπίνοια τῆς καρδίας σου (Ac. 8:22). It may be used either elliptically or absolutely (Mk. 4:12; 11:25 f.; Mt. 6:14 f.; 12:32 and par.). The usage of the post-apostolic fathers is similar.

The noun ἄφεσις almost always means "forgiveness" (God's), usually with the gen. ἁμαρτιῶν (Mk. 1:4 and par.; Mt. 26:28; Lk. 1:77; 24:47; Ac. 2:38; 5:31; 10:43; 13:38; 26:18; Col. 1:14; cf. Hb. 10:18), and once with τῶν παραπτωμάτων (Eph. 1:7), either elliptically or absolutely. Even where ἄφεσις is meant in the sense of "liberation" (twice in Lk. 4:18 quoting Is. 61:1 and 58:6), this at least includes the thought of forgiveness. The usage in the post-apostolic fathers is again the same.

The same sense is borne by πάρεσις, [9] found only once at R. 3:25 : διὰ τὴν πάρεσιν τῶν προγεγονότων ἁμαρτημάτων ἐν τῇ ἀνοχῇ τοῦ θεοῦ. This word, which is not found in the LXX, has the same legal meaning as the verb παριέναι (→ 509) and is attested in this sense [10] in Dion. Hal. Ant. Rom., VII, 37, p. 1393, 13 ff.: τὴν μὲν ὁλοσχερῆ πάρεσιν οὐχ εὕροντο, τὴν δὲ εἰς χρόνον ὅσον ἠξίουν ἀναβολὴν ἔλαβον. [11]

The forgiveness denoted by ἄφεσις (ἀφιέναι) and πάρεσις is almost always that of God. In the Synoptists (cf. also Ac. 8:22; Jm. 5:15) this is mostly a forgiveness to which man is continually referred and which he can receive on request so long as he is ready to forgive others (Mt. 6:12, 14 f.; 18:21-35; Lk. 17:3 f.; Mk. 11:25). To this extent, the concept is the same as the OT and Jewish idea of forgiveness. [12] Yet there is a new and specifically Christian feature. For the community realises that it has to receive from God the forgiveness which is offered to men through the saving act which has taken place in Jesus Christ. As it tells

---

[8] Cf. Blass-Debr. § 364, 1 and 2; and Pr.-Bauer.

[9] παρίημι → 509.

[10] Perhaps also BGU, 624, 21, cf. Deissmann NB, 94.

[11] The same antith. of full release and postponement is found in Philo Flacc., 84 : ἄφεσις παντελής and ὑπέρθεσις. Trench, 69-74 defends the distinction between ἄφεσις and πάρεσις.

[12] On the terminology and understanding of forgiveness in Judaism, cf. Bousset-Gressmann, 388 ff.; W. Staerk, *Sünde u. Gnade nach der Vorstellung des älteren Judentums* (1905); O. Schmitz, *Die Opferanschauung des späteren Judentums und die Opferaussagen des NT* (1910); Moore, I; A. Büchler, *Studies in Sin and Atonement* (1928); Dalman WJ, 1, 334 ff.; Schl. Mt., 213 f., 289, 559; Str.-B., I, 421 f., 424 ff., 495, 795 f.; II, 585 f. Jos. uses ἀφιέναι for "to forgive" (cf. Schl. Mt., 213); it also occurs in Test. G. 6:3, 5; 7:5. Philo often uses ἄφεσις in the sense of forgiveness (ἁμαρτημάτων, Vit. Mos., II, 147; Spec. Leg., I, 190 ; ὧν ἐξήμαρτεν, Spec. Leg., I, 237; πάντων ἁμαρτημάτων καὶ παρανομημάτων, Spec. Leg., I, 215); but he also uses it for liberation, Spec. Leg., II, 39, 67 and 122; Vit. Mos., I, 123; Det. Pot. Ins., 144; and often figur. for the liberation of the ψυχή from the σῶμα and the πάθη (Rer. Div. Her., 273; Congr., 89 and 107-109; Mut. Nom., 228; Sacr. AC, 122), or of the νοῦς from its own strivings (Migr. Abr., 32).

us that Jesus Himself dispensed forgiveness (Mk. 2:5 ff. and par.), so it, too, dispenses forgiveness through Him (Col. 1:14; Eph. 1:7; Ac. 13:38), through His name (Lk. 24:47; Ac. 10:43; 1 Jn. 2:12), on His commission (Jn. 20:23), esp. in baptism (Ac. 2:38; Hb. 6:1 f.; cf. Mk. 1:4 and par.) and the Lord's Supper (Mt. 26:28). To the extent that the community is established by the act of salvation as the holy community of the last age (→ ἐκκλησία), forgiveness is an eschatological blessing and is expressly described as such in Lk. 1:77 (cf. 4:18); the same view obviously underlies both Paul and Hb. If the thought of forgiveness is of fundamental significance in the NT, its terminological explication is not highly developed, and ἄφεσις (or ἀφιέναι and πάρεσις) are rare in Paul and John, being found only at R. 3:25; Col. 1:14; Eph. 1:7; Jn. 20:23; 1 Jn. 1:9 and 2:12. Yet in Paul the thought is expressed in such terms as → δικαιοσύνη and → καταλλαγή, in Hb. by → ἁγιάζειν and → καθαρίζειν, which are also found in Jn., as also by such cognate or related concepts as → ἱλασμός, → (ἀπο)λύτρωσις, → ἀπολούεσθαι, → χαρίζεσθαι etc. (cf. the linking of ἀφιέναι with related concepts in R. 3:24 f.; 4:7; Col. 1:14; Eph. 1:7; 1 Jn. 1:9; Hb. 9:22 f.).

All this makes it plain a. that the OT conception of God as the Judge to whom man is responsible is maintained; b. that God's forgiveness is not deduced from an idea of God or His grace, but is experienced as His act in the event of salvation, so that preaching does not consist in illuminating instruction regarding the idea of God but in the proclamation of the act of God; c. that forgiveness as an eschatological event renews the whole man, in whom sin was not just something isolated and occasional but the power which determined his whole being; d. that forgiveness can be received only when man affirms God's judgment on himself, tho old man, in the confession of sins (1 Jn. 1:9; Jm. 5:16; Ac. 19:18; cf. Mk. 1:5 and par.) and penitence (Lk. 24:47; Ac. 2:38; 5:31; 8:22; Hb. 6:1, 6; cf. Mk. 1:4 and par.), which corresponds to → πίστις in Paul and John. There is thus avoided the legal understanding of the thought of forgiveness as a remission of punishment related only to past events; the future is included in eschatological forgiveness.

Bultmann

ἀφιλάγαθος → 18

ἀφίστημι, ἀποστασία, διχοστασία

ἀφίστημι.

Trans. "to remove," either spatially or from the context of a state or relationship (τινά τινος or τινὰ ἀπό τινος), or from fellowship with a person = "to seduce," "to win away" from someone, ether privately or politically. Hence also the intrans. sense "to remove oneself," "to resign," "to desist," "to fall away."

Of these different meanings the only ones which are important theologically are those which concern alienation from persons.

In the LXX, with the most diverse equivalents in the Mas., ἀφίστασθαι is used of political (Gn. 14:4; 2 Ch. 21:8; Tob. 1:4) and religious (Dt. 32:15; Jos. 22:18 f., 23; Da. 9:9; Gr. Sir. 10:12) apostasy. In the latter sense it has become a tech. term, so that we can read in Jer. 3:14: ἐπιστράφητε υἱοὶ ἀφεστηκότες (cf. Is. 30:1: τέκνα ἀποστάται). Normally it is ἀπὸ θεοῦ or ἀπὸ κυρίου, but also ἀπὸ διαθήκης ἁγίας (1 Macc. 1:15) and ἀπὸ λαρτείας πατέρων (1 Macc. 2:19). The material equivalents are λατρεύειν θεοῖς ἑτέροις Dt. 7:4); οὐκ εἰσακούειν (Dt. 9:10); καταλιπεῖν τὸν θεόν (Dt. 32:15). The apostasy finds expression in a disobedient cultic and ethical worship of other gods.

In the NT the religious sense is at least found alongside others. In Ac. 15:38; 5:37; 19:9 the word seems to acquire increasingly the emphatic sense of religious apostasy. In Hb. 3:12 it is used expressly of religious decline from God. The opposite here is: τὴν ἀρχὴν τῆς ὑποστάσεως μέχρι τέλους βεβαίαν κατέχειν (3:14). This apostasy entails an unbelief which abandons hope. [1] According to 1 Tm. 4:1 apostasy implies capitulation to the false beliefs of heretics. [2] This apostasy is an eschatological phenomenon: ἐν ὑστέροις καιροῖς. The same view is found in Lk. 8:13, where ἀφίστασθαι is used absolutely. The reference is to the situation of Rev. 3:8. ἀφίστασθαι thus approximates to → ἀρνεῖσθαι, as may be seen in Herm. s., 8, 8, 2 : τινὲς δὲ αὐτῶν εἰς τέλος ἀπέστησαν ... ἐβλασφήμησαν τὸν κύριον καὶ ἀπηρνήσαντο λοιπόν. [3]

ἀποστασία.

A later construction for ἀπόστασις. [1] The word presupposes the concept ἀποστάτης "to be an apostate," and thus signifies the state of apostasy, whereas ἀπόστασις denotes the act. Politically an ἀποστάτης is a "rebel" (Polyb., V, 41, 6; 57, 4 : τοῦ βασιλέως; Diod. S., XV, 18 : τῆς πατρίδος), and this sense is retained in ἀποστασία (Plut. Galb., 1 (I, 1052e): τὴν ἀπὸ Νέρωνος ἀποστασίαν; Jos. Vit., 43 : διὰ τὴν ἀποστασίαν τὴν ἀπὸ ʽΡωμαίων; Ap., 1, 135 f.; Ant., 13, 219.

In the LXX it also occurs in the political sense in 1 Esr. 2:23. It is particularly employed, however, in the religious sense, Jos. 22:22; Jer. 2:19; 2 Ch. 29:19 (the apostasy of Ahaz); 33:19 (of Manasseh). Cf. 1 Macc. 2:15 (used absol.); Asc. Is. 2:4. ἀποστάτης has also retained this religious sense, cf. Is. 30:1; 2 Macc. 5:8 : Jason ὡς τῶν νόμων ἀποστάτης καὶ βδελυσσόμενος; Nu. 14:9; Jos. 22:16, 19 : ἀποστάτης ἀπὸ τοῦ κυρίου.

In the NT Ac. 21:21 may be compared with 2 Macc. 5:8. Here the reproach is brought against Paul: ἀποστασίαν διδάσκεις ἀπὸ Μωυσέως. Materially this implies the rejection of the Torah. [2] In 2 Th. 2:3 ἀποστασία is used in the absol. sense as an event of the last days alongside or prior to (?) the appearance of the ἄνθρωπος τῆς ἀνομίας. Here a Jewish tradition [3] is adopted which speaks of complete apostasy from God and His Torah shortly before the appearance of the Messiah. This is applied to the apostasy of Christians from their faith to error and unrighteousness (v. 11 f.) in the last days (Mt. 24:11 f.). Again we have the situation of Lk. 8:13. [4]

ἀφίστημι. [1] Cf. Herm. v., 2, 3, 2; 3, 7, 2.
[2] Cf. Herm. s., 8, 9, 1: ἐνέμειναν τῇ πίστει; Just. Dial., 8, 2 : ἀφίστασθαι τῶν τοῦ σωτῆρος λόγων; 20, 1: ... τῆς γνώσεως (θεοῦ); 111, 2 : τῆς πίστεως (Χριστοῦ).
[3] Cf. Just. Apol., I, 50, 12 : οἱ γνώριμοι αὐτοῦ πάντες ἀπέστησαν, ἀρνησάμενοι αὐτόν.

ἀποστασία. [1] C. A. Lobeck on Phryn. Ecl., 528.
[2] Cf. Str.-B., II, 753 f.; G. Kittel, "Paulus im Talmud," in *Rabbinica* (1920), 14.
[3] Str.-B., III, 637.
[4] Dob. Th., 270 f. thinks that the reference is to the religious and moral declension, not "of the community of Christians but of the non-Christian world." But the term ἀποστασία is against this, for it includes a prior turning to God. To be sure, the ἀποστάται and the appearance of the ἄνθρωπος τῆς ἀνομίας are to be differentiated, but only in such a way

In Just. Dial., 110, 2 the ἄνθρωπος τῆς ἀνομίας of 2 Th. 2:3 is called ὁ τῆς ἀποστασίας ἄνθρωπος. He comes in the power of Satan, who in Just. Dial., 103, 5 is brought into etymological connection with ἀποστάτης. Cf. Act. Thom., 32 D.

† διχοστασία.

"Division," "disunity," "contention" : Hdt., V, 75; Plut. Aud. Poet., 4 (II, 20c). Esp. "political revolt" or "party dissension" : Solon Fr., 3, 37 (Diehl, I, 24); Theogn., 78 (Diehl, I, 121). LXX, 1 Macc. 3:29 : καὶ οἱ φορολόγοι τῆς χώρας ὀλίγοι χάριν τῆς διχοστασίας καὶ πληγῆς ἧς κατεσκεύασεν ἐν τῇ γῇ ...

In the NT it signifies "objective disunity" in the community. In R. 16:17 it occurs in connection with the σκάνδαλα περὶ τὴν διδαχήν; in 1 C. 3:3 in 𝕭𝕽 alongside ζῆλος καὶ ἔρις = τὰ σχίσματα of 1:10; in Gl. 5:20 between ἐριθεῖαι and αἱρέσεις to denote general parties within the church. Probably in these passages, too, διχοστασία has a limited "political" sense. It is within the ἐκκλησία that διχοστασίαι arise.

This political character is plain in 1 Cl., cf. 46, 5 : Ἱνατί ἔρεις καὶ θυμοὶ καὶ διχοστασίαι καὶ σχίσματα, πόλεμός τε ἐν ὑμῖν; 51, 1 ἀρχηγοὶ στάσεως καὶ διχοστασίας ἐγενήθησαν. On the other hand, in Herm. s., 8, 7, 5; v., 3, 9, 9; m., 2, 3 διχοστασία has the more general sense of "contentiousness," and in s., 8, 10, 2 of "cleavage."

Schlier

ἀφομοιόω → ὅμοιος   ἀφορίζω → ὅρος

---

† Βαβυλών

1. Apart from references to the Babylonian captivity in Mt. 1:11, 12, 17 and Ac. 7:43, and the single mention in 1 Pt. 5:13 (→ 2.), the term Βαβυλών is found only in the Apocalypse, where it is applied in a most significant manner as a symbolical name for the ungodly power of the last time : Βαβυλών ἡ μεγάλη (14:8; 16:19; 17:5; 18:2, 10, 21), the great city[1] (17:18; 18:10, 16, 18, 19, 21). The destruction of Babylon is proclaimed by an angelic voice in 14:8. The place of the fall of Babylon in the apocalyptic drama (with the outpouring of the 7th vial) is indicated in 16:19. Then in 17:1 to 19:10 the divine expressly portrays this city and its fall in 7 visions.[2] He paints it in the symbolical form of a harlot : the great whore (17:1; 19:2), the mother of harlots and the abomination of the earth

---

that the apostasy makes possible the power of the man of sin, and this in turn increases the apostasy. The same applies in the passage quoted from Justin.

Β α β υ λ ώ ν. Comm. on Rev. 17 and 18. Also Hastings DB, I, 213 f.; A. Schlatter, *Das AT in der Apk.* (1912), 90 ff.; *Gesch. d. ersten Christenheit* (1926), 301 ff.; T. Zahn, *Einl. i. d. NT*, II³ (1906), 17 ff. (on 1 Pt. 5:13); A. H. Blom, "De Ondergang van Rome naar de Apk.," ThT, 18 (1884), 541 ff.; J. Sickenberger, "Die Johannesapk. und Rom," BZ, 17 (1926), 270 ff.

[1] Cf. Strabo, XVI, 1, 5 (of the historical Bab.): ἐρημία μεγάλη 'στὶν ἡ μεγάλη πόλις; and Rev. 18:19 : ἡ πόλις ἡ μεγάλη ... μιᾷ ὥρᾳ ἠρημώθη.

[2] v. Loh. Apk., 135.

(17:5).³ She sits on a beast with 7 heads and 10 horns, strikingly adorned.⁴ Her name is written on her forehead.⁵ She is drunk with the blood of the saints slain within the city⁶ (17:3-6).⁷ The interpretation of the image (17:7-18) bursts its framework; its plastic fixity yields to dramatic movement. In union with 10 kings, the beast on which the city sits — the antichrist of c. 13 — will destroy the city and burn it with fire (17:16). It is God who will thus bring judgment on the city (17:17; 18:8; 19:2). At its fall there is jubilation in heaven but sorrow among the inhabitants of earth (c. 18).

The most important features of this picture are taken from the OT prophets. This is true even of the name Babylon. The historic city and empire of Babylon were always depicted by the prophets as the ungodly power *par excellence*. Thus even after the fall of Babylon, Babel, as they saw it, represented for later Jewish readers of Scripture, and also for early Christians (→ 517), the very epitome and type of an ungodly and domineering city,⁸ the localisation of which might vary with the current historical situation.⁹ The image of the whore also comes from the OT. Tyre is thus named in Is. 23:15 ff.,¹⁰ and Nineveh in Na. 3:4.¹¹ In addition, the same picture is often used in connection with the idolatry of Israel.¹² The image of the beast is taken even in detail from Da. 7. Thus we might well say that the whole depiction of the Apocalypse, esp. c. 18, is made up of OT thoughts and expressions rather after the manner of a mosaic.¹³

---

³ The mode of expression is Jewish. Cf. the use of אָב in Rabb. writings: אֲבוֹת מְלָאכוֹת, Shab., 7, 2 ff.: "The 39 chief activities (forbidden on the Sabbath)"; אֲבוֹת נְזִיקִין, BQ, 1, 1: "The 4 main forms of injuries" etc. Above all S. Nu., 134 on 27:12 : Moses אבי הנביאים, "the greatest prophet," "the main prophet." Thus μήτηρ πορνῶν means the chief whore in the world. Cf. also Jn. 8:44 where the devil is the "father of lies." The μυστήριον of the name in Rev. 17:5 does not lie, then, in the expression "mother," as supposed in Loh. Apk., 139, but in the name Βαβυλών. It is a μυστήριον in the sense that it cannot be understood literally, but only πνευματικῶς (Bss. Apk., 404), as a symbolical name.

⁴ This denotes the harlot, but there is also a hint of the wealth and power of the city.

⁵ It is attested of Roman harlots that they bore their names on their foreheads, Sen. Rhet. Contr., I, 2, 7; Juv., 6, 122 f.

⁶ The divine feels so strongly the unity of the images (harlot, beast) with what they depict (city, antichrist) that he can easily pass from the one to the other in his statements. Cf. 17:16; 17:6 with 18:24; esp. 17:3 : καθημένην ἐπὶ θηρίον ... γέμοντα.

⁷ In the whole apocalyptic drama Βαβυλών is the great antitype of the new Jerusalem which comes down from heaven (21:2) as the holy city. In place of the πόρνη Babylon in this world there will come the νύμφη Jerusalem (21:2) in the new world.

⁸ Cf. Schlatter, *Gesch. d. erst. Chr.*, 301.

⁹ Other features of the city are taken over with the type, e.g., that it is situated on many waters (Rev. 17:1 on the basis of Jer. 51:13), even though they apply only to the historical Babylon and are no longer relevant in the current situation (hence the allegorical interpretation in 17:15).

¹⁰ Since Babel has become a type of the ungodly city, all the OT warnings and judgments concerning such cities are applied to it even though originally pronounced against other powers. Thus the complaint of kings, merchants and sailors at its fall in Rev. 18:9-19 is largely influenced by Ez. 27, where the reference is to Tyre.

¹¹ In these two passages the harlotry does not denote idolatry, as normally in the OT, but the trading activity of the city. We are to remember this in relation to the whore Babylon in Rev. 17; cf. 18:11-19.

¹² Cf. esp. Ez. 16. To bring in Mandaean par. to explain the image (e.g., Loh. Apk., 142) is thus unnecessary, quite apart from more general critical objections to this course.

¹³ The form of the quotations shows that the divine knew his Bible in the original Heb. rather than the Gk. trans. Yet he never quotes exactly; he rather makes free use from memory of OT expressions and clauses, often intermingling different passages, as one who has learned much of the Bible by heart.

The sayings of Jesus have also had their influence on the shaping of the visions. Thus, for the heavenly command to depart from Babylon we have models in Is. 48:20; 52:11; Jer. 50:8; 51:6 etc. on the one hand, but also in Mt. 24:15 ff. and par. on the other. In Rev. 18:21 we have a mixture of Jer. 51:63 f. and Mt. 18:6 and par. Perhaps we are also to see an influence of Mt. 23:25 (cf. 23:27) on Rev. 17:4 (the golden cup full of abomination and impurity).

Many other traditional features must have passed into the visions of the divine which we cannot now track down in detail. Thus the fact that the woman sat on the beast (which is disregarded in the interpretation in 17:7 ff. and even contradicted in 17:16, → 515), probably derives from the writer's acquaintance with pictures of a goddess or god riding on a beast. [14] Again, she holds a cup in her hand, and the question arises whether this feature is suggested by depictions of goddesses with the horn of plenty. [15]

All these different elements are arranged by the divine in his visions into a great and uniform whole in which he sees part of what is going to take place in the immediate future (Rev. 1:1). He knows that the city which is to be destroyed is already present, Rev. 17:18: ἡ γυνὴ ... ἔστιν ἡ (article) πόλις ἡ μεγάλη ἡ ἔχουσα (present) βασιλείαν ἐπὶ τῶν βασιλέων τῆς γῆς. This can only be Rome. [16] The main arguments for this are a. Rev. 17:9: the city lies on 7 hills, and Rome is almost proverbially known as the city of 7 hills; [17] b. it was common for later Judaism to apply to Rome the title Babel as a type of ungodly power (→ 515). [18] Cf. Apc. Bar. 67:7; Sib., 5, 143 and 159, and many Rabbinic passages. [19]

2. In 1 Pt. 5:13 also, where we have greetings from the Christian church ἐν Βαβυλῶνι to the churches of Asia Minor, the reference can only be to Rome. The essential reasons for this, apart from those already mentioned, are a. the general application to Rome in early exegesis, with only a few dwindling exceptions; [20] the lack of even a hint that Peter ever stayed or worked in the land of Babylon, as distinct from the fairly solid historicity of his stay and martyrdom in Rome. [21]

---

[14] E.g., the depiction of Attis sitting on the lion in Haas, No. 9-11, Leipoldt (1926), No. 146; further examples may be found in Loh. Apk., 136. More commonly the deity stands on the beast, as in Haas-Leopoldt, No. 117, 119, 121, 122 (Zeus of Doliche and goddesses); also Haas, No. 5 Zimmern (1925), No. 1 and 2 (Hittite); v. also 9-11, p. XV b f. and XVII a.; also H. Gunkel, *Schöpfung und Chaos* (1895), 365.

[15] On the use of the popular belief in Nero *redivivus* in interpretation of the beast of 17:8 ff., cf. Bss., 411 ff.

[16] This is the view of all the more recent expositors apart from Loh. His thesis is that the reference to Rome is impossible because Babylon and the beast are obviously demonic or satanic rather than political powers. This is true. But it is a feature of the Apoc. that the world in which the divine actually lives, and the forces which determine it, are regarded as demonic.

[17] Loh., 140, with examples. The cogency of this argument is shown by the fact that Loh. himself can hardly escape it.

[18] It is to be noted that in the prophets and Judaism generally בָּבֶל denotes both the city and the state; the former is the epitome of the power of the latter. The equation with Rome is later understood in the same way. Indeed, in Rabb. writings רומי (= ῾Ρώμη) often means the empire rather than the city.

[19] In addition to the passages mentioned in Str.-B., III, 816, cf. also Nu. r., 7 on 5:2 ff.; Midr. Ps. 121 (ed. Buber, 507).

[20] Zn., *Einleitung*[3], II, 17 ff. In two minusc. this interpretation has even made its way into the text.

[21] Zn., *op. cit.*; H. Lietzmann, *Petr. u. Pls. in Rom*[2] (1927). On the whole subject, cf. Wnd. Kath. Br.[2], 82.

If we accept this reference to Rome in 1 Pt. 5:13, then we must follow Schlatter [22] in his deduction "not merely that Peter expects the destruction of Rome and sees it in the prophetic utterances against Babylon, but that the whole Church both in Rome and Asia Minor shared this view."

Kuhn

---

† βάθος	(→ ὕψος).

"External depth." a. The depth of a stratum (= mass or greatness), Mt. 13:5; τῆς γῆς, Jos. Ant., 8, 63; or the direction (downward), Ez. 32:24: εἰς γῆς βάθος; Lk. 5:4: εἰς τὸ βάθος, not necessarily suggesting how great is the depth. Often with ὕψος, as in Is. 7:11: εἰς βάθος ἢ εἰς ὕψος; Dg., 7, 2; Corp. Herm., XI, 20b. b. Depth as one dimension of a σῶμα or στερεόν, and indeed the dimension τὸ πρόσθεν καὶ τὸ ἀντικείμενον, Arist. Cael., II, 1, p. 284b, 25; the opp. of ἐπιπολή, Gen. Corr., II, 2, p. 330a, 18. Hence βάθος comes to denote the spatial depth, e.g., of the earth, Cael., II, 13, p. 294a, 26, or of the sea, Barn., 10, 10, or of the outermost sphere, Philo Som., I, 21, or of cosmic space, Preis. Zaub., IV, 575; 662 f., or of the ἄβυσσος, Wis. 10:19; Gr. Sir. 24:5.

"Depth" or "depths" figuratively in many different senses, mostly to denote the inscrutability or hiddenness as well as the vastness or greatness of something. It may denote the general character of man, Plat. Theaet., 183e; Plut. Fab. Max., 1 (I, 174c). It is also used of ἐπιστήμη, Philo Poster. C., 130; Som., II, 271; of σοφία, Ebr., 112; of γραφή, Orig. in Joh. XX, 10, 74; of ψυχή, Philo Som., I, 200; Orig. in Joh. VI, 58, 297; of καρδία, Jdt. 8:14; Just. Dial., 121, 2.

In the NT it is used of this figurative depth only [1] in relation to God or the world. Thus in R. 11:32 [2] God's depth of riches, wisdom and knowledge is distinguished first by His unsearchability to human judgment and then by His character as the God who meets us in hidden ways and judgments. [3] Similarly in 1 C. 2:10 the depth of the activity of God is concealed from the world in principle; it is accessible only to the πνεῦμα τοῦ θεοῦ. The opposite is to be found in τὰ βαθέα τοῦ σατανᾶ (Rev. 2:24) which disclose themselves to libertine practice. [4] Analogies are to be found especially in Gnostic terminology: Tert. Val., 1; Iren., I, 21, 2; Hipp. Ref., V, 6, 4: ἐπεκάλεσαν ἑαυτοὺς γνωστικούς, φάσκοντες μόνοι τὰ βάθη γινώσκειν. Yet it should be noted that in Gnosticism God and His βάθος are understood in the sense of being. For this reason there is not merely reference to the βάθος of the πατήρ (Orig. in Joh. II, 2, 18; Hipp. Ref., V, 9, 1), but God Himself can be βάθος (Act. Thom., 143; Hipp. Ref., VI, 30, 7). In the NT even the world as a hostile depth does not disclose its depth as a given quantity but as a power which withdraws and which thus threatens in virtue of its unfathomable nature. In R. 8:39 βάθος is a κτίσις like δύναμις etc. The τόπος is known as a power, whereas in Gnosticism [5] the power (of God) is understood as

---

[22] *Gesch. d. erst. Chr.*, 303.

β ά θ ο ς. [1] Apart from 2 C. 8:2, cf. Wnd., *ad loc.*

[2] On the Hellenistic form cf. E. Norden, *Agnostos Theos* (1913), 243, 3.

[3] Cf. Apc. Bar. 14:8 (1 Cl., 40, 1).

[4] Cf. the sacrament of the ἀπολύτρωσις ἡ εἰς τὸ βάθος κατάγουσα αὐτούς (Iren., I, 21, 2).

[5] Cf. C. Schmidt, "Gnostische Schriften in koptischer Sprache," TU, 8 (1892), 336, 358.

τόπος. [6] In Eph. 3:18 [7] βάθος stands in a series — πλάτος, μῆκος, ὕψος, βάθος — which denotes the heavenly κλῆσις or κληρονομία. These first express the three dimensions, the third dividing into ὕψος/βάθος. The heavenly inheritance is thought of as a cube, like the heavenly Jerusalem in Rev. 21:16, bBB, 75b and the heavenly ἐκκλησία in Herm. v., 3, 2, 5. They then denote the four quarters of the earth. [8] The inheritance is thus comprehensively indicated.

Cf. Iren. Epid., 1, 34: (Christ) "embraces the whole world, its breadth and length, its height and depth . . . illumining the heights (i.e., heaven) and penetrating to the depths, to the foundations of the earth, spreading out the expanses from morning to evening and directing the spaces from north to south . . ." Iren., V, 17, 4: ἐπιδεικνύων τὸ ὕψος καὶ μῆκος καὶ πλάτος καὶ βάθος ἐν ἑαυτῷ (= τὰ πέρατα τῆς γῆς). Preis. Zaub., IV, 965 ff.: the οἶκος τοῦ θεοῦ (or God Himself) represents salvation as an embracing cube. Pist. Soph., 133: "To wander through the portions of the earth . . . from without inwards and from within outwards, from above downwards . . . and from the heights to the depths . . . and from the length to the breadth . . ." (ibid., 130, 148). [9]

Schlier

> (βαίνω,) ἀναβαίνω,
> καταβαίνω, μεταβαίνω

(βαίνω).

This word is not found in the NT nor in Philo. It occurs only twice in Jos: Ant., 1, 20: τοὺς ἔξω βαίνοντας ἀρετῆς μεγάλαις περιβάλλει συμφοραῖς, and Ant., 19, 220: οὐ πάνυ τοῖς ποσὶ βαίνειν δυνάμενον (Claudius). In the LXX we find it in no more than 4 passages: Dt. 28:56; Wis. 4:4; 18:16; 3 Macc. 6:31. Even on inscriptions (Ditt. Syll.[3], 540, 163) and pap. (BGU, IV, 1192, 10) it is rare.

Class. Gk. is dominated by the intrans. sense of "to go," "to stride," "to stretch the legs" ("to ride"); and then "to go away," "to come" and "to go on before." [1]

The term acquires another meaning in the cultic texts of the mysteries. In the Mithr. Liturg., 2, 7 it denotes the heavenly journey of the soul: ὅπως ἐγὼ μόνος αἰητὸς οὐρανὸν βαίνω. [2] With few exceptions, [3] however, ἀναβαίνειν rather than βαίνειν is used for the soul's ascent to heaven.

In the secular sphere there is an analogous use of βαίνειν in Anth. Pal., XVI, 6: ἁ δὲ Φιλίππου δόξα πάλιν θείων ἄγχι βέβακε θρόνων.

---

[6] The depth of the world is always spoken of according to the understanding and access to it. In ψ 129:1 βάθη is an image for a difficult situation (= τὰ βάθη τῆς θαλάσσης in ψ 68:3). In Qoh. 7:24 (25) it is used ethically; in Porphyr. Vit. Plot, 16 speculatively; in Mak. Homil., 8, 1 (MPG, 34, 528c) mystically.

[7] Ad loc. Dib. Gefbr.; A. Dieterich, Jbch. f. Phil., Suppl., XVI (1888), 766, 802 ; Reitzenstein Poim., 25 f.; E. Peterson, Εἷς Θεός (1926), 250, 3.

[8] J. Hehn, Siebenzahl und Sabbath (1907), 13 f., 76 f.; J. Lewy, OLZ, 26 (1923), 538 f.

[9] Without the full formula, Pogn. Inscr. Sém., 48.

βαίνω. [1] It is also used trans. a. "to make go" (only fut. βήσω and aor. ἔβησα); b. "to mount" (a horse). This trans. sense is of no importance in the NT or indeed elsewhere.

[2] Cf. on this pt. A. Dieterich-O. Weinreich Mithr.-Liturg., 220: "The Mythras initiate of the eagle's degree 'strides' up to heaven."

[3] Cf. Luc. Pergr. Mort., 39: ἔλιπον γᾶν, βαίνω δ' ἐς Ὄλυμπον. Also the epigram in Anth. Pal., VII, 62 wrongly ascribed to Plato: Αἰετὲ τίπτε βέβηκας ὑπὲρ τάφον; (cf. Mithr. Liturg., 220).

ἀναβαίνω.

1. The basic meaning is spatial, i.e., "to rise from the depths to the heights." It is used for climbing aboard a ship, mounting a horse or climbing a mountain. Geographically it denotes mounting from a plain to a city, [1] from the coast inland, from the mouth of a river upstream, from the street over the threshold, up the steps of a house, from the lower storey of a house to the upper. The orator mounts the rostrum (εἰς τὸ βῆμα) ar appears on an elevated place before the people (εἰς [ἐπὶ] τὸ πλῆθος). The advocate rises to address the court (εἰς τὸ δικαστήριον). [1] Sometimes ἀναβαίνειν is used with the simple acc. and no prep. [2] The spatial use of ἀναβαίνειν in the LXX is similar. It is mostly a rendering of עָלָה. [3] In the NT it has this sense mostly in the Gospels. To avoid the crowds or to pray, Jesus climbs a hill (Mt. 5:1; 14:23; 15:29 and par.). He joins His disciples in the boat (Mt. 14:22 and par.). He goes up with them to Jerusalem (Mt. 20:17 f. and par.). It is said of Joseph in Lk. 2:4: ἀνέβη ἀπὸ τῆς Γαλιλαίας ἐκ πόλεως Ναζαρὲθ εἰς τὴν Ἰουδαίαν εἰς πόλιν Δαυείδ. The men who bring the sick of the palsy to Jesus do so ἀναβάντες ἐπὶ τὸ δῶμα (Lk. 5:19). Zacchaeus climbs a sycomore to see Jesus (Lk. 19:4). Even though the goal is not stated, ἀναβαίνειν can be understood from the context. [4]

In the spatial sense ἀναβαίνειν is also used intrans. in the NT. The seed grows up from the earth as a plant; it springs up (ἀνέβησαν αἱ ἄκανθαι, Mt. 13:7; Mk. 4:7, 32).

2. Much more important is the use of ἀναβαίνειν in statements related to the cultic life or cultic actions. Here the NT follows the usage of the Heb. OT, [5] the LXX, [6] and Rabbinic writings. [7] עָלָה = ἀναβαίνειν is a "standing formula for going to Jerusalem" (Schlatter) and the temple.

In the life of Jesus the moment of His going up from the water of baptism (Mt. 3:16; Mk. 1:10) acquires significance from the descent of the Spirit. Going into the sanctuary is ἀναβαίνειν εἰς τὸ ἱερόν (Lk. 18:10). [8] ἀναβαίνειν is so typical an expression for this that further indication need not be given (Jn. 12:20). The cultic sense is especially common in John's Gospel: ἀναβαίνειν εἰς Ἱεροσόλυμα (2:13; 5:1; 11:55); [9] εἰς τὴν ἑορτήν (7:8, 10); [10] εἰς τὸ ἱερόν (7:14; cf. Ac. 3:1). [11] For Paul and the other apostles, too, the statement that they went up to Jerusalem [12] had rather more than a topographical significance. Jerusalem meant the mother community. This is clearest in Ac. 18:22: καὶ κατελθὼν εἰς Καισάρειαν, ἀναβὰς καὶ ἀσπασάμενος τὴν ἐκκλησίαν, κατέβη εἰς Ἀντιόχειαν. Naturally the basic meaning in all these expressions is the topographical. Sanctuaries

---

ἀ ν α β α ί ν ω. [1] Examples are given in Liddell-Scott and Moult.-Mill., s.v. ἀναβαίνειν. V. on this pt. Class. Philol., 22 (1927), 240.

[2] Cf. W. Schmid, Philol. Wochenschr., 46 (1926), 137.

[3] On עָלָה in the spatial sense, v. Ges.-Buhl, s.v.

[4] Mk. 15:8; Ac. 8:31; Rev. 8:4; 9:2.

[5] V. Ges.-Buhl, s.v. עָלָה.

[6] V. Hatch-Redpath, s.v. ἀναβαίνειν.

[7] For Rabb. usage, v. Schl. Mt., 594; Schl. J., 74 f.

[8] Cf. BCH, 11 (1887), 375, 1, 14: τοὺς ἀνερχομένους εἰς τὸ ἱερόν; 379, 2, 9: τοὺς ἀνιόντας ἐς τὸ ἱερόν.

[9] V. also Jos. Ant., 14, 270; Bell., 2, 40: ἀναβαίνειν εἰς Ἱεροσόλυμα; Ant., 20, 164: ἀνέβησαν εἰς τὴν πόλιν ὡς προσκυνήσοντες τὸν θεόν.

[10] Blass suggests that in Jn. 7:8 we delete εἰς τὴν ἑορτήν, along with Chrysost. Minusc. 69 Lat. q (Bl.-Debr. § 323, 3).

[11] Cf. Jos. Ant., 12, 164 and 362; 13, 304; Bell., 2, 340 and 405; 6, 285,

[12] Ac. 11:2; 15:2; 21:12, 15; 24:11; 25:1, 9; Gl. 2:1 f.

were usually located on hills, and Jerusalem is the holy city on a hill. Yet there is also a cultic nuance, especially when the word is used without object.

That ἀναβαίνειν was a cultic term may be seen in non-biblical writings. Steinleitner [13] has pointed out that, though ἀναβαίνειν became the usual expression by reason of the elevated situation of temples, it became a technical term for cultic action in the sense of going to the temple.

Thus we have ἀναβαῖ ᾿Αντιγόνη [14] and ἀ[ν]α(β)αῖ μετὰ τῶν ἰδίων πάντων [15] on inscriptions from Cnidos. Again, we find ἀναβάντες ἐπὶ τὸν βωμὸν τῆς ᾿Αρτέμιδος τῆς Λευκοφρυηνῆς [16] on a Cretan inscription. Since the immediate environs of the temple are also holy, the expression ἀναβαίνειν ἐπὶ τὸ χωρίον also has a cultic ring. [17] There is attestation in the pap. too. In P. Par., 49, 34 we read: ἐὰν ἀναβῶ κἀγὼ προσκυνῆσαι, and 47, 19 f.: ὁ στρατηγὸς ἀναβαίνει αὔριον εἰς τὸ Σαραπιῆν. [18] Even clearer are the accounts of the Caric Panamaros cult on the Panamara inscr. [19] In the festival of Comyrion, held in honour of Zeus, there is reference to a ceremony called the ἄνοδος or ἀνάβασις τοῦ θεοῦ. [20] The idol, which leaves the temple at appointed times and then stays in Stratonikeia, is at the time of the main celebration of the mystery cult brought back to the temple, which lay on a hill near Stratonikeia. In the mystical sense ἀναβαίνειν is found in P. Oxy., 41, 5, which refers to the divine power flowing into man to salvation: ἰσιην φιλῖ σε καὶ ἀναβαίνι εὐτυχῶς τῷ φιλοπολίτῃ.

3. The culmination of ἀναβαίνειν in the religious sphere is the ἀναβαίνειν εἰς τὸν οὐρανόν. This corresponds to the Heb. עָלָה הַשָּׁמַיִם (Dt. 30:12; Am. 9:2; 2 K. 2:11. Cf. 1 S. 2:10 עָלוּ בַשָּׁמַיִם (LXX: κύριος ἀνέβη εἰς οὐρανούς). [21]

In Peter's first address in Ac. 2:34 there is reference to the ἀναβαίνειν εἰς τοὺς οὐρανούς. Ps. 110:1 is adduced in proof of the resurrection and exaltation of Jesus. Here, according to the argument, the prophecy is not fulfilled in the person of David. It has been fulfilled, however, in Jesus. The author of Acts says expressly: οὐ γὰρ Δαυεὶδ ἀνέβη εἰς τοὺς οὐρανούς. In Rabbinic literature this Psalm is interpreted both non-Messianically and Messianically. [22] The Messianic interpretations either refer it to the Messiah, or to David as prince in the last time of salvation, or to the Messianic age with no mention of the Messiah. [23] It is just possible that in Ac. 2:34 Luke consciously polemicises against the reference of the Ps. to David. In relation to the ascension Luke thinks exclusively of Jesus.

---

[13] F. Steinleitner, *Die Beicht im Zusammenhange mit der sakralen Rechtspflege in der Antike* (Diss. München, 1913), 41.

[14] C. T. Newton, *A History of Discoveries at Halicarnassus, Cnidus and Branchidae* (1862 f.), II, 2, 719, No. 81, 19.

[15] *Ibid.*, 735, No. 85.

[16] Ditt. Syll.³, 685, 26.

[17] Cf. Steinleitner, 40 and 41, where further examples are given.

[18] Moult.-Mill., I, 29 f., *s.v.* ἀναβαίνω here refers to Lk. 18:10 as a par.

[19] The inscr. may be found in BCH, 11 (1887), 373 ff.; 12 (1888), 82 ff.; 15 (1891), 169 ff. Cf. H. Oppermann, "Zeus Panamaros," RVV, 19 (1924), 73-75.

[20] BCH, 15, 185, No. 130, n. 15 f.; 11, 383, No. 3, 10; 15, 203, No. 144, 10. O. Weinreich (Mithr.-Liturg., 225) refers the expression ἀνέβη Ζεὺς εἰς ὄρος χρυσοῦν (Mithr.-Liturg., 20, 13 f.) to the Panamaros cult on account of the word αμαρα (20, 14). Oppermann (*op. cit.*, 207) rejects this special interpretation and takes the phrase generally, since many temples of Zeus were located on hills.

[21] Schl. J., 93.

[22] *V.* Str.-B., IV, 452 ff. Excursus: "Der 110. Ps. in der altrabbinischen Literatur."

[23] Examples in Str.-B., IV, 457 f.

He alone is exalted to the right hand of God and has thus been given a share in the divine rule. He alone is the Messiah. Perhaps in such statements early Christianity was rejecting the "ascensions" of Jewish apocalyptic. In later Judaism we have many depictions of the heavenly journeys of famous heroes of faith (*v.* 1 En. 70-71; 2 En.; Test. L. 2-5; 4 Bar.; Vis. Is.; Vit. Ad., 25 ff.; Apc. Abr.).[24] The notion of the heavenly journey of the soul, often depicted after the manner of these ascensions, is later found in Gnostic circles.[25]

In the conception of Christ in John's Gospel ἀναβαίνειν, with καταβαίνειν, plays an important part. The Johannine Christ has come down from heaven. He thus knows of heavenly things (3:12 f.).[26] He will be lifted up again to heaven, to the place where He was before (6:62). His ascension is His going up to the Father (20:17). As a heavenly being who has taken flesh and concealed His δόξα, the Johannine Christ on earth is constantly in touch with the heavenly world. The angels maintain His uninterrupted intercourse with God. By their descending and ascending (Gn. 28:12) they mediate this contact with the heavenly world and "support the work of the Son of Man on earth"[27] (Jn. 1:51).[28] The same thought is present in Eph. 4:8-10. Here Ps. 68:18, referred by the Rabbinic tradition to Moses,[29] is reinterpreted christologically. The author uses καταβαίνειν and ἀναβαίνειν of the descent and ascent of the Redeemer. He aims to show that the One who ascends is identical with the One who descended. After the completion of His earthly work Christ returns to His original place. Schlier[30] has rightly pointed out that καταβαίνειν and ἀναβαίνειν are technical terms for the coming down of the Redeemer to earth and His going up from earth to heaven.

The questions in R. 10:6 f.: τίς ἀναβήσεται εἰς τὸν οὐρανόν; and τίς καταβήσεται εἰς τὴν ἄβυσσον; formulated according to Dt. 30:11-14 and certain passages from the Psalms (ψ 70:19; 106:26 etc.), are probably only a rhetorical way of using a proverbial saying which denotes something quite impossible.[31] If so, the meaning is that it is not necessary to fetch the Messiah either from heaven or hell. The righteousness which is by faith, unlike the Jews who do not believe in Christ, knows that He is already present. At the back of Paul's thinking there is naturally the idea of the descent of the pre-existent Christ and His resurrection from the dead.

In Revelation the demand is made of the seer (4:1): Ἀνάβα ὧδε. The state of prophetic rapture is denoted by these words. A door is opened in heaven, and the divine looks into the throne room of heaven.

There is an important par. in the Mithras-Liturg., 10, 22. The initiate is promised that he will see the doors of heaven opened and that he will thus see the world of the gods

---

[24] Cf. Bouss.-Gressm., 297 f.

[25] Much material is to be found in H. Schlier, *Christus u. d. Kirche im Eph. Brief* (1930), 1 ff.

[26] Cf. Schl. J., 93 f. and H. Odeberg, *Fourth Gospel* (1929), 72 ff.

[27] H. Windisch, "Angelophanien um den Menschensohn auf Erden," ZNW, 30 (1931), 215. Cf. Joachim Jeremias, *Angelos*, 3 (1928/30), 2 ff.; Odeberg, *Fourth Gospel*, 33 ff.; H. E. Weber, *"Eschatologie" und "Mystik" im NT* (1930), 169.

[28] A similar view is found in the Mithr.-Liturg., 6, 11: ὄψει θείαν θέσιν, τοὺς πολεύοντας ἀναβαίνοντας εἰς οὐρανὸν θεούς, ἄλλους δὲ καταβαίνοντας.

[29] Str.-B., III, 596 ff.

[30] *Christus u. d. Kirche im Eph. Brief*, 3.

[31] So b BM, 94a; b Git., 84a; cf. Str.-B., III, 281; Ltzm. R. on 10:6.

within, so that his spirit will be enraptured by the joy and delight of his vision and will mount up on high. [32]

In other non-biblical passages [33] we also read of the ascent εἰς τὸν οὐρανόν, [34] ἐπὶ τὸν Ὄλυμπον. [35]

In Ac. 10:4 Cornelius is told by an angel who appears to him that his prayers and good deeds have ascended up for a memorial before God (ἀνέβησαν εἰς μνημόσυνον ἔμπροσθεν τοῦ θεοῦ). In Ac. 7:23 we have the peculiar expression ἀνέβη ἐπὶ τὴν καρδίαν αὐτοῦ, modelled on the Heb. עָלָה עַל־לֵב [36] Similarly we read in Lk. 24:38 : διὰ τί διαλογισμοὶ ἀναβαίνουσιν ἐν τῇ καρδίᾳ ὑμῶν;

καταβαίνω.

1. This word is the complete opp. of ἀναβαίνω, both spatially and geographically and also cultically. Cf. the altar of the descending Demetrius (Δημητρίου καταβάτου) in Plut. Demetr., 10 (I, 893, Kleinknecht). In the LXX it is usually the rendering of יָרַד. [1] There are no essential differences between its use in the OT and the NT.

It is often used of leaving Jerusalem or Palestine or other places. Usually the place which one leaves or to which one goes is mentioned. [2] But is also occurs absolutely. Another usage is in relation to natural phenomena. Rain, storm, hail and fire come down from heaven.

2. In the religious sphere καταβαίνειν is mostly used in close conjunction with ἀναβαίνειν. In many passages (Jn. 3:13; 6:33 ff.), and especially in the self-declarations of Jesus, the Fourth Gospel stresses the fact that the Son of Man is ὁ ἐκ τοῦ οὐρανοῦ καταβάς. He has come down from heaven to do the will of the Father who has sent Him (6:38). [3] The gifts which He offers are also gifts from heaven. Jesus calls Himself ὁ ἄρτος ὁ καταβὰς ἐκ τοῦ οὐρανοῦ (6:41 f.). [4] Those who partake of Him, the Bread of God (6:33), will partake of heavenly being and nature. Those who feed on Him will never die but live to eternity (6:50 f., 58). For the true Bread from heaven has two features : the καταβαίνειν ἐκ τοῦ οὐρανοῦ and the ζωὴν διδόναι τῷ κόσμῳ. [5]

According to Jm. 1:17 every good and perfect gift comes down from God, the Father of lights. [6] At the baptism of Jesus the Baptist sees the Spirit like a dove coming down on Him (Jn. 1:32). Baptism itself is described as a καταβαίνειν εἰς

---

[32] ὥστε ἀπὸ τῆς τοῦ θεάματος ἡδονῆς καὶ τῆς χαρᾶς τὸ πνεῦμά σου συντρέχειν καὶ ἀναβαίνειν.

[33] Cf. Porphyr. Ad Marc., 27: κατανοητέον οὖν πρῶτόν σοι τὸν τῆς φύσεως νόμον, ἀπὸ δὲ τούτου ἀναβατέον ἐπὶ τὸν θεῖον.

[34] Dio C., 59, 11, 4 : Λίουιός τέ τις Γεμίνιος βουλευτὴς ἔς τε τὸν οὐρανὸν αὐτὴν (Drusilla) ἀναβαίνουσαν καὶ τοῖς θεοῖς συγγιγνομένην ἑωρακέναι ὤμοσεν.

[35] In parody Luc. Icaromen., 11: ἐπὶ τὸν Ὄλυμπον ἀναβάς.

[36] Cf. Bl.-Debr., § 130, 1 and p. 291.

κ α τ α β α ί ν ω. [1] On the detailed meanings of יָרַד v. Ges.-Buhl, s.v. On καταβαίνειν in the LXX, cf. Hatch-Redpath, s.v.

[2] Jn. 5:4, which is not authentic, has the prep. ἐν instead of the usual εἰς : κατέβαινεν ἐν τῇ κολυμβήθρᾳ. Cf. BCH, 15, 185, No. 130, n. 15 f.: τῇ ἀνόδῳ τῇ ἐν τῷ ἱερῷ (= εἰς τὸ ἱερόν). On this pt. v. Oppermann, "Zeus Panamaros," loc. cit. (→ 520, n. 19). In P. Par., 42, 10 we read : ἐὰν ... καταβῶσι ἐκτὸς τοῦ ἀσύλου. Cf. on this pt. Moult.-Mill., IV, 324, s.v. καταβαίνω.

[3] On the alternation of ἀπό and ἐκ with καταβαίνειν in Jn., v. Schl. J., 175; cf. Schl. Mt., 268.

[4] Cf. Schl. J., 176.

[5] Ibid., 173.

[6] On this pt. v. Dib. Jk. on 1:17 and A. Meyer, Das Rätsel des Jk. Briefes (1930), 184, 205 etc.

(τὸ) ὕδωρ in Ac. 8:38. [7] Contact with the heavenly world is mediated for Jesus by the καταβαίνειν and ἀναβαίνειν of the angels (Jn. 1:51; → 521). In Eph. 4:9 f. κατέβη εἰς τὰ κατώτερα μέρη τῆς γῆς refers to the earthly journey of the Redeemer, [8] not to His descent into Hades. [9] Yet motifs from the journey into the underworld are transferred to this earthly journey. [10] For κατάβασις is a technical term for descent to the underworld. [11]

3. καταβαίνειν is also used of eschatological events, esp. in Rev. These start in heaven and come down from it upon the earth and men. The *parousia* in particular is a descent of the κύριος from heaven (1 Th. 4:16). The new Jerusalem also comes down from God out of heaven to earth (Rev. 3:12; 21:2, 10).

4. καταβαίνειν is used in a philosophical sense in Heraclitus Hom. Alleg., 3 : οὐδ' εἰς τὰ μύχια τῆς ἐκείνου σοφίας καταβεβήκασιν. Philo speaks of the Spirit descending from heaven [12] and of joy coming down from heaven to earth. [13] The souls which enter human bodies also come down from heaven. [14]

5. Finally, outside the NT καταβαίνειν is a commercial term for a fall in the value of money. Thus in P. Oxy., 1223, 33 we read : ὁ ὁλοκόττινος νῦν μυ(ριάδων) β'κ ἐστίν· κατέβη γάρ.

μεταβαίνω.

The usual meaning of μεταβαίνειν is "to move from one place to another," especially "to change one's dwelling," [1] though also in speaking and writing "to move on to a new subject," [2] and "to attain from one state to another."

In the NT the word occurs predominantly in the topographical sense. [3] Only in the Johannine literature is it used metaphorically. Thus in Jn. 5:24 and 1 Jn. 3:14 we have the expression : μεταβεβηκέναι ἐκ τοῦ θανάτου εἰς τὴν ζωήν. [4] Believers are removed from the sphere of death. By acceptance of the divine Word in faith they have crossed the frontier between death and life even in their earthly existence. In Jn. 13:1 there is a sharp distinction between this world and the heavenly world of the Father. For Jesus the hour of death means a change of scene and therefore transition into the state of δόξα which He enjoyed as the Pre-existent prior to His incarnation.

There is a par. in Ditt. Or., 458, 7: εἰς ἀτυχὲς μεταβεβηκὸς σχῆμα. [5]

Schneider

---

[7] Cf. Barn., 11, 8 and 11; Herm. m., 4, 3, 1; s., 9, 16, 4 and 6.

[8] Cf. Schlier, op. cit., 3.

[9] So, e.g., W. Bousset, *Kyrios Christos*³ (1926), 30 f.

[10] Schlier, op. cit., 4, n. 2.

[11] Pauly-W., X (1919), 2359 ff. (Ganschinietz); v. also Anth. Pal., XI, 23 : εἰς ἀίδην μία πᾶσι καταίβασις; cf. ibid., 92 : καὶ πέρας εἰς ἀίδην καταβάς, and 274 : πῶς κατέβαινεν Λολλιανοῦ ψυχὴ δῶμα τὸ Φερσεφόνης; Ps.-Plut. Vit. Poes. Hom., 126 : εἰς ἄδου κάτεισιν.

[12] Rer. Div. Her., 274 : ἄνωθεν ἀπ' οὐρανοῦ καταβὰς ὁ νοῦς.

[13] Abr., 205 : χαρὰν ἀπ' οὐρανοῦ καταβαίνειν ἐπὶ τὴν γῆν.

[14] Gig., 12; Sacr. AC, 48.

μ ε τ α β α ί ν ω. [1] P. Tebt., 316, 20 and 92 ; cf. Lk. 10:7. Also Mart. Pol., 6, 1.

[2] E.g., Plat. Phaedr., 265c; Crat., 438a. Cf. also Barn., 18, 1: ἐπὶ ἑτέραν γνῶσιν καὶ διδαχὴν μεταβαίνειν.

[3] Mt. 8:34; 11:1; 12:9; 15:29; Lk. 10:7; Jn. 7:3; Ac. 18:7. In the LXX only Wis. 7:27; 19:19 and 2 Macc. 6:1, 9, 24.

[4] There is a similar expression in Wis. 7:27: (σοφία) καὶ κατὰ γενεὰς εἰς ψυχὰς ὁσίας μεταβαίνουσα.

[5] Cf. also Anth. Pal., IX, 378 : καὶ κοιμῶ μεταβάς (= *transgressus*) ἀλλαχόθι.

---

† Βαλαάμ

1. The OT gives us two different accounts of Balaam. The first is in Nu. 22-24 (J and E); Jos. 24:9-10; Mi. 6:5; also Dt. 23:5-6 (quoted in Neh. 13:2). Balak the king of Moab summons him to curse Israel. Instead, he blesses the people according to the command of God. The emphasis of the story is on the blessing of the people. Balaam himself is simply an instrument of the will of God. No question of personal merit or personal guilt arises. The second is in Nu. 31:16 (P). On the advice of Balaam the Midianite women (or Moabite in Nu. 25:1) entice the Israelites into licentiousness and therefore into apostasy from Yahweh to Baal Peor.[1] Because of this, Balaam is killed in the campaign of revenge against the Midianites (Nu. 31:8 = Jos. 13:22).

2. Later Judaism found the kernel of the story of Balaam in 31:16 and interpreted the older account (Nu. 22-24) in the light of it. Balaam, who enticed Israel into licentiousness and apostasy (S. Nu., 157 on 31:8 and 16; S. Nu., 131 on 25:1, with the par. Tanch. B בלק, 74a; bSanh., 106a)[2] is the "wrongdoer" (Tanch. B בלק 69a, twice ; 70a, several times ; Ab., 5, 19; bZeb., 116a etc.). He was envious and malicious acc. to Nu. 24:2; proud acc. to Nu. 22:13;[3] covetous acc. to Nu. 22:18 (Tanch. B בלק, 68b; Nu. r., 20;[4] Ab., 5, 19).[5] What he said to the angel who stopped him in the way (Nu. 22:34) was hypocrisy and deceit which marked him as thoroughly bad (Tanch. B בלק, 70a). In Sanh., 10, 2 he is expressly numbered among those who have no part in the future world.[6] Philo depicts him in exactly the same colours (Vit. Mos., I, 264-300; Migr. Abr., 113-115).[7] On the other hand, Josephus is more restrained in his judgment (Ant., 4, 100-158). He does not censure him even in respect of his counsel (Nu. 31:16). He stresses all the favourable aspects and either ignores[8] or quickly passes over the rest. Josephus must have had some interest in putting him in the best possible light.[9]

Β α λ α ά μ. W. Smith and H. Wace, *Dict. of Christ. Biography* (1877 ff.), I, 239 f.; DAC, I, 127; Jew. Enc., II, 466 ff.; EJ, IV, 790 ff.; Comm. on 2 Pt. 2:15 f.; Jd. 11; Rev. 2:14.

[1] This story of P perhaps arose out of the fact that in J and E the account of licentiousness and idolatry immediately follows the Balaam story (Nu. 25:1 ff.), so that an inner connection was sought between the two. Cf. Akiba's declaration concerning Nu. 25:1 (S. Nu., 131): "Every section which is directly connected with what precedes (as Nu. 25:1 with the Balaam story) must be interpreted in the light of it."

[2] Str.-B., III, 793.

[3] For he says here : "God has not permitted me to go with *you*," i.e., He will permit me to go with greater than you (Tanch., *ad loc.*).

[4] Str.-B., III, 771.

[5] A. Geiger (*Jüd. Zeitschr. Wiss. u. Leben*, 6 [1868], 31-37) has advanced the view (followed by Str.-B., IV, 1218, Index *s.v.*) that in Ab., 5, 19 Balaam is a concealed name for Jesus. Only in 2 passages — and nowhere else in Rabb. literature — is this at all likely, namely, in bSanh., 106a in R. Levi's (3rd cent. A.D.) exposition of Nu. 24:23 and bSanh., 106b in the debate between R. Chanina (3rd cent. A.D.) and a heretic on the age of Balaam (33 yrs.).

[6] The passages might easily be multiplied. For later Rabb. views of the story, *v.* EJ and Jew. Encyc. (and esp. bSanh., 105 f.; Tg. J., I on Nu. 22-24).

[7] Cf. esp. Migr. Abr., 113: ὁ μάταιος Βαλαάμ ... ἀσεβὴς καὶ ἐπάρατος; *ibid.*, 114: τοῖς γὰρ πολεμίοις φησὶν αὐτὸν ἐπὶ μισθῷ συνταχθέντα μάντιν γενέσθαι κακὸν κακῶν.

[8] E.g., the fact that the Israelites slew Balaam in revenge for his evil action (Nu. 31:8). He gives names to the Midianite kings slain acc. to Nu. 31:8, but does not mention Balaam (Ant., 4, 161).

[9] For he can hardly have failed to know the later Jewish assessment, attested by Philo as well as the Rabbis and already present in germ in P Nu. 31:16. Cf. the strange con-

3. This later Jewish assessment of Balaam (e.g., by Philo and the Rabbis) was adopted *in toto* by Christianity too. In 2 Pt. 2:15; Jd. 11; Rev. 2:14 Balaam is an OT model of the licentious Gnostic whose errors disrupt the Christian community. The true point of comparison is indicated in Rev. 2:14. As Balaam seduced the Israelites by his counsel, so the Nicolaitans, as Rev. calls the Gnostics, [10] entice the churches by their teaching to idolatry (the eating of flesh sacrificed to idols) and licentiousness. [11, 12] Another less central point of comparison is mentioned in Jd. 11 [13] (as also 2 Pt. 2:15), namely, that like Balaam the Gnostics carry on their destructive activity out of covetousness and for gain. [14] 2 Pt. 2:16 sees in the episode in Nu. 22:22-33 a proof that Balaam was hostile to God, inferring that the heretics who are like him are similarly hostile. It may be seen that in early Christian polemics Balaam, the dreadful example, became a catch-word and stock comparison. The comparison did not have to be worked out in detail; it was enough simply to make it, as in Jd. 11.

Kuhn

† βαλλάντιον   (→ πήρα).

The spelling of this word varies in antiquity. [1] In so far as βάλλειν is the basic word, βαλάντιον is the more correct. Yet βαλλάντιον is the better attested. Textually the two forms occur alongside, e.g., in Teleclides, 41 (CAF, I, 219), Job 14:17 LXX (B: ἐν βαλαντίῳ; א A: ἐν βαλλαντίῳ) and the three NT passages (Lk. 10:4; 12:33; 22:35 f.) where the older and more important witnesses (including א ABD) favour βαλλάντιον.

The term, first used in Epicharmus, 10 (5th cent. B.C.), [2] always [3] means "pocket" or "purse," and esp. a "purse for money," whether with (Aristoph. Eq., 1197: ἀργυρίου βαλλάντια) or without the explanatory addition (Telecl., 41: ἐκ βαλλαντίου, [4] etc.). To this there corresponds the explanation of βαλλάντιον by μάρσιπος in Suidas,

---

cluding sentence on the Balaam story in Ant., 4, 158: καὶ ταῦτα μὲν ὡς ἂν αὐτοῖς τισι δοκῇ οὕτω σκοπείτωσαν, which seems almost to be an excuse for his depiction to those who think otherwise.

[10] Certainly based on a Νικόλαος as the founder of the sect, since the name cannot be understood in terms of popular etymology as a transl. of בְּלְעָם = בֶּלַע עַם ("devourer of the people," bSanh., 105a). Cf. R. Knopf, *Das nachapostolische Zeitalter* (1905), 293, n. 1; A. v. Harnack, *Journal of Religion,* 3 (1923), 413 ff. (where sources and bibl. are given).

[11] πορνεῦσαι in Rev. 2:14 is to be taken lit. and not therefore as "syncretistic strivings" (as in Loh. Apk., 29).

[12] The διδαχὴ Βαλαάμ of Rev. 2:14 is to be compared with תַּלְמִידָיו שֶׁל־בִּלְעָם (Ab., 5, 19), i.e., the disciples of Balaam, or those who act like him, as the opp. of תַּלְמִידָיו שֶׁל־אַבְרָהָם, i.e., those who are similar in character to Abr. It is erroneous to conclude that there was a sect of Balaamites.

[13] The πλάνη τοῦ Βαλαάμ naturally denotes the διδάσκειν φαγεῖν εἰδωλόθυτα καὶ πορνεῦσαι, as Rev. 2:14.

[14] Cf. ἐπὶ μισθῷ in Philo Migr. Abr., 114 (→ n. 7). There is no comparison with Balaam in respect of the despising of angels (as against Wnd. on Jd. 11).

βαλλάντιον. [1] On the question of spelling v. Thes. Steph. s.v.; Bl.-Debr. § 11, 2; Helbing, 15 f.; Winer-Schmiedel, 55, n. 51; Liddell-Scott, 304.

[2] CGF, I, 1, p. 92, Kaibel.

[3] The only apparent exception is in a quotation of the older Dionysius of Syracuse in Athen., III, 98d (I, p. 226, Kaibel); in a "witty" play on words βαλλάντιον is here claimed for the javelin (ἀκόντιον) (ὅτι ἐναντίον βάλλεται).

[4] Cf. Kock, *ad loc.*

though in Gr. Sir. 18:33 the readings ἐν βαλλαντίῳ (אᶜᵃ) and ἐν μαρσίππῳ (AC) or ἐν μαρσιππίῳ (א*B) etc. are found alongside. It occurs 6 times in the LXX (though only in א at Tob. 1:14; 8:2); it is a translation of צְרוֹר at Job 14:17 and כִּיס at Pr. 1:14. [5] In later Judaism the latter became the usual word for a money-bag. [6] As a bag or purse βα(λ)λάντιον is also found in Philo Jos., 180 (βαλάντιον ὑπόμεστον ἀργυρίου); 207 (τὴν τιμὴν [purchase price] ἐν βαλαντίοις καταθεῖναι). It does not occur in Josephus. It is found once as an alien word in S. Lv., 109c on 25:39 : "... that he should not follow with the purse (בלנטיא) like a slave."

The 4 NT occurrences are all in Lk. (10:4; 12:33; 22:35 f.) and always signify a purse in the sense also found in Jewish Hellenism. At 10:4 it is linked directly with → πήρα, and is not therefore an equivalent, an important point in fixing the basic meaning of this term. Materially Jesus' exhortation to the seventy (→ ἑβδομήκοντα): μὴ βαστάζετε βαλλάντιον, is the same as that to the twelve, which reads in Mt. 10:9 : μὴ κτήσασθε χρυσὸν μηδὲ ἄργυρον μηδὲ χαλκὸν εἰς τὰς ζώνας ὑμῶν, and in Mk. 6:8 : μὴ εἰς τὴν ζώνην καλκόν, whereas in this case Lk. (9:3) simply has : μήτε ἀργύριον. [7] On both occasions the point is that the disciples are not to rely on greater or smaller sums of money which travellers usually carry [8] to meet their needs. Matthew and Mark, however, think of the native custom of tying coins into the girdle, [9] while Luke assumes the possession of a special purse and is thus thinking in terms of a greater amount. It is possible, however, that Luke mentions the purse because it was part of the equipment of the well-to-do towsman (→ supra). If the disciples were not to carry it, this would imply renunciation of the financial security of civic society as elsewhere indicated in Lk. [10] The second passage (12:33) is certainly relevant in this connection, while the third (22:35 f.) refers back to 10:4, though regard is now had to the alteration in the situation of the disciples with the approaching death of Jesus.

Rengstorf

βάλλω, ἐκ-, ἐπιβάλλω

βάλλω.

a. trans. the powerful [1] movement of "throwing" or "propelling," e.g., βέλος, Hom. Od., 9, 495; σπόρον, Theocr., 25, 16; κόπρια, P. Oxy., 934, 9; κλήρους, Jos. Ant., 6, 61; ὀργὴν ἐπὶ τὴν γῆν, Jos. Ant., 1, 98; τινὰ ἔξω γῆς, Soph. Oed. Tyr., 622; εἰς φυλακήν, Epict. Diss., I, 1, 24; vulg. "to throw out" : εἰς κόρακας, Aristoph. Vesp., 835; σφᾶς αὐτοὺς ἀπὸ τῶν δωμάτων, "to cast oneself down," Jos. Bell., 4, 28; εἰς (τὸν θησαυρόν), Jos. Ant., 9, 163; pass.: βεβλημένος πρὸ τῶν ποδῶν, Jos. Bell., 1, 629. b. "to bring to a place," "to lay down," "to pour in": οἶνον ... εἰς πίθον, Epict. Diss., IV, 13, 12; ἐνὶ θυμῷ βάλλειν, "to lay up a thought in the heart," Hom. Od., 1, 201; mid. :

---

[5] כִּיס, which here means purse or bag generally, is sometimes rendered μαρσίππιον in the LXX, as in Is. 46:6, where it clearly means "money-bag."

[6] No importance is to be attached to passages like Bek., 6, 6, where כִּיס has a special meaning derived from the basic sense of purse.

[7] Kl. Lk., ad loc.

[8] Cf. e.g., Lk. 10:35 : ἐκβαλὼν δύο δηνάρια, an expression behind which Thes. Steph., II, 74 (Dindorf) sees the possession and use of a βαλλάντιον.

[9] V. the examples in Str.-B., I, 564 f., where Billerbeck also calls attention to the fact that "the girdle is often called פונדא, פונדה or אפונדה, i.e., funda = purse."

[10] With the sayings against riches, cf. esp. 12:13 ff., but also Ac. 2:45 f.; 4:34 ff.; 5:1 ff.

β ά λ λ ω.   [1] A passionate book like Rev. uses βάλλειν no less than 26 times.

κρηπῖδα (foundation stone), Pind. Pyth., 7, 4 (cf. *fundamenta iacere*). c. intr.[2] "to cast onself on," εἰς ὕπνον, "to sink into sleep," Eur. Cyc., 574.

In the LXX βάλλειν is the counterpart of נפל hiph : κλήρους, 1 Βασ. 14:42; ψ 21:18; שלך hiph Qoh. 3:5; Is. 19:8; ירה 2 Ch. 26:15; Is. 37:33; Job 38:6 : λίθον γωνιαῖον.

In the NT βάλλειν is first used trans. for "to throw" or "to cast," e.g., Mt. 4:18 :[3] ἀμφίβληστρον εἰς θάλασσαν; Mt. 17:27: ἄγκιστρον; Mk. 4:26 : σπόρον; Mk. 15:24 : κλῆρον; Rev. 6:13 : "to cast off fruit." Often in the NT βάλλειν is used in different ways in connection with the thought of judgment, partly as committal to the element which exercises it : εἰς πῦρ, Mt. 3:10; 13:42; εἰς γέενναν, 5:29 and par., partly of expulsion from the community of salvation, as with the adv. ἔξω in the sense of → ἐκβάλλειν, Mt. 5:13 and par.; 13:48; Lk. 14:35; Jn. 15:6. In Mt. 18:9 and par. βάλε ἀπὸ σοῦ expresses resolute separation from what entices to sin.

On the pass. "to lie," used of the sick man in Mt. 8:6, 14, cf. T. Ket., 4, 15 : היה חולה מוטל במיטה etc.[4]

Again, βάλλειν in the NT simply means, as under b., "to lay down," "to set in a place" : Mk. 2:22 and par. : wine in the wineskin ; Mk. 7:33 : the finger in the ears ; Jn. 20:25 : the finger in the wounds ; Jn. 13:2 : a thought in the heart. On the expression εἰρήνην or μάχαιραν βάλλειν εἰς τὴν γῆν, cf. the Rabb. הטיל שלום (M. Ex. 20:25; S. Nu., 16 on 5:23; 42 on 6:26).

Intr. (cf. c.) in Ac. 27:14 of the breaking of the storm.

ἐκβάλλω.

a. "To throw out," "to expel," "to repel," e.g., of invading enemies, Demosth., 60, 8; of expulsion from the government, Thuc., II, 68, 6; of the expulsion of demons, cf. Preis. Zaub., IV, 1227: πρᾶξις γενναία ἐκβάλλουσα δαίμονας; of exclusion from the house, P. Oxy., I, 104, 17; λόγους, Plat. Crito, 46b (of the bandying of the name). b. "To send forth," without the accompanying sense of violence, P. Ryl., 80, 1 (1st cent. A.D.): ὑδροφύλακας, "to lead forth," "to release": ἐκ τῆς φυλακῆς;[1] "to leave aside" : τὸ ἀναγνωσθὲν δάνειον, Mitteis-Wilcken, No. 372, col., 6, 23 (2nd cent. A.D.); "to cause to break forth from within" : δάκρυα, Hom. Od., 19, 362.

In the LXX ἐκβάλλειν in the sense of "to eject" or "to repel" is the usual equivalent of גרש (Gn. 3:24; Ex. 6:1; Lv. 21:7, γυναῖκα; Ju. 6:9; Prv. 22:10, ἐκ συνεδρίου; also of שלך hiph (Is. 2:20, βδελύγματα); of ירש hiph; "to eject from possession" (Ex. 34:24, τὰ ἔθνη; Dt. 11:23 etc.).

In the NT ἐκβάλλειν has particularly 1. the sense of "to expel" or "to repel," esp. in the case of demons, who have settled in men as in a house (Mt. 12:44) into which they have unlawfully penetrated (Mk. 1:34, 43; 3:15, 22 f.; 9:38 etc.). By ancient custom demons were ejected by pronouncing against them the name of a more powerful spirit (cf. Mt. 12:29). Thus there had been constructed, esp.

---

[2] Radermacher, 23; H. Ljungvik, *Studien z. Sprache d. apokryphen Apostelgeschichten* (1926), 77 f.
[3] Mk. 1:16 : ἀμφιβάλλειν without obj.
[4] Schl. Mt., 274.

ἐκβάλλω. [1] Μαρτύριον τῆς ἁγίας Αἰκατερίνας, 18, p. 17, Viteau ; D. Tabachovitz, *Sprachl. und textkrit. Studien zur Chronik des Theophanes Confessor* (Uppsala, 1926), 32; Wien. Stud., XX (1898), 159.

by Judaism in the time of Jesus, a whole apparatus of formulae and measures which were supposed to be effective against demons.[2] Yet a demon can be expelled simply by the word of command, e.g., R. Simeon.[3] Jesus,[4] who accepts the current view of demons, ignores in His expulsions the whole apparatus constructed by Judaism. His majesty finds expression in His accomplishment of expulsions by the Word (Mt. 8:16). He has full power over demons, so that they cannot evade His command (Mk. 1:27). He brings the power of God to bear against them (Lk. 11:20).[5] The distinctive feature in His exorcisms is to be found not merely in the powerful and majestic sovereignty therein displayed but in the appraisal of His actions and their results. The latter are for Him a sign that the kingdom of God is being inaugurated (Mt. 12:28). He thus engages in exorcism in conscious connection with His preaching of the coming of the kingdom. Hence He charges His messengers (→ ἀπόστολος) to exorcise as part of their commission (Mt. 10:1, 8). In the assessment of His successes against demons as devilish (ἐν τῷ Βεελζεβούλ, Mt. 12:24; 9:34) He sees a blasphemous misrepresentation of the holy war which He wages in the name of God (Mt. 12:22 ff., 31). A result of His successes is that soon His own "name" (→ ὄνομα) comes to be used as a means of driving them out (Mk. 9:38; 16:17).

2. In the NT ἐκβάλλειν is also used of the expulsion of the wife or secondary wife in Gl. 4:30 (cf. Gen. 21:10); of the plucking out of the eye (Mk. 9:47); of expulsion from the community, as in the case of the Jews driving out those who confess Christ (Jn. 9:34 f.).[6] In contrast, Jesus excludes from His fellowship none of those whom the Father causes to come to Him (Jn. 6:37).[7] It is used of the expulsion from the community exercised by the φιλοπρωτεύων Διοτρέφης (3 Jn. 10) and also of the casting out of the Christian name (Lk. 6:22).

3. "To send out,"[8] Mt. 9:38 and par.: ἐργάτας εἰς τὸν θερισμόν; Jn. 10:4; Jm. 2:25; Ac. 16:37: "to let go," "release"; Mk. 1:12: "to lead out"; Mt. 7:4 and par.: "to pull out" (κάρφος, δοκόν); Mt. 12:35; 13:52; Lk. 10:35: "to take forth"; Mt. 12:20: "to lead forth εἰς νῖκος, unto victory"; Rev. 11:2: "to leave out." Pass. Mt. 15:17: "to let fall εἰς ἀφεδρῶνα."

ἐπιβάλλω.

a. trans. "to throw over" (χλαῖναν), Hom. Od., 14, 520; "to lay on" (χεῖρα), Aesch. Choeph., 395; (χεῖράς τινι), Aristoph. Lys., 440; "to add to" (γάλα ἐπὶ τὸ ὕδωρ), Theophr. Ign., 49. b. intrans. "to cast oneself on something," Hom. Od., 15, 297, ἐπέβαλε τερετίζειν, Diog. L., VI, 27; ἐπιβαλὼν συνέχωσεν, P. Tebt., 50, 12; in the hostile sense, "to break in," Diod. S., XVII, 64, 3; "to dedicate oneself to something,"

---

[2] Cf. e.g., Jos. Ant., 8, 45 ff. Cf. also Str.-B., IV, 501-535 on older Jewish demonology, esp. 533 ff.; RE³, IV, 411 ff. s.v. "Dämonische"; W. Ebstein, Die Medizin im NT u. im Talmud (1903), 173 ff.; A. Jirku, Die Dämonen und ihre Abwehr im AT (1912), 41 ff.; J. Tambornino, De antiquorum daemonismo, RVV, VII, 3 (1909), 9 ff., 16 f.

[3] Me'ila, 17b: "He said: Ben Telamjon, go forth (צֵא), Ben Telamjon!" (Str.-B., IV, 534 f.).

[4] O. Bauernfeind, Die Austreibung der Dämonen im MkEv. (1926); W. Grundmann, Der Begriff d. Kraft in d. nt.lichen Gedankenwelt (1932), esp. 45 ff., 54 f., 66 f.

[5] ἐν δακτύλῳ θεοῦ. This is undoubtedly older than the ἐν πνεύματι θεοῦ of Mt. 12:28, which is a more spiritual way of expressing the same thought.

[6] The meaning is twofold, as so often in Jn., i.e. out of the hall of judgment and also out of the Jewish community, cf. 9:22.

[7] ἐκβάλλειν is used absol. in both cases and strengthened by ἔξω.

[8] Cf. E. Löfstedt, Symbolae philol. Danielsson (1932), 179 ff.

Diod. S., XX, 43, 6; "to follow": ἐπιβαλὼν ἔφη, Polyb., I, 80, 1; "to belong to": τὸ ἐπιβάλλον sc. μέρος, Hdt., IV, 115; τοῦ ἐπιβαλλόντος τῷ ἀδελφῷ μέρους οἰκίας, P. Flor., 50, 100 (3rd cent. A.D.). A current legal term. c. mid. "earnestly to desire," Hom. Il., 6, 68; "to undertake," Thuc., VI, 40, 2.

In the LXX ἐπιβάλλειν is used for נפל hiph in Gn. 2:21; for שׁלך hiph in ψ 107:10 vl.; for שׁלה in Dt. 12:7, 18; Is. 11:14; for נשׂא in Gn. 39:7; נתן in Ex. 7:4; פרשׂ in Nu. 4:6 f.; ἱμάτιον שׂים in Lv. 10:1; Nu. 16:18 θυμίαμα etc.

In the NT the word depicts trans. a. the violent movement of "casting on or over," as in 1 C. 7:35 (βρόχον), and especially "hostile seizure," as in Mk. 14:46 and par.; Ac. 4:3; 5:18. The Fourth Gospel shows that the Jews cannot use force against Jesus until His hour comes (Jn. 7:30, 44). It can be used of the putting of one's hand to work (Lk. 9:62) or the putting of a patch on a garment (Mt. 9:16 and par.).

Intrans. "to cast oneself on something" (Mk. 4:37: κύματα). So also Mk. 14:72: ἐπιβαλὼν ἔκλαιεν, "he began to weep bitterly"; [1] Lk. 15:12 of the portion which lawfully accrues.

Hauck

| βάπτω, βαπτίζω, βαπτισμός |
| βάπτισμα, βαπτιστής |

βάπτω, βαπτίζω.

A. The meaning of βάπτω and βαπτίζω.

βάπτω, "to dip in or under" (trans.): Hom. Od., 9, 392; Aesch. Prom., 863: ἐν σφαγαῖσι βάψασα ξίφος; "to dye," used in Josephus only in this sense, Bell., 4, 563; Ant., 3, 102; βάμμα, "dyed material," Ant., 3, 129; P. Par., 52, 10; 53, 5 (163/2 B.C.): βαπτά, "dyed or coloured clothes."

ἐ π ι β ά λ λ ω. [1] Cf. Bl.-Debr. § 308, Suppl., p. 308; Theophyl. MPG, 123, p. 661d, ad loc.: ἐπικαλυψάμενος τὴν κεφαλὴν ἢ ἀντὶ τοῦ ἀρξάμενος μετὰ σφοδρότητος. The reference is obviously also to Mk. 14:72, cf. the trans. in sy[s] it: "began," D: ἤρξατο κλαίειν. H. Ljungvik, Studien z. Sprache d. apokr. Ap. Gesch. (1926), 77 f.

β ά π τ ω κ τ λ. RE[8], XIX, 396 ff. (with older bibl.); Cr.-Kö., 194 ff.; RGG[2], V, 1002 ff.; Pauly-W., 2 Series, IV, 2501 ff.; NT Theology: H. Weinel[4] (1928), esp. 63, 202 f., 247, 356, 467 f.; H. J. Holtzmann[2] (1911), esp. I, 171 ff., 448 ff., 501; II, 195 ff., 244, 268, 317, 554 ff.; P. Feine[4] (1922), Index, s.v. Taufe; A. Schlatter, Gesch. d. Chr.[2] (1923), 69 ff.; Theol. d. Ap.[2] (1922), 35 ff., 515 ff. P. Althaus, Die Heilsbedeutung der Taufe im NT (1897); W. Heitmüller, Im Namen Jesu (1903); E. v. Dobschütz, "Sakrament und Symbol im Urchristentum," ThStKr., 78 (1905), 1-40, cf. 461 ff.; F. Rendtorff, Die Taufe im Urchristentum im Lichte der neueren Forschungen (1905); H. Windisch, Taufe und Sünde im ältesten Christentum (1908); W. Koch, Die Taufe im NT[3] (1921). Religious History: J. Leipoldt, Die urchristl. Taufe im Lichte der Religionsgesch. (1928); E. Rohde, Psyche[9, 10] (1925), II, 405 ff.; F. Cumont, Die Mysterien des Mithra[3] (1923), 144; Die orientalischen Religionen im römischen Heidentum[3] (1931), Index, s.v. taurobolium; M. Dibelius, "Die Isisweihe des Apuleius und verwandte Initiationsriten," SAH (1917); H. Gressmann, "Tod und Auferstehung des Osiris nach Festbräuchen und Umzügen," AO, 23 (1923), 3; Reitzenstein Hell. Myst., esp. 16, 20, 41, 81, 88, 143 f., 165; Die Vorgeschichte der christl. Taufe (1929), and on this H. H. Schaeder, Gnomon, 5 (1929), 353 ff. and Reitzenstein, ARW, 27 (1929), 241 ff.; H. Lietzmann, "Ein Beitrag zur Mandäerfrage," SAB (1930), 596 ff.; F. Dölger, Antike u. Christentum, I (1929), 143 ff.; 150 ff.; 156 ff.; 174 ff.; II (1930), 57 ff.; 63 ff.; 117 ff. Judaism (Proselyte Baptism): W. Brandt, Die jüdischen Baptismen (1910);

The intens. βαπτίζω occurs in the sense of "to immerse" (trans.) from the time of Hippocrates, in Plato and esp. in later writers. a. strictly, act. βαπτίζειν τὸ σκάφος, "to sink the ship," Jos. Bell., 3, 368, ὁ κλύδων (τὰς ναῦς) ἐβάπτιζεν, Bell., 3, 423; pass. "to sink": ἐν ὕλῃ (in the mud), Plot. Enn., I, 8, 13 (I, p. 112, 6, Volkmann; → 532), "to suffer shipwreck," "to drown," "to perish": Jos. Bell., 3, 525; Epict. Gnom. Stob. Fr. 47, p. 489, Schenkl; ἀβάπτιστος ναῦς, schol. in Luc. Jup. Trag., 47, p. 83, Rabe). In magic a part is played by water ἀπὸ νεναυαγηκότος πλοίου or ἀπὸ πακτῶνος βεβαπτισμένου, Preis. Zaub., V (London), 69 (4th cent. A.D., under Christian influence ✹). b. figur., act. βαπτίζειν τὴν πόλιν, "to bring the city to the border of destruction," Jos. Bell., 4, 137; ἡ λύπη βαπτίζουσα τὴν ψυχήν, Lib. Or., 18, 286; of desires which destroy the soul, Philo Leg. All., III, 18; Det. Pot. Ins., 176; Migr. Abr., 204; pass. "to go under" with the same double meaning as in Eng., "to sink into" sleep, intoxication, impotence: Hippocr. Epid., 5, 63 (or meaning a. ?); Jos. Ant., 10, 169; "to be overwhelmed" by faults, desires, sicknesses, magical arts: Plut. Galb., 21 (I, 1265c); Philo Vit. Cont., 46; Max. Tyr., XVIII, 44; Plot. Enn., I, 4, 9 (I, p. 73, 5, Volkmann); ἰσχύειν ψυχὴν λύπῃ βεβαπτισμένην, Lib. Or., 64, 115; also absol. without specification: βαπτίζῃ "thou lettest thyself be overborne," Lib. Or., 45, 24; opp. αἴρεσθαι, Lib. Or., 18, 18.

The sense of "to bathe" or "to wash" is only occasionally found in Hellenism, Menand. Fr., 363, 4 (CAF, III, 105), usually in sacral contexts, → 531. The idea of going under or perishing is nearer the general usage.

The NT uses βάπτω only in the literal sense, in Lk. 16:24; Jn. 13:26 for "to dip in," and in Rev. 19:13 for "to dye"; on the other hand it uses βαπτίζω only in the cultic sense, infrequently of Jewish washings (Mk. 7:4 ℵ D for ῥαντίσωνται in Lk. 11:38), and otherwise in the technical sense "to baptise." This usage shows that baptism is felt to be something new and strange. The use of → βάπτισμα, βαπτιστής is similar.

B. Religious Washings in Hellenism.

1. The General Facts.

Sacral baths are found in the Eleusinian and similar cults, [1] in Bacchic consecrations, [2] in Egyptian religion [3] and the worship of Isis outside Egypt, [4] in the

---

Schürer, III, 181 ff.; Str.-B., I, 102 ff.; J. Jeremias, ZNW, 28 (1929), 312 ff.; G. Polster, *Angelos,* 2 (1926), 2 ff. Jüd. Lex., IV, 177 ff., 1146 ff.; V, 876 f. John the Bapt.: M. Dibelius, *Die urchristliche Überlieferung von Joh. d. T.* (1911); C. A. Bernoulli, *Joh. d. T. und die Urgemeinde* (1918); R. Bultmann, ZNW, 24 (1925), 139 ff.; on the Slav. Fr. of Josephus ed. in Germ. by A. Berendts and K. Grass (*Acta et comm. Univ. Dorpat,* 1924 ff.): R. Eisler, ᾿Ιησοῦς βασιλεὺς οὐ βασιλεύσας (1928) (imaginative; → βασιλεύς n. 63). Also F. Büchsel, *Der Geist Gottes im NT* (1926), Index, s.v. *Taufe*; H. v. Baer, *Der hl. Geist in den Lk.schriften* (1926), 153 ff.; E. Sommerlath, *Der Ursprung des neuen Lebens nach Pls.*[2] (1927), 100 ff.; A. Schweitzer, *Die Mystik des Ap. Pls.* (1930), esp. 222 ff.; H. v. Soden, "Sakrament und Ethik bei Pls.," *Marb. Theol. Stud. Rudolf Otto Fest-Gruss* (1931), 1-40, esp. 35. For the latest discussions of the origin of infant baptism, → n. 72.

[1] Eleusinian relief (5th cent. B.C.), *Angelos,* 1 (1925), 46, No. 1; cf. *Annuario della regina scuola archeologica di Athene e delle missione italiene in Oriente,* IV/V (1921/22), Bergamo (1924), Plate III. Myst. inscript. of Andania, Ditt. Syll.[3], 736, 107 [βαλανεύε]ιν ἐν τῷ ἱερῷ. ὑδρανός = ὁ ἁγνιστὴς τῶν ᾿Ελευσινίων, Hesychius (1867), 1486. On the other hand, Tert. Bapt., 5 is not relevant in this connection, → n. 6.

[2] Liv. XXXIX, 9, 4: *pure lautum.* A stucco relief from the Roman house in the garden of the Villa Farnese Rom., Museo nazionale, *Angelos, loc. cit.,* also Haas, No. 9/11, Leipoldt (1926), No. 169, 188.

[3] H. Bonnet, *Angelos,* 1 (1925), 103 ff.; also Leipoldt, *Taufe,* 45 ff. (as also for most of the other cults).

[4] Apul. Met., XI, 23; Juv., VI, 522 ff.; Tib., I, 3, 23 ff.; Tert. Bapt., 5.

Mithras mysteries,[5] in the Apollinarian games and in the festival of Pelusium.[6] The *taurobolium* and *criobolium* attested in the worship of Attis and Mithras are[7] post-Christian sacral baptisms of blood, perhaps by way of rivalry to Christianity. Hard to integrate are certain baptismal customs in the upper Jordan valley.[8] They certainly illustrate that ancient religion, especially in the Orient, is carried beyond the circle of direct perception by lustrations in which water is used. On Mandaean baptism → 536. There are many early examples of sacral water ceremonies in Babylon,[9] Persia[10] and India.[11] With the Ganges the Euphrates came to have a religious significance comparable with that of the Jordan among Jews and Christians.[12] It is impossible to trace all these customs to a common root.

2. βαπτίζειν in Sacral and Similar Contexts.

This usage is comparatively infrequent. The most important passages are as follows.

a. P. Lond., 121, 441 (3rd cent. A.D.; app. wholly pagan): One should live in vegetarian fashion, keep silence, throw something in the river, καὶ λουσάμενος καὶ βαπτισάμενος ἀνάβα παρὰ σαυτόν. There then follows an incantation. The synon. is worth noting. Cf. also Preis. Zaub., IV, 44 (4th cent. A.D.): ἐνάλλου τῷ ποταμῷ. μεθ' ἧς ἔχεις ἐσθῆτος βαπτισάμενος ἀναποδίζων ἄνελθε.

b. Cl. Al. Strom., III, 12, 82, 6: οὐδὲ μὴν τὸν ἀπὸ τῆς κατὰ συζυγίαν κοίτης ὁμοίως ὡς πάλαι βαπτίζεσθαι καὶ νῦν προστάσσει ἡ θεία διὰ κυρίου πρόνοια. Cf. Jos. Ap., 2, 203: καὶ μετὰ τὴν νόμιμον συνουσίαν ἀνδρὸς καὶ γυναικὸς ἀπο-

---

[5] Tert. Bapt., 5. Mithr. shrine in S. Maria Capua *vetere*; cf. A. Minto, *Notizie degli scavi di antichità* (1924), 353 ff. Springs in the neighbourhood of the Mithr. shrines in Treves, on the Saalburg, etc. V. Cumont, *Myst. d. Mithra*, 144.

[6] Tert. Bapt., 5, p. 12, 4 ff., Lupton reads, as against the majority of ed.: *Ceterum uillas, domos, templa totasque urbes aspergine circumlatae aquae expiant. Passim certe ludis Apollinaribus et Pelusiis tinguntur idque se in regenerationem et impunitatem periuriorum suorum agere praesumunt.* "*Eleusiniis*" is a correction for which there are no real grounds. The Apoll. games are a Roman institution dating from the 3rd cent. B.C. (Hist. Aug. Alex. Sev., 37, 6; Liv., XXV, 12; Macrobius Sat., I, 17, 25 ff.; Pauli excerpt. ex lib. *Pomp. Festi*, p. 21, Lindsay); the Pelusian feast was originally an Egyptian festival, later associated with the name of Peleus, which became very popular in the time of Marcus Aurelius and in which lustrations in the Nile or a neighbouring lake played a part (Joh. Lyd., IV, 57; Hist. Aug. M. Anton, 23, 8; Amm. Marc., XXII, 16, 3). Cf. Dölger, *Antike und Chrtt.*, I (1929), 143 ff., 150 ff., 156 ff. The bath on the morning of the Saturnalia seems not to have had any sacral significance. On the other hand, the bathings at Ostia on the occasion of the Maiumas festival were originally sacral whatever their later development (Joh. Lyd., IV, 80; Dölger, 147).

[7] F. Cumont, *Orient. Rel.*[3] (1931), Index, *s.v.*; Prud., X, 1011 ff.; CIL, VI, 510: *in aeternum renatus.* There are *taurobolium* pits in Treves (S. Loeschcke, *Die Erforschung des Tempelbezirkes im Altbachtale zu Trier* [1928] No. 9) and Dieburg (F. Behn, *Das Mithrasheiligtum zu Dieburg* [1928]).

[8] Reitzenstein, *Taufe*, 18 ff.

[9] Chant. de la Saussaye, I, 572.

[10] *Ibid.*, II, 241.

[11] On the Vedic *dīkshā* (consecration of Brahmins), *ibid.*, II, 49, 55 and Reitzenstein, *Taufe*, 46, 120, 211 ff.

[12] Cf. the Naassenes in Hipp. Ref., V, 9, 21: ἡμεῖς δ' ἐσμέν, φησίν, οἱ πνευματικοί, οἱ ἐκλεγόμενοι ἀπὸ τοῦ ζῶντος ὕδατος τοῦ ῥέοντος Εὐφράτου διὰ τῆς Βαβυλῶνος μέσης τὸ οἰκεῖον, διὰ τῆς πύλης ὁδεύοντες ἀληθινῆς, ἥτις ἐστὶν 'Ιησοῦς ὁ μακάριος. This is an echo of older motifs in Gnosticism. It is noteworthy that later Judaism did not regard the Jordan as suitable for certain bathings (Str.-B., I, 109).

λούσασθαι. Here, too, we have the same synon. If Clement does not regard washing as necessary after marital intercourse, it may be assumed that he is repudiating the expression of the heathen past.

c. Plut. Superst., 3 (II, 166a) censures a superstitious remedy against fear: ἀλλ᾽ εἴτ᾽ ἔνυπνον φάντασμα φοβεῖ χθονίας δ᾽ Ἑκάτης κῶμον ἐδέξω, τὴν περιμάκτριαν κάλει γραῦν καὶ βάπτισον σεαυτὸν εἰς θάλασσαν καὶ καθίσας ἐν τῇ γῇ διημέρευσον. He adduces as par. exercises: πηλώσεις, καταβορβορώσεις, σαββατισμούς, [13] ῥίψεις ἐπὶ πρόσωπον, αἰσχρὰς προκαθίσεις, ἀλλοκότους προσκυνήσεις.

d. Corp. Hermet., IV, 4 : All men have the *logos,* but the *nus* is an ἆθλον which God gives only to some as He causes to come down on earth a mixing vessel filled therewith and then causes to be preached to the hearts of men: βάπτισον σεαυτὴν ἡ δυναμένη εἰς τοῦτον τὸν κρατῆρα, γνωρίζουσα ἐπὶ τί γέγονας <καὶ> πιστεύουσα ὅτι ἀνελεύσῃ πρὸς τὸν καταπέμψαντα τὸν κρατῆρα. ὅσοι μὲν οὖν συνῆκαν τοῦ κηρύγματος, καὶ ἐβαπτίσαντο τοῦ νοός, οὗτοι μετέσχον τῆς γνώσεως. Of these it is then said in 5 : ἀθάνατοι ἀντὶ θνητῶν εἰσι.

e. P. Par., 47 = Wilcken Ptol. No. 70 (I, 330 ff.) [14] (152/1 B.C.), however, belongs to a different context. The pap., in a letter of Apollonius to his brother, the κάτοχος → κατέχω) Ptolemy, contains the words :

<table>
<tr><td>

[6] ὅτι ψεύδηι [7] πάντα καὶ οἱ παρὰ σὲ [8] θεοὶ ὁμοίως, ὅτι ἐν-[9] βέβληκαν ὑμᾶς (= ἡμᾶς) εἰς ὕλην [10] μεγάλην καὶ οὖ δυνάμε-[11]θα ἀποθανεῖν, κἂν ἴδῃς [12] ὅτι μέλλομεν σωθῆναι, [13] τότε βαπτιζώμεθα (= βαπτιζόμεθα).

</td><td>

[6] For thou liest [7] and the [8] gods likewise, for they have cast us [9] into a great morass [10] wherein we may [11] die, and if thou hast seen in a dream [12] that we shall be saved from it, [13] then we shall be plunged under.

</td></tr>
</table>

Following the reading of Brunet de Presle, [15] Reitzenstein earlier saw in the letter the complaint of a Serapis novice impatiently awaiting his calling to baptism (i.e., dedication) [16] in accordance with the vision of the mystagogue. Apollonius had received news from Ptolemy that the dedication was now no longer possible and the gods had thus cast him into much ὕλη. He thus complains that he has been deceived and that he cannot now die (i.e., be baptised). But he adds hopefully : "If, however, thou seest in a dream that we shall be saved, then we shall let ourselves be baptised." In this case the three terms ἀποθανεῖν, σωθῆναι and βαπτίζεσθαι (in the sacral sense) would be essentially synon. and we should have proof of the understanding of baptism as a voluntary dying two hundred years before Paul, as a concept of the Mysteries. Yet, as Reitzenstein himself has partly admitted, this interpretation is untenable. βαπτίζεσθαι is used either in the sense of A.a. (where we also have the connection with ὕλη), or in that of A.b. In either case, its use is purely secular, as is also that of ἀποθανεῖν and σῴζεσθαι.

We may thus conclude that, while βαπτίζειν, βαπτίζεσθαι are occasionally found in a religious or similar context in Hellenism, they do not acquire a technically sacral sense.

3. The Meaning of the Rites.

In two of the three examples given (a.-c.), the underlying motif is that of bathing, washing or cleansing. In Hellenism, this is to be regarded as the basic feature, as many of the rites mentioned (→ 530) show and as many critical voices

---

[13] As against Bentley's conjecture (βαπτισμούς). Dölger, *Antike u. Christentum,* I, 154. On the use of σαββατισμός in pagan writers, cf. Dölger, *Ichthys,* II (1922), 94, n. 8, 288 f.

[14] To the literature given here we should add Reitzenstein Hell. Myst., 206 f.; Dölger, *Antike u. Christentum,* II, 57 ff.

[15] Line 9 : ὑμᾶς (2nd per.); line 10 : οὐ δυνάμεθα; line 13 : βαπτιζώμεθα (conj.).

[16] Cf. Apul. Met., XI, 21 and 22.

recognise. If we are to understand, we must begin with the primitive notion, later spiritualised, that what is unclean before God, whether physically or morally, and without any clear distinction, may be washed away like dirt, even though it consist in blood-guiltiness (cf. Heracl. Fr., 5, Diels). Along with other means, such as the urine of cattle, blood, clay, mud and filth, water may also be used, especially from a river or the sea. On the other hand, d. seems to indicate a ritual background and thus to point in a different direction. Here it is a matter of the enhancement of life, of immortality. It is no accident that this line of thought arises in the Hermes Mystery, i.e., in Egypt, one of the great river kingdoms of the ancient world. In the other, i.e., Babylon, water, as the water of life, is regarded as a chief means of incantation. [17] So in Egypt there may be distinguished an older (?) form of the baptism of kings and of the dead with a view to renewal of life, as may be seen from the accompanying hieroglyphics ♀ (life) and 𝟙 (health), which are perhaps used in symbolical depiction of the drops of water. [18] In this respect there is no clear distinction between the departed vitality of the dead, which must now be replaced, the miraculous water of the Nile and the divine seed. The dead Osiris is also sprinkled, and out of his body there sprout blades of corn. [19] The god is identical with the Nile, and the dead man, rightly treated, is identical with the god (Osiris N N). The thought of revivification flows into that of regeneration among all peoples. [20] But this often rests on the idea of a dying which is only symbolical. All these lines come together in the belief in an apotheosis effected by drowning in the Nile. [21] Herodotus tells us in II, 90 : "When an Egyptian or a foreigner is dragged into the water by a crocodile and killed, or destroyed by the water itself, and it is known, then the inhabitants of the city where he comes to shore have the solemn obligation of embalming him, of arraying him in the most gorgeous robes and of placing him in a sacred sarcophagus. No one may touch him, whether relatives or friends, apart from the priests of the Nile, who must tend him with their own hands and treat him as one who is more than an ordinary being." A man drowned in this way was called one who had been "immersed" (Boh. ЄСІЄ, Gk. Ἐσιῆς, Lat. esietus). [22] To link

---

[17] Chant. de la Saussaye, I, 572.

[18] H. Bonnet, Angelos I (1925), 103 ff.; Leipoldt, Taufe, 45 ff. A conception of the baptism of the sun-god which leads us particularly close to the idea of regeneration is espoused by A. M. Blackman, Receuil de Travaux relatifs à la Philologie et l'Archéologie égyptiennes et assyriennes, 39 (1921), 44 ff.; Proc. Soc. Bibl. Arch., 40 (1918), 57 ff., 86 ff.; but this view has met with opposition. In Sib., 5, 478 βαπτίζεσθαι is used of the eschatological disappearance of the sun.

[19] J. F. Champollion, Monuments de l'Egypte, I (1835), Plate 90 ; Haas, No. 2/4, Bonnet (1924), No. 155.

[20] → παλλιγγενεσία, γεννάω, ἄνωθεν; Mith. Liturg., Erläuterungen ; J. G. Frazer, The Golden Bough (1911 ff.), esp. III, 422 ff.

[21] F. L. Griffith, Herodotus, II, 90, "Apotheosis by Drowning," Ztschr. f. ägypt. Sprache und Altertumsk., 46 (1909/10), 132-134 ; W. Spiegelberg, ibid., 53 (1917), 124 f. We have apotheosis by a stroke of lightning in the Nabataic inscript. (225 A.D.) published in the Acad. des inscr. et des belles lettres, Comptes rendus (1931), 144 ff.; → n. 26.

[22] W. Spiegelberg, Koptisches Lexikon (1921), 246. Preis. Zaub., III, 1: λαβὼν αἴ[λου-ρον [ἐκποί]ησον Ἐσιῆν ἐ[μβαλὼν τὸ σ]ῶμ[α ἐς] τὸ ὕδωρ, "Take a tom-cat and make him Osiris by putting his body in the water." The transl. of ἐσιῆς in Gk. texts is ὑπο-βρύχιος; in Tert. Bapt., 5 esietos = quos aquae necaverunt. Dölger, Antike u. Christentum, I (1929), 174 ff.

this with the *hsjj* of the Pyramid texts, which means "extolled" or "highly estimated" or "valued"[23] (= μακάριος, "blessed"?) is materially interesting but can
hardly be sustained philologically. Yet the term can be traced back to the Demotic.
It has a technical meaning. Thus it serves as an address to Osiris as he is given up
to the Nile.[24] Osiris is thought of in conjunction with the river. To be drowned
in the river is to enter into connection with the god and thus to be divinised.
When Antinous, the favourite of Hadrian, was drowned in the Nile, there arose
a cult which lasted for centuries.[25] In this light it thus seems possible that the
baptisms of the Mysteries were understood as a voluntary dying and deification.[26]
Yet it would be rash to generalise. In Apuleius the true dedication conducted in
the temple, and cultically representing dying and deification,[27] is preceded by
another washing which takes place in the public baths and is sacral only in its
second part.[28] Thus the thought of purification is the important one in the
"baptism." Except to the degree that the similarity of the rites favours a conjunction, there is no very close connection between purification and vivification.
Apart from unimportant tendencies, both are understood, not in a moral, but in
a ritual and a magically natural sense.[29]

Within paganism itself profounder thinkers were conscious of this deficiency.
Diogenes in Plut. (Aud. Poet., 4 [II, 21 f.]) says sarcastically: "Pataicion the thief
will enjoy a better fate after death than Epaminondas, for he has received the
rites." Cf. Plat. Resp., II, 364 f. and Ovid Fast., II, 45 f. :

> *A! nimium faciles, qui tristia crimina caedis*
> *fluminea tolli posse putatis aqua!*

Even when it took a moralistic direction, the rationalistic protest was often feeble
enough. But when it took sharper weapons from another arsenal, it presented the
dominant practice in a most unfavourable light. The Jew Philo reproaches the
heathen: "They remove dirt from their bodies by baths and means of purification,[30] but they neither desire nor seek to wash away the passions of their souls
by which life is soiled" (Cher., 95). In Josephus, too, there shines through the

---

[23] A. Erman-H. Grapow, *Ägypt. Wörterbuch*, III (1928), 156. In later Egyptian we have
the concept of "waters" under the roots *hsw* and *hsj*, sometimes in connection with "magic."
[24] On the address to Osiris Ἐσιῆς καὶ ποταμοφόρητος, cf. Preis. Zaub., IV, 875 f.,
V, 270, 273.
[25] Haas, 9/11, No. 10, 11 Leipoldt; cf. W. Weber, *Drei Unters. z. ägypt.-griech. Rel.*
(1911), 22. A parallel from the purely popular sphere is the burial altar of the five-year old
Aesculapius on the Sarapeion of Memphis with the inscription (Louvre): Ἀσκληπιὰς L
(= ἐτῶν) ε' ἐσιῆς ἀπῆλθε, *Jahrb. d. Deutsch. Archäol. Inst.*, 32 (1917), 200 f.
[26] The inscription of El Burdj quoted in Reitzenstein, *Taufe*, 18: ... Νετείρου, τοῦ
ἀποθεωθέντος ἐν τῷ λέβητι δι' οὗ οἱ αἱορταὶ ἄγωνται ..., does not prove this in spite
of ZNW, 26 (1927), 61, n. 3, since it concerns an unusual and unique process, perhaps
drowning or self-drowning in a watercourse arranged for ritual purposes. C. Clermont-
Ganneau, *Recueils d'Archéol. Or.*, II (1898), 64 ff. → 533. On P. Par., 47 → 532. Again,
it does not point unconditionally in the direction indicated if ritual washings are appointed
from the standpoint of asceticism (cf. Plut. → 532 and also Juv., VI, 520 ff.
[27] M. Dibelius, *Die Isisweihe bei Apuleius*, 19 ff.
[28] Apul. Met., XI, 23 : *iamque tempore, ut aiebat sacerdos, id postulante stipatum me
religiosa cohorte deducit ad proximas balneas et prius sueto lavacro traditum, praefatus
deum veniam, purissime circumrorans abluit.*
[29] Bonnet, *op. cit.*, 111. Most interesting are the Lydian and Phrygian inscriptions in-
vestigated by F. S. Steinleitner (→ ἁμαρτάνω, 301).
[30] On Egypt. depictions of sacral sprinklings we can see the vessels with natron ; Bonnet,
op. cit., 111.

shell of rational Stoicism something of the moral earnestness of the prophets when he writes of John the Baptist (Ant., 18, 117): "Herod put him to death although he was a good man and directed the Jews to come to baptism in the exercise of virtue and righteousness towards one another and piety towards God. Thus baptism is acceptable to God when used, not for the purification of the soul, but for sanctification of life, the soul being already cleansed by righteousness."

This brief review has shown us how little cultic significance the word βαπτίζειν has in Hellenism. Yet it has also disclosed many connections which might become significant either positively or negatively if some stronger emphasis were given from without to the term and to that which it represents.

C. טבל and βαπτ(ίζ)ειν in the OT and Judaism.

In the LXX βάπτειν (βαπτίζειν occurs only at 4 Βασ. 5:14) as a rendering of טבל, "to dip," is used for the dipping of the morsel in wine at Ju. 2:14, of feet in the river at Jos. 3:15, of the finger in blood in the Torah of sacrifices at Lv. 4:6, 17 etc., of the dipping of unsanctified vessels in water in the laws of purification at Lv. 11:32 (בא hiph). In the latter case, however, πλύνω (כבס) and λούομαι (רחץ) are more common, as in Lv. 15:11, 13 etc. The sevenfold dipping of Naaman (2 K. 5:14) perhaps suggests sacramental ideas and illustrates the importance of the Jordan. In the later Jewish period טבל (bBer., 2b of the bathing of priests; Joma, 3, 2 ff. etc.) and βαπτίζειν become tech. terms for washings to cleanse from Levitical impurity, as already in Jdt. 12:7; Gk. Sir. 31(34):30. The טְבִילָה of proselytes belongs to this context.

Yet the origin of this special washing is hard to fix, since in the first instance it does not seem to differ from other washings and is not linked to any special ritual. [31] On inner grounds it is likely that it was already customary in the NT period, since the purity demanded of every Jew could not be relaxed in the case of an impure Gentile. Again, it is hardly conceivable that the Jewish ritual should be adopted at a time when baptism had become an established religious practice in Christianity. After 70 A.D. at least the opposition to Christians was too sharp to allow of the rise of a Christian custom among the Jews. Proselyte baptism must have preceded Christian baptism.

The most important external witnesses are as follows. a. Epict. Diss., II, 9, 19 ff. says that mere appearance does not make a Stoic just as mere talk does not make a Jew: ὅταν δ' ἀναλάβῃ τὸ πάθος (uncomfortable manner of life? persecution?) τὸ τοῦ βεβαμμένου καὶ ᾑρημένου, τότε καὶ ἔστι τῷ ὄντι καὶ καλεῖται Ἰουδαῖος. οὕτω καὶ ἡμεῖς παραβαπτισταί, λόγῳ μὲν Ἰουδαῖοι, ἔργῳ δ' ἄλλο τι. b. Sib., 4, 165 (soon after 79 A.D.), in a warning to the heathen to repent in view of the threatening destruction of the world: ἐν ποταμοῖς λούσασθε ὅλον δέμας ἀενάοισιν. c. Casuistical definitions of proselyte baptism were debated in the schools of Shammai and Hillel. These controversies are attested in the Mishnah (Pes., 8, 8; Ed., 5, 2; Str.-B.,

---

[31] Earlier the pre-Christian origin of proselyte baptism was disputed in the interests of the originality of Christian baptism. There is a survey and criticism of the older treatments in Schürer, III, 181 ff. Reitzenstein, Taufe, 231 ff. contests the age of proselyte baptism in order to be able to deduce the baptism of John and Christian baptism from syncretism. Yet witnesses a. and b. cannot be explained in terms of oddities like Bannus (→ n. 40), and Reitzenstein has completely missed the Rabb. evidence. Against his view, in addition to Schürer, cf. W. Brandt, Die jüdischen Baptismen, 57 ff.; Leipoldt, Taufe, 2 ff.; A. Oepke, Ihmelsfestschrift (1928), 96 and ThLBl, 51 (1930), 35.

I, 102 f.) and date from the 1st cent. A.D. if not from the B.C. period. d. According to bJeb., 46a, Str.-B., I, 106, R. Eleazer and R. Joshua (both around 90-130 A.D.) discussed the necessity of circumcision and baptism to make a full proselyte. In this discussion some part is played by the question of a baptism of the fathers prior to the covenant at Sinai. The line of argument in 1 C. 10:1 ff. is best explained if similar traditions were known to Paul. [32] Probably even earlier than the middle of the 1st century A.D., and under the influence of the many women proselytes who could not be circumcised, the existing washing of proselytes came to have the significance of an independent rite of reception. [33]

Genealogically the Jewish washings, including proselyte baptism, are linked with existing rites of purification. In consequence, however, of the strongly transcendental Jewish conception of God, they did not develop along the lines of sacral magic, but exclusively along legalistic lines. Their one goal was ritual purity. [34] If the proselyte could be described as a "new-born child," [35] this relates only to his theocratic and casuistic position. As a heathen he did not understand the Torah. Hence sufferings which might afflict him after his conversion are not punishments for earlier transgressions. It is from this point on that he must keep the commandments. There is no thought of any natural, let alone ethical, death and regeneration.

The meanings "to drown," "to sink" or "to perish" seem to be quite absent from the Heb. and Aram. טבל and therefore from βαπτίζειν in Jewish Greek. If the spontaneous construction of such connections cannot be contested a priori, the rise of metaphors based on them has thus far seemed to be most unlikely in the purely Semitic field of speech. The usage of Josephus (→ 530) is not specifically Jewish Greek.

D. The Baptism of John.

Cf. Mk. 1:4-11 and par.; 11:27 ff. and par.; Jn. 1:25-33; 3:23 ff.; 10:40; Ac. 1:5; 11:16; 13:24; 18:25; 19:4. The baptism of John introduced a powerful Messianic awakening from which Christianity sprang. This indicates its geometric position within religious history, namely, Palestinian Judaism. There is no suggestion in the Gospels that it is a child of oriental syncretism. This must be contested until every possible closer analogy has been explored.

Attempts have been made to find the original form of John's baptism in that of the Mandaeans, [36] whose sacred writings have been made generally accessible by M. Lidz-

---

[32] Joachim Jeremias, ZNW, 28 (1929), 312 ff.

[33] Str.-B., I, 102-108. On the following pages are assembled individual directions for the fulfilment of washing by immersion, which also apply to proselyte baptism. G. Polster, "Der kleine Talmudtraktat über die Proselyten," Angelos, 2 (1926), 2 ff. draws attention to the distinction between proselyte baptism with and without ritual.

[34] We cannot deduce from Joma, 8, 9, even in conjunction with 3, 6, that special expiatory significance attached to immersion on the day of atonement, particularly in the case of the high-priest (W. Bacher, Agada der Tanaiten, I [1903], 280 f.). Rabb. Judaism thinks of washing only in terms of purification from cultic uncleanness (cf. Lv. 14:8; 15:5 ff.; 15:11; Nu. 31:23, and on this the whole Mishnah tractate Miqvaot). Forgiveness can be compared to this, but neither it, nor especially ethical purity, can be mediated by it.

[35] For examples, v. Str.-B., II, 423; K. H. Rengstorf, Mishnah Jebamot (1927), 138 f.

[36] Reitzenstein, Taufe; cf. the criticism in H. H. Schaeder, Gnomon, 5 (1929), 353 ff. and Reitzenstein's reply, ARW, 27 (1929), 241 ff.; A. Oepke, ThLBl, 51 (1930), 33 ff.; J. Jeremias, ZNW, 28 (1929), 312 ff.

barski. [37] In the Mandaean ritual the thought of purification is subsidiary and the strongest emphasis rests on the sacramental or magical power of vivification. Every baptismal stream, invested with heavenly fire by incantations, counts as the Jordan. Yet in spite of their veneration of the Baptist and the Jordan, the Mandaeans probably had little dealings with the disciples of John and arose only centuries later as a Gnostic sect. In detail their baptismal ritual is dependent on that of the Nestorians, particularly in the description of the water as Jordan, and on the Peshitta. The honouring of the Baptist came into their writings only in the Islamic period. [38] Even from the much older practices in the upper Jordan valley (→ 531) there is no solid bridge to the Baptist. It would be easier to suppose that syncretistic influences through the Essenes [39] or odd individuals like Bannus [40] affected the Baptist. But the completely different attitude to ritualism, demonstrated by the daily repetition of washings on the one side and the uniqueness of baptism on the other, denotes an unbridgeable distinction.

The nearest analogies to the baptism of John are the baptisms of official Judaism, and especially proselyte baptism. John's baptism, like that of proselytes, is once and for all. It makes a great demand on the members of the elect people in ranking them with the defiled Gentiles who were apparently admitted on the same conditions (Lk. 3:14). In contrast to proselyte baptism, however, its orientation is not political or ritualistic, but distinctively ethical, with a close relation to eschatology. To be sure, proselyte baptism can also be eschatologically grounded and linked with a summons to polytheists to repent, Sib., 4, 165 (→ 535 f.). This application is native to Judaism. Yet in John the relationship is more essential and urgent. His concern is not to defer the destruction of the world, but to prepare the people for the imminent coming of Yahweh. The baptism of John is an initiatory rite for the gathering Messianic community. Linking up with prophetic passages like Is. 1:15 f.; Ez. 36:25 (cf. Is. 4:4; Jer. 2:22; 4:14; Zech. 13:1; Ps. 51:7), it is to be regarded as a new development. The very fact that in prophetic power John baptised others is striking. From now on there occurs the active, and in Christianity the predominantly passive, use of βαπτίζειν, whereas elsewhere on both Jewish and Gentile soil the mid. or refl. use is most common (though → 535, βεβαμμένος, 2nd cent. A.D.; → βαπτιστής). The basic conception is still that of the cleansing bath. Bound up with confession of sin, baptism is in the first instance an expression of repentance, i.e., of sorrow for sin and the desire to be free from it (βάπτισμα μετανοίας, Mk. 1:4; Lk. 3:3; εἰς μετάνοιαν, Mt. 3:11). Nevertheless, the thought of a sacramental purification for the coming aeon is at least suggested (εἰς ἄφεσιν ἁμαρτιῶν, Mk. 1:4; Lk. 3:3). As compared with Christian baptism, of course, that of John is mere water baptism. The saying about

---

[37] Johannesbuch (1905/15); Mand. Liturg. (1920); Ginza (1925).

[38] For the extensive liter. on the Mandaean controversy, v. RGG², III, 1956 f. Cf. F. C. Burkitt, JThSt, 29 (1928), 225 ff.; M. J. Lagrange, Rev. Bibl. NS, 36 (1927), 321 ff., 481 ff.; 37 (1928), 1 ff.; E. Peterson, ZNW, 25 (1926), 236 ff.; 27 (1928), 55 ff.; ThBl, 7 (1928), 317 ff.; C. H. Kraeling, "The Origin and Antiquity of the Mandaeans," Journal of the Americ. Orient. Soc., 49 (1929), 195 ff.; H. Odeberg, Die mand. Religionsanschauung, Uppsala Universitets Arsskrift (1930); H. Lietzmann, SAB (1930), 596 ff. Peterson and Lietzmann in particular have decisively proved the post-Christian character of the relevant Mandaean passages.

[39] On these cf. Schürer, II, 651 ff.; RE³, V, 524 ff.; RGG², II, 374 ff.

[40] Jos. Vit., 11: "When I had learned that a man named Bannus was in the desert, using clothing from trees (wool ?), eating only food which grew of itself, and often washing in cold water day and night with a view to cultic purity (λουόμενον πρὸς ἁγνείαν), I became his enthusiastic follower." This example is of course, from a later period.

baptism with the Spirit (Mk. 1:8 and par.; cf. Jn. 1:26; Ac. 1:5; 11:16; cf. Ac. 19:2 ff.; cf. baptism with fire, Mt. 3:11; Lk. 3:16; Ac. 2:3), if it arose on Palestinian soil and was not put on the lips of the Baptist later, [41] shows, however, that in the baptism of John, if only as a picture of things to come, there is at least some influence of the idea of a life-giving inundation already familiar in Hellenism. This is not completely unknown on the soil of OT Judaism (cf. Jl. 3:1 ff.; Is. 44:3; 32:15; Ez. 47:7 ff.). The eschatological context prevents us from assuming that the individualistic notion of regeneration espoused in syncretism had penetrated the circle of ideas of the Baptist, or even given essential shape to his baptism. That John conceived of his baptism as a voluntary dying cannot be deduced from the immersions current in Judaism generally.

E. Christian Baptism.

1. Jesus allows Himself to be baptised by John but does not Himself baptise (Mk. 1:9 ff. and par.; Jn. 3:22 is uncertain, cf. also 4:2). This raises a two-sided problem. The question, acutely felt by the early Church according to Mt. 3:14 f.; Hebr. Ev. 5, [42] whether the baptism of Jesus included a confession of sin, is solved by the suggestion that the sinlessness of Jesus was not something static and apart, that He could not exclude Himself from the wonderful awakening, and that baptism was for Him a dedication as the Messiah. It was in keeping with His conception of the Messiah, based on Deutero-Isaiah, that He should not withdraw from sinners but identify Himself with them. Thus, whether or not they are historical in the literal sense, Mt. 3:14 f. and Jn. 1:29 (→ ἀμνός, 338) rightly interpret the matter. If Jesus did not Himself baptise, we can see from Mk. 11:30 and par. and Mt. 11:7 ff. and par., in spite of Mk. 7:14 ff. and par., that this was not due to any objections to baptism in principle as an external action. It corresponds rather to the expectant manner of Jesus in movement towards His atoning death. [43]

According to Mk. 10:38 f.; Lk. 12:50, Jesus described His own death as a βαπτισθῆναι. It is hard to suppose that we are to see already at this point an influence of the later conception of martyrdom as baptism in blood. [44] On the other hand, these isolated sayings hardly give us grounds for concluding that He takes as His point of departure the conception of the baptism of John (and future Christian baptism?) as a voluntary dying. [45] Indeed, this is unlikely in view of what was said on p. 536. It is not impossible, however, that in a bold and profound image, hardly understandable to the men of his day, He anticipates the results of the religious development of decades. The only alternative is that a popular expression, already used figuratively in the OT (cf. Ps. 42:7; 69:1; Is. 43:2; Cant. 8:7; though never transl. βαπτίζειν in the LXX), has here come to be associated with baptism by way of the linguistic possibilities described on p. 530 — something which could only happen on Hellenistic soil (→ 536) and which cannot, then, be

---

[41] Cf. Meyer, *Ursprung*, I, 39; Bultmann, *Trad.*, 261 f.; W. Michaelis, *Täufer, Jesus, Urgemeinde* (1928), 19 ff.
[42] Acc. to Jer. Pelag., III, 2 (Hennecke, 44).
[43] Well worked out, if rather one-sidedly, by Michaelis, *op. cit.*
[44] It can be proved from the time of Iren., Dölger, *Antike u. Christentum*, II, 117 ff. Hck. Mk., *ad loc.*, following Wellhausen: "As water baptism represented the consecration of Jesus to secret Messianic dignity, so blood baptism represented consecration to the dignity of the Exalted."
[45] Reitzenstein Hell. Myst., 229 f.

attributed to Jesus Himself. This would give us a point of departure for interpreting baptism in terms of the Mysteries. [46]

2. In the Christian community baptism was undoubtedly practised from the very first (Ac. 2:38, 41; 8:12 etc.; R. 6:3; 1 C. 12:13 : ἐβαπτίσθημεν, understood biographically, leads us back to something like 33 A.D.). [47] It would be wrong to attribute this fact exclusively to an influx of the disciples of John. [48] The community must have been aware that in baptising it was fulfilling the intention of the Lord. Quite irrespective of the ceaseless critical objections to Mt. 28:18-20 and Mk. 16:16, we may conclude from the very existence and significance of the apostolate (→ ἀπόστολος, 431) that there was knowledge of a missionary command, or many such commands, of the risen Lord, and that in accordance with the new situation this command was understood as a command to baptise. The distinctive feature of Christian baptism is that it is administered εἰς Χριστόν or εἰς τὸ ὄνομα Χριστοῦ.

3. The syntactical connections of βαπτίζειν in the NT are as follows. The link with the inner object βαπτίζειν or βαπτίζεσθαι βάπτισμα occurs in Ac. 19:4; Mk. 10:38 f.; Lk. 7:29; 12:50. The means by which it is administered is expressed by the dat. instr. (ὕδατι, Mk. 1:8; Lk. 3:16; Ac. 1:5; 11:6; πνεύματι ἁγίῳ, Mk. 1:8), or more commonly by ἐν (ἐν ὕδατι, Mt. 3:11; Mk. 1:8 vl.; Jn. 1:26, 31, 33; ἐν τῷ Ἰορδάνῃ, Mt. 3:6; Mk. 1:5; ἐν πνεύματι ἁγίῳ [καὶ πυρί], Mt. 3:11; Lk. 3:16; Jn. 1:33; Ac. 1:5; 11:16; in 1 C. 12:13, however, ἐν ἑνὶ πνεύματι means "embraced by one spirit"), [49] and only once by → εἰς (Mk. 1:9; cf. Plut. Superst., 3 [II, 166a] → 532; Corp. Herm., IV, 4 → 532). Elsewhere εἰς is mostly used finally to denote the aim sought and accomplished by baptism: εἰς μετάνοιαν, Mt. 3:11; εἰς ἄφεσιν τῶν ἁμαρτιῶν, Ac. 2:38; εἰς ἓν σῶμα, 1 C. 12:13. Weakened spatial notions are present where εἰς denotes the constitutive element of a form of baptism : εἰς Χριστόν, Gl. 3:27; R. 6:3 with εἰς τὸν θάνατον αὐτοῦ; εἰς τὸν Μωυσῆν, 1 C. 10:2; εἰς τί ἐβαπτίσθητε; ... εἰς τὸ Ἰωάννου βάπτισμα, Ac. 19:3. The idea of a mystically understood medium of baptism ("to be immersed in Christ etc.") [50] is always and in every respect wide of the mark. βαπτίζειν means technically "to baptise in water." Hence it is unnecessary to specify a medium. Where this is done for some reason in the NT, it is hardly ever introduced by εἰς. In Gl. 3:27 Χριστὸν ἐνεδύσασθε is a heightened form of εἰς Χριστὸν ἐβαπτίσθητε. The notion of being baptised in Moses would be meaningless and would clash with a second spatial indication in 1 C. 10:2 (ἐν τῇ νεφέλῃ καὶ ἐν τῇ θαλάσσῃ). A trinitarian name-mysticism in Mt. 28:19, hypothetically extended to Paul in 1 C. 1:13, 15, is quite out of the question. The formula εἰς τὸ ὄνομα seems rather to have been a tech. term in Hellenistic commerce [51] ("to the account"). In both cases the use of the phrase is understandable, since the account bears the name of the one who owns it, and in baptism

---

[46] In the mind of the Evangelist it is hardly accidental that baptism is mentioned alongside the cup in Mk. 10:38 f.

[47] It cannot be concluded from 1 C. 1:17 that baptism was not at first generally practised in the Pauline communities, nor from Ac. 18:24 ff. that it might be excluded if there had already been Johannine baptism and there was also possession of the Spirit. Cf. H. Preisker, ZNW, 23 (1924), 298 ff.; 30 (1931), 301 ff.

[48] Reitzenstein Ir. Erl., 124 f.; Taufe, 266; C. Bernoulli, Joh. d. T. u. d. Urgem. (1918), 153 ff.

[49] Joh. W. 1 C., ad loc.

[50] E. Wissmann, Das Verhältnis von πίστις und Christusfrömmigkeit bei Paulus (1926), 101: "We are baptised into Christ, i.e., immersed into His pneumatic mode of being."

[51] Ostrakon from Thebes, Deissmann LO, 97. Cf. Deissmann B, 143 ff.; NB, 25; ThLZ, 25 (1900), 73 f.; also W. Heitmüller, Im Namen Jesu (1903), 100 ff.; F. Preisigke, Girowesen im griech. Ägypten (1910), 149 ff.

the name of Christ is pronounced, invoked and confessed by the one who baptises or the one baptised (Ac. 22:16) or both. The question and answer in Ac. 19:3 have more of a legal than a mystical flavour. The thought is elucidated by the addition of → πιστεύειν εἰς. [52] This does not mean that we are to deny pneumatic union with the crucified and risen Christ. It means that this is not basic to the expression βαπτίζειν εἰς; it is not, therefore, its primary implication (→ εἰς, → ὄνομα).

4. The Saving Significance of Baptism into Christ.

Christian baptism certainly has as its final goal new and eternal life. Yet even in this respect it is not to be understood primarily or directly in terms of the idea of vivification or regeneration. Of the passages adduced Mk. 10:38 f. may be dismissed at once (→ 538). Again, 1 Pt. 3:20 f. does not form the starting-point for the Christian view of baptism, but contains an isolated theologoumenon which is comparatively late even on the assumption that it was composed by Silvanus on the direct commission of Peter. Jn. 3:5 f. and Tt. 3:5 also belong to a younger stratum of NT tradition which was under stronger Hellenistic influence. For the most part, however, expressions used in the context (λουτρόν, οὐ σαρκὸς ἀπόθεσις ῥύπου, πιστεύειν) show even here that the new life stands in firm causal connection with purification from the guilt of sin. This is particularly clear, though often overlooked, in Paul. Because God is the only source of real life, and His holiness excludes sin, the basic conception both of Paul and of the NT generally in relation to baptism is that of the cleansing bath (1 C. 6:11; Eph. 5:26; Hb. 10:22; cf. Ac. 2:38; 22:16). The significance of baptism thus depends on the fact that it is a real action of the holy God in relation to sinful man. Hence both a superstitious and also a purely symbolical understanding are excluded.

Rightly to evaluate the efficacy of baptism in the NT sense, it must be remembered that criticism of a purely external, materialistic and magical evaluation of religious objects and actions belongs to the very essence of biblical piety from the days of the prophets (Dt. 10:16; 30:6; 1 S. 15:22 f.; Am. 5:21 ff.; Hos. 6:6; Is. 1:10 ff.; Jer. 2:22; 4:4; 7:3 ff.; 9:25; 31:31 ff.; Ez. 18:31; 36:26; Jl. 2:13; Ps. 51:10, 16, 17; Mk. 7:14 ff. and par.; R. 2:17-29; 1 C. 10:1-11). This does not mean that we are to depreciate the realism of references to the saving significance of baptism. Nor are detailed inconsistencies excluded. The point is that if we leave out of account this basic presupposition, we are from the very first in danger of distorting the picture. To baptism as a mere rite or realistically developed symbol no such incomparable efficacy could be ascribed in the NT world of thought. This is indicated, not merely by the relative unimportance of the action as such (cf. 1 C. 1:17; Mk. 16:16b), but also by express statements (Hb. 9:9 f.; 1 Pt. 3:21; 1 Jn. 5:6 : οὐκ ἐν ὕδατι μόνον. Hb. 10:22 reminds us of Jos. Ant., 18, 117, → 535, but may be understood as a parallelism). Though mediated by men, baptism is the action of God or Christ (Eph. 5:26). Hence baptism by others rather than se-baptism, and hence also the predominance of the passive. The mid. is used of Christian baptism in the NT only in Ac. 22:16 (cf. 1 C. 6:11: ἀπελούσασθε), and the reflex. (→ 531) never. Standing in a definite and absolutely indispensable historical context, baptism derives its force from the reconciling action of God in Christ, or more exactly from the atoning death of Christ (1 C. 6:11; Eph. 5:25 f.; Tt. 3:4 f.; 1 Jn. 5:6 [→ διά, → αἷμα, 174, → ὕδωρ]; cf. Jn. 19:34; 1 Pt. 1:2; Hb. 10:22). It places us objectively in Christ, the second Adam; it thus removes us from the sphere of

---

[52] J. Böhmer, Das biblische "Im Namen" (1898), 15.

death of the first Adam to the δικαίωσις ζωῆς and divine sonship (Gl. 3:26 f. → ἐνδύω, cf. R. 5:18 f.).

It is characteristic, however, that the thought of imputative purity, righteousness and holiness impels us to that of effective, i.e., to the new ethical life (1 C. 6:11 as a basis of exhortation, and Eph. 5:26 ff.). In Paul there is no suggestion of cleavage between a forensic and a mystical mode of thought. Forensic justification leads to pneumatic fellowship with Christ. The *iustitia Christi extra nos posita* aims ceaselessly to become the *iustitia Christi intra nos posita*. There is here no leap, and a transition only in so far as justification is not conditioned by the new life, but the new life by justification, so that a distinction of thought is demanded. [53] As imparted in baptism, δικαίωσις is δικαίωσις ζωῆς (R. 5:18). The new life, however, necessarily bears an ethical character. For it is life from God, the life of Christ. Baptism implies participation in the death and resurrection of Christ (R. 6:1-14; Col. 2:11-15; 3:1 ff.; and materially Gl. 2:19 f.; 5:24; 6:14 etc., though characteristically with no mention of baptism). [54] The break with sin is thereby accomplished and attachment to the life of the new creation effected, yet in such a way that in this aeon the translation into empirical reality of what God has posited remains, or rather becomes, a task for the baptised. In the theology of the 19th century these statements were misunderstood in terms of the almost completely dominant idealistic and symbolical conceptions of the age. Thanks to research into the history of religion, and also to other factors, [55] this misunderstanding has now been dispelled. What is at issue is an objective process which can be fixed in time. The appeal to the will is merely a consequence. In this respect Paul seems to approximate to the Hellenistic notion of participation in the death and resurrection of the Mystery deities. Indeed, it is not improbable that his vocabulary was influenced by Hellenistic mysticism with its dying and rising gods. Perhaps there underlies his expositions a borrowed interpretation of the rite of baptism like that of the Mysteries. [56] Nevertheless, the material difference must not be missed. On the one side, we have a timeless and naturalistic individualism of regeneration, on the other a spiritual historical relationship, a new creation of the totality, eschatologically understood. [57] Baptism is the "prodromal manifestation of the coming world"; it is a "lift" not a "staircase." [58] The close connection between the resurrection of Christ and forensic and completely non-mystical justification, as also the basic significance of this justification, is supremely safeguarded in relation to baptism by Col. 2:12 ff. [59] Every interpretation of Paul's view of baptism is thus mistaken which takes as its starting-point the subjective and

---

[53] The attempt, most recently undertaken by A. Schweitzer in his *Mystik*, esp. p. 201 ff., to show that the forensic doctrine of justification is to be understood as a "subsidiary crater" in the main crater of a mystical and naturalistic doctrine of redemption, breaks down not merely on the obvious importance of forensic lines of thought in Romans and the missionary preaching of Paul, but also on a correct understanding of Galatians.

[54] For an understanding of these statements, → ἐγείρω and the bibl. given there.

[55] The first significant opposition came from P. Althaus the elder, *Die Heilsbedeutung d. Taufe im NT* (1897).

[56] Dibelius, *Isisweihe*, 45 f.

[57] Clearly proved by A. Schweitzer, *op. cit.*, 12 ff., 22 ff., 27 ff. According to v. Soden, *op. cit.*, 35, R. 6 "rests on a hylozoistic understanding only as a metaphysics of the age. This is merely the form into which a historical, christological and eschatological content is poured. The death of Christ is the sacrament; baptism is sacramental confession of Him in which there is attained participation in Him, i.e., incorporation into the body of Christ."

[58] A. Schweitzer, *Gesch. d. pl. Forsch.* (1911), 169, 175.

naturalistic experience of baptism and not the objective situation in salvation history. The death and restoration of nature-gods take place again and again at the appropriate seasons. The consecration of the Mystery religions is renewed every twenty years or so. Baptism, however, shares with Christ's death a strictly once-for-all character (ἐφάπαξ, R. 6:10, → 383). The phrase "Christ metaphysics" [60] more correctly expresses the existential character of the Pauline statements than the unhappy "Christ mysticism." On the other hand, a place must be found for the plenitude of pneumatic interconnections which are here felt by Paul and which may even be comprehended psychologically and empirically. [61] Nevertheless, it must be emphasised that an immediate and almost magical transformation of human nature, in which sin is eradicated, is no more a part of Paul's logic than an immediate destruction of suffering and death.

In 1 C. 10:1-13 Paul energetically combats a materialistic and superstitious estimation of baptism and the Lord's Supper which would have it that their recipients are set free from every possibility of the divine wrath — a view which differs essentially from the objective and genuinely sacramental understanding. [62] There is no contradiction in 1 C. 15:29 as Paul sees it (cf. R. 2:28), even though this refer to a groping attempt, unconditionally accepted by him, to apply salvation in Christ to the unbaptised dead. [63] It is more likely, however, that the argument is purely tactical; Paul is referring ironically to the inconsistency of the Corinthians. Indeed, he may even be alluding to a non-Christian practice of the Mysteries.

Many Gnostic sects are reported to have held vicarious baptisms. [64] It is thus legitimate to seek a pagan origin (cf. even 2 Macc. 12:39-45). Plat. Resp., II, 364bce; 365a, contains reference to expiations for the dead. Orph. Fr., 232, p. 245, Kern (ὄργια τ' ἐκτελέσουσι, λύσιν προγόνων ἀθεμίστων μαιόμενοι) also seems to speak of substitutionary dedications. [65] In the same connection we may mention the oriental inscription: Μεγάλη Μήτηρ Ἀναεῖτις. Ἀπολλώνιος Μηνοδώρου ὑπὲρ Διονυσίου τοῦ ἀδελφοῦ, ἐπεὶ κατελούσετο καὶ οὐκ ἐτήρησε τὴν προθεσμίαν τῆς θεοῦ, ἀπετελέσετο αὐτόν (163 A.D.). [66] After the death of Scyllos, severely punished by the gods for perjury, his daughter Tatias redeems the vow. [67] It may be presumed that baptisms were linked with such consecrations. Wild speculations concerning substitutionary baptisms of angels for men are to be found in Cl. Al. Exc. Theod., 22.

---

[59] By Gk. usage the aorists χαρισάμενος, ἐξαλείψας, προσηλώσας denote neither an accompanying circumstance nor a preceding act but the means by which what is expressed in the main verb is effected.

[60] E. Lohmeyer, Grundlagen paul. Theol. (1929), 145.

[61] These are not recognised by the dialectical theology. For a correct view, cf. K. Mittring, Heilswirklichkeit bei Pls. (1929), 43, 71 ff., 120; and for greater detail, ZNW, 29 (1930), 104 ff.

[62] Cf. esp. v. Soden, op. cit., 23 ff., 31, though it may be asked whether Paul is not the "true" sacramental thinker.

[63] Joh. W. 1 K., ad loc. All interpretations which seek to evade vicarious baptism for the dead (most recently Bchm. 1 K.) are misleading. Cf. H. Preisker, ZNW, 23 (1924), 298 ff.

[64] For material, cf. Ltzm. 1 K., ad loc.

[65] Cf. E. Rohde, Psyche, II, 128. P. Tannery, Rev. d. Phil., 23 (1899), 126 ff. suggests the atonement of the sins of earlier existences. The above understanding is confirmed by Plat. Resp., II, 364 bc : ... δύναμις ... θυσίαις τε καὶ ἐπῳδαῖς, εἴτε τι ἀδίκημά του γέγονεν αὐτοῦ ἢ προγόνων, ἀκεῖσθαι (cf. 364e ; 365a).

[66] Jahresh. d. Öst. Arch. Inst. Wien, 23 (1926), Beibl., 23 f. Cf. also Reitzenstein, Taufe, 43. It is open to dispute whether καταλούεσθαι means a baptism or a forbidden washing which would defile the holy water.

[67] F. S. Steinleitner, Die Beicht, 28, No. 6.

We cannot know how far Paul is the author of the line of thought concerning dying and rising again with Christ, or how far he keeps to the common stock of Christian thinking. It is beyond question, however, that the close interrelating of baptism and the reception of the Spirit is both general and primitive. Christian baptism is thus represented as the completion of that of John. In a few cases the πνεῦμα ἅγιον is imparted prior to baptism (Ac. 10:44 ff.; 18:25), [68] but in the majority either at baptism or shortly afterwards, [69] often by the laying on of hands (→ πνεῦμα, → χείρ). In Luke [70] there are traces of Hellenistic influence on the pneumatic conception of baptism, but these are not constitutive, and do not crowd out either the thought of the forgiveness of sins or the basic ethical understanding. Deutero-Pauline (Tt. 3:5) and Johannine (Jn. 3:5) theology approximates rather more closely to the Hellenistic thought of regeneration from which Paul holds fundamentally aloof, but it does not abandon the main line of a theology of faith linked with salvation history. So far as leading circles are concerned, it is only with the older Catholic Church that baptism becomes a means of grace which is not specifically eschatological or christological, but physical or hyper-physical.

The preconditions for baptism of infants in apostolic Christianity are to be weighed in the light of the presuppositions developed above. It cannot be proved nor disproved that children were baptised with their families, [71] though this is likely enough by contemporary analogies. Even then a distinction would have to be made between children and infants. Infant baptism, however, represents a departure from apostolic Christianity only where it is linked with superstitious views of the sacrament. [72]

F. Baptism as a Syncretistic Mystery.

Already in the later strata of the NT we can see indications of an approach to Hellenism. These were not followed up in the NT itself, but increasingly so from the post-apostolic period onwards. The eschatological context in which baptism had been rooted from the very first thus came to lose its significance. It was not forgotten. It ceased, however, to be the basis or leaven. It simply became the concluding chapter or appendix. In its place, alien elements came in from the outside world. Hitherto these had been carefully held in check by the filter of prophetic and NT religion. But now, using external agreement as a channel, they came in full flood. Baptism became a syncretistic mystery.

For such the first essential is the matter. Ignatius (Eph., 18, 2) already speaks of Jesus purifying the water by His baptism in Jordan and His passion. Barn., 11 assembles several OT passages which speak of water as intimations of baptism. This sacramental materialism reaches a first climax with Tertullian, who in Bapt., 4 and 9 introduces considerations concerning the nature of the water which deviate

---

[68] ζέων τῷ πνεύματι of the supernatural but pre-Christian possession of the Spirit as in Lk. 2:25; τὰ περὶ τοῦ Ἰησοῦ is a misunderstanding. For a partially different view, cf. A. v. Stromberg, *Studien zur Theorie und Praxis der Taufe in der altchristl. Kirche* (1913), 141 ff., 148 ff.

[69] Ac. 2:38; 8:16 f.; 9:17 f.; 19:1 ff., cf. Mk. 1:8 and par.; Ac. 1:4 f.; 11:16. For Paul, cf. 1 C. 12:13 : ἓν πνεῦμα ἐποτίσθημεν, and Gl. 3:2; 4:6; R. 8:15.

[70] H. v. Baer, *Der hl. Geist in den Lukasschriften* (1926).

[71] 1 C. 7:14 hardly affects the question, since it is restricted to the children of mixed marriages.

[72] Leipoldt, *Taufe*, 73-78; H. Windisch, ZNW, 28 (1929), 118-142; Oepke, *Ihmelsfestschrift*, 84-100; ZNW, 29 (1930), 81-111.

widely from the true point at issue. Since the time when the Spirit of God hovered over the water at creation, this has been invested with supernatural powers.

Moreover, the rite as such is significant. As before the Isis consecration, so now before baptism a fast of many days is enjoined both on the one who baptises and on those baptised (Did., 7, 4). A magical transformation is expected through the fulfilment of the action. "We go down into the water full of sins and impurity, but then rise out again laden with fruits" (Barn., 11, 11). Similarly Herm. s., 9, 16, 4 : ἡ → σφραγὶς [73] τὸ ὕδωρ ἐστίν· εἰς τὸ ὕδωρ καταβαίνουσι νεκροί, καὶ ἀναβαίνουσι ζῶντες. Various ceremonies such as exorcism, anointing, first communion, confirmation, investiture and candles are added to the originally simple action. Relics of the Mysteries and OT allusions surround the action ever more closely. If the water of baptism was formerly regarded as an antitype of the Flood (1 Pt. 3:21) and the Red Sea (1 C. 10:1 f.), it now flows as "Jordan" into the font. [74] The baptism of blood, with which martyrdom is now equated, sheds an explanatory light on water baptism. [75] The thought of remission is not forgotten (Herm. m., 4, 3, 1), but it is almost submerged under that of vivification and regeneration. There thus arise complicated constructs like the Mandaean ritual, which it would be a strange *Quidproquo* of religious history to regard as the original form of Christian baptism. [76]

The new approach finally comes to expression in the fact that baptism links the baptised with the organised Church and is thus requisitioned by the Church. Ignatius already forbids baptism without the bishop (Sm., 8, 2) and Tertullian will not allow women to baptise (Bapt., 17).

Two forces are at work in relation to the time of baptism. On the one hand, since baptism as a mode of attaining eternal bliss is absolutely efficacious but can be used only once, it is postponed even to the point of death notwithstanding Christian conviction. This does not preclude a certain seriousness in the understanding of the Christian life. The best known example is that of Constantine. On the other hand, since one cannot come to participate too soon in sacramental grace, it seems to be a duty to baptise infants at a tender age, and if possible on the day of birth. It cannot be proved that infant baptism was an innovation adopted in the middle of the 2nd century under the influence of a superstitious sacramental conception and an accomodation to the surrounding world. It is incontestable, however, that the sacramental thinking of the older Catholic Church contributed to the triumph of general infant baptism over previous obstacles. The famous saying of Tertullian : *Quid festinat innocens aetas ad remissionem peccatorum?* (Bapt., 18) occupies middle ground between the two trends. It can hardly be used as a witness to original practice on account of its practical bent and its sporadic character even in Tertullian.

The question whether there is any second repentance for those who have fallen again after being washed — there never seems to have been any thought of a

---

[73] On this term for baptism, which is borrowed from the language of the Mysteries, cf. A. v. Stromberg, *Studien zur Theorie und Praxis der Taufe* (1913), 89 ff.; F. Dölger, *Sphragis* (1911), 51 ff.; W. Heitmüller in *Studien G. Heinrici dargebracht* (1914), 40 ff.; Pr.-Bauer, *s.v.*

[74] F. Dölger, *Antike u. Christentum*, II (1930), 63 ff.; 70 ff.; H. Lietzmann, SAB (1930), 599.

[75] Dölger, *op. cit.*, 117 ff.

[76] On the detailed development of the ritual, RGG², V, 1016 ff., also Reitzenstein, *Vorgeschichte, passim.*

second baptism — gradually became an urgent problem for the whole Church. There seem to be negative answers even in the NT (Hb. 6:4 ff.; 10:26; though cf. 2 C. 12:21). The more magical conception of baptism increased the problem. Later, however, a milder or even laxer view came to predominate.

† βαπτισμός, † βάπτισμα.

"Immersion" or "baptism," βαπτισμός signifying the act alone and βάπτισμα the act with the result, and therefore the institution. There are no instances of βάπτισμα outside the NT. Even βαπτισμός used to be regarded as a new Jewish and Christian term,[1] though cf. Antyllus Medicus (2nd century A.D.) in Oribasius, X, 3, 9, of lethargic sleep, Archigenes Medicus (2nd cent. A.D.) and Posidonius Medicus (3/4 cent. A.D.) in Aetius, 6, 3 (ed. Aldina [1534], p. 100b, 11), of the frenzy of wickedness, Iambl. Theol. Arithm., 30; → βαπτίζω, 530. Technically only in Jos. Ant., 18, 117 with βάπτισις for the baptism of John.[2] Neither word occurs in the LXX. On Plut. Superst., 3 (II, 166a) → βάπτω, n. 13.

βαπτισμοί are Levitical "cleansings" of vessels or of the body at Mk. 7:4 (8 vl.); Hb. 9:10. βαπτισμῶν διδαχή denotes instruction on the difference between Jewish (and pagan?) "washings" (including John's baptism?) and Christian baptism (Hb. 6:2). βάπτισμα is the specific NT word for "baptism." It is used for John's baptism in Mt. 3:7; Mk. 11:30 and par.; Lk. 7:29; Ac. 1:22; 10:37; 18:25; 19:3; βάπτισμα μετανοίας, Mk. 1:4; Ac. 13:24; 19:4; βάπτισμα μετανοίας εἰς ἄφεσιν ἁμαρτιῶν = a baptism of repentance which gives remission of sins. βάπτισμα is also Christian baptism, which as βάπτισμα εἰς τὸν θάνατον (Χριστοῦ) unites the baptised with the buried Christ, that in accordance with His resurrection they should walk in newness of life, R. 6:4; cf. Col. 2:12 : συνταφέντες αὐτῷ ἐν τῷ βαπτίσματι, ἐν ᾧ (sc. βαπτίσματι) καὶ συνηγέρθητε. → βαπτίζω, 541. In 1 Pt. 3:21 the thoughts of washing and quickening are particularly clearly linked on the basis of the atonement (cf. 1:2). According to Eph. 4:5 ἒν βάπτισμα is one of the seven constitutive factors of Church unity. The word is used of the death of Christ in Mk. 10:38 f.; Lk. 12:50.[3]

Since the NT either coins or reserves for Christian baptism (and its precursor) a word which is not used elsewhere and has no cultic connections, and since it always uses it in the sing. and never substitutes the term employed elsewhere, we can see that, in spite of all apparent or relative analogies, it understands the Christian action to be something new and unique.

† βαπτιστής.

The "Baptist," nickname of John, found in the NT only in the Syn : Mt. 3:1; 11:11 f.; 14:2; 17:13; Mk. 6:25 and par. (6:14, 24 : Ἰωάννης ὁ βαπτίζων); 8:28 and par.; Lk. 7:20, 33. It is a Jewish habit to differentiate in this way those who bear the same name (cf. Σίμων ὁ λεγόμενος Πέτρος, Mt. 10:2 and par., Σίμων ὁ Καναναῖος, Mk. 3:18 and par., Σίμων ὁ λεπρός, Mk. 14:3 and par., Σίμων βυρσεύς, Ac. 10:6, 32). Yet this description, specially coined for the precursor of Jesus and used only of him, shows that his appearing was felt to be new and unique, especially as he did not baptise himself but, contrary to all Jewish tradition, baptised others. For a baptism to which the Word gave content a baptist was indispensable.[1]

β α π τ ι σ μ α κτλ. [1] Cr.-Kö., Pr.-Bauer, s.v.
[2] → 535. On the genuineness of the Josephus passage, v. Schürer, I, 436 ff.
[3] In Mt. 20:22 f. the secondary text has been later brought into line with the Syn. par.
β α π τ ι σ τ ή ς. [1] Schl. Mt., 53 f.

Acc. to Jos. Ant., 18, 116 (→ βάπτισμα, n. 2) βαπτιστής is also a Jewish Greek and therefore a popular name for John. The word is not found elsewhere, though cf. παρα-βαπτισταί → 535. It corresponds to a mainly active (and passive) use of βαπτιζειν → 540 which only commences with Jn. and is then found esp. in Christianity. That Mk. prefers ὁ βαπτίζων, while Lk. generally avoids the addition in his account, shows the stronger Gk. orientation of these two Evangelists.

The Mysteries have instances of baptisms by gods or priests.[2] The disciples of the scribes who officiate at proselyte baptisms go down with the baptised into the water in order to repeat the Jewish obligations, but they are witnesses rather than baptisers. At a later period we find the predic. part. hiph הַאִישׁ מַטְבִּיל אֶת הָאִישׁ וְהָאִשָּׁה מַטְבֶּלֶת אֶת הָאִשָּׁה.[3] This is distinguished from βαπτιστής as "one who causes another to immerse himself" from "one who immerses another." ἡμεροβαπτισταί in Epiph. Haer., 17 does not wholly correspond to the plur. of the Rabb. טְבוּל יוֹם (v. the Mishnah tractate of this name). We should rather compare טוֹבְלֵי שַׁחֲרִין in T. Jad., 2, 20. Originally the name of a sect, this term characterises the distinctiveness of strictly Jewish circles (cf. Mk. 7:3 f.).[4] βάπται[5] was a name in Athens for the effeminate devotees of the Thracian Cotys (the title of a comedy of Eupolis [416/15 B.C.]; Luc. Indoct., 27; Schol. in Juv., II, 92; Plin. Hist. Nat., XXXVII, 10, 55); they are not "baptists" but "dyers," because they paint themselves.

Oepke

---

† βάρβαρος

A. The Greek Usage.

1. The basic meaning of this word, which is so important in the history of civilisation, is "stammering," "stuttering," "uttering unintelligible sounds."

Etymology: reduplication of sound, cf. Sansk. *barbara* = "stammering"; plur. to denote non-Aryans; Sloven. *brbrati* "to babble."[1]

Thus βάρβαρος (like the verb βαρβαρίζειν) is used of the twittering of birds: Aesch. Ag., 1003 f.; Aristoph. Av., 199; Hdt., II, 54-58, the story of the priestesses of Dodona called πελειάδες (doves): διότι βάρβαροι ἦσαν, ἐδόκεον δέ σφι ὁμοίως ὄρνισι φθέγγεσθαι (57).

2. Here we have already the transition to the most important usage, i.e., "of a strange speech," or "the one who speaks a strange language" (i.e., other than Greek).

The oldest example is Hom. Il., 2, 867: Καρῶν ... βαρβαροφώνων, where naturally we also have an indirect instance of the simple βάρβαρος; cf. the exposition in Strab.,

---

[2] On the murals mentioned in n. 1 and 2 of → βάπτω; cf. n. 28.

[3] Gerim, 1, 8. The dative constr. mentioned by G. Polster in *Angelos,* 2 (1926), 4 does not appear in the only MS which has come down to us. The sources from which the relevant tractate are compiled derive from the 1st and 2nd cent. A.D. The custom of having assistants at baptism may be traced back to this period.

[4] We are reminded of the Essenes or Bannus (→ βάπτω, n. 40). Schürer, II, 672[6].

[5] Not βαπτισταί, Reitzenstein, *Taufe,* 233.

β ά ρ β α ρ ο ς. A. Eichhorn, Βάρβαρος quid significaverit (Diss. Leipzig, 1904); H. Werner, "Barbarus," NJbch. Kl. Alt., 21 (1918), 389-408; J. Jüthner, *Hellenen und Barbaren* (1923); *ibid.,* 122 f. for addit. bibl. J. Vogt, "Herodot in Ägypten" in *Genethliakon für W. Schmid* (1929), 136 f.; Pauly-W., II (1896), 2858.
[1] Cf. A. Walde-J. Pokorny, *Vergl. Wörterb. d. indogerm. Spr.,* II, 106 [Debrunner].

XIV, 2, 28 ff., esp. : πάντων δὴ τῶν παχυστομούντων οὕτω βαρβάρων λεγομένων, ἐφάνη τὰ τῶν ἀλλοεθνῶν στόματα τοιαῦτα· λέγω δὲ τὰ τῶν μὴ ῾Ελλήνων; again, they were called βαρβάρους, at first κατὰ τὸ λοίδορον, ὡς ἂν παχυστόμους ἢ τραχυστόμους· εἶτα κατεχρησάμεθα ὡς ἐθνικῷ κοινῷ ὀνόματι ἀντιδιαιροῦντες πρὸς τοὺς ῞Ελληνας (28). A further synon. ἀγριόφωνος is first found in Hom. Od., 8, 294. What Herodotus says of the Egyptians (II, 158): βαρβάρους δὲ πάντας οἱ Αἰγύπτιοι καλέουσι τοὺς μὴ σφίσι ὁμογλώσσους, also explains the Gk. βάρβαρος. The word is also found in this sense among the Romans ;[2] the classical example, and also the best parallel to 1 C. 14:11, is in Ovid Tristia, V, 10, 37: *barbarus hic ego sum, qui non intelligor ulli ; et rident stolidi verba Latina Getae.* In Plat. Crat., 421cd the pred. βαρβαρικόν is also applied to archaic Gk. words (cf. the Pauline λαλεῖν → γλώσσαις).

3. From the sense "of strange speech" there naturally develops the geographical and ethnographical sense "of a strange race," "non-Greek," as in the antithesis ἡ ῾Ελλάς/ἡ βάρβαρος (γῆ), "foreign parts,"[3] and esp. the juxtaposition ῞Ελληνες καὶ βάρβαροι. This does not merely denote the totality of all peoples ; it also brings out the distinction, which implies the whole of Greek history, between Greeks and non-Greeks or barbarians. οἱ βάρβαροι are the other peoples who are different in nature, poor in culture, or even uncultured, whom the Greeks hold at arm's length, and over whom they are destined to rule, esp. such national enemies as the Persians and the Egyptians etc.[4]

For the political and national antithesis expressed in βάρβαρος cf. Plat. Menex., 242d ;[5] Livius, XXXI, 29, 15 : *Aetolos Acarnanas Macedonas, eiusdem linquae homines, leves ad tempus ortae causae disiungunt coniunguntque : cum alienigenis, cum barbaris aeternum omnibus Graecis bellum est eritque* (speech of a Macedonian); cf. Ex. 17:16; Eur. Iph. Aul., 1379 f., 1400 f.: βαρβάρων δ᾽ ῞Ελληνας ἄρχειν εἰκός, ἀλλ᾽ οὐ βαρβάρους, μῆτερ, ῾Ελλήνων· τὸ μὲν γὰρ δοῦλον, οἱ δ᾽ ἐλεύθεροι, approvingly quoted by Aristot. Pol., I, 2, p. 1252b, 8. There is a criticism of this distribution, in view of the numerical disparity of the two parts, in Plat. Polit., 262de.

The antithesis of cultures is esp. expressed in Dion. Hal. Ant. Rom., I, 89, 4 : Many Hellenes who dwelt ἐν βαρβάροις very quickly unlearned τὸ ῾Ελληνικόν, ὡς μήτε φωνὴν ῾Ελλάδα φθέγγεσθαι; again in the prayer of thanksgiving of Thales (Diog. L, I, 7, 33): ἔφασκε γάρ, φησί, τριῶν τούτων ἕνεκα χάριν ἔχειν τῇ Τύχῃ· πρῶτον μὲν ὅτι ἄνθρωπος ἐγενόμην, καὶ οὐ θηρίον· εἶτα ὅτι ἀνήρ, καὶ οὐ γυνή· τρίτον ὅτι ῞Ελλην, καὶ οὐ βάρβαρος.[6] Acc. to Isoc., 4, 157, by pious proclamation βάρβαροι were excluded from the Mystery rites of initiation in exactly the same way as ἀνδροφόνοι.[7]

The Hellenistic world established by Alexander fulfilled the ancient Greek ideal of the dominion of the ῞Ελληνες over the βάρβαροι, but it also led to a certain removal of the distinction, to a Hellenisation of the βάρβαροι. This had been prepared by the Sophists with their insight into the essential likeness of all

---

[2] Thes. Ling. Lat., *s.v. barbarus.*
[3] Aesch. Pers., 186 f.; Soph. Trach., 1060, we have instead οὔθ᾽ ῾Ελλάς, οὔτ᾽ ἄγλωσσος (= βάρβαρος γῆ).
[4] Persians, Aesch. Pers. *passim* ; Hdt., VIII, 142 and *passim.* Thuc. : Eichhorn, *op. cit.,* 41; Xenoph. : Eichhorn, 45. Egyptians, examples in Pape, Pass., Jüthner, 13 ff.
[5] Cf. Werner, 395.
[6] For a variant, referred to Plato, *v.* Plut. Marius, 46 (I, 433a), Lact. Inst., III, 19, 17.
[7] Cf. Luc. Demon., 4, Pseudolog., 5.

men, sharply formulated by Antiphon (Diels, II³, *Nachträge*, XXXVI, col. 2, 10 ff.): [8] ἐπεὶ φύσει πάντα πάντες ὁμοίως πεφύκαμεν καὶ βάρβαροι καὶ Ἕλληνες εἶναι. The new view found classical form in the cosmopolitanism of the Stoics. In this connection it should be noted that the older proponents of the Stoa were partly of barbarian origin; they not merely assimilated Greek culture but became teachers of the Greeks. [9]

For comprehensive witness, *v.* Plut. Alex. Fort. Virt., 6 (II, 329b-d), where Alexander is lauded as the divinely sent reconciler of humanity, the destroyer of the previous enmity between Hellenes and barbarians (cf. Eph. 2:11 ff.); hence the restriction of the term βάρβαρος to the wild peoples on the frontier of Hellenistic and Roman civilisation. [10] For differentiation among the barbarians, *v.* Plut. Cons. ad Apoll., 22 (II, 113a).

Naturally the Romans were at first reckoned among the βάρβαροι. [11] The more Hellenised they became, the more they earned the right to be listed with the Ἕλληνες in the formula: Ἕλληνες καὶ βάρβαροι. The relationship remained obscure. One solution was to include a third division, i.e., Greeks, Romans and barbarians, but this was never fully adopted. [12] Even in the Epistle to the Romans Paul uses the older formula Ἕλληνες καὶ βάρβαροι. Sometimes this was abandoned altogether in favour of Romans and non-Romans. [13]

4. The ethnographical sense 3. which equates βάρβαροι with non-Greeks who are destitute of Greek culture and full of all vices, leads quickly to the general moral sense of "wild," "crude," "fierce," "uncivilised."

Aristoph. Nu., 492: ἄνθρωπος ἀμαθὴς ... καὶ βάρβαρος; Polyb., I, 65, 7: πρὸς δὲ τούτοις τί διαφέρει καὶ κατὰ πόσον ἤθη σύμμικτα καὶ βάρβαρα τῶν ἐν παιδείαις καὶ νόμοις καὶ πολιτικοῖς ἔθεσιν ἐκτεθραμμένων. P. Oxy., 1681, 5. Cf. in Latin Cic. Mil., 30, where the *docti* are set in antithesis to the *barbari*: *sin hoc et ratio doctis et necessitas barbaris et mos gentibus et feris etiam beluis natura ipsa praescripsit.* Cic. Verr., IV, 112. Sen. Marc., 7, 3: *magis barbaros quam placidae eruditae-que gentis homines, magis indoctos quam doctos eadem orbitas volnerat.* βάρβαρος is here synon. with σκληρός, ὠμός, ἄγριος, μανικός, ἄπιστος, ἀνόητος, σκαιός, ἀμαθής, ἀπαίδευτος, ἀναίσθητος. [14] How the change of meaning from 3. to 4. is linked with the great historical work of Alexander is shown by Plut. Alex. Fort. Virt., 6 (II, 329cd): τὸ δ' Ἑλληνικὸν καὶ βαρβαρικὸν μὴ χλαμύδι ... διορίζειν, ἀλλὰ τὸ μὲν Ἑλληνικὸν ἀρετῇ, τὸ δὲ βαρβαρικὸν κακίᾳ τεκμαίρεσθαι; cf. also Cic. Resp., I, 58 (→ n. 11).

---

[8] Cf. H. Diels in SAB (1916), 931 ff.; W. Nestle, "Politik u. Moral im Altertum," *NJbch. Kl. Alt.,* 21 (1918), 228 f.

[9] Cf. M. Pohlenz, "Stoa u. Semitismus," *NJbch. Wiss. u. Jugendbildung,* 2 (1926), 257 ff. I have not so far encountered any Stoic statement anal. to that of Antiphon. The word βάρβαρος is not found in v. Arnim's Index, nor in Epict.

[10] Cf. Preisigke Wört., 255.

[11] Jüthner, 60 ff.; Werner, 397 ff. Cato in Plinius Hist. Nat., XXIX, 7, 14: *nos quoque dictitant barbaros* (sc. *Graeci*) *et spurcius nos quam alios* Ὀπικῶν *appellatione foedant;* Livius, XXXI, 29, 30: *qui Romanos alienigenas et barbaros vocet;* Cic. Resp., I, 58: *Si, ut Graeci dicunt, omnis aut Graios esse aut barbaros, vereor ne* (*Romulus*) *barbarorum rex fuerit; sin id nomen moribus dandum est, non linguis, non Graecos minus barbaros quam Romanos puto.*

[12] Cic. Fin., II, 49: *non solum Graecia et Italia, sed etiam omnis barbaria;* Divin., I, 84; cf. also Philo Vit. Cont., 48. Cf. further, Jüthner, 140, n. 202.

[13] So Ael. Arist., XIV, p. 347, 15 ff., Dindorf; Jüthner, 85 f.

[14] For examples, *v.* Eichhorn, 62 ff. For ἀνόητος, apart from R. 1:14 cf. Dion. Hal. Ant. Rom., V, 4, 3. Cf. also Plut. Pelop., 21 (I, 289c); Apophthegm. (Caesar), II, 205 f.

5. Within the new cosmopolitanism the barbarians, or some outstanding barbarians, came to be highly estimated in certain circles of Hellenes. Individual barbarian peoples were idealised and the intellectual greatness of some of their kings highly valued (Xenoph. Cyrop.), as also that of individual sages of barbarian origin (the Scythian Anacharsis) and the philosophy of the barbarians, e.g., Chaldeans and Jews. [15]

Christianity found a place in this movement. Yet it was the Apologists who first asserted the barbarian origin of this new religion or philosophy and of its Founder, thus deducing the superiority of Christian philosophy.

Just. Apol., I, 5, 4; 7, 3; 46, 3; 60, 11; the new state of affairs is denoted by the expression: ἰδιωτῶν μὲν καὶ βαρβάρων τὸ φθέγμα, σοφῶν δὲ καὶ πιστῶν τὸν νοῦν ὄντων, Dial., 119, 4; esp. Tatian, 1, 1 etc. [16]

B. βάρβαρος in the LXX, Jewish Hellenism and the Rabbis.

In the true LXX βάρβαρος occurs only twice, at Ez. 21:31 (36) and ψ 113:1: ἐν ἐξόδῳ Ἰσραὴλ ἐξ Αἰγύπτου, οἴκου Ἰακὼβ ἐκ λαοῦ βαρβάρου, where λαὸς βάρβαρος (עַם לֹעֵז) [17] means a people with a stammering or alien tongue (sense 1. or 2.), and holy people of Yahweh (ψ 113:2) has a sense of superiority over barbarian Egypt. At Ez. 21:31 (36), in an oracle against the Ammonites, we read: καὶ ἐκχεῶ ἐπὶ σὲ ὀργήν μου ... καὶ παραδώσω σε εἰς χεῖρας ἀνδρῶν βαρβάρων κτλ. Here אֲנָשִׁים בֹּעֲרִים means "stupid and brutish men" [18] and βάρβαρος is thus used in sense 4.

This is its usual meaning in the Apocrypha: 2 Macc. 4:25: θυμοὺς δὲ ὠμοῦ τυράννου καὶ θηρὸς βαρβάρου ὀργὰς ἔχων; 5:22, where it is not as a Phrygian, but in character, that Philip is βαρβαρώτερος than his· king; cf. also 10:4: μὴ βλασφήμοις καὶ βαρβάροις ἔθνεσι παραδίδοσθαι (cf. Ez. 21:36); 15:2 and 3 Macc. 3:24, where the Egyptians do not want the Jews at their back as προδότας καὶ βαρβάρους πολεμίους, i.e., "fierce" enemies, though "foreign" enemies is also possible. The latter sense is to be preferred in 2 Macc. 2:21, where the reference of τὰ βάρβαρα πλήθη is to Syrian Hellenistic troops. Here the Jews speak of the Syrians as the Greeks of the Persians. Their fight against them is one against barbarians, and we almost seem to have the formula Ἰουδαῖοι καὶ βάρβαροι in opposition to Ἕλληνες καὶ βάρβαροι. [19]

On the other hand, in Ep. Ar., 122 the description of the 70 chosen by the high-priest is in Gk. terms: ἀποτεθειμένοι τὸ τραχὺ καὶ βάρβαρον τῆς διανοίας, i.e., as men of Jewish and Greek culture they have put off the crudity of uncivilised Jews (or men).

Philo took over the Greek usage. [20] Ἑλλάς and (ἡ) βάρβαρος (γῆ) is for him the world, and in Leg. Gaj. esp. the Roman Empire (cf. 141, 145 and 147) in which Augustus and Tiberius disseminated their blessings. Wholly Hellenistic is the expression in the hymn to Καῖσαρ Σεβαστός (ibid., 145 ff.): ὁ τὴν μὲν Ἑλλάδα Ἑλλάσι πολλαῖς παραυξήσας, τὴν δὲ βάρβαρον ἐν τοῖς ἀναγκαιοτάτοις τμήμασιν ἀφελληνίσας, i.e., by the spreading of Gk. culture the Roman Augustus has enlarged Hellas and hellenised great areas of barbarian territory (147). He is also extolled,

---

[15] So Celsus in Orig. Cels., I, 2: ἱκανοὺς εὑρεῖν δόγματα τοὺς βαρβάρους, and on the other side κρῖναι καὶ βεβαιώσασθαι καὶ ἀσκῆσαι πρὸς ἀρετὴν τὰ ὑπὸ βαρβάρων εὑρεθέντα ἀμείνονές εἰσιν Ἕλληνες. In any case, the judgment of Celsus on Christianity: βάρβαρον ἄνωθεν εἶναι τὸ δόγμα (namely, of Jewish origin), implies no defect.

[16] Cf. R. C. Kukula, "Was bedeuten die Namen Ἕλληνες und Βάρβαροι in der altchristl. Apologetik?" Festschrift f. T. Gomperz (1902), 359-363.

[17] Ges.-Buhl, s.v. לֹעֵז.

[18] Ibid., s.v. בֹּעֵר.

[19] C. L. W. Grimm, Handbuch zu den Apokryphen d. AT, 4 (1857), 61.

[20] H. Leisegang, Index, s.v.

however, as ὁ τὰς κοινὰς νόσους Ἑλλήνων καὶ βαρβάρων ἰασάμενος (145), and therefore, as one might say, as the saviour of both Hellenes and barbarians. Here the idea of cultural distinction is levelled down, and even more so in Omn. Prob. Lib., 72 ff., where, in proof that the frugal or wise man still exists, appeal is made both to ἡ Ἑλλὰς καὶ ἡ βάρβαρος, the former with its 7 sages and the latter with its magi and gymnosophists; [21] when later (75 ff.) ἡ Παλαιστίνη Συρία is also adduced with its Essenes, there is room for doubt whether Judaism is classed with the barbarians or regarded as a third group. The latter view is certainly found in Spec. Leg., II, 165 f.: Ἕλληνες ὁμοῦ καὶ βάρβαροι have associated other deities with the one God, the πατὴρ θεῶν τε καὶ ἀνθρώπων; this fault has been made good by τὸ Ἰουδαίων ἔθνος; the Jewish people is thus set in antithesis to others in virtue of its unique possession of true knowledge of God. In addition to the Persians and Indians, Philo reckons the Egyptians and esp. the → Σκύθαι as barbarians (Vit. Mos., II, 19). [22] Acc. to Vit. Mos., II, 19 f. the Jewish laws are also able to unite all groups where the laws of other peoples divide, namely, βαρβάρους, Ἕλληνας, ἠπειρώτας, νησιώτας κτλ. The destiny of Jewish religion is to overcome the differences between Hellenes and barbarians and thus to become the universal religion. In Philo the sense of "non-Greek" thus predominates, though we have sense 4. in Spec. Leg., III, 163: βάρβαροι τὰς φύσεις, ἡμέρου παιδείας ἄγευστοι.

Josephus, [23] too, followed Gk. usage. The question is whether he included the Jews among the βάρβαροι. Mostly he excluded them. Thus he characterises as βάρβαροι the Midianites in Ant., 2, 263, the Parthians in Bell., 1, 264 and 268, Ant., 18, 328, the branch of the Scythians known as the Sarmates, Bell., 7, 94, the non-Jewish inhabitants of East Jordania, Ant., 12, 222, and the Arabs, Ant., 15, 130. [24]

It is accordingly charged against the Zealots that they rejoiced in the destruction of their Jewish opponents as if they were barbarians (Bell., 5, 345), and against the Idumeans that zeal in assisting the Zealots against other Jews was greater than if the metropolis summoned them ἐπὶ βαρβάρους, i.e., non-Jews (4, 239).

Even when Josephus uses the expression Ἕλληνες καὶ βάρβαροι, he excludes the Jews, [25] though he does not emphasise the fact that they are a *tertium genus*. For Josephus Ἕλληνες καὶ βάρβαροι simply denotes non-Jews.

On the other hands, and rather surprisingly, he speaks of the Parthian Jews, for whom he first wrote his *War* in their Syrian Aramaic, as τοῖς ἄνω βαρβάροις (Bell., 1, 3). This is an accommodation to Roman and Gk. usage, and he sets over against these ἄνω βάρβαροι τοῖς κατὰ τὴν Ῥωμαίων ἡγεμονίαν (sc. οἰκοῦσιν) to whom he now presents his *War* Ἑλλάδι γλώσσῃ. We see the same thing when he opposes to witnesses (about the Jews) παρ' ἡμῖν τε αὐτοῖς καί τισιν ἄλλοις τῶν βαρβάρων (the Persians and Macedonians) τὰ ὑπὸ Ῥωμαίων δόγματα (Ant., 14, 178 f.). The malicious saying ἀφυεστάτους εἶναι τῶν βαρβάρων (τοὺς Ἰουδαίους) in Ap., 2, 148, is a quotation from Apollonius Molon.

In Rabbinic lit. [26] בַּרְבָּר, בַּרְבְּרָאָה, plur. בַּרְבְּרִים, בַּרְבְּרַיָּא occurs only as a loan word to denote a. Jews as spoken of by nations which subjugate them, like the Babylonians, Medes and Romans, [27] and b. non-Jewish peoples and uncultured individuals. [28]

---

[21] Cf. Abr., 181 ff.

[22] Similarly in Op. Mund., 128 Moses the law-giver of the Jews is compared with the mathematicians of the Ἕλληνες καὶ βάρβαροι.

[23] Most of these examples are from material kindly placed at my disposal by A. Schlatter.

[24] Their παρανομία is so great ὡς εἰκὸς ἔχειν τὸ βάρβαρον καὶ ἀνεννόητον θεοῦ.

[25] Mostly Ἕλληνες καὶ βάρβαροι relates to Gk. and oriental writers, Ant., 1, 93 and 107; Ap. 1, 58 and 161, though cf. Ant., 4, 12; 15, 136; Ap. 1, 201 (in a quotation from Hecataeus).

[26] Str.-B., III, 27 ff.

[27] E.g., in the acclamation for Nebuchadnezzar as for Titus: נְקִיטָא בַּרְבְּרַיָּא = νικητὴς βαρβάρων (Str.-B., III, 28).

[28] Str.-B., III, 28 f.

The true Rabbinic equivalent to the Gk. Ἕλληνες καὶ βάρβαροι is יִשְׂרָאֵל and אֻמּוֹת הָעוֹלָם or יִשְׂרָאֵל and הַגּוֹיִם == oἱ Ἰουδαῖοι καὶ ἔθνη. It is only in these expressions that we can see the similarity of the Gk. and Jewish feeling in relation to other peoples. A typical example is the Rabb. par. to the prayer of thanksgiving of Thales (→ 547), T. Ber., 7, 18 (R. Jehuda as author): "Praised be He who hath not made me a Gentile ... a woman ... a barbarian !" There is a variant in bMen., 43b: The three beatitudes of R. Meir, that He hath made me an Israelite and not a *Goy*, ... that He hath not made me a woman ... that He hath not made me a fool (בּוּר). [29]

The distinction between βάρβαρος and גּוֹי is that the former applies only to race, language and culture, whereas גּוֹי (== → ἔθνη, → ἁμαρτωλός, 328, cf. also → ἀκροβυστία, 226) is a cultic and religious term which only secondarily refers to differences of race and culture. Thus βάρβαρος and גּוֹי are not equivalents, and Heb. and Aram. adopt "barbarous" as a loan word. The cleft between Jews and non-Jews is deeper than that between Gks. and barbarians, the more so as the distinction between Jews and non-Jews, between circumcised and uncircumcised, has an eschatological significance with implications for the world to come and for eternity. [30]

C. βάρβαρος in the NT.

The term occurs only 4 times in the NT, [31] at Ac. 28:2, 4; 1 C. 14:11; R. 1:14 and Col. 3:11.

In 1 C. 14:11 Paul gives us a classical example of sense 1. in the general statement which he makes in his discussion of tongues: ἐὰν οὖν μὴ εἰδῶ τὴν δύναμιν τῆς φωνῆς, ἔσομαι τῷ λαλοῦντι βάρβαρος καὶ ὁ λαλῶν (ἐν) ἐμοὶ βάρβαρος. βάρβαρος here is the ἀλλόγλωσσος who speaks a language which I do not understand. Paul thus emphasises the two-sided nature of the relationship; the Hellene is a "barbarian" to non-Hellenes, as was Ovid to the "barbarian" Getae (→ 547).

Similarly in Ac. 28:2, 4 οἱ βάρβαροι are those of alien, non-Greek race, i.e., the Maltese who speak Punic, "natives" who use their own tongue. [32]

When Luke says: οἵ τε βάρβαροι παρεῖχον οὐ τὴν τυχοῦσαν φιλανθρωπίαν ἡμῖν, he means that we met with friendly treatment which as shipwrecked travellers we had not expected, or had never met with elsewhere, from such "barbarians." Hence there is either a contrast between βάρβαρος and φιλανθρωπία, or else a protest against the dominant contempt for βάρβαροι.

In R. 1:14 f. Paul describes the universality of his apostolic commitment: Ἕλλησίν τε καὶ βαρβάροις, σοφοῖς τε καὶ ἀνοήτοις ὀφειλέτης εἰμί, and thus deduces his readiness to preach also to the Romans. The saying is a parallel to 1:5 f.; the reference is to πάντα τὰ ἔθνη. [33] The expression is wholly in line with Gk. usage. The apposition σοφοῖς τε καὶ ἀνοήτοις shows that Paul has also a cultural distinction in view. βάρβαρος thus means "non-Greek," whether in respect

---

[29] Bousset-Gressm., 426 f.; J. Leipoldt, *Jesus u. d. Frauen* (1921), 3 f., 115 f.

[30] Ac. 15:2; Str.-B., IV, 1, 37 ff.

[31] βάρβαρος is not found at all in the post-apostolic fathers and only recurs in the Apologists.

[32] This is the best rendering of βάρβαροι in this passage. Some of them must have known a little Greek, for Luke made out and passed on one or two of their sayings (28:4b and 6b). Paul probably conversed with them Ἑβραΐδι διαλέκτῳ, i.e., in Aram. Zn. Ac., *ad loc.*

[33] Cf., e.g., Cl. Al. Prot., 12, 120, 2.

of descent or culture. [34] Yet Hellenes and barbarians are alike in the fact that the new Gospel must be proclaimed to both, as Philo had also believed in respect of the law of the Jews (→ 550).

As mostly in Philo, the formula includes the Romans. [35] The fact that Paul writes a Greek letter τοῖς ἐν 'Ρώμῃ means that he classifies them with the "Ελληνες. Among the βάρβαροι to whom he also owes the Gospel he perhaps groups the Spaniards to whom he plans to journey from Rome (R. 15:24), the Celts, who were related to his hellenised ἀνόητοι Γαλάται (Gl. 3:1), the Germans, the Scythians, and all non-Hellenistic peoples either within or without the Roman Empire. [37] In general, the Roman Empire was for Paul co-extensive with Greek society both linguistically and culturally.

According to R. 1:14 the apostle's calling has in view the two groups of Hellenes and barbarians, i.e., the non-Jewish world (τὰ ἔθνη). [38] The Jews are not counted here, and thus constitute a *tertium genus*. Occasionally Paul uses in close proximity the alternative 'Ιουδαῖος καὶ "Ελλην (1:16), which denotes the totality of the human race from the Jewish and biblical standpoint. Both formulae are construed along the same lines; 'Ιουδαῖος is the equivalent of "Ελληνες and "Ελλην of βάρβαρος. The one elect people is contrasted with all others. In the Jewish formula "Ελλην necessarily includes the βάρβαροι and thus equals ἔθνη. We may thus put the two together to produce the three-pronged synthesis: 'Ιουδαῖοι, "Ελληνες, βάρβαροι, which is hinted at by Paul in Col. 3:11.

In this verse we have a fourfold grouping, in pairs, of the race as it has been united in Christ (cf. Gl. 3:28). The first two pairs are "Ελλην καὶ 'Ιουδαῖος and περιτομὴ καὶ ἀκροβυστία, in which we have division from the standpoint of nationality and of salvation history and religion. The final pair is δοῦλος/ἐλεύθερος; the sociological division (ἄρσεν/θῆλυ) is not found in the original. [39] The third pair, namely, βάρβαρος/Σκύθης, is rather more difficult to understand. On the analogy of the others, an antithesis is intended. It has been suggested that Σκύθης here stands for a noble northern people corresponding to the idealised Germania of Tacitus and others, and that this is set over against the βάρβαρος. [40] The Σκύθης, however, is almost always thought of as a particularly uncivilised barbarian. [41] Again, in some later travel stories the word Βαρβαρία is used for the Somali coast and part of Ethiopia (the inhabitants are οἱ Βάρβαροι); hence it has been thought that the contrast is between southern and northern peoples or even black and white. [42] It is unlikely, however, that in view of the widespread use of the formula "Ελληνες/βάρβαροι Paul would adopt so specialised and little known a sense in such close proximity to the term "Ελληνες. It has also to be remembered that the attestation, and perhaps the designation, is post-

---

[34] Cf. also Zn. R., *ad loc.*

[35] Cf. Ps.-Clem. Recg., I, 7: *audite me, o cives Romani;* and then 9: *vos o omnis turba Graecorum* (they are thus described as supposed *philosophi*).

[37] Lycaonian in Ac. 14:11 is for Paul just as much a barbarian language as Celtic or Punic Maltese.

[38] Gl. 2:7 f.; R. 3:29; 1 Tm. 2:7.

[39] For a formal par. *v.* Plat. Theaet., 175a: πάππων καὶ προγόνων μυριάδες ..., ἐν αἷς πλούσιοι καὶ πτωχοί, καὶ βασιλεῖς καὶ δοῦλοι, βάρβαροί τε καὶ "Ελληνες πολλάκις μύριοι γεγόνασιν ὁτῳοῦν.

[40] Jüthner, 55, 143.

[41] For examples → 550; cf. also Cic. Verr., V, 150. The word περισκυθίζειν occurs in 2 Macc. 7:4. Cf. Wettstein and Loh. on Col. 3:11.

[42] Another possible distinction is between βάρβαροι subject to the Roman Empire and those outside. Again, there is the possibility of a distinction from Berber if this designation, common in older Arab writers, is pre-Arab, as seems possible according to information received from G. Jacob.

Pauline. We are thus forced to explain the formula in relation to βάρβαρος/Ἕλλην. Paul began with the Jewish formula. Obviously, therefore, he was taking Ἕλλην in the narrower sense of non-Jews of Greek origin and culture, i.e., in the sense of the rival formula Ἕλλην καὶ βάρβαρος. He thus found it necessary to make specific mention of the βάρβαροι in order to supply the missing section of the race. But there was no available antithesis as the style of the passage demanded. To make good the deficiency he contrasted the barbarians generally with a particularly notorious barbarian people. The expression is thus a stylistic device.

In general, then, Paul uses the Hellenistic βάρβαρος in the same way as Philo and Josephus and with a conscious exclusion of the Ἰουδαῖος. The new thing is his desire to lead the βάρβαροι to the εὐαγγέλιον θεοῦ, and the doctrine that Greeks, Jews, Scythians and barbarians are all fashioned into a totality in Christ.

Windisch

βάρος, βαρύς, βαρέω

† βάρος.

Apart from the basic meaning, i.e., "bodily weight" in the wider sense, the word is used figuratively to denote two important and ineluctable characteristics of existence, namely, oppressive suffering and significant power. This is the imortant point for a comparison of the secular and the NT usage.

A. In the Greek and Hellenistic World.

1. The first sense of "physical weight" provides a neutral basis. Thus βάρος is used in cosmological discussion for the weight of the elements: Diod. S., I, 7, 1; Philo Rer. Div. Her., 146. It is also used for the weight of men or animals (Polyb., XVIII, 30, 4) and hence for pregnancy (Preisigke Sammelbuch, 5718). It is used of scales (βάρεσιν ἀνίσοις, Philo Jos., 140), of the freight of ships (Polyb., I, 39, 4) and of the baggage of an army (Ju. 18:21 B, Mas. כְּבֹד).[1]

When used metaphorically of the (reduced) weight of an enclitic word[2] or of depth of tone,[3] the idea is that by emphasis a special "stress" is laid on a syllable or note.

The following nuances may be noted as leading to, though not yet expressing, the complexes of suffering and power. 2. The element of pressure occurs when the word is used to denote the "thrust" of active movement. The basis of "weight" may still be seen, but it is now given emotional content to signify "force" or "violence." Thus the violence of hail does damage (Diod. S., XIX, 45, 2; Philo Vit. Mos., I, 119); or there is reference to the ponderous movement of troops or ships or elephants (Jdt. 7:4; Polyb.,

---

β ά ρ ο ς. Bibl. on the content of the term: E. Balla, "Das Problem des Leides in der Gesch. der isr.-jüd. Religion" in *Eucharisterion,* I (1923), 214 ff.; A. Beyer, "Was sagen Jesus und Paulus über das Leid?" Pr. M., 20 (1916), 321 ff., 371 ff.; R. Liechtenhan, "Die Überwindung des Leides bei Pls. und in der zeitgenössischen Stoa," ZThK, NF, 3 (1922), 368 ff.; O. Schmitz, *Das Lebensgefühl des Pls.* (1922), 105 ff.; H. Weinel, *Bibl. Th. d. NT*[4] (1928), 266 ff.; J. Schneider, *Die Passionsmystik des Pls.* (1929), 17 ff., 73 ff.; O. Kietzig, *Die Bekehrung des Pls.* (1932), 193 ff.; RGG², III, 1565.

[1] In the LXX, where it occurs only infrequently, βάρος is always used for כָּבוֹד. It is striking that סֵבֶל, מַשָּׂא (1 K. 11:28), מוּעָקָה (Ps. 66:11) and similar words are not rendered βάρος.

[2] Apollon Dyscol. Synt., 98, 1. Cf. P. Hanschke, *De accentuum graecorum nominibus* (Diss. Bonn, 1914), esp. "De vocibus ὀξύς et βαρύς."

[3] Aristides Quintil. Musicus, 1, 11.

X, 12, 8; Diod. S., XX, 52, 3; Polyb., I, 74, 5), or to the baying of dogs (Alciphr. Ep., 3, 18).

3. To some extent distinct from the basic meaning of weight, though not entirely figurative, is the sense of "fulness" or "superfluity" or "ripeness." The significant feature here is not just weight, though this is included, but fulness or content. This approximates closely to the usage in which emphasis falls on the complex of power. There is reference to the plenitude of riches in Eur. El., 1287: καὶ δότω πλούτου βάρος, cf. also Plut. Alex., 48 (I, 692b); to the fulness of well-being in Eur. Iph. Taur., 416: ὄλβου βάρος. In the image of the scales in Philo Rer. Div. Her., 46 ἄχθος is used for weight and βάρος for mass. The state is described in the image of the fulness and maturity of the body in Jos. Bell., 1, 507.

But we have not yet reached the main figurative meaning. 4. βάρος comes into significant use for suffering through the emphasis on its oppressive or burdensome nature. It applies a. to afflictions of the body: Aristot. Hist. An., VIII, 21, p. 603b, 8: κεφαλῆς πόνος καὶ βάρος; Hippocr. Acut., 4; to the smart of wounds, Plut. Alex. Fort. Virt., II, 13 (II, 345a); Diod. S., XVI, 12, 4; to exposure to an intolerable smell, 2 Macc. 9:10.

It also applies b. to afflictions of the soul, to oppression, dejection, depression, misery: Soph. Oed. Col., 409: ἔσται ποτ᾽ ἆρα τοῦτο Καδμείοις βάρος; P. Oxy., VII, 1062, 14: εἰ δὲ τοῦτό σοι βάρος φέρει; Ditt. Syll.³, 888, 67 (238 A.D.): ἐπεὶ οὖν οὐκέτι δυνάμεθα φέρειν τὰ βάρη.

In relation to Mt. 20:12 it may be mentioned that βάρος is very common with gen. apposit. Similar constructions to τὸ βάρος τῆς ἡμέρας are the burden of fate in Soph. Trach., 325: ἀλλ᾽ αἰὲν ὠδίνουσα συμφορᾶς βάρος; official burdens in Jos. Bell., 4, 616: βάρος τῆς ἡγεμονίας; Bell., 1, 461: τῶν πραγμάτων; Philo Spec. Leg., II, 102: πραγματειῶν; the burden of sorrows in Philo Vit. Mos., I, 14: βάρος τῶν φροντίδων; cf. also Philo Vit. Mos., I, 39: ἀνάγκης βάρος.

c. A specialised use, very common in the pap., is to denote the burden, e.g., of taxation, as in P. Giess., I, 7, 13 f. (117 A.D.) in relation to conditions of tenure; BGU, I, 159, 3 ff. (216 A.D.) in relation to national expenditure (βάρος τῆς λειτουργίας); and Polyb., I, 67, 1 in relation to taxes (τὸ βάρος τῶν φόρων).

5. Hardly less common than the use for suffering is the use of βάρος for power, i.e. weight, dignity, influence, power or presence. The reference may be a. to personal influence, dignity or appearance: Plut. Pericl., 37 (I, 172c); Plut. Cat., 1 (I, 336d), 20 (I, 347 f.); Demetr., 2 (I, 889e); Diod. S., XIX, 70, 8; or b. to the power of a state: Diod. S., XVI, 8, 5 etc.; or c. to the strength of an army or the power of arms, as sometimes in the historians and frequently in Polyb.: I, 16, 4; II, 68, 9; V, 104, 2.

B. The NT Usage.

It is to be noted that, if faith in Christ involves a change in the use of the word, this is particularly instructive because it illustrates the new attitude of early Christianity to suffering, to depression, to the yoke of the Law, and to the question of power.

In the NT use there is first reflected 1. the unchanged participation of the Christian in earthly oppression (→ n. 4). In spite of the new position of the recipient of grace, this will continue until the final redemption of the body, to use the Pauline phrase. If in Mt. 20:12: τοῖς βαστάσασι τὸ βάρος τῆς ἡμέρας, we have a simple and non-accentuated reference to the daily burden of work, we are led into a profound evaluation of suffering in 2 C. 4:17. To be sure, the primary reference is to apostolic suffering. Yet a glance at R. 8:18 shows that the same standards apply to the Christian life in general. The βάρος of affliction is in no way denied or minimised. But in relation to what is to come it is an ἐλαφρὸν βάρος. [4] The formula αἰώνιον βάρος δόξης naturally reminds us that the Heb. כבד expresses both the weight and the glory. The distinctive feature in this view of suffering is that the present burden is conceived to be productive in the eschatological sense (κατεργάζεται). From the burden of suffering comes the fulness of δόξα. If this reminds us of Mandaean parallels, where the mounting soul carries a pure burden, it should not be overlooked that the Mandaean view is linked with ideas of merit. [5] The result is the same if we attempt a comparison with Wis., the Macc. and post-Pauline apocalyptic as regards the connection between suffering and glory. Wis., too, connects the brief sufferings of this aeon with the glory of the future world at 3:5 : ὀλίγα παιδευθέντες μεγάλα εὐεργετηθήσονται. It does so, however, on the express basis of the idea of merit : ὅτι ὁ θεὸς ἐπείρασεν αὐτοὺς καὶ εὗρεν αὐτοὺς ἀξίους ἑαυτοῦ. Similarly, the θεία μερίς will be won by the representative suffering of martyrs in 4 Macc. 18:3. Again, suffering will safeguard against eternal pain according to S. Bar. 78:6. On the other hand, at 2 Cor. 4:17 the significant feature is the new glory of the Christian life which is already assured in affliction on the basis of grace in Christ. Far more profoundly influenced by the later Jewish views already mentioned is the usual Hellenistic conception, e.g., in Jos. Bell., 7, 346 (the speech of Eleazar), where it is only through suffering that the soul — ἐπειδὰν ἀπολυθεῖσα τοῦ καθέλκοντος αὐτὴν βάρους ἐπὶ γῆν — attains its home, its effectiveness and its unrestricted power. Here we are expressly told that this life has no true connection with the hoped for immortality; it is quite simply a misfortune. Mysticism goes on to seek a sloughing off of human nature by the ascetic and ecstatic liberation of soul, but fails to do justice to the reality of the continuing existence of suffering.

2. As regards the task of love in relation to suffering (→ n. 4), Gl. 6:2 describes it as the sum and substance of the Christian life to bear one another's burdens. The context shows us that the primary reference of βάρη here is to moral lapses, temptations and guilt. [6] Nevertheless, it is obvious that this saying offers us a basic thesis in description of the total task of love, so that we cannot restrict the application of βάρος to a particular sphere. [7] This is proved above all by the sentence which follows : καὶ οὕτως ἀναπληρώσετε τὸν νόμον τοῦ Χριστοῦ. [8] The distinctive nature of the conception emerges from a comparison with Stoic teaching. Here there are altruistic impulses. The demands of humanity, of κοινω-

---

[4] With P. W. Schmiedel, ad loc. (cf. the Zurich Bible, 1931), we should expand this to ἐλαφρὸν βάρος. This does not necessarily demand the obliteration of the play of meanings, i.e., "burden" in the first clause and "fulness" in the second, since this is preserved if "weight" is used as the rendering in both cases.

[5] Lidz. Joh., 204, 24 ff.; Reitzenstein Hell. Myst., 355; Ir. Erl., 54. Cf. also G. Flügel, Mani (1862), 105, and for the thought of reward Lidz. Joh., 204, 28 : Men of "tested piety" have trodden "the way of reward and almsgiving," 23 f.

[6] Gl. 6:1: παραπτώματι μὴ πειρασθῇς. The burden to be borne in 6:5 is primarily that of personal responsibility, i.e., of the decisions which have to be taken in the fight against temptations.

[7] For Rabb. par. cf. Ab., 6, 5 f. : "to bear the yoke with one's neighbour," Str.-B., III, 577 and Gn. r., 1 (2b): "The great of the land share the king's burden," cf. Str.-B., I, 731.

[8] Though νόμος τοῦ Χριστοῦ is put in place of the νόμος, we have here a par. to R. 13:10. The statement is understood in the widest sense in Dg., 10, 6 : ὅστις τὸ τοῦ πλησίον ἀναδέχεται βάρος.

νικόν, εὔνοια and εὐμένεια, are emphasised. Yet everything remains in the sphere of intellectualistic ethics. For there is no ἐκκλησία in which this "bearing" can be realised as the true and concentrated content of life.

3. In relation to freedom from the yoke of the Law (→ n. 4), we may refer to Ac. 15:28 [9] and Rev. 2:24, which resist the view that a burden in laid on the community. This is in harmony with Mt. 11:29 f., where personal commitment to Christ replaces the yoke of statutes. The yoke of the Torah and ordinances is part of the earthly βάρος which is lifted from the community. [10]

4. It is certainly not for nothing, nor accidental, that in all the passages in which βάρος is used in the sense of earthly influence, importance or power, this element is opposed, whereas βάρος as suffering is profoundly indicated by βαρεῖσθαι. At 1 Th. 2:7: δυνάμενοι ἐν βάρει εἶναι, the reference can hardly be to financial cost, [11] i.e., the material burden the apostle might be to the community; it is rather to conscious self-assertion. [12] Though the apostle maintains his apostolic authority, he does not think it necessary to support it by a particularly imposing appearance.

† βαρύς.

In ordinary Gk. the use of βαρύς is wholly par. to that of βάρος. The division under A. may thus be accepted as still applicable, and our attention concentrated on the NT passages with biblical and extra-biblical par. [1]

1. Outside the NT βαρύς is often used for "heavy" in the corporal sense, for "awkward," "pregnant," "heavy with wine" (opp. κοῦφος), or figur. "deep," e.g., in tone (opp. ὀξύς) and accent, a. of syllables (musically "deep") or b. of words (the place of the accent in words). This usage does not occur in the NT, but the τοῖς ὠσὶ βαρέως ἤκουσαν of Mt. 13:15; Ac. 28:27 belongs directly to this category. The quotation is from Is. 6:10 (Mas. וְאָזְנָיו הַכְבֵּד); Their ears have become "dull of hearing." Without τοῖς ὠσί, βαρέως ἤκουον elsewhere denotes an unfavourable reception, Polyb., XVIII, 39, 1; Xenoph. An., II, 1, 9. [2]

2. To the sense of βάρος which emphasises thrust or force or violence there corresponds that of βαρύς as "forceful" or "violent," as in 2 C. 10:10 : ἐπιστολαὶ βαρεῖαι καὶ ἰσχυραί — the accusation made against Paul by his opponents. This is the usage which applies the term to natural forces. It is used of the wind : νότος βαρύς, Paus., X, 17, 11; of thunder : βαρεῖα βροντή, Poll. Onom., I, 118; of storms : βαρὺς χειμών, Philo Gig., 51; of hail : χάλαζα βαρεῖα, Philo Vit. Mos., I, 118; or of the baying of

---

[9] In elucidation Ac. 15:10 is important : ἐπιθεῖναι ζυγόν (common LXX alternatives are βαρύνειν τὸν ζυγόν or τὸν κλοιόν, 3 Βασ. 12:4; 12:14; Hab. 2:6; 1 Macc. 8:31) ἐπὶ τὸν τράχηλον τῶν μαθητῶν. ζυγόν and βάρος are here rejected, for the few decisions in the decree cannot be understood thus. Zn. Einl., II, 445, n. 10 links Rev. 2:24 with the apostolic decree, but the formal agreement may well be accidental ; cf. Loh. Apk., ad loc.

[10] On "yoke of the Torah" עֹל תּוֹרָה or עֹל מִצְוֹת, cf. Ab., 6, 5 f. (the 48 demands on those occupied with the Torah), Str.-B., III, 577, also I, 608 and 912; II, 728.

[11] Like ἐν προφάσει πλεονεξίας in 2:5 and ἐπιβαρῆσαί τινα in 2:9; so Thdrt. But just before we have : οὔτε ζητοῦντες ἐξ ἀνθρώπων δόξαν. We are given the impression that the financial theme does not recur in this instance.

[12] With Chrys., Dob., Dib., ad loc.; Pr.-Bauer, s.v.

β α ρ ύ ς. [1] Cf. Hanschke, De accentuum nominibus (→ βάρος, n. 2).
[2] On Is. 6:9 f. in Rabb. lit., cf. Str.-B., I, 662 f. Very common is βαρέως φέρειν, Aristoph. Vesp., 114; Polyb., I, 7, 9; I, 38, 5 etc.; βαρέως ἔχειν, P. Lond., 42, 29 (168 B.C.); βαρὺ ἡγεῖσθαι, Philo Leg. All., III, 90 etc.

dogs, Alciphr. Ep., 3, 11. But it can also be used of violent anger, Soph. Phil., 368; 3 Macc. 5:1, ὀργὴ βαρεῖα; and of violent hostility, Plat. Ap., 23a.

3. To βάρος as fulness or maturity there corresponds the adjectival "full of age" or the common LXX use for "numerous" (of the people, an army or a following). This does not appear in the NT.

4. The usage in relation to suffering is most common in the NT. Investigation shows that βαρύς, too, is most often used to denote that which presses heavily, or is burdensome or painful. This may be painful sickness, as in Soph. Phil., 1330; Philo Op. Mund., 125; P. Lond., 1676, 15 (6th cent. A.D.); or oppressive care, bad news, painful service, severe warfare, heavy affliction or misfortune. Thus the Jews in Ac. 25:7 bring before Festus βαρέα αἰτιώματα ("grievous complaints"). Cf. βαρυτέρα τιμωρία in Diod. S., XIII, 30, 7.

From the standpoint of biblical theology the passages which deal with freedom from the yoke of the Law are most important. a. In Mt. 23:4 Jesus accuses the Pharisees of binding and laying φορτία βαρέα, "heavy burdens," on the shoulders of men.

In illustration of this phrase, we may refer to φορτίον in Diod. S., XIII, 20, 1: τὴν εὐτυχίαν ὥσπερ βαρὺ φορτίον οὐ φέροντες. In ψ 37:4, of misdeeds, we have: ὡσεὶ φορτίον βαρὺ (A om) ἐβαρύνθησαν ἐπ' ἐμέ. Cf. also φόρτον, Philo Poster C, 148: βαρύτατον φόρτον (of the beast of burden). Most common is ἄχθος. This is first used physically: Philo Vit. Mos., I, 231: βαρύτατον ἄχθος (the fruits brought by the spies); Agric., 20, of work on the land; Deus Imm., 15, of the soul; Agric., 49: πολλαῖς ὑπακούειν ἀρχαῖς ἀναγκάζεσθαι βαρύτατον ἄχθος; of the burden of cares of state, Plant., 56. Migr. Abr., 14: βαρύτατον ἄχθος — that perspicacity is dulled by carnal desires. βάσταγμα is used in Jos. Ant., 19, 362: καὶ τελείῳ δ' οὖν εἶναι βαρὺ βάσταγμα βασιλείαν; βαρὺς ζυγός in 2 Chr. 10:4: ἀπὸ τοῦ ζυγοῦ αὐτοῦ τοῦ βαρέος οὗ ἔδωκεν ἐφ' ἡμᾶς (כָּבֵד, of Solomon); Sir. 40:1: ζυγὸς βαρὺς ἐπὶ υἱοὺς (א υἱοῖς) 'Αδάμ (of human tribulation); Jos. Ant., 8, 213. Orders or demands (προστάγματα, ἐπιτάγματα) are described as "heavy" in Polyb., I, 31, 7; XV, 8, 11; Philo Vit. Mos., I, 37; Conf. Ling., 92. λειτουργία βαρυτάτη is used of state taxes in BGU, 159, 4 (3rd cent. A.D.).

b. The same theme of liberation from the yoke of the Law underlies 1 Jn. 5:3. The phrase: ἐντολαὶ αὐτοῦ βαρεῖαι οὐκ εἰσίν, signifies removal of the category of difficult commands viewed by men as demanding extraordinary achievement. [3] Mt. 11:30 is important for the light it sheds, since it is the coming of Jesus which makes the change, as the continuation in 5:4 shows (→ βάρος B. 3). But in itself this reference is not enough, since in Mt. the contrast is between burdensome and light. The form and content of the saying are influenced by Dt. 30:11 ff., a passage often used by Philo. [4] As he sees it, the love of God as the sum of the commandments is not burdensome or complicated or exaggerated. He emphasises that especially the patriarchs, the embodiment of the laws of reason, prove that it is no great effort for those who have a ready mind to live according to written laws. As in Dt., so in 1 Jn. 5:3 there is reference to love of God. Love of God is essentially directed to the keeping of His commands. But if it is then said that these are not heavy, this is not an optimistically rational reference to human ability

---

[3] On the Rabb. distinction between מִצְוָה חֲמוּרָה and מִצְוָה קַלָּה = ἐντολὴ βαρεῖα, ἐντολὴ ἐλαφρά, cf. Str.-B., I, 901 ff. For 1 Jn. 5:3, cf. jKid., 61b, 58 (Str.-B., I, 902).
[4] Wnd. 1 Jn., ad loc.

and good will. The basis of the statement is that the one who is born of God overcomes in virtue of faith in the Son of God, who has already won the victory over the κόσμος, this κόσμος which threatens the keeping of the commands. The commands are not hard to keep because the believer can draw on the perfect triumph of Christ.

5. a. On the other hand, καὶ ἀφήκατε τὰ βαρύτερα τοῦ νόμου in Mt. 23:23 does not mean the harder commands as distinct from the easier, but the weightier as district from the trifling, such as those dealing with the tithing of herbs. We should compare the question as to the ἐντολὴ πρώτη πάντων in Mk. 12:28. This use of βαρύς corresponds, therefore, to the sense of βάρος which we have discussed under the complex of power (→ A. 5). [5]

βαρύς often means "forceful" or "significant," [6] not merely in relation to such concrete things as princes (Polyb., V, 55, 2) or cities (Polyb., I, 17, 5; I, 38, 7), but also to abstract things, Polyb., V, 14, 3 : μερίς of the most important share (praecipuus); Herodian Hist., II, 14, 3 : βαρυτάτην εὐδαιμονίαν.

b. In Ac. 20:29 εἰσελεύσονται λύκοι βαρεῖς εἰς ὑμᾶς refers to dangerous, rending wolves. Here βαρύς denotes the violent man.

Cf. Poll. Onom., V, 164; 2 Ch. 25:19 : ἡ καρδία σου ἡ βαρεῖα, "insolent"; 3 Macc. 6:5 of arrogant speech : βαρέα λαλοῦντα κόμπῳ καὶ θράσει.

† βαρέω.

1. βαρεῖσθαι [1] in the sense of being physically burdened, in the first instance without any suggestion of a basic view of earthly existence, is found in the NT

---

[5] In the Rabb., cf. the quotations in Str.-B., I, 901 f. (No. 2 under d and e), esp. S. Dt., 79 on 12:28. Cf. also Schl. Mt., 679.

[6] Philology supplies some important par. for this sense. The Sansk. gurú-, which means "imposing" as well as "heavy," is particularly used as a term of respect for teachers. The Lat. gravis is related etym., and denotes "severe," "dignified."

β α ρ έ ω. Anz., Subsidia, 10 f.; Moult.-Mill., 103 f. On 2 C. 5:4 : E. Teichmann, Die paulin. Vorstellungen von Auferstehung u. Gericht (1896); E. Haupt, "Einführung in das Verständnis der Briefe des Pls. an die Kor.," Dtsch. Ev. Bl. (1903), 107 ff.; E. Kühl, Über 2 C. 5:1-10 (1904); F. Tillmann, Die Wiederkunft Christi nach den paulin. Briefen (1909); K. Deissner, Auferstehungshoffnung und Pneumagedanke bei Pls. (1912); J. Weiss, Das Urchristentum (1917), 418 f.; Reitzenstein Hell. Myst., 356; W. Mundle, "Das Problem des Zwischenzustandes in dem Abschn. 2 K. 5:1-10," in Festg. f. A. Jülicher (1927), 93 ff. (where older lit. is also listed). Cf. also the Comm. of Heinrici, Schmiedel, Bousset, Bachmann, Wnd. and Ltzm., ad loc.

[1] βαρέω (esp. βεβαρημένος since Hom.) instead of βαρύνω is found already in Plato, Dion. Hal., Lucian, Herodot. For Atticising crit. of βαρέω, cf. Luc. Soloec., 7. Cf. further Schol. on Thuc., II, 16. Thom. Mag., p. 62, 15, Ritschl, and Suid. Except in Ex. 7:14 and 2 Macc. 13:9 the LXX uses only the older βαρύνω, and βαρέω only in βεβαρημένος (never βεβαρυσμένος); cf. Bl.-Debr. § 101, s.v.; Thackeray, I, 261. The NT, however, has only βαρέω except for Mk. 14:40 ℵ c ABKLN etc. and some later and obviously classicising emendations : Lk. 21:34 D H Method. Bas. Cyr. (βαρυνθῶσιν instead of βαρηθῶσιν, ℵ ABCL etc.) and the replacement of ἠρνήσασθε by ἐβαρύνατε in Ac. 3:14 in D d Ir. Aug. In Philo βαρέω is rare as in the LXX. Yet βαρέω has come right down into modern Gk. along with βαρύνω : G. N. Hatzidakis, Einleitung in die neugriech. Grammatik (1892), 396 (for the islands and the Peloponnese); A. Thumb, Handb. der neugriech. Volkssprache (1910), 310. In modern Gk. there are two trends : 1. act. βαρῶ, "strike" or "hit"; 2. dep. βαρειοῦμαι "to be satiated." Cf. βαρύνω "to trouble" and dep. (= βαρειοῦμαι). On βαρέεται, first used by Hippocr. Morb., 4, 49 (VII, 578, Littré), and βεβαρηώς instead of βεβαρημένος (Hom. Od., 3, 139), cf. Anz., 10.

at Mt. 26:43: ἦσαν γὰρ αὐτῶν οἱ ὀφθαλμοὶ βεβαρημένοι, and Mk. 14:40 CEFGH (→ n. 1.). Lk. expands ὕπνῳ to βεβαρημένοι in 9:32.

Cf. Anth. Pal., VII, 290: πυμάτῳ βεβαρημένου ὕπνῳ; Heliodor. Aeth., I, 7: καμάτῳ τε τῆς ὁδοιπορίας βαρούμενος.

The hortatory reference in Lk. 21:34 goes deeper. It speaks of the pressure of worldly desires and cares on the heart, to be resisted by disciples with resolute hope: προσέχετε δὲ ἑαυτοῖς μήποτε βαρηθῶσιν ὑμῶν αἱ καρδίαι ἐν κραιπάλῃ καὶ μέθῃ καὶ μερίμναις βιωτικαῖς. In this case we are not to think of the hardening of the heart as in LXX Ex. 7:14, but of the intoxication which drags it down and oppresses it. [2]

For this usage, cf. Hom. Od., 3, 139: οἴνῳ βεβαρηότες; 19, 122: βεβαρηότα με φρένας οἴνῳ; Plut. Mar., 19 (I, 416c): τὰ σώματα πλησμονῇ βεβαρημένοι; Plat. Symp., 203b of the drunkenness of Poros: βεβαρημένος ηὗδεν; Philo Ebr., 104: βεβαρημένων καὶ πεπιεσμένων οἴνῳ.

Much of the use of βαρύνεσθαι in the LXX does not recur in the NT. Thus we do not find "to afflict" (2 Macc. 9:9); "to torment" (Na. 3:15, βαρυνθήσῃ for כָּבֵד hithp); nor the common ἐβαρύνθη ὁ πόλεμος of the "outbreak of war" (Ju. 20:34 A; 1 Βασ. 31:3; 1 Ch. 10:3; 1 Macc. 9:17 (always כָּבֵד kal); nor "to rage," "to be severe" (Zech. 11:8: βαρυνθήσεται for קָצַר; Mal. 3:13: ἐβαρύνατε ἐπ' ἐμὲ τοὺς λόγους ὑμῶν, חָזַק, "You speak insolently against me"; 2 Macc. 13:9 A: τοῖς δὲ φρονήμασιν ὁ βασιλεὺς βεβαρημένος ἤρχετο, of violent hatred). Above all, we do not find the favourite ἐβαρύνθη ἡ χεὶρ ἐπί (Jos. 19:47a; Ju. 1:35; 1 Βασ. 5:3, 6; ψ 31:4, always in rendering of כָּבֵד kal).

2. a. The investigation of the NT conception of affliction, commenced in relation to βάρος, is carried an important stage further by the use of βαρεῖσθαι in 2 C. It is conceded quite undisguisedly in 2 C. 1:8 that the experience of affliction in Asia was beyond anything that could be borne in one's own strength: καθ' ὑπερβολὴν ὑπὲρ δύναμιν ἐβαρήθημεν. [3] On this occasion it is made clear that the strength to endure is not to be sought in one's own will or reserves (1:9). Those who are beset by θλῖψις, seeing their situation is so hopeless, cannot trust in themselves but only in the God who raises them from the dead (R. 4:17 f.). While in Epictetus (→ 560) βαρεῖσθαι is either denied or explained away by hypothetical thinking, the faith which despairs of itself here experiences deliverance again in the midst of βαρεῖσθαι. This is the norm as the lasting attitude of faith (καὶ ῥύσεται); an important place is left for intercession, but in such a way (v. 11) that the gift of grace which is sought leads finally to the glory and praise of God alone.

The discussion in 2 C. 5:4 digs deepest of all. For here affliction is shown to

---

[2] βαρύνειν is very common in the LXX for the hardening of the heart, esp. of Pharaoh, Ex. 7:14 BA; 8:15 (11); 9:7; 8:32 (28); 9:34; 10:1 A; 1 Βασ. 6:6, always in transl. of כָּבֵד kal or hiph. The same idea of hardening or dulling is found in respect of the dimming of the eyes in 1 Βασ. 3:2: βαρύνεσθαι (כָּהָה) and the making deaf of the ears in Is. 59:1; 33:15: βαρύνων (אָטַם); Zech. 7:11: τὰ ὦτα αὐτῶν ἐβάρυναν τοῦ μὴ εἰσακούειν (כָּבֵד hiph); Sir. 21:24: ὁ δὲ φρόνιμος βαρυνθήσεται ἀτιμίᾳ (א AC: -ίαν).
[3] Cf. Plut. Aem. Paul., 34 (I, 273d): βεβαρημένων τὰ πρόσωπα πένθει. P. Tebt., I, 23, 5 (c. 119 B.C.): καθ' ὑπερβολὴν βεβαρυμμένοι; P. Oxy., III, 525, 3 (early 2nd cent. A.D.): καθ' ἑκάστην ἡμέραν βαροῦμαι δι' αὐτόν. Cf. also Moult.-Mill., 103. In the NT we never find βαρεῖσθαι with sins (ψ 37:4; Σ Gn. 18:20; Is. 1:4).

be a divinely willed expression of our as yet imperfect existence as one of hope : καὶ γὰρ οἱ ὄντες ἐν τῷ σκήνει στενάζομεν βαρούμενοι. As in R. 8, Paul is not ashamed of anxious sighing. He sees in it a symptom of life in the Spirit (v. 5). If we cannot deal fully with all the eschatological questions relating to this passage, we can at least say that there is little probability of any basic change in Paul's view of the *parousia* as between 1 C. and 2 C.[4] For all the problems, there is little doubt as to the basis of the sighing. The ἐκδύσασθαι should not[5] be related to the φθορά of the non-Christian, for in Paul the foundation is assurance of σωτηρία. The sighing is caused rather by shrinking before the act of physical dying, which seems to be the immediate possibility awaiting the soul rather than reclothing at the *parousia* (v. 4).[6] If instead we refer the στενάζειν to fear of being without a body in the intervening state,[7] this makes of the utterance a rather querulous[8] reflection, and also seems to involve a strange eschatological specialisation. In any case, the assumption of being without a body in the intervening state is exegetically insecure. The εἴ γε καὶ ἐνδυσάμενοι οὐ γυμνοὶ εὑρεθησόμεθα is quite satisfactorily explained by reference to the purely judicial divine judgment which tests the truth of his pneumatic being, of his fellowship with Christ.[9] If this is correct, then the point of the βαρεῖσθαι is that for all his assurance of faith Paul still shrinks before death as an expression of this present imperfect existence. The earnest of the Spirit is the only guarantee of perfection. It is on this ground that he who is so triumphantly born again in the power of Christ can still honestly admit the oppressive yoke of death.

b. The uniqueness of this attitude is shown by comparison with similar utterances in Hellenism or in Judaism which came under Hellenistic influence. Wis. 9:15 : φθαρτὸν γὰρ σῶμα βαρύνει ψυχὴν καὶ βρίθει τὸ γεῶδες σκῆνος νοῦν πολυφρόντιδα, is very like 2 C. 5:1 ff.[10] even in its conjunction of βαρύνειν and σκῆνος. Yet this similarity does not overcome the basic fact that there is here a Hellenistic cleavage or dualism between σῶμα and ψυχή or νοῦς. In Paul it is the new pneumatic orientation which both brings out the true severity of the cleavage and yet reveals a power which increases hope. The same is to be said of Philo, e.g., Migr. Abr., 204, where the νοῦς is burdened (βαρύνουσα) and overwhelmed by expenditure in satisfaction of the senses. A similar statement may be found in Jos. Bell., 7, 346 (→ βάρος B. 1).[11]

The view of βαρεῖσθαι in Epictetus claims independent consideration. According to Diss., I, 1, 15 it denotes the state in which we forge heavy fetters out the body, possessions, love of places, the family, friends, society and all the outward things which do not belong to us but are so attractive (βαρούντων, I, 9, 14 f.). The closer the attachment, the more these things drag us down. The required conquest of them takes place through skilful accommodation, through sitting loose to

---

[4] So finally Wnd. 2 K.

[5] Mundle, *op. cit.*, 104.

[6] A simple reference to the process of suffering and death (Haupt) hardly does justice to the context.

[7] Kühl, Lietzmann and most commentators.

[8] Wnd. 2 C., 161.

[9] Cf. Reitzenstein Hell. Myst., 356. It makes no difference whether we read εἴπερ with the Alex. text or εἴγε with the Western. Either way a precondition is mentioned.

[10] E. Grafe, "Das Verhältnis der paulin. Schriften zur Sap. Sal" in *Theol. Abh. f. C. v. Weizsäcker* (1892), 251 ff.

[11] Of later writers, cf. Porphyr. Abst., I, 54 (the burden of unnecessary wealth).

them, through patiently remaining at the post to which one is commanded (I, 9, 14 f.), through autosuggestive exercise of the will, leading after the model of hypothetical deduction to the persuasion that the evil does not really exist (I, 25, 17), that basically it is not the thing itself which oppresses us, but our own view of it, which can be controlled (II, 16, 24). βαρεῖσθαι is thus rejected as a state unworthy of the sage. The concern of the Stoic is merely with the psychological question whether or not he has an awareness of oppression in his own spiritual life. All στενάζειν is rejected as inward bondage. The concern of Paul, however, is with the final question of the new existence, and it is recognised that this is provisionally linked with the mortal body. By faith in Christ and the hope of the parousia εἶναι ἐν τῷ σκήνει is given its determination, tension and solution at one and the same time. Hence Paul does not need to deny βαρεῖσθαι, for in faith and hope he is certain of the newness of life.

3. In 1 Tm. 5:16: μὴ βαρείσθω ἡ ἐκκλησία, the reference is to the financial burdening of the church. There are many instances of this usage: Ditt. Or., 595, 16 (174 A.D.): ἵνα μὴ τὴν πόλιν βαρῶμεν; of the burden of taxes: Polyb., V, 94, 9: ὑπὲρ τοῦ μὴ βαρυνθήσεσθαι ταῖς εἰσφοραῖς. Jos. Bell., 2, 273: (Albinus) τὸ πᾶν ἔθνος ἐβάρει ταῖς εἰσφοραῖς; Dio C., 46, 32: ταῖς εἰσφοραῖς βαρούμενοι; Ditt. Or., 669, 5 (1st century A.D.): μὴ βαρυνομένην καιναῖς καὶ ἀδίκοις εἰσπράξεσι. P. Giess., I, 4, 11 (118 A.D.): αὐτοί τε βεβαρημένοι πολλῶι χρόνωι δημοσίοις (costs of state); of the burden of the account: P. Oxy., I, 126, 8 (572 A.D.): βαρέσαι τὸ ἐμὸν ὄνομα. [12]

Schrenk

βάσανος, βασανίζω,
βασανισμός, βασανιστής

---

1. The βάσανος originally belongs to the calling of the inspector of coins. It is linked with the Heb. root בחן ("to test") and the Egyptian *bhn* ("basalt"). According to K. Sethe,[1] *bhn* is the word which underlies the Heb. בחן [2] and the Gk. βάσανος. βάσανος is generally accepted to be a loan word. βασανίτης is most closely related to it. Βασανίτου λίθου ὄρος is the mountain of the *bhn* stone. R. Herzog[3] thinks that he may deduce from the etymological development that the *ars spectandi*, the testing of gold and silver as media of exchange by the proving stone, was first developed by the Babylonians,[4] then came to the Aramaeans and Hebrews by way of Lydia (Λυδία λίθος [Bacchyl. Fr., 14, 1, Blass]; βάσανος, Bacchyl., 8, 58), and from them to the Gks. In non-biblical Gk. βάσανος is a commercial expression, or is used in relation to government. It then acquires the meaning of the checking of calculations, which develops naturally out of the basic sense of βάσανος, βασανίζειν (P. Oxy., 58, 25 [288 A.D.]).

---

[12] Cf. also Preisigke Wört. and Moult.-Mill. *s.v.* for further examples.

β ά σ α ν ο ς κτλ. [1] Pauly-W., III, 39, *s.v.* Βασανίτου λίθου ὄρος.

[2] בחן is especially used of the testing of metal. Cf. Jer. 6:27 ff., where בָּחוֹן is used in the sense of "one who tests" or "one who tests metal" (בָּחֹן = δοκιμαστής, LXX).

[3] R. Herzog, "Aus der Geschichte des Bankwesens im Altertum," *Abh. d. Giessener Hochschulgesellsch.,* 1 (1919), 29 f.

[4] According to Herzog the stems בחן and צרף are synon.; the derivat. of the stem *srp* are borrowed from Accadian. But צרף means "to purify" rather than "to test." Thus the thesis of Herzog is not solidly grounded. V. on צרף and *srp* F. Delitzsch, *Assyr. Handwörterbuch* (1896), 574, *s.v.*

In the spiritual sphere it has the figur. sense, which is closely related to the original concrete meaning, of a means of testing (Anth. Pal., VII, 54 : ἀνδρῶν κρινομένων ἐν βασάνῳ σοφίης).

The word then undergoes a change in meaning. The original sense fades into the background. βάσανος now comes to denote "torture" or "the rack," espec. used with slaves (P. Lille, I, 29, 22; Ditt. Syll.³, 356, 12). βάσανος occurs in the sense of "torment" in Theocr. Idyll., 13, p. 13, 5, Meineke ; Thom. Mag., p. 94, 4, Ritschl ; Demetr. Eloc., 201, 4. An inscription from Cyprus (Salamis), BCH, 51 (1927), 148, 18, contains the malediction : ἐν βασάνοις ἀπόλοιτο. Vet. Val., IV, 13, p. 182, 19, Kroll has a reference to torments of soul (ψυχικὰς βασάνους). [5]

The change in meaning is best explained if we begin with the object of treatment. If we put men instead of metal or a coin, the stone of testing become torture or the rack. The metal which has survived the testing stone is subjected to harsher treatment. Man is in the same position when severely tested by torture. In the testing of metal an essential role was played by the thought of testing and proving genuineness. The rack is a means of showing the true state of affairs. In its proper sense it is a means of testing and proving, [6] though also of punishment. Finally, even this special meaning was weakened and only the general element of torment remained.

2. In the LXX [7] the word βάσανος and deriv. are seldom found except in the originally Gk. books, or those preserved only in Gk. A corresponding basis in the Heb. is lacking in almost every case. The word group is most common in 4 Macc. With βάσανος and βασανίζειν we here find βασανισμός, βασανιστήριον (*tormentum*) and προβασανίζειν. In general two groups of meaning may be discerned : a. testing afflictions which the righteous have to suffer in the world at the hands of the ungodly ; and b. judicial sufferings which by reason of his conduct the ungodly will receive from the righteous in time and eternity. The martyrdom which the righteous have to suffer can consist in spiritual or physical torments (Wis. 2:19). In a few passages (e.g., Wis. 3:1) βάσανος is to be understood eschatologically. In Ez. 12:18, where we have βάσανος with ὀδύνη and θλῖψις, it has the meaning of eschatological affliction. In Ez. 32:24, 30 βάσανος refers to future torments. In Ez. 3:20; 7:19 (Heb. מִכְשׁוֹל), the LXX has altered the original meaning of the text; βάσανος is suffering in the sense of punishment. There is a similar alteration in 1 Βασ. 6:3, 4, 8, 17, where the Heb. has אָשָׁם and refers to guilt to be atoned, whereas the LXX speaks of trouble for which payment must be made. The same is probably true in Ez. 16:52, 54; 32:24, 30 (Heb. כְּלִמָּה), where instead of shame or disgrace the LXX has affliction in the sense of punishment. The reference in Sir. 30:35 (33:27) is to the punishment of a wicked slave. Here στρέβλη (στρέβλαι καὶ βάσανοι) is par. to βάσανος. In one passage (Wis. 2:19) βάσανος is par. to ὕβρις (mockery).

With βασανίζειν we sometimes have the basic meaning of testing genuineness, as in Sir. 4:7. The predominant meaning, however, is "to torment" or "to torture." In Wis. 11:9 (10) βασανίζειν and πειράζειν are set in juxtaposition.

Of the other translators 'Α in Qoh. 1:18 and 2:23 has βάσανος [8] for מַכְאוֹב, whereas the LXX uses ἄλγημα. In 'Ιερ. 20:2 Σ according to Jerome has βασανιστήριον *sive* στρεβλωτήριον, which in the LXX is found only in 4 Macc.; the LXX and Θ here have καταράκτης. At Prv. 10:8 (LXX : ὑποσκελίζειν) Σ has βασανίζειν, obviously in the sense of punishing with plagues ; cf. 'Α : δέρω (δαρήσεται); the לִבֵּט (יִלָּבֵט) of the Heb., however, means to bring to pass. Θ at 1 Βασ. 15:33 has ἐβασάνισεν in the sense of penal torments ('Α Σ : διέσπασεν, LXX : ἔσφαξε, Heb. שִׁסַּף).

---

[5] Cf. also Vett. Val., IV, 25, p. 201, 32; V, 2, p. 211, 28, Kroll.
[6] Cf. the common NT thesis that buffetings and sufferings serve to test our faith.
[7] We are indebted to G. Bertram for the section on the LXX.
[8] In 2 Ch. 6:29 Cod. 93 also has βάσανος for מַכְאוֹב.

3. βάσανος occurs in the NT only in Mt. and Lk. At Mt. 4:24 νόσοι and βάσανοι are co-ordinated. [9] At Lk. 16:23, 28 the plur. βάσανοι refers to the torments of hell. [10] Hell is called ὁ τόπος τῆς βασάνου.

βασανίζειν means strictly "to test by the proving stone" (βάσανος), i.e., "to rub against it," "to test the genuineness of," "to examine or try," then "to apply means of torture to find the truth," "to harry or torture" in a hearing or before a tribunal. [11] In the NT it is found only in the general sense of "to plague" or "to torment." The centurion's servant lying sick of a palsy is grievously tormented (Mt. 8:6). [12] To those possessed with demons encounter with Jesus is a tormenting experience (Mt. 8:29; Mk. 5:7; Lk. 8:28). At Rev. 12:2 βασανίζειν, like βάσανος in Anth. Pal., IX, 311, is used of the pains of labour. [13] At 2 Pt. 2:8 there is reference to the inner torment of soul at the sight of the acts of the ungodly; Lot suffers as he sees the licentiousness of the inhabitants of Sodom. [14] This is the only passage in the NT in which βασανίζειν is connected with the suffering of the righteous. In Rev. βασανίζειν is used of the torments of the last time. At Mt. 14:24; Mk. 6:48 it is used to depict the serious situation of the disciples on the lake; their boat is hard pressed by the waves. [15] The suggestion that βασανίζεσθαι denotes the torture of the disciples rowing [16] is artificial. In both passages it must be taken passively. [17]

βασανισμός occurs only in Rev. In 9:5 it is used actively of the torment which will come on men as the first woe after the fifth trumpet. In 18:7 ff., however, it is used passively and denotes the suffering of Babylon when deprived of its power. This torment strikes the once powerful city in retribution for its wicked conduct.

βασανιστής does not occur in the NT in the original sense of a "tester" but it is found once in Mt. 18:34 in the sense of a "tormentor." [18]

Schneider

---

[9] Cf. P. Leid., 7, 26 ff. (Preis. Zaub., II, 102; XIII, 290), where we have together ἐν βασάνοις, ἐν ἀνάγκαις, and ἐν ὥραις.

[10] Cf. the similar linking of κόλασις and βάσανος in P. Oxy., 840, 6, βάσανος having the sense of penal torment.

[11] Thuc. VIII, 92, 2. Thom. Mag., p. 62, 12 ff.; 93, 17; 94, 2, Ritschl. Cf. also Preisigke Wört., 257; and further pap. material in Moult.-Mill., II, 104, s.v. βασανίζω.

[12] δεινῶς βασανιζόμενος. Cf. Ps.-Luc. Asin., 25: τῆς βασάνου τὸ δεινόν. V. also Luc. Soloec., 6; Thom. Mag., p. 62, 13, Ritschl; Jos. Ant., 2, 14; 9, 101; 12, 413.

[13] On βασανιζομένη τεκεῖν (Rev. 12:2), cf. T. Jeb., 9, 4: האשה שמקשה לוולד (simil. S. Nu., 76 on 10:9) and Gn. 35:17.

[14] Cf. also Herm. m., 4, 2, 2.

[15] On βασανίζεσθαι (of the ship), cf. S. Nu., 76 on 10:9: "When a ship is tossed to and fro" (מְטֹרֶפֶת = βασανιζόμενος).

[16] Zn. Mt. on 14:24 and B. Weiss Mk. on 6:48.

[17] Kl. Mk. on 6:48.

[18] Cf. Thom. Mag., p. 93, 17; 94, 4, Ritschl.

βασιλεύς, βασιλεία, βασίλισσα, βασιλεύω,
συμβασιλεύω, βασίλειος, βασιλικός

A. βασιλεύς in the Greek World.

βασιλεύς[1] denotes the king as the lawful and usually hereditary priestly ruler of the people in the good sense. In later political practice and theory he was distinguished from the τύραννος as an usurper.[2] In the well-known verses in Od., 19, 108 ff. Homer gives us a mythical picture and ἔπαινος of the good king and associated blessings. For the justice or otherwise of the βασιλεύς works itself out on the people inasmuch as the people must either suffer or flourish and prosper with him. The power of the king is traced back to Zeus (τιμὴ ἐκ Διός ἐστιν, Il., 2, 197); this connection is especially denoted by the common epithet διοτρεφής (Il., 2, 196 etc.), i.e., "sustained by Zeus." In Hesiod, where the βασιλεύς is essentially regarded in judicial terms, we are given a developed picture of the royal wisdom which is the norm of knowledge. Not merely bards but kings

---

βασιλεύς κτλ. On A.: Pauly-W., III (1899), *s.v.* Basileus; E. Lohmeyer, *Christuskult und Kaiserkult* (1919), 11 ff. and n.; Deissmann LO, 310 f. There is a histor. and systemat. analysis of the 5 different forms of the βασιλεύς or βασιλεία concept in the class. Gk. period by Aristot. in Pol., III, 14, p. 1284b, 35 ff. On B.: H. Gressmann, *Der Messias* (1929); E. Sellin, *Die isr.-jüd. Heilandserwartung* (1909); *Der at.liche Prophetismus* (1912); L. Dürr, *Ursprung u. Ausbau der isr.-jüd. Heilandserwartung* (1925); S. Mowinckel, *Psalmenstudien* II: *Das Thronbesteigungsfest Jahwes u. der Ursprung der Eschatologie* (1922); O. Eissfeldt, "Jahwe als König," ZAW, 50 (1928), 81 ff. A. v. Gall, Βασιλεία τοῦ θεοῦ (1926); M. Buber, *Königtum Gottes = Das Kommende, Untersuchungen zur Entstehungsgesch. des messianischen Glaubens,* I (1932); R. Kittel, *Die hellenist. Mysterienreligion und das AT* (1924); Bousset-Gressm., 222 ff. On C.: Dalman WJ, I, 75-119 (cf. ²[1930], 375 ff.); Str.-B., I, 172-184 etc.; Moore, I, 401, 432 ff.; II, 346 f.; 371-375. On E.: Cf. the books mentioned. Of the vast lit., esp. on the NT βασιλεία, we can only mention the most recent works. Naturally the concept of the kingdom of God plays a decisive role in all studies of early Christianity, and esp. of Jesus. Cf. P. Feine, *Theol. d. NT*⁵ (1931), 73 ff. (with full bibl.); K. L. Schmidt, "Jesus Christus," RGG², III, 110-151. For more specialised lit, cf. W. Mundle, "Reich Gottes," *ibid.,* IV, 1817-1822. In discussion, cf. the report of the first British and German Theological Conference at Canterbury: "Das Wesen des Reiches Gottes und seine Beziehung z. menschlichen Gesellschaft," ThBl, 6 (1927), 113 ff. (NT contributions by C. H. Dodd, E. C. Hoskyns, G. Kittel, A. E. J. Rawlinson, K. L. Schmidt). Of recent monographs, cf. G. Holstein, *Die Grundlagen des ev. Kirchenrechts* (1928), 5 ff.; W. Michaelis, *Täufer, Jesus, Urgemeinde, die Predigt Jesu vom Reiche Gottes vor und nach Pfingsten* (1928); J. Köster, *Die Idee d. Kirche beim Ap. Pls.* (1928); G. Gloege, *Reich Gottes und Kirche im NT* (1929); H. E. Weber, *"Eschatologie" und "Mystik" im NT* (1930); H. D. Wendland, *Die Eschatologie des Reiches Gottes bei Jesus* (1931).

[1] It is now generally accepted that βασιλεύς is a loan word from an Aegean, pre-Gk. language, *v.* Debrunner, *Reallex. für Vorgesch.,* IV, 2 (1926), 526. For earlier etym. explanations, *v.* Pauly-W., 55 f.

[2] On this contrast cf. Aristot. Eth. Nic., VIII, 12, p. 1160b, 3 and the formulation in Suidas, *s.v.*: βασιλεὺς μὲν γὰρ ἐκ προγόνων κατὰ διαδοχὴν ἔχει τὴν ἀρχὴν ἐπὶ ῥητοῖς λαβὼν πέρασι· τύραννος δέ, ὃς τὴν ἀρχὴν βιαίως σφετερίζεται. The antithesis does not apply to the earlier period, for the two words were often used as synon., and it was only with the emergence of Gk. democracy and its contrasting of νόμος and τύραννος that τύραννος acquired the bad odour which still clings to it to-day. Cf. Pindar, who addresses Hieron as βασιλεύς in Olymp., 1, 23; Pyth., 3, 70; and as τύραννος, Pyth., 3, 85. Cf. K. Stegmann v. Pritzwald, *Zur Gesch. der Herrscherbezeichnungen von Homer bis Plato* (1930), 93, 136 (Herodot.), 156 f. (Isocrates).

as well are inspired by the Muses: Calliope βασιλεῦσιν ἅμ' αἰδοίοισιν ὀπηδεῖ, Theog., 80. Infallible utterance (ἀσφαλέως ἀγορεύειν, 86) is the ἱερὴ δόσις of the Muses to kings. Linked with this Greek ideal of kingship is the philosophical discussion of the nature of the ideal βασιλεύς[3] in Plato's Politicus. Knowledge of the ideas is a royal art, and the man who has it is the royal man (Polit., 292e; cf. the famous statement in Plat. Resp., V, 473d: ἐὰν μὴ ... ἢ οἱ φιλόσοφοι βασιλεύσωσιν ἐν ταῖς πόλεσιν ἢ οἱ βασιλεῖς τε νῦν λεγόμενοι καὶ δυνάσται φιλοσοφήσωσι γνησίως ... οὐκ ἔστι κακῶν παῦλα ... ταῖς πόλεσι, δοκῶ δ' οὐδὲ τῷ ἀνθρωπίνῳ γένει ...). Reacting against a long process of development, Plato is also the forerunner of Hellenism with its very different concept of the king. "There arises the ideal figure of the benevolent king[4] moving god-like above men and sustaining them as the shepherd his sheep. He knows no law but the personal one of his own will, which is not subject to a social order; and his will is the norm, not merely of a particular land or state, but of all things in general. The nature and task of the king may be summed up in the fact that he is a benefactor to the whole world."[5] From these philosophical ideas of the 4th century there developed, under the dominating impress of Alexander the Great, the monarchy of Hellenism. The early Greek idea of the divinity of a politically creative personality linked up in Hellenism with the views of divine kingship current among different civilised peoples of the Orient. Thus βασιλεύς comes to denote the Hellenistic God-king, who after the Persian pattern might be called βασιλεὺς μέγας or even sometimes βασιλεὺς βασιλέων, as, for example, Antiochus I of Commagene: βασιλεὺς μέγας Ἀντίοχος θεός ..., Ditt. Or., 383, 1, and later the Roman Emperor.[6] The βασιλεία of such rulers is an ἀνυπεύθυνος ἀρχή (Suid., s.v.).

> Alongside the use of βασιλεύς for earthly or divinised kings the word is also used of the ancient gods, esp. of Zeus as the θεῶν βασιλεύς or the βασιλεύς absolutely, Hes. Theog., 886; Op., 668, both as an epithet and as a cultic name, IG, VII, 3073, 90, Lebadeia; Ditt. Syll.³, 1014, 110, Erythrae. For other βασιλεύς deities (e.g., Hades in Aesch. Pers., 627; IG, I, 872; Poseidon, Apollo, Dionysus, Heracles), cf. Pauly-W., 82.

Kleinknecht

B. מֶלֶךְ and מַלְכוּת in the OT.

מֶלֶךְ is a common Semitic word from the verb מָלַךְ. The original meaning of the root is doubtful ("possessor" or "arbiter"). It is seldom used metaph. in the OT (Job 18:14).

1. It denotes national or civic monarchy. In Israel the monarchy arose under Philistine pressure. Saul, who in the first instance was a charismatic leader like

---

[3] On the Platonic ideal, v. G. Heintzeler, "Das Bild des Tyrannen bei Platon," *Tüb. Beitr. z. Altertumswissensch.*, 3 (1927), 81 ff. and *passim*.

[4] εὐεργέτης is a favourite and striking name for the Hellenistic kings; Antigonus and Demetrius, for example, are celebrated as θεοὶ σωτῆρες καὶ εὐεργέται.

[5] E. Lohmeyer, *op. cit.*, 12. Cf. again Plat. Polit., 267d and 275b; or Aristotle's picture of the ideal ruler who cannot be set under the νόμοι because he himself is νόμος, Pol., III, 13, p. 1284a, 13, and also of the ideal παμβασιλεία, *ibid.*, III, 10, p. 1225b, 32 ff. On this pt., cf. E. Meyer, *Kl. Schr.*, I² (1924), 289 f.; again Xenoph. Cyrop., VIII, 2, 14, in which the office of the king is compared with that of the shepherd. For examples of the resultant Stoic and Cynic concept of the king, cf. Lohmeyer, *op. cit.*, 48 f., n. 28, 29.

[6] For its use as a title and divine predicate of Hellenistic rulers at the time of the transition from B.C. to A.D., v. Deissmann LO, 310 f.

others before him, was chosen to be king over Israel. After his death his captain David first became king of Judah and then of Israel, which in his person was thus united with Judah. David ruled the two kingdoms from his new royal capital of Jerusalem, and protected the complicated national structure from disintegration by substituting a dynasty for the previous *ad hoc* designation of leaders by Yahweh. The definitive religious legitimation of the house of David he found in the Davidic covenant (2 S. 7 and 23:1-7) which Yahweh had concluded with himself and his successors. After the dissolution of the personal union with the death of Solomon, there were only shortlived dynasties in the Northern Kingdom and the designation of the king by Yahweh again became predominant. In Judah, however, the house of David occupied the throne for 400 years, and in theory the line was followed even further from the genealogical standpoint. [7]

The relationship of the monarchy to the world of religious thought in Israel is determined by the circumstance that the monarchy came at a time when the faith of Israel had already developed strongly along its own original lines. Thus, in contrast to most oriental peoples, it had not developed the monarchy as an institution alongside religion. The monarchy was not a basic element in its religion. It was brought into secondary connection with an established religious heritage. Yahwism brought to bear upon it an independent criticism and very definite claims, yet also adopted it with some degree of tension into its faith and especially its hope.

At oriental courts, where a divine-human person stood at the centre, the presuppositions were present for the fashioning of a distinctive courtly language, i.e., of a style of addressing the king according to tradition and etiquette, of greeting him on his mounting the throne, of extolling him in exaggerated felicitations and songs, etc. There thus developed a definite stock of stereotyped titles, comparisons, epithets and styles of address, and we can see clearly how strongly Israel, too, shared these common oriental forms. [8] If in the so-called Royal Psalms (Ps. 2; 20 f.; 45; 72; 101; 110; 132) divine sonship and the ends of the earth are assured to the king, if he is magnified as the king with whom a new era of peace and righteousness dawns, this shows us that Israel has adopted many thoughts and formulations and incorporated them into its circle of Yahwistic ideas. The king, who according to ancient ideas embodied the people, was necessarily in Israel a preeminent object of the gracious promises of Yahweh. Nevertheless, it is an important truth that Israelite religion remained stronger than these adopted forms. The king was still a man. There is in the OT no hint of the deification which lay at the heart of the court-styles of Babylon and Egypt. [9]

2. The word is also used for the Redeemer King. A sharp distinction is to be made between even the most extravagant statements of the courtly language of Israel and faith in the Messiah. None of the Royal Psalms is Messianic, for the ruler is always conceived to be present, and the reference is to present enemies. There is no indication of eschatological expectation of a Royal Deliverer. Nevertheless, as we can now see, the language of court forms the bridge to faith in the Messiah. The whole complex of religious and political ideas linked with the

---

[7] Cf. A. Alt, *Die Staatenbildung der Israeliten in Palästina, Leipziger Reformationsprogramm* (1930).

[8] Perhaps through the medium of older traditions from Canaanite Jerusalem, cf. Ps. 110.

[9] The one relic of this view which escaped the strict censorship is in Ps. 45:7. The declarations of divine sonship are formulae of adoption.

empirical king ; what was expected of him ; how he was addressed ; what wonderful deeds were ascribed to him — all these form the soil for Messianic belief.
The connection is natural, for the expected king was of the house of David. Yet
it is still a question how the eschatological element came into the simple language
of court. Thus far there has been no satisfactory explanation of the rise in Israel
of this mysterious projection into the ἔσχατον. [10] We must never forget that there
is no similar eschatology, no comparable expectation of a Deliverer King at the
end of the age, in Babylon or Egypt, the classical lands of courtly address.

If Messianic belief was formally nourished by the world of courtly formulae,
materially the true point of connection, or starting-point, was the person of David
and especially the Davidic covenant (2 S. 7). It was not David who was to build
a house for Yahweh ; Yahweh would build David a house, and his monarchy
would be for ever. This was a great promise which, it was increasingly seen, still
awaited its full realisation in a manner worthy of Yahweh. It could not fail ; if it
did not correspond to the present, it must be projected into the future. Thus the
hope of salvation rests on the restoration of the house of David, which in Amos
(9:11) is implicitly linked with the still unfulfilled prophecy of Nathan (2 S. 7).

If David is thus to be seen as the *terminus a quo* for the awakening of faith in
the Messiah, the hope still has elements whose seeds are not to be found in the
empirical monarchy. Already in the difficult prophecy of Gen. 49:8 ff. there are
sounded paradisial motifs, as also in Am. (9:11-15). These are not to be taken as
an unimportant symbolical form, for they occur most strongly of all in the prophet
of the Messiah *par excellence*, namely, Isaiah. The shoot of the stump of Jesse
awaited in Is. 9 and 11 introduces a new aeon [11] of righteousness and paradisial
peace. This is preceded by the destruction of his enemies. He is a being endowed
with supernatural gifts. A similar expectation of the scion of David who brings
deliverance is found in Micah (5:1 ff.). [12] Less vivid, but more clearly delineated,
is Jeremiah's hope for the branch (23:5 f.) or Ezekiel's for the tender twig (17:22 ff.;
34:23 f.; 37:24 f.). Deutero-Isaiah regarded the Persian Cyrus (Is. 45:1 ff.) and
Zechariah the Davidic Zerubbabel (6:9 ff.) as the king of the last time. This
projection of the Messianic belief upon contemporary historical figures denotes an
important change in eschatological conception. With the failure of such hopes,
Messianic voices became very rare ; they were hardly heard at all in the post-
canonical literature [13] and reappeared only in the period directly prior to the NT.

Apart from the enthusiastic phraseology of courtly style and the specific
eschatological element, both of which characterise Messianic belief in Israel, we

---

[10] The best is still that of Dürr, 52 f., namely, that Israel's unique view of God, its belief
in the strong and trustworthy God who can help Israel, is the root of the religious expectation.

[11] עַד is "aeon," cf. R. Kittel, Hell. Mysterienrel., 73 ff.

[12] Here we see plainly opposition to Jerusalem, which is not only not mentioned, but
which is to be destroyed, so that the Davidic dynasty will again originate in Bethlehem.

[13] The Messianic hope seems to have displayed remarkable vitality in the Levitical
circles which gave rise to the Books of Chronicles, cf. G. v. Rad, *Geschichtsbild des chronist.
Werkes* (1930), 119 ff. Zech. 9:9 f. is hard to date. In the symbol. material in Da. 7:13
there is reference to a Messiah, but the author has reshaped it. The Servant Songs of
Dt.-Is. do not refer to a Messiah. For a recent discussion, cf. J. Fischer, *Wer ist der Ebed
in den Perikopen Jes. 42 ...?* (1922); ZAW, 47 (1925), 90 ff.; 48 (1926), 242 ff.; 50 (1928),
156 ff.; 51 (1929), 255 ff. In any case, the OT never uses the title מָשִׁיחַ for the King of
the last time.

have important remnants of mythological ideas which were certainly not introduced by the prophets and which it is very difficult to trace back to older Israelite belief. In particular, the notion of the pre-temporal existence of this Redeemer King [14] and the linking of this figure with an aeon of paradisial fruitfulness suggest that non-Israelite mythical [15] elements concerning a returning king of the past or the first man of Paradise have fused with the strong promises of the Davidic covenant. If the expectations linked with the Messiah take many forms, all witnesses are agreed that the Messiah will be for His own people a figure of peace, and that His appearance will follow, though rather strangely it will not be related to, the wars and conquests which precede the Messianic era. The transition to the new aeon will not be won by Him; [16] He will be the Ruler in a paradisial aeon after the final conflict. Most of the witnesses to the coming of the Messiah avoid the title מֶלֶךְ; "it has an irreligious and much too human sound, suggesting force and suppression." [17] Most of the Messianic statements display hostility to the empirical monarchy.

3. A further concept is that of Yahweh as King. It is easy to see that the hope of a Messiah does not dominate the OT. Indeed, its appearances are comparatively isolated in relation to the whole. Better attested is faith in another supraterrestrial kingdom determining the present and the future, namely, that of Yahweh. The relationship of this sequence of thought to belief in a Messianic kingdom is difficult to reduce to a single formula. [18] It will not do to assume two independent traditions, for Isaiah, the most powerful Messianic prophet, also calls Yahweh a King (6:5), and the same is true of Micah and Jeremiah. On the other hand, the Psalter, to which the figure of the eschatological King is quite alien, has the most numerous and important references to the kingship of Yahweh. [19]

The application of the term מֶלֶךְ to the Godhead is common to all the ancient Orient (cf., in the immediate environs of Israel, Melkart, Milcom, Chemosh-melech); indeed, this usage is probably pre-Semitic. One of the best descriptions of the relationship between God and man is that of God as the Lord who demands obedience but in return gives help and protection. In Israel the emergence of this view may be fixed with some precision. As is only natural, references are first found only after the rise of the empirical monarchy; Nu. 33:21; Dt. 33:5; 1 K. 22:19 and Is. 6:5 are among the earliest.

The idea of Yahweh's kingship, however, is given a very different emphasis in the OT. Some statements underline the timeless element in the kingly being of Yahweh as this embraces equally both past and future as well as present (Ex. 15:18;

---

[14] Esp. Mic. 5:1; cf. Sellin, *Prophetismus,* 178 f.

[15] R. Kittel (*op. cit.,* 64 ff.) seeks the roots of the Isaianic view of the Messiah in the Egyptian Osiris myth.

[16] Is. 11:4 is hardly an exception, for without any weapon He miraculously fights His enemies with the breath of His mouth.

[17] W. Caspari, *Echtheit, Hauptbegriff u. Gedankengang der messianischen Weissagung Jes. 9* (1908), 14.

[18] Unfortunately this question has been almost completely ignored in the present lively discussion of OT eschatology. Caspari (*op. cit.,* 12 ff.) pertinently notes that the Messianic figure of Is. 9 is not an autonomous Ruler. Both שַׂר and יוֹצֵץ show that He is responsible to a higher figure, and thus a kind of vizier; in Jeremiah (and Ezekiel), however, the Messiah is מֶלֶךְ (cf. Jer. 23:5; Ez. 37:24).

[19] Here, as elsewhere, Deuteronomic theology takes an independent line, with no mention either of the kingship of Yahweh or of a Messianic hope.

1 S. 12:12; Ps. 145:11 ff.; 146:10). In others, the accent is placed on the element of expectation (Is. 24:23; 33:22; Zeph. 3:15; Ob. 21; Zech. 14:16 f.). The present alone cannot meet this claim, and the concept of the kingship of Yahweh is thus drawn increasingly into the stream of eschatology towards which it has an inherent tendency; [20] hope is set on the fact that Yahweh will show Himself to be the King. Nevertheless, even the most strongly eschatological utterances do not question the present kingship of Yahweh. There is expectation merely of the final manifestation of His total kingly power. A third group of statements is found in Psalms 47, 93, 96, 97 and 99, and possibly many others. In these the distinctive feature lies in the use of the verb מָלַךְ in relation to Yahweh (Yahweh has become King). The Psalms are coronation Psalms probably sung in the middle of a festival to celebrate cultically, and perhaps even dramatically, the enthronement of Yahweh. [21] These Psalms do not proclaim an eschatological event but a present reality experienced in the cult.

Only the final group contains a truly concrete view of the kingship of Yahweh, and the exponents of this cultic life may actually have felt that expectation of a King of the last time was incompatible with their belief. In contrast, the other statements belong to traditional poetic usage and can thus be linked relatively easily with faith in a coming Messiah. That the two lines of thought, which undoubtedly developed in original independence, could later come together quite peacefully, may be seen in Chronicles, which makes powerful use of the as yet unfulfilled promise to David. The meaning of the Davidic covenant as understood by the later Chronicler is that the Davidic King rules in the *malkut* of Yahweh (1 Ch. 17:14; 28:5; 29:23; 2 Ch. 9:8; 13:8).

In what the kingship of Yahweh consists the majority of passages do not tell us more precisely. Most of the hymnal salutations of Yahweh as King do not even tell us whether He is understood as King of Israel or King of the world. [22] Predominantly in the pre-exilic period He is described as the King of Israel, and, whether for the present or the future, help, deliverance, righteousness and joy are promised to His chosen people. [23] On the other hand, in the exilic and post-exilic period He is also described as King of the world. [24] The description of Yahweh as King impressively depicts His power, greatness and readiness to help, but this thought is so general, and so little related to the specific concept of "king," that there is little hesitation in combining it with other lines of thought. Thus Micah intermingles the idea of Yahweh as Shepherd (5:3) and Deutero-Isaiah introduces the parallelism of Creator, Redeemer and King (43:14 f.). The nature of the *malkut* of Yahweh is seldom delineated with any greater precision. It may be said, however, that it is always immanent. Even according to later pronouncements like Is. 24:23 and Zech. 14:9, 16 Yahweh rules over the whole earth, is enthroned in Jerusalem and is magnified by all nations (cf. Ob. 21).

---

[20] Eissfeldt, *op. cit.,* 96.

[21] Cf. Mowinckel, *Psalmenstudien,* II. Mowinckel, however, overestimates the importance of this festival, and the brilliant deduction of Isr. eschatology from it has been weakened by the more recent discussion in ZAW, 52 (1930), 267, n. 3.

[22] Cf. Jer. 46:18; 48:15; 51:57; Ps. 5:2; 24:7 ff.; Da. 4:34.

[23] Nu. 23:21; Jer. 8:19; Zeph. 3:15; Mi. 2:12 f.; 4:6 ff.; but also Is. 41:21; 43:15; 44:6.

[24] Jer. 10:7, 10 ff. (Jer. 10:1-16 hardly seems to be by Jeremiah); Zech. 14:9, 16 f.; Mal. 1:14; Ps. 22:28; 47:2, 7.

In recent years Martin Buber has dealt with this problem in his well documented work on the kingship of God.[25] His theses are artificial inasmuch as no general theological significance is attached to the attestation of Yahweh as *melek* in the OT, as he presupposes. Even if we do not follow Eissfeldt,[26] who regards Is. 6:5 as the first example, on the ground that he narrows the field unduly to lexical considerations, the fact remains that Yahweh is never called *melek* prior to the monarchy. There is certainly no exegetical basis in the text for regarding the Sinaitic covenant as a royal covenant. The description of Yahweh as King is usually found in hymnic flights, so that there is no cause to view it as representative of a basic attitude of faith. Buber contrasts the *malk*, the divine Leader, most sharply with Baal. If he had said Yahweh instead of *malk*, we could agree. But in all the serious conflict with Baal religion — we think of Hosea and Deuteronomy — where is any use made of the theological slogan that Yahweh is *malk*? Buber adduces passages which refer to Yahweh's leading of Israel, but this hardly gives us the theologoumenon *malk* in the accepted sense. The word is simply deprived of its specific force in the passages where it really belongs, i.e., in the cultic and eschatological sense.

4. מַלְכוּת. The noun מַלְכוּת is one of the few older Heb. abstract terms from which the many others come.[27] It is to be rendered "kingdom" or "kingship." There is a slight departure from the original sense when it is used with reference to a concrete sphere of power.[28]

Mostly in the OT the word מַלְכוּת is used in the secular sense of a political kingdom (1 S. 20:31; 1 K. 2:12). Prior to Daniel the religious world made little use of it. In analogy to the description of Yahweh as a מֶלֶךְ, His sphere of power is sometimes called His מַלְכוּת.[29] Small emendations of the original text in Chronicles form a smooth transition to the eschatological conception which became so important in the post-canonical writings. If David was confirmed in his מַמְלָכָה in 2 S. 7:16, מַמְלָכָה was here meant in a much more secular sense than in 1 Ch. 17:14, where David is shown to be set over Yahweh's מַלְכוּת. Again, in 1 Ch. 28:5 Solomon sits on the throne of the מַלְכוּת of Yahweh. Nevertheless, this way of speaking is not to be understood eschatologically. The Davidic kingdom is here conceived of as the מַלְכוּת of Yahweh and the descendants of David sit on the throne of Yahweh (1 Ch. 29:23; 2 Ch. 9:8). Yet the nuance is significant, for the Chronicler, who belonged to an age when the Davidic kingdom was only a distant memory, thereby displays a true, though not an eschatological, interest in the realisation of Yahweh's מַלְכוּת.

The sharp apocalyptic distinction between the present and the future aeon, first apparent in Daniel, carries with it a much more precise delineation of the kingdom

---

[25] M. Buber, *Königtum Gottes* (1932).

[26] *Op. cit.,* 104.

[27] L. Gulkowitsch, *Die Bildung von Abstraktbegriffen in den hebräischen Sprachgeschichte* (1931), *passim*. There is here a discussion of the possible derivation of the word from official Accadian terminology, 130 f.

[28] מַמְלָכָה differs only slightly in meaning from מַלְכוּת, except that there is less yielding of the abstract reference to the institutional side of monarchy (עִיר הַמַּמְלָכָה, בֵּית מַמְלָכָה) for royal city, national temple, 1 S. 27:5; Am. 7:13). In the religious sense all Israel is required to be a kingdom of priests, esp. in Ex. 19:6, though there is here no particular emphasis on מַמְלָכָה as such. (Cf. a par. saying in Nu. 11:29: "Would that all the people were prophets!") However, it certainly means "kingdom." In the true religious sense it is found only at Ps. 22:28 and Ob. 21 in relation to Yahweh's present and final dominion.

[29] Ps. 103:19; 145:11, 13; Da. 3:33. Cf. also Ps. 22:28 (מְלוּכָה).

of God. If in Da. 7 the kingdom which comes from above is described as מַלְכוּ the term has a particular stamp when applied to the final kingdom of the saints. God can give the מַלְכוּ to whom He will (Da. 2:44; 4:22); He gives it to His people and thus establishes an eternal kingdom (Da. 7:27). Yet the reference is not to God's מַלְכוּת, nor is He the king in question. The reference is to a succession of human kingdoms until finally the מַלְכוּ of the saints — this is how the coming Son of Man is interpreted (Da. 7:16 ff.) — is inaugurated. This strongly nationalistic hope of the מַלְכוּ frequently recurs in later apocalyptic [30] literature (Eth. En. 84:2; 90:30; 92:4; 103:1; Ass. Mos. 10:1 ff. etc.). [31]

von Rad

C. מַלְכוּת שָׁמַיִם in Rabbinic Literature. [32]

1. The later Jewish term מלכות שמים owes its origin to the general tendency of later Judaism to avoid verbal statements about God such as we find in the OT, and to replace them by abstract constructions. It is closely related to the term שכינה. As this is a simple substitute for the OT saying שָׁכַן יהוה: "God dwells," "God is present," [33] so later Judaism uses מלכות שמים for "God is King" (→ 568 f.). [34]

Thus the Targumim often replace the OT expression by מלכותא דיי "the kingdom of God," e.g., Tg. O. Ex. 15:18 : יי מלכותיה קאים ("the kingdom of God stands fast") for the Mas. יהוה ימלך; Tg. Is. 24:23 : תתגלי מלכותא דיהוה ("manifest is the kingdom of God") for the Mas. מלך יהוה; cf. also Is. 31:4; 40:9; 52:7; Mi. 4:7; Zech. 14:9, [35] though the OT expression is retained in Ez. 20:33; Ps. 47:8; 93:1; 96:10; 97:1; 146:10.

Since the divine name יהוה was replaced by אדוני in the cultic use of later Judaism, i.e., in the Synagogue readings, the Targumim consistently have מלכותא דיהוה, [36] read as מ'' דאדוני. In freer use, the divine name is avoided by using שמים ("of heaven") instead. Hence in Rabb. literature outside the Targumim we always have מלכות שמים; the slavishly literal transl. in Gk. is βασιλεία τῶν οὐρανῶν (Mt.) but the material equivalent βασιλεία τοῦ θεοῦ (Mk., Lk.). At a later point in Rabbinic usage, probably at the end of the 1st cent. and beginning of the 2nd., even שמים as a divine name was replaced by the very general המקום, "the place" (→ ἅγιος, 98). Only in a few fixed expressions and formulae [37] did it continue in use as a divine name, as in מלכות שמים.

The derivation of the term makes it immediately apparent that מלכות שמים can never mean the kingdom of God in the sense of the territory ruled by Him. For

---

[30] On the use of מַלְכוּת in Rabb. Judaism, → *infra*.

[31] Cf. Bousset-Gressm., 214 ff.

[32] מֶלֶךְ in Rabb. lit. hardly needs separate treatment, since here, in contrast to the OT, the significance of the word group is wholly in terms of מַלְכוּת. Any important features in the use of מֶלֶךְ (God as King or the Messiah King) will be noted in the next section, so far as they have not been brought out in that on the OT.

[33] V. on this pt. Str.-B., II, 314; S. Nu., 1 on 5:3 (K. G. Kuhn, S. Nu. [1933] 12 f.) = S. Nu., 161 on 35:34.

[34] A third later Jewish abstract construction of the same kind is מֵימְרָא דיי, which the Targumim use for אָמַר יהוה, — and nothing more, no "hypostasis"), v. Str.-B., II, 302 ff.

[35] Cf. Dalman WJ, I, 79 and 83.

[36] Or מלכותא דיי, יי being an abbrev. for יהוה (properly י, but usually written יי on account of the smallness of the letter, or even ','', or 'יי).

[37] Enumerated in Str.-B., I, 172 under A and I, 862 ff.

the expression denotes the fact that God is King, i.e., His kingly being or kingship. [38] Thus from the very first מלכות שמים is a purely theological construction in
later Judaism and not an application of the secular concept מלכות to the religious
sphere. [39] In Rabb. writings the absol. מלכות always denotes earthly or worldly
government, i.e., the Roman Empire, [40] not so much in the sense of the state as of
Roman rule or the Roman authorities as seen from the standpoint of the subject. [41]
With this secular מלכות, the מלכות שמים, which derived from very different roots,
was sometimes contrasted in later writings when it had come to have a fixed
meaning. [42] The true and original sense of מלכות שמים, as an abstract construction
to denote the fact that God is King, always persisted, however, in spite of the
Rabbis. This is shown in the fact that in the Rabbis the verses in which God is
called King are always known as מלכיות, i.e., מלכות or kingship verses. [43]

2. The development of the term in detail need not be followed in this context,
since the whole of the Rabbinic material has already been collected many times
(→ Bibl.). Rather we should seek to present the essential aspects for an understanding of the range of the concept. It must be emphasised first that in relation
to the whole Rabbinic corpus מלכות שמים is comparatively infrequent and not by
a long way of such theological importance as in the preaching of Jesus. In the
main, the phrase occurs properly only in two expressions which span the whole
compass of its theological significance. The one is קיבל עול מלכות שמים "to accept
the yoke of the kingdom of God," [44] i.e., in accordance with the above definition,
"to acknowledge God as one's King and Lord," "to confess the one God as the
King, and to forswear all other gods." The expression thus serves to denote the
monotheism of Judaism as daily declared by every adherent of the Jewish faith
in God in the Sch*ema* (Dt. 6:4: "Hear, O Israel, the Lord our God is one Lord").
Hence קיבל עול מלכות שמים is often used quite simply for reciting the Sch*ema*. [45]

Here, then, מלכות שמים is something which a man must freely decide either to
be for or against. He always has the possibility of rejecting God as King and
Lord ("to throw off the yoke of the kingdom of God"). This possibility implies
that the kingdom is not manifest in the world. For otherwise, willingly or un-
willingly, there could only be recognition of the obvious fact that God is King.
Again, real decision is demanded, i.e., the decision which each must make for
himself and which is binding and valid only if the possibility of decision is limited

---

[38] This is also stressed by Dalman WJ, I, 77 ("the rule of a king rather than the territory
of a king"). Yet he finds an empirical reason for this: "An oriental 'kingdom' is ... not a
state in our sense, i.e., a constituted people or country, but a 'dominion' comprising a certain
territory" — whereas it actually lies in the nature of the term itself. It is better not to put
this in terms of "more" and "less" as in RGG², IV, 1817 (Mundle): "... denotes less the
geographical concept of a kingdom than the fact of the dominion of a king."

[39] This transference took place much earlier and at a different point, namely, under the
Israelite monarchy (*terminus a quo*, David) and in relation to מֶלֶךְ; → 568.

[40] Cf. Str.-B., I, 183 for many examples.

[41] It is thus legitimate to use "more or less" (n. 38) in relation to this מלכות.

[42] In only three passages, all from the 3rd cent. A.D., is מלכות שמים contrasted with
מלכות הארץ: Gn. r., 9 (7b); Pesikt., 51a (and par.); bBer., 58a (Str.-B., I, 175 f. under h).

[43] So, e.g., RH, 4, 5; S. Nu., 77 on 10:10; v. on this pt. Moore, II, 210, 373.

[44] For examples, v. Str.-B., I, 173 ff. *passim*.

[45] For examples, v. Str.-B., I, 177 f. under n.

and therefore finite. This brings us to the second expresson in which מלכות שמים ordinarily occurs. For the boundary or end (קץ, → τέλος) which removes the possibility of accepting or rejecting the kingdom of God by a free decision of the will is the manifestation of the kingdom of God. This manifestation is a recurrent object of Jewish petition, [46] and the Targumim often speak of the end of time (→ τέλος) when the kingdom of God will be revealed (איתגליאת מלכותא דיהוה).[47] Hence in the theology of later Judaism מלכות שמים is a purely eschatological concept in the strict sense of the word.

3. It should be noted especially that the people of Israel does not figure in this whole train of thought. National membership, then, is not in any way an element which determines religious position. At this point man stands before God as an individual who must make his own decision, i.e., simply as man, and not as the member of a particular people. In Rabbinic theology there is thus developed to its conclusion a line of thought which commences in the OT prophets. The other line of OT piety, i.e., religion which is determined by nationality and finds its vitality especially in the Law and the cultus, has not entirely disappeared from Rabbinic theology. On the contrary, the Rabbis constantly emphasise the religious prerogatives of the people of Israel, according to which nationality does determine the position of a man before God. [48] Even in the concept of the מלכות שמים this thought plays a certain role. Often in Jewish prayers God is addressed as the King of Israel. [49] The same thought is present when it is said that the progenitor of the people, Abraham, made God King on earth [50] as the first to acknowledge the one God as King and Lord, or when it is said that Israel, i.e., the people as such, "accepted the yoke of the kingdom of God" at the Red Sea and Sinai with its confession of the true God and its adoption of the Torah. [51]

These two lines, religion as determined by nationality and the religion of the individual, are thus found together in later Judaism. This juxtaposition arises from the fact that both occur in the different OT writings, so that when the OT was canonised both were the authoritative Word of God for Judaism, and both with equal force. But the distinctive feature is that nowhere in Rabbinic theology do we find any attempt to bring together into a unitary theological system these concurrent lines which are sanctioned by Holy Scripture. The Rabbis apparently see no need to do this. They apparently find no tension or *aporia* in the coexistence of these two lines.

In the case of מלכות שמים any incidental link with the thought of nationality simply denotes a traditional attachment to the OT statements which emphasise this factor (→ n. 49), whereas the true vitality and significance of the concept in later Judaism were along the strictly religious lines already indicated. מלכות שמים is thus one of the few, if not the only strict and pure concept in later Judaism; the ἔσχατον of the manifestation of the מלכות שמים demands an individual decision

---

[46] Cf. the two petitions from the tractate *Soferim* in Str.-B., I, 179. For further examples, *ibid., passim.*

[47] Cf. the passages adduced above (→ 571, mostly transl. in Str.-B., I, 179 under c). Cf. also Moore, II, 374, n. 3; Sib., 3, 47 f. (φανεῖται) and Lk. 19:11 (μέλλει ἡ βασιλεία τοῦ θεοῦ ἀναφαίνεσθαι).

[48] Sanh., 10:1: All Israel has a part in the future world.

[49] Str.-B., I, 175 under e. Also Ps. Sol. 5:18 f.; 17:3. Dependence on the cultic piety of the Royal Psalms is here apparent.

[50] S. Dt., 313 on 32:10 (Str.-B., I, 173 under c).

[51] Str.-B., I, 172 under d and 174; S. Lv., 18:6 (Shim'on ben Joḥai).

either to accept or to reject "the yoke of the מלכות שמים."

4. This enables us to fix unequivocally the difference between this concept and expectation of the Messiah King at the end of the age. מלכות שמים is a purely eschatological concept. It does not emerge in the course of a historical process. Expectation of the Messiah King, however, develops out of the originally secular expectation of an Israelite king who will revive the monarchy in all its greatness and restore the splendour of the idealised Davidic kingdom. This hope becomes a hope for the end of the age. It is not, therefore, eschatological in the strict sense. The coming of the Messiah precedes the ἔσχατον in Jewish thinking.[52] The difference may be stated as follows. In later Judaism the thought of the Messiah is always the expression of a hope for the last times which knows God primarily as the King of Israel, and which consequently links the final establishment of the kingdom of the people of Israel, as the goal of God's plan of salvation, with the Messiah as a King to whom all other peoples will be subject. In מלכות שמים, on the other hand, the purely religious concept of the ἔσχατον achieves its full stature (God as All in All), so that there is no more place for the special thought of a national link with Israel.

Thus the two concepts are heterogeneous. To be sure, they often appear together as the two things on which the hope of Israel, both national and religious, is set.[53] But they are nowhere brought into an inner relationship. Nowhere do we have the thought that the kingdom of the Messiah is the מלכות שמים, or that the Messiah by His operation will bring in the מלכות שמים, or vice versa. Such a link with the thought of the Messiah is quite impossible in terms of the strict concept of the מלכות שמים.

Kuhn

D. βασιλεία (τοῦ θεοῦ) in Hellenistic Judaism.

In the few passages in which it speaks of the kingdom of God, the LXX is in essential agreement with the Heb. or Aram. (Da.) original. Yet there are also some passages in the LXX which are specifically Greek or Hellenistic, and have no Heb. original in the canonical OT. Thus Wis. 6:20 : ἐπιθυμία σοφίας ἀνάγει ἐπὶ βασιλείαν. This deals comprehensively with the high value and the accessibility of wisdom. Regard for wisdom leads to dominion. This sixth chapter of the Book of Wisdom also speaks of the βασιλεία τοῦ θεοῦ. In 6:4 the kings of the earth will be claimed as the ὑπηρέται τῆς αὐτοῦ (i.e., God's) βασιλείας; in 10:10 it is said of wisdom that it has shown the righteous the kingdom of God. But the absolute use of βασιλεία in 6:20 (cf. 10:14) indicates the dominion of the wise. In this respect we may also refer to 4 Macc. 2:23 : God has given man a law by the following of which he βασιλεύσει βασιλείαν σώφρονά τε καὶ δικαίαν καὶ ἀγαθὴν καὶ ἀνδρείαν; the βασιλεία is identified with the four cardinal virtues. This ethicising of the βασιλεία concept in terms of popular philosophy was carried through more even comprehensively and clearly by Philo. So far as concerns the general use of βασιλεία, the sense of kingdom, kingship and then lordship is predominant. The actor assumes the παράσημα (insignia) τῆς βασιλείας in Flacc., 38. This meaning is also found in the plural; the possessors of military rank are set alongside those who enjoy royal dignity, οἱ τὰς βασιλείας καὶ

---

[52] Cf. Str.-B., IV, 968 f.
[53] E.g. at the beginning of the Kaddish prayer : "May He set up His royal dominion ... and bring His Messiah." Cf. on this whole train of thought esp. Moore, II, 371-375.

ἡγεμονίας ἀναψάμενοι (Plant., 67). Nimrod had Babylon as the ἀρχὴ τῆς βασιλείας (Gig., 66). Philo gives many definitions. By way of hendiadys it is linked with ἀρχή, Mut. Nom., 15; Vit. Mos., I, 148; Omn. Prob. Lib., 117; it is set alongside πολιτεία, Plant., 56; it is more than ὀχλοκρατία, Fug., 10; earthly βασιλεία has two tasks, ποιμενικὴ μελέτη καὶ προγυμνασία, Vit. Mos., I, 60. In addition, βασιλεία is constantly linked, and even identified, with ἀρχή. The βασιλεία of Moses, as his leadership, is parallel to his νομοθεσία, προφητεία and ἀρχιερωσύνη in Praem. Poen., 53, to his νομοθετικὴ ἕξις, ἱερωσύνη and προφητεία in Vit. Mos., II, 187. We can see this also if we refer back to the whole of Bk. I of the Vita, which makes it evident that the theme of this book is the βασιλεία of Moses (Vit. Mos., I, 333 f.; cf. II, 66). In a special discussion, the distinction between βασιλεία as human monarchy, and ἀρχιερωσύνη as the high-priesthood, is explained in such a way that the second takes precedence of the first. For it amounts to a θεοῦ θεραπεία whereas βασιλεία is an ἐπιμέλεια ἀνθρώπων; the distinction is thus found in the objects, i.e., θεός or ἄνθρωποι (Leg. Gaj., 278; cf. on this Virt., 54). The ἱερωσύνη is worthy of an εὐσεβὴς ἀνήρ and should be preferred to freedom and even to βασιλεία, Spec. Leg., I, 57. In a definition of βασιλεία, of which the δόγματα and νόμοι are to be observed, we read : βασιλείαν ... σοφίαν εἶναι λέγομεν, ἐπεὶ καὶ τὸν σοφὸν βασιλέα, Migr. Abr., 197. A similar expression (ἡ τοῦ σοφοῦ βασιλεία) is to be found in Abr., 261; cf. Som., II, 243 f. Similarly, Saul is to learn from Samuel τὰ τῆς βασιλείας δίκαια, Migr. Abr., 196. That the first man gives names to the animals is understood as σοφίας καὶ βασιλείας τὸ ἔργον (a linking of wisdom and power), Op. Mund., 148. The true sense of βασιλεία is thus defined as simply dominion in the rule of the wise man as the true king, Sacr. AC, 49. In relation to the wise king Abraham ἀρετή is defined as ἀρχή and βασιλεία, Som. II, 244. In the same way it is said of νοῦς that its advocates attribute to it τὴν ἡγεμονίαν καὶ βασιλείαν τῶν ἀνθρωπείων πραγμάτων, Spec. Leg., I, 334. The opposite of all this is τὸ ἡδέως ζῆν, which it is an illusion to regard as ἡγεμονία and βασιλεία, Ebr., 216.

Is Philo speaking of the kingdom of God, or also of the kingdom of God, in these passages ? Does he ever speak of the kingdom of God ? Yes and no ! Τοῦ θεοῦ is once found as an attribute when the dominion of a king is compared with the βασιλεία τοῦ θεοῦ, Spec. Leg., IV, 164; and it is once used as a predicate : ἡ βασιλεία τίνος; ἆρ' οὐχὶ μόνου θεοῦ; Mut. Nom., 135. There is perhaps an allusion to the kingdom of God when the building of the tower is regarded as the καθαίρεσις τῆς αἰωνίου βασιλείας, Som., II, 285. God is invested with the ἀνανταγώνιστος (invincible) and ἀναφαίρετος (impregnable) βασιλεία, Spec. Leg., I, 207. Abraham as a true king, the king of wisdom, comes from God, because God τὴν τοῦ σοφοῦ βασιλείαν ὀρέγει, Abr., 261. Moses confronts circumstances as a superior being directing the world χρώμενον αὐτεξουσίῳ καὶ αὐτοκράτορι βασιλείᾳ, Rer. Div. Her., 301.

The only occasion when Philo looks to a future βασιλεία is in Vit. Mos., I, 290, where he quotes the LXX of Nu. 24:7 (the Messianic prophecy of Balaam): ἡ τοῦδε βασιλεία καθ' ἑκάστην ἡμέραν πρὸς ὕψος ἀρθήσεται. Here as elsewhere he construes the kingdom ethically.

Our general assessment of the βασιλεία passages [54] in Philo can only be that royal dominion is never conceived of as an eschatological magnitude. Rather, the

---

[54] Cf. H. Leisegang's Indexes. The ref. V, 142, 1 should read V, 14, 21. In V, 230, 8 we should derive τῶν βασιλείων from τὰ βασίλεια rather than ἡ βασιλεία.

βασιλεία constitutes a chapter in his moral doctrine.[55] The true king is the wise man. Thus Philo adds his voice to the ancient chorus in praise of the wise. The wise man as the true βασιλεύς (→ 565) is distinguished from ordinary earthly kings, and is to be extolled as divine. This view also determines what Philo has to say philosophically and religiously concerning the βασιλεία τοῦ σοφοῦ. Materially this term also derives from ancient philosophy, though formally it comes from the Greek Bible, which Philo interprets as in the LXX passages mentioned. It should be noted that there were in later Judaism generally certain impulses towards this ethicising and anthropologising. In spite of an obvious synergism, however, apocalyptic and Rabbinic Judaism maintained the thought of the kingdom of God which rests on God's free decision.[56] Philo, on the other hand, has completely reconstructed the original βασιλεία concept, though as an exegete, unlike Josephus, he is not afraid to speak of the βασιλεία τοῦ θεοῦ.[57]

Josephus never uses the expression. Only in Ant., 6, 60 is βασιλεία mentioned in connection with God. While the Palestinian Judaism from which he came used the phrase שָׁמַיִם מַלְכוּת, for all its present reference, in an eschatological sense as well, Josephus uses the word θεοκρατία of the present constitution of the community in Ap., 2, 165. Instead of βασιλεύς and βασιλεία he has ἡγεμών and ἡγεμονία; he ascribes ἡγεμονία rather than βασιλεία to the Roman emperor.[58] The reason may be that on the one side Josephus is one of those who avoided referring to the Messianic and eschatological hope of his people which was linked with the word βασιλεία, and on the other that as a historian living and writing in Rome he is an adherent of Hellenism and is yet wholly dependent on his sources.[59]

E. The Word Group βασιλεύς κτλ. in the NT.

† βασιλεύς.

βασιλεύς, "king," is applied in the NT to men, to gods (or God) and to intermediary beings. From the standpoint of biblical theology, it is an important fact that in the NT, in close dependence on OT and Jewish usage and in full agreement with it, God as well as Christ (the Messiah Jesus) bears this title, and men are restricted and depreciated as kings.

1. a. Earthly kings mentioned in the NT, either generally without name or more particularly by name, are explicitly or implicitly contrasted with God or the Messiah as King, or at any rate regarded as subordinate. In the non-biblical world the following are given the title: Pharaoh in Ac. 7:10, who is followed by another

---

[55] It is striking that in the index to E. Bréhier, *Les Idées philosophiques et religieuses de Philon d'Alexandrie* (1908), there is a whole list of references under *vertu*, but *royaume de Dieu* is not even mentioned. We gain a similar impression from I. Heinemann, *Philons griechische und jüdische Bildung* (1932).

[56] As correctly noted by G. Gloege, *Reich Gottes und Kirche im Neuen Testament* (1929), 19 ff. Philo is not discussed in the section on later Judaism in this work.

[57] Cf. A. Schlatter, *Die Theologie des Judentums nach dem Bericht des Josephus* (1932), 49, n. 1.

[58] So A. Schlatter, *Wie sprach Josephus von Gott?* (1910), 11 f.

[59] Cf. G. Hölscher in his art. "Josephus" in Pauly-W., IX, 1955: "J. in his presentation of biblical history renounces any independent use of the biblical text, whether in the Gk. or Heb. form, and creates his material almost completely, and even to the smaller details, from biblical models."

king in 7:18; Hb. 11:23, 27; Herod the Great in Mt. 2:1, 3, 9; Lk. 1:5; also Herod Antipas, though he was not king in the strict sense, in Mt. 14:9; Mk. 6:14, 22, 25, 26, 27; Herod Agrippa I, Ac. 12:1, 20; Herod Agrippa II, Ac. 25:13, 14, 24, 26; 26:2, 7, 13, 19, 26, 27, 30; also the Nabataean king Aretas in 2 C. 11:32. According to oriental usage the Roman emperor is also king [60] in 1 Tm. 2:2; 1 Pt. 2:13, 17; Rev. 17:9 f. (cf. 1 Cl., 37, 3). All such kings are kings of the earth or the Gentiles (τῆς γῆς, Mt. 17:25; Ac. 4:26; Rev. 1:5; 6:15; 17:2, 18; 18:9; 19:19; 21:24; τῶν ἐθνῶν, Lk. 22:25; τῆς οἰκουμένης ὅλης, Rev. 16:14). The description and evaluation of the kings of the earth are taken from Ps. 2:2, ψ 88:27 and similar passages. As in the OT, divine rank is not ascribed to the earthly king after the manner of oriental court style; this dignity is ascribed only to Yahweh or His Messiah. In Revelation this distinction is given particular emphasis by the fact that, in contrast to the contemporary style of the Roman emperors and their oriental predecessors, [61] only the one Almighty God is called βασιλεὺς τῶν ἐθνῶν (Rev. 15:3) and only the Messiah King the βασιλεὺς βασιλέων καὶ κύριος κυρίων (Rev. 19:16; cf. 17:14). The sons of the kingdom of God are set by God or by Christ above earthly kings with their power. They are strictly taken out of the sphere of earthly power and serve one another as brethren (Mt. 17:25 f.; Lk. 22:25). As the kingdom of God draws near, Christians will be brought to judgment by ἡγεμόνες καὶ βασιλεῖς for the sake of Christ (Mt. 10:18; Mk. 13:9; Lk. 21:12). Ἐν τοῖς οἴκοις τῶν βασιλέων (vl. βασιλείων) those are at home who wear soft clothing, but not a prophet like John the Baptist (Mt. 11:8). That which will be revealed to the children of the kingdom is hidden from earthly kings and even from the prophets (Lk. 10:24). Kings, whose business is war (Lk. 14:31), must hear the Gospel like Jews and Gentiles (Ac. 9:15; cf. Rev. 10:11). At the end of the days the kings of the East (→ ἀνατολή) will be the scourge of God and will then be destroyed (Rev. 16:12; cf. 16:14; 17:2, 9, 12, 18; 18:3, 9; 19:18 f.). On the other hand, there is also the possibility that they will make obedient submission (Rev. 21:24).

b. No more and no less than an earthly king is an intermediary being like → Ἀβαδδών, the ruler of the spirits of the underworld (Rev. 9:11).

c. It is another matter that earthly figures like David and Melchisedec are also invested with royal dignity. As in the period of the Israelite monarchy (cf. Ac. 13:21: "Afterward they desired a king, and God gave unto them Saul"), so on the NT view David as the ancestor of Jesus Christ is a divinely recognised king (Mt. 1:6; Ac. 13:22). [62] And Melchisedec, by allegorical interpretation, is a type of Christ as the king of Salem, of peace and righteousness (Hb. 7:1, 2).

2. a. It is thus natural that in the NT Jesus Christ should be regarded as "the King." As the Messiah Jesus is first the βασιλεὺς τῶν Ἰουδαίων (Mt. 2:2; 27:11, 29, 37; Mk. 15:2, 9, 12, 18, 26; Lk. 23:3, 37 f.; Jn. 18:33, 37, 39; 19:3, 14 f., 19, 21). Yet the usage is somewhat ambivalent. A disinterested contemporary like Pilate can only accept the designation from the Jewish accusers (Lk. 23:2 f.). For the hardened Jewish enemies of Jesus, in this case both the Pharisees and the Sadducees, the designation is the blasphemous claim of a false Messianic pretender. According

---

[60] Cf. Deissmann LO, 310 f.

[61] *Loc. cit.*

[62] The difficult incident concerning the Davidic sonship in Mk. 12:35-37 and par. cannot finally affect our judgment at this point.

to Jewish opinion Jesus is a man who makes himself a king (Jn. 19:12). The vacillating mob, detecting but not understanding the Messianic claim of Jesus, takes the title "King of the Jews" for the most part in a political sense. Even the disciples taught by Jesus share this view. The people thus wish to make Jesus a king, but do not see what this really implies (Jn. 6:15). In short, the fact that Jesus is King raises the question in what the Messiahship of Jesus consists. If the true Messianic claim linked with the royal title is to be underlined, then He should be called the King of → 'Ισραήλ rather than the Jews. In fact, even though infrequently, we do find this designation βασιλεὺς (τοῦ) 'Ισραήλ (Mt. 27:42; Mk. 15:32; Jn. 1:49; 12:13). At any rate, the Jew who really knows the promise given to his people ought to speak of the King of Israel. The promise of Zech. 9:9 : "Behold, thy King cometh unto thee" (Mt. 21:5; Jn. 12:15), is given to the daughter of Jerusalem as the true Israel. By divine commission this Messiah King will hold the last assize (Mt. 25:34, 40). According to ψ 117:26 Jesus on His entry into Jerusalem is the anointed King who comes in the name of the Lord (Lk. 19:38). Is is only thus that Jesus is the Messiah King (χριστὸς βασιλεύς), in an antithesis to the Roman emperor which is not understood either by Jews or Gentiles (Lk. 23:2).[63] It seems rather strange at a first glance that apart from the Evangelists the authors of the NT describe Jesus Christ neither as the King of the Jews nor the King of Israel. This title is lacking in the original kerygma in Acts, and also in Paul. Yet there is no reason to conclude that the early community, to which the Evangelists also belong, did not know or use the title. There is a concealed indication that it is not alien to the kerygma at Ac. 17:7, where the Jews in Thessalonica denounce the Christians for high treason on the ground that they maintain that there is another king, namely, Jesus. On the other hand, the restraint in this respect is striking. We may surmise that the difficulty (already mentioned) concerning the Messiahship of Jesus brought with it some measure of uncertainty and caution. We may also see here an indication that the whole complex of the Messianic secret, which the early community hesitated to take up, really belongs to the history of Christ on earth, i.e., that Jesus Himself as the King of the Jews or of Israel understood Himself to be the Messiah of His people. At this point the Fourth Evangelist is in full agreement with the others, except that in the answer to Pilate's question he goes on to give a christological definition of the kingdom of Jesus (Jn. 18:37). A distinctive position is occupied by the Apocalypse, which gives to the royal title a cosmological implication. The Messiah King of the last time finally exercises His office in relation to the world. In the so-called Synoptic Apocalypse the case is materially the same, as also in Paul's depiction of the judgment by Christ at 1 C. 15:24, where Christ restores royal dominion to God at the end of the days. It is in this sense that at 1 Tm. 6:15, in line with the hymnic style of Revelation, Jesus Christ is the βασιλεὺς τῶν βασιλευόντων καὶ κύριος τῶν κυριευόντων.

---

[63] On the theme of this antithesis in the framework of the Messianic secret there is a good deal of useful material in the comprehensive work of R. Eisler, 'Ιησοῦς βασιλεὺς οὐ βασιλεύσας, I (1929), II (1930), cf. esp. II, 374 and 688. On the other hand, the detailed presentation, while apparently perspicacious, is often obscure and unreliable. On Eisler as a whole, cf. the discussions of his book by H. Windisch, Gnomon, 7 (1931), 289-307; H. Lewy, DLZ, 51 (1930), 481-494; W. Windfuhr, Philol. Wochenschr., 53 (1933), 9 ff.; they unanimously reject Eisler's methods as unscientific.

In the post-apostolic fathers Christ is called βασιλεὺς μέγας in Did., 14, 3 after the pattern of Mal. 1:14. He is preceded by a Messianic and apocalyptic enemy, the βασιλεὺς μικρός, according to Barn., 4, 4; cf. Da. 7:24. If Christ is called King, this helps to confirm the dignity of the Incarnate, who is instituted King by God the King (Dg., 7, 4). In the light of the results of the incarnation, and the example thereby given, the attribute σώσας (Mart. Pol., 9, 3) and the title διδάσκαλος (Mart. Pol., 17, 3) are added to His style as βασιλεύς.

b. When royal dominion is restored to God by His Christ, God is described by Paul as God the Father, the eternal King. This is clearly expressed in 1 Tm. 1:17, where God is called the βασιλεὺς τῶν αἰώνων (cf. Tob. 13:6, 10; → αἰών). Only in one passage in Mt. is God extolled as the μέγας βασιλεύς (5:35). It is worth noting that Mt., who follows the OT more closely than the other Evangelists, adduces this quotation. Similarly, Mt. gives more parables of the kingdom of God than the others. And in the details of these parables God is the King in His different functions; cf. Mt. 14:9; 18:23; 22:2, 7, 11, 13.

It is in keeping with the piety and theology of the post-apostolic fathers that in them, as in the philosophically influenced Judaism of the *diaspora,* more epithets are applied to God than in the NT. As in 1 Tm. 1:17, which almost belongs to this group, so in 1 Cl., 61, 2 God is βασιλεὺς τῶν αἰώνων, also δεσπότης ἐπουράνιος. He is also lauded as ὁ βασιλεὺς ὁ μέγας in Herm v., 3, 9, 8; cf. ψ 47:2; Tob. 13:15. God is also βασιλεύς in Dg., 7, 4.

c. According to some not too well attested readings of Rev. 1:6; 5:10, Christians, too, may be called βασιλεῖς. The verbs → βασιλεύω and → συμβασιλεύω are certainly used of Christians. [64]

† βασιλεία. [65]

In relation to the general usage of βασιλεία, usually translated "kingdom," it is to be noted first that it signifies the "being," "nature" and "state" of the king. Since the reference is to a king, we do best to speak first of his "dignity" or "power." This is true in the oldest known use of the word: τὴν βασιληίην (Ionic for βασιλείαν) ἔχε τὴν Λυδῶν, Hdt., I, 11. Similarly in Xenoph. Mem., IV, 6, 12 : βασιλείαν ... καὶ τυραννίδα ἀρχὰς μὲν ἀμφοτέρας ἡγεῖτο εἶναι, διαφέρειν δὲ ἀλλήλων ἐνόμιζε (cf. what was said about the difference between βασιλεύς and τύραννος, → 564, n. 2). Almost spontaneously there then intrudes a richly attested second meaning ; the dignity of the king is expressed in the territory ruled by him, i.e., his "kingdom." [66] This transition is no less obvious in the Eng. "principality," or "empire," or indeed "dominion." On the other hand, it did not wholly replace the original meaning of dignity. Both

---

[64] There is a formal analogy to this figur. and improper use of βασιλεύς, in the sense of a distinguished person, in Philostr. Vit. Soph., II, 10, 2, where Herodes Atticus appears as ὁ βασιλεὺς τῶν λόγων [Kleinknecht].

[65] Against Holstein and Gloege (→ 564, Bibl.), it should be pointed out that a primary lexical investigation of the word as used, such as is attempted here on the foundation and in development of that of Cr.-Kö., is particularly fruitful in questions of biblical theology, esp. when we avoid such dubious modern categories, used esp. by Gloege, as "dynamic," "supratemporality" and "otherworldliness." Neither directly nor indirectly should exegesis make use of such modern terminology — better though it may be than that which preceded — in attempts to free itself from the long dispute concerning the transcendence or immanence of the kingdom of God — a dispute which has been inevitably fruitless.

[66] Well expounded by Suid., *s.v.* : τὸ ἀξίωμα καὶ τὸ ἔθνος βασιλευόμενον.

meanings are present in βασιλεία. In Rev. 17:12 and 17:17 we seem to have the two meanings almost directly alongside one another. [67]

Investigation of the canonical OT (both Heb. and Aram. originals and the LXX, → 565 ff.), of the pseudepigraphical and apocryphal liter. (including also the Rabbinic writings, → 571 ff.) and of Hellenistic authors (esp. Philo, → 574 ff.), shows that the sense of dignity or power is still predominant. This is quite definitely so in the NT. [68]

1. The Earthly βασιλεία.

a. To the earthly → βασιλεύς there corresponds the earthly βασιλεία, the kingdom of men. The two meanings mentioned in the introduction merge into one another at this point, though in certain NT passages the context enables us to distinguish them. Thus in the parable of the pounds in Lk. 19:12, 15 it is said of a certain nobleman that he journeyed into a far country λαβεῖν ἑαυτῷ βασιλείαν, and then returned λαβόντα τὴν βασιλείαν. The reference here is obviously to royal dignity. [69] The same verb is to be found in Rev. 17:12 : δέκα βασιλεῖς ... βασιλείαν οὔπω ἔλαβον. [70] To this there corresponds shortly afterwards Rev. 17:17: δοῦναι τὴν βασιλείαν τῷ θηρίῳ, [70] and also 17:18 : ἡ πόλις ἡ μεγάλη ἡ ἔχουσα βασιλείαν ἐπὶ τῶν βασιλέων τῆς γῆς. [71] In other passages the reference is no less plainly to the territory. Thus in Mt. 4:8 = Lk. 4:5, where in the temptation story the devil shows Jesus πάσας τὰς βασιλείας τοῦ κόσμου or τῆς οἰκουμένης, the use of the plural and the assumption of visibility imply kingdoms in the territorial sense. [72] When Jesus in His defence against the Pharisees says : πᾶσα βασιλεία μερισθεῖσα καθ᾽ ἑαυτῆς ἐρημοῦται (Mt. 12:25; cf. Mk. 3:24 and Lk. 11:17), the statement itself, and the comparison with a πόλις or οἰκία (οἶκος), clearly incline in the same direction. Again, in the apocalyptic discourse : ἐγερθήσεται ἔθνος ἐπ᾽ ἔθνος καὶ βασιλεία ἐπὶ βασιλείαν (Mt. 24:7 and par.), the link with ἔθνος points to the territory ruled. The same meaning is found in the promise of Herod to his daughter : ἕως ἡμίσους τῆς βασιλείας μου (Mk. 6:23), and also in Rev. 16:10 : ἐγένετο ἡ βασιλεία αὐτοῦ (sc. τοῦ θηρίου) ἐσκοτωμένη.

Such earthly βασιλεία is almost always seen in emphatic opposition, or at least subjection, to the βασιλεία of God, just as the κόσμος (Mt. 4: 8) or the οἰκουμένη (Lk. 4:5) as the βασιλεία τοῦ κόσμου (Rev. 11:15) is against God, having given itself to "the" hostile king, i.e., the devil. This is seen particularly in the fact that the world power of the Roman Empire (θηρίον in the Apoc.), understood apocalyptically and therefore regarded as devilish, seeks to represent the βασιλεία and to spread light, even though it is in distress and darkness (ἐσκοτωμένη, Rev. 16:10). That the devil raises the claim to have a βασιλεία may be seen from the fact that as the tempter he seduces the βασιλεῖαι of the world, and that Jesus,

---

[67] In modern Greek βασιλεία means "kingship", "royal dominion" or "reign" ; the word for territorial "kingdom" is βασίλειον.

[68] Cf. A. E. J. Rawlinson, *The Gospel according to St. Mark* (1925), 111, who interprets "God's rule or sovereignty, the reign of God" ; A. Deissmann, *The Religion of Jesus and the Faith of St. Paul* (1923), 108 ff. "kingdom or sovereignty, kingly rule of God" ; J. Warschauer, *The Historical Life of Christ* (1927): "What we translate 'the kingdom of God' means thus rather His 'kingship,' His 'reign' rather than His 'realm'."

[69] So, e.g., Kl. Lk., ad loc.

[70] Loh. Apk., ad loc.: "Königtum."

[71] *Ibid.,* freely rendered : "The great city is queen over the kings of the earth."

[72] Kl. Mt. and Kl. Lk., ad loc.: "Reiche der Welt."

when speaking to the Pharisees of earthly kingdoms in general, then goes on at once to speak specifically of the βασιλεία of the devil.

b. In this defence there is express reference to the βασιλεία of the devil: πῶς οὖν σταθήσεται ἡ βασιλεία αὐτοῦ (sc. τοῦ σατανᾶ), whether in the sense of "realm" or "reign" (Mt. 12:26 = Lk. 11:18).

c. Apart from the earthly, human or devilish βασιλεία, there is the βασιλεία of the men or people elected by God. A legitimate possessor or representative of the βασιλεία is king David: εὐλογημένη ἡ ἐρχομένη βασιλεία τοῦ πατρὸς ἡμῶν Δαυίδ (Mk. 11:10). Only to Israel as the divine people of the old and new covenant (Ἰσραὴλ κατὰ πνεῦμα) does there belong this βασιλεία, concerning which the disciples hopefully ask: κύριε, εἰ ἐν τῷ χρόνῳ τούτῳ ἀποκαθιστάνεις τὴν βασιλείαν τῷ Ἰσραήλ; (Ac. 1:6).

2. The βασιλεία of Christ.

We have seen already that on the basis of the OT Jesus Christ is the King of the true Israel in the NT. Hence we must now consider the βασιλεία of Christ. The Son of Man will send His angels and they will gather ἐκ τῆς βασιλείας αὐτοῦ all seducers and evildoers (Mt. 13:41). Jesus says that some standing with Him will not taste of death until they see the Son of Man coming ἐν τῇ βασιλείᾳ αὐτοῦ (Mt. 16:28). It is said of the King Jesus Christ: τῆς βασιλείας αὐτοῦ there will be no end (Lk. 1:33). This King promises His disciples that they shall eat and drink ἐν τῇ βασιλείᾳ μου (Lk. 22:30). The thief crucified with Him asks the suffering and dying Messiah King to remember him when He comes εἰς τὴν βασιλείαν σου (vl. ἐν τῇ βασιλείᾳ σου) (Lk. 23:42). Of the manner of this kingdom Jesus says that ἡ βασιλεία ἡ ἐμή is not of this world (Jn. 18:36). The apostle of Christ attests τὴν ἐπιφάνειαν αὐτοῦ καὶ τὴν βασιλείαν αὐτοῦ (2 Tm. 4:1). He knows that his Lord will deliver him εἰς τὴν βασιλείαν αὐτοῦ τὴν ἐπουράνιον (2 Tm. 4:18). To us Christians entrance is given εἰς τὴν αἰώνιον βασιλείαν τοῦ κυρίου ἡμῶν καὶ σωτῆρος Ἰησοῦ Χριστοῦ (2 Pt. 1:11).

This βασιλεία of Jesus Christ is also the βασιλεία of God. In various passages there is reference to the kingdom of God and of Christ. The unbeliever has no inheritance ἐν τῇ βασιλείᾳ τοῦ Χριστοῦ καὶ θεοῦ (Eph. 5:5). At the end of the times the βασιλεία τοῦ κόσμου has become the βασιλεία τοῦ κυρίου ἡμῶν καὶ τοῦ Χριστοῦ αὐτοῦ (our Lord and His Anointed, Rev. 11:15). Thus God and Christ are linked; sometimes the one is mentioned, sometimes the other. On the other hand, there is no reference to the βασιλεία of Christ apart from that of God. This is attested by Jesus Himself: My Father hath made over to Me βασιλείαν (Lk. 22:29). It is God who has delivered us εἰς τὴν βασιλείαν τοῦ υἱοῦ τῆς ἀγάπης αὐτοῦ (Col. 1:13). Having thus received the kingdom from the Father, at the end of the days Christ gives it back to Him (1 C. 15:24). He can only give Him what belongs to Him. This brings us to the dominant NT concept of the βασιλεία (τοῦ) θεοῦ which we have already been discussing implicitly, just as we shall be explicitly discussing the βασιλεία (τοῦ) Χριστοῦ as well in the section which follows.

3. The βασιλεία of God.

a. As regards the usage, four points are to be noted: 1. the alternative βασιλεία τῶν οὐρανῶν; 2. the references to βασιλεία in the absolute; 3. the attributive and predicative statements; and 4. the synonyms.

Except for the textually uncertain Jn. 3:5, the expression βασιλεία τῶν οὐρανῶν ("kingdom of heaven") is found only in Mt. In Ev. Hebr. Fr., 11 it recurs as *regnum coelorum*. On three occasions Mt. also uses the term which is customary in Mk., Lk. and elsewhere, i.e., βασιλεία τοῦ θεοῦ ("kingdom of God"). To these we should probably add a fourth in Mt. 6:33 (though not all the MSS have τοῦ θεοῦ), and perhaps even a fifth in Mt. 19:24, if we are not to read τῶν οὐρανῶν. The question arises why Mt. has this double usage. Does he intend a distinction in meaning between his usual τῶν οὐρανῶν and his less frequent τοῦ θεοῦ? In general, the very fact that the expressions are interchangeable both in the MSS and in the Synoptic parallels forces us to the conclusion that they are used *promiscue* and have exactly the same meaning. It is open to dispute whether Jesus used the one or the other in the original Aramaic. The possibility must also be taken into account that there is at least a nuance in the kingdom of heaven in so far as this refers to the lordship which comes down from heaven [73] into this world. If so, this gives us two important insights. The first is a plain reassurance that the essential meaning is reign rather than realm. The second is the related indication that this reign cannot be a realm which arises by a natural development of earthly relationships or by human efforts, but is one which comes down by divine intervention. Since heaven can be substituted for God by later Jewish usage, what is true of βασιλεία τῶν οὐρανῶν is also true of βασιλεία τοῦ θεοῦ. The same holds good also of βασιλεία τοῦ πατρός ("kingdom of the Father") in Mt. 13:43; 26:29 (cf. Mt. 6:10: "Thy kingdom come," i.e., the kingdom of "our Father"); 25:34 and Lk. 12:32 ("It hath pleased your Father to give you the kingdom").

Quite a number of passages speak of the βασιλεία without addition and therefore in the absolute, namely, Mt. 4:23; 9:35; 13:19; 24:14 (εὐαγγέλιον, or λόγος τῆς βασιλείας); 8:12; 13:38 (υἱοὶ τῆς βασιλείας); Hb. 11:33 (διὰ πίστεως κατηγωνίσαντο βασιλείας); 12:28 (βασιλείαν ἀσάλευτον παραλαμβάνοντες); Jm. 2:5 (κληρονόμους τῆς βασιλείας); perhaps also Ac. 20:25 (κηρύσσων τὴν βασιλείαν). [74] It need hardly be proved that in all these passages the reference is to the kingdom of God, since this is unambiguously shown both by the context and by the specific attributes and predicates. [75]

Whether directly by the addition τοῦ θεοῦ or τῶν οὐρανῶν, or indirectly in the absolute use, the being and action of God supply the necessary qualification. Hence any other direct attributes are extremely rare. We have referred already to ἀσάλευτος in Hb. 12:28, and to this we may add ἐπουράνιος in 2 Tm. 4:18 and αἰώνιος in 2 Pt. 1:11. In relation to the kingdom of God, however, such attributes are largely formal and rhetorical, and add hardly anything from the material or theological standpoint. The NT is also sparing in direct predicates. Whose is the kingdom? It is the kingdom of God, and also the kingdom of men, but only of men who are poor in spirit (Mt. 5:3 = Lk. 6:20) and persecuted for righteousness' sake (Mt. 5:10).

---

[73] The plur. is a Semitism, unlike 2 C. 12:2.

[74] To which many MSS add τοῦ [κυρίου] Ἰησοῦ or τοῦ θεοῦ.

[75] In the course of centuries such absolute usage has led to a religious or ostensibly religious, but also immanent, worldly and pseudo-theological way of speaking of the kingdom in the sense of an earthly realm. We find this even in religious Socialism on the one side and the Third Reich of National Socialism on the other (in connection with the belief in the Holy Roman Empire, which for its part may be traced back to this absolute usage).

More extended attributes and predicates lead us into a sphere of synonyms well adapted to bring out the complexity of the proclamation of the kingdom of God. In this respect it makes no difference whether the synon. expressions are introduced by a καί (hendiadys) or as predicates. Again, it makes no difference in what order they stand or are treated. The reference is always to the manifold yet unitary being and work of God and His appeal to man and claim upon him. Men are to seek the kingdom of God and His δικαιοσύνη (Mt. 6:33). This δικαιοσύνη and εἰρήνη and χαρά ἐν πνεύματι ἁγίῳ make up the kingdom of God (R. 14:17). This does not imply a native quality, or one attained or to be attained, but the παλιγγενεσία referred to in Mt. 19:28 (Jn. 3:3 ff.) where the Lucan parallel has βασιλεία (Lk. 22:30). In this context the writer of Revelation addresses his fellow-Christians as their brother and companion ἐν τῇ θλίψει καὶ βασιλείᾳ καὶ ὑπομονῇ ἐν 'Ιησοῦ (Rev. 1:9). There has come to him ἡ σωτηρία καὶ ἡ δύναμις καὶ ἡ βασιλεία τοῦ θεοῦ ἡμῶν καὶ ἡ ἐξουσία τοῦ χριστοῦ αὐτοῦ (Rev. 12:10). In other places, too, there is allusion to this δύναμις of God in attempted definition of the kingdom of God. It comes ἐν δυνάμει (Mk. 9:1). It does not consist ἐν λόγῳ (of men), but ἐν δυνάμει (of God) (1 C. 4:20). [76] Again, to the kingdom of God there belongs δόξα as the glory of God (1 Th. 2:12); indeed, βασιλεία and δόξα may be used interchangeably, as shown by ἐν τῇ δόξῃ σου in Mk. 10:37, where Mt. 20:21 has ἐν τῇ βασιλείᾳ σου. The kingdom of Christ as the One sent by God coincides with His ἐπιφάνεια (2 Tm. 4:1). This βασιλεία ἀσάλευτος is for believers χάρις (Hb. 12:28), or ἐπαγγελία, as MSS א A have for βασιλεία in Jm. 2:5, or ζωή, into which one enters as into the kingdom in Mt. 18:9; the par. in Mk. 9:47 has βασιλεία. The Pharisees and scribes have tried to take this kingdom from the men thereto invited by God according to Mt. 22:13, but the fact that the parallel in Lk. 11:52 speaks of the κλεῖς τῆς γνώσεως shows us that βασιλεία (θεοῦ) is the same as γνῶσις (θεοῦ).

From all these synonyms we may see that the concern of the βασιλεία as God's action towards man is soteriological, so that our explanation of it stands or falls with our explanation of soteriology generally in the preaching of Jesus Christ and His apostles.

b. The last statement makes it plain that the kingdom of God implies the whole of the preaching of Jesus Christ and His apostles. If the whole of the NT message is εὐαγγέλιον, this is the εὐαγγέλιον of the kingdom of God. For → εὐαγγέλιον τοῦ θεοῦ in Mk. 1:14 many MSS have εὐαγγέλιον τῆς βασιλείας τοῦ θεοῦ. This summarised account corresponds to many others (cf. Mt. 4:23; 9:35 and also 24:14). Like εὐαγγέλιον, εὐαγγελίζεσθαι, too, refers to the kingdom of God (Lk. 4:43; 8:1; 16:16; Ac. 8:12). So, too, do related verbs like κηρύσσειν (Mt. 4:23; 9:35; Lk. 9:2; Ac. 20:25; 28:31; or διαμαρτύρεσθαι: Ac. 28:23; or διαγγέλλειν: Lk. 9:60; or πείθειν: Ac. 19:8; or λαλεῖν: Lk. 9:11; or finally λέγειν: Ac. 1:3). Like εὐαγγέλιον, → μυστήριον or μυστήρια (revelation) is also mentioned in relation to the kingdom of God in Mt. 13:11 and par., or the λόγος in Mt. 13:19, where the par. passages in Mk. 4:15 and Lk. 8:12 simply speak of the

---

[76] This saying of Paul is completely misconstrued if we see in it merely the common antithesis between word and work, or speaking and acting. The reference is not to the fact that men should act rather than speak. It is to the fact that the work of man is valueless in comparison with the power of God. We catch the sense if we paraphrase: The kingdom of God does not consist in the power of man but in the Word of God. The whole emphasis falls on the kingdom of God as the dominant and unambiguously logical subject.

λόγος as the Word of God. The whole of this proclamation is expressly attested by the linking of word and deed which is emphasised in decisive passages. Thus with the direction of Jesus to His disciples to proclaim the kingdom of God, we also have the direction: καὶ ἰᾶσθαι (Lk. 9:2; cf. Mt. 10:7 f.; Mk. 3:13 f.). Jesus sees in the fact that He expels demons the dawn of the kingdom of God (Mt. 12:28 = Lk. 11:20). Hence we are concerned not merely with the word of the kingdom of God but also with the coincident act of the kingdom of God. This is expressly stated in the summarised accounts of the Gospels, following the original *kerygma* (cf. Mk. 4:23).

c. What is the point of contact for this NT proclamation? Jesus of Nazareth was not the first to speak of the kingdom of God. Nor was John the Baptist. The proclamation of neither is to the effect that there is such a kingdom and its nature is such and such. Both proclaim that it is near. This presupposes that it was already known to the first hearers, their Jewish contemporaries. This concrete link is decisive. It gives us a positive relationship of Jesus and the Baptist with apocalyptic and the Rabbinic writings in which there are points both of agreement and of distinction to these two movements, which for their part derive from OT prophecy. Details emerge from a comparison with the points already made in sections on the OT and the Rabbinic writings. For the NT authors, who all wrote in Greek, the Greek translation of the OT has to be taken into account in this respect. If in Hb. 1:8 we have reference to the ῥάβδος τῆς βασιλείας αὐτοῦ (LXX: σου) in the middle of a long quotation from the OT, there can be no doubt that this derives from ψ 44:6. [77] On the other hand, as we have seen, there are certain Hellenistic passages in the LXX, and these form a point of contact for the NT preaching of the kingdom of God. The same holds good of Philo and Josephus.

d. If, as the linguistic usage has shown, the kingdom of God implies the state of kingly rule, this emerges logically in the description of this state. The predominant statement is that the kingdom of God is near, that it has drawn near, that it has attained to us, that it comes, that it will appear, that it is to come: ἤγγικεν, Mt. 3:2; 4:17 = Mk. 1:15; Mt. 10:7; Lk. 10:9, 11; ἐγγύς ἐστιν, Lk. 21:31; ἐρχομένη, Mk. 11:10; ἔρχεται, Lk. 17:20; ἔφθασεν, Mt. 12:28 = Lk. 11:20; μέλλει ἀποφαίνεσθαι, Lk. 19:11; ἐλθάτω, Mt. 6:10 = Lk. 11:2.

In the preaching of Jesus of Nazareth, which is linked with that of John and which He passes on to His disciples, the nature of this state of divine kingship is described both negatively and positively, or in the first instance negatively and therewith positively. [78]

Negatively, it is opposed to everything present and earthly, to everything here and now. It is thus absolutely miraculous. Hence we cannot understand it as a *summum bonum* to which man strives and gradually approximates. From the direction in the summarised account at the beginning of the proclamation of the

---

[77] The author of Hebrews is a theologian who, arguing from the LXX, writes the best Gk. in the NT.

[78] For what follows, cf. R. Bultmann, *Jesus* (1926), 28-54; K. L. Schmidt, "Jesus Christus" in RGG², III, 129-132; "Das überweltliche Reich Gottes in der Verkündigung Jesu," ThBl, 6 (1927), 118-120; "Die Verkündigung des Neuen Testaments in ihrer Einheit und Besonderheit," ThBl, 10 (1931), 113 ff.

Gospel: μετανοεῖτε· ἤγγικεν γὰρ ἡ βασιλεία τῶν οὐρανῶν (Mt. 4:17), there arises the only question which can be and is relevant. This is not the question whether or how we men may have the kingdom of God as a disposition in our hearts, or whether we may represent it as a fellowship of those thus minded. The question is whether we belong to it or not. To try to bring in the kingdom of God is human presumption, self-righteous Pharisaism and refined Zealotism. From this standpoint, the supremely hard thing required of man is the patience by which alone may be achieved readiness for the act of God. We can see this in the preaching of the apostle Paul, for whom the νήφειν and the μὴ σβεννύναι τὸ πνεῦμα are coincident (1 Th. 5:8, 19). The parables of the kingdom are spoken to drive home this point. The man who does not display a patient openness for God is like a man who sows, and then like an impatient and curious child — the seed grows he knows not how — he cannot allow it to germinate and grow of itself (the parable of the seed which grows of itself, Mk. 4:26-29). A pure miracle takes place before our eyes when without any co-operation of our own, and beyond all our understanding, the fruit-bearing head develops out of the tiny seed. That modern man has done something to solve this riddle does not affect the decisive *tertium comparationis*. The parables of the mustard seed (Mt. 13:31 f. and par.) and the leaven (Mt. 13:33 = Lk. 13:20 f.) carry the same lesson. It is also present, though rather less obviously, in the other parables, except that there is now a second meaning which we have still to consider, e.g., in the parables of the wheat and the tares in Mt. 13:24-30, of the treasure hid in the field in Mt. 13:44, of the pearl of great price in Mt. 13:45 f., of the drag-net in Mt. 13:47-50, of the wicked servant in Mt. 18:23-35, of the labourers in the vineyard in Mt. 20:1-16, of the marriage feast in Mt. 22:2-14 and of the ten virgins in Mt. 25:1-13. The purpose of all these parables is to make it plain that the order in God's kingdom is different from all human order, and that this kingdom is incalculably and over-whelmingly present within the signs in which it lies enclosed in the activity of Jesus.

From this standpoint, the kingdom of God is a cosmic catastrophe depicted in certain events which constitute the eschatological drama of Jewish apocalyptic. Jesus is at one with those of His Jewish contemporaries whose hope is not set on a visionary political kingdom but who look for the Son of Man coming on the clouds of heaven (Da. 7:13). Even though the community, in its intoxication with apocalyptic visions, might have made some addition, esp. in the so-called Synoptic Apocalypse in Mk. 13 and par., there can be no doubt that Jesus spoke of eating and drinking in the kingdom of God (Mk. 14:25 and par.). Nevertheless, the decisive point is not that Jesus shared or even surpassed the ideas of his con-temporaries in this respect. The decisive point is that He was far more reserved, and consciously so. In contrast to genuine Jewish and early Christian apocalyptic, He neither depicted the last things nor enumerated the signs. The scorn of the Sadducees, who put before Him a problem implied in the apocalyptic and re-surrection hopes which they rejected (as distinct from the Pharisees), was ir-relevant (Mk. 12:25 f.). Particularly striking is His rejection of any enumeration of signs. In the Lucan story in Lk. 17:20 f. Jesus tells us that the divine kingship does not come with observation, or with "external show," as Luther freely but excellently translates οὐ μετὰ παρατηρήσεως. One cannot say, Lo here! or, Lo there! for the reign of God is among you — not "within you," as in the mis-leading AV and Luther.

The whole point of this much quoted and much wrested saying is that we are not to look for signs. The question whether there is an emphasis on the presence of the kingdom

of God at the moment of speaking is irrelevant, since in the original Aramaic there is
no copula "is" or "will be." It has also to be considered that the Syriac translation
demands a rendering back of the Greek ἐντός into the cognate Aramaic which would
give us "among you." The saying of Jesus concerning the dating of the day of the Son
of Man (Mt. 24:26 f.; cf. Lk. 17:23 f.) is in full agreement. Those around Jesus had
very different views of the signs and nature of the kingdom of God. Thus the sons of
Zebedee, or their mother, ask concerning the best places in the kingdom, and Jesus
answers that this is a matter for God alone (Mk. 10:40 = Mt. 20:23). The apostolic
preaching of Paul also agrees, as in R. 14:17, where he tells us that the kingdom of
God does not consist in eating and drinking etc.

Jesus was also more reserved in another respect. Even where national and
political hopes were not to the fore, but salvation was expected for the whole
world in the last time, His contemporaries still thought it important that there
should be a place of privilege for Israel. Israel was to arise with new glory, and
the scattered tribes, and indeed the Gentiles, were to stream towards the new
Jerusalem. Jesus shares this hope. He gives to His disciples, the twelve, as representatives of the twelve tribes of the people of God, the holy people, judicial
and administrative office in the reign of God (Mt. 19:28 = Lk. 22:29 f.). But like
the Baptist Jesus also emphasises the negative fact that the Jew as such has no
particular claim before God. In the day of judgment he can and will be ashamed
in face of the Gentiles. The role of the Jew is viewed as it was later by Paul
(R. 2: the rejection of Israel; R. 9-11: the salvation of Israel). This concern for
Israel is not directed against Rome. In this respect we should compare the Jewish
Sheمone Esre and its fervent nationalism with the Lord's Prayer and its complete
absence of any such particularism. Similarly, immanence is never preached at the
expense of transcendence in the proclamation of the kingdom of God. The kingdom
of God is beyond ethics. To orientate oneself by ethics is to think of the individual. In Jesus and the apostles, however, the individual does not stand under
the promise as an individual. It is the community which stands under the promise ;
the individual attains to salvation as its member.

The proclamation of the kingdom is misunderstood if we overlook these differences from Judaism. It is completely misunderstood, however, if we conceive
of the differences in Greek terms. The Greek view, mostly followed to-day, sees in
man a self-evolving character in which the bodily and sensual element withers
and the spiritual grows. Individualism cannot be replaced by universalism. This
ideal is alien to Jesus and His apostles, as also to later antiquity. To see the proclamation of the kingdom of God in the context of this popular philosophy is to
sublimate it, substituting a refined humanism for the phantasy of human apocalyptic
and visionary political aspirations. Where God breaks in with His kingdom, where
God speaks and acts, no training of the soul, no mysticism, no ecstaticism, can
give access to Him. The cruder Jewish conceptions of heaven and hell make quite
impossible the subtler human possibilities of communion with God imagined by
the Greeks. Anthropomorphic concepts of God and His kingdom do far less
violence to God the Lord in His supraterrestrial majesty than a sublime philosophy.
It has also to be considered that expressions like supraterrestriality, transcendence,
cosmic catastrophe or miracle lose their point if they are used to fashion a higher
world. The negative point that the kingdom of God is a miracle must be maintained in its strict negativity. For this negative, i.e., that the kingdom of God is
wholly other, that it is absolutely above the world and distinct from it, is the
most positive thing that could be said of it. The actualisation of the rule of God

is future. And this future determines man in his present. The call for conversion comes to the man who is set before God and His rule. Where man responds to this call in faith, i.e., in obedience, he is in touch with the kingdom of God which comes without his co-operation, and the Gospel is glad tidings for him.

e. Many terms are used to show how man comes to have dealings with this kingdom. The basic note is that he receives it as the gift of God. God gives His kingdom: εὐδόκησεν ὁ πατὴρ ὑμῶν δοῦναι ὑμῖν τὴν βασιλείαν (Lk. 12:32). Jesus Christ promises the confessing Peter: δώσω σοι τὰς κλεῖδας τῆς βασιλείας τῶν οὐρανῶν (Mt. 16:19). The kingdom is taken from the obdurate Jews and given to believers: ἀρθήσεται ἀφ' ὑμῶν ἡ βασιλεία τοῦ θεοῦ καὶ δοθήσεται ἔθνει ποιοῦντι τοὺς καρποὺς αὐτῆς (Mt. 21:43). Christ makes over the kingdom as the Father has made it over to Him: διατίθεμαι ὑμῖν καθὼς διέθετό μοι ὁ πατήρ μου βασιλείαν (Lk. 22:29). God calls Christians into His kingdom and glory: τοῦ θεοῦ τοῦ καλοῦντος ὑμᾶς εἰς τὴν ἑαυτοῦ βασιλείαν καὶ δόξαν (1 Th. 2:12). God has set us in the kingdom of the Son of His love: μετέστησεν εἰς τὴν βασιλείαν τοῦ υἱοῦ τῆς ἀγάπης αὐτοῦ (Col. 1:13). Believers are made worthy of the kingdom of God: καταξιωθῆναι ὑμᾶς τῆς βασιλείας τοῦ θεοῦ (2 Th. 1:5). The Lord will deliver believers into His heavenly kingdom: ... ῥύσεταί με ὁ κύριος ... σώσει εἰς τὴν βασιλείαν αὐτοῦ τὴν ἐπουράνιον (2 Tm. 4:18). God has promised His kingdom: ἐπηγγείλατο (Jm. 2:5). God does not act like the Pharisees who presume to close the kingdom to men: οὐαὶ ... ὅτι κλείετε τὴν βασιλείαν τῶν οὐρανῶν ἔμπροσθεν τῶν ἀνθρώπων (Mt. 23:13; cf. Lk. 11:52). To these expressions there correspond many correlatives on the side of the believer. He receives the kingdom of God like a child: ὃς ἂν μὴ δέξηται τὴν βασιλείαν τοῦ θεοῦ ὡς παιδίον (Mk. 10:15 = Lk. 18:17). Joseph of Arimathea is in the attitude of one προσδεχόμενος τὴν βασιλείαν τοῦ θεοῦ (Mk. 15:43 = Lk. 23:51). Similarly παραλαμβάνειν at Hb. 12:28. Especially common, and corresponding to the διαθήκη of the kingdom of God, is the expression κληρονομεῖν, e.g., in Mt. 25:34; 1 C. 6:9, 10; 15:50; Gl. 5:21; also ἔχει κληρονομίαν ἐν τῇ βασιλείᾳ ... in Eph. 5:5 and κληρονόμους τῆς βασιλείας in Jm. 2:5. To be thus distinguished by God is to see the kingdom. Some are privileged to see it before their death (Mk. 9:1 and par.). Only the regenerate is worthy of this vision (Jn. 3:3). Particularly common, too, is the idea of entering the kingdom: εἰσέρχεσθαι or εἰσπορεύεσθαι in Mt. 5:20; 7:21; 18:3 and par.; 19:23 f. and par.; 23:13, cf. Lk. 11:52; Mk. 9:47; Jn. 3:5; Ac. 14:22; εἴσοδος in 2 Pt. 1:11. In this connection we should also refer to the passages which speak of ἐν τῇ βασιλείᾳ ... (Mt. 5:19; 8:11 = Lk. 13:28 f.; Mt. 11:11 = Lk. 7:28; Mt. 13:43; 18:1, 4; 20:21; 26:29 and par.; Lk. 14:15; 22:16, 30; 23:42 [alternative reading: εἰς]; Eph. 5:5; Rev. 1:9). The publicans and harlots will go into the kingdom before the self-righteous Pharisees: προάγουσιν ὑμᾶς εἰς τὴν βασιλείαν τοῦ θεοῦ (Mt. 21:31). The Jews should be υἱοὶ τῆς βασιλείας (Mt. 8:12), but because of their hardness of heart they are not (cf. Mt. 13:38). The scribe who is concerned for the cause of God is οὐ μακρὰν ἀπὸ τῆς βασιλείας τοῦ θεοῦ (Mk. 12:34). The true scribe, as God will have him, is μαθητευθεὶς τῇ βασιλείᾳ τῶν οὐρανῶν (Mt. 13:52). Whosoever truly decides for God is εὔθετος τῇ βασιλείᾳ τοῦ θεοῦ (Lk. 9:62). If this is so, there is an appeal for true concern for the cause of God. Like the fellow-workers of Paul, we should be συνεργοὶ εἰς τὴν βασιλείαν τοῦ θεοῦ (Col. 4:11). It should be noted that the text does not say: συνεργοὶ τῆς βασιλείας. ... Thus in spite of the phrase there is no real synergism.

Since, however, faith is obedience to the command of God, our concern and effort are demanded. Through faith we should fight for the kingdom of God like the elect under the old covenant: διὰ πίστεως κατηγωνίσαντο βασιλείας (Hb. 11:33). In short, we should seek earnestly the divine rule: ζητεῖτε ... πρῶτον τὴν βασιλείαν (Mt. 6:33 = Lk. 12:31). This ζητεῖν is rather different from the → βιάζεσθαι and → ἁρπάζειν of Mt. 11:12 = Lk. 16:16. To whom does the kingdom of God belong? To whom is it allotted and assigned? To the poor (in spirit) according to Mt. 5:3 (= Lk. 6:20); to those who are persecuted for right-eousness' sake according to Mt. 5:10; to children according to Mt. 19:14 and par. These passages make it plain how great and inexpressible is the decision required of us. The invitation to the kingdom of God must be accepted in μετάνοια. For the sake of it all the other things of this world, its riches and fame, must be abandoned. We are not to be like those invited to the wedding who pleaded all kind of obstacles (Mt. 22:1-14 = Lk. 14:16-24). Again there are various parables which emphasise this with particular sharpness. For the sake of the kingdom of God, which is like the treasure hid in a field or the goodly pearl for which all else will be exchanged (Mt. 13:44-46), we must pluck out the treacherous eye or cut off the treacherous hand (Mt. 5:29 f.). The most startling saying is that we must reflect that many have made themselves eunuchs for the sake of the kingdom of God (Mt. 19:12).

> In contrast to isolated instances such as that of Origen in the early Church, this is not to be taken as a moral injunction but as a striking and arresting call to consider what it implies to take seriously the divine dominion, namely, that it may even demand self-emasculation, which is here neither praised nor blamed, and certainly not praised. This interpretation is preferable to the weaker, though not impossible, suggestion that some men, like John the Baptist and Jesus Himself, voluntarily renounce the sexual life.

At any rate, true regard for the kingdom of God requires the most serious decision, the most serious weeding out of the few from the many (Mt. 22:14). [79] A sharp alternative demands a pitiless decision. "No man, having put his hand to the plough, and looking back, is fit for the kingdom of God" (Lk. 9:62). This decision is no mere matter of enthusiasm. It is not taken in a wave of emotion. It is a matter for cool and sober consideration, as when an architect makes his plans before beginning to build or a king considers his strategy before going to war (Lk. 14:28-32). Those who are invited by God to His kingdom must reflect whether they can really accept the invitation. Those who do so without realising what it implies, or who hear without obeying, are like a man building his house on sand (Mt. 7:24-27 = Lk. 6:47-49). Not everyone who says "Lord, Lord!" will enter into the kingdom of heaven, but those who do the will of God (Mt. 7:21). Supreme readiness for sacrifice is demanded, even to the point of sacrifice of self, or of hatred of one's own family (Mt. 10:37 = Lk. 14:26). Who is really capable of this? Who judges that he obeys God thus? No one but Jesus Christ Himself.

f. This brings us to the clamant question of the special and particularly close connection between the kingdom of God and Jesus Christ Himself. It is not merely

---

[79] Cf. the sayings about the strait gate and the broad way in Mt. 7:13 f. = Lk. 13:23 f.

that in speaking of the kingdom of God we also speak of that of Christ (→ 581 f.). Certain passages presuppose the actual identity of the kingdom with Christ. Thus in Mk. 11:10 the coming kingdom of our father David is extolled, but Mt. 21:9 and Lk. 19:38 refer only to the person of Jesus Christ (in par. with Mk. 11:9). Even more plain is the Synoptic comparison of ἕνεκεν ἐμοῦ καὶ ἕνεκεν τοῦ εὐαγγελίου (Mk. 10:29), ἕνεκα τοῦ ἐμοῦ ὀνόματος (Mt. 19:29) and εἵνεκεν τῆς βασιλείας τοῦ θεοῦ (Lk. 18:29). The name and message of Jesus Christ, or Jesus Christ Himself, are thus equated with the kingdom of God. This equation goes rather beyond the identification of the Son of Man as a representative of the people of God. While Mk. 9:1 (= Lk. 9:27) speaks of the coming of the kingdom of God in power, the parallel passage in Mt. 16:28 speaks of the coming of the Son of Man with His kingdom. Christians wait for this Son of Man and Lord as for the kingdom of God itself; e.g., Mt. 25:1 and Lk. 12:35 f. As parallelisms we have: εὐαγγελιζομένῳ περὶ τῆς βασιλείας τοῦ θεοῦ καὶ τοῦ ὀνόματος Ἰησοῦ Χριστοῦ (Ac. 8:12) and: κηρύσσων τὴν βασιλείαν τοῦ θεοῦ καὶ διδάσκων τὰ περὶ τοῦ κυρίου Ἰησοῦ Χριστοῦ (Ac. 28:31). Cf. also the parallelism: ἡ βασιλεία τοῦ θεοῦ ἡμῶν καὶ ἡ ἐξουσία τοῦ χριστοῦ αὐτοῦ (Rev. 12:10). There is thus linguistic support for the obvious material fact that for Jesus the invading kingdom of God has come into time and the world in His person, as expressed by John in the statement ὁ λόγος σὰρξ ἐγένετο (Jn. 1:14). What is still to come and is still awaited by the Christian is only in Jesus Christ a σήμερον (Lk. 4:21; cf. Mt. 11:5 f. = Lk. 7:22). [80] It is on this decisive fact of the equation of the incarnate, exalted and present Jesus Christ with the future kingdom of God that the christological κήρυγμα depends with its understanding of the mission of the Messiah as a → ἅπαξ or ἐφάπαξ event, as a unique event which cannot be repeated, as once and for all (→ 381 ff.). Christ ἀπέθανεν ἐφάπαξ (R. 6:10, cf. Hb. 6 ff.; 1 Pt. 3:18). If we seek a brief formula in which to comprehend this equation, there suggests itself the distinctive αὐτοβασιλεία of Origen (in Mt. tom. XIV, 7 on Mt. 18:23 [III, p. 283, Lommatzsch]), [81] though not necessarily Origen's own understanding of it. [82] Before Origen Marcion in his emphatic Panchristismus [83] had said: In evangelio est dei regnum Christus ipse (Tert. Adv. Marc., IV, 33 [III, p. 532, 6 f.]). [84] Jesus Christ alone obeyed the Law and believed (cf. Phil. 2:5 ff.), both preaching the word of the kingdom of God and doing miracles as its signs (Mt. 11:2 ff. = Lk. 7:18 ff.).

We can thus see why the apostolic and post-apostolic Church of the NT did not speak much of the βασιλεία τοῦ θεοῦ explicitly, but always emphasised it implicitly by its reference to the κύριος Ἰησοῦς Χριστός. It is not true that it now substituted the Church (→ ἐκκλησία) for the kingdom as preached by Jesus of Nazareth. On the contrary, faith in the kingdom of God persists in the post-Easter experience of Christ.

---

[80] Cf. G. Kittel, "Das innerweltliche Reich Gottes in der Verkündigung Jesu" ThBl, 6 (1927), 122 f.

[81] So P. Feine, Theol. d. NT¹ (1910), 100 (⁵[1931], 80); Kittel Probleme, 130 f.

[82] Cf. R. Frick, Die Geschichte des Reich-Gottes-Gedankens in der alten Kirche bis zu Origenes u. Augustin (1928), 101, n. 2.

[83] Cf. A. v. Harnack, Marcion² (1924), 223 ff.

[84] It is justly observed by R. Frick (op. cit., 52, n. 1) that there are no good grounds for deleting Christus ipse as a scribal error.

4. As the NT witness is plain and unequivocal in relation to the αὐτοβασιλεία of Christ, it is understandably reserved in its linking of the βασιλεία τοῦ θεοῦ with Christian believers. The only relevant verse in this connection is Rev. 1:6 : Christ ἐποίησεν ἡμᾶς βασιλείαν. [85] It hardly need be shown or proved, however, that in this verse Christians may be understood as βασιλεία only in a derivative sense, i.e., as linked with Christ.

† βασίλισσα.

The "queen" of the south, of Sheba, a heathen ruler who will confront the impenitent Jews on the day of judgment because she came from the ends of the earth to hear the wisdom of Solomon (Mt. 12:42; Lk. 11:31). The Ethiopians have laid claim to this queen [86] (cf. Ac. 8:27). [87] Her antithesis is the great harlot Babylon which is enthroned as a queen and is judged (Rev. 18:7).

† βασιλεύω.

This word, meaning "to be king," "to reign," is used with the emphatic article of the βασιλεύς Jesus Christ (→ 577 ff.) and of the βασιλεύς God (→ 579). Christ βασιλεύσει ἐπὶ τὸν οἶκον ᾿Ιακὼβ εἰς τοὺς αἰῶνας (Lk. 1:33). With more restricted reference to the rule of God Himself we read in 1 C. 15:25 : δεῖ αὐτὸν (sc. Χριστὸν) βασιλεύειν ἄχρι οὗ θῇ πάντας τοὺς ἐχθροὺς ὑπὸ τοὺς πόδας αὐτοῦ. Rev. 11:15 speaks of God and His Anointed as rulers to all eternity. God's rule in the past and the future is often treated in Rev., cf. 11:17 and 19:6. With Him will reign those who are called by Him (Rev. 5:10). They will reign with Christ in the millennial kingdom (Rev. 20:4, 6). They will reign to all eternity (Rev. 22:5). This specific emphasis on the rule of Christians with Christ is probably present also in 1 C. 4:8, where Paul says ironically : χωρὶς ἡμῶν ἐβασιλεύσατε (behind ἡμῶν we see the apostle of the Gospel as the one commissioned by Christ). The following wish : καὶ ὄφελόν γε ἐβασιλεύσατε ἵνα καὶ ἡμεῖς σὺν ὑμῖν συμβασιλεύσωμεν, points us to the goal of Christian hope anticipated by the Corinthians in egotistic arrogance. Linked with the thought of the Christian reigning with Christ is that of his reigning through Him (R. 5:17).

Grace as the gift of Christ rightly occupies the place of rule (R. 5:21) when the usurpers death and sin are destroyed (R. 5:14, 17, 21; 6:12).

Alongside this specialised use there is also reference to the reign of Archelaus in Mt. 2:22, to reigning monarchs in 1 Tm. 6:15 and to the rule of men among themselves in Lk. 19:14, 27.

---

[85] We may take it that this text — a quotation from the OT — is more certain than the alternatives βασίλειον or βασιλεῖς.

[86] Kl. Mt., ad loc.

[87] Cf. S. Lösch, "Der Kämmerer der Königin Kandake (Apg. 8:27)," Theol. Quart., 111 (1930), 477-519.

† συμβασιλεύω.

It has already been mentioned that as a reigning together the reigning of Christians stands under a σύν (Χριστῷ), 1 C. 4:8. This rule implies service, obedience and patience : εἰ ὑπομένομεν, καὶ συμβασιλεύσομεν (2 Tm. 2:12).

† βασίλειος.

This word, meaning "royal," is found in an uncertain reading in Mt. 11:8 (→ 577), better attested in the parallel Lk. 7:25 : τὰ βασίλεια, in the sense of the royal palace or royal palaces. In the rich and pregnant saying at 1 Pt. 2:9, βασίλειον ἱεράτευμα is the expression, deriving from the LXX, for מַמְלֶכֶת כֹּהֲנִים in Ex. 19:6, cf. Ex. 23:22. The reference here might be to the priesthood as invested with royal dignity. But the Hebrew text has Israel in view as the people whose king is God. Perhaps βασίλειος is meant in a rather weaker sense at 1 Pt. 2:9 to signify royal priesthood in the manner in which one speaks of royal service. It must certainly be considered, as we have shown above, that in the case of men a βασιλέα εἶναι or βασιλεύειν does not denote an inherent quality; we are to understand it rather as a συμβασιλεύειν with God and His Christ. The logical subject of the ἐκκλησία as the βασίλειον ἱεράτευμα is God who calls and Christ through whom the call comes.

† βασιλικός.

Having the same meaning "royal" (v. Ac. 12:20 f.), this word is not so common as βασίλειος; yet it is more common in the NT.

Theologically important is Jm. 2:8 : νόμον τελεῖτε βασιλικόν. The phrase νόμος βασιλικός is a common literary expression, esp. in ancient philosophy (e.g., Philo passim). It signifies the law as given by the βασιλεύς. This controls access to him, and it thus invests with royal dignity, though extending beyond, e.g., mere differences in rank (cf. the whole tenor of James). More generally it might refer to the predominant significance of law. Yet it is better to give it the more specific sense and thus to see in it a reference to God as the βασιλεύς who makes law. [88]

In Jn. 4:46, 49 the concrete sense of βασιλικός is debatable. [89] The probable reference is to a royal official. The variant βασιλίσκος, supported by D it^var, would denote a petty king.

F. Βασιλεία (τοῦ θεοῦ) in the Early Church. [90]

Relationship between the statements concerning the kingdom of God in the post-apostolic fathers and those in the NT is first established by the presence of certain

---

[88] Dib. Jk., ad loc.; Wnd. Jk., ad loc.
[89] Bau. Jn.³, ad loc.
[90] For βασιλεύς in the post-apostolic fathers, → 579.

quotations, such as Mt. 5:3, 10 or Lk. 6:20 in Pol., 2, 3; Mt. 6:10 in Did., 8, 2; 1 C. 6:9 f. (cf. Eph. 5:5) in Ign. Eph., 16, 1; Ign. Phld., 3, 3; Pol., 5, 3.

The usage in relation to the kingdom of God is in general the same as in the NT. Βασιλεία τοῦ Χριστοῦ is often used as well as βασιλεία τοῦ θεοῦ, e.g., in 1 Cl., 50, 3; 2 Cl., 12, 2; Barn., 4, 13; 7, 11; 8, 5 and 6; Mart. Pol., 22, 1 and 3. Βασιλεία also occurs in the absolute in 1 Cl., 61, 1; 2 Cl., 5, 5. Among direct attributes we may mention αἰώνιος in Mart. Pol., 20, 2; οὐράνιος in Mart. Pol., 22, 3; ἐπουράνιος in Mart. Pol. epil., 4. With regard to synonyms it is to be noted that in 2 Cl., 5, 5 the ἐπαγγελία τοῦ Χριστοῦ is understood as the ἀνάπαυσις τῆς μελλούσης βασιλείας καὶ ζωῆς αἰωνίου. That the μέλλειν ἔρχεσθαι refers to the kingdom of God may be seen also in 1 Cl., 42, 3. There are many ways of stating the manner in which man comes to have dealings with this kingdom. The basic thought of the NT remains: he receives it as God's gift. It is said of God: ἔδωκας τὴν ἐξουσίαν τῆς βασιλείας (1 Cl., 61, 1); τὴν ἐν οὐρανῷ βασιλείαν ἐπηγγείλατο καὶ δώσει τοῖς ἀγαπήσασιν αὐτόν (Dg., 10, 2); He can πάντας ἡμᾶς εἰσαγαγεῖν εἰς τὴν αὐτοῦ βασιλείαν (Mart. Pol., 20, 2); prayer is made to Him: συναχθήτω σου ἡ ἐκκλησία ἀπὸ τῶν περάτων τῆς γῆς εἰς τὴν σὴν βασιλείαν (Did., 9, 4; cf. 10, 5); or it is said of Christ: ἵνα κἀμὲ συναγάγῃ εἰς τὴν βασιλείαν αὐτοῦ (Mart. Pol., 22, 3). As in the NT there are on man's side many correlatives to this mode of expression. The believer receives, encounters, sees and inherits the kingdom of God; he dwells, is found and is glorified in it; he enters into it: ἐκδέχεσθαι (2 Cl. 12, 1); ἅπτεσθαι (Barn., 7, 11); ὁρᾶν (Herm. s., 9, 15, 3); κληρονομεῖν (Ign. Eph., 16, 1; Ign. Phld., 3, 3); κατοικεῖν (Herm. s., 9, 29, 2); εὑρεθῆναι (Herm. s., 9, 13, 2); δοξασθῆναι (Barn., 21, 1); ἔρχεσθαι (2 Cl., 9, 6); εἰσέρχεσθαι (Herm. s., 9,12, 3; 4; 5; 8; 15, 2, 3; 16, 2; 3; 4; 20, 2; 3; Dg., 9, 1); εἰσήκειν (2 Cl., 11, 7).

In this usage the post-apostolic fathers are wholly at one with the NT. [91] The final coming will take place with the return of Christ (1 Cl., 50, 3). The entry of the Christian is linked with the sacrament (Herm. s., 9, 16, 2) and good works (2 Cl., 6, 9). The ethical imperative is strongly underlined: ἐὰν οὖν ποιήσωμεν τὴν δικαιοσύνην ἐναντίον τοῦ θεοῦ εἰσήξομεν εἰς τὴν βασιλείαν αὐτοῦ (2 Cl., 11, 7); ὁ γὰρ ταῦτα (sc. τὰ δικαιώματα τοῦ κυρίου) ποιῶν ἐν τῇ βασιλείᾳ τοῦ θεοῦ δοξασθήσεται (Barn., 21, 1). To this there corresponds the stress on the thought of judgment in hope of the kingdom of God (cf. 2 Cl., 17, 5). It is decisive, however, that God Himself brings in the kingdom and that He calls believers in Christ: εἰς τὴν βασιλείαν τοῦ θεοῦ ἄλλως εἰσελθεῖν οὐ δύναται ἄνθρωπος εἰ μὴ διὰ τοῦ ὀνόματος τοῦ υἱοῦ αὐτοῦ τοῦ ἠγαπημένου ὑπ' αὐτοῦ (Herm. s., 9, 12, 5; cf. 9, 12, 8). While there is here formal and verbal agreement with the NT, in contrast to the preaching of Jesus Christ and His apostles the coming of the kingdom is now made dependent on the conduct of the community, as in 2 Cl., 12, 2 ff., where the Lord is asked: πότε ἥξει αὐτοῦ ἡ βασιλεία, and answers: ὅταν ἔσται τὰ δύο ἕν, καὶ τὸ ἔξω ὡς τὸ ἔσω, καὶ τὸ ἄρσεν μετὰ τῆς θηλείας οὔτε ἄρσεν οὔτε θῆλυ. The saying here presupposed is also found in the apocryphal Egypt. Ev. and denotes an ethicising of the idea of the kingdom of God in the direction of an ascetic and dualistic ethics of perfection. In Herm. the coming of the kingdom of God does not depend on man, but entry into it is linked with a specific degree of moral perfection. In this connection faith and the moral life are not completely divorced, but they are certainly distinguished. In the catalogue of virtues in Herm. s., 9, 15, 2 ff. ἐγκράτεια and other moral qualities are mentioned after πίστις. [92]

---

[91] Cf. R. Frick, op. cit., 27-35.
[92] Cf. on this pt., E. Fuchs, Glaube und Tat in den Mandata des Hirten des Hermas (Diss. Marburg, 1931).

The post-apostolic writings are not clear in relation to the distinction between the kingdom and the Church, which is so characteristic of the NT. In Barn. the kingdom is a purely eschatological magnitude ; hence it cannot be the Church. It is a distinctive feature of Barn. that in 8, 5 f. the beginning of the reign of Christ is set at the cross : ἡ βασιλεία 'Ιησοῦ ἐπὶ ξύλου, and that in a way which is almost chiliastic days of conflict and misfortune are spoken of even in the kingdom of Christ : ἐν τῇ βασιλείᾳ αὐτοῦ ἡμέραι ἔσονται πονηραὶ καὶ ῥυπαραί, ἐν αἷς ἡμεῖς σωθησόμεθα. While the eucharistic prayer in the Did. distinguishes plainly between the kingdom and the ἐκκλησία which Christ gathers into His kingdom, the distinction has faded in 2 Cl., 14, 3 to the extent that the ἐκκλησία must be received like the βασιλεία τοῦ θεοῦ. Similarly the two approximate closely in Herm.

Influenced by the metaphysics of Plato and the ethics of the Stoics, the Christian Apologists [93] make little use of the concept of the kingdom of God. In so far as they have an eschatology, it is dominated by the idea of the perfection of the individual Christian. The conception of God asserting a claim to lordship over man with His kingdom is alien to them. The Christian has the task of imitating God and striving towards him ; he hopes for the βασιλεία μετὰ θεοῦ (Just. Apol., I, 11, 1). The ἐπου-ράνιος βασιλεία is conceived by Athen. Suppl., 18, 1 and 2 as the Creator's power over everything that happens. Yet neither in Athen. nor the Apologists is the idea common. Justin uses the word βασιλεία chiliastically of the millennium, but does not distinguish this clearly from the eternal kingdom. The kingdom is promised as an eternal reward for the righteous, and is the opposite of the torments of hell (Just. Dial., 117, 3) ; βασιλείαν κληρονομεῖν means the same as τὰ αἰώνια καὶ ἄφθαρτα κληρο-νομεῖν (Just. Dial., 139, 5). As distinct from these isolated references, there is frequent mention of the βασιλεία τοῦ θεοῦ in the quotations in Justin's Dialogue and Apology. OT sayings and λόγια 'Ιησοῦ are quoted to clarify the relation between promise and fulfilment and to give point to the demand of God on man, who will then be rewarded. Yet this link with the teaching of Jesus and the apostles is more formal than material. The starting-point is not the efficacy of divine grace, but the freedom for virtuous living in connection with the claim to reward. Thus the theological and philosophical work of the Apologists makes an ambiguous impression. On the one side, Greek concepts of immortality, eternal life and knowledge are more important than the biblical concept of the βασιλεία τοῦ θεοῦ. On the other, the words of Jesus and the apostles, even though they are only quoted and not fully explored, preserve the Christian teaching from transmutation into religious philosophy.

This introduces us to the theme of further development in ecclesiastical and theological history. [94] The one-sided ethicising of the thought of the kingdom of God is accompanied from the 2nd cent. onwards by a one-sided eschatologising expressed as popular religion in the early Christian apocalypses with their Gnostic trend (cf. Asc. Is., 4 Esr., Sib.), in stories of martyrdom and especially in burial inscriptions and pictures in the catacombs. As against this, Greek philosophical thinking becomes predominant in Clement of Alex., as in the Apologists ; the βασιλεία concept of this religious philosopher is in terms of Platonism and Stoicism. It is striking that Clement turns to Stoic definitions in this field (Strom., II, 4, 19, 3 f.). Faith in gradual progress (προκοπή) replaces the biblical conception of the last judgment. Similarly in Origen, in spite of the formally excellent term αὐτοβασιλεία (→ 589), there is almost no place at all for the biblical message of the kingdom of God. As distinct from this Greek mode of thought predominant in the East, the Latin theology of the West believes in the active realisation of the kingdom of God on earth ; this development finds its climax in the identification of the kingdom with the Church as found in Augustine.

Karl Ludwig Schmidt

---

[93] Cf. R. Frick, *op. cit.*, 35-45.
[94] *Ibid.*, 73 ff.

---

† βασκαίνω

Denominative construction of βάσκανος[1] ("defamatory," "bewitching"), which is linked with (βάσκω[2] and) βάζω.[3] The original meaning, (cf. the related *fascinare,* root *fa(ri)*), though the connection with βασκαίνω is not wholly clear)[2] is "to do hurt to someone through unfavourable words." According to the sense in which this was taken in the ancient world (→ ὄνομα), the damage might be the result of envious praise or of denigration. These could have the same effect as direct witchcraft. Hence we have three senses: a. "to bewitch," b. "to revile" and c. "to envy."[4] So far as concerns a., there came to be added to the original meaning that of harm through hostile looks, so that a. denotes "specifically the simple but all the more sinister" witchcraft "exercised through hostile looks or words," even though it might be unintentional.[5] It thus indicates amongst other things a harmful magic exercised independently of the subjective will and with no particular technique.

The ancient world, except in so far as better instructed by the philosophical enlightenment,[6] was conscious of being surrounded by invisible and hostile beings which sought power over it. A particular way of attaining this was by the naming of the name[7] (→ ὄνομα). This in why in letters the writer adds to the name of those he greets, or whose greetings he sends on, an ἀβασκάντους (-οι), or to the wish an ἀβασκάντως (e.g., P. Oxy., II, 300, 9 [1st cent. B.C.]: ἀσπάζου [five names are given] τοὺς ἀβασκάντους; or for the latter, cf. P. Oxy., III, 930, 23: ἀσπάζονταί σε ... καὶ τὰ ἀβάσκαντα παιδία ...).[8] We should thus render: "Heaven preserve us!"[9] In all these cases, of course, it is not merely a question of magic through the evil eye but of any bewitching or hurting through men or non-human forces. Hence it is clear that,

---

β α σ κ α ί ν ω. E. Kuhnert in Pauly-W., VI (1909), 2009 ff.; O. Jahn, *Ber. Sächs. Gesellsch. d. Wiss.,* 1855, 28 ff. has some good material, though mainly in relation to the warding off of the evil eye.

[1] Debr. Griech. Wortb., 109 (§ 219). Boisacq., *s.v.;* from βάσκανος (which does not occur).

[2] I owe this to Debrunner. Acc. to Pass., *s.v.* βάσκω = "I speak" is used only by grammarians to deduce βασκαίνω from it.

[3] Originally guttural; cf. fut. βάξω, perf., pass. βέβακται — from βάκσκειν (not found). Boisacq, *s.v.* βάζω.

[4] Cf. the lexicons. βάσκανος is attested from the 5th cent. B.C., βασκανία since Plato, βασκαίνω since Aristotle.

[5] Kuhnert, *op. cit.,* 2009 on *fascinari.*

[6] For reference to the superiority of the educated man over belief in the operation of the βάσκανος, though without support for the view, cf. Plut. Quaest. Conv., V, 1 (II, 680c).

[7] This closely related meaning is also to be found in Preisigke Wört., *s.v.* ἀβάσκαντος.

[8] Where there is a list of those sending or receiving greetings, and children are included, ἀβάσκαντος seems (mostly?) to apply to the children, since they are particularly endangered (Plut. Quaest. Conv., V, 1 [II, 680de]). Cf. also P. Oxy., IX, 1218, 11; VIII, 1159, 27; P. Giess., 23, 10; 25, 3; BGU, 714, 11; 811, 4. The application can be so fully to children that even in the gen. ἀβάσκαντα may denote children without τέκνα or παιδία. Is a child meant also in P. Giess., 76, 8? Or why is Heracleides alone thought of with an apotropaic wish?

[9] This is the rendering selected by Preisigke, *op. cit.*

unless βασκαίνειν is given this narrower sense by the context, it does not have to denote the evil eye but may equally well refer to other means of harming by magic.

Thus in Aristot. Fr., No. 271, p. 1527a, 29 we find the strange assertion that the pigeon spits on its young three times after hatching out, ὡς μὴ βασκανθῶσι (this is an attested means of protecting men against βασκαίνεσθαι, Theocr. Idyll., 6, 39). Harm can also come from suspicious foods (Aristot. Probl., XX, 34, p. 926b, 20 ff.), or from the breath, the sound of words or touch (Plut. Quaest. Conv., V, 1 [II, 680ef]). It is to be noted, however, that βασκαίνειν is never used of other magic which employs certain external means that acquire magical power by conjuration. The magical power of the βάσκανος lies always in his look or touch etc. This is the meaning of Plut., op. cit. (V, 3 [II, 681d]) when he describes βασκαίνειν as primarily a psychical and even bodily process. Of course, in popular belief the energy in question is not that of the man himself; it is suprahuman and often demonic. [10]

That βασκανία may be unintentional is shown, e.g., by belief in the unintentional harming of children by parents endowed with the power of the βάσκανος (Plut., op. cit., V, 4 [II, 682a]), or of friends by one another (Heliodor. Aeth., III, 8), or even of the possibility that a man might αὐτὸν βάσκαινεν (Plut., op. cit., 682b).

In the LXX it means only "to be unfavourably disposed to" (even at Dt. 28:54, 56; the only other instance is at Sir. 14:6, 8).

In the NT the word occurs only at Gl. 3:1 in the sense of "to bewitch" (by words). This is not merely an exaggerated metaphor, for behind magic stands the power of falsehood (→ γόης) [11] and this has been exercised by the τίς (or the group behind the τίς) to do real harm to the νοῦς of the Galatians (ἀνόητοι). [12] This is certainly not to be understood in a naively realistic way as mechanical magic. The dangerous feature is that the Galatians have willingly yielded to these magicians and their influence without realising to what powers of falsehood they were surrendering. The characteristic point of the βασκανία is that it exerts its influence without extraordinary means.

Delling

---

[10] We already have a rationalising view, differing from the popular conception, when Plut., op. cit., II, 681 f. suggests that the bodily process of βασκαίνειν (connected in Plut. with the evil eye) receives its power from the underlying energy of soul.

[11] Cf. the passages from Philo Praem. Poen., 25; Spec. Leg., I, 315; Praem. Poen., 8; Op. Mund., 165, 2; Som., II, 40.

[12] Or does ἀνόητοι mean that like children those addressed have proved incapable of resisting the βάσκανος ?

βαστάζω

Found in the NT 27 times, 8 in Luke, often par. with αἴρω or φέρω. Relatively rare in the LXX, the equivalent of נָשָׂא as βάσταγμα is of מַשָּׂא. Corresponding Heb. terms acc. to Schlatter are סבל and טען.[1] The basic meaning is uncertain.[2] In the NT it means a. "to lift up" (Jn. 10:31), b. "to bear away" (Jn. 20:15), "to pilfer" (Jn. 12:6; cf. Jos. Ant., 1, 316 : Laban to Jacob : ἱερά τε πάτρια βαστάσας οἴχῃ).

Since carrying is an exertion of power and thus includes an exercise and application of will, the word takes on ethical and religious significance, as in Epict. Diss., III, 15, 9 : ἄνθρωπε ... τί δύνασαι βαστάσαι;[3] The metaphor τὸν → σταυρὸν βαστάσαι originally denotes the outward carrying of the cross by Jesus (Jn. 19:17), then the personal attitude of the disciples (Lk. 14:27).[4] Similarly ζυγὸν βαστάσαι at Ac. 15:10.[5] Often the meaning is "to bear" (Jn. 16:12; R. 15:1; Gl. 5:10; 6:2, 5).[6] In → στίγματα βαστάζω (Gl. 6:17) βαστάζω means the same as ἔχω "to have on oneself"; cf. Rev. 7:2; 9:14; 13:17; 14:1; 16:2, where the reference is to the bearing of the seal (sign) or name of God (or Christ) or Antichrist. In Ac. 9:15 βαστάσαι τὸ ὄνομά μου is the service of the missionary for Jesus, the steadfast confession of Him as the Lord. Here again βαστάσαι is very close to ἔχειν. In spite of v. 16 there is no idea of a burden.[7]

Büchsel

β α σ τ ά ζ ω. Pass., Preisigke Wört., *s.v.*; A. Schlatter, *Sprache u. Heimat des 4 Evglst.* (1902), 132.

[1] *Op. cit.*, 111, 132, 139; Schl. J., 313. סבל originally means "to carry," though in the Rabb. it often has the figur. sense of "to suffer" or "endure" (cf. βαστάζειν in Jn. 16:12); used of God in relation to the world it denotes His preserving, cf. Str.-B., III, 673 on Hb. 1:3. טען means 1. trans. "to burden someone with something," figur. "to accuse or to engage someone"; 2 intrans. "to be burdened with something," "to bear," cf. βαστάζειν (Jn. 19:17 — not figur.).

[2] The etymology does not help us. The first attested meaning is "to lift up." "To bear" is derived from this, as with the Lat. *tollere*. The meaning "to take away" is Hellen. and may have been influenced by the Lat. *tollere*.

[3] Also in the pap., Preisigke Wört., *s.v.*

[4] In magic the Mith. Liturg., 18, 11: βαστάξας κεντρῖτιν, Reitzenstein Poim., 227: σοῦ δὲ τὸ πνεῦμα βαστάξας εἰς ἀέρα, Deissmann B., 270 : βαστάξω τὴν ταφὴν τοῦ Ὀσίρεως.

[5] The expression ζυγὸν βαστάσαι was traditional; cf. Did., 62 : βαστάσαι ὅλον τὸν ζυγὸν τοῦ κυρίου and ζυγὸν ... ὑπενεγκεῖν; Jos. Ant., 8, 213 and Schl. Mt. on 11:29; also Lam. 3:27 etc. The Rabb. קבל עול (Schl., *op. cit.*; Dalman WJ, I, 80) is δέχεσθαι ζυγόν and is thus to be distinguished from βαστάζειν ζυγόν. קבל = δέχεσθαι denotes the resolve to subject oneself to God's will; its opp. is פרק עול (to throw off the yoke, Dalman, *op. cit.*), whereas βαστάζειν implies the constant attitude of submission.

[6] Cf. already Is. 53:11 (A) and Is. 53:4 in Mt. 8:17.

[7] ὄνομα βαστάσαι also in Herm. s., 8, 10, 3 (of loyal confession as distinct from apostasy); 9, 28, 5; similarly φορεῖν τὸ ὄνομα in s., 9, 13, 2 and 3 (= "to confess oneself a Christian"). Cf. also κεκλημένοι τῷ ὀνόματι κυρίου in s., 8, 1, 1. Since it is in baptism that the name of the Lord is first invoked over a man (Jm. 2:7), the βαστάζοντες τὸ ὄνομα κυρίου are the baptised (cf. W. Heitmüller, *Im Namen Jesu* [1903], 92, 297); yet the reference to baptism is not essential in the formula.

† βατταλογέω

This occurs only at Mt. 6:7 in the sense of "to babble." The non-Christian, and non-Jew, thinks that by heaping up the names of God, of which he does not know the true and relevant one, he can include the deity which will grant his request, and that he can weary God — this includes Jews too — by constant repetition. Jesus, on the other hand, advises a calm trust in the Father (→ ἀββᾶ) who need only be addressed as such and who will give all necessary things to His children if they prove themselves to be such by praying first for His kingdom (6:33).

The attestation of this stem, even in substantive constructions, is so meagre that no sure solution of the etymol. problem is possible. βαττολογέω occurs in Epict. Ench., 37 (p. 340, Schweighäuser), Vita Aesopi, 46, 21 Westermann, [1] and in eccles. liter.; βαττο-λογία in Hesych. [1] and the fathers; βαττολόγος in the fathers and Corp. Gloss. Lat., III, 334, 13. Least likely are the solutions of Blass (and earlier scholars), [2] namely, that we have a hybrid construction from λογο- and Syr. בטל (Aram. = "empty," "vain"), thus giving βαττολογέω, "to speak futilities"), and of Zahn and Schlatter: [3] "Branches of the Batta tree run together to signify futile exertion." The question which has to be put to both these suggestions is whether such a saying would have arisen in the Palestinian Gospel. Could the editor of Mt. expect the Greeks to grasp the meaning of a semi-Semitic word?

It must be granted that there is no satisfactory solution purely in Gk. terms. Hesych. (s.v.) claims knowledge of a word βάττος [4] which he renders "stammerer" or "stutterer," but if in βαττολογέω we really have the addition of λογ- to a stem βαττο-, it is hard to explain the vl. βατταλογ- in Cod. א B. According to the available material, the form βατταλ- is the older. [5] The most probable solution is that, irrespective of the rules of grammatical composition, βατταλογέω has been constructed in analogy with the better known βατταρίζω, "to stammer or stutter," in a free manner echoing the common stem λογ-; [6] there is certainly little doubt that both constructions are onomato-poeic. [7] Such words sometimes defy exact linguistic analysis.

Delling

β α τ τ α λ ο γ έ ω. Bibl. in Pr.-Bauer, s.v.; Dausch Synpt.[4], 122.

[1] As suggested by Debrunner.

[2] Since the 2nd. ed. of the Gramm., and still in Bl.-Debr.[6] (§ 40), though Debrunner later abandoned it.

[3] Both on Mt. 6:7.

[4] Debrunner has pointed out that Liddell-Scott have it, though elsewhere it occurs only as a proper name.

[5] Hence also in the Corp. Gloss. Lat., III, 73, 55 *battalago* (*sic !*) *delero* : βατταλογῶ *deliro* (Debrunner).

[6] This seems to be the view of Liddell-Scott, who simply compare it with βατταρίζω and render "to stammer," "to repeat the same thing again and again."

[7] So Pass., Boisacq, s.v. βατταρίζω, and already Hesych., s.v. βατταρίζω. For this reason no significance can be attached to the vl. βατολογία in Hesych. Hence a connection of the word with βάτ(τ)αλος is impossible, since in the grammars this is construed very differently (cf. the lexicons). As shown by Debrunner, the same point emerges from Aeschin., 2, 99 : Demosthenes ἐν παισὶ ... ὢν ἐκλήθη δι᾽ αἰσχρουργίαν τινὰ καὶ κιναιδίαν Βάταλος ; it thus denotes the paederast.

**† βδελύσσομαι, † βδέλυγμα,
† βδελυκτός**

From the basic stem with its sense of causing abhorrence. [1] βδελυρός and its derivatives βδελυρεύομαι and βδελυρία are often found in the secular field to denote an improper attitude, often in connection with such related expressions as ἀναίσχυντος, μιαρός, θρασύς. In particular this word group denotes a shameless attitude. [2] Also deriving from this stem are the words βδελύσσομαι, βδελυγμία, βδέλυγμα, βδελυκτός, βδελυγμός; the last three are not found at all in Jewish and Christian literature; [3] βδελύσσομαι is a middle pass. with acc. in the sense of "to loathe," "to abhor," though it later takes on the more intensive meaning of "to censure" or "to reject." [4]

βδελυρός and its derivatives are not found in biblical usage, [5] but the word group associated with βδελύσσομαι emerges the more strongly in the LXX. The act. form seems to take on the sense of "to make abhorrent" or "to cause to be abhorred" (Ex. 5:21; Lv. 11:43; 1 Macc. 1:48) with the class. sense of the mid. and the further common sense of "to abhor," "to reject," as also with the true pass. of "to come to be abhorred" (Is. 49:7; 2 Macc. 5:8; Sir. 20:8). The perf. pass. has the sense of "to be abhorrent or unclean" (Hos. 9:10; Lv. 18:30; Job 15:16 [with ἀκάθαρτος]; Prv. 8:7; 28:9; Is. 14:19; 3 Macc. 6:9). There are also examples of the pass. in the sense of "to act abominably" (3 Βασ. 20:26; ψ 13:1; 52:1). Corresponding to the sense of "to abhor" is βδέλυγμα, "the subject of abhorrence," βδελυκτός as a verbal adj. "abhorrent," "unclean," βδελυγμός (Na. 3:6) = βδελυκτὸς νομίζεσθαι.

The constructions deriving from the stem βδελυρ- are not found in the Bible because the Bible is not concerned to emphasise the abhorrent nature of things but to describe in a plastic and anthropomorphic expression the attitude and judgment of God in relation to things which He hates. Fundamental to the concept βδέλυγμα, βδελύττεσθαι in the LXX is the fact that God has a contrary mind and rejects; this is the guiding rule for the people Israel. In the legal parts of the Bible the reference may be to things which are cultically (= aesthetically?) "unclean," "repugnant" or "abhorrent," and especially to certain pagan things which are particularly abominable to the God of the OT. Thus idols themselves (= שִׁקּוּצִים) may be called βδελύγματα. This usage is found in the writing prophets ('Ιερ. 13:27; 39:35; 51:22; Ez. 5:9, 11; 6:9 etc.), but in them there is an extension which makes βδέλυγμα parallel to ἀνομία (Jer. 4:1; Ez. 11:18; 20:30; Am. 6:8; ψ 5:7; 13:1; 52:1; 118:163; Job 15:16). In the Wisdom literature this development leads to the point where the opposition to paganism disappears and the word simply denotes God's hostility to evil (Prv. 8:7; 11:1, 20; 12:22; 15:8 f., 26; 20:17; 21:27).

βδελύσσομαι κτλ. [1] Cf. E. Kieckers, *Indogerm. Forsch.*, 30 (1912), 190-192.
[2] For examples, v. Liddell-Scott, *s.v.*, esp. Aristoph. Ra., 465, Nu., 446, Demosth., 25, 27: βδελυρὸς καὶ ἀναιδής, similarly Aeschin., 1, 41.
[3] βδελυκτός is present in βδελύκτροπος.
[4] Polyb., XXXIV, 14, 1: γεγονὼς ἐν τῇ πόλει βδελύττεται τὴν τότε κατάστασιν.
[5] Cf. Philo Det. Pot. Ins., 95: ὁ τοῦ βδελυρῶς καὶ ἀσελγῶς ζῆν αἴτιος.

This mode of expression persists in the Rabbinic lit. (M. Ex. 20:21: כל גבהי לבב קרוים תועבה), [6] though the older usage is also found, cf. the reference to the command to abstain from certain meats in terms of "abhorring" them (bAZ, 66a = bChul., 114b; bShab., 145b אוכלין שקוצים). The word group תעב is also used of those who are permanently or temporarily forbidden to marry (bNidd., 70a; jJeb., 4, 6b and bJeb., 11b; in 44b מתועב לפני המקום means abhorred by God.

In many passages of the Torah especially the question might be raised how far there is perhaps a natural aesthetic as well as a religious element in the word group βδελυκ-, [7] as, for example, when the eating of certain animals is described as an abomination, or incest or pagan ways of life are called abominable. Probably for the OT, which recognises God as the Creator of the world which is good, the two elements are inseparable on profounder theological reflection, so that even in respect of what is abhorrent the view of God is basic.

The word group βδελυκ- in the LXX [8] is a. a regular translation of the word group תעב (92 times). There are 6 exceptions in Jer., Ezr., Chr., Ez. and Prv. In Ez. the word group תעב occurs 44 times, and 30 times βδελυκ- is not used; ἀνομέω and derivatives are used in 24 of these. On 8 occasions out of 21 תעב is not rendered βδελυκ- in Prv., ἀκάθαρτος, ἀκαθαρσία are used 5 times. Again, b. βδελυκ- is used relatively infrequently for certain Heb. terms for idols, along with other attempted renderings such as εἴδωλον, γλυπτόν, χειροποίητον, μάταιον, δαιμόνιον, ἔνθυμα, ἐπιτήδευμα. c. It is used quite often for the word group שקץ (9 times in Lv., 20 in the prophets incl. Da., elsewhere only 3 times), along with such renderings as προσοχθίζειν, προσόχθισμα.

The LXX continued the extension of the term begun in the prophets, and helped to liberate it from natural and aesthetic connections (→ 598), partly by equating it with ethical concepts like ἀνομία (for תּוֹעֵבָה, 599), and partly by pouring into it the purely ethical content acquired by תּוֹעֵבָה especially in Prv. (→ 598), and thus giving it a completely new orientation. This is particularly plain in Sir. 15:13, where the LXX has πᾶν βδέλυγμα for the double term רעה ותעבה. As an expression of the dualistic antithesis between the will of God and that of man, βδέλυγμα can also denote the repugnance of the ungodly to the will of God (Prv. 29:27; Sir. 1:25; 13:20).

In the use of the word group βδελυκ- in the OT, there is reflected some part of the obligation of Israel to separate itself from everything pagan in the natural life of the people. In the NT this conflict is loosed from its national and natural foundation. Hence the word is not much used. At R. 2:22: ὁ βδελυσσόμενος τὰ εἴδωλα ἱεροσυλεῖς, there is correspondence to the secular use, though also a hint of paganism. In Rev. we are more in the sphere of OT and Rabbinic usage, as shown by the fact that βδελύγματα in 17:4 f. are "abominations linked with heathenism," and by the similar allusion in 21:8: τοῖς δὲ δειλοῖς καὶ ἀπίστοις καὶ ἐβδελυγμένοις καὶ φονεῦσιν καὶ πόρνοις καὶ φαρμακοῖς καὶ εἰδωλολάτραις καὶ πᾶσιν τοῖς ψευδέσιν τὸ μέρος ... ἐν τῇ λίμνῃ ..., and 21:27: πᾶν κοινὸν καὶ ὁ ποιῶν βδέλυγμα καὶ ψεῦδος ... In Tt. 1:16: βδελυκτοὶ ὄντες καὶ

---

[6] Schl. Lk., 379.

[7] The use of נִדָּה in relation to idols (2 Ch. 29:5) would be similar.

[8] What follows is according to Bertram.

ἀπειθεῖς, the reference is more general. Jesus follows the prophetic use and that of the Wisdom literature in Lk. 16:15 : τὸ ἐν ἀνθρώποις ὑψηλὸν βδέλυγμα ἐνώπιον τοῦ θεοῦ. While βδέλυγμα has here its very concrete significance, and thus denotes the object of the strongest (because natural) aversion among men, it also serves to express the reaction of the holy will of God to all that is esteemed among men ; it thus breaks quite free from the natural and aesthetic and also the cultic connotation.

In Mk. 13:14 and par. : ὅταν δὲ ἴδητε τὸ βδέλυγμα τῆς ἐρημώσεως ἑστηκότα ὅπου οὐ δεῖ, [9] the expression βδέλυγμα ἐρημώσεως is taken from Da. 12:11, where it denotes the desecration of the temple by an image or altar of Zeus. It thus refers to Antichrist, as shown by the masc. construction and a comparison with 2 Th. 2:3 f.

Foerster

> † βέβαιος, † βεβαιόω
> † βεβαίωσις

A. βέβαιος κτλ. outside the NT. [1]

βέβαιος [2] means "standing firm on the feet," "steadfast," "maintaining firmness or solidity," "steadfast for ..." Thuc., IV, 67: καὶ τοῖς τῶν Ἀθηναίων ὁπλίταις ἐπι-φερομένοις βεβαίους τὰς πύλας παρέσχον. Hence "firm" in the sense of having inner solidity. [3] In respect of abstract things and persons βέβαιος thus comes to mean "steady," "sure," "reliable" "steadfast," or "certain." Xenoph. Hier., 3, 7; βεβαιόταται φιλίαι; Stob. Ecl., IV, 625, 2 : βεβαιοτέραν ἔχε τὴν φιλίαν πρὸς τοὺς γονεῖς; Plut. Anton., 3 (I, 917a): ἅμα καὶ τὴν ὁδὸν ἀσφαλῆ τῷ στρατεύματι καὶ τὴν ἐλπίδα τῆς νίκης τῷ στρατηγῷ βέβαιον; Pseud.-Isoc., 1, 36: τὴν παρ' ἐκείνων εὔνοιαν βεβαιοτέραν ἔχειν; Philo Quaest. in Ex. 2:45 : ὡς ἥκοντος εἰς βεβαιοτάτην πίστιν τῶν μελλόντων νομοτεθεῖσθαι; Plant., 82: διὰ τοῦθ' ὅρκος ὠνομάσθη προσ-φυέστατα τὸ πίστεως βεβαιότητος σύμβολον μαρτυρίαν θεοῦ περιεχούσης; Epict. Diss., II, 11, 20 : ἀβεβαίῳ οὖν τινι θαρρεῖν ἄξιον; Οὔ. μή τι οὖν βέβαιον ἡ ἡδονή; IV, 13, 15 : δεῖξόν μοι σεαυτὸν πιστόν, αἰδήμονα, βέβαιον, δεῖξον ὅτι δόγματα ἔχεις φιλικά. [4] What is meant by βέβαιος emerges clearly in Philo Vit. Mos., II, 14 : τὰ δὲ τούτου μόνου (νόμου) βέβαια, ἀσάλευτα, ἀκράδαντα, κα-θάπερ σφραγῖσι φύσεως αὐτῆς σεσημασμένα, μένει παγίως, ἀφ' ἧς ἡμέρας ἐγράφη μέχρι νῦν καὶ πρὸς τὸν ἔπειτα πάντα διαμενεῖν ἐλπὶς αὐτὰ αἰῶνα ὥσπερ ἀθάνατα ... In practice, though not originally, it is close to → πιστός.

βέβαιος is often found with reference to λόγος. Α βέβαιος λόγος is a firm, sure, well-grounded λόγος. It denotes one which rests on an insight into things and grants insight. Hence Plat. Tim., 49b: πιστῷ καὶ βεβαίῳ χρήσασθαι λόγῳ; Phaed., 90c:

---

[9] On βδέλυγμα ἐρημώσεως: E. Nestle in ZAW, 4 (1884), 248; Schl. Mt., 702 f.; Str.-B., I, 945, 951; Moore, I, 367, 6; EB, II, 2148-50.

β έ β α ι ο ς κ τ λ. [1] → also, however, 602.

[2] βεβαυῖα: βεβαύσιος, cf. E. Schwyzer, *Indog. Forsch.*, 45 (1927), 252 f.

[3] To be distinguished from στερεός = "hard."

[4] There can hardly be any question of an ἐλπὶς στερεά.

λόγος βέβαιος καὶ ἀληθὴς καὶ δυνατὸς κατανοῆσαι (earlier: οὔτε τῶν πραγμάτων οὐδενὸς οὐδὲν ὑγιὲς οὐδὲ βέβαιον οὔτε τῶν λόγων). The opposite is seen in Tim., 37b: δόξαι καὶ πίστεις γίγνονται βέβαιοι καὶ ἀληθεῖς.

The same meanings are also seen in βεβαιοῦν and βεβαίωσις. βεβαιοῦν (act. and mid.) means "to make firm": Thuc., VI, 10: μὴ ... ἀρχῆς ἄλλης ὀρέγεσθαι πρὶν ἣν ἔχομεν βεβαιωσώμεθα; Plut. Sulla, 22 (I, 466e); Plat. Crito, 53b: βεβαιώσεις τοῖς δικασταῖς τὴν δόξαν ("to strengthen"); Polyb., III, 111, 10: βεβαιώσειν ἡμῖν πέπεισμαι τὰς ἐπαγγελίας ("to fulfil"). It is also used absol. in Xenoph. Cyrop., VIII, 8, 2 ("to keep troth," "to verify"); Thuc., I, 23: τά τε πρότερον ἀκοῇ μὲν λεγόμενα, ἔργῳ δὲ σπανιώτερον βεβαιούμενα ("to confirm"); Thuc., II, 42: δοκεῖ δέ μοι δηλοῦν ἀνδρὸς ἀρετὴν πρώτη τε μηνύουσα καὶ τελευταία βεβαιοῦσα ἡ νῦν τῶνδε καταστροφή ("to seal"); Epict. Diss., II, 18, 32; Plat. Gorg., 489a: ἵνα ... βεβαιώσωμαι ἤδη παρὰ σοῦ ("I will cause it to be confirmed"): Philo Som. I, 12: τὰ ἐνδοιαζόμενα τῶν πραγμάτων ὅρκῳ διακρίνεται καὶ τὰ ἀβέβαια βεβαιοῦται καὶ τὰ ἄπιστα λαμβάνει πίστιν ("to give validity or force"). It is also used in the more general sense of a strengthened ποιεῖν: Xenoph. An., VII, 6, 17: ἐὰν μὴ βεβαιῶ τὴν πρᾶξιν αὐτῷ ("to achieve"). In the mid. it means "to assure for oneself": Thuc., VI, 78: τὴν ἐκείνου φιλίαν οὐχ ἧσσον βεβαιώσασθαι βούλεσθαι; Polyb., II, 21, 5: τὰ περὶ βοηθείας βεβαιώσασθαι. For. βεβαίωσις, cf. Vett. Val., I, 1 (p. 2, 28, Kroll): ὁ δὲ τοῦ Διὸς σημαίνει ... κοινωνίαν, εἰσποίησιν, ἀγαθῶν βεβαίωσιν, κακῶν ἀπαλλαγήν. In relation to λόγος the meaning of βεβαιοῦν (and βεβαίωσις) is again "to establish": Plat. Resp., V, 461e: δεῖ δὴ τὸ μετὰ τοῦτο βεβαιώσασθαι παρὰ τοῦ λόγου; Lach., 200b: καὶ ἐπειδὰν βεβαιώσωμαι αὐτά, διδάξω καὶ σέ ...; Epict. Diss., II, 11, 24: καὶ τὸ φιλοσοφεῖν τοῦτο ἐστιν, ἐπισκέπτεσθαι καὶ βεβαιοῦν τοὺς κανόνας.

In the LXX βέβαιος is rare: 3 Macc. 5:31: ἀποδεδειγμένων ... βεβαίαν πίστιν ... 'Ιουδαίων, a sure and unshakeable loyalty; 3 Macc. 7:7: βέβαια εὔνοια; Wis. 7:23: πνεῦμα βέβαιον. In βεβαιοῦν the original meaning is again apparent: ψ 40:12: ἐμοῦ δὲ διὰ τὴν ἀκακίαν ἀντελάβου καὶ ἐβεβαίωσάς με ἐνώπιόν σου εἰς τὸν αἰῶνα. R translates ἐστερέωσάς με. The Heb. equivalent is נצב hiph ("to set"), elsewhere trans. ἔστησεν (Gn. 21:28; Dt. 32:8), ἐστήρισεν (Prv. 15:25), ἐστήλωσεν (Lam. 3:12). What is meant in ψ 40:12 is the experience of being eternally established by God. ψ 118:28: βεβαίωσόν με ἐν τοῖς λόγοις σου "give me a basis in thy word" (Heb. equiv. קום pi). 3 Macc. 5:42: ἀτελέστατον βεβαίως ὅρκον ὁρισάμενος, acc. to R.: ἀτ. ἐβεβαίωσεν ὅρκον, ὁρισάμενος ...

βεβαιοῦν τὸν λόγον does not occur. Instead we have ἀναστῆσαι λόγον in Ez. 13:6 = "to validate in the fulfilment" (קום pi).

Symmachus is interesting. Instead of ἀληθὲς ἔσται τὸ ῥῆμα τὸ παρὰ τοῦ θεοῦ in Gn. 41:32, he has βέβαιον ... The history of God is βέβαιος in the sense that it can be relied on, that it comes to pass, that it is proved true. In ψ 88:24, instead of καὶ ἡ ἀλήθειά μου καὶ τὸ ἔλεός μου μετ' αὐτοῦ, he has καὶ ἡ βεβαίωσίς μου καὶ τὸ ἔλεός μου ... The underlying word is אֱמוּנָה, so that βεβαίωσις is the true rendering. We cannot merely translate "assurance," but "establishment," or "assurance" in the sense of true security (→ ἀλήθεια).

B. βέβαιος κτλ. in the NT.

In the NT we first find a. the ordinary meanings in the more original sense: Hb. 6:19: ἄγκυραν ... ἀσφαλῆ τε καὶ βεβαίαν ("reliable," "certain," "firm"); 2 Pt. 1:10: ... σπουδάσατε βεβαίαν ὑμῶν τὴν κλῆσιν καὶ ἐκλογὴν ποιεῖσθαι = "to make firm and valid the calling and election already present," i.e., in the development of → ἀρετή; Hb. 3:14 (3:6): ἐάνπερ τὴν ἀρχὴν τῆς ὑποστάσεως μέχρι τέλους βεβαίαν κατάσχωμεν. Participation in Christ is actualised for us when we grasp and hold the establishment[5] of ourselves as firm and valid in its firmness (validity). In 2 C. 1:7 ἐλπίς is called βεβαία in the sense that it is firm and does not waver. On the other hand, the ἐπαγγελία is firm in R. 4:16 in the sense that it is valid and will be fulfilled. In general, βέβαιος maintains its original character in the NT, i.e., that a thing is firm in the sense of being solidly grounded, though it acquires the note of validity in connection with certain substantives.

This is true of βεβαιοῦν in Col. 2:6 f., where ἐρριζωμένοι καὶ ἐποικοδομούμενοι ἐν αὐτῷ (sc. Χριστῷ) is extended and made more concrete by καὶ βεβαιούμενοι τῇ πίστει καθὼς ἐδιδάχθητε, i.e., in instruction there followed assurance through πίστις. The assuring took place as a rooting and grounding in Christ. In 1 C. 1:8 : ὃς καὶ βεβαιώσει ὑμᾶς ... denotes the establishment and assurance known in Christ. There is a similar expression in oriental Gnosticism, e.g., O. Sol. 38:16 : "I was confirmed and won life and salvation ; my foundation was established at the side of the Lord." Mostly, however, we should expect στηρίζειν here rather than βεβαιοῦν, for the former had become a technical term. Yet the two words are interchangeable, as may be seen from a comparison of 2 Th. 2:17 with Hb. 13:9. In R. 15:8 the original meaning is not so prominent. The link with the ἀλήθεια θεοῦ, however, is worth noting. The truth of God is daily fulfilled, i.e., in the establishment, i.e., validation, of the promises of the Father through the ministry of Christ. Similarly in 2 Pt. 1:19 the προφητικὸς λόγος is βέβαιος, i.e., sure, reliable, but also valid ; its declarations are fulfilled for faith by their enactment. Here a λόγος is βέβαιος, not in so far as it maintains an insight, but in so far as it shows itself to be grounded in an event. This, and therefore the distinction from the Greek view, becomes even clearer in Hb. 2:2, which is to be rendered : "For if what was once spoken by angels showed itself to be valid, and every transgression and disobedience receives the appropriate punishment..." The λόγος proves its "certainty" and "foundation" by its efficacy. It is βέβαιος, not as perspicacious, but as actual, effective and forceful.

b. This usage, however, is closely related to a special meaning of βέβαιος, βεβαιοῦν, βεβαίωσις present in both the Gk. and the Jewish world and developed in the legal sphere.[6] It was said of a seller who confirmed a purchase to the buyer in face of the claims of third parties that he accepted a βεβαίωσις, i.e., a legally valid confirmation of the sale and therefore a guarantee (auctoritas, evictio). The buyer could demand of the seller : βεβαιῶσαι, and if he did not do so could plead βεβαιώσεως against him. This legal commercial term is also found in the LXX. Lv. 25:23 : καὶ ἡ γῆ οὐ πραθήσεται εἰς βεβαίωσιν· ἐμὴ γάρ ἐστιν ἡ γῆ, διότι προσήλυτοι καὶ πάροικοι ὑμεῖς ἐστε ἐναντίον μου. Εἰς βεβαίωσιν is a serviceable translation of לִצְמִתֻת in the sense of totally and for ever. What is meant in both the Heb. and the Gk. is that the land could not be sold definitively, i.e., with a legal guarantee. On this pt. cf. Lv. 25:30 : κυρωθήσεται ἡ οἰκία ἡ οὖσα ἐν πόλει τῇ ἐχούσῃ τεῖχος βεβαίως τῷ κτησαμένῳ αὐτήν. Βεβαίως here means definitive, legally guaranteed (excluding the right of redemption or lapse in the year of jubilee). This legal sense remains even where there is no longer any question of a commercial transaction, and in such cases βεβαίωσις has the sense of legal guarantee. So Wis. 6:18 and perhaps 3 Macc. 5:42.

---

[5] Cf. also A. Schlatter, Der Glaube im NT⁴ (1927), 614, 617.
[6] Deissmann B., 100-105; NB, 56; Cr.-Kö., 218; Mitteis-Wilcken, II, 1, 188 ff., 269; O. Eger, Rechtsgeschichtliches z. NT (1918), 38 f.

The technical sense persists in the NT. Hb. 6:16 : καὶ πάσης αὐτοῖς ἀντιλο-γίας πέρας εἰς βεβαίωσιν (guaranteed, definitive) ὁ ὅρκος. Phil. 1:7: ἔν τε τοῖς δεσμοῖς μου καὶ ἐν τῇ ἀπολογίᾳ καὶ βεβαιώσει τοῦ εὐαγγελίου ... ἀπολογία, too, has a technical legal sense. [7] The apostle understands his εὐαγγε-λίζεσθαι in prison as an apology, and at the same time as the fulfilment of a legally valid witness. The Gospel is legally validated in εὐαγγελίζεσθαι. That this does not apply only in this situation, but that preaching the Gospel is a kind of legal act, is shown by Hb. 2:2 ff. The νόμος is βέβαιος (of legal force, one might almost say), and how much more the σωτηρία first spoken by the κύριος and then ὑπὸ τῶν ἀκουσάντων εἰς ἡμᾶς ἐβεβαιώθη, made effective and shown to be valid by the apostles. The legal terminology is retained in v. 4 : συνεπιμαρ-τυροῦντος τοῦ θεοῦ σημείοις ... To the legal act of εὐαγγελίζεσθαι belongs the witness of God in miracles and signs ; the σωτηρία constitutes itself legally effective by signs and wonders in the λόγος of the apostles. This is also the meaning in Mk. 16:20, except that here the saying is more pregnant ; κηρύττειν is accomplished under the operation of the Lord as He gives force to the λόγος in σημεῖα. The σημεῖα do not prove the validity of the λόγος ; they are a way in which the valid Logos is more forcefully put into effect. This gives us the clue to 1 C. 1:6 : In the Corinthian community the μαρτύριον τοῦ Χριστοῦ has been given legal force by the apostles, even to the institution of rich χαρίσματα. It is open to question whether 2 C. 1:21 should not also be adduced here. As the dictionaries and catenae listed by Deissmann show, → ἀρραβών is a legal term which stands materially in some relation to βεβαίωσις. [8] On the other hand, the personal reference (ἡμεῖς) and the connection with χρίειν and σφραγίζεσθαι seem to point to a baptismal terminology such as is also found in 1 C. 1:8. It may be that Paul found himself forced by the legal term ἀρραβών to use βεβαιοῦν instead of στηρίζειν, so that in this indirect way we have the intrusion of a legal character even in recollection of the sacrament. Cf. Ign. Phld., Intr. : οὓς (the deacons) κατὰ τὸ ἴδιον θέλημα ἐστήριξεν ἐν βεβαιωσύνῃ τῷ ἁγίῳ αὐτοῦ πνεύματι.

In post-apostolic lit. βεβαιοῦν etc. is used in the ordinary sense of "firm" or "in-wardly secure," cf. 1 Cl., 6, 2 : βέβαιος δρόμος; 1, 2 : βεβαία πίστις; Just. Dial., 69, 1 : βεβαία γνῶσις; of "firm" or "well-grounded," cf. 1 Cl., 47, 6 : βεβαιοτάτη ... ἐκκλησία; Ign. Mg., 13, 1 : βεβαιωθῆναι ἐν τοῖς δόγμασιν τοῦ κυρίου καὶ τῶν ἀποστόλων ...; of "valid," 1 Cl., 22, 1, and esp. Ign., where the sense of "legally valid" recurs : Mg., 4, 1; 11, 1; Sm., 8, 1 and 2.

Schlier

---

[7] Loh. Phil., 24, n. 2.
[8] Cf. Athenag. Suppl., 22, where in formal similarity we have ἀπολογεῖσθαι and βεβαιοῦν alongside one another, though not identical in sense.

βέβηλος, βεβηλόω

† βέβηλος.

βέβηλος denotes a. the place which may be entered by anyone as distinct from ἄβατον [1] and ἄδυτον, i.e., "accessible." It corresponds exactly to the Lat. *profanus.* Soph. Fr., 109 : ἔς τε τἄβατα καὶ πρὸς βέβηλα. [2] It then acquires the further sense of what may be said publicly in contrast to what must not be uttered on religious grounds : Eur. Heracl., 404 : ἤλεγξα καὶ βέβηλα καὶ κεκρυμμένα λόγια, Philostr. Heroic., p. 266, Boissonade : βεβήλῳ τε καὶ ἀπορρήτῳ ... λόγῳ. It is used b. of persons in the sense of "unsanctified" or "profane" = ἀμύητος. Soph. Fr., 154; Anth. Pal., IX, 298 : βέβηλος τελετῆς ; Plut. Def. Orac., 16 (II, 712d) : with ἀμύητος; Orpheus in Tat. Or. Graec., 8, 4 : θύρας ἐπίθεσθε βεβήλοις.

In the LXX βέβηλος is used of things, predominantly as the equivalent of חֹל, in the sense of that which is "loosed" and may be "used freely," e.g., meats (1 Βασ. 21:4 f. [ἄρτοι]; Ez. 4:14 vl.), vessels etc. It is the opp. of ἅγιος and is par. to the antithesis of clean and unclean. [3] This use is still within a material conception of holiness. Then, as in b., there is an application to persons in the sense of "unclean" (Ez. 21:25, alongside ἄνομος; 3 Macc. 2:2, alongside ἀνόσιος; 2:14, alongside θρασύς; 4:16 βεβήλῳ στό- ματι, alongside πεπλανημένη φρενί; everywhere in the sense of moral and religious depreciation of an enemy of God.

In Philo βέβηλος is used figur. of a "profane disposition," esp. in relation to the covetousness which remains even in disciplined action ; [4] it is then used of persons, e.g., (with πόρνη) of the raped and thereby profaned virgin who in consequence cannot become the wife of the holy high-priest. [5]

In the NT βέβηλος occurs only in the Past. (4 times) and Hb. (once). This is in keeping with NT religion, which no longer distinguishes between holy and un-holy things, nor, as in the esoteric Hellenistic religions, between sacred and profane persons. The repeated occurrence in the Past. and Hb. attests the stronger Hellenistic influence on the religious language of these Epistles, and especially the ethical and religious content which the term took on in the sphere of Hellenistic Judaism (→ *supra*).

1. As applied to material things in the Past., the word refers to Gnostic teachings which are scornfully described as profane and unholy μῦθοι (1 Tm. 4:7)

β έ β η λ ο ς. Trench, 350 f.; *Glotta,* 18 (1930), 235; A. Merx, *Die 4 kanon. Ev.,* II, 2, 1 (1905), 67 f.; Meinertz Past.[4], 79, 107.

[1] Etym. either "accessible" from βη- (ἔβην), or "outside the threshold (βηλός)," *v.* E. Schwyzer, *Indog. Forsch.,* 45 (1927), 252 ff. In both cases *profanus* = *quod pro fano est.*

[2] Eustath. Thessal. Comm. in Hom. Il., p. 1003, 40 f. : ὁ βηλός, ἐξ οὗ καὶ βέβηλος κυρίως τόπος ὁ καὶ τῷ τυχόντι βάσιμος καὶ ἀβέβηλος ὁ μὴ τοιοῦτος.

[3] The task of the priests in Ez. 44:23 : διδάξουσιν ἀνὰ μέσον ἁγίου καὶ βεβήλου καὶ ἀνὰ μέσον ἀκαθάρτου καὶ καθαροῦ, cf. Lv. 10:10; Ez. 22:26.

[4] Spec. Leg., I, 150 : ἐπιθυμία μὲν οὖν βέβηλος καὶ ἀκάθαρτος καὶ ἀνίερος οὖσα; Sacr. AC., 138 : τὸ γὰρ αἰσχρὸν βέβηλον, τὸ δὲ βέβηλον πάντως ἀνίερον.

[5] Fug., 114, cf. Lv. 21:7: βεβηλωμένη (חֲלָלָה).

and κενοφωνίαι (1 Tm. 6:20; 2 Tm. 2:16). In opposition to their claim to offer an inward truth of religion inaccessible to others, the Gnostic statements concerning God are actually seen to be outside the sphere of the holy God and His Gospel. [6]

2. As applied to persons, βέβηλος in Hb. 12:16 (alongside πόρνος) and 1 Tm. 1:9 (alongside ἀνόσιος, → supra) denotes profane men who are far from God; their unholiness includes ethical deficiency in accordance with the NT approach. Esau, with whom the βέβηλος is compared in Hb. 12:16, is in Judaism a type of the common mind which is unreceptive to God. [7]

† βεβηλόω.

"To desecrate": Heliod. Aeth., II, 25 (p. 64, 25, Bekker): τεμένη θεῶν, ibid., X, 36 (p. 308, 22, Bekker): τέμενος.

Common in the LXX, usually as a rendering of חלל pi: thus of God Himself in Ez. 13:19, of His name in Lv. 18:21; 19:12; of the temple of God in Ez. 23:39, of the holy day of God in Neh. 13:17 f., of His land in Jer. 16:18, of His covenant in ψ 54:20; 88:34, of the name of the priest in Lv. 21:9, and in the last passage (only in the LXX) with reference also to the violation of a virgin (cf. Sir. 42:10, supra, Heliod. Aeth., II, 25). [1]

In the NT the only use is at Mt. 12:5 of the violation of the Sabbath and at Ac. 24:6 of that of the temple, in both cases in the sense of the OT view of holiness which is basically transcended in the NT. [2]

Hauck

---

† Βεεζεβούλ   (→ δαίμων).

On the lips of the Pharisees in Mk. 3:22 and par.; Mt. 12:27 and par.; Lk. 11:18, this is a name for the prince of demons alluded to by Jesus in Mt. 10:25. It is with his help that Jesus is supposed to expel demons. In His answer Jesus tacitly substitutes Satan, since for Him the kingdom of demons stands under the one Satan. Only in Mt. 10:25 does Jesus Himself use this name with reference to the accusation of His enemies.

The orthography [1] and meaning are disputed. The main forms attested are Βεελζεβούλ, Βεεζεβούλ and Βεελζεβούβ. The third of these is assimilated to 2 K. 1:2, 3, 6,

---

[6] Cf. 3 Macc. 4:16 (→ supra).

[7] Gn. r., 63 on 25:29; bBB, 16b in Str.-B., III, 749.

β ε β η λ ό ω. [1] With an ethical significance ψ 9:26 speaks of the ways of the sinner and ψ 88:31 of the violation of the divine statutes.

[2] Herm. s., 8, 6, 2: βεβηλόω of the name of God.

Β ε ε ζ ε β ο ύ λ. For bibl. apart from the works listed in Pr.-Bauer, v. Ges.-Buhl, s.v. זבוב; Zn. Mt. and Schl. Mt. on 10:25; Kl. Mk. on 3:22; Hck. Mk., 48; Str.-B., I, on Mt. 12:24; Dausch Synpt.⁴, 195.

[1] The form Βελζεβούλ is no longer considered, being a variation of Βεελζεβούλ, nor yet the obvious singularities of individual MSS.

the second is a popular Palestinian form [2] and may thus be regarded as local colour in B and usually in א, as opposed to most MSS which have Βεελζεβούλ. The latter is the normal form. It alone is found outside the NT, [3] and if all the OT passages originally had Βεεζεβούλ, it must rest on an independent tradition which penetrated into most of the NT MSS. The meaning of the name [4] is of little importance in the NT, for even Jos. did not understand that there probably underlay it the name of the god of Ekron, called בַּעַל זְבוּב in the OT. [5] After the NT we find the name in Origen [6] and Hipp. (as Valentinian), [7] more frequently in the Test. Sol., [8] where the reference is to the prince of demons but there is no necessary equation with Satan. Only at Rev. 12:9 does the Armenian version substitute Βεελζεβούλ for διάβολος. Elsewhere the name appears in a Jewish prayer to the planets which is obviously strongly syncretistic. [9] For the NT passages it is significant that, in agreement with the usage described, Beelzebul is for the Jews the name of one of the demon princes according to Mt. 12:24 (ἄρχων τῶν δαιμωνίων) and Mk. 3:30 (where the accusation of a league with Beelzebul is equal to the charge of πνεῦμα ἀκάθαρτον ἔχει). [10] This view is strengthened by the fact that in contemporary Judaism the conception of Satan as the accuser was not linked with that of demons and their princes (→ διάβολος, δαίμων).

Foerster

---

[2] Cf. the assimilation of the Arabic art. before the sibilant.

[3] → n. 6-9.

[4] The possibilities considered are a. that Βεελζεβούλ is an easier expression or cacophemy for Βεελζεβούβ, the god of Ekron, in the latter case with the sense of the lord of filth = of idolatrous sacrifice; less probably b. that Βεελζεβούλ means the lord of habitation, i.e., the one who dwells in the possessed, or the lord of the heavenly abode on high; and c. that Βεελζεβούβ is בַּעַל דְּבָב, i.e., the lord of enmity = ἐχθρός. It may be mentioned that more recently the designation Zbl (= Zebûl?) has been found in religious texts. In a poem from Ras Shamra the dying and rising god Alein is called Zbl B'l, Syria, 12 (1931), 195 = Col., I, line 14 f.; 213 = Col. III/IV, 3, 9, 21, 29 and 40. The editor C. Virolleaud regards Zbl as part. kal. and thus translates: "celui qui habite le zbl du Baal de la terre"; he sees a similarity to such expressions as Zbl B'l sdmt, Zbl B'l snt, Zbl B'l im (Syria, 12 [1931] 350). W. F. Albright, however, in the Bulletin of the American Schools of Oriental Research, 46 (Apr. 1932), 17, thinks that Zbl (= Zebûl) is a name for the god.

[5] LXX in 4 Βασ. 1:2, 3 has ἐν τῷ Βάαλ μυῖαν θεὸν 'Ακκάρων, but in v. 6 it has ἐν τῇ Βάαλ, which should require αἰσχύνη instead of Βάαλ, as with the OT בֹּשֶׁת for בַּעַל (cf. R. 10:4 and comm. ad loc.). Jos. did not understand this, cf. Ant., 9, 19: πρὸς τὴν 'Ακάρων θεὸν Μυῖαν, τοῦτο γὰρ ἦν ὄνομα τῇ θεῷ.

[6] Orig. Cels., VIII, 25: οὐ γὰρ ἄρχων αὐτῶν (sc. τῶν δαιμόνων) ὁ θεὸς ἀλλ', ὥς φασιν οἱ θεῖοι λόγοι, ὁ "Βεελζεβούλ."

[7] Hipp. Ref., VI, 34, 1: καλεῖται ... ὁ διάβολος δὲ ὁ ἄρχων τοῦ κόσμου, Βεελζεβούλ (δ') ὁ τῶν δαιμόνων. It is worth noting that in this passage the devil and the prince of demons Βεελζεβούλ are distinguished.

[8] C. C. McCown, The Test. of Solomon, UNT, 9 (1922), Index, II. Here, too, Βεελζεβούλ is the prince of demons. Some MSS have secondary forms of the name with -el, in approximation to the names of angels.

[9] Reitzenstein Poim., 75 f.

[10] Cf. Zn. Mt. on 12:24.

| † Βελίαρ | (→ διάβολος).

This name for the devil is found in the NT only at 2 C. 6:15 : τίς δὲ συμφώ-νησις Χριστοῦ πρὸς Βελίαρ. It cannot be determined with any certainty whether Paul had particular reasons for the choice of this unusual name. Though it might be a title for Antichrist, this is not likely.

It is widely assumed that it derives from the name of a god of the underworld, cf. 2 S. 22:5 and Ps. 18:4. In the OT the phrase בְּלִיַּעַל or more often אִישׁ הַבְּלִיַּעַל and בְּנֵי בְלִיַּעַל is used to denote wrongdoers. The LXX renders the Heb. (ἀνὴρ etc.) λοιμός (1 Βασ. 1:16; 2:12; 10:27; 25:17, 25; 30:22), παράνομος (Dt. 13:13; Ju. 19:22; 20:13; 2 Βασ. 16:7; 20:1; 23:6; 3 Βασ. 20:10; 2 Ch. 13:7; ψ 40:8), or παρανομεῖν (Job 34:18), ἄφρων (Prv. 6:12; 16:27; 19:28), ἀσεβής (Ju. 20:13 A), ἁμαρτωλός (Sir. 11:32), ἀνόμημα, ἀνομία (Dt. 15:9; 2 S. 22:5; Ps. 18:4), and ἄνδρες τῆς ἀποστασίας in 3 Βασ. 20:13 acc. to A. Occasionally individual MSS retain the Heb. expression, as Ju. 19:22 Θ; Ju. 20:13a (AG : Βελιαμ); Prv. 16:22, where Εβρ. has Βέλιαλ for אֱוִיל. The brooks of Belial in 2 S. 22:5; Ps. 18:4 are rendered χείμαρροι ἀνομίας. In parts of the Asc. Is.,[1] Jub. 1:20 (15:33 ?) and always in Test. XII Βελίαρ is the name of the devil, as in Damasc., 4, 13 and 15; 5, 18; 8, 2, where at least in 5, 18 it is not the name of Antichrist. It is first used as such in Sib., 2, 167; 3, 63 and 73, and in the Lives of the Prophets, 17 (not 21).[2] In the Rabb. the use of the expression (בְּנֵי) בְלִיַּעַל is par. to that of the OT (bSanh., 111b; bQid, 66a),[3] though it must be remembered that they understood בְּלִיַּעַל as בְּלִי עֹל,[4] and that of the later translators of the OT 'A almost always rendered it ἀποστασία, while Σ and Θ translate it variously as ἀνυπότακτος, ἀνυπόστατος, ἀπαίδευτος, ἄνομος.[5] Yet this does not justify us in speaking of a Rabb. doctrine of the Antichrist Beliar, since there seem to be only isolated and obscure references to the doctrine of Antichrist in the Rabbis[6] (→ Χριστός/ἀντίχριστος).

Foerster

Β ε λ ί α ρ. Comm. *ad loc.* : Wnd., Bchm., Str.-B., Bousset-Gressm., 255, n. 1, 334 f., 341; M. Friedländer, *Der Antichrist* (1901), 118 ff.; W. Bousset, ERE, I, 578 ff.; Sickb. K.⁴, 118 f. Further lit. in Pr.-Bauer, *s.v.*

[1] Cf. J. Kroll, "Gott und Hölle," *Stud. d. Bibl. Warburg*, 20 (1932), 105.
[2] Transl. by P. Riessler, *Altjüdisches Schrifttum ausserhalb d. Bibel* (1928), 871 ff.
[3] Examples in Friedländer, 122, n. 2 and 3.
[4] S. Dt., 117 on 13:14; further examples in A. Büchler, *Studies in Sin and Atonement* (1928), 83, n. 2 and 3 ; cf. Moore, II, 166, n. 2.
[5] Dob. Th.⁷, 270, 3 (2).
[6] As against Friedländer. אִישׁ בליעל is also found in Sir. 11:32, and Friedländer also suspects it in the orig. Heb. of 1 Macc. 1:11; 10:61; 11:21; 2 Macc. 4:11, p. 121, 1-4.

---

† βέλος

"Pointed weapon," "javelin," esp. "arrow," [1] Ps.-Apollod. Bibl., II, 4 : βέλεσι πεπυρωμένοις (burning arrows). In the LXX it is used for יְרִי e.g., Is. 5:28; 7:24; 37:33; Sir. 19:12; figur. Sir. 26:12.

In myths it is used for lightning, Hdt., IV, 79; Pind. Nem., 10, 15; of the rays of the sun, Aesch. Choeph. 286, or of the moon or fire, Hipp., 531; El., 1159. Thus many gods are armed with the βέλος in Gk. mythology, esp. Zeus, Apollo, Artemis, Aphrodite and Eros. [2] When the god shoots his arrow, the result is death or mortal sickness, Hom. Il., 1, 45 ff.; 24, 758. Great spiritual agitation might also be caused in this way, Eur. Med., 628. ἱμέρου βέλος, Aesch. Prom., 649 (of passionate love). The arming of deity with bows and arrows is also common in the world of Semitic religion [3]

Similarly, the OT speaks of the divine armament. The rainbow is originally the bow with which God shoots in the storm and which He then hangs up in the clouds. The original mythical conception is present in weakened form at Gn. 9:13. [4] The lightning is His burning arrow, Ps. 7:13; ψ 143:6; Hab. 3:9 ff. Sunstroke and drought are traced back to the deadly arrows of the burning midday sun at ψ 90:5. God shoots the ungodly with His arrows, Dt. 32:23, 42; ψ 63:7. The sufferer bemoans the fact that he has been the target of God's arrows, Lam. 3:12; Job 6:4; 34:6. Joash shoots an arrow of victory from Yahweh (βέλος σωτηρίας τῷ Κυρίῳ) against Aram in 4 Βασ. 13:17. The servant of the Lord is compared to a chosen arrow in Is. 49:2. The picture of the divine armament is carried into the ethical and spiritual realm in Is. 59:17. In later Judaism En. 17:3 speaks of the place where God's weapons (bow, arrows, fiery sword and lightnings) are stored. Philo, on the other hand, characteristically uses the old image in a psychological context. [5]

The NT βέλος occurs only in Eph. 6:16. The righteous is here addressed as God's warrior. As in ancient mythology God strives against hostile chaos, so here the righteous is challenged to a spiritual but very real battle against Satan. The picture of his equipment is taken from Is. 59:17; [6] cf. also 4 Βασ. 13:17: βέλος σωτηρίας (→ supra). The menace of Satan's weapons is brought out by the fact

---

βέλος. HW, s.v. "Bogen," I, 197; E. Kalt, Bibl. Reallex. (1931), II, 350; Meinertz Gefbr.⁴, 103.

[1] Examples may be found in Liddell-Scott, s.v.; on the etymology, v. Walde-Pokorny, Vergl. Wört., I, 689 f.; on βάλλω, root βελ-, βαλ-, βλη-.

[2] For examples, v. O. Gruppe, Griech. Mythologie u. Rel.gesch. (1906), Index, s.v. "Pfeil," e.g., 1071, 1; 1226, 1; 1309, 17.

[3] A. Jeremias, D. AT im Lichte des AO³ (1916), 421 f.; thus, e.g., Ramman-Adad is portrayed with a bundle of lightning and double-headed axe, cf. A. Jeremias, Handbuch der altoriental. Geisteskultur (1929), 370 f., No. 200, 202 J. Leipoldt, D. Religionen in d. Umwelt d. Urchristent. (1926), No. 116 ff.

[4] Cf. O. Procksch, Genesis, ad loc.

[5] Det. Pot. Ins., 99 : κάλλος ἰδὼν ἔρωτος ἐτρώθη δεινοῦ πάθους βέλεσιν.

[6] Cf. Dib. Gefbr., ad loc. (Excurs.: "Das Bild v. d. Waffenrüstung d. Frommen"); A. Harnack, Militia Christi (1905); Reitzenstein Hell. Myst., 214 f.; H. Junker, "Über iran. Quellen der hell. Aionvorstellung" = Vortr. Bibl. Warburg, I (1923), 125 ff., esp. 140 (Persian examples of the motif of the spiritual armour in the fight against evil); Roscher, I, 1770, 4.

that his arrows are called πεπυρωμένα.[7] But whereas in the OT use of the image man has no defence against the arrows of God, in the NT the real defence (→ θυρεός, v. 16) of the righteous against satanic attacks lies in his union with God (→ πίστις).

Hauck

βιάζομαι, βιαστής

† βιάζομαι.

A. βιάζομαι in Ordinary Greek.

Like βία and its Sanskrit cognates,[1] βιάζομαι always denotes a forced as distinct from a voluntary act. πείθειν is expressly contrasted with it; Dio C., 36, 3 : πείθεται πᾶς ἥδιον ἢ βιάζεται. The βιαζόμενος acts as an unwilling conscript. The exercise of force does not have to be by an external act, but may find expression in self-willed utterance (Demosth., 21, 205) or the heretical representation of views (Gelas. Hist. Eccl., II, 17, 1; 20, 1). Yet in the use of the word these refinements are exceptional. The active is rare. The mid., which easily passes over into the pass., has usually the sense of "to force," "to compel," "to overpower" (sometimes militarily and sometimes sexually); the pass. means "to be constrained or oppressed." Whether the reference is to compulsion by higher powers (nature or fate), or whether man compels himself or natural forces, there is always the effective achievement of an act of force, or an attempt at such. In the rich use in relation to military action, maltreatment, compulsion of various kinds and even religious constraint, we can see clearly this basic sense of the exercise of hostile force.

B. βιάζομαι in the NT.

The two NT passages in which βιάζομαι is used (Mt. 11:12; Lk. 16:16) demand special treatment in virtue of their differences in linguistic structure and context.

1. Mt. 11:12 belongs to a series of related sections dealing with John the Baptist, his position in relation to the merciful readiness of Jesus to help as the heart of His Messianic action (11:1-6), his human character (v. 7-8), his place in the divine history of revelation (v. 9-15), his reception by the people (v. 16-19).

---

[7] For allegorical interpr., Orig. Hom. in Ex., I, 5 (p. 153, 5): *cogitationes iniicit malas et concupiscentias pessimas* ; Orat., 30, 3 : temptations ; Eus. Hist. Eccl., X, 4, 58 : πάθη.

βιάζομαι κτλ. Apart from the comm., Kühner-Blass-Gerth, I, 2³ (1892), 382 f.; II, 1³ (1898), 120 f., 293, 325 ; Cr.-Kö., 219 f.; Deissmann NB, 85 f.; Moult.-Mill., *s.v.*; Pr.-Bauer, *s.v.*; Str.-B., I, 598 f.; 601 ff. M. Schneckenburger, *Beitrag z. Einleitung i. NT* (1832), 48 ff.; Alex. Schweizer, ThStKr., 9 (1836), 90-122; A. Meyer, *Jesu Muttersprache* (1896), 88 f., 157 f.; Dalman WJ, I, 113 ff.; J. Weiss, *Die Predigt Jesu v. Reiche Gottes²* (1900), 192 ff.; A. Merx, *Evgl. Mt.* (1902), 189 f.; *Evgl. Lk.* (1905), 331; A. Harnack, SAB, 1907, 947 ff.; H. Windisch, *D. mess. Krieg u. das Urchristent.* (1909), 35 f.; ZNW, 27 (1928), 166; M. Dibelius, *Die urchristl. Überlieferung v. Joh. d. Täufer* (1911), 23 ff.; H. Scholander, ZNW, 13 (1912), 172 ff.; M. Goguel, *Jean Baptiste* (1928), 60 ff.; A. Pallis, *Notes on St. Luke and the Acts* (1928); W. Bussmann, *Synpt. Stud.,* II (1929), 170 ff. I aim to present the comparative linguistic material and history of exposition in an independent treatise the results of which are briefly summarised in this art. For defin. cf. Hesych: βιάζεται = βιαίως κρατεῖται; Thomas Mag., p. 35, 14 f., Ritschl : ἀναγκάζειν ἐπὶ ἐμψύχου μόνον· βιάζειν δὲ καὶ ἐπὶ ἀψύχου, οἷον ἐβιάσατο τὸ ῥεῦμα τοῦ ποταμοῦ [τὴν ναῦν].

[1] Walde-Pokorny, *Vergl. Wört.,* I, 666 ff.

The concluding woes on the cities of the lake (v. 20-24) are part of the call to repentance issued to the people, who in these sayings are shown to be fickle and impenitent sensation-mongers. The greatness of the Baptist is first indicated ; he is more than a prophet, for he is the ἄγγελος (v. 10) who precedes the Messiah according to Mal. 3:1 and Ex. 23:20, he is Elias (v. 14), and he is greater than any born of women (v. 11). His limitation is that he does not belong to the age in which the βασιλεία deploys its power. Rather, in v. 13 f. he is set in the time of the Law and the prophets, which comes to its conclusion in him. Hence, when it is said in this context : ἀπὸ δὲ τῶν ἡμερῶν Ἰωάννου τοῦ βαπτιστοῦ ἕως ἄρτι ἡ βασιλεία τῶν οὐρανῶν βιάζεται καὶ βιασταὶ ἁρπάζουσιν αὐτήν, these words obviously characterise the dominion of heaven as it has presented itself since the turn given to affairs by John.

A first possibility a. is to take βιάζεται in the sense of an intr. mid. : "the rule of God breaks in with power, with force and impetus." [2, 3] It might be argued against this interpretation that it truncates the basic eschatological reference of the βασιλεία concept. But shortly after the same Mt. has ἄρα ἔφθασεν (12:28, as at Lk. 11:20). The triumphs against demons are regarded by the Synoptists as decisive indications of the new situation which consists in the coming into effect of the divine rule. At the same time, the καὶ βιασταὶ ἁρπάζουσιν αὐτήν causes difficulty, since it is construed most naturally as an interpretation of the first part of the statement, βιασταί agreeing with βιάζεται. Since the reference (→ βιαστής) is obviously to a powerful hostile action, it seems better to seek an explanation which will better harmonise the two parts of the saying.

b. This is not achieved with the mid. : "The kingdom of heaven compels or forces" ; indeed, this is out of keeping with the whole conception of the βασιλεία in the Synoptists.

c. The pass. is hardly more successful. Adopted since Cl. Al., its interpretation in bonam partem was popularised by Luther. βιάζεσθαι is here taken to denote the ardent pressure of needy souls from the time of the Baptist to "seize the kingdom as a prey". [4] βιάζεσθαι, however, is not used for laudable striving, but for hostile acts of force. [5] Again, we have already seen that in the whole series of sayings (Mt. 11:1-24) the assessment of the relation of the people to the kingdom of God is exactly the opposite. Against this interpretation, however, the main argument is provided by the other sayings of Jesus concerning entry into the kingdom. In view of Mk. 10:17 ff.; Mt. 5:3 ff.; 7:21, and also the present chapter (27-29), it is hardly conceivable that He should have spoken of men deliberately and successfully seeking to wrest the kingdom to themselves. The Synagogue can certainly speak of the forceful initiation of the days of the Messiah by penitence, the keeping of the commandments and especially the study of the Torah

---

[2] So Melanchthon, F. C. Baur, Zahn and Harnack.

[3] In the pres., we find this use in Aesch. Ag., 1510 : βιάζεται μέλας Ἄρης (he rages); Demosth., 55, 17: κἂν βιάσηταί ποτε, of an inrushing flood ; often of compelling ἀνάγκη : Diod. S., IV, 11, 3; Jos. Ant., 2, 114; 3, 5. Joh. Malalas (Corp. Script. Byz. [Dindorf], 686): εἴς με βιάζεται οὐράνιον φῶς.

[4] Cl. Al. Strom., IV, 2, 5; V, 3, 16; VI, 149, 5; VI, 17, 149; Quis Div. Salv., 21, 3; Iren., IV, 37, 7 (MPG, 7, 1103c); Orig. in Joh., VI, 19, 105; Erasmus, Luther and many moderns.

[5] We might adduce as similar Theocr. Idyll., 22, 9 : βιάζεσθαι ἄστρα; Hdt., IX, 41: τὰ σφάγια; cf. Max. Tyr., V, 1g; though always mid., not pass. In these passages, however, we have the pagan conception that the one who prays or sacrifices can exert pressure on the deity. This applies to the bold expression in Cl. Al. Quis Div. Salv., 21, 3 : θεὸν βιάσασθαι. Paus., II, 1, 5 shows that even in the Gk. sphere, however, there is still a feeling that this is presumption : τὰ θεῖα βιάσασθαι; the reference is to the transgression of divinely ordained natural restrictions.

and almsgiving. [6] But this is diametrically opposed to all that is said by the Synoptists concerning entry into the kingdom of God (→ βασιλεία, 588). It can be required in Lk. 13:24: ἀγωνίζεσθε εἰσελθεῖν διὰ τῆς στενῆς θύρας. But this is hardly βιάζεσθαι in the sense of pious seizure. The inner difficulty is only increased by the second part of the verse. ἁρπάζειν can certainly mean to attain something by resolute appropriation. But when it is linked with βιάζεσθαι and βιασταί, it merely serves to give added emphasis to the basic thought of hostile seizure by violence. [7] d. It would be linguistically possible to decide for a pass. *in bonam partem* as follows: "The dominion is powerfully advanced by God." [8] Materially, this would amount to much the same as a. But the second part of the verse then confronts us with the same difficulty.

e. The only option is to consider the possibilities of a pass. *in malam partem*. This would at least correspond to current usage. The saying might be pronounced against the Zealots: [9] the rule of heaven is sought by unprincipled enthusiasts in violent action. The difficulty here is that Mt. is concerned with the prophets, the Law, the Baptist, Jesus and the βασιλεία. It is thus hard to see the point of a special reference to an irrelevant subject when we naturally expect an important insight on the situation depicted. In any case the Zealot movement had already been started before the appearance of John. The conjecture that something of this kind is in view, at least in the source of the utterance, is perhaps better supported by the form of the saying in Lk., which draws on the same source (→ 612).

We are thus brought f. to the pass. interpretation *in malam partem* which refers the βιάζεσθαι to the enemies of the divine rule, i.e., that it is contested, attacked or hampered [10] by contentious opponents. [11] This explanation has a twofold advantage. It corresponds to most of the linguistic parallels. And the second part of the saying can be construed in the same sense as an elucidation of the hostile βιάζεσθαι, namely, that it is taken from men by the violent. [12] The surest key to what is meant by ἁρπάζειν is given by Mt. himself in the only other place in his Gospel in which this word occurs: ὁ πονηρὸς ἁρπάζει τὸ ἐσπαρμένον ἐν τῇ καρδίᾳ αὐτοῦ (13:19). In this context it means taking the seed away from someone. Hence in our present saying, if we are to use a similar instance for the purpose of interpretation, the meaning is that by ἁρπάζειν violent enemies close the kingdom to men, not allowing those who desire to enter to do so (Mt. 23:13). [13] If this is correct, then in the description of the present state of the divine rule we have urgent emphasis on the fact that it is hampered by all the hostile forces which in the days of Jesus seek to foil His work. The strongly negative tone of the utterance is striking. It is partly explained, however, by the first passage in this whole series of sayings concerning John the Baptist; for we are told at the outset

---

[6] H. Scholander, 172 ff.; Str.-B., I, 599 f.

[7] When ἁρπάζειν is linked with βιάζεσθαι, it usually denotes hostile plundering: Plut. Apophth. (Pompeius), II, 203c; Luc. Hermot., 22; Luc. Nec., 20; Herodian Hist., II, 3, 23. There is a surprising par. in Tg. Is., 21, 2, where אנס is linked with בזז in a statement that the oppressors will be oppressed and the robbers robbed.

[8] *Magna vi praedicatur*: C. A. F. Fritzsche Mt., *ad loc.*

[9] Alex. Schweizer; B. Weiss; J. Weiss; Wellhausen; Windisch.

[10] βιάζεσθαι as "hamper": Ju. 13:15 Θ; 13:16 A; Jos. Ant., 1, 261.

[11] So esp. the Syr. sys syc; Eth. and old Latin; It.: *vim patitur*; Wulf. Of the moderns, Bretschneider, Schneckenburger, Hilgenfeld, Merx, Dalman, Schlatter; M. Dibelius suggests regents in the spirit world.

[12] On ἁρπάζειν, → 472 f.

[13] That men may hamper and delay the Messianic age by their sin is also taught by the Rabbis: b.Ket., 111a; Midr. HL, 2, 7; cf. H. Scholander, ZNW, 13 (1912), 172 ff.; Str.-B., I, 599 ff.

that John as a βιαζόμενος is in the prison of the βιαστής, and this dominates the whole section. Indeed, as we have seen already, the note of repentance is found right on into the story of the sulking children, so that in the context there is a special reason for this reference to the forces which hamper the βασιλεία. All that we read elsewhere in Mt. shows that Jesus has in view the forces which were opposed to Him in the Judaism of His day.

2. Lk. 16:16 stands in a chain of sayings which can hardly be compared with Mt. 11 for closeness of theme. Yet there is a common link provided by the words Φαρισαῖοι and especially νόμος. Thus the theme in Lk. 16:14-18 is not John the Baptist but the righteousness of the Pharisees and the validity of the Law. Without any preparation we suddenly come upon the saying: ὁ νόμος καὶ οἱ προφῆται μέχρι Ἰωάννου· ἀπὸ τότε ἡ βασιλεία τοῦ θεοῦ εὐαγγελίζεται καὶ πᾶς εἰς αὐτὴν βιάζεται. Even here, however, John is put in the time of the Law and the prophets, whereas the new era is characterised by the εὐαγγελίζεσθαι — this is a distinctive feature in Lk. The subject of the saying with βιάζεται is not βασιλεία, as in Mt., but πᾶς.

> If we first try to interpret the saying as under f. in Mt., we must take it in the mid. a. : "Every man exerts force against it." [14] In this case, however, if there were a contrast with εὐαγγελίζεται, we should expect an advers. ἀλλά instead of καί. But in any case, this rendering is impossible, because in Gk. βιάζεσθαι εἰς does not mean "to exert force against" but "forcefully to press into"; "to fight against" would be βιάζεσθαι with the accus., and if a preposition were used it would be πρός or ἐπί. [15] b. Philologically possible is the pass.: "Every man is pressed into," [16] along the lines of Lk. 14:23 : ἀνάγκασον εἰσελθεῖν. But this is artificial and is not supported by Gk. parallels.

With full assurance we can thus assume that this time we have a mid. act. : "Every man presses in." [17] The picture, which reminds us of the ἀγωνίζεσθε εἰσελθεῖν of 13:24, expresses the resolute and directed movement of crowding masses. It is thus in keeping with the missionary basis of Luke's historical work, for which εὐαγγελίζεσθαι is a characteristic of the new age with its conversion of the heathen. With joyful pathos the character of the εὐαγγέλιον is revealed through this πᾶς, which can only be meant hyperbolically if what is considered is evident success and not a basic universalism. It assures to every one an entry unhampered by any restrictions.

Thus in the source common to Mt. and Lk. it must have been said of John the Baptist that he marked a turning-point in the times ; the old comes to an end in him and the βασιλεία is inaugurated with the work of Jesus. As regards the βιάζεσθαι, however, the more difficult Mt. text gives the impression of being more original. Lk. seems to be secondary, since things are smoothed and simplified, the βιασταί clause is omitted, and the whole is incorporated into the missionary interest of Lk. [18] Consideration of the Aram. background seems to support even

---

[14] Jerome : omnis in illud vim facit. More recently Schl. Lk., 549.

[15] For extended references, v. my special study. Here we might mention Thuc., I, 63, 4; Demosth., 7, 32; Polyb., I, 74, 5; Diod. S., XL, 50, 4; Jos. Bell., 2, 262; Philo Vit. Mos., I, 108; Plut. Otho, 12 (I, 1072c). βιάζεσθαι with accus., Jos. Ant., 4, 121; 14, 173; with πρός or ἐπί, Polyb., II, 67, 2; III, 43, 6; Diod. S., II, 19, 7.

[16] Pesh.; Wulf. More recently Schneckenburger, Cr.-Kö., Wellhausen.

[17] Ephr., cf. Merx Lk., 331; other Syr. and the Old Latin. More recently Harnack, Dalman, Zahn, Windisch, Pr.-Bauer.

[18] Cf. Harnack, op. cit., 949.

more strongly the priority of Mt. אנס is probably the Aram. original of βιά-ζεσθαι. [19] אנס can mean both to exert force and to rob. On the other hand, neither the pass. εὐαγγελίζεται nor the εἰς αὐτὴν βιάζεται of Lk. can be traced back to an Aram. use of אנס

3. The significance of the saying from the standpoint of biblical theology is primarily as follows. In both Mt. and Lk. the βασιλεία is viewed in such a way that after the work of the Baptist it dawns with the work of Jesus. Thus, whatever the basic eschatological convictions, it is seriously thought to be present in Jesus. In the Synoptists the presence and future of the divine rule are brought together in Jesus, who is the Bearer of salvation both present and future. Jesus speaks here as He who inaugurates the new epoch which replaces and transcends all that has gone before, the Law, the prophets and the Baptist. To this degree the saying underlies that of Paul in R. 10:4, i.e., that Christ is the τέλος of the Law (cf. Jn. 1:17). If, however, the βασιλεία is also shown to be under the pressure of violent men which stand in its way, this means that serious account is taken of the fact that the rule of God does not playfully disarm all opposition with self-evident directness. On the contrary, it enters a way of suffering irrespective of the divine sovereignty, which is indeed expressed in this basic concept of faith. It is not for nothing that the βιάζεσθαι experienced by Jesus is also referred to the βασιλεία. Coming effectively into this temporal world, it is exposed to acts of hostility and violence. The secondary form in Lk. does not have merely the same conception of the times; it also has the same view of the present lordship and Messiahship of Jesus. Jesus is the decisive turning-point. For Lk., however, the true characteristic of the βασιλεία in the present situation is to be seen in the pressing into it of those for whom the collective πᾶς triumphantly discloses the missionary horizon. Yet there is here no final divergence. The varied attempts of the Evangelists to solve the meaning of the βασιλεία derive basically from their fundamental concern with the great reality of the fact of Christ. In content both the persecution of enemies and the addition of those who are no longer impeded by the old barriers are negative and positive signs of the one reality that the decisive change has been forcefully initiated and that this necessarily implies a state of conflict.

† βιαστής.

βιαστής is an extremely rare word. So far as we know, as a subst. in the pregnant sense of "violent men," it occurs for the first time in Mt. 11:12. To be sure, we often find βιατάς in Pindar in the sense of "strong," "bold" or "brave." [1] Thus in Pyth., 1, 10 βιατάς Ἄρης denotes the wild god of war (cf. Anth. Pal., VII, 492, 3, Anyte). We also find it as an attribute in Pind. Pyth., 4, 419 f.: βιατάς ἀνήρ; 6, 28: Ἀντίλοχος βιατάς; Olymp., 9, 75: μαθεῖν Πατρόκλου βιατὰν νόον; Nem., 9, 51 (of wine): βιατὰν παῖδα. Apart from Pyth., 1, 42: σοφοὶ καὶ χερσὶ βιαταί, its use is always adjectival and it hardly sheds much light on the meaning of the NT word. The classical

---

[19] Cf. Dalman, WJ, I, 113 ff., after rejection of אֲהֵסֶן and תָּקַף (which has no pass.). A. Meyer, 88 f. favoured חֲסַן, "to take in possession." Schl. Mt., 368 inclines like Dalman to אֲנַס, adducing Tanch. (Buber) כי תשא, 6, 108. Tg. Is., 21, 2 especially might also be mentioned (→ n. 7).

[1] βιατάς (-ής) is *nomen agentis* for βιᾶσθαι, as βιαστής for βιάζομαι.

writers, also LXX and Jos., the main Hellenistic authors, give us no further help. Nor do the pap. In Philo there is only one doubtful reference, namely, Agric., 89, which speaks of the stormy waves of the passions beating against the ship of the soul, and in which the cod. MH read: τῆς ψυχῆς ὑπὸ βιαστῶν καταπνεόντων εἰς αὐτὴν παθῶν τε καὶ ἀδικημάτων ἀντιρρεπούσης καὶ κλινομένης ἐξαιρόμενον ἐπιβαίνῃ τὸ κῦμα. Cod. G (and with it Cohn-Wendl.), however, rightly has the vl.: ὑπὸ βίας τῶν.[2] Elsewhere βιαστής is used medically in Aretaeus, IV, 12, 12 of gout. It then occurs in patristic expositions of Mt. 11:12;[3] and later still in Eustathius Macrembolites (12th cent. A.D.) De Ismeniae et Ismenes amoribus, 5 as a link in the series: μοιχός, ἀκόλαστος, βιαστής.

Directed by this later development, we do better not to follow the harmless lyrical conception of Pindar but to be guided by the analogy of similar βία derivatives. Thus βιαστέον calls for consideration. A saying of Epict. runs:[4] οὐ βιαστέον τὴν φύσιν ἀλλὰ πειστέον. Or again, βιαστός: Choricius in Lib. Or. (IV, p. 793, 13, Reiske): βιαστὰ πράγματα. Or again, βιαστικός: Philo Spec. Leg., III, 35: συνηθείας, βιαστικωτάτου πράγματος, of the compulsion of habit. Or again, the subst. βιασμός: Plut. Amat., 11 (II, 755d): ἁρπαγὴ καὶ βιασμός. Everywhere it is obvious that the idea of a violent act is predominant. As a first substitute for the subst., ὁ βιαζόμενος is common: Diod. S., IV, 12, 5: τοῖς βιαζομένοις, of the violent centaurs; XVI, 27, 1: ἡ ὑπεροχὴ τοῦ βιαζομένου, of the overwhelming power of the violent. Mostly adj., but in the same sense, is βίαιος: Hom. Od., 2, 236: ἔρδειν ἔργα βίαια, of violent crime; Soph. Ant., 1140: βιαίας νόσου; Thuc., III, 36, 6: βιαιότατος τῶν πολιτῶν, of the most violent; Hdt., VII, 170: ἀποθανεῖν βιαίῳ θανάτῳ, cf. Plat. Resp., VIII, 566b; Tim., 64d: τὸ παρὰ φύσιν καὶ βίαιον γινόμενον πάθος (at least "forceful"); Plat. Resp., III, 399a, where we have ἐν πάσῃ βιαίῳ ἐργασίᾳ alongside ἐν πολεμικῇ πράξει; Resp., X, 603c, where there is a distinction between βίαιοι and ἑκούσιαι πράξεις. Josephus, too, uses βίαιος in this way, so that the element of hostile violence is emphasised.[5]

Thus the βιαστής is the *violator,* the man of force who achieves his desires by theft. In Mt. 11:12 the word corresponds to the preceding βιάζεσθαι, which, as we have shown, must be referred to the violence of the foes of Jesus in the persecution and hampering of the rule of God. It is worth noting that Origen in his Hom. in Lev., IV, 4 (p. 320, 7 ff.), restrained by the obvious meaning of βιαστής, gives an ambiguous interpretation of the second clause in Mt. 11:12: among the *raptores* are both the *boni* who desire and therefore take the kingdom and the *mali* who usurp it. As the Memphitic rendering perceived, however, the latter is the only correct choice. Thus in the case of βιασταὶ ἁρπάζουσιν we must reject the exposition *in bonam partem.*[6] The meaning indicated by the βία is "violently to assault the divine rule, and to rob those who come to it of its blessing."[7]

Schrenk

[2] Strictly speaking, these are not variants but scribal interpretations.
[3] Suic. Thes., *s.v.* adduces Basil, Chrysostom and Isidore of Pelusium, who all support the exposition of Cl. Al. (→ βιάζομαι, n. 4).
[4] C. Wotke, "Epikur Spruchsammlung," No. 21, *Wiener Studien,* 10 (1888), 193.
[5] Cf. Schl. Mt., 368.
[6] In Cl. Al., Bengel, Zn. and Harnack the βία is explained to mean that the "children of wisdom" (Bengel) use force to enter the divine kingdom.
[7] For all other pts. → βιάζεσθαι.

βίβλος, βιβλίον

† βίβλος.

1. The general use. βίβλος is a loan-word from the Egyptian. It denotes in the first instance the shrub of the papyrus and then its bark ;[1] βίβλινος is what is prepared from this shrub.[2] The original form is βύβλος, βυβλίον. βιβλίον arises from the second word by assimilation, and βίβλος is formed accordingly. From the 1st cent. B.C. βιβλ- is crowded out by βυβλ-, which is the norm according to Attic judgment. βιβλ-, however, is revived by itacism. There are vacillations from the 1st cent. A.D. Thus Josephus usually has βίβλος, but occasionally employs the older form.[3]

Writing material made of papyrus replaces the wooden tablet in Greece as early as the 6th cent. B.C.[4] The term thus comes to be applied to inscribed paper.[5] In particular it is used for a roll of papyrus. But it also comes to be used of other writing materials such as tablets, leather, skin and parchment, and of what is written on them.[6]

It thus comes to denote a book, a letter, a record, or a statute.[7] In the LXX βιβλίον is more common. Like βίβλος, it is almost always used for סֵפֶר. It is impossible to establish any material distinction between the two terms. There is simply a preference in certain formulae. When an author refers to an earlier volume of his work or quotes the volume of another writer, he may use either.[8] In the LXX, too, βιβλίον does not have any distinctive meaning which is not in certain circumstances expressed by βίβλος at least in some MSS.

2. βίβλοι ἱεραί. According to Jos. Bell., 2, 159 the Essene prophets are βίβλοις

βίβλος, βιβλίον. L. Löw, "Graph. Requisiten u. Erzeugnisse bei d. Juden" in *Beitr. z. jüd. Altertskde.*, I (1870). S. Krauss, *Talmud. Archäologie*, III (1912), 132 ff.; RE³, XVII, 766 ff.; T. Birt. *Das antike Buchwesen* (1882), 12 ff.; *Handbuch der klass. Altertumswiss.³*, I, 3 (1913), 247-382; K. Dziatzko, in Pauly-W., III (1899), 939 ff., *s.v.* "Buch"; *Untersuchungen über ausgewählte Kapitel des antiken Buchwesens* (1900); W. Schubart, *Das Buch bei den Griechen u. Römern* (1921), 32 f. On βυβλ-, βιβλ- : Moiris, *Lex Atticum* (1830), p. 88, Pierson-Koch ; K. Meisterhans-E. Schwyzer, *Gramm. der att. Inschr.³* (1900), 28; Kühner-Blass-Gerth, I, 70; A. Maidhof, *Zur Begriffsbestimmung der Koine* (1912), 303 ff. On βιβλαρίδιον, βιβλιδάριον, BZ, 6 (1908), 171. J. Hänel, "D. Schriftbegriff Jesu," BFTh, 24 (1919). Book of Life etc. : Weber, 242, 282 f.; Dalman WJ, I, 171; P. Volz, *Jüd. Esch.* (1903), 93 f.; Bousset-Gressm., 258; H. Zimmern in E. Schrader, KAT³, II (1903), 400 ff.; B. Meissner, *Babylonien u. Assyrien*, II (1925), 124 ff.; L. Ruhl, "De mortuorum judicio," RVV, II, 2 (1903), 68, 101 ff.; J. Weiss, *D. Offb. d. Joh.* (1904), 57 ff.; Zahn Einl., II, 600, 608 f.; A. Schlatter, *D. AT i. d. joh. Apk.* (1912), 61 f.; W. Sattler, "D. Buch mit 7 Siegeln," II, ZNW, 21 (1922), 43 ff.; W. Brückner, *Die grosse und die kleine Buchrolle in d. Offb. Kp. 5 u. 10* (1923); Rohr Off.⁴, 129.

[1] Jos. Ant., 2, 246.

[2] *Ibid.*, 2, 220 : πλέγμα βίβλινον.

[3] LXX : 1 Esr. 1:31 B; Jos. : Ant., 12, 113; Vit., 365; Polyb., III, 34, 3; Diod. S., XVI, 3, 8. On the other hand Aristeas always has βίβλος, βιβλία.

[4] The wooden tablet πυξίον (לוּחַ) is distinguished from βιβλίον in Is. 30:8.

[5] Is. 18:2 : ἐπιστολαὶ βίβλιναι.

[6] The Torah was preferably written on leather rolls. In the Mishnah סֵפֶר is always used only of animal skins, Löw, 115. Cf. also S. Nu., 16 on 5:23. On the other hand Jehoiakim in Jer. 43(36):20 ff. obviously cuts paper and not leather (LXX : χαρτίον).

[7] For examples, *v.* Preisigke Fachwörter, 40 and Wört., *s.v.*; Mitteis-Wilcken, I, 1, p. XXXI, n. 2.

[8] βίβλος : Jos. Ant., 1, 94; 4, 74 etc.; Philo Ebr., 1. βιβλίον : Jos. Ant., 20, 267; Bell., 1, 30; Philo Sacr. AC, 51. Both writers often use the words interchangeably : Jos. Ant., 8, 44; 10, 93-95; Philo Leg. All., I, 19 and 21.

ἱεραῖς ἐμπαιδοτριβούμενοι καὶ διαφόροις ἁγνείαις καὶ προφητῶν ἀποφθέγμα-
σιν. This refers to the OT but perhaps embraces more than the Canon, for
according to 2, 142 the Essenes must swear: συντηρήσειν τὰ τῆς αἱρέσεως αὐτῶν
βιβλία. This use of βίβλοι ἱεραί corresponds to the observation that occasionally
in the imperial period this expression is chosen for the hieratic book. [9] We can
thus understand why the Ephesian books of magic are called βίβλοι in Ac. 19:19.

It is thus a mere transfer of ordinary usage to the OT when we meet αἱ ἱεραὶ
βίβλοι countless times in Josephus and Philo, not only for the books of Moses,
but for the whole collection of canonical writings. [10] Philo, who limits himself to
the Torah, uses the expression of the Pentateuch. [11] Already in Daniel the OT
is referred to as αἱ βίβλοι. [12]

3. βίβλος is also used to denote the individual writings of the Canon. In view
of the later ecclesiastical term "the Bible," it is to be noted that the singular has
its historical origin in the description of the Torah as βίβλος. This seems to be
grounded in the custom of writing it on a particular roll. [13] But βίβλος can also
be used of other parts of the Canon or related religious books, though not in the
LXX (→ βιβλίον, n. 8). [14] In the NT Mk. 12:26 corresponds to the general usage:
ἐν τῇ βίβλῳ Μωϋσέως, as do also Lk. 20:42 and Ac. 1:20: ἐν βίβλῳ ψαλμῶν, [15]
Lk. 3:4: ἐν βίβλῳ λόγων Ἠσαΐου, and Ac. 7:42: ἐν βίβλῳ τῶν προφητῶν. [16]
It is worth noting that Luke, the most Hellenistic of all the writers, is very free
in his use of the LXX formula (though cf. Lk. 4:17, → βιβλίον, 618).

4. βίβλος γενέσεως. This expression in Mt. 1:1 is taken from Gn. 5:1 (for
סֵפֶר תּוֹלְדֹת), [17] As in Gn., it relates only to the succeeding genealogy and not [18] to
the whole Gospel or even to the infancy stories up to Mt. 2:23. Otherwise we do
violence to the traditional formula.

---

[9] Diod. S., I, 44, 4; 73, 4; 82, 3; Philo Conf. Ling., 3; 8 book of Moses in A. Dieterich,
Abraxas (1891), 169. For further examples from Luc. and Pap., *v.* Nägeli, 19.

[10] Joseph.: ἱεραὶ βίβλοι for the Torah: Ant., 1, 26; 1, 82; 2, 347; 3, 81 and 105; 4, 326;
10, 58; for the whole collection: Ant., 1, 139; 9, 28 and 46; 16, 164; 20, 261; Ap., 1, 1 and
91; 2, 45. Rarely βιβλία ἱερά: Vit., 418. Other expressions for the Canon: αἱ Ἑβραικαὶ
βίβλοι, Ant., 9, 208; similarly, 10, 218; Ap., 1, 154. Cf. also → βιβλίον, n. 8, 9 and 11.

[11] Decal., 154; Spec. Leg., II, 150; Abr., 157; Vit. Mos., II, 10; II, 45 (αἱ ἱερώταται
βίβλοι); Ebr., 208; Rer. Div. Her., 258.

[12] Da. (LXX and Θ) 9:2: ἐν ταῖς βίβλοις, with reference to Jer. Cf. τὰ βιβλία,
Ep. Ar., 46.

[13] For the sing. with reference to the Torah, cf. Tg., II, Est., 4, 2: בְּסִפְכָּא דְמֹשֶׁה; jTaan.,
66d: הָדֵין סֵפֶר אוֹרַיְתָא: Sota, 7, 9 and often in Rabb. lit.: סֵפֶר תּוֹרָה. 1 Esr. 5:48; 7:6, 9: ἡ
Μωυσέως βίβλος. 2 Macc. 8:23: ἡ ἱερὰ βίβλος, similarly Jos. Ant., 4, 303 (never in the
sing. elsewhere in Jos.); Bar. 4:1: βίβλος τῶν προσταγμάτων τοῦ θεοῦ; Philo Det. Pot.
Ins., 139: ἡ θεοῦ βίβλος. On the other hand, in Jos. Ant., 12, 256 βίβλος ἱερά with
νόμος means any individual book. Worth noting is Ep. Ar., 316: ἐν ᾗ βίβλῳ, apparently
used of the whole OT. But one would need to know whether Theodectes borrowed only
from the Torah.

[14] Tob. 1, 1: βίβλος λόγων Τωβίτ; Test. L. 10:5: ἡ βίβλος Ἐνὼχ τοῦ δικαίου;
Jos. Ant., 11, 337: ἡ Δανιήλου βίβλος; Philo Migr. Abr., 14: ἱερά βίβλος Ἐξαγωγή;
Plant, 26: ἐν Λευιτικῇ βίβλῳ; Conf. Ling., 128: ἐν τῇ τῶν κριμάτων βίβλῳ, 149: ἐν
βασιλικαῖς βίβλοις.

[15] Cf. סֵפֶר תִּילִּים, Tanch. (Buber) מצורע, 5, 46 and jMeg., 72a. In LXX B as a title:
βίβλος ψαλμῶν.

[16] That βίβλος as distinct from βιβλίον embraces several individual writings (Cr.-Kö.)
is difficult to prove, → βιβλίον n. 8, 9, 11.

[17] Cf. Philo Abr., 11.

[18] Zn. Mt., *ad loc.*

† βιβλίον.

1. The general use. βιβλίον was first a diminutive of βίβλος, but soon it came to be conceived differently. Other diminutives replaced it, like βιβλίδιον and βιβλαρίδιον, Rev. 10:2, 8 (א P), 9 f. ¹ βιβλιόν is the most common word for the "roll of a book," a "book," or a "writing" in the *koine*. In the LXX (βίβλος, n. 13, 14), for example, it is used when there is reference to non-biblical writings. ² Elsewhere it is used with reference to libraries, archives and chronicles. ³ The historical work of Josephus is called τὰ βιβλία. ⁴ Like βίβλος, however, the word can also denote an epistle ⁵ or document. Thus in Tob. 7:13 it means the record of marriage; in Dt. 24:1 and 3 βιβλίον ἀποστασίου (סֵפֶר כְּרִיתֻת), as in Mk. 10:4 and Mt. 19:7, is the bill of divorce given to the wife on her release. ⁶

2. βιβλίον and βιβλία for the Canon.

Often in the OT we meet the demand to write down what is said בַּסֵּפֶר. ⁷ This can mean any surface or sheet adapted for writing, but the translators, who have βιβλίον, would naturally think of the papyrus roll. Rolls are actually meant in ψ 39:7: ἐν κεφαλίδι βιβλίου (בִּמְגִלַּת־סֵפֶר), quoted in Hb. 10:7; also Ez. 2:9, cf. the metaphor in Is. 34:4.

With reference to the OT, τὸ βιβλίον is first the more or less solemn expression of the LXX for the book of the Law. ⁸ Thus Gl. 3:10 : πᾶς ὃς οὐκ ἐμμένει πᾶσιν τοῖς γεγραμμένοις ἐν τῷ βιβλίῳ τοῦ νόμου (LXX Dt. 27:26 follows the Mas. and has: ἐν πᾶσι τοῖς λόγοις τοῦ νόμου) is in full keeping with this usage. So is Hb. 9:19 (Ex. 24:7), where the Torah is meant, even though the τῆς διαθήκης of the LXX is not added to βιβλίον.

It is worth noting that Josephus, who almost always has the plural ἱεραὶ βίβλοι (→ βίβλος, 616), uses βιβλία rather than βιβλίον for the Torah and the Canon. ⁹ On this usage 2 Tm. 4:13 might well refer to rolls of the OT. If from the time of

---

β ι β λ ί ο ν. ¹ βιβλαρίδιον according to BZ, 6 (1908), 171, hitherto attested only in Herm. v., 2, 1, 3 and 4, 3. C* and many min have βιβλιδάριον (cf. Aristoph. Fr., 490, CAF, I, 518), H. C. Hoskier, *Concerning the Text of the Apoc.*, II (1929), 275. But there are other readings. On βιβλίδιον = *libellus*, which does not occur in the NT, cf. Preisigke Fachwörter, 40; Wört., *s.v.*; Mitteis-Wilcken, I, 1, p. XXXI; APF, 5 (1909), 262 f., 441. On the use in the post-apost. fathers, *v.* Pr.-Bauer, *s.v.*

² Nu. 21:14; 2 Βασ. 1:18; 3 Βασ. 8:53; 3 Βασ. 11:41; 2 Ch. 13:22 (for מִדְרַשׁ); Est. 10:2; Job, 42:18 A — in some MSS βίβλος.

³ Libraries : Ep. Ar., 9,10 and 29; Jos. Ant., 1, 10; 12, 12. Archives : Ant., 8, 55 and 159. Genealogies : 2 Εσδρ. 17:5 : βιβλίον τῆς συνοδίας. Chronicles of the fathers : 2 Ezr. 4:15 AB, cf. Mal. 3:16; Est. 10:2.

⁴ Jos. Vit., 361 and 364.

⁵ 2 Βασ. 11:14; 3 Βασ. 20:8; 4 Βασ. 10:1; 'Ιερ. 36:1.

⁶ In the pap. it is used for many official, commercial and legal papers and documents, cf. Preisigke, *op. cit.* (→ n. 1).

⁷ Ex. 17:14; Nu. 5:23; Dt. 17:18; Tob. 12:20; Is. 30:8 etc.

⁸ For the Law as τὸ βιβλίον: Dt. 25:58; 29:20 (19); 4 Βασ. 22:8 B (βίβλος, 4 Βασ. 22:16). βιβλίον τοῦ νόμου: Dt. 28:61; 29:21 (20), 27 (26); 30:10; 31:26; 4 Βασ. 22:8; 22:11; 2 Εσδρ. 18:3; βίβλος τοῦ νόμου: Jos. 1:8; βιβλίον Μωυσῆ : 2 Ch. 35:12; βιβλίον τοῦ νόμου Μωυσῆ : Jos. 23:6; βιβλίον νόμου τοῦ θεοῦ : 2 Εσδρ. 18:8; βιβλίον νόμου κυρίου : 2 Ch. 34:14; βιβλίον ἐντολῶν κυρίου : 2 Ezr. 7:11; βιβλίον τῆς διαθήκης : Ex. 24:7; 4 Βασ. 23:2, 21; 2 Ch. 34:30; Sir. 24:23.

⁹ Jos. for the Torah: Ant., 3, 74; 4, 304; 12, 36, 89 and 114. For the whole collection : Ant., 1, 15; 8, 159. Ep. Ar., 28 and 30 also speaks of the Jewish βιβλία. Cf. on the other hand the prol. to Sir.: τὴν τοῦ νόμου καὶ τῶν προφητῶν καὶ τῶν ἄλλων πατρίων βιβλίων ἀνάγνωσιν; 2 Cl., 14, 2 : τὰ βιβλία τῶν προφητῶν καὶ οἱ ἀπόστολοι.

Chrysostom [10] the canonical collection of both OT and NT has been called τὰ βιβλία, this follows the usage found in Josephus except that it is now extended to cover the NT Canon as well.

Even in the LXX the individual books of the OT apart from the Torah are sometimes called βιβλίον. [11] This usage is found at Lk. 4:17. In the synagogue at Nazareth there is handed to Jesus βιβλίον τοῦ προφήτου Ἡσαΐου. The πτύξας in v. 20 shows that it was a roll. [12] If in Jn. 20:30 [13] the author calls his Gospel βιβλίον, this certainly does not imply any formal claim (cf. 21:25).

3. The Apocalyptic Use and the Other NT Passages concerning the Book of Life.

The word "book" acquires a special sense in the Apocalypse as an image for the divine secret which is declared and developed as a firmly sketched entity, [14] and also as an expression for the impregnable foundation of the divine counsel. The author of Rev. prefers βιβλίον to βίβλος; he uses it 23 times. He is much more influenced by OT than imperial usage. Apart from the quotation in 6:14: βιβλίον ἐλισσόμενον (Is. 34:4), which merely strengthens the impression that he has the idea of a roll in view, the term is applied in 5 different connections.

a. The βιβλίον of the Apocalypse, which according to 1:11 is to be sent to the churches of Asia, contains λόγοι προφητείας which are to be observed (22:7, 9 f., 18 f.). It is not sealed (22:10), as distinct from Da. 12:4, 9, because the time is near, i.e., the message will be wholly worked out in the community of Jesus Christ and is not to be set aside as a closed secret (as in 10:4). The divine has to mediate effective instruction, consolation and direction to true hope.

b. The βιβλίον with seven seals (5:1-5, 7 f.) is again in the form of a roll, and indeed of an ὀπισθόγραφον, [15] not a codex. This is shown decisively by the close relation of the text to Ez. 2:9 f., where there is also a roll inscribed on both sides and indicating the inscrutable fulness of events. According to the image, however, there is also an influence of the Roman testament with its seven seals. [16] The contents of the βιβλίον must be brought into relation to the whole chain of judicial

---

[10] Hom. in Col. 9:1 (MPG, 62, 361). Cf. also Suic. Thes., s.v.

[11] So in the numerous ref. to books of chronicles and kings: βιβλίων ῥημάτων τῶν ἡμερῶν τῶν βασιλέων Ἰσραήλ, 3 Βασ. 14:19 A etc.; 1 Ch. 27:24 (for מִסְפָּר); Nah. 1:1: βιβλίον ὁράσεως Ναούμ; cf. 2 Macc. 6:12. Cf. also Jos. Ant., 10, 210: τὸ βιβλίον τὸ Δανιήλου; 11, 5: βιβλίον δ τῆς αὐτοῦ προφητείας δ Ἡσαΐας κατέλιπεν. According to Ap., 1, 38 he numbers in the Canon δύο πρὸς τοῖς εἴκοσι βιβλία.

[12] On ἀνοίξας in v. 17, cf. 2 Εσδρ. 18:5. On the other hand, cf. 1 Macc. 3:48: ἐξεπέτασαν τὸ βιβλίον τοῦ νόμου.

[13] On ἃ οὐκ ἔστιν γεγραμμένα ἐν τῷ βιβλίῳ τούτῳ, cf. M. Ex. 17:14; Lv. r., 35.

[14] On Herm., v. Pr.-Bauer, s.v.

[15] For examples, v. Bss. Apk., 254; esp. Luc. Vit. Auct., 8; Grotius, Zahn, Nestle: codex. J. Weiss, Offb. Joh., 57 ff.: bound tables. The objection of Zahn that we could partially read a roll which is also written on the back goes beyond what is admissible in the Apocalypse. The roll is so bound and sealed that it cannot be read. That ἐπὶ τὴν δεξιάν demands a codex founders on the use of the prep. in 20:1. Nor is the ἀνοῖξαι of v. 4 decisive, as shown by Lk. 4:17. Cf. Charles Apc., I, 136 ff.

[16] The oldest text of 5:1 (A, Cypr., Orig.: βιβλίον γεγραμμένον ἔσωθεν καὶ ὄπισθεν κατεσφραγισμένον σφραγῖσιν ἑπτά, Hoskier, II, 141 f.; Zn. Apk., 328, n. 19) enables us to link ἔσωθεν καὶ ὄπισθεν with γεγραμμένον (Orig., as Ez. 2:10) or to take ὄπισθεν κατεσφραγισμένον etc. separately (Grotius: intus scriptum, extra signatum; Zn., J. Weiss). Either way there might well be reference to the official will sealed on the back by 7 witnesses, J. Marquardt, D. Privatleben d. Römer² (1886), 805 f.; E. Huschke, D. Buch mit 7 Siegeln (1860). For further bibl., v. Zahn Einl., II, 609, n. 8. It should be

acts which unfold from c. 6 on and from which there develop organically the visions of the trumpets and bowls. Hence we are not concerned merely with the 6 or 7 seals themselves, but with all the last events up to the consummation, and indeed with the direction and goal given to the community. The βιβλίον is thus the book of the sacredly established divine decrees concerning the future of the world and the community. We do not find the expression "book of destiny" because the eternal basis of the sovereign and historically determinative counsel of God is fundamentally different from εἱμαρμένη. As the roll of Ez. contained lamentations and cries and woes concerning Israel and the nations, so the book with seven seals declares the ways of God in judgment as ordained by His ruling power. [17] In the first instance they are sealed, i.e., withdrawn from human knowledge, yet also laid down inviolably. To open them is to fulfil the will of the testator and thus to initiate the train of events. That no one in all creation is qualified for this task directs attention to the fact, which is to be described as a main christological motif in the Apoc., [18] that only the ἀρνίον on the throne (5:6), the Crucified who as the Lamb has gained the Lion's victory and is now enthroned, is worthy to open the seals. Triumphant in His sacrificial death, Christ can execute the divine will up to the final consummation. Thus the cross is the basis of His ruling power, which can bring the divine lordship to its goal. [19]

c. The βιβλαρίδιον which the divine has to swallow in Rev. 10:9 f. in order fully to assimilate news of the final events (Ez. 2:8-3:3) obviously contains the vision of the temple and the two witnesses and therefore of God's dealings with Israel in the last time (11:1-14). [20] Here, as in all the divine books of Revelation, the book is a sum of the active will of God. It can be read only in such a way that, translated at once into action, it unfolds the divine will before the community.

d. τὸ βιβλίον τῆς ζωῆς (Rev. 13:8; 17:8; 20:12; 21:27), also called ἡ βίβλος τῆς ζωῆς — like Phil. 4:3 except that there it has no article — at 3:5; 13:8 א*; 20:15, is based on OT sayings which speak of all the saints and faithful, and of all who fear God or await salvation, being inscribed in God's book. [21] In the OT

---

remembered, however, that the idea of a sealed book derives from Is. 29:11 and Da. 12:4 (cf. 8:26: καὶ σὺ σφράγισον τὴν ὅρασιν); cf. Eth. En. 89:71. The sevenfold sealing is also in keeping with the symbolism of numbers in Rev. For sealing in Judaism: Str.-B., III, 800; cf. Tanch. (Buber) ויחי 1, 211, the book sealed by God: וַיְחִי. In Gnosticism a great role is played by the sealed letter (O. Sol. 23) which the son of truth, who inherits all things, brings as a message from God. Cf. H. Gressmann, SAB, 37 (1921), 616 ff. The sealed letter also occurs in Lidz. Ginza, 552, 34; Liturg., 111 and 118; the letter in Lidz. Joh., 241, 20; 94, 19; Ginza, 339, 16 etc. Reitzenstein Ir. Erl., 66 ff.; Loh. Apk., 49.

[17] For apocal. par. to this "book of the divine world plan," v. Str.-B., II, 174 ff.

[18] Cf. J. Behm, "Joh. Apk. u. Geschichtsphilosophie," ZSTh, 2 (1925), 323 ff.

[19] That world destinies are the content of the book is to be maintained against Orig. and Victorinus (the OT fulfilled in Christ) and W. Sattler, ZNW, 21 (1922), 43 ff. (identification of the sealed book with the book of life). Both these views disrupt the forward looking view of history in Rev. On this whole question, cf. A. Schlatter, Das AT i. d. joh. Apk., 62.

[20] W. Brückner would also include 12:1-9; 13:1-7, 11-18.

[21] Ex. 32:32 f., which is the basis of Rev. 3:5; Is. 4:3, which refers to all those in Jerusalem written among the living; ψ 68:28: ἐξαλειφθήτωσαν ἐκ βίβλου ζώντων; ψ 86:6, the list of Jewish proselytes in heaven; cf. 1 Βασ. 25:29: ἐνδεδεμένη ἐν δεσμῷ τῆς ζωῆς; Da. 12:1: πᾶς ὁ γεγραμμένος ἐν τῇ βίβλῳ; Jub. 19:9, inscribed on heavenly tables as the friend of God; Eth. En. 47:3: books of the living; philosophically attenuated, Philo Gig., 61. On ἐξαλείψω in Rev. 3:5, cf. Neh. 13:14; Is. 48:19; Jos. Ant., 6, 133 (based on Ex. 17:14); Eth. En. 108:3. Tg. jer. on Ex. 32:32 f.: סְכַר צַדִּיקַיָּא דִכְתִיבְתָּא שְׁמֵי בְּגַוֵּיהּ. For the use in the post-apostolic fathers, v. Pr.-Bauer, s.v.

this is to be differentiated from the book in which God has laid down in advance all human destinies, sorrows and joys (Ps. 56:8; 139:16). [22]

The same image of the writing of names in heaven is found at Lk. 10:20 (the disciples of Jesus); Phil. 4:3 (those who stand in the service of the Gospel); Hb. 12:23 (the community of the first-born, i.e., of the NT). The idea may have been fostered by the establishment of genealogies, family lists and national registers in Israel (Neh. 7:5 f., 64; 12:22 f.; Ez. 13:9; this is also the reference in Ps. 87:6), but also by the royal "note-book" (cf. → e.). Yet the belief in heavenly tables of destiny on which the fates of the living are inscribed, to which they are added, and from which they are erased, is an ancient oriental heritage. [23] In the NT the image is freed from fatalism and becomes an expression of the assurance of salvation of the Christian community, which knows that it is elected on the impregnable basis of the divine counsel of grace (2 Tm. 2:19). When Rev. 13:8 calls this βιβλίον the book of life of the crucified Lamb, it again makes the act of redemption on the cross the foundation, as in the case of the sealed book. The reference, however, is not now to the consummation ; it is to the salvation of individuals. The opposite is eternal perdition (20:14). This ordination to eternal life goes back behind the crucifixion to the καταβολή κόσμου (13:8; 17:8), [24] but only the names of those who overcome are not erased (3:5). The divine foreordination is thus linked with the human readiness to carry the conflict to victory. The thought of predestination is not unaccompanied by an emphasis on the cohortative motive for ready obedience ; 13:8; 17:8 (not worshipping the beast) and 21:27 (shunning abomination and falsehood) are also to be seen in this light.

e. τὰ βιβλία, the books of judgment, are expressly distinguished in 20:12 from the book of life. The phrase goes back to Da. 7:10 : βίβλοι ἠνεῴχθησαν, and is also based on Is. 65:6; Jer. 22:30 and Mal. 3:16 : βιβλίον μνημοσύνου = סֵפֶר זִכָּרוֹן, "note-book," cf. Est. 6:1. [25] It is a mark of the NT view, as distinct from that of the Synagogue, that all ἔργα are inscribed in these books. The thought of reckoning and counting, and restriction to the purely negative side of transgressions, are alien to the NT. On the contrary, the reference is to a judgment on all men's works.

Schrenk

---

[22] For Jewish par., *v.* Str.-B., II, 173 f.

[23] KAT³, II, 400 ff. In Judaism there develops out of this the idea that all words and acts are written in heaven in 2 books, i.e., of the righteous and the wicked, the friends of God and the enemies. Cf. Lev. r., 26 on 21:1; Gn. r., 81 on 35:1; Jub. 30:20 ff.; 36:10. According to the strict Synagogue view fulfilments of the Law are put in one book and infringements in another : bTaan., 11a. The idea of counting or reckoning thus comes into use : Wis. 4:20; Eth. En. 63:9; Qoh. r., 77c.; S. Lev., 26, 9. The angels, archangels, Michael, Elias or Enoch are the recorders. Str.-B., II, 169 ff.; III, 840; IV, 1037.

[24] This can hardly mean the "sowing of humanity" (A. Schlatter, *Das NT übersetzt,* 1931), but the "foundation of the world."

[25] Cf. S. Bar. 24:1. The books of judgment occur particularly frequently in Eth. En.: 81:4; 89:61-64, 68, 70 f., 76; 90:17, 20; 97:6; 98:7 f.; 104:7; 108:7. Transgressions especially are noted in them → n. 23. In 4 Esr. 6:20 (Vis. II § 10, p. 102 f., Violet) the reference is to the books of the world plan, → n. 17. For further examples of e., cf. Str.-B., II, 171 ff.

βίος → ζωή.

---
† βλασφημέω, † βλασφημία,
  † βλάσφημος

βλασφημία is always the act committed in βλασφημεῖν, βλάσφημος the quality either of the doer or his attitude.

A. βλασφημία in Greek Literature.

In secular Gk. βλασφημία is a. "abusive speech" (misuse of words) in contrast to εὐφημία: Demosth., 25, 26: βλασφημίαν ἀντὶ τῆς νῦν εὐφημίας; Democ. Fr., 177 (II, 97, 3 ff., Diels): οὔτε λόγος ἐσθλὸς φαύλην πρῆξιν ἀμαυρίσκει οὔτε πρῆξις ἀγαθὴ λόγου βλασφημίῃ λυμαίνεται. In Eur. Ion., 1189: ἐν χεροῖν ἔχοντι δὲ σπονδὰς μετ' ἄλλων παιδὶ τῷ πεφηνότι βλασφημίαν τις οἰκετῶν ἐφθέγξατο. J. Wackernagel translates βλασφημία as a "word of evil sound." [1] b. The word means further the strongest form of "personal mockery and calumniation." It almost amounts to the same as λοιδορεῖν: Isoc., 10, 45: ἤδη τινὲς ἐλοιδόρησαν αὐτόν, ὧν τὴν ἄνοιαν, ἐξ ὧν ἐβλασφήμησαν περὶ ἐκείνου, ῥᾴδιον ἅπασι καταμαθεῖν. Mostly, however, it is stronger than λοιδορεῖν and ὀνειδίζειν, e.g., Demosth., 18, 10; 19, 210. The living and the dead can be derided: Demosth., 18, 95: τὰς βλασφημίας, ἃς κατὰ τῶν Εὐβοέων καὶ τῶν Βυζαντίων ἐποιήσατο; Luc. Alex., 4: τὰ χείριστα καὶ βλασφημότατα τῶν ἐπὶ διαβολῇ περὶ τοῦ Πυθαγόρου λεγομένων; Herodian Hist., VII, 8, 9: βλάσφημα πολλὰ εἰπὼν εἰς τὴν Ῥώμην καὶ τὴν σύγκλητον; Demosth., 40, 17: περὶ τεθνεώτων αὐτῶν βλασφημοῦντες. c. It then means "blasphemy of the deity" by mistaking its true nature or violating or doubting its power. Ps.-Plat. Alc., II, 149c: βλασφημούντων οὖν αὐτῶν ἀκούοντες οἱ θεοὶ οὐκ ἀποδέχονται τὰς πολυτελεῖς ταυτασὶ πομπάς τε καὶ θυσίας. Plat. Leg., VII, 800c: (εἴ τις) βλασφημοῖ πᾶσαν βλασφημίαν. Myths which presuppose an anthropomorphic form of the gods become βλασφημεῖν εἰς θεούς: Plat. Resp., II, 381e. Vett. Val., I, 22 (p. 44, 4, Kroll); ibid., II, 2 (p. 58, 12, Kroll): εἰς τὰ θεῖα βλασφημοῦντες; ibid., II, 13 (p. 67, 20, Kroll): πολλὰ βλασφημήσει θεοὺς ἕνεκεν τῶν συμβαινόντων αὐτῷ πραγμάτων.

B. βλασφημία in the LXX and Judaism.

The root βλασφημ- in the LXX [2] has nothing clearly corresponding in the original. The word is used for the pi of גדף, the pi of נאץ and the root שׁלו or שׁלה: βλασφημία corresponds to words formed from these roots and βλάσφημος once to מְבָרֵךְ אָוֶן. In the translations of the Hexapla βλασφημ- is also used for חרף, לעג, ברך and קלל. All these terms are rendered variously and with widely varying emphases in the Greek translations, and no firm rules can be distinguished. Alternatives to βλασφημεῖν are particularly ὀνειδίζειν and παροξύνειν, which often occur for גדף, חרף, לעג and נאץ. As distinct from these synonyms, βλασφημ- always refers finally to God, whether in the sense of the disputing of His saving power (4 Βασ. 19:4, 6, 22), the desecrating of His name by the Gentiles who capture and enslave His people (Is. 52:5), the violation of His glory by derision of the mountains of Israel (Ez. 35:12) and His people (2 Macc. 15:24), all ungodly speech and action, espe-

---

β λ α σ φ η μ έ ω κτλ. [1] *Zeitschr. f. vergl. Sprachforsch.*, 33 (1895), 42.
[2] For what follows, I am indebted in part to Bertram.

cially on the part of the Gentiles (Is. 66:3; 1 Macc. 2:6; 2 Macc. 8:4; 10:34 ff.; 12:14; Tob. 1:18 א), or human arrogance with its implied depreciation of God (Lv. 24:11 in marg Codd 58, 85, 130 βλασφημεῖν, Codex X in marg ἐνυβρίζειν for קלל, which at 2 Βασ. 19:43 LXX is rendered ὑβρίζειν; 4 Βασ. 19:22 : ἐβλασφή-μησας ... ἦρας εἰς ὕψος τοὺς ὀφθαλμούς σου, cf. also Sir. 48:18, where גדל is translated μεγαλαυχεῖν ὑπερηφανίᾳ). The very fact that they do not believe in Yahweh makes the Gentiles βλασφήμοις καὶ βαρβάροις ἔθνεσιν (2 Macc. 10:4). With this direct or indirect reference to God, βλασφημ- also occurs in other translations of the OT: Σ 2 Βασ. 12:14 (Field, I, 563); ᾽ΑΣ ψ 43:16 (Field, II, 159); ᾽ΑΣΘ Is. 37:6, 23 (Field, II, 502 f.); 43:28 (Field, II, 519).

> The varying significance of the term in Philo is best shown by considering the words with which he associates it, συκοφαντεῖν in Leg. Gaj., 169, κατηγορεῖν in Migr. Abr., 115, κακηγορεῖν in Spec. Leg., IV, 197, ὕβρις in Decal., 86, Jos., 74, διαβολή in Flacc., 33, ἀσέβεια in Decal., 63. βλασφημ- is sharpest when it is linked with κατάρα in antithesis to εὐλογία and εὐχή in Migr. Abr., 117. It here denotes abuse to the point of cursing. The religious sense is predominant, obviously under the influence of the LXX. There is the general statement ὅπως μηδεὶς μηδένα βλασφημῇ in Spec. Leg., IV, 197. But mostly there is reference to the divine : τῶν εἰς τὸ θεῖον βλασφη-μιῶν, Leg. Gaj., 368; Decal., 63; Fug., 84. The Jew should not blaspheme other gods according to LXX Ex. 22:28 in order that the name of God should not be brought into jeopardy : Spec. Leg., I, 53 : προστάττει δὲ μὴ ... στομαργίᾳ χρήσασθαι καὶ ἀχαλίνῳ γλώσσῃ βλασφημοῦντας οὓς ἕτεροι νομίζουσι θεούς. Similarly Jos. Ant., 4, 207 and Ap., 2, 237. [3] The real sin, however, is τὸν τῶν ὅλων πατέρα καὶ ποιητὴν βλασφημεῖν, Philo Fug., 84; Vit. Mos., II, 206. In Josephus, with the secular use, blasphemy is equated with attacks on the Jews as the people of God (Ap., 1, 59; 1, 223), or on Moses (Ant., 3, 307; Ap., 1, 279), or on the law of the fathers (Ap., 2, 143).
>
> In the Damascus Document, 5, 11 ff. [4] it is said of the opponents of the new covenant : "They desecrate the Holy Spirit, blaspheming with their tongue and opening their mouths against the laws of the divine covenant." Here we have the thought, specifically reminiscent of Mk. 3:28 f., that blasphemy is a transgression against the Holy Spirit, who is here viewed as the divinely given inner purity of men.
>
> The Rabbis [5] in their concept of blasphemy start with the divinely ordained stoning of the blasphemer (Lv. 24:10-16) and the similar saying in Nu. 15:30 f. They find the substance of this capital offence in one "who speaks impudently of the Torah" (S. Nu., 112 on 15:30), in the idolater (S. Nu., 112 on 15:31) and in the one who brings shame on the name of Yahweh (bPes., 93b). The formal exposition of the concept by later Rabbinic law, which finds fulfilment of the substance of blasphemy in such things as the clear enunciation of the name of God (Sanh., 7, 5), is not yet present in the time of Jesus. [6] The decisive thing in the concept of blasphemy is here, too, violation of the majesty of God. βλασφημέω is introduced as a loan-word into Rabb. Heb. [7]

C. βλασφημία in the NT.

1. In the NT the concept of blasphemy is controlled throughout by the thought of violation of the power and majesty of God. Blasphemy may be directed im-mediately against God (Rev. 13:6; 16:11, 21; Ac. 6:11), [8] against the name of God (R. 2:24, quoting Is. 52:5 LXX, → 621; 1 Tm. 6:1; Rev. 16:9), against the Word

---

[3] Cf. also Str.-B., I, 1009 f.
[4] Cf. W. Staerk, Die jüdische Gemeinde des Neuen Bundes in Damaskus (1922), 23; L. Ginzberg, Eine unbekannte jüdische Sekte (1922), 33 ff.
[5] On the whole section, v. Str.-B., I, 1009 f.
[6] Dalman WJ, I, 258. Cf. also G. Dalman, Der Gottesname Adonaj (1889), 44 ff.
[7] Levy Wört., I, 235.
[8] But also against the goddess Artemis in Ac. 19:37.

of God (Tt. 2:5), against Moses and God and therefore against the bearer of revelation in the Law (Ac. 6:11).

Distinctive is the idea of a blaspheming of angelic powers by Gnostic errorists in Jd. 8-10: ὁμοίως μέντοι καὶ οὗτοι ἐνυπνιαζόμενοι σάρκα μὲν μιαίνουσιν, κυριότητα δὲ ἀθετοῦσιν, δόξας δὲ βλασφημοῦσιν. ὁ δὲ Μιχαὴλ ὁ ἀρχάγγελος, ὅτε τῷ διαβόλῳ διακρινόμενος διελέγετο περὶ τοῦ Μωϋσέως σώματος, οὐκ ἐτόλμησεν κρίσιν ἐπενεγκεῖν βλασφημίας, ἀλλὰ εἶπεν· ἐπιτιμήσαι σοι κύριος. οὗτοι δὲ ὅσα μὲν οὐκ οἴδασιν βλασφημοῦσιν. The verse is somewhat altered in 2 Pt. 2:10-12. [9] The blaspheming of heavenly beings ἐπὶ τὰς ἐν οὐρανῷ θείας φύσεις is also found in Philo: Conf. Ling., 154; Som., II, 131: ἥλιον καὶ σελήνην καὶ τοὺς ἄλλους ἀστέρας βλασφημεῖν. In Jd. and 2 Pt. the reference is undoubtedly to angelic powers. [10] In Jd. 8, and even more strongly in 2 Pt. 2:10, their blaspheming is brought into connection with what the Sodomites did to the divine commandments and with the libertine immorality of the false teachers. By the spotting of the flesh they repudiate the claim to lordship of the κύριος and blaspheme the δόξαι, which are here to be understood as powers of good, in close connection with the κυριότης. [11] How seriously we are to refrain from such blasphemy (→ the passages from Philo and Jos. *supra*) is shown by the fact that not even the archangel Michael dares to utter a railing accusation against the devil.

The NT assumes this strict concept of blasphemy to be that of the Jews — an assumption supported by the LXX, Philo and Josephus (→ 621). It is thus easy to see why Jesus should bring down on Himself the charge of blasphemy, not unjustly from the Jewish standpoint, when He claims to be the Messiah and assumes the prerogatives of God. As soon as Jesus forgives the sins of the man sick of the palsy — the prerogative of God alone — the scribes suspect Him of blasphemy (Mk. 2:7 and par.). The reason for the anger of the Jews is clearly given in Jn. 10:33-36: λιθάζομέν σε ... περὶ βλασφημίας, καὶ ὅτι σὺ ἄνθρωπος ὢν ποιεῖς σεαυτὸν θεόν. The blasphemy which brings about His death is His assertion that He is the Messiah and His statement that He will be seen as the Son of Man seated at the right hand of the Almighty, together with His apparent inability to give any convincing proof of His omnipotence to His judges (Mk. 14:64; Mt. 26:65). [12]

2. On the other hand, for Christians it is blasphemy to throw doubt on the lawful Messianic claim of Jesus, to deride Christ in His unity with the Father and as the Bearer of divine majesty. When the men who guard the captive Jesus mock His prophetic gift (Lk. 22:64 f.), this is just as blasphemous for the Evangelists as when the crowd at the cross (Mk. 15:29; Mt. 27:39) or the impenitent thief (Lk. 23:39) contemptuously challenge His divine sonship.

The fate of being slandered and attacked in their basic faith passed from Christ to His community in its union with the Lord. [13] For this cause Paul as a persecutor of Christians was a blasphemer (1 Tm. 1:13). Suffering blasphemy is one of the sufferings laid on the community (Rev. 2:9; 1 C. 4:13; [14] 1 Pt. 4:4). The opposition

---

[9] J. Sickenberger, "Engel- oder Teufelslästerer im Judas- und im 2. Petrusbrief," *Mitteilungen d. Schlesischen Gesellschaft f. Volkskunde*, 13/14 (1911), 621 ff.

[10] → δόξαι = angels, LXX Ex. 15:11. Cf. Wnd. Jd., *ad loc.*

[11] *Schriften d. NT*³, II (1917), 298, 310.

[12] From Rabb. writings it would seem that the mere claim to be the Messiah was not enough for condemnation, Dalman WJ, I, 257.

[13] Though βλασφημεῖν is not used, this is sharply expressed in Mt. 5:11.

[14] V.l. inℵ c BDEFGL it vg, otherwise δυσφημούμενοι.

of the Jews to the preaching of Paul is necessarily blasphemy because it attacks its basic content, the proclamation of the Messiah (Ac. 13:45; 18:6).

3. But the Christian, too, is in danger of giving cause for blasphemy. Denial of Christ in persecution would be such. Hence Paul can say of his activity as a persecutor : αὐτοὺς ἠνάγκαζον βλασφημεῖν. Even in partaking of idol meats Christians in bondage could see blasphemy (1 C. 10:30), as distinct from Paul. Violation of the obligation of love even in such matters ὑμῶν τὸ ἀγαθόν (R. 14:16) could expose to scandal. False teaching is blasphemy when it perverts from the way of truth (2 Pt. 2:2; R. 3:8). The blasphemy does not have to find verbal expression. Any bad or unloving action can contain it, either because it resists the holy will of God or because it causes the enemies of Christianity to calumniate it (1 Tm. 6:1; Jm. 2:7; R. 2:24; Tt. 2:5). The basis is clearly set out in 2 Cl., 13, 2-4.

According to Mk. 3:28, 29 and par. any blasphemy can be forgiven, even though it be against the Son of Man (Mt. 12:32), but not against the Holy Spirit. This can hardly refer to the mere utterance of a formula in which the word πνεῦμα appears. It denotes the conscious and wicked rejection of the saving power and grace of God towards man. Only the man who sets himself against forgiveness is excluded from it. In such cases the only remedy is to deliver up to Satan that he may learn not to blaspheme (1 Tm. 1:20). [15] βλασφημεῖν is related to the Spirit in an addition to 1 Pt. 4:14 in some MSS. [16]

The opposition to God of the beast of the last days is βλασφημία (Rev. 13:1, 5, 6), as is also that of the Babylonian harlot (17:3).

The predominantly religious connotation is present even where it is not expressed, e.g., when βλασφημ- occurs in the lists of offences in Mk. 7:22; Mt. 15:19; Eph. 4:31; Col. 3:8; 1 Tm. 6:4; 2 Tm. 3:2, also Herm. m., 8, 3; Did., 3, 6, or when the general command is given in Tt. 3:2 : μηδένα βλασφημεῖν.

D. βλασφημία in the Early Church.

The different nuances in the NT recur in the fathers. The concept is made more inward when Orig. says in Joh., XXVIII, 15 : βλασφημεῖ γὰρ ἔργοις καὶ λόγοις ἁμαρτίας εἰς τὸ παρὸν πνεῦμα ἅγιον ὁ καὶ παρόντος αὐτοῦ ἐν τῇ ψυχῇ ἁμαρτάνων. Tertullian in his Montanist days seeks to make it as strict as possible, as in Pud., 13, 17: incestum vero atque blasphemia totos homines in possessionem ipsi Satanae, non angelo eius tradidisse meruerunt. In his view, Hymenaeus and Alexander (1 Tm. 1:19 f.) were eternally lost (Pud., 13, 19 ff.). The concept was sharpened in rather a different direction in the dogmatic struggles of the 4th century, when opposing theological views were stigmatised as blasphemy. Gelas. Hist. Eccl., II, 22, 4 : ὁ ἀσεβὴς ἐβλασφήμησεν Ἄρειος ἕνα θεὸν ἄκτιστον καὶ ἄλλον κτιστὸν εἰρηκὼς καὶ τὸ πνεῦμα τοῦ θεοῦ ὁμοίως κτιστὸν κεκηρυχώς ...; II, 20, 6 : τὰ Ἀρείου βλάσφημα ῥήματα, κτίσμα καὶ ἐργαλεῖον τὸν υἱὸν τοῦ θεοῦ ἀποκαλῶν.

Already the fathers had difficulty in expounding Mt. 12:32. It was seriously discussed how blasphemies against Christ could be forgiven, but not against the Spirit. Chrys. Hom. in Mt., 41, 3 (MPG, 57, 449) makes the Lord answer : ὅσα μὲν οὖν ἐβλασφημήσατε κατ' ἐμοῦ πρὸ τοῦ σταυροῦ ἀφίημι· ... ἃ δὲ περὶ τοῦ πνεύματος εἰρήκατε, ταῦτα οὐχ ἕξει συγγνώμην· ... ὅτι τοῦτο γνώριμον ὑμῖν ἐστι καὶ πρὸς

---

[15] Dib. Past., ad loc.; Ltzm. Exc. on 1 C. 5:5.
[16] KLP sah.

τὰ δῆλα ἀναισχυντεῖτε· εἰ γὰρ καὶ ἐμὲ λέγετε ἀγνοεῖν, οὐ δήπου κἀκεῖνο ἀγνοεῖτε, ὅτι τὸ δαίμονας ἐκβάλλειν καὶ ἰάσεις ἐπιτελεῖν τοῦ ἁγίου πνεύματος ἔργον ἐστίν. If the solution is still found here externally in the knowledge or ignorance of the blasphemers, Augustine has a very profound view of blasphemy against the Spirit when he says of it in Ep., 185, 49, Goldbacher: *hoc est autem duritia cordis usque ad finem huius vitae, qua homo recusat in unitate corporis Christi, quod vivificat spiritus sanctus, remissionem accipere peccatorum ... huic ergo dono gratiae dei quicumque restiterit et repugnaverit vel quoquo modo ab eo fuerit alienus usque in finem huius temporalis vitae, non remittetur ei neque in hoc saeculo neque in futuro.*

Beyer

βλέπω → ὁράω.

> † βοάω   (→ κράζω).

"To cry," "to call." Commonly attested from the time of Hom., also in inscr. and pap. Often expanded, e.g., ἀναβοάω ("to cry out"), ἐπιβοάω ("to call to"), καταβοάω ("to raise a complaint"). βοή, "outcry." [1] LXX makes considerable use of this word group in translation of קרא, צעק, רוע, of the subst. צעקה and numerous other expressions — often strengthened by φωνῇ μεγάλῃ.

a. "To exult," Gl. 4:27, quoting Is. 54:1: ῥῆξον καὶ βόησον (צהל "to rejoice"), [2] which is also quoted in 2 Cl., 2, 1.

b. "To proclaim the message of God," קרא. So Is. 40:6: φωνὴ λέγοντος· βόησον. καὶ εἶπα· τί βοήσω, and Is. 40:3: φωνὴ βοῶντος. By adding the words ἐν τῇ ἐρήμῳ, Mk. 1:3 (Mt. 3:3; Lk. 3:4) makes this refer to the desert preacher, John. In Jn. 1:23 it is put on the lips of John as his own witness to himself: ἐγὼ φωνὴ βοῶντος ... καθὼς εἶπεν Ἠσαΐας ... In Barn., 9, 3 it is changed into a saying about hearing which has typical validity: Ἀκούσατε, τέκνα, φωνῆς βοῶντος ἐν τῇ ἐρήμῳ.

c. "To call to," "to call out." Lk. 9:38: ἰδοὺ ἀνὴρ ἀπὸ τοῦ ὄχλου ἐβόησεν λέγων. [3] Cf. Is. 36:13: וַיִּקְרָא בְקוֹל־גָּדוֹל וַיֹּאמֶר, in Codd. A and S. rendered: ἐβόησε φωνῇ μεγάλῃ καὶ εἶπεν, while B has ἀνεβόησεν. 1 Macc. 13:45: ἐβόησαν φωνῇ μεγάλῃ, 4 Macc. 6:16; 10:2: ἀναβοάω ("to answer with a raised voice").

d. "To raise an outcry," mostly by way of complaint, as in Gn. 39:14 of the wife of Potiphar: ἐβόησα (קרא) φωνῇ μεγάλῃ; or tumultuously: Ac. 17:6; 25:24. In the same sense the Syr. and Byz. etc. have ἀναβοήσας (instead of ἀναβάς) at Mk. 15:8. [4] At Ac. 18:13 the West. adds καταβοῶντες καί between κατεπέστησαν ὁμοθυμαδόν and λέγοντες. In Mart. Pol., 12, 2 f. ἐπιβοάω occurs 3 times in the sense of "to cry out against someone."

e. Only once in the NT is βοάω used of the cries with which demons go out of the sick (Ac. 8:7). Elsewhere κράζω is preferred in such accounts (e.g., Mk. 9:26). [5]

βοάω as Crying in Need to God.

Most significant theologically is the use of βοάω and cognates for the needy

---

β ο ά ω. [1] *V.* Preisigke Wört., *s.v.*
[2] Cf. also Apc. Mos., 37. By contrast, cf. the terrified outcry in 1 Βασ. 28:12: ἀνεβόησε (רוע) φωνῇ μεγάλῃ.
[3] The situation is different in Mk. 9:17 (ἀπεκρίθη) and Mt. 17:14 (προσῆλθεν ... λέγων).
[4] Cf. Mk. 15:14: περισσῶς ἔκραξεν.
[5] Cf. H. Leisegang, *Pneuma Hagion* (1922), 23 f., n. 4.

cry of the oppressed and downtrodden to God. [6] In the LXX we often meet with expressions like ἐβόησαν (זעק) υἱοὶ Ἰσραὴλ πρὸς κύριον (Ju. 10:10), ἀνεβοήσαμεν (צעק) πρὸς κύριον (Nu. 20:16); cf. also βοή in 1 Βασ. 9:16 (צעקה), Ex. 2:23 (שַׁוְעָה, "call for help"). Innocent blood crying out to heaven for vengeance is referred to in Gn. 4:10 (צעק, βοάω) and 2 Macc. 8:3 : τῶν καταβοώντων πρὸς αὐτὸν αἱμάτων [7] εἰσακοῦσαι. Similarly the OT warns concerning the cry of labourers vainly waiting for their wages and bringing their complaint to God (Dt. 24:15). The field itself can cry out (ἐστέναξεν) against exploiters, and the furrows complain in Job 31:38. Yahweh is a swift witness and judge against oppressors of labourers, widows and orphans (Mal. 3:5). The book of the covenant demands (Ex. 22:21 ff.): "Thou shalt not vex a stranger, nor oppress him : for ye were strangers in the land of Egypt. Ye shall not afflict any widow, or fatherless child. If thou afflict them in any wise, and they cry at all unto me, I will surely hear their cry ; and my wrath shall wax hot, and I will kill you with the sword ; and your wives shall be widows, and your children fatherless." The old Midrash on Exodus (M. Ex., 18 on 22:22) asks here : "Will God punish only when appeal is made to Him ?" and answers : "I will make haste to punish the oppressor when the oppressed cries more than when he does not (צעק)." [8]

The צעקה, the cry of innocent blood for vengeance, which cannot be silenced, reaches to heaven and finds there its witness (Job 16:18 ff.) and avenger ; God Himself in the day of vengeance undertakes to execute the penalty (Is. 26:21; cf. 1 K. 21:19 ff.). [9] In Eth. En. the blood-drenched earth raises a cry concerning the act of violence committed (7:5, ἐνέτυχεν; cf. 87:1). [10] The souls of those innocently slain charge that their cry rings out over the earth and ascends to the gate of heaven, the angels finally bringing it to the throne of the Most High. [11] The lament of those who have suffered violence cannot be silenced until God has brought a flood on the perpetrators (8:4, βοή; 9:1 ff.). The souls of Abel and other suppliants await in special chambers the day of judgment (22:7, 12). Even the souls of beasts complain acc. to Slav. En. 58:6; they accuse their masters, i.e., men, of abusing them and offering them violence. In the Bundehesh (IV, 12, Justi) the soul of the slaughtered bullock departs its body, and as though 1000 men were crying at once it complains to Ahura Mazda, the heaven of the stars and moon and sun, calling upon the deliverer of creation. The same theme is found in a very different form in Rev. 6:9 ff.; 8:3 ff. etc.

To the same circle of ideas belongs the threat against rich exploiters in Jm. 5, as also the parable of the widow who seeks justice in Lk. 18. The injustice done to the labourers cries to heaven, and the complaint of those who are deprived of their rights comes before God in evidence for the judgment of the ἐσχάται

---

[6] Cf. βοη-θόος, "hastening on the cry of need," βοηθεῖν: W. Schulze, SAB, 1918, 550 f. → βοηθέω n. 1.

[7] For the same plur. cf. A. Dürer, Tageb. d. Reise i. d. Niederlande (1521), Bergemann, p. 58 ff.: "the innocent bloods which they (the priests) have shed."

[8] Cf. also צוח in Levy Wört., IV, 177.

[9] Cf. Ass. Mos. 9:7; 4 Esr. 15:8 : sanguis innoxius et iustus clamat ad me, et animae iustorum clamant perseveranter.

[10] Eth. En. 88:15 : "The sheep began to cry out … and to complain to the Lord." Test. Jos. 19:3 f.: ἀμνοὶ … ἐβόησαν πρὸς Κύριον. For the complaint of the earth in the last judgment, cf. Apc. Elias, ed. Buttenwieser (1897), p. 65.

[11] 9:2, 10 (φωνὴ βοώντων, ἐντυγχάνειν, στεναγμός). The same terminology is found in Syncellus, v. J. Flemming-L. Radermacher, D. Buch Hen. (1901), 27 f. Cf. the complaint of the advocate in 89:57, 69; Hb. En. 44:10 (צווח); Apc. Elias 16:15 ff., Steindorff (TU, 17 [1899], 62 f.; 154; Syr. Schatzhöhle (Bezold), p. 21.

ἡμέραι. Ἰδοὺ ὁ μισθὸς τῶν ἐργατῶν ... ὁ ἀφυστερημένος ἀφ' ὑμῶν κράζει καὶ αἱ βοαὶ τῶν θερισάντων εἰς τὰ ὦτα κυρίου σαβαὼθ εἰσελήλυθαν ... κατεδικάσατε, ἐφονεύσατε τὸν δίκαιον· οὐκ ἀντιτάσσεται ὑμῖν (Jm. 5:4 ff.; cf. Wis. 2:20). In the parable, the emphasis is wholly on the penetrative quality of the prayer for vengeance in the sense of M. Ex. on 22:22. The widow does not rest, and leaves the judge no rest, until he helps her to her rights against her adversary, i.e., just because she is so persistent. The more surely will God hear the unwearied crying of His elect: τῶν βοώντων αὐτῷ ἡμέρας καὶ νυκτός. The cry of need of the persecuted hastens [12] the day of recompense: λέγω ὑμῖν ὅτι ποιήσει τὴν ἐκδίκησιν αὐτῶν ἐν τάχει (Lk. 18:8). [13]

A different note is sounded in the prayer of Jesus on the cross in Mk. 15:34: καὶ τῇ ἐνάτῃ ὥρᾳ ἐβόησεν [14] ὁ Ἰησοῦς φωνῇ μεγάλῃ· ἐλωῖ ἐλωῖ λαμὰ σαβαχθάνι· [15] Here, too, the elect is in extreme need, delivered up to the fury of the ungodly. But the reference of the prayer is to God alone and not to enemies. The Son of Man goes through the lowest depth of human need. [16] This depth, however, is the inferno of dereliction. From it He cries as only a man can cry, with full and final force. Yet the ἐβόησεν is no longer a crying to God for help and recompense; it is a crying after God Himself. The biblical βοᾶν finds its deepest meaning in prayer. Prayer, however, finds its extreme expression in the cry of the dying Christ for God — a cry in which a new relationship to God, a new form of being, is already intimated.

Three things are made quite clear in this respect. The first is that prayer, as understood in biblical and esp. NT religion, is an elementary crying in which the final reserves of man are concentrated. [17] It is a cry in which the shattering and impotence of his whole being are manifested. It is finally a mortal cry: נַפְשִׁי אָשִׂים בְּכַפִּי (Job 13:14). [18]

---

[12] Cf. M. Ex., loc. cit., and the shortening of the days διὰ τοὺς ἐκλεκτούς at Mk. 13:20; cf. Eth. En. 80:2; S. Bar. 20:1; Barn., 4, 3: εἰς τοῦτο γὰρ ὁ δεσπότης συντέτμηκεν τοὺς καιροὺς ... ἵνα ταχύνῃ ὁ ἠγαπημένος αὐτοῦ ... (cf. Lk. 18:8b). God shortens the period up to the coming of the Son of Man out of regard for the elect whose crying comes to Him. Perhaps this is the meaning of the much contested saying in Lk. 18:7: καὶ μακροθυμεῖ ἐπ' αὐτοῖς.

[13] Cf. Dt. 32:43 and the martyrs of Rev. 6:10: καὶ ἔκραξαν φωνῇ μεγάλῃ λέγοντες· ἕως πότε ὁ δεσπότης ... οὐ κρίνεις καὶ ἐκδικεῖς τὸ αἷμα ἡμῶν ἐκ τῶν κατοικούντων ἐπὶ τῆς γῆς ... καὶ ἐρρέθη αὐτοῖς, ἵνα ἀναπαύσωσιν ἔτι χρόνον μικρόν. Similarly the Jewish prayer for vengeance from Rheneia in Deissmann LO, 352 ff., 359: ἐπικαλοῦμαι καὶ ἀξιῶ τὸν θεόν ... ἵνα ἐγδικήσῃς τὸ αἷμα τὸ ἀναίτιον ζητήσεις καὶ τὴν ταχίστην.

[14] Mt. 27:46 acc. to א AD etc. has ἀνεβόησεν. Luke introduces the softer πάτερ, εἰς χεῖράς σου ... with the softer φωνήσας φωνῇ μεγάλῃ (Lk. 23:46). Mk. 15:37 refers to the death cry of Jesus in the words: ἀφεὶς φωνὴν μεγάλην ἐξέπνευσεν; Mt. 27:50 has: κράξας φωνῇ μεγάλῃ ἀφῆκεν τὸ πνεῦμα; Lk. 23:46 is again the mildest: τοῦτο δὲ εἰπὼν ἐξέπνευσεν.

[15] The Evangelist naturally does not mean that he prayed the whole of Ps. 22, cf. Mk. 15:35.

[16] Cf. Hb. 5:7 f.: ὃς ἐν ταῖς ἡμέραις τῆς σαρκὸς αὐτοῦ δεήσεις ... μετὰ κραυγῆς ἰσχυρᾶς καὶ δακρύων προσενέγκας ... ἔμαθεν ἀφ' ὧν ἔπαθεν τὴν ὑπακοήν. Phil. 2:8: ὑπήκοος μέχρι θανάτου; 2 C. 13:4: ἐσταυρώθη ἐξ ἀσθενείας.

[17] The much weaker βοάω is used for the eschatological supplication of the Church in 1 Cl., 34, 7: ὡς ἐξ ἑνὸς στόματος βοήσωμεν πρὸς αὐτὸν ἐκτενῶς εἰς τὸ μετόχους ἡμᾶς γενέσθαι τῶν ... ἐπαγγελιῶν, and in Barn., 3, 5, quoting Is. 58:9: τότε βοήσεις καὶ ὁ θεὸς ἐπακούσεταί σου.

[18] Cf. also Ps. 119:109; also, e.g., bTaan, 8a: "The prayer of a man is heard only when he yields up his soul"(נפשו בכפו); v. Lam. 3:41.

Secondly, this βοᾶν does not ring out unheard in cold and empty space. The man who relies on himself and his own power is silenced in his distress. The man who knows that he confronts a divine Thou presses on to God in his distress and brings all his need before Him. The man who does not know this kind of prayer is overwhelmed by loneliness. Biblical man knows a profounder solitariness, namely, the abyss of isolation from God. But this despairing and mortal loneliness wrings from him the cry in which he confesses for good or ill the Thou of God : מִמַּעֲמַקִּים קְרָאתִיךָ יְהֹוָה: "Out of the depths cry I unto thee, O God" (Ps. 130:1). Thirdly, this cry in which man surrenders his all to God, this mortal cry of the old man, is also the first cry of the new according to Christian conviction, namely, the cry of the man whose life emerged in the hour of the death of the Son of God (cf. 2 C. 13:4; Gl. 4:4 ff.). It is the πνεῦμα υἱοθεσίας, ἐν ᾧ κράζομεν· ᾽Αββά ... ὡσαύτως δὲ καὶ τὸ πνεῦμα συναντιλαμβάνεται τῇ ἀσθενείᾳ ἡμῶν· τὸ γὰρ τί προσευξώμεθα καθὸ δεῖ οὐκ οἴδαμεν, ἀλλὰ αὐτὸ τὸ πνεῦμα ὑπερεντυγχάνει στεναγμοῖς ἀλαλήτοις (R. 8:16, 26).

                                                                                        Stauffer

---

> ## βοηθέω, βοηθός,
> ## βοήθεια

† βοηθέω.

Like the par. βοη-δρομέω, βοη-θέω originally means "to run on a call to help," "to hasten to the help of the oppressed," and then "to help." [1] Attested from the time of Herodotus, it is found also in inscr. and pap. is common in the LXX and Josephus, [2] less common in Philo (e.g., Som., II, 265) and rare in the post-apost. fathers.

The basic meaning may still be seen in Ac. 21:28 : ἄνδρες ᾽Ισραηλῖται βοηθεῖτε (cf. Aristoph. Vesp., 433 : ὦ Μίδα καὶ Φρύξ, βοηθεῖτε δεῦρο). It is often used of the physician, e.g., Plut. Alex., 19 (I, 674e); Epict. Diss., II, 15, 15 : νοσῶ, κύριε, βοήθησόν μοι; and cf. also the healings of Jesus (Mk. 9:22, 24; Mt. 15:25). Similarly in Ac. 16:9; Rev. 12:16. Of God as the One who helps it is used only at 2 C. 6:2, quoting Is. 49:8. It is used of help in religious need at Mk. 9:24; Hb. 2:18. The expression οὐ βοηθεῖν (1 Cl., 39, 5; 2 Cl., 8, 2) is not found in the NT.

† βοηθός.

The adj. βοηθός is formed from βοηθέω. It may also be used as a noun for "helper." Attested from the time of Herodotus, it occurs in inscr. and pap., is common in the LXX (often of God, esp. in the Ps.), is also found in Joseph. and Philo (e.g., Som., II, 265), but is rare in the post-apostolic fathers.

In the NT it occurs only at Hb. 13:6, quoting ψ 117:6, in relation to God as the Helper of the righteous.

† βοήθεια.

"Help," constructed from βοηθέω like ἀσέβεια from ἀσεβέω, from the time of Thuc., also in inscr. and pap., common in the LXX, rarer in Philo (e.g., Rer. Div. Her.,

---

β ο η θ έ ω. [1] The oldest construction in the word group is βοήθοος (Homer, e.g., Il., 13, 477; 17, 481): "hastening on the call for help" (from θέω, "to run"). Cf. W. Schulze, SAB, 1918, 550 f. From this comes βοηθοόω, preserved in Lesb. βαθόημι, elsewhere βοηθέω.
[2] Cf. A. Schlatter, *Wie sprach Josephus von Gott?* (1910), 66.

58 and 60 of divine help), more frequent in Joseph., not found at all in the post-apost. fathers. In the NT it occurs only at Hb. 4:16 (of God); Ac. 27:17. In Hb. βοηθεῖν and its cognates, in accord. with the more literary form of expression, are relatively common. On the phrase εἰς εὔκαιρον βοήθειαν (Hb. 4:16), cf. Ditt. Or., 762, 4 : ὁ δῆμος τῶν Κιβυρατῶν τῷ δήμῳ τῶν Ῥωμαίων βοηθεῖτο κατὰ τὸ εὔκαιρον; Ditt. Syll.³, 693, 12. In Ac. 27:17 it is a nautical term, as shown by Philo Jos., 33 : κυβερνήτης ταῖς τῶν πνευμάτων μεταβολαῖς συμμεταβάλλει τὰς τῆς εὐπλοίας βοηθείας. [1]

The sparing use of βοηθεῖν and cognates in the NT, as in Josephus, causes Schlatter[2] to observe that it "distinguishes the language of the early Church from the synergism of rational piety, which likes to speak of divine help."

Büchsel

┌─────────────────────────┐
│ βούλομαι, βουλή,   │
│   βούλημα   │
└─────────────────────────┘

βούλομαι.

A. βούλομαι outside the NT.

The original difference in meaning between βούλομαι and (ἐ)θέλω is disputed in philological investigation. Two diametrically opposing views confront one another. a. The one finds in θέλειν impulsive and unconscious desire, and in βούλεσθαι rational and conscious.[1] ἐθέλειν thus signifies volition by inclination or natural instinct, the *proclivitas animi e desiderio,* while βούλεσθαι denotes a decision of will based on deliberate resolve, the *consilium secundum deliberationem.*[2] b. On the other hand, ἐθέλειν is understood to mean the resolution of the spirit, and βούλεσθαι as desire or inclination, as the wish of the soul.[3]

The first view is supported by the fact that βούλεσθαι is related to βουλή, βουλεύειν, βουλεύεσθαι.[4] The second view argues amongst other things that it is often

---

β ο ή θ ε ι α. [1] E. Nestle (ZNW, 8 [1907], 75 f.) suggests "shoring," but this is hardly likely on a voyage.
[2] Mt., 490.
β ο ύ λ ο μ α ι. R. Rödiger, *Glotta, 8* (1917), 1 ff.; W. Fox, *Berl. Phil. Wochenschr., 37* (1917), 597 ff., 633 ff.; P. Kretschmer, *Glotta, 3* (1910), 160 ff., cf. 8 (1917), 5, n. 2; Bl.-Debr. § 101, *s.v.* θέλειν; 392, 1a; 359, 2; 366, 3.
[1] The Alexandrian Ammonius Περὶ ὁμοίων καὶ διαφόρων λέξεων (Valckenaer² [1822]) 31, 70 gives the definition : βούλεσθαι μὲν ἐπὶ μόνου λεκτέον τοῦ λογικοῦ, τὸ δὲ θέλειν καὶ ἐπὶ ἀλόγου ζῴου. Similarly Maximus Confessor, John Damascene and the Scholastics call θέλησις an ὄρεξις φυσική and βούλησις an ὄρεξις λογική, on the basis of comparison, of λογισμός. Cf. W. Fox, *op. cit.*
[2] From the time of Dindorf, who introduced this view into modern philology, it has been disputed among others by G. Hermann, Ellendt, Pape, Rehdantz-Blass, Sandys, Adam and Rödiger. Cf. Demosth., 2, 20 : ἂν οἵ τε θεοὶ θέλωσι (are inclined) καὶ ὑμεῖς βούλησθε (Athenians — be resolved); Plat. Resp., IV, 437bc, and on this Rödiger, 2.
[3] Buttmann Lexilogus, Passow, Benseler-Kägi, Franke; J. H. H. Schmidt, *Synon. d. griech. Spr.* (1879), 3, 602 ff. Cf. Fox, *op. cit.*
[4] Thus Ps.-Plat. Def., 413c describes βούλησις as ἔφεσις μετὰ λόγου ὀρθοῦ, as ὄρεξις εὔλογος, ὄρεξις μετὰ λόγου κατὰ φύσιν. Aristot. does not distinguish between βούλεσθαι and (ἐ)θέλειν, but calls βούλησις α λογιστική ὄρεξις as distinct from ἐπιθυμία, which is called an ὄρεξις ἄνευ λόγου, Rhet., I, 10, p. 1369a, 2 ff.

used synon. with ἐπιθυμεῖν. [5] It is difficult to decide between them because at a very early date the two groups overlap. Hence the only course is to study the usage in different periods. [6] The following results accrue from such historical investigation. In Homer there are 38 instances of βούλομαι and 294 of ἐθέλω. [7] βούλομαι always has here the sense of "to prefer," "to choose," whereas ἐθέλω is used for all the other nuances of volition. Thus ἐθέλω is the older and more comprehensive term. It is particularly loved by the poets, [8] whereas βούλομαι is preferred by the prose writers and predominates from the time of Herodotus. In time it replaces ἐθέλειν so fully that always in Thuc., Isocr. and Lycurg., and mostly in Plato, Lysias, Andocides, Aeschines and Demosth., this is restricted to its original sense of being ready or inclined. [9] In Polybius, and also Diodorus, ἐθέλειν notably retreats into the background. Yet in the NT, and also in Epict., the relationship is reversed and ἐθέλειν is more common. In modern Gk. βούλομαι has been almost completely crowded out by θέλω.

If a decision must be made concerning the original meaning, the fact that "to prefer" or "to choose" (often with ἤ) seems to be the first sense of βούλομαι in Homer and Herodotus strongly favours the view, inaugurated by Ammonius, that βούλομαι originally means volition on the basis of choice, preference or decision. [10] Later there develops the general sense of desiring, wishing, [11] purposing [12] and striving, with an emphasis on the active element. A weaker sense sometime attested is "to mean" or "to think." [13] But so far as concerns the exposition of the NT, there can be no establishing of a dogmatic distinction on the basis of earlier usage, because the NT writings belong to a period when the high tide of ἐθέλειν has overwhelmed all the territory previously reserved for βούλεσθαι. Even at an earlier date [14] both words could be used to denote conscious, decided and resolute volition. There is a widespread alternation between the two on stylistic grounds. [15] Thus the most important task in NT exegesis is to study the use of the word in contemporary Hellenistic Judaism.

In the LXX the two words are almost equal numerically; βούλομαι is very slightly in the lead. This is not merely due to the fact that the LXX belongs to the age when the distinctions were being obliterated by the struggle between the terms. It also owes something to the fact that the Canon includes both historical and poetical sections, so that the words preferred by both the prose authors (→ supra; Polyb., Diod. S.) and the poets are accepted. The frequent use of θέλειν in the Ps. is particularly noteworthy. βούλεσθαι is usually the rendering of חָפֵץ and אָבָה, or, in the negative "to refuse," of

---

[5] Xenoph. An., II, 6, 21; Lys., 13, 16; Demosth., 5, 21 and 23; 13, 26; 27, 45; 29, 45. Cf. Plat. Prot., 340ab. On the other hand, in Plat. Resp., 437bc both ἐθέλειν and βούλεσθαι are contrasted with ἐπιθυμεῖν as sensual desire.

[6] Rödiger has been the first to attempt this difficult task on a big scale. I have carried through a comparison in the LXX, Philo, Josephus, also Polyb., Diod. S., and Epict., and have come to much the same conclusions.

[7] Acc. to Rödiger, βούλομαι ἤ in Il., 1, 117; 11, 319; 17, 331; 23, 594; Od., 3, 232; 11, 489. Cf. also Rödiger, 5. Hdt., III, 40, 8; 124, 10. Less frequent without ἤ, as in Il., 1, 112; Od., 15, 88.

[8] Rödiger, 4 has shown that Aristoph. is closer to prose usage in his fuller use of βούλομαι.

[9] Rödiger, 3, 14.

[10] This fits in well with the etymol. explanation of Kretschmer, which links βούλομαι with βάλλομαι. For the same sense, though ironically, cf. Plat. Crat., 420c (βάλλω).

[11] Already in Il., 23, 682; Hes. Op., 647; later Polyb., I, 1, 5; Epict. Diss., II, 1, 23 f.

[12] Soph. Ai., 681; Trach., 486; Polyb., I, 7, 12. Arrian Praef., in Epict. Diss., 7.

[13] Plat. Parm., 128a; Aristot. Eth. Nic., III, 2, p. 1110b, 30.

[14] Thus βούλομαι can mean "to resolve": Eur. Iph. Taur., 61; Aristot. Pol., V, 9, p. 1309b, 17; Corp. Herm., IV, 6b (βούλομαι, "I am resolved").

[15] To the instances given by Rödiger, 24, which illustrate their parallel use from another angle, I add some in which the grounds are stylistic: Plat. Gorg., 522e; Polyb., X, 40, 5; Plut. Tranq. An., 13 (II, 472e); Epict. Diss., I, 2, 12 f.; 12, 13; III, 22, 100; 24, 54; IV, 1, 89 f.; Jos. Ant., 1, 233; 3, 67; 6, 226; 9, 240; 10, 29 and 156 f.; 11, 242 f.; Philo Rer. Div. Her., 158; Corp. Herm., I, 3; XIII, 15; XVIII, 7b.

מֵאֵן pi and adj. It is often used for determined refusal, [16] but also for the royal will, [17] caprice [18] and especially the divine resolve and will. [19] This shows that it is not thought of as merely the desire of the heart or wish of the soul. [20] Like θέλειν, it often has also the sense of "having a desire for," [21] of "desiring something," or "seeking," [22] "wanting," [23] or "purposing." [24] Indeed, in some instances the sense is simply that of "being ready or inclined." [25]

Occasionally Josephus has the older meaning of "to prefer," mostly without ἤ. [26] For the most part, however, the meanings "to have a desire, an inclination," "to have an inner intention," [27] or "to wish" [28] are predominant. In the case of "to purpose," [29] it is instructive that βούλεσθαι can denote an intention which is never fulfilled. [30] The word is often used of literary projects. [31] As in the LXX we have (neg.) the sense of refusal. [32] More positively, however, resolute religious volition can be expressed by βούλομαι. [33] When Joseph. says that at 16 he resolved to test the Jewish αἱρέσεις, he can use βούλομαι for this active resolve. [34] It is in keeping that a great role is played by the βούλομαι of the royal will, or permission, or rule — more so than in the LXX. [35] Related is the solemnly declared intention of such fathers as Moses and Nehemiah. [36] Joseph. uses the term quite often for the divine will. [37] But he also uses it in the weaker sense of "to mean" or "to think," [38] cf. also ὁ βουλόμενος in the sense of one who has the will or desire. [39]

The basic sense of "to prefer" occurs also in Philo. [40] There are many examples of the sense of inner intention or striving. [41] Above all, the ideas of wishing and intending

---

[16] E.g., Pharaoh in Ex. 4:23; 8:21 etc.; of the refusal of Israel to listen to God in Ex. 16:28; 1 Βασ. 8:19; Jdt. 5:7; ψ 77:10; Is. 30:9 etc.

[17] 2 Βασ. 6:10; 1 Macc. 15:3 א; 2 Macc. 11:23.

[18] 1 Macc. 8:13; 11:49.

[19] Tob. 4:19; ψ 113:10 (115:3); Wis. 12:6; Is. 53:10; Da. LXX 4:28 etc.; Ep. Ar., 269. This usage is very old: Hom. Od., 4, 353; Eur. Iph. Aul., 33; later Corp. Herm., I, 31; BGU, 248, 11.

[20] Religious volition is particularly plain, ψ 39:9: τοῦ ποιῆσαι τὸ θέλημά σου, ὁ θεός μου, ἐβουλήθην. The resolute prosecution of a goal, Ep. Ar., 250.

[21] Ex. 36:2; Job 9:3; Jer. 49(42):22; Da. LXX, 11:3.

[22] 3 Βασ. 20:6. βούλομαι ἐν: 1 Βασ. 18:25; 2 Βασ. 24:3. θέλειν ἐν is more common.

[23] 1 Βασ. 2:25; Wis. 16:21; 1 Macc. 4:6; Ep. Ar., 5; 40; 207.

[24] 1 Macc. 3:34; 11:45; 15:4. With acc. of obj. ψ 69(70):2; cf. Prv. 12:20; Ep. Ar., 38; 53; 180.

[25] 1 Βασ. 24:11; esp. ψ 39:8. Cf. on the other hand for the classical writers, Rödiger, 13, though against this we may set Plat. Crat., 384a and Gorg., 448d. Cf. in Philo Abr., 102; Jos., 55; Rer. Div. Her., 44.

[26] Ant., 2, 272; 12, 161.

[27] Ant., 1, 102: βούλεσθε alongside τὰς ὀρέξεις ἔχετε; 1, 260 and 266.

[28] Ant., 1, 91; 2, 99; 4, 167; 6, 226 etc.

[29] Ant., 1, 165; 4, 96; 7, 208 etc.

[30] Ant., 12, 358. Cf. Aristot. Pol., I, 6, p. 1255b, 3: nature usually wills it, but cannot always do it.

[31] Ant., 1, 1; 4, 196; 18, 10; Vit., 27; 345.

[32] Ant., 2, 197; 12, 181; Bell., 7, 51.

[33] Ant., 3, 203, with πιστεύειν.

[34] Vit., 10; cf. Ant., 11, 63.

[35] Ant., 2, 80; 11, 17; 12, 150; 13, 51; 14, 230 and 315 etc.; 16, 167 f.; 19, 291; Bell., 2, 184. But θέλω, too, can be used of official rule, as in Ant., 14, 233.

[36] Ant., 1, 268; 2, 163; 4, 57; 11, 170.

[37] Ant., 1, 192; 2, 145; 3, 45; 4, 119; 5, 218; 7, 294 etc.

[38] Ant., 2, 14; 3, 152; cf. Philo Leg. All., II, 36.

[39] Jos. Ap., 1, 182; cf. Hdt., I, 54.

[40] Rer. Div. Her., 290; "to prefer" without ἤ, Abr., 216.

[41] Leg. All., II, 32; βούλονται alongside ἐπιτηδεύουσι: Cherub., 95.

are again to the fore. [42] Here, too, we often have the sense of zealous and resolute volition, especially in terms of religious aspiration. [43] On innumerable occasions it is used of the divine will, of God's goal in creation, [44] of His purpose in Scripture, [45] of His providence, [46] of His guidance of the soul. [47] It can also be stated, however, of τὸ ὄν [48] or ἡ φύσις. [49] Especially common are statements concerning the intention of Scripture, the Lawgiver and the Law. [50] The εἰ βούλει at Lk. 22:42 is much less emphatic and much more colourless in Philo than in this passage. [51]

B. βούλομαι in the NT.

In the NT we have only a remnant, as it were, of βούλομαι; the alternative ἐθέλω has carried the day. It occurs mostly in Ac., less in the Gospels, least in the Epistles. This is linked with the fact that Ac. is stylistically more akin to narrative prose such as that of Polybius, Diod. S. and Josephus, who still like βούλομαι even in the period of transition to ἐθέλω. a. In most of the NT passages, as in LXX, Aristeas, Josephus and Philo, the sense is that of "wishing," "desiring" [52] or "intending," [53] often with something of all three (27 times out of a total of 37). b. Three times βούλομαι is used in the Past. with reference to ordering by apostolic authority. [54]

c. The most important point in terms of biblical theology is the emphasising of the will of God, His Son and the Spirit (7 times). In the sense of the economy of salvation it is argued in Hb. 6:17 that God willed to manifest more fully to the heirs of promise the immutable nature of His counsel. Here βούλομαι expresses the eternal divine purpose. Similarly in 2 Pt. 3:9 the word expresses the divine will to save. In Jm. 1:18 βουληθεὶς ἀπεκύησεν ἡμᾶς λόγῳ ἀληθείας (used absol.) denotes the resolute will of God as the motive force which gives new life by the

---

[42] "To wish" : Migr. Abr., 99; Abr., 129; Vit. Mos., I, 16; alongside εὔχομαι, Deus Imm., 164. On Jm. 3:4 : Leg. All., III, 223. "To purpose" Vit. Mos., I, 144; Jos., 181; Det. Pot. Ins., 1; Deus Imm., 153 etc.

[43] Spec. Leg., I, 36; Leg. All., III, 134; Deus Imm., 144.

[44] Op. Mund., 16; 44; 77; 138; 149; Plant., 14; Conf. Ling., 166; 196.

[45] Abr., 5; 9; Decal., 9; Leg. All., III, 210; Cherub., 60; Gig., 60; Deus Imm., 21; Ebr., 85.

[46] Jos., 99; 165; Poster C., 145.

[47] Vit. Mos., I, 164; 198; Migr. Abr., 2.

[48] Det. Pot. Ins., 154.

[49] Spec. Leg., II, 48.

[50] Of Scripture, Leg. All., I, 4; 35; 63; 90; III, 45-55; Cher., 14; Det. Pot. Ins., 168; Plant., 94; Migr. Abr., 46; of the Lawgiver, Vit. Mos., I, 220; Spec. Leg., I, 96; of the Law, Spec. Leg., I, 116; 203 etc.

[51] Abr., 251; Leg. All., III, 69; Decal., 86. It is common as a milder form of the imperative: "If thou desirest, or if it please thee," or simply as : "May it be that — or" : Soph. Ant., 1168; Xenoph. An., III, 4, 4; Plat. Gorg., 448d; Symp., 201a; Phaed., 95e.

[52] "To wish" : Jn. 18:39 : βούλεσθε ἀπολύσω, before a question, cf. Bl.-Debr. § 366, 3. Otherwise almost always with inf.: Ac. 15:37; 17:20; 18:15 (have no pleasure); 22:30; 23:28; 25:20, 22 (ἐβουλόμην, adding to Bl.-Debr. § 66, 3); 1 Tm. 6:9; Phlm. 13 (cf. Bl.-Debr. § 359, 2); Jm. 4:4; 2 Jn. 12. With acc. c. inf.: Phil. 1:12; Jd. 5.

[53] Mt. 1:19 : Joseph purposed to release her privately; Mk. 15:15; Ac. 5:28, 33; 12:4; 19:30; 2 C. 1:15. Thus far all with inf. With acc. c. inf.: Ac. 12:4; 27:43; 28:18 (or "to wish"). In Jm. 3:4 the reference is to resolute purpose ; there is an implied μετάγειν or κυβερνᾶν. In 3 Jn. 10 τοὺς βουλομένους implies ἐπιδέχεσθαι ἀδελφούς. Thus these passages, too, belong to this category. With the acc. of object : 2 C. 1:17. For par. from the post-apost. fathers, v. Pr.-Bauer, 229.

[54] Always with acc. c. inf. : 1 Tm. 2:8; 5:14; Tt. 3:8. Cf. Plat. Symp., 184a (the Law demands); the examples from the LXX cited above are linked particularly with this usage, as also those from Josephus, i.e., when the reference is to the disposition of the royal will or the lawgiver.

word of truth.[55] In Lk. 22:42 Jesus with His εἰ βούλει[56] appeals to the divine will, design and counsel, and makes Himself dependent on it at the very moment when the humanly anxious request for help and deliverance presses for utterance.

The reference in the solemn declaration in Mt. 11:27 (Lk. 10:22): ᾧ ἐὰν βούληται ὁ υἱὸς ἀποκαλύψαι, is to the omnipotence of the Son. Here the βούλεσθαι of the Son is His faithful execution of the divine βουλή.

Of the Spirit, too, Paul can say in 1 C. 12:11: διαιροῦν ἰδίᾳ ἑκάστῳ καθὼς βούλεται (in the absol.). The distribution of spiritual gifts by the Spirit takes place, analogously to the divine will, through free resolve according to a determinative selection.

† βουλή.

A. βουλή outside the NT.

βουλή denotes "deliberation" and "taking counsel" in all its stages and effects up to "resolve" and "decree." In the LXX the term is mostly used for עֵצָה, but also for סוֹד, דֵּעָה, מַחֲשָׁבָה etc.

1. βουλή as the first stage of inward "deliberation." Sir. 37:16 : πρὸ πάσης πράξεως βουλή. Hence in many cases it simply means "thought," as at Is. 55:7; 1 Macc. 4:45. The element of clever and reasoned wisdom and deliberation is usually emphasised : Prv. 2:11; 8:12; 11:14 etc.; Sir. 35(32):19; 1 Macc. 8:4. Here the connection with the inner movement of βουλεύεσθαι is very clear. Jos. Ant., 1, 338 : Ἰακὼβ ἠξίωσεν ἐπιτρέψαι αὐτῷ βουλὴν ἀγαγεῖν. Epict. Diss., II, 16, 15 : τίς βουλευόμενος αὐτῆς τῆς βουλῆς. Yet βουλή is often used, not merely for the individual process in man, but as a characteristic of wise and thoughtful deliberation : Dt. 32:28; 4 Βασ. 18:20; Sir. 21:13; 25:4. In Is. 11:2 the spirit of counsel is a gift ; cf. Ep. Ar., 270. βουλή is sometimes a gift of age : Philo Migr. Abr., 201: πρεσβύτεροι βουλαῖς; Plant., 168. In Test. L. 4:5 it occurs along with σύνεσις, and in Vit. Mos., I, 242 we have πράξεις with βουλαί. In some cases βούλομαι affects the usage as well as βουλεύομαι, so that we should often render simply as "will," "expression of will," or "wish" : Philo Poster. C., 11, 36; Jos. Ant., 19, 314.

2. Secondly, βουλή denotes the final result of inner deliberation. a. As "resolve" : Tob. 4:19 AB; Sir. 22:16; Ep. Ar., 42; Jos. Ant., 2, 18; 9, 76; Philo Spec. Leg., III, 29 along with πράξεις; Abr., 101. b. As "intention" : 2 Macc. 14:5 : ἐν τίνι διαθέσει καὶ βουλῇ, "design," "purpose" : 3 Macc. 3:11; Philo Conf. Ling., 153; 198. c. As "plan" or "project," e.g., the plan in the divine message, Is. 44:26; the project of alliance with a heathen power, Is. 30:1; the plans of the nations, ψ 32:10 AB א²; Is. 8:10; of kings, Wis. 6:3; of war, 1 Macc. 9:60, 68. Closely related is βουλή as a cunning and wicked design, Job 5:12; 18:7; Neh. 4:15 (9) = 2 Εσδρ. 14:15; 1 Macc. 7:31; 3 Macc. 5:8; Jos. Ant., 2, 23. d. As "counsel" given to someone : Gn. 49:6; the counsel of Ahithophel, 2 Βασ. 15:31; of the old men, 3 Βασ. 12:8; the stupid counsel of the wise men of Pharaoh, Is. 19:11; the righteous man as he who does not follow the counsels of the ungodly, Ps. 1:1; cf. Job 22:18; according to Sir. 37:13 the conscience has a part in

---

[55] Cf. Schl. Jk., 136. A. Meyer, Rätsel des Jk. (1930), 76, n. 4; 268 sees a reference to Reuben after the manner of an ancient onomastic. On the pt. that in Philo βουληθείς is always at the beginning with an inf. when used of God, cf. Hck. Jk., 70, n. 17. The following instances are relevant : Op. Mund., 16; 77; Cher., 60; Plant., 14; Migr. Abr., 2; Rer. Div. Her., 112; 225; 243 (of Abraham). Cf. the construction in Jos. Ant., 1, 21 and 260; 12, 350; Bell., 1, 311. For further details, cf. Hck. and Schl., ad loc.

[56] On the form βούλει instead of Att. βούλη, Bl.-Debr. § 27, Mayser, 328 for the pap. Par. to εἰ βούλει (→ n. 51) are no help to the elucidation of this passage, in which the reference is to the revealed nature of the specific will of God.

βουλή; according to 39:7 a just scribe gives βουλή and ἐπιστήμη. In the prophecy of the child who will be the bearer of divine counsel (Is. 9:6), the LXX reads : μεγάλης βουλῆς ἄγγελος. Cf. Test. Jud. 9:7, fatherly counsel ; Test. Jos. 17:7, Joseph's counsel ; Jos. Ant., 7, 44, military counsel ; Philo Vit. Mos., I, 294 : our counsels and the λόγια of God.

3. βουλή also denotes the official machinery of counsel and resolution. Thus it can be used a. for the process in general : 1 Ch. 12:19, where the princes of the Philistines hold counsel ; Jdt. 2:2, where Nebuchadnezzar holds secret counsel ; cf. Jos. Vit., 204; with reference to public gatherings in 1 Macc. 14:22 : ἐν ταῖς βουλαῖς τοῦ δήμου. Advising is called βουλὴν προτίθεσθαι in Diod. S., II, 24, 4, or ἄγειν in Jos. Ant., 14, 361, or ποιεῖσθαι in Polyb., XIV, 6, 9; Jos. Ant., 15, 98. b. Then βουλή is used for the council of a city. Diod. S., XIII, 2, 4 of the council of Athens ; XVI, 15, 8 : ἡ βουλὴ καὶ οἱ πρυτάνεις; the senate in Rome : Jos. Ant., 13, 164 f.; 18, 1 etc.; Bell., 1, 284 f.; 2, 209; the council in Samaria : Jos. Ant., 11, 117; in Tiberias : Vit., 64; 284. In the edict of Claudius, Ant., 20, 11: Ἱεροσολυμιτῶν ἄρχουσι, βουλῇ, δήμῳ. Later, at the time of Septimius Severus in 202 A.D., βουλή is the council of a city with an autonomous constitution.[1] c. Of a resolution of state : Polyb., XXI, 32, 3 : δημοσίᾳ βουλῇ; cf. 3 Macc. 7:17: κοινὴ βουλή, of the common resolution of the Jewish people.

4. βουλή as the "divine counsel" : Job 38:2; 42:3; ψ 32(33):11; 72(73):24; Prv. 19:18 (21); Wis. 9:17; Mich. 4:12; Is. 5:19; 14:26; 25:1; 46:10; Jer. 29:21 (49: 20); the counsel of wisdom, Prv. 1:25; 8:14. Josephus prefers βούλησις (cf. βού-λημα), and though we might mention Ant., 4, 42 the ethical concept is here characteristically weakened.

In Hellenistic mysticism the emphasis on the βουλή of God, though not so prominent as πρόνοια, ἀνάγκη, εἱμαρμένη, indicates a notable penetration of the divine transcendence. According to Corp. Herm., I, 8b the στοιχεῖα τῆς φύσεως are ἐκ βουλῆς θεοῦ. According to I, 31 this counsel is executed by inherent forces. The willing is also accomplishing : I, 14 (with reference to the God Anthropos): ἅμα δὲ τῇ βουλῇ (or βουλήσει) ἐγένετο ἐνέργεια. At the end of the period the all-encompassing fetter will be loosed by God's decree (I, 18). This βουλή can also be called θέλημα (XIII, 19; 20, cf. 2). It is, however, viewed as a goddess and is separated from God Himself.[2] It is debatable whether the theory[3] is correct which would have it that the λόγος θεοῦ in I, 8 is received by βουλή as divine seed to bear the κόσμος αἰσθητός, or whether βουλή, with the help of the Logos representing the world of ideas, creates the κόσμος αἰσθητός by μίμησις.[4] Either way, we have a divine triad with the linking of βουλὴ θεοῦ, λόγος and κόσμος.[5] Everything is pantheistically ordained. In favour of the first view it might be argued that even in Philo Poster. C., 175 there is reference to the pregnancy of βουλή. The two daughters of Lot, βουλὴ καὶ συγκατάθεσις, ἐκ τοῦ νοῦ τοῦ πατρὸς αὐτῶν ἐθέλουσι παιδοποιεῖσθαι, cf. Ebr., 165; 203, where the younger daughter is called συναίνεσις ("agreement"). Naturally both concepts serve only to represent psychological processes and there is no hypostatising of βουλή. In Philo βουλή does not mean counsel so much as wish or will. The ἐπιστήμη and σοφία of God are more closely related to the divine counsel (Ebr., 30).[6]

βουλή. [1] Preisigke Fachwörter, 41; Wört., III, 100; Mitteis-Wilcken, I, 1, 41.
[2] J. Kroll, Die Lehren des Hermes Trismegistos (1914), 27 ff.
[3] Reitzenstein Poim., 45.
[4] Kroll, 28.
[5] Ibid., 71.
[6] E. Bréhier, Les Idées philosoph. et relig. de Philon d'Alex.[2] (1925), 117, 4; 119.

B. βουλή in the NT.

1 C. 4:5 : τὰς βουλὰς τῶν καρδιῶν. Since "heart" implies the hiddenness of the βουλαί, the meaning is to be sought under 1. or 2. We might simply translate "thoughts," though this would lose the element of striving. "Desires" or "impulses"[7] is too weak, but "plans" or "purposes"[8] is not absolutely necessary. The reference is to the "intents" of the heart, i.e., the most inward intentions of the inner life (2. b.). Ac. 5:38 : ὅτι ἐὰν ᾖ ἐξ ἀνθρώπων ἡ βουλὴ αὕτη ("design"), certainly belongs under 2. b.

Ac. 27:12, 42 must be placed under 3. a. In both cases the βουλή of the soldiers on the ship is the result of agreement, and they propose a plan based on deliberation.

In the NT, however, βουλή is mostly used of the divine counsel. The writings of Luke favour such usage. All the Lucan statements are elements in a total conception of the divine βουλή. This rules over the preceding OT history. According to Ac. 13:36 the death of David took place according to God's βουλή.[9] It manifested itself in the message of the Baptist. According to Lk. 7:30 the Pharisees and scribes rejected the counsel of God to them[10] when they did not accept John's baptism. Again, it ordains the self-sacrifice of Jesus. According to Ac. 2:23 Jesus is delivered up τῇ ὡρισμένῃ βουλῇ καὶ προγνώσει τοῦ θεοῦ. This counsel is predetermined and inflexible. Both phrases emphasise the resolute and inviolable determinateness of the decree. Similarly Ac. 4:28 treats of the fact that Herod, Pilate, the Gentiles and Israel all conspired against Jesus to do ὅσα ἡ χείρ σου καὶ ἡ βουλὴ προώρισεν γενέσθαι. Here the ὁρίζειν and πρόγνωσις, separated in 2:23, are combined in a single word, thus showing that Luke wishes to emphasise the elements both of impregnability and of foreordination. The related χείρ stresses the thought of the providential guidance of the world. The βουλή fills the whole content of apostolic preaching. In Ac. 20:27 Paul tells the Ephesian elders that he has declared to them the whole counsel of God.

In the magnifying of the divine economy of salvation in Eph. 1, which is shot through with references to the will of God (cf. the recurrent θέλημα and εὐδοκία), the expositions of the foreordination and election of the community within a Christological universalism which embraces both heaven and earth (v. 10), lead finally to a solemn climax in the statement (v. 11): ἐν ᾧ καὶ ἐκληρώθημεν προορισθέντες κατὰ πρόθεσιν τοῦ τὰ πάντα ἐνεργοῦντος κατὰ τὴν βουλὴν τοῦ θελήματος αὐτοῦ. The inheritance of the community, which consists in the final revelation and has its provisional seal in the Spirit (cf. what follows), is rooted in the προορισθῆναι κατὰ πρόθεσιν. Everything is mediated and present once and for all in Christ (ἐν αὐτῷ) and everything finally derives from the βουλὴ τοῦ θελήματος αὐτοῦ which finally effects the whole fulness of the event of salvation. It is quite plain that this βουλὴ τοῦ θελήματος αὐτοῦ has the final word, that it not merely overarches the ἐξελέξατο (v. 4), προορίσας (v. 5, 11) and πρόθεσις (v. 11), but that it also sets in movement everything which in this whole section is described as the grace present in Christ and granted to the community as the

---

[7] J. Weiss 1 K., *ad loc.*

[8] The latter is suggested by Ltzm. 1 K., *ad loc.*

[9] The context demands that τῇ τοῦ θεοῦ βουλῇ be related to ἐκοιμήθη, because in contrast to David Jesus has not seen corruption. It is also easier to understand the first dat. ἰδίᾳ γενεᾷ on this view.

[10] The εἰς ἑαυτούς qualifies the βουλή.

reality of salvation. This helps us to see that in the formula "counsel of his will" the inflexible ordination of His will finds a full-orbed pleonastic expression. Nowhere else does Paul use βουλή. [11] Instead, he has θέλημα and once βούλημα (R. 9:19). But θέλημα is strengthened here by βουλή, and behind it stands a rich LXX usage (→ 633). [12] The peculiarity of Eph. 1:11 lies in the linking of the whole οἰκονομία of God with His βουλή. To this degree there is a close relationship in content with Ac. 20:27.

Finally, in Hb. 6:17 there is reference to the fact that God confirms τὸ ἀμετά-θετον τῆς βουλῆς αὐτοῦ with an oath to the heirs of the promise. Here the unbreakable and unchangeable nature of the counsel is underlined.

βούλημα.

1. The comparatively rare βούλημα occurs e.g., in the LXX only in 3 (4) passages for דַעַת. The reading in Prv. 9:10 א* (βούλημα for βουλή א ᶜᵃ) shows by the vacillation how closely linked it is to βουλή. Yet it is not very difficult to discover a basic meaning which gives the word its own nuance. It denotes the "will as plan, project, purpose, goal, intention or tendency." The question of purpose or intention is predominant even where, as in the pap., it is used sometimes for the last will and testament. [1] When we turn particularly to the sphere of Hellenistic Judaism, or to Polybius and Epictetus, this basic element seems to be less prominent in some passages. Thus in Philo Leg. All., 62 τὸ κακὸν ἀποτέλεσμα διὰ τῶν ἔργων is compared with κακὸν βού-λημα as reflection on what is odious, which is called a τροπὴ τῆς ψυχῆς. Yet even here, although there is less emphasis on active efforts and a stronger intellectual colouring, the idea of "purpose" is still present. In Vit. Mos., I, 59 it is said of Reguel that he was at once filled with astonishment at the appearance of Moses and at his βούλημα, which is later listed among the μεγάλαι φύσεις. What is meant is the will and purpose expressed in him.

Apart from such easily explicable generalisings in derivatives of βουλ-, one can almost always find the common factor in the element of purpose. At 2 Macc. 15:5 τὸ σχέτλιον βούλημα is a shameful project. In Polyb., X, 18, 13 : λαβὼν ἐν νῷ τὸ βούλημα τῆς γυναικός has reference to the intention of the wife. Serious striving is meant in Ep. Ar., 322. Often in Phil. "purpose" is the only possible rendering, e.g., in Spec. Leg., I, 323; II, 132; III, 85; Vit. Mos., II, 31; Det. Pot. Ins., 72. In Spec. Leg., III, 121 the βουλήματα are the inner tendencies which are laid bare. Hence βούλημα can also mean "plan," e.g., in Jos. Ant., 1, 278. Also favouring the basic meaning is a phrase much used by Philo and Epictetus : βούλημα τῆς φύσεως, i.e., that which nature discloses of planning and purposeful will (Philo Spec. Leg., III, 136; 176; Op. Mund., 3; Epict. Diss., I, 17, 13-17; II, 20, 15; III, 20, 13).

Even when the reference is to the βούλημα of the ruler we find confirmation of this nuance. Thus Ep. Ar., 283 speaks of the plans and purposes of kings. In Jos. Ant., 16, 173, after τοῖς τοῦ Σεβαστοῦ καὶ ᾿Αγρίππα βουλήμασιν, there follows at once a description of the purpose, i.e., that the Jews should live according to the customs of the fathers. Jos. Ant., 13, 425 is more general. But in Bell., 1, 178 : (Gabinius) πρὸς τὸ ᾿Αντιπάτρου βούλημα κατεστήσατο τὴν πολιτείαν, the meaning might well be "plan." Since these purposes are not always pressed, the sense of preference or opinion or even whim sometimes suggests itself. Thus in 4 Macc. 8:18 the βουλήματα κενά are empty whims, and in Epict. Diss., II, 1, 25 the reference is to being chased hither and thither πρὸς τὸ βούλημα τοῦ κυρίου (preference or opinion). In Polyb., VI, 15, 4;

---

[11] H. J. Holtzmann, *Kritik der Eph. und Kol.-briefe* (1872), 257; A. Klöpper Eph. (1890), 47, n. 2, see here a reason against authenticity.
[12] Cf. J. Schmid, *Der Eph. des Ap. Pls.* (1928), 203.
β ο ύ λ η μ α. [1] Cf. Preisigke Wört., s.v.

17, 8: τὸ τῆς συγκλήτου βούλημα, the resolution of the senate (as compared with XXIII, 2, 10: κατὰ τὴν τῆς συγκλήτου βούλησιν, the will of the senate), βούλημα denotes the result of βουλή.

2. It may be asked whether passages which speak of the βούλημα of God should be construed in terms of resolve or whether the thought of purpose should again predominate. There seems to be good evidence for the latter view. Thus in Jos. Ant., 1, 232, in the story of the sacrifice of Isaac, Isaac is prepared to subject himself τοῖς ἀμφοτέρων βουλήμασιν (of God and his father). The reference is to the plan and purpose of the divine will which Isaac cannot fathom. According to Ant., 2, 304 Pharaoh is disobedient τοῖς τοῦ θεοῦ βουλήμασιν, to the true intention of God, in refusing to let the children of Israel go. According to Philo Leg. All., III, 239, works are ordained for the temperate θεοῦ βουλήματι (plan and purpose). According to Vit. Mos., I, 95 God reveals His βούλημα, His previously undisclosed purpose, by oracles and wonders. In Rer. Div. Her., 272 the reference is plainly to the βούλημα θεοῦ as the divine purpose to alleviate innate evils. Most convincing, however, is Vit. Mos., I, 287, in which the βούλημα of God in Balaam's oracle is described as contrary to the purpose of the king (προαίρεσις). [2]

3. βούλημα in the NT merely confirms these findings. In Ac. 27:43 the captain frustrates the design of the soldiers to kill the prisoners. In 1 Pt. 4:3: τὸ βούλημα τῶν ἐθνῶν κατειργάσθαι — there follows a catalogue of vices — the community is told that in the past it followed the tendency and direction of the Gentiles. Finally in R. 9:19: τῷ γὰρ βουλήματι αὐτοῦ τίς ἀνθέστηκεν, what is meant is the purposeful intention of God which has been previously (v. 18) described as the twofold will of mercy and severity. The instances adduced for "opinion" or "preference" only help to make clearer the sense of the term in this passage.

Schrenk

βραβεύω, βραβεῖον

Among the technical terms of the arena introduced by Paul into the theological speech of early Christianity (→ ἀγωνίζεσθαι, ἀθλεῖν), βραβεύω and especially βραβεῖον deserve mention.

† βραβεύω.

Common from the time of Euripides, [1] this word refers originally to the activity of the umpire (βραβεύς, βραβευτής) whose office at the games is to direct, arbitrate and decide the contest. In the wider sense it then comes to mean "to order," "rule," or

---

[2] In Josephus (cf. A. Schlatter, *Wie sprach Josephus von Gott?* [1910] 26 f.) the divine will is very often called βούλησις, predominantly in the sense of the purposeful guidance and direction of Israel and its history both as a whole and in detail. It is used along with ἐντολαί in Ant., 6, 147, cf. 7, 39. Since Jos. also uses βούλησις (with ἰδία, οἰκεία, Ant., 5, 179; 6, 143; also 3, 319; 13, 41) of capricious opinion, or of the whim of a ruler (Ant., 6, 61; cf. Polyb., IV, 82, 5; V, 26, 13; Diod. S., III, 16, 3), it is clearly linked with the thought of free and sovereign self-determination when applied to God.

β ρ α β ε ύ ω κτλ. [1] For class. examples of βραβεύειν, βραβεύς etc., cf. J. Wieneke, *Ezechielis Judaei poetae Alexandrini fabulae quae inscribuntur Ἐξαγωγή* (Diss. Phil. Münster, 1931), 68.

"control." The LXX uses the term only once in a later passage under Hellenistic influence, i.e., at Wis., 10:12, where wisdom is the umpire who directed and decided the bitter contest of Jacob with the angel (Gn. 32:24 ff.): ἀγῶνα ἰσχυρὸν ἐβράβευσεν αὐτῷ. Βραβεύειν without obj. is used of God in Philo Vit. Mos., I, 16: παρ' ἑκόντων ἔλαβε τὴν ἀρχήν, βραβεύοντος καὶ ἐπινεύοντος θεοῦ. In the sense of "to rule" it is used of Moses in Ez. Ἐξαγωγή, 86 (→ n. 1): αὐτὸς βραβεύσεις καὶ καθηγήσῃ βροτῶν.

Paul uses the verb of the peace which settles all strife and preserves the unity of the Christian community: ἡ εἰρήνη τοῦ Χριστοῦ βραβευέτω ἐν ταῖς καρδίαις ὑμῶν (Col. 3:15); the community is a kingdom of peace. Otherwise the simple βραβεύω does not occur in the NT.[2] In the analogous expression in Phil. 4:7 Paul uses another verb: ἡ εἰρήνη τοῦ θεοῦ ... φρουρήσει τὰς καρδίας ὑμῶν ... ἐν Χριστῷ Ἰησοῦ. Obviously both terms have much the same sense of "to control" or "to rule," as finely attested for βραβεύειν and φυλάττειν by a Christian papyrus of the 6th century: δικαία ἡ διαθήκη ... ὑπὸ Χριστοῦ ... βραβευομένη καὶ [φυλαττομένη].[3]

† βραβεῖον.

The subst. βραβεῖον, "the prize of conflict," equated by Hesych. (s.v.) with ἐπινίκιον, ἔπαθλον, νικητήριον, ἀμοιβή,[4] is rare in secular Gk.[5] It is used already by Menander in a figur. sense: βραβεῖον ἀρετῆς ἐστιν εὐπαιδευσία (Menand. Mon., 653 [IV, p. 359, Meineke]). Later there came to be linked with the word the thought of the warring confusion of life: ὀψὲ βροτοῖσιν ἔδωκε βραβήϊα πάντα μόθοιο,[6] and of the completion and crown of life's work: τὸ βραβεῖον τοῦ ἀποτελέσματος.[7] In a similar sense the LXX uses the image of the ἆθλον (→ ἀθλεῖν), but never βραβεῖον. On the other hand, Gr. Bar. 12 speaks of the βραβεῖα which the righteous gain by fighting. As an alternative to ἆθλον, βραβεῖον appears in Philo's work περὶ ἄθλων καὶ ἐπιτιμίων, which carries through most consistently the image of the ἀγών of life from which the righteous emerges victorious: οἱ ... ἀθληταὶ ... ἀρετῆς ... βραβείων καὶ κηρυγμάτων καὶ τῶν ἄλλων ὅσα νικῶσι δίδοται μετελάμβανον (Praem. et Poen., 5 f.).

In the NT Paul is again the only one to use βραβεῖον in two closely related passages: 1 C. 9:24 ff.: Οὐκ οἴδατε ὅτι οἱ ἐν σταδίῳ τρέχοντες πάντες μὲν τρέχουσιν, εἰς δὲ λαμβάνει τὸ βραβεῖον (στέφανον ἄφθαρτον); οὕτως τρέχετε ἵνα καταλάβητε ... ἐγὼ τοίνυν οὕτως τρέχω ὡς οὐκ ἀδήλως ("aimless"), and Phil. 3:13 f.: τὰ μὲν ὀπίσω ἐπιλανθανόμενος τοῖς δὲ ἔμπροσθεν ἐπεκτεινόμενος κατὰ σκόπον διώκω εἰς τὸ βραβεῖον τῆς ἄνω κλήσεως. Βραβεῖον is here the prize of conflict which a man can win only if he throws in his whole self and all his resources, namely, the resurrection to eternal life (Phil. 3:11). This certainly does not mean that man decides his own destiny by his own willing and running (R. 9:16). The prior decision is made by God alone, who issues the call: διώκω

---

[2] Paul once uses καταβραβεύειν "to decide against someone" in a very striking manner at Col. 2:18: μηδεὶς ὑμᾶς καταβραβευέτω (cf. 2:16: κρινέτω).

[3] P. Masp., II, No. 67151, 221 ff.

[4] As βραβεύω can take on the sense of "to rule" (βραβεύς, "prince"), so βραβεῖον can denote a "sceptre," v. Mithr. Liturg., 12, 19: οὐρανοῦ Τύχαι κρατοῦσαι χρύσεα βραβία.

[5] Insc. Priene, 118, 3; cf. further Moult.-Mill., s.v.; Nägeli, 37; Reisch in Pauly-W., V, 801; equivalent in meaning to βράβευμα, v. Wieneke, op. cit.

[6] Ps.-Oppian Cyn., 4, 197.

[7] Vett. Val., VII, 5 (p. 288, 8), cf. IV, 9 (p. 174, 21, Kroll): τὸ βραβεῖον ἀπονέμειν.

δὲ εἰ καὶ καταλάβω, ἐφ' ᾧ καὶ κατελήμφθην (Phil. 3:12; cf. 1 C. 8:3; Gl. 4:9; 1 C. 13:12). The final decision is also made by God (1 C. 3:15). God is He who in vocation sets for man the goal which at once gives meaning to his work and direction to his life. By this divine act, however, man is summoned to supreme activity. He must break with all the things which are behind (Phil. 3:7 ff., 13) and bend all his thoughts and actions to the divinely appointed goal (1 C. 9:16 ff. — note the sevenfold "that," and cf. 1 C. 9:27 and Gl. 2:2 : μή πως). He must keep in step with the march of the divine revelation (Phil. 3:15; Gl. 5:7 f.). He must resolutely integrate his own will into the divine will : εἰ γὰρ ἑκὼν τοῦτο πράσσω, μισθὸν ἔχω (1 C. 9:17). The will of man is thus made free and strong, and God reaches His goal as man does (Phil. 2:12 f.). The βραβεῖον is the point in eternity in which the two parallel lines meet. It is the goal beyond this age and its possibilities. It is the meeting-place of divine and human action.

1 Clement perspicaciously sums up the life and death of Paul in terms of this guiding concept : Παῦλος ὑπομονῆς βραβεῖον ἔδειξεν ... τὸ γενναῖον τῆς πίστεως αὐτοῦ κλέος ἔλαβεν ... ἀπηλλάγη τοῦ κόσμου καὶ εἰς τὸν ἅγιον τόπον ἐπορεύθη (5, 5 ff.). And in the Mart. Pol., 17, 1 βραβεῖον has become an alternative expression for the martyr's crown : ἐστεφανωμένον ... τὸν τῆς ἀφθαρσίας στέφανον καὶ βραβεῖον ἀναντίρρητον ἀπενηνεγμένον. In the same sense βραβεῖον is adopted by Tertullian with all the terminology of the arena : *Bonum agonem subituri estis, in quo agonothetes deus vivus est, xystarches spiritus sanctus, corona aeternitatis, brabium angelicae substantiae, politia in coelis, gloria in saecula saeculorum* ... (Ad Mart., 3). [8] But the weaker use of βραβεῖον as an expression for the profit and reward of our action in the sense of popular Hellenistic philosophy is still found, e.g., in Tatian's Or. Graec., 33, 4 : μοιχείας καὶ ἀκρασίας βραβεῖον ἀπηνέγκατο.

Stauffer

---

† βραχίων   (→ χείρ).

This word appears in the NT only in the expression the "arm of God" and only in quotations from the LXX or similar modes of speech (Lk. 1:51; Jn. 12:38; Ac. 13:17).

In the OT or LXX זְרוֹעַ = βραχίων is in this connection an expression for the mighty works of God. The anthropomorphic figure is plainest in Is. 30:30: וְנַחַת זְרוֹעוֹ יַרְאֶה, which the LXX renders : καὶ τὸν θυμὸν τοῦ βραχίονος αὐτοῦ δεῖξαι (cf. also the Tg. Is. 30:30). Cf. Is. 51:9 Mas. and LXX. Mostly the image is softened and ὁ βραχίων τοῦ θεοῦ simply means the "power of God." Thus plainly in Is. 62:8; Jer. 28:14 : Yahweh swears by His arm, or Is. 59:16; 63:5, Yahweh's arm comes to help. In Ez. 30:21 ff.; Da. 11:22, it means concretely the "host of the Lord." The different terms associated with βραχίων [1] show what is meant by the arm of the Lord. [2] Thus there is reference to μέγεθος (Ex. 15:16), ἰσχύς (Dt. 9:26, 29; 33:27; 2 Macc. 15:24 etc.), κράτος (Wis. 11:22; 16:16), μεγαλωσύνη (ψ 78:10), δύναμις (ψ 88:10 etc.). Or

---

[8] The Test. of the 40 Mart. begins with quotations from Hb. 12:1 and Phil. 3:14 : ἐπειδὰν ... τὸν προκείμενον [ἡμῖν] ἀγῶνα τελέσωμεν καὶ ἐπὶ τὰ βραβεῖα τῆς ἄνω κλήσεως φθάσωμεν. 2, 1 moves in the same complex of images : πλοῦτον ... ἀνελλιπῆ παρέχει [ὁ θεὸς] τοῖς εἰς αὐτὸν προστρέχουσι, ζωὴν δὲ αἰώνιον βραβεύει τοῖς εἰς αὐτὸν πιστεύουσι. Cf. also βραβεῖον (and ἄθλησις) in Euseb. Hist. Eccl. (Schwartz), Index, *s.v.*

βραχίων is used along with σημεῖα, τέρατα, πόλεμος, ὁράματα (Dt. 4:34; 7:19; 26:8; 'Ιερ. 39:21; Bar. 2:11). The arm of God describes in a concrete image the miraculous demonstration of the power of God. Apart from a few passages where God's arm acts on behalf of the individual righteous (2 Ch. 6:32; Wis. 5:17; Ps. Sol. 13:2), it is used only in relation to the world and with reference to the people of God. Thus it relates a. to creation, which is understood as a conflict with Rahab and her company at ψ 88:10; Is. 51:9 f.; [3] 'Ιερ. 39:17. What is active in creation is not the arm of a τεχνίτης but of the warring God Himself. Especially, however, it relates b. to the election and redemption of the people by the wonderful exodus from Egypt (Dt. 4:34); Ex. 6:1, 6; 15:16; Dt. 3:24; 7:19 etc.; 4 Βασ. 17:36; Is. 65:12; 'Ιερ. 39:21 etc. It relates c. to the direction and preservation of the people : Dt. 33:27; ψ 78:10; Is. 26:11 etc. It relates finally d. to the bringing of eschatological salvation at ψ 97:1; Is. 40:10; 51:9 ff.; 52:10; 53:1; 63:5; Ez. 20:33 f.

This arm of God, miraculously put forth for the salvation of His people, has shown its power and fulfilled the ancient promise in the birth of the Messiah (Lk. 1:51). The words which previously referred to the praise of creation, and which in the LXX are already related to the redemption out of Egypt, are now used to magnify the fulfilment in the birth of the Messiah. In Jn. 12:37 f. the arm of God is the experienced demonstration of the power of God, the σημεῖα 'Ιησοῦ.

Cf. Just. Apol., I, 32, 12, where Nu. 24:17 and Is. 11:1, 10 are combined and the βραχίων τοῦ θεοῦ is implicitly (with ἄστρον and ἄνθος explicitly) referred to Χριστός.

Schlier

---

† βροντή

"Thunder." At Jn. 12:29 and Rev. 6:1; 14:2; 19:6, this word is used to denote overwhelming power of voice, as also at Rev. 10:3 f., where there can hardly be reference to the thunderous course of the planets. [1] It occurs with other natural phenomena in Rev. 4:5; 8:5; 11:19; 16:18 (→ ἀστραπή).

In the LXX it is often used of the terrifying revelation of God ; except in Job 40:4 (9) the verb βροντᾶν is always used in this way. Cf. also the magic texts, e.g., Preis. Zaub., V (London, 4th cent. A.D.), 151: ἐγώ εἰμι ὁ ἀστράπτων καὶ βροντῶν. [2] On Phrygian inscriptions βροντῶν is a common name for the deity of heaven. [3]

The only other instance is in Mk. 3:17: ἐπέθηκεν αὐτοῖς (the sons of Zebedee) ὀνόματα Βοανηργές, ὅ ἐστιν υἱοὶ βροντῆς. Both the orthography of the Aram.

β ρ α χ ί ω ν. [1] βραχίων is often an altern. for χείρ (Ex. 6:1; Dt. 4:34; 7:19 etc.). In the LXX βραχίων is used for יָד in Ex. 6:1, where זְרוֹעַ is to be presupposed as original in the Heb.; 32:11; Is. 26:11; Da. 9:15. It is also used in a secular sense for יָד at Gn. 24:18; 27:16; Ju. 15:14.

[2] Common attributes are ὑψηλός and ἅγιος (ψ 97:1; Is. 52:10).

[3] Here creation is seen together with the redemption out of Egypt and both are related to eschatological salvation.

β ρ ο ν τ ή. [1] F. Boll, Aus d. Offb. Joh. (1914), 22; H. E. Weber in Aus Schrift u. Geschichte, Festschr. f. A. Schlatter (1922), 47 ff.

[2] Deissmann LO, 113.

[3] Moult.-Mill., s.v.

name and its meaning, together with that of the Gk. translation, are contested. [4] The passage acquired particular importance when in some MSS [5] the name was applied to all the apostles, as though to describe them as revolutionaries. But this weakly attested reading is more of an attempt to smooth the awkward Marcan text than *vice versa*, and there is no reason why the name should have been later restricted to the sons of Zebedee.

Foerster

βρύχω, βρυγμός

† βρύχω.

The co-existence of several roots βρυχ- [1] makes it extraordinarily difficult to review the development of the term. To be sure, we already find a perf. βέβρυχα used by Hom. (Il., 13, 393; 16, 486; cf. Od., 12, 242 etc.) to describe the breaking out of sufferers into open lamentation ; cf. also Soph. Trach., 1072 (ὥστε παρθένος βέβρυχα κλαίων) etc., and again Ps.-Oppian Cyn., 2, 273 of the cry of pain of a stag mortally wounded by snake-bite. Here, however, we must insert the βρύχειν from which there developed the common post-Homeric βρυχάομαι for loud outcry. As "to gnash" it first occurs in the expression βρύχειν (τοὺς ὀδόντας) with which Hippocrates (Mul., 1, 2, 120 [VIII, 16, 262]; Epid., 5, 86 [V, 252, Littré]) characterises especially the ague. [2] In the LXX there are 5 instances of βρύχειν (τοὺς) ὀδόντας (ἐπί) [3] ('Ιωβ 16:10; ψ 34:16; 36:12; 111:10; Lam. 2:16) in the sense of "to gnash with the teeth," always as an expression of hate (usually that of the → ἁμαρτωλός for the → δίκαιος) and as a translation of חָרַק שִׁנַּיִם עַל or חָרַק בְּשִׁנָּיִם (Job 16:9), in which it is linked with a desire to destroy the opponent ; cf. also the Rabb. liter. (Tanch. [Buber] בלק 15, 140; jKil., 32c, 37 f. etc.). [4]

The only NT passage (Ac. 7:54) may be classified with the OT and Rabbinic examples both formally and materially. When the opponents of Stephen heard his speech before the Sanhedrin, it is said of them : ἔβρυχον τοὺς ὀδόντας ἐπ' αὐτόν. This attests their hatred and desire to destroy him. It does so in such a way that, according to OT usage, they are at once set in the camp of sinners who are opposed to the righteous, even though they think they are doing God service in removing him. It is possible that there is a direct allusion to Ps. 35:11 ff.

† βρυγμός.

From the time of Eupolis (CAF, I, 349) in the general sense : ἡ σύντομος ἐδωδή (Etym. Gud., 290, 18, Steph.) etc., esp. of the chattering of the teeth in the ague, sometimes without τῶν ὀδόντων (Hippocr. Vict., 3, 84 [VI, 634]; Mul., 3, 214 [VIII, 416,

---

[4] Apart from the Comm. and the bibl. in Pr.-Bauer, *s.v.* Βοανηργές, *v.* Had. Apk., 224; Joach. Jeremias, *Jesus als Weltvollender* (1930), 71, n. 4; W. Erbt, *Der Anfänger unseres Glaubens* (1930), 5 f.

[5] The Cod. W and some Ital. MSS (bceq).

β ρ ύ χ ω. Thes. Steph., *s.v.*; Liddell-Scott, 331 f., *s.v.*; Str.-B., IV, 1040; Schl. Mt., 279 f.; W. K. Hobart, *The Medical Language of St. Luke* (1882), 208.

[1] Cf. L. Meyer, *Handbuch d. griech. Etymologie,* III (1901), 134 ff., but also K. Brugmann (A. Thumb), *Griech. Gramm.*[4] (1913), 133.

[2] Cf. also βρυχή, "gnashing of the teeth," βρυχετός, "cold fever."

[3] ψ 36:12 Σ : καὶ βρύχει κατ' αὐτοῦ τοὺς ὀδόντας αὐτοῦ.

[4] Schl. Mt., 279 f.

β ρ υ γ μ ό ς. Bibl. → under βρύχω; Clemen, 153; Zn. Mt. on 8:12.

Littré]).[1] In the LXX it is used in Prv. 19:9 for נָהַם of the snarling of the lion, in ψ 37:9 'A for נְהָמָה of the groaning of the heart[2] (LXX : ἀπὸ στεναγμοῦ τῆς καρδίας μου), Σιρ. 51:3 of the bloodthirsty gnashing of the enemies of the righteous against them in a favourite OT image (→ βρύχω), though in wide deviation from the Heb. Only this passage is linked linguistically with the non-biblical attestation, while the other two display a usage which seems to be more under the influence of βρυχάομαι (→ 641) than βρύχω ("to gnash").[3] There are no later Jewish parallels.

In the NT the only relevant use is in the saying : ἐκεῖ ἔσται ὁ κλαυθμὸς καὶ ὁ βρυγμὸς τῶν ὀδόντων (Mt. 8:12; 13:42, 50; 22:13; 24:51; 25:30; Lk. 13:28), in which Jesus describes the state of those who are excluded from the → βασιλεία (→ σκότος) even though they were called to it. In spite of the Greek parallels, the formula βρυγμὸς τῶν ὀδόντων does not denote despairing rage,[4] and it is certainly not used to describe the bodily reaction of the excluded to the extreme cold of their place of punishment.[5] It simply denotes the despairing remorse[6] which shakes their whole body and is linked also with → κλαυθμός.[7]

The NT usage is thus independent both of the general Gk. and also of the OT attestation. It cannot be understood directly in the light of the phrase → βρύχω τοὺς ὀδόντας, but takes its meaning from its context. The solid place of the formula in Mt. suggests that it is really peculiar to him,[8] though there can be no certainty on this point. To assume that it has been taken over from religious history[9] obscures rather than elucidates the matter.

Rengstorf

---

† βρῶμα, βρῶσις

1. "Food" in the Strict Sense.

Mt. 14:15 and par.; Lk. 3:11 (Hb. 12:16), with reference to cultic and ascetic prescriptions of Judaism which are declared to be religiously indifferent by Jesus and early Christianity. Mk. 7:19 : καθαρίζων (sc. Jesus) πάντα τὰ βρώματα :[1] the distinction between clean and unclean meats is done away (→ καθαρός, → καθαρίζω, → κοινός, → κοινόω). In his discussion of the eating of idol meats

---

[1] Cf. also Apoll. Rhod., 2, 83 : βρυχὴ ὀδόντων (in boxing).
[2] Unless we adopt another reading (לְבִיא), v. BHK², ad loc.
[3] Cf. ἐβρυχώμην ἀπὸ βρυγμοῦ ... ψ 37:9 'A and Zn. Mt. on 8:12.
[4] So Zn., H. J. Holtzmann, Kl. etc.
[5] So esp. Clemen on the basis of Mazdaist conceptions of the place of punishment ; cf. also O. Holtzmann.
[6] Cf. also En. 108:3, 5, 15.
[7] Schl. Mt., 280.
[8] Bultmann Trad., 352.
[9] Clemen : Mazdaism.
β ρ ῶ μ α, β ρ ῶ σ ι ς. Pr.-Bauer, 232.
[1] There is here no ground for adopting the modern Gk. sense of "filth" (Radermacher, 12, Bl.-Debr. § 126, 3; cf. in opposition Pr.-Bauer, ad loc. and Moult.-Mill., 118), since καθαρίζων ... βρώματα is to be understood as an observation of the Evangelist in the sense of R. 14:14, 20 (cf. Orig. in Mt. tom. XI, 12 [III, p. 97, Lommatzsch]); it succinctly denotes the "new and basic religious conception" of Jesus that "the religious relationship of man to God ... is not decided in the external and bodily sphere of man" (Hck. Mk., 92). Cf. also Kl. Mk., 80.

in 1 C. 8, and in the controversy between the strong and the weak in R. 14, Paul describes βρῶμα as of no significance for the relationship with God : 1 C. 8:8 : βρῶμα ἡμᾶς οὐ → παραστήσει τῷ θεῷ (cf. 6:13; R. 14:15), cf. R. 14:17: οὐ γάρ ἐστιν ἡ → βασιλεία τοῦ θεοῦ βρῶσις καὶ πόσις. [2] Only regard for the weaker brother can require voluntary renunciation of offending meats, 1 C. 8:13; R. 14:15, 20 f. [3] According to Hb. 9:10 βρώματα and → πόματα belong to the → δικαιώματα → σαρκός which were given for the time of the incomplete older covenant but which have lost their validity in the perfect new order of things brought in by Christ. Hb. 13:9 relegates βρώματα to the sphere of things which cannot confirm the → καρδία, so that even those concerned about them can derive no profit therefrom. The ordinances referred to here, being reckoned with the διδαχαὶ ποικίλαι καὶ ξέναι, need not be restricted to the ancient Jewish statutes, e.g., the forbidding of unclean foods or the rules for what is to be eaten on the occasion of sacrifices, but include the syncretistic customs of the surrounding world. [4] There is no point in laying special emphasis on βρώματα. At 1 Tm. 4:3 it is insisted, in opposition to heretics who, along the lines of Gnostic asceticism (cf. Col. 2:16, 21 ff.), advance the demand → ἀπέχεσθαι βρωμάτων, [5] that meats are gifts of the Creator to be enjoyed by Christians with thanksgiving. [6]

2. "Food" in the Figurative Sense.

a. The word is used of the miraculous food which is not of this world but which comes down from heaven, 1 C. 10:3 : → πνευματικὸν βρῶμα, i.e., the manna of Ex. 16 (ψ 77:24; 104:40 : ἄρτον οὐρανοῦ; 77:25 : ἄρτον ἀγγέλων; Wis. 16:20 : ἀγγέλων τροφήν ... ἄρτον ἀπ᾽ οὐρανοῦ : → ἄρτος) as a type of the eucharistic bread.

b. It is also used of spiritual food, 1 C. 3:2 : → γάλα ὑμᾶς ἐπότισα, οὐ βρῶμα. Milk (γάλα → 645) was the first missionary instruction which declared the facts of the revelation of salvation ; solid food (cf. Hb. 5:12 ff.: → στερεός) was the word of wisdom which disclosed its meaning and was addressed to the πνευματικοί (3:1), though Paul did not think the Corinthians were as yet mature enough to understand it. [7]

---

[2] To assess βρῶσις καὶ πόσις (a formula from the time of Hom.) both here and in Col. 2:16, cf. bBer., 17a : "In the future world there is neither eating nor drinking" ; Philo Vit. Mos., I, 184 : ἐπιστάμενον ... τὰς τοῦ σώματος ἀνάγκας ἐκ τροφῆς, ἠρτημένου καὶ δεσποίναις χαλεπαῖς συνεζευγμένου, βρώσει καὶ πόσει; Ign. Tr., 2, 3 (the deacons) οὐ ... βρωμάτων καὶ ποτῶν διάκονοι, ἀλλ᾽ ἐκκλησίας θεοῦ ὑπηρέται. Qoh. r., 2, 24 (15b), Str.-B., II, 485, allegorises : Eating and drinking denote the study of the Torah and good works.

[3] Cf. Did., 6, 3 : περὶ δὲ τῆς βρώσεως, ὃ δύνασαι βάστασον, where there is no compulsion to refrain from certain meats.

[4] For an understanding of the passage, cf. Wnd. Hb.², 117 f.; Rgg. Hb.², ³, 436 ff.; A. Seeberg, Hb. (1912), 142 f.

[5] Dib. Past.³, 40 ff.; R. Bultmann, RGG², IV, 995; E. Hennecke, RGG², II, 1569 f.

[6] On the question of asceticism in the NT and the surrounding world of religion, cf. in general E. v. Dobschütz, Die urchristl. Gemeinden (1902), 93 ff., 274 ff.; H. Strathmann, RGG², I, 575 ff.; Ltzm. R.³, 114 f.; Loh. Kol., 121 f.; Str.-B., II, 523; III, 307 f.; Reitzenstein Hell. Myst., 329 f.; P. R. Arbesmann, "Das Fasten bei den Griechen und Römern," RVV, 21, 1 (1929).

[7] These metaphors are common in Philo, e.g., Congr., 19 : οὐχ ὁρᾷς, ὅτι καὶ τὸ σῶμα ἡμῶν οὐ πρότερον πεπηγυίαις καὶ πολυτελέσι χρῆται τροφαῖς, πρὶν ἢ τοῖς ἀποικίλοις καὶ γαλακτώδεσιν ἐν ἡλικίᾳ τῇ βρεφώδει; Omn. Prob. Lib., 160 : τὸ μὲν πρῶτον ἀντὶ γάλακτος ἀπαλὰς τροφάς ... εἶτ᾽ αὖθις κραταιοτέρας ... ἐξ ὧν ἀνδρωθεῖσαι καὶ εὐεκτήσασαι πρὸς τέλος αἴσιον ... ἀφίξονται. On their derivation from the diatribe,

Jn. 4:34 : ἐμὸν βρῶμά ἐστιν ἵνα ποιῶ τὸ θέλημα τοῦ πέμψαντός με καὶ τελειώσω αὐτοῦ τὸ ἔργον, is the answer of the Johannine Jesus to the question of the disciples whether anyone has given Him to eat (v. 33). What nourishes and satisfies Him belongs to another sphere than that of physical life, namely, the sphere of His divinely given calling (cf. Mt. 4:4). [8] Obediently to do the will of God and to finish His work is for Him "as necessary and indispensable as daily bread." [9] It is His spiritual food (βρῶσις) of which the disciples are ignorant (4:32). There is, of course, no question of a Gnostic devaluation of the earthly and material in Jn. 4:34. It does not say that Jesus either will or can dispense with earthly nourishment. [10] It is voluntaristic and active, and as such is characteristic of the biblical history of salvation.

We read of spiritual food as the gift of the Son of Man to men in Jn. 6:27: μὴ τὴν βρῶσιν τὴν → ἀπολλυμένην, ἀλλὰ τὴν βρῶσιν τὴν → μένουσαν εἰς → ζωὴν → αἰώνιον, v. 55 ἡ → σάρξ μου → ἀληθῶς (ℵ: ἀληθής) ἐστιν βρῶσις. The link with the miracle of feeding (cf. v. 26) and the goal of the address (v. 32 ff.) in v. 51 make it plain that for Jesus the food which nourishes to incorruptible and eternal life is Himself, His presence in the Lord's Supper. Man is fed in faith in Him (v. 29, 35). He is nourished in the Lord's Supper, the concrete representation of the spiritual fellowship of faith with Him (v. 51, 53 ff., 63).

βρῶμα is rare in the figur. sense, e.g., Aristoph. Fr., 333 (CAF, I, 480): ἦν μέγα τι βρῶμ' ἔτι τρυγῳδοποιομουσική (the art of sound which underlies comedies). It does not occur at all in the LXX and is alien to the koine. But the thought of heavenly or spiritual food (Gr. τροφή etc. → ἄρτος, → γάλα) is common in Gk. and oriental religion. [11] Nectar and ambrosia (= ἀθανασία) are the food of the Homeric gods, and when they are given as a gift of divine grace to man they invest him with immortality and eternal youth (Hom. Il., 5, 342; Od., 5, 135). [12] We may also think of the OT manna (→ ἄρτος), not merely in Ex. 16 but also in Dt. 8:3 (the words of God are food necessary to life, cf. Am. 8:11 f.). According to Rabb. deliberations manna is the food of the heavenly world. [13] Along the lines of Ps. 63:5 (the satisfying of the soul) and Prv. 9:5: φάγετε τῶν ἐμῶν (sc. of wisdom) ἄρτων καὶ πίετε οἶνον ὃν ἐκέρασα ὑμῖν, Philo goes further when he explain that manna, as τροφή ἀπ' οὐρανοῦ, τροφὴ θεία etc., is wisdom: Mut. Nom., 259: τὸν οὐράνιον ἀρετῆς λόγον; cf. Rer. Div. Her., 79: τὸ μάννα ... τὸν θεῖον λόγον, τὴν οὐράνιον ψυχῆς ... ἄφθαρτον τρο-φήν; Fug., 137; Sacr. AC, 86 etc. In Eth. En. 69:24 it is said of angels that "their food consists of pure thoughts." As in early Christian texts the Lord's Supper is described as πνευματικὴ τροφή (Did., 10, 3), ἄρτος θεοῦ (Ign. R., 7, 3; opp. τροφὴ φθορᾶς) or εὐχαριστηθεῖσα τροφή, ἐξ ἧς αἷμα καὶ σάρκες κατὰ μεταβολὴν τρέφονται

---

cf. the material in Ltzm. K., ad loc.; Wnd. Hb., ad loc.; cf. more generally R. Bultmann, Der Stil der paul. Predigt u. die kynisch-stoische Diatribe (1910), 35 ff., 88. On the differences, cf. Joh. W. 1 K., 72; A. Bonhöffer, Epiktet u. d. NT (1911), 61 f. On the whole question, → γάλα. V. also Cl. Al. on 1 C. 3:2 (Strom., V, 66, 2): γάλα μὲν ἡ κατήχησις οἱονεὶ πρώτη ψυχῆς τροφὴ νοηθήσεται, βρῶμα δὲ ἡ ἐποπτικὴ θεωρία· σάρκες αὗται καὶ αἷμα τοῦ λόγου, τουτέστι κατάληψις τῆς θείας δυνάμεως καὶ οὐσίας.

[8] There is an echo of this thought in Herm. s., 9, 11, 8 : ἐδείπνησα ... ῥήματα κυρίου ὅλην τὴν νύκτα.

[9] W. Heitmüller, ad loc. (Schriften d. NT³, IV [1918], 79).

[10] On the other hand, cf. Act. Thom., 5 : διὰ μεῖζόν τι τῆς βρώσεως καὶ τοῦ πότου ἦλθον ἐνθάδε, καὶ ἵνα τὸ θέλημα τοῦ βασιλέως τελέσω.

[11] Cf. Bau. J.³, 100 f. For further religious material, cf. N. Söderblom, La Vie future (1901), 330 ff.

[12] Cf. Roscher, I, 280 ff.; K. Wernicke, in Pauly-W., I (1894), 1809 ff.

[13] Str.-B., IV, 1246, s.v.; H. Odeberg, The Fourth Gospel (1929), 239 ff.

ἡμῶν (Just. Apol., I, 66, 2), and as in the legend of Joseph and Asenath [14] both enjoy heavenly food which makes them immortal : ἄρτον εὐλογημένον ζωῆς καὶ ... ποτήριον εὐλογημένον ἀθανασίας (p. 49, cf. 61, 64), [15] so texts from the world of later syncretism speak of foods which impart divine qualities and incorruptible life etc., or of foods for the regenerate. Cf. the rich though partly disputed material in the Mithr. Liturg., 100 ff.; 241 f., [16] e.g., Sallust. De Deis, 4 (p. 8, 19 ff., Nock): (of Phrygian initiates) πρῶτον μὲν ... σίτου τε καὶ τῆς ἄλλης παχείας καὶ ῥυπαρᾶς τροφῆς ἀπεχόμεθα· ἑκατέρα γὰρ ἐναντία ψυχῇ ... ἐπὶ τούτοις γάλακτος τροφή, ὥσπερ ἀναγεννωμένων. [17] Lidz. Ginza, 357, 6 : "I impart strength to thee in virtue of the Pihta" (the sacramental food of the Mandaeans), cf. 239, 27 ff.; Lidz. Lit., 70 f. According to Act. Thom., 36 there also belongs to the "greater than these earthly things," which includes the Gospel, περὶ τῆς ἀμβροσιώδους τροφῆς καὶ τοῦ ποτοῦ τῆς ἀμπέλου τῆς ἀληθινῆς, 61: κορεσθῶμεν τῆς αὐτοῦ τροφῆς τῆς θεϊκῆς, 120 : γενοῦ μοι κοινωνὸς τῆς αἰωνίου ζωῆς, ἵνα δέξωμαι παρὰ σοῦ τροφὴν τελείαν. In the song of the daughter of light (ibid., 6), the divine king is enthroned τρέφων τῇ ἑαυτοῦ ἀμβροσίᾳ τοὺς ἐπ᾽ αὐτὸν ἱδρυμένους. Ibid. 7 the eternal ones at the feast linger in the presence of their Lord, οὗ τὴν ἀμβροσίαν βρῶσιν ἐδέξαντο μηδὲν ὅλως ἀπουσίαν ἔχουσαν. In Mandaism, as distinct from the "food of the children of Tibil" (Lidz. Ginza, 306, 35, cf. 320, 15), the "food of the 12 gates" (298, 19) "wherein the planets concealed themselves" (320, 15), and the "pilgrim nourishment of the children of men" (246, 28), a great part is played by the "nourishment" for the ascent of the soul which "the father of the Uthras imparts to his friends" (96, 13 f.); they are "victorious in virtue of their nourishment for the way" (247, 2 f., cf. 246, 29 f.). In 252, 9 ff. the "once begotten" receives from the father the command : "Up, provide thy Uthras ... with the nourishment which I have given thee"; cf. 273, 13 : "My nourishment for the journey comes from the strange man." If the nourishment of the wicked is their works (540, 11 f.), the summons goes out to the elect : "Do good works, and lay up nourishment for your way" (23, 1 f., cf. 141, 20 f.); to good works belongs perseverance in faith (377, 20; 392, 32; 584, 21). Kuštā, true faith, is the provision for the soul : "The Uthras of light ... provided themselves with the nourishment of Kuštā and armed themselves with all its wisdom" (509, 28 ff. = Lidz. Lit., 161, 5 f.); "When he wished to eat, he prepared himself a table with Kuštā" (Lidz. Joh., 106). There is a similar reference in Manichean literature (from the Gospel of Mani): "And the food of wisdom was proffered." [18]

Behm

---

† γάλα

1. 1 C. 3:1 f. ... οὐκ ἠδυνήθην λαλῆσαι ὑμῖν ὡς πνευματικοῖς ἀλλ᾽ ὡς σαρκίνοις, ὡς νηπίοις ἐν Χριστῷ. γάλα ὑμᾶς ἐπότισα, οὐ βρῶμα· οὔπω γὰρ ἐδύνασθε. Γάλα is here a figure for the *kerygma* brought to Corinth by Paul. Its opposite is → βρῶμα, which is the σοφία (the γνῶσις) which he cannot yet give to them as νήπιοι ἐν Χριστῷ.

---

[14] P. Battifol, *Studia patristica,* 1 (1889).
[15] Cf. on this point Schürer, III, 400 f.
[16] Cf. further Bau. J.³, 100 f.
[17] Cf. apart from Reitzenstein Hell. Myst., 329 f., H. Schlier, *Religionsgeschichtl. Untersuchungen zu den Ignatiusbriefen* (1929), 150 f.
[18] F. W. K. Müller, *Handschriften-Reste ... aus Turfan,* II (AAB, 1904), M, 17 (p. 26) and M, 172 (p. 101).
γ ά λ α. H. Usener, *Rhein. Mus.,* 57 (1902), 177 ff.; R. Perdelwitz, "Die Mysterienreligion u. das Problem des 1 Pt.," RVV, 11, 3 (1911), 56 ff.; K. Wyss, "Die Milch im Kultus der Griechen u. Römer," RVV, 15, 2 (1914); Mithr. Liturg., 171 ff.

Similarly, yet more rhetorically, Hb. 5:12 ff. says : ... πάλιν χρείαν ἔχετε τοῦ διδάσκειν ὑμᾶς τινα τὰ στοιχεῖα τῆς ἀρχῆς τῶν λογίων τοῦ θεοῦ, καὶ γεγό- νατε χρείαν ἔχοντες γάλακτος, οὐ στερεᾶς τροφῆς. πᾶς γὰρ ὁ μετέχων γά- λακτος ἄπειρος λόγου δικαιοσύνης, νήπιος γάρ ἐστιν· τελείων δὲ ἐστιν ἡ στερεὰ τροφή ... In this passage γάλα is a figure for the basic elements of divine teaching, for the elementary Christian instruction described in 6:1 f. It is for νήπιοι. The στερεὰ τροφή is the λόγος δικαιοσύνης, a kind of gnosis presented by the author in 6:13 ff. This is for τέλειοι.

For both figures, i.e., the comparison of milk with initial instruction suitable for children, and of solid food with profounder teaching more serviceable to the mature, there is a similar usage in both Epictet. and Philo. [1] E.g., Epict. Diss., III, 24, 9 : οὐκ ἀπογαλακτίσομεν ἤδη ποθ᾽ ἑαυτοὺς καὶ μεμνησόμεθα ὧν ἠκούσαμεν παρὰ τῶν φιλοσόφων. In Epict., however, there must be weaning from the milk. Philo gives a clearer parallel, e.g., in Congr., 19 : οὐχ ὁρᾷς, ὅτι καὶ τὸ σῶμα ἡμῶν οὐ πρότερον πεπηγυίαις καὶ πολυτελέσι χρῆται τροφαῖς, πρὶν ἢ ταῖς ἀποικίλοις καὶ γα- λακτώδεσιν ἐν ἡλικίᾳ τῇ βρεφώδει; τὸν αὐτὸν δὴ τρόπον καὶ τῇ ψυχῇ παιδικὰς μὲν νόμισον εὐτρεπίσθαι τροφὰς τὰ ἐγκύκλια καὶ τὰ καθ᾽ ἕκαστον αὐτῶν θεωρήματα, τελειοτέρας δὲ καὶ πρεπούσας ἀνδράσιν ὡς ἀληθῶς τὰς ἀρετάς. Cf. Ign. Tr., 5, 1; Act. Joh., 45. The image is the same, though different objects of teaching are denoted by milk or solid food.

That the terminology of the Mysteries occurs in 1 C. 3:1 is no reason why we should link this image with the ideas of the Mystery religions. These are present only in the third [2] and very different passage.

2. 1 Pt. 2:2 : ἀποθέμενοι οὖν πᾶσαν κακίαν ... ὡς ἀρτιγέννητα βρέφη τὸ λογικὸν ἄδολον γάλα ἐπιποθήσατε, ἵνα ἐν αὐτῷ αὐξηθῆτε εἰς σωτηρίαν, εἰ ἐγεύσασθε ὅτι χρηστὸς ὁ κύριος. Again in the environment of the terminology of the Mysteries, τὸ ῥῆμα τὸ εὐαγγελισθὲν εἰς ὑμᾶς (1:25b) denotes here the pure, pneumatic (divine) milk by which the new born are nourished and may grow to σωτηρία. Hence τὸ γάλα is not set in opposition to τὸ βρῶμα, but is itself the *gnosis* provided for Christians in the Gospel.

This comparison derives from a pneumatic mode of speech which has its ultimate basis in a mystery rite. We need not discuss in this context the disputed question whether τὸ γάλα (often in connection with μέλι and less frequently with οἶνος) owes its sacramental significance to a mythological conception (the food of the gods), an eschatological (the food of Paradise), or a magical (the mediatrix of life). All three elements probably played some part in making milk a sacramental food and causing a particular sacramental power to be ascribed to it. Many examples show us that it is in fact a sacramental element.

The LXX, of course, does not attest this. In it milk is a characteristic of the holy land (Ex. 3:8, 17 etc.) and stands for blessing in general (Job 29:6). Similarly, it will mark the eschatological marriage (Jl. 3:18; Is. 60:16). On the other hand, the Egyptian king enjoys the milk of Isis and becomes immortal. As μελαίνης βοὸς γάλα, when enjoyed, it is the beginning of immortality, as wine is the end. [3] In the Berlin magic

---

[1] Joh. W., 1 K., 72; Ltzm. K., *ad loc.*; Wnd. Hb. on 5:13; Rgg. Hb. on 5:12, n. 76.
[2] Elsewhere in the NT it occurs only at 1 C. 9:7 in the literal sense.
[3] A. Dieterich, *Abraxas* (1891), 172, 12; 181, 2.

pap., 5025, we read: [4] καὶ λαβὼν τὸ γάλα σὺν τῷ μέλιτι ἀπόπιε πρὶν ἀνατολῆς ἡλίου καὶ ἔσται τι ἔνθεον ἐν τῇ σῇ καρδίᾳ. In the Dionysus cult of Southern Italy it seems likely that the ἔριφοι (the highest class of initiates) underwent a baptism in milk: ἔριφος ἐς γάλ' ἔπετον. [5] As the sacramental drink of the ἀναγεννωμένων, γάλακτος τροφή is distinguished from all other food (σίτου τε καὶ τῆς ἄλλης παχείας καὶ ῥυπαρᾶς τροφῆς ἀπεχόμεθα: ἑκάτερα γὰρ ἐναντία ψυχῇ), Sallust. De Deis, 4. Porphyr. Antr. Nymph., 28, Macrob. in Cic. Som. Scip., I, 12 report a γαλακτηφόρος priestess who dispenses milk in the cult. In the Coptic and Ethiopian churches the custom still persists of handing mingled milk and honey to the newly baptised. Already in the Canon Hipp., 144 [6] we read: *et presbyteri portant alios calices* (after bread and wine) *lactis et mellis, ut doceant eos qui communicant, iterum se natos esse ut parvuli, quia parvuli communicant lac et mel ... 148, postea autem sumant lac et mel in memoriam saeculi futuri* (cf. for the latter explanation, 4 Esdr. 2:19; Apc. Pl. 23 ff.; Barn., 6, 17).

This conception of milk as the sacramental element, the drinking of which procures ἀθανασία, passed over to the word of *gnosis* as the mysterious sacramental means of salvation in circles where the sacrament was dissolved by *gnosis* and the sacramental element was replaced by the λόγος of *gnosis*. Cf. Hipp. Ref., V, 8, 30: τοῦτο (τὰ μυστήρια) ... ἐστὶ τὸ μέλι καὶ τὸ γάλα, οὗ γευσαμένους τοὺς τελείους ἀβασιλεύτους γενέσθαι καὶ μετασχεῖν τοῦ πληρώματος. In the Od. Sol. this usage becomes very common. Cf. 8:16: "I have formed them limbs (i.e., the Gnostics) and prepared them breasts to drink my holy milk (γάλα λογικόν) and to live thereby." Like a child of the Lord Himself the Gnostic is nourished with His milk, i.e., *gnosis*. Cf. also 19:1-5: The Gnostic, like the aeons, as one who in the pleroma is already on the right hand, drinks milk, i.e., the Son (cf. 1 Pt. 2:3: εἰ ἐγεύσασθε ὅτι χρηστὸς ὁ κύριος), who is milked by the Holy Spirit from the breasts of the Father. "A cup of milk was handed to me, and I drank it with the soft sweetness of the Lord ..." Cf. 4:10; 35:5. The *gnosis* of the Gnostic is itself milk, e.g., 40:1: "As honey drips from the honeycomb, and milk from the woman giving suck to her children, so does my praise to Thee, my God. As the fountain gushes forth its water ..."

This terminology is also found in 1 Pt. 2:2 f. The difference between this passage and Gnosticism lies in the matter related to such pneumatic language, namely, the Gospel on the one side and the revelation of the Mysteries on the other. Naturally, the choice of this terminology is not accidental. It reveals certain tendencies in the concept of the Gospel, a. its character as → μυστήριον, and b. its sacramental character.

That the pneumatic mode of speaking of the Christian ῥῆμα as milk persisted on the basis of 1 C. 3 and 1 Pt. 2, and even underwent a certain semi-speculative expansion, may be seen from Iren., IV, 38, 1 f. (MPG, 7, 1105 ff.) and Cl. Al. Paed., I, 6, 25 ff.

Schlier

---

[4] Preis. Zaub., I, 20.
[5] Kern Orph., 32c, 11.
[6] TU, 6, 4 (1891), 100 f.

| γαμέω, γάμος | → (νυμφίος).

γαμεῖν "to marry" and γάμος "marriage," "wedding," from the time of Homer. Common in the plur. for "wedding festivities" (Ditt. Syll.³, 1106, 100). γαμίζειν acc. to the grammarian Apollonius [1] means "to give a maiden or woman in marriage," though this is the only instance in secular Gk. More common is γαμίσκω, "to give in marriage," mid. "to get married." [2] In the LXX the word group is rare, though common in Philo and Josephus.

1. Marriage Customs in the NT.

In the writings of the Heb. Canon the LXX has γάμος only 3 times : Gn. 29:22 : ἐποίησε γάμον; Est. 2:18 : ὕψωσεν τοὺς γάμους and Est. 9:22 : ἡμέρας γάμων, always for מִשְׁתֶּה "marriage feast" (orig. "carousal," Est. 9:22). γάμος is very common in Tobit, e.g., 11:19 : καὶ ἤχθη ὁ γάμος Τωβία μετ' εὐφροσύνης, ἑπτὰ ἡμέρας. The equivalent משתה occurs frequently in Rabb. works, [3] e.g., Halla, 2, 7 = S. Nu., 110 on 15:21: בעל הבית שעושה משתה לבנו a master of the house who arranges the wedding-feast for his son (cf. also S. Dt., 343). [4]

The ancient Jewish custom of extending the marriage over several days (a whole week in the case of a virgin), and also of celebrating far into the night, is reflected in the parable at Lk. 12:36, where it may be well after midnight before the κύριος returns ἐκ τῶν γάμων. At Lk. 14:8 Jesus speaks of the marriage-feast and warns : ὅταν κληθῇς ὑπό τινος εἰς γάμους, μὴ κατακλιθῇς εἰς τὴν πρωτοκλισίαν. Again at Jn. 2:1 ff. the reference is to a wedding (γάμος) in which Jesus Himself took part and revealed τὴν δόξαν αὐτοῦ by the changing of water into wine (v. 11).

2. The New Ideal of Early Christianity.

The firm starting-point for the early Christian evaluation of marriage is Gn. 2:24, the saying concerning the *henosis* of the partners in which the original unity of man and woman is restored. Marriage is the continuation of the divine work of creation in the history of the human race (cf. also Gn. 1:28). [5] This thought always persisted in the Jewish community. [6] Thus Tobias prays with his young wife : σὺ ἐποίησας τὸν 'Αδάμ

γ ά μ ο ς. H. Preisker, *Christentum u. Ehe in den ersten drei Jahrhunderten* (1927); G. Delling, *Paulus' Stellung zu Frau und Ehe* (1931).

[1] *De Constructione,* III, 153 : ἔστι γὰρ τὸ μὲν πρότερον (= γαμῶ) γάμου μεταλαμβάνω, τὸ δὲ "γαμίζω" γάμου τινὶ μεταδίδωμι. On the linguistic form, v. Bl.-Debr., § 101, 314.

[2] V. Aristot. Pol., VII, 16, p. 1335a, 20 f.; Preisigke Wört., *s.v.*; Sickb. K.⁴, 37 f., which also gives the most recent Roman Catholic literature.

[3] Rich material on Jewish customs is to be found in Str.-B., I, 500 ff., also 45 f.; II, 398 f. The institution of the 7 day feast is traced back to Moses himself in jKet, 25a, 26.

[4] For further examples, cf. Str.-B., I, 879 on Mt. 22:2; other and less frequent terms for the feast may also be found there.

[5] Since the Fall, however, marriage stands under a curse. Genesis refers to tensions in the relationship between man and woman, and to the indissoluble conflict between the self-giving and surrender of the wife, Gn. 3:16. But Judaism also speaks of a unique fellowship of the patriarchs under the sign of the commonly incurred curse, e.g., Vit. Ad., 3; 20; 25.

[6] Almost always in the Jewish tradition there is exhortation to marry and bear children, together with an attack on exogamy and licentiousness ; e.g., Jub. 25:3; 30:7 ff.; Test. L. 9:9 ff.; Bodleiana Frag., 16 f. (Charles, Test. XII, p. 247); Ps.-Phocylides, 175-205; Jos. Ap., 1, 31 ff.; 2, 199. On everyday practice, v. the Jewish burial inscription from the catacomb of Monteverde (Müller-Bees, No. 145; Deissmann LO, 387 ff.).

καὶ ἔδωκας αὐτῷ βοηθὸν Εὕαν ... καὶ σὺ εἶπας· οὐ καλὸν εἶναι τὸν ἄνθρωπον μόνον ... καὶ νῦν, κύριε, σὺ γινώσκεις ὅτι οὐ διὰ πορνείαν λαμβάνω τὴν ἀδελφήν μου ταύτην, ἀλλὰ κατὰ δικαίωμα τοῦ νόμου σου ἐπὶ τῷ ἐλεηθῆναι ἡμᾶς ... καὶ δὸς ἡμῖν, κύριε, τέκνα καὶ εὐλογίαν (Tob. 8:6 ff.; cf. 7:12). [7] The Jewish ideal of marriage, however, reaches its climax in the rich circle of legends which clustered around the marriage of Akiba and Rahel. Rahel allows Akiba to go to the house of instruction while she remains behind in shame and poverty. After twice 12 years Akiba returns as a great rabbi with the confession: All that we have we owe to her. Rahel has sacrificed her hair to make study possible for him. Instead, he brings her a diadem representing the pinnacles of the holy city which is now so dreadfully destroyed. [8] This is the symbol of a marriage which has led two persons ceaselessly in service of their God and people under the sign of the divine calling and the historical moment. [9]

Pointing in the same direction is the ideal of marriage which Zarathustra wins from his dualistic and eschatological understanding of life. In the marriage liturgy composed by the prophet for the marriage of his youngest daughter (Yasna, 53), [10] marriage is the alliance of two persons who set the will and blessing of Ahura Mazda above all else and would strengthen their front against the evil forces which threaten catastrophe: "Soon it will come to pass." Parseeism maintained this high view of marriage, as may be seen from the last sentence of the Bundehesh: "He who hath thrice drawn near (to his spouse), cannot be separated from fellowship with Ahura Mazda and the immortal saints." [11]

Jesus sees in marriage the original form of human fellowship. It has its basis and norm in God's act of creation. It has a history which divides into three periods. It has its time, and will end with this aeon.

᾽Απὸ ἀρχῆς κτίσεως ἄρσεν καὶ θῆλυ ἐποίησεν αὐτούς ... καὶ ἔσονται οἱ δύο εἰς σάρκα μίαν, Mk. 10:6 ff. This is the original state in Paradise, i.e., marriage as God intended it. Jesus emphasises the event, the henosis, which marks it as belonging to creation: οὐκέτι εἰσὶν δύο ἀλλὰ μία σάρξ, Mk. 10:8b. The practical consequence is clear and is drawn by Jesus Himself in a new word of institution: ὃ οὖν ὁ θεὸς συνέζευξεν, ἄνθρωπος μὴ χωριζέτω, Mk. 10:9 f. To be sure, Jesus realises that the primitive order has been shattered by the corruption of the human heart. He sees the historical justification and necessity of the Mosaic law of divorce which introduces the second period in the history of marriage, the period of compromise: πρὸς τὴν σκληροκαρδίαν ὑμῶν ἔγραψεν ὑμῖν τὴν ἐντολὴν ταύτην, i.e., the direction to give a bill of divorcement. Jesus Himself, however, introduces a new period in the history of marriage. This third and decisive period is characterised by a new conception of the law of divorce, a deepened ideal of marriage and finally a fourfold reservation in respect of it.

Jesus begins by recalling the original order of creation, thus assuring the elementary unity and inviolability of marriage, and overthrowing the lax interpretation and practice of the Mosaic law with the corresponding Jewish Halacha and

---

[7] From the same awareness of the henosis and historical function of marriage as rooted in creation there also develops here and there in Judaism a sense that the destruction of a marriage is a mortal assault on the total life of creation, Pirke R. Eliez., 34. Certain of the basic concepts of Mt. 5:27 ff. may be seen already in Job 31:1, 7 ff.: ὀφθαλμός, καρδία, γυνή.

[8] V. esp. b.Ned., 50a; also the art. "Akiba" in EJ.

[9] For the procreation of children as an act of faith, cf. Ps.-Philo Ant. Bibl., 9, 6 ff.; cf. also Is. 8:1 ff.

[10] C. Bartholomae, Die Gathas des Avesta (1905), 115 ff.

[11] F. Justi, Der Bundehesh (1868), 47.

practice of divorce : [12] μὴ χωριζέτω ! But Jesus is no fanatic dreaming of a new Paradise. In all sobriety He creates practical conditions for carrying out the ancient divine order in the present aeon. In place of Jewish traditions He sets a sharper interpretation of Moses which handles the problem of divorce according to the principle of the lesser evil, a new Halacha which can sometimes allow legal divorce but leaves intact the *henosis* of the marriage partners : ὃς ἂν ἀπολύσῃ τὴν γυναῖκα αὐτοῦ καὶ γαμήσῃ [13] ἄλλην, μοιχᾶται ἐπ᾽ αὐτήν. καὶ ἐὰν αὐτὴ ἀπο-λύσασα τὸν ἄνδρα αὐτῆς γαμήσῃ ἄλλον, μοιχᾶται (Mk. 10:11 ff.). This means quite clearly and unambiguously that dissolution of marriage may be conceded at a pinch, but that there must be no contracting of a new marriage. The replacement of one spouse by another is adultery. For it affects the fundamental unity of the partners. This unity is posited and actualised in accordance with creation. It remains even when human σκληροκαρδία causes a rift which leads to legal divorce. Hence it must not be violated by any law of divorce permitting another union. [14]

Again, Jesus finds the starting-point of marital failure in σκληροκαρδία only with a view to establishing in the καρδία the base of a new ethos of marriage (Mt. 5:27 f.). It is in the heart that the decision is taken respecting the continuance of *henosis*. If it is abandoned in the heart, the marriage is broken. The meaning of *henosis* is fulfilled, according to Jesus, only where persons become and remain one inwardly as well as outwardly, in a fusion which is total and all-comprehensive. Physical fellowship must have and maintain its centre in moral. Copulation without communion is fornication.

> The words of Jesus permit neither free love nor double standards. Yet complete equality is not the ideal of Jesus. The linguistic usage in Lk. 17:27 etc. proves this (→ n. 15). The husband is the active partner in the conclusion and direction of marriage. This is self-evident for Jesus.

Finally, Jesus shows that marriage is historically conditioned with a view to making His fourfold reservation in respect of the present state of things. There are times of threatened judgment in which careless and self-confident γαμεῖν and

---

[12] The Jewish law of marriage and divorce is treated in the tractates Git., Kid., Sota and Ket. There are excellent reviews in Str.-B., II, 372 ff.; I, 303 ff. On the hesitation in basic attitude, *v*. Kittel Probleme, 98 ff. On the demand for monogamy, *v*. Damasc., 4, 20 ff., where there is an attack on the licentiousness of having two wives, and where the basis is found in creation : "Male and female created he them," and in the ark : "There went in two and two into the ark," so that it is written concerning the prince that he shall not multiply wives to himself (Dt. 17:17). Cf. also Staerk, *ad loc*. For further details, *v*. K. H. Rengstorf, *Jebamot* (1929), 30 ff.

[13] In the LXX cf. Est. 10:6 (F 3): ἣν ἐγάμησεν ὁ βασιλεύς. γαμεῖν occurs without obj. in 4 Macc. 16:9 (οἱ μὲν ἄγαμοι, οἱ δὲ γαμήσαντες); 2 Macc. 14:25 (γῆμαι καὶ παιδοποιήσασθαι).

[14] Lk. 16:18 gives us from the Q tradition a saying with the same meaning in another form : πᾶς ὁ ἀπολύων τὴν γυναῖκα αὐτοῦ καὶ γαμῶν ἑτέραν μοιχεύει, καὶ ὁ ἀπο-λελυμένην ... γαμῶν μοιχεύει. Mt. uses both Mk. and Q, but in both cases introduces a qualification which blunts the saying and is obviously designed to justify the practice of the Early Church : Mt. 19:9 : μὴ ἐπὶ πορνείᾳ, and Mt. 5:32 : παρεκτὸς λόγου πορ-νείας. (On → πορνεία, cf. Tob. 8:7: οὐ διὰ πορνείαν ἐγὼ λαμβάνω τὴν ἀδελφήν μου ταύτην sc. to wife). These casuistic clauses can hardly derive from Jesus and were obviously not known to Pl. in 1 C. 7:10 ff.

γαμίζεσθαι [15] indicate a culpable blindness to the seriousness of the situation and can thus be frivolous and irresponsible. One such time was in the days of the flood; another such time [16] has now dawned (Lk. 17:27). There are situations in which γυναῖκα ἔγημα can be wrong and obstructive, [17] because marriage hampers a man's unconditional readiness for the call of God (Lk. 14:20, cf. Mt. 22:14). There are men [18] who have the gift and task of refraining from marriage διὰ [19] τὴν βασιλείαν (Mt. 19:12). [20] And a new age is coming in which there will be no more marrying : ὅταν γὰρ ἐκ νεκρῶν ἀναστῶσιν, οὔτε γαμοῦσιν οὔτε γαμίζονται, ἀλλ᾽ εἰσὶν ὡς ἄγγελοι ἐν τοῖς οὐρανοῖς (Mk. 12:25 and par.). Marriage, too, is one of the forms of life in the present aeon which are to pass away. The history of marriage will terminate with the end of this age.

Jesus Himself never married. But He is not a pessimist in relation to it like the Christ of the apocryphal Acts. He does not go into houses to warn against it. He attends weddings. He has a deep joy in children. He knows the legitimacy, meaning and glory of marriage, as He knows the glory of the lilies which tomorrow will have faded. One day the form of marriage will pass. But this day has not yet come. To-day, and especially to-day, the word of institution from the time of creation is still in force (→ 649 on Mk. 10:6 ff.). Hence a general abstinence from marriage would be an anachronism in this aeon.

Paul in 1 C. honours all the motifs introduced by Jesus. For him, too, the saying in Genesis concerning *henosis* denotes the metaphysical range of every sexual union (1 C. 6:16 f.). Yet the thought is not developed positively in an understanding of marriage. It is used polemically in an attack on πορνεία. Free love is sin against the body (6: 18b). [21] In 1 C. 7 Paul refers expressly to the saying of the κύριος in his radical rejection of divorce, or at any rate his prohibition of the remarriage of a divorced wife (10 f.). [22] Once a marriage is contracted, it must be carried

---

[15] Jesus keeps closely to the traditional modes of Jewish thought and expression when here and in Mk. 12:25 He uses the act. (γαμεῖν) for the man and the mid. (γαμίζεσθαι) for the woman. γαμίζειν does not occur in the LXX. Mt. 24:38 has γαμίζοντες in אD and 33. B, as so often, has a more archaic reading of its own — the more refined γαμίσκοντες; the Byzantines have ἐκγαμίζοντες. The case is much the same in Lk. 20:35.

[16] Cf. also S. Bar. 10:13a : "Ye who are free, do not enter the marriage chamber."

[17] Cf. Mt. 5:29 f. (συμφέρει as in 19:10).

[18] The Baptist is obviously one of these. Peter was married acc. to Mk. 1:30, and even if he was alone at the time of Lk. 18:28 and par., he later had an ἀδελφή to wife ; the same is true of the other apostles, v. 1 C. 9:5.

[19] Cf. Rev. 2:3 : ἐβάστασας διὰ τὸ ὄνομά μου.

[20] The Evangelist here develops the problem of marriage in exactly the same way as the ensuing problem of judging. The disciples are roused and startled by the stringent demand of Jesus and say to the Master : εἰ οὕτως ἐστὶν ἡ αἰτία τοῦ ἀνθρώπου μετὰ τῆς γυναικός, οὐ συμφέρει γαμῆσαι, 19:10 (cf. 19:25: τίς ἄρα δύναται σωθῆναι;). Then Jesus reveals a final point to them in the separate saying : οὐ πάντες χωροῦσιν τὸν λόγον τοῦτον ἀλλ᾽ οἷς δέδοται ... ὁ δυνάμενος χωρεῖν χωρείτω, 19:11 f. (cf. 19:28 : ἀμὴν λέγω ὑμῖν ὅτι ὑμεῖς οἱ ἀκολουθήσαντές μοι ...). This is the way of the called : εἰσὶν εὐνοῦχοι οἵτινες εὐνούχισαν ἑαυτοὺς διὰ τὴν βασιλείαν τῶν οὐρανῶν (cf. Mt. 19:29; Lk. 18:29 : ὃς ἀφῆκεν οἰκίαν ἢ γυναῖκα ... εἴνεκεν τῆς βασιλείας τοῦ θεοῦ ...). Cf. also T. Jeb., 8, 4.

[21] It is not an occasion for the κοιλία, which is a prey to corruptibility, but an offence against the body, which is given a new consecration by the πνεῦμα and assured of a new future by the fact of the resurrection (1 C. 6:14, 19). Sin against the body is thus an offence against the coming life and the ongoing work of divine creation.

[22] A new problem is whether marriage with an unbeliever should be dissolved. Paul's answer is that the initiative should come only from the ἄπιστος (v. 15; cf. 1 Pt. 3:1 f.; for a different view cf. Jer. 8:2 ff.).

out in full both physically and spiritually. Periods of withdrawal should be brief (3 ff.; cf. 24, 27a and Col. 3:18 f.). The basis given by Paul is, however, somewhat pessimistic : διὰ ... τὰς πορνείας ἕκαστος τὴν ἑαυτοῦ γυναῖκα ἐχέτω ... ἵνα μὴ πειράζῃ ὑμᾶς ὁ σατανᾶς διὰ τὴν ἀκρασίαν (v. 2, 5). [23] If Jesus explained divorce as a necessary evil, Paul seems almost to see marriage in the same light. He thus presses even more strongly the fourfold reservation already encountered in Jesus. Marriage can be a hindrance to final dedication to God (v. 5, 32 ff.; cf. Lk. 14:20 → 651). Basically, it is not consonant with this καιρὸς συνεσταλμένος (1 C. 7:26, 28 f.); παράγει γὰρ τὸ σχῆμα τοῦ κόσμου τούτου (v. 31; cf. Mk. 12:25 → 651). Hence celibacy is the true demand of the hour διὰ τὴν ἐνεστῶσαν ἀνάγκην (1 C. 7:26, 29; cf. Lk. 17:27 → 651). To be sure, Paul has no use for ascetic experiments, and if they lead to tense situations resolute marriage [24] is for him the lesser evil. Yet it is still an evil. A widow is free to remarry ; μακαριωτέρα δέ ἐστιν ἐὰν οὕτως [25] μείνῃ (39 f., cf. 8; R. 7:2). Finally, he could wish that all γαμεῖν and γαμίζειν were at an end (1 C. 7:1, 7 f.) — ἀλλὰ ἕκαστος ἴδιον ἔχει χάρισμα ἐκ θεοῦ (v. 7). He himself has the charisma of remaining unmarried for the sake of his unique situation and commission (cf. 1 C. 9:5, 12, 15 ff.). [26] It may be seen that this is no accident but a demonstration. Paul is conscious of being one of the εὐνοῦχοι διὰ τὴν βασιλείαν (→ 651, on Mt. 19:12). [27]

In later writings the battle for the inviolability of marriage is prominent. 1 Cl. warns against the discord which can even shatter marriage : ζῆλος ἀπηλλοτρίωσεν γαμετὰς ἀνδρῶν καὶ ἠλλοίωσεν τὸ ῥηθὲν ὑπὸ πατρὸς ἡμῶν Ἀδάμ : τοῦτο νῦν ... σάρξ ἐκ τῆς σαρκός μου. [28] Hb. 13:4 admonishes : τίμιος ὁ γάμος ἐν πᾶσιν, and Ign. writes in the same vein to Polycarp (5, 1). Hence a Christian marriage should not be contracted without the blessing of the Church : πρέπει δὲ τοῖς γαμοῦσιν καὶ ταῖς γαμουμέναις μετὰ γνώμης τοῦ ἐπισκόπου τὴν ἕνωσιν ποιεῖσθαι, ἵνα ὁ γάμος ᾖ κατὰ κύριον καὶ μὴ κατ' ἐπιθυμίαν. ἁγνεία should not be made a law ; it becomes a curse if it puffs up the ascetic ; εἴ τις δύναται ἐν ἁγνείᾳ μένειν εἰς τιμὴν τῆς σαρκὸς τοῦ κυρίου, ἐν ἀκαυχησίᾳ μενέτω (Ign. Pol., 5, 2). And while the thought of mere co-habitation becomes more prevalent (v. Herm. v., 1, 1 and esp. s., 9, 11, 3), the Pastorals condemn the shunning of marriage and the questionable activities of young widows, laying down the principle : βούλομαι οὖν νεωτέρας γαμεῖν (1 Tm. 4:3; 5:11, 14). Here, too, of course, the principle of the lesser evil lurks in the background, namely, in the motive : μηδεμίαν ἀφορμὴν διδόναι τῷ ἀντικειμένῳ. The ideal is again that the widow should manage without a second marriage (5:5 ff.). It is

---

[23] On a similar basis Akiba (bSan., 76a) advises the marriage of daughters at the right time. Cf. also Sir. 7:25 : ἔκδου θυγατέρα; but cf. 1 C. 7:36 ff. for another aspect.

[24] γαμίζειν act. in 1 C. 7:38 (twice) and Mt. 24:38; Lk. 20:35 γαμίζεσθαι (the later Byzant. have ἐκγαμίζω in all four instances). The meaning of γαμίζειν is consistent throughout the NT, i.e., "to marry" = γαμεῖν and γαμίσκειν. It seems likely that in 1 C. 7:36 ff. the reference is to mere co-habitation. On the linguistic and material problem, cf. Ltzm., ad loc.; A. Juncker, Ethik des Paulus, II (1919), 191 ff.

[25] Note the οὕτως. If Paul were a widower, we should expect a ὡς κἀγώ, as in 7:7 f. There, however, the ἄγαμοι are to the fore, so that it is most likely that he himself was an ἄγαμος.

[26] On the debated issue whether Paul was a widower, cf. Joach. Jeremias, ZNW, 30 (1929), 321 ff. On the problem "Ehe und Charisma bei Paulus," v. W. Michaelis, ZSTh, 5 (1928), 426 ff.; H. Preisker, ibid., 6 (1928), 91 f.

[27] Even the συμφέρει of Mt. 19:10 recurs in Paul in order to show the meaning and pre-eminence of celibacy : τοῦτο ... πρὸς ... σύμφορον λέγω (1 C. 7:35). It is a technical term for the orientation of ethics to the final goal of calling. Cf. Mt. 5:29 f.; 1 C. 6:12; 10:23; 10:33.

[28] γαμετή, the wife, found only here in early Christian literature.

demanded of the bishop in particular that he should remain ἑνὸς ἀνδρὸς γυνή (3:2). It is evident that the demands of Paul are increasingly restricted; they are now limited to bishops as the ecclesiastical successors of the apostles and charismatics.

Only in one passage in the early Christian treatment does the principle of celibacy find a place, namely, in the picture given in Revelation of those who followed the Lamb, [29] of the 144,000 παρθένοι: οὗτοί εἰσιν οἳ μετὰ γυναικῶν οὐκ ἐμολύνθησαν ... οὗτοι οἱ ἀκολουθοῦντες τῷ ἀρνίῳ ὅπου ἂν ὑπάγῃ. οὗτοι ἠγοράσθησαν ἀπὸ τῶν ἀνθρώπων ἀπαρχὴ τῷ θεῷ καὶ τῷ ἀρνίῳ (Rev. 14:4). There is here no suggestion either of human impotence on the one side or of successful monkish achievement on the other. The reference is to the genuine heroism of those who are called for the sake of a unique situation and commission.

Yet early Christianity does not speak only of the difficulty of marriage in this *kairos*. It also speaks in strict and lofty terms of the inviolability of the marriage bond. Jesus in His saying concerning the heart (→ 650 on Mt. 5:27 f.) laid the new foundation for a positive understanding and ethos of marriage. The house tables [30] of the NT build on this foundation when they base the whole fellowship of marriage and the family on → ἀγάπη. ἀγάπη and not ἔρως creates marital fellowship. Again, the fellowship of the family is the organic centre of the actualisation of ἀγάπη, which sustains all fellowship. In the NT, however, the ground and measure of all human ἀγάπη are to be found in the love of God. The Epistle to the Ephesians carries this thought further. The basis of all marital love is for the Christian the love of Christ for His community. [31] This gives marriage its place in the new world situation. The Christian ideal of marriage is thus brought into a wider theological context.

3. The Messianic Wedding and Christian Marriage.

γάμος acquires its greatest religious significance where it is used of the union or close connection between God and man. The thought of a divine being having sexual intercourse with a human woman is common in the ancient Orient. It is the presupposition of the ruler ideology of Egypt, of the fertility rites of the Near East and of the Greek Mysteries both in classical and Hellenistic times. The δρώμενον of Eleusis represented the ἱερὸς γάμος between Zeus and Demeter, between the lord of heaven and mother earth. [32] The climax of the Feast of Flowers consisted in the γάμος of Dionysus, who came in human form to his earthly bride. [33] Again, the heavenly wedding is a sign set over the marriage of the earthly couple. Thus in the "bridal chamber" of the Villa Item the wedding of Dionysus and Ariadne is perhaps represented as a model for the future marriage of devotees. [34] In Plato (Resp., V, 459 ff.), where the mythical and cultic realism is less evident, the idea of the heavenly ἱερὸς γάμος gives both form and meaning to earthly marriage.

In the world of Israel and Judah, too, there is reference to the marriage between God and the land or people of Israel. The OT, however, has no hint of any actualisation of this relationship in mysteries, or of any sensually perceptible union with the deity. [35]

---

[29] ἀκολουθοῦντες in Rev. 14:4 as in Mt. 19:28: ἀκολουθήσαντες (→ n. 20 and 214). They form the central corps of the people of God, cf. ἀπαρχή (Rev. 14:4).

[30] Col. 3:18 ff.; Eph. 5:22 ff.; 1 Pt. 2:18 ff.

[31] On Eph. 5 → 656.

[32] V. O. Kern, *Die griech. Mysterien d. klass. Zeit* (1927), 71 f.

[33] V. O. Kern in Pauly-W., *s.v.* Dionysos, V (1905), 1010 ff.; L. Deubner, "Dionysos u. d. Anthesterien," *Jahrb. Deutsch. Arch. Inst.*, 42 (1927), 172 ff. On the sacrament of the bridal chamber, *v.* Mith. Liturg., 126 f.; on the wedding feast, *ibid.*, 244.

[34] V. M. Bieber, "Das Mysteriensaal der Villa Item," *Jahrb. Deutsch. Arch. Inst.*, 43 (1928), 298 ff.; 314 f.; 320.

[35] J. Hempel, ZSTh, 9 (1931), 18.

On the contrary, marriage is simply a symbol for the covenant between God and the people as this is to be kept in all fidelity and renewed with all passion [36] (Hos. 2:19; Is. 54:4 ff.; 62:4 f.; Ez. 16:7 ff.).

With the same strictness with which prophecy fought the ancient fertility cults, Hellenistic Judaism damps the erotic impulse of the Mysteries, e.g., in Wis. 14:23 ff.: ἢ γὰρ τεκνοφόνους τελετὰς ἢ κρύφια μυστήρια ἢ ἐμμανεῖς ἐξάλλων θεσμῶν κώμους ἄγοντες ... οὔτε γάμους καθαροὺς ἔτι φυλάσσουσιν ... γάμων ἀταξία, μοιχεία καὶ ἀσέλγεια. [37] Philo uses the imagery of the Hellenistic Mysteries together with the OT stories of Sarah and Leah to depict in a varied allegory the truth that the ἀγέννητος θεὸς καὶ τὰ σύμπαντα γεννῶν is the πατήρ who in the ἀρεταί gives birth to beautiful and perfect works. [38]

Wholly along the lines of the OT the Rabbis extolled the conclusion of the covenant at Sinai as the marriage of Yahweh with Israel. The Torah is the marriage contract, Moses is the friend of the bridegroom and Yahweh comes to Israel as a bridegroom to his bride. [39] Acc. to Akiba the bride of the Song of Songs is Israel as the bride of God. "I belong to my friend, and my friend belongs to me. You have no part in him (God)." Thus speaks the people of God in a great dialogue between Israel and the Gentiles composed by Akiba on the basis of this text (M. Ex. on 15:2). But the final renewal of the covenant between God and the people, intimated by the prophets, was expected by the Rabbis in the days of the Messiah. Thus we often find the view that in these days there will take place the true marriage feast. [40] In this connection the present age is that of engagement, the seven years of Gog will be the period immediately prior to the marriage, the marriage itself will dawn with the resurrection and the great marriage feast will be eaten in the future world. [41]

Jesus moves wholly within the circle of ideas of His contemporaries when He expresses the meaning and glory of the Messianic period in the images of the wedding and wedding feast. The virgins will wait until a late hour of the night to accompany the bridal pair with lamps to the marriage house, where at a brightly illuminated table the seven day feast will begin: [42] καὶ αἱ ἕτοιμοι εἰσῆλθον μετ᾽ αὐτοῦ εἰς τοὺς γάμους. So the community of disciples hastens to the coming of the Lord, fully alert: γρηγορεῖτε οὖν, ὅτι οὐκ οἴδατε τὴν ἡμέραν οὐδὲ τὴν ὥραν (Mt. 25:10 ff.). This point, cf. Lk. 12:36 ff., is undoubtedly the chief one. But the rich imagery is chosen deliberately. This is shown by Mk. 2:19 and par., where Jesus describes Himself as the Bridegroom. [43] Here (and in Jn. 3:29), the

---

[36] H. Schmidt, "Die Ehe des Hosea," ZAW, 42 (1924), 245 ff.

[37] Jos. Ant., 18, 66 ff. gives us a crass example frequently quoted.

[38] Cherub., 13. Cf. also γάμος in Abr., 100 f. and Som., I, 200. The wedding of the king with wisdom, Wis. 8:2, 9 (Sir. 15:2).

[39] Dt. r., 3 (200d); Pirke R. Eliez., 41; M. Ex. on 19:17 in Str.-B., I, 969 f.; II, 393.

[40] V. Ex. r., 15 on 12:2; Lv. r., 11 on 9:1 and jShebi, 35c, 25, in Str.-B., I, 517. The image of the eschatological feast, already found in Is. 25:6, is united with the thought of mother Israel, called back by God to Himself, in the wholly Jewish verses in 4 Esr. 2:15, 38. On the feast as a form and means of fellowship with God, v. Joachim Jeremias, Jesus der Weltvollender (1930), 75 ff.

[41] In a typical Rabb. attempt to find a theological origin for even secular marriages, it is suggested that Yahweh is the first Bridegroom (Gn. r., 18 on 2:22).

[42] Cf. b.Sukk., 25b; Pesikt., 20 (95a); 43 (180b); Ter., 11, 10 etc. in Str.-B., I, 504 ff. For the rather different torch procession leading the bridal couple to their home or to the bridal chamber, cf. M. Est., 1, 4, Str.-B., I, 511; also Str.-B., I, 969 (in the land of Ishmael) and Kl. Mt. on 25:1 ff. (in Trans-jordania). Torches are also mentioned in relation to the home-coming of the bride in M. Bieber, op. cit., 318, 6; 320, 1.

[43] The same thought is also found in Jn. 3:29, and possibly even in Jn. 2:7 ff. in the original form of the Cana story; so H. Schmidt, Die Erzählung v. d. Hochzeit zu Kana. Eine rel.-gesch. Untersuchung (1931), 25.

days of wedding festivity fall in the life of Jesus, whereas in Mt. 25:1 ff. they await His return — an obvious tension. Even more important is another shift in conception. In Jewish eschatological expectation God is the One who renews the marriage bond with His people. In the NT Christ takes the place of God as the heavenly Bridegroom. According to Mt. 22:1 ff. He is the King's Son for whom the βασιλεύς holds the great wedding feast (ἐποίησεν γάμους). Again, the image can hardly be accidental. Jesus often speaks of the Messianic feast. [44] The βασιλεία τῶν οὐρανῶν is the great Messianic banquet to which the people of God is invited. But those invited refuse when the γάμος ἕτοιμός ἐστιν. The call δεῦτε εἰς τοὺς γάμους goes out to those outside, and they hear and stream in (Mt. 22:3 ff.; cf. Lk. 14:8 ff.).

Who is the bride in the Messianic feast? In Jewish tradition it is the people of the covenant brought home to its Lord. In the Synoptic parables, however, the community of disciples is invited as a guest, and the bride is not mentioned. Yet the thought readily suggests itself that the new community of the covenant is the bride. The first traces of this view are to be found in Paul, probably in 1 C. 6:14 ff., where Paul sees an analogy between pneumatic union with Christ and the *henosis* of Gn. 2:24. It emerges more clearly in R. 7:4, and especially in 2 C. 11:2: ζηλῶ γὰρ ὑμᾶς θεοῦ ζήλῳ, ἡρμοσάμην γὰρ ὑμᾶς ἑνὶ ἀνδρὶ παρθένον ἁγνὴν παραστῆσαι τῷ Χριστῷ. Paul here thinks of himself as occupying a similar role to that of the Moses of the Haggada (→ 654). He is the one who conducts the bride to the heavenly Bridegroom, presenting the community to Him pure and chaste. The same imagery is found in Jn. 3:29, where the Baptist has the office of friend and therefore the community must again be the bride of the Messiah. The image of the bride is most powerfully used in the final visions of the Apocalypse, which brings together all the varied imagery of the Messianic banquet. [45] The bride waits with longing: ἔρχου! (22:17). But the divine already catches the final Hallelujah which intimates the day of consummation: ἦλθεν ὁ γάμος τοῦ ἀρνίου καὶ ἡ γυνὴ αὐτοῦ ἡτοίμασεν ἑαυτήν; and at the same time a voice declares: μακάριοι οἱ εἰς τὸ δεῖπνον τοῦ γάμου τοῦ ἀρνίου κεκλημένοι (19:7 ff.). It may thus be seen that the thought of the community as the bride includes rather than excludes the further thought that the individual members are invited to the wedding as guests. The sustaining thought, however, is that of the community as bride. The words which Trito-Isaiah [46] sets in the mouth of the divine bride Jerusalem as an eschatological hymn are seen by the divine to be fulfilled after the final cosmic upheavals. He sees the new city of God ἡτοιμασμένην ὡς νύμφην κεκοσμημένην τῷ ἀνδρὶ αὐτῆς (21:2). [47]

In contrast to Jn. 3:29 Jesus is not the bridegroom in the Cana story. The couple is of only subsidiary interest in this episode. [48] Jesus stands at the centre. Again, the conjunction of the wedding and wine is not mythologically determined in the sense of

---

[44] V. the par. in Lk. 14:16 ff., and much more concretely in Mk. 14:25 and par.
[45] On the harlot Babylon as the opp. of the Messianic bride, cf. Sib., 3, 356 ff.: ὦ χλιδανή ... παρθένε, πολλάκι σοῖσι πολυμνήστοισι γάμοισιν οἰνωθεῖσα (→ n. 53; → Βαβυλών, 515).
[46] In the misplaced section 61:10, which must be understood in the light of 62:5.
[47] In the Syr. *Schatzhöhle* (p. 67, Bezold) a bill of divorce is given to the Jewish community after the crucifixion of Jesus.
[48] H. Schmidt, *op. cit.*, suspects an original form of the Cana story in which Jesus was perhaps the bridegroom.

the Mysteries.[49] It simply arises out of the situation. The marriage as such is not important to the narrator (cf. 4:46), but the σημεῖον which points beyond itself to the δόξα of the Son. The miracle is a miracle of revelation, like that of the bread (6:26) and all the Johannine miracles. It is the first step on the way of the historical manifestation of the glory of the Son.

This conception of Christ as the Bridegroom underlies the house table of Ephesians (5:22 ff.). Already in 2 C. 11:3 (cf. 1 C. 6:16 f.) the marriage bond between Christ and the community as His bride had been set in analogy to the marriage bond between the first human couple. In Eph. 5:31 f. the thought is worked out typologically, and the Genesis saying[50] concerning the impulse of the man to the woman and the *henosis* of the two is explained as a μυστήριον μέγα and referred εἰς Χριστὸν καὶ εἰς τὴν ἐκκλησίαν. This relationship between Christ and the community, however, is necessarily normative for that between husband and wife in a Christian marriage. Thus Eph., developing Pauline motifs (cf. 1 C. 11:3; 6:15 ff.), offers a christological basis for the two main parts of the early Christian marriage catechism,[51] for the subordination of the wife to the husband and the overriding love of the husband for the wife: ὡς ἡ ἐκκλησία ὑποτάσσεται τῷ Χριστῷ, οὕτως καὶ αἱ γυναῖκες τοῖς ἀνδράσιν ἐν παντί (5:24, cf. 22 f.). Οἱ ἄνδρες, ἀγαπᾶτε τὰς γυναῖκας, καθὼς καὶ ὁ Χριστὸς ἠγάπησεν τὴν ἐκκλησίαν καὶ ἑαυτὸν παρέδωκεν ὑπὲρ αὐτῆς, ἵνα ... (5:25 ff.; cf. 29 f.). The tensions in the relationship between husband and wife, recognised already in Genesis, are resolved ἐν Χριστῷ. For the self-giving of the wife acquires a new dedication, and the impulse of the husband a new content and standard, in ἀγάπη.[52] The wife is no longer surrendered to the husband; she is entrusted to him. He does not have rights of lordship over her; he takes responsibility for her. Sometimes the execution of this thought has been as artificial as its exegetical basis. But the enterprise is magnificent and bold. It is the only attempt of early Christianity to set marital duty definitely under the sign of the fact of Jesus.

> The starting-point is obviously the old idea of the imitation of Jesus which first arose in Judaism as the *imitatio Dei* (→ ἀκολουθέω), which then came to control Christian ethics, and which played a great role from the time of Ignatius. It is no accident that it is in Ign. that the ideas of Eph. 5 find their first echo (Ign. Pol., 5, 1). On the other hand, there is no doubt that the thought of Christian marriage is here referred much more strongly to that of the ἱερὸς γάμος, to the analogy between heavenly and earthly wedding which is so important in Gk. thinking.
>
> In the later development of early Christian ideas of marriage and celibacy there is

---

[49] E.g., M. Bieber, *op. cit.,* 319. H. Schmidt sees in Jn. 2:1 ff. the reconstruction of a story which originally treated of the epiphany of a wine-god, *op. cit.,* 30, 33. W. Bauer, too, recalls the wine miracles of Dionysus and interprets the story as a rich allegorising of the wine of the Lord's Supper, *v.* Bau. Jn., *ad loc.* The specifically Johannine impress and character of the story are especially worked out, and made fruitful for interpretation, by K. L. Schmidt in "Der Johanneische Charakter der Erzählung vom Hochzeitswunder zu Kana," *Harnackehrung* (1921), 32 ff.

[50] The Roman Catholic view starts with the application of the term μυστήριον (*sacramentum*) to the marital relationship established in Eph. 5:31 = Gn. 2:24, and thus declares marriage to be a sacrament. For further details, cf. Meinertz Gefbr.⁴, *ad loc.*

[51] → 650. Cf. 1 C. 14:34; 1 Th. 4:4; Col. 3:18 f.; 1 Pt. 3:1, 7. Cf. also Jos. Ap., 2, 201: γυνὴ χείρων ... ἀνδρὸς εἰς ἅπαντα. τοιγαροῦν ὑπακουέτω, μὴ πρὸς ὕβριν, ἀλλ᾽ ἵν᾽ ἄρχηται. θεὸς γὰρ ἀνδρὶ τὸ κράτος ἔδωκεν. Christian sensibility could not possibly approve a crude saying like that of Sir. 36:26: πάντα ἄρρενα ἐπιδέξεται γυνή, ἔστιν δὲ θυγάτηρ θυγατρὸς κρεῖσσον.

much contact and conflict with Hellenistic motifs. Gnostics speculate on heavenly syzygies, mystics revel in the imagery of the Song of Songs, ascetics despise the body and ecstatic women experience the union of the soul with the heavenly Bridegroom. Two texts stand out in the welter of literature. The Jewish legend of Joseph and Asenath, [52] which deals with the marriage of Joseph to a daughter of the Egyptian king, is obviously interpreted and allegorically exploited in Judaism with reference to the marriage of the Messiah to the city of God (p. 15; 16; 17; 19); and Christians, too, work it out in the same way, the virgin Asenath being fearfully opposed to all men until the great stranger comes (υἱὸς θεοῦ, 6; 13) who converts her to the true God and imparts the Spirit of God to her in a kiss (19). She gives herself to him. She is affianced to him from eternity, and their marriage bond will last to eternity (21). Similar ideas and motifs recur frequently in the apocryphal legends of the apostles, esp. the Acts of Thomas. Here, too, there is an evident ascetic tendency. Jesus enters the bridal chamber and wins the newly espoused for the ideal of continence. A higher marriage takes the place of carnal union: ἑτέρῳ γάμῳ ἡρμόσθην ... ἀνδρὶ ἀληθινῷ συνεζεύχθην (Act. Thom., 14). And an ecstatic hymn of Thomas lauds the mystical wedding, the dance of the seven male and female attendants and the eternal joys of the marriage feast (6 f.). [53] In the story of Joseph and Asenath the reference is still to the relationship between the Messiah and the community, but here it is to the sensual and supra-sensual experiences of the individual soul. Mysticism has triumphed.

Stauffer

---

† γέεννα   (→ αἰώνιος, πῦρ).

1. γέεννα (γέενα, [1] γέννα [2]) is a Gk. form of the Aram. גֵּיהִנָּם (bErub., 19a), [3] which for its part derives from the Heb. גֵּי־הִנֹּם (Jos. 15:8; 18:16), an abbreviation of the original גֵּי בֶן־הִנֹּם (Jos. 15:18) [4] or גֵּי בְנֵי הִנֹּם (2 K. 23:10, Ketib). This name was given to the Wādi er-rabābi in South Jerusalem, which later acquired a bad reputation [5] because sacrifices were offered in it to Moloch in the days of Ahaz and Manasseh (2 K. 16:3; 21:6). The threats of judgment uttered over this sinister valley in Jer. 7:32; 19:6; cf. Is. 31:9; 66:24, are the reason why the Valley of Hinnom came to be equated with the hell of the last judgment in apocalyptic literature from the 2nd cent. B.C. (the oldest instances are in Eth. En. 90:26; 27:1 ff.; 54:1 ff.; 56:3 f.). The name *gehinnom* thus came to be used for the eschatological fire of hell (NT; bRH, 16b; 4 Esr. 7:36; S. Bar. 59:10; 85:13; Sib., 1, 103; 2, 291; 4, 186, *vl.*). This is the stage of development reflected

---

[52] Ed. P. Batiffol, *Studia Patristica,* 1 (1889).

[53] Cf. O. Sol. 42:11 f. (wedding couch); 38:9 ff. (bride of Satan). Cf. also Reitzenstein, *Hellenistische Wundererzählungen* (1906), 134 ff.

γ έ ε ν ν α. G. Dalman, RE³, VI, 418 ff.; Str.-B., IV, 1022-1118; Schl. Mt., 171; Dausch Synpt.⁴, 105.

[1] Sib., 1, 103 : εἰς γέεναν. The one ν is supported by the metre. In the NT cf. Mk. 9:45 E al 47 D.

[2] Preis. Zaub., IV, 3072 : γέννα πυρός.

[3] Cf. the popular etym. in bErub., 19a : Gehenna means the valley to which one descends by reason of frivolity (הִינָם). In the Gk. form the final ם- is omitted, as in Μαρία (Lk. 2:19 = מִרְיָם) in order to make Gk. inflection possible.

[4] Also written גֵּיא בֶן־הִנֹּם (Jer. 7:32).

[5] Cf. Joach. Jeremias, *Jerusalem zur Zeit Jesu* (1923), 17.

in the NT. In the 1st cent. A.D. the term was further extended[6] to cover the place where the ungodly were punished in the intermediate state (→ ᾅδης), but this is not so in the NT.

The LXX does not have γέεννα. Joseph. mentions neither the term not the matter, probably because he was a Pharisee and thus denied the resurrection of the ungodly (Bell., 3, 374 f.; Ap., 2, 218). Philo does not know the word and uses τάρταρος instead (Exsecr., 152).[7]

2. Fundamental for an understanding of the γέεννα passages in the NT, which occur only in the Synoptists and John, is the sharp distinction made by the NT between → ᾅδης and γέεννα. This distinction is a. that Hades receives the ungodly only for the intervening period between death and resurrection, whereas Gehenna is their place of punishment in the last judgment; the judgment of the former is thus provisional but the torment of the latter eternal (Mk. 9:43 and par.; 9:48). It is then b. that the souls of the ungodly are outside the body in Hades, whereas in Gehenna both body and soul, reunited at the resurrection, are destroyed by eternal fire (Mk. 9:43 and par., 45, 47 and par., 48; Mt. 10:28 and par.).

γέεννα is pre-existent (Mt. 25:41).[8] It is manifested as the fiery abyss (Mk. 9:43 etc.; cf. ἡ κάμινος τοῦ πυρός, Mt. 13:42, 50) only after the general resurrection (→ ἀνάστασις) and the last judgment (→ κρίσις) (cf. βάλλεσθαι, Mk. 9:45, 47 and par.; ἐμβάλλειν, Lk. 12:5). Those whose fall victim to divine judgment at the last day (Mt. 5:22; 23:33) will there be destroyed by everlasting fire. The ungodly are the υἱοὶ γεέννης (Mt. 23:15), together with Satan and the demons (Mt. 25:41; 8:29; cf. ἡ λίμνη τοῦ πυρός, Rev. 19:20; 20:10, 14 f., into which the ungodly, Satan, the beast and his prophet, death and hell are thrown).

In the NT there is no description of the torments of hell as in apocalyptic literature. If they are mentioned, it is only to rouse consciences to fear of the wrath of the heavenly Judge (Mt. 10:28 and par.). The κρίσις (sentence)[9] τῆς γεέννης (Mt. 23:33) is a κρίσις τῆς ὀργῆς (Mt. 3:7 and par.). The severity of the judgment of God on sin is expressed by Jesus in His threatening of γέεννα even to disciples who wound their brothers with contemptuous words (Mt. 5:22). No sacrifice is too costly in the war against sin (Mt. 9:43 ff.).

It is significant that the oldest Rabbinic reference to Gehenna (T. Sanh., 13, 3 and par.) tells us that the disciples of Shammai, as distinct from those of Hillel, ascribe to Gehenna a purgatorial as well as a penal character, namely, in the case of the שְׁקוּלִים or בֵּינוֹנִים, i.e., those whose merits and transgressions balance one another. It may be that this conception of a purificatory character of the final fire of judgment underlies such passages as Mk. 9:49; 1 C. 3:13-15; cf. 2 Pt. 3:10.

Joachim Jeremias

┌─────────────────────────────┐
│ † γελάω, † καταγελάω,   │
│   † γέλως   │
└─────────────────────────────┘

1. The Word Group Applied to Men.

γελάω and γέλως are common from the time of Homer in all shades of their basic meaning, whether for "free and joyous laughter" or for that of "triumph or scorn."

---

[6] The oldest attestation is in b.Ber., 28b; Jochanan b. Zakkai (d.c. 80 A.D.).
[7] Cf. Str.-B., IV, 1034, ad loc.
[8] Cf. 4 Esr. 7:36. Even in Rabb. lit. the pre-existence of Gehenna is solidly maintained.
[9] Schl. Mt., 686.

γέλως means not merely "laughter" itself but also the "occasion for or object of laughter" (e.g., Soph. Oed. Col., 902 f.: ... γέλως δ' ἐγὼ ξένῳ γένομαι τῷδε; Test. Sol. 26:7 [p. 74 McCown]: καὶ ἐγενόμην γέλως τοῖς εἰδώλοις καὶ δαίμοσιν). καταγελάω, attested from the time of Aeschylus (Ag., 1236), is a strengthened form denoting "hearty or loud laughter," or "ridicule." The word as applied to men has no particular connections with religion or morality in the Gk. and Hellen. world, even in Hesychius, s.v. Σαρδόνιος γέλως: οἱ τὴν Σαρδόνα κατοικοῦντες τῷ Κρόνῳ ἔθυον γελῶντα καὶ ἀσπαζόμενοι ἀλλήλους. Here γελᾶν simply means the rather forced merriment expected of the sacrifice and those participating in it.

Things are different in the LXX. Here γελάω as a rendering of צחק [1] is used exclusively for the true or supposed superiority towards another expressed in scorn or laughter (cf. Abraham in relation to God in Gn. 17:17; Sarah in relation to God in Gn. 18:12, 13, 15; the narrator (J) found a sharp contrast between the attitude of the former in Gn. 15:6 (הֶאֱמִין/πιστεύειν) and that of the latter in Gn. 18:12 ff. (צחק/γελᾶν).

The word means much the same when שׂחק is rendered γελάω (of the enemies of Jerusalem laughing at the stricken city in Lam. 1:7, or the righteous laughing at a man of deceitful tongue in ψ 51:6), or when it is rendered καταγελάω (e.g., the man who trusts in God laughing at destruction and famine in Job 5:22, or the ostrich at the horse and rider who pursue it in Job 39:18). [2] Except in Job 17:6, where there is a softening, γέλως is used for צחק (11 times), [3] and so far as meaning goes corresponds to the verb, though the neutral sense has not completely disappeared (e.g., Prv. 10:23; Ἐκκλ. 7:4, 7). Except in Gn. 21:6 it is certainly never used for righteous joy. [4] In Jesus Sirach (Σιρ. 21:20; 27:13) γέλως is a mark of the fool (μωρός); Prv. 10:23 and Ἐκκλ. 7:7 speak emphatically of the γέλως of the ἄφρων. It should not be overlooked that in both these cases the opposite is the σοφός, who is thus the equivalent of the righteous.

The Rabbis seldom speak of laughter. It is worth noting that both the צחק of Gn. 21:6 and the לצחק of Ex. 32:6 are referred to idolatry, adultery and blood-shed (Gn. r., 53, 11 on 21:9 or Ex. r., 42, 1 on 32:7). [5] Hence it is not surprising to read in Gn. r., 22, 6 on 4:7 that R. Chanina bar Papa (c. 300 A.D.) [6] said: "When you have an impulse [7] towards frivolity (לַהֲשׂתִּיקְךָ), then resist it with the words of the Torah." Here שׂחק is undoubtedly used for the attitude which is the exact opposite of serious application to the Torah. Things are not quite so blunt, but take much the same course, in the

---

γελάω κτλ. Moult.-Mill., 122; E. Kornemann, Klio, 7 (1907), 285 ff. (on γέλως, P. Giess., I, 3, 8 ff.); E. Norden, Die Geburt des Kindes (1924), 59 ff.

[1] The pi'el צחק is translated παίζω (Gn. 21:9; 26:8; Ex. 32:6; Ju. 16:25) or ἐμπαίζω (Gn. 39:14, 17).

[2] καταγελάω is used for שׂחק 2 times in the LXX, and 22 times in all, but only 4 times for לעג, once for עלל and once for היה לבוז.

[3] Not counting Ez. 23:32 A.

[4] In Gn. 21:6 matters are complicated, since there seem to be two different interpretations of the name צחק, and the one can be taken in a pious sense (E) whereas the other has the profane. Yet this is not necessary; the verse may perhaps be taken to imply that Sarah herself has now become the object of sceptical laughter. In the LXX this thought is suppressed and the whole verse is given a positive meaning: γέλωτά μοι ἐποίησεν κύριος· ὃς γὰρ ἐὰν ἀκούσῃ συγχαρεῖταί μοι (I owe this to G. Bertram). Perhaps there is here a desire to free the mother of the people from the charge of צחק/γέλως — hence συγχαρεῖται, though γέλως itself could not be avoided in view of the existing Haggadic explanation of the name צחק.

[5] These interpretations are already Tannaitic (Akiba): T. Sot., 6, 6.

[6] The sentence derives from an older tradition, since it also seems to be linked with R. Simon (c. 280 A.D.) in the same connection.

[7] Naturally a bad impulse.

Tannaitic tradition (bBer., 31a). Here we are not only warned against praying מִתּוֹךְ שְׂחוֹק as an unworthy attitude — the formula occurs in a kind of catalogue of vices — but also against parting from one's neighbour מִתּוֹךְ שְׂחוֹק; Here, too, שְׂחַק is contrasted with a pious sense of dependence on God which is well-pleasing to Him. In שְׂחַק, then, there is seen a rejection of God as the reality which determines all things and an affirmation of man as an autonomous being.

This linguistic background is most important for an understanding of the NT passages in which there is reference to laughter. Everywhere we can see a distinction from Greek usage and dependence on the more religious Jewish usage צָחַק (שָׂחַק)/γελάω. This is true even in Mt. 9:24 and par., the only passage where καταγελάω is used. Here it is said of those assembled in the house of Jairus that in face of the καθεύδει of Jesus: καὶ κατεγέλων αὐτοῦ. This obviously denotes scornful laughter on the basis of supposedly better information and therefore of a superiority which is not slow to make itself felt. [8]

In Lk. 6:25 a Woe is pronounced by Jesus on the γελῶντες νῦν; [9] a prospect of future πενθεῖν and κλαίειν is held out for them, whereas it is said of the κλαίοντες νῦν that they shall laugh (6:21). The old antithesis γελᾶν/κλαίειν (Qoh. 3:4) is thus filled with new content in relation to the eschatological division and decision of men (though → 662). In this connection it is to be noted that the γελῶντες νῦν are set directly alongside the πλούσιοι and the ἐμπεπλησμένοι νῦν (6:24 f.); the comprehensive reference of Jesus is to those who find satisfaction in the present aeon in contrast to the needy. If there is no immediate thought of sin or righteousness in the original sayings (cf. Mt. 5:6), the interpretation of Matthew is right in so far as Jesus here threatens with judgment an attitude which no longer reckons seriously with God and which one part of Palestinian Christianity saw to be connected, either as a danger or as a reality, with wealth. Thus for James (4:9) it is part of the conversion from worldliness, however religiously embellished, that γέλως [10] should disappear and give place to humility before God if God Himself is not finally to make it πένθος, i.e., complaint at the loss of worldly goods, [11] which must ultimately be wrested from man's control (4:8 ff.).

2. The Word Group applied to the Deity.

γελάω and γέλως are particularly important for the Gks. when brought into connection with the gods. [12] Merry laughter is a divine characteristic (cf. perhaps φιλομμειδής, a name for Aphrodite as early as Homer, Od., 9, 362), and is thus inseparable from theophany. [13] We have a particularly good example of this in the epiphany hymn to Demetrius Poliorketes from the year 307 B.C., where it is said of the god Demetrius on his bodily manifestation (Athen., VI, 253d): ὁ δ' ἱλαρός, ὥσπερ τὸν θεὸν δεῖ, καὶ καλὸς καὶ γελῶν πάρεστι. [14] Alongside this we might set the legend in Plin.

---

[8] The same usage is found in Jos. Ant., 5, 144: the men of Gibeah ὠλιγώρουν τοῦ δικαίου καὶ κατεγέλων; cf. also Jos. Ap., 1, 69 and Schl. Mt., 319. There is an instance of διαγελάω to express scepticism towards a miracle in R. Herzog, Die Wunderheilungen von Epidauros (1931), 10.

[9] In Joseph. γελάω is used only in connection with mockery and witticisms, without religious content; cf. Schl. Lk., 247 f.

[10] Joseph. uses γέλως of frivolous or scornful laughter: Vit., 323; Ant., 4, 276.

[11] Cf. Hck. Jk., 204.

[12] I owe much of this section to the work of H. Kleinknecht.

[13] Cf. on this pt., Norden, 58 and 61 ff.

[14] V. Ehrenberg, Antike, 7 (1931), 290 f. refers the hymn to Dionysus: "Only to a Demetrius assimiliated to him could this hymnal form apply."

Hist. Nat., VII, 15, 72, that the only man to laugh on the day of his birth was Zoroaster, or the demand made of the boy hymned in Verg. Ecl., 4, 60 ff.: *Incipe, parve puer, risu cognoscere matrem ... incipe, parve puer, cui non risere parenti, nec deus hunc mensa, dea nec digita cubili est;* the underlying thought here is that laughter immediately after birth declares the divine character of this child. [15] γέλως is a mark of the deity, which also spreads γέλως in the world around: [ἐστι] ... Ἥλιός τε γέλως. τούτῳ γὰρ ἅπασα δικαίως / καὶ θνητὴ διάνοια γελᾷ καὶ κόσμος ἀπείρων (Stob. Ecl., I, 781 f.). It is perhaps in this light that we should explain the difficult passage in P. Giess., I, 3, 8 ff., where in connection with the coronation of Hadrian there is reference to a γέλως of the people. This is the laughter which breaks out with the *parousia* of the god (here the emperor), denoting the age of joy which he introduces. [16]

From the examples adduced it may be seen that γέλως is intrinsic to the god in antiquity, even though it is not a trait which is regularly emphasised. The material explanation lies in a fact which calls for attention, namely, that in contrast to the Orient Greek religion stresses the gracious presence of deity and its union with man. [17] It hardly need be said that the term cannot be brought into any essential connection with the biblical view of God. This would be true even if a certain odium did not attach to it in biblical usage. To be sure, it is said of God 4 times in the OT that He laughs (שָׂחַק, Ps. 2:4; 37:13; 59:8; Prv. 1:26). [18] This does not imply, however, that laughter is a divine characteristic. It simply expresses His absolute superiority over the ungodly who will not accept Him as God even though they are nothing beside Him. [19] The use of שָׂחַק thus falls materially under the biblical usage mentioned in → 1., and it is in keeping that in the first 3 cases the LXX has ἐκγελάομαι and in Prv. ἐπιγελάομαι. Yet it should not be overlooked that the Rabbis were astonished even to read of this fourfold laughter of God in Scripture. Otherwise they would not have assembled the passages, let alone tried to take ישׂחק in Ps. 2:4 as pi'el and thus taken it to mean that God will make His enemies the objects of mutual derision [20] (Midr. Ps. 2 § 6). Thus it is not God Himself who laughs, and it is clear that laughter is seen to be something unworthy, or, more correctly, that the content of שָׂחַק is thought to be out of keeping with God and His world. Why this is so cannot be pursued in the present context. Possible the basic concern was to maintain the majesty of God. It is enough, however, that there is this distinction from the Greek view of God, that laughter is not ascribed to God, and that this has a bearing on the linguistic expression of the joy which He gives to man.

In Ps. 126:2 it is said with reference to the coming time of salvation [21] that "the mouth will be full of laughter (שְׂחֹק)." [22] From the context it is obvious that this laughter expresses superiority over previous opponents. In this case, there is here nothing un-

---

[15] Cf. Norden, 64 ff.

[16] E. Kornemann, *op. cit.,* attempted to explain this in terms of a triumphal procession. This is near the mark, since a merry procession is part of the *parousia*. → ἀπάντησις, 381.

[17] Cf. J. Leipoldt, *War Jesus Jude?* (1923), 47 ff.

[18] The subject in Prv. 1:26 is really wisdom, but behind this is God.

[19] It is in accordance with the sense that except at Ps. 37:13 שָׂחַק is a par. of לָעַג.

[20] Another explanation of יושב בשמים ישחק is: "Thus saith the Holy One, blessed be He: The ones shall laugh at the others."

[21] It makes no material difference whether the verse is taken as recollection or expectation.

[22] Cf. Str.-B., IV, 965 f.

godly, since God is gratefully praised for His liberating act (v. 2b). It is thus the more instructive that in its rendering of רָנַן the LXX does not use γέλως but χαρά; it thus imports into the text the thought of the righteous joy which has reference to God alone. [23] What the translator has done is to set the expectation of salvation under the thought of God. It is in keeping that in the descriptions of the time of salvation in later Judaism there is constant reference to joy (שִׂמְחָה, Test. Jud. 25) but not to laughter. It is to be noted finally that Rabbinic ethics, with its thought of rewards, rejected laughter in relation to the coming aeon because this is something for God to give, not for man to give himself; this is perhaps indicated by the use in this context of Ps. 126:2 with reference to the future world (Midr. Ps. 126:2 [p. 511, Buber]; bBer., 31a). [24] We may thus say that even in the eschatological terminology and thinking of Judaism רָנַן /γελᾶν does not belie its ungodly character.

This is not without bearing on NT usage, since in the future world laughter is the prospect of the κλαίοντες νῦν according to the definitely eschatological saying at Lk. 6:21. We could explain this easily if we might assume that Hellenistic ideas that the time of salvation is the time of γέλως had had some influence on the formation of the saying. This is excluded, however, by the Jewish character of the whole section. Nor can we think of a future triumph of the oppressed over their oppressors in the original sense of Ps. 126:2. This leaves us only two possible ways of explaining the γελάσετε of Lk. 6:21. On the one hand, it is just possible that Luke himself deliberately selected γελᾶν, in ignorance of Jewish usage, in order to maintain the strongest possible parallelism with 6:25. On the other hand, it is possible that the saying in 6:21 was pronounced by Jesus under the influence of Ps. 126:2 (cf. also Mt. 5:4 with Ps. 126:5), and that רָנַן or חִדּוּ (cf. חֶדְוָא Tg. Ps. 126:2) was thus adopted in conscious allusion, but this was not perceived or regarded (cf. the χαρά of the LXX) when the saying was put into its present Greek form. [25] Which of the two possibilities is the more likely and compelling, it is hard to say.

Rengstorf

γενεά, γενεαλογία, γενεαλογέω, ἀγενεαλόγητος

γενεά.

In general usage, this means a. "birth," "descent" : Αἰτωλὸς γενεήν, Hom. Il., 23, 471: ἀπὸ γενεᾶς, "from birth," Xenoph. Cyrop., I, 2, 8; b. "what is born," "progeny," "descendant" : χρήματα καὶ γενεὰν ὑποδιδόναι = "to deliver up possessions and children," Polyb., XX, 6, 6; c. "race" in the sense of those bound by common descent : ἀνδρῶν γενεή (opp. φύλλων γενεή), Hom. Il., 6, 146; d. "generation" : τρεῖς γενεαὶ ἀνδρῶν ἑκατὸν ἔτη εἰσίν, Hdt., II, 142; ἐπὶ πολλὰς γενεάς, Plat. Tim., 23c; also in

---

[23] For a similar process → n. 4.

[24] The tradition seems to be linked with the name of R. Shimon b. Jochai (c. 150 A.D.), a pupil of Akiba.

[25] Cf. as the closest par. Test Jud. 25:4 (αβ S¹ Charles): καὶ οἱ ἐν λύπῃ τελευτήσαντες ἀναστήσονται ἐν χαρᾷ.

γ ε ν ε ά. Pass., Pape, Pr.-Bauer, *s.v.*; Schl. Mt. on 18:15.

the sense of age: ἡ ἀνθρωπίνη λεγομένη γενεά (in distinction from the heroic age), Hdt., III, 122. The sense of the totality of those living as contemporaries is not found in Gk., though it must be presupposed in explanation of d.

The LXX uses the term mostly for דּוֹר, rarely for עַם or מִשְׁפָּחָה. דּוֹר means "age" or "age of man," or "generation" in the sense of contemporaries; [1] Aram. דָּר.

In the NT γενεά is common in the Synoptics, rare in Paul, absent from Jn., including Rev. As a purely formal concept it is always qualified. It mostly denotes "generation" in the sense of contemporaries.

We often have the formule ἡ γενεὰ αὕτη, as at Mk. 8:12 (Lk. 11:29, 30); 13:30 (Mt. 24:34; Lk. 21:32); Mt. 11:16 (Lk. 7:31); 12:41, 42 (Lk. 11:31, 32); 23:36 (Lk. 11:50, 51); Lk. 17:25; Hb. 3:10. [2] This generation is to be understood temporally,. but there is always a qualifying criticism. Thus we read of an "adulterous" generation (→ μοιχαλίς, Mk. 8:38), or an "evil" generation (Mt. 12:45; Lk. 11:29), or an "evil and adulterous" generation (Mt. 12:39; 16:4), or an "unbelieving and corrupt" generation (Mt. 17:17, cf. Lk. 9:41; Mk. 9:19, which has only ἄπιστος). There is a combination at Ac. 2:40: σώθητε ἀπὸ τῆς γενεᾶς τῆς σκολιᾶς ταύτης. Phil. 2:15: μέσον γενεᾶς σκολιᾶς καὶ διεστραμμένης, derives from the Song of Moses (Dt. 32:5). So too, perhaps, does Mt. 17:17 (Dt. 32:20): γενεὰ ἐξεστραμμένη ἐστίν, υἱοὶ οἷς οὐκ ἔστιν πίστις ἐν αὐτοῖς. This Song is related to the Messianic age in S. Dt., 318 on 32:15. [3] γενεά in this critical sense is also found in Jos. Bell., 5, 442: μὴ γενεὰν ἐξ αἰῶνος γεγονέναι κακίας γονιμωτέραν. As shown by the usual addition of αὕτη, [4] the phrase ἡ γενεὰ αὕτη is a rendering of the Rabbinic הַדּוֹר הַזֶּה. [5] In the role played by γενεά in the sayings of Jesus we can see His comprehensive purpose — He is aiming at the whole people and not at individuals — and His view of solidarity in sin. πᾶσαι αἱ γενεαί occurs in the sense of all future men at Lk. 1:48, 50. [6]

γενεά in the sense of "age" or "period" is found in Mt. 1:17; Ac. 13:36; 14:16; 15:21; Eph. 3:5; Col. 1:26. It occurs in the sense of "manner" in Lk. 16:8. In Ac. 8:33 there is allusion to Is. 53:8: τὴν γενεὰν αὐτοῦ τίς διηγήσεται is a literal rendering of the obscure Hebrew text. [7]

† γενεαλογία.

"Genealogical tree." Attested from the time of Plat. Crat., 396c: τὴν Ἡσιόδου γενεαλογίαν, τίνας ἔτι τοὺς ἀνωτέρω προγόνους λέγει τούτων (of the gods). Solon's attempt to recount the origin of the race is described in Plat. Tim. 22a as περὶ Δευκαλίωνος καὶ Πύρρας μυθολογεῖν καὶ τοὺς ἐξ αὐτῶν γενεαλογεῖν. Among other forms of historical writing Polybius mentions a γενεαλογικὸς τρόπος which he himself does not follow (IX, 1, 4). In a formula similar to that of Plato he refers to

---

[1] Ges.-Buhl, s.v.
[2] ψ 94:10. We should read ταύτῃ; ἐκείνη is an assimilation to the LXX.
[3] Cf. Schl. Mt. on 17:17.
[4] Bl.-Debr., 306.
[5] Cf. Schl. Mt. on 18:15.
[6] There is an obvious uncertainty in v. 50, but the meaning is "for all generations." Bl.-Debr., 322: "to many generations." The basis is the Heb. דּוֹר וָדוֹר or דּוֹר דּוֹרִים (Is. 51:8; Ps. 102:24).
[7] γενεά can here mean spiritual progeny (in the members of the Christian community), or the present evil generation, or even ancestry (cf. Preisigke Wört., s.v.). I owe this reference to G. Bertram.
γ ε ν ε α λ ο γ ί α. Wbg. Past., 31 ff.; Dib. Past., ad loc.; G. Kittel, ZNW, 20 (1921), 49 ff. Cf. also bibl. in → n. 3.

many who have concerned themselves with τά τε περὶ τὰς γενεαλογίας καὶ μύθους (IX, 2, 1). Thus the formula μῦθοι καὶ γενεαλογίαι at 1 Tm. 1:4 may be regarded as traditional. The LXX does not have the word.

In the NT it is found only at 1 Tm. 1:4; Tt. 3:9. The meaning is contested. The total understanding of the Past. with the alternatives of authentic or unauthentic or Gnostic or Jewish opponents, makes interpretation difficult. We should thus start with the term itself in the context. From 1 Tm. 1:4 we learn that γενεαλογίαι cannot be separated from μῦθοι. Tt. 1:14 mentions μῦθοι 'Ιουδαϊκοί. It thus follows that the γενεαλογίαι, too, are Jewish in content. This also corresponds to the fact that in Tt. 3:9 they are associated with the μάχαι νομικαί, men (Tt. 1:14), questions their claim to be teachers of the Law (1 Tm. 1:7) and attacked in a discussion of the Law in v. 8 ff. [1] The νομοδιδάσκαλοι are neither Judaists nor Nomists; they are Jews. The issue is not the same as in Gl. [2] But they are not Antinomians in the bad sense. They represent a Gnostic Judaism which uses the Law (of the OT) to spread ascetic demands ("Halachot") and speculative doctrines ("Haggadot"). Hence the author emphasises the need for a true keeping of the Law (1 Tm. 1:8), calls their teaching the commandments of men (Tt. 1:14), questions their claim to be teachers of the Law (1 Tm. 1:7) and demands that real teachers should be provided for the communities (Tt. 3:13). There is no longer any reason to question the possibility or probability of a Gnostic Judaism. [3]

We can only guess as to the nature of the γενεαλογίαι. They can hardly have been lists of aeons similar to those found in the classical Gnosticism of the Valentinians and forced into the text of the OT by violent exegesis. Such lists are never called γενεαλογίαι. [4] More likely, they are the genealogies of men. G. Kittel has shown [5] that the Rabbis had a lively interest in both their own genealogies and those of others, but especially those taken from the OT, and that these played a role in the debates between the Jews and Jewish Christians. The errorists of the Past., however, are not just Jews but syncretists. [6] Again, μῦθοι καὶ γενεαλογίαι is a traditional Greek formula. [7] Hence it is probable that the expression denotes the biblical history enriched by interpretations and additions. [8] If so, the γενεαλογίαι of Tt. 3:9 are the same as the μῦθοι καὶ γενεαλογίαι of

---

[1] The idea that the Judaism of the false teachers is simply feigned in order to make it appear that Paul, the chief opponent of the Jews, is the author (cf. Dib. Past. on 1 Tm. 1:7) attributes an unlikely subtlety to the writer. He would hardly make his task more difficult by substituting Jewish for pagan-Christian Gnosticism and by linking it with the OT.

[2] Cf. Dib. Past. on 1 Tm. 1:7 and W. Lütgert, "Die Irrlehrer der Past.," BFTh, 13 (1909), 16 ff.

[3] Cf. Lütgert, 22; Schlatter Gesch. Isr.³, 313-316, 397, n. 48, 443, n. 305; Schürer, III, 407-420; H. Gressmann, ZAW, 43 (1925), 1 ff.; also M. Friedländer, Der vorchristliche jüdische Gnostizismus (1897). Cf. esp. Colossians.

[4] Irenaeus opens his work against heresies by referring 1 Tm. 1:4 to the Gnostics. Similarly Tertullian (Praescr. Haer., 7 and 33) refers it to heresies, esp. the Valentinians. But neither of them says that the Gnostics spoke of γενεαλογίαι.

[5] Cf. also 1 Ch. 5:1: οὐκ ἐγενεαλογήθη, in the Mas. hithp. of יחש (in the Rabbis יחסם), elsewhere translated καταλοχία, καταλοχισμός. In bPes., 62b Ch. is probably described as ספר יוחסין (Str.-B., I, 6). I owe this reference to G. Bertram.

[6] Cf. the prohibition of marriage in 1 Tm. 4:3.

[7] Chrysostom ad loc. sees here an allusion to the Gks., i.e., to the myths and genealogies of the gods; cf. Wbg., 31.

[8] Wbg., 31 points to the embellishment of the biblical narrative in the Book of Jubilees, which an unenthusiastic critic might well have called ἀπέραντος as in 1 Tm. 1:4.

1 Tm. 1:4. For Philo in his review of the work of Moses (Vit. Mos., II, 45) describes as τὸ γενεαλογικόν the total ἱστορικόν (the historical parts of the Pentateuch in distinction from the legal) apart from the story of creation, i.e., the whole historical narrative of the Pentateuch. [9]

† γενεαλογέω.

Like γενεαλογία, this derives from γενεαλόγος, the one who gives an account of descent or draws up a genealogy. In the LXX it occurs only at 1 Ch. 5:1 (→ γενεαλογία, n. 5). In the NT it is found only at Hb. 7:6 with reference to Melchisedec: ὁ δὲ μὴ γενεαλογούμενος ἐξ αὐτῶν, "who does not derive his descent from them (the sons of Levi)."

† ἀγενεαλόγητος.

This occurs only at Hb. 7:3. It means "without descent," i.e., without having a place by derivation in the human series, in this case as a priest. [1] How important descent was for priests on Jewish soil may be seen from Ezr. 2:61-63; Phil. Spec. Leg., I, 110 ff.; Jos. Ap., 1, 30-37; Ant., 11, 71. That all those who wished to discharge priestly functions were examined as to their descent is attested by Mid., 5, 4; T. Sanh., 7, 1; Qid., 4, 4. [2]

Büchsel

> γεννάω, γέννημα, γεννητός,
> ἀρτιγέννητος, ἀναγεννάω

γεννάω.

Like τίκτω, this term is used of the "begetting" of the father and the "bearing" of the mother, not only in Gk. generally, [1] but also in the LXX and NT. Figur. it is used of producing without birth, as at 2 Tm. 2:23 and also Joseph.: γεννᾶται ἐν αὐτῇ φοῖνιξ ὁ κάλλιστος (Ant., 9, 7, cf. Bell., 4, 469); in the religious sense of the old covenant (Gl. 4:24), of Paul in the self-protestations at 1 C. 4:15; Phlm. 10. γεννᾶν with God as subj., Prv. 8:25; Ps. 2:7 (quoted in Lk. 3:22 [west. reading]; Ac. 13:33; Hb. 1:5; 5:5). γεννᾶσθαι (pass.) in Jn. 1:13; [2] 3:3, 5, 6, 8; 1 Jn. 2:29; 3:9; 4:7; 5:1, 4, 18.

A. "Begetting" as an Image of the Relationship of Master and Disciple.

The use of the terms father and son with reference to the master and disciple may be seen already in 2 K. 2:12. [3] At the time of Jesus it was customary for the

---

[9] Hipp. Ref., IX, 8, 1 describes as τῆς γενεαλογίας αὐτῶν τὴν διαδοχήν the history of Noetus and his followers in distinction from the δόγματα.
ἀ γ ε ν ε α λ ό γ η τ ο ς. [1] Cf. Rgg. Hb., ad loc.
[2] Schürer, II³, 227 ff.; Str.-B., I, 2 ff.
γ ε ν ν ά ω. Pass., Pape, Pr.-Bauer, s.v.; Zn. J., 74, n. 67; Str.-B., III, 339 f.; Joh. W., Ltzm. on 1 C. 4:15; H. Gunkel, *Psalmen* (1926), 6 f.; Str.-B., II, 287; K. H. Rengstorf, *Jebamot* (1929), 138 f.; F. Büchsel, *Joh. u. d. hellenist. Synkretismus* (1928), 59 ff.; Wnd. 1 Jn., Excurs. after 3:9. Cf. also the bibl. under → n. 15.
[1] For examples, cf. Pr.-Bauer, s.v. and Zn. Jn., 74, n. 64.
[2] Cf. Zn., ad loc.
[3] אָבִי is indeed used as a general title of honour in addressing a prophet, cf. 2 K. 6:21; 13:14. In Ju. 17:10 אָב seems to be the title of a priest. In 1 S. 24:12 אָבִי is used in addressing the king, who for his part uses בְּנִי (1 S. 26:17).

rabbi to call his pupil and the ordinary member of the community "my son," cf. the style of address used by Jesus and Mt. 23:8-10. There was here no thought of begetting, as shown by the application to favoured members of the community. It was simply designed to emphasise the superiority and warmth of the "father" on the one side and the reverence of the "son" on the other. The more significant the achievement of the master and his relation to the disciple, the more he is compared to a father. bSan., 19b : "When a man teaches the son of another the Torah, the Scripture treats him as if he had begotten him" ; cf. also bSanh., 99b. [4] Paul goes further than this when he not only calls himself father but speaks of his γεννᾶν (cf. Gl. 4:19). This is usually derived from the Mysteries. [5] But the mode of expression does not really imply more than that of the Rabbis. Again, though the mystagogue is called the father of the initiates, the word γεννᾶν is not actually used. [6] Moreover, Paul begets through the Gospel (1 C. 4:15), through public preaching, not through a mystery. [7] Furthermore, he begets whole communities and not just individual believers. In 1 C. 4:15 and Phlm. 10 we simply have a rhetorical development of the usual Jewish expression. It is wholly in line with the emotional strength, forcefulness and metaphorical power of the language of Paul. Perhaps some of his contemporaries used similar phrases.

Büchsel

B. The Idea of New Birth by Conversion to the True Religion in Later Judaism.

The idea of "new birth" or "becoming new" by conversion to Judaism is common in the Rabbis. [8] Instead of giving several examples, we shall prove the point by adducing two which are particularly clear. In Cant. r. 1 on 1:3 we read : "When someone brings a creature (i.e., a man) under the wing of the Shekinah (i.e., wins him to Judaism according to Cant. r., 1 on 1:1), then it is counted to him (i.e., by God) as though he had created and fashioned and formed him." Similarly, we read in bJeb., 22a etc. : " A proselyte just converted is like a child just born." The two statements give us a glimpse into the world of thought from which they sprang and which was given its linguistic stamp by expressions connected with generation.

The first statement compares the one who wins a non-Jew to Judaism directly with God. This is shown by the expressions used to extol his work. They are the words used in the OT to describe God as the Creator *ex nihilo* (ברא, Gn. 1:1, 27), as the One who gives man his form (יצר, Gn. 2:7; Ps. 139:16) and as the One who holds His creative hand over him from his mother's womb (cf. רקם, Ps. 139:15). The winning of a proselyte is an achievement of unsurpassable greatness, since it can be compared with the creative work of God (→ 418). Yet this is not the essential point in the present context. More important is the fact that the Jew who wins another to his faith satisfies in an ideal manner the command to be

---

[4] Cf. Str.-B., III, 339 on 1 C. 4:14 under 1 and III, 340 on 1 C. 4:15 under c.

[5] Joh. W., 1 K., 116 f.; Ltzm., 1 K. on 4:15.

[6] This is proved by the collection of materials in A. Dieterich Mithr. Liturg., 146, cf. Reitzenstein Hell. Myst., 40 f. That we have *parens* rather than *pater* in Apul. Met., XI, 25 is of no significance. Apuleius displays a good deal of preciosity in his style. In Gk. the old and honoured often address the young as τέκνον.

[7] That baptism establishes a spiritual relationship is not at all the thought of Paul (as against Dieterich, *op. cit.*, 153). It would contradict the estimation of baptism in 1 C. 1:17.

[8] Cf. on this pt. Rengstorf, 138 f.

fruitful and multiply, which, according to the Rabbinic understanding, is laid on all male Jews as a supreme command. [9] It should not be forgotten, of course, that the whole idea remains in the realm of comparison. This fact prevents us from finding in the statement, for which there are many parallels, [10] echoes of the terminology of the Mysteries. In it we find ourselves within the sphere of rational considerations. This is not altered in the very least by the final saying with its reference to the creation of life in the narrowest sense, i.e., in the embryo.

The totally unmystical character is fully seen, however, only in the concluding observation that the proselyte does not become a true man until his conversion to Judaism. Previously he has been a mere creature. This is the point at which the second sentence links up with and augments the first. The proselyte is reckoned a child because he has only just entered into the presuppositions of true humanity. These are found in Judaism alone because here alone, through the Law, is there the possibility of doing the will of God and thus leading a life commensurate with the being of man as God's image. This is the link between the two statements. This is what links them to all similar statements. This is what brings them into the great nexus of statements which separate the Jewish people from second-class nations on the ground of the presence and use of the Law. [11] The whole circle of thought illustrated here thus stands in close connection with the central concern of Judaism in sanctification. In fact the conversion to Judaism which is here compared with becoming new or becoming a genuine man is characterised in another connection as the entry into a state of holiness, or more accurately of being sanctified. [12] We may thus say that "new" and "holy" are related to the extent that "new" marks off the new state of the proselyte as compared with his previous profane life and "holy" marks him off from his previous hopeless religious situation. "Holy" is thus the religious and moral counterpart of the more forensic "new." At any rate, the two terms are not schematically disparate, as might appear from what has been said. Only in the closest relationship do they describe the situation of the proselyte as it appears in the light of the Law, which is now the predominant factor in his life.

The forensic and rational character of the regeneration of the proselyte is revealed by the implications of his conversion to Judaism. These may be briefly summarised in the statement that the past has now ceased to exist for him. This is true of his previous relations. Since Judaism denies the existence of a solid sexual morality outside the sphere of the Law (→ 325), it recognises no degree of relationship prior to the coming of the Law. The proselyte is literally a new born child in his new environment. He has no previous father, mother or brethren. [13] It is literally true of him that the old has passed away and all things are made new, as Paul says in a rather different sense in 2 C. 5:17.

This is the point of transition to the corresponding terms and thought forms of the NT. To be sure, the Rabbinic material adduced does not exclude the possibility of some Hellenistic influence as well, especially on Paul. Yet this material has also to be taken into account in relation to Paul's statements concerning the

---

[9] Cf. Jeb., 6, 6; T. Jeb., 8, 4, and Rengstorf, *ad loc.*

[10] Cf. Rengstorf, *loc. cit.*

[11] → 324.

[12] Cf. Jeb., 11, 2; T. Jeb., 12, 2 and Rengstorf, *ad loc.*

[13] This has serious consequences in the sphere of family rights and rights of inheritance, though we cannot pursue these in the present context.

γεννηθῆναι of Christians. This is suggested by the existence of an unmistakeable line of development from the Rabbinic קדוש to the NT → ἅγιος; the two complexes of thought are obviously inseparable. We thus do well to take into serious account the later Jewish ideas attested in our attempt to understand Gl. 4:19; 1 C. 4:15; Phlm. 10 and in the last resort even 1 Th. 2:11. [14] At any rate, these are a safeguard against too strong an emphasis on the influence of the Mysteries. We are the less exposed to this danger the more we see how strongly in Paul the forensic element, which controls the thinking of the Rabbis, yields before the purely religious claiming of man by God, which is at once posited for Paul by the fact that in his thinking Christ takes the place of the Law, so that all human strivings and achievements are surpassed and set aside by Christ's sanctification of His people. This is the real reason why existence "through the Gospel" (1 C. 4:15) is for the NT a new being which is not a burdensome duty but a grateful response to the divine action in Jesus.

Rengstorf

C. Generation by the Deity.

1. Generation from God in the OT and Judaism.

γεννᾶν is used very rarely of God in the OT, but it occurs in significant passages. Thus the king addressed in Ps. 2 is begotten of God, as also the king in ψ 109 : ἐκ γαστρὸς πρὸ ἑωσφόρου ἐξέγεννησά σε. Finally, wisdom is begotten of God in Prv. 8:25. In Ps. 2:7 the generation is no more than institution to the position of son and heir; "I have begotten thee" is probably no more than a stereotyped formula. [15] To be sure, Ps. Sol. 17:23 ff. takes it rather differently, but it does not infer the begetting of the Messiah by God. The Targum paraphrases: "Thou art as dear to me as a son to his father, and innocent as though I had this day created thee." In the Midrash on Ps. 2 § 9 (14b) Rabbi Huna elucidates the thought of generation by that of a new creation out of previous troubles. [16] In ψ 109:3 the ἐξεγέννησά σε was probably in the original, but owing to corruption of the Hebrew text, not perhaps unintentional, these words had no influence in Judaism. [17] Prv. 8:22 is clearly adopted and expounded in Sir. 24. It is noteworthy that the γεννᾷ με of Prv. 8:25 is translated ἔκτισέν με in Sir. 24:6 (10). But the thought of the generation of wisdom from God did not disappear in Judaism. What Prv. 8:22 says of wisdom is referred to the Law in Sir. 24:23. Jos. Ant., 4, 319 also says of the Law: νόμοι οὓς αὐτὸς γεννήσας ἡμῖν ἔδωκεν, though it is to be noted that Josephus does not use γεννᾶν elsewhere of God. [18] Thus, even though the Jews do not say that any man is begotten of God, [19] the thought of a generation from God has not completely perished.

Philo makes extensive and varied use of γεννᾶν in relation to God. He can call all God's creating (ποιεῖν) a "begetting" (γεννᾶν) in Leg. All., III, 219. Everything is begotten of God, the λόγος (Conf. Ling., 63), but also animals and

---

[14] Cf. on this pt. Rengstorf, 262.

[15] Cf. H. Gunkel, *Psalmen* (1926), 6 f.

[16] Cf. Str.-B., II, 287 under g.; also III, 21, where a serious weakening of בני אתה is adduced from the Warsaw edition (1875). Cf. on this whole pt., Dalman WJ, 219 ff. and Str.-B., III, 673 ff.

[17] Cf. the material in Str.-B., IV, 453 ff.

[18] A. Schlatter, *Wie sprach Josephus von Gott?* (1910), 15.

[19] Str.-B., II, 421-423.

plants (Mut. Nom., 63). The divine sonship of the Israelites, however, does not rest on a γεννᾶν of God. In the allegorising of Philo the idea of a marriage of God with wisdom or knowledge plays an important role. He also speaks of a σπείρειν of God in man in Migr. Abr., 35 etc. Behind all this stands the wisdom of the Mysteries.[20] But for him the righteous are not γεννηθέντες of God.[21]

2. Generation or Adoption in the Mysteries.

In the Mysteries ideas and processes from sex life play an important part,[22] e.g., the ἱερὸς → γάμος, phallic celebrations etc. A *renasci,* ἀναγεννᾶσθαι, μεταγεννᾶσθαι, mediating a relationship to deities, constitutes the true meaning of the rites. On the other hand, there seems to be no reference to the birth of the initiate through a goddess or to his begetting by a god. In pre-Christian times, at least, the real thought is that of adoption.[23] Now it may be that in the rites the distinction between adoption and birth through a goddess was dimmed. But in the B.C. period there is certainly no reference in the Mysteries to a γεννηθεὶς ἐκ τοῦ θεοῦ.[24]

A. Körte has claimed[25] that in the Eleusinian Mysteries the initiate became a physical child of the earth mother.[26] But he has not proved this from the sources. It may be granted that the *pudendum* which was contained in the κίστη, and with which the initiate undertook a mysterious action (Cl. Al. Prot., II, 21, 2: σύνθημα Ἐλευσινίων μυστηρίων: ἐνήστευσα, ἔπιον τὸν κυκεῶνα, ἔλαβον ἐκ κίστης, ἐργασάμενος ἐπεθέμην εἰς κάλαθον καὶ ἐκ καλάθου εἰς κίστην), did not represent a phallos[27] but the womb of the goddess. But this does not mean that birth rather than adoption is the meaning of the rite. For the Greeks had a form of adoption which imitated birth, yet was not designed to mediate physical sonship, but only the corresponding legal position, cf. Diod. S., IV, 39: Hera adopted Heracles (υἱοποιήσασθαι) by getting on a bed, taking Heracles to her body and letting him down to the earth through her garments μιμουμένην τὴν ἀληθινὴν γένεσιν. Thus, although Heracles seems to pro-

---

[20] Cf. Reitzenstein Hell. Myst., 245 ff.

[21] Cf. F. Büchsel, *Joh. u. d. hellen. Synkretismus* (1928), 59-61; Wnd. 1 J., Excurs. after 3:9.

[22] Cf. Windisch, *op. cit.* and the bibl. there given, esp. Mithr. Liturg., 134 ff.; Reitzenstein Hell. Myst., 245 ff.; F. Cumont, *Die orient. Rel. im röm. Heidentum*³ (1931); M. Dibelius, "Die Isisweihe," SAH, 1917.

[23] γεννήτης τῶν θεῶν in Ps.-Plat. Ax., 371d is not one who is conceived of the gods but a fellow of the gods. γεννήτης is an Athenian technical term for the citizens who together make up a γένος. Cf. E. Rohde, *Psyche*⁵, ⁶ (1910), II, 421, who shows that here as elsewhere in the Gk. Mysteries the thought is that of adoption and not of conception or generation. The καὶ γὰρ ἐγὼν ὑμῶν γένος ὄλβιον εὔχομαι εἶναι of the tablets from Sybaris (Mith. Liturg., 37) is no help. The Eleusinian ἱερὸν ἔτεκε πότνια κοῦρον Βριμὼ Βριμόν (Hipp. Ref., V, 8) refers originally to Iakchos or Pluto, not to an initiate. That the (Naassenic) reference to an initiate is pre-Christian cannot be proved. On the contrary, we have to remember the point made by Dibelius "that syncretistic religions appropriate and assimilate the Christian heritage" (*op. cit.,* 51; cf. also 52). On the touching of the womb of the goddess, cf. what follows.

[24] It is not true that *renasci,* ἀναγεννᾶσθαι, implies a goddess to give birth. The Isis initiate is called *renatus* in Apul. Met., XI, 21, and yet Dibelius (*op. cit.,* 27) rightly explains the rite as follows: "The union with Isis — so far as one can speak of such — is thus effected in this rite, not in the sacrament of the feast, of the ἱερὸς γάμος, of adoption, as practised elsewhere, but in that of migration through the cosmos." Cf. on this whole pt., Büchsel, *op. cit.,* 61-62.

[25] ARW, 18 (1915), 11-126.

[26] *Ibid.,* 12, cf. 126.

[27] Mithr. Liturg., 125 f.

ceed from her body, he is the adopted, not the physical, son of Hera. In the same way the touching of the womb of the earth mother need not signify more than adoption in the Eleusinian Mysteries. Adoption is by a process which imitates birth. The well-known δεσποίνας ὑπὸ κόλπον ἔδυν χθονίας βασιλείας of the Orphic tablets proves that adoption was practised in the Mysteries in the way attested by Diodorus. E. Rohde [28] came near to the correct reading. But instead he substituted a feeble modernisation ("I seek protection in her motherly bosom [or lap]"). He overlooked the fact that in Diod. Heracles was adopted by the divine mother after his death in order to be assured of her favour ; he also failed to note that adoption can be the goal of the initiate in the hereafter even though he does not possess it in virtue of the rite. The ὑπὸ κόλπον ἔδυν can only be a mysterious formulation in the first person of that which Diod. recounts as Hera's action in respect of Heracles. That a formula like ὑπὸ τοῦ κόλπου ἐξῆλθον is not chosen seems to make it quite evident to me that the thought was that of adoption and not of physical birth. The Eleusinian rite is analogous. Körte seems to have been extremely rash in his exposition of ἱερὸν ἔτεκε πότνια κοῦρον Βριμὼ Βριμόν. [29] Even if the κοῦρος were the initiate, this would not prevent the action from being adoption, since this was an imitation of birth and had an equivalent result. The passages adduced by O. Kern add nothing of material significance. [30]

3. Ps. 2:7 in the NT.

Ps. 2:7 is much used in the NT. At Ac. 13:33 the "to-day" of the generation of the Son of God is the resurrection. At Lk. 3:22 (west. reading) it is the baptism as an impartation of the Spirit. At Hb. 1:5; 5:5 it may be doubted whether any specific point of time is in view. If we think of His coming into the world (cf. 1:6: πάλιν εἰσαγάγῃ), or of the beginning of His high-priesthood in the days of His flesh, it is again doubtful whether the reference is to His birth or to His baptism. The birth stories in Mt. and Lk. do not quote Ps. 2:7. There is only a distant contact between this verse and Lk. 1:35: τὸ γεννώμενον ἅγιον κληθή-σεται υἱὸς θεοῦ. In any case, however, we can see from Ac. 13:33 that quite early, and independently of the idea of the Virgin Birth, Ps. 2:7 was used in interpretation of the divine sonship of Jesus. Jesus is accepted as the Begotten of God because the Word of God speaks thus of Him. This begetting is more than adoption. For the resurrection, in which it was consummated, is the beginning of a new and pneumatic, i.e., divine, mode of being ; the impartation of the Spirit is the earnest of the gifts of this mode of being. On the basis of the resurrection and the endowment of the Spirit, Jesus was for the community much more than a mere man in whom the religious life of humanity reached a new level, He was the man in whom the new αἰών began. Generation from God in a very real sense was here perceived by the community. The idea that this generation must be thought of either in the sense of adoption or in that of the Virgin Birth [31] rests on a misconception of the early Christian belief in Christ and understanding of Scripture, and especially of the basic significance of the resurrection of Jesus and the resultant beginning of the new αἰών, in short, of the eschatological impulse in early Christian thinking. [32] Only where this element is correctly evaluated can we correctly understand the divine sonship and generation of Jesus and therefore the

---

[28] *Psyche,* II, 421.
[29] *Op. cit.,* 123 ff.
[30] ARW, 19 (1916-19), 433-435.
[31] In this false alternative there is merely reflected the unresolved antithesis between the traditional understanding of the person of Christ and that of the Enlightenment.
[32] Cf. Zn. and Kl., *ad loc.*

significance of Ps. 2:7 in the NT. But then we can also understand how believers who were sure of the resurrection, and had the pledge of it in themselves in the Spirit, could also believe themselves to be begotten of God. [33]

4. γεννηθῆναι in John.

In John γεννηθῆναι is always used with a reference to the point of origin, mostly ἐκ τοῦ θεοῦ or ἐξ αὐτοῦ (1 Jn. 2:29; 3:9; 4:7; 5:1, 4, 18; Jn. 1:13; ἐκ πνεύματος (Jn. 3:5, 6, 8); ἐξ ὕδατος (3:5); ἐκ τῆς σαρκός (3:6); ἐκ θελήματος (1:13); → ἄνωθεν (3:3, 7). The seed mentioned in 1 Jn. 3:9 is the Spirit of Jn. 3:5 rather than the Word of 1 Jn. 2:14. This birth is thus everything which it is in virtue of its origin. As a birth from God, it is a reality but also a mystery (3:8). Even as a birth of water and the Spirit it is a mystery, because these are what they are through God. For Jn. the authenticity of his statements concerning birth from God cannot rest on experiences and the like, for what he says about birth from God contradicts all experience (1 Jn. 3:9; cf. 1 Jn. 1:8-10). His statements are statements of faith. They are true in virtue of the fellowship with God enjoyed by the believer (1 Jn. 1:3, 6 ff.). Jn. emphasises particularly the ethical or religious and ethical consequences of the birth. These emerge in the doing of righteousness (1 Jn. 2:29), in not sinning (3:7 ff.), in love (4:7), in the overcoming of the world (5:4), in faith in Jesus as the Christ (5:1). They cannot be understood as investiture with a power or position appropriated by man. Divine sonship is all that it is as the fellowship with God which depends on the will of God. There is a parallel in the devilish sonship of the Jews referred to in Jn. 8:38-47. This, too, is essentially ethical; it finds expression in lying and murder. It, too, is a personal relationship of fellowship or dependence.

We can only guess at the origin of the Johannine view. [34] John attributes this divine generation both to Jesus (1 Jn. 5:18; 1:13) and to believers. The former is obviously primary. The description of Jesus as γεννηθεὶς ἐκ τοῦ θεοῦ corresponds to belief in His divine sonship on the one side and to Messianic prophecy, which always includes Ps. 2:7, on the other (→ 668). It is not difficult to transfer the thought from Jesus to believers. For believers are members of the αἰὼν μέλλων in which the promises of Scripture are fulfilled. They participate in the divine Spirit. They share in the eternal divine life. They have passed from death to life (1 Jn. 3:14; Jn. 5:24). Through the Spirit they are in some sense essentially united to Jesus. That the γεννᾶν, applied to God's relationship to Jesus and believers, has originally an eschatological sense may be seen in John only to the degree that the kingdom of God, the seeing of which depends on the birth (3:3; cf. 3:5), is an eschatological magnitude. The terms ἀνάστασις and ζωὴ αἰώνιος, which Jn. uses in the present tense, have also an original eschatological meaning. [35]

It is unlikely that the idea of the divine γεννᾶν in Jn. derives from the Mysteries. There can be no doubt that the application of the idea to Jesus in Ac. 13:33 is completely independent of the Mysteries. And the Johannine γεννηθῆναι ἐκ τοῦ θεοῦ has little in common with what is called ἀναγεννηθῆναι, renasci, μετα-

---

[33] In Paul Jesus is the First-born of many brethren who will be fashioned according to His image and will be co-heirs with Him (R. 8:17, 29). In Rev. 2:25-28 power over the heathen is transferred in Him to believers on the basis of Ps. 2:8 ff. (cf. 19:15), and in Rev. 3:21 session on the throne of God is also transferred to them on the basis of Ps. 110:1.

[34] Cf. Wnd. 1 J., Excurs. after 3:9.

[35] Büchsel, op. cit., 56.

γεννηθῆναι, in the Mysteries. [36] There is a completely different view of both the attitude and possession of piety. Even the link with baptism in Jn. 3:5-8 is no argument for dependence on the Mysteries. [37]

† γέννημα. [1]

"What is born," "fruit." Common, and often used in Philo and the LXX. In the NT only in the phrase γεννήματα ἐχιδνῶν, Mt. 3:7 (Lk. 3:7); Mt. 12:34; 23:33. The par. ὄφεις in Mt. 23:33 gives us the sense. There are no examples in the Rabbis. Nor is this construction found in Joseph. [2] or the LXX. In the post-apost. fathers it occurs only in Did., 13, 3 : ἀπαρχὴν γεννημάτων ληνοῦ καὶ ἅλωνος, βοῶν τε καὶ προβάτων.

† γεννητός.

Often in Philo etc. In the NT only in the phrase γεννητοὶ γυναικῶν, Mt. 11:11 (Lk. 7:28). The formula derives from the OT אִשָּׁה יְלוּד (Job 14:1; 15:14; 25:4). A common Jewish expression, [1] this denotes men as distinct from angels and God, i.e., as earthly creatures. It does not occur in Josephus or Philo. [2] Par. are found in the OT: γεννήματα γυναικῶν (Sir. 10:18); in the NT: γενόμενος ἐκ γυναικός (Gl. 4:4); in Herodot., VII, 141 f.: τέκνα γυναικῶν; in the Mithr. Liturg., 12, 2 : γενόμενος ἐκ θνητῆς ὑστέρας. In 1 Cl., 30:5 we have γεννητὸς γυναικός in a literal quotation from Job 11:2,3.

† ἀρτιγέννητος (→ νεόφυτος).

"New born," rare, though attested in Luc. Alex., 13; Longus, 1, 9; 2, 4.

In the NT it occurs in the phrase ἀρτιγέννητα βρέφη (1 Pt. 2:2), which is a customary expression, as may be seen from Luc. Dial. Marit., 12, 1: βρέφος αὐτῆς ἀρτιγέννητον. On the underlying idea of regeneration in 1 Pt. → ἀναγεννάω; on the comparison of a new proselyte with a new born child → γεννάω, 666. Whether the readers are newly converted or whether the epistle, or at any rate 1:3-4:11, is a baptismal address, [1] is an open question. For in relation to the eternal Word of God (cf. 1:23-25) all men are only just born.

Par. words are ἀρτιγενής in Nicand. Alexipharm., 357, ἀρτίγονος in Philo Aet. Mund., 67, ἀρτίτοκος in Jos. Ant., 5, 11 and βόας ἀρτιτόκους in IG, XIV, 2068, 3.

---

[36] *Ibid.,* 62-64.

[37] What Jn. says about baptism does not confirm the view that he conceived of it as did the Mysteries their rites. On the contrary, in Jn. 3:5 (birth of water and the Spirit as the precondition of entry into the kingdom of God) there is an unmistakeable connection of baptism with that of John the Baptist. In addition, it is no accident that in 1 Jn., as also in 1 Pt. 1:23 and Jm. 1:18, the thought of birth is not linked with baptism. Baptism is not essential in these passages.

γ έ ν ν η μ α. Zn., Schl. on Mt. 3:7.
[1] On the relation of γέννημα and γένημα → γένημα, 685 n. 1.
[2] Schl. Mt., 68.

γ ε ν ν η τ ό ς. Schl. Mt., 364, 486; Str.-B., I, 597; Pr.-Bauer, *s.v.*
[1] For examples, *v.* Str.-B., I, 597 and Schl. Mt. 364, 486.
[2] Schl. Mt., 364.

ἀ ρ τ ι γ έ ν ν η τ ο ς. Comm. of Kn., Wnd., Wbg. on 1 Pt. 2:2.
[1] R. Perdelwitz, "D. Mysterienr. u. d. Problem d. 1 Pt.," RVV, 11, 3 (1911), 16 ff.; W. Bornemann, "D. 1 Pt. eine Taufrede des Silvanus," ZNW, 19 (1919/20), 143-165; also Wnd., Excurs. after 1 Pt. 5:14.

† ἀναγεννάω (→ παλιγγενεσία, 686).

A. The Non-Biblical Usage.

This word is usually derived from the linguistic usage of the Mysteries. The verb, however, occurs in only one passage, which is later than the NT. This is Sallust. De Deis, 4 (p. 8, 24, Nock) in a description of the Mysteries ἐπὶ τούτοις γάλακτος τροφή ὥσπερ ἀναγεννωμένων. Since *renati* can be shown to be used of the *tauroboliati*[1] and in the Isis Mysteries (Apul. Met., XI, 21), the ἀγαγεννω-μένων of Sallust. may rest on a pre-Christian tradition.

In the prologue to Sirach (Swete, line 17), the *vl.* ἀναγεννηθείς א* is an error. In Jos. Ant., 4, 13 we should not read ἀναγεννώμενα δεινά but ἂν γενόμενα δεινά. In the so-called regeneration Mystery in Corp. Herm., XIV ἀναγεννᾶν is not in the traditional text but is only conjectured by Reitzenstein and Scott. The text has ἐγεννή-θη, so also Parthey. To conjecture ἀνεγεννήθης (Reitzenstein) or ἀναγεννηθείη ἄν (Scott) would be legitimate only if these words occurred at least once in some other passage. But we have only γεννᾶσθαι (Reitzenstein Poim., 340, 3; 4; 15) and παλιγγε-νεσία (339, 4 and 6; 340, 12; 341, 5; 342, 15; 343, 12; 344, 12 and 14; 345, 10; 348, 8). It is obvious that Reitzenstein, and Scott after him, must have been influenced by the NT in their conjectures. This is an instructive example of the way in which material is sometimes gathered for the historical interpretation of the NT. The claim of Reitzenstein that ἀναγεννᾶσθαι and μεταγεννᾶσθαι are interchangeable in the Mithras Liturgy is also incorrect.[2] ἀναγεννᾶσθαι does not occur at all in the so-called Mithras Liturgy.

Though Philo borrows not a little from the Mysteries, he does not use this verb. On the other hand, Josephus uses it in a general sense, with no evident dependence on the Mysteries. Bell., 4, 484: ἔτι δὲ κἀν τοῖς καρποῖς (at the Dead Sea) σποδιὰν (ashes) ἀναγεννωμένην (the fruits look edible, but turn to dust and ashes when plucked, thus attesting the judgment of God on Sodom etc.). Thus at the time of the NT ἀναγεννάω was not common, but it was used generally and not merely in the Mysteries, like the Lat. *renasci.*[3] This is confirmed by the use of the substant. ἀναγέννησις. Philo employs this for the Stoic doctrine of the rejuvenation of the world after the ἐκπύρωσις (Aet. Mund., 8: οἱ δὲ Στωικοὶ κόσμον μὲν ἕνα ... ἐξ ἧς πάλιν ἀναγέννησιν κόσμου συνίστασθαι). Elsewhere he has the term παλιγγενεσία for the same thing, e.g., Aet. Mund., 9. ἀναγέννησις cannot be proved to be a technical term of the Stoics. It was a current word (→ παλιγγενεσία). The mere mention of ἀναγεννᾶν does not prove any de-pendence on the Mysteries; this applies equally to 1 Pt. 1:3, 23.

B. ἀναγεννάω in 1 Pt.

In 1 Pt. regeneration is God's act on man (1:3). It is effected by the resurrection of Jesus (1:3) or by the Word of God (1:23), i.e., the Gospel (cf. v. 25). The result of man's regeneration is a living hope (1:3). The hope is here considered only as a personal attitude. The regenerate are thus summoned to what they have as such (1:13).[4] It is not said that regeneration is a static and observable state, nor that it is a psychological factor, an experience. On the contrary, this seems

---

ἀναγεννάω. Kn. 1 Pt., 41 f.; Wnd. 1 Pt., Excurs. after 2:2; Str.-B., II, 421 ff.; III, 840 ff.; Reitzenstein Hell. Myst., 262. → γεννάω, n. 7.

[1] F. Cumont, *Orient. Rel. im röm. Heident.*[3] (1931), 63.

[2] Hell. Myst.[3], 262.

[3] E.g., its use in Cicero, K. Georges, *Lat.-deutsches Hdwört.* (1880), *s.v.*

[4] τελείως ἐλπίσαι cannot be either more or less than the ἐλπὶς ζῶσα.

to be very different from what is said here of regeneration and the regenerate.[5] Nor is it said that the regenerate have acquired a capability or power. On the contrary, the power of God keeps them to salvation. They are posited on faith as those born again (1:5). Their commitment is not a capability which they should have but that to which they are referred (1:23; 2:2). Regeneration has posited a beginning, not something complete (2:2). It is not mystical. The tension between present and future, and therefore the antithesis between God and man, is not removed for the regenerate; it is sharpened. They hope for an inheritance and live in fear of God (1:17). They stand under God's judgment (4:17). There is no question of regeneration being effected in a cultic act or through a magically operative sacrament.[6] Baptism in 1 Pt. is simply an act of faith in which man is cleansed by the fact that he prays God for a good conscience and receives this on the basis of the resurrection of Jesus Christ (3:21). Regeneration consists basically in the fact that one may hope because of the resurrection of Jesus. We do not understand the thought of new birth in 1 Pt. if we fail to see its eschatological character. Not the experience of Christians, but the resurrection of Jesus Christ, i.e., His penetration to a new stage of being, enables us to speak of regeneration as it is proclaimed and believed and as it is thus the foundation of a hope which embraces and refashions the whole life of believers. There is a profound gulf between the religion of the Mysteries, in which man is deified by magical rites, and this religion of faith (2:6, 7; 1:5, 9, 21; 5:9), of hope (1:3; 3:15) and of the fear of God (1:17; 2:18; 3:2, 15).[7]

As the OT and Jewish elements are very much alive in this religion, so the origin of the thought of regeneration is to be sought in Judaism. It is true that the Jews did not describe themselves or others as regenerate. Yet they hoped for a new life for the world and themselves, and they did not speak of this merely as resurrection or new creation,[8] but also thought in terms of παλιγγενεσία and πάλιν γενέσθαι when speaking Greek.[9] The thought of regeneration was adopted as an expression of their hope, though not, of course, of their experience.[10] The great difference between Jewish and Hellenistic religion is that the Jews could only hope for what was already reality and experience in the Mysteries, i.e., the elevation of man to a new level of being. For Christians the resurrection was not merely an object of hope. After the resurrection of Jesus it was a present reality. In the resurrection it was revealed that the Messianic age, the αἰὼν μέλλων, had begun. Believers were now linked with the risen Lord by His

---

[5] The view of Knopf, p. 41 ff. that there is "a feeling of new joy, certainty and blessedness, but also of will, moral power and religious knowledge," is to be radically rejected. So, too, is that of Windisch (Excurs. after 2:2), who refers to "salvation experience" and "realistic feeling." It is worth noting that 1 Pt. speaks of the regenerate only in the plur., whereas Kn. has the sing. (42).

[6] Windisch's statement that "according to the whole context baptism is to be assumed already as the background" is not only unsupported but incorrect.

[7] Perdelwitz, D. Mysterienrel. (→ ἀρτιγέννητος, n. 1) merely discusses the words and does not achieve any living conception of the religion of 1 Pt.

[8] Cf. Str.-B., II, 421 ff.; III, 840 ff.

[9] → παλιγγενεσία. Even though there is no known Heb. equivalent for παλιγγενεσία, it is not accidental that παλιγγενεσία occurs in Joseph. and Mt., both of whom are rooted in Palestinian Judaism. It probably became current among the Gk. speaking Jews of Palestine to express the hope of resurrection.

[10] Cf. Schl. J., 89.

Spirit. [11] They had tasted the powers of the αἰὼν μέλλων (Hb. 6:5). The new birth for which the Jews hoped was for them in some way a present reality. God had already assured them of an eternal inheritance in His Word by the raising of the Shepherd and Bishop of their souls (2:25). This lifted them up already to the παλιγγενεσία. The πολὺ ἔλεος of the Father of their Lord Jesus Christ (1:3) gave them the right to believe this of themselves. [12]

We can never be sure where the author of 1 Pt. found the word ἀναγεννᾶν to express this belief. He certainly did not take it from the Mysteries, even though these may have influenced his use of it. Most likely it came from general usage. The main point, however, is that the term acquired a new significance when used by Christians to denote what God had granted to them.

Büchsel

---

† γεύομαι [1]

1. Strictly "to taste," e.g., Plat. Resp., VIII, 559d; Job 12:11; 34:3 (for טָעַם, as throughout the LXX); Jos. Ant., 3, 26; Ign. Tr., 11, 1; P. Oxy., 1576, 4 f.: τοῦ οἴνου; Iambl. Vit. Pyth., 28 (100, Nauck): φρέατος; Preisigke Sammelbuch, 1106 : συμπόσιον. [2] "To enjoy," "to eat," Hippocr. Epid., III, 1 β : γεύεσθαι οὐκ ἠδύνατο ; 1 Βασ. 14:43; 2 Macc. 6:20; Jos. Ant., 6, 126 and 338; Ael. Arist., III, 39 : οὐδ' ἀνάγκη γεύεσθαι (of sacrifice); P. M. Meyer [3] *passim* : τῶν ἱερείων ἐγευσάμην (a fixed formula in the *libelli libellaticorum* of the Decian persecution). εἰδωλοθύτων ἀπογεύεσθαι is found already in 4 Macc. 5:2; cf. also 4:26; 5:6; 6:15; 10:1. οὐ γεύεσθαι, fasting as a form of mourning : 2 Βασ. 3:35; 1 Ἔσδρ. 9:2; Jos. Ant., 6, 377; 7, 42; cf. 7, 359; of penitence, Jon. 3:7; of a vow, 1 Βασ. 14:24; Tob. 7:11; of ascetic practice, Herm. s., 5, 3, 7 etc. 2. Figur. "to come to feel," "to learn in one's own experience," "to come to an inward awareness of" both good and beautiful things, but also adverse and difficult. Cf. on the one side Hdt., IV, 147: ἀρχῆς; VI, 5 : τῆς ἐλευθερίης; Pind. Isthm., 1, 21: στεφάνων; *ibid.*, 5, 20 : ὕμνων; Pind. Pyth., 9, 35 : ἀλκᾶς ἀπειράντου; Soph. Ant., 1005 : ἐμπύρων (fire gazing of the diviner), Leonidas (Anth. Pal., VI, 120): θηλείης ἔρσης ἱκμάδα; ψ 34:8 : ὅτι χρηστὸς ὁ κύριος; Prv. 31:18 (29:36): ὅτι καλόν ἐστιν τὸ ἐργάζεσθαι; Jos. Ant., 4, 321: τῆς ἀρετῆς (sc. Moses); Bell., 2, 158 : τῆς σοφίας αὐτῶν (sc. the Essenes); Ant., 2, 240 : τῶν ἀγαθῶν (of the fruits of victory); 4, 140 : ξενικῶν ἐθισμῶν; Philo Som., I, 165 : θείων ἐρώτων; 48 : φρονήσεως; Abr., 89 : ἀρετῆς; Spec. Leg., I, 176 : μηδ' ὄναρ ἀληθοῦς ἐλευθερίας; Virt., 188 : σοφίας; Spec. Leg., I, 37; IV, 92; Leg. Gaj., 310 : φιλοσοφίας; Decal., 80 : παιδείας ὀρθῆς;

---

[11] Everywhere in the NT the Spirit is God-given, not immanent and therefore apprehensible in psychological or sociological terms. The religion of early Christianity was from the very first pneumatic. It was from the risen rather than the historical Jesus, however, that the disciples received the Spirit.

[12] Cf. A. Schweitzer's derivation of mysticism from eschatology (*Mystik des Apostels Paulus* [1930], 98 f.). Here the significance of the resurrection of Jesus for early Christian faith is excellently depicted.

γ ε ύ ο μ α ι. Cr.-Kö., 230 f.; Pr.-Bauer, 245 f.; Moult.-Mill., 125; Liddell-Scott, 346.

[1] The mid. is original. γεύω, "to provide for," "to feed," is a rare reconstruction back from it, cf. Walde-Pokorny Vergl. Wört., I, 568 (Debrunner).

[2] On the gen. and acc. with γεύομαι, cf. Bl.-Debr. § 169, 3, also Suppl., p. 300. Cf., too, R. Helbing, *Die Kasussyntax der Verben bei den Septuaginta* (1928), 135. → n. 7.

[3] AAB (1910), Append., 5.

Som., II, 149 : εἰρήνης ἀκράτου; Vit. Mos., I, 190 : ὁσιότητος; II, 192 : εὐσεβείας; Corp. Herm., X, 8 : ψυχὴ εἰς ἀνθρώπου σῶμα εἰσελθοῦσα, ἐὰν κακὴ μείνῃ, οὐ γεύεται ἀθανασίας; 1 Cl., 36, 2 : ἀθανάτου γνώσεως. On the other side, Hom. Il., 21, 60 : δουρὸς ἀκωκῆς; Od., 21, 98 : ὀιστοῦ; Pind. Nem., 6, 24 : πόνων; Soph. Trach., 1101: ἄλλων μόχθων μυρίων; Eur. Alc., 1069 : πένθους τοῦδε πικροῦ; Plat. Resp., II, 358e : ἀμφοτέρων (sc. to do and suffer wrong); Plat. Leg., VI, 752c : οἱ παῖδες τῶν νόμων; Leonidas (Anth. Pal., VII, 662): ἀστόργου θανάτου. The expression "to taste death" is often found, esp. in Sem. languages, [4] though not in the OT (cf., however, 1 S. 15:32 : "The bitterness of death" ; and cf. Sir. 41:1). It occurs at 4 Esr. 6:26 : "the translated men who have not tasted death," and often in Aram. and later Rabbin. Heb. texts : מִיתָה [טַעַם] טָעַם, טָעִים מִיתוּתָא e.g., Gn. r., 9 on 1:31; 21 on 3:22; Tg. J. I Dt., 32, 1; bJoma, 78b; Midr. Qoh., 12, 5 (53a). [5] In these we also have the phrase : טַעַם מֵעֵין הָעוֹלָם הַבָּא, "to taste something of the future world," BB., 15b (Job); 16b (Abraham, Isaac and Jacob). [6]

In the NT γεύομαι means 1. literally "to taste," as at Mt. 27:34; Jn. 2:9. [7] It also means "to enjoy," "to eat," Ac. 10:10; 20:11; Lk. 14:24 (→ δεῖπνον). At Ac. 23:14 the voluntary abstinence which the Jewish conspirators against the life of Paul took on themselves is called μηδενὸς γεύσασθαι (cf. v. 12) until the fulfilment of their project ; this is part of a strict vow (→ 675 ; → ἀνάθεμα, 355). The rules of purity of the syncretistic teachers alluded to by Paul in Col. 2:21: μὴ ἅψῃ μηδὲ γεύσῃ μηδὲ θίγῃς, are taboos linked with the worship of the → στοιχεῖα. These include some rules about food, and according to the apostle they are beneath the dignity of Christians, who are freed by Christ from angelic powers and are thus no longer under obligation to cosmic ordinances (v. 20). [8]

2. It is used figur. at 1 Pt. 2:3 : εἰ ἐγεύσασθε ὅτι χρηστὸς ὁ κύριος (= ψ 34:9 — καὶ ἴδετε). The quotation, with the image of tasting the sweetness of the Lord, is occasioned by the figures used in v. 2 (new born babes and milk → γάλα). As in the latter the author has in view the Word of God as the means of further growth (1:23 ff.), so there is reference here to personal experience of the goodness of Christ which Christians have enjoyed by regeneration through the Word (1:23; cf. Hb. 6:5). On the other hand, there is no recollection of enjoying the Lord in the Lord's Supper. [9] Hb. 6:4 f. : τοὺς ἅπαξ ... γευσαμένους ... τῆς δωρεᾶς τῆς ἐπουρανίου ... καὶ καλὸν γευσαμένους θεοῦ ῥῆμα δυνάμεις τε μέλλοντος αἰῶνος, describes vividly the reality of personal experiences of salvation enjoyed by Christians at conversion (baptism). They have had a taste of the heavenly gift (→ δωρεά, → ἐπουράνιος) of the forgiveness of sins accomplished for them

---

[4] Cf. J. D. Michaelis, *Abhandlung v. d. syrischen Sprache*² (1786), 52 ff. In the OT we find טַעַם figur. for "insight" or "understanding," e.g., Ps. 119:66; Job 12:20, corresponding to the Accadian *têmu*. Cf. A. Jeremias, *Das AT im Lichte des alten Orients*⁴ (1930), 755.

[5] Str.-B., I, 751 f. Cf. R. Wünsche, *Neue Beiträge zur Erläuterung der Evang. aus Talmud u. Midrasch* (1878), 200; A. Schlatter, *Die Sprache u. Heimat des vierten Evangelisten* (1902), 35, 1; Schl. Mt., 524.

[6] Str.-B., III, 690.

[7] The acc. with γεύεσθαι here is perhaps influenced by the construction of טַעַם. Cf. S. Nu. 86 on 11:4 : טְעָמוּ אוֹתוֹ. "they have tasted it."

[8] Dib. Gefbr.², 20 f., 27 f.; Loh. Kol., 128.

[9] With Kn. Pt., 88; Clemen, 190; Wnd. Pt.², 59 as opposed to Wbg. Pt. 53 etc. (cf. already the sacramental interpretation of Ps. 34:8 in Cl. Al. Strom., V, 66, 3). There can hardly be a reference to the Lord's Supper in 1 Cl., 36, 2. For ἀπογεύεσθαι and ἀπόγευσις in magic ritual, which perhaps goes back to the Mysteries, cf. Preis. Zaub., XIII, 359 f., 377, 378; cf. also A. Dieterich, *Abraxas* (1891), 171, 12 f.; 172, 12 ff.

by the heavenly High-priest Christ (5:1 ff.; 9:24 ff.), of the good Word of God (→ καλός, → ῥῆμα), the Gospel, and of the wonderful powers of the future aeon (→ δύναμις, → αἰών) already operative in the present (2:4). [10]

The formula γεύεσθαι → θανάτου (→ 676) in Mk. 9:1 and par.; Jn. 8:52 (cf. the logion, P. Oxy., 654, 5); Hb. 2:9 ("to experience death as what it is"), [11] like ἰδεῖν or θεωρεῖν θάνατον (Hb. 11:5; Lk. 2:26; Jn. 8:51), is a graphic expression of the hard and painful reality of dying which is experienced by man and which was suffered also by Jesus (cf. Hb. 2:9 : τὸ πάθημα τοῦ θανάτου). [12]

Behm

γῆ, ἐπίγειος

γῆ. [1]

1. The Earth, Land as a Dwelling-place of Man.

a. "Land" (in the geographical sense). A definite land which is not named : ὅλη ἡ γῆ ἐκείνη, "the whole district," Mt. 9:26, 31; σκότος ... ἐφ' ὅλην (Mt. : πᾶσαν) τὴν γῆν, "darkness ... over the whole land," Mk. 15:33 and par., cf. Lk. 4:25; ἐκ τῆς γῆς σου, "from thine own land," Ac. 7:3; εἰς τὴν γῆν ταύτην, "into this land" (Palestine), Ac. 7:4; ἐν γῇ ἀλλοτρίᾳ, "in a foreign land," Ac. 7:6. A land which is named : γῆ Ἰούδα, "the land of Judah," Mt. 2:6, following the Heb. st. c ; similarly Israel in Mt. 2:20 f.; Zabulon and Naphthali in Mt. 4:15; Midian in Ac. 7:29; Canaan in Ac. 13:19; γῆ Αἴγυπτος or Αἰγύπτου, "the land of Egypt" in quotations from the LXX in Ac. 7:36, 40; 13:17; also Jd. 5; with the gen.: γῆ Σοδόμων καὶ Γομόρρων, Mt. 10:15; cf. 11:24; with gen. of inhabitants : γῆ Χαλδαίων, Ac. 7:4; with adj.: ἡ Ἰουδαία γῆ, "the land of Judah," Jn. 3:22.

b. "The land of promise." The land promised to Abraham : εἰς τὴν γῆν ἣν ἄν σοι δείξω, Ac. 7:3 (Gn. 12:1 LXX); εἰς γῆν τῆς ἐπαγγελίας, Hb. 11:9; in the eschatological sense : κληρονομήσουσιν τὴν γῆν, "the land will be their inheritance," Mt. 5:5 (ψ 36:9, 11). The land which Ps. 37:11 promises the ענוים is Palestine perfected in the Messianic glory. In this and similar promises (e.g., Gn. 28:13 f.; Is. 60:21), later Judaism took the land to mean either the whole earth (e.g., Jub. 32:18 f.)[2] or the future world. [3]

---

[10] For a closer definition of the gifts of salvation enumerated, cf. the catenae *ad loc.*, and among newer expositors esp. Hofmann, B. Weiss, Seeberg, Riggenbach and Windisch, *ad loc.* The γεύεσθαι δυνάμεις μέλλοντος αἰῶνος is characteristically distinguished in substance from the par. Rabb. passages (→ 676).

[11] Cf. Rgg. Hb., 44.

[12] The ancient attempt at interpretation (cf. J. A. Cramer, *Catenae in St. Pauli epistolas ... ad Hebraeos* [1843], 147 ff., 394 ff.) in terms of the shortness of the death of Jesus rests on a misunderstanding both of the formula and of the context, *v.* Hb. 2:9.

γ ῆ. Cr.-Kö., 231; Pr.-Bauer, 246.

[1] We cannot deal with the meanings of γῆ which have no bearing on the theological understanding of the N'l'. For γῆ in the sense of a. "the ground," b. "the fruitful earth" and c. "land as distinct from water," reference should be made to Pr.-Bauer.

[2] So often in the LXX, in which we find the same universalism of world outlook. Cf. Hos. 4:1. In v. 3 (later acc. to Guthe in Kautzsch) the universalistic concept is already in the Mas. At ψ 94:3 the ἐπὶ πᾶσαν τὴν γῆν has found its way into a number of important MSS from ψ 46:3. In other passages, e.g., Ex. 9:5, 14, 16, ארץ certainly refers to a specific land, but γῆ would be taken universalistically, at least by LXX readers [G. Bertram].

[3] *Pereq ha-shalom,* 21b, Str.-B., I, 199; in the latter there are further examples with reference to Mt. 5:5.

It is hard to say how Jesus or the early Palestinian community understood the אֶרֶץ of Ps. 37:11. Readers of the Gk. Mt., as of ψ 36:9, 11, could only think of it in terms of the earth.

c. "The inhabited earth" (→ οἰκουμένη). Men as the inhabitants of earth : οἱ κατοικοῦντες ἐπὶ τῆς γῆς, Rev. 3:10 etc.; καθήμενοι ἐπὶ τῆς γῆς, Rev. 14:6; cf. Lk. 21:35[4] (Is. 24:17); Ac. 17:26;[4] πᾶσαι αἱ πατριαὶ τῆς γῆς, Ac. 3:25 (Gn. 22:18); πᾶσαι αἱ φυλαὶ τῆς γῆς, Mt. 24:30; Rev. 1:7 (following Zech. 12:10 ff., where the original, however, means land and not earth); οἱ βασιλεῖς τῆς γῆς, οἱ ἔμποροι τῆς γῆς, Rev. 18:3 etc.; αἴρειν ἀπὸ τῆς γῆς, "to remove from the earth (as the place of the living)," Ac. 22:22; cf. 8:33 (Is. 53:8).

d. The earth as the theatre of history : of the past : οὐκ ἐγένετο ἀφ' οὗ ἄνθρωπος ἐγένετο ἐπὶ τῆς γῆς, Rev. 16:18, cf. Da. 12:1; πᾶν αἷμα ἐκχυννόμενον ἐπὶ τῆς γῆς, Mt. 23:35 (Nu. 35:33), cf. Rev. 18:24 (Jer. 51:49); of the activity of Jesus : ἐξουσίαν ἔχει ὁ υἱὸς τοῦ ἀνθρώπου ἀφιέναι ἁμαρτίας ἐπὶ τῆς γῆς, Mk. 2:10; Lk. 5:24; πῦρ ἦλθον βαλεῖν ἐπὶ τὴν γῆν, Lk. 12:49; μὴ νομίσητε ὅτι ἦλθον βαλεῖν εἰρήνην ἐπὶ τὴν γῆν· οὐκ ἦλθον βαλεῖν εἰρήνην ἀλλὰ μάχαιραν, Mt. 10:34, cf. Lk. 12:51; ἐγώ σε ἐδόξασα ἐπὶ τῆς γῆς, Jn. 17:4. In these passages the concept of the earth merges into that of the world or the human world. Cf. the parallelism of γῆ and κόσμος in ὑμεῖς ἐστε τὸ ἅλας τῆς γῆς ... τὸ φῶς τοῦ κόσμου (Mt. 5:13 f.; → κόσμος). Many passages in Rev. speak of the earth as the theatre of eschatological history ; cf. Lk. 18:8; 21:23, 25.

2. The Earth as Part of the World.

The OT and ancient oriental description of the world in terms of heaven and earth persists in the NT (→ κόσμος). Heaven and earth (= the world) will pass away (Mk. 13:31 and par.; cf. Mt. 5:18; Lk. 16:17; Hb. 1:10 f.; 2 Pt. 3:7; Rev. 21:1), and in place of this world, of the first heaven and earth (ἡ πρώτη γῆ, Rev. 21:1; cf. 2 Pt. 3:7) God will create a new heaven and earth (οὐρανὸν καινὸν καὶ γῆν καινήν, Rev. 21:1; καινοὺς οὐρανοὺς καὶ γῆν καινήν, 2 Pt. 2:13; cf. Is. 65:17; 66:22). It would be wrong to emphasise the word γῆ in exegesis of these passages, or to read into them the metaphysical antithesis of heaven and earth discussed below (→ 679). New heaven and new earth is merely the older way of denoting what is meant by αἰὼν μέλλων in terms of the → αἰών concept, namely, the future world of eschatological expectation. Heaven and earth together constitute the cosmos.[5] Together with them, according to the OT view (Ex. 20:11; ψ 145:6), the sea is a third constituent part of the world; the word γῆ is thus restricted to the totality of solid land, which is thought of as a single unit surrounded by and resting on the sea (Ac. 4:24; 14:15; Rev. 10:6; 14:7; 21:1). A further restriction is that the waters of earth are sometimes separated from the dry land (Hb. 11:29): τὸ τρίτον τῆς γῆς ... τῆς θαλάσσης ... τῶν ποταμῶν (Rev. 8:7 ff.; cf. 14:7). Another division is between what is in heaven, on the earth, and under the earth (→ ἐπίγειος, καταχθόνιος). Here the earth is the middle of the cosmos, cf. Rev. 5:3 : οὐδεὶς ... ἐν τῷ οὐρανῷ οὐδὲ ἐπὶ τῆς γῆς οὐδὲ ὑποκάτω τῆς γῆς.[6] The NT, especially in eschatological passages, presupposes definite though not very consistent cosmological conceptions. Nevertheless, in contrast to Jewish apocalyptic (e.g., the books of Enoch), it does not contain any true cosmological

---

[4] On ἐπὶ πρόσωπον (προσώπου) τῆς γῆς, cf. Dt. 7:6; Ez. 38:20; Da. 4:19 LXX.

[5] Cf. also Lk. 12:56; Ac. 2:19; 1 C. 8:5; Col. 1:16, 20; Eph. 1:10; 3:15; Hb. 12:26 (Hag. 2:6).

[6] On the threefold division of the cosmos, v. E. Peterson, Εἷς Θεός (1926), 241, n. 2; 259, n. 2; 261, n. 1; 326.

teaching. Even in Revelation the cosmological ideas are wholly subordinate to the theological.

Detailed points to be noted are as follows. ἐκ τῶν περάτων τῆς γῆς, "from the ends of the earth," is used hyperb. at Mt. 12:42; Lk. 11:31, for "from a foreign land." ἕως ἐσχάτου τῆς γῆς, "to the ends of the earth," occurs in the spatial sense at Ac. 1:8; 13:47 (quoting Is. 49:6 LXX; cf. Jer. 6:22; ᾿Ιερ. 27:41; 28:16; 38:8); ἐν ταῖς τέσσαρσιν γωνίαις τῆς γῆς, "in the four corners of the earth" (Rev. 20:8), the earth being here four-sided (cf. Ez. 7:2; 38:15; Is. 11:12; 24:16; Job 37:3; 38:13; Mk. 13:27; Mt. 24:31; Rev. 7:1); ἐπισυνάξει τοὺς ἐκλεκτοὺς ἐκ τῶν τεσσάρων ἀνέμων ἀπ' ἄκρου γῆς ἕως ἄκρου οὐρανοῦ, "he will gather his elect from the margin of earth to the margin of heaven" (Mk. 13:27), is a rather obscure picture and is thus omitted by Lk. and amended in Mt. 24:31 to ... ἐκ τῶν τεσσάρων ἀνέμων ἀπ' ἄκρων οὐρανῶν ἕως ἄκρων αὐτῶν; what is meant here is "from one end of the world to the other"; the two possible ways of expressing this, namely, ἀπ' ἄκρου τῆς γῆς ἕως ἄκρου τῆς γῆς (Dt. 13:7) and ἀπ' ἄκρου τοῦ οὐρανοῦ ἕως ἄκρου τοῦ οὐρανοῦ (Dt. 4:32; 30:4 and ψ 18:6) are combined in Mk.

There is an echo of personification of the earth at Rev. 12:16 (and Gn. 4:11; Nu. 16:30; Ex. 15:12, Tg. J., II), cf. Rev. 20:11.

3. The Earth in Its Relation to God.

As a part of the world created by God (Ac. 4:24; 14:15; 17:24; Hb. 1:10; Rev. 10:6), the earth shares in the relation of the cosmos to God, of what is created to the Creator. It is "creature" (→ κτίσις), not "nature" in the sense of the philosophical concept of nature. That is to say, it exists only by the will of the Creator and the creative Word of almighty God. Its existence is bordered by an absolute beginning and an absolute end like that of the whole world of heaven and earth. As a creature, the earth is God's possession (1 C. 10:26, quoting ψ 23:1), and God, the κύριος τοῦ οὐρανοῦ καὶ τῆς γῆς (Mt. 11:25; Lk. 10:21; Ac. 17:24) is κύριος τῆς γῆς (Rev. 11:4; cf. Zech. 4:14) as He is θεὸς τοῦ οὐρανοῦ (Rev. 11:13 → οὐρανός). [7] His omnipotence, in which Christ shares as the κύριος (1 C. 8:6; Col. 1:16; Mt. 28:18), [8] extends over the whole world, over heaven and earth. Nevertheless, the earth does not stand in the same relation to God as heaven. As in the OT, the idea of heaven and earth as the two parts of creation is both augmented and broken by the idea of a distinction between them. Already in the image of heaven as God's throne and earth as His foot-stool (Mt. 5:35; Ac. 7:49 on the basis of Is. 66:1) the superiority of heaven is expressed. Heaven and earth are viewed both in their indissoluble connection and also in their differentiation in the NT. This twofold conception appears in passages like Mt. 6:10; 23:9; Lk. 2:14, as also in places where it is said of an event on earth that it has validity and force in heaven, e.g., Mt. 16:19; 18:18, where binding and loosing are both on earth and in heaven, → δέω, or in Mt. 18:19, where there is prayer on earth and hearing in heaven, or in Mk. 2:10 = Lk. 5:24, of the forgiveness of sins on earth. The same is true in passages which refer to earthly things which are ὑπόδειγμα καὶ σκιὰ τῶν ἐπουρανίων (Hb. 8:5), e.g., Hb. 8:1, 4 (the high-priest in heaven and on earth) or Hb. 12:25. In such cases the earth, in comparison with heaven, is regarded as the place of the imperfect (Mk. 9:3; Hb. 8:4), of the transitory (Mt. 6:19), of sin (Mk. 2:10; Rev. 17:5) and of death (1 C. 15:47 → ἐπίγειος). The difference can be stressed to such a degree that γῆ

---

[7] Attention should be paid to the difference in the use of κύριος and θεός.
[8] On the formula πᾶσα ἐξουσία ἐν οὐρανῷ καὶ ἐπὶ (τῆς) γῆς, cf. Da. 7:14 LXX.

and οὐρανός (→ ἄνω and κάτω) are almost understood dualistically as two different worlds, particularly in the Pauline Epistles and John.

Christ is the Redeemer because He is not ἐκ τῆς γῆς but ἄνωθεν, ἐκ τοῦ οὐρανοῦ (Jn. 3:31), not ἐκ γῆς but ἐξ οὐρανοῦ (1 C. 15:47). He is ὁ καταβάς who has come down from heaven εἰς τὰ κατώτερα μέρη τῆς γῆς (Eph. 4:9 f.) and who has thus ascended far above all heavens, lifted up ἐκ τῆς γῆς (Jn. 12:32). At this point the NT conception and terminology are influenced by an oriental myth, based on Persian dualism, of the redeemer who descends from the upper world of light to the depths of the world of darkness. [9] But the ambiguity of τὰ κατώτερα μέρη τῆς γῆς (Eph. 4:9), which can mean either "the lowest parts of the earth," i.e., "the underworld," or (γῆς as gen. epexeget.) "the spheres of the deep, namely, the earth," means that καταβαίνειν (→ 522) might refer either to the descent into Hades or to the incarnation in the sense of Phil. 2:7. We thus see the difficulty of applying the terminology of this dualistic redeemer myth to the biblical Christian faith. For the NT, too, there is a metaphysical distinction between heaven and earth. But for all the sharpness of emphasis on this distinction, the unity of the divine creation is maintained, as is also the identity of the God of creation and the God of redemption and the interconnection of creation and redemption. The contrast between heaven and earth is finally in terms of sin. It is because the earth is the setting of a fallen creation, the theatre of sin, [10] that it stands in a different relation to God from heaven. [11] It is for this reason that the Son of Man has come to forgive sins on earth (Mk. 2:10), that the redeemed are οἱ ἠγορασμένοι ἀπὸ τῆς γῆς, "those who are ransomed from the earth" (Rev. 14:3), that believers are ξένοι καὶ παρεπίδημοι ἐπὶ τῆς γῆς "strangers and pilgrims on earth" (Hb. 11:13, of the believers of the OT; [12] cf. Phil. 3:20) who must be exhorted: τὰ ἄνω φρονεῖτε, μὴ τὰ ἐπὶ τῆς γῆς, "set your mind on what is above, not on what is on the earth" (Col. 3:2), νεκρώσατε οὖν τὰ μέλη τὰ ἐπὶ τῆς γῆς, "mortify your earthly members" (Col. 3:5).

† ἐπίγειος.

In Gk. from the time of Plato in the sense a. "existing on earth," "belonging to it," "earthly," in contrast to what is not on earth; e.g., Plat. Resp., VIII, 546a: ἐπίγεια ζῷα in contrast to ἔγγεια φυτά. [1] Then in the sense b. of "earthly" esp. in contrast to what is more than earthly, or heavenly (→ ἐπουράνιος), e.g., Plut. Ser. Num. Pun., 22

---

[9] W. Bousset, Hauptprobleme der Gnosis (1907); Kyrios Christos[2] (1921), 26-33; 201-206: Reitzenstein Ir. Erl., 56 ff.; 84 ff.; 92; 113 ff.; H. Schlier, Christus und die Kirche im Epheserbrief (1930), 27 ff.

[10] Gn. 3:17: ἐπικατάρατος ἡ γῆ (Mas. הָאֲדָמָה, "the field") ἐν τοῖς ἔργοις σου (בַּעֲבוּרֶךָ = ἕνεκέν σου ['Α], Θ: ἐν τῇ παραβάσει σου).

[11] On the question of the relation of evil to heaven, → οὐρανός, ἐπουράνιος.

[12] This dualistic view came into the OT only at a later stage. Originally God is the possessor of earth (though cf. Jer. 14:8) and men are strangers and newcomers (Lv. 25:23; so also 1 Ch. 29:15; Ps. 39:12; 119:19 [Syr.]), though in these passages there is already a dualistic ring which is expressed in Ps. 119:19 by the substitution of בָּאָרֶץ for עִמָּךְ and in the LXX ψ 38:12; 118:19 by the rendering of עִמָּךְ as ἐν τῇ γῇ. Sometimes in a dualistic sense the term γῆ characterises the vanity of everything earthly, i.e., where it is linked with σποδός in rendering of אפר and עפר as in Σιρ. 10:9 (cf. 17:32). In Gn. 3:14 and Ἰωβ 30:23 (not the Mas.), too, the term γῆ expresses earthly corruptibility [G. Bertram].

ἐπίγειος. Cr.-Kö., 232; Pr.-Bauer, 452; Tillm. J.[4], 111; Meinertz Kath. Br.[4], 41.

[1] Cf. τὰ ἐπίγεια πάντα, ζῷά τε αὖ καὶ φυτά, Philo Op. Mund., 113; similarly Jos. Ant., 8, 44.

(II, 566d). So often in Philo, e.g., Migr. Abr., 178 : Χαλδαῖοι ... τὰ ἐπίγεια τοῖς μετεώροις καὶ τὰ οὐράνια τοῖς ἐπὶ γῆς ἁρμοζόμενοι. ἐπίγειος does not occur in the LXX.

In terms of the three divisions of the world, heaven and earth and what is under the earth (→ γῆ), Phil. 2:10 describes the totality of beings which will bow before the Κύριος Χριστός as heavenly, earthly and under the earth : πᾶν γόνυ ... ἐπουρανίων καὶ ἐπιγείων καὶ καταχθονίων. [2] In the NT, too, ἐπίγειοι does not refer only to men (cf. 1 C. 8:5). In the first instance the earthly are simply beings which exist on earth. Only in trains of thought in which there is strong emphasis on the distinction of earth from heaven does ἐπίγειος comes to mean what is earthly in the sense of what is completely opposed to the heavenly. Thus in 2 C. 5:1 ἡ ἐπίγειος ἡμῶν οἰκία τοῦ σκήνους is distinguished from the οἰκοδομὴ ἐκ θεοῦ, from an οἰκία ... αἰώνιος ἐν τοῖς οὐρανοῖς. [3] The contrast between the earthly and heavenly body (→ σῶμα) here under discussion is developed further in 1 C. 15:40 ff.: καὶ σώματα ἐπουράνια, καὶ σώματα ἐπίγεια· ἀλλὰ ἑτέρα μὲν ἡ τῶν ἐπουρανίων δόξα, ἑτέρα δὲ ἡ τῶν ἐπιγείων. To the contrasting terms ἐπίγειος/ἐπουράνιος there correspond the terms φθορά/ἀφθαρσία, ἀτιμία/δόξα, ἀσθένεια/δύναμις, ψυχικός/πνευματικός, χοϊκός (of earthly material)/ἐξ οὐρανοῦ. To the degree that earth is the place of sin, ἐπίγειος acquires a subsidiary moral sense, as in Phil. 3:19 (cf. Col. 3:2): τὰ ἐπίγεια φρονοῦντες, "earthly minded." In Jm. 3:15 earthly wisdom is distinguished from the wisdom which is from above: οὐκ ἔστιν αὕτη ἡ σοφία ἄνωθεν κατερχομένη (cf. ἡ ἄνωθεν σοφία, v. 17), ἀλλὰ ἐπίγειος, ψυχική, δαιμονιώδης. With this we may compare the idea of the πνεῦμα ἐπίγειον of false prophets in Herm. m., 11, 6, 11-19, and cf. also ibid., 9, 11: πίστις ἄνωθέν ἐστι παρὰ τοῦ κυρίου ... ἡ δὲ διψυχία ἐπίγειον πνεῦμά ἐστι παρὰ τοῦ διαβόλου, and Dg., 7, 1: εὕρημα ἐπίγειον. The equation of the earthly with the demonic does not exclude the fact that demonic powers may also be thought of as heavenly (→ ἐπουράνιος), cf. πᾶς πόλεμος καταργεῖται ἐπουρανίων καὶ ἐπιγείων, Ign. Eph., 13, 2. The meaning of ἐπίγειος in the statement in Jn. 3:12 : εἰ τὰ ἐπίγεια εἶπον ὑμῖν καὶ οὐ πιστεύετε, πῶς ἐὰν εἴπω ὑμῖν τὰ ἐπουράνια πιστεύσετε; cannot be determined merely from the context. We are probably to think of the contrast between speaking in earthly parables and direct instruction on heavenly things, as in 16:25 and Mt. 4:11 ff.

Sasse

| γίνομαι, γένεσις, γένος, γένημα, |
| ἀπογίνομαι, παλιγγενεσία |

γίνομαι.

In the NT we have this Ionic and Hellenistic form rather than γίγνομαι. [1] Usually the term has no particular religious or theological interest in the NT.

---

[2] Cf. Ign. Tr., 9, 1: τῶν ἐπουρανίων καὶ ἐπιγείων καὶ ὑποχθονίων; Rev. 5:3; or again the neut. form : ᾧ ὑπετάγη τὰ πάντα ἐπουράνια καὶ ἐπίγεια, Pol. 2, 1; cf. Dg., 7, 2. There is reference to demons in the different regions of the world on the magic pap., e.g., Preis. Zaub., IV (Paris), 3038 ff., esp. 3043; V (London), 167 (v. Pr.-Bauer, 452).

[3] Cf. Philo Cher., 101: οἶκον οὖν ἐπίγειον τὴν ἀόρατον ψυχὴν τοῦ ἀοράτου θεοῦ λέγοντες.

γίνομαι. [1] On the construction and meanings, cf. Pr.-Bauer, s.v., where there is also a bibl. on the grammatical questions.

Only at Jn. 8:58 is there any special distinction between γίνεσθαι and εἶναι (→ εἶναι, ὁ ὤν), though there is also an emphasis on that between death and eternal life, or between perishing and abiding. The formulation of faith and of the knowledge of God is not abstract and speculative; even Hb. 11:3 speaks of βλεπόμενον rather than γενόμενον.

In the OT we often find a type of construction like וַיְהִי בְ (אַחֲרֵי) . . . וַ, e.g., in Gn. 4:8. [2] Essentially this begins with וַיְהִי, which is then followed by the indication of time either adverbially or in a subsidiary clause, and then the main clause is usually introduced by וַ consecutive. This is not a Greek construction, and in the LXX it is mostly translated καὶ ἐγένετο . . . καί, e.g., Gn. 4:8: καὶ ἐγένετο ἐν τῷ εἶναι αὐτοὺς ἐν τῷ πεδίῳ καὶ ἀνέστη Κάϊν. In some cases the LXX alters the construction completely. In the Aram. it is found only in the Tg. as a translation from the Heb. [3] It is rare in the Apocrypha. We do not find it at all in Tobit and 2, 3 and 4 Maccabees. [4] It recurs only in the Synoptic Gospels and Acts (not in Jn.), and here in its typical form, e.g., Lk. 5:12: καὶ ἐγένετο ἐν τῷ εἶναι αὐτὸν ἐν μιᾷ τῶν πόλεων καὶ ἰδοὺ ἀνήρ, or 5:17: καὶ ἐγένετο ἐν μιᾷ τῶν ἡμερῶν καὶ αὐτὸς ἦν διδάσκων . . . The form is not always strictly preserved. In Mk. and Mt. we have the less Hellenised form without the καί of the second clause, and sometimes without the opening καί. There are 4 instances in Mk., 5 in Mt. and 39 in Lk. In Ac. there is only one instance at 5:7, though a more strongly Hellenised construction is found 12 times, i.e., ἐγένετο with the following acc. c. inf., ἐγένετο having an ensuing δέ rather than a preceding καί (which is better Gk.!), e.g.: ἐγένετο δὲ . . . εἰσελθεῖν αὐτοὺς εἰς τὴν συναγωγήν (14:1). This construction is possible in Gk., being found in the pap. [5] But the construction καὶ ἐγένετο ἐν . . . καὶ . . . cannot be accepted as good Gk. and is to be regarded as a conscious imitation of the style of the Bible. It shows that the Synoptists did not merely use the common or literary speech of the everyday world but sometimes adapted at small points the style of the OT Bible. [6] Even though we cannot make it the basis of our understanding of the language of the NT, there is still something to be said for the discarded concept of "biblical Greek."

γένεσις.

1. The basic meaning is "birth" or "genesis" (Mt. 1:18; Lk. 1:14). Derivative meanings are a. "what has come into being" as distinct from the Creator, Plat. Tim., 29c: γενέσεως καὶ κόσμου ἀρχήν; Phaedr., 245e: πάντα τε οὐρανὸν πᾶσάν τε γένεσιν; cf. Philo Poster. C., 29, where God in His rest is set in antithesis to the γένεσις creation in its movement; b. "life," e.g., Jdt. 12:18: πάσας τὰς ἡμέρας τῆς γενέσεώς μου, corresponding to Ps.-Ael. Aristid., 30, 27 (Keil): οἱ . . . τῆς γενέσεως ἐνιαυτοί; Jm. 1:23: τὸ πρόσωπον τῆς γενέσεως αὐτοῦ can be explained along these lines as the appearance posited with life. This is not very satisfactory, but there is no better alternative.

---

[2] Cf. the collection of material by M. Johannessohn, Ztschr. f. vergl. Sprachforschung, 23 (1925), 161 ff.; also the bibl. in Bl.-Debr., p. 317; esp. M. Dibelius, Gnomon, 3 (1927), 646-650.
[3] Dalman WJ, I, 25 f.
[4] Johannessohn, 191 ff.
[5] Pr.-Bauer, s.v. γίνομαι.
[6] Cf. Bl.-Debr. § 4.
γ έ ν ε σ ι ς. Zn., Kl., Schl. Mt. on 1:1; Dib., Wnd., Hck., Schl. Jk. on 3:6; Kittel Probleme, 141 ff.

2. βίβλος γενέσεως for Genealogy in Mt. 1:1.

This expression goes back to סֵפֶר תּוֹלְדֹת or אֵלֶּה ת׳ (Gn. 2:4; 5:1; 6:9; 10:1; 11:10, 27; 37:2; Ju. 4:18); LXX : αὕτη ἡ βίβλος γενέσεως or αὗται αἱ γενέσεις. The formula is used to introduce genealogies or historical narratives (Gn. 6:9; 37:2) or the two together. The question whether Mt. 1:1 is a heading for the whole book or just for the genealogy in 1:2-17 [1] cannot be decided from OT parallels. The OT βίβλοι γενέσεως are not always the same, and as genealogies they are named after the ancestors rather than the descendants. The OT usage is undoubtedly changed here. Since, however, v. 17 refers back to v. 1 with its mention of Abraham and David, v. 1 is obviously meant to introduce vv. 2-17. Again, such a heading is clearly needed, since otherwise no one would know what the reference was in v. 2.

3. ὁ τροχὸς τῆς γενέσεως as the Wheel of Life in Jm. 3:6.

This expression, which is surprising in the context, has now been shown by the study of religious history to be a technical term in Orphic teaching. [2] Simplicius (6th cent.A.D.) gives us the phrase ἐν τῷ τῆς εἱμαρμένης καὶ γενέσεως τροχῷ. He alludes to Orpheus in this connection, [3] and we find similar expressions among the Orphic writers, e.g., κύκλος τῆς γενέσεως, κύκλος χρόνοιο, κύκλος, ὁ τῆς μοίρας τροχός. [4] Philo too, under Orphic influence, speaks of the κύκλος καὶ τροχὸς ἀνάγκης ἀτελευτήτου (Som., II, 44). But there is a significant difference between the Orphic τροχός and that of Jm. 3:6. The latter is set alight ; the former rolls, but has nothing to do with fire. [5] It is indisputable that the wheel idea is not used in Jm. as among the Orphics. If it derives from Orphism, it is certainly not taken from it directly. [6]

Among the Greeks the comparison of life with the wheel which in its turning brings the bottom to the top and *vice versa* is often found in proverbial sayings. [7] The best known is a follows : κοινὰ πάθη πάντων, ὁ βίος τροχός, ἄστατος ὄλβος. [8] Behind this idea of the wheel stands the popular insight into the uncertainty of human circumstances rather than the Orphic theory of finitude as a recurrence of birth and death and what is enclosed by the two. [9] It is occasionally said of this wheel that it turns irregularly. [10] In this sense it can even be said that it burns, i.e., that the inversions of life bring searing pain because of guilt. If,

---

[1] Certainly not for 1:2-25 (2:23).

[2] Wnd. and Dib., *ad loc.*; Kittel is unconvinced (Probleme, 141 ff.). So, too, is Hck., *ad loc.*

[3] Simplicius Comm. on Aristot. Cael., 168b, 24 ff.; cf. Orph. Fr., Kern, No. 229 and 230.

[4] E. Rohde, *Psyche* II [5, 6] (1910), 123 f.; Dib., 182.

[5] To establish the dependence of Jm. 3:6, it has been stated that the Orphic τροχός burns ; but this is incorrect (cf. Kittel, 162). The wheel of Ixion burns because it serves as a torch for the individual hero in the underworld. But, although Simplicius compares the cosmic τροχός with the wheel of Ixion, he does not equate the two, and neither he nor any Orphic says that the Orphic τροχός burns.

[6] "The expression had already lost its Orphic character and become a current saying for the ups and downs of life," Dib., 183; cf. Pr.-Bauer, *s.v.* γένεσις, 4.

[7] Hck., 162, n. 63 gives many illustrations from the Paroemiographi Graeci, I, p. 458, II, p. 87, 223, 695.

[8] Phocylides, 27; similarly Sib., 2, 87.

[9] Though the two merge into one another, there is an essential difference.

[10] γέλα, τοῦ βίου τὸν τροχὸν ὁρῶν ἀτάκτως κυλιόμενον, Anecdota Graec., I, p. 19; 50; 87 (Boissonade).

then, there is a greater similarity of expression between Jm. and the passage in Simplicius, since both refer to the τροχὸς γενέσεως or γενέσεως τροχός, there is a greater similarity of substance between Jm. and the popular saying. We may thus trace back Jm. to the popular saying rather than to Orphic teaching. [11] Probably there had long since been an interfusion of the Orphic and the popular conception, so that by the time of Jm. an Orphic formulation could be used in the popular and not the Orphic sense. We have also to take into account a Jewish saying that "there is a wheel in the world" or that "the world is a wheel." [12] On the other hand, we can hardly derive the ὁ τροχὸς τῆς γενέσεως of Jm. 3:6 from this, since it is not original in Judaism (including the OT), [13] but itself derives from Greek proverbs. For in the Jewish statement the wheel means exactly the same as in the Greek sayings, namely, the uncertainty of human fortune. [14] Perhaps the best solution is to derive Jm. 3:6 from the Jewish saying. But this means that we must still find its ultimate origin in the Greek proverbs which lie behind the Jewish saying, and perhaps in the Orphic view with which the proverbs have interfused. It is less likely that Jm. 3:6 derives directly from the Greek proverbs, i.e., without the mediation of the Jewish saying, since the tradition of Palestinian Judaism obviously underlies Jm. [15]

In Buddhism there is much reference to the wheel, e.g., the wheel of rotation, becoming and time. [16] The most striking feature is that this wheel is set on fire by self-consciousness. [17] But the speculative nature of this view is too alien to justify any direct connection with Jm. [18] Here again the similarity of phrase should not blind us to the material difference. There may be connections between Buddhism and Orphism, but they cannot be shown, and it is hardly likely that they will be. [19]

γένος.

1. "Posterity," "family" : common in the NT. In Ac. 17:28 the quotation from Arat. Phaen., 5 follows Stoic belief in ascribing relationship with God to all men

---

[11] That γένεσις in Jm. 3:6 cannot mean "becoming" rather than "life" is also shown by comparison with 1:23, where γένεσις cannot possibly mean "becoming."

[12] Cf. Kittel, 142-151.

[13] Kittel, 152.

[14] This argues against a derivation of the Jewish saying from Orphic or Buddhist sources, in which the wheel has cosmic significance.

[15] Schl., op. cit., 219-224 thinks that in view of 1:23 : τὸ πρόσωπον τῆς γενέσεως, the gen. in ὁ τροχὸς τῆς γενέσεως must be understood as a gen. of origin. He does not relate γενέσεως to the origin of man but to that of nature. Hence ὁ τροχὸς τῆς γενέσεως is the sun which according to the Rabb. view burns up the sinner on the Day of Judgment. Yet Schl. fails to give a convincing interpretation of ὁ τροχὸς τῆς γενέσεως in terms of the sun on p. 221. The sun can be described as a wheel, but not as ὁ τροχὸς τῆς γενέσεως; τῆς γενέσεως is surely a gen. of elucidation.

[16] R. Garbe, Indien u. d. Christentum (1914), 60, n.; Kittel, 152-158; Hck., 164, n. 69.

[17] Mahâvagga, I, 21; cf. Kittel, 165.

[18] The flaming of the tongue (Mahâvagga, I, 21) can hardly be connected with φλογιζομένη ὑπὸ τῆς γεέννης in Jm. 3:6. For the former reference is to the tongue as an organ of touch (i.e., taste), whereas in the latter it is an organ of speech.

[19] The vl.: τὸν τροχὸν τῆς γενέσεως ἡμῶν is for the most part rejected, but in the concurrence of the Western tradition (vg) and the Alexandrian (א) it has such good attestation (aeth syP) that it must be seriously considered. Certainly it does not fit in with the derivation of τροχὸς τῆς γενέσεως from Orphic and Buddhist sources. For the wheel of the latter rolls through the world, whereas that of the Gk. and Jewish proverb rolls through our own lives.

γ έ ν ο ς. Pass., Pape, Pr.-Bauer, s.v.

on the basis of their existence. In Rev. 22:16 γένος (ἐγὼ ἡ ῥίζα καὶ τὸ γένος Δαυίδ) is used of the individual, not so much in the sense of Lohmeyer :[1] "Christ represents the whole house of David and is thus its Consummator," but rather in the simple sense of υἱός according to poetic usage (Hom. Il., 19, 124; 6, 180; also in Pindar and the tragic dramatists).

2. In the sense of "people": often in the NT for the Jewish people, e.g., at Gl. 1:14; Phil. 3:5; 2 C. 11:26; Ac. 7:19 (cf. the LXX). It is used of Christians in the NT only at 1 Pt. 2:9, quoting Is. 43:20. At a later date it is used more often of Christians, as in Mart. Pol., 3, 2; 17, 1; Dg., 1; *tertium genus,* Tert. Nat., I, 8.[2] In the NT λαός, too, is used of Christians only in quotation from or allusion to the OT.

3. In the sense of "kind" or "species": the species of living beings, animals and plants, but also of voices and "tongues" (1 C. 12:10, 28).

γένημα.

"Product," esp. "increase of harvest," "fruit." γένημα is not found in the class. age but occurs for the first time in the Hellen. The oldest examples are in the LXX, where it is common in connection with γένημα τῆς γῆς, in the pap.,[1] of which the oldest dates back to 230 B.C.,[2] on inscriptions (CIG, 4757, 62) and finally in Polyb., I, 1, 1; 79, 6; III, 87, 1.

γένημα "fruit of the earth" (lit. what has become), from γεν- (γίνομαι; cf. ἐ-γενή-θην), must be distinguished from γέννημα "offspring of man or beast (plant ?)," from γεννᾶν,[3] though the spelling is uncertain and γέννημα is sometimes written with one ν in the pap.[4] It is debatable whether γέννημα may be correctly used of the products of plants.[5] Philo sometimes speaks of γεννᾶν in relation to plants as well as animals; Op. Mund., 113: ζῷά τε αὖ καὶ φυτὰ καρποὺς γεννῶνται. Josephus has γεννᾶται... φοίνιξ (palms), Ant., 9, 7. Did., 13, 3 refers to the γεννήματα ληνοῦ καὶ ἅλωνος. It is misleading that Hatch-Redpath combine γένημα and γέννημα, πρωτογένημα and πρωτογέννημα, in their concordance to the Septuagint.

In the NT 2 C. 9:10: τὰ γενήματα τῆς δικαιοσύνης (here in the special sense of "well-doing") ὑμῶν, follows Hos. 10:12. Mk. 14:25 (Mt. 26:29; Lk. 22:18): γένημα τῆς ἀμπέλου, is to be equated with פְּרִי הַגֶּפֶן,[6] which occurs in the blessing of the paschal cup in Ber., 6, 1 and T. Ber., 4, 3.[7] The LXX has γένημα τοῦ ἀμπελῶνός σου at Dt. 22:9; the pap. οἴνου γένημα in BGU, 774, 3 (2nd cent. A.D.) and οἰνικὸν γένημα (BGU, 1123, 9 1st cent. A.D.). The expression of the Evangelists is particularly close, therefore, to that of contemporary Judaism.[8]

---

[1] Loh. Apk., *ad loc.*
[2] Cf. Harnack, *Mission und Ausbreitung* (1924), 259 ff., esp. 263, n.

γ έ ν η μ α. Pape, Pr.-Bauer, *s.v.*; Bl.-Debr. § 11, 2; Radermacher, 49.
[1] Cf. Preisigke Wört., I, 286.
[2] Deissmann B., 105 f. and NB, 12.
[3] Cf. Radermacher, 49.
[4] Deissmann NB, 12.
[5] Cf. Bl.-Debr. § 11, 2.
[6] Cf. G. Dalman, *Jesus-Jeschua* (1922), 137, 164.

[7] γένημα τῆς ἀμπέλου corresponds more exactly, of course, to הַיּוֹצֵא מִן הַגֶּפֶן (S. Nu. 23 on 6:3; cf. K. G. Kuhn, S. Nu. [1933], 79, n. 40).

[8] At Lk. 12:18 we should read πάντα τὰ γενήματά μου with א D it sys.c. rather than τὸν σῖτον καὶ τὰ ἀγαθά μου with B etc.

† ἀπογίνομαι.

A rare expression, not in the LXX, though found in the pap.[1]

In the NT it occurs only at 1 Pt. 2:24. Since ἀπογενόμενοι is here contrasted with ζήσωμεν, it means "dead."

Similarly Teles, p. 45, 16, Hense: διὰ τοὺς ἀπογενομένους τῶν ζώντων ὀλιγωρεῖν; Mithr. Liturg., 14, 31: πάλιν γενόμενος ἀπογίνομαι; Dion. Hal. Ant. Rom., IV, 15 (p. 675, 14 f.): τὸ πλῆθος τῶν τε γεννωμένων καὶ ἀπογινομένων.

1 Pt. 2:24 refers to the goal of the death of Jesus, and thus to the divine purpose revealed and fulfilled in the death of Jesus. The words can hardly be taken to indicate an inner experience underlying the Christian, for there is no experience of the full separation from sin, both as guilt and habit, which is expressed in death. Nor is the reference to sacramental experience. Otherwise baptism would be mentioned. 1 Pt. is here expressing faith in redemption (→ ἀναγεννάω, 673 ff.).

Since the ἀπογενόμενοι plainly corresponds to the ἀναγεγεννημένοι of 1:23, the root of both ideas is naturally the same, namely, the Christian interpretation of the death and resurrection of Jesus in terms of the Jewish belief in the destruction and renewal of the world. Even though the term ἀπογίνομαι may occur in the Mithras Liturgy, the origin of the concept does not have its locus here, since the term was in general use.[2]

† παλιγγενεσία.

This word derives from πάλιν and γένεσις[1] and thus means "new genesis"[2] either in the sense of a. "return to existence," "coming back from death to life," or of b. "renewal to a higher existence," "regeneration" in the usual sense.[3]

A. The Usage outside the NT.

The word first seems to have acquired significance in Stoicism and its doctrine of the renewal of the world following the ἐκπύρωσις. It probably received its distinctive impress from the Stoics. It is not attested in the Orphic[4] or Pythagorean writings,[5] though one would expect it in view of the importance for them of re-

---

ἀ π ο γ ί ν ο μ α ι. Kn., Wbg., Wnd. 1 Pt. on 2:24.
[1] Cf. Preisigke Wört., s.v.
[2] Cf. the occurrence in the pap.

π α λ ι γ γ ε ν ε σ ί α. Zn., Kl., Schl. Mt. on 19:28; Wbg., Dib. Past. on Tt. 3:5; Pr.-Bauer, s.v. Cf. also → γεννάω, 668.
[1] Acc. to the rule established by E. Fraenkel, Ztschr. f. vergleichende Sprachforschung, 45 (1913), 160 ff., the fem. -σία replaces the simple -σις in compounds, as θέσις becomes νομοθεσία, νουθεσία, υἱοθεσία and κάθαρσις ἀκαθαρσία. The koine often has παλινγενεσία, Debr. Griech. Wortb., 125, n.
[2] The original notion was not that of human birth, nor esp. of birth on the basis of sexual conception; whether and how far this later penetrated into it calls for investigation.
[3] Related words are παλιγγενής, "regenerate" (first attested in Nonnus Dionys., II, 650 [c. 400 A.D.]), which is formed analog. to ἀγενής, εὐγενής, and παλιγγενέσιος "concerning regeneration" (attested in Cl. Al. Paed., II, 9, 81, 3). The oldest term seems to be παλιγγενεσία rather than παλιγγενής or παλιγγενέσιος.
[4] Cf. Orph. Fr., Kern, Index.
[5] The much quoted passage from E. Zeller, Philosophie d. Griechen I⁵ (1892), 442, can adduce from Porphyr. Vit. Pyth, 19 as the view of Pyth. only τὰ γενόμενα πάλιν γίνεται, not παλιγγενεσία. It cannot be stated with any certainty that the formula was genuinely Pythagorean. The description of the many incarnations of Pythagoras quoted in Diog. L., VIII, 4 from Heracleides Pont. (I, 24, 21 ff., Diels) uses other terms.

incarnation. [6] In the exposition of the Stoic view of the world in Philo Aet. Mund., 89 ff. we often find παλιγγενεσία. Its opposite is ἐκπύρωσις (47 and 76). παλιγγενεσία is more often linked with περίοδοι. Epictetus does not have it. Marc. Aurel. says of the soul : τὴν περιοδικὴν παλιγγενεσίαν τῶν ὅλων ἐμπεριλαμβάνει (M. Ant., XI, 1). Plutarch uses the word in his account of the myths of Dionysus and Osiris (Ei. Delph., 9 [II, 389a]) : τὰς ἀποβιώσεις καὶ παλιγγενεσίας (Is. et. Osir., 35 [II, 364 f.]) : τοῖς λεγομένοις 'Οσίριδος διασπασμοῖς καὶ ταῖς ἀναβιώσεσι καὶ παλιγγενεσίαις (Carn. Es., I, 7 [II, 996c]). He speaks of the παλιγγενεσίαι of souls in Carn. Es., II, 4 (II, 998c); cf. Def. Or., 51 (II, 438d) : χρῆσθαι μεταβολαῖς καὶ παλιγγενεσίαις. Lucian states the Platonic doctrine of souls as follows : ἀποθανοῦσα ... ἀνίσταται καὶ παλιγγενεσία τις αὐτῇ καὶ βίος ἄλλος ἐξ ὑπαρχῆς γίνεται (Enc. Mus., 7). In a fragment of Terentius Varro (in Aug. Civ. D., 22, 28) παλιγγενεσία is used for the new birth of individuals in a new period of the world, and this is accepted as the general Gk. usage. [7] Thus the word has an individual as well as the original cosmic sense.

It seems quite early to have come into use outside the Stoic schools and to have become part of the heritage of the educated world, thus acquiring a more general sense. This is shown by Cic. Att., 6, 6, where return from banishment is described as παλιγγενεσία.

It cannot be finally proved whether παλιγγενεσία played any role in the Mysteries of the 1st cent. A.D. The word occurs only in the so-called birth mystery in Corp. Herm., XIII, where it is used 10 times (Reitzenstein Poim., 339, 4 and 6; 340, 12; 341, 5; 342, 15; 343, 12; 344, 12 and 14; 345, 16; 348, 8). But here the word does not have the meaning hitherto found in pagan Gk., i.e., return to existence. It signifies renewal to a higher existence by means of an incantation. The mystery of regeneration is certainly later than the NT. When Plutarch uses the term in his description of the Dionysus and Osiris myths, it is an open question whether he takes it from the Mysteries or from his philosophical heritage. The latter is more probable, since this is almost certainly the derivation of the parallel ἀναβίωσις. In the 1st cent. B.C., then, παλιγγενεσία is in general use in educated circles, and its use in the Mysteries may thus be presumed.

παλιγγενεσία occurs in magic : Antike Fluchtafeln, 4, 18, Wünsch² : ὁ θεὸς ὁ τῆς παλιγγενεσίας Θωβαρραβαυ. The Mithr. Liturg., 14, 31 has πάλιν γενόμενος.

In Jewish literature παλιγγενεσία is found from the time of Philo. The LXX merely has the phrase ἕως πάλιν γένωμαι at Job 14:14. This is a free rendering of the Hebrew to denote life after death, which is doubtful in this passage. Philo uses παλιγγενεσία of the restoration to life of individuals, e.g., of Abel in Seth, Poster. C., 124, or more generally : μετὰ τὸν θάνατον ... εἰς παλιγγενεσίαν ὁρμήσομεν, Cherub., 114 (cf. also Leg. Gaj., 325 : ἐκ παλιγγενεσίας ἀνήγειρας);

---

[6] The passage from Plutarch Quaest. Conv., VIII, 3, 5 (II, 722d) quoted in Pr.-Bauer, s.v. gives us as a saying of Democritus only νέα ἐφ' ἡμέρῃ φρονέοντες. The preceding καθάπερ ἐκ παλιγγενεσίας is from Plutarch and not Democr., as easily shown from the other version of the saying in Lat. Viv., 5 (II, 1129e); cf. II, 91, 19 ff., Diels. The other passage quoted in Pr.-Bauer from P. Lond., 878, III, 42 proves nothing, since we cannot assert with any precision the meaning of δῶρον παλιγγενεσίας in this pap. of the 3rd or 4th cent. A.D. The pap. has not been printed because it is not legible.

[7] Genethliaci quidam scripserunt ... esse in renascendis hominibus, quam appellant παλιγγενεσίαν Graeci : hac scripserunt confici in annis numero quadringentis quadraginta, ut idem corpus et eadem anima, quae fuerint coniuncta in homine aliquando, eadem rursus redeant in coniunctionem. W. Weber, Der Prophet und sein Gott (1925), 91 f. regards these nativity fixers as ultimately of Babylonian origin, though without explaining their particular doctrine.

and also of the reconstitution of the world after the Flood: Noah and his family παλιγγενεσίας ἐγένοντο ἡγεμόνες καὶ δευτέρας ἀρχηγέται περιόδου, Vit. Mos., II, 65. [8] Josephus calls the re-establishment of his people after the exile ἀνάκτησιν καὶ παλιγγενεσίαν τῆς πατρίδος, Ant., 11, 66. He thus uses in a national sense a word previously found only in the cosmic or individual. For the resurrection he has the formula: ἔδωκεν ὁ θεὸς γενέσθαι τε πάλιν καὶ βίον ἀμείνω λαβεῖν, Ap., 2, 218. This is a paraphrase for παλιγγενεσία.

When παλιγγενεσία passes from Stoicism into Judaism its meaning changes. The new existence to which the world and man come in the new aeon is not just a repetition of the former, as in Stoicism. It is an existence in which righteousness dwells (2 Pt. 3:13). In Judaism the cosmic catastrophe is the Last Judgment, and in contrast to that expected in Stoicism this is definitive. The παλιγγενεσία for which the Jews hoped posited a different moral nature. Even if this does not appear in the language of Philo and Josephus, it is a self-evident presupposition. This change with the transition of the concept from Stoicism to Judaism is of great importance. The word is filled with a new religious content. It should be noted in this connection that in both Stoicism and Judaism παλιγγενεσία lies in the future. In the former it follows the future ἐκπύρωσις; in the latter it belongs to the future judgment. The well-known passage in Cicero (→ 687), however, shows that even toward the end of the 1st century B.C. a present experience could also be called παλιγγενεσία.

B. παλιγγενεσία in the NT.

1. In Mt. 19:28: ἐν τῇ παλιγγενεσίᾳ, the use of παλιγγενεσία is in full agreement with that of Philo and Josephus. The Jewish faith in the resurrection of the dead and the renewal of the world is clothed in this term. The parallel saying in Lk. 22:30 has ἐν τῇ βασιλείᾳ μου. In Mk. 10:30 and Lk. 18:30 the phrase ἐν τῷ αἰῶνι τῷ ἐρχομένῳ has the same meaning. The Stoic usage obviously stands behind this Jewish or Jewish Christian expression, but in the sense of Jewish and Christian eschatology. There is no influence of the Mysteries. [9]

2. Tt. 3:5: διὰ λουτροῦ παλιγγενεσίας καὶ ἀνακαινώσεως πνεύματος ἁγίου. Here παλιγγενεσία is the result of baptism and parallel to ἀνακαίνωσις. It does not mean only attainment to a new life with the end of the old life, nor does it mean only moral renewal; it embraces both. [10] The former, however, is the more important, as shown by ἔσωσεν and κληρονόμου (v. 7). The idea is basically eschatological, though moral renewal is included. No moral change is denoted, for the epistle demands of the regenerate that they should deny ungodliness and worldly lusts. The grace of God is ethically efficacious by way of instruction, i.e., by personal fellowship, and not magically by material means. There is no thought of παλιγγενεσία by magical incantation (Corp. Herm., XIII, 1, 1) in Tt. 3:5. The term is rather to be explained as a further Christian development of the Jewish form of the Stoic concept. Derivation from the Mysteries would

---

[8] The word is used in the same sense in 1 Cl., 9, 4: Νῶε ... παλιγγενεσίαν κόσμῳ ἐκήρυξε ...

[9] So far no Heb. or Aram. equivalent for παλιγγενεσία has been found, cf. Dalman WJ, I, 145. Zn. Mt.³, 601, n. 76 merely gives us a postulate. Schl. Mt., 582 constructs חִדּוּשׁ הָעוֹלָם from similar expressions.

[10] As ἀνακαίνωσις; cf. 2 C. 4:16, where ἀνακαινοῦσθαι is the opp. of διαφθείρεσθαι, and R. 12:2, where the νοῦς is the object of renewal in the ethical sense.

presuppose its earlier use in the Mysteries, which cannot be shown.[11] On the other hand, Mt. 19:28 proves with absolute clarity that the cosmic Stoic view of regeneration came into early Christianity by way of Judaism.[12] And Cic. Att., 6, 6 (→ 687) shows that we do not have to go to the Mysteries for the term; it had long since been used by the educated. Obviously we cannot exclude the possibility that the usage of the Mysteries also lies behind λουτρὸν παλιγγενεσίας; its true home, however, is in Stoicism.

Büchsel

γινώσκω, γνῶσις, ἐπιγινώσκω, ἐπίγνωσις,
καταγινώσκω, ἀκατάγνωστος,
προγινώσκω, πρόγνωσις, συγγνώμη,
γνώμη, γνωρίζω, γνωστός

γινώσκω, γνῶσις, ἐπιγινώσκω, ἐπίγνωσις.

A. The Greek Usage.

γινώσκειν (older form: γιγνώσκειν) denotes in ordinary Greek the intelligent comprehension of an object or matter, whether this comes for the first time, or comes afresh, into the consideration of the one who grasps it ("to come to know," "to experience," "to perceive [again]") or whether it is already present ("to perceive"). The inchoative construction shows that, while the ingressive aspect of the act of comprehension is originally emphasised, this can fade into the background, and the meaning can be simply "to know" or "to understand." This is shown on the one hand by the common use of οἶδα for the perf. ἔγνωκα, and on the other by the almost exclusive use of γνῶσις or γνώμη for the subst. εἴδησις.[1]

---

[11] Tert. Bapt., 5 (*certe ludis Apollinaribus et Pelusiis tinguuntur idque se in regenerationem et impunitatem periuriorum suorum agere praesumunt*) seems to come very near to explaining the λουτρὸν παλιγγενεσίας (Vulg. *lavacrum regenerationis*) from the language of the Mysteries. It should be remembered, however, that the thought of baptism giving deliverance in the Day of Judgment is undoubtedly much older than the contacts of early Christianity with the Mysteries, and also that certain expressions like ἔσωσεν and κληρονόμοι ζωῆς αἰωνίου point more to Jewish Christian eschatology than to the teaching of the Mysteries. It must also be taken into account that *regeneratio* came to Tertullian from the Christian tradition, so that he rather explains it in the light of the Mysteries than creates it from their usage. In any case, the *taurobolium* is not baptism but a blood rite, cf. F. Büchsel, *Joh. u. d. hell. Synk.* (1928), 63, n. 1.

[12] → also what is said under ἀναγεννάω (672 ff.) concerning the rise of the belief in new birth.

γ ι ν ώ σ κ ω, γ ν ῶ σ ι ς. B. Snell, *Die Ausdrücke für den Begriff des Wissens in der vorplaton. Philosophie* (*Philol. Unters.*, 29 [1924]); G. Anrich, *Das Antike Mysterienwesen* (1894); W. Bousset, GGA (1914), 740 ff.; also in Pauly-W., VII (1912), 1503 ff.; Reitzenstein Hell. Myst., esp. 66 ff. and 284 ff.; *Historia Monachorum u. Historia Lausiaca* (1916), esp. 146 ff.; J. Kroll, *Die Lehren des Hermes Trismegistos* (1914), 350 ff.; A. Schlatter, *Der Glaube im NT*⁴ (1927), 214 ff.; 316 ff.; 388 ff.; H. Jonas, *Der Begriff der Gnosis* (Diss. Marburg, 1930). For OT usage: E. Baumann, "ידע und seine Derivate," ZAW, 28 (1908), 22 ff.; 110 ff.

[1] Cf. Snell, *op. cit.*, 30 f. For examples of the ingressive sense of γινώσκειν, *v.* Hom. Il., 17, 333 f.: ὣς ἔφατ᾽, Αἰνείας δ᾽ ἑκατήβολον Ἀπόλλωνα ἔγνω ἐσάντα ἰδών ("per-

The basic meaning of γινώσκειν, and the specifically Greek understanding of the phenomenon of knowledge, are best shown by a twofold differentiation. The term is to be distinguished a. from αἰσθάνεσθαι, which denotes perception with no necessary emphasis on the element of understanding. Since some degree of understanding is present in all perception, too sharp a distinction is not to be made between γινώσκειν and αἰσθάνεσθαι. Indeed, αἰσθάνεσθαι can describe understanding perception in so far as it is unreflective and instinctive.[2] Yet in discussion of the problem of knowledge we must insist on the difference between αἴσθησις as sensual perception and γνῶσις, or ἐπιστήμη which is acquired through γινώσκειν as knowledge deriving from the νοῦς or λόγος; the emphasis will sometimes fall on the contrast and sometimes on the connection. The word is also to be distinguished b. from δοκεῖν and δοξάζειν, which signify having an opinion (δόξα) of some object or matter with no guarantee that it really is as supposed. In contrast, γινώσκειν embraces things as they really are, i.e., the ὄν or the ἀλήθεια.[3] To be sure, an opinion can also be correct (ἀληθής), but only the γινώσκων has the certainty that he grasps the ἀλήθεια, that he has ἐπιστήμη. Thus γνῶσις is related to ἐπιστήμη (Plat. Resp., V, 476c ff.; 508e), but (as distinct from ἄγνοια, → 116) it is not used absolutely like ἐπιστήμη. It needs an obj. gen., and in the first instance denotes the act of knowing rather than knowledge.[4]

The execution of γινώσκειν is not primarily related to a particular organ or limited to any particular mode. It takes place in man's dealings with his world, in experience. It denotes close acquaintance with something (Hom. Od., 21, 35 f.: οὐδὲ τραπέζῃ γνώτην ἀλλήλων). It relates to the knowledge acquired in experiences both good and bad (Hom. Il., 18, 270; Od., 15, 537; Plat. Resp., V, 466c; Xenoph. An., I, 7, 4). It is achieved in all the acts in which a man can attain knowledge, in seeing and hearing, in investigating and reflecting (γνῶθι σαυτόν). Thus γινώσκειν can also mean personal acquaintance and friendship with persons (Xenoph. Cyrop., I, 4, 27; Hist. Graec., V, 3, 9).[5] This is a sense which developed particularly in relation to the adj. γνωστός and γνώριμος. It is also possible that γινώσκειν may simply mean "to be or to become aware of," and that a γινώσκων is almost a σοφός, i.e., not a formal teacher but one who has an understanding of life[6] (Plat. Resp., I, 347d). Yet this use developed

---

ceive"); Xenoph. An., I, 7: αἰσχυνεῖσθαί μοι δοκῶ οἵους ἡμῖν γνώσεσθε τοὺς ἐν τῇ χώρᾳ ὄντας ἀνθρώπους ("come to know"); Soph. Ant., 1089: (ἵνα) γνῷ τρέφειν τὴν γλῶσσαν ἡσυχωτέραν ("learn"). Examples of the wider use may be found in Heracl. Fr., 97 (I, 97, 5 f., Diels): κύνες γὰρ καταβαΰζουσιν ὧν ἂν μὴ γινώσκωσι ("know"); Plat. Crat., 435a: εἰ γιγνώσκεις ἐμοῦ φθεγγομένου ("understand"); Democr. Fr., 198 (II, 102, 6 f., Diels): τὸ (the beast) χρῇζον οἶδεν, ὁκόσον χρῄζει, ὁ δὲ (man) χρῄζων οὐ γινώσκει (almost "know").

[2] Αν αἰσθανόμενος ἀγαθῶν τε καὶ καλῶν is one who can discern between right and wrong (Xenophon Mem., IV, 5, 6; cf. αἴσθησις, Phil. 1:9); the αἰσθανόμενος is the intelligent or perspicacious man (Thuc., I, 71, 5), whereas the ἀναίσθητος is the foolish or stupid.

[3] Heracl. Fr., 5 (I, 78, 11 f., Diels): ... οὐ̈ τι γινώσκων θεοὺς οὐ δ' ἥρωας, οἵτινές εἰσιν. The object of knowledge is the ὄν, Parm. Fr., 4, 7 f. (I, 152, 12 f., Diels); Plat. Resp., V, 477a ff., where δόξα as μεταξὺ is placed between γνῶσις and ἄγνοια; Plat. Resp., IX, 581b, where it is ἀλήθεια. It is the opp. of δοκεῖν or δοξάζειν in Heracl. Fr., 7 (II, 59, 17 ff., Diels), Plat. Men., 97a ff.; Resp., V, 476d ff.

[4] Isolated examples of γνῶσις in the absol. are Plat. Resp., VI, 508e (→ 693); Epicur. (cf. Philodem., Περὶ κακιῶν, ed. Jensen, Col. VIII, 33 f.: ἄλυπον [εἶν]αι [τὴν γ]νῶσιν; Plut. Col., 3 (II, 1108e): ἅψασθαι τῆς ὀρθῆς γνώσεως.

[5] This is where the apparent parallels belong which are adduced by Wettstein in relation to Mt. 7:23; these show that γινώσκειν (and γνωρίζειν) with the negative can mean the same as "to ignore."

[6] Snell, op. cit., 5 ff.

less in respect of γινώσκειν than εἰδέναι, which can mean quite generally "to have an understanding or capacity." [7]

The main question, however, is which mode of knowledge primarily determines the Greek concept of knowledge. Since γινώσκειν denotes knowledge of what really is, it comes to have the sense of "to verify"; and since for the Greeks the eye is a more reliable witness than the ear (Heracl. Fr., 101a [I, 97, 15 ff., Diels]; Hdt., I, 8), and sight is ranked above hearing (Plat. Phaedr., 250d; Resp., VI, 507c, → ἀκούω, 216), this verification is primarily by observation; indeed, the link between the verbs γινώσκειν and εἰδέναι shows that knowledge is regarded as a mode of seeing, for εἰδέναι means "to know on the basis of one's own observation." [8] This is the guiding conception even when γινώσκειν results from the weighing of circumstances or reflection on facts (Democr. Fr., 285 [II, 119, 13 ff., Diels]; Aristoph. Nub., 912; Pl., 944; Thuc., I, 25, 1; 43, 2; 102, 4; Plat. Ap., 27a; Phaed., 116c etc.). Knowledge in such cases implies disclosure and is thus insight; its result is that something is δῆλον or φανερόν (Philol. Fr., 11 [I, 313, 5 ff., Diels]; Archyt. Fr., 1 [I, 334, 12, Diels]; Plat. Crat., 435a). Knowledge is achieved by inspection from without. Its object is thought of as something present and open to the scrutiny of the observer. The observer is himself there, and his knowledge is thus objective; any participation in what is known is limited to seeing. Naturally, γινώσκειν is not restricted to a present object or fact. Whatever can be the object of enquiry can also be an object of γινώσκειν, e.g., the καιρός at which something should be done (καιρὸν γνῶθι, Pittac., 1 [II, 216, 10, Diels]), or what should be done (ἔγνω δεῖν ..., Xenoph. Hist. Graec., III, 1, 12). Hence γινώσκειν etc. can mean "to decide" (Democr. Fr., 229 [II, 107, 1 f., Diels]; cf. κρίσις ἐγνωσμένη, Isoc., 6, 30; ἡ γνωσθεῖσα διαλλαγή, Demosth., 59, 47); and in the language of politics and jurisprudence it can mean "to resolve" [9] and even "to give legal recognition" (Plut. Ages., 3 [I, 597a]). Nowhere, however, is there a complete abandonment of the basic idea of visual and objective verification.

---

[7] This may relate to skill like τόξων or αἰχμῆς εὖ εἰδώς, πολεμήια ἔργα εἰδέναι, Hom. Il., 2, 718; 15, 525; 7, 236, but also to all aspects of human conduct, e.g., φίλα εἰδέναι, "to be friendly disposed" (Hom. Od., 3, 277), or χάριν εἰδέναι, "to be grateful" (frequently, though cf. also χάριν γινώσκειν), or θέμιστα or ἀθεμίστια (Hom. Il., 5, 761; Od., 9, 189), though also θέμιστας γινώσκειν (Theogn., 1141 f.). Similarly γνώμη can mean "reason," "reasonableness" or "insight" (Theogn., 1171 f.; Heracl. Fr., 41 [I, 86, 4 f., Diels]; Epich. Fr., 4 [I, 120, 17 ff., Diels]; Hdt., III, 4: γνώμην ἱκανός; Thuc., I, 75, 1; Xenoph. An., II, 6, 9; Plat. Resp., V, 476d (opp. δόξα), or a good or evil disposition (Theogn., 60; 396; 408; Pind. Ol., 3, 41: εὐσεβὴς γνώμη; Aristoph. Ra., 355: καθαρεύειν γνώμη; cf. Snell, op. cit., 34). From a later period, cf. Porphyr. Marc., 11; 20; 21, p. 281, 19; 287, 17; 288, 4, Nauck; Albin. Isag., 1, p. 152, Hermann; Ditt. Syll.³, 983, 4 ff.: χεῖρας καὶ γνώμην καθαροὺς καὶ ὑγιεῖς ὑπάρχοντας καὶ μηδὲν αὐτοῖς δεινὸν συνειδότας καὶ τὰ ἐκτός. Alone, γνώμη may also connote a clever opinion, a good counsel, a rule of life, or a pronouncement (cf. the definition of such γνώμη in Aristot. Rhet., II, 21, p. 1394a, 19 ff.). Cf. also → n. 9.

[8] On the connection of γινώσκειν with seeing and the verbs of seeing, cf. Snell, op. cit., 20 ff.

[9] Thus γνώμη (→ n. 7) can be "will" or "decision" (Pind. Nem., 10, 89; Thuc., II, 55, 2) in the sense of popular or judicial resolutions (cf. Snell, op. cit., 35; so also inscr. and pap.), just as γνῶσις can be judicial knowledge (Snell, 38, 2). We must be careful, however, not to interpret this in the light of modern ideas of the will, but rather to see that the Greek concept of will and resolve is to be interpreted in the light of seeing. Cf. E. Wolff, "Platos Apologie," NPhU, 6 (1929), 34 ff. on προαίρεσις and B. Snell, "Das Bewusstsein von eigenen Entscheidungen im frühen Griechentum," Philol., 85 (1930), 141 ff.; also on γνώμη, E. Schwartz, Gnomon, 2 (1925), 68; J. Stenzel, GGA. 1926, 200 f. and Pauly-W., 2, Reihe III (1927), 829.

In the Greek world the question of truth implies that of the reality underlying all appearances as true reality (→ ἀλήθεια, 239). The understanding of knowledge as that which comprises this ἀλήθεια is shaped accordingly. The meaning and significance of the Greek ideal of knowledge are plain when we remember that knowing is understood as a kind of seeing. To this understanding of knowledge there corresponds the understanding of what constitutes reality. Reality consists of forms and figures, or rather of the elements and principles which shape these forms and figures. Thus the γινώσκειν of the investigator and philosopher has reference to these; the εἶδος (or ἰδέα) is what makes possible the knowledge of things, as it also makes them what they are. [10] Hence knowing has the character of seeing (θεωρεῖν, σκοπεῖν and σκέπτεσθαι become terms for enquiry) and seeing the character of grasping or comprehending in the original sense. In this light we can also understand the importance of mathematics for knowledge (cf. Plat. Gorg., 508a) and the fact that γινώσκειν can be an equivalent of καταλαμβάνειν and γνῶσις of κατάληψις. On the one side, therefore, the truly real, which is to be comprehended in such knowledge, is thought of as the eternal and timeless reality which is constant in all change and is seen by the ὄμμα ψυχῆς. On the other hand, the one who sees really "has" this reality, and is thus assured that he can control as well as know it. As distinct from δόξα, ἐπιστήμη is "bound" (Plat. Men., 98a); it confers possession (Plat. Theaet., 209e: τὸ γὰρ γνῶναι ἐπιστήμην που λαβεῖν ἐστιν; Phaed., 75d: τὸ γὰρ εἰδέναι τοῦτ' ἔστιν, λαβόντα του ἐπιστήμην ἔχειν καὶ μὴ ἀπολωλεκέναι). The reality of what is known, however, is constituted by the essential content of what is known as this is appropriated in knowledge. Hence the knowledge of what really is can be the supreme possibility of existence, for in it the one who knows encounters the eternal and participates in it. Though the ideal of this γνῶσις is largely identical with the ideal of the βίος θεωρητικός, [11] there are naturally differences. For knowledge relates not merely to the elements or ideas which form the world of nature but also to those which give form and consistency to the human βίος and πόλις, i.e., ἀρετή and the καλόν (e.g., Plato Resp., V, 476cd: The man who has the capacity for the καθορᾶν of the καλόν is a γιγνώσκων). Thus for Plato γνῶσις or ἐπιστήμη is the presupposition of right political action. Knowing is here a seeing, and action a fashioning of the τέχνη, of the artist, who gives form to matter as he contemplates the idea. Similarly, for Aristotle existence achieves its supreme possibility in disinterested scientific consideration, in θεωρία. [12]

B. The Gnostic Usage.

The usage of Hellenism, and especially of Gnosticism, is to some extent pre-

---

[10] It obviously makes no difference when instead of the εἴδη (apart from Plato, cf. e.g., Antiphon Fr., 1 [II, 292, 5 ff., Diels]) the Pythagoreans speak of the ἀριθμοί, for these are what make knowledge possible by giving things form and limit (Philol. Fr., 3; 4; 6; 11 [I, 310 ff., Diels]); cf. also J. Stenzel, *Zahl u. Gestalt bei Platon u. Aristoteles*[2] (1932). Similarly the atoms of Democritus, which are different in their σχήματι or εἴδει (Aristot. Phys., I, 2, p. 184b, 21), serve to explain differences of quality as differences of form, order and situation; indeed, he seems to have called the atoms ἰδέαι as well (Diels, II, 26, 35).

[11] Cf. on this pt. F. Boll, "Vita contemplativa" (SAH, 1920); W. Jaeger, "Über Ursprung und Kreislauf des philos. Lebensideals" (SAB, 1928, 390 ff.).

[12] It is worth noting, and is perhaps to be explained as a Semitism, that from the Hellenistic period γινώσκειν is also used in the sexual sense, *v.* Moult.-Mill. and Pr.-Bauer, *s.v.*

pared by classical development.[13] Yet it also derives from other sources : from the Mystery religions, which mediate secret knowledge leading to salvation ; and from magic, whose knowledge confers supernatural powers.[14] Our present concern, of course, is simply to describe the technical use of γινώσκειν (γνῶσις) and not the general use, which remains unchanged in its religious application.[15] The γνῶσις which is the goal of the Hellenistic piety which (both outside and inside Christianity) we describe as Gnostic, is characterised by the following elements.

a. Γνῶσις here connotes knowledge as well as the act of knowing, and it can thus be used in the absolute without any supplementary genitive, though what is meant is not knowledge generally (ἐπιστήμη) but the knowledge of God. There is a formal similarity when Plato says (Resp., VI, 508e) that the idea of the ἀγαθόν is more lofty than γνῶσις (in the absol.) and ἀλήθεια. And if it is self-evident for Plato that γνῶσις in its concern for what really is attains to the divine, in Gnostic sources God is regarded much more exclusively as the self-evident object of γνῶσις. He is so, indeed, against the background of a dualism[16] which does not accept the Greek view that the deity is beyond the world of becoming in the sense of a reality that underlies all becoming, but which conceives of this transcendence in terms of an absolute separation from all becoming, so that we cannot discover the Godhead by a "recognitive" contemplation of the world but only by turning away from it (cf. Corp. Herm., X, 5 and → ἄγνωστος). This

---

[13] Empedocles and Plato already describe philosophy by analogy with mystical initiation (for Plato cf. Rohde, *Psyche,* II, 281 ff.; Anrich, *Das antike Mysterienwesen,* 63); but for Plato this is only a metaphor, whereas Neo-Platonism takes it seriously (cf. Anrich, 66 ff.; P. Friedländer, *Platon* I [1928] 68 ff.; cf. also on the whole pt. J. Stenzel, *Platon der Erzieher* [1928]). The important expositions in Plut. Is. et Os., 1; 2 (II, 351de) are still essentially Greek ; the blessedness of God consists in ἐπιστήμη and φρόνησις. Οἶμαι δὲ καὶ τῆς αἰωνίου ζωῆς, ἣν ὁ θεὸς εἴληχεν, εὔδαιμον εἶναι τὸ τῇ γνώσει μὴ προαπολιπεῖν τὰ γινόμενα ("not to be behind reality in knowledge," Parthey) τοῦ δὲ γινώσκειν τὰ ὄντα καὶ φρονεῖν ἀφαιρεθέντος οὐ βίον ἀλλὰ χρόνον εἶναι τὴν ἀθανασίαν. Διὸ θειότητος ὄρεξίς ἐστιν ἡ τῆς ἀληθείας, μάλιστα τὲ τῆς περὶ θεῶν ἔφεσις, ὥσπερ ἀνάληψιν ἱερῶν τὴν μάθησιν ἔχουσα καὶ τὴν ζήτησιν ("especially concern for the knowledge of the gods, which both learning and investigation serve in the attainment of what is holy," Parthey). Worth commending is a σώφρων δίαιτα, abstemiousness and participation in the cult of the temple, ὧν τέλος ἐστὶν ἡ τοῦ πρώτου καὶ κυρίου καὶ νοητοῦ γνῶσις, ὃν ἡ θεὸς (Isis) παρακαλεῖ ζητεῖν παρ' αὐτῇ καὶ μετ' αὐτῆς ὄντα καὶ συνόντα. Τοῦ δ' ἱεροῦ τοὔνομα καὶ σαφῶς ἐπαγγέλλεται καὶ γνῶσιν καὶ εἴδησιν τοῦ ὄντος· ὀνομάζεται γὰρ Ἰσεῖον, ὡς εἰσομένων τὸ ὄν, ἂν μετὰ λόγου καὶ ὁσίως εἰς τὰ ἱερὰ παρέλθωμεν τῆς θεοῦ.
[14] Cf. Reitzenstein Hell. Myst., 295 f.; 300 ff.; Kroll, *Die Lehren des Hermes Trismegistos,* 326 ff.; esp. 366 f.; 382 f.; Anrich, *op. cit.,* 78 ff.; W. Bousset, Pauly-W., VII (1912), 1521 ff. The connection with the view of the Mysteries (cf. also → n. 13) is illustrated by the esoteric character of γνῶσις and by its description as λόγος ἀπόρρητος καὶ μυστικός, Hipp. Ref., V, 7, 22. The connection with magic is shown, e.g., in Epiph., 31, 7, 8 (I, p. 397, 9): τὸ δὲ τάγμα τὸ πνευματικὸν ἑαυτοὺς λέγουσιν, ὥσπερ καὶ γνωστικούς, καὶ μηδὲ καμάτου ἐπιδεομένους ἢ μόνον τῆς γνώσεως καὶ τῶν ἐπιρρημάτων τῶν αὐτῶν μυστηρίων. As the magician can address God: δῶρόν μοι ἐδωρήσω τὴν τοῦ μεγίστου σου ὀνόματος γνῶσιν (Preis. Zaub., II, 128), so he himself can be addressed : ὦ μακάριε μύστα τῆς ἱερᾶς μαγείας (*ibid.,* I, 127); thus μαγεία and γνῶσις are equivalent. Similarly, Philo can call ὀπτικὴ ἐπιστήμη, which means the same as γνῶσις, an ἀληθὴς μαγική, Spec. Leg., III, 100.
[15] On the knowledge of God in Stoicism → ἄγνωστος.
[16] Cf. on this pt. W. Bousset, *Kyrios Christos*[2] (1921), 183 ff.; NGG (1914), 706 ff. and Pauly-W., VII (1912), 1507 ff.; 1518 ff.

means, however, that the knowledge with which the Gnostics were concerned, in contrast to that of the Greeks, was distinct from all other kinds of knowledge ; and this is in keeping with the restriction of ἀλήθεια (→ 240) and οὐσία to the divine reality and nature.

b. While γινώσκειν is for the Greeks the cultivated methodical activity of the νοῦς or λόγος, fulfilled in science and particularly philosophy, the γνῶσις of the Gnostic, both as process and result, is a χάρισμα which is given by God to man. It is thus radically distinguished from rational thought ; it is illumination. [17] God is inaccessible to man as such (→ ἄγνωστος). But he knows men, i.e., the pious, and reveals Himself to them : γνωσθῆναι βούλεται καὶ γινώσκεται τοῖς ἰδίοις (Corp. Herm., I, 31; cf. VII, 2; X, 4 and 15 : οὐκ ἄρα ἀγνοεῖ τὸν ἄνθρωπον ὁ θεός, ἀλλὰ καὶ πάνυ γνωρίζει καὶ θέλει γνωρίζεσθαι; Ascl., 29b [Hermetica, I, 370, 6 f., Scott]; Cl. Al. Exc. ex Theod., 7; Porphyr. Adv. Marc., 13 and 21 [p. 283, 9; 288, 14, Nauck]; Cl. Al. Strom., V, 11, 71; O. Sol. 6:6 f.; 7:12 f.; 8:8 ff.; 15:1 ff. etc.). [18] Such γνῶσις is ecstatic or mystical vision, [19] and to this extent knowing is still understood as a kind of seeing, though in the sense of mystic vision rather than the older Greek sense. It does not make what is seen a possession of the one who sees. On the contrary, he must pray that he may be kept in γνῶσις. [20] Not merely the culmination of the divine vision is described as γνῶσις, but more often the way which leads to it and whose goal is θεωρία in

---

[17] If γνῶσις is often traced back to νοῦς or λόγος, this does not imply a human capacity but the supernatural power which flows into man and enlightens him, e.g., Corp. Herm., I, 2, 22 f.; IV, 3 ff. (the divine νοῦς is here distinguished from the human λόγος). In such cases νοῦς or λόγος really stands for πνεῦμα, cf. Reitzenstein Hell. Myst., 328 ff.

[18] Cf. for γνῶσις as χάρισμα R. Liechtenhan, Die Offenbarung im Gnosticismus (1901), 98 ff.; E. Norden, Agnostos Theos (1913), 287 f.; Kroll, Die Lehren des Hermes Trismegistos, 354, and esp. Reitzenstein Hell. Myst., 285 ff., with the thanksgiving of the Logos teleios which is found there and in Scott, I, 374 ff. Cf. also H. Schlier, Religionsgesch. Unters. z. d. Ignatiusbriefen (1929), 58 f.

[19] For a description of the vision, cf. esp. Corp. Herm., I, 30; X, 4-6; XIII, 13 ff.; Stob. Ecl., I, 189, 21 (Hermetica, I, 418, 12 ff., Scott); Kroll, Die Lehren des Herm. Trism., 355 f. On the use of ὁρᾶν, θεᾶσθαι, etc. as synon. of γινώσκειν, cf. Kroll, 352; Reitzenstein Hell. Myst., 352. Plotinus avoids the expression γνῶσις for the mystical vision. He calls it θέα, while γνῶσις is the scientific knowledge which helps prepare for it (Enn., VI, 7, 36 [II, p. 469, 20 ff.]). γνῶσις has to do with the εἴδη (VI, 9, 3; II, p. 510, 26 f.), and in the θέα of the ἕν the soul must be ἀνείδεος (VI, 9, 7 [II, p. 518, 6 ff.]). Even the ἕν itself has no γιγνώσκειν, though ἄγνοια is not on this account to be ascribed to it (VI, 9, 6 [II, p. 515, 20 f.]). The scientific grasp of the concept of the ἕν can, of course, be described as γινώσκειν (VI, 9, 5 [II, p. 515, 3 ff.]). Cf. Norden, Agnostos Theos, 89, 1.

[20] Corp. Herm., I, 32; Logos teleios, Herm., I, 376, 12 ff., Scott; Cl. Al. Strom., VII, 7, 46. In Cl. γνῶσις can, of course, become ἕξις through ἄσκησις, Strom., IV, 22, 139; VI, 9, 71; 74; 78 (ἡ γνῶσις ... οὕτως ἐν ἕξει τελειωθεῖσα τῇ μυστικῇ ἀμετάπτωτος δι᾽ ἀγάπην μένει).

[21] On γνῶσις as way, cf. Corp. Herm., IV, 8; 11; VII, 1 ff.; X, 15 (γνῶσις as εἰς τὸν Ὄλυμπον ἀνάβασις). In the Naassene hymn (Hipp. Ref., V, 10, 2 the Redeemer says :
σφραγῖδας ἔχων καταβήσομαι,
αἰῶνας ὅλους διοδεύσω,
μυστήρια πάντα δ᾽ ἀνοίξω,
μορφὰς δὲ θεῶν ἐπιδείξω·
[καὶ] τὰ κεκρυμμένα τῆς ἁγίας ὁδοῦ,
γνῶσιν καλέσας, παραδώσω.
Iambl. Myst., 10, 5, p. 291, 7 ff., Parthey on γνῶσις : σῴζει τὴν ἀληθινὴν ζωὴν ἐπὶ τὸν πατέρα αὐτῆς ἀνάγουσα. It is thus τῆς εὐδαιμονίας ὁδός, a θύρα πρὸς θεὸν τὸν δημιουργὸν τῶν ὅλων. Cl. Al. Strom., IV, 6, 39. Cf. Kroll, op. cit., 380 ff.; Reitzenstein Hell. Myst., 295; R. Bultmann, ZNW, 29 (1930), 173 ff.

the sense of ecstatic mystical vision (Cl. Al. Strom., VI, 7, 61). [21] Since on this way there is imparted a knowledge which can be possessed, a medley of mythological and philosophical tradition penetrates into Gnosticism, and in certain types and strata it is hard to distinguish Gnosticism from philosophical speculation. In Philo and Plotinus true scientific philosophy precedes mystical vision. But in consistent Gnosticism the fiction is maintained that all knowledge preparatory to vision is a gift of divine revelation imparted to the believer by tradition (→ παράδοσις). It is an esoteric knowledge, and the instruction is more like the teaching of initiates than philosophical instruction. The prerequisite is not a controlling enquiry but the hearing of faith. [22] At the primitive stage the knowledge imparted to the Gnostic by sacred παράδοσις guarantees the ascent of his soul after death (Iren., I, 21, 5 [MPG, 7, 665 ff.]); at a higher stage the regeneration of the initiate takes place with the hearing of the λόγος παλιγγενεσίας as an efficacious mystical or magical formula (Corp. Herm., XIII).

The content of the doctrine is cosmology and anthropology, but wholly from the standpoint of soteriology. The teaching can thus embrace τὰ ἐπὶ γῆς, τὰ ἐν οὐρανῷ, καὶ εἴ τί ἐστιν ὑπὲρ οὐρανόν (Corp. Herm., IV, 5; cf. I, 3 and 27), particularly astrological secrets; [23] but all knowledge serves the knowledge of self which is the condition of redemption and the vision of God. Self-knowledge, however, does not mean becoming perspicuous to oneself in the Gk. sense (ἑαυτὸν ἐξετάζειν, Plat. Ap., 38a), i.e., as reflection on one's spiritual endowment and abilities. It is knowledge of the tragic history of the soul, which, coming from the world of light, is entangled in matter. It is knowledge of the Whence and Whither. [24] He who knows that he originally comes from ζωή and φῶς will return thither (Corp. Herm., I, 21). Thus although this γνῶσις includes cosmological speculation, it is not a theoretically dogmatic faith. Knowledge of self implies a definite life decision (Corp. Herm., IV, 6) and is followed by a distinctive attitude to life. Knowledge of the καλόν, however, does not serve the shaping of the world as in Plato, but rather aversion from it; the ἀναγνωρίσας ἑαυτόν is contrasted with the ἀγαπήσας ἐκ πλάνης ἔρωτος τὸ σῶμα. γνῶσις is a definite εὐσέβεια, [25] and ἄγνοια (ἀγνωσία) is not merely ignorance but also κακία

---

[22] For πίστις in Gnosticism, cf. Corp. Herm., I, 32; IX, 10; XI, 1; esp. IV, 4 f.; 9; Ascl., III (Herm., I, p. 366, 7; 9; 20; 370, 12 and 15, Scott); Porphyr. Adv. Marc., 21; 22; 24 (p. 288, 7; 22 f.; 289, 18 ff., Nauck). Cf. Reitzenstein Hell. Myst., 234 f.; 385 ff.

[23] Cf. Kroll, op. cit., 367 ff.

[24] Cl. Al. Exc. ex Theod., 78: ἔστιν δὲ οὐ τὸ λουτρὸν μόνον τὸ ἐλευθεροῦν, ἀλλὰ καὶ ἡ γνῶσις, τίνες ἦμεν, τί γεγόναμεν· ποῦ ἦμεν ἢ ποῦ ἐβλήθημεν· ποῦ σπεύδομεν, πόθεν λυτρούμεθα· τί γέννησις, τί ἀναγέννησις. Acc. to Hipp. Ref., V, 16, 1 the Peratae say: μόνοι δὲ ... ἡμεῖς οἱ τὴν ἀνάγκην τῆς γενέσεως ἐγνωκότες καὶ τὰς ὁδούς, δι' ὧν εἰσελήλυθεν ὁ ἄνθρωπος εἰς τὸν κόσμον, ἀκριβῶς δεδιδαγμένοι διελθεῖν καὶ περᾶσαι τὴν φθορὰν μόνοι δυνάμεθα. Ibid., V, 6, 6: νομίζουσιν εἶναι τὴν γνῶσιν αὐτοῦ (of the ἄνθρωπος) ἀρχὴν τοῦ δύνασθαι γνῶναι τὸν θεόν, λέγοντες οὕτως· "ἀρχὴ τελειώσεως γνῶσις ἀ<νθρώπου, θεοῦ δὲ> γνῶσις ἀπηρτισμένη τελείωσις." Act. Thom., 15, p. 121, 12 f. Corp. Herm., I, 19; 21; IV, 4 f. (ἀγνοοῦντες ἐπὶ τί γεγόνασι καὶ ὑπὸ τίνος). Lidz. Joh., 170, 18; 171, 17; 180, 15 f. Cf. Norden, op. cit., 102 ff.; Kroll, op. cit., 372 ff.; Bousset, Kyrios Christos, 201 f.; Reitzenstein Hell. Myst., 291; G. P. Wetter, ZNW, 18 (1917/18), 49 ff. The thought of self-knowledge is developed rather more philosophically, e.g., in Hierocl. Carm. Aur., p. 137 ff., Mullach (esp. p. 141, 2 ff.; 142, 1 ff.); Plotin. Enn., VI, 9, 7 (II, p. 518, 28 f.): ὁ δὲ μαθὼν ἑαυτὸν εἰδήσει καὶ ὁπόθεν (cf. also V, 1, 1); Porphyr. Abst., III, 27 (p. 226, 15 ff., Nauck): (the wicked man) εἴκει τε τῷ θνητῷ τῆς φύσεως αὐτοῦ, ἕως τὸν ὄντως ἑαυτὸν οὐκ ἐγνώρισεν. There is a moralistic turn in Cl. Al. Paed., III, 1, 1, 1; Strom., III, 6, 44.

[25] Corp. Herm., I, 22; 27; IX, 9; X, 21; Hermet. Fr. in Lact. Inst., II, 15, 6 (I, 536, No. 10, Scott): ἡ γὰρ εὐσέβεια γνῶσίς ἐστιν τοῦ θεοῦ; Cl. Al. Strom., II, 10, 46; III, 6, 43 f. (on the connection between γνῶσις and πολιτεία τοῦ βίου); VII, 12, 71: γνῶσις as a λογικὸς

τῆς ψυχῆς. [26]

c. If γινώσκειν as the investigation of truth brings the Greek into proximity to deity, because in intellectual consideration of true reality he finds his own true being, γνῶσις invests the Gnostic with the divine nature, and therefore in the first instance with immortality. By his vision he is transformed from a man into God. [27] Indeed, the very γνῶσις which leads to this is regarded as a divine δύναμις which flows into man and, along with other powers, drives death out of him. For Plato, too, γνῶσις or ἐπιστήμη was a δύναμις (Resp., V, 477d ff.); but here δύναμις has the sense of a possibility native to man, of a capacity. In Gnosticism it means magical power. [28] Like the πνεῦμα, it is a mysterious divine fluid (mana), and can be linked and even equated with ζωή and φῶς. [29] Thus γνῶσις gives the Gnostic ἐξουσία and grants him freedom from εἱμαρμένη. [30] In this sense γνῶσις is a possession, though it is always in jeopardy and must be made secure by asceticism. It is so as a mysterious quality of the soul which is regarded as a substance, not as knowledge which in the act of comprehension controls the content of what is comprehended.

C. The OT Usage.

1. A further presupposition of NT usage, however, is the LXX use of γινώσκειν and εἰδέναι, or the OT concept of knowledge. This comes out most clearly

---

θάνατος which frees from πάθη; VI, 9: γνῶσις as ἀπάθεια; IV, 6, 39: ἡ γνῶσις τοῦ ἡγεμονικοῦ τῆς ψυχῆς κάθαρσίς ἐστι καὶ ἐνέργειά ἐστιν ἀγαθή; Chairemon in Porphyr. Abst., IV, 6 (p. 237, 3 f., Nauck): τὸ γὰρ ἀεὶ συνεῖναι τῇ θείᾳ γνώσει καὶ ἐπιπνοίᾳ πάσης μὲν ἔξω τίθησι πλεονεξίας, καταστέλλει δὲ τὰ πάθη, διεγείρει δὲ πρὸς σύνεσιν τὸν βίον. So also the Mandaeans, cf. Lidz. Ginza, 58, 36 f. Cf. Kroll, op. cit., 353 f.; W. Jaeger, GGA (1913), 584 and 587.

[26] → ἄγνοια.

[27] Corp. Herm., I, 27-29; IV, 4 f. (ὅσοι μὲν οὖν συνῆκαν τοῦ κηρύγματος ... οὗτοι μετέσχον τῆς γνώσεως ... ὅσοι δὲ τῆς ἀπὸ τοῦ θεοῦ δωρεᾶς μετέσχον, οὗτοι ... ἀθάνατοι ἀντὶ θνητῶν εἰσί), 11 (ἔχει γάρ τι ἴδιον ἡ θέα· τοὺς φθάσαντας θεάσασθαι κατέχει καὶ ἀνέλκει καθάπερ φασὶν ἡ Μαγνῆτις λίθος τὸν σίδηρον; VII, 1-3; X, 4-6; XIII (the γένεσις τῆς θεότητος is described as παλιγγενεσία; 10: ἐθεώ[ρη]θημεν τῇ <ταύτης> γενέσει); Iren., I, 21, 4 (MPG, 7, 665a): the ἔσω ἄνθρωπος is freed (λυτροῦσθαι) by γνῶσις; Plotin. Enn., V, 8, 10; VI, 9; Porphyr. Abst., II, 34; Hierocl. Carm. Aur., p. 180 f., Mullach on ἀποθέωσις (p. 181, 13 f.: ταῖς μὲν γνώσεσιν ἑνοῦται τῷ παντὶ καὶ πρὸς αὐτὸν ἀνάγεται τὸν θεόν); Cl. Al. Strom., IV, 6, 40; IV, 23, 149: τούτῳ δυνατὸν τῷ τρόπῳ τὸν γνωστικὸν ἤδη γενέσθαι θεόν; V, 10, 63: τὸ δὲ ἀγνοεῖν τὸν πατέρα θάνατός ἐστιν, ὡς τὸ γνῶναι ζωὴ αἰώνιος κατὰ μετουσίαν τῆς τοῦ ἀφθάρτου δυνάμεως κτλ. Cf. Kroll, op. cit., 360 ff.; Reitzenstein Hell. Myst., 288 ff., on the Christian Gnostics, 302 ff.; Bousset, op. cit., 165 f. It is characteristic that in terminology describing the relation to the object, verbs of touching and tasting are used rather than καταλαμβάνειν.

[28] Corp. Herm., XIII, 7 ff.; Iambl. Myst., 10, 5 (p. 292, 1 ff., Parthey) on γνῶσις as δύναμις; it leads εἰς μετουσίαν καὶ θέαν τοῦ ἀγαθοῦ ..., μετὰ δὲ ταῦτα πρὸς τοὺς τῶν ἀγαθῶν δοτῆρας θεοὺς ἕνωσιν. Cf. K. Müller, NGG (1920), 181 f.; as ὄνομα = γνῶσις, so ὄνομα and δύναμις are used synon., Act. Thom., 27, p. 142, 13 f. Cf. again K. Müller, 225: "(γνῶσις) is wherever divine being is; indeed, one may say that it is divine being." For γνῶσις as aeon among the Barbelognostics, cf. Iren., I, 29, 3 (MPG, 7, 693a). The γνωστικοί are πνευματικοί, cf. Reitzenstein Hell. Myst., 289; 292; 301; 305.

[29] Corp. Herm., XIII, 7 ff. (esp. in the hymn, XIII, 18: γνῶσις ἁγία, φωτισθεὶς ἀπὸ σοῦ, διὰ σοῦ τὸ νοητὸν φῶς ὑμνῶ[ν] ... ζωὴ καὶ φῶς, ἀφ' ὑμῶν εἰς ὑμᾶς χωρεῖ ἡ εὐλογία); Logos teleios, I, 374 ff., Scott. Cf. Kroll, op. cit., 375 f.; Reitzenstein Hell. Myst., 292.

[30] On γνῶσις and ἐξουσία, cf. Reitzenstein Hell. Myst., 301 f.; on liberation from εἱμαρμένη, ibid., 300 f.; Kroll, op. cit., 382 ff.; cf. Iambl. Myst., 10, 5.

in the use of יָדַע, for which γινώσκειν and εἰδέναι are the normal renderings in the LXX. That these are possible renderings shows that in ידע the element of perception is to be maintained. Indeed, the Greek and Hebrew words may be equated to the degree that both γινώσκειν and ידע denote primarily the original phenomenon of existence, i.e., the act in which man comprehends the objects and circumstances of his world. Like γινώσκειν, ידע is not originally linked with any specific organ, but means "coming to know" in the process of things, i.e., in experience. [31] Similarly ידע, like εἰδέναι, can also mean understanding in the sense of ability. [32] Again, it can signify knowledge of what ought to be done. [33] Yet the OT usage is much broader than the Greek, and the element of objective verification is less prominent than that of detecting or feeling or learning by experience. [34] Hence ידע can govern objects which are seldom if ever found with the Greek word, such as blows (1 S. 14:12), childlessness (Is. 47:8), sickness (Is. 53:3), divine punishment and divine retribution (Jer. 16:21; Ez. 25:14). The LXX usually has γινώσκειν in such cases, but αἰσθάνεσθαι would be better Greek, [35] and it is characteristic that no distinction is seen between γινώσκειν and αἰσθάνεσθαι. It is in this connection that we are to understand the use of ידע for sexual intercourse (Gn. 4:1, 17, 25 etc.), not only of the man but also of the woman (Nu. 31:18, 35; Ju. 21:12). In ידע the element of mere information can, of course, be emphasised (Ps. 94:11; 139:1), and דעת, especially in the Wisdom literature, can mean the contemplative perception or knowledge possessed by the wise man (Prv. 1:4; 2:6; 5:2; Qoh. 1:18). The distinctive feature, however, is that the concept of knowledge in the OT is not determined by the idea that the reality of what is known is most purely grasped when personal elements are obliterated between the subject and object of knowledge, and knowledge is reduced to contemplation from without. On the contrary, the OT both perceives and asserts the significance and claim of the knowing subject. Hence knowledge is understood more as a way of hearing than of seeing, and it is to be noted that seeing, too, is understood otherwise than in the Greek world, → ὁρᾶν. It is in keeping with this that we do not find in Israel any knowledge which objectively investigates and describes reality. It is also in keeping that for the OT reality is not constituted by the ἀεὶ ὄν, by the timeless and permanent forms and principles which give shape to things, but by that which constantly takes place in time. Events, however, are not understood as the unfolding of a causal nexus of processes; they are a qualified action of God, or of men in relation to God. God is not

---

[31] ידע means "to know," or "to learn to know," by personal dealings at Ex. 1:8; Dt. 9:2, 24; 1 S. 10:11 etc.; through good or bad experience at Is. 42:25; Jer. 16:21; 44:28 etc. (In both cases the LXX has γινώσκειν or εἰδέναι). Hence the pass. part., like the Gk. γνωστός, can mean an acquaintance, friend or confidant, e.g., Ps. 31:11; 55:13; 88:8, 18.

[32] Gn. 25:27: אִישׁ יֹדֵעַ צַיִד = a cunning hunter (LXX: εἰδὼς κυνηγεῖν); 1 S. 16:16; 1 K. 9:27; Is. 29:12 (here the LXX has ἐπίστασθαι, otherwise εἰδέναι). The act. part. with דעת as object can have the same sense as the Gk. γινώσκων, namely, a man of insight or understanding (Prv. 17:27; Da. 1:4). But the absol. ידע can also mean "to be perceptive" (Ps. 73:22; 82:5).

[33] Ju. 18:14; 1 S. 25:17 (LXX γινώσκειν).

[34] Characteristic is the use of ידע in the hiph with God as subject: He causes His power to be known in punishment or blessing (Jer. 16:21; Ps. 77:14; 98:2; 106:8; LXX γνωρίζειν).

[35] αἰσθάνεσθαι is comparatively rare in the LXX. It is used for ידע only at Is. 49:26 (elsewhere γινώσκειν). αἴσθησις, however, is often used in Prv. for דעת.

regarded as that which always is; He is the will which has a specific goal, demanding, blessing and judging. The reference, then, is not to knowledge in a general sense but to knowledge in a special sense. This knowledge is the knowledge of God (רעת יהוה). This does not mean that it is a knowledge of God's eternal essence. On the contrary, it is a knowledge of His claim, whether present in direct commands or contained in His rule. It is thus respectful and obedient acknowledgment of the power and grace and demand of God. This means that knowedge is not thought of in terms of the possession of information. It is possessed only in its exercise or actualisation. For this reason the ideal of the βίος θεωρητικός is just as alien to the OT as the ideal of a πόλις or κοσμοπολιτεία, i.e., of an image of human society which is grounded in a theory of philosophy and which is then to be fulfilled in action. No less alien is the thought of mystical contemplation of the Godhead.

Thus knowledge has an element of acknowledgment. But it also has an element of emotion, or better, of movement of will, so that ignorance means guilt as well as error. Linguistically this is expressed primarily in the fact that knowledge, as a grasping of the significance and claim of what is known, can have the connotation of an anxious concern about something, whether in relation to God or man. [36] Above all, however, ידע is used for acknowledgment of the acts of God (Dt. 11:2; Is. 41:20; Hos. 11:3; Mi. 6:5). And it bears the same sense when used of the recognition that Yahweh is God (Dt. 4:39; 8:5; 29:5; Is. 43:10; Ps. 46:10). To know Him or His name is to confess or acknowledge Him, to give Him honour and to obey His will (1 S. 2:12; Is. 1:3; Jer. 2:8; 9:2-5; Ps. 9:10; 36:10; 87:4; Job 18:21; Da. 11:32). The "knowledge of God" (Hos. 4:1; 6:6; Is. 11:2, 9), or "knowledge" in the absolute (Hos. 4:6; Prv. 1:7; 9:10), is almost identical with the fear of God with which it is linked in Is. 11:2, and it implies the doing of what is right and just (Jer. 22:16). We can thus read of the knowledge, i.e., the confession and acknowledgment, of guilt on the part of man (Jer. 3:13; Ps. 51:3) and of the knowledge or recognition of innocence on the part of God (Job 31:6). "Known" men are those who are recognised and respected (Dt. 1:13, 15; Prv. 31:23). Finally, the element of will in ידע emerges with particular emphasis when it is used of God, whose knowing establishes the significance of what is known. In this connection ידע can mean "to elect," i.e., to make an object of concern and acknowledgment. [37]

2. In the LXX [38] we find special nuances in certain passages. Thus γινώσκειν occurs only 6 times in Lv. (Mas. יָדַע 8 times), and the reference in each is to sin. This usage forms the basis for a view of knowledge which awakens man, which threatens

---

[36] Of man, Gn. 39:6, 8; Dt. 33:9; Prv. 12:10; Job 9:21; Ps. 101:4 (obj. רָע); Ps. 119:79 (obj. "God's witnesses"). In the LXX the rendering is usually γινώσκειν or εἰδέναι, though ἐπίστασθαι occurs, and in Prv. 12:10 οἰκτείρειν. Of God, Ps. 50:11; 73:11; 144:3; γινώσκειν in the LXX. Particularly striking are the cases in which the character of דע is illustrated by a parallel verb, e.g., Jer. 8:7 (שָׁמַר), Prv. 27:23 (יָדֹעַ תֵּדַע) par. שִׁית לִבְּךָ). Cf. also esp. Ps. 1:6; 31:7; 37:18.

[37] Gn. 18:19; Ex. 33:12; Am. 3:2; Hos. 13:5; Jer. 1:5. I doubt whether this usage rests on the sexual, and therefore whether we should translate Am. 3:2: "With you alone is my marriage bond," or Hos. 13:5: "Thee alone have I married," as K. Cramer maintains in his Amos (1930), 32; 57; 60. In any case, the meaning is clarified by related or alternative expressions such as קָרָא בְשֵׁם (Is. 43:1, followed by לִי אָתָּה!; 45:3 f.; 49:1) or לָקַח and בָּחַר. In such instances the LXX often has → συνιέναι as well as γινώσκειν and εἰδέναι.

[38] I am indebted to G. Bertram for this whole section.

his whole existence, but which leads him to repentance and salvation if accepted. Apart from the many instances in which γινώσκειν in this sense simply follows the Heb. original, the LXX often has it independently, e.g., in revelations, introduced by an imperative, which contradict human hope and expectation. Here the irrational element in such knowledge is stressed from the very outset (Ju. 4:9; ᾽Ιωβ 19:3 [cf. v. 6 Mas.]; 36:5; Prv. 29:20; Is. 8:9; [39] 44:20; [40] 47:10; 51:12). We are also to understand Is. 15:4 in this way, where the LXX wrongly reads יִרְעָה (from ירע) as יִדְעָה. [41] In Is. 30:15 salutary self-knowledge is demanded independently of the Mas. γινώσκειν as a disturbing knowledge is the opp. of the οὐ γινώσκειν with which sinners and the Gentiles are reproached (Wis. 2:22; 5:7). The same reproach is in view in the pregnant use of οὐ γινώσκειν at Zech. 7:14 : τὰ ἔθνη, ἃ οὐκ ἔγνωσαν. The LXX speaks of peoples which have no knowledge of God, whereas the Mas. is simply referring to peoples unknown to the Jews. The Mas. means that even the remotest peoples will serve the Jews ; it thus emphasises the power of God and the future greatness of His people. Relating the thought to the heathen, the LXX turns the passage into religious propaganda. Something of the same is to be seen at ψ 17:43 according to ᾽Α. At Is. 26:11 the LXX uses γινώσκειν to express the shattering knowledge of the power of God's wrath. According to the view of Guthe, who omits וַיֵּבֹשׁוּ, the weaker חֹזֶה is designed to express the thought of salvation. [42] The case is otherwise when all knowledge of divine overruling in the world is denied to the natural man, e.g., many times in Qoh. (cf. also Wis. 9:13, 17). From this standpoint the LXX in Is. 40:13 has γινώσκειν for the Heb. תכן pi, which in the LXX is usually equated with כון and thus translated ἑτοιμάζειν, κατευθύνειν etc. From the idea of the incommensurability of God the Greek moves to that of His unknowability for man ; the theological statement of the Mas. is thus replaced by an anthropological. Similarly in ᾽Ιωβ 38:31 A the incapacity of man's knowledge is substituted for the transcendence of the creative power of God. The Mas. asks a rhetorical question. It is debatable whether the question of the Greek text was always answered in the negative by Hellenistic Jews who came under astrological influences. [43]

In many instances γινώσκειν or γινώσκεσθαι signifies the divine self-revelation as such. In this sense it is often used for the Heb. verb ידע, which is rightly rendered in different ways in the LXX. In the relevant passages in Ex. this verb is incorrectly emended to ידע in BHK. For though ועד is once translated γνωσθήσομαι and once τάξομαι in Ex. 29:42, 43, the distinction is intentional. γνωσθήσομαι, τάξομαι and ἁγιασθήσομαι are three words which supplement one another in relation to God's revelation. Man, however, is always the logical subject, so that the LXX maintains its anthropocentric view in opposition to the Heb. ועד, which in the niphal indicates self-revelation.

---

[39] The LXX reads דְּעוּ instead of רֹעוּ from רעע.

[40] The LXX reads דְּעִי instead of רֹעֶה from רעה.

[41] The LXX also has ד for ר, ידע for רעה at Hos. 9:2. Guthe in Kautzsch wrongly brings the Mas. into line with the LXX. That the threshing-floor and the wine-press will know the chosen people no more, signifies divine condemnation. Cf. also Jer. 2:16 and 1 Βασ. 10:24 where וַיְרְעוּ from רוע is read as וַיֵּדְעוּ.

[42] H. Guthe in Kautzsch, ad loc. Duhm, ad loc. disagrees. Elsewhere the LXX occasionally has γινώσκειν for verbs of hearing and seeing (→ 697 with reference to → ὁρᾶν). Thus it is used for ראה in Nu. 11:23 and Ju. 2:7 (cf. also Gn. 39:23 and Ex. 22:10; 33:13) in the sense of a saving knowledge of revelation. At Is. 48:8 γινώσκειν is used for שמע synon. with the ἐπίστασθαι which follows for ידע. Cf. also Neh. 4:9 (15) ᾽Α.

[43] Cf. A. Jeremias, Handbuch der altorientalischen Geisteskultur² (1929), 213 and Index, s.v. "Plejaden," also Str.-B., IV, 1046 and 1048 (the Zodiac allegory in Pesikt. r., 203a, 31 and its cultic application in Tanch. האזינו 27b, 33). From this to an astral analogy magic is only a short step which a ψευδώνυμος γνῶσις was always ready to take.

There are far more passages in which man is the logical subject of γινώσκειν than there are references to the knowledge, recognition or acknowledgment of man by God. When used in the latter sense, γινώσκειν implies standing the divine test (Gn. 22:12, cf. γινώσκειν =תכן kal, Prv. 24:12); or election (Nu. 16:5; ψ 1:6; 36:18; Hos. 11:12). In the last example the LXX goes its own way, introducing the thought of election rather than that of the knowledge of God which threatens the sinful people with judgment. The same idea is present in Hos. 5:3; Am. 3:2; Nah. 1:7. Closely related is the thought of the divine omniscience, which in γινώσκειν can be linked no less with the idea of the love of the Creator for His creatures than with the thought of election (Gn. 20:6; 44 4 Βασ. 19:27; 1 Ch. 28:9; ψ 39:9; 43:21; 49:11; 68:5, 19; 102:14; 137:6; 138; 141:3; Am. 5:12; Bar. 2:30). In the Psalms especially, we have also to take into account both confidence in the mercy of God and the thought of the Judge and Saviour who knows and expiates the wrong which has been done.

The noun γνῶσις is much rarer in the LXX than the verb. On the other hand, it is used comparatively much more often in a religious and ethical sense to denote a revealed knowledge whose author is God or *sophia*. God is the God of knowledge (דֵּעָה = γνῶσις, 1 Βασ. 2:3; ψ 72:11 Σ: ἐπίγνωσις, cf. Sir. 35:8; Prov. 3:20 Ἀ), i.e., of the omniscience which is the foundation of His dealings with His creature in judgment and grace (1 Ch. 4:10; 45 Wis. 1:7; Est. 14:14; 2 Macc. 6:30; Is. 40:14, ἈΣΘ, the LXX has κρίσιν). The *gnosis* of the righteous derives from God. It is a spiritual possession resting on revelation. Prv. 24:26: θεὸς δεδίδαχέν με σοφίαν καὶ γνῶσιν ἁγίων ἔγνωκα. Sir. 1:19; Ἰωβ 32:6; 46 Prv. 16:8 (diff. from the Mas.); Prv. 2:6; Wis. 7:17; cf. 10:10; ψ 93:10; 118:66. The bearer and teacher of *gnosis* is the pious sage, the παῖς θεοῦ (Is. 53:11), the δίκαιος (Wis. 2:13; 16:22), the σοφός (Sir. 21:13; Prv. 15:7 Σ), the πανοῦργος (Prv. 13:16; 47 14:18 48), the φρόνιμος (Prv. 14:6 ἈΣΘ; 19:25 ἈΣΘ).

At many points in the Wisdom literature of the OT, of course, we merely have secular wisdom, and the concept of *gnosis* is used in this sense too. On the other hand, the obvious trend of the LXX is towards a religious interpretation. This is seen in the fact that all capacity for knowledge is denied to the worldly minded, to the ἀσεβής (Prv. 13:19; 49 29:7), to the ἀνόητος (Prv. 1:22 Ἀ); to the μωρός (Sir. 21:14), to the ἀσύνετος (Sir. 21:18; Prv. 1:22 Ἀ) and to the ἄφοβος (Prv. 19:20) — all these are terms used for the ungodly or the sinner. This is true even of the holy people if they turn from God. 50 It is also the verdict on the idolater (Wis. 14:22) and the man who is far from God (Jer. 10:14; 28:17). It applies to the σοφός in the sense of this world. At least, this is how the LXX seems to understand the Heb. in Ἰωβ 15:2: True spiritual

---

44 In Gn. 18:19 the LXX has the thought of omniscience instead of that of election (Mas. → 698, n. 37).

45 The LXX reads מַדָּע or מֹדַעַת and translates γνῶσις in the sense of favourable judicial knowledge. Another rendering (Cod. 53) has βόσκησις on the assumption of מִרְעֶה. The Mas. has מֵרֵעַ (→ n. 39-41).

46 Ἀθ γνῶσιν; LXX ἐπιστήμην. Cf. 32:8 and 33:3, 4: πνοὴ δὲ παντοκράτορος ἡ διδάσκουσά με.

47 In Prv. 13:16 Mas. the reference is to secular wisdom. But the LXX inserts Prv. 9:10 (in a different form) into v. 15 and thus gives the verse a religious turn, as often happens.

48 LXX: πανοῦργοι κρατήσουσιν αἰσθήσεως· Ἀ: ... ἀναμένουσι γνῶσιν· Θ: στεφθήσονται γνῶσιν. The Mas. is usually understood in the sense of Θ.

49 Here, too, we have a misreading of מֵרֵעַ as מַדָּע. Ἀ translates literally: ἀπὸ κακοῦ. The same mistake is found in Sir. 8:6 and 40:5. → also n. 45.

50 The summons to conversion in Hos. 10:12 is formulated accordingly in the LXX: φωτίσατε ἑαυτοῖς φῶς γνώσεως. The Mas. reads: נִירוּ לָכֶם נִיר וְעֵת ("Break up your fallow ground, for it is time ..."). The changing of וְעֵת into דַּעַת, as suggested by Guthe in Kautzsch, hardly corresponds to the original sense of the Heb.

knowledge is concealed from the wise of this world. [51] Γνῶσις here is a technical religious term in antithesis to the secular σοφός. But the usage is not unambiguous. γνῶσις and σοφία are frequently related, and σοφία can even be the superior principle. This is so in the definition of σοφία at 4 Macc. 1:16: [52] σοφία δὴ τοίνυν ἐστὶν γνῶσις θείων ἀνθρωπίνων πραγμάτων καὶ τῶν τούτων αἰτιῶν. Cf. also Prv. 8:12. Gnosis is certainly also divine revelation of an objective character, but under Hellenistic influence there is a plain subjective element of profound religious knowledge in the mystical and Gnostic sense. Thus gnosis may be insight into the world plan of God (Da. 12:4 Θ and Mas., where the LXX presupposes רֵעַ rather than יָדַע). Gnosis is knowledge concerning God and His work which goes beyond all human comprehension (ψ 138:6) and which is proclaimed for believers by the whole of creation (ψ 18:3).

D. The Jewish Usage.

1. The OT conception of knowledge persists in Judaism, and in the LXX and other Graeco-Jewish sources (apart from Josephus) the use of γινώσκειν is greatly modified thereby. In Judaism, with the exception of Philo, knowledge as such is not a problem. When the Rabbis speak of knowledge (דֵּיעָה) in the absolute, they mean knowledge of the requirements of the Law, [53] as they do when knowledge is extolled (דַּעַת).[54] Yet knowledge can also have a general sense for the Rabbis. A man who has דַּעַת is a. one who is capable of thinking, as distinct from the child or the feeble-minded (שֶׁאֵין בּוֹ דַּעַת); b. one who is gifted as contrasted with the stupid; c. one who has acquired learning in contrast with a man of the people (עַם הָאָרֶץ) who has had no education. For the Rabbis, however, the Torah and tradition are the only source and theme of knowledge and instruction. Hence all the meanings amount to very much the same in fact. Again, according to the Rabbinic view the fulfilment of the commands present in the Torah and tradition is possible only when they have been studied and are known. Hence the distinction between the educated, i.e., the Rabbi and the עַם הָאָרֶץ is the same as that between the righteous and the sinner (→ ἁμαρτωλός). If in the OT the thought of obedience is regulative in the equation of the knowledge of God and the fear of God, and if this obedience is rooted in knowledge, then the idea of the knowledge which is the presupposition of obedience is dominant for the Rabbis. Nevertheless, the specifically OT view of the knowledge of God is not wholly lost in Judaism. [55] In the liturgy the Jewish community praises God for endowment with knowledge, and this custom is taken over by the Christian Church. [56]

---

[51] The Mas. reads: הֶחָכָם יַעֲנֶה דַעַת־רוּחַ ("Will a wise man propose windy knowledge as an answer?", Steuernagel in Kautzsch). The σύνεσις πνεύματος (B) πνεῦμα (A) in the LXX, and the γνῶσις πνεύματος in ᾽Α and Σ, have nothing to do with wind, as shown by the continuation in the LXX.

[52] Cf. Trench, 188 f., where almost exactly the same definition of σοφία is quoted from Cl. Al. Paed., II, 2, 25, 1 ff.; cf. Strom., I, 5, 30, 1 f.

[53] Str.-B., I, 191 f.; Test. L. 13:3.

[54] Str.-B., III, 378 on 1 C. 8:1.

[55] Cf. Schl.-Mt., 384. Again, S. Dt., 6, 6 § 33 (74a); 11, 22 § 49 (85a) in Str.-B., III, 778, 776. To know God is to hear Him (Gn. r., 64, 4 on 26:5, Str.-B., III, 34). Knowledge as acknowledgment is also found, whether of a person (Str.-B., I, 469 on Mt. 7:23) or of guilt (Test. S. 2:13 f.; 4:3; Test. Iss. 7:1; Test. Jos. 3:9). Naturally "to know" also continues to be used in the sexual sense (cf. Str.-B., I, 75 f.; Schl. Mt., 24; Jdt. 16:22; Wis. 3:13; Test. Jud. 10:3 f. etc.; Philo Poster. C., 33 and 134).

[56] Apart from Midr. Sm., 5 § 9 (30b) in Str.-B., III, 378, cf. W. Bousset, NGG (1915), 466 ff. (on Const. Ap., VII, 33-39) and the prayers from Jewish sources in Did., 9 and 10. Cf. the request for knowledge in the fourth petition of the Schᵉmone Esre.

Hellenistic Judaism has the same usage, cf. Wis. 15:3 : τὸ γὰρ ἐπίστασθαί σε ὁλόκληρος δικαιοσύνη, καὶ εἰδέναι σου τὸ κράτος ῥίζα ἀθανασίας. There is reference to acknowledgment of the power and acts of God in Sir. 36:22 (19); Bar. 2:15, 31; 1 Macc. 4:11; 2 Macc. 1:27; Tob. 14:4 (אּ); Jdt. 9:7; Sib., 3, 693; and to the knowledge of His ὁδός (ὁδοί) etc. in Wis. 5:7; 9:10; 10:8; Bar. 3:9, 14, 20; cf. Sir. 18:28; 24:28.[57] Yet along with the older usage there is also modification (as seen already in Dt.-Is.). The monotheistic motif is stressed in opposition to heathenism, so that the knowledge of God also means, or means specifically, recognition of the fact that there is only one God and that the gods of the heathen are not gods (cf. Jdt. 8:20; Ep. Jer. 22, 28, 50, 64, 71; Wis. 12:27; Sib. Fr., 1, 31 f.). In this respect there also arises a question quite alien to the Rabbis, namely, that of the possibility of the knowledge of God (cf. already 2 Macc. 7:28; Test. N. 3:4 and esp. Wis. 13-15, and also the whole apologetic and propagandist literature of Hellenistic Judaism).[58] Thus both the concept of knowledge and the concept of God are to some extent hellenised in either a Stoic or a Gnostic direction.[59]

2. Philo's view of knowledge and his use of γινώσκειν etc. are wholly Hellenistic, i.e., rationalist or Gnostic. He can speak generally of ἐπίγνωσις ἀληθείας (Omn. Prob. Lib., 74) but also of γνῶναι τὸ ὄν (Virt., 215). Nevertheless, what he finally means is the knowledge of God. On the one hand he speaks of the knowledge of the one God in opposition to polytheism (Virt., 178 f.; Ebr., 44 f.) or to scepticism (Ebr., 19) and in so doing uses the Stoic theory of the knowledge of God (Virt., 215 f.; Poster. C., 167). On the other hand this knowledge, as Philo sees it, leads only to the fact of God and not His nature (Som., I, 231; Spec. Leg., I, 32 ff.; Praem. Poen., 39 and 44); or it leads only to a knowledge of His δυνάμεις (Spec. Leg., I, 43 ff.; cf. Fug., 165; Mut. Nom., 17). Beyond this, however, there is a knowledge of God which consists in direct vision, described by Philo as the ecstasy in which the soul is both ὁρῶσά τε καὶ ὁρωμένη (Som., II, 226). This is not attained by study; it is given by God (Op. Mund., 70 f.; Abr., 79 f.; Praem. Poen., 37 and 41 ff. etc.).[60] This obviously Gnostic view of the knowledge of God appears again in the fact that it is a γνῶσις εὐσεβείας (Abr., 268), i.e., it is linked with dualistic piety (Leg. All., III, 48; Deus Imm., 4 and 143). Since this conception carries with it a depreciation of man, Philo can also adopt OT ideas

---

[57] For ἐπιγινώσκω → 703.

[58] Cf. Ltzm. R. on 1:20 and Excurs. on 1:25; also → ἄγνωστος, n. 3. The Rabbis do not discuss the problem (Str.-B., III, 33); when they speak of the unknowability of God, they refer to the inscrutability of His providence (Str.-B., III, 294 f.); → ἄγνωστος.

[59] For Stoic influence → n. 58, also Ep. Ar., 195; 210; 254 and (for Philo) R. Bultmann, ZNW, 29 (1930), 189 ff. Symptomatic is the proximity of ἔμφυτος γνῶσις to ἔμφυτος νόμος in Const. Ap., VII, 33, 3 (→ n. 40). For Gnostic influence there may be adduced the combination of γνῶσις with ζωή and ἀθανασία in eucharistic prayers (Did., 9, 3; 10, 2), cf. R. Knopf, ad loc. (Handbuch z. NT, Supplement). On Philo → 2. In the Test. XII frequent use of γινώσκειν for secret eschatological knowledge may perhaps be traced back to the same influence (e.g., Test. D. 5:6; Test. N. 4:1; Test. G. 8:2; Test. A. 7:5), and also the φῶς γνώσεως of Test. L. 4:3; 18:3; Test. B. 11:2. Yet the genuine Jewish view of knowledge is also found, e.g., Test. L. 18:5, 9; Test. G. 5:7. Joseph. uses γνῶσις only in the sense of the knowledge of events (Ant., 8, 171 etc.).

[60] Cf. Bousset-Gressmann, 450 f.; Bousset, Kyrios Christ., 167; H. Windisch, Die Frömmigkeit Philos (1909), 60 ff.; Reitzenstein Hell. Myst., 317 f.; H. Leisegang, Der hl. Geist, I (1919), 223, 4; R. Bultmann, ZNW, 29 (1930), 189 ff. Like Plotinus (→ n. 16), Philo avoids γινώσκειν and γνῶσις (though not consistently) for the vision of God, preferring ὁρᾶν, ὅρασις, θέα etc.; similarly he speaks of ὁρατικοί and φιλοθεάμονες rather than γνωστικοί.

according to which γνῶσις is also τιμὴ τοῦ ἑνός (Leg. All., III, 126). The rather obscure mixture of philosophical, Gnostic and OT ideas may be seen especially in his interpretation of the γνῶθι σαυτόν. He certainly takes this to mean ἐξετά-ζειν ἑαυτόν (Fug., 46 f.; cf. Leg. Gaj., 69), but for the most part he interprets it dualistically as aversion from the earthly together with the knowledge of God (Migr. Abr., 8 f.; 137 f.; Spec. Leg., I, 10; 44; 263 ff.; Mut. Nom., 54 and 186). The OT motif can thus be introduced (Deus Imm., 161; Rer. Div. Her., 30), especially in Som., I, 54-60 (cf. 211 f.; 220), where γινώσκειν ἑαυτόν is followed by ἀπο-γινώσκειν, and this in turn by γινώσκειν τὸν ὄντα. No less syncretistic is the use of ἄγνοια, which is sometimes depicted in Greek fashion as κακοδαιμονίας αἰτία (Leg. Gaj., 69; cf. Ebr., 6), sometimes in that of Gnosticism or the OT as πάντων ἁμαρτημάτων αἰτία (Ebr., 154 ff.; Som., I, 114).

E. The Early Christian Usage.

1. Popular Usage.

The early Christian use of γινώσκειν (and γνῶσις) raises no problems where the reference is to knowledge in the ordinary sense and there is no question of an OT or Greek or specifically NT concept. Thus γινώσκειν can mean "to detect" (Mk. 5:29; Lk. 8:46), or "to note" (Mk. 8:17; 12:12; Mt. 26:10; 2 C. 2:4; Jn. 5:42; 8:27), or "to recognise" (Lk. 7:39; Mt. 12:15; 22:18; Gl. 3:7; Jm. 2:20; Jn. 4:1; 5:6; 6:15), with no clear-cut lines of differentiation. Naturally it can also mean "to learn" (Mk. 5:43; 15:45; Lk. 9:11; Ac. 17:13, 19; Phil. 1:12; 2:19; Jn. 11:57; 12:9; 1 Cl., 12, 2; Ign. Tr., 1, 1 f.; or in the pass. Mt. 10:26 and par.; Ac. 9:24; Phil. 4:5). Sometimes it can shade into the sense of "to confirm" (Mk. 6:38; 13:28 f.; Lk. 1:18; 1 C. 4:19; 2 C. 13:6; Jn. 4:53; 7:51; Did., 11, 8; esp. common in 1 Jn. in the phrase ἐν τούτῳ γινώσκομεν etc.). It can also mean "to know" in the sense of awareness (Mt. 24:50 and par.; Lk. 2:43; 16:4; Hb. 10:34; Rev. 3:3; Jn. 2:24 f.; 7:27; 1 Jn. 3:20; Ign. R., 5, 3) [61] or acquaintance (Mt. 25:24; Lk. 12:47 f.; 16:15; Ac. 1:7; R. 2:18; 7:1; 2 C. 5:16; Jn. 1:48; 7:49; 1 Cl., 31, 3; 35, 3) [62] or even understanding (Lk. 18:34; Ac. 8:30; 1 C. 14:7, 9; Jn. 3:10).

γινώσκειν in the sense of mastery is found only in the interpolated Mt. 16:3, where the original Lk. par. 12:56 has εἰδέναι, which is better Gk. We are probably to interpret 2 C. 5:21 along these lines (τὸν μὴ γνόντα ἁμαρτίαν) in accordance with OT usage, though there is nothing corresponding in Rabbinic literature according to Str.-B. The practical sense of familiarity is what is primarily meant in R. 7:7: τὴν ἁμαρτίαν οὐκ ἔγνων εἰ μὴ διὰ νόμου. Cf. Herm. m., 2, 1: τὰ νήπια τὰ μὴ γινώσκοντα τὴν πονηρίαν; s., 9, 29, 1: οὐδὲ ἔγνωσαν, τί ἐστιν πονηρία. The Gk. use of γινώσκειν for "to resolve" is not found in the NT, though it is common in Joseph. (e.g., Ant., 5, 22; 15, 284) and Philo (e.g., Spec. Leg., I, 176; Det. Pot. Ins., 27, also γνῶσις in Spec. Leg., IV, 63 and 70).

ἐπιγινώσκειν is often used instead of γινώσκειν with no difference in meaning. In Gk. ἐπιγινώσκειν can mean "to observe" if the prepos. is emphasised, but this means much the same as "to perceive," so that any distinction disappears. In fact the simple and compound forms are used interchangeably in the pap., where ἐπιγινώσκειν really means "to affirm" or "to confirm" rather than "to test," as Preisigke maintains. Only in the sense of "to (re-)cognize," or, in law, "to reach a further conclusion," does the compound have a special sense, but this does not affect early Christian usage, nor do

---

[61] γινώσκειν and εἰδέναι can be used as full equivalents, cf. Mk. 12:15 with 8:17; Mk. 15:10 with Mt. 27:18; Mt. 7:23 with 25:12; Ac. 1:7 with Mk. 13:32; Jn. 8:55 with 7:28; 8:19. Further passages in which the two alternate are Mk. 4:13; 1 C. 2:11 f.; 2 C. 5:16; Gl. 4:8 f.; Jn. 7:27; 14:7; 21:17; 1 Jn. 2:29. There are variant readings at Rev. 2:17.

[62] γινώσκειν can be used interchangeably with ἐπίστασθαι for "to know" (cf. Ac. 19:15).

certain special uses in the pap. In the LXX the two terms are often used as equivalents, and they occur as par. in Hab. 3:2; cf. Ez. 25:14 with Is. 43:10; Hos. 14:10 with Jer. 3:13; ψ 78:6 with ψ 86:4; 1 Macc. 3:42 with 3:11 etc. Sometimes ἐπιγινώσκειν seems to be used intentionally for "to perceive" (Gn. 27:23; 31:32; Ju. 18:3 etc.; so also Jos. Bell., 5, 262; Ant., 6, 138; 8, 417 etc.). There is often an alternation in readings, as in Gn. 42:8; Ex. 14:4; Hos. 7:9; Jer. 4:22; 1 Macc. 16:22 etc. Philo, too, uses ἐπιγινώσκειν with no perceptible difference from γινώσκειν, e.g., Det. Pot. Ins., 176; cf. Som., I, 231 with I, 60 or Leg. All., III, 48 with III, 126 (the noun). That there is no general distinction between the simple and compound forms in early Christian writings is shown by a comparison of Mk. 2:8 with 8:17; Mk. 5:30 with Lk. 8:46; Mk. 6:33, 54 with Lk. 9:11; Mt. 7:16, 20 with Lk. 6:44; Mt. 11:27 with Lk. 10:22; Lk. 24:31 with 24:35; Col. 1:6 with 2 C. 8:9. Similar interchange between the two is found in Herm. s., 4, 3; 9, 18, 1 f.; Dg., 12, 6 and the variant readings at Ac. 23:28; 24:11. Even in 1 C. 13:12 the alternation is purely rhetorical ; the compound is also an equivalent of the simple form at 1 C. 8:3; Gl. 4:9. Thus ἐπιγινώσκειν τὸ δικαίωμα τοῦ θεοῦ at R. 1:32 corresponds to γινώσκειν τὸ θέλημα at 2:18.

The general meaning of ἐπιγινώσκειν is "to perceive," and only infrequently is it intentionally selected instead of the simple form (e.g., Lk. 1:22; 24:16, 31, though cf. v. 35; Ac. 3:10; 4:13; 12:14; Herm. v., 5, 3 f.). It can also mean "to learn" (Lk. 7:37; 23:7; Ac. 9:30; 22:29), "to understand" (2 C. 1:13 f., where the supplementary ἕως τέλους shows that in itself the compound does not have any additional meaning), and "to know" (Ac. 25:10; 2 C. 13:5). Too narrow a sense should not be read into ἐπιγινωσκόμενοι when set in rhetorical antithesis at 2 C. 6:9 (ὡς ἀγνοούμενοι). If it has the primary sense of "known," it can also mean "understood" in the sense of 1:13 f. Nor does this mean only known by man ; it can also mean known by God (cf. 5:11). The compound is perhaps chosen intentionally sometimes for "to confirm" (Lk. 1:4; Ac. 22:24; 23:28 vl.; 24:8 vl.). Other meanings corresponding to those of γινώσκειν will be discussed later. [63]

2. The OT and Jewish Usage and Its Influence.

There is no special sense even in cases where there is admonition to embrace a special knowledge. Yet the usage diverges at this point from that which characterises the Greek world. It approximates to the OT view in which knowledge is also a movement of the will, so that γινώσκετε means : "Let it be told you." That is to say, it is no mere question of objective confirmation but of a knowledge which accepts the consequences of knowledge. Thus already in the parable in Mt. 24:43 and par. : ἐκεῖνο δὲ γινώσκετε, εἰ ᾔδει ὁ οἰκοδεσπότης ... Again, Lk. 10:11: πλὴν τοῦτο γινώσκετε ὅτι ἤγγικεν ἡ βασιλεία τοῦ θεοῦ; Eph. 5:5 : τοῦτο γὰρ ἴστε γινώσκοντες, ὅτι πᾶς πόρνος ... οὐκ ἔχει κληρονομίαν. Cf. also Jm. 1:3; 5:20; 2 Tm. 3:1; 2 Pt. 1:20; 3:3; 1 Cl., 7, 4; 59, 1; 2 Cl., 5, 5; 9, 2; 16, 3; Barn., 19, 11; Pol., 4, 3; Herm. v., 3, 6, 7; m., 6, 2, 3 and 5. ἐπιγινώσκειν is used in the same way at 1 C. 14:37. Yet there is here no conflict with Greek usage, [64] nor at Ac. 2:36 : γινωσκέτω πᾶς οἶκος Ἰσραήλ, ὅτι καὶ κύριον αὐτὸν ... ἐποίησεν ὁ θεός, even though we should certainly understand this knowledge also in the OT sense of acknowledgment.

In other passages, however, we clearly see the OT view that knowledge is insight into the will of God in command and blessing. It is primarily acknow-

---

[63] Cf. Moult.-Mill. s.v. and A. Robinson, St. Paul's Epistle to the Ephesians (1904), 248 ff.

[64] γινώσκειν is, of course, meant in the same way in Epict. Diss., I, 25, 24; II, 18, 5; IV, 1, 13; 9, 2. Cf. also Philo Cher., 29; Ebr., 160; Som., I, 54 ff.

ledgment, and obedient or grateful submission to what is known. [65] This is naturally found in quotations like R. 3:17 (Is. 59:8): ὁδὸν εἰρήνης οὐκ ἔγνωσαν, and Hb. 3:10 (Ps. 95:10): αὐτοὶ δὲ οὐκ ἔγνωσαν τὰς ὁδούς μου. In the same connection we may also mention Lk. 19:42, 44 : εἰ ἔγνως ... τὰ πρὸς εἰρήνην σου ... οὐκ ἔγνως τὸν καιρὸν τῆς ἐπισκοπῆς σου, and R. 10:19; for 2 Pt. 2:21 → 706. Similarly, there is reference to the knowledge of God's θέλημα in R. 2:18 and Ac. 22:14, [66] and to the knowledge of Christian salvation in 2 C. 8:9 : γινώσκετε γὰρ τὴν χάριν τοῦ κυρίου ἡμῶν Ἰησοῦ Χριστοῦ, ὅτι δι' ἡμᾶς ἐπτώχευσεν (cf. ἐπιγινώσκειν in Col. 1:6), or to knowledge of a special grace of God in Gl. 2:9 and Rev. 3:9. [67]

In the same sense we read of the knowledge of God Himself at Rev. 2:23 : καὶ γνώσονται πᾶσαι αἱ ἐκκλησίαι ὅτι ἐγώ εἰμι ὁ ἐρευνῶν νεφροὺς καὶ καρδίας; cf. Hb. 8:11, quoting Jer. 31:34. Elsewhere there is some difference in the conception of the knowledge of God as compared with the OT. Unlike the preaching of the prophets, Christian missionary proclamation is not directed primarily against the practical denial of God in Israel; it is addressed to the heathen who do not honour the one God. Thus in the concept of the knowledge of God the element of knowledge emerges alongside and sometimes prior to that of acknowledgment. The two are obviously linked in R. 1:18-23 (esp. 21: διότι γνόντες τὸν θεὸν οὐχ ὡς θεὸν ἐδόξασαν ἢ ηὐχαρίστησαν). Cf. 1 C. 1:21: ἐπειδὴ γὰρ ἐν τῇ σοφίᾳ τοῦ θεοῦ οὐκ ἔγνω ὁ κόσμος διὰ τῆς σοφίας τὸν θεόν. Gl. 4:8 f.: ἀλλὰ τότε μὲν οὐκ εἰδότες θεὸν ἐδουλεύσατε τοῖς φύσει μὴ οὖσιν θεοῖς· νῦν δὲ γνόντες θεόν ... (→ infra). That there is no thought of a speculative knowledge of God may be seen also from R. 11:34; 1 C. 2:16 : τίς γὰρ ἔγνω νοῦν κυρίου (quoting Is. 40:13; → n. 69), where γινώσκειν means theoretical comprehension. That the knowledge of God attained in Christianity is a service of God, is illustrated by the material parallel in 1 Th. 1:9 : πῶς ἐπεστρέψατε πρὸς τὸν θεὸν ἀπὸ τῶν εἰδώλων δουλεύειν θεῷ ζῶντι καὶ ἀληθινῷ. Similarly, 1 C. 8:4-6 shows that, while the knowledge of God includes a theoretical element, this is not decisive. The same is true of Jn. 1:10 : ὁ κόσμος αὐτὸν οὐκ ἔγνω, though → 711 on Jn. Similarly, theoretical and practical conversion to monotheism is meant in 1 Cl., 59, 3 : (God as the) ἀνοίξας τοὺς ὀφθαλμοὺς τῆς καρδίας ἡμῶν εἰς τὸ γινώσκειν σε τὸν μόνον ὕψιστον ἐν ὑψίστοις. The practical element is dominant in

---

[65] γινώσκειν also has the sense of "to acknowledge" in some cases where neither God nor His will is the object, e.g., Hb. 13:23 (?); 1 Cl., 61, 1: εἰς τὸ γινώσκοντας ἡμᾶς τὴν ὑπὸ σοῦ (God) αὐτοῖς (earthly rulers) δεδομένην δόξαν καὶ τιμὴν ὑποτάσσεσθαι αὐτοῖς; Ign. Pol., 5, 2 : ἐὰν γνωσθῇ (sc. the ascetic) πλέον τοῦ ἐπισκόπου, ἔφθαρται. Cf. ἐπιγινώσκειν at 1 C. 16:18. The sense of "concern" often borne by the OT ידע is not found in the early Christian use of γινώσκειν except to the degree that it is implied in "acknowledgment." γινώσκειν is used in the sexual sense at Mt. 1:25 and Lk. 1:34.

[66] When Epict. Diss., IV, 7, 17 says: ἠλευθέρωμαι ὑπὸ τοῦ θεοῦ, ἔγνωκα αὐτοῦ τὰς ἐντολάς, γινώσκειν means "to know" (cf. Mk. 10:19 : τὰς ἐντολὰς οἶδας); nevertheless, Epict. means that he is "letting it be told him."

[67] In this connection we might adduce Did., 5, 2; Barn., 20, 2 : οὐ γινώσκοντες μισθὸν δικαιοσύνης, for verbs of will are parallel. There is also a par. in 2 Pt. 2:15 : ὃς μισθὸν ἀδικίας ἠγάπησεν. Again, the reference in Herm. s., 9, 10 and 4 : γινώσκοντες τὰς πράξεις αὐτῶν, is to acknowledgment of guilt (cf. ἐπιγινώσκειν in Herm. s., 8, 6, 3; 11, 2). On the other hand, the (εἰδέναι and) γινώσκειν of 2 C. 5:16 does not mean acknowledge in the first instance; it simply means "to know" with a suggestion of understanding. Paul's concern from 1:13 f. is with the way in which he is to be understood as an apostle and made manifest to the community (5:11), namely, in such sort that he is known as a bearer of ζωή and not κατὰ σάρκα (2:14-16; 3:7 ff.; 4:7 ff.).

Did., 5, 2; Barn., 20, 2 (οὐ γινώσκοντες τὸν ποιήσαντα αὐτούς, cf. Herm. s., 4, 4). The theoretical aspect of conversion is more strongly emphasised in 2 Cl., 3, 1; 17, 1, where γινώσκειν (τὸν θεόν) means conversion to Christianity. The same is true in Herm. s., 9, 18, 1 f.; 16, 7 (obj. τὸ ὄνομα τοῦ υἱοῦ τοῦ θεοῦ) and v., 3, 6, 2 (obj. the ἀλήθεια). Cf. also Kerygma Petri Fr., 2 and 3. ἐπιγινώσκειν is used in the same way at 1 Tm. 4:3 (obj. τὴν ἀλήθειαν); this is used interchangeably with γινώσκειν in Herm. s., 9, 18, 1 f. (cf. Col. 1:16), while 2 Pt. 2:21 (μὴ ἐπεγνωκέναι τὴν ὁδὸν τῆς δικαιοσύνης ἢ ἐπιγνοῦσιν ὑποστρέψαι) unites the practical and theoretical elements. Cf. also Epict. Diss., I, 6, 42 ff.; 9, 11; P. Masp., 4, 9 (6th cent. A.D.): τὸν ἀΐδιον ἐπιγινώσκειν θεόν.

The corresponding use for knowledge on God's part in the sense of election, which is so characteristic of the OT, is occasionally found, most clearly at 2 Tm. 2:19: ἔγνω κύριος τοὺς ὄντας αὐτοῦ (= Nu. 16:5; cf. also Mt. 7:23), but also 1 C. 8:3; 13:12; Gl. 4:9 (→ infra). This usage is the furthest from ordinary Greek and was later abandoned.

The noun γνῶσις occurs in the same OT sense as γινώσκειν. γνῶσις (τοῦ θεοῦ) is obedient acknowledgment of the will of God. When Paul in R. 2:20 characterises the Jews as ἔχοντα τὴν μόρφωσιν τῆς γνώσεως καὶ τῆς ἀληθείας ἐν τῷ νόμῳ, γνῶσις, even though it does not have the supplementary gen., is equivalent to the OT דַּעַת, i.e., knowledge of the will of God as declared ἐν τῷ νόμῳ. Yet there is also a suggestion of the theoretical knowledge of monotheism; this is emphasised by the addition καὶ τῆς ἀληθείας. For at this point the Jew is contrasted with the Gentile who is engulfed by the σκότος of polytheism. Obedience is plainly meant by the γνῶσις τῶν δικαιωμάτων of Barn., 21, 5 and the γνῶσις ὁδοῦ δικαιοσύνης of Barn., 5, 4. The same is true of 2 Cl., 3, 1: τίς ἡ γνῶσις ἡ πρὸς αὐτόν (God), ἢ τὸ μὴ ἀρνεῖσθαι δι' οὗ ἔγνωμεν αὐτόν (i.e., Christ); the required ὁμολογία, however, consists ἐν τῷ ποιεῖν ἃ λέγει (2 Cl., 3, 4). We have already seen (→ 702) that the Christian liturgy takes over the OT and Jewish concept of דַּעַת (Did., 9, 3; 10, 2; Const. Ap., VII, 33-39). In the NT itself the concept also occurs with distinctive shades of meaning at 2 C. 2:14; 4:6; 10:5 (→ 710). Whether Lk. 11:52 has this דעת in view in its alteration of Q (cf. Mt. 22:13) is not certain; there might be a reference to theoretical knowledge of God in the Hellenistic sense. There can be no doubt, however, that Lk. 1:77: τοῦ δοῦναι γνῶσιν σωτηρίας τῷ λαῷ αὐτοῦ, is meant in the OT sense; the content of σωτηρία is here elucidated by the ἐν ἀφέσει ἁμαρτιῶν αὐτῶν. Naturally, γνῶσις here is not theoretical impartation, but either the divinely fashioned acknowledgment of the new order of salvation (cf. Is. 59:7 f.; Lk. 19:42, 44, → supra) or more likely an inward appropriation or experience. [68] God Himself is the Subject of γνῶσις in R. 11:33: ὦ βάθος πλούτου καὶ σοφίας καὶ γνώσεως θεοῦ. The expression is OT and Jewish, though there is no direct parallel. [69] It

---

[68] On this pt. cf. ψ 15:11: ἐγνώρισάς μοι ὁδοὺς ζωῆς and 97:2: ἐγνώρισεν κύριος τὸ σωτήριον αὐτοῦ ἐναντίον τῶν ἐθνῶν. Cf. also Lidz. Joh., II, XVII, n. 2 on γνῶσις σωτηρίας.

[69] Cf. the descriptions of the divine transcendence and inscrutability in Is. 40:12 ff.; 55:8 f.; Prv. 30:1 ff.; Job 9:1 ff.; 28:23 ff.; for Judaism cf. Bar. 3:29 ff.; Sir. 42:18 ff.; 43:15 ff.; Wis. 9:13 ff. and Str.-B., III, 294 f. on R. 11:33. The OT and Judaism like to heap up expressions for knowledge and wisdom: Ex. 31:3; 35:31 (both in the secular sense); Dt. 4:6; Is. 11:2; Prv. 1:4; 2:6; 8:12; Qoh. 1:18; 2:26; Bar. 3:14; Sir. 1:19; S. Nu., 41 on 6:25; Barn., 2, 3 (cf. Windisch in the Supplement to the Handb. z. NT); 21, 5. Cf. also Phil. 1:9; Col. 1:9; Eph. 1:17.

best fits the context to take it on the analogy of יָדַע in the sense of election. That is, the reference is to the gracious will of God directing history according to His plan.

Rather curiously, the compound ἐπίγνωσις has become almost a technical term for the decisive knowledge of God which is implied in conversion to the Christian faith. The verb, too, is often used in this sense (→ supra). To be sure, there is no technical use in R. 1:28 (τὸν θεὸν ἔχειν ἐν ἐπιγνώσει, → 703). This is plain, however, in the Past.; cf. 1 Tm. 2:4 (θεοῦ) ὃς πάντας ἀνθρώπους θέλει σωθῆναι καὶ εἰς ἐπίγνωσιν ἀληθείας ἐλθεῖν; Tt. 1:1; 2 Tm. 2:25; 3:7. In the last two passages the meaning is true doctrine as opposed to false. Similarly, Hb. 10:26 speaks of the ἐπίγνωσις τῆς ἀληθείας, while 1 Cl., 59, 2; Mart. Pol., 14, 1; 2 Pt. 1:3, 8; 2:20 mention God or Christ as object. [70] The theoretical element is present in all these cases, yet it is assumed that Christian knowledge carries with it a corresponding manner of life.

Judaism already makes frequent use of ἐπιγ- (both verb and noun) for the knowledge of God: Ex. 14:4; Hos. 2:20; 4:1, 6; 5:4; 6:6; Ez. 25:14; ψ 78:6; Prv. 2:5; Sir. 23:27; 33(36):5; Test. N. 4:3; 2 Macc. 3:28; 9:11; Jdt. 9:14; Wis. 5:7 (vl.); 12:27; Sib., 3, 557; Philo Leg. All., III, 48; Som., I, 230; Omn. Prob. Lib., 74 (πρὸς ἐπίγνωσιν ἀληθείας). It is just as hard to find any strict distinction between γνῶσις and ἐπίγνωσις in the NT as it is in the LXX and Philo (→ 703). The same holds good of Justin Dial., 3, 5; Iren., I, 21, 4 (MPG, 7, 665a). The γνόντες τὸν θεόν of R. 1:21 corresponds to the τὸν θεὸν ἔχειν ἐν ἐπιγνώσει of 1:28; and the τὴν ἁμαρτίαν οὐκ ἔγνων εἰ μὴ διὰ νόμου of 7:7 to the διὰ γὰρ νόμου ἐπίγνωσις ἁμαρτίας of 3:20. Similarly, ἐπίγνωσις in Phil. 1:9 has exactly the same meaning as γνῶσις in 1 C. 1:5; R. 15:14. Again, if γνῶσις can mean inward appropriation (→ 706), so, too, can ἐπίγνωσις in R. 3:20. Again, ἐπιγινώσκειν as well as γνῶσις can have the sense of obedient recognition and insight into the will of God (R. 10:2; cf. v. 3: οὐχ ὑπετάγησαν and 11:30-32). It is in vain that Origen tries to make a distinction at Eph. 1:15 ff.: [71] εἰ γὰρ μὴ ταὐτόν ἐστι γνῶσις θεοῦ καὶ ἐπίγνωσις θεοῦ, ἀλλ' ὁ ἐπιγνώσκων οἱονεὶ ἀναγνωρίζει ὃ πάλαι εἰδὼς ἐπελέληστο, ὅσοι ἐν ἐπιγνώσει γίνονται θεοῦ πάλαι ᾔδεσαν αὐτόν (ψ 21:27 being adduced in support). [72] Epict. uses ἐπιγινώσκειν of the knowledge of God in Diss., I, 6, 42; 9, 11, but γινώσκειν has the same meaning, e.g., I, 3, 2. He uses ἐπίγνωσις τῆς ἀληθείας in the same general sense as Philo (→ supra). Ἐπίγνωσις τῶν ἁπάντων is found in Ep. Ar., 139 and γινώσκειν ἅπαντα in Chrysipp. (III, 60, 28, Arnim). According to Iren., I, 21, 4 (MPG, 7, 665a) the Marcosites teach: εἶναι δὲ τελείαν ἀπολύτρωσιν αὐτὴν τὴν ἐπίγνωσιν τοῦ ἀρρήτου μεγέθους, and in Jul. Conv., p. 336c (Hertlein) Hermes says: σοὶ δέ ... δέδωκα τὸν πατέρα Μίθραν ἐπιγνῶναι. Cf. also Porphyr. Abst., II, 53: ἐπιγνῶναι τὸ ἐν τοῖς ὅλοις τιμιώτατον καὶ πᾶν τὸ ἐν τῷ ὅλῳ ἀγαθὸν φίλον καὶ προσήγορον.

The Christian view of knowledge is thus largely determined by the OT. An obedient and grateful acknowledgment of the deeds and demands of God is linked with knowledge of God and what He has done and demands. It is in keeping that this Christian knowledge is not a fixed possession but develops in the life of the Christian as lasting obedience and reflection. For this reason γνῶσις is regarded as a gift of grace which marks the life of the Christian by determining its ex-

---

[70] Philo Omn. Prob. Lib., 74 and Epict. Diss., II, 20, 21 are only formal parallels; for here ἐπίγνωσις (τῆς) ἀληθείας means knowledge of truth or reality in general.
[71] JThSt, 3 (1902), 399, 26 ff.
[72] Cf. M. Dibelius, Nt.liche Studien f. G. Heinrici (1914), 176 ff., and on 1 Tm. 2:4 (Dib. Past.); Wnd. Hb. on 10:26.

pression (1 C. 1:5; 12:8; [73] 2 C. 8:7; 1 Cl., 1, 2; if there is here no supplementary gen., this does not mean that we are to assume a technical Hellenistic usage). This explains the many desires and demands for (ἐπι-)γνῶσις and other statements concerning it. Intrinsically the usage is that of popular Greek, and we may always translate "knowledge." If the theoretical element determines the concept, the practical consequences are always implied. It is characteristic that the guiding factor is not interest in Christian learning but the edification of the community which is to be advanced by the γνῶσις of the individual (R. 15:14; 1 C. 14:6; 1 Cl., 48, 5; Did., 11, 2). Phil. 1:9 f. shows plainly that reflective enquiry is involved, but it is grounded in love and thus leads to right action : ἵνα ἡ ἀγάπη ὑμῶν ... περισσεύῃ ἐν ἐπιγνώσει καὶ πάσῃ αἰσθήσει, εἰς τὸ δοκιμάζειν ὑμᾶς τὰ διαφέροντα, ἵνα ἦτε εἰλικρινεῖς καὶ ἀπρόσκοποι. Cf. also Phlm. 6 : ὅπως ἡ κοινωνία τῆς πίστεώς σου ἐνεργὴς γένηται ἐν ἐπιγνώσει παντὸς ἀγαθοῦ τοῦ ἐν ἡμῖν εἰς Χριστόν. The faith which Phlm. shares is to be effectual in his recognition of all that is given to the believer and of what must foster union with Christ when it is expressed. That this knowledge of the ἀγαθόν must result in action may be seen from what follows. In Col. 1:9 f. ἐπίγνωσις leads to περιπατῆσαι ἀξίως τοῦ κυρίου. The new man, who has put away heathen vices, is renewed εἰς ἐπίγνωσιν (Col. 3:10). The Christian husband lives with his wife κατὰ γνῶσιν (1 Pt. 3:7). In Barn., 18, 1 ethical instruction is a distinctive form of γνῶσις and διδαχή, and the description of the ὁδὸς τοῦ φωτός in 19:1 is introduced as follows : ἔστιν οὖν ἡ δοθεῖσα ἡμῖν γνῶσις τοῦ περιπατεῖν ἐν αὐτῇ τοιαύτη· ἀγαπήσεις τὸν ποιήσαντά σε ... Cf. also 2 Pt. 1:3, 5 f.; 3:18; Barn., 2, 3; 21, 5.

Nevertheless, the theoretical element can be more strongly emphasised. γινώσκειν (or γνῶσις) can be specifically theological knowledge. This grows, e.g., out of the study of Scripture. γινώσκειν is used in this way in Gl. 3:7; Jm. 2:20; Barn., 7, 1; 14, 7; 16, 2; and γνῶσις, which in Barn., 1, 5 means primarily Christian knowledge in general, later denotes the knowledge attained by allegorical exposition of Scripture (6, 9; 9, 8; 13, 7). Similarly, in 1 Cl., 32, 1; 40, 1 (ἐγκεκυφότες εἰς τὰ βάθη τῆς θείας γνώσεως); 41, 4, γνῶσις is used for the Christian knowledge won from Scripture. In Herm. v., 2, 2, 1 understanding of the mysterious βιβλαρίδιον is γνῶσις. The understanding of parables or allegories (ibid., 3, 1, 2; 4, 3; s., 5, 3, 1; 9, 5, 3 etc.) is γινώσκειν. Realisation that faith implies knowledge of τὰ μυστήρια τῆς βασιλείας τοῦ θεοῦ (Mt. 13:11 and par.; cf. Wis. 2:22) leads to the idea of γινώσκειν as systematic theological knowledge. Paul introduces his theological interpretation of baptism at R. 6:6 with the words τοῦτο γινώσκοντες. Col. shows how faith leads εἰς ἐπίγνωσιν τοῦ μυστηρίου τοῦ Χριστοῦ, ἐν ᾧ εἰσιν πάντες οἱ θησαυροὶ τῆς σοφίας καὶ γνώσεως ἀπόκρυφοι (2:2); and the author of Eph., who desires such γνῶσις for his readers (1:17; 3:19; 4:13), gives more than one example of it (→ γνωρίζω).

3. The Influence of Gnostic Usage.

a. Early Christianity had to develop such γνῶσις in conflict not only with

---

[73] It does not seem possible to me to make a precise distinction between the λόγος γνώσεως and the λόγος σοφίας in 1 C. 12:8 (cf. the comm.), whether in respect of form or of content. Certainly I do not agree with C. Weizsäcker, Das apostol. Zeitalter der christl. Kirche³ (1902), 580, that both forms of λόγος, as forms of διδαχή, are to be distinguished from ἀποκάλυψις and προφητεία. According to 13:2 and also 14:6 such a sharp differentiation cannot be made.

polytheism but especially with heathen Gnosticism, which in conjunction with the Mystery religions competed with its preaching. The result, however, was to bring the Christian message into some analogy with heathen Gnosticism and to expose it to the acute danger of penetration not merely by Gnostic terminology but by Gnostic problems and conceptions. The danger was the more acute in view of the current infection of Jewish circles by Gnosticism. Jd., 2 Pt. and 1 Jn. are not the first writings to oppose Gnostic teachers in the Christian communities. Rev. 2:24 is not the first statement to the effect that they ἔγνωσαν τὰ βαθέα τοῦ Σατανᾶ. [74] The Past. are not the first epistles to contend against ψευδώνυμος γνῶσις (1 Tm. 6:20). The terminology of Col. and Eph. is not the first to be fashioned in opposition to Gnosticism. [75] Already at Corinth there had been a movement of Gnostic pneumatics, and Paul had had to resist their influence. The struggle for speculative wisdom (1 C. 1:17 ff.), the insistence on γνῶσις, on the ἐξουσία with which it invested them in matters of personal conduct (6:12 ff.; 8:1 ff.), and on demonstrations of a pneumatic quality (2 C. 10-13), shows that the opponents were Gnostics; so, too, does the tendency towards asceticism (1 C. 7) and the denial of the resurrection of the body (1 C. 15). Paul for his part maintains the uniqueness of genuine Christian knowledge, but in so doing he appropriates to some extent the vocabulary and approach of the Gnostics. [76] This is shown by the use of γνῶσις in the absolute at 1 C. 8:1, 7, 10 f.; 13:8. But this brings the antithesis into clear focus. He concedes (1 C. 2:6 ff.) that the Christian, too, has a σοφία which makes possible for him a γινώσκειν of the divine plan of salvation which is concealed from rulers — a knowledge which penetrates the βάθη τοῦ θεοῦ because it rests on the divinely given πνεῦμα. He concedes that the → πνευματικός is exalted above the → ψυχικός and is judged of no man. But the theme of this γινώσκειν is simply the divine act of salvation (τὰ ὑπὸ τοῦ θεοῦ χαρισθέντα ἡμῖν, 2:12). Hence there is no question of vague speculation. Again, this γινώσκειν is achieved only by those who walk according to the πνεῦμα (3:1 ff.). That the Gnostic does not have a mysterious quality which he can enjoy is shown plainly by 1 C. 8:1 ff.: ... εἴ τις δοκεῖ ἐγνωκέναι τι, οὔπω ἔγνω καθὼς δεῖ γνῶναι· εἰ δέ τις ἀγαπᾷ τὸν θεόν, οὗτος ἔγνωσται ὑπ' αὐτοῦ ... Here it is plain 1. that the knowledge of the one God is not theoretical speculation, which allows the one who has it to live according to his own caprice (ἐξουσία, v. 9), but is genuine only when there is corresponding ἀγάπη; 2. that ἀγαπᾶν τὸν θεόν is not a mystical relationship to God but finds expression in brotherly love; and 3. that γινώσκειν does not arise from within man but is grounded in God's knowledge of man (note the surprising substitution of the passive for the active). That this knowledge of God is His election of grace, and that ἔγνωσται (ὑπ' αὐτοῦ) is thus to be understood in terms of OT ידע, is beyond

---

[74] It is surely obvious that we have here a formula of Gnostic teaching. Probably those under rebuke were taking Satan mythology seriously (Ophites, Cainites) and drawing licentious deductions from Gnosticism. This is preferable to the view that the author is simply twisting the slogan of opponents who really spoke of the βαθέα τοῦ θεοῦ.

[75] The conflict in Col. is against a false syncretistic and Gnostic teaching. Not merely the vocabulary but the cosmological speculation applied in Christological exposition is influenced by this antithesis. In Eph. there is no polemic, the vocabulary is applied in a different direction and ecclesiological conceptions replace the cosmological; cf. esp. Dib. Gefbr.; H. Schlier, *Christus u. d. Kirche im Epheserbrief* (1930).

[76] Cf. esp. Reitzenstein Hell. Myst., 258 ff.; 333 ff.; Bousset, *Kyrios Chr.*², 113 ff.; 130 ff. For a different view, cf. K. Deissner, *Pls. u. d. Mystik seiner Zeit*² (1921); A. Schweitzer, *Die Mystik des Apostels Pls.* (1930).

question. There is an analogous case in Gl. 4:9 : νῦν δὲ γνόντες θεόν, μᾶλλον δὲ γνωσθέντες ὑπ' αὐτοῦ. Since knowledge here is the wholly non-mystical knowledge imparted by missionary preaching, γνωσθῆναι can only have the same sense as κλῆσις and ἐκλογή elsewhere. Opposition to Gnosticism may also be seen in 1 C. 13. The γνῶσις given to faith is not to be equated here with OT דעת. The absolute use in v. 8 shows that it is viewed, on the Gnostic analogy, as a pneumatic capacity for knowledge. This much is conceded. Nevertheless, 1. this γνῶσις is set under ἀγάπη, without which it is worthless ; and 2. it is described as something provisional and inadequate which will pass away, whereas πίστις, ἐλπίς and ἀγάπη remain. Gnostic piety is surpassed by ἀγάπη and eschatological faith. γνῶσις is not the true relationship to God. Indeed, there is no direct relationship to God as Gnosticism claims, at any rate in this life. When Paul uses ἐπιγνώσομαι for the future relationship, he is certainly adopting Gnostic usage. [77] But the term is robbed of its Gnostic significance by the phrase καθὼς καὶ ἐπεγνώσθην, which is to be understood as in 1 C. 8:3 and Gl. 4:9. [78]

Similarly it might be shown that in the struggle against Gnostic pneumatics in 2 C. Paul adopts the Gnostic approach and describes his own calling in terms of the dissemination of γνῶσις. But the objective genitives used with γνῶσις show that it is primarily acknowledgment (2:14; 4:6; 10:5). In the passage Phil. 3:8 ff., which also contains Gnostic expressions, Paul undoubtedly borrows from the Gnostics in describing the γνῶσις Χριστοῦ Ἰησοῦ as a distinctive mark of the Christian. But this γνῶσις corresponds to the resolve to renounce πεποιθέναι ἐν σαρκί (v. 4 ff.) and consists in the knowledge of Christ as the Lord. The existential character of this emerges plainly in the fact that this resolve is not made once and for all but must be continually renewed (v. 12 ff.). In v. 9 f. γνῶσις is explained as εὑρεθῆναι, i.e., being drawn into God's saving act in virtue of πίστις, which never possesses its object but looks to God on the one side and to the future on the other. Hence γνῶναι (v. 10) is not withdrawal from existence in earthly history but experience of the δύναμις τῆς ἀναστάσεως αὐτοῦ and the κοινωνία τῶν παθημάτων αὐτοῦ within historical life (cf. 2 C. 4:7 ff.), which for the Christian is changed by the event of salvation and behind which stands the ἐξανάστασις ἐκ νεκρῶν (v. 11). That all this is very different from Gnosticism

---

[77] A Rabbi would have spoken of "seeing" God, thought not in the sense of ecstatic and mystical vision, cf. R. Bultmann, ZNW, 29 (1930), 186 ff. Paul does indeed begin : βλέπομεν γὰρ ἄρτι, but the continuation : ἄρτι γινώσκω, shows that in the chapter he is discussing the Gnostic problem.

[78] Reitzenstein Hell. Myst., 383 ff. seems to me to be right in his view that in 1 C. 13:13 Paul is wrestling against a formula of Gnostic origin, in which γνῶσις is a divine power which in company with other powers (πίστις, ἐλπίς, ἀγάπη) constitutes the pneumatic man and establishes his immortality. Paul not only rejects the description of such magnitudes as δυνάμεις (or στοιχεῖα) but reduces the number to three by the exclusion of γνῶσις. On this discussion, cf. also R. Reitzenstein, *Historia Monachorum u. Historia Lausiaca* (1916), 100 ff.; 242 f.; *Histor. Zeitschr.*, 116 (1916), 189 ff.; NGG (1916), 367 ff.; (1917), 130 ff.; E. Norden, *Agnostos Theos* (1913), 352 ff.; A. v. Harnack, *Preuss. Jahrb.*, 161 1916), 1 ff.; M. Dibelius, *Wochenschr. f. klass. Phil.*, 30 (1913), 1041 f.; P. Corssen, *Sokrates, NF*, 7 (1919), 18 ff. On the other hand, Reitzenstein is obviously wrong in his derivation of the correspondence between knowing God and being known by Him (1 C. 8:3; 13:12; Gl. 4:9) from mystic usage. Corp. Herm., X, 15 (→ 694) is no true analogy, for the οὐκ ἄρα ἀγνοεῖ τὸν ἄνθρωπον ὁ θεός does not really refer, as Paul does, to the act of God which in its concrete fulfilment (κλῆσις) is the foundation of the knowledge of the individual ; it is conceived very generally. Similarly, there is no material parallel in Porphyr. Marc., 13 (σοφὸς δὲ ἄνθρωπος ... γινώσκεται ὑπὸ θεοῦ), since God's knowledge is here grounded in the conduct of the σοφός.

is finally illustrated by the fact that Paul is not describing individual experiences but the character of Christian existence in general.

b. A greater role is played by γινώσκειν in John's Gospel and 1 John (ἐπιγινώσκειν does not occur, nor, perhaps intentionally, γνῶσις) than in any other early Christian writings. Apart from its ordinary use, the word here denotes emphatically the relationship to God and to Jesus as a personal fellowship in which each is decisively determined by the other in his own existence. As the relationship between the Father and the Son, which elsewhere can be described as εἶναι ἐν (Jn. 10:38; 14:11; 17:21; cf. esp. 1 Jn. 2:3, 5; 5:20) and even ἐν εἶναι (Jn. 10:30), is a mutual γινώσκειν, so is the relationship between Jesus and His own (Jn. 10:14 f., 27; cf. 7:29; 8:55), which can also be described as εἶναι ἐν (Jn. 15:1 ff.; 17:21). But if the one who knows is determined in his existence by the one who is known, the meaning of knowledge is determined by the nature of the one who is known. Because God and the Son are and have ζωή (5:26), it is αἰώνιος ζωή to know God and Jesus Christ (17:3), and it "sufficeth" to be shown the Father (14:8). Thus it is obvious that γινώσκειν is the supreme and true mode of being. But it is also obvious that materially this is understood to be ἀγάπη. God is ἀγάπη, so that the man who is related to Him is related as one who loves (1 Jn. 4:8, 16). To be determined by love is thus a criterion of the knowledge of God (1 Jn. 4:7 f.; cf. 4:20 f.), as also of belonging to Jesus (Jn. 13:35). Like γινώσκειν, ἀγαπᾶν determines the relationship between the Father and the Son (Jn. 3:35; 10:17; 15:9; 17:23 f., 26 and 14:31), and also between Jesus and His own (13:1, 34; 14:21 ff.; 15:12, 17). Hence it is plain that γινώσκειν does not mean the knowledge of investigation, observation or speculation, nor of mystical vision remote from historical contacts or action; it achieves concrete expression in historical acts. The ἀγάπη of God for the κόσμος is actualised in the sending of the Son (Jn. 3:16; 1 Jn. 4:9 f.), and the ἀγάπη of Jesus in obedience to the Father and service for the world or for His own (Jn. 14:31; 13:1 ff.; 15:9, 12 f.). Since the knowledge of Jesus or of God expresses itself accordingly in ἀγαπᾶν, observing the commandments (which have in ἀγάπη their content) might also be called a criterion of γινώσκειν (1 Jn. 2:3-5; cf. 3:6). Yet γινώσκειν, as determination by God or Jesus, is ἀγάπη not merely in ἀγαπᾶν as loving action but also in awareness of being loved. The saying: μείνατε ἐν τῇ ἀγάπῃ τῇ ἐμῇ (15:9) can signify abiding both in being loved and in loving (cf. 17:26; 1 Jn. 4:16). Indeed, the former, and awareness of it, are the basis of the latter (1 Jn. 4:10). The phrase καθὼς ἠγάπησα ὑμᾶς (Jn. 13:34; 15:12) means "on the basis of the fact that I have loved you." This means that γινώσκειν has primarily the sense of the recognition and reception of love, i.e., πίστις. But this shows again that the γινώσκειν which is orientated to God, which thus brings ζωή to man (17:3; 14:8 → supra) and which the Son has been sent to make possible (1:18; 17:4 ff.), does not connote a direct relationship to God but has its object in revelation, in Jesus. Direct knowledge of God is excluded (1:18), and all pretended knowledge is tested by the appearance and claim of Jesus (5:37 f.; 7:28 f.; 8:19). God does not exist apart from revelation. [79] Jesus, however, is revelation for the sinful κόσμος. To see and confess Him is to see the Father (14:7-9; cf. 14:20; 1 Jn. 5:20). To know Him, however, is

---

[79] This is absolutely true, and is the meaning of Jn. 1:1 ff. God was never without the → λόγος, so that it has always been true: ὁ κόσμος αὐτὸν οὐκ ἔγνω (Jn. 1:10). Since σάρξ ἐγένετο this is true in a special sense: there is no knowledge of God apart from Jesus. Cf. R. Bultmann, Z.d.Z., 6 (1928), 11 ff.

not merely to have information concerning the circumstances of His life (6:42; 7:28). It is to know His unity with the Father (10:38; 14:20; 16:3). Nor does this mean a mystical relationship with Jesus. It means understanding Him in His obedience and love. It means seeing in Him the ἅγιος τοῦ θεοῦ, i.e., the One whom God has sent and who has sanctified Himself for the world (14:31; 6:69; 17:3, 18 f.). He is also present as such in the proclamation of the community, so that it may be said: ὁ γινώσκων τὸν θεὸν ἀκούει ἡμῶν, ὃς οὐκ ἔστιν ἐκ τοῦ θεοῦ οὐκ ἀκούει ἡμῶν (1 Jn. 4:6; cf. 3:1). The same is true of the ἄλλος παράκλητος, i.e., of the Spirit who is at work in the Church's preaching. The world does not know Him, but the community does, because He determines its being (14:17).

Since γινώσκειν thus means acceptance of the divine act of love in Jesus, and obedience to its demand, it might appear that Johannine γινώσκειν corresponds to OT ידע. There is indeed a relationship, but we can also see the distinctiveness of the Johannine view when we realise that it is paradoxically building on the γινώσκειν of Hellenistic Gnosticism. This emerges 1. in the way in which it can be combined or used interchangeably with verbs of seeing (e.g., Jn. 14:7-9, 17, 19 f.; 1 Jn. 3:6; 4:14). The author is obviously opposed to those who allege a non-historical vision and knowledge of God.[80] But he accepts their approach. What they seek will be accomplished, but very differently. It also emerges 2. in the apparently dogmatic way in which ὅτι- statements describe the content of γινώσκειν. There is battle for a dogma (a διδαχή, Jn. 7:16 f.), i.e., the dogma of the divine sonship of Jesus (7:26; 10:38; 14:20; 16:3; 17:7 f., 23, 25 etc.). Certainly what is at issue is the historical nature of revelation. But this leads to the offence of dogmatic knowledge. We cannot omit this trait in our depiction of Johannine γινώσκειν. It emerges 3. in the fact that obedience (ἀγαπᾶν) is called the *criterion* of γινώσκειν (→ 711). This means that the author does not identify it with γινώσκειν (cf. ידע). His polemical thesis that γινώσκειν is actualised in obedience (esp. in 1 Jn.) is paradoxical in relation to the presupposed concept. Finally, it emerges 4. in the distinctive interrelating of πιστεύειν and γινώσκειν. That γινώσκειν denotes a full and true relation to the object may be seen from the fact that only γινώσκειν and not πιστεύειν is used of the mutual relationship of the Father and the Son. In the relationship of man to God, or to revelation, πιστεύειν denotes the first movement which, if maintained, has promise of γινώσκειν (Jn. 8:31 f. → ἀλήθεια; 10:38; cf. 14:20). Faith alone, which is constantly required by Jesus, is the doing of the will of God which is followed by γινώσκειν (Jn. 7:17). γινώσκειν is impossible where the Word is not heard (8:43), i.e., where faith is refused (cf. Jn. 5:24; 6:60 with 6:64, 69; 12:46-48; 17:8 : to hear or to receive the Word is to believe). In John, therefore, πιστεύειν corresponds to the OT ידע, while γινώσκειν lies beyond. Far from signifying obedience or grateful submission, it is promised to these acts.[81] This does not mean, of course,

---

[80] 1 Jn. makes it quite evident that the opponents are Gnostics.

[81] For this reason Jn. differs from Paul in not using γινώσκειν for God's electing, though he has the thought of election (6:70; 13:18; esp. 15:16, 19). In 10:14 f., 27, the knowledge of Jesus does not precede or underlie that of His disciples (note the difference in tense from Paul). It corresponds to theirs and is contemporary with it. The relationship is that of mutual γινώσκειν. In this respect he obviously follows Gnostic usage (→ 694, and R. Bultmann, ZNW, 24 (1925), 117 f.). Only in 8:32; 14:31; 17:23 may we see the OT concept of ידע. The world will one day realise to its horror (cf. the ἐλέγχειν which the παράκλητος will exercise, 16:8-11) that Jesus is the Revealer ; cf. Is. 41:20; 43:10: → 698.

that the object of γινώσκειν is different from that of πιστεύειν. Nor does it mean that γινώσκειν is a higher stage of development at which there is possession of what is known. The normal movement from πιστεύειν to γινώσκειν (6:69; 8:31 f.; 10:38) can be reversed. γινώσκειν gives πιστεύειν new power (16:30; 17:7 f.; cf. 1 Jn. 4:16; cf. Tob. 14:4 א). True faith, i.e., the faith which "abideth," contains γινώσκειν within itself (cf. 1 Jn. 2:4 with 6). γινώσκειν is a constitutive element in πιστεύειν. It is faith's own understanding, identical with the χαρά which no longer needs to "ask" (Jn. 15:11; 16:22-24) but for which the Word of Jesus has the character of παρρησία rather than παροιμία (16:25, 29).

On the basis of his distinctive conception of the knowledge of God John can both vary and deepen the traditional use (→ 705) of γινώσκειν (τὴν ἀλήθειαν) for conversion to Christianity.

c. There has been much dispute concerning the interpretation of Mt. 11:27 and par.: πάντα μοι παρεδόθη ὑπὸ τοῦ πατρός μου, καὶ οὐδεὶς ἐπιγινώσκει τὸν υἱὸν εἰ μὴ ὁ πατήρ, οὐδὲ τὸν πατέρα τις ἐπιγινώσκει εἰ μὴ ὁ υἱὸς καὶ ᾧ ἐὰν βούληται ὁ υἱὸς ἀποκαλύψαι (the Lucan version differs only in style). Apart from Mk. 13:32, this verse, with its reference to the Son in the third person, stands quite alone in the Synoptists, though it has affinities with Johannine usage. It hardly seems to have any original connection with the neighbouring verses (25 f.; 28-30); the latter have no par. in Lk. [82] The text is uncertain, since the order of the statements which describe the mutual knowledge of Father and Son varies in the tradition, and the statement that no one knows the Father but the Son is perhaps a later addition. If it is original, then the relationship between the Father and the Son is here described as in John, and the view of knowledge is necessarily the same. But even if it is not genuine, the ἐπιγινώσκειν can be understood only in the Johannine sense, for in view of the καὶ ᾧ ἐὰν — ἀποκαλύψαι, the ἐπιγινώσκειν cannot be equivalent to the OT דעת י. Here then, as in Jn., we have Gnostic terminology, and the question whether this is an authentic saying of Jesus must be discussed along the same lines as the relation of the Johannine sayings to the Synoptic. [83]

F. The Later Development of the Usage.

The works of the Apologists yield nothing distinctive. Except in quotations from the OT, they follow popular usage, i.e., γινώσκειν and γνῶσις (or ἐπιγινώσκειν and

---

[82] Bultmann Trad., 171 f.

[83] It is worth noting that Str.-B. on Mt. 11:27 cannot adduce any par., and that the Rabb. par. in Schl. Mt., 384 merely illustrate the OT and Jewish concept of דעת י. The Hellenistic nature of ἐπιγινώσκειν in Mt. 11:27, with which we may compare the par. Jul. Conv., 336c mentioned on → 707, is strongly felt by the Jewish exegete C. G. Montefiore, *The Synoptic Gospels*,[2] II (1927), 175 f. Dalman WJ, I, 158 f., who also regards the οὐδὲ ὁ υἱὸς εἰ μὴ ὁ πατήρ of Mk. 13:32 as an addition, feels that the absolute use of "the Father" and "the Son" is non-Jewish, and therefore regards the statement as a very general one, i.e., as "reference to something which is true of every father and son, and which may thus be applied to Jesus and His Father as well." This is quite impossible. Perhaps there is a suggestion of Gnostic terminology in the πάντα μοι παρεδόθη, cf. Corp. Herm., I, 32: εὐλογητὸς εἶ πάτερ· ὁ σὸς ἄνθρωπος συναγιάζειν σοι βούλεται, καθὼς παρέδωκας αὐτῷ τὴν πᾶσαν ἐξουσίαν. Apart from the comm., cf. A. Harnack, "Sprüche und Reden Jesu" in *Beitr. z. Einl. in d. NT*, II (1907), 189 ff.; Norden, *Agnostos Theos*, 277 ff.; J. Weiss, *Nt.liche Studien für G. Heinrici* (1914), 120 ff.; Bousset, *Kyrios Christ.*,[2] 45 ff.

ἐπίγνωσις) always denote theoretical knowledge, primarily as knowledge of God or of the ἀλήθεια or Christ, [84] then as knowledge attained from Scripture [85] and finally as theological knowledge. [86] The battle against Gnosis and wrestling with Greek philosophy led the Alexandrians to reconstruct the view of *gnosis* and to distinguish between πίστις and γνῶσις, not as John does, but in such sort that γνῶσις is regarded as a higher stage of Christian life; the γνωστικός is the τέλειος. Here we have a distinctive but obscure combination of the Greek conception of knowledge and the Gnostic view of the vision of God.

That πίστις and γνῶσις are linked is often stated incidentally and with no attempt at delimitation (Corp. Herm., IV, 4; IX, 10; Porphyr. Marc., 21-24; Just. Dial., 69, 1). The Christian Gnostics were the first to attempt a clear formulation. They were forced to do this because they wished to maintain their own position within the Church and had thus to recognise the ordinary Christians who were not γνωστικοί (πνευματικοί, τέλειοι) as those who had πίστις but not γνῶσις. In this connection the word → ψυχικός, originally the opposite of πνευματικός, came to denote a new category midway between the πνευματικός and the σαρκικός. According to Cl. Al. Strom., II, 3, 10, the use of πίστις and γνῶσις for two different stages goes back to Valentinus. Cl. and Orig. accepted it as a basis for their scientific and speculative theology in the Church. If πίστις is a γνῶσις σύντομος τῶν κατεπειγόντων, γνῶσις is the ἀπόδειξις τῶν διὰ πίστεως παρειλημμένων τῇ πίστει ἐποικοδομουμένη (Cl. Al. Strom., VII, 10, 57; cf. 55 f.). πίστις is ἡ πρώτη πρὸς σωτηρίαν νεῦσις (*ibid.*, II, 6, 31), but πλέον δέ ἐστι τοῦ πιστεῦσαι τὸ γνῶναι (*ibid.*, VI, 14, 109). The movement is ἐκ πίστεως εἰς γνῶσιν, but always in such a way that πίστις is never wholly without γνῶσις and γνῶσις is never ἄνευ πίστεως (*ibid.*, II, 6, 31; V. 1, 1), so that it is possible to speak of πίστις γνωστική or ἐπιστημονική (*ibid.*, VI, 9, 76; II, 11, 48). γνῶσις leads to fulfilment, to vision (*ibid.*, VI, 7, 61; 12, 98), and when it is said that it leads to ἀγάπη (*ibid.*, VII, 10, 55 and 57) this ἀγάπη γνωστική (*ibid.*, VI, 9, 73 and 75) is identical with θεωρία. This γνῶσις can never be lost: οὔποτε οὖν ἄγνοια γίνεται ἡ γνῶσις οὐδὲ μεταβάλλει τὸ ἀγαθὸν εἰς κακόν (*ibid.*, VII, 12, 70). [87]

καταγινώσκω, ἀκατάγνωστος.

In Gk. usage καταγινώσκειν means "to note," "to see something (bad) in someone," "to catch someone" (cf. the pap.), "to see accurately," especially "to know to be guilty," "to judge" (as often in the pap.), sometimes in the sense of self-judgment (cf. Moult.-Mill), and then "to take a low view of," "to despise" (cf. the pap.). [1]

The word is rare in the LXX. It means "to condemn" at Dt. 25:1 (for רשע hiph in antith. to δικαιοῦν, "to acquit") and Sir. 14:2: μακάριος οὗ οὐ κατέγνω ἡ

---

[84] E.g., Aristid., 15, 3; Athenag. Suppl., 13, 1; Just. Apol., I, 19, 6; Dial., 14, 1; 20, 1; Tat. Or. Graec., 12, 4; 13, 1; 19, 2; 42, 1; γινώσκειν τὰ τοῦ Χριστοῦ διδάγματα, Just. Apol., II, 2, 2; absol. of Christian knowledge, Just. Dial., 39, 5. On the possibility of philosophical knowledge of God, cf. Just. Dial., 3 ff.

[85] E.g., Just. Dial., 27, 4; 69, 1; 99, 3; 112, 3.

[86] Cf. Just. Dial., 74, 3: τοὺς ... γνόντας τὸ σωτήριον τοῦτο μυστήριον, τουτέστι τὸ πάθος τοῦ Χριστοῦ.

[87] On the mysterious conception of γνῶσις in Cl. Al. → 694-696, cf. Anrich, *Das antike Mysterienwesen,* 133 ff. In its practical exercise, γνῶσις is for him theological science or speculation as κατὰ τὴν ἐποπτικὴν θεωρίαν γνῶσις which follows the κανὼν τῆς παραδόσεως (Strom., I, 1, 15). In Orig. who distinguishes between πίστις and γνῶσις in the same way as Cl. Al. (e.g., Comm. in Joh., XIX, 3, 16 f.), there is a greater emphasis on the scientific character of γνῶσις. Cf. also the discussion τί πρότερον, ἡ γνῶσις ἤ ἡ πίστις in Bas. Ep., 235 (MPG, 32, 872).

κ α τ α γ ι ν ώ σ κ ω. Apart from the lex., cf. Deissmann NB, 28 f.; Nägeli, 47; F. W. Mozley Exp., 8, Ser. IV (1912), 143 f.; Dib. Past. on Tt. 2:8.

[1] On the different forms of construction, cf. the lex. and grammars.

ψυχὴ αὐτοῦ (Heb. חסר pi). It apparently means "to scorn" at Prv. 28:11 and Sir. 19:5. It is used of self-judgment at Sir. 14:2 and Job 42:6 Σ (for מאס); Ez. 16:61 Σ (for כלם), and also Test. G. 5:3 : οὐχ ὑπ' ἄλλου καταγινωσκόμενος ἀλλ' ὑπὸ τῆς ἰδίας καρδίας. This usage recurs in the NT at 1 Jn. 3:20 f.: ὅτι ἐὰν κατα-γινώσκῃ ἡμῶν ἡ καρδία, ὅτι μείζων ἐστὶν ὁ θεὸς τῆς καρδίας ἡμῶν καὶ γινώσκει πάντα, where the play of words shows that some element of knowledge is still felt to be present. ἀγαπητοί, ἐὰν ἡ καρδία μὴ καταγινώσκῃ παρρησίαν ἔχομεν πρὸς τὸν θεόν. Cf. also Act. Thom., 94, p. 207, 11 f.: μακάριοι οἱ ἅγιοι, ὧν αἱ ψυχαὶ οὐδέποτε ἑαυτῶν κατέγνωσαν. [2] The meaning in Gl. 2:11 is hard to determine : κατὰ πρόσωπον αὐτῷ ἀντέστην ὅτι κατεγνωσμένος ἦν. The Vet. Lat. has *reprehensus,* the Vg. and Ambstr. *reprehensibilis.* We might render "detected," or better "condemned" or "judged," though the reference is not to official judgment but to what is meant in R. 14:23 : ὁ δὲ διακρινόμενος ἐὰν φάγῃ κατακέκριται (Jn. 3:18 is different) or in Jos. Bell., 2, 135, where the Essenes reject the oath : ἤδη γὰρ κατεγνῶσθαί φασιν τὸν ἀπιστούμενον δίχα θεοῦ.

> The meaning is "to condemn" or "to despise" in Dg. , 10, 7: τότε τῆς ἀπάτης τοῦ κόσμου καὶ τῆς πλάνης καταγνώσῃ, ὅταν τὸ ἀληθῶς ἐν οὐρανῷ ζῆν ἐπιγνῷς.
>
> ἀκατάγνωστος means "one against whom no fault can be alleged, and therefore no accusation alleged or sustained." In Gk. it is found only in inscriptions and pap. of the imperial period (Nägeli, 47), where it is often linked with ἄμεμπτος. In the LXX it occurs only at 2 Macc. 4:47: οἵτινες ... ἀπελύθησαν ἀκατάγνωστοι, and in the NT only at Tt. 2:8 : (παρεχόμενος) ... λόγον ὑγιῆ ἀκατάγνωστον.

προγινώσκω, πρόγνωσις.

> προγινώσκειν usually means "to know beforehand" as human foresight or cleverness makes this possible (Eur. Hipp., 1072 f.; Thuc., II, 64, 6; Plat. Resp., IV, 426c; Hippocr. Progn., 1), though any real foreknowledge of destiny is concealed from man (Hom. Hymn. Cer., 256 f.). In the LXX προγινώσκειν is ascribed to σοφία at Wis. 8:8. Similarly Philo speaks of a προγινώσκειν τι τῶν μελλόντων (through dreams) in Som., I, 2. There is a peculiar passive use at Wis. 6:13 : φθάνει (sc. σοφία) τοὺς ἐπιθυμοῦντας προγνωσθῆναι, "it comes to those who long for it, letting itself be known beforehand." Cf. 18:6 : ἐκείνη ἡ νὺξ (of the destruction of the firstborn) προεγνώσθη πατράσιν ἡμῶν.

In the NT προγινώσκειν is referred to God. His foreknowledge, however, is an election or foreordination of His people (R. 8:29; 11:2) or Christ (1 Pt. 1:20) (→ γινώσκω, 698; 706). [1] In Herm. m., 4, 3, 4 it simply means God's foreknow-ledge (cf. προγνώστης in 2 Cl., 9, 9). On the basis of prophecy the word προ-γινώσκειν can be used of believers in 2 Pt. 3:17, as also in Herm. s., 7, 5 → ἐκ-λέγω.

Another possible meaning in Gk. is that of knowing earlier, i.e., than the time speaking (cf. Demosth., 29, 58; Aristot. Rhet., II, 21, p. 1394b, 11; Jos. Bell., 6, 8).

---

[2] There is a materially instructive par. to the use of καταγινώσκω for self-criticism in Stob. Ecl., III, 558, 1 f.: Δημῶναξ ἐρωτηθεὶς πότε ἤρξατο φιλοσοφεῖν "ὅτε κατα-γιγνώσκειν" ἔφη "ἐμαυτοῦ ἠρξάμην."

π ρ ο γ ι ν ώ σ κ ω, π ρ ό γ ν ω σ ι ς. L. Edelstein, περὶ ἀέρων (*Problemata,* IV), 1931, 60 ff.; E. F. K. Müller, *Die göttliche Zuvorersehung und Erwählung* (1892).

[1] On the underlying apocalyptic world view in 1 Pt. 1:20 (προεγνωσμένου μὲν πρὸ καταβολῆς κόσμου φανερωθέντος δὲ ἐπ' ἐσχάτου τῶν χρόνων), cf. esp. 4 Esr. 6:1 ff. and the comm. of R. Knopf and H. Windisch, *ad loc.*

This is found in Ac. 26:5, where the meaning is strengthened by the addition of ἄνωθεν.

In Justin God's προγινώσκειν is His foreknowledge (Apol., I, 28, 2 etc.) and the προεγνωσμένοι are believers (Apol., I, 45, 1 etc.). The polemic against determinism, however, shows that the OT view has been abandoned (Dial., 140, 4). As One who simply knows beforehand, God is called προγνώστης in Apol., I, 44, 11 etc., as is also Christ in Dial., 35, 7; 82, 1. There is also reference to prophetic foreknowledge in Apol., I, 43, 1; 49, 6 etc. Tat. Or. Graec., 19, 3 speaks of Apollo in the same terms, so that what we have here is the Gk. understanding.

πρόγνωσις in Greek means "advance knowledge" (a technical term in medicine from the time of Hippocrates). It is found in the LXX at Jdt. 9:6 with reference to the predeterminative knowledge of God.

The reference is to prophetic foreknowledge at Jdt. 11:19; Jos. Ant., 8, 234 and 418; 15, 373 (the Essene Menaem πρόγνωσιν ἐκ θεοῦ τῶν μελλόντων ἔχων) etc. For Justin God's πρόγνωσις is His foreknowledge (Dial., 92, 5; 134, 4); and among the gifts of the Spirit he lists the πνεῦμα προγνώσεως instead of prophecy (Dial., 39, 2). There is a similar definition in Cl. Al. Strom., II, 12, 54, 1: ἡ προφητεία πρόγνωσίς ἐστιν, ἡ δὲ γνῶσις προφητείας νόησις. That the Greek Christians understood the concept in mantic terms may be seen from Tat. Or. Graec., 1, 1, where the πρόγνωσις διὰ τῶν ἀστέρων is parallel to δι᾽ ὀνείρων μαντική (cf. Preis. Zaub., VII, 294), and from Cl. Al. Strom., I, 21, 133, 1 f., where μαντική and πρόγνωσις are parallel. The miraculous element in prophetic πρόγνωσις is described in Ps.-Clem. Hom., II, 11: ἄγνοια γὰρ γνῶσιν οὐκ ὀρθῶς κρίνει, ἄτε δὴ οὔτε γνῶσις πρόγνωσιν ἀληθῶς κρίνειν πέφυκεν. ἀλλ᾽ ἡ πρόγνωσις τοῖς ἀγνοοῦσιν παρέχει τὴν γνῶσιν.

συγγνώμη.

In Gk. the verb συγγινώσκειν means "to think the same as someone," "to agree," then "to yield," "to recognise," "to accept," "to be aware," and "to pardon."[1] It is found in the LXX only in 2 Macc. 14:31 in the sense of "to perceive" or "to be aware," and in 4 Macc. 8:22 in the sense of "to pardon" (cf. συγγνωμονεῖν in 4 Macc. 5:13, as also Ign. Tr., 5, 1). Jos. has συγγινώσκειν for "to know (with others)" and "to pardon" (Ant., 6, 93; Bell., 1, 167) and συγγινώσκειν ἑαυτῷ for "to be aware (in conscience)" (Ant., 1, 46). συγγνωστός is used in Wis. 6:6; 13:8 of one who deserves pardon; cf. Jos. Ant., 7, 285 etc.; Just. Dial., 65, 2. In Christian literature the verb is first found in Ign. R., 6, 2 in the sense of "to agree"; then in Athen. Suppl., 18, 1 in the sense of "to pardon," "to forbear."

The noun συγγνώμη in Gk. means "agreement," "forbearance," "pardon" (often with ἔχειν, "to pardon", though also "to deserve pardon"). Aristot. defines it in Eth. Nic., IV, 11, p. 1143a, 23 as γνώμη κριτικὴ τοῦ ἐπιεικοῦς ὀρθή. That it was highly valued is shown by the saying (Diog. L., I, 76) quoted in Cl. Al. Strom., II, 15, 70: συγγνώμη τιμωρίας κρείσσων. In the LXX it occurs in 2 Macc. 14:20 as "patience", also in Sir. Prol., 11, Swete and 3:13 in the expression συγγνώμην ἔχειν, "to exercise patience." Cf. also Ign. R., 5:3. In Joseph. it is used for "pardon" in Ant., 6, 144 etc.; also in Philo Spec. Leg., II, 196 (the opp. of κόλασις), sometimes, as also the verb, with reference to sins κατὰ ἄγνοιαν, Spec. Leg., III, 35; Vit. Mos., I, 273; Flacc., 7; and cf. on this pt. Aristot. Eth. Nic., III, 2, p. 1111a, 2; Polyb., XII, 7, 6: τοῖς μὲν γὰρ κατ᾽ ἄγνοιαν ψευδογραφοῦσιν ἔφαμεν δεῖν διόρθωσιν εὐμενικὴν καὶ συγγνώμην ἐξακολουθεῖν, τοῖς δὲ κατὰ προαίρεσιν ἀπαραίτητον κατηγορίαν (cf. XV, 19, 3)

συγγνώμη. [1] Cf. Eur. Ion, 1440: συγγνώσεται γὰρ ὁ θεός.

and Max. Tyr., 33, 3a : the ψυχή is ἐλεεινὴ μὲν τοῦ πάθους, συγγνωστὸς δὲ τῆς ἀγνοίας.

In the NT it occurs only at 1 C. 7:6 : τοῦτο δὲ λέγω κατὰ συγγνώμην, οὐ κατ' ἐπιταγήν, obviously in the sense of "forbearance" or "concession." Though the context might support "personal opinion," there is no example of this ; γνώμη is the word used in such cases.

Cf. κατὰ συγγνώμην in Tat. Or. Graec., 20, 1. In Just. Dial., 9, 1 συγγνώμη means "pardon" (συγγνώμη σοι ... καὶ ἀφεθείη σοι).

γνώμη.

On the Gk. usage, → 691, n. 7 and 9. Most of the senses, apart from "reason," are attested in Jewish and Christian literature, though the term is comparatively rare in the LXX. It is hard to differentiate the various nuances with any precision.

1. "Disposition," "will." As we find δικαία and εὐγενὴς γνώμη in the LXX (Prv. 2:16; 4 Macc. 9:27), so we find ἀγαθὴ γνώμη in Barn., 21, 2 (cf. Ditt. Syll.³, 75, 28 [428/7 B.C.]: γνώμας ἀγαθὰς ἔχειν). Here the meaning is "disposition," as in Jos. Ant., 2, 97; 13, 416. The same rendering best fits the εἰς θεὸν γνώμη of Ign. R., 7, 1; Phld., 1, 2, or the ἐν θεῷ γνώμη of Ign. Pol., 1, 1, also the γνώμη of God in Ign. Eph., 3,2; R., 8, 3 etc. or of Jesus Christ in Eph., 3, 2 (here He is also called the γνώμη τοῦ πατρὸς), while κατὰ θεοῦ γνώμην (Jos. Ant., 15, 144; cf. Ap., 2, 166) means "according to the will of God." In 2 Macc. 9:20, and often in the salutations in pap. letters, the meaning of κατὰ γνώμην is "as desired." In the NT we find ἐν τῇ αὐτῇ γνώμῃ at 1 C. 1:10 (linked with ἐν τῷ αὐτῷ νοΐ and hardly to be differentiated from it ; cf. τὸ αὐτὸ or τὸ ἓν φρονεῖν at Phil. 2:2; 4:2; R. 12:16 etc.); cf. Thuc., I, 113, 2 : ὅσοι τῆς αὐτῆς γνώμης ἦσαν. [1] The sense is the same in Rev. 17:13 : οὗτοι (the 10 kings) μίαν γνώμην ἔχουσιν and 17:17 (though → infra): ὁ γὰρ θεὸς ἔδωκεν εἰς τὰς καρδίας αὐτῶν ποιῆσαι τὴν γμώμην αὐτοῦ καὶ ποιῆσαι μίαν γνώμην; cf. the μία γνώμη in Demosth., 10, 59 (ὁμοθυμαδὸν ἐκ μιᾶς γνώμης) and elsewhere, [2] also in Philo Vit. Mos., I, 235; Spec. Leg., II, 165; III, 73 (ἀπὸ μιᾶς καὶ τῆς αὐτῆς γνώμης) and Jos. Ant., 7, 60 and 276. The idea of "consent" [3] is present in 2 Macc. 4:39; Jos. Ant., 20, 202; Phlm. 14; Ign. Pol., 4, 1; 5, 2. Cf. also the self-description of Isis on the Kyme inscription : [4] ἐγὼ ποταμῶν καὶ ἀνέμων καὶ θαλάσσης εἰμὶ κυρία· οὐδεὶς δοξάζεται ἄνευ τῆς ἐμῆς γνώμης.

2. "Resolve," "decision." It often has this meaning in inscr. and pap. We may also construe Rev. 17:17 in this sense (→ supra). In 2 Esr. the LXX often uses γνώμη for טְעֵם (resolve or edict of the king), also in Da. 2:14, cf. Θ, which has γνώμη for דָּת (royal command) in Da. 2:15 and δόγμα for טְעֵם in 13:10 etc. In Philo Som., I, 81 γνώμη means much the same as νόμος, and in Jos. Ant., 13, 196 it means resolve or intention. Only at Ac. 20:3 : ἐγένετο γνώμης, "he resolved," does it have this sense in the NT ; cf. Ign. Phld., 6, 2.

3. "Counsel," "opinion." Cf. LXX ψ 82:3 (for סוֹד "proposal"); Gr. Sir. 6:23; Wis. 7:15 (?); 2 Macc. 11:37 etc. In 1 C. 7:25; 2 C 8:10 γνώμην διδόναι means "to give

---

γ ν ώ μ η. [1] Bl.-Debr. § 162, 7.
[2] Pr.-Bauer, s.v.
[3] Nägeli, 33.
[4] BCH, 51 (1927), 380, 40 f.; W. Peek, Der Isishymnus von Andros u. verw. Texte (1930), 124, 40.

counsel"; cf. also Jos. Ant., 8, 379; 11, 253; 1 C 7:40 : κατὰ τὴν ἐμὴν γνώμην, "according to my opinion."

γνωρίζω.

1. "To make known." In this sense the word is common in the LXX (mostly for ידע, hiph.) both in secular contexts (3 Βασ. 1:27; Neh. 8:12; Prv. 9:9 etc.) and in cases where it has an emotional ring.

The priest, teacher or prophet may be the subject (1 Βασ. 6:2; 10:8; 28:15; Ez. 43:11), or God Himself, who causes His power or grace to be known (→ γινώσκω, 698; cf. Jer. 16:21; ψ 15:11; 76:14; 97:2 etc.), or declares His will (ψ 24:4 : τὰς ὁδούς σου; Ez. 20:11: τὰ δικαιώματά μου, etc.), or grants secret knowledge (Jer. 11:18; Da. 2:23, 28 ff. Θ etc.). The cultic declaration of the acts of Yahweh is called γνωρίζω in 1 Ch. 16:8 (ἀπ- or ἀναγγέλλειν in ψ 104:1; Is. 12:4), and also the confession of sin in ψ 31:5. In Θ Da. 4:3 f.; 5:8 etc. γνωρίζω is used of the interpretation of dreams and visions.

The NT use of γνωρίζω corresponds to that of the LXX. The word often occurs in a secular sense (1 C. 12:3; 15:1; Col. 4:7, 9). Even here God is frequently the subject, making known His power and salvation (R. 9:22 f.; Ac. 2:28, quoting Ps. 16:11; Lk. 2:15). Above all, the term is used for God's declaration of His secret counsel of salvation (His μυστήριον), e.g., in Col. 1:27; Eph. 1:9; 3:5, 10; 6:19 (cf. → φανεροῦν in R. 16:25 f.; Ign. Eph., 19, 2 f. and elsewhere). Even the declaration of God's acts by men (Lk. 2:17), especially through preaching (R. 16:26; 2 Pt. 1:16), can be called γνωρίζω. In John, Jesus is the subject of γνωρίζειν as the Revealer (15:15; 17:26). But the making known of our requests to God is also γνωρίζεσθαι at Phil. 4:6 (cf. γνωρίζεσθαι θεῷ in Philo Sacr. AC, 132; Det. Pot. Ins., 56; also Congr., 18; Fug., 38).

2. "To perceive," "to know." This sense is common not only in the pap. but also in the LXX (Am. 3:3; Prv. 3:6; 15:10; Job 34:25; at Job 4:16 Σ has ἐγνώρισα and the LXX ἐπέγνων). The term is found in this sense in both Philo and Joseph. in both the act. and the pass. In the pass. it is hard to distinguish between the senses "to be made known" and "to be known." When we turn to the NT we find this meaning only at Phil. 1:22 : τί αἱρήσομαι οὐ γνωρίζω. γνωρίζω is used of the knowledge of God in Philo (Poster. C., 167; Mut. Nom., 17); Corp. Herm., X, 15 (here of God's own knowledge); the λόγος τέλειος; [1] Dg., 8, 5; Act. Andr., 6 (p. 41, 7). It is also used of being known by God in Act. Andr., 1 (p. 38, 7 and 20), cf. 9 (p. 42, 3 f.).

γνωστός.

In Gk. γνωστός means both "knowable" and "known" (cf. the inscr. and pap., though as a more select term). [1] In the LXX it is esp. used as a part. pass. in the sense of "acquaintance," "confidant," or "relative" (4 Βασ. 10:11; ψ 30:11; 54:13; 87:8, 18). It is not found in Joseph., but Philo uses it in Leg. All., I, 60 f., where the LXX has γινώσκειν. In Rabb. usage relatives (קְרוֹבִין) are distinguished from acquaintances (מְיֻדָּעִין). [2] So in Lk. 2:44 : ἐν τοῖς συγγενεῦσιν καὶ τοῖς γνωστοῖς, though in Lk. 23:49

γ ν ω ρ ί ζ ω. [1] Hermetica, I, 376, Scott ; Reitzenstein Hell. Myst., 286.
γ ν ω σ τ ό ς. [1] Cf. Nägeli, 19.
[2] Str.-B., II, 149 on Lk. 2:44; Schl. J., 332 on Jn. 18:15.

relatives are included among γνωστοί. In Jn. 18:15 f. γνωστός obviously means acquaintance.

In the more general sense of "made known," as in the LXX Is. 19:21; Ez. 36:32; ψ 75:1 and Θ Da. 3:18 (where the LXX has φανερόν), the word is often used in Ac. in expressions such as γνωστὸν ἐγένετο (1:19; 2:14; 4:10; 9:42 etc.). In Ac. 4:16 (γνωστὸν σημεῖον) the meaning is perhaps "clearly recognisable." "Recognisable" (in the LXX only at Sir. 21:7) is certainly the sense in R. 1:19 : τὸ γνωστὸν τοῦ θεοῦ φανερόν ἐστιν ἐν αὐτοῖς, though it is debatable whether the gen. τοῦ θεοῦ should be understood as a partit., thus giving us "what may be known of God," [3] or whether we should follow the analogy of such expressions as τὰ κρυπτὰ τοῦ σκότους in 1 C. 4:5 or τὸ χρηστὸν τοῦ θεοῦ in R. 2:4 etc. and thus translate "God in His knowability." [4] In v. 20 the τὰ ἀόρατα αὐτοῦ certainly does not mean "what is invisible to Him" but "He the Invisible." Cf. → γινώσκω, 705 and → ἄγνωστος.

Bultmann

γλῶσσα, ἑτερόγλωσσος

γλῶσσα.

A. The General Use of γλῶσσα.

As regards the NT, the following principal meanings may be distinguished :

1. The strict physiological meaning of "tongue" : [1] Hom. Il., 5, 292, as the organ of taste : Philo Op. Mund., 159 : γλώττῃ τῇ χυλοὺς δικαζούσῃ, or more particularly of speech : Eur. Suppl., 203 f.: ἄγγελον γλῶσσαν λόγων; Philo Conf. Ling., 36 : διὰ στόματος καὶ γλώττης καὶ τῶν ἄλλων φωνητηρίων ὀργάνων; cf. Agric., 53 : τῇ διὰ γλώττης καὶ στόματος ῥεούσῃ φωνῇ; Vit. Mos., II, 239 : ὦ δέσποτα, πῶς ἂν σέ τις ὑμνήσειε, ποίῳ στόματι, τίνι γλώττῃ, ποίᾳ φωνῆς ὀργανοποιίᾳ; Sir. 28:18 : οἱ πεπτωκότες διὰ γλῶσσαν (cf. 19 ff.). Figur. it can be used of the speaker, e.g.,

---

[3] Cf. Bl.-Debr. § 263, 2.

[4] Cf. ψ 75:1: γνωστὸς ... ὁ θεός; Is. 19:21: γνωστὸς ... κύριος; Ex. 33:13 : γνωστῶς (vl. γνωστός) ἴδω σε (θεός).

γ λ ῶ σ σ α. Moult.-Mill., 128; Cr.-Kö., 260 ff.; Liddell-Scott, 353; Pr.-Bauer, 254. On glossolalia, P. Feine, RE³, 21, 749 ff.; E. Mosiman, *Das Zungenreden geschichtlich und psychologisch untersucht* (1910, with bibl. on p. VII ff.); E. Lombard, *De la glossolalie chez les premiers chrétiens* ... (1910); Joh. W. 1 K., 335 ff.; Wdt. Ag., 83 ff.; T. K. Oesterreich, *Einführung in die Religionspsychologie* (1917), 49 ff.; W. Reinhard, *Das Wirken des hl. Geistes* (1918), 120 ff.; K. L. Schmidt, *D. Pfingsterzählung u.d. Pfingstereignis* (1919); P. W. Schmiedel, "Pfingsterzählung u. Pfingstereignis," Pr. M., 24 (1920), 73 ff.; F. Jackson-K. Lake, *The Beginnings of Christianity,* I (1920), 323 ff.; Bchm. 1 K., 422 f.; H. Güntert, *Von der Sprache der Götter u. Geister* (1921), 23 ff.; Reitzenstein Poim., 55 ff.; Hell. Myst., 323 f.; H. Leisegang, *Pneuma Hagion* (1922), 113 ff.; Zn. Ag., I, 99 f.; E. F. Scott, *The Spirit in the NT* (1923), 92 ff.; Clemen, 157 f.; H. Rust, *Das Zungenreden* (1924); *Wunder der Bibel,* 2 and 3 (1924 f.); RGG², V, 2142 f.; Schlatter, *Geschichte d. erst. Chr.,* 21 ff., 215 f.; F. Büchsel, *Der Geist Gottes im NT* (1926), 242 ff.; 321 ff.; W. Bauer, *Der Wortgottesdienst der ältesten Christen* (1930), 33 ff.; Ltzm. K.³, 68 ff.; *Das NT Deutsch,* II (1933), 13 ff. (H. W. Beyer); *ibid.,* 362 ff. (H. D. Wendland); R. M. Pope, DAC, II, 598 f.

[1] On δεσμὸς τῆς γλώσσης in Mk. 7:35, cf. Ditt. Syll.³, 1169, 43; Deissmann LO, 258 ff.

in Cratinus (CAF, I, 98): μεγίστη γλῶττα τῶν Ἑλληνίδων; Jos. Ant., 3, 85 : γλῶττα ἀνθρωπίνη πρὸς ὑμᾶς λέγει; P. Oxy., XI, 1381, 198 ff.: Ἑλλην<ι>ς δὲ π<α>σα γλῶσσα τὴν σὴν λαλ<ή> ... σε<ι> ἱστορίαν κ<αὶ> πᾶς Ἑλ<λ>ην ἀνὴρ τὸν τ<ο>ῦ Φθᾶ σεβήσεται Ἰμού <θ>ην; Preis. Zaub., XII (Leiden), 187 f.: ἀκουσάτω μοι πᾶσα γλῶσσα καὶ πᾶσα φωνή.

2. "Speech," "manner of speech": Hom. Il., 2, 804 : ἄλλη δ᾽ ἄλλων γλῶσσα πολυσπερέων ἀνθρώπων; Xenoph. Mem., III, 14, 6 : ἐν τῇ Ἀθηναίων γλώττῃ; Aen. Tact., 42, 2 : ἐὰν κατὰ γλῶσσάν (dialect) τις παραγγέλλῃ <μᾶλλον> ἢ κοινόν τι ἅπασιν; P. Giess., I, 99, 8 f.: ὕμνοι ... ἅι<δονται> γλώττῃ ξενικῇ, Schol. in Dion. Thr. Art. Gramm. (Tryph.) (Gramm. Graec., I, 3, p. 302 H): Δωρὶς ... διάλεκτος μία ὑφ᾽ ἥν εἰσι γλῶσσαι (sub-dialects) πολλαί; Philo Vit. Mos., II, 40 : τὴν Ἑλληνικὴν γλῶτταν ... τὴν Χαλδαίων; Decal., 159 : πατρίῳ γλώττῃ, Gn. 11:7: καταβάντες συγχέωμεν αὐτῶν ἐκεῖ τὴν γλῶσσαν; cf. Philo Conf. Ling., 9 : τὴν γε φωνῆς εἰς μυρίας διαλέκτων ἰδέας τομήν, ἣν καλεῖ (Scripture) γλώττης σύγχυσιν. Figur. of a "people with its own language": Da. 3:7: πάντες οἱ λαοί, φυλαί, γλῶσσαι; Is. 66:18; Jdt. 3:8; cf. M. Ex., 14, 5 : כָּל־אֲשֶׁר רְוּחֲךָ; Skylax Geogr., 15 (Geogr. Graec. Min., I, 24, Müller): ἐν τούτῳ τῷ ἔθνει (sc. the Σαυνῖται) γλῶσσαι ἤτοι στόματα τάδε Λατέρνιοι κτλ. (interpolation ?).

3. "An expression which in speech or manner is strange and obscure and needs explanation" : [2] Aristot. Poet., 21, p. 1457b, 1 ff.: ἅπαν ... ὄνομά ἐστιν ἢ κύριον (properly) ἢ γλῶττα ... λέγω δὲ κύριον μὲν ᾧ χρῶνται ἕκαστοι, γλῶτταν δὲ ᾧ ἕτεροι, ὥστε φανερὸν ὅτι καὶ γλῶτταν καὶ κύριον εἶναι δυνατὸν τὸ αὐτό, μὴ τοῖς αὐτοῖς δέ· τὸ γὰρ "σίγυνον" Κυπρίοις μὲν κύριον, ἡμῖν δὲ γλῶττα; ibid., 22, p. 1458a, 22 ff.: ξενικὸν ... λέγω γλῶτταν ... καὶ πᾶν τὸ παρὰ τὸ κύριον· ἀλλ᾽ ἄν τις ἅμα ἅπαντα τοιαῦτα ποιήσῃ, ἢ αἴνιγμα ἔσται ἢ βαρβαρισμός· ... ἐκ τῶν γλωττῶν βαρβαρισμός; cf. Rhet., III, 10, p. 1410, 12 ff.: αἱ μὲν οὖν γλῶτται ἀγνῶτες, τὰ δὲ κύρια ἴσμεν; Sext. Emp. Gramm., 313 : τῆς κατὰ γλῶσσαν προενεχθείσης (sc. λέξεως) ὁμοίως οὔσης ἀσυνήθους ἡμῖν; Plut. Is. et Os., 61 (II, 375e): ὁ δὲ Ὄσιρις ἐκ τοῦ ὁσίου καὶ ἱεροῦ τοὔνομα μεμιγμένον ἔσχηκε ... οὐ δεῖ δὲ θαυμάζειν τῶν ὀνομάτων εἰς τὸ Ἑλληνικὸν ἀνάπλασιν· καὶ γὰρ ἄλλα μυρία τοῖς μεθισταμένοις ἐκ τῆς Ἑλλάδος συνεκπεσόντα μέχρι νῦν παραμένει καὶ ξενιτεύει παρ᾽ ἑτέροις, ὧν ἔνια τὴν ποιητικὴν ἀνακαλουμένην διαβάλλουσιν ὡς βαρβαρίζουσαν οἱ γλῶτταις τὰ τοιαῦτα προσαγορεύοντες. Or again, "archaic expression" : Diod. S., IV, 66, 6 : τὸ γὰρ ἐνθεάζειν κατὰ γλῶτταν (according to the old expression) ὑπάρχειν "σιβυλλαίνειν"; Galen Ling. Hippocr. Expl. prooem (XIX, 62 f., Kühn): ὅσα τοίνυν τῶν ὀνομάτων ἐν μὲν τοῖς πάλαι χρόνοις ἦν συνήθη, νυνὶ δ᾽ οὐκέτι ἐστί, τὰ μὲν τοιαῦτα γλώττας καλοῦσι; M. Ant., IV, 33 : αἱ πάλαι συνήθεις λέξεις νῦν γλωσσήματα. Finally, "select poetic expression" : Plut. Pyth. Or., 24 (II, 406 f.): (God has caused the Pythia in its oracles to pass from obscure poetic expression to understandable prose) ἀφελὼν δὲ τῶν χρησμῶν ἔπη καὶ γλώσσας καὶ περιφράσεις καὶ ἀσάφειαν οὕτω διαλέγεσθαι παρεσκεύασε τοῖς χρωμένοις ὡς νόμοι τε πόλεσι διαλέγονται καὶ βασιλεῖς ἐντυγχάνουσι δήμοις καὶ μαθηταὶ διδασκάλων ἀκροῶνται, πρὸς τὸ συνετὸν καὶ πιθανὸν ἁρμοζόμενος; cf. Anecd. Graec., I, 87, 12 : γλώττας τὰς τῶν ποιητῶν ἢ ἅς τινας ἄλλας ἐξηγούμεθα; also Quintilian Inst. Orat., I, 1, 35, cf. 8, 15 : voces minus usitatae of the lingua secretior quas Graeci γλώσσας vocant.

---

[2] Cf. on this pt. F. Lübker, Reallexikon d. klass. Altertums[8] (1914), 418 f.

B. The Use of γλῶσσα in the NT and Its Background.

1. "Tongue," esp. as an organ of speech: Lk. 16:24; 1:64; demonically bound, Mk. 7:35 : ὁ δεσμὸς τῆς γλώσσης αὐτοῦ (→ n. 1); author of many sins, Jm. 3:1-12 (cf. also Jm. 1:26; 1 Pt. 3:10 = Ps. 34:13). [3]

The striking emphasis on sins of the tongue is characteristic of practical Jewish wisdom, though we also meet with similar warnings in other ancient oriental traditions [4] and they become a common-place of ethical exhortation in the Hellenistic period. [5] In the OT such references occur mainly in the Psalter, Job and Proverbs, and cf. also Sir. Yet there are also references in the prophets, and Jer. uses the term γλῶσσα almost exclusively in this connection. Among individual sins, mostly against the 9th commandment, arrogance and boasting may be specifically mentioned (ψ 11:3, 4; Mi. 6:12, where the LXX with its tendency to emphasise the sin of pride reads the רְמִיָּה of the Mas. as a form of רוּם; 3 Macc. 2:17; 6:4).

No one escapes these sins of the tongue (Sir. 19:16), though with the thought that man becomes a sinner through the tongue (ψ 38:1; Prv. 6:17; cf. Herm. v., 2, 2, 3) there is the further thought that the offender with the tongue gives rise to fresh evil (Prv. 10:31; 17:4). Indeed, the tongue hatches evil (ψ 51:4 LXX; cf. Is. 59:3). The mischief done is incalculable (Sir. 28:14 ff.). As a scourge ('Ιωβ 5:21; Sir. 28:17), or a sword (ψ 56:4; 63:3; Sir. 28:18), or a bow and arrow (Jer. 9:3, 8), or the sharp tongue of a serpent (ψ 139:3), the tongue is a terrible weapon which can destroy men (ψ 63:8; Jer. 18:18). Hence we must be on the watch against rashness in our use of it (Sir. 4:29). But only → παιδεία, i.e., a moral and religious attitude and culture, can give power over it (Prv. 27:20; Hos. 7:16; cf. Sir. 4:24; Is. 50:4). This must be attained or prayed for (Sir. 22:27). For life and death depend upon the tongue (Prv. 18:21). Indeed, Cod. A has θάνατος ζωῆς at this point, cf. Sir. 5:13 : γλῶσσα ἀνθρώπου πτῶσις αὐτῷ. Thus all the consequences of sinning with the tongue recoil on those who commit it. It hovers as a scourge over all men (Sir. 26:6). To ward it off means security and happiness (Sir. 22:27; 25:8).

In the OT the purely ethical exhortation with regard to sins of the tongue has a religious significance even though there is no direct reference in most cases. For in the last resort deception and falsehood and arrogance and boasting are directed against God (Hos. 7:16, → ψεύστης; 3 Macc. 2:17; 6:4, → ὕβρις). Again, in the sections dealing with this form of sin there is an unmasking of even the inner details and the final consequences of the sin of man which, as a call to repentance, attains a profundity that can hardly be surpassed in the soil of the practical wisdom of Judaism. It stands at the place occupied by sins of thought in the Christian summons to repent (Ps. 51:2 LXX: ἀδικίαν ἐλογίσατο ἡ γλῶσσά σου, though the Mas. differs; cf. Is. 59:3). [6]

In a figurative sense the tongue can be the subject of jubilation: Ac. 2:26 (ψ 15:9): ἠγαλλιάσατο ἡ γλῶσσά μου, and praise: Phil. 2:11 (Is. 45:23): πᾶσα γλῶσσα ἐξομολογήσηται. At Ac. 2:3 : ὤφθησαν αὐτοῖς διαμεριζόμεναι γλῶσσαι ὡσεὶ πυρὸς καὶ ἐκάθισεν ἐφ᾽ ἕνα ἕκαστον αὐτῶν ("there appeared unto them tongues as of fire, which parted and one of which alighted on each of them"),

---

[3] On the background of Jm. 3:1 ff.; 1:26, cf. the Jewish and Hell. material in J. Geffcken, Kynika u. Verwandtes (1909), 45 ff.; A. Meyer, Das Rätsel des Jakobusbriefes (1930), 260 f.; 309 f. etc.; Dib., Hck., Wnd. and Str.-B., ad loc.; cf. also Philo Spec. Leg., IV, 90 : (ἐπιθυμία) ἤδη δὲ καὶ ἐπὶ γλῶτταν φθάσασα μυρία ἐνεωτέρισεν; Mut. Nom., 244 : προπετεία ... γλώττης; Som., II, 165 : γλῶτταν ἀχαλίνωτον; cf. 132 and 267; Abr., 20 : τὴν μὲν γλῶτταν ἀνιεὶς πρὸς ἄμετρον καὶ ἀπέραντον καὶ ἄκριτον διήγησιν; Congr., 80 : ἐγκράτειαν ... καὶ γλώττης; Som., II, 51: τιθασεύουσι γλῶτταν.

[4] For the Babylonian material, cf. AOT, 291 and 293; cf. also the proverbs of Amen-(em)ope, ibid., → 38 ff.

[5] → n. 3 for bibl.

[6] I am indebted to G. Bertram for this section.

tongue is an image for flame (Is. 5:24 שֶׁן יְוֹשֹׁב; cf. Tg. II Est., 6, 13); the reference
is to the heavenly power of God descending on each of the disciples assembled
on the day of Pentecost (→ 724; → πῦρ).

2. "Language," Ac. 2:11: ἀκούομεν λαλούντων αὐτῶν ταῖς ἡμετέραις γλώσσαις = v. 8 : ἀκούομεν ἕκαστος τῇ ἰδίᾳ διαλέκτῳ ἡμῶν cf. v. 6. Figur. (→ 720)
it means "people" in Rev. 5:9; 7:9; 10:11; 11:9; 13:7; 14:6.

3. Glossolalia.

The peculiar phenomenon of λαλεῖν (ἐν) γλώσσῃ (γλώσσαις) (1 C. 12-14;
Ac. 10:46; 19:6), with which we should link the λαλεῖν γλώσσαις καιναῖς of
Mk. 16:17 and the λαλεῖν ἑτέραις γλώσσαις of Ac. 2:4, may be understood only
in the light of the vivid depiction in 1 C. 14:2 ff. Speaking with tongues, like
→ προφητεύειν, is a → χάρισμα, a spiritually effected speaking (14:2 ff., 14 ff.,
37 ff.; cf. 12:10, 28, 30), not to men, but to God (14:2, 28), in the form of a prayer,
possibly of praise and thanksgiving and possibly sung (14:2, 14-17; cf. Ac. 10:46);
its value is for the individual concerned rather than for the community as a whole
(14:4 ff., 16 f., 28). In this inspired utterance the → νοῦς is swallowed up (14:14,
19), so that mysterious words, obscure both to the speaker and to the hearers,
are spoken in the void (14:2, 9, 11, 15 f.). There is an unarticulated sound as of
an instrument played with no clear differentiation of notes (14:7 f.). An impression
is left of speaking in foreign languages (14:10 f., 21). The uncontrolled use of
tongues might thus make it appear that the community is an assembly of madmen
(14:23, 27). Yet tongues are a legitimate sign of overwhelming power (14:22).
There are various kinds (12:10, 28; cf. 14:10); some are tongues of men and
others of angels (13:1). To make glossolalia serviceable to the community, however, either the speaker or another brother must be able to give an interpretation
(14:5, 13, 27 f.; 12:10, 30). In Corinth, therefore, glossolalia is an unintelligible
ecstatic utterance. One of its forms of expression is a muttering of words or
sounds without interconnection or meaning. Parallels may be found for this phenomenon in various forms and at various periods and places in religious history. [7]

In Gk. religion [8] there is a series of comparable phenomena from the enthusiastic cult
of the Thracian Dionysus with its γλώττης βακχεῖα (Aristoph. Ra., 357) to the
divinatory manticism of the Delphic Phrygia, of the Bacides, the Sybils etc. Heracl. Fr.
(I, 96, 7 ff., Diels): Σίβυλλα ... μαινομένῳ στόματι ἀγέλαστα καὶ ἀκαλλώπιστα
καὶ ἀμύριστα φθεγγομένη. Cf. also Plato on μάντις and προφήτης in Tim., 71e-
72a : οὐδεὶς ... ἔννους ἐφάπτεται μαντικῆς ἐνθέου καὶ ἀληθοῦς, ἀλλ' ἢ καθ'
ὕπνον τὴν τῆς φρονήσεως πεδηθεὶς δύναμιν ἢ διὰ νόσον ἢ διά τινα ἐνθουσιασμὸν
παραλλάξας. ἀλλὰ ξυννοῆσαι μὲν ἔμφρονος τά τε ῥηθέντα ἀναμνησθέντα ὄναρ
ἢ ὕπαρ ὑπὸ τῆς μαντικῆς τε καὶ ἐνθουσιαστικῆς φύσεως, καὶ ὅσα ἂν φαντάσ-
ματα ὀφθῇ, πάντα λογισμῷ διελέσθαι, ὅπῃ τι σημαίνει καὶ ὅτῳ μέλλοντος ἢ
παρελθόντος ἢ παρόντος κακοῦ ἢ ἀγαθοῦ· τοῦ δὲ μανέντος ἔτι τε ἐν τούτῳ
μένοντος οὐκ ἔργον τὰ φανέντα καὶ φωνηθέντα ὑφ' ἑαυτοῦ κρίνειν, ἀλλ' εὖ καὶ
πάλαι λέγεται τὸ πράττειν καὶ γνῶναι τά τε αὑτοῦ καὶ ἑαυτὸν σώφρονι μόνῳ
προσήκειν· ὅθεν δὴ καὶ τὸ τῶν προφητῶν γένος ἐπὶ ταῖς ἐνθέοις μαντείαις
κριτὰς ἐπικαθιστάναι νόμος· οὓς μάντεις αὐτοὺς ὀνομάζουσί τινες, τὸ πᾶν
ἠγνοηκότες, ὅτι τῆς δι' αἰνιγμῶν οὗτοι φήμης καὶ φαντάσεως ὑποκριταί, καὶ
οὔ τι μάντεις, προφῆται δὲ μαντευομένων δικαιότατα ὀνομάζοιντ' ἄν. Cf. also

---

[7] Cf. the material in Lombard, Mosiman, Oesterreich, Güntert, op. cit.
[8] Cf. E. Rohde, Psyche[9-10] (1925), II, 20 ff., 51, 58 ff., 68 etc.; Reitzenstein Poim., 55 ff.;
Joh. W. 1 K., 338 f.; H. Leisegang, Der Hl. Geist, I, 1 (1919), 168 ff.; cf. 125 ff.; Pneuma
Hagion, 118 ff.; Ltzm. K., 68 f.

Philo Spec. Leg., IV, 49 : προφήτης μὲν γὰρ οὐδὲν ἴδιον ἀποφαίνεται τὸ παράπαν, ἀλλ' ἔστιν ἑρμηνευτὴς ὑποβάλλοντος ἑτέρου πάνθ' ὅσα προφέρεται, καθ' ὃν χρόνον ἐνθουσιᾷ γεγονὼς ἐν ἀγνοίᾳ, μετανισταμένου μὲν τοῦ λογισμοῦ καὶ παρακεχωρηκότος τὴν τῆς ψυχῆς ἀκρόπολιν, ἐπιπεφοιτηκότος δὲ καὶ ἐνῳκηκότος τοῦ θείου πνεύματος καὶ πᾶσαν τῆς φωνῆς ὀργανοποιῖαν κρούοντός τε καὶ ἐνηχοῦντος εἰς ἐναργῆ δήλωσιν ὧν προθεσπίζει. Cf. further I, 65; Rer. Div. Her., 265; Iambl. Myst., III, 4 (p. 109), 11 (p. 126) etc. Nor is there lacking a connection between Hellenistic prophecy and what Irenaeus (I, 13, 3) can tell of the Christian Gnostic Marcos, [9] whose demonic prophetic gift is transferred to a woman : ἡ δὲ ... ἀποτολμᾷ λαλεῖν ληρώδη, καὶ τὰ τυχόντα πάντα κενῶς καὶ τολμηρῶς, ἅτε ὑπὸ κενοῦ τεθερμαμένη πνεύματος, or Celsus' description of the impulse of Christian ecstatics (Orig. Cels., 7, 8 f.), namely, after prophetic utterances, which are intelligible even though uttered with the claim to be spoken by a divine Ego, προστιθέασιν ἐφεξῆς ἄγνωστα καὶ πάροιστρα καὶ πάντη ἄδηλα, ὧν τὸ μὲν γνῶμα οὐδεὶς ἂν ἔχων νοῦν εὑρεῖν δύναιτο· ἀσαφῆ γὰρ καὶ τὸ μηδέν, ἀνοήτῳ δὲ ἢ γόητι παντὶ περὶ παντὸς ἀφορμὴν ἐνδίδωσιν, ὅπη βούλεται, τὸ λεχθὲν σφετερίζεσθαι (7, 9). The unintelligible lists of magical names and letters in the magic pap. (*voces mysticae*), which are used in the invoking and conjuring of gods and spirits, [10] may also be analogous to this obscure and meaningless speaking with tongues. With these mystical divine names etc., in which there are echoes of all the various oriental languages, [11] we may certainly couple the view that they derive from supraterrestrial tongues used by the gods and spirits in heaven, each class having its peculiar φωνή or διάλεκτος, e.g., in the Hermetic prayer in Preis. Zaub., XIII (Leiden), 139 ff.: ἐπικαλοῦμαί σε, τὸν τὰ πάντα περιέχοντα, πάσῃ φωνῇ καὶ πάσῃ διαλέκτῳ, ὡς πρ<ώ>τως ὕμνησέ σε ὁ ὑπό σου ταχθεὶς καὶ πάντα πιστευθεὶς τὰ αὐθεντικά. Cf. the utterance which is falsely ascribed to Plato, but which reflects the Hellenistic view, in Cl. Al. Strom., I, 143, 1: ὁ Πλάτων δὲ καὶ τοῖς θεοῖς διάλεκτον ἀπονέμει τινά, μάλιστα μὲν ἀπὸ τῶν ὀνειράτων τεκμαιρόμενος καὶ ἀπὸ τῶν χρησμῶν, ἄλλως δὲ καὶ ἀπὸ τῶν δαιμονώντων, οἳ τὴν αὑτῶν οὐ φθέγγονται φωνὴν οὐδὲ διάλεκτον, ἀλλὰ τὴν τῶν ὑπεισιόντων δαιμόνων; or Corp. Herm., I, 26a : The soul which has mounted to the intermediate kingdom of the Ὀγδοάς ὑμνεῖ σὺν τοῖς <ἐκεῖ> οὖσι τὸν πατέρα ... καὶ ὁμοιωθεὶς τοῖς συνοῦσι ἀκούει καὶ τῶν δυνάμεων ὑπὲρ τὴν ὀγδοαδικὴν φύσιν οὐσῶν φωνῇ τινι ἰδίᾳ ὑμνουσῶν τὸν θεόν. Similarly, there is reference to the tongues of angels in the Test. Job (48 ff.), [12] which is a Jewish work that has undergone Christian revision. Here the three daughters of Job are given magic girdles by their father shortly before his death : the first puts on her girdle καὶ παραχρῆμα ἔξω γέγονε τῆς ἑαυτῆς σαρκός ... καὶ ἀνέλαβεν ἄλλην καρδίαν ὡς μηκέτι φρονεῖν τὰ τῆς γῆς, ἀπεφθέγξατο <δὲ> τοὺς ἀγγελικοὺς ὕμνους ἐν ἀγγελικῇ φωνῇ καὶ ὕμνον ἀνέμελπε τῷ θεῷ κατὰ τὴν ἀγγελικὴν ὑμνολογίαν; the second speaks the διάλεκτος τῶν ἀρχόντων (ἀρχῶν?); the third the διάλεκτος τῶν Χερουβίμ. The content of the ecstatic song of praise of the second daughter is τοῦ ὑψηλοῦ τόπου τὸ ποίημα, and it is added by way of explanation : διότι εἴ τις βούλεται γνῶναι τὸ ποίημα τῶν οὐρανῶν, δυνήσεται εὑρεῖν ἐν τοῖς ὕμνοις Κασίας. The third extols τὸν δεσπότην τῶν ἀρετῶν ἐνδειξαμένη τὴν δόξαν αὐτῶν (with the explanatory addition : καὶ ὁ βουλόμενος λοιπὸν ἴχνος ... καταλαβεῖν τῆς πατρικῆς δόξης εὑρήσει ἀναγεγραμμένα ἐν ταῖς εὐχαῖς τῆς Ἀμαλθείας κέρας). All three ᾖδόν τε καὶ ἔψαλλον καὶ ηὐλόγησαν καὶ ἐδοξολό-

---

[9] Cf. Reitzenstein Poim., 220 ff.

[10] E.g., Preis. Zaub., XIII (Leiden), 588 ff.: ἐπικαλοῦμαί σε, κύριε, ὡς οἱ ὑπό σου φανέντες θεοί, ἵνα δύναμιν ἔχωσιν· Ἀχεβυκρων, οὗ ἡ δόξα· ααα, ηηη, ωωω· ιιι: ααα· ωωω· Σαβαώθ, Ἀρβαθιάω, Ζαγουρῆ, ὁ θεὸς Ἀραθ, Ἀδωναί, Βασυμμ, Ἰάω.

[11] The magician boasts (Preis. Zaub., VIII [London], 20 ff.): οἶδά σου καὶ τὰ βαρβαρικὰ ὀνόματα.

[12] M. R. James, *Apocrypha Anecdota*, II (*Texts and Studies*, V, 1 [1897]), 135 ff.; Reitzenstein Poim., 57. So far as possible I follow Reitzenstein's collation of the text.

γησαν τὸν θεόν, ἑκάστη ἐν τῇ ἐξαιρέτῳ διαλέκτῳ ... τὰ μεγαλεῖα τοῦ θεοῦ. The voices of the four archangels, which in their different ways magnify the Lord of glory, are already referred to in Eth. En., 40.

Paul is aware of a similarity between Hellenism and Christianity in respect of these mystical and ecstatic phenomena. The distinguishing feature as he sees it is to be found in the religious content (1 C. 12:2 f.). He can accept speaking with tongues as a work of the Holy Spirit, as a charisma (1 C. 14:39; 1 Th. 5:19). Indeed, he can lay claim to it himself (1 C. 14:18; 13:1; 2 C. 12:4). But he demands that its exercise before the assembled community should be subordinated to the principles of general exhortation, order, limitation and testing (1 C. 14:26 ff., 40; 1 Th. 5:21 f.). Higher than the gift of tongues, which in view of their pagan background the Corinthians are inclined to view as the spiritual gift *par excellence* (1 C. 14:37; → πνευματικός), is the gift of prophecy, and superior to all the gifts of the Spirit, which in themselves are valueless and transitory, is ἀγάπη (1 C. 13).

b. If the judgment of Paul on glossolalia raises the question whether this early Christian phenomenon can be understood merely in the light of the ecstatic mysticism of Hellenism, the accounts of the emergence of glossolalia or related utterances of the Spirit in the first Palestinian community (Ac. 10:46; 8:15 ff.; 2:2 ff.) make it plain that we are concerned with an ecstatic phenomenon which is shared by both Jewish and Gentile Christianity and for which there are analogies in the religious history of the OT and Judaism. [13]

The ecstatic fervour of the נְבִיאִים, who seem to be robbed of their individuality and overpowered by the Spirit (cf. 1 S. 10:5 ff.; 19:20 ff.; also 1 K. 18:29 f.), finds expression in broken cries and unintelligible speech which might be derided as the babbling of madmen (2 K. 9:11). Indeed, drunkards can still mock Isaiah's ecstatic babbling of obscure words, and he can give the sharp answer: "Yea verily, with stammering lips and another tongue will Yahweh speak to this people" (Is. 28:10 f.). Even in the case of the elders upon whom the Spirit imparted by Moses descends (Nu. 11:25 ff.) the endowment finds primary expression in ecstatic frenzy, i.e., in raving gestures and outcries after the manner of the נְבִיאִים. However, this did not last, for "it was followed by more sober endowment for office." [14] The later literature gives us many examples of ecstatic speech, though not necessarily of speaking in tongues, esp. in the apocalypses, e.g., Eth. En. 71:11, where Enoch, having been taken up into heaven, says: "I then fell on my face, and my whole body melted, and my spirit was transformed, and I cried with a loud voice, with the spirit of power, and I praised and extolled and magnified (Him)"; Da. 4:16 LXX: καὶ φοβηθεὶς τρόμου λαβόντος αὐτὸν καὶ ἀλλοιωθείσης τῆς ὁράσεως αὐτοῦ κινήσας τὴν κεφαλὴν ὥραν μίαν ἀποθαυμάσας ἀπεκρίθη ... φωνῇ πραείᾳ. For additional Hellenistic Jewish material from Philo and the Test. Job, → 722 f.

c. The event of Pentecost, as recorded in Ac. 2, belongs to the same context. This λαλεῖν ἑτέραις γλώσσαις bears essentially the same characteristics as the glossolalia depicted by Paul. It is an endowment of the Spirit (v. 4 f.; cf. v. 16 f.). It takes ecstatic forms (v. 4: → ἀποφθέγγομαι; v. 2 f.: the visionary accompanying phenomena of the wind from heaven and fiery tongues) which arouse astonishment (v. 7, 12). The awareness of the speakers seems to be lost as in the case of drunkards (v. 13). There is neither an orderly succession of individual speakers nor an overriding concern for the hearers. The λαλεῖν τὰ μεγαλεῖα

[13] Cf. P. Volz, *Der Geist Gottes* (1910), Index, *s.v.* "Glossolalie"; Bousset-Gressm., 394 ff.
[14] Volz, *op. cit.*, 28.

τοῦ θεοῦ (v. 11) seems to consist in praise of God (cf. 10:46 : μεγαλύνειν τὸν θεόν). As distinct from Paul and Ac. 10 and 19, however, this event is depicted in terms of speaking in foreign tongues (γλῶσσα, v. 11 = διάλεκτος, v. 6, 8). In the assembled crowd of Jews and proselytes of the *diaspora* each can detect his mother tongue on the lips of these Galilean disciples (v. 8, 11). This philological miracle, which is no mere miracle of hearing, is the unique feature in this out-pouring of the Spirit as recorded in Ac. All attempts, however, either to establish its historicity or to explain its meaning, including that of Zahn, [15] come up against the difficulty that for each to hear his own tongue presupposes something which both here and elsewhere seems to be excluded, namely, a multiplicity of languages. The Ἰουδαίαν (v. 9), which is surely authentic, makes quite impossible the idea of foreign tongues. In addition, there would be no occasion for scorn if unknown languages were spoken intelligibly (cf. v. 11, 13). Finally, in 10:44 f., cf. 11:15, 17, particular stress is laid on the similarity between glossolalia in Caesarea and the Pentecost incident in Jerusalem. It thus seems that, perhaps due to two sources, the tradition in Ac. 2 is confused, and we are not given any very reliable picture of what really happened. The historical kernel is a mass ecstasy on the part of the disciples which includes outbreaks of glossolalia. This first experience of the presence of the Spirit in the early community leads to enthusiastic possession, which is quickly followed, however, by the orderly prophetic witness of Peter (v. 14 ff.) and missionary enterprise. Reflection on the basic significance of the reception of the Spirit at Pentecost led the community to see a parallel with the establishment of the Jewish community as depicted in Jewish tradition, namely, that in the giving of the Law at Sinai the Word of God was distributed into 70 languages, so that each nation receives the commandments in its own tongue. [16] The miracle of tongues by which the Gospel is transmitted to the nations at Pentecost thus corresponds to the miracle by which the Law is published to the world. The result of this reflection, which sees in Christianity a new world religion as distinct from Judaism, is contained in the Lucan account of Pentecost, which is a legendary development of the story of the first and significant occurrence of glossolalia in Christianity.

d. The question how the word γλῶσσα came to be a technical term for this ecstatic mode of expression has received different answers. Of the three main meanings of γλῶσσα, "tongue" (→ 719, 720) is the least adapted to furnish an explanation. It is an intrinsically unlikely assumption that glossolalia simply means speaking with the tongue as an instrument of the Spirit, i.e., to the exclusion of human consciousness. Such a view would do justice neither to the expressions of Paul (the individual pneumatic has γένη γλωσσῶν in 1 C. 12:10 and is called ὁ λαλῶν γλώσσαις (plur.) in 14:5, cf. v. 18 and 13:1) nor to those of Ac. (in 2:11, cf. v. 6, 8, the meaning "tongue" is quite impossible, and logically the same is true in v. 4). Nor is there any support in the sources for the conjecture that Ac. 2:3 f. led to the early Christian use of γλῶσσα as a technical term for ecstatic utterance. [17] The sense of a "strange, unintelligible or mysterious word" [18] (→ 720)

[15] Ac., I, 102 f. Zn. sees here the antithesis to the confusion of tongues at Babel and an indication that the Spirit-filled community of believers is to proclaim the Gospel to all nations.

[16] Examples are given in Str.-B., II, 604 f.; cf. Philo Spec. Leg., II, 189; Decal., 32 ff., 46 f. Cf. also Schl., *Gesch. d. erst. Chr.*, 21 ff.

[17] Bchm. 1 K., 422, n. 1.

[18] So esp. F. Bleek, ThStKr, 2 (1829), 3 ff.

fits one essential aspect of γλῶσσα in Paul (1 C. 14:2, 9, 11), but it is the aspect which the apostle most sharply criticises, so that it could hardly be the most prominent aspect even in the Corinthian church — *a potiori fit denominatio!* Obviously γλῶσσα is for Paul more than an isolated oracle (1 C. 14:26 : γλῶσσαν ἔχει along with ψαλμὸν ..., διδαχὴν ..., ἀποκάλυψιν ..., ἑρμηνείαν ἔχει). The fact that he calls the charisma γένη γλωσσῶν (1 C. 12:10, 28; cf. 14:10) indicates that in his view the distinctive feature is to be found in the wealth and variety of γλῶσσαι. The words ἕτεραι (Ac. 2:4) and καιναί (Mk. 16:17) are a further indication that the essence of the gift lies in the fact that it is implies the new and unusual. It thus seems most likely that the word γλῶσσα has here the sense of "language" (→ 720, 722), and that it is used as a "technical expression for a peculiar language," [19] namely, the "language of the Spirit," a miraculous language which is used in heaven between God and the angels (1 C. 13:1) and to which man may attain in prayer as he is seized by the Spirit and caught up into heaven (2 C. 12:2 ff.; cf. 1 C. 14:2, 13 ff.; Ac. 10:46; 2:11). The heavenly origin of the phenomenon is certainly given strong emphasis in Ac. 2:2 ff. This interpretation, [20] which does not give any final answer to the question whether γλώσσαις λαλεῖν is an abbreviated expression for ἑτέραις γλώσσαις λαλεῖν (Ac. 2:4, cf. 1 C. 14:21), [21] meets the facts of the case both in Paul and in Ac., even though it is not always possible to give a strict rendering of γλῶσσα. It is also in keeping with Hellenistic usage and syncretistic modes of thought, yet not to the detriment of its link with Jewish conceptions (Eth. En. 40).

Like other ecstatic phenomena in early Christianity, glossolalia is more than a tribute to the century of its origins. In the Spirit the young community learned by experience "that decisive experiences begin with a powerful act as with an upwelling spring." [22] But the first enthusiastic surge quickly assumed fruitful forms of spiritual activity. Ecstatic egoism was harnessed to general edification (Paul). We can thus see that the divine power of the Spirit did in fact rule in the community. Any subsequent phenomena of glossolalia in Church history can only be hollow imitations of this first springtime of the Spirit. [23]

† ἑτερόγλωσσος.

a. "Speaking another language," "of an alien tongue" (synon. → βάρβαρος), e.g., Polyb., XXIII, 13, 2 : πλείστοις ἀνδράσιν ἀλλοφύλοις καὶ ἑτερογλώττοις χρησάμενος; Onosander, 26, 2 : τὰς ἑτερογλώσσους συμμαχίας τῶν ἐθνῶν; Strabo, VIII, 1, 2. b. "Speaking different languages," Philo Conf. Ling., 8 (opp. ὁμόφωνος). In both senses it is the equivalent of ἀλλόγλωσσος (cf. Philo Poster. C., 91; Jos. Ant., 1, 117). ἑτερόγλωσσος does not occur in the LXX but is found in 'A at ψ 113:1; Is. 33:19.

In the NT it occurs only at 1 C. 14:21: ἐν ἑτερογλώσσοις ("men of foreign speech") καὶ ἐν χείλεσιν ἑτέρων λαλήσω τῷ λαῷ τούτῳ καὶ οὐδ' οὕτως εἰσακούσονταί μου. Here Paul is expounding Is. 28:11 f., apparently according

---

[19] Mosiman, *op. cit.,* 35, cf. 130 ff.
[20] Cf. W. Bousset, GGA (1901), 773 : "Utterance with tongues is the speech of angels in which the secrets of the heavenly world are revealed."
[21] Bl.-Debr. § 480, 3.
[22] Volz, *op. cit.,* 28, n. 5.
[23] Cf. Mosiman, Lombard, Oesterreich, *op. cit.*

to a text related to ᾿Α; [1] LXX : διὰ φαυλισμὸν χειλέων, διὰ γλώσσης ἑτέρας, ὅτι λαλήσουσι τῷ λαῷ τούτῳ ... καὶ οὐκ ἠθέλησαν ἀκούειν. He sees in it a prophecy of early Christian glossolalia which does not aim at the edification of the community and is thus unprofitable (cf. v. 22). Glossolalia in this sense is a miraculous divine sign which works in unbelievers to "bring about a final and decisive repudiation of God." [2] In Is., of course, the men of another speech are Assyrians, whereas for Paul they are men who speak the language of heavenly spirits (→ γλῶσσα, 726). But this is simply an example of Paul's sovereign re-interpretation of the OT, for which there are many parallels among the Rabbis, and of which this is an instructive instance. [3]

Behm

† γνήσιος

This does not derive from γένος but from the old part. γνητός, "born," as in διόγνητος, κασίγνητος. It originally denotes the true son as opposed to the adopted, [1] or the legitimate as opposed to the νόθος. It thus means "true born." In a wider sense it may be used for the wife as distinct from the παλλακίς. Figur. it means "regular," "unfalsified," "genuine," or "pure." It is a favourite word in the pap., common in Philo and Joseph., but in the LXX occurs only in the apocryphal writings (Sir. 7:18; 3 Macc. 3:19).

In the NT it is not found in the Synopt. or Jn. (including Rev.). Jn. uses → ἀληθινός instead. The NT always uses it of persons by way of recognition. Thus in Phil. 4:3 the σύζυγος has shown himself to be a true fellow-worker, and in 1 Tm. 1:2; Tt. 1:4 Timothy and Titus are genuine sons of Paul because they have a true faith. [2] In relation to 2 C. 8:8 : τὸ τῆς ὑμετέρας ἀγάπης γνήσιον δοκιμάζων, cf. the Sestos inscr., 7: πρὸ πλείστου θέμενος τὸ πρὸς τὴν πατρίδα γνήσιον καὶ ἐκτενές. [3] Phil. 2:20 : γνησίως μεριμνᾶν τὰ περὶ ὑμῶν, is to be compared with 2 Macc. 14:8 : γνησίως φρονῶν (in 3 Macc. 3:23 the adverb is used in a different sense) and P. Lond., 130, 3 (1/2 cent. A.D.): γνησίως τε περὶ τὰ οὐράνια φιλοπονήσαντες. [4]

Büchsel

ἑτερόγλωσσος. Cr.-Kö., 263; Pr.-Bauer, 490; Liddell-Scott, 701; comm. on 1 C. 14:21.
[1] Cf. the note on 1 C. 14:21 in Orig. Philocal., 9, 2 (p. 55, Robinson): εὗρον γὰρ τὰ ἰσοδυναμοῦντα τῇ λέξει ταύτῃ ἐν τῇ τοῦ ᾿Ακύλου ἑρμηνείᾳ κείμενα; also H. Vollmer, *Die at.lichen Citate bei Pls.* (1895), 27 f.; Ltzm. K.³, 73; O. Michel, *Pls. u. s. Bibel* (1929), 64 f.
[2] Bchm. 1 K., 420.
[3] Michel, *op. cit.*, 168.
γνήσιος. Pr.-Bauer, *s.v.*
[1] Cf. γόνῳ γεγονός in explanation of γνήσιον, Demosth., 44, 49.
[2] Cf. γνήσιος υἱός εἰμι in Reitzenstein Poim., 13, 3; 340.
[3] *Wiener Studien,* I (1879), 33 ff., c. 120 B.C.
[4] I owe this to Bertram.

γογγύζω, διαγογγύζω
γογγυσμός, γογγυστής

† γογγύζω.

A. The Greek Usage.

1. Acc. to Phrynichus, 336 this is an Ionic word, used by Phocylides of Miletus (c. 540 B.C.); but this derivation is debatable. [1] Like the synon. Attic τονθυρίζω it is probably onomatopoeic, [2] but it is less correct and elegant, appearing in literature only in the post-Christian epoch. The oldest incontestable attestation is in P. Petr., III, 43, col. 3, 20 in a letter dated the 7th year of Ptolemy III (241/39 B.C.), where we read in 1, 19 ff.: ... ὅτι Μέγητος πλήρωμα [3] ἀναβέβηκεν καὶ τὰ λοιπὰ τὰ ἐνταῦθα, ὥστε μηθένα εἶναι ἐνταῦθα ἀλλ' ἢ ἡμᾶς, καὶ τὸ πλήρωμα γογγύζει φάμενοι ἀδικεῖσθαι ἐν τῷ ἔργῳ ἤδη μῆνας ι', τοῦτο δὲ πάσχειν διὰ τὸ μὴ παρεῖναι αὐτοῖς τὸν τριήραρχον. The meaning here is "to be dissatisfied" or "to express dissatisfaction," justifiably, as it appears, in this instance. There is a similar use in P. Oxy., I, 33, col. 3, 14 (2nd cent. A.D.), where it denotes "expressions of displeasure": ʽΡωμαῖοι γονγύζουσιν at the procession of someone condemned to death whom they disliked.

To the few examples from the pap. [4] we may add one or two literary attestations. Epict. Diss., I, 29, 55: οὐ θέλεις τὰ μὲν λογάρια τὰ περὶ τούτων ἄλλοις ἀφεῖναι, ἀταλαιπώροις ἀνθρωπαρίοις, ἵν' ἐν γωνίᾳ καθεζόμενοι μισθάρια λαμβάνωσιν ἢ γογγύζωσιν, ὅτι οὐδεὶς αὐτοῖς παρέχει οὐδέν, σὺ δὲ χρῆσθαι παρελθὼν οἷς ἔμαθες. Here the word has the sense already noted, as also in IV, 1, 79: ἄφες, μὴ ἀντίτεινε μηδὲ γόγγυζε, where γογγύζειν, used with ἀντιτείνειν in the sense of active opposition, indicates verbal protest against a distasteful action, i.e., the enforcing of military service on the sage. In M. Ant., 2, 3 we have the admonition: τὴν δὲ τῶν βιβλίων δίψαν ῥῖψον, ἵνα μὴ γογγύζων ἀποθάνης, ἀλλὰ ἵλεως ἀληθῶς καὶ ἀπὸ καρδίας εὐχάριστος τοῖς θεοῖς. Here γογγύζειν denotes "grumbling at disappointed hopes." It is important that the last example gives us much the same meaning as the first in 241/39 B.C.

2. In relation to the general use of γογγύζειν in non-Jewish and non-Christian Greek [5] we can easily discern its basic sense in spite of variations. It carries with it the thought of a legal claim and the view that no satisfaction has been or is being done to this claim. Both the claim and the opinion are, of course, subjective. This aspect is not affected by the possibility that both may sometimes seem to be fully justified. The examples also show us that from the very first γογγύζειν has no particular religious associations. To be sure, in M. Ant. it is used as the

---

γ ο γ γ ύ ζ ω. Pr.-Bauer, 257; Liddell-Scott, 355; P. Melcher, *De sermone Epicteteo quibus rebus ab Attica regula discedat* (= Diss. phil. Hal., 17 [1907], 1-114), 61.

[1] Cf. the bibl. in Pr.-Bauer, 257.

[2] γογγύζω is used of the cooing of doves in Poll. Onom., V, 89.

[3] This means here a column of workers.

[4] Cf. Preisigke Wört., 303. The most important examples are mentioned above.

[5] So far as I can see, the only literary example apart from those mentioned is Ps.-Luc. Ocyp., 44 f.:

νεωτέρῳ γὰρ αἶσχος ἐν πεσήμασι
ὑπηρέτης ἀδύνατα γογγύζων γέρων.

opposite of the fitting attitude of thankfulness to the gods. This does not mean, however, that it is in any sense a technical term. It should be noted that the personal reaction denoted by γογγύζειν is not represented as directed against the gods, but simply as a personal reaction. At most in this passage we could only say that it is a reaction which as such imputes injustice to the gods, and even this is perhaps saying too much. The statement thus helps to clarify a point which is not always quite so clear, namely, that behind γογγύζειν stands man in his totality; γογγύζειν describes a basic personal attitude and the external conduct shaped by the temperament and situation of the individual.[6] We have here a presupposition for the use of the word in the LXX to the extent that in biblical religion man is always a distinct and self-contained whole.

The unilateral character of the term perhaps gives us a second presupposition. A strong word was needed to describe a particular attitude of the people of Israel in certain circumstances (→ 730). γογγύζειν is such a word. This may be seen from all the examples. Nor should we ignore the subsidiary element of censure. The attitude denoted by it is not seemly in those who display it. We can see this already in the first example in the pap. The writer of the letter uses the γογγύζειν of his workers as a means of pressure, but he makes it plain that their attitude is unusual and therefore that attention should be paid to it, though he does not identify himself with it but merely reports it. It is in keeping with this aspect that the term is always used of others. In other words, this is a trait which even on Greek soil marks one as a ἁμαρτωλός (→ 320). As with the latter term, we thus have here an important presupposition in respect of the biblical usage. Indeed, it is one which greatly facilitates its incorporation into the biblical world of thought and utterance as this is shaped by the concept of God, and as it does not merely depict man, but condemns him.

B. γογγύζω among Greek Jews.

1. In the LXX γογγύζειν occurs 15 times, and διαγογγύζειν (→ 735) 10 times.[7] In 12 cases it is based on the Sem.; it is used 7 times for לוּן, once for נָלוֹז (לוּז: Is. 30:12), 3 times for הִתְאֹנֵן (Nu. 11:1; Lam. 3:39 : Σιρ. 10:25) and twice for רָגַן (kal : Is. 29:24; niph : ψ 105:25). Among the passages which do not use a form of לוּן, Is. 30:12 imports into ἐγόγγυσας an interpretation of the original by the translator, i.e., in respect of the disobedience and deficient trust of the people along the lines of the traditional national sin, though it is also possible that he had a corrupt text, or made a mistake, and thus presumed a form of לוּן for נָלוֹז. In Is. 29:24 again it is obvious that there is an element of interpretation, as we can see especially in the rendering of לֶקַח as ὑπακούειν. Thus we have οἱ δὲ γογγύζοντες μαθήσονται ὑπακούειν for וְרוֹגְנִים יִלְמְדוּ־לֶקַח. In this way the promise is accentuated; every apparent intellectual element is excluded.[8] Those who have previously murmured against God will learn to obey Him. The two terms γογγύζειν and ὑπακούειν, both controlled by the concept of God, are thus seen to be opposites. This goes much beyond the original on a presupposition which is in full keeping with the use of γογγύζειν. There is a similar

---

[6] This is true even in P. Oxy., I, 33, col. 3, 14, where one might most easily assume a different usage.

[7] As counted by Hatch-Redpath. In the LXX לוּן is always rendered either γογγύζειν or διαγογγύζειν, and הִתְאֹנֵן always γογγύζειν.

[8] Is. 29:24a reads : וְיָדְעוּ תֹעֵי־רוּחַ בִּינָה.

development of the original in Nu. 11:1, where וַיְהִי הָעָם כְּמִתְאֹנְנִים רַע בְּאָזְנֵי יְהוָה is translated καὶ ἦν ὁ λαὸς γυγγύζων πονηρὰ ἔναντι Κυρίου. The attitude of the people is thus lifted out of the realm of mere mood and seen as culpable guilt. It is best to take Lam. 3:39 in the sense that the γογγύζειν, i.e., dissatisfaction, is really against oneself (ἁμαρτία) rather than against God.

A closer analysis of these passages brings out two factors. The first is the inner consistency of the word even where it derives from different Semitic roots. We are not to attribute this to the translators, but to the fact that they found here an established term adapted to express both the concern of the text and their own concern. The second is the theological character of the term. Here already γογγύζειν always signifies an ungodly attitude on the part of man and not merely dissatisfaction at an unfulfilled promise, as in ordinary Greek. Yet the latter contributes in full measure the suggestion that the whole man shares in the attitude thus described.

2. The term which colours γογγύζειν in the LXX, and which is normally translated γογγύζειν, is לוּן. It occurs only in Ex. 15-17 and Nu. 14-17, apart from Jos. 9:18. Similarly, the derivates תְּלֻנָּה and תְּלוּנָה are found only in these passages. The root לוּן is always rendered γογγ-. It is thus in the light of this stem that we are to understand γογγύζειν in the LXX.

לוּן means "to murmur," and except in Jos. 9:18 it refers to the attitude of the people when delivered from Egypt but not yet brought into the promised land, and therefore discontented with its lot. Usually the murmuring is against Moses (Ex. 15:24; [9] 17:3), or Moses and Aaron (Ex. 16:2; Nu. 14:2; 17:6, 20), though there can be no doubt that it is finally against God, at whose commission these men led the people out of Egypt (cf. Ex. 16:7, 8; Nu. 14:27, 29, 36). [10] The murmuring always has some concrete ground, namely, hunger or thirst in the desert (Ex. 15:24; 16:3), or the proximity and yet apparent unattainability of the promised land (Nu. 14:1). There is, of course, a certain justification for it. The presupposition of the whole attitude is the election of the people in the exodus. This is grace no less than the promise of the land. But the people makes of it a claim, i.e., a claim to be cared for in every respect and to be brought to the goal without effort. When the people murmurs, it is always because it thinks that justice has not been done or is not being done to its claim. The texts leave us in no doubt that the claim and this assessment of the situation are both wholly subjective. Yet they also leave us in no doubt that in such an attitude God is reduced to human standards and is robbed, or is in process of being robbed, of His sovereignty in relation to the people. This is why the murmuring of the people is a tempting of God (Ex. 17:2 etc.) or a scorning of God (נִאֵץ, Nu. 14:11). This is why it is severely punished. For murmuring is an attitude of the whole man. Hence it incurs guilt which must be punished. Finally, this helps us to see why the right attitude, in contrast to murmuring, is הֶאֱמִין, i.e., unconditional acceptance (Nu. 14:11) or obedience, hearkening to the voice of God (Nu. 14:22).

In keeping with what has been said, we can appreciate that γογγύζειν was peculiarly fitted by its presuppositions to express the point at issue in לוּן, but that

---

[9] Here, of course, we have → διαγογγύζειν, as in Ex. 16:2, 7, 8; Nu. 14:2, 36; 16:11.
[10] Cf. esp. Nu. 16:11: "What is Aaron, that ye murmur against him?" Moses and Aaron are representatives (שְׁלוּחִים) of God to the people. Cf. → 414 and esp. 415.

in so doing it received a distinctly religious accentuation which was not present in the Greek world. It now suggests the judgment and condemnation of God by the man whom God has bound to Himself, who therefore owes Him trust, gratitude and obedience, but who instead constitutes himself His judge. It also suggests God's judgment on this man.

At this point we can easily fit the γογγύζειν passages already mentioned (→ 729) into the history and usage of the term. This is true of ψ 105:25, where רָגַן is the original, and Dt. 1:27, where we have → διαγογγύζειν, since both passages refer to the murmuring of the people after the return of the spies (Nu. 14:1 ff.). [11] In Σιρ. 10:25 there is no historical allusion, but the usage is the same, especialy when we consider the Heb.: καὶ ἀνὴρ ἐπιστήμων οὐ γογγύσει == וְחָכָם נוֹסָר לֹא יִתְאוֹנֵן [12]; chastisement will not cause the man who knows God to become embittered.

Of the remaining passages (Ju. 1:14; Jdt. 5:22 and ψ 58:16), the last is the only one to have a Heb. original, but it is too textually uncertain to be of much help. Perhaps the translator had another text, [13] or perhaps he tried to enhance the severity of the verse by referring the γογγύζειν to ungodly enemies. [14] It is impossible to say. In Ju. 1:14 γογγύζειν is linked with κράζειν and is designed to strengthen a request. In Jdt. 5:22 the word expresses indignation and lively protest. In these two cases the usage is the same as that of secular Greek both before and after Christ. [15] There are thus examples of this in the LXX too.

3. To complete the history of the term we should take a brief glance at later Jewish usage, and also at that of Philo and Josephus. In this case the findings are particularly instructive. For we find confirmation of the fact that, notwithstanding certain variations in detail, the meaning of the word as determined by the underlying לוּן in Ex. 15-17 and Nu. 14-17 becomes the main sense of the term in all later Judaism. The Rabbis, Philo and Josephus are here at one. It does not affect the thesis that good care is often taken to avoid the word. For since we can understand the reasons for this, the affirmation only acquires the greater weight.

a. The Rabbis engage in exegesis and systematic declaration of the Law among those who know the texts which are expounded or taken as a starting-point. Hence there is no evading the murmuring of the people; it is attested in the Torah. But this means that there is no evading the word which the Torah uses for it (לוּן). It is thus the more instructive to see the attempts made to divest this murmuring of its ungodly and hostile character and to render it harmless. A common way of doing this is to interpret the OT word in terms of the less pregnant הִתְרַעֵם or (Aram.) אִתְרַעַם.

הִרְעִים in the OT means "to cause to thunder," and in 1 S. 1:6 "to provoke to anger." Materially, then, it is not related to לוּן. On the other hand, in Syr. רעם means "to lift up one's voice," and אתרעם can sometimes mean "to make oneself disagreeable" etc. The latter became the usual rendering of לוּן in the Targums; [16] לוּן itself never

---

[11] The translator of ψ 105:24 f. seems to have been familiar with Δτ. 1:19 ff.; cf. ψ 105:24b with Δτ. 1:32.

[12] This word, or perhaps נָבוֹן, is not in the original and must be supplied; cf. R. Smend, *Die Weisheit des Jesus Sirach* (1906), *ad loc.*

[13] Cf. BHK², *ad loc.* According to G. Bertram ψ 58:16 rests on a confusion of לוּן and לִין?

[14] The word hardly fits the comparison of the ungodly with hungry dogs.

[15] → 728.

[16] E.g., Tg. O., Ex. 15:24; 16:2, 7 etc.

occurs. [17] Even more important is the fact that the Rabbis, when they have occasion to refer to the murmuring of the people, do not use the term suggested by the text, but הִתְרַעֵם, e.g., M. Ex. on 16:7 (p. 162, 10, Horovitz-Rabin): "What then are we, that ye murmur against us?" They (i.e., Moses and Aaron) say : "Why do you pay such particular regard to us, that you rise up and murmur against us (שֶׁאַתֶּם . . . . מִתְרַעֲמִים עָלֵינוּ". הִתְרַעֵם, however, is not an exact equivalent of לוּן. If it were, all would be in order and the specific meaning and theological thrust of לוּן would be maintained in a new form. In fact, however, הִתְרַעֵם is the word used by later Judaism for grumbling dissatisfaction in general. Unlike לוּן, it is not related specifically to the concept of God. Cf. M. Ex. on 20:2 (p. 221, 21): "He murmured (והיה מתרעם) (against the king) because he had not been set over the treasure of silver and gold" ; jBer., 5c, 24 f.: [18] "A worker who works only a short time but shows particular skill is given the same wage as his fellows who had to work the whole day ; hence the workers murmured (והיו מתרעמין) etc. Most pertinent of all, however, is the use of תַּרְעוֹמֶת in place of the OT תְּלֻנָּה to express Israel's murmuring against God (M. Ex. on 15:24 [p. 155, 3 ff., Horovitz-Rabin]; cf. תִּרְעָמְתָּא, Tg. O., Ex. 16:12; תִּרְעֲמוּתָא Tg. O., Ex. 16:7 f.), like the protest of someone who has been cheated in wages, business etc. (BM, 4, 6; 6, 1). In other words, we are brought back to the situation which obtained prior to the adoption of γογγύζειν by the translators of the OT to express the specific attitude of the covenant people of Israel denoted by לוּן.

The weakening of the sinful element in Israel's murmuring against God can be accomplished in another way. The texts leave us in no doubt as to the true character of this murmuring even where it is not expressly stated to be against (עַל) God (→ 730). The Rabbis could hardly avoid the force of this, and in M. Ex. on 15:24 (p. 155, 4 f., Horovitz-Rabin), for example, murmuring against Moses is recognised to be also against God (עַל הַגְּבוּרָה). But mitigation is found by representing this as a murmuring before God, so that it loses most of its character as guilt. [19]

M. Ex. on 16:8 (p. 162, 15): ". . . and lo, you stand up and murmur (מִתְרַעֲמִים), before (לִפְנֵי) the One who lives and continues to all eternity." S. Nu., 84 on 10:35 (p. 80, 14 f., Horovitz): ". . . then began the Israelites to murmur (מִתְרַעֲמִים) before God (לִפְנֵי הַמָּקוֹם" etc.

b. The situation is even clearer in Philo and Josephus. They are writing for non-Jews, and in so far as they record the history of their people they are concerned to make it as glorious and impressive as possible. Hence they must either suppress any conflicts between God and His people or represent them rather differently from Scripture. The repeated murmuring of the people is part of the scriptural record of these conflicts. It is noticeable, however, that, while the Rabbis make mention of this in other terms, Philo and Josephus do not merely avoid the word γογγύζειν but depict the events themselves from a very different angle. We can understand this only if the word was so repugnant both to the authors and readers that it had to be avoided on apologetic grounds. [20]

---

[17] Levy does not have the root either in Chald. Wört. or Wört.
[18] → γογγυσμός.
[19] There is something of a par. in the efforts made by the Rabbis to rob David of blame in the affair with Bathsheba (→ 325, including n. 58 f.).
[20] In view of the extent to which Josephus quotes his sources in the Ant., and esp. the LXX, his attitude at this point is doubly striking.

Josephus makes the murmuring of Israel against Moses at Marah (Ex. 15:23 f.) an urgent appeal for help (Ant., 3, 6),[21] that in the wilderness of Sinai (Ex. 16:2 f.) a complaint (Ant., 3, 11) and movement (Ant., 3, 13) against Moses,[22] that in Rephidim (Ex. 17:1 ff.) a δι' ὀργῆς τὸν Μωυσῆν ποιεῖσθαι (Ant., 3, 33), that after leaving Sinai (Nu. 11:1)[23] a στασιάζειν against Moses (Ant., 3, 295), and that after the return of the spies (Nu. 14:1 ff.) ill-advised complaint linked with βλασφημίαι against Moses and Aaron (Ant., 3, 306). At every point the aspect of complaint against God is ignored. This is true even on the last occasion when Moses speaks of the ὕβρις and ἁμαρτήματα of the people (Ant., 3, 311), for neither word presupposes the thought of God to Gk. ears.

In Philo we find such words as μεμψιμοιρεῖν, τὰς ψυχὰς ἀναπίπτειν used in respect of Ex. 15:23 f. (Vit. Mos., I, 181 f.), ἀθυμεῖν, followed by an ὀνειδίζειν of Moses, in respect of Ex. 16:1 ff. (ibid., 192), ἀπόγνωσις σωτηρίας in respect of Ex. 17:1 ff. (ibid., 196). The murmuring of Nu. 14:1 ff. is represented as cowardice (δειλία) and is ascribed to only 80% of the people (ibid., 233 f.). Everything is a matter of mood and concerns only the people and not God. There is a certain exception in Vit. Mos., I, 236, where Moses describes the attitude of the cowards as ἀπιστεῖν τοῖς χρησμοῖς and of the brave as καταπειθεῖς τοῖς λογίοις, but this does not alter the basic picture nor affect its rationalistic character.

We may thus conclude that the unanimity of the theological judgment on Israel expressed in לון/γογγύζειν is not maintained in later Judaism. By choosing γογγύζειν, the LXX reaches a high point of usage and understanding which is never again reached in Judaism.

C. γογγύζω in the NT.

For a true grasp of the NT usage we must see it against the LXX background and also take into account the deviations of later Judaism. Three groups call for notice.

1. In Mt. 20:11 γογγύζειν amounts to little more than the הִתְרַעֵם of later Judaism. The Rabbis, too, can speak of the grumbling of workers who do not think that they are properly paid (→ 732). The word is used in its strict secular sense in Lk. 5:30, where it denotes the dissatisfaction of the religious leaders at Jesus' dealings with publicans and sinners, which as they see it are quite improper. The two instances of διαγογγύζειν in Lk. 15:2 and 19:7 (→ 735) may be placed in the same category.

2. There is a direct connection with לון/γογγύζειν at 1 C. 10:10 : μηδὲ γογγύζετε, καθάπερ τινὲς αὐτῶν ἐγόγγυσαν, καὶ ἀπώλοντο ὑπὸ τοῦ ὀλεθρευτοῦ. This statement recalls the historical murmuring of the people and by its adoption of the special OT term accepts the fact of its guilt. To this degree it testifies to the readoption of the theological assessment of murmuring which was abandoned by Judaism. This was probably a direct result of the deepening of the concept of God by Jesus.[24] No less significant is the transfer of the word, and the judgment

---

[21] Materially, cf. also Wis. 11:4.

[22] Here we also have a warning against the threatened stoning of Moses on the ground that it would be a τοῦ θεοῦ κατακρίνειν (3, 21).

[23] Here the LXX has γογγύζειν even though there is no לון in the original.

[24] The 1st chapter of 4 Esr. gives us another example which is almost certainly Christian in origin. In 1:15 f. (p. 2, Bensly-James) God says : Coturnix vobis in signo fuit, castra vobis ad tutelam dedi, et illic murmurastis, et non triumphastis in nomine meo de perditione inimicorum vestrorum, sed adhuc nunc usque murmuratis.

contained in it, to the Christian community, at least as a possibility. At this point we can see on the one side the consistency with which Paul carries through the thought of the new covenant people ('Ισραὴλ τοῦ θεοῦ: Gl. 6:16) and on the other the danger which threatens this people if it allows its own desires and cravings to shape its expectations and is not content with what God promises and gives. It was along such lines that the ancient covenant people was betrayed into murmuring disappointment, and therefore into sin against God, and therefore into ἀπώλεια.

3. In the Gospel of John γογγύζειν is used at 6:41, 43 for the rejection of Jesus by the Jews and at 6:61 for the sceptical attitude of the disciples, [25] while at 7:32 it is used of the ὄχλος in its speculation whether Jesus is after all the Christ. The question thus arises whether there is any fixed usage in Jn. The first three passages agree, but the fourth seems to stand apart.

a. What γογγύζειν means at 6:61 may be seen from v. 61b: τοῦτο ὑμᾶς σκανδαλίζει; In the γογγύζειν of His own, Jesus sees the danger of sinning against Him, and perhaps even the act. Immediately preceding are His words concerning the eating of His body and drinking of His blood as a presupposition for the reception of eternal life. The disciples cannot accept this saying. It makes no odds whether they call it σκληρός because of its boldness or because of their deficient insight (6:60). The essential point is that they measure Jesus by their own expectations, which are also those of their people, and that on this basis they criticise Him, i.e., they express dissatisfaction, which materially is criticism of God and dissatisfaction with Him, since Jesus is the υἱὸς τοῦ ἀνθρώπου (6:62). Thus the group of disciples, like Israel in the desert, reaches a necessary point of division and decision. It is no accident, but belongs to the heart of the matter, that there follows the parting from Jesus of those οἳ οὐ πιστεύουσιν (6:64, cf. 66) and that in the case of those who remain γογγύζειν gives way to confession (68 f.). This contrast makes it plain that the whole man is again at stake in γογγύζειν.

b. The most important aspects of the use of the word in 6:41, 43 are the same. The hearers of Jesus among the people measure Jesus by their own standards and reject Him on this ground. In so doing they display *mutatis mutandis* the same attitude as that of their fathers in the wilderness. It has often been noted that John refers here to 'Ιουδαῖοι though in the whole passage Jesus is obviously addressing Galileans (6:22 ff.). The point is that 'Ιουδαῖοι is used for the Jewish people as officially [26] represented. [27] Yet the author seems to have something more in his mind in his choice of this word. He is perhaps indicating that the attitude of the hearers derives from a "Jewish mode of thought." [28] He is particularly influenced, however, by the connection between 'Ιουδαῖοι and γογγύζοντες which is so familiar to him from the history of the Jewish people. The Galilean hearers of Jesus show themselves to be 'Ιουδαῖοι by the fact that they are γογγύζοντες and that they withhold πίστις at the decisive moment. The Evangelist thus sees disaster overtaking the people a second time because it cannot resolve to recognise

---

[25] John means disciples in the widest sense (→ μαθητής).
[26] Bau. J. on 1:19.
[27] Bau. J., *ad loc.*; H. J. Holtzmann, *Das Ev. des Joh.*[2] (1893), on 2:19.
[28] Schl. J., 175 f. Zn., *ad loc.* is content with the purely formal explanation that the Galileans are called Jews in characterisation of their hostile mood.

God as God but insists that God must be guided by itself and its own opinions and expectations. This thought runs though the whole Gospel from 1:11 onwards. It helps us to see why 'Ιουδαῖοι is selected to sum up and to delineate the circles which treat Jesus with chilly reserve or even with open rejection.

c. Perhaps Jn. 7:32 is to be viewed in the same light. Comparison with 7:12 (→ γογγυσμός) shows us that γογγύζειν does not denote mere discussion of Jesus, or secret approval of His claim, but vacillation. It is in keeping that the religious leaders find this dangerous, since there is the possibility of the ὄχλος turning from them. On the other hand, the Evangelist can use γογγύζειν in the sense of a. and b. because vacillation is not acceptance and thus falls under the divine judgment (ἀπιστία). Moreover, the story of the relationship between Jesus and the ὄχλος up to the σταύρωσον provides external justification for ascribing OT γογγύζειν to vacillating hearers. The word thus includes a judgment, as accounts of the fact always carry the implied judgment of their author (→ 728). [29]

† διαγογγύζω.

Among Gk. writers this word occurs only in Heliod. Aeth., 7, 27 in the sense of "to whisper (a message or task)." It is found 10 times in the LXX and sometimes as a textual alternative for γογγύζω. Except in Dt. 1:27 (רָגַן niph) [1] and Σιρ. 34:24 [2] it is always used for לוּן [3] and cannot be distinguished in sense from γογγύζω.

In the NT it is found only at Lk. 15:2; 19:7, where it denotes the dissatisfaction of the Φαρισαῖοι and γραμματεῖς at the conduct of Jesus. There is no direct link with LXX usage. We best take it in terms of Hellenistic usage. To attempts to find here the Johannine application (→ 734) there is the objection that Luke does not present the same group of ideas as John, so that it is most unlikely that there should be this isolated example.

† γογγυσμός.

Acc. to Phrynichus, 336 this is an Ionic word like γογγύζω, and it is supposed to have been used by Anaxandrides (c. 375 B.C.) for τονθορυσμός (Fr., 31, CAF, II, 146) in the sense of "murmuring" (→ 728). Thus far the only literary example known is in M. Ant., 9, 37: ἅλις τοῦ ἀθλίου βίου καὶ γογγυσμοῦ καὶ πιθηκισμοῦ ... ἀλλὰ καὶ πρὸς τοὺς θεοὺς ἤδη ποτὲ ἁπλούστερος καὶ χρηστότερος γενοῦ — a thought similar to that expressed in 2, 3 (→ 728), i.e., grumbling dissatisfaction at disappointed expectations. In Catal. Cod. Astr. Graec., VII, 139, 11 it is found in the same sense alongside δυσαρεστία, and in P. Masp., 67159, 27 it is used in the articles of association of two builders (Dec. 16, 568) alongside ῥᾳδιουργία, ὑπέρθεσις and ἀναβολὴ ἔργων διόλου.

It occurs 11 times in the LXX (not counting γόγγυσις in Nu. 14:27). Of these

---

[29] Later Christian usage can be ignored, since it is never more than formal, e.g., Ev. Pt., 28, where it occurs along with κόπτεσθαι τὰ στήθη as a sign of penitence, or Test. Sol., 9, 3 (p. 35*, 11, McCown), where it is used of the lamentation (οἴμοι) of an imprisoned demon.

δ ι α γ ο γ γ ύ ζ ω. Pr.-Bauer, 284.

[1] → on this passage 731.

[2] The Heb. has ירגן for διαγογγύσει.

[3] Cf. Jos. 9:18, where it is not so easy to integrate לוּן with the normal OT usage.

Ex. 16:7, 8 (twice), 9, 12; Nu. 17:5, 10 (20, 25) use it for תְּלֻנֹּת or תְּלוּנֹת to sum up the murmurings of Israel. The sense is exactly the same as that of לוּן/γογγύζειν. Relevant, too, is Sir. 46:7: γογγυσμὸς πονηρίας (original: דִּבָּה רָעָה); the reference is to the γογγύζειν of Nu. 14:1 ff. So, too, Ps. Sol. 16:11, where a righteous man, in the same situation as that of the people in the desert, prays: γογγυσμὸν καὶ ὀλιγο-πιστίαν [1] ἐν θλίψει μάκρυνον ἀπ᾽ ἐμοῦ. On the other hand, in Wis. 1:10, [2] 11 the word denotes the misue of the tongue in the widest sense, as also in Is. 58:9, where the LXX makes [3] the דַּבֶּר־אָוֶן a ῥῆμα γογγυσμοῦ. [4] In Ps. Sol. 5:15 the reference is simply to the grumbling attitude of a "benefactor."

The case is much the same as with γογγύζειν. A more general use goes hand in hand with the more specific. The Rabbis substitute תַּרְעֹמֶת (or corresponding Aram. con-structions) for תְּלֻנֹּת, and this is as little adapted as הִתְרַעֵם to bring out the true point at issue in לוּן/γογγύζειν, as illustrated by the contemporary use of the term both in theological and secular contexts. [5] Thus it can mean no more than "evil report" or "calumniation," e.g., b.Ber., 12a: תַּרְעֹמֶת הַמִּינִין "calumniation by heretics," etc. At the very most, therefore, we can speak of only a formal and not a material par. between γογγυσμός/תְּלֻנָּה and תַּרְעֹמֶת. [6]

In the NT it is found 4 times: Jn. 7:12; Ac. 6:1; Phil. 2:14; 1 Pt. 4:9. a. In Jn. 7:12 there is no direct adoption of the theological use of γογγυσμός in the LXX as this was shaped by the thought of God. That is to say, the word is not used to depict the murmuring of Israel. On the other hand, there is a link with it as the Evangelist considers the situation in the primitive community (cf. γογγύζειν in Jn. 7:32). γογγυσμός is used here to denote the vacillation of the people towards Jesus as already discussed (→ 735).

b. At Ac. 6:1 there is obviously no connection with OT γογγυσμός. The reference here is simply to the dissatisfied grumbling of one part of the community at claims which are not met (cf. M. Ant., 9, 37 and the Lucan use of → γογγύζω and → διαγογγύζω). The same is even more true of 1 Pt. 4:9, where there is the admonition: φιλόξενοι εἰς ἀλλήλους ἄνευ γογγυσμοῦ, which will free hospitality from either inward or outward unfriendliness (cf. Ps. Sol. 5:15; → supra).

c. Phil. 2:14 probably stands somewhere between a. and b.: πάντα ποιεῖτε χωρὶς γογγυσμῶν καὶ διαλογισμῶν. It is possible that Paul is here thinking of the murmuring of Israel, as in 1 C. 10:10, [7] and that this leads him to the admoni-tion. Understood in this way, the admonition — cf. the verses which follow — would tally with the general thought of the epistle, which is one long appeal for unconditional self-surrender to God in Christ.

γ ο γ γ υ σ μ ό ς. Pr.-Bauer, 257, Liddell-Scott, 356.

[1] Cf. Wis. 1, where γογγυσμός is used with πειράζειν, ἀπιστεῖν in v. 2 and βλάσφη-μος in v. 6. Cf. also Did., 3, 6, where it is linked with βλασφημία; also → 733.

[2] The only plur. in the LXX, or anywhere apart from Phil. 2:14.

[3] This is quoted in Barn., 3, 5 — the only instance of γογγυσμός in the post-apost. fathers. γογγύζειν does not occur at all, but we have γόγγυσος in Did., 3, 6 and γόγ-γυσις in Did., 4, 7 and Barn., 19, 11 (neither in the NT).

[4] The thought of God is always present in אָוֶן, and this may well affect the meaning of γογγυσμός.

[5] → 732.

[6] The list of par. in Schl. J., 189 might well leave this impression, but it is wrong.

[7] The use of διαλογισμοί/διαλογίζεσθαι perhaps points in the same direction with its suggestion of secret doubt; cf. Loh., ad loc.

† γογγυστής.

Apart from the NT this word occurs only at Prv. 26:22 Σ for נִרְגָּן ('A : τονθρυστής);
Prv. 26:20 Θ for נִרְגָּן (LXX : δίθυμος; Σ : δόλιος; 'A : τονθρυστής); Is. 29:24 (LXX :
οἱ γογγύζοντες).

In the NT it is used only at Jd. 16 : γογγυσταὶ μεμψίμοιροι, to describe false
teachers as men who are "dissatisfied with their lot[1] and therefore with God,"
though not giving to God what they owe to Him as such. Even though there is
no direct connection with the LXX usage, there is an obvious similarity.

Rengstorf

---

† γόης   (→ μάγος)

This mostly has a. the strict sense of a "magician," esp. one who works with verbal
formulae. Those who believe in demons take him quite seriously, though he is sometimes
detested, esp. by the educated. Cf. Philostr. Vit. Ap., 5, 12 : Apollonius does not prophesy
on the basis of γοητεία, but on that of divine revelation, inspiration.[1] To be sure,
μάγος can give rise to the same antithesis between conjuring and true revelation which
is free and for that reason full. The only distinction between μάγος and γόης is that
the latter is mostly used for the lower practitioner. "To *goetia* belong conjurations,
since it normally works with the help of evil, lower and stupid material demons."[2]
Thus Aristot. Fr., 30 expressly refuses to ascribe γοητικὴ μαγεία to the μάγοι. This
is not a hard and fast distinction, but when strictly used γόης usually bears this
derogatory sense. b. It is thus used for the "false magician" — this is never true of
μάγος in more precise usage. c. It thus comes to denote the "charlatan" in a more
general sense, as in Herodot. Cf. γοητεία in 2 Macc. 12:24 for "pretence." This is the
only occurrence of the root γοη- in the LXX. γοητικός is found in 'A Prv. 26:22 in
the sense of "deluding."

The use of the word group in Philo is instructive. In the primary sense we only have
γοητεύειν (Som., I, 220, where all magical practices are repudiated). Yet γόης is also
used figur. to denote the confusion and delusion of idolatry in Praem. Poen., 25. The
man who abuses the divine gift of speech is grouped with charlatans (γόητες) in
Rer. Div. Her., 302. The φιλήδονος or sensual man is also called a γόης ("charlatan")
in the list of vices in Sacr. A.C., 32. Most important is Spec. Leg., I, 315, where προφήτης and γόης are contrasted. The one is the bearer of true revelation, whereas the
other composes his own alleged divine sayings. For Philo γοητεία is basically the
opposite of truth (cf. esp. Praem. Poen., 8; Som., II, 40). It may thus be used as an
equivalent of falsehood or deception (with ἀπάτη in Op. Mund., 165), even where
there is not the slightest suggestion of magic (as in Plant., 106). It can thus signify
hypocritical conduct (Decal., 125; cf. Leg. Gaj., 162), deception (of ἡδονή in
Post. C., 101) or the natural sensual magic of woman (Vit. Mos., I, 301). In the figur.

γογγυστής. [1] Cf. Philo Vit. Mos., I, 18.
γόης. T. Hopfner in Pauly-W., XIV (1928), 373 ff.; F. Pfister, *ibid.,* Suppl. IV (1924),
324 ff.; O. Weinreich, "Gebet und Wunder," *Genethliakon f. W. Schmid* (1929), Index,
s.v., p. 350 f.; occasional remarks by A. D. Nock in F. Jackson-K. Lake, *Beginnings of
Christianity,* IV (1932), 516-54.
[1] Weinreich esp. (*op. cit.*) emphasises this distinction, but his material does not justify
any clear differentiation between μάγος and γόης.
[2] Hopfner, 378.

sense it can also be used, of course, with reference to the world of thought of alien religions (Op. Mund., 2; Praem. Poen., 8). Philo is not thinking only of harmless deception ; γοητεία (like γόης) always carries with it the thought of deliberate deceit.

In the NT the only occurrence is at 2 Tm. 3:13. In Eur. Ba., 234 Dionysus is called a γόης, obviously in the sense of one who entices to impious action by apparently pious words, [3] and this is the meaning in 2 Tm. 3:13. The γόητες are here identical with those described in v. 6 f. There is no contrast here between magic and revelation. As in Philo, the word is used figuratively, yet in such a way that the danger and evil effects of these γόητες are fully appreciated (→ βασκαίνω).

Delling

---

† γόνυ, † γονυπετέω   (→ προσκυνέω).

A. Genuflection in the NT.

Except in Hb. 12:12 (cf. Is. 35:3; Prv. 4:26; Gr. Sir. 25:23; also Polyb., XX, 10, 9) γόνυ is used in the NT only in connection with genuflection. We have a. τιθέναι τὰ γόνατα in Mk. 15:19; Lk. 22:41; Ac. 7:60; 9:40; 20:36; 21:5. Equivalents are γονυπετεῖν in Mt. 27:29 = Mk. 15:19; Mt. 17:14; Mk. 1:40; 10:17; προσκυνεῖν in Mt. 8:2 = Mk. 1:40; though in Mk. 15:19 the sense is "to do homage" ; πίπτειν ἐπὶ πρόσωπον or ἐπὶ τῆς γῆς, Lk. 22:41 = Mt. 26:39 = Mk. 14:35; Mt. 8:2 = Lk. 5:12. b. κάμπτειν τὰ γόνατα in liturgical style at R. 11:4 (LXX : ὤκλασαν); R. 14:11; Eph. 3:14; Phil. 2:10. The equivalents make it clear that no distinction is intended between bowing the knee and full prostration. Genuflection is linked with prayer to God (Lk. 22:41; Ac. 7:60 etc.; Eph. 3:14), with requests to the *Kyrios* (Mt. 17:14; Mk. 1:40), with greeting of the διδάσκαλος (Mk. 10:17), with homage to the βασιλεύς (Mt. 27:29) or to Baal (R. 11:4), or to God the Judge (R. 14:10 f.), or to the *Kyrios* at His enthronement and proclamation as Lord of the world (Phil. 2:10). The gesture thus expresses supplication, abasement, worship, subjection etc.

B. Genuflection outside the NT.

The history of this term belongs to that of the wider concept of προσκυνεῖν. τιθέναι (κάμπτειν) τὰ γόνατα and γονυπετεῖν (as an independent gesture) are seldom mentioned among the Greeks and Romans, Eur. Tro., 1305. Mostly we have a Latinism (cf. *genua ponere*, Curtius, VIII, 7, 13, Quintil., IX, 4, 11; *genua submittere*, Ovid. Fast., 4, 317; Plin. Hist. Nat., VIII, 1, 3; *genua inclinare*, Ps.-Vergil Anthol., 172, 10b etc.). γονυπετεῖν is found in Polyb., XV, 29, 9; XXXII, 25, 7; Cornut. Nat. Deor., 12 (though Eur. Phoen., 293 : γονυπετής). Equivalents are προσπίπτειν, Hdt., I, 134; VII, 136; ἐς γόνυ ἵζεσθαι, Ps.-Luc. Dea Syr., 55; προσκυνεῖν, Suid. etc. In Gk. and Lat. there is usually no distinction between

---

[3] Weinreich obviously takes a different view (283, 295).

genuflection and full prostration. [1] It is practised a. by a slave before his lord, Nonnus Dionys., 25, 2, though not among citizens, Hdt., VII, 136; Isoc., 4, 151. This custom came to Greece and Rome from the East, Liv., XXX, 16, 48. The ἱκέτης falls on his knees before his patron and thus acknowledges himself to be his slave, Heliod. Aeth., X, 16; Nonnus Dionys., 22, 374 f. b. There is genuflection before the gods in prayer (Liv., XXVI, 9, 6; Plut. C. Gracch., 16 [I, 482c]), esp. before chthonic deities (Eur. Tro., 1303 ff.), in popular religion (Aristoph. Av., 501 ff.), or in cults which stand under unofficial or oriental influence [2] such as the cult of Helios (Soph. Fr., 672; Plat. Leg., X, 887e) or in a hymn to Dionysus Lysios (Ael. Arist., 50, 39). In the normal worship of the official gods there was no bowing of the knee.

In the LXX genuflection is rendered ὀκλάζειν (ἐπὶ τὰ) γόνατα, 3 Βασ. 8:54; 19:18 (distinguished from προσκυνεῖν in the sense of throwing a kiss with the hand), κάμπτειν (ἐπὶ) τὰ γόνατα, 4 Βασ. 1:13 (cf. 9:24); Da. 6:10; 1 Ch. 29:20 (with προσκυνεῖν = to cast oneself to the ground); 1 Esr. 8:70; 3 Macc. 2:1 (R) 20; κάμπτειν, Is. 45:23; πίπτειν, κλίνειν ἐπὶ τὰ γόνατα, 2 Ch. 6:13; 2 Esr. 9:5. The Heb. equivalents are (עַל־בִּרְכַּיִם) בֶּרֶךְ, Ps. 95:6 with שָׁחָה hithp προσκυνεῖν and כָּרַע προσπίπτειν; (עַל־בִּרְכַּיִם) כָּרַע, Is. 45:23; 1 K. 8:54; 19:18; 2 Esr. 9:5; קָדַד, 1 Ch. 29:20 (Gn. 43:28; Ex. 4:31; 12:27 = κύπτειν with προσκυνεῖν, שָׁחָה hithp, but Gn. 24:26, 48 = εὐδοκεῖν). The gesture of genuflection occurs as a sign of humility and worship in the prayer of the individual or the community to God at 1 Ch. 29:20; 1 K. 8:54; 1 Esr. 8:70; 2 Esr. 9:5; Da. 6:10; 3 Macc. 2:1 (R), and as a sign of abasement, acknowledgment and homage before God at 3 Βασ. 19:18; Is. 45:23, before the king at 1 Ch. 29:20, and before the ἄνθρωπος τοῦ θεοῦ at 4 Βασ. 1:13. Standing, however, is more usual in prayer (Gn. 18:22; 19:27; 1 S. 1:26; Ps. 134 f.).

In the Rabbis there is a systematic differentiation between individual gestures. a. כְּרִיעָה denotes brief falling on the knee; b. קִידָה signifies falling on one's face; c. הִשְׁתַּחֲוָיָה is used for prostration with outstretched hands and feet. Bar Qappara speaks of four prostrations: a. כְּרִיעָה, inclining; b. כְּפִיפָה, bowing; c. הִשְׁתַּחֲוָיָה, casting oneself down; d. בְּרִיכָה, kneeling. [3]

In the Christian Church kneeling was customary both in individual prayer and public worship. Although various terms are used (τιθέναι τὰ γόνατα, Mart. Andr., 8; Act. Thom., 167; Herm. v., 1, 1, 3; 2, 1, 2; 3, 1, 5; ὀκλάζειν, Just. Dial., 90, 5; κάμπτειν, 1 Cl., 57, 1), γονυκλινεῖν is the commonest, [4] and becomes a technical term for kneeling in divine service (e.g., Const. Ap., VIII, 10, 2; Orig. Orat., 31, 3). Bending the knee expresses a. subjection (1 C., 57, 1); b. abasement in confession and sorrow (Chrysost. Serm. de Anna, 4, MPG, 54, 667 f.; Bas. Spir. Sct., 27, MPG, 32, 192c; c. petition, Const. Ap., II, 22, 14. There is an obvious intermingling of pagan and Christian custom in Act. Joh., 12. (the people after the crash of the temple of Artemis in Ephesus (καὶ οἱ μὲν αὐτῶν ἐπ᾽ ὄψιν κείμενοι ἐλιτάνευον· οἱ δὲ τὰ γόνατα κλίνοντες ἐδέοντο· οἱ δὲ τὰς ἐσθῆτας διαρρήξαντες ἔκλαιον· οἱ δὲ φυγεῖν ἐπειρῶντο. [5] The meaning

---

γόνυ κτλ. C. Sittl, *Die Gebärden der Griechen u. Römer* (1890), 177 ff.; H. Bolkestein, "Theophrastus Charakter der Deisidaimonia" (RVV, 21, 2 [1929]), 25 ff.; J. Leipoldt, *War Jesus Jude?* (1923), 44 ff.

[1] Sittl, 156.
[2] Cf. O. Walther, *Östr. Jhft.*, 13 (1910), *Beiblatt*, 229 ff.
[3] Str.-B., II, 260, I, 401; cf. also S. Krauss, *Synagogale Altertümer* (1922), 401 f.
[4] Cf. Eustath. Thessal. Comm. in Il., 669, 32: κάμπτεται δὲ γόνυ ἔστιν ὅτε καὶ ἱκετευτικῶς· ὃ καὶ γονυπετεῖν λέγεται καὶ γόνυ κλίνειν καὶ συνθέτως γονυκλινεῖν.
[5] Cf. F. J. Dölger, *Sol Salutis*,[2] (1925), 78, n. 3.

of the symbolical gesture of kneeling in prayer may be gathered from Ps.-Just. Quaest. et Resp. ad Orth., 115 : If kneeling is more efficacious in prayer than standing, why do not worshippers kneel on the Lord's Day and between Easter and Pentecost ? Ἐπειδὴ ἀμφοτέρων ἐχρῆν ἡμᾶς ἀεὶ μεμνῆσθαι, καὶ τῆς ἐν ταῖς ἁμαρτίαις πτώσεως ἡμῶν καὶ τῆς χάριτος τοῦ Χριστοῦ ἡμῶν, δι' ἧς ἐκ τῆς πτώσεως ἀνέστημεν. On 6 days γονυκλισία is the σύμβολον of the fall, and on the 7th μὴ κλίνειν γόνυ is the σύμβολον ... τῆς ἀναστάσεως.

In modern Synagogue worship there is still genuflection to the degree that on the Day of Atonement, at the point in the liturgy which corresponds to the utterance of the name of Yahweh in the worship of the temple (when there was prostration, cf. Joma 6, 2), [6] and also on New Year's Day, at a certain point in the liturgy, there is kneeling and then full prostration.

Schlier

γραμματεύς

1. Scribes in the NT Period.

Only once in the NT (Ac. 19:35) is γραμματεύς used as the title of a higher Ephesian official in the ordinary Greek sense of "clerk" or "secretary." [1] The normal Jewish use, however, is very common. [2] According to this use, first attested in the LXX in 2 Esr. and 1 Ch., γραμματεύς is a translation of the Heb. סוֹפֵר (Aram. סָפְרָא) which means a "man learned in the Torah," [3] a "rabbi," an "ordained theologian."

סוֹפֵר "scribe" or "secretary," was a title of royal officials, [4] and only from the time of Ezra, [5] Neh., 1 Ch. and Sir. did it come to denote a man learned in the Torah, cf. also the earliest Rabbinic traditions (13 Berakha of the 18 petitions in Meg. Taan., 12). [6] Apart from a few isolated occurrences in the Tannaitic

---

[6] Str.-B., II, 311 ff.

γραμματεύς. Schürer, II, 372-447; Str.-B., I, 79-82; 691-695; II, 647-661; Joach. Jeremias, *Jerusalem zur Zeit Jesu,* II, A (1924), 27-32; II, B (1929), 101-114; 122-127; J. Hoh, "Der christ. γραμματεύς," BZ, 17 (1929), 256-269; Schl. Mt., 33, 163 f., 686 f.; A. Schlatter, *Die Theologie des Judentums nach dem Bericht des Josefus* (1932), 199 ff.; E. Sellin, *Israelit.-jüdische Religionsgeschichte* (1933), 140 f.

[1] Moult.-Mill., 132a; Pr.-Bauer, 259.

[2] Synpt., Ac., elsewhere only 1 C. 1:20 (Jn. 8:3).

[3] Cf. the synon. νομικός (Mt. 22:35); νομοδιδάσκαλος (Lk. 5:17); in Joseph. ἐξηγηταὶ τῶν πατρίων νόμων (Ant. 17, 149), ἱερογραμματεῖς (Bell., 6, 291).

[4] Acc. to official lists from the time of David and Solomon (2 S. 8:15 ff.; 20:23 ff.; 1 K. 4:1 ff.), the sōfēr was one of the 6 or 8 highest officials ; cf. K. Galling, "Die Halle des Schreibers," PJB, 27 (1931), 56.

[5] The transition may be seen in the Book of Ezra. In the royal decree in Ezra 7:12-26 "scribe of the law of the God of heaven" is still an official title (R. Kittel, *Geschichte des Volkes Israel,* III [1929], 577 ff.; H. H. Schaeder, *Esra der Schreiber* [1930], 48 f.: "secretary or minister of the law of the God of heaven" — a first step towards the later dignity of the exilarch ; E. Sellin, *Geschichte des israelitisch-jüdischen Volkes,* II [1932], 137). In Ezra 7:6, 11, however, it is given its later meaning.

[6] In both passages פְּלֵיטַת סוֹפְרִים or פ״ סָפְרַיָּא (the rest of the scribes) is a fixed expression taken over from an earlier period (Str.-B., I, 80).

period, [7] the NT is our final witness for this use of סוֹפֵר /γραμματεύς. Neither Philo nor Josephus [8] uses the term for biblical scholars of their own day. In post-Christian Rabbinic literature the rabbis of the day are called חֲכָמִים, while סוֹפְרִים is used for scholars of an earlier period, and in everyday life for biblical instructors and secretaries (cf. γραμματεύς in Josephus). [9]

The rabbis formed a closed order. Only fully qualified scholars, who by ordination had received the official spirit of Moses, mediated by succession [10] (cf. Mt. 23:2), were legitimate members of the guild of scribes. The high reputation of the rabbis among the people (Mk. 12:38 f.; Mt. 23:6 f.) rested on their knowledge of the Law and oral tradition, and also of secret theosophic, cosmogonic and eschatological doctrines concealed by an esoteric discipline. [11] Sociologically the rabbis were the direct successors of the prophets, i.e., men who knew the divine will and proclaimed it in instruction, judgment and preaching. [12] As incumbents of the teaching office, they questioned Jesus on His message and His transgression of the Halacha. As members of the Sanhedrin, on which the leading rabbis sat as leaders of the Pharisaic communities [13] and thus constituted one of the three parties of which this supreme assembly of the Jews consisted, they took part in the prosecution and condemnation of Jesus.

2. The Judgment of Jesus on the Scribes.

To understand the judgment of Jesus on the theologians of his age, we must distinguish them sharply from the Pharisees, whose societies were mostly composed of small people with no theological mastery. [13] A certain obscurity has been caused by the expression "scribes and Pharisees" (used only in Mt. and Lk.). It is helpful to compare Mt. 23:1-36 with the parallel tradition in Lk., for this shows us that a distinction is to be made between the sayings against the scribes (Lk. 11:46-52; 20:46) and those against the Pharisees (Lk. 11:39-42, 44). [14] It is only in this light that we can understand the accusations against the scribes. As distinct from those made against members of the Pharisaic communities, they refer wholly to the theological learning of the scribes and the resultant social claims and privileges. The Sermon on the Mount in Matthew, like Mt. 23, contains a section against the scribes and Pharisees. Both groups are mentioned in Mt. 5:20, and then the theologians are singled out in 5:21-48 and members of the Pharisaic societies in 6:1-18.

The charges of Jesus are levelled against the conduct and teaching of the theologians of His time. As regards the former, Jesus sees a lack of humility (Mt. 23:5 ff. etc.), of selflessness (Mk. 12:40a) and of sincerity (Mk. 12:40b etc.). His most serious accusation, however, is that they do not practise what they demand in their teaching and preaching (Lk. 11:46 etc.). The main reproach against their doctrine is that their casuistry defeats the true will of God contained

---

[7] Str.-B., I, 80.
[8] An exception in Joseph. is ἱερογραμματεῖς in Bell., 6, 291.
[9] For examples, cf. Str.-B., I, 79 ff.
[10] Str.-B., II, 654 f.
[11] Joach. Jeremias, *Jerusalem zur Zeit Jesu,* II B, 106 ff.
[12] *Ibid.,* 110 f.
[13] *Ibid.,* 115-140, esp. 122-130.
[14] Lk. 11:43 is to be seen in the light of Mk. 12:38 f.; Lk. 20:46, where the desire for honour rightly refers to the rabbis rather than the Pharisees.

in the law of love. This is stated particularly clearly in the example of the fictional dedication in Mk. 7:9 ff. and par. In contrast, Jesus brings out the full seriousness of the true will of God in the powerful antitheses of the Sermon on the Mount (Mt. 5:21-48).

3. Paul, himself an ordained scribe, [15] saw in the rejection of the preaching of the cross by Jewish theologians a fulfilment of the saying in Is. 33:18 (ποῦ γραμματεύς;), which according to his exposition prophesied the futility of human wisdom and the paradox of divine election (1 C. 1:20).

4. There is reference to the Christian γραμματεύς [16] in Mt. 13:52; cf. 5:19; 16:19; 18:18; 23:8-12. The First Gospel, especially in its proof from Scripture, shows us this scribe at work.

Joachim Jeremias

γράφω, γραφή, γράμμα, ἐγγράφω,
προγράφω, ὑπογραμμός

γράφω.

A. The General Use of γράφω.

1. The word is found in Homer. It is used of the tearing of the flesh by a lance, and of engraving in tables. [1] The sense of "carving," "engraving," is probably the original. In the LXX, where it is almost always used for כָּתַב (predominantly kal, occasionally niph) or for כְּתַב, it is very common. It is used of ἁγίασμα κυρίῳ on the plate of the high-priest (ἐπί with gen., Ex. 36:39 [39:30]); of the carved figures in

---

[15] This may be deduced, e.g., from his part in capital prosecutions (Ac. 26:10).
[16] Cf. Hoh, op. cit., 256-269; Schl. Mt., 449-451.

γ ρ ά φ ω κ τ λ. Deissmann B, 108-111; NB, 77 f. F. R. Montgomery Hitchcock, "The Use of γράφειν," JThSt, 31 (1929 f.), 271-275; E. Majer-Leonhard, ᾿Αγράμματοι (Diss. Marburg, 1913); W. Bussmann, Synopt. Studien, III (1931), 184 ff.; H. G. Meecham, ExpT, 44 (1933), 384 f. γέγραπται: G. Thieme, D. Inschriften von Magnesia am Mäander u. d. NT. (1906), 22; J. F. Marcks, Symbola critica ad epistolographos Graecos (1883), 27. On 1 C. 4:6 : W. Lütgert, "Freiheitspredigt und Schwarmgeister in Korinth," BFTh., 12 (1908), 97 ff.; A. Schlatter, "D. kor. Theologie," BFTh., 18 (1914), 7 ff. On the autographed endings : Deissmann LO, 133 and 137; G. Milligan, The NT Documents (1913), 24 f.; H. Erman, Mélanges Nicole (1905), 130 ff.; JThSt, 31 (1929 f.), 271 ff. (→ supra). O. Roller, D. Formular der paulin. Briefe (1933). ἱερὰ γράμματα : Deissmann LO, 321 f.; A. Wilhelm, Oestr. Jhft., 3 (1900), 77. On the Canon : Schürer, II, 363 ff.; F. Buhl, Kanon u. Text des AT (1891); G. Wildeboer, D. Entstehung des at.lichen Kanons (1891); B. Poertner, D. Autorität der deuterokan. Bücher des AT (1893); G. Hölscher, Kanonisch. u. Apokryph. (1905); E. König, "Kanon u. Apokryphen," BFTh, 21 (1917), 409 ff.; W. Staerck, "D. Schrift- u. Kanonbegriff der jüd. Bibel," ZSTh, 6 (1928), 101-119. Rabbinic designation and view of Scripture : G. Surenhusius, Βίβλος καταλλαγῆς (1713), 1-36; Bousset-Gressm., 153 ff.; Schürer, II, 390-414; Weber, 80-118; Moore, I, 233-250; A. Schlatter, D. Theologie des Judentums nach d. Bericht d. Josefus (1932), 64-72, 151 f.; G. Aicher, "Das AT i. d. Mischna," BSt, 11 (1906). Jesus and Paul and the OT : De Vet. Test. locis a Paulo apostolo allegatis, Diss. Leipzig (1869); H. Vollmer, D. at.lichen Citate bei Paulus (1895); J. Hänel, "D. Schriftbegriff Jesu," BFTh, 24 (1919); Ltzm. Gl., Excurs. on 4:31; E. v. Dobschütz, "The Attitude of Jesus and St. Paul toward the Bible," The Bible Mag. (1914); P. Bratsiotes, Ὁ ἀπόστολος Παῦλος καὶ ἡ μετάφρασις τῶν Ὁ (1925); W. Windfuhr, "D. Ap. Paulus als Haggadist," ZAW, 44 (1926), 327 ff.; E. v. Dobschütz, "Zum paulin. Schriftbeweis," ZNW, 24 (1925), 306; A. v. Harnack, "D. AT i. d. paulin. Briefen u. i. d. paulin. Gemeinden," SAB (1928), 124 ff.; O. Michel, Paulus und seine Bibel

1 K. 6:28 (29): ἔγραψε γραφίδι χερουβείν; of the hewing out of a chamber in the rock in Is. 22:16; of the engraving of the Law on the stones of Jordan in Dt. 27:3; Jos. 9:5 (8:32); of inscribing on bronze tablets in 1 Macc. 14:18 (with the dat.). Writing on tablets may be meant in this context, since it is often hard to determine how far the original idea of engraving or inscribing is still present: εἰς τόμον or πυξίον or ἐπὶ πυξίου, Is. 8:1; Hab. 2:2; Is. 30:8; figur. 'Ιερ. 38:33 (31:32): ἐπὶ καρδίας, Prv. 3:3 'Α: ἐπὶ τὸ πλάτος τῆς καρδίας σου. Simple writing is certainly meant in Da. 5:5 LXX: ἐπὶ τοῦ τοίχου τοῦ οἴκου.

In the NT, apart from ἐγγράφειν, we have the original sense of engraving in Jesus' καταγράφειν or γράφειν εἰς τὴν γῆν in Jn. 8:6, 8, also in Lk. 1:63, where Zacharias writes the name of John on a waxed tablet (πινακίδιον),[12] and finally in Rev. 2:17 (→ 745).

2. γράφειν is commonly used for "painting" or "drawing," e.g., Aristoph. Ra., 537; Hdt., II, 41; Xenophanes, 13 (I, p. 59, 1, Diehl); Plat. Gorg., 453c; Jos. Ap., 2, 252.

3. It is used of the activity of writing generally. When Paul dictates his letters (in R. 16:22 Tertius is the true γράψας), he usually appends a greeting in his own hand, as in 2 Th. 3:17: οὕτως γράφω; Gl. 6:11 [3] (→ 764). There can be no doubt that the dictating is also called γράφειν, for γράφειν does not mean only to write with one's own hand. Thus in 1 C. 4:14 or 14:37 all that is meant is that Paul now imparts this to the community, whether by dictation or in his own hand. In the light of this incontrovertible fact it may be asked whether the ὁ γράψας ταῦτα of Jn. 21:24 might not simply mean that the beloved disciple and his recollections stand behind this Gospel and are the occasion of its writing. This is a very possible view so long as we do not weaken unduly the second aspect. Indeed, it would be difficult to press the formula to imply more than an assertion of spiritual responsibility for what is contained in the book. [4]

When Paul refers to an earlier letter, he can say, e.g., in 1 C. 5:9: ἔγραψα ὑμῖν ἐν τῇ ἐπιστολῇ.[5] γράφειν can be used both of an earlier writing of the community

---

(1929); G. Schrenk, "Die Geschichtsanschauung des Paulus auf d. Hintergrund s. Zeitalters," *Jahrbch. d. Theol. Schule Bethel*, 3 (1932), 74 ff. Florilegia: E. Hatch, *Essays in Biblical Greek* (1889); R. Harris, *Testimonies* I/II (1916-20); Ltzm. Gl. Relations to Hellenism: R. Bultmann, *D. Stil der paulin. Predigt u. d. kynisch-stoische Diatribe* (1910), 94 ff.; R. Hirzel, Νόμος ἄγραφος, ASG, XX, 1 (1900), 27 f.; E. Fascher, Προφήτης (1927), 152 ff.; E. v. Dobschütz, "Vom vierfachen Schriftsinn," *Harnack-Ehrung* (1921), 1-13. Post-Apost. Fathers: A. v. Harnack, *op. cit.*; Wnd. Barn., 313-316; A. v. Ungern-Sternberg, *D. traditionelle at.liche Schriftbeweis* de Christo u. de evangelio *i. d. alten Kirche* (1913). The Doctrine of Scripture in the Gk. Fathers: Suic. Thes. (dogmatic standpoint). For further liter., v. Michel, *op. cit.*

[1] Il., 17, 599; 6, 169: ἐν πίνακι πτυκτῷ (both aor.).

[2] λέγων = לֵאמֹר is added (4 Βασ. 10:6); cf. on this Sem. expression Bl.-Debr., 420, 2; E. Kieckers, *Indogerm. Forsch.*, 35 (1915), 34 ff. On this whole question, cf. Str.-B., II, 108 ff.

[3] The πηλίκοις γράμμασιν ἔγραψα τῇ ἐμῇ χειρί (Zn. Gl., *ad loc.*) might be related to the whole letter, but also to an autographed conclusion. Cf. 1 C. 16:21. Whether or not Paul dictated all his epistles can hardly be decided so long as the authenticity of 2 Th. and R. 16 is debated. Cf. JThSt, 31 (1930), 273 f., where there is additional material on the endings and dictation in the case of Romans.

[4] Cf. J. H. Bernard, *Joh.* (1929), II, 713; JThSt, *loc. cit.* Appeal to Ju. 8:14 LXX and the writing of the τίτλος by Pilate (→ *infra* and n. 10) hardly touches the heart of the matter. The question of writing with one's own hand is quite subsidiary in Jn. 21:24.

[5] On γράφειν ἐπιστολήν in Ac. 23:25; 2 Pt. 3:1, cf. 2 Ch. 30:1; 2 Esr. 4:6; 1 Macc. 13:35; 2 Macc. 9:18; 3 Macc. 3:11, 30 (where we have τύπος as in Ac. 23:25); M. Ex., 18, 6: Moses כָּתַב לוֹ בְּאִגֶּרֶת (to Jethro); Tanch. וישלח, 5, 164. γράφειν βιβλίον can also be used for writing a letter, as in Hdt., I, 125; cf. 4 Βασ. 10:1; 2 Ch. 32:17. In Ac. 18:27 the reference is to a letter of the brethren commending Apollos.

(1 C. 7:1) and also of preceding material in the letter of the apostle (1 C. 9:15). For sending a communication by delegates Ac. 15:23 has: γράφειν διὰ χειρός τινος (of the decree sent by Barnabas and Silas). Διὰ Σιλουανοῦ ἔγραψα (1 Pt. 5:12) might be taken in the same way, [6] but the reference could also be to the scribe [7] or to an associate in composition. [8]

4. "To set down" or "to draw up." Thus in Plat. Leg., XI, 923c; 924a, διαθήκην γράφειν means "to make testamentary disposition." [9] Again, in Jer. 39:25 ἔγραψα βιβλίον refers to a bill of sale.

In the NT γράφειν is used in this way in relation to the βιβλίον ἀποστασίου (→ βιβλίον, 617) in Mk. 10:4 and the debt in Lk. 16:6 f. The writing, or more strictly the order for the writing of the τίτλος [10] on the cross by Pilate in Jn. 19:19, together with the objection and the striking answer: ὃ γέγραφα γέγραφα, in v. 21 f., obviously refers to a similar public document. A voluntary putting on record of debt is also to be seen in Phlm. 19: ἐγὼ Παῦλος ἔγραψα τῇ ἐμῇ χειρί.

It is obviously from this usage, with its sense of public accusation, that there develops in Attic judicial terminology the phrase γράφεσθαι τινά τινος in the sense of "to accuse someone." [11] Cf. Aristoph. Nu., 1482; Demosth., 18, 103; Plat. Euthyphr., 2b. This is not found in the NT. Nor is the sense of "to enter as," "to inventory". Jos. 18:9 (recording of the land); 1 Ch. 4:41; Jer. 22:30; 1 Macc. 8:20; and often in an ideal figurative sense in Philo: Rer. Div. Her., 245, 250. "To characterise someone as": Hdt., VII, 214; Philo Poster. C., 80; Leg. All., III, 198; Spec. Leg., II, 132. "To be viewed or treated as": Det. Pot. Ins., 141; Vit. Mos., I, 35.

5. Composition of a Writing or Inscription in a Roll or Book.

Mal. 3:16; Bar. 1:1: γράφειν εἰς βιβλίον Ἰερ. 39(32):10; Tob. 12:20; ἐν: Ἰερ. 43(36):18; Da. Θ 12:1; ἐπί (with acc.): ψ 138(139):16; Ἰερ. 43(36):2. For the NT → βίβλος, βιβλίον. For γράφειν in the sense of "to describe" in Polyb., II, 56, 4 there is a par. in Rev. 22:18 f.

In the OT writing down is an important mark of revelation. Thus God Himself writes down in Ex. 24:12; 31:18; 32:15, 32; 34:1; Dt. 4:13; 9:10 etc. Moses writes down the commandments of the Lord in Ex. 24:4; 34:27; Joshua in Jos. 24:26, Samuel in 1 S. 10:25. The king is to cause the Law of God to be written down (Dt. 17:18). The people is to write the words of God on the door-posts (Dt. 6:9; 11:20). The authoritative significance of writing in the OT, in so far as it mediates

---

[6] For examples from the post-apost. fathers, cf. Wnd. 1 Pt., ad loc.

[7] Eus. Hist. Eccles., IV, 23, 11: ἐπιστολὴν διὰ Κλήμεντος γραφεῖσαν. A different sense is borne by the τὰ γεγραμμένα διὰ τῶν προφητῶν of Lk. 18:31, where the διά has much the same force as an ὑπό. In Est. 8:10 ἐγράφη διὰ τοῦ βασιλέως means in the name of the king.

[8] On the common NT phrase γράφειν τινί, τινί τι "to write to someone" (R. 15:15; 2 C. 2:4; 1 C. 14:37; Gl. 1:20 etc.), cf. Pr.-Bauer, where some LXX examples are given. Cf. Jos. Ant., 12, 16. With inf., Ac. 18:27. On γράφειν περί τινος in Jn. 5:46; Ac. 25:26 (Festus of litterae dimissoriae to Caesar); 1 C. 7:1; 2 C. 9:1; 1 Th. 4:9; 5:1; Jd. 3; 1 Jn. 2:26, cf. Jos. Ant., 17, 81; 18, 262; 20, 154; Vit., 62. → γέγραπται, 748.

[9] For the varied use in the pap., cf. Preisigke Wört.

[10] On τίτλος (Mt. 27:37: αἰτία; Lk. 23:38: ἐπιγραφή), which might be used either of the tablet with the name of the delinquent or of the inscription itself (Columella, 9: scribere titulum), cf. Suet. Calig., 32: praecedente titulo qui causam poenae indicaret; and perhaps also ibid., Domit., 10: cum hoc titulo; Eus. Hist. Eccl., V, 1, 44: πίνακος αὐτὸν προάγοντος ἐν ᾧ ἐγέγραπτο Ῥωμαϊστί κτλ. In Tac. Ann., II, 22 Caesar sets up a pile of weapons with a titulus (inscription). For older liter., cf. O. Zöckler, D. Kreuz Christi (1875), 441. Cf. also JThSt, op. cit., 272 f. On γεγραμμένον Ἑβραϊστί κτλ. in Jn. 19:20, cf. Schl. J., ad loc. with examples from Joseph. and the Rabbis.

[11] Cf. Suid., s.v. γράφεται: ἀντὶ τοῦ γράφει, ἢ κατηγορεῖ.

the declaration of the will of God, is fully endorsed in the NT, even though the meaning of the authority is very different, cf. the ἐγράφη of Paul when he discusses the purpose of OT Scripture in 1 C. 9:10; 10:11; R. 4:23; 15:4.[12] On the other hand, from the standpoint of the history of revelation the significance of γράφειν is given a remarkably different emphasis in the NT generally. Thus Jesus Himself is never presented as One who wrote down revelation, nor even as One who caused others to write, except in the case of the Apocalypse. We may also remember the natural tone of the ἔδοξε κἀμοὶ γράψαι of Lk. 1:3 in this connection. There is certainly an awareness that writing in the service of the Gospel is undertaken for a supreme purpose and before God (Gl. 1:20; R. 15:15). But neither in the Synoptists nor in Paul is there the emphatic claim to be writing sacred literature. In this regard the Johannine writings stand apart. In the Fourth Gospel the proclamation of the kingship of Christ in the τίτλος on the cross is particularly significant (→ 744), and so, too, is the concluding statement that the goal of the work is faith in Christ the Son of God (20:30 f.) and the emphatic equation of μαρτυρεῖν and γράφειν in the witness of the author (21:24 f.). When quoting the OT, John almost always uses the introductory γεγραμμένον (→ 749), and in 20:31, when speaking of the aim of his own writing, i.e., to awaken faith, he can use a word which elsewhere he reserves for OT Scripture, namely, γέγραπται. Indeed, in the previous verse (v. 30) we already find the expression: ἃ οὐκ ἔστιν γεγραμμένα ἐν τῷ βιβλίῳ τούτῳ. This solemn statement is striking. Naturally, it does not imply that the unheard of wealth of the activity of Jesus can be adequately presented in literature (21:25). Yet there is a no less solemn emphasis on the testimony of writing in 1 Jn.[13]

Even more emphatic, in accordance with the sense of apocalyptic declaration, is the conviction of the revelatory significance of writing in the Apocalypse. The writing of the divine stands under the promise and direction of God. This refers to the whole book (1:11, 19). Blessed is the man who keeps τὰ ἐν αὐτῇ γεγραμμένα (1:3, cf. 22:19). With equal solemnity the exalted Lord requires of the ἄγγελος of the seven churches that he should write: γράψον (2:1-3:14).When it is important to emphasise the sacred validity and import of certain sayings, the divine receives the specific command: γράψον (14:13; 19:9; 21:5),[14] and there is a corresponding prohibition in 10:4. The fact that what is written has a hypostatic background in the heavenly world testifies to the significance of the roll written on both sides in 5:1 etc.[15] and the repeated mention of those whose names are written in the book of life or of the Lamb throughout the Apocalypse (→ βιβλίον, 617). Apart from this use of γράφειν for literary inscription, however, the word γράφειν is often linked with ὄνομα in images which have a strong personal reference. In 2:17, for example, there is the promise to the one who overcomes, as by strenuous effort in the games, that he will receive the white stone with a

---

[12] For reasons of convenience this Pauline ἐγράφη is treated under → γραφή, 759. Cf. on this ἐγράφη Philo Rer. Div. Her., 172: μεθόριος δ' ὁ θεσμὸς οὗτος ἐγράφη.

[13] Cf. the → ἵνα- statements in 1 Jn. 1:4; 2:1; 5:13 and the repeated γράφω and ἔγραψα in 2:12-14.

[14] On καὶ λέγει· γράψον (Rev. 21:5), cf. 'Ιερ. 37:2 and the אָמַר לוֹ כְּתוֹב and similar expressions in T. Sanh., 2, 6; S. Dt., 357 on 34:5; M. Ex., 22, 24.

[15] In relation to the art. → βιβλίον, it may be added that the tables of the Law are written on both sides, also the roll in Ez. 2:10 (cf. Ex. 32:15). They are also written by the finger of God (Ex. 31:18; Dt. 9:10).

name engraven on it, i.e., a new name. [16] Again, in 3:12 the fact that the victor belongs wholly to God is expressed in the writing upon him of the sacred name. Again, the 144.000 bear on their foreheads the divine name (14:1). [17] Again, there is reference to a name on the forehead of the whore (17:5). Finally, we read of the secret and manifest name of the returning Logos. In all such cases γράφειν or γεγραμμένον is used. The God of revelation proclaimed by the divine declares Himself in readable signs. He does not merely manifest Himself ; He also gives forceful expression to His will to save. Nor is the sacred book the final thing. The perfect expression of the divine will consists in writing on and in persons.

6. γράφειν in Legislative Activity.

Already in Pind. Nem., 6, 7 γράφειν is used in the sense of "to prescribe" or "to decree" : γράφειν νόμους means "to give or lay down laws." In Demosth., 24, 48 γράφειν is used with νομοθετεῖν; in Xenoph. Mem., I, 2, 42 we read : νόμοι οὓς τὸ πλῆθος ἔγραψε; I, 2, 44 refers to the legislative activity of the usurper. The same usage is found in the OT, e.g., of God in 4 Βασ. 17:37 (τὰς ἐντολάς); of Darius and Cyrus in 1 Esr. 4:55, 56; 6:16 (17); of the instruction of officials by Demetrius in 1 Macc. 13:37. Josephus and Philo have the same expression. Thus in Jos. Ant., 3, 213 we find νόμους ἔγραψε; in 11, 92, with reference to the written order of Cyros, οἰκοδομῆσαι with the infin.; also 12, 201. Cf. also with ἵνα : 11, 127 and cf. 216. Philo Ebr., 64 : γράφειν with νομοθετεῖν. γράφειν νόμους : Conf. Ling., 112; Som., I, 92 and 95; Vit. Mos., I, 300; II, 14; Decal., 132. Of the codification of laws in the Chaldean language, Vit. Mos., II, 26; ὁ γραφεὶς νόμος, Conf. Ling., 160; Congr., 137 νόμος ἐγράφη; of the issuance of the divine decree (κήρυγμα): Conf. Ling., 197; of the judicial sentence : Decal., 40.

In the NT, too, we have Μωυσῆς ἔγραψεν [18] in the sense of legislative prescription : Mk. 10:5 : τὴν ἐντολὴν ταύτην; 12:19, par. Lk. 20:28 : Μωυσῆς ἔγραψεν ἡμῖν ὅτι, followed by Dt. 25:5 f. The meaning of R. 10:5 [19] is similar. In Jn. 1:45; 5:46, [20] however, the γράφειν of Moses signifies his prophesying of the Messiah. Yet formally 1 Jn. 2:7 f.: οὐκ ἐντολὴν καινὴν γράφω (cf. 2 Jn. 5), again suggests legislative activity, except that the nomistic character of the new law is changed by the fact that the commandment is true in Him (Jesus). In R. 2:15 : ἔργον τοῦ νόμου γραπτὸν ἐν ταῖς καρδίαις, the reference is to the counterpart of the Mosaic codification. Heathen doers of the Law make it clear that the required work of the Law is codified in their hearts.

B. The Special Use of γέγραπται and γεγραμμένον.

γραπτός, -όν is always "that which is fixed in writing." P. Amh., 78, 17 (2nd cent. A.D.): ἀσφάλεια γραπτή, "written bond of indebtedness." It is often used as the opp. of non-written or verbal, cf. APF, IV, 259 f. So also Ep. Ar., 56 : διὰ γραπτῶν, previously ἄγραφα; γραπτὸς λόγος, "written utterance" : P. Petr., III, 219, 38. V. further Moult.-Mill., s.v. In the LXX (always for מִכְתָּב), 2 Ch. 36:22; 2 Esr. 1:1: ἐν γραπτῷ, and 1 Esr. 2:2 : διὰ γραπτῶν, for the written decree of Cyrus, and 2 Macc.

---

[16] Zn. Apk., I, 276 ff.; Had. Apk., 50.
[17] On Rev. 3:12, cf. b.Joma, 8a; Ex. r., 15 on 12:2.
[18] Cf. Jos. Ant., 3, 74; 4, 326; 17, 159; Philo Op. Mund., 163. On the other hand, cf. Jos. Ant., 1, 95 : Μωυσῆς ἀνέγραψεν, "has reported." Tanch. ויקרא 18 and 10 : Jeroboam says : משֶׁה כָּתַב בַּתּוֹרָה. Similarly Philo Sobr., 68 : ὁ προφητικὸς λόγος ἔγραψεν (Gn. 49:22).
[19] BG lat syr Chrys Ambrst Pelag : γράφει τὴν δικαιοσύνην, acc. of object.
[20] 1:45 : ὃν ἔγραψεν (acc. of person); 5:46 : περὶ ἐμοῦ.

11:15 : διὰ γραπτῶν περὶ τῶν Ἰουδαίων, memorandum on the Jews laid before Lysias by Maccabeus.

A stock expression for written laws is τὰ γεγραμμένα (→ 748). There is a striking similarity between the use of γράφειν as a legal expression in the Greek sphere and its legal use in the Israelite and Jewish sphere. The innumerable references to τὰ γεγραμμένα in the OT correspond to the view that the written Law is authoritatively binding. The same is to be said of γέγραπται. This denotes not merely the appeal in Greek law to the impregnable authority of the law but also the validity of what is written for Israel both in the absolute religious sense and also in the juridical. [21] What is quoted as γέγραπται is normative because it is guaranteed by the binding power of Yahweh the King and Lawgiver. This is basically true of the Law of Moses, but is then applied also to the prophets and *ketubim*. If the assertion that the νόμος has legal validity in Israel does not express the whole meaning of the embracing authority of the divine work of revelation, the usage can hardly be understood apart from the legal element. In the Rabbis the legal view of the written word is developed in isolation. The NT conception of γέγραπται and γεγραμμένον, however, is rather different (→ γραφή, 757).

1. The Specific Use of γέγραπται.

a. On the simple use as in Mt. 4:4-10; Lk. 4:8; 19:46; 1 C. 9:9 (ἐν τῷ Μωυσέως νόμῳ); 14:21 (ἐν τῷ νόμῳ), [22] cf. 2 Esr. 5:7; Gk. addition to Job 42:17a; ψ 39:7; 1 Macc. 16:24; Test. Zeb. 3:4 : ἐν γραφῇ νόμου Μωυσέως γέγραπται. Josephus : Ap., 1, 154 : γέγραπται ἐν αὐταῖς (our books). Elsewhere Joseph. prefers ἀναγέγραπται ἐν ταῖς ἱεραῖς βίβλοις, Ant., 3, 81; 9, 28 (Philo Vit. Mos., II, 188) or ἐν τοῖς Μωυσέως νόμοις, Ant., 13, 297. [23] The same formula is used of bronze tablets with Jewish rights, Bell., 7, 110; of Phoenician annals, Ap., 2, 18; of the memoirs of Vespasian, Vit., 342; of the historical books of Tyre, Ant., 9, 283. In Philo : Rer. Div. Her., 102; Congr., 126; Decal., 47. In the Rabbis the simple γέγραπται is כָּתוּב Tanch. לְ לֶךְ 9 and 67; Gen. r., 11, 1 on 2:3. [24] In the inscr. and pap. the reference is very often to a normative record, as in Inschr. Priene, 105, 83 (9 B.C.): ὡς καὶ ἐν τῷ Κορνηλίωι νόμωι γέγραπται, P. Hal., 1, 96 (3rd cent. B.C.).

b. The confirmatory formula καθὼς γέγραπται is found in Mk. 1:2 (ἐν τῷ Ἠσαΐᾳ τῷ προφήτῃ, as in 2 Ch. 32:32); Lk. 2:23 (ἐν νόμῳ κυρίου); Ac. 7:42 (ἐν βίβλῳ τῶν προφητῶν); 15:15. It occurs 14 times in Paul, 10 times in R. and 4 in C. [25] In the LXX, cf. 4 Βασ. 14:6 (ἐν βιβλίῳ νόμων Μωυσῆ A al); 2 Ch. 23:18; Test. L. 5:4 (ἐν πλαξὶ τῶν πατέρων); Tanch. לֶךְ לְ, 16, 73 כְּמוֹ שֶׁכָּתוּב בַּתּוֹרָה; Pes. Kah., 5; 50a; Tanch. תֹּזְרִיעַ 12, 41 and in countless other passages : כְּדִכְתִיב; Ditt. Syll.³, 736, 44 (92 B.C.); CPR, 154, 11; 1 Cl., 48, 2.

c. On ὅτι γέγραπται, Gl. 3:13 : καθότι, P. Par., 13, 13 (157 B.C.); P. Leid. O., 19 (89 B.C.). [26]

---

[21] In the debate between Cr.-Kö., 264 and Deissmann B., 108 ff. both are really right. Cf. Schl. Mt., 35.
[22] On πάλιν γέγραπται, Mt. 4:7, cf. → γραφή, 758, n. 43. For μὴ ὑπὲρ ἃ γέγραπται in 1 C. 4:6, cf. → 760, and n. 55. For the striking expression in Jn. 20:31, cf. → 745.
[23] Cf. H. Drüner, *Untersuchungen über Josefus* (Diss. Marburg, 1896), 54, n. 1; 85. For ἀναγέγραπται in Arrian, cf. H. Wilcken, *Philol.*, 53 (1894), 117 f.
[24] On Jn. 8:17: ἐν τῷ νόμῳ τῷ ὑμετέρῳ γέγραπται (the outsider quotes the Law), cf. the Rabbin. par. in Schl. J., 206 f.
[25] For lists of formulae in Pl., cf. Michel, 72; for examples from Barn., *ibid.*, 209, n. 1; from 1 Cl., *ibid.*, 201, n. 2.
[26] *V.* further Deissmann B., 110.

d. ὡς γέγραπται, Mk. 7:6; Lk. 3:4 (ἐν βίβλῳ λόγων Ἡσαΐου τοῦ προφήτου); Ac. 13:33 (ἐν τῷ ψαλμῷ τῷ δευτέρῳ); ὥσπερ, 1 C. 10:7; cf. 2 Ch. 35:12 (ἐν βιβλίῳ A, *vl.*); 2 Εσδρ. 20:36 AR (ἐν τῷ νόμῳ); Ditt. Syll.³, 45, 44.

e. καθάπερ γέγραπται, R. 3:4; 9:13 etc. Cf. Tegea building inscr. (c. 3rd cent. B.C.) in P. Cauer, *Delectus Inscriptionum Graec.* (1883), 457, 50 f.; Inschr. Perg., 251, 35 (2nd cent. B.C.); καθά, Jos. 9:4 (8:31) (ἐν τῷ νόμῳ Μωυσῆ); BGU, 252, 9 (98 A.D.); Inscr. Mar. Aeg., 761, 41 (Rhodos, 3rd cent. B.C.): καθὰ καὶ ἐν τοῖς νόμοις γέγραπται; P. Par., 7, 6 (2nd or 1st cent. B.C.).

f. οὕτως γέγραπται, Mt. 2:5 (διὰ τοῦ προφήτου); Tanch. בחקתי 4; 110: שֶׁכָּךְ כָּתִיב; Cant. r., 8, 14 (on Mi. 5:2): כָּךְ כְּתִיב; 1 Cl., 17, 3. ²⁷

g. On γέγραπται ὅτι, Mt. 4:6; Mk. 11:17, cf. Phil. Post. C., 24.

h. γέγραπται γάρ, Mt. 4:10; Ac. 1:20 (ἐν βίβλῳ ψαλμῶν); R. 12:19; 14:11; 1 C. 1:19; Gl. 3:10 etc., cf. Tanch. לְךָ לְךָ 8, 66 and often elsewhere דִּכְתִיב; Phil. Post. C., 102; 176; 179; 1 Cl., 36, 3; 39, 3 etc.

i. On περὶ οὗ γέγραπται, Mt. 11:10; Mk. 14:21 and Mt. 26:24: περὶ αὐτοῦ, cf. מִי שֶׁכָּתוּב בּוֹ in T. Sota, 6, 6 and 7 of Abraham and Moses. ²⁸ Cf. also Pes. Kah., 28, 185b: זֶה מָשִׁיחַ דִּכְתִיב בֵּיהּ; Tanch. וישב, 13, 184.

2. The Specific Use of γεγραμμένον.

In illustration of the class. use of τὰ γεγραμμένα for "written laws" we may refer to Demosth., 58, 24; Plat. Leg., VI, 754e : παρὰ τὰ γεγραμμένα; Aristot. Rhet., I, 10, p. 1368b, 7 ff.: γεγραμμένον, opp. ἄγραφα. There is a similar use of γραφέντα for a medical prescription in Plat. Polit., 295d.

Of the countless references to the OT as τὰ γεγραμμένα in the LXX we may mention ἐν (τῷ) νόμῳ or ἐν τῇ βίβλῳ Μωυσέως, 3 Βασ. 2:3 (A al); Da. Θ 9:11; Tob. 7:12 א; ἐν νόμῳ κυρίου, 2 Ch. 35:26; τοὺς λόγους τοῦ νόμου τοὺς γεγραμμένους ἐπὶ τοῦ βιβλίου, 2 Ch. 35:19; ἐπὶ τῷ βιβλίῳ, 4 Βασ. 23:24. Of the many references to the words of the written Law, cf. Dt. 28:58; 30:10; Jos. 9:7 (8:34); 1 K. 2:3; cf. 2 Ch. 31:3; 2 Εσδρ. 18:14. There are also innumerable references to specific books, e.g., 1 K. 14:10 A; 2 Ch. 9:29; 26:22 etc.

The findings are similar in the case of Aristeas, Josephus and the Rabbis. Ep. Ar., 311: τὰ γεγραμμένα; Jos. Ant., 11, 6; Ant., 13, 297, of the divergent attitude of the Sadducees to τὰ γεγραμμένα and παράδοσις τῶν πατέρων. Elsewhere Joseph. prefers the ἀναγεγραμμένα ἐν ταῖς ἱεραῖς βίβλοις (Ant., 1, 26) or ἐν τοῖς λογίοις (Bell., 6, 311); cf. Ant., 9, 208. In the Rabbis there is a regular occurrence of the formula מַה שֶׁכָּתוּב, e.g., בַּנְּבִיאִים in M. Ex., 17, 14.

ˈ In the NT γεγραμμμένον is used less frequently of Scripture. It is most common in Lk. and Jn., rarer in Pl. Cf. Lk. 4:17; 20:17; 22:37. It should be emphasised that with respect to Jesus Lk. gives prominence to πάντα τὰ γεγραμμένα in connection with the thought of fulfilment (τελέω, πληρόω, → γραφή, 758), e.g., in 18:31; 21:22; 24:44; Ac. 13:29; 24:14 (cf. Lk. 24:27, ἐν πάσαις ταῖς γραφαῖς), and most completely in Lk. 24:44 (the Law of Moses, the Prophets and the Psalms). It is he who most strikingly and impressively underlines the fact that all the Scriptures bear witness to Christ.

---

²⁷ In the LXX ἰδοὺ γέγραπται is often used for non-biblical sources, e.g., in 2 Βασ. 1:18; 3 Βασ. 8:53a; 11:41; 2 Ch. 33:19; Est. 10:2; though also for biblical, e.g., in 3 Βασ. 22:39; 4 Βασ. 8:23 etc.
²⁸ Acc. to Schl. Mt., 363.

On this πάντα, cf. Jos. 9:7 (8:34) → *infra* ; 23:6; Tanch. צו, 5, 16; ויקרא, 15, 9 : כָּל־מָה שֶׁכָּתוּב בַּתּוֹרָה.

Only at 8:17 does Jn. speak of the νόμος as γέγραπται. He prefers γεγραμμένον. Thus he has the simple ἔστιν γεγραμμένον (ἐν τοῖς προφήταις) at 6:45, or as a question at 10:34 (ἐν τῷ νόμῳ ὑμῶν), or with the succeeding ὅτι at 15:25. Or he has καθώς ἐστιν γεγραμμένον at 6:31; 12:14 or ὅτι γεγραμμένον ἐστίν at 2:17.

Paul uses γεγραμμένος only in 1 C. 15:54 : ὁ λόγος ὁ γεγραμμένος (Is. 25:8) and 2 C. 4:13 : κατὰ τὸ γεγραμμένον.

On the latter, cf. Jos. 9:7 (8:34): κατὰ πάντα τὰ γεγραμμένα ἐν τῷ νόμῳ Μωυσῆ; 4 Βασ. 22:13; 1 Ch. 16:40 (ἐν νόμῳ κυρίου); 2 Ch. 34:21 (ἐν τῷ βιβλίῳ τούτῳ, of the book of the covenant); 1 Εσρ. 1:10 (ἐν βιβλίῳ Μωυσῆ); 2 Εσρ. 3:2 (ἐν νόμῳ Μωυσῆ); Bar. 2:2. In the sing., 2 Εσδρ. 18:15; 2 Εσρ. 3:4. For the plur., cf. Inschr. Priene, 12, 12 (300 B.C.); Ditt. Syll.³, 955, 22; 1016, 6. For the sing., cf. Gn. r., 79 on 33:18 לְפִי שֶׁכָּתוּב; Taan., 3, 3 : כַּכָּתוּב; Ditt. Syll.², 438, 13; 84; Orig. Comm. in Joh., 1, 17, p. 494.

Sometimes γεγραμμένα or γέγραπται is used in relation to Jesus. This is expressed by a dat. or ἐπί. Cf. Lk. 18:31: τελεσθήσεται πάντα τὰ γεγραμμένα διὰ τῶν προφητῶν τῷ υἱῷ τοῦ ἀνθρώπου, where the dat. belongs to γεγραμμένα in the sense of "concerning" or "with reference to"; [29] cf. 1 Εσρ. 4:47; 3 Macc. 6:41. In Jn. 12:16 the same thought is expressed in the phrase ἦν ἐπ᾽ αὐτῷ γεγραμμένα. Another example is Mk. 9:12 f., where the γέγραπται is linked with ἐπί with the acc.

τὰ γεγραμμένα is also found in Church usage, as in Orig. Princ., IV, 2, 6 (p. 316). γέγραπται refers to the sayings of Jesus in Barn., 4, 14; 14, 6, and the sayings of the apostles in Orig. Princ., III, 1, 19 (p. 232, 6), a quotation from 1 C. 3:6 f.; cf. Jn. I, 3, 18 : τὰ ὑπὸ τῶν ἀποστόλων γεγραμμένα. This is in keeping with the consolidation of the NT Canon.

γραφή.

A. γραφή in Secular Greek.

1. In the first instance γραφή means inscribed "writing," or "written characters," or in a rather wider sense the "art of writing." Soph. Trach., 683 : χαλκῆς ἐκ δέλτου γραφήν. Hence, as in the case of γράφειν, it may be used for "what is inscribed," i.e., "inscription" ; this is still very close to the original meaning: Thuc., I, 134; IG, XII, 5, No. 679 (Syros); Epigr. Graec., 347 (Chios). So, too, in the LXX : 3 Macc. 2:27 of the inscription on the pillar at Alexandria ; Sir. 45:11 (בִּכְתָב) of the engraven inscription on the breastplate of the high-priest. Jos. Ant., 15, 417 of the inscription in the temple warning aliens ; Philo Poster. C., 113. Of the divine characters on the tables of the Law : Ex. 32:16 : ἡ γραφὴ γραφὴ θεοῦ κεκολαμμένη ἐν ταῖς πλαξί; Dt. 10:4 (in both cases מִכְתָּב); cf. Jos. Ant., 3, 101; Philo Vit. Mos., I, 287. The mysterious inscription on the wall at Babylon, Da. LXX Θ 5:6-26 (כְּתָב).

In the LXX γραφή is always the rendering of כָּתוּב, כְּתָב, מִכְתָּב and once מִדְרָשׁ (2 Ch. 24:27). On the other hand, סֵפֶר is never γραφή but βιβλίον, βίβλος (→ βίβλος, 614).

---

[29] With Kl. Lk., *ad loc.* and Pr.-Bauer, Zurich Bible. For a different view, cf. Zn., Cr.-Kö., who relate the dat. to τελεσθήσεται.

The reference in Plat. Phaedr., 274b is to the "art of writing."

2. "Copy" or "drawing": Hdt., II, 73; IV, 36; Plat. Symp., 193a: κατὰ γραφήν. Philo uses this in a platonising sense of the original plan of the tabernacle which Moses saw on the mount: Vit. Mos., II, 74; of the exemplar of the works of nature: Spec. Leg., IV, 55; of the virtuous life as γραφὴ ἀρχέτυπος: Virt., 51; Jos., 87; Omn. Prob. Lib., 62 and 94. The term is used for "picture" or "painting" in Hdt., III, 24; Philo Vit. Mos., I, 158; Spec. Leg., I, 33; Leg. Gaj., 151 (γραφαί with ἀνδριάντες); Abr., 11 (with μνήμη); Cher., 104 (κονιάματα καὶ γραφαὶ καὶ πινάκια); Eus. Vit. Const., III, 3. It is used for "art" in Jos. Ant., 19, 7; Bell., 7, 159.

3. It can also mean "written statement in personal or official dealings." In the widest sense it means "what is written" or "writing." Hence a written report is a report διὰ τῆς γραφῆς: Polyb., I, 56, 11; cf. 1 Ch. 28:19: πάντα ἐν γραφῇ χειρὸς κυρίου ἔδωκε Δαυὶδ Σαλωμών (כְּתָב); Sir. 39:32: ἐν γραφῇ ἀφῆκα (בִּכְתָב), "I put it down in writing"; 42:7 of the writing down of what is received and spent. a. "Letter": 2 Ch. 2:10, ἐν γραφῇ "by letter" (בִּכְתָב); 2 Ch. 21:12 (מִכְתָב); [5] Jos. Ant., 12, 226. Also in modern Gk. b. "Piece of writing": P. Hibeh, 78, 18 (3rd cent. B.C.); [1] Philo Leg. Gaj., 276. c. "Record," "document": 1 Macc. 14:48: τὸ ἀντίγραφον τῆς γραφῆς; "copy" 8:22 A; 14:27; "genealogy": 2 Esr. 2:62; 1 Esr. 5:39 (γενικὴ γραφή); 2 Εσδρ. 17:64 (γραφὴ τῆς συνοδίας). "Contract": CPR, 224, 6; P. Amh., 43, 13 (2nd cent. B.C.). Of the state archives as a repository for documents: IG, XI, 203 B, 100 (Delos, 3rd cent. B.C.). d. "List," "inventory," "survey" · Polyb., III, 33, 18; Ez. 13:9: γραφὴ οἴκου Ἰσραήλ (כְּתָב). [2] e. "Decree," "edict": Da. Θ 6:8 (9) of royal edicts (כְּתָב). Eus. Eccl. Hist., VIII, 4, 5; IX, 7, 2 of imperial edicts. [2] f. "Accusation" in legal Attic, and hence more generally. [3] Cf. Philo Poster. C., 38; Sacr. AC, 71: γραφὴ ἀσεβείας.

4. "Published work" in the literary sense. In Jos. Ap., 1, 236 γραφὴν καταλείπειν does not have this literary sense, but in Sir. 44:5 διηγούμενοι ἔπη ἐν γραφῇ bears this meaning. In Jos. Ant., 20, 261; Ap., 1, 20; 58 ἀναγραφή is used in a literary connection. The word is used of non-biblical books in 1 Macc. 12:21; of the historical work of Nikolaos in Jos. Ant., 16, 185; of philosophical writings in Philo Abr., 23; Migr. Abr., 34; cf. γραφῆς καὶ μνήμης ἄξιος in Abr., 11. It is also used of the present work of the author in Jos. Ant., 3, 74; Ap., 2, 147; Philo Ebr., 11 etc., or with reference to previous volumes in Jos. Ant., 19, 298; Philo Som., I, 1. It is used for "authorship" in Jos. Vit., 361, esp. Josephus' own authorship in Bell., 5, 20: ὁ νόμος τῆς γραφῆς; Eus. Hist. Eccl., I, 1, 5.

5. "Written law or statute." Plat. Leg., XI, 934c of written law; κατὰ γραφάς with ref. to laws: BGU, 136, 10 (135 A.D.). The sing. is sometimes used in this sense in the LXX, perhaps with something of the suggestion of "Holy Scripture." At 2 Esr. 7:22: καὶ ἅλας οὗ οὐκ ἔστι γραφή (כְּתָב) the meaning is simply "prescription," but sometimes there seems to be a certain influence of the use in the sing. for "Holy Scripture": 1 Ch. 15:15: ὡς ἐνετείλατο Μωυσῆς ἐν λόγῳ θεοῦ κατὰ τὴν γραφήν (כִּדְבַר יְהֹוָה); 2 Ch. 30:5: ὅτι πλῆθος οὐκ ἐποίησε κατὰ τὴν γραφήν (כַּכָּתוּב), 30:18: ἀλλ' ἔφαγον τὸ φάσεκ παρὰ τὴν γραφήν (בְּלֹא כַכָּתוּב) "in a contrary manner to that prescribed." In all such cases, however, we ought to render γραφή as "legal regulation," since the Mas. never gives any reason for thinking of it as a title for Scripture. Cf. 2 Ch. 35:4: κατὰ τὴν γραφὴν Δαυὶδ βασιλέως Ἰσραήλ (וּבִכְתָב); also 1 Esr. 1:4. In Philo Vit. Mos., II, 203 γραφή can mean "account of the divine order." Cf. the medical use in Galen, XII, p. 293; XIII, p. 638; XV, p. 918, Kühn, where γραφὴ φαρμάκου means "medical prescription."

γ ρ α φ ή. For bibl. → γράφω, 742 f. The definitions of Hesych. and Suid. emphasise the official and judicial usage (→ supra).

[1] V. further Preisigke Wört., s.v.
[2] On d. and e., ibid.
[3] On f. v. Liddell-Scott, s.v.

B. γραφή as Holy Scripture.

1. γραφαί of the (Holy) Scriptures, or the Collection of Individual Books.

It is to be noted that αἱ ἱεραὶ γραφαί is a specifically Rabbinic mode of expression which is also found in Philo and Hellenistic Judaism but not in the OT. In the Rabbis the formula is כִּתְבֵי הַקֹּדֶשׁ. [4] The usage in Josephus falls short of this. It is infrequent, e.g., Ap., 2, 45: Ptolemy Philadelphus demands ταῖς τῶν ἱερῶν γραφῶν βίβλοις ἐντυχεῖν. Here the concept of book is contained in βίβλοι, but the βίβλοι contain sacred utterances (→ 752). Philo, on the other hand, often speaks of αἱ ἱεραὶ γραφαί and he obviously means the OT, esp. the Pentateuch: Abr., 61; Congr., 34; 90; Decal., 8; 37; Fug., 4; Op. Mund., 77; Rer. Div. Her., 106; 159; 286; Spec. Leg., I, 214; II, 104; 134. Very occasionally the superlative is used: Abr., 4: ἐν ταῖς ἱερωτάταις γραφαῖς. There is also a use of the sing. in Vit. Mos., II, 84 with reference to the curtains frequently mentioned in Ex. 26: ἃς διὰ τῆς ἱερᾶς γραφῆς ὠνόμασεν. The sing. in Test. N. 5:7: ἰδοὺ γραφὴ ἁγία ὤφθη ἡμῖν, does not refer to the OT but to a visionary apocalyptic oracle (→ 752). [5]

It is worth noting that in the NT holiness is very rarely applied to Scripture. It is not found at all in the Gospels, though used there of the Father, the Spirit, and the angels (→ ἅγιος). [6] There is thus no formula to denote the perfection of Scripture in the sense of the concept of divine holiness. Paul does once say in R. 1:2: ὃ προεπηγγείλατο διὰ τῶν προφητῶν αὐτοῦ ἐν γραφαῖς ἁγίαις [7] (not ἱεραῖς) when speaking of the Gospel. We may also think of R. 7:12 with its reference to the νόμος ἅγιος. ἱερός is used in relation to γράμματα only at 2 Tm. 3:15 (→ γράμμα, 765).

We may thus conclude that the phrase αἱ ἱεραὶ γραφαί perpetuates in the Church a Jewish and Hellenistic rather than a specifically early Christian usage.

αἱ ἱεραὶ γραφαί occurs in 1 Cl., 45, 2; 53, 1. It is used of the books burnt in persecution in Eus. Hist. Eccl., VIII, 2, 1. Cf. Philostorg. Hist. Ecc., VIII, 11 (p. 112, 13); Gelas. Hist. Eccl., II, 21, 14; sing.: ἡ ἱερὰ ἡμῶν γραφή, III, 9; without ἡμῶν: Thdrt. Ep., 14, MPG, 83, 1188c. αἱ θεῖαι γραφαί is often found in the early Church: Gelas., II, 16, 14, cf. II, 20, 5; Method. Symp., IV, 3, 99; Philostorg. Vit. et Mart. Luc., 2 (185, 18); sing. of the OT: Chrysostom Hom. in Gn. X, 3 (MPG, 53, 84); αἱ θεῖαι γραφαί in relation to a NT passage: Eus. Marcell. Fr., p. 186, No. 6; p. 192, No. 43; p. 212, No. 121 etc. ἡ θεία γραφή of the NT: p. 192, No. 42. Elsewhere αἱ κυριακαὶ γραφαί is used: Cl. Al. Strom., VII, 1, 4; 16, 94, 1; Method. Resurrect., I, 62, 4 (of the OT, Levit.).

---

[4] Tanch. addition to קרח, 1, 95; T. Shab., 13, 1; B 1, 6. Cf. Levy Chald. Wört., I, 395; Levy Wört., II, 435 f.; G. Aicher, D. AT i. d. Mischna (1906), 22; Str.-B., III, 14.

[5] Hänel, 18, has advanced the thesis that in Jewish usage כתביא without attribute does not have the pregnant sense of "Scripture κατ' ἐχοχήν", but that for this purpose הקדש is always added like ἱεραί to αἱ γραφαί in Hellenistic Judaism. In face of the Rabbinic הַכְּתוּבִים, הַכָּתוּב, however, this thesis can hardly be sustained (→ infra; 749).

[6] It is noteworthy that in Mt. 7:6 τὸ ἅγιον is used of the message which the disciples have to deliver.

[7] Cf. Hipp. Ref., I, praef. 8, also without art. That the lack of article is of no significance may be seen from R. 16:26, or in the sing. 1 Pt. 2:6; 2 Pt. 1:20.

Of the OT as a whole the simple plur. αἱ γραφαί is equally well established, though this may refer to the statements therein contained. In the Rabbis we find הַכְּתוּבִים (S. Dt. 1 on 1:1) or בַּכְּתוּבִים (M. Ex., 19, 19). Philo occasionally has αἱ γραφαί (Abr., 236), or ἀμφότεραι αἱ γραφαί with reference to the Mas. and the Gk. translation (Vit. Mos., II, 40). In the NT, too, αἱ γραφαί is constantly used of the OT Canon. It cannot be shown that the reference is only to individual passages. To be sure, in Mt. 21:42 the phrase is followed by οὐδέποτε ἀνέγνωτε ἐν ταῖς γραφαῖς (Ps. 118:22 f.) and in Mt. 22:29 those who scoff at the resurrection are answered by the phrase πλανᾶσθε μὴ εἰδότες τὰς γραφάς, and then by a quotation from Ex. 3:6.[8] On the other hand, in Mt. 26:54 : πῶς οὖν πληρωθῶσιν αἱ γραφαὶ ὅτι οὕτως δεῖ γενέσθαι, there is no mention of any particular writer (par. Mk. 14:49), and the same is true of Mt. 26:56, except that here one portion of the Scriptures is specifically mentioned (αἱ γραφαὶ τῶν προφητῶν). A particularly plain argument for the view that αἱ γραφαί can mean Scriptures and not just passages of Scripture is the elucidation of ἐν πάσαις ταῖς γραφαῖς in Lk. 24:27 by ἀρξάμενος ἀπὸ Μωυσέως καὶ ἀπὸ πάντων τῶν προφητῶν. This expository instruction of the risen Lord is described in Lk. 24:32, 45 as a διανοίγειν[9] of the γραφαί. Similarly, it is highly doubtful whether the reference in Jn. 5:39 : ἐρευνᾶτε τὰς γραφάς, is to passages or oracles[10] and not to the Scriptures. In Ac. 17, 2, 11; 18:24; 28, the reference is to something comprehensive, either in terms of searching the OT or seeking proofs for Christ from the Scriptures. The four passages in which Paul uses αἱ γραφαί (without ἁγίαι), i.e., 1 C. 15:3 f.,[11] the repeated κατὰ τὰς γραφάς; R. 15:4 : διὰ τῆς παρακλήσεως τῶν γραφῶν; R. 16:26 : διὰ γραφῶν προφητικῶν, all point in the same direction; they link the saving act of Christ, His suffering, death and resurrection, and the Gospel in general, with all the OT Scriptures and their prophetic witness.

2. γραφή of Individual Passages of Scripture.

It is incontestable that in the Syn., Ac. and Jn. ἡ γραφή is also used for individual biblical statements, though we cannot say that it is used only in this sense.[12]

Cf. 4 Macc. 18:14, where obviously the ὑπεμίμνησκε τὴν Ἠσαίου γραφὴν τὴν λέγουσαν refers to the verse from Is. which is then cited (Is. 43:2 LXX). In the Rabbis :

---

[8] Par. Mk. 12:24. Schl. Mt., 653 quotes in this connection the related expression in S. Nu., 112.

[9] On this expression, cf. the פָּתַח in jChag., 77d (Schl. Lk., 459).

[10] Schl. on Jn. 5:39; Hänel, 15.

[11] Bultmann, III, 186 ff. has advanced the interesting hypothesis that Paul's κατὰ τὰς γραφάς refers to early stories of the passion and resurrection which underlie the present Gospels. Jülicher has suggested that R. 16:26 refers to current prophetic works. But in face of the broad tradition in the use of the formula these theories are quite untenable. An erstwhile Rabbi can only have had the OT in view in using such a phrase as κατὰ τὰς γραφάς. There are good reasons for the fact that this traditional formula occurs only in 1 C. 15:3 f., namely, that he is here dealing with a formulation handed down by the early community. On the other hand, there was no reason why he should not vary the current formula ; there are countless examples of such variation from the time of the OT itself right on into the Gk. Church.

[12] Hänel, 14, claims that this is so in the case of the Gospels, but it seems to me to be highly debatable in that of Jn.

כָּתוּב אַחֵר אוֹמֵר, M. Ex., 14, 3; Tanch. וייצא, 20, 158. Philo Rer. Div. Her., 266 : τὸ δὲ ἀκόλουθον τῇ γραφῇ (the particular verse Gn. 15:13); Abr., 131: ἀλλὰ καὶ τῆς ῥητῆς γραφῆς τάδε περιεχούσης.

The following individual references may be noted in the NT : Mk. 12:10 : τὴν γραφὴν ταύτην; Lk. 4:21: ἡ γραφὴ αὕτη; Jn. 19:37: καὶ πάλιν ἑτέρα γραφή; Ac. 1:16 : ἔδει πληρωθῆναι τὴν γραφὴν ἣν προεῖπεν τὸ πνεῦμα τὸ ἅγιον διὰ στόματος Δαυίδ (there follows ψ 69:25; 109:8); Ac. 8:32, where ἡ περιοχὴ τῆς γραφῆς which the treasurer reads is Is. 53:7 f.; and Ac. 8:35 : ἀρξάμενος ἀπὸ τῆς γραφῆς ταύτης. On the basis of these findings it is also likely, though not certain, that γραφή denotes an individual saying whenever followed by a quotation, e.g., in Mk. 15:28 ℵ lat syp; Jn. 7:38; [13] 13:18; 19:24, 36. Yet even in such cases there may well be a reference to Scripture as a whole.

How does it stand with Paul ? Our best starting-point is Gl. 3:8, 22 (→ 754), where the personification of γραφή makes it quite inconceivable that Paul should simply have in view an individual text. On the other hand, the reference may well be to a single saying in the 5 instances (or 6 if we include 1 Tm. 5:18) of λέγει ἡ γραφή [14] (Gl. 4:30; R. 4:3; 9:17; 10:11; 11:2), for here we have a quotation following. The situation is complicated, however, by R. 11:2 : ἐν Ἠλίᾳ τί λέγει ἡ γραφή. For it is better to take this to signify the utterance of all Scripture in Elias, or in the story of Elias, rather than this particular passage in Elias. Again, we can see from R. 11:4 : τί λέγει ὁ χρηματισμός, [15] that Paul can use other expressions to emphasise a particular passage. Hence it is more likely that he is using ἡ γραφή for the OT as a whole. There is even the possibility that when he uses the phrase λέγει ἡ γραφή he has no fixed conception in his own mind, as often happens when there is a variation in usage. We can certainly trace this twofold use of γραφή right on into the early Church (→ infra ; 755).

In Jm. 2:23 the situation is much the same as in Paul's general use of λέγει ἡ γραφή. Followed by Lv. 19:18, κατὰ τὴν γραφήν (2:8) obviously refers to a single passage. Thus the true parallel is not 2 Esr. 6:18 : κατὰ τὴν γραφὴν βίβλου Μωυσῆ, but the כַּכָּתוּב of the Rabbis. In Jm. 4:5, however, the δοκεῖτε ὅτι κενῶς ἡ γραφὴ λέγει must surely be with reference to Scripture as a whole.

The post-apost. fathers have instances of both forms of usage. Thus there is reference to all Scripture in, e.g., 1 Cl., 42, 5 : ποῦ λέγει ἡ γραφή; 2 Cl., 6, 8 : λέγει ἡ γραφὴ ἐν τῷ Ἰεζεκιήλ; Barn., 6, 12 (where ἡ γραφή is equated with God). There is dubiety in 1 Cl., 34, 6; 35, 7; 2 Cl., 14, 1 f.; Barn., 4, 7; 5, 4; 13, 2. On the other hand, individual passages are plainly in mind in 1 Cl., 23, 3: ἡ γραφὴ αὕτη (apocryphal) and 2 Cl., 2, 4 : ἑτέρα δὲ γραφή (a NT verse). This twofold usage persists in later writers. Cf. Hipp. Ref., V, 7, 24 : τὸ εἰρημένον ἐν τῇ γραφῇ, VI, 10, 2 : εἴρηκεν ἡ γραφή, with Orig. Comm. in John., X, 14, 81 : ἐν τῇ προκειμένῃ τοῦ εὐαγγελίου γραφῇ, though he, too, can elsewhere use both γραφή and γραφαί of Scripture as a whole. Method. Symp., VIII, 8, 191 can still say : ἔν τινι γραφῇ.

---

[13] We cannot be sure whether the reference here is to a combination of OT passages (Schl. J., 200 f. : Moses' dispensing of water along with Is. 44:3; Ez. 47:1; Zech. 14:8, cf. Akiba, S. Dt., 48 on 11:22), or to a particular verse in the Canon (Hänel, 13 : Tg. Cant., 4, 15), or perhaps even an apocryphal saying. Cf. Bau. J., ad loc.

[14] On "saying of Scripture" in Rabb. usage, cf. Schl. J. on 7:38, 42 (p. 200, 202). The formulae שֶׁאָמַר הַכָּתוּב or הַכָּתוּב אוֹמֵר are fixed.

[15] On χρηματισμός in Jos. : Schl. Theol. d. Judt., 67; λόγιον and χρησμός, 66.

3. γραφή is never used in the NT of a single book of the Bible, though this usage is elsewhere common in Hellenistic Judaism. The only possible example is 2 Tm. 3:16: πᾶσα γραφὴ θεόπνευστος, but according to current analogies this obviously means every passage of Scripture. [16]

Instances of its use for individual books are 2 Esr. 6:18: κατὰ τὴν γραφὴν βίβλου Μωυσῆ (כְּתָב); 2 Ch. 24:27: ἡ γραφὴ τῶν βασιλέων (מִדְרַשׁ); Test. Zeb. 3:4: ἐν γραφῇ νόμου Μωυσέως. Of the Torah at least: Jos. Ant., III, 38; Philo Vit. Mos., II, 51; of the Decalogue: Spec. Leg., I, 1; of the first table of the Law: Decal., 51: ἡ μία γραφή. In the Gk. fathers, Orig. Cels., I, 12: ἡ τοῦ νόμου καὶ τῆς Ἰουδαϊκῆς ἱστορίας γραφή; VI, 49: ἡ περὶ ἀνθρώπων γενέσεως γραφή (Genesis); Eus. Marcell. Fr. No. 23: ἡ τῆς Ἐξόδου γραφή; of the Gospel: Orig. Cels., II, 27: ἡ πρώτη γραφή; cf. I, 59: ἡ εὐαγγελικὴ γραφή.

4. γραφή emphasising the Unity of Scripture: the Totality of OT Scripture.

In Test. Zeb., IX, 5 it is said of the OT: ἐν γραφῇ τῶν πατέρων μου. Again, in Ep. Ar., 155; 168: διὰ τῆς γραφῆς, the term is synon. with νόμος and denotes Scripture as a whole. [17] This usage might well have developed out of the Rabbin. הַכָּתוּב. We certainly do not have it in Joseph. or Philo, where the plur. alone is used for all Scripture. [18]

At this point we must resume our discussion of γραφή in Paul. It has been briefly mentioned (→ 753) that in Gl. 3:8: προϊδοῦσα ἡ γραφή, and Gl. 3:22: συνέκλεισεν ἡ γραφὴ τὰ πάντα ὑπὸ ἁμαρτίαν, Paul takes the unity of Scripture so seriously that he can personify it. But there is no sense in this unless he has in view its identification with God's own speaking (cf. R. 11:32, where συνέκλεισεν is used of God Himself). The only point of Paul's hypostatising of Scripture is that he regards it in its essential unity as a declaration of the divine will. [19] In this respect, of course, he is simply using a customary Rabbinic mode of expression. [20]

Our findings with regard to Paul have an important bearing on the understanding of the post-pauline Gospel of John. If there can be no doubt (→ 753) that the meaning in Jn. 19:17 is "saying," and if this is at least a possible, though not a necessary, rendering in 7:38, 42; 13:18; 19:24, 28, 36 — in fact the ἵνα ἡ γραφὴ πληρωθῇ or τελειωθῇ seems to refer more naturally to the fulfilment of all Scripture, including its individual utterances — there can hardly be any doubt

---

[16] Cf. Pr.-Bauer, Schlatter, as against Cr.-Kö., Meecham.

[17] ψ 86:5: ἐν γραφῇ λαῶν, does not refer to the OT, cf. H. Gunkel, Psalmen⁴ (1926), 379 (and → βιβλίον, 620). Nor does Da. 10:21 Θ: ἐν γραφῇ ἀληθείας (LXX: ἀπογραφῇ) (כְּתָב), where the reference is to the secret apocalyptic book of God in which future events and national destinies are written.

[18] Though cf. BGU, 5273 (5th cent. A.D.): ἡ καλλίνικος καὶ ἀθάνατος γραφή; P. Lond., 981, 4 (4th cent. A.D.): γέγραπται ἐν τῇ γραφῇ.

[19] The λέγει, φησίν of Paul in 1 C. 6:16; R. 15:10 f., and the λέγει γάρ in 2 C. 6:2, have little bearing on the question. They naturally refer to Scripture, but in a general sense which is also common in the diatribe and Philo. The Rabbis have שנאמר or ואומר. Cf. Epict. Diss., I, 28, 4: ὡς λέγει Πλάτων; III, 24, 99: ὡς λέγει ὁ Σωκράτης (cf. IV, 1, 41).

[20] For examples of Rabbinic personification of the Torah, cf. Str.-B., III, 538, with reference to the formula מה ראתה תורה: "How, or on what grounds, does the Torah come to say this or that?" TBQ, 7, 2 (357); the same of Scripture, S. Lv., 23, 22 (410a); b.BQ, 79b: "Why has the Torah threatened a more severe punishment?" Cf. further S. Lv., 5, 17; S. Nu., 151 on 29:35; Tanch. פנחס, 3, 151; שופטים, 7, 30.

whatever that in 2:22: ἐπίστευσαν τῇ γραφῇ, and 10:35: οὐ δύναται λυθῆναι ἡ γραφή (cf. 7:23 of the νόμος: ἵνα μὴ λυθῇ), and also in 17:12: ἵνα ἡ γραφὴ πληρωθῇ (with no particular citation) and 20:9: οὐδέπω γὰρ ᾔδεισαν τὴν γραφήν, we are to think of the unified totality of Scripture. Similarly, it is impossible to take 1 Pt. 2:6: περιέχει ἐν γραφῇ, or 2 Pt. 1:20, [21] in any other way.

Cf. this use of γραφή in the early Church, which also included the NT Canon: [22] Orig. Comm. in Joh., X, 23, 131: τὰ κεκρυμμένα τῆς γραφῆς; Philostorg. Hist. Eccl., III, 8; Gelas., II, 17, 16. Orig. can say of the OT: ἡ παλαιὰ γραφή, Cels., VII, 24; Method. Symp., III, 1, 52; 8, 69; V, 2, 110 (including the apostolic writings as well as the OT); Gelas., II, 19, 3 (of the Gospel of Mt.).

C. The Question of Scripture.

1. The Judaistic View of Scripture.

According to the later Jewish view, Scripture has sacred, authoritative and normative significance. It is of permanent and unassailable validity. As the dictate of God, it is given by His Spirit. This view referred originally to the Pentateuch but was then transferred to the Prophets and Writings. The implication of the doctrine of inspiration is that the revealed truth of God characterises every word. The Alexandrian synagogue devoted particular attention to the question of inspiration and interpreted it along the lines of Greek ecstaticism. The author becomes the organ of God's dictation in ἔκστασις. [23] In ἑρμηνεία Moses, the prophet κατ᾽ ἐξοχήν, interprets the will of God in human speech. προφητεία is distinguished from this inspiration, however, and may be experienced by the sage speaking in rapture. [24]

The use of Scripture in the Rabbinic synagogue is determined by the concern to rediscover and prove the παράδοσις which had established itself alongside Scripture. This demands literal attention to the wording, as does also the casuistical nomism and the onesidedly legal conception of Scripture. Already in the Pirke Aboth Moses is viewed as the first to pass on the tradition of the Torah received at Sinai (Ab., 1, 1). If the whole Halacha is to be spun out of Scripture and established by it, there is naturally demanded a minute treatment of the text which goes rather beyond exegesis. Hillel's 7 rules (מִדּוֹת) are only the beginning of a system of schematic, syllogistic and scholastic wresting of the text in which justifiable concerns are immediately choked by a tendentious over-minuteness which cannot possibly do justice to the living realities of the statements. [25] The Alexandrian treatment of the text, which is rather freer in relation to the παράδοσις but surrenders the more easily to a whole host of Hellenistic motifs, is particularly influential by reason of its allegorising. The Palestinian synagogue had already adopted this to some degree (the Midrash and older Targumim). This method is the unavoidable consequence of forcing the text into a schema imported from without.

---

[21] Without the art. → n. 7.
[22] For the post-apost. fathers, Pr.-Bauer, s.v. γραφή.
[23] Philo Spec. Leg., IV, 49; Rer. Div. Her., 265.
[24] Philo Vit. Mos., II, 191; Mut. Nom., 126.
[25] For the later 13 rules, cf. Weber, 109 ff. On this whole section, cf. Str.-B., IV, 415-451 (Excurs.: "Der Kanon des AT u.s. Inspiration").

2. The Early Christian Canon.

Hand in hand with the consolidation of the Pharisaic movement, which is particularly concerned to erect a dam of law and tradition against the Hellenistic flood, there goes the formation of the Canon, which is shaped to a surprising degree by this anti-Hellenistic tendency.[26] The absolute normativity of a binding text demands a carefully differentiated and integrated number of books.

The NT helps us to understand this development at many points. Thus we can see from Mt. 23:35 that Chronicles (2 Ch. 24:20 f.) was then the last book.[27] Again, in Lk. 24:44 we have the same threefold division as in the Prologue to Sir. (c. 130 B.C.).[28] The fact that the prophecies of Jeremiah are presupposed in Da. 9:2 shows us that the prophetic writings were already in use at this period, and the fact that the *Corpus propheticum* was then closed makes it plain that Da. was not included in it. The Bible of Jesus must certainly have included the כתובים and early Christian tradition records that Jesus quoted especially from Da., the Twelve, Is., Ps. and Dt.[29] Paul quotes most heavily from Is. and Ps., then the Torah (especially Gn. and Dt.).[30] He uses the LXX[31] in older recensions or strata no longer extant.[32]

There is little apocryphal citation in the NT, and the same solemnity does not attach to it as to canonical citation.[33]

The fact that Test. N. 2:14, Test. S. 5:4 introduce the Book of Enoch as (ἡ) γραφή 'Ενώχ does not imply more than that it is literature. In 2 Macc. 2:4 there is a similar reference to apocryphal material: ἐν τῇ γραφῇ (cf. 2:1: ἐν ταῖς ἀπογραφαῖς), but no particular claim is involved.

In the NT we have to consider Lk. 11:49 (ἡ σοφία τοῦ θεοῦ εἶπεν, a book of wisdom?); Jn. 7:38; 1 C. 2:9;[34] 9:10 (doubtful); Eph. 5:14 (διὸ λέγει);[35] Jm. 4:5 (ἡ γραφὴ λέγει);[36] Jd. 14 ff. ('Ενώχ λέγων, a reference to Eth. En.; cf. the allusion

---

[26] Acc. to Jos. Ap., 1, 40 the 22 (or 24 in 4 Esr. 14:44) books of the Canon derive from the period from the death of Moses to Artaxerxes. They receive their authority from Moses and the prophets who follow him. On the difference between the concept of Scripture and that of the Canon in the Synagogue, cf. Staerk, *op. cit.*

[27] As against Hänel, 96.

[28] Lk. 24:44: ἐν τῷ νόμῳ Μωυσέως καὶ τοῖς προφήταις καὶ ψαλμοῖς; the last is *pars pro toto* for כתובים. Elsewhere Lk. likes the expression ὁ νόμος καὶ οἱ προφῆται, Lk. 16:16, 29, 31; Ac. 13:15; 28:31; cf. 24:14; 28:23. The tripartite division is found in Philo Vit. Cont., 25: νόμους καὶ λόγια θεσπισθέντα διὰ προφητῶν καὶ ὕμνους. Philo expounds the Pentateuch but occasionally quotes from all three parts (Ps., Prv., Job from the 3rd). Paul (1 C. 14:21 — a saying from Is. as νόμος) and Jn. (10:34; 15:25 — of verses from the Ps.) follow Jewish custom in using νόμος for Scripture as a whole.

[29] Cf. Hänel, 35-44. Hänel links his findings from the Gospels directly with Jesus, though his views really apply to the early Christian tradition inaugurated by the influence of Jesus.

[30] Michel, 11. Of the כתובים Pl. quotes Ps., Prv., Job. For his following of the threefold division, → 758, n. 43. It is likely that he knew Wis., but the allusions are not quotations and his basic orientation is different.

[31] Particularly striking is his acceptance of the 430 years in Gl. 3:17 acc. to the LXX and not the Mas. (Ex. 12:40). On Joseph. and the LXX, Schl., *Theol. d. Judt.,* 151 f.

[32] Ltzm. Gl., 32-34; A. Rahlfs, ZNW, 20 (1921), 182 ff.

[33] The judgment of B. Poertner, 31 and E. König, 43 is to be modified in the light of Jm. 4:5.

[34] Acc. to Orig. on Mt. 27:9 (Lommatzsch, V, 29), Ambrosiast., Euthalius, from an Elias Apoc.; Jerome on Is. 64:4 regards this verse or 65:16 as the original of the quotation.

[35] Acc. to Epiph. Haer., 42, 12. 3 this παρὰ τῷ 'Ηλίᾳ was to be found in an Elias Apoc.

[36] The interpretation in Cr.-Kö., 265, where v. 5b is not regarded as a quotation, is forced.

to the Ass. Mos. in v. 9). The situation is basically the same in the post-apost. fathers. In 1 Cl., 23, 3 there is an apocryphal citation introduced by ἡ γραφὴ αὕτη, ὅπου λέγει (Eldad and Modad, or Ass. Mos. ?), which is also found in 2 Cl., 11, 2 as προφητικὸς λόγος. In Barn., 16, 5 there is a saying from En. 89:56 ff. introduced by λέγει γὰρ ἡ γραφή. Apocryphal sayings are also quoted in terms of γέγραπται in Herm. v., 2, 3, 4; Barn., 4, 3.

The Pauline Epistles are already called γραφαί in 2 Pt. 3:16. A saying of the Lord is called γραφή in 2 Cl., 2, 4.

3. The Belief of the Early Church as regards Scripture.

a. Inspiration. In Jn. 5:39 : ἐρευνᾶτε τὰς γραφάς, it is acknowledged that Judaism takes great pains to investigate the Scriptures with a view to attaining eternal life. [37] Early Christianity did not free itself from the Jewish doctrine of inspiration nor even from the influence of its exposition at certain points. It is a matter of far-reaching significance, however, that παράδοσις was no longer accepted as an equally important magnitude. In addition, the sayings of the Lord came to be given the same authority as the OT (cf. the Sermon on the Mount, also 1 C. 7:10; 9:14; 11:23), thus modifying the original authority. For the "I say unto you" caused great changes in the whole concept of authority, especially in relation to the validity of Scripture (→ 760). The γραφαί were still the basic expression of the will of God. This is established by the fact that the divine Spirit was said to speak in Scripture, though this formulation is rare as compared with all that is said concerning the non-capricious charismatic utterances of the Spirit. [38] Thus David in the Psalms speaks by the Spirit (Mt. 22:43; Mk. 12:36; [39] Ac. 1:16). Again, the prophets speak by the Spirit (Ac. 28:25; 1 Pt. 1:11, the Spirit of Christ ; 2 Pt. 1:21: ὑπὸ πνεύματος ἁγίου φερόμενοι ἐλάλησαν ἀπὸ θεοῦ ἄνθρωποι). Hb. especially emphasises the fact that the Spirit speaks in the sayings of the OT (3:7; 9:8; 10:15). The true doctrinal formulation of inspiration is most comprehensively given in 2 Tm. 3:16 : πᾶσα γραφὴ θεόπνευστος. But Eph. 6:12 presupposes the same conviction, and all emphasis upon the fact that God speaks in Scripture (Mk. 12:26; par. Mt. 22:31; Mt. 15:4; 19:5), or that the κύριος speaks by the prophets (Mt. 1:22; 2:15; cf. λέγει κύριος as an introductory formula in Pl. : 1 C. 14:21; 2 C. 6:17; R. 12:19; cf. also 2 C. 6:2, 16; R. 9:15, 25, where λέγει presupposes ὁ θεός), testifies at root to exactly the same point as is at issue in the doctrine of inspiration. Naturally, when we ask concerning the relation between Scripture and Spirit, we again come up against the new norm of the words of Jesus, which acc. to Jn. 6:63 are spirit and life ; and in Jn. 14:26 it is the Paraclete who will bring to the minds of the disciples what was said to them by Jesus.

We may perhaps conclude that there is a greater sense of the persons of the authors in early Christianity than in Judaism, [40] and therefore a greater regard for the natural and historical mediation of the divine utterance. Yet this does not in

---

[37] On → ἐρευνᾶν in Joseph. the Rabb., Philo, cf. Schl. J., 158; on Philo cf. Leg. All., III, 84; Congr., 44.

[38] Rather surprisingly, Paul never lists true exposition of Scripture among the gifts of the Spirit.

[39] This does not weaken the doctrine of inspiration (Hänel) by suggesting that there are in the Ps. things which David did not speak by inspiration.

[40] This is esp. striking in Mt. (2:5, 17, 23; 3:3; 4:14; 8:4, 17; 12:17; 13:14, 35; 22:24; 24:15; 27:9). For a Pauline list, v. Michel, 69. The difference from Hb. is palpable, cf. Michel, 68.

any way weaken the basic conviction that it is God who speaks in Scripture. The fact that Paul, for example, sometimes handles his texts very freely shows us that his belief in inspiration does not entail slavery to the letter. But in comparison with the liberties and capricious alterations which are made by Josephus in spite of his insistence on the sanctity of the very letter of Scripture, [41] Paul is by far the more reverent, especially in his high regard for the fact of what is reported in the OT. [42]

Rabbinic influence [43] may still be seen in Paul's allegorising (→ ἀλληγορέω, 263 f.): ἅτινά ἐστιν ἀλληγορούμενα, Gl. 4:24; cf. Gl. 3:16 (σπέρματα, σπέρμα); [44] Gl. 3:19 (διαταγεὶς δι' ἀγγέλων); [45] 4:25 (Hagar, Sinai); [46] 4:30 (Ishmael); [47] 1 C. 10:4 (the rock which is Christ—Haggadic). [48] Yet if we compare Paul with Philo, it is instructive that τὸ ῥητόν, the literal sense, does not have for Philo [49] the same value as for Paul when compared with the allegorical. [50] The allegories of Paul are relics of Rabbinism. Allegorising is not his predominant mode of exposition. [51]

On the inspiration of Scripture in the Gk. fathers: Chrysost. De Lazaro, IV, 3 (MPG, 48, 1010): ἃ αἱ γραφαὶ φθέγγονται, ταῦτα ὁ Δεσπότης ἐφθέγξατο.
Great use was made of the term θεόπνευστος: Cl. Al. Strom., VII, 16, 101, 6; Orig. Comm. in Joh., VI, 48, 248; on John. 1:17 (p. 494); Cels., IV, 17; Hom. in 1 S. 28:3-25 (p. 286, 2 f.); Thdrt. Interpret., 2 Tm. 3:16 (MPG, 82, 849b).

b. The Thought of Fulfilment as the Heart of the Early Christian Understanding of Scripture. All the writings of the NT display a conviction of the πληρωθῆναι or τελειωθῆναι of Scripture in and through Jesus Christ. In the Gospels this is a main theme in Christian edification. γραφή, γραφαί are particularly related to this thought in Mk. 14:49; 15:28 𝔎 lat sy^p; Mt. 26:54, 56; Lk. 4:21; Ac. 1:16; Jn. 17:12; 19:24, 28 (ἵνα τελειωθῇ), 36. It is also to be noted that this thought underlies the whole emphasis on the fact that there is Messianic prophecy in the OT, and that the life and work of Jesus, His mission as Christ, His suffering and resurrection, may be found in the Law, Prophets and Writings. [52]

---

[41] Schl., Theol. d. Judt., 65.
[42] On Paul's handling of Scripture, v. Michel, 74 f. (list), 76 ff. Hb. is more literal. On the license of Joseph. and the influence of legends on him, cf. Schl., Theol. d. Judt., 68-72. On Paul's attitude to the historical element in Scripture, cf. G. Schrenk, Geschichtsanschauung des Paulus, 74 f. (→ 743 n.).
[43] That Paul derives from the Rabb. tradition may be seen formally from the fact that like the Rabb. he combines quotations from all 3 groups (Michel, 83), and that he likes to heap up key sayings and to draw up catenae (Windfuhr). This is Rabb., as is also the πάλιν γέγραπται of Mt. 4:7. On florilegia, which are not definitely found prior to Barn., cf. Hatch; Vollmer; Harris; Michel; Ltzm. Gl., 33; for Barn., cf. Wnd. (→ 743 n.).
[44] Philo Mut. Nom., 145.
[45] Str.-B., III, 554 ff.
[46] Philo Leg. All., III, 244; Mut. Nom., 66, 77.
[47] Str.-B., III, 575.
[48] Philo Leg. All., II, 86; Det. Pot. Ins., 115-118.
[49] Philo Abr., 68; 131; 236; Praem. Poen., 65.
[50] G. Schrenk, op. cit., 74 ff.
[51] How a true disciple of Philo allegorises is shown by Orig. On the alleg. and liter. meaning of Scripture, cf. Princ., IV, 2, 2; IV, 3, 4; IV, 3, 11. For the Gnostic view of the harmony of the organic whole of Scripture, cf. Comm. in Joh., X, 18, 107.
[52] On πληρόω, which corresponds to the Rabb. םײק, "to sustain," "to prove valid," cf. Str.-B., I, 74 and Schl. Mt., 21. In any case, the final realisation or "bringing to pass" is in view (cf. the τελειόω of Jn.), even in Mt. 5:17, where the opp. is καταλῦσαι, said in relation to the νόμος. Joseph. does not have the concept of the fulfilment of Scripture.

The great message of Scripture is confirmed by its actualisation in Christ, e.g., in His passion. In Lk. 24:27, 32, 45 the risen Lord Himself shows this. Paul takes the same line in Ac. 17:2; 28:23. Apollos finds proof from the Scriptures in Ac. 18:28. Indeed, the same conception underlies the whole of the NT even when we do not have the κατὰ τὰς γραφάς of 1 C. 15:3 f.

This thought of fulfilment does not imply only that individual passages provide scriptural proof for various concrete facts or features relating to what took place in Christ. Paul especially has a larger understanding in view when he describes the purpose of the OT for the Christian community in terms of ἐγράφη δι' ἡμᾶς, ἐγράφη ἵνα. He is claiming no less than that OT Scripture finally belongs to the Christian community rather than the Jewish. [53] All that is written (R. 15:4) was written for the instruction of Christians and the fostering of their hope by the patience and comfort of the Scriptures. He applies this in all its breadth. Thus in R. 16:26 he says that the εὐαγγέλιον for the nations was revealed by prophetic Scriptures. Again, in R. 4:23 he emphasises that the λογίζεσθαι in the case of Abraham δι' ἡμᾶς ἐγράφη, or in 1 C. 10:11 that the true aim of every OT story depicting the visitation of divine judgment is to serve as an example, or in 1 C. 9:10 that the saying concerning the ox which treads out the corn, and which is not to be muzzled, δι' ἡμᾶς ἐγράφη, disclosing the mind and principle of the divine rule in the instruction of the servants of the Gospel concerning their attitude to the question of support. Everywhere, then, the thought of fulfilment is conceived in such a way that the profoundest sense of Scripture is effectively realised in the community of Christ.

Along the same lines Jn. argues that the γραφαί bear witness to Christ (5:39-47), and that they do so in their totality. Abraham is a prophet of Christ (8:56). Moses wrote concerning Him (5:46 f.). The cross and resurrection are prophesied in Scripture (19:37; 20:9), but so, too, is the freedom of Jesus in relation to the Sabbath (7:22). Indeed, His Sonship is proved from Scripture (10:34 ff.).

Hb. gives us the most penetrating and consistent detailed exegesis in homiletical form. In it apologetic value in ascribed to the word of Scripture. Hence it is not surprising that everything is here brought under the conception of fulfilment; the events and institutions of the OT are applied typologically as shadows of the higher future reality of the Christ revelation. Everything, then, is lit up by Christ. His superiority to the angels, to Moses, to Aaron and to Melchisedec is established by proofs from Scripture. The main theme, however, in this outworking of the thought of fulfilment is that of His superiority to the cultus. In Hb. 11, a meditation which has obvious links with the homiletic traditions of the Synagogue, the wit-

---

[53] From the observation that solemn scriptural proof is adduced with remarkable one-sidedness only in Gl., R., and 1 and 2 C., but plays very little part in 1 and 2 Th., Phil., Col. and Eph., Harnack (op. cit.) has concluded that the OT was not used for purposes of edification in the community, and that Paul turned to it only in conflict with Judaism. Yet R. is surely written to a predominantly Gentile community, and the same is probably true of Gl. and 1 and 2 C. as well. Paul presumes a fair knowledge of Scripture in his churches. That searching the Scriptures played a great part in them is rightly noted in Ac. 18:24; 17:11. Cf. further Hb. 4:12; Jn. 19:7. It is impossible to conceive either of the missionary preaching of Paul or of the instruction of the communities without the proof from Scripture. This is attested by the saying in 2 Tm. 3:16 concerning the value of Scripture — which is surely more than pious moralising. διδασκαλία, ἐλεγμός, ἐπανόρθωσις, παιδεία ἐν δικαιοσύνῃ are words which describe the total service of γραφή to the community.

nesses of the OT generation of faith must again proclaim the content of Christian faith in terms of hope.

In Rev. the OT provides an instructive treasury of images for the portrayal of the final denouement to which the community looks forward, except that there is now an undreamed of heightening of what is therein narrated. Scripture is thus an authority to the extent that it is interpreted in the light of the event of salvation accomplished in Christ. It is a transparency in which Christ may be seen, and its office is to advance Christianity. There may be difficulties to-day as regards some aspects of this understanding, but basically the detailed interpretation is not the new thing but the rule that the fact of Christ is normative and regulative for the whole use of Scripture. Early Christianity no longer has Scripture without Christ. It has Scripture only to the extent that in it the Christ event has been fulfilled. It is characteristic of the NT conception of faith that there is no reference to belief in Scripture. The phrase πιστεύειν τῇ γραφῇ in Jn. 2:22, and the question πιστεύεις τοῖς προφήταις in Ac. 26:27, imply believing Scripture, but not belief in it. [54]

c. The Twofold Attitude to Scripture in Early Christianity. The thought of fulfilment carries with it a negative conception in so far as it conceives of Scripture in terms of something which is fulfilled, which does not therefore exist alone, which is nothing apart from the fulfilment. Yet the concept of authority remains unshaken. This is the real problem in the early Christian understanding of Scripture. Jn. states the principle of authority in the saying in 10:35 : καὶ οὐ δύναται λυθῆναι ἡ γραφή. Scripture is of unimpeachable validity. The same point is emphasised in Mt. 5:18. On the other hand, the Law and the Prophets are only until John (Lk. 16:16), and ἕως ἂν πάντα γένηται is an integral part of Mt. 5:18. Thus the thought of fulfilment both sustains and modifies that of authority. According to the Synoptic record, even though Jesus sees the will of God in the Torah, He opposes to it His own decisions in such matters as marriage, retribution, hatred, the law of the Sabbath, the law of purification, the Messianic ideal of Israel, and other questions. He does not merely transcend the older statement; He can set it aside in virtue of His own incomparable authority, which is superior both to tradition and to the written OT. Jesus' criticism of the word of Scripture may be seen most clearly in His distinction between the original will of God and the concession of Moses as regards divorce. He maintains that the Word of God has been added to by men. If Scripture is an authoritative declaration of the divine will, its authority is not valid apart from the "I say unto you." In other words, the concept of authority is changed by that of fulfilment.

In Paul we find the same duality of the unbroken and the broken attitude, of bondage and freedom. In 1 C. 4:6 the principle of μὴ ὑπὲρ ἃ γέγραπται φρονεῖν [55] is polemically established. But this can never mean Scripture apart from Christ, just as νόμον ἱστάνομεν in R. 3:31 can never mean Law apart from the fulfilment of its final purpose in Christ. For Paul, the νόμος and γράμμα are transcended by

---

[54] Acc. to Jn. 20:30 f. the goal of the Fourth Gospel (ταῦτα δὲ γέγραπται, ἵνα πιστεύητε is not faith in what is written but faith in the fact that Jesus is the Christ, the Son of God. Cf. Orig. Hom. in 1 S. 28:3-25 (p. 287, 1 f.): ἡ γραφὴ ᾗ δεῖ πιστεύειν.

[55] Whether or not this is to be viewed as the slogan of a libertine theology in Corinth (Lütgert, 97 ff.; Schlatter, Kor. Theol., 7 ff.) — and it may be that too much is read into the saying — there can be no doubt that the norm of Scripture is emphasised.

Christ and the Spirit, and are thus given their true validity. We read this from the Law or from Scripture itself. The lasting soteriological, ethical and eschatological truths [56] which Paul still takes from Scripture are of great significance even though the same Scripture tells him that the Law which is its kernel is overcome.

In the great discussion of Christ and the OT in Hb., Scripture serves to prove that Christ is incomparably more than the OT. The NT represents a higher stage. Yet the OT — as shown, e.g., by the chain of witnesses — reveals also the continuity of the whole revelation; the OT demands the NT as a link and continuation.

This duality in the early Christian view reveals a truth which is first brought clearly to light by Paul in his discussion of the γράμμα. For early Christianity Scripture is no longer just what is written, nor is it just tradition; it is the dynamic and divinely determined declaration of God which speaks of His whole rule and therefore of His destroying and new creating, and which reaches its climax in the revelation of Christ and the revelation of the Spirit by the risen Lord. Because Scripture serves and attests Christ, it can contain the most diverse elements, including some which disturb the old concept of authority or contradict the new. If the historical rule of God in creation and redemption is His foreshadowing and fulfilment, His prophesying and realisation, then basically the full revelation in Christ and the Spirit is more than what is written. The latter has its true force only in this event and not in codification.

γράμμα.

A. γράμμα in Greek and Hellenistic Usage.

The use of γράμμα is par. to that of γραφή. γράμμα is properly what is "inscribed" or "engraven" and then what is "written" in the widest sense.

1. The primary sense is most clearly seen in the prohibition of γράμματα στικτά, tattooing, (כְּתֹבֶת קַעֲקַע) in Lv. 19:28; cf. Philo Spec. Leg., I, 58. The word is thus often used for "inscription": Hdt., I, 187; Plat. Phaedr., 229e; Charm., 164d; Xenoph. Mem., IV, 2, 24; Plut. Lucull., 10, 4 (I, 498b); Polyb., IV, 33, 2. Engraven symbols like those on the headband of gold in Ex. 36:39 (39:30): γράμματα ἐκτετυπωμένα (מִכְתָּב); Ep. Ar., 98; Jos. Ant., 3, 178; Bell., 5, 235; or the names of the sons of Jacob inscribed on the breastplate: Jos. Ant., 3, 169; Philo Rer. Div. Her., 176 are ἱερά or ἅγια or θεῖα γράμματα. Here the γράμματα are symbols (→ infra), but the idea of engraving is still preserved.

2. γράμμα can also mean "picture," like γραφή (Plat. Resp., V, 472d; Crat., 430e), or "geometrical figure." [1]

3. γράμματα can also be "symbols" or "letters" without the idea of engraving. It is used a. of "writing in characters," e.g., by the Phoenicians, Hdt., V, 58; Jos. Ap., 1, 28; or by the Jews, Jos. Ant., 12, 15; or by the Gks., Jos. Ap., 1, 11. Egyptian hieroglyphics are called ἱερά γράμματα, Diod. S., I, 27, 3; 45, 2; 55, 7; Philo Vit. Mos., I, 23; Ditt. Or., 56, 36 (3rd cent. B.C.); 90, 54 (2nd cent. B.C.). It is also used b. of the "individual letter," as when γράμματα is linked with συλλαβαί in Plat. Crat., 390e; Philo Mut. Nom., 64. In this sense it may signify the letters used for the quarters of a

---

[56] Cf. Ltzm. Gl., 33 in an excellent summary.

γ ρ ά μ μ α. For bibl. → γράφω, 742, n. The def. of Hesych.: τὰ γεγραμμένα, καὶ συλλαβαί, καὶ τὰ ζωγραφήματα. καὶ τὰ ἐν ταῖς δικασταῖς ψήφοις. καὶ ἀπογραφαί is instructive when compared with our findings in the NT, and esp. Paul, for it gives prior significance to what is written rather than to συλλαβαί.

[1] Cf. Liddell-Scott, s.v.

city,[2] or for numbers : Barn., 9, 7 f. (cf. the Hellenistic mysticism of letters).[3] It may also be used c. for the "letters of a book" : Jos. Ant., 12, 83 : χρυσοῖς γράμμασιν on the rolls of the Torah; Epict. Diss., II, 23, 1: βιβλίον εὐσημοτέροις γράμμασι γεγραμμένον. It is used d. for "handwritten characters" : Jos. Bell., 1, 529; Method. Symp., V, 4, 117.

Lk. 23:38 א* AD it : γράμμασιν ἑλληνικοῖς (καὶ) ῥωμαϊκοῖς (καὶ) Ἑβραϊκοῖς (cf. Jn. 19:20) should be compared with Hdt., IV, 87 on an inscription in two languages : ἐνταμὼν γράμματα ἐς μὲν τὴν Ἀσσύρια, ἐς δὲ τὴν Ἑλληνικά; Ep. Ar., 4 on the Law : διὰ τὸ γεγράφθαι παρ' αὐτοῖς ἐν διφθέραις Ἑβραϊκοῖς γράμμασιν; 176 : Ἰουδαϊκοῖς γράμμασι; P. Lond., 43, 3 (2nd cent. B.C.). In Joseph. it is used of the inscriptions on the temple barriers, Bell., 5, 194 : αἱ μὲν Ἑλληνικοῖς αἱ δὲ Ῥωμαϊκοῖς γράμμασιν; 6, 125 : γράμμασιν Ἑλληνικοῖς καὶ ἡμετέροις κεχαραγμένας (στήλας); Hipp. Ref., IV, 28, 2 : Ἑβραϊκοῖς γράμμασι.

e. In such cases as that of translation γράμματα can also have the sense of "language" : Ep. Ar., 38; Jos. Ant., 12, 48; cf. 14, 319; 197; 20, 263.

4. It will be seen that γράμμα always connotes "what is written." Logically, then, it can be used in antithesis to the spoken word : Philo Plant., 131 and 173. It is no contradiction that in Plat. Phileb., 18c; Philo Mut. Nom., 63 γράμματα ἄφωνα are mute sounds. Here, as in the sense of musical notes (Anth. Pal., 11, 78, Lucill.), the reference is to the notation rather than the phonetic aspect. Often κατὰ γράμματα is used to emphasise the literal sound, as in Aristot. Polit., III, 14, 4, p. 1286a, 12; III, 16, 5, p. 1287a, 33 f.; P. Giess., 30, 6, 15 (2nd cent. A.D.): τὰ τῆς συγγραφῆς γράμματα of the wording of the contract. In keeping with this is the etymological observance of the γράμμα in Aristot. Eth. M., I, 6, p. 1185b, 39.

5. "What is written" and "writing" are basic elements in education. "Grammar," γραμματικὴ ἐμπειρία (Jos. Ant., 20, 263, or γράμματα, Philo Spec. Leg., I, 336; II, 230; cf. Epict. Diss., I, 12). Yet γράμματα can also be used for "academic disciplines" and all that pertains to academic education : Xenoph. Cyrop., I, 2, 6; Plat. Ap., 26d : ἀπείρους γραμμάτων; Diod. S., V, 40, 2; Jos. Ant., 10, 187: τὰ τῶν Χαλδαίων γράμματα. This γράμματα can be so used in the Israelite sphere that the reference is to the Law: Test. L. 13:2: διδάξατε δὲ καὶ ὑμεῖς τὰ τέκνα ὑμῶν γράμματα, ἵνα ἔχωσι σύνεσιν ἐν πάσῃ τῇ ζωῇ αὐτῶν, ἀναγινώσκοντες ἀδιαλείπτως τὸν νόμον τοῦ θεοῦ. The learning of γράμματα is especially related to knowledge of the Law, cf. Test. R. 4:1. In the first instance, however, γράμματα διδάσκειν or μανθάνειν etc. simply means "learning to read and write." Demosth., 18, 265. Da. 1:4 LXX and Θ; γράμματα παιδεύειν : Jos. Ap., 2, 204, μανθάνειν : Plat. Alc., I, 106e; Prot., 325e; P. Flor., III, 382, 79 (3rd cent. A.D.): ὁ δεῖνα μανθάνων γράμματα. Rabbin. : Ex. r., 20, 15 on 13:17: עַד שֶׁיִּלְמֹד בְּנֵי בְּנֵי כְתָבִין. The ἐπιστάμενος γράμματα or γραμμάτων ἐπιστήμων is one who can read and write : Is. 29:11 f. (יָדַע סֵפֶר); Jos. Ant., 12, 209; P. Amh., 82, 4 (3/4 cent. A.D.). The opp. is γράμματα μὴ ἐπίστασθαι or εἰδέναι : Plat. Leg., III, 689d; Ditt. Syll.[2], 844, 5; BGU, 351. Hence ἀγράμματος for an "unlettered man" (Ac. 4:13).[4]

6. γράμμα, γράμματα are most commonly used for various kinds of "written pieces." Especially a. τὰ γράμματα means a "letter," Hdt. I, 124; Polyb., II, 6, 4; 1 Macc. 5:10; Est. 8:5; Ep. Ar., 43; Jos. Ant., 7, 137; Epict. Diss., III, 24, 26; Alex. Erot. Fr., 30, 5 (Grenfell, 2nd cent. B.C.); P. Amh., II, 143, 10 (4th cent. A.D.). "Letters of recommendation" are called γράμματα συστατικά in Epict. Diss., II, 3, 1. It also means b. a "report" or "document," as generally in Aristoph. Nu., 772 : τὰ γράμματα τῆς δίκης. "City records" are called τὰ δημόσια γράμματα in Jos. Bell., 7, 61, also "acts" in Jos. Ant., 14, 255 (though cf. Ap., 1, 116), or the "archives" in which they are de-

---

2 Preisigke Wört., s.v.
3 F. Boll, Sphaira (1903), 469 ff.; Reitzenstein Poim., 260 ff.. 288 ff.
4 Cf. E. Majer-Leonhard, Ἀγράμματοι; Pr.-Bauer Wört.

posited in Ant., 14, 243 and 253. In Vit., 337 πλαστὰ γράμματα refers to falsified accounts of a treaty. In Philo Spec. Leg., IV, 30 the reference is to records of loans on interest. The word is used of a "deed of gift" in Euseb. Vit. Const., II, 21: τὸ τῆς δωρεᾶς γράμμα; [5] of a "bill of indebtedness" in Jos. Ant., 18, 156 (sing.); P. Tebt, II, 397, 17 (198 A.D.); of "proofs" in a law-suit in Philo Dec., 140 ; [6] of an "accusation" in Jos. Ant., 17, 145 : γράμματα ἐπὶ κατηγορίᾳ; of "national rolls" in Jos. Ap., 1, 35 and of "guard rosters" in Ditt. Syll.[2], 569, 21 (Cos, 3rd cent. B.C.). Again, it means c. an "official report" in Jos. Ant., 17, 133; 19, 292. It means d. the "decree" or "decision" of the king in Est. 4:3, 8; 8:10; 9:1; Jos. Ant., 11, 222 and 224; 14, 265 etc.; Bell., 7, 433; Eus. Hist. Eccl., IX, 1, 1; 9, 13; of the governor in P. Oxy., 1104, 9 (4th cent. A.D.). Joseph. often uses πρόγραμμα for "edict," e.g., in Ant., 12, 145; Vit., 370.

Worth noting is the use of ἱερά or θεῖα γράμματα for "royal letters and decrees," esp. in the eastern world : CIG, 2943, 10 (age of Augustus); Ditt. Or., 502, 13 f. (age of Hadrian); IG, XII, 5, No. 132; Ditt. Syll.[3], 881 (both 3rd cent. A.D.); θεῖα γράμματα, P. Herm. (Wessely, 1905), 119 B, III, 19 (3rd cent. A.D.); Ditt. Syll.[3], 888, 95. [7]

7. "Laws fixed in writing," Plat. Polit., 302e : ἐν γράμμασιν ἀγαθοῖς, οὓς νόμους λέγομεν; cf. *ibid.*, 293a for the contrast between κατὰ γράμματα and ἄνευ γραμμάτων ἄρχειν. κατὰ γράμματα and κατὰ νόμους are synon. in Aristot. Pol., II, 9, p. 1270b, 30 in the sense of legal statutes. The same sense is found in Plat. Ep., 7, 325d. The contrast between written law and unwritten national custom may be seen in Aristot. Pol., III, 16, p. 1287b, 5 f. : ἔτι κυριώτεροι καὶ περὶ κυριωτέρων τῶν κατὰ γράμματα νόμων οἱ κατὰ τὰ ἔθη εἰσίν. Philo uses γράμμα both for 1. commandment and 2. table of the Law (Spec. Leg., III, 8), and also for the power of nature as a divine law (Migr. Abr., 85 : γράμμα θεῖον). For further material details on written and unwritten law, → 768. The sing. can be used in Thuc., V, 29, 3 of the individual clause in a contract.

8. γράμμα, γράμματα as "literature." Joseph. uses γράμματα for his sources, the records of Egypt, Phoenicia, Chaldea, Tyre and Greece, in Ap., 1, 21 f.; 59; 73; 104 f. etc.; cf. Philo Vit. Mos., I, 23 : τὰ Ἀσσύρια γράμματα (though the reference here may be to sciences rather than literature). It may thus be used for "books" or "individual writings," Xenoph. Mem., IV, 2, 1; Philo Sacr. AC, 79; Jos. Ap., 1, 12; Eus. Vit. Const., I, 10 of his biography of Constantine.

9. As a Term for the Sacred Scriptures of the OT and NT.

a. It is not quite accurate [8] that in the Jewish sphere γράμματα is used of Holy Scripture only with the addition ἱερά etc. Joseph. in Ant., 5, 61 can say : δηλοῦται διὰ τῶν ἀνακειμένων ἐν τῷ ἱερῷ γραμμάτων. Here of course the epithet is hardly necessary, since it is said that Scripture is preserved in the sanctuary. But in relation to a specific book of the Canon we find γράμματα alone in Est. 6:1 (of Chronicles); in Jos. Ant., 3, 322 (of the Pentateuch : τὰ καταλειφθέντα ὑπὸ Μωυσέως γράμματα; cf. Philo Conf. Ling., 50 : κατὰ τὸ Μωυσέως γράμμα, in introducing quotations); in Jos. Ant., 10, 79 of the prophecies of Jeremiah : he left them ἐν γράμμασι.

Elsewhere γράμματα is more common with an epithet : Ep. Ar., 121: τὰ Ἰουδαϊκά; Jos. Ant., 1, 5 : τὰ Ἑβραϊκὰ γράμματα or τὰ ἴδια, τὰ ἡμέτερα γράμματα; Ap., 1, 42 and 128; cf. 160. The most common formula is τὰ ἱερὰ γράμματα. The Synagogue furnished the original with its recurrent כִּתְבֵי הַקֹּדֶשׁ. We find it in Jos. Ant., 10, 210; 13, 167; 16, 168; 20, 264; Ap., 1, 54; 127; 228; Philo Praem. Poen., 79; Spec. Leg.,

---

[5] Cf. Jos. Ant., 17, 115 : γράμμασιν προησφαλισμένος of the will set out in writing. Much additional material may be found from the pap. in Preisigke Wört., *s.v.*

[6] K. Latte in Pauly-W., XIV (1930), 2032 ff. *s.v. martyria.*

[7] *V.* further Deissmann LO, 321 f.

[8] Cr.-Kö., 266.

II, 159; 238; Vit. Mos., II, 290 : τὸ τέλος τῶν ἱερῶν γραμμάτων (Dt. 34 of the Pentateuch); II, 292; Leg. Gaj., 195; Vit. Cont., 28; cf. 75 and 78.

The term ἱερὰ γράμματα passes into the usage of the early Church. Orig. has θεῖα γράμματα in Cels., IV, 9, but more often ἱερὰ γράμματα, e.g., in Cels., IV, 27; II, 4 : τὰ ἱερὰ Μωυσέως καὶ τῶν προφητικῶν γραμμάτων; VI, 18 : τὰ ἱερὰ τῶν προφητῶν γράμματα; Method. Symp., V, 1, 109 of the NT. For Orig. the OT and NT are the γράμματα θεοῦ in Princ., III, 1, 16 : πάντα ἡγεῖσθαι ἑνὸς εἶναι γράμματα θεοῦ. He often uses κατὰ τὸ γράμμα, esp. for the Law (Cels., II, 1, 386; II, 2, 387; II, 4, 390; VII, 18, 707; Comm. in Joh., XXVIII, 12, 95), but can also use it for the NT (Comm. in Joh., XIII, 8, 47). Along with τὰ νομικὰ γράμματα etc. in Cels., II, 76; II, 6 and τὰ προφητικὰ γράμματα in Cels., II, 28 we also have τὰ εὐαγγελικὰ γράμματα in Cels., I, 70 (or sing. Comm. in Joh., XXVIII, 24, 211) and τὰ γράμματα Παύλου, Cels., III, 76, 497. Together with τὰ παλαιὰ γράμματα in Cels., III, 46, 478 we may mention τὸ καινὸν γράμμα in Comm. in Joh., X, 29, 179 (opp. τὸ πρεσβύτερον). Method. likes (τὰ) θεόπνευστα γράμματα, Resurr., I, 28, 4; Symp., II, 6, 45 (of the NT).

b. Like γραφή, γράμμα can also be used with reference to "what is written in a specific place." Est. 6:2 : in the Book of Chronicles εὗρε τὰ γράμματα τὰ γραφέντα περὶ Μαρδοχαίου (כָּתוּב). Philo in Migr. Abr., 195 quotes a saying from Homer's Od. : κατὰ τὸ ποιητικὸν γράμμα; and in Leg. Gaj., 69 he refers to the γνῶθι σεαυτόν as τὸ Δελφικὸν γράμμα. Cf. Conf. Ling., 50 in a quotation from Nu. 16:15 : κατὰ τὸ Μωυσέως γράμμα; also Deus Imm., 6 (Nu. 28:2); Migr. Abr., 139 (Nu. 31:28 etc.); Rer. Div. Her., 258 : γράμμα ῥητόν of an express saying ἐν ἱεραῖς βίβλοις.

B. γράμμα in NT Usage.

1. In Lk. 23:38 א* AD it (→ 744) γράμματα are "written characters," and in Gl. 6:11 they denote "letters in the handwriting" of Paul (→ 743). [9]

2. In Jn. 7:15 linguistic par. show that the question : πῶς οὗτος γράμματα (without art.) οἶδεν μὴ μεμαθηκώς simply means: Whence hath this man learning, seeing he has never received any instruction ? (→ 762). In the context, however, the reference is to the whole διδάσκειν and διδαχή of Jesus. The examples from Test. XII on → 762, esp. Test. L. 13:2, illustrate the obvious fact that schooling and schooling in the Law are very closely related in Judaism, and even identical. Thus we need not interrupt the train of thought on the one side [10] nor deviate from the customary meaning of γράμματα εἰδέναι on the other. On the contrary, we have a parallel to Test. L. 13:2. The unity of education and instruction in the Law is in view, and the disparagement of Jesus [11] as ἀγράμματος implies that He is not fit to teach. A very different estimate of learning is found in the saying of Festus to Paul in Ac. 26:24 : τὰ πολλά σε γράμματα εἰς μανίαν περιτρέπει; the reference is to much studying or great learning, more specifically in Scripture.

3. Ac. 28:21: οὔτε γράμματα περὶ σοῦ ἐδεξάμεθα ἀπὸ τῆς Ἰουδαίας. The reference here is to "communications by letter" (→ 762). Lk. 16:6 f. : δέξαι σου

---

[9] On the debated question whether this refers to the whole letter (Hofm., Zn.), or simply to the conclusion, → γράφω (743, n. 3).

[10] Bau. J., ad loc. There is only one learning, i.e., that of the Torah. In Rabb. Judaism, there is only one discipline from the first beginnings of childish learning, i.e., the study of the Torah. This embraces all knowledge.

[11] In view of the exaggerated scorn, it is not unlikely that the education of Jesus is deliberately ignored.

τὰ γράμματα καὶ καθίσας ταχέως γράψον πεντήκοντα. This obviously refers to a bill of indebtedness (→ 763). [12]

4. Jn. 5:47: εἰ δὲ τοῖς ἐκείνου γράμμασιν οὐ πιστεύετε, πῶς τοῖς ἐμοῖς ῥήμασιν πιστεύετε; here the γράμματα are the Books of Moses or the Pentateuch (→ 763). Presupposed is the conviction of the early Church, which underlies all the Gospels (→ γραφή, 758), that the γράμματα, the authoritative Scriptures established among the Jews and accepted as Mosaic, bear witness to Christ. If the Jew does not give credence to the γράμματα, he will certainly not believe the ῥήματα of Christ. γράμμα, then, denotes a palpable authority for the Jew. If this authority, with its prophetic witness, is resisted, then the living Word of Christ will obviously be resisted. (On the interrelationship of Scripture and Word, → 762.) 2 Tm. 3:15 : ὅτι ἀπὸ βρέφους ἱερὰ γράμματα οἶδας refers to the OT as a whole (→ 763). The lack of article makes no difference in what is clearly a technical term. [13]

5. γράμμα/πνεῦμα.

There are important passages in Paul in which we see a significant antithesis between γράμμα and πνεῦμα. In R. 2:27 γράμμα is the Law as what is demonstrably written, just as περιτομή is a demonstrable sign. Neither can guarantee fulfilment of the Law. Without this doing of the Law, however, the two gifts of the older phase of revelation confer no advantage as compared with the ἔθνη. When we are told in v. 27 that the Jew διὰ γράμματος καὶ περιτομῆς is a transgressor of the Law, the διά cannot just be translated "in spite of" as though to denote an accompanying circumstance ; [14] it must also be given an instrumental significance. It is precisely through what is written and through circumcision that the Jew is a transgressor. He is to see that his true position involves possession of the γράμμα and περιτομή, but with no genuine fulfilment of the Law, since neither what is written nor circumcision leads him to action. The word γράμμα does not mean "letter" in this context. It characterises the Law in its quality of what is written or prescribed. The true meaning is "prescription of the Law" (→ 763); this goes far beyond the customary "letter" of exegetical tradition. The choice of the term is partly influenced by the similarity of sound which it has to πνεῦμα, for an impressive antithesis is thus created. In 2:29 the περιτομή καρδίας introduces a theme which dominates all the γράμμα/πνεῦμα passages in Paul. The fashioning of the καρδία afresh to obedience is the antithesis not merely to a false use of the Law but to every pre-Christian use. This renewal, however, is effected by the Spirit. In v. 28 f., where it is emphasised that this working of the Spirit on the καρδία makes the true Jew, γράμμα and περιτομή, already linked in v. 27, are brought more closely together by the use of the phrase περιτομή ἐν γράμματι for the περιτομή which is a purely legal happening, and the opposing to it of περιτομή ἐν πνεύματι. In both cases the ἐν is to be taken strictly instrumentally. [15] As the one takes place only through the Spirit, the other does so

---

[12] The δέξαι compels us (against Zn., ad loc.) to assume falsification.

[13] Without τά : ℵ CᵇD*G 33 Clem. Epiph. τά : AC*ℵ is a correction. For γράμματα or ἱερὰ γράμματα without the art., cf. Est. 6:1; Jos. Ant., 16, 168; Orig. Princ., III, 1, 16 (γράμματα θεοῦ); Method. Symp., II, 6, 45 : ἐν θεοπνεύστοις γράμμασιν; Philo Rer. Div. Her., 258 : ἐν ἱεραῖς βίβλοις. Cf. also on Philo, Dib. Past., ad loc.

[14] Ltzm. R., ad loc.

[15] With Zn. R., ad loc.

only through the γράμμα, there being merely an execution of the prescription or written Law. The opposing of σάρξ to καρδία and of ἐν τῷ φανερῷ to ἐν κρυπτῷ underlines the fact that the truly decisive invasion of the personal life is opposed to purely external prescription and the mere affecting of the physical life in terms of the sign. The antithesis is absolute in so far as the γράμμα can never accomplish what is done by the πνεῦμα. What is merely written does not have the power to produce observance. It is not even remotely suggested that the πνεῦμα might use the γράμμα to bring about this observance. The whole point of the argument (cf. R. 7 and 8) is that the Spirit alone makes possible the true circumcision and true observance which the Jew cannot achieve by his Holy Scripture. The point of the passage is perhaps alien to us. It is hampered by the ecclesiastical understanding of Scripture. But we can appreciate it once we recognise that Paul is speaking of the inadequacy of the νόμος, which is here used synonymously with γράμμα. The νόμος as here understood is that which is merely written in contrast to the πνεῦμα.

R. 7:6 makes it particularly plain that in its character as γράμμα, as a Law which does not rule in the καρδία, the νόμος cannot accomplish δουλεύειν in relation to God. Here again we have confirmation of the fact that when Paul speaks of the Law he always raises the question how there may be fulfilment of the will of God. If the present passage teaches that we are now dead to the Law, the continuation shows that this means our death to the character of the Law as γράμμα, to its quality as what is merely written. This character belongs to what is past (→ παλαιότης); it is done away. Only in the being of the Spirit can the goal of δουλεύειν be attained. Without Christ and the Spirit what is written is absolutely ineffective. The question again arises whether there is not a γράμμα sustained by the Spirit. Do Scripture and Spirit stand in unconditional antithesis? Paul's view of γραφή has to be taken into account in this connection. His expositions, however, are no less difficult than all that he says concerning the Law to which we are dead but which is still holy. There can certainly be no doubt that Scripture as what is merely written has no power to give new life. Behind these deliberations concerning the "past being of the Bible" [16] (παλαιότης γράμματος) stands his experience of the futility of the religion of the Synagogue, for all its emphasis on Scripture, in virtue of its inability to press on to the service of God (cf. Jn. 5:39-47, where this is equated with its failure to press on to Christ).

The most comprehensive discussion of this question is found in 2 C. 3:6 f., where γράμμα is linked with παλαιὰ διαθήκη. The statements concerning Scripture and Judaism in vv. 12-18, and especially vv. 14-16, are particularly valuable in our attempt to see the relationship of the γράμμα/πνεῦμα antithesis to the total Pauline view of Scripture. The gen. of quality γράμματος and πνεύματος in 3:6 are closely related to καινὴ διαθήκη. The new covenant is not characterised by what is merely written and prescribed, but by the Spirit. The use of the term shows us that the whole antithesis γράμμα/πνεῦμα in Paul derives from his understanding of 'Ιερ. 38:33 (31:33). For Paul, therefore, the nature of the new covenant lies in the fact that this διδοὺς δώσω νόμους μου (Mas. sing.) εἰς τὴν διάνοιαν αὐτῶν καὶ ἐπὶ καρδίας αὐτῶν γράψω αὐτούς is now fulfilled. There is no stronger argument for the interrelating of νόμος and γράμμα than the fact that in 'Ιερ. 38:33 what Paul in his exposition always calls γράμμα is the plur.

---

[16] Schl. Erl., ad loc.

νόμοι, but the new activity of God is described as His inscribing on the heart. If, then, the apostle goes on to say that the γράμμα kills, this is to be compared with what he elsewhere says concerning the νόμος. Thus in R. 7:9 f. he argues that in virtue of its character as ἐντολή the νόμος brings sin and death to fruition. The meaning in the present passage is exactly the same. The killing is a consequence of the fact that this Law is only what is written or prescribed (= ἐντολή). Neither here nor in R. 7 can this killing be attributed only to a false use of the Bible or the Law. As always when Paul speaks radically of the negative operation of the Law, he is thinking in terms of the divine purpose. The disposing of God is with a view to the exercise of judgment by Scripture as Law. What is merely written or prescribed can only kill. The Spirit alone can make alive and not Scripture. The new covenant, however, is wholly determined by the Spirit.

In 2 C. 3:7: εἰ δὲ ἡ διακονία τοῦ θανάτου ἐν γράμμασιν ἐντετυπωμένη λίθοις, [17] the plur. γράμματα undoubtedly means inscribed on stones in the form of letters (→ 761). The reference is to the tables of the Law. The verse does not conflict, however, with our previous findings. If the old is described in the sing., it does not imply that only the "letter" is meant. The letters of the tables of the Law bear eloquent witness to the fact that the νόμος is only what is written. To translate "letter" is to miss the deep seriousness of what is said. The sing., strengthened by the plur., introduces an antithesis which embraces what is written as such. Paul is not merely saying that Judaism has a literal exposition of Scripture, though this would be correct enough in fact. [18] He is claiming that the whole of the older phase of revelation is not yet determined by Christ and the Spirit. Nevertheless, there is a glory even in this ministry of death engraven in letters of stone.

To translate γράμμα as "letter" is to foster an idealistic interpretation of Paul's argument. Any suggestion is to be rejected which would have it that the spirit of Scripture is here opposed to its letter, or its true or richer sense to the somatic body. The Alexandrians rightly perceived that in 2 C. 3 the reference is to the νομικὸν γράμμα. [19] But their whole conception of Scripture depended upon an opposition of the νοητὴ ἐκδοχὴ to the αἰσθητὴ ἐκδοχὴ τῶν θείων γραμμάτων. [20]

A related conception, no less incongruent with Paul, dominates the Platonic statements which would have it that what is written is an inadequate means to express spiritual insights. Here the problem is that of the interrelation of what is written to intellectual truth as the perception of the soul. [21]

That the solemn antithesis γράμμα/πνεῦμα does not refer merely to a false use of Scripture may be seen particularly clearly from 2 C. 3:14-16. For it is only here that consideration is given to the Jewish use, which is characterised by the

---

[17] Following Ex. 36:39 LXX: καὶ ἔγραψεν ἐπ᾽ αὐτοῦ γράμματα ἐντετυπωμένα (→ 762).
[18] Cf. on this pt. Gelas. Symp., IX, 1, 235.
[19] Orig. Cels., VII, 20, 708 f. Theophylact. Expos. in 2 C. 4:6 (MPG, 124, 829a) also speaks at this pt. of the working of the Law.
[20] Orig. Cels., VI, 70 (p. 140, 16 ff.); cf. Thdrt. Hist. Eccl., IV, 29, 4 of Didymus: τῆς θείας γραφῆς μεμάθηκεν οὐ μόνον τὰ γράμματα, ἀλλὰ καὶ τὰ τούτων νοήματα. We often find in Orig. the antithesis κατὰ τὸ γράμμα / κατὰ τὸ πνεῦμα: Comm. in Joh., XIII, 10, 61; 49, 325; XX, 3, 10; cf. X, 26, 161: οἱ ἐπὶ τοῦ γράμματος ἱστάμενοι pay attention to σωματικὸν μόνον.
[21] Plat. Phaedr., 276a; Ep., 7, 341, esp. d. That the antithesis wholly concerns understanding, and that it is a question of the distinction between γράφειν and ἐκμανθάνειν, is shown especially by Ep., 2, 314bc.

fact that the twofold veil, i.e., on Scripture and on the heart, conceals the truth in Christ. This is a consequence of the present obstinacy of the Jews (v. 14). It is not said that this use alone is characterised by γράμμα. This is true of the older revelation of Law in general.

6. γράμμα/γραφή.

In sum, it may be said that the antithesis is not directed absolutely against γραφή as such. We have seen that Paul affirms the lasting significance of Scripture and he does not intend in any way to weaken its authority. As for him the νόμος is ἅγιος (R. 7:12), so, too, is γραφή. Whatever he may say concerning the inferiority of the Law does not affect its divine nature. Similarly, whatever he may say about the supersession of the γράμμα does not dispute its value as revelation. It is plain that Paul does not use γράμμα as a title for Scripture in the same way as he uses γραφή. He uses it rather to characterise the Law. γράμμα is not used when he speaks of the positive and lasting significance of Scripture. This positive task is always stated in terms of γραφή. When the reference is to γράμμα, Paul is always thinking of the legal authority which has been replaced. The relationship between γραφή and γράμμα in Paul is thus to be stated as follows. γράμμα represents the legal authority which has been superseded, while γραφή is linked with the new form of authority determined by the fulfilment in Christ and by His Spirit, the determinative character of the new no longer being what is written and prescribed. The word which is near (R. 10:8) is not the γράμμα but Scripture, which is self-attesting through the Spirit of Christ. To this extent we can say that Paul is contending against a religion of the book. [22] Mere concentration on the book is set aside. This does not mean, however, that we have a "purely Marcionite antithesis." [23] The *diversitas instrumentorum* is not meant in such a way that the supersession of the γράμμα involves that of the γραφή. On the contrary, the latter becomes an authority regulated by Christ and His Spirit. In particular, there does not develop out of the *diversitas instrumentorum* a *diversitas deorum* as in the case of Marcion. What we can say, however, is that these discussions imply that the external writing is not to be described as the distinctive mark of the revelation of the new covenant (→ γράφειν, 745). This does not live only by what is written. For the Church's use of Scripture there is the solid norm that all legal use kills, even though it is use of the NT. It may be questioned, however, whether Paul would have formulated it in this way, since the καινὴ διαθήκη of his time had not yet been committed to written records. [24] His basic position has reference finally to the Law.

The Pauline antithesis is in no sense parallel to the Greek distinction between written law and νόμος ἄγραφος. [25] Here it is a matter of the relationship of written law to the law of nature and reason. When Sophocles [26] speaks of ἄγραπτα κἀσφαλῆ θεῶν νόμιμα, he has in view the distinction between transgression of the written law and protection by the unwritten law of the gods. In Paul, however, we have something unwritten, i.e., the Spirit, giving power to fulfil the innermost intentions of what is

---

22 Harnack, *D. AT,* 141; Wnd. 2 K., 111.
23 Wnd. 2 K., 110.
24 Wnd. 2 K., *ad loc.*
25 R. Hirzel, Νόμος ἄγραφος, *op. cit.*; Wnd. 2 K., 111 f.
26 Soph. Ant., 450 ff., esp. 454.

written. Acc. to Hippias of Elis, [27] the ἄγραφος νόμος, which represents what is universally valid, e.g., worship of the gods, the honouring of parents, upbringing of children etc., is in agreement with φύσις, while positive law is a τύραννος [28] compelling men to do many things which are against nature. In both Plato [29] and Philo [30] the antithesis is between natural law and written political law. The πνεῦμα of Paul, however, is a miraculous power which has nothing whatever to do with these considerations of natural law.

† ἐγγράφω.

1. On Lk. 10:20.

ἐγγράφειν is not merely used a. of "writing in a letter or petition": Thuc., I, 128; Jos. Ant., 11, 271; P. Oxy., 237, 5, 14 (2nd cent. A.D.): τὰ τῷ βιβλιδίῳ ἐνγεγραμμένα, the "contents of a petition", but also b. of solemn "entry in a document." Thus in Jos. Ant., 17, 226 Archelaus is mentioned as king in his father's will, ἐγγεγραμμένος βασιλεύς; in Bell., 1, 625 Antipater is named as successor; in Philo Spec. Leg., III, 72 the word is used of a marriage contract; in Polyb., III, 21, 4 ἔγγραφον means written in a peace treaty; Polyb., III, 24, 6 εἰρήνη ἔγγραπτος; III, 25, 3 etc. συμμαχία ἔγγραπτος, always with the sense of something firmly laid down in a written compact. This use, which emphasises the element of documentation, leads to the sense of "to prosecute" in penal law: Aristoph. Pax, 1180; Demosth., 37, 24. Also determined by penal law is the image or matter in Jer. 17:13 א c.a.: ἀπὸ τῆς γῆς ἐγγραφέτωσαν (AB א al) (כָּתַב niph); cf. also Ps. 149:9: κρίμα ἔγγραπτον; Ep. Ar., 110. c. Also deserving of notice is the popular use of ἐγγράφειν for "to inscribe in a list, an inventory, or a public register": P. Hal., 1, 247 (3rd cent. B.C.); Isaeus, 7, 1; Ditt. Syll.³, 921, 97: ἐγγράφειν ἐς τὰ κοινὰ γραμματεῖα; Demosth., 18, 261: εἰς τοὺς δημότας; Ps.-Plat. Ax., 366e: εἰς τοὺς ἐφήβους; Ditt. Syll.³, 736, 163: εἰς τοὺς πολεμάρχους. Related, though rather more generally, is Jos. Ant., 16, 225: through circumcision ἐγγραφῆναι τοῖς τῶν Ἰουδαίων ἔθεσι; 1 Macc. 13:40: to be enrolled in the bodyguard. Philo makes extraordinarily heavy use of the image of being inscribed on the list of citizens (non-figur. in Omn. Prob. Lib., 7); he metaphorically applies the ἐγγράφεσθαι τῷ πολιτεύματι or τῇ πολιτείᾳ, πόλει, πατρίδι to the civic list of virtue: Conf. Ling., 109; Op. Mund., 143; Gig., 61; Leg. All., III, 244; Vit. Mos., I, 157, etc. This type of expression is quite essential to an understanding of Lk. 10:20. Here, however, the well-known image from civic life is combined with the biblical conception of inscription in a book, for d. in the LXX, Jos., and Philo ἐγγράφειν is used quite simply for the "inscribing of divine words in the Bible": 3 Βασ. 22:46; 2 Ch. 34:31 A; Ἰερ. 28:60 A; Jos. Ant., 10, 35; 12, 89; Philo Det. Pot. Ins., 139; in a free rationalisation, Leg. All., I, 19: the figures inscribed in the book of divine reason. On the other hand, it is not this sacred book which is in view in Lk. 10:20, but e. the "book of life" (→ βιβλίον, 619). Da. LXX, 12, 1: ἐγγεγραμμένος ἐν τῷ βιβλίῳ (כָּתַב kal), cf. Ez. 13:9, the book in which God writes His people. [1]

---

27 Xenoph. Mem., IV, 4, 19; Plato Prot., 337c.
28 For tyrants as the originators of written laws: Plat. Leg., IV, 722e: τυραννικὸν ἐπίταγμα; Seneca Ep., 90, 3 ff.; cf. further Wnd. 2 K., 111.
29 Plat. Gorg., 484a.
30 Philo Abr., 5: τὰ τεθειμένα διατάγματα τῆς φύσεως οὐκ ἀπάδει; 60: Abraham follows not merely God's verbal and written commands, but also φύσις; 275: he observes the Law, not merely as taught by Scripture, but ἀγράφῳ τῇ φύσει. Philo conceives of laws as additions τοῦ τῆς φύσεως ὀρθοῦ λόγου: Jos., 31; cf. Spec. Leg., I, 31.
ἐ γ γ ρ ά φ ω. 1 Cf. Herm. v., 1, 3, 2. Elsewhere Herm. has ἐγγράφειν εἰς ἀριθμόν; v. Pr.-Bauer.

When, therefore, the Lord says to the returning 70 disciples in Lk. 10:20 : χαίρετε δὲ ὅτι τὰ ὀνόματα ὑμῶν ἐγγέγραπται² ἐν τοῖς οὐρανοῖς, we have a particularly solemn image which carries with it the thought of the ancient custom of inscribing in a list of citizens, but which is also linked with the idea of the book of life. The meaning is that by ὄνομα, i.e., as persons of individual worth, those who belong to Jesus are God's inalienable possession and citizens of the heavenly πολιτεία. The opposite is stated in ᾿Ιερ. 17:13 as follows : πάντες οἱ καταλιπόντες σε καταισχυνθήτωσαν, ἀφεστηκότες ἐπὶ τῆς γῆς γραφέτωσαν.³

2. When Paul in 2 C. 3:2 f. describes the Corinthians as a letter inscribed on his heart : ἐπιστολή, ἐγγεγραμμένη ἐν ταῖς καρδίαις ἡμῶν, ἐγγεγραμμένη οὐ μέλανι ἀλλὰ πνεύματι θεοῦ ζῶντος, οὐκ ἐν πλαξὶν λιθίναις ἀλλ᾿ ἐν πλαξὶν καρδίαις σαρκίναις, the word ἐγγράφω is used in the sense of "engrave," which is the original meaning of γράφω, γραφή, γράμμα.

Thus ἐγγράφειν can often be used for "inscribing on a tablet" : Soph. Trach., 157; Jos. Ant., 3, 101 (cf. 8, 104); Epict. Diss., III, 16, 9. Hence Lys., 30, 2 : ἐγγράφειν νόμους, "to codify." Or of "inscribing on pillars" : Hdt., II, 102; Ditt. Syll.³, 966, 38; Philo Spec. Leg., III, 36; Jos. Ant., 1, 70. Hence ἐγγράφεσθαι as the public "posting up of an edict" : ibid., 19, 291. Cf. also inscription on the altar in Jos. Ant., 4, 308; on the crown in 11, 331; on the breastplate in Ex. 36:21 (39:14) B; Jos. Ant., 3, 166.

The Pauline expression "to inscribe on the heart" etc. is widespread in the ancient world. Cf. already Aesch. Prom., 789 : ἣν ἐγγράφου σὺ μνήμοσιν δέλτοις φρενῶν; Xenoph. Cyr., III, 3, 52 : μέλλουσι ... διάνοιαι ἐγγραφήσεσθαι ἀνθρώποις. The ἐν στήθει ὀστέων ἐγγέγραπται ἐνώπιον Κυρίου in Test. Jud. 20:4 β AS¹ has basically the same meaning (cf. Jos. Ant., 4, 213 : on the forehead and arm); Jos. Ant., 4, 210 : ταῖς ψυχαῖς ἐγγραφέντας, of impressing laws on the soul. According to Philo Spec. Leg., 106 the soul of a woman who has had sexual intercourse with a man is no longer adapted like wax to receive τῶν ἐγγραφησομένων δογμάτων. The simple γράφειν is used for "to inscribe in the heart or soul" in Soph. Phil., 1325; Philo Rer. Div. Her., 294 (in the soul of the new-born child, which is like wax); Op. Mund., 78 (the impressions of the heavenly music of the spheres in the soul).

In 2 C. 3:2 f., however, Paul is building on the expression in ᾿Ιερ. 38:33 : ἐπὶ καρδίας γράψω and Prv. 3:3 A : γράψον (7:3 : ἐπίγραψον) δὲ αὐτὰς ἐπὶ τὸ πλάτος τῆς καρδίας σου, except that in the LXX we do not find ἐγγράφειν either in these or any of the passages which exerted a formal and material influence on 2 C. 3:2 f.: Ex. 24:12; 31:18; 34:1 (the γράφειν on the tables of stone) and Ez. 11:19; 36:26 (the influencing of the heart).

† προγράφω.

1. Eph. 3:3 : καθὼς προέγραψα, "as I have written above, in the same writing." This usage for something already mentioned is very common. Hence προγραφή can be used for the heading of a work intimating and preceding the contents : Polyb., XI, 1 ff.;¹ in Da. LXX 3:3, 87 Syr. the οἱ προγεγραμμένοι are "the persons already mentioned," as in P. Amh., 42, 10 (2nd cent. B.C.) sing. The word is often used in this sense in the pap. and inscr. : BGU, 1131, 55 (1st cent. B.C.); P. Petr., III, 104, 11 (3rd cent. B.C.); τὰ προγεγραμμένα : P. Oxy., I, 79, 17 (2nd cent. A.D.); P. Lips., 26,

---

² ἐγγέγραπται is found in ℵ BLX ; ἐνεγράφη, 157; ἐγράφη (Blass) is secondary ; cf. Zn. Lk.
³ Cr.-Kö. draws attention at this pt. to γράφειν εἰς ὕδωρ or ἐν ὕδατι : Plat. Phaedr., 276c; Luc. Tyr., 21 (καθ᾿ ὕδατος).
π ρ ο γ ρ ά φ ω. ¹ Preisigke Wört.; APF, III, 504; Mitteis-Wilcken, I, 2, 540.

13, 14 (4th cent. A.D.). κατὰ τὰ προγεγραμμένα is often used to introduce quotations: P. Petr., III, 179 (3rd cent. B.C.); BGU, 1107, 30 (1st cent. B.C.). Sometimes we have καθότι προγέγραπται: P. Tebt., 104, 38 (1st cent. B.C.); BGU, 189 (7 A.D.). [2]

2. R. 15:4: ὅσα γὰρ προεγράφη, εἰς τὴν ἡμετέραν διδασκαλίαν ἐγράφη; here the reference is to "things previously written," i.e., in times past.

Cf. P. Oxy., 291, 7 (1st cent. A.D.): προέγραψά σοι, "I have written you once before"; P. Hal., 7, 3 (3rd cent. B.C.): τὸν δεῖνα κομίζοντα τὰ προγεγραμμένα, "of which I wrote before."

3. Gl. 3:1: οἷς κατ' ὀφθαλμοὺς Ἰησοῦς Χριστὸς προεγράφη. There are here two possibilities. a. We can take προγράφειν as "public promulgation." [3] It is often used for published placards and notices.

Aristoph. Av., 450: ἐν τοῖς πινακίοις. Plut. Demetr., 46 (I, 912b), where a soldier writes the beginning of Oed. Col. on the tent of Demetr. Plut. Pyth. Orac., 29 (II, 408e); Epict. Diss., III, 1, 28 f.; 24, 80, of the posting of an advertisement referring to an object of interest. For the publication of a notice, cf. BGU, 1046, II, 17 (2nd cent. A.D.); IG, X, 4, 24; for summoning by such: Plut. Camill., 11 (I, 134 f.); P. Amh., 135, 12 (2nd cent. A.D.); for following up with a warrant: P. Tebt., II, 411, 8 (2nd cent. A.D.). Cf. the use of πρόγραμμα for "edict," "decree," "official notice," "proclamation" or "governmental order": Jos. Ant., 10, 254; 12, 145; Vit., 370. [4]

b. The second possibility is the usually adopted rendering "to depict before your eyes," in the sense of making the image of the Crucified as vividly as possible (κατ' ὀφθαλμούς) the object of this proclamation. Linguistically this is possible, but the fact remains that the word is never attested in this sense, though γράφειν (→ 743) is often used for "to draw" or "to paint." Furthermore, there is nothing in Paul to suggest that in his proclamation of the cross he gave centrality to a heart-rending depiction in the sense of later homiletical and lyrical understanding and practice. Is it likely, then, that his missionary preaching would differ from the κήρυγμα of the word of the cross in the epistles, which is certainly important and central, which undoubtedly extols the saving act of God, but which never even attempts to impress by physical depiction?

Evaluation of the meaning of προγράφειν thus brings into focus the distinction between the Pauline proclamation of the act of salvation and the later ecclesiastical understanding of depiction after the influential manner of the *salve caput cruentatum* of Arnulf von Löwen. The linguistic findings themselves compel us to adopt the surest translation: "Before whose eyes Jesus Christ has been set as the Crucified like a posted proclamation." In this sense the saying helps us to understand the missionary preaching of Paul as solemn announcement by divine commission, which is comparable to an edict.

4. Jd. 4: οἱ πάλαι προγεγραμμένοι εἰς τοῦτο τὸ κρίμα.

This corresponds to a usage found in Polyb., 32, 5, 12; cf. 6, 1, where προγράφειν has the sense of the publication of lists of influential people who are proscribed. The προγεγραμμένοι of 6, 1 are *proscripti* or outlaws, cf. Luc. Tim., 51: προὐγράφην ἐν τῷ καταλόγῳ, "I was put on the list." To fill out the picture we should also note the

---

[2] Cf. further Moult.-Mill.; for the post-apost. fathers, v. Pr.-Bauer.
[3] Lightfoot Gl., *ad loc.*; F. Field, *Notes on the Translation of the New Testament* (1899), 189; Moult.-Mill. on προγράφειν.
[4] Cf. further Preisigke Wört., Moult.-Mill.

sense of "to enlist," e.g., in the army of the king : 1 Macc. 10:36, or "to appoint" : ἡ προγεγραμμένη ἡμέρα, "the appointed day," Jos. Ant., 11, 283; τὸ προγεγραμμένον κεφάλαιον, "the appointed ransom," Ant., 12, 30 (cf. 12, 33).

It is thus indisputable that the reference in Jd. 4 is to the divine appointment of false teachers to judgment, though with no suggestion of eternal reprobation. [5] They are "long since" appointed εἰς τοῦτο τὸ κρίμα, and are thus entered as proscribed offenders [6] in the judgment book of God (→ βιβλίον, 620). When this entry took place, however, is not stated.

† ὑπογραμμός (ὑπογράφω).

ὑπογραμμός is very rare. Thus it is not found in Polyb., Diod. S., Joseph., Philo, Epict. or the pap. Is it attested only in "biblical and post-Christian Greek" ? [1] The earliest known instance is certainly in 2 Macc. 2:28, where the epitomist says that he will leave the minuter detail to the author and simply give an abridgment of the books of Jason. This abridgment, however, will deserve the name of ὑπογραμμοί : τὸ δὲ ἐπιπορεύεσθαι τοῖς ὑπογραμμοῖς τῆς ἐπιτομῆς διαπονοῦντες. There is little doubt that what is in mind is a model or example, as more clearly in Cl. Al. Strom., V, 8, 49, 1, where for the purposes of instruction a word is proposed (several examples are given) which contains all the letters of the alphabet in a form in which children can remember them, so that a model is given which is called ὑπογραμμὸς παιδικός.

a. To this there corresponds the use of ὑπογράφειν as an academic expression. In Plat. Prot., 326d : ὑπογράψαντες γραμμὰς τῇ γραφίδι, is used for the drawing of lines by the elementary teacher in order to guide children who are learning to write. Along the same lines is the figur. use by Origen when in Orat., 18, 1 he says of the Lord's Prayer : τὴν ὑπογραφεῖσαν ὑπὸ τοῦ κυρίου προσευχήν. It is the model prayer, the example of instruction in prayer. [2] Thus ὑπογράφειν comes to mean rather more generally "to give an example." Acc. to Plat. Leg., IV, 711b the tyrant should win influence over the citizens in this way : αὐτὸν πρῶτον πάντα ὑπογράφοντα τῷ πράττειν.

b. From the original pedagogic sense we can trace the common use of the term in Diod. S., Polyb. and Philo for "to show," [3] "to describe," "to represent," "to depict," "to denote," "to signify," "to set in view," "to ascribe." In Philo Spec. Leg., I, 65 ὑπογράφει is used of Moses, who "indicates" in his description ; in Polyb., II, 14, 3 it is used of describing the distinctive features of the land ; in Polyb., III, 47, 9; Philo Leg. All., I, 21 and 56; II, 6; Op. Mund., 67 of depicting or representing. Hence ὑπογραφή for "description" in Polyb., V, 21, 7. The sense of "to denote" is found in Philo Deus Imm., 95; of "to signify" in Jos., 92; Conf. Ling., 67; of "to set in view" in Conf. Ling., 166; of "to ascribe something to someone" in Gig., 66; cf. Deus Imm., 70. c. It can also take on the sense of "to demand," as in 1 Macc. 8:25, 27; 3 Macc. 6:41. Again, d. it can have the sense of "dazzling," cf. Diod. S., XIX, 46, 3; Polyb., V, 62, 1; Jos. Ant., 13, 399; Bell., 6, 287, usually in respect of disappointed hopes. Related is its use in Philo

---

[5] Calvin, ad loc. : aeternum Dei consilium.

[6] 𝔅g : qui olim praescripti sunt in hoc iudicium. It might equally well have been rendered proscripti.

ὑπογραμμός. Defin. Ps.-Ammon. Adfin. Vocab. Diff., 134 (Valckenaer): ὑπογραμμὸν ἀντὶ τοῦ προγραμμόν. Hesych.: = τύπος, μίμημα. Schol. in Aristoph. Ra., 874, where it is used synon. with προγραμμός.

[1] Cr.-Kö., 268.

[2] Cf. Eus. Hist. Eccl., VIII, 10, 2 where with ὑποδείγματα ("examples") we have ὑπογραμμοί ("models") and καλὰ γνωρίσματα, ("marks"). They are laid down in Holy Scripture.

[3] Cf. Suid. ὑπογράφεται : δείκνυται. He quotes Diod. S., XIX, 46, 3.

Vit. Mos., I, 69 for "counting on something." e. ὑπογραφή can also be used for painting e.g., under the eyes in the case of women trying to adorn themselves : Jos. Bell., 4, 561; Philo Leg. All., III, 62, where there is a close approximation to the first sense. f. It can even be used for literary reference and official protocol, i.e., "that which follows or is written below" in Polyb., III, 22, 3; 1 Esr. 2:5, 25; 2 Macc. 9:18; 3 Macc. 6:41; Jos. Ant., 12, 57 and 258; and therefore quite often for "subscribing," [4] as in P. Oxy., 136, 10 (6th cent. A.D.), though this is a somewhat remote development.

In 1 Pt. 2:21: ὑμῖν ὑπολιμπάνων ὑπογραμμὸν ἵνα ἐπακολουθήσητε τοῖς ἴχνεσιν αὐτοῦ, the reference is to Christian slaves. They are told that Christ in His suffering has left footprints which we must takes as models or examples in the way that the scholar follows the guiding lines of his teacher. This does not mean that there is to be a copying or *imitatio* of Christ. The point is that we must accept the vocation of suffering laid down for the community by the passion of its true and legitimate Lord. The ὑπογραμμός does, however, express commitment to the lines (steps) traced out by Him.

The further development of ὑπογραμμός in the early Church is closely linked with this passage. Thus Pol. Phil., 8, 2; 1 Cl., 16, 17; 33, 8 make a similar statement about Christ and 1 Cl., 5, 7 about Paul. Cl. Al. Paed., I, 9, 84, 2 explains Ez. 34 in terms of the thought that God as the true παιδαγωγός has given the πρεσβύτεροι a model in His saving concern for the sheep. Along the lines of Christ as example we may also mention Mac. Hom., 19, 2 (MPG, 34, 64b); Custodia Cordis, *ibid.*, 837a; Joh. Damasc. Hom. in Sabb. Sanct., 24 (MPG, 96, 624a); Fid. Orthod., III, 1 (MPG, 94, 984c). The word is linked with Dion. Areop. in Mich. Syncellus, Vita Dion. Areopag. (MPG, 4, 632d).

Worth noting is the constant interrelating of ὑπογραμμός and → τύπος. [5] In Eus. Dem. Ev., IV, 16, 55 the term seems to be synon. for the typological significance of the OT cultus. Ps.-Athan. Hom. in S. Patr. et Proph., 8 (MPG, 28, 1072a), in accordance with his symbolical conception of the Lord's Supper, conceives of the Eucharist as an action εἰς ὑπογραμμόν. Joh. Damasc. Fid. Orthod., III, 18 (MPG, 94, 1076) says of the Son that He is τύπος and ὑπογραμμός. The same words are used in Rhet. Graeci (ed. C. Walz), I (1832), 643, 27. There is a similar use of ὑπογραμμός with σκιογράφοι in Eustathius De oboedientia magistratui christ. debita, 18, 1 and 24 (MPG, 136, 313, 317). There is thus no doubt as to the sense of "example" or "model."

Schrenk

γρηγορέω → ἐγείρω.

γυμνός, γυμνότης, γυμνάζω, γυμνασία

---

† γυμνός.

Attested since Hom.; common in the LXX : Gn. 3:7; Job 1:21 etc.; a favourite word of Philo.

1. "Naked" in the strict sense. a. "Unclothed," Anth. Pal., X, 58 (Pallades): γῆς ἐπέβην γυμνός, γυμνός θ' ὑπὸ γαῖαν ἄπειμι· | καὶ τί μάτην μοχθῶ, γυμνὸν ὁρῶν τὸ τέλος. In the NT : Mk. 14:51, 52. b. "Badly clothed" : BGU, 846, 9 (2nd cent.

---

[4] Preisigke Wört.; Fachw., 175 f. On ὑπογραφή as the completion of a document by subscription, cf. Mitteis-Wilcken, II, 1, 56.

[5] Cf. Hesych. (→ 772, n.).

A.D.): (the lost son to his mother) αἴγραψά σοι ὅτι γυμνός εἰμει. Tob. 1:17; 4:16; Job 22:6; Is. 58:7. In the NT: Mt. 25:36, 38, 43, 44; Jm. 2:15. c. "Unclothed or stripped by force": P. Fay., 12, 20 (c. 103 B.C.): ἐξέντες γυμνόν 2 Ch. 28:15. In the NT: Ac. 19:16; Rev. 17:16. d. "Without an upper garment," "not fully clothed": Aristoph. Nu., 498; P. Magd., 6, 7 (3rd cent. B.C.); Is. 20:2. In the NT: Jn. 21:7 (→ n. 6).

2. Naked in the Figurative Sense.

a. "Unconcealed," "disclosed," "manifest": Diod. S., I, 76: γυμνῶν τῶν πραγμάτων θεωρουμένων; Philo Migr. Abr., 192: γυμνά ... τὰ ὄντα ὁρᾶν. In the NT: Hb. 4:13: πάντα γυμνὰ καὶ τετραχηλισμένα τοῖς ὀφθαλμοῖς αὐτοῦ.

b. "Without bodily form": Hadrian at death addressed his *animula nudula*:[1] ἡ ψυχὴ γυμνὴ τοῦ σώματος, Plat. Crat., 403b; γυμνὸς καὶ ἀσώματος (to salvation), Philo Leg. All., II, 59; Porphyr. Abst., I, 31: the soul must fight naked like the boxer. In the NT, 1 C. 15:37 ff.: The contrast between the γυμνὸς κόκκος and the plant which it receives as a body on dying illustrates the glory of the resurrection body in comparison with the earthly. The detailed exposition of the image is difficult, not merely because of our different scientific understanding, but because the naked seed represents both the body which is buried and also the bearer of individuality, i.e. the soul in the current and not the Pauline sense. Nevertheless, the comparison is both meaningful and illuminating. In 2 C. 5:3 we should accept the reading: εἴ γε[2] καὶ ἐνδυσάμενοι[3] οὐ γυμνοὶ εὑρεθησόμεθα. It is arguable whether what Paul wishes to avoid is the temporary loss of the body by believers prior to the *parousia*[4] or the final destiny of unbelievers for whom there will be no heavenly body.[5] It is hardly conceivable that Paul should have thought of the intervening state as one of dreadful nakedness, cf. Phil. 1:23 (σὺν Χριστῷ εἶναι).[6] On the other hand, the damned were often thought of as naked. Thus in the Samaritan liturgy for the eve of the Day of Atonement the *goyim* will be raised naked, whereas the righteous will rise again with the clothes (?) in which they were buried (יְקוּמוּ בְּסַבְלוֹתָם דְּבוֹן הָיוּ מִקְבָּרִי).[7] It thus seems that there is little

---

γ υ μ ν ό ς. [1] Deissmann LO, 249, 1.

[2] BDG: εἴπερ.

[3] D*G it Mcion, Chrys.: ἐκδυσάμενοι, in correction of the apparent tautology.

[4] For current exposition, cf. the NT theologies of H. J. Holtzmann and P. Feine; cf. also E. Kühl, *Über 2 K. 5:1-10* (1904); H. E. Weber, *"Eschatologie" und "Mystik"* (1930), 88. → βαρέω, 559.

[5] Wnd. 2 K.; on rather different but better grounds, W. Mundle, *Jülicherfestschrift* (1927), 93-109, esp. 101. → ἐκ-, ἐν-, ἐπενδύω.

[6] Wnd. 2 K. recalls the cultic horror of nakedness, e.g., in Ex. 20:26; Jn. 21:7; Rev. 3:18; 16:15; Jos. Bell., 2, 148; T. Ber., II, 14 and 15 (*Angelos,* 3 [1930], 159 f.); cf. also the ordinances for the *flamen dialis* in Gell., X, 15, 20; Plut. Aet. Rom., 40 (II, 274a ff.). J. Heckenbach, *"De nuditate sacra,"* RVV, 9, 3 (1911), 1 ff., 55 f.

[7] A. Merx, *Der Messias oder Ta'eb der Samaritaner* (1909), 15, 13. Ištar puts off an article of clothing at each gate of hell and appears naked before the queen of hell. On her ascent she resumes the garment. There would be a fine illustration of the shrinking of the apostle on a Gnostic fresco in Rome (the catacomb on the Viale Manzoni) if only we could be sure that the three naked figures before the weaver's loom were among the damned. Wilpert, however, thinks of those who are naked in the sense of Mt. 25:36, while Bendinelli is reminded of a scene in the Odyssey. Cf. J. Wilpert, *Atti della pontificia academia Romana di archeologia* (Ser. III, 1, 2 [1924]), 26-30, Plate 16, the best reproduction; G. Bendinelli, *Notizie degli scavi,* 17 (1920), 135; O. Marucchi, *Nuovo bullettino di archeologia christiana,* 27 (1921), 44-47; J. Sauer, *Neues Licht auf dem Gebiet der christlichen Archäologie* (1925), 31 ff. On the idea of the clothing of souls in general, cf. the source material and bibl. in F. Cumont, *Orient. Relig.*[3] (1931), 290 f. Cf. also Ltzm. 2 K., *ad loc.*

place in 2 C. 5:3 for any thought of the intervening state. The second explanation is right. [8]

c. "Without the preparedness of the inner man." Philo knows a nakedness of the soul which is to perdition as well as one which is to salvation (Leg. All., II, 60 : γυμνὸς ἀρετῆς; cf. Leg. All., III, 55). In the NT : Rev. 3:17; 16:15.

† γυμνότης.

Rare in secular Gk. In the good sense, M. Ant., 11, 27 syn. : τάξις, καθαρότης, οὐδὲν γὰρ προκάλυμμα ἄστρου; Philo Leg. All., II, 59 : γυμνότης ψυχική; on the other hand cf. Ps.-Dion. Hal. Art. Rhet., X, 6 (II, p. 363, 9 f., Usener): γυμνότης τῶν προτάσεων = the poverty of assertions. Not found in Joseph., and in the LXX only Dt. 28:48 A.

In the NT : "nakedness," "emptiness," "poverty" (R. 8:35; 2 C. 11:27; figur. in Rev. 3:18 : ἡ αἰσχύνη τῆς γυμνότητός σου (→ γυμνός, supra).

† γυμνάζω.

"To exercise naked." Ps.-Isoc. Demon., 21: γύμναζε σεαυτὸν πόνοις ἑκουσίοις; Jos. Ant., 6, 185 : David οὐκ ἐγεγύμναστο; cf. 16, 400; Bell., 3, 73; 2 Macc. 10:15 : Ἰδουμαῖοι ... ἐγύμναζον τοὺς Ἰουδαίους (kept them occupied); figur. Ditt. Syll.[3], 578, 29 (2nd cent. B.C.): ὅπως δὲ ἐπιμελῶς ἐν τοῖς μαθήμασιν γυμνάζωνται οἱ παῖδες; Gern. Epict. Diss., I, 26, 3 : πρῶτον οὖν ἐπὶ τῆς θεωρίας γυμνάζουσιν ἡμᾶς οἱ φιλόσοφοι; II, 18, 27: οὗτός ἐστιν ὁ παῖς ἀληθείαις ἀσκητὴς ὁ πρὸς τὰς τοιαύτας φαντασίας γυμνάζων ἑαυτόν; III, 12, 7 etc. Philo Virt., 18 : γυμνάσαι ψυχήν; similarly Vit. Mos., I, 48; Jos. Ant., 3, 15 of God : ὃν εἰκὸς δοκιμάζοντα τὴν ἀρετὴν αὐτῶν ... γυμνάζειν αὐτοὺς τοῖς ἄρτι χαλεποῖς.

In the NT it occurs only figur. and in writings under Hell. influence. 1 Tm. 4:7: γύμναζε σεαυτὸν πρὸς εὐσέβειαν, demands concentration on what is inward instead of externally dualistic asceticism (→ γυμνασία). Cf. materially 1 C. 9:24-27; Phil. 2:12; 3:12 ff. In Hb., too, there is a faint echo of Greek perfectionism : 5:14 : τελείων ... τῶν διὰ τὴν ἕξιν τὰ αἰσθητήρια γεγυμνασμένα ἐχόντων πρὸς διάκρισιν καλοῦ τε καὶ ἀγαθοῦ; 12:11: (παιδεία) καρπὸν εἰρηνικὸν τοῖς δι' αὐτῆς γεγυμνασμένοις ἀποδίδωσιν δικαιοσύνης; 2 Pt. 2:14 : καρδίαν γεγυμνασμένην πλεονεξίας (vl. πλεονεξίαις), might be meant sarcastically, though it reflects a later and weaker usage.

Cf. P. Masp., 20, 16 (6th cent. A.D.): γυμνάζεσθαι τῷ ἐπιτηδεύματι, "to devote oneself to one's calling." On the constr. with the gen., cf. Philostr. Heroic., 2, 15; 3:1; 10, 1: γεγυμνασμένος θαλάσσης, πολέμων, σοφίας.

† γυμνασία.

From the time of Plato and Aristotle (Pol., IV, 13, p. 1297a, 17: law concerning the palaestra); militarily, Polyb., IV, 7, 6; Jos. Bell., 2, 649. Figur. "exercise" in political concerns, Polyb., I, 1; "philosophical disputation," Plat. Theaet., 169c etc.; "martyrdom," 4 Macc. 11:20 (only here in the LXX).

1 Tm. 4:8 : ἡ σωματικὴ γυμνασία πρὸς ὀλίγον ἐστὶν ὠφέλιμος. The antithetical ἡ εὐσέβεια allows the linguistically most obvious rendering "physical

---

[8] L. Brun has restated the argument of Mundle in ZNW, 28 (1929), 207 ff., but he does not reject the dominant opinion (209).

exercise." The context, however, makes it clear that there is no attack on Hellenic development of the body, as lexical association might seem to demand (cf. v. 7), but rather a rejection of narrow encratitic strivings (cf. 4:3; 5:23; Tt. 1:15).

More common in this technical sense is → ἄσκησις : Philo Spec. Leg., IV, 99 : ἄσκησις τῆς ἐγκρατείας; Strab., XV, 1, 61; XVII, 1, 29; Jos. Bell., 2, 150. γυμνασία does not seem to occur elsewhere.

Oepke

γυνή

In general Gk. from the time of Homer, as also in the LXX and the NT, γυνή denotes a. the "female" as distinct from the male : ἄνδρες καὶ γυναῖκες, Ac. 5:14; 8:3 etc.; γυναικὸς ἅπτεσθαι, 1 C. 7:1; ἡ γυνὴ ὅταν τίκτῃ, Jn. 16:21; γεννητοὶ γυναικῶν, Mt. 11:11, cf. Gl. 4:4; Mk. 5:25 par.; Lk. 15:8 etc.; b. the "wife" : γυναῖκες καὶ παρθένοι, Xenoph. An., III, 2, 25; Opp. : ἑταίρα, Isaeus 3:13; Dt. 13:6; Mal. 2:14 etc.; Lk. 1:5; 1 C. 7:2; Eph. 5:22 ff.; Col. 3:18 f.; 1 Pt. 3:1. So also Mt. 5:28 : "the wife of another," and 1 C. 9:5 : ἀδελφὴν γυναῖκα περιάγειν, "to take a fellow-Christian around with one as wife." [1] Similarly in 1 C. 7:27 the reference is to a wife rather than one who is spiritually affianced. 1 C. 5:1: γυνὴ τοῦ πατρός, "step-mother" (cf. Lv. 18:8, 11). By Semitic marriage law the bride is already called γυνή, Gn. 29:21; Dt. 22:24; Rev. 21:9; cf. 19:7; Mt. 1:20, 24. In Lk. 2:5, however, τῇ μεμνηστευμένη αὐτῷ γυναικί [2] is a later conflation. On γυνή χήρα for "widow" in 3 Βασ. 17:9; Lk. 4:26, cf. BGU, 522, 7 (2nd cent. A.D.): γυνὴ χήρα καὶ ἀβοήθητος.

γυνή. RGG², II, 25 ff., 718 ff.; RE³, IV, 616 ff.; V, 184 ff., 738 ff.; H. Weinel, *Nt.liche Theol.*⁴ (1928), 304 f., 490 f., Index *s.v.* "Ehe"; H. Jacoby, *Nt.liche Ethik* (1899), 123 ff.; 230 ff., 348 ff., 369 ff.; E. Grimm, *Ethik Jesu*² (1917), 207 ff.; A. Juncker, *Ethik des Apostels Pls.*, II (1919), 167 ff., 181 ff. H. Preisker, *Christentum und Ehe in den ersten drei Jahrhunderten* (1927); J. Leipoldt, *Jesus und die Frauen* (1921); G. Delling, *Pls.' Stellung zu Frau u. Ehe* (1931). In these books a good deal of older theological and historical material is listed. Cf. also F. Lübker, *Reallexikon d. klass. Altertums* (1914), 318 ff.; Pauly-W., V (1905), 2011 ff., 481; 1241 ff.; XIV (1930), 2259 ff.; H. Blümner, *Die römischen Privataltertümer* (1911), 341 ff.; L. Friedländer, *Darstellungen aus der Sittengesch. Roms*¹⁰, II (1922), 267 ff.; K. Hermann-H. Blümner, *Griech. Privatsaltertümer*³ (1882), 64 f.; T. Birt, *Frauen der Antike* (1932); L. Radermacher, "Die Stellung der Frau innerhalb der griech. Kultur," *Mittlgen. d. Freunde d. humanist. Gymnas. Wien*, 27 (1929), 6 ff.; E. Hruza, *Beiträge z. Gesch. des griech. Familienrechts,* I (1892); S. G. Huwardas, *Beiträge z. griech. u. gräkoägypt. Eherecht der Ptolemäer- und frühen Kaiserzeit* (1931). H. Holzinger, "Frau und Ehe im vordeuteronomischen Israel," in *Wellhausen-Festschrift* (1914), 227 ff.; A. Bertholet, *Kulturgesch. Israels* (1920); I. Benzinger, *Hebr. Archäologie*³, (1927), 112 ff.; G. Beer, *Die soziale und relig. Stellung der Frau im israel. Altertum* (1919); U. Türck, "Die Stellung der Frau in Elephantine," *ZAW*, 41 (1928), 166 ff.; S. Krauss, *Talmud. Archäologie,* II (1911), 1 ff.; H. Norden, *Die eheliche Ethik der Juden z. Zt. Jesu* (1911); R. H. Charles, *The Teaching of the NT on Divorce* (1921); A. Ott, "Die Auslegung der nt.lichen Texte über die Ehescheidung," *Nt.liche Abhdlgen*, III (1911). L. Zscharnack, *Der Dienst der Frau in den ersten Jdten. d. christ. Kirche* (1902); E. Goltz, *Der Dienst der Frau in der christl. Kirche*² (1914); A. Kalsbach, *Die altkirchl. Einrichtung der Diakonissen bis zu ihrem Erlöschen* (1926), with full bibl.

[1] Roman Catholic exegesis usually interprets ἀδελφὴν γυναῖκα in terms of the very different ἄνδρες ἀδελφοί of Ac. 15:7 as a single concept denoting either *matrona serviens* (Jer., Aug., A. Maier [1857], *ad loc.*) or spiritual marriage for the support of women's work (Cl. Al. Strom., III, 6; Vulg.). F. Gutjahr (1907), *ad loc.* tries to combine the two. The real meaning seems obvious enough. Cf. Sickb. K., *ad loc.,* also A. Bisping (1855), *ad loc.,* though cf. K. Pieper, *Paulus* (1926), 137.

[2] ΑΔΘ min lat as against γυναικὶ αὐτοῦ it syˢ, ἐμνηστευμένη αὐτῷ ℵ BDLW min Tat.

The address (ὦ) γύναι in Mt. 15:28; Lk. 13:12; 22:57; Jn. 2:4; 4:21 (8:10 vl.); 19:26; 20:13, 15; 1 C. 7:16 is in no way disrespectful or derogatory. When Jesus addresses His mother in this way in Jn. (2:4; 19:26), however, it excludes the filial relationship.

Cf. Eur. Med., 290; Menand. Fr., 363, 1 (CAF, III, 105); Dio C. LI, 12, 5 (Octavian to Cleopatra); Jdt. 11:1; Jos. Ant., 1, 252 : Abraham's servant to Rebekah's mother ; Hom. Od., 7, 347: γυνή with δέσποινα. Derekh Ereç, 6 : a beggar to the wife of Hillel, אִשָּׁה. [3]

A. Woman in the Contemporary NT World.

Characteristic of the traditional position and estimation of woman is a saying current in different forms among the Persians, Greeks and Jews in which man gives thanks that he is not an unbeliever or uncivilised, that he is not a woman and that he is not a slave. [4] The Greek versions are in the field of anecdotes. The proverb is undoubtedly of oriental origin. Correctly to understand it, we must take into account the low level of woman in the oriental world. The general rule in this matter is that the further west we go the greater is the freedom of woman. In detail, however, there are the widest possible variations.

1. The Greek World and Hellenism.

Athenian woman is of inferior status. She is guarded by dogs in a separate chamber (Aristoph. Thes., 414 ff.; 790 ff.). With some exceptions, Attic tragedy treats her as an inferior being. γυναιξὶ κόσμον ἡ σιγὴ φέρει (Soph. Ai., 293). ὅρκους ἐγὼ γυναικὸς εἰς ὕδωρ γράφω (Soph. Fr., 742). Comedy, which draws its spectators mostly from men, is frequently insulting and spiteful. Woman is fickle (οὐ πάνυ | εἴωθ᾽ ἀληθὲς οὐδὲ ἓν λέγειν γυνή, Menand. Fr., 746 [CAF, III, 210]), contentious (Fr., 754, ibid., p. 212), nature's greatest misfit (πολλῶν κατὰ γῆν καὶ κατὰ θάλατταν θηρίων | ὄντων μέγιστόν ἐστι θηρίον γυνή [Fr. 488, ibid., p. 141]; ὅπου γυναῖκές εἰσι, πάντ᾽ ἐκεῖ κακά [Fr. 804, ibid., p. 220]), with no claim to culture. To instruct a woman is simply to increase the poison of a dangerous serpent (Fr., 702, ibid., p. 201). Only the hetaera is cultivated. A house in which woman has the final say will inevitably perish (Fr., 484, ibid., p. 140). Aristophanes satirises a communistic regime of women in Ecclesiazusai. This presupposes that there were women who could assert themselves. But this was unusual. The normal fate of woman was to be despised and oppressed, especially if she did not enjoy male protection (cf. P. Flor., 58, 14 [3rd cent. A.D.]: [κατα-φρονο]ῦντές μου ὡς γυναικὸς ἀσ[θ]ε[νο]ῦς). The principle of the comedy of Poseidipp : υἱὸν τρέφει πᾶς κἂν πένης τις ὢν τύχῃ | θυγατέρα δ᾽ ἐκτίθησι, κἂν ᾖ πλούσιος (CAF, III, 338), was followed even at the beginning of the present era (P. Oxy., IV, 744, 9 f.). Women occupied a position of more freedom and influence in the Doric world. We are given a vivid impression of the proud and heroic nature of the women of Sparta in Plutarch's collection Lacaenarum Apophthegmata (II, 240c ff.).

In spite of all this, the Greek ideal of woman is a lofty one. Greek poetry offers a wealth of impressive and imperishable types of womanhood both in the physical

---

[3] J. Wackernagel, Über einige antike Anredeformen (1912), 25 f.; Str.-B., II, 401; Schl. Mt., 491; Schl. J., 67.

[4] Among the Rabb. it is traced back to R. Jehuda b. Elaj (c. 150 A.D.) T. Ber., 7, 18; jBer., 13b, 57 ff.; bMen., 43b; among the Gks. to Thales, Socrates, Plato (Diog. L., I, 33; Lact. Inst., 19, 17; cf. Plut. Mar., 46 (I, 433a)). D. Kaufmann, MGWJ, 37 (1893), 14 ff. It is still found in the modern Jewish prayer-book (ed. E. Cohn), with the consoling addition for women : "Praised be Thou, Eternal One, Lord of the world, who hast made me according to Thy will."

and the spiritual sense : Niobe, Helena, Nausicaa, Penelope, Andromache, Antigone, Cassandra, Clytaemestra, Iphigenia etc., and not forgetting the careful Eurycleia. There are nobler strains even in the mocker Menander : ταμιεῖον ἀρετῆς ἐστιν ἡ σώφρων γυνή (Fr., 1109 [CAF, III, 269]). Plato in the Republic makes the demand, revolutionary in the Attic world though common in the Doric, that there should be an equality of women, even in respect of exercise in arms. In fact the capable woman, especially in Hellenistic Asia Minor but also in Greece, could occupy a surprisingly independent and influential role even in public life. [5] Plutarch wrote : ὅτι καὶ γυναῖκα παιδευτέον (Stob. Ecl., III, 520, 10 ff.; IV, 89, 9 ff.). His work *consolatio ad uxorem* is a notable testimony to his own close personal relationship to his wife Timoxena.

Marriage is the rule except in so far as freer forms of sexual intercourse replace it. A vivid light is thrown on the various relationships by the speech of Ps.-Demosth. against Neaira (59, 122): "We have harlots for our pleasure, concubines (παλλακάς) for daily physical use, wives to bring up legitimate children and to be faithful stewards in household matters." In Homeric days there was concubinage with slaves, or with prisoners of war who were sometimes of royal blood, but this was no longer a recognised practice in the classical period. There are cases of bigamy to a late period, though very rarely among citizens. [6] No legal restrictions existed. In practice, however, Greek marriage was strictly monogamous in the later period. A man might freely resort to a harlot, but if he married her he must leave his first wife. To the Greeks, Egyptian concubinage was very lax. In Graeco-Egyptian marriage contracts we often find clauses like the following : μὴ ἐξέστω δὲ Ἡρακλείδηι γυναῖκα ἄλλην ἐπεισάγεσθαι ἐφ' ὕβρει Δημητρίας μηδὲ τεκνοποιεῖσθαι ἐξ ἄλλης γυναικός. [7]

According to the pap. the mutual relations of married couples were often affectionate, especially in middle class circles. Thus the wife of an officer who for reasons of service is left alone at nights assures him that she has no more pleasure in food or drink. [8] In such letters there is often evidence of gentle manners. The more blatant, however, are the many bitter complaints. Divorces were not uncommon. They occurred by common consent, or by the unilateral action of the husband (ἀποπέμπειν) or the wife (ἀπολείπειν τὸν ἄνδρα) after the sending of an official notice, or by simple declaration before a judge, or even through third parties. There were looser forms of marriage, e.g., synchoresis and homology in Egypt, or the γάμος ἄγραφος which appeared under Roman influence and which was a marriage with no official status yet not always without a written contract. Full marriage was often the goal. How far these looser forms contributed to the incidence of divorce is hard to say. The need to divide possessions was always a restraining factor. The φερνή forfeited at divorce was a kind of conventional punishment. [9]

In Sparta childlessness was a ground for divorce (or for taking a second wife, Hdt., V, 39 f.), though it is not clear whether the cowardice of the husband might also be considered such, as among the Parthians (Jos. Ant., 18, 360 f.).

---

[5] Cf. the material in Delling, *op. cit.,* 8 ff.
[6] Dionysius the Elder married two wives on the same day (Diod. S., XIV, 44). Hruza, *op. cit.,* II, 31. On polygamy, *loc. cit.*; on concubinage, p. 93.
[7] P. Eleph., 20, No. 1, 7 ff.
[8] P. Giess., I, 19 (early in the 2nd cent. A.D.).
[9] Huwardas, *op. cit.,* 47 f. It is almost a tragi-comedy when in the dissolution of the *gamos agraphos* the wife receives a few earrings and a little money.

Repeated divorce might lead to a form of polygamy. Though there is satirical exaggeration, there are also grains of truth in the picture of Menander Fr., 547/8 (CAF, III, 166), that eleven and even twelve wives were not uncommon and those who had only had four or five were regarded as καταστροφὴ γῆς, unmarried and deserving of pity. The epithet μόνανδρος, often found on the gravestones of faithful wives, is generally designed as a protest against this looser practice, and obviously so when the widower makes the inscription. We should not assume any opposition to second marriage when the first was broken by death. [10] In such a case to remain unmarried was regarded as the sign of special continence and sometimes even had cultic significance, as in the cult of Ge in Aegira : γυνὴ δὲ ἡ ἀεὶ τὴν ἱερωσύνην λαμβάνουσα ἁγιστεύει μὲν τὸ ἀπὸ τούτου, οὐ μὴν οὐδὲ τὰ πρότερα ἔσται πλέον ἢ ἑνὸς ἀνδρὸς ἐς πεῖραν ἀφιγμένη (Paus., VII, 25, 13), though it may be that the opposition is here to remarriage after divorce. [11] That there is no counterpart in the case of the male is characteristic of the prevailing double standard of morality.

There were always varying estimates of marriage. Stobaeus collected a number of statements under the double heading : ὅτι κάλλιστον ὁ γάμος and : ὅτι οὐκ ἀγαθὸν τὸ γαμεῖν (Ecl., IV, 494, 2 and IV, 513, 2). It is cynicism rather than asceticism which informs the suspicion of marriage in Menand. Fr., 650 (CAF, III, 191): ὅστις πενόμενος βούλεται ζῆν ἡδέως, | ἑτέρων γαμούντων αὐτὸς ἀπεχέσθω γάμου. The older Stoicism displays a high sense of the value of marriage. Antipater of Tarsus (d. 151/150 B.C., Fr. in v. Arnim, III, 254 ff.) describes it as κρᾶσις, the full union of man and woman. Already in Epictetus, however, it is regarded as better not to marry, at least for the Cynic in his exercise of supervision over all men (Diss., III, 22, 77). Neo-Platonism adopted a fully ascetic view. The marriage of Porphyry with the sickly widow Marcella was completely non-sexual. Even in early Greek thinking a certain antithesis was found between sexual intercourse and cultic approach to the godhead. Continence was demanded of the Eleusinian hierophants before and during the fasts, and of some other priests more generally. The growing influence of the Mysteries strengthened this tendency. In a simultaneous protest against widespread excesses both in and outside marriage, the ideal of absolute continence spread in wide circles. [12] Spiritual marriage was adopted in paganism even earlier than in Christianity. [13] In face of the older eroticists, Heliodorus of Emesa (3rd cent. A.D.) gives evidence of the changed view in his Ethiopian romance when he concludes the work with a marriage of the lovers from which all sexual elements are strictly excluded.

2. Rome.

Among the Romans, as among primitive peasant peoples, the position of the housewife was relatively high. The husband had only a mild superiority (*manus*) which constantly diminished. Corporal chastisement was sometimes recommended but rarely practised. In comedy the wife, too, could sometimes box the ears. The

---

[10] The only instance is in J. B. Frey, "La signification des termes ΜΟΝΑΝΔΡΟΣ et *univira*," *Recherches de Science Religieuse*, 20 (1931), 48 ff.

[11] Cf. on this pt. and on what follows E. Fehrle, "Die kultische Keuschheit im Altertum," RVV, 6 (1910).

[12] For further details on the religious and philosophical basis of the movement of sexual abstinence and on its effects, cf. Preisker, *op. cit.*, 32 ff., 45 ff.; Delling, *op. cit.*, 19 f., 26, 72 and 90.

[13] R. Reitzenstein, *Hellenistische Wundererzählungen* (1906), 146 ff., *Historia monachorum* (1916), 55; A. Harnack, *Mission und Ausbreitung*[4] (1924), I, 232 ff. (where a reference to Galen's testimony concerning the continence of Christians, preserved by the Arabs, finely illustrates the parallelism of views).

respectful *domina* was used even by the husband. In the conduct of the household the *matrona* had equality. There was no special chamber for women. They could move about freely (Corn. Nep. Vit. prooem., 6 f.). Even among the Roman Stoics there were exertions on behalf of equal education. Both male and female horses and hounds were trained for racing and the chase. Why, then, should not daughters be educated as well as sons (Mus. Ruf. in Stob. Ecl., II, 235, 24 ff.)? Juvenal can already satirise the bluestocking (Sat., 6, 434 ff.), as also Martial, II, 90, 9 : *sit non doctissima coniux!* (cf. XI, 19).

Roman history is rich in noble women as well as reprobate. Cornelia, the mother of the Gracchi, and Livia, the wife of Augustus, are good examples. Prop. celebrated another Cornelia in the "queen" of his elegies (IV, 11). In the Roman Stoic Musonius, a contemporary of Paul, the antique estimation of woman and marriage reaches its climax. All sexual intercourse either outside or prior to marriage is frowned upon. In marriage the physical union is for the purpose of producing good citizens. It is to be sustained, however, by the spiritual communion of the partners, who are fully equal. [14]

Roman marriage had always been monogamous. This did not exclude intercourse with slaves or harlots. In general this was not regarded as reprehensible. [15] But Roman law could admit only one *mater familias*. A characteristic of the legal development is its progressive softening.

> In the older period *manus* marriage was contracted either without form and by *usus,* or by ceremonial purchase (*coëmptio*), or by a religious ceremony of *confarreatio*. This meant that the wife joined the family circle of her husband. Increasingly, however, this was replaced by marriage without *manus* contracted sometimes by *mutuus consensus* without any preceding betrothal, festivities, or written agreement. In such cases the wife remained in the household of her father and did not become *mater familias* but *uxor*. In addition, there were looser forms such as the concubinage which was practised in the army and which Christianity refused to countenance, or the *contubernium* which was not accepted as marriage, i.e., the more lasting union between slaves, often at the wish of their master. These could be concluded and dissolved quite freely. Divorce was also possible in other cases by mutual repudiation. In the imperial period marriage by *confarreatio,* which had previously been indissoluble, became dissoluble by *diffarreatio.* The only exception was the marriage of the *flamen dialis*. Grounds of divorce were the rise of the husband to a higher social class, childlessness, the use of false keys, poisoning of the children, or *si quid perverse taetreque factum est a muliere,* often merely the desire for another marriage.

In the increase of divorces we have an expression of the moral corruption of the later period. The moralists strove against them, but in vain. Wives counted the years by their husbands rather than by the consuls (Sen. Ben., III, 16, 2 and 3). Eight marriages could be contracted in the course of five autumns (Juv. Sat., 6, 229 f.). Ovid speaks cynically of his three wives (Trist., IV, 10, 69 ff.). In contrast to this degeneracy burial inscriptions sing the praises of the *univira*. [16] Characteristically, there is nothing corresponding in the case of the husband. Prop. (IV, 11, 91 f.) regards it as the ideal for the widower not to remarry, but is not so sure of its feasibility.

---

[14] For further details, cf. Delling, *op. cit.,* 24 f.

[15] Liv., XXXIX, 9, 5 f. calls Hispala a *scortum nobile* and intercourse with her *minime adulescentis aut rei aut famae damnosa.*

[16] Blümner, *Privataltertümer,* 350 and 364; Frey, *op. cit.*

3. Woman in the OT.

In spite of certain rather doubtful relics of matriarchate, woman was legally more a chattel than a person in Israel. In marriage she passed from the dominion of her father to that of the husband to whom he gave her in marriage (1 S. 18:17, 19, 27 etc.). In the process such matters as the dowry played a part. If her husband died or she was put away, she came under the protection of her grown-up son or of her own family. Levirate marriage could be rejected by the man concerned, but not by the woman (Dt. 25:5 ff.). Rest was made a duty for all on the Sabbath, but not for the woman (Ex. 20:8 ff.; Dt. 5:12 ff.; though she did in fact rest, 2 K. 4:22 f.). In every respect the husband was her lord (Gn. 3:16). He determined her portion at the sacrificial meal (1 S. 1:5). Fidelity was demanded of her alone, though the husband had to avoid adultery. Betrothal was equivalent to marriage (Nu. 5:11 ff.; Ex. 22:15 f.; Dt. 22:23 ff.; Gn. 38:15 ff.). Polygamy was a heavy burden on the wife. Above all, if she did not enjoy the blessing of children and especially sons, she occupied an unenviable position in relation to more fortunate wives or concubines. She was particularly lucky if she did not forfeit the affection of her husband in consequence (1 S. 1:5 ff.; Gn. 16:4 ff.).

There were, however, more favourable aspects. Wives and girls could appear publicly in everyday life, at festivals and on sacral occasions (Gn. 24:13 ff.; Ex. 2:16; Dt. 12:12; Ju. 21:21; 2 S. 6). Where there were no sons, the daughters had rights of inheritance (Nu. 27:8). In these and even in other cases (Nu. 36:6) the inclination and will of the girl could also be consulted in marriage (Gn. 24:39, 58). The woman had almost incalculable influence, especially when she had sons and when she could act adroitly. Figures like Sarah, Rebekah, Michal, Abigail and especially the evil Jezebel, offer convincing proof. Indeed, a woman like Deborah can even attain to an extraordinary position in public life. The basic biblical tradition, which emphasises the secondary position of woman by creation and her greater susceptibility to temptation (Gn. 2:22; 3:6 ff.), also shows a fine and profound appreciation of her position as the helpmeet of man, of her divine likeness even if only by derivation, and of the close relationship of the one man and the one woman.

4. Woman in Judaism.

Judaism, however, involves more reaction than progress. Woman is openly despised. "Happy is he whose children are males, and woe to him whose children are females" (bQid, 82b). The honourable title of "daughter of Abraham" is rare in Rabbinic literature as compared with the corresponding "son of Abraham." [17] Women are greedy, inquisitive, lazy, vain (Gn. r., 45 on 16:5) and frivolous (bShab., 33b). "Ten qab of empty-headedness have come upon the world, nine having been received by women and one by the rest of the world" (bQid., 49b). "Many women, much witchcraft" (Hillel, c. 20 B.C., 2, 7). The custom of women preceding corpses in many places finds aetiological explanation in their assumed responsibility for death (Slav. En. 30:17; Vit. Ad., 1, 3 etc.; jSanh., 20b, 44). [18] Conversation should not be held with a woman (cf. Jn. 4:9, 27), even though she be one's own (bErub., 53b; Ab., 1, 5). "May the words of the Torah be burned, they should not be handed over to women" (jSota, 10a, 8). "The man who teaches

---

[17] Str.-B., II, 200.
[18] Ibid., IV, 581.

his daughter the Torah teaches her extravagance" (Sota, 3, 4; cf. bSota, 21b). The wife should neither bear witness, instruct children, nor pray at table; she is not even bound to keep the whole Torah. [19] In the synagogues women are assigned special places behind a screen. Special chambers are provided for them not only in Palestine but even in Alexandria (Philo Flacc., 89). Hellenistic Judaism generally shows little enlightenment on this question. Philo says (Op. Mund., 165): "In us the attitude of man is informed by reason (νοῦς), of woman by sensuality (αἴσθη-σις)." And Josephus, if the passage be genuine, says quite succinctly: γυνὴ χείρων ἀνδρὸς εἰς ἅπαντα (Ap., 2, 201).

Nevertheless, other notes are also sounded in Judaism. Thus the Wisdom literature, while it speaks bluntly of the malign influence of ambitious, talkative and undisciplined wives (Prv. 6:24; 7:5; 9:13; 11:22; 19:13; 21:9; 25:24; 27:15; Sir. 25:16 ff.; 19:2; 9:3 ff.), can also sing enthusiastically the praises of a virtuous woman (Prv. 12:4; 18:22; 19:14; 31:10-31; Sir. 36:27 ff.; 26:13 ff.: "As the sun rises on the heavenly hill of the Lord, so does the beauty of a righteous woman in the well-ordered household of her husband"). Even in Rabbinic writings we occasionally hear similar notes. "Her husband is adorned by her, but she is not adorned by her husband" (Gn. r., 47 on 17:15). [20] Before God wives have equal if not greater promise than their husbands (Ex. r., 21 on 14:15; Tanna debe Eliahu Rabba, 9; Rab. gest., 247 A.D.; bBer., 17a). Particular mention may be made of Beruria (Veluria? Valeria?), the daughter of R. Chanina ben Teradion, and wife of R. Meïr (c. 150 A.D.) as an outstanding and quick-witted woman, or of Rahel, the wife of Akiba (→ 649), as an example of one who manifested an extra-ordinary piety and readiness for sacrifice in the Jewish sense.

Marriage was a duty for loyal Jews and therefore a presupposition of ordination as rabbi. [21] Not to further propagation of the species was tantamount to shedding blood or despising the image of God. [22] If there were no children after ten years, another marriage had to be contracted, and the husband had liberty whether or not to divorce the first wife. [23]

Polygamy remains legitimate. In relation to the practice of Herod, Joseph. explains that it is a patriarchal custom in an attempt to neutralise the alienation of Greek and Roman readers (Ant., 17, 14). Of two high-priestly families in Jerusalem it was known that they descended from double marriages (bJeb., 15b). In a famine (according to T. Ket., 5, 1) a prominent rabbi, R. Tarfon, married 300 wives in order to care for them (as a wealthy priest), though the marriages were only temporary and formal. The question of the treatment of the children of rival wives formed a subject of dispute between the schools of Shammai and Hillel. The community of the new covenant at Damascus (1st cent. B.C.?) attacked polygamy on the basis of Gn. 1:27. [24] R. Ami also championed monogamy in principle. But the first formal prohibition of polygamy was issued only by R. Gershom ben Jehuda in Mainz c. 1000 A.D., and it applied only to the West. In practice, of course, the expense and the problems entailed constituted a strong barrier, especially in the lower middle classes. [25] The NT thus seems to assume

---

[19] *Ibid.,* 1226, Index.
[20] *Ibid.,* III, 610 f.
[21] For material, cf. ZNW, 25 (1926), 310 ff.; 28 (1929), 321 ff.
[22] bJeb., 63b.
[23] Jeb., 6, 6. Divorce seems to have been the rule (bJeb., 64a; T. Jeb., 8, 4 249; cf. Str.-B., I, 317).
[24] S. Schechter, *Documents of Jewish Sectaries,* I (1910), IV, 21.
[25] Cf. S. Krauss, *Talmudische Archäologie,* II (1911), 26 ff.; RGG², III, 481.

that monogamy is the general rule. The real evil in the Jewish and the Hellenistic world, together with divorce and prostitution, was successive polygamy (→ 779; 780; 783).

Marital intercourse was demanded by the Rabbis, though not to excess. [26] It was emphasised that it should not be for reasons of carnal desire, especially where there was Hellenistic influence (Tob. 8:7; Philo Spec. Leg., I, 112; Virt., 207 etc.; Jos. Ap., 2, 199). The smaller married sect of Essenes refrained from intercourse during pregnancy (Jos. Bell., 2, 161). Strict Judaism opposed not only adultery and unnatural licence, but also extramarital intercourse, with an energy inexplicable to paganism, though these evils were never completely overcome. In relation to them, the main odium fell on the woman (Mt. 21:31 f.; Lk. 7:39). Ascetic ideas were for the most part alien to Judaism, [27] though they made occasional inroads under Hellenistic influence. The didactic poem of Ps.-Phokylides combines insistence on the duty of marriage with a certain restraint in the sense of popular Hellenistic philosophy (175 f.; 193 f.). There are also ascetic trends in the Testaments of the Twelve Patriarchs (Test. R. 6; Iss. 2; Jos. 9 f.). Philo obviously sympathises with the asceticism of the Therapeutae, [28] but he himself was married and had many things to say in praise of marriage.

Though the main emphasis in Judaism is on the physical side of marriage, there is not lacking a more spiritual and personal relationship between the partners and an appreciation of this factor. Even after ten years of childlessness Philo cannot conceive of the unconditional dissolution of a marriage because the bond of love is too strong (Spec. Leg., III, 35). He depicts a restrained courtship under the impulse of affection in terms which are almost modern (Spec. Leg., III, 67). Even the Talmud claims in relation to the betrothal of children that a grown-up daughter alone can say that "she will have the one proposed." [29]

The Jews staunchly maintained their singular law of divorce. At bottom, this gave the initiative only to the husband. The distinctive feature was that he could give a bill of divorcement conferring freedom to marry again. [30] Apart from childlessness, the main ground was "something scandalous" (עֶרְוַת דָּבָר, Dt. 24:1). The school of Shammai took this to mean only licentiousness, but the school of Hillel included a variety of lesser matters from salting food to the mere finding of someone else more beautiful. [31] The fact that Salome herself dissolved her marriage according to Gk. custom is described as repugnant to Jewish law in Jos. Ant., 15, 259. To be sure, there were times when the Jewish wife could and should ask for divorce, e.g., when her husband forced her into a morally doubtful vow. [32] But this, too, could be made into a stratagem by men seeking divorce. Hence even divorces on trivial grounds were hardly less common among the Jews than among pagans. Joseph. speaks quite dispassionately and complacently of his many marriages in Vit., 414 f.; 426 f.

---

[26] Cf. the material in Str.-B., III, 371.

[27] In bJeb., 64ab sexlessness is claimed for Abraham and Sarah. If this is supposed to illustrate the power of God and the effectiveness of prayer, then it may be that there are underlying ascetic tendencies (of Hellenistic origin ?).

[28] The work De vita contemplativa is now accepted as authentic in spite of Schürer, III, 687 ff. Cf. H. Leisegang, RGG², IV, 1197.

[29] bQid, 41a; Str.-B., II, 381.

[30] סֵפֶר כְּרִיתוּת, Gk. ἀποστάσιον. The word first takes on this special significance in Jewish Gk. In the pap. the phrase ἀποστασίου συγγραφή means a document of renunciation in financial matters. For the form of a Jewish bill of divorcement, cf. Str.-B., I, 311 f. The best material on divorce is to be found in the tractate Gittin.

[31] For examples, cf. Str.-B., I, 312 ff.; also Schürer, II, 494.

[32] Str.-B., I, 318 f.

In Judaism, too, the real evil was successive polygamy. What was originally designed to protect the wife and to prevent cruelty became an aid to injustice and oppression. Individual rabbis protested against divorce, but the evil was not tackled at the root.

Commenting on Mal. 2:13 f. R. Eleazar said : "If a man divorces his first wife, even the altar sheds tears over him." It is expressly stated, however, that this applies only to the first wife. [33]

B. Woman in Christianity.

The foundations of the Christian view are to be found in the two factors, 1. that it is an order of creation that man and woman should become one in inviolable monogamous marriage, and 2. that the lordship of God radically removes all the differences which separate them. On the other hand, primitive Christianity did not deduce from these two factors an absolutely new and predominantly spiritual ideal of woman and marriage, nor did it champion any such view with revolutionary vigour. In practice it showed itself to be conservative and even perhaps reactionary from the standpoint of Hellenistic culture. To this degree, it offered a corrective to the desire of antiquity for complete emancipation. On the other hand, for all its reserve Christianity showed itself to be most adaptable and capable of transforming inwardly both the old which it had inherited and the new which it added to it.

1. Jesus. [34]

At this point, too, Jesus is not the radical reformer who proclaims laws and seeks to enforce a transformation of relationships. He is the Saviour who gives Himself especially to the lowly and oppressed and calls all without distinction to the freedom of the kingdom of God. Characteristic is the small trait that in His parables Jesus turns frequently and with such tenderness to the everyday life of the woman with its anxieties and joys (Mt. 13:33; 25:1 ff.; Lk. 15:8 ff.; 18:1 ff.). The Rabbinic parables are much poorer in such references. Where necessary, Jesus seems to observe the Jewish proprieties. Thus he does not approach the bed of Jairus' daughter without witnesses (Mk. 5:40). On the other hand, to fulfil His calling in relation to women He can break rigid Jewish custom with matter-of-fact boldness. Thus He does not hesitate to speak with a woman (Jn. 4:27 etc.), to teach a woman (Lk. 10:39) or to call a woman the daughter of Abraham (Lk. 13:16). He speaks on behalf of women (Mk. 12:40 and par., 41 ff. and par.; 14:6 and par.) and helps the needy among them more than any Rabbinic thaumaturge had ever done (Mk. 1:29 ff. and par.; 5:21-43 and par.; 7:24-30 and par.; Lk. 13:10-17; 8:2; 7:11-17; Jn. 11:1-44). On behalf of a sick woman, He breaks the Sabbath (Lk. 13:10 ff.) and He does not shun contact with unclean women (Mk. 1:31 and par.; 5:27 ff. and par., 41 and par.; Lk. 7:38 ff.). Whatever our view of the historical details, John paints a similar picture when he shows Jesus wrestling for the soul of the Samaritan woman (Jn. 4:7 ff.). Jesus is surrounded by a band of women (Lk. 8:2 f.) who are with Him in His suffering (Mk. 15:40 f. and par., 47 and par.) and glorification (Mk. 16:1 ff. and par.; Jn. 20:1, 11 ff.). Even on

---

[33] bGit., 90b; Str.-B., I, 320, where other examples are given.
[34] On the attitude of Jesus to marriage, monogamy and divorce, → 648 ff.

women who stand at a greater distance He exercises an extraordinary influence which He can also deepen (Lk. 11:27 f.; 23:27 ff.; cf. Mt. 27:19). We never hear from the lips of Jesus a derogatory word concerning woman as such. In holding out the prospect of sexless being like that of the angels in the consummated kingdom of God (Mk. 12:25 and par.; on the very different Jewish views → ἐγείρω), He indirectly lifts from woman the curse of her sex and sets her at the side of man as equally a child of God.

2. The Community.

In the early community there was no doubt as to the full membership of women (Ac. 1:14; 12:12). After the Jewish pattern, but without succumbing to the feminism of Jewish and Gnostic propaganda (Ac. 13:50; 17:4, 12; 2 Tm. 3:6; Act. Pl. et Thecl., 41), the Christian mission wins women from the very outset (Ac. 16:13 f.; 17:4, 12, 34; 18:18). As men are called brothers, so women are called sisters (R. 16:1; 1 C. 9:5 etc. → ἀδελφή).

a. In Paul there is perhaps a stronger tension than one might have expected between a progressive and a Jewish reactionary tendency. The same Paul who can write Gl. 3:28 can also emphasise that it was Eve who was seduced (2 C. 11:3) and that by creation woman was a stage further removed from God than man (1 C. 11:3, 7). The tension is not to be resolved by referring some statements to woman as a sexual being by nature and others to woman as sexually neutralised in Christ. [35] It is removed by understanding and therefore transcending the differences in the light of God and the new aeon. Although this is of immediate and radical significance, however, it does not lead to practical consequences of a revolutionary kind. Thus woman is still subject to man in spite of her equality in divine sonship (1 Cor. 11:10 → ἐξουσία; Col. 3:18; Eph. 5:21 f.). It is the duty of man, however, to exercise his leadership, not selfishly, but with love and consideration. The full removal of sexual distinction must await the coming aeon (1 C. 6:13). [36]

b. The later apostolic and post-apostolic periods manifest the same tendency as is seen in Paul. The fall of Eve is emphasised in almost Jewish fashion in 1 Tm. 2:13 f. On the other hand, 1 Pt. 3:7 demands full recognition of woman as a joint heir of life. The ideal of woman, however, differs in practice from the thought of emancipation and remains conservative. This does not exclude Hellenistic influences in the house-tables, as already in Paul. [37] The positive tendency emerges especially in the Pastorals (→ 652; 1 Tm. 2:15). By contrast, the apocryphal Acts, which essentially follow the traditions of later Hellenistic Rome, [38] extol the ascetic ideal and especially that of spiritual marriage (Act. Ptr., 33 f.; Act. Jn., 63; Act. Pl. et Thecl., 9 ff., Act. And., 4 ff.; Act. Thom., 12 ff.; 88 ff.; 117 etc.). There is evidence of non-sexual co-habitation in Hermas (s., 9, 11) and perhaps in the Didache (11, 11), and later this became increasingly common until the synods began to take action against it. → παρθένος, also 652.

---

[35] Delling, op. cit., 120 on Gl. 3:28: "In the community of Christ, sexual differences cease only when men themselves no longer exercise them, when woman no longer tempts man either directly or indirectly." Paul, however, warns against ascetic experiments in marriage (1 C. 7:3, 5), and he does not forbid Christians to marry (1 C. 7:28, 36, 39). The exposition in 1 C. 11:3 ff. is with reference to Christians.

[36] On virginity, marriage and divorce → παρθένος; 651.

[37] On these passages, cf. K. Weidinger, Die Haustafeln (1928).

[38] F. Pfister in Hennecke, 163 ff.

C. Sacral and Social Functions of Woman.

1. Non-Christian Antiquity. Throughout antiquity the participation of woman is customary not merely in the family cultus [39] but also in the public cultus [40] and the celebration of the Mysteries. [41] There are some festivals which are only for women, [42] whether for all, or for the blameless wives of citizens, who are to prepare by a nine day period of abstinence, e.g., the Thesmophoria, Scirophoria, Brauronia and Adonia [43] in Attica and a seven day festival of Demeter Mysia in Pellene. [44] On the other hand, women are excluded from some sacred rites, such as that of Aphrodite Acraia on the Cypriot Olympus. [45] In the Dionysus cult women play a very prominent part as maenads and the thyads. [46] Priestesses are very common both in public cults (→ 779, the Vestals etc.) and in those of the Mysteries (the hierophants in Eleusis, the priestesses of Isis etc.). Their ministry is not in the least restricted to women. [47] Outstanding ecstatic endowment assures women of prophetic rank as sybils. [48] The best known specific instance is the Pythia in Delphi. [49]

2. The OT. In characteristic distinction from pagan antiquity there are no priestesses of Yahweh in Israel. In the strict sense sacral ministry is reserved for men. This does not mean the exclusion of women from the religious community or from the cultus. Women take part in national festivals (2 S. 6:19; Dt. 12:12; cultic שמחה). They are also active in cultic dancing (Ju. 21:21) and in the sacrificial meal (1 S. 1:4 f.), especially the passover. Not merely the men, but the whole community, including women and children and aliens, is brought into covenant with Yahweh (Dt. 29:10 f.). Women are even admitted to lower offices at the entrance to the tent of revelation (Ex. 38:8). A religious significance almost equivalent to that of men is achieved by prophetically gifted women like Miriam, Huldah and Noadiah.

3. Judaism. Judaism not only conferred no new rights on women but curtailed the earlier rights. The older piety, orientated to the natural side of life, retreated

---

[39] Cf. the Aesculapius and Hygieia family sacrifices, Paris (Louvre), Photo. Alinari, 22, 767.

[40] P. Stengel, *Die griechischen Kultusaltertümer,* (1920), 235 f. etc. Women appear, e.g., in the Panathenean processions (Eastern Parthenon frieze, Photo. Girandon, 1018).

[41] For women in the Eleusis Mysteries on the Niinnionpinax, Haas, No. 9/11, Leipoldt (1926), 6. L. Deubner, *Attische Feste* (1932), 5, 1. The Andania inscr. prescribes the dress for women who are to be or are already consecrated (ἱεραί) (Ditt. Syll.³, 736, 15 ff.). Mithra excludes women from its mysteries, but in its missionary work associates with Cybele. On women in the Isis cult, Apul. Met., XI, 9.

[42] Stengel, *op. cit.,* 231, 235, 247, 250 f.

[43] For pictures of the Adonis rites on vases, cf. Haas, 9/11; Leipoldt, 105 ff.; Deubner, *op. cit.,* 25.

[44] Stengel, 257.

[45] Strab., XIV, 6, 3.

[46] Part. impressive is the depiction in Eur. Ba., 1050 ff. Depictions of maenads are so common that enumeration is unnecessary. On the other hand, reference may be made to the Bacchic frieze of the Villa Item at Pompeii, Photo. Anderson, 26 380-26 387, cf. M. Bieber, *Jbch. d. Deutsch. Arch. Inst.,* 43 [1928], 298 ff.; J. Leipoldt, *Dionysos* [1931], 28 ff.; the best coloured reproduction with the text is in A. Maivri, *La villa dei Misteri* [1931]). It probably represents the consecration of brides in the Dionysiac mysteries.

[47] This was certainly true of the Eleusinian Haloa (L. Deubner, *Attische Feste* [1932], 63). On the other hand, cf. the Choa festival, at which the sacred marriage of Dionysus is commonly celebrated with the *Basilinna,* whom the *Archon Basileus* must have married as a virgin (*ibid.,* 100).

[48] E. Rohde, *Psyche*⁹⁻¹⁰ (1925), 63 ff.

[49] H. Leisegang, *Pneuma Hagion* (1922), 32 f.

more and more into the background. The destruction of the temple made it impossible to carry out most of the earlier practices, including the passover. The nomistic piety of the Rabbis was wholly a matter for men.

In Herod's temple women were limited to the eastern part of the inner court, the "court of women" (Jos. Ap., 2, 104). In the synagogue they sat in special places, often a gallery, behind screens as mere spectators. They were committed to only partial observance of the Torah and had no right to study it (→ 781 f.). There were exceptions, like Valeria or the mother of Rabina. [50] Like slaves and children, they did not have to recite the sch^ema' nor carry phylacteries, though they had the obligation of daily prayer, the mezuza and saying grace (Ber., 3, 3). On the other hand, they were not to say grace publicly. "Cursed is the man whose wife and children say grace for him" (bBer., 20b). In principle there seems to have been the possibility of women being summoned to read the Torah in the synagogue. But custom demanded that they should refuse. [51] We are reminded of the ministry of women in the Christian church when we read of the niece of R. Eliezer the elder (c. 90 A.D.) offering to wash the feet of his disciples. [52] The true practice of charity, however, was in the hands of men. [53]

4. The NT.

a. Jesus had women followers who ministered to Him of their substance and by their labour (Lk. 8:2 f.). No women, however, were admitted to the circle of the twelve (→ δώδεκα).

b. In the early Christian and Pauline churches women were not merely the objects (Ac. 6:1; 9:39) but also the subjects of charitable practice (Ac. 9:36 ff.). Both in Palestine and the Gentile Christian world this practice seems, however, to have had a voluntary and purely charismatic character. In addition to Lydia (Ac. 16:15), we may mention the women who are particularly noted in R. 16:6, 12 f. for their zeal in the Lord — Mary, Tryphena, Tryphosa, Persis and the mother of Rufus. The description of Phebe as the διάκονος of the church at Cenchrea indicates the point where the original charisma is becoming an office (R. 16:1). [54] The general usage of the NT (διάκονος), however, is a reminder that, in spite of προστάτις in v. 2, we are not to think exclusively or even predominantly of works of charity in this connection, but of all kinds of service rendered to the community. Women like Prisca (Ac. 18:26; R. 16:3; 1 C. 16:19), Euodia and Syntyche (Phil. 4:2 f.) give suitable support to Paul in his evangelistic work. They can even minister to men, e.g., Apollos. In 1 C. 11:3 ff. Paul confers on prophetically gifted women the unfettered right to speak and pray (before the assembled community?), so long as they do so in an appropriate manner. There is a certain tension between this and the famous mulier taceat in ecclesia (1 C. 14:34 f.). This saying it not beyond suspicion on textual grounds. [55] On the other hand, there is no necessary contradiction. The apostle is simply preventing women from taking the initiative in speaking, but allows exceptions where there is genuine pneumatic endowment.

---

[50] Leipoldt, op. cit., 13.

[51] Str.-B., III, 467; IV, 157 f.

[52] Ab. R. Nat., 16 (6a), Str.-B., III, 653.

[53] Cf. Der talmudische Traktat Pea übersetzt ... nebst einer Abhdlg. von Versorgung der Armen bei den Juden, J. J. Rabe (1781); Str.-B., IV, 536 ff., Exc. 22.

[54] Esp. if καί (אBC* against D*G it) is genuine.

[55] DG 88 it Ambst put v. 34 f. after v. 40. Perhaps we have here a later ordinance deriving from 1 Tm. 2:12.

c. In the later apostolic and post-apostolic periods the charismatic element fades increasingly into the background. As regards the work of women, this has three consequences. In some cases it dies away. In others it takes a heretical form (Rev. 2:20), so that the sober sense of the Church is against it (1 Tm. 2:11 ff., and perhaps also 1 Tm. 5:13, → infra). In others again it is integrated into the regulated life of the community. The loosest form of organisation is the division of the community into the groups apparently recommended in Tt. 2:2 ff. In these the elder women have the duty of exhorting the younger to family life as Christians. In 1 Tm. 3:11: γυναῖκας ὡσαύτως σεμνάς κτλ., [56] there is reference to official deaconesses with much the same duties as their male counterparts. Their work is designed to support that of the bishops or presbyters. It is certainly not limited to charitable endeavour, but consists rather in organisational or even pastoral work among women. Nothing is said concerning their family relationships. This suggests that they are single and elderly ladies who devote all their energies to the community. Their relationship to the widows in 1 Tm. 5:3 ff. creates problems. There can be little doubt that in the first instance the latter receive support (v. 4, 16). It is generally assumed that in return they rendered charitable and pastoral services, but this cannot be deduced with certainty from the text. For v. 10 does not speak of the future tasks of widows put on the roll, but of their worthiness, which is also determined by the free exercise of mercy. Again, the reference in v. 13 is not to pastoral visitation but more generally to the wanton and gossipy curiosity and busybodying of younger widows who desire to remarry and for whose support the community should no longer accept responsibility. The position of widows on the list, however, is an honourable one. If they were too old for physical work, e.g., nursing the sick (v. 9), they might well be used for the tasks outlined in Tt. 2:3 ff. The further development of the institution of widows certainly points in a semi-clerical direction (→ infra ; → χήρα).

Among the requirements for such widows we read in 1 Tm. 5:9 : ἑνὸς ἀνδρὸς γυνή. The usual view is that this is aimed against second marriage after the death of the first husband [57] but there are several arguments against this. [58] First, there is the meaning of μόνανδρος and univira in common usage (→ 779; 780). Again, the right of second marriage in such a case is taken for granted in the NT. Only rarely do we get hints that it is better to refrain from it (R. 7:3; 1 C. 7:39 f., 8 f.; cf. Lk. 2:36 f.). [59] Again, the Pastorals favour marriage (→ 785), everywhere assuming a married clergy (1 Tm. 3:2, 12) and recommending the younger widows to marry again (1 Tm. 5:14). The objection in v. 11 is against subsequent relapse from widowhood. In v. 12 the πρώτη πίστις has nothing to do with fidelity to their first husband but refers to the loyalty to Christ of a life wholly devoted to Him in widowhood. We may thus conclude that the phrase ἑνὸς ἀνδρὸς γυνή, in addition to excluding common licentiousness, is aimed specifically against successive polyandry, i.e., against those who are divorced, or even repeatedly divorced.

---

[56] So also W. Brandt, Dienst u. Dienen im NT (1931), 177. The arguments against a reference to the wives of deacons are convincingly assembled by G. Uhlhorn, Die christliche Liebestätigkeit, I (1882), 396 f. Dib. Past., ad loc. does not come to any clear decision but inclines to the rejected view.

[57] So finally Preisker, 148; Frey, op. cit.; Delling, 136 ff.

[58] Dib. Past., ad loc. and on 3:2 rightly contests the reasons for the other view but hardly gives sufficient consideration to successive polygamy.

[59] The vl. ἡμέρας sys Ephr. probably derives from Tatian's Diatessaron.

5. Further Development in the Church.

The work of women teachers is for the most part found only in sectarian circles, e.g., Thecla,[60] or Priscilla, Maximilla and Quintilla among the Montanists, or women in Gnosticism.[61] In some places the Church took over from the sects the practice of having women's choirs in divine service, though this was much opposed.[62] More widely developed was the participation of women in works of charity and in pastoral visitation, especially among women. The younger Pliny mentions Christian *ancillae* called *ministrae* (διάκονοι) in Ep., 96. In Rome Grapte, herself a widow, is to exhort widows and orphans with the visions of Hermas (v. 2, 4, 3). Very early young unmarried women come to be enrolled on the official lists (Ign. Smyrn., 13, 1: παρθένους, τὰς λεγομένας χήρας), sometimes being under twenty years old (Tert. Virg. Vel., 9). These "widows" are reckoned among the officers of the community in the West and Egypt, but stand under the bishops, presbyters and deacons and are not ordained by laying on of hands. In the East there is fuller development of deaconesses. According to the Syrian Didascalia (14 and 15) the institution of widows comprises all the widows of the community above the age of fifty. But these have only modest functions and are more strictly the poor of the community. Women who bear office are called deaconesses. It is debatable whether this is only a difference in terminology or whether a new order had been formed consisting of ascetic virgins. With the passage of time these women clergy were more and more restricted to activity in divine service, assistance at the baptism of women, visitation of women, the bringing of the elements for the Lord's Supper etc. The true sacral functions ardently desired by some were not granted to them.[63] Even the right of baptising in emergency cannot be proved in the early Church.[64] Tertullian expressly forbade it (Bapt., 17). In both East and West the decisions against women exercising priestly functions became increasingly stricter. The history of the ministry of women finally ended for the time being in the convent; the title of deaconess was borne by the abbess in the early Middle Ages (→ διάκονος, παρθένος, χήρα).

Oepke

---

† Γὼγ καὶ Μαγώγ

In the NT this occurs only at Rev. 20:8-9 as a mythical name for the heathen host which, after the Messianic period of the millennial reign, will wage final conflict against the people of God and will be destroyed by God with fire. Both the name and the whole idea are taken by the divine from the prophecy of Ezekiel

---

[60] The Act. Pl. lie inside the Church, but their anti-Gnostic purpose does not mean that they are not under Gnostic influence.
[61] For more details, cf. Zscharnack, *op. cit.*, 156 ff.
[62] J. Quasten, *Musik und Gesang in den Kulten der heidnischen Antike und christlichen Frühzeit* (1930), 114 ff.
[63] The Arabic tradition of the *canones* of the apostles mentions women readers (Quasten, *op. cit.*, 120).
[64] Zscharnack, 93. Appeal to the se-baptism of Thecla allowed by Paul (Act. Pl. et Thecl., 40 f.) was a weak argument.
Γὼγ καὶ Μαγώγ. Comm. on Rev. 20:8 f.; also A. Schlatter, *Das AT in der joh. Apk.* (1912), 93 ff.; Bousset-Gressm., 205 ff.

(Ez. 38-39). [1,2] The order especially is taken from Ezekiel. In Ezekiel we have the Messianic reign in 37, Gog and Magog and their destruction in 38-39, and the new Jerusalem in 40 ff.; in Rev. the millennial kingdom in 20:4-6, Gog and Magog in 20:7-10, the resurrection of the dead and the last judgment in 20:11-15, [3] and the new heaven, the new earth and the new Jerusalem in 21:1 ff.

The same schema, i.e., Gog after the Messianic age, is found elsewhere, e.g., most of the relevant passages, and all the earliest, in the Rabbinic literature (esp. S. Nu., 76 on 10:9; M. Ex. 16:30 [4] and Pesikt., 181b-182a). [5] Cf. also Sib., 3, 652-701, where, although the names Gog and Magog do not occur, we have the sequence : Messianic kingdom, attack of the nations on it, their destruction by God. On the other hand there could obviously be no place for the Ez. tradition where the Messianic period was regarded as the period of the absolute consummation of salvation, as in Test. XII and Enoch. [6] For the same reason it is not found in the Apc. Bar. or 4 Esr., though these distinguish between the Messianic period and the future world [7] and thus allow space for the interposition of the war of Gog and Magog. On the other hand, if the Messianic period was seen in this light, in spite of the Ez. tradition the Gog and Magog episode might well be put before the time of the Messiah, as in some Rabbinic writings. [8] Cf. Enoch 56:4-8, where there is reference to an attack of the Parthians and Medes prior to the Messianic kingdom, though Gog and Magog are not mentioned. [9]

It is striking that in the apocalyptic and pseudepigraphical literature, apart from the fruitless references in Sib., 3, 319 ff. and 3, 512 ff., there is no mention whatsoever of Gog and Magog. [10] Several individual themes are taken from Ezekiel 38 f. [11] (as in Sib., 3, 652 ff. and Enoch 56:4 ff.), but the prophecy of Ezekiel as such, which is so closely linked with the names of Gog and Magog, is not incorporated into the schema. On the other hand, among the Rabbis the war of Gog and Magog, on the basis of

---

[1] The destruction by fire is taken from Ez. 38:22; 39:6.

[2] Our present concern is simply with the literary dependence of the divine on the prophetic Scripture. Hence we are not pursuing the various questions which arise in relation to Ez. (the origin of the names, their reference to specific princes or peoples etc.), nor the later, post-Johannine development of the saga, which displayed a certain independence of Rev. 20. On the first point, cf. the art. of H. Gunkel in RGG², II, 1303 and the bibl. there given ; on the second, cf. the art. of F. Pfister in the *Handwört. d. dtsch. Aberglaubens*, III, 910 ff. with references to liter.; also M. J. de Goeje, *De muur van Gog en Magog* (1888); A. R. Anderson, *Alexander's Gate, Gog and Magog, and the inclosed Nations* (= *Monographs of the Medieval Academy of America*, XII [1932], with full bibl.); cf. also E. Littmann in DLZ, 54 (1933), 1276 ff.

[3] The introduction of resurrection and judgment at this point comes from another schema which the divine has here combined with that of Ez. and which is given in a pure form in Syr. Bar and 4 Esr. : Messianic kingdom, resurrection, last judgment, new creation.

[4] Here we have the correct sequence of the three judgments : woes of the Messianic period, the day of Gog and Magog, the great day of judgment. In the par. M. Ex. 16:25 the sequence is wrong.

[5] Cf. A. Schlatter, *Das AT in der Apk.*, 93 f.; further refs. in Str.-B., III, 833 f. under d. In so-called 3 Enoch, which belongs to the Rabbinic literature, we have in § 45, 5 (ed. Odeberg), the sequence : Messiah ben Josef, Messiah ben David, Gog and Magog (with the rather inconsistent addition "in the days of the Messiah"), their destruction by God (not by the Messiah, whose day is already past).

[6] Cf. Str.-B., IV, 802 ff.

[7] *Ibid.*, 808 ff.

[8] *Ibid.*, III, 832 f. under a. and b.

[9] Cf. Bss. Apk., 440, n. 1.

[10] The passages Jub. 7:19; 8:25; 9:8 are not relevant, since they have nothing to do with Ez. 38 f.; they are based on Gn. 10:2.

[11] These are mostly linked with the very different motif, which derives from other sources, of the war of the Messiah against the nations and His victory over them.

Ez. 38 f., is a constituent part of apocalyptic thinking.[12] In this respect, therefore, the Johannine Apocalypse, which rests on the prophetic sayings of the OT, stands much closer to the more scriptural apocalyptic of the Rabbis than to the apocryphal and pseudepigraphical writings.[13]

There is one characteristic difference between Rev. 20:8 f. and Ez. 38 f. For all the fantastic depiction, Ez. is offering real prophecy. He is referring to future historical events. In Rev. 20:8 f., however, the whole conception is mythical. Prophecy has become apocalyptic. Thus Ezekiel gives precise names to the princes, peoples and kingdoms which make this attack on the people of God; he makes a more or less clear geographical and political identification. Even when he describes the destruction of the invaders in the land of Israel he mentions the place and gives a detailed account. In Rev. 20:8 f., however, the armies come from the four corners of the earth ἐπὶ τὸ πλάτος τῆς γῆς (→ infra).

Hand in hand with this there is an altered understanding of the names. In Ezekiel Gog is the prince who leads the invaders and Magog the territorial name. Elsewhere in the OT Gog is a personal name (1 Ch. 5:4)[14] and Magog that of the people or of the land in which he dwells (Gn. 10:2; 1 Ch. 1:5). In Rev. 20:8 f., however, the two very similar[15] names are brought together as a mythical double name for the hostile host, and this name still has a sinister ring for the receptive reader.

The divine did not create this form of the name. It was common to the whole of later Judaism. The Rabbis have it in this form,[16] and cf. also Sib., 3, 319 and 3, 512. Since the name in this form reflects the mythicising of the whole conception, the latter, too, is a feature which the Apocalypse has in common with all later Judaism.

Kuhn

γωνία, ἀκρογωνιαῖος,
κεφαλὴ γωνίας

---

† γωνία.

"Corner" (Mt. 6:5; Ac. 26:26), hence of the four corners of the earth (Rev. 7:1; 20:8). The two passages from Rev. throw light on the cosmology of the author. In oriental and OT cosmology[1] the earth[2] is thought to have four corners. To these

---

[12] Cf. also the Rabbinic 3 Enoch (→ n. 5).

[13] Cf. Schlatter, *op. cit.* (→ n. 5).

[14] In the textual variants in Nu. 24:7 (LXX, Samarit. etc. מָגוֹג instead of Mas. מֵאֲגַג) it is hard to say whether Gog is a personal or territorial name. In any case, this passage ("the kingdom of the Messiah will be higher than Gog") is the oldest instance of the incorporation of the prophecy of Ez. into the schema of later Jewish eschatology.

[15] There are many instances of the formation of like-sounding words of no particular significance by the addition of the prefix ma-; cf. the "hocus, pocus, malocus" of children. [I owe this to H. A. Winkler.]

[16] Here, however, Gog is more common alone, though as a national rather than a personal name, cf. Str.-B., III, 832.

γ ω ν ί α. [1] A. Jeremias, *Handbuch der altorientalischen Geisteskultur*² (1929), 142 ff.
[2] The four ends of the earth: Jer. 49:36 (= LXX 25:16); P. Lond., 122, 8: ἐν ταῖ[ς] δ' γωνίαις τοῦ οὐρανοῦ. The four parts of the underworld: Eth. En. 22; spurious Joh. Apc. 25:2: τὰ τέσσαρα μέρη τῆς ἀβύσσου.

correspond the four winds (Rev. 7:1),[3] which are here controlled by four angels (7:1). From the four corners blow the winds of destruction over the godless world (7:1). From them come also the anti-Christian nations (Rev. 20:8) to attack the holy city, which stands on a mountain in the centre of the earth (20:9).[4]

† ἀκρογωνιαῖος (→ κεφαλὴ γωνίας).

The "final stone" in a building, probably set over the gate. In the NT the word is found only in 1 Pt. 2:6 (= Is. 28:16) and Eph. 2:20, in both cases with reference to Christ.

The meaning may be gathered from Test. Sol. 22:7 (McCown, 66*): καὶ ὁ ναὸς συνεπληροῦτο. καὶ ἦν λίθος ἀκρογωνιαῖος μέγας, ὃν ἐβουλόμην θεῖναι εἰς κεφαλὴν γωνίας τῆς πληρώσεως τοῦ ναοῦ τοῦ θεοῦ (= εἰς τὸ πτερύγιον τοῦ ναοῦ, 22:8 = εἰς τὴν ἀρχὴν τῆς γωνίας ταύτης τῆς οὔσης ἐν τῇ εὐπρεπείᾳ τοῦ ναοῦ, 23:2); 23:3 (69* f.) καὶ ἀνῆλθεν εἰς τὸν (sic) κλίμακα βαστάζων τὸν λίθων (sic) καὶ ἔθετο αὐτὸν εἰς τὴν ἄκραν τῆς εἰσόδου τοῦ ναοῦ.[1] These sentences depict the conclusion of the building of Solomon's temple. Confirmation is found in 4 Βασ. 25:17, where ἀκρογωνιαῖον is used for כֹּתֶרֶת (the head of a pillar). Again, the Pešiṭṭa describes the stone of Is. 28:16 as the "head of the wall" and Aphrahaṭ (I, 6 f., p. 17, Parisot) calls it the final stone. The LXX of Is. 28:16: Ἰδοὺ ἐγὼ ἐμβάλλω εἰς τὰ θεμέλια Σειὼν λίθον πολυτελῆ ἔκλεκτον ἀκρογωνιαῖον ἔντιμον εἰς τὰ θεμέλια αὐτῆς identifies ἀκρογωνιαῖος with the foundation stone, but this usage is not found except in LXX Is. 28:16 and quotations from it.

Eph. 2:20, like 1 Pt. 2:1, describes the community as a spiritual temple. The apostles and prophets are the foundation, and Christ is the corner-stone who binds the whole building together[2] and completes it (Eph. 2:20 f.). Underlying the image is the lofty declaration of Jesus that He is the final stone in the heavenly sanctuary (→ κεφαλὴ γωνίας).

† κεφαλὴ γωνίας (→ ἀκρογωνιαῖος).

The Hebraism κεφαλὴ γωνίας is produced by a literal rendering of רֹאשׁ פִּנָּה (Ps. 118:22). The phrase occurs only in LXX ψ 117:22: λίθον ὃν ἀπεδοκίμασαν οἱ οἰκο-δομοῦντες, οὗτος ἐγενήθη εἰς κεφαλὴν γωνίας, and the derived literature. The sense of "final stone in the building" may be most clearly deduced from Test. Sol. 22:7 ff. (→ ἀκρογωνιαῖος) and Pešiṭṭa Ps. 118:22 ("head of the building").

In the NT κεφαλὴ γωνίας (Mk. 12:10 and par.; Ac. 4:11; 1 Pt. 2:7; all quoting LXX ψ 117:22) is consistently used of Christ. According to Mk. 12:10 and par. Jesus described Himself as the stone, rejected by the builders, which has been chosen by God as the chief corner-stone in the heavenly sanctuary. The saying

---

[3] Jer. 49:36; Ez. 37:9; Zech. 6:5; Da. 7:2; Mk. 13:27 and par.

[4] Joach. Jeremias, Golgotha (1926), 43 ff.; 51 ff.

ἀ κ ρ ο γ ω ν ι α ῖ ο ς. Joach. Jeremias, "Der Eckstein," Angelos, 1 (1925), 65 ff.; Golgotha (1926), 77 ff.: "κεφαλὴ γωνίας — ἀκρογωνιαῖος," ZNW, 29 (1930), 264 ff.

[1] Hs. E. 7:6 (113*): εἰς τὴν πρώτην κεφαλαίαν τοῦ ναοῦ.

[2] The term συναρμολογεῖσθαι (Eph. 2:21) occurs elsewhere in the NT only at Eph. 4:16, where it is used of Christ as the Head by which the whole body is integrated (cf. Col. 2:19). Eph. 4:16 confirms the fact that the integration is from above, so that the ἀκρογωνιαῖος of 2:20 is to be sought high up in the building.

κ ε φ α λ ὴ γ ω ν ί α ς. For bibl. → ἀκρογωνιαῖος.

is one of the lofty declarations of Jesus in which He relates Himself to the heavenly sanctuary. [1] He is not merely the final stone, i.e., the Consummator, but also the Builder of the new temple (Mk. 14:58 and par.; cf. Mt. 16:18). Hence He can say of Himself that He stands above the earthly temple (Mt. 12:6). [2] With this description we are to link very closely the lofty predicates which describe Jesus as the cosmic rock dispensing the water of life [3] (→ λίθος).

The early community found in Ps. 118:22 scriptural evidence for the death and resurrection of Jesus. The Crucified is the rejected stone which in the resurrection is made by God the chief corner-stone in the heavenly sanctuary (Ac. 4:11), to be manifested as such in the *parousia*.

1 Pt. 2:7 interprets Ps. 118:22 in terms of the σκάνδαλον which Jesus is for unbelievers. In other words, the κεφαλὴ γωνίας is not so much the final stone but a sharp stone at the corner of the building against which men stumble and fall. This interpretation is suggested by the quotation from Is. 8:14 which immediately follows (1 Pt. 2:8).

Joachim Jeremias

---

[1] J. Jeremias, *Jesus als Weltvollender* (1930), 79 ff.
[2] It is also significant that Jesus refers Ps. 110 to Himself (Mk. 12:36 and par.), for here the Lord of David is called a "priest after the order of Melchizedek."
[3] J. Jeremias, *Golgotha* (1926), 80-85.